FICTION CORE COLLECTION

SIXTEENTH EDITION

CORE COLLECTION SERIES

Formerly

STANDARD CATALOG SERIES

JOHN GREENFIELDT, GENERAL EDITOR

CHILDREN'S CORE COLLECTION
MIDDLE & JUNIOR HIGH CORE COLLECTION
SENIOR HIGH CORE COLLECTION
PUBLIC LIBRARY CORE COLLECTION: NONFICTION
FICTION CORE COLLECTION

On WilsonWeb only:
GRAPHIC NOVELS CORE COLLECTION
NONBOOK MATERIALS CORE COLLECTION

FICTION CORE COLLECTION

SIXTEENTH EDITION

Former Title:

Fiction Catalog

EDITED BY

JOHN GREENFIELDT

NEW YORK AND DUBLIN

THE H. W. WILSON COMPANY

2010

Printed in the United States of America

ISBN 978-0-8242-1103-5

Library of Congress Cataloging-in-Publication Data

Fiction core collection.— 16th ed. / edited by John Greenfieldt.
    p. cm. — (Core collection series)
    Includes index.
    Previous ed. under title: Fiction catalog.
    ISBN 978-0-8242-1103-5 (alk. paper)
    1. Fiction—Indexes. 2. Best books—United States.
I. Greenfieldt, John.
    Z5916 .F5 2010
    [PN3451]
    016.80883—dc22

                                  2009027909

CONTENTS

CONTENTS

PREFACE

Fiction Core Collection is a selective list of classic and contemporary works of adult fiction either written in or translated into English. This sixteenth edition includes 11,300 titles, including 4,100 analytical entries for novelettes and novels contained in composite works. This is an increase of nearly 1,300 titles over the fifteenth edition. This edition of the Collection will be updated by three annual Supplements, containing approximately 2,000 new titles over the next four years.

New in this edition

Of the 11,300 fiction titles listed in this volume, 2,680 are new to this edition, mostly titles published in the past four years. New editions and new translations of classic fiction are added as they are published. In preparing this edition the editor and advisors have made an extensive review of genre fiction: mystery, romance, western, and science fiction, in particular, in an attempt to establish a core list in those areas. As with other types of fiction, both literary quality and popularity are taken in to consideration in preparing these lists.

For the first time in this edition the most highly recommended titles are identified with a rosette (an asterisk *) in the bibliographic record, following the ISBN.

Scope and Coverage

Books listed are both hardcover and paperback editions published in the United States, or published in Canada or the United Kingdom and distributed in the United States. Out-of-print titles have been retained in the belief that good fiction is not obsolete simply because it happens to go out of print. Information about an out-of-print title that is reissued between editions of the Collection will be included in a Supplement.

Fiction Core Collection is a guide only to works of fiction. Users who seek literary criticism, literary history, biographies of authors, and books on the writing of fiction are referred to *Fiction Core Collection*'s companion publication, *Public Library Core Collection: Nonfiction*.

Organization

The Core Collection consists of two parts. The first part lists works alphabetically by author. Following the bibliographic information are notes about related works, a descriptive summary for novels and a contents note for story collections, and, in most cases, an evaluative comment from a quoted source.

The second part of the Collection is a Title and Subject Index. Access is provided by subject or theme, and by genre, form, and literary technique. This access is one of the Collection's most important features and is especially valued by readers' advisors.

More detailed information about the arrangement and content of the Collection will be found in the Directions for Use.

Acknowledgments

The H. W. Wilson Company is indebted to the following librarians, who played an essential role in the selection of titles for this Collection, in many cases with the participation of their colleagues:

Beth Anderson
Reference Librarian
Ann Arbor District Library
Ann Arbor, MI

Jennifer Baker
Fiction and Readers'
  Advisory Librarian
Seattle Public Library
Seattle, WA

Megan McArdle
Library Services Manager
Berkeley Public Library
Berkeley, CA

Richard Oloiza
Assistant Manager
Fiction and Young Adult Department
Enoch Pratt Free Library
Baltimore, MD

Kaite Mediatore Stover
Head of Readers' Services
Kansas City, Kansas, Public Library
Kansas City, KS

Don Wentworth
Senior Staff Librarian
Reference Service Department
Carnegie Library of Pittsburgh
Pittsburgh, PA

DIRECTIONS FOR USE

Fiction Core Collection is arranged in two parts as follows:

  Part I lists works of fiction in alphabetical order by the last name of the author or by title, if the title is the main entry. The following bibliographical information is provided: author, title, publisher, date of publication, paging, illustration note, price, out-of-print status, ISBN designation, and, when available, Library of Congress control number. Notes regarding sequels, publication history, and contents of story collections are also supplied. A descriptive summary and, in most instances, an excerpt from a reviewing source conclude the entry. References are made from variant forms of authors' names, from names of joint authors, and from names of editors or compilers of short story collections. Analytical entries, identified by the words *"In"* or *"also in,"* provide title and author access to novels and novellas contained in composite works.

  Part II is a Title and Subject Index. Each book is listed under title, which is followed by the name of the author under which the entry for the book will be found in Part I. Books are also listed under their main subjects or themes, as well as under headings for genre, form, or literary technique, if appropriate. Among specific headings are those for persons, places, events, historical periods, lifestyles, and legendary characters. Subject headings and subject cross references are printed in capital letters.

FICTION CORE COLLECTION
Sixteenth Edition

200 years of great American short stories; edited by Martha Foley. Houghton Mifflin 1975 968p

ISBN 0-395-20447-X

Contents: A pretty story, by F. Hopkinson; Rip Van Winkle, by W. Irving; Peter Rugg, the missing man, by W. Austin; The grey champion, by N. Hawthorne; The big bear of Arkansas, by T. B. Thorpe; The cask of Amontillado, by E. A. Poe; Bartleby the scrivener, by H. Melville; Tennessee's partner, by B. Harte; Captain Kidd's money, by H. B. Stowe; Marjorie Daw, by T. B. Aldrich; The lady or the tiger, by F. Stockton; Over on the T'other Mounting, by C. E. Craddock; The revolt of mother, by M. W. Freeman; One of the missing, by A. Bierce; The return of a private, by H. Garland; The real thing, by H. James; The courting of Sister Wisby, by S. O. Jewett; The open boat, by S. L. Crane; The man that corrupted Hadleyburg, by S. L. Clemens; The furnished room, by O. Henry; To build a fire, by J. London; The strength of God, by S. Anderson; The teacher, by S. Anderson; The diamond as big as the Ritz, by F. S. Fitzgerald; Haircut, by R. Lardner; Double birthday, by W. Cather; Spring evening, by J. T. Farrell; Masses of men, by E. Caldwell; The gilded six-bits, by Z. N. Hurston; Silent snow, secret snow, by C. Aiken; An odor of verbena, by W. Faulkner; The daring young man on the flying trapeze, by W. Saroyan; The snows of Kilimanjaro, by E. Hemingway; A tooth for Paul Revere, by S. V. Benét; Noon wine, by K. A. Porter; The leader of the people, by J. Steinbeck; Lily Daw and the three ladies, by E. Welty; Fire and cloud, by R. Wright; The patterns of love, by W. Maxwell; The ballad of the sad café, by C. McCullers; Cass Mastern's wedding ring, by R. P. Warren; The wedding: Beacon Hill, by J. Stafford; Rain in the heart, by P. Taylor; Gunners' passage, by I. Shaw; The lottery, by S. Jackson; February 1999: Ylla, by R. Bradbury; The country husband, by J. Cheever; A good man is hard to find, by F. O'Connor; The Mexican girl, by J. Kerouac; The Pedersen kid, by W. H. Gass; Seven say you can hear corn grow, by K. Boyle; Where are you going, where have you been? by J. C. Oates; Tell me how long the train's been gone, by J. Baldwin; Son, by J. Updike; Yellow woman, by L. Silko

A

Abani, Christopher

GraceLand. Farrar, Straus, and Giroux 2004 321p $24

ISBN 0-374-16589-0   LC 2003-12705

"The city of Lagos, Nigeria, provides the backdrop to the story of Elvis, a teenage Elvis impersonator hoping to make his way out of the ghetto. Broke, beset by floods, and beatings by his alcoholic father, and with no job opportunities in sight, Elvis is tempted by a life of crime. Thus begins his odyssey into the dangerous underworld of Lagos, guided by his friend Redemption and accompanied by a . . . hybrid of voices including The King of Beggars, Sunday, Innocent and Comfort." Publisher's note

"This book works brilliantly in two ways. As a convincing and unpatronizing record of life in a poor Nigerian slum, and as a frighteningly honest insight into a world skewed by casual violence, it's wonderful." N Y Times Book Rev

Abbott, Lee K.

All things, all at once; new and selected stories. Norton 2006 365p $26.95

ISBN 0-393-06137-X   LC 2005-27348

Contents: Ninety nights on Mercury; As fate would have it; Category Z; Dreams of distant lives; Gravity; How love is lived in paradise; Love is the crooked thing; Martians; Men of rough persuasion; One of Star Wars, one of Doom; Revolutionaries; Sweet cheeks; The eldest of things; The end of grief; The final proof of fate and circumstance; The talk between the worms; The human use of inhuman beings; The valley of sin; The view of me from Mars; The way sin is said in Wonderland; The who, the what, and the why; What Y was; When our dream world finds us, and these hard times are gone; X

"With his distinctive literary voice, Abbott claims the short story as his own territory and populates it with 40-ish men with bellies going soft who are products of their pasts—which may include duty in Vietnam—trying to make their best of the present. In these sometimes loosely linked stories, which fall into the author's categories of boy-girl, buddy-buddy, father-son, and futuristic or wacky, Abbot virtually grabs the reader by the neck with his opening sentences and doesn't let go. His territory is the Southwest, often small-town Deming, New Mexico, the hometown to which his protagonists tend to return as adults." Booklist

Abbott, Megan E., 1971-

The song is you; [by] Megan Abbott. Simon & Schuster 2007 242p $23

ISBN 978-0-7432-9171-2; 0-7432-9171-9
                               LC 2006-51229

The author uses a "real-life crime—the disappearance of actress Jean Spangler from Los Angeles in 1949—as her hook to spin a downbeat tale about a journalist-turned-studio-flack, Gil 'Hop' Hopkins. Hop was with Spangler, a stunner but a second-rate acting talent, the last night she was seen, and harbors guilt over leaving her in the company of a famous acting and singing duo, Marv Sutton and Gene Merrel, who have a reputation for rough play. Hop's efforts at amateur sleuthing unearth a

Abbott, Megan E., 1971-—*Continued*

blackmail ring and a possible mob connection to Spangler's disappearance. Abbott deserves credit for resurrecting this virtually forgotten case and concocting a plausible fictional solution to a true crime." Publ Wkly

Abe, Kōbō, 1924-1993

The woman in the dunes; translated from the Japanese by E. Dale Saunders; with drawings by Machi Abé. Knopf 1964 239p il o.p.

Original Japanese edition, 1962

The protagonist of this novel "is Niki Jumpei, an amateur entomologist who, on a weekend trip from the city, discovers a bizarre village in the dunes where residents live in deep sand pits. Imprisoned with a widow in one of the pits, he must shovel the omnipresent sand that threatens to bury the community. The novel relates Niki's attempts to escape the pit, his relationship with the woman, and his gradual acceptance of a new identity." Merriam-Webster's Ency of Lit

Abercrombie, Joe

Before they are hanged. Pyr Books 2008 543p pa $15.98

ISBN 978-159102-641-9; 1-59102-641-5

LC 2007-51694

Sequel to: The blade itself

"As savage Northmen invade Angland, the northernmost province of the unwieldy Union, honorable, hardworking Union soldier Colonel West watches his notions of civilized warfare erode in one horrible battle after another. In Dagoska, a southern city threatened by Gurkish soldiers and left undefended as Union troops head to Angland, dreadfully maimed Inquisitor Glokta employs tortures and deceptions to ferret out conspiracies against the king. Ignoring these worldly concerns, disreputable magus Bayaz of Calcis drives a squabbling little band through a wasteland in search of a relic that can open a gate to the realm of demons. Abercrombie leavens the bloody action with moments of dark humor, developing a story suffused with a rich understanding of human darkness and light." Publ Wkly

Followed by: Last argument of kings

Last argument of kings. Pyr Books 2008 639p pa $15.98

ISBN 978-1-59102-690-7; 1-59102-690-3

LC 2008-482104

Concluding title in the author's First Law sword & sorcery trilogy that began with The blade itself and Before they are hanged

"Abercrombie is a fresh new talent, presenting a dark view of life with wit and zest, and readers will mourn the end of this vivid story arc." Publ Wkly

Abercrombie, Joe, 1974-

The blade itself. Pyr 2007 531p pa $15

ISBN 978-1-59102-594-8; 1-59102-594-X

LC 2007-28499

"Logen Ninefingers, a barbarian on the run from an ex-employer who's now king of the North, finds his loyalties complicated when he switches sides and becomes a valuable source of intel to the beleaguered Union.

Glokta, a torture victim turned torturer, gets roped into securing the Union's position against both the invading Northmen and the incompetent Union king and council, and ruthlessly wields his skills in attempts to weed out traitors. Foppish Jezal, a preternaturally excellent swordsman, manages to win the contest to become the Union champion, thanks to a little help from Bayaz, a mage with his own agenda." Libr J

This is a "fantasy novel full of enough ironic and slightly self-deprecating humor and Scorcese-esque violence to make the average hipper than thou non-fantasy reader want to learn more about the genre . . ., yet filled with enough touchstones to make your average Tolkien weaned fantasy reader quite happy indeed." Blade & Thruster

Followed by: Before they are hanged

Ablow, Keith R.

Compulsion; {by} Keith Ablow. St. Martin's Press 2002 321p

ISBN 0-312-26641-3   LC 2001-58861

"Battle-scarred Boston forensic psychiatrist Frank Clevenger is reluctantly drawn into the Nantucket murder case of five-month-old twin Brooke Bishop. All evidence points to the younger of the victim's two adopted Russian-born brothers, 16-year-old problem child Billy." Publ Wkly

"Clevenger does not spout jargon, and if you can get past the unnerving glibness, he comes across with fascinating clinical insights into murderers and other psychos." N Y Times Book Rev

Abraham, Daniel

An autumn war. Tor 2008 366p $25.95

ISBN 978-0-7653-1342-3; 0-7653-1342-1

LC 2008-16974

"A Tom Doherty Associates book"

Third volume in the author's Long Price Quartet; earlier titles: A shadow in summer; A betrayal in winter

In this fantasy, "powerful elementals called andat are enslaved by poets to work for the city-states of the Khaiem. The ongoing struggles of familiar, aging characters-poet Maati, his ex-lover Liat, the mercenary Sinja, and Otah, now the reluctant ruler of his Khaiem city-occupy much of the story, but a new voice drives the plot. Gen. Balasar Gice, of the rival Galt Empire, is convinced that the andat are a threat to mankind and wants to eliminate them for good. As Gice's plan comes to fruition, everyone must confront changes in their world that go beyond anything they'd ever imagined. New readers will find Abraham's deft storytelling style accessible, but returning fans will most appreciate the growth of the world and the characters." Publ Wkly

A shadow in summer. Tor 2006 331p $24.95

ISBN 0-765-31340-5   LC 2005-16832

"A Tom Doherty Associates book"

This first volume in the author's projected Long Price Quartet is "set in a world where poets create and bind powerful shape-shifting creatures called 'andat.' The Empire hangs on, literally, by a thread; the cloth industry depends on the ability of andat Seedless to magically remove seeds from cotton plants to keep commerce flowing and the barbarians in check. Seedless, who can also remove unborn children from their mother's womb, aims

Abraham, Daniel—*Continued*

to drive his poet-creator, Heshai-kvo, mad with grief. A love triangle develops among a threesome—Heshai's apprentice, Maati; Itani, a laborer with a past; and the beautiful scribe Liat—as they unknowingly assist the andat in his plot to abort a wanted child. When Liat's master, Amat Kyaan, uncovers the plan, Amat must flee and live as a bookkeeper in a brothel. The complex characters all struggle to navigate a path between their duty to their Empire and to themselves." Publ Wkly

This is a "fine example of high fantasy that, in its presentation of the poet-andat relationship, offers a new and striking take on the age-old question of the power of magic and the responsibilities of the magician. But what is most stisfying about the book is the degree to which it bends the conventions of the genre in interesting ways." Sci Fic Wkly

(jt. auth) Martin, G. R. R. Hunter's run

Abraham, Pearl, 1960-

The romance reader. Riverhead Bks. 1995 296p
ISBN 1-573-22015-9   LC 95-964

"Rachel, romance reader and the oldest of seven children is only 12 as the novel opens and grows into a 19-year-old married woman in the course of . . . {this} novel. This surreptitious reader of romance novels breaks the rules of her Hasidic parents with her visits to libraries and growing independence of mind. Rachel and her sister take advantage of their mother's visit to Israel to take lifesaving lessons and apply for jobs at a private pool. These adventures leave Rachel totally unsuited to the conventional arranged marriage she finds herself in near the novel's end." Booklist

"Abraham's intense, sensitive prose and her ability to create vivid scenes and memorable characters augment this authentic, often disturbing, look at Hasidic home life and beliefs." Publ Wkly

Abrahams, Peter, 1947-

Dog on it; a Chet and Bernie mystery; [by] Spencer Quinn. Atria Books 2008 305p $25
ISBN 978-1-4165-8583-1; 1-4165-8583-4

"Chet the Jet is a dog who failed K-9 school (cats in the open country played a role in his demise), but now he is a dedicated PI and works with Bernie, owner of the Little Detective Agency. The story is told entirely from Chet's point of view, which will delight dog-loving mystery readers, but the book is also an excellent PI tale, dogs aside, as Chet and Bernie investigate the disappearance of a teenage girl whose developer dad may be up to no good. . . . Excellent and fully fleshed primary and secondary characters, a consistently doggy view of the world, and a sprightly pace make this a not-to-be-missed debut." Booklist

Hard rain. Dutton 1988 374p
ISBN 0-525-24581-2   LC 87-18947

"A sinister deal struck at the Woodstock festival in 1969 sends a poor young man to Vietnam in the place of a rich young man, who finds a new life in California. Nearly 20 years later, the now-divorced man and his daughter have disappeared, and Jessie Shapiro, the child's mother, begins a cross-country hunt. Jessie's search ends in Vermont, the home of her husband's fam-

ily and the location of a commune in which he once lived. Jessie also finds the home of the man who took her husband's place, thought to be killed in action but now returned." Booklist

"Jessie is an appealingly ordinary heroine, a resilient working mother. And each of the characters she encounters on her descent into a violent world of personal and political deception is vividly drawn. 'Hard Rain,' which takes its title from a Bob Dylan song, is infused with a knowing, affectionate feeling for the pop culture of the 1960's." N Y Times Book Rev

Nerve damage. William Morrow 2007 304p $24.95
ISBN 978-0-06-113797-6; 0-06-113797-9
     LC 2006-47092

"Sculptor Roy Valois has never recovered from the tragic death of his beloved wife, Delia, in a helicopter accident while on a humanitarian mission to Honduras. Delia worked for the Hobbes Institute, 'a think tank specializing in third-world economic problems.' Roy's internal scars have kept him at a distance from others, even as the effects of asbestos exposure in his youth begin to ravage his body. When a chance remark leads Roy to search out the text of his already written obituary for the New York Times, he finds a minor error concerning the Hobbes Institute. That niggling loose thread obsesses the artist, but his efforts to set the record straight reveal that much of what he knew about his wife was a lie." Publ Wkly

"The care with which Abrahams brings his characters to life sets him apart from most thriller writers working today." New Yorker

Abu-Jaber, Diana

Crescent. Norton 2003 349p hardcover o.p. pa $13.95
ISBN 0-393-05747-X; 0-393-32554-7 (pa)
     LC 2002-152907

"Sirine's now-deceased missionary parents were Iraqi and American; she's been raised since she was nine by her beloved Iraqi uncle. Her world is his house, the cafe where she is chef, and the air of Los Angeles. She's nearly 40, and inside her pale skin and green eyes she feels the rhythms of her uncle's Arabic stories and the scent of Eastern spices. Hanif ('Han'), a professor of Arabic literature at the local university comes to the cafe for the tastes of home, and he and Sirine fall into an affair of wild, sweet tenderness. . . . Abu-Jaber's language is miraculous, whether describing the texture of Han's skin or Sirine's way with an onion. It is not possible to stop reading." Booklist

Origin; a novel. W.W. Norton & Co. 2007 384p $24.95
ISBN 978-0-393-06455-1; 0-393-06455-7
     LC 2007-4963

"Set in wintry Syracuse and narrated by Lena Dawson, a reclusive fingerprint expert working in a gossipy city crime lab, Abu-Jaber's complex drama revolves around a baffling string of infant deaths. Is the culprit SIDS, something environmental, or the work of a serial killer? Separated from her police-officer husband, Lena is assaulted by painful questions and bizarre flashbacks." Booklist

"For all its internal chill, the drama that unfolds

Abu-Jaber, Diana—*Continued*

around fingerprint expert Lena Dawson is a struggle toward spring and the light. Haunting and compelling, Origin combines the traditions of the crime novel with an examination of Lena's unusual upbringing. It's a little film noir, a bit independent-woman-detective thriller, and winningly fresh in its approach." PopMatters

Achebe, Chinua, 1930-

Things fall apart. Astor-Honor 1959 215p $15.95

ISBN 0-8392-1113-9

First published 1958 in the United Kingdom; first United States edition published by McDowell, Obolensky

"The novel chronicles the life of Okonkwo, the leader of an Igbo (Ibo) community, from the events leading up to his banishment from the community for accidentally killing a clansman, through the seven years of his exile, to his return. The novel addresses the problem of the intrusion in the 1890s of white missionaries and colonial government into tribal Igbo society. It describes the simultaneous disintegration of its protagonist Okonkwo and of his village. The novel was praised for its intelligent and realistic treatment of tribal beliefs and of psychological disintegration coincident with social unraveling." Merriam-Webster's Ency of Lit

Aciman, André A.

Call me by your name; [by] André Aciman. Farrar, Straus and Giroux 2007 248p $23

ISBN 0-374-29921-8   LC 2006-11720

"When Oliver, a handsome young American philosopher, arrives in a seaside town in Italy to work on a book about Heraclitus, as the guest of an Italian professor, the son of the house, Elio—seventeen, studious, moody, and ravenous—falls for him. Elio's edgy rapture as he forms himself in relation to another plays out against the background of a scorching Mediterranean summer, and Aciman introduces a small universe of characters who are themselves altered by the charged air that surrounds the lovers: Elio's mother, who calls Oliver il cauboi (the cowboy); his generous, hazy father; and the households cantankerous cook, who every morning carefully cracks open the American's soft-boiled eggs." New Yorker

Ackroyd, Peter

The fall of Troy. Nan A. Talese 2007 212p $23

ISBN 978-0-385-52290-8   LC 2007-7208

First published 2006 in the United Kingdom

"In telegram- and steamboat-era Athens, the Greek Sophia Chrysanthis hastily weds German archeologist Johann Ludwig Heinrich Julius Obermann, mainly out of desire for an Indiana Jones–style adventure. Sophia quickly finds, however, that life with Johann approximates the Trojan excavation site (outside the Turkish village of Hissarlik) that Johann mines so lovingly: one jaw-dropping discovery follows another. But while Johann interprets the antiquities he finds using the Iliad, Sophia is left without a guide to her enigmatic husband's true self." Publ Wkly

Ackroyd's "evocation of the landscape, the weather and the conditions of the Hissarlik dig are brilliant, and his minor charactersSare deftly brought to life. Above all, he manages to suggest, in a book which is less slight than it may appear, that men who meddle with the gods do so at their peril." Sunday Telegraph

The trial of Elizabeth Cree; a novel of the Limehouse murders. Talese 1995 261p

ISBN 0-385-47707-4   LC 94-37348

First published 1994 in the United Kingdom with title: Dan Leno and the Limehouse Golem

"Well-known but incidental Victorian 'characters'— Karl Marx and the novelist George Gissing—converge in this mystery/anti-suspense fiction about a former music-hall actress, Elizabeth Cree, and her husband, an apparent serial killer. Chapters of Mr. Cree's diary alternate with transcripts of Mrs. Cree's trial for his murder and sections of third-person narrative." New Yorker

"Mr. Ackroyd's methods are both subtle and outrageous. Everything and everyone in this novel is so intimately connected that one reads with a sense of the world becoming progressively smaller and tighter; a kind of anguished claustrophobia sets in. The tone is agitated and compelling, by turns macabre and inventive." N Y Times Book Rev

Adams, Alice, 1926-1999

After the war; a novel. Knopf 2000 305p $25

ISBN 0-375-40683-2   LC 99-47104

Adams' final novel, set in 1940s North Carolina, "picks up where her previous book, 'A Southern Exposure,' left off. Cynthia Baird, a transplanted Yankee, is floating from one affair to another while her husband, Harry, is off fighting in Europe; her housekeeper, Odessa, the moral center of this particular universe, keeps turning out her ham biscuits; the local girls, including Melanctha Byrd, who is heading North to Radcliffe . . . are growing sly and eager to leave town. There are so many subplots—about race relations, sex, politics, and adolescence—that it's as if Adams wanted both to capture an era entirely and to make things, this once, come out right. The result is lovely, tender, and a little hokey, like that moment just before the birthday candles are blown out." New Yorker

A southern exposure; a novel. Knopf 1996 305p

ISBN 0-679-44452-1   LC 95-16109

This novel takes place "during the Great Depression. Harry and Cynthia Baird and their daughter, Abigail, run from their New England roots to Pinehill, North Carolina, hoping to escape from debt, social obligations, and boredom. Instead, they stumble into a small-town soap opera with its own rules of conduct they struggle to understand. The mystery of the Southern way of life unravels as they settle into its rhythms." Libr J

"Though this plot teeters on the edge of soap opera, it never slips into the slush, thanks in part to the sobering imminence of war, which casts an air of gravity over all these amorous proceedings. Ms. Adams's breezy, wistful lyricism perfectly captures this lovely place and golden time, just before things got so damn serious forever." NY Times Book Rev

The stories of Alice Adams. Knopf 2002 622p $30

ISBN 0-375-41285-9

     * LC 2002-70940

Adams, Alice, 1926-1999—*Continued*

Contents: Verlie I say unto you; Winter rain; Ripped off; The swastika on our door; Flights; Beautiful girl; Home is where; A pale and perfectly oval moon; Roses, rhododendron; For good; Snow; Greyhound people; By the sea; An unscheduled stop; The girl across the room; Lost luggage; Berkeley house; Legends; At the beach; Truth or consequences; To see you again; Alaska; Return trips; La señora; New best friends; A public pool; Waiting for Stella; Barcelona; Separate planes; Molly's dog; Mexican dust; Elizabeth; Sintra; My first and only house; 1940: fall; The end of the world; Fog; Tide pools; Favors; Ocracoke Island; Your doctor loves you; After you've gone; His women; The haunted beach; Great sex; Raccoons; Old love affairs; A very nice dog; The visit; The last lovely city; The islands; The drinking club; Earthquake damage

"Taken together, these stories betray the changing mores of the past half-century; taken in sequence, they trace the changes in the American short story over the past 40 years, some of those changes wrought by Adams herself." Publ Wkly

Adams, Douglas, 1952-2001

The hitchhiker's guide to the galaxy. 25th anniversary illustrated collector's ed. Harmony Books 2004 271p il $35

ISBN 1-4000-5293-9   LC 2004-558987
First published 1980
"Based on a BBC radio series, . . . this is the episodic story of Arthur Dent, a contemporary Englishman who discovers first that his unpretentious house is about to be demolished to make way for a bypass, and second that a good friend is actually an alien galactic hitchhiker who announces that Earth itself will soon be demolished to make way for an intergalactic speedway. A suitably bewildered Dent soon finds himself hitching . . . rides throughout space, aided by a . . . reference book, The Hitchhiker's Guide to the Galaxy, a compendium of 'facts,' philosophies, and wild advice." Libr J

Life, the universe, and everything. Harmony Bks. 1982 227p hardcover o.p. pa $12.95

ISBN 0-517-54874-7; 0-345-41890-6 (pa)
     LC 82-15470
Third volume in The hitchhiker's series
In this volume, "Arthur finds himself in a cave on prehistoric earth, awaiting the arrival of his extraterrestrial friend Ford Perfect so that they may resume their travels in time and space. Their mission: to save the universe from a cataclysm."
"Arthur Dent and his motley crew do tie up most of the loose ends and manage to prevent the destruction of the universe, but the first two novels . . . 'must' be read to understand the situation, and even then it's confusing." Libr J
Followed by So long, and thanks for all the fish

Mostly harmless. Harmony Bks. 1992 277p hardcover o.p. pa $12.95

ISBN 0-517-57740-2; 0-345-37933-0 (pa)
     LC 92-25457
"A Grebulon reconnaissance ship with faulty programming, a news reporter suffering from a bad case of missed opportunities, a fugitive from the new 'improved' offices of the Hitchhiker's Guide to the Galaxy, and a hitchhiker lost in a parallel universe come together in grand style in the fifth installment of Adams's best-selling 'trilogy.'" Libr J

The restaurant at the end of the universe. Harmony Bks. 1981 c1980 250p hardcover o.p. pa $12.95

ISBN 0-517-54535-7; 0-345-41892-1 (pa)
     LC 81-6563
Second volume in The hitchhiker's series
First published 1980 in the United Kingdom
"Poor uprooted Arthur Dent finds himself swept along in the wake of Zaphod Beeblebrox, former President of the Galaxy, as Zaphod searches for the man who rules the Universe. They and their companions tumble from one scrape into another, with the erratic aid of Zaphod's dead great-grandfather and Marvin, their perpetually depressed robot. Adams's lively sense of the ridiculous has concocted many hilarious episodes, though the inspired lunacy of the first book has become rather uneven here. Still, this is one of the best pieces of sf humor available." Libr J
Followed by Life, the universe, and everything

So long, and thanks for all the fish. Harmony Bks. 1985 204p hardcover o.p. pa $7.99

ISBN 0-517-55439-9; 0-345-39183-4 (pa)
     LC 84-19350
Fourth volume in The hitchhiker's series
Arthur Dent "returns to a supposedly destroyed Earth to build a hyperspace bypass. The night of his return, Arthur falls in love with a sedated girl (her brother says she's 'barking mad'), only to lose her, then accidentally find her twice more. She is Fenchurch, the girl who in . . . 'Guide' . . . discovered the secret of Earth's potential happiness moments before it was demolished. Her 'madness' stems from the time when Earth should have been destroyed, and wasn't, but when all the dolphins disappeared. . . . The humor is still off-the-wall, but less forced and more gentle than the other books. . . . The series seems to be winding down, but it is still an addictive commodity to its fans." SLJ
Followed by Mostly harmless

Adams, Henry, 1838-1918

Democracy; an American novel; introduction by Arthur Schlesinger, Jr. Modern Library 2003 xx, 209p pa $12.95

ISBN 0-375-76058-X
     * LC 2002-19645
First published anonymously 1880
"A social and political satire based on the corruption of the second Grant administration, the book includes characters modeled on President Hayes and James G. Blaine. A charming and intelligent young widow, Madeleine Lee, moves to Washington 'to touch with her own hands the massive machinery of society.' She finally rejects an offer of marriage from a senator who has compromised his moral integrity for political advantage." Reader's Ency. 3d edition

Adams, John Joseph, 1976-

(ed) The living dead. See The living dead

Adams, Lorraine

Harbor. Knopf 2004 291p $23.95

ISBN 1-4000-4233-X   LC 2004-40916

This novel "tells the story of Aziz Arkoun, a twenty-four-year-old Arab Muslim from Algeria who enters America illegally by hiding for fifty-two days in the hold of a tanker and swimming into Boston Harbor. Aziz falls in with a group of young Algerians in East Boston, including Rafik, a childhood friend who is now a petty criminal. Hopes for prosperity and safety are dashed: Aziz takes low-paying jobs, is beset by chaotic living arrangements, and, after stumbling across some suspicious secret dealings of Rafik's, gets caught up in the F.B.I. investigation of an international terrorist cell. Though the premise of the novel may seem too topical for its own good, Adams displays a gift for detail and character that takes us fully inside the complex systems of survival, kinship, and religious ideology which form Aziz's world." New Yorker

Adams, Poppy, 1972-

The sister; a novel. Alfred A. Knopf 2008 273p $23.95

ISBN 978-0-307-26816-7; 0-307-26816-0

LC 2008-1882

Published in the United Kingdom with title: The behaviour of moths

"Ginny and her younger sister Vivien lead an idyllic childhood in West Dorset, England, until Vivien nearly dies in an accident . . . when Ginny is 11 and Vivien is eight. Later, after the pair is expelled from school, a 15-year-old Vivien moves to London, and Ginny stays behind, covering up her mother Maud's alcoholism while trying to assist her father, Clive, with his research on moths and butterflies. After Maud's death and Clive's subsequent dementia, Ginny lives alone in the massive house, a brilliant but increasingly reclusive scientist whose insular world is cracked open when Vivien announces her desire to return and live out her days with Ginny. Long-buried secrets float to the surface as Ginny narrates with scientific precision her life's slow disintegration. Though the lepidopterological jargon and asides can slow things down, Adams expertly captures Ginny's voice and the dynamics of a deeply troubled family as the book barrels toward its chilling conclusion." Publ Wkly

Adams, Richard, 1920-

Watership Down. Scribner Classics 1974 c1972 429p $27.50 o.p.

ISBN 0-684-83605-4

First published 1972 in the United Kingdom; first United States edition 1974 by Macmillian

"Faced with the annihilation of its warren, a small group of male rabbits sets out across the English downs in search of a new home. Internal struggles for power surface in this intricately woven, realistically told adult adventure when the protagonists must coordinate tactics in order to defeat an enemy rabbit fortress. It is clear that the author has done research on rabbit behavior, for this tale is truly authentic." Shapiro. Fic for Youth. 3d edition

Adams, Sheila Kay

My old true love; a novel. Algonquin Books of Chapel Hill 2004 289p $23.95

ISBN 1-565-12407-3   LC 2003-70809

"Hackley and Larkin are rivalrous cousins raised as brothers in the North Carolina mountains and bred on the songs of their ancestors. Predictably, they both fall for Mary, a singular Appalachian beauty. Hackley soon wins her affections and marries, only to be whisked away by the Confederate draft. Left in Larkin's care, Mary swoons for the other cousin, inviting tragedy into their country lives." Publ Wkly

"Paying keen attention to the nuances of relationships between individuals as well as between people and their geographical and temporal contexts, Sheila Kay Adams writes a uniquely private and complex Civil War novel. Adams elegantly interweaves folk songs and nature into her narrative in ways that never stray from her purpose, which is to tell a family's story." Hist Fic Rev

Adamson, Gil, 1961-

The outlander; a novel. Ecco 2008 389p $25.95

ISBN 978-0-06-149125-2; 0-06-149125-X

LC 2007-41062

First published in 2007 in Canada

"A picaresque tale in the style of Charles Frazier's Cold Mountain. Set in 1903, it reveals Mary Boulton's life with her cruel husband, John, in jagged flashbacks reflecting her sporadic delirium from hunger and the harsh elements. After their sickly newborn son dies, Mary takes the only way out she knows: she kills John with his hunting rifle and escapes West, with John's two angry brothers in pursuit. Various eccentrics help her along her harrowing journey, including William Moreland, a rough mountain man who eventually leaves her to return to the wilderness. Mary barely survives until a Crow Indian finds and takes her to a nearby mining town, where she recuperates. The brothers eventually track her down there, arriving just after a calamitous landslide." Libr J

"Of course, the Girl Being Chased is one of the most enduring figures of chivalric and chauvinistic literature, a staple of television dramas and horror films. . . . But Gil is short for Gillian, and her strange and complicated heroine has nothing in common with Hollywood's wornout damsels in distress. . . there are pages here you can't read slowly enough to catch every word." Washington Post Book World

Adichie, Chimamanda Ngozi, 1977-

Half of a yellow sun. Alfred A. Knopf 2006 435p $24.95

ISBN 978-1-4000-4416-0; 1-4000-4416-2

LC 2005-57784

"Set in Nigeria during the turbulent years of the 1960s, this . . . work follows the stories of twin sisters Olanna and Kainene, their lovers, their family, and others who inhabit their privileged worlds, soon to be transformed by civil war." Libr J

The author has a "gift for capturing the rhythms of African middle-class life: not just its political awareness but the aspirations and cultural imperatives that lend it its varied character. . . . For its portrayal of Nigeria's political and cultural past, [this book] is a welcome addition to the corpus of African letters." Times Lit Suppl

Adichie, Chimamanda Ngozi, 1977-—_Continued_

The thing around your neck. Alfred A. Knopf 2009 240p $24.95

ISBN 978-0-307-27107-5; 0-307-27107-2

LC 2008-41271

Contents: Cell one; Imitation; A private experience; Ghosts; On Monday of last week; Jumping Monkey Hill; The thing around your neck; The American embassy; The shivering; The arrangers of marriage; Tomorrow is too far; The headstrong historian

"The stories are set both in the United States and in Nigeria, where things continue to fall apart. . . . Adichie, a brilliant writer whose characters stay with you for a long time, deserves to be more widely known." Libr J

Adiga, Aravind

The white tiger; a novel. Free Press 2008 336p $24

ISBN 978-1-416-56259-7; 1-416-56259-1

LC 2007-45527

"In this darkly comic début novel set in India, Balram, a chauffeur, murders his employer, justifying his crime as the act of a 'social entrepreneur.' In a series of letters to the Premier of China, in anticipation of the leader's upcoming visit to Balram's homeland, the chauffeur recounts his transformation from an honest, hardworking boy growing up in 'the Darkness'—those areas of rural India where education and electricity are equally scarce, and where villagers banter about local elections 'like eunuchs discussing the Kama Sutra'—to a determined killer. He places the blame for his rage squarely on the avarice of the Indian élite, among whom bribes are commonplace, and who perpetuate a system in which many are sacrificed to the whims of a few. Adiga's message isn't subtle or novel, but Balram's appealingly sardonic voice and acute observations of the social order are both winning and unsettling." New Yorker

Adler, Elizabeth

All or nothing. Delacorte Press 1999 327p

ISBN 0-385-33380-3

LC 99-31965

This suspense novel features retired New Orleans homicide detective, now Hollywood Hills private investigator Al Giraud and his partner, law professor and ex-DA Marla Cwitowitz. The wife of electronics executive Steve Mallard hires the duo when her husband becomes the prime suspect in the disappearance of realtor Laurie Martin

Fortune is a woman. Delacorte Press 1992 433p

ISBN 0-385-30529-X

LC 91-24977

"Francie Harrison is the poor little rich girl with a misogynistic father in turn-of-the-century San Francisco. She escapes the doll's world he plans for her and finds love, only to have it disintegrate in the earthquake of 1906. Amidst the destruction, she meets Lai Tsin, an illegal Chinese immigrant, and the strong Yorkshirewoman Annie Aysgarth who, together, help her build a world for herself. All three profit from the alliance and emerge on top of the business world, rich in friendship as well as treasure. . . . Writing and characterization are tight, depictions of Nob Hill and Oriental influence ring true, and pacing is superb." Booklist

Now or never. Delacorte Press 1997 346p

ISBN 0-385-31592-9

LC 96-24146

"A serial killer is stalking young women in Boston, and the police are at a loss for clues. The best they've come up with so far are a composite drawing of the killer and some educated hunches. Totally frustrated, Detective Harry Jordan turns to Mallory Malone, the beautiful star of a prime-time investigative TV show, in hopes of obtaining some air time from her for the case." Libr J

"Predictably, romantic sparks fly, but there's something mysterious about the beautiful Mallory. Eventually Harry pries his lover's deepest secrets out of her and finds she may hold the clue to the murderer's identity. Nerve-jangling suspense, steamy sex, glamorous characters, and graphic descriptions of the victims' last moments will grab readers' attention." Booklist

Adrian, Chris

The children's hospital. McSweeney's Books 2006 615p $24

ISBN 1-932416-60-9

In this novel, the "world comes to an end, drowned beneath seven miles of water. All that is preserved is a solitary children's hospital and its occupants. Presiding over the apocalypse are four angels who often are indistinguishable from demons: one to chronicle and one to accuse, one to protect and one to punish. Within the floating hospital, medical student Jemma Claflin discovers that a fearsome healing fire burns within her, a fire that she uses to cleanse the hideously diseased children of their 'wrongness.' It is useless, however, against the greater wrongness of the rest of her ark mates, who struggle to maintain some semblance of normalcy amidst the confounding swirl of the end-time." Booklist

"Adrian's vast floating world of a novel is a marvel. The Children's Hospital is intelligent, seductive and beautifully realized." Hartford Courant

Agee, James, 1909-1955

A death in the family. McDowell, Obolensky 1957 339p o.p.

*

"Six-year-old Rufus Follet, his younger sister Catherine, his mother, and various relatives all react differently to the unexpected announcement that Rufus's father has been fatally injured in an automobile accident. The poignancy of sorrow, the strength of personal beliefs, and the comforting love and support of a family are all elements of this compassionate novel." Shapiro. Fic for Youth. 3d edition

also in Agee, J. Let us now praise famous men; A death in the family, and shorter fiction

Let us now praise famous men; A death in the family, and shorter fiction; . Library of America 2005 818p il $35

ISBN 1-931082-81-2

LC 2005-45098

Contents: Let us now praise famous men; The morning watch; A death in the family; Stories: Death in the desert; They that sow in sorrow shall reap; A mother's tale

Let us now praise famous men (1941) is a journalistic collaboration with photographer Walker Evans that depicts the lives of Alabama sharecroppers. A death in the

Agee, James, 1909-1955—*Continued*

family is entered separately. The morning watch (1951) is an autobiographical novella where a twelve-year-old school boy in Tennessee wrestles with religious issues. Several short stories are also included.

The morning watch
In Agee, J. Let us now praise famous men; A death in the family, and shorter fiction

Agnon, Shmuel Yosef, 1888-1970

Only yesterday; [by] S.Y. Agnon; translated by Barbara Harshav. Princeton Univ. Press 2000 652p
　ISBN 0-691-00972-4　　　　　LC 00-21147
In this "novel, first published in 1945 and now translated into English for the first time, Agnon paints the panorama of the second Aliya, or immigration, of Jews to Palestine, which occurred between the turn of the century and WWI. Isaac Kumer is a young, fervent but feckless young Zionist in the Austrian province of Galicia, whose disappointed father gives him the money to emigrate to Israel. Once Isaac reaches the Land, he becomes a housepainter. . . . In Jaffa, Isaac tastes his first experience of love with Sonya, a modern woman, but in Jerusalem he meets Shifra, the daughter of a strict religionist, and he is torn between the two. . . . Impulsively, Isaac one day paints 'Crazy Dog' on the back of a friendly stray. The scruffy canine then wanders around Jerusalem, causing the population to panic. This fantastical subplot 'dogs' Isaac's stay in Jerusalem and is interwoven with his fate and that of Shifra's father." Publ Wkly

"Though Agnon would go on to write much of compelling interest during his remaining 25 years, this would be his masterpiece—a novel that deserves comparison with Kafka's The Trial, Mann's The Magic Mountain and Hermann Broch's The Sleepwalkers as a deployment of the resources of fiction for plumbing those abysses of cultural and personal crisis that haunted so many imaginations in the modernist period." Los Angeles Times Book Rev

Aira, César, 1949-

An afternoon in the life of a landscape painter. New Directions 2006 87p $12.95
　ISBN 978-0-8112-1630-2; 0-8112-1630-6
　　　　　　　　　　　　LC 2005-35053
Original Spanish edition, 2000
"This novella-cum-artistic meditation is about Johann Moritz Rugendas, a 19th century German artist and colleague of explorer Alexander von Humboldt. Rugendas visited Chile, Argentina and Mexico in the hope of recording the flora and fauna through an art conceived as 'physiognomic totality.' During a trip to the Pampas, he is electrified by a convergence of nature and spirituality. The impact of his experience handicaps him physically and psychologically. And his quest to see the Indians of the region ultimately crowns his descent to hell. More than fiction, it is an imaginative chronicle based on Rugendas' correspondence and other historical sources from the era. To which Aira adds the novelistic touch: el beso de la fantasía—the kiss of fantasy. That his protagonist is a European attempting to scientifically codify what he sees—Rugendas is a child of positivism—allows

for an unforgettable opportunity to see Latin America from the eyes of a foreigner. Better yet, the foreigner, Rugendas, is re-imagined a la Russian doll by a native, Aira, thus inviting the reader to be simultaneously outsiders and insider." San Francisco Chronicle

Ghosts; translated by Chris Andrews. New Directions 2008 139p pa $12.95
　ISBN 978-0-8112-1742-2 (pa); 0-8112-1742-6 (pa)
　　　　　　　　　　　　LC 2008-47193
Original Spanish edition, 1990
A "novel about a migrant Chilean family living in an apartment house under construction in Buenos Aires. New Year's Eve finds the hard-drinking Chilean night watchman, Raúl Vinas, hosting a party with his wife, Elisa, their four small children and Elisa's pensive 15-year-old daughter, Patri. Moreover, ghosts reside in the house: naked, dust-covered floating men, mostly unseen except by Elisa and Patri. The novel engineers a clever layering of metaphorical details about the building, but gradually focuses on Elisa's preparations for the party and her conversations with her daughter about finding a 'real man' to marry. Prodded perhaps by her isolation within the family, Patri accepts the ghosts' invitation to a midnight feast, at her life's peril." Publ Wkly

Akst, Daniel

The Webster chronicle; a novel. Putnam 2001 311p $24.95
　ISBN 0-399-14812-4　　　　　LC 2001-25679
Protagonist Terry Mathers "struggles with the declining financial stability of the small-town newspaper he co-owns and edits, his failing marriage, and his long-suffering relationship with his successful television journalist father. While he fights his own demons, he must objectively cover crucial matters in the village of Webster—including the threatened takeover of a local department store by a big chain and allegations of sexual abuse and Satanism at the local preschool." Libr J

"Akst vividly illustrates the rocky road from ethical journalism to tabloid sensationalism." Booklist

Akunin, Boris, 1956-

Murder on the Leviathan; a novel; translated by Andrew Bromfield. Random House 2004 223p il $21.95
　ISBN 1-400-06051-6　　　　　LC 2003-70379
Original Russian edition, 2000
"In 1878, a horrible murder shakes Paris; Lord Littleby's skull has been cracked open, a precious statue is missing, and seven servants and two children in the household lie supine, dispatched by poison. Blustery 'Papa' Gauche deduces that the killer will board the Leviathan, a luxurious cruise ship making its maiden voyage to India, and he arranges passage. In short order, he collects suspect passengers in a salon and attempts to entrap them, only to be quietly shown up by a young Russian diplomat named Erast Fandorin." Libr J

"Snappishly witty in Andrew Bromfield's crisp translation, Akunin's dry observations on the moral poverty of the upper classes are drolly set off by his lush descriptions of the material luxuries by which they measure the value of life itself." N Y Times Book Rev

Alam, Saher, 1973-

The groom to have been. Spiegel & Grau 2008 399p pa $14

ISBN 978-0-385-52460-5; 0-385-52460-9

LC 2007049047

"Inspired by Edith Wharton's The Age of Innocence, the narrative transports readers back and forth between Canada and New York as Nasr, a successful young professional, indulges his mother by allowing the family to look for a wife for him, despite his second-generation immigrant's ambivalence about the practice. Readers who enjoyed Vikram Seth's A Suitable Boy, set in India, will find familiar themes in this classic story of love found too late. But there's a considerable twist. We know from the novel's start who Nasr's bride-to-be is but not how the events of 9/11 and its aftermath affect their plans or how a series of misunderstandings with Jameela, the rebellious, contradictory family friend, will change everything for Nasr." Libr J

Alarcón, Daniel, 1977-

Lost City Radio; a novel. HarperCollins 2007 257p $24.95

ISBN 0-06-059479-9

LC 2006-046498

"For ten years, Norma has been the voice of consolation for a people broken by violence. She hosts Lost City Radio, the most popular program in their nameless South American country, gripped in the aftermath of war. Every week, the Indians in the mountains and the poor from the barrios listen as she reads the names of those who have gone missing, those whom the furiously expanding city has swallowed. Loved ones are reunited and the lost are found. Each week, she returns to the airwaves while hiding her own personal loss: her husband disappeared at the end of the war. But the life she has become accustomed to is forever changed when a young boy arrives from the jungle and provides a clue to the fate of her long-missing husband." Publisher's note

This "is a fable for an entire continent, and is no less pertinent in other parts of the world where different languages are spoken in different climates but where the same ruinous dance is played out." Washington Post Book World

Albert, Elisa, 1978-

The book of Dahlia; a novel. Free Press 2008 276p $23

ISBN 978-0-7432-9129-3; 0-7432-9129-8

LC 2007-33839

"Dahlia Finger, the heroine of this début novel, is a sarcastic, self-absorbed Jewish American Princess, twenty-nine years old and living in a desirable bungalow in Venice, California, bought for her by her lawyer father. She's also, thanks to Albert's control of tone and timing, one of the most likable characters in recent fiction, as self-aware about her bad habits (smoking pot, wallowing in hopelessness, refusing to engage with her broken family) as she is incapable of changing them, even when diagnosed with a 'level four' tumor in the left temporal lobe of her brain. Basing her chapters on a self-help book that Dahlia buys ('It's Up to You: The Cancer To-Do List'), Albert writes with the black humor of Lorrie Moore and a pathos that is uniquely her own, all the more blistering for being slyly invoked." New Yorker

Albert, Susan Wittig

Rosemary remembered; a China Bayles mystery. Berkley Prime Crime 1995 296p

ISBN 0-425-14937-4

LC 95-15062

In this mystery China Bayles "discovers a dead woman—who resembles herself—in a pick-up truck. China interrupts her herb-shop business to investigate the woman's past and uncovers a small host of likely suspects. The best of small-town Texas." Libr J

Alcott, Louisa May, 1832-1888

Jo's boys

In Alcott, L. M. Little women; Little men; Jo's boys

Little men

In Alcott, L. M. Little women; Little men; Jo's boys

Little women

In Alcott, L. M. Little women; Little men; Jo's boys

Little women; Little men; Jo's boys; [Elaine Showalter, editor] Library of America, Distributed to the trade in the U.S. by Penguin Putnam 2005 1092p il (The library of America) $40

ISBN 1-931082-73-1

* LC 2004-48828

Contents: Little women; Little men; Jo's boys

"Little Women (1868-69), set in New England during the Civil War, introduces the charming, unforgettable March sisters Meg, Jo, Amy, and Beth as they begin to make their way into the world. Little Men (1871) follows the intellectual tomboy Jo, now married, into adulthood, as she finds herself the caretaker of a houseful of rambunctious children at Plumfield school. Jo's Boys (1886) returns to Plumfield a decade later. Now grown, Jo's children recount adventures of their own." Publisher's note

Aldiss, Brian Wilson, 1925-

Helliconia spring; [by] Brian W. Aldiss. Atheneum Pubs. 1982 361p

ISBN 0-689-11196-9

* LC 81-66036

"In this first of a trilogy, Aldiss presents Helliconia, a dual-star system planet that is beginning to thaw from its centuries-long winter. Humans, humanoid protognostics, and the animal-like phagors contend for its sparse resources, and Aldiss relates episodes from the lives of several of the inhabitants." Libr J

"Aldiss has not only written a science fiction novel about another world, he has created another universe complete with it's own language and flavor, peopled with colorful characters (both human and otherwise) who engage sympathy and interest." Best Sellers

Followed by Helliconia summer

Helliconia summer; [by] Brian W. Aldiss. Atheneum Pubs. 1983 398p

ISBN 0-689-11388-9

* LC 83-45062

Aldiss, Brian Wilson, 1925—*Continued*

"In this second novel in Aldiss's trilogy, the planet Helliconia . . . is presented as an epic miniature of humanity's loftiest aspirations and basest shortcomings. The action takes place on two levels, represented by the geometrical symbol of the planet's supreme god Akhanaba. Some events proceed along the inner rim, driven by incessant racial wars between the cohabitant Helliconian humans and the 'ahuman' Phagors. Along the outermost rim are the concerns of the king of Borlien . . . and the nefarious intrigues of court hangers-on ranging from chancellors to child prostitutes." Publ Wkly

Followed by Helliconia winter

Helliconia winter. Atheneum Pubs. 1985 281p
ISBN 0-689-11541-5

* LC 84-45607

In this concluding volume of the "trilogy, the planet Helliconia begins its descent into a winter that will last for centuries. Nonhuman phagors, better suited to the changing climate, begin to reclaim their ancient lands, and the plague they bring panics the Oligarchy into ever more repressive measures to stave off a new dark age. As young Luterin Shokerandit learns, however, such civilized willfulness only subverts the grand, interdependent cycles of the natural world." Publ Wkly

"This conclusion to the Helliconia trilogy ranks as a landmark of fictional world-building." Libr J

Aleichem, Shalom *See* Sholem Aleichem, 1859-1916

Aleichem, Sholem *See* Sholem Aleichem, 1859-1916

Alexander, Margaret Walker *See* Walker, Margaret, 1915-1998

Alexie, Sherman, 1966-

Flight; a novel. Black Cat 2007 181p pa $13
ISBN 978-0-8021-7037-8; 0-8021-7037-4

LC 2006-52656

This novel's protagonist, Zits, is a fifteen-year-old orphaned half-Indian who has lived in a series of foster homes and juvenile jails. "About to commit a devastating act, the young man finds himself shot back through time on a [journey] . . . through moments of violence in American history. He resurfaces in the form of an FBI agent during the civil rights era, inhabits the body of an Indian child during the battle at Little Big Horn, and then rides with an Indian tracker in the 19th century before materializing as an airline pilot." Publisher's note

"Many of [the] allegorical, action-packed vignettes tread familiar thematic territory—the continuing fight for survival, the anger of racial divides, the absence of fathers—of Mr. Alexie's earlier works. . . . But with 'Flight,' he takes these themes a step further: he skillfully explores both sides of the proverbial war. Zits witnesses brutal violence through the eyes of whites and Indians, fathers and sons, and he begins to understand what it means to be the hero, the villain and the victim." N Y Times (Late N Y Ed)

Indian killer. Atlantic Monthly Press 1996 420p
ISBN 0-871-13652-X   LC 96-27996

"Bodies in trendy Seattle have been turning up scalped and decorated with owl feathers, prompting anti-Indian rhetoric from a vitriolic shock jock and leading to a spate of street violence, white against Indian and Indian against white. The killer, John Smith, is an Indian without a tribe. Adopted by a white couple, John quickly slips into a delusional fantasy life in which he dreams of righting all the wrongs inflicted on Native Americans." Booklist

"Sherman Alexie is too good a writer, too devoted to the complexities of a story, to settle for a diatribe. His vigorous prose, his haunted, surprising characters and his meditative exploration of the sources of human identity transform into a resonant tragedy what might have been a melodrama in less assured hands." N Y Times Book Rev

Reservation blues. Atlantic Monthly Press 1995 306p
ISBN 0-871-13594-9   LC 94-46132

This novel relates the "whimsical tale of Coyote Springs, an all Indian-Catholic 'four-and-a-half chord' rock band formed after a chance encounter with none other than the legendary—and long dead—Delta bluesman Robert Johnson, who happens onto the Spokane Indian Reservation looking for the woman in his dreams to save him from the mysterious 'Gentleman' on his trail." Libr J

"Hilarious but poignant, filled with enchantments yet dead-on accurate with regard to modern Indian life, this tour de force will leave readers wondering if Alexie himself hasn't made a deal with the Gentleman in order to do everything so well." Publ Wkly

Algren, Nelson, 1909-1981

The man with the golden arm; a novel. Doubleday 1949 343p o.p.

*

"Set in the slums of Chicago, the novel, which won a National Book Award in 1950, tells the story of Frankie Machine (Francis Majcinek) who is said to have a 'golden arm' because of his sure touch with pool cues, dice, his drumsticks, his heroin needle, and his deck of cards. Unable to free himself from his slum environment, Frankie is finally driven to suicide." Reader's Ency. 4th edition

A walk on the wild side. Farrar, Straus & Cudahy 1956 346p o.p.

A novel about the residents of a slum street in New Orleans during the early years of the Depression

"Algren's vivid writing gives this degenerate cast the power to shock or appall, and if a glimmer of compassion leaks through occasionally it is slapped down before it gets out of hand." Libr J

Ali, Monica

Brick lane; a novel. Scribner 2003 369p $25
ISBN 0-7432-4330-7

* LC 2003-42795

"Nazeen, a young Bangladeshi woman, moves to London's Bangla Town (around the street of the title) in the mid-nineteen eighties after an arranged marriage with an older man. Seen through Nazeen's eyes, England is at first utterly baffling, but over the seventeen years of the

Ali, Monica—*Continued*
narrative (which takes us into the post-September 11th era), she gradually finds her way, bringing up two daughters and eventually starting an all-female tailoring business. . . . In Ali's subtle narration, Nazeen's mixture of traditionalism, and adaptability, of acceptence and restlessness, emerges as a quiet strength." New Yorker

In the kitchen; a novel. Scribner 2009 436p $25.99
ISBN 978-1-4165-7168-1; 1-4165-7168-X
LC 2009-01551
This is "the story of Gabriel Lightfoot, a 42-year-old executive chef at London's Imperial Hotel who aspires to open his own restaurant. The novel is set in motion with the death of a Ukrainian porter who's been living in the basement of the restaurant to save money. The incident forces Gabriel to consider his staff as individuals for the first time. It also leads him to question his own identity — and his profession." NPR
"Gabriel plans to serve "Classic French, a modern twist, cooked with precision" in his restaurant. Translated into literary terms, it's a fair description of what Ali herself dishes up in this rich, classically structured novel that tackles big social issues." San Francisco Chron

Allan, John B.
For works written by this author under other names see Stark, Richard; Westlake, Donald E.

Allen, Sarah Addison

The sugar queen. Bantam Books 2008 276p $22
ISBN 978-0-553-80549-9; 0-553-80549-5
LC 2007-48178
"At 27, Josey Cirrini is 'plain and just this side of plump' and trying to make up for her legendary childhood temper tantrums by caring for her aging, widowed mother Margaret. Her closet features neatly stacked junk food packages and romance novels, and her life chugs along. But as the book opens, Della Lee Baker, waitress at the local greasy spoon, shows up in Josey's closet, having propped a ladder against the house and climbed silently in overnight. She's hiding from someone or something, and has no intention of leaving anytime soon. Instead, the very direct Della Lee sends Josey on a series and missions and misadventures that encourage our low self-esteem heroine to step outside her box and away from her snack-filled closet." Publ Wkly
"Allen's characters are darling, and even the bad guys are charming and charismatic in this novel written as a modern-day fairy tale. In Allen's town of Bald Slope, magic lets books choose their owners and passion fry eggs in their carton. Best of all, it lets friends discover one another in the most mysterious ways." St. Petersburg Times

Allende, Isabel

Daughter of fortune; a novel; translated from the Spanish by Margaret Sayers Peden. HarperCollins Pubs. 1999 399p hardcover o.p. pa $7.99
ISBN 0-06-019491-X; 0-380-82101-X (pa)
LC 99-26021

Original Spanish edition, 1999
A "historical novel flavored by four cultures—English, Chilean, Chinese and American—and set during the 1849 California Gold Rush. The . . . tale begins in Valparaiso, Chile, with young Eliza Sommers, who was left as a baby on the doorstep of wealthy British importers Miss Rose Sommers and her prim brother, Jeremy. Now a 16 year-old, and newly pregnant, Eliza decides to follow her lover, fiery clerk Joaquin Andieta, when he leaves for California to make his fortune in the gold rush. Enlisting the unlikely aid of Tao Chi'en, a Chinese shipboard cook, she stows away on a ship bound for San Francisco." Publ Wkly
"This novel has pretensions, but they are overridden by Allende's riproaring girl's adventure story. . . . Throughout it all, Allende projects a woman's point of view with confidence, control and an expansive definition of romance as a fact of life." Time

Eva Luna; translated by Margaret Sayers Peden. Knopf 1988 271p hardcover o.p. pa $14
ISBN 0-394-57273-4; 0-553-38382-5 (pa)
* LC 88-45272
Original Spanish edition, 1987
This novel "gives us successive episodes in Eva's life, from illegitimate birth and orphanhood through drifting adolescence to relative stability and success, but also recounts in parallel the biography of Rolf Carle, from his wartime childhood in Austria to his emigration to Latin America, subsequent fame as a controversial documentary film-maker, and finally his encounter and love affair with Eva herself. A third narrative strand deals with the fortunes of Huberto Naranjo . . . guerrilla fighter and [Eva's] transient lover." Times Lit Suppl
This "wonderful novel, crammed with the strange and fantastical, the sensuous and the erotic, also speaks powerfully in the cause of freedom." Publ Wkly

The house of the spirits; translated from the Spanish by Magda Bogin. Knopf 1985 368p $29.95
ISBN 0-394-53907-9
* LC 84-48516
Original Spanish edition, 1982
This novel "tells the story of the Trueba family, with its deep loves and hates, following them from the turn of the century to the violent days of the overthrow of the Salvador Allende government in 1973." Christ Sci Monit
"The style is superbly controlled (and/or the translation is marvelously sensitive), balancing detail rich in associations with a deadpan humor that completely demystifies things that would be otherwise inexplicable. In other words, sentimentality never intrudes on the emotions you develop for these hopelessly well-meaning people and their equally errant children." Best Sellers

Portrait in sepia; translated from the Spanish by Margaret Sayers Peden. HarperCollins Pubs. 2001 304p
ISBN 0-06-621161-1
LC 00-54127
Sequel to Daughter of fortune
Original Spanish edition, 2000
The narrator of this novel "is a photographer named Aurora del Valle, who tells the story of her life as she reconstructs it with the help of old pictures and family gossip. She learns that her mother died during childbirth and that she was only 5 when sent to live with her pater-

Allende, Isabel—*Continued*

nal grandmother, one of many bigger-than-life women who would instill a sense of independence in her despite the inchoate feminism of 19th-century South America." N Y Times Book Rev

"Through Aurora, Allende exercises her supreme storytelling abilities, of which strong, passionate characters are paramount." Publ Wkly

Allingham, Margery, 1904-1966

Crime and Mr. Campion. Doubleday 1959 575p o.p.

"Published for the Crime Club"

An omnibus volume containing the complete texts of three mystery novels all starring the British detective Albert Campion. Death of a ghost (1934) is based on art forgery, Flowers for the judge (1936) is about the murder of a publisher and Dancers in mourning (1937) concerns a group of theatrical characters

Dancers in mourning
  In Allingham, M. Crime and Mr. Campion p363-575

Death of a ghost
  In Allingham, M. Crime and Mr. Campion p7-175

The fashion in shrouds
  In Allingham, M. Three cases for Mr. Campion p9-255

Flowers for the judge
  In Allingham, M. Crime and Mr. Campion p177-362

The Gyrth chalice mystery
  In Allingham, M. Three cases for Mr. Campion p421-604

Three cases for Mr. Campion. Doubleday 1961 604p o.p.

"Published for the Crime Club"

"The Gyrth chalice mystery" unravels Mr. Campion's solution to the secret in the locked room of Gyrth Tower; "The fashion in shrouds" involves the theft of dress designs, sixty cages of canaries, and blackmail, as Albert Campion investigates a three-year-old murder; "Traitor's purse" finds Albert Campion, an amnesia victim haunted by an urgency to do something of immense consequence before time runs out

Traitor's purse
  In Allingham, M. Three cases for Mr. Campion p257-420

Allison, Dorothy, 1949-

Bastard out of Carolina. Dutton 1992 309p hardcover o.p. pa $16

ISBN 0-525-93425-1; 0-452-28705-7 (pa)

* LC 91-34607

"Set in the rural South, this tale centers around the Boatwright family, a proud and closeknit clan known for their drinking, fighting, and womanizing. Nicknamed Bone by her Uncle Earle, Ruth Anne is the bastard child of Anney Boatwright, who has fought tirelessly to legitimize her child. When she marries Glen, a man from a good family, it appears that her prayers have been answered. However, Anney suffers a miscarriage and Glen begins drifting. He develops a contentious relationship with Bone and then begins taking sexual liberties with her. . . . Unaware of her husband's abusive behavior, Anney stands by her man. Eventually, a violent encounter wrests Bone away from her stepfather." Libr J

Altschul, Andrew Foster

Lady Lazarus. Harcourt 2008 561p $25

ISBN 978-0-15-101484-2; 0-15-101484-1

LC 2007-28550

"The center of this novel, Calliope Bird Morath, is a young poet. The daughter of a Kurt Cobain-like rock god and a minimally talented but outrageously self-promoting rock goddess, Calliope is destined for stardom. Then, when she is 4, her father kills himself in front of her. . . . Calliope is struck silent for years. When she begins to speak, it's in poetry." Sacramento News & Rev

"A sort of Gen X answer to Don DeLillo's boomer epic Underworld; it uses alt rock as a springboard to address all of the human condition." Minneapolis Star Tribune

Alvarez, Julia, 1950-

How the García girls lost their accents. Algonquin Bks. 1991 290p $18.95

ISBN 0-945575-57-2

* LC 90-48575

This novel "tells the story (in reverse chronological order) of four sisters and their family, as they become Americanized after fleeing the Dominican Republic in the 1960s. A family of privilege in the police state they leave, the Garcias experience understandable readjustment problems in the United States, particularly old world patriarch Papi. The sisters fare better but grow up conscious, like all immigrants, of living in two worlds." Libr J

"This is an account of parallel odysseys, as each of the four daughters adapts in her own way, and a large part of Alvarez's accomplishment is the complexity with which these vivid characters are rendered." Publ Wkly

Yo!. Algonquin Bks. 1997 309p $18.95

ISBN 1-56512-157-0

LC 96-24611

Sequel to How the Garcia girls lost their accents

"Yolanda Garcia's mother and sisters are furious at her for having plagiarized their lives in her all-too-celebrated novel. The balance of *this* novel is a rebuttal of sorts, narrated by her defenders. For everyone else who has come into contact with Yo and her storytelling prowess—from her repressed professor to her downtrodden landlady—life has changed for the better. These high-spirited accounts indulge the pleasing fantasy that we are the heroes not only of our own lives but of everyone else's as well." New Yorker

Amado, Jorge, 1912-2001

Dona Flor and her two husbands; a moral and amorous tale; translated from the Portuguese by Harriet de Onís. Knopf 1969 553p o.p.

*

Original Portuguese edition published 1966 in Brazil
"Dona Flor has such a harridan of a mother (Dona Rozilda) that you would like her to have her cake and eat it, too, and she very nearly does. Dona Flor's first husband, Vadinho, is a scamp, a prevaricator, and a 'shameless lover.' On Carnival Sunday, at the height of the gaiety, filled with rum, he drops dead. Dona Flor is desolate but cuts a handsome figure as a widow. She lives through the wake (a gem of a scene) and her mourning quite well, with memories and her cooking school to sustain her. Then suitors appear. None appeal but Dr. Teodoro Madureira, pharmacist and bassoonist, a pillar of propriety. Dona Rozilda is ecstatic, but the well-rounded Dona Flor has her troubles, for alas, Dr. Teodoro is no lover. Dreams haunt her and strange things begin to happen. Thanks to a Yoruba charm, Vadinho returns to ravish our bewildered heroine, and then the fun begins. Bahia in Brazil is the setting for this delectable rum cake of a novel." Publ Wkly

Gabriela, clove and cinnamon; translated from the Portuguese by James L. Taylor and William L. Grossman. Knopf 1962 425p o.p.
Original Portuguese edition published 1958 in Brazil
"Ilhéus, a Brazilian town near Bahia, is fortunate in the wealth it is realizing from its cacao crop. Money flows freely and is spent in cabarets, in bordellos, and on gambling during the period 1925-1926. . . . The removal of a sand bar blocking the harbor is the basis of this fascinating portrait of politics in a provincial Brazilian town. Amado also tells the love story of Nacib, the Arab owner of the most popular café in town, and Gabriela, a child of nature. Amoral rather than immoral, with skin the color of cinnamon and smelling of cloves, Gabriela gives her love readily and freely. Her skillful cooking makes her more valuable to Nacib as a mistress than as a wife. The atmosphere of this entertaining novel is lusty, sensual, and humorous." Shapiro. Fic for Youth. 3d edition

American fantastic tales: terror and the uncanny from Poe to the pulps; Peter Straub, editor. Library of America 746p $35
ISBN 978-1-59853-047-6   LC 2009-927073

Contents: Somnambulism: a fragment, by C. B. Brown; The adventure of the German student, by W. Irving; Berenice, by E. A. Poe; Young Goodman Brown, by N. Hawthorne; The tartarus of maids, by H. Melville; What was it?, by F.-J. O'Brien; The legend of Monte del Diablo, by B. Harte; The moonstone mass, by H. P. Spofford; His unconquerable enemy, by W. C. Morrow; In dark New England days, by S. O. Jewett; The yellow wall paper, by C. P. Gilman; The black dog, by S. Crane; Ma'ame Pélagie, by K. Chopin; Thurlow's Christmas story, by J. K. Bangs; The repairer of reputations, by R. W. Chambers; The dead valley, by R. A. Cram; The little room, by M. Y. Wynne; The striding place, by G. Atherton; An itinerant house, by E. F. Dawson; Luella Miller, by M. W. Freeman; Grettir at Thorhall-stead, by F. Norris; Yuki-Onna, by L. Hearn; For the blood is life, by F. M. Crawford; The moonlit road, by A. Bierce; Lukundoo, by E. L. White; The shell of sense, by O. H. Dunbar; The jolly corner, by H. James; Golden baby, by A. Brown; Afterward, by E. Wharton; Consequences, by W. Cather; The shadowy third, by E. Glasgow; Absolute evil, by J. Hawthorne; Unseen-unfeared, by F. Stevens; The curious case of Benjamin Button, by F. S. Fitzgerald; The curse of Everard Maundy, by S. Quinn; The king of the cats, by S. V. Benét; The jellyfish, by D. H. Keller; Mr. Arcularis, by C. Aiken; The black stone, by R. E. Howard; Passing of a god, by H. S. Whitehead; The panelled room, by A. Derleth; The thing on the doorstep, by H.P. Lovecraft; Genius Loci, by C. A. Smith; The cloak, by R. Bloch
"A valuable collection of excellent, often deeply disturbing stories." Kirkus

American fantastic tales: terror and the uncanny from the 1940s to now; Peter Straub, editor. Library of America 2009 713p $35
ISBN 978-1-59853-048-3   LC 2009-927074

Contents: Evening primrose, by J. Collier; Smoke ghost, by F. Leiber; The mysteries of the Joy Rio, by T. Williams; The refugee, by J. Rice; Mr. Lupescu, by A. Boucher; Miriam, by T. Capote; Midnight, by J. Snow; Torch Song, by J. Cheever; The daemon lover, by S. Jackson; The circular valley, by P. Bowles; I'm scared, by J. Finney; The Vane sisters, by V. Nabokov; The April witch, by R. Bradbury; Black country, by C. Beaumont; Trace, by J. Bixby; Where the woodbine twineth, by D. Grubb; Nightmare, by D. Wandrei; I have no mouth, and I must scream, by H. Ellison; Prey, by R. Matheson; The events at Poroth Farm, by T.E.D. Klein; Hanka, by I. B. Singer; Linnaeus forgets, by F. Chappell; Novelty, by J. Crowley; Mr. Fiddlehead, by J. Carroll; Family, by J. C. Oates; The last feast of Harlequin, by T. Ligotti; A short guide to the city, by P. Straub; The general who is dead, by J. VanderMeer; That feeling, you can only say what it is in French, by S. King; Sea Oak, by G. Saunders; The long hall on the top floor, by C. Kiernan; Nocturne, by T. Tessier; The God of Dark Laughter, by M. Chabon; Pop art, by J. Hill; Pansu, by P. Z. Brite; Dangerous laughter, by S. Millhauser; The chambered fruit, by M. Rickert; The wavering knife, by B. Evenson; Stone animals, by K. Link; Pat Moore, by T. Powers; The little stranger, by G. Wolfe; Dial tone, by B. Percy
This volume's "contents reflect confused and perturbed reactions to radical changes in people's daily lives and the larger world around them during periods of instability beginning around the time of World War II and extending into the dizzying technological changes of the past quarter-century. . . . A terrific, must-have collection." Kirkus

American West: twenty new stories from the Western Writers of America; edited with an introduction by Loren D. Estleman. Forge 2001 367p $25.95
ISBN 0-312-87317-4   LC 00-48446

"A Tom Doherty Associates book"
This collection of stories about the West includes works by Don Coldsmith, Jory Sherman, Elmer Kelton,

American West: twenty new stories from the Western Writers of America—*Continued*

Richard S. Wheeler, Johnny D. Boggs, and Max Evans

"Uniformly fine writing makes this a welcome addition to any western collection." Booklist

Amidon, Stephen

Security. Farrar, Straus and Giroux 2009 276p $25

ISBN 978-0-374-25711-8; 0-374-25711-6

LC 2008-13850

"Stoneleigh is the 'nuclear-free, dolphin-safe' New England town where Edward Inman outfits the homes of skittish yuppies with motion sensors, panic rooms and CCTV. Doyle Cutler is one of his clients—a wealthy man with a seedy mien, an aversion to shaking hands and a recessive chin (always a bad sign.) These men, respectively, are hero and villain of [the novel] . . . . The book is part campus tale, part mystery, part police procedural. The proportions are well mixed. Stoneleigh's customary tranquility is stirred when Mary Steckl, a local college student, accuses Doyle Cutler of sexually assaulting her. Cutler rebounds with an accusation that Mary's father, a drunk with a criminal record, is the real perp. The town is divided. . . . For all its plot twists, Security is a book stitched of sensible prose. There are no flourishes, no embroidery." N Y Observer

Amirrezvani, Anita

The blood of flowers; a novel. Little, Brown and Co. 2007 377p $23.99; pa $13.99

ISBN 978-0-316-06576-4; 0-316-06576-5; 978-0-316-06577-1 (pa); 0-316-06577-3 (pa)

LC 2006-23034

This novel is "narrated by a nameless teenager whose life in 17th-century Iran is derailed by misfortune following her father's death. With no means of support, she and her mother move to the city of Isfahan to live as servants with relatives. There, despite the obstacle of gender, the young woman learns the art of carpet design. An even greater hurdle is her poverty; dowryless, she is pressured into a sigheh, or temporary marriage, in which the woman offers sexual favors in return for money." Libr J

The author "has crafted a lush and sensuous story, where betrayal is common, wealth is unequally distributed, and temporary marriages allow prosperous men to take advantage of impoverished virgins without the burden of a full-time wife. . . . Though the trajectory of this novel seemed sure to lead toward a full marriage in a society where this is expected, Amirrezvani provides more than that: a wonderful man might exist in fairytales, but a woman can be self-sufficient and happy without him." PopMatters

Amis, Kingsley, 1922-1995

Lucky Jim; a novel. Doubleday 1954 c1953 256p o.p.

First published 1953 in the United Kingdom

"The title is ironic, since the story is about the comic misfortunes of Jim Dixon, a young lower-middle-class instructor at an English university. The book satirizes the academic 'racket' and cultural pretensions." Reader's Ency. 4th edition

The Russian girl. Viking 1994 c1992 296p

ISBN 0-670-85329-1

First published 1992 in the United Kingdom

"Dr. Richard Vaisey is an esteemed scholar at the London Institute of Slavonic Studies whose wife, Cordelia, has perfected the art of manipulation. When Anna Danilova, an obscure Russian poet, asks his help in freeing her brother from a Russian jail by making her 'famous' and thus calling world attention to the brother's plight, Richard finds himself torn between his growing passion for her and his outright dislike of her poetry. Realizing what is going on between her husband and 'the Russian girl,' Cordelia, plots revenge." Libr J

"What makes 'The Russian Girl' such a jolly good read is precisely {its} scathing level of insight, to say nothing of Amis's dazzling virtuosity with the old bons mots. They litter the floor. He also manages to be very, very funny, even when he's being very, very serious." NY Times Book Rev

Amis, Martin

House of meetings. Alfred A. Knopf 2007 256p $23

ISBN 1-400-04455-3

LC 2006-47397

First published 2006 in the United Kingdom

"There were conjugal visits in the slave camps of the USSR. Valiant women would travel continental distances, over weeks and months, in the hope of spending a night, with their particular enemy of the people, in the House of Meetings. The consequences of these liaisons were almost invariably tragic. [This novel] is about one such liaison. It is a triangular romance: two brothers fall in love with the same girl, a nineteen-year-old Jewess, in Moscow, which is poised for pogrom in the gap between the war and the death of Stalin. Both brothers are arrested, and their rivalry slowly complicates itself over a decade in the slave camp above the Arctic Circle." Publisher's note

"In previous novels Amis has been something of a meta-fictioneer, but the outstanding virtue of House of Meetings is its traditional psychological realism. Its themes of the camps, the misery, the overwhelming sense of sin, and the presentation of Russia as an emblem of human fate all recall Dostoyevsky, and, like Dostoyevsky, Amis fails to offer any answer to the question of human evil that the book raises." New Yorker

London fields. Harmony Bks. 1989 470p

ISBN 0-517-57718-6

* LC 89-49558

This novel, set in 1999 London, follows the exploits of Nicola Six, who has the "knack of knowing what will happen next, and what is going to happen on the morning of November the Sixth—her thirty-fifth birthday—is her own murder. One day she walks into a pub where the palely loitering aristocrat Guy Clinch and the {drunken} tabloid dartsman Keith Talent are separately drinking (as is our narrator, a terminally ill American) and recognizes her future murderer. For the rest of the book she manipulates Guy (through a parody of love) and Keith (through a parody of sex) to bring about the end she requires." Times Lit Suppl

"Amis's technical virtuosity is extraordinary. . . . {This is} the most intellectually interesting fiction of the year, and a work beyond the reach of any British con-

Amis, Martin—*Continued*

temporary. Amis's figures, like those of Dickens, are caricatures that have their own gigantic reality." London Rev Books

Time's arrow; or, The nature of the offense. Harmony Bks. 1991 168p
    ISBN 0-517-58515-4   LC 91-4144
This novel "shoots us into the past as it reveals the true identity of a man called Tod Friendly. As Tod lies in a hospital bed, his consciousness distances itself from the present and assesses his life in reverse, like a film run backwards. Every action is reversed and every conversation inverted. This voice, this estranged soul, watches Tod create food and beverages at meals, get paid for bringing items into stores, and grow younger. As his American identity is stripped away, his hideous past as a German doctor and executioner at a Nazi extermination camp is revealed." Booklist

"With Time's Arrow, Amis takes another look at our diseased world. This time he pares the story down to essentials. Though his writing is as fizzy as ever, it doesn't call attention to itself. His artfully contrived structure serves a purpose: to present the horror in a way so unfamiliar it can't be anesthetized." Voice Lit Suppl

Anatoli, A., 1929-1979

Babi Yar; a document in the form of a novel; {by} A. Anatoli (Kuznetsov). Translated by David Floyd. Farrar, Straus & Giroux 1970 477p
    ISBN 0-374-10761-0
Original Russian edition published 1966 in censored form under author's former name A. Kuznetsov; English translation by Jacob Guralsky of this version published 1967 by Dial Press
A documentary novel about the period from 1941 to 1943 in which the Germans systematically murdered some 2,000,000 people, including 50,000 Jews, at the ravine on the outskirts of Kiev known as Babi Yar. The author, who was twelve years old at the time, based his work on interviews, newspaper clippings, diaries and other documents

Anaya, Rudolfo A.

The man who could fly and other stories. University of Oklahoma Press 2006 197p (Chicana & Chicano visions of the Américas) $19.95
    ISBN 0-8061-3738-X   LC 2005-51426
Contents: Thr road to Platero; Children of the desert; The village that the gods painted yellow; A story; The silence of the llano; The place of the swallows; The apple orchard; B. Traven is alive and well in Cuernavaca; Jerónimo's journey; Iliana of the pleasure dreams; Devil deer; The man who found a pistol; Message from the Inca; Absalom; The captain; In search of Epifano; Dead end; The man who could fly
"The stories showcase 30 years of Anaya's Chicano literary voice, simultaneously innocent and omniscient and always rooted in the landscape, especially the windswept llanos of New Mexico. . . . The characters' passionate force radiates from Anaya's simple prose as they confront ethical dilemmas in varied regional settings." Libr J

Andersen Nexø, Martin, 1869-1954

Pelle the conqueror: v1 Childhood; translated from the Danish by Steven T. Murray; edited and with an afterword by Tiina Nunnally. Fjord Press 1989 244p o.p.   LC 89-7837
"The first of a four-volume Danish classic follows the fortunes of Lasse Karlsson, an impoverished, aging Swede, and his young son, Pelle. Attracted by legendary prosperity . . . they migrate to Denmark in the late 19th century." Publ Wkly
"Andersen Nexo, who was born in the slums of Copenhagen, ultimately developed Pelle into a proletarian epic hero. In this first, largely autobiographical volume, however, there's scant evidence of his strict social realism. Rather, Andersen Nexo's robust sense of life, his convincing evocation of childhood, his moral vision—and, above all, his brave young hero—make this novel generous and grand." N Y Times Book Rev

Pelle the conqueror: v2 Apprenticeship; translated from the Danish by Steven T. Murray & Tiina Nunnally; with an afterword by Niels Ingwersen. Fjord Press 1991 224p o.p.
In this volume "Pelle begins the journey the European proletariat undertook when the modern capitalistic society was formed; he goes from rural misery and poverty to the same or worse in an urban setting. As a shoemaker's apprentice in the nearest town, he retains some ties with the past but grows into adolescence in a milieu of different values and new people, establishing solidarity with the poorest. . . . With his faults and virtues, endurance and optimism, Pelle is one of literature's most charming heroes." Libr J

Anderson, Alison

(tr) Barbery, M. The elegance of the hedgehog

Darwin's wink; a novel of nature and love. Thomas Dunne Books/St. Martin's Press 2004 288p $23.95
    ISBN 0-312-33199-1   LC 2004-17763
"Christian, a disenchanted, 30-something Swiss man haunted by his experiences as a Red Cross worker in Bosnia, comes to Egret Island, . . . off the coast of Mauritius, to work for Fran, a middle-aged, outwardly brusque American naturalist seeking to restore the island to its original, untouched state and the endangered mourner-bird to its previous strength. Like Christian, who left behind a pregnant lover, Fran has also loved and lost; she tries to confine herself to a cerebral approach to work and life, blunting her sexual frissons and painful flashbacks through Darwinian logic. . . . Readers will find the plot distantly secondary to the novel's rich emotional palette, as Anderson captures the expansive beauty of Mauritius and the nuances of human character with languid, sensual and occasionally violet prose." Publ Wkly

Anderson, Edward, 1905-1969

Thieves like us
    In Crime novels: American noir of the 1930s and 40s

Anderson, Kevin J., 1962-

(jt. auth) Herbert, B. Dune: House Atreides

(jt. auth) Herbert, B. Dune: House Corrino

(jt. auth) Herbert, B. Dune: House Harkonnen

(jt. auth) Herbert, B. Dune: The Butlerian jihad

(jt. auth) Herbert, B. Paul of Dune

(jt. auth) Van Vogt, A. E. Slan hunter

Anderson, Poul, 1926-2001

Genesis. TOR Bks. 2000 253p

ISBN 0-312-86707-7   LC 99-58829

"A Tom Doherty Associates book"

"Christian Brannock agrees to have his personality uploaded into a computer so that his mind can explore the stars long after the death of his body. When his billion-year journey brings him back to an Earth that has undergone many cosmic changes, Brannock encounters another uploaded personality who restores to him the wonder of being 'human.' The lyrical approach of this sf master to the meaning of human existence gives his latest effort a surreal, allegorical feel." Libr J

Goat song

In The Hugo winners p330-64

Hunter's moon

In The Hugo winners p510-50

The longest voyage

In The Hugo winners p279-310

The Queen of Air and Darkness

In The Hugo winners p143-90

The Saturn game

In The Hugo winners p269-325

The sharing of flesh

In The Hugo winners p558-94

War of the Gods. TOR Bks. 1997 304p

ISBN 0-312-86315-2   LC 97-19383

"In this historical fantasy about the little-known Viking king Hadding, Anderson . . . fleshes out extant Norse literature to create an epic tale of a young man raised in secret by giants after his parents are killed. The heir to the Danish throne grows up and gathers armies to support his effort to reclaim his kingdom." Libr J

"Anderson writes with a spare style, often relying on the alliterative, rhythmic prose of Scandinavian folklore, giving this epic tale an original spirit and tone. Readers bored with Tolkien-clone fantasies will be enthralled by the intricately detailed world and characters Anderson brings to life here." Publ Wkly

Anderson, Sherwood, 1876-1941

Winesburg, Ohio. Modern Lib. 1995 231p

ISBN 0-679-60146-5

          * LC 94-23229

A reissue of the title first published 1919 by B.W. Huebsch

"A series of twenty-three vignettes, *Winesburg, Ohio* is a character study of a small town. It highlights individual residents and scrutinizes who they are and why this reality often conflicts with their dreams. The short stories are

linked through George Willard, a young newspaper reporter who is disenchanted with the narrow-mindedness of small towns." Shapiro. Fic for Youth. 3d edition

Anderson-Dargatz, Gail, 1963-

A recipe for bees. Harmony Bks. 2000 305p

ISBN 0-609-60451-1   LC 99-25269

First published 1999 in the United Kingdom

"Having lost her mother at 14, Augusta was no stranger to hardship when she married at 18. Still, life with the much-older Karl and his miserly father on a remote {Canadian} farm that had not seen a woman's touch in decades was initially almost too much to bear. But, finally, after she had found tenderness with another man and borne his child, Augusta was able to lure Karl from his father to a farm of their own. There, Augusta started keeping bees to earn a little extra money and began to find some sweetness in her marriage." Libr J

"Augusta is a headstrong heroine with prismatic perspectives; her long, never-dull life as told by the gifted Anderson-Dargatz is both charming and impressive in its quiet, cumulative power." Publ Wkly

Andrews, Cecily Isabel Fairfield *See* West, Dame Rebecca, 1892-1983

Andrews, Chris

(tr) Bolaño, R. Last evenings on Earth

(tr) Bolaño, R. Nazi literature in the Americas

(tr) Bolaño, R. The skating rink

Andrews, Colin *See* Wilson, F. Paul (Francis Paul)

Andrews, Mary Kay, 1954-

Every crooked nanny. HarperCollins Pubs. 1992 286p

ISBN 0-06-017923-6   LC 91-58359

This novel introduces "J. Callahan Garrity, a former cop and failed gumshoe who now runs a cleaning service in Atlanta, Ga. While cleaning the home of snooty society lady Lilah Rose Beemish, Callahan is hired to trace Kristee, the family's Mormon nanny, who has absconded with furs, jewels and, Callahan learns, incriminating business secrets gleaned from Lilah's husband Bo during their affair." Publ Wkly

"This quick-paced thriller provides an intriguing introduction to a delightfully down-to-earth sleuth." Booklist

Irish eyes; a Callahan Garrity mystery. HarperCollins Pubs. 2000 296p $24

ISBN 0-06-019421-9   LC 99-55680

"Former Atlanta cop Garrity returns to crime solving when her ex-partner, Bucky Deavers, is shot on the way home from a party he finagled her into attending at the Shamrock Society. With the help of the eccentric staff of her housecleaning business, Garrity vows to get to the bottom of the shooting. This is an entertaining, suspenseful romp." Booklist

Andrézel, Pierre, 1885-1962

For works written by this author under other names see Dinesen, Isak, 1885-1962

Angell, Roger

(ed) Nothing but you. See Nothing but you

Ansa, Tina McElroy, 1949-

The hand I fan with. Doubleday 1996 462p
ISBN 0-385-47601-9   LC 96-6256
Sequel to Baby in the family (1989)
This novel is set in Mulberry, a small central Georgia town, where Lena McPherson, "a single, 40-ish African American, is regarded with awe. Vested with psychic powers as a result of being born with a caul, Lena enjoys 'an abundance of blessings' (good real estate investments, a beautiful house, prestige cars, designer clothes). . . . Within days of conducting a ritual to bring a man into her life, Lena is knocked down by an invisible force while inspecting one of her properties." Publ Wkly

"Ansa writes believably of the spirit world; on the other hand, her inventories of Lena's many material possessions can be overlong and jarring. Yet a strong sense of place and an engagingly eccentric cast of characters keep the narrative moving—and ultimately bring Lena's two worlds together." N Y Times Book Rev

Ansay, A. Manette, 1964-

River angel. Morrow 1998 243p
ISBN 0-688-15243-0   LC 97-31006
"A rural legend—of an angel watching over a river—provides the framework for this . . . novel about faith and its power to transform individuals and a community. When odd, overweight Gabriel Carpenter comes to Ambient, Wisconsin, he's taunted by other children and instantly disliked by his fifth-grade teacher. One night, teenagers, drinking and up to no good, take Gabriel to the bridge, where he somehow jumps, slips, or is pushed into the river; then his body is found, warm and fragrant, lying in a distant barn, presumably delivered there by the river angel. The legend is reborn, the barn becomes a shrine, and a small town struggling with progress is given new life." Booklist

"With 'River Angel,' A. Manette Ansay has moved beyond her prior mastery of the family scene to a lucid, eloquent representation of the commingled and conflicting lives of a town." N Y Times Book Rev

Anthony, Evelyn, 1928-

The Janus imperative. Coward, McCann & Geoghegan 1980 275p
ISBN 0-698-11016-1   LC 79-20768
"Political journalist Max Steiner is interviewing a German politician in Paris when the man is assassinated. His dying word is 'Janus.' As a Hitler Youth 25 years earlier, Steiner had heard another dying man utter the same word in Hitler's Berlin bunker in 1945. He persuades his boss to let him do an in-depth story on the assassination and hurries to Germany to dig into Bunker archives for connections between the two Januses. But as he starts interviewing survivors, a terrorist group is proceeding to murder the same survivors. German intelligence and the CIA become involved, and Steiner's quest ends in a convent in Munich, where some unholy violence takes place." Publ Wkly

This novel has "strong, believable characters, clear prose and good description." West Coast Rev Books

Anthony, Piers

Split infinity. Ballantine Bks. 1980 372p il (Apprentice Adept)
ISBN 0-345-28645-6   LC 79-20282
"A Del Rey book"
In this first volume of the author's Apprentice Adept series "Stile, the principal character . . . takes his turns between two parallel worlds. His home world of Proton is a strictly regulated mechanized society where wealthy Citizens own serfs who work and compete for them in the Games. These Games are a central feature of the novel and range from tiddlywinks to marathon racing. The fantasy land of Phaze is an organic world into which he escapes to avoid a mysterious killer. There he meets a unicorn, . . . who changes into a woman, and a man who changes into a werewolf, among others. Here he discovers that he can cast magic spells and sets out to find his alter ego." Voice Youth Advocates

Followed by: Blue Adept (1981); Juxtaposition (1982); Out of phaze (1987); Robot Adept (1988); Unicorn point (1989); Phaze doubt (1990)

Virtual mode. 1991 304p (Mode)
ISBN 0-399-13661-4   LC 90-42919
"An Ace/Putnam book"
In this first volume of the author's Mode series "Darius, a Cyng of Hlahtar, had traveled to earth in order to meet his true love, a suicidal teen named Colene, and bring her back to his universe. But in proving to her that other worlds exist, Darius uses up the power of the artifact that would have permitted them to travel, and they must try a slower, more dangerous method: the creation of a four-dimensional universe." Publ Wkly

"Anthony's 'realism' manages to avoid sleaze, and the lighter parts of the narrative, while indeed light, are seldom frivolous. In addition, Anthony's pacing and world building are up to standard." Booklist

Followed by: Fractal mode (1992); Chaos mode (1993); DoOon mode (2001)

Antunes, António Lobo, 1942-

The inquisitors' manual; translated by Richard Zenith. Grove Press 2003 435p $25
ISBN 0-8021-1732-5   LC 2002-33858
Original Portuguese edition, 1997
"Antonio de Oliveira Salazar is not the best known of 20th-century dictators, but he was as cruel and ruthless as any of them in his rule over Portugal from 1932 to 1968 . . . . [The author] recreates the harrowing story of Salazar's regime, building gradually from the petty problems and thoughts of a host of characters, related in stream of consciousness, to blunt exposition of the inhuman inner workings and brutal violence of authoritarianism." Publ Wkly

"Lobo Antunes, one of the most skillfull psychological portraitists writing anywhere, renders the turpitude of an entire society through an impasto of intensely individual voices." New Yorker

Appelfeld, Aharon *See* Appelfeld, Aron

Appelfeld, Aron

Badenheim 1939; [by] Aharon Appelfeld; translated by Dalya Bilu. Godine 1980 148p

ISBN 0-879-23342-7

* LC 80-66192

Originally published in Hebrew

"Year after year the regular summer guests, most of them comfortably wealthy middle-class Jews, come to the little resort town Badenheim near Vienna to be entertained, to eat strawberry tarts, to find love. Even in 1939, with the Nazis firmly ensconced in Vienna, no one is allowed to worry, and the few who do are declared mad. In the end, Badenheim is closed off; all its people—guests, musicians, pastry chefs, even the dogs and goldfish of the town—are packed into cattle cars. Still the people delude themselves into thinking that they are going 'home,' back to their origins in Poland, and anyone who doubts this is argued down. The novel ends with the closing of the cattle cars' sliding doors." Libr J

"The most shocking thing about this novel is not its satirical humor, but its charm. Appelfeld manages to treat his appalling theme with grace." N Y Rev Books

Apple, Max

The Jew of Home Depot and other stories. Johns Hopkins University Press 2007 170p $19.95

ISBN 978-0-8018-8738-3; 0-8018-8738-0

LC 2007-18864

Contents: Yao's chick; Indian giver; Proton decay; Stabbing the elephant; Peace; Stepdaughters; Sized up; Threads; House of the lowered; Strawberry shortcake; Adventures in dementia; Talker; The Jew of Home Depot

"Comic movies don't often get Oscar nods. In fiction, too, tragedy wears the capital L for Literature, whereas comedy—good luck, happy endings, pleasure itself—is deemed to be the fluffy stuff of chick lit and beach books. With The Jew of Home Depot, his first collection of stories in two decades, Max Apple challenges the canard that misery reveals more about our identity than joy does. . . . The 13 delightful, utterly cynicism-free stories collected here are mostly tales of courtship, and as the title not so shyly suggests, they often star Jews." Washington Post Book World

Archer, Jeffrey, 1940-

As the crow flies. HarperCollins 1991 617p

ISBN 0-06-017914-7

LC 90-56105

This novel "tells the story of a poor barrow boy or street peddler, Charlie Trumper, born in the year 1900 in the slums of London's Whitechapel district. Charlie . . . rises to become the founder of Britain's first and most prestigious department store, {and} a member of the peerage." N Y Times Book Rev

This novel has the "usual Archer signature: fast-moving plot, romance, high finance, and good natured mockery of Britain. It uses the conventions of the classic revenge tale, featuring a feud that continues through two generations and the stock characters of the genre: the resourceful hero, the clever childhood sweetheart, the bastard son, the nefarious mother. . . . Archer knows what fast-reading light fiction is all about and dishes it up with panache." Quill Quire

A matter of honor. Linden Press 1986 399p

ISBN 0-671-62434-2

LC 86-7405

"Adam Scott is left a most unorthodox bequest in his father's will that takes him on a terrifying chase across Europe pursuing a priceless icon and being pursued by Soviet, American, and British intelligence forces. Archer cagily impels his well-crafted characters straight into action, then ever so slowly fills in all the dimensions of the struggle in which they are engaged. . . . Scott's steely determination to uphold his family's honor holds the reader's interest, and his skill at eluding the enemy culminates in a master stratagem that gives the story its final twist. A fast-paced and exciting, though corpse-riddled, thriller." Booklist

Arends, Marthe *See* MacAlister, Katie

Armstrong, Kelley

Bitten. Viking 2001 342p

ISBN 978-0-670-89471-0

LC 00-68590

This is the first title in the author's Women of the Otherworld series. "Elena Michaels is a self-described 'mutt,' a werewolf who left her secretive pack in upstate New York for a life among humans. In the year since she relocated to Toronto, she's embarked on a career as a journalist and begun a pleasingly mundane relationship with a decent man. All this is jeopardized when she agrees to help her old packmates hunt some troublesome mutts who are converting common criminals to werewolves and leaving a trail of conspicuous carnage. . . . Filled with romance and supernatural intrigue, this book will surely remind readers of Anne Rice's sophisticated refurbishings of the vampire story." Publ Wkly

Followed by: Stolen (2002); Dime store magic (2004); Industrial magic (2004); Haunted (2005); Broken (2006); No humans involved (2007); Personal demon (2008); Living with the dead (2008); Frostbitten (2009)

Arnaldur Indriðason, 1961-

The draining lake; translated from the Icelandic by Bernard Scudder. Thomas Dunne Books 2008 312p $24.95

ISBN 978-0-312-35873-0; 0-312-35873-3

LC 2008-21257

Original Icelandic edition, 2004

In this entry in the crime series starring detective Erlendur Sveinsson, "a human skeleton surfaces in the bed of a lake near Reykjavik that's been mysteriously draining away. The bones are tied to some kind of Russian listening device, presumably a remnant of the Cold War. As Erlendur and his colleagues, Elinborg and Sigurdur Oli, go about checking on people who went missing around 1970, Erlendur is reminded of the disappearance of his younger brother when they were children." Publ Wkly

"Indridason keeps readers guessing as to the identities of the snitch and the skeleton until the very last pages of this moody investigation into the fatal follies of youth, politics and memory. By novel's end, fittingly, the lake waters begin to rise again, obscuring all." Washington Post Book World

Arnow, Harriette Louisa Simpson, 1908-1986

The dollmaker; [by] Harriette Simpson Arnow. Macmillan 1954 549p o.p.

"Gertie Nevels, a courageous and unselfish Kentucky countrywoman who has a talent amounting to a passion for whittling small objects out of wood, is forced by the war to leave the happy, although poverty-stricken, community where she has spent her life and go to Detroit, where her husband has found work in a factory. The meanness, squalor, and lack of privacy of her new surroundings, and the debasing effect of the city on her husband and on some of their children, oppress her, but she maintains her integrity and her fatih in her fellow human beings." New Yorker

"It is hard to believe that anyone who opens its pages will soon forget [Gertie] and her sufferings as traced in Harriette Arnow's long, heavily packed masterwork." NY Times Book Rev

Arouet, François Marie *See* Voltaire, 1694-1778

The **Art** of the story; an international anthology of contemporary short stories. Viking 1999 667p

ISBN 0-670-88761-7   LC 99-13816

Contents: A gift from somewhere, by A. A. Aidoo; The keeper of the virgins, by H. Al-Shaykh; Amor divino, by J. Alvarez; The immortals, by M. Amis; The glass tower, by R. Arenas; Wilderness tips, by M. Atwood; Gorilla, my love, by T. C. Bambara; My mother's memoirs, my father's lie, and other true stories, by R. Banks; G-string, by N. Barker; Evermore, by J. Barnes; Aren't you happy for me? by R. Bausch; In Amalfi, by A. Beattie; Rara avis, by T. C. Boyle; Mr. Green, by R. O. Butler; The fat man in history, by P. Carey; The courtship of Mr. Lyon, by A. Carter; Are these actual miles? by R. Carver; The old man slave and the mastiff, by P. Chamoiseau; Dharma, by V. Chandra; Never marry a Mexican, by S. Cisneros; The prospect from the silver hills, by J. Crace; Night women, by E. Danticat; The house behind, by L. Davis; All because of the mistake, by D. del Giudice; Ysrael, by J. Diaz; Betrayal, by P. Duncker; Reflections of spring, by Thu Huong Duong; The girl who left her sock on the floor, by D. Eisenberg; The twenty-seventh man, N. Englander; The parakeet, by V. Erofeyev; Roberto narrates, by P. Esterházy; My father, the Englishman, and I, by N. Farah; Optimists, by R. Ford; The story of the lizard who had the habit of dining on his wives, by E. Galeano; The Hammam, by H. Guibert; Escort, by A. Gurnah; Midnight and I'm not famous yet, by B. Hannah; Portrait of the avant-garde, by P. Høeg; Moving house, by P. Huelle; A family supper, by K. Ishiguro; Encounter, by R. Jacobsen; The first day, by E. P. Jones; Remember young Cecil, by J. Kelman; Intimacy, by H. Kureishi; The stump-grubber, by T. Lindgren; Wish, by B. A. Mason; Everything in this country must, by C. McCann; Pornography, by I. McEwan; Behind the blue curtain, by S. Millhauser; Willing, by L. Moore; The lifeguard, by M. Morris; The canebrake, by M. Mrabet; The management of grief, by B. Mukherjee; Muradhan and Selvihan; or, the tale of the crystal kiosk, by M. Mungan; The elephant vanishes, by H. Murakami; Mark of Satan, by J. C. Oates; In the shadow of war, by B. Okri; Where the

Jackals howl, by A. Oz; The life and adventures of Shed Number XII, by V. Pelevin; Talking dog, by F. Prose; The free radio, by S. Rushdie; Africa kills her sun, by K. Saro-Wiwa; The ring, by I. Schulze; Learning to swim, by G. Swift; A riddle, by A. Tabucchi; Minutes of glory, by Ngugi wa Thiong'o; On the golden porch, by T. Tolstaya; John-Jin, by R. Tremain; Who, me a bum? by L. Valenzuela; Cinnamon skin, by E. White; You can't get lost in Cape Town, by Z. Wicomb; Doc's story, by J. E. Wideman; The farm, by J. Williams; Dirt angel, by J. Wilmot; The green man, by J. Winterson; The night in question, by T. Wolff; The child who raised poisonous snakes, by Ts'an-hsüeh; Helix, by B. Yoshimoto

Asaro, Catherine, 1955-

Primary inversion. Tor 1995 317p

ISBN 0-312-85764-0   LC 94-47207

"A Tom Doherty Associates book"

"In a distant future where three empires battle for control of the galaxy, Sauscony Valdoria, the heir apparent of the Skolian Empire, finds herself inexplicably attracted to Jaibriol Qox, the son of the Emperor of Tarnth and the symbol of everything Sauscony has been taught to despise. Asaro's sf debut features strong male and female protagonists and a well-realized far-future world. Blending hard science with a familiar tale of star-crossed lovers." Libr J

Asch, Sholem, 1880-1957

The Apostle; translated by Maurice Samuel. Putnam 1943 804p o.p.

"Around the life of St. Paul the author has built a picture of the early spread of Christianity. The novel opens soon after the crucifixion when Paul with others in Jerusalem became aware of the disciples' preachings, and it follows Paul to his death. Religious and social conditions important in the development of Christianity are portrayed, but Paul's work is always the dominant theme." Booklist

In "'The Apostle,' Sholem Asch has written a book which should stand beside 'The Nazarene.' Its erudition, its essential reverence for the two faiths concerned, its scholarly and dramatic portrayal of the Jew who spread the gospel to the gentiles will call forth the respect of every civilized and intelligent reader." N Y Her Trib Books

The Nazarene; translated by Maurice Samuel. Putnam 1939 698p o.p.

A novel based on the life of Christ told from three different points of view. First there is the narrative as a modern Polish Jewish scholar hears it from lips of one who claims to be the reincarnation of the Roman military governor of Jerusalem. Then there is the 'fifth gospel' written by Judas Iscariot, and finally there is the story as the young Jew remembers it when he realizes that he himself is the reincarnation of a disciple of the Pharisee, Rabbi Nicodemon

"Judged purely as a novel, The Nazarene is a superb achievement. Even on the factual side, a work such as Papini's Life is thin beside it. This is because Mr. Asch has taken an infinite amount of trouble to build up an historical background against which the figure of Jesus may move authentically, with that sense of reality which we should expect of fiction as of life." Atlantic

Asimov, Isaac, 1920-1992

The Bicentennial Man
In The Hugo winners p259-99

The caves of steel
In Asimov, I. The rest of the robots p165-362

The complete stories. Doubleday 1990-1992 2v
v1 pa $19.95; v2 o.p.
ISBN 0-385-41627-X; (v1 pa)   LC 90-3136
"A Foundation book"
Contents: v1 The dead past; Franchise; Gimmicks
three; Kid stuff; The watery place; Living space; The
message; Satisfaction guaranteed; Hell-fire; The last
trump; The fun they had; Jokester; The Immortal Bard;
Someday; Dreaming is a private thing; Profession; The
feeling of power; The dying night; I'm in Marsport without Hilda; The gentle vultures; All the troubles of the
world; Spell my name with an S; The last question; The
ugly little boy; Nightfall; Green patches; Hostess;
"Breeds there a man . . . ?"; C-Chute; "In a good
cause—"; What if—; Sally; Flies; "Nobody here but—";
It's such a beautiful day; Insert knob A in
hole B; The up-to-date sorcerer; Unto the fourth generation; What is this thing called love?; The machine that
won the war; My son, the physicist; Eyes do more than
see; Segregationist
This set contains all of Asimov's science fiction stories
including the "collections 'Earth Is Room Enough' and
'Nine Tomorrows' from the 1950s as well as . . .
'Nightfall and Other Stories.'" SLJ

Forward the Foundation. Doubleday 1993 415p
(Foundation)
ISBN 0-385-24793-1
                                    * LC 92-46655
"A Foundation book"
This volume and Prelude to Foundation predate the
other Foundation novels in terms of internal chronology
"As a galactic empire struggles to hold onto the million worlds it purports to rule, one man conceives of an
idea that will preserve human knowledge during the dark
ages that will follow the empire's inevitable fall. The
man is Hari Seldon. His idea: psychohistory." Libr J
Although "Asimov leans rather heavily on dialogue to
carry the story, we are privileged to learn something
more of Seldon, whom Asimov regards as his alter
ego—intellectually vigorous, witty, vulnerable, and deeply concerned about the fate of his fallible species." Christ
Sci Monit

Foundation. Gnome Press 1951 255p
(Foundation) o.p.
                                    *
"A story of a Galactic Empire of the future, and its
successor in the government of the Milky Way." Publ
Wkly
Followed by Foundation and empire

Foundation and earth. Doubleday 1986 356p
(Foundation)
ISBN 0-385-23312-4
                                    * LC 86-2130
In the fifth novel of the Foundation series "Golan
Trevize rejects the vaunted Selden Plan of Foundation
and Empire in favor of a bold experiment in galactic uni-
ty. To ferret out the reason for his instinctive decision,

Trevize embarks on a journey through uncharted space in
search of a legendary planet known as Earth. Asimov's
latest entry in his epic series features his usual cast of intelligent, likeable characters and just enough action to
give substance to this novel of lucid speculations." Libr
J

Foundation and empire. Gnome Press 1952 247p
(Foundation) o.p.
                                    *
In this second volume of the Foundation series "two
groups struggle for control of the world's destiny in a fu-
ture time when mankind has settled in the Milky Way.
Then a mutant appears bringing with him a new threat
for everyone." Chicago Public Libr
Followed by Second Foundation

Foundation's edge. Doubleday 1982 366p
(Foundation)
ISBN 0-385-17725-9
                                    *
The fourth novel in the Foundation series "shows us
the Seldon Plan at midpoint and still surprisingly on tar-
get in spite of the passage of time and unforeseen events.
The focus has narrowed to power struggles between the
Foundations, both wishing to be the controlling element
in the planned Second Galactic Empire, quite unlike
Seldon's idealistic vision. And new players have been in-
troduced into the game." Libr J
Followed by Foundation and earth

The gods themselves. Doubleday 1972 288p o.p.
"A three-level tale of the 21st century. The first level
is told from the point of view of the Earth Scientists who
are receiving mysterious messages from the para-
Universe that matches Earth's in some unfathomable
realm of time and space. The messages have to do with
the Electron Pump that transfers matter back and forth
between the two Universes. The second level of the story
is told from viewpoints of the nonhumans in the 'other'
Universe, where the messages are coming from. The
third level is many years later at a time when scientists
on a moon colony are grappling with the problems of the
two Universes." Publ Wkly
"Imagination is the fount of Isaac Asimov's mastery.
The suspense he generates . . . is low-key and subtle,
and he has a gifted knack for making wild and indescribable superbeings (for he never quite describes them)
seem lifelike, though scarcely human." Best Sellers

I, robot. Bantam hardcover ed. Bantam Books
2004 224p (Robot series) $24; pa $7.99
ISBN 0-553-80370-0; 0-553-29438-5 (pa)
                                    * LC 2003-69139
First published 1950 by Gnome Press
Contents: Robbie; Runaround; Reason; Catch that rabbit; Liar!; Little lost robot; Escape!; Evidence; The evita-
ble conflict
"These loosely connected stories cover the career of
Dr. Susan Calvin and United States Robots, the industry
that she heads, from the time of the public's early distrust of these robots to its later dependency on them.
This collection is an important introduction to a theme
often found in science fiction: the encroachment of technology on our lives." Shapiro. Fic for Youth. 3d edition

The naked sun
In Asimov, I. The rest of the robots

Asimov, Isaac, 1920-1992—*Continued*

Prelude to Foundation. Doubleday 1988 403p (Foundation)

ISBN 0-385-23313-2

* LC 87-33086

"A Foundation book"

This novel and Forward the Foundation are set chronologically prior to other volumes in the Foundation series

"On Trantor, capital world of the Empire, the 32-year-old Seldon, a mathematician of promise who knows nothing of history or politics, attracts the unwelcome attention of the Imperial Government with his speculations about the predictive power of his equations. Before the Imperials can turn the new tool of psychohistory to their own purposes, a journalist named Chetter Hummin helps Seldon disappear into the cultural maze of Trantor—an experience that provides the naïve academic with an education in human diversity and duplicity." N Y Times Book Rev

This "is vintage Asimov, a novel that places ideas ahead of all its other elements but doesn't stint on characterization or entertaining plot lines. It also contains a fair number of mysteries, and . . . all of this is handled in a simple, direct style that never gets between the reader and the story." West Coast Rev Books

The rest of the robots. Doubleday 1964 556p o.p.

"Doubleday science fiction"

Short stories included are: Robot A1-76 goes astray; Victory unintentional; First Law; Let's get together; Satisfaction guaranteed; Risk; Lenny; Galley slave

Second Foundation. Gnome Press 1953 210p (Foundation) o.p.

*

Third book of the Foundation series about the efforts of a group of scientists who are trying to subdue the chaos and conflict of the galactic world. The story centers on fourteen-year-old Arkady Darrell's search for this secret group

Followed by Foundation's edge

Aslam, Nadeem

The wasted vigil. Alfred A. Knopf 2008 319p $25

ISBN 978-0-307-26842-6; 0-307-26842-X

LC 2008-17772

"English-born doctor James Marcus has made Afghanistan his home, having married an Afghan woman named Qatrina, also a doctor. Qatrina was stoned to death by the Taliban (she's an adulteress, having married an infidel), and their daughter has been abducted and is known to be dead, though there's rumor of a grandson. The gentle, saintly James shelters Lara, who's come from Russia to look for a brother lost during the Soviet incursion, and welcomes old friend David, an American jewel dealer and disaffected CIA spy. Also entering their midst is Casa, an injured (and angry) young man who claims to be a laborer but in fact is committed to jihad." Libr J

"The prose in The Wasted Vigil is usually so generous with startling perceptions that the reader rarely feels overwhelmed by the social and historical facts that Aslam, writing about a country largely unknown to his readers, has to constantly smuggle into his narrative. . . . Aslam's determination to gaze resolutely at the darkest side of our many cold and hot wars is what gives The Wasted Vigil its depth and power." N Y Rev Books

Atherton, Nancy

Aunt Dimity digs in. Viking 1998 275p

ISBN 0-670-87061-7

LC 97-34633

"Living in the cottage left to Lori by her mother's close friend, Dimity Westwood, Lori is thankful for the arrival of the local and unmarried Francesca Sciaparelli to aid with the double joys of motherhood. In this corpseless tale, the mystery concerns a document stolen from the vicarage. . . . Asked to resolve the dilemma, Lori, a rare book expert, is aided by Aunt Dimity who communicates with her ghostly handwriting in a special blue journal." Publ Wkly

Atkins, Ace

Devil's garden. G.P. Putnam's Sons 2009 354p $24.95

ISBN 978-0-399-15536-9; 0-399-15536-8

LC 2008-46361

"The 1921 rape/manslaughter trial of silent film star Roscoe 'Fatty' Arbuckle provides the gritty backdrop for Atkins's outstanding crime novel, in which Dashiell Hammett, then a Pinkerton operative living in San Francisco, plays a significant role. A wild party Arbuckle throws at San Francisco's posh St. Francis Hotel results in tragedy after an actress, Virginia Rappe, is mysteriously injured and later dies. . . . With enviable ease, Atkins . . . brings to life Hammett, Arbuckle, William Randolph Hearst and other real figures of the period. Those familiar with the historical case will be impressed by how well the book meshes fact and fiction. Genre fans who enjoy the grim realism of James Ellroy's post-WWII Los Angeles will find a lot to like in Atkins's Prohibition-era San Francisco." Publ Wkly

White shadow. Putnam 2006 370p $24.95

ISBN 0-399-15355-1

LC 2005-56683

"It's 1955, and the Ybor City area of Tampa is a melting pot of Cuban and Sicilian immigrants liberally laced with gangsters vying for control of the city's gambling, prostitution, drug, and liquor concessions. When vice don Charlie Wall, affectionately known as The White Shadow, is murdered gangland style in his home, all of Tampa takes notice. . . . [This novel is a] fictionalized history of the affair told from a variety of perspectives–those of the prime suspects, the investigating police detective, an investigative reporter for the Tampa Times, and an elusive Cuban girl who was a prime mover in the case." Libr J

This novel "slowly unfurls itself, strolling along with the readers, as it evokes the heat and humidity of a setting where the languorousness stands in sharp contrast to the life and death stakes at hand. Murder, corruption, and organized crime are all present, but the heat seems to suck the speed out of them, so even death is dispatched in slow motion. Ultimately, the atmosphere of this novel is the star. Atkins nails all the period details and describes the city perfectly." PopMatters

Wicked city. G. P. Putnam's Sons 2008 336p $24.95

ISBN 978-0-399-15457-7

LC 2007-32774

Atkins, Ace—*Continued*

"It's 1954, and the attorney-general-elect of Alabama has been assassinated near a downtown street. Among the gathering crowd stands a young teen still wearing 3-D glasses from the John Wayne movie he's just seen. So begins Ace Atkins' novel, Wicked City, a vivid depiction of the real-life Phenix City, a den of gambling, prostitution and corruption that rivaled any Hollywood creation. Atkins provides a 3-D view through two narrators, an omniscient teller and Lamar Murphy, an ex-boxer enlisted to help solve Albert Patterson's murder. . . . A character warns that the sweetness of Phenix City moonshine masks the embalming fluid that provides its kick. Atkins has likewise crafted a smart tale of a decadent place; Southern sweetness laced with poison." Paste

Atkinson, Kate

Case histories; a novel. Little, Brown 2004 312p $23.95

ISBN 0-316-74040-3 (Little, Brown); 0-385-60799-7 (Doubleday)

* LC 2004-2379

"Cambridge P.I. and Francophile Jackson Brodie serves as the link among three interwoven tales. Red herrings abound as Jackson plows through the sad cases of a missing toddler, a young woman brutally killed while temping at her father's law firm, and an overwrought mother driven to ax murder." Libr J

"The novel is packed with women whose appetites are large, and Atkinson's prose is correspondingly loose and louche: no single point of view predominates, and everyone's thoughts effortlessly rollick along." N Y Times Book Rev

Not the end of the world; stories. Little, Brown 2002 244p il $23.95

ISBN 0-316-61430-0　　　　　LC 2003-40117

Contents: Charlene and Trudi go shopping; Tunnel of fish; Transparent fiction; Dissonance; Sheer big waste of love; Unseen translation; Evil dopplegangers; The cat lover; The bodies vest; Temporal anomaly; Wedding favors; Pleasureland

"While not as intense or unified as Atkinson's full-length work, this is a sharp and wholly original collection." Publ Wkly

When will there be good news? Little, Brown & Co. 2008 388p $24.99

ISBN 978-0-316-15485-7; 0-316-15485-7

* LC 2008-14738

This is the author's third mystery featuring former police officer and private detective Jackson Brodie. "Set mostly around Edinburgh, Scotland, the tale begins with a six-year-old girl escaping an attacker who kills her mother, eight-year-old sister, and baby brother. Atkinson then weaves a plot that connects Brodie to the girl, now an adult, through coincidence and more tragedy, this time a train wreck. Detective Chief Inspector Louise Morse, who has a thing for Brodie, returns to his life, and a new character appears: Reggie, an orphaned 16-year-old girl with a criminal for a brother and a desire to study for her A-levels even though she has dropped out of school." Libr J

"As always, Atkinson inhabits her characters with fluency, clarity and a good eye and ear for quirks and habits of mind." Times Lit Suppl

Attebery, Brian, 1951-

(ed) The Norton book of science fiction. See The Norton book of science fiction

Atwood, Margaret, 1939-

Alias Grace. Talese 1996 468p il

ISBN 0-385-47571-3　　　　　LC 96-21689

This "novel is based on the case of Grace Marks, who in 1843 was sentenced to life imprisonment for her role in the murders of her employer and his mistress. In this fictional rendition, three men try to spring the beautiful alleged murderess from prison, by way of religion, pre-Freudian analysis, and chicanery." New Yorker

"Always a powerful writer, Atwood outdoes herself with compelling prose, expert control of the material, and fine attention to historical detail." Libr J

The blind assassin. Talese 2000 521p $26

ISBN 0-385-47572-1　　　　　LC 99-462109

"Dying octogenarian Iris Chasen's narration of the past carefully unravels a haunting story of tragedy, corruption, and cruel manipulation. Iris and her younger sister, Laura, are born into the privileged Canadian world of Port Ticonderoga in the early part of the 20th century. At 18, Iris is the marital pawn in a business deal between her financially desperate father and the ruthless, much-older industrialist Richard Griffen. When the father dies, the rebellious Laura is forced to move into Richard's controlling household, accelerating the tangled mess of relentless tragedy. At this point, Atwood . . . overlays a second story, an sf novel-within-a-novel, credited to Laura Chasen, that features nameless lovers trysting in squalor." Libr J

"Within the novel, stories produce anguish and arousal, charges and vindications, guilt and vengeance. For readers of the novel, all this may foster something like delight, although the fictional universe is hardly a pleasant one." Women's Rev Books

Cat's eye. Doubleday 1989 c1988 446p

ISBN 0-385-26007-5

* LC 88-24345

First published 1988 in Canada

Elaine Risley, the narrator of this novel, "is a Canadian painter of some renown who, at 50, has returned to her childhood city of Toronto for a retrospective of her work. The dull, provincial city of her youth has become world class in the intervening years . . . but in the week she is there her interest in the city's new galleries and restaurants and shops and, in many ways, in the retrospective itself, is only glancing. Her focus, and the novel's, is all on the past." N Y Times Book Rev

"Atwood's achievement is the decoding of childhood's secrets, and the creation of a flawed and haunting work of art." Time

The Handmaid's tale; with an introduction by Valerie Martin. Everyman's Library 2006 xxxiii, 350p $24

ISBN 0-307-26460-2

* LC 2006-42618

First published 1986 by Houghton Mifflin

"The time is the near future, the place is the Republic of Gilead—formerly known as the United States. A coup d'etat by religious fundamentalists has left the President and Congress dead, The Constitution suspended, and the

Atwood, Margaret, 1939——*Continued*

borders sealed. . . . Atwood's storyteller, a 33-year-old woman known only as Offred, serves as a handmaid to one of the ruling Commanders of the Faithful, Fred, from whom she takes her name. . . . Her sole function . . . is to carry out a . . . version of Old Testament lore and bear a child for the aging Commander, with the collusion of his barren wife." Christ Sci Monit

"A gripping suspense tale, The Handmaid's Tale is an allegory of what results from a politics based on misogyny, racism, and anti-Semitism." Ms

Life before man. Simon & Schuster 1980 317p
ISBN 0-671-25115-5   LC 79-20281
This novel set in Toronto in the mid-1970's is "about the entangled relationship of three characters: Elizabeth, aggressive and intimidating, mourning the suicide of her lover; Nate, her husband, helpless within and without the marriage, and Lesje, whose work with fossils at the museum is more absorbing and safer than the present, than her affair with Nate." Libr J

This "is a powerful, introspective view of contemporary marriage and the changing roles of the sexes. . . . {This novel} returns to the survival and identity theme of Atwood's early thematic guide to Canadian literature, but at a level that transcends the national. With men and mores rooted in the prehistoric past, Atwood forces us to confront a harrowing present that anticipates an ecologically and culturally doomed future." Choice

The year of the flood; a novel. Nan A. Talese/Doubleday 2009 448p $26.95
ISBN 978-0-385-52877-1; 0-385-52877-9
LC 2009-05901
A novel set in the "nightmarish future first envisioned in Oryx and Crake. Contrary to expectations, the waterless flood, a biological disaster predicted by a fringe religious group, actually arrives. In its wake, the survivors must rely on their wits to get by, all the while reflecting on what went wrong. Atwood wins major style points here for her framing device, the liturgical year of the God's Gardeners sect." Libr J

"Structurally, the book can be overwhelming. The story begins with the end and is told from the disparate points of view of Ren, a young sex-club trapeze dancer; Toby, who becomes one of God's Gardeners; and Adam One, the leader of the Gardeners. Narratives jump back and forth in time to show how and why the destruction came about. Keeping the story line straight can be challenging because of the multiple narrators, but it's easy enough to tell the good guys from the bad guys. The good guys are green. (Not literally, although in a book like this, that is a possibility.) Atwood gives each main character an imaginative life history." Dallas Morning News

Aubert, Rosemary, 1946-

The ferryman will be there; an Ellis Portal mystery. Bridge Works 2001 258p $22.95
ISBN 1-882593-44-8   LC 00-52900
"Middle-aged detective Ellis Portal, a former judge who fell from grace through drink and drugs, wound up homeless on the streets and re-ascended to the edge of respectability, helps his friend, Det. Sgt. Matt West, to locate a young woman, Carrie Simm. Her father, a Toronto movie producer, was murdered in front of her, in full view of hundreds of people, at a film premiere. Possibly fearing for her own life, Carrie disappeared." Publ Wkly

"Portal's indomitable integrity and checkered past make his ministrations to the troubled girls utterly believable and moving. This is quickly becoming a very special series." Booklist

Auchincloss, Louis

The book class. Houghton Mifflin 1984 212p
ISBN 0-395-36138-9   LC 84-522
"In 1908 a group of Park Avenue debutantes begins to meet once a month to discuss books, past and present. 'The Book Class' endures for 64 years, creating a lasting and telling impression on the son of one of its members, the novel's narrator, Christopher Gates. These pampered and seemingly fragile women, whose lives are filled with great passion, disappointment, and tragedy, exude an aura of power and mystery which fascinates Gates and which he probes throughout his life." Libr J

"Auchincloss may work on a small canvas, but no one excels his finely etched portraits of sophisticates of good breeding and inherited wealth." Publ Wkly

Her infinite variety. Houghton Mifflin 2000 224p $25
ISBN 0-618-02191-4   LC 99-47302
This novel "relates how a Depression-era Vassar graduate named Clara Longcope—the shrewd and beautiful daughter of a Yale professor—charms and manipulates her way to the pinnacle of New York society." N Y Times Book Rev

"An astute and witty novel about a woman who disdains the old values of money and class in favor of a feminine meritocracy in the world of business." Publ Wkly

The young Apollo and other stories. Houghton Mifflin 2006 237p $24
ISBN 0-618-55115-8; 978-0-618-55115-6
LC 2005-19899
Contents: The young Apollo; Other times, other ways; A case history; Lady Kate; The attributions; An hour and a lifetime; The artist's model; Pandora's box; Her better half; The grandeur that was Byzantium; Pa's darling; Due process

"The world depicted here is one of 'old money' in which appearance and social status are everything and social climbing is the sport of choice. For all the privilege and monetary advantage they enjoy, however, most of the characters end up living tragically compromised lives. Many of the stories focus on marriage, and Auchincloss shows us again and again how the naïve and well intentioned are routinely betrayed by the ambition and selfishness of others." Libr J

Auel, Jean M.

The Clan of the Cave Bear; a novel. Crown 1980 468p (Earth's children)
ISBN 0-517-18918-6
* LC 80-14581
"Young Cro-Magnon orphan Ayla is adopted into the Neanderthal Clan of the Cave Bear and grows up mothered by medicine woman Iza and protected by magician Creb. However, her different characteristics and abilities

Auel, Jean M.—*Continued*

bring her into conflict with the clan time and again. Broud, clan-leader's son, is her chief adversary: to him Ayla is an intolerable threat to tradition who must be subdued or die." Libr J

"It's subject matter, its vast research . . . make this fictional excursion into prehistory a thing of wonder. But it's an enjoyable story, too, though leisurely and not notable for the quality of its prose. . . . The depiction of how the cave-dwelling Neanderthals lived—how they performed their totemistic rituals, gathered medicinal plants, slew mammoths and other animals—is solid, convincing and sometimes exciting." Publ Wkly

Followed by The Valley of Horses

August, David

(jt. auth) Lutz, J. Final seconds

Austen, Jane, 1775-1817

Emma; with an introduction by Marilyn Butler. Knopf 1991 xlvii, 498p $19
ISBN 0-679-40581-X

      * LC 91-52988

"Everyman's library"

First published 1815

"Emma is a pretty girl of sterling character and more will than she can properly manage. She thinks she knows what is best for everybody, and is a prey to many deceptions. She is imposed upon, and imposes upon herself; it is a long while before she sees things as they are, and recognizes where her own happiness lies. Her hero is one of Jane's sober, clear-eyed, and perfect men. The Fairfax and Churchill subplot furnishes a comedy of dissimulation contrasting didactically with Emma's honesty. A formidable snob and vulgarian, Mrs. Elton, and a good-natured bore, Miss Bates, who would be insufferable outside these pages, are among the more laughable characters." Baker. Guide to the Best Fic

Mansfield Park; with an introduction by Peter Conrad. Alfred A. Knopf 1992 xxxvii, 488p $21
ISBN 0-679-41269-7

      * LC 91-58689

"Everyman's library"

First published 1814

"Presents a household of young people in love with the right or the wrong person. Thru the device of marrying off three sisters into different ranks, upper middle-class distinctions come in for amusing comparisons." Lenrow. Reader's Guide to Prose Fic

"Her most considerable piece of work, not in mere dimensions, but in the mastery of a difficult problem. . . . In truth, nowhere is the difference between true comedy and satire better exemplified." Baker. Guide to the Best Fic

Northanger Abbey. Vintage Classics 2007 241p pa $6.95
ISBN 978-0-307-38683-0; 0-307-38683-X

      LC 2007-281091

First published 1818

"The heroine is a girl in the first innocent bloom of youth, whose entry into life is attended by the collapse of many illusions." Lenrow. Reader's Guide to Prose Fic

"Though not published until 1818, this was written

1798-9 and entitled 'Susan', revised in 1803 and sold for publication; it may perhaps have been rewritten or touched up later, before it appeared posthumously. Begun as a parody of sentimentalism and the romantics, it developed into the genre which was to be peculiarly Jane Austen's—the portrayal in sober and faithful tints of the quiet middle-class life she knew; the satire restrained, the comedy all-pervasive." Baker. Guide to the Best Fic

Persuasion. Alfred A. Knopf 1992 xxxvii, 260p $18
ISBN 0-679-40986-6   LC 91-53181

"Everyman's library"

First published 1818

"The heroine, Anne Elliott, and her lover, Captain Wentworth, had been engaged eight years before the story opens but Anne had broken the engagement in deference to family and friends. Upon his return he finds her 'wretchedly altered,' but after numerous obstacles have been overcome, the lovers are happily united." Gerwig. Handb for Readers and Writers

Pride and prejudice; introduction by Anna Quindlen. Modern Library 1995 281p $14.95
ISBN 0-679-60168-6

      * LC 95-6310

First published 1813

"Concerned mainly with the conflict between the prejudice of a young lady and the well-founded though misinterpreted pride of the aristocratic hero. The heroine's father and mother cope in very different ways with the problem of marrying off five daughters." Good Read

"The characters are drawn with humor, delicacy, and the intimate knowledge of men and women that Miss Austen always shows." Keller. Reader's Dig of Books

Sense and sensibility; with an introduction by Peter Conrad. Knopf 1992 xxxix, 367p $16
ISBN 0-679-40987-4

      * LC 91-53182

"Everyman's library"

First published 1811

A story "in which two sisters, Elinor and Marianne Dashwood represent 'sense' and 'sensibility' respectively. Each is deserted by the young man from whom she has been led to expect an offer of matrimony. Elinor bears her deep disappointment with dignity and restraint while Marianne violently expresses her grief." Reader's Ency. 4th edition

"A study of character and manners in a very delicate, precise, miniature style; the characters just everyday people, drawn as they are without exaggeration; the minute differences of human nature delicately penciled; the satire directed against mere commonplace foolishness, conceit, and vulgarity, rather than vice or eccentricity. In truth, the social failings and personal foibles are self-revealed rather than satirized and make spontaneous comedy." Baker. Guide to the Best Fic

Auster, Paul, 1947-

The Brooklyn follies. Holt 2006 306p $24
ISBN 0-8050-7714-6   LC 2005-40201

"Nathan Glass has come to Brooklyn to die. Divorced, estranged from his only daughter, the retired life insurance salesman seeks only solitude and anonymity. Then Nathan finds his long-lost nephew, Tom Wood, working

Auster, Paul, 1947-—*Continued*

in a local bookstore–a far cry from the brilliant academic career he'd begun when Nathan saw him last. Tom's boss is the charismatic Harry Brightman. . . . Through Tom and Harry, Nathan's world gradually broadens to include a new set of acquaintances—not to mention a stray relative or two—and leads him to a reckoning with his past." Publisher's note

This "is a departure for Auster. Instead of tight plotting and theoretical figure work, there is domestic realism. The result is a novel far more passionately American than Auster's previous ones." Times Lit Suppl

In the country of last things. Viking 1987 188p
ISBN 0-670-81445-8   LC 86-40257
"Imagine an American city in the near future, populated almost wholly by street dwellers, squatters in ruined buildings, scavengers for subsistence. Suicide clubs offer interesting ways to die, for a fee, but the rich have fled with their jewels, and those who are left survive on what little cash trade-in centers will give them for the day's pickings. This . . . dreamlike fable about a peculiarly recognizable society, now in the throes of entropy, focuses on the plight of a young woman, Anna Blume." Publ Wkly

This novel "is distinguished by an uncanny grasp of the day-to-day realities of homelessness. This is a scary but highly relevant book." Libr J

Invisible. Henry Holt and Co. 2009 308p $25
ISBN 978-0-8050-9080-2; 0-8050-9080-0
                            * LC 2009-02237
"A Frances Coady book"
This novel "novel opens in New York City in the spring of 1967, when twenty-year-old Adam Walker, an aspiring poet and student at Columbia University, meets the enigmatic Frenchman Rudolf Born and his silent and seductive girfriend, Margot. Before long, Walker finds himself caught in a perverse triangle that leads to a sudden, shocking act of violence that will alter the course of his life. Three different narrators tell the story of Invisible, a novel that travels in time from 1967 to 2007 and moves from Morningside Heights, to the Left Bank of Paris, to a remote island in the Caribbean." Publisher's note

"To be blunt, as a writer of sentences, Auster isn't anything special; reading this book after reading Roth or Richard Yates, for example—or, to draw upon a couple of comparisons that are even more unfair, Bellow or Nabokov—one is aware of how neutral and unremarkable, and occasionally even plodding, Auster's prose can be. What Auster is, instead, is a spellbinding storyteller, sometimes thanks to, and other times in spite of, his post-modern narrative trickery. Even more important, he is a writer of high moral seriousness. Indeed, this novel, like some of his others, could best be described as a moral suspense story. As such, it succeeds brilliantly." PopMatters

Oracle night. Holt 2003 243p $23
ISBN 0-8050-7320-5
"One morning in September 1982, a struggling novelist recovering from a near-fatal illness purchases, on impulse, a blue notebook from a new store in his Brooklyn neighborhood. . . . Reflecting on a past conversation and armed with his new notebook, Sidney Orr is compelled to write about a man who walks away from his comfort-

able, staid life after a brush with death. . . . Orr's description of his fictional project takes over for a while, but through a framing narrative and a series of long, occasionally digressive footnotes, he teasingly reveals himself, his lovely wife, Grace, and their mutual friend, the famous novelist John Trause. While Orr's hero finds himself locked in a bomb shelter, Grace begins behaving strangely, the stationery shop is shuttered, John's drug-addicted son looms menacingly in the background and the blue notebook exerts a troubling power." Publ Wkly

"A novelist writing about a novelist writing about an editor reading a novel: these Russian dolls might come across as merely cute, were it not for the fact that the lucid Mr Auster is a natural storyteller, with a seemingly inexhaustible trove of yarns at his disposal. All of the stories within stories are compelling in their own right." Economist

Axton, David, 1945-

For works written by this author under other names see Koontz, Dean R., 1945-

B

Babel´, I. (Isaac), 1894-1940

The complete works of Isaac Babel; edited by Nathalie Babel; translated with notes by Peter Constantine; introduction by Cynthia Ozick. Norton 2001 1072p il maps $39.95
ISBN 0-393-04846-2
                            * LC 2001-44036
Contains the following short stories: Old Shloyme; At grandmother's; Elya Isaakovich and Margarita Prokofievna; Mama, Rimma, and Alla; The public library; Nine; Odessa; The aroma of Odessa; Inspiration; Doudou; Shabos-Nakhamu; On the field of honor; Thedeserter; Papa Marescot's family; The Quaker; The sin of Jesus; An evening with the empress; Chink; A tale about a woman; The bathroom window; Bagrat-Ogly and the eyes of his bull; Line and color; You missed the boat, captain!; The end of St. Hypatius; The king; Justice in parentheses; How things were done in Odessa; Lyubka the Cossack; The father; Froim Grach; The end of the almshouse; Sunset; Crossing the river Zbrucz; The church in Novograd; A letter; The reserve cavalry commander; Pan Apolek; Italian sun; Gedali; My first goose; The rabbi; The road to Brody; The Tachanka theory; Dolgushov's death; The commander of the Second Brigade; Sashka Christ; The life of Matvey Rodionovich Pavlichenko; The cemetery in Kozin; Prishchepa; The story of a horse; Konkin; Berestechko; Salt; Evening; Afonka Bida; At Saint Valentine's; Squadron commander Trunov; Ivan and Ivan; The continuation of the story of a horse; The widow; Zamosc; Treason; Czesniki; After the battle; The song; The rabbi's son; Makhno's boys; A hardworking woman; Grishchuk; Argamak; The kiss; And then there were nine; And then there were ten; A letter to the editor; The story of my dovecote; First love; Karl-Yankel; The awakening; In the basement; Gapa Guzhva; Kolyvushka; The road; The Ivan and Maria; Guy de Maupassant; Petroleum; Dante Street; Di Grasso; Sulak; The trial; My first fee; Roaming stars: a movie tale; A story; Information; Three in the afternoon; The

Babel', I. (Isaac), 1894-1940—*Continued*

Jewess

In addition to the stories this volume contains sketches, journalistic pieces, a diary, plays, and screenplays

"Few writers possess Babel's level of genius and temerity, and this first complete collection should acquaint more readers with his unjustly neglected work." Publ Wkly

Babel', Isaac *See* Babel', I. (Isaac), 1894-1940

Babson, Marian

Canapes for the kitties. St. Martin's Press 1997 220p

ISBN 0-312-16929-9   LC 97-16232

"A Thomas Dunne book"

"When Lorinda Lucas, a well-known mystery writer in Brimful Coffers, kills off her popular fictional heroines, neighboring writers rebel. Old and new resentments (that even involve local cats Had-I, But-Known, and Roscoe) lead to murder." Libr J

Babson's "lighthearted good humor and skewed view of the world enliven every page of this charming morsel of a mystery." Publ Wkly

Baca, Jimmy Santiago, 1952-

The importance of a piece of paper. Grove Press 2004 225p $22

ISBN 0-8021-1765-1   LC 2003-57089

Contents: Matilda's garden; The three sons of Julia; The importance of a piece of paper; The Valentine's Day card; Enemies; Mother's ashes; Bull's blood; Runaway

"The rural Southwest landscape of Baca's short stories is inhabited by outsiders: drug addicts and convicts, absentee mothers and runaways. Baca's first collection of fiction . . . paints a picture of Chicano life that is at once cruel and sweetly redemptive." Publ Wkly

Bachman, Richard *See* King, Stephen, 1947-

Bacon, Charlotte, 1965-

Split estate. Farrar, Straus and Giroux 2008 290p $25

ISBN 978-0-374-28183-0; 0-374-28183-1

LC 2007-42856

"The story opens shortly after Laura King—wife, mother of two teenagers and longtime depressive—jumps to her death from an Upper East Side apartment. Shocked and devastated, Arthur, her doting lawyer husband, decides to move his family back to his childhood home in the small town of Callendar, Wyoming—a place where he never quite fit in, being more comfortable with a book than astride a horse. Bacon adeptly captures the less obvious and less pretty aspects of the King family's grief, particularly Arthur's complete loss of confidence—as if his wife's decision to end her life has exposed him as inadequate. Lucy, Arthur's salty, independent mother, might be grateful for the company that Arthur and the kids provide, but she also struggles to overcome her frustration with her only child's nebbishy ways—as well as her own sense of culpability. . . . There are no easy resolutions here, just haunting meditations on character that are as compelling as they are austere." Time Out N Y

Bahr, Howard, 1946-

The Judas Field; a novel of the Civil War. H. Holt 2006 292p $25

ISBN 978-0-8050-6739-2   LC 2005-055011

"A middle-aged salesman in 1885 Mississippi, Cass Wakefield is a Civil War veteran of the Army of Tennessee, which saw action far from the leadership of Robert E. Lee, and ended, badly, at the battle of Franklin in 1864. Cass agrees to accompany a neighbor, 54-year-old terminally ill widow Alison Sansing, to Tennessee to recover the bodies of her father and brother, killed at Franklin. As they travel north, Cass's memories return with painful vividness, culminating as he walks over the scene of his army's disastrous defeat." Publ Wkly

The author "recreates this seminal moment in American history with prose that is vivid, unflinching and often incantatory. The book's pace and detail are wrenching, and it is starkly devoid of romanticism. Within the battlefield scenes, Bahr's accomplishment is magnificent: a fully realized depiction of controlled mass butchery on a field of blood, body parts and utterly obliterated human beings. The reader puts down the book with a sense of shock to find he is not actually inside a level of hell." Washington Post Book World

Bail, Murray, 1941-

Eucalyptus; a novel. Farrar, Straus & Giroux 1998 255p

ISBN 0-374-14857-0   LC 98-5880

"In this contemporary Australian fairy tale, a widower named Holland acquires a sprawling property in New South Wales and plants it with hundreds of varieties of eucalyptus . . ., when it is time for his daughter, Ellen, to wed, he offers her hand to the suitor who can name each specimen on his estate. In the meantime, Ellen encounters a handsome stranger under a coolabah who courts her with stories that prove to be less random than they appear. The novel's categorizations and mysteries become a playful inquiry into the nature of storytelling, with an unpredictable conclusion." New Yorker

Bailey, Blake

(ed) Cheever, J. Collected stories and other writings

(ed) Cheever, J. Complete novels

Bailey, Charles W. (Charles Waldo), 1929-

(jt. auth) Knebel, F. Seven days in May

Bainbridge, Beryl, 1933-

The birthday boys. Carroll & Graf Pubs. 1994 c1991 189p

ISBN 0-7867-0071-8   LC 94-1264

First published 1991 in the United Kingdom

"The story of Capt. Robert Scott's second expedition is narrated by Scott himself and the four men who perished along with him in the frigid weather and miserable conditions of Antarctica. Beginning with their June 1910 departure from Cardiff on the 'Terra Nova,' and ending with the terrible journey by sled back to the ship in

Bainbridge, Beryl, 1933-—*Continued*
March 1912, the five men consecutively recount their
journey through an emotional as well as physical landscape." Libr J

"These five monologues, which contain some of the
most convincing and slyly revealing first-person narrative
I've ever read, span a remarkable range of voices and
dispositions, but what they share is a mesmerizing readability. . . . They present us with a microcosmic society
of flawed individuals, pushed and pulled even in a frozen
wilderness by the subtle dictates of class, personality and
ambition." N Y Times Book Rev

Every man for himself. Carroll & Graf Pubs.
1996 224p
ISBN 0-786-70349-0   LC 96-32518
This novel "takes place on the ill-fated Titanic. The
story is narrated by Morgan, a young American, and follows the events between boarding and rescue by the
Carpathia." Libr J

"Bainbridge hits a tremendous pace as her story reaches its climax. In a remarkably concise book, shot through
with laconic wit, she establishes complex characters who
engage first the reader's curiosity, then affection. The elegiac theme extends far beyond the historical event."
New Statesman (1913)

Baker, Dorothy, 1907-1968

Young man with a horn. Houghton Mifflin 1938
243p o.p.
                                                        *
"Rick Martin is not interested in school but is intrigued
by music. Learning how to play the jazz trumpet from
black musicians, Rick becomes a genius in the art of
'swing' and quickly rises to fame in the Phil Morrison
orchestra. The inability to cope with success, as well as
a bad marriage and gin, lead to his fatal end." Shapiro.
Fic for Youth. 3d edition

Baker, Kage

The graveyard game. Harcourt 2000 298p
ISBN 0-15-100449-8   LC 00-27790
"When the cyborg known as Mendoza disappears out
of grief for her murdered lover, fellow operatives Joseph
and Lewis begin a search through time for her and dis-
cover some unpleasant secrets about their employer–Dr.
Zeus Incorporated, otherwise known as The Company.
. . . [This installment] spans centuries and includes stops
in late 20th-century Hollywood and early 21st-century
London, among other times and places." Libr J

The house of the stag. Tor 2008 350p $25.95
ISBN 978-0-7653-1745-2; 0-7653-1745-1
                                                    LC 2008-30212
"A Tom Doherty Associates Book"
"The peaceful, primitive Yendri tribe is no match for
the Riders who conquered and enslaved them. Only
Gard, a half-demon foundling, bears enough anger to
fight back but finds himself cast out of the tribe. Captured by mages who rule an underground realm, Gard secretly learns their magic to try to escape and redeem
himself in the eyes of his people." Libr J

"Baker's fantasy is completely different from her science fiction, but it's just as good. Gently humorous and
ironic, Gard is a character readers will pull for as he

moves from foundling to outcast to slave to ruler. Baker's worldbuilding is consistently topnotch, and the various supporting characters are just as well drawn as her
antihero." Romantic Times

In the garden of Iden; a novel of the company.
Harcourt Brace & Co. 1998 329p
ISBN 0-15-100299-1   LC 97-23284
"The initial assignment for 18-year-old Mendoza,
transformed into an immortal cyborg by the 24th-century
Company, is to retrieve from Renaissance England an
endangered plant that cures cancer. Posing as a Spanish
lady accompanying her doctor father, she falls in love
with the mortal Nicholas Harpole, secretary to the owner
of Iden Hall and its exotic gardens. Amidst the raging
Catholic/Protestant powerplays revolving around the English throne and the fervent religious bloodlust of common folk, Mendoza is torn between her task and her
love. Baker's story comments powerfully on religious hypocrisy and xenophobia." Libr J

The life of the world to come. TOR Books 2004
334p $25.95
ISBN 0-7653-1132-1   LC 2004-49574
"Cyborg biologist Mendoza has been exiled to the extremely distant past to live her immortal span farming
maize and lettuce for wealthy tourists of the twenty-
fourth century. She occasionally reminisces about the
man she loved in, first, the sixteenth, and then, the nineteenth century. Then, one day, he crash-lands in her
cornfield. It isn't precisely he, of course, but someone
from the same Company project named Alec
Checkerfield. . . . Most of the story is his, from childhood
spent on a sailing ship to his youth and education in
London to growing wealth and power. As he discovers
ever more about his parentage and the power of Dr.
Zeus, Inc., to manipulate people and the world, he determines to bring the Company down. Mendoza provides
him the key tidbit that, after 2355, Dr. Zeus' knowledge
is blank. That time will be Alec's window of opportunity. Alec is quite a character, especially for the sedate
twenty-fourth century, and in Baker's skillful hands, his
story is well told and engrossing." Booklist

Mendoza in Hollywood; a novel of the company. Harcourt 2000 334p
ISBN 0-15-100448-X   LC 99-14949
"Assigned, along with other time-traveling members of
the Company, to Cahuenga Pass, CA, in 1862, Mendoza
discovers firsthand the dangers and pleasures of living in
the American West during the Civil War. Haunted by
dreams of a long-lost lover and pursued by his ghost,
Mendoza struggles to come to terms with her personal
past while fulfilling her duties to the future–with mixed
results. Baker's latest tale of the wisecracking cyborg
mercenaries from the 24th century combines historical
detail and fast-paced action with a good dose of ironic
wit and a dollop of bittersweet romance." Libr J

Mother Aegypt and other stories. Night Shade
Books 2004 249p $27
ISBN 1-892389-75-4
"Told with splendid clarity, the 13 tales in this collection . . . are deceptively simple and seem, at first, to be
comfortably folkloric. Each then takes a distinctive turn,
often an O. Henry twist, and becomes indelibly the author's own." Publ Wkly

Baker, Kage—*Continued*

Sky coyote; a novel of the company. Harcourt Brace & Co. 1999 310p

ISBN 0-15-100354-8   LC 98-16833

"Fresh from a cushy R&R after a supervisory stint in the Inquisition, time-hopping cyborg Facilitator Joseph jaunts to 16th-century Alta California. There, cybernetically outfitted with fur and paws, he apotheosizes to the cannily entrepreneurial Chumash Indian tribe so he can collect them and their entire biosystem for Company studies in the remote future." Publ Wkly

The author "blends accurate historical research and arch comedy to produce an entertaining tale of time travel and mythic adventure." Libr J

The sons of heaven. Tor 2007 430p $25.95

ISBN 978-0-7653-1746-9; 0-7653-1746-X

     LC 2007-9541

"A Tom Doherty Associates book"

This is the concluding volume of the "saga of The Company and its immortal, time-traveling minions. As this volume opens, it is very nearly July 9, 2355, the end of recorded time, after which there is only silence regarding the fate of humankind. Various factions of cyborgs, mortals and other mysterious entities have differing opinions about what should occur after that date, and some of their plans involve armed insurrection and genocide. From the first volume, 'In the Garden of Iden,' Botanist Mendoza has always been at the center of the narrative, and for a certain subset of Baker's readers, Mendoza's star-crossed love affairs with three eerily similar men across literally countless centuries inspire the most devotion to the series. Others may find Mendoza something of an annoying pill and prefer the adventures of the supporting cast, especially Preservationist Lewis and Facilitator Joseph, two secret agents never sure of who their true enemies might be. No matter. 'The Sons of Heaven' gives equal time to both Mendoza and her subordinates, and Baker resolves the apocalyptic conflict with flair and enviable skill." San Francisco Chronicle

Baker, Kevin, 1958-

Strivers Row. HarperCollins 2006 550p $26.95

ISBN 0-06-019583-5   LC 2005-52679

In this "novel—the final volume of a New York trilogy called 'City of Fire' [previous titles: Dreamland and Paradise Alley]—Kevin Baker plunges into the world of Harlem in the early 1940's to imagine the lives of two African-American men. . . . One of his main characters was known in the 'real' world of 1943 as Malcolm Little, a rootless 18-year-old who would later become famous as Malcolm X. The other is the invention of Baker: a young, bourgeois, light-skinned Harlem clergyman named Jonah Dove. Malcolm is poor. Jonah is comfortably middle-class. In different ways, each is tormented by the world. . . . In the end, Baker has written a brave, honorable work, taking us into a vanished world that should be better known. More important, he imagines his human subjects with a sense of pity and compassion and embrace, thus making them visible in ways that are fresh and new." N Y Times Book Rev

Baker, Nicholson

The anthologist. Simon & Schuster 2009 243p $25

ISBN 978-1-4165-7244-2; 1-4165-7244-9

     LC 2009-01205

"The narrator, Paul Chowder, is a poet who is struggling to write the introduction to an anthology of rhyming poems he's collected. He's also trying to win back Roz, the woman who has just left him. These dilemmas make for some enlightening, absorbing reflections on poetry, the creative process, and life itself. While Chowder admits that he despises teaching, the narrative offers a wonderful explanation of what poetry is and the relationship between form and meaning. In the process, Chowder comes to understand himself better and pulls out of a slump. The novel's subtle sense of humor comes through as Chowder deals with injured fingers, a misbehaving dog, and the perils of reading his poetry in public." Libr J

Baker, Tiffany

The little giant of Aberdeen County; a novel. Grand Central Pub. 2009 341p $24.99

ISBN 978-0-446-19420-4; 0-446-19420-4

     LC 2008-774

"In an upstate New York backwater, Truly, massive from birth, has a bleak existence with her depressed father and her china-doll-like sister, Serena Jane. Truly grows at an astonishing rate—her girth the result of a pituitary gland problem—and after her father dies when Truly is 12, Truly is sloughed off to the Dyersons, a hapless farming family. Her outsize kindness surfaces as she befriends the Dyersons' outcast daughter, Amelia, and later leaves her beloved Dyerson farm to take care of Serena Jane's husband and son after Serena Jane leaves them. Haunting the margins of Truly's story is that of Tabitha Dyerson, a rumored witch whose secrets afford a breathtaking role reversal for Truly." Publ Wkly

"Baker enters Alice Hoffman territory in this parable about beauty and ugliness, meanness and mercy and magic, and does it with considerable dark humor." Hartford Courant

Baldacci, David

Absolute power. Warner Bks. 1996 469p

ISBN 0-446-51996-0   LC 95-22956

"The action begins when a grizzled professional cat burglar gets trapped inside the bedroom closet of one of the world's richest men, only to witness, through a one-way mirror, two Secret Service agents kill the billionaire's trampy young wife as she tries to fight off the drunken sexual advances of the nation's chief executive. Running for his life, but not before he picks up a blood-stained letter opener that puts the president at the scene of the crime, the burglar becomes the target of a clandestine manhunt orchestrated by leading members of the executive branch. Meanwhile, Jack Graham, once a public defender and now a high-powered corporate attorney, gets drawn into the case." Publ Wkly

Divine justice. Grand Central Pub. 2008 387p $27.99

ISBN 978-0-446-19550-8; 0-446-19550-2

     LC 2008-33072

Baldacci, David—*Continued*

In this installment in the author's Camel Club series, "Oliver Stone (aka John Carr, ex-CIA assassin) is wanted dead by his enemies and alive by his friends. Stone is on the run after assassinating the two men responsible for the death of his family and his friend Milton. Now Stone's former superior, Gen. Macklin Hayes, enlists tracker Joe Knox to locate Stone so Hayes can silence Stone forever. During Stone's flight from the law, a random act of kindness by Stone forces him on an unwanted detour to Divine, VA. There, Stone's continued good deeds might end up costing him his life as he quickly gets tangled in the hidden web of deceit to which the town owes its prosperity. . . . Fans will welcome this latest tale about the charismatic Stone and his exceedingly loyal friends with its fast-paced action and intriguing plot twists." Libr J

The simple truth. Warner Bks. 1998 470p
ISBN 0-446-52332-1   LC 98-22548
In this legal thriller "the principals are Rufus Harms, a slow-witted black giant who, after decades in a military prison, realizes that, for reasons revealed only at the novel's end, he is morally innocent of the murder for which he's doing time; John Fiske, a cop-turned-lawyer who's drawn into Harms's quest for justice after his younger brother, a Supreme Court clerk interested in Harms's case, is murdered; and Sara Evans, another Supreme Court clerk who joins forces—and beds—with Fiske." Publ Wkly
"The crime being covered up is stale beer compared to the Supreme Court setting, but as with a scenic drive, the destination of a Baldacci cliff-hanger is less important than the route taken." Booklist

Total control. Warner Bks. 1997 520p
ISBN 0-446-52095-0   LC 96-32869
"Sidney Archer is devastated when she hears that the plane carrying her husband to Los Angeles has crashed. But her nightmare begins when she learns he'd traded identities and flown to Seattle instead. Evidence suggests that Jason Archer was selling corporate secrets to a high-tech rival. Soon Sidney herself is caught in a web of intrigue as wealthy men vie for more power and money." Libr J

Baldick, Chris

(ed) The Oxford book of gothic tales. See The Oxford book of gothic tales

Baldwin, Alex

For works written by this author under other names see Griffin, W. E. B.

Baldwin, James, 1924-1987

Another country. Dial Press (NY) 1962 436p o.p.

                                                    *

This novel is set in "New York City and focuses mainly on Harlem society. The death—perhaps suicide—of the main character, Rufus Scott, is representative of the treatment individuals receive in an environment which is essentially hostile and which erects barriers to their desire for love." Camb Guide to Lit in Engl

also in Baldwin, J. Early novels and stories

Early novels and stories. Library of Am. 1998 970p $35
ISBN 1-88301-151-5   LC 97-23028
Contents: Go tell it on the mountain; Giovanni's room; Another country; Going to meet the man

Giovanni's room; a novel. Dial Press (NY) 1956 248p o.p.

                                                    *

"We meet the narrator, known to us only as David, in the south of France, but most of the story is laid in Paris. It develops as the story of a young American involved both with a woman and with another man, the man being the Giovanni of the title. When a choice has to be made, David chooses the woman, Hella." N Y Times Book Rev
"Mr. Baldwin has taken a very special theme and treated it with great artistry and restraint." Saturday Rev

also in Baldwin, J. Early novels and stories

Go tell it on the mountain. Knopf 1953 303p $15.95; pa $6.99
ISBN 0-679-60154-6; 0-440-33007-6 (pa)

                                                    *

This novel is an "autobiographical story of a Harlem child's relationship with his father against the background of his being saved in the pentecostal church." Benet's Reader's Ency of Am Lit

also in Baldwin, J. Early novels and stories

Going to meet the man. Dial Press (NY) 1965 249p o.p.
Contents: The rockpile; The outing; The man child; Previous condition; Sonny's blues; This morning, this evening, so soon; Come out the wilderness; Going to meet the man

also in Baldwin, J. Early novels and stories

If Beale Street could talk. Dial Press (NY) 1974 197p hardcover o.p. pa $12.95
ISBN 0-803-74169-3; 0-307-27593-0 (pa)
"Tish, aged 19, and Fonny, 22 years old, are in love and pledged to marry, a decision hastened by Tish's unexpected pregnancy. Fonny is falsely accused of raping a Puerto Rican woman and is sent to prison. The families of the desperate couple search frantically for evidence that will prove his innocence in order to reunite the lovers and provide a safe haven for the expected child. There is some explicit sex but it is not treated in a sensational manner, nor is the use of street language gratuitous." Shapiro. Fic for Youth. 3d edition

Tell me how long the train's been gone; a novel. Dial Press (NY) 1968 484p o.p.
Leo Proudhammer, a successful black "actor has a serious heart attack on stage. Barbara King, his leading lady . . . and in a strange way his inamorata, stays by his side. In a series of flashbacks . . . Leo relives his past from his Harlem boyhood on. Although he learned early to hate 'the man,' Leo's own betrayal as a man and as a human being is not limited to the white man's corruption. It encompasses his painful relationship with his brother, who lures him into homosexuality. Paralleling this story is the tale of Leo's career. The third thread is his bisexual private life in which the two main figures are white Barbara, his true but unattainable love, and black Christopher, worshipful and available." Publ Wkly

Balfour, Janice

(tr) Bragi Ólafsson. The pets

Ball, John Dudley, 1911-1988

In the heat of the night; by John Ball. Harper & Row 1965 184p o.p.

"Virgil Tibbs is found with a full wallet in the waiting room of a railroad station in Wells, a small town in the Carolinas. Because he is black he becomes the prime suspect for the murder of the town's musical director. The local police chief learns that Tibbs is a homicide expert from the Pasadena police department and enlists his assistance. Tibbs solves the crime, despite the bigotry to which he is exposed." Shapiro. Fic for Youth. 2d edition

Ball, Margaret

(jt. auth) McCaffrey, A. Acorna

(jt. auth) McCaffrey, A. Acorna's quest

Ballard, J. G., 1930-2009

The day of creation. Farrar, Straus & Giroux 1988 254p

ISBN 0-374-13527-4   LC 87-37525

First published 1987 in the United Kingdom

The narrator of this novel, Dr. Mallory, "is a physician with the World Health Organization, working in a mythical central African country, who launches what appears to be a vain search for water to forestall the desertification of the region. He accidentally releases the flow-and in fact thinks he is the creator-of a new river. . . . {He later} embarks on a dangerous journey to find its source and destroy it." Books Can

"Had Conrad been more inclined to fantasy, or less to fact and discipline, this is a novel he might have written. A blend of animated reverie, myth and adventure story, The Day of Creation imprints itself on the mind by its acid sweetness." Times Lit Suppl

Empire of the Sun; a novel. Simon & Schuster 1984 279p hardcover o.p. pa $13

ISBN 0-671-53051-8; 0-7432-6523-8 (pa)

LC 84-10630

"The day after Pearl Harbor, Shanghai is captured by the Japanese, and 11-year-old Jim is separated from his parents and spends some months living on his own. Then he is captured and interned in a Japanese prison camp with other civilians. The story of the next four years is one of struggling to stay alive by any means possible." Libr J

"This novel is much more than the gritty story of a child's miraculous survival in the grimly familiar setting of World War II's concentration camps. There is no nostalgia for a good war here, no sentimentality for the human spirit at extremes. Mr. Ballard is more ambitious than romance usually allows. He aims to render a vision of the apocalypse, and succeeds so well that it can hurt to dwell upon his images." N Y Times Book Rev

Followed by The kindness of women (1991)

Balogh, Mary

More than a mistress. Delacorte Press 2000 343p

ISBN 0-385-33531-8   LC 99-462117

"When Jane Ingleby tries to stop a duel, Jocelyn Dudley, Duke of Tresham, is wounded. So it's surprising that she ends up employed as his nurse—and ultimately his mistress as well. But as their relationship blossoms, Jocelyn commits the unpardonable sin of falling in love. In this refreshingly unconventional romance, which boasts an outspoken, memorable heroine, the author again pushes the edges of the genre." Libr J

Seducing an angel. Delacorte Press 2009 325p $23

ISBN 978-0-385-34105-9   LC 2009-01662

"Cassandra Belmont, the widowed Lady Paget, is in London on a desperate mission. Rumored to have killed her husband and banished penniless from his estate by the heir, Cassie has no option but to find a protector for herself and her small household—and wealthy, young, angelically handsome Stephen Huxtable, Earl of Merton, seems the perfect choice. Marriage is definitely not her goal, nor is it his, until an impulsive public kiss changes everything. The gradually developing relationship between these fully realized, three-dimensional characters is complex, believable, and exquisitely rendered." Libr J

Simply love. Delacorte Press 2006 311p $22

ISBN 978-0-385-33883-7; 0-385-33883-X

LC 2005-58262

This novel brings "together lovely Anne Jewell, a teacher at Miss Martin's School for Girls in Bath, and Sydnam Butler, the horribly disfigured steward for the Wales estate of the Duke of Bewcastle. Anne and her son have been invited on holiday with the Bedwyn clan. Neither Anne nor Sydnam is comfortable in company, he because of the injuries he sustained in the Peninsular Wars and she because as a rape victim she is the unwed mother of a nine-year-old. The two connect, and Anne soon discovers that she is pregnant. They marry, but that is only the beginning of their story. Both have had so much pain in their lives, neither one feels worthy of love. Balogh has once again crafted a sensuous tale of two very real people finding love and making each other's lives whole and beautiful." Booklist

Simply magic. Delacorte Press 2007 326p $22

ISBN 978-0-385-33823-3; 0-385-33823-6

LC 2006-48480

"Susanna Osbourne is enjoying a perfectly lovely holiday in the countryside until she meets the wealthy nobleman Peter Edgeworth. Despite Susanna's best efforts to let Peter know she has no interest whatsoever in him, the viscount, who is visiting a friend at a neighboring estate, insists on flirting with her. Peter's persistent charm gradually melts Susanna's icy reserve, and the two end up sharing one wonderfully romantic afternoon together. But then Susanna disappears, forcing Peter to solve the mystery of her past if he is to have any chance at all of a life with her. . . . Balogh continues her superb Simply romance series featuring four teachers from Miss Martin's School for Girls with another exquisitely crafted Regency historical that brilliantly blends deliciously clever writing, subtly nuanced characters, and simmering sensuality into a simply sublime romance." Booklist

Simply perfect. Delacorte Press 2008 343p $22

ISBN 978-0-385-33824-0   LC 2007-24314

A title in the authors's Regency series centering on Miss Martin's School for Girls. "Falling in love with the heir to a dukedom is the last thing practical, compassion-

Balogh, Mary—*Continued*

ate headmistress Claudia Martin has in mind when she agrees to take her charity students to spend part of the summer at a country estate. But fate has a way of shaking things up, and as Claudia and Joseph, the Marquess of Attingsborough, are thrown together, a wary friendship and respect expand into a love that for all its passion seems doomed from the start. Class lines are clearly drawn in this emotionally rich romance that pits a pair of beautifully delineated, appropriately conflicted protagonists against the snobbish rigidity of the social structure of the times." Libr J

Slightly dangerous. Delacorte Press 2004 344p
ISBN 0-385-33811-2   LC 2003-70091
This is the "culmination of Balogh's wonderfully entertaining Bedwyn series, in which each sibling in the aristocratic family finds the love of his or her life. Wulfric, the eldest brother, is known for his icy reserve, and, in fact, the formidable duke effectively stopped marriage-minded pursuits and was content with his mistress until she died. Invited to a house party, he unhappily finds himself in the company of Christine Derrick, the klutzy, impoverished widow of a viscount's brother. Two more unsuitable lovers have never been imagined, but Balogh, famous for her believable characters and finely crafted Regency-era settings, forges a relationship that leaps off the page and into the hearts of her readers. The sixth title in a series would seem an unlikely point to begin, but Balogh includes the other five Bedwyn siblings and their loves in such a way as to delight readers familiar with them, and entice readers new to the series to read the previous installments." Booklist

Balzac, Honoré de, 1799-1850

The country doctor; Translated by Ellen Marriage; introd. by Marcel Girard. Dutton 1961 xxv, 290p o.p.
"Everyman's library"
Original French edition, 1833. Part of the series: Scenes of provincial life
The device with which this character study is held together concerns the visit of Pierre Joseph Genastas, an ex-soldier, who is searching for the saintly doctor Benassis. "A minute description of country life in the hilly region about Grenoble; the agricultural doings, the wretchedness of the peasantry, and M. Benassis' persevering attempts to ameliorate their condition, furnish a good example of Balzac's indefatigable realism. In this practical philanthropist, the reformed sinner who becomes a public benefactor, an ideal figure is created, a great soul, unselfish, full of love for man, unconquerably patient." Baker. Guide to the Best Fic

Cousin Bette; translated from the French by James Waring. Knopf 1991 xliii, 484p
ISBN 0-679-40671-9   LC 91-52964
"Everyman's library"
Original French edition, 1846. Part of the series: Scenes of Parisian life
"This powerful story is a vivid picture of the tastes and vices of Parisian life in the middle of last century. Lisbeth Fischer, commonly called Cousin Bette, is an eccentric poor relation, a worker in gold and silver lace. The keynote of her character is jealousy, the special object of it her beautiful and nobel-minded cousin Adeline,

wife of Baron Hector Hulot. The chief interest of the story lies in the development of her character, of that of the unscrupulous beauty Madame Marneffe, and the base and empty voluptuary Hulot. . . . Gloomy and despairing . . . [it is] yet terribly powerful." Keller. Reader's Dig of Books

Père Goriot (Old Goriot); a new translation: responses, contemporaries and other novelists, twentieth-century criticism; translated by Burton Raffel; edited by Peter Brooks. W.W. Norton & Co. 1998 370p map pa $11.25
ISBN 0-393-97166-X
                                         * LC 97-19938
Original French edition, 1835. Part of the series: Scenes of Parisian life
"Goriot, a retired manufacturer of vermicelli, is a good man and a weak father. He has given away his money in order to ensure the marriage of his two daughters, Anastasie and Delphine. Because of his love for them, he has to accept all kinds of humiliations from his sons-in-law, one a 'gentilhomme,' M. de Restaud, and the other a financier, M. de Nucingen. Both young women are ungrateful. They gradually abandon him. He dies without seeing them at his bedside, cared for only by young Rastignac, a law student who lives at the same boarding house, the pension Vauquer." Haydn. Thesaurus of Book Dig

Bambara, Toni Cade

Gorilla, my love. Random House 1972 177p
ISBN 0-394-48201-8
Contents: My man Bovanne; Gorilla, my love; Raymond's run; The hammer man; Mississippi Ham Rider; Happy birthday; Playin with Punjab; Talkin bout Sonny; The lesson; The survivor; Sweet town; Blues ain't no mockin bird; Basement; Maggie of the green bottles; The Johnson girls

The salt eaters. Random House 1980 295p
ISBN 0-394-50712-6   LC 79-4806
"Velma Henry has tried suicide and survived and now sits on a stool in the Southwest Community Infirmary in Clayborne (a Southern city) listening to faith healer Minnie Ransom ask a hard question about what she wants. Fitfully she asks herself some questions, too, and in the process remembers what happened, fingers the past, absents herself from her own healing to recollect other times, other places, other folks, as she mentally travels abroad in Clayborne in search of answers." Publ Wkly
This novel "with its beautiful, difficult prose, is a work at once intensely personal and political that will assure Bambara's place in black American fiction." Libr J

Bank, Melissa

The girls' guide to hunting and fishing. Viking 1999 288p $23.95
ISBN 0-670-88300-X   LC 98-48590
This novel traces the love life of its central character, Jane, "episodically from the time she is 14 through her 20s and 30s as she orbits Manhattan's publishing world." Time
"Often funny, poignant, and well sprinkled with razor-sharp wit, Jane's search for love (usually in all the wrong places) is going to be familiar to many." Booklist

Banks, Iain

Matter; a Culture novel; [by] Iain M. Banks. Orbit 2008 593p $25.99

ISBN 9780316005364; 0316005363

LC 2007-941828

This novel in the author's series about "the Culture, an interstellar posthuman civilization of incredible wealth and technological sophistication, centers on three siblings: Ferbin and Oramen, the misfit heirs of conquering King Hausk of the Sarl, who rules a backward and patriarchal realm deep beneath the surface of the artificial 'Shellworld' Sursamen, and their exiled sister, Djan, now a powerful agent of the Culture's Special Circumstances division. When King Hausk is murdered, Ferbin narrowly avoids the conspirators and sets out across the galaxy to ask Djan's help with revenge against the killer, now serving as Oramen's regent. Soon they learn of the horrific forces a hidden enemy is about to unleash on Sursamen, and must race to save the home that has rejected them both. Beautifully written and filled with memorable characters and startling technology" Publ Wkly

Banks, Oliver T.

The Caravaggio obsession; a novel; by Oliver Banks. Little, Brown 1984 230p

ISBN 0-316-08022-5

LC 83-17497

"When a friend in the art auction business is killed in New York, Amos {Hatcher} tracks art and murder to Rome. There he is thwarted by the police and threatened by quasi-radical thugs. Amos soon realizes that his friend's murderer, the ringleader of the robberies, is obsessed with that earlier dark genius, the painter Caravaggio. Banks crams his story with history and lore in ways that are essential to the plot and fascinating to even the most culture-resistant reader. The spirit of Caravaggio and the desperate, beautiful city of Rome haunt this superlative thriller." Wilson Libr Bull

Banks, Russell, 1940-

Affliction. Harper & Row 1989 355p

ISBN 0-06-016142-6

* LC 89-45075

"Wade Whitehouse is a small-town policeman in his early forties made crazy-desperate by a life of chronic failure and intractably self-destructive behavior. Like his father, he's moody, abusive, and a mean drunk. Wade's got a good heart, and he'd like to change his ways, but his desire to reform is thwarted by his baser male instincts. Things just keep getting worse until he finally can't take it anymore, whereupon he snaps and literally runs amok in a mad and murderous rage of Oedipal annihilation before vanishing, ghostlike, into the snow-covered New Hampshire countryside. Wade's tragic saga is related by his younger brother, Rolfe, a bookish history teacher who suppresses his own self-destructive tendencies by submerging himself in scholarly pursuits." Booklist

This novel is "psychological portraiture of a high order, and like all profound portraits it finds in its subject astonishing contradictions." N Y Times Book Rev

Cloudsplitter; a novel. HarperCollins Pubs. 1998 758p

ISBN 0-06-016860-9

LC 97-22163

In 1859, five insurrectionists escaped Harpers Ferry, "including Brown's son Owen. In 'Cloudsplitter' Owen decides to tell his tale. He has fled . . . to a California mountaintop, there to remain in seclusion until the end of the century, when one Miss Mayo requests an audience for a biography of John Brown she's researching. Owen responds with this book, a very long suicide note addressed to her but, as he explains, also to his father, his brothers, and others among the already dead. It is Owen's brief for Purgatory, where he expects to meet all those who devoted their lives to John Brown." New Yorker

"To rise above period costume and stately diction, a historical novel must have a saving tincture of anachronism, a point of forced contact with the unfinished business of the present. Cloudsplitter, is brought alive by Owen's ambivalent, recognizably modern consciousness." Nation

The sweet hereafter. HarperCollins Pubs. 1991 257p

ISBN 0-06-016703-3

* LC 90-56404

In this novel the story "is told by four people: Dolores Driscoll, a school-bus driver in a small town; Billy Ansel, father of two of the children on the bus; Mitchell Stephens, a lawyer; and Nichole Burnell, a student. In the accident on which the story is centered, Ansel loses his children and Nichole is paralyzed. Dolores survives the accident—the plunge of the bus through the guardrail and into the water-filled quarry—and then tries to survive survival. Mitchell Stephens becomes the attorney for the group of parents who mount a lawsuit." Christ Sci Monit

"Banks handles his dark theme with judicious restraint, empathy and compassion." Publ Wkly

Bannister, Jo

No birds sing. St. Martin's Press 1996 297p $21.95

ISBN 0-312-14382-6

LC 96-7296

This procedural "about the Castlemere, England, police department boasts a wonderful cast of multidimensional characters: Detective Superintendent Frank Shapiro, Detective Inspector Liz Graham, and the department's wild Irishman, Detective Sergeant Cal Donovan. In this . . . installment in the series, Castlemere is hit by a smash-and-grab gang, train hijackers, and a rapist. Watching Bannister weave these disparate elements together to produce another gripping tale is half the fun." Booklist

Banville, John

The book of evidence. HarperCollins Pubs. 1990 219p

ISBN 0-684-19180-6

* LC 89-10985

First published 1989 in the United Kingdom

"Freddie Montgomery is a schizophrenic 38-year-old ex-scientist. . . . After study in America, Freddie returns to Ireland to find that his disowning mother has sold what he believes is part of his inheritance from his late father, some paintings that include an Old Dutch master of a woman he thinks regards him with caring, benevolent authority. As he steals it, he murders a maid who

Banville, John—_Continued_

catches him in the act. His lawyer advises him to plead manslaughter to quash evidence. Instead . . . Freddie writes the 'book of evidence' that we read." Libr J

"This novel, the inventive testimony of a murderer more interested in making an impression than escaping conviction, is . . . hauntingly beautiful and original. . . . Mr. Banville shows his uncanny ability to make everything he describes seem new and rare, yet instantly recognisable." Economist

Christine Falls; a novel; [by] Benjamin Black. H. Holt 2006 340p $25
ISBN 978-0-8050-8152-7; 0-8050-8152-6
* LC 2006-43581

In this "debut thriller from Irish author Black (the pseudonym of Booker Prize–winner John Banville), pathologist Garret Quirke uncovers a web of corruption in 1950s Dublin surrounding the death in childbirth of a young maid, Christine Falls. Quirke is pulled into the case when he confronts his stepbrother, physician Malachy Griffin, who's altering Christine's file at the city morgue. Soon it appears the entire establishment is in denial over Christine's mysterious demise and in a conspiracy that recalls the classic film Chinatown. And the deeper Quirke delves into the mystery, the more it seems to implicate his own family and the Catholic church." Publ Wkly

"As the story moves from Ireland to Boston, the push and pull of the novel's dual existence as 'literary thriller' becomes almost as absorbing as the plot; the tension between the two halves of that troublesome equation regularly rippling the book's surface. . . . At its best, the prose here is every bit as acute as one would expect from John Banville, even Banville in disguise—the baroque flourishes are held in check . . ., but the stern elegance remains, and its marriage to a thriller's momentum can have startling results." Times Lit Suppl

Followed by: The silver swan (2008)

The sea. Knopf 2005 195p $23
ISBN 0-307-26311-8
LC 2005-50418

"When Max Morden returns to the coastal town where he spent a holiday in his youth he is both escaping from a recent loss and confronting a distant trauma. The Grace family appear that long ago summer as if from another world. Drawn to the Grace twins, Chloe and Myles, Max soon finds himself entangled in their lives, which are as seductive as they are unsettling. What ensues will haunt him for the rest of his years and shape everything that is to follow." Publisher's note

"What's strangest about 'The Sea' is that the novel somehow becomes simpler and clearer as it gets more selfconscious: a consequence, I suppose, of its author dropping the pretense of being one kind of writer and giving in to his authentic and much more complicated creative nature. This misshapen but affecting novel turns out to be about something even more familiar than the loss of innocence: it's about grief, the misery and confusion the narrator feels on losing his wife." N Y Times Book Rev

The silver swan; a novel; [by] Benjamin Black. Henry Holt and Co. 2008 290p $25
ISBN 978-0-8050-8153-4; 0-8050-8153-4
LC 2007-31567

"After a young woman's corpse is fished from the sea, Dublin pathologist Quirke delves into a 'grimy little suburban melodrama' of kinky sex, drugs, and murder." Entertainment Wkly

"Black has created a wonderful protagonist in Quirke. Tortured and guilt-ridden, six months sober and aching to drink, and just a bit more curious and perceptive than he would choose to be, Quirke is a natural detective. Even when he wants to cover up the truth, he can't. No one will thank him, he knows from the start. But that's just another burden he must carry." Boston Globe

Bao Ninh, 1952-

The sorrow of war; a novel of North Vietnam; translated from the Vietnamese by Phan Thanh Hao; edited by Frank Palmos. Scribner 1995 233p
ISBN 0-679-43961-7
LC 94-22390
Original Vietnamese edition, 1991

This novel is based on the experiences of a North Vietnamese soldier who fought in the South for over ten years. "The tale is told in a series of flashbacks by the novel's hero, Kien, who is writing his story as an act of therapy in the late 1980s. As a young man, Kien had been led to believe that a patriotic war was being waged as an example to future generations. He gradually comes to believe that the three golden rules of preparedness he had learnt at school were empty sloganeering. To the common soldier in this story, the realities of war are a frenzied, dehumanising aggression, and the creation of an unnatural thirst for killing and wanton cruelty." Economist

"The word classic is bandied about with ridiculous laxity, but in this case it is hard not to fall back on it. Nothing else really fits the elemental simplicity of theme and treatment: love, war, death, disillusionment, betrayal." New Statesman (1913)

Barbash, Thomas _See_ Barbash, Tom

Barbash, Tom

The last good chance; a novel. Picador USA 2002 440p $24
ISBN 0-312-28796-8
LC 2002-25847

"Steven Turner is a young journalist exiled at a paper in Lakeland, a decaying port town in rural upstate New York. His best friend, Jack Lambeau, is the Lakeland town planner. An ambitious Ivy League graduate, Lambeau had had difficulty advancing his experimental urban planning ideas in New York City. When Lakeland's mayor, William Hickey, promised him carte blanche for his New Urbanist—style visions, Lambeau agreed to return to his hometown. With evangelical fervor, he tries to revive Lakeland through a glittering lakefront development project. What he doesn't know, and what the mayor does, is that there are tubs of toxic materials illegally dumped under the lakefront. . . .This is a taut, intricate vision of ambition, corruption and love in the postindustrial era." Publ Wkly

Barbery, Muriel, 1969-

The elegance of the hedgehog; translated from the French by Alison Anderson. Europa Editions 325p pa $15
ISBN 978-1-933372-60-0; 1-933372-60-5

Barbery, Muriel, 1969-—*Continued*
Original French edition, 2006
In this novel, "the unschooled middle-aged concierge of an upper-class Paris apartment building acts like a stereotypical concierge, leaving the television on all day and sharing her quarters with an old, fat cat, but she secretly consumes vast quantities of literature. A few floors above her, the brilliant and prematurely disillusioned twelve-year-old daughter of a 'holier-than-thou-left-wing-intellectual' family is planning arson and suicide, unless she can find something worth living for beyond the 'vacuousness of bourgeois existence.' Unbeknown to each other, the two autodidacts share an allergy to grammatical errors (the concierge considers a misplaced comma an 'underhanded attack') and a love of tea and moments of ineffable beauty. Barbery's sly wit, which bestows lightness on the most ponderous cogitations, keeps her tale aloft." New Yorker

Barfoot, Joan

Critical injuries. Counterpoint 2002 336p $25
ISBN 1-58243-208-2   LC 2002-23845
"At 49 Isla revels in her second marriage and loves her advertising career, a happy life forever changed when she walks in on a robbery and the startled gunman, 17-year-old Roddy, shoots. . . . As Isla lies frozen in a hospital bed and Roddy emotionally freezes everyone out as he lies hopeless in jail, their thoughts are remarkably similar as they revisit the people and events that shaped their lives and worry about each other." Booklist

Barker, Clive

The books of blood. Putnam 1988 c1984 462p
ISBN 0-399-13343-7   LC 88-2404
"An Ace/Putnam book"
Omnibus edition of volumes 1-3 of Books of blood originally published 1984 in the United Kingdom; 1986 in paperback in the United States. Volumes 4 and 5 of Books of blood published with title: The inhuman condition and In the flesh
Contents: Volume one: The Book of Blood; The midnight meat train; The Yattering and Jack; Pig blood blues; Sex, death and starshine; In the hills, the cities
Volume two: Dread; Hell's event; Jacqueline Ess: her will and testament; The skins of the fathers; New murders in the Rue Morgue
Volume three: Son of celluloid; Rawhead Rex; Confessions of a (pornographer's) shroud; Scape-goats; Human remains; The Book of Blood (a postscript): on Jerusalem Street

Coldheart Canyon. HarperCollins Pubs. 2001 676p
ISBN 0-06-018297-0   LC 2001-279145
Years ago, many film stars and "their colleagues were drawn by the beautiful, rapacious film star Katya Lupi to her magnificent home in Los Angeles's Coldheart Canyon. What kept them at the house, even after death, is the incredible room in its lowest story. Assembled from thousands of painted tiles, that room—brought to California in the 1920s from an ancient monastery in Romania—is literally alive with evil. . . . The room's powers bestow timeless youth on some, including Katya, but give rise to monstrous entities as well. In the present day, into this horrific place enter several modern sorts,

most notably A-list film hero Todd Pickett and a dowdy woman, head of Todd's fan club, whose courage and good sense mark her as the novel's hero." Publ Wkly

Imajica. HarperCollins Pubs. 1991 824p
ISBN 0-06-017922-8
                                        * LC 90-56405
This fantasy "begins when a rich gent hires a peculiar assassin to off his estranged wife, the tome's female protagonist, whom he'd . . . stolen a while back from the professional art forger who's the male protagonist. The attempt fails but starts the romance's personae plunging back and forth between 'Dominions,' of which there are at least five, the Earth upon which we all dwell being the fifth and seemingly least developed of the lot." Booklist
"Barker's prodigious imagination delivers magicians, doppelgängers, Boschean creatures of staggeringly various descriptions and a pantheon of gods and goddesses seduced by power and redeemed by love in a story of violence, occasional unconventional eroticism and mesmerizing invention." Publ Wkly

Weaveworld. Poseidon Press 1987 584p
ISBN 0-671-61268-9
                                        * LC 87-18602
This fantasy concerns "the Fugue, a magical land inhabited by descendants of supernatural beings who once shared the earth with humans. The Fugue has been woven into a carpet for protection against those who would destroy it; the death of its guardian occasions a battle between good and particularly repulsive evil forces for control of the Fugue." Libr J
Barker "creates a fantastic romance of magic and promise that is at once popular fiction and utopian conjuring. . . . There is great wit in the struggle that ensues, and keen attention to the facts of poverty and exile." NY Times Book Rev

Barker, Nicola, 1966-

Darkmans. Harper Perennial 2008 c2007 838p pa $16.95
ISBN 978-0-06-157521-1; 0-06-157521-6
                                        LC 2007-40012
First published 2007 in the United Kingdom
"Darkmans is set in Ashford, the Kent town now best known as the home of the Channel Tunnel's International Passenger Station. But in becoming a 'geographical hub', the town in Barker's imagination is robbed of its history, sterilised in the present, and abandoned to an uncertain future. . . . [The central character, Daniel] Beede is a diligent local worthy turned Puritan avenger by, and against, the brash homogenisation of his hometown. The novel introduces the reader to a remarkable cast of characters: one circle encompasses Beede's drug-dealing son Kane, his ex-girlfriend Kelly Broad (of the infamous Broad clan) and Gaffar, a Kurdish refugee mildly besotted with Kelly and 'employed' by Kane, who has a morbid fear of salads. Another circle links Beede's chiropodist Elen and her husband, the paranoid, narcoleptic Isidore, and their eerie child-prodigy son Fleet. . . . [The plot] is twisted and braided with an intricacy so delicate you barely notice the links until the whole web engulfs you." Scotland on Sunday

LIST OF FICTIONAL WORKS

Barker, Pat, 1943-

Double vision. Farrar, Straus & Giroux 2003
258p $23

ISBN 0-374-20905-7 LC 2003-54736

"Kate Frobisher, a sculptor working on a monumental figure of Jesus, is recovering from a car accident and grieving for her husband, Ben, a war photographer killed in Afghanistan. Stephen Sharkey, a journalist (and friend of Ben's) suffering from post-traumatic stress syndrome after covering Bosnia, Rwanda and other conflicts, has left London and a failed marriage to write a book about 'the way wars are represented.' An ensemble cast gathers around these two haunted figures: Stephen's brother Robert and his family; Alec Braithewaite, the friendly vicar, and his Cambridge-bound daughter Justine; and Peter Wingrave, Kate's studio assistant and Justine's ex." Publ Wkly

Barker "writes superbly, with economy and a lovely talent for darting images. The subject matter is dark, and much is left unsaid, but the reader is drawn on, from page to page." Economist

The eye in the door. Dutton 1994 c1993 280p
ISBN 0-525-93808-7

* LC 93-43833

First published 1993 in the United Kingdom

"Revisiting World War I England to explore war and its effects on individuals and society, Barker brings back characters . . . from *Regeneration*, including bisexual war hero Billy Prior and psychiatrist William Rivers. In 1918, the war was not going well for the Allies, and hysteria took root—the targets being pacifists and homosexuals, who were allegedly open to blackmail. Prior has connections to a group of pacifists who are being persecuted, and he also suffers from psychological episodes in which his personality alters dramatically. Dr. Rivers treats both Prior and other homosexuals on 'The 47,000,' a list of all purported gays in Britain." Libr J

This work "succeeds as both historical fiction and as sequel. Its research and speculation combine to produce a kind of educated imagination that is persuasive and illuminating about this particular place and time. . . . The novel's greatest success, however, has to do with the insight it provides into its central doctor-patient relationships." N Y Times Book Rev

Followed by The ghost road

The ghost road. Dutton 1996 c1995 278p
ISBN 0-525-94191-6

* LC 95-46863

"A William Abrahams book"
First published 1995 in the United Kingdom

This novel's main protagonists "are Dr. William H. Rivers, the English psychologist who treated the poets Siegfried Sassoon and Wilfred Owen, among others, for shell shock, and the fictional Billy Prior, a former 'cured' patient who insists on returning to the front in France even though the war is winding down to its bloody finale. In the late summer of 1918, ghosts—of the dead and of the soon-to-be-dead—roam the land. . . . Rivers, facing the moral dilemma of healing men so that they might be killed, recalls an anthropological trip he made to a Melanesian tribe whose head-hunting practices were banned by the British." Libr J

"The Ghost Road is a startlingly good novel in its own right. With the other two volumes of the trilogy, it forms one of the richest and most rewarding works of fiction of recent times. Intricately plotted, beautifully written, skillfully assembled, tender, horrifying and funny, it lives on in the imagination, like the war it so imaginatively and so intelligently explores." Times Lit Suppl

Regeneration. Dutton 1992 c1991 251p
ISBN 0-525-93427-8

* LC 91-41264

"A William Abrahams book"
First published 1991 in the United Kingdom

This novel "blends fact and fiction in relating a pivotal incident in the tragic life of noted English poet Siegfried Sassoon. In 1917, Sassoon, an army officer who had been decorated for his gallantry, was sent to a military sanitarium at Craiglockhart, diagnosed as suffering from shell shock. In fact, he had been assigned to the hospital less for medical reasons than political ones. No longer believing in the government's vaguely stated war aims and haunted by memories of the victims of the carnage he experienced, he had issued a declaration condemning the war. Only the intervention of his friend, poet Robert Graves, prevented a court-martial." Publ Wkly

"'Regeneration' is an antiwar war novel, in a tradition that is by now an established one, though it tells a part of the whole story of war that is not often told—how war may batter and break men's minds—and so makes the madness of war more than a metaphor, and more awful." N Y Times Book Rev

Followed by The eye in the door

Barnard, Judith

For works written by this author in collaboration with Michael Fain see Michael, Judith

Barnard, Robert

Death of a literary widow. Scribner 1980 c1979
192p

ISBN 0-684-16648-8 LC 80-13128

First published 1979 in the United Kingdom with title: Posthumous papers

"Two elderly women, Viola and Hilda, live in the same house, avoiding each other like the plague. Both have been married to the same man, the late writer Walter Mackin, who is the object of a sudden, intense renewal of interest—articles are written about him, his books are reissued. The great concern of the two wives is who will profit from Mackin's posthumous reputation. One of the old ladies dies in a fire, leaving everyone wondering whether she went out in an accidental blaze or as the result of someone's murderous rage." Booklist

A fall from grace. Scribner 2007 261p $24
ISBN 978-0-7432-7220-9; 0-7432-7220-X

LC 2006-51427

Leeds cop Charlie Peace is a "newly made inspector, relocating with his wife to the village of Slepton Edge, a move somewhat darkened by the parallel move of Peace's detested father-inlaw to a house nearby. . . . Peace and his wife, Felicity, learn that her father had to leave his former village hurriedly, after he struck a young woman. And now the old man is hitting on a teenage girl. Before the Peaces have a chance to figure out how to protect her, the old man is found dead at the bottom of a quarry. Suspects abound, including a clutch

Barnard, Robert—*Continued*

of murderous children and Felicity herself. Peace moves into full detective mode with a murder on his doorstep and his wife a prime suspect. This very satisfying riff on the traditional village mystery finds Barnard at the top of his game." Booklist

A murder in Mayfair. Scribner 2000 270p

ISBN 0-684-86445-2   LC 99-46962

"When Colin Pinnock becomes a junior minister in the new Labor government, he is full of promise and resolve, until a curt message on a grubby postcard—'Who do you think you are?'—challenges all his assumptions about himself. . . . Barnard is meticulous about building up the suspense as Colin is hounded by the faceless fury bent on ending, or at least ruining, his blameless life. But there's more nasty fun in reading the story as the revenge of the ousted Tories on the cheeky whippersnappers who think they can keep their integrity, not to mention their sanity, once they start playing politics for real." N Y Times Book Rev

Out of the blackout. Scribner 1985 c1984

ISBN 0-684-18282-3   LC 85-1694

"An unusual piece of detection in that the central character is searching for himself—who was he before he was taken, with other children, to foster homes in the country during the London blitz? Though the tale is not wholeheartedly crime fiction, a murder is discovered and its ramifications elucidated by the self-searching hero." Barzun. Cat of Crime. Rev and enl edition

Barnes, Djuna, 1892-1982

Nightwood. Modern Lib. 2000 c1937 xxxii, 169p

ISBN 0-679-64024-X

     * LC 99-56308

First published 1936 in the United Kingdom; first United States edition 1937 by Harcourt, Brace

"An account of the tangled sexual and psychological relationships between various expatriates in Paris and Berlin. Narrated in part through an alcoholic haze of stream of consciousness, it owes its reputation as an avant-garde work partially to its frank treatment of lesbianism." Benet's Reader's Ency of Am Lit

Barnes, John, 1957-

The armies of memory. Tor 2006 429p $25.95

ISBN 0-7653-0330-2   LC 2005-18807

"A Tom Doherty Associates book"

"Giraut Leone, secret agent for the Thousand Cultures, is approaching retirement. One final mission remains, however: to track down a repository of deadly secrets established by a dissident group far beyond the frontier of settlement." Booklist

"Set in the same far-future universe as A Million Open Doors and A Sky So Big and Black, Barnes's novel concludes the adventures of one of the genre's most distinctive 'special agents,' the cultured, talented, and deadly Giraut Leones. At the same time, the author depicts a future in which the coexistence of divergent human cultures remains a major force in the development of human society. A superb blending of adventure and scientific speculation." Libr J

The sky so big and black. TOR Bks. 2002 315p $24.95

ISBN 0-7653-0303-5   LC 2002-22307

"A Tom Doherty Associates book"

As Terpsichore (Teri) Murray and her eco-prospector father "escort a group of students from Mars's highlands to their school in Wells City, a catastrophic solar phenomenon occurs, decimating many of the human colonies and disrupting communication planet-wide. Left to her own devices to rescue herself and the survivors in her group, Teri is forced to compromise her principles and make an alliance with a force that could mean the end of Martian independence." Libr J

"As always, Barnes's character are beautifully natural. His sense of how the conditions of a place can create a culture and individual sensibilities is outstanding, and here he even allows his slang to evolve." Publ Wkly

Barnes, Jonathan

The somnambulist. William Morrow & Co. 2008 c2007 353p $23.95

ISBN 978-0-06-137538-5; 0-06-137538-1

First published 2007 in the United Kingdom

In this Victorian pastiche "the slumberer of the title is a mute giant of a man who assists the hero, Edward Moon, in his magic acts and detective work. The novel begins with Moon and his drowsy partner at the fag end of an illustrious career. As the 19th century fades, so does the public's taste for the sorts of entertainments that Moon supplies. With his reputation falling—and a spot of arson at his theater—Moon agrees to assist the police in solving a pair of unlikely murders. He finds at their root a fiendish and far-reaching utopian plot." Village Voice

"There is much that is strange, magical and darkly hilarious in this book, at least if one savors the sardonic and the bizarre. At various points it recalls Dickens, Alice in Wonderland and Frankenstein, but it remains an original and monumentally inventive piece of work." Washington Post Book World

Barnes, Julian

A history of the world in $10\frac{1}{2}$ chapters. Knopf 1989 307p

ISBN 0-394-58061-3

     * LC 89-45266

"A revisionist view of Noah's Ark, told by the stowaway woodworm. A chilling account of terrorists hijacking a cruise ship. A court case in 16th-century France in which the woodworm stands accused. A desperate woman's attempt to escape radioactive fallout on a raft. An acute analysis of Géricault's 'Scene of Shipwreck.' The search of a 19th-century Englishwoman and of a contemporary American astronaut for Noah's Ark. An actor's increasingly desperate letters to his silent lover. A thoughtful meditation on the novelist's responsibility regarding love. These and other stories make up Barnes's . . . retelling of the history of the world." Libr J

This book "shapes up not only as Barnes's funniest novel but also his most richly cargoed and imaginatively designed. . . . As satirist and story-teller he has few equals at present." New Statesman Soc

Barnes, Linda

Cold case. Delacorte Press 1997 385p
ISBN 0-385-30614-8   LC 96-38216
"Adam Mayhew shows up on PI Carlyle's Cambridge, Mass., doorstep with the first chapter of a manuscript that he says could only have been penned by Thea Janis, who disappeared so long ago. When her clothes were later found on a beach, Thea Janis was presumed to be a suicide. But Mayhew, a relative of the author, insists that the manuscript—which makes reference to the fall of the Berlin Wall—proves she is alive and writing. Carlyle's task is to find the writer." Publ Wkly

"Carlotta isn't as smooth an operator as some of her colleagues . . . but her gung-ho technique works for her and it's easy to get caught up in her enthusiasm." N Y Times Book Rev

The snake tattoo. St. Martin's Press 1989 290p
ISBN 0-312-02643-9   LC 88-30525
Private eye Carlotta Carlyle "is faced with two equally difficult cases: finding a missing teenage girl, who seems to have traded posh suburbia for the moral sewer of Boston's Combat Zone, and helping Beantown cop and longtime friend Mooney, who stands accused of assaulting a supposedly unarmed man in a bar fight." Booklist
"Bright, witty, and a touch sarcastic." Libr J

Barnes, Steven

(jt. auth) Niven, L. Saturn's race

Barone, Sam

Dawn of empire. William Morrow 2006 483p map $25.95
ISBN 978-0-06-089244-9; 0-06-089244-7
     LC 2005-58374
"In the fertile land of Mesopotamia circa 3000 B.C.E., the first cities arose, threatening the existence of nomads who depended on raiding small, defenseless farmsteads and villages for food and slaves. When news reaches the people of one of these cities that the barbaric Alur Meriki have targeted them for their next raid, Eskkar, a nomadic warrior exiled from his clan, assumes the role of war leader and devises a plan to save Orak and its people. . . . Readers will find it hard to put down this dramatic tale of conflict between cultures, bloody warfare, and early diplomacy and statehood as seen through the eyes of a man born to conquer and rule." Libr J

Empire rising. William Morrow 2007 465p $25.95
ISBN 978-0-06-089246-3   LC 2007-40485
In this sequel to Dawn of empire, "Lord Eskkar, a former barbarian who earlier saved the city of Akkad from almost-certain defeat, and Lady Trella, an erstwhile slave and his wife, now rule the 'biggest city on the Tigris.' Hoping to crush the bandits marauding in the countryside and extend Akkadian rule, Eskkar dispatches one band of soldiers south from Akkad and leads another north. In Eskkar's absence, Korthac, a newly arrived Egyptian warrior posing as a trader, schemes to infiltrate the city with his followers and seize power. . . . The frenetic action might be predictable, but it's never boring. The setting is convincingly rendered, and the characters—heroes and villains—are sharply drawn. Fans of ancient historical fiction will enjoy this instructive journey to the dawn of civilization." Publ Wkly

Barr, Nevada

High country. Putnam 2004 323p $24.95
ISBN 0-399-15144-3   LC 2003-47243
This mystery finds Ranger Anna Pigeon "undercover as a waitress at the famous Ahwahnee Hotel in Yosemite National Park. Four seasonal workers have been missing for two weeks, and not even a professional rescue team can scrounge up a clue. Are they AWOL, or is it foul play? Anna waits tables, plays mom to a couple of twentysomething roommates, takes flak from the dining room manager, and deals with bullies before striking out on her own to figure out what has happened. The gossip among hotel staff and visitors is that there's a gold mine in the Sierra Mountains. Barr's even pace and deft characterizations will please series fans while winning her new readers." Libr J

Winter study. Putnam 2008 370p $24.95
ISBN 978-0-399-15458-4; 0-399-15458-2
Park ranger Anna Pigeon has been sent to Michigan's Isle Royale National Park "from her current assignment, Rocky Mountain National Park, to observe wolves, the stars of a longstanding scientific research study made possible because the park is closed from fall to late spring. Trouble is, Homeland Security wants to open up the facilities year-round owing to perceived border-security issues. When wolf researcher Katherine Huff turns up dead one night, attacked by the wolves she loved, all bets are off as to which human let her fall victim." Libr J
"The blizzards, the dangerous ice and the manhunts through the frozen woods are described with crisp, hard-edged beauty. And the wolves, those maligned 'ogres of childhood,' are magnificent." N Y Times Book Rev

Barrett, Andrea

Ship fever and other stories. Norton 1996 254p $21
ISBN 0-393-03853-X   LC 95-14562
Contents: The behavior of the hawkweeds; The English pupil; The littoral zone; Rare bird; Soroche; Birds with no feet; The Marburg sisters; Ship fever
Barrett "tells her stories through alternating voices, diaries, letters—whatever seems to hint at the most promising results. Seen against a larger fictional landscape overpopulated with the sensational and affectless, her work stands out for its sheer intelligence, its painstaking attempt to discern and describe the world's configuration." N Y Times Book Rev

Barrett, William E.

The lilies of the field; drawings by Burt Silverman. Doubleday 1962 92p o.p.

"Homer Smith is an amiable Southern black man. Driving through the Southwest after getting out of the Army, he stops to help four German refugee nuns build a church. After teaching them English and survival skills, he disappears, leaving behind the legend of his faithful help." Shapiro. Fic for Youth. 3d edition

Barron, Stephanie

See also Mathews, Francine

Barrows, Annie

(jt. auth) Shaffer, M. A. The Guernsey Literary and Potato Peel Pie Society

Barry, Brunonia

The lace reader. William Morrow 2008 c2006 390p $24.95

ISBN 978-0-06-162476-6; 0-06-162476-4

Self-published 2006

"Set in Salem, Mass., the story is that of a 32-year-old woman who fled when she was 17 to California but returns when her 85-year-old great-aunt, Eva, is reported missing. Like Eva, Towner Whitney is a 'reader,' though she suppresses the talent. Eva could see a picture in a piece of Ipswich lace that would foretell what was to come. . . . Towner ran off after an extended stay in a high-end looney bin, where she ended up following the suicide of her twin sister, Lyndley. It was that, more than anything, that caused her to reject the family heritage of reading minds as well as lace, though such gifts certainly hold a respected place in Salem. Or did until her Uncle Cal, a wife batterer who sexually abused Lyndley, form a fundamentalist cult to torment and harass the modern-day wiccans? That includes Great-Aunt Eva, a wise and knowing woman, who is found dead and may have been murdered. Cal is a suspect, and it seems he also may have killed a young woman carrying his child. This time it's not so easy for Towner to run, but in staying she confronts pervasive menace." N Y Daily News

Barry, Max

Company. Doubleday 2006 338p $22.95

ISBN 0-385-51439-5   LC 2005-48498

The setting is "the Seattle corporate headquarters of Zephyr Holdings. . . . [Stephen] Jones wonders why his salary has been hidden within the budget for office expenses ('I'm copy paper?') just because he arrived in the midst of a hiring freeze. And he begins to wonder why Zephyr, though a hive of activity, seems to have no real customers and no real work to do." N Y Times (Late N Y Ed)

"As bitter as break-room coffee, the novel eviscerates demeaning modern management techniques that treat workers as 'headcounts.' Though Barry's primary target is corporate dehumanization, he's at his funniest lampooning the suits that tread the stage, consumed by the sound and fury of office politics that signify nothing." Publ Wkly

Bart, André Schwarz- See Schwarz-Bart, André, 1928-

Barth, John

Giles goat-boy; or, The revised new syllabus. Doubleday 1966 xxxi, 710p o.p.

                                                          *

"The novel's protagonist, Billy Bockfuss (also called George Giles, the goat-boy), was raised with herds of goats on a university farm after being found as a baby in the bowels of the giant West Campus Automatic Computer (WESCAC). The WESCAC plans to create a being called GILES (Grand-Tutorial Ideal, Laboratory Eugeni-cal Specimen) that would possess superhuman abilities. Billy's foster father, who tends the herd, suspects Billy of being GILES but tries to groom him to be humanity's savior and to stop WESCAC's domination over humans." Merriam-Webster's Ency of Lit

The sot-weed factor. Doubleday 1967 806p o.p.

Picaresque novel "originally published in 1960 and revised in 1967. A parody of the historical novel, it is based on and takes its title from a satirical poem published in 1708 by Ebenezer Cooke, who is the protagonist of Barth's work. The novel's black humor is derived from its purposeful misuse of conventional litarary devices." Merriam-Webster's Ency of Lit

Barthelme, Donald

Sixty stories. Putnam 1981 457p

ISBN 0-399-12659-7

                                      * LC 81-8646

Contents: Margins; A shower of gold; Me and Miss Mandible; For I'm the boy; Will you tell me; The balloon; The President; Game; Alice; Robert Kennedy saved from drowning; Report; The dolt; See the moon; The Indian uprising; Views of my father weeping; Paraguay; On angels; The Phantom of the Opera's friend; City life; Kierkegaard unfair to Schlegel; The falling dog; The Policemen's Ball; The glass mountain; Critique de la vie quotidienne; The sandman; Träumerei; The rise of capitalism; A city of churches; Daumier; The party; Eugénie Grandet; Nothing: a preliminary account; A manual for sons; At the end of the mechanical age; Rebecca; The captured woman; I bought a little city; The sergeant; The school; The great hug; Our work and why we do it; The crisis; Cortés and Montezuma; The new music; The zombies; The king of jazz; Morning; The death of Edward Lear; The abduction from the Seraglio; On the steps of the conservatory; The leap; Aria; The emerald; How I write my songs; The farewell; The emperor; Thailand; Heroes; Bishop; Grandmother's house

Barthelme, Frederick

Waveland; a novel. Doubleday 2009 240p $24.95

ISBN 978-0-385-52729-3; 0-385-52729-2

                                      LC 2008-13511

"The cast: Vaughn Williams, a retired architect in his late fifties, recently divorced after 15 years of marriage. Greta Del Mar, 10 years Vaughn's junior, whose first husband was murdered five years before, a crime for which Greta was indicted but exonerated. Gail, Vaughn's ex-wife, who remains in their home while Vaughn briefly rents a garage apartment from Greta before moving in with her. Eddie, a one-armed Operation Desert Storm vet, who moves into the garage apartment vacated by Vaughn. Newton, Vaughn's successful and resented younger brother, living on the West Coast off the fortune he made selling his computer startup. Tony, Gail's lover, young and dangerous. And in cameo flashbacks, the Williams brothers' father, whose memory haunts his eldest son. The setting: Waveland and environs, on the Mississippi Gulf Coast, still littered with wreckage a year after it was ravaged by Hurricane Katrina." Providence J

"In this powerfully atmospheric story of loneliness and risk, Barthelme slyly conceals emotional and philosophi-

Barthelme, Frederick—*Continued*

cal intensity beneath the peculiarity of circumstance, the dazzle of hilarious repartee, and the luster of gorgeous prose." Booklist

Barton, Emily, 1969-

Brookland. Farrar, Straus & Giroux 2006 478p $25

ISBN 0-374-11690-3   LC 2005-16269

"Since her girlhood, Prudence Winship has gazed across the tidal straits from her home in Brooklyn to the city of Manhattan and yearned to bridge the distance. Now, established as the owner of the enormously successful gin distillery she inherited from her father, she can begin to realize her dream. Set in eighteenth-century Brooklyn, this is the story of a . . . woman who is consumed by a vision of a bridge: a gargantuan construction of timber and masonry she devises to cross the East River in a single, magnificent span." Publisher's note

"So much modern fiction thinks small, feels small. Emily Barton will never be accused of either. The large and complex storytelling in 'Brookland' is divided between a traditional third-person narrative and the much older Prudence's letters to her daughter. Both feature a large and complex cast." N Y Times Book Rev

Bassani, Giorgio, 1916-2000

The garden of the Finzi-Continis; translated from the Italian by William Weaver; with an introduction by Tim Parks. Everyman's Library 2005 xxxiii, 246p $23

ISBN 978-1-4000-4422-1; 1-4000-4422-7

     LC 2004-63119

Original Italian edition, 1962; first published in the United States 1965 by Atheneum

"The Finzi-Continis, a wealthy Jewish Italian family, lived in a beautiful and seemingly secure environment and enjoyed intellectual pursuits. The narrator remembers the family, his unrequited love for the beautiful but cold Micol, and his friendship with her brother, Albert. The novel describes the assimilation of Jews into Italian society and then the changes effected when fascism overtakes Italy and anti-Semitism destroys the family." Shapiro. Fic for Youth. 3d edition

Bastable, Bernard

See also Barnard, Robert

Bates, H. E. (Herbert Ernest), 1905-1974

Fair stood the wind for France. Little, Brown 1944 270p o.p.

     *

"An Atlantic Monthly Press book"

A British bomber, returning from a mission over Italy, crashed in occupied France. The members of the crew managed to escape via the underground route, all but the pilot who was too ill. He was cared for by a family of French peasants, whose innate goodness made such an impression on him that when he finally left France he took with him the daughter of the family, as his wife.

"An almost unbearable suspense, the romance of the two young people and a true portrait of the little people

of France, defenseless but possessed of an enduring power, all these go to make an unforgettable story, beautifully told." Bookmark

Bates, Herbert Ernest *See* Bates, H. E. (Herbert Ernest), 1905-1974

Battle, Lois

Bed & breakfast. Viking 1996 372p

ISBN 0-670-86074-3   LC 96-17258

"Josie Tatternall, the septuagenarian widow of an unfaithful martinet of an army officer and owner of a bed and breakfast in upscale Beaufort, S.C., is determined that all three of her daughters will be reunited for the upcoming Christmas holidays. That will be no easy task after years of real and imagined affronts among the siblings and their mother." Publ Wkly

"The story introduces a cast of memorable characters, primarily Josie herself, who fully reminds us that life, love, and growth are not limited to any particular age." Libr J

Southern women. St. Martin's Press 1984 404p

ISBN 0-312-74747-0   LC 83-22999

This novel "depicts three generations of Southern women represented by the female line of a prominent Savannah family. Eunnonia Grace Hampton, known as Nonnie, is matriarch of the clan; over 70 when widowhood permits her her first real independence. . . . Lucille Hampton Simpkins, her youngest daughter, has devoted her life to cultivating those traditional feminine charms that only fleetingly satisfy her vanity and leave her vulnerable at 50 to a consummate roué. Lucille's daughter, Cordy, 30, wants more from life than her marital bed can provide, and has become a romance novelist. The book begins when Cordy, after leaving Chicago and her husband, returns home to Savannah." N Y Times Book Rev

"The author's characters are the type that readers of light fiction enjoy: they possess ordinary urges and desires overlaid with tinges of nobility, tragedy, and/or glamour. The plot unravels quickly but logically, with no artificial twists and turns." Booklist

Bausch, Richard, 1945-

Peace; a novel. Knopf 2008 171p $19.95

ISBN 978-0-307-26833-4; 0-307-26833-0

     LC 2007-37096

"It is the winter of 1944. Italy has fallen, but the retreating German army is still very much a lethal force, hidden in the mountains near Cassino. When an American patrol encounters an old Italian on the road, he agrees to lead them to where the Germans are. So Robert Marson, a corporal, is put in charge of two other soldiers, Saul Asch and Benny Joyner, to follow the old man into the hills. It is a miserable climb. Freezing rain turns to snow as they go higher. Marson, the novel's central character, suffers the agony of a blistered foot. Asch and Joyner bicker constantly. And when they find where the Germans are — or have been — they come under sniper fire. Has the old man led them into a trap?" Houston Chron

"A story cleanly told — void of trickery or plot shifting, without the faux drama of point-of-view shifts or uninvited monologue on the state of the cultural land-

Bausch, Richard, 1945-—*Continued*

scape — well, that's a thing to behold. . . . Bausch, among the most prolific and accomplished story writers of the last two decades, provides a gift to those who like to swallow their stories whole, in one sitting, without digression or narrative handstands." Esquire

The stories of Richard Bausch. HarperCollins 2003 651p $29.95

ISBN 0-06-019649-1

* LC 2003-42318

Contents: Nobody in Hollywood; Valor; Riches; Self knowledge; Glass meadow; Par; Someone to watch over me; Fatality; The voices from the other room; Two altercaations; 1951; The man who knew Belle Starr; What feels like the world; Ancient history; Contrition; Police dreams; Wise men at their end; Wedlock; Old West; Design; The fireman's wife; Consolation; The brace; The eyes of love; Luck; Equity; Letter to the lady of the house; Aren't you happy for me?; Not quite final; Weather; High-heeled shoe; Tandolfo the Great; Evening; Billboard; The person I have mostly become; 1-900; "My mistress' eyes are nothing like the sun"; The weight; Accuracy: Unjust: Guatemala; The last day of summer

"Failure and its exactions this is Bausch's big subject. These 42 stories test the play of hope and disappointment in the lives of spouses and lovers, of parents and children and siblings. And while Bausch does in several instances write with insight and authority from a woman's perspective, it is the sons, fathers and husbands in their daily trials that he registers most memorably. Indeed, so alive are these characters, with their credible flaws, their complaints and loud excitements, that closing the book feels like pushing the door shut on some clamorous party." N Y Times Book Rev

Thanksgiving night; a novel. HarperCollins Publishers 2006 403p $24.95

ISBN 978-0-06-009443-0; 0-06-009443-5

LC 2006-41222

"Caught in the middle of two pairs of warring relatives, middle-aged Will Butterfield feels helpless to control much of anything in his life. The 'Crazies' are two old women who happen to be Will's mother and great-aunt. Their late-night calls, fueled by alcohol, give neither used-bookstore owner Will nor his much-younger second wife, Elizabeth, much rest. When the Crazies aren't tearing up his household, his adult children from his first marriage are. Still, Will and Elizabeth's solid, loving marriage weathers the squalls—that is, until Will allows himself to be seduced by his unstable neighbor, which destroys the fragile balance of everyone around him." Libr J

"For all its alternately antic and sly humor, Bausch's novel is also filled with sudden displays of emotion. . . . Old-fashioned novelists tend to be generous, and 'Thanksgiving Night' comes with broad swaths of detail, abundant quirks and lots of human suffering, as well as low-key lyricism." N Y Times Book Rev

Baxter, Charles

The feast of love. Pantheon Bks. 2000 308p

ISBN 0-375-41019-8

LC 99-53088

"An insomniac Mid-western novelist named Charlie Baxter becomes the unwitting audience of a neighbor's midnight confession, and is drawn into a tale of love in

its manifold guises—confused, ecstatic, unrequited. We hear the story of Kathryn, who left her husband for the female shortstop of a local softball team; of Diana, a capricious lawyer who doesn't want anyone to want her too much; and of Chloé, a pierced teenager with a strong sense of justice and a doomed passion for a former drug addict. Baxter's novel is a modern Symposium, unexpectedly hilarious in its attempt to get at the evasive truths of love; unlike Plato's treatise, though, its strength lies in its recognition that such truths aren't universal." New Yorker

Saul and Patsy. Pantheon Bks. 2003 317p $24

ISBN 0-375-41029-5

LC 2003-42027

"Young-marrieds Saul and Patsy move to Five Oaks from Evanston, Ill., when Saul is hired to teach at the local high school. They rent a farmhouse, where they make love in every room and even in the backyard, settling into the rhythms of domestic life. Patsy, a former modern dancer who finds work as a bank teller, gives birth to a daughter, and with infinite patience tolerates her 'professional worrier' of a husband. The narrative is dense with quotidian detail, precisely charted shifts of consciousness and pitch-perfect moments of emotional truth." Publ Wkly

"Baxter's prose is succulent, his characters magnetic, his humor incisive, his decipherment of the human psyche felicitous, and his command of the storyteller's magic absolute." Booklist

The soul thief. Pantheon Books 2008 210p $20

ISBN 978-0-375-42252-2; 0-375-42252-8

LC 2007-18119

"Nathaniel Mason is a graduate student in early 1970s Buffalo. At a beer party one autumn night, he meets the mysterious Jerome Coolberg, 'a virtuoso of castoff ideas.' Coolberg quickly becomes obsessed with Mason, going so far as to steal his notebooks, his clothes, his girlfriend, and, finally, his memories and identity. . . . Several decades on, in the book's second half, Mason is living a colorless existence in the Midwest, while Coolberg has transformed himself into a National Public Radio star who encourages people to narrate personal stories on the air. In a surprise ending, we learn that Coolberg played a much bigger role in Mason's life than we'd originally been led to believe." Libr J

"Baxter's evocation of the mindset of Vietnam-era students and the 'hysterical intellectualism' of their parties is gloriously done, especially in its attention to era-specific details." N Y Times Book Rev

Baxter, Stephen

Evolution; a novel. Del Rey/Ballantine Bks. 2003 578p $25.95

ISBN 0-345-45782-X

LC 2002-31422

"As a group scientists gathers in the South Pacific for a conference to save the human race from extinction, their actions represent the culmination of millions of years of struggle by their primate ancestors to survive in an ever-changing world. . . . [Baxter] uses a modern-day story as a frame within which he relates a series of vignettes tracing the history of the evolution of intelligent life on Earth, from its mammalian beginnings in the Cretaceous era to the present. Spanning more than 165 million years and encompassing the entire planet, Baxter's ambitious saga provides both an exercise in painless paleontology and superb storytelling." Libr J

Bayard, Louis

The black tower. William Morrow 2008 352p $24.95

ISBN 978-0-06-117350-9; 0-06-117350-9

LC 2008-5059

The author sets his "historical adventure in the streets of Paris as the blood lust of the revolution subsides. It is 1818 when Vidocq, a former convict and the (real-life) founder of the newly created plainclothes investigative force known as the Sûreté, tracks down obscure medical student Hector Carpentier, whose name was found in the pocket of a dead man. As they work through the clues together, they move from the slums of Paris out to the royal gardens of Saint-Cloud. The duo soon realizes that the murders they are investigating may be connected to the whereabouts of Marie Antoinette's lost son, said to have died in the Black Tower." Libr J

"Bayard makes brilliant application of Vidocq in this fanciful adventure. . . . No snatch-and-run researcher, Bayard takes care to capture Vidocq's roguish voice and grandiose affectations, as well as the melodramatic substance of his published memoirs." N Y Times Book Rev

Bayley, Iris *See* Murdoch, Iris

Beach, Edward Latimer, 1918-2002

Run silent, run deep; [by] Edward L. Beach. Holt & Co. 1955 364p o.p.

"Commander Beach has taken the exciting material of a submarine war patrol in the Pacific in World War II and woven it into a novel. The author speaks and sees through the eyes of the book's central character, an Annapolis two-and-a-half striper with his first fleet submarine command, the Walrus." N Y Trib Books

"If ever a book has the ring of reality, this is it. From the moment the reader steps aboard a training boat in New London, Conn., to the time when the submarine Walrus dives deeply to avoid the depth charges of the enemy's destroyers, there is awe and respect for the author who created them." N Y Times Book Rev

Beagle, Peter S.

The last unicorn. Viking 1968 218p hardcover o.p. pa $14.95

ISBN 0-670-41908-7; 0-451-45052-3 (pa)

*

"A beautiful and previously happy unicorn learns she may be the last unicorn left on earth. Wanting not to believe it, she sets off in quest of her fellows. In the course of her journey, she meets a carnival magician of little ability, has encounters with a Robin Hood-like band, a king presiding over a hate-filled and miserable land, with the aid of the mysterious Red Bull, and a glamorous, if previously ineffectual prince." Publ Wkly

"Beagle is a true magician with words, a master of prose and a deft practitioner in verse. He has been compared, not unreasonably, with Lewis Carroll and J. R. R. Tolkien, but he stands squarely and triumphantly on his own feet." Saturday Rev

Bear, Elizabeth

All the windwracked stars. Tor 2008 368p (The edda of burdens) $24.95

ISBN 978-0-7653-1882-4; 0-7653-1882-2

LC 2008-34076

"A Tom Doherty Associates book"

A "postapocalyptic melodrama based loosely upon Norse mythology. On the Last Day, the historian Muire fled the battle, leaving her sibling Valkyries to die. More than 2,300 years later, only a single city, Eiledon, has survived as the dying world slowly turns into ice. Ashamed of her cowardice, Muire now vows to keep the last humans safe, but as she slowly pieces together the horrific truth behind the magic that has kept Eiledon standing, she must decide whether it's worth the price." Publ Wkly

The author's "ability to create breathtaking variations on ancient themes and make them new and brilliant is, perhaps, unparalleled in the genre." Libr J

Blood and iron. ROC 2006 432p pa $7.99

ISBN 978-0-451-46092-9; 0-451-46092-8

LC 2005-33954

"Ancient grudges and ruthless schemes are simply business as usual to the Faerie court in Bear's complex and involving contemporary fantasy. Seeker, formerly Elaine Andraste, is a changeling bound to the Mebd, the queen of the Daoine Sidhe, to find other changelings and bring them to the Faerie court. There, like legendary Tam Lin, and Seeker's own son, Ian, they entertain the queen until she tires of them. Now the queen needs Seeker to find—and win the heart of—the new Merlin, latest incarnation of a being who, in the hands of the Prometheans, could be used to destroy the Fae. Pragmatic college professor Carel Bierce, the first female Merlin, is not easily swayed by Fae—or Promethean—advances. Long-forgotten rivalries and unsuspected blood ties arise to tug at Seeker's loyalties, even as the queen promises to free Ian when she succeeds." Publ Wkly

Ink and steel; a novel of the Promethean Age. Roc 2008 427p pa $14

ISBN 978-0-451-46209-1

LC 2008-746

"Bear reveals the secret war between fae and the Elizabethan court in this dramatic prequel to Blood and Iron and Whiskey and Water. Framed with the intrigues of queens and courtiers, the story focuses on the mutual respect and growing love of Kit Marley (aka Christopher Marlowe) and Will Shakespeare. As Morgan le Fey rescues Kit from assassins, various factions recruit Will to bolster their political machinations with the magic of poetry. Kit pulls Will into Faerie and both are forced to face their own deepest desires and fears, which cannot be resolved until they deal with a power even higher than mortal Queen Elizabeth or fae Queen Mab. Copious quotes and intelligent speculation about their lives and works mark this sensitive and sensual look at the two supreme playwrights of the English Renaissance." Publ Wkly

Bear, Greg, 1951-

Anvil of stars. Warner Bks. 1992 434p

ISBN 0-446-51601-5

* LC 91-50411

Bear, Greg, 1951-—*Continued*
Sequel to The forge of God
"One alien culture has destroyed Earth; another, called the Benefactors, has offered the survivors a chance for revenge by building a spaceship for a group of young volunteers whose goal is the extermination of their enemy." Libr J
"Bear is superlatively competent in the English language and a master of both technical wizardry and powerful scenes. Throughout the book, he addresses the question of an ethical basis for genocide, leaving the matter sufficiently open to make one wonder whether the story is yet completed." Booklist

Blood music
In Bear, G. The collected stories of Greg Bear

The collected stories of Greg Bear. TOR Bks. 2002 653p hardcover o.p. pa $17.95
ISBN 0-7653-0160-1; 0-7653-0161-X (pa)
LC 2002-20466
"A Tom Doherty Associates book"
Contents: Blood music [novelette]; Sisters; A Martian Ricorso; Schrodinger's plague; Heads; The wind from a burning woman; The venging; Perihesperon; Scattershot; Plague of conscience; The white horse child; Dead run; Petra; Webster; Through road, no whither; Tangents; The visitation; Richie by the sea; Sleepside story; Judgment engine; The fall of the house of Escher; The way of all ghosts; MDIO ecosystems increase knowledge of DNA languages (2215 C.E.); Hardfought
In addition to Blood music (1985), a novelette where a genetic engineer injects himself with experimental intelligent microorganisms with disasterous results, this "volume subsumes Bear's earlier collections, The wind from a burning woman (1983) and Tangents (1989), while also including more recent work." Anatomy of Wonder 5

The forge of God. TOR Bks. 1987 474p
ISBN 0-312-93021-6
* LC 87-50482
"Three geologists discover an alien artifact in Death Valley and set off a chain of events leading to the discovery that Earth is about to be invaded by two alien races. One race sends out planet-wrecking machines; . . . the other is trying to enlist the survivors of humanity in tracking down and destroying the planet wreckers. The battle over Earth is seen through the eyes of a large cast of well-drawn characters, crowned by a climax of enormous power." Booklist
Followed by Anvil of stars

Beaton, M. C.

Death of a hussy. St. Martin's Press 1990 164p
ISBN 0-312-05071-2
* LC 90-36883
"The Scottish village of Lochdubh has a problem: the beloved police constable, Hamish Macbeth has been transferred to Strathbane because of a dearth of local crime. In a successful bid to get him back, the villagers, led by newcomer Maggie Baird, organize a crime wave. On his return Hamish is confronted with a possible murder." Publ Wkly
"Maggie is a devil, all right, but splendid fun as a

character. And the mischief she makes in Lochdubh is resolved by Hamish in an easygoing Highland fashion that is no less canny for being so droll." N Y Times Book Rev

Death of a macho man. Mysterious Press 1996 216p
ISBN 0-89296-531-2
LC 96-7268
"Scottish constable Hamish MacBeth, finding his reputation on the line, agrees to a public fight with a tattooed stranger who claims to be a professional wrestler. When someone prevents the match by murdering the stranger, suspicion falls on Hamish, who then investigates." Libr J
"Befuddled, earnest and utterly endearing, Hamish makes his triumphs sweetly satisfying." Publ Wkly

Love, lies, and liquor; an Agatha Raisin mystery. St. Martin's Minotaur 2006 231p $22.95
ISBN 0-312-34910-6
LC 2006-43407
Agatha Raisin's "ex-husband, James, from whom she has never fully recovered, has given Agatha reason to believe he may want to reconcile. He invites her to join him at the beloved scene of his childhood summer vacations, Snoth-on-Sea. The resort is rundown, the food miserable, and the guests obnoxious. Agatha's shouting match in the dining room with a boorish, insulting woman comes back to haunt her when the woman is found strangled to death, Agatha's scarf around her pudgy neck. Agatha must investigate to clear herself. More murder follows. Another highly satisfying Beaton cozy, this one is long on the kind of social comedy that uses character, plot, and atmosphere to produce the laughter." Booklist

Beattie, Ann

Chilly scenes of winter. Doubleday 1976 280p
ISBN 0-385-11658-6
*
Charles, the protagonist "loves Laura and is waiting for her, as he must; she is married, not well, and he can only wait for her to return to him, if she will. Waiting, he turns 27, works at the dull job he can't afford to leave, endures his grotesquely crazy mother and his well-meaning but stupid stepfather and kills time with his old buddy Sam." N Y Times Book Rev
"Beattie has an instinct for the grotesque that verges on the edge of real wit and pain. She is obviously a first-rate craftswoman with an eye for idiosyncratic detail." Saturday Rev

Follies; new stories. Scribner 2005 305p $25
ISBN 0-743-26961-6
LC 2004-65087
Contents: Fléchette follies; Find and replace; Duchais; Tending something; Apology for a journey not taken:how to write a story; Mostre; The garden game; The rabit hole as likely explanation; Just going out; The last odd day in L. A.
"The tales in this volume showcase a newly flexible voice that accommodates both the author's patented gift for social observation and her more recent interest in her characters' inner lives, a voice that allows her to move fluently back and forth in time, back and forth from memory to rumination." N Y Times (Late N Y Ed)

My life, starring Dara Falcon. Knopf 1997 307p
ISBN 0-679-45502-7
LC 96-36679

LIST OF FICTIONAL WORKS

Beattie, Ann—*Continued*

"Raised after her parents' death by an unloving maiden aunt, young Jean Warner has struggled to leave the loneliness of her childhood behind: she dropped out of college, rushed into marriage and lost herself as best she could in the bosom of her husband's large, close-knit New Hampshire family. But when she falls under the spell of Darcy Fisher, aka Dara Falcon, a seductive aspiring actress with a mysterious past, Jean's marriage begins to reveal its flaws, and Jean is forced to taste the bitterness that permeates her new family's claustrophobic self-involvement." Publ Wkly

"Dara is a fascinating character, and though she finally gets on the reader's nerves, Beattie has crafted a fine study of obsessive relationships with her usual aplomb." Libr J

Picturing Will. Random House 1989 230p
ISBN 0-394-56987-3

* LC 89-42781

"Aspiring photographer Jody, abandoned by husband Wayne—now on his third wife—is deeply devoted to her young son Will but hesitant to commit to lover Mel. Still, she visits Mel in faraway New York City, where Mel's friend, gallery owner Haverford (whose name she can recall only as Haveabud), takes a shine to her work—or to her. When Mel takes Will to visit his father in Florida, Haveabud goes along for the ride, bringing Spencer, a former protegé's son. . . . Meanwhile Wayne demonstrates his continued instability by cheating flagrantly on his new wife, Corky." Libr J

Beattie "has almost as many narrative voices as characters in this book, yet the result is never confusing. . . . 'Picturing Will' would be admirable for its technique alone; what makes it Beattie's best novel is her new and fearless way with emotional complexity." Newsweek

Beatty, Paul

Slumberland; a novel. Bloomsbury 2008 256p
ISBN 978-1-59691-240-3; 1-59691-240-5

LC 2007-45049

"The protagonist of the novel, DJ Darky, is a Los Angeles DJ who comes to Berlin to be a jukebox sommelier. He is in search of a virtuoso saxophonist, Charles Stone nicknamed the Shuwa who is in many ways his doppelgänger. DJ Darky has created a sonic masterpiece, layering nearly every sound he can find into a flawless testament, a musical ars poetica. Now, despite offers from the gangsta rap community, he wants the Shuwa to play some avant-garde mystical voodoo music over the beat. DJ Darky arrives in Germany, having already declared the end of blackness, to find himself once more the subject of racism amid constant reminders of his obsolete ethnicity. His real quest, we soon learn, is for meaning and a place in the increasingly chaotic post-Cold War world. 'Slumberland' is laugh-out-loud funny in many places, and its wit and satire can be burning, regardless of where they are pointed: blackness or whiteness." Los Angeles Times Book Rev

Beauvoir, Simone de, 1908-1986

The mandarins; a novel. World Pub. 1956 610p
o.p.

*

Original French edition, 1954

This "semiautobiographical novel addressed the attempts of post-World War II leftist intellectuals to abandon their elite, 'mandarin' status and to engage in political activism. The characters of psychologist Anne Dubreuilh and her husband Robert were roughly based on de Beauvoir and her lifelong associate Jean-Paul Sartre; de Beauvoir's account of Anne's affair with the American Lewis Brogan was a thinly veiled account of her own relationship with novelist Nelson Algren." Merriam-Webster's Ency of Lit

Beckett, Samuel, 1906-1989

Malone dies
In Beckett, S. Molloy, Malone dies, The unnamable

Molloy
In Beckett, S. Molloy, Malone dies, The unnamable

Molloy, Malone dies, The unnamable; with an introduction by Gabriel Josipovici. Knopf 1997 xliii, 476p $22
ISBN 0-375-40070-2

* LC 98-119494

"Everyman's library"

A reissue of the title first published 1959 by Grove Press; Original French editions of Molloy and Malone dies published 1951; The unnamable, 1953. These translations published separately 1955, 1956 and 1958, respectively

The trilogy "is concerned with the search for identity, for the true self which can rest from self-caricature; and as a parallel it is concerned with the true silence which is the end of speech. Molloy, Malone and their final unnamable incarnation are paradigms of humanity in general and of the artist in particular. . . . The trilogy seen as a whole composes one of the most remarkable, most original and most haunting prose-works of the century." Times Lit Suppl

Murphy. Grove Press 1957 282p o.p.

*

First published 1938 in the United Kingdom

"The story concerns an Irishman in London who yearns to do nothing more than sit in his rocking chair and daydream. Murphy attempts to avoid all action; he escapes from a girl he is about to marry, takes up with a kind prostitute, and finds a job as a nurse in a mental institution, where he plays nonconfrontational chess. His disengagement from the world is shattered when his fiancée, with a detective and two new lovers in tow, discovers him. He is killed when someone accidentally turns on the gas in his apartment." Merriam-Webster's Ency of Lit

The unnamable
In Beckett, S. Molloy, Malone dies, The unnamable

Bell, Albert A., 1945-

The blood of Caesar; a second case from the notebooks of Pliny the younger. Ingalls Pub. Group 2008 pa $15.95

ISBN 978-1-932158-82-3; 1-932158-82-0

LC 2007-51907

"When the body of a mason is found in the library of current Princeps (first citizen) Domitian, Pliny the Younger is asked by his mother to find the killer. At the same time, Domitian orders Pliny and his friend Tacitus to find out if there is a real heir to the throne. . . . Readers will delight in the duo's tracing of Caesar's blood line; walking with Pliny through his daily routine is entertaining, too. Outstandingly researched and laden with suspense." Libr J

Bell, Anthea, 1936-

(tr) Stanišic, S. How the soldier repairs the gramophone

Bell, Christine, 1951-

The Perez family. Norton 1990 256p

ISBN 0-393-02798-8

LC 89-25569

This is a "novel about a Cuban ex-prisoner's arrival in America in the Mariel boatlift. . . . Juan Raul Perez was imprisoned 20 years ago for his political views in his native Cuba, while his wife and young daughter fled to Miami. Few letters have gotten through in the ensuing 20 years, and Juan doesn't know what to expect when he finds them again. But before the reunion, Juan must survive the dizzy world of refugee relocation." Libr J

"Christine Bell is much more than a lighthearted comic novelist. She's one of those writers like Flannery O'Connor or Isak Dinesen: she doesn't so much write stories as spin tales. . . . What may have seemed cartoonish in the middle of the book, you now realize, was mythic, archetypal. What you have been reading turns out to be a profound little parable about the redemptive power of love." N Y Times Book Rev

Bell, Currer *See* Brontë, Charlotte, 1816-1855

Bell, Ellis *See* Brontë, Emily, 1818-1848

Bell, Ian

(ed) Stevenson, R. L. The complete short stories

Bell, Madison Smartt

All souls' rising. Pantheon Bks. 1995 530p

ISBN 0-679-43989-7

LC 95-12339

"Set during the struggle for Haiti's independence in the late 1700s, this intensely imagined epic novel of racial hatred and bloody upheaval illuminates the enmities among the astonishingly complex ethnic populations of the Caribbean island. Bell evokes a society caught in the crucible of violence with superb characterizations, ranging from the arrogant *grand blanc* plantation owners to the black slaves—including Toussaint L'Ouverture, the leader of the black revolt." Publ Wkly

Ten Indians. Pantheon Bks. 1996 264p

ISBN 0-679-44246-4

LC 96-14357

The protagonist of this novel is "Mike Devlin, a middle-aged white child-therapist who, for somewhat murky reasons, decides to open a Tae Kwon Do school in the black projects of inner-city Baltimore. Unbeknownst to him, Devlin's school attracts members of two drug gangs increasingly caught up in a murderous rivalry. Meanwhile, the singularly oblivious Devlin lets his daughter, Michelle, come down to the projects to train; she soon launches an affair with the leader of one of the gangs." Publ Wkly

The novel, "told partly from Devlin's viewpoint and partly, in convincing street language, from that of the drug dealers and their women, is spare and cinematic. Devlin, far out on a lonely voyage, saves his honor. Saves his daughter too. But it is the neighborhood that wins. Good ending, good novel." Time

Bellow, Saul, 1915-2005

The adventures of Augie March; with an introduction by Martin Amis. Knopf 1995 xxxvii, 616p

ISBN 0-679-44460-2

"Everyman's library"

A reissue of the title first published 1953 by Viking

"It is a picaresque story of a poor Jewish youth from Chicago, his progress, sometimes highly comic, through the world of the 20th century, and his attempts to make sense of it." Merriam-Webster's Ency of Lit

also in Bellow, S. Novels, 1944-1953

The Bellarosa connection. Penguin Bks. 1989 102p

ISBN 0-14-012686-4

LC 89-32936

"This is the story of clubfooted, multilingual Harry Fonstein, a lucky refugee from Holocaust Europe, and his grandly obese wife, Sorella. Arrested in Mussolini's Rome, Harry was imprisoned and awaiting deportation when his escape was arranged by an underground group, bankrolled by Broadway bigshot Billy Rose. Harry wants personally to thank Rose, but all his efforts are rebuffed. Finally, Sorella confronts Rose in Jerusalem, ready to blackmail him into meeting with Harry." Libr J

"The end of 'The Bellarosa Connection' is abrupt, matter-of-fact, almost offbeat. It is a conclusion, perhaps, in which nothing is concluded, . . . but it is appropriate to the overall pitch and voice of this cannily resourceful entertainment." N Y Times Book Rev

Dangling man. Vanguard Press 1944 191p o.p.

This story purports to be the journal of a young man living in Chicago, who gives up his job, expecting to be inducted into the army. Owing to technicalities Joseph is left dangling for almost a year. His journal explains his psychological reactions to idleness, how he passes his time, his growing unrest, and finally the relief when the call comes

"The book is an excellent document on the experience of the non-combatant in time of war. It is well written and never dull—in spite of the dismalness of the Chicago background and the undramatic character of the subject. It is also one of the most honest pieces of testimony on the psychology of a whole generation who have grown up during the depression and the war." New Yorker

also in Bellow, S. Novels, 1944-1953

Bellow, Saul, 1915-2005—*Continued*

Henderson the rain king; a novel. Viking 1959 341p o.p.

*

This novel, "designed on a grand and mythic scale, records American millionaire Gene Henderson's quest for revelation and spiritual power in Africa, where he becomes rainmaker and heir to a kingdom." Oxford Companion to Engl Lit

also in Bellow, S. Novels, 1956-1964

Herzog. Viking 1964 341p o.p.

"Beleaguered by the intensity of his introspection, Herzog worries over his life: an intellectual stumped in the middle of his second book—tellingly, an inquiry into Romanticism—a husband brooding over his second failed marriage, and above all a man trying to think his way into clarity, all the while wryly aware that he is the creator of his own paralysis. The epitome of this condition is the spate of letters that Herzog writes—to the living and the dead, to the famous and to his own circle of friends and enemies—but never sends. The letters document Herzog's detailed, vivid, and anxious apprehensions of contemporary American life in Chicago, in New York, and in the more pastoral setting of his retreat in the Berkshires. They also serve as a wonderfully colloquial venue for his irreverent, chatty, but also profound reflections on the fate of the individual in modern society." Benet's Reader's Ency of Am Lit

also in Bellow, S. Novels, 1956-1964

Humboldt's gift. Viking 1975 487p
ISBN 0-670-38655-3

*

"The story of Charlie Citrine, a successful writer and academic plagued by women, lawsuits, and mafiosi, whose present career is interwoven with memories of the early success, failing powers, and squalid death of his friend Von Humboldt Fleischer, whose poetic destiny he fears he may inherit, together with his manuscripts." Oxford Companion to Engl Lit

Mr. Sammler's planet. Viking 1970 313p
ISBN 0-670-33319-0

"Artur Sammler, in his seventies and an escapee from the horrors of Nazi atrocities and the memory of having had to dig himself out of his own grave, theorizes about the possibility of finding a similar escape from the assaults of life in New York City, its muggings, crime, dirt, noise. Living with his bizarre daughter, Shula, also saved from death in Europe but somewhat deranged, perhaps the result of traumas suffered, is not possible, and living with his niece Margotte also has its drawbacks. The most important person to Sammler is his nephew Elya, by whose generosity Sammler and Shula are able to exist. But Elya's escape from the horrors of his own life—his son Wallace's irresponsible behavior and his daughter Angela's sexually promiscuous behavior—is by way of death. For our desire to find relief from the outrages of life in this decade, Bellow has made a metaphor of man's desire to go to the moon." Shapiro. Fic for Youth. 3d edition

Novels, 1944-1953. Library of America 2003
1029p $35
ISBN 1-931082-38-3   LC 2003-40144

Contents: Dangling man; The victim; The adventures of Augie March

Dangling man and The adventures of Augie March are entered separately. The victim (1947) tells the story of Asa Leventhal, who once held a position on a New York trade journal, and had won a certain security, but a few sultry weeks while his wife was away almost wrecked him. The remembrance of his insane mother, and the constant harrying of a Gentile friend, who insisted that Asa had ruined his career, brings him to the verge of insanity.

Novels, 1956-1964. Library of America 2007
794p $35
ISBN 978-1-59853-002-5; 1-59853-002-X
          LC 2006-46687
Contents: Sieze the day; Henderson the rain king; Herzog, each entered separately

Seize the day; with three short stories and a one-act play. Viking 1956 211p o.p.

Anthology composed of one novella: Seize the day; three short stories: A father-to-be, Looking for Mr. Green, and The Gonzaga manuscripts; and a one-act play: The wrecker

"Seize the Day gives contemporary literature a story which will be explained, expounded, and argued, but about which a final reckoning can be made only after it ripples out in the imagination of the generations of readers to come. I suspect that it is one of the central stories of our day." Nation

also in Bellow, S. Novels, 1956-1964

Seize the day [novelette]
  In Bellow, S. Seize the day

The victim
  In Bellow, S. Novels, 1944-1953

Belzer, Richard

I am not a cop!; Richard Belzer with Michael Black. Simon & Schuster 2008 260p $24
ISBN 978-1-4165-7066-0; 1-4165-7066-7
          LC 2008-9534
A murder mystery that features an actor named Richard Belzer who plays John Munch, a TV detective. "When an old friend of Belzer's, New York City assistant medical examiner Rudy Markovich, disappears under suspicious circumstances, Belzer decides to investigate. After the actor finds a clue referring to four recent deaths, he and Kalisha Carter, the attractive woman his producer assigns to keep an eye on him, dig into those cases." Publ Wkly

"Deft comic timing, the gruff persona, and a lively, if predictable, story will satisfy fans." Libr J

Benchley, Peter, 1940-2006

Jaws. Random House 2005 311p $15.95
ISBN 1-4000-6456-2   LC 2005-46451
First published 1974
This is a "story about what happens when a great white shark terrorizes a small Long Island town. . . . A woman swimmer is devoured by the shark, and Police Chief Martin Brody insists on closing the beaches. But he's overruled by the town fathers who remind him that

Benchley, Peter, 1940-2006—*Continued*

the community is dependent on summer visitors for economic survival. Two deaths later, the news can no longer be suppressed and Brody, an oceanographer and a fisherman go after the monster in an exciting chase." Publ Wkly

Benét, Stephen Vincent, 1898-1943

The Devil and Daniel Webster; illustrated by Harold Denison. Farrar & Rinehart 1937 61p il o.p.

"Jabez Stone, a New Hampshire farmer, receives a decade of material wealth in return for selling his soul to the Devil—Mr. Scratch. When the Devil comes to claim Stone's soul, the farmer has the statesman and orator Daniel Webster argue his case at midnight before a jury of historic American villains." Merriam-Webster's Ency of Lit

Benford, Gregory, 1941-

Foundation's fear. HarperPrism 1997 425p (Second Foundation trilogy)

ISBN 0-06-105243-4   LC 96-45296

"Set thousands of years in the future, this novel begins the Second Foundation Trilogy, a prequel to Isaac Asimov's famous original." Publ Wkly

"Mr. Benford picks up the story as Seldon is about to become First Minister to Emperor Cleon I, who rules the 25 million inhabited planets of the galaxy from the imperial capital of Trantor. I have no idea whether anyone unfamiliar with the original Foundation series—which spells out what happened to Seldon and his predictions—will be able to make sense of 'Foundation's Fear.' But for the legions of readers who have long been tantalized by Asimov's cryptic references to psychohistory, Mr. Benford provides some fascinating insights into its development." N Y Times Book Rev

Followed by Foundation and chaos, by Greg Bear

Timescape. Simon & Schuster 1980 412p

ISBN 0-671-25327-1

                                     *

"As the world lurches toward disaster, scientists in 1998 try to transmit a warning message to 1962 by means of tachyons. Their story is told in parallel with that of the scientists trying to decode the transmission, and the two plots converge on the possibility of paradox. Unusual for the realism of its depiction of scientists at work; admirably serious in handling the implications of its theme." Anatomy of Wonder 4

Benioff, David

City of thieves; a novel. Viking 2008 258p $24.95

ISBN 978-0-670-01870-3; 0-670-01870-8

                           LC 2007-42784

In this novel, a writer depicts his grandfather's experiences during the siege of Leningrad. "Having elected to stay in Leningrad during the siege, 17-year-old Lev Beniov is caught looting a German paratrooper's corpse. The penalty for this infraction (and many others) is execution. But when Colonel Grechko confronts Lev and Kolya, a Russian army deserter also facing execution, he

spares them on the condition that they acquire a dozen eggs for the colonel's daughter's wedding cake. Their mission exposes them to the most ghoulish acts of the starved populace and takes them behind enemy lines to the Russian countryside. There, Lev and Kolya take on an even more daring objective: to kill the commander of the local occupying German forces." Publ Wkly

Benjamin, Paul *See* Auster, Paul, 1947-

Benn, James R., 1949-

Billy Boyle; a World War II mystery. Soho Press 2006 284p $23

ISBN 1-569474-33-8   LC 2006-42300

"Billy Boyle is a Boston cop, from a family of Boston cops, but he is a reluctant soldier who prefers walking the beat in Southie to fighting Nazis. Using her cousin by marriage, a certain General Eisenhower, Billy's mother lands her son a seemingly soft job with Ike's staff in London. But Ike wants Billy to use his investigative knowhow to sniff out a possible spy in the Allies' inner circle. Young Billy, oversold by his mother as a crackerjack detective, is definitely in over his head, especially when it turns out that the apparent suicide of a Norwegian dignitary may have been the work of the spy." Booklist

"Benn provides historically accurate background and appealing characters, spices the narrative with romance and emotion, and ruminates about the consequences of actions, all in a suitably straightforward prose style. A solid addition to mystery collections." Libr J

The first wave; a Billy Boyle World War II mystery. Soho Press 2007 294p $24

ISBN 978-1-56947-471-6; 1-56947-471-0

                           LC 2007-5314

"Take a young Irish cop. Turn him into a lieutenant on Eisenhower's personal staff—one charged with being 'Ike's investigator.' Set him ashore on the coast of French North Africa along with the first wave of invading American troops. And watch the mayhem, mystery, and murder that are bound to follow. Corrupt Vichy French officers steal a shipment of American penicillin, killing a supply sergeant in the process. Benn . . . delivers a cross-genre tale that is at once spy story, soldier story, and hard-Boyled detective. Bullets, babes, and bombs give Billy Boyle a bad time before he solves the case, but you'll have a good time reading about it." Libr J

Benson, E. F. (Edward Frederic), 1867-1940

Lucia in London

In Benson, E. F. Make way for Lucia p179-358

Make way for Lucia. Harper & Row 1986 c1977 1119p

ISBN 0-06-015678-3

                              * LC 86-45639

A reissue of the omnibus edition of six novels and one short story published 1977 by Crowell

These novels were originally published in the United States by George H. Doran Company and Doubleday, Doran & Company

Benson, E. F. (Edward Frederic), 1867-1940—
Continued

Contents: Queen Lucia (1920); Lucia in London (1928); Miss Mapp (1923); The male impersonator (1929); Mapp and Lucia (1931); The worshipful Lucia (1935) [published in England with title: Lucia's progress]; Trouble for Lucia (1939)

The male impersonator
In Benson, E. F. Make way for Lucia p535-48

Mapp and Lucia
In Benson, E. F. Make way for Lucia p549-762

Miss Mapp
In Benson, E. F. Make way for Lucia p359-534

Queen Lucia
In Benson, E. F. Make way for Lucia p1-178

Trouble for Lucia
In Benson, E. F. Make way for Lucia p941-1119

The worshipful Lucia
In Benson, E. F. Make way for Lucia p763-940

Benson, Edward Frederic *See* Benson, E. F. (Edward Frederic), 1867-1940

Berg, Elizabeth, 1948-

Home safe; a novel. Random House 2009 260p $25
ISBN 978-1-4000-6511-0; 1-4000-6511-9
LC 2008-49247
"Helen Ames is a popular and prolific writer living in Oak Park, Illinois. . . . But Helen has lost her ability to write. Her inner world is as stunned and hushed as her cherished home in the wake of her husband's sudden death. Dan took care of everything, leaving Helen free to dwell in her imaginary worlds. Now she is bereft and confused. Tessa, her beautiful, patient, funny daughter, a beauty editor at a woman's magazine, is trying to help, as is Helen's outspoken best friend, Midge. And at least Helen is financially secure. Or not. Where has her money gone? Did Dan have a secret life? Or was he planning a glorious surprise? Berg is a tender and enchanting storyteller who wisely celebrates the simple, sustaining elements of life, from comfort food to birdsong to a good laugh." Booklist

We are all welcome here; a novel. Random 2006 187p $22.95
ISBN 1-4000-6161-X
LC 2005-48956
"It is the summer of 1964. In Tupelo, Mississippi, the town of Elvis's birth, tensions are mounting over civil-rights demonstrations occurring ever more frequently—and violently—across the state. But in Paige Dunn's small, ramshackle house, there are more immediate concerns. Challenged by the effects of the polio she contracted during her last month of pregnancy, Paige is

nonetheless determined to live as normal a life as possible and to raise her daughter, Diana, in the way she sees fit—with the support of her tough-talking black caregiver, Peacie." Publisher's note
"Full of humor, devoid of self-pity, with lively characters that rise above their circumstances, this is the story of an adolescent accepting adult responsibilities, encountering the temptations of boys and booze, and experiencing the tensions between race and class in the 1960s." SLJ

What we keep; a novel. Random House 1998 272p
ISBN 0-375-50099-5
* LC 97-42070
As the novel "opens, Ginny is flying to California to join her sister in a meeting with their mother, whom neither daughter has seen for 35 years. Ginny uses her travel time to reflect upon her memories of the summer when her mother withdrew from the family and became an outsider in her daughters' lives. Berg's precise, evocative descriptions create vivid images of Ginny's physical world, while Berg's understanding and perception are an eloquent testimony to Ginny's emotional turmoil." Libr J

Berger, Thomas, 1924-

Arthur Rex. Delacorte Press/Seymour Lawrence 1978 499p
ISBN 0-440-00362-8
LC 78-7241
A "modernization of Malory's 'Morte d'Arthur.' The setting remains ancient Britain, but King Arthur, Merlin, Launcelot, and the knights of the Round Table suffer from 20th-Century maladies; Guinevere and other fair ladies are liberated. Sex and introspection abound. Embellishing the basic tale, Berger adds seriocomic twists, fantasies, and exaggerations." Libr J
This is a "splendid, satiric retelling of the legend of Camelot. . . . The curious truth is that Mr. Berger's revisions are most authentic, most profound, when the admixture of parody is strongest. At those times—a good three-fourths of the book—he is never merely a parodist after all, but also a compelling yarnspinner in his own right." N Y Times Book Rev

Being invisible; a novel. Little, Brown 1987 262p
ISBN 0-316-09158-8
* LC 86-20897
"Things are not going well for Fred Wagner, a typical Berger victim. His wife has left him, his job as a catalog copywriter is becoming increasingly unsatisfying, and his novel, after six years, has not progressed beyond the opening pages. Wagner discovers, however, that he does have a talent—he can make himself invisible—and the novel recounts his struggle to make the best of this unique gift. But surprisingly, Wagner finds that whether he is trying to bypass a long line, steal from a bank, or avoid his co-workers, invisibility has its drawbacks; rather than improving his situation, each invisible adventure leads to a further mishap." Libr J
"There is much in 'Being Invisible' to celebrate—the pleasures of invention, humor, surprise, of Mr. Berger's enraged, unforgiving view. That so much of his vision seems neither freakish nor admonitory but rather, oddly tonic, says something about the era in which we live.

Berger, Thomas, 1924-—*Continued*

. . . It is a sign of the times that we feel such affection for Thomas Berger's dogged, cranky courage, and for the denizens of his unwelcoming and chaotic corner of the fictional world." N Y Times Book Rev

Little Big Man. Dial Press (NY) 1979 1964 xxii, 440p o.p.

"The author purports to write the story of Jack Crabb, adopted Cheyenne, gunfighter, buffalo hunter, and survivor of Custer's last stand, whom he has located at the Marville Center for Senior Citizens. In the few months before his death at the self-professed age of 111, Crabb recounts *his* version of life in the Old West." Shapiro. Fic for Youth. 3d edition

Followed by The return of Little Big Man (1999)

Neighbors. Delacorte Press/Seymour Lawrence 1980 275p

ISBN 0-440-06556-9

* LC 79-20307

"The new neighbors drop in for a drink and chaos breaks loose, as Berger records the nightmarish distractions of a day and night among the American middle class. Existential reverses skewer the suburban lifestyle of the bourgeoisie and unleash unkempt fantasies on manicured lawns as a man's mind, life, and home are boldly and cunningly invaded and violated." Booklist

Berger "quickly conditions the reader to expect the unexpected but manages to be consistently surprising nevertheless, introducing new twists and outrages that not even the most warped spectator could have foreseen. The novel adopts a formal, almost fussy style to convey lunacy, as if Berger were describing low deeds to a maiden aunt. . . . {The book} is not at all interested in being socially redeeming, and those who read books to gain warm feelings or philosophic nuggets will come away from this one empty-handed and probably angry. . . .What Berger has produced is a tour de force." Time

Berlinski, Mischa, 1973-

Fieldwork. Farrar, Straus and Giroux 2007 320p $24

ISBN 978037429916-3; 0-374-29916-1

LC 2006-16214

The narrative "focuses on Martiya van der Leun, who has committed suicide in a Thai women's prison, where she was serving a 50-year sentence for murdering an American missionary. A young farang (white and foreign) journalist named Mischa Berlinski learns that Martiya was an American anthropologist who for years lived with a tribe called the Dyalos to study its mysterious culture. Mischa finds Martiya's story—and exactly why she committed the crime—so oddly compelling that he dedicates his life to understanding Martiya's fate." Libr J

"With its offbeat style, Berlinski's consummate fieldwork—fictional though it may be—produces an intricate whodunit, both disturbing and entertaining." Washington Post Book World

Berne, Suzanne, 1961-

A perfect arrangement; a novel. Algonquin Bks. 2001 301p $23.95

ISBN 1-56512-261-5

LC 00-69451

"A Shannon Ravenel book"

A domestic novel set in the small New England town of New Aylesbury. "Mirella and Howard Cook-Goldman are fortunate to have found Randi Grill, who seems like the perfect nanny. Not only does she take care of their two children but she also cooks, cleans, and sews. Yet something is wrong with the flawless Midwesterner and her charges." Libr J

The author provides a "probing, intelligent exploration of a contemporary family with a strong sense of entitlement, whose future turns out to be anything but certain." N Y Times Book Rev

Bernhard, Thomas, 1931-1989

Frost; translated from the German by Michael Hofmann. Alfred A. Knopf 2006 341p $25.95

ISBN 1-4000-4066-3

LC 2006-40886

Original German edition, 1963

"A student's increasingly erratic dispatches over 27 days comprise this obsessive first novel by Bernhard. . . . An unnamed medical student is sent from Vienna by his supervisor, an eminent surgeon named Strauch, to undertake 'precise observation' of the surgeon's brother, a famous painter who has suddenly left the city for the 'dismal' village of Weng. After 'systematically inveigling' himself into the company of the painter under the pretense of being a vacationing law student, the student slowly feels his own mood and mental attitudes being subsumed by the painter's paranoid outbursts and disjointed monologues. Weng itself, located in a grim valley still bearing the grisly traces of WWII, is a hotbed of murky scandal. . . . Bernhard's glorious talent for bleak existential monologues is second only to Beckett's, and seems to have sprung up fully mature in his mesmerizing debut." Publ Wkly

The loser; translated from the German by Jack Dawson; afterword by Mark M. Anderson. Knopf 1991 189p

ISBN 0-394-57239-4

* LC 90-45942

Original German edition, 1983

This is an "account of an imagined relationship among three men who meet in 1953 to study with Vladimir Horowitz. In the face of Glenn Gould's incomparable genius as a piano virtuoso, his two fellow students renounce their musical ambition, but in very different ways." Midwest Book Rev

"Dawson's translation is superb. . . . The Loser is undoubtedly one of the most fascinating works of contemporary Austrian literature, and given its extraordinary meditations on art, the artist, and the reception of the creative process, it is a work that should find international readership." American Book Rev

Woodcutters; translated from the German by David McLintock. Knopf 1987 {i.e. 1988} 181p

ISBN 0-394-55152-4

LC 87-45123

Original German edition, 1984

A "tour de force in which the narrator, during the course of a Viennese dinner party, relives nonstop 20 years of his life. As he whines about the bourgeois rituals he is forced to observe at his hosts' table, he also exposes the past. The dark revelations in the story revolve around the recent suicide of a mutual friend and how this woman's death has affected the people at the dinner par-

Bernhard, Thomas, 1931-1989—*Continued*

ty. The world of the artist also comes alive in the book as the narrator/writer discourses wittily and ruthlessly on the multiple forms of aesthetic hypocrisy on display around the table." Booklist

"Mr. Bernhard's portrait of a society in dissolution has a Scandinavian darkness reminiscent of Ibsen and Strindberg, but it is filtered through a minimalist prose of obsessive repetition and ever so slight modulations." N Y Times Book Rev

Bernhardt, William, 1960-

Dark justice. Ballantine Pub. Group 1999 389p
ISBN 0-345-40738-5   LC 98-28182
On a book-signing tour in Washington State attorney Ben Kincaid "inadvertently gets involved in a group called Green Rage, a conservationist organization wrestling with the local logging industry in a life-or-death struggle. One of the members of the group has been charged with a horrible murder—and who is the alleged perp? None other than [a] man Ben defended six years ago. To defend him again, Ben has to go up against prosecutor Granville 'Granny' Adams, who, despite her moniker, is attractive and tough as nails. She is bound and determined to win this case. In the meantime, subplots swirl and crash around Ben's feet, but these only serve to enrich the entertainment value of this wonderfully riveting read." Booklist

Bernofsky, Susan

(tr) Erpenbeck, J. The book of words

Berry, Jedediah

The manual of detection. Penguin Press 2009 278p $25.95
ISBN 9781594202117   LC 2008-44753
"Charles Unwin, a meek detective-agency clerk, is set on the trail of a legendary adversary after the disappearance of a colleague. He's handed the rulebook of the title, but it gets him only so far; the vast bureaucratic agency and the nightmarish villain remain mysterious, and the nameless nocturnal city in which the story takes place presents its own series of surrealistic bewilderments. When the central conflict eventually clarifies, it's somewhat disappointing that it is a 9/11 allegory. More valuable is Berry's ability to create the feeling of inhabiting a strange and haunting dream, with its own persuasive logic and somnambulant pacing." New Yorker

Berry, Michael, 1974-

(tr) Wang Anyi. The song of everlasting sorrow

Berry, Steve, 1955-

The Charlemagne pursuit; a novel. Ballantine Books 2008 509p il $26
ISBN 978-0-345-48579-3; 0-345-48579-3
                                        LC 2008-28357
"Using his connections in the federal government, Cotton [Malone] asks to see a classified file that details the mission that resulted in his father's death. He knew his father died on a submarine but none of the shocking details about where or why he died. But Cotton is not the only person who wants this file, and they kill to get it. Nazi missions to the Antarctic, ancient societies, and a valuable artifact from Charlemagne's tomb all play key roles as Malone uncovers the truth. So much is going on that there is enough material for two good books, let alone one great one." Libr J

Berry, Wendell, 1934-

Jayber Crow; a novel. Counterpoint 2000 363p
ISBN 1-58243-029-2   LC 00-35889
"Orphaned at 4 by the flu epidemic of 1918, and again at 10, when age claims the elderly relatives who took him in, Jonah 'Jayber' Crow finds a valued place as a humble barber in a Kentucky river township. He finds love, too, though he never speaks of it." Booklist

"The richly portrayed community unfolds delicately and surely, with the human dramas of its inhabitants revealed from Jayber's perspective. A moving, lyrical work on a small canvas." Libr J

That distant land; the collected stories of Wendell Berry. Shoemaker & Hoard 2004 440p $26
ISBN 1-593-76027-2
                                    * LC 2003-25213
Contents: The hurt man; Don't send a boy to do a man's work; A consent; Pray without ceasing; Watch with me; A half-pint of Old Darling; The lost bet; Thicker than liquor; Nearly to the fair; The solemn boy; A jonquil for Mary Penn; Turn back the bed; Making it home; Where did they go?; The discovery of Kentucky; It wasn't me; The boundary; That distant land; A friend of mine; The wild birds; Are you all right?; Fidelity; The inheritors

"Set in a small Kentucky farming village, this collection of Berry's Port William stories illuminates the evolution of rural American life over the course of the 20th century. In 23 stories, Berry chronicles Port William from the 1880s to the 1980s, evoking the connectedness of the small town's denizens to each other and to the land." Publ Wkly

Best American mystery stories [date]; Otto Penzler, series editor. Houghton Mifflin
ISSN 1094-8384
Annual. First published 1997. Editors vary
An annual volume of mystery stories culled from a variety of magazines, collections, and anthologies. Loren D. Estleman, Lawrence Block, Michael Connelly, Joyce Carol Oates, Bill Pronzini, Hannah Tinti, James Lee Burke, and Holly Goddard Jones are among the authors represented

The **Best** American mystery stories of the century; Tony Hillerman, editor; Otto Penzler, series editor; with an introduction by Tony Hillerman. Houghton Mifflin 2000 813p $28; pa $17.95
ISBN 0-618-01267-2; 0-618-01271-0 (pa)
"Dating from 1904 to the present, these stories provide a rough chronology of 20th-century crime fiction. . . . All the great writers of the genre are here—Raymond Chandler, Ellery Queen, Sue Grafton, etc.—but so are writers not normally associated with crime fiction, e.g.,

The Best American mystery stories of the century—*Continued*

Flannery O'Connor, John Steinbeck, and Harlan Ellison." Libr J

"This anthology is a cornerstone volume for any mystery library." Publ Wkly

The **Best** American short stories; selected from U.S. and Canadian magazines. Houghton Mifflin
ISSN 0067-6233
This annual series began in 1915 under the editorship of Edward J. O'Brien with title: Best short stories. Editors vary
An annual anthology of stories by American and Canadian writers culled from a variety of magazines. Authors represented include: Alice Munro, Tobias Wolff, John Updike, Rick Bass, Jamaica Kincaid, Steven Millhauser, Allegra Goodman, and A. M. Homes

The **Best** from Fantasy & Science Fiction; 1st-20th, 22nd-24th series. Doubleday 1952-1982 23v o.p.
24th series published by Scribner. No volume bearing 21st series designation published; Special 25th anniversary volume published instead
Collection culled from a journal, founded in 1949, that "continues to publish an unusual number of first stories and award winners, to discover new, literary writers, to maintain a circulation of about half to two-thirds that of the most popular magazines, and to remain the most consistently reliable magazine in the field." New Ency of Sci Fic

The **Best** from fantasy & science fiction: the fiftieth anniversary anthology; edited by Edward L. Ferman and Gordon Van Gelder. Doherty Assocs. 1999 381p $24.95
ISBN 0-312-86973-8   LC 99-40560

"A TOR book"
"This anthology includes 22 stories published . . . between 1993 and 1998. . . . Their authors include such luminaries as Ursula Le Guin, Gene Wolfe, and Ray Bradbury, and the distinguished if less conspicuous likes of Paul Di Filippo, Terry Bisson, and Esther Friesner." Booklist

Best of the Best American short stories, 1915-1950; edited by Martha Foley. Houghton Mifflin 1952 369p o.p.
Contents: How the Devil came down Division Street, by N. Algren; I'm a fool, by S. Anderson; The blue sash, by W. Beck; Nothing ever breaks except the heart, by K. Boyle; Horse thief, by E. Caldwell; Sex education, by D. Canfield; The enormous radio, by J. Cheever; The wind and the snow of winter, by W. V. Clark; Boys will be boys, by I. S. Cobb; Christ in concrete, by P. Di Donato; Hand upon the waters, by W. Faulkner; My old man, by E. Hemingway; The peach stone, by P. Horgan; Haircut, by R. Lardner; Man on a road, by A. Maltz; Prince of darkness, by J. F. Powers; Resurrection of a life, by W. Saroyan; Search through the streets of the city, by I. Shaw; The interior castle, by J. Stafford; How beautiful with shoes, by W. D. Steele; The women on the wall, by

W. Stegner; Dawn of remembered spring, by J. Stuart; A wife of Nashville, by P. Taylor; The catbird seat, by J. Thurber; A curtain of green, by E. Welty

Betts, Doris, 1932-

Souls raised from the dead; a novel. Knopf 1994 339p
ISBN 0-679-42621-3   LC 93-30900
"Still clearing the emotional debris left after his selfish, narcissistic wife, Christine, decamped three years earlier, North Carolina state trooper Frank Thompson is lovingly raising their 12-year-old daughter, Mary Grace. Mary is a typical adolescent, masking her insecurities with a nonchalant air. When she becomes obsessed with horses, Frank begins a romance with her young riding instructor, but the balance of all their lives goes askew when Mary develops kidney disease." Publ Wkly
"Mary's life and death are superbly and unsentimentally accomplished. . . . Yet none of this should sound grim, only appropriately sad, because Ms. Betts seems to be possessed of high spirits and a generous wisdom. And that is what buoys up her characters and makes a lot of the proceedings very funny even as her people struggle with their anger and bewilderment." N Y Times Book Rev

Beyle, Marie Henri *See* Stendhal, 1783-1842

Bierce, Ambrose, 1842-1914?

The complete short stories of Ambrose Bierce; compiled with commentary by Ernest Jerome Hopkins. Doubleday 1970 496p o.p.
                                                                    *

Contents: Haita the shepherd; The secret of Macarger's Gulch; The eyes of the panther; The stranger; An inhabitant of Carcosa; The applicant; The death of Halpin Frayser; A watcher by the dead; The man and the snake; John Mortonson's funeral; Moxon's master; The damned thing; The realm of the unreal; A fruitless assignment; A vine on a house; The haunted valley; One of twins; Present at a hanging; A wireless message; The moonlit road; An arrest; A jug of sirup; The Isle of Pines; At old Man Eckert's; The Spook House; The middle toe of the right foot; The thing at Nolan; The difficulty of crossing a field; An unfinished race; Charles Ashmore's trial; Staley Fleming's hallucination; The night-doings at "Deadmans"; A baby tramp; A psychological shipwreck; A cold greeting; Beyond the wall; John Bartine's watch; The man out of the nose; An adventure at Brownville; The suitable surroundings; The boarded window; A lady from Redhorse; The famous Gilson bequest; A holy terror; A diagnosis of death; One of the missing; A baffled ambuscade; The affair at Coulter's Notch; A son of the gods; One kind of officer; A tough tussle; An occurrence at Owl Creek Bridge; Chickamauga; The coup de grâce; One officer, one man; The story of a conscience; Parker Adderson, philosopher; An affair of outposts; Jupiter Doke; Brigadier-General; A horseman in the sky; The mockingbird; George Thurston; Killed at Resaca; Three and one are one; Two military executions; The Major's tale; A resumed identity; A man with two lives; The other lodgers; A bivouac of the dead; An imperfect conflagration; A bottomless grave; The City of the Gone Away; Curried cow; A revolt of the Gods; Oil of dog;

Bierce, Ambrose, 1842-1914?—*Continued*

The widower Turnmore; The baptism of Dobsho; The race at Left Bower; The failure of Hope & Wandel; A providential intimation; Mr. Swiddler's flip-flap; The little story; My favorite murder; The hypnotist; Mr. Masthead, journalist; Why I am not editing "The Stinger"; Corrupting the press; "The bubble reputation"; A shipwreckollection; The captain of the "Camel"; The man overboard; A cargo of cat

Binchy, Maeve

Circle of friends. Delacorte Press 1991 c1990 565p

ISBN 0-385-30149-9

* LC 90-3944

First published 1990 in the United Kingdom

The author "explores the intertwining bonds of three women as they travel from a small Irish village to university life in Dublin." Libr J

"There is nothing fancy about 'Circle of Friends.' There is no torrid sex, no profound philosophy. There are no stunning metaphors. There is just a wonderfully absorbing story about people worth caring about. And that is a rare pleasure." N Y Times Book Rev

The glass lake. Delacorte Press 1995 584p

ISBN 0-385-31354-3   LC 94-36104

First published 1994 in the United Kingdom

This novel "focuses on the inhabitants of a small town in Ireland. Helen, wife and mother of the McMahon household, is presumed to have drowned in a nearby lake. Actually, she shook off her dull, staid life and fled to London with her lover. Successful at business, she yearns for some communication with her now teenaged daughter, Kit. She begins a casual correspondence with Kit under the guise of being an old friend of her mother." Libr J

"If some aspects of the plot are contrived and the narrative overtold, the richness of Binchy's characters makes these drawbacks easy to forgive. A weeper of an ending brings this compelling saga to an unforgettable climax." Publ Wkly

Silver wedding. Delacorte Press 1989 306p

ISBN 0-385-29826-9

* LC 89-1276

The author "uses the story-within-a-story device to introduce the long-absent, oddball friends and relatives who will reunite at Deirdre and Desmond Doyle's silver anniversary in the couple's suburban London home. Among these are the Doyles' three grown children—a failed Irish nun, the much-put-upon eldest daughter, and the prodigal sheepherder son—the snooty yet tragically unmarried maid of honor, and the corporately well-positioned best man (who happens to be both Desmond's friend and nemesis). As celebratory preparations begin, the skeletons in this dysfunctional network are unearthed." Booklist

"An elegant literary construction, a comedy of manners as well as a soap opera. Each chapter has its own story, yet each story connects with all the others to produce a satisfying whole. Add to this a sly, understated tone and you have a book that's an effortless pleasure to read." NY Times Book Rev

Whitethorn Woods. A.A. Knopf 2007 c2006 339p $25.95

ISBN 978-0-307-26578-4; 0-307-26578-1

LC 2006-48803

First published 2006 in the United Kingdom

"Nestled outside the once sleepy Irish village of Rossmore in a copse known as Whitethorn Woods is the shrine of St. Ann's Well, which attracts so many of the faithful and hopeful that the little town overflows with visitors. This prompts a controversial proposal to construct a bypass highway that would divert traffic, ironically, right through the Woods, thus destroying the source of the town's popularity. Worried that the shrine's days are numbered, villagers flock to the Well, where they plead for everything from the restoration of a faltering love affair to the recognition of an ancestor's legacy." Booklist

"Story by story, voice by voice, Binchy builds the fictional community of Rossmore so that, by the end of the novel, we know Rossmore's inhabitants better than our own neighbours . . . . Few contemporary novelists match Binchy's gift for giving us the world through her characters' eyes." Toronto Globe and Mail

Bird, Sarah

The Yokota Officers Club; a novel. Knopf 2001 367p

ISBN 0-375-41214-X   LC 2001-89763

Set in the late 1960s, this novel "is narrated by 18-year-old Bernie, the eldest of six children in the peripatetic Root family. After her freshman year in college, Bernie joins her nomadic kin at their current home, an Okinawan air force base. They have changed: her younger sister, Kit, is out of control and 'now being played by Lolita'; her once glamorous mother, Moe, is overweight and depressed; her father, who was a heroic and swaggering fighter pilot, has become a distant, self-loathing 'ground pounder.' And Bernie can't stop thinking of Fumiko, the family's former maidservant, whom no one is allowed to mention." Publ Wkly

The author "nails the voice of Bernie in a delicate balance of confused, shy child vs. the bright emerging woman she has become. Bird's masterly use of the tricky technique of children revealing adult subtleties is breathtaking." Libr J

Birdwell, Cleo *See* DeLillo, Don

Black, Benjamin *See* Banville, John

Black, Lisa

Takeover. William Morrow 2008 341p $24.95

ISBN 978-0-06-154445-3; 0-06-154445-0

LC 2007-45606

As this thriller "opens, thirty-eight year old forensic scientist Theresa MacLean is working a murder scene along with her cousin, homicide detective Frank Patrick, and his partner, Theresa's fiancé, Paul Cleary. The deceased is a middle-aged man whose head had been bashed in. His name is Mark Ludlow, and he had worked as an examiner for the Federal Reserve Bank of Cleveland. Coincidentally, two armed men later enter that same bank in an apparent robbery attempt. Since the

Black, Lisa—*Continued*
Federal Reserve is no ordinary savings and loan, the perpetrators fail to get their hands on any ready cash. Knowing that they cannot escape without being gunned down by snipers, the two criminals, Lucas Parrish and Bobby Moyers, take hostages while they consider their options. Much to Theresa's horror, her future husband, Paul, is among the people being held captive. . . . Black skillfully creates a claustrophobic and tension-laden atmosphere." Mostly Fiction

Black, Mansell, 1920-1995
For works written by this author under other names see Hall, Adam, 1920-1995

Blackmore, R. D. (Richard Doddridge), 1825-1900

Lorna Doone; a romance of Exmoor; edited with an introduction and notes by Sally Shuttleworth. Oxford University Press 2009 c1994 xxix, 680p (Oxford world's classics) pa $13.95
ISBN 978-0-19-953759-4; 0-19-953759-3
First published 1869
A romantic love-story of Exmoor and the North Devon Coast of England, telling of the outlaw Doones, the maid brought up in the midst of them, and plain John Ridd's herculean power and his service to James II during Monmouth's Rebellion
"The scenic descriptions of the lovely region befits the tale, and many local worthies have their lineaments preserved here. Though 'Lorna Doone' made little stir at the time of its appearance, it has had innumerable imitations since, and it initiated a return to . . . romanticism in historical fiction." Baker. Guide to the Best Fic

Blackmore, Richard Doddridge *See* Blackmore, R. D. (Richard Doddridge), 1825-1900

Blackwell, Elise, 1964-

Grub. Toby Press 2007 353p $24.95
ISBN 978-1-59264-199-4; 1-59264-199-7
In this contemporary retelling of George Gissing's 'New Grub Street' set in New York City, Blackwell "focuses on a smoothie out for money and fame but intrigued by the daughter of a bitter, fading man-of-letters: Jackson Miller, Margot and her father Andrew Yarborough. Equally important are a novelist struggling to sell a second novel, produce a third and not lose his ambitious wife, and the wife, who turns to her own pragmatic pen: Eddie and Amanda Renfros." PopMatters
"A mordantly witty, thoroughly stimulating absolutely wonderful, satire of the New York literary world and of the price of being a literary success in America." Islamorada Free Press

Blair, Eric *See* Orwell, George, 1903-1950

Blaisdell, Anne, 1921-
For works written by this author under other names see Shannon, Dell, 1921-

Bland, Eleanor Taylor

See no evil; a Marti MacAlister mystery. St. Martin's Press 1998 274p
ISBN 0-312-16910-8   LC 97-39642
"Detective Marti MacAlister, of the Lincoln Prairie police department, wonders how she and her partner will find the murderer of a young woman who 'fell' to her death on the rocky shores of Lake Michigan. A homeless black man has not seen his best friend in days and wonders what has happened. And a crafty stalker wonders how best to massacre Marti, her kids, and her housemates." Libr J
"Bland tightens the suspense with realistic details and subplot twists before wrapping the narrative up in a satisfying solution." Publ Wkly

Blatty, William Peter

The exorcist. Harper & Row 1971 340p
ISBN 0-06-010365-5
                                                    *
Set in Georgetown, "the central figure is Regan MacNeil . . . the sweet 'normal' eleven-year-old daughter of a famous actress, Chris MacNeil. . . . Overnight, Regan turns from that normal little girl into a grotesque, unrecognizable monster, possessed by a demonic force that has locked her in a life-and-death struggle. Her weird and ugly behavior baffles the best medical experts. . . . {Chris} turns to the Jesuits. Perhaps exorcism will succeed where science has failed. Father Damien Karras, who is a trained psychiatrist, is skeptical, despite his deep knowledge of Satanism and possession. That is, until the last resort is the Church ritual." Saturday Rev
"Blatty has done his homework. He discourses, a bit bookishly, on the history of possession and the relation of autosuggestion to masked guilt. . . . Blatty maintains headlong thrust, slowly increasing Regan's agony until the reader winces; no more, a part of us says, but of course we want more because Blatty handles the horror so well." Newsweek

Bleeck, Oliver *See* Thomas, Ross, 1926-1995

Blew, Mary Clearman, 1939-

Jackalope dreams. University of Nebraska Press 2008 390p (Flyover fiction) $24.95
ISBN 978-0-8032-1588-7; 0-8032-1588-6
                                        LC 2007-23271
"Corey Henry is fired from her Montana middle school teaching job after striking a taunting student, 13-year-old Ariel Doggett. Heading into her 60s with diminished hopes, Corey faces further trials when her 80-year-old father, a decorated WWII vet and former rodeo star named Loren, commits suicide. Then Ariel's opportunistic father, Hailey Doggett, sues Corey for assaulting his daughter and turns out to be a lot more than merely greedy. Corey's lifelong passion to paint helps keep her grounded during the strife. When the tables turn on the Doggetts, Corey has a further role to play in their lives." Pub Wkly
"Blew's prose is as hardscrabble and finely whittled as her Montana subjects. . . . [She has woven] disparate elements—the death of the old West, the crazed militiamen, women both weak and strong, all-seeing children, the creeping destruction of drugs—into a tautly beautiful book." PopMatters

Blixen, Karen, 1885-1962

For works written by this author under other names see Dinesen, Isak, 1885-1962

Block, Lawrence, 1938-

All the flowers are dying. Morrow 2005 288p $24.95

ISBN 0-06-019831-1   LC 2004-53643

"In a Virginia prison, a man awaits execution for the torture and murder of three young boys, a crime he denies to the very end. After the execution, one of the witnesses—the sole person who knows the truth—heads back to Manhattan to attend to unfinished business. Meanwhile, ex-cop and investigator Matthew Scudder is semiretired, content with the fact that his toughest battles are now with his own sobriety. But the killing of his wife's best friend, along with a series of seemingly random murders, leads Scudder head-on into a confrontation with a killer he ran out of town years earlier." Libr J

"Although Scudder's hunt for the killer turns into a companionable tour of colorful neighborhoods, his thoughts on the city run deep and reflect real feelings about its humanity." N Y Times Book Rev

The burglar in the library; a Bernie Rhodenbarr mystery. Dutton 1997 342p

ISBN 0-525-94301-3

* LC 96-37537

"Panting after a copy of 'The Big Sleep' inscribed by Raymond Chandler for Dashiell Hammett ('the ultimate association copy in American crime fiction'), Bernie drags Carolyn to an inn, 'a genuine English country house' in the Berkshires, so he can relieve the unsuspecting owners of this treasure. But before he can pull the heist, the inn is snowbound, the phone lines are cut, the bridge is down and Bernie's ex-girlfriend shows up with her new husband. What next? A body in the library? Yes, and, even better, the drollest sendup of a murder-in-a-teacup mystery that you will ever hope to beg, borrow—or steal." N Y Times Book Rev

Eight million ways to die. Arbor House 1982 319p

ISBN 0-87795-405-4   LC 81-71698

This "novel is both a rousing private-eye story and an extended meditation on the whimsical ways of death—through freak accident, premeditated murder, and self-destruction. Private eye Matthew Scudder solves murders while he battles his own alcoholism. . . . In {this} tale, a 23-year old prostitute, Kim Dakkinen, wants out of 'the life' and asks Scudder to speak to her pimp, Chance. Scudder does, and a few days later Kim is found stabbed to death. Chance does the unexpected by hiring Scudder to find Kim's murderer, and while Scudder investigates, another one of Chance's prostitutes commits suicide; then another slashing occurs. A magnificently plotted, sensitive portrayal of two kinds of death—the kind that comes as an intruder and the kind that comes as an invited guest." Booklist

Killing Castro. Hard Case Crime 2009 c1961 204p pa $6.99

ISBN 978-0-8439-6113-3; 0-8439-6113-9

First published 1961 by Monarch under the pseudonym Lee Duncan with title: Fidel Castro assassinated

An "absorbing yarn about five men vying for a $100,000 prize put on Fidel Castro's head by a mysterious guy named Hiraldo. Bounty hunter Ray Garrison only works on his own; hardened murderer Michael Turner is paired with 19-year-old Jim Hines, avenging his brother's execution; and Earl Fenton, longing to do some good before he dies of cancer, teams up with jack-of-all-trades Matt Garth, who just wants the money. As they make their way to the Cuban coast, sympathetic locals support the five would-be killers in their titular goal despite their penchant for rape and mayhem. Passages discussing Castro's life and times add depth to this intense, taut thriller, just as good now as it was in 1961." Publ Wkly

(ed) Master's choice [v1]-2: mystery stories by today's top writers and the masters who inspired them. See Master's choice [v1]-2: mystery stories by today's top writers and the masters who inspired them

The sins of the fathers; a Matthew Scudder novel; introduction by Stephen King. Dark Harvest 1992 179p

ISBN 0-913165-66-2

First published 1976 in paperback

This novel introduced the then-hard-drinking ex-cop Matt Scudder. "The father of murdered Wendy Hanniford comes to Scudder to try to find out more about his errant daughter—not to find her killer, who was apparently her living partner, a brittle young man who was found in the street raving and covered with her blood and who killed himself shortly after he was arrested. In his dour, methodical, oddly empathetic way, Scudder finds out a great deal, altering several lives in the process. . . . This is a fine opportunity to get in on the start of what has become one of the most rewarding PI series currently in progress." Publ Wkly

A ticket to the boneyard; a Matthew Scudder novel. Morrow 1990 302p

ISBN 0-688-09070-2   LC 90-5710

"This time, former cop, recovering alcoholic, and dick-without-a-license Matthew Scudder is his own case. Twelve years past, in order to protect himself and a hooker friend, Scudder framed a man, James Leo Motley, who had it coming. Motley's out of prison now, and guess what? He hasn't mellowed." Booklist

The author "has a fine nose for the pungencies of New York's after-dark street life, and he gives his hero wonderful opportunities to swap syllables with the city's most articulate riffraff. This is primo stuff, and Scudder doesn't get any sharper than when he's interviewing transvestite hookers, desk clerks in fleabag hotels and bouncers in gay leather bars." N Y Times Book Rev

When the sacred ginmill closes. Arbor House 1986 239p

ISBN 0-87795-774-6

* LC 85-18682

In this novel "Scudder solves a New York City bar holdup by prying into the underworld of the city's taverns. Scudder deals with the IRA, murder, and the 'Westies,' a mob of toughs from the west of Ireland that has ruled Hell's Kitchen since the Great Potato Famine." Booklist

"The writing is realistic in the best sense of the word.

Block, Lawrence, 1938—*Continued*

There are no artificial heroics, forced lines of dialogue or false moves. Mr. Block knows his New York and the way people speak." N Y Times Book Rev

Bock, Charles

Beautiful children; a novel. Random House 2008 417p $25

ISBN 978-1-4000-6650-6; 1-4000-6650-6

LC 2007-4166

"Set in the sex-charged city of Las Vegas, the . . . plot centers on missing 12-year-old Newell Ewing, covering both the hours surrounding his disappearance and the situation's devastating effect on his parents. Complex characters playing a role in Newell's disappearance occasion a stark look into the grimy world of hustling, strip clubs, and a porn industry drawing transient and desperate teens. Among these characters are the spoiled Newell; Kenny, whose low self-esteem makes him hook up with a younger boy; Cheri, a high-class stripper involved with a skuzzy predator named Ponyboy; a pitiful comicbook artist named Bing; and a host of homeless teenagers like Danger-Prone Daphney—pregnant, doped up, and from an upper-middle-class family." Libr J

"In the no-man'sland of Bock's Vegas there remain only the survival strategies of the hopelessly inept young. I cannot think of another novelist who has dared to attack this most pressing and complex issue so ferociously." Washington Post Book World

Bock, Dennis

The ash garden; a novel. Knopf 2001 281p $23

ISBN 0-375-41302-2 LC 2001-29872

This "novel considers the legacy of the bombing of Hiroshima through the lives of Emiko, a young Hiroshima native who lost part of her face in the attack and is now a documentary filmmaker, and Anton, a German physicist who worked in Los Alamos and now lives in Canada with his wife, an Austrian refugee from World War II." Booklist

"Bock's writing is both dense and immensely readable, as engaging when it focuses on life's minutiae as when it explores life's catastrophes. The Ash Garden is difficult to forget and it rewards repeated readings in a way that few novels can." Quill Quire

Bohjalian, Christopher A., 1960-

Skeletons at the feast; a novel; by Chris Bohjalian. Shaye Areheart Books 2008 372p map $25

ISBN 978-0-307-39495-8; 0-307-39495-6

LC 2007-40800

"Inspired by the World War II diary of an East Prussian woman, Skeletons describes the horrific final months of the war as a motley crew of characters struggle to make their way across the Polish countryside to reach British and American lines. With Russian troops on their flanks and remnants of the Third Reich dotted dauntingly here and there, their journey is a daring and terrifying exodus. Key to the group are Uri Singer, a German Jew who dove to freedom from a train headed to Auschwitz and thereafter assumes the identity of various dead German soldiers; Anna Emmerich, a daughter of Prussian

aristocrats who is fleeing with her family; and Callum Finnella, a Scottish prisoner of war who hides in the Emmerich family wagon and has become Anna's lover." Rocky Mountain News

Bolaño, Roberto, 1953-2003

2666; translated from the Spanish by Natasha Wimmer. Farrar, Straus and Giroux 2008 898p $30

ISBN 978-0-374-10014-8; 0-374-10014-4

LC 2008-18295

Original Spanish edition, 2004

"More vast and more lurid than his previous novels that have been translated into English, '2666' is not Roberto Bolaño's masterpiece but almost a compendium, in individual scenes, of the qualities that made him a great writer. His themes are violence, dislocation, and the sexiness of literature, and here these strands are recombined endlessly, in Europe, Detroit, and Mexico, through multiple narrators and prose styles. The action converges on the Sonoran desert, where Bolaño anatomizes, in brutal and eerie detail, the true-life murders of hundreds of women, most of which remain unsolved. By the end, after close to nine hundred pages, the reader will be impressed by the range and power on display but might wish that the novel cohered, rather than merely concluding." New Yorker

Amulet; translated from the Spanish by Chris Andrews. New Directions 2006 184p $19.95

ISBN 978-0-8112-1664-7; 0-8112-1664-0

LC 2006-23507

Original Spanish edition, 1999

"Originally from Montevideo, poet Auxilio Lacouture cleans house in Mexico City for two wellknown poets and hangs about the university literary scene doing odd jobs. In September 18, 1968, as the army occupies the campus, arresting and killing people, Auxilio is in the deserted bathroom stalls, obliviously reading poetry; later she becomes famous for being the only one who resists arrest that fateful day." Publ Wkly

This is a "curiously joyful novel that delights in its storytelling even as it struggles with the question of how art might be sustained under conditions resolutely opposed to it." Harper's

By night in Chile; translated from the Spanish by Chris Andrews. New Directions 2004 130p pa $13.95

ISBN 0-81121-547-4 (pa)

*

Original Spanish edition, 2000

"During the course of a single night, Father Sebastian Urrutia Lacroix, a Chilean priest who is a member of Opus Dei, a literary critic and a mediocre poet, relives some of the crucial events of his life. He believes he is dying, and in his feverish delirium various characters, both real and imaginary, appear to him as icy monsters, as if in sequences from a horror film. Among them are the great poet Pablo Neruda, the German novelist Ernst Junger, and General Augusto Pinochet whom Father Lacroix instructs in Marxist doctrine as well as various members of the Chilean intelligentsia whose lives, during a period of political turbulence, have touched his own." Publisher's note

"Postwar Chilean politics and literature infuse this

Bolaño, Roberto, 1953-2003—*Continued*

densely learned, richly evocative novel. In Chris Andrews's lucid translation, Bolano's febrile narrative tack and occasional surreal touches bring to mind the classics of Latin American magic realism; his cerebral protagonist and nonfiction borrowings are reminiscent of Thomas Bernhard and W. G. Sebald." N Y Times Book Rev

Distant star; translated from the Spanish by Chris Andrews. New Directions 2004 149p pa $14.95

ISBN 0-8112-1586-5   LC 2004-19033

Original Spanish edition, 1996

"'The melancholy folklore of exile' pervades this novel, which describes the divergent paths of three young Chilean poets around the time of Pinochet's coup. At university, the unnamed narrator and his friend are fascinated by a mysterious new member of their poetry workshop. Alberto Ruiz-Tagle is 'serious, well mannered, a clear thinker,' but his poems seem false, as if his true work were yet to be revealed. It becomes apparent that this is literally the case when Allende's government falls: as an Air Force officer for the new regime, he becomes famous for writing nationalist slogans in the sky. (The left-wing narrator, now in jail, reads them from his prison yard.) Bolano's spare prose lends his narrator's account a chilly precision—as if the detachment of his former classmate had become his country's, and his own." New Yorker

Last evenings on Earth; translated from the Spanish by Chris Andrews. New Directions 2006 219p $23.95

ISBN 978-0-8112-1634-0; 0-8112-1634-9

       LC 2006-3819

Contents: Sensini; Henry Simon Leprince; Enrique Martín; A literary adventure; Phone calls; The grub; Anne Moore's life; Mauricio ("the Eye") Silva; Gómez Palacio; Last evenings on Earth; Days of 1978; Vagabond in France and Belgium; Dentist; Dance card

"These 14 bleakly luminous stories are all told in the first person by men (usually young) who yearn for something just out of their grasp (fame, talent, love) and who harbor few hopes of attaining what they desire. . . . The stories are similar, in theme and voice (though not in locale), and they are perfectly calibrated: Bolaño limns the capacity of a voice to carry despair without shading into bitterness." Publ Wkly

Nazi literature in the Americas; translated from the Spanish by Chris Andrews. New Directions 2008 227p $23.95

ISBN 978-0-8112-1705-7; 0-8112-1705-1

       * LC 2007-37800

Original Spanish edition, 1996

This novel, "a wicked, invented encyclopedia of imaginary fascist writers and literary tastemakers, is Bolaño playing with sharp, twisting knives. As if he were Borges's wisecracking, sardonic son, Bolaño has meticulously created a tightly woven network of far-right litterateurs and purveyors of belles lettres for whom Hitler was beauty, truth and great lost hope. Cross-referenced, complete with bibliography and a biographical list of secondary figures, Nazi Literature is composed of a series of sketches, the compressed life stories of writers in North and South America who never existed, but all too

easily could have. Goose-stepping caricatures a la 'The Producers' they are not; instead, they are frighteningly subtle, poignant and plausible." N Y Times Book Rev

The savage detectives; translated from the Spanish by Natasha Wimmer. Farrar, Straus & Giroux 2007 577p il $27

ISBN 978-0-374-19148-1; 0-374-19148-4

       * LC 2006-22176

Original Spanish edition, 1998

"New Year's Eve, 1975: Arturo Belano and Ulises Lima, founders of the visceral realist movement in poetry, leave Mexico City in a borrowed white Impala. Their quest: to track down the obscure, vanished poet Cesarea Tinajero. A violent showdown in the Sonora desert turns search to flight; twenty years later Belano and Lima are still on the run. . . . The Savage Detectives follows Belano and Lima through the eyes of the people whose paths they cross in Central America, Europe, Israel, and West Africa." Publisher's note

"Though the fragmented narrative can be frustrating at times, the late-20th-century panorama emerging from the cacophony is simultaneously frightening and spectacular. At every turn, Bolaño examines the individual lives history discards. The result is a large, sprawling and—most of all—sublime novel." Paste

The skating rink; translated by Chris Andrews. New Directions 2009 182p $21.95

ISBN 978-0-8112-1713-2; 0-8112-1713-2

       LC 2009-10724

Original Spanish edition, 1993

"Set in the fictional Spanish seaside town of 'Z' and told from the points-of-view of an alternating trio of narrators—Remo Morán, former poet-turned-businessman; Enric Rosquelles, corrupt civil servant; and Gaspar Heredia, illegal immigrant, campground nightwatchman and our authorial stand-in—the novel revolves around Nuria Martí, an aspiring Olympic skater whose beauty will compel Morán and Rosquelles in ways neither had previously imagined. To help Martí in her training, Rosquelles embezzles city funds to transform a dilapidated mansion on the outskirts of the city into a fully operational regulation-sized skating rink. Meanwhile, Martí begins a casual romance with Morán, the more physically attractive (and apparently well-endowed) of the two rivals. And here, the initial pieces are set. Add in Heredia's fixation with two of the campground's residents, Carmen, a former opera singer, and Caridad, a mysterious, taciturn girl, and it seems inevitable that these actions will culminate in disaster. . . . The novel traverses territories of escalating and unstable passion, but not without occasional comedy." Faster Times

Böll, Heinrich, 1917-1985

The clown; translated from the German by Leila Vennewitz. McGraw-Hill 1965 247p o.p.

Original German edition, 1963

This novel revolves around the loss of meaning in the life of Hans Schnier, a twenty-seven-year-old clown and mime who returns home to Bonn after a disastrous performance tour. Flashbacks reconstruct Schnier's life in Hitler's Germany and his bitter experiences of the postwar period

"What Schnier (and the author) seem to be asking is: How can an honest man profess Christianity when Chris-

Böll, Heinrich, 1917-1985—*Continued*

tian culture in the West failed to stop the rise of Nazism . . . and when the Church thrives in a society that worships nothing but the values of the marketplace? Hard questions but embodied in a bitter and brilliant book." NY Times Book Rev

The silent angel; translated by Breon Mitchell. St. Martin's Press 1994 182p

ISBN 0-312-11064-2   LC 94-2052

Written in 1950; first German edition, 1992

"Amid the charred rubble of Germany just days after World War II ends, cynical, numbed soldier Hans Schnitzler returns to Cologne under an alias to deliver a dead soldier's will to the widow, Elisabeth Gompertz. Hans was supposed to be shot as a deserter, but military court stenographer Willy Gompertz switched jackets with him and was killed instead. So begins what was Nobel-winner Böll's first novel." Publ Wkly

"While the bleakness Böll portrays might have made German publishers wary in 1950, the artistry of his portrayal makes 'The Silent Angel' a rich novel, one still pertinent to our own hunger for the bread of meaning amid the rubble of history. Heinrich Böll's gift to us is the skill with which he captures its first pangs." NY Times Book Rev

Bond, Michael, 1926-

Monsieur Pamplemousse. Beaufort Bks. 1985 191p

ISBN 0-8253-0267-6   LC 84-24444

First published 1983 in the United Kingdom

Pamplemousse is a "gastronomic detective, an undercover critic for a prestigious Gallic dining guide. With his faithful bloodhound, Pommes Frites, Pamplemousse—a former inspector with the Sureté—investigates the cuisine of his favorite hotel-restaurant, La Langoustine. There, misfortune strikes: the specialty of the house is served to him with a man's head inside. . . . Mystery takes a back seat to fine food and hilarious characters in this ribald, side-splitting farce." Publ Wkly

Borchardt, Alice

The silver wolf. Ballantine Bks. 1998 451p

ISBN 0-345-42360-7   LC 98-4802

"A Del Rey book"

"As Charlemagne consolidates his empire through a combination of wars and strategic marriages, a young girl who possesses the power to transform herself into a silver wolf becomes a reluctant pawn in a game of politics and survival. Against the decadent and barbaric backdrop of Rome in the Dark Ages, the author . . . spins a love-story tinged with the supernatural. Borchardt's sensual prose and period detail provide a lush setting for her tale of a woman struggling to reconcile her human and wolf natures." Libr J

Borges, Jorge Luis, 1899-1986

Collected fictions; translated by Andrew Hurley. Viking 1998 565p

ISBN 0-670-84970-7

                    * LC 98-21217

This is a collection of all the stories written by Borges over a 50-year period

"A Borges invention . . . always takes the reader on a roller-coaster ride into some previously unsuspected dimension. This collection of the great magician's work is a new translation and includes one piece never before put into English." Atl Mon

Borland, Hal, 1900-1978

When the legends die. Lippincott 1963 288p pa $6.50 hardcover o.p.

ISBN 0-553-25738-2

"Thomas Black Bull, a Ute Indian, is being reared in the traditional Native American way when his parents are forced to flee from the world of the white man. After the death of his parents Tom is returned to the white world, where he suffers the disintegration of his native heritage and traditions as he experiences school, sheep herding, and rodeo life. Following a serious accident at a rodeo he returns to the mountains and is drawn back into his past." Shapiro. Fic for Youth 3rd edition

Bosse, Malcolm J., 1934-2002

The warlord. Simon & Schuster 1983 717p

ISBN 0-671-44332-1

"In the violent, disorganized China of 1927 four people are thrown together. Tang Shan-teh, a successful general, desires unity and modernization but respects and preserves the old values of Confucianism and tradition; Vera Rogacheeva is a sometime prostitute, a White Russian refugee; Erich Luckner sells German guns to bandits and warlords; and Philip Embree is an American missionary who has gone native to the point of enlisting in Tang's army as an axeman." Libr J

"This book is a must for the student of China as well as those interested in human nature. It is a complicated story and cannot be skimmed or read between loads at the laundromat. This story is for those who enjoy 'hunkering down' in the sun and traveling to exotic places, where they must deal with contradictions, love and hate, peace and violence, confusions, and Marxist loyalty, and ultimately betrayal." Best Sellers

Followed by Fire in heaven

Boswell, Robert, 1953-

Century's son. Knopf 2002 307p $24

ISBN 0-375-41237-9   LC 2001-38101

"Morgan, whose first name has fallen away 'from disuse,' was once a fearless labor organizer for his fellow sanitation workers; it was his uncompromising idealism that led Zhenya, his college-professor wife, to fall in love with him. But, ten years later, Morgan has abandoned his activism; he spends his days collecting garbage and contemplating his decline, which began when his son hanged himself, at the age of twelve. As if the Morgan marriage didn't have enough to deal with, Zhenya's father, the famous Russian writer Peter Ivanovich Kamenev, is coming to visit. . . . A moving portrait of a family both torn apart and united by grief." New Yorker

The heyday of the insensitive bastards; stories. Graywolf Press 2009 258p $24

ISBN 978-1-55597-524-1; 1-55597-524-0

                    LC 2008-941562

Boswell, Robert, 1953-—_Continued_

Contents: No river wide; Smoke; Miss Famous; A walk in winter; A sketch of highway on the nap of a mountain; Supreme beings; In a foreign land; City bus; Guests; Almost not beautiful; Skin deep; Lacunae; The heyday of the insensitive bastards

"Some of the stories are very short sketches or vignettes of brief encounters of a sexual or violent nature, while the longer stories are more novelistic and include large casts of characters and complex narratives. Boswell, whose style and subject matter is somewhat reminiscent of Tobias Wolff and Robert Stone, is a virtuoso of descriptive prose, and handles the psychological and emotional imagery with skill." Libr J

Boucolon, Maryse _See_ Condé, Maryse, 1937-

Boulle, Pierre, 1912-1994

The bridge over the River Kwai; translated by Xan Fielding. Vanguard Press 1954 224p o.p.

        *

Original French edition, 1952

"In 1942 the Japanese military under the command of Col. Saito orders its British prisoners of war to construct a bridge over the 400-foot-wide River Kwai in the Siamese jungle. Complications arise when prisoner Col. Nicholson insists that officers not be treated like regular lower-class soldiers. Medical officer Clipton is much more humane, and this difference brings the two fellow prisoners into frequent conflict. When the bridge is finally completed, a British demolition team prepares to destroy it." Shapiro. Fic for Youth. 3d edition

Planet of the apes; translated by Xan Feilding. Ballantine 2001 c1991 268p pa $6.99

ISBN 0-345-44798-0

        *

"A Del Rey book"

First published 1963 by Vanguard Press; published in the United Kingdom with title: Monkey planet

"Ulysse Merou writes of his experiences on an unusual planet where the roles of humans and apes are reversed. Gorillas wear clothing and run businesses, while humans are caged in zoos and are the subjects of scientific experiments. In the year 2500 a vacationing couple cruising through space spot a bottle-encased message, retrieve it, and soon become absorbed in Merou's tale." Shapiro. Fic for Youth. 3d edition

"In this Swiftian fable Boulle gives full play to his not inconsiderable gift for irony and satire." Libr J

Bourne, Joanna

My lord and spymaster. Berkley Sensation 2008 324p pa $7.99

ISBN 978-0-425-22246-1; 0-425-22246-2

"Jess Whitby, daughter of suspected spy Josiah Whitby, is doing everything in her power to exonerate her imprisoned father. In order to free him, she must prove that someone other than her father is the Cinq, a notorious mole. But Jess has met her match in Capt. Sebastian Kennett, wealthy bastard son of an English nobleman, equally as clever at keeping tabs on Jess as she is at tracking him. Sebastian is responsible for Josiah's arrest; Jess believes that Sebastian may be the Cinq; their

mutual attraction proves a lovely foil for their suspicious minds. Glimpses of the leads' sordid pasts add depth, and Bourne's consummate way with a story line and an explosive denouement do the rest." Publ Wkly

The spymaster's lady. Berkley Publishing Group 2008 373p pa $7.99

ISBN 978-0-425-21960-7

"Annique Villiers, the elusive spy known as the Fox Cub, has outwitted, outmaneuvered and outfoxed every man she's ever met, until British spymaster Robert Grey steps into a French prison. Grey's mission is to capture the Cub and uncover exactly what she knows and who she works for. As enemies, they hate one another; as fellow prisoners they must band together to escape. Their truce is filled with suspicion, but there's also a spark of something more a forbidden passion that threatens their missions." Romantic Times

Bova, Ben, 1932-

Jupiter. TOR Bks. 2001 368p

ISBN 0-312-87217-8   LC 00-48021

"A Tom Doherty Associates book"

"Assigned by the New Morality, Earth's conservative ruling coalition, to act as its agent at a research station in orbit around the planet Jupiter, astrophysicist Grant Archer finds himself torn between his faith in God and his loyalty to science. . . . {This is a} first-rate adventure that combines hard science with human drama to create a challenging and compelling tale of courage and conviction." Libr J

Mars. Bantam Bks. 1992 502p

ISBN 0-553-07892-5

        * LC 91-29466

"A Native American geologist finds himself the center of political controversy as he becomes one of the first humans to set foot on the red planet. Bova's imaginary chronicle of the first human mission to Mars offers a field day for science buffs as his characters experience the challenges of exploring Earth's nearest neighbor." Libr J

Followed by Return to Mars

Mars life. Tor 2008 432p $24.95

ISBN 978-0-7653-1787-2; 0-7653-1787-7

        LC 2008-20388

"A Tom Doherty Associates book"

Sequel to: Return to Mars (1999)

"Two scientists add up fossil evidence to conclude that Mars once supported intelligent life and that Martians colonized Earth—conclusions that run them into the religious buzz saw of New Morality conservatives." Booklist

"Bova deftly captures the excitement of scientific discovery and planetary exploration. This compelling story, balancing action and plausible political intrigue, will easily be enjoyed by both fans and newcomers." Publ Wkly

Return to Mars. Avon Bks. 1999 403p

ISBN 0-380-97640-4   LC 99-21635

Sequel to Mars

"Determined to prove that his sighting of a pueblo-like cliff dwelling on Mars was not a delusion born of false hopes, Navaho geologist Jamie Waterman returns to the Red Planet as part of a controversial second mission to exploit the resources of the solar system. Strained relations among the crew lead to the growing suspicion of

Bova, Ben, 1932--—*Continued*

a saboteur in their midst as Waterman sees his dreams fade in the face of political short-sightedness and human greed." Libr J

"Where Bova shines is in making science not only comprehensible but entertaining." N Y Times Book Rev

Followed by: Mars life (2008)

Saturn. TOR Bks. 2003 412p $24.95

ISBN 0-312-87218-6   LC 2003-40216

"A Tom Doherty Associates book"

"When Earth's leadership decides to 'encourage' its dissidents to leave the planet aboard an interstellar habitat destined for Saturn, Susan Lane joins the expedition, eager to begin a new life. Attracted to Malcolm Eberly, the charismatic director of the habitat, Susan (now calling herself Holly) dedicates herself to the task of helping Malcolm organize life aboard the habitat, remaining blissfully unaware of the sinister politics going on among the habitat's leaders and blinding herself to Malcolm's real agenda." Libr J

"Bova is definitely the man to do justice to the astronomical marvels of the Saturnian system with its enormous potential as a second home for humanity, especially in the complex environments of its moons. Loud, prolonged applause, then, for the strengths of this book." Booklist

Bowen, Elizabeth, 1899-1973

The heat of the day. Knopf 1949 c1948 372p o.p.

Essentially this novel presents character studies of Stella Rodney, and the two men who loved her. The background is London after Dunkirk, a London of blitzes and buzz bombs; and peaceful Ireland. The two men are Robert Kelway, Stella's lover, and the mysterious Harrison, who betrays Kelway's secret in order to gain Stella for himself

"Miss Bowen's novel expertly flicks the rawness of several unsolved queries concerning loyalty and love and ponders the degree to which human beings are strangers to each other. More densely written than her earlier work, this study of behavior is a soberly shocking, compassionate baring of the confused and vulnerable human heart." N Y Her Trib Books

Bowen, Peter, 1945-

Badlands. St. Martin's Minotaur 2003 250p $23.95

ISBN 0-312-26252-3   LC 2002-37196

Montana sheriff Gabriel Du Pré's "suspicions are aroused when the Host of Yahweh immediately destroys the ranch buildings, sells the livestock and erects a makeshift metal chapel for secret rites. Soon, reportsof mass murders and suicides bring in cautious FBI agents ever mindful of the Waco debacle. Du Pré's blunt speech and sometimes opaque thought patterns can be hard to follow, but his pursuits of wrongdoers over cliffs, canyons and arid river beds are truly riveting." Publ Wkly

Bowen-Judd, Sara Hutton *See* Woods, Sara

Bowles, Paul, 1910-1999

Collected stories & later writings. Library of America 2002 1062p $40

ISBN 1-931082-20-0   LC 2002-19452

Fifty-two of the short stories in this volume have appeared in the five books: The delicate prey (1950); A hundred camels in the courtyard (1962); The time of friendship (1967); Things gone and things still here (1977); and Midnight mass (1981). Six selected later stories are also included. Up above the world (1966) is a novella where an American couple visiting Central America have a frightening experience with an apparently wealthy local couple. Their heads are green and their hands are blue (1963) is a collection of travel essays.

Contents: The delicate prey and other stories; A hundred camels in the courtyard; New stories from The time of friendship; Things gone and things still here; Midnight mass; Selected later stories; Their heads are green and their hands are blue; Up above the world

The delicate prey and other stories
In Bowles, P. Collected stories & later writings

A hundred camels in the courtyard
In Bowles, P. Collected stories & later writings

Let it come down
In Bowles, P. The sheltering sky; Let it come down; The spider's house

Midnight mass
In Bowles, P. Collected stories & later writings

The sheltering sky. New Directions 1949 318p o.p.

                                              *

"Port and Kit Moresby, an American couple of independent means, have been traveling aimlessly for 12 years. By the time they reach Morocco they have become disaffected and alienated. They take up with a series of unreliable, rootless wanderers. On a trip to the interior Port contracts typhoid fever—out of apathy he has neglected to be vaccinated—and dies. Kit has an affair with an Arab and joins his household, but their relationship soon falls apart. Kit is found and returned to Oran. She is teetering on the brink of insanity and finds an opportunity to disappear into the crowded bazaar." Merriam-Webster's Ency of Lit

also in Bowles, P. The sheltering sky; Let it come down; The spider's house

The sheltering sky; Let it come down; The spider's house. Library of America 2002 938p $35

ISBN 1-931082-19-7   LC 2002-19453

Contents: The sheltering sky; Let it come down; The spider's house

The sheltering sky is entered separately. "In Let It Come Down (1952), Bowles plots the doomed trajectory of Nelson Dyar, a New York bank teller who comes to Tangier in search of a different life and ends up giving in to his darkest impulses. . . . The Spider's House (1955) . . . is set against the end of French rule in Morocco. Its characters—ranging from a Moroccan boy gift-

Bowles, Paul, 1910-1999—*Continued*

ed with spiritual healing power to an American writer who regrets the passing of traditional ways—are caught up in the clash between colonial and nationalist factions, and are forced to confront cultural gulfs widened by political violence." Publisher's note

The spider's house

In Bowles, P. The sheltering sky; Let it come down; The spider's house

The stories of Paul Bowles; introduction by Robert Stone. Ecco Press 2001 657p $39.95

ISBN 0-06-621273-1   LC 2001-51231

Contents: By the water; The echo; A distant episode; Call at Corazón; The scorpion; Under the sky; At Paso Rojo; You are not I; Pages from Cold Point; Pastor Dowe at Tacaté; Tea on the mountain; How many midnights; The circular valley; The delicate prey; Señor Ong and Señor Ha; The fourth day out from Santa Cruz; Doña Faustina; The successor; If I should open my mouth; The hours after noon; The frozen fields; Tapiama; A thousand days for Mokhtar; The story of Lahcen and Idir; He of the assembly; A friend of the world; The hyena; The wind at Beni Midar; The garden; The time of friendship; Afternoon with Antaeus; Mejdoub; The fqih; Reminders of Bouselham; Istikhara, Anaya, Medagan and the Medaganat; Things gone and things still here; Midnight mass; Here to learn; The eye; The waters of Izli; You have left your lotus pods on the bus; Allal; The dismissal; Madame and Ahmed; Kitty; The husband; At the Krungthep plaza; Bouayad and the money; The little house; The empty amulet; Rumor and a ladder; In the red room; Massachusetts 1932; Tangier 1975; Julian Vreden; Hugh Harper; Unwelcome words; New York 1965; An inopportune visit; In absentia; Dinner at Sir Nigel's; Too far from home

"Earthy, violent and comfortable with corruption, these deeply affecting stories are distinguished by their lyrical rhythms and meticulous regard for language." Publ Wkly

Things gone and things still here

In Bowles, P. Collected stories & later writings

Up above the world

In Bowles, P. Collected stories & later writings

Box, C. J.

Blood trail. G.P. Putnam's Sons 2008 301p $24.95

ISBN 978-0-399-15488-1; 0-3991-5488-4

LC 2007-44776

"When a hunter is butchered in Wyoming, game warden Joe Pickett and his boss, Randy Pope, set off to investigate. Soon, it becomes clear that someone is systematically killing hunters. Caught between the people who hunt and those who are opposed to hunting, not to mention facing one of the most dangerous cases of his career, Pickett must find a way to bring the killer to justice before more deaths occur. . . . [Box's] sense of place and talent for character development are on a par with those of James Lee Burke." Libr J

Savage run. Putnam 2002 272p

ISBN 0-399-14887-6   LC 2001-57872

"Two creepy, coldhearted guys carry out orders from an unseen other as they murder a famous environmental activist, a noted environmental writer, and the country's most powerful 'green' congressman. Called in after the first murder (by explosion), which also killed several animals in his part of the Wyoming wilderness, game warden Joe Pickett begins to suspect a broader conspiracy. With a few clues from his part-time librarian wife, Pickett moves the investigation forward." Libr J

"The 'outdoor mystery' was a thriving subgenre before Box arrived on the scene, but he has taken it to new levels of substance and style." Booklist

Boyd, Jerry *See* Toole, F. X., 1930-2002

Boyer, Richard *See* Boyer, Rick

Boyer, Rick

The Daisy Ducks; a Doc Adams suspense novel. Houghton Mifflin 1986 276p

ISBN 0-395-35289-4   LC 86-3016

In this novel dentist-cum-detective Doc Adams' "soldier-for-hire pal Liantis Roantis . . . gives the adventurous surgeon a reason to take a brief hiatus from impacted wisdom teeth. Roantis needs Doc's help in finding a Vietnam buddy who has become a fanatic survivalist and is ensconced in the North Carolina mountains preparing for Armageddon. Amid the action, Boyer effectively ponders the not-so-romantic reality of life on the edge versus the sometimes somnambulant comforts of home." Booklist

"If you like action-suspense novels, Doc Adams could become addictive. Boyer's smooth style creates a character with charisma and a story that moves like a freight train at full throttle—powerfully swift." Best Sellers

Boyle, T. Coraghessan

Road to Wellville; a novel. Viking 1993 476p il

ISBN 0-670-83766-0   LC 92-50731

This social satire provides a portrait of 1907 Battle Creek, Michigan "from three perspectives. The first and most central is that of Dr. Kellogg himself, high priest of a sanitarium where the rich and powerful go to be cured of physical and spiritual 'autointoxication' brought about by meat eating and sexual activity. Possessed of a Napoleon complex and an abiding hatred of Post, he is saluted around the clinic as 'the Chief.' The second is that of Will Lightbody, a patient at the clinic who has trouble getting the Kellogg religion. The third viewpoint is that of Charlie Ossining, a shady businessman who tries to get a piece of the breakfast-cereal action a little too late." Booklist

The author "evokes the world of the senses with remarkable skill. As always, his prose is a marvel, enjoyable from beginning to end, alive with astute observations, sharp intelligence and subtle musicality. Possibly as an effect of his highly developed style, Mr. Boyle's vision has been one of the most distinctive and original of his generation." N Y Times Book Rev

The tortilla curtain. Viking 1995 355p

ISBN 0-670-85604-5

* LC 95-1970

Boyle, T. Coraghessan—*Continued*

"The lives of two couples living in Topanga Canyon (Los Angeles) intersect when Delaney Mossbacher slams his car into Cándido Rincón. But the couples couldn't be more disparate: Delaney is a nature writer ('Pilgrim at Topanga Canyon') whose wife, Kyra, is a successful realtor; the Rincóns are illegal aliens camping out, looking for any work at all, and América {is} pregnant." Libr J

"What Boyle does, and does well, is lay on the line our national cult of hypocrisy. Comically and painfully he details the snug wastefulness of the haves and the vile misery of the have-nots. . . . Americans of every stripe will find themselves rooting for Cándido and América, right up to the riproaring *deus ex machina* ending that screams out that we are all in this together." Nation

The women; a novel. Viking 2009 451p $27.95
ISBN 978-0-670-02041-6; 0-670-02041-9
LC 2008-42462

"Boyle's latest novel takes on the architect Frank Lloyd Wright by examining his notoriously tumultuous relationships with four women, each unique in her own histrionic way. Narrated in reverse chronological order by a fictional Japanese apprentice, the book is extremely readable and deftly builds a portrait of the artist as pure egoist. Unfortunately, the novel avoids any sustained consideration of Wright's relationship to his art—a passion arguably more important in forming his genius than any of the women in his life were. Still, it proves an effective showcase for Boyle's own strengths as a craftsman. His prose is full of vivid descriptions and turns of phrase that pop with a preternatural precision." New Yorker

World's end; a novel. Viking 1987 456p
ISBN 0-670-81489-X
LC 87-40023

"The sins of the fathers—along with physical afflictions and other worries—are visited on their children as one generation relives in contemporary terms the experiences of the past. Boyle's novel—partly a historical tale and partly a modern-day re-creation of the same story—switches from past to near present and mixes seventeenth-century Dutch settlers and their landlords with hippie motorcyclists and Indians intent on reclaiming their territory in the Hudson River valley." Booklist

"The themes Mr. Boyle develops as his story shuttles between epochs make us grasp in new terms their connection with the American social and political experiment. His mastery of history is the secret of the accomplishment here. Mr. Boyle has lost none of the qualities that marked him a wit writer before, but now he has challenged his own disengagement; passion, need and belief breathe with striking force and freedom through this smashing good novel." N Y Times Book Rev

Boyne, John, 1971-

Crippen; a novel of murder. Thomas Dunne Books 2006 337p $24.95
ISBN 978-0-312-34358-3; 0-312-34358-2
LC 2005-56011

First published 2004 in the United Kingdom

The author "blends fact, fiction, and supposition in a suspenseful tale based on the 1910 transatlantic pursuit of Dr. Hawley Crippen for the murder and brutal dismemberment of his wife, Cora." Libr J

"Boyne starts with the basic facts. . . but he has al-

tered the story to suit his dramatic needs and authorial whims. The result of his reinvention is a dark comedy that is supremely readable, always suspenseful, sometimes laugh-out-loud funny and, finally, a monumental piece of misogyny. In Boyne's sardonic telling, Cora Crippen was a monster who richly deserved to die, and her long-suffering husband was a man more sinned against than sinning." Washington Post Book World

Boz *See* Dickens, Charles, 1812-1870

Bradbury, Malcolm, 1932-2000

To the Hermitage. Overlook Press 2001 498p $27.95
ISBN 1-58567-131-2
LC 00-50147

A "dual narrative that compares Denis Diderot's *Age of Reason* to the postmodern 1990s. The first story follows the French encyclopedist as he travels from Paris to Catherine the Great's court in St. Petersburg. The acquisitive Catherine has just purchased Diderot's personal library. Now she wants to hire him as her librarian. In the second narrative, a British novelist attends an international Diderot conference held in St. Petersburg in 1993, just as the military coup against Boris Yeltsin is unfolding. When an American deconstructionist in a baseball cap refutes the very notion of an Age of Reason, the conference collapses into drunken anarchy." Libr J

"The book is overextended, but it is also lively, thought provoking and, in its portrait of contemporary Russia, vividly chilling. For patient readers of a scholarly inclination and with a liking for the stranger corners of history, this will be a treat." Publ Wkly

Bradbury, Ray, 1920-

Bradbury stories; 100 of his most celebrated tales. Morrow 2003 893p $29.95; pa $17.95
ISBN 0-06-054242-X; 0-06-054488-0 (pa)
* LC 2003-42189

Contents: The whole town's sleeping; The rocket; Season of disbelief; And the rock cried out; The drummer boy of Shiloh; The beggar on O'Connell Bridge; The flying machine; Heavyset; The first night of Lent; Lafayette, farewell; Remember Sascha?; Junior; That woman on the lawn; February 1999: Ylla; Banshee; One for his lordship, and one for the road!; The Laurel and Hardy love affair; Underderseaboat doktor; Another fine mess; The dwarf; A wild night in Galway; The wind; No news, or what killed the dog?; A little journey; Any friend of Nicholas Nickleby's is a friend of mine; The garbage collector; The visitor; The man; Henry the ninth; The messiah; Bang! you're dead!; Darling Adolf; The beautiful shave; Colonel Stonesteel's genuine homemade truly Egyptian mummy; I see you never; The exiles; At midnight, in the month of June; The witch door; The watchers; 200405: the naming of names; Hopscotch; The illustrated man; The dead man; June 2001: and the moon be still as bright; The burning man; G.B.S.—Mark V; A blade of grass; The sound of summer running; And the sailor, home from the sea; The lonely ones; The Finnegan; On the Orient, North; The smiling people; The fruit at the bottom of the bowl; Bug; Downwind from Gettysburg; Time in thy flight; Changeling; The dragon; Let's play "poison"; The cold wind and the warm; The meadow; The Kilimanjaro device; The man in the Ror-

Bradbury, Ray, 1920-—*Continued*

schach shirt; Blees me, father, for I have sinned; The pedestrian; Trapdoor; The swan; The sea shell; Once more, Legato; June 2003: way in the middle of the air; The wonderful death of Dudley Stone; By the numbers!; April 2005: Usher II; The square pegs; The trolley; The smile; The miracles of Jamie; A far-away guitar; The cistern; The machineries of joy; Bright phoenix; The wish; The lifework of Juan Diaz; Time intervening/interim; Almost the end of the world; The great collision of Monday last; The poems; April 2026: the long years; Icarus Montgolfier Wright; Death and the maiden; Zero hour; The Toynbee convector; Forever and the earth; The handler; Getting through Sunday somehow; The Pumpernickel; Last rites; The watchful poker chip of H. Matisse; All on a summer's night

"This massive retrospective of self-selected Bradbury stories offers a compendium of his eccentrics, misfits, losers, and small-town dreamers, who typically inhabit an uncanny setting or confront a strange, unsettling situation." Libr J

Dandelion wine; a novel. Avon Books 1999 267p $15.95

ISBN 0-380-97726-5
* LC 98-93914

First published 1957 by Doubleday

A novel about one summer in the life of a twelve-year-old boy, Douglas Spaulding: the summer of 1928. The place is Green Town, Illinois, and Doug and his brother Tom wander in and out among their elders, living and dreaming, sometimes aware of things, again just having a wonderful time. Doug's big discovery that summer was that he was alive.

"The writing is beautiful and the characters are wonderful living people. A rare reading experience—highly recommended to all libraries." Libr J

Followed by Farewell summer (2006)

Fahrenheit 451. Simon & Schuster 2003 190p $23

ISBN 0-7432-4722-1
* LC 2003-66160

First published 1953 in paperback by Ballantine Bks.

Dystopian novel about a bookburner official in a future fascist state.

The illustrated man. Doubleday 1951 251p o.p.

Contents: The veldt; Kaleidoscope; The other foot; The highway; The man; The long rain; The Rocket Man; The fire balloons; The last night of the world; The exiles; No particular night or morning; The fox and the forest; The visitor; The concrete mixer; Marionettes, Inc.; The city; Zero hour; The rocket

In this work "the stories are given a linking framework; they are all seen as magical tattoos becoming living stories, springing from the body of the protagonist." Sci Fic Ency

The Martian chronicles. Avon Books 1997 268p $15.95

ISBN 0-380-97383-9
* LC 96-95071

First published 1950 by Doubleday

This book's "closely interwoven short stories, linked by recurrent images and themes, tell of the repeated attempts by humans to colonize Mars, of the way they bring their old prejudices with them, and of the repeated, ambiguous meetings with the shape-changing Martians." Sci Fic Ency

Something wicked this way comes. Avon Bks. 1999 293p $15.95; pa $7.99

ISBN 0-380-97727-3; 0-380-72940-7 (pa)
*

A reissue of the title first published 1962 by Simon and Schuster

"We read here of the loss of innocence, the recognition of evil, the bond between generations, and the purely fantastic. These forces enter Green Town, Illinois, on the wheels of Cooger and Dark's Pandemonium Shadow Show. Will Halloway and Jim Nightshade, two 13-year-olds, explore the sinister carnival for excitement, which becomes desperation as the forces of the dark threaten to engulf them. Bradbury's gentle humanism and lyric style serve this fantasy well." Shapiro. Fic for Youth. 3d edition

Bradford, Barbara Taylor, 1933-

The Ravenscar dynasty. St. Martin's Press 2007 484p $25.95

ISBN 978-0-312-35460-2; 0-312-35460-6
LC 2006-50979

This is the "first installment of a projected trilogy centering on internecine power struggles within the early 20th century incarnation of the centuries-old Deravenel clan and their London-based family business. A suspicious hotel fire causes the death of patriarch Richard Deravenel along with that of one of his sons, his brother-in-law and his young nephew, forcing tall, handsome, bright, seductive, 17-year old Edward Deravenel out of Oxford into the world of commerce. He and cousin Neville Watkins (a successful businessman in his own right) plot to avenge their fathers' and brothers' deaths and seize the company, currently under the stewardship of a delusional absentee executive whose ambitious (and French) wife is behind the skullduggery. Edward's longtime friend, Will Hasling, also joins the fray, and Neville has his own motivations." Publ Wkly

A woman of substance. Doubleday 1979 755p

ISBN 0-385-12050-8
* LC 77-9231

"A poor Yorkshire girl rises from the servant class to found a department store and eventually head an important business dynasty. As the aged Emma recalls how she has sacrificed love and happiness for success and power, she repudiates the past for the simpler and more enduring pleasures of life." Booklist

"It's a life worth the telling, and Ms. Bradford has told it well, sparing no detail. She writes competently, if not extraordinarily, against an accurate and well drawn historical background." West Coast Rev Books

Followed by Hold the dream

Bradley, Marion Zimmer

The mists of Avalon. Ballantine Pub. Group 2000 876p $30; pa $16.95

ISBN 0-345-44118-4; 0-345-35049-9 (pa)
LC 00-712415

Bradley, Marion Zimmer—*Continued*

"A Del Rey book"

A reissue of the title first published 1982 by Knopf

This retelling of the Arthurian legend is dominated by the character of Morgan le Fay (here called Morgaine), the powerful sorceress who symbolizes the historical clash betweeen Christianity and the early pagan religions of the British Isles." Publ Wkly

Other novels in the Avalon series written with Diana L. Paxson are: The forest house (1993); Lady of Avalon (1997); Priestess of Avalon (2000). Following Bradley's death Paxson continued the series with: Ancestors of Avalon (2004); Ravens of Avalon (2007); Sword of Avalon (2009)

Bradshaw-Isherwood, Christopher William *See* Isherwood, Christopher, 1904-1986

Brady, William S., 1938-

For works written by this author under other names see Harvey, John, 1938-

Bragg, Melvyn, 1939-

The soldier's return. Arcade Pub. 2002 384p $25.95

ISBN 1-55970-639-2   LC 2002-21558

First published 1999 in the United Kingdom

"In 1946, Englishman Sam Richardson returns to his wife and young son after fighting the the 'Forgotten War' in Burma. Like so many who fought beside him and lived to return, Sam feels suffocated by life in tiny rural Wigton. The men who were left behind ask too many painful questions, and nightmares rob Sam of sleep. Work is scarce and demeaning, and rebuilding his life with his wife, Ellen, and young son, Joe, is fraught with awkwardness, misunderstanding, and frustration." Libr J

"Bragg weaves a powerful, deeply moving story of a family and a society torn apart by war. His straightforward prose and the measured pace of his writing allow readers to savor every nuance of life in a small town in postwar England, and the depth and reality of his characters and his ability to bring the horrors of war alive are nothing short of brilliant." Booklist

A son of war; a novel. Arcade Pub. 2003 426p $25.95

ISBN 1-559-70686-4   LC 2002-44058

This sequel to A soldier's return "finds Sam and Ellen Richardson and their son, Joe, still in the dreary slums of Wigton, waiting for their chance for a new council house in a developing outskirt. Times are tough, and they are barely scraping by." Libr J

"A hauntingly evocative slice of postwar life." Booklist

Bragi Ólafsson, 1962-

The pets; a novel; translated from the Icelandic by Janice Balfour. Open Letter 2008 157p $14.95

ISBN 978-1-934824-01-6; 1-934824-01-1

    * LC 2008-926608

Original Icelandic edition, 2001

"Back in Reykjavik after a vacation in London, Emil Halldorsson is waiting for a call from a beautiful girl, Greta, that he met on the plane ride home, and he's just put on a pot of coffee when an unexpected visitor knocks on the door. Peeking through a window, Emil spies an erstwhile friend—Havard Knutsson, his onetime roommate and current resident of a Swedish mental institution—on his doorstep, and he panics, taking refuge under his bed and hoping the frightful nuisance will simply go away. Havard won't be so easily put off, however, and he breaks into Emil's apartment and decides to wait for his return. . . . While Emil hides under his bed, increasingly unable to show himself with each passing moment, Havard discovers the booze, and he ends up hosting a bizarre party for Emil's friends, and Greta." Publisher's note

"A horribly amusing tale about a man who is stuck under a bed, a semiliterate translation of R Kelly's Trapped in the Closet writ small. It's a witty and comical trifle." Brick Wkly

Brand, Max, 1892-1944

Beyond the outposts. Five Star 1997 254p

ISBN 0-7862-0745-0   LC 97-9308

"Five Star standard print western series"

Earlier version of this story was serialized in 1925 in Western Story magazine

This western adventure follows the "journeys of young Lew Dorset as he searches for his father, an escaped convict. His skill with firearms gets him a job as a hunter with a trader's freight train heading onto the prairies to barter with the Indians. There he meets young Chuck Morris, and together they take on a Cheyenne attack party. Finding shelter in a Sioux village, they absorb the native culture. . . . Lew goes on to play a decisive role in a battle between the Sioux and Pawnee, but returns to find that Chuck has deserted his wife and son. His attempts to reconcile them culminate in great danger and, ultimately, a threat to his life." Publisher's note

Chinook; a north-western story. Five Star 1998 271p

ISBN 0-7862-1155-5   LC 98-22718

"Five Star standard print western series"

"Joe Harney heads to Alaska during the great gold rush of 1898 and finds himself impressed by a great wolf dog owned by Andrew Steen, a crusty, bad-tempered loner. When Harney saves Steen's life, Steen grudgingly agrees that they can travel overland together. On that harsh journey, they meet Kate Winslow and learn that she's headed for Circle City to meet up with a man who wants her dead. This is a tale of the tough and often ruthless folks who risked their lives to get to the frozen north and, with any luck, to find their fortune." Publisher's note

The collected stories of Max Brand; edited, with story prefaces, by Robert and Jane Easton; introduction by William Bloodworth. centennial ed. University of Neb. Press 1994 xx, 342p $40

ISBN 0-8032-1244-5

    * LC 93-43938

Contents: John Ovington returns; Above the law; The wedding guest; A special occasion; Outcast breed; The sun stood still; The strange villa; The claws of the tigress; Internes can't take money; Fixed; Wine on the desert; Virginia creeper; Pringle's luck; The silent witness; Miniature; Our daily bread; Honor bright; The king

Brand, Max, 1892-1944—*Continued*

Dark Rosaleen

In Brand, M. Max Brand's best western stories

Dust across the range

In Brand, M. Max Brand's best western stories

Fugitives' fire. Putnam 1991 184p

ISBN 0-399-13587-1   LC 90-8478

This novel originally appeared 1928 in Western story magazine as two novelettes: Prairie pawn and Fugitive's fire

This novel features fugitive plainsman Paul Torridon. "A prisoner of the mighty Cheyenne Nation, young Torridon lives in pampered misery. The Cheyenne, who call him 'White Thunder,' are convinced of his supernatural talents and expect him to deliver good luck in battle and rain in drought. He is richly rewarded for his 'mystical favors,' but he dreads the day his good luck and horse sense will fail, revealing him as only too mortal— and losing him his scalp in the bargain." Publisher's note

The gentle desperado. Dodd, Mead 1985 195p

ISBN 0-396-08715-9   LC 85-10321

"Silver star westerns"

This novel is comprised of three stories originally published in Western Story Magazine under the pseudonym, George Owen Baxter

"Robert Fernald was a deadly fighter, but he didn't really believe it, not even when he outgunned his opponents. To his enemies, he looked like a kid, too mild-mannered to be a threat. But then he went after Tom Gill and his men who were preying on the Larkin ranch, forcing handsome young Beatrice Larkin into bankruptcy. Everyone said it would take an army to stop the rustlers from driving the stolen cattle through the mountain passes—until Fernald faced tough Tom Gill himself in a showdown." Publisher's note

In the hills of Monterey; a western story. Five Star 1998 239p

ISBN 0-7862-0988-7   LC 97-38421

"Five Star standard print western series"

"The wealthiest landowner in the province of Spanish-controlled Alta California has sent away to Spain for a suitable bridegroom for his beautiful daughter, Ortiza Tarabal. Francisco Valdez arrives with his slave, an Englishman known as El Rojo, a courageous man who has made some enemies among the ruling class, but has the devotion of the Indians. El Rojo also has the very dangerous love of Ortiza Tarabal, despite her betrothal to Francisco Valdez and the wrath of her father." Publisher's note

Max Brand's best western stories; edited with a biographical introduction by William F. Nolan. Dodd, Mead 1981-1987 3v o.p.   LC 81-3204

Contents v1 Wine on the desert; Virginia creeper; Macdonald's dream; Partners; Dust across the range [novelette]; The bells of San Carlos

v2 Outcasts [novelette]; The fear of Morgon the Fearless; Dark Rosaleen [novelette]; Cayenne Charlie; The golden day

v3 Reata's peril trek; Crazy rhythm; Dust storm; A lucky dog; The third bullet; Half a partner; The sun stood still

Outcasts

In Brand, M. Max Brand's best western stories

Sheriff Larrabee's prisoner

In Brand, M. Stolen gold: a western trio

A shower of silver

In Brand, M. Stolen gold: a western trio

The Stingaree. Dodd, Mead 1968 c1930 216p o.p.

"Silver star westerns"

"Jimmy Green is a wild, half-Indian, half-civilized, thirteen-year-old who is undisputed king of the small village of Fort Anxious. One day, a tramp wanders into the village, and ultimately into the life of Jimmy, changing it from the complacent existence of a boy into the desperate flight of a fugitive. The stranger, also known as the Stingaree, has come from Alabama to revenge the death of his partner by the leading citizen of Fort Anxious. Although he succeeds in forcing the man to confess, he is thwarted by the police in his attempt to kill Stanley Parker. The Stingaree, along with Jimmy Green, an Indian companion, and a wild dog is forced to flee into the wilderness, beginning one of the best chase episodes." Libr J

Stolen gold

In Brand, M. Stolen gold: a western trio

Stolen gold: a western trio. Five Star 1999 255p

ISBN 0-7862-1333-7   LC 98-52067

"Five Star standard print western series"

"The three short novels collected here were all published in pulp magazines during the 1920s. . . . In the title piece, former convict Reata is duped into abandoning his hard-won domestic bliss to search for treasure. The second tale finds a drifter accused of murder. His only hope for justice is the daughter of the sheriff who captured him. The third tale features a good samaritan drawn into a web of duplicity when he tries to help a newlywed whose husband is suddenly seized by a local lawman." Booklist

The survival of Juan Oro. Five Star 1999 259p

ISBN 0-7862-1325-6   LC 98-42372

"Five Star standard print western series"

This tale "was born as a magazine serial in 1925. Now published in book form with the author's original material restored, the story tells of Juan Oro, who, raised by Yaquis and captured by the forces of Don José Fontana, is apprenticed to outlaw Matias Bordi after promising to murder Bordi once he has learned the ways of a killer. But Juan's feelings for Bordi are such that he cannot keep his promise. . . . Mainstream western fare from a master of the genre." Booklist

Brandon, John

Arkansas. McSweeney's Books 2008 230p $22

ISBN 978-1-932416-90-9

This novel relates the "misadventures of two young drug runners, Kyle and Swin. With boss Pat Bright, they work for a mysterious man named Frog out of a neglected Arkansas state park. . . . Bright, whose past is littered with despicable activities, suffers a ghastly death at

Brandon, John—*Continued*

the hands of Nick, the nephew of a drug customer. After Kyle kills Nick, they dump his body in a swamp and take charge of Bright's operation. The only positive influence in their lives is Swin's girlfriend, Johnna, a nurse who adds a woman's touch to their dumpy trailer. After Johnna gets pregnant, Swin realizes there is no future in what they've been doing and dreams of something better." Libr J

"The novel jumps from perspective to perspective—even dabbling in the second person to tell Frog's story—and at times it can be difficult to keep track of a narrative that is constantly slipping in time to provide back story on different characters. Brandon's writing is so sparse it sometimes feels blasé, but the tension between his hardboiled prose and his characters' appealing naïveté makes the novel work." Portland Mercury

Braun, Lilian Jackson

The cat who ate Danish modern. Dutton 1967 192p o.p.

The "adventure of Koko, The Siamese, and his Watson, Jim Qwilleran. The 'Daily Fluxion' assigns Jim to mastermind a new Sunday supplement called, of all things, 'Gracious Abodes.' But the shocking consequences of the first few issues makes Jim realize that he is back in his own field, crime reporting, and that only Koko can help with the answers." Libr J

"The mystery is mild, the satire on interior decorating fads and fancies amusing, and the Siamese cat who helps play detective delightful." Publ Wkly

The cat who brought down the house. Putnam 2003 228p

ISBN 0-399-14942-2   LC 2002-68138

"Thelma Thackery, in her 80s, comes back to Pickax after a long Hollywood career in food. She's turning the old opera house into a revival movie theater, sparks a few other local delights, but can't seem to get her ne'erdowell nephew to do well at all. Qwill plugs away at old lies and a death in Thelma's family. We learn stuff through his newspaper column and his journal entries, and through the responses of his Siamese cat, KoKo. All the murders are offstage: the fun part is in food, clothing, and the quotidian joys of small-town life." Booklist

The cat who sang for the birds. Putnam 1998 244p

ISBN 0-399-14333-5   LC 97-19094

In this mystery featuring Jim Qwilleran and his sleuthing Siamese cats, "the crime—involving fraud, bribery, and arson—centers on the murders of a 93-year-old woman and a young butterfly painter. Equally important to the story and to reader enjoyment are an adult spelling bee (developed and promoted as a baseball game complete with competing teams and pinch spellers), the painting of librarian Polly Duncan's portrait, and Qwill's brief experience with lepidopterology." Booklist

The cat who smelled a rat. Putnam 2001 229p

ISBN 0-399-14665-2   LC 00-34198

"Jim 'Qwill' Qwilleran is still enjoying life in the small town of Pickax in Moose County. . . . Having moved into his winter residence, a condominium near his ladylove, head librarian Polly, the wealthy Qwill and his

Siamese cats, Koko and Yum Yum, are awaiting the 'Big One'—the first blizzard of the season. A drought has caused a series of fires in the abandoned mine shafts around Pickax-or is it arson? When a member of the citizens' firewatch patrol is killed, a sinister plot unfolds." Booklist

The cat who went underground. Putnam 1989 223p

ISBN 0-399-13431-X

* LC 88-32185

"Koko and Yum Yum . . . lead their guardian, Jim ('Qwill') Qwilleran, on a subterranean chase for a psychotic plumber. When Qwill decides to spend a restful summer at his cabin in Mooseville, he does not anticipate endless home-repair crises. But he is genuinely astonished when Koko reveals why the carpenter never finished the room addition." Booklist

"Qwill's saving grace is that he is properly humble before the superior intelligence of his pets, while the author is shrewd enough to balance the cats' amazing antics with many amusing character studies of the Mooseville natives." N Y Times Book Rev

Braybrooke, June, 1920-1994

Every eye; [by] Isobel English; with an introduction by Neville Braybrooke. David R. Godine 2006 151p $23.95

ISBN 1-57423-199-5; 978-1-57423-199-1

LC 2006-2858

"A Black Sparrow book"

First published 1956 in the United Kingdom

"Hatty, the narrator of this exquisite 1956 novel, is a piano teacher who was born with a lazy eye. Though her vision has been repaired, a lingering feeling of isolation makes it seem that 'this outward sign was only the visible proof of inward impediment.' Hatty's voice on the page vividly conveys her sense of 'discordancy' with others, as the action shifts between recollections of adolescence and young-adulthood in grim, gray England and her considerably cheerier present, travelling through a Technicolor Spain with a new, much younger husband. The true marvel of the novel lies in the taut interweaving of these narratives: past informing present and present recasting past. Enlightenment is kept satisfyingly in abeyance until a rapturous conclusion on a mountaintop in Ibiza." New Yorker

Brennan, John *See* Welcome, John, 1914-

Breslin, Jimmy

The gang that couldn't shoot straight. Viking 1969 249p

ISBN 0-670-33396-4

*

"The only trouble with the Palumbo Mafia 'Family' of Brooklyn is that it isn't very well organized. Kid Sally Palumbo is trying to take over from the big Mafia boss, Baccala. Baccala has his wife start his car for him every morning in case explosives are wired in. Big Mama Palumbo's watchword is 'be sure to steal-a-da license plates.' Into this happy milieu wanders Mario, imported from Italy to ride in a six-day bike race that flopped. A natural-born con man himself, Mario has a brief love af-

Breslin, Jimmy—*Continued*
fair with young Angela Palumbo, and acts as finger-man for the gang in the big attempt to wipe out Baccala." Publ Wkly

"By no means a great work, this is still a strong indictment of American society—police, politicians, criminals, and the 'silent'—that deserves to offend more than Sicilians." Choice

Table money. Ticknor & Fields 1986 435p
ISBN 0-899-19312-9   LC 85-28880
This "saga concerning the Morrisons of Queens, New York—from their late-nineteenth-century arrival in the U.S. to the present day—is painfully stereotypical in its depiction of the men (a long line of hard-drinking, male chauvinistic, and irresponsible tunnel workers) and their beleaguered, long-suffering women. Generation after generation repeats the same mistakes—dying too soon from alcoholism, giving birth too early in life—and even when Owen Morrison, the latter-day lad whose story takes up most of the book, wins the Congressional medal of honor in Vietnam, he finds that his hero's badge is virtually worthless on the gray borough streets and in the perilous tunnel that epitomizes his clan's plight." Booklist

Brett, Simon, 1945-

Mrs. Pargeter's package. Scribner 1991 224p
ISBN 0-684-19286-1   LC 90-27463
First published 1990 in the United Kingdom
"On a tour of Greece, the mature and spirited Melita Pargeter . . . takes on a case more substantial than her earlier challenges. When she agreed to join recently widowed Joyce Dover on holiday, Melita knew she was apt to encounter the moodiness of the freshly bereaved. But Joyce appears to be importing a bottle of the Greek liqueur ouzo *from* England, and talks about her husband controlling her from the grave. When she is found dead, an apparent suicide, Melita has even more on her hands than she bargained for." Publ Wkly

"Avoiding the treacly simpering typical of so many British cozy mysteries, Brett keeps us chuckling with a steady stream of dryly noted cultural tidbits, while still supplying a wide-ranging plot that hangs together elegantly." Booklist

Murder unprompted; a Charles Paris novel. Scribner 1982 160p
ISBN 0-684-17659-9
                            * LC 82-5578
"Here Paris is less drunk than usual, which enables us to believe that he can think as shrewdly as he does. And the situation is delightful: he gets at last a chance to act in a play that may move to a big West End theater if all goes well in the tryouts. The interplay among the cast is splendid, funny, and also touching. Murder in full view, on the first night, might bring good publicity, but other troubles develop—the whole mess handled in masterly fashion." Barzun. Cat of Crime. Rev and enl edition

The torso in the town; a Fethering mystery. Berkley Prime Crime 2002 340p
ISBN 0-425-18502-8   LC 2002-18482
"A dinner party in a richly restored country house in a Sussex village that is 'riddled with class consciousness' is interrupted by a scream. A body, arms and legs neatly removed, has been discovered in the cellar. There to witness the discovery is an outsider, a middle-aged woman from the seaside village of Fethering. The woman, Jude brings news of the grisly find back to her pal Carole Seddon another middle-aged woman from Fethering, in hopes that a little mystery will pull her out of a depression brought on by a lapsed love affair. . . . The ladies from Fethering once again proceed totally outside the bumbling police investigation in a somehow utterly credible way, gaining access and insight where the police can't." Booklist

Brin, David, 1950-

Brightness reef. Bantam Bks. 1995 514p
ISBN 0-553-89015-8
                            * LC 95-17601
The first volume of a trilogy "set in the universe of Brin's Hugo-winning *The Uplift War* [1987]. It's a multivoice narrative concerning the six diverse cultures living on the banned planet Jijo—and what happens to their peaceful society when more humans arrive there via starship, searching for species to 'uplift' by bringing them to the next level of sentience." Publ Wkly

"Brin's rich world-building easily equals that displayed in classic series such as Herbert's Dune and Asimov's Foundation. Brin's resumption of Uplift is most welcome." Booklist
Followed by Infinity's shore

Earth. Bantam Bks. 1990 601p
ISBN 0-553-05778-2
                            * LC 90-4
"In the mid-21st century, as the world is attempting to reconcile humanity's furious technological progress with its depletion of the planet's vanishing resources, the discovery of a pair of singularities (miniature black holes) deep in the Earth's core abruptly transforms an ongoing struggle for preservation into a desperate battle to prevent the Earth's imminent destruction. Combining the fast pacing of a techno-thriller with a unique array of characters, the author . . . delivers a thoughtful, persuasive message of hope and warning that embraces today's issues and tomorrow's possibilities." Libr J

Heaven's reach. Bantam Bks. 1998 447p
ISBN 0-553-10174-9
                            * LC 98-4914
Final volume in the Uplift trilogy. "The narrative, which unfolds at frenzied speed, opens with the Earth under attack by an alliance of evil aliens, the essence of space itself shaking apart and the beleaguered *Streaker*, captained by Dr. Gillian Baskin, trying to outrun a Jophurian battleship that seeks to destroy it." Publ Wkly

"Brin's intellectual fertility is as prodigious as ever; indeed, readers coming to his work for the first time may feel a bit daunted. Brin doesn't fill all parts of his vast canvas with equal skill but manages enough of it at the top of his form to please all Uplift followers and many others as well." Booklist

Infinity's shore. Bantam Bks. 1996 524p
ISBN 0-553-10173-0   LC 96-32346
Second volume in the Uplift trilogy. "On the planet Jijo, the painfully developed cooperation among six sapient races (humans included) is rapidly crumbling under the impact of contact from space. The visitors include the dolphin crew of the ship *Streaker* and the Rothen, the

Brin, David, 1950——*Continued*

race who may have 'uplifted' to intelligence most of the races of Jijo, except the humans, who because of their unique status are in greater peril than ever. The ensuing tale is well paced, immensely complex {and} highly literate." Publ Wkly

Followed by Heaven's reach

Brink, André Philippus, 1935-

The other side of silence; [by] André Brink. Harcourt 2003 c2002 311p

ISBN 0-15-100770-5
                                        * LC 2002-32748
First published 2002 in the United Kingdom

This novel "takes as its point of departure a German program at the turn of the twentieth century whereby women were shipped out to Germany's colonies in South-West Africa (now Namibia) to be wives—or, failing that, sexual fodder—for the colonizers. Brink's protagonist, Hannah X., an abused orphan from Bremen, is eager for the imagined romance of the desert, but life in the colonies turns out to be even worse than what she has known before. . . .Brink's powerful and brutal story is an effective response to those who suspected that the end of apartheid would leave him without a subject, and a shrewd meditation on the dehumanizing power of hatred." New Yorker

Bristow, Gwen, 1903-1980

Jubilee Trail. Crowell 1950 564p o.p.

The Jubilee Trail was the traders' name for the great Spanish Trail, which in the 1840's led from Santa Fé to Los Angeles. This long novel describes the trek of a gently bred New York girl and her trader husband, along that trail. When she was left a widow and penniless, Garnet and the variety girl she had befriended managed to make their living. The story closes about the time of the California gold discovery

Brockmeier, Kevin

The brief history of the dead; Kevin Brockmeier. Pantheon Books 2006 252p $22.95

ISBN 0-375-42369-9   LC 2005-48882
"The City is inhabited by the recently departed, who reside there only as long as they remain in the memories of the living. Among the current residents of this afterlife are Luka Sims, who prints the only newspaper in the City, with news from the other side; Coleman Kinzler, a vagrant who speaks the cautionary words of God; and Marion and Phillip Byrd, who find themselves falling in love again after decades of marriage. On Earth, Laura Byrd is trapped by extreme weather in an Antarctic research station." Publisher's note

"Although it never quite lives up to its promising premise, the novel's Borges-like spirit will appeal to select readers." Booklist

The view from the seventh layer. Pantheon Books 2008 267p $21.95

ISBN 978-0-375-42530-1; 0-375-42530-6
                                        LC 2007-23404

Contents: A fable ending in the sound of a thousand parakeets; The view from the seventh layer; The lives of the philosophers; The year of silence; A fable with a photograph of a glass mobile on the wall; Father John Melby and the ghost of Amy Elizabeth; The human soul as a Rube Goldberg device: a choose-your-own-adventure story; The lady with the pet tribble; A fable containing a reflection the size of a match head in its pupil; Home videos; The air is full of little holes; Andrea is changing her name; A fable with slips of white paper spilling from the pockets

"This work compiles 13 wondrous tales—four fables, eight stories, and one choose-your-own-adventure. . . . [Brockmeier's] stories have a bit less of the troubling, possibly ironic distancing that can be a pitfall in the fiction of peers like David Foster Wallace. Instead, we're invited to empathize with the characters via his clean lines and attentive crafting. The comparisons to Italo Calvino are certainly valid (Calvino's novel The Baron in the Trees is even referenced), and yet Brockmeier's tales feel distinctly contemporary." Libr J

Bromfield, Andrew

(tr) Pelevin, V. The sacred book of the werewolf

Brontë, Anne, 1820-1849

The tenant of Wildfell Hall. Modern Lib. 1997 510p

ISBN 0-679-60279-8   LC 97-14200
First published 1848

"This epistolary novel presents a portrait of debauchery that is remarkable in light of the author's sheltered life. It is the story of young Helen Graham's disastrous marriage to the dashing drunkard Arthur Huntingdon—said to be modeled on the author's wayward brother Branwell—and her flight from him to the seclusion of Wildfell Hall. Pursued by Gilbert Markham, who is in love with her, Graham refuses him and, by way of explanation, gives him her journal. There he reads of her wretched married life. Eventually, after Huntingdon's death, they marry." Merriam-Webster's Ency of Lit

Brontë, Charlotte, 1816-1855

Emma; by Charlotte Brontë and "Another Lady". J.M. Dent 1980 201p

ISBN 0-460-00467-2
                                        *

Fragments of a story left unfinished at Brontë's death form the opening two chapters of this novel completed by Constance Savery

"In the full-blown literary manner and circuitous storytelling characteristic of Charlotte Brontë, . . . an intriguing melodrama unrolls in this tale of wrongs finally righted. Most wronged is adolescent Martina, deprived of her natural mother by the machinations of her stepbrothers, led on by their sister, the cruel, enigmatic beauty Emma. The events that lead to familial reconciliation include Martina's sentence to ladies' boarding school, abduction to a French convent and graveyard visitations before some fancy detective work by an old friend unravels the ingenious but dastardly plot. The author of this Goth-

Brontë, Charlotte, 1816-1855—*Continued*
ic romp is obviously steeped in the period and felicitous
style of the brilliant English novelist, providing entertainment on the same grand scale." Publ Wkly

Jane Eyre; Charlotte Brontë with an introduction
by Lucy Hughes-Hallet. Knopf 1991 xxxviii, 284p
$20
    ISBN 0-679-40582-8
                          * LC 91-52968
"Everyman's library"
First published 1847
"In both heroine and hero the author introduced types
new to English fiction. Jane Eyre is a shy, intense little
orphan, never for a moment, neither in her unhappy
school days nor her subsequent career as a governess,
displaying those qualities of superficial beauty and charm
that had marked the conventional heroine. Jane's lover,
Edward Rochester, to whose ward she is governess, is a
strange, violent man, bereft of conventional courtesy, a
law unto himself. Rochester's moodiness derives from
the fact that he is married to an insane wife, whose existence, long kept secret, is revealed on the very day of his
projected marriage to Jane. Years afterward the lovers
are reunited." Reader's Ency. 4th edition

Brontë, Emily, 1818-1848

Wuthering Heights; with an introduction by
Katherine Frank. Knopf 1991 xxxiii, 385p $22
    ISBN 0-679-40543-7
                          * LC 91-52969
"Everyman's library"
First published 1847
Forced by a storm to spend the night at the home of
the somber and unsociable Heathcliff, Mr. Lockwood has
an encounter with the spirit of Catherine Linton. He
gradually learns that Catherine's father, Mr. Earnshaw,
had taken in Heathcliff as a young orphan. Heathcliff
and Catherine began to fall in love, but after Mr.
Earnshaw's death Catherine's brother treated Heathcliff
in a degrading manner and Catherine married rich Edgar
Linton. Heathcliff gradually worked his revenge against
those who injured him.

Brookner, Anita

Brief lives. Random House 1991 c1990 260p
    ISBN 0-394-58548-8
                          * LC 90-38904
First published 1990 in the United Kingdom
This "novel covers the nearly 40 years of intertwining
lives of two dissimilar, incompatible women. Flamboyant, selfish Julia was once a glamorous actress. Fay arranges her life around men—first her father, then her
husband, then her lover—and eventually her friend, none
of them her ideal; finally, she is alone." Libr J
"This short, subtle, beautifully organised and orchestrated novel positively gains from the deliberate restraint
and detachment of the writing." London Rev Books

Family and friends. Pantheon Bks. 1985 187p
    ISBN 0-394-54616-4   LC 85-6373
"We first see the widowed Sofka Dorn and her children—Frederick, Alfred, Mimi, and Betty—in London
between the wars, after they have come from Eastern Europe, and we follow them from the children's adolescence through their middle age." N Y Times Book Rev
"Anita Brookner's prose is impeccably elegant and she
is unsentimental with it. . . . There is a closeness of atmosphere, almost claustrophobic, in Family and Friends,
as if we were alternating between a discreetly perfumed
lady's boudoir and the smoking room of a superior gentleman's club. There is no mistaking the originality as
well as the skill and consistency with which the novel so
beautifully conforms to its genre and its intentions." N Y
Rev Books

Hotel du Lac. Pantheon Bks. 1985 c1984 184p
    ISBN 0-394-54215-0
                          * LC 84-20641
First published 1984 in the United Kingdom
"A sedate Swiss Hotel at end-of-season is the scene of
Edith Hope's brief, melancholy exile (she's in disgrace
for having jilted her fiancé on their wedding day). Edith
observes her fellow guests with sympathy and amusement; writes long, unposted letters to her married lover;
and works at her latest romantic novel, her life suspended and uneventful. When the worldly Mr. Neville plumbs
her 'unused capacity' for mischief, she nearly acquiesces,
at 39, to his quaintly treacherous proposal of marriage
and respectability without the promise of love." Libr J
The tone of this novel is "oddly detached, very small-scale, faintly humorous. . . . It is by means of this very
remoteness that Edith manages to hold our interest
throughout this achingly uneventful holiday, with its
empty chasms of time, its murmuring respectability, its
dining room scattered sparsely with people who mean
nothing to her. . . . There are some uncomfortable
patches. . . . But generally, the writing is graceful and
attractive." N Y Times Book Rev

Undue influence; a novel. Random House 2000
231p $24 o.p.
    ISBN 0-375-50334-X   LC 99-36282
"Having come through her father's long illness and her
mother's recent death, [Londoner] Claire Pitt faces mid-life longing for a significant attachment. She works in a
used bookshop, sorting through the papers of the owner's
father, which chronicled his largely uneventful life and
observations. Into her musty basement one morning
comes a handsome stranger, Martin Gibson, seeking out
a novel by Fontane. On the pretext of delivering the
book to his home, Claire becomes enmeshed in his life
and his marriage to a sickly wife. The weird and wealthy
Gibsons begin to occupy a new corner of Claire's life
and provide a spark of previously unknown drama." Libr
J
"The novel contains a fine brace of supporting characters whose behavior implicitly reflects on Claire's fall
into limbo, and Brookner's narrative skill works like a
scalpel exposing the complexity of each of their lives."
Publ Wkly

Brooks, Geraldine

People of the book. Viking 2008 372p $25.95
    ISBN 978-0-670-01821-5   LC 2007-18082
"When an Australian rare-book conservator named
Hanna Heath finds a butterfly wing, a salt crystal, a
white hair, and bloodstains in the recently rediscovered
Sarajevo Haggadah, a late-medieval illuminated codex of
uncertain provenance, she sets out to solve the mystery
of the book's origins. To her disappointment, analysis of

Brooks, Geraldine—*Continued*

the specimens reveals little. . . . Brooks, beginning where science leaves off, uses Hanna's finds as entry points to richly imagined historical landscapes peopled by the Haggadah's creators, protectors, and would-be destroyers—a female Muslim slave in Convivencia Spain, a Jewish doctor in fin-de-siècle Vienna, an alcoholic priest in seventeenth-century Venice. Their narratives alternate with Hanna's own, and the final, multilayered effect is complex and moving." New Yorker

Year of wonders; a novel of the plague. Viking 2001 308p

ISBN 0-670-91021-X   LC 00-52757

"In 1665, the intense young pastor of a plague-stricken Derbyshire village persuades his parish to quarantine itself from the outside world. This selfless decision leads to the deaths of two-thirds of the inhabitants but saves the surrounding towns, as it did in the case of the historical village that inspired the tale. The novel glitters with careful research into such arcana as seventeenth-century lead-mining, sheep-farming, and of course, medicine, but its true strength is a deep imaginative engagement with how people are changed by catastrophe. . . . A rare few—including the narrator, a young widow who is a servant of the pastor—discover new strengths and abilities." New Yorker

Brooks, Max

World War Z; an oral history of the zombie war. Crown 2006 342p $24.95

ISBN 0-307-34660-9

                                     * LC 2006-9517

"Brooks tells the story of the world's desperate battle against the zombie threat with a series of first-person accounts 'as told to the author' by various characters around the world. A Chinese doctor encounters one of the earliest zombie cases at a time when the Chinese government is ruthlessly suppressing any information about the outbreak that will soon spread across the globe. The tale then follows the outbreak via testimony of smugglers, intelligence officials, military personnel and many others who struggle to defeat the zombie menace. Despite its implausible premise and choppy delivery, the novel is surprisingly hard to put down." Publ Wkly

Brooks, Terry, 1944-

The druid of Shannara. Ballantine Bks. 1991 423p (Heritage of Shannara)

ISBN 0-345-36298-5   LC 90-42424

"A Del Rey book"

In the second novel in the Heritage of Shannara tetralogy "Walker Boh, the 'Dark Uncle,' embarks on a perilous journey to recover the black Elfstone and restore the lost druid keep of Paranor." Libr J

"Broadening the landscape of his magic world, Brooks has produced a deep and thoughtful fantasy." Publ Wkly

Followed by The elfqueen of Shannara

First king of Shannara. Ballantine Bks. 1996 489p

ISBN 0-345-39652-9   LC 95-52321

"A Del Rey book"

"To defend his followers and escape subjugation from the evil Warlock Lord, Druid Bremen must possess the magical Black Elfstone. This . . . answers fans' questions about the early history of the Shannara family." Libr J

The sword of Shannara; illustrated by the Brothers Hildebrandt. Random House 1977 726p il

ISBN 0-394-41333-4   LC 77-151532

"Humans, trolls, dwarfs, elves, gnomes, sorcerers both good and evil, and battalions of knights and knaves populate this sweeping adult epic-fantasy. At the urging of a mysterious sorcerer, an adopted orphan named Shea reluctantly takes up the quest for the Sword of Shannara, a legendary elvin blade that alone can defeat the forces of evil engulfing the world." Booklist

"Reminiscent of Tolkien's fantasies though lacking the originality of his vision and the beauty of his language, this is still an engrossing saga of hardship and adventure with well-maintained action that will keep readers captive right up to a nicely-wrought finish." SLJ

Followed by The Elfstones of Shannara

Brower, Brock, 1931-

Blue dog, green river. Godine 2005 107p $23.95

ISBN 1-56792-280-5   LC 2004-16528

This novella tells the "tale of a dog's redemption. A former chicken thief, Blue Dog finds herself locked up in the pound with her hindquarters full of buckshot. Enter Paul Nozik, a river guide who decides to reform the canine criminal. A year later, while rafting a string quartet down Utah's Green River, Nozik becomes separated from his pal. Bitten by a rattlesnake and shot at by angry drunks, Blue Dog is knocked into the river toward the rapids. Struggling ashore, she sees a campfire and a naked man playing a flute. Is it Kokopelli, the ancient rock-art deity, come to life? Or is Blue Dog merely hallucinating from the snake venom? In alternating chapters, Brower weaves together the dual threads of Blue Dog's odyssey and Nozik's search. Brower does a good job capturing the life and culture of raftsmen; Blue Dog's thoughts are pure delight, and by the time Blue Dog is reunited with Nozik, the line between reality and the supernatural has become comfortably blurred." Booklist

Brown, Carrie, 1959-

The hatbox baby; a novel. Algonquin Bks. 2000 333p $22.95

ISBN 1-56512-299-2   LC 00-44208

"Confirmed bachelor Dr. Leo Hoffman is a pioneer in neonatal intensive care who finances his research into and medical care of destitute babies by charging admission to his educational programs at fairs and amusement parks. During the summer of 1933, while working at his premature baby exhibit at the Chicago World's Fair, he saves the life of a special 'premie'—and finds love in the process. . . . This is a moving story about complex, interesting characters who love deeply." Libr J

Lamb in love; a novel. Algonquin Bks. 1999 336p $21.95

ISBN 1-56512-203-8

                                     * LC 98-44580

Norris Lamb, "thought of as a confirmed bachelor at 55, is the postmaster of Hursley, a tiny village in rural England. Vida, at 41, has been the caretaker of severely retarded Manford Perry for 20 years, ever since his

Brown, Carrie, 1959-—*Continued*
mother died giving birth to him. In July 1969, on the
very day of the Apollo moon landing, Norris' perception
of Vida, and ultimately himself, is suddenly, dramatically, and forever changed." Booklist

The author "reveals her characters not as others perceive them but as they are able to see one another, and
as they come to understand themselves. Norris and Vida
are full of depth and longing, passion and poetry, that
continually startle and delight." N Y Times Book Rev

Brown, Charles Brockden, 1771-1810

Arthur Mervyn
In Brown, C. B. Three Gothic novels

Edgar Huntly
In Brown, C. B. Three Gothic novels

Three Gothic novels. Library of America 1998
914p $40
ISBN 978-1-88301-157-4   LC 97-46701
"Wieland; or The Transformation (1798) is a novel of
a religious fanatic preyed upon by a sinister ventriloquist.
. . . A relentlessly dark exploration of guilt, deception,
and compulsion, it creates a sustained mood of irrational
terror in the midst of the Pennsylvania countryside. In
Arthur Mervyn; or Memoirs of the Year 1793 (1799),
Brown draws on his own experiences to create indelible
scenes of Philadelphia devastated by a yellow fever epidemic, while telling the story of a young man caught in
the snares of a professional swindler. Edgar Huntly; or
Memoirs of a Sleepwalker (1799) fuses traditional Gothic
themes with motifs drawn from the American Wilderness
in a series of eerily unreal adventures that test the limits
of the protagonist's self-knowledge." Publisher's note

Wieland
In Brown, C. B. Three Gothic novels

Brown, Dale, 1956-

Hammerheads. Fine, D.I. 1990 478p
ISBN 1-556-11170-3   LC 89-46026
"Hammerheads are an elite force, part U.S. Coast
Guard and part customs service, that use a powerful array of weapons, including a V-22C tilt-rotor Sea Lion (a
combination helicopter and fixed-wing aircraft). The
force is stationed on offshore platforms and led by General Brad Elliott and Major Mac McLanahan, and its purpose is to stop the operations of the South American
drug cartels." Booklist

"This smooth blend of plot, action and gadgetry supports the debatable argument that drug smuggling can be
checked by military methods. But forget ideologies—
Hammerheads is a reader's delight from first page to
last, a model of the genre." Publ Wkly

Storming heaven. Putnam 1994 399p
ISBN 0-399-13931-1   LC 94-12213
"Henri Cazaux is a terrorist with a grudge against the
United States because MPs mistreated him in an army
jail. In retribution, he decides to destroy the entire coun-
try by blowing up airports and, eventually, the Capitol.
He is opposed by misunderstood retired Coast Guard ad-
miral Ian Hardcastle." Libr J

"Over the top? Sure. But the author's view about the
vulnerability of U.S. airports to aerial attack reads almost
plausibly, and Cazaux is a fascinating monster." Booklist

Brown, Dan, 1964-

The Da Vinci code; a novel. Doubleday 2003
454p $24.95
ISBN 0-385-50420-9   LC 2002-40918
"In a two-day span, American symbologist Robert
Langdon finds himself accused of murdering the curator
of the Louvre, on the run through the streets of Paris and
London, and teamed up with French-cryptologist Sophie
Neveu to uncover nothing less than the secret location of
the Holy Grail. It appears that a conservative Catholic
bishop might be on the verge of destroying the Grail,
which includes an alternate history of Christ that could
bring down the church. . . .The story is full of brain-
teasing puzzles and fascinating insights into religious history and art." Booklist

The lost symbol; a novel. Doubleday 2009 509p
$29.95
ISBN 978-0-385-50422-5; 0-385-50422-5
As this novel opens Harvard University symbologist
Robert Langdon is "quietly brewing a cup of coffee at
home in Cambridge one Sunday morning when he gets
a call asking him, in the name of his dear friend and
mentor, Peter Solomon, to fly immediately to Washington to fill in for a canceled guest speaker at an illustrious
gathering. Many of the attendees at the meeting are expected to be Freemasons and they are gathering in a
building rich with Masonic history. So it makes sense
that Langdon will be addressing the group on the symbolism found in the architecture of the US capital. Eager
to be of service to Solomon, Langdon jumps on a private
jet and speeds to Washington only to discover that his
mentor, who is a high-level Mason, is in serious trouble,
threatened by a deranged loner who hopes to learn the
inner secrets of the Masonic world." Christ Sci Mon

"Brown has never been lauded for his deft handling of
the written word. As in his other books, here his prose
can be clumsy, flowery and heavyhanded. But, to his
credit, he tells an action-packed story filled with fascinating history, myths, math, science, madmen and philosophers." USA Today

Brown, Dee Alexander

Creek Mary's blood; a novel; [by] Dee Brown.
Holt, Rinehart & Winston 1980 401p il
ISBN 0-03-044281-8
                                                 * LC 79-9060
"Through the words and memories of Dane, grandson
of Creek Mary (or Akusa Amayi), we follow the history
of the men, children, and grandchildren in the life of that
indomitable exemplar of the American Indian. The action—and there is plenty of it—takes place in the period
after the Revolutionary War and continues through the
nineteenth century. The customs, rituals, courting, fighting, and celebrating are all described in detail. One of
the most painful sections of the book depicts the forced
removal west of the Mississippi of Indian tribes. . . .
The relationships among the various tribes—Creek,
Cheyenne, Cherokee, and others—is of great interest.
Many famous names are recalled, among them Tecumseh, Andrew Jackson, Teddy Roosevelt, and the great
chiefs Crazy Horse and Sitting Bull." Shapiro. Fic for
Youth. 3d edition

Brown, Elizabeth Inness- *See* Inness-Brown, Elizabeth, 1954-

Brown, Joe David, 1915-1976

Addie Pray; a novel. Simon & Schuster 1971 313p

ISBN 0-671-20962-0

"Set during the Depression this . . . picaresque novel follows the adventures of two con artists—the narrator Addie Pray, an eleven-year-old orphan, and Long Boy, her presumptive father. The pair travel the South selling gold-initialed Bibles to new widows, working a wallet-switching trick, and trading in nonexistent cotton, among other outrageous ploys, until they join Major Carter E. Lee in more sophisticated swindles culminating in a slick scheme to set Addie up as heiress to an enormous fortune." Booklist

"Brown has a special feeling for the Depression-era South. . . . {Addie's speech} is vulgar, pungent country talk, which adds greatly to the book's easygoing charm. Looking at Long Boy with his floozy, she observes that 'he got that silly, dazed grin like a tom cat being choked to death with cream.' Like that extravagant expression, the book is a long tall, oldtime tale. But as Addie might put it, in the right hands that kind of yarn has a lot of prance left." Time

Brown, Larry, 1951-2004

Joe; a novel. Algonquin Bks. 1991 345p

ISBN 0-945575-61-0   LC 91-12026

A novel about "poor 'white trash' in rural Mississippi. Joe Ranson is a middle-aged redneck with a soul. He fights and spits, drinks beer by the gallon from a cooler embedded in his truck, and endures bad relationships with women. But within the society he inhabits, he is a moral man, more or less following the rituals and established 'codes' of fair play. Unfortunately, he is involved in a classic feud, the roots of which are never revealed, that threatens to destroy him. Also destined to cross paths with Joe is the nomadic Jones family. Gary Jones is a hardworking and painfully naive teenager. His father is pure evil, his mother nearly insane, and his siblings barely human. Joe offers Gary work, fueling hope that these two very different men will learn enough from each other to save themselves." Booklist

Brown is a "talented fiction writer in the whiskeyish, rascally Southern tradition of Faulkner and Erskine Caldwell. . . . The new novel is clear, simple and powerful, and it is great, rowdy fun to read." Time

Brown, Rita Mae

Dolley; a novel of Dolley Madison in love and war. Bantam Bks. 1994 382p o.p.

LC 93-44429

The author re-creates a "critical year in the life of the fourth president's wife, who loved politics and her husband and who had a great gift for friendship. In 1814, Napoleon's war with Britain spilled into its former colonies, and redcoats marching toward under-defended Washington constitute the backdrop of Brown's slice of Dolley Madison's life. Brown vivifies the capital hostess and covert political manipulator's doings by interspersing snippets from an imaginary diary with the main narrative. . . . Brown's Dolley Madison is full-blown and vibrant." Booklist

Murder at Monticello; or, Old sins; [by] Rita Mae Brown & Sneaky Pie Brown; illustrations by Wendy Wray. Bantam Bks. 1994 298p il

ISBN 0-553-08140-3   LC 94-16711

"Tiger cat Mrs. Murphy and corgi Tee Tucker . . . help Mary Minor 'Harry' Haristeen, postmistress of Crozet, Virginia, solve a nearly 200-year-old mystery. It begins with a skeleton discovered in a slave cabin during restorations at Monticello—and continues with the present-day murder of Kimball Haynes, head of archaeology there, who has discovered secrets of miscegenation recorded in a doctor's long-hidden journals. . . . An entertaining treat for animal-loving mystery/history fans." Booklist

Southern discomfort. Harper & Row 1982 249p

ISBN 0-06-014928-0   LC 81-47683

In this novel "the focus is on the rigid class and racial divisions of Montgomery, Ala., society during the early decades of this century. . . . Hortensia Banastre, ice goddess, model society matron, falls passionately in love with a young black boxer, and she bears and secretly raises his daughter. . . . Paris, Hortensia's beautiful and hateful son, figures it out—knowledge that figures in his shocking death." Publ Wkly

The author "seems to understand the way in which dark passions and unspeakable desires become magnified among a people segregated by unnatural laws concerning race, class and social position. She portrays well the suffering incurred by trying to defy such a system; she also captures the earthy quality of those who do what they must to get by." Best Sellers

Wish you were here; [by] Rita Mae Brown & Sneaky Pie Brown; illustrations by Wendy Wray. Bantam Bks. 1990 242p il

ISBN 0-553-05881-9   LC 90-1071

"Mary Minor ('Harry') Haristeen, divorce in the works, runs the post office in Crozet, Virginia, with a pet cat and dog at her side. After two spectacularly gruesome murders rock the community, Harry attempts to gather helpful clues, while the pets (who converse with each other) do their best to protect her." Libr J

"Ms. Brown writes with wise, disarming wit about her country-bred characters and their not-always-neighborly ways." N Y Times Book Rev

Brown, Rosellen

Before and after. Farrar, Straus & Giroux 1992 354p

ISBN 0-374-10999-0

* LC 92-81571

This novel begins "on the day that Carolyn Reiser, a New Hampshire pediatrician with two teenage kids, gets called to the emergency room. A girl has been bludgeoned to death. The chief suspect is Carolyn's son and he has disappeared." Newsweek

Brown is "tenacious in her examination of each major character. Deftly, artfully, she strips away the delicate shelter of conventional relationships." N Y Times Book Rev

Half a heart. Farrar, Straus & Giroux 2000 402p

ISBN 0-374-44013-1   LC 00-22926

Brown, Rosellen—*Continued*

"Miriam, a rich Houston housewife with three children, has a secret in her past: during a teaching stint at a black college in the Sixties, she had an affair with a black professor and gave birth to a daughter. When the baby's father challenged her for custody of the child, Miriam gave up without a fight and fled to Houston, soon marrying a rich doctor. For years she suffered feelings of guilt and loss yet felt smug that she wasn't as superficial or racist as her friends. As her own mother's health deteriorates, Miriam suddenly tracks down her daughter, Veronica, now 17 and entering Stanford. Veronica, for her part, intends to milk her new family for money for college." Libr J

"The situation is an intriguing one rendered all the more so by Brown's skillful and sympathetic handling of her two central characters." Time

Tender mercies. Knopf 1978 259p

ISBN 0-394-42741-6 LC 78-1315

"In a moment of high spirits, vacationing Dan Courser took the wheel of a powerboat, gunned the motor, and sucked his swimming wife {Laura} into its blades. Nine months later, Dan goes back home with his family—son Jon, daughter Hallie, and quadriplegic Laura, plucked abruptly from a rehabilitation institute—to come to terms with life. Now bright, lovely Laura must live in her head, her most intimate needs attended to by others. And Dan, weighed down with guilt, longs for pain to exceed hers but still needs some space of his own to keep himself and his family on an even keel." Libr J

"What impresses one most about Tender Mercies is its dignity and restraint. While we learn a great deal about the physical details of paralysis, catheters and such, Brown makes no case for any horror of the body, nor does Laura's suffering prompt a garish loathing of the universe. . . . The language is spare and clean, with flashes of quiet poetry, perfectly suited to the plain but by no means simple New Englanders it portrays." Saturday Rev

Brown, Sandra, 1948-

The alibi. Warner Bks. 1999 490p

ISBN 0-446-51980-4 LC 99-31444

"When Charleston real estate developer Lute Pettijohn is murdered in the penthouse suite of the posh hotel he recently built, there is no shortage of likely suspects; Pettijohn is one of the most hated men in town. On the same night that the murder occurs, assistant district attorney Hammond Cross attends a county fair, where he meets a mysterious woman who refuses to tell him her name. . . . Later, when a witness places the woman, now identified as respected psychologist Dr. Alex Ladd, at the scene of the crime, she becomes the number one suspect. . . . A web of labyrinthine relationships becomes ever more intricate until the identity of the killer is revealed, a shock that would be implausible in a less carefully constructed tale." Publ Wkly

The crush. Warner Bks. 2002 474p

ISBN 0-446-52704-1 LC 2002-25896

"Dr. Rennie Newton thought she was doing the right thing when she voted to acquit contract killer Ricky Lozada while serving on a jury. After all, the prosecution had not proved its case. But when Lozada is released, he begins calling her and leaving her flowers. When a rival

doctor at Rennie's hospital is murdered, suspicion falls on Rennie, and the police suspect she has a connection to Lozada. Detective Wick Threadgill, who has deeply personal reasons to hate Lozada, begins to investigate Rennie. . . . This novel delivers a menacing villain and page-turning suspense." Booklist

The witness. Warner Bks. 1995 422p

ISBN 0-446-51631-7 LC 94-42733

"This story pivots on the relationship between Kendall Deaton Burnwood, an idealistic public defender, and U.S. Marshal John McGrath, who is returning her to Prosper, S.C., as a material witness when their car crashes into a ravine in Georgia. With her three-month-old in tow, Kendall tries repeatedly to abandon John, who's hobbled by temporary amnesia and a leg injury. Kendall fears the town of Prosper for good reason: it's where she witnessed her husband and father-in-law, ringleaders of a white-supremacist vigilante group, ritualistically execute one of her clients. . . . The push-pull generated by John's memory loss and Kendall's terror sparks a sexual tension that is deftly and vividly consummated, and secrets keep popping out until the last page." Publ Wkly

Browne, Marshall, 1935-

Eye of the abyss. Thomas Dunne Bks. 2003 c2002 290p $23.95

ISBN 0-312-31156-7 LC 2003-47297

"Franz Schmidt, chief auditor for a family-owned bank in an unnamed south German city, loses his eye defending a Jew attacked by Nazi thugs in 1935. A quiet and meticulous man, he apparently bears no grudges, though his wife and best friend aren't so sure. Three years later, when his bank is chosen as a repository for large amounts of Nazi Party cash, the other shoe drops, and Schmidt becomes a man of action. First, he takes great risks trying to help a female bank employee whose mother was Jewish. Then he dreams up a plan to punish Dietrich, the sleek and seductive party operative placed inside the bank." Publ Wkly

"Like the shifting reality of Schmidt's life, the changes in his character are as subtle as they are harrowing, a triumph of Browne's clean, exacting style." N Y Times Book Rev

Brownjohn, John

(tr) Glavinic, T. Night work

Brownrigg, Sylvia

The delivery room. Counterpoint 2008 399p pa $14.95

ISBN 978-1-58243-424-7; 1-58243-424-7 LC 2008-13102

First published 2006 in the United Kingdom

"Sixty-something Mira Braverman, a Serbian immigrant with a successful psychotherapy practice in London, is enduring seismic stresses in the late 1990s as her country descends ever deeper into unspeakable violence under Slobodan Milosevic. Mira's patients, mostly women with motherhood issues (thus, the title, which refers to her office), value her professional guidance even as they uneasily tread the topic of the country of her birth. Add to the story Mira's gravely ill beloved husband, Pe-

Brownrigg, Sylvia—*Continued*

ter, and Peter's son from a casual college liaison, Graham, who is struggling with his own fear of fatherhood with his much younger bride and who has viewed his stepmother with civil distance until Peter's illness shifts family dynamics." Libr J

"The Delivery Room is, despite its contemporary themes, an old-fashioned novel, one full of texture and detail, in which character and plot are patiently dissected and illuminated so that a larger picture might become apparent." Times Lit Suppl

Morality tale; a novel; drawings by Monica Scott. Counterpoint 2008 224p il $24

ISBN 978-1-58243-404-9; 1-58243-404-2

LC 2007-43783

Narrator Pan "has come to realize the truth in the old saying, 'What goes around comes around.' It's been five years since her husband, Alan, left his wife for her, and she's disenchanted that their married lovemaking isn't as passionate as their adulterous action was. Plus, Alan barely helps around the house, Pan's not exactly enamored of her stepsons, and Alan is still hopelessly entangled with his combative ex, Theresa. So when Richard, a kindhearted envelope salesman, walks into the stationery store where Pan clerks, a harmless one-sided romance blooms in the form of letters Richard leaves for her. Of course, when Alan finds Richard's letters, he's less than understanding." Publ Wkly

"Contemplating Sylvia Brownrigg's short new novel, the adjective 'quirky' comes to mind. Bold, dry, eccentric, 'Morality Tale' cries out for a descriptive term that can pinpoint its oddness along with its likability. 'Quirky' it will have to be, for this curious, teasing, idiosyncratic and strangely charming book." San Francisco Chron

Bruccoli, Matthew Joseph, 1931-2008

(ed) Fitzgerald, F. S. The short stories of F. Scott Fitzgerald

Bruen, Ken

Cross. St. Martin's Minotaur 2008 288p $23.95

ISBN 978-0-312-34142-8; 0-312-34142-3

LC 2007-42421

First published 2007 in the United Kingdom

"As a result of a shooting meant to kill Galway PI Jack Taylor . . ., Cody, his young apprentice and surrogate son, lies comatose and close to death in the hospital. Meanwhile, Taylor tries to make sense of the brutal murder by crucifixion of a young man and the burning death of the victim's sister." Libr J

"Bruen riffs on different meanings and implications of the word cross throughout, and his insights into pain, loss and Irishness are unforgettable." Publ Wkly

The guards. St. Martin's Minotaur 2003 291p $23.95

ISBN 0-312-30355-6

LC 2002-35855

"Ousted from Ireland's police force, the Garda Siochana (or Guards), Jack Taylor ekes out a living on the unmodernized margins of Galway. . . .When Ann Henderson walks into the pub that serves as Taylor's office, asking him to prove that her daughter Sarah was not

a suicide but a murder victim, Taylor finds himself investigating a sex-and-murder tangle—and in love." Booklist

"Bruen's astringent prose and death's-head humor keep this quest for redemption from getting maudlin, just as his 'tapestry of talk' makes somber poetry of the barstool laments that serve as dialogue." N Y Times Book Rev

Brulard, Henry *See* Stendhal, 1783-1842

Brunner, John, 1934-1995

Stand on Zanzibar. Grove Press 1968 505p o.p.

*

"Doubleday science fiction"

"Extrapolating from current politics, social and sexual mores, the communications revolution, the use of computers, brainwashing, drug use, psychology, philosophy, and sociology, Brunner has fashioned a mammoth work that is an intricate tapestry depicting a possible future. The dozens of characters interspersed in a complex fashion make the novel difficult to read but well worth the effort. Brunner's brand of cynicism and radical social commentary may not appeal to the taste of all readers, but in the time that has elapsed since the publication of the book, we have seen changes that bear startling similarities to several of Brunner's predictions." Shapiro. Fic for Youth. 3d edition

Buchan, John, 1875-1940

The thirty-nine steps. Doran, G.H. 1915 231p o.p.

*

"A bored, well-to-do Englishman, Richard Hannay, returns home to England after growing up in South Africa. Drifting between his club and the sights of London, he is drawn into the confidences of a secret agent in the thick of espionage. The agent is murdered in Hannay's apartment and Richard finds himself on the run from Scotland Yard and the cult of the 'Black Stone.'" Shapiro. Fic for Youth. 3d edition

Buchanan, Edna

Love kills; a Brit Montero novel. Simon and Schuster 2007 308p $25

ISBN 978-0-7432-9476-8; 0-7432-9476-9

LC 2006-39050

"Miami crime reporter Britt Montero, on the mend emotionally after losing her fiance in a shootout . . ., decides work is the best medicine. Her first case is actually an old one. The body of Nathan York is excavated by construction workers. Years earlier York was the subject of Britt's first big story. He was a militant advocate for men's rights in custody cases and would snatch children from their mothers and deliver them to their estranged fathers. Britt is also trying to track down Marsh Holt, the Honeymoon Killer. A hunky thirtysomething lothario operating with aliases in various states, Holt married a string of women across the country who all suffered fatal 'accidents' while on their honeymoons." Booklist

"A novel full of vitality with sophisticated plotting, expert tensions and characters who leap off the page." PopMatters

Buchanan, Edna—*Continued*

Suitable for framing. Hyperion 1995 243p

ISBN 0-7868-6047-2   LC 94-33133

Miami News crime reporter Britt Montero "confronts a mystery that cuts close to the bone: why she's suddenly losing her journalistic edge. Chance puts her on the spot to see a young woman killed and her toddler injured in the most horrible of a recent string of carjackings. Since then, however, the scoops have been gravitating toward young Trish Tierney, Britt's protégé and the *News's* newest reporter. Britt doggedly works her contacts in the Miami Police, especially Det. Bill Rakestraw, who is investigating the juvenile ring apparently responsible for the car thefts." Publ Wkly

"Busy, busy plot but Buchanan's streamlined prose and genuine affection for Miami's weirdness make it a quick and entertaining read." Booklist

You only die twice; a Britt Montero mystery. Morrow 2001 292p $24

ISBN 0-380-97655-2   LC 00-49543

"When the body of a beautiful woman is found floating offshore, seaweed in her hair, veteran *Miami News* police-beat reporter Britt Montero gets the call. . . . Britt senses a good story in the making, and when the body remains unclaimed and foul play is established, she is sure of it. A fingerprint check identifies the well-cared-for mermaid as Kaithlin Jordan of the prominent department store family. One problem: she's been dead for 10 years, and her husband is scheduled to be executed for her murder." Publ Wkly

"A fascinating amalgam of red herrings, misdirection, and guilt by personality. . . . An intelligent, thoroughly entertaining crime novel." Booklist

Buck, Pearl S. (Pearl Sydenstricker), 1892-1973

The good earth. Washington Square Press 2004 357p (Contemporary classics) pa $14

ISBN 0-7432-7293-5

                                            *

First published 1931 by Day

This novel set in prerevolutionary China "describes the rise of Wang Lung, a Chinese peasant, from poverty to the position of a rich landowner, helped by his patient wife, O-lan. Their vigor, fortitude, persistence, and enduring love of the soil are emphasized throughout. Generally regarded as Pearl Buck's masterpiece, the book won universal acclaim for its sympathetically authentic picture of Chinese life." Reader's Ency. 4th edition

Buckley, William F., 1925-2008

Elvis in the morning. Harcourt 2001 328p il $25

ISBN 0-15-100643-1   LC 00-54484

In 1959 Orson Killere, whose mother works for the U.S. Army in Wiesbaden, "decides to 'liberate' two dozen Elvis records from the PX for German teens who can't afford them. His crime is reported in *Stars and Stripes*, and PFC Presley, stationed nearby, holds a private concert at Orson's home. Orson and Priscilla are soon regular visitors to Presley's off-base quarters. She ultimately moves to Memphis and, years later, becomes Mrs. Presley; Orson is expelled from the University of Michigan as a premature college radical, wanders the country, stumbles into the computer business, and

throughout the 1960s and 1970s, plays a small but important role in the King's often troubled life." Booklist

"This is a low-key pleasure of a read, a nostalgic tale that eschews mush and a heartfelt tribute to the tragic figure who touched so many lives." Publ Wkly

Mongoose, R.I.P; a Blackford Oakes novel; [by] William F. Buckley, Jr. Random House 1988 322p

ISBN 0-394-55931-2

                             * LC 87-28344

This Blackford Oakes novel is a "retelling of the Kennedy assassination, which links Oswald to the Castro regime. Learning that the Soviets have secretly left behind a single missile after the U.S. challenge, Castro masterminds a scenario that will see Kennedy dead whether by bullet or ballistic missile." Libr J

"The best of the Blacky books, this is an entertainment of the Graham Greene order that truly entertains, excites, and edifies. . . . The story builds with considerable suspense up to Blackford's horrendous dilemma on the day of JFK's assassination." Natl Rev

Buffett, Jimmy, 1946-

A salty piece of land. Little, Brown and Co 2004 462p $27.95

ISBN 0-316-90845-2   LC 2004-16508

"Waking from a ganja buzz on the beach in Tulum, [Cowboy Tully Mars] can't believe his eyes when a 142-foot schooner emerges out of the ocean mist. At its helm is Cleopatra Highbourne, the eccentric 102-year-old sea captain who will take him to a lighthouse on a salty piece of land that will change his life forever." Publisher's note

"Perhaps it is because Buffett has long been a writer of lyrics that his prose style now seems to flow in a fresh, fanciful, finely imagined fashion. . . . What makes the incredible so credible to the reader, what makes the old lighthouse shine again, is the spiritual savvy Buffett has gleaned from the beach of life as he's wandered in the raw poetry of time." N Y Times Book Rev

Bujold, Lois McMaster

The paladin of souls. Eos 2003 456p hardcover o.p. pa $7.99

ISBN 0-380-97902-0; 0-380-81861-2 (pa)

                                LC 2003-40884

Sequel to The curse of Chalion

"Three years free of the madness that kept her imprisoned in her family's castle, Ista is finally released from her last remaining duties by the death of her mother. She undertakes a pilgrimage, but doesn't get far before she is overtaken by trouble, sorrow, need, and a host of other adversities. Chalion is in trouble again, thanks to the plots, counterplots, machinations, and follies of men and of gods. . . . What really keeps one turning the pages is the fascinating cast of characters—not that the plot is anything to sneeze at." Booklist

Bulgakov, Mikhail Afanas´evich, 1891-1940

The master and Margarita; translated from the Russian by Michael Glenny. Knopf 1992 c1967 xxvii, 446p $19

ISBN 0-679-41046-5

                                * LC 91-53220

Bulgakov, Mikhail Afanas´evich, 1891-1940—
Continued

"Everyman's library"

Written in the 1930s. Original Russian edition published 1966-67 in censored form. This translation, first published 1967 by Harper, is based on the unexpurgated version that was subsequently published 1973 in the Soviet Union

This novel "juxtaposes two planes of action—one set in Moscow in the 1930s and the other in Jerusalem at the time of Christ. The three central characters of the contemporary plot are the Devil, disguised as one Professor Woland; the 'Master,' a repressed novelist; and Margarita, who, though married to a bureaucrat, loves the Master. The Master has burned his manuscript and gone willingly into a psychiatric ward when critics attacked his work—a portrayal of the story of Jesus. Margarita sells her soul to the Devil in order to obtain the Master's release from the psychiatric ward. A parallel plot presents the action of the Master's destroyed novel, the condemnation of Yeshua (Jesus) in Jerusalem." Merriam-Webster's Ency of Lit

Bull, Emma, 1954-

Territory. Tor 2007 318p $24.95

ISBN 978-0-312-85735-6; 0-312-85735-7

LC 2007-9534

"A Tom Doherty Associates book"

"In 1881, the Arizona town of Tombstone, rich in minerals for the taking, becomes a magnet for men and women possessing special gifts or hungry for more power than they already have. To this region of natural magic come Wyatt Earp, a master of sorcery; Doc Holliday, whose power belongs to those who can take it; Chow Lung, a Chinese doctor with his own strange abilities; Mildred Benjamin, a writer of Western adventure and a true visionary; and Jesse Fox, a man with a talent for taming horses, among other gifts." Libr J

"Mixing fantasy with Old West lore is risky, but Bull takes time to make the place and the people real before undeniably supernatural forces appear. The magic is less flashy than in many fantasy novels, but it's vivid and deeply felt." Publ Wkly

War for the Oaks. Orb 2001 332p pa $14.95

ISBN 978-0-765-30034-8; 0-765-30034-6

LC 2001-27117

"A Tom Doherty Associates book"

First published 1987 by Ace

"Guitarist and singer Eddi McCandry has just left a floundering band and is organizing a new one when a phouka, a man who at times is a talking dog, becomes her guardian at the behest of the Faerie Folk. Eddi soon finds herself involved with warring Faerie groups, the Seelie Court and its noble queen versus the Unseelie Court, ruled by the evil Queen of Air and Darkness. The Seelie Court has chosen Eddi because there's 'power in a mortal soul that all of Faerie cannot muster.' Eddi's tart humor helps lend reality. . . . For many readers, the fey qualities of the wispy fantasy may be enough; Eddi even labels her new band Eddi and the Feys. The strength of the novel, however, is in the nonfantasy scenes. These demonstrate a sure knowledge of rock music and the field, and contribute to the climax, a struggle between Eddi and the dark queen at a concert." Publ Wkly

Bulwer-Lytton, Edward *See* Lytton, Edward Bulwer Lytton, Baron, 1803-1873

Bunyan, John, 1628-1688

The pilgrim's progress; edited with an introduction and notes by W.R. Owens. Oxford University Press 2003 lvi, 333p il (Oxford world classics) pa $8.95

ISBN 0-19-280361-1

LC 2003-283122

First published 1678

"The 'immortal allegory,' next to the Bible the most widely known book in religious literature. It was written in Bedford jail, where Bunyan was for twelve years a prisoner for his convictions. It describes the troubled journey of Christian and his companions through this life to a triumphal entrance into the Celestial city. Bunyan 'wrote with virgin purity utterly free from mannerisms and affectations; and without knowing himself for a writer of fine English, produced it.'" Pratt Alcove

Burdett, John

Bangkok 8. Knopf 2003 317p $24

ISBN 1-400-04044-2

LC 2002-40658

"The narrator, a Buddhist cop named Sonchai Jitplecheep, finds himself plunged into a dangerous investigation of the deaths of his partner Pichai Apiradee and U. S. Embassy Sgt. William Bradley. Sonchai is an unusual character on several levels, from the mysteries of his violent past to his conversations with the ghost of Pichai. His ambiguous feelings toward Kimberley Jones, an American FBI agent brought in to work the case, reflect his upbringing as the child of a Thai mother and an unknown American father. . . .The mix of detective work, Bangkok street life, the Thai sex trade and drug smuggling forms a powerful mélange of images and insight." Publ Wkly

Bangkok haunts. Alfred A. Knopf 2007 305p $24.95

ISBN 978-0-307-26318-6; 0-307-26318-5

LC 2007-61472

In this installment featuring Buddhist Bangkok police detective Sonchai Jitpleecheep, "a murdered prostitute proves to be—even more in death than she was in life—a femme fatale of special magnitude. As in previous episodes, the pleasures derive less from Burdett's baroque plotting (in this case including former Khmer Rouge hired killers, a pornography ring debased even by Bangkok standards, and a death by torture involving elephants) than from the vivid portrait he paints of contemporary Thai life and mores." New Yorker

Bangkok Tattoo. Knopf 2005 301p $24

ISBN 1-400-04045-0

LC 2005-5593

A mystery featuring Rayal Thai police detective Sonchai Jitpleecheep. "A devout Buddhist, Sonchai makes complex karmic calculations to justify his roles as law-bending cop and part-time papasan at his mother's gogo bar. When the bar's biggest moneymaker is suspected of killing her john, who turns out to be C.I.A., Sonchai initiates a coverup that eventually involves Muslim separatists in southern Thailand and American operatives eager to exploit post-9/11 paranoia for career advancement. The plot showcases Burdett's sly riffs on

Burdett, John—*Continued*

Third World stereotypes, Buddhism, and the gustatory pleasures of fried grasshoppers. It's a giddy, occasionally over-the-top performance, but mesmerizing: a comic tour of the underbelly of Bangkok in pursuit of both a murderer and the sublime." New Yorker

Burdick, Eugene

Fail-safe; by Eugene Burdick & Harvey Wheeler. McGraw-Hill 1962 286p o.p.

"With mounting tension this gripping thriller tells of a possible nuclear holocaust. An American attack squadron is accidentally and irretrievably launched to obliterate Moscow. The frantic U.S. president and the Russian premier begin a dramatic hotline race against time to halt the bombers' flight and prevent disaster. The crisis is seen through the eyes of several characters, and their differing perceptions provide an effective story-telling technique." Shapiro. Fic for Youth. 3d edition

Burford, Eleanor, 1906-1993

For works written by this author under other names see Holt, Victoria, 1906-1993; Plaidy, Jean, 1906-1993

Burgess, Anthony, 1917-1993

A clockwork orange. [New American ed.] Norton 1988 192p hardcover o.p. pa $13.95

ISBN 0-393-02439-3; 0-393-31283-6 (pa)

         * LC 86-23843

First published 1962 in the United Kingdom

"A compelling and often comic vision of the way violence comes to dominate the mind. The novel is set in a future London and is told in curious but readable Russified argot by a juvenile deliquent whose brainwashing by the authorities has destroyed not only his murderous aggression but also his deeper-seated sense of humanity as typified by his compulsive love for the music of Beethoven. It is an ironic novel in the tradition of Zamiatin's and Orwell's anti-Utopias." Sci Fic Ency

Burgess, Trevor, 1920-1995

For works written by this author under other names see Hall, Adam, 1920-1995

Burke, Alafair

Angel's tip. Harper 2008 342p il $23.95

ISBN 978-0-06-156102-3; 0-06-156102-9

         LC 2008-3071

Rookie New York City police detective Ellie Hatcher "is out on her morning run when she discovers the corpse of a teenage girl who's been strangled, stabbed, and shorn of her blond hair. The 19-year-old had been visiting the Big Apple with friends and hitting all the clubs while on break from college. Her murder creates a whirlwind of bad publicity for the city, but the NYPD breaks the case very quickly-or have they? Turns out there are weird similarities to some cold cases that Hatcher's deceased partner had been checking out, and she is unconvinced they have the right perp. . . . Lots of suspense and plot twists galore keep the pages turning, but the story lines about Hatcher, her boyfriend, her brother, and her partner deserve the credit for making this novel a winner." Libr J

Burke, James Lee, 1936-

Black cherry blues. Little, Brown 1989 290p

ISBN 0-316-11699-8

         * LC 89-7977

"A former homicide cop is trying to run his fishing business, care for six-year-old orphan Alafair, and come to terms with the violent death of his wife, Annie. A chance encounter with an old friend haunted by a troubling secret sets off a chain of events that leaves Dave framed for murder. Desperate to prove his innocence and protect Alafair, Robicheaux is forced to conduct his own investigation." Libr J

"A stunning novel that takes detective fiction into new imaginative realms. . . . All the main characters in this darkly beautiful, lyric saga carry heavy emotional baggage, and Robicheaux's sleuthing is a simultaneous exorcism of demons of grief, loss, fear, rage, vengeance." Publ Wkly

Heaven's prisoners. Holt & Co. 1988 292p

ISBN 0-8050-0665-6

         * LC 87-26878

"Ex-New Orleans cop Dave Robicheaux and his wife, Annie, are fishing in the Gulf one afternoon when a small plane crashes nearby. All of the plane's passengers—Nicaraguan refugees attempting to enter the U.S. illegally—are killed except one, a young girl whom Dave rescues. This chance encounter lands the Robicheaux family in the midst of an immigration squabble and then a vicious drug war." Booklist

"There is a pronounced streak of poetry in Mr. Burke's prose. He has the knack of combining action with reflection; he has pity for the human condition, and even his villains can have some sympathetic and redeeming qualities. Mr. Burke writes in an unhurried manner, but the book never loses tension because he is so wrapped up in his characters and their locale." N Y Times Book Rev

Last car to Elysian Fields; a Dave Robicheaux novel. Simon & Schuster 2003 335p $25

ISBN 0-7432-4542-3   LC 2003-54386

"Dave Robicheaux, an Iberia Parish homicide detective with an 'abiding anger' for the corrupters of innocence and the despoilers of beauty, is roped into investigating [legendary R & B guitarist Junior] Crudup's fate by Jimmie Dolan, a priest whose moral crusades cause mobsters to put out a hit on him. Burke's heavies make great showpieces, but Max Coll, a stone killer who repents of his sins and causes all kinds of mayhem trying to do penance, knocks them all off the shelf. In the absence of plagues of locusts, a good hit man can really clean up a dirty town." N Y Times Book Rev

Rain gods. Simon & Schuster 2009 434p $25.99

ISBN 978-1-4391-2824-4; 1-4391-2824-3

         LC 2009-12166

Hackberry Holland "is the sheriff of a sleepy Texas town near the Mexican border, the last stop for the aging Hack after a tumultuous personal life and an up-and-down career as a politician and lawyer. His downshifted lifestyle is torn asunder when Hack discovers the bodies of nine illegal aliens, buried in a shallow grave behind a church. The trail leads to a troubled Iraq vet, who knows something about the killings, and his country-singer girlfriend, both now on the run from various baddies who want to make sure the kids don't tell anyone what they know. Hack and his deputy, Pam Tibbs,

Burke, James Lee, 1936-—_Continued_

who has a romantic interest in her boss despite his insistence that he is much too old for her, join the chase. . . . Burke fans will notice much that is familiar here—the lyricism, the minor key, the elegiac refrain—but the melody is new and haunting. And, besides, you just have to love a guy with a name like Hackberry." Booklist

A stained white radiance. Hyperion 1992 305p
ISBN 1-562-82980-7   LC 91-34213
"Sadistic villains and interior demons plague Cajun police detective Dave Robicheaux as the murder of a local cop draws him into the painful conflicts of the Sonnier family, with whom he grew up near the bayous." Publ Wkly

In this novel "the 'venal and meretricious' bear the unmistakable stench of the modern world: a drug-dealing mobster out to settle scores, a trio of swastika-sporting members of the Aryan Brotherhood, and, lurking on the respectable fringe, an impeccably coiffed former Klansman intent on snagging a senate seat. . . . Dave tackles them all, of course, and in the end establishes a tenuous calm into which he and his family are able to retreat. But the elegiac tone dominates." Booklist

The tin roof blowdown; a Dave Robicheaux novel. Simon & Schuster 2007 373p $26
ISBN 978-1-4165-4848-5; 1-4165-4848-3
LC 2007-4847
In this Dave Robicheaux novel, "Hurricane Katrina and its aftermath provide the backdrop for an account of sin and redemption in New Orleans. When Detective Robicheaux's department is assigned to investigate the shooting of two looters in a wealthy neighborhood, he learns that they had ransacked the home of New Orleans's most powerful mobster. Now he must locate the surviving looter before others do, and in the process he learns the fate of a priest who disappeared in the ill-fated Ninth Ward trying to rescue his trapped parishioners." Publ Wkly

"In Mr. Burke's universe, some of the saddest storm victims are those who committed terrible sins in a time of crisis and wish they could undo the transgressions. But like George Pelecanos's Washington, Mr. Burke's New Orleans is a place where the destinies of ghetto-bred young black men are all but determined at birth. Mr. Burke sometimes shows an overheated, lyrical bent, and the extremes of Hurricane Katrina make it especially pronounced. . . . Whether invoking William Blake's tiger or Voltaire's Candide, Dave thinks big. He reaches for literary as well as biblical terms to convey the apocalyptic magnitude of New Orleans's collapse." N Y Times (Late N Y Ed)

Burke, Jan

Remember me, Irene; an Irene Kelly mystery. Simon & Schuster 1996 303p
ISBN 0-684-80343-7   LC 95-52186
In this episode Southern California news reporter Irene Kelly is "married to her longtime lover, cop Frank Harriman. One day at a bus stop, Irene has a disturbing encounter with a homeless wino, only later discovering that the man, Lucas, was once her close friend, a gifted statistician who managed to get even the math-impaired Irene excited about numbers. Lucas has obviously fallen on hard times, so when Irene gets a cryptic message asking her to meet him, she's curious to learn more. But when she goes to the rendezvous, she discovers his dead body—and opens a Pandora's box of troubles. . . . Exciting action, clever dialogue, solid writing, and a smart, likable heroine produce a well-deserved thumbs-up." Booklist

Burke, Shannon

Black flies. Soft Skull Press 2008 185p pa $14.95
ISBN 978-1-59376-191-2; 1-59376-191-0
LC 2007-46762
A "novel about Harlem paramedics in the mid-1990s. . . . Oliver Cross graduated from Northwestern as a middle-class do-gooder. But he and his partner, Rutkovsky, a jaded Vietnam veteran and one of the city's best medics, see enough massive trauma to put Cross on the fast track to deep disillusionment." Publ Wkly

"It would have been easy for Black Flies to slip into slumming mode, or a voyeuristic inventory of gruesome catastrophes and macho heroism. But Burke's gripping prose, as unadorned as the book's burned-out backdrop, calmly builds toward a larger conundrum: What happens when horrors become commonplace? A gifted stylist, the author makes a thoughtful stab at showing what constant danger can do to an ambulance worker and to a neighborhood's inhabitants." Time Out N Y

Burnford, Sheila, 1918-1984

Bel Ria. Little, Brown 1978 c1977 215p
ISBN 0-316-77139-2   LC 77-21082
"An Atlantic Monthly Press book"
First published 1977 in the United Kingdom
"A British soldier who is fleeing before the advancing German troops first comes upon a small trick dog in a circus caravan. When its owners are killed he takes on the responsibility for it and a monkey that makes a habit of riding on its back. When he is evacuated from France, even when the ship is sunk and they must remain in the water for hours, the three stick together. Sinclair, however, is badly wounded and must be hospitalized, so he entrusts the animals to a sick berth attendant on the ship. The dog, who soon is named Ria, at first is lonely and afraid, while the monkey quickly adapts, though every effort is made to keep them apart. Back on shore briefly, Ria is left with someone who will return him to Sinclair. That night, however, the town is bombed and Ria winds up saving the life of a 76-year-old woman who has been entombed by the debris. She takes him under her wealthy wing and he changes her life." Publ Wkly

"A realistic portrayal of wartime life, and an unsentimental but delightful picture of a remarkable animal, self-reliant, independent, and loving." Libr J

The incredible journey; with illustrations by Carl Burger. Little, Brown 1961 145p il o.p.
*

"A half-blind English bull terrier, a sprightly yellow Labrador retriever, and a feisty Siamese cat have resided for eight months with a friend of their owners, who are away on a trip. Then their temporary caretaker leaves them behind in order to take a short vacation. The lonely trio decides to tackle the harsh 250-mile hike across the

Burnford, Sheila, 1918-1984—*Continued*
Canadian wilderness in search of home, despite the human and wild obstacles the group will encounter." Shapiro. Fic for Youth. 3d edition

Burns, Olive Ann

Cold Sassy tree. Ticknor & Fields 1984 391p $28
ISBN 0-89919-309-9
* LC 84-8570
"Young Will Tweedy lives in a small Georgia town called Cold Sassy in the early 1900s. He is hard working (when pushed) because he has chores to do at home and work to do at his Grandpa Blakeslee's store. That still leaves him time to plan practical jokes with his pals and to overhear family dramas. The biggest drama begins when Grandpa, only three weeks after the death of his wife whom he had dearly loved, marries Miss Love Simpson—young enough to be his daughter. Miss Love has to face not only the town gossip, but also rejection from Will's Mother and Grandpa's other daughter. The story has humor, excitement, and realistic family confrontations." Shapiro. Fic for Youth. 3d edition
Followed by Leaving Cold Sassy: the unfinished sequel (1992)

Burns, Tex, 1908-1988
For works written by this author under other names see L'Amour, Louis, 1908-1988

Burnside, John, 1955-

Glister. Nan A. Talese/Doubleday 2008 375p $25.95
ISBN 978-0-385-52764-4; 0-385-52764-0
"In recent years, five teenage boys have disappeared from the coastal village of Innertown, where an abandoned chemical plant deep in the forest is slowly poisoning its rapidly declining population. The official line is that the missing boys are seeking a better life away from the town whose 'sole business is slow decay.' A 15-year-old lad, who's found solace in books and foreign films that he can barely understand, is determined to find out what happened to his friends and why the town's lone cop spends so much time in those tarnished woods." Publ Wkly
"What is most beautiful, and most frightening, about the novel itself is its melancholy awareness of how desperate our acts of devotion can be in places like this toxic town, how terrible the things we can learn to love." N Y Times Book Rev

Burroughs, William S., 1914-1997

Naked lunch; the restored text edited by James Grauerholz and Barry Miles. Grove Press 2003 c2001 289p pa $14
ISBN 978-0-8021-4018-0; 0-8021-4018-1
* LC 2001-23190
First published 1959 in France; first published 1962 in the United States
"An autobiographical novel that discards . . . conventional narrative prose . . . to present a surrealistic vision of a liberated, hallucinatory counterculture set in opposi-

tion to a mass-produced, technological society bent on mass destruction. In this and the books of the next few years, Burroughs relied on such techniques as random cutting and pasting to create an extreme montage effect. Surviving obscenity trials in the U. S., Naked Lunch became an icon of the emancipated sixties." Benet's Reader's Ency Am Lit

(jt. auth) Kerouac, J. And the hippos were boiled in their tanks

Burroway, Janet, 1936-

Bridge of sand. Houghton Mifflin Harcourt 2009 328p $25
ISBN 978-0-15-101543-6; 0-15-101543-0
LC 2008-22758
"Dana is at a loss after burying her husband, a Pennsylvania senator, a few miles from the United 93 crash on 9/11. Her marriage had almost ended when Graham was diagnosed with cancer, and she nursed him to the end before beginning the task of selling her home. Originally from the South, she heads back to Georgia, aimlessly driving and thinking about her future. She decides to visit her grandmother's house, only to find it has been turned into a strip mall. Once again at loose ends, she looks up old friend Cassius Huston, and they begin an affair, which is problematic because she is white, and he is black. . . . [Burroway] crafts memorable characters while challenging readers' assumptions about race, love, and family." Libr J

Buruma, Ian

The China lover. Penguin Press 2008 392p $26.95
ISBN 978-1-594-20194-3; 1-594-20194-3
LC 2008-18201
"A teenage singer and actress, Yoshiko Yamaguchi rose to stardom in Japanese-occupied Manchuria in the 1930s, appearing in a series of propaganda films. After the war, she worked in pro-American movies in occupied Japan, before switching to Hollywood and reinventing herself there as a diplomat's wife, a journalist and a prominent Japanese politician. Her career forms the narrative thread of Ian Buruma's evocative novel, which spans roughly 50 years of Japan's tumultuous modern history. Buruma uses Yamaguchi's bizarre story as a metaphor for Japan's own shifting identity, from militaristic dictatorship to America-besotted, postwar ruin, to economically rejuvenated modern nation. . . . Yamaguchi's story is divided into three parts, each narrated by a different man and each paralleling a different phase of Japan's reinvention. This ambitious approach brings her world vividly to life." Scotsman

Busch, Frederick, 1941-2006

The night inspector; a novel. Harmony Bks. 1999 278p il $23
ISBN 0-609-60235-7
LC 99-11890
The narrator of this novel "William Bartholomew, served as a Union sniper in the Civil War until an explosion maimed his face; now it's 1867, and Bartholomew works as an investor in New York City, hiding his scars behind a pasteboard mask. The Civil War may be over, but slavery isn't: slave children are stuck at a Florida

Busch, Frederick, 1941-2006—*Continued*

school, and Jessie, a Creole prostitute romantically involved with Bartholomew, entangles him in a plot to bring them North to freedom. Bartholomew seeks help from Herman Melville, once a bestselling novelist, now a customs inspector . . . in Manhattan's shipyards." Publ Wkly

The novel "is a marvelously dark-hued story by a master craftsman, and watching mastery at work provides at least a part of the pleasure of reading it." N Y Times Book Rev

Rescue missions; stories. W.W. Norton & Co. 2006 316p $24.95

ISBN 978-0-393-06252-6; 0-393-06252-X

LC 2006-13011

Contents: The rescue mission; Good to go; Frost line; Last time for old times' sake; The small salvation; The bottom of the glass; Now that it's spring; Manhattans; The hay behind the house; I am the news; Something along those lines; Metal fatigue; Patrols; The barrens; Sense of direction

"'Need trumps love,' in the words of one of Busch's indelible characters, and need in all its permutations infuses the final collection of stories from this master of the genre. Whether it's the obligation of a son to his dying father, the unfulfilled duty of a soldier fresh from the war in Iraq, or the demand for revenge of a former lover, the drive for recognition, connection, and affirmation is revealed as an essential life force. In Busch's hands, it thrums with an elegiac cadence, so subtle at times as to be barely perceptible, so strong at others as to take one's breath away." Booklist

Bushnell, Candace

Lipstick jungle. Hyperion 2005 353p $24.95

ISBN 0-7868-6819-8

LC 2005-46379

"Victory Ford, Wendy Healy, and Nico O'Neilly are three movers and shakers in Manhattan who still find time to lunch at the hottest restaurants. . . . Victory is a world-famous fashion designer whose spring collection failed to impress at New York's all-important fashion week. As the president of Parador Pictures, Wendy is gearing up for the film she hopes will finally snag her the coveted Best Picture Oscar. Nico, editor in chief of Bonfire magazine, is working her way up the corporate ladder. The ladies' love lives are just as interesting as their careers. Victory is being courted by an eccentric billionaire; Wendy's handsome, lazy husband has just demanded a divorce; and married Nico finds herself drawn into a fling with a handsome, younger male model. Readers who want to immerse themselves in the trendy world of New York's high society will find themselves at home in this scintillating novel." Booklist

Butcher, Jim, 1971-

Small favor; a novel of the Dresden files. Roc 2008 423p $23.95

ISBN 978-0-451-46189-6; 0-451-46189-4

LC 2007-42136

Supernatural crime noir featuring Harry Dresden. "A friendly snowball fight opens the Chicago-based wizard-detective's latest tale, but it's not long before a host of more dangerous foes are out for Harry's blood. A miss-ing human mobster is said to be seeking greater influence among Chicago's extranormal population, but the true threat proves both more subtle and of much greater consequence." Publ Wkly

"There is a lot going on in this book, which is the tenth installment in the bestselling series about that other wizard named Harry. With so many factions, and so many agendas involved, it's easy to get a little lost in the chaos and confusion, but Jim Butcher clearly has it all mapped out, and he's obviously moving around a growing number of pieces on the board as he positions them for the inevitable final conflict at some point down the road. . . . New relationships are forged and old ones tested, some plans are thwarted while others are set into motion, and at the end, there's the distinct sensation of change and growth in Harry Dresden's world." SF Site

Butler, Gwendoline

Death lives next door; the first Inspector Coffin mystery. St. Martin's Press 1992 c1960 191p

ISBN 0-312-08175-8

LC 92-1581

"A Thomas Dunne book"

First published 1960 in the United Kingdom

"Keeping her detective in the wings, {Butler} begins by focusing her narrative on a gang of shabby, bitter academic types in Oxford, at the center of which dysfunctional clique is the famous and slightly mysterious Marion Manning, watched by a man who in time will claim to be her long lost husband. Everything in Marion's past is weird, and as Coffin is drawn out of London into this narrow little world, it is the investigation of this mysterious past that forms the heart of the book. Butler's regulars shouldn't pass up the chance for this peek at Coffin's past." Booklist

Butler, Octavia E., 1947-2006

Adulthood rites. 1988 277p (Xenogenesis)

ISBN 0-446-51422-5

LC 87-34620

In the second novel in the Xenogenesis trilogy "the alien Oankali have rescued the dying remnants of humanity after Earth's nuclear war. Now, though, the children of the two races, called constructs, are resented and feared by the original survivors. This is the story of one such construct, Akin, who possesses an adult mind and voice before he is two years old. Stolen by a barren human community, he grows up knowing both races." Publ Wkly

Followed by Imago

Dawn; [by] Octavia Butler. Warner Bks. 1987 264p (Xenogenesis)

ISBN 0-446-51363-6

* LC 87-6195

In this first volume in the Xenogenesis trilogy "a band of nuclear holocaust survivors is in the hands of an alien race that offers to save them. The price is high though: the survivors must participate in the evolution of the aliens by bearing children that incorporate some of the aliens' characteristics. Butler is one of the few sf writers who can handle effectively a slow-moving plot that emphasizes characters' emotions. Her command of the language is superior, and her aliens are quite convincing creations." Booklist

Followed by Adulthood rites

Butler, Octavia E., 1947-2006—*Continued*

Imago. Warner Bks. 1989 c1985 264p (Xenogenesis)

ISBN 0-446-51472-1   LC 88-27975

First published 1985 in the United Kingdom

The concluding volume of the Xenogenesis trilogy "considers a post-holocaust humanity whose only chance for survival is to be absorbed by the alien Oankali. Totally uninterested in domination, this race thrives on a symbiosis that Earthlings find difficult to credit. That distrust hampers the narrator, an ooloi (neuter) named Jodahs, as it tries to find life partners in the same ratio as its five parents: a human couple, an Oankali couple and itself, the essential ooloi who joins all five and melds their genetic legacy. Butler's achievement here is less the abstract reassignment of sexual roles than a warmth and urgency that dramatizes and personalizes these conflicts and transformations." Publ Wkly

Kindred. 25th anniverary ed. Beacon Press 2003 287p (Black women writers series) pa $14

ISBN 0-8070-8369-0

          * LC 2003-62862

First published 1979 by Doubleday

"Dana, a well-educated contemporary African American woman, suddenly finds herself pulled into the past to save the life of a distant ancestor, an early-19th-century southern white boy named Rufus Weylin. Although she returns to the present moments later, she soon finds herself saving Rufus again and again. Although only a short time passes for her between each bout of time travel, years pass for Rufus, who gradually grows into adulthood and becomes a slave owner. This sometimes painful novel features superb character development." Anatomy of Wonder 5

Butler, Robert Olen

Hell; a novel. Grove Press 2009 232p $24

ISBN 978-0-8021-1901-8; 0-8021-1901-8

"Set in the not-too-distant future, this short novel finds protagonist Hatcher McCord in Hell—which tends to resemble Earth, with the addition of midday sulfur storms. A network news anchor in life, he's in the same role in the afterlife, hosting the Evening News from Hell. He's involved with Anne Boleyn, who still longs for the man who done her wrong, and encounters a variety of famous personages, from Virgil and Humphrey Bogart to various U.S. presidents (Richard Nixon is the Devil's chauffeur). Along the way, he hears that a new harrowing of Hell may be imminent and sets about trying to be included by making amends with those he wronged in life (primarily his three ex-wives)." Libr J

"Butler's lust for the tabloid romp and his stream of the never-ending punch line both irritates and illuminates. The reader's taste will have to be the final arbiters of worth." Publ Wkly

Butler, Samuel, 1835-1902

The way of all flesh. Knopf 1992 374p $17

ISBN 0-679-41718-4

          * LC 92-52916

"Everyman's library"

First published posthumously 1903; first Everyman's library edition 1933

The theme of this semi-autobiographical novel "is the hypocrisy and smug complacency of English middle-class life, and particularly the relationship between parents and children, which is traced through several generations of the Pontifex family. . . . 'The Way of All Flesh' is generally regarded as a very original work: it exercised considerable influence on later English writers. 'It contains records of the things I saw happening rather than imaginary incidents,' said the author. Undoubtedly this novel has a strong vein of autobiography." Haydn. Thesaurus of Book Dig

Butters, Dorothy Gilman *See* Gilman, Dorothy, 1923-

Butterworth, W. E., 1929-

For works written by this author in collaboration with H. Richard Hornberger see Hooker, Richard;

For works written by this author under other names see Griffin, W. E. B.

Byatt, A. S. (Antonia Susan), 1936-

Angels and insects; two novellas. Turtle Bay Bks. 1993 c1991 339p

ISBN 0-679-40512-7   LC 92-56806

First published 1991 in the United Kingdom

"In 'Morpho Eugenia' penniless young entomologist William Adamson has just returned from a 10-year expedition in the Amazon. William is taken in by a titled clergyman with scientific pretensions, and soon marries his benefactor's beautiful daughter. Unable to undertake another Amazon adventure, he studies domestic ant colonies and discovers indecent parallels between the insects and his new family. 'The Conjugial Angel' involves a circle of spiritualists, chief among them Alfred Tennyson's sister Emily, in her youth engaged to Arthur Hallam, the man immortalized in Tennyson's *In Memoriam.* Emily has been branded faithless for having married years after Hallam's death, . . . but she is uncompromising in her pursuit of Hallam's ghost. . . . Complex and captivating, this fluid volume recasts itself on every page." Publ Wkly

The children's book; a novel. Alfred A. Knopf 2009 675p $26.95

ISBN 978-0-307-27209-6; 0-307-27209-5

          LC 2009-16334

"Olive Wellwood and her banker husband are founding members of the Fabian Society, a precursor to Britain's Labour Party. They also have many children, who are looked after by Olive's sister, Violet, so Olive can create the stories that keep the family in their beloved home, Todefright. Not having to cook or clean, Olive concocts never ending stories, 'like segmented worms,' for each of her children. . . . Into this imagination-driven society stumbles Phillip Warren, a runaway teen with an artistic spirit. After Olive plays good fairy for the weekend, Phillip is apprenticed to a family friend, a potter of uncertain temper and undoubted genius, who has two fragile-looking daughters. The Fabians believed in giving children room to explore, and Olive's most beloved child, Tom, disappears into the woods for days at a time. Prickly Dorothy longs to be a doctor; and proto-Goth

Byatt, A. S. (Antonia Susan), 1936-—*Continued*

Hedda ferrets out family secrets and rages at being ignored. Meanwhile, Olive's bourgeois-raised nephew flirts with anarchy, and her golden niece longs to be allowed to think." Christ Sci Monit

"This is a moving book. Its words are beautifully chosen. . . . Everything connects. A S Byatt is Gaudi and Christopher Wren rolled into one." Scotsman

The conjugial angel

In Byatt, A. S. Angels and insects

Morpho Eugenia

In Byatt, A. S. Angels and insects

(ed) The Oxford book of English short stories. See The Oxford book of English short stories

Possession; a romance. Modern Lib. 2000 605p ISBN 0-679-64030-4

* LC 99-56297

A reissue of the edition first published 1990 by Random House

The protagonist of this novel, Roland Mitchell, "is a postdoctoral research student. Working in the London Library of the Victorian poet Ash, he comes upon an interchange of letters between Ash and an unknown woman. . . . A series of clues lead him to believe the recipient of Ash's affections might be Christabel Lamotte, a Victorian poet of much interest . . . to feminist critics, and his quest for information about Lamotte leads him to the beautiful scholar Dr. Maud Bailey. Together Roland and Dr. Bailey unearth letters which establish the details of an intense and hitherto unsuspected relationship between these poets, and form one of their own." New Statesman Soc

"Intelligent, ingenious and humane, [this] bids fair to be looked back upon as one of the most memorable novels of the 1990s." Times Lit Suppl

Byatt, Antonia Susan *See* Byatt, A. S. (Antonia Susan), 1936-

Bynum, Sarah Shun-Lien

Ms. Hempel chronicles. Harcourt 2008 193p $23 ISBN 978-0-15-101496-5; 0-15-101496-5

LC 2008-08924

"Eight interconnected stories about Beatrice Hempel, a middle school English teacher. Ms. Hempel is the sort of teacher students adore, and despite feeling disenchanted with her job, she regards her students as intelligent, insightful and sometimes fascinating. Bynum . . . weaves stories of the teacher's childhood with the present—reminiscences about Beatrice's now deceased father and her relationship with her younger brother, Calvin—while simultaneously fleshing out the lives of Beatrice's impressionable students." Publ Wkly

"Ms. Hempel's consciousness is a joy to inhabit. Kind, scrupulous, curious, wistful, and odd, she has the vitality of a bright, nervous child, overlaid by the premature world-weariness of someone in their late twenties. . . . This is not a saccharine novel, and heartache, sexual confusion, and resignation rear their heads." Bookforum

Byrd, Max

Grant; a novel. Bantam Bks. 2000 362p $23.95 ISBN 0-553-09633-8

LC 99-56577

"As he covers Grant's potential candidacy and approaching death for the *Washington Post*, Nicholas Trist, a veteran of the Civil War who lost an arm at the battle of Cold Harbor (in which Grant was the commanding general), interacts with the major political and literary lights of the time. Washington in the 1880s resembles Washington of the 1990s: love affairs, leaks to the newspapers, jockeying for advantages, and even a best-selling anonymous novel purporting to give the inside scoop on Washington politicos. Historical fiction doesn't get any better than this." Booklist

C

Cadwalladr, Carole

The family tree. Dutton 2005 384p il $23.95 ISBN 0-525-94842-2   LC 2004-52756

"Set in late-20th-century Britain, the novel is narrated by Rebecca Monroe, a pop culture researcher who tells of her marriage to Alistair, a behavioral geneticist; her childhood leading up to her mother's suicide; and her grandmother's doomed biracial romance with Cecil, a Jamaican immigrant. In an effort to better understand herself, the child she can't decide whether or not to have, and the people she still can't believe make up her family, Rebecca considers both sides of the nature/nurture debate, with any romantic notions she might be on the brink of reaching debunked by her husband's passionless scientific postulations. Cadwalladr explicates her tale with a slew of definitions, scientific charts and graphs, detailed family anatomies, examples of deductive fallacies and footnotes expounding on such essential '70s pop culture references as Dallas and The Sale of the Century. Her mastery of time and place, wry humor and sporadic bouts of self-doubt will endear her to readers, while her fascination with the choices people make combined with a morbid curiosity about her own fate add depth and texture to this utterly winning tale of one lovable, dysfunctional family." Publ Wkly

Cain, Chelsea

Heartsick. St. Martin's Minotaur 2007 326p $23.95 ISBN 978-0-312-36846-3; 0-312-36846-1

LC 2007-18005

"When someone starts dumping the bodies of teenage girls around Portland, Ore., after soaking them in tubs of bleach, Archie Sheridan, a police detective addicted to pain killers, turns for help to Gretchen Lowell, an imprisoned serial killer who once tortured him . . . . Covering the crimes is reporter Susan Ward, a smart-alecky punk with pink hair and authority issues." Publ Wkly

"In addition to spiky characters, Cain has a crisp voice, a wicked sense of humor, and an imagination for all the horrors that can unfold in a locked basement." Entertainment Wkly

Cain, James M. (James Mallahan), 1892-1977

Double indemnity

In Cain, J. M. The postman always rings twice, double indemnity, Mildred Pierce and selected stories

Cain, James M. (James Mallahan), 1892-1977—
Continued

Mildred Pierce
> *In* Cain, J. M. The postman always rings twice, double indemnity, Mildred Pierce and selected stories

The postman always rings twice
> *In* Crime novels: American noir of the 1930s and 40s
> *In* Cain, J. M. The postman always rings twice, double indemnity, Mildred Pierce and selected stories

The postman always rings twice, double indemnity, Mildred Pierce and selected stories. Alfred A. Knopf 2003 xxxix, 594p (Everyman's library) $25
    ISBN 978-0-375-41438-1; 0-375-41438-X
                          LC 2003-277292
The postman always rings twice, (1934) is the tale of a drifter who stumbles into a job, into an erotic obsession, and into a murder. Double indemnity (1934) is a story of blind passion, duplicity, and murder. Mildred Pierce (1943) is the tale of a woman with a taste for shiftless men and an unreasoned devotion to her monstrous daughter. Also included here are five stories:Pastorale; The baby in the icebox; Dead man; Brush fire; The girl in the storm

Caldwell, Erskine, 1903-1987

God's little acre. Viking 1933 303p o.p.
                                             *
"A Georgia 'cracker,' Ty Ty Walden, has devoted 15 years to digging for gold on his farm. Always a 'religious man,' he has set aside one acre whose income shall go to the church, but has had to shift 'God's little acre' constantly, so as not to interfere with the digging. Ty Ty's sincere but adaptable morality appears also in the shiftless lives of his children." Oxford Companion to Am Lit. 6th edition

Tobacco road. Scribner 1932 241p o.p.
                                             *
"Jeeter Lester is an impoverished Georgia sharecropper who lives on Tobacco Road with his starving old mother, his sickly wife, Ada, and his two children, sixteen-year-old Dude and Ellie May, who has a harelip. A third child, Pearl, has been married at the age of twelve to Lov Bensey, a railroad worker. When Jeeter's widowed preacher sister, Bessie Rice, induces Dude to marry her by buying him a new automobile, Dude accidentally wrecks the car and kills his grandmother. Pearl runs away from Lov Bensey; Ellie May happily goes to live with him; and Jeeter and Ada, left alone one night, perish when their shack burns down." Reader's Ency. 4th edition

Caldwell, Ian

The rule of four; [by] Ian Caldwell & Dustin Thomason. Dial Press 2004 372p $24
    ISBN 0-385-33711-6   LC 2003-70124

"A Princeton student has only twenty-four hours to complete his senior thesis—hardly the nail-biting stuff of thrillers, except that the thesis in question purports to solve the mystery of an erotic fifteenth-century allegory littered with ciphers and algorithms. . . . As the student races to meet his deadline, mayhem engulfs the campus: a chase through steam tunnels beneath the grassy quads, an inferno at the school's toniest eating club, and nude frolics in the snow (this last not fiction but a real Princeton tradition). The authors . . . keep up a frantic, somewhat exhausting pace, but the most riveting action sequences take place inside the mind, as the hero wrestles with the manuscript." New Yorker

Caldwell, Taylor, 1900-1985

Captains and kings. Doubleday 1972 640p o.p.
This novel follows the growth of an Irish immigrant family from complete poverty to a position of wealth and political power. Joseph Armagh is ruled by the desire for money and overcome by ambition for his children. Along the way the family seems to have acquired a curse, so that the second generation of Armaghs reaps only misfortune and destruction
"Through all this saga one cannot help but find some parallels with the Kennedy saga, set back to the period 1850-1915. Portraits of some characters, rather bitterly slanted, are certainly more than coincidental." Publ Wkly

Dear and glorious physician. Doubleday 1959 574p o.p.
This novel about Lucanus, or Luke, "physician and author of one of the Gospels, depicts him as an individual apart, plainly marked out for the service of God in spite of his almost lifelong protest against a deity who inflicted pain on men. Antioch, scene of his boyhood; Rome, where he visited his family in the intervals between his restless travels; Alexandria, where he was educated; and Judaea, where he learned the story of Jesus from his mother Mary and acknowledged him as the Christ, provide a background." Booklist
"Gripping and absorbing reading that illuminates a period and highlights the development of a man being prepared for God's purpose. The sweep and greatness of the story dwarf any defects in style." Wis Libr Bull

Testimony of two men. Doubleday 1968 605p o.p.
"Jonathan Ferrier is the central character. He is dedicated to perfection—to perfect asepsis when few doctors yet acknowledged or even knew the need for it in 1901, and to perfect truth in human relations. Ironically, he himself has been tried for the murder of his wife and justly acquitted. The verdict was not acceptable to his community. Since they are incapable of the perfection he vocally demands, the people around him hate him and are delighted by an apparent opportunity to condemn him." Libr J
"Caldwell combines incisive characterization with an absorbing description of nineteenth-century medical practices." Booklist

Calisher, Hortense

The collected stories of Hortense Calisher. Arbor House 1975 502p
    ISBN 0-87795-115-2

Calisher, Hortense—*Continued*

Contents: In Greenwich there are many gravelled walks; Heartburn; The night club in the woods; Two colonials; The hollow boy; The rehabilitation of Ginevra Leake; The woman who was everybody; A Christmas carillon; Il ploe:r dã mõ koe:r, If you don't want to live I can't help you; A wreath for Miss Totten; Time, gentlemen; May-ry; The Coreopsis Kid; A box of ginger; The pool of Narcissus; The watchers; The gulf between; The sound of waiting; Old stock; The rabbi's daughter; The middle drawer; The summer rebellion; What a thing, to keep a wolf in a cage; Songs my mother taught me; So many rings to the show; One of the chosen; Point of departure; Letitia, Emeritus; The seacoast of Bohemia; Mrs. Fay dines on zebra; Saturday night; Little did I know; Night riders of Northville; In the absence of angels; The scream of Fifty-seventh Street

Calling the wind; twentieth century African-American short stories; edited and with an introduction by Clarence Major. HarperCollins Pubs. 1993 xxv, 622p hardcover o.p. paperback available $17

ISBN 0-06-018337-3   LC 92-52620

"An Edward Burlingame book"

"Fifty-nine African American authors, including Terry McMillan, Arna Bontemps, Richard Wright, Langston Hughes, James Baldwin, Toni Morrison, Alice Walker and Rosa Guy, have each contributed one short story to this collection." Book Rep

This "could become *the* anthology of black American short fiction for wide use in the high school and college classroom as well as by the general reading public." Booklist

Calvino, Italo

Baron in the trees; translated by Archibald Colquhoun. Harcourt 1977 c1959 217p pa $12

ISBN 0-15-610680-9

* LC 76-039704

Original Italian edition, 1957; this translation first published 1959 by Random House

Calvino's "status as one of Italy's greatest writer's was confirmed by the acclaim which met the fantasy, The baron in the trees (1957), in which a nineteenth-century nobleman opts to pursue life without ever setting foot on the ground. The story examines the meeting-points of reality and imagination." Good Fiction Guide

If on a winter's night a traveler. Knopf 1993 c1981 254p $18

ISBN 0-679-42025-8

* LC 92-54302

"Everyman's library"

Original Italian edition, 1979; this is a reissue of the edition published 1981 by Harcourt Brace Jovanovich

The novel "begins with a man discovering that the copy of a novel he has recently purchased is defective, a Polish novel having been bound within its pages. He returns to the bookshop the following day and meets a young woman who is on an identical mission. They both profess a preference for the Polish novel. Interposed between the chapters in which the two strangers attempt to

authenticate their texts are 10 excerpts that parody genres of contemporary world fiction, such as the Latin-American novel and the political novel of eastern Europe." Merriam-Webster's Ency of Lit

Invisible cities; translated from the Italian by William Weaver. Harcourt Brace Jovanovich 1974 165p

ISBN 0-15-145290-3

"A Helen and Kurt Wolff book"

Original Italian edition, 1972

"Marco Polo, the traveler, describes to Kublai Khan (his patron) the various cities of the Khan's vast empire. The cities, which all have women's names, are metaphors for different kinds of people and the varied relationships they may form. . . . They progress from medieval to modern times, growing steadily in complexity and malignancy." Libr J

"Italo Calvino is recognized as one of the consummate stylists among writers today, a novelist whose superbly imaginative mind conjures up metaphorical fables of exquisite beauty to transcribe his personal visions of man and the universe." Choice

Mr. Palomar; translated from the Italian by William Weaver. Harcourt Brace Jovanovich 1985 c1983 130p

ISBN 0-15-162835-1   LC 85-5490

"A Helen and Kurt Wolff book"

Original Italian edition, 1983

"'A nervous man who lives in a frenzied and congested world, Mr. Palomar tends to reduce his relations with the outside world; and, to defend himself against the general neurasthenia, he tries to keep his sensations under control insofar as possible.' . . . Calvino [seeks to] lead the reader into three levels of experience—visual, cultural, speculative—in the life of Mr. Palomar. We watch Mr. Palomar on vacation, in the city, and silently thinking." Libr J

"There is an almost perfect sense of complementary relationships: Calvino is delicate and strong, his precision is lyric and mathematic; the equation between perceiver and perceived is made infinitely and effortlessly complex but remains exact. The care which Calvino has lavished on the formal arrangement of his book should not, however, lead us to think that it offers only a formal resolution of compositional intricacies, for Mr. Palomor is a work of cunning dialectics that goes beyond the delight in paradoxes for which Calvino is lazily praised." New Statesman (1913)

Cameron, Peter, 1959-

The city of your final destination. Farrar, Straus & Giroux 2002 312p $24

ISBN 0-374-28197-1

* LC 2001-51127

In this "novel, Omar Razaghi, a graduate student in Kansas by way of Iran and Canada, travels to Uruguay to research a biography of Jules Gund, a critically ignored expatriate writer who published only a single novel before his death. In an attempt to obtain permission to proceed with his work, Omar finds himself entangled in, and even falling a bit in love with, the family Jules left behind: his homosexual brother, Adam; Jules's wife, Caroline; and his mistress Arden. . . . The characters discover themselves not through the books they have read

Cameron, Peter, 1959—— *Continued*
(as Omar first believes) or the places they have been (as the title would suggest) but through Cameron's precisely rendered conversations." New Yorker

Camp, John, 1944-
See also Sandford, John, 1944-

Campbell, Bebe Moore

Brothers and sisters. Putnam 1994 476p
ISBN 0-399-13929-X   LC 94-14196
"Set in the heart of a Los Angeles still troubled by the aftermath of the April riots, the novel draws a . . . portrait of the internal and external conflicts regarding race experienced by characters of varied backgrounds. The story centers on Esther Jackson, an African American with a promising career in banking who is torn between her need to succeed professionally and her loyalty to other people of color." Libr J
"What makes 'Brothers and Sisters' different from the traditional potboiler is Ms. Campbell's genuine attempt to address the complexities of race in the modern age." N Y Times Book Rev

Your blues ain't like mine. Putnam 1992 332p
ISBN 0-399-13746-7   LC 91-45518
"In Ms. Campbell's story, a young black man, Armstrong Todd, visiting from Chicago in 1955, is murdered in Hopewell, Miss., by a white man. Reporters from New York are secretly summoned by an influential citizen of Hopewell, and as a consequence of the resulting news media attention there is, uncharacteristically, a trial. After the trial, the novel follows the lives of Armstrong's relatives in Mississippi—and in Chicago, where Armstrong's mother, Delotha Todd, starts a new and difficult life, raising another son. The novel also follows the lives of the murderer, Floyd Cox, and his family." N Y Times Book Rev
"Written in poetic prose, filled with masterfully drawn and sympathetic characters that a less able hand might have rendered in stereotypes, this first novel blends the irony of Flannery O'Connor's fiction and the poignance of Harper Lee's." Publ Wkly

Camus, Albert, 1913-1960

The fall; translated from the French by Justin O'Brien. Knopf 1957 147p o.p.

*

Original French edition, 1956
"A former Parisian lawyer explains to a stranger in an Amsterdam bar his current profession of judge-penitent. His bitter honesty prevented him first from winning his own self-esteem through good deeds, then from exhausting his own self-condemnation through debauchery. Knowing that no man is ever innocent, he is still trying to forestall personal judgment by confession, by judging others, and by avoiding any situation demanding action." Reader's Ency. 4th edition

The plague; translated from the French by Stuart Gilbert. Knopf 1948 278p hardcover o.p. pa $12.95
ISBN 0-394-44061-7; 0-679-72021-9 (pa)

Original French edition, 1947
"Using an epidemic of bubonic plague in an Algerian city as a symbol for the absurdity of man's condition, Albert Camus has in this novel articulated his firm belief in mankind's heroism in struggling against the ultimate futility of life. The plague makes everyone in the city intensely aware both of mortality and of the fact that cooperation is the only logical consolation anyone will find in the face of certain death. Though each character, from doctor to priest, represents some aspect of mankind's attempts to deal with the absurd, none is a cardboard figure. The reader cares what happens to the men depicted here. One takes pleasure in the moments of deep human connection that leave us with the conviction that men are, on the whole, admirable." Shapiro. Fic for Youth. 3d edition

The stranger; translated from the French by Matthew Ward. Knopf 1988 123p $25
ISBN 0-394-53305-4
* LC 83-48885
Original French edition, 1942; published in the United Kingdom with title: The outsider
"The new translation of Camus's classic is a cultural event. . . . With the domestications pruned away from the text, students will be as close to the original as another language will allow." Libr J
This novel "reveals the 'Absurd' as the condition of man, who feels himself a stranger in his world. Meursault refuses to 'play the game,' by telling the conventional social white lies demanded of him or by believing in human love or religious faith. The unemotional style of his narrative lays naked his motives—or his absence of motive—for his lack of grief over his mother's death, his affair with Marie, his killing an Arab in the hot Algerian sun. Having rejected by honest self-analysis all interpretations which could explain or justify his existence, he nevertheless discovers, while in prison awaiting execution, a passion for the simple fact of life itself." Reader's Ency. 4th edition

Canin, Ethan

America America; a novel. Random House 2008 458p $27
ISBN 978-0-679-45680-3; 0-679-45680-5
LC 2008-2341
"In the early 1970s, Corey Sifter, the son of working-class parents, becomes a yard boy on the grand estate of the powerful Metarey family. Soon, through the family's generosity, he is a student at a private boarding school and an aide to the great New York senator Henry Bonwiller, who is running for president of the United States. Before long, Corey finds himself involved with one of the Metarey daughters as well, and he begins to leave behind the world of his upbringing." Publisher's note
"Sifter is, at times, too perfect a lead, and his Saline coming-of-age is an idealized yesteryear, a mythic America encased in amber. But it is so passionately imagined that it is hard to resist Mr. Canin's retreat to simpler times and his vision of those who would forfeit comfort for the possibility of unknown highs (or lows)." N Y Sun

The palace thief. Random House 1994 205p
ISBN 0-679-41962-4   LC 93-26888

Canin, Ethan—*Continued*

Contents: Accountant; Batorsag and Szerelem; City of broken hearts; The palace thief

This "book presents us with four beautifully told long short stories. In each, a man muses over his past and realizes how little control he has had over pivotal moments in his life. . . . Canin proves himself adept at articulating moments of profound embarrassment followed by flashes of self-knowledge that are either invigorating or demoralizing. Moving and memorable." Booklist

Cannell, Dorothy

How to murder your mother-in-law. Bantam Bks. 1994 261p

ISBN 0-553-07493-8   LC 93-31149

"After insisting that husband Ben's parents celebrate their anniversary with them at Merlin's Court, Ellie {Haskell} is dismayed when her in-laws reveal that their religious differences (she's Catholic, he's Jewish) prevented their legal marriage. . . . Then Ellie's father-in-law is caught skinny-dipping with a female friend, prompting mother-in-law Magdalene to leave him. Ellie seeks solace from friends in the village and discovers that everyone is suffering from a surfeit of mothers-in-law. A commiseration session among the afflicted daughters-in-law results in several vividly imagined murder scenarios—which, unfortunately, begin to happen." Booklist

Cannell, Stephen J.

Vertical coffin. St. Martin's Press 2004 335p $24.95

ISBN 0-312-30425-0   LC 2003-58567

A thriller featuring LAPD cop, Shane Scully. "In this latest outing, he finds himself in the middle of a law enforcement territorial war when he begins to investigate the murder of one of his friends from the Los Angeles County Sheriff's Department. It seems as if both the sheriff and the feds arrived at the scene of the crime even though neither of their communications systems were compatible with the LAPD frequency. Shane is teamed with a female sheriff, and together they find themselves without friends in any law enforcement agencies. . . . Cannell is, quite simply, one of the best police procedural writers today." Libr J

Capote, Truman, 1924-1984

Breakfast at Tiffany's

In Capote, T. Breakfast at Tiffany's: a short novel and three stories

Breakfast at Tiffany's: a short novel and three stories. Random House 1958 179p

ISBN 0-394-41770-4

*

Short stories included are: House of flowers; A diamond guitar; A Christmas memory

"'Breakfast at Tiffany's' tells the story of haunting and neurotic Holiday Golightly, Texan child-bride, girl-about-New York and friend of gangster czar, Sally Tomato, in a remarkable novelette that bears the Capote trademark of neat prose, multiple dimensions and unusual atmosphere." Ont Libr Rev

The complete stories of Truman Capote; introduction by Reynolds Price. Random House 2004 300p $24.95

ISBN 0-679-64310-9

* LC 2004-46876

Contents: The walls are cold; A mink of one's own; The shape of things; Jug of silver; Miriam; My side of the matter; Preacher's legend; A tree of night; The headless hawk; Shut a final door; Children on their birthdays; Master misery; The bargain; A diamond guitar; House of flowers; A Christmas memory; Among the paths to Eden; The Thanksgiving visitor; Mojave; One Christmas

"Now, for the first time, all of Capote's short stories are being published together, an event that signifies a renewed appreciation of his overall contribution to literature, for evidence is presented in this one volume that he should be ranked as a major American short story writer." Booklist

The grass harp. Random House 1951 181p o.p.

*

"After the death of his parents, Collin goes to live with his two aunts, Verna and Dolly. The former is wealthy and practical, the latter, whimsical and romantic. Dolly produces a cure for dropsy that she bottles and sells through the mail. Verna is ready to take over the operation and realize a large profit. To avoid this scheme, Collin, Dolly, and Catherine, a servant, go off to live in a treehouse, where they are joined by other eccentric characters. When Dolly dies, Collin is ready for his independence, having learned a valuable lesson about love and nonconformity." Shapiro. Fic for Youth. 3d edition

Caputo, Philip

Acts of faith. Knopf 2005 669p $26.95

ISBN 0-375-41166-6   LC 2004-48982

"An evangelical Christian, a woman with a colonial past, and a crusading, multiracial Kenyan all have their reasons for joining Douglas Braithwaite as he flies supplies to the war-ravaged Sudan." Libr J

"Mr. Caputo writes with such authority that he's able to invest events that might seem improbable in another novelist's hands with an uncommon degree of verisimilitude, delineating not only the viewpoints of his Western visitors, but also those of the Sudanese rebels and their Islamic opponents with equally sure-handed drama and psychological ballast" N Y Times (Late N Y Ed)

Horn of Africa. Holt & Co. 1980 487p

ISBN 0-03-042136-5

* LC 79-27513

"Three men, two Americans and one Englishman, embark on a mission as mercenaries in Africa, involving gun-running and clandestine warfare. Their capacity for violence is related to events and drives in their own lives. Nordstrand, the most amoral of them, is a character that is indelibly drawn as are the horrible experiences lived through in desert treks. This author has been compared to Joseph Conrad and Graham Greene in his exploration of the deepest recesses of man's soul." Shapiro. Fic for Youth. 3d edition

Caras, Roger A.

(ed) Roger Caras' Treasury of great cat stories. See Roger Caras' Treasury of great cat stories

Caras, Roger A.—*Continued*

(ed) Roger Caras' Treasury of great dog stories.
See Roger Caras' Treasury of great dog stories

Carcaterra, Lorenzo, 1954-

Apaches. Ballantine Bks. 1997 336p
ISBN 0-345-40101-8
This novel opens with the "brutal kidnapping of an innocent 12-year-old girl. But the kidnapper has made a deadly mistake. He has brought Boomer Frontieri back to life, back to the streets. And back into action. A New York City detective forced to retire after being wounded in a drug bust, Boomer thirsts to return to the life he loved—the life of a cop. When an old friend turns to him for help, Boomer has the excuse he needs." Publisher's note

Card, Orson Scott

Alvin Journeyman. TOR Bks. 1995 384p (Tales of Alvin Maker)
ISBN 0-312-85053-0　　　　LC 95-22693
"A Tom Doherty Associates book"
Fourth title in the Tales of Alvin Maker series. "Driven from the Wobbish country by a girl's false accusation, [Alvin] returns to his birthplace in Hatrack River and promptly finds himself on trial for stealing the golden plough from Makepiece Smith and also facing lynching for helping fugitive slaves. Meanwhile, Alvin's younger brother, Calvin, is peddling his own Maker's skills with more profit if many fewer scruples, both in America and in Europe. . . . From beginning to end, this novel is full of riches." Booklist
Followed by Heartfire

Earthfall. TOR Bks. 1995 350p (Homecoming, v4)
ISBN 0-312-93039-9　　　　LC 94-41993
"A Tom Doherty Associates book"
"The fourth volume of Homecoming, Card's grand saga of the human race's far-future return to Earth, takes the characters on a century-long starship voyage back to the old planet. They find it inhabited by two sapient races, one evolved from rats, the other from bats. The two are constantly hostile to each other but also symbiotically linked by their reproductive process. Meanwhile, the long-standing rivalry between the statesmanlike Nafai and the dictatorial Elemak nearly wrecks the voyage, then leads to open violence on Earth, with consequences for relations with the other two sapient Earth races." Booklist
"This action-packed, plot-rich installment features Card's typical virtues—well-drawn characters and a story driven by complex moral issues." Publ Wkly
Followed by Earthborn

Ender's game. TOR Bks. 1991 c1985 xxi, 226p $24.95; pa $6.99
ISBN 0-312-93208-1; 0-8125-5070-6 (pa)
"A Tom Doherty Associates book"
A reissue of the title first published 1985
"Chosen as a six-year-old for his potential military genius, Ender Wiggin spends his childhood in outer space at the Battle School of the Belt. Severed from his family, isolated from his peers, and rigorously tested and trained, Ender pours all his talent into the war games that will one day repel the coming alien invasion." Libr J
"The key, of course, is Ender Wiggin himself. Mr. Card never makes the mistake of patronizing or sentimentalizing his hero. Alternately likable and insufferable, he is a convincing little Napoleon in short pants." N Y Times Book Rev

Ender's shadow. Doherty Assocs. 1999 379p (Ender Wiggin) $24.95; pa $7.99
ISBN 0-312-86860-X; 0-812-57571-7 (pa)
　　　　　　　　　　　　　　LC 99-35824
In this fifth installment "Card has added a parallel novel that occupies the same time frame as *Ender's Game*, and chronicles many of the same events. Children are being tested, the best and the brightest being placed into a school where they will be trained for the eminent and final fight to the death between humanity and the insectlike 'Buggers.' *Shadow* shifts from Ender to Bean as the protagonist and presents the events from Bean's perspective, with his own unique viewpoints. Complex three-dimensional characters, a strong story line, and vivid writing all combine to make this an exceptional work." SLJ
Followed by Shadow of the Hegemon

Keeper of dreams. TOR 2008 656p $27.95
ISBN 978-0-7653-0497-1; 0-7653-0497-X
　　　　　　　　　　　　　　LC 2007-46720
"A Tom Doherty Associates book"
Contents: The elephants of Poznan; Atlantis; Geriatric ward; Heal thyself; Space boy; Angles; Vessel; Dust; Homeless in Hell; In the dragon's house; Inventing lovers on the phone; Waterbaby; Keeper of lost dreams; Missed; 50 WPM; Feed the baby of love; Grinning man; The Yazoo queen; Christmas at Helaman's house; Neighbors; God plays fair once too often; Worthy to be one of us
"These short science fiction, fantasy and 'literary' stories, along with a handful of Hatrack River tales (related to the Alvin Maker series) and four stories 'written by a Mormon, about Mormon culture, for Mormon readers,' illustrate Card's fascination with complex child protagonists. . . . Card intended several of the included stories, like the powerful 'In the Dragon's House,' to open novels not yet written, but even on their own they provide significant examples of his perennial themes: morality, salvation and redemption." Publ Wkly

Maps in a mirror; the short fiction of Orson Scott Card. TOR Bks. 1990 675p $19.95
ISBN 0-312-85047-6
　　　　　　　　　　　　　　* LC 90-38896
"A Tom Doherty Associates book"
Contents: Eumenides in the fourth floor lavatory; Quietus; Deep breathing exercises; Fat farm; Closing the timelid; Freeway games; A sepulchre of songs; Prior restraint; The changed man and the king of words; Memories of my head; Lost boys; A thousand deaths; Clap hands and sing; Dogwalker; But we try not to act like it; I put my blue genes on; In the doghouse; The originist; Unaccompanied sonata; A cross-country trip to kill Richard Nixon; The porcelain salamander; Middle woman; The bully and the beast; The princess and the bear; Sandmagic; The best day; A plague of butterflies; The monkeys thought 'twas all in fun; Mortal gods; Saving grace; Eye for eye; St. Amy's tale; Kingsmeat; Holy;

Card, Orson Scott—*Continued*

Ender's game; Mikal's songbird; Malpractice; Follower; Hitching; Damn fine novel; Billy's box; The best family home evening ever; Bicicleta; I think Mom and Dad are going crazy, Jerry; Gert Fram

This collection features "46 pieces by an exceptional writer. Card's talents are represented by fantasy, science fiction, horror, poetry, and the stories that launched his sagas of Alvin Maker and Ender Wiggins. A substantial amount of autobiographical discussion of each story's origin enhances the volume's high value." Booklist

Seventh son. Doherty Assocs. 1987 241p (Tales of Alvin Maker) pa $6.99

ISBN 0-312-93019-4; 0-812-53305-4 (pa)

LC 86-51490

"A TOR book"

This first novel of the Tales of Alvin Maker series is a "fantasy set in early nineteenth century of an alternate-world America. Settlers beyond the Appalachians have brought with them powerful folk magic—charms, hexes, petitions—to ease the hard work and danger of everyday life. Into this world is born Alvin Miller, a seventh son carrying powerful magic. Unfortunately, Somebody or Something is determined that Alvin won't grow up." Booklist

"This beguiling book recalls Robert Penn Warren in its robust but reflective blend of folktale, history, parable and personal testimony, pioneer narrative." Publ Wkly

Followed by Red prophet

Carduff, Christopher

(ed) Maxwell, W. Early novels and stories

Carey, Edward, 1970-

Alva & Irva; the twins who saved a city. Harcourt 2003 207p il map $24

ISBN 0-15-100782-9   LC 2002-13701

"Entralia, the fictitious metropolis at the heart of Edward Carey's. . . novel, exists not only in our imagination and in the pages of 'Alva & Irva' (which serves as Entralia's one and only guidebook) but in the form of tiny plasticine models of its streets and houses, seen in the appealingly smudgy photographs that punctuate the novel. A re-creation of Entralia also appears in the story of 'Alva & Irva,' since the twins of the book's title are the designer and sculptor, respectively, of their native city in miniature." N Y Times Book Rev

This novel is "mock epical in its consequential-ridiculous tone. . .and comedically symphonic in the precision and daffy chasteness of its diction. For all its ludicrousness, it is honorably pathetic, too—a genuine human comedy," Booklist

Carey, Jacqueline, 1964-

Kushiel's dart. Tor 2001 701p

ISBN 0-312-87238-0   LC 2001-21945

"A Tom Doherty Associates book"

"Trained from childhood to a life of servitude and espionage, Phèdre nò Delaunay serves her master, Anafiel, as a courtesan and spy, ferreting out the dangerous secrets of the noble houses of Terre d'Ange. When she uncovers a treasonous conspiracy, however, her life takes on a new and deadly purpose. Set in a world reminiscent of late medieval and early Renaissance Europe, Carey's first novel portrays a society based upon political and sexual intrigue." Libr J

"Making a marvelous debut, Carey spins a breathtaking epic starring an unflinching yet poignantly vulnerable heroine. The tale blends Christianity and paganism with fascinating results." Booklist

Followed by Kushiel's chosen (2002) and Kushiel's avatar (2003)

Carey, Peter

His illegal self. Alfred A. Knopf 2008 272p $24.95

ISBN 978-0-307-26372-8; 0-307-26372-X

LC 2007-42862

"Raised by his boho-turned-bourgeois grandmother on New York's Upper East Side, Che Selkirk, seven years old in 1972, hasn't seen his Weathermenesque parents since he was a toddler, but when a young woman who calls herself Dial walks into Che's apartment one afternoon, he believes his mother has finally come. Within two hours, Dial and Che are on the lam and heading for Philly as Che's kidnapping hits the news. Unexpected trouble strikes, and soon the boy and Dial, who doesn't know how or if to tell Che that she is only a messenger who was supposed to escort him to meet his mother, land in a hippie commune in the Australian outback." Publ Wkly

"Hippie communal disintegration has been done before, and better by T.C. Boyle in 'Drop City,' but Carey keeps us reading with his vivid lyricism, his finely tuned sense of the ridiculous and his focus on two very specific characters: a boy aching for mother love and a woman who is trying to make sense of having maternal love thrust upon her. In the end, this is a love story, an unconventional but emotionally compelling one." St. Louis Post-Dispatch

My life as a fake. Knopf 2003 266p $24

ISBN 0-375-41498-3

* LC 2003-52746

A novel told through the "eyes of Lady Sarah Wode-Douglass, editor of a struggling but prestigious London poetry journal, who one day in the early 1970s finds herself accompanying an old family friend, poet and novelist John Slater, out to Malaysia. There they encounter an eccentric Australian expatriate, Christopher Chubb, who concocted, Slater says, a huge literary hoax in Australia just after the war, creating an imaginary genius poet, Bob McCorkle, whose publication by a litle magazine led to the suicide of the magazine's editor. Now Chubb offers Lady Sarah a page of poetry that shows undoubted genius and claims it is from a book in his possession. Lady Sarah's every acquisitive instinct is inflamed, but to get her hands on the book she has to listen, as Chubb inflicts on her, Ancient Mariner-like, the amazing story of his own epic struggle with McCorkle." Publ Wkly

This work "is so confidently brilliant, so economical yet lively in its writing, so tightly fitted and continuously startling in its plot that something, we feel, must be wrong with it. It ends in a bit of a rush, and left several questions dangling in this reader's mind. Unfortunately, to spell out those questions would be to betray too much of an intricate fictional construct where little is as it first seems and fantastic developments unfold like scenes on a fragile paper fan." New Yorker

Carlson, Ron, 1947-

Five skies. Viking 2007 244p $23.95

ISBN 978-0-670-03850-3; 0-670-03850-4

LC 2006-51760

"High in the desert plains of southern Idaho, three men gather for a summer of hard work: an aging rancher, whose wife was killed in a freak accident; a nineteen-year-old fleeing both family and law; and an engineer whose career is built on precision but whose brother died in a poorly planned stunt. Time and talk, so often friends to Carlson's characters, slowly heal the wounds, but the men's commission, a ramp for a Knievel-style canyon jump, makes hazardous any hope for moral uplift and serves, in the end, as the stage for tragedy." New Yorker

The signal. Viking 2009 184p $25.95

ISBN 978-0-670-02100-0; 0-670-02100-8

LC 2008-46690

"Following his dad's sudden death, Mack, who comes from a long line of Wyoming ranchers, takes to muling drugs to raise fast cash to save the family homestead. Add months of constant drinking and a fling with an even more damaged woman, and Mack finds himself despondent, divorced, and jailed. Free again, he convinces ex-wife Vonnie to come on one final fishing trip high in the mountains they both love. For him, it's both an attempt to win her back and a secret, high-paying job to locate a classified government object that fell from a military plane. Vonnie simply wants closure and a last good-bye." Libr J

Carlson "evokes the rugged solace of nature with grace and simplicity, his unadorned prose reminiscent of Cormac McCarthy's. He's as adept at describing the stark beauty of the wild as he is at reflecting the contradictory nature of human interaction. And on the treacherous ground between passion and sentimentality, he never loses his footing." PopMatters

Carr, Caleb, 1955-

The alienist. Random House 1994 496p

ISBN 0-679-41779-6

* LC 93-32766

"A society-born police reporter and an enigmatic abnormal psychologist—the 'alienist' of the title—are recruited in 1896 by New York's reform police commissioner Teddy Roosevelt to track down a serial killer who is slaughtering boy prostitutes. The investigators are opposed at every step by crime bosses and city's hidden rulers (including J. Pierpont Morgan); they distrust the alienist's novel methods and would rather conceal evidence of the murders than court publicity." Libr J

"This story boasts a veracious historical feel and a tight plot that keeps open the murderer's identity to the end. An original that fits no established mystery niche." Booklist

Followed by The angel of darkness

Carr, Philippa, 1906-1993

For works written by this author under other names see Holt, Victoria, 1906-1993; Plaidy, Jean, 1906-1993

Carroll, James

Fault lines. Little, Brown 1980 248p

ISBN 0-316-13012-5

LC 80-36756

The title of this novel "alludes to the complexities of strained human relationships. David Dolan, once a notorious, draft-dodging radical, returns to the States after eight years in Canada and Sweden teaching contemporary American literature. Disappointment, remorse, guilt, and longing complicate his search for a new beginning as he confronts an old lawyer friend (who cannot help), his aging mother (who can), and his dead (in Vietnam) brother's widow, Eddie, a writer now married to, and estranged from, ultra-movie star Cheney McCoy. The three principals and their lines of fault and guilt converge on Hunter's Island, Maine, where Eddie has sent her son." Libr J

"Mr. Carroll has told his story from all the characters' points of view—which is to say that the narrator's voice jumps from one character's mind to another's even within a single conversation. And by doing so he's made his people too strong and complex to be reduced to mere agents of the action." Books of the Times

Carroll, Jonathan, 1949-

The ghost in love. Sarah Crichton Books/Farrar, Straus and Giroux 2008 308p $25

ISBN 978-0-374-16186-6; 0-374-16186-0

LC 2008-7877

"Ben Gould hits his head on the sidewalk in an accident that should have killed him. Somehow he survives, but he's changed in ways that he cannot understand. So starts a magical tale in which Ben talks to his dog, Pilot; the ghost sent to monitor Ben falls in love with his girlfriend; and a mysterious knife-wielding man threatens them all. . . . Love, memory, and balancing the needs of our many selves are themes in this occasionally scary, often luminous work of unconventional fantasy." Libr J

Carter, Angela, 1940-1992

Burning your boats; the collected short stories; with an introduction by Salman Rushdie. Holt & Co. 1996 462p

ISBN 0-8050-4462-0

* LC 95-26312

"A John Macrae book"

Contents: The man who loved a double bass; A very, very great lady and her son at home; A Victorian fable; A souvenir of Japan; The executioner's beautiful daughter; The loves of Lady Purple; The smile of winter; Penetrating to the heart of the forest; Flesh and the mirror; Master; Reflections; Elegy for a freelance; The bloody chamber; The courtship of Mr. Lyon; The tiger's bride; Puss-in-boots; The Erl-King; The snow child; The lady of the house of love; The werewolf; The company of wolves; Wolf-Alice; Black Venus; The kiss; Our Lady of the Massacre; The cabinet of Edgar Allan Poe; Overture and incidental music for *A midsummer night's dream*; Peter and the wolf; The kitchen child; The Fall River axe murders; Lizzie's tiger; John Ford's *'Tis pity she's a whore*; Gun for the Devil; The merchant of shadows; The ghost ships; In Pantoland; Ashputtle; Alice in Prague; Impressions: The wrightsman Magdalene; The Scarlet House; The snow pavilion; The quilt maker

"Gathered from 30 years of Carter's writing life, this collection is arranged chronologically to reveal her evolution as a writer as well as her consistent preoccupation with the Gothic. . . . As her friend Salman Rushdie

Carter, Angela, 1940-1992—*Continued*

writes in his moving introduction, Carter is not an easy read, but there are many rewards for the persistent." Libr J

Nights at the circus. Viking 1985 294p
ISBN 0-670-80375-8
* LC 84-40459

The protagonist of this novel is "a six-foot-two-inch woman aerialist with wings. The setting is turn of the century London, St. Petersburg, and Siberia. An American journalist, Jack Walser, has been sent to interview Sophia, known as Fevvers to her friends, and is so intrigued by her account of her childhood that he joins the circus as a clown." Libr J

"Carter describes a locale as exotic to the traditional reader as her women are to Walser and, by implication, all men; and she undercuts accepted Western history as she goes." New Republic

Carter, Stephen L.

The emperor of Ocean Park. Knopf 2002 657p
$26.95
ISBN 0-375-41363-4   LC 2001-38227

This "tale of ambition, revenge and the power of familial obligations is set in the privileged environs of an Ivy League law school, Martha's Vineyard, and Washington, D.C. Oliver Garland is the demanding but emotionally distant patriarch of an elite, affluent African American family used to special privileges and close relationships with the powerful in government, business, and the criminal underworld. Oliver's death sparks renewed interest in his political career—as a vitriolic conservative, embittered by a failed bid for the U.S. Supreme Court—and concern in many quarters about 'arrangements' he has made in the event of his demise. Garland's son Talcott, a law professor, is very reluctantly drawn into the intrigue. . . . An elegantly nuanced novel, with finely drawn characters, a challenging plot, and perfect pacing." Booklist

Jericho's fall. Alfred A. Knopf 2009 355p
$25.95
ISBN 978-0-307-27262-1   LC 2009-03814

"When Beck, now a single mom with a responsible career, hears that old flame Jericho Ainsley is dying, she drops her child with grandma and flies to the bedside. Suddenly, her life is on the line. Her ex-lover is also ex-CIA, ex-Department of Defense, and an ex-investment wizard. He has desperate secrets to protect even in the face of death itself. His family and associates warn Beck that Jericho has lost his marbles, but he drafts her into the front line to guard his intel. In a remote mountain hideaway, the characters battle for mastery of Jericho's assets—psychological, emotional, and tangible." Libr J

"I'm not sure how much of 'Jericho's Fall' is possible or even makes sense. Characters occasionally make decisions that seem driven more by plot than by reason. Yet it's all great fun — and I couldn't help but smile as I watched a CIA director being stalked for a change." Boston Globe

New England white. Alfred A. Knopf 2007 555p $24.95
ISBN 978-0-375-41362-9; 0-375-41362-6
LC 2006-19721

This novel focuses on Lemaster and Julia Carlyle, two characters first introduced in the author's The emperor of Ocean Park. "Lemaster, one of the country's most influential African-Americans, has recently begun his tenure as president of a prestigious New England university. As he and Julia, who serves as a dean in the university's divinity school, drive home one snowy night, they happen upon the corpse of Professor Kellen Zant, a brilliant economist as well as Julia's former lover. The murder threatens to shatter not only the Carlyles' marriage but also the fragile psyche of their precocious but troubled daughter, Vanessa—and may affect the upcoming, bitterly contested race for the White House. Julia proves an unlikely but dogged investigator, who looks beyond the official verdict that Zant was killed in a chance encounter with a robber." Publ Wkly

Carter "creates an invigorating and often scathing portrait of the Carlyles' community. He refutes political correctness, preferring to explore the contradictions warring within Julia. . . . [He] is equally intense in his portrayal of the Carlyles' outwardly perfect, inwardly turbulent marriage, a delicate balance of duty and endurance, even love of a sort." PopMatters

Palace council. Alfred A. Knopf 2008 513p
$26.95
ISBN 978-0-307-26658-3; 0-307-26658-3
LC 2007-52134

"Set primarily in the years between 1954 and 1974—what Carter calls the 'two decades' of the sixties—this political thriller leaves virtually no important person or event unturned. Richard Nixon, Langston Hughes, and dissident groups all play roles as the action shifts from Harlem to Washington and Saigon. After Eddie Wesley stumbles upon the body of a prominent lawyer who died clutching the talisman of a secret society in his fist, he finds himself caught up in the machinations of spies and assassins. Untangling the so-called Palace Council's purpose gains new urgency when Eddie's sister suddenly vanishes. At the same time, Aurelia, the ex-girlfriend for whom he still carries a torch, is on her own path to discovering the enigmatic group's secrets. . . . Carter offers a finely drawn picture of the complicated black social world." New Yorker

Cartwright, Justin

The promise of happiness. Thomas Dunne Books/St. Martin's Press 2006 c2004 308p $23.95
ISBN 0-312-34880-0   LC 2005-49381
First published 2004 in the United Kingdom

"Former golden girl Juliet Judd has just been released after serving two years in a New York prison for art fraud. Her homecoming offers her distraught family a chance to reunite and, at long last, to feel a sense of normalcy. Her 68-year-old father is failing, recently forced out of his job and into retirement in the Cornish village of Trebetherick. Her mother obsesses over cooking classes, as if it's her bad cooking that landed her daughter in jail. Meanwhile, Juliet's sister, Sophie, distracts herself with drugs and a married lover, while brother Charlie, soon to become a millionaire after founding a company that sells socks over the Internet, feels that his impending marriage to a glamorous Brazilian is something of a sham." Booklist

"Cartwright's novel is wonderfully well written. The savage irony and probing moral questioning nicely bal-

Cartwright, Justin—*Continued*

ance each other out, and as an exploration of contemporary Englishness—'proud, ironic and ridiculous all at once'—it is unsurpassed." N Y Times Book Rev

Carver, Raymond

Collected stories; [edited by William L. Stull and Maureen P. Carroll] Library of America 2009 $40

ISBN 978-1-59853-046-9

*

Contents: Fat; Neighbors; The idea; They're not your husband; Are you a doctor?; The father; Nobody said anything; Sixty acres; What's in Alaska?; Night school; Collectors; What do you do in San Francisco?; The student's wife; Put yourself in my shoes; Jerry and Molly and Sam; Why, Honey?; The ducks; How about this?; Bicycles, muscles, cigarets; What is it?; Signals; Will you please be quiet, please?; Pastoral; Furious seasons; Why don't you dance?; Viewfinder; Mr. Coffee and Mr. Fixit; Gazebo; I could see the smallest things; Sacks; The bath; Tell the women we're going; After the denim; So much water so close to home; The third thing that killed my father off; A serious talk; The calm; Popular Mechanics; Everything stuck to him; What we talk about we talk about love; One more thing; The lie; The cabin; Harry's death; The pheasant; Feathers; Chef's house; Preservation; The compartment; A small, good thing; Vitamins; Careful; Where I'm calling from; The train; Fever; The bridle; Cathedral; Boxes; Whoever was using this bed; Intimacy; Menudo; Elephant ; Blackbird pie; Errand; The hair; The aficionados; Poseidon and company; Bright red apples; Kindling; What would you like to see?; Dreams; Vandals; Call if you need me; Beginners (The manuscript version of What we talk about when we talk about love): Why don't you dance?; Viewfinder; Where is everyone?; Gazebo; Want to see something?; The fling; A small, good thing; Tell the women we're going; If it please you; So much water so close to home; Dummy; Pie; The calm; Mine; Distance; Beginners; One more thing

"The Library of America Collected Stories is a fascinating event . . . if you haven't read it you cannot claim, in the fullest sense, to have read Raymond Carver." Tmes Lit Suppl

Cary, Arthur Joyce Lunel *See* Cary, Joyce, 1888-1957

Cary, Joyce, 1888-1957

The horse's mouth; a novel. Harper & Row 1950 311p o.p.

*

The third volume in the trilogy that began with Herself surprised (1948) and To be a pilgrim (1949)

First published 1944 in the United Kingdom

Gulley Jimson is an "artist newly released from prison. At 67, he has finally gained some critical acclaim. His aspirations to paint and live comfortably off the fruits of his achievements are thwarted, however, by his own desire to change artistically and by his accidental killing of a former model, Sara Monday. Gulley is a charming and humorous hero, constanly spouting his ideas on art and London and vividly describing the people around him."

Shapiro. Fic for Youth. 3d edition

"The book is crammed with characters and picaresque episodes, and its fire and gusto never once flag. It is a comic hymn to life, but it has nobility as well. Depicting low life, it blazes with an image of the highest life of all—that of the creative imagination." Burgess. 99 Novels

Casey, John, 1939-

Spartina. Knopf 1989 375p

ISBN 0-394-50098-9

* LC 88-45765

"Dick Pierce is an angry man because he has seen property belonging to his family in his fishing village in Rhode Island bought up by affluent people for their summer homes. He works hard, not really making enough for his family, going out for crabs, lobsters, and swordfish. Pierce's relationship with his wife and his two sons is uneasy and his love for the boat he is building (Spartina—named for the tough grass that thrives on salt in marshy water) crowds out all other considerations. His discontent and need for money lead him to dangerous disregard for the law and into a passsionate affair with Elsie Buttrick, an unconventional and independent young woman. A stunning episode in the novel is Pierce's exposing his new boat to the force of a violent hurricane because there is no safe harbor for it." Shapiro. Fic for Youth. 3d edition

It is the author's "fearless romantic insistence on lyric, even mythic symbolism, coupled with the relentless salt-smack clarity of realistic detail, that makes 'Spartina' just possibly the best American novel about going fishing since 'The Old Man and the Sea,' maybe even 'Moby-Dick.'" N Y Times Book Rev

Cassirer, Nadine Gordimer *See* Gordimer, Nadine, 1923-

Castellanos Moya, Horacio, 1957-

Senselessness; translated from the Spanish by Katherine Silver. New Directions 2008 142p pa $15.95

ISBN 978-0-8112-1707-1; 0-8112-1707-8

* LC 2008-2235

Original Spanish edition, 2005

"The book's narrator, a hapless copy editor, arrives in an unnamed Central American country in order to 'manicure' an exhaustive, 1,100-page report on the military's abuses of the indigenous population." Time Out N Y

"A chaptered but nearly paragraphless 142 pages, Senselessness reads like a vicious, novella-length rant by the Austrian writer Thomas Bernhard—had Bernhard spent his developmental years drinking mescal in a corrupt, oppressively Catholic Latin America and having sex with passionate Spanish women. Bernhard's influence is obvious, like Joyce's influence on Flann O'Brien and J.P. Donleavy, but never burdensome. By filtering Bernhard's addled consciousness through his own, and steeping it in the humidity of a thinly disguised Guatemala, the novel provides a kind of meta-analysis of the neurotic Austrian master—though it stands alone, too, as an innovative and invigoratingly twisted piece of art." Village Voice

Cather, Willa, 1873-1947

Death comes for the archbishop. Knopf 1992
xxvii, 297p $17; pa $11.95
    ISBN 0-679-41319-7; 0-679-72889-9 (pa)

*

"Everyman's library"
First published 1927
"Bishop Jean Latour and his vicar Father Joseph Vaillant together create pioneer missions and organize the
new diocese of New Mexico. . . . The two combine to
triumph over the apathy of the Hopi and Navajo Indians,
the opposition of corrupt Spanish priests, and adverse climatic and topographic conditions. They are assisted by
Kit Carson and by such devoted Indians as the guide Jacinto. When Vaillant goes as a missionary bishop to Colorado, they are finally separated, but Latour dies soon after his friend, universally revered and respected, to lie in
state in the great Santa Fe cathedral that he himself created." Oxford Companion to Am Lit. 6th edition

    also in Cather, W. Later novels

Early novels and stories. Library of Am. 1987
1336p $40
    ISBN 0-940450-39-9   LC 86-10704
    The troll garden contains the following stories: Flavia
and her artists; The sculptor's funeral; The garden lodge;
"A death in the desert"; The marriage of Phaedra; A
Wagner matinée; Paul's case
    Omnibus edition of four novels: O pioneers! (1913);
The song of the lark (1915); My Antonia (1918); One of
ours (1922) and the story collection—The troll garden
(1905)

Later novels. Library of Am. 1990 988p
    ISBN 0-940450-52-6   LC 89-64130
    Contents: The lost lady (1923); Death comes for the
archbishop (1927); Shadows on the rock (1931); Sapphira and the slave girl (1940); The professor's house
(1925); Lucy Gayheart (1935)

A lost lady. Knopf 1923 173p o.p.
    "The story of Marian Forrester is told by Niel Herbert,
a Midwestern youth. Married to rugged old empire-
builder Captain Forrester, Marian's graciousness sets her
much above her commonplace neighbors. She becomes
the lover of his friend, Frank Ellinger, however; and after
the Captain's death due to a stroke, the lover of Ivy Peters, the man who acquires her home. Peters marries, and
the impoverished Marian returns to the West, a 'lost
lady' in the eyes of her youthful admirer, Niel. He later
hears that Marian, married to a wealthy Englishman, won
the respect and admiration of all in her new surroundings." Haydn. Thesaurus of Book Dig

    also in Cather, W. Later novels

Lucy Gayheart
    In Cather, W. Later novels

My Antonia; with an introduction by Lucy
Hughes-Hallett. Knopf 1996 xxxiii, 272p $20
    ISBN 0-679-44727-X
                                    * LC 96-223945
"Everyman's library"
First published 1918 by Houghton Mifflin
"Told by Jim Burden, a New York lawyer recalling his
boyhood in Nebraska, the story concerns Antonia

Shimerda, who came with her family from Bohemia to
settle on the prairies of Nebraska. The difficulties related
to pioneering and the integration of immigrants into a
new culture are clearly portrayed." Shapiro. Fic for
Youth. 3d edition

    also in Cather, W. Early novels and stories
        p707-938

O pioneers!; edited with an introduction and
notes by Marilee Lindemann. Oxford University
Press 1999 xxxi, 179p (Oxford world's classics) pa
$9.95
    ISBN 0-19-283216-6
                                    * LC 98-35944
First published 1913 by Houghton Mifflin
"The heroic battle for survival of simple pioneer folk
in the Nebraska country of the 1880's. John Bergson, a
Swedish farmer, struggles desperately with the soil but
dies unsatisfied. His daughter Alexandra resolves to vindicate his faith, and her strong character carries her weak
older brothers and her mother along to a new zest for
life. Years of privation, are rewarded on the farm. But
when Alexandra falls in love with Carl Linstrum, and her
family objects because he is poor, he leaves to seek a
different career. After Alexandra's younger brother Emil
is killed by the jealous husband of the French girl Marie
Shabata, however, Carl gives up his plans to go to the
Klondike, returns to marry Alexandra and take up the
life of the farm." Haydn. Thesaurus of Book Dig

    also in Cather, W. Early novels and stories

One of ours
    In Cather, W. Early novels and stories

The professor's house
    In Cather, W. Later novels

Sapphira and the slave girl. Knopf 1940 295p
o.p.
    This novel "centers on the family's matriarch, Sapphira
Colbert, and her attempt to sell Nancy Till, a mixed-race
slave girl. Sapphira's plot is foiled by her husband Henry
and their widowed daughter Rachel Blake. A confident,
strong-willed invalid, Sapphira has earned the respect of
many of her slaves despite her subtle cruelty toward
Nancy. Henry is a pious miller whose simple upbringing
and passivity contrast with the aristocratic and manipulative nature of his wife. Henry's nephew Martin, a suave
but lecherous ex-soldier, tries to seduce Nancy. Rachel,
who helps Nancy flee to Canada, remains at odds with
Sapphira over the issue of slavery until the death of Rachel's daughter reconciles the pair." Merriam-Webster's
Ency of Lit

    also in Cather, W. Later novels

Shadows on the rock. Knopf 1931 280p o.p.
    "A product of Cather's interest in Catholicism, this
work is an episodic narrative of life in Quebec during
the last days of Frontenac, centered upon the life of Cé-
cile Auclair, a child recently emigrated from Old
France." Benet's Reader's Ency of Am Lit

    also in Cather, W. Later novels

The song of the lark. Houghton Mifflin 1915
580p o.p.
    This novel "tells the story of Thea Kronborg, a Colora-
do girl, the daughter of a Swedish clergyman, who has
a talent for music. She goes to Chicago to study, has an

Cather, Willa, 1873-1947—*Continued*
unhappy love affair with Fred Ottenburg, a wealthy young man who cannot obtain a divorce to marry her, and eventually becomes a soprano at the Metropolitan Opera House in New York City, famous for her Wagnerian roles." Reader's Ency. 3d edition

In Cather, W. Early novels and stories

The troll garden
In Cather, W. Early novels and stories
In Cather, W. Willa Cather's collected short fiction, 1892-1912

Willa Cather's collected short fiction, 1892-1912. University of Neb. Press 1970 3v in 1
ISBN 0-8032-0770-0
First published 1965. This edition includes an attributed unsigned story: The elopement of Allen Poole
Contents: v 1 The Bohemian girl; v2 The troll garden {published separately, 1905}; v3 On the Divide
Short stories included are: v 1 The Bohemian girl; Behind the Singing Tower; The joy of Nelly Deane; The enchanted bluff; On the gulls' road; Eleanor's house; The willing muse; The profile; The namesake; v2 The troll garden; Flavia and her artists; The sculptor's funeral; The garden lodge; "A death in the desert"; The marriage of Phaedra; A Wagner matinee; Paul's case; v3 On the Divide; The treasure of Far Island; The Professor's commencement; El Dorado; A Kansas recessional; Jack-a-Boy; The conversion of Sum Loo; A singer's romance; The affair at Grover Station; The sentimentality of William Tavener; Eric Hermannson's soul; The westbound train; The way of the world; Nanette: an aside; The prodigies; A resurrection; The strategy of the Were-Wolf Dog; The Count of Crow's Nest; Tommy, the unsentimental; A night at Greenway Court; On the Divide; "The fear that walks by noonday"; The clemency of the court; A son of the Celestial; A tale of the white pyramid; Lou, the prophet; Peter

Caunitz, William J.

Chains of command. Dutton 1999 323p $23.95
ISBN 0-525-94514-8   LC 99-28778
"The book begins with the murder of a cop (with $5000 in his pocket) and his mistress (who has ties to the Cali drug cartel) in Washington Heights. Their deaths signal serious trouble for First Deputy Police Commissioner Suzanne Albrecht, who is in line to become the next commissioner and is worried that a scandal in the Heights will ruin her chances. So she enlists the aid of Matt Stuart, a lieutenant in the NYPD's intelligence division. When two street dealers are murdered, threatening to set off a territorial battle over the area's drug market, Albrecht and Stuart must act fast to avert a blood bath and save a political career." Libr J
"Christopher Newman deserves a hunk of credit for finishing the last book of his good friend William J. Caunitz, who died before he could complete the job himself. Whoever did what, this is one of the best police procedurals you're likely to read this season. The procedures are impeccable, the dialogue gleefully flouts all rules of grammar and the characters are poster children for their representative neighborhoods." N Y Times Book Rev

One Police Plaza. Crown 1984 369p
ISBN 0-517-55029-6   LC 83-14323

"This story details the tenacious search of a New York police detective for the murderer responsible for a heinous crime. Lt. Dan Malone is called in on the murder and is caught up in the apparent inconsistencies of the case. Despite threats, direct orders and attempts on his life, Malone refuses to back off. His tenacity pays off, . . . and he is able to solve the murder. The murder, though, includes elements of international terrorism and espionage as well as internal departmental vigilante activities." Best Sellers
The author "expertly depicts the stark reality of the police officer's life and work, and his hard-edged prose drives the story to a stunning conclusion." Booklist

Cavallo, Evelyn *See* Spark, Muriel

Céline, Louis-Ferdinand, 1894-1961

Journey to the end of the night; translated from the French by John H. P. Marks. Little, Brown 1934 509p o.p.
*

Original French edition, 1932
"Ferdinand Bardamu, the cynical, disillusioned hero, wanders aimlessly through war-torn Europe, surrounded by destruction and putrefaction. Man, as Céline portrays him, attempts to flee from the solitude of his existence and the impossibility of helping his fellow humans but succeeds only in embracing evil and death. The novel caused a scandal when it was published because of the coarsness of its language and the unrelieved blackness of its pessimism. Yet the language is a highly original attempt to reproduce the proletarian *argot* that reflects the horror and intimacy of war, and the pessimism shows Céline's desire to arouse the reader and make him aware of his condition." Reader's Ency. 4th edition

A **Century** of great Western stories; edited by John Jakes. Forge 2000 525p $27.95; pa $18.95
ISBN 0-312-86986-X; 0-312-86985-1 (pa)
LC 99-462096

"A Tom Doherty Associates book"
This anthology of 30 short stories includes pieces by such writers as Owen Wister, Zane Grey, Max Brand, Bill Pronzini, Elmer Kelton and Marcia Muller
"Romance, murder, action, mystery and suspense are mixed with hefty doses of moral dilemma, guilt and redemption in these carefully plotted tales. . . . Many of the stories are appearing here for the first time since they were published in the pulps of the '30s, '40s and '50s, but their appeal is as fresh as ever." Publ Wkly

Cervantes Saavedra, Miguel de, 1547-1616

The colloquy of the dogs
In Cervantes Saavedra, M. d. Three exemplary novels p125-217

Don Quixote de la Mancha; [by] Miguel de Cervantes; translated, with a critical text based on the first editions of 1605 and 1615, and with variant readings, variorum notes, and an introduction by Samuel Putnam. Modern Library 1998 xl, 1239p $25.95
ISBN 0-679-60286-0
* LC 97-47415

Cervantes Saavedra, Miguel de, 1547-1616—
Continued

Original Spanish edition, published in two parts, 1605 and 1615

"Originally conceived as a comic satire against the chivalric romances then in literary vogue, the novel describes realistically what befalls an elderly knight who, his head bemused by reading romances, sets out on his old horse Rosinante, with his pragmatic squire Sancho Panza, to seek adventure. In the process, he also finds love in the person of the pleasant Dulcinea. Contemporaries evidently did not take the book as seriously as later generations have done, but by the end of the 17th century it was deemed highly significant, especially abroad. It came to be seen as a mock epic in prose, and the 'grave and serious air' of the author's irony was much admired. In the history of the modern novel the role of *Don Quixote* is recognized as seminal." Merriam-Webster's Ency of Lit

Man of glass
    In Cervantes Saavedra, M. d. Three exemplary novels p75-121

Rinconete and Cortadillo
    In Cervantes Saavedra, M. d. Three exemplary novels p9-71

Three exemplary novels; translated by Samuel Putnam; illustrated by Luis Quintanilla. Viking 1950 xxi, 232p il o.p.

Part of a collection first published 1613 in Spain
Rinconete and Cortadillo is a picaresque novella about thieves in early 17th century Seville. Man of glass is a philosophical tale set in 17th century Italy about a man intent on exposing the lie upon which human existence is based. The colloquy of the dogs describes life in 17th century Spain

Chabon, Michael

The amazing adventures of Kavalier and Clay; a novel. Random House 2000 639p $26.95

ISBN 0-679-45004-1
                                    * LC 00-29063
"Joe Kavalier, a Czech war refugee, and his American-born cousin Sammy Clay are {this} novel's protagonists. They create a comic-book crusader known as the Escapist. . . . A young artist with Harry Houdini's ability to pick locks while holding his breath, Kavalier has escaped Nazi-occupied Czechoslovakia by hiding in a coffin containing the mythic Golem of Prague." Time

"Themes are masterfully explored, leaving the book's sense of humor intact and characters so highly developed they could walk off the page." Newsweek

The Yiddish policemen's union; a novel. HarperCollins Publishers 2007 414p $26.95

ISBN 978-0-00-714982-7; 0-00-714982-4
                                    LC 2006-49751
An "alternate-history saga of Jewish life since World War II. The premise draws on an obscure historical fact: FDR once proposed that Alaska, not Israel, become the homeland for Jews after the war. In Chabon's telling, that's exactly what happened, except, inevitably, it hasn't gone as planned: the U.S. government now has enacted a policy that will evict all Jews without proper papers

from Sitka, the center of Jewish Alaska. In the midst of this nightmare, browbeaten police detective Meyer Landsman investigates the murder of a heroin-addicted chess prodigy who happens to be the disgraced son of Sitka's most powerful rabbi." Booklist

"Though the ultimate secret behind the murder that kick-starts the story involves a religious-political scheme that tips over clumsily into surreal satire, the remainder of the book is so authoritatively and minutely imagined that the reader, absorbed in the plight of [the author's] shambling hero, really doesn't mind. . . . Mr. Chabon has so thoroughly conjured the fictional world of Sitka—its history, culture, geography, its incestuous and byzantine political and sectarian divisions—that the reader comes to take its existence for granted." N Y Times (Late N Y Ed)

Challans, Mary *See* Renault, Mary, 1905-1983

Chandler, Raymond, 1888-1959

The big sleep. Knopf 1939 277p o.p.
                                                            *
"A tale of degeneracy in southern California, in which two Hollywood heiresses become mixed up in blackmail and murder; and Philip Marlowe is the private detective, who tells the story." Washington, D.C. Public Libr

    also in Chandler, R. Stories and early novels p587-764

Farewell, my lovely
    In Chandler, R. Stories and early novels p765-984

The high window. Knopf 1942 240p o.p.
"This early exploit of Philip Marlowe's is certainly high in the merit list. The Pasadena scene, the characterization, the tough-yet-literate style match the complex plot, involving counterfeiting and blackmail. Just how the photograph of the victim was obtained is glossed over, but all other details are clearly etched." Barzun. Cat of Crime. Rev and enl edition

    also in Chandler, R. Stories and early novels p985-1177

The lady in the lake. Knopf 1943 216p o.p.
"A young wife has been missing for a month and Marlowe is hired by the husband whom she is about to leave for another man. The exposition of situation and character is done with remarkable pace and skill. . . . The scene shifts to Little Fawn Lake, where talk between a local woman, the caretaker of the missing wife's cabin, and Marlowe produces speculation about the absent girl, her lover, and also the missing wife of the caretaker; whereupon comes the dramatic discovery of the corpse in the lake. It is 'not' Marlowe's quarry. From then on this superb tale moves through a maze of puzzles and disclosures to its perfect conclusion. Marlowe makes a greater use of physical clues and ratiocination in this exploit than in any other. It is Chandler's masterpiece and true detection." Barzun. Cat of Crime. Rev and enl edition

    In Chandler, R. Later novels and other writings

Later novels and other writings. Library of Am. 1995 1076p $35

ISBN 1-883011-08-6   LC 94-43705

Chandler, Raymond, 1888-1959—*Continued*

Contents: The lady in the lake; The little sister; The long goodbye; Playback; Double indemnity; Selected essays and letters

The lady in the lake and The long goodbye are entered separately. In The little sister (1949), Marlowe takes on a case set in Hollywood involving a young starlet and her brother. In Playback (1958), "Marlowe is weakening (by his own standards), since he takes on an impossible girl who is running away from a quite imaginary threat and forces her to trust him. There is some silly back-and-forth with $5,000 of traveler's checks, a double fornication without much zest, and at last a transatlantic phone call summoning Marlowe to marry his true love." Barzun. Cat of Crime. Rev and enl ed

The little sister
In Chandler, R. Later novels and other writings

The long goodbye. Houghton Mifflin 1953 316p o.p.

Detective Philip Marlowe provides moral support for Terry Lennox who is running away to Mexico because he thinks he committed a murder

This novel is one of Chandler's "most meticulously plotted and by some stretches his most corrosive. What he gives us here is painful if exciting pleasure." N Y Her Trib Books

also in Chandler, R. Later novels and other writings

Playback
In Chandler, R. Later novels and other writings

Raymond Chandler; collected stories; with an introduction by John Bayley. Knopf 2002 xxxvii, 1299p $27.50

ISBN 0-375-41500-9

"Everyman's library"

Contents: Blackmailers don't shoot; Smart-aleck kill; Finger man; Killer in the rain; Nevada gas; Spanish blood; Guns at Cyrano's; The man who liked dogs; Pick-up on Noon Street; Goldfish; The curtain; Try the girl; Mandarin's jade; Red wind; The king in yellow; Bay City blues; The lady in the lake; Pearls are a nuisance; Trouble is my business; I'll be waiting; The bronze door; No crime in the mountains; Professor Bingo's snuff; The pencil; English summer

"To read these 25 stories, 22 of which were originally published in the 1930s, consecutively is to watch Chandler's craft develop. . . . Only Chandler fanatics will want to read every word of this encyclopedic volume, but anyone with any interest in the history of hard-boiled fiction should sample its groundbreaking wares." Booklist

Stories and early novels. Library of Am. 1995 1199p $35

ISBN 1-883011-07-8 LC 94-45462

Contents: Pulp stories; The big sleep; Farewell, my lovely; The high window

The big sleep and The high window are entered separately. Pulp stories includes the following titles: Blackmailers don't shoot; Smart-aleck kill; Finger man; Nevada gas; Spanish blood; Guns at Cyrano's; Pick-up on Noon Street; Goldfish; Red wind; The king in yellow; Pearls are a nuisance; Trouble is my business; I'll be waiting

Farewell, my lovely (1940), a mystery featuring Philip Marlowe, is a "model of complexity kept under control, with a holocaust at the end. Its contents are the now familiar ones of political and personal corruption, double-crossing, and the woman killer." Barzun. Cat of Crime. Rev and enl edition

Chaon, Dan

Await your reply; a novel. Ballantine Books 2009 324p $25

ISBN 978-0-345-47602-9; 0-345-47602-6

LC 2009-21245

"Lucy is a recent high school graduate who leaves a small town in Ohio with her high-school teacher after her parents are killed. Only just above-average in intelligence, she's led to believe she's a stellar thinker by her witty, Maserati-driving, Yale-educated history teacher, George Orson. Miles is searching for his long-gone twin brother, Hayden, a probable schizophrenic. Flashbacks to the twins' childhoods reveal that Miles feels inferior to Hayden, who antagonized him throughout childhood. . . . College student Ryan, who was adopted, leaves a structured life in small-town Iowa to live with his biological father. . . . These stories, at first, present a lot of detail but not a lot of direction, but all the ink spent on backstory and character development prove to be worth it when the characters' lives intersect, and the novel turns from stories about people trying to find themselves to a page-turning mystery." Pittsburgh Post-Gazette

Charyn, Jerome, 1937-

Johnny One-Eye; a tale of the American Revolution. W.W. Norton & Co. 2008 479p $25.95

ISBN 978-0-393-06497-1; 0-393-06497-2

LC 2007-34343

A "comic novel set during the American Revolution. At its center is young double agent John Stocking, known as Johnny One-Eye after an injury he received fighting for Benedict Arnold in Canada. Johnny, his mother — Mrs. Gert Jennings, a flame-haired, freckle-faced bordello queen — and a stunning young prostitute named Clara form an odd little family to whom George Washington himself grows ever attached." Entertainment Wkly

"What 'Johnny One-Eye' lacks in narrative momentum it handily supplies in antics and atmosphere. Here are the founding fathers on a lark; here is the Revolution waged at the gaming table and in the bedroom. . . . Charyn hasn't woven a taut narrative from a lurching plot. What he has done is to create a rollicking tale in which — true to the dictates of the genre — our hapless rogue makes good. That he should do so in Washington's 'runt of a republic' isn't such a stretch. When you think about it, the American Revolution was something of a picaresque too." International Herald Tribune

Chase, Loretta Lynda, 1949-

The last hellion; [by] Loretta Chase. Five Star 1999 393p (Five Star standard print romance series)

ISBN 0-7862-1989-0 LC 99-26433

Chase, Loretta Lynda, 1949-—*Continued*

"When Vere Mallory, the seventh Duke of Ainswood and the last of the infamous 'Mallory Hellions,' ends up in the mud after being properly slugged by an outspoken, crusading journalist of Amazonian proportions, he decides to teach her a lesson—and ends up learning a few things himself. Well-matched, appealing protagonists, a lively, witty writing style, and excellent dialog complement this compelling story that addresses some of the more relevant social issues of the Regency era." Libr J

Lord of scoundrels. Five Star 1999 352p (Five Star standard print romance series)
ISBN 0-7862-2252-2   LC 99-45472

"A young woman sets out to save her brother from the influence of the wicked Marquess of Dain and falls under the 'Devil's' spell herself in this classic Regency-set historical." Libr J

Chase-Riboud, Barbara, 1939-

Sally Hemings; a novel. Viking 1979 348p
ISBN 0-670-61605-2   LC 78-12682

"A Seaver book"

A novel about the relationship between Thomas Jefferson and his mistress Sally Hemings, a slave, whom he lived with for thirty-eight years

"If it indeed existed, the relationship must have been much as the author depicts it in this fine first novel: a mixture of love and hate, of tenderness and cruelty, and of freedom and bondage. The book is well researched, well written, insightful, and entertaining." Libr J

Followed by The President's daughter

Chatterjee, Upamanyu

English, August; an Indian story; introduction by Akhil Sharma. New York Review Books 2006 326p (New York Review Books classics) pa $14.95
ISBN 1-59017-179-9   LC 2005-22842

First published 1988 in India

"This satiric novel chronicles the reluctant coming of age of a privileged young man who has just entered the prestigious Indian Administrative Service. Posted to a small town deep in the interior, he finds himself a foreigner in his own country, wary of cholera, defenseless against mosquitoes, and shocked by the sight of a tribal woman: 'They exist, he shrieked silently, outside arty films about tribal exploitation and agrarian reform.' In revolt, he sneaks out of meetings, pretends to be the son of Antarctic explorers, and smokes copious amounts of pot. He's an avatar of the Western slacker: overeducated, bored, plagued with doubts, and incapable of action. Still, Chatterjee's story is uniquely Indian, as he plumbs his hero's fear of being 'just one more urban Indian bewitched by America's hard sell in the Third World.'" New Yorker

Chatwin, Bruce

Utz. Viking 1989 154p
ISBN 0-670-82497-6   LC 88-40310

This novel details the "existence of one Kaspar Utz, owner of a superb private collection of Meissen porcelain in Prague. The novel is narrated by a writer who goes to the Czech capital in 1967 to research the Holy Roman Emperor Rudolph II's passion for collecting objets d'art. His research—which he hopes will lead him to conclusions about the psychology of the compulsive collector—first leads him to the door of Kaspar Utz. What develops from this meeting affords the narrator a rich opportunity to observe and attempt to fathom human nature." Booklist

"The hero of Mr. Chatwin's provocative short novel is a successful survivor. He is part Jewish but has managed to survive Hitler. . . . {Utz is} required to bequeath the collection to the state, and what he does about that insult to his elegant eighteenth-century companions becomes his own peculiar final solution. Mr. Chatwin has created an intriguing proposition—that obedient passivity can amount to successful rebellion." Atlantic

Chaudhuri, Amit, 1962-

The immortals. Alfred A. Knopf 2009 333p $25.95
ISBN 978-0-307-27022-1; 0-307-27022-X
                              LC 2009-24461

This novel, "set in Bombay during the nineteen-seventies and eighties, traces the relationship between the middle-class Senguptas and their music teacher, Shyamji. Nirmalya Sengupta, a son of privilege, urges purity in art—the ustads, ragas, and shrutis of Indian classical music—while Shyamji succumbs to the exigencies of the marketplace and Hindi film music. . . . Not much happens—Sengupta's father ascends the corporate ladder, his mother takes part in recitals and shyly hopes for a record contract, and Sengupta himself discovers philosophy—but Chaudhuri lovingly evokes a fractious, contradictory city caught between tradition and modernization." New Yorker

Chayefsky, Paddy, 1923-1981

Altered states; a novel. Harper & Row 1978 184p
ISBN 0-06-010727-8   LC 77-11542

This novel tells the "story of an experiment in genetic regression. . . . Edward Jessup is a psychophysiologist with 'an extraordinary if monomaniacal mind'. His wife suspects that her coldly passionate husband may be a genius. . . . After numerous descents into the black water of an isolation tank he at last succeeds in regressing into a small, hairy, proto-human creature that eats gazelles in the university park and experiences 'the primal unity'. He smashes his way out of the laboratory and exults in the taste of warm blood." New Statesman (1913)

"What makes this shocking fantasy work is not only Chayefsky's dramatic skill . . . but also the authority of his prodigious research in chemistry, biology, and medicine. . . . The result is a marvelous and exciting work of the imagination." Saturday Rev

Chazin, Suzanne

Flashover. Putnam 2002 332p
ISBN 0-399-14850-7   LC 2001-48772

"Fire marshal Georgia Skeehan and her veteran sidekick, Randy Carter, are called to investigate a fire that took the life of a retired doctor with a history of denying pensions to firefighters disabled in the line of duty. To

LIST OF FICTIONAL WORKS

Chazin, Suzanne—*Continued*

complicate matters, Georgia's best friend, NYPD detective Connie Ruiz, confirms that there is talk of a bomb threat to a fuel pipeline under the city and that whoever is behind it knew the retired doctor." Publ Wkly

"Fans of Patricia Cornwell will appreciate the gritty, realistic details Chazin provides concerning the techniques used to investigate suspicious fires. The appealing main character and the fast pace will keep readers turning the pages into the wee hours." Booklist

Cheever, John, 1912-1982

Bullet Park; a novel. Knopf 1969 245p o.p.
* LC 69-14730

"The interplay between [suburbanites] Eliot Nailles, Paul Hammer, and Naille's son Tony forms the structure of a novel . . . embodying many contemporary issues and problems. Using the third person, Cheever depicts Nailles as an open-faced, conscientious man, driven to desperation when his son is ill. Hammer, in a first-person account, is revealed as criminally insane beneath his [middle-class] neighborly exterior. The third part portrays Hammer's attempt to murder Tony Nailles, an act narrowly averted by his father." Booklist

The author "mixes compassion and high comedy brilliantly, holding up to view an America that is fatally schizoid in many of its manifestations. The confrontation that finally comes between Hammer and Nailles is a horrifying dark allegory of our times." Publ Wkly

also in Cheever, J. Complete novels

Collected stories and other writings. Library of America 2009 1040p $35
ISBN 978-1-59853-034-6   LC 2008-935565
Contents: Goodbye, my brother; The common day; The enormous radio; O city of broken dreams; The Hartleys; The Sutton Place story; The summer farmer; Torch song; The pot of gold; Clancy in the Tower of Babel; Christmas is a sad season for the poor; The season of divorce; The chaste Clarissa; The cure; The superintendent; The children; The sorrows of gin; O youth and beauty!; The day the pig fell into the well; The five-forty-eight; Just one more time; The housebreaker of Shady Hill; The bus to St. James's; The worm in the apple; The trouble of Marcie Flint; The bella lingua; The Wrysons; The country husband; The duchess; The scarlet moving van; Just tell me who it was; Brimmer; The golden age; The lowboy; The music teacher; A woman without a country; The death of Justina Clementina; Boy in Rome; A miscellany of characters that will not appear; The chimera; The seaside houses; The angel of the bridge; The brigadier and the golf widow; A vision of the world; Reunion; An educated American woman; Metamorphoses; Mene, mene, tekel, upharsin; Montraldo; The ocean; Marito in città; The geometry of love; The swimmer; The world of apples; Another story; Percy; The fourth alarm; Artemis, the honest well-digger; Three stories; The jewels of the Cabots; Summer theatre; Forever hold your peace; Of love: a testimony; The brothers; Publick house; When grandmother goes; These tragic years; Expelled; The autobiography of a drummer; In passing; Play a march; Town house; Roseheath; The national pastime

In addition to the stories, this volume appends several short essays on writers and writing, including a previously unpublished speech on Saul Bellow.

Complete novels. Library of America 2009 933p $35
ISBN 978-1-59853-035-3   LC 2008-935642
The Wapshot chronicle (1957) depicts a "venerable Massachusetts family in decline. . . . The Wapshot scandal [1964] continues their story by moving beyond the archetypal Yankee village of St. Botolphs and taking its characters abroad and into the planned communities of postwar America, quietly teetering on the brink of nuclear Armageddon. . . . The taut satire Bullet Park (1969), with its scathing indictment of suburbia, shows Cheever taking his novelistic gifts in a new, darker direction. But it scarcely could have prepared readers for the stunning achievement of Falconer [1977], a prison novel unlike anything in Cheever's fiction. . . . At the novel's center is Ezekiel Farragut, a college professor and drug addict serving time for murdering his brother. Within the dehumanizing confinement of the prison, he falls in love with a hustler named Jody. . . . Oh What a Paradise It Seems (1982), the novella with which the volume concludes, is a tale of a May–December relationship that also sounds an elegiac note of protest against the degradation of the environment." Publisher's note

Falconer. Knopf 1977 211p
ISBN 0-394-41071-8
                                                                    *

The novel's protagonist, Ezekiel Farragut, "is a well-read college professor, a drug addict convicted of murdering his brother, Falconer. Prison breaks Zeke Farragut of his addiction but embroils him in all the coarse, desperate gambits of prison life." Libr J

"John Cheever uses prison as an emblem for the world in this stunning novel about love, mysticism, and man's relationship with God. . . . The surface events include a prison riot, a massacre of prison cats by an enraged guard who had his steak stolen by one of them, a homosexual love affair, and a couple of breathtaking escapes, one by Farragut's lover, who dons a cassock to escape in a helicopter with a visiting bishop. Woven in and out are threads of Farragut's past life, his relationship to his wife and the other women in his life, the secret behind his hatred for his brother." Choice

also in Cheever, J. Complete novels

Oh, what a paradise it seems. Knopf 1982 99p
ISBN 0-394-51334-7   LC 81-48109
"In a novella that focuses on an aging man's regret and anger at the erosion of time on the human body and the environment, John Cheever attempts a modern fable. Lemuel Sears, elegantly elderly, is rejuvenated via an impromptu, lively and offbeat love affair. His energy is galvanized to mount a legal attack on the despoilment by landfill of a once jewel-like pond near the home of his youth. A series of bizarre but somehow connected events, including a homosexual encounter, enhance Sears' appreciation of the mystery of life and the need for renewal in the waning of the 20th century." Publ Wkly

"Ever more boldly the celebrant of the grand poetry of life, Cheever, once a taut and mordant chronicler of urban and suburban disappointments, now speaks in the cranky, granular, impulsive, confessional style of our native wise men and exhorters since Emerson. The pitch of his final page is positively Transcendental." New Yorker

also in Cheever, J. Complete novels

Cheever, John, 1912-1982—*Continued*

The Wapshot chronicle. Harper & Row 1957
307p o.p.

"Based in part on Cheever's adolescence in New England, the novel takes place in a small Massachusetts fishing village and relates the breakdown of both the Wapshot family and the town. Part One focuses on Leander, a gentle ferryboat operator harried by his tyrannical wife and his eccentric sister; he eventually swims out to sea and never returns. Part Two chronicles the disastrous lives of Leander's sons, Coverly and Moses. Told in a comic rather than a tragic vein, the novel uses experimental prose techniques to convey a nostalgic vision of a lost world." Merriam-Webster's Ency of Lit

Followed by The Wapshot scandal

also in Cheever, J. Complete novels

The Wapshot scandal. Harper & Row 1964
309p o.p.

This sequel to The Wapshot chronicle "continues the tale of the decline of the fortunes of the Wapshot family and of the mythical New England town of St. Botolphs. The 'scandal' is the discovery that Aunt Honora has never paid her income taxes, and the principal disaster stems from the long-standing oversight. The novel also traces the misfortunes of two Wapshot nephews, Coverly, a public relations man at a missile site, and Moses, an alcoholic. Despite the somberness of the main line of events, the book is not depressing; it is lighted by the high gloss of Mr. Cheever's style, by glints of humor, and especially by the warm glow of human fortitude under stress." Libr J

also in Cheever, J. Complete novels

Chekhonte, Antosha *See* Chekhov, Anton
Pavlovich, 1860-1904

Chekhov, Anton Pavlovich, 1860-1904

Complete short novels; translated from the Russian by Richard Pevear and Larissa Volokhonsky; with an introduction by Richard Pevear. Alfred A. Knopf 2004 548p (Everyman's Library) $23

ISBN 1-400-04049-3   LC 2003-64595

The steppe is "an account of a nine-year-old boy's frightening journey by wagon train across the steppe of southern Russia. The Duel sets two decadent figures–a fanatical rationalist and a man of literary sensibility–on a collision course that ends in a series of surprising reversals. In The Story of an Unknown Man, a political radical spying on an important official by serving as valet to his son gradually discovers that his own terminal illness has changed his long-held priorities in startling ways. Three Years recounts a complex series of ironies in the personal life of a rich but passive Moscow merchant. In My Life, a man renounces wealth and social position for a life of manual labor." Publisher's note

The duel
   In Chekhov, A. P. Complete short novels

Early short stories, 1883-1888; edited by Shelby Foote; translated by Constance Garnett. Modern Lib. 1999 642p

ISBN 0-679-60317-4   LC 98-20049

Contents: Joy; The death of a government clerk; A daughter of Albion; Fat and thin; The bird market; Choristers; Minds in ferment; A chameleon; In the graveyard; Oysters; The marshal's widow; The fish; The huntsman; A malefactor; The head of the family; A dead body; The cook's wedding; Overdoing it; Old age; Sorrow; Mari d'elle; The looking-glass; Art; A blunder; Children; Misery; An upheaval; The requiem; Anyuta; The witch; A joke; Agafya; A story without an end; Grisha; Love; A gentleman friend; The privy councillor; A day in the country; The chorus girl; A misfortune; A trifle from life; Difficult people; In the court; An incident; A work of art; Vanka; On the road; Easter eve; The beggar; An inadvertence; Verotchka; Shrove Tuesday; A bad business; Home; Typhus; The cossack; Volodya; Happiness; Zinotchka; The doctor; The runaway; The cattle-dealers; In trouble; The kiss; Boys; Kashtanka; A lady's story; A story without a title; The steppe; Lights

Following his introduction Foote presents seventy of Chekhov's early stories

Later short stories, 1888-1903; edited by Shelby Foote; translated by Constance Garnett. Modern Lib. 1999 628p

ISBN 0-679-60316-6   LC 98-20048

Contents: Sleepy; The beauties; The party; The shoemaker and the devil; The bet; A nervous breakdown; The princess; The horse-stealers; Gusev; Peasant wives; The grasshopper; After the theatre; In exile; Neighbours; Terror; The helpmate; The two Volodyas; Rothschild's fiddle; The student; The teacher of literature; At a country house; The head-gardener's story; Whitebrow; "Anna on the neck"; Ariadne; An artist's story; The Petchenyeg; At home; The schoolmistress; The man in a case; Gooseberries; About love; Ionitch; A doctor's visit; A dreary story; The darling; The new villa; On official duty; The lady with the dog; At Christmas time; The bishop; Betrothed

Longer stories from the last decade; {by} Anton Chekhov; translated by Constance Garnett. Modern Lib. 1993 611p

ISBN 0-679-60063-9   LC 93-14536

Contents: The duel; The wife; Ward no. 6; An anonymous story; The black monk; A woman's kingdom; Three years; The murder; My life; Peasants; In the ravine

My life
   In Chekhov, A. P. Complete short novels

The steppe
   In Chekhov, A. P. Complete short novels

The story of an unknown man
   In Chekhov, A. P. Complete short novels

Three years
   In Chekhov, A. P. Complete short novels

Chen, Da, 1962-

Brothers; a novel. Shaye Areheart Books 2006
421p $25

ISBN 1-4000-9728-2   LC 2005-36267

Chen, Da, 1962——*Continued*

This saga, "set against the backdrop of the Chinese Cultural Revolution revolves around two half brothers separated by fate. As the legitimate son of a general, Tan Long enjoys every advantage his father's rank provides. Shento, the military leader's bastard child, is not so lucky. His mother, the general's mistress, commits suicide mere moments after his birth; his father denies his existence. The two boys approach manhood with no knowledge of one another. Tan is groomed to become a leader, while Shento is sent to an orphanage run by sadists. When the Long family falls out of favor after Chairman Mao's death, they leave Beijing for their rural ancestral home, where Tan plants the seeds of his career as an entrepreneur. Shento, meanwhile, rises to the head of the new president's security detail, determined to exact revenge on his father. The two brothers have similar taste in women—both fall in love with the beautiful orphan Sumi Wo—but vastly different views on democracy." Booklist

"Da Chen has achieved something that sounds simple but is, in fact, close to impossible: he brings the Western reader into the guts of the conflict, the agonies and the revelations of events that shook the world's largest population in the 35 years after 1960, when Shento and his brother were born. Make no mistake, this is not contemporary history retold. This is magnificent fiction. It transcends the events it chronicles and does what fiction at its best should do: it changes our internal landscape." Washington Post Book World

Chenoweth, Emily

Hello goodbye; a novel. Random House 2009 273p $25

ISBN 978-1-4000-6517-2; 1-4000-6517-8

LC 2008-38496

"Elliott is the headmaster of a shabby private school in Ohio; his wife, Helen, is a juvenile-court counsellor. When a doctor tells Elliott that his wife has a terminal brain tumor, he plans a vacation at a grand New England hotel. . . . Old friends are invited, for what they learn will be their final visit with Helen, but neither she nor her daughter, Abby, is told how sick Helen really is. Chenoweth writes with a restraint that allows minor gestures to become elegantly weighted with meaning." New Yorker

Cherryh, C. J., 1942-

The collected short fiction of C.J. Cherryh. DAW Bks. 2004 642p $23.95

ISBN 0-7564-0217-4

Contents: The only death in the city; The haunted tower; Ice; Nightgame; Highliner; The general; MasKs; Cassandra; Threads of time; Companions; A theif in Korianth; The last tower; The brothers; The dark king; Homecoming; The dreamstone; Sea Change; Willow; Of law and magic; The unshadowed land; Pots; The scapegoat; A gift of prophecy; Wings; A much briefer history of time; Gwydion and the dragon; Mech; The Sandman, the Tinman, and the BettyB

"Cherryh demonstrates a fine flair for compact storytelling that encompasses science, fantasy, and myth." Libr J

Finity's End. Warner Bks. 1997 471p

ISBN 0-446-52072-1

LC 96-37992

In this Merchanter universe novel, "The ship *Finity's End*, seriously shorthanded after the Union-Alliance War, returns to the Pell station to reclaim Fletcher Neihart, who grew up on the station after his mother was left there during the war. Young Fletcher, however, has a real gift for dealing with Pell's native inhabitants and no interest in being frog-marched aboard *Finity's End* or adjusting to the role of a new crew member." Booklist

"Despite an abundance of exciting action, this is character-driven drama that represents old-fashioned SF at its very best." Publ Wkly

Foreigner; a novel of first contact. DAW Bks. 1994 378p

ISBN 0-88677-590-6

* LC 94-179662

"Set on an alien world where the descendants of humans marooned in a long-ago starship accident live segregated from the indigenous *atevi* on a remote island, this {novel} . . . addresses the complicated issue of how humans might have to compromise to survive on a planet where they are barely tolerated by the original, humanoid inhabitants." Publ Wkly

"Cherryh plays her strongest suit in this exploration of human/alien contact, producing an incisive study-in-contrast of what it means to be human in a world where trust is nonexistent." Libr J

Followed by Invader

Chesterton, G. K. (Gilbert Keith), 1874-1936

Father Brown mystery stories; selected and edited with an introduction by Raymond T. Bond. Dodd, Mead 1962 246p o.p.

Contents: The blue cross; The queer feet; The flying stars; The invisible man; The sins of Prince Saradine; The absence of Mr. Glass; The dagger with wings; The oracle of the dog; The insoluble problem

The Father Brown omnibus; with a preface by Auberon Waugh. Dodd, Mead 1983 993p

ISBN 0-396-08159-2

First omnibus edition published 1933; this is a reissue of the 1951 edition analyzed in Short story index, with a new preface by Auberon Waugh

Contents: The wisdom of Father Brown: The absence of Mr. Glass; The paradise of thieves; The duel of Dr. Hirsch; The man in the passage; The mistake of the machine; The head of Caesar; The purple wig; The perishing of the Pendragons; The God of the Gongs; The salad of Colonel Cray; The strange crime of John Boulnois; The fairy tale of Father Brown

The incredulity of Father Brown: The resurrection of Father Brown; The arrow of heaven; The oracle of the dog; The miracle of Moon Crescent; The curse of the golden cross; The dagger with wings; The doom of the Darnaways; The ghost of Gideon Wise

The secret of Father Brown: The secret of Father Brown; The mirror of the magistrate; The man with two beards; The song of the flying fish; The actor and the alibi; The vanishing of Vaudrey; The worst crime in the world; The red moon of Meru; The chief mourner of Marne; The secret of Flambeau

The scandal of Father Brown: The scandal of Father Brown; The quick one; The blast of the book; The green man; The pursuit of Mr. Blue; The crime of the communist; The point of a pin; The insoluble problem; The vampire of the village

Chesterton, G. K. (Gilbert Keith), 1874-1936—
Continued

The incredulity of Father Brown
In Chesterton, G. K. The Father Brown omnibus p433-630

The innocence of Father Brown. Lane 1911 334p o.p.
Contents: The blue cross; The secret garden; The queer feet; The flying stars; The invisible man; The honour of Israel Gow; The wrong shape; The sins of Prince Saradine; The hammer of God; The eye of Apollo; The sign of the broken sword; The three tools of death

also in Chesterton, G. K. The Father Brown omnibus p1-226

The scandal of Father Brown
In Chesterton, G. K. The Father Brown omnibus p815-974

The secret of Father Brown
In Chesterton, G. K. The Father Brown omnibus p631-811

The wisdom of Father Brown
In Chesterton, G. K. The Father Brown omnibus p227-431

Chesterton, Gilbert Keith *See* Chesterton, G. K. (Gilbert Keith), 1874-1936

Chevalier, Tracy, 1962-

Burning bright. Dutton 2007 311p $24.95
ISBN 978-0-525-94978-7; 0-525-94978-X
LC 2006-26898
A novel set in late 17th-century London. "After a tragic death in the family, the Kellaways are persuaded by a traveling circus owner to move to the bustling city, where they discover that they live next door to the famous William Blake: printer, poet, and political radical. A streetwise girl named Maggie befriends the youngest boy, Jem, and their coming-of-age adventures eventually provide material for Blake's Songs of Innocence and Experience. In addition, the French Revolution has made everyone jittery, and the family is soon caught up in the excitement and uncertainty of political unrest; they also face economic hardship, struggling daily to earn enough to stay together. Chevalier's vivid descriptions and unusual mix of characters make this story an easy pleasure to read." Libr J

Girl with a pearl earring. Dutton 2000 240p $21.95
ISBN 0-525-94527-X
* LC 99-32493
Chevalier examines the world of artist Johannes Vermeer and the city of Delft in the 17th century through the eyes of Griet, an illiterate 17-year-old. In this novel the fictional character of Griet, a servant in the Vermeer household, acts as the model for the artist's portrait Girl With a Pearl Earring
The author "has done very well in creating the feel of a society with sharp divisions of status and creed. . . . Griet is a memorable character—reserved, wary, obser-

vant, and, although she does not know it, afflicted with a serious and ultimately dangerous crush on her employer. The situation makes a fine story, which is exceptionally well told." Atl Mon

Child, Lee

Bad luck and trouble; a Jack Reacher novel. Delacorte Press 2007 377p $26
ISBN 978-0-385-34055-7; 0-385-34055-9
LC 2006-31931
When Jack Reacher "withdraws money from an ATM, he discovers that his account has unexpectedly grown. The amount is a code that takes him to California, where a friend and former colleague from his military days tells him that another member of their former unit has been murdered. A group of people who could trust one another with their lives is now being picked off one by one." Libr J
"Throughout the book, Reacher remains fanatically interested in codes, fractions, cube roots and probabilities. The [author] who devises all this must also be acutely aware of formulas, because he is smart enough to avoid them. . . . In the world of Mr. Child's novels, what matters, and dazzles, is what works on the page." N Y Times (Late N Y Ed)

Echo burning. Putnam 2001 354p
ISBN 0-399-14726-8
LC 00-45910
Jack Reacher is "hitching a ride in Lubbock, Tex., when the Mexican wife of a sadistic landowner picks him up and gets his macho dander up with an ugly tale of physical abuse and mental torture. Although he refuses to play hit man for Carmen Greer, he agrees to hang around the family spread, keep the nasty in-laws at bay and see what happens when her husband gets out of prison for tax evasion. But things go wrong, and soon Reacher is looking for a criminal lawyer." N Y Times Book Rev
"Reacher is a one-man wrecking crew nourished only by the hunt. For anyone who thinks the hard-boiled genre is growing soft around the edges." Booklist

The enemy; a Jack Reacher novel. Delacorte Press 2004 393p $25
ISBN 0-385-33667-5
LC 2003-65282
This novel sends the military detective Jack "Reacher back to 1990. The Berlin Wall is being dismantled, and the United States Army's anti-Communist outlook is in disarray. . . . As the cold war winds down, Reacher finds himself embroiled in a Army scandal even as he wonders whether he has a future in uniform." N Y Times (Late N Y Ed)
"Known for his hold-your-breath action scenes, Child proves equally adept at portraying how a criminal investigation uses the smallest of building blocks . . . to construct a compelling circumstantial case." Booklist

The hard way; a Jack Reacher novel. Delacorte Press 2006 371p $25
ISBN 0-385-33669-1
LC 2005-51946
Former military cop Jack Reacher is "having an espresso in Greenwich Village when a man walks across the street, gets in a car, and drives away. It happens every day, but it's not always a kidnapper picking up the ransom. Soon Reacher is involved in helping a ruthless mercenary find his wife and stepdaughter before the kid-

Child, Lee—*Continued*

nappers tie up loose ends." Booklist

"The imperfections Child adds to his protagonist's character this time out, such as Reacher's not catching onto all of the questionable dealings early on in the novel, give Reacher a much-needed vulnerability. . . . [This is a] breathless, well-paced thriller that will satisfy diehard fans and newcomers." Denver Post

Nothing to lose. Delacorte Press 2008 407p $27
ISBN 978-0-385-34056-4; 0-385-34056-7
LC 2007-43735
Jack Reacher "hitchhikes into Colorado, where he finds himself crossing the metaphorical and physical line that divides the small towns of Hope and Despair. Despair lives up to its name; all Reacher wants is a cup of coffee, but what he gets is attacked by four thugs and thrown in jail on a vagrancy charge. After he's kicked out of town, Reacher reacts in his usual manner—he goes back and whips everybody's butt and busts up the town's police force. In the process, he discovers, with the help of a good-looking lady cop from Hope, that a nearby metal processing plant is part of a plan that involves the war in Iraq and an apocalyptic sect bent on ushering in the end-time. With his powerful sense of justice, dogged determination and the physical and mental skills to overcome what to most would be overwhelming odds, Jack Reacher makes an irresistible modern knight-errant." Publ Wkly

One shot; a Jack Reacher novel. Delacorte Press 2005 376p $25
ISBN 0-385-33668-3
LC 2004-58246
"Accused of five murders in what looks like an open-and-shut case, the bad guy fires his last shot: he wants to speak to Jack Reacher." Libr J

"Mr. Child's idea of heroism has nihilism around the edges but a fierce, fighting spirit at its core. In marked contrast to the brooding figures who otherwise dominate contemporary detective stories, Reacher is not one for self-doubt. His is a two-fisted decency. But Mr. Child also gives him amazing powers of deduction, a serious conscience and the occasional touch of tenderness. It's a wildly improbable mixture, one that can't be beat." N Y Times (Late N Y Ed)

Persuader; a Jack Reacher novel. Delacorte Press 2003 342p $24.95
ISBN 0-385-33666-7
LC 2002-34965
"Beginning with a stunning set-piece involving the apparent kidnapping of a college student, the novel offers the brooding Reacher, a former military policeman, the chance to settle a score with an old nemesis, renegade army intelligence officer Quinn, whom Reacher believed was dead until a chance encounter on a Boston street." Booklist

"What makes the novel really zing, though, is Reacher's narration—aunique mix of the brainy and the brutal, of strategic thinking and explosive action, moral rumination and ruthless force, marking him as one of the most memorable heroes in contemporary thrillerdom." Publ Wkly

Without fail. Putnam 2002 374p
ISBN 0-399-14861-2
LC 2001-48849

In this thriller Jack Reacher "is given the assignment of his career: to assassinate the newly elected vice president. Well, not exactly. More accurately, a nervous official high up in the Secret Service wants him to figure out . . . how the V.P. *might* be killed. When Reacher and a female confederate obligingly illustrate, the Secret Service contact reveals what Reacher has already surmised—that a serious assassination plot is under way and must be foiled." N Y Time Book Rev

This "novel is a stunner, packed with extraordinary detail regarding executive protection and overlaid with a genuine mystery that will baffle even the most astute armchair crime buffs." Booklist

Child, Lincoln, 1957-
(jt. auth) Preston, D. Brimstone
(jt. auth) Preston, D. The cabinet of curiosities
(jt. auth) Preston, D. Reliquary
(jt. auth) Preston, D. Riptide
(jt. auth) Preston, D. Still life with crows

Childress, Mark, 1957-

Crazy in Alabama. Putnam 1993 383p
ISBN 0-399-13855-2
LC 92-38334
"Peejoe, a successful screenwriter living in San Francisco, gets a call from his Aunt Lucille, who wants a part in the movie he's writing. Her request launches Peejoe into remembering the series of incredible events in both his and his aunt's lives in the summer of 1965, 'when everybody went crazy in Alabama.'" Booklist

"It is a measure of Mr. Childress's skill as a novelist—not to mention a triumphant example of style over content—that he soon had me eating out of his hand. I don't know how he did it but he managed to confront every cliché, every convention of the genre head on and pound it into submission, so that his novel seems not only fresh and original but also positively inspired." NY Times Book Rev

Chisholm, P. F., 1958-
See also Finney, Patricia, 1958-

Chkhartishvili, Grigory See Akunin, Boris, 1956-

Choi, Susan, 1969-

A person of interest; a novel. Viking 2008 356p $24.95
ISBN 978-0-670-01846-8; 0-670-01846-5
LC 2007-19873
"Lee is a surly Asian-American mathematics professor, who, twice divorced and estranged from his only daughter, has spent his life at a drab state school in the Midwest, a place 'only recently somewhat renowned' for a popular computer-science professor, Rick Hendley, whose office is next door to Lee's. When Hendley is killed by a mail bomb, Lee becomes a 'person of interest' to the F.B.I., and a suspenseful confrontation in the Idaho mountains ensues. But the story's true focus is Lee's fraught sense of his past: a friend whose wife he stole, his failure to achieve youthful ambitions, his 'immigrant's sense of hopeless illegitimacy and impending exposure.'" New Yorker

Chopin, Kate, 1851-1904

At fault
In Chopin, K. Complete novels and stories

The awakening
In Chopin, K. Complete novels and stories

Complete novels and stories. Library of America 2002 1071p $40
ISBN 1-931082-21-9   LC 2002-19450
Includes the novels At fault and The awakening; the story collecions Bayou folk and A night in Acadie; and fifty-five uncollected stories

Bayou folk (1894): A no-account Creole; In and out of old Natchitoches; In Sabine; A very fine fiddle; Beyond the bayou; Old Aunt Peggy; The return of Alcibiade; A rude awakening; The Benitous' slave; Desiree's baby; A turkey hunt; Madame Celestin's divorce; Love on the Bon-Dieu; Loka; Boulot and Boulotte; For Marse Chouchoute; A visit to Avoyelles; A wizard from Gettysburg; Ma'ame Pelagie; La belle Zoraide; A gentleman of Bayou Teche; A lady of Bayou St. John

A night in Acadie (1897): A night in Acadie; Athenaise; After the winter; Polydore; Regret; A matter of prejudice; Caline; A Dresden lady in Dixie; Neg Creol; The lilies; Azelie; Mamouche; A sentimental soul; Dead men's shoes; At Cheniere Caminada; Odalie misses mass; Cavanelle; Tante Cat'rinette; A respectable woman; Ripe figs; Ozeme's holiday

The uncollected stories included are: Emancipation. A life fable; Wiser than a god; A point at issue!; Miss Witherwell's mistake; With the violin; Mrs. Mobry's reason; The going away of Liza; The maid of Saint Phillippe; A shameful affair; A harbinger; Doctor Chevalier's lie; An embarrassing position: comedy in one act; Croque-Mitaine; A little free-mulatto; Miss McEnders; An idle fellow; The story of an hour; Lilacs; The night came slowly; Juanita; The kiss; Her letters; Two summers and two souls; The unexpected; Two portraits; Fedora; Vagabonds; Madame Martel's Christmas Eve; The recovery; A pair of silk stockings; Aunt Lympy's interference; The blind man; Ti Frere; A vocation and a voice; A mental suggestion; Suzette; The locket; A morning walk; An Egyptian cigarette; A family affair; Elizabeth Stock's one story; A horse story; The storm; The godmother; A little country girl; A reflection; Ti Demon; A December day in Dixie; Alexandre's wonderful experience; The gentleman from New Orleans; Charlie; The white eagle; The wood-choppers; Polly; The impossible Miss Meadows

At fault (1890) is a melodrama set in Louisiana centered on a love triangle between a young widow, a St. Louis businessman who purchases timber rights to her plantation, and his alcoholic wife. The awakening (1899) depicts a Southern woman's revolt against her husband and her quest for sexual and emotional fulfillment

Christensen, Inger, 1935-2009

Azorno; translated from the Danish by Denise Newman. New Directions 2009 104p pa $13.95
ISBN 978-0-8112-1657-9   LC 2009-16786
Original Swedish edition, 1967
"The book's central drama is also its opening one. It is the question of which woman meets Azorno on page eight, page eight being that of the mysterious novel within the novel ostensibly. The eponymous Azorno is cited as the protagonist of Sampel's book, yet Sampel is also called Azorno, both by himself and by the women who may or may not surround him in reality. . . . The novel's kaleidoscope of females—Xenia, Louise, Randi, Katarina, Bathsheba—all write novels or letters, but beyond existing on the page to the reader at hand (which is to say Christensen's) they are themselves written by one another in turn, defined as characters within each others' dramas. . . . It is to the novel's credit that it asks more questions than it ever answers. Just whose daydream this is we never know for sure, but at Christensen and Newman's combined best it feels like our own." Harvard Crimson

Christensen, Kate, 1962-

The great man; a novel. Doubleday 2007 305p $23.95
ISBN 978-0-385-51845-1; 0-385-51845-5
                                  LC 2007-5927
"At the center of this snippy comedy of manners is a New York-based painter and philanderer, Oscar Feldman, whose oeuvre consists of boldly rendered female nudes. That Oscar has been dead for a few years barely matters to the constellation of elderly women in his orbit: his long-suffering wife, Abigail, who rarely leaves her Upper West Side apartment; Teddy, his soignée bohemian mistress, moldering in Greenpoint; his sister Maxine, an abstract painter who is equally preoccupied with female flesh, and considered by some a greater talent. When two feckless biographers descend, looking for the inside scoop, Oscars big secret, hanging in plain view, becomes a vehicle for both rapprochement and revelation." New Yorker

Trouble; a novel. Doubleday 2009 320p $26
ISBN 978-0-385-52730-9; 0-385-52730-6
                                  LC 2008-31416
"Josie Dorvillier, a Manhattan therapist, is trapped in a loveless marriage to an academic. When her best friend from college, a rock star whose best days are behind her, draws ridicule on a celebrity blog for her affair with a much younger television actor, the two friends decide to escape to Mexico City for an uncharacteristically debauched vacation of mescal, marijuana, and men. The subject matter teeters on the edge of tabloid, and the sex scenes with Latin lovers are sometimes just cheesy, but Christensen . . . generally eschews sentimentality, spinning a stylish, even occasionally suspenseful story of middle-aged sexual awakening and female friendship." New Yorker

Christensen, Lars Saabye, 1953-

The half brother; a novel; [translated by Kenneth Steven] Arcade Pub. 2004 682p $27
ISBN 1-559-70715-1   LC 2003-19905
Original Swedish edition, 2001; this translation first published 2003 in the United Kingdom
This novel "charts 50 years in the life of an unconventional Oslo family. . . . Narrator Barnum, an award-winning screenwriter, retraces his family's history, which begins with the rape of his mother, Vera, as a young girl at the end of World War II. From this crime, Barnum's half-brother, Fred, is conceived. Fred is angry, prone to mood swings and outbursts of verbal cruelty. But he is

Christensen, Lars Saabye, 1953—*Continued*

also street-smart, self-reliant and fiercely-if erratically-protective of Barnum, a small, sensitive boy who never grows to full height. The boys live with Vera and an extended family of spirited, loving women, including the Old One, Barnum's great grandmother (a former silent movie actress), and his beer-drinking grandmother, Boletta. Barnum's father is Arnold Nilsen, an itinerant con man, who woos and marries Vera. When Barnum is almost grown up, unpredictable Fred goes to sea and disappears, leaving Barnum angry and confused." Publ Wkly

"The Half Brother combines the meticulousness of a short story and the ambition of an epic and in doing so shows time passing in a new way. By favouring event over explication and imagination over analysis it allows readers to draw any appropriate conclusions. Kenneth Steven has helped by translating the novel superbly into precise, fluent English." Times Lit Suppl

Christie, Agatha, 1890-1976

The A.B.C. murders; a Hercule Poirot mystery. Black Dog & Leventhal Publishers 2006 252p $12
ISBN 1-57912-624-3; 978-1-57912-624-7
     * LC 2006-45734
First published 1936 by Dodd, Mead & Company
This novel is "about a serial killer who announces his apparently unmotivated killings in advance to Poirot; the only clue is a railway guide left at the scene of each crime. In the opinion of many critics, this is one of Dame Agatha's greatest detective novels." Ency of Mystery & Detection

And then there were none. St. Martin's Griffin 2004 264p pa $12.95
ISBN 0-312-33087-1
     * LC 2004-41165
First published 1939 in the United Kingdom with title: Ten little niggers; first United States edition, 1940, by Dodd, Mead. Variant title: Ten little Indians
"A tour de force on the following trapeze: invitations go out to a group of people, all of whom have been responsible for the death of someone by negligence of intent. The island on which the party is gathered is owned by the would-be avenger of all those deaths. The events and the tension produced by the gradual polishing off of the undetected culprits are beautifully done. One improbability, well hidden, makes the whole thing plausible." Barzun. Cat of Crime. Rev and enl edition

The body in the library. Dodd, Mead 1942 245p o.p.
"The body that turns up in the married colonel's library is that of a dancing hostess from a neighboring seaside hotel. The setting is St. Mary Mead, whence Miss Marple has drawn her knowledge of human evil and duplicity and applies it to the case at hand, predicting a second murder and averting a third." Barzun. Cat of Crime. Rev and enl edition

Curtain. Dodd, Mead 1975 238p
ISBN 0-396-07191-0
            *
"In this her last book, which contrives Poirot's death *proprio motu*, the old grand master shows that her powers of invention and execution remained strong and fresh till the end. Her villain acts villainous in an entirely new way and from an original yet convincing motive. As for Poirot's performance, it is charged with a new purposefulness, ending in a fine display of moral conscience. The story may have one or two moments of weak writing and even an unparsable sentence, but it is an astonishing piece of work nevertheless." Barzun. Cat of Crime. Rev and enl edition

Endless night. Dodd, Mead 1968 o.p.
First published 1967 in the United Kingdom
"A sharp break with all her previous work: none of her usual detectives. No résumé would be fair since the impact of the book depends upon a skillfully worked-out *volte-face* involving two characters. The creator of Roger Ackroyd has done it again, in a different way, but without any pretense at detection." Barzun. Cat of Crime. Rev and enl edition

The Hollow. Putnam 1992 c1974 296p
ISBN 0-399-13727-0   LC 91-31855
"A Winterbrook edition"
First published 1946; copyright renewed 1974
"A triumph of Christie's art, not so much of characterization—for the detective story does not really permit true character study—but of *motive-building*. That is where A.C. is unrivaled. She knows how to make plausible the divergence between action and motive that maintains uncertainty until the physical clues, the times, and other objective facts mesh with motive to disclose the culprit. The great art is to multiply the ambiguities of feeling, action, and gesture without falling into obvious patterns about greed, revenge, and the like. Here the familiar figure of the able, virile, brilliant man whom women go for is admirably sketched and provided with three possible women murderers and their possibly jealous men. In addition, an elderly *femme folle* very well done—and Poirot." Barzun. Cat of Crime. Rev and enl edition

Mrs. McGinty's dead. Dodd, Mead 1952 c1951 243p o.p.
First published 1951 in the United Kingdom with title: Blood will tell
"A Poirot story with Mrs. Oliver thrown in for humor, otherwise, an ingenious plot involving the discovery of one of the offspring of some scandals of 20 years earlier, so as to account for the murder of a charwoman who presumably found an incriminating photograph. Complex and well handled, as well as amusing." Barzun. Cat of Crime. Rev and enl edition

The murder at the vicarage; a detective story. Dodd, Mead 1930 319p o.p.
Colonel Protheroe, the heartily disliked squire of St Mary Mead, is the victim. The fact that his wife is desperately in love with another man seems to have supplied motive for murder on the part of two people at least. But shrewd Miss Marple points out several other possibilities
"The plot of this tale is intricate. . . . But it is well constructed and holds the reader's attention on the problem of who wanted Col. Protheroe out of the way. The byplay between the vicar and his flirtatious wife is also an amusing innovation." Barzun. Cat of Crime. Rev and enl edition

Christie, Agatha, 1890-1976—*Continued*

Murder in the Calais coach. Dodd, Mead 1934 302p o.p.

          *

A man is murdered on a train going from Istanbul to Calais. The famous detective Hercule Poirot happens to be on board and unravels the mystery

"This is the tour de force in which Agatha makes conspiracy believable and enlivens it by a really satisfying description of the Taurus Express (part of the Orient system)." Barzun. Cat of Crime. Rev and enl edition

A murder is announced. Dodd, Mead 1950 248p o.p.

"A well-told story—her 50th—of blackmail and murder in an English village. Miss Marple does the detecting, and the author plays very fair with the reader in the laying down of a trail leading to the unmasking of a most satisfactory least likely person." Barzun. Cat of Crime. Rev and enl edition

The murder of Roger Ackroyd. Dodd, Mead 1926 306p o.p.

"Roger Ackroyd, a retired business man, is found dead in his study shortly after the suicide of the woman he was to have married. Suspicion and the police point to Ackroyd's adopted son as the murderer, but the outcome of the story is a complete surprise. As in others of Miss Christie's tales, the mystery is solved by . . . M. Poirot." Booklist

The pale horse. Dodd, Mead 1962 c1961 242p o.p.

          *

First published 1961 in the United Kingdom

A story of a Catholic priest who was murdered after hearing a dying woman's confession. "On his body was discovered a list of names, mysterious in that the people had nothing in common; yet when Mark Easterbrook came to inquire into the circumstances of the people named, he began to discover a connection between them, and an ominous pattern." Publisher's note

"This story relies on Mrs. Oliver without Poirot: detection is carried out by an oldish-young scholar called Mark Easterbrook, and what he investigates is superbly organized murder compounded with black magic. A classic treatment of the paralytic suspect-cum-wheelchair is thrown in for good measure." Barzun. Cat of Crime. Rev and enl edition

Three blind mice

  In Christie, A. Three blind mice and other stories p1-91

Three blind mice and other stories. Dodd, Mead 1950 c1948 250p o.p.

Contents: Three blind mice; Strange jest; Tape-measure murder; The case of the perfect maid; The case of the caretaker; The third-floor flat; The adventure of Johnnie Waverly; Four and twenty blackbirds; The love detectives

A collection of eight stories and one novelette most of the puzzles solved either by Miss Marple or Hercule Poirot. The title story is a novelette, first published 1948, which was also published with the title: The mousetrap, and appeared as a play with that title. It involves a murder at a boarding-house where several people have taken shelter during a snowstorm. After a policeman arrives on skis, another murder takes place

Towards zero. Blakiston 1944 o.p.

"Agatha has always liked the combination of the big house on the cliff, the large party composed of relatives and in-laws at odds with one another, plus a couple of mysterious and possibly good-for-nothing male visitors. All these give sufficient reason for fastening the murder(s) upon almost any one of the group. The present brew is one of her best servings, enhanced by almost too many cleverly arranged clues, some of them laid by the murderer to bring off a double bluff. Poirot functions only to the extent of being wished for by Insp. Battle, who is solid and acceptable." Barzun. Cat of Crime. Rev and enl edition

Chute, Carolyn

The Beans of Egypt, Maine. Ticknor & Fields 1985 215p

  ISBN 0-899-19314-5   LC 84-8840

"The Beans are the unworthy poor with a vengeance, and the novel is a sequence of their dismal, cozy or audacious moments with one another and their angry or hapless encounters with outsiders. Between chapters about the Beans, Mrs. Chute narrates the life of the Beans' neighbor, Earlene Pomerleau. . . . Her story—in its entirety—consists of her progress from a childhood dominated by God-fearing Gram and Gram-fearing Daddy to a worse subjugation—through marriage—as a woman among the Beans." N Y Times Book Rev

The author "vividly evokes the substitutions rural poverty must make for everything from drinking glasses to romance, yet her imaginary Egypt can also echo with Old Testament allusions. The writing is uneven: sometimes striking and provocative, but mainly hovering uncomfortably between (perfectly caught) rural Maine speech patterns and a more literary spareness." Libr J

Other titles about the inhabitants of Egypt, Maine are: Letourneau's Used Auto Parts (1988) and Merry men (1994)

The school on Heart's Content Road. Atlantic Monthly Press 2008 384p $24

  ISBN 978-0-87113-987-0; 0-87113-987-1

This novel, set in rural Egypt, Maine, focuses on "a 15-year-old boy, Mickey Gammon, who has been ground down by poverty and the public schools. He earns money working odd jobs for the Border Mountain Militia, patriots with an equal love of Bible and country, and commanded by Vietnam veteran Rex York. Through Rex, Mickey meets, and ultimately joins, a utopian community called The Settlement — home-schoolers, radical agrarians and anti-corporate types living where even Google Maps can't find them. They're led by the polygamous Gordon St. Onge with such a religious fervor that his followers refer to him as 'the prophet.' Gordon collects lost children just as he does wives; he also has taken in a 6-year-old named Jane, whose mother has been arrested on trumped-up drug charges. In a plotline with shades of Waco and the YFZ Ranch, authorities pressure Jane to act as a spy inside the Settlement. Characters and plotlines burst forth and multiply . . . . But get past the political screeds and Chute's disdain for the media and capitalism, and this is a profoundly human novel. Her language is both down-home and inventive, idiosyncratic and real." USA Today

LIST OF FICTIONAL WORKS

Cisneros, Sandra

The house on Mango Street. Knopf 1994 134p $24
  ISBN 0-679-43335-X
                                    * LC 93-43564
"Originally published by Arte Público Press in 1984."
Verso of title page
  Composed of a series of interconnected vignettes, this
"is the story of Esperanza Cordero, a young girl growing
up in the Hispanic quarter of Chicago. For Esperanza,
Mango Street is a desolate landscape of concrete and
run-down tenements, where she discovers the hard realities of life—the fetters of class and gender, the specter
of racial enmity, the mysteries of sexuality, and more."
Publisher's note
  This is "a composite of evocative snapshots that manages to passionately recreate the milieu of the poor quarters of Chicago." Commonweal

Clancy, Tom, 1947-

Clear and present danger. Putnam 1989 656p
  ISBN 0-399-13440-9   LC 89-10287
  "A president decides that drug smuggling has become
a 'clear and present danger' to national security. The response is a complex and covert military campaign
against the 'Colombian Cartel.' Clancy presents the technology of special operations and the details of light infantry warfare with his usual flair. Superior even to
his descriptions of tools and techniques, however, is
Clancy's analysis of the legal and moral problems of operating in a twilight zone, where the rules are ambiguous
and an open society makes secrecy impossible." Publ
Wkly

The hunt for Red October. Naval Inst. Press
1984 387p $27.95
  ISBN 0-87021-285-0
                                    * LC 84-16569
  "Based on a true incident—the attempted defection of
a Soviet destroyer in 1975—the plot concerns the defection of the 'Red October', a Soviet submarine carrying
26 Seahawk missiles able to destroy 200 cities. Russia's
fleet is ordered to find and destroy the sub; the U.S.
Navy wants to find it and get it to an American port. An
18-day, 4,000-mile hunt across the Atlantic ensues."
Booklist

Patriot games. Putnam 1987 540p $27.95
  ISBN 0-399-13241-4   LC 87-6910
  "On a visit with his wife and daughter in London,
Ryan stumbles onto an attempt by a new Irish revolutionary group to kidnap the Prince and Princess of Wales
and their eldest son. Using his Marine Corps training,
Ryan saves the royals (which leads to several visits between the Ryans and the residents of Buckingham Palace), but Ryan becomes the target of the surviving terrorists." Publ Wkly

Clark, Carol Higgins

Decked; a Regan Reilly mystery. Warner Bks.
1992 230p
  ISBN 0-446-51549-3   LC 91-50639

This mystery, finds "private detective Regan Reilly returning to Oxford for her tenth reunion. Discovery of a
dead classmate's body on the estate of a former professor
and his eccentric aunt, however, dampens any festivity.
Regan accompanies the aunt on a week-long cruise to
New York after someone poisons the original companion,
but stays in touch with police. Danger lurks on the boat,
of course, and Regan figures things out just in time."
Libr J

Clark, Curt

*For works written by this author under other
names see* Stark, Richard; Westlake, Donald E.

Clark, Martin

The legal limit. Knopf 2008 356p $24.95
  ISBN 978-0-307-26835-8; 0-307-26835-7
                                  LC 2007-042861
  "While Gates Hunt chose to fight his abusive father
head-on, his younger brother, Mason, eventually escaped
their bitter, impoverished circumstances by earning a free
ride to college and law school. And while Gates became
an intransigent, compulsive felon, Mason met and married the love of his life, had a spitfire daughter, and returned to his rural hometown as the commonwealth's attorney. But Mason's idyll is abruptly pierced by a wicked tragedy, and soon afterward his life further unravels
when Gates, convinced that his brother's legal influence
should spring him from prison, attempts to force his cooperation by means of a secret they'd both sworn to take
with them to the grave." Publisher's note
  This is a "model for how to write a literary thriller
with a wry sense of humor. . . . Compelling characters,
surprising twists, rich details, all told in a knowing voice
that will affect the way you view destiny, God, the human condition and the heady concept of justice." Oregonian

Clark, Mary Higgins

The Anastasia syndrome
  In Clark, M. H. The Anastasia syndrome and
    other stories p9-157

The Anastasia syndrome and other stories.
Simon & Schuster 1989 318p
  ISBN 0-671-67367-X   LC 89-38841
  Contents: The Anastasia syndrome; Terror stalks the
class reunion; Lucky day; Double vision; The lost angel
  In the title novella a "noted woman historian sets to
work on a study of the British Civil War, juggling her
research schedule with a love affair with a rising politician. But her writing is interrupted by strange mental sequences that seem to transport her back to Cromwell's
time and involve her in plots against the monarchy.
Moreover, these troubling events out of the past are mirrored in the present as a series of terrorist bombings
seems to follow the historian's path around England."
Booklist

Before I say goodbye. Simon & Schuster 2000
332p
  ISBN 0-684-83598-3   LC 00-266596

Clark, Mary Higgins—*Continued*

"Nell MacDermott, a Manhattan political columnist with her eye on her grandfather's Congressional seat, has been hearing voices since she was 10 years old. But she doesn't tap into her gifts until her husband, Adam, dies in a boating accident and a sympathetic aunt takes her to a medium. Suddenly Nell is seeing black auras and having insights into her husband's shady character and dodgy business deals. There are limits to her powers, however, and she fails to spot the villain who is setting her up to die." N Y Times Book Rev

"The elements of Clark's plot masterfully converge to reveal the killer. A fast-paced, fun ride that leaves the reader guessing until the end." Booklist

The cradle will fall. Simon & Schuster 1980 314p

    ISBN 0-671-25268-2   LC 80-121

"The story centers on what assistant prosecutor Katie De Maio may have seen when she was recovering in the hospital from a car accident. Katie believes, but isn't sure, that she saw a doctor load the body of a young woman into the trunk of a car. Katie has seen clearly, but she doesn't know it. The doctor, a fertility expert who murders his unsuccessful experimental subjects, has seen Katie and determines to get rid of her." Booklist

A cry in the night. Simon & Schuster 1982 317p

    ISBN 0-671-43128-5   LC 82-10289

"After divorce from a callow actor, Jenny McPartland works hard at a Manhattan art gallery to support her two young daughters. At an exhibition of the works of Erich Krueger, the painter is thunderstruck when he meets Jenny. He is handsome, mature, kind, and he loves her children, so when he proposes, Jenny accepts. At first she is impressed with Erich's magnificent mansion in rural Minnesota; but her new husband soon displays odd traits and jealous possessiveness. When Jenny's ex-husband shows up to scrounge, he quickly disappears; a too friendly stable boy nearly dies of poison; Jenny gives birth to Erich's child, which dies mysteriously—and all signs point to Jenny as either mad or criminal." Publ Wkly

In this neo-Gothic thriller "the clues are so subtle, so delicately woven into the fabric of the heroine's life, that even the reader begins to believe, with the heroine, that she herself is either criminal or insane." West Coast Rev Books

Daddy's little girl. Simon & Schuster 2002 291p
    ISBN 0-7432-0604-5   LC 2002-21112

This novel's "heroine is Atlanta investigative journalist Ellie Cavanaugh, who was seven when her sister, Andrea, 15, was beaten to death by 20-year-old Rob Westerfield, scion of the wealthiest family in a small Westchester town. Now Westerfield is up for parole, so Ellie, now 30, returns home to speak out against him. When Westerfield is released, Ellie begins to write a book aimed at re-proving his guilt. . . . With its textured plot, well-sketched secondary characters, strong pacing and appealing heroine, this is Clark at her most winning." Publ Wkly

Loves music, loves to dance. Simon & Schuster 1991 319p
    ISBN 0-671-67364-5
                           * LC 91-10757

This novel focuses "on two friends, Erin and Darcy, who'd been college roommates and now, in their late twenties and each engrossed in her own profession, remain close. Thinking little of it, they become involved in a research project concerning people who utilize personal ads to meet people of potential romantic interest; but their efforts result in the murder of Erin." Booklist

"This Cinderella story turned sour reaffirms that Mary Higgins Clark deserves her reputation for creating splendid suspenseful fiction. Though the novel's characters are simple in more ways than one . . . the plot—surprisingly upbeat and thoroughly engaging—more than makes up for this flaw." N Y Times Book Rev

Nighttime is my time. Simon & Schuster 2004 370p $25.95
    ISBN 0-7432-0607-X   LC 2004-273751

This book features "three females in peril, all targets of a serial killer who fancies himself a night-hunting predator. . . . The Owl kills his first victim, then it's off to attend his 20th high school reunion at Stonecroft Academy in Cornwall-on-Hudson, where he intends to do in the last several women who humiliated him when he was a geeky high school student. . . . The game here is figuring out which of the men who come to the reunion, all former nerds, is the Owl." Publ Wkly

No place like home. Simon & Schuster 2005 368p $25.95
    ISBN 0-7432-6489-4   LC 2005-42535

"At One Old Mill Lane, in Mendham, N.J., 10-year-old Liza Barton wakes to find her stepfather, Ted Cartwright, attacking her mother, Audrey. Liza grabs a gun in defense, but in the ensuing melee Audrey is killed and Ted is wounded. Dubbed 'Little Lizzie Borden,' Liza is taken away and almost convicted of murdering her mother and attempting to kill the lying, scheming Ted. Twenty-four years later, Liza, now known as Celia Foster Nolan, has just been presented with a surprise birthday present from her new husband, Alex: the house at One Old Mill Lane." Publ Wkly

On the street where you live. Simon & Schuster 2001 317p $26
    ISBN 0-7432-0602-9   LC 2001-272623

"In the 1890s, three young women in the upscale seaside village of Spring Lake died at the hands of an unidentified killer. In the present day, two young women have disappeared from town—and their killer, whose first-person ruminations vein the third-person narrative, is preparing to strike again. His final target will be Emily Graham, an ambitious young attorney just moved to Spring Lake from upstate New York, where she'd been victimized by a stalker. . . . Clark's prose ambles as usual, but it takes readers where they want to go—deep into an old-fashioned tale of a damsel in delicious distress." Publ Wkly

Remember me. Simon & Schuster 1994 306p
    ISBN 0-671-86708-3   LC 94-8762

"Just what is the mysterious presence that seems to haunt Menley Nichols and baby Hannah in their spectacular rented Cape Cod mansion? Menley is still trying to recover from the horror of her two-year-old son Bobby's death on the railroad crossing. Lawyer husband Adam is too busy dashing to and from New York, and defending a local hunk suspected of doing away with his wealthy

Clark, Mary Higgins—*Continued*

bride, to be much help. And so the presence moves in on Menley, *Rebecca* style, with eerie middle-of-the-night sound effects and rocking cradles. As always with Clark, there are several plots going on at once, which are miraculously blended and resolved in the finale." Publ Wkly

The second time around. Simon & Schuster 2003 302p $26

ISBN 0-7432-0606-1   LC 2003-271798

"Financial columnist Marcia 'Carley' DeCarlo finds herself squarely in the middle of a bizarre story about the mysterious disappearance of Nick Spencer, founder of the medical research firm Gen-stone, which had been on the brink of developing a cancer vaccine. When it's discovered that Spencer apparently stole thousands of investment dollars and either lied about or sabotaged the progress of the vaccine's development, Carley can't believe it. . . . Under the guise of doing an in-depth story on Nick Spencer, Carley conducts her own investigation, discovering dark forces behind Gen-stone's demise. The prolific and ever-popular Clark isn't the subtlest crime writer, but she knows how to spin an intriguing tale, and this time she's created a convincing heroine in Carley." Booklist

Stillwatch. Simon & Schuster 1984 302p

ISBN 0-671-46952-5   LC 84-14058

"Pat Traymore arrives in the nation's capital to produce a TV documentary on Sen. Abigail Jennings, rumored to be the President's choice to succeed the ailing, retired Vice-President. Disregarding dire warnings, Pat moves back into the house where, when she was a baby, her father had killed her mother and himself and tried to kill her too. The young woman begins to suspect something not quite admirable in Jenning's background as her research gets under way." Publ Wkly

A stranger is watching. Simon & Schuster 1978 c1977 314p

ISBN 0-671-23071-9

"When Steve Peterson's son and girl friend disappear, there is no apparent connection between this event and the murder of Steve's wife several years earlier. The latter crime had supposedly been solved, and, indeed, the convicted murderer is about to be executed. However, the kidnapping, the murder, and the execution are linked, as it turns out, and the common denominator is an expert mechanic and full-time psychopath named Arty." Best Sellers

Two little girls in blue. Simon & Schuster 2006 322p $25.95

ISBN 0-7432-6490-8

＊ LC 2006-42254

"Before leaving for a black-tie affair in New York City, Margaret and Steve Frawley celebrate the third birthday of their twin girls, Kathy and Kelly, with a party at their new home in Ridgefield, Conn. Later that night, when Margaret can't reach the babysitter, she contacts the Ridgefield police. The frantic couple return home to find the children missing and a ransom note demanding $8 million. Though the Frawleys meet all the conditions, only Kelly turns up in a car along with a dead driver and a suicide note saying that Kathy has died. But Kelly's telepathic messages from her sister

keep telling her differently, and Margaret won't give up hope. Even the most skeptical law enforcement officers and the FBI, who pursue suspects from New York to Cape Cod, begin to believe Kelly is on to something. Clues from ordinary people lead to a riveting conclusion. Rivaling Clark's debut–Where Are the Children?–this suspense thriller is certain to send terror into the heart of any parent." Publ Wkly

Weep no more, my lady; a novel. Simon and Schuster 1987 315p

ISBN 0-671-55664-9   LC 87-4760

This novel "is a throwback to the romantic suspense of the thirties and forties. A beautiful leading actress, Leila LaSalle, dies in a fall from her high-rise terrace, leaving behind a wealthy fiancé who is arrested for her murder. Various 'friends' jockey for money and power and alibis, while her inconsolable little sister wanders around unaware that she is next on the killer's hit list." Wilson Libr Bull

"Although this novel is not quite as tightly plotted as other of Clark's best-sellers, . . . the author's legions of fans will find much to enjoy here—characters aplenty, multiple motives, and enough surprises to keep the action chugging along." Booklist

Where are the children? Simon & Schuster 1975 223p

ISBN 0-671-21942-1

This tale is "set against a background of Cape Cod in the dead of winter. Nancy Eldredge's past hides a terrible secret. She was once tried and almost convicted of the murder of her two young children from a first marriage. . . . She is now happily married again with another little boy and girl. When these children vanish from their front yard in a snowstorm, Nancy's past is raked up and the local police are certain she has killed again." Publ Wkly

Clark, Nancy, 1952-

The Hills at home. Pantheon Bks. 2003 481p $25

ISBN 0-375-42203-X   LC 2002-72314

"In the summer of 1989, septuagenarian Lily Hill's serenely solitary life in her ramshackle family home in Towne, MA, comes to a screeching halt. A torrent of Hill relatives with a richly diverse menu of dysfunctional quirks pours into her life, and they forget to leave." Libr J

"The plot is mild and ambling, and the darker emotions are kept strictly offstage, but plot and angst are not the point. The point is the revelation of a particular kind of life, and at that the book succeeds brilliantly." N Y Times Book Rev

Clark, Walter Van Tilburg, 1909-1971

The Ox-bow incident. Random House 1940 309p o.p.

＊

"Rustlers are systematically stealing cattle near Bridger's Gulch, Nevada, in the late 1880s. After a cattleman is killed, an illegal posse is formed to apprehend the criminals. In a remote valley they surprise three men, hold a makeshift trial, and hang the three. Soon after-

Clark, Walter Van Tilburg, 1909-1971—Continued

ward it is discovered that the wrong men have been punished. This is a western with psychological insight." Shapiro. Fic for Youth. 3d edition

Clarke, Arthur C., 1917-2008

2001: a space odyssey. New Am. Lib. 1968 221p pa $7.99 hardcover o.p.

ISBN 0-451-45799-4 (pa)

*

Astronauts of the spaceship Discovery, aided by their computer, HAL, blast off in search of proof that extraterrestrial beings had a part in the development of intelligent life forms on Earth millions of years ago.

"By standing the universe on its head, the author makes us see the ordinary universe in a different light. . . . [This novel becomes] a complex allegory about the history of the world." New Yorker

2010: odyssey two. Ballantine Bks. 1982 291p

ISBN 0-345-30305-9   LC 82-6850
"A Del Rey book"
"The Soviet Union and the United States send a joint mission, which includes Dr. Heywood Floyd, to find out what happened to David Bowman, HAL, and the 'Discovery'. . . . Clarke has written a sequel to the movie, not the book, but it doesn't matter. This is another gripping adventure for which there is bound to be much demand." Libr J

2061: odyssey three. Ballantine Bks. 1987 279p

ISBN 0-345-35173-8   LC 87-47811
"A Del Rey book"
"Fifty years after the alien message forbidding humans to approach the moon Europa, an expedition to Halley's Comet is forced to violate the prohibition in the name of mercy." Libr J
"Clarke transforms his grasp of science into informed speculation while unleashing, with the understated skill of a master storyteller, several stunning narrative twists." Booklist

3001: the final odyssey. Ballantine Bks. 1997 263p

ISBN 0-345-31522-7   LC 96-49490
"*2001* astronaut Frank Poole, presumed dead and adrift in deep space near Jupiter, is recovered alive in the year 3001. Intent on saving humanity, he returns to Jupiter's satellite, Europa, to contact partner Dave Bowman, whose mind has become absorbed by a third monolith." Libr J
"3001 can stand alone from its predecessors in Clarke's Space Odyssey saga and is an intelligent romp, distinguished by Clarke's usual and inimitable wit and an unusual (perhaps unwelcome) strain of grumpiness about religion." Booklist

Childhood's end. Ballantine Bks. 1953 214p pa $13.95 hardcover o.p.

ISBN 0-345-44405-1 (pa)

*

This novel is "paradigmatic of Clarke's more speculative, transcendental novels. Structured as a succession of apocalytic revelations, it depicts the sudden metamorphosis of humanity, under the protective midwifery of the

alien Overlords, into the next evolutionary stage, a group mind that ultimately merges with the cosmic Overmind, destroying the Earth in the process. . . . The alien other that transcends humanity yet paradoxically represents humanity's destiny is a recurring theme in the author's speculative novels." New Ency of Sci Fic

The collected stories of Arthur C. Clarke. TOR Bks. 2001 c2000 966p $29.95; pa $19.95

ISBN 0-312-87821-4; 0-312-87860-5 (pa)

*

"A TOR book"
First published 2000 in the United Kingdom
Contents: Travel by wire!; How we went to Mars; Retreat from Earth; Reverie; The awakening; Whacky; Loophole; Rescue party; Technical error; Castaway; The fires within; Inheritance; Nightfall; History lesson; Transience; The wall of darkness; The lion of Comarre; The forgotten enemy; Hide-and-seek; Breaking strain; Nemesis; Guardian angel; Time's arrow; A walk in the dark; Silence please; Trouble with the natives; The road to the sea; The sentinel; Holiday on the moon; Earthlight; Second dawn; Superiority; 'If I forget thee, oh Earth . . .'; All the time in the world; The nine billion names of God; The possessed; The parasite; Jupiter five; Encounter in the dawn; The other tiger; Publicity campaign; Armaments race; The deep range; No morning after; Big game hunt; Patent pending; Refugee; The star; What goes up; Venture to the moon; The pacifist; The reluctant orchid; Moving spirit; The defenestration of Ermintrude Inch; The ultimate melody; The next tenants; Cold war; Sleeping beauty; Security check; The man who ploughed the sea; Critical mass; The other side of the sky; Let there be light; Out of the sun; Cosmic Casanova; The songs of distant Earth; A slight case of sunstroke; Who's there?; Out of the cradle, endlessly orbiting . . .; I remember Babylon; Trouble with time; Into the comet; Summertime on Icarus; Saturn rising; Death and the senator; Before Eden; Hate; Love that universe; Dog Star; Maelstrom II; An ape about the house; The shining ones; The secret; Dial F for Frankenstein; The wind from the sun; The food of the gods; The last command; Light of darkness; The longest science-fiction story ever told; Playback; The cruel sky; Herbert George Morley Robert Wells, Esq.; Crusade; Neutron tide; Reunion; Transit of Earth; A meeting with Medusa; Quarantine; 'SiseneG'; The steampowered word processor; On golden seas; The hammer of God; The wire continuum; Improving the neighbourhood

"Although most of these stories date from between 1946 and 1970, seven earlier tales, rescued from what would now be called fanzines, extend coverage back to 1937, and a few snippets stretch it toward the present. At least two dozen stories bear titles that are household words among sf readers. . . . The stories demonstrate Clarke's dazzling and unique combination of command of the language, scientific and other kinds of erudition, and inimitable wit." Booklist

The Garden of Rama; by Arthur C. Clarke and Gentry Lee. Bantam Bks. 1991 441p (Rama)

ISBN 0-553-07261-7

* LC 91-2888
This is the third title in the Rama saga. "Trapped aboard the massive Raman spacecraft as it leaves Earth's solor system, three cosmonauts begin a 13-year voyage toward an unknown destination. Combining the best of

Clarke, Arthur C., 1917-2008—*Continued*
space adventure (as the spacefarers encounter other life forms within the multi-habitat vessel) with human drama (as children are born and raised in an unearthly environment), this third novel in the Rama cycle asks as many questions as it answers." Libr J
Followed by Rama revealed

The hammer of God. Bantam Bks. 1993 226p
ISBN 0-553-09557-9   LC 93-22096
Expanded version of a short story that appeared 1992 in Time magazine
"As an asteroid named 'Kali' hurtles toward earth on a collision course that spells the end to life on the planet, a lone spaceship armed with a weapon to alter the asteroid's path attempts to carry out its perilous mission—unaware that others are simultaneously working for earth's destruction." Libr J
This is "vintage Arthur C. Clarke. While he takes pains to persuade readers that the threat of destruction from outer space is real, he is optimistic about humanity's ability to meet any challenge if its keeps its collective head." N Y Times Book Rev

Rama II; by Arthur C. Clarke and Gentry Lee. Bantam Bks. 1989 420p (Rama)
ISBN 0-553-05714-6   LC 89-15152
In this second installment in the Rama saga "another *Rama* appears in our galaxy with the same shape, the same unearthly vistas, and even more creatures running wild over its spacescapes. A childlike genius, a beautiful medical officer, and a deeply religious military man form the nucleus of the good guys, anxious to explore, befriend the creatures, and discover the true purpose of the spacecraft." Booklist
Followed by The Garden of Rama

Rama revealed; {by} Arthur C. Clarke and Gentry Lee. Bantam Bks. 1994 466p (Rama)
ISBN 0-553-09536-6   LC 93-31459
In this conclusion of the Rama saga "Cosmonaut Nicole Wakefield, the former governor of the human colony housed within the globe-shaped spaceship Rama III, is awaiting execution for opposing the fascistic powers that now run the colony. She is rescued from her cell by small robots sent by her husband Richard, whom she had thought dead. . . . Along with friends and family from the Earth sector, they begin traveling through the different alien environments housed in the vast Raman world." Publ Wkly
"Fans of skillfully crafted hard sf . . . will find plenty of Clarke and Lee's fascinating scientific speculations vividly given form in the marvels of Raman technology." Booklist

Rendezvous with Rama. Harcourt Brace Jovanovich 1973 303p (Rama)
ISBN 0-15-176835-8
                                              *
A massive space capsule "is discovered approaching earth in the 22nd century. A team of scientists sent into space to make contact with and explore the monster at first believe it to be a dead artifact launched from an unknown galaxy a million years before. But as the machine approaches solar orbit it comes alive—with light, oxygen and biological life—and human reactions to it are mixed. A religious cult thinks Rama is a rescue ship come to

save the faithful, while colonists on Mercury start making a bomb to keep the thing away." Publ Wkly
This work contains "flights of prose where the language fairly purrs. And here too one finds the questioning and probing of man and his place in the cosmos that marks good fiction and good science fiction." Libr J
Followed by Rama II

Clarke, Brock

An arsonist's guide to writers' homes in New England; a novel. Algonquin Books Of Chapel Hill 2007 303p $23.95
ISBN 978-1-56512-551-3; 1-56512-551-7
                                              LC 2006-100732
"When Sam Pulsifer's parents separated for three years during his childhood, his mother lied about his father's whereabouts and also told Sam ghost stories about the Emily Dickinson House in his hometown of Amherst, MA. At age 18, he broke into the house one night to verify these stories, got spooked by a noise, dropped a lit cigarette, burned down the house, and unwittingly killed its two occupants. After ten years in a minimum security prison, Sam moved to the nearby suburbs to live an anonymous life, attend college, marry, and raise children. All is well until the son of the couple who died in the fire shows up on his doorstep, and fires begin breaking out at the homes of other New England writers." Libr J
"This straight-faced, postmodern comedy scorches all things literary, from those moldy author museums to the excruciating question-and-answer sessions that follow public readings. There are no survivors here: women's book clubs, literary critics, Harry Potter fans, bookstores, English professors, memoir writers, librarians, Jane Smiley, even the author himself—they're all singed under Clarke's crisp wit." Washington Post Book World

Clarke, Susanna, 1959-

Jonathan Strange & Mr. Norrell; illustrations by Portia Rosenberg. Bloomsbury; distributed by Holtzbrinck 2004 782p il $27.95
ISBN 1-582-34416-7
                                              * LC 2004-2402
"This fantasy novel is set in early-nineteenth-century England, where two men, Gilbert Norrell and his pupil Jonathan Strange, revive the once-thriving practice of the dark arts. After aiding the British against Napoleon, the magicians fall out over interpretations of wizardly philosophy. Meanwhile, a malevolent fairy accidentally set loose by Norrell enchants, among others, Strange's wife. Clarke's ability to construct a fully imagined world-much of it explained in long, witty footnotes-is impressive." New Yorker

Classic lines: more great racing stories. See The New treasury of great racing stories

Claudine, Sidonie Gabrielle *See* Colette, 1873-1954

Clavell, James

Gai-Jin; a novel of Japan. Delacorte Press 1993 1038p
ISBN 0-385-31016-1   LC 92-42129

Clavell, James—*Continued*

The sixth volume in the author's Asian saga depicts the political and social intrigue that resulted when Japan slowly opened its doors to foreigners or gai-jin. This novel "opens in 1862 with a fictionalized version of the assassination of a British citizen, Charles Richardson, by samurai traveling with the rebellious lord of Satsuma on the great national highway known as the Tokaido. It ends with the British bombardment of Kagoshima in 1863, a seminal event on the road to the Meiji Restoration, which brought feudal Japan into the modern era." N Y Times Book Rev

Clavell "melds plot-driven storytelling and colorful characterization in vibrant collaboration with an exotic, dynamic setting." Publ Wkly

King Rat; a novel. Little, Brown 1962 406p o.p.
Third novel in the author's Asian saga
"A novel about corruption, fear and despair among the prisoners in a Singapore prison camp in World War II. 'King Rat,' so called because he breeds the prison rats and sells them for food, is an American corporal turned gambler and black marketeer. He has bribed his way into a position as real though unofficial ruler of the camp." Publ Wkly

This novel "is strong in narrative detail, penetrating in observation of human nature under stress, and thought-provoking in its analysis of right and wrong." Cincinnati Public Libr

Noble house; a novel of contemporary Hong Kong. Delacorte Press 1981 1206p
ISBN 0-440-06456-2   LC 80-26889
Fourth novel in the author's Asian saga
"Ian Dunross, head of Struan's, an old and respected China trade firm in Hong Kong, makes his appearance in the middle of a typhoon, and from there to the very end of this . . . saga the action never lets up. This action takes place during one week of 1963, with two plots going, and dozens of participants. . . . Along the way we are treated to the sights, sounds, smells, and history of Hong Kong. There is international finance and banking, the workings of multinational companies, smuggling of narcotics and gold, insight into how the Chinese regard sex, and their marvelously pragmatic view of how the world works." Libr J

Shogun; a novel of Japan. Atheneum Pubs. 1975
ISBN 0-689-10565-7
                                                    *
First novel in the author's Asian saga
East and West meet in this "epic of feudal seventeenth-century Japan. When a gale casts John Blackthorne's ship ashore here, the English sea pilot and his crew must learn to sink or swim in an alien culture. Blackthorne's mentor is a feudal lord locked in a power struggle with another for control of all Japan. How Blackthorne makes himself useful and is rewarded with samurai status forms the bulk of this swashbuckler." Booklist

"Clavell creates a world: people, customs, settings, needs and desires all become so enveloping that you forget who and where you are. 'Shōgun' is history infused with fantasy. It strives for epic dimension and occasionally it approaches that elevated state. It's irresistible, maybe unforgettable." N Y Times Book Rev

Tai-Pan. Delacorte Press 1983 c1966 590p
ISBN 0-440-08724-4   LC 82-18339

Second novel in the author's Asian saga
A reissue of the title first published 1966 by Atheneum
"The time is 1841. England has just won the first Opium War with China and is determined to advance her interests there. Dirk Struan is tai-pan (supreme ruler) of the Noble House, the most powerful trading company in the orient. Struan realizes with a prophetic vision the value of Hong Kong and her port. He feels that England must use this area to branch out over the far East. Opposition to his plan comes from the apathy of politicians in England. Struan must also deal with Chinese pirates and with the multiple entity that is China and her people." Best Sellers

"The backgrounds—Hong Kong, the sailing ships, the trading preserve in Canton—surge with life, and the plot is neatly dovetailed with history. Superb storytelling; an utterly absorbing book." Publ Wkly

Whirlwind. Morrow 1986 1147p
ISBN 0-688-06663-1   LC 86-11293
Fifth novel in the author's Asian saga
"Andrew Gavallan, based in Scotland, runs a helicopter company operating in Iran during the Shah's reign. When Khomeini comes to power, Gavallan must get his pilots and their families, and his valuable helicopters, out of the riot-torn country. Complicating matters is his power struggle with his company's secret owner, the Noble House of Hong Kong. The pilots' escape efforts form the basic story {of the novel}." Libr J

"Clavell has done a fine job . . . of delineating the geography and politics of a country in turmoil. He seems less successful with the characters, however, as many of his Iranians are thinly disguised stereotypes. Still, the novel is rife with corporate and multinational intrigue, political drama, and romance." Booklist

Cleage, Pearl

Babylon sisters; a novel. Ballantine Books/One World 2005 292p $23.95
ISBN 0-345-45609-2   LC 2004-51909
"For more than 17 years, Catherine Sanderson has not revealed the identity of her daughter's father and has kept the child's existence hidden from him. However, the universe, teenage curiosity, and two new work assignments conspire to put Catherine's past and present on a collision course. The plot is spun around a tale of women's empowerment, modern-day slavery, betrayal, and the survival of African American community institutions." Libr J

The author's "intelligent, lively narrative hits numerous notes–domestic drama, romance, thriller–right in tune." Publ Wkly

I wish I had a red dress. Morrow 2001 323p $24
ISBN 0-380-97733-8   LC 00-54620
"Joyce Mitchell is the social-worker founder of the Sewing Circus and Community Truth Center, dedicated to guiding young women from teenage pregnancies and violent relationships with the 'babydaddies' to free and independent adulthood. Joyce herself, five years a widow, longs for enough safety and assurance to wear a red dress, an ultimate symbol of freedom and abandon. When she meets former Detroit cop Nate Anderson, the new counselor at the high school, long-repressed feelings are awakened." Booklist

Cleage, Pearl—*Continued*

"With humor and sparkling dialog, Cleage balances the dark, abusive relationships of Joyce's clients with the delightfully healthy love between Joyce and Nate and the strength of women's friendships." Libr J

What looks like crazy on an ordinary day—; a novel. Avon Bks. 1997 244p
ISBN 0-380-97584-X   LC 97-17708
This novel "focuses on an HIV-positive woman who seeks solace and refuge for the summer in her hometown with her widowed sister." Libr J
"Despite the early bad news, Cleage's funny, irreverent, and hopeful novel is stunningly real and evocative of the conditions behind the high unemployment, aimlessness, and drug culture that permeate the urban landscape and have invaded smaller towns as well." Booklist

Cleave, Chris

Little Bee. Simon & Schuster 2009 c 2008 271p $24
ISBN 978-1-4165-8963-1; 1-4165-8963-5
                     LC 2008-30689
First published 2008 in the United Kingdom with title: The other hand
"The novel begins in the middle of the story when Little Bee is illegally released from a prison outside of London after two years of incarceration for attempting to sneak into the country. . . . Without any papers, legal documentation or identification, Little Bee is forced to visit the only person she knows in England—Sarah Summers. . . .Sarah Summers and her husband, Andrew O'Rourke, met Little Bee on a beach in Nigeria. Having grown apart in their marriage, Andrew and Sarah traveled to Nigeria to get away from city life. Inadvertently, the couple stumbles across Little Bee and her sister while taking a romantic walk on the beach, only to be surrounded by a group of mercenaries intent on killing the girls. . . . In a gruesome twist, the soldiers agree to let the girls live if Andrew will cut off his middle finger. As Andrew is unable to comply with their terms, Sarah picks up a machete and slices off her own finger—effectively dooming their marriage. The soldiers initially take both girls away, but in the end spare Little Bee. When she appears at Sarah and Andrew's household outside of London, a series of tragic, beautiful and emotionally turbulent events unfold which will change all of their lives forever." PopMatters

Clemens, Samuel Langhorne *See* Twain, Mark, 1835-1910

Clement, Hal, 1922-2003

Heavy planet; the classic Mesklin stories. Orb 2002 414p il pa $20.99
ISBN 978-0-765-30368-4; 0-765-30368-X
                     LC 2002-32481
"A Tom Doherty Associates book"
This volume includes the novel Mission of gravity (1954) and its sequel, Star light (1971), as well as the short stories Under and Lecture Demonstration. Also included is Whirligig world, the essay Clement published in Astounding in 1953 that describes the process he used to create the high-gravity planet Mesklin

Mission of gravity is a "first-rate story of First Contact between explorers from Earth and a most unhuman sentient native species, to the benefit of both, rejecting the cliché that one still sees in movie and TV SF that alienness equals evil. . . . A major work." Anatomy of Wonder 4

Noise. TOR Bks. 2003 252p $23.95
ISBN 0-7653-0857-6   LC 2003-55987
"Linguist Mike Hoani arrives on the water planet Kainui to study the evolution of the language of its original Polynesian colonists. His travels on a planet with no fixed land except for floating artificial cities plunge him into a maritime adventure that tests his knowledge of both language and human nature." Libr J
"Clement skillfully weaves together challenging science, a unique familial society, and an encounter with a 'lost' city in a narrative that allows the reader to puzzle out Mike's questions along with him." Booklist

Clinch, Jon

Finn; a novel. Random House 2007 287p $23.95
ISBN 978-1-4000-6591-2; 1-4000-6591-7
                     LC 2006-45802
The author "fleshes out the shadowy figure of Huckleberry Finn's father, known as Finn. In Clinch's version, Finn is the black sheep of his family—a barely literate drunkard who supports his habit by trading catfish for whiskey. His father is a bigoted circuit court judge, and his brother is an unctuous attorney. Finn lives in a rundown cabin on the riverbank with his beautiful black mistress and their pale mulatto child, Huck, but he knows that to reconcile with his father he must sever all ties with the woman." Libr J
"Shocking and charming. Clinch creates a folk-art masterpiece that will delight, beguile and entertain as it does justice to its predecessor. . . . In Finn, Clinch expands the bloodlines and scope of the original story and casts new light on the troubled legacy of our country's infamous past." N Y Post

Cline, Rachel, 1957-

What to keep; a novel; Rachel Cline. 1st ed. Random House 2004 290p $23.95
ISBN 1-400-06183-0   LC 2003-54810
"Divided into three sections, the story follows the life of Denny Roman, a daughter of brilliant but socially dysfunctional parents, and her relationship with Maureen, the family's de facto life secretary, who teaches Denny how to accept the good parts of herself and her parents and not obsess over the bad." Libr J
"This is a wryly funny novel that feels completely fresh. It has an odd but effective structure; depicts offbeat, memorable characters; and offers a perceptive, nuanced take on familial relationships." Booklist

Clute, John

Appleseed. TOR Bks. 2002 337p $25.95
ISBN 0-765-30378-7

                                                *

Clute, John—*Continued*

"Nathaniel 'Stinky' Freer captains his ship, the Tile Dance, through space with the aid of a conjoined AI. . . . On a seemingly routine mercantile contract to the planet Trencher, he's nearly killed by the rampaging, cannibalistic, self-devouring alien, Opsophagos. On returning to his ship, Stinky discovers that he's somehow acquired two new AIs and that he has a stowaway: a topiary parthogenete, Mamselle Cunning Earth Link, who holds the key to the location of the planet where there are plaque-eating lenses. Opsophagos remains in hot pursuit as Stinky meets the mythic Johnny Appleseed, rediscovers his lady love and has a sexual encounter that just might save the universe." Publ Wkly

Clynes, Michael

For works written by this author under other names see Doherty, P. C.

Coben, Harlan, 1962-

Darkest fear. Delacorte Press 2000 285p
ISBN 0-385-33433-8   LC 99-89788
"Manhattan sports agent Myron Bolitar is shocked when his former college lover informs him he is the father of her 13-year-old son, who has anemia. But the girlfriend—now inimically divorced from her husband—only uses that fact to convince him to locate the boy's bone-marrow donor, who has disappeared." Libr J
"The Bolitar thrillers are always leavened with humor, no matter how grim the content, and this one is no exception. Even so, the darkness of the plot and the seriousness of the theme—the reponsibilities of parenthood—give this installment added impact." Booklist

Gone for good. Delacorte Press 2002 340p
ISBN 0-385-33558-X   LC 2001-55292
"Will Klein was a nice Jewish boy from a nice Jersey suburb until his ex-girlfriend was found strangled next door and his brother became an international fugitive. Eleven years later, as his mother succumbs to cancer, Will gets the deathbed confession that his brother, Ken, is alive." Publ Wkly
"Through Klein, the psychological suspense turns on the question of guilt, surely but also on the transcendence of familial love and forgiveness. Watching Klein decide among dangerous alternatives, as the clockwork plot keeps picking up speed, is breathtaking." Booklist

Hold tight. Dutton 2008 416p $26.95
ISBN 978-0-525-95060-8; 0-525-95060-5
                                       LC 2007-51582
"The story is about Tia and Mike Baye, whose son, Adam, has been somewhat isolated since his best friend killed himself. The parents, not knowing where he is going and what he is doing, consider putting some sophisticated spyware on their son's computer. Even though troubled by their invasion of his privacy they do so, anyway, using their worries about his welfare as an excuse. Once they find out where Adam is going and what he is doing, Mike all but abandons his medical practice to search for him and interact with some very dangerous people. Coben's style is laid back initially, but it builds into a strong, smart, suspenseful novel including at least five different storylines. " Deseret News

The innocent. Dutton 2005 388p $26.95
ISBN 0-525-94874-0   LC 2005-1627

"A paralegal, devoted husband and soon-to-be father, Matt Hunter has a not-so-secret past: when he was 20, in an attempt to break up a fistfight, he killed a man and served four years in prison for it. He's been out five years, living in his New Jersey hometown, and life is pretty good. But when his beloved wife, Olivia, goes away on a business trip, he receives 15 seconds of digital video on his camera phone showing her in a hotel room with another man. Meanwhile, Loren Muse, Essex County homicide investigator, is working on an unusual case: an autopsy of a nun reveals breast implants, which hint at a previous, not so holy life. After the FBI is called in, evidence links Matt to the nun killing. . . . All the characters have extensive, interesting histories, which makes their actions believable under the extreme circumstances that engulf them." Publ Wkly

Just one look. Dutton 2004 370p $25.95
ISBN 0-525-94791-4   LC 2004-2329
"While flipping through a set of newly developed photographs, Grace Lawson comes across an old picture of four people, one of whom resembles her husband, Jack. When she shows him the photo, he denies being the person or knowing anyone involved. Later that night, with the photo in his possession, Jack flees the house and promptly vanishes. When Grace uncovers proof that one of the strangers in the picture is now dead, her picture-perfect life starts to unravel. With each thriller, Coben just gets better and better." Libr J

No second chance. Dutton 2003 338p $24.95
ISBN 0-525-94729-9   LC 2002-192530
"Marc Seidman, a plastic surgeon near New York City, wakes up in a hospital to learn that he has been gravely wounded, his wife shot dead and his infant daughter, Tara, snatched. The ensuing narrative, which shuttles between third person and Marc's first person, covers more than a year in Marc's hunt for Tara." Publ Wkly
"The novel, spanning 18 months and jumping between the father and the kidnappers, sets off depth charges of meets, double-crosses, near-misses, and vengful acts. Coben holds it together with his hero's determination and smarts." Booklist

One false move. Delacorte Press 1998 322p
ISBN 0-385-32369-7   LC 97-51206
"Sports agent Myron Bolitar handles everything with panache: his relationships, his clients, and this search for two missing people. When a sports store mogul asks him to 'watch over' basketball star Brenda Slaughter, Myron winds up looking for her father, who disappeared a week ago, and her mother, who deserted the family some 20 years earlier. Myron not only discovers mob interest in female basketball but also a connected suspicious death in a high-profile political family." Libr J
"After four paperback appearances, sports agent/sleuth Myron Bolitar makes his hardcover debut in a stylish mystery distinguished by memorably quirky characters and smart, tough narration." Publ Wkly

The woods. Dutton 2007 404p $26.95
ISBN 978-0-525-95012-7; 0-525-95012-5
                                       LC 2007-8329
"Paul 'Cope' Copeland, acting county prosecutor for Essex County, N.J., and Lucy Gold, his long-lost summer camp love, are still haunted by a fateful night, decades earlier, when their nighttime tryst allowed some younger campers, including Cope's sister, to venture into

Coben, Harlan, 1962---—*Continued*
the nearby forest, where they apparently fell victim to
the Summer Slasher, a serial killer. Cope's intense focus
on a high-profile rape prosecution of some wealthy college students shifts after one of the Slasher's victims,
whose body was never found, turns up as a recent corpse
in Manhattan, casting doubt on the official theory of the
old case." Publ Wkly
The author "has created another surprising and emotional story that will remain with the reader long after
the last page is finished. One of Coben's best." Libr J

Cockey, Tim

Hearse case scenario. Hyperion 2002 338p
ISBN 0-7868-6711-6   LC 2001-24188
In this mystery "Hitchcock Sewell, Baltimore's wisecracking mortician/sleuth, sets out to exonerate his hapless childhood friend, Lucy, accused of murdering her
low-life boyfriend, Shrimp Martin. Sure, Lucy shot him,
but she wasn't the one who killed him." Publ Wkly
"Cockey effectively grounds Hitch's high jinks in the
real world, placing his hero squarely in the comic-
realistic tradition of Lawrence Block's Bernie
Rhodenbarr and Janet Evanovich's Stephanie Plum."
Booklist

Murder in the hearse degree. Hyperion 2003
324p $22.95
ISBN 0-7868-6712-4   LC 2002-27458
Wisecracking undertaker Hitchcock Sewell "finds out
that his former squeeze, Libby Gellman, is back in town
with her two children but sans husband and nanny. The
nanny, surprisingly pregnant, is more than geographically
distant: she's fallen from a very high bridge and
drowned. Or was she pushed? The police support a knee-
jerk suicide theory. The nanny's loyal mother doesn't. So
Hitch sets off to see exactly what happened. . . . Brimming with humor—much of it dark—this book is perfect
for the reader who has finished all the books by Janet
Evanovich or Sue Grafton and doesn't know what to
read next." Libr J

Cocteau, Jean, 1889-1963

The impostor; translated from the French by
Dorothy Williams. Noonday Press 1957 132p o.p.
Original French edition, 1923; first English translation
published 1925 by Appleton with title: Thomas the imposter
The setting of Cocteau's short novel "is the First
World War; his imposter, a French youth, too young for
the services, who in a borrowed uniform and under a
borrowed name succeeds in obtaining a post in a curious
nursing unit run by a Polish princess and her daughter.
He plays the part he has adopted so well that in the end
he succeeds in convincing even himself of his authenticity, and having finally been adopted as their mascot by a
unit of Marines dies in the end a gallant death." Times
Lit Suppl

Coe, Jonathan, 1961-

The closed circle. Knopf 2005 367p $25
ISBN 0-375-41415-0   LC 2004-57789

In this sequel to The Rotters' Club, " which was set
in the 1970s, the circle of British teenagers is now teetering on the brink of middle age and struggling with infidelity and failed ambition. Benjamin Trotter is an accountant who has been working for decades on a novel
that runs to thousands of pages and is to be accompanied
by his own music; he is a victim of self-doubt and a paralyzing obsession with his first love. He becomes infatuated with young Malvina, who falls hard for Benjamin's
brother, Paul, a rising political star. Coe interweaves the
personal with the political as key developments over the
past four years run continually in the background—the
threatened closure of the Rover car factory, England's
role in the war on terrorism." Booklist
"While Coe's political sensibility is readily apparent,
this novel, with its incredibly well developed characters
and its immensely engaging narrative, is no polemical
tract. It's a compelling, dramatic and often funny depiction of the way we live now—both savage and heartfelt
at the same time." Publ Wkly

The rain before it falls. Alfred A. Knopf 2008
c2007 240p $23.95
ISBN 978-0-307-26803-7; 0-307-26803-9
LC 2007-43487
First published 2007 in the United Kingdom
"Following the death of her Aunt Rosamond, niece
Gill is named executrix of her estate and inherits a series
of cassettes that Rosamond recorded on the eve of her
demise. The cassettes detail Rosamond's tumultuous connection with her cousin Beatrix, as well as Beatrix's
daughter Thea and granddaughter Imogen. Rosamond intended the tapes for Imogen, but Gill can't locate her.
Gradually, the tapes reveal the unhappiness of these relationships and the tragedies of these women's lives. In the
recordings, Rosamond often displays an irritating passivity, while the manipulative, volatile Beatrix is revealed as
a bitch—not that this genteel novel makes use of such a
term. . . . If Rosamond's temperament makes for a
somewhat mannered novel, it's nevertheless an absorbing
one." Village Voice

The Rotters' Club. Knopf 2002 419p
ISBN 0-375-41383-9
* LC 2001-42523
First published 2001 in the United Kingdom
"It is Birmingham, England, in the '70s and amidst
IRA pub bombings, labor strikes, and immigration-
related racism, Benjamin, Philip, and Doug are going
about the business of adolescence. This means, among
other things, changing their theoretical band's name from
'Gandalf's Pikestaff' to 'The Maws of Doom' and sneaking as much satire into the school paper as possible. . . .
The narrative switches occasionally from third person to
first (Benjamin), and includes diary excerpts, the boy's
ridiculously pretentious attempts at music and theatre reviews, and other formatting diversions." SLJ
"The Rotter's Club, for all its occassional overegging
and its selfconscious deployment of issues, is a superior
entertainment. The pages seem to turn themselves, and
Coe's oblique humor allows the romantic and satirical to
combine without undercutting each other." New Statesman (1913)

Coe, Tucker
*For works written by this author under other
names see* Stark, Richard; Westlake, Donald E.

Coel, Margaret, 1937-

Blood memory. Berkley Prime Crime 2008 305p
$24.95

ISBN 978-0-425-22345-1; 0-425-22345-0

LC 2008-22197

This mystery intoduces Denver investigative reporter
Catherine McLeod. "After an attempt on her life, Catherine realizes she was far from a random target when
Arapaho elder Norman Whitehorse informs her that she's
'one of us.' Adopted as a child and still unsure of her
identity and heritage, Catherine begins to understand the
deep connection she feels to her latest story, about the
1864 Indian massacre at Sand Creek. Whitehorse and
Cheyenne leaders call for the tribes' further compensation for Sand Creek, but when Catherine starts digging,
she realizes that there's more to the land fight than meets
the eye, and the trail leads all the way to Washington."
Publ Wkly

"The story sails along like an eagle riding the wind,
and Coel provides plenty of plausible misdirection before
revealing the surprising hand behind the plot to take her
life. . . . Coel does a nice job of making Denver and the
nearby environs into a charming 'character'—not the eas-
iest task." Daily Camera (Boulder, Co.)

The dream stalker. Berkley Prime Crime 1997
244p

ISBN 0-425-15967-1   LC 96-54797

"Arapaho lawyer Vicky Holden opposes the plan to
construct a nuclear waste facility on the Wind River Reservation, but she receives death threats and the enmity of
her people for her pains. Good friend John O'Malley, Jesuit priest at the local mission, believes that a murdered
Indian he found has some connection to Vicky's troubles, so he investigates—against police advice. Financial
problems at the mission, the personal crises of the new
assistant, and O'Malley's own temptations of the flesh
lend realistic touches to the author's usual commendable
plotting and characterization." Libr J

The ghost walker. Berkley Prime Crime 1996
243p

ISBN 0-425-15468-8   LC 95-26164

In this mystery, "Father John O'Malley discovers a
body dumped in a frozen ditch near his small church on
the Arapaho reservation in Wyoming. His own truck disabled, Father John gets a ride from an edgy, evasive
stranger. When police arrive at the snow-covered roadside, the body has vanished. The Arapahos say the ghost
is walking around somewhere, causing trouble until the
body is properly buried and the spirit can rest. Sure
enough, Marcus Deppert, a troubled young Indian, disappears." Publ Wkly

"Coel's Catholic Irish Jesuit priest and his Arapaho
friends and neighbors, each with individual worldviews
and sensibilities, make for interesting contrasts in this excellent mystery that focuses on the strange place Native
Americans occupy in their own land." Booklist

Coetzee, J. M., 1940-

Age of iron. Random House 1990 198p
ISBN 0-394-58859-2

* LC 90-8310

This novel "takes the form of a letter-diary from Mrs.
Curren, a former classics professor dying of cancer, to
her daughter in America. She details a series of strange
events that turn her protected middle-class life upside
down. A homeless alcoholic appears at her door, eventually becoming her companion and confessor. Her liberal
sentiments and her very humanity are tested as she experiences directly the horrors of apartheid. She comes to
recognize South Africa as a country in which the rigidity
of both sides has led to barbarism and to acknowledge
her complicity in upholding the system." Libr J

"The word 'shame' throbs through the text like a recurrent pain. The principal character thinks she is dying
of it. . . . One can, of course, read her death as a metaphor for the doom of liberalism in South Africa. . . .
But Age of Iron is about dying as much as it is about
apartheid, and that raises it above the level of a political
novel or a *roman à thèse*, and gives resonance to the political message." N Y Rev Books

Diary of a bad year. Viking 2007 231p $24.95
ISBN 978-0-670-01875-8; 0-670-01875-9

LC 2007-27378

"Señor C, an aging and ailing writer in Australia, has
been asked by his publisher to contribute political essays
to a book called Strong Opinions. Having become infatuated with Anya, a beautiful young woman who lives in
his apartment building, he hires her to type his manuscript. While Señor C is writing his essays on politics
and morality, a morality tale of a different sort is playing
out in his apartment, as the young woman's boyfriend
tries to tap into the old writer's online bank account. The
result reads like a literary hybrid of fiction and nonfiction, with each page alternating between Señor C's observations for Strong Opinions and dialog among him,
Anya, and her boyfriend, Alan." Libr J

The "essays create a compelling, even lovable, portrait
of a chilly and curmudgeonly aging writer. . . . Anya, in
the last 90 pages, transcends her gestural, schematic
treatment, and becomes a complex, compassionate individual." Boston Globe

Disgrace. Viking 1999 220p
ISBN 0-670-88731-5

*

"At fifty-two, Professor David Lurie is divorced, filled
with desire, but lacking in passion. An affair with one of
his students leaves him jobless, shunned by his friends,
and ridiculed by his ex-wife. He retreats to his daughter
Lucy's isolated smallholding, where a brief visit becomes
an extended stay as he tries to find meaning from this
one remaining relationship. David's attempts to relate to
Lucy and to a society with new racial complexities are
disrupted by an afternoon of violence that shakes all his
beliefs and threatens to destroy his daughter." Publisher's
note

"A novel that not only works its spell but makes it impossible for us to lay it aside once we've finished reading it. . . . Coetzee's sentences are coiled springs, and
the energy they release would take other writers pages to
summon." New Yorker

Elizabeth Costello. Viking 2003 230p S21.95
ISBN 0-670-03130-5   LC 2003-60849

"Elizabeth Costello, a fictional aging Australian novelist who gained fame for a Ulysses-inspired novel in the
1960s, reveals the workings of her still-formidable mind

Coetzee, J. M., 1940-—*Continued*

in a series of formal addresses she either attends or delivers herself (an award acceptance speech, a lecture on a cruise ship, a graduation speech)." Publ Wkly

"There is no justice in the ability of youth to shame age, and yet it's a fundamental fact of the embodied life. Coetzee's unflinching exploration of this desolate and strangely beautiful terrain represents the cruelest and best use to which literature can be put." N Y Times Book Rev

Foe. Viking 1987 c1986 157p
ISBN 0-670-81398-2   LC 86-40267
First published 1986 in the United Kingdom
"Cast adrift by a mutinous crew, Susan Barton washes ashore on an isle of classic fiction. For the next year, Robinson Cruso sculpts the land while Friday mutely watches Susan intrude upon their loneliness. Life is mere pattern for the two unquestioning castaways, but Susan is not of their story and she pushes Cruso for rationales that don't exist in a world of imagination. Finally rescued and returned to London, Susan leads Friday to Daniel Foe, the author who will write their tale. Foe, however, sees a different story and seeks 'to tell the truth in all its substance.'" Libr J

"In adding to Defoe's repertory company, Coetzee has introduced urgencies that are neither fresh nor illumined, only brilliantly disguised. Flashing back and forward, scattering allusions, adopting a series of poses and styles, the author is less reminiscent of a prior novelist than of contemporary street mimes who build hints until the audience shouts in recognition." Time

Life & times of Michael K. Viking 1984 c1983 184p
ISBN 0-670-42789-6
            * LC 83-47860
First published 1983 in the United Kingdom
"Born with a harelip and brought up in an uncaring orphanage, Michael K. struggles through a desperate life in South Africa. When his sick mother persuades him to bring her back to her homeland, he must endure not only the terrible journey, pulling her in a cart he has made, but also risk the dangers of military checkpoints since he does not have the necessary permits. His undying attachment is to the land, but he is not allowed to remain the gardener he wishes to be. The details of Michael's suffering in camps, hospitals, and labor gangs are harrowing and underscore a courage that never forsakes him." Shapiro. Fic for Youth. 3d edition

Slow man. Viking 2005 265p $24.95
ISBN 0-670-03459-2   LC 2005-54693
"When photographer Paul Rayment loses his leg in a bicycle accident, his solitary life is irrevocably changed. Stubbornly refusing a prosthesis, Paul returns to his bachelor's apartment in Adelaide, uncomfortable with his new dependency on others. He is given to bouts of hopelessness as he looks back on his sixty years of life, but his spirits rise when he finds himself falling in love with Marijana, his practical, down-to-earth Croatian nurse who is struggling to raise her family in a foreign land. As Paul contemplates how to win her heart, he is visited by the mysterious writer Elizabeth Costello, who challenges Paul to taken an active role in his own life." Publisher's note

"What saves Slow Man from being a sterile, self-referential literary exercise is the vividness of the characters who animate it. Coetzee writes in a degree-zero style, purposely flat and unemphatic-he must be a translator's dream-yet in this book he has found a new access of warmth and humor, and displays a vivifying fondness for his characters. It is his triumph in Slow Man to bring a world into being with a minimum of literary effects." New Republic

Coffey, Brian, 1945-
For works written by this author under other names see Koontz, Dean R., 1945-

Coghlan, Peggie, 1920-
See also Stirling, Jessica

Cohen, Janet *See* Neel, Janet, 1940-

Cohen, Leah Hager

Heart, you bully, you punk. Viking 2003 $23.95p $23.95
ISBN 0-670-03167-4   LC 2002-69191
"Cohen offers a bittersweet love story involving a 31-year-old math teacher at a Brooklyn private school, her star pupil, and the student's father. Ann James, the star student, breaks both heels when she slips (or jumps?) from the top of the bleachers. Her injuries render her immobile for a time; to help her keep up in math, Ann's teacher, Esker, volunteers to tutor her at home. After meeting Ann's father, Wally, Esker begins, despite herself, to fall in love with him. . . . Cohen demonstrates that there can be beauty even in sadness." Booklist

House lights. W. W. Norton 2007 302p $24.95
ISBN 978-0-393-06451-3; 0-393-06451-4
            LC 2007-06910
"Beatrice Fisher-Hart should be in college, but her parents, who are both psychologists, allow her to defer higher education while she takes acting classes. After all, her maternal grandmother is Margaret Fourcey, grande dame of the American theater. Even though they both live in Boston, Beatrice hardly knows her grandmother owing to some lingering family estrangement. When Beatrice's father, whom she has always adored, is accused of sexual misconduct, the family starts to fall apart. Just in time, Beatrice gains entry to her grandmother's salon and is given a part in a summer production. She harbors a fierce crush on the director, and her sense of family contracts and expands as she finds her footing on stage and in matters of love." Libr J

The novel is "artfully constructed. By virtue of their length, novels forgive undisciplined descriptive flights, but Cohen writes with the scrupulousness of someone fashioning a short story, in which even the smallest details must bear their weight of significance." N Y Times Book Rev

Cohen, Robert, 1957-

Inspired sleep; a novel. Scribner 2001 399p $25
ISBN 0-684-85079-6   LC 00-57337
"Bonnie Saks, divorced with two sons, a filmmaker ex-husband off in South America, an unfinished dissertation the point of which she has lost, an unsatisfactory job,

Cohen, Robert, 1957---—*Continued*

and an unwanted pregnancy, finds her most debilitating problem to be an insurmountable case of insomnia. Her story is paralleled by that of Ian Ogelvie, a hapless sleep researcher." Booklist

"Smartly observed and stylishly written, Cohen's new novel is crammed with incidental pleasures. Yet underneath its clever examination of our current love affair with pharmaceuticals lie unsettling questions about the myths we choose to live by: it's not the interpretation of dreams but the meaning of our waking hours that is up for grabs here." New Yorker

Coldsmith, Don, 1926-

The long journey home. Forge 2001 400p $24.95

ISBN 0-312-87617-3   LC 00-48459

"A Tom Doherty Associates book"

"John Buffalo is a Lakota Sioux sent to a government school as a young boy in the 1890s. Proud of his Native American heritage, he vows to outdo the white man at his own game. Although he is a bright student, John's real success comes as an athlete—he plays football, baseball and track, and dreams of competing in the Olympics and later becoming a coach. Racism, however, derails his Olympic hopes and disrupts his budding romance with a U.S. senator's daughter. John later becomes a horse trainer and actor with a traveling Wild West show, performing around the world." Publ Wkly

Coldsmith portrays a "Native American athlete who bears an intentional resemblance to the great Jim Thorpe. . . . This well-researched piece of historical fiction interweaves a compelling life story with many of the pivotal events of the early twentieth century." Booklist

Tallgrass; a novel of the Great Plains. Bantam Bks. 1997 454p

ISBN 0-553-10632-5   LC 96-19672

Coldsmith's saga concerns "the opening of the Santa Fe Trail. Starting with the coming of the Spanish conquistadors in 1541, his work spans 300 years to a time when the fur trade has died, Eastern Native Americans have been relocated onto lands west of the Mississippi, and conflict is building between the Plains Indians and Eastern interlopers, both Indian and white. Coldsmith focuses on a tribe of Pawnee and the devastation that contact with whites brings. This powerful novel demonstrates the diversity of the Native American culture while treating the tribes and their history with dignity and understanding." Libr J

Colegate, Isabel

The shooting party. Viking 1981 c1980 195p

ISBN 0-670-64064-6

     * LC 80-54194

First published 1980 in the United Kingdom

"The time is October 1913, the place an estate in Oxfordshire where Sir Randolph Nettleby and his wife are hosting the biggest shoot of the season. Brought together are the privileged in pursuit of pleasure. For these guests shooting is a special ritual with the shooters, gamekeepers, beaters, and servants all playing specific roles, and the sport is marvelously and meticulously described. Woven through the story are the portrayals of the gentry,

the allusions to romantic and adulterous affairs, the relationship between the classes, and the feeling of the vast changes soon to overtake the Edwardian period. The rising tension that accompanies the final hours of the shooting on this day explodes into unexpected tragedy." Shapiro. Fic for Youth. 3d edition

Winter journey. Counterpoint 2001 199p

ISBN 1-58243-122-1   LC 00-64449

First published 1995 in the United Kingdom

This "is the story of a brother and sister in late middle age who spend a few quiet days together at their childhood home between late December 1992 and early January 1993. . . . Alfred Ashby is 60, a well-known photographer who lives in the stone farmhouse in Somerset where he and his sister grew up. Edith, slightly older, is a former member of Parliament who runs a language school in London. . . . Neither is aware of the pain and disillusionment the other has suffered." N Y Times Book Rev

"Colegate employs a varied cast of background characters who, in addition to their fully dimensional portrayals, provide insight into Britain's still potent class system. In Colegate's assured hands, the natural landscape is rendered as clearly as her characters' interior landscapes, and she accomplishes this in a slim text remarkable for its lucidity, humor and precise observation." Publ Wkly

Coleridge, Nicholas, 1957-

Godchildren. Thomas Dunne Books 2008 551p $25.95

ISBN 978-0-312-38258-2; 0-312-38258-8

     LC 2008-19639

First published 2002 in the United Kingdom

"This wickedly enjoyable novel about a venal British billionaire and his godchildren shows a moribund class society being rapidly dismantled by global wealth. The property and shipping tycoon Marcus Brand's six godchildren include a Scottish aristocrat whose snobbery outstrips his dwindling inheritance, a debonair London gigolo, and a socialist Birmingham boy who pulls himself up by his bootstraps to become a capitalist with a heart of gold. While the story of who triumphs is predictable, Coleridge dissects the social mores of Cap Ferrat and Lyford Cay with skill, noting sartorial codes with the precision of Tom Wolfe." New Yorker

Colette, 1873-1954

Chéri

     In Colette. Six novels p411-534

Claudine and Annie

     In Colette. The complete Claudine p516-632

Claudine at school

     In Colette. The complete Claudine p1-206

     In Colette. Six novels p1-234

Claudine in Paris

     In Colette. The complete Claudine p209-364

Claudine married

     In Colette. The complete Claudine p367-510

Colette, 1873-1954—*Continued*

The collected stories of Colette; edited, and with an introduction, by Robert Phelps; translated by Matthew Ward, et al. Farrar, Straus & Giroux 1983 605p
ISBN 0-374-12629-1
* LC 83-16449
Contents: The other table; The screen; Clouk alone; Clouk's fling; Chéri; The return; The pearls; Literature; My goddaughter; A hairdresser; A masseuse; My corset-maker; The saleswoman; An interview; A letter; The Sémiramis Bar; "If I had a daughter . . ."; Rites; Newly shorn; Grape harvest; In the boudoir; The "master"; Morning glories; What must we look like; The cure; Sleepness nights; Gray days; The last fire; A fable: the tendrils of the vine; The halt; Arrival and rehearsal; A bad morning; The circus horse; The workroom; Matinee; The starveling; Love; The hard worker; After midnight; "Lola"; Moments of stress; Journey's end; "The strike, oh Lord, the strike"; Bastienne's child; The accompanist; The cashier; Nostalgia; Clever dogs; The child prodigy; The misfit; "La Fenice"; "Gitanette"; The victim; The tenor; The quick-change artist; Florie; Gribiche; The hidden woman; Dawn; One evening; The hand; A dead end; The fox; The judge; The omelette; The other wife; Monsieur Maurice; The burglar; The advice; The murderer; The portrait; The landscape; The half-crazy; Secrets; "Châ"; The bracelet; The find; Mirror games; Habit; Alix's refusal; The seamstress; The watchman; The hollow nut; The patriarch; The sick child; The rainy moon; Green sealing wax; In the flower of age; The rivals; The respite; The bitch; The tender shoot {novella}; Bygone spring; October; Armande; The rendezvous; The kepi {novella}; The photographer's wife; Bella-Vista; April
"Includes two novellas that rank as classics, not only in Colette's canon, but in all of 20th century French literature. The Tender Shoot is the story of a singularly nasty middle-aged roué's pursuit of a 15-year-old peasant girl. Upon this squalid tale, Colette lavished her most lyrical language and poetic fancies, heightening the sense of evil. . . . As Colette remarked of her writing, her 'great landscape was always the human face.' No work demonstrates this better than The Kepi, the portrait of a doomed 46-year-old French lieutenant." Time

The complete Claudine; Claudine at school, Claudine in Paris, Claudine married, Claudine and Annie; translated by Antonia White. Farrar, Straus & Giroux 1976 632p o.p.
*
Omnibus edition of four semi-autobiographical novels written by Colette in 1900-1903. The first three appeared under the pen name of her husband and the fourth novel was published under both their names. These translations have copyright dates 1956, 1958, 1960 and 1962 respectively. Variant title for English translation of third volume: Indulgent husband; of final volume: Innocent wife
In the first novel we meet Claudine as a precocious school girl peeping and spying on both her contemporaries and her boarding school teachers. The second novel depicts a girl approaching womanhood discovering the exciting world of Paris and meeting a varied assortment of escorts. Claudine married is not so much the story of the heroine's marriage as the story of Claudine's love affair with Rézi, another married woman. The final volume has Claudine as one of its principal characters, but it is largely the story of an innocent young wife, who during the absence of her domineering husband begins to see more of her sister-in-law and her sophisticated friends and her eyes open to the true ways of life and love

Gigi
In Colette. Six novels p649-97

The kepi
In Colette. The collected stories of Colette p498-531

The last of Chéri
In Colette. Six novels p535-648

Mitsou
In Colette. Six novels p339-410

Music-hall sidelights
In Colette. Six novels p237-337

Six novels. Modern Lib. 697p o.p.
Contents: Claudine at school; Music-hall sidelights; Mitsou; Chéri; The last of Chéri; Gigi

The tender shoot
In Colette. The collected stories of Colette p421-48

Coll, Susan

Acceptance; a novel. Farrar, Straus and Giroux 2007 286p $23
ISBN 978-0-374-23719-6; 0-374-23719-0
LC 2006-15896
"Sarah Crichton books"
This "sendup of the college admissions process is set in a tony suburb of Washington, D.C. A group of overachieving students . . . fight for what seems an ever-narrowing pool of Ivy League spots (the only ones that matter), state-university scholarships (for the rare student who is financially challenged), and liberal-arts places ('safeties'). The view from the other side of the desk is provided by a character in the admissions department of a newly popular college in upstate New York, which is trawling for kids whose parents can pay for new campus facilities. Coll is alert to the comedy—and the pathos—of a system that leads highschool seniors to solicit recommendation letters from their pediatricians." New Yorker

Collins, James, 1958 May 8-

Beginner's Greek; a novel. Little, Brown, and Co. 2008 441p
ISBN 9780316021555; 0-316-02155-5
LC 2007-11690
"Whenever Peter [Russell] boards a plane, which is often, due to his Wall Street job, he wonders whether this will be the flight on which he meets the woman of his dreams. Then, on a trip from New York to Los Angeles, it actually happens: A woman sits next to him who is not only beautiful, but on page 500 of one of Peter's favorite books. They talk (or rather, Holly talks and a smitten Peter tries his best to answer intelligibly). They learn about each other's favorite books, their families, their jobs. It looks as if this might be love at first sight. . . . Five

Collins, James, 1958 May 8——_Continued_
hours later, they land in L.A. and promise to meet for dinner. But when Peter gets to his hotel, her phone number has vanished from his shirt pocket. Years later, when he and Holly meet again, she's on the arm of a womanizing but charming author who also happens to be Peter's closest friend. The two eventually marry, and, resigned, Peter marries the dull but sweet Charlotte." BookPage

Collins "has a rare ability to satirize without becoming nasty, and periodically gives romantic clichés a good tweak." Christ Sci Monit

Collins, Max Allan

Black hats; a novel of Wyatt Earp and Al Capone; [by] Patrick Culhane. William Morrow 2007 304p $24.95

ISBN 978-0-06-089253-1; 0-06-089253-6

LC 2006-48611

This novel "has the young and reckless son of the late "Doc" Holliday being protected and guided by a 70-year-old Wyatt Earp in a New York City gangland war over a large supply of hard liquor. Did Johnny Holliday Jr. give gangster Al Capone the three knife scars on his cheek responsible for the "Scarface" nickname? That's just part of the story. Collins has outdone himself in this tale of bad guys, bullets, and booze set at the start of the Prohibition era." Libr J

(jt. auth) Spillane, M. The Goliath bone

Collins, Michael, 1964-

Death of a writer; a novel. Bloomsbury Pub. 2006 307p $24.95

ISBN 978-1-59691-229-8; 1-59691-229-4

LC 2006-1950

"E. Robert Pendleton's heralded first novel secures him a teaching position at exclusive Bannockburn College in the Midwest, but his career is on the skids because he hasn't published recently. When an old friend, acclaimed writer Allen Horowitz, arrives at Bannockburn for a lecture, the despondent Bob attempts suicide but fails. While helping Bob recuperate, graduate student Adi Wiltshire discovers cartons of a self-published novel, Scream, in his basement; recognizing its brilliance, she and Allen arrange its reissue without the incapacitated Bob's knowledge. The successful new edition of Scream attracts the attention of cold case detective Jon Ryder, who notices close parallels between its story and a local unsolved murder." Publ Wkly

This novel is as "caustic as it is brilliant, a concoction of academic satire, German philosophy and literary criticism mixed up as a haunting murder mystery that will leave you disoriented—and deeply amused." Washington Post Book World

Lost souls; Michael Collins. 1st American ed. Viking 2004 260p $23.95

ISBN 0-670-03328-6   LC 2003-64535

"On Halloween night in a dead-end town in Indiana, local cop Lawrence discovers the body of a three-year-old girl, dressed as an angel, who appears to be the victim of a hit-and-run accident. Called into a private meeting with the mayor, Lawrence is told to steer the investigation away from a star athlete, who is set to quarterback

a championship game. But as the investigation spirals out of control, the body count mounts, and Lawrence discovers an astounding level of hypocrisy at work among the town's most prominent citizens." Booklist

"Collins's style, which alternates between the clipped prose of a cop novel and some surreally introspective passages, gives the book the prose feel of a David Lynch film." Publ Wkly

Collins, Wilkie, 1824-1889

The moonstone. Knopf 1992 473p $19

ISBN 0-679-41722-2

* LC 92-52918

"Everyman's library"

First published 1868

This novel "concerns the disappearance of the Moonstone, an enormous diamond that once adorned a Hindu idol and came into the possession of an English officer. The heroine, Miss Verinder, believes her lover, Franklin Blake, to be the thief; other suspects are Blake's rival and three mysterious Brahmins. The mystery is solved by Sergeant Cuff, possibly the first detective in English fiction." Reader's Ency. 4th edition

The woman in white. Knopf 1991 xxxvii, 569p $20

ISBN 0-679-40563-1

* LC 91-52971

"Everyman's library"

First published 1860; first Everyman's library edition 1910

"Practically the first English novel to deal with the detection of crime. The plot is based on the resemblance between the heroine and a mysterious woman in white, and involves an infamous attempt to obtain the heroine's money." Lenrow. Reader's Guide to Prose Fic

Coltman, Derek

(tr) Kadare, I. The general of the dead army

Colwin, Laurie

A big storm knocked it over; a novel. HarperCollins Pubs. 1993 259p

ISBN 0-06-017019-0   LC 92-56219

"For Jane Louise, even Teddy—her wonderful, new, rock-solid husband—and a baby on the way are not enough to stave off plenty of free-floating anxiety. Luckily, she shares her joy and her distress with best friends Edie and Mokie, who have decided to embark on parenthood at the same time. The extended family formed by these two couples must suffice emotionally for each of the four individuals, since not one of the four fits within his or her own family." Booklist

"The novel makes the idea of happy endings for decent people seem entirely plausible, almost inevitable—no small feat for a writer these days and no small pleasure for a reader." N Y Times Book Rev

Family happiness; a novel. Knopf 1982 271p

ISBN 0-394-52511-6   LC 82-23

"Polly Solo-Miller is the mainstay of an attractive, well-to-do New York Jewish family, a family so ensconced in society, so sure of itself and its eminently

Colwin, Laurie—*Continued*

proper, aristocratic view of life that there is never a doubt in the minds of any of them but what the Solo-Miller way of doing things is the best. Polly loves her husband and two children, her parents, her siblings. She is, in fact, the perfect wife, mother, daughter. But underneath there is more than a hint of rebellion seething and when Polly falls headlong in love with a painter, Lincoln, and takes to spending long and very cozy afternoons in his studio, thoroughly enjoying the adulterous affair, her Solo-Miller conscience is sorely beset." Publ Wkly

"What is so striking about this wrenching novel is not the plot itself . . . but, rather, the absolutely convincing way that Colwin portrays Polly's slow awakening to selfhood." Booklist

Goodbye without leaving. Poseidon Press 1990 253p
ISBN 0-671-70706-X   LC 90-6797
This novel follows the "progress of Geraldine Coleshares' life, from mediocre graduate student to rock 'n' roll backup singer to wife and mother. She seems happily married to Johnny Miller, a lawyer but a music fanatic at heart. She worries (but not too much) about what she is doing with her life, and what it all means." Libr J

"The tone here is disarmingly light, the humor intimate, and the plot inventive. A cheerfully irreverent look at an identity crisis and its unexpected resolution." Booklist

Happy all the time; a novel. Knopf 1978 213p
ISBN 0-394-50190-X   LC 78-2425
Set in New York City, this love story involves four quite normal people, "two men, two women. The men are cousins and close friends, the women are very different from each other, but full of spunk and individuality. Guido and Holly come together first, Vincent and Misty meet later. The men, long-time associates, are terribly nervous about their women liking each other. The women, in turn, eye each other warily. What we, as readers are treated to, however, is one of the most engaging and funniest dual courtships in a long time. The dialogue is sparkling and crisp, the encounter situations perfectly believable and perfectly ridiculous, as these four people, who really are 'happy all the time,' go through the 'angst' of realizing it." Publ Wkly

Condé, Maryse, 1937-

I, Tituba, black witch of Salem; translated by Richard Philcox; foreword by Angela Y. Davis; afterword by Ann Armstrong Scarboro. University Press of Va. 1992 227p
ISBN 0-8139-1398-5   LC 92-8134
"A Caraf book"
Original French edition, 1986
This historical novel attempts to re-create the life story of the Barbadian slave who was arrested in 1692 "for witchcraft in Salem, Massachusetts. . . . As a child, Tituba sees her mother executed. She is then raised by an old woman who teaches her the African art of healing and communicating with spirits. As a young woman, she is sold to a Puritan minister who leaves Barbados for America. Tituba uses her powers for good purposes, including the healing of her master's family. But her pow-

ers are misunderstood by the [Puritans]." Libr J

"Part historical novel, part literary fable, part exploration of the clash of irreconcilable cultures, [this] is most of all an affirmation of a courageous and resourceful woman's capacity for survival." N Y Times Book Rev

Conley, Robert J.

Mountain windsong; a novel of the Trail of Tears. University of Okla. Press 1992 218p
ISBN 0-8061-2452-0   LC 92-54150
The author "chronicles the Trail of Tears—the forced removal of the tribe in the 1830s from its homelands in the southeastern U.S. to alien territory in Oklahoma. He gives this epic drama a human scale by focusing on the story of Oconeechee, daughter of a famous Cherokee chief, and Waguli (Whippoorwill), the young man she loves. Separated by the genocidal march—one-quarter of the participants died en route to Oklahoma—the pair spend much of the novel searching for each other. A young Native American named LeRoy . . . narrates their saga, related to him by his grandfather after he asks about the beautiful 'windsong' he has heard on a North Carolina reservation occupied by descendants of the Cherokees who escaped relocation." Publ Wkly

"Its historical accuracy and its political correctness aside, the novel is a timeless love story about young people buffeted by a changing world over which they have no control." Booklist

Connell, Evan S., 1924-

Deus lo volt!; chronicle of the Crusades. Counterpoint 2000 462p
ISBN 1-58243-065-9   LC 99-54831
A chronicle "of the crusades from the point of view of a French knight. Jean Joinville, a participant in the disastrous second crusade under Louis IX, begins his chronicle with the first crusade, in 1095, and ends with the taking of Acre in 1290 by the forces of Ashraf Khalil, which effectively ended the mad attempt to make Palestine a Christian protectorate." Publ Wkly

What enlivens Connell's historial fiction "is first, his boyish fascination with how much has been buried alongside the victims: lost books and alphabets, artworks, cities, enigmatic treasures of all kinds. Second, there is the glittering anger of his style." Yale Rev

Lost in Uttar Pradesh; new and selected stories. Counterpoint 2008 359p $27
ISBN 978-1-59376-175-2; 1-59376-175-9
                                      LC 2007-43829
Contents: Lion; Hooker; Nan Madol; Proctor Bemis; The walls of vila; Arcturus; The land where lemon trees bloom; Caribbean provedor; Octopus, the Sausalito Quarterly of new writing, art & ideas; Election eve; St. Augustine's pigeon; Bowen; Assassin; Mrs. Proctor Bemis; Noah's ark; Puig's wife; Guadalcanal; Yellow raft; The Cuban missile crisis; Ancient musick; The palace of the Moorish kings; Lost in Uttar Pradesh

"The stories in 'Lost in Uttar Pradesh' — seven of which are published here for the first time — vary in setting and length, but it is not hard to identify the common thread running through them: Connell's characters, whether recurring or simply enjoying a walk-on, find themselves suddenly shellacked by the realization that

Connell, Evan S., 1924-—*Continued*
the world is not as it appears — moral, ordered, progressing toward some comprehensible end but is, in fact, the opposite. . . . If these narratives sometimes feel less like fully realized stories and more like fragments of an ongoing conversation Connell is having with the world, so be it — what he's working to do here is express both rage and its futility, and it's fascinating to watch this theme morph and play out in various scenarios." Star Tribune (Minneapolis, Minn.)

Mr. Bridge; [by] Evan S. Connell, Jr. Knopf 1969 369p o.p.

*

This novel is made up "of fragments of experience from the life of a middle-aged suburban couple between the world wars. Brief episodes are juxaposed to reveal the stereotyped values and emotional and spiritual aridity of the prosperous, proper Bridges." Libr J
"Mr. Connell's art is one of restraint and perfect mimicry. His chapters are admirably short, his style is brevity itself. . . . Rarely has a satirist damned his subject with such good humor." N Y Times Book Rev

Mrs. Bridge; [by] Evan S. Connell, Jr. Viking 1959 254p o.p.

*

"India Bridge is a country club matron in Kansas City. Her husband, a successful lawyer, is seldom home so Mrs. Bridge copes—not too well—with her children, who are very different from one another. Ruth, the eldest, keeps aloft; Douglas, the youngest, is mostly off on his own projects and not interested in the fine rules of behavior that Mrs. Bridge finds essential. She seems able to communicate most easily with Carolyn, the middle child. We follow the family as the children grow. Mrs. Bridge, eager to be a proper upper-middle-class wife and mother, finds no happiness despite her affluence and good intentions." Shapiro. Fic for Youth. 3d edition

Connell, Joe, 1963-

Crumbtown. Knopf 2003 259p $23
ISBN 0-375-41364-2   LC 2002-72930
"Set in a phantasmagoric dreamscape that is part New York City slum and part absurd parallel universe, Crumbtown is a place in which little is as it appears. The story centers on Don Reedy, in prison for a Robin Hood-style bank robbery, who is freed from jail to act as a consultant on a TV show based on his life. Once out, he quickly falls for Rita, a Russian émigré bartender, and teams up with half twins Tim and Tom, his former partners-in-crime, who sold him out to the police 15 years earlier. With them, he plots a new robbery set to take place during the filming of the bank robbery scene of the TV show. The result is a wildly inventive and darkly satiric take on a world constantly shifting and media image." Libr J

Connelly, Karen, 1969-

The lizard cage. Nan A. Talese 2007 430p $26
ISBN 978-0-385-51818-5; 0-385-51818-8
          LC 2006-44565
First published 2005 in Canada
This novel, a political thriller set in Burma, centers "on Teza, a nonviolent, prodemocracy activist in solitary con-

finement because of his participation in the 1988 demonstrations against the government. Enduring brutality and betrayal, Teza develops a friendship with Zaw Gyi, a 12-year-old orphan who serves food to the prisoners, and becomes determined to help the boy escape the inhumane environment." Libr J
"A thrilling, vital excoriation of the military junta that has ruled Burma for decades. . . . Karen Connelly's language and imagery evoke the short stories and poems that trickle out of Burma, by turns fearful and violent, beautiful and rancid." Wall Street J

Connelly, Michael, 1956-

The black ice. Little, Brown 1993 322p
ISBN 0-316-15382-6   LC 92-33500
Harry Bosch is a "smart, determined LAPD homicide detective who's driven by an inner sense of justice. This time out he arrives early on the scene of a fellow officer's suicide; then he's told it's not his case: back off. Fat chance. Harry senses the officer may have gone over to the bad guys and was killed when he tried to tiptoe back to the right side of the tracks. At every turn, Harry is confronted by dirty cops struggling to save their collective butts by lying and misdirecting the investigation. . . . A powerful novel." Booklist

Blood work. Little, Brown 1998 393p
ISBN 0-316-15399-0   LC 97-28240
"Terry McCaleb was an FBI profiler specializing in serial killers until his heart gave out. After waiting two years for a heart transplant, he's just happy to be alive—until Graciela, a beautiful woman with a disturbing story, draws him back into the game. Graciela's sister Glory was killed in a convenience story robbery, and she's come to seek McCaleb's help in solving the crime. . . . High suspense, masterful plotting, and smart prose make this a superior thriller." Libr J

The brass verdict; a novel. Little, Brown and Company 2008 422p $26.99
ISBN 978-0-316-16629-4; 0-316-16629-4
          LC 2008-19374
Mickey Haller "returns to the courtroom in an unusual way here. Former colleague Jerry Vincent is murdered, and his caseload is dropped in Haller's lap. One of Vincent's high-profile cases involved a movie mogul accused of killing his wife and her lover in a jealous rage. As Haller prepares the mogul's defense, he discovers that Vincent's killer might have chosen him as the next target. Haller must trust Harry Bosch, the police officer investigating Vincent's murder, if he is going to survive and trust his instincts if he is going to succeed in convincing a jury of his client's innocence." Libr J
"If this were no more than a standard legal thriller, it would still be hard to put down. But for all the glee we might take in watching Mickey in action—psychoanalyzing the jury pool, shredding the credibility of a prosecution witness or faking civility to a powerful judge—The Brass Verdict is not just a conventional legal thriller but also a complicated morality play." N Y Times Book Rev

City of bones; a novel. Little, Brown 2002 393p
ISBN 0-316-15405-9   LC 2001-38399
This mystery opens with "the discovery of a human bone in the densely wooded hills around Laurel Canyon. Once the recovered skeleton is identified as that of a 12-

LIST OF FICTIONAL WORKS

Connelly, Michael, 1956—_Continued_

year-old boy who had been repeatedly abused before his death, some 20 years earlier, Harry Bosch, the Los Angeles homicide detective . . . can go on the hunt for the killer. But before he does, Connelly works those initial scenes into a taut mini-drama in which even minor characters, like the elderly doctor whose dog dug up the first bone, play standout roles that burn with conviction." N Y Times Book Rev

The closers; a novel. Little, Brown 2005 403p $26.95

ISBN 0-316-73494-2

* LC 2005-00076

"In Los Angeles in 1988, a sixteen-year-old girl disappeared from her home and was later found dead of a gunshot wound to the chest. The death appeared at first to be a suicide but some of the evidence contradicted that scenario, and detectives came to believe this was in fact a murder. Despite a by-the-book investigation, no one was ever charged. Now Detective Harry Bosch is back with the LAPD with the sole mission of closing unsolved cases, and this girl's death is the first he's given." Publisher's note

"Like James Ellroy and John Fante, both of whose work is referred to here, Mr. Connelly continues to make his doomy, secretive Los Angeles a living, breathing character in his stories." N Y Times (Late N Y Ed)

A darkness more than night; a novel. Little, Brown 2001 418p

ISBN 0-316-15407-5   LC 00-31025

This mystery pits L.A.P.D. detective Harry Bosch and former FBI profiler Terry McCaleb against each other. "When approached by an old L.A.P.D. pal, McCaleb jumps at the chance to help on a baffling murder case, the ritualistic details of which suggest a serial killer. It doesn't take McCaleb long to focus in on a prime suspect: Bosch. . . . Readers familiar with Bosch's bend-but-don't-break morality won't be stumped for long, but Connelly's . . . novel is otherwise flawless, cleverly conceived, superbly plotted and morally complex." Publ Wkly

Echo Park; a novel. Little, Brown and Co. 2006 405p $26.99

ISBN 978-0-316-73495-0; 0-316-73495-0

LC 2006-9809

In this case, "the elusive quarry is the man who abducted a 22-year-old equestrian, Marie Gesto, in 1993. Having returned to active duty as a member of the LAPD Open-Unsolved Unit, Bosch repeatedly pulls the file to see if he can discover something new and give some small solace to the victim's parents. When a chance police stop of a suspicious vehicle nets serial killer Raynard Waits, who's carrying body parts in his van, Bosch assesses the murderer's claim that he was responsible for killing Gesto, too. The weary and cynical detective soon suspects that Waits is trying to barter information for a reduced sentence of life imprisonment. Political motivations connected with the upcoming DA election also cloud the investigation." Publ Wkly

"What puts Connelly in the top rank of modern procedural writers and, perhaps, into the ranks of the better modern L.A. writers of any genre is his willingness to accept that there aren't always easy answers in Bosch's life, or sometimes any answers at all. . . . That sense of uncertainty and dread, combined with Bosch's going from middle age to the precipice of old age, informs every page of this novel." Washington Post Book World

The Lincoln lawyer; a novel. Little, Brown 2005 404p $26.95

ISBN 0-316-73493-4

* LC 2005-12863

"Mickey Haller defends low-life criminals who seem to offend habitually. With no actual office in which to hang his law degree, he works out of the backseat of his car. When a wealthy client lands in Mickey's lap, he thinks he has found a dream case. The evidence indicates a frame, and Mickey believes he might actually be defending his first truly innocent client. While he manipulates the system to his advantage, Mickey discovers that he is being maneuvered as well." Libr J

"The book is haunted by Mickey's worst nightmare: the thought of having to defend an innocent man. He starts out without the foggiest idea of what to do with someone like that. But by the end of the story an Honest Abe conscience has begun to kick in. That's when Mickey becomes a Connelly character through and through." N Y Times (Late N Y Ed)

Lost light; a novel. Little, Brown 2003 360p $25.95

ISBN 0-316-15460-1   LC 2002-36848

"The cop who failed to collar the person who strangled Angela Benton on her 24th birthday can't do much about it now; having taken a bullet in the spine, he's paralyzed from the neck down. But the man can talk, and he talks Harry Bosch into taking the cold case. . . . Despite some shockingly sunny developments in his personal life, Bosch wears his depression like armour, making him the perfect hero for our paranoid age." N Y Times Book Rev

The narrows; a novel. Little, Brown 2004 404p $25.95

ISBN 0-316-15530-6   LC 2003-25681

Private investigator Harry Bosch "confronts the most terrifying killer he's ever known—the monster known to millions as the Poet. FBI agent Rachel Walling finally gets the call she's dreaded for years. The Poet has returned. Years earlier she worked on the famous case tracking the serial killer who wove lines of poetry into his . . . crimes. Rachel has never forgotten the Poet-and apparently he has not forgotten her. Former LAPD detective Harry Bosch gets a call, too, from an old friend whose husband recently died. The death appeared natural, but this man's ties to the hunt for the Poet make Harry dig deep." Publisher's note

"Expertly juggling the narrative between Bosch's brooding, hardboiled voice and a broader third-person perspective that takes in the points of view of Walling and the Poet, Connelly builds tension exponentially through superb use of dramatic irony." Booklist

The overlook; a novel. Little, Brown and Co. 2007 225p $21.99

ISBN 978-0-316-01895-1; 0-316-01895-3

LC 2007-1954

This novel, which was originally serialized in the New York Times magazine, reunites Harry Bosch "with his former flame, FBI agent Rachel Walling. Bosch must break in a new partner, rookie Iggy Ferras, when they're called to look into the execution of physicist Stanley

Connelly, Michael, 1956--—*Continued*

Kent on a Mulholland Drive overlook. When a special FBI unit, headed by Walling, arrives and tries to usurp his case, claiming it's a matter of national security, Bosch refuses to back down. Walling's focus on the potential theft of radioactive material from the hospital where Kent was lending his expertise to cancer treatment and her unwillingness to share information only make Bosch more determined to solve the case. . . . The scramble to investigate threats to national security, justified or otherwise, is a timely subject and one on which Connelly puts a brilliant new spin." Publ Wkly

The scarecrow; a novel. Little, Brown and Co. 2009 419p $27.99

ISBN 978-0-316-16630-0   LC 2009-00855

This novel "begins with Jack McEvoy — the crime reporter who was the hero of Connelly's 1996 The Poet— being given two weeks' notice at the Los Angeles Times. He's expected to spend his last days training his replacement: a young reporter whose real advantage, for the bosses, is that her salary is much lower than Jack's. . . . Jack decides that the ultimate 'fuck you' to the paper will be a final story so good that the suits will look like fools to fire him. He decides on the case of a teen gangbanger charged with a stripper's rape and murder. It doesn't take long for Jack to suss out that the police have the wrong man, and to link the murder with another that makes it clear both are the work of a serial killer. The Scarecrow is swift and engrossing, and it marks a development that has needed to happen in Connelly's novels for a while." Boston Phoenix

Void moon; a novel. Little, Brown 2000 391p $32

ISBN 0-316-15406-7   LC 99-37054

"Cassie Black, a crack burglar whose specialty is stealing from high rollers who break the bank in Las Vegas, ignores the astrological warning of a bad moon and inadvertently rips off a courier for the Chicago mob. 'Sometimes you can steal too much,' Cassie tells her panicked accomplice when they finish counting the mob's $2.5 million down payment for the Cleopatra Casino. 'We just did.' Connelly makes shrewd work of the manhunt, cranking up the suspense to keep Cassie a whisker ahead of her pursuer, a techno-savvy psycho named Jack Karch, who is so adept at ruining a perfectly good hand that they call him the Jack of Spades." N Y Times Book Rev

Connolly, John, 1968-

Bad men; a thriller. Atria Books 2004 392p $25

ISBN 0-7434-8784-2   LC 2003-69639

"The small island of Sanctuary, off the coast of Maine, was once the scene of a bloody massacre. Now, three centuries later, evil has again come to the island, a modern-day evil with strange, eerie connections to the events of the late 1600s. Do two police officers have even a remote chance of stopping the carnage? This is one of those novels that refuses to be pigeonholed. It's a thriller; it's a mystery; it's a tale of the supernatural (sort of). At its center is Joe Dupree, the (literal) gentle giant of a cop, a man whose kindness and compassion would appear to make him a bad choice to defend the citizens of Sanctuary from the marauding evil that approaches." Booklist

The book of lost things. Atria Books 2006 339p $23

ISBN 978-0-7432-9885-8; 0-7432-9885-3

LC 2006-049340

A "novel about a 12-year-old English boy, David, who is thrust into a realm where eternal stories and fairy tales assume an often gruesome reality. Books are the magic that speak to David, whose mother has died at the start of WWII after a long debilitating illness. His father remarries, and soon his stepmother is pregnant with yet another interloper who will threaten David's place in his father's life. When a portal to another world opens in time-honored fashion, David enters a land of beasts and monsters where he must undertake a quest if he is to earn his way back out. Connelly echoes many great fairy tales and legends (Little Red Riding Hood, Roland, Hansel and Gretel), but cleverly twists them to his own purposes." Libr J

The unquiet; a novel. Atria Books 2007 418p $25.95

ISBN 978-0-7432-9893-3; 0-7432-9893-4

LC 2006-101541

"Daniel Clay, a psychiatrist alleged to have worked with a child-abuse ring, is missing and presumed dead. His grown daughter, Rebecca, is being stalked by an excon whose own daughter is missing. Rebecca hires Portland, Maine, investigator Charlie Parker to protect her and dissuade her stalker, a former contract killer named Merrick who is intent on either finding his daughter or avenging her death. The case leads to a very dark chapter in Maine's rural history and to the still-operational remnants of a syndicate of highly organized child abusers. Connelly weaves elements of the supernatural into a disturbing, very dark tale. . . . The disquieting subject, coupled with Connolly's dark, lyrical prose, will leave unshakable images lurking on the edge of the reader's consciousness." Booklist

Conrad, Joseph, 1857-1924

The complete short fiction of Joseph Conrad; edited with an introduction by Samuel Hynes. Ecco Press 1991-1992 2v

ISBN 0-88001-307-9 (v1); 0-88001-308-7 (v2)

LC 91-27115

Contents: v1 The idiots; The lagoon; An outpost of progress; Karain: a memory; The return; Youth: a narrative; Amy Foster; To-morrow; Gaspar Ruiz: a romantic tale

v2 An anarchist: a desperate tale; The informer: an ironic tale; The brute: an indignant tale; The black mate; Il conde: a pathetic tale; The secret sharer: an episode from the coast; Prince Roman; The partner; The Inn of the Two Witches: a find; Because of the dollars; The warrior's soul; The tale

Great short works of Joseph Conrad. Harper & Row 1966 378p o.p.

"A Harper perennial classic"

Contents: The lagoon [short story]; The Nigger of the Narcissus (1914); Youth (1903); Heart of darkness (1899); Typhoon (1902); The secret sharer [short story]

Heart of darkness; with an introduction by Verlyn Klinkenborg. Knopf 1993 110p $15

ISBN 0-679-42801-1

* LC 93-1855

Conrad, Joseph, 1857-1924—*Continued*

"Everyman's library"

Originally published 1902 in the United Kingdom in the collection Youth, and two other stories

"Marlow tells his friends of an experience in the (then) Belgian Congo, where he once ran a river steamer for a trading company. Fascinated by reports about the powerful white trader Kurtz, Marlow went into the jungle in search of him, expecting to find in his character a clue to the evil around him. He found Kurtz living a depraved and abominable life, based on his exploitation of the natives. Without the pressures of society, and with the opportunity to wield absolute power, Kurtz succumbs to atavism." Reader's Ency. 4th edition

> *also in* Conrad, J. Great short works of Joseph Conrad p175-256
> *also in* Conrad, J. The portable Conrad p490-603

Lord Jim; a tale. Knopf 1992 xxxiii, 437p $19
ISBN 0-679-40544-5
                                * LC 91-53223
"Everyman's library"

First published 1899; first Everyman's library edition 1935

"The title character is a man haunted by guilt over an act of cowardice. He becomes an agent at an isolated East Indian trading post. There his feelings of inadequacy and responsibility are played out to their logical and inevitable end." Merriam-Webster's Ency of Lit

The Nigger of the Narcissus; edited, with an introduction and notes, by Cedric Watts. Penguin Books 1989 151p map pa $12.95
ISBN 0-14-018094-X

First published 1897 with title: Children of the sea

"All life on board the *Narcissus* revolves around James Wait, a dying black sailor. Other members of the crew include the strong Captain Allistoun; Craik, an Irish religious fanatic; and Donkin, an arrogant, lazy Cockney. The superstitious sailors cater to Wait, even steal food for him, and rescue him when the ship capsizes during a fierce storm. However, he is also the cause of dissension aboard ship, leading to a near mutiny. The novel is notable not only for its vivid picture of life at sea but also as a study of evolving relationships among men amid the most extreme circumstances." Merriam-Webster's Ency of Lit

> *also in* Conrad, J. Great short works of Joseph Conrad p21-140
> *also in* Conrad, J. The portable Conrad p292-453

Nostromo; a tale of the seaboard. Knopf 1992 532p $20
ISBN 0-679-40990-4
                                * LC 91-53185
"Everyman's library"

First published 1904; first Everyman's library edition 1957

"Set in the South American republic of 'Costaguana,' it is an exciting, complicated story about capitalist exploitation and revolution on the national scene and about personal morality and corruption in individuals. Charles Gould's silver mine helps to maintain the country's sta-

bility and its reactionary government. Gould's idealistic preoccupation with the mine warps his character and makes him neglect his gentle wife, Dona Emilia. When the revolution comes, Gould puts a consignment of silver in the charge of Nostromo, the magnificent, 'incorruptible' *capataz de cargadores* ('foreman of the dock workers'). A chance happening makes Nostromo decide to bury the silver and pretend that it was lost at sea. He is eventually killed on the island where his riches are buried, when he is mistaken by his fiancée's father for a prowler. . . . Conrad's characterization is strong, his narration is complex and oblique. The story starts halfway through the events of the revolution and proceeds by way of flashbacks and glimpses into the future." Reader's Ency. 4th edition

The portable Conrad; edited, and with an introduction and notes, by Morton Dauwen Zabel. Viking 1947 760p o.p.
"Viking portable library"

Contains two novels: The Nigger of the 'Narcissus,' and Typhoon; three long stories; six shorter stories; and a selection from Conrad's prefaces, letters and autobiographical writings

Short stories included are: Prince Roman; Warrior's soul; Amy Foster; Outpost of progress; Il Conde; The lagoon; The secret sharer. The novelettes are: Youth; Heart of darkness

Typhoon
> *In* Conrad, J. Great short works of Joseph Conrad p259-328
> *In* Conrad, J. The portable Conrad p192-287

Victory; an island tale; with an introduction by Tony Tanner. Knopf 1998 lxi, 385p $20
ISBN 0-375-40047-8   LC 98-27677
"Everyman's library"

First published 1915

"The novel's "central character, Axel Heyst, a Swedish aristocrat, lives on an island in the Malay Archipelego. Influenced by the sceptical philosophy of his father, and trying to avoid forming any attachments, his way of life is challenged when he rescues Lena, who has been touring the islands as part of a Ladies' Orchestra, from the sexual harassment of the hotelkeeper, Schomberg. The novel explores their relationship and the difficulties precipitated by the arrival of the devilish 'Mr Jones' and his two companions." Oxford Companion to 20th-century Lit in Engl

Youth
> *In* Conrad, J. The complete short fiction of Joseph Conrad p151-80
> *In* Conrad, J. Great short works of Joseph Conrad p143-71
> *In* Conrad, J. The portable Conrad

Conroy, Pat

Beach music. Talese 1995 628p $32.50
ISBN 0-385-41304-1   LC 95-13563

This novel tells "the story of Jack McCall of Waterford, South Carolina, his five brothers, drunken father, . . . [his] mother, and Holocaust-surviving in-laws." Booklist

Conroy, Pat—*Continued*

This "is an absolute attic of a book. It's overstuffed. Seemingly every memory, character, place, and event from not only Conroy's life, but from the lives of most of the people he's ever met are in it. And as in a proper attic, you wander through 'Beach Music' dazed and fascinated by the odd, clashing richness of the several lifestyles it contains." Christ Sci Monit

The lords of discipline. Bantam Books 2002 c1980 561p pa $15

ISBN 0-553-38156-3

A reissue of the title first published 1980 by Houghton Mifflin

The story is set in the late sixties at the time of the Vietnam War. The narrator, "Will McLean, recounts his four years at 'Carolina Military Institute.' . . . We follow the fates of four roommates and their reactions to the Institute. Will has been given the responsibility of helping the Institute's first black cadet make it through the first year. In doing that Will runs into a mysterious secret society." Libr J

The novel "is engrossing and well written. Pat Conroy . . . writes dialogue that reeks of witty Hollywood repartee, but his descriptions and characterizations are both sensitive and entertaining. He carefully draws Will as the young man who disdains military formalities and defends plebes." Saturday Rev

The prince of tides. Houghton Mifflin 1986 567p $35

ISBN 0-395-35300-9

* LC 86-10689

"Savannah Wingo, a successful feminist poet who has suffered from hallucinations and suicidal tendencies since childhood, has never been able to reconcile her life in New York with her early South Carolina tidewater heritage. Her suicide attempt brings her twin brother, Tom, to New York, where he spends the next few months, at the request of Savannah's psychiatrist . . . helping to reconstruct and analyze her early life." Libr J

South of Broad; a novel. Doubleday 2009 514p $29.95

ISBN 978-0-385-41305-3; 0-385-41305-X

LC 2008-45681

In this novel "Charleston, S.C., gossip columnist Leopold Bloom King narrates a paean to his hometown and friends. . . . In the late '60s and after his brother commits suicide, then 18-year-old Leo befriends a cross-section of the city's inhabitants: scions of Charleston aristocracy; Appalachian orphans; a black football coach's son; and an astonishingly beautiful pair of twins, Sheba and Trevor Poe, who are evading their psychotic father. The story alternates between 1969, the glorious year Leo's coterie stormed Charleston's social, sexual and racial barricades, and 1989, when Sheba, now a movie star, enlists them to find her missing gay brother in AIDS-ravaged San Francisco." Publ Wkly

"In the great Southern tradition of storytelling, the city of Charleston, S.C., is the principal 'character' in Pat Conroy's new novel. . . . Like the Southern Gothic masters, William Faulkner and Flannery O'Connor, Conroy understands that a compelling sense of place will lend grace to his narrative, inhabiting the minds of his readers like the mournful strains of an old folk song." Boston Globe

Constantine, K. C.

Blood mud. Mysterious Press 1999 375p

ISBN 0-89296-647-5

LC 98-34909

Retired Rocksburg, Pennsylvania police chief Mario Balzic "is hired by an insurance lawyer to investigate a claimed loss of 40-plus handguns and 30,000 rounds of ammunition stolen from a firearms company. Bored with retirement, trying to ignore his wife's suggestions that he exercise more and they move to Florida, and the self-described 'old geezer' eagerly takes the job." Publ Wkly

"Constantine knows that Faulkner was right: the only subject truly worth writing about is the human heart in conflict with itself. The evocation of Mario's fears and inner conflicts, told through agonizingly wonderful dialogue between husband and wife, raises this latest Balzic novel to the level of the best contemporary literature." Booklist

Brushback. Mysterious Press 1998 278p $29

ISBN 0-89296-646-7

LC 97-10130

In this mystery set in Rocksburg, Pennyslvania "Ruggiero 'Rugs' Carlucci is investigating the brutal murder of Brushback Bobby Blasco, a local hero who once beaned the immortal Ted Williams, even though Williams was his Red Sox teammate. Blasco, who has a history of beating wives and girlfriends, has been bludgeoned to death with a Louisville Slugger autographed by the Splendid Splinter. But Rugs has many competing concerns: his mother's nightly anxiety attacks; his duties as acting police chief; byzantine city politics; undertrained, overworked cops; and summoning the courage to ask a beautiful woman for a date." Booklist

"This is another near-perfect game from Constantine. His working-class dialogue is always exacting and evocative, and his detective is a great guy with a good heart and a mouth that just never quits." Publ Wkly

Family values. Mysterious Press 1997 216p

ISBN 0-89296-545-2

LC 96-23330

Retired Rocksburg, Pa. police chief Mario Balzic is "working on special assignment for the state's Deputy Attorney General, who is bedeviled by a 17-year-old murder case that won't roll over and die. The plot isn't much: Balzic goes around interviewing people involved in the trial of Lester Walczinsky, who is doing serious prison time for killing a couple of no-good drug dealers, and digging up evidence of past perjury and police corruption. Plot doesn't really count for much in Mr. Constantine's books. Character does." N Y Times Book Rev

Grievance. Mysterious Press 2000 279p

ISBN 0-89296-648-3

LC 99-41380

This mystery, set in Rocksburg, Pa., begins with "the murder of J. D. Lyon, C.E.O. of the local steel outfit that pulled up stakes and relocated to Brazil, tossing this company town into an economic sinkhole. Ruggiero (Rugs) Carlucci, the young police sergeant who recently took over the peacekeeping chores . . . does his best to conduct a fair investigation. But he is driven to distraction by his mother's deteriorating mental state, and his work ethic is compromised by his compassion for the families whose lives were so casually destroyed by the murdered man. . . . The anguished voices of the broken people in this beat-up town would make a saint weep." N Y Times Book Rev

Constantine, K. C.—*Continued*

Saving room for dessert. Mysterious Press 2002 294p

ISBN 0-89296-763-3   LC 2002-20096

This mystery "focuses on three Rocksburg cops who patrol the Flats, an area of the city known for domestic disputes that often become deadly. Officer William Rayford prays for a thunderstorm that will keep the feuding Bucyks and Hornyaks, not to mention the certifiable Scavellis, indoors. His prayers aren't answered, however, and Rayford and fellow cops Reseta and Canozza all find themselves drawn into a lunatic situation that ends tragically." Booklist

"Constantine is as eloquent as ever in speaking out on the inevitability of violence when people can't find the language to express themselves." N Y Times Book Rev

Cook, Elizabeth, 1952-

Achilles. Picador 2002 115p

ISBN 0-312-28884-0   LC 2001-52398

First published 2001 in the United Kingdom

"This forceful re-creation of the life of Achilles sacrifices nothing to modernity: gods mate violently with mortals, ghosts feast on sheep's blood, and Achilles rages and slays, unburdened by psychology. At the same time, this brief, intense novel is unmistakably modern in intent, turning a war epic into a meditation on the limits of human perfectibility." New Yorker

Cook, Robin, 1940-

Coma; a novel. Little, Brown 1977 306p

ISBN 0-316-15510-1

* LC 76-52951

"A female medical student uses her charms and femininity to obtain forbidden charts and computer read-outs on certain patients who have gone into coma on the operating table and never come out of it, remaining like vegetables due to extensive brain damage. Susan feels there is something wrong and sets out to find what it is. As a second-year med student, she knows practically nothing of medical terms or practices, so spends all of her class time in the library trying to learn the terminology before she can try to solve a mystery that has puzzled the finest surgeons in the hospital. She does manage to uncover a ring of doctors who are selling various organs for transplant from the coma victims as soon as they can declare them dead, and is almost a victim herself for her pains." West Coast Rev Books

Crisis. G.P. Putnam's Sons 2006 468p $25.95

ISBN 0-399-15357-8   LC 2006-46231

"Dr. Craig Bowman is irritated when problem-patient Patience Stanhope calls him on what he assumes is yet another false alarm. But Craig makes a house call and discovers Patience near death. He rushes her to the hospital but not in time to save her, and the result is a malpractice suit that could cost Craig his livelihood. Alexis, the wife Craig recently reunited with, calls her brother, New York City medical examiner Jack Stapleton . . ., and asks him to come to Boston for advice. Jack, who is less than a week away from his wedding to fellow ME Laurie Montgomery, agrees, despite the fact that he's never liked Craig. But when he travels to Boston and starts to attend Craig's trial, Jack worries that the case is being railroaded by the plaintiff's sleazy lawyer. When Jack performs the autopsy, the results are shocking." Booklist

Godplayer. Putnam 1983 368p

ISBN 0-399-12764-X   LC 83-4507

"Someone is playing God on the surgery floor of Boston Memorial Hospital, causing unexplained patient deaths. Pathologist Robert Sieber, with the help of Dr. Cassandra Kingsley, is investigating these 'SSD's,' sudden surgical deaths. Meanwhile Cassi's husband, a top surgeon, is becoming estranged from her, and seems headed for a breakdown. When Cassi herself must be admitted for an eye operation, she isn't aware that she is the Godplayer's next target." Libr J

Marker; Robin Cook. Putnam 2005 533p $25.95

ISBN 0-399-15293-8   LC 2005-45812

This book "revisits medical examiners Jack Stapleton and Laurie Montgomery, whose romantic relationship has hit a major bump. Approaching her forty-third birthday, Laurie wants a family and has grown impatient with Jack's reluctance to commit. She walks out on Jack, but she can't avoid him at work. She soon finds herself absorbed in a puzzling case: 28-year-old Sean McGillan has landed on her table, and she can't determine what killed him. Sean had just undergone routine knee surgery, but she can't find any reason why he went into cardiac arrest in his hospital bed. When another young, seemingly healthy patient dies, she suspects foul play." Booklist

"True love runs a rocky course, and the plot thickens before the denouement crackles to an electric edge-of-the-seat finale." Publ Wkly

Seizure. Putnam 2003 464p $24.95

ISBN 0-399-14876-0   LC 2003-43225

This "medical thriller centers around two men—Daniel Lowell, a brillant researcher and Ashely Butler, a powerful southern senator. Daniel and his girlfriend, Stephanie D'Agostino, are the cofounders of CURE, a medical research company, the existence of which relies heavily on biotechnology legislation that Butler is trying to block. . . . Cook is at his best when focusing on fascinating cutting-edge biotechnology procedures." Booklist

Vector. Putnam 1999 404p

ISBN 0-399-14471-4   LC 98-49058

In this "novel, the People's Aryan Army (PAA) is planning a major terrorist attack against a big government building in New York, hoping that will spark nationwide revolution. PAA founder Curt recruits immigrant Russian technician Yuri to prepare bioweapons for the attack. Yuri sets up a basement lab to produce anthrax, and a package 'bomb' becomes the vector for the anthrax when Yuri tries it out on a Greek rug dealer. Desiring proof of the merchant's death, Yuri meets Jack Stapleton from the medical examiner's office, and Jack's sidekick, Laurie, gets involved. . . . *Vector* is Cook at his best, providing both thrills and an urgent message." Booklist

Cook, Thomas H.

Breakheart Hill. Bantam Bks. 1995 264p

ISBN 0-553-09651-6   LC 94-26639

Cook, Thomas H.—*Continued*

"The narrator is Ben Wade, the town doctor of Choctaw, Alabama: the story he tells is of 1962, his senior year in high school, and his unrequited love for Kelli Troy, the new girl in town, whose shattered body is found on Breakheart Hill at the end of that year. Ben's narration shuttles back and forth between an innocent past and a blighted present, where Ben and his former classmates struggle to free themselves of the sense of loss." Libr J

"Cook has crafted a novel of stunning power, with a climax that is so unexpected the reader may think he has cheated. But there is no cheating here, only excellent storytelling." Booklist

The Chatham School affair. Bantam Bks. 1996 292p
ISBN 0-553-09652-4   LC 96-4021
"The aged storyteller, a lawyer named Henry Griswald, was just a schoolboy when Elizabeth Channing arrived in his seacoast village in Massachusetts to teach art at his father's private school. But like more than one man in this staid community, young Henry was fascinated by Miss Channing, so unconventional and exotic by local standards, and by romanticizing her relationship with a married teacher, he contributed to her downfall. But did he also drive her to murder?" N Y Times Book Rev

"Cook is a marvelous stylist, gracing his prose with splendid observations about people and the lush, potentially lethal landscape surrounding them. Events accelerate with increasing force, but few readers will be prepared for the surprise that awaits at novel's end." Publ Wkly

The cloud of unknowing. Harcourt 2007 320p $24
ISBN 978-0-15-101260-2; 0-15-101260-1
                                         LC 2006-13951
"An Otto Penzler book"
"David and Diana Sears, the children of a paranoid schizophrenic father, were left deeply scarred by the abuse that resulted from his illness. David, too, is anxious about the genetic legacy of his father's condition, a legacy that seems to play itself out when Diana's son, Jason, is born with schizophrenia. Her ambitious scientist husband, Mark, is never able to reconcile himself to Jason's condition, and after Jason drowns, Diana can't accept the authorities' conclusion that his death was accidental. She becomes obsessed to the point of madness with the notion of Mark's involvement an obsession that will ultimately have disastrous consequences." Libr J

"Although Cook is maddeningly coy about who actually killed whom, he writes eloquently about the fears that lead people to equate intelligence with madness, suppressing the imagination and taking refuge in mediocrity." N Y Times Book Rev

The fate of Katherine Carr. Houghton Mifflin Harcourt 2009 276p $25
ISBN 978-0-15-101401-9; 0-15-101401-9
                                         LC 2008-49203
"George Gates has been completely broken by the kidnapping and murder of his eight-year-old son seven years ago. Gates is a former travel writer, much given to writing about places where people disappeared. Now he salves his psyche by writing totally innocuous small features for the local paper. A chance meeting at a bar with

the detective who organized the search parties when Gates' son went missing leads Gates into a new interest, a cold case that has obsessed the detective for two decades. Retired missing-persons detective Arlo McBride shows Gates the poems and journal that the 31-year-old missing woman left behind, and both men are pulled into reopening the case." Booklist

"Adept at merging past and present plot lines, Cook eloquently examines the often cathartic act of storytelling." Publ Wkly

Instruments of night. Bantam Bks. 1998 293p
ISBN 0-553-10554-X   LC 97-52760
"Paul Graves, the author of a popular series of thrillers, is hired to write about an unsolved murder that took place half a century ago in the small town of Riverwood. And the crime—a young girl was tortured and killed—bears a frightening resemblance to an incident from Paul's own past." Booklist

"Although it's easy to miss the very real clues that Cook drops so artfully into the story, there's no ignoring his savage imagery, or escaping the airless chambers of his disturbing imagination." N Y Times Book Rev

The interrogation. Bantam Bks. 2002 286p $23.95
ISBN 0-533-80095-7   LC 2002-280882
"It's 1952. Three cops take turns grilling one suspect in interrogation Room Number Three. They have 12 hours to solve the murder of a little girl, found strangled to death in a park, before the suspect must be released. . . . The ticking clock, in addition to the economy of scene, makes this an incredibly intense read, culminating in a true shocker of an ending." Booklist

Master of the delta. Harcourt 2008 367p $24
ISBN 978-0-15-101254-1; 0-15-101254-7
                                         LC 2007-26506
"An Otto Penzler book"
A "tale of suspense set in 1954. Jack Branch, who's returned to his hometown of Lakeland, Miss., and taken a job at the same high school where his father once taught, is dismayed to learn that one of his students in his class on historical evil is the son of the town's infamous Coed Killer. Eddie Miller's father confessed to torturing and killing a local girl when Eddie was five, but died in jail before he could stand trial. Hoping to help Eddie step out of his father's shadow, Jack proposes that the boy write a research paper on the Coed Killer. Eddie is soon immersed in the project, which grows in scope until it encompasses the entire town's sordid past." Publ Wkly

"Cook writes in a multiplicity of voices and time frames, and with a profusion of literary references that in another context might seem showy. But from the perspective of a learned narrator who has lived long enough to rue the day he tried to play God, the convolutions of both plot and thought—so tortured and twisted and ultimately so futile—are entirely in character." N Y Times Book Rev

Places in the dark. Bantam Bks. 2000 245p
ISBN 0-553-10563-9   LC 99-89644
A village on the coast of Maine "is torn apart by the arrival of a young woman, Dora March, who seems to bring death in her path. Dora awakens the interest and passions of two brothers. Central to the brothers' fascination with Dora is their half-knowledge of the childhood

Cook, Thomas H.—*Continued*

trauma that has maimed her spirit. One brother is murdered; Dora flees; the older brother embarks on a quest to find her and rid himself of obsession." Booklist

This novel "is swept along by Cook's artistry, his insights into broken people, his austere imagery of the barren landscapes that attract them." N Y Times Book Rev

Cooley, Martha

The archivist; a novel. Little, Brown 1998 328p
ISBN 0-316-15872-0   LC 97-38385
Matthias Lane, a widower in his 60's, is an archivist and guardian to a collection of letters between T. S. Eliot and his friend Emily Hale. "This invaluable correspondence is off-limits until 2019, but Roberta, an attractive poet, is determined to gain access to it and draws Matthias into a tense tango of negotiations that unfreezes painful memories of his poet-wife's suicide." Booklist

The novel "treats serious questions in a humane and passionate manner, and leaves one thinking about these questions long after one has read the last page. Cooley is an accomplished stylist—there's scarcely a graceless or unintelligent sentence in the book—and a subtle chronicler of the inner life." N Y Times Book Rev

Coonts, Stephen, 1946-

America; a Jake Grafton novel. St. Martin's Press 2001 390p
ISBN 0-312-25341-9   LC 2001-34899
"*America*—the U.S. Navy's most advanced submarine—is pirated on her shakedown cruise by a mysterious crew of terrorists, just two months after the newly launched first satellite in an orbital antimissile system mysteriously disappeared. The missing sub then dispatches its Tomahawk missiles with magnetic pulse warheads to Washington and New York, devastating the government and Wall Street. Jake Grafton thinks these dire deeds are connected, and with various allies, he sets out to prove it and retrieve sub and satellite." Booklist

Final flight. Doubleday 1988 387p
ISBN 0-385-24555-6   LC 88-12001
Capt. Jake Grafton's "night-flying's over, thanks to failing eyesight. But the fate of the Middle East is hanging in the balance when his F-14 tears off into Mediterranean air-space. Coonts has cast the hero of his first novel, *The Flight of the Intruder,* as a wing commander aboard an aircraft carrier. He has also thrust him into the bulls-eye of an Arab plot to steal the ship's nuclear weapons. . . . The backdrop is Naples, and the well-detailed lives of Navy pilots. *Final Flight* has a long fuse, but its detonation is well worth the wait." Publ Wkly

Flight of the Intruder. Naval Inst. Press 1986 329p $26.95
ISBN 0-87021-200-1
                             * LC 86-16440
"In the autumn of 1972, despite rumors of peace, United States Navy pilots flew A-6 Intruder attack planes in bombing raids over North Vietnam. Some of these pilots were angered by the relative insignificance of their targets—road intersections, sampan repair yards—which mocked the loss of life incurred carrying out the missions. So when the pilot Jake Grafton's best friend, a

bombardier, is killed by a rifle bullet fired randomly from the ground, he decides 'to bomb something worth the trip' and plans a solo, unauthorized raid on Communist Party headquarters in downtown Hanoi." N Y Times Book Rev

Cooper, J. California

The future has a past; stories. Doubleday 2000 265p $23.95
ISBN 0-385-49680-X   LC 00-34602
Contents: A shooting star; A filet of soul; The eagle flies; The lost and the found
Stories about "African-American women struggling to make something of their smalltown lives. . . . Navigating poverty, unwanted pregnancy, single motherhood and inexperience, all Cooper's heroines triumph, to lesser and greater degrees, finding 'real love' despite being surrounded by 'no good men'." Publ Wkly

The wake of the wind. Doubleday 1998 373p
ISBN 0-385-48704-5   LC 98-21594
"Two good friends in Africa, Kola and Suwaibu, are taken from Africa and brought to America as slaves. The story of their great-great-great grandchildren, Mordecai (Mor) and Lifee, reunites these friends' families through marriage. Mor and Lifee's life together is chronicled through their marriage, freedom from slavery, the birth of their children and grandchildren, and their deaths." Booklist

Wild stars seeking midnight suns. Doubleday 2006 209p
ISBN 0-385-51133-7   LC 2005-56004
Contents: As time goes by; The eye of the beholder; Success; Rushing nowhere; Just-life politics; Wait a minute, world!; The party; Catch a falling heart
"Cooper's talent for capturing the lives of ordinary people penetrates this collection of short stories. These are simple stories about personal struggles in settings from small towns to urban centers. An awkward young woman, pushed into a loveless marriage by her mother, eventually finds her own way professionally and emotionally. Two successful urban professionals cross paths in a nightclub, and neither is satisfied when the evening ends as so many have–in disappointment. A 14-year-old in love with her best friend's much older brother observes the sexual tensions he stirs in others. Many of the stories are told from the perspective of a narrator, close but far away enough for sharp discernment. Cooper fans will enjoy this collection, and those who are new to her work will appreciate her character development and artful storytelling." Booklist

Cooper, James Fenimore, 1789-1851

The Deerslayer; or, The first war-path, a tale; with an introduction by Donald E. Pease. Penguin Books 1987 xxvii, 548p il (Penguin classics) pa $12
ISBN 0-14-039061-8   LC 88-104322
This is the first title of the author's Leatherstocking saga featuring Natty Bumppo
First published 1841 in two volumes by Lea & Blanchard
Set in New York State this "is a record of Natty Bumppo's early days as a young hunter brought up

Cooper, James Fenimore, 1789-1851—*Continued*
among the Delaware Indians, engaged in warfare against
the Hurons. He helps defend the family of Tom Hutter,
a settler, from attack. Judith, who is really not Tom's
daughter, but a girl of noble birth, loves Natty Bumppo
and begs him not to return to the Iroquois, who have released him on parole from capture. Bumppo does return,
but is rescued by the intervention of Judith, who thereafter disappears, and the Delaware Chief Chingachgook,
who remains a lifelong friend." Haydn. Thesaurus of
Book Dig

Followed by The last of the Mohicans

> *also in* Cooper, J. F. The Leatherstocking
> tales

The last of the Mohicans; introduction by Leslie
A. Fiedler. Modern Library 2001 xxxii, 350p (The
Modern Library classics) pa $9.95

ISBN 0-375-75764-3   LC 00-68105
First published 1826
This Leatherstocking tale "presents Chingachgook and
his son Uncas as the last of the Iroquois aristocracy. Natty Bumppo, the scout Hawkeye, is in the prime of his
career in the campaign of Fort William Henry on Lake
George under attack by the French and Indians. The
commander's daughters, Cora and Alice Munro, with the
latter's fiancé Major Duncan Heyward, are captured by
a traitorous Indian but rescued and conveyed to the fort
by Hawkeye. Later Munro surrenders to Montcalm, and
the girls are seized again by Indians. Uncas and Cora are
killed, and the others return to civilization." Haydn. Thesaurus of Book Dig

> *also in* Cooper, J. F. The Leatherstocking
> tales

The Leatherstocking tales. Library of Am. 1985
2v ea $40

ISBN 0-940450-20-8 (v1); 0-940450-21-6 (v2)
                                    * LC 84-25060
Contents: v1 The pioneers; or, The sources of the Sus-
quehanna, a descriptive tale; The last of the Mohicans;
a narrative of 1757; The prairie; a tale; v2 The Pathfinder; or, The inland sea; The Deerslayer; or, The first war-
path

These novels "are linked together by the career of Natty Bumppo, or Hawkeye, Cooper's inimitable back-
woodsman, a romantic embodiment of the virtues of both
races, and of Chingachgook, his Indian counterpart,
equally idealized. . . . There is little historical background; but the vivid descriptions of wood, lake, and
prairie, and of the daily life of Indian and huntsman,
gives the finest imaginable picture extant of natural
scenes and human conditions that have long passed
away." Baker. Guide to the Best Fic

The Pathfinder; or, The inland sea; edited with
an introduction and notes by William P. Kelly.
Oxford University Press 1992 xxxv, 484p pa
$11.95

ISBN 0-19-283989-6
First published 1840
The third in the Leatherstocking tales "finds Natty
Bumppo at the age of forty. A small outpost on Lake
Ontario is under attack. Mabel Dunham helps in the de-
fense, and with the aid of Pathfinder, Chingachgook, and
Jasper Western, a young sailor, the Iroquois are routed.

Lieutenant Muir . . . arrests Jasper as a traitor, but when
Muir is revealed as the guilty one, he is killed by Arrowhead, a Tuscarora Indian. Jasper wins the love of Mabel." Haydn. Thesaurus of Book Dig

Followed by The pioneers

> *also in* Cooper, J. F. The Leatherstocking
> tales

The pilot; a tale of the sea; edited with an his-
torical introduction and explanatory notes by Kay
Seymour House. State University of New York
Press 1986 xlvii, 479p il $59.50

ISBN 0-8739-5415-7   LC 84-8765
First published 1823
John "Paul Jones's adventures suggested the plot;
which is, in brief, an attempt during the Revolutionary
War to abduct some prominent Englishmen for exchange
against American prisoners." Keller. Reader's Dig of
Books

> *also in* Cooper, J. F. Sea tales: The pilot, The
> red rover

The pioneers; edited with an introduction and
notes by James D. Wallace. Oxford University
Press 1999 465p map pa $10.95

ISBN 0-19-283667-6
First published 1822
In this fourth of the Leatherstocking tales Natty "first
appears as an older man. The story takes place in the village of Templeton, founded by Judge Temple. The central conflict is between the laws of nature, upheld by
Natty, and the laws of civilization. Symbolic of this opposition are two incidents, the first being the settler's
hypocritical effort to punish Natty for killing a deer out
of season for food, despite their own slaughter of pigeons purely for sport. The second is over the true ownership of the Judge's lands, which is resolved by the
marriage of Elizabeth Temple and Edward Effingham,
heir of the true owner. Natty, like Huck Finn, heads for
the Far West to escape confining civilization." Reader's
Ency. 4th edition

Followed by The prairie

> *also in* Cooper, J. F. The Leatherstocking
> tales

The prairie; with an introduction by Blake
Nevius. Penguin 1987 xxvi, 386p pa $13

ISBN 0-14-039026-X   LC 87-2891
Sequel to The pioneers
First published 1827
This final installment in the Leatherstocking tales cen-
ters on the death of Natty Bumppo. "Cooper contrasts
the noble, disinterested Natty with the squatter Ishmael
Bush and his family. Lawless and self-seeking, the squat-
ters portend ill for the future of democracy. Cooper's
prairie descriptions . . . are derived from the *Journals* of
Lewis and Clark." Reader's Ency. 4th edition

> *also in* Cooper, J. F. The Leatherstocking
> tales

The red rover
> *In* Cooper, J. F. Sea tales: The pilot, The red
> rover

Cooper, James Fenimore, 1789-1851—*Continued*

Sea tales: The pilot, The red rover. Library of America, Distributed to the trade in the U.S. and Canada by Viking Press 1991 902p $35

ISBN 0-940450-70-4   LC 90-52923

Contents: The pilot; The Red Rover

The pilot is entered separately. In The red rover (1827 in United Kingdom and France, 1828 in the United States), "Lt. Henry Ark, an officer in the British Navy about the middle of the 18th century, . . . takes the name Wilder and enlists as a common sailor on board the Dolphin in the hope of tracking down a mysterious pirate, the Red Rover." Reader's Ency. 2nd edition

The spy; a tale of the neutral ground. Wiley & Halsted 1821 2v o.p.

A story of the American Revolution. The hero, the spy, is a cool, shrewd, fearless man, who is employed by General Washington in service which involves great personal danger and little glory

Covers "the locality 'between the royal barracks in New York City and the American outposts on the Hudson' where a mixed population of loyalists and British sympathisers mistrusted one another. Not many historic figures or events are introduced . . . but the tale well illustrates the later Revolution period, and is full of allusions to such men as Burgoyne, Gates, Tarleton, Sumter, etc." Nield. Guide to the Best Hist Novels & Tales

Coover, Robert

Briar Rose. Grove Press 1996 86p

ISBN 0-8021-1591-8   LC 96-4917

This work of fiction is Coover's "retelling of the story of Sleeping Beauty. In this dark and unromantic world, a prince hacks his way through the briar hedge surrounding the castle, ever aware that the bodies of dead princes who went before him are swinging in the wind, and the princess dreams of the men who come and assault her as she lies helpless." Libr J

"Coover doesn't just spit in the eye of happily-ever-after; he gouges it out. But what makes Briar Rose more than a cynical tale for adult children is the startling complexity of its vision." Nation

Ghost town; a novel. Holt & Co. 1998 147p

ISBN 0-8050-5884-2   LC 98-5713

This novel "retails the fever-dream misadventures of a nameless rider . . . as he moves back and forth through the gravity field of an archetypal Western frontier town, a place at times populated by . . . staple figures (the gruff barkeep, the saloon bawd, the grizzled drunk), at other times inexplicably stripped back to the tumbleweed streets and banging shutters suggested by the book's title." N Y Times Book Rev

"Genre isn't the only target of Coover's perversity: the goings on are often hilariously obscene, and perhaps truer to the old West than what we want to imagine. 'Ghost Town' is both warped and scintillating, a cross between 'No Exit' and 'The Canterbury Tales'." New Yorker

Pinocchio in Venice. Linden Press/Simon & Schuster 1991 330p

ISBN 0-671-64471-8   LC 90-45706

"Pinocchio in Mr. Coover's novel has become an elderly professor of aesthetics and philosophy, . . . winner of two Nobel prizes and recipient of enough honors for an entire faculty. He returns to Venice, hoping that the scenes of his youth will inspire him to compose an adequate ending to the book he is writing, which is a tribute to the fairy with the blue hair, his mentor and lifelong inspiration. He encounters old friends in Venice, and even more old enemies; he blunders through nightmarish disasters; he is robbed, abused, and humiliated; and he gradually reverts to his original condition as a wooden puppet." Atlantic

"The ribaldry and the 'fun' are a lot more strenuous and obsessive than self-denial ever was. But then, that is Coover's specialism–the joke on the joker, that the world without soul, far from being easy, is absurdly hard." Times Lit Suppl

Cornwell, Bernard

The archer's tale. HarperCollins Pubs. 2001 374p

ISBN 0-06-621084-4   LC 2001-24333

First published 2000 in the United Kingdom with title Harlequin

"Set in the early 1400s at the beginning of the Hundred Years War between England and France, this novel depicts one of the most bloody and violent periods in the history of conflict between these two nations. After the theft of the treasure of Hookton, a broken lance thought to have been the weapon St. George used to slay the dragon, young Thomas, the bastard son of the village priest and a skilled longbowman, joins the English army in hopes of recovering the relic. Instead, he finds himself caught up in the invasion of France." Libr J

"Authentically detailed and appropriately gruesome, the medieval battle scenes fairly crackle with tension; however, what sets Cornwell's work apart from most run-of-the-mill military adventures are his meticulously developed story lines and his razor-sharp characterizations." Booklist

Enemy of God; a novel of Arthur. St. Martin's Press 1997 396p (Warlord chronicles, bk2)

ISBN 0-312-15523-9   LC 96-51740

In the second volume of the Warlord Chronicles trilogy, "having secured the throne of Dumnonia for the infant King Mordred, Arthur seeks to bring peace to the kingdom by uniting the various rival Celtic factions into the 'Brotherhood of Britain.' Derfel, one of Arthur's warriors and the book's narrator, sardonically notes that 'the Round Table, of course, was never a proper name, but rather a nickname.' But Arthur's good intentions are gradually undone: by Merlin's quest for the Thirteen Treasures of Britain; by Lancelot's and Guinevere's ambitions; by Mordred, now an unpleasant young man incapable of wise rule; and by the growing conflict between the old Druid religion and the new Christianity." Libr J

"This complex and superbly wrought narrative easily eclipses the more sanitized and tepid versions of Arthur's exploits." Booklist

Followed by Excalibur

Excalibur; a novel of Arthur. St. Martin's Press 1998 340p (Warlord chronicles, bk3)

ISBN 0-312-18575-8   LC 98-10247

Cornwell, Bernard—*Continued*

In the concluding volumes of the Warlord Chronicles "Arthur temporarily halts the invading Saxons at the battle of Mynydd Baddon (during which Lancelot meets a coward's death and Guinevere is reconciled with her husband), [but] his dream of a unified Celtic kingdom is doomed. Thwarting him is the vicious Mordred who makes a pact with Nimue to bring back the old Druid gods and destroy the new Christian deity." Libr J

"The action is gripping and skillfully paced, cadenced by passages in which the characters reveal themselves in conversation and thought, convincingly evoking the spirit of the time. Ways of ancient ritual, battle and daily life are laid out in surprising detail." Publ Wkly

Gallows thief. HarperCollins Pubs. 2002 297p
ISBN 0-06-008273-9   LC 2001-58334
First published 2001 in the United Kingdom

"After successfully defending his country at Waterloo, Captain Rider Sandman returns to England to face bankruptcy and disgrace. . . . Looking for any type of honest work that will enable him to live and to pay off some of his father's creditors, he accepts an assignment to investigate the circumstances of the brutal rape and murder of the countess of Avebury. Though a hapless young portrait painter has already been convicted of the crime, Sandman begins to suspect well-connected members of the aristocracy have framed him." Booklist

Rebel. HarperCollins Pubs. 1993 308p (Starbuck chronicles)
ISBN 0-06-017713-6
                              * LC 92-53344

This first volume of the Starbuck chronicles "follows the adventures of Nathaniel Starbuck, the rebellious and discredited son of a famous Boston abolitionist preacher. Nate flees the North after helping a *femme fatale* steal money she claimed was hers, winding up in Richmond as Fort Sumter falls and the Civil War begins. Unable to return home, distrusted by Southerners because of his parentage, Nate is taken under the wing of the mercurial and megalomaniacal Washington Faulconer, obsessed with building an independent army, answerable only to him, to fight for the Confederacy. Spanning the period from Sumter's capitulation in April 1861 to the First Battle of Bull Run in July, the book is well paced and filled with the historical details genre fans demand." Publ Wkly

Followed by Copperhead

Sharpe's battle; Richard Sharpe and the Battle of Fuentes de Oñoro, May 1811. HarperCollins Pubs. 1995 304p il
ISBN 0-06-017677-6   LC 95-10347

This adventure finds Sharpe "fighting the French and the hierarchy of Wellington's army. The encounter takes place in 1811, shortly after the destruction of Almeida (recounted in *Sharpe's Gold*. It is still Almeida that is under contention, for the French have mounted a massive campaign to supply the scant forces that still hold the fort. On another front, Sharpe is waging a private battle (which nearly gets him court-martialed) against the ferocious French Wolf Brigade. Vintage Cornwell." Booklist

Sharpe's devil; Richard Sharpe and the Emperor, 1820-1821. HarperCollins Pubs. 1992 280p
ISBN 0-06-017977-5   LC 91-58360

Sequel to Sharpe's Waterloo

In this episode Richard Sharpe "finds himself in the Spanish colony of Chile during its fight for independence in 1820-21. Hired by the wife of a Spanish nobleman to locate her kidnapped husband, the captain-general of Chile, Sharpe and friend Patrick Harper sail halfway around the world on a mission complicated by political intrigue and corruption." Libr J

This is a "rousing read, full of invincible characters, deafening broadsides, roaring cannons, and smoking pistols as Cornwell writes of old-fashioned battles, blazing with glory." Booklist

Sharpe's fortress; Richard Sharpe and the Siege of Gawilghur, December 1803. HarperCollins Pubs. 2000 294p
ISBN 0-06-019424-3   LC 00-59703

This installment in the Richard Sharpe saga finds "Sharpe, a junior officer in Her Majesty's army, stationed in India in 1803. Struggling to earn the respect of both his superiors and his troops, he . . . runs up against the unscrupulous Sergeant Obadiah Hakeswill. Uncovering an act of treason by Hakeswill, Sharpe must confront his sworn enemy in order to protect himself and recover a cache of stolen jewels. Set against the backdrop of the Maharatta War and the siege of the fortress of Gawilghur, this fast-paced historical adventure features plenty of electrifying military action." Booklist

Sharpe's fury; Richard Sharpe and the Battle of Barrosa, March 1811. HarperCollins 2006 337p $24.95
ISBN 0-06-053048-0

In this adventure "Capt. Richard Sharpe, upstart rifleman, performs a sensitive mission for Henry Wellesley, the duke of Wellington's younger brother and special envoy to Spain in Cadiz. . . . A secret cabal of Spaniards who favor a rapprochement with France threatens the alliance between England and Spain in the fight against Bonaparte. The conspirators, who include a murderous priest, Fr. Salvador Montseny, have stolen some unfortunate love letters Wellesley wrote to his prostitute amour, Caterina Blazquez, and plan to use them to embarrass the British. It's up to Sharpe to recover the letters and save the alliance." Publ Wkly

"As in the other Sharpe novels, there is a lot of action here, played out in sturdy prose." Libr J

Sharpe's havoc; Richard Sharpe and the campaign in northern Portugal, spring 1809. HarperCollins Pubs. 2003 306p $25.95
ISBN 0-06-053046-4   LC 2002-191284

"It is 1809, and Napoleon has plans to annex the Iberian Peninsula; British troops are sent to help the Portugese in their battle against the French. Sharpe and his small regiment of riflemen are separated from the main body of British troops, and once again find themselves in the thick of the action, which centers in and around the city of Oporto. Complicating matters is Kate Savage, the daughter of a British wine mechant in Oporto, whom Sharpe must find and escort to to safety. Meanwhile, a French spy marries Kate solely to get his hands on her fortune. The action shifts between battle scenes and the spy, whom Sharpe unmasks. Although the outcome is never in doubt, this nevertheless makes for a rousing story." Libr J

Cornwell, Bernard—*Continued*

Sharpe's prey: Richard Sharpe and the Expedition to Copenhagen, 1807. HarperCollins Pubs. 2002 262p

    ISBN 0-06-000252-2   LC 2001-46501

"Richard Sharpe, though stuck in the lowly role of regimental quartermaster, finds himself in the thick of the 1807 British campaign to destroy the Danish navy anchored in Copenhagen before the French can seize the ships and pose another invasion threat. As ever, the story starts fast, here with the murder of an English army officer in London by Captain John Lavisser—a traitor working for the French and as vile a villain as any Sharpe has faced—and scarcely lets up until Sharpe's final confrontation with Lavisser during the British bombardment of Copenhagen." Publ Wkly

Sharpe's Trafalgar; Richard Sharpe and the Battle of Trafalgar, October 21, 1805. HarperCollins Pubs. 2001 293p

    ISBN 0-06-019425-1   LC 00-53871

First published 2000 in the United Kingdom

"Sharpe finds himself on a homeward-bound ship to England after duty in India. He has some problems adjusting to sea life but learns quickly. When his ship is attacked by the French, Sharpe finds out that the French ship contains a treaty that could cause a new outbreak of hostilities between India and the British. The result is the 1805 Battle of Trafalgar. . . . Cornwell satisfyingly delivers action, adventure, and a great gallery of villains and heroes, plus the usual beautiful lady." Libr J

Sharpe's Waterloo; Richard Sharpe and the Waterloo campaign, 15 June to 18 June 1815. Viking 1990 378p o.p.   LC 89-40661

    Sequel to Sharpe's revenge

"At Waterloo, Lieutenant-Colonel Sharpe serves as military adviser to the Dutch prince of Orange—a hapless military strategist who sends legions to their deaths before Sharpe takes matters into his own hands. . . . Along the way, Sharpe settles an old score with Lord John Rossendale, who previously cuckolded him and helped deprive him of his hard-earned fortune. Cornwell graphically depicts the grime and horror of the battlefield, including cavalry charges, cannon bombardments, and infantry attacks. A sublime work of historical fiction." Booklist

    Followed by Sharpe's devil

Stonehenge, 2000 B.C.; a novel. HarperCollins Pubs. 2000 433p

    ISBN 0-06-019700-5   LC 00-24288

A "novel that imagines the history behind Stonehenge. At the story's center are three brothers: Lengar, a warrior who takes the leadership of his tribe through patricide; Camaban, a crippled outcast who transforms himself into a sorcerer and seizes power from Lengar; and Saban, a craftsman who longs for the peaceful days of his father's reign. . . . Cornwell's depictions of the herculean efforts needed to move, shape and raise the stones of Stonehenge sound plausible, and his portrayal of the vitality and brutality of a society slowly creeping toward civilization is deft." N Y Times Book Rev

Vagabond. HarperCollins Pubs. 2002 405p $25.95

    ISBN 0-06-621080-1   LC 2002-68884

"In this sequel to The Archer's Tale, gifted archer Thomas of Hookton continues his quest to avenge his father's murder and to find the Holy Grail, which King Edward III believes will help England defeat the French. Thomas finds himself embroiled in a series of events beginning with the Battle of Neville's Cross (October 1346) and ending with the English victory at La Roche—Derrien (spring 1347)." Libr J

"Cornwell is meticulous about historical facts and period detail, and his descriptions of butchery with arrow, mace and battleaxe are nothing if not convincing. As expected, the book culminates with battlefield slaughter on an epic scale." Publ Wkly

The winter king; a novel of Arthur. St. Martin's Press 1996 431p (Warlord chronicles, bk1)

    ISBN 0-312-14447-4

                          * LC 96-1421

First published 1995 in the United Kingdom

"Cornwell's Arthur is fierce, dedicated and complex, a man with many problems, most of his own making. His impulsive decisions sometimes have tragic ramifications, as when he lustfully takes Guinevere instead of the intented Ceinwyn, alienating his friends and allies and inspiring a bloody battle. The secondary characters are equally unexpected, and are ribboned with the magic and superstition of the times." Publ Wkly

    Followed by Enemy of God

Cornwell, David John Moore *See* Le Carré, John, 1931-

Cortázar, Julio, 1914-1984

Hopscotch; translated from the Spanish by Gregory Rabassa. Pantheon Bks. 1966 564p o.p.

                                   *

Original Spanish edition published 1963 in Argentina

"Considered to be Cortázar's masterwork, it is an open-ended novel; after reading the first 56 chapters, the reader is asked to reread the chapters in a different order. . . . The novel's antihero is Horacio Oliveira, an Argentine existentialist who lives among cultured expatriates in Paris while searching for his telepathic mistress. Returning to Buenos Aires, Oliveira meets Traveler and Talita, who are the doubles of his mistress and himself. None of the characters understands or cares more than superficially about the others, and impulse motivates their choices and actions. Narrative progress in the story is insignificant and its end is inconclusive." Merriam-Webster's Ency of Lit

Costa, Margaret Jull

    (tr) Marías, J. The man of feeling

    (tr) Saramago, J. The cave

    (tr) Saramago, J. Death with interruptions

Costello, Mark, 1936-

Big if. Norton 2002 315p $24.95

    ISBN 0-393-05116-1   LC 2002-512

Costello, Mark, 1936-—*Continued*

This novel focuses on the "world of Vi Asplund, a Secret Service agent assigned to protect the vice-president. As the daughter of an accident investigator, she saw things . . . that prepared her well for the tense uncertainties she faces on a daily basis. . . . Meanwhile, her brother, Jens, a computer genius who writes code for a war game, is starting to question the ethics of his creations, namely, the too-lifelike villains who are armed to the teeth." Booklist

"The novel ends not with a bang but a shiver—in a masterfully orchestrated scene that is vividly cinematic. But true to his materials and vision—and to life— Costello slyly defuses the emotional catharsis in a manner that would be anathema to the feel-good demands of a major Hollywood production." N Y Times Book Rev

Coulter, Catherine

The maze. Putnam 1997 373p

ISBN 0-399-14264-9   LC 97-12343

"San Franciscan Lacey Sherlock was just a teenager, dreaming of studying piano at Berkeley, when her older sister's life was brutally ended by the serial murderer that the media dubbed the String Killer. Now, seven years and one brief mental breakdown later, her career plans have changed. Having completed FBI training and learned to be addressed by her surname, she's assigned to agent Dillon Savich's Criminal Apprehension Unit, which, utilizing Dillon's specialized computer program for profiling, is responsible for pursuing serial killers. This places the obsessed Sherlock exactly where she wants to be when the String Killer strikes again, this time in Boston. It also puts her in position to become romantically involved with her attractive superior." Publ Wkly

The target. Putnam 1998 372p

ISBN 0-399-14395-5   LC 98-10563

"Federal Judge Ramsey Hunt is eluding the press in the mountains when he finds a frightened, injured little girl. When her mother locates them, she accuses Ramsey of kidnapping Emma. Soon, however, the three join forces to flee the bad guys, who attack again and again. FBI agents Sherlock and Savich, last seen in *The Maze* drop in occasionally, usually by telephone, to lend moral support." Libr J

"Coulter's plot doesn't always add up, and she can overdo her penchant for quirky characters . . . but her central figures—wary, quietly resilient Molly, musically gifted Emma and tough, decent Ramsey—make this an absorbing read." Publ Wkly

Coupland, Douglas

Eleanor Rigby; a novel. Bloomsbury 2005 249p $22.95

ISBN 1-582-34523-6   LC 2004-46437

"Liz Dunn is fat, lonely and has no friends. . . . The only exciting incident ever to brighten Liz's life was a class trip to Rome when she was 16, during which she attended a party where she drank so much she can't remember what happened. Nine months after she returned home, she gave birth to a son, an event hidden from her family because of her natural rotundness. Liz gave the child up for adoption and then launched into a life of perpetual loneliness (hence the title's nod to the lonely

lady of Beatles fame). All this changes when her now 20-year-old son, Jeremy, shows up. He's a great kid, but his story is tragic-he bounced around foster homes until he could take care of himself, he has multiple sclerosis and his body is rapidly deteriorating. Coupland . . . avoids the pitfalls of weepy melodrama with sarcastic humor, inspired treatment of the weirdness of everyday life and dark mystical interludes." Publ Wkly

Couto, Mia, 1955-

Sleepwalking land; translated by David Brookshaw. Serpent's Tail 2006 213p pa $14.95

ISBN 1-85242-897-X

Original Portuguese edition, 1992

"As the civil war rages in 1980s Mozambique, an old man and a young boy, refugees from the war, seek shelter in a burnt-out bus. Among the effects of a dead passenger, they come across a set of notebooks that tell of his life. As the boy reads the story to his elderly companion, this story and their own develop in tandem." Publisher's note

"Many great novels have shown a world torn to shreds by the brutality of war. To do so, their authors ground their texts in the details of destruction and decay. But Couto's novel stands apart: it shows the world that war creates, a dreamscape of uncertainty where characters and readers alike marvel not at the abnormal becoming normal but at the way we come to accept the impossible as reality." N Y Times Book Rev

Coward, Noel

Bon voyage

In Coward, N. The collected stories of Noël Coward p562-630

The collected stories of Noël Coward. Dutton 1983 630p

ISBN 0-525-24207-4   LC 83-5704

Contents: The wooden Madonna; Traveler's joy; Aunt Tittie; What mad pursuit; Cheap excursion; The kindness of Mrs. Radcliffe; Nature study; A richer dust; Mr. and Mrs. Edgehill; Stop me if you've heard it; Ashes of roses; This time tomorrow; Star quality; Pretty Polly; Mrs. Capper's birthday; Me and the girls; Solali; Mrs. Ebony; Penny dreadful; Bon voyage {novelette}

Cox, Michael, 1948-2009

The glass of time; the secret life of Miss Esperanza Gorst; narrated by herself. W. W. Norton 2008 586p $24.95

ISBN 978-0-393-06773-6; 0-393-06773-4

LC 2008-23909

"When orphaned 19-year-old Esperanza Gorst is hired as a lady's maid by Baroness Tansor of Evenwood in 1876, she does not understand her role in a complex plan to restore the Duport family succession. Lady Tansor, the former Emily Carteret, still mourns for her fiancé, Phoebus Daunt, murdered two decades earlier. Through clever spying, Esperanza uncovers information about the murders of Emily's father and Daunt and about Emily's marriage and children. Letters and documents from Esperanza's guardian and others reveal the stories of her own parents and how she had been cheated of her inheri-

Cox, Michael, 1948-2009—*Continued*

tance. Yet, despite realizing that she cannot trust Emily or her unscrupulous associates, Esperanza feels affection and sympathy for the beleaguered Lady. Jealousies among Emily's sons and Esperanza fuel more misunderstandings." Libr J

An "entirely wonderful mock Victorian novel. . . . It's a melodrama, of course, chock-full of revenge, romance, duplicity, concealed identities and murder most frequent—but melodrama on a grand scale." Washington Post Book World

The meaning of night; a confession. W. W. Norton 2006 703p $25.95

ISBN 978-0-393-06203-8; 0-393-06203-1

LC 2006-18941

This novel "opens with a murder on a misty night in 1854 London. The perpetrator, Edward Glyver, is an erudite bibliophile and resourceful detective who assumes different names and personas with disquieting ease. He stabs a total stranger as a precursor to murdering his cunning adversary, Phoebus Daunt, a literary genius who expects to be adopted as heir by the wealthy Lord Tansor. When Glyver discovers that Daunt has destroyed the only evidence that Glyver, in fact, is Tansor's real son, he becomes obsessed with seeking revenge and claiming his rightful inheritance." Libr J

"Cox has delivered almost everything Victorian readers might have expected (mystery, wit, romance, an evil double) and some (explanatory footnotes) they might not. Throughout [the book], he winks slyly at the era's literary conventions while twisting story lines back on one another. The result is a narrative as beguiling as it is intelligent, full of great country houses, epic loves, fierce anger and vicious habits of every sort." N Y Times Book Rev

(comp) The Oxford book of English ghost stories. See The Oxford book of English ghost stories

(ed) The Oxford book of spy stories. See The Oxford book of spy stories

(ed) The Oxford book of twentieth-century ghost stories. See The Oxford book of twentieth-century ghost stories

Cozarinsky, Edgardo

The bride from Odessa; translated from the Spanish by Nick Caistor. Farrar, Straus and Giroux 2004 161p $22

ISBN 0-374-11673-6

Original Spanish edition, 2001

Contents: The bride from Odessa; Literature; Real estate; Days of 1937; View of dawn over a lake; Budapest; Christmas '54; Obscure loves; Émigré hotel

"Any exploration of the past is necessarily incomplete and Cozarinsky has found the perfect form in these fragmentary stories. . . . His prose, as translated by Nick Caistor, is elegant, cool and precise. Occasionally the amassing of clauses might suggest the original Spanish, . . . but this is a book about moving between cultures, between continents and between generations; to be aware of the movement between languages is not necessarily a bad thing." Times Lit Suppl

Cozzens, James Gould, 1903-1978

By love possessed. Harcourt Brace & Co. 1957 570p o.p.

This novel concerns "49 hours in the life of Arthur Winner, . . . New England lawyer. The stability of Arthur's private and professional worlds is suddenly shaken both by repercussions of unhapppy and indiscreet episodes from his supposedly well-ordered past and by present events involving himself and those close to him." Booklist

"Cozzens is no peripheral observer of the human situation in which the Man of Reason finds himself; and all the vignettes of life in small-town Brocton involving the noble and the mean, the serious and the ridiculous, are viewed with sheer objectivity, boldly at one time, sensitively and delicately at another." Best Sellers

Crace, Jim

Being dead. Farrar, Straus & Giroux 2000 193p

ISBN 0-374-11013-1   LC 99-45082

First published 1999 in the United Kingdom

This novel's two central characters, Joseph and Celice, are biologists. "The story is told in two directions. As it opens, Joseph and Celice are recently dead, victims of a senseless murder. Subsequent chapters alternate between a counterclockwise retracing of the route they took to meet their bloody fate, and . . . descriptions of their physical decomposition." N Y Rev Books

"The style is agile, precise, and vigorous. Words hit their target directly and unerringly. Images are colorful, evocative, forceful." Commonweal

The devil's larder. Farrar, Straus & Giroux 2001 165p $20

ISBN 0-374-13859-1   LC 2001-23625

Crace has "written a set of teasing tales about how we are never so ignorantly alive as when we are eating ourselves to death. The 64 brief fictions that make up 'The Devil's Larder' are parables and parodies of knowingness. . . . Reading a collection of 64 apparently unconnected brief fictions, numbered and untitled and held together only by the odd title of the book, may not necessarily appear to be a tempting prospect. The form of the book is experimental in that it toys with the reader's willingness (or unwillingness) not to make too much sense of what is going on." N Y Times Book Rev

The gift of stones. Scribner 1989 c1988 169p

ISBN 0-684-19070-2

* LC 88-31587

First published 1988 in the United Kingdom

"The protagonists of this novel are workers of flint in the Stone Age, chipping and hammering tools and arrowheads in a coastal village, exact time and place unspecified. They grow easy and complacent with the trading successes their skills bring them, and care little about the world without-though marauding bands of men on horseback sometimes come by. They are thus quite unprepared to discover, when ships appear from the great beyond and land on their coast, that bronze has been manufactured, and that their livelihood is gone." Publ Wkly

"As the fabulist tale unwinds, Crace looks into the role of the artist in society-here, a storyteller-considering both the impact and limits of imagination in guiding us toward new horizons. A marvelous literary effort." Libr J

Crace, Jim—_Continued_

The pesthouse; a novel. Nan A. Talese 2007 255p $24.95

ISBN 978-0-385-52075-1; 0-385-52075-1

LC 2006-26555

"After a forgotten eco-reaction in the distant past, the U.S. government, economy and society have collapsed. The illiterate inhabitants ride horses, fight with bows and swords and scratch a meager living from farming and fishing. But with crop yields and fish runs mysteriously dwindling, most are trekking to the Atlantic coast to take ships to the promised land of Europe, gawking along the way at the ruins of freeways and machinery yards, which seem the wasteful excesses of giants. Heading east, naïve farm boy Franklin teams up with Margaret, a recovering victim of the mysterious 'flux' whose shaven head (mark of the unclean) causes passersby to shun her. Their love blossoms amid misadventures in an anarchic landscape." Publ Wkly

"The story is a gripping, harrowing adventure tale and Crace's language is extraordinary: he has immersed himself in his own kind of variant American idiom . . . which is simple, often beautiful, as tough and workable as leather." New Statesman

Quarantine. Farrar, Straus & Giroux 1998 c1997 242p

ISBN 0-374-23962-2

* LC 97-61489

First published 1997 in the United Kingdom

"Five people come to the desert of Judea, for a quarantine, a fast of forty days. For four of them, the standard daytime fast will be enough. . . . They are Shim, part-Jew, part-Greek, sophisticate, religious dilettante, sceptic; Aphas, an old man with a new growth, looking for a simple miracle; Marti, the childless wife of a barren marriage, about to be cast off by her philoprogenitive husband; a nameless, perhaps Tourettic nomad, whose hopes remain unintelligible. And Jesus, a callow young man from Galilee with Messianic ambitions. He intends a total fast." Times Lit Suppl

Crace's "prose is startlingly specific about ancient life and Judea's harsh, terrible beauty. Unlike many authors of biblical fiction, he blends his research smoothly into his narrative and adds a leavening pinch of humor." Time

Crafts, Hannah

The bondswomans narrative; edited by Henry Louis Gates Jr. Warner Bks. 2002 lxxiv, 338p il $24.95

ISBN 0-446-53008-5

LC 2001-98325

This autobiographical novel "follows a female slave in her circumscribed existence on a North Carolina plantation and her flight to freedom in the North." Booklist

"Published from a manuscript bought at auction by Henry Louis Gates Jr., [this] is quite probably the first novel written by a black woman, as well as the only novel written by a female fugitive slave. It is also one of the few purely firsthand accounts of the slave experience available." N Y Times Book Rev

Craig, Alisa _See_ MacLeod, Charlotte

Craig, Amanda, 1959-

Love in idleness; a novel. Talese 2003 340p $23.95

ISBN 0-385-50776-3

LC 2002-43570

"When eight adults and three children vacation together in a rented Italian villa, the children discover fairies, and the adults discover truths about themselves as they reunite with old lovers or find themselves changed and ready for new relationships." Libr J

"The novel reprises Shakespeare's mercurial farce about Athenian lovers and fairy royalty wandering around a forest at night, falling in and out of besottedness at the instigation of the mischievous Puck." N Y Times Book Rev

Craig, Kit, 1932-

See also Reed, Kit, 1932-

Craig, Patricia

(ed) The Oxford book of travel stories. See The Oxford book of travel stories

Craig, Philip R., 1933-

A shoot on Martha's Vineyard; a Martha's Vineyard mystery. Scribner 1998 285p map $22

ISBN 0-684-83454-5

LC 97-51141

When "J.W. Jackson's long-time nemesis arrives in town and is murdered, J.W. can avoid suspicion only by finding the murderer. A handsome Hollywood movie scout, meanwhile, takes a shine to Jackson's new wife. A lively and entertaining addition to the series." Libr J

Third strike; a Brady Coyne/J.W. Jackson mystery; [by] Philip R. Craig and William G. Tapply. Scribner 2007 323p $24

ISBN 978-1-4165-3256-9; 1-4165-3256-0

LC 2007-9103

"Tapply's Boston lawyer, Brady Coyne, responds to an anguished call for help from an old client living on Martha's Vineyard, where the late Philip Craig's ex-cop, J.W. Jackson, is being urged by his wife to investigate the death of a striking ferry boat worker. . . . The two friends pursue their cases separately and together as tensions caused by the ferry strike mount and a murder raises the stakes. This marks the highly enjoyable and poignant end to a short, sweet series." Publ Wkly

Vineyard enigma; a Martha's Vineyard mystery. Scribner 2002 242p $24

ISBN 0-7432-0523-5

LC 2001-57809

"The arrival on Martha's Vineyard of a strange man in search of two African soapstone eagles creates turmoil for series star J. W. Jackson. Murder, art-world intrigue, and jealousy of his wife's attraction to the man all complicate J. W.'s life." Libr J

A vineyard killing; a Martha's Vineyard mystery. Scribner 2003 229p $24

ISBN 0-7432-0524-3

LC 2002-42878

This installment "begins with a bang: an unknown assailant shoots someone outside the delicatessen where series private investigator J. W. Jackson is eating with his wife. Jackson is soon embroiled in a murder case involving grabby real estate developers and recalcitrant islanders. Off-season atmosphere and the usual high-caliber sleuthing." Libr J

Craig, Philip R., 1933-—*Continued*
(jt. auth) Tapply, W. G. First light

Crais, Robert, 1953-

Chasing darkness; an Elvis Cole novel. Simon & Schuster 2008 273p $25.95
ISBN 978-0-7432-8164-5; 0-7432-8164-0
LC 2008-10709
"While clearing houses in the path of a forest fire in Laurel Canyon, police officers find the body of Lionel Byrd, an apparent suicide. Three years earlier, Cole, working for Byrd's attorney, uncovered evidence that cleared Byrd of a murder charge. Now new evidence suggests that he was guilty of that murder and six others, two of them committed after Cole helped exonerate him. Torn by guilt, Cole plunges into his own investigation, which leads in startling directions." Publ Wkly

Demolition angel; a novel. Doubleday 2000 386p
ISBN 0-385-49584-6
LC 00-29054
"Carol Starkey, an LAPD bomb-squad technician who nearly died in a blast three years earlier, is emotionally burned out. When a partner is killed by a bomb in what Starkey realizes is an assassination, she finds herself caught up in a deadly game with a serial bomber who targets individuals—including her." Libr J
"The book features one of the most complex heroines to grace a thriller since Clarice Starling locked eyes with Hannibal Lecter, a deliciously spooky villain in the person of a mad bomber known as Mr. Red, and an aggressively involving plot." Publ Wkly

The forgotten man; a novel. Doubleday 2005 352p $24.95
ISBN 0-385-50428-4
LC 2004-61857
"When an apparently homeless man is found shot in an alley, the first officer on the scene tells private investigator Elvis Cole that the dying man claimed to be Cole's father. Cole has never known the identity of his father. His mother was mentally unstable and would often go missing for extended periods. Cole was conceived during such a disappearance, and the only clue his mother gave him was the cryptic comment that his father was a 'human cannonball' in a circus. Long obsessed with finding his father, Cole backtracks through the years to learn the dead man's true identity. As he searches, Cole is unaware that he is the target of an associate of the dead man. . . . A deeply moving, heartfelt mystery." Booklist

Indigo slam; an Elvis Cole novel. Hyperion 1997 288p
ISBN 0-7868-6261-0
LC 97-966
In this mystery L.A. shamus Elvis Cole is "approached by three resourceful young children who would like their missing father located. That dad, Clark Hewitt, is soon revealed as a mystery man, a master printer and a possible junkie who fled the witness protection program he entered after informing on a counterfeiting operation run by Russian and Ukrainian mobsters. While Clark's kids clearly revere him, Elvis is suspicious. The feds want Clark back in their care and the Russians want revenge for his squealing." Publ Wkly

L.A. requiem. Doubleday 1999 382p
ISBN 0-385-49583-8
LC 98-52921

In this episode L.A. PI Elvis Cole, "drops his adolescent swagger in the heroic act of helping his friend and partner, Joe Pike, to stop the vengeful killer who is framing Pike for his own crimes. The writing doesn't fool around, either, and what starts as a routine search for a rich man's pampered daughter becomes a tense face-off with a killer and a serious examination of the limits of friendship." N Y Times Book Rev

The last detective; a novel. Doubleday 2003 302p $24.95
ISBN 0-385-50426-8
LC 2002-41507
This Elvis Cole thriller finds the "Los Angeles P. I. racing the clock to rescue his girlfriend's 10-year-old son, Ben, from a team of kidnappers who claim to be paying Cole back for atrocities they say he committed in Vietnam." N Y Times Book Rev
"Fast action, though guys, vivid Los Angeles details, and snappy dialog are Craig's trademarks, and this tale has them all." Libr J

The two minute rule. Simon & Schuster 2006 325p $24.95
ISBN 0-7432-8161-6
LC 2005-57476
"Career criminal Max Holman, a.k.a. the 'Hero Bandit,' has just finished serving ten years in prison for bank robbery and at middle age finally understands that he has to change his ways. On the day of his release, Holman's estranged police officer son is killed along with three other cops—a tragedy that shatters any hope of reconciliation. When the LAPD quickly closes the case by blaming a junkie who killed himself after the crime, Holman is unconvinced. He persuades the now retired FBI agent who originally arrested him to help him, and the story takes off at breakneck speed. In this superb tale with a likable ex-con protagonist, Crais creates a totally believable world in which good and evil are turned upside down." Libr J

The watchman. Simon and Schuster 2007 292p $25.95
ISBN 978-0-7432-8163-8; 0-7432-8163-2
LC 2006-38775
"Larkin Barkley, a troubled L.A. woman from a wealthy family, finds herself under the protection of federal agents after emerging uninjured from a serious car accident. Something she saw warrants her death. The bad guys came close to success, probably with an assist from someone charged with her safety. Joe Pike, a former marine, LAPD officer, and mercenary, is hired to protect her on the word of his former police partner. Pike and the girl go underground after another attempt on her life leaves three would-be assassins dead. Pike then enlists his partner, private investigator Elvis Cole, to do the digging while he does the shooting. Cole targets a drug cartel's money-laundering network as the source of the death squads and identifies Barkley's father as the possible link. . . . Fans of the Elvis Cole series have long wished for an installment focusing on sidekick Pike, and their wish is more than granted with this stunningly emotional thriller." Booklist

Crane, Elizabeth, 1961-

You must be this happy to enter; stories. Punk Planet Books 2008 183p pa $14.95
ISBN 978-1-933354-43-9
LC 2007-926133

Crane, Elizabeth, 1961——*Continued*

Contents: My life is awesome! And great!; Betty the zombie; Banana love; Notes for a story about people with weird phobias; Clearview; What our week was like; The glistening head of Ricky Ricardo begs further experimentation; Donovan's closet; Sally (featuring: Lollipop the rainbow unicorn); What happens when the mipods leave their milieu; Emmanuel; Varieties of loudness in Chicago; Blue girl; You must be this happy to enter; The most everything in the world; Promise

"Zombies, time travelers, reality TV contestants and even a few normalish folks populate the pages of Elizabeth Crane's quirky, charming new collection. . . . Crane writes like she's running out of air: fast and a little babbly, but she's endlessly entertaining." PopMatters

Crane, Stephen, 1871-1900

Active service
In Crane, S. The complete novels of Stephen Crane p429-592

The complete novels of Stephen Crane; edited with an introduction by Thomas A. Gullason. Doubleday 1967 821p o.p.

Includes: Maggie: a girl of the streets (1893); The red badge of courage (1895); George's mother (1896); The third violet (1897); Active service (1899); The O'Ruddy (1903)

The complete short stories & sketches of Stephen Crane; edited with an introduction by Thomas A. Gullason. Doubleday 1963 790p o.p.

Contains the following short stories: The king's favor; The camel; Dan Emmonds; Four men in a cave; Travels in New York; The broken-down van; The octopush; A ghoul's accountant; The black dog; Killing his bear; The Captain; A tent in agony; The cry of a huckleberry pudding; An explosion of seven babies; The mesmeric mountain; The holler tree; Why did the young clerk swear; The pace of youth; The reluctant voyagers; A desertion; An experiment in misery; An experiment in luxury; An ominous baby; A dark brown dog; Billie Atkins went to Omaha; Mr. Binks' day off; The men in the storm; Coney Island's failing days; In a Park Row restaurant; Stories told by an artist; When every one is panic stricken; When a man falls a crowd gathers; The duel that was not fought; A Christmas dinner won in battle; A lovely jag in a crowded car; A mystery of heroism; A gray sleeve; One dash—horses; A tale of mere chance; Three miraculous soldiers; A freight car incident; The little regiment; The veteran; The snake; Raft story; An Indiana campaign; In the Tenderloin; The voice of the mountain; Yen-Nock Bill and his sweetheart; Diamonds and diamonds; The auction; A poker game; A man and some others; The open boat; How the donkey lifted the hills; The victory of the moon; Flanagan and his short filibustering adventure; An old man goes wooing; A fishing village; The bride comes to Yellow Sky; Death and the child; The five white mice; The wise men; The monster; His new mittens; The blue hotel; The price of the harness; A self-made man; The clan of no-name; God rest ye, merry gentlemen; The lone charge of William B. Perkins; The angel child; Lynx-hunting; The revenge of the 'Adolphus'; The sergeant's private madhouse; The battle of Forty Fort; The surrender of Forty Fort; "Ol'

Bennett" and the Indians; The lover and the telltale; "Showin' off"; Virtue in war; Making an orator; Twelve o'clock; The second generation; An episode of war; Shame; The carriage-lamps; The Kicking Twelfth; The shrapnel of their friends; "And if he wills, we must die"; The upturned face; The knife; The stove; Moonlight on the snow; The trial, execution, and burial of Homer Phelps; An illusion in red and white; The fight; This majestic lie; The city urchin and the chaste villagers; Manacled; A little pilgrimage; At the pit door; The squire's madness; The man from Duluth; A man by the name of Mud

George's mother
In Crane, S. The complete novels of Stephen Crane p301-47
In Crane, S. The portable Stephen Crane p89-146
In Crane, S. Prose and poetry

Maggie: a girl of the streets (a story of New York); an authoritative text, backgrounds and sources, the author and the novel, reviews and criticism, edited by Thomas A. Gullason. Norton 1979 258p

ISBN 0-393-01222-0

          * LC 78-24596

"A Norton critical edition"

First published privately in 1893 under the pseudonym Johnston Smith

"Maggie Johnson is the daughter of a brutal father and a drunken mother. She goes to work in a collar factory, falls in love with Pete, a bartender who is a friend of her brother Jimmie, and is seduced by him. Her mother disowns her, she becomes a prostitute; and in despair she finally kills herself. Her final degeneration becomes almost an allegory." Reader's Ency. 4th edition

also in Crane, S. The complete novels of Stephen Crane p99-155
also in Crane, S. The portable Stephen Crane p3-74
also in Crane, S. Prose and poetry

The monster
In Crane, S. Prose and poetry

The O'Ruddy
In Crane, S. The complete novels of Stephen Crane p593-790

The portable Stephen Crane; edited, with an introduction and notes, by Joseph Katz. Viking 1969 xxvi, 550p

ISBN 0-670-01068-5

"Viking portable library"

Short stories included are: A great mistake; An ominous baby; A dark-brown dog; The men in the storm; An experiment in misery; An experiment in luxury; An episode of war; The veteran; Flanagan and his short filibustering adventure; The open boat; The bride comes to Yellow Sky; The five white mice; The blue hotel; The monster; His new mittens; The knife

Prose and poetry. Library of Am. 1984 1379p $40; pa $15.95

ISBN 0-940450-17-8; 1-883011-39-6 (pa)

          LC 83-19908

Crane, Stephen, 1871-1900—*Continued*

Maggie: a girl of the streets and The red badge of courage are entered separately. George's mother (1896) focuses on a woman who sacrifices everything for her own son, whom she mistakenly believes to be destined for greatness. The third violet (1896-97) deals with an artist and his bohemian life. In The monster (1898) "Henry Johnson, a black servant in the home of Dr. Trescott, rescues the physician's son from a fire. He is terribly disfigured and loses his sanity, so that no home can be found for him in the town. Horrified by the 'monster,' the townspeople ostracize the doctor and his family because they harbor the man." Oxford Companion to Am Lit. 6th edition

The red badge of courage; an episode of the American Civil War; [by] Stephen Crane, with an introduction by Shelby Foote. Modern Library 1993 li, 246p $17.95
ISBN 0-679-60296-8
            *

First published 1895
"A young Union soldier, Henry Fleming, tells of his feelings when he is under fire for the first time during the battle of Chancellorsville. He is overcome by fear and runs from the field. Later he returns to lead a charge that re-establishes his own reputation as well as that of his company. One of the great novels of the Civil War." Cincinnati Public Libr

 also in Crane, S. The complete novels of Stephen Crane p197-299
 also in Crane, S. The portable Stephen Crane p189-318
 also in Crane, S. Prose and poetry
 also in Crane, S. The red badge of courage and other stories

The red badge of courage and other stories; with biographical illustrations and pictures of the settings of the stories together with an introduction and captions by Max J. Herzberg. Dodd, Mead 1957 409p il o.p.
"Great illustrated classics"
Contents: The red badge of courage; The veteran; A mystery of heroism; An episode of war; Ouida's masterpiece; The gratitude of a nation

The third violet
 In Crane, S. The complete novels of Stephen Crane p349-428
 In Crane, S. Prose and poetry

Crayencour, Marguerite De *See* Yourcenar, Marguerite

Crews, Harry, 1935-

A feast of snakes. Atheneum 1976 177p
ISBN 0-689-107293
         * LC 76-8206
The novel is set in the backwoods hamlet of Mystic, Georgia, where the annual festival "begins with the crowning of the high-school Rattlesnake Queen, continues with a pit-bull championship fight, and ends with a Rattlesnake Roundup. The festival this year is a total nightmare: a black girl with a razor emasculates Sheriff Buddy Matlow, Big Joe Mackey kicks his losing dog to death, and Joe Lon Mackey–aged twenty-two, practically illiterate, miserably married, with two screaming babies, his years of glory as an all-around athlete . . . behind him–goes out of control with a twelve-gauge shotgun." New Yorker

Crichton, Michael, 1942-2008

The Andromeda strain. Avon Books 2003 c1969 331p pa $7.99
ISBN 0-06-054181-4
            *

First published 1969 by Knopf
"In these days of interplanetary exploration, this tale of the world's first space-age biological emergency may seem uncomfortably believable. When a contaminated space capsule drops to earth in a small Nevada town and all the town's residents suddenly die, four American scientists gather at an underground laboratory of Project Wildfire to search frantically for an antidote to the threat of a worldwide epidemic." Shapiro. Fic for Youth. 3d edition

Jurassic Park; a novel. Knopf 1990 399p $28.95; pa $7.99
ISBN 0-394-58816-9; 0-345-37077-5 (pa)
         * LC 90-52960
This novel "tells of a modern-day scientist bringing to life a horde of prehistoric animals." N Y Times Book Rev
"Crichton is a master at blending technology with fiction. . . . Suspense, excitement, and good adventure pervade this book." SLJ
Followed by The lost world (1995)

Prey; novel. HarperCollins Pubs. 2002 376p $26.95
ISBN 0-06-621412-2   LC 2002-32338
"Jack Forman has been laid off from his Silicon Valley job as a senior software programmer and has become a househusband, while his wife continues her career with a biotech firm involved in defense contracting. Jack is called in as a consultant to debug one of their products, and finds himself confronting a full-blown emergency, about which his wife and others in the organization have been suspiciously deceptive." SLJ
"Despite its absurd moments, 'Prey' is irresistibly suspenseful. You're entertained on one level and you learn something on another, even if the two levels do ultimately diverge." N Y Times Book Rev

Sphere; a novel. Knopf 1987 385p
ISBN 0-394-56110-4   LC 86-46321
The author "sends a team of civilian experts to the floor of the Pacific to investigate an enormous spaceship that appears to have rested there for some 300 years. In it, they discover a huge sphere, made of a mysterious metal, which they cannot force open despite its having a door. Then, when one of the group inspects the ship on his own, it opens, he enters, and the real fun begins. . . . Crichton's prose, pedestrian but not clumsy, lets the story spin itself out, and few readers who grab its thread will let go until the web is broken in a 'Wizard of Oz'-style ending." Booklist

Crichton, Michael, 1942-2008—*Continued*

Timeline. Knopf 1999 449p

ISBN 0-679-44481-5   LC 99-461985

In this novel, a billionaire planning a theme park uses time travel to send historians working on an excavation in the Dordogne back to the France of 1357, where they become involved in a war

"Crichton is a master of an odd hybrid: entertaining novels that educate. 'Timeline' is a page turner *and* a very lucid look at life in the late Middle Ages. He teaches you how to think like a knight during a joust by putting you in the saddle." Newsweek

Crime from the mind of a woman. See A moment on the edge

Crime novels: American noir of the 1930s and 40s; [edited by Robert Polito] Library of Am. 1997 990p il $35

ISBN 1-88301-146-9   LC 97-2485

Contents: The postman always rings twice, by J. M. Cain; They shoot horses, don't they? by H. McCoy; Thieves like us, by E. Anderson; The big clock, by K. Fearing; Nightmare alley, by W. L. Gresham; I married a dead man, by C. Woolrich

The postman always rings twice (1934) is a novel of murder and adultery along the California highway. The big clock (1946) portrays the neurotic inner world of a giant publishing corporation run by a murderous chief executive. They shoot horses, don't they? (1935) explores the turbulent world of a Hollywood dance marathon. Thieves like us (1937) follows a fugitive band of Oklahoma bank robbers. Nightmare alley (1946) presents a psychological portrait of a doomed carnival hustler. I married a dead man (published 1948 under pseudonym William Irish) is a tale of switched identities set in suburbia

Crime novels: American noir of the 1950s; [edited by Robert Polito] Library of Am. 1997 892p $35

ISBN 1-883011-49-3   LC 97-2487

Contents: The killer inside me, by J. Thompson; The talented Mr. Ripley, by P. Highsmith; Pick-up, by C. Willeford; Down there, by D. Goodis; The real cool killer, by C. Himes

The killer inside me (1952) portrays a small town Texas deputy sheriff who is a psychopathic killer. The talented Mr. Ripley (1955) is about an opportunistic social parasite. Pickup (1955) explores the seedy world of an alcoholic African American painter. Down there (1956; variant title: Shoot the piano player) is a psychological portrait of a barroom pianist. The real cool killers (1959) features Harlem police officers Coffin Ed Johnson and Grave Digger Jones

Cristofano, David

The girl she used to be. Grand Central Pub. 2009 241p $22.99

ISBN 978-0-446-58222-3; 0-446-58222-0

LC 2008-03280

"After 20 years in the Federal Witness Protection Program (WITSEC) and eight aliases, Melody Grace McCartney hardly knows who she is. On the run since she and her parents stumbled on a gruesome murder by mobster Tony Bovaro when she was six years old, Grace saw WITSEC's promised protection fail her mother and father when they were killed 12 years later. Now she feigns personal danger to be relocated just because she's bored and wants a change. But before her new case officer can move her from suburban Maryland to rural Wisconsin, Tony's son, Jonathan, tracks her down to present an alternative: protection from his family and a life of more safety and freedom than she has ever known. While federal officials pressure her to stay in WITSEC and show her Jonathan's violent side, her attraction to him grows, and she must decide a course for the rest of her life." Booklist

"The novel is told from Melody's point of view, and Cristofano is largely able to pull off the female perspective. . . . Snappy dialogue and scenes with unpredictable outcomes keep the novel going at a steady pace." PopMatters

Crombie, Deborah

And justice there is none. Bantam Bks. 2002 318p

ISBN 0-553-10973-1   LC 2002-21459

In this "police procedural featuring Scotland Yard Superintendent Duncan Kincaid and Inspector Gemma James, the pair's relationship deepens. With the progression of Gemma's pregnancy . . . they consolidate households while working together to solve three murders. Dawn Arrowood, wife of prominent Notting Hill antiques dealer Karl, 25 years her senior, is newly pregnant and is having an affair when she is killed (her throat cut, her lung pierced) outside her home. It's no longer an isolated case when Kincaid finds similarities in the murder of antiques dealer Marianne Hoffman two months earlier, and police lose a prime suspect when Karl himself is found dead." Libr J

"For all the picturesque charms of its setting, . . . this is another hard-nosed piece of social criticism from Deborah Crombie, an American author with serious designs on the British cozy mystery." N Y Times Book Rev

Kissed a sad goodbye. Bantam Bks. 1999 322p $23.95

ISBN 0-553-10943-X   LC 98-50186

"The murder of a beautiful businesswoman in London's Isle of Dogs neighborhood calls both local police and Scotland Yard into play. The Yard's Duncan Kincaid and Gemma James . . . create a psychological profile of the victim and thoroughly investigate the thriving family tea concern." Libr J

Water like a stone. William Morrow 2007 407p $24.95

ISBN 978-0-06-052527-9; 0-06-052527-4

LC 2006-46841

"After Duncan Kincaid and Gemma James arrive at the Cheshire home of Duncan's parents, he must leave to help his sister, who has found the body of a small child walled up in a barn she is renovating. Because both Kincaid and James are high-ranking police detectives in London, it is natural that they feel the pull of the investigation, but the Kincaid family requires their attention as

Crombie, Deborah—_Continued_

well." Libr J

"As in books by Elizabeth George and P. D. James, the intriguing personal relationships and family dynamics drive this well-crafted, impressive mystery-drama." Booklist

Cronin, A. J. (Archibald Joseph), 1896-1981

The citadel. Little, Brown 1937 401p o.p.

*

"In 1921 Andrew Manson, newly graduated at the top of his medical-school class, accepts his first position as assistant to a dying physician in an impoverished Welsh mining town. Hard-working and conscientious at first, Andrew is promoted to a more socially desirable post in London, where he abandons his principles. A faulty operating-room procedure magnifies his increasing incompetence and jolts him back to a career of integrity." Shapiro. Fic for Youth. 3d edition

The keys of the kingdom. Little, Brown 1941 344p

ISBN 0-316-16189-6

*

"A child of Scottish fisher folk, Father Francis Chisholm, even as a young lad, yearned to enter the Catholic priesthood. After graduation from the seminary and a few years of parish work at home, he was sent to China as a missionary. With the years of toil he acquired saintliness and tolerance. Pestilence and famine, bandits and flood, and unappreciative superiors only served to strengthen his character and fortitude. Excellent character delineation." Libr J

Cronin, Archibald Joseph _See_ Cronin, A. J. (Archibald Joseph), 1896-1981

Cross, Amanda, 1926-2003

The collected stories of Amanda Cross. Ballantine Bks. 1997 184p

ISBN 0-345-40817-9   LC 96-42006

Contents: Tania's nowhere; Once upon a time; Arrie and Jasper; The disappearance of Great Aunt Flavia; Murder without a text; Who shot Mrs. Byron Boyd?; The proposition; The George Eliot play; The Baroness

"Kate Fansler, a university professor normally involved with things academic, also dabbles in solving mysteries. In these short stories, she deals with cases ranging from missing persons to murder. Cross presents a complex jumble of seemingly enigmatic clues that Kate proceeds to study and resolve into a simple answer based on logic and deduction. The author camouflages the clues, facts, and answers by placing them in total view during the entire story." SLJ

Honest doubt. Ballantine Bks. 2000 259p $22

ISBN 0-345-44011-0   LC 00-41445

In this mystery Kate Fansler serves "as a consultant to private eye Estelle 'Woody' Woodhaven, who is investigating the murder of misogynistic Tennyson scholar Charles Hancock. Woody, a down-to-earth, overweight sleuth, is a likable foil to the elegant, erudite Kate. . . . Devotees of the series may be disappointed at Kate's relatively minor role, but they will be amply compensated by the delightful Woody." Libr J

An imperfect spy. Ballantine Bks. 1995 228p

ISBN 0-345-38917-4   LC 94-25357

Academic sleuth Kate Fansler "and husband Reed have each agreed to teach a course at New York's third-rate, racist, and chauvinistic Schuyler Law School, where they investigate the accidental death of the school's only woman professor and try to assist an imprisoned faculty wife who murdered her abusive husband. Highly sophisticated tone, carefully constructed prose, and nicely contrived plot make this a winner." Libr J

The puzzled heart. Ballantine Bks. 1998 257p

ISBN 0-345-41883-2   LC 97-22686

This "Kate Fansler mystery starts with the kidnapping, just outside his Manhattan office, of attorney Reed Amhearst, the husband of English professor and amateur sleuth Kate. Told that her husband will be released after she publicly renounces feminism, Kate is frustrated by her unfamiliar powerlessness. She turns to Harriet Furst . . . now part-owner of a detective agency. The innocuous-looking but feisty Harriet and her businesslike partner, Toni, almost effortlessly rescue Reed. The remainder of this entertaining intellectual puzzle concerns the discovery of who kidnapped him and why." Publ Wkly

Cross, Mary Ann Evans _See_ Eliot, George, 1819-1880

Crouch, Katie

Girls in trucks. Little, Brown 2008 241p $21.99

ISBN 978-0-316-00211-0; 0-316-00211-9

          LC 2007-30639

"An unenthusiastic Southern debutante copes with the cruelties of postcollege New York life in Crouch's amusing debut. Sarah Walters is neither a misfit nor the queen of the Camellia Society cotillion scene growing up in Charleston, S.C. But when she and her fellow Camellias try to make a life in New York City, they find themselves coping in unexpectedly dangerous ways — from standard substance addictions to Sarah's fixation on preppy ex-boyfriend Max, a smooth and sadistic child of wealth." Publ Wkly

"Occasionally allowing us glimpses of the inner lives of her fellow debutantes, Sarah Walters has a fresh and winning voice, and Crouch easily maintains the reader's interest in her funny, painful journey all the way to the last page despite the lack of a conventionally laid-out plot. Girls in Trucks is not exactly experimental fiction— it's told in the linked-short-story format used in books like The Girls' Guide to Hunting and Fishing—but it's not your grandmother's Southern saga either." BookPage

Crowley, John, 1942-

Four freedoms. William Morrow 2009 389p $25.99

ISBN 978-0-06-123150-6; 0-06-123150-9

          LC 2008-46338

"Although nominally about life at an American aircraft factory during World War II, Crowley's complex and subtle novel is much grander. He explores the minds and hearts of people compelled by history to radically change their lives. Unaccountably optimistic Prosper Olander, orphaned as a child and crippled by a failed surgery, discovers that even he can find important work at a distant

Crowley, John, 1942-—*Continued*

aircraft company in rural Oklahoma. Connie Wrobleski, frightened of nearly everything except her infant son, also travels to Oklahoma to reunite with her domineering husband, only to see him desert his family by enlisting. Prosper, Connie, and half a dozen other characters are developed in intricate detail and used as lenses on the massive relocation, dislocation, and societal change caused by the war." Booklist

Little, big. HarperPerennial 2006 538p (Harper Perennial modern classics) pa $16.99

ISBN 978-0-06-112005-3; 0-06-112005-7

First published 1981 by Bantam

The "story of Smoky Barnable, an anonymous young man who travels by foot from the City to a place called Edgewood—not found on any map—to marry Daily Alice Drinkwater, as was prophesied. It is the story of four generations of a singular family, living in a house that is many houses on the magical border of an otherworld." Publisher's note

"One of the authentic masterpieces of modern imaginative literature. Painstakingly composed and elegantly structured, it is the sort of book that defies categorization yet lodges permanently in the memories of readers fortunate enough to encounter it." Barnes and Noble

Lord Byron's novel; the evening land. William Morrow 2005 465p $25.95

ISBN 0-06-055658-7

* LC 2004-63575

"Documents discovered in a rotting old trunk in an English storage room prove that the manuscript of a novel by Byron once existed, and that it was saved from destruction, read, and annotated by Ada, Countess of Lovelace, a brilliant mathematician and Byron's abandoned daughter, during the final, agonizing months of her young life. While the mystery of what became of the manuscript itself is explored, we are permitted to read it—the whole of Byron's only novel—beginning to end." Publisher's note

"Crowley's real achievement in Lord Byron's Novel is not a convincing imitation of Byron—not even Byron, who was pudgy and pale and walked with a limp, could always pull that off. More persuasive by far is the suffocating world of encryption and code, coincidence and conspiracy, paranoia and parapsychology that Crowley summons from his 19th-century documents and 21st-century decoders." N Y Times Book Rev

The translator. Morrow 2002 295p

ISBN 0-380-97862-8

* LC 2001-40324

In this novel, set during the Cuban missile Crisis of 1962, "Kit Malone, an aspiring writer at a small midwestern college, develops a relationship with exiled Russian poet Innokenti Falin. . . . Their friendship turns to romance as the international crisis builds. The world survives the Soviet-American crisis, but their relationship does not. Finally, on a trip to Russia years later, Kit can come to terms with their relationship." Booklist

"The fears 'The Translator' conjures seem eerily familiar, like a bad dream we've had before. At the same time, the novel gives us a world so suffused with beauty that its inhabitants manage to speak in fragments of poetry without sounding pompous or absurd." N Y Times Book Rev

Crumey, Andrew, 1961-

Mr. Mee. Picador 2001 344p

ISBN 0-312-26803-3

Mr. Mee is an English scholar who, late in life, has become fascinated with computers. On his screen is a picture of a naked woman reading a book, but Mr. Mee is excited mainly "by the title of the book she is reading, 'Ferrand and Minard,' which was written by a member of the faculty at the local university, one Dr. A.B. Petrie. . . . The book also goes back in time to meet Ferrand and Minard themselves. These are real-life figures who appear briefly in Book 10 of Rousseau's 'Confessions.'" N Y Times Book Rev

"Musing on Rousseau, the French encyclopedists and the vagaries of chance and identity, Crumey . . . has written another novel of ideas in the grand tradition of Calvino, Borges and Kundera." Publ Wkly

Crumley, James, 1939-2008

Bordersnakes. Mysterious Press 1996 320p

ISBN 0-89296-573-8   LC 96-34405

"Milo Milodragovitch and Sonny Sughrue are former partners bent on revenge. . . . Milodragovitch, ex-lawman, p.i., and bartender in his mid-fifties, vows to locate the weasely banker who absconded with his inheritance. Sughrue is a leathery cowboy looking for the men who tried to do him in. They crisscross Texas in Milo's new Cadillac, drinking hard, throwing money and punches, tricking bad guys, and coming upon a gruesome murder." Libr J

"The plot, such as it is, takes the pair from one violent encounter to the next, each with its separate cast of sublimely weird characters. . . . Mr. Crumley saves his fiercest prose for El Paso, where the villains of the piece have their day; but the sheer originality of his style tears up every pit stop on this hellishly funny adventure." NY Times Book Rev

The final country. Mysterious Press 2001 310p

ISBN 0-89296-666-1   LC 2001-30640

"Texas is no place for an old reprobate like Milo Milodragovitch to sober up and settle down. Except for laundering a little money through the bar he owns in the Hill Country, James Crumley's saddle-sore private eye is keeping faithful to his woman and living a blameless life . . . when the payback murder of a drug dealer gives him an excuse to oil his gun, pack some drugs, jump in his black cherry El Dorado and hit the road again." N Y Times Book Rev

"Plot twists and details seem loose and easy, yet every thread is sewn tight as a hardball. This is a brilliant achievement, with Crumley returned to his full powers, seeming to say with each assured sentence, Yeah, I'm an old dog, but I still wag the baddest bone." Publ Wkly

The last good kiss; a novel. Random House 1978 259p

ISBN 0-394-41946-4

* LC 77-90286

"C. W. Sughrue is hired to trace the missing and drunken writer Abraham Trahearne by the man's divorced first wife, Catherine. Catherine Trahearne is sexy, elegant, and ice-cold. She lives with Trahearne's ancient mother, Edna, across the creek from the house where Trahearne lives with Melinda, his second wife. The plot

Crumley, James, 1939-2008—*Continued*
is episodic and keeps one bleary eye loosely focused on Trahearne's dysfunctional extended family." Murphy. Ency of Murder and Mystery

The wrong case; a novel. Random House 1975 272p
ISBN 0-394-49198-3
* LC 74-29598
Milton "Milo" Milodragovitch is a private detective in Meriwether, Montana. This case involves the suicide of a homosexual heroin pusher

This is "an exceptionally good example of the genre. Properly deferring to hallowed conventions, Crumley writes about damaged people seen through a haze of jaded romanticism, but he asserts his own tone of voice . . . . Crumley is a vivid writer. He makes Milo much more vulnerable, more involved in this sordid case than Hammett or Chandler would have done." Newsweek

Crusie, Jennifer

Bet me. St. Martin's Press 2004 337p $22.95
ISBN 0-312-30346-7
LC 2003-58182
"Minerva Dobbs thought David Fisk might be the one she's been waiting for, until he dumps her three weeks before her sister Diana's wedding. Min soon realizes just how lucky she is to be rid of David when she overhears him at her favorite bar betting a handsome stranger, Calvin Morrisey, that Cal couldn't bed Min in a month. At first Min debates the idea of giving them both a piece of her mind, but then she remembers she still needs a date for the wedding. Why not use the all-too charming Cal just like he was going to use her, and then dump him? Of course, Min never expected that Cal might turn out to be the 'one.' . . . Finding exactly the right balance between cynicism and optimism, Crusie deftly blends snappy dialogue; quirky, irrepressible secondary characters; and two beautifully matched protagonists struggling against their romantic fate." Booklist

Faking it. St. Martin's Press 2002 340p $24.95
ISBN 0-312-28468-3
"Matilda Goodnight has put her days of forging art behind her, but when her niece accidentally sells one of the six paintings she did as the fictitious daughter of a reclusive painter, she fears her secret past will be discovered. Tilda determines to steal the painting from Clea Lewis, the conniving social climber who brought it. But when she sneaks into the house Clea shares with wealthy Mason Phipps, she runs right into Davy Dempsey, who is there to steal back the money Clea took from him. Sparks fly instantly between the two. . . . [This] is an entertaining, fast-paced romp with a pleasing love story at its heart." Booklist

Cullin, Mitch, 1968-

A slight trick of the mind; a novel. Nan A. Talese 2005 272p $23.95
ISBN 0-385-51328-3
* LC 2004-46038
"It is 1947, and the long-retired Holmes, now 93, lives in a remote Sussex farmhouse, where his memories and intellect begin to go adrift. He lives with a housekeeper and her young son, Roger, whose patient, respectful demeanor stirs paternal affection in Holmes. Holmes has

settled into the routine of tending his apiary, writing in journals, and grappling with the diminishing powers of his razor-sharp mind, when Roger comes upon a case hitherto unknown. It is that of a Mrs. Keller, the long-ago object of Holmes's deep-and never acknowledged-infatuation." Publisher's note
"Cullin is an unusually sophisticated theorist of human nature, and this book is first and foremost an analysis of Holmes—both as a fictional character and as an embodiment of the human drive to make fictions. . . . As the conclusion of this beautiful novel makes plain, lives aren't like cases or, for that matter, like narratives. They are never solved or resolved: they just one day come to an end." N Y Times Book Rev

Undersurface; a novel; art by Peter I. Chang. Permanent Press 2002 166p il $24
ISBN 1-57962-077-9
LC 2001-36621
An "account of a Tucson teacher's descent into the lurid, furtive world of illicit gay sex, which lands him in the wrong place at the wrong time when a murder is committed. John Connor is the ordinary, sensitive narrator whose descent begins when he finds himself frequenting adult video stores after his sex life with his wife sours. . . . As a crime narrative based on a true story, the book is a chilling if somewhat dated tale of a misstep morphing into free fall; as a literary character study, Connor's attempt to come to terms with his situation is both haunting and compelling." Publ Wkly

Culver, Timothy J.
For works written by this author under other names see Stark, Richard; Westlake, Donald E.

Cummins, Ann

Yellowcake. Houghton Mifflin Co. 2007 303p $24
ISBN 978-0-618-26926-6; 0-618-26926-6
LC 2006-23453
"Ryland Mahoney, Sam Behan, and Woody Atcitty are more than three decades away from the New Mexico uranium mine where they all worked and breathed in the radioactive yellow dust ('yellowcake') that has now sickened Ryland and Woody, who is Navajo. Rumblings of lawsuits and settlements accompany Woody's daughter, Becky, and an entourage of lawyers to the Mahoneys' home, where preparations are being made for daughter Maggie's wedding. When Sam arrives in town for the event, he finds that his ex-wife, Lily, has a legal issue of her own regarding their divorce proceedings and that the son he fathered with his longtime mistress is just out of prison." Libr J
"By fusing suspenseful love entanglements with family angst, Native American concerns, grief over the poisoning of the land, penetrating compassion, and ironic humor, Cummins brilliantly conflates the insidious damage wrought by radiation sickness with the maladies of the soul caused by prejudice, poverty, nature's abuse, and love's betrayal." Booklist

Cumyn, Alan, 1960-

Losing it. St. Martin's Press 2003 365p $24.95
ISBN 0-312-30691-1
LC 2002-31882

Cumyn, Alan, 1960-—_Continued_

"The Sterlings are ordinary members of the educated middle class living in Ottawa, but turmoil lurks beneath their surface calm. Bob Sterling, a professor of literature specializing in Edgar Allan Poe, is secretly obsessed with women's underthings; Julia, Bob's much younger wife and former student, is quietly losing her mind from the exhaustion of caring for Matthew, their two-year-old, and her mother, Lenore, who is tormented by Alzheimer's." Publ Wkly

"The nuanced persuasive characterization propels the story forward and provides depth and texture. . . . A bonus is that Cumyn spices up this essentially sad story with some horrifyingly funny scenes." Booklist

Cunningham, Elaine

Shadows in the starlight. Tor 2006 286p $23.95

ISBN 0-7653-0971-8   LC 2005-44639

"A Tom Doherty Associates book"

"Fired from the vice squad when a failed bust becomes a bloodbath, Gwen Gelman opens her own P.I. business focused on domestic problems and runaways. Called to investigate a missing-persons case involving the wife and son of someone she dislikes immensely, Gelman begins questioning her own cloudy past and slowly awakens to her changeling heritage. The second installment in a series that began with Shadows in the Darkness [2004] features a wise-cracking, gun-toting heroine and a fast-paced story of an elven legacy rediscovered." Libr J

Cunningham, Michael, 1952-

Flesh and blood. Farrar, Straus & Giroux 1995 465p

ISBN 0-374-18113-6   LC 94-24628

This family chronicle begins "in 1935 in Greece, where a boy suffers poverty and neglect. Constantine Stassos eventually immigrates to the U.S., where he marries a lovely and industrious young woman, amasses a fortune, and turns his attractive home into a living hell. No one goes unscathed, from his suffocating wife, Mary, through his self-negating eldest daughter, his acerbic gay son, and his younger daughter, Zoe, a strangely feral child. As the years go by and abrupt social changes become the rack upon which families are wrenched and broken, each member of the Stassos clan struggles to achieve love and respect." Booklist

"Fairly brief episodes, often occuring years apart, recount key moments in the establishment, disintegration, and reconfiguration of the family. Thoroughly realized action, vivid character delineation, and the splendid control of language guarantee both the unity and powerful impact of this successful novel." Libr J

The hours. Farrar, Straus & Giroux 1998 229p $23

ISBN 0-374-17289-7

                              * LC 98-34188

In alternating chapters, "three stories unfold: 'Mrs. Woolf,' about Virginia's own struggle to find an opening for *Mrs. Dalloway* in 1923; 'Mrs. Brown,' about one Laura Brown's efforts to escape, somehow, an airless marriage in California in 1949 while, coincidentally, reading *Mrs. Dalloway*; and 'Mrs. Dalloway,' which is set in 1990s Greenwich Village and concerns Clarissa

Vaughan's preparations for a party for her gay—and dying—friend, Richard, who has nicknamed her Mrs. Dalloway." Publ Wkly

"After a brief prologue, the stories alternate in an intricate sequence, rather like a rhyme scheme. . . . The whole book does sound a little fussy in description, an exercise in echoes, but it doesn't read that way." N Y Times Book Rev

Specimen days. Farrar, Straus and Giroux 2005 308p $25

ISBN 0-374-29962-5

                              * LC 2005-40518

"In 'In the Machine,' the first of three interrelated tales set in New York City, 13-year-old Lucas, who almost involuntarily spouts lines of Whitman's verse, confronts grief and the ambiguity of love as he tries to take his dead brother Simon's place. The setting, the Industrial 1920s, melds into the early 21st century in the second tale, 'The Children's Crusade,' in which African American police detective Cat investigates a band of Whitman-quoting children terrorizing the city. In the futuristic final story, 'Like Beauty,' an android with Whitman's poetry implanted in his circuits embarks on a journey with a young boy named Luke to meet his manufacturer." Libr J

"As much as Cunningham's novel is haunted by the ghost of Whitman's prophecies, it is profoundly informed by the events of September 11, 2001. . . . Cunningham's brilliantly imagined dystopian future represents the final betrayal of Walt Whitman's joyously democratic America." New Leader

Cusk, Rachel, 1967-

Arlington Park. Farrar, Straus and Giroux 2007 256p $23

ISBN 978-0-374-10080-3; 0-374-10080-2

                              LC 2006-7952

First published 2006 in the United Kingdom

A novel about the "not-so-quiet desperation of young mothers in the well-to-do London suburb Arlington Park. The book's single day begins with an epic rainstorm that wakes part-time private-school English teacher Juliet Randall, who spent the previous evening at a wealthier neighbor's home and was told, in front of husband Benedict, 'You want to be careful. . . . You can start to sound strident at your age.' As Amanda Clapp strains to maintain her house's empty perfection, a multi-kid play date gets out of control. Maisie Carrington feels 'imprisoned for life' by her frosty, upper-crust childhood, and can barely contain her violent feelings toward her own daughters. Christine Lanham, a newcomer to the class distinction her marriage has brought her, abhors the hypocrisy that surrounds her, but knows she will never leave her family. The story line coils around each woman's home until it gathers the group for a drunken dinner party." Publ Wkly

"The microscopic detail of daily life offered here could be excruciating for some readers, but for anyone who enjoys an original and imaginative writing style and wry observations of the way people live, it's well worth the read." Rocky Mountain News

In the fold; a novel. Little, Brown and Co. 2005 262p $23.95

ISBN 0-571-22813-5   LC 2005-02589

Cusk, Rachel, 1967-—*Continued*

"As a college student Michael visited Egypt Hill, the curiously named estate of his roommate's family, for a garden party, and in one afternoon met a host of eccentric characters who have stayed with him ever since. Years later he decides a return to Egypt Hill would be an ideal sojourn—a place where he can escape the chaos at home that is destroying his marriage, his fashionably old townhouse, and possibly his worrisomely taciturn young son, Hamish. But now nothing in Egypt Hill is as it was, or at least how it once seemed." Publisher's note

This novel is the "cleverest portrait of narcissism since Charles Allen Gilbert's 1892 painting 'All Is Vanity.' Like that image, an optical illusion that can be seen either as a young woman at her mirror or as a human skull, 'In the Fold' is at once a shimmering vision of privilege and a wise meditation on disillusionment." N Y Times Book Rev

Cussler, Clive

Atlantis found. Putnam 1999 534p $26.95

ISBN 0-399-14588-5   LC 99-39883

The threat in this Dirk Pitt suspense novel "comes from a family of genetically engineered superhumans that just may have Hitler as an ancestor. Basing a plan on relics discovered from an ancient civilization, the evilly insane Wolf family plans to split the Antarctic ice shelf, flooding the world. Then their superbreed can take over the world and bring about the creation of a Nazi 'Fourth Empire.' Dirk and sidekick Al Giordano are aided by a beautiful archaeologist and the NUMA staff in unraveling clues stretching back to 7000 B.C., in order to beat a doomsday countdown." Booklist

"This is a fascinating story with exotic locations, high-tech wizardry, heart-pounding suspense, the threat of a cataclysmic disaster, resourceful heroes, and an action-packed conclusion—all backed by meticulous research to make this a truly grand adventure." Libr J

Black wind; [by] Clive Cussler and Dirk Cussler. Putnam 2004 530p il $27.95

ISBN 0-399-15259-8   LC 2004-53536

"The story begins toward the end of World War II, and the Japanese have sent two submarines to the West Coast of the U.S. They are carrying a lethal new strain of biological virus, but neither vessel makes it to the designated target. Then, in 2007, a number of sea-lion deaths are reported along the western Alaska Peninsula, and birds and people in the area become sick and die, although no known environmental catastrophe or human-induced culprit is suspected. Called to the scene is Dirk Pitt, the head of the National Underwater Marine Agency, and his two sons, one a marine biologist, the other a marine engineer. Their task is to locate and recover the two subs from the ocean floor. There are the usual harrowing encounters, close calls, daring exploits, and—in the end—annihilation of the bad guys. Another win for NUMA." Booklist

The chase. G.P. Putnam's Sons 2007 404p il $26.95

ISBN 978-0-399-15438-6; 0-399-15438-8

LC 2007-17291

"In 1906, the American West is still expanding. With the cities still distant from one another, a ruthless criminal nicknamed 'The Butcher Bandit' takes advantage, robbing banks, killing all witnesses, and seemingly disappearing into thin air. Recruited to end the crime spree is Isaac Bell, one of the best outlaw hunters in the country. His adversary proves to be exceptionally cunning, and Bell will have a tough time not only proving the identity of the killer but also staying alive long enough to catch him. Cussler clearly had a lot of fun writing this. The details of early 20th-century America and the novel's thrill-a-minute pace will add another best seller to his résumé." Libr J

Fire ice; a novel from the NUMA® files; {by} Clive Cussler, with Paul Kemprecos. Putnam 2002 434p

ISBN 0-399-14872-8   LC 2002-19050

Previous titles in the Kurt Austin series: Serpent (1999) and Blue Gold (2000), published in paperback

In this thriller Kurt Austin and "the men from NUMA (Native Underwater & Marine Agency) team up with former KGB spies to face down a Russian mobster with czarist aspirations and a zealot's hatred for the 'corruption and materialism' of the Western lifestyle. . . . Cussler is in top form here, working in a role for Old Ironsides and Czar Nicholas II's crown while throwing in enough derringdo and eco-lore to leave his fans breathless." Publ Wkly

Flood tide; a novel. Simon & Schuster 1997 511p

ISBN 0-684-80298-8   LC 97-26660

In this thriller, Dirk Pitt and "his sidekick, Al Giordino, are out to catch a Chinese shipping magnate who smuggles illegal Chinese immigrants into countries around the world to be worked as indentured slaves. On a lake near Seattle, Pitt stumbles across Qin Shang's heavily guarded compound. Pitt is the special projects director for the National Underwater & Marine Agency. . . . Searching the lake with a robotic observation device, Pitt finds heaps of mass-executed Chinese bodies. He then rescues a dozen still-living captives, including beautiful Immigration and Naturalization Service agent Julia Lee." Publ Wkly

Inca gold; a novel. Simon & Schuster 1994 537p

ISBN 0-671-68156-7   LC 94-6577

"A chance rescue of two divers trapped in a Peruvian sinkhole leads series hero Dirk Pitt . . . into a search for lost treasure that involves grave robbers, art thieves and ancient curses. Cussler's latest adventure novel features terrorists who aren't really terrorists and a respected archeologist who is not what he seems: it all boils down to a race between Pitt and some unscrupulous crooks for a cache of Inca gold hidden away from the Spanish and lost since the 16th century. . . . It's pure escapist adventure, with a wry touch of humor and a certain self-referential glee." Publ Wkly

Lost city; a novel from the NUMA files; [by] Clive Cussler with Paul Kemprecos. Putnam 2004 420p $26.95

ISBN 0-399-15177-X   LC 2004-50556

"A body is discovered frozen in the Alps, scientists begin disappearing from a Greek lab, and death greets anyone intent on recovering a life-prolonging enzyme discovered deep in the ocean. . . . [These are some of the problems facing protagonist] Kurt Austin, leader of the

Cussler, Clive—*Continued*

National Underwater Marine Agency's (NUMA) Special Assignments Team." Libr J

"Kidnappings, hair's breadth escapes, fierce battles, strange science, beautiful women and plenty of action add up to vintage Cussler." Publ Wkly

Plague ship; a novel of the Oregon files; [by] Clive Cussler; with Jack Du Brul. G.P. Putnam's Sons 2008 515p $26.95

ISBN 978-0-399-15497-3   LC 2008-5426

"Capt. Juan Cabrillo, who heads the Corporation, a co-vert military company for hire, and the multifaceted crew of the Oregon, a high-tech ship disguised to look like a tramp steamer, take on a group known as the Responsivists. The Responsivists publicly espouse a pro-gram of global population control, but are secretly plan-ning a devastating attack on the human race utilizing a virulent virus found aboard an ancient ship that may be Noah's Ark. The authors are up to their usual high stan-dards when in fighting mode." Publ Wkly

Sahara; a novel. Simon & Schuster 1992 541p

ISBN 0-671-68155-9   LC 92-5100

"In West Africa, a vicious plot launched by a military dictator and a French industrialist is killing thousands of people and threatening all the creatures in the world's seas with extinction. As Cussler's perennial hero Dirk Pitt hikes off across the Sahara to bring the world news of these evil doings, he discovers the secret behind Lin-coln's assassination, hidden aboard a lost Confederate ironclad, and the disappearance of British aviatrix Kitty Mannock in 1931." Libr J

"Pepper the plot with human-rights abuse, cannibalism, state-of-the-art weaponry, espionage, and the evil General Zateb Kazim—and you've got more than enough action to keep the Cussler's thrill-craving fans satiated." Booklist

Shock wave; a novel. Simon & Schuster 1996 537p

ISBN 0-684-80297-X   LC 95-30057

Protagonist Dirk Pitt "leads a National Underwater and Marine Agency expedition to discover why seals and dolphins have been disappearing on Seymour Island in the Antarctica. But the novel actually begins in 1859, when a British ship carrying convicts to Australia sinks. Eight survivors reach land, a deserted island. In the year 2000, naturalist Maeve Fletcher, one of the descendants of two of the survivors who'd married, is stranded on Seymour Island with passengers of a cruise ship and is rescued by Pitt." Booklist

"Readers will love this ripsnorting, old-fashioned sea adventure based on only slightly futuristic science. Cussler writes with tremendous confidence, creating bold characters to love or hate. They all act in situations of gripping intensity and palpable reality." Libr J

Valhalla rising. Putnam 2001 531p

ISBN 0-399-14787-X   LC 2001-19516

Dirk Pitt's "current nemesis is a timely one: Curtis Merlin Zale, an oil tycoon bent on taking over the U.S. by making it dependent on him for all its oil supplies. . . .He starts out by sinking an ocean liner with a revo-lutionary new propulsion system, and then he hijacks the research vessel sent to investigate the disaster. Fate keeps dropping Dirk Pitt in the middle of the action." Booklist

"Historical asides of submarine lore, Jules Verne minu-tiae and references to Viking runes in America add touches of real-life oddity to the mix, and nothing will prepare even longtime Cussler fans for the major surprise he drops at the end." Publ Wkly

White death; a novel from the NUMA files; [by] Clive Cussler with Paul Kemprecos. Putnam 2003 419p $26.95

ISBN 0-399-15041-2   LC 2003-46501

This thriller "chronicles the exploits of Kurt Austin, leader and hero of NUMA's Special Assignment Team. The plot involves Austin and his partner Zavala, who are investigating a feud between a radical environmentalist group and a Danish cruiser. Austin and Zavala must come to the rescue of men trapped on the ship. They find that a giant multinational corporation is seeking to kill anyone who attempts to stop its efforts to control the seas." Booklist

Cussler, Dirk

(jt. auth) Cussler, C. Black wind

Czaczkes, Shmuel Josef *See* Agnon, Shmuel Yosef, 1888-1970

D

Dahl, Roald

Collected stories; edited and introduced by Jere-my Treglown. Everyman's Library/Alfred A. Knopf 2006 xxxvii, 850p $30

ISBN 978-0-307-26490-9; 0-307-26490-4

First published 1991 in the United Kingdom with title: The collected stories of Raold Dahl. The introduction is new to this volume

Contents: An African story; Only this Katina; Beware of the dog; They shall not grow old; Someone like you; Death of an old old man; Madame Rosette; A piece of cake; Yesterday was beautiful; Nunc Dimittis; Skin; Man from the South; The soldier; The sound machine; Mr Botibol; Vengeance is Mine Inc.; The wish; Poison; Taste; Dip in the pool; The great automatic grammatizator; Claud's dog; The ratcatcher; Claud's dog: Rummins; Claud's dog: Mr Hoddy; Claud's dog: Mr Feasey; My lady love, my dove; Neck; Lamb to the slaughter; Galloping Foxley; Edward the Conqueror; The way up to Heaven; William and Mary Parson's pleasure; George Porgy; Mrs. Bixby and the Colonel's coat; Royal jelly; The champion of the world; Genesis and catastro-phe; Pig; The landlady; The visitor; The last act; The great switcheroo; The butler; Bitch; Ah, sweet mystery of life; The hitchhiker; The umbrella man; The booksell-er; The surgeon

"With the inventive power of a Thomas Edison and the imagination of a Lewis Carroll . . . Roald Dahl is a wiz-ard of comedy and the grotesque, an artist with a marvel-ously topsy-turvy sense of the ridiculous in life." Cleve-land Plain Dealer

Dai Sijie, 1954-

Once on a moonless night; translated from the French by Adriana Hunter. Alfred A. Knopf 2008 277p $24.95

ISBN 978-0-307-27158-7   LC 2008-41089

Original French edition, 2007

"The plot hinges on an ancient silk manuscript written in a mysterious tongue, torn in half by the teeth of the last Chinese emperor, Puyi, in a fit of rage, and destined to be a source of fascination and mystery thereafter. This scroll serves as a narrative device that leads the novel through the centuries from Imperial China to 1979, where it piques the interest of a Western student in China. And here enters the love story." BookPage

"This strange and beautiful novel ponders the nature of language, the history of China, filial and romantic love, and intellectual passion. . . . Though it plays with ideas, the novel is most impressive as a stream of striking images and vignettes." N Y Times Book Rev

Daley, Robert

Nowhere to run. Warner Bks. 1996 460p

ISBN 0-446-52063-2   LC 96-3146

"When New York detective Jack Dilger's marriage to an interior designer deteriorates, he decides to bust one of her art-world pals who is dealing stolen paintings to South American drug lords. But it all goes bad: cops die, bad guys (including one of the infamous Zaragon brothers) die, and Jack is severely wounded. Forced to retire, he flees to France, the surviving Zaragon brother on his tail. There he meets Madeleine Leclerq, also a cop in deadly trouble." Booklist

"Daley's leads are likable and believable, his French local color is first-rate and his complicated plot turns, buoyed by tension and splashed with violence, work beautifully. The ending isn't happy, but it rings true." Publ Wkly

Wall of brass; a novel. Little, Brown 1994 409p

ISBN 0-316-17206-5   LC 94-14185

"When New York City Police Commissioner Harry Chapman is shot while jogging on Manhattan's Upper West Side, his former patrol-car partner, Bert Farber, now chief of detectives, is assigned to find the killer. Farber is also one of three top contenders to replace Chapman as commissioner, and his two chief rivals are doing their best to roadblock him in his search for the killer. Complicating the situation . . . [is] Farber's torrid romance with Chapman's wife, Mary Alice." Publ Wkly

"A tightly plotted, involving tale of law and disorder." Booklist

Dallas, Sandra

The diary of Mattie Spenser. St. Martin's Press 1997 229p

ISBN 0-312-15515-8   LC 96-53926

"Beginning in 1865, a week after her wedding in Fort Madison, Iowa, Mattie Spenser confides to her diary as she and her new husband travel by Conestoga wagon to the Colorado Territories. The building of a sod house; the births and deaths of children; the melting of narrow attitudes toward 'loose' women, Indians, and Negroes; and the growth of Mattie as a person are all visible in these pages, full of what seems like genuine details of prairie life." Booklist

The Persian Pickle Club. St. Martin's Press 1995 196p

ISBN 0-312-13586-6   LC 95-31032

"Hard times in Depression-era Harveyville, Kansas, are softened by the conviviality of a weekly quilting circle called the Persian Pickle Club. Queenie Bean, the 'talkingest' member of the group, narrates the novel. . . . When Queenie forms a fast friendship with the newest 'Pickle,' a flashy, big-city gal named Rita, the equilibrium of the group changes, for Rita is a novice newspaper reporter intent on making a name for herself. The story Rita most wants to crack involves the mysterious death of one of the club ladies' husbands." Libr J

This is a "simple but endearing story that depicts small-town eccentricities with affection and adds dazzle with some latebreaking surprises. Dallas hits all the right notes, combining an authentic look at the social fabric of Depression-era life with a homespun suspense story." Publ Wkly

Tallgrass. St. Martin's Press 2007 305p $23.95

ISBN 978-0-312-36019-1; 0-312-36019-3   LC 2006-51271

"Rennie Stroud looks back to 1942, when she was 13, to tell a powerful coming-of-age story. That year, the U.S. government opened a Japanese internment camp outside Ellis, CO, less than a mile from where Rennie and her family farmed sugar beets. Rennie observes the prejudice of some of the townspeople as well as her parents' strong moral code and their entanglement in the emotions of the time. Her father, Loyal, not only shows open support for the Japanese, whom he views as Americans, but offers to hire them to work on the farm. When a young girl is murdered, suspicion naturally turns to the camp, and the town is divided by fear. Dallas's strong, provocative novel is a moving examination of prejudice and fear that addresses issues of community discord, abuse, and rape." Libr J

D'Amato, Barbara

Hard evidence; a Cat Marsala mystery. Scribner 1999 255p

ISBN 0-684-83354-9   LC 98-31785

Cat Marsala "tosses her dog a bone bought from an expensive food store, but the bone turns out to be human. What a way to end a pleasant dinner and begin sleuthing." Libr J

"A vivid supporting cast, sprightly yet controlled wit and some fine cooking advice . . . combine to make for another delightful mystery from the ever-reliable author." Publ Wkly

Hard road; a Cat Marsala mystery; [by] Barbara D'Amato; and an essay by Brian D'Amato, [The wooden gargoyles: evil in Oz] Scribner 2001 286p $24

ISBN 0-7432-0095-0   LC 2001-31393

"As freelance journalist Cat is squiring her young nephew, Jeremy, around a mythical Oz festival in Chicago's Grant Park . . . two people die before her eyes, one a stabbing victim. When bullets start to fly, Cat and Jeremy flee through a system of dark and dank tunnels." Publ Wkly

"Fans of L. Frank Baum's Oz books and all the history, controversy, and minutiae surrounding them will re-

D'Amato, Barbara—*Continued*

joice in D'Amato's merry weaving of all things Oz into this innovative mystery. Oz references are no mere gloss, however, but provide a satirical, sometimes spooky commentary on the action." Booklist

White male infant. Forge 2002 333p
ISBN 0-7653-0024-9   LC 2002-25029
"A Tom Doherty Associates book"

In this thriller about a baby-selling cartel D'Amato mixes "together a couple who are fighting against their suspicions that their greatly loved adopted son is not who they thought he was; a CNN reporter and her cameraman who see, firsthand, the deplorable conditions in European and Russian orphanages; and an FBI investigation into a highly profitable and corrupt international adoption agency. The separate strands of this complex but riveting story start coming together when the couple find evidence suggesting their son was not orphaned but kidnapped at the same time the CNN reporter discovers her cameraman brutally slain in their Russian hotel. Another D'Amato stunner." Booklist

D'Ambrosio, Charles, Jr.

The dead fish museum. Knopf 2006 236p $22
ISBN 1-4000-4286-0   LC 2005-44672

Contents: The high divide; Drummond & Son; Screenwriter; Up north; The scheme of things; The dead fish museum; Blessing; The bone game

"A gemlike set of eight stories in which wayward, self-deceiving characters set out to make order of their customary chaos–and realize they are more likely to find unhappy company than catharsis." Publ Wkly

Dams, Jeanne M.

Death in lacquer red; a Hilda Johansson mystery. Walker & Co. 1999 255p
ISBN 0-8027-3329-8   LC 98-45223

"With its fine churches and stately homes, its new industries and bustling downtown, South Bend, Ind., in 1900 looks like paradise to Hilda Johansson, a young Swedish maid who keeps house for the prominent Studebaker family. . . . When Hilda finds the battered body of a missionary lady, the sister of the grand political personage who lives next door, . . . [she] takes it upon herself to solve the crime before people look for a scapegoat among the city's immigrant population." N Y Times Book Rev

Daniel, Margaret Truman *See* Truman, Margaret, 1924-2008

Danielewski, Mark Z.

Only revolutions. Random House 2006 384p $26
ISBN 0-375-42176-9; 0-385-61138-2
LC 2006-40996

This novel "consists of the dual free-verse narratives of 16-year-old Hailey and Sam, which are meant to be read in tandem; eight pages of Hailey's story are to be read first, then the volume needs to be flipped upside down and read in reverse for Sam's story, until the two narratives meet in the middle. With a Jack Kerouac-like rever-

ence for the open road and a Dr. Seuss-like feel for wordplay, Danielewski tells an epic love story as the two teens travel across time, from the Civil War to the year 2063, in vehicles ranging from a Model T to a Mustang. Though outside forces threaten to undermine them, the two remain forever 16 and madly in love. . . . This creative paean to the velocity of young lovers and the vibrancy of American culture is sure to wow the experimental-fiction camp." Booklist

Dann, Jack

Jubilee. TOR Bks. 2003 441p $27.95
ISBN 0-7653-0676-X   LC 2002-73275

Contents: The diamond pit; Going under; Voices; Fairy tale; Marilyn; The black horn; Bad medicine; Tattoos; Camps; Da Vinci rising; Kaddish; The extra; A quiet revolution for death; Jumping the road; Blind shemmy; Tea; Jubilee

"The 17 stories in this collection illustrate the varied talents of one of the genre's most flexible and enduring writers." Libr J

Dannay, Frederic, 1905-1982

For works written by this author in collaboration with Manfred Lee see Queen, Ellery

Danticat, Edwidge, 1969-

The dew breaker. Knopf 2004 244p $22
ISBN 1-400-04114-7

This novel "focuses on the lives affected by a 'dew breaker,' or torturer of Haitian dissidents under Duvalier's regime. Each chapter reveals the titular man from another viewpoint, including that of his grown daughter, who, on a trip she takes with him to Florida, learns the secret of his violent past and those of the Haitian boarders renting basement rooms in his Brooklyn home. This structure allows Danticat to move easily back and forth in time and place, from 1967 Haiti to present-day Florida, tracking diverse threads within the larger narrative." Publ Wkly

"Beautifully written fiction about the real-life horror that is Haiti. Seamlessly blending the personal and political, it deals with what happens to a country and its people when mothers and fathers disappear for their political transgressions." USA Today

The farming of bones; a novel. Soho Press 1998 312p $23
ISBN 1-56947-126-6   LC 98-3655

"The book is based on a historical incident in 1937, when Dominican dictator Trujillo ordered the massacre of 15,000 to 20,000 Haitian emigrants living in his country. The Farming of Bones recounts the story through the eyes of Amabelle Désir, a young Haitian woman who is working in the Dominican Republic as the servant to a patrician family." Time

"It's a testament to Danticat's skill that Amabelle's musical, sorrowing voice never falters, even during her stark descriptions of the bloodbath." New Yorker

Krik? Krak!. Soho Press 1995 224p
ISBN 1-56947-025-1   LC 94-41999

Danticat, Edwidge, 1969-—*Continued*

Contents: Between the pool and the gardenias; Caroline's wedding; Children of the sea; The missing peace; New York day women; Night women; Nineteen thirty-seven; Seeing things simply; A wall of fire rising

The author "touches upon life both in Haiti and in New York's Haitian community, though we spend most of our time in Port-au-Prince and the country town of Ville Rose. The best of these stories humanize, particularize, give poignancy to the lives of people we may have come to think of as faceless emblems of misery, poverty and brutality." N Y Times Book Rev

Danvers, Dennis

The fourth world. Avon Eos 2000 336p $23

ISBN 0-380-97761-3   LC 99-52345

"When virtual reporter Santee St. John joins forces with the woman he loves in order to fight for a people's revolution in 21st-century Mexico, he uncovers a conspiracy that introduces a new element into the perennial battle between the First and Third Worlds. The author . . . crafts a mind-bending tale of paranoia, adventure, and unexpected love set in a near-future filled with web addicts deceived by powerful manipulators of the truth." Libr J

Dargatz, Gail Anderson- *See* Anderson-Dargatz, Gail, 1963-

Dark, Alice Elliott

Think of England; a novel. Simon & Schuster 2002 271p $24

ISBN 0-684-86522-X   LC 2002-17554

"While the MacLeod family anxiously awaits the Beatles performance on the *Ed Sullivan Show*, nine-year-old Jane is painfully aware of the escalating tensions between her parents. When a tragedy occurs later that night, Jane will relive every nuance of that evening, twisting the events like a set of rusty keys hoping to unlock the truth." Booklist

"Everything in this spare, eccentrically paced book is a pleasure to read, from the exposition of nine-year-old Jane MacLeod's home life in Pennsylvania to a family reunion, thirty-six years later. . . . It's almost impossible to write about the kind of subtle, inward sorrows and tensions that animate this story, and the author manages the challenge handsomely." New Yorker

The **dark**; new ghost stories; edited by Ellen Datlow. TOR Bks. 2003 378p $25.95

ISBN 0-7653-0444-9   LC 2003-54336

Contents: The Trentino Kid, by Ford, J.; The ghost of the clock, by Lee, T.; One thing about the night, by Dowling, T.; The silence of the fallinf stars, by O'Driscoll, M.; The dead ghost, by Wilson, G.; Seven sisters, by Cady, J.; Subway, by Oates, J. C.; Doctor Hood, by Gallagher, S.; An amicable divorce, by Abraham, D.; Feeling remains, by Campbell, R.; The gallows necklace, by McCrumb, S.; Brownie, and me, by Grant, C. L.;Velocity, by Koja, Kathe; Limbo, by Shepard, L.; The hortlak, Link, K.; Dancing men; Hirshberg, G.

"Datlow has cast her net beyond the horror genre's usual names and pulled in contributors whose stories are the equal of their best work, as well as mystery, fantasy and SF writers whose tales seem to be the ghost story they've always wanted to tell." Publ Wkly

Dark matter; a century of speculative fiction from the African diaspora; edited by Sheree R. Thomas. Warner Bks. 2000 427p

ISBN 0-446-52583-9   LC 00-22288

This volume contains five essays and the following stories: Sister Lilith, by H. F. Jeffers; The comet, by W. E. B. DuBois; Chicago 1927, by J. Gomez; Black no more, by G. S. Schuyler; Separation anxiety, by E. Shockley; Tasting songs, by L. Ross; Can you wear my eyes, by Kalamu ya Salaam; Like daughter, by T. Due; Greedy choke puppy, by N. Hopkinson; Rhythm travel, by A. Baraka; Buddy Bolden, by Kalamu ya Salaam; Aye, and Gomorrah . . ., by S. R. Delany; Ganger (Ball Lightning), by N. Hopkinson; The becoming, by A. L. Hope; The goophered grapevine, by C. W. Chesnutt; The evening and the morning and the night, by O. E. Butler; Twice, at once, separated, by L. Addison; Gimmile's songs, by C. R. Saunders; At the huts of Ajala, by N. Shawl; The woman in the wall, by S. Barnes; Ark of bones, by H. Dumas; Butta's backyard barbecue, by T. Medina; Future Christmas, by I. Reed; At life's limits, by K. I. Salaam; The African origins of UFO's, by A. Joseph; The astral visitor delta blues, by R. Fleming; The space traders, by D. Bell; The pretended, by D. A. Smith; Hussy Strutt, by A. Patterson

"Ranging in variety from the lilting cadence of Nalo Hopkinson ('Greedy Choke Puppy') to the understated bleakness of Derek Bell ('The space traders'), this collection of 28 tales by African American sf and fantasy authors showcases a wealth of talent that spans over 100 years." Libr J

Darnton, John

Black and white and dead all over. A. A. Knopf 2008 351p $24.95

ISBN 978-0-307-26752-8; 0-307-26752-0

     LC 2007-50902

"The assistant managing editor of the New York Globe, a broadsheet newspaper based in midtown Manhattan, is murdered in his office. Suspects include disgruntled beat reporters, ambitious editors, and conniving board members, and the only person who really seems to know what's going on is Bashir, the Afghan coffee-cart guy. Darnton, a forty-year veteran of the Times, precisely plots an old-fashioned murder mystery while also considering the changing nature of modern journalism. . . . Darnton's villain is ultimately undone by a penchant for cliché. Being a psychopathic killer is one thing, but at the Globe hackneyed writing is the real crime." New Yorker

The experiment. Dutton 1999 421p

ISBN 0-525-94517-2   LC 99-28860

"One way to achieve longer life might be to clone people who could provide body parts when yours wear out; clandestine research might reveal better but equally diabolical ways to extend life for those willing to pay large sums. When reporter Jude Harley discovers his apparent twin, a man raised in a mysterious island colony, he

Darnton, John—*Continued*

joins forces with a beautiful expert on twins, and the three uncover a genetic engineering plot of monstrous proportions, extending into the government and backward into their own childhoods as part of a secret project deep in an Arizona cavern." Libr J

"The central anxieties of 'The Experiment' strongly reflect the velocity of our technologies and the godlike desires of our nature." N Y Times Book Rev

Mind catcher. Dutton 2002 387p $25.95

ISBN 0-525-94662-4   LC 2002-25540

"When 13-year-old Tyler Jessup suffers profound brain injury, two neurosurgeons see conflicting opportunities. One wants to replace damaged brain cells with regenerated ones, the other wants to use a machine to separate the mind from its physical surroundings. Tyler's father, desperate to rescue his son, ultimately subjects himself to the latter experiment in order to find his son's psyche and bring it back." Libr J

"This is a dazzling, fast-paced novel that taps into issues about mind-body duality, cyberspace, artificial intelligence, and stem cell research. Well-drawn characters, tense emotions, and philosophical debates provide additional depth to this exciting scientific thriller." Booklist

Neanderthal. Random House 1996 368p

ISBN 0-679-44978-7   LC 96-11045

"Mat Morrison and Susan Arnot, archaeologists and ex-lovers, are summoned to investigate an odd find: an apparently new Neanderthal skull. They rush to Tadjikistan and foray into some of the least hospitable terrain in Asia. Not too unexpectedly, they find their quarry only to discover a long-lost mentor who is guarding unsettling moral, political, and archaeological secrets that threaten their lives and those of the reclusive Neanderthals. . . . When government agents intrude and threaten the scientific find, the two scientists must survive, rescue their old friend, deceive American and Russian intelligence gatherers, and balance a study of an astounding archaeological find with the interests of the tribes." Libr J

Datlow, Ellen

(ed) The dark. See The dark

(ed) Snow white, blood red. See Snow white, blood red

(ed) The Year's best fantasy and horror. See The Year's best fantasy and horror

Davenport, Diana *See* Davenport, Kiana

Davenport, Kiana

House of many gods; a novel. Ballantine Books 2006 330p $24.95

ISBN 0-345-48150-X   LC 2005-48174

"Left by her beautiful, tortured mother to be raised by her extended family, little Ana must survive by her wits in a small village on the west coast of Oahu. All the while, she keeps a tight hold on her anger at this abandonment, using it as fuel to fight her way to a good education and to medical school. . . . Davenport mines the depths of emotion and does not shy away from themes of madness and cruelty. Here she follows both Ana and her mother as they encounter love, illness, and redemption, all woven with the mysticism of island lore." Libr J

Davidar, David

The house of blue mangoes. HarperCollins Pubs. 2002 421p

ISBN 0-06-621254-5

A multigenerational family saga set on the "Dorai estate in a tiny village in southern India. Tamil Christians, the Dorais are fortunate to have the contemplative patriarch Solomon at the helm in 1899, a time of violent unrest. Solomon has high hopes for his good-looking and athletic son, Aaron, but the heir apparent gets drawn into a radical terrorist group, so it's shy and studious Daniel, who makes a fortune in cosmetics, who takes his father's place. An avid student of the history and cultures of India, Davidar tracks the fortunes of the Dorai clan over the course of five turbulent decades as the independence movement coalesces, British rule ends, and India is drawn into two world wars." Booklist

Davidson, Andrew

The gargoyle. Doubleday 2008 468p $25.95

ISBN 978-0-385-52494-0; 0-385-52494-3

The "the unnamed narrator, a coke-addled pornographer, drives his car off a mountain road in a part of the country that's never specified. During his painful recovery from horrific burns suffered in the crash, the narrator plots to end his life after his release from the hospital. When a schizophrenic fellow patient, Marianne Engel, begins to visit him and describe her memories of their love affair in medieval Germany, the narrator is at first skeptical, but grows less so. Eventually, he abandons his elaborate suicide plan and envisions a life with Engel, a sculptress specializing in gargoyles." Publ Wkly

"Likely to ignite the passion of anyone who loves a mix of romance and the macabre. . . . Nothing [the narrator]—or you—can assume about this spectacularly imaginative journey will help navigate its twists and turns. Before it's all over, like Dante before him, our narrator must visit Hades, and like every chapter of The Gargoyle, that's a hell of a story, too." Washington Post Book World

Davidson, Diane Mott

Killer pancake. Bantam Bks. 1995 301p

ISBN 0-553-09588-9   LC 95-10852

"Careful planning for a cosmetics firm's lowfat luncheon fails to prepare Goldy [Schulz] for the sudden death of a gorgeous sales associate who was caught in the midst of an animal-rights demonstration." Libr J

The author "includes recipes as she brings events to a proper boil in this latest lively and satisfying outing for Goldy, who not only solves the mystery but also finds, much to her delight, that coffee can save your life." Publ Wkly

The last suppers. Bantam Bks. 1994 283p il

ISBN 0-553-09587-0   LC 94-18886

"Caterer Goldy Bear's wedding would have been perfect except for two minor problems—the priest is killed shortly before the wedding and her fiancé, homicide detective Tom Schultz, is kidnapped from the scene of the

LIST OF FICTIONAL WORKS

Davidson, Diane Mott—*Continued*

crime. Frustrated with waiting for updates from the police, Goldy attempts to find out who ruined her wedding." Booklist

"An appealing mixture of food and crime." Libr J

Prime cut. Bantam Bks. 1998 305p
ISBN 0-553-10001-7   LC 98-33736

In this mystery "Aspen Meadows, Colo., caterer Goldy Schulz is ousted from her kitchen. Bilked, like many other residents, by local contractor Gerald Eliot, her workplace in a shambles, she agrees to help her old teacher, Chef André, as he caters a Christmas catalogue fashion shoot. On the way home from the acrimonious set, she stops by to visit her friend Cameron Burr, whose house has also been ravaged by Eliot. Searching for a coffee pot, she discovers Eliot's dead body." Publ Wkly

Davies, Peter Ho, 1966-

The Welsh girl; a novel. Houghton Mifflin 2007 338p $24
ISBN 978-0-618-00700-4; 0-618-00700-8
         LC 2006-15358

This novel is "set during World War II in northern Wales, where German POWs are held in a low-security prison. The intertwining stories involve a farm girl named Esther, who becomes pregnant after being raped by an English soldier; German POW Karsten, who is ashamed of surrendering in battle; and Jewish interrogator Rotheram, who is trying to refute captured Hitler deputy Rudolf Hess's claims of amnesia. From behind the prison fence, Karsten becomes friendly with Esther. He later escapes and hides at Esther's farm. Karsten and Esther share their fears, humiliation, and shame, which eventually leads to an affectionate sexual episode before Karsten gives himself up and returns to prison. . . . The characters are heartfelt and real and events vividly and memorably described." Libr J

Davies, Robertson, 1913-1995

The cunning man; a novel. Viking 1995 469p
ISBN 0-670-85911-7   LC 94-31874

This novel's "protagonist, Dr. Jonathan Hullah, is a holistic physician—a cunning diagnostician who is often able to get to the root of problems that have baffled others. A young reporter's query about the circumstances surrounding an Episcopalian priest's death at the high altar on Good Friday leads the doctor to reflect on his own life and career." Libr J

Robertson "entertains with an old-fashioned fictional mixture that he seems to have invented anew: keen social observations delivered with wit, intelligence and free-floating philosophical curiosity." Time

Fifth business. Viking 1970 308p o.p.
The first volume in the Deptford trilogy, followed by The manticore and World of wonders

"In the year 1908 in the Canadian Midwest, a woman is struck by a poorly aimed snowball. Her son is born prematurely as a result of her fright. Dunstan Ramsay describes his connection with four of his friends whose lives were affected by the incident: Boy Staunton who threw the snowball; Mrs. Amasa Dempster, who was hit by it; Paul, the son born prematurely; and Leola Cruikshank, a local beauty whom Staunton marries. The inter-

twining of their lives spans 60 years, three continents, and two wars." Shapiro. Fic For Youth. 3d edition

This novel "achieves a richness and depth that are exceptional in a modern novel and rare at any time. On its simplest and most obvious level it is a remarkably colorful tale of ambition, love and weird vengeance. At its deepest, it is a work of theological fiction that approaches Graham Greene at the top of his form." Book World

The lyre of Orpheus. Viking 1989 472p
ISBN 0-670-82416-X   LC 88-40311
Concluding volume of the Cornish trilogy

"This fable about the nature of artistic creation has two major plot lines. One thread concerns the production of an unfinished opera said to have been written by E.T.A. Hoffmann. The other concerns the discovery that the famous art collector Francis Cornish actually passed off one of his own paintings as a 16th-century masterpiece." Merriam-Webster's Ency of Lit

The manticore. Viking 1972 310p
ISBN 0-670-45313-7
The second volume in the Deptford trilogy

"The central figure is a highly successful Canadian lawyer, David Staunton, son of a Canadian millionaire, who is compelled to submit himself to the Jung Institute in Zurich for analysis when he feels insecure and no longer in command of his actions. Staunton himself relates the course of his Jungian analysis, revealing significant incidents and aspects of his past life and commenting from a different point of view on persons and actions." Booklist

This book "reflects in its style the buoyancy of the quick mind of its hero as well as his pomposity, his over confidence, and egotism. No doubt about it: Robertson Davies is a manipulator of words and he entrances the reader with a flowing flurry of dialogue and narrative. His book is well written, insightful, and a delightful psychological excursion." Best Sellers

Murther & walking spirits; a novel. Viking 1991 357p
ISBN 0-670-84189-7   LC 91-29844

"Connor Gilmartin ('Gil') is murdered in the novel's first sentence by a co-worker he discovers in bed with his (Gil's) wife. The indignity of being snuffed by 'the Sniffer,' a theater-cum-movie critic, is compounded when Gil is seemingly condemned to spend his after-life seated next to his nemesis at a film festival. But what Gil sees—unlike the rest of the audience—is a series of highly personal films starring an assortment of ancestors." Libr J

"The films convey more than sight and sound, making our hero eerily privy to his relatives' thoughts and feelings. Davies has great fun with this device, giving full rein to his sense of drama, love of gritty, historical detail, and delight in satire." Booklist

The rebel angels. Viking 1982 c1981 326p
ISBN 0-670-59063-0
         * LC 81-51907

First volume in the Cornish trilogy, followed by What's bred in the bone and The lyre of Orpheus
First published 1981 in Canada

"Set in a prominent Canadian university, the novel examines the dual themes of the distinction between knowledge and wisdom and the role of the university in contemporary society." Merriam-Webster's Ency of Lit

Davies, Robertson, 1913-1995—*Continued*

"The names of Rabelais and Paracelsus are not gratuitously invoked by the plot. There is a Rabelaisian quality . . . in Mr. Davies's own writing; while the hermetic and heterodox ideas associated with the name of Paracelsus are exploited in a fashion that is at once playful and serious." New Repub

What's bred in the bone. Viking 1985 436p
ISBN 0-670-80916-0   LC 85-40550
"An Elisabeth Sifton book"
Second volume in the Cornish trilogy
"Born in 1909 in the Canadian town of Blairlogie, Francis [Cornish] inherits a religious and cultural dichotomy: his mother is Canadian Catholic, his father English; both are also secret agents, and mostly absent. After college at Oxford and art school in Paris, Francis too becomes a spy, gathering intelligence in Hitler's Germany while apprenticed to a brilliant and devious art restorer. Three ill-fated loves leave Francis alone at the end, his life a puzzle to his descendants but not to his 'Daiman' and an Angel of Biography who unravel Francis's character and destiny." Libr J
"This novel nourishes the brain while it beguiles the senses. Even those who dislike its message must keep it in mind while they scramble for a rebuttal." Time

World of wonders. Viking 1976 c1975 358p
ISBN 0-670-78812-0
Final volume in the Deptford trilogy
"The world's premier illusionist, Magnus Eisengrim, tells his story to an audience of friends and filmmakers: his solitary childhood in a small, deeply Calvinistic village in rural Canada; his abduction by a carnival magician and his years of labor as a huckster; his initiation into the British theater by a grande dame and her husband, an egotistical star whom Magnus all but absorbs into himself; his work as a master repairman of gadgets, clocks, and mechanical toys; and finally his triumphant career on stage." Libr J
"If there is a single dominating theme, it is that we can never escape the consequences of our actions, and to ignore them is to be destroyed. . . . Among contemporary novelists, only Graham Greene has trod this ground and gleaned it so successfully. He and Davies stand alone, each in his own quarter of the field." New Repub

Davies, Valentine, 1905-1961

Miracle on 34th Street. Harcourt Brace & Co. 1947 120p
ISBN 0-15-160239-5
"Old Mr. Kringle believed he was Santa Claus, and he looked the part, but the home for the aged decided the delusion made him ineligible as a permanent resident so he went to stay with a friend who was a keeper of Central Park zoo. Quite by accident he became the official Santa Claus in Macy's department store where he inaugurated a new and profitable policy of good will between stores, but an irritated personnel manager tried to have him committed to a mental hospital. The case went to court and the judge was in a dilemma—what would happen to his political career if he declared Santa Claus a myth?" Booklist
"Nice blend of fantasy, fun and humor with the universal and wholesome appeal of the Christmas spirit." Libr J

Davies, William Robertson *See* Davies, Robertson, 1913-1995

Daviot, Gordon, 1896-1952

For works written by this author under other names see Tey, Josephine, 1896-1952

Davis, Amanda

Wonder when you'll miss me. William Morrow 2003 259p $24.95; pa $12.95
ISBN 0-688-16781-0; 0-06-053426-5 (pa)
LC 2002-24118
"After she is sexually assaulted under the school bleachers, 16-year-old Faith runs away from home, accompanied by the Fat Girl, a taunting, imaginary former self. At the circus, Faith finds a safe haven and a healing environment." Booklist
"Davis's writing is at its finest when the protagonist is struggling through the constant trials with her distant mother, her ineffectual teachers, and her one true friend's suicide. . . . The author succeeds in making this character unique, with flaws that teens will relate to. Readers will root for Faith, and the heartwarming conclusion will leave them satisfied." SLJ

Davis, Claire, 1949-

Winter range. Picador 2000 262p $23
ISBN 0-312-26140-3   LC 00-34701
"Winters are hard on the eastern edge of Montana, and a couple of bad ones in a row can force a rancher to sell his herd. But Chas Stubblefield refuses to unload his cattle, or even to slaughter them; he is letting them starve to death out on the range as a reproach to the merchants, the banks, and God, who he believes has turned against him. Local wisdom dictates that property is property: if Stubblefield wants to lose his reputation along with his farm, that's his business. But Ike Parsons, the sheriff, is an outsider, and he decides to intervene—a decision that has dire consequences for both his marriage and his community. This fine first novel—part thriller, part love story—explores the gradations between pity and mercy." New Yorker

Davis, Kathryn

The thin place. Little Brown 2006 277p $23.95
ISBN 0-316-73504-3   LC 2005-07981
"In the opening pages of this . . . book, three small-town girls discover a man's corpse at the edge of a lake, and one of them, Mees Kipp, mysteriously brings him back to life. Davis writes hallucinatory, literate prose, and adopts a cosmic perspective: she is concerned with nothing less than describing the town's every waking moment. The experiences of Mees's dog, trotting through a clearing that smells of porcupine, stand alongside those of a minister's wife reading her morning paper and 'confronting whatever form the devil had chosen to assume overnight.' In any other book, a magical resurrection would be a central event; for Davis, it's just another moment in a particular place." New Yorker

Versailles. Houghton Mifflin 2002 206p $21
ISBN 0-618-22136-0
* LC 2002-510048

Davis, Kathryn—*Continued*

This "idiosyncratic novel begins when Marie Antoinette, née Maria Antonia Josephina Johanna, Archduchess of Austria, aged fourteen, is riding in a blue-satin-lined carriage on her way to be married to the Dauphin of France. It ends with her death. Except for the brief, witty playlets studded throughout the narrative (in which various minor actors try to figure out what's going on), the Queen tells her own story, and the voice Davis has given her is by turns sage, mercurial, and ravishing. It is also edged with doom, each word bordered in black by the reader's own premonitions." New Yorker

Davis, Lindsey

The accusers. Mysterious Press 2004 c2003 368p il map $25
ISBN 0-89296-811-7   LC 2003-65008
In this installment Marcus Didius Falco matches his "wits against two sleek lawyers intimately involved with the evident suicide of a Roman senator accused of corruption. Did he or didn't he? Of course, Falco uncovers the truth, though just barely; the ending is a surprise and surprisingly affecting. Meanwhile, the brothers of Falco's beloved Helen continue learning how hard the life of an informer can be and grow up just a little. Topnotch work in a topnotch series." Libr J

Last act in Palmyra. Mysterious Press 1996 c1994 476p
ISBN 0-89296-625-4   LC 95-1612
First published 1994 in the United Kingdom
Court investigator Marcus Didius Falco "was denied a promised promotion into the upper class by the emperor Vespasian after his last escapade, a promotion required for him to marry his lover, the patrician Helena Justina. To get out of town with Helena, he takes on a job for one of the emperor's less trustworthy underlings, heading for Syria to do a little snooping. . . . While sightseeing, Falco and Helena discover, in a cistern, the body of a playwright who had been with an acting troupe out of Rome." Publ Wkly
"A delightful adventure that's charming, witty, intriguing, and clever." Booklist

Poseidon's gold; a Marcus Didius Falco mystery. Crown 1994 336p
ISBN 0-517-59241-X   LC 94-13060
First published 1993 in the United Kingdom
In this mystery Marcus Didius Falco "is challenged to locate both the art treasure hidden by his deceased brother as well as to clear his own name from a murder charge. His father, an auctioneer of (sometimes fine) art, and Helena, his fiancee, are able assistants. The first-person narrative immediately draws readers into the story. Falco's dry wit surfaces with puns and satirical asides, and the conversations are especially realistic—often with half sentences. Details of Roman art, architecture, military, etc. appear throughout." SLJ

Three hands in the fountain. Mysterious Press 1999 351p $30
ISBN 0-89296-691-2   LC 98-45058
First published 1997 in the United Kingdom
In this "mystery featuring Marcus Didius Falco, the Roman gumshoe teams with old friend Petronius Longus to discover who is assaulting and murdering young wom-en during festival time and then tossing their chopped-up remains into the city's reservoirs." Libr J
"Davis weaves an intricate, irreverent plot filled with wittily imagined characters." Publ Wkly

Venus in copper; a Marcus Didius Falco novel. Crown 1992 c1991 277p
ISBN 0-517-58477-8   LC 91-37297
First published 1991 in the United Kingdom
A "mystery set in the Rome of Vespasian. Falco, the ancient equivalent of a private detective, ferrets out information for two nouveau-riche women about a 'professional bride' who wants to marry their husbands' business partner. When someone murders the partner, the fiancée hires Falco to find the murderer." Libr J
This novel "demonstrates Davis' solid historical knowledge as well as his quick wit." Booklist

Davis, Lydia

The collected stories of Lydia Davis. Farrar, Straus and Giroux 2009 733p $30
ISBN 978-0-374-27060-5; 0-374-27060-0
                                    * LC 2009-25451
Includes the collections: Break it down (1986); Almost no memory (1997); Samuel Johnson is indignant (2001); Varieties of disturbance (2007)
This volume presents a "body of work probably unique in American writing, in its combination of lucidity, aphoristic brevity, formal originality, sly comedy, metaphysical bleakness, philosophical pressure, and human wisdom. I suspect that The Collected Stories of Lydia Davis will in time be seen as one of the great, strange American literary contributions, distinct and crookedly personal, like the work of Flannery O'Connor, or Donald Barthelme, or J. F. Powers." New Yorker

Davis-Goff, Annabel

This cold country. Harcourt 2002 348p $31
ISBN 0-15-100847-7   LC 2001-3817
A "tale about a young English woman adjusting to new social, political and class demands when she moves to Ireland during World War II. A volunteer in England's Land Army, Daisy Creed works on a farm in Wales. Given the rare wartime occasion to meet an eligible bachelor, she quickly marries Patrick Nugent, a distant Anglo-Irish cousin of her employer. In a matter of days, Patrick is called on duty and Daisy joins Patrick's family in Ireland. Gothic touches abound; the Nugents are eccentrics, their home full of mysteries and reminders of better days." Publ Wkly
"A satisfying story told without sentimentality or melodrama but with a fine eye for detail." Booklist

Day, Cathy

The circus in winter; Cathy Day. 1st ed. Harcourt 2004 274p il $23
ISBN 0-15-101048-X   LC 2003-25033
Contents: Wallace Porter; Jennie Dixianna; The last member of the Boela tribe; The circus house; Winnesaw; The Lone Star Cowboy; The Jungle Goolah Boy; The King and His Court; Boss man; The bullhook; Circus people
In this "collection of interrelated short stories, [Day]

Day, Cathy—*Continued*
succeeds in appropriating much of the garish pungency
of the world of freaks, geeks and sideshow Houdinis
without succumbing to its ready banalities. Although
once or twice she treads close to cliche must the revelations of two-bit fortunetellers in fiction always turn out
to be true? most of the time she steers clear of tired expectations. This is one circus act that doesn't rely on dependable gimmicks to keep the audience amused." N Y
Times Book Rev

De Balzac, Honoré *See* Balzac, Honoré de, 1799-
1850

De Beauvoir, Simone *See* Beauvoir, Simone de,
1908-1986

De Bernières, Louis, 1954-

Birds without wings; Louis de Bernieres. 1st
American ed. Knopf 2004 553p $25.95
ISBN 1-400-04341-7 LC 2004-14529
"This novel tells of the inhabitants of a small coastal
town in South West Anatolia in the dying days of the
Ottoman empire: Iskander the Potter and fount of proverbial wisdom; Philothei, a Christian girl of legendary
beauty who is courted almost from infancy by Ibrahim
the Goatherd; . . . {and} Karatavuk and Mehmetcik,
childhood friends who play in the hills above the town.
. . . When jihad is declared against the Allies the young
men of the town are sent to war. Karatavuk soon finds
himself at Gallipoli where he experiences the . . . brutality of trench warfare, the loss of many comrades and of
his own innocence." Publisher's note
"This epic about the tragedy of borders is likely to
cross all borders, moving readers everywhere as it describes the harrowing cost of remaking faraway places in
the image of our dreams." Christ Sci Monit

Corelli's mandolin. Pantheon Bks. 1994 437p
ISBN 0-679-43644-8
* LC 94-4783
"Set on the Greek island of Cephallonia, this . . . nov-
el spans five decades beginning in the late 1930s just before the Axis forces occupy the island. . . . Corelli is an
Italian army captain, a member of the first extraneous
forces to occupy Cephallonia, and the lover of Pelagia
Iannis. It is through Pelagia's voice that much of the story is revealed, but the chorus includes her father, various
Greek villagers, Italian and Greek soldiers, and a goatherd." Libr J
The novel "has at times the rangy, expansive feeling
of legend or saga, at other times the cozy intensities of
chamber drama. The piece of Greek history it represents
is composed of sufferings large and small, of national catastrophes and household agonies." N Y Times Book
Rev

A partisan's daughter. Alfred A. Knopf 2008
193p $23.95
ISBN 978-0-307-26887-7; 0-307-26887-X
LC 2008-17773
This novel's main "characters are Chris and Roza.
He's a 40-year-old English pharmaceuticals salesman,
locked in a loveless suburban marriage; she's an
undocumented Yugoslav girl, scraping out an existence

amid the economic hardship of pre-Thatcher 1970s London. They meet when, on an impulse—and for the first
time in his life—Chris approaches a girl he believes to
be a streetwalker. Roza protests she is not a 'working
girl,' but she accepts a ride from him because she judges
him, rightly, to be safe and kind. Before they part, she
admits that she was once a prostitute, and charged 500
pounds for her services. Obsessed with the idea of sleeping with her, Chris begins to squirrel away money, but
in the meantime he regularly visits Roza as friend rather
than client, enjoying her company and listening to her
stories. . . . Roza shocks Chris with the revelation that
she once seduced her father, who was a comrade of Tito,
and details her rape at the hands of a British thug. But
Chris, like readers of the novel, is never quite sure when
Roza is telling the truth or when she is weaving a tale
to make herself more fascinating—to this humdrum man
who so obviously adores her, and to herself." BookPage

De Crayencour, Marguerite *See* Yourcenar, Marguerite

De Gramont, Nina

Gossip of the starlings; a novel. Algonquin
Books of Chapel Hill 2008 276p $22.95
ISBN 978-1-56512-565-0; 1-56512-565-7
LC 2008-5883
"Catherine Morrow and Skye Butterfield both end up
at Esther Percy School for Girls after landing in trouble
at their previous schools for the well-to-do. Catherine's
dad pulled her from the exclusive Waverly after she was
caught in bed with her lower-crust boyfriend, John Paul.
Skye was expelled from her previous school after a couple of offenses. . . . Both of Skye's transgressions, however, are of the noble variety, which provides convenient
campaign spin for her father, the famed and charming
U.S. Sen. Douglas Butterfield. Skye chooses Catherine as
her closest (and only) friend at Esther Percy, and the two
take to toking like it's going out of style (the novel is
set in 1984, so in fairness, maybe it was). After a failed
excursion to the Butterfields' summer estate, during
which Catherine unsuccessfully tries to meld Skye with
her old friends, frissons of tension crackle between the
two, leading to the sort of high-drama tragedy that only
the privileged get to partake in. De Gramont writes with
uncommon grace about the hypnotizing effect of fame on
Catherine." Time Out Chicago

De Hartog, Jan, 1914-2002

The peaceable kingdom; an American saga.
Atheneum Pubs. 1972 c1971 677p o.p.
*
This first volume in the author's trilogy about Quaker
life "is set in England in 1652-53 and Pennsylvania in
1754-55. . . . In the first section, Margaret Fell, who
falls in love with the Quaker preacher George Fox, must
exorcise the passion of sexual desire in order to achieve
grace. In her encounters she begins the work of reform
in prisons, schools and mental institutions; in her progress she loses her property and possessions and is forced
into prison. . . . In the second part of the novel, which
takes place in colonial Pennsylvania, (there occur) Indian
uprisings, massacres of Indians by whites, several mur-

De Hartog, Jan, 1914-2002—*Continued*
ders of black slaves and ritual retribution by the blacks
for the murders." N Y Times Book Rev
Followed by The lamb's war

De Hériz, Enrique *See* Hériz, Enrique de, 1964-

De Kretser, Michelle

The Hamilton case. Little, Brown and Co 2004
307p $24.95
ISBN 0-316-73548-5   LC 2003-60759
"Having come of age on the island nation of Ceylon,
Sam Obeysekere is a lawyer whose life is guided by the
British culture that dominates his homeland. . . . Sam's
undoing arrives in the form of the Hamilton case, a scandalous murder that shakes the upper echelons of island
society. Guided by grandiose visions of Sherlock
Holmes, he becomes convinced he can solve the mysterious case-and that his good standing with the English will
insulate him from the unrest the case has exposed." Publisher's note
"This is a miniature masterpiece of a mystery. . . .
Obeysekere fancies himself a Holmesian observer in his
own right and an instrument of English justice, but he
can't see the treacherousness . . . of the territory he's
treading. De Kretser's prose is stunning and subtle in depicting his downfall, evoking the glittering excesses of
colonial life . . . and the tropical fecundity of Ceylon
with equally irresistible power." Time

The lost dog; a novel. Little, Brown and Co.
2008 326p il $24.99
ISBN 978-0-316-00183-0; 0-316-00183-X
                           LC 2007-43331
First published 2007 in Australia
"While staying in a remote cabin trying to finish his
book on Henry James, divorced college professor Tom
Loxley loses his dog and sets out to find him in the Australian outback. Accompanying him is Nellie Zhang, a
highly regarded contemporary artist with a scandal in her
past—and a woman with whom Tom would like to be
more than just friends. Tom's search for the dog is mirrored by multiple needs: to understand his past as an immigrant from India, to grasp both Nellie's art and her
personal history (information about which is doled out in
fragments), to be sensitive to his mother's growing disabilities, and to anchor himself in the present." Libr J
This is "an uncompromisingly literary (and literate)
book: ferociously intelligent, highbrow, allusive and unflinching." Time

De la Mare, Walter, 1873-1956

Collected tales; chosen, and with an introduction, by Edward Wagenknecht. Knopf 1950 xxi,
467p o.p.
Contents: The riddle; The almond tree; In the forest;
The talisman; Miss Duveen; The bowl; The tree; Ideal
craftsman; Seaton's aunt; Lispet, Lispett and Vaine;
Three friends; Willows; Missing; The connoisseur; The
map; All Hallows; The wharf; The orgy; Cape Race;
Physic; The trumpet; The creatures; The vats; Strangers
and pilgrims

De la Roche, Mazo, 1879-1961

Jalna. Little, Brown 1927 347p o.p.
"An Atlantic Monthly Press book"
Jalna is the family home of the Whiteoaks. Gathered
under its roof are representatives of each generation from
the time the grandparents drifted to Canada, via England
from India and there built their homestead on a lavish
scale. Renny, 37, is the present head of the household
which includes Gran—a formidable old lady of 99—two
uncles, an aunt, an elderly sister, and four half-brothers.
An affectionate, warring group of strong personalities
from the old lady down to Wakefield, the youngest, aged
nine. Two of the boys marry and bring their wives home

De Lint, Charles, 1951-

Memory and dream. TOR Bks. 1994 400p
ISBN 0-312-85572-9   LC 94-21752
"A Tom Doherty Associates book"
"This is the story of a young Canadian artist whose
paintings free (or unleash) ancient spirits into the modern
world. The story moves from the spirit world into the everyday during a 20-year panorama of contemporary Ontario history." Booklist
The author's "multi-voiced, time-shifting narrative . . .
beautifully evokes a sense of creative community, making it almost possible to believe that the rarified aesthetic
atmosphere might well be capable of conjuring up a spirit or two." Publ Wkly

Someplace to be flying. TOR Bks. 1998 380p
ISBN 0-312-85849-3   LC 97-37443
"A Tom Doherty Associates book"
"A cab driver and a freelance photographer come together in the town of Newford to explore the existence
of the mythical 'animal people' and discover the hidden
world that lurks outside their normal perceptions. . . .
DeLint's elegant prose and effective storytelling continue
to transform the mundane into the magical at every
turn." Libr J

Trader. TOR Bks. 1997 352p
ISBN 0-312-85847-7   LC 96-30646
"A Tom Doherty Associates book"
An urban fantasy set in the fictional "city of Newford.
When quiet, responsible luthier Max Trader and egotistical loser Johnny Devlin wake up in each other's bodies,
Max has a harder time dealing with it than Johnny, who
had desperately wished for a change. Now homeless,
Max receives help from a Native American fortune teller
to get his life back." Libr J
"De Lint is a master at world building, at creating the
apt image, and at making grippingly suspenseful a story
in which the fate of the characters may have no cosmic
significance but is vitally important to them and their
closest friends." Booklist

Widdershins. Tor Books 2006 560p $27.95
ISBN 0-765312-85-9   LC 2005-34475
"A Tom Doherty Associates book"
"On her way home from a gig in the small Canadian
town of Sweetwater, Celtic fiddler Lizzie Mahone disrupts the feasting of a band of faerie thugs and becomes
a target for their hostility, also winning the respect of a
pair of Native American spirits. These new complications
bring her into the orbit of Jilly Coppercorn, a brilliant
painter and a favorite of the many faerie folk who dwell

De Lint, Charles, 1951—_Continued_

unseen in the nearby town of Newford, and Jilly's friend, master fiddler Geordie Riddell. As familiarly as though he were chronicling the lives of old friends, de Lint . . . spins yet another magical story of the intersections between reality and the faerie and spirit world in this latest addition to the Newford opus." Libr J

De los Santos, Marisa, 1966-

Belong to me. William Morrow 2008 390p $24.95

ISBN 978-0-06-124027-0; 0-06-124027-3

LC 2007-43197

This sequel to Love walked in follows Cornelia Brown and "her oncologist husband, Teo Sandoval, to suburban Philadelphia. Piper Truitt lives across the street with her husband and two young children. She considers herself the arbiter of style and local propriety. Add to the mix waitress Lake and her son, Dev, who is enrolled in a private academy far superior to his previous California public school. From the outset, Cornelia and Piper are traveling down different paths, while Cornelia and Lake seem to hit it off. . . . But there is more beneath the surface of these women and their motivations than the lovely locale can mask." Libr J

"Smart, funny writing about the risks we take for love." Redbook

Love walked in; a novel. Dutton 2006 c2005 307p $23.95

ISBN 0-525-94917-8   LC 2005-3281

"Cornelia is a sprightly little thing who's stuck in a rut managing a coffee shop and watching her beloved film classics in her spare time. Then, right out of the movies, 'love walked in,' looking just like a modern-day incarnation of Cary Grant. Martin seems to be perfect for Cornelia, until she meets his ten-year-old daughter, Clare, whom he had failed to mention. When Cornelia learns that Clare's mother, Martin's ex-wife, has disappeared, she steps right into the situation. Narrated by Cornelia and Claire in alternating chapters, this is the story of how two lives intersect and a great relationship blooms from an unexpected seed." Libr J

De Onís, Harriet, 1899-1969

(tr) Amado, J. Dona Flor and her two husbands

De Saint-Aubin, Horace _See_ Balzac, Honoré de, 1799-1850

De Saint-Exupéry, Antoine _See_ Saint-Exupéry, Antoine de, 1900-1944

Dean, Debra, 1957-

The madonnas of Leningrad; a novel. William Morrow 2006 231p $23.95

ISBN 0-06-082530-8   LC 2005-50233

"Her granddaughter's wedding should be a time of happiness for Marina Buriakov. But the Russian emigre's descent into Alzheimer's has her and her family experiencing more anxiety than joy. As the details of her present-day life slip mysteriously away, Marina's recollec-

tions of her early years as a docent at the State Hermitage Museum become increasingly vivid. When Leningrad came under siege at the beginning of World War II, museum workers—whose families were provided shelter in the building's basement—stowed away countless treasures, leaving the painting's frames in place as a hopeful symbol of their ultimate return." Booklist

"Like her adoring museum audiences 60 years earlier, readers will absorb Marina's glorious, lush accounts of classical beauties as she traces them in her mind. Dean eloquently depicts the ravages of Alzheimer's disease and convincingly describes the inner world of the afflicted." Libr J

Dean, Louise

Becoming strangers. Harcourt 2006 c2004 307p $24

ISBN 0-15-101174-5   LC 2005-2400

First published 2004 in the United Kingdom

"At a Caribbean resort, elderly Britishers Dorothy and George Davis are thrown together with a younger and more urbane Belgian couple, Annemieke and Jan De Groot. Although this is the Davises' first trip abroad (courtesy of their pushy daughter), it may well be the unhappily married De Groots' last, for Jan is slowly dying of cancer. Although he hopes the holiday will help them become better friends, Annemieke spends most of her time in pursuit of extramarital sexual adventure. George and Dorothy, meanwhile, are coming to terms with the fact that Dorothy is in an increasingly advanced stage of Alzheimer's." Booklist

"Dean peels back the skin of these marriages with an unflinching lack of sentimentality and an immense talent for close observation and evocative, often poetic detail." Atlantic

This human season. Harcourt, Inc. 2007 374p $23

ISBN 978-0-15-101253-4; 0-15-101253-9

LC 2006-16217

First published 2005 in the United Kingdom

"Christmas is coming in bleak and lawless 1979 Belfast, but there is little cheer for the families of IRA political prisoners or for their prison guards. Alternating chapters follow the stories of Sean Moran, a young man in prison for his part in a car bombing gone awry, and John Dunn, a former British soldier and recent guard recruit." Libr J

"Dean mercilessly heightens the suspense while managing at the same time to confer complexity and even grace on her characters and on their forbidding city." Boston Globe

Dean, Margaret Lazarus, 1972-

The time it takes to fall. Simon & Schuster 2007 305p $24

ISBN 978-0-7432-9722-6; 0-7432-9722-9

LC 2006-52213

"This first novel looks at the tragedy of the Challenger space shuttle from the unique perspective of a teenage girl named Dolores, whose father works for NASA. Dolores is obsessed with becoming an astronaut and keeps a scrapbook of stories associated with the space program that includes a journal of her attendance at the successful

Dean, Margaret Lazarus, 1972-—*Continued*

launches. After Dolores befriends a schoolmate named Eric, she comes to suspect that his father, the director of launch safety, is having an affair with her mother. Dolores is forced to consider the wobbly direction her young life is beginning to take when her mother leaves the family and when her father is involved in the investigation of the space program's cover-ups after the Challenger disaster. . . . A gripping judgment of American culture with a harrowing depiction in the epilog of the last few minutes in the lives of the Challenger's seven astronauts." Libr J

Dean, S. F. X.

It can't be my grave. Walker & Co. 1984 222p
ISBN 0-8027-5596-8   LC 84-13192
First published 1983 in the United Kingdom
Professor Neil Kelly "is in London for the British publication of his surprise bestseller on the life of John Donne. There an old Oxford chum, now a famous thespian, and his actress wife tell Kelly of the possibility of running their own theater company devoted to lost plays by women writers and funded by tycoon Gordon Fairly. Sir Gordon, a man of power and charm, believes a 16th century female ancestor to have been the author of a newly found play attributed to Shakespeare or Marlowe, and wants to confirm her authorship. He offers Kelly a huge sum to play devil's advocate and prove his theories wrong, but before research can get under way, the rich man is murdered. . . . This mystery is worth reading for the sheer pleasure of its language." Publ Wkly

Deane, Seamus, 1940-

Reading in the dark. Knopf 1997 245p
ISBN 0-394-57440-0
                              * LC 96-49635
First published 1996 in the United Kingdom
"A Catholic boy growing up hard by the border between Donegal and Derry is fascinated by the local ghost stories and neighborhood lore, and this fascination leads him to secrets at the heart of a family feud. His search for the truth runs through a labyrinth of Irish detours and delights: elaborate catechisms, mad poets, mute idiots, drunken hyperbole, deathbed revelations, and a clever reprisal involving an unwitting bishop." New Yorker

Deaver, Jeff

The bodies left behind; [by] Jeffery Deaver. Simon & Schuster 2008 350p $26.95
ISBN 978-1-4165-9561-8; 1-4165-9561-9
                              LC 2008-30682
"When two masked men break into the isolated lakeside weekend house of Steven Feldman, who works for the Milwaukee Department of Social Services, and his wife, Emma, an attorney who may have stumbled on union corruption in the course of some corporate research, Steven has just enough time to phone 911 before the intruders shoot him and Emma dead. That interrupted plea for help brings Deputy Brynn McKenzie . . . to the scene." Publ Wkly
"Deaver plays gotcha with readers so many times you begin to anticipate his tricks, but the biggest twist of all, you'll never see coming. Very engrossing story." Fort Worth Star-Telegram

The broken window; a Lincoln Rhyme novel; [by] Jeffery Deaver. Simon & Schuster 2008 417p $26.95
ISBN 978-1-4165-4997-0; 1-4165-4997-8
                              LC 2007-48867
"Quadriplegic forensics whiz Lincoln Rhyme and his Glock-toting girlfriend, Amelia Sachs, track a serial killer who uses an all-knowing computer database to frame fall guys. . . . Rhyme still intrigues in his eighth outing, while Deaver's scarily believable depiction of identity theft in a total-surveillance society stokes our paranoia." Entertainment Wkly

The Coffin Dancer; [by] Jeffery Deaver. Simon & Schuster 1998 358p
ISBN 0-684-85285-3   LC 98-13537
Quadriplegic forensic specialist Lincoln Rhyme "is called in to track down a contract killer, known as the Coffin Dancer, who has been hired to eliminate three witnesses in the upcoming federal trial of Philip Hansen. The trial is set to begin just 48 hours from the novel's (literally) explosive beginning. Rhyme and his beautiful assistant, detective Amelia Sachs, have just that much time to ID the Dancer and keep him from murdering the remaining witnesses. . . . The pace, energized by Deaver's precise attention, never flags." Publ Wkly

Garden of beasts; a novel of Berlin 1936; {by} Jeffery Deaver. Simon & Schuster 2004 404p $24.95
ISBN 0-7432-2201-6   LC 2004-45206
"Paul Schumann, a German American living in New York City in 1936, is a conscientious Mafia hit man known for agreeing to dispose of only the true dregs of society. When he is captured by the Feds, he is given an alternative to prison-travel to Berlin to assassinate Reinhardt Ernst, the man behind Nazi Germany's rearmament. Getting to know many of the locals while posing as a reporter covering the Olympics, Paul glimpses firsthand the horrors perpetrated by Hitler and his National Socialist Party. Finding himself the victim of a double-cross, Paul must choose between saving himself and completing his mission." Libr J
"Top Nazis, including Hitler, Himmler and Göring, make colorful cameos, but it's the smart, shaded-gray characterizations of the principals that anchor the exciting plot." Publ Wkly

Roadside crosses; [by] Jeffery Deaver. Simon & Schuster 2009 399p $26.95
ISBN 978-1-4165-4999-4   LC 2009-02294
In this mystery Kathryn Dance, "an agent with the California Bureau of Investigation, gets an eye-opening education in some of the hottest areas of the cyberworld. After an auto accident kills two teens, vicious smears of Travis Brigham, the teen driver deemed responsible but not charged in the accident, appear on the Chilton Report, a popular blog. After one of the accusing bloggers barely survives an assault, Brigham becomes a "person of interest." Brigham disappears, and attacks, each preceded by a crude roadside cross, spread to other Chilton bloggers." Publ Wkly
"The web sites mentioned throughout the book are actual live links and add to the fun. Though a couple of subplots get glossed over, the main story resonates. Dance is another exciting series character, and though

Deaver, Jeff—*Continued*

this series has a ways to go before it achieves the devotion accorded Deaver's Rhyme/Sachs series, it has unlimited potential." Libr J

The vanished man; a Lincoln Rhyme novel; [by] Jeffery Deaver. Simon & Schuster 2003 399p $25.95

ISBN 0-7432-2200-8   LC 2002-42826

In this thriller the "killer is a master magician who murders his victims in the style of classic magic acts. He is also able to change his appearance at will and plants evidence at the murder scenes to mislead the police. It is up to Rhyme and his paramour, cop Amelia Sachs, to sort out the few clues from manufactured ones." Libr J

"Among the crimes rendered with Deaver's customary grace and wit are sadistic variations on Houdini's Water Torture Cell, P. T. Selbit's neat trick of sawing a woman in half and one of Howard Thurston's animal acts, in which he brought a dead bird back to life." N Y Times Book Rev

Deaver, Jeffery *See* Deaver, Jeff

Deb, Siddhartha, 1970-

The point of return. Ecco Press 2003 304p $24.95

ISBN 0-06-050151-0   LC 2002-35300

This novel explores "what it was like to come of age in a provincial town during the nationalistic fervor in the time of Indira Gandhi's rule. Babu, the inquisitive son of a Bengali civil servant, grows up in a remote northeastern Indian state. His father, Dr. Dam, the director of the veterinary and dairy department of the state, was a principled, devoted government official who grew up in the time of India's partition and fled with his family from East Pakistan, which became Bangladesh." Booklist

"To allow Dr. Dam to evolve through most of the book in a self-generated fog of benevolence and to shatter it in the last pages is a brilliant stroke. . . . Storytelling of the kind Deb lavishes, for most of his book, on Dr. Dam is rare and precious and uplifting." N Y Times Book Rev

Dee, Ed

The con man's daughter. Mysterious Press 2003 279p $23.95

ISBN 0-89296-794-3   LC 2003-50976

"Eddie Dunne's hands are swollen from fighting, his cell phone rings to the tune of 'When Irish Eyes Are Smiling,' and his spending money is in a metal box above his bathroom ceiling. Banished from the NYPD and retired from his job with the Russian mob, Eddie plays the ponies and baby-sits his six-year-old grandchild. Then, in the blink of an eye, his life is invaded when someone kidnaps his thirty-five-year-old daughter." Publisher's note

"Dee proves a sure hand when depicting the rough life of cops and criminals—and especially when creating Eddie Dunne, an amalgam of good and bad." Libr J

Defoe, Daniel, 1661?-1731

A journal of the plague year; edited with an introduction and notes by Cynthia Wall. Penguin Books 2003 xxxviii, 289p (Penguin classics)

ISBN 0-14-043785-1   LC 2003-276684

First published 1722

An account "of the epidemic of bubonic plague in England during the summer and fall of 1665." Reader's Ency. 4th edition

Moll Flanders; with an introduction by John Mullan. Knopf 1991 xxxiii, 338p $19

ISBN 0-679-40548-8

                                        * LC 91-52994

"Everyman's library"

First published 1722. Variant title: The fortunes and misfortunes of the famous Moll Flanders

"This purports to be the autobiography of the daughter of a woman who had been transported to Virginia for theft soon after her child's birth. The child, abandoned in England, is brought up in the house of the compassionate mayor of Colchester. The story relates her seduction, her subsequent marriages and liaisons, and her visit to Virginia, where she finds her mother and discovers that she has unwittingly married her own brother. After leaving him and returning to England, she is presently reduced to destitution. She becomes an extremely successful pickpocket and thief, but is presently detected and transported to Virginia in company with one of her former husbands, a highwayman. With the funds that each has amassed they set up as planters, and Moll moreover finds that she has inherited a plantation from her mother. She and her husband spend their declining years in an atmosphere of prosperity and ostensible penitence." Oxford Companion to Engl Lit. 6th edition

Robinson Crusoe; edited with an introduction by Thomas Keymer and notes by Thomas Keymer and James Kelly. Oxford University Press 2007 368p (Oxford world's classics) pa $7.95

ISBN 0-19-283342-1; 978-0-19-283342-6

                                        * LC 2006-26022

First published 1719

"A minutely circumstantial account of the hero's shipwreck and escape to an uninhabited island, and the methodical industry whereby he makes himself a comfortable home. The story is founded on the actual experiences of Alexander Selkirk, who spent four years on the island of Juan Fernandez in the early 18th century." Lenrow. Reader's Guide to Prose Fic

Deford, Frank

The entitled; a novel. Sourcebooks 2007 318p $24.95

ISBN 978-1-4022-0896-6; 1-4022-0896-0

                                        LC 2007-10914

"Howie Traveler is the manager of the Cleveland Indians, and Jay Alcazar is his star player. Never quite good enough as a player, Traveler spent two decades in the minors as a coach and manager, building his resume oh so slowly. Alcazar, on the other hand, is the son of a wealthy Cuban immigrant. Even if he hadn't become a baseball star, he would have enjoyed myriad opportunities. The pair share a mundane player-manager relationship until one night Traveler inadvertently spies Alcazar

Deford, Frank—*Continued*

in a physical dispute with a woman trying to escape the star's hotel room. When the woman comes forward with a rape charge, Traveler must balance his career against doing the right thing. In a parallel plot, Alcazar tries to unravel the mystery surrounding his real parents and his birth in Castro's Cuba." Booklist

"More than a terrific baseball book. It's a terrific book, period." Sports Illustrated

Deighton, Len, 1929-

Berlin game. Knopf 1984 c1983 345p
ISBN 0-394-53407-7
* LC 83-48104
The first volume of an espionage trilogy; other volumes are Mexico set and London match

British agent Bernard Samson must "help an undercover agent known as Brahms Four escape from East Berlin; unfortunately, a security leak high in the British organization threatens the continued success of the Brahms Four network." Libr J

This novel "is a decent entertainment that rattles swiftly along to its payoff. Two things especially recommend it—a devious contrivance of plot that has probably never been used before in an espionage novel; and the city of Berlin, mecca to spies and spy novelists. The second is the greater asset. Although the book is elaborately plotted, its best moments derive from the setting and from the force of this particular setting upon behavior and psychology." N Y Times Book Rev

City of gold. HarperCollins Pubs. 1992 375p
ISBN 0-06-017937-6
LC 92-52565
"City of Gold is Cairo, and the time is 1942. Rommel is on the move, and the city waits to see what will happen when he arrives. He has conquered Allied forces because somebody is feeding him information about their plans. A British captain is put in charge of an investigation to dig out the mole." N Y Times Book Rev

"Story lines concern not just the war but also black-market activities and the efforts of Jewish operatives to arm themselves for the anticipated battle for a homeland. Directing his varied characters and juggling his many subplots, Deighton demonstrates enviable legerdemain." Publ Wkly

Funeral in Berlin; a novel. Putnam 1965 c1964 312p o.p.
*
First published 1964 in the United Kingdom
A spy story in which a British agent is involved in smuggling a Russian scientist out of East Berlin with the connivance of a Russian security officer and a German contact man whose loyalties and motives are questionable

The author "writes well of the circles within circles at international crossroads where enemies can be closer than friends, and where horror and humor follow the agent." Libr J

The Ipcress file. Simon & Schuster 1963 c1962 287p o.p.
*
First published 1962 in the United Kingdom
"A British secret-service agent is assigned to help recover a kidnapped biochemist. The international intrigue, involving brainwashing, spies, and counter-spies of uncertain loyalties, takes the agent from London to the Far East, to an atomic test site in the Pacific, and behind the Iron Curtain." Shapiro. Fic for Youth. 3d edition

London match. Knopf 1985 i.e. 1986 407p
ISBN 0-394-54937-6
LC 85-40454
In this concluding volume of the Berlin-based trilogy "Agent Bernie Samson is faced with yet another problem. While one mole—Bernie's former wife—has been flushed from the London office, the Soviet defector's debriefing indicates there may be yet another double agent still operating. Bernie, of course, is a likely suspect, but this would be too obvious and, besides, there are numerous candidates for the office turncoat. Who could it be? Or could it be a cunning piece of subterfuge to further disrupt British intelligence gathering?" Booklist

"The strength of (this novel) is not in its plot but its characterization. . . . Mr. Deighton portrays each character of his large cast fully and sympathetically. However, the best character is the city of Berlin. It is a living presence, and in some of the descriptions one can almost hear the stones breathing." N Y Times Book Rev

Mexico set. Knopf 1985 373p
ISBN 0-394-53525-1
LC 84-48500
The second volume of the spy trilogy that began with Berlin game

"Fiona Samson—wife of our hero, British agent Bernard Samson—has defected to the KGB and become a diabolical alter ego to her husband, anticipating his moves and countermoves in ways only a spouse can do." Booklist

"Deighton displays prodigious talent here: while portraying sharply defined, sympathetic, and down-to-earth characters, he slowly but inexorably revs up the plot for a thoroughly exciting and satisfying conclusion." Libr J

Delany, Samuel R.

Stars in my pocket like grains of sand. Bantam Bks. 1984 384p
ISBN 0-553-05053-2
* LC 84-45180
This far future novel is the "dual story of Rat Korga, a slave and the last survivor of his devastated world, and Marq Dyeth, an industrial diplomat who introduces Korga to a future galaxy consisting of 6,000 human- and alien-inhabited planets." Booklist

"Reading this novel is like learning another language, only to realize how much it teaches you about your own, and how relative it makes your cultural assumptions." Publ Wkly

Delargy, Marlaine

(tr) Theorin, J. Echoes from the dead

Delbanco, Nicholas

What remains. Warner Bks. 2000 200p
ISBN 0-446-52416-6
LC 00-39895
The author presents a "portrait of a Jewish family with artistic and intellectual inclinations. The story encompasses several generations: Elsa, the proud and slightly eccentric matriarch; her sons Karl, who takes over the family business when his father dies, and Gustave, who

Delbanco, Nicholas—*Continued*

is more interested in art; Karl's wife, Julia; and their little son, Jacob. Forced to leave their comfortable life in Hamburg when Hitler comes to power, they settle first in London. Not long after the war, Karl moves his family again, this time to America, and he sets up a branch of the family business." Booklist

"The mood is elegiac, meditative, yet delicate: a Chopin nocturne, perhaps, played out in words. The horror, the melodrama, is always held back. The memory and effects of the Holocaust are ever present but never dwelled on." N Y Times Book Rev

Delderfield, R. F. (Ronald Frederick), 1912-1972

To serve them all my days. Simon & Schuster 1972 638p

ISBN 0-671-21371-7

        *

Concerns "the boys and masters of a West Country English public school in the years between World War I and II. . . . The central character is David Powlett-Jones, a shell-shocked youngster fresh from the Western Front, when we first meet him; a compassionate headmaster, whose personal life has known its full share of drama, sorrow and love, when we part company with him. In between, Mr. Delderfield has some eminently sane and sensible points to make about what education for life is really like. Academic rivalries, some bitter and vengeful; the loneliness of a small boy whose parents have no real feeling for him, and of a small girl whose mother and twin have died tragically; the development of an intense love affair between a mature man and woman are all elements in the storytelling." Publ Wkly

"Here is a schoolmaster's cavalcade of England between World Wars, told in the author's best stand-up style, and rife with episodes designed to pluck at the heartstrings." N Y Times Book Rev

Delderfield, Ronald Frederick See Delderfield, R. F. (Ronald Frederick), 1912-1972

DeLillo, Don

The body artist; a novel. Scribner 2001 124p

ISBN 0-7432-0395-X   LC 00-58842

"A young widow discovers that a dishevelled, vaguely autistic man has somehow taken up residence in her spare room—and that her dead husband's spirit may or may not be inhabiting her new boarder. This is a fertile premise—the novel plays with questions of identity, presence, ritual, memory, and sanity, and uses those questions to investigate the larger mystery of death—but the book's brevity forces DeLillo to treat his themes sketchily, and at times with an uncharacteristic sentimentality." New Yorker

Cosmopolis; a novel. Scribner 2003 209p $25

ISBN 0-7432-4424-9   LC 2002-30540

"Most of the action takes place inside a 'prousted' (cork-lined) stretch limo, as the reclusive financial wizard Eric Packer is chauffeured across Manhattan for a haircut. Thanks to a presidential visit, antiglobalization demonstrations, and a celebrity funeral, this journey takes up most of the day." Libr J

"DeLillo, master novelist and seer, tells the surreal,

electrifying story of this dehumanized moneyman in English scrubbed so clean and assembled so exquisitely it seems like a new language." Booklist

Falling man; a novel. Scribner 2007 246p $26

ISBN 978-1-416-54602-3; 1-416-54602-2

        LC 2006-52306

This 9/11 novel's "opening pages follow lawyer Keith Neudecker, who has just emerged from the World Trade Center, as he makes his way up the street, fighting raining debris and 'seismic tides of smoke.' It's not until he's almost there that he realizes where he's heading-the apartment of his ex-wife and son. And over the succeeding months, we are made privy to the family's reactions to that heartbreaking day. Keith's young son plays a game with his friends in which they search the sky with binoculars, looking for signs of planes and for Bill Lawton (their misheard name for bin Laden); meanwhile, Keith's ex-wife is both mesmerized and horrified by a performance artist dubbed the Falling Man, who, dressed in a blue suit and tethered by a bungee cord, launches himself headfirst off train tracks and balconies." Publ Wkly

"Scenes are laid out like cards face up in some mysterious game of solitaire, except that each card, each sequence, seems to carry some larger import. It's not clear even at the novel's end what its finishing up might mean. On one narrative level, the game is already over — the characters are living in an unknown afterworld. But on another level — DeLillo inserts several timejumps into the pre-Sept. 11 past — we see his terrorist preparing himself. . . . Though the setup feels stylized, it is also riveting." Los Angeles Times Book Rev

Libra. Viking 1988 456p

ISBN 0-670-82317-1

        * LC 87-40649

DeLillo's "novel is his own personal vision—though anchored well enough in historical actuality—of what really was behind Lee Harvey Oswald's gun blasts from the book depository that day in Dallas. DeLillo follows Oswald through the marines and during his defection to the Soviet Union, as well as positing a scenario for how he came to be the vehicle for delivering the anti-Castro blow that resulted in Kennedy's death." Booklist

This novel "provokes the reader with its clever use of history, its dramatic pacing and its immaculate and detailed construction." Publ Wkly

The names. Knopf 1982 339p

ISBN 0-394-52814-X   LC 82-48012

"Self-absorbed, rootless James Axton is a 'risk analyst' for insuring multinational corporations against political hazards. His ambiguous world—defined by an estranged family and the Iranian revolution—is bizarrely highlighted by the advent of an elusive ritual murder cult, 'The Names.' His compulsion to track down the meaning of the cult (it matches the initials of victims and place names) leads him as far off as India, and deep into 'memory, solitude, obsession, death.'" Libr J

"Nearly every page testifies to DeLillo's exceptional gifts as a writer." New Republic

Ratner's star. Knopf 1976 437p

ISBN 0-394-40083-6

        * LC 75-36808

DeLillo, Don—*Continued*

This is a "grim, surreal novel, it's protagonist a 14-year-old mathematical genius and Nobel laureate, Billy Twillig, whose mission is to decode the message of a star and to invent a mathematical language to answer it." Oxford Companion to Am Lit. 6th edition

Underworld. Scribner 1997 827p

ISBN 0-684-84269-6   LC 97-13825

"On October 3, 1951, there occurred two 'shots heard round the world'—Bobby Thomson's last-minute homer, which sent the N.Y. Giants into the World Series, and a Soviet atomic bomb test. The fallout from these two events provides the nexus for this sagalike rumination on the last 50 years of American cultural history." Libr J

"The dialogue is a rockingly comic attack on our mental excreta: the distortions and sound bites of the television age. DeLillo was absent from his fiction before, an unbodied intelligence, but here is an undertow of personal pain he has never touched. This is his most demanding novel and yet his most transparent, giving the reader the privileged intimacy that comes from seeing a writer whole." N Y Times Book Rev

White noise. Viking 1985 326p

ISBN 0-670-80373-1

                                      * LC 84-40375

"An Elisabeth Sifton book"

"The chairperson of the department of Nazi studies at a midwestern college aches to escape the inevitable path of decline and death; a 'toxic event' that releases a dangerous cloud of pollution gives him the chance to break free in previously uncontemplated ways." Booklist

This "is a stunning performance from one of our finest and most intelligent novelists. DeLillo's reach is broad and deep, combining acute observation of the textures of American life and analytic rigor." New Repub

Delinsky, Barbara, 1945-

Flirting with Pete; a novel. Scribner 2003 355p $26

ISBN 0-7432-4642-X   LC 2003-42721

"Therapist Casy Ellis knew she was a product of a one-night stand between her mother (now comatose) and her renowned psychologist father. But she never met him, and he never acknowledged her until after his death, when he left her his mortgage-free townhouse in Boston's upscale Beacon Hill. Casey has every intention of selling it and reaping a sizable nest egg, but circumstances cause her to linger. When she discovers writings about a young woman named Jenny Clyde among her father's belongings, she is determined to find out more about Jenny and to understand the father she never knew." Libr J

"Seamlessly and compassionately weaving Jenny's unsettling past with Casey's uncertain future. Delinsky delivers a scintillating study of each woman's search for answers and absolution." Booklist

Lake news. Simon & Schuster 1999 380p

ISBN 0-684-86432-0

"Falsely implicated in a scandal by an unscrupulous reporter, Lily Blake returns to Lake Henry, her small New England hometown. She is devastated by the loss of her job, privacy, and reputation and struggles to regain control of her life. Although distrustful of the media, she is drawn to John Kipling, the editor of the local *Lake News*. A wounded soul himself, Kip has also returned home to exorcise personal demons. Together they find justice for Lily and healing for themselves." Libr J

The author "plots this satisfying, gentle romance with the sure hand of an expert, scattering shady pasts and dark secrets among some of her characters, while giving others destructive family patterns and difficult family dynamics to contend with." Publ Wkly

The summer I dared; a novel; Barbara Delinsky. Simon & Schuster 2004 355p $24.95

ISBN 0-7432-4643-8   LC 2004-45339

The "tale of three people quite literally thrown together following a boating accident off the Maine coast that spares them while taking the lives of nine others. At 40 Julia is an obedient wife, dutiful daughter, and devoted mother, and has planned a visit to her aunt Zoe to reflect on her obligation to herself versus her ties to her family. Rescued by fellow passenger Noah Prine, Julia feels connected to him by virtue of their shared tragedy while also being drawn to Kim Colella, the other survivor, whose whereabouts at the time of the crash provide a shadowy subplot. As a gentle romance blossoms between Julia and Noah, each evaluates who they were before the accident and who they hope to become in its aftermath. Once again, Delinsky excels at combining a compelling mystery with an insightful portrayal of captivating people facing challenges both ordinary and dramatic." Booklist

Delson, Rudolph, 1975-

Maynard and Jennica. Houghton Mifflin 2007 300p $24

ISBN 978-0-618-83448-8; 0-618-83448-6

                                      LC 2007-8520

This is a "giddy boy-meets-girl (twice) fable that evolves into an astute portrait of a relationship. The lovers are an odd couple—she a workaholic Princeton grad from California, he an indie filmmaker and New York native who loathes everything outside his home town. Their story is told documentary style, with thirty-five characters taking turns narrating. Each character has an appealing voice, and the chatty arrangement highlights Delson's comic timing. Best is his portrait of New York, which emerges as both fantastical and hilariously recognizable, a unique place defined by its possibilities and worthy of the dreams it inspires." New Yorker

DeMarinis, Rick, 1934-

Borrowed hearts; new and selected stories. Seven Stories Press 1999 322p $24

ISBN 1-88836-398-3   LC 98-55233

Contents: Under the wheat; Billy Ducks among the pharaohs; Life between meals; The smile of a turtle; Weeds; The handgun; Disneyland; Romance: a prose villanelle; Your story; Pagans; Your burden is lifted, love returns; Medicine man; Safe forever; Paraiso: an elegy; An airman's goodbye; Aliens; Horizontal snow; Wilderness; The Voice of America; Insulation; Borrowed hearts; A romantic interlude; Experience; Fault lines; Feet; Hormone X; Novias; On the lam; Sieze the day; The boys we were, the men we became; The singular we

"Dark humor, cosmic danger, and unglamorous romance snake through DeMarinis' compelling short stories." Booklist

DeMarinis, Rick, 1934—*Continued*

Sky full of sand. Dennis McMillan 2003 250p $30

ISBN 0-939767-47-3

In this novel, set in El Paso, Uriah Walkinghorse is "suspended somewhere between a 'normal' existence and a descent into the bizarre and desperate world that surrounds him. Strained but strong ties still bind him to his odd assortment of adopted siblings—black and white and Korean—who include a school principal, an addict, a delivery driver and a corporate lawyer. At 42, he has lost his wife, abandoned his quest for a master's and manages derelict apartments of derelicts in exchange for rent. His one accomplishment was a bodybuilding title, Mr. West Side, and he still maintains a diet and exercise program. DeMarinis's exceptionally sharp wit slashes through the prose as Uri undertakes an odyssey through a world of kinky sex, drugs, high finance and the most vicious, most wasted dregs of humanity on either side of the border." Publ Wkly

Demetz, Hanna

The house on Prague Street; translated from the German by the author. St. Martin's Press 1980 186p

ISBN 0-312-39322-9   LC 79-27312

Original German edition, 1970

This autobiographical novel tells the story of Helene Richter whose "adolescence in wartime Czechoslovakia coincides with the Holocaust, which intrudes more and more insistently into her life until its . . . violence destroys her romantic dreams. The house on Prague Street symbolizes her loss of innocence. At first the serene family homestead, it eventually shelters survivors of Auschwitz whose only familial ties are their shared memories of horror." SLJ

DeMille, Nelson

The charm school. Warner Bks. 1988 533p

ISBN 0-446-51305-9   LC 87-34637

"On an unorthodox vacation trip to Russia, Gregory Fisher, a young American tourist, stumbles onto a secret. . . . In a place called Mrs. Ivanova's Charm School, young Russians are being taught to imitate American citizens. And their instructors, none of whom have volunteered for the job, are Americans. . . . *The Charm School* offers much in the way of action and adventure, but the novel is more than an 'Us vs. Them' shoot 'em up. It is also a fascinating psychological study, one that forces the reader to ponder the true roles of good and evil, in connection with the individual mind as well as with international relations." West Coast Rev Books

The gate house. Grand Central Pub. 2008 677p $27.99

ISBN 978-0-446-53342-3; 0-446-53342-4

LC 2008-26065

A "sequel to The Gold Coast (1990), in which Susan Sutter, then the wife of tax attorney John Sutter, had a torrid affair with Frank Bellarosa, a powerful Mafia boss and the Sutters' neighbor on Long Island's tony Gold Coast, with fatal results for Bellarosa. After divorcing Susan, John sailed the world for three years, then built himself a new life in London. Now John has returned to the small gatehouse that was once part of his ex-wife's family estate, only to find Bellarosa's thuggish son, Anthony, living next door. In another coincidence, Susan has just reacquired the six-bedroom guest cottage where she and John lived as a married couple on her family's former property. Susan and John soon begin to explore an improbable reconciliation, even as they suspect she may be in Anthony's gun sights. The plot more than takes its time getting to its violent and predictable resolution, but DeMille devotees should have plenty of fun along the way." Publ Wkly

The general's daughter. Warner Bks. 1992 454p

ISBN 0-446-51306-7   LC 91-51174

"Paul Brenner, a warrant officer in the army's criminal investigation unit, reluctantly teams with an old flame, Cynthia Sunhill, to investigate the murder of Captain Ann Campbell. Ann's body has been staked down with tent pegs on a rifle range; she's naked but she hasn't been brutalized. She's the daughter of a famous general, just back from the Gulf War, and she's also the Army's poster girl, a graduate with honors from West Point. And yet her chosen specialty, psychological operations, has raised some eyebrows, and Brenner and Sunhill soon discover other dark secrets about her." Booklist

"Characterization in general is fuzzy, though DeMille captures the often unquestioning regimen of life on a military base." Publ Wkly

The Gold Coast. Warner Bks. 1990 500p

ISBN 0-446-51504-3   LC 89-40465

"What happens to a priggish, WASPy, disillusioned Wall Street lawyer when a Mafia crime boss moves into the mansion next door in his posh Long Island neighborhood? He ends up representing the gangster on a murder rap and even perjures himself so the mafioso can be released on $5 million bail. . . . Attorney John Sutter has problems that would daunt even Fitzgerald's Jay Gatsby. His marriage is crumbling, despite kinky sex games with his self-centered wife, Susan, who's the mistress of his underworld client Frank Bellarosa. The IRS is after Sutter, and his law firm wants to dump him." Publ Wkly

"What makes 'The Gold Coast' glitter is Nelson DeMille's sharp evocation of the vulpine Bellarosa and of Sutter, a wonderfully sardonic, self-mocking man betrayed by a midlife crisis. In his way, Mr. DeMille . . . is as keen a social satirist as Edith Wharton." NY Times Book Rev

The lion's game; a novel. Warner Bks. 2000 677p $36

ISBN 0-446-52065-9

NYPD homicide detective John Corey, "now a special contract agent for the Federal Anti-Terrorist Task Force, is on the trail of a Libyan terrorist known as the Lion who vanished after arriving at New York's JFK Airport on a 747 filled with corpses. While the FBI and CIA think Asad Khalil has returned to Europe, Corey believes otherwise and teams up with Kate Mayfield, a leggy blonde FBI agent, to track Khalil down." Libr J

"DeMille artfully constructs a compulsively readable thriller around a troubling story line, slowly developing his villain from a faceless entity into a nation's all-too-human nemesis." Publ Wkly

Plum Island. Warner Bks. 1997 511p

ISBN 0-446-51506-X   LC 97-7221

DeMille, Nelson—*Continued*

"On Long Island's North Fork, . . . roguish NYPD bad-boy detective John Corey assists the local police chief at a crime scene that features a house deck garnished with a married couple dead of clean head shots. Investigators suppose that the pair, researchers at a heavily guarded lab on Plum Island, were involved in smuggling a viral antidote. But Corey, unpersuaded, soon discovers that local history and buried-treasure lore fascinated the victims." Booklist

"Key to the novel's sway is its boisterous plot, as DeMille expertly melds medical mystery, police procedural and nautical adventure, adding assorted love interests and capping matters with a ferocious storm at sea." Publ Wkly

Wild fire; a novel. Warner Books 2006 519p $26.99

ISBN 978-0-446-57967-4; 0-446-57967-X

LC 2006-20982

This thriller features "John Corey, the ex-NYPD detective who now works on a government anti-terrorism task force. . . . Bain Madox, a brilliant and probably insane villain, has hatched a fiendishly clever plot to force the U.S. to launch an all-out nuclear attack against the entire Islamic world. It's up to Corey, with the help of his FBI agent wife, to stop Madox before he can detonate nuclear weapons on American soil. Set in 2002, barely a year after 9/11, the novel presents a what-if scenario that's so plausible we have to remind ourselves that DeMille is making the whole thing up. Or is he? As usual, DeMille appears to have done a ton of research; what sets his thrillers apart from those of some of his competitors is the way he seamlessly incorporates real technology and real government organizations into his stories." Booklist

Word of honor. Warner Bks. 1985 518p

ISBN 0-446-51280-X   LC 85-40005

A fictional version of the "My Lai massacre and the trial of Lieutenant William F. Calley. Calley's counterpart in this fictional account is Ben Tyson, a much-decorated Vietnam veteran and former Army lieutenant. One morning, on the way to work as an electronics executive in New York City, Tyson learns that a book has just been published about a military massacre at a French hospital in Hue, Vietnam. The book unhesitatingly accuses Tyson of staging the attack against nuns, children, and other civilians, and wounded soldiers on February 15, 1968. Based on evidence contained in the book and on testimony given by two of Tyson's former platoon members, the Army recalls Tyson to active duty in order to try him for murder." Booklist

"The flashbacks to Hue, the pre-trial investigation (involving an attractive female major), the court-martial proceedings, the emotions of the principal characters and the soul-sickness wrought by war (which is the story's effective subtext)—all are depicted with marvelous vividness." Publ Wkly

Dennis, Patrick, 1921-1976

Auntie Mame; an irreverent escapade. Vanguard Press 1955 280p o.p.

"A fond and somewhat baffled nephew reminisces about the aunt who guided his young footsteps in her unorthodox, inimitable fashion. Auntie Mame lived wholeheartedly in phases; whether she was being show girl, shopgirl, Southern belle, tweedy authoress, college widow, or society matron, she played each part to the hilt. Life with Auntie Mame was infinitely entertaining and unpredictable." Booklist

Followed by Around the world with Auntie Mame (1958)

DePoy, Phillip

The drifter's wheel. St. Martin's Minotaur 2008 276p $24.95

ISBN 978-0-312-36203-4; 0-312-36203-X

LC 2008-13401

"The arrival of a young man at Fever Devilin's house in Blue Mountain, GA, upsets the folklorist's quiet life. The stranger ends up dead, but Fever is convinced that the deceased man is not the one who visited him. Investigating this puzzle leads Fever to unraveling the secrets held by a reclusive but influential family in the area and the possibility that the stranger is really a time traveler come back to murder again. . . . DePoy's latest concocts a delicious brew of Southern culture laced with a dollop of the supernatural, topped by unexpected denouements leaving readers wanting more." Libr J

D'Erasmo, Stacey

The sky below. Houghton Mifflin 2009 320p $24

ISBN 978-0-618-43925-6; 0-618-43925-0

LC 2008-25673

This "novel tells the story of a misanthropic obituary writer for a dying New York newspaper, who views his life through a series of memory boxes modelled on the assemblage art of Joseph Cornell. 'I assiduously collected interesting junk, filling my pockets with pebbles and wire and old nails: the stuff of transformation,' he says. He narrates the drudgery of the daily grind and scrutinizes his dysfunctional, fatherless childhood, during which he rebelled against his mother by dealing drugs and engaging in sex with men for money. Now nearing forty and spiritually broken, he is given a diagnosis of cancer and travels to a commune in Mexico, where he reluctantly receives the help of a clairvoyant eight-year-old girl. Although the book strays into portentous magic realism, its lyrical prose and telling detail create a powerful atmosphere." New Yorker

Desai, Anita, 1937-

Clear light of day. Houghton Mifflin 2000 182p pa $13

ISBN 0-618-07451-1

* LC 00-61326

"A Mariner book"

First published 1980 by Harper & Row

"The novel begins with the triennial visit of the younger sister Tara and her diplomat husband to the old family home, a decaying suburban mansion on the banks of the Jumma outside Old Delhi. Here Bim the older sister, lives with the youngest brother, Baba. Baba is autistic, a childlike, speechless whisp of a man who spends his days playing 'I'm Dreaming of a White Christmas' and 'Donkey Seranade' on an ancient windup gramophone. The oldest brother, Raja, has moved away. The book divides itself equally between the present of Tara's visit

Desai, Anita, 1937—*Continued*

and the sisters' memories of the past. . . . The visit is a strain—a series of under-the-surface estrangements and rapprochements, with sisterly love ebbing and flowing." Times Lit Suppl

This work "does what only the best novels can do: it totally submerges us. It takes us so deeply into another world that we almost fear we won't be able to climb out again." N Y Times Book Rev

Fire on the mountain. Harper & Row 1977 145p
ISBN 0-06-011066-X   LC 77-3788

"In this novel set in the hill country of India, Nanda Kaul's great-granddaughter is sent to spend the summer with her, thus breaking the solitude of the old and withdrawn woman, shattering the privacy she prizes most. But Raka, too, is clearly an outsider, a child living in and through her imagination, and one with a talent for disappearing. As Nanda Kaul finds herself attempting to draw out and communicate with the strange and unfathomable Raka, she discovers in the girl more of herself than she would have believed possible. Meanwhile, Nanda Kaul's lone friend, Ila Das, appears and hovers always on the brink of hysteria until that hysteria leads to a shocking rape and murder that is the book's climax." Publ Wkly

"This is a delicate wisp of a story that nevertheless possesses great tensile strength." Booklist

Desai, Kiran, 1971-

The inheritance of loss. Atlantic Monthly 2006 324p $24
ISBN 0-87113-929-4   LC 2005-52416

This "novel is set in the nineteen-eighties in the northeast corner of India, where the borders of several Himalayan states—Bhutan and Sikkim, Nepal and Tibet—meet. At the head of the novel's teeming cast is Jemubhai Patel, a Cambridge-educated judge who has retired from serving a country he finds 'too messy for justice.' He lives in an isolated house with his cook, his orphaned seventeen-year-old granddaughter, and a red setter, whose company Jemubhai prefers to that of human beings. The tranquillity of his existence is contrasted with the life of the cook's son, working in grimy Manhattan restaurants, and with his granddaughter's affair with a Nepali tutor involved in an insurgency that irrevocably alters Jemubhai's life. Briskly paced and sumptuously written, the novel ponders questions of nationhood, modernity, and class, in ways both moving and revelatory." New Yorker

Destouches, Henri-Louis *See* Céline, Louis-Ferdinand, 1894-1961

Deutermann, Peter T., 1941-

Darkside. St. Martin's Press 2002 406p maps $24.95
ISBN 0-312-28120-X   LC 2002-68393

An "account of some creepy goings-on at the U.S. Naval Academy in Annapolis. As the book opens, the school is buzzing with the news that a plebe has plummeted from a sixth-story window and died. Amid questions of suicide, a new twist emerges; the plebe was wearing a pair of panties belonging to Midshipman First

Class Julie Markham, a perky senior at the academy and an acquaintance of the dead plebe, who then gets drawn into the investigation. Her father, a retired former fighter pilot and academy history professor, hires crack defense lawyer Liz DeWinter, fearing that Markham will somehow be scapegoated by the Navy Criminal Investigation Service." Publ Wkly

DeVido, Brian

Every time I talk to Liston. Bloomsbury 2004 276p $22.95
ISBN 1-58234-458-2

"Aging and not as quick as he used to be, Amos 'Scrap Iron' Fletcher has finally arrived in Las Vegas, capital city of boxing. His years of slugging it out as a sparring partner for heavyweight contenders are about to pay off. But after his first big-league fight ends in defeat and when he's falsely accused of offering to sell secrets to his sparring partner's opponent he heads back home to Trenton to figure out his next move. It's there at his uncle's boxing gym that he's reunited with TNT, another boxer down on his luck. TNT is a reckless but kindhearted kid who just happens to throw some of the toughest punches Amos has ever seen. TNT's hunger for vindication rekindles Amos's passion for the sport, and he agrees to take the neglected young fighter under his wing." Publisher's note

The "writing shows quiet purpose in every move, carrying its insider knowledge with easy confidence. DeVido, at his best when showing how men tell stories about themselves with their bodies, pulls off the tricky feat of using boxing action to express character." N Y Times Book Rev

Dew, Robb Forman

The evidence against her; a novel. Little, Brown 2001 327p
ISBN 0-316-89019-7   LC 2001-29101

This novel is "set in the small town of Washburn, Ohio. The story begins with three children born on the same September day in 1888, and it ends with those same three, grown and with children of their own, in the summer of 1927. Lily Scofield, her cousin Warren Scofield and Robert Butler, son of the Methodist pastor, grow up as an inseparable group. . . . Even after Lily marries Robert in June 1913, she assumes that Warren will still somehow always be close by. . . . {But he meets} Agnes Claytor, who was a 14-year-old guest at Lily's wedding." N Y Times Book Rev

"A marvel of lyrical understatement, the narrative flows like a river—smooth, with surprising depths, some turbulence and the inexorability of time's passing." Publ Wkly

The truth of the matter; a novel. Little, Brown 2005 327p $24.95
ISBN 0-316-89004-9   LC 2005-03841

Second title in a trilogy about the Scofield family of Washburn, Ohio; begun with: The evidence against her.

"Agnes Scofield has raised her children as a widow, having lost husband Warren in a car accident in 1930. This loss permeates the way in which Agnes recalls her life–she does not feel, she represses–and affects the relationships she has with her children. During World War

Dew, Robb Forman—*Continued*

II, her children leave home, and Agnes adjusts to single life only to have to readjust when they return to their small Ohio town with spouses and children in tow. The family ultimately finds the homecoming unsettling, as if they are just meeting one another for the first time. Dew's plain writing highlights the characters' inner lives and the wartime environment, yet it carries the reader along effortlessly." Libr J

DeWitt, Patrick, 1975-

Ablutions; notes for a novel. Houghton Mifflin Harcourt 2009 164p $23

ISBN 978-0-15-101498-9; 0-15-101498-1

LC 2008-37772

The "story of an alcoholic, pill-popping, 32-year-old Hollywood bartender in the midst of a slow and steady downward spiral. Told deftly in the second person—a potentially annoying conceit—deWitt's portrayal of the drinking life is staunchly unromantic. (Consider him the anti-Bukowski.) The author, an ex-barman himself, poses the book as 'notes on a novel,' arranged in short, anecdotal snippets that read like the outline for a future, more elaborate project. This risk could have resulted in an underrealized mess, but the result is an accessible, side-splitting story that never buckles under its apparently haphazard structure. The cast of characters—which include a former child star and various tawdry, L.I.I.T.-slurping women—adds background to the main narrative of a man whose life and ambition are drowning in an ocean of Jamesons. . . . Despite its messy topic, the book becomes a welcome rarity: an experimental novel that's also a page-turner." Time Out N Y

Dexter, Colin

The daughters of Cain. Crown 1995 c1994 295p

ISBN 0-517-70067-0

*

First published 1994 in the United Kingdom

In this Inspector Morse case "the crime is the murder of a retired Oxford don, and the stratagem is to make the homicide seem easy to solve. . . . Mr. Dexter is a superb technician who torments the reader with logistical details that contradict every previously established point in his puzzle. Red herrings are a specialty. But the canny author also strews the path with literary quotations to think on, polysyllabic words to look up and characters whose lives are so complicated they turn into richly distracting mini-dramas." N Y Times Book Rev

Death is now my neighbor; an Inspector Morse novel. Crown 1996 347p

ISBN 0-517-70786-1

LC 96-31781

This mystery "involves two senior Oxford dons and their ambitious wives in the death of a young woman with no obvious connections to any of them. Despite a medical scare that leaves him feeling 'unmanned' and has him behaving with uncharacteristic charity, Morse is brilliant at finding the links, filling in the blanks and coming up with the answers to this complicated case—if not to the ultimate questions that trouble his soul." N Y Times Book Rev

The jewel that was ours. Crown 1992 c1991 275p il

ISBN 0-517-58847-1

LC 91-45245

First published 1991 in the United Kingdom

This mystery finds British Inspector Morse "stymied by the theft of a rare artifact bound for the Ashmolean Museum and by the sudden deaths of both the American woman who owned it and the curator for whom it was intended. Challenged to keep track of several sneaky academics and frisky elderly tourists, the detective noses over British Rail timetables, handwritten notes and a smelly assortment of red herrings." N Y Times Book Rev

"The watertight solution is as tricky as it is dazzling." Booklist

Morse's greatest mystery and other stories. Crown 1995 c1993 242p

ISBN 0-517-79992-8

First published 1993 in the United Kingdom

Contents: As good as gold; Morse's greatest mystery; Evans tries an O-level; Dead as a dodo; At the Lulu-Bar Motel; Neighborhood watch; A case of mis-identity; The inside story; Monty's revolver; The carpet-bagger; Last call

The remorseful day. Crown 2000 363p

ISBN 0-609-60622-0

LC 99-59840

First published 1999 in the United Kingdom

"A two-year-old murder has baffled the police in Burford, a rural English village. Inspector Morse, who excels at this sort of puzzle, refuses to touch it, despite anonymous phone calls offering new evidence. Then his sidekick, Sergeant Lewis, discovers that the inspector knew the murdered woman." Libr J

"This finale to a grand series presents a moving elegy to one of mystery fiction's most celebrated and popular characters. . . . Dexter has fashioned another brilliantly intricate puzzle, one of his finest, with the valedictory tone of the narrative lending a particularly rich texture to the tale. Morse leaves us on the highest possible note, perfectly pitched." Publ Wkly

The secret of annexe 3. St. Martin's Press 1987 c1986 218p

ISBN 0-312-01089-3

LC 87-17590

First published 1986 in the United Kingdom

"Inspector Morse and Sergeant Lewis investigate a murder committed on New Year's Eve at a hotel in Oxford. Three couples are housed in the hotel annex, and one man, winner of the prize in the fancy-dress contest, is found dead in his room. The first problem facing Morse and Lewis is locating the other five guests, including the victim's wife, all of whom have fled, having registered under fake names and addresses. . . . Engrossed in the story that Dexter tells in his witty and stylish fashion, readers will savor the mystery of the masquerade and the detecting partners' ultimate triumph." Publ Wkly

The way through the woods. Crown 1993 c1992 296p

ISBN 0-517-59444-7

LC 92-40762

First published 1992 in the United Kingdom

"A student disappears, and Inspector Morse's only clue is a cryptic poem that the murderer might have sent." Libr J

"To say that the investigation is tricky is only to hint at the technical density of the plot, which, once all the tantalizing enigmas have been packed up, hinges on the most basic human frailties. Dazzling." N Y Times Book Rev

Dexter, Colin—*Continued*

The wench is dead. St. Martin's Press 1990
c1989 200p il
ISBN 0-312-04444-5   LC 89-77807
First published 1989 in the United Kingdom

A mystery featuring Chief Inspector Morse of the Oxford police force. "In the hospital for an ulcer made
worse by drink, and frustrated by the proximity of so
many pretty young nurses, he finds distraction in an apparent case of gang rape and murder unsolved for over
a hundred years." Booklist

"Mr. Dexter has fashioned a taxing brainteaser for
Morse, whose superior wits and famously foul temper
tug the reader into the detective's hospital bed to share
his single-minded pursuit of the truth." N Y Times Book
Rev

Dexter, Pete, 1943-

Deadwood. Random House 1986 365p
ISBN 0-394-53669-X
                              * LC 85-19635
"Deadwood (is) a vibrant, squalid late-nineteenth-
century boomtown nestled in the forbidding Black Hills
of the untamed Dakota Territory. When the legendary
Wild Bill Hickok guides a wagon train full of prostitutes
into the virtually lawless town, he becomes the target of
Al Swearingen, a vengeful and cowardly pimp who hires
an addlepated sot to kill him. Wild Bill's disquieted final
days are spent in the company of a score of rough characters (including a riotously off-color Calamity Jane),
each of whom is later bitterly haunted by the freakish
circumstances of his murder." Booklist

This novel "is unpredictable, hyperbolic and, page after
page, uproarious; a joshing book written in high spirits
and a raw appreciation for the past." N Y Times Book
Rev

The paperboy. Random House 1995 307p
ISBN 0-679-42175-0   LC 94-21523
"Set in the fetid swamps of northern Florida, the novel
concerns the legal case of Hillary Van Wetter, who has
been condemned to death for the murder of the county
sheriff. Nineteen-year-old Jack James, son of the local
newspaper publisher and delivery boy for the daily edition, narrates the story, which begins with Charlotte
Bless, an interloping southern floozy just past her prime
who takes an obsessive interest in Van Wetter's case.
Jack's elder brother, Ward, a reporter in Miami, also detects a story in Van Wetter's predicament and returns to
his native Moat County to investigate. He brings along
the handsome, ambitious writer Yardley Acheman, whose
stylistic flash is matched by his willingness to cut ethical
corners. The group's inquiry drives this novel's action,
taking them through the swamp, to death row, and on to
Daytona Beach." Booklist

"Dexter's writing is rock-solid, he offers acute observations about the nature of reporting and his grip on the
Southern male psyche is unquestionable." Publ Wkly

Paris Trout. Random House 1988 306p
ISBN 0-394-56370-0
                              * LC 87-43314
"Paris Trout, the small-town Georgia store owner . . .
sleeps with a sheet of lead under his mattress. He's
afraid someone is going to hide under his bed and shoot

him in the middle of the night—and for no good reason,
as Trout sees it. He was only taking care of business,
trying to collect on Henry Ray Boxer's debt. That little
black girl, Rosie Sayers, who got shot and killed in the
scuffle, shouldn't have got in his way, or the woman
with Rosie, who still walks around with Trout's bullet in
her chest. . . . Mr. Dexter has created a character whose
racism is a blunt, unregenerate fact, as primitive and
willful as an earthquake or a rainstorm—and just as
sealed off from argument, examination or questions of
mercy. What the town's polite society takes care to disguise in Sunday-go-to-meeting euphemisms, Paris sets in
defiant, ugly relief; he makes it easy for them to believe
they are innocent of racism." N Y Times Book Rev

Spooner. Grand Central Pub. 2009 469p $26.99
ISBN 978-0-446-54072-8; 0-446-54072-2
                              LC 2009-06087
"The title character is one Warren Spooner, a kid
dogged by the fact that his mother's favorite child,
Spooner's twin brother, died at birth. Spooner's dad dies
soon afterward. Into the family's life arrives Ottosson,
[a] disgraced young naval officer turned schoolteacher.
He is a man of great virtues: smart, tough, capable and
wreathed in infinite patience. He will need the latter
quality in spades to deal with his troubled stepson. . . .
Despite the autobiographical elements in 'Spooner,' the
book lacks a narrative arc that permits a complete picture
of the protagonist's life. This is not cited as a fault. It
is a function of how this picaresque novel serves as a
work of memory, real or imagined." Denver Post

Train; a novel. Doubleday 2003 280p $26
ISBN 0-385-50591-4   LC 2003-51946
Lionel "Train" Walk is a "young black caddy at an exclusive L.A. country club in 1953. Train is a self-taught
golfer, too, and his natural ability catches the eye of an
enigmatic cop, Miller Packard (or 'Mile-Away-Man,' as
Train dubs him). As the stories of Train, Packard, and
Norah Still, the survivor of a yacht hijacking (and eventually, Packard's wife), interject and ultimately implode,
Dexter painstakingly reminds us that noir is all about disappointment, too." Booklist

Dezenhall, Eric

Money wanders. Thomas Dunne Bks. 2002 338p
$24.95
ISBN 0-312-28275-3   LC 2001-54335
A "comic caper about a Jewish pollster put to work for
an aging South Jersey/Philly Mafia don. Middle-aged Jonah Eastman, a D.C. spin doctor for hire whose business
is in the doldrums, is summoned back to his Jersy home
by his ailing grandfather Mickey, an old-school Jewish
capo for the local Cosa Nostra kingpin, Mario Vanni.
Mickey's cryptic deathbed missive to his nervous grandson directs Jonah to take on the don as a client." Publ
Wkly

Diamant, Anita, 1951-

Last days of Dogtown; a novel. Scribner 2005
263p il $25
ISBN 0-7432-2573-2   LC 2005-45191
This novel "weaves together seemingly disparate stories of a dying Massachusetts town. . . . In the early
1800s, Dogtown is a village on Cape Ann populated by

Diamant, Anita, 1951——*Continued*

spinsters, free slaves, and prostitutes, all of whom are reviled by the surrounding communities. Beginning with
the death of a town patriarch and ending when the last
resident expires, Dogtown's final days are filled with all
the secrets a town can keep. Several characters stand out,
including Tammy Younger, the town pariah, and Judy
Rhines, whose affair with a free African is kept secret to
heartbreaking effect. Diamant has a gift for storytelling
and breathes life into this dying town and its eccentric
inhabitants." Libr J

The red tent. St. Martin's Press 1997 321p
$24.95; pa $16.95
ISBN 0-312-16978-7; 0-312-35376-6 (pa)
* LC 97-16825
This biblical tale "re-creates the life of Dinah, daughter
of Leah and Jacob, from her birth and happy childhood
in Mesopotamia through her years in Canaan and death
in Egypt." Libr J
"Diamant's fiction debut links the passions of the early
Israelites to the ongoing traditions of modern Jews, while
the red tent of her title (where women retreat for men-
struation, childbirth and illness) becomes a resonant symbol of womanly strength, love and wisdom. Despite a
few unprofitable digressions, Diamant succeeds admirably in depicting the lives of women in the age that engendered our civilization and our most enduring values."
Publ Wkly

Díaz, Junot, 1968-

The brief wondrous life of Oscar Wao.
Riverhead 2007 339p $24.95
ISBN 978-1-59448-958-7; 1-59448-958-0
In this novel "Díaz presents a slice of the vast history
of Santo Domingo and the intricate past and present of
a doomed family. . . . Oscar de León [is] Díaz's sci-fi
obsessed, overweight, romantic hero who hopes to someday be the 'Dominican Stephen King.' Oscar is the ultimate outcast both at home and at school. This 'ghetto
nerd' lacks the philandering, macho finesse expected of
a Dominican male. His bookish manner and unappealing
looks relegate his high school experience to the level of
'a medieval spectacle,' an experience 'like being put in
the stocks and forced to endure the pelting and outrages
of a mob of deranged half-wits.' But this is more than
a tale of mere adolescent anguish. Oscar and his family
appear to be the hapless victims of a so-called Dominican curse, or the 'fukú,' that has followed them for generations from the shores of their homeland to New Jersey. Díaz weaves the stories of Lola, his troubled but
supportive sister, and Belicia, his hardened mother, along
with various other family members, to portray a colorful
and complex portrait of mad love, old-world superstition,
and the continual strivings of a diaspora." Christ Sci
Monit

Drown. Riverhead Bks. 1996 208p
ISBN 0-573-22041-8   LC 96-18362
Includes the following stories: Ysrael; Fiesta, 1980;
Aurora; Aquantando; Drown; Boyfriend; Edison, New
Jersey; How to date a browngirl, blackgirl, whitegirl, or
halfie; No face; Negocios
"The 10 tales in this intense debut collection plunge us
into the emotional lives of people redefining their Ameri-
can identity. Narrated by adolescent Dominican males

living in the struggling communities of the Dominican
Republic, New York and New Jersey, these stories
chronicle their outwardly cool but inwardly anguished attempts to recreate themselves in the midst of eroding
family structures and their own burgeoning sexuality."
Publ Wkly

Dibdin, Michael

And then you die; an Aurelio Zen mystery.
Pantheon Bks. 2002 183p
ISBN 0-375-42188-2   LC 2002-283086
"Zen has been given a new identity and use of a
beachfront home in Versilia, a Tuscan coast resort town,
while he awaits the beginning of a Mafia trial in America—a trial where he's supposed to be a surprise, and
key, witness. . . . Zen's enforced idleness chafes, then
evaporates as people too near him begin to die and the
new strategies developed to conceal him seem to have
(almost) fatal flaws." Publ Wkly
"You have to read between the lines—in scenes about
a broken marriage, an empty home, a discredited occupation—to understand why Zen is really running for his
life." N Y Times Book Rev

Blood rain; an Aurelio Zen mystery. Pantheon
Bks. 2000 c1999 273p
ISBN 0-375-40915-7   LC 99-46938
First published 1999 in the United Kingdom
Posted to Sicily, Aurelio Zen's "nominal assignment,
spying on the State Police's anti-Mafia operation for the
rival Interior Ministry, is another example of corruption
at work, and soon enough, he blunders into a lethal
crossfire of power-hungry politicians, bureaucrats, and
crime bosses. When his mother dies a suspicious death
in Rome, and the woman he considers his daughter is
killed in Sicily, Zen must ask himself a familiar question: Will finding the truth only make matters worse?"
Booklist
Dibdin "uses the somber tones, circuitous locutions and
dense plot structure appropriate to a region where every
gesture—from a chess game to a political assassination—
sends a subtle and dangerous message." N Y Times
Book Rev

A long finish; an Aurelio Zen mystery.
Pantheon Bks. 1998 261p
ISBN 0-375-40429-5   LC 98-15764
When a leading Piedmontese "vintner is murdered and
his son is charged with the gruesome deed, Zen is dispatched from Rome by a notable personage fearful that
'one of the great vintages of the century' will be compromised. . . . The all-embracing sense of place in
Dibdin's mysteries extends here to the earthy sights and
smells of dark woods (where the truffles grow) and lush
vineyards (where the grapes ripen) and ancient farm-
houses (where murder is done). Only when Zen learns to
look past the beauty of these pastoral scenes can he identify the evil that lives in this village." N Y Times Book
Rev

Medusa; an Aurelio Zen mystery; Michael
Dibdin. Pantheon Books 2003 259p $22
ISBN 0-375-42269-2   LC 2003-60893
"A long-dead body found in a mountain tunnel piques
the interest of veteran Italian police officer Aurelio Zen
(Blood Rain), who is especially intrigued by the inordi-

Dibdin, Michael—*Continued*

nate attention paid to the case by the Defense Ministry and his own superior in the Interior Ministry. The corpse turns out to be that of Lt. Leonardo Ferraro, reportedly killed in a plane crash 30 years earlier. Its discovery brings to light a secret right-wing military group that prepared to overthrow the government in the 1970s. . . . Dibdin does a superb job of creating a complex background of Italian politics and society." Libr J

Dick, Philip K.

The collected stories of Philip K. Dick. Underwood/Miller 1987 5v
ISBN 0-88733-053-3

*

Contents: Beyond lies the wub: Stability; Roog; The little movement; Beyond lies the wub; The gun; The skull; The defenders; Mr. Spaceship; Piper in the woods; The infinites; The Preserving Machine; Expendable; The variable man; The indefatigable frog; The crystal crypt; The short happy life of the brown oxford; The builder; Meddler; Paycheck; The great C; Out in the garden; The king of the elves; Colony; Prize ship; Nanny

Second Variety: The cookie lady; Beyond the door; Second Variety; Jon's world; The cosmic poachers; Progeny; Some kinds of life; Martians come in clouds; The commuter; The world she wanted; A surface raid; Project: Earth; The trouble with bubbles; Breakfast at twilight; A present for Pat; The hood maker; Of withered apples; Human is; Adjustment team; The impossible planet; Impostor; James P. Crow; Planet for transients; Small town; Souvenir; Survey team; Prominent author

The father-thing: Fair game; The hanging stranger; The eyes have it; The golden man; The turning wheel; The last of the masters; The father-thing; Strange Eden; Tony and the beetles; Null-o; To serve the master; Exhibit piece; The crawlers; Sales pitch; Shell game; Upon the dull earth; Foster, you're dead; Pay for the printer; War veteran; The chromium fence; Misadjustment; A world of talent; Psi-man heal my child!

The days of Perky Pat: Autofac; Service call; Captive market; The mold of yancy; The minority report; Recall mechanism; The unreconstructed M; Explorers we; War game; If there were no Benny Cemoli; Novelty act; Waterspider; What the dead men say; Orpheus with clay feet; The days of Perky Pat; Stand-by; What'll we do with Ragland Park?; Oh, to be a Blobel!

The little black box: The little black box; The war with the fnools; A game of unchance; Precious artifact; Retreat syndrome; A terran odyssey; Your appointment will be yesterday; Holy quarrel; We can remember it for you wholesale; Not by its cover; Return match; Faith of our fathers; The story to end all stories for Harlan Ellison's anthology *Dangerous visions*; The electric ant; Cadbury, the beaver who lacked; A little something for us tempunauts; The pre-persons; The eye of the sibyl; The day Mr. Computer fell out of its tree; The exit door leads in; Chains of air, web of aether; Strange memories of death; I hope I shall arrive soon; Rautavaara's case; The alien mind

The divine invasion
In Dick, P. K. VALIS and later novels

Do androids dream of electric sheep? Ballantine Books 1996 244p pa $13.95
ISBN 0-345-40447-5

         * LC 96-96117

"A Del Rey book"
First published 1968
"In a future where technological sophistication has made the ersatz virtually indistinguishable from the real, the hero is a bounty hunter who must track down and eliminate androids passing for human. . . . A key novel in Dick's canon." Anatomy of Wonder 5

also in Dick, P. K. Four novels of the 1960s

Dr. Bloodmoney
In Dick, P. K. Five novels of the 1960s & 70s

Five novels of the 1960s & 70s; Martian time-slip; Dr. Bloodmoney; Now wait for last year; Flow my tears, the policeman said; A scanner darkly. Library of America 2008 1128p $40
ISBN 978-1-59853-025-4
"Martian Time-Slip (1964) unfolds on a parched and thinly colonized Red Planet where the unscrupulous seek to profit from a troubled child's time-fracturing visions. Dr. Bloodmoney, or How We Got Along After the Bomb (1965) chronicles the interwoven stories of a multiracial community of survivors, including the scientist who may have been responsible for World War III. . . . Now Wait for Last Year (1966) explores the effects of JJ-180, a hallucinogen that alters not only perception, but reality. In Flow My Tears, the Policeman Said (1974), a television star seeks to unravel a mystery that has left him stripped of his identity. A Scanner Darkly (1977), the basis for the 2006 film, envisions a drug-addled world in which a narcotics officer's tenuous hold on sanity is strained by his new surveillance assignment: himself." Publisher's note

"Wild unevenness is the price a reader pays for Dick's two great virtues: a blazing fecundity of imagination (the science part of science fiction didn't interest him that much, but the sheer fictiveness of it certainly did) and a quality of claustral despair that only Theodore Dreiser can match in American fiction. . . . 'A halfway land' isn't a bad way to summarize Dick's fictional world. Past and future merge. Technological might and personal frailty mock each other. Life on Mars feels a lot like life on Earth: Both are equally grim (there's just less water on Mars, and the air is a lot thinner). The truly unsettling thing about Dick's novels isn't how dystopian they are; it's how comfortable he feels in dystopias. It's almost as if, his suspicions confirmed, Dick can now relax and get on with things—however grim those things might be." Chicago Tribune

Flow my tears, the policeman said
In Dick, P. K. Five novels of the 1960s & 70s

Four novels of the 1960s; The man in the high castle; The three stigmata of Palmer Eldritch; Do androids dream of electric sheep?; Ubik. Library of America 2007 830p $35
ISBN 978-1-59853-009-4; 1-598-53009-7

         * LC 2006-48776

Dick, Philip K.—*Continued*

"These novels grapple with spirituality, rather than science. In The Man in the High Castle [1962], set in a United States that has been defeated by the Axis powers in World War II, the characters use the ancient Chinese text I Ching to determine their actions. In The Three Stigmata [1965], hallucinogenic drugs provide virtual reality experiences that lead to discussions of the existence and nature of God. Do Androids Dream [1968] features a religion, Mercerism, in which adherents experience real suffering through a machine that registers their empathy for a sacrificial victim. Ubik [1969] utilizes the Tibetan Book of the Dead to examine the existence and consciousness of an afterlife. I don't want this to sound as if Dick is some dry-as-bones, proselytizing prophet. These novels are also funny, thrilling and stimulating. There are shootouts with renegade androids and undercover spies. There are parodies of consumer culture. There are debates about historicity and drug use. Each novel offers a reading experience that is cathartic while reading, yet offers fruit for continued thought afterward." Philadelphia Inquirer

The man in the high castle. Vintage Books 1992 259p pa $12
ISBN 0-679-74067-8
* LC 91-50895
First published 1962 by Putnam
"An alternate history in which Germany and Japan won World War II and partitioned the U.S., except for the Rocky Mountain States, which were left in a kind of political limbo. Faction-ridden Nazism oppressively rules the eastern U.S. In the west, the Japanese overlords are reconciling Oriental and American cultural values. . . . This is Dick's most important early book." Anatomy of Wonder 5

also in Dick, P. K. Four novels of the 1960s

Martian time-slip
In Dick, P. K. Five novels of the 1960s & 70s

A maze of death
In Dick, P. K. VALIS and later novels

The minority report. Pantheon Bks. 2002 103p $12.95
ISBN 0-375-42187-4
LC 2002-72313
Originally published posthumously as a short story
"Police Commissioner John Anderton finds himself at the mercy of his own crime-prevention system when the prescient precogs he's hired to stop crime before it starts peg him as a soon-to-be murderer." Publ Wkly

Now wait for last year
In Dick, P. K. Five novels of the 1960s & 70s

A scanner darkly
In Dick, P. K. Five novels of the 1960s & 70s

The three stigmata of Palmer Eldritch
In Dick, P. K. Four novels of the 1960s

The transmigration of Timothy Archer
In Dick, P. K. VALIS and later novels

Ubik
In Dick, P. K. Four novels of the 1960s

Valis
In Dick, P. K. VALIS and later novels

VALIS and later novels. Library of America 2009 849p $35
ISBN 978-1-59853-044-5
"The collection opens with A Maze of Death (1970). . . . Mysteriously summoned to the planet Delmak-O, a motley group of colonists attempts to survive together in a hostile new world. . . . . [VALIS (1981) is a] self-portrait of a man confronting a 'Vast Active Living Intelligence System,' torn between conflicting interpretations of what might be gnostic illumination or mental collapse. In The Divine Invasion (1981), the life of a solitary off-world colonist is hijacked by a local alien, who turns out to be the Yahweh of Judeo-Christian tradition. Returning to Earth with his pregnant wife in tow, Dick's hapless Herb Asher finds himself thrust into the middle of an apocalyptic war between Good and Evil. . . . The Transmigration of Timothy Archer (1982), Dick's last novel, is by turns a theological mystery story, a roman à clef, and a starkly disillusioned portrait of contemporary California life. Based loosely on the career of Bishop James Pike, Dick's close friend and a kindred spirit, the novel's title character gives up his comfortable place in the church hierarchy in a tragic quest for enlightenment." Publisher's note

The **Dick** Francis treasury of great racing stories; edited and introduced by Dick Francis and John Welcome. Norton 1990 c1989 221p
ISBN 0-393-02879-8
LC 89-72151

First published 1989 in the United Kingdom with title: Great racing stories
Contents: The dream, by R. Findlay; Silver Blaze, by A. C. Doyle; A glass of port with the proctor, by J. Welcome; Carrot for a chestnut, by D. Francis; The look of eagles, by J. T. Foote; Prime rogues, by M. Keane; The coop, by E. Wallace; The splendid outcast, by B. Markham; I'm a fool, by S. Anderson; Had a horse, by J. Galsworthy; The major, by C. Davy; What's it get you?, by J. P. Marquand; Harmony, by W. Fain; The bagman's pony, by E. de Somerville

Dickens, Charles, 1812-1870

Barnaby Rudge; a tale of the riots of 'eighty; with 76 illustrations by George Cattermole and Hablot K. Browne "Phiz" and an introduction by Kathleen Tillotson. Oxford Univ. Press 1961 634p il
ISBN 0-19-254513-2
First published 1841
"Gives a lurid account of the mad orgies and incendiarism of the 'No Popery' riots, introducing Lord George Gordon as an actor, the principal events being founded on fact. Intertwined with this is a private story containing a few characteristic traits." Baker. Guide to Hist Fic
"The plot is one of Dickens' weakest. The novel's chief interest lies in its depiction of the riots, shown to have been caused by a government heedless of the needs of its poor." Reader's Ency. 4th edition

Dickens, Charles, 1812-1870—*Continued*

Bleak House; with the original illustrations by Phiz; introduced by Barbara Hardy. Knopf 1991 xlix, 891p il $23

ISBN 0-679-40568-2

* LC 91-52974

"Everyman's library"

First published 1853

"The heroine is Esther Summerson or rather Esther Hawdon, the illegitimate child of Lady Dedlock and Captain Hawdon. Esther, whom Lady Dedlock believes dead, is the ward of Mr. Jarndyce of the interminable case of Jarndyce and Jarndyce in Chancery Court, and lives with him at Bleak House. Lord Dedlock's lawyer, Mr. Tulkinghorn, gets wind of Lady Dedlock's secret past; and when Tulkinghorn is murdered, Lady Dedlock is suspected, disappears and is later found dead." Univ Handbk for Readers and Writers

"In this novel, Dickens attacks the delays and archaic absurdities of the courts, which he knew about firsthand." Reader's Ency. 4th edition

A Charles Dickens Christmas; A Christmas carol; The Chimes; The cricket on the hearth; with illustrations by Warren Chappell. Oxford Univ. Press 1976 308p il o.p.

Omnibus edition of the titles first published 1843, 1845 and 1846 respectively, the first and third of which are entered separately. The chimes is a fable about the fears and aspirations of the London poor. A porter and runner of errands, under the influence of the goblins of the church bells and/or a dish of tripe, has a nightmare or vision of awful misfortunes befalling his daughter, but conditions are ameliorated after he awakens

The chimes

In Dickens, C. A Charles Dickens Christmas p101-202

A Christmas carol; with illustrations by Arthur Rackham. Knopf 1994 155p il $13.95

ISBN 0-679-43639-1

* LC 95-163031

"Everyman's library children's classics"

Written in 1843

"This Christmas story of nineteenth century England has delighted young and old for generations. In it, a miser, Scrooge, through a series of dreams, finds the true Christmas spirit. . . . The story ends with the much-quoted cry of Tiny Tim, the crippled son of Bob Cratchit, whom Scrooge now aids: 'God bless us, everyone!'" Haydn. Thesaurus of Book Dig

also in Dickens, C. A Charles Dickens Christmas p3-98

also in Dickens, C. The complete ghost stories of Charles Dickens p89-151

The complete ghost stories of Charles Dickens; edited by Peter Haining. Watts 1983 c1982 341p il

ISBN 0-531-09885-0   LC 82-13481

First published 1982 in the United Kingdom

Contents: Captain Murderer and the Devil's bargain; The lawyer and the ghost; The queer chair; The ghosts of the mail; A madman's manuscript; The story of the goblins who stole a sexton; Baron Koëldwethout's appa-

rition; A Christmas carol; The haunted man and the ghost's bargain; To be read at dusk; The ghost chamber; The haunted house; Mr Testator's visitation; The trial for murder; The signalman; Four ghost stories; The portrait-painter's story; Well-authenticated rappings

The cricket on the hearth; a tale of home; with illustrations by C. E. Brock. Dutton 171p il o.p.

First published in 1846; this is a reissue of an edition first published 1905

"In this short Christmas fairy tale of a happy English home, the cricket chirps when all is well, and is silent when sorrow enters. Mr. and Mrs. Perrybingle (John and Dot) give refuge to an old stranger, Edward Plummer. John sees the stranger, as a young man, without his disguise, put his arm around Dot. The cricket takes the form of a fairy and counsels him. John does not judge his young wife and is ready to forgive her. However, Edward bursts in with his bride, May Fielding, and explains everything." Haydn. Thesaurus of Book Dig

also in Dickens, C. A Charles Dickens Christmas p205-308

David Copperfield; with the original illustrations by "Phiz"; introduced by Michael Slater. Knopf 1991 xlii, 891p il $25

ISBN 0-679-40571-2

* LC 91-52995

"Everyman's library"

First published 1850

This novel "incorporates material from the autobiography Dickens had recently begun but soon abandoned and is written in the first person, a new technique for him. Although Copperfield differs from his creator in many ways, Dickens uses many early personal experiences that had meant much to him—his own period of work in a factory while his father was jailed, his schooling and reading, his passion for Maria Beadnell (a woman much like Dora Spenlow), and (more cursorily) his emergence from parliamentary reporting into successful novel writing." Merriam-Webster's Ency of Lit

Dombey and Son; with forty illustrations by 'Phiz'; introduced by Lucy Hughes-Hallett. Knopf 1994 xlvii, 889p il $23

ISBN 0-679-43591-3   LC 94-4778

"Everyman's library"

First published 1848

"The proud, unfeeling Mr. Dombey has but one ambition: to have a son so that his firm might be called Dombey and Son. When his son Paul is born, he promises to fulfill this ambition, which overrides even grief at the death of Mrs. Dombey. Young Paul, a delicate, sensitive boy, is quite unequal to the great things expected of him; he is sent to Mr. Blimber's school and gives way under the strain of the discipline. . . . Mr. Dombey is embittered by Paul's death. Florence, his daughter, lives on with him, trying desperately to win his love, but she has succeeded only in incurring his hatred because she lives while her brother died. Dombey marries again, but his second wife, Edith Granger, runs off with Mr. Carker, his business manager. Florence marries the kind young Walter Gay. Dombey's firm fails, and alone and miserable, he finds himself longing for the sweet and kind daughter whom he treated so coldly. The two are reconciled, and Dombey tries to expiate his past through his grandchildren." Reader's Ency. 4th edition

Dickens, Charles, 1812-1870—*Continued*

Great expectations; illustrated by F.W. Pailthrope with an introduction by Michael Slater. Knopf 1992 xxxiv, 469p il $21

ISBN 0-679-40579-8

* LC 91-53219

"Everyman's library"

First published 1861

"The first-person narrative relates the coming-of-age of Pip (Philip Pirrip). Reared in the marshes of Kent by his disagreeable sister and her sweet-natured husband, the blacksmith Joe Gargery, the young Pip one day helps a convict to escape. Later he is sent to live with Miss Havisham, a woman driven half-mad years earlier by her lover's departure on their wedding day. . . . When an anonymous benefactor makes it possible for Pip to go to London for an education, he credits Miss Havisham. . . . Pips benefactor turns out to have been Abel Magwitch, the convict he once aided, who dies awaiting trial after Pip is unable to help him a second time. Joe rescues Pip from despair and nurses him back to health." Merriam-Webster's Ency of Lit

Hard times. Knopf 1992 299p $19

ISBN 0-679-41323-5   LC 91-58704

"Everyman's library"

First published 1854. Variant title: Hard times for these times

The proprietor of an experimental private school in an English manufacturing town, "Thomas Gradgrind, a fanatic of the demonstrable fact, has raised his children Tom and Louisa in an atmosphere of grimmest practicality. Louisa marries the banker Josiah Bounderby partly to protect her brother who is in Bounderby's employ, and partly because her education has resulted in an emotional atrophy that makes her indifferent to her fate. Tom, shallow and unscrupulous, robs Bounderby's bank and contrives to frame Stephen Blackpool, an honest and long-suffering mill hand. Meanwhile, Louisa's dormant emotions began to awaken, stimulated by disgust for the vulgar Bounderby and the attentions of the charming, amoral James Harthouse. When she runs away to her father and when Tom's guilt is discovered, Gradgrind realizes how his principles have blighted his children's lives. . . . The novel is Dickens's harshest indictment of practices and philosophical justifications of mid-19th-century industrialism in England." Reader's Ency. 4th edition

Little Dorrit. Knopf 1992 xxxvii, 836p il $22

ISBN 0-679-41725-7   LC 92-52919

"Everyman's library"

First published 1857

"Little Dorrit was born and brought up in the Marshalsea prison, Bermondsey, where her father was confined for debt; and when about fourteen years of age she used to do needlework to earn a subsistence for herself and her father. . . . Her father, coming into a property, was set free at length, and Little Dorrit married Arthur Clennam, the marriage service being celebrated in the Marshalsea, by the prison chaplain." Univ Handbk for Readers and Writers

"Satirizes the Civil Service under the style of the Circumlocution Office. Also pictures prison life. Little Dorrit's father being Father of the Marshalsea. The melodramatic element appears in the history of the House of Clennam: with the usual complement of originals: Mr.

F.'s Aunt, the Meagles, Pancks, Mr. Nanby, Mr. Casby, Flora Finching, Miss Wade, Tallycoram." Baker. Guide to the Best Fic

Martin Chuzzlewit; with forty illustrations by "Phiz"; introduced by William Boyd. Knopf 1994 xlvii, 851p il $20

ISBN 0-679-43884-X   LC 95-136833

"Everyman's library"

"The story's protagonist, Martin Chuzzlewit, is an apprentice architect who is fired by Seth Pecksniff and is also disinherited by his own eccentric, wealthy grandfather. Martin and a servant, Mark Tapley, travel to the United States, where they are swindled by land speculators and have other unpleasant but sometimes comic experiences. Thoroughly disillusioned with the New World, the pair returns to England, where a chastened Martin is reconciled with his grandfather, who gives his approval to Martin's forthcoming marriage to his true love, Mary Graham." Merriam-Webster's Ency of Lit

The mystery of Edwin Drood; with 12 illustrations by Luke Fildes and 2 by Charles Collins, and an introduction by S. C. Roberts. Oxford Univ. Press 1956 278p il

ISBN 0-19-254516-7

"New Oxford illustrated Dickens"

First published 1870

"This novel Dickens left unfinished at his death. The striking opening scene shows John Jasper, precentor of Cloisterham cathedral, in an opium den. He is the uncle of Edwin Drood, and persecutes with his evil passion Rosa Bud, to whom Drood is betrothed by an arrangement made by the late respective fathers of the two orphans. Actually Edwin is cool to Rosa, and it is another orphan, Neville Landless, who is attracted to her. The sinister Jasper foments a quarrel between Edwin and Neville, not knowing that the engagement has already been broken off. The same night Edwin disappears, and there is circumstantial evidence pointing to Neville as his murderer. The latter is arrested, but as no body has been found, is released. There turns up in the neighborhood a white-haired stranger who calls himself Datchery and acts like a detective on the trail of Jasper. Here the story breaks off with no indication as to how it would have ended." Haydn. Thesaurus of Book Dig

Nicholas Nickleby; with an introduction by John Carey. Knopf 1993 lvii, 843p il $24

ISBN 0-679-42307-9

* LC 93-1856

"Everyman's library"

First published 1839

After Nicholas Nickleby's father dies bankrupt, Nicholas, his sister and their mother go to London to seek aid from Nicholas' uncle, a moneylender. At the scheming miser's insistence, Nicholas "first serves as usher to Mr. Wackford Squeers, schoolmaster at Dotheboys Hall; the brutality of Squeers and his wife, especially toward a poor, half-witted boy named Smike, causes Nicholas to leave in disgust. Smike runs away from school to follow Nicholas, remaining his follower until he dies. Next Nicholas joins the theatrical company of Mr. Crummles, and finally he secures a good post in a counting house owned by the benevolent Cheeryble brothers, Ned and Charles, self-made merchants ready to help those struggling against ill fortune." Reader's Ency. 4th edition

Dickens, Charles, 1812-1870—*Continued*

The old curiosity shop; with seventy-five illustrations by Cattermole and 'Phiz'; introduced by Peter Washington. Knopf 1995 569p il $24

ISBN 0-679-44373-8　　　　　　LC 95-75208

"Everyman's library"

First published 1841; first Everyman's library edition 1907

This is the "story of Little Nell Trent and the evil dwarf Quilp. When Little Nell's grandfather gambles away his curiosity shop to his creditor Quilp, the girl and the old man flee London. Nell's friend Kit Nubbles and a mysterious Single Gentleman (who turns out to be the wealthy brother of Nell's grandfather) attempt to find them but are thwarted by Quilp, who drowns while fleeing the law. Little Nell dies before Kit and the Single Gentleman arrive, and her brokenhearted grandfather dies days later." Merriam-Webster's Ency of Lit

Oliver Twist; with twenty-four illustrations by George Cruikshank; introduced by Michael Slater. Knopf 1992 xlvi, 427p il $20

ISBN 0-679-41724-9　　　　　　LC 92-52899

"Everyman's library"

First published 1837-1838

"A boy from an English workhouse falls into the hands of rogues who train him to be a pickpocket. The story of his struggles to escape from an environment of crime is one of hardship, danger and the severe obstacles overcome." Natl Counc of Teachers of Engl

Our mutual friend; with an introduction by Andrew Sanders. Knopf 1994 xliii, 832p $22

ISBN 0-679-42028-2　　　　　　LC 93-81033

"Everyman's library"

First published 1865

"John Harmon, 'our mutual friend,' will inherit a fortune if he marries Bella Wilfer. He assumes the names of Julius Handford and later John Rokesmith, and his supposed death helps him conceal his identity. John's father's foreman, Nicodemus Boffin, and his wife, Henrietta, help him with the ruse. He enters the employ of Boffin, who has adopted Bella. Bella has had her head turned by wealth, but reforms when her eyes are opened to its evils; she marries Harmon. Other characters are: Jesse Hexam; his son Charley, and daughter, Lizzie; Bradley Headstone, schoolmaster, who is jealous of Eugene Wrayburn's love for Lizzie Hexam; Fanny Cleaver (Jenny Wren), a doll's dressmaker; one-legged Silas Wegg, the villain in the main plot, as Headstone is in the secondary one. Here again Dickens protests against the poor laws through the character Betty Hidger, who fears the workhouse." Haydn. Thesaurus of Book Dig

The posthumous papers of the Pickwick Club; with forty-three illustrations by Seymour and 'Phiz' and an introduction by Bernard Darwin. Oxford Univ. Press 1959 xxiii, 801p il

ISBN 0-19-254501-9

"New Oxford illustrated Dickens"

First published 1837

"Episodes of the doings and foibles of the Pickwick Club. . . . The book is made up of letters and manuscripts about the club's actions. Among the incidents are: the army parade; trip to Manor Farm; the saving of Rachel Wardle from the villain, Alfred Jingle; trip to Eatonsville; Mrs. Leo Hunter's party of authors, including Count Smorltork and Charles FitzMarshall; ice skating. Pickwick's landlady, Mrs. Bardell, faints in his arms and compromises the unsophisticated gentleman. She sues him for breach of promise and an amusing court trial follows. Pickwick refuses to pay damages and is put in Fleet prison. Sam Weller, his faithful servant, accompanies him. Mrs. Bardell is also incarcerated for not paying the costs of the trial. When Pickwick is released he retires to a house outside London, with Weller, and the latter's new bride, Mary, as housekeeper. He dissolves the club and spends his time arranging its memoranda." Haydn. Thesaurus of Book Dig

A tale of two cities; with an introduction by Simon Schama and sixteen illustrations by Phiz. Knopf 1993 xxviii, 413p il $20

ISBN 0-679-42073-8

　　　　　　　　　　　　　* LC 92-73542

"Everyman's library"

First published 1859

"Although Dickens borrowed from Thomas Carlyle's history, The French Revolution, for his sprawling tale of London and revolutionary Paris, the novel offers more drama than accuracy. The scenes of large-scale mob violence are especially vivid, if superficial in historical understanding. The complex plot involves Sydney Carton's sacrifice of his own life on behalf of his friends Charles Darnay and Lucie Manette. While political events drive the story, Dickens takes a decidedly antipolitical tone, lambasting both aristocratic tyranny and revolutionary excess." Merriam-Webster's Ency of Lit

Dickey, James

Deliverance. Houghton Mifflin 1970 278p o.p.

　　　　　　　　　　　　　　　　　　　*

"The plot revolves around a canoe trip undertaken by four city men as a break in routine and to see a wilderness river before it is dammed. Early in the journey two of the men are attacked by brutal mountaineers and another member of the quartet is killed. Dickey probes the diverse personalities of each man, showing clearly that leadership devolves on the one most able to solve a problem rationally rather than the one most given to theorizing about how to cope with the issue of basic survival." Booklist

This "is a thriller—or, more strictly, a suspense story—that transcends its genre. . . . Dickey is to be praised for resisting the temptation of the poet to write 'poetical' prose. . . . He writes in a neat, terse, matter-of-fact prose, level in pitch and perfectly suited to carry the burden of the action." New Yorker

To the white sea. Houghton Mifflin 1993 275p

ISBN 0-395-47565-1　　　　　　LC 93-1247

"A Marc Jaffe book"

WWII Air Force gunner Muldrow is shot down over Tokyo shortly before the "fire raid on that city. His position should be hopeless, but the man comes from a remote region of Alaska, where he grew up hunting, trapping, and studying game. His object is to find similarly cold country, and as he lurks and dodges his way north to Hokkaido, he uses every trick of camouflage and predation that he has learned from hare and wolverine." Atlantic

This novel "allows no easy assumption about nature or

Dickey, James—*Continued*

violence or war. What makes it so haunting, though, what keeps you reading, is the beauty of the prose." Newsweek

Dickinson, Charles, 1951-

A shortcut in time. Forge 2003 288p $24.95

ISBN 0-7653-0579-8   LC 2002-34688

"A Tom Doherty Associates book"

"Josh Winkler's settled life changes when he chooses a shortcut to town and ends up 15 minutes in the past. On the same path, he meets Constance, another bewildered time traveler from the year 1908. No one believes them, especialy Josh's doctor wife, who orders neurological tests. To validate their experiences, Josh researches Constance's disappearance in the local library's newspaper archives and discovers that Constance's boyfriend, a suspect in her disappearance, was hanged by an angry mob; Constance needs to find her way back to 1908 to prevent his death." Libr J

"Dickinson conjures a notably mundane environment, then makes it extraorinary" Booklist

Dickinson, Peter, 1927-

Some deaths before dying. Mysterious Press 1999 251p $27

ISBN 0-89296-696-3   LC 98-37535

"Rachel Matson was a talented photographer and the devoted wife of Jocelyn, a World War II prisoner of war. Now a 90-year-old widow dying of an illness that has paralyzed her, Rachel is determined to hang on to her mental powers. When she discovers that Jocelyn's treasured antique pistol is missing, a long-buried secret comes back to torment her. With the help of her loyal nurse, Dilys, Rachel uses her photographs to come to terms with her past, piecing together a series of events that tore her family apart 39 years ago." Libr J

Dickinson's "radiant portrait of Rachel does honor to 'her long and steadfast campaign to keep hold of her mind,' just as he dignifies the other aged or inarticulate characters in his story by lending them the clarity of voice to express the thoughts they feared they'd lost forever." N Y Times Book Rev

The yellow room conspiracy. Mysterious Press 1994 261p

ISBN 0-89296-556-8

                              * LC 94-1980

"The yellow room was one of about 50 in Blatchards, an old mansion near Bury St. Edmonds. Owned by Lord Vereker, Blatchards was dominated by his five striking daughters whose politics and personal lives in the 1930s and '40s are at the heart of Dickinson's . . . tale. Flashbacks told in alternating chapters by Lucy Vereker, the third daughter, and her lover Paul Ackerley, now near the end of their lives, describe events that culminated in the 1956 fire that destroyed the house, an event that each one thought the other may have, in different ways, engineered. The fire covered up evidence about the death—accident, suicide or murder?—of Gerry Grantworth, the eldest daughter's husband." Publ Wkly

"Like the labyrinthine route one must take to the Yellow Room, the resolution of the mystery is lengthy and winding and delightfully disorienting." N Y Times Book Rev

Dickson, Gordon R., 1923-2001

The cloak and the staff

In The Hugo winners p209-43

Lost Dorsai

In The Hugo winners p137-206

Didion, Joan

A book of common prayer. Simon & Schuster 1977 272p

ISBN 0-671-22491-3   LC 76-50067

Charlotte Douglas, the novel's heroine, "is the quintessential American innocent. . . . Nothing alters her self-centered perception of events—not two disastrous marriages nor the fact that her daughter has turned overnight into a political outlaw. . . . Charlotte retires to Boca Grande, a shabby banana republic, to wait for things to turn out 'all right.' There she meets Grace Strasser-Mendana, the narrator of the novel, like Charlotte a 'norte-americana,' an anthropologist by training, and a local political power by marriage. Grace unwittingly involves Charlotte in a coup d'état. Charlotte in turn provides the subject matter for Grace's final inquiry into human behavior." Atlantic

Didion's "exposition of situations and details adroitly conceals their significance—until much later their meaning flares before our eyes. This is a remarkably good novel." Newsweek

The last thing he wanted. Knopf 1996 227p

ISBN 0-679-43331-7   LC 96-17084

"The year is 1984, and Elena McMahon is burned out. She has survived a bout with cancer, a divorce, and the death of her mother and has already reinvented herself several times over, but she is forced, once again, to adopt a false identity when her father, a quintessential fixer plugged into the deadly world of arms trading, takes ill. A journalist, Elena had been covering the presidential campaign, but she walks off the job, flies to Miami, and lands in the eye of a hurricane of deals, counterdeals, and political subterfuge, a storm of lies and power plays set in motion by the war in Nicaragua." Booklist

"There's an animating tension in Didion's fiction between her achingly sure control as storyteller and stylist and the numbing vagueness of the people she depicts. . . . Didion's novels are thus simultaneously lucid and surreal." New Yorker

Play it as it lays; a novel. Farrar, Straus & Giroux 1970 214p o.p.

                                                    *

"Using a phrenetic millieu of drugs, pills, sexual aberrancy, Didion elliptically etches the self-destructive life of Maria Wyeth. Didion with authorial legerdemain skillfully controls the suspense as Maria dangerously exists: she cannot relate and adjust. Her father has told her life was a crap game and to play it as it lays, not the hard way. But Maria plays it the hardest way, trying to anesthetize herself against pain (almost everyone, anything) and pleasure (Kate, her neurally damaged child), and trying to lose herself in the dead-end life around her." Choice

Diehl, William, 1924-2006

Primal fear. Villard Bks. 1993 418p
ISBN 0-679-40211-X   LC 92-5728
This thriller "focuses on the maneuvers of Chicago defense attorney Martin Vail, a prosecutor's worst nightmare. . . . After discovering the mutilated body of Archbishop Richard Rushman in the rectory of his church, police find Aaron Stampler cowering in a confessional, blood-soaked and gripping the murder weapon. It seems like an iron-clad case—psycho slasher carves up 'the Saint of Lakeview Drive'—and a hostile judge appoints Vail as pro bono defense attorney, hoping to publicly humble him." Publ Wkly
"Taking the best elements of horror fiction, the psychological thriller, and the legal novel, best-selling author Diehl concocts an especially exciting chiller. . . . The ending may not hold up under a psychiatrist's professional scrutiny, but the general reader will find it an immensely successful finis!." Booklist

Reign in hell. Ballantine Bks. 1997 437p
ISBN 0-345-41144-7   LC 97-18214
"Illinois state attorney general Vail is called upon by President Lawrence Pennington to seek a trial case against one of the largest militia outfits in the country. The leader of this outfit, Gen. Joshua Engstrom, just happens to be an old adversary of the president, putting Vail in the middle of a dangerous situation. Vail must also relive the past when unwillingly faced with his nemesis from years ago, serial killer Aaron Stampler, who has now become blind Brother Transgression. The meshing of these storylines is intricate yet easily followed as the tension mounts." Libr J

Show of evil. Ballantine Bks. 1995 483p
ISBN 0-345-37535-1   LC 94-24112
"Defense attorney-turned-district attorney Martin Vail comes to regret having saved a murderer, Aaron Stampler, from the death penalty; Stampler wasn't suffering from multiple personality disorder but was merely a vicious killer who has many more scores to settle. When Stampler proves smart enough to convince an egotistical psychiatrist that he is now sane and can return to society, Vail has to out-think him to save not only his own life but the lives of everyone who contributed to the killer's ten years in a mental institution. The action is gripping, and the characters are well drawn." Libr J

Dierbeck, Lisa, 1963-

One pill makes you smaller. Farrar, Straus & Giroux 2003 312p $24
ISBN 0-374-22649-0   LC 2002-44675
This novel revolves around "11-year-old Alice Duncan, a Manhattan girl of declining privilege who has been left in the slipshod care of her 16-year-old half sister. Her young mother, Rain, has long since disappeared; her father, a 60-year-old failed artist, is in a mental institution. It's 1976. Alice and her sister, known as Aunt Esme, rattle around a tattered Upper East Side brownstone in a haze of nonsupervision, drugs, rock music and Esmes hippie boyfriends." N Y Times Book Rev
"This unsettling and disorienting—but also deliciously pop—account of deplorable actions and shattered innocence is a tour de force, a meshing of the myths of the counterculture with the fantastic universe of Lewis Carroll. It's a genuinely original, compulsively readable first novel, sure to stir up controversy." Publ Wkly

Dikty, Julian May See May, Julian, 1931-

Dillard, Annie

The Maytrees; a novel. HarperCollinsPublishers 2007 216p $24.95
ISBN 978-0-06-123953-3; 0-06-123953-4
LC 2006-52599
This book, "set on Cape Cod, is a fictional account of a broken family. The plot follows the courtship and marriage of Toby Maytree and Lou Bigelow, who fall in love and settle near Provincetown shortly after World War II. Good-looking, unconventional, and brainy, Toby and Lou share an intense appreciation of the natural world—the Cape's wild sand dunes are major players in the novel—yet husband and wife live most vividly within their own minds, a trait strongly reflected in Pete, their only child. When Toby impulsively leaves with another woman to settle in Maine, none of the Maytrees really knows how to cope." Libr J
"The good news is that in The Maytrees, despite the big words and the name-dropping . . . there is also good old straight narrative and prose that is often, yes, breathtakingly illuminative." N Y Times Book Rev

Dinesen, Isak, 1885-1962

Seven Gothic tales; with an introduction by Dorothy Canfield. Modern Lib. 1994 c1934 422p
ISBN 0-679-60086-8
* LC 91-50030
First published 1934 by H. Smith and analyzed in Short story index
Contents: The deluge at Norderney; The old chevalier; The monkey; The roads round Pisa; The supper at Elsinore; The dreamers; The poet
"Distinguished by a romantic style and an aura of mystery, these tales of nineteenth-century aristocratic life in northern Europe remain favorites of a wide audience. A major plot device in some stories is the revealing of illegitimacy (sometimes of legitimacy), while a strong element of the supernatural is to be found in others." Shapiro. Fic for Youth. 3d edition

Winter's tales. Random House 1942 313p o.p.
Contents: The sailor-boy's tale; The young man with the carnation; The pearls; The invincible slaveowners; The heroine; The dreaming child; Alkmene; The fish; Peter and Rosa; Sorrow-acre; A consolatory tale

Disch, Thomas M., 1940-2008

The wall of America. Tachyon Publications 2008 245p pa $14.95
ISBN 978-1-892391-82-7; 1-892391-82-1
Contents: White man; Wall of America; Ringtime; Owl and the pussycat; Canned goods; Abduction of Bunny Steiner, or, A shameless lie; Jour de Fete; Voices of the kill; Nights in the gardens of the Kerhonkson prison for the aged and infirm; Family of the post-apocalypse; In praise of older women; Painting eggplants; Three chronicles of Xglotl and Rwang; In Xanadu; Torah! Torah! Torah!: three bible tales for the third millennium; One night, or, Scheherazade's bare minimum; Knight at the opera; Man who read a book; First annual performance art festival at the Slaughter Rock Battlefield

Disch, Thomas M., 1940-2008—*Continued*

"Decrying but not despairing, this collection of 19 later short pieces by author and poet Disch (1940-2008) lovingly tears into the realities and fantasies of American life. . . . Though sometimes light and slight, these tales show Disch at his masterful, acerbic best." Publ Wkly

Word of God: or, Holy writ rewritten. Tachyon 2008 180p $14.95

ISBN 978-1-892391-77-3; 1-892391-77-5

"Wearying of the world's religious schisms, doctrinal heresies, and manifold sins, Thomas M. Disch has taken it upon himself to embrace divine authority, unless his outlandish enemies emerging from the depths of a dissatisfying hell manage to prevent him. [This book reveals] the hidden conspiracies that link the author with Philip K. Dick, Mel Gibson, Santa, L. Ron Hubbard, and eternity itself." Publisher's note

"The book is a memoir and a novel at the same time; spoof and jeremiad; reportage and alternate-world fantasy; the confessional chrestomathy of a lonely man and the card sharpery of a devilish fine grinning God guy, all at the same time. It is a parable of the making of the work of art; it is the work of art." Sci Fi Wkly

Dische, Irene

The Empress of Weehawken. Farrar, Straus and Giroux 2007 307p $24

ISBN 978-0-374-29912-5; 0-374-29912-9

LC 2006--101574

"As a German army nurse in WWI, Elizabeth Gierlich meets wealthy Jewish surgeon Carl Rother and marries him once he converts to Catholicism. They have a 'racially impure' daughter, Renate, whom Elizabeth mocks and chastises relentlessly, even as she dotes on her. After the Nazis rise to power in Germany, life for Elizabeth's in-laws becomes precarious . . . and Carl's 'honorary Aryan' status can't protect him from the SS. . . . The Rothers flee to the 'less-civilized world' of Weehawken, N.J., where Renate grows up, marries Jewish professor Dische, becomes a successful pathologist and has two children, a boy too intelligent for his own good and a rebellious daughter, Irene, whose adventures, tracked via letters and collect calls home, take her across the Middle East and Africa. Elizabeth dies in 1989, still outspoken and bigoted, and continues to meddle in her beloved daughter's life from Heaven." Publ Wkly

"Incredibly witty, beautifully written. . . 'The Empress of Weehawken' is a potent stew of class, sex and religion, as well as cultural and generational clashes, and Dische crafts a glorious misanthrope in her fictionalized version of her grandmother." Newark Star-Ledger

Ditzen, Rudolf *See* Fallada, Hans, 1893-1947

Dixon, Keith, 1971-

The art of losing. St. Martin's Press 2007 243p $24.95

ISBN 978-0-312-35868-6; 0-312-35868-7

LC 2006-50972

"New York City filmmaker Mike Jacobs is so tired of being broke that it seems like a good idea when his friend and producer, Sebby Laslo, suggests they strike it rich by fixing a horse race. Sebby enlists two jockeys to do the heavy lifting, but Mike will have to place the bets with a string of shady bookmakers because Sebby has run out of credit. First, he needs to establish his credentials by losing a few bets—that's the easy part. The hard part comes when the horses who are supposed to win the fixed race collide and fall en route to the big payoff. One jockey is left paralyzed, the other is overcome by a need to confess, and Mike is left holding the bag for thousands in debts that he has no way of repaying. Just to survive, he'll need to do things he wouldn't have thought himself capable of doing, but he does them all the same. It is a descent into darkness that can only end in calamity, but the reader, swept up in the narrative momentum, can no more look away than Mike can avoid damnation, if not death. Dixon has written a cautionary tale that is not easy to enjoy but even harder to forget." Booklist

Dixon, Stephen, 1936-

Frog. British Am. Pub. 1991 769p

ISBN 0-945167-43-1; 0-945167-41-5 (pa)

LC 91-12639

This fictional work presents stories about the life of a writer named Howard Tetch. He is "a New Yorker by birth and temperament, a teacher living in Baltimore who has come to academia late and almost by accident. . . . In the chapter 'Frog Remembers,' in which Howard seems to be elderly, divorced, and on his own, he tries to recall how he met Denise, his ex-wife, at a friend's house. Later in the text, however, in 'Frog Dances,' the story of the meeting is completely different, and in 'Frog Restarts,' in which it seems his wife has died, there is another version." Am Book Rev

"'Frog' is a narrative that leaps forward and lands sideways and flops over backward, croaking in dissonant pitches from chapter to chapter and contradicting itself whenever it pleases. . . . [The book], though billed as a novel, looks very much like a crazy quilt of short stories. Does that matter? Surprisingly, not very much. For no reader can fail to grasp that these often mutually exclusive scenarios for the family of a writer called Howard Tetch convey the jumpy landscape of that writer's mind." N Y Times Book Rev

I; a novel. McSweeney's Books 2002 338p $18

ISBN 0-9719047-07-0

"Reading this novel made up of interlinked stories can feel like being trapped in a small room with someone who insists on telling you every damn thing that crosses his mind. I., the hero, is an older writer stuck in a life that seems increasingly hard to endure: his wife is chronically ill, his two daughters find him difficult at best, and he is often gripped by an unfocussed and uncontrollable anger. But from this grim material emerges a moving and oddly funny book, as I. takes refuge in reveries of the past, recounting stories of Thanksgiving Day parades, meals in Paris, family quarrels, and the courtship of his wife. He also imagines myriad scenarios that might have happened but didn't; these unlived possibilities underscore the contingency of even our deepest relationships, and the ways in which we can be haunted by the alternatives." New Yorker

Followed by: End of I (2006)

Interstate; a novel. Holt & Co. 1995 374p

ISBN 0-8050-2654-1

LC 94-40174

Dixon, Stephen, 1936-—*Continued*

In this novel, "eight narratives are alternative replays of a . . . moment that transpires in the book's opening pages: an act of random violence in which a man [Nathan Frey]and his two daughters are shot at by punks in a passing van, and one of the girls is killed." Libr J

"Italo Calvino and Alain Robbe-Grillet have also written novels that begin again and again, revising themselves, but the subjects of these novels are only themselves. Neither of them has brought off anything like the broken eloquence of Nathan's voice, which is as distinct and original and American as Mark Twain's, if otherwise very different. . . . Neither Italo Calvino nor Alain Robbe-Grillet ever brought off anything so cruelly audacious (although they tried) or so upsetting as 'Interstate' – or even attempted the muted beauty of the novel's last few pages, as Nathan performs the ordinary rituals of fatherhood, haunted by everything that has gone before." N Y Times Book Rev

Old friends; a novel. Melville House Pub 2004 220p $22.95

ISBN 0-9749609-2-6   LC 2004-16101

"Dixon follows the lives of two writers from the time they meet as young men until late middle age. Neither Irv nor Leonard has achieved any great fame, and though there's a good deal of writerly chatter, it's really background music to the story of the daily struggles of two aging men and their families. Their lives are tragic, but not dramatically so—Leonard slowly fades into Lyme disease-induced dementia while Irv is busy caring for his crippled wife. What makes this book so good is Dixon's ability to invent characters just average enough that readers can identify with the banality of their pain." Publ Wkly

Dobyns, Stephen, 1941-

Saratoga strongbox; a Charlie Bradshaw mystery. Viking 1998 198p $21.95

ISBN 0-670-87692-5   LC 98-2886

This Bradshaw racetrack adventure "begins when his sometime partner, Vic Plotz, agrees to pick up a mysterious suitcase in Montreal for a wealthy Saratoga entrepreneur. Ex-cop Charlie is soon investigating an assortment of strange characters, looking for a murderer." Libr J

"Dobyns keeps a grip on his farcical plot and gives his rambunctious characters plenty of room to win, place and show off." N Y Times Book Rev

Doctorow, Cory

Down and out in the Magic Kindgom. TOR Bks. 2003 208p $22.95

ISBN 0-7653-0436-8   LC 2002-73277

"A Tom Doherty Associates book"

"Jules, a relative youngster at more than a century old, is a contented citizen of the Bitchun Society that has filled Earth and near-space since shortage and death were overcome. . . . What Jules wants to do is move to Disney World, join the ad-hoc crew that runs the park and fine-tune the Haunted Mansion ride to make it even more wonderful. When his prudently stored consciousness abruptly awakens in a cloned body, he learns that he was murdered; evidently he's in the way of somebody else's dreams. . . . Doctorow has served up a nicely understated dish: meringue laced with caffeine." Publ Wkly

Overclocked; stories of the future present. Thunder's Mouth Press 2007 285p pa $15.95

ISBN 978-1-56025-981-7; 1-56025-981-7

Contents: Printcrime; When sysadmins ruled the earth; Anda's game; I, robot; I row-boat; After the siege

"As these stories illustrate, [Doctorow] has a knack for identifying those seminal trends of our current landscape that will in all likelihood determine the shape of our future(s). Add in a recursive affection for past landmarks of SF . . ., and a gentle empathy for the underdogs in such scenarios, and you get a winning narrative and ideational combination." Sci Fi Wkly

Doctorow, E. L., 1931-

Billy Bathgate; a novel. Random House 1989 323p

ISBN 0-394-52529-9

          * LC 88-42820

"Having grown up poor but ambitious on the Bronx's Bathgate Avenue during the Depression, young Billy is now being educated in the ways of the world. . . . [He] is a gangster-in-training employed by [Dutch Schultz]. . . . Billy falls for 'the Dutchman's' latest lady—a beauty named Drew Preston who eventually reciprocates his youthful passion. Soon Billy is questioning the actions of the mob he was so eager to join as he seeks to protect Drew from its vengeance." Libr J

This is the "story of Billy's education, conducted on an extravagant scale. Doctorow brings a nice sense of moral ambiguity and creates characters who develop or deteriorate at an appropriate pace. His fecund run-on sentences are a pleasure to read. It all adds up to that rarity: a formal literary work that's also hugely entertaining." Newsweek

The book of Daniel; a novel. Random House 1971 303p

ISBN 0-394-46271-8

          *

"The trial of Julius and Ethel Rosenberg in 1950-51 for espionage was a cause célèbre during the fifties. The justice of administering the death penalty to that pair is still argued, particularly by the sons of the Rosenbergs. In this novel, which is based on that case, Daniel Isaacson tells of the effect of that execution on his childhood, marriage, and career. The whole period of pre-World War II radicalism, the tyranny of the McCarthy era, the peace march on the Pentagon in 1967, the nature of left-wing politics in the United States are the elements that make this a provocative sociopolitical novel." Shapiro. Fic for Youth. 3d edition

City of God; a novel. Random House 2000 272p

ISBN 0-679-44783-0   LC 99-53215

"In fall 1999, a brass cross disappears from St. Timothy's Episcopal Church in Manhattan and reappears at an Upper West Side synagogue, forcing clergy deep into a religious mystery." Libr J

This is Doctorow's "most vital—and most difficult—work yet. . . . Without linear plot or unified voice, City of God is tessellated, a mosaic touching on love and loneliness, faith and physics. It glints and glimmers, reflecting off rather than building upon itself, and adding up to a sum greater than its multifarious parts." Nation

Doctorow, E. L., 1931-—*Continued*

Homer & Langley; a novel. Random House 2009 208p $26

ISBN 978-1-4000-6494-6; 1-4000-6494-5

LC 2009-06959

"Toward the end of E.L. Doctorow's novel 'Homer & Langley,' narrator Homer Collyer, the real-life Manhattanite notorious for his and his brother Langley's reclusive lifestyle and hoarding of sundry objects, frets about their legacy: 'For what could be more terrible than being turned into a mythic joke? How could we cope, once dead and gone, with no one available to reclaim our history?' In attempting to recover the Collyer brothers' history from those who would reduce their existence to eccentricities, Doctorow probes the inner workings of the brothers' minds and extends their lives well beyond 1947, when the real Collyers died." San Antonio Express-News

"Cunningly panoramic. . . . Doctorow has packed this tale with episodes of existential wonder that capture the brothers in all their fascinating wackiness." Elle

Loon Lake. Random House 1980 c1979 258p

ISBN 0-394-50691-X LC 79-5526

Set in the 1930's the narrative "covers several picaresque years in the life of a young roughneck from Paterson, the son of wretchedly poor mill hands, who runs away from home, joins a gang of hobos, becomes a carnival roustabout, and stumbles accidentally onto Loon Lake, the vast Adirondack estate of the steel tycoon F. W. Bennett. One of the old industrialist's toys is a gangster's moll who sneaks out of Loon Lake with Joe, and the two settle down for a while in a steel town owned by one of Bennett's many companies. She leaves him, and Joe goes back to Loon Lake [and] is taken in by the old man." Commentary

"Doctorow has written a myth about the inheritance of America. Many techniques enhance the epic feeling. The novel is set in 1936, yet ranges across the first half of the century, even as it shifts viewpoints from the young man's memories to the poet's verses." Books of the Times

The march. Random House 2005 363p $25.95

ISBN 0-375-50671-3 LC 2005-46452

"The march in question is that of General William Tecumseh Sherman and his Union soldiers as they slash and burn their way through Georgia and the Carolinas, and the 'march to freedom' as liberated slaves fall in step with the liberating army. But it is also, given the poetic depth of Doctorow's vision, the great march of time and of humanity in all its cruelty and glory. As Doctorow dramatizes the fury, conviction, and chaos of the Civil War, he portrays historical figures, as he is wont to do, most electrifyingly Sherman himself. But he focuses most on brilliantly imagined characters who embody the epic conflicts of that cataclysmic era, including Pearl, the smart and courageous daughter of a slave and slave owner; an excessively clinical military surgeon; the valiant daughter of a Southern judge; a freed slave who becomes a war photographer; and Arly, a scheming Rebel soldier who provides shrewdly comic relief. Doctorow writes with blazing clarity about the 'brutal romance' of war and its gruesome realities, with lyrical splendor about nature, and with wry wisdom and nimble satire about human folly." Booklist

Ragtime. Modern Library 1997 320p $18.95

ISBN 0-679-60297-6

* LC 97-42251

This is a reissue of the title first published 1975 by Random House

"The lives of an upper-middle-class family in New Rochelle; a black ragtime musician who loses his love, his child, and his life because of bigotry; and a poor immigrant Jewish family are interwoven in this early-twentieth-century story. There are cameo appearances by wellknown figures of that period: Houdini, anarchist Emma Goldman, actress Evelyn Nesbit, Henry Ford, and J.P. Morgan, whose magnificent library plays an important part in the story. The book mingles fact and fiction in portraying the era of ragtime." Shapiro. Fic for Youth. 3d edition

Sweet land stories. Random House 2004 147p $22.95

ISBN 1-400-06204-7 LC 2003-58780

Contents: A house on the plains; Baby Wilson; Jolene: a life; Walter John Harmon; Child, dead, in the rose garden

"As one might expect of Doctorow, the title is ironic. In settings that range across the U.S., most of the alienated characters in the five stories here find life anything but sweet as they struggle to surmount the stigmas of poverty, lack of education and their instincts to gamble against the odds. . . . In this knowing treatment of the cynical abuse of power, Doctorow uses the spare, laconic style endemic to thrillers and builds suspense with sure strokes. Boring like a laser into the failures of the American dream, he captures the resilience of those who won't accept defeat." Publ Wkly

The waterworks. Random House 1994 253p

ISBN 0-394-58754-5 LC 93-44735

"Martin Pemberton, renegade son of rich, unscrupulous Augustus Pemberton and favorite freelance of the persevering editor of the New York *Telegram*, . . . narrates this tale. First, Martin claims to have seen his dead father on a horse-drawn omnibus, and then he disappears. The worried editor contacts Inspector Edmund Donne—the only honest cop in 1870s New York, where the Tweed Ring holds sway—and eventually they discover that the ailing Augustus is part of an experiment by the brilliant Dr. Sartorius to prolong the lives of several old men rich enough to foot the bill." Libr J

Welcome to Hard Times. Simon & Schuster 1960 180p o.p.

"A novel about a small town in the barren West at the close of the last century. . . . The tale revolves around a bad-man who destroys the town of Hard Times in one day, causally and cruelly; a mayor who is too weak to kill the bad-man but who is hopeful enough to rebuild the town; and a woman of easy virtue who waits, in terror and hatred, for the return of the bad-man." Springfield Repub

Docx, Edward

The calligrapher. Houghton Mifflin 2003 360p $24

ISBN 0-618-34397-0 LC 2003-51149

Docx, Edward—*Continued*

The novel's "protagonist, Jasper Jackson, is a Londoner whose current job is to transcribe the Songs and Sonnets of John Donne for a wealthy client. Like Donne, Jasper is also a relentless womanizer, a charming cad who lives for love affairs. When the woman of his dreams appears in his own garden, Jasper succumbs to real love for the first time and slowly begins to realize what it feels like to be the pursuer rather than the pursued." Publ Wkly

Pravda. Houghton Mifflin Co. 2007 395p pa $13.95

ISBN 978-0-618-53440-1; 0-618-53440-7

LC 2007-8523

Published in Great Britain with title: Self help

"Twins Gabriel and Isabella Glover, both 32 and leading lackluster lives—she at a New York PR firm, he the editor in London of Self-Help! magazine—see another crack form in their perennially tortured existences when their mother, Maria, who defected to marry their British father, dies alone in St. Petersburg. . . . All are unaware of an additional family member: Arkady Artamenkov, their mother's first son, who had been kept afloat by Maria's financial assistance and the guiding hand of his junkie friend, Henry Whey. After the checks stop, Henry hatches a plan to send Arkady to plead for money from the family that doesn't know he exists." Publ Wkly

The author's "ability to evoke the atmosphere of a city is almost Dickensian. . . . Docx can place you within each heart-stopping moment, speed up and slow down time from one sentence to the next. . . . A gripping read that will engage, delight, and engross." Guardian (London)

Doenges, Judy, 1959-

God of gods

In Doenges, J. What she left me: stories and a novella p116-73

What she left me: stories and a novella. Middlebury College Press 1999 173p $22.95

ISBN 0-87451-937-3   LC 99-30945

"The Katharine Bakeless Nason literary publication prizes"

Contents: What she left me; MIB; Crooks; Solved; The money stays, the poeple go; Occidental; Disaster; The whole numbers of families; Incognito; God of Gods [novella]

"Marginal may be the best overall descriptor for these characters, who, whether working class or elite, and despite outward appearances, roil with inner turmoil. Certainly, the sad poignancy and the dark humor of their lives touch us deeply." Booklist

Doerr, Harriet

Consider this, señora. Harcourt Brace & Co. 1993 241p

ISBN 0-15-193103-8   LC 93-21471

This "novel focuses on expatriate Americans in Mexico searching for love, connection and meaning. Three women buy land on the hillside hard by a poverty-stricken village whose inhabitants view them with gentle bewilderment." Publ Wkly

"Doerr instills each of her memorable characters with great dignity and resilience, and bestows upon her entranced readers a deep sense of peace and wonder." Booklist

Stones for Ibarra. Viking 1984 214p

ISBN 0-670-19203-1

* LC 83-47861

"When Sara and Richard Everton pack up their belongings and mortgage themselves to leave California for a small village in Mexico, their friends think they are crazy. Many of the Mexican natives in the village of Ibarra also consider the two gringos incredible. While Sara restores the house that had belonged to Richard's grandparents, Richard restores a copper mine that had been his family's, and thereby gives employment to many of the villagers. We learn that Richard has leukemia and has been given just a few years to live, but it is the lives of the villagers that are more full of tragedy, religious commitment, and reliance on talismans and prayers. There is a strength among these people and an acceptance of all that life brings which make them memorable. Learning from them, perhaps, Sara finally accepts the inevitability of her husband's death." Shapiro. Fic for Youth. 3d edition

The tiger in the grass; stories and other inventions. Viking 1995 210p

ISBN 0-670-86471-4   LC 95-32391

Contents: The flowering stick; Carnations; The extinguishing of Great-Aunt Alice; The seasons; Sun, pure air, and a view; The local train; Way stations; The watchman at the gate; Saint's Day; Please; Low tide at four; Like heaven; A sleeve of rain

"In this elegant collection of stories and 'inventions,' never before published in book form, Doerr opens the window on her own past: childhood in California, marriage, . . . child-rearing experiences and the bold decision to return to school after the death of her husband. These are revelatory tales full of tenderness, humor, and gratitude, but the jewels of the collection are Doerr's stories about life in Mexico, the place dearest to her heart." Booklist

Doherty, P. C.

The Anubis slayings; a story of intrigue and murder set in ancient Egypt. St. Martin's Minotaur 2001 c2000 308p

ISBN 0-312-27658-3

First published 2000 in the United Kingdom

An historical mystery set in ancient Egypt "where principal judge Amertoke must solve a series of gruesome murders. It is 1497 B.C.E. and the Pharaoh Queen Hatusu (Hatshepsut) is in the process of consolidating power and taking over as ruler after her husband's death. She has just defeated the Mitanni, and formal peace negotiations are in progress. Someone wearing a jackal mask that resembles the god Anubis is poisoning people." Booklist

"Although he's essentially working with the elements of a locked-room mystery, Doherty cloaks his technique in the morbid trappings of the Theban death industry." N Y Times Book Rev

Doherty, P. C.—*Continued*

The gates of hell; a mystery of Alexander the Great; [by] Paul Doherty. Carroll & Graf Pubs. 2003 292p il $24

ISBN 0-7867-1157-4

This mystery revolves "around the military exploits of Alexander the Great and the behind-the-scenes adventures of Telamon, his boyhood friend and personal physician. When Alexander's determination to invade and conquer Halicarnassus, a city inextricably linked to his infamous father, is threatened by an unsettling series of murders within his own inner circle, Telamon must use his considerable powers of detection in order to uncover a treasonous plot linked to the legendary Pythian manuscript. Booklist

The godless man; a mystery of Alexander the Great; [by] Paul Doherty. Carroll & Graf Pubs. 2002 303p $25

ISBN 0-7867-0995-2   LC 2002-67397

"After his mighty victory at the Granicus in 334 B.C., Alexander the Great sweeps deeper into Persia in this multilayered and entertaining mystery, but when his army captures the city of Ephesus, the march of conquest seems doomed to halt in the face of intrigue and multiple murders." Publ Wkly

The house of death; a mystery of Alexander the Great; {by} Paul C. Doherty. Carroll & Graf Pubs. 2001 276p

ISBN 0-7867-0853-0   LC 2001-28828

"Anxious to dominate the Persian empire in 334 B.C.E., Alexander the Great awaits a sign from the gods. He instead finds intrigue, secret agendas, spies, and murder. The appearance of boyhood friend Telamon gives him a trusted ear—he hopes." Libr J

"Fans of ancient historical mysteries will find themselves in superbly practiced hands." Publ Wkly

Doig, Ivan

Bucking the sun; a novel. Simon & Schuster 1996 412p

ISBN 0-684-81171-5   LC 96-3814

The author "begins this saga with adultery and death, then moves backward to examine the causes. Just as the building of the mammoth Fort Peck Dam transforms the Montana countryside, it radically alters the lives of its Depression-era inhabitants. In particular, members of the Duff clan abandon subsistence farming and move to the construction boomtowns. There a father, three brothers, and their wives confront the task of building the largest earthen dam in the world, brave the dangers of such labor, and battle among themselves. . . . This richly detailed narrative offers comedy, passion, and adventure." Libr J

Dancing at the Rascal Fair. Atheneum Pubs. 1987 405p

ISBN 0-689-11764-7

* LC 87-18672

Chronologically the first in the author's Montana trilogy

"The settlement of Montana between 1890 and 1919 is recounted through the quiet but compelling life of Angus McCaskill, a young Scotsman who travels with his friend Rob Barclay to Montana's Two Medicine Country to homestead." Libr J

"If the thorny individualism of Rob and Angus results in lives that are never easy, they are rich in incident and growth, beautifully described in Doig's strong, savory prose. America's frontier history comes vividly to life in this absorbing saga filled with memorable characters." Publ Wkly

The eleventh man. Harcourt 2008 406p $26

ISBN 978-0-15-101243-5; 0-15-101243-1

LC 2008-10046

In this novel, "11 starters of a close-knit Montana college championship football team enlist as the U.S. hits the thick of WWII and are capriciously flung around the globe in various branches of the service. Ben Reinking, initially slated for pilot training, is jerked from his plane and more or less forced to become a war correspondent for the semisecret Threshold Press War Project, a propaganda arm of the combined armed forces. His orders: to travel the world, visiting and writing profiles on each of his heroic teammates. The fetching Women's Airforce Service Pilot who flies him around, Cass Standish, is married to a soldier fighting in the South Pacific, which leads to anguish for them both . . . . Meanwhile, Ben's former teammates are being killed one by one, often, it seems, being deliberately put into harm's way. Doig adroitly keeps Ben on track, offering an old-fashioned greatest generation story, well told." Publ Wkly

English Creek. Atheneum Pubs. 1984 339p

ISBN 0-689-11478-8   LC 84-45051

This volume in the Montana trilogy chronologically follows Dancing at the Rascal Fair

"In the summer of 1939, in the high country of western Montana, 14-year-old Jick McCaskill wants to understand who he is and why. He lives in a boy's dream of wilderness, mountains, sheep ranches, national forests, and an amazing variety of small-town characters. His father is a forest ranger, his mother a practical, hard-nosed local woman; his brother wants to forego college for a girl and a cowboy's life. The summer climaxes in a forest fire that leads Jick and his father to discuss and understand some painful hidden events of their personal histories." Libr J

This "is a sensitive coming-of-age story as well as a portrait of a society still looking to its frontier past, but about to be engulfed by the future. The result is both highly personal and deeply engaging." Best Sellers

Mountain time; a novel. Scribner 1999 316p

ISBN 0-684-83295-X   LC 99-14324

This novel focuses on "sisters Lexa and Mariah McCaskill. Lexa's marriage to a forest ranger and her days as cook in Alaska are behind her; now sturdy, capable Lexa runs a catering service in Seattle. She lives with rugged environmental journalist Mitch Rozier, another escapee from rough life in northern Montana. At 50, Mitch is facing a double crisis: the newspaper where his column appears is about to fold, and his foxy, rapacious father, Lyle, a notorious land despoiler, is dying of leukemia and has summoned him back to Twin Sulphur Springs. Lexa goes back to Montana, too, bringing her sexy sister, Mariah, just returned to the States after a year-long photographing expedition around the world. Lyle's illness and death unleash complex memories and future shocks." Publ Wkly

"A worthy addition to Doig's impressive saga of the twentieth-century West." Booklist

Doig, Ivan—*Continued*

Prairie nocturne; a novel. Scribner 2003 371p $26

ISBN 0-7432-0135-3 LC 2003-50385

"Susan Duff, ever the recalcitrant singer, is now approaching middle age and living alone after a love affair with the wealthy Wesley Williamson. When Williamson's chauffeur, former rodeo clown Montgomery Rathbun, comes to him with the idea of honing his vocal talents, Williamson brings him to Susan. But Monty is black, and when he and Susan begin late-night voice lessons in a secluded cabin, thinking no one the wiser, its revelation incites the local Ku Klux Klan. Monty flees to New York, where he establishes a brilliant career as a singer of spirituals. On a concert tour back out west, however, old feuds reignite." Libr J

"By multiplying, deepening and texturing the genealogy of the Two Medicine country in the course of six novels, Doig has staked his claim as one of Montana's essential literary witnesses. . . . And no other writer since A.B. Guthrie has been more determined to evoke the supersized grandeur of Big Sky country, especially in a time when it was emptier and more suited to mythologizing than it is today." Washington Post Book World

Ride with me, Mariah Montana. Atheneum Pubs. 1990 324p

ISBN 0-689-12019-2 LC 90-35834

Concluding volume of the author's Montana trilogy

"To explore the meaning of Montana's century of statehood, 65-year-old Jick McCaskill, his photographer daughter Mariah, and her newspaper columnist ex-husband Riley Wright tour the Treasure State in Jick's Winnebago. While Riley writes on-the-scene dispatches and Mariah takes photos of the places they visit, Jick, the narrator, recounts the state's—and his family's—good and bad times. A lengthy picaresque with innumerable well-crafted vignettes, this leisurely novel could easily serve as a tour guide of Montana's historic places. As the miles go by, Riley and Mariah again fall in and out of love, and Jick, a widower, unexpectedly finds a new mate." Libr J

The whistling season. Harcourt 2006 345p $25

ISBN 978-0-15-101237-4; 0-15-101237-7

LC 2005-25457

"Set in the early 1900s, this novel is a nostalgic, bittersweet story about a widower, his three sons, and the year these boys spend in a one-room country schoolhouse. The novel begins with the father, Oliver, hiring a widowed housekeeper named Rose from Minneapolis (her advertisement reads 'Can't Cook but Doesn't Bite'). She arrives with her unconventional brother, Morrie, in tow. Morrie is something of a scholar, and he soon finds himself pressed into service as a replacement teacher. During the course of the novel, these intriguing and unpredictable characters come together in surprising and uplifting ways. This is an affectionate, heartwarming tale that also celebrates a vanished way of life and laments its passing." Libr J

Dolan, Harry

Bad things happen. Amy Einhorn Books/G. P. Putman's Sons 2009 338p $24.95

ISBN 978-0-399-15563-5 LC 2008-54628

"Shortly after a man who calls himself David Loogan arrives in Ann Arbor, he gets a job as assistant editor to Tom Kristoll and begins sleeping with Tom's wife, Laura. Then Tom asks him to help bury a body lying in the office of Gray Streets, the mystery magazine they edit. When Tom is found dead six floors below his office window, Det. Elizabeth Waishkey begins to investigate—and so does Loogan. Several other murders occur, all of which seem linked somehow to Gray Streets and to its various authors." Libr J

"Although the plot is fairly outlandish, the narrative comes with startling developments and nicely tricky reversals. There's also something appealingly offbeat about the wry, dry tone of its academic humor, which has much to do with the self-important authors who figure in the hectic plot ." N Y Times Book Rev

Domínguez, Carlos María, 1955-

The house of paper; illustrations by Peter Sís; translated from the Spanish by Nick Caistor. Harcourt 2005 103p il $18

ISBN 0-15-101147-8 LC 2005-02401

Original Spanish edition, 2004

"Bluma Lennon, distinguished professor of Latin American literature at Cambridge, is hit by a car while crossing the street, immersed in a volume of Emily Dickinson's poems. Several months after her untimely demise, a package arrives for her from Argentina—a copy of a Conrad novel, encrusted in cement and inscribed with a mysterious dedication. Bluma's successor in the department (and a former lover) travels to Buenos Aires to track down the sender, one Carlos Brauer, who turns out to have disappeared." Publisher's note

The author has "written a wonderfully amusing account of how books can dominate the life of the inveterate collector. It is itself a small book, beautifully translated by Nick Caistor and charmingly illustrated by Peter Sis, and you may buy it without worrying about finding room for it on your shelves. I have already found such a place–between a copy of a novel by Italo Calvino and a collection of the stories of Dino Buzzati. It should be happy there, with its Italian cousins, a jewel of whimsy supported on each side by authors from roughly the same tradition." N Y Times Book Rev

Donaldson, Stephen R.

The Illearth war. Holt, Rinehart & Winston 1977 407p il (Chronicles of Thomas Covenant, the Unbeliever)

ISBN 0-03-022776-3 LC 77-8621

In this second volume, Lord Foul the Despiser continues his attack against the Land with the Illearth Stone. Covenant and the daughter of the High Lord, Elena, undertake a mission into a mountain region, where they hope they will find the ancient gnostic power that will combat the Stone

Lord Foul's bane. Holt, Rinehart & Winston 1977 369p il (Chronicles of Thomas Covenant, the Unbeliever) o.p. LC 77-73868

Thomas Covenant, a man burdened with a stigma that has isolated him, is suddenly sent to a mysterious magic world known as the Land. The Land has an immortal enemy—Lord Foul the Despiser—who wishes to destroy it.

Donaldson, Stephen R.—*Continued*
In Thomas, who does not believe in the Land's life-restoring powers, Lord Foul thinks he has found the perfect tool for his purpose

The One Tree. Ballantine Bks. 1982 475p (Chronicles of Thomas Covenant, the Unbeliever)
ISBN 0-345-29898-5   LC 81-17596
"A Del Rey book"
This is the central volume of the second trilogy about the Land
"Covenant finds that his role as savior of the Land must be shared with another from our world, Dr. Linden Avery. . . . To stop Lord Foul's terrible concatenation of plagues, the Sunbane, they sail with giants on a granite ship in search of the One Tree. Covenant hopes to fashion from it a new Staff of the Law to restore the natural order Foul has overturned." Publ Wkly

The power that preserves. Holt, Rinehart & Winston 1977 379p il (Chronicles of Thomas Covenant, the Unbeliever)
ISBN 0-03-022781-X   LC 77-10814
In this final volume of the first trilogy Covenant makes his way to the stronghold of Lord Foul the Despiser. He is accompanied by his friend Saltheart Foamfollower, a Giant. But it is Covenant who must meet Foul in final combat, to ensure survival for the Land and to achieve salvation for himself
"Below the stirring adventure tale is a poignant and profoundly religious chronicle of a quest for self-esteem and peace." Booklist

The runes of the earth. G.P. Putnam's Sons 2004 xx, 532p (Last chronicles of Thomas Covenant) $26.95
ISBN 0-399-15232-6   LC 2004-50526
"It is 10 years since Thomas Covenant's death, and Linden Avery runs the small mental hospital in which Covenant's widow, Joan, is confined. Roger Covenant, newly turned 21, visits Avery and tries to get his mother released. Failing at that, he kidnaps Joan as well as Avery's adopted son, then commits several murders and flees to the Land, the other world of Covenant sagas. Roger is clearly doing Lord Foul's bidding, and Avery has no choice but to follow him. She discovers that in the Land three and a half millennia have passed. The Haruchai are now called the Masters and distrust Earthpower, and an old man, Anele, who is full of Earthpower, is key to finding the lost and essential Staff of Law. . . . Expect readers to swarm." Booklist

White gold wielder. Ballantine Bks. 1983 485p il (Chronicles of Thomas Covenant, the Unbeliever)
ISBN 0-345-30307-5   LC 82-20640
"A Del Rey book"
This is the concluding volume of the second trilogy about the Land
"At the end of 'The One Tree,' Covenant failed to create a new Staff of Law to deliver the Land from the Sunbane, so he, Linden Avery, and their companions set out across the northern wastes to Revelstone, where Covenant extinguishes the Banefire. The paradox of white gold and venom has set him against his friends, however; when he faces Lord Foul at Mount Thunder, they believe that he will betray the Land, until that enigmatic created being, Vain, achieves his destiny." Libr J

The wounded Land. Ballantine Bks. 1980 497p il (Chronicles of Thomas Covenant, the Unbeliever)
ISBN 0-345-28647-2   LC 79-20644
"A Del Rey book"
This is the first volume of the second trilogy about the Land
"In the first of the second trilogy of his adventures, leper Thomas Covenant returns to the mysterious Land after nearly 4000 years have passed there (ten years in earth time). Dr. Linden Avery unexpectedly joins him and goes through the same denial and disbelief he had suffered before. Now the Land is suffering from unending plagues called the Sunbane, inflicted by the evil Lord Foul whom Covenant had defeated but not destroyed on his last visit. Although it is not necessary to have read the previous three to appreciate the breadth and scope of this grim fantasy, for those who have 'The Wounded Land' is absolutely compelling." SLJ

Donoghue, Emma, 1969-

The sealed letter. Harcourt 2008 396p $26
ISBN 978-0-15-101549-8; 0-15-101549-X
          LC 2008-14677
"In Victorian England, spinster Emily 'Fido' Faithfull is earnestly engaged in the emerging women's movement. But her orderly life is disrupted when she becomes reacquainted with Helen, a former friend just returning from Malta, where her admiral husband has been posted for seven years. Though Helen is Fido's polar opposite in temperament and approach to life, they quickly reestablish a close friendship. Helen—selfish, manipulative, and thoroughly disenchanted with her husband—engages in risky behavior that results in a scandalous divorce trial, and Fido is caught in the middle of a struggle between the friend she so blindly believes in and the admiral, whom she respects." Libr J
Donoghue "has sifted through court records, newspapers, correspondence, and even Faithfull's later novels. She makes 150-year-old events immediate. . . . What could have been mere Victorian melodrama resonates here with emotional truth." Quill Quire

Slammerkin. Harcourt 2001 336p $30
ISBN 0-15-100672-5   LC 00-49867
First published 2000 in the United Kingdom
"Mary Saunders's mother scratches out a meager living as a seamstress in 1760s London, but Mary longs for a more luxurious life with fine ribbons and clothes. At 13, she sneers at her mother's suggestion that she take up the needle, then makes a fateful mistake that leads her into prostitution." Libr J
"In her storytelling, the author shrewdly alternates the point of view, a technique that, rather than feeling gratuitous and shticky as it so often does these days, works to put Mary in a delicious pickle, since the satisfaction of her deepest desires, and the revelation of her secret career, could crush those for whom she—and we—come to feel real affection." N Y Times Book Rev

Touchy subjects; stories. Harcourt 2006 280p $24
ISBN 978-0-15-101386-9; 0-15-101386-1
          LC 2005-26170

Donoghue, Emma, 1969-—*Continued*

Contents: Touchy subjects; Expecting; The man who wrote on beaches; Oops; Through the night; Do they know it's Christmas?; Lavender's blue; The cost of things; Pluck; Good deed; The sanctuary of hands; WritOr; Team men; Speaking in tongues; The welcome; The dormition of the virgin; Enchantment; Baggage; Necessary noise

Donoghue "exhibits adeptness in the short story form in this collection of 19 tales that, without a hint of pretension but with wisdom extending far beyond the placidness of her prose style, isolates aspects of a character or a moment of revelation for a character. . . . Her stories find secure footing where poignancy and humor intersect, and their geniality will prove an asset to librarians encouraging readers exclusively devoted to the novel to–come on–try some short stories." Booklist

Donohue, John J., 1956-

Sensei. Thomas Dunne Bks. 2003 258p $23.95
ISBN 0-312-28812-3   LC 2002-32507
"Someone who calls himself Ronin—masterless Samurai—is apparently killing off martial-arts masters across the U.S., and Connor Burke, a university professor and martial-arts student, is brought into the investigation by his brother, a New York detective assigned to the case. Connor recruits his own sensei, Yamshita, and this unusual pair uncover the facts with a combination of mental skill and good, old-fashioned (amateur) detective work." Booklist

Donohue, Keith, 1959-

Angels of destruction; a novel. Shaye Areheart Books 2009 347p $24
ISBN 978-0-307-45025-8; 0-307-45025-2
                              LC 2008-21277
"One night in the middle of winter, widow Margaret Quinn hears a tiny rap on her door. To her surprise, she finds a 9-year-old girl shivering in the cold. She shuffles the child into her home and, soon enough, into her heart. Margaret has grown reclusive with the years. A decade earlier, in 1975, her daughter, Erica, ran off with a high school sweetheart to join a West Coast revolutionary group called Angels of Destruction. Not long after, her husband, Paul, died. . . . When the beguiling 9-year-old says she has no family and no home, Margaret's mind races. She names the girl Norah and decides to pass her off as a granddaughter. Norah is her conniving equal, and their bond deepens at breakneck speed. Enrolled in elementary school, Norah befriends a boy named Sean, whose father abandoned him and his mother. Naturally withdrawn, given the circumstances of his life, Sean warms to Norah, who quickly reveals — first to him and later to classmates and adults — ethereal displays of magic." Pittsburgh Post-Gazette

"The book's coda is beautiful and wrenching, yet still leaves its protagonists and readers open to the possibility that the miraculous, once glimpsed, might recur." Washington Post Book World

The stolen child; a novel. Nan A. Talese 2006 319p $23.95
ISBN 0-385-51616-9   LC 2005-53828

"Inspired by a W.B. Yeats poem, [this novel] is a modern retelling of the changeling myth, in which a child is stolen away by fairies who leave one of their own in its place. In this case, seven-year-old Henry Day is the changeling; the real Henry is now called Aniday and lives in the woods with a group of other stolen-away children. We follow Henry and Aniday in alternating chapters as Henry grows up and Aniday, forever seven, does not. Henry tries to fit into his new life, but traces of his previous existence keep revealing themselves . . . . Meanwhile, Aniday struggles to hold on to his humanity even as he forgets who he was." Libr J

"On the surface, Donohue may seem to have written a clever debut novel about fairies. But the real triumph of the book is that, while our backs were turned, he has performed a switch and delivered a luminous and thrilling novel about our humanity." Washington Post Book World

Donovan, Anne, 1961-

Buddha Da. Carroll & Graf Publishers 2004 330p pa $14
ISBN 0-7867-1336-4 (pa)   LC 2004-45770
"Anne Marie's dad, a Glaswegian painter and decorator, has always been game for a laugh. So when he first takes up meditation at the Buddhist Center, no one takes him seriously. But as Jimmy becomes more involved in a search for the spiritual, his beliefs start to come into conflict with the needs of his wife, Liz. Cracks appear in their apparently happy family life, and the ensuing events change the lives of each family member." Publisher's note

"The transcribed brogue and gag-rich premise initially lend Buddha Da a slapstick feel. But as Jimmy's engagement with Buddhism deepens, the novel matures into an astute exploration of Donovan's enormously appealing characters." N Y Times Book Rev

Donovan, Gerard

Young Irelanders; stories. Overlook Press 2008 223p $24.95
ISBN 978-1-59020-030-8
Contents: Morning swimmers; How long until; Shoplifting in the USA; Country of the grand; By Irish nights; Archeologists; Glass; Another life; The summer of birds; The receptionist; New deal; Harry Dietz; Visit

Donovan "writes convincingly about loss and survival in an Ireland where big gaps remain between what his characters want and what they have." Publ Wkly

Dorris, Michael

Cloud chamber; a novel. Scribner 1997 316p
ISBN 0-684-81567-2   LC 96-42544
Dorris's "first novel, 'A Yellow Raft in Blue Water,' traced the experiences of three generations of modern American Indian women. 'Cloud Chamber' stretches back farther still, to the 19th-century Irish immigrants whose descendants eventually fall in love with some of the black and Indian characters in that earlier book. . . . It tells the stories of five generations who live in Ireland, Kentucky and Seattle and on a Montana reservation." N Y Times Book Rev

"Though not unflawed—a few voices sound confusing-

Dorris, Michael—_Continued_
ly similar and a few characters are more types than people—this is a compellingly readable and emotionally satisfying novel, full of secrets and surprises." Booklist

The crown of Columbus; a novel; {by} Michael
Dorris, Louise Erdrich. HarperCollins Pubs. 1991
382p
ISBN 0-06-016079-9 LC 90-55964
"Told in the very different voices of college professor
lovers Vivian Twostar, Native American single mother,
and Roger Williams, poet of an old New England family,
the collaborative effort flows smoothly. Although estranged during Vivian's pregnancy, both are working on
academic projects concerning the 500th anniversary of
the discovery of North America by Columbus. The collision of their two lives is funny, vivid, and life-
affirming." Libr J

A yellow raft in blue water. Holt & Co. 1987
343p hardcover o.p. pa $14
ISBN 0-8050-0045-3; 0-312-42185-0 (pa)
* LC 86-26947
"The bitter rifts and inevitable bonds between generations are highlighted as a teenaged daughter, mother, and
grand matriarch of an American Indian family tell their
life stories. Humorous and poignant, with unique characters." SLJ

Dorst, Doug

Alive in Necropolis. Riverhead Books 2008
437p $25.95
ISBN 978-1-594-48987-7; 1-594-48987-4
LC 2008-05817
This novel "novel maps the landscape and lives of a
small town where ghosts and the living are sometimes
indistinguishable from one another. That's what police
officer Michael Mercer discovers the night he saves the
life of a teenage boy left unconscious and at the mercy
of the elements in a Colma, Calif., cemetery. Later, Michael witnesses nocturnal incidents that turn out to be the
afterlife activities of local residents who've been dead for
decades." Publ Wkly
"Like Dashiell Hammett, Dorst conveys a hard-bitten
love of the physical San Francisco, the fog-swallowed
town, the sun after rain, the mineshaft drops in temperature. Scenes are rooted in surroundings and the weather.
The fiction seems to possess, and be possessed by, its
beloved Bay. . . . The ghosts are a prime pleasure here.
The prose picks up a quickness in their presence. They
are figures out of newsreels, colorful, iconic." N Y
Times Book Rev

Dos Passos, John

The 42nd parallel. Harper 1930 426p o.p.
First volume of the author's U.S.A. trilogy
The characters "include Fainy McCreary ('Mac'), who
eventually joins the Mexican Revolution; the ruthless J.
Ward Moorehouse; Eleanor Stoddard, with whom he has
an affair; and Charley Anderson, who later becomes a
war hero and airplane manufacturer. These various interlocking strands are designed to show the U.S. on the eve
of the First World War, rather than the development of
particular individuals." Reader's Ency. 3d edition
Followed by 1919
also in Dos Passos, J. U.S.A.

1919. Harcourt Brace & Co. 1932 473p o.p.
In this second volume of the trilogy, the author continues his chronicle of life in America through the war
years, giving glimpses of the lives and characters of five
young Americans—a low caste sailor, the daughter of a
Chicago minister, a young girl from Texas, a radical
Jew, a young poet
"'1919' is literally what so many books are erroneous-
ly called, 'a slice of life.' With infinite skill that slicing
is done by the author, and the raw surface which meets
the reader's eye is the actual living, breathing record of
a period in its most intense manifestation." Chicago Daily Trib
Followed by The big money (1936)
also in Dos Passos, J. U.S.A.

The big money
_In_ Dos Passos, J. U.S.A.

Manhattan transfer. Harper 1925 404p o.p.
"Dos Passos creates a portrait of New York City in the
first quarter of this century by telling the stories of many
people. They include the daughter of an accountant, who
loses hope for any future happiness when her first love
commits suicide; a milkman who rises in status to become a union boss; and an immigrant sailor who starts
as a bartender and becomes a wealthy bootlegger during
Prohibition. There are happy and unhappy endings to
these stories, but always the city plays an important
role." Shapiro. Fic for Youth. 3d edition
also in Dos Passos, J. Novels, 1920-1925

Novels, 1920-1925. Library of America 2003
873p (The library of America, 142) $35
ISBN 1-931082-39-1
* LC 2003-47529
Contents: One man's initiation, 1917; Three soldiers;
Manhattan transfer
One man's initiation, 1917 (1920) focuses on a young
American's experiences in France during a time of war.
Three soldiers (1921) describes the lives of three men
with three different backgrounds—an Indiana farmboy,
an Italian-American store clerk, and a musician hoping to
become a composer—and how they cope with life both
on and off the battlefield. Manhattan transfer is entered
separately.

One man's initiation: 1917
_In_ Dos Passos, J. Novels, 1920-1925

Three soldiers
_In_ Dos Passos, J. Novels, 1920-1925

U.S.A. Library of Am. 1996 1288p $40
ISBN 1-883011-14-0
* LC 95-49282
An omnibus volume containing the trilogy titles: The
42nd parallel, first published 1930; 1919, first published
1932 and The big money, first published 1936
"U.S.A. tries to capture, through a diversity of fictional
techniques, the variety and multiplicity of American life
in the first decades of the 20th cent.; it presents various
interlocking and parallel narratives, against a panoramic
collage of real-life events, snatches of newsreel and popular song, advertisements, etc., with a commentary by the
author as 'The Camera Eye.'" Oxford Companion to
Engl Lit

Doss, James D.

The night visitor; a shaman mystery. Avon Twilight 1999 392p

ISBN 0-380-97721-4   LC 99-25049

Ute lawman Charlie Moon and Shaman Daisy Perika are featured in this "blend of modern murder and ancient beliefs, set on the Southern Ute Reservation in Colorado. Charlie investigates a murder associated with a paleontological dig, while Daisy senses a much older injustice. An excellent addition to the series." Libr J

The shaman's bones. Avon Bks. 1997 276p

ISBN 0-380-97424-X   LC 96-52148

"Even though Ute police officer Charlie Moon's elderly aunt, a well-known visionary and shaman, warns him of impending violence on the Colorado reservation, he is ill prepared for what happens. Events begin with an Indian's bad check but escalate to child abandonment, a vicious attack on a female police trainee, murder, and the theft of another shaman's sacred objects. Doss uses setting and atmosphere to heighten the mystical aspects of his subject and astute characterization to enforce its credibility." Libr J

Dostoevskiĭ, Fedor Mikhaĭlovich   *See* Dostoyevsky, Fyodor, 1821-1881

Dostoyevsky, Fyodor, 1821-1881

The best short stories of Dostoevsky; translated with an introduction by David Magarshack. Modern Lib. 1992 xxvii, 348p

ISBN 0-679-60020-5   LC 92-50214

First Modern Library edition 1955

Contents: White nights; The honest thief; The Christmas tree and a wedding; The peasant Marey; Notes from the underground; A gentle creature; The dream of a ridiculous man

The brothers Karamazov; translated by Constance Garnett. Modern Library 1996 xxi, 880p $21

ISBN 0-679-60181-3

     *

Written 1880

"The main plot involves Fyodor Pavlovich 'Karamazov' and his four sons: Dmitry, Ivan, Alyosha, and the bastard Smerdyakov. Fyodor Pavlovich, a depraved buffoon, is Dmitry's rival for the affections of the local siren, Grushenka, despite her checkered past and blemished reputation. Fyodor Pavlovich is a model of animation and irrationalism, who enjoys his depravity and is only encouraged by the shock and disapproval of others. After violent quarrels over Grushenka and over Dmitry's disputed inheritance, Fyodor Pavlovich is murdered. Dmitry is arrested and brought to trial for the crime. This basic line of action is complicated throughout the novel by a host of other factors masterfully linked to the main plot. . . . The literal, religious, social, and ethical levels of the novel are buttressed by the psychological probings for which Dostoyevsky is well known." Reader's Ency. 4th edition

Crime and punishment; translated from the Russian by Constance Garnett; with an introduction by Ernest J. Simmons. Modern Library 1994 xxiv, 629p $19.95

ISBN 0-679-60100-7

     *

Written 1866

"The novel is a psychological analysis of the poor student Raskolnikov, whose theory that humanitarian ends justify evil means leads him to murder a St. Petersburg pawnbroker. The act produces nightmarish guilt in Raskolnikov. The narrative's feverish, compelling tone follows the twists and turns of Raskolnikov's emotions and elaborates his struggle with his conscience and his mounting sense of horror as he wanders the city's hot, crowded streets. In prison, Raskolnikov comes to the realization that happiness cannot be achieved by a reasoned plan of existence but must be earned by suffering." Merriam-Webster's Ency of Lit

The gambler; translated by Constance Garnett; edited, with an introduction and notes, by Gary Saul Morson. Modern Library 2003 xlvii, 188p (Modern Library classics) pa $13

ISBN 978-0-8129-6693-0; 0-8129-6693-7

     LC 2002-32566

Written 1866

"The gambling mania of the tale's hero, Aleksey Ivanovich, is a reflection of the author's own weakness. The heroine of the story, Polina, is based on Polina Suslova, Dostoevski's lover in 1862-63." Reader's Ency. 4th edition

The idiot; translated from the Russian by Richard Pevear and Larissa Volokhonsky; with an introduction by Richard Pevear. Everyman's Library 2002 xxxiii, 633p $23

ISBN 0-375-41392-8

     * LC 2001-33561

Written 1868

"Dostoevsky puts into a world of foolishness, vice, pretence, and sordid ambitions, a being who in childhood had suffered from mental disease, and who with an intellect of more than ordinary power retains the simplicity and clear insight of a child. . . . The deeply absorbing drama in which he is a protagonist turns on the salvation of a woman, Nastasya Filipovna who had been corrupted in young girlhood." Baker. Guide to the Best Fic

Notes from underground; translated from the Russian by Richard Pevear and Larissa Volkhonsky [sic]; with an introduction by Richard Pevear. Knopf 2004 xxxi, 126p $18

ISBN 1-4000-4191-0   LC 2003-59216

"Everyman's library"

Written 1864. Variant titles: Letters from the underworld and Memoirs from underground

"The work, which includes extremely misanthropic passages, contains the seeds of nearly all of the moral, religious, political, and social concerns that appear in Dostoyevsky's great novels. Written as a reaction against Nikolay Chernyshevsky's ideological novel What Is to Be Done? (1863), which offered a planned utopia based on 'natural' laws of self-interest, Notes from the Underground attacks the scientism and rationalism at the heart of Chernyshevsky's novel. The views and actions of

Dostoyevsky, Fyodor, 1821-1881—*Continued*

Dostoyevsky's underground man demostrate that in asserting free will humans often act against self-interest." Merriam-Webster's Ency of Lit

also in Dostoyevsky, F. The best short stories of Dostoevsky p115-260

The possessed; a novel in three parts; from the Russian by Constance Garnett. Macmillan Pub. Co. 1913 637p o.p.

Original Russian edition, 1892. Variant titles: Demons; The devils

"Loosely based on sensational press reports of a Moscow student's murder by fellow revolutionists, The possessed depicts the destructive chaos caused by outside agitators who move into a moribund provincial town. The enigmatic Stavrogin dominates the novel. His magnetic personality influences his tutor, the liberal intellectual poseur Stepan Verkhovensky, and the teacher's revolutionary son Pyotr, as well as other radicals. Stavrogin is portrayed as a man of strength without direction, capable of goodness and nobility. When Stavrogin loses his faith in God, however, he is seized by brutal desires he does not fully understand. In the end, Stavrogin hangs himself in what he believes is an act of generosity, and Stepan Verkhovensky is received into the church on his deathbed." Merriam-Webster's Ency of Lit

Douglas, Carole Nelson

Cat in a midnight choir; a Midnight Louie mystery. Forge 2002 350p

ISBN 0-312-85797-7   LC 2001-58281

"A Tom Doherty Associates book"

In this adventure Vegas cat sleuth "Louie's human roommate, Temple Barr, and her boyfriend, Max, are interested in a group of mysterious magicians called the Synth. Matters are complicated when a stripper is murdered, and police lieutenant C. R. Molina, a recurring character, identifies Max, also a magician, as a prime suspect. Alternating chapters—third-person human narration playing off against first-person Louie—move the action along briskly." Booklist

Cat in a neon nightmare; a Midnight Louie mystery. Forge 2003 365p $24.95

ISBN 0-7653-0680-8   LC 2002-45491

"A Tom Doherty Associates book"

In this episode sleuth and supercat Midnight Louie "and his human associates, Temple Barr and Max Kinsella, tangle with the Synth, a gang of outlaw magicians up to no good. Tracking down the elusive renegades takes Louie to a private magic club called Nightmare—imagine the bar in Star Wars but not quite as friendly." Booklist

Douglas, Michael *See* Crichton, Michael, 1942-2008

Douglass, Billie, 1945-

For works by this author see Delinsky, Barbara, 1945-

Dovey, Ceridwen

Blood kin. Viking 2008 183p $23.95

ISBN 978-0-670-01856-7; 0-670-01856-2

LC 2007-019876

In this "novel, the deposed president of an unnamed country is imprisoned in his residence with, among others, his chef, his barber, and his portraitist. These three servants, awaiting their fate, reveal, in alternating chapters, their ties to the president and their reasons for serving his corrupt regime. Dovey connects her main characters to the president first through their work—their tasks of feeding, grooming, and painting give them an uneasy intimacy with the president—and then through various women in their lives. The narratives of these women, halfway through the book, expose the full extent of the president's depravity. In lively, straightforward prose, Dovey gets to the heart of the complicit nature of the master-servant relationship." New Yorker

Downie, Ruth, 1955-

Medicus; a novel of the Roman Empire. Bloomsbury Pub. 2006 386p $23.95

ISBN 978-1-59691-231-1; 1-59691-231-6

LC 2006-13179

"Gaius Petrius Ruso, a military medicus (or doctor), transfers to the 20th Legion in the remote Britannia port of Deva (now Chester) to start over after a ruinous divorce and his father's death. Things go downhill from there. His quarters are filthy and vermin-filled, and his superior at the hospital is a petty tyrant. Gaius rescues and buys an injured slave girl, Tilla, from her abusive master, but she refuses to talk, can't cook and costs more to keep than he can afford. Meanwhile, young women from the local bordello keep turning up dead, and nobody is interested in investigating. Gaius becomes a reluctant detective, but his sleuthing threatens to get him killed and leaves him scant time to work on the first-aid guide he's writing to help salvage his finances." Publ Wkly

"The plot is suspenseful and fluidly told, but the evolving bond between master and servant is at the heart of this excellent first work, as Downie carefully details the pained conscience of the former and the latter's sorrow that both her family and her country have been ravaged." Libr J

Terra incognita; a novel of the Roman Empire. Bloomsbury 2008 384p $23.95

ISBN 978-1-59691-232-8; 1-59691-232-4

LC 2007-44474

"Having just solved the mysterious deaths of several prostitutes . . ., Ruso accepts a posting to the northern border of Roman Britain in the hopes of getting a much-deserved rest and a return to actual medical practice. Instead, he finds himself at the center of an investigation into the death of a Roman soldier. The murder victim's missing head, an overzealous military aide who doesn't hesitate to use torture to force confessions from the local natives, a drug-addled fellow medic who has confessed to the murder, a stag-headed rabble-rouser, and Ruso's housekeeper all play a part in the drama. Saving this novel from a certain gritty grimness often found in mysteries is Downie's wry and witty humor." Libr J

Doyle, Sir Arthur Conan, 1859-1930

The best science fiction of Arthur Conan Doyle; edited by Charles G. Waugh and Martin H. Greenberg; with an introduction by George E. Slusser. Southern Ill. Univ. Press 1981 190p (Alternatives) o.p.   LC 81-8884

Contents: The American's tale; The Los Amigos fiasco; The great Keinplatz experiment; The adventure of the devil's foot; The adventure of the creeping man; The terror of Blue John Gap; Through the veil; The last galley; The great Brown-Pericord motor; The horror of the heights; Danger; The lift; The disintegration machine; When the world screamed

"The 14 pieces inevitably include a couple of Sherlock Holmes stories. They also include 2 of the not-so-readily-available Professor Challenger tales . . . and 10 other stories spread over more than 40 years of the author's career." Booklist

The complete Sherlock Holmes; with a preface by Christopher Morley. Doubleday 1960 c1930 1122p $27.95

ISBN 0-385-00689-6

First published 1930

This book contains the following four Sherlock Holmes novels: A study in scarlet (1887); The sign of the four (1890); The hound of the Baskervilles (1902); The valley of fear (1915). It also contains fifty-eight Sherlock Holmes stories which were originally published in the following separate volumes: Adventures of Sherlock Holmes (1892); Memoirs of Sherlock Holmes (1894); The return of Sherlock Holmes (1905); His last bow (1917); The case book of Sherlock Holmes (1927).

The hound of the Baskervilles; introduction by Laurie R. King; notes by James Danly. Modern Library 2002 xx, 181p pa $7.95

ISBN 0-8129-6606-6   LC 2002-29505

First published 1902

This is the "case of the eerie howling on the moor and strange deaths at Baskerville. Sir Charles Baskerville is murdered, and Holmes and Watson move in to solve the crime." Haydn. Thesaurus of Book Dig

"By a miracle of judgment, the supernatural is handled with great effect and no letdown. The plot and subplots are thoroughly integrated and the false clues put in and removed with a master hand. The criminal is superb, Dr. Mortimer memorable, and the secondary figures each contribute to the total effect of brilliancy and grandeur combined. One wishes one could be reading it for the first time." Barzun. Cat of Crime. Rev and enl edition

The lost world; being an account of the recent amazing adventures of Professor George E. Challenger, Lord John Roxton, Professor Summerlee, and Mr. E.D. Malone of the Daily gazette; edited with an introduction and notes by Ian Duncan. Oxford University Press 2008 xxxi, 199p pa $10.95

ISBN 978-0-19-953879-9; 0-19-953879-4
                    LC 2009-290488

"Two professors and two other Englishmen come across a region in the Amazon valley where the Jurassic period still persists, with its flora and fauna, pterodactyls,

dinosaurs, iguanodons, and other beasts that we know only in fossil form, still flourishing. The scientific squabbles of Challenger and the other professor provide incidental comedy." Baker. Guide to best Fic

The sign of four; with an introduction by Graham Greene. Doubleday 1977 134p o.p.

First published 1890 in the United Kingdom. Variant title: The sign of the four

Mary Morstan, the future wife of Dr. Watson, engages Holmes to trace her vanished father. Four years after his disappearance, Miss Morstan began receiving an annual gift of a large and lustrous pearl. Now her unknown benefactor has summoned her to a rendezvous outside the Lyceum Theater. As Holmes unravels the mystery, the Agra pearls are seen to be the center of a grim tale of murder and duplicity, which begins in India and ends in a chase through London's dockland

A study in scarlet; with an introduction by Hugh Greene. Doubleday 1977 145p o.p.

First published 1887

"A sensational story in two parts: the first deals with adventures in Utah and the wrong committed by two brutal Mormons on a girl and her lover; the second is the history of a mysterious double murder committed in London and, by the agency of Sherlock Holmes, shown to be the work of the wronged lover, who thus, after many years, attains his revenge." Baker. Guide to the Best Fic

The valley of fear; a Sherlock Holmes novel; illustrated by Arthur I. Keller. Doran, G.H. 1915 320p il o.p.

First published 1914

"With the exception of 'The Hound of the Baskervilles,' our favorite among the long tales of Sherlock Holmes. Chapter 1 has in its ten pages some of the best wit and humor to be found anywhere, plus the solution of a cipher, and a stunning punch ending. Nor is there any serious letdown as Holmes, Watson, and Inspector MacDonald investigate the murder of John Douglas at Birlstone Manor in Sussex. The shadow of Moriarty appears early and comes into sharper focus at the end of the story after the long—and gripping—interlude dealing with Douglas' life among the 'scowrers' of the Pennsylvania coalfields." Barzun. Cat of Crime. Rev and enl edition

The White Company; by A. Conan Doyle; pictures by N. C. Wyeth. Morrow 1988 366p il $24.99

ISBN 0-688-07817-6   LC 87-62625

First published 1891; this is a reissue of the edition published 1922 by Cosmopolitan Book Corporation

"The Hampshire hero joins an English Free Company, and, in the course of much wandering through France and the Pyrenees, meets with stirring adventures and performs many a deed of valour. The historical situation is that arising out of the Black Prince's decision to espouse the cause of Pedro the Cruel of Castile. Edward III, the Black Prince, Chandos, Sir William Felton, Bertrand du Guesclin, Don Pedro and others appear." Nield. Guide to the Best Hist Novels & Tales

Doyle, Conan See Doyle, Sir Arthur Conan, 1859-1930

Doyle, Roddy

The deportees and other stories. Viking 2008 c2007 242p

ISBN 978-0-670-01845-1   LC 2007-17659

Contents: Guess who's coming for the dinner; The deportees; New boy; 57% Irish; Black hoodie; The pram; Home to Harlem; I understand

"Sure, Doyle's characters' voices are to the line pitch-perfect, taut and precise. But in the best of these stories it isn't the dialogue. It's the pacing. It's the velocity. As the author explains in an introduction to the book, the stories in The Deportees were serialized in a Dublin newspaper, eight-hundred words per segment, and each story is broken down into sections that can leave them a tad choppy, creating a kind of Doppler Effect. But Doyle's stories are always compressed the way the best short story writers compress." Esquire

Paddy Clarke, ha ha ha. Viking 1993 282p o.p.
                                  *

"Set in the working-class environment of an Irish town in the late 1960s, the story is related by bright, sensitive 10-year-old Paddy Clarke, who, when we first meet him, is merely concerned with being as tough as his peers. Paddy and his best friend Kevin are part of a neighborhood gang that sets fires in vacant buildings, routinely teases and abuses younger kids and plays in forbidden places. In episodic fashion, Doyle conveys the activities, taboos and ceremonies, the daring glee and often distorted sense of the world of boys verging on adolescence." Publ Wkly

Doyle's "triumph in this novel is to replenish our sense of how children think and speak and explain the adult world to themselves." London Rev Books

Paula Spencer. Viking 2007 281p $24.95

ISBN 978-0-670-03816-9; 0-670-03816-4
                           LC 2006-41370

In this novel "novel, Doyle revisits the life of Paula Spencer, the heroine of his 1996 book, 'The Woman Who Walked Into Doors.' A decade on, Paula has been off the bottle for four months and five days, her abusive husband has been shot while robbing a bank, and her four children are—almost—grown: a daughter with a job in sales buys Paula one appliance after another in an effort to make her mom's life work; a son, recovering from heroin addiction, shows up after an absence of nine years, competent and silent; her younger daughter is drinking herself senseless at twenty-two; and her younger son, worried and self-contained, is still in high school. Doyle's depiction of a seething home life is penetrating, and Paula, as she patches a self together from remnants, emerges as an inspiring heroine without a hint of smarminess." New Yorker

A star called Henry. Viking 1999 343p

ISBN 0-670-88757-9   LC 99-25310

"The story is told in the voice of Henry Smart, born into harsh poverty in 1901 in Dublin. By age five, Henry was on his own, living in the streets of the city with his younger brother Victor in tow. . . . Fearless, more man than boy at 14, Henry was among the Irish rebels at the 1916 Easter Rising, pitching his own personal rage into the onset of Ireland's long and bloody battle for independence. Haunted by memories of a mother ravaged by poverty and repeated childbirths and by the fate of young Victor and his other siblings, Henry throws himself into

the fight for the Republic." Booklist

"In Doyle's hands, the grand patriotic narrative is tempered with a sharp sense of humanity and human frailty." Times Lit Suppl

The woman who walked into doors. Viking 1996 226p o.p.
                          * LC 95-41850

"Proud of her early-developed breasts, Paula O'Leary 'went with' lots of boys from her working-class Dublin neighborhood. With perfectly timed dance moves to 'My Eyes Adored You,' Charlo Spencer takes her. But he changes after their honeymoon. When Charlo first strikes her, she is stunned. His violent outbursts increase as slaps and bruises become yanked-out hair, broken fingers, and knocked-out teeth. While raising four children, she continues to be abused; she loses self-respect, denies how bleak things are, and drinks heavily." Booklist

Doyle "is a very, very good writer. 'The Woman Who Walked Into Doors' honors not the female experience in the abstract, but the experience of this one woman, Paula Spencer; it examines it with tenderness, but with fearless clearsightedness. And it's funny in places too. Paula Spencer is neither a victim nor a flawless Madonna; she inhabits the complexity of her mind and history; she acts to buy a better future for her children." N Y Times Book Rev

Dozois, Gardner R.

(ed) The new space opera. See The new space opera

(ed) Year's best science fiction. See Year's best science fiction

(jt. auth) Martin, G. R. R. Hunter's run

Drabble, Margaret, 1939-

The radiant way. 1987 407p

ISBN 0-394-56143-0   LC 87-45126

This first volume of a trilogy covers five years in the lives of three women who "met at Cambridge in the '50s. Liz Headleand is a Harley Street psychotherapist and mother of a large family; Alix Bowen teaches 'the poor, the dull and the subnormal' in government sponsored programs; Esther Breuer is an art scholar who has pared her life to minimal terms. Among them these women experience divorce, the death of a parent and of a lover, the loss of a job and a resulting sense of dislocation, an intimation of vulnerability as a ghastly murder affects their lives." Publ Wkly

Drabble "charts every hill and dale in the increasingly brighter landscape of middle-class women's roles (a progression that takes place, ironically, as Britain's economic power erodes). Drabble is a master of delicate phrasing set amid a big, robust narrative." Booklist

Followed by A natural curiosity (1989) and The gates of ivory (1992)

The sea lady; a late romance. Harcourt, Inc. 2007 c2006 345p $24

ISBN 978-0-15-101263-3; 0-15-101263-6
                           LC 2006-23778

First published 2006 in the United Kingdom

"Two British academic celebrities who have avoided each other for decades after their early passion crashed and burned are brought together again to receive honor-

Drabble, Margaret, 1939—_Continued_
ary degrees in the North Sea locale where they spent
memorable childhood moments. Staid Humphrey and
flamboyant Ailsa, now in their sixties, rediscover feelings
in need of resolution." Libr J

The author "has a keen sense of the past and the ways
in which intellectual fashions evolve. She is pitiless—and
very funny—about the flimsiness of Ailsa's various pos-
turings. Where Humphrey craves knowledge, Ailsa
craves exposure. Their love affair mirrors the age they
are living through. . . . Drabble writes beautifully about
the passing of time and the sad, incomplete experience
of human love." New Staesman

The witch of Exmoor. Harcourt Brace & Co.
1997 281p
   ISBN 0-15-100363-7   LC 97-10952
First published 1996 in the United Kingdom
"The witch of Exmoor is Frieda Haxby Palmer, a writer 'social analyst, prophet, sage and sybil,' reluctant matriarch, and determined lone wolf. Bored with her three
self-important and ambitious children and with all but
one of her five grandchildren, and irritated by the viper-
ish reviews of her last book, a historical novel about
Queen Christina, she sold the family estate and bought
a great, rotting mansion perched precariously above the
sea. Here Frieda resides in eccentric solitude, working
fitfully on her memoirs and enjoying her scheming family's increasing discomfort and concern over her sanity
and her last will and testament." Booklist

"Can politics ever amount to more than the conspiracies we hatch against our parents and the spells we cast
on our children? The humbling surprise of Drabble's
novel is not that it refuses to resolve this question but
that we gradually lose our lofty perspective and begin to
have an emotional stake in the answer." New Yorker

Dragomán, György, 1973-

The white king; translated from the Hungarian
by Paul Olchváry. Houghton Mifflin 2007 263p
$24
   ISBN 978-0-618-94517-7; 0-618-94517-2
                  LC 2007-36124
"In a rushing stream of . . . language, 11-year-old
Djata narrates a coming-of-age tale from somewhere behind the Iron Curtain, sometime before glasnost. Many of
his preteen traumas are universal — e.g., disorienting
jolts of feeling for a classmate emitting ''that big-girl
smell'' — while others are painfully specific to growing
up in a dictatorship: Dad's doing hard labor in a prison
camp, and radioactive winds from Chernobyl have a way
of screwing up soccer practice." Entertainment Wkly

"Political and geographical ambiguities are what allow
the novel to hover between bildungsroman and historic
documentation. The novel swirls between polarities and
it is the dichotomous tension that brings joy, freedom
and adventure to the story. Dragomán's prose is exuberant and sputters with youthful truthfulness." PopMatters

Drake, Bonnie, 1945-
   For works by this author see Delinsky, Barbara, 1945-

Drake, David, 1945-

Grimmer than hell. Baen Bks. 2003 373p $24
   ISBN 0-7434-3590-7   LC 2002-34194
Contents: Rescue mission; When the devil drives;
Team effort; The end; Smash and grab; Mission accom-
plished; Facing the enemy; Failure mode; The tradesmen;
Coming up against it; With the sword he must be slain;
Nation without walls; The predators; Underground

"Fourteen short stories and an introduction make up
the latest, highly recommended collection from a leading
light of military sf. . . . The intoduction puts everything
in perspective with a minimum of apologetics, compress-
ing Drake's psychological history since the Vietnam War
into a short essay valuable to new and old fans alike."
Booklist

Drayson, Nicholas

Guide to the birds of East Africa. Houghton
Mifflin 2008 201p $22
   ISBN 978-0-547-15258-5; 0-547-15258-2
                  LC 2008-17183
"Mr. Malik, a short, round, aging Indian man with a
horrendous comb-over, is in love with Mrs. Rose
Mbikwa, who is attractive, Scottish, and the leader of the
Tuesday morning bird walks. Both have lost their
spouses and both are devoted to Kenya, birds, and politics, but beyond that, they couldn't be more different.
Nevertheless, Mr. Malik intends to invite Mrs. Mbikwa
to the Hunt Club Ball. Alas, Harry Khan, a flashy playboy on holiday in Nairobi, also has his sights set on Mrs.
Mbikwa. A contest is staged that grants the man who can
sight the most bird species in one week the right to invite the lady to the ball." Libr J

"With captivating character sketches and glimpses into
Kenyan life and politics, Drayson meets the inevitable
comparisons to Alexander McCall Smith without breaking a sweat." Publ Wkly

Dreiser, Theodore, 1871-1945

An American tragedy. Boni & Liveright 1925
2v o.p.
                                 *

"Clyde Griffiths, product of a poor and pious home, is
driven by ambition to acquire money and social status.
He is loved by Roberta, a factory coworker, but is daz-
zled by Sondra, who would be a passport to the country-
club set. When Roberta, pregnant and no longer desirable, becomes an obstacle to Clyde's fulfilling his dream,
he plans her death, for which he is caught and convicted." Shapiro. Fic for Youth. 3d edition

Jennie Gerhardt; a novel. Harper 1911 430p o.p.
                                 *

"The fortunes of two families, German and Irish immigrants. Jennie, child of an unsuccessful German, falls a
prey to the pleasure-loving son of the enterprising Irishman. Whether of deep-laid purpose or not, the book illustrates the rottenness of a complex social fabric resting
on materialism." Baker. Guide to the Best Fic

   also in Dreiser, T. Sister Carrie; Jennie
      Gerhardt; Twelve men

Dreiser, Theodore, 1871-1945—*Continued*
Sister Carrie; historical editors, John C. Berkey, Alice M. Winters; textual editor, James L.W. West III; general editor Neda M. Westlake; introduction by Alfred Kazin. Penguin Books 1994 499p pa $12.95
ISBN 0-14-018828-2

First published 1900
"A powerful account of a young working girl's rise to the 'tinsel and shine' of worldly success, and of the slow decline of her lover and protector Hurstwood." Oxford Companion to Engl Lit
also in Dreiser, T. Sister Carrie; Jennie Gerhardt; Twelve men

Sister Carrie; Jennie Gerhardt; Twelve men. Library of America 1987 1168p il $40
ISBN 0-940450-41-0
Contents: Sister Carrie; Jennie Gerhardt; Twelve men
Sister Carrie and Jennie Gerhardt are entered separately. Twelve men (1919) presents brief biographical sketches of twelve men that have influenced the author's life

Drew, Flora

(tr) Ma Jian. Beijing coma

Drummond, Laurie Lynn, 1956-

Anything you say can and will be used against you; stories. HarperCollinsPublishers 2004 250p $23.95
ISBN 0-06-056162-9   LC 2003-51133
Contents: Something about a scar; Cleaning your gun; Taste, touch, sight, sound, smell; Finding a place; Under control; Katherine's elegy; Where I come from; Keeping the dead alive; Lemme tell you something; Absolutes
"Combining Southern grace and urban brutality, ex-cop Drummond debuts with 10 short stories grouped into five blistering fictional portraits of Baton Rouge policewomen. Each lady is tough even without her bulletproof vest, and all are plagued by death and corruption as they undertake the bracing, dehumanizing enforcement of justice." Publ Wkly

Drury, Allen

Advise and consent; drawings by Arthur Shilstone. Doubleday 1959 616p il o.p.

"Robert A. Leffingwell, a liberal intellectual, is nominated by the President of the United States to be Secretary of State. The lives of four politicians are affected by the fight for his approval in the Senate. A suicide, a surprise witness at the hearings, a vote of censure, and some chicanery highlight the Washington political scene depicted in this novel." Shapiro. Fic for Youth. 3d edition

Drury, Tom

The driftless area. Atlantic Monthly Press 2006 215p $22
ISBN 0-87113-943-X   LC 2006-40787

In this novel, "24-year-old Pierre Hunter leads a rather aimless life in the small town of Shale, IA. His parents have died, and he works as a bartender, hanging out with the few high school friends who haven't left town. A chance encounter with a mysterious old man on New Year's Eve sets in motion a series of events involving a bag of money and a young woman with a secret who saves Pierre's life." Libr J
"Deadpan wit, cosmic melancholy, characters both ethereal and down and dirty, predicaments a Beckett character would accept as inevitable, and a porous divide between the living and the dead add up to a delectably unnerving outlaw fairy tale." Booklist

D'Souza, Tony

The Konkans. Harcourt 2008 320p $25
ISBN 978-0-15-101519-1; 0-15-101519-8
                              LC 2007-15303
"Narrator Francisco D'Sai descends partially from a small group of Konkans, former Hindus converted to Catholicism by the Portuguese in the 16th century. His American mother, Denise, met and married his father, Lawrence, while working as a Peace Corps volunteer in the 1960s. The couple moves to Chicago, where Francisco is born and where Lawrence is obsessed with assimilation and achieving the American dream. In contrast, Francisco's uncle Sam, whom Denise insists they sponsor to America, is a much more soulful man who retains his Indian identity. Sam tells fabulous tales of Konkan culture and is adored by both Francisco and Denise, whose infatuation with India persists even as her love for Lawrence dwindles." Publ Wkly
This is "more than an ethnographic study—D'Souza stays character-focused throughout the novel, gently mixing irony and fatalism with a warm affection for humans and the stupid things they do." Washington City Paper

Whiteman. Harcourt 2006 279p $22
ISBN 0-15-101145-1   LC 2005-25459
This is a "novel about a maverick American relief worker deep in the West African bush. When his funding is cut off, Jack Diaz refuses to leave his post, a Muslim village in the Ivory Coast where Christians and Muslims are squaring off for war." Publisher's note
"One significant virtue of D'Souza's storytelling rests in his ability to present Jack's experiences of African life with a vividness that reveals the continent's allure without sentimentalizing its exoticism. . . . Much of the drama that unfolds in the 12 loosely chronological parts of 'Whiteman' (each a story that could stand on its own) rests in the gentle progression that ferries Jack away from a form of blindness to a new kind of sight." N Y Times Book Rev

Du Brul, Jack B.
(jt. auth) Cussler, C. Plague ship

Du Maurier, Dame Daphne, 1907-1989

Daphne du Maurier's classics of the macabre; illustrated by Michael Foreman. Doubleday 1987 284p il $18.95
ISBN 0-385-24302-2   LC 87-9108

Du Maurier, Dame Daphne, 1907-1989—*Continued*

Contents: Don't look now; The apple tree; The blue lenses; The birds; The alibi; Not after midnight

"Six of du Maurier's best stories admirably illustrated by a watercolorist, Michael Foreman, well able to catch their atmosphere. . . . Careful readers will notice that most of the creepy situations in these stories develop from marital stress and that sexual undertones sound everywhere. All readers ought to savor du Maurier's peerless narrative gift." Booklist

Frenchman's Creek. Doubleday, Doran 1942 310p o.p.

"The lovely Lady St. Columb fled by coach from the boredom of London society, and an unloved husband to their wild and unused Cornish coast estate. There she discovered an aristocratic French pirate who secreted his ship and crew in the hidden creek and as a game preyed gaily upon the dull Cornish gentry. [The book describes] the love between the two and the thrilling adventure they shared." Booklist

Jamaica Inn. Doubleday, Doran 1936 332p o.p.

"A stirring tale of an old inn on the desolate moors of Cornwall, where Mary Yellan, left alone in the world at her mother's death, took refuge with her aunt. Her uncle, the landlord, directed smugglers who wrecked ships on the nearby coast, and the inn was a place of horror and mystery. Mary's hope of rescuing her aunt, and escaping, was soon complicated by her unwilling interest in the landlord's brother, who stole horses but drew the line at murder." Booklist

Rebecca. Doubleday 1938 457p $29.95
ISBN 0-385-04380-5

*

"Rebecca, lovely and charming wife of English aristocrat Maxim de Winter, dies unexpectedly, and the mystery surrounding her death haunts all who remain at the Manderley country estate. Eight months after the sailing accident in which Rebecca lost her life Maxim remarries. Through his new wife's writing, the reader learns the truth about Rebecca's death and character." Shapiro. Fic for Youth. 3d edition

Dubus, Andre, 1959-

The garden of last days; a novel; [by] Andre Dubus III. W.W. Norton 2008 537p $24.95
ISBN 978-0-393-04165-1; 0-393-04165-4
LC 2008-1294

The "narrative mostly unfolds at a Florida strip club, and the evening is spent with a terrorist who drives a leased Neon, a stripper who brings her toddler to work, a patron who gets bounced for innocently touching a dancer, and a landlord who, had he not taken ill, might have saved everyone. . . . When the critics weigh in, there will be plenty of chatter about how Dubus so deeply inhabits even the most disturbing characters. And rightly so. But the book's most profound achievement is a far more difficult one: the omnipresence of hope in a hopeless place. [The novel] is riveting and disturbing, as beautiful as it is bleak, and if there are cowards among the cast of broken characters, I couldn't find them." Esquire

Ducker, Bruce

Dizzying heights; the Aspen novel. Fulcrum Pub. 2008 362p il $25.95; pa $16.95
ISBN 978-1-55591-685-5; 978-155591-658-9 (pa)
LC 2007-51817

"This satirical comedy takes place in Aspen, Colorado, second home to billionaires and corporate titans, as well as the ski bums and service staff who keep the town running. Waddy Brush, a young computer programmer, stumbles into a new life in Aspen, falling in with Mortimer Dooberry, a bestselling author/psychologist who lives from scam to scam." Publisher's note

The satire "works well, staying lighthearted, with just enough plot twists to keep things interesting, and characters unraveling from stereotypes to more sympathetic individuals over the course of the book. But it's Ducker's use of language that separates his spin on the well-worn form and makes the book his own. Not only does Ducker display a keen sense of intelligence in breaking down the various structures of business, investment, and law and makes them both real and understandable for the reader, but he displays a far more poetic sense of his setting than most comedic writers. The Colorado Ducker describes is in the details, from understandings of local history to the precise and intricate descriptions of the flora and fauna." PopMatters

Ducornet, Rikki

Gazelle. Knopf 2003 189p $21
ISBN 0-375-41124-0
LC 2002-34000

"Recounts the sexual awakening of Elizabeth, a 13-year-old American girl in 1950's Cairo. While her father, an academic, plays war games with tiny toy soldiers and her mother moves out to satisfy her extramarital appetites, Elizabeth devours—and is awakened by—a provocatively illustrated edition of 'The Arabian Nights.'" N Y Times Book Rev

"Lushly detailed yet swiftly paced, this mythic coming-of-age novel archly traces the plexus of sensuality, intelligence, and imagination that defines the human soul." Booklist

Dudevant, Amantine Lucile Aurore Dupin *See* Sand, George, 1804-1876

Dudevant, Mme *See* Sand, George, 1804-1876

Due, Tananarive, 1966-

Blood colony; a novel. Atria Books 2008 422p $25
ISBN 978-0-7432-8735-7; 0-7432-8735-5
LC 2008-12403

"There's a new drug on the street: Glow. Said to heal almost any illness, its main ingredient is blood—the blood of immortals. A small but powerful underground railroad of immortals is distributing the blood, slowly wiping out the AIDS epidemic. But the Glow peddlers are being murdered by a violent, hundred-year-old sect with ties to the Vatican. And the only immortal born with the Living Blood is being hunted to fulfill an ancient blood prophecy that could lead to countless deaths" Publisher's note

Due "expertly mixes genres and intertwines sociopoliti-

Due, Tananarive, 1966-—*Continued*

cal issues into the framework of a story about a group of ancient African immortals who are battling to end the AIDS/HIV epidemic. Like the late, great Octavia Butler, Due fearlessly tackles contemporary issues." Baltimore Sun

The good house. Atria 2003 482p $25

ISBN 0-7434-4900-2

"After her 15-year-old son Corey's suicide, Angela Toussaint spent several months in a mental hospital. Now, divorced and focused on her work, she receives word of potential buyers of her grandmother's house in Sacajawea, Washington, in which Corey died. Realizing that she must put the tragedy to rest, Angela decides to go to the house to try to understand exactly what happened. Sacajawea is, however, a town beset by evil." Booklist

"Due handles the potentially unwieldy elements of her novel with confidence, cross-cutting smoothly from past to present, introducing revelatory facts that alter the interpretation of earlier scenes and interjecting powerfully orchestrated moments of supernatural horror that sustain the tale's momentum." Publ Wkly

My soul to keep. HarperCollins Pubs. 1997 346p o.p.   LC 97-4992

"Dawit's story spans 400 years and several countries. Yet, it is his current life, with wife Jessica and daughter Kira, that he wants to hold on to forever. His lives as a warrior, slave, jazz musician, teacher, husband, and father have all ended amid sorrow and extreme human conditions. He seeks to balance his mortality and immortality, yet with each mortal experience his perceptions of life are more human than wizardly." Booklist

"Smart psychological renderings, particularly of familial bonds, and a memorable set of African American protagonists highlight Due's . . . horror novel. Centering around the potent theme of immortality, this briskly told tale adds fresh blood—literally and figuratively—to a genre currently on life support." Publ Wkly

Dufossé, Christophe, 1963-

School's out; translated by Shaun Whiteside. Penguin Books 2007 c2006 326p pa $14

ISBN 978-0-14-303811-5

Original French edition, 2002; this translation first published 2006 in the United Kingdom

"At a middle school in Clerval, the teacher of class 9F jumps to his death, in an apparent suicide. Pierre Hoffman, a thirty-two-year-old melancholic literature instructor, is told to take his place and immediately senses something 'unsettling' about the students. Gossip reveals that the entire staff is spooked by 9F, but Hoffman, disregarding warnings, is drawn into a series of creepy events. . . . At its heart, the novel is a subtle and disconcerting meditation on the relationship between teachers and students (Dufossé is a former teacher), and, despite digressive subplots, the central mystery—what's wrong with the students?—enthralls." New Yorker

Dufresne, John, 1948-

Deep in the shade of paradise. Norton 2002 364p $25.95

ISBN 0-393-02020-7   LC 2001-44487

A novel set in the "Louisiana bayous and byways. Conceived the day his daddy Billy Wayne died in 1988, Boudou Fontana (short for Bergeron Boudeleaux deBastrop) has an eidetic memory and the knowledge that he's the last of the Fontana line. His mother, hillbilly songwriter Earlene deBastrop Fontana, is a cousin of Grisham Loudermilk, who is marrying Ariane Thevenot at Paradise, the family plantation in Shiver-de-Freeze (*chival de frise*), a small political subdivision outside Monroe, La." Publ Wkly

"The people in this small town are surprisingly endearing, despite their quirks. Numerous asides sprinkled throughout the novel make for a clever and memorable narrative style." Booklist

Requiem, Mass.; a novel. W. W. Norton & Co. 2008 316p $24.95

ISBN 978-0-393-05790-4; 0-393-05790-9

LC 2008-1343

"The story is of a man named Johnny, a writer of some renown who has at the book's outset written the tale of his own life in the guise of a novel. His wife doesn't like the book and confronts him with the idea of telling the truth, urging him to 'strip away the pretense' and let Johnny's family be who they were and are so as to tell the truest truth he can about these people he loves. Ostensibly seeing the light, he embarks on writing a memoir instead of a novel: the book 'Requiem, Mass.'" Boston Globe

"The book unfolds like a series of nesting dolls: John meanders around his coastal Florida home, writing his novel, visiting with friends and going on appointments for teaching jobs, while Johnny lives with his mother's worsening condition, his father's absences, his mother's hospitalization and a momentous trip South. Then there are stories within the memoir within the story, including the one a woman tells about her friend, Ginger Rae, who talks of writing a neighbor's suicide note, then claims it's part of a story she herself is writing. John is a very amusing unreliable narrator, and Dufresne's witty, sardonic take on life's fictions leaps off the page." Publ Wkly

Duisberg, Kristin Waterfield

The good patient; a novel. St. Martin's Press 2003 328p $23.95

ISBN 0-312-30039-5   LC 2002-36877

"Darien Gilbertson is a 28-year-old Manhattan advertising executive known for her biting sarcasm, morbid humor and party-girl tendencies. But beneath the sleek facade, she hides the scars, bumps and bruises of her secret life—she enjoys violently hurting herself. Her husband, Robert, knows of her penchant for pain, but Darien can't seem to stop and refuses to get help. Then she goes too far and breaks her hand. . . . Robert forces her to see a psychiatrist, and despite herself, Darien begins to trust cool Dr. Rachel Lindholm." Publ Wkly

"From the facile duplicity of Darien's counseling sessions to the innocence of her interior dialogues, Duisberg's first-person narrative is electrifying in its unfeigned candor, harrowing in its unnerving vulnerability." Booklist

Dukthas, Ann

For works written by this author under other names see Doherty, P. C.

Dumas, Alexandre, 1802-1870

The Count of Monte Cristo. Modern Library 1996 1462p $25.95

ISBN 0-679-60199-6

                               * LC 96-3397

Original French edition, 1844

"Edmond Dantes, a young sailor unjustly accused of helping the exiled Napoleon in 1815, has been arrested and imprisoned in the Chateau d'If, near Marseille. After fifteen years, he finally escapes by taking the place of his dead companion, the Abbe Faria; enclosed in a sack, he is thrown into the sea. He cuts the sack with his knife, swims to safety, is taken to Italy on a fisherman's boat. From Genoa, he goes to the caverns of Monte Cristo and digs up the fabulous treasures of which the dying Faria had told. He then uses the money to punish his enemies and reward his friends." Haydn. Thesaurus of Book Dig

The last cavalier; being the adventures of Count Sainte-Hermine in the age of Napoleon; translated by Lauren Yoder. Pegasus Books 2007 751p $32

ISBN 978-1-93364-831-6; 1-93364-831-7

Original French edition, 2005

Originally serialized in a newspaper, this unfinished novel, "nominally concerns a young velvet-suited nobleman 'whose pallor bespoke a strange destiny': to redeem his family's Royalist past, he must serve as a common sailor on a corsair. But Dumas seems only intermittently interested in his hero, lingering instead on Napoleon, still an emperor-in-waiting, bemoaning his marriage to spendthrift Josephine ('I shall keep divorce legal in France, if only so I can leave that woman'). Amid stagecoach heists, assassination attempts, and the occasional tiger hunt, sudden details gleam: a condemned aristocrat requests the services of a barber en route to the scaffold; a lovelorn girl conspires to commit suicide by snakebite." New Yorker

The man in the iron mask; translated by Joachim Neugroschel ; introduction by Francine du Plessix Gray. Penguin Books 2003 xxv, 470p (Penguin classics) pa $16

ISBN 978-0-14-043924-3; 0-14-043924-2

                           * LC 2002-193017

Original French edition published 1850 as part of Le Vicomte de Bragelonne

The identity of the man in the iron mask—is an unsolved mystery. Dumas' "iron mask episode is found toward the end . . . of the third volume of 'Vicomte De Bragelonne'. . . . The present volume remains essentially the story of the . . . closing years of those four men who had performed such prodigies—attacking armies, assaulting castles, terrifying death itself—Athos, Porthos, Aramis, and their captain, D'Artagnan." Preface for the reader

Short stories. Black, W.J. 1927 10v in 1 o.p.

Contents: v1 Courtship of Josephine and Napoleon; Drowner; Blood union; Lady Hamilton and Admiral Nelson; Honor of Von Bulow; Gaetano and gorger; Provisional government; Cannibals; Confession of the district attorney; Vindication; Mme Dubarry; Storming the Bastile; Aurora; Branded; Tragedy of Nantes; Cripple and giant; Louis XIII; Death of Mirabeau; Anne of Austria; Black pearl

v2 Female defender; Great Copt; Scarlet sphynx; Real Bonaparte; Corneille; Wedding night; Bouquet; Tactics of love; Pipe and a man; Marat and Rousseau; Fate of a regicide; Scar of de Guise; Hollow voice; King and courtiers; Frankfort-on-Main; Bitter cup; Smuggler's in; Prodigal's favor; Sword of the Swiss; French breed

v3 Vive le roi; Mademoiselle; Uninvited visitors; Death of Richelieu; Vicomte's breakfast; Drum-head marriage; Sword and pistol; It rains; Melancholy tale; Isabella; Ransom of Isabella; Bridals; On to Rome; His oath; Legend; Some Prussian history; Count von Bismarck; Chalice; Avalanche; Little dog Jet

v4 King cobbler; Sweet smell; Citizen Bonaparte; Grecian slave-girl; Glove of Conde; Luisa San Felice; Chevalier San Felice; Martyr San Felice; Mad method; Historic fete; D'Orsay; Chimney-back; Modern Aspasia; Royal criminologist; Tenth muse; Ball of the victims—a sketch; Conquest of Circe; Inscription; Statistics; Birds of prey

v5 Caracciolo's capture; Wild boar hunt; Historic Banquo; Daughter of the Caesars; Three madames—a portrait; Vertigo; La Fontaine's first fable; Glimpse of Paris; Odoardo, the prisoner; Odoardo, the gentleman; Marseillaise; D'Artagnan, the Gascon; D'Artagnan meets the musketeers; Musketeers meet D'Artagnan; Voice of liberty; Dowry; Black tulip; Perennial Venus; Straw; Carnot and conspiracy

v6 Burgomaster; Sack of the Tuileries; Murat; Diana de Castro; Champion of beauty; Glory of love; D'Artagnan, detective; Narcotic dream; Instinct; Moliere; Moreau; View of the terror; Bismarck—his offer; Spanish surprise; Prison; Madam; Substitute; Man in the iron mask; Lame mendicant; Andre Chenier

v7 Career of a courtesan; Strange ending; People; Crossing the Alps; Battle of Langensalza; Diana de Meridor; Assassination; Fruit, a torch and a bouquet; Gourmand; Surprise; Cabaret; Picture; Bastard of Waldeck; Word of a king; Marie Touchet; Remember; Queen's perfumer; Madame de Sauve's chamber; Boxes; To Rusconise

v8 Saint Jean d'Acre; Men from Marseilles; Regent's letter; Regent's revenge; Marengo; Byron sees Kean; Son of a courtesan; Destiny; Call; Dock fight; Regal love; Balmasque; Chateau d'If; Story of no.27; Story of no.34; Cemetery of Chateau d'If; Madness; Paradise for hell; Battle of Charenton; Mercedes

v9 Death of the king's mistress; Theory of war; Two fugitives; Chastelard; Big spider; Count of Monte-Cristo; Slaughter; Italian lover; Dormice; First consul; Death of Hercules; Act of faith; Bernadotte; Pilgrimage; Conscience's dream; Mariettes dream; Vision of Athos; Le terrain de Dieu; Weird costume; Three against three

v10 Goddess of reason; Portrait; Thief; Jean Ouillier—a study; Eight long days; Gay prince; Remark; Augereau; Sacrifice of beauty; D'Artagnan-Marechal; Duel; Corsican mother; Corsican son; Corsican brother; Printing house—a sketch; Milan; Source of money: Hannibal; Brigand's faith; Mercy and Brigand; Reverses

The three musketeers; translated with an introduction by Richard Pevear. Viking 2006 704p $35

ISBN 0-670-03779-6

                           * LC 2005-58468

Original French edition, 1844

"D'Artagnan arrives in Paris one day in 1625 and manages to be involved in three duels with three musketeers . . . Athos, Porthos and Aramis. They become

Dumas, Alexandre, 1802-1870—*Continued*

d'Artagnan's best friends. The account of their adventures from 1625 on develops against the rich historical background of the reign of Louis XIII and the early part of that of Louis XIV, the main plot being furnished by the antagonism between Cardinal de Richelieu and Queen Anne d'Autriche." Haydn. Thesaurus of Book Dig

"Richard Pevear's brisk, agile new translation succeeds, I think, because it does justice to the pure nuttiness of Dumas's writing: the nonindustrial, nonformulaic, downright peculiar qualities that make a work of popular fiction memorable." N Y Times Book Rev

Twenty years after; edited with an introduction and notes by David Coward. Oxford University Press 1998 xxv, 845p il pa $15.95

ISBN 0-19-283843-1   LC 99-188043

Sequel to The three musketeers

Original French edition, 1845; first United States edition published 1846 by Taylor, Wilde and Company

"Anne of Austria's regency, the insurrection of the Fronde, and the execution of Charles I of England mark out the period (1648-9)." Baker. Guide to the Best Fic

Followed by The Vicomte de Bragelonne (1848-1850)

Dumas, Alexandre, 1824-1895

Camille; the lady of the camellias; by Alexandre Dumas fils; translated by Edmund Gosse; with a new introduction by Toril Moi. Signet Classic 2004 255p il pa $6.95

ISBN 978-0-451-52920-6; 0-451-52920-0

*

Original French edition, 1848; first United States edition published 1857 by E.J. Hincken with title: The camelia-lady. Variant title: Lady with the camellias

Camille "is a beautiful courtesan who has become part of the fashionable world of Paris. Scorning the wealthy Count de Varville, who has offered to relieve her debts should she once more become his mistress, she escapes to the country with her penniless lover Armand Duval. Here Camille makes her great sacrifice. Giving Armand, whom she truly loves, the impression that she has tired of their life together, but actually at the request of his family, she returns to Paris and her life of frivolity. The tale concludes with the ultimate tragic reunion of Armand and the dying Camille." Reader's Ency. 4th edition

Dunant, Sarah, 1950-

The birth of Venus; a novel. Random House 2004 394p $21.95

ISBN 1-400-06073-7   LC 2003-46932

"In this novel, the fictional narrator is Alessandra Cecchi, 14, the daughter of a wealthy cloth merchant in the Florence of Michelangelo and Botticelli. Alessandra yearns to live with a brush in her hand. For that matter, she would be happy just to get out of the house. But it's the 1490s, so her best hope is an agreeable arranged marriage." Time

"Part feverish thriller, part historical romance, the story of the outspoken heroine's sentimental education—a comprehensive curriculum including every conceivable transgression—sometimes comes off as a heady blend of Browning's My Last Duchess and Anaïs Nin. But Dunant's skill lies in combining these elements with a finely textured and pertinent depiction of a cultured citizenry in the grip of rampant fundamentalism." New Yorker

In the company of the courtesan; a novel. Random House 2006 371p $23.95

ISBN 1-4000-6381-7   LC 2005-51649

This historical novel "follows the fortunes of a beautiful, flame-haired courtesan, Fiammetta Bianchini, who, after escaping from the 1527 pillage of Rome, sets up shop in Venice. The novel, narrated by Fiammetta's servant, a dwarf, chronicles the pair's horrific scrapes and their dizzying triumphs, which include Fiammetta's becoming Titian's model for his 'Venus of Urbino.' Along the way, Dunant presents a lively and detailed acccount of the glimmering palaces and murky alleys of Renaissance Venice, and examines the way the city's clerics and prostitutes alike are bound by its peculiar dynamic of opulence and restraint." New Yorker

Duncan, Glen

Death of an ordinary man; Glen Duncan. Grove Press 2005 304p pa $13

ISBN 0-8021-7004-8   LC 2004-56727

"As this novel opens, Nathan finds himself falling into darkness and emerges to float above his own funeral. . . . Along with the reader, Nathan pieces together his life and death mosaiclike as he hovers around his family after the funeral, able to sense their feelings and falling into the memories thus invoked. We see his passion for his edgy, intense wife, who ultimately betrayed him with his best friend; we register his concern for his floundering son and budding, tough-as-nails older daughter. We learn that a younger daughter has died and are eventually rubbed raw by the details of her horrific death. Duncan layers on brilliant prose—sometimes a little heavily, as the narrative seems to slow halfway through. In the end, however, he has produced an arresting story, and he writes convincingly and affectingly of the consequences of a child's death, which is pretty rare indeed." Libr J

Dunn, Katherine

Geek love. Knopf 1989 347p

ISBN 0-394-56902-4

* LC 88-45776

"The narrator is a bald female albino hunchback dwarf, raised in her family's carnival show, Binewski's Fabulon. (By using drugs and other methods, her parents succeeded in producing children with physical 'attributes' perfect for performance in a freak show.) This picaresque tale follows the life of the narrator during her family's carnival existence, through times both strange and awful." Booklist

"This raw, shocking view of the human condition, a glimpse of the tormented people who live on the fringe, makes readers confront the dark, mad elements in every society. . . . A brilliant, suspenseful, heartbreaking tour de force." Publ Wkly

Dunn, Sarah

The big love. Little, Brown 2004 228p $21.95

ISBN 0-316-73815-8

Dunn, Sarah—*Continued*

"Alison Hopkins is devastated when her live-in boy-friend, Tom, walks out of their dinner party and back into the arms of his ex-girlfriend, Kate. Tom is only 33-year-old Alison's second lover, and she wonders if she wouldn't be better off if she had slept with more men. So when Henry, her handsome new boss at the free daily Philadelphia paper for which she writes a relationship column, seems interested in her, Alison seizes the opportunity. . . . Musing on everything from her evangelical Christian upbringing to men behaving badly . . . Alison's engaging voice carries this thoughtful, introspective, smart novel along and raises it far above the average novel about a young woman looking for love in the big city." Booklist

Dunne, Dominick

An inconvenient woman. Crown 1990 458p o.p.
LC 90-1602

This novel "concerns billionaire financier and presidential adviser Jules Mendelson; his high-society wife, Pauline, and fractious stepson, Kippie; a bunch of other gangsters and Hollywoodites who are either business associates, friends or antagonists; and Flo March, Jules' curvacious, decidedly nonblueblood mistress, who comes to know too much about everyone else's less-than-licit dealings for her own good." Booklist

"This is a smart novel because Dominick Dunne understands the distance between Los Angeles society and the spicy bazaars of Hollywood. And what makes Mr. Dunne not only first-rate, but also different from other writers who write about the very rich in late 20th-century America, is his knowledge that there's more to it than getting the labels and the street names right." N Y Times Book Rev

People like us; a novel. Crown 1988 403p o.p.
LC 88-353

In this novel about upper-crust New York life, "Loelia Manchester is leaving her husband for shoe designer Micki Mindaros; Hubie Altemous is dying of AIDS; Matilde Stewart is broke. Trying to break into this world are Elias and Ruby Renthal, the richest people in Cleveland, who soon become the toast of the Upper East Side by watching carefully and spending excessively. The story's two culminating events, Elias Renthal's Boesky-like fall and Gus Bailey's thirst for vengeance, shake the fabric of a world where custom and manners rule." Booklist

"Engaging us in his characters' concerns and then pulling multiple story strands into a tight knot, Dominick Dunne demonstrates with wit and accuracy the delicate, merciless distinction between 'people like that' and 'people like us'." N Y Times Book Rev

A season in purgatory. Crown 1993 377p o.p.
LC 92-42352

This novel "begins with the jury deliberating in the murder trial of Constant Bradley, a charming, handsome Congressman from an affluent Irish Catholic family in New England. He has been charged with a crime from his prep school days: the death of Winifred Utley, a pretty 15-year-old neighbor of the Bradleys who was clubbed to death with a baseball bat after a dance at the country club." N Y Times Book Rev

"The unforgettable Bradley family, their skeletons . . . and peccadillos offer an allure similar to a sidelong glance at tabloid headlines, though here told with wit and skill. Their machinations prove both fascinating and appalling—and always hypnotically readable." Publ Wkly

The two Mrs. Grenvilles; a novel. Crown 1985 374p o.p.

* LC 85-445

"Basil Plant, a semisuccessful novelist tenuously clinging to the fringes of high society, narrates this haunting tale of two women destroyed by the virulence of their own twisted emotions. Alice Grenville, a respected woman of means, is initially appalled when her only son chooses to marry considerably beneath their fashionable set; still, rather than risk Junior's disaffection, Alice grudgingly accepts second-rate actress Ann Arden into her upper-crust family. The pathetic fates of the two Mrs. Grenvilles are sealed when Ann, in a jealous rage, murders her disenchanted husband. In order to avoid the sensationalism of a highly publicized scandal, Alice helps cover up the crime, forever binding herself to the woman she despises most. An affecting and disturbing tragedy replete with vivid portraits of spiritually crippled souls desperately struggling to inject some substance into their empty lives." Booklist

Dunne, John Gregory, 1932-2003

Nothing lost. Knopf 2004 335p $24.95
ISBN 1-4000-4143-0

This novel begins with the "torture-murder of a black man named Edgar Parlance, who has been skinned alive. It is also a detective story about its characters' pasts, {an} . . . inquiry into the lives of Edgar Parlance; his accused murderer, Duane Lajoie; and especially Duane's brilliant but tortured lawyer Teresa Kean. . . . Finally, it is a modern-day story about the media madness that routinely ensues with notorious trials, a story about celebrity and its consequences." N Y Times (Late N Y Ed)

The author "adeptly skewers the pretensions of the politicians, pundits, and celebrities who descend upon the trial, ready to use it to further their own agendas. This is a violent, sexually charged, and, at times, acidly funny tale of power and paranoia in contemporary America." Libr J

True confessions. Dutton 1977 341p o.p.
*

"A Henry Robbins book"

This novel is "about brotherhood, the loss of innocence, and the frailty of the human condition. Corruption-ridden LA in the late 1940s provides the backdrop for this tale of two brothers, a cop and a priest, who are unable to detach themselves from their Irish Catholic milieu. The bizarre murder of a prostitute provides the focal point but not the main subject matter of this work, which is concerned with policeman Tom's investigation and his discovery of seemingly universal weakness among the multitude of characters." Libr J

Dunnett, Dorothy, 1923-2001

Caprice and Rondo. Knopf 1998 c1997 xxix, 539p (House of Niccolò)
ISBN 0-679-45477-2
LC 97-49458

First published 1997 in the United Kingdom

This seventh book in the House of Niccolo series "opens in 1474 as self-exiled Nicholas, holed up in Dan-

Dunnett, Dorothy, 1923-2001—*Continued*

zig with rowdy Polish cronies, licks his wounds from the family feud that destroyed his Scottish bank and alienated him further from his estranged wife (the obdurate, sharp-witted Gelis van Borselen). To protect Europe from the Turks, and to rebuild his financial empire, the globetrotting Nicholas . . . mixes it up with Crimean Tartars, negotiates with the Shah of Persia and parries with Moscow traders before confronting Gelis in Ghent, where family skeletons tumble out of the closet. As usual, Dunnett brings her early modern financiers and aristocrats glitteringly to life." Publ Wkly

Checkmate. Putnam 1975 581p il o.p.

This concluding volume of the Francis Crawford saga "resolves Lymond's final mystery, the prophecy of astrologer John Dee: 'It is not one thing you seek, I fancy, but two. . . . The first you will have: the second you shall never have, nor would it be just that you should.' Lymond, an aggressive player in the political chess game of royalty, is also a key pawn in the quirky game of family bloodlines." Publ Wkly

"A thoroughly romantic action yarn which isn't an insult to the intelligence. Intricately plotted, atmospheric, and peopled with characters of magnetic complexity, this series combines literary quality with can't-put-down entertainment." Libr J

Gemini. Knopf 2000 xxxii, 672p il (House of Niccolò) $27.50

ISBN 0-679-45478-0   LC 00-25027

This "eighth and final installment of the 'House of Niccolò' series has as its backdrop the late 15th-century rift between King James III of Scotland and his brothers. Nicholas de Fleury has decided to return to Scotland to face two enemies: his family, the St. Pols, who still refuse to recognize him, and David Simpson, who stole the African gold in an earlier adventure. Nicholas immediately gets swept up in the fraternal strife of the royal family." Libr J

"It's remarkably easy for the neophyte to enter Dunnett's adventurous world, for the author does an outstanding job of keeping each personality distinct and each of the innumerable subplots coherent. . . . Dunnett's work sits triumphantly at the top of a crowded field: it is a sensational, emotionally resonant epic." Publ Wkly

Niccolò rising. Knopf 1986 470p (House of Niccolò)

ISBN 0-394-53107-8

* LC 86-45306

In the first volume of the House of Niccolò series we meet Claus, later known as Niccolò, "an apprentice at the Bruges branch of the Charetty company, run by the widowed owner. Claus is an enigma, seemingly a buffoon getting into scrapes with Felix, the Charetty heir, but also capable of initiating a courier service in connection with the Charetty commercial and mercenary ventures. In an era of economic and political intrigue, Claus makes the most of all opportunities—romantic and business." Libr J

This novel "displays all the author's strengths: strong characterization, subtle wit (with a dash of slapstick), lively action, and labyrinthine plot." Wilson Libr Bull

Followed by The spring of the ram

Pawn in frankincense. Putnam 1969 486p o.p.

Previous titles in this series of interlocking novels about Scottish adventurer Francis Crawford are: The game of kings (1961); Queen's play (1964) and The disorderly knights (1966)

This installment of Crawford's adventures finds him in "the eastern Mediterranean region searching for his bastard son, who is being held hostage. Plots and counterplots, blood and gore lead to an excruciating climax in the form of a chess contest (a game this is not), in which Crawford and his old adversary Graham Mallett play with living pieces, themselves included. Penalty for capture is death, and Crawford's son, whom he can't recognize, is involved." Libr J

Followed by The ringed castle (1971)

Race of scorpions. Knopf 1990 534p (House of Niccolò)

ISBN 0-394-57107-X   LC 89-45292

Third volume in the Niccolò series. "At age 21, fifteenth-century Dutch adventurer Niccolò has lost his wife and her inheritance, but he has the rich resources of his personality and potential wealth in a trading business based in Venice to restore his fortunes in short order. Indeed, a dynastic power struggle over control of Cyprus draws him to that island, where both sides eagerly enlist his support and talents. Meanwhile, there are old wounds and debts to settle with the rulers of Anjou who have previously thwarted his ambitions." Booklist

"Through precisely rendered scenes, whether depicting a battle on the high seas, the operations of a dye works, a cleverly plotted ambush (using insects) or the gruesome tactics employed to destroy a proud city under siege, Dunnett furnishes fascinating images while spinning her admirable narrative web." Publ Wkly

Followed by Scales of gold

Scales of gold. Knopf 1992 519p (House of Niccolò)

ISBN 0-394-58627-1   LC 91-58554

First published 1991 in the United Kingdom

Fourth book in the House of Niccolò series. "In 1464, adventurer and merchant banker Nicholas van der Pole . . . returns to Venice to find his financial empire in jeopardy due to the Crusades and the onslaught of powerful, unscrupulous competitors. Closely guarding the specifics of his mission, Nicholas sets out for Africa and its gold trade." Publ Wkly

"Set within a rich tapestry of fifteenth-century Europe and Africa that is woven by a master of historical fiction, Nicholas' travels are constantly endangered by the greedy and vengeful figures he has tangled with in the past as well as by the natural hazards of the period." Booklist

Followed by The unicorn hunt

The spring of the ram. Knopf 1988 469p (House of Niccolò)

ISBN 0-394-56437-5   LC 87-37847

In the second volume of the House of Niccolò saga "Plucky 19-year-old Nicholas, fleeing his bitter foe Simon de Pol, journeys via Florence—where he gets funding from the Medicis—to the East. There he hopes to trade with the Emperor of Trebizond. . . . But the seductive Princess Violante, in diaphanous déshabillé, offers Nicholas protection—and much more." Publ Wkly

"Dunnett tells this story of love and money against a

Dunnett, Dorothy, 1923-2001—*Continued*
well-researched background of historical and cultural detail, taking her readers from Europe to Byzantium."
Booklist
Followed by Race of scorpions

To lie with lions. Knopf 1996 xxiv, 626p
(House of Niccolò)
ISBN 0-394-58629-8   LC 95-50422
First published 1995 in the United Kingdom
This sixth book in the House of Niccolo series focuses
on 15th century adventurer Nicholas de Fleury's "marriage to quick-witted, self-sufficient Gelis van Borselen.
It's a war of wills, egos and attrition that erupts in 1471
as de Fleury (aka Nicholas vander Poele) snatches his infant son, Jordan, from Gelis's arms and kidnaps the boy,
a pawn in a bitter power struggle that will take the lives
of friends and rivals. . . . With her usual dramatic flair,
Dunnett mixes historical and fictive characters in a tale
that sweeps from Venice to Antwerp, Edinburgh, Iceland,
France and Cyprus." Publ Wkly
Followed by Caprice and Rondo

The unicorn hunt. Knopf 1994 656p (House of
Niccolò)
ISBN 0-394-58628-X   LC 93-35692
First published 1993 in the United Kingdom
In the fifth volume of the saga fifteenth century banker/knight Nicholas vander Poele "sails to Scotland, where
he confronts his archenemy, Simon de St. Pol, who may
be the father of the child whom Nicholas's wife, Gelis
van Borselen, is carrying. Months later, back in Flanders,
vengeful Gelis, in order to punish Nicholas for fathering
an illegitimate child by her sister, hides her newborn
boy. Intrigue, betrayal and adventure follow as hardened
Nicholas journeys from Florence, full of Medici machinations, to the Tyrol, where he uses a divining rod to
find silver." Publ Wkly
"Dunnett's writing style is somewhat complex but rich
in information. The reader can feel immersed in the environment she creates; the characters (there are many) have
well-developed, unique identities." Libr J
Followed by To lie with lions

Dunning, John, 1942-

Booked to die; a mystery introducing Cliff
Janeway. Scribner 1992 321p $24
ISBN 0-684-19383-3
                                    * LC 91-26889
Homicide detective and rare book collector Cliff
"Janeway turns in his badge, opens a shop called Twice
Told Books on Denver's Book Row and for a time becomes preoccupied with the enchanting lore of his trade.
But Janeway discovers that not all book folk are gentlefolk. Two inoffensive book scouts are murdered after
making a rare find, and the young clerk in Twice Told
Books is dispatched with equal brutality. Thinking like a
cop again, Janeway starts suspecting all his new friends
on Book Row, including the woman with whom he has
fallen in love. . . . This is a soundly plotted, evenly executed whodunit in the classic mode." N Y Times Book
Rev

The bookman's wake; a mystery with Cliff
Janeway. Scribner 1995 351p
ISBN 0-684-80003-9   LC 94-34328

"Unexpected danger and chilling intrigue attend a Denver bookstore owner's trip to Seattle for the purpose of
escorting a purported book thief to jail. Ex-cop Cliff
Janeway . . . agrees to act as bounty hunter because of
his interest in rare books; he soon realizes, however, that
his employer has a hidden agenda involving the years-ago murder of two brothers who were owners of a publishing company known for its limited editions." Libr J
The author "can't resist writing lengthy, luxurious passages about the craftsmanship of the great print men.
Strictly speaking, these eloquent lectures on the art of the
printer and the beauty of the book get in the way of the
action; but that shouldn't bother anyone who loves
books—and their covers." N Y Times Book Rev

The sign of the book; a Cliff Janeway novel;
John Dunning. Scribner 2005 353p $25
ISBN 0-7432-5505-4   LC 2004-51190
"Rare books dealer Cliff Janeway agrees to help a
friend of a friend, who's accused of murdering her husband. Coincidentally, the victim had an amazing book
collection." Libr J
"It's great fun thumbing the pages with Janeway, who
knows his business and takes a keen, almost sensual
pleasure in a virgin edition." N Y Times Book Rev

Two o'clock, eastern wartime; a novel. Scribner
2001 478p $26
ISBN 0-7432-0195-7   LC 00-32218
"In 1942, writer/drifter Jack Dulaney breaks out of jail
when he gets a mysterious message that his long-lost
love, Holly, may be in trouble. He traces her to a small
New Jersey shore town, changes his name, and finds
work as a writer at the local radio station. Holly's father
has vanished and is somehow linked to the disappearance
of a famous radio actor six years ago. Dulaney quickly
adapts to radio and discovers his true talent—writing
scripts. But his life is ever in danger as he hunts for
pieces to the puzzle." Libr J
"Dunning masterfully re-creates that brief moment
when radio seemed to offer a means of changing the nature of artistic expression. Superb entertainment and fascinating media history." Booklist

Dupin, Amantine Aurore Lucile *See* Sand,
George, 1804-1876

Durham, David Anthony, 1969-

Acacia; book one: The war with the Mein.
Doubleday 2007 576p $26.95
ISBN 978-0-385-50606-9; 0-385-50606-6
                                    LC 2006-29726
"Leodan Akaran wants only to be a devoted father and
political reformer, but his Acacian empire is based on
forced labor, drugged pacification, and a dark deal that
trades children into slavery. His chance for reform ends
abruptly when the Meins, a fierce people subjugated by
the Acacians, revolt through assassination, warfare, and
biological terror. The four Akaran children scatter to
their respective hiding places—and destinies—around the
empire. . . . A series opener that combines the moral
ambiguity and brutality of George R.R. Martin's Song of
Ice and Fire with Guy Gavriel Kay's emotional sweep
and Ursula K. Le Guin's ethnic diversity." Libr J

Durham, David Anthony, 1969-—*Continued*

Gabriel's story. Doubleday 2001 291p hardcover o.p. pa $13.95

ISBN 0-385-49814-4; 0-385-72033-5 (pa)

* LC 00-25291

In this "novel, set in the eighteen-seventies, Gabriel, a fifteen-year-old black boy from Baltimore, resents his new life on the Kansas plains when his widowed mother marries a homesteader. But then he falls in with a charismatic cowpunch and horse thief, and as they travel west to New Mexico a series of violent episodes brings Gabriel to swift maturity. The moral gravity of Durham's narrative is offset by his attentiveness to the primacy of nature in the Western landscape." New Yorker

A walk through darkness. Doubleday 2002 292p

ISBN 0-385-49925-6 LC 2001-47673

Durham "tells the parallel tales of two men in antebellum America: William, a young fugitive slave, and Morrison, a white man hired to track him. William escapes from Maryland and makes his way toward Philadelphia in search of his pregnant wife, Dover. Morrison, an older Scottish immigrant, has lived a hard, violent life he's not proud of, whose dark secrets—such as his responsibility for the death of his brother—slowly emerge as the story unwinds." Publ Wkly

Durham, Marilyn

The man who loved Cat Dancing. Harcourt Brace Jovanovich 1972 246p o.p.

"The man who loved Cat Dancing is John Wesley [Jay] Grobart, an ex-army officer who married Cat, a Shoshone squaw, when she was only 14. . . . When we meet Grobart, he is about to rob a train: recently released from prison after serving a 10-year term for the killing of three Indians believed to have raped and killed his wife, he wants money to regain his son. . . . At the same time, we meet Catherine Crocker who is on her way to catch the same train to expedite flight from her husband. Instead of catching the train she is kidnapped by the robbers. . . . The story . . . takes place in the Wyoming Territory of the 1880s." New Repub

Durrell, Lawrence

The Alexandria quartet: Justine; Balthazar; Mountolive [and] Clea. Dutton 1962 884p o.p.

Omnibus edition of four titles entered separately

Balthazar; a novel. Dutton 1958 250p o.p.

*

The second volume of the Alexandria quartet

"Once again [Durrell] writes of Justine, Melissa, Clea, Nessim, Pursewarden, Scobie, Pombal—but from a fresh point of view. The new insights are provided by the psychiatrist, Balthazar, who convinces the narrator that the first volume of the story was almost wholly inaccurate. . . . So this second volume is a correction and an expansion of the first." N Y Times Book Rev

Followed by Mountolive

also in Durrell, L. The Alexandria quartet: Justine; Balthazar; Mountolive [and] Clea p205-390

Clea; a novel. Dutton 1960 287p o.p.

*

Final volume of the Alexandria quartet

"In this novel events are seen from the point of view of the Englishman Darley who, returning to Alexandria to see old friends and lovers, has a passionate affair with Clea, one of the women in the circle of friends. Again, the tone is philosophic, the language frequently overripe, and the characters, though individualistic, are symbolic. Heterosexual and homosexual affairs are prominent in each of the novels." Booklist

"'The Alexandria Quartet' is one of the major achievements of fiction in our time, distinguished not only by its power of language, by its evocation of a place, by its creation of character, by the drama of many of its incidents, but also by its boldly original design. 'Clea' perfects the work, as a spire crowns a cathedral, but the spire is not to be judged in isolation." Saturday Rev

also in Durrell, L. The Alexandria quartet: Justine; Balthazar; Mountolive [and] Clea p653-884

Justine. Dutton 1957 253p o.p.

*

First volume of the Alexandria quartet

"Set in Alexandria the story concerns the amorous adventures of a penniless young man, a prostitute who lives with him, the rich and beautiful Justine with whom he has an affair, and Justine's husband." Publ Wkly

Followed by Balthazar

also in Durrell, L. The Alexandria quartet: Justine; Balthazar; Mountolive [and] Clea p11-203

Mountolive; a novel. Dutton 1959 c1958 318p o.p.

*

Third volume of the Alexandria quartet

First published 1958 in the United Kingdom

The perspective is "that of David Mountolive, the British ambassador: and what appeared to be 'the intrigues of desire' are shown to be intrigues motivated by politics. We learn that the beautiful Jewess, Justine, and her Coptic (Christian) husband, Nessim, are passionately united by a common cause: he believes that the formation of a Jewish state will save other minorities in the Arab world from Muslim domination and he is the leader of a group which is smuggling arms to the Jews in Palestine. The discovery of this conspiracy by Nessim's loyal English friends, Pursewarden and the ambassador, and their reactions to it form the plot line of Mountolive." Atlantic

Followed by Clea

also in Durrell, L. The Alexandria quartet: Justine; Balthazar; Mountolive [and] Clea p391-652

Dwyer, K. R., 1945-

For works written by this author under other names see Koontz, Dean R., 1945-

Dybek, Stuart

I sailed with Magellan. Farrar, Straus and Giroux 2003 307p $24

ISBN 0-374-17407-5 LC 2003-49052

Dybek, Stuart—*Continued*

Contents: Song; Live from Dreamville; Undertow; Breasts; Blue boy; Orchids; Lunch at the Loypla Arms; We didn't; Qué quieres; A minor mood; Je reviens

The "episodes that intersect and surround young Perry Katzek's upbringing in the Polish-Mexican ghetto of Chicago's South Side are simultaneously daring and compassionate, intimate in detail and mythic in scale. Dybek has the rare ability to dart back and forth in time and slide around recklessly in space while carrying the reader effortlessly with him." Washington Post Book World

Dyer, Geoff, 1958-

Jeff in Venice, death in Varanasi. Pantheon Books 2009 296p $24

ISBN 978-0-307-37737-1; 0-307-37737-7

LC 2008-23759

"Here's the initial setup: two distinct parts with a few overlapping similarities. In the first, 'Jeff in Venice,' London journalist Jeff Atman is sent to the Venice Biennial to chase down an elusive subject for an article. Amid the booze and drug-filled parties (with a few forays into checking out a bit of art), he meets the attractive Laura and has the time of his life. In the second, 'Death in Varanasi,' an unnamed London journalist (also Jeff, we would assume) is sent to Varanasi as a last-minute replacement to write a travel piece. He is initially overwhelmed upon arrival in the holiest of India's holy cities, home to the ultimate in Hindu cremations along the Ganges River. He makes friends, files his article and decides to stay." San Francisco Chron

This novel is "zany and deceptively light, even as Atman explores the meaning of life and enlightenment. Does it matter whether the unnamed hero of the second part is Jeff or Geoff? Or whether the stories in Venice and Varanasi are the same story? You can read this novel as if you're munching a burger or savoring a ribeye." St. Louis Post-Dispatch

E

Eagles, Cynthia Harrod- *See* Harrod-Eagles, Cynthia

Earley, Tony, 1961-

The blue star; a novel. Little, Brown 2008 286p $23.99

ISBN 978-0-316-19907-0; 0-316-19907-9

LC 2007-9921

Sequel to: Jim the boy

"It's late summer 1941, and Jim Glass, now a high school senior, has an earnest, unshakable passion for classmate Chrissie Steppe. But as straightforward as his feelings are, the circumstances of his nascent romance are complex: Chrissie's family is indebted to their landlord, whose sailor son Bucky claimed Chrissie as his girl before shipping out to serve on the USS California at Pearl Harbor. Throughout Jim's fraught final year at school, he relies on the advice of his uncles, but after Pearl Harbor is bombed, they can't protect him from the war's toll. Questions of patriotism, sexuality and poverty weave their way into a narrative that's deceptive in its simplicity: the growing pains that Jim and his friends experience pack a startling emotional punch." Publ Wkly

Jim the boy; a novel. Little, Brown 2000 227p $23.95

ISBN 0-316-19964-8

LC 99-42901

This novel is set in "the Depression-era town of Aliceville, N.C. . . . The story opens on Jim's 10th birthday and ends a year later. In that time, Jim sees the ocean for the first time, plays ball in front of a stopped passenger train that might or might not have Ty Cobb on board, visits his dying grandfather and watches a traveling salesman court his widowed mother." Newsweek

"The genius of a novel like this is Earley's trust in the purity of his style and the plainness of his story. Perhaps all things done very well look simple." Christ Sci Monit

Easton, Jane Faust

(ed) Brand, M. The collected stories of Max Brand

Easton, Robert Olney

(ed) Brand, M. The collected stories of Max Brand

Ebershoff, David

The 19th wife; a novel. Random House 2008 514p $26

ISBN 978-1-4000-6397-0; 1-4000-6397-3

LC 2008-00074

This "novel tells two parallel stories of polygamy. The first recounts Brigham Young's expulsion of one of his wives, Ann Eliza, from the Mormon Church; the second is a modern-day murder mystery set in a polygamous compound in Utah. Unfolding through an impressive variety of narrative forms—Wikipedia entries, academic research papers, newspaper opinion pieces—the stories include fascinating historical details. . . . Ebershoff demonstrates abundant virtuosity, as he convincingly inhabits the voices of both a nineteenth-century Mormon wife and a contemporary gay youth excommunicated from the church, while also managing to say something about the mysterious power of faith." New Yorker

Echevarría, Roberto González *See* González Echevarría, Roberto

Eco, Umberto

Baudolino; translated from the Italian by William Weaver. Harcourt 2002 522p $27

ISBN 0-15-100690-3

LC 2002-2345

Original Italian edition, 2000

An "adventure about a 12th-century Italian peasant gifted in learning languages, telling lies and putting himself in the middle of genuine historical situations." N Y Times Book Rev

"In this whimsical yet deadly earnest tale, Eco puts forth the question that perpetually beguiles him and with which he beguiles the rest of us: If a teller of tales tells us he's telling the truth, how can we know for sure what really happened?." New Yorker

Foucault's pendulum; translated from the Italian by William Weaver. Harcourt Brace Jovanovich 1989 641p $33

ISBN 0-15-132765-3

LC 89-32212

Eco, Umberto—*Continued*

"A Helen and Kurt Wolff book"
Original Italian edition, 1988

A "student of philology in 1970s Milan, Casaubon is completing a thesis on the Templars, a monastic knighthood disbanded in the 1300s for questionable practices. At Pilades Bar, he meets up with Jacopo Belbo, an editor of obscure texts at Garamond Press. Together with Belbo's colleague Diotallevi, they scrutinize the fantastic theories of a prospective author, Colonel Ardenti, who claims that for seven centuries the Templars have been carrying out a complex scheme of revenge. When Ardenti disappears mysteriously, the three begin using their detailed knowledge of the occult sciences to construct a Plan for the Templars—only to discover too late that the Plan they have invented is in fact real." Libr J

This book "is not meant to be easy. . . . [But] great are the rewards for those who actually manage to read it. For while it is not a novel in the strict sense of the word, it is a truly formidable gathering of information delivered playfully by a master manipulating his own invention—in effect, a long, erudite joke." N Y Times Book Rev

The island of the day before; translated from the Italian by William Weaver. Harcourt Brace & Co. 1995 515p
ISBN 0-15-100151-0 LC 95-7594
Original Italian edition, 1994

In this novel, "set in 1643, Roberto della Griva is shipwrecked on a ship. His own ship has been rent apart by a storm, and, tied to a plank, he has drifted to the Daphne, anchored in the bay of a South Pacific island. The deserted Daphne has no boat, and Roberto can't swim, so he is effectively a prisoner. As he explores the Daphne, he recalls his life as a young man at the siege of Casale, his years spent in hot philosophical debate in Paris, and his devotion to an adored but unapproachable woman. But there is an intruder on board, which brings to mind Ferrante, the evil twin Roberto imagines he has. The intruder turns out to be a monk obsessed with issues of time and the meridians." Libr J

"Umberto Eco's narrative surface is sensually alluring, cool and glittery, but for all its lucidity and charm, there is always something else going on. . . . This novel is really a book about telling, reminding us that the only clarity we are capable of reaching is the story we tell to compel time and the universe to take on meaning." N Y Times Book Rev

The mysterious flame of Queen Loana; translated from the Italian by Geoffrey Brock. Harcourt, Inc. 2005 469p il $27
ISBN 0-15-101140-0 LC 2004-29105
Original Italian edition, 2004

"Giambattista Bodoni is an antiquarian book dealer, who has just lost all memory of his existence, except for his reading. . . . Bodoni discovers that he is a happily married, if philandering, husband, knowledge that quickly renders him eager to learn whether, before his recent neurological calamity, he was having an affair with his attractive assistant, Sibilla." N Y Times Book Rev

"Those who don't enjoy the occasional ramble through 'Bartlett's Quotations' may quickly lose patience with 'Queen Loana,' but bookworms will get an added kick out of puzzling out the dozens of literary allusions." Christ Sci Monit

The name of the rose; translated from the Italian by William Weaver. Harcourt Brace Jovanovich 1983 502p $35
ISBN 0-15-144647-4
* LC 82-21286
"A Helen and Kurt Wolff book"
Original Italian edition, 1982

This mystery set in 14th century Italy "centers on William of Baskerville, a 50-year-old monk who is sent to investigate a death at a Benedictine monastery. During his search, several other monks are killed in a bizarre pattern that reflects the Book of Revelation. Highly rational, Baskerville meets his nemesis in Jorge of Burgos, a doctrinaire blind monk determined to destroy heresy at any cost." Merriam-Webster's Ency of Lit

This novel "is an antidetective-story detective story; as a semiotic murder mystery it is superbly entertaining; it is also an extraordinary work of novelistic art." Harpers

Edge, Arabella

The god of spring. Simon & Schuster 2007 340p $24
ISBN 978-0-7432-9484-3; 0-7432-9484-X
LC 2006-46952
First published 2005 in Australia; published in the United Kingdom with title: The raft

"In 1818, Romantic painter Théodore Géricault had just returned to France from a trip meant to distract him from an obsessive love affair with his stepaunt. He wanted to paint but was immobilized by love and could find no subject that moved him. Then he heard about the wreck of the French frigate Medusa, which set 150 souls adrift on a raft; only 15 survived. Realizing that his own misery was nothing in comparison, he soon forgot his love affair and was able to think of little else but the frigate's unfortunates. No one but the survivors knew exactly what happened aboard the raft, so Géricault sought them out, determined to discover and tell the truth. The story within the story is of the creation of Géricault's masterwork, which was eventually to be called The Raft of the Medusa." Libr J

This "brilliant and original . . . novel explores the mechanism of creativity through the story of a single painting. . . . The narrative zips along at such a terrific pace that only at the end is there time for reflection upon the all-consuming nature of real art. Page-turning and substantial, a rare combination." London Daily Mail

Edgerton, Clyde, 1944-

The Bible salesman; a novel. Little, Brown and Co. 2008 241p $23.99
ISBN 978-0-316-11751-7; 0-316-11751-X
LC 2007-45410

"Preston and Henry make an odd couple. Henry is an innocent, 20-year-old Bible salesman whom Preston picks up hitchhiking one day in postwar North Carolina. Preston has been looking for a new patsy to help him with his car theft ring. Of course he tells Henry that he is with the FBI and that they are out to catch the criminals behind the crimes. The earnest young Henry loves the idea of being a G-man and serving the Lord. As the two travel around the South, the reader learns not only about their escapades but also about Henry's upbringing, his first romance, and, finally, his questioning of the very

Edgerton, Clyde, 1944-—Continued

religion that had him out on the road in the first place." Libr J

"Edgerton is a master of comic timing, and 'The Bible Salesman' is a font of wildly creative comedy. . . . But it's the novel's quiet, introspective moments that are most memorable." Richmond Times-Dispatch

Walking across Egypt; a novel. Algonquin Bks. 1987 216p $17.95

ISBN 0-912697-51-2

* LC 86-20645

"Mattie Rigsbee, at 78, is slowing down. She plans her funeral so as not to be a burden; she supports the local Baptist church and entertains herself with hymns at the parlor piano; she tries not to meddle in her children's lives, though she does wish they'd marry; she longs for grandchildren. Then comes Wesley. Reared in an orphanage until he graduated to the reformatory, Wesley touches her heart, revives a life gone to seed. Just as he needs a grandmother's love and stability, so Mattie needs his challenge, dependence, and love." Libr J

This novel is "warm, innocent, and has a charming central character." Booklist

Followed by Killer diller

Edgeworth, Maria, 1767-1849

Castle Rackrent; edited by George Watson; with an introduction by Kathryn J. Kirkpatrick. Oxford University Press 2000 c1995 xliii, 127p (Oxford world's classics) pa $11.95

ISBN 0-19-283563-7

* LC 94-48873

First published 1800 in the United Kingdom

"This work may be regarded as the first fully developed historical novel and the first true regional novel in English. Set, according to the title-page, 'Before the year 1782', the characters, the life of the country, and the speech, are unmistakably Irish. It is a brief, high-spirited work, narrated in his old age by the devoted Thady Quirk, steward to three generations of Rackrents." Oxford Companion to Engl Lit. 6th edition

Edghill, India

Queenmaker; a novel of King David's Queen. St. Martin's Press 2002 376p

ISBN 0-312-28918-9

LC 2001-48603

"When Saul, a simple farmer, is crowned the first king of Israel, his youngest daughter, Michal, thus becomes a princess. She meets and falls in love with a devastatingly handsome charmer, David." Booklist

"With its excellent writing, dynamic characters, and galloping pace, Edghill's work is highly recommended for all historical fiction collections." Libr J

Edmonds, Walter D., 1903-1998

Drums along the Mohawk. Little, Brown 1936 592p o.p.

A "regional novel about early settlers in the Mohawk river valley in New York state during the Revolutionary war. The little community is made up of . . . individuals to whom Indian raids, British invasions, and militia gatherings are evidences of a distraught world outside. Their own understanding of the difficulties is rather vague. Gil Martin and his wife, clearing their home in the forest, and their not-very-near neighbors, are the main characters." Booklist

Effinger, George Alec, 1947-2002

George Alec Effinger live! from planet Earth; featuring contributions by Neal Barrett Jr. ... {et al.}. Golden Gryphon Press 2005 360p $25.95

ISBN 1-930846-32-0   LC 2004016935

Contents: The aliens who knew, I mean, everything; All the last wars at once; Two sadnesses; Target: Berlin!; One; My old man; Everything but honor; Solo in the spotlight; At the bran foundry; Housebound; Glimmer, glimmer; From downtown at the buzzer; The wooing of Slowboat Sadie; The man outside; Afternoon under glass; Two bits; The day the invaders came; The wisdom of having money; Put your hands together; Seven nights in Slumberland

"Effinger was one of the acknowledged masters of satirical sf and a prolific short story writer whose prodigious stylistic gifts are showcased in this unusual collection selected by his fellow writers and editors. In tribute to Effinger's genius, 16 veteran authors, from Michael Bishop and Jack Dann to Mike Resnick and Neil Gaiman, introduce each selection with personal reflections on Effinger's character and legacy. . . . Constituting a special treat for Effinger's fans are the O. Niemand stories, here introduced by Gardner Dozois, in which Effinger mimics, without caricature, the styles of such literary legends as Steinbeck, Hemingway, and Twain, while in each tale exploring an sf theme." Booklist

Egan, Greg, 1961-

Incandescence. Night Shade Books 2008 250p $24.95

ISBN 978-1-59780-128-7; 1-59780-128-3

A hard SF novel about the "efforts of the Arkmakers, who live in a neutron star's accretion disk at the center of the galaxy, to develop orbital physics from first principles and save the artificial world created by their more sophisticated ancestors. Meanwhile, Rakesh, a more or less human member of a distant posthuman society, sets off on an unrelated quest to find the Arkmakers and is soon trying to save them from their current danger." Publ Wkly

Egan "writes clearly and vividly about the cutting edge of science yet doesn't forget that characters are the windows through which the world is viewed." Libr J

Schild's ladder. Eos 2002 342p $25.95

ISBN 0-06-105093-8   LC 2001-55583

First published 2001 in the United Kingdom

A novel "set some 20,000 years in the future. . . . At the start, an experiment in quantum physics goes badly astray, creating another universe with physical laws that differ from our own. Its border expanding at half the speed of light, this new universe swallows planetary systems whole. Fortunately, humanity is so highly developed that entire populations can be quickly evacuated with little if any loss of life. Soon the scientific community divides into two groups, those who would destroy the new universe, and those who would study it." Publ Wkly

Egan, Greg, 1961—*Continued*

"Egan writes rather forbidding novels, always grounded in real science and imbued with serious scientific speculations. This is his most uncompromising book to date." Booklist

Egan, Jennifer

The keep. Alfred A. Knopf 2006 239p $23.95
ISBN 1-4000-4392-1   LC 2006-11573

"The story of two cousins, Danny and Howard, who reunite to renovate an eastern European castle Howard has purchased, is narrated by Ray, a tormented convict who is desperate to make a connection with his writing teacher in the prison. Insisting the story is one that has merely been passed on to him by another man, Ray tells about how Danny leaves New York ambivalent about the prospect of helping Howard with his project. When Danny and Howard were boys, Danny and his other cousins played a cruel prank on Howard, and Danny worries that Howard, now a powerful man, hasn't forgiven him." Booklist

This novel "makes us think hard about one of the murkiest mysteries of all: the mystery of perception, that uncertain border where reality and imagination meet. . . . In a novel full of unexpected shifts and interruptions, it's amazing how deftly Egan builds a logic for her characters." Los Angeles Times

Egan, Lesley, 1921-

For works written by this author under other names see Shannon, Dell, 1921-

Egan, Susan Chan

(tr) Wang Anyi. The song of everlasting sorrow

Eggers, Dave, 1970-

What is the what; the autobiography of Valentino Achak Deng: a novel. McSweeney's 2006 475p $26
ISBN 1-932416-64-1

Valentino Achak Deng, the real-life hero of this autobiographical novel, "was a refugee from the Sudanese civil war—the bloodbath before the current Darfur bloodbath—of the 1980s and 90s. . . . Separated from his family when Arab militia destroy his village, Valentino joins thousands of other 'Lost Boys,' beset by starvation, thirst and man-eating lions on their march to squalid refugee camps in Ethiopia and Kenya, where Valentino pieces together a new life. He eventually reaches America, but finds his quest for safety, community and fulfillment in many ways even more difficult there than in the camps: he recalls, for instance, being robbed, beaten and held captive in his Atlanta apartment." Publ Wkly

Eggers "has made the outlines of the tragedy in East Africa—so vague to so many Americans—not only sharp and clear but indelible. An eloquent testimony to the power of storytelling, What Is the What is an extraordinary work of witness, and of art." N Y Times Book Rev

Egolf, Tristan, 1971-2005

Skirt and the fiddle; a novel. Grove Press 2002 199p $23
ISBN 0-8021-1722-8   LC 2002-16442

"Narrator Charlie Evans, a violin virtuoso and orphan of Asian-Afro-American parentage, ends up in a skid-row boarding house in Philth Town, somewhere near New York City. Among the residents is Tinsel Greetz, an anarchist and troublemaker with whom Charlie reluctantly forms a friendship. . . . This energetic and entertaining work seems more like an expanded short story, but the author's vibrant writing and lunatic vision might be especially appealing to a younger . . . audience." Libr J

Ehrenreich, Ben

The suitors; a novel. Counterpoint Press 2006 295p $23
ISBN 978-158243-335-6   LC 2005-29772

A "novel loosely based on Homer's Odyssey. . . . The suitors of the title are the parade of prospective lovers who line up on the doorstep of heroine Penny (i.e., Penelope) after her husband, Payne, abandons her. As the novel's Odysseus figure, Payne has built a protective palace around his wife, then promptly assembled an army to fight overseas. In his absence, Penny becomes surrounded by lustful ne'erdowells but pines only for Payne until a mysterious stranger appears to capture her fancy and set the stage for her husband's dramatic return. Ehrenreich's odd mixing of psychological insight and full-blooded characterizations with frivolous plot twists and riotous action may not be to everyone's taste, yet it makes for some delicious occasional black comedy." Booklist

Eisenberg, Deborah

Twilight of the superheroes. Farrar, Straus & Giroux 2006 225p $23
ISBN 978-0-374-29941-5; 0-374-29941-2
          LC 2005-42659

Contents: Twilight of the superheroes; Some other, better Otto; Like it or not; Window; Revenge of the dinosaurs; The flaw in the design

"Using her playwright's ear for dialogue and a journalistic eye for the askew detail, Ms. Eisenberg gives us—in just a handful of pages—a visceral sense of these characters' daily routines, the worlds they inhabit and the families they rebel against or allow to define them. . . . Instead of forcing her characters' stories into neat, arbitrary, preordained shapes, she allows them to grow asymmetrical narratives—narratives that possess all the surprising twists and dismaying turns of real life." N Y Times (Late N Y Ed)

Eliot, Alice *See* Jewett, Sarah Orne, 1849-1909

Eliot, Alice C. *See* Jewett, Sarah Orne, 1849-1909

Eliot, George, 1819-1880

Adam Bede. Knopf 1992 xxxiii, 612p $20
ISBN 0-679-40991-2
          * LC 91-53187

"Everyman's library"
First published in 1859

"The title character, a carpenter, is in love with a woman who bears a child by another man. Although Bede tries to help her, he eventually loses her but finds happiness with Dinah Morris, a Methodist preacher.

Eliot, George, 1819-1880—*Continued*

Adam Bede was Eliot's first long novel. Its masterly realism—evident, for example, in the recording of Derbyshire dialect—brought to English fiction the same truthful observation of minute detail that John Ruskin was commending in the Pre-Raphaelites. But what was new in this work of English fiction was the combination of deep human sympathy and rigorous moral judgment." Merriam-Webster's Ency of Lit

Middlemarch; a study of provincial life; with an introduction by E.S. Shaffer. Knopf 1991 xxxix, 888p $22
    ISBN 0-679-40567-4
                              * LC 91-52976

"Everyman's library"
First published 1872

A novel "with a double plot interest. The heroine, Dorothea Brooke, longs to devote herself to some great cause and, for a time, expects to find it in her marriage to Rev. Mr. Casaubon, an aging scholar. Mr. Casaubon lives only eighteen months after their marriage, a sufficient period to disillusion her completely. He leaves her his estate, with the ill-intentioned proviso that she will forfeit if she marries his young cousin Will Ladislaw, whom she had seen frequently in Rome. Endeavoring to find happiness without Ladislaw, whom she has come to care for deeply, Dorothea throws herself into the struggle for medical reforms advocated by the young Dr. Lydgate. Finally, however, she decides to give up her property and marry Ladislaw. The second plot deals with the efforts and failure of Dr. Lydgate to live up to his early ideals." Reader's Ency. 4th edition

The mill on the Floss. Knopf 1992 xxxi, 597p $22
    ISBN 0-679-41726-5
                              * LC 92-52920

"Everyman's library"
First published 1860

"Deeply significant tragedy of the inner life, enacted amidst the quaint folk and old-fashioned surroundings of a country town (St. Ogg's is Gainsborough). The conflict of affection and antipathy between a brother and sister, and again in the family relations of their father, is a dominant motive; but the emotional tension rises to a climax in Maggie's unpremeditated yielding to an unworthy lover and betrayal of her finer nature. Brother and sister . . . are purified and reconciled only in death." Baker. Guide to the Best Fic

Romola; introduction by George Kiely; notes by Kimberly VanEsveld Adams and Emily Sohmer Tai. Modern Library xxii, 621p pa $11.95
    ISBN 978-0-375-76121-8; 0-375-76121-7
                            LC 2002-40788

First published in book form 1863

"Based on a special study of Florentine history in the epoch 1492-1509, the days of Lorenzo de' Medici, and the saintliness and all-conquering energy of Savonarola are finely portrayed. 'Romola' is a sternly tragic novel of temptation, crime and retribution." Baker. Guide to the Best Fic

Silas Marner; the weaver of Raveloe. Knopf 1993 xxx, 206p $18
    ISBN 0-679-42030-4
                              * LC 92-54293

"Everyman's library"
First published 1861

"Silas Marner is a handloom weaver, a good man, whose life has been wrecked by a false accusation of theft, which cannot be disproved. For years he lives a lonely life, with the sole companionship of his loom: and he is saved from his own despair by the chance finding of a little child. On this baby girl he lavishes the whole passion of his thwarted nature, and her filial affection makes him a kindly man again. After sixteen years the real thief is dicovered, and Silas's good name is restored. On this slight framework are hung the richest pictures of middle and low class life that George Eliot has painted." Keller. Reader's Dig of Books

Elkin, Stanley, 1930-1995

The MacGuffin. Linden Press 1991 283p
    ISBN 0-671-67324-6
                              * LC 90-13233

In this novel, Elkin "unleashes a Hitchcockian MacGuffin (the narrative spirit) which takes over the ebbing life of Bobbo Druff, 58, the fairly honest but bribable street commissioner of a mid-size American city. Kafkaesque unseen enemies and their supposed spies, perhaps including Bobbo's newly acquired mistress, Meg Glorioso, may be trying to nail him for an unspecified crime linked somehow to the hit-and-run death of the Lebanese Moslem Shiite girlfriend of his son Mikey, a 30-year-old ninny." Publ Wkly

"Here, MacGuffins of adultery, smuggling, and drug abuse merely provide a context for inspired, Joycean wordplay based on cliches, shoptalk, and technical jargon. Language itself is the real topic." Libr J

Stanley Elkin's The magic kingdom. Dutton 1985 317p
    ISBN 0-525-24304-6   LC 84-21109

"When seven terminally ill English children [go] on a visit to Disney World . . . in the charge of five ostensibly healthy but odd adults, highly comic, and deeply tragic, things happen." Publ Wkly

"This is a book by an extraordinary artist in language. It is also extremely funny and its effect is often that of a strong emetic. That combination leaves the reader wondering which way to turn—not perhaps the worst position for a thoughtful reader to be left in. . . . Elkin is gentle yet tough with his forlorn children, funny yet kind with his distrait adults; as a whole, he has written a sensitive book. . . . His book challenges a resilient and imaginative reader." N Y Rev Books

Elkins, Aaron J.

Good blood; [by] Aaron Elkins. Berkley Prime Crime 2004 293p $23.95
    ISBN 0-425-19411-6   LC 2003-62799

In this mystery, forensic anthropologist Gideon Oliver and his park ranger wife, Julie, "are on holiday in Italy, helping a friend host a tour featuring canoeing and bicycle riding. Since neither activity is Gideon's idea of fun, he lounges around the picturesque town of Stresa and is pulled, consequently, into the investigation of recently uncovered bones, which turn out to be connected to a 40-year-old secret baby swap. In turn, the swap is tied to a recent kidnapping involving the wealthy, influential family to which Gideon's tour guide friend is related.

Elkins, Aaron J.—*Continued*

. . . This is vintage Elkins: well-drawn supporting characters, lovely scenery, and a bit of interesting science." Libr J

Little tiny teeth; [by] Aaron Elkins. Berkley Prime Crime 2007 292p $23.95

ISBN 978-0-425-21530-2; 0-425-21530-X

LC 2006-103154

In this installment, forensic anthropologist Gideon Oliver takes an "expedition up the Amazon River with his friends Phil Boyajian, who heads a budget travel agency, and FBI agent John Lau. While Phil rates the boat's amenities, Gideon and John marvel at the natural wonders. But before long, they pick up on tension among the other passengers, who include world-famous ethnobotanist Arden Scofield and two of his colleagues—a ghostwriter and a bug researcher—plus a mysterious guide known only as Cisco. As the travelers go deep into the jungle, fearful of the rarely seen Chayacuro headhunters, Gideon and his pals find themselves in the middle of a decades-old blood feud, along with drug smuggling, greed and murder." Publ Wkly

"Elkins totally avoids the sin of sloth represented by some mystery writers who habitually underresearch their topics. Elkins always presents a rich buffet of fascinating scientific facts." Booklist

Skeleton dance; a novel; [by] Aaron Elkins. Morrow 2000 246p $23

ISBN 0-688-15928-1

LC 00-23278

"Celebrated Seattle 'skeleton detective' Gideon Oliver travels to the quaint French village of Les Eyzies to aid police in the identification of some human bones. At first, the bones were thought to be prehistoric fossils, common enough in a town famous for its Paleolithic caves and the world-class Institut de Préhistoire. But closer examination reveals the deceased to have been murdered sometime within the past five years, possibly by someone linked to the institute." Publ Wkly

"But for all the breezy humor, the satirical treatment of squabbling scientists respectfully illuminates their fascinating work, and in the end it is the scholarship that dazzles." N Y Times Book Rev

Unnatural selection. Berkley Prime Crime 2006 281p $23.95

ISBN 0-425-21005-7

LC 2006-2173

In this installment, "forensic sleuth Gideon Oliver accompanies his second wife, Julie, to an unusual gathering of conservation experts in the Scilly Isles. . . . Frustrated by his passive role and forced to bite his tongue when opinions are voiced that strike him as lacking intellectual rigor, Oliver leaps at a chance to examine some human remains stored at the local museum. His casual look becomes something more when he determines that one humerus bone is a recent relic, leading to his rousing the sleepy local constabulary to a murder probe. When the victim turns out to have belonged to the conservation group, the circle of suspects centers on the surviving members." Publ Wkly

"Elkins keeps things moving with plenty of local atmosphere, compelling characterization, and a refreshingly low level of violence." Natural Hist

Ellis, Bret Easton, 1964-

Lunar Park. Alfred A. Knopf 2005 308p $24.95

ISBN 0-375-41291-3

LC 2005-40923

"At a fateful Halloween party [the protagonist] glimpses a disturbing (fictional) character driving a car identical to his late father's, his stepdaughter's doll violently 'malfunctions,' and their house undergoes bizarre transformations both within and without. Connecting these aberrations to graver events—a series of grotesque murders that no longer seem random and the epidemic disappearance of boys his son's age—Ellis struggles to defend his family against this escalating menace even as his wife, their therapists, and the police insist that his apprehensions are rooted instead in substance abuse and egomania." Publisher's note

"The whole book swirls, surreally, pushing the limits of tolerable confusion while sending up laughably familiar horror story shticks. For a while, it looks as if nothing will be resolved. It works precisely because it is a ghost story, replete with eviscerated livestock, freshly dug graves, and messages written in ash—and because everything, ultimately, is resolved." New Criterion

Ellis, David

Life sentence. Putnam 2003 390p $24.95

ISBN 0-399-14979-1

LC 2002-68137

"Jon Soliday and Grant Tully share a dirty secret from their teenage years: after a night of drinking and drugs, Soliday climbed through the bedroom window of a beautiful young woman and then blacked out. Consequently, he doesn't remember anything after that—not even how she ended up dead. Via family connections, Soliday eludes prosecution, and 20 years later he is chief legal counsel to Senator Tully, who is running a fierce campaign for governor. . . . Elegant prose skillfully impels Soliday through a haze of deadly deceit, where no one is who he appears to be." Libr J

Ellis, Warren

Crooked little vein. William Morrow 2007 280p $21.95

ISBN 978-0-06-072393-4; 0-06-072393-9

"Private Detective Michael McGill's gritty life takes a turn for the bizarre when a drug-addicted White House chief of staff enlists him to recover the Constitution. The real Constitution, of course, not the one in the National Archives. This one was handed to the Founding Fathers by aliens, lost in the 1950s, and since traded among the nation's sexual deviants. McGill hits the road with sexpot Trix to track down its current holder." Libr J

"The home of the free and the land of the brave has rarely looked so creepy in this snappily paced homage to William Burroughs's Naked Lunch." Publ Wkly

Ellison, Harlan

Adrift just off the Islets of Langerhans: latitude 38° 54′ N, longitude 77° 00′ 13″ W

In The Hugo winners p547-81

The deathbird

In The Hugo winners p437-68

Ellison, Ralph

Invisible man; preface by Charles Johnson. Modern Lib. 1994 xxxiv, 572p $19.95; pa $12
ISBN 0-679-60139-2; 0-679-73276-4 (pa)
* LC 94-176953
A reissue of the title first published 1952 by Random House

"Acclaimed as a powerful representation of the lives of blacks during the Depression, this novel describes the experiences of one young black man during that period. Dismissed from a Negro college in the South for showing one of the founders how Negroes live there, he is used later as a symbol of repression by a Communist group in New York City. After a Harlem race riot, he is aware that he must contend with both whites and blacks, and that loss of social identity makes him invisible among his fellow beings." Shapiro. Fic for Youth. 3d edition

Ellroy, James

American tabloid; a novel. Knopf 1995 571p
ISBN 0-679-40391-4　　　　　　　　LC 94-42898
This novel presents a "view of the American underworld from the late 1950s to the assassination of JFK. . . . The story hinges on the entanglements of three 40-something government mercenaries who play major, behind-the-scenes roles in such events as the Bay of Pigs and the assassination of the president." Publ Wkly

"The dizzying number of covert alliances and compromised loyalties that link the Mob, the C.I.A., Howard Hughes, J. Edgar Hoover, and the Kennedys comes across less like a cancer of epic proportions that like a kind of institutional dyspepsia. Ellroy's tabloidization of this chapter of American history makes it all the more queasy and real." New Yorker

Because the night
In Ellroy, J. L.A. noir p207-425

The black dahlia. Mysterious Press 1987 325p o.p.
* LC 87-7952
"Using the basic facts concerning the 1940s' notorious and yet unsolved Black Dahlia case, Ellroy creates a kaleidoscope of human passion and dark obsession. A young woman's mutilated body is found in a Los Angeles vacant lot. The story is seen through the eyes of Bucky Bleichert, ex-prize fighter and something of a boy wonder on the police force." Libr J

"The author manages a gripping re-creation of LA street life in the 1940s, and his characters are powerfully written and terrifyingly real. The bare-bones plot, the slew of false conclusions, and the hazy evocation of the murder victim give the narrative a dreamlike atmosphere, ideal for a tale of immoral heroes and wasted lives." Booklist

Blood on the moon
In Ellroy, J. L.A. noir p1-206

Blood's a rover; a novel. Alfred A. Knopf 2009 633p $28.95
ISBN 978-0-679-40393-7; 0-679-40393-0
LC 2009-24460

"The final novel of Ellroy's 'Underworld U.S.A.' trilogy, following 'American Tabloid' and 'The Cold Six Thousand,' is a fittingly crazed and violent account of the years 1968 to 1972. Alternating chapters follow three henchmen with ties to a labyrinth of interconnected schemes—one cooks dope for Howard Hughes while facilitating his Vegas hotel takeover; another subverts black militant groups for J. Edgar Hoover; and the third kills revolutionaries in Cuba. Ellroy employs a huge cast and hyper-pulp prose to create a convincingly horrific universe run by the F.B.I., the Mob, and a host of other sinister organizations." New Yorker

The cold six thousand. Knopf 2001 672p $25.95
ISBN 0-679-40392-2
Sequel to American tabloid
A look "at the dark side of American life during the 1960s, focusing on a Las Vegas police officr, Wayne Tedrow Jr., and his inadvertent role in the cover-up of John F. Kennedy's assassination. The narrative spans a five-year period and traces Tedrow's dealings with the Mafia, the Ku Klux Klan, and various political and cultural icons of that time period." Libr J

"Ellroy's prose is easy to absorb sentence by sentence, thanks to his simple subject-verb-object constructions, but monstrous as it acquires cumulative force over hundreds of pages. . . . The novel is an exhausting, masochistic, often revelatory rereading of the allegedly idealistic sixties—an assassination, finally, of the decade rather than of its leaders." New Yorker

L.A. confidential. Mysterious Press 1990 496p $32
ISBN 0-89296-293-3
* LC 89-40523
This novel focuses on three L.A. policemen: "Trashcan Jack Vincennes, a narcotics cop who makes a little cash on the side by setting up indiscreet celebrities for exposure in a Hollywood scandal sheet; Bad Bud White, whose favorite crime-stopping technique is to 'shoot everyone involved, then look for somebody a bit more intelligent to sort out the bodies'; and Ed Exley, a well-connected officer who believes in 'stern, absolute justice, whatever the price,' provided it doesn't impede his political ambitions." N Y Times Book Rev

The author "merges raw-edged period detail with sleazy celluloid lore, producing a dark and dazzling descent into the criminal underworld of the 1950s." Booklist

L.A. noir. Mysterious Press 1998 644p o.p.
LC 98-15470
Contents: In Blood on the moon (1984) Hopkins unearths a serial killer; Because the night (1984) concerns the disappearence of a hero cop and a multiple murder; Suicide hill (1986) explores corruption and betrayal when a kidnapping leads to an orgy of violence

Suicide hill
In Ellroy, J. L.A. noir p427-644

White jazz; a novel. Knopf 1992 349p o.p.
LC 92-52890
This novel unfolds in "the murky, decadent world of Los Angeles in the late 1950s, as seen through the cynical eyes of David Klein, age 42, the commanding officer of the LAPD's vice division. Klein makes up his own rules as he goes along, rules that involve money, mayhem, and murder as necessary. Klein isn't the only one

Ellroy, James—*Continued*

to follow such rules, which apparently are the 'norm' for other members of the force as well. But Klein suffers the unthinkable when he becomes the scapegoat so that other officers can protect their own dirty laundry from the probing eyes of federal agents." Libr J

"Ellroy's clipped, telegraphic style, his use of real people and real events, and his creation of a world horrifyingly devoid of any conventional morality make *White Jazz* a harrowing, remarkable read." Booklist

Elward, James, 1928-1996

(jt. auth) Van Slyke, H. Public smiles, private tears

Emerson, Earl W.

Pyro. Ballantine Bks. 2004 307p $24.95
ISBN 0-345-46288-2

"Paul Wollf is a veteran Seattle firefighter whose firefighter father died in an arson blaze when Wollf was four. Fueled by his hatred for the killer, he achieves heroics that protect him from political infighting within the department. Work gets more complicated, however, when a new pattern of fires is detected, each one closer to Wollf's station; evidence points to the arsonist who caused his father's death." Libr J

This is a "fast-paced, smoke-filled, gripping story loaded with plot twists, snappy and graphic dialogue, and firefighting lore." Publ Wkly

Vertical burn; by Earl Emerson. Ballantine Bks. 2002 340p
ISBN 0-345-44589-9   LC 2001-35969

"One day, life is dandy for John Finney, . . . a veteran of Seattle's fire department. The next day he loses his friend and partner in a fire he suspects was set, and shortly after that he is being framed for arson and targeted for murder by conspirators who are planning to burn down the city's tallest building. . . . Emerson combines an intimate knowledge of fires and fire fighting with an intricate plot played out by characters you can love or hate." Booklist

Emmons, Cai

His mother's son. Harcourt 2003 366p $25
ISBN 0-15-100734-9   LC 2002-2990

"Dr. Jana Thomas has a secret that no one knows—not even her husband. Fifteen years before, she had a different life and a different name, which she abandoned when her younger brother murdered their parents and went on a killing spree at his school. Now Jana has a young son, and she begins to panic when she sees the warning signs that no one noticed in her brother." Libr J

"Those looking for domestic drama and hidden lives will enjoy Emmons' book and find the anxious and troubled character of Jana interesting." Booklist

Emshwiller, Carol

The secret city. Tachyon 2007 209p pa $14.95
ISBN 978-1-892391-44-5; 1-892391-44-9

"The city of the title . . . is a mountainous retreat, concealed by vines and tree roots, where alien tourists now stranded on Earth may assuage nostalgia for their home world, Betasha. It is to this now largely abandoned hideout that one particular alien, Lorpas, goes to seek fellowship after being arrested for vagrancy and escaping to the hills. There he meets and falls for Allush, a female Betashan who, like Lorpas, was born on Earth and has blended in so well that rescue is no longer appealing. Emshwiller alternates between Lorpas' account of his growing friendship with a bumbling rescuer whom he overpowers and Allush's tale of return to Betasha as the two meet, separate, and finally reunite to establish Earth as their new home world." Booklist

"First and foremost, Emshwiller is a poet—with a poet's sensibility, precision, and magic. She revels in the sheer taste and sound of words, she infuses them with an extraordinary vitality and sense of life." Newsday

Endō, Shūsaku, 1923-1996

Deep river; translated by Van C. Gessel. New Directions 1995 216p
ISBN 0-8112-1289-0
                                        * LC 94-38913

"A trip to India becomes a journey of discovery for a group of Japanese tourists playing out their 'individual dramas of the soul.' Isobe searches for his reincarnated wife, while Kiguchi relives the wartime horror that ultimately saved his life. Alienated by middle age, Mitsuko follows Otsu, a failed priest, to the holy city of Varanas." Libr J

This is a "beautifully wrought, lyrically suggestive story. . . . If Christianity holds up to us the lonely individual challenged by a God who entered history, Buddhism gives us people who are ready to surrender, finally, a measure of their human and spiritual particularity and who, with acceptance, join their fellow creatures as part of the great tide of humanity. Mr. Endo manages to merge both of these streams of faith, bringing them together in a flow that is, indeed, deep. His work is a soulful gift to a world he keeps rendering as unrelievedly parched." N Y Times Book Rev

The final martyrs; translated by Van C. Gessel. New Directions 1994 199p $21.95
ISBN 0-8112-1272-6   LC 94-746

Contents: The final martyrs; Shadows; A fifty-year-old man; Adieu; Heading home; Japanese in Warsaw; Life; A sixty-year-old man; The last supper; A woman called Shizu; The box

"This deftly translated collection, comprised of stories written as early as 1959 and as late as 1985, also includes semi-autobiographical tales in which Endo deals with the traumatic impact that his parent's divorce had on his boyhood. He also writes with grace, compassion and gentle humor about old age, love betrayed, Japanese tourists and the marks we leave on the lives of others." Publ Wkly

Silence; translated by William Johnston. Taplinger 1979 c1976 294p o.p.
                                        * LC 78-27168

Original Japanese edition, 1966; this translation first published 1969 in Japan

"The story is based on events in early 17th-century Japan, when Japanese Christians and Christian missionaries

Endō, Shūsaku, 1923-1996—*Continued*

were brutally persecuted. In the novel, Sebastian Rodrigues, a Portuguese seminarian, journeys to Japan to investigate why his former teacher, a missionary to Japan, has chosen apostasy over martyrdom. Pervading the novel is the belief that Christianity is incomparable with Japanese culture. In the end, seeing the selfishness of martyrdom, Rodrigues also chooses apostasy." Merriam-Webster's Ency of Lit

Eng, Tan Twan

The gift of rain. Weinstein Books 2008 435p $23.95

ISBN 978-1-60286-024-7; 1-60286-024-6

First published 2007 in the United Kingdom

"Set in Penang in the years just before and during the Second World War, this début novel explores the consequences of love and duty. Philip Hutton, born to a British father and a Chinese mother, finds himself drawn to a mysterious Japanese diplomat and aikido master, and soon becomes his devoted student. But their friendship—described in romantic, even erotic terms—is called into question when the Japanese invade the island and Philip must decide whether to join the resistance or collaborate with the occupying army." New Yorker

"Eng's characters are as deep and troubled as the time in which the story takes place, and he draws on a rich palette to create a sprawling portrait of a lesser explored corner of the war. Hutton's first-person narration is measured, believable and enthralling." Publ Wkly

Engel, Howard, 1931-

The Cooperman variations; a Benny Cooperman mystery. Overlook Press 2002 279p $24.95

ISBN 1-58567-233-5   LC 2002-70410

"Canadian-Jewish P.I. Benny Cooperman . . . goes to work for Vanessa Moss, a former acquaintance who now heads the entertainment division of a television network. After a friend is murdered in her house, Vanessa fears for her own life." Libr J

"Readers new to Benny's world may find themselves a little confused from time to time, but this is only a minor inconvenience. Benny is a wonderful narrator, and once readers have spent a few minutes with him, they will feel like they've known him all their lives." Booklist

Engel, Mary Potter

Strangers and sojourners; stories from the lowcountry. Counterpoint 2004 222p $23

ISBN 1-582-43264-3   LC 2003-20892

Contents: Queen Esther Coosawaw; You got to learn how to read things right; All that we need; Let them big animals come back; Lowcountry cold; Why; A soldier's disease; Rat; Who calls each one by name; Philosophy of education; Unnatural acts; Redeeming the dead; Tongues of angels; What Addie wants; M to F; A better man; What we ought to be; Dis aliter visum; Those who shine like the stars; Epiphany; Strangers and sojourners

"Subtly interweaving the tale of each character, from a 114-year-old black woman to a cross-dressing outcast, Engel allows each to speak in his or her own distinctive voice, each of which she renders with pinpoint accuracy and astounding versatility. Their eccentricities notwith-

standing, these are extraordinary characters, endowed by Engel with a sublime grace and humbling spirituality that is both penetrating and poignant." Booklist

Enger, Lin

Undiscovered country. Little, Brown and Co. 2008 308p $23.99

ISBN 978-0-316-00694-1; 0-316-00694-7

LC 2007-30138

"A modern-day Hamlet story set in rural northern Minnesota. Teenage Jesse's father, the mayor of Battlepoint, apparently committed suicide with his own hunting rifle. But Jesse suspects his Uncle Clay, who had more than one motive for murder. Is Jesse's suspicion simply his inability to accept his father's senseless act? Or is Clay really guilty—and how complicit is Jesse's mother? If Clay is guilty, what should he do about it? The obvious parallels with Shakespeare's play are even acknowledged by some of the characters, but Enger doesn't let this conceit overwhelm the story. He skillfully draws a portrait of small-town life and all its barely concealed secrets and effectively narrates Jesse's torment." Libr J

Englander, Nathan

The Ministry of Special Cases. Alfred A. Knopf 2007 339p $25

ISBN 978-0-375-40493-1; 0-375-40493-7

LC 2006-48731

"The time is the mid-1970s, and the place is Argentina. The widow of Juan Peron (Isabella, that is, not his 1940s wife, Eva) has just been given the boot from the presidential office by the military, which has inaugurated an internal terrorist program that came to be known as the dirty war. Kaddish Pozman, a Jewish resident of Buenos Aires, works for hire as a midnight eraser of names from tombstones of Jews whose living families do not want any connection to their dear departed's past dubious behavior, now that an uncertain regime governs the land. Of course, one of the major characteristics of the military government is its widespread program of making people who just might be revolutionaries or insurrectionaries or even free thinkers disappear into the regime's system of detention centers, and Pozman's son becomes one such desaparecido . The bulk of this . . . novel, then, is Pozman's and his wife's attempt to locate their missing son." Booklist

The author "bravely wrangles the themes of political liberty and personal loss with the swift style and knowing humor of folklore. In the spirit of the simple ambiguity of its title, The Ministry of Special Cases is carefully contradictory, wise and off-kilter, funny and sad." N Y Observer

English, Isobel, 1920-1994 *See* Braybrooke, June, 1920-1994

Enquist, Per Olov, 1934-

The book about Blanche and Marie; translated from the Swedish by Tiina Nunnally. Overlook Press 2006 218p $24.95

ISBN 1-58567-668-3   LC 2005-58523

Enquist, Per Olov, 1934-—*Continued*

Original Swedish edition, 2004

The author depicts the "working friendship between Marie Curie and her lab assistant, Blanche Wittman. . . . After working with the uranium-rich ore called pitch-blende, Blanche got radiation poisoning; she eventually had both legs and one left arm amputated. She moved around on a wagon and lived in Marie's Paris apartment, where she died in 1913. . . . Blanche kept several note-books, collectively entitled The Book of Questions, in which she revealed her obsession with love, first stoked years before by the doctor who treated her for hysteria at age 18, J.M. Charcot-the renowned head of Salpetriere Hospital (Paris's asylum for mad women) whose public experiments were duly absorbed by the young Sigmund Freud." Publisher's note

"As Enquist fancifully, lugubriously and rapturously riffs on, extends, and wonders after the notebooks (which really exist), Blanche, Marie (suffering the scandal of her adulterous relationship with Paul Langevin) and the con-flicted Charcot get alternating POV chapters, and the modern sensibility that sprang from her body—scientifi-cally scrutinized and dissected, but ever resistant to being known or possessed—emerges beautifully." Publ Wkly

Enright, Anne, 1962-

The gathering. Black Cat 2007 261p pa $14

ISBN 978-0-8021-7039-2; 0-8021-7039-0

"Middle-aged Veronica Hegarty, the middle child in an Irish-Catholic family of nine, traces the aftermath of a tragedy that has claimed the life of rebellious elder brother Liam. As Veronica travels to London to bring Liam's body back to Dublin, her deep-seated resentment toward her overly passive mother and her dissatisfaction with her husband and children come to the fore. Tempers flare as the family assembles for Liam's wake, and a se-cret Veronica has concealed since childhood comes to light." Publ Wkly

"You will love this book or loathe it. It doesn't take prisoners, it doesn't simper or seek to be liked. Abrasively honest and toweringly moving, it grabs and shakes you, rabbiting on in a manic monologue, comical, tragic, lost and profound." Scotsman

Yesterday's weather. Grove Press 2008 308p $24

ISBN 978-0-8021-1874-5; 0-8021-1874-7

Contents: Until the girl died; Yesterday's weather; Wife; Caravan; The cruise; Natalie; Here's to love; Hon-ey; Switzerland; What you want; The bad sex weekend; Della; Green; Shaft; In the bed department; Little sister; Pillow; Pale hands I loved, beside the Shalimar; Taking pictures; The house of the architect's love story; Men and angels; (She owns) every thing; The portable virgin; Indifference; Historical letters; Luck be a lady; Revenge; What are cicadas?; Mr Snip Snip Snip; Seascape; Felix

"Enright's subjects are family, children, love, domestic horror. The stories are strong and hard bitten. Something in them is always snagging and catching on grief, large or small. She is a confident writer, letting stories unfold at their own speed. Her best pieces have a fluid shape that feels close to the way we actually think, choose, muse." Washington Post Book World

Epstein, Joseph, 1937-

Fabulous small Jews; stories. Houghton Mifflin 2003 339p $23

ISBN 0-395-94402-3   LC 2002-27621

Contents: Felix emeritus; Artie Glick in a family way; The third Mrs. Kessler; Moe; Love and The Guinness book of records; Family values; The executor; Saturday afternoon at the zoo with dad; Freddy Duchamp in ac-tion; Don Juan Zimmerman; Dubinsky on the loose; Coming in with their hands up; The master's ring; Howie's gift; A loss for words; My little Marjie; Post-cards; Uncle Jack

"Like his emotionally candid, low-key protagonists, Epstein is intrinsically honest. Gratifying and genuine, this collection examines all sorts of respones to the en-croachment of old age on human dignity." Publ Wkly

Epstein, Leslie

The eighth wonder of the world; a novel. Handsel Books/Other Press 2006 461p $25.95

ISBN 978-1-59051-250-0; 1-59051-250-2

LC 2006-895

This novel "imagines a wisecracking American archi-tectural genius, Amos Prince, who, after fleeing America, wows Mussolini with the design for a mile-high sky-scraper. . . . The novel soon focuses on Amos's young Jewish-American acolyte, Maximilian Shabilian, who shares Prince's obsessive dream of completing the tower and becomes entangled with the architect's dysfunctional family (and, predictably, his beautiful daughter). As World War II intensifies, Amos descends into livid antiSemitism and anti-Americanism, while Max launches a tragic attempt to save the Jews of Rome by enlisting them to work on the skyscraper." Publ Wkly

In this work, " the tragic and the inane are slyly spliced together, with inflated delusions punctured by sharp barbs of satire." Washington Post Book World

San Remo Drive; a novel from memory. Handsel Press 2003 238p il $26

ISBN 1-59051-066-6   LC 2002-35547

This novel "portrays one talented but troubled Holly-wood family through the eyes of the elder son, Richard, who becomes a famous artist. His director father, Nor-man Jacobi, wittily mocks the HUAC during his tele-vised hearing, his mother, Lotte, is beautiful and a bit of a loose cannon; and his strange little brother, Barton, is given to fits and visions, serving as a trickster figure, the fool who reveals the truth." Booklist

"There is something of 'The Winter's Tale' in the way Epstein pulls it all together, something of the miraculous second chance. Losing and finding, he shows us love be-tween fathers and sons as the most powerful and endur-ing in life. . . . In doing so he has given us, along with F. Scott Fitzgerald's 'Last Tycoon,' Budd Schulberg's 'What Makes Sammy Run?' and his own 'Pandaemonium,' one of the four best Hollywood novels ever written." N Y Times Book Rev

Erdrich, Louise

The Beet Queen; a novel. Holt & Co. 1986 338p

ISBN 0-8050-0058-5

* LC 86-4788

Erdrich, Louise—Continued

Second installment in the author's North Dakota Quartet

This novel "concerns a brother and sister, Karl and Mary Adare, who are abandoned by their mother, who runs away with a barnstorming pilot. Flight is a recurring theme in this . . . tale of loneliness set against a stark North Dakota landscape. Karl spends his life as an itinerant salesman, running from his troubled family and his own sexual ambivalence; Mary, who grows up with her aunt and uncle, uses self-reliance as a way of hiding from the pain of human relationships; and Sita, Mary's cousin, retreats into insanity to avoid facing the realization that her idealized dreams of a glamorous life have evaporated. Only Celestine, Mary's friend and the mother of Karl's child, accepts reality on its own terms as she struggles to protect her daughter from the suffering that has engulfed those around her." Booklist

Four souls. HarperCollins Publishers 2004 210p $23.95

ISBN 0-06-620975-7   LC 2003-65243

"Fleur Pillager takes her mother's name, Four Souls, for strength and walks away from her Ojibwe reservation to the cities of Minneapolis and Saint Paul. She is seeking restitution from and revenge on the lumber baron who has stripped her reservation." Publisher's note

"The shifting of voices and stories, ranging back and forth in time and place, may sound dauntingly complicated; luckily, it doesn't read that way. In fact, the progression of events feels natural and unforced, full of satisfying yet unexpected twists. The book begins with clean, spare prose, but finishes in gorgeous incantation and poetry." N Y Times Book Rev

The last report on the miracles at Little No Horse; a novel. HarperCollins Pubs. 2001 361p hardcover o.p. pa $13.95

ISBN 0-06-018727-1; 0-06-093122-1 (pa)
                                        LC 00-47198

This novel features characters who have appeared previously in Erdrich's work: Father Damien Modeste and Agnes DeWitt. "Now these two merge into one person. . . . From 1912 to 1996, Agnes, disguised as Damien and thus a sham as both man and priest, tries to bring Roman Catholicism to the Ojibwas of Little No Horse Reservation on a loney patch of North Dakota." Time

"Even the small incidents in this novel are moments of tremendous power, stripped of sentimentality or pretension. Erdrich has developed a style that can sound as serious as death or ring with the haunting simplicity of ancient legend." Christ Sci Monit

Love medicine; new and expanded version. Holt & Co. 1993 367p

ISBN 0-8050-2798-X

* LC 93-15166

Original version published 1984

"The story opens in 1981 when June Kashpaw, an attractive, leggy Chippewa prostitute who has idled away her days on the main streets of oil boomtowns in North Dakota, decides to return to the reservation on which she was raised. Before leaving Williston, N.D., however, June takes on one more client and, afterward, decides to walk back to her home. En route she dies in the freezing Dakota countryside. But her memory and the legacy she

passes on to her family prompt various relatives and acquaintances to recall their relationships with her and to reminisce about their own lives." N Y Times Book Rev

The Master Butchers Singing Club. HarperCollins Pubs. 2002 289p $25.95

ISBN 0-06-620977-3   LC 2002-68501

"Erdrich tells the story of Fidelis Waldvogel, a WWI sniper and master butcher with a 'talent for stillness' and for singing. After marrying Eva, the pregnant fiancée of his best friend, who was killed in the war, he emigrates to America. Settling in Argus, N. Dak., he and Eva establish a butcher shop known for its Old World expertise and for housing Fidelis's beloved singing club." Publ Wkly

"Erdrich is demonstrably capable of pursuing a potent image or theme throughout a narrative. And although this novel's leitmotif of violent, gruesome death is a bit too obvious, its smaller symbols succeed better, perhaps because they're accompanied by less fanfare." N Y Times Book Rev

The painted drum. HarperCollins 2005 277p $25.95

ISBN 0-06-051510-4   LC 2005-40227

"Faye Travers, who narrates the first section, is a woman in her 50's who has come home to live with her mother in rural New Hampshire. Together they run the family's estates business, sorting through and selling the accumulations left behind by acquisitive lifetimes. . . . Faye, herself one-quarter Ojibwa, discovers a ceremonial drum among the possessions of an old New Hampshire family whose ancestor was an Indian trader. The drum begins to obsess her, as she increasingly questions her sense of self. The rest of the novel, told from various perspectives, follows the history of the drum in several episodes." N Y Times Book Rev

"There is searing pain and loss aplenty in this book, but one of Erdrich's strengths as a writer is the way in which she controls emotion. . . . Readers familiar with her works will recognize characters from the North Dakota native families who populate other of her works. But again, it doesn't really matter. Her themes transcend that terrain." Christ Sci Monit

The plague of doves. HarperCollins 2008 313p $25.95

ISBN 978-0-06-051512-6; 0-06-0515512-0
                                        LC 2007-33626

This novel is about the unsolved murder of a farm family, "but it is also an allegory about blood (and bloody) connections that develop as the descendants of killers and victims continue to live alongside one another near the Ojibwe reservation in North Dakota. As always with Erdrich, the bloodlines are both white and Native American, churned by the passions of characters with wonderful names like Mooshum Milk and Holy Track, whose lives and stories make the question of whodunit seem like an afterthought. Mooshum, one of three Indians falsely accused of the 1911 crime and the only one who survives the lynch mob tells of finding the murdered farm family and the infant who lived. Evelina, his granddaughter, becomes the central narrator of Mooshum's story amidst the intertwining tales of 'deathless romantic encounters' that follow. Evelina and others detail the dramas of her family, including her own budding romantic

Erdrich, Louise—*Continued*
encounters with the descendant of the murdered family
and a nun whose lineage goes back to the lynch mob."
N Y Daily News

The red convertible; selected and new stories,
1978-2008. HarperCollins 2009 496p $27.99

ISBN 978-0-06-153607-6; 0-06-153607-5

Contents: The red convertible; Scales; The world's
greatest fishermen; Saint Marie; The plunge of the brave;
The blue velvet box; Pounding the dog; Knives; Destiny;
The little book; The dress; Snares; Fleur; A wedge of
shade; The fat man's race; The leap; The bingo van;
Fuck with Kayla and you die; The crest; Best Western;
Anna; Tales of burning love; The antelope wife; Father's
milk; The gravitron; History of the Puyats; Le mooz; Na-
ked woman playing Chopin; Shamengwa; The shawl;
The butcher's wife; Revival Road; The painted drum;
Hasta namaste, baby; Future home of the living god;
Beauty stolen from another world

"Louise Erdrich is an immensely satisfying storyteller
who molds her novels from the clay of her short fiction.
. . . This anthology returns 30 of those stories, which
eventually became parts of 11 novels, to their original,
unentangled forms. The book also includes six other stories, some of which are being published for the first
time. Like Faulkner, Erdrich has created a fictional community an Ojibwe reservation in North Dakota from
which her work can unfold. Her stories stretch back 100
years or more and venture as far away as New Hampshire, looping elliptically, intersecting through a priest, a
place, a hidden parentage. But where her novels develop
these relationships, 'The Red Convertible,' in dislodging
the stories, creates a new arc between them." Los Angeles Times Book Rev

Tracks; a novel. Holt & Co. 1988 226p

ISBN 0-8050-0895-0   LC 88-9321

This third installment in the author's North Dakota
Quartet depicts "the escalating conflict between two
Chippewa families, a conflict begun when hapless Eli
Kashpaw—who has passionately pursued the fiery, ele-
mental Fleur Pillager—is made to betray her with young
Sophie Morrissey through the magic of the vengeful Pau-
line." Libr J

"Ms. Erdrich is, as always, the generous kind of storyteller, passing along not only everything her characters
know, but the story of the stories as well. Giving life and
shape and sense to what's happened, she lets the designs
spring clear." N Y Times Book Rev

(jt. auth) Dorris, M. The crown of Columbus

Erickson, Steve

Zeroville. Europa Editions 2007 329p pa $14.95

ISBN 978-1-933372-39-6; 1-933372-39-7

"Vikar Jerome, whose almost deranged film fixation
manifests itself in the images of Elizabeth Taylor and
Montgomery Clift tattooed on his bald head, wanders
around Hollywood, where he gets mistaken for a perp in
the Charles Manson murders and is robbed by a man
who turns out to be a fellow film buff. After Vikar becomes a film editor, he's kidnapped by revolutionaries in
Spain who want him to edit their propaganda film. Later,
he wins a Cannes Film Festival award in France and receives an Oscar nomination, with strange consequences.
Vikar repeatedly crosses paths with actress Soledad

Palladin and her daughter, Zazi." Publ Wkly

"Over his entire career Erickson has challenged readers
with a fiercely intelligent and surprisingly sensual brand
of American surrealism that can, at times, seem impenetrable. For this reason, it surprised me that almost everything in Erickson's new novel Zeroville entertains so
readily without seeming watered down or slight.
Zeroville is funny, sad and darkly beautiful, built around
short chapters that allow the author to capture the essential moment and move effortlessly through time." Washington Post Book World

Eriksson, Kjell, 1953-

The princess of Burundi; translated from the
Swedish by Ebba Segerberg. St. Martin's Press
2006 300p $23.95

ISBN 0-312-32767-6   LC 2005-50965

Original Swedish edition, 2002

"When the badly mutilated body of John Harald
Jonsson—a working-class family man and an expert on
the tropical fish known as cichlids—is found in the snow
in the provincial Swedish town of Libro, homicide detective Ola Haver and his colleague, Ann Lindell, quickly
identify a suspect, an embittered sociopath. The brilliance
of Eriksson's richly detailed crime novel, . . . lies in its
psychological and even sociological insights. Eriksson
not only reveals a deep, sympathetic understanding for
his large cast of characters but also evokes a pervasive
sense of despair, reminiscent of Henning Mankell's, in
the face of the violent, amoral nature of contemporary
society and the challenges it places on the police." Publ
Wkly

Erpenbeck, Jenny, 1967-

The book of words; translated, with an
afterword, by Susan Bernofsky. New Directions
2007 96p pa $14.95

ISBN 9780811217064; 0-8112-1706-X

LC 2007-23569

"Erpenbeck's narrator speaks in the language and consciousness of a little girl, attending school, going on day
trips with her wet nurse though she's long past the age
of breastfeeding, and living in a beautiful country 'where
the sun almost always shines'. Darker hints begin to appear. Playmate Alice casually refers to the gunshots
heard outside the schoolyard. The wet nurse's young
daughter doesn't return home one day, and other people
start to disappear, too. There is a nightmare coming, revealed finally when the narrator's father, a high-ranking
government official, takes her on a trip into the countryside and calmly tells her of horror upon horror.
Erpenbeck . . . eschews specific geographical detail, letting the eeriness rise to the universal. Susan Bernofsky's
remarkably fluid translation does a seamless job of capturing Erpenbeck's swirl of language as the voice of her
narrator trips along like uninterrupted thought. . . . This
is writing so intense you don't even notice the brevity."
Guardian

Eskridge, Kelley

Solitaire. Eos 2002 353p $24.95

ISBN 0-06-008857-5   LC 2002-25381

Eskridge, Kelley—*Continued*

"As one of the elite members of society on Ko Island, the world's first corporate country, Jackal Seguro is destined for political greatness until she discovers a secret that places her on the wrong side of the government. Arrested and sentenced to virtual solitary confinement, Jackal undergoes a social and psychological transformation that eventually leads her in a direction unforeseen by those who want to control her." Libr J

"Eskridge's evocation of Jackal's time in hightech solitary confinement is a stylistic and psychological tour de force. The horrors she confronts, the defenses she mounts, the things she learns are treated with a painful but bracing clarity." N Y Times Book Rev

Esquivel, Laura

Like water for chocolate; translated by Carol Christensen and Thomas Christensen. Doubleday 1992 245p $26; pa $13.95

ISBN 0-385-42016-1; 0-385-42017-X (pa)

* LC 91-47188

Original Spanish edition published 1989 in Mexico

Set in turn-of-the-century Mexico, this novel relates the story of Tita, "the youngest of three daughters. Practically raised in the kitchen, she is expected to spend her life waiting on Mama Elena and never to marry. Her habitual torment increases when her beloved Pedro becomes engaged to one of her sisters. Tita and he are thrown into tantalizing proximity and manage to communicate their affection through the dishes she prepares for him and his rapturous appreciation. Eventually, Tita's culinary wizardry unleashes uncontrollable forces, with surprising results." Booklist

"A poignant, funny story of love, life, and food which proves that all three are entwined and interdependent." Libr J

Swift as desire. Crown 2001 207p $22

ISBN 0-609-60870-3   LC 2001-28351

"Júbilo, a former telegraph operator, is suffering from Parkinson's disease; he has gone mostly blind and mute. His daughter, Lluvia, has the ingenious idea of installing telegraph equipment in Júbilo's bedroom. Now her father can tap out his thoughts in Morse code, which a computer program translates into written words. Flashbacks show us the glories and sorrows of Júbilo's life: his discovery of the power of words, his realization that people hardly ever say what they mean and his choice of telegraphy as a career." N Y Times Book Rev

Essex, Karen

Kleopatra. Warner Bks. 2001 385p

ISBN 0-446-52740-8   LC 00-44930

The author places "Kleopatra in the center of a deadly family controversy that pits her firmly against her brother. Forced into exile, she must raise an army in order to make her bid for the throne of Egypt. Unable to mount a successful assault on her own, she ultimately joins forces with the crafty Julius Caesar." Booklist

Essex's "rendering of the ancient world's culture and political machinations make this fast-paced treatment of Kleopatra's adventures particularly engaging. Exhaustive research is evident throughout." Publ Wkly

Leonardo's swans; a novel. Doubleday 2006 344p $21.95

ISBN 0-385-51706-8   LC 2005-048468

This historical novel revolves around "15th-century Italian sisters Isabella and Beatrice d'Este. Isabella, the elder, more accomplished sister, is engaged to handsome Francesco Gonzaga, a minor aristocrat, while Beatrice is intended for the future duke of Milan, Ludovico Sforza, who's powerful, unscrupulous and already in possession of a pregnant mistress. It seems, at first, that Isabella will enjoy domesticity with Francesco, while unhappy Beatrice is useful to her husband only as a vehicle for breeding sons—a situation further complicated by Ludovico's infatuation with the more beautiful Isabella. While Isabella encourages her brother-inlaw's overtures, she's actually desperate to sit for his resident artist, Leonardo da Vinci." Publ Wkly

"Readers of Tracy Chevalier's Girl with a Pearl Earring or Sarah Dunant's The Birth of Venus will welcome this novel, which brings Renaissance Italy vividly to life." Libr J

Pharaoh. Warner Bks. 2002 408p

ISBN 0-446-53025-5   LC 2002-16802

Sequel to Kleopatra

This second volume in the series, "which picks up as the 22-year-old queen of Egypt returns from exile in Rome, overflows with war, sex, political intrigue and the fruits of Essex's assiduous research on everything from ancient Egyptian religious ceremonies to traffic laws in Julius Caesar's Rome. . . . The careful balance Essex strikes between Kleopatra's intimate emotional life and her statecraft makes this a satisfyingly nuanced and approachable portrait." Publ Wkly

Esterházy, Péter, 1950-

Celestial harmonies; a novel; translated by Judith Sollosy. Ecco 2004 846p $29.95

ISBN 0-06-050104-9   LC 2003-53139

Original Hungarian edition, 2000

This Hungarian family saga is "divided into two books, the first containing fragmented glimpses of five centuries of the aristocratic Esterházy family, the second a somewhat more conventional narrative of the family's fortunes under Communism. Animating the book are a number of father figures—among them Esterházy's actual father—that owe much to the Central European literary tradition of the foolish, magical paterfamilias, and perhaps even more to Donald Barthelme's (dead) version. Ultimately, Esterházy's attempt to explode epic until it resembles the shards and mirrors of his own style doesn't quite live up to its ambition, though it yields many extraordinary moments." New Yorker

Esteves, Carmen C., 1952-

(ed) Green cane and juicy flotsam. See Green cane and juicy flotsam

Estleman, Loren D.

The adventures of Johnny Vermillion. Forge 2006 269p $24.95

ISBN 978-0-765-30914-3   LC 2006-42532

Estleman, Loren D.—*Continued*

"A Tom Doherty Associates book"

"Johnny Vermillion, operator and featured performer of the Prairie Rose Repertory Company, travels the Wild West putting on plays in towns like Lockjaw, Diablo, and Purgatory. But that's just his cover: in fact, he and his small troop are bank robbers. And when a determined Pinkerton agent tips to what Johnny has been up to, an all-out pursuit results, culminating in a wickedly clever trap. Once again, Estleman proves why he is among the best of our contemporary western novelists . . . . Johnny and his merry band of thieves are thoroughly delightful characters, a bunch of good-natured rogues, colorful without being cartoony." Booklist

American detective; an Amos Walker novel. Forge 2007 254p $24.95

   ISBN 978-0-765-31224-2; 0-765-31224-7

"A Tom Doherty Associates book"

"Walker is hired by Darius Fuller, a legendary retired Detroit Tigers pitcher facing substantial financial pressure from the IRS. Fuller's daughter Deirdre is several weeks away from gaining access to her $2 million trust fund, and her father fears that her sleazy boyfriend, Hilary Bairn, is wooing her just to get her money. Before Walker can fulfill his assignment to attempt to bribe Bairn to back off, Deirdre is found dead in Bairn's apartment, a death that may be connected to a smuggling ring and a local gangster." Publ Wkly

"Besides yielding the usual gunplay and fisticuffs, along with choice baseball metaphors . . . the well-oiled plot is supple enough to handle the newfangled criminal enterprises that a big-city shamus has to contend with nowadays. But Estleman also delivers some outstanding stuff on the hazards of the profession, including a bone-chilling stakeout on a lonely lake in the dead of night, that could come only from an old pro." N Y times Book Rev

(ed) American West: twenty new stories from the Western Writers of America. See American West: twenty new stories from the Western Writers of America

Black powder, white smoke. Forge 2002 318p $24.95

   ISBN 0-7653-0189-X   LC 2002-69266

"A Tom Doherty Associates book"

Honey Boutrille is a "freed slave who kills a white man to save a working girl in the New Orleans brothel he owns. 'Twice' Emerson is a career criminal on the run after a botched train robbery. Most of the time, Honey travels in Texas, while Twice hides out in the West. We know that they will eventually cross paths, but part of this story's charm is how it will happen." Libr J

Frames; a Valentino mystery. Forge 2008 269p $23.95

   ISBN 978-0-7653-1575-5; 0-7653-1575-0

                LC 2008-4505

"A Tom Doherty Associates book"

"Valentino is a UCLA film archivist with a passion for the silent screen. When he buys a decrepit movie theater in West Hollywood, he gets much more than he expects—a skeleton in a hidden Prohibition-vintage basement and a stack of priceless film reels of Erich von Stroheim's legendary Greed. The sale of the film to UCLA's archives will finance his theater's restoration, but the LAPD confiscates it as evidence when Valentino reports the skeleton. Fearing the cops will destroy the fragile film, he enlists the help of his mentor, the famed scholar Broadhead, and the two play detective to identify the skeleton and retrieve Greed." Libr J

"Estleman first introduced Valentino in a series of short stories for Ellery Queen Mystery Magazine and promises that 'Frames' is the first in a series of novels featuring the 'film detective.' As with every Estleman novel, 'Frames' is written in crisp, vivid prose, the characters well-drawn. And the author's meticulous research of movie history adds another layer of richness." San Francisco Chron

Gas City. Forge 2008 c2007 299p $24.95

   ISBN 978-0-7653-1956-2; 0-7653-1956-X

               * LC 2007-34927

"A Tom Doherty Associates book"

"The shades of Frank Norris and Upton Sinclair must have been looking over Loren D. Estleman's shoulder when he wrote Gas City. Set in a Midwestern metropolis that grew up around a refinery, his muscular novel initially takes a long view of the cynical bargain struck between civic leaders and organized crime—and only moves in for the kill when a key figure in this devil's dance decides to reform. Like earlier muckraking writers, Estleman is always looking for the tipping point where our frontier values of independent entrepreneurship and community justice tumble into criminality. And his characters never stop asking whether it's possible to go back and get it right." N Y Times Book Rev

The hours of the virgin. Mysterious Press 1999 296p $23

   ISBN 0-89296-683-1   LC 98-48001

"Detroit private eye Amos Walker acts as bodyguard during a blackmail transaction involving a 15th-century illuminated manuscript. During the exchange, however, someone tries to kill him." Libr J

"Estleman doesn't write pretty travelogues; the pavements of his mean streets are always slippery with bodily fluids. But for all the noir trappings of his style, with its moody nightscapes of lonely streets and empty rooms, this is one genre author who follows the procedures without debasing the language or insulting the intelligence." N Y Times Book Rev

Jitterbug; a novel of Detroit. Forge 1998 303p

   ISBN 0-312-86360-8   LC 98-21185

"A Tom Doherty Associates book"

In World War II Detroit "the heat is on Racket Squad leader Lieutenant Maximilian Zagreb and his three detectives . . . when someone starts killing people for hoarding ration coupons. Using some artful manipulation and some very unsubtle pressure, Zagreb leans on a couple of unlikely sources for help. Frankie 'The Conductor' Orr, a local mob boss, and Dwight Littlejohn, a black riveter in an airplane factory, are unwilling participants in Zagreb's efforts to smoke out the killer dubbed Kilroy by the newspapers." Publ Wkly

"This is historical crime drama at its highest level done by a consummate craftsman." Booklist

The master executioner. Forge 2001 270p $23.95

   ISBN 0-312-86970-3

               * LC 2001-23181

Estleman, Loren D.—*Continued*

"A Tom Doherty Associates book"

This novel set in the 19th century American West follows "Oscar Stone, a professional hangman, as he dispenses justice to axe murderers and army deserters. . . . Stone's calling causes his lovely young wife to flee in revulsion. But [he] is driven to exploit a gift that marries professionalism with mercy." Economist

"Estleman has created an unforgettable character in Stone. . . . A dark, compelling journey into a previously unexplored facet of the old West." Booklist

Poison blonde; an Amos Walker novel. Forge 2003 269p $24.95

ISBN 0-7653-0447-3   LC 2002-35242

"Latin singer Gilia Cristobal, the hottest commodity in show business, hires Detroit private eye Amos Walker to get to the bottom of a scam involving the singer's designer gowns, but her real problem is blackmail. It turns out she's not really who she claims to be. . . . Walker is a classic hard-boiled private eye. He breathes air heavy with smoke and cordite, he delivers his dialogue through clenched teeth, and he operates by a murky moral code only he understands." Booklist

Port hazard; a Page Murdock novel. Forge 2004 301p $24.95

ISBN 0-7653-0190-3   LC 2003-49425

"Deputy U.S. Marshal Page Murdock usually roams the open trails and cow towns of the West in his dead-or-alive search for outlaws and miscreants. Federal judge Harlan Blackthorne has a different venue for Murdock's next assignment: California's Barbary Coast. A militant wing of the Sons of the Confederacy, located in San Francisco, is assassinating anyone who impedes its efforts to revive interest in secession from the union. . . . Estleman, at home in many genres, here mixes noir and the Old West, as Murdock literally walks off the trail and onto the mean streets. A wildly entertaining read with great period atmosphere and dialogue." Booklist

Retro; an Amos Walker novel. Forge 2004 286p $24.95

ISBN 0-7653-0448-1   LC 2003-71103

"When time ran out on legendary Detroit madam Beryl Garnet, PI Amos Walker, a longtime acquaintance of Garnet, was asked to deliver her ashes to her son. The only problem was that the son, Delwayne, a Vietnam protestor implicated in a botched bomb plot, had been underground for 30 years. Walker finds Delwayne easily enough, but moments after meeting with him, he is murdered, and Walker becomes the prime suspect. Walker investigates to clear himself and learns the gun that killed Delwayne was the same gun used to kill his biological father in a celebrated but unsolved Motor City case 50 years earlier." Booklist

"Estleman makes his strongest stand for the pure, unvarnished glory of the classic American private eye in Retro, whose tongue-in-cheek title tells you what you need to know about Amos Walker." N Y Times Book Rev

A smile on the face of the tiger. Mysterious Press 2000 295p $24.95

ISBN 0-89296-706-4   LC 00-22284

Detroit gumshoe Amos Walker, "a serious drinker-thinker who lives by a tough-guy code that went out of fashion with the Edsel, is sick of hearing that he looks as if he just slouched out of a 1950's paperback novel. But when a publisher hires him to find Eugene Booth, a has-been pulp legend who skipped out on a lucrative contract to reissue his best book, Walker finds himself staring at a streaky mirror image of himself—if he lives so long. . . . Estleman pays handsome homage to Goodis and Woolrich and all the other 'paper tigers' to whom he dedicates this wonderful book." N Y Times Book Rev

Something borrowed, something black; a Peter Macklin novel. Forge 2002 236p $24.95

ISBN 0-312-87863-X

* LC 2001-54752

"A Tom Doherty Associates book"

Peter Macklin "has retired from the hit-man business and married Laurie, a young woman who knows nothing of his former career. They're on their honeymoon in Los Angeles when Macklin is forced back into his old calling by a Midwestern crime lord who's interested in expanding his territory. . . . Back in L.A., Laurie is being held hostage. At first she thinks the lanky cowboy named Abilene is just keeping her company while her husband is away 'on business,' but a fist in the face changes her take on things. . . . The story vibrates with letter-perfect details, and the plot, with changing locations and changing points of view, is deftly handled." Publ Wkly

Estrin, Marc

Insect dreams; the half life of Gregor Samsa. BlueHen Bks. 2002 468p

ISBN 0-399-14836-1   LC 2001-35941

This novel follows Kafka's Gregor Samsa "from post-World War I Vienna through the Manhattan Project in Los Alamos, NM. In numerous behind-the-scenes actions, Gregor befriends historical figures like Charles Ives, President Franklin D. Roosevelt, and Robert Oppenheimer, as well as numerous other highly fascinating fictional characters." Libr J

Where the book "succeeds is in taking Kafka's character, and the knowledge and ideas we have about him, and using him for its own un-Kafkan purposes. The novel draws us in by offering us something we know, but keeps us there by giving us something new." Am Book Rev

Eugenides, Jeffrey

Middlesex. Farrar, Straus & Giroux 2002 529p $26

ISBN 0-374-19969-8   LC 2002-19921

A coming of age story about Cal, a hermaphrodite, born in 1960 Detroit as a baby girl and reborn in 1974 as a teenage boy

"Eugenides pitches a big tent, but one of the delights of 'Middlesex' is how soundly it's constructed, with motifs and characters weaving through the novel's various episodes, pulling it tight." N Y Times Book Rev

(ed) My mistress's sparrow is dead. See My mistress's sparrow is dead

The virgin suicides. Farrar, Straus & Giroux 1993 249p

ISBN 0-374-28438-5   LC 92-33466

Eugenides, Jeffrey—*Continued*

"The Lisbon girls, all five of whom committed suicide in the early 1970s, haunt the memories of boys next door in a wealthy Detroit suburb. A nameless narrator, one of the boys, 20 years later collects and weaves together the impressions that friends, neighbors, and parents had of the dead girls. Except for school and group outings to two ill-fated parties, the girls' lives played out confined to their dwelling, a cloistered existence protected by a mother vigilant for their virtue and by a meek father cowed by his feminized surroundings." Booklist

The author's "engrossing writing style keeps one reading despite a creepy feeling that one shouldn't be enjoying it so much. A black, glittering novel that won't be to everyone's taste but must be tried by readers looking for something different." Libr J

Eustace, Robert

(jt. auth) Sayers, D. L. The documents in the case

Evanovich, Janet

Eleven on top. St. Martin's Press 2005 310p $26.95

ISBN 0-312-30626-1   LC 2005-47846

Stephanie Plum "no longer wants to work for her cousin Vinnie, the bail bondsman in the Burg, a section of Trenton, New Jersey. Her first three tries at new gainful employment–the button factory, the local dry cleaner, and the infamous Cluck in a Bucket fast-food joint–engender firebombings, exploding cars, and even the death of a local everyone is way too happy to see go. Meanwhile, several local businessmen have disappeared, and a lowlife Stephanie has known since high school is leaving lurid and scary notes in her apartment. Although brimming with lines that will have readers howling with laughter, this installment also allows flashes of insight into the men in Stephanie's life, Morelli the cop and Ranger the bounty hunter, as well as into Stephanie herself and her (over)extended family." Booklist

Hard eight. St. Martin's Press 2002 311p $25.95
ISBN 0-312-26585-9   LC 2002-21290

In this adventure Jersey bounty hunter Stephanie Plum drops "everthing to search for a missing child when Mabel Markowitz's granddaughter, Evelyn, skips town with her little girl, Annie, forfeiting Mabel's house as collateral on a child custody bond. . . . For all its zany elements, the plot turns logically on its own comically warped axis." N Y Times Book Rev

Hot six. St. Martin's Press 2000 294p
ISBN 0-312-20540-6   LC 00-25208

"Stephanie Plum, Jersey Girl and bounty hunter extraordinaire, is on the hunt for Ranger, her mysterious and sexy co-worker, who has been implicated in a murder. At the same time, she is tracked by thugs Habib and Mitchell, who threaten bodily harm if she doesn't find Ranger for them." Libr J

One for the money. Scribner 1994 290p $25
ISBN 0-684-19639-5   LC 93-50733

"Stephanie Plum, a New Jersey native, is a laid-off discount lingerie buyer. Desperate for bucks, she decides to pursue a career as an 'apprehension agent,' tracking down scofflaws for her bail bondsman cousin, Vinnie.

Her first mission: to bring in Joe Morelli, a cop accused of murder." Booklist

"A wonderful sense of humor, an eye for detail, and a self-deprecating narrative endow Stephanie Plum with the easy-to-swallow believability that accounts for her appeal as heroine. . . . A witty, well-written, and gutsy debut." Libr J

Three to get deadly. Scribner 1997 300p $25
ISBN 0-684-82265-2   LC 96-42176

"Hunting for a local candy-store owner who jumped bail, Trenton's most famous bounty hunter, Stephanie Plum . . . is knocked out on the job. She awakens beside a dead man who happens to be in violation of a bond agreement with her cousin Vinnie, so homicide wants to give her the third degree." Libr J

"Stephanie Plum stands apart from the female series characters who are so popular in crime fiction. She's funnier, tougher, politically incorrect, and just loves her job to death." Booklist

To the nines; a Stephanie Plum novel. St. Martin's Press 2003 312p il $25.95
ISBN 0-312-26586-7

"Bounty hunter Stephanie Plum is at it again. Singh has jumped ship, abandoning his fianceé, stealing her dog, and owing his landlord back rent. Through their sleuthing, Stephanie and Ranger track him down in Vegas. Unfortunately, owing to a previous problem with the law, Ranger isn't allowed to go to Vegas. This leaves Stephanie with Lulu and Connie as her traveling companions." Libr J

Two for the dough. Scribner 1996 301p
ISBN 0-684-82592-9   LC 95-23888

In this novel bounty hunter Stephanie Plum tracks "a bond jumper through her blue-collar neighborhood known as the 'burg.' A local funeral home, a slimy undertaker and mutilated corpses figure large in the search for Kenny Mancuso, who, having shot an old high school friend in the knee, posted bail with Stephanie's boss, her cousin, and then disappeared. When the old friend is shot again, fatally, Stephanie reluctantly joins forces with her sexy enemy and love interest, Trenton homicide cop Joe Morelli. . . . Readers will likely stay a few steps ahead of the sleuths, but the sharp repartee and Stephanie's slightly cynical but still fond relationship with her family and the burg hold a treasury of urban-style charms." Publ Wkly

Evans, Nicholas

The horse whisperer. Delacorte Press 1995 404p $24.95
ISBN 0-385-31523-6

                              * LC 95-17742

"The narrative begins with a frightful accident: teenage Grace Maclean, daughter of nice-guy lawyer Robert and tough, English-born magazine editor Annie, is out riding near their country home in upstate New York on a snowy day, and she and her beautiful horse Pilgrim are hit by a skidding tractor-trailer. Grace is crippled, Pilgrim desperately injured and mentally shattered. Annie takes things firmly in hand, finds a cowboy, Tom Booker, who is a wizard with horses and, with Grace and Pilgrim in tow, heads out to Montana in search of healing for the horse and ultimate recovery of Grace."

Evans, Nicholas—Continued

Publ Wkly

"Evans can give equally clipped but clear descriptions of a prosthetic device or a Montana vista, and the lead characters emerge through carefully constructed, seemingly effortless scenes and dialog, not in histrionics." Libr J

Evaristo, Bernardine, 1959-

Blonde roots. Riverhead Books 2009 269p $24.95

ISBN 978-1-59448-863-4; 1-59448-863-0

LC 2008-46308

First published 2008 in the United Kingdom

An "alternative history that goes back several centuries to flip the slave trade, with 'Aphrikans' enslaving the people of 'Europa' and exporting many of them to 'Amarika.' The plot revolves around Doris, the daughter of a long line of proud cabbage farmers who live in serfdom. After she's kidnapped by slavers, she experiences the horror and inhumanity of slave transport, is sold and works her way back to freedom. The narrative cuts back and forth through time, contrasting the journey to freedom with the journey toward slavery." Publ Wkly

"The whole story is a riotous, bitter course in the arbitrary nature of our cultural values. Don't be fooled; slavery might have ended 150 years ago, but you've still got time to be enlightened by this bracing novel." Washington Post Book World

Eve, Nomi, 1968-

The family orchard. Knopf 2000 316p $25

ISBN 0-375-41076-7

LC 00-40566

This is "a six-generation family memoir recast as fiction. . . . Set almost entirely in Israel, the book spans 160 years of tumultuous Israeli and family history, from the 1830's, when Palestine was part of the Turkish Empire, through the three major waves, or aliyahs, of Jewish immigration, the British mandate, modern statehood and warfare, up to the present. Historical figures and events flit past in the background of the characters' lives." N Y Times Book Rev

"This fascinating novel not only acknowledges that much of family history is imagined or embellished but glories in it." Booklist

Evenson, Brian, 1966-

The open curtain; a novel. Coffee House Press 2006 223p pa $14.95

ISBN 978-1-56689-188-2; 1-56689-188-4

LC 2006-12060

The author "makes a murder committed in 1902 by a grandson of Mormon prophet Brigham Young one of the central plot strands of his latest novel. Raised in a troubled but strict religious home, teenage misfit Rudd gradually pulls away from his oppressive mother, inventing a new family and new world for himself. When he is found at the scene of a double murder with little memory of the preceding events, he forms a unique bond with 19-year-old Lyndi, the daughter of the victims. The two, barely recovered from the gruesome events, start to lose track of time and to call each other by the names of the perpetrators of the 1902 murder. The Mormon angle is not what is most interesting about this uncompromising novel; instead, it's the convincing portrayal of a disturbed young man pushed to the breaking point by social isolation and religious extremism." Booklist

Everett, Percival L.

American desert; [by] Percival Everett. Hyperion 2004 291p $24.95

ISBN 0-7868-6917-8

LC 2003-056757

"While on his way to commit suicide, Ted Street, an untenured English professor and philandering husband, is beheaded in a car accident. Worse, he wakes up at his own funeral, his head clumsily stitched on his neck and his mouth sewn closed. From there, Ted embarks on a wide-ranging cruise through the American landscape, as he is kidnapped by a cult convinced that he is a devil; picked up by the military to be experimented on as a prototype of the perfect soldier; and sheltered by another cult, which worships him as a messiah." New Yorker

"Thoughtful, darkly comic and full of heart, the novel offers a wonderfully unusual story about retrospection and forgiveness." Publ Wkly

I am Not Sidney Poitier; a novel; [by] Percival Everett. Graywolf Press 2009 234p pa $16

ISBN 978-1-55597-527-2; 1-55597-527-5

"Everett's latest tells the story of a young man named Not Sidney Poitier who bears an uncanny resemblance to the famed actor and is adept at deploying a hypnotic technique called Fesmerism. When Not Sidney is young, his mother dies, but not before becoming an early investor in Ted Turner's enterprises. The boy then moves to Atlanta, into the home of Ted Turner. Despite his vast wealth and celebrity looks, when Not Sidney ventures out into the world as a young adult, he faces bizarre, stinging and potentially deadly forms of racism. . . . Not only is the novel smart and without a trace of pretentiousness, it shows Everett as a novelist at the height of his narrative and satirical powers." Publ Wkly

The water cure; [by] Percival Everett. Graywolf Press 2007 216p $22

ISBN 978-1-55597-476-3; 1-55597-476-7

LC 2007-924763

"Ishmael Kidder, eccentric enough to bring his own food to restaurants, has made a fortune writing romance novels under an assumed name. He divides his time between California and a remote house, with no telephone, in the hills of Taos, N.M. He is also a kidnapper and torturer. . . . If you think Kidder makes an unlikely hero, please take into consideration that the man he kidnaps, transports across state lines, and ties up in his basement is responsible, or so he believes, for the rape and murder of Kidder's 11-year-old daughter, Lane. The Water Cure takes the form of journal in which Kidder reports his wide-ranging thoughts. The terrible sadness is made all the more acute by an underlying dark humor. The text jumps around from Socratic dialogues with his prisoner to silly jokes to meditations on ancient philosophy and aesthetics to memories of his daughter." PopMatters

Evison, Jonathan

All about Lulu; a novel. Soft Skull Press 2008 340p pa $14.95

ISBN 978-1-59376-196-7; 1-59376-196-1

LC 2007-46761

Evison, Jonathan—*Continued*

"William Miller Jr. is a scrawny loner whose mother dies of cancer when he is seven years old, leaving him an awkward vegetarian with an ominously macho father and idiot twin brothers in mid-1970s Santa Monica. William's father, Big Bill, remarries a grief counselor named Willow, and Will spends the following decades in love with Louisa (Lulu, as she prefers to be called), his new stepsister. They are close throughout adolescence, but after a summer at cheerleading camp, Lulu returns home distant and hostile, leaving Will to pine for her in solitary desperation. Will finally appears to be on the path to normalcy in the early 1990s when he lucks into a radio talk-show hosting gig, but the stroke of good fortune is short-lived, as he discovers things about Lulu he'd rather not know. Evison provides readers a viciously funny and deeply felt portrayal of a blended family and one man's thwarted longing." Publ Wkly

Exupéry, Antoine de Saint- *See* Saint-Exupéry, Antoine de, 1900-1944

F

Faber, Michel

The courage consort; three novellas. Harcourt 2004 232p $23.00
ISBN 0-15-101061-7   LC 2004-5912
"In 'The Courage Consort,' the soprano of a vocal quintet her husband directs progresses from suicidal anxiety to relative equanimity as the group rehearses a difficult new piece that sudden death prevents them from premiering. In 'The Hundred Ninety-Nine Steps,' a woman resolves her trauma over losing a leg and her lover because of a senseless accident; by means romantic and eerie, a handsome young doctor, his late father's dog, and a manuscript in a bottle are the catalysts of her transformation. In the entrancing 'The Fahrenheit Twins'—perhaps a coming-of-age parable—brother and sister Marko'cain and Tainto'lilith, born and reared in arctic isolation, quest far from home for a signal from the universe telling them what to do with their mother's corpse. Faber's literary artistry in all three pieces is consummate." Booklist

The courage consort [novelette]
In Faber, M. The courage consort

The crimson petal and the white. Harcourt 2002 838p $26
ISBN 0-15-100692-X   LC 2002-24138
The protagonist of this novel, set in 1870s London, is a "young prostitute named Sugar. Intelligent and ambitious, Sugar yearns to escape from the livelihood forced on her at age 13. Enter William Rackham, a besotted philanderer and idle heir to a family perfume business, who installs Sugar as his secret mistress in a fashionable hideaway. When the incompetent William is forced into managing the family firm, he initially seeks advice from Sugar, who, fearful of losing his affection, schemes to gain closer proximity to the Rackham family. She succeeds by becoming governess to William's only child, young Sophie, who is cruelly ignored by her father and

his insane and sickly wife, Agnes." Libr J
"The large themes that interwine the characters with one another—religion, health, sexuality, death, and, reluctantly, love—are juxtaposed against the most minute and intimate details of Victorian life. . . . This massive work is startling and absorbing." Booklist

The Fahrenheit twins
In Faber, M. The courage consort

The hundred and ninety-nine steps
In Faber, M. The courage consort

Vanilla bright like Eminem; stories. Harcourt 2007 246p $23
ISBN 978-0-15-101314-2   LC 2006-103560
First published 2005 in the United Kingdom with title: The Fahrenheit twins
Contents: The safehouse; Andy comes back; The eyes of the soul; Serious swimmers; Explaining coconuts; Finesse; Flesh remains flesh; Less than perfect; A hole with two ends; The smallness of the action; All black; Mouse; Someone to kiss it better; Beyond pain; Tabitha Warren; Vanilla bright like Eminem
"A cunning, sui generis talent. . . . Mr. Faber's clinical detachment serves well the deprivations and frustrations of postindustrial near-manhood. . . . [His] style provides the fun-house unheimlich of an unedited newswire; comas and infanticide evince the same mannered anxiety as train rides and daydreams." N Y Observer

Fain, Michael
For works written by this author in collaboration with Judith Barnard see Michael, Judith

Fairstein, Linda

Bad blood. Scibner 2007 400p $26
ISBN 978-0-7432-8748-7; 0-7432-8748-7
          LC 2006-51168
"An explosion that rocks the construction site of Water Tunnel #3 in New York also rocks the courtroom where Alexandra Cooper aims to prove that a young businessman did in his wife." Libr J
"While Cooper may engage in a few too many action sequences for legal purists, the crisp writing and Fairstein's enviable capacity to translate her own experience as a prosecutor into an accessible plot puts this series a cut above most entries in this crowded subgenre." Publ Wkly

The bone vault; a novel. Scribner 2003 386p $25
ISBN 0-7432-2354-3   LC 2002-26686
A thriller starring Alexandra Cooper, "a Manhattan assistant district attorney. This time out, she and her sidekick, cop Mike Chapman, are drawn into a particularly mysterious case: a Metropolitan Museum of Art intern is found dead in a sarcophagus, and though she's been dead for months, her body is perfectly preserved. When it is discovered that she died of arsenic poisoning, the plot thickens. This is fun reading." Libr J

Entombed; [by] Linda A. Fairstein. Scribner 2005 400p $26
ISBN 0-7432-5488-0   LC 2004-52189

Fairstein, Linda—*Continued*

"Alexandra Cooper returns in another case featuring two seemingly unrelated crimes that the talented sex-crimes prosecutor is hell-bent on connecting. A serial rapist is terrorizing Manhattan's tony Upper East Side. Dubbed the Silk Stocking rapist, his usual M.O. is to terrorize the victim but not kill her. When one girl winds up dead, Alex and her trusted detective partners, Mercer Wallace and Mike Chapman, believe that perhaps a copycat perpetrator is out there who takes his crimes one step further. At the same time, Alex becomes obsessed with the stories of Edgar Allan Poe, especially after a young person's skeleton is found in an old home Poe once inhabited." Booklist

"It's a tribute to Fairstein's integrity and her clear, measured prose that the novel never tips into prurience. Her methodical presentation of authentic detail engages reader interest more than narrative flourish or cheap thrills." Publ Wkly

Killer heat; a novel. Doubleday 2008 370p $26
ISBN 978-0-385-52397-4; 0-385-52397-1
LC 2007-20286

Assistant DA Alexandra Cooper "alternates between the courtroom and crime scenes amid the sweltering summer heat of Manhattan. As she works to convict a serial rapist accused of over 50 rapes in a 35-year-old cold case, verbal and physical threats from vengeance-seeking drug-gang members heat up the courtroom. Alex is called to a crime scene in an abandoned government building, and soon two other young women vanish. Similarities in the cases suggest the possibility of a serial killer, and Alex and colleagues Mike Chapman and Mercer Wallace brave rising temperatures and isolated locations in hot pursuit of the killer. Partly based on a 2006 crime, the novel delivers taut suspense, action-packed chases, historical glimpses of Manhattan, and a smattering of romance." Libr J

Falconer, Colin, 1953-

Feathered serpent; a novel of the Mexican conquest. Crown 2002 374p $22.95
ISBN 0-609-61029-5
LC 2002-24711

"Born an Aztec princess and sold into slavery after her father's death, Malinali was at 15 given to conquistador Herman Cortes. A highly intelligent woman gifted in several languages, she made herself indispensable as an interpreter to the Spaniards. Her desire for revenge against Montezuma II, whom she held responsible for the murder of her father, and her belief that Cortes was actually the god Feathered Serpent, coupled with the Spaniards' overwhelming greed for gold, initiated a disastrous sequence of events that led to the fall of the Aztec empire." Libr J

"This enthralling reconstruction of the birth of modern Mexico is rooted in both genuine history and cultural myth." Booklist

Falconer, Delia, 1966-

The lost thoughts of soldiers. Soft Skull Press 2006 151p $16
ISBN 1-933368-17-9
LC 2006-4052

This is an "imagined portrait of the last days of Frederick Benteen, a real-life survivor of the Battle of Little Bighorn whose reputation in history has changed somewhat over the decades. . . . As the novel opens, Benteen is in retirement in Georgia, living out his days quietly and reflecting on the circle of men he knew under Custer's command, when he receives a letter from an admirer in Chicago, who wants his help in setting the record straight about his service during the fateful battle. As Benteen recalls those days, sliding in and out of the past like a man exploring a house he's not been inside for many years, Falconer gently leads the reader through Benteen's life, giving equal weight to his longstanding marriage to his wife Kate and his days on the prairie with the men of the Seventh Cavalry. Despite the subject matter, Falconer writes with a soft touch, mixing subtly poetic images with the occasional burst of crudity and bawdy humor one might expect of hard-bitten military men in 1876." Boise Wkly

Fallada, Hans, 1893-1947

Every man dies alone; translated by Michael Hofmann, with an afterword by Geoff Wilkes. Melville House Pub. 2009 543p il $27
ISBN 978-1-933633-63-3; 1-933633-63-8
LC 2008-27489

Original German edition, 1947

A novel "inspired by the true story of Otto and Elise Hampel, who scattered postcards advocating civil disobedience throughout wartime Nazi-controlled Berlin. Their fictional counterparts, Otto and Anna Quangel, distribute cards during the war bearing antifascist exhortations and daydream that their work is being passed from person to person, stirring rebellion, but, in fact, almost every card is immediately turned over to authorities." Publ Wkly

This is a "readable, suspense-driven novel from an author who a) knew what he was doing when it came to writing commercial fiction, and b) had lived through, and so knew intimately, the period he was writing about. This is an extraordinary combination. I hesitate to use a word like 'serendipity,' but cruelly enough, that's exactly what it was. Thus, the characters — and what characters they are, the good, the bad and the ugly of the Berlin working class during the war — are drawn from life. They are alive." Globe and Mail

Fallenberg, Evan

(tr) Leshem, R. Beaufort

Fallon, Martin, 1929- *See* Higgins, Jack, 1929-

Farah, Nuruddin, 1945-

Knots. Riverhead Books 2006 422p $25.95
ISBN 978-1-59448-924-2; 1-59448-924-6
LC 2006-23107

Second book of a trilogy started with Links. "A decade after 'the collapse,' Somalian-born Cambara, who has spent most of her life in Canada, leaves Toronto for Mogadishu, intending to mourn the death of her nine-year-old son (caused by the negligence of her philandering husband), reclaim a family home from a marauding warlord, and try to make peace for herself and her coun-

Farah, Nuruddin, 1945-—*Continued*
try." Booklist
"Despite its weaknesses, there is beauty in this story of reclamation and resurrection. When Farah's heroine sheds her veil of conformity, it is as if Somalia itself is emerging from a cocoon of despair." Time Out New York

Links. Riverhead Books 2004 336p $24.95
ISBN 1-573-22265-8   LC 2003-65969
First published 2003 in South Africa
"Jeebleh, settled in the United States with an American wife and grown children, returns to Mogadishu with two purposes. One is to find the burial place of his mother; the other is to try to rescue the kidnapped niece of Bile, an old friend and onetime comrade in the early fight against the dictator Mohammed Siad Barre." N Y Times Book Rev
This novel is "both alien and familiar, a haunting exploration of the desire to help and the attendant costs of doing so." Christ Sci Monit

Farmer, Philip José, 1918-2009

The classic Philip José Farmer, 1952-1964—1964-1973; edited and introduction by Martin H. Greenberg; foreword by Isaac Asimov. Crown 1984 2v o.p.
"Classics of modern science fiction"
Contents: 1952-1964: Sail on! Sail on; Mother; The God business; The Alley Man; My sister's brother; The king of beasts
1964-1973: The shadow of space; Riders of the purple wage [novelette]; Don't wash the carats; The jungle rot kid on the nod; The oogenesis of Bird City; The sliced-crosswise only-on-Tuesday world; Sketches among the ruins of my mind; After King Kong fell

The dark design. Berkley Pub. Group 1977 412p (Riverworld)
ISBN 0-399-12031-9   LC 77-5138
The third volume of the Riverworld series
This volume "continues the adventures of explorer Sir Richard Burton, Mark Twain, and scores of others who are resurrected along the banks of the multimillion-mile-long River. . . . In dirigibles and riverboats, through heroism and treachery, a band of restless explorers attains the headwaters home of the mysterious Ethicals, who apparently are responsible for creating the Riverworld and resurrecting its confused populace." Booklist
"Some threads in the design are loose or overknotted, but the dash and grand scope of the project and this installment of it are compellingly fascinating." Publ Wkly
Followed by The magic labyrinth

The fabulous riverboat; a science fiction novel. Putnam 1971 253p o.p.
This second novel in the Riverworld series "is set in an 'after-Earthlife' of resurrected people over the age of five from time immemorial. The main character is . . . Sam Langhorne Clemens, alias Mark Twain, who attempts to build a metal riverboat. His goal, not obtained in this novel, is to sail upriver to reach the Misty Tower and discover the secret of its guardians, the Ethicals." Libr J
Followed by The dark design

Gods of Riverworld. Putnam 1983 331p (Riverworld)
ISBN 0-399-12843-3   LC 83-9552
The fifth volume of the Riverworld series
"The members of the intrepid band that achieved its quest for the end of the River in the previous books now find themselves in command of the Ethicals' polar control center. When they're not trying to track down an unknown enemy, they're building private worlds and resurrecting a few friends. . . . It's the two varieties of god-playing, culminating in a disastrous tea party in Alice Pleasance Liddell's Wonderland, that give the book its interest." Publ Wkly

The magic labyrinth. Berkley Pub. Group 1980 339p (Riverworld)
ISBN 0-399-12381-4   LC 80-144
In this fourth volume in the Riverworld series "Farmer brings his large and bizarre cast of characters (including King John Lackland of England, Samuel Clemens, Sir Richard Burton, Hermann Göring, and Alice Liddell, who inspired 'Alice in Wonderland') to the end of their quest and reveals the secret of the Riverworld. For readers prepared to accept it on its own terms, this book will be rewarding, even exciting. Farmer's imagination does not flag from beginning to end." Booklist
Followed by Gods of Riverworld

Riders of the purple wage
In The Hugo winners p388-459
In Farmer, P. J. The classic Philip José Farmer, 1952-1964—1964-1973 p30-103

To your scattered bodies go; a science fiction novel. Putnam 1971 221p (Riverworld) o.p.
The first volume of the Riverworld series
"The fabulous Riverworld, site of the resurrection of every human being who has died, is one of the great fictional creations. Sir Richard Burton, Victorian explorer and rogue, finds himself reborn and sets off on an epic journey to learn the truth of its existence." Shapiro. Fic For Youth. 3d edition
Followed by The fabulous riverboat

Farrell, James T. (James Thomas), 1904-1979

Judgment day
In Farrell, J. T. Studs Lonigan

Studs Lonigan; a trilogy. Library of America 2004 988p (The library of America, 148) $35
ISBN 1-931082-55-3   LC 2003-44207
First published as a trilogy 1935 by Vanguard Press
Contents: Young Lonigan; The young manhood of Studs Lonigan; Judgment day
A trilogy "about life among lower-middle-class Irish Roman Catholics in Chicago during the first third of the 20th century. . . . As a boy, William Lonigan (always referred to as 'Studs') makes a slight effort to rise above his squalid urban environment. However, the combination of his own personality, unwholesome neighborhood friends, a small-minded family, and his schooling and religious training all condemn him to the life of futility and dissipation that are his inheritance." Merriam-Webster's Ency of Lit

Young Lonigan
In Farrell, J. T. Studs Lonigan

Farrell, James T. (James Thomas), 1904-1979—
Continued

The young manhood of Studs Lonigan
In Farrell, J. T. Studs Lonigan

Faulkner, William, 1897-1962

Absalom, Absalom!; corrected text. Random House 1986 313p
ISBN 0-394-55634-8

* LC 86-6488

First published 1936

"During the summer of 1910, prior to Quentin Compson's leaving the South for his first year at Harvard, old Rosa Coldfield insists upon a private conference with the youth to divulge her recollections of Thomas Sutpen. Driven by a great plan to become a Southern aristocrat, Sutpen builds a mansion, only to see his life ruined. The title of the book reveals the story's basic tragedy: Sutpen's disappointment in his children. One is a spinster and thus has no offspring to continue the family lineage; the other is a son who has disappeared. Sutpen himself falls victim to a murder for retribution. Faulkner depicts the South before and after the Civil War in this powerfully written novel." Shapiro. Fic for Youth. 3d edition

also in Faulkner, W. Novels, 1936-1940 p1-315

As I lay dying. Modern Lib. 2000 $16.95
ISBN 0-375-50452-4

*

This is a reissue of the title first published 1930 by H. Smith

"Experimental in both subject and narrative structure, this novel treats the events surrounding the illness, death and burial of Addie Bundren, wife of Anse and mother of Cash, Darl, Jewel, Dewey Dell, and Vardaman. It is divided into 59 short interior monologues, predominantly in the present tense, spoken both by the seven members of the family and by various other characters, including the Reverend Whitfield, Dr. Peabody, and the Bundrens' neighbours, Vernon and Cora Tull." Camb Guide to Lit in Engl

also in Faulkner, W. Novels, 1930-1935

Collected stories of William Faulkner. Random House 1950 900p pa $19.95 hardcover o.p.
ISBN 0-679-76403-8 (pa)

Contents: Barn burning; Shingles for the Lord; The tall men; A bear hunt; Two soldiers; Shall not perish; A rose for Emily; Hair; Centaur in brass; Dry September; Death drag; Elly; Uncle Willy; Mule in the yard; That will be fine; That evening sun; Red leaves; A justice; A courtship; Lo!; Ad astra; Victory; Crevasse; Turnabout; All the dead pilots; Wash; Honor; Dr. Martino; Fox hunt; Pennsylvania Station; Artist at home; The brooch; My Grandmother Millard; Golden land; There was a queen; Mountain victory; Beyond; Black music; The leg; Mistral; Divorce in Naples; Carcassonne

"Forty-two short stories, including all from These Thirteen (1931), all but two from Doctor Martino and other stories (1934) and seventeen published in magazines, 1932-1948. . . . Many of the stories deal with characters and incidents related to those in his novels set in the mythical Yoknapatawpha County, Mississippi." Libr J

A fable. Random House 1954 437p
ISBN 0-394-42400-X

"Set in France a few months before the end of World War I, 'A Fable' is both an allegory of the passion of Christ and a study of a world that has chosen submission to authority and the secular values of power and chauvinism instead of the individuality and the exercise of free will. The novel centers on the fate of a young corporal . . . [who] with the aid of twelve companions, incites a mutiny in the trenches which results in a temporary armistice. Betrayed by a member of his own regiment, the corporal is executed for cowardice along with two other military criminals, becoming a martyr to his principles and his belief in humanity." Benet's Reader's Ency of Am Lit

also in Faulkner, W. Novels, 1942-1954 p665-1072

The Faulkner reader; selections from the works of William Faulkner. Random House 1954 682p o.p.

Contains the following: The sound and the fury [complete] (1929); The bear, excerpt from Go down, Moses; Old man, excerpt from The wild palms; Spotted horses, excerpt from The hamlet; A rose for Emily; Barn burning; Dry September; That evening sun; Turnabout; Shingles for the Lord; A justice; Wash; An odor of verbena, excerpt from The Unvanquished; Percy Grimm, excerpt from Light in August; The courthouse, excerpt from Requiem for a nun

Flags in the dust; edited and with an introduction by Douglas Day. Random House 1973 370p o.p.

This is the uncut and complete version of Sartoris. "The introduction describes the bibliographic history of the narrative and makes clear that the present work is as complete a reproduction as possible of the extant composite typescript. Emphasis of 'Flags in the dust' is extended from the Sartoris family featured in the later novel to the full range of Faulkner's Yoknapatawpha social structure, resulting in a complete fictional documentation of the intense Faulknerian world which saturated all his writings." Booklist

also in Faulkner, W. Novels, 1926-1929

Go down, Moses; introduction by Stanley Crouch. Modern Lib. 1995 xxii, 367p
ISBN 0-679-60174-0

* LC 95-4715

A reissue of the Random House edition published 1942 with title: Go down Moses, and other stories which was analyzed in Short story index

"The voices of Faulkner's South—black and white, comic and tragic—ring through this sprawling tale of the McCaslin clan. The tone ranges from the farcical to the profound. As the title suggests, the stories are rife with biblical themes. Although the seven stories were originally published separately, *Go Down, Moses* is best read as a novel of interconnecting generations, races, and dreams." Merriam-Webster's Ency of Lit

also in Faulkner, W. Novels, 1942-1954 p1-281

The hamlet. 3rd ed. Random House 1964 366p
ISBN 0-394-42759-9

Faulkner, William, 1897-1962—*Continued*

First published 1940

First volume in the trilogy about the "Snopes family who descended upon Yoknapatawpha County, Mississippi in the latter years of the nineteenth century. It "tells how Ab Snopes, ex-bushwhacker, horse trader and sharecropper won immunity in Frenchman's Bend because of his reputation as a barn burner and how his son Flem became a clerk in Will Varner's store. Before long other members of the family descend like swarming locusts on the village. . . . Led by Flem, who has set himself up in the world by marrying Eula Varner when she was pregnant with another man's child, they then move on to Jefferson, the county seat." Magill. Masterpieces of World Lit in Dig Form

Followed by The town

also in Faulkner, W. Novels, 1936-1940 p727-1075

also in Faulkner, W. Snopes p1-349

If I forget thee, Jerusalem
In Faulkner, W. Novels, 1936-1940 p493-726

Intruder in the dust. Random House 1948 247p
ISBN 0-394-43074-3

"When Lucas, an elderly Negro, is accused of murdering a white man, Charles, a 16-year-old white boy, works to save him from being lynched. Charles gets the help he needs in his sleuthing from an old aristocratic lady and a young black boy. The trio visits the church graveyard at night to dig up the corpse of the supposed victim. The book can be read as a mystery and, on a deeper level, as a social commentary on the South." Shapiro. Fic for Youth. 3d edition

also in Faulkner, W. Novels, 1942-1954 p283-470

Light in August; the corrected text. Modern Library 2002 512p $21.95
ISBN 0-679-64248-X   LC 2001-57933

First published 1932 by Harrison Smith & Robert Haas, Inc.

The novel "reiterates the author's concern with a society that classifies men according to race, creed, and origin. Joe Christmas, the central character and victim, appears to be white but is really part black; he has an affair with Joanna Burden, a spinster whom the townsfold of Jefferson regard with suspicion because of her New England background. Joe eventually kills her and sets fire to her house; he is captured, castrated, and killed by the outraged townspeople, to whom his victim has become a symbol of the innocent white woman attacked and killed by a black man. Other important characters are Lena Grove, who comes to Jefferson far advanced in pregnancy, expecting to find the lover who has deserted her, and Gail Hightower, the minister who ignores his wife and loses his church because of his fanatic devotion to the past." Reader's Ency. 4th edition

also in Faulkner, W. Novels, 1930-1935

The mansion. Random House 1959 436p o.p.

The mansion completes the trilogy of the Snopes family. Using his techniques of flashbacks and recombining earlier themes, Faulkner "covers a time span linking Jack Houston's murder with Flem's violent death at the hands of Mink Snopes thirty-eight years later. In this novel,

however, much of Flem's trickery and greed for money and power fade into the background and Linda, Eula's daughter becomes the central figure." Magill. Masterpieces of World Lit in Dig Form

"Sometimes the reader grows tired of the tough repetitive monologues and the revelations of Southern decay, but in Faulkner there is a massiveness and even a majesty not easily found elsewhere in the American fiction of this century. . . . Turgid and difficult as he is, Faulkner is worth the trouble." Burgess. 99 Novels

also in Faulkner, W. Novels, 1957-1962 p327-721

also in Faulkner, W. Snopes p673-1065

Mosquitoes
In Faulkner, W. Novels, 1926-1929

Novels, 1926-1929. Library of Am. 2006 1182p $40
ISBN 1-931082-89-8   LC 2005-49444

Contents: Soldiers' pay; Mosquitoes; Flags in the dust; The sound and the fury

Soldiers' pay (1926) explores the disillusionment provoked by World War I. Mosquitoes (1927) is a satire of artistic poseurs. In Flags in the dust (published in truncated form in 1929 as Sartoris) Faulkner began his exploration of Yoknapatapha County, Mississippi. The sound and the fury (1929) tells of the decline of the Compson clan

Novels, 1930-1935. Library of Am. 1985 1034p $35
ISBN 0-940450-26-7   LC 84-23424

Contents: As I lay dying; Sanctuary; Light in August; Pylon

Novels, 1936-1940. Library of Am. 1990 1117p map $37.50
ISBN 0-940450-55-0   LC 89-62931

Contents: Absalom, Absalom!; The unvanquished; If I forget thee, Jerusalem (The wild palms); The hamlet

Absalom, Absalom!, The unvanquished, and The hamlet are entered seperately. If I forget thee, Jerusalem (published 1939 with title The wild palms) depicts, in alternating narratives, the "effects of a Mississippi flood on the lives of a hillbilly convict and a New Orleans doctor and his mistress." Oxford Companion to Am Lit. 6th edition

Novels, 1942-1954. Library of Am. 1994 1115p $35
ISBN 0-940450-85-2   LC 94-2942

Contents: Go down, Moses; Intruder in the dust; Requiem for a nun; A fable

Novels, 1957-1962. Library of Am. 1999 1008p $35
ISBN 1-88301-169-8   LC 99-18348

Contents: The town; The mansion; The reivers

Pylon. H. Smith and R. Haas, Inc. 1935 315p o.p.

The scene is a Southern city where a Mardi Gras celebration is in progress. The action covers four days in the lives of a strange set of people, all of them connected in some way with the airplane contests which are being held in celebration of the opening of a new airport. The

Faulkner, William, 1897-1962—*Continued*
main characters are: Shumann, an airplane pilot; Jiggs, his mechanic; Jackson, a parachute jumper; Laverne, Shumann's wife; and a nameless reporter who adopts the group for the time being

also in Faulkner, W. Novels, 1930-1935

The reivers; a reminiscence. Vintage Books 1992 305p pa $12.95

ISBN 0-679-74192-5   LC 92-50095

First published 1932 by Harrison Smith & Robert Haas, Inc.

"Told to his grandson as 'A Reminiscence,' Lucius Priest's monologue recalls his adventures in 1905 as an 11-year-old, when he, the gigantic but childish part-Indian Boon Hogganbeck, and a black family servant, Ned William McCaslin, become reivers (stealthy plunderers) of the automobile of his grandfather, the senior banker of Jefferson, Miss." Oxford Companion to Am Lit. 5th edition

also in Faulkner, W. Novels, 1957-1962 p722-971

Requiem for a nun. Random House 1951 286p o.p.

"Written in three prose sections, which provide the background, and three acts which present the drama in the courthouse and the jail, the novel centers on Temple Drake, one of the main characters of *Sanctuary*. In the interval of the eight years separating the events of the two books, Temple has married Gowan Stevens and borne two children; she is being blackmailed by Pete, brother of her lover in *Sanctuary*, and is planning to run away with him when Nancy Manningoe, her black servant, kills Temple's youngest child. Her attempts to gain a pardon from the governor for Nancy finally bring out Temple's own involvement in and responsibility for the crime." Reader's Ency. 4th edition

also in Faulkner, W. Novels, 1942-1954 p471-664

Sanctuary. J. Cape & H. Smith 1931 380p o.p.

"Horace Benbow, an ineffectual intellectual, becomes involved in the violent events centering on Temple Drake, a provocative, irresponsible young coed. Temple is raped by Popeye, who murders a man trying to protect her. Popeye is a figure of evil, but is also a victim of his environment. Carried off to a Memphis brothel by Popeye, Temple later protects him and testifies against Lee Goodwin, who is accused of the murder. Benbow defends Goodwin at the trial and unsuccessfully tries to give shelter to Goodwin's common-law wife. Temple's perjured testimony ends all hope for Goodwin, who is lynched by the townspeople." Reader's Ency. 4th edition

also in Faulkner, W. Novels, 1930-1935

Sartoris. Harcourt Brace & Co. 1929 380p o.p.

"A saga of the Sartoris family, the novel deals primarily with young Bayard Sartoris' urge for self-destruction. His beloved twin brother, John, having been killed in World War I, Bayard returns home haunted by the memories of his brother, and becomes involved in a number of accidents. Because of his reckless driving, his grandfather, old Bayard Sartoris, rides with him in an attempt to force him to drive carefully, but young Bayard runs the

car off a cliff and his grandfather dies of a heart attack. Unable to face either himself or his family, Bayard goes to Ohio to become a test pilot and is killed. . . . Faulkner picks up the beginnings of the Sartoris family in 'The Unvanquished.'" Benet's Reader's Ency of Am Lit

A more complete version of this novel was published with title: Flags in the dust

Snopes; The hamlet, The town, The mansion; introduction by George Garrett. Modern Lib. 1994 1065p $27.95

ISBN 0-679-60092-2

An omnibus volume of three novels entered separately

Soldiers' pay. Boni & Liveright 1926 319p o.p.

"Lieutenant Donald Mahon, an American in the British air force during World War I, is discharged from the hospital where he has been treated for a critical head wound, and makes his way home to Georgia. The wound leaves a horrible scar, and causes loss of memory and later blindness. On the train from New York he is aided by Joe Gilligan, an awkward, friendly, footloose ex-soldier, and Margaret Powers, an attractive young widow whose husband was killed in the war. Margaret, strangely attracted to the dying, subhuman Donald, decides to go home with him, as does Gilligan, who is in love with her. Their reception in the Georgia town reveals the character of the fickle people." Oxford Companion to Am Lit. 6th edition

also in Faulkner, W. Novels, 1926-1929

The sound and the fury. New, corrected ed. Random House 1984 326p

ISBN 0-394-53241-4

* LC 84-42626

First published 1929

"The story is told in four parts, through the stream of consciousness of three characters (the sons of the Compson family, Benjy, Quentin, and Jason), and finally in an objective account. The Compson family, formerly genteel Southern patricians, now lead a degenerate, perverted life on their shrunken plantation near Jefferson, Miss. The disintegration of the family, which clings to outworn aristocratic conventions, is counterpointed by the strength of the black servants, who include old Dilsey and her son Luster." Oxford Companion to Am Lit. 6th edition

also in Faulkner, W. The Faulkner reader p5-251

also in Faulkner, W. Novels, 1926-1929

The town. Random House 1957 371p

ISBN 0-394-42452-2

This second volume in the Snopes trilogy "relates through two narrators of varying reliability the story of Flem Snopes' rise to prominence in the fictional Yoknapatawpha County. Flem's coldly calculated vengeance on his wife, Eula, and her lover culminates in Eula's suicide and Flem's rise to power in Jefferson, the county seat. Because Flem longs for respect as well as money, he turns against the clan of shiftless Snopes cousins who have followed him to town and forces them to leave Jefferson. In his hunger for social validation, he denies his own origins, and the book ends with a hint that the cousins' revenge will follow." Merriam-Webster's Ency of Lit

Followed by The mansion

Faulkner, William, 1897-1962—*Continued*
also in Faulkner, W. Novels, 1957-1962
p1-326
also in Faulkner, W. Snopes p351-671

Uncollected stories of William Faulkner; edited by Joseph Blotner. Random House 1979 716p
ISBN 0-394-40044-5 LC 78-21803
Contents: Ambuscade; Retreat; Raid; Skirmish at Sartoris; The unvanquished; Vendée; Fool about a horse; Lizards in Jamshyd's courtyard; The hound; Spotted horses; Lion; The old people; A point of law; Gold is not always; Pantaloon in black; Go down, Moses; Delta autumn; The bear; Race at morning; Hog pawn; Nympholepsy; Frankie and Johnny; The priest; Once aboard the Lugger (I); Once aboard the Lugger (II); Miss Zilphia Gant; Thrift; Idyll in the desert; Two dollar wife; Afternoon of a cow; Mr. Acarius; Sepulture South; Gaslight; Adolescence; Al Jackson; Don Giovanni; Peter; Moonlight; The big shot; Dull tale; A return; A dangerous man; Evangeline; A portrait of Elmer; With caution and dispatch; Snow

The unvanquished; drawings by Edward Shenton. Random House 1938 293p il o.p.
Contents: Ambuscade; Retreat; Raid; Riposte in tertio; Vendée; Skirmish at Sartoris; An odor of verbena
This is "a collection of interlocking stories. . . . Set during the Civil War, these stories deal with the Sartoris family, whose modern history Faulkner recounted in Sartoris. Composed of seven stories, which first appeared separately in magazines, the book centers primarily on the adventures of Bayard Sartoris and his black companion, Ringo. Colonel John Sartoris and Miss Rosa, Bayard's grandmother, also figure prominently." Reader's Ency. 3d edition
also in Faulkner, W. Novels, 1936-1940
p317-492

Faulks, Sebastian

Birdsong. Random House 1996 c1993 402p o.p.
* LC 95-23721
First published 1993 in the United Kingdom
"In 1910, England's Stephen Wraysford, a junior executive in a textile firm, is sent by his company to northern France. There he falls for Isabelle Azaire, a young and beautiful matron who abandons her abusive husband and sticks by Stephen long enough to conceive a child. Six years later, Stephen is back in France, as a British officer fighting in the trenches. Facing death, embittered by isolation, he steels himself against thoughts of love. But despite rampant disease, harrowing tunnel explosions and desperate attacks on highly fortified German positions, he manages to survive, and to meet with Isabelle again. . . . [The author] proves himself a grand storyteller here." Publ Wkly

Charlotte Gray; a novel. Random House 1999 399p
ISBN 0-375-50169-X LC 98-33658
First published 1998 in the United Kingdom
Charlotte Gray is a "young woman who, in 1942, leaves her home in Scotland to find work in London. Because of her fluency in French, she soon is recruited by G Section and sent to France to deliver a set of wireless

crystals to the Resistance. Her personal mission is to find Peter Gregory, a missing RAF pilot with whom she had a brief but intense affair. Posing as Dominique Gulbert, Charlotte makes her way to the village of Lavaurette. Her official task accomplished, she decides to stay on, and her life becomes enmeshed with the lives of the villagers—in particular Julien Levade, a young architect who also works for the Resistance, and his father, a painter." Booklist
Faulks "has written one of those rare books that is adventurous enough to attract a popular audience while thoughtful enough to sustain the more serious reader." Libr J

Devil may care; [by] Sebastian Faulks, writing as Ian Fleming. Doubleday 2008 278p $24.95
ISBN 978-0-385-52428-5; 0-385-52428-5
LC 2007-43052
This novel was written to mark the centenary of Ian Fleming's birth. At it's start "an Algerian drug runner is savagely executed in the desolate outskirts of Paris. This seemingly isolated event leads to the recall of Agent 007 from his sabbatical in Rome. . . . The head of MI6, M, assigns him to shadow the mysterious Dr. Julius Gorner, a power-crazed pharmaceutical magnate, whose wealth is exceeded only by his greed. Gorner has lately taken a disquieting interest in opiate derivatives, both legal and illegal, and this urgently bears looking into. Bond finds a willing accomplice in the shape of a glamorous Parisian named Scarlett Papava." Publisher's note
"Mr. Faulks-writing-as-Fleming does not fall short of the rest of Fleming's posthumous output. Nor does he tinker with the series's surefire recipe for success. What he delivers is a serviceable madeleine for Bond nostalgists and a decent replica of past Bond escapades." N Y Times (Late N Y Ed)

Engleby; a novel. Doubleday 2007 319p $24.95
ISBN 978-0-385-52405-6 LC 2007-16044
Readers are "plunged without introduction into the journals of Mike Engleby, a fiercely intelligent, acerbic and curiously disturbing young man who's studying natural sciences at Cambridge University in the early 1970's. . . . Engleby drinks and smokes a lot, and skulks, and does drugs—but not in a way that could be described as recreational. He pops little blue pills (also unnamed) but never seems to lose his capacity for lucid, almost clinical analysis of his surroundings. . . . Then there's his creepy infatuation with a pretty fellow student, Jennifer Arkland, who disappears in their final year—missing and presumed dead. Has Engleby killed her? The novel generates an unusual kind of suspense, a nagging puzzlement. Jennifer's fate is a worry, of course, but the persistent question is, What's his problem? . . . . The best way to enjoy Engleby is to concentrate, as the bizarre suspense percolates, on Mr. Faulks' exceptionally precise writing." N Y Observer

Human traces; a novel. Random House 2006 c2005 563p $25.95
ISBN 0-375-50226-2 LC 2005-46683
First published 2005 in the United Kingdom
"An epic novel about the rise of the disciplines of psychology and psychiatry from the late 19th century to the years after World War I. The story revolves around two men: Jacques Rebiere, a precociously talented youth with a scientific bent, and Thomas Midwinter, also intellectu-

Faulks, Sebastian—*Continued*

ally gifted and naturally curious but with more of a leaning toward literature. The two meet by chance in a French resort town and together dedicate their lives to finding a solution to the problems of insanity and reaching a basic understanding of consciousness, personality, and memory. Thomas's older sister, Sonia, also figures in the story, as the novel follows the course of her tragic first marriage, her later espousal to Jacques, and her involvement in her husband and brother's quest." Publ Wkly

"Faulks understands the difficulties inherent in using fiction to convey these complex arguments. He offsets his characters' earnestness—and his own—through attention to settings and plot details. He sends his protagonists to California and Tanzania to fill in pieces of the puzzle. He allows Rebiere to indulge in titillating sexual obsessions. Generally, the effort to entertain succeeds. And Human Traces can be moving, as its characters grapple with the limitations of knowledge and reason. Despite its shortcomings, the book should serve as a popular vehicle for reassessing the history of psychiatry and confronting the mystery of consciousness." Washington Post Book World

On Green Dolphin Street; a novel. Random House 2002 351p

ISBN 0-375-50225-4   LC 2001-41753

"It is 1960, and Mary and Charlie van der Linden are an English couple posted to Washington, where Charlie serves at the British Embassy. Mary is an exceptionally loyal wife—while Charlie, disillusioned by his own and the world's failures, is destroying himself through drink and pills, Mary uncomplainingly shores him up. Then she meets Frank Renzo, an American newspaper reporter, and enters into an affair." N Y Times Book Rev

"The outline of this archetypal love story may sound familiar, but everything about Faulks' telling of it is fresh. . . . It is a love story above all, but it is also a New York story, the sights, sounds, and smells of the city perfectly evoked to capture one of those moments when the forces of change collide with the proprieties of the past." Booklist

Faust, Christa

Money shot. Hard Case Crime 2008 250p pa $6.99

ISBN 978-0-8439-5958-1

"Former porn star Angel Dare (nee Gina Moretti), who stopped acting to establish Daring Angels, a firm that manages women in the business, is lured to perform once more by a hot young male star. Instead, she's beaten, raped, shot, and left for dead in the trunk of a car, and that's just the start—all because of money from the international sex trade. With the help of her company's ex-cop security escort, Lalo Malloy, Angel untangles the plot and players, depending finally on nothing but her own resources for the vengeance she craves. A rip-roaring story with nonstop action and an inside look at X-rated movie making, this is clearly not for all readers or collections; but the title (which originated in the porn industry) and cover art are indicators of its contents." Libr J

Faust, Frederick *See* Brand, Max, 1892-1944

Faust, Frederick, 1892-1944
See also Brand, Max, 1892-1944

Fearing, Kenneth, 1902-1961

The big clock
In Crime novels: American noir of the 1930s and 40s

Feeling very strange; the Slipstream anthology; James Patrick Kelly & John Kessel, editors. Tachyon Publications 2006 288p pa $14.95

ISBN 978-1-892391-35-X; 1-892391-35-X

Contents: Al, by C. Emshwiller; The little magic shop, by B. Sterling; The healer, by A. Bender; The specialist's hat, by K. Link; Light and the sufferer, by J. Lethem; Sea Oak, by G. Saunders; Exhibit H: torn pages discovered in the vest pocket of an unidentified tourist, by J. VanderMeer; Hell is the absence of God, by T. Chiang; Lieserl, by K. J. Fowler; Bright morning, by J. Ford; Biographical notes to "A discourse on the nature of causality, with airplane," by Benjamin Rosenbaum, by B. Rosenbaum; The god of dark laughter, by M. Chabon; The rose in twelve petals, by T. Goss; The lions are asleep this night, by H. Waldrop; You have never been here, by M. Rickert

"Is slipstream just science fiction and fantasy that doesn't know that it's science fiction or fantasy? Or is it more than that? Decide for yourself by slipping into short stories that are superb, whatever you choose to call them." SciFi.com

Feldman, Ellen
See also Villars, Elizabeth, 1941-

Ferber, Edna, 1887-1968

Cimarron. Doubleday, Doran 1930 388p o.p.

"Yancey Cravat was a big, handsome man who quoted Shakespeare and the Bible and knew the law. He started a newspaper in Wichita, Kansas, in whose pages he protested the government's treatment of the Indians. Against the wishes of her family he married Sabra Venable, daughter of an aristocratic Southern family. Then, lured by the newly opened frontier, he took off with her to help settle Oklahoma, where he was instrumental in establishing law and order. Although he could have been governor of the state, his restlessness took him away for weeks, months, and finally years, leaving Sabra with the responsibility for the newspaper. In the lives of these two strong-willed people, and of their son, Cim, Ferber has captured the drama, conflicts, and rewards of life in pioneer America." Shapiro. Fic for Youth. 3d edition

So Big. Doubleday, Page 1924 360p o.p.

Selina DeJong would look up from her work and say, 'How big is my man?' Then little Dirk DeJong would answer in the time-worn way, 'So-o-o big!' And he was so nicknamed. Though So Big gives the book its title his mother is the outstanding figure. Until Selina was nineteen she traveled with her gambler-father. At his sudden death she secured a teacher's post in the Dutch settlement of High Prairie, a community of hardworking farmers and their thrifty, slaving wives—narrow-minded people indifferent to natural beauty. Soon Selina married

Ferber, Edna, 1887-1968—*Continued*

Pervus DeJong, a plodding, goodnatured boy. With her marriage the never-ending drudgery of a farmer's wife began. Through all the years of hardship she never lost her gay indomitable spirit. Unfortunately, she was unable to transmit these qualities to her son

Fergus, Jim

The wild girl: the notebooks of Ned Giles, 1932; a novel. Hyperion 2005 355p $23.95

ISBN 1-401-30054-5   LC 2004-54161

"After the death of his parents, 17-year-old Giles leaves behind his job at a Chicago country club to join the Great Apache Expedition, a journey organized by citizens of the U.S and Mexico to recover the kidnapped son of a Mexican rancher. Exploring Mexico's Sierra Madres is an opportunity too rich to resist for Giles, who lucks into a job as one of the expedition's photographers. But when he captures the chilling image of a wild Apache girl in a Mexican jail, the young man cannot, in good conscience, turn his back and walk away. . . . Fans of both Larry McMurtry and Louis L'Amour will relish this deftly rendered tale of survival, self-discovery, and the precarious boundaries between man and beast. " Booklist

Ferman, Edward L.

(ed) The Best from fantasy & science fiction: the fiftieth anniversary anthology. See The Best from fantasy & science fiction: the fiftieth anniversary anthology

Ferrante, Elena

The lost daughter; translated from the Italian by Ann Goldstein. Europa 2008 125p pa $14.95

ISBN 978-1-933372-42-6; 1-933372-42-7

Original Italian edition, 2006

"In this brutally frank novel of maternal ambivalence, the narrator, a forty-seven-year-old divorcée summering alone on the Ionian coast, becomes obsessed with a beautiful young mother who seems ill at ease with her husband's rowdy, slightly menacing Neapolitan clan. When this woman's daughter loses her doll, the older woman commits a small crime that she can't explain even to herself. Although much of the drama takes place in her head, Ferrante's gift for psychological horror renders it immediate and visceral." New Yorker

Troubling love; translated from the Italisn by Ann Goldstein. Europa 2006 139p pa $14.95

ISBN 1-933372-16-8

Original Italian edition, 1995

"Delia, a cartoonist living in Rome, receives three incoherent phone calls from her mother, who is supposed to be on her way from Naples; the next day, her mother's nearly naked body washes up onshore at a seaside resort town. In Naples for the funeral, Delia is confronted with the past she tried to disown as she struggles to make sense of the events leading to her mother's drowning. A shadowy figure named Caserta, the man Delia, as a five-year-old, accused her mother of having an affair with, reëmerges as possibly the last person to see her

alive. Ferrante's polished language belies the rawness of her imagery, which conveys perversity, violence, and bodily functions in ripe detail. Delia's discovery of the secret of her childhood is made all the more jarring by the story's disorienting mixture of fantasy and reality." New Yorker

Ferraris, Zoe

Finding Nouf. Houghton Mifflin 2008 305p $24

ISBN 978-0-618-87388-3; 0-618-87388-0

LC 2007-38411

"Sixteen-year-old Nouf ash-Shrawi, daughter of a wealthy Saudi Arabian family, mysteriously disappears and is eventually found drowned in the desert. . . . Nouf's brother, Othman, asks his friend Nayir Sharqi, a local desert guide, to find out what happened to his sister. Nayir's investigation leads him into unknown territory—notably, the secret realm of women in a segregated Middle Eastern society. In an unusual partnership that challenges his traditional ideas, Nayir works on the case with Othman's fiancée, a laboratory technician in the medical examiner's office. Ferraris's debut novel gives a fascinating peek into the lives and minds of devout Muslim men and women while serving up an engrossing mystery." Libr J

Ferrell, Monica

The answer is always yes. Dial Press 2008 382p $24

ISBN 978-0-385-33929-2   LC 2008-6627

In this "novel, Matthew Acciaccatura, a bullied nerd from Teaneck, New Jersey, in his freshman year at N.Y.U. and hungry to be cool, is spotted by a Manhattan nightclub owner and given the chance to become a promoter. Ferrell chronicles Matt's ascent in the nineties rave culture and his downfall—brought about by his need, when he is faced with someone who symbolizes his childhood torturers, 'to deal a blow here for all loserkind.' Ferrell's . . . inclusion of a 'Pale Fire'-like commentary by a German sociologist seems unnecessary, given the ease with which her exuberant narration evokes her likable protagonist's world." New Yorker

Ferrigno, Robert

Prayers for the assassin; a novel; Robert Ferrigno. Scribner 2006 397p $24.95

ISBN 0-7432-7289-7   LC 2005-51590

This novel is set "in the year 2040. The U.S. has been rent by civil strife and a nuclear attack that leveled New York and Washington, D.C. The nation is now divided into the Islamic States of America, whose capital is in Seattle, and the Bible Belt, located in the South. Young and fearless researcher Sarah Dougan, a moderate Muslim who frequently chafes at the restrictions placed on women, discovers that the nuke attacks long blamed on Israel were in fact carried out by a fanatical Muslim billionaire who intends to take over the nation by launching an unprecedented attack on the Christian South. Intending to verify her explosive findings, Sarah must go into hiding, where she is joined by her lover, former elite Muslim warrior Rakkim Epps. The two zigzag their way across an unrecognizable U.S., dogged by a psychopathic rogue assassin named Darwin." Booklist

Ferrigno, Robert—Continued

"Ferrigno raises important questions about religious freedom while handling the subject of Islamic faith with great insight and evenhandedness. If the plot sometimes overwhelms character development, he still allows his creations to air their own opinions without moralizing. In sum: a fast-paced thriller with timely appeal." Bookmarks Magazine

Fesperman, Dan, 1955-

The amateur spy. Alfred A. Knopf 2008 367p $24.95

ISBN 978-1-4000-4467-2; 1-4000-4467-7

LC 2007-47313

First published 2007 in the United Kingdom

"Freeman Lockhart, the Arabic-speaking titular spy, is burdened by guilt for his unwitting participation in horrific blunders as an aid worker in Africa. As Lockhart attempts to retire with his new wife to a Greek island, mysterious strangers play on that guilt to blackmail him into spying on a Palestinian ex-colleague in Jordan. The plot is complex, the sense of place powerful, and the characterization memorable. A parallel plot features an Arab American woman whose story at last converges with Lockhart's." Libr J

The warlord's son; a novel. Knopf 2004 319p $23

ISBN 0-375-41473-8

LC 2004-11841

"A burned-out war correspondent hoping for a last hurrah in Afghanistan, Skelly arrives on the Afghan border just as American bombs begin falling on the ruling Taliban. Seeking the scoop of a lifetime as witness to the capture of 'the biggest fish of them all,' he links up with an exiled warlord's quixotic expedition. Guiding Skelly's way is Najeeb, a tribal Pakistani with his own objective—U. S. visas for his girlfriend and himself, promised by Pakistani intelligence if he acts as an informant." Publisher's note

Fever, Buck See Anderson, Sherwood, 1876-1941

Fforde, Jasper

The Eyre affair; a novel. Viking 2002 374p hardcover o.p. pa $14

ISBN 0-670-03064-3; 0-14-200180-5 (pa)

LC 2001-43775

First published 2001 in the United Kingdom

"It's 1985 in England, at least on the calendar; the Crimean War is in its hundred-and-thirty-first year; time travel is nothing new; Japanese tourists slip in and out of Victorian novels; and the literary branch of the special police, led gamely by the beguiling Thursday Next, are pursuing Acheron Hades, who has stolen the manuscript of 'Martin Chuzzlewit' and set his sights on kidnapping the character Jane Eyre, a theft that could have disastrous consequences for Bronte lovers who like their story straight. This rambunctious caper could be taken as a warning about what might happen if society considered literature really important—like, say, energy futures or accounting." New Yorker

Thursday Next in Lost in a good book; a novel. Viking 2003 399p il $24.95

ISBN 0-670-03190-9

LC 2002-71304

Companion volume to: The Eyre affair

First published 2002 in the United Kingdom with title: Lost in a good book

"Thursday Next, who literally jumps into books to do her detective work, must locate a surprise enemy in Poe's 'The Raven' to save her beloved." Libr J

"Time flies—and leaps and zigzags—while reading this wickedly funny and clever fantasy. Would-be wordsmiths and mystery fans will find the surreal genre-buster irresistible." Publ Wkly

Thursday Next in Something rotten; a novel. Viking 2004 383p $24.95

ISBN 0-670-03359-6

LC 2004-49497

Published in the United Kingdom with title: Something rotten

"Detective Thursday Next has had her fill of her responsibilities as the Bellman in Jurisfiction. . . . Packing up her son, Friday, Thursday returns to Swindon accompanied by none other than the dithering Danish prince Hamlet. Caring for both is more than a full-time job and Thursday decides it is definitely time to get her husband Landen back, if only to babysit. Luckily, those responsible for Landen's eradication, The Goliath Corporation-formerly an oppressive multinational conglomerate, now an oppressive multinational religion-have pledged to write the wrong." Publisher's note

The author's "penchant for plotting knows no bounds. . . . It's easy to be delighted by a writer who loves books so madly." N Y Times (Late N Y Ed)

Thursday Next in The well of lost plots; a novel. Viking 2004 c2003 375p il $24.95

ISBN 0-670-03289-1

LC 2003-62150

First published 2003 in the United Kingdom with title: The well of lost plots

Thursday Next "has beaten a strategic retreat into BookWorld, where as part of the Character Exchange Program, she hides out in an unpublished, by-the-numbers police procedural. She's pregnant, her husband has been killed before he really existed, and her memories of him are being eaten away by a mindworm. She can't rest for long, however; she's still a trainee agent in the BookWorld police force, JurisFiction, and soon fiction itself is under a greater threat than ever before." Booklist

Fielding, Helen

Bridget Jones: the edge of reason. Viking 2000 338p

ISBN 0-670-89296-3

LC 99-86499

Sequel to Bridget Jones's diary

First published 1999 in the United Kingdom

A novel in diary form. "The familiar cast is gathered. There are Bridget's friends Magda, Jude and Shaz, who compete in giving her disastrous advice from self-help books about dealing with Mark's apparently cavalier behavior and his involvement with a minx named Rebecca." Publ Wkly

"How can a reader not love this woman—not in spite of her faults but because of them? Bridget tries so hard. Her days are made up of glorious surges of hope followed by instant defeat or rash interpretations, or both." N Y Times Book Rev

Fielding, Helen—*Continued*

Bridget Jones's diary; a novel. Viking 1998 271p $22.95

ISBN 0-670-88072-8   LC 98-18687

First published 1996 in the United Kingdom

This novel is the "purported diary, complete with daily entries of calories consumed, cigarettes smoked, 'alcohol units' imbibed and other unsuitable obsessions, of a year in the life of a bright London 30-something." Publ Wkly

"Brimming with a deliciously irreverent sense of humor and a keen sense of women's deepest insecurities, *Bridget Jones's Diary* is a must-read." Booklist

Fielding, Henry, 1707-1754

The history of the adventures of Joseph Andrews and of his friend Mr. Abraham Adams and, An apology for the life of Mrs. Shamela Andrews; edited by Douglas Brooks-Davies. Oxford University Press 2008 xliv, 410p (Oxford world's classics) pa $9.95

ISBN 978-0-19-953698-6; 0-19-953698-8

       LC 2009-290678

"Henry Fielding wrote both Joseph Andrews (1742) and Shamela (1741) in response to Samuel Richardson's book Pamela (1740), of which Shamela is a splendidly bawdy travesty. Joseph Andrews begins as a parody, too, but soon outgrows its origins, and its deepest roots lie in Cervantes and Marivaux. In both stories, Fielding demonstrates his concern for the corruption of contemporary society, politics, religion, morality, and taste. This revised and expanded edition follows the text of Joseph Andrews established by Martin C. Battestin for the definitive Wesleyan Edition of Fielding's works. The text of Shamela is based on the first edition, and two substantial appendices reprint the preliminary matter from the second edition of Richardson's Pamela and Conyers Middleton's Life of Cicero, which is also closely parodied in Shamela." Publisher's note

The history of Tom Jones, a foundling. Knopf 1991 xxxvi, 408, 427p $20

ISBN 0-679-40569-0

       * LC 91-52996

"Everyman's library"

First published 1749. Variant title: Tom Jones

"Squire Allworthy suspects that the infant whom he adopts and names Tom Jones is the illegitimate child of his servant Jenny Jones. When Tom is a young man, he falls in love with Sophia Western, his beautiful and virtuous neighbor. In the end his true identity is revealed and he wins Sophia's hand, but numerous obstacles have to be overcome, and in the course of the action the various sets of characters pursue each other from one part of the country to another, giving Fielding an opportunity to paint an incomparably vivid picture of England in the mid-18th century." Merriam-Webster's Ency of Lit

Fielding, Joy

Charley's web; a novel. Atria Books 2008 437p $24.95

ISBN 978-0-7432-9601-4; 0-7432-9601-X

       LC 2007-32674

When Jill Rohmer, a convicted child killer, invites Charlotte "Charley" Webb, a single mom and columnist for the Palm Beach Post, "to collaborate on the 'true story' of what really happened to the three children she was convicted of murdering, Charley at first thinks it sounds like a great idea. Her sister Anne is, after all, a bestselling romance author, so why couldn't Charley have a nonfiction bestseller? Charley meets with Jill's attractive lawyer, Alex Prescott, who secures a book contract. After committing to the project, Charley begins dating Alex. Then Charley learns Jill had an accomplice, someone on the loose whom Jill calls 'Jack.' Fielding pulls out all the stops as the identity of the ruthless murderer becomes obvious, and Charley must race against time to catch the horrible Jack and save his next target— her son." Publ Wkly

Don't cry now; a novel. Morrow 1995 356p o.p.

       LC 94-42095

Protagonist "Bonnie Wheeler has a wonderful life wth handsome husband Rod and preschool daughter Amanda even though Rod's ex-wife, Joan, is a pest and Rod's children from his former marriage are less than warm to Bonnie. One of Joan's annoying phone calls leads Bonnie to an empty house where Joan is seated at the kitchen counter, dead. . . . Bonnie turns sleuth, questioning Joan's psychiatrist and anyone who befriended the dead woman." Libr J

"Just when things appear to be all worked out, new evidence points Bonnie in a different direction. With Fielding, nothing is as it appears, and like Bonnie, we can't help brooding on the vulnerability of what we all take for granted." Quill Quire

Heartstopper; a novel. Atria Books 2007 387p $24.95

ISBN 978-0-7432-9598-7; 0-7432-9598-6

       LC 2006-50801

In this "suspense novel set in tiny Torrance, Florida, a serial killer's journal entries are interspersed with the stunned reactions of various of the town's citizens when two teenage girls go missing. Sandy Crosbie, a highschool English teacher and the mother of two teenagers, has relocated to remote Torrance from Rochester, New York, at the urging of her handsome doctor husband. But his reasons for the move soon become apparent when he leaves her for Kerri Franklin, a 'Barbie clone and Internet paramour extraordinaire.' Sandy, along with the rest of the town's citizens, is jolted out of her self-absorption when the body of the most popular girl in school is found buried in a shallow grave. Now it's up to exhausted, overweight Sheriff John Weber, unhappily married to the TV-addicted Pauline, to calm residents' fears and find out what happened to the pretty blonde teen. But even as he fends off the town's obnoxious mayor, intent on calling in the FBI, Sandy's daughter goes missing. Fielding crafts a suspenseful plot, with a stunner of a twist, while giving her characters a depth of humanity not frequently found in formula fiction." Booklist

Missing pieces. Doubleday 1997 368p o.p.

       LC 96-40901

"Practical Kate Sinclair, 47, a family therapist married for 24 years and the mother of two teenaged daughters, is losing control of her orderly, settled life. She fights with her rebellious elder daughter, Sara, who's 17. Her

Fielding, Joy—*Continued*

mother is diagnosed with Alzheimer's. Even her body is betraying her, as hot flashes startle her metabolism. Meanwhile, a chance encounter with an old high-school sweetheart inflames her in a totally different way. Worst of all, though, is the infatuation of her sexy half-sister, Jo Lynn, with a man on trial for the murder of 13 women." Publ Wkly

"As outlandish as the relationship between sister Jo Lynn and the serial killer seems, Fielding's talent makes it all quite credible." Booklist

See Jane run. Morrow 1991 364p
ISBN 0-688-08867-8   LC 90-22603

"Jane finds herself in downtown Boston, her dress covered with blood, nearly $10,000 in her coat pocket, and absolutely no idea of who she is. She seeks help at Boston City Hospital, where she discovers that she is the wife of handsome Michael Whittaker, a renowned surgeon. The doctor seems to be the perfect husband, and as Jane learns the details of their ideal life together she is unable to understand her suspicions of him. However, as Jane's amnesia persists, it becomes clear that her model husband is threatening her sanity in order to conceal a sinister secret." Libr J

"Fielding handles her material with finesse; suspense is maintained at a high level, and the narrative is enriched by Jane's bracing sense of humor and a cast of sharply drawn, articulate characters." Publ Wkly

Tell me no secrets. Morrow 1993 352p o.p.
                                      LC 92-43692

"Prosecutor Jess Koster is still distressed at the disappearance of her mother eight years before, but then her client disappears, and she starts receiving death threats in the mail." Libr J

"When Jess' ex rescues, or seems to rescue, her from the predictably sadistic stalker/rapist, her comment that 'it's just like in the movies' may seem like self-parody. Jess escapes this formula—and becomes not only real, but touching—when she visits her suburban sister and the brother-in-law she despises, when she talks with a woman juror in a rape trial about why the verdict was not guilty, and when we visit with her in her private fear." Booklist

Fifty years of the best from Ellery Queen's Mystery Magazine; edited by Eleanor Sullivan. Carroll & Graf Pubs. 1991 642p o.p.
                                      LC 90-23928

Contents: The clue of the red wig, by J. D. Carr; Lost star, by C. D. King; The Bloomsbury wonder, by T. Burke; Dressing-up, by W. R. Burnett; Malice domestic, by P. MacDonald; I can find my way out, by N. Marsh; The fourth degree, by H. Pentecost; Midnight adventure, by M. Arlen; A study in white, by N. Blake; The phantom guest, by F. I. Anderson; As simple as ABC, by E. Queen; Money to burn, by M. Allingham; The gentlest of the brothers, by D. Alexander; One-way street, by A. Armstrong; Murder at the dog show, by M. G. Eberhart; Always trust a cop, by O. R. Cohen; The withered heart, by J. Potts; The girl who married a monster, by A. Boucher; Between eight and eight, by C. S. Forester; Knowing what I know now, by B. Perowne; Change of climate, by U. Curtiss; Life in our time, by R. Bloch; The

special gift, by C. Fremlin; A neat and tidy job, by G. H. Coxe; Run—if you can, by C. Armstrong; Line of communication, by A. Garve; Danger at Deerfawn, by D. B. Hughes; The man who understood women, by A. H. Z. Carr; Revolver, by A. Davidson; The eternal chase, by A. Gilbert; Reasons unknown, by S. Ellin; Three ways to rob a bank, by H. R. Daniels; The perfect servant, by H. Nielsen; The marked man, by D. Ely; Flowers that bloom in the spring, by J. Symons; A nice place to stay, by N. Tyre; Paul Broderick's man, by T. Walsh; When nothing matters, by F. V. Mayberry; This is death, by E. Westlake; Woodrow Wilson's necktie, by P. Highsmith; The jackal and the tiger, by M. Gilbert; The fix, by R. Twohy; One moment of madness, by E. D. Hoch; Loopy, by R. Rendell; The plateau, by C. Howard; The butchers, by P. Lovesey; Burning bridges, by J. Powell; A good turn, by R. Barnard; Clap hands, there goes Charlie, by G. Baxt; Big Boy, Little Boy, by S. Brett

Finch, Charles

The September Society. St. Martin's Minotaur 2008 310p $26.95
ISBN 978-0-312-35978-2; 0-312-35978-0
                                      LC 2008-3452

"When Oxford student George Payson goes missing, his mother asks Charles Lennox to find him. All avenues of investigation point to foul play, and then Payson's garroted body is found in the Christ Church Meadow. Wealthy, intelligent, Oxford-educated, and a detective of some repute, Charles seeks to determine what role the little-known student club, the September Society, might have played in Payson's death and what lies behind the threats against Payson's friends and now Lennox's beloved Lady Jane Grey. . . . Finch, a superb hand at plotting, gives nothing away, and even the most astute reader will be guessing to the end." Libr J

Finch, Sheila, 1935-

The guild of xenolinguists; with a foreword by Ian Watson. Golden Gryphon Press 2007 281p $24.95
ISBN 978-1-930846-48-7; 1-930846-48-7
                                      LC 2007-6550

Contents: First was the word; A flight of words; A world waiting; The roaring ground; No brighter glory; Out of the mouths; Stranger than imagination can; Babel interface; The naked face of God; Communion of minds; Reading the bones

A collection of tales about "the Guild of Xenolinguists (later called lingsters), a formal organization devoted to translating the languages of other worlds. Much as Asimov did with the Three Laws of Robotics, Finch creatively examines the conflicts stemming from adherence to the guild's strict rules. The stories span a wide range, from First Was the Word, a brief tale setting the stage for the development of the guild, to the moving A World Waiting and A Flight of Words, which present their protagonists with morally difficult situations—tortured prisoners, conflicting religious beliefs, abortion—that hold significant contemporary resonance." Publ Wkly

Finder, Joseph

Company man. St. Martin's Press 2005 520p
$24.95

ISBN 0-312-31916-9

"Nick Conover, the youngish CEO of the Stratton Corporation, in Fenwick, Mich., has fired half of the high-end office furniture company's 10,000 employees at the bidding of new ownership in Boston. As a result, much of Fenwick hates Nick, including the person who has been breaking into his mansion and scribbling 'No Hiding Place' on the walls, and who then kills the Conover family dog—presumably Andrew Stadler, a fired employee and erstwhile mental patient. When Stadler accosts Nick one night, Nick, panicking, shoots him dead, and then, under the influence of his shady corporate security director, covers up the crime. The two cops assigned to the murder prove dogged, sending Nick into a generally beleaguered state that's slightly alleviated by his new romance with, of all people, the daughter of the murdered man, but exacerbated considerably by his discovery that his Boston masters intend to sell Stratton to Chinese government interests." Publ Wkly

This is "as much a novel about the chicanery of the business world as it is a mystery story. Takeovers and outsourcing are not news, but Mr. Finder weaves these prospects menacingly throughout the story, as Nick finds himself increasingly undermined by his colleagues." N Y Times (Late N Y Ed)

Killer instinct. St. Martin's Press 2006 406p
$24.95

ISBN 0-312-34747-2   LC 2006-40501

"Jason Steadman is a cog in a huge company that specializes in plasma TVs. He wants to move up the corporate ladder but lacks the ruthlessness necessary to reach the next level. When he meets Kurt Semko, a former Special Forces officer, the two of them strike up a friendship, and Jason helps Kurt get a job in the company's security office. Prospects immediately start turning around for Jason, but he's ignorant of the inside help he's getting from his new friend, who could just as easily become his enemy." Libr J

This is a "superb story that dazzles with its heart-pounding suspense, even while posing deeper questions about the ethics of business and what we're willing to do to get ahead." Boston Globe

Power play. St. Martin's Press 2007 371p
$24.95

ISBN 978-0-312-34748-2; 0-312-34748-0
        LC 2007-16178

A thriller set in the aerospace industry. "Although he's low on the corporate food chain, Jake Laundry receives an invitation to the annual company retreat far from civilization. With his boss abroad, Jake doesn't have much of a choice. The others at the rustic lodge include the new female CEO, who is despised by most of the company, and Jake's ex-girlfriend, who now works as the CEO's assistant. Before he has a chance to prove that he deserves to be at the lodge as well, their isolated location becomes a source of terror as a group of local hunters take them hostage." Libr J

The author's "strong suit is technical expertise, and he fills this book with seductive bits of inside information. . . . Power Play starts cleverly and later devolves into

more conventional suspense tactics. But its premise is enough to send chills through corporate boardrooms, and through civilian readers too." N Y Times (Late N Y Ed)

Vanished. St. Martin's Press 2009 388p $25.99

ISBN 978-0-312-37908-7; 0-312-37908-0
        LC 2009-13029

The first title in a "new series featuring Nick Heller, a high-powered international investigator and corporate security consultant. Through a brilliant piece of detection, Heller has just tracked down 12 cargo containers packed with $1 billion in cash when he gets a call from his nephew Gabe in Washington, DC. Heller's brother Roger, the kid's stepfather, has vanished, and the boy's mother, Lauren, is in the hospital, the victim of a late-night attack. Both Roger and Lauren work for Gifford Industries, a multibillion-dollar corporation where Roger mostly handled mergers and acquisitions. . . . Using his Special Forces skills and the latest high-tech wizardry, Heller counters lethal adversaries as he peels back layers of secrets that hide not only high-level corporate crimes but the troubled affairs of his own family." Libr J

Findley, Timothy

The piano man's daughter. Crown 1996 461p il
o.p.   LC 96-171372

First published 1995 in Canada

"Set in turn-of-the-century Canada, the story tells, in a series of evocative flashbacks, the engaging tale of Lily Kilworth, and her son, Charlie. Conceived when her mother, Ede, falls in love with a musician, Lily is born in a field of flowers and grows into an odd, lonely child whose world is exotically tip-tilted. As she matures, she becomes more and more alienated from real life, but this doesn't keep her from having a brief, mysterious affair while she's a student in wartime England. The result is her son, Charlie, who has perfect musical pitch and a high tolerance for his mother's eccentric ways. . . . Brilliantly told, powerfully affecting." Booklist

Finney, Jack

From time to time; a novel. Simon & Schuster
1995 303p il o.p.   LC 94-24497

In this sequel to Time and again, "time traveler Simon Morley leaves his voluntary exile in the 19th century to visit the 20th century of his origins and finds himself drawn into a desperate attempt to alter the events of history and prevent the onset of World War I." Libr J

"This mind-stretching escapist adventure is studded with period photos and news clippings that function as an integral part of the story." Publ Wkly

Time and again. Simon & Schuster 1970 399p
o.p.

                    *

The author "re-creates the world of nineteenth-century New York City and at the same time critically appraises modernity. His hero, Simon Morley, agrees to live in the Dakota apartments and, assisted by hypnosis, to share a series of experiences in the year 1882. Eager to cooperate with the U.S. governmental agencies conducting the test Simon observes the manners and mores of the past and falls in love with Julia, a girl of the period. Simon's enthusiasm palls, however, when he is asked to alter his-

Finney, Jack—*Continued*

torical events in the interest of the agency's evidently nefarious designs." Booklist

Followed by From time to time

Finney, Patricia, 1958-

Gloriana's torch. St. Martin's Press 2003 452p $24.95

ISBN 0-312-31285-7   LC 2003-58454

This "tale is set on the eve of the sailing of the Spanish Armada in 1588. David Becket, clerk of the ordnance and sometime spy for Elizabeth I, is ordered by the queen to discover the details of a top-secret Spanish plot dubbed the 'Miracle of Beauty.' In addition, Becket is commanded to rescue his fellow English spy and friend, Simon Ames, who has been condemned by the Spanish Inquisition as a heretic. . . . The various threads of this wide-ranging tale of intrigue do not come together neatly, but Finney's vivid prose and the high level of historical imagination on display make for a satisfying read." Publ Wkly

Fishburne, Rodes

Going to see the elephant; a novel. Bantam Dell 2009 293p $22

ISBN 978-0-385-34239-1; 0-385-34239-X

LC 2008-28465

"On a windy September day, twenty-five-year-old Slater Brown stands in the back of a bicycle taxi hurtling the wrong way down the busiest street in San Francisco. Slater has come to 'see the elephant,' to stake his claim to fame and become the greatest writer ever. . . . Out of money and prospects, he applies for a job at a moribund weekly newspaper called the Morning Trumpet—and, as if by fate, is given a very special parting gift from a moonlighting mystic. Suddenly Slater has an exclusive on every story in the city. With his uncanny knack for finding scoops, he's bringing the Trumpet back to life, infuriating a corrupt mayor and falling in love with the woman destined to become his muse. But it is the astonishing inventor Milo Magneta—a man obsessed with harnessing the weather—who will force Slater to navigate the most dangerous straits." Red Room

"At times Fishburne has trouble maintaining so many moving parts; the inventor story line can feel extraneous, and the love story takes a while to get going. But what saves the book is its sweetness and innocence, and the depiction of Slater in the big city is a pleasure." Publ Wkly

Fitch, Janet 1955-

White oleander; a novel. Little, Brown 1999 390p $24.95

ISBN 0-316-28526-9   LC 98-50371

In this novel, "the title flower triggers a savage turn of events when the poet Ingrid Magnussen poisons her lover, consigning herself to jail life and her 12-year-old daughter to Los Angeles' foster-care system. Young Astrid gets off to a shaky start at the home of a born-again Christian who shoots her in a fit of righteous jealousy." Time

"This sensitive exploration of the mother daughter terrain . . . offers a convincing look at what Adrienne Rich has called 'this womanly splitting of self,' in a poignant, virtuosic, utterly captivating narrative." Publ Wkly

Paint it black; a novel. Little, Brown & Co. 2006 387p $24.99

ISBN 978-0-316-18274-4   LC 2006-10211

"Opting for the antithesis of beauty, Josie Tyrell exists within the punk club scene of 1980s Los Angeles, and, unfortunately, she finds familiar terrain in that subculture's harshness and brutal sexuality. Not until she meets Michael Faraday, a child of affluence and privilege, does Josie know that there is such a thing as true beauty in the world. He teaches her about the beauty of the night sky; of music, art, and poetry. But his obsession becomes his undoing as he cannot find enough of this transcendent beauty to protect him from his demons. Giving in to the inescapable lure of his family's ghosts, he commits suicide. Michael was the sole source of light for Josie and his tortured, tortuous mother: now both women engage in a dangerous struggle to survive in a world of darkness." Libr J

"Fitch has given us a courageous and interesting young woman who handles the bad cards she has been dealt with grace and resolve. No one, not even Cinderella, knows better than Josie Tyrell that life isn't fair—and no one, despite some very long odds, seems more likely to transcend the role of victim and succeed with or without her fairy-tale prince." Washington Post Book World

Fitzalan, Roger, 1920-1995

For works written by this author under other names see Hall, Adam, 1920-1995

Fitzgerald, F. Scott (Francis Scott), 1896-1940

The beautiful and damned. Scribner 449p

ISBN 0-684-15153-7

*

"Hudson River editions"

First published 1922; copyright renewed 1950

"Anthony Patch pursues and wins the beautiful and sought-after Gloria Gilbert. He decides that they can survive on his limited income until he comes into a large fortune he stands to inherit from his grandfather. Through the ensuing years, their lives deteriorate into mindless alcoholic ennui. Anthony's grandfather makes a surprise appearance at one of their wild parties and, in disgust, disinherits him. After his grandfather's death, Anthony institutes a lawsuit that takes years to settle. Although the Patches eventually win, by then Anthony's spirit is broken, he and Gloria have grown apart, and they care about nothing." Merriam-Webster's Ency of Lit

also in Fitzgerald, F. S. Novels and stories, 1920-1922 p435-795

The Fitzgerald reader; edited by Arthur Mizener. Scribner 1963 xxvii, 509p o.p.

Contents: The short stories are: Winter dreams; Absolution; "The sensible thing"; Basil and Cleopatra; Outside the cabinetmaker's; Babylon revisited; Crazy Sunday; Family in the wind; Afternoon of an author; "I didn't get over"; The long way out; Financing Finnegan; The lost decade

This representative selection of Scott Fitzgerald's work "includes the whole of his best novel, 'The Great Gatsby,' and considerable parts of his other two important novels, 'Tender Is the Night, and 'The Last Tycoon.'

Fitzgerald, F. Scott (Francis Scott), 1896-1940—
Continued
It also includes two novelettes ('May Day' and 'The Rich Boy'), the four or five best short stories from each period of his career, and his four most famous essays." Foreword

Flappers and philosophers
In Fitzgerald, F. S. Novels and stories, 1920-1922 p249-433

The great Gatsby; preface by Matthew J. Bruccoli. Scribner Classics 1996 170p $25
ISBN 0-684-83042-6
* LC 96-16596
First published 1925
"The mysterious Jay Gatsby lives in a luxurious mansion on the Long Island shore. . . . Nick Carraway, the narrator, lives next door to Gatsby, and Nick's cousin Daisy and her crude but wealthy husband Tom Buchanan live directly across the harbor. Gatsby reveals to Nick that he and Daisy had a brief affair before the war and her marriage to Tom. . . . He persuades Nick to bring him and Daisy together again but ultimately he is unable to win her away from Tom. Daisy, driving Gatsby's car, runs over and kills Tom's mistress Myrtle, unaware of her identity. Myrtle's husband traces the car and shoots Gatsby, who has remained silent in order to protect Daisy. Gatsby's friends and business associates have all deserted him, and only Gatsby's father, and one former guest attend the funeral." Reader's Ency. 4th edition
"The power of the novel derives from its sharp and antagonistic portrayal of wealthy society in New York City and Long Island. . . . The 'Jazz Age,' Fitzgerald's constant subject, is exposed here in terms of its false glamor and cultural barrenness." Benet's Reader's Ency of Am Lit

also in Fitzgerald, F. S. The Fitzgerald reader p105-238

The last tycoon; an unfinished novel. Scribner 163p
ISBN 0-684-15311-4
*
"Hudson River editions"
First published 1941 with The Great Gatsby, and selected stories; copyright renewed 1969
In addition to providing a foreword to this unfinished novel "Edmund Wilson has assembled a tentative outline of the rest of the story as Fitzgerald intended to develop it, and has appended passages from the author's notes dealing with the characters and scenes." Publisher's note
"The work is an indictment of the Hollywood film industry, where Fitzgerald had had a disappointing career as a screenwriter. Monroe Stahr is a studio executive who has worked obsessively to produce high-quality films without regard to their financial prospects. He takes a personal interest in every aspect of the studio. At age 35 he is almost burned out, and the novel is the story of how he loses control of the studio and his life." Merriam-Webster's Ency of Lit

May Day
In Fitzgerald, F. S. The Fitzgerald reader p3-53

Novels and stories, 1920-1922. Library of Am. 2000 1082p $35
ISBN 1-88301-184-1
LC 00-24287
Contents: This side of paradise (1920); Flappers and philosophers (1920); The beautiful and the damned (1922); Tales of The jazz age (1922)
Flappers and philosophers includes the following stories: The offshore pirate; The ice palace; Head and shoulders; The cut-glass bowl; Bernice bobs her hair; Benediction; Dalyrimple goes wrong; The four fists
Tales of the jazz age includes the following stories: The jelly bean; The camel's back; May day; Porcelain and pink; The diamond as big as the ritz; The curious case of Benjamin Button; Tarquin of cheapside; "O russet witch!"; The lees of happiness; Mr. Icky; Jemina, the mountain girl

The rich boy
In Fitzgerald, F. S. The Fitzgerald reader p239-75

The short stories of F. Scott Fitzgerald; edited and with a preface by Matthew J. Bruccoli. Scribner Classics 1998 797p $37.50
ISBN 0-684-84250-5
* LC 98-121806
Reissue of the 1989 edition analyzed in Short story index
Contents: Head and shoulders; Bernice bobs her hair; The ice palace; The offshore pirate; May Day; The jelly-bean; The curious case of Benjamin Button; The diamond as big as the Ritz; Winter dreams; Dice, brassknuckles & guitar; Absolution; Rags Martin-Jones and the Pr-nce of W-les; 'The sensible thing'; Love in the night; The rich boy; Jacob's ladder; A short trip home; The bowl; The captured shadow; Basil and Cleopatra; The last of the belles; Majesty; At your age; The swimmers; Two wrongs; First blood; Emotional bankruptcy; The bridal party; One trip abroad; The hotel child; Babylon revisited; A new leaf; A freeze-out; Six of one—; What a handsome pair!; Crazy Sunday; More than just a house; Afternoon of an author; Financing Finnegan; The lost decade; 'Boil some water—lots of it'; Last kiss; Dearly beloved

Six tales of the jazz age, and other stories. Scribner 1960 192p o.p.
Contents: The jelly-bean; The camel's back; The curious case of Benjamin Button; Tarquin of Cheapside; "O'Russet witch"; The lees of happiness; The adjuster; Hot and cold blood; Gretchen's forty winks

The stories of F. Scott Fitzgerald; a selection of 28 stories; with an introduction by Malcolm Cowley. Scribner 1951 xxv, 473p
ISBN 0-684-15366-1
Contents: The diamond as big as the Ritz; Bernice bobs her hair; The ice palace; May Day; Winter dreams; "The sensible thing"; Absolution; The rich boy; The baby party; Magnetism; The last of the belles; The rough crossing; The bridal party; Two wrongs; The scandal detectives; The freshest boy; The captured shadow; A woman with a past; Babylon revisited; Crazy Sunday; Family in the wind; An alcoholic case; The long way out; Financing Finnegan; Pat Hobby himself; Three hours between planes; The lost decade

Fitzgerald, F. Scott (Francis Scott), 1896-1940—
Continued

"The editor has attempted to make the best selection from all stages of Fitzgerald's career; the stories are arranged in chronological groups." Booklist

Tales of the jazz age
In Fitzgerald, F. S. Novels and stories, 1920-1922 p797-1054

This side of paradise. Scribner 282p
ISBN 0-684-15601-6

*

"Hudson River editions"
First published 1920; copyright renewed 1948
"Immature though it seems today, the work when it was published was considered a revelation of the new morality of the young in the early Jazz Age; and it made Fitzgerald famous. The novel's hero, Amory Blaine, is a handsome, spoiled young man who attends Princeton, becomes involved in literary activities, and has several ill-fated romances. A portrait of the Lost Generation, the novel addresses Fitzgerald's later theme of love distorted by social climbing and greed." Merriam-Webster's Ency of Lit

also in Fitzgerald, F. S. Novels and stories, 1920-1922 p1-248

Fitzgerald, Francis Scott *See* Fitzgerald, F. Scott (Francis Scott), 1896-1940

Fitzgerald, Penelope

The blue flower. Houghton Mifflin 1997 225p pa $13
ISBN 0-395-85997-2 (pa)   LC 96-52911
First published 1996 in the United Kingdom
This "is a historical novel based on the life of the poet, aphorist, novelist, Friedrich von Hardenberg, a Saxon nobleman who wrote under the name of Novalis. . . . Novalis had a vision of a unique blue flower as the goal of a quest. . . . In the waking life of Fritz von Hardenberg the part of the flower was played by Sophie von Kuhn. She is 12 years old when he meets her and at once designates her his future bride and his incarnation of Wisdom. Reluctant parental permission is obtained for their betrothal, but Sophie (as well as not being noble) is tubercular. . . . Their relationship, and Fritz's dealings with his own family and Sophie's, are the main business of the novel." London Rev Books
This novel "ranges far beyond itself. It is an interrogation of life, love, purpose, experience and horizons, which has found its perfect vehicle in a few years from the pitifully short life of a German youth about to become a great poet." N Y Times Book Rev

The means of escape. Houghton Mifflin 2000 117p $18
ISBN 0-618-07994-7   LC 00-38914
Contents: The means of escape; The prescription; Desideratus; Beehernz; The axe; The red-haired girl; Not shown; At Hiruharama
"Strange, whimsical, sometimes gothic or bizarre, these tales demonstrate Fitzgerald's cool and civilized wit and the merciless eye she casts on worldly pretensions." Publ Wkly

Flagg, Fannie

Fried green tomatoes at the Whistle-Stop Cafe. Random House 1987 403p
ISBN 0-394-56152-X

* LC 87-12813
This novel is "set in a rural hamlet outside of Birmingham, Alabama. Bulletins from a gossipy town newsletter produced in the 1940s by Dot Weems are interspersed with the recollections of Mrs. Cleo (Vinnie) Throughgoode uttered (40 years later) in a nursing home to a depressed, menopausal visitor, Evelyn Couch (whose life is rejuvenated by these Sunday afternoon chats). Flagg also supplies basic narrative passages illuminating the news shared by Dot and Vinnie. The pace of the novel is as swift as the life of the small town is slow— at least it seems slow until Vinnie drops hints of a murder and of riotous pranks played upon the local minister. The story is carefully plotted, with the moods and people of pre- and post-World War II Alabama splendidly evoked." Booklist

Standing in the rainbow; a novel. Random House 2002 493p
ISBN 0-679-42615-9   LC 2002-21977
"We first met many members of this cast in *Welcome Back to the World, Baby Girl* (1998), one of whom is Dorothy Smith, the host of the daily radio show *Neighbor Dorothy*. The story begins in 1945. The war is over, the American economy is booming, and there is no better place in the world than Elmwood Springs, Missouri. At least that's what Bobby Smith thinks. He is the 10-year-old son of Neighbor Dorothy, and he's got the world wrapped around his little finger." Booklist
"Beneath the sentimentality, there's a real celebration of life here, an affirmation that success and happiness are the results of simple kindness gratituder and courage." Sci Monit

Flanagan, Richard 1961-

Wanting. Atlantic Monthly Press 2009 256p $24
ISBN 978-0-8021-1900-1; 0-8021-1900-X
First published 2008 in Australia
The novel's protagonist is "a young aborigine girl known as Mathinna, who was adopted and later abandoned by the governor of Van Diemen's Land (now Tasmania), the famed polar explorer Sir John Franklin, and his wife, Lady Franklin. . . . It is a story about an innocent caught in the gears of the British imperial machine; a story about two famous Victorian men — Sir John and Charles Dickens — and the odd connections between their lives." N Y Times (Late N Y Ed)
This novel is a "meditation on the nature and character of the Tasmanian landscape and its bloody history; and it is an exploration of the ways human beings imprison themselves emotionally, and label their prisons reason, science, religion; and it is a musing on illusions and lies, on the awful and wonderful implications of desire." Portland Oregonian

Gould's book of fish; a novel in twelve fish. Grove Press 2002 404p il
ISBN 0-8021-1711-2   LC 2001-55747

Flanagan, Richard, 1961---*Continued*

The novel "tells the story of William Buelow Gould, a convict sent to a penal colony in Van Diemen's Land in the nineteenth century. Gould recounts his life story as he paints the island's native fish, a task given him by the fatuous prison doctor, convinced that such a taxonomic achievement will launch him into British society. As he completes each painting, Gould's story dips into his past, recalling his grim childhood and ill-fated life of crime." Booklist

"This remarkable novel is a meditation on colonialism—indeed, on history itself—couched in the story of an English guttersnipe." New Yorker

The unknown terrorist. Grove Press 2007 c2006 320p $24

ISBN 978-0-8021-1851-6; 0-8021-1851-8

First published 2006 in Australia

"Gina Davies, a 26-year-old nightclub pole dancer (referred to throughout as 'the Doll'), leads a provincial life in Sydney, Australia, spends $2,000 a month on clothes and is given to the occasional racist rant. But after a one-night stand with a man named Tariq, she turns on the TV and learns she's been pegged as the accomplice in an attempted terrorist attack on Sydney's Olympic stadium. She's instantly the most-wanted woman in Australia and the source of a raging tabloid media feeding frenzy led by sleazy TV journalist Richard Cody." Publ Wkly

A "page-turning thriller worthy of John le Carré, with a plot so credible a reader might feel it's nonfiction, except for a few too many coincidences. But even those can't dampen the chilling effect of the story, written in a fresh, exhilarating prose style in which the author makes each sentence a small work of art." Seattle Times

Flanagan, Thomas, 1923-2002

The tenants of time. Dutton 1988 824p o.p.

* LC 87-13632

"A William Abrahams book"

"Set during three pivotal decades of Irish history, the narrative focuses on four men who participate in the short-lived Rising of 1867 and the irrevocable effects on their lives of the battle of Clonbrony Wood. . . . Except for Hugh, who is one of the narrators of this moving story, tragedy stalks each of the veterans of Clonbrony Wood." Publ Wkly

This "novel is enormously long and unfalteringly rich in its delineation of the sometimes thorny connection between the public associations and private needs and loyalties of people who live energetically, and even recklessly, through times of political turbulence." Commonweal

The year of the French; a novel. Holt, Rinehart & Winston 1979 516p o.p.

* LC 78-23539

This historical novel is based on actual events. The year is 1798, when a band of "Irishmen rise up in County Mayo against their English rulers. The French, secure in the success of their own revolution, decide to come to the aid of the Irish, less for the sake of an ideal than to harass the English. Three shiploads of troops, under the brilliant General Humbert, set sail from France. Their arrival in Kilcummin Bay is the signal for the war of liberation to begin. . . . But by fall, disappointed in their hope for more troops from France and confronted by vastly superior forces under Lord Cornwallis, the Irish are doomed." Publisher's note

The author "writes well, taking care to approximate . . . the spoken and written language of the time. The result is, I'm convinced, not only a serious book, free of the irony and satire that informs so many of the more literary historical fictions written today, but a distinguished one as well." Newsweek

Flaubert, Gustave, 1821-1880

Madame Bovary; patterns of provincial life; translated from the French by Francis Steegmuller; with an introduction by Victor Brombert. Alfred A. Knopf 1993 xxxviii, 330p $17

ISBN 0-679-42031-2

* LC 92-54294

Original French edition, 1857

A novel about the "life and fate of the Norman bourgeoise Emma Bovary. Unhappy in her marriage to a good-hearted but stupid village doctor, Emma finds her pathetic dreams of romantic love unfulfilled. A sentimental, discontented, and hopelessly limited person, she commits adultery, piles up enormous debts, and finally takes her own life in desperation. The novel's subject, the life of a very ordinary woman, and its technique, the amassing of precise detail, make Madame Bovary one of the crowning works in the development of the novel." Reader's Ency. 4th edition

Sentimental education; or, The history of a young man. Magee c1904 2v o.p.

*

Original French edition, 1869

"The background of this novel is the decline and fall of the Monarchy of Louis Philippe and the Revolution of 1848. . . . The hero, Frederic Moreau, has many of the traits of young Flaubert. Madame Arnous, with whom he falls in love, is very like Madame Schlesinger whom Flaubert had admired at Trouville as early as 1836. The subject of the novel is really the futility of existence." Haydn. Thesaurus of Book Dig

Fleishman, Jeffrey

Promised virgins; a novel of jihad. Arcade Pub. 2009 253p $24.95

ISBN 978-1-55970-897-5; 1-55970-897-2

LC 2008-31205

"Jay Morgan is a veteran journalist who has seen it all. Stationed in Kosovo—and breaking a cardinal rule by sleeping with his beautiful translator, Alijah—he is in hot pursuit of the dateman, an Osama bin Laden–like figure who has recently set up camp in the mountains. Meanwhile, Alijah, the survivor of violence, hopes to find her missing brother who she suspects has enlisted with the guerrillas. As Jay and Alijah inch closer to their goals, it becomes clear that the individuals they pursue are more entwined than they could have imagined." Publ Wkly

This novel "does what a good novel is supposed to do. It creates a real, textured, believable world, and it sweeps the reader along at a fast pace that nevertheless doesn't seem hurried. And it's clear that for the characters, what's real is the here and now, and their own memories, not what's happening in a prosperous, peaceful

Fleishman, Jeffrey—*Continued*
world away. Fleishman's writing captures what war must be like—a startling mix of the mundane, the extraordinary and the ominous." PopMatters

Fleming, Ian, 1908-1964

Casino Royale. Macmillan 1954 c1953 176p o.p.

*

"Against the background of a French resort the book describes Bond's destruction of the French branch of SMERSH, the Soviet espionage ring. The climax of the story is a tense game of baccarat in which Bond ruins the leader of the ring, Le Chiffre. The girl in the case is a compliant Soviet agent named Vesper Lynd, and there is much closely described violence." Wakeman. World Authors, 1950-1970

Doctor No. Macmillan 1958 256p o.p.
The setting is the Caribbean, where James Bond is trying to trace the disappearance of two agents who had trespassed on the isolated island kingdom of the Eurasian Dr. No. The maniacal doctor, equipped with two pairs of steel pincers for hands, dreams of world conquest and is stockpiling a deadly arsenal for that time. Bond, with female companion in tow, survives a manhunt through the island's mangrove swamps to foil the doctor's plans

From Russia, with love. Macmillan 1957 253p o.p.
James Bond, the British secret agent here meets the Soviet murder organization SMERSH once more. His execution has been ordered but Bond's counter activities seem successful—until the last page

Goldfinger. Macmillan 1959 318p o.p.

*

"James Bond, British Secret Service Agent 007, must retrieve British gold from a Mr. Auric Goldfinger whose ruthless obsession is suggesting in his goal—personal possession of half the supply of mined gold in the world." Publ Wkly
"All this is, in some measure, a great joke, but Fleming's passion for plausibility, his own naval intelligence background, and a kind of sincere Manicheism, allied to journalistic efficiency in the management of his récit, make his work rather impressive." Burgess. 99 Novels

The man with the golden gun. New Am. Lib. 1965 183p o.p.
This adventure "begins with a brainwashed Bond ready to do the bidding of the K.G.B. in headquarters of the Secret Service, and thrashes through to a climax in Jamaica where the adversary is Scaramonga, the most ruthless death-dealing instrument forged in the 20th century." Libr J

On Her Majesty's Secret Service. New Am. Lib. 1963 299p o.p.
James Bond, British secret agent 007, forsakes his bachelorhood for Countess Teresa di Vicenzo, who involves him in another adventure with Ernst Stavro Blofeld, head of an international crime syndicate and architect of an atomic blackmail scheme. The story is set against an Alpine background

You only live twice. New Am. Lib. 1964 240p o.p.
"Bond, near-prostrate from his bride's death, is given a Japanese assignment to snap him out of his torpor. . . . {The story} involves Bond's making up as a Japanese and venturing into the den of a foreign 'death collector,' a madman who has set up a poisonous garden complete with noxious plants, volcanic geysers, snakes, and, in a lake, piranha fish. Very grisly and chilling. The ending is an epitome of horror." Publ Wkly

Fleming, Julia Spencer- *See* Spencer-Fleming, Julia

Fleming, Oliver *See* MacDonald, Philip, 1899-1981

Fleming, Thomas J., 1927-

Dreams of glory; {by} Thomas Fleming. Forge 2000 301p $24.95
ISBN 0-312-87743-9   LC 00-31810
"A Tom Doherty Associates book"
"Set during the frigid, bone-creaking winter of January 1780, when the Revolutionary War had seemingly quieted down, this . . . tale is based on an actual British plot to kidnap George Washington. . . . At the heart of the novel is the elusive British spy Twenty-Six, whose activities touch all the other characters. Meanwhile, Fleming gives us an almost tactile sense of that cold winter and the desperate living conditions of the American troops in contrast to the near luxury of the British." Libr J

When this cruel war is over; [by] Thomas Fleming. Forge 2001 301p $24.95
ISBN 0-312-87204-6   LC 00-48444
"A Tom Doherty Associates book"
"In the last year of the Civil War, headstrong southern belle Janet Todd secretly works to rally support for the Sons of Liberty, a revolutionary conspiracy aiming to turn the northwest Union states into a second Confederacy. Her chief recruiting prospect is the dashing Major Paul Stapleton, a battle-scarred Union officer who is disillusioned by the grisly tactics of his army." Booklist
"Appearances by such historical figures as John Wilkes Booth and Mary Surratt and reprints of actual letters between President Lincoln and Colonel Gentry foster suspense." Publ Wkly

Flying Officer X *See* Bates, H. E. (Herbert Ernest), 1905-1974

Flynn, Gillian, 1971-

Dark places. Shaye Areheart Books 2009 349p $24
ISBN 978-0-307-34156-3; 0-307-34156-9
                                      LC 2008-40244
"Libby Day, the protagonist of Flynn's disturbing second novel, was, as a seven-year-old, the only survivor of her family's brutal murder by her older brother, an event dubbed by the media the 'Satan Sacrifice of Kinnakee, Kansas.' Twenty-five years later, she has become a hardened, selfish young woman with no friends or family. Since the tragedy, her life has been paid for by donations

Flynn, Gillian, 1971——_Continued_
of well-wishers, but, with that fund now empty, Libby
must find a way to make money. Her search leads her
to The Kill Club, a secret society of people obsessed
with the details of notorious murders. As Libby tries to
gather artifacts to sell to The Kill Club (whose members,
it turns out, doubt the guilt of her brother), she is forced
to reëxamine the events of the night of the murder.
Flynn's well-paced story deftly shows the fallibility of
memory and the lies a child tells herself to get through
a trauma." New Yorker

Sharp objects; a novel. Shaye Areheart Books
2006 245p $24
ISBN 0-307-34154-2   LC 2005-35046
"Troubled newspaper reporter Camille Preaker is sent
back to her Missouri hometown in a bid to get the inside
scoop on the murders of two preteen girls-both were
strangled and had their teeth removed. Almost as nasty
as the brutal crimes are Camille's twisted family dynamics. She intends to stay with her zombie-like mother,
whom she has hardly spoken to in 8 years; her cipher of
a stepfather; and her twisted, overly precocious 13-year-
old half sister. Wading back into the insular social dynamics of the town proves to be a stressful experience
for Camille, a reformed cutter whose body is riddled
with the scars of words such as wicked and cupcake."
Booklist
The author "offers up a literary thriller that's a
doozy. . . and she does it with wit and grit, a sort of
Hitchcock visits Stephen King, with plenty of the former's offstage and often only implied violence, and the
latter's sense of pacing and facility with dialogue. . . .
This is not a comfortable novel of touchy-feely family
fun. Rather, it is a tough tale told with remarkable clarity
and dexterity." Denver Post

Flynn, Michael

Eifelheim. Tor Book 2006 320p $25.95
ISBN 0-7653-0096-6   LC 2006-5468
"A Tom Doherty Associates book"
"Tom, a young historian, obsesses about Eifelheim, a
German village that mysteriously disappeared from all
maps in 1349. His lover Sharon, a theoretical physicist,
occupies herself with testing the limits of conventional
theories of time and space. Their interests merge when
they discover the remarkable story of Father Dietrich,
Eifelheim's parish priest during the Black Death and a
believer in travelers from the stars. With a sure grasp of
both speculative science and medieval history, Flynn
. . . compellingly weaves past and present together in a
dialog of faith and science." Libr J

The January dancer. Tor 2008 350p il $24.95
ISBN 978-0-7653-1817-6; 0-7653-1817-2
                                      LC 2008-29772
"A Tom Doherty Associates book"
"Forced to land for repairs on an unnamed, remote
planet, Captain Amos January and crew discover a cache
of artifacts left by a cryptic alien race 'long before humans went to space.' They soon retrieve the Dancer, a
shape-changing stone that defies analysis. Possibly the
scepter of a legendary prehuman king, certainly unique,
the priceless trophy is desired by diverse governments,
military powers, plutocrats and cabals throughout human-
settled space." Publ Wkly

"The characters zip through so many worlds that it's
hard to keep track of them, but Flynn includes enough
clever references to the long-abandoned Earth to keep the
journey amusing. . . . The balladic framework can be
heavy-handed at times, but it adds a mythical quality to
what could have been run-of-the-mill space fantasy."
Washington Post Book World

Foe, Daniel _See_ Defoe, Daniel, 1661?-1731

Foer, Jonathan Safran, 1977-

Everything is illuminated; a novel. Houghton
Mifflin 2002 276p il $24
ISBN 0-618-17387-0   LC 2001-51610
"There are two plots here. The first is the story of Jonathan Safran Foer, who travels to the Ukraine hoping to
find Augustine, the woman who helped save his grandmother from the Nazis. Jonathan; his Ukranian translator,
Alexi (who narrates much of the novel in a hilarious broken English); Alexi's grandfather; and the family dog,
Sammy Davis Junior Junior, all grow to love Augustine
on their mad and hopeless search for her. The second
story follows the history of one family in Trachimbrod,
the shtetl for which Alexi and Jonathan are searching."
Booklist
"Foer deftly handles the intricate story-within-a-story
plot, and the layers of suspense build as the shtetl hurtles
toward the devastation of the 20th century while Alex
and Jonathan and Grandfather close in on the object of
their search. An impressive, original debut." Publ Wkly

Extremely loud & incredibly close. Houghton
Mifflin 2005 326p il $24.95; pa $13.95
ISBN 0-618-32970-6; 0-618-71165-1 (pa)
                                      LC 2004-65131
"Oskar Schell is an inventor, Francophile, tambourine
player, Shakespearean actor, jeweler, pacifist. He is nine
years old. And he is on an urgent, secret search through
the five boroughs of New York to find the lock that fits
a mysterious key belonging to his father, who died in the
attacks on the World Trade Center." Publisher's note
The author's "depiction of Oskar's reaction to phone
messages left by his father as he awaited rescue in the
burning World Trade Center, his description of Oskar's
grandfather's love affair . . . and his experiences during
the bombing of Dresden—these passages underscore Mr.
Foer's ability to evoke, with enormous compassion and
psychological acuity, his characters' emotional experiences, and to show how these private moments intersect
with the great public events of history." N Y Times
(Late N Y Ed)

Foley, Martha, 1897-1977

(ed) 200 years of great American short stories.
See 200 years of great American short stories

(ed) Best of the Best American short stories,
1915-1950. See Best of the Best American short
stories, 1915-1950

Follett, Ken, 1949-

Eye of the needle; a novel. Arbor House 1978 313p o.p.

* LC 77-90670

"It is 1944 and the Allies are preparing to invade France. Part of the preparations call for a vast deception that will draw the bulk of the German defending forces to the Calais area while the Allies go in at Normandy. Only one of the enemy smells out the fakery, a German spy called Die Nadel (for the stiletto which is his favorite murder weapon). Called variously Faber or Baker, the only spy Hitler trusts, he must get his information back to the homeland. The race by British Intelligence to thwart Die Nadel provides the story drive of the book." Best Sellers

"An absolutely terrific thriller, so pulse-pounding, so ingenious in its plotting, and so frighteningly realistic that you simply cannot stop reading, this World War II espionage tale is right up there with the best of them." Publ Wkly

Hornet flight. Dutton 2002 420p $26.95

ISBN 0-525-94689-6   LC 2002-37903

"Tale of amateur spies pursued by Nazi collaborators in occupied Denmark in 1941. Harald Olufsen is an 18-year-old physics student who stumbles into espionage when he accidentally discovers a secret German radar installation on the island where he lives. . . . Follett starts out fast and keeps up the pace, revealing how ordinary people who want to do the right thing are undone by their own enthusiasm and inexperience. He also paints a vivid and convincing picture of life in occupied Denmark, of easy collaboration with the Nazis and of the insidious, creeping persecution of the Jews. Publ Wkly

Jackdaws. Dutton 2001 451p

ISBN 0-525-94628-4   LC 2001-37087

This thriller is about a mission "to take out a German telephone exchange near Reims in the last few hours before D-Day. A full-frontal assault led by British SOE (Special Operations Executives) Felicity 'Flick' Clariet and her husband, a French Resistance leader, has failed, leaving the Allies with only a last-minute desperation plan: a team of six women, posing as a cleaning detail, will infiltrate the exchange and dismantle it. . . . The assembled team includes two lesbians, a German transvestite, and a gypsy. All of this may sound like cliched melodrama, but when Follett starts the clock and slips the narrative gearshift into synchromesh, one's literary misgivings are abandoned in the wake of the plot's forward thrust." Booklist

Lie down with lions. Morrow 1986 333p o.p.

LC 85-25876

This novel is set in "Afghanistan, where the farmers and nomads are battling their Russian invaders. Jean-Pierre, a doctor fresh from residency, has volunteered two years to tend the wounded and offer general medical aid in the Valley of Five Lions; his real motive, however, is to spy on the rebels for the 'KGB'. Jane, his newly pregnant wife, serves as his nurse and his contact with the women of the villages. When local caravans bringing munitions are repeatedly attacked and the men killed, Ellis Thaler, a 'CIA' expert in explosives, arrives to consolidate the rebel's efforts, that he and Jane had been lovers complicates the situation. Separately they deduce Jean-Pierre's treachery. . . . This is fine adventure filled with passion, violence, and tension." Best Sellers

Pillars of the earth. Morrow 1989 973p o.p.

LC 89-9405

This novel "chronicles the vicissitudes of a prior, his master builder, and their community as they struggle to build a cathedral and protect themselves during the tumultuous 12th century, when the empress Maud and Stephen are fighting for the crown of England after the death of Henry I." Libr J

"Follett has skillfully crafted an extraordinary epic buttressed by a succession of suspenseful subplots. A towering triumph of romance, rivalry, and spectacle from a major talent." Booklist

Triple; a novel. Arbor House 1979 377p o.p.

LC 78-73869

"The Egyptians are making nuclear weapons and the Israelis, in order to do the same, are obliged to steal 100 tons of uranium. A group of old acquaintances at Oxford in 1947 come together again in different roles: the Mossad agent who organizes the theft, the disgruntled Palestinian spying for Egypt, the Russian bureaucrat (actually a KGB colonel), and the American become a Mafia don. The hijacking plot is elaborate beyond description." Libr J

World without end. Dutton 2007 1014p $35

ISBN 978-0-525-95007-3; 0-525-95007-9

LC 2007-26639

"Some 200 years after Pillars, the town of Kingsbridge is still dominated by its magnificent cathedral. But times have changed. War and plague have dramatically affected the infrastructure of the Middle Ages, shifting the base of power from the noble and religious to the rising merchant and artisan classes. Populated with an immense cast of truly remarkable characters-the rich and powerful, the weak and downtrodden, clergy, guildsmen and nobility-this novel explores the lives and fortunes of the ancestors of the original inhabitants of Kingsbridge." Libr J

Folsom, Allan R.

The day after tomorrow; a novel; by Allan Folsom. Little, Brown 1994 596p o.p.

LC 93-30344

"A young American doctor haunted by his father's murder stumbles into a chilling international conspiracy and crosses paths with, among others, a weary L.A. cop investigating a series of surgically precise decapitations, a naive physical therapist and a hypercompetent German assassin." Publ Wkly

"In this ambitious and impressive first novel, Folsom covers vast amounts of territory at breakneck speed. . . . That Folsom manages to instill some genuine tension amidst all this is testimony to his skill." Libr J

Day of confession; a novel; [by] Allan Folsom. Little, Brown 1998 566p $35

ISBN 0-316-28755-5   LC 98-5470

"Four days after Cardinal Rosario Parma is assassinated in Rome, hotshot L.A. entertainment lawyer Harry Addison gets a frantic phone message from his estranged brother, Danny, a Vatican priest. Shortly thereafter, Harry hears that Danny has died in a bus explosion. When he flies to Rome to claim the body, he discovers that Danny is the prime suspect in Parma's murder-and that he's still alive. The novel then follows two parallel plots. Harry tries to find Danny and clear his name; mean-

Folsom, Allan R.—*Continued*

while, the sinister Cardinal Umberto Palestrina, who thinks he's the reincarnation of Alexander the Great, plots to make China the site of a new Holy Roman Empire." Publ Wkly

Fonseca, Isabel

Attachment. Knopf 2008 305p $23.95
ISBN 978-0-307-26691-0; 0-307-26691-5
LC 2007-42860

"The novel begins with Jean Hubbard, a freelance columnist, and her advertising exec husband Mark living happily on a remote tropical island, taking a break of indeterminate length from life in London; the respite is ruined for Jean when she intercepts a sexually explicit letter addressed to Mark, which she chooses not to confront him about. Months later, Jean receives abnormal mammogram results that prompt her and Mark to return home, where their daughter attends college and takes care of the family house. She soon learns that her father will undergo serious surgery in New York, where she grew up, so she hops on another plane and, back in America, winds up growing close to an old flame." N Y Sun

"If all this sounds soap-operatic—well, it kind of is, but the bubbles have heft as well as loft. Except for her clumsy effort to integrate Sept. 11 into the narrative—and, as a sort of dramatic bonus, the 2003 blackout—Ms. Fonseca's exploration of middle-aged displacement, both mental and physical, is intelligent, nuanced and immensely satisfying." N Y Observer

Forbes, Charlotte

The good works of Ayela Linde; a novel in stories. Arcade Pub. 2006 227p $24
ISBN 1-55970-807-7
LC 2005-29294

"We meet the beautiful and enigmatic 17-year-old Ayela Linde in 1950, in the Texas border town of Santa Rosalia, where she lives with her dressmaker mother and suffers the stigma of illegitimacy with unconcerned defiance. We see her through the eyes of her friend Druanne as they meet their respective suitors at the local pool and dance hall. In the next 15 chapters, different narrators outline their encounters with Ayela, chronicling everything from her tumultuous young marriage to her death in 1999. . . . Forbes presents a delicate gem of a novel in which she moves deftly from narrator to narrator to produce a rich and moving portrait of Ayela in all phases of her adult life against the colorful backdrop of a town with ever-shifting mores and priorities." Libr J

Ford, Elbur, 1906-1993

For works written by this author under other names see Holt, Victoria, 1906-1993; Plaidy, Jean, 1906-1993

Ford, Ford Madox, 1873-1939

The good soldier; a tale of passion. Knopf 1991 (Everyman's library, 20) $24
ISBN 0-679-40665-4
* LC 91-52977

First published 1915 in the United Kingdom

This novel "consists of the first-person narration of American John Dowell (an archetypally unreliable narrator), who relates the history of relationships that begin in 1904, when his wife Florence meet Edward and Leonora Ashburnham in a hotel in Nauheim. The two couples form a foursome, and meet regularly. In August 1913 the Ashburnhams take their young ward Nancy Rufford to Nauheim with them, and Florence commits suicide. Later that year the Ashburnhams send Nancy to India (where she goes mad) and Edward also commits suicide. Dowell becomes Nancy's 'male sick nurse'; Leonora remarries. The substance of the novel lies in Dowell's growing understanding of the intrigues that lay behind the orderly Edwardian façade both couples had presented to the world." Oxford Companion to Engl Lit. 6th edition

The last post
In Ford, F. M. Parade's end

A man could stand up
In Ford, F. M. Parade's end

No more parades
In Ford, F. M. Parade's end

Parade's end. Knopf 1992 906p $22
ISBN 0-679-41728-1
* LC 92-52922

"Everyman's library"

A reissue of the title first published 1950; A one volume edition of the author's tetralogy that includes: Some do not (1924); No more parades (1925); A man could stand up (1926); and The last post (1928)

This series of novels "describes the adventures in love and war of Christopher Tietjens, an old-fashioned gentleman of the English governing class. Ford draws a brilliant picture of the social changes brought about by the First World War. Before the war, Tietjens is nobly faithful to his impossible wife. But trench warfare seems to him a symbol of the disintegration of his whole society. He has a mental breakdown, goes to live with a woman he loves, and gives up his position, wealth, and historic family ties." Reader's Ency. 4th edition

Some do not
In Ford, F. M. Parade's end

Ford, Jeffrey, 1955-

The drowned life. Harper Perennial 2008 290, 16p pa $14.95
ISBN 978-0-06-143506-5; 0-06-143506-6
LC 2008-13181

Contents: The drowned life; Ariadne's mother; The night whiskey; A few things about ants; Under the bottom of the lake; Present from the past; The manticore spell; The fat one; The dismantled invention of fate; What's sure to come; The way he does it; The scribble mind; The bedroom light; In the house of four seasons; The dreaming wind; The golden dragon

"This collection of short stories from the author of The Shadow Year contains some of the most unusual and provocative settings and plots this reviewer has ever encountered, which will make it perfect for book talking to patrons. . . . Sometimes shocking, sometimes mesmerizing, sometimes humorous, this collection will please fans of Raymond Carver and Flannery O'Connor." Libr J

Ford, Jeffrey, 1955-——*Continued*

The empire of ice cream; with an introduction by Jonathan Carroll. Golden Gryphon Press 2006 319p $24.95

ISBN 1-930846-39-8   LC 2005-24035

Contents: The annals of Eelin-Ok; Jupiter's skull; A night in the tropics; The empire of ice cream; The beautiful Gelreesh; Boatman's holiday; Botch Town; A man of light; The green word; Giant Land; Coffins on the river; Summer afternoon; The weight of words; The Trentino kid

"Giants and unidentifiable alien creatures, fairy tales, the intertwining of wonder and terror, and fantastic views of both the strange and the ordinary all appear in this marvelous collection, with Ford's comments on his inspiration and motivations appended to each story. Ford is nothing if not versatile, as this collection confirms to great effect." Booklist

The shadow year. William Morrow 2008 289p $25.95

ISBN 978-0-06-123152-0; 0-06-123152-5

LC 2007-37319

"Strange things are happening in a small Long Island community-a child disappears, a large, white car no one recognizes is seen creeping around, there's a smell of pipe smoke at odd times, and a Peeping Tom is scaring women at night. When the narrator, an introspective sixth-grade boy who likes detective stories, and his older brother decide to track the culprit, they set up a model of their town in the basement only to discover that their younger sister is predicting future events by moving the figures around." Libr J

"A masterly literary adventure that is at once a hypnotically compelling mystery and a stunningly evocative portrait of small-town adolescence." Pittsburgh Press

Ford, Richard, 1944-

Independence Day. Knopf 1995 451p

ISBN 0-679-49265-8

* LC 95-3126

This novel "picks up the story of Frank Bascombe where it left off in a previous novel, *The Sportswriter* (1986). The time is now the late 1980s, and Frank, divorced, is no longer sportswriting but selling real estate. Within the time span of preparing and participating in a Fourth of July weekend, Frank tells us in . . . detail about the Sisyphean boulders he has been forced to push uphill throughout his life: career, kids, ex-wife, current girlfriend, and the unpleasant people occupying his rental property. Frank's plan is to take his teenage son on the road over the Fourth to visit sports halls of fame, but, more significantly, to try to get the troubled youth somewhat straightened out." Booklist

One is "constantly struck by the rich, dense mixture of Ford's narrative. No one writes better—and with more inventive brio—about the bland wasteland of US suburbia; that shopping-malled, subdivisioned terrain that has rapidly become the true defining landscape of late 20th-century America." New Statesman (1913)

The lay of the land. Alfred A. Knopf 2006 496p $26.95

ISBN 978-0-679-45468-7; 0-679-45468-3

LC 2006-25570

This third novel featuring sports journalist Frank Bascombe, who appeared previously in The Sportswriter (1986) and Independence Day (1995), finds the protagonist facing health problems (prostate cancer), the end of the Clinton era, and family issues.

This is as "as vibrant a book as any that Richard Ford has written. It bristles with energy, with a natural assurance on the part of its writer. . . . And what a slice of life at the turn of the century and millennium this novel is. There is so much trenchant criticism of what is wrong with American society: the economic royalism, the greed, the lack of common decency and civility in so many walks of life, and above all perspective. . . . As people today read Theodore Dreiser for his acute portraits of industrialized America in its gilded age and Sinclair Lewis for his insights into his nation's struggles to come to terms with 20th-century changes in its social structures, one day readers will turn to Richard Ford to discover just what the United States was like on the homefront during his particular fin de siecle." Christ Sci Monit

A multitude of sins; stories. Knopf 2002 286p

ISBN 0-375-41212-3   LC 2001-38402

Contents: Privacy; Quality time; Calling; Reunion; Puppy; Crèche; Under the radar; Dominion; Charity; Abyss

"Tracing the blueprint of human interaction in this latest collection . . . Ford signals the master text of lust standing behind the multitude of small sins he so tersely and poignantly chronicles. To err is human, and, in Ford's worldview, little is so human as the act of cheating on a wife or husband." Publ Wkly

(ed) Welty, E. Stories, essays & memoir

Women with men; three long stories. Knopf 1997 255p o.p.   LC 97-5832

Contents: The womanizer; Jealous; Occidentals

In these "three powerful long stories, the author explores precarious and complicated relationships between men and women. Each tale revolves around the fractured emotions aroused by the dissolution of a marriage: feelings of failure and the dizzying sense of spinning unsteadily and off course through life, like a wheel without an axle. . . . All of Ford's magnetic characters seem permanently jet-lagged, woozy with displacement and disappointment, and their troubles escalate accordingly, with surreal and sickening inevitability." Booklist

Ford, Robert

The student conductor. Putnam 2003 289p $24.95

ISBN 0-399-15037-4   LC 2003-46514

"Eight years after dropping out of Juilliard, 30-year-old Cooper Barrow makes a bid to restart his career, going to work with Karlheinz Ziegler, a legendary conductor from prewar days who now teaches at a provincial music school. A strongly antagonistic relationship develops between them, exacerbated by Barrow's continuing anxiety, Ziegler's brusquely authoritarian manner and the young American's romantic interest in Petra Vogel, a young oboist in the student orchestra, a refugee from East Germany." Publ Wkly

"This is finally a novel about power—the power of a great conductor driving a well-trained orchestra, the power of the past to enslave us, the power of the future to

Ford, Robert—*Continued*

free us, and the power of the individual to love and to forgive. There is hardly a wrong note, from the moment Ford lifts his baton to the final refrain." Booklist

Forester, C. S. (Cecil Scott), 1899-1966

Admiral Hornblower in the West Indies. Little, Brown 1958 329p o.p.

A collection of Horatio Hornblower's adventures set in the West Indies. "The first belongs chronologically with 'Lieutenant Hornblower.' The rest are set nearly 15 years later when, as rear admiral in command of His Majesty's fleet in the West Indies, he faces a new Bonapartist uprising, suppresses the slave trade, stamps out piracy, and maintains British diplomacy during the South American revolutions." Booklist

"Recounted with taste, with psychological insight, and with a sure sense of story. This is top grade adventure fiction." N Y Her Trib Books

The African Queen. Little, Brown 1935 275p
ISBN 0-89244-065-1
          *

"At her brother's death Rose Sayer is left alone in an isolated African mission. She is determined to fight against the Germans, who have taken her brother's black converts into custody. She joins forces with a Cockney, Alnutt, and they take a long and dangerous trip downriver in Alnutt's dilapidated launch in order to reach the German boat they intend to blow up. The journey points up the differences between this ill-matched pair, and their bravery as well." Shapiro. Fic for Youth. 3d edition

Beat to quarters. Little, Brown 1937 324p o.p.
          *

A sea story of the British navy in the early nineteenth century. Essentially it is a portrait of a man, captain of an English frigate. Hornblower, son of a country doctor, is a man uncertain of his own powers, of his technical skill and of the admiration of his men, yet when he is sent under sealed orders to the Pacific coast of Central America, he accomplishes his mission brilliantly, and fights two successful battles with the same Spanish warship

"There is plenty of action. But there is also an unusual character study." N Y Times Book Rev

Followed by Ship of the line

Commodore Hornblower. Little, Brown 1945 384p o.p.

"Hornblower returns to sea in command of a squadron on a delicate mission to the Baltic, reluctantly taking leave of his lovely wife Lady Barbara. In this expedition he combines brilliant naval strategy with diplomatic cunning to out-maneuver his old, unseen enemy Napoleon." Ont Libr Rev

"It is a spirited piece of work, and full of interesting detail where matters naval, military, and diplomatic in that year of decision are concerned." Times Lit Suppl

Followed by Lord Hornblower

Flying colours. Little, Brown 1939 294p o.p.

Third book in a series which began with Beat to quarters and Ship of the line. Captain Hornblower, his crippled first mate, Bush, and his servant, Brown, escape from their escort on the way to Paris to be tried for pira-

cy. The story is of their recapture of an English vessel and return to England, where they are covered with honors

Followed by Commodore Hornblower

Hornblower and the Atropos. Little, Brown 1953 325p o.p.

This is a series of episodes in the early life of the Captain; a journey across England from Gloucester to London by canal; his part in the funeral of Nelson; and his battles on the coast of Turkey, where he recovers a huge treasure from a sunken English ship

Hornblower and the Hotspur. Little, Brown 1962 344p
    ISBN 0-316-28899-3

"From the standpoint of sequence, this . . . title in the Hornblower saga follows 'Lieutenant Hornblower.'" Wis Libr Bull

"The story opens just before Horatio sails on a cruise in his first command. His rank is Commander; his ship something less than a frigate but something more than a sloop; his task to act as the eyes of the Channel Fleet which is to be in position to blockade Brest upon the imminent declaration of hostilities with France. In the course of action Hornblower is detained at sea for almost two years as, in his own inimitable and logically necessary style, he helps cripple the Napoleonic effort to invade England, the last block to conquest of Europe." Best Sellers

Hornblower during the crisis, and two stories: Hornblower's temptation and The last encounter. Little, Brown 1967 174p
    ISBN 0-316-28915-9

"Posthumous novel fragment and two slender stories. The former concerns Hornblower's eventful voyage to London on another man's ship for reassignment on a spy mission to Spain. . . . In one story Mr. Hornblower is almost taken in by a seemingly harmless mission entrusted to him by a young Irishman before his shipboard execution. In the other tale a stranded traveler in distress, helped by Admiral Hornblower and wife, proves to be Napoleon Bonaparte." Booklist

"Because Forester died before completing this novel, the reader is left with a summary sketch and his own imagination for final details of the plot. For Forester devotees, this will not detract from the essential verve and dash of Hornblower's last chase." Christ Sci Monit

The last nine days of the Bismarck. Little, Brown 1959 138p o.p.

"Forester describes the pursuit and epic bombardment at sea in World War II when the German battleship 'Bismarck' broke into the Atlantic and sailed toward Brest with the whole British Home Fleet after her. Scenes on board the 'Bismarck' and the British ships have been given dialog to make the telling more vivid." Publ Wkly

Lieutenant Hornblower. Little, Brown 1952 306p
    ISBN 0-316-28907-8

This novel details "Horatio's adventures as a Lieutenant until his promotion to Commander during the early years of the Napoleonic Wars." Best Sellers

The author "interprets the navy, certainly in its Napoleonic period, with the help of a character that represents

Forester, C. S. (Cecil Scott), 1899-1966—*Continued*

the navy at its best and action that is grandly exciting without being melodramatic; helped, too, by a sense of order and a mastery of technique that puts his work on a high plane of artistry." Christ Sci Monit

Lord Hornblower. Little, Brown 1946 322p
ISBN 0-316-28908-6

In this "Hornblower novel Horatio continues his adventures and helps defeat Napoleon by aiding the heir to the Bourbon throne to enter France. Barbara goes to the Congress of Vienna to act as hostess for her brother while Horatio returns to France to visit old friends and renew an old love. When Napoleon escapes from Elba danger threatens Hornblower as he forms a guerrilla band in the south of France. But, saved by the defeat of the French at Waterloo, he returns to the arms of Barbara and new honors as Lord Hornblower." Booklist

Mr. Midshipman Hornblower. Little, Brown 1950 310p
ISBN 0-316-28909-4

Contents: Hornblower and the even chance; Hornblower and the cargo of rice; Hornblower and the penalty of failure; Hornblower and the man who felt queer; Hornblower and the man who saw God; Hornblower, the frogs, and the lobsters; Hornblower and the Spanish galleys; Hornblower and the examination for lieutenant; Hornblower and Noah's Ark; Hornblower, the duchess, and the devil

Ship of the line. Little, Brown 1938 298p o.p.

In this sequel to Beat to quarters, Captain Hornblower is given command of the ship Sutherland and sent to join the forces blockading the Spanish coast in the war with Napoleon

Followed by Flying colours

To the Indies. Little, Brown 1940 298p o.p.

"The story of Narciso Rich who is lifted suddenly from his quiet life as a successful lawyer to join the swaggering, gold-hungry hidalgos who went with Columbus on his third voyage. He fights Indians at San Domingo, is kidnapped by renegades, shipwrecked off the coast of Cuba, and finally makes his way back to the settlement in time to return on the ship that carried Columbus in chains." Ont Libr Rev

Forester, Cecil Scott *See* Forester, C. S. (Cecil Scott), 1899-1966

Forna, Aminatta

Ancestor stones. Atlantic Monthly Press 2006 317p $24
ISBN 0-87113-944-8   LC 2006-47708

"Abie, a West African woman who has lived in London for years, learns that she has inherited the family coffee plantation in her native village. Abie returns to consider her inheritance and visits with four of her aunts, daughters of four of the 11 wives of her great-grandfather. The aunts tell Abie their life stories, which span nearly a century. They describe the founding of the village and the coffee plantation, what it was like seeing a white man for the first time, the end of colonialism, the first elections, political and religious upheaval, and

the social implications of polygamous families." Libr J

This is an "optimistic, truthful novel and if we accept Ben Okri's notion of writers as 'the barometer of the vitality of the spirit of the nation', then we should be optimistic about an indisputably talented young novelist and for the future of Africa too." Times Lit Suppl

Forrest, Katherine V., 1939-

Apparition alley; a Kate Delafield mystery. Berkley Prime Crime 1997 248p o.p.
                                LC 96-53688

"Wounded by 'friendly fire' during a burglary arrest gone awry, lesbian LAPD homicide detective Kate Delafield must undergo routine—but intrusive—psychological counseling before returning to duty. Meanwhile, officer Luke Taggart, a pariah among their colleagues, wants Kate to represent him at his disciplinary hearing. Luke believes that he has been set up by vindictive cops and that Kate's 'accident' could be part of the same conspiracy. Aptly described West Hollywood and L.A. settings, great counseling dialog, and subtle plot machinations underscore the author's talent." Libr J

Liberty Square; a Kate Delafield mystery. Berkley Prime Crime 1996 242p
ISBN 0-425-15467-X   LC 95-46809

This mystery "featuring lesbian LAPD homicide detective Kate Delafield is also a moody meditation on the Vietnam War and the conflicted loyalties it engendered. For ex-marine Delafield begrudgingly attends a reunion with her military buddies from a quarter-century past, an event that not only stirs up troubled memories but also sets the scene for a grisly murder whose motives stem from the time when America's Southeast Asia involvement was bloodiest." Booklist

Sleeping bones. Berkley Prime Crime 1999 260p $21.95
ISBN 0-425-17029-2   LC 98-54294

This Kate Delafield "adventure takes her to the famous La Brea tar pits, where she breaks in new partner Joe on a bizarre case of murder. An excellent novel." Libr J

Forstchen, William R.

(jt. auth) Gingrich, N. Gettysburg

(jt. auth) Gingrich, N. Grant comes east

Forster, E. M. (Edward Morgan), 1879-1970

The collected tales of E. M. Forster. Knopf 1947 308p o.p.

The celestial omnibus: The story of a panic; The other side of the hedge; The celestial omnibus; Other kingdom; The curate's friend; The road from Colonus

The eternal moment: The machine stops; The point of it: Mr. Andrews; Co-ordination; The story of the siren; The eternal moment

Howards End. Knopf 1991 xxxiii, 359p $19
ISBN 0-679-40668-9
                                * LC 91-52997

"Everyman's library"

First published 1910

This novel "deals with an English country house called Howards End and its influence on the lives of the mate-

Forster, E. M. (Edward Morgan), 1879-1970—
Continued

rialistic Wilcoxes, the cultural and idealistic Schlegel sisters, and the poor bank clerk Leonard Bast. The Schlegels try to befriend Bast. Mr. Wilcox, whom Margaret Schlegel later marries, gives him financial advice which ruins him. Helen Schlegel becomes his mistress for a short time and bears his son; thereupon Charles Wilcox thrashes and accidentally kills him. The house passes from intuitive, half-mystical Mrs. Wilcox to her husband's second wife Margaret Schlegel, to Margaret's nephew, Leonard Bast's son. Illustrating Forster's motto 'Only connect,' the house brings together three important elements in English society: money and successful business in the Wilcoxes, culture in the Schlegels, and the lower classes in Leonard Bast." Reader's Ency. 4th edition

also in Forster, E. M. A room with a view and Howards End

Maurice. Norton 1971 256p o.p.

This novel was written between 1913 and 1914. It depicts the steps by which Maurice Hall, a shy, conventional young man, while a student at Cambridge, first discovers and then gradually comes to accept the fact that he is, by nature, sexually attracted to men, not women. "He enjoys a romantic friendship—idyllic, sentimental, chaste—with Clive, a fellow undergraduate at Cambridge. When Clive turns abruptly to women . . . the unhappy Maurice consults his family doctor and a hypnotist who fail to help him. On a visit to the now-married Clive's country estate he falls in love, physically this time, with a young gamekeeper to whom he commits his future on a brief acquaintance." Newsweek

"This posthumous novel with a homosexual theme would have been sensational had it been published when written in 1913. Appearing in the 1970's, it is not sensational, but it is an interesting novel—well written as all of E. M. Forster's works are. . . . It is filled with keen insight and sympathetic character analysis, valuable for an understanding of the author and his works." Choice

A passage to India; with an introduction by P.N. Furbank. Knopf 1991 xxxix, 293p $18
ISBN 0-679-40549-6

"Everyman's library"
First published 1924
"Politics and mysticism are potent forces in India just after World War I. Ronald Heaslop, magistrate of Chandrapore, has asked his mother, Mrs. Moore, to visit him along with his fiancee, Adela Quested. To add to their knowledge of the real India, Dr. Aziz, a young Moslem doctor, offers to take them to the Marabar Caves outside the city. The visit is a shattering experience. Mrs. Moore is struck by the thought that all her ideas about life are no more than the hollow echo she hears in the cave. Adela, entering another cave alone, emerges in a panic and accuses Dr. Aziz of having attacked her in the gloom of the cave. The trial that results from her accusation divides the groups in the city so acutely that a reconciliation appears impossible." Shapiro. Fic for Youth. 3d edition

A depiction of the "clash between East and West, and of the prejudices and misunderstandings that foredoomed goodwill. Criticized at first for being anti-British and possibly inaccurate bias, it has been praised as a superb character study of the people of one race by a writer of another." Oxford Companion to Engl Lit

A room with a view. Putnam 1911 364p

First published 1908
The novel "is set mostly in Italy, a country which represents for the author the forces of true passion. The heroine, upper-class Lucy Honeychurch, is visiting Italy with a friend. When she regrets that her hotel room has no view, lower-class Mr. Emerson offers the friends his own room and that of his son. Lucy becomes caught between the world of the Emersons and that of Cecil Vyse, the shallow, conventional young man of her own class to whom she becomes engaged on her return to England. Finally, she overcomes her own prejudice and her family's opposition and marries George Emerson." Reader's Ency. 4th edition

also in Forster, E. M. A room with a view and Howards End

A room with a view and Howards End. Modern Lib. 1993 533p
ISBN 0-679-60069-8   LC 93-15340
A combined edition of two titles, both entered separately

Forster, Edward Morgan *See* Forster, E. M. (Edward Morgan), 1879-1970

Forsyth, Frederick, 1938-

Avenger. Thomas Dunne Bks. 2003 370p $24.95
ISBN 0-312-31951-7   LC 2003-53163
"World War II, Vietnam, Bosnia, and Cambodia take turns commanding center stage, held together by two protagonists: a middle-age lawyer and an aging business tycoon, who have both suffered devastating losses. The tycoon's loss, that of his grandson on a relief mission in Bosnia, becomes subsumed in the mission of attorney Calvin Dexter, grieving father and former 'Nam tunnel rat, whose mission in life is to bring justice to those who have gotten away with murder. . . . Forsyth's extraordinary care with detail, his solid voice, and his exquisite pacing make this a totally engrossing thriller." Booklist

The day of the jackal. Viking 1971 380p o.p.

"Dissident OAS officers hire a mercenary, known by the code name 'Jackal', to assassinate General Charles deGaulle. The officers hope to cash in on the political chaos that would follow. The methodical, ingenious preparations of 'Jackal' are paralleled by the attempts of the combined French law-enforcement agencies to uncover and stop the plot. The suspense is acute." Shapiro. Fic for Youth. 3d edition

The dogs of war. Viking 1974 408p o.p.

A "novel about the carefully planned overthrow of the small African state of Zangaro. Behind the coup is a British multimillionaire, seeking control of the mining rites to the platinum within Zangaro's Crystal Mountain. He hires top mercenary Cat Shannon to do most of the planning and to carry out the attack. The bulk of the

Forsyth, Frederick, 1938——*Continued*
novel is devoted to each of the detailed transactions of
the 100-day operation, from purchasing and smuggling
arms to arranging a multitude of clandestine business
deals." Libr J

The fourth protocol. Viking 1984 389p o.p.
LC 83-40646
"The narrative reveals a Soviet plan to control England
and destroy NATO by swaying the popular vote in England's election: the Russian's best undercover man will
detonate a small nuclear device near an American base
in Britain, thereby ensuring a wave of antinuclear sentiment." Libr J
This novel "succeeds magnificently on at least two
. . . levels: as a scrupulously detailed study of spy
'tradecraft' and as a testament to the virtues of a well-
constructed plot. We want to know what happens in this
book not only because of the inherently dramatic situation, but also because we anticipate the sense of resolution that comes when the puzzle's last piece clicks se-
curely into place." Booklist

The Odessa file. Viking 1972 337p o.p.
*
"Young German reporter Peter Miller comes upon the
diary of a survivor of a World War II extermination
camp at Riga. Its revelations lead him into the deadly
pursuit of commandant Roschmann, known as the Butcher of Riga. Roschmann is engaged in an international
scheme to destroy the Jewish state. The plan is promoted
by the Odessa, a secret organization that protects the
identities and fortunes of former SS members. Miller infiltrates the organization to find and expose Roschmann."
Shapiro. Fic for Youth. 3d edition
"Forsyth skillfully blends fact and fiction into a suspenseful and detailed story which is often downright
chilling in its credibility." Libr J

The veteran. St. Martin's Press 2001 367p
ISBN 0-312-28691-0
Contents: This collection contains the novella The
whispering wind and the following short stories: The veteran; The art of the Matter; The miracle; The citizen
Whispering wind, set during the Indian wars in 1876,
focuses on a frontier scout who survived the massacre at
the Little Bighorn
These stories "showcase the author's ability to capture
character and generate suspense in remarkably few
words." Booklist

The whispering wind
In Forsyth, F. The veteran

Foster, Alan Dean, 1946-

Dinotopia lost. Turner Pub. (Atlanta) 1996 318p
o.p.
LC 95-41352
"The plot revolves around a band of pirates whose ship
miraculously survives the reefs around Dinotopia and
who set out to turn what they find there to profit. Will
Denison, the nineteenth-century discoverer of the symbiotic human-saurian society, is dragged into taking a leading part in defeating the pirates, most of whom are converted to the Dinotopian way of life. . . . Although the
saurian characters are better limned than the human ones,
Foster's addition to Dinotopiana will agreeably reward
the fantastic place's many fans." Booklist

Kingdoms of light. Warner Bks. 2001 372p
$24.95
ISBN 0-446-52667-3   LC 00-43501
"The fearsome sorcerer Khaxan Mundurucu has laid
waste to the Gowdlands. While a host of goblins terrorize the land, leaching it of all color and destroying the
will of the conquered populace, a dying wizard's final
spell transforms his pets into a company of human heroes who possess the only chance of restoring hope and
freedom to their world." Libr J
"Foster's brand of storytelling, lighthearted even at the
darkest moments, doesn't leave much room for doubt
about how it's all going to turn out. Fans of swift-
moving plots and imaginative settings will overlook the
thin characters and enjoy this pleasant fantasy tale." Publ
Wkly

The mocking program. Warner Bks. 2002 279p
ISBN 0-446-52774-2   LC 2002-22851
"Angel Cardenas of the Namerican States Federales is
a police inspector whose beat is the Strip, a megalopolis
that encompasses Mexico and part of what used to be the
United States. A routine investigation of what appears to
be a mugging death soon leads to something unlike anything Cardenas has ever encountered." Libr J
"Like Anthony Burgess' *A Clockwork Orange,* this
novel comes with a glossary to help readers translate the
characters' slang (a combination of English and Spanish,
mostly). Peppered with clever new technology and offbeat characters, the book successfully crosses genres and
will appeal to both mystery and sf fans." Booklist

A triumph of souls. Warner Bks. 2000 406p
$24.95
ISBN 0-446-52218-X   LC 99-41376
Concluding volume in the author's Journeys of the
Catechist trilogy; previous titles Carnivores of light and
darkness (1998) and Into the thinking kingdoms (1999)
"Bound by his promise to a dying stranger, the good-
hearted herdsman and unlikely hero Etjole Ehomba continues his journey through strange and treacherous lands
filled with odd creatures and marvelous sights." Libr J
"Set in a magical world with prehistoric overtones, the
novel offers more wit and wandering than plot, but the
inventive situations are engaging and the characters far
more complex than they first appear. The ending is clever and will satisfy those who have made the fantastic
trek through Foster's whimsical world." Publ Wkly

Fowler, Karen Joy

The Jane Austen book club. Putnam 2004 288p
$23.95
ISBN 0-399-15161-3   LC 2003-47244
This novel is "essentially a character study of six people who meet regularly over several months to discuss
six of Austen's works. Jocelyn, in her 50s and never
married, is the originator of the club, a control freak who
handpicked all the members; Sylvia, her good friend, is
in a funk because her husband of 32 years has just left
her for another woman; Sylvia's daughter, Allegra, is an
attractive 30-year-old lesbian who recently broke up with
her lover; Prudie is a twentysomething high school
French teacher; the much-married Bernadette, 67, is now
single; and Grigg, in his 40s, would love to get married."
Libr J
"In her portrait of a California reading group, Karen

Fowler, Karen Joy—*Continued*

Joy Fowler turns a mirror on the gawking, voyeuristic presence that lurks in every story: the reader. What results is Fowler's shrewdest, funniest fiction yet, a novel about how we engage with a novel." N Y Times Book Rev

Sarah Canary. Holt & Co. 1991 290p

ISBN 0-8050-1753-4   LC 91-9746

"Chin Ah Kin is the reluctant hero of this search across Washington Territory for Sarah Canary. The year is 1873, one that holds promise for the emancipation of women, yet things couldn't be worse for Sarah. Chin first encounters her when she suddenly appears on the periphery of his camp. Because Sarah only speaks nonsense, Chin decides she is crazy and sets off with her to an asylum in Stellacoom. But because of her inability to communicate, Sarah soon becomes separated from Chin. Without her to justify his presence in the wilderness, Chin becomes the scapegoat for all the evil deeds around him." Libr J

"This novel is similar in scope to E. L. Doctorow's 'Ragtime,' and yet Ms. Fowler's book is as much a dreamscape as a panorama. Each of her 19 chapters has a contemporaneous and often cryptic epigraph from Emily Dickinson's poetry that, amazingly, seems to dictate the narrative that follows." N Y Times Book Rev

Sister Noon; a novel. Putnam 2001 321p $24.95

ISBN 0-399-14750-0   LC 00-46025

"A Marian Wood book"

"In Gilded Age-era San Francisco, fortyish spinster Lizzie Hayes is by any measure a good woman. She busies herself with worthy, conservative projects, especially her role as volunteer treasurer and fund-raiser for the Ladies' Relief and Protection Society Home. She does what is expected when it is expected. None in her circle suspects that a risk-taking spirit hides just beneath the surface. But when Lizzie crosses paths with the influential—and notorious—Mrs. Mary Ellen 'Mammy' Pleasant, opportunities for intrigue, passion, and subversion abound, and Lizzie plunges in with enthusiasm. This witty novel is a deft blend of historical fact, urban myth, social satire, and romance." Libr J

Fowles, John, 1926-2005

The French lieutenant's woman. Little, Brown 1969 467p o.p.

*

"The setting is Victorian England. The hero is Charles, respectable, well-to-do, thoughtful, progressive. He is engaged to Ernestina, a rich, attractive, but highly conventional girl, but he falls in love with the beautiful, tragic, mysterious Sarah who is known to Lyme Regis (where the action begins) as 'the French lieutenant's woman' because of some disreputable but romantic episode in her past life. The situation, that of the amorous triangle, is familiar in fiction. What makes this book highly original is that it has three possible endings, all different. . . . We have here a highly readable and informative book, compelling, thrilling, erotic, but we are not permitted to relax as if we were reading Dickens or Thackeray. A very modern mind is manipulating us as well as the characters." Burgess. 99 Novels

The magus; a revised version; with a foreword by the author. Little, Brown 1978 c1977 656p

ISBN 0-440-35162-6   LC 77-17343

Originally published 1966; this version first published 1977 in the United Kingdom

"This novel follows the harrowing misadventures of Nicholas Urfe, a young British schoolmaster who takes a teaching post on a remote Greek island, Phraxos, where he is drawn into an emotional maelstrom of high intrigue." Newsweek

"With the narrative skill and literary sleight of hand . . . Fowles again provides hours of engrossing entertainment for an audience susceptible to a massive blend of sensuous realism, suspenseful romanticism, hypertheatrical mystification, psychic intervention, and a gallery of unusual or exotic characters in the vivid setting of the golden, craggy, threatening beauty of an isolated Greek island." Booklist

Frame, Janet

Towards another summer. Counterpoint 2009 216p $24

ISBN 978-1-58243-476-6; 1-58243-476-X

LC 2008-50515

Written in 1963; first published 2007 in New Zealand

"New Zealander Grace Cleave is a writer living in London. Single, 30, and introverted, she copes dreamily with the outside world, her grasp of reality tenuous at best. When she accepts an invitation to spend the weekend with an acquaintance, Philip, and his wife, Anne, she is hoping that the trip will be good for both her and her stalled novel." Libr J

"Like every writer worth remembering, Frame exploits—or creates on the page, to be absolutely puristic about it—her peculiar sensibility, her private window into the universal. . . Frame's sad, slyly comic fish-out-of-water story . . . looks back to Virginia Woolf in its focus on the tortuous internal positionings beneath the surface of apparently casual conversation." N Y Times Book Rev

Frame, Ronald

The lantern bearers; a novel. Counterpoint 2001 224p $24

ISBN 1-58243-155-8   LC 2001-28897

"A Cornelia and Michael Bessie book"

First published 1999 in the United Kingdom

"Neil Pritchard, told that he will die of cancer within two years, presses forward with his book on the Scottish composer Euan Bone. He also tells in this book the story of his encounter with Bone shortly before the composer's death. Neil, 14 then and a superb boy soprano, was summering with his aunt in a southern Scottish coastal town when Bone enlisted him to help prepare a vocal score based on a Robert Louis Stevenson essay. All went beautifully, and Neil was falling in love with Bone; then his voice changed, ending the collaboration. . . . In a resentful funk, he told the lie that Bone had molested him, which led, Neil came to think, to Bone's demise." Booklist

"Subtly developed characters, a unique and enchanting setting, suspense, and lovely writing make this an exceptional work." Libr J

Francis, Clare

Wolf winter. Morrow 1988 c1987 558p
ISBN 0-688-06376-4   LC 87-24209
First published 1987 in the United Kingdom
"When Norwegian mountain climber Jan Johansen is killed in an incident on the Russian-Finnish border, his widow, Ragna, is drawn into a series of events with roots in World War II which set the stage for espionage in the Cold War of the 1960s. Ragna's attraction for two men, Jan's best friend and an Oslo journalist, brings them all together in a violent struggle for truth and survival in Lapland's frozen wastes." Libr J

"The skill with which the author counterpoints her several plot lines to create a mounting sense of tension is exemplary. . . . 'Wolf Winter' has a sure dramatic sense, minutely realized settings and—most important— the sort of casual style that easily delivers the large amounts of information that are essential to this sort of entertainment." N Y Times Book Rev

Francis, Dick

10 lb. penalty. Putnam 1997 273p $24.95
ISBN 0-399-14302-5   LC 97-28020
"As the action begins, Ben Juliard, a teen-age apprentice jockey, is tipped out of his job to find himself helping his father, George, win a seat in the House of Commons. Five years later, George Juliard is headed for national prominence when vicious rumors about an old crime are bruited about by his enemies and Ben, now an insurance investigator, returns to help solve it, risking his life in the process." N Y Times Book Rev

"As usual in a Francis novel, the sweetest parts are about family; here, especially the growing love and understanding between father and son. The villains aren't particularly scary, but this smooth, nimbly paced charmer isn't really about bad people anyway, but about how the rest of us cope and live, sometimes in their shadow." Publ Wkly

Bolt. Putnam 1987 318p o.p.
                                   * LC 86-25167
Jockey-sleuth Kit Fielding "must help his employer, Princess Casilia and her husband overcome pressure to convert their large industrial holdings to a munitions works. Murder and physical threats against his fiancée, the Princess's niece, force Kit to adopt a dangerous plan of action." Libr J

"As adept on a race-course as he is in an Eaton Square drawing room, Fielding is a match for any menace. . . . In mystery circles, Francis again demonstrates that he is both a win and a nice read." Time

(ed) The Dick Francis treasury of great racing stories. See The Dick Francis treasury of great racing stories

Even money; [by] Dick Francis and Felix Francis. G.P. Putnam's Sons 2009 350p $26.95
ISBN 978-0-399-15591-8; 0-399-15591-0
                                      LC 2009-24109
"Bookmaker Ed Talbot is struggling with his wife's mental illness, even as technology threatens to give the big bookmaking outfits an insurmountable advantage over his small family business. Soon after a man shows up at Ascot and identifies himself as Ed's father, Peter, whom Ed believed long dead, a thug demanding money stabs Peter to death. Ed is in for even more shocks when he learns his father was the prime suspect in his mother's murder—and that Peter's killing, rather than a random act of violence, may be linked to a mysterious electronic device used in some horse-racing fraud." Publ Wkly

"Ever since he started writing with his son Felix, Dick Francis seems to have found fresh inspiration at the racetrack." N Y Times Book Rev

Field of thirteen. Putnam 1998 287p $24.95
ISBN 0-399-14434-X   LC 98-28720
Contents: Raid at Kingdom Hill; Dead on red; Song for Mona; Bright white star; Collision course; Nightmare; Carrot for a chestnut; The gift; Spring fever; Blind chance; Corkscrew; The day of the losers; Haig's death

"Many of the stories were written in the 1970s and originally appeared in British and American sporting magazines, but a few have never been published before, thus offering a rare and unexpected treat for Francis' legions of loyal fans." Booklist

Longshot. Harper & Row 1990 320p o.p.
                                      LC 90-41145
John Kendall "is an expert on survival, having written several books on the subject before turning to fiction: when Longshot opens, he is awaiting the publication of his first novel, living very frugally, and (with many reservations) about to accept a commission for a biography . . . [of racehorse trainer] Tremayne Vickers." Times Lit Suppl

"Francis remains one of the most incandescent talents in the mystery game. His plot positively shimmers, and his sleuth easily hurdles that always difficult jump from credible character to believable amateur detective. Perhaps best of all, Francis extracts a wealth of weird and wonderful shadings from his suspects." Booklist

Nerve. Harper & Row 1964 273p o.p.
"Rob Finn, a young steeplechase jockey, had been near Art Mathews when Mathews shot himself at the Dunstable races. When asked why the man had killed himself, Finn replied, 'Mr Kellar might know.' Then other jockeys began having trouble and finally Finn was involved." Publisher's note

(ed) The New treasury of great racing stories. See The New treasury of great racing stories

Proof. Harper & Row 1985 334p o.p.
                                      LC 84-15940
"Wine merchant Tony Beach is engaged to supply a horse trainer's garden party. During the party a horse van careens into the marquee, bringing disaster. One of the casualties is a restaurant owner suspected of serving cheap liquor under false labels, and Beach, as an expert taster, is enlisted to track the bootleggers. Francis gives the same fascinating and authoritative detail about the liquor trade as he does about the racing world (which figures intermittently in this book as background)." Libr J

Shattered. Putnam 2000 289p $25.95
ISBN 0-399-14660-1   LC 00-55937
It was young glassblower Gerard Logan's "misfortune to have been entrusted with the videotape of a valuable medical secret by his best friend, a jockey who dies in a dreadful racing accident at Cheltenham. Not having the slightest clue as to the contents of the tape, which is stolen before he can blink, Logan enlists the aid of some

Francis, Dick—*Continued*

brave and burly friends to trace the tape. . . . Francis' formula is made for excitement, not subtlety, so the eerie serenity of the glass blower's studio provides a nice breather from the choreographed displays of bruising action that keep the author on his toes." N Y Times Book Rev

Smokescreen. Harper & Row 1973 c1972 213p o.p.

"A Joan Kahn-Harper novel of suspense"

First published 1972 in the United Kingdom

"An English film star is persuaded by a dying friend to go to South Africa to see what is the matter with her eleven race horses—horses that could win races if they did not mysteriously collapse just before the finish." Newsweek

"Even given Francis's high standards [this novel is] an elegant construction, in which we see the parts and their potentialities, and are as much excited to discover how he put them together as what happens when he does. . . . A symphony tumultuous with thrills." Times Lit Suppl

Whip hand. Harper & Row 1980 c1979 293p o.p.

"A Joan Kahn book"

First published 1979 in the United Kingdom

In this novel "Sid Halley, a famous ex-jockey crippled in an accident, is laboriously putting his life back together as a private investigator and making do with an artificial hand. Professionally he is successful. A top trainer's horses are failing in the home stretch; the jockey's repellent ex-wife gets caught in a fraudulent mail-order scheme; an aged peer is trapped as a front man in a crooked consortium. The jockey reluctantly agrees to investigate these mysteries, and they lead him into confronting his deepest fears." Libr J

"The book contains moments of breathless suspense, much information about the sport of kings, and perceptive insights into Halley's character that explain some of the reasons for the breakdown of his marriage." Shapiro. Fic for Youth. 3d edition

Francis, Felix

(jt. auth) Francis, D. Even money

Frank, Pat, 1907-1964

Alas, Babylon; a novel. Lippincott 1959 253p o.p.

"Survival after a submarine nuclear attack is the focus of this story of a small group of people in Fort Repose, Florida. Rationing food, reestablishing law and order, and pondering whether there will be any future for the survivors are some of the concerns of organizer-leader Randy Bragg." Shapiro. Fic for Youth. 3d edition

"This is an extraordinarily real picture of human beings numbed by catastrophe but still driven by the unconquerable determination of living creatures to keep on being alive. The writing is simple and straightforward and practical." New Yorker

Franklin, Ariana

Mistress of the art of death. Putnam 2007 384p $25.95

ISBN 978-0-399-15414-0; 0-399-154140

LC 2006-24710

"It is 1171 in Cambridge, England, and Henry II is beside himself. Four children have been found murdered and mutilated, and the townsfolk of Cambridge are blaming the Jews, who have taken shelter in the castle. King Henry is less concerned about the murderer than the tax revenue he is losing while the Jewish community languishes in the fortress. He appeals to the king of Sicily to send him a master of the art of death—one who can look at the deceased and determine how he or she died. Adelia, a mistress of this art, arrives with a group of returning pilgrims. Along with a eunuch escort named Mansur and Simon of Naples, a Jew with an affinity for detection, she must piece together the mystery of these hideous crimes before the monster kills again. I. . . . This novel will surely please mystery fans as well as lovers of historical fiction." Libr J

The serpent's tale. G. P. Putnam's Sons 2008 371p $25.95

ISBN 978-0-399-15464-5

LC 2007-38585

"When Rosamund Clifford, Henry II's mistress, is poisoned, Dr. Vesuvia Adelia Rachel Ortese Aguilar must draw on her formidable forensic skills to try to uncover the killer. The prime suspect is Henry's estranged wife, Queen Eleanor of Aquitaine, who once plotted to overthrow the king. Adelia reunites with Rowley Picot, now a bishop as well as the father of Adelia's child, and the two set out on a dangerous journey, during which they brave a blizzard and Eleanor's band of ruthless mercenaries." Publ Wkly

"This excellent adventure delivers high drama and lively scholarship from its heroine's feminist perspective." N Y Times Book Rev

Franklin, Miles, 1879-1954

The end of my career; the sequel to My brilliant career; with a foreword by Verna Coleman. Harper & Row 1981 234p o.p.

First published 1946 in Australia with title: My career goes bung

Protagonist "Sybylla Melvyn, the Australian country girl who narrated My Brilliant Career, explains that while the earlier work was fiction, she will now tell the truth about how she came to write her book and the events that followed. The adventures of her fictional namesake have created a furor. Beyond her rural circle, whose members are indignant about their apparent depiction in My Brilliant Career, are others eager to fete the young author. They prompt a visit to Sydney, where Sybylla finds the supposedly cultured class just as flawed as those left behind." Libr J

"This book is at times a delicious satire on morals and manners. At other times it is a heart-rending tract for feminism. Always it is entertaining and filled with wisdom and universal truths." Christ Sci Monit

My brilliant career. Putnam 1980 232p o.p.

First published 1901 in Scotland

"The novel's heroine, Sybylla Melvyn, a girl of sixteen, rebels against the stagnant life on her parents' dairy

Franklin, Miles, 1879-1954—*Continued*

farm at Possum Gully and against the inevitable fate of teaching or marriage that awaits her; both forms of 'slavery' are distasteful to her but she sees marriage as particularly degrading. Rescued temporarily by a period with her affluent grandmother at the congenial station homestead, Caddagat, she faces interwoven problems—her sexual ambivalence which is characterized by strong physical attraction to eligible young squatter, Harold Beecham, and an equally strong physical revulsion." Oxford Companion to Australian Lit

Followed by The end of my career

Franklin, Stella Maria Miles Lampe *See* Franklin, Miles, 1879-1954

Franklin, Tom

Hell at the breech; a novel. Morrow 2003 520p $23.95

ISBN 0-688-16741-1   LC 2002-40982

"When a storekeeper campaigning for the state legislature is assassinated, Mitcham Beat is swept by a wave of violence that includes lynchings and shootings, barn burnings, and robberies. A gang of hooded men known as the Hell-at-the-Breech gang is terrorizing the community, and the only man to stop them is an aging sheriff ready to retire with his whiskey bottle. It sounds like the wild, wild West, but Franklin. . . has taken a little-known event in Alabama history, the Mitcham Beat War, and transformed it into a Faulknerian tale of bloody revenge and vigilante justice." Libr J

Smonk; or, Widow town; being the scabrous adventures of E.O. Smonk & of the whore Evavangeline in Clarke County, Alabama, early in the last century. . . William Morrow 2006 254p $23.95

ISBN 978-0-06-084681-7; 0-06-084681-X

       LC 2006-43835

"E.O. Smonk is an ugly, unwashed, murdering rapist who has terrorized the small town of Old Texas, Ala., for years. In 1911, the town summons Smonk to stand trial, and a nonstop blood-orgy of brutality and destruction is the result. . . . After Smonk's goons assault the Old Texas courthouse and kill the town's menfolk, reformed former Smonk associate turned lawman Will McKissick pursues Smonk. Meanwhile, a posse of Christian deputies chase teenage whore Evavangeline through the Gulf Coast, but the girl is a skilled killer, too, and the trail of her victims spans the region. . . Fast-paced and unrelentingly violent, Franklin's western isn't for everyone, but readers looking for a strange and savage tale can't go wrong." Publ Wkly

Franzen, Jonathan

The corrections. Farrar, Straus & Giroux 2001 568p $25

ISBN 0-374-12998-3

       * LC 2001-33478

This work "follows the delamination of the Lambert family—Alfred, once a rigid disciplinarian, flounders against Parkinson's-induced dementia; Enid, his loyal and embittered wife, lusts for the perfect Midwestern Christmas; Denise, their daughter, launches the hippest restau-

rant in Philly; and Gary, their oldest son, grapples with depression, while Chip, his brother, attempts to shore his eroding self-confidence by joining forces with a self-mocking, Eastern-Bloc politician." Publ Wkly

The novel "has the absorbing treacheries of married life, the comic squalors of cruise-shop travel and the shenanigans of global capitalism. It also has language that builds in powerful, rolling strides. And it has characters, the separately unraveling Lamberts, who get very deeply under your skin." Time

Fraser, George MacDonald, 1925-2008

The reavers. Alfred A. Knopf 2008 267p $24

ISBN 978-0-307-26810-5; 0-307-26810-1

       LC 2007-50904

First published 2007 in the United Kingdom

"Set on the border between England and Scotland, the plot (if it can be called that) revolves around a Spanish effort, led by the mysterious La Infamosa, to kidnap King James and replace him with an impostor. Attempting to foil her are the ravishing Lady Godiva Dacre and her dimwitted companion, Kylie, along with Gilderoy, part-time highwayman and Scotland's best-known secret agent, and Archie Noble, English 'double-nought' secret agent and ostensible hero of the tale. After a series of hilarious complications, the unlikely foursome finds itself at La Infamosa's cave just as the coup is about to take place. A piece of inspired silliness and a worthy companion to the Flashman tales." Libr J

Frayn, Michael

Headlong; a novel. Metropolitan Bks. 1999 342p

ISBN 0-8050-6285-8   LC 99-20717

Martin Clay "seems to have all he might reasonably wish for: a new career as an art historian, a loving wife, an adorable baby daughter, and a summer cottage in the English countryside, where he is supposed to be completing his book on fifteenth-century Netherlandish art. Instead, he stumbles upon an unsigned Brueghel (at least, he's almost positive it's a Brueghel) stashed in a fireplace of his neighbor's crumbling estate. Overwhelmed by high-minded professional curiosity and base greed, Martin resolves to acquire it by whatever means necessary. What follows is part detective story, part art-history lesson, part cautionary tale, and entirely funny." New Yorker

Spies; a novel. Metropolitan Bks. 2002 261p

ISBN 0-8050-7058-3   LC 2001-39840

"Stephen Wheatley, now a grandfather living abroad, is drawn back to London to revisit his boyhood home, to deal with the complexities and eventual tragedy engendered by what seemed a harmless game of spy when he was just a schoolboy during WWII. His best friend at the time was Keith Hayward, the bright son of rather standoffish parents; Keith and Stephen embark on a childish adventure after Keith announces that his British mother is a German spy." Publ Wkly

"A compelling story about secrecy and betrayal. . . . What is truly remarkable about this novel, though, is the way Frayn perfectly captures the dynamics of childhood friendships." Booklist

Frazier, Charles, 1950-

Cold Mountain. Atlantic Monthly Press 1997
356p $19.95

ISBN 0-87113-679-1

* LC 97-275

"After Inman, a Confederate soldier, is gravely wounded outside Petersburg, he decides to flee the war. With his fearsome LeMat's pistol for protection, he sets out for Cold Mountain, where he was raised and where he left Ada, the woman he loves, on uncertain terms four years earlier. In the meantime, Ada, a preacher's daughter transplanted to the country from Charleston, has begun to learn the hard reality of a farmer's life. This novel's landscape is finely drawn, full of dark beauty and presentiment, and so are its characters. They give voice to a classical, peculiarly American feeling of nostalgia—the pain of returning home" New Yorker

Thirteen moons; a novel. Random House 2006
422p $26.95

ISBN 0-375-50932-1   LC 2007-270081

In this novel, an old man remembers his glory days. "As a teenager during the James Monroe administration, Will Cooper is sent off, in an indentured situation, into the wilderness of the Indian Nation to run a trading post. From a mixed-race Indian, he wins a girl with whom he will be besotted for the rest of his life, and his passion will extend into personal involvement in Indian affairs, to the highest level of politics. Thus Frazier also remains faithful to the theme of his previous novel: the odyssey, especially one man's path through trials and tribulations to be by the side of the woman he loves." Booklist

The author "uses his sense of time and place and his lyrical, pointillist prose to give the reader an aching appreciation of the Indians' plight. . . . [He] recounts Will's melancholy adventures with plenty of narrative brio, giving the reader a succession of suspenseful—and in some cases touching—set pieces." N Y Times (Late N Y Ed)

Freda, Joseph, 1951-

The patience of rivers; a novel. Norton 2003
351p $24.95

ISBN 0-393-05176-5   LC 2002-13330

"It is 1969, and Nick Lauria is spending his final summer before college hanging out with his best friend, Charlie Miles, while working at his family's campgrounds in Delaware Ford, a small New York town just up the road from the farm where Woodstock is to be held. Nick spends his spare time trying to bed Darlene Van Vooren, the youngest of the three gorgeous Van Vooren sisters. But beneath the surface of Nick's idyllic existence, his family is in trouble." Publ Wkly

"This is an appealing coming-of-age tale set to a classic rock soundtrack." Libr J

Freed, Lynn

The curse of the appropriate man. Harcourt 2004 188p pa $13

ISBN 0-15-602994-4   LC 2004-5914

"A Harvest original"

Contents: Under the house; Foreign student; The widow's daughter; Family of shadows; An error of desire; Liars, cheats, and cowards; The curse of the appropriate

man; The mirror; Twilight; Selina comes to the city; William; Songbird; The first rule of happiness; Ma: a memoir; Luck

Freed is "expertly equipped to dissect the defiant longings and treacherous pleasures of the daughters and mothers, lovers and adventurers whom she imagines in her fiction." Washington Post Book World

Freedgood, Morton, 1912-2006

See also Godey, John, 1912-2006

Freedman, Benedict

Mrs. Mike; the story of Katherine Mary Flannigan; by Benedict and Nancy Freedman; drawings by Ruth D. McCrea. Coward-McCann 1947 312p o.p.

"At 16, Boston-reared Katherine Mary O'Fallon is sent north to Alberta, Canada, to find relief for the pleurisy from which she has been suffering. While residing with her Uncle John, she falls in love with Mike, a handsome Canadian Mounted Policeman. Life in the wilderness in the early 1900s is harsh, but the newly married couple finds joy and challenge in their adventures." Shapiro. Fic for Youth. 3d edition

Freedman, Nancy, 1920-

(jt. auth) Freedman, B. Mrs. Mike

Freeling, Nicolas

A dwarf kingdom. Mysterious Press 1996 213p

ISBN 0-89296-615-7   LC 96-11954

In this mystery Inspector Henri Castang "retires from the Brussels police force. Recoiling from the savage murders of two dear friends, Castang and his wife, Vera, retreat to a villa they have inherited in Biarritz. The living is easy, but Castang is too curmudgeonly to fall into a mental stupor. . . . Sure enough, someone kidnaps his infant granddaughter, and the real estate mogul who has been buzzing around his well-situated property grows increasingly menacing. For Castang, there is no escape, after all, from the 'dwarfish greed' or the gnomish values of his constant nemesis, the ruthless power elite of the abominable bourgeoisie." N Y Times Book Rev

One more river. Mysterious Press 1998 214p

ISBN 0-89296-616-5   LC 97-52323

"John Charles, a 70-year-old English expatriate living in the south of France, is jolted out of his complacency (as 'a writer of acknowledged distinction, with an individual prose style') when someone takes a shot at him in the garden of his secluded cottage—which his attackers later burn down. 'Pleased to find himself excited' by the violent turn his placid life has taken, Charles thinks he can escape danger by keeping on the move, in a trek that returns him to scenes (and secrets) of his youth in the Netherlands, Germany and England. . . . Despite the fatalism of the bleak ending, this is a wondrous, strange trip through a very fine mind." N Y Times Book Rev

Sand castles. Mysterious Press 1990 c1989 209p

ISBN 0-89296-372-7   LC 89-43144

First published 1989 in the United Kingdom

The author "restores to life his well-beloved Dutch detective, Commissaris Piet van der Valk, whom he killed

Freeling, Nicolas—*Continued*

off in 'Auprès de Ma Blonde' (1972). . . . In Groningen (a 'dusty corner of a tight, righteous little land'), van der Valk comes across a sordid child-pornography racket that confirms his belief in the moral hypocrisy beneath the 'stuffy sinless atmosphere' breathed by the Dutch." N Y Times Book Rev

"Like his idiosyncratic hero and heroine—he bashes the Dutch, she the French, for example—Freeling rewards with his oblique, subtly comic style." Publ Wkly

Freely, Maureen, 1952-

Enlightenment. Overlook Press 2008 398p $24.95

ISBN 978-1-59020-074-2; 1-59020-074-8

First published 2007 in the United Kingdom

"In 1970 Istanbul, Jeannie, the daughter of an American CIA agent, falls in love with Sinan, a student radical who is alienated from America by its persistent support of Turkish corruption. Sinan is imprisoned on trumped-up charges, but years later, the lovers reunite and marry, living peacefully for a while. Then, without warning, on a visit to the States, Sinan is arrested by Homeland Security as a suspected terrorist, leaving Jeannie scrambling to reach her husband and recover their child from foster care. When Jeannie, too, disappears, a reporter unearths truths that alter our perception of all that has transpired." Libr J

"Byzantine in structure, mischievous in intent, [this novel] is as concerned with the garbled and provisional nature of truth as with the minutiae of repression." Times Lit Suppl

Freeman, Brian, 1963-

Stripped. St. Martin's Minotaur 2006 368p $24.95

ISBN 978-0-312-34044-5   LC 2006-045827

"Detective Jonathan Stride has left his northern Minnesota roots to follow his lover, Detective Serena Dial, to her home turf of Las Vegas, where he joins her on the Metro Homicide Division. In Stride's first case, a wealthy playboy is murdered in what appears to be an assassination. Stride soon discovers that someone is killing people connected to the 40-year-old murder of a showgirl. Meanwhile, Dial is investigating the seemingly senseless hit-and-run death of a ten-year-old boy. As the two cases converge, additional murders ensue." Libr J

"Freeman strengthens his plot with well-shaped characters with complex personalities. . . . His new lieutenant resents Jonathan and has saddled him with Amanda Gillen, a thoughtful cop with quite a few secrets. We hope Freeman will have years to excavate Stride's flawed and complicated personality. But Freeman doesn't just invest in his series hero. Each character gets a full-court press. There's not a character that Freeman doesn't make the reader care about." PopMatters

Freeman, Castle, 1944-

All that I have; a novel; [by] Castle Freeman Jr. Steerforth Press 2009 164p pa $13.95

ISBN 978-1-58642-151-9; 1-58642-151-4

LC 2008-43223

"Sheriff Lucian Wing, the narrator of Freeman's wonderfully wry fourth novel, is a laconic, old-fashioned lawman who discovers an outpost of nefarious Russians in his sleepy Vermont county. Wing's Fargo-esque delivery is hysterical, but what makes this spare tale a standout is Freeman's keen ear for dialogue and his affection for the quietly complex characters of small-town life." People

Go with me; [by] Castle Freeman, Jr. Steerforth Press 2008 160p $21.95

ISBN 978-1-58642-139-7; 1-58642-137-9

* LC 2007-42572

"In a Vermont logging town, a young woman recruits a musclebound kid and a wily old man to help her track down the vicious former cop who's been stalking her. Over a day, their travels lead from a hot-sheet motel to a hardcore bar to the forest primeval, while a chorus of beer-drinking locals comment on the action." Entertainment Wkly

"This nimble thriller is the literary equivalent of a fierce bantamweight fighter: Short but muscular and lightning quick, it packs a surprising punch . . . . Freeman has a flawless ear for dialogue and a sharp eye for quirky detail." People

Freemantle, Brian

Bomb grade. St. Martin's Press 1997 407p

ISBN 0-312-14565-9   LC 96-48769

"A Thomas Dunne book"

First published 1996 in the United Kingdom with title: Charlie's chance

"The cold war is over, and Britain's spy agencies are being dismantled. Agent Charlie Muffin expects to be fired any day, so he's flabbergasted when the director-general gives him a plum assignment in Moscow: to help the Russian government curb the illegal smuggling of uranium from Russian nuclear silos. Charlie's delighted with the opportunity to revisit his beloved Moscow and possibly see Natalia, the Soviet agent he loved and then lost in a spy game gone wrong." Booklist

"Mr. Freemantle suggests that what makes Charlie's personal life so precarious is exactly what makes him so successful in his profession, since talk filled with deception and evasion is a basic tool of his trade. Watching this spy at work is like watching a stunted genius play Mozart perfectly, even as the rest of his life threatens to crumble around him." N Y Times Book Rev

Dead men living. St. Martin's Press 2000 345p

ISBN 0-312-24379-0   LC 99-462044

"A Thomas Dunne book"

"British agent Charlie Muffin is surviving just fine in the new Russia, living with his lover, former KGB agent Natalia, and juggling his expense account to cover a snazzy Moscow apartment. Then three bodies turn up after a Siberian thaw, and the Cold War is jump-started. Two of the bodies—one American, one English—are wearing remarkably well-preserved World War II uniforms." Booklist

"Siberia's harsh climate and Moscow's volatile politics are in clear focus as slippery, upper-class Brits and powerful Americans toss monkey wrenches into Charlie's plans." Publ Wkly

Mind/reader. St. Martin's Press 1998 475p

ISBN 0-312-18654-1   LC 98-4484

Freemantle, Brian—*Continued*

"A Thomas Dunne book"

"Criminal profiler Claudine Carter has joined Europol, Europe's version of the FBI, after her husband's tragic suicide. Hoping to escape her grief, Claudine throws herself into a horrifying case involving a serial killer who is leaving bloody body parts at public sites across Europe. . . . Freemantle is at the top of his form, with a cunningly devious plot, riveting suspense, strong characters, and enough stunning twists to keep even seasoned readers from guessing the shocking conclusion." Booklist

French, Albert

Billy. Viking 1993 214p

ISBN 0-670-85013-6

* LC 93-14676

"In 1937, in the small town of Banes, Miss., 10-year-old Billy Lee Turner lives with his mother in one of the miserable shanties of the black ghetto called the Patch. Headstrong Billy convinces another youngster to enter the white area of town, where they are attacked by teenaged cousins who are enraged to see black boys in 'their' pond. Seeking to escape, Billy impulsively stabs one of the girls; she dies, and the white community works itself into a paroxysm of rage and violence. Though Billy is too young to comprehend what he has done, he is sentenced to the electric chair." Publ Wkly

"The story, once in motion, gathers momentum like a landslide. . . . 'Billy' is tragedy in the classical mode, mythic in the sense that instead of the surprise, the twists of plot we might discover in a more typical contemporary novel, here we are confirmed in our worst dreads as destiny immutably and shockingly unfolds." NY Times Book Rev

French, Marilyn, 1929-2009

Her mother's daughter; a novel. Summit Bks. 1987 686p il o.p.

LC 87-7061

"Anastasia narrates her life experiences by blending them with those of her grandmother, mother, and daughter. Each woman has been determined not to make the sacrifices her mother made, instead seeking joy, freedom, and independence. And in doing so, each has become like her mother—emotionally drained, alienated from her children, and alone." Libr J

The author "continues to imbue what used to be dismissed as 'women's issues' with the significance they deserve. . . . Ms. French continues to write about the inner lives of women with insight and intimacy. What she's given us this time is a page-turner with a heart." N Y Times Book Rev

The women's room. Summit Bks. 1977 471p o.p.

* LC 77-24918

"Dealing with the interlocking lives of dozens of American women, who know each other at some point of time between the 1950s and the 70s, and concentrating in particular on the evolution of Mira from petted baby girl wife to independent womanhood, it speaks from the heart to women everywhere. . . . [The author's] dialogue, her characterizations, her knowledge of the changing relationships, sexual and otherwise, between men and women in a complex world of shifting values, are all extraordinary. Mira, the suburban housewife and mother, the unexpected divorcee groping her way out of a marriage that she never understood, going back to Harvard at 38 as a graduate student, meeting other women, some tougher, some weaker, coming to terms with herself against all odds, even if it means a bleak and lonely parting from a man she loves, is memorable." Publ Wkly

French, Nicci

Beneath the skin. Mysterious Press 2000 378p $24.95

ISBN 0-89296-726-9   LC 00-101483

Londoners "Zoe Haratounian (a pre-school teacher), Jennifer Hintlesham (a former model and mother of three) and Nadia Blake (a children's entertainer) are all petite, uniquely pretty women. They also are all involved in, or getting out of, bad relationships with men, and they are all the targets of a murderous stalker who haunts his victims through disturbingly personal letters." Publ Wkly

French "gives the killer terrifying presence through the perverse 'love' letters he sends to his victims. . . . But, in a stylistic twist that is rare for this genre, the focus of the suspense remains locked on his victims, smart, articulate women who reveal their escalating fears in intimate first-person narratives that are insightful and also sad, because the lessons learned come too late." N Y Times Book Rev

Land of the living. Warner Bks. 2003 341p $23.95

ISBN 0-446-53151-0   LC 2002-33149

In the "opening scenes, 25-year-old Abbie Devereaux finds herself blindfolded and shackled in some filthy hole, the victim of a kidnapping she can't recall. Through sheer luck Abbie escapes her prison, only to realize that no one in authority believes her story. . . . Although the thwarted killer who is still stalking Abbie is too real for us to share her terror of going mad, we're with her all the way in her gritty quest to forge a new identity and discover what went wrong with the old one." N Y Times Book Rev

French, Paul *See* Asimov, Isaac, 1920-1992

French, Tana

In the woods. Viking 2007 429p $24.95

ISBN 978-0-670-03860-2; 0-670-03860-1

LC 2006-33498

"When Katy Devlin, a 12-year-old girl from Knocknaree, a Dublin suburb, is found murdered at a local archeological dig, Det. Rob Ryan and his partner, Cassie Maddox, must probe deep into the victim's troubled family history. There are chilling similarities between the Devlin murder and the disappearance 20 years before of two children from the same neighborhood who were Ryan's best friends. Only Maddox knows Ryan was involved in the 1984 case." Publ Wkly

French "sets a vivid scene for her complex characters, who seem entirely capable of doing the unexpected. Drawn by the grim nature of her plot and the lyrical ferocity of her writing, even smart people who should know better will be able to lose themselves in these dark woods." N Y Times Book Rev

French, Tana—*Continued*

The likeness. Viking 2008 448p $25.95

ISBN 978-0-670-01886-4; 0-670-01886-4

LC 2008-003940

"Cassie Maddox, the partner of the self-destructing detective who narrated 'In the Woods,' is drawn into a ménage à cinq of college students living a seeming charmed existence in an Irish country house. One of the five, a girl who is Cassie's doppelgänger and has been living under an alias Cassie once used as an undercover narcotics agent, turns up murdered in a ruined cottage. Cassie is given the unlikely task of pretending to be a woman who was pretending to be a woman whom Cassie once pretended to be. As you might expect, 'The Likeness' wrestles with matters of identity and intimacy as its heroine comes to prefer this triply false life to her real one. The hypnotic prose and eerie atmosphere conspire to make this ostensible mystery novel much, much more than it appears to be." Salon.com

Fresán, Rodrigo, 1963-

Kensington Gardens; translated from the Spanish by Natasha Wimmer. Farrar, Straus and Giroux 2006 c2005 370p $25

ISBN 0-571-22280-3   LC 2006-11391

Original Spanish edition, 2004; this translation first published 2005 in the United Kingdom

This novel takes the form of a monologue by "Peter Hook, pseudonymous author of a hit series of children's novels featuring time-traveling boy bicyclist Jim Yang. Its audience is the actor chosen to star in the first Jim Yang movie. He is bound and gagged, abducted to hear the harangue and join Hook in out-the-window flight a la Peter Pan. Hook's discourse interweaves his life as the early-orphaned son of aristocratic English musicians who participated in the 1960s British rock efflorescence, and the life of J. M. Barrie, creator of Peter Pan." Booklist

"For all its interest in the Peter Pan story, the novel is principally a homage to the 1960s. . . . Fresan is a consummate fan of pop culture . . . as well as a rank Anglophile, and his breathless rendition of an imaginary guest list at the ultimate Swinging Sixties party is the literary equivalent of an episode of the Rock'n'Roll Years television series." Times Lit Suppl

Freud, Esther

Love falls. Harper Perennial 2007 279p pa $13.95

ISBN 978-0-06-134961-4; 0-06-134961-5

"An Ecco book"

"It's the summer of 1981, a mere week before Diana Spencer and Prince Charles are to be married. Lara, just turned 17, is embarking on a trip from London to Tuscany with her scholarly, travel-phobic father, Lambert, whom she has seen only sporadically since her early childhood. They are off to stay with one of Lambert's oldest friends. The expectation is obvious: this girl will come to know her elusive father; she will break out from her troubled, tentative girlhood and become a confident woman. Will she find a fairy-tale love as well? . . . [While the author's novel] follows this all-too-familiar arc, her depiction of Lara is so charming and observant, her writing so dynamic, that all the cliches of a youthful summer of self-discovery are transcended." N Y Times Book Rev

Freudenberger, Nell

The dissident. Ecco 2006 427p $25.95

ISBN 978-0-06-075871-4; 0-06-075871-6

LC 2006-42617

This "novel centers on a Chinese performance artist and former political prisoner, who travels to Los Angeles to accept a teaching fellowship at a prestigious girls' school. His hosts are a well-off family whose matriarch, Cece Travers, is trapped in a loveless marriage with Gordon, a psychiatrist obsessed with tracing his genealogy back to 'the crossing ancestor.' A large cast of secondary characters includes Gordon's sister Joan, an accomplished but discontented novelist who stays skinny 'by worrying,' and his charming but irresponsible brother Phil, who is single-mindedly in love with Cece. Freudenberger demonstrates great talent for capturing the subtleties of cross-cultural and intergenerational relationships, as the dissident's struggles with his past and with his art intersect with Cece's unravelling." New Yorker

Lucky girls; stories. HarperCollins Pubs. 2003 225p $22.95

ISBN 0-06-008879-6   LC 2003-44875

Contents: Lucky girls; The orphan; Outside the Eastern gate; The tutor; Letter from the last bastion

"A remarkably poised collection of stories about Americans abroad." N Y Times Book Rev

Freundlich, Jeffry P. *See* Lindsay, Jeffry P., 1952-

Frey, James, 1969-

Bright shiny morning. Harper 2008 501p $26.95

ISBN 978-0-06-157313-2; 0-06-157313-2

LC 2008-09273

"When not resurrecting L.A.'s history or making lists of gangs, museums, universities, nationalities, homicides and artists, Frey focuses on four main stories: Old Man Joe, a homeless alcoholic whose attempt to help a meth addict goes terribly wrong; Amberton, a top actor whose obsession with a young man almost shatters his perfectly constructed life; Esperanza, a first-generation Latina who finds herself denying her intelligence and her family's dreams for her future just to survive; and Dylan and Maddie, a young couple fleeing abuse and violence in the Midwest who come looking for a house by the ocean only to find a new brand of horror." Newsday

"The worst bits of Morning are probably worse than anything else you'll read this year, but Frey is such a relentlessly entertaining storyteller that you just won't care." Time

Friedman, Michael, 1960-

Martian Dawn. Turtle Point Press 2006 149p pa $14.95

ISBN 1-885586-44-2   LC 2005-926844

This first novel "offers a playful imagining of the lives of a fictional movie-star couple, Richard and Julia, who are reminiscent of the millionaire and prostitute played on-screen by Richard Gere and Julia Roberts in the Pygmalion update Pretty Woman. While they are involved in shooting the science-fiction movie Martian Dawn, their lives intersect with those of an unlikely assortment of

Friedman, Michael, 1960——*Continued*
other characters, including a would-be sea captain, a film
producer and his therapist, a cosmonaut and her astronaut
boyfriend, two members of the Biosphere team, and a Tibetan Buddhist rinpoche." Publisher's note

The author "skewers Hollywood pomposity, environmental idealism, spiritual empowerment—and the surprising banality of a human outpost on Mars—with prose
that's a marvel of economy, sardonic without excess sarcasm and rife with deadpan humor. Slight but sly, this
is a scrumptious literary trifle." Publ Wkly

Fromm, Pete, 1958-

As cool as I am. Picador 2003 388p $24
    ISBN 0-312-30775-6   LC 2003-49869
This "coming-of-age story follows Lucy Diamond of
Great Falls, Mont., for two years, from 14 o 16. They're
turbulent years, but more so for Lucy because her parents, themselves married as teenagers, are both self-
centered, trying to recapture the youth they feel they
missed. Chuck, her father, appears only for a few days
every few months; he is a charmer, and Lucy has inherited his humor and smart mouth. Though he claims to be
a logger, it becomes clear that there must be other reasons for his long disappearances. Lucy's mother, Lainee,
frustrated by her absent husband, has a long string of
boyfriends, all of whom, like her husband, eventually
disappear. Lucy, meanwhile, drifts into an affair with her
best friend, scrawny, funny Kenny, whose divorced
mother is an alcoholic." Publ Wkly

"Fromm explores the sexual evolution of a cynical
teenage girl who has the spunk and wit to survive two
flaky parents and the urges of unbridled adolescence."
Booklist

Fuentes, Carlos, 1928-

The campaign; translated by Alfred Mac Adam.
Farrar, Straus & Giroux 1991 246p o.p.
                                        LC 91-9723
Original Spanish edition, 1990
The focus of this novel is "on Argentina's complicated
transition from colonial to free status. The protagonist is
one Baltasar Bustos, a young man of certain privilege—
the son of a wealthy ranchowner on the pampas—who
performs an amazing act of defiance against the Spanish
colonial regime. He sneaks into the house of the judge
of the superior court of the viceroyalty of La Plata and
substitute's the magistrate's newborn child with the child
of a black prostitute. In the process, he not only causes
the house to catch on fire, killing one of the babies, but
also catches a glimpse of the judge's wife and falls in
love with her. To assuage himself of guilt and to attempt
to gain her love, Baltasar joins the independence army
and follows the lady of his dreams all over South America." Booklist

"The novel takes on huge themes: revolution versus
justice, the illusion of human perfectibility, the value of
tradition against the appeal to reason. Though set in the
past, it is not trapped in it. Mr Fuentes might equally be
writing about modern revolutions." Economist

The crystal frontier; a novel in nine stories;
translated from the Spanish by Alfred Mac Adam.
Farrar, Straus & Giroux 1997 266p
    ISBN 0-374-13277-1   LC 97-11230

Original Spanish edition published 1995 in Mexico
Contents: A capital girl; Pain; Spoils; The line of
oblivion; Malintzin of the maquilas; Las amigas; The
crystal frontier; The bet; Rio Grande, Rio Bravo

"Leonardo Barroso is an unscrupulous Mexican oli-
garch whose fortress of a villa is only a short drive from
the 'crystal frontier' of the title, and each one of the nine
stories comprising this work explores the life of someone
touched by him." Libr J

The death of Artemio Cruz; translated from the
Spanish by Alfred MacAdam. Farrar, Straus &
Giroux 1991 307p o.p.
                                    * LC 90-43280
Original Spanish edition published 1962 in Mexico;
first English translation by Sam Hileman published 1964
"As the novel opens, Artemio Cruz, former revolutionary turned capitalist, lies on his deathbed. He drifts in
and out of consciousness, and when he is conscious his
mind wanders between past and present. The story reveals that Cruz became rich through treachery, bribery,
corruption, and ruthlessness. As a young man he had
been full of revolutionary ideals. Acts committed as a
means of self-preservation soon developed into a way of
life based on opportunism. A fully realized character,
Cruz can also be seen as a symbol of Mexico's quest for
wealth at the expense of moral values." Merriam-
Webster's Ency of Lit

The eagle's throne; translated by Kristina
Cordero. Random House 2006 336p $26.95
    ISBN 1-4000-6247-0   LC 2006-40806
Original Spanish edition, 2003
The title of this "novel refers to the office of the Mexican presidency; the plot centers on the question of who
is to succeed an ineffective incumbent in that office. The
time is the 2020s, and a disagreement with the U.S. has
led to the severance of satellite power to Mexico, leaving
communications defunct. People must rely on an old-
fashioned medium: letter writing. And that is the conceit
of the novel: it is in epistolary format, as a host of politicos discuss what is wrong with the regime and what
should be done about it—each person, of course, holding
an opinion based on their own preservation and advancement. The tension builds inexorably as letters are fired
off, revealing political and personal secrets, private ambitions, and sexual liaisons." Booklist

While Fuentes is "concerned, as always, about the destiny of his native country, his story focuses more on
down-and-dirty political means than serious political
ends, leaving us to draw our own conclusions about what
sort of good can possibly come of his characters' byzantine strategies and counterstrategies—their opportunistic
alliances, their calculated secret-keeping and secret-
leaking, their posturing, their watchful waiting, their sly
brutalities. What results is the most wickedly entertaining
novel of Fuentes's career." N Y Times Book Rev

Happy families; stories; translated by Edith
Grossman. Random House 2008 331p $26
    ISBN 978-1-4000-6688-9; 1-4000-6688-3
                                        LC 2008-02335
Original Spanish edition, 2006
Contents: A family like any other; The disobedient
son; A cousin without charm; Conjugal ties (1); Mater
Dolorosa; The mariachi's mother; Sweethearts; The
armed family; The gay divorcee; The official family; The

Fuentes, Carlos, 1928-—_Continued_

father's servant; The secret marriage; The star's son; The discomforting brother; Conjugal ties (2); Eternal father

"Certainly, there aren't many 'happy families' to be found in these pages — more like miniature cyclones of emotion that oscillate between loyalty and betrayal, devotion and rebellion. These 16 stories, like most of the author's fiction, spotlight his home country, though more often than not it's portrayed in less-than-rose-colored hues." San Francisco Chron

The old gringo; translated by Margaret Sayers Peden. Farrar, Straus & Giroux 1985 199p

ISBN 0-374-22578-8

* LC 85-16266

Original Spanish edition published in Mexico

"Fuentes fictionalizes the last days of the life of American journalist and author Ambrose Bierce, involving a mythic figure to the Mexican revolutionaries with whom Bierce fights and representing Bierce of the novel as an implanted, recurrent memory for the young American schoolteacher who witnesses his final passages through time." Choice

"We have in this novel a fastidious American governess stranded in Pancho Villa's revolution, where she attracts the erotic interest of an intellectual fellow countryman and a nature-boy Mexican general. On this inanely trite foundation Mr. Fuentes has erected a narrative of brilliant complexity and sophistication, describing brisk military action and philosophically contrasting national character, or social tradition, or styles of revolt, or regional strengths, weaknesses, and prejudices." Atlantic

The years with Laura Diaz; translated by Alfred MacAdam. Farrar, Straus & Giroux 2000 516p

ISBN 0-374-29341-4 LC 00-37648

"The novel begins in 1999 when photographer Santiago Lopez-Alfare arrives in Detroit to film a documentary about Mexican muralists in the U.S. There he comes across the image of an unnamed woman immortalized on the mural of the famous Diego Rivera. He soon realizes that 'those almost golden eyes, mestizo, between European and Mexican' belonged to his great-grandmother, Laura Diaz. Thereafter, the novel recounts the life of Diaz, from the settlement of her German grandparents in Mexico in the late 1800s . . . to her experience of the Mexican Revolution and its aftermath." Booklist

"Fuentes's emotional commitment to his subject shows in the lucidity of the book's underlying intellectual dialogues—the opposition of communism and fascism, the corrosion of individual identities by historical processes—which Fuentes is able to animate with a learned lyricism that should make this volume one of his most admired and memorable." Publ Wkly

Fugard, Lisa

Skinner's drift; a novel. Scribner 2006 304p $25

ISBN 0-7432-7299-4 LC 2005-44145

"Ten years after leaving South Africa, Eva von Rensburg returns to her homeland because her estranged father is dying. Reluctant to visit him, owing to a dark secret she discovered as a child, Eva spends most of her time drinking in her hotel room, making arrangements for his care, and preparing to sell the family farm. Avoiding the past, however, only serves to bring it to the surface, and Eva remembers with guilt and shame the

pain and isolation of growing up in a time of political unrest and class distinction. Set against the vivid landscape and wildlife of the African landscape, this first novel conveys a message of redemption and forgiveness that holds true whether it's concerning a country and its people or a father and his daughter." Libr J

Fujiwara, Murasaki _See_ Murasaki Shikibu, b. 978?

Fuller, David, 1953-

Sweetsmoke; a novel. Hyperion 2008 310p $24.95

ISBN 978-1-40132-331-8; 1-40132-331-6

LC 2008-01939

"The year is 1862, and the Civil War rages through the South. On a Virginia tobacco plantation, another kind of battle soon begins. There, Cassius Howard, a skilled carpenter and slave, risks everything-punishment, sale to a cotton plantation, even his life-to learn the truth concerning the murder of Emoline, a freed black woman, a woman who secretly taught him to read and once saved his life." Publisher's note

"In a bizarre bit of literary artifice, Fuller uses quotation marks for white dialogue but not black. (Aren't all men punctuated equal?) And within this framework, Fuller gives Cassius a mostly plain, vaguely bookish vernacular. . . . Yet if you read Fuller's novel mainly for its fast-paced plot, 'Sweetsmoke' can be captivating." N Y Times Book Rev

Fulmer, David

The blue door. Harcourt 2008 325p $25

ISBN 978-0-15-101181-0; 0-15-101181-8

LC 2007-19423

A mystery set in 1962 Philadelphia. "Eddie Cero, a welterweight boxer with too many serious injuries, meets up with Sal Giambroni, who hires him to tail a businessman. Eddie discovers he has a natural bent for this work and is soon taking on a three-year-old cold case involving a rising soul singer. Offering a vivid portrait of Philly's heyday as a music scene (think American Bandstand), Fulmer's latest mystery is an excellent choice for patrons who like George Pelecanos and a good dollop of music in their mysteries." Libr J

Fulton, Alice, 1952-

The nightingales of Troy; stories of one family's century. W.W. Norton 2008 254p $23.95

ISBN 978-0-393-04887-2; 0-393-04887-X

LC 2008-13206

Contents: Happy dust; Queen Wintergreen; A shadow table; The nightingales of Troy; Dorothy loves Maleman; The glorious mysteries; The real Eleanor Rigby; Centrally isolated; It's not too much to ask; L'air du temps

"These 10 linked short stories by MacArthur fellow Fulton track the lives of four generations of women from Troy, N.Y., where 'love comes to die.' The first story begins in 1908, and subsequent stories are spaced approximately a decade apart, creating a colorful patchwork of the 20th century. . . . Fulton's strengths are in elaborate detail and delicate construction. And many stories also contain moments of blunt violence and unthinking

Fulton, Alice, 1952—*Continued*
cruelty, providing the tension at the heart of a book
that's rich with feeling for its characters yet willing to
expose their faults." Publ Wkly

Furnivall, Kate

The red scarf; a novel. Berkley Books 2008
470p pa $15
ISBN 978-0-425-22164-8; 0-425-22164-4
LC 2007-40037
"Sophia Morozova's relationship with fragile Anna
Fedorina begins through a small act of kindness at a
1930s Siberian labor camp. As the two inmates struggle
daily to survive, they increasingly rely on each other for
hope and comfort; when Anna falls ill, Sophia escapes,
intending to find Anna's lifelong love, Vasily, and rescue
Anna. Beautiful and charismatic, Sophia quickly becomes
a force to reckon with in the town of Tivil, where she
hopes to find Vasily, and her connections with powerful
gypsy Rafik, the handsome factory director Mikhail
Pashin and the stern but unreadable Aleksei Fomenko become satisfying sources of danger and desire. Furnivall
. . . paints a stark picture of rampant scarcity, grim regi-
mentation and blaring propaganda in pre-WWII Soviet
Russia." Publ Wkly

Furst, Alan

Blood of victory; a novel. Random House 2002
237p
ISBN 0-375-50574-1
LC 2002-21312
This thriller "revolves around a plan to disrupt the
flow of Romanian oil to the Third Reich. As usual, Furst
adheres strictly to the rules of the genre: the protagonist,
a Russian expatriate writer, is seduced into service both
by the prospect of heroism and by a mysterious
Frenchwoman, and embarks on a globetrotting, spy-
versus-spy adventure. But his debts to convention work
in his favor. Densely atmospheric and genuinely romatic,
the novel is most reminiscent of the Hollywood films of
the forties, when moral choices were rendered not in
black-and-white but in smoky shades of gray." New
Yorker

Dark voyage; a novel. Random House 2004
256p $24.95
ISBN 1-400-06018-4
LC 2004-46674
The protagonist of this novel is "E. M. DeHaan, the
captain of the Dutch tramp freighter Noordenham, a ship
without a home since the Nazis invaded Holland. It's
1941 when DeHaan accepts . . . his new assignment:
disguised as a Spanish freighter, the Noordendam will be
deployed on secret assignments for the British." Booklist
The author "lulls us into the atmosphere, allows us to
imbibe his descriptions and then, in the last 50 pages,
turns the screws. The denouement of Dark Voyage is
both breathless and utterly relaxed, not so pellmell that
Furst can't stop to be amused at the ironies of shifting
alliances. If he ever breaks a sweat, it doesn't show." N
Y Times Book Rev

The foreign correspondent; a novel. Random
House 2006 273p $24.95
ISBN 1-4000-6019-2
LC 2006-40417

This novel "opens in Paris in December 1938. Journalist Carlo Weisz, an expatriate Italian who's half Slav, is
fighting the Mussolini regime by writing for the Paris-
based underground opposition newspaper, the
Liberazione. When agents of the OVRA, the Italian secret police, murder the Liberazione's editor in the arms
of his mistress, Weisz assumes greater responsibility for
keeping the paper running. OVRA also targets Weisz and
his surviving colleagues, forcing him to scramble to stay
alive while continuing his subversive work." Publ Wkly
"In an interview in 2002, Furst said that he had difficulty understanding why none of his bestselling novels
had yet been filmed. With no apparent preciousness
about what might be lost in a transfer to the screen, he
added, 'These really are movies.' In a sense, this is true.
He has the ability to invent plots that work all on their
own, which is, as Somerset Maugham once pointed out,
a very rare gift indeed." Atlantic Monthly

Kingdom of shadows; a novel. Random House
2001 272p
ISBN 0-375-50337-4
LC 00-32344
"In Paris in 1938, Nicholas Morath, a Hungarian aristocrat, enjoys the benefits of his wealth and breeding—
benefits that include the company of a beautiful young
Argentine girlfriend and control of a successful advertising firm. But the rumblings of the Third Reich are drawing nearer, and when Morath's uncle and benefactor,
Count Janos Polanyi enlists Nicholas to help fight Fascism back in Hungary the playboy becomes a political
operative. . . . The novel's most attractive feature is its
matter-of-fact suspense: Furst vigilantly restricts Nicholas's perspective, refusing to allow him anachronistic insight into the history being made around him, and this
strategy helps reinvigorate one of the century's frequently told stories." New Yorker

Red gold. Random House 1999 258p
ISBN 0-679-45186-2
LC 98-24409
Sequel to The world at night (1996)
"It's 1941, and Jules Casson is back in Paris, on the
run from the Gestapo and trying to stay alive without attracting attention. Drawn back into the resistance by an
intelligence officer he knows from Dunkirk, Casson soon
finds himself in the middle of an ill-advised plot to
smuggle arms to the Communists. It all goes wrong, of
course, as Casson and a Jewish girl he falls in love with
struggle to tell the good guys from the bad." Booklist
"Furst proves himself a master at capturing the bleak
and mean mood of wartime Paris." N Y Times Book
Rev

The spies of Warsaw; a novel. Random House
2008 266p $25
ISBN 978-1-4000-6602-5; 1-4000-6602-6
"The novel opens in the fall of 1937, when the assembly of the next great war machine from Germany is resonating throughout Europe. There can be no doubt that
war is coming. Enter our hero, a military attaché from
the French embassy, Col. Jean-Francois Mercier, suave
and dapper, a decorated hero of World War I with the
requisite amount of courage and testosterone. As if an
imminent war weren't enough to keep Mercier busy, he
is in love with a Parisian woman of Polish heritage,
Anna, who is a lawyer for the League of Nations. Matters get sticky when one of his lower-level spies becomes
convinced the Gestapo is on to him. " BookPage

Furst, Alan—_Continued_

"Rather than Eric Ambler thrillers or Graham Greene entertainments, the comparisons Mr. Furst's novels most often draw, they might more accurately be seen as extended series of Talk of the Town pieces. There's the same soupSon of irony, the expert deployment of detail and, above all, a thick helping of knowingness—only with military secrets, machine pistols and Gestapo agents instead of celebrity quirks or outer-borough oddities." N Y Observer

Fyfield, Frances, 1948-

Blind date. Viking 1998 264p
ISBN 0-670-87889-8

* LC 98-21218

First published 1992 in the United Kingdom

"Haunted by her sister's murder and humiliated by her failure, as a police officer on the case, to find the killer, [Elizabeth Kennedy] retreats to her womblike quarters in a London church belfry to recover from a near-fatal mugging that just about destroyed whatever strength and dignity she had left. Here she rages over her miserable condition . . . unaware of how close the killer is to her and to her family, and without a clue of the danger to three of her friends." N Y Times Book Rev

The plotting is "masterly, and Fyfield's critique of society—the real concern of the best crime thrillers—is seriously unsettling." Times Lit Suppl

Undercurrents. Viking 2001 278p $23.95
ISBN 0-670-89636-5   LC 00-43806

First published 2000 in the United Kingdom

American pharmacist Harry Evans "travels to the soaked seaside town of Warbling [England] to discover what happened to his lover from 20 years in the past. . . . Evans learns that his old girlfriend is serving time for the murder of her five-year-old son." Booklist

"Dark humor occasionally flashes through the narrative, but Fyfield's latest is primarily a grim, tense story about regret, loneliness and leaving well enough alone. In Warbling, she's created a memorable setting. It's a harsh, foreboding town populated by people—disappointed, judgmental, distrustful—who deserve such a place." Publ Wkly

G

Gabaldon, Diana

A breath of snow and ashes. Delacorte Press 2005 979p $28
ISBN 0-385-32416-2   LC 2005-51948

Previous titles in the Oulander series: Outlander (1991); Dragonfly in amber (1992); Voyager (1994); Drums of autumn (1997); The fiery cross (2001)

In this sixth title in the Outlander series, the author "unfolds the continuing story of the Frasers, heartbreakingly heroic highlander Jamie and his time-traveling wife Clare. Set during the three years leading up to the American Revolution, this . . . [novel] maps both violent loss and strong family ties. On the eve of war much is changing on Fraser's Ridge and Jamie and Claire encounter much harm. This vivid and haunting novel, therefore, brings an aching sadness, but it is bal-anced with sheer joy, revelation, and solace. The large scope of the novel allows Gabaldon to do what she does best, paint in exquisite detail the lives of her characters." Booklist

Followed by: An echo in the bone

An echo in the bone. Delacorte Press 2009 820p $30
ISBN 978-0-385-34245-2; 0-385-34245-4

This seventh Outlander title "covers approximately two years during the heart of the Revolutionary War, beginning in July 1776. Brianna and Roger Mackenzie have traveled back through the stones to 1980 to get the health care for their infant daughter that was unavailable in the 18th century. Jamie Fraser and his beloved time-traveling wife Claire, having survived the fire that burned down their home in the hills of North Carolina, are making plans to sail back to Scotland to retrieve Jamie's printing press so he can fight on the American side with the pen instead of the sword. Meanwhile rich, powerful but tormented homosexual Lord John Grey finds himself in coastal North Carolina catching up with his adoptive son William Ransom, who is anxiously waiting to prove his worth in the British army. . . . There's no lack of action in the novel, and the Revolutionary War setting provides an opportunity for the characters to cross paths with such notable luminaries as Benjamin Franklin, Nathan Hale and Benedict Arnold." Romance Reader

Gaddis, William, 1922-1998

Agapé agape; afterword by Joseph Tabbi. Viking 2002 113p
ISBN 0-670-03131-3   LC 2002-20676

"Gaddis has compressed 50 years of research on the social history of the player piano into a novel narrated by a dying elderly man who is as concerned with his own physical collapse as he is with his piano-based literary project. . . . As usual, Gaddis's avant-garde style requires patience and staying power from readers, who must parse long, elliptical sentences that wander from idea to idea while barely advancing the narrative. But his thoughts and ruminations remain fascinating and challenging." Publ Wkly

A frolic of his own; a novel. Poseidon Press 1994 586p
ISBN 0-671-66984-2   LC 93-26098

In this novel "Oscar Crease, middle-aged college instructor, savant, and playwright, is suing a Hollywood producer for pirating his play _Once at Antietam_, based on his grandfather's experiences in the Civil War, and turning it into a gory blockbuster called _The Blood in the Red White and Blue_. Oscar's suit, and a host of others—which involve a dog trapped in an outdoor sculpture, wrongful death during a river baptism, a church versus a soft drink company, and even Oscar himself after he is run over by his own car—engulf all who surround him." Publisher's note

"The medium is exceptionally dense. The mere effort of sorting out the voices, of tracking them, can be exhausting. . . . In any case, I hope the reader will persevere. 'A Frolic of His Own' is an exceptionally rich, even important novel." N Y Times Book Rev

Gaddis, William, 1922-1998—*Continued*

The recognitions; a novel. Harcourt Brace & Co. 1955 956p o.p.

*

"A novel about forgery. In it William Gaddis has attempted a full-scale portrait of our chaotic contemporary world, in all its hypocrisy and lack of love—a world in which the genuine is continually being discarded in favor of a successful facsimile. . . . Scores of characters move back and forth within the design, each one busy in pursuing his own desired deception." Publisher's note

"Rangy in settng, (New England, Greenwich Village, Paris, Spain, Italy, Central America), aswim in erudition, semi-Joycean in language, glacial in pace, irritatingly opaque in plot and character. The Recognitions is one of those eruptions of personal vision that will be argued about without being argued away." Time

Gaffney, Patricia

Circle of three; a novel. HarperCollins Pubs. 2000 421p $24

ISBN 0-06-019375-1 LC 00-33521

This tale "follows three generations of women through one tumultuous year. The book centers on recently widowed Carrie, who sees the grieving process as a chance to reinvent herself. But for Ruth, her 15-year-old daughter, it simply precipitates the onset of parent/child separation. Dana, Carrie's 70-year-old mother, isn't grieving; she's too busy trying to direct her daughter's life." Libr J

"Gaffney has each woman narrate in turn, providing added dimension to this poignant story of growing up and growing old." Booklist

Flight lessons; a novel. HarperCollins Pubs. 2002 388p

ISBN 0-06-018528-7 LC 2001-51934

"At 36, Anna Catalano is going home to the Eastern Shore of Maryland after finding her boyfriend in bed with her boss and best friend. For some reason she is more upset with her friend than with her boyfriend, maybe because history seems to be repeating itself. Anna walked in on her father and her aunt Rosa in the same position 20 years ago, and even though her mother was dead, Anna could never forgive Rosa, the guiding force in her life, although she did absolve her father. Now Anna is returning to help Rosa run the family restaurant, having flitted from job to job and man to man all this time. . . . The novel is filled with touching insights into family relationships." Booklist

Gaiman, Neil, 1960-

American gods; a novel. Morrow 2001 465p $26

ISBN 0-380-97365-0

* LC 2001-30407

"A noirish sci-fi road trip novel in which the melting pot of the United States extends not merely to mortals but to a motley assortment of disgruntled gods and deities. Early in 'American Gods' we are introduced to Shadow, a man who has been released from prison only to learn that his wife has died in a car crash. With nothing to return home to, Shadow accepts a job protecting Mr. Wednesday, an omniscient one-eyed grifter. . . .

Soon the ex-convict finds himself in an alternate universe, where he is haunted by prophetic nightmares and visited by his dead wife." N Y Times Book Rev

Anansi boys. William Morrow 2005 336p il $26.95; pa $7.99

ISBN 978-0-06-051518-8; 0-06-051518-X; 978-0-06-051519-5 (pa); 0-06-051519-8 (pa)

* LC 2005-47176

"Fat Charlie's life is about to be spiced up–his estranged father dies in a karaoke bar, and the handsome brother he never knew he had shows up on his doorstep with a gleam in his eye. Next thing he knows, Fat Charlie is being investigated by the police, his fiancée's falling in love with the wrong brother, and he finds out that his father was the god Anansi, Trickster and Spider, and that the beast gods of folklore are plotting their own revenge upon his family bloodline. A fun book with a little of everything–horror, mystery, magic, comedy, song, romance, ghosts, scary birds, ancient grudges, and trademark British wit." Libr J

Fragile things; short fictions and wonders. William Morrow 2006 xxxi, 360p $26.95

ISBN 978-0-06-051522-5; 0-06-051522-8

LC 2006-48135

In addition to nine selections of poetry, the following short stories are included: A study in emerald; October in the chair; Forbidden brides of the faceless slaves in the secret house of the night of dread desire; The flints of memory lane; Closing time; Bitter grounds; Other people; Keepsakes and treasures; Good boys deserve favors; The facts in the case of the departure of Miss Finch; Strange little girls; Harlequin valentine; The problem of Susan; Instructions; How do you think it feels?; My life; Fifteen painted cards from a vampire tarot; Feeders and eaters; Diseasemaker's group; Goliath; Pages from a journal found in a shoebox left in a Greyhound bus somewhere between Tulsa, Oklahoma, and Louisville, Kentucky; How to talk to girls at parties; Sunbird; The monarch of the glen

In the novella The monarch of the glen, "set two years after the events of American gods, Shadow pays a visit to an ancient Scottish mansion, and finds himself trapped in a game of murder and monsters." Publisher's note

"Gaiman follows no overarching theme, but that is what makes these stories charming, at times creepy, and good fun. They read like dreams and meditations, with a stream-of-consciousness quality to their presentation. Gaiman also explains some of the inspiration behind the stories to help put them in perspective." Libr J

Good omens; the nice and accurate prophecies of Agnes Nutter, witch: a novel; [by] Neil Gaiman and Terry Pratchett. Workman 1990 354p

ISBN 0-89480-853-2 LC 90-50362

"The end of the world is nigh! At least according to the prophecies of Agnes Nutter, a witch whose predictions are usually accurate but seldom heeded. Eleven years before the deadly Last Saturday Night, the ancient rivals of good and evil personified by the angelic Aziraphale (otherwise living as a London book dealer) and the demonic devil and former serpent Crowley clash in substituting the Antichrist during the birth of a baby. But the babies are switched as an unexpected third child enters the picture. The confusion picks up pace as witch hunters Sgt. Shadwell and Newton Pulsifer pursue mod-

Gaiman, Neil, 1960-—Continued

ern Nutter follower Anathema Device. Along the way, countless puns, humorous footnotes, and satirical illusions enliven the story." SLJ

The monarch of the glen
In Gaiman, N. Fragile things

Stardust. Avon Bks. 1999 238p hardcover o.p. pa $13.95
ISBN 0-380-97728-1; 0-06-114202-6 (pa)
LC 98-8773
"Young Tristran Thorn has grown up in the isolated village of Wall, on the edge of the realm of Faerie. When Tristran and the lovely Victoria see a falling star during the special market fair, Victoria impulsively offers him his heart's desire if he will retrieve the star for her. Tristran crosses the border into Faerie and encounters witches, unicorns, and other strange creatures." Libr J
"Grounding his narrative in mythic tradition, Gaiman employs exquisitely rich language, natural wisdom, good humor and a dash of darkness to conjure up a fairy tale in the grand tradition." Publ Wkly

Gaines, Ernest J., 1933-

The autobiography of Miss Jane Pittman. Dial Press (NY) 1971 245p pa $6.99 hardcover o.p.
ISBN 0-553-26357-9 (pa)
* LC 77-144380
"In the epic of Miss Jane Pittman, a 110-year-old ex-slave, the action begins at the time she is a small child watching both Union and Confederate troops come into the plantation on which she lives. It closes with the demonstrations of the sixties and the freedom walk she decides to make. This is a log of trials, heartaches, joys, love—but mostly of endurance." Shapiro. Fic for Youth. 3d edition

A gathering of old men. Knopf 1983 213p hardcover o.p. pa $11.95
ISBN 0-394-51468-8; 0-679-73890-8 (pa)
* LC 82-49000
"The story opens with the murder of Beau Boutan, a Cajun farmer, on the Louisiana plantation of Candy Marshall, a headstrong white owner. She claims to have done the shooting because she wished to protect one of her black workers, Mathu, who has been like a guardian to her following the death of her parents. In the plan to stand between Mapes, the local sheriff, and Mathu, Candy has set into motion an idea that has brought together a group of old black men with shotguns (unloaded), all claiming to have done the shooting. The threat of the South's way of punishing blacks by lynching hangs over the story like a pall. It meets opposition from Beau's young brother who has been friends with a black fellow-student and team-mate at his university." Shapiro. Fic for Youth. 3d edition

A lesson before dying. Knopf 1997 c1993 256p $26; pa $12.95
ISBN 0-679-45561-2; 0-375-70270-9 (pa)
* LC 92-20335
First published 1993
"The story of two African American men struggling to attain manhood in a prejudiced society, the tale is set in Bayonne, La. . . in the late 1940s. It concerns Jefferson,

a mentally slow, barely literate young man, who, though an innocent bystander to a shootout between a white store owner and two black robbers is convicted of murder, and the sophisticated, educated man who comes to his aid. When Jefferson's own attorney claims that executing him would be tantamount to killing a hog, his incensed godmother, Miss Emma, turns to teacher Grant Wiggins, pleading with him to gain access to the jailed youth and help him to face his death by electrocution with dignity." Publ Weekly
"YAs who seek thought-provoking reading will enjoy this glimpse of life in the rural South just before the civil rights movement." SLJ

Gaitskill, Mary, 1954-

Don't cry; stories. Pantheon Books 2009 226p $23.95
ISBN 978-0-375-42419-9; 0-375-42419-9
LC 2008-25231
Contents: College town, 1980; Folk song; Old virgin; Agonized face; Mirror ball; Today I'm yours; Little boy; Arms and legs of the lake; Description; Don't cry
"There is always a moment in a Mary Gaitskill story when you wince. And then you shrug. The wince means, 'Wow, that's a pretty creepy aspect of human nature to point out,' while the shrug is a way of acknowledging, 'But it's true. Life's really like that, isn't it?' The Gaitskill two-step — that wince-and-shrug maneuver that her work inspires — is what elevates her above other fiction writers who, though talented, are content to give us surfaces. Gaitskill never stops at surfaces. She's too adventurous for that, too reckless. " Newsday

Veronica. Pantheon 2005 227p $23
ISBN 0-375-42145-9
LC 2005-43143
Narrator Alison "discovers at an early age that her prettiness gives her power and leaves her vulnerable. She stumbles into modeling, barely survives a decadent interlude in Paris, then ends up in New York, worried that her modeling days are over. She takes a night-shift temp job and meets Veronica, who is older, unbeautiful, not hip, and joltingly cynical. Duncan, the love of Veronica's life, is a rampantly unfaithful bisexual who infects her with AIDS." Booklist
The author's "fierce, night-blooming new novel is about a close friendship between two women. But it should not be confused with anything cozy. Imagine a buddy story from the mind of William S. Burroughs, illustrated with images by Robert Mapplethorpe or David Cronenberg, and you get some idea of the tenderness to be found here. . . . Ms. Gaitskill writes so radiantly about violent self-loathing that the very incongruousness of her language has shocking power." N Y Times (N Y Late Ed)

Galbraith, Douglas

The rising sun. Atlantic Monthly Press 2001 535p
ISBN 0-87113-781-X
LC 00-45336
A novel about pioneering "Scots of the 17th century seeking to establish a colony in modern-day Panama. Based on fact, the story is told from the viewpoint of the rather naive young Roderick Mackenzie, who signs on as a cargo supervisor of the *Rising Sun*, flagship of five vessels bound for the New World." Libr J

Galbraith, Douglas—*Continued*

"Galbraith's greatest achievement is in finding a voice for his narrator, a tone and a vocabulary that sound plausibly like those of a 17th century clerk without resorting to the more onerous clichés and archaisms of historical fiction." N Y Times Book Rev

Galchen, Rivka, 1976-

Atmospheric disturbances. Farrar, Straus and Giroux 2008 240p il $24

ISBN 978-0-374-20011-4; 0-374-20011-4

LC 2007-47327

"Leo Liebenstein, a middle-aged shrink, becomes convinced that the woman who returns to his apartment one day is not his wife, Rema, but an 'impostress.' Thereafter, he refers to her as 'the simulacrum' and struggles to learn what has befallen the real Rema, just as we struggle to figure out what exactly has befallen Leo." Entertainment Wkly

It is on the "level of psychological realism rather than postmodern invention, that 'Atmospheric Disturbances' succeeds, and where Ms. Galchen displays her real gifts as a writer. As we come to learn, in a series of dropped hints, the real story of Leo and Rema and their marriage, it becomes clear that the particular form of Leo's delusion is anything but accidental." N Y Sun

Galdós, Benito Pérez *See* Pérez Galdós, Benito, 1843-1920

Galgut, Damon, 1963-

The impostor. Black Cat 2009 c2008 249p pa $14

ISBN 978-0-8021-7053-8 (pa); 0-8021-7053-6 (pa)

First published 2008 in South Africa

"Set in post-apartheid South Africa, this gripping novel explores the seamier aspects of reconciliation. Adam, adrift after losing his job to a young black candidate, moves to an isolated town to write poetry. Boredom sets in, relieved only by the appearance of an old school acquaintance, Canning, who invites Adam to spend weekends on his nearby game farm. There Adam meets Canning's wife, Baby, who is both alluring and chillingly aloof, and begins to realize that no one's motives are as pure as they appear. Galgut gives even seemingly innocuous details sinister overtones: the clicking of peacocks on a roof, the shuffling steps of Canning's elderly black servants. Beneath a fairly standard thriller plot (affairs, corruption) runs a critique of contemporary South Africa, from the venality of those enriched by a reinvigorated economy to the stale pieties of the white liberal class." New Yorker

Gallagher, Michael

(tr) Mishima, Y. Runaway horses

(tr) Mishima, Y. Spring snow

Gallagher, Stephen

The kingdom of bones; a novel. Shaye Areheart Books 2007 366p $24.95

ISBN 978-0-307-38280-1; 0-307-38280-X

LC 2007-13288

"Set mainly in late 19th-century England, Gallagher's . . . horror thriller revolves around the extraordinary life—and death—of Tom Sayers, a real-life bare-knuckle fighter who, after retiring, briefly traveled the country staging reenactments of his most memorable bouts. While working as a manager for a touring theatrical company, Sayers falls in love with the troupe's leading lady, 22-year-old Louise Porter, who unfortunately doesn't share his feelings. Sayers also becomes the prime suspect in a series of mutilation murders and, while barely evading arrest, embarks on a quest to save Porter, who's become hopelessly entangled in an all-too-real occult legend. Bram Stoker and Aleister Crowley play minor roles." Publ Wkly

"Vividly set in England and America during the booming industrial era of the late 19th and early 20th centuries, this stylish thriller conjures a perfect demon to symbolize the age and its appetites, an entity that inhabits characters eager to barter their souls for fame and fortune." N Y Times Book Rev

Galloway, Janice

Clara. Simon & Schuster 2003 425p $25

ISBN 0-684-84449-4

LC 2002-26800

First published 2002 in the United Kingdom

This work focuses on the life of "18th century composer and piano virtuoso, Clara Schumann. Schumann, better known as the wife of Robert Schmann, and the musical associate of such greats as Brahms and Mendelssohn, was a true artist in her own right. She was also the mostly submissive daughter of an egomaniacal and manipulative father and the long-suffering spouse to a mentally disturbed genius." Libr J

"The Schumanns' marriage was forged of perfectly dissonant material, and Galloway allows the collisions to speak for themselves." N Y Times Book Rev

Galsworthy, John, 1867-1933

End of the chapter. Scribner 1934 897p o.p.

"The Forsyte chronicles"

Sequel to A modern comedy

Also known as the Cherrell saga (after family connections of the Forsytes) this book contains volumes 7-9 of the larger series, The Forsyte chronicles: Maid in waiting (1931), Flowering wilderness (1932), and Over the river (1933; published with title: One more river)

In Maid in waiting, Denny Cherrell undertakes the vindication of her brother whose army career has been ruined by an American archeological expedition leader's unjust accusations

In Flowering wilderness, Denny falls in love with Wifred Desert, a young poet back from the East. A meddlesome traveler spreads the rumor that Wilfred accepted Mohammedanism in order to escape death at the hands of Arab fanatics; English club and society people see this as an outrage to the British ruling class' code of honor. Ostracized and tortured by pride, the sensitive poet becomes in truth a coward and disappears, leaving his still loyal fiancée only her memories

In the final volume, Over the river, Denny's chief concern is her younger sister Clare's divorce from a sadistic husband. After learning of Wilfred's drowning in Siam, Denny decides to marry Dornford

Galsworthy, John, 1867-1933—*Continued*

Flowering wilderness

In Galsworthy, J. End of the chapter p331-592

The Forsyte saga; with a preface by Ada Galsworthy. Scribner 1922 xx, 921p o.p.

        *

Contains volumes 1-3 of the Forsyte chronicles: The man of property (entered separately), In chancery (1920), and To let (1921). Two interludes are included: Indian summer of a Forsyte (1918) and Awakening (1920)

In chancery relates the further fortunes of the Forsyte family. Irene Forsyte's first effort toward emancipation from her husband Soames ended with the accidental death of the architect who loved her. Meeting Irene again, after a separation of fifteen years, awakens in Soames the old desire to possess her, and failing of her consent, files for divorce. This action forces his cousin Jolyon into the role of correspondent. Soames eventually marries Annette Lamotte, who presents him with a daughter, Fleur, instead of a longed-for male heir. Jolyon and Irene marry and have a son, Jon

The first interlude, Awakening, is about little Jon until he is eight years old. The second interlude, Indian summer of a Forsyte, goes back in time to the secret visit of Irene to old Jolyon at Robin Hill, the country place Soames had built for her before their separation. She captivates the older man by her gentleness, and he dies quietly one summer day

To let centers on the romance of Jon and Fleur who are brought together by chance and are ignorant of the enmity between Soames, and Irene and Jolyon. When Fleur proposes a hasty marriage to Jon, his father reluctantly discloses the reason for the feud. After Jolyon's death, Irene and Jon leave for America, and Fleur, disappointed, marries Michael Mont.

Followed by A modern comedy

In chancery

In Galsworthy, J. The Forsyte saga p363-639

The Indian summer of a Forsyte

In Galsworthy, J. The Forsyte saga p313-59

Maid in waiting

In Galsworthy, J. End of the chapter p1-330

The man of property

   also in Galsworthy, J. The Forsyte saga p3-309

A modern comedy. Scribner 1929 798p o.p.

"A Scribners/Macmillan Hudson River edition"

Sequel to The Forsyte saga

A reissue of the title first published 1929

This book contains volumes 4-6 of the Forsyte chronicles: The white monkey (1924); The silver spoon (1926); Swan song (1928)

The white monkey concerns Fleur and Michael Mont, and Fleur's father Soames. A son is born to the couple, thus strengthening the marriage which had been weakened by Fleur's affair with an artist and her unrequited love for her cousin Jon

The silver spoon, picks up the story line three years later in 1924 as Soames challenges a rival of Fleur's for calling his daughter a snob. A disagreeable libel suit

evolves

As Swan song opens, Soames has mellowed. He guards with special tenderness the welfare of his daughter and son-in-law, but all his watchfullness and devotion are powerless to avert the tragedy of Fleur's deliberate revival of her love affair with Jon Forsyte when he returns to England with his American wife, Anne. The story ends as Soames saves Fleur from death, and in doing so, is killed himself. This sobers the girl and she returns to her husband.

Followed by End of the chapter

Over the river

In Galsworthy, J. End of the chapter p593-897

The silver spoon

In Galsworthy, J. A modern comedy

Swan song

In Galsworthy, J. A modern comedy

To let

In Galsworthy, J. The Forsyte saga p665-921

The white monkey

In Galsworthy, J. A modern comedy

Gander, Forrest, 1956-

As a friend. New Directions Pub. 2008 106p pa $13.95

ISBN 978-0-8112-1745-3; 0-8112-1745-0

        LC 2008-23125

"Les is the magnetic, godlike protagonist of this reflective four-part narrative: introduced at the time of his difficult birth to a teenage mother, he is put up for adoption. Years later, he is observed by Clay, a colleague on his land-surveying team in a small town in Arkansas, who finds his friend's mannerisms and dissembling so compelling that he apes Les and eventually betrays him. Les, a part-time poet and practical joker, is beloved for his eccentricities, especially by his second wife, Cora, and mistress, Sarah, whose poetic remembrances of Les after his suicide make up the novel's third section and reveal hopelessly guilt-ridden Sarah to be angry, grieving for her tender, quirky lover." Publ Wkly

"The story is a small one, with no ambitions to be the Great American Novel or to chronicle our time. It sets itself the task of seeing up close the lines of one man's very particular life, and how those lines are walked and read, stumbled over and misread, by those nearby." N Y Times Book Rev

Gao Xingjian, 1940-

Buying a fishing rod for my grandfather; stories; translated from the Chinese by Mabel Lee. HarperCollins Pubs. 2004 127p $17.95

ISBN 0-06-057555-7   LC 2003-51138

Original Chinese edition, 1989

Contents: The temple; In the park; Cramp; The accident ; Buying a fishing rod for my grandfather; In an instant

"Though few in number, the stories in this collection are richly diverse. One is a bittersweet reflection of a newlywed on his honeymoon; another a Pinteresque dia-

Gao Xingjian, 1940——*Continued*

logue in a park; a third a traffic accident recounted in realtime with all its voyeuristic detail and authentic philosophical questioning, and still another, a strong memory-driven, first-person tale that follows the mental trail of a man who passes a fishing equipment shop and begins to remember his grandfather. For variety of content, stylistic experimentation, graceful language, and poignant insight, Xingjian is a writer who does it all beautifully." Booklist

Soul mountain; translated from the Chinese by Mabel Lee. HarperCollins Pubs. 2000 510p
ISBN 0-06-621082-8   LC 2001-269378
In this novel "a character called 'I' learns that he does not have lung cancer, as previously diagnosed, and embarks on a journey through China in search of spiritual tranquility." Time
"It is not easy to say what the novel is about—and yet the marvel is that somehow it is still both engaging and elegant." N Y Times Book Rev

García, Cristina, 1958-

The Aguero sisters. Knopf 1997 299p
ISBN 0-679-45090-4   LC 96-52204
"The story of the middle-aged Agüero sisters—independent Reina, an electrician living in Havana, and thoroughly urbanized Constancia, a successful cosmetics salesperson living in New York—is also the story of how personal tragedy and the legacy of Castro's revolution impact one family's history and collective memory. The narrative is filtered through many voices, both past and present, including the women's parents, famous naturalists, and Reina's daughter, a sometime prostitute who is sick to death of poverty-stricken Havana." Booklist
"Unmoored by the reverberating effects of the revolution, Garcia's characters search for stability and meaning in a world where fatalism is their only belief. They all endure 'the fidelity of certain, unshakable pain,' but sudden insights illuminate their different routes to salvation." Publ Wkly

Dreaming in Cuban; a novel. Knopf 1992 244p o.p.
                                        * LC 91-20755
Shifting back and forth between Cuba and Brooklyn, this novel "centers on three generations of a family torn apart by Fidel Castro's revolution. Celia del Pino is the matriarch whose passions alternate between a long-lost Spanish lover and service to El Lider. In Brooklyn, Celia's daughter Lourdes runs the Yankee Doodle Bakery. Haunted by the memory of being raped by a revolutionary soldier back home, she is obsessed by her hatred for Castro and communism and her mother's devotion to both. Lourdes's daughter, Pilar, scoffs at her mother's belief that she can 'fight Communism from behind her bakery counter' and plots a return to the island." Newsweek
"While taking very seriously those ideas that have truly riven so many families in recent years, leaving many obsessed with the politics of Cuba, Ms. Garcia also portrays the costliness of such an obsession and the fading of the light between mothers and daughters, between lovers, as communication fails." N Y Times Book Rev

A handbook to luck. Knopf 2007 259p $24
ISBN 978-0-307-26436-7; 030726436X
                                        LC 2006-48736
The author "writes from several points of view as she tells unpredictably linked stories of people in flight from oppression during the 1970s and 1980s. Young Enrique Florit accompanies his exuberantly flamboyant and talented Cuban magician father, Fernando, as he flees Castro and the wrath of his late wife's family, seeking fame and fortune in Hollywood and Las Vegas. As war ravages El Salvador, Marta Claros, whose brother lives in a tree, leaves her abusive husband and bravely makes her way to California, where she finds sanctuary with a kind Korean factory owner. Leila Rezvani allows herself a brief interlude of pleasure in Las Vegas before returning to Tehran and a disastrous arranged marriage." Booklist
"García's characters have a lot to teach us about playing life's odds, and about resilience . . . . With an ear for language and its cadence, García writes with humor, tenderness and an intuitive sense of how ordinary people weather fortune's turns. If you long for a 'handbook' that reveals how ordinary people become extraordinary, you are in luck." N Y Daily News

Monkey hunting. Knopf 2003 251p $23
ISBN 0-375-41056-2   LC 2002-35916
This novel "chronicles the fortunes of Chen Pan, a Chinese who is enslaved in the Cuban sugar fields in 1857 and later becomes a prosperous businessman in Havana; the mulata slave Lucrecia, whose relationship with Chen Pan is poignantly rendered; and their descendants: Lorenzo, a doctor of herbal medicine in Havana; lesbian Chen Fang, a teacher imprisoned for counter-revolutionary activities in Mao's China; and Domingo Chen, an immigrant to New York City who serves in the U.S. Army in Vietnam." Libr J
"For all the ground Garcia covers, the most beautiful and moving parts of her novel are the chapters on Chen Pan's youthful sufferings. Here, horror and wonder alternate unblinkingly, as if they are random occurrences in a dark once-upon-a-time." N Y Times Book Rev

García Márquez, Gabriel, 1928-

The autumn of the patriarch; translated from the Spanish by Gregory Rabassa. Harper & Row 1976 269p o.p.
                                        *
Original Spanish edition, 1975
"A highly sophisticated novel about an unnamed dictator (the patriarch), who, at the time of his death, is somewhere between 107 and 232 years of age. The patriarch embodies the archtypal evils of despotism, but even more significant is his extreme, and often pathetic, solitude, which becomes increasingly evident with his advancing age and which emerges as the principal theme. Despite its political and psychological overtones, the autumn of the patriarch can best be described as a lyrical novel, whose plot and character development are subordinate to formal design and symbolic imagery." Ency of World Lit in the 20th century

Big Mama's funeral
In García Márquez, G. Collected stories p97-200

García Márquez, Gabriel, 1928-—*Continued*

Chronicle of a death foretold; translated from the Spanish by Gregory Rabassa. Knopf 1983 c1982 120p $25

    ISBN 0-394-53074-8   LC 82-48884

Original Spanish edition published 1981 in Colombia; this translation first published 1982 in the United Kingdom

Set in a provincial Colombian town, this novella "is a reconstruction of an actual episode in which the people of a whole neighborhood, if not in fact a whole town, stood by and did nothing while a couple of drunks planned, announced, and finally carried out a murder. The killers alleged motive was revenge for their sister's loss of honor and this claim, together with normal languor and stupidity, appears to have brought on collective paralysis and even collective complicity among their fellow citizens." Atlantic

This "investigation of an ancient murder takes on the quality of a hallucinatory exploration, a deep groping search into the gathering darkness of human intentions for a truth that continually slithers away." N Y Rev Books

    also in García Márquez, G. Collected novellas p167-249

Collected novellas. HarperCollins Pubs. 1990 249p o.p.   LC 89-46106

English translations of the three novellas included in this volume were first published 1972, 1968 and 1982 respectively

    Contents: Leaf storm; No one writes to the colonel; Chronicle of a death foretold

Collected stories. Harper & Row 1984 311p o.p.
                              LC 84-47826

This volume includes stories from the author's three previous collections: No one writes to the colonel, and other stories; Leaf storm, and other stories, and Innocent Eréndira, and other stories

The general and his labyrinth; translated from the Spanish by Edith Grossman. Knopf 1990 285p

    ISBN 0-394-58258-6   LC 90-52957

Original Spanish edition, 1989

This novel attempts to portray the last days of Simon Bolivar. "Ousted from the presidency of Colombia while once adoring crowds jeer him as a tyrant, a dying 46-year-old Bolivar journeys to supposed exile. His route on the Magdalena River is a tropical Via Dolorosa, lined by war-ravaged towns, grieving widows, scheming generals and long-ago romances. What Bolivar encounters most, however, are delirious dreams and memories that expose his life's epic contradictions." Newsweek

"Seldom has there been a more fitting match between author and subject. Mr. Garcia Márquez wades into his flamboyant, often improbable and ultimately tragic material with enormous gusto, heaping detail upon sensuous detail, alternating grace with horror." N Y Times Book Rev

In evil hour; translated from the Spanish by Gregory Rabassa. Harper & Row 1979 183p o.p.

Original Spanish edition, 1968

This novel "is set in a squalid river town. . . . The village is weighed down by an immense inertia, the result of the natives' hatred of a corrupt dictatorship and of the seasonal rains that dampen their spirits. The mayor, a hired assassin of the new central government, dreams of wealth, not war. . . . Lampoons begin to haunt the town, in the form of slanderous posters that appear overnight on doors and walls. No one can trace the authors. . . . Prominent citizens become so upset by the ghostly terrorism that the mayor is forced to impose a curfew, which in turn triggers a resurgence of political opposition." Newsweek

"The reader is carried along effortlessly in the current of this gifted storyteller's prose. Both heroes and villains elicit sympathy because their basic human foibles, while true to local circumstances, can be recognized by people of any culture." Libr J

The incredible and sad tale of innocent Eréndira and her heartless grandmother

    In García Márquez, G. Collected stories p262-311

Leaf storm

    In García Márquez, G. Collected novellas p1-106

    In García Márquez, G. Leaf storm, and other stories p1-97

Leaf storm, and other stories; translated from the Spanish by Gregory Rabassa. Harper & Row 1972 146p o.p.

Short stories included are: The handsomest drowned man in the world; A very old man with enormous wings; Blacamán the Good, vendor of miracles; The last voyage of the ghost ship; Monologue of Isabel watching it rain in Macondo; Nabo

The title novella (originally published 1955) covers three generations of boom and decline in the mythical Colombian town Macondo. "The small river town changes with the leaf storm of people—strangers who come there as a result of civil war and the establishment of a banana company. Marquez begins with the end, the death of one mysterious wanderer, a doctor who . . . withdraws from the world. As the narrators, a man, his daughter, her young son, reveal the doctor's story, so too do the tellers' own melancholy lives emerge, symbolic yet specific, representing the everlasting variety of man's inhumanity to man." Publ Wkly

Love in the time of cholera; translated from the Spanish by Edith Grossman; with an introduction by Nicholas Shakespeare. Knopf 1997 xxxiii, 422p $22

    ISBN 0-375-40069-9

"Everyman's library"

Original Spanish edition published 1985 in Colombia, this is a reissue of the 1988 edition

"The story, which concerns the themes of love, aging, and death, takes place between the late 1870s and the early 1930s in a South American community troubled by wars and outbreaks of cholera. It is a tale of two lovers, artistic Florentino Ariza and wealthy Fermina Daza, who reunite after a lifetime apart. Their spirit of enduring love contrasts ironically with the surrounding corporeal decay." Merriam-Webster's Ency of Lit

Memories of my melancholy whores; translated from the Spanish by Edith Grossman. Knopf 2005 115p $20

    ISBN 1-4000-4460-X   LC 2005-43591

García Márquez, Gabriel, 1928-—*Continued*

Original Spanish edition, 2004

"The unnamed protagonist, an unmarried man, is a columnist for the local newspaper, but until this point in time, he has never written anything of lasting value. This memoir, this recollection of the past year, is to be his literary legacy. 'The year I turned ninety, I wanted to give myself the gift of a night of wild love with an adolescent virgin,' he boldly–and, perhaps, in a delusion of potency–declares. It is soon revealed–sadly–that he has never loved, that his sexual gratification has always been bought and paid for. What his brazen plan to celebrate this milestone birthday comes to entail is a confrontation with a heretofore unrealized aspect of his 'inner self'– namely, that without love is an empty house in which to dwell." Booklist

"Measured by the highest standards, Memories is not a major achievement, but its goal is brave: to speak on behalf of the desire of older men for underage girls, or, in other words, pedophilia. The conceptual strategy that Garcia Marquez uses toward this end is to break down the barrier between erotic passion and the passion of veneration." N Y Rev Books

No one writes to the colonel

In García Márquez, G. Collected novellas p107-66

One hundred years of solitude; translated from the Spanish by Gregory Rabassa. Harper & Row 1970 422p

ISBN 0-06-011418-5

*

Original Spanish edition published 1967 in Argentina

This novel "relates the founding of Macondo by Jose Arcadio Buendia, the adventures of six generations of his descendants, and, ultimately, the town's destruction. It also presents a vast synthesis of social, economic, and political evils plaguing much of Latin America. Even more important from a literary point of view is its aesthetic representation of a world in microcosm, that is, a complete history, from Eden to Apocalypse, of a world in which miracles such as people riding on flying carpets and a dead man returning to life tend to erase the thin line between objective and subjective realities." Ency of World Lit in the 20th Century

Strange pilgrims; twelve stories; translated from the Spanish by Edith Grossman. Knopf 1993 188p

ISBN 0-679-42566-7   LC 93-12257

Contents: Bon voyage, Mr. President; The saint; Sleeping beauty and the airplane; I sell my dreams; "I only came to use the phone"; The ghosts of August; Maria dos Prazeres; Seventeen poisoned Englishmen; Tramontana; Miss Forbes's summer of happiness; Light is like water; The trail of your blood in the snow

"Exile and loss are the principal subjects of these 12 stories . . . which capture with lyrical precision the emotions of disorientation and fear, coupled with a sense of new possibility, experienced by Latin Americans in Europe." Publ Wkly

García-Roza, Luiz Alfredo, 1936-

Alone in the crowd; an Inspector Espinosa mystery; translated by Benjamin Moser. Henry Holt and Co. 2009 225p $23

ISBN 978-0-8050-7959-3; 0-8050-7959-9

LC 2008-50135

Original Portuguese edition published 2007 in Brazil

"At a bank in Rio de Janeiro, pensioner Dona Laureta withdraws her money from the same teller Hugo Breno every month like clockwork. She leaves the bank, goes to the grocery and pharmacy, and then she travels to the police of the Twelfth Precinct in Copacabana. She asks to speak with the chief, but Espinoza is tied up in a meeting. She decides to leave and come back later, but instead is run over by a bus; bystanders believe she was deliberately pushed. The police interrogate Breno who remains a person of interest. Espinosa has him under surveillance. . . . Espinosa is unaware that Breno has been watching him for decades and even came to the same park when they were children. A memory of a child's death makes the cop wonder if the teller was involved. They meet at a restaurant and Hugo tells his story to Espinosa. A day later Laureta's friend is killed. Espinosa is sure that Breno killed both women, but has no evidence. Both adversaries risk their lives with similar yet differing purposes." Mystery Gazette

December heat; translated by Benjamin Moser. Holt & Co. 2003 273p $23

ISBN 0-8050-6890-2   LC 2002-38825

Original Portuguese edition published 1998 in Brazil

"This time the plot concerns Espinosa's friend, a retired policeman who appears to be the likely suspect when his hooker girlfriend is murdered. Confusing the issue, though, is a series of subsequent murders whose tenuous links to the first are fading as precious time passes." Booklist

"An exciting procedural, infused with exotic ambience, sympathetic detectives, and a little romance." Libr J

The silence of the rain; a mystery; translated by Benjamin Moser. Holt & Co. 2002 261p

ISBN 0-8050-6889-9   LC 2001-51523

Original Portuguese edition published 1996

In this mystery "Inspector Espinosa of the Rio de Janeiro police department, a jaded intellectual who'd rather visit a used bookstore than a crime scene, must catch the murderer of Richardo Carvalho, a corporate executive found shot to death in a parking garage, his briefcase and wallet missing. . . . The sultry Rio setting, whose exotic neighborhoods add definition to the action, and a most unorthodox detective should appeal to police procedural fans with a taste for the offbeat." Publ Wkly

Garcia y Robertson, R.

Firebird. Tor Books 2006 320p $24.95

ISBN 978-0-7653-1356-0; 0-7653-1356-1

LC 2006-40363

"A Tom Doherty Associates book"

"In the fictitious European country of Markovy, which borders on the Iron Wood, a young girl named Aria rescues Sir Roye de Roye, a knight bearing the precious egg of the Firebird and fleeing from his pursuers. Falling in love with Sir Roye, Aria joins him on his journey to return the egg to its proper nest. Along the way, the pair

Garcia y Robertson, R.—*Continued*

encounters a host of mythical creatures, from witches to murderers to beasts of the kind in which people no longer believe." Libr J

"Bawdy and bloody, magical and mythic, this joyous novel is sure to please heroic fantasy fans." Publ Wkly

Gardam, Jane

Faith Fox. Carroll & Graf 2003 416p $25
ISBN 0-786-71221-X
First published 1996 in the United Kingdom
In this novel set in the Britain of the early 1990s, Faith Fox's mother dies in childbirth. Her father won't take care of her and her grandmother "refuses to acknowledge the baby whose birth killed the daughter she loved. And so an extraordinary group of family, friends, and strangers converge to make sure that Faith Fox ends up raised well in the right hands." Publisher's note
Gardam's "characters, Dickensian in their number, variety, and abounding eccentricities, carry on so convincingly that she seems to be channeling, rather than creating, these people." Atl Mon

The flight of the maidens. Carroll & Graf Pubs. 2001 278p $25
ISBN 0-7867-0879-4   LC 00-343383
First published 2000 in the United Kingdom
"It is the summer of 1946 in Yorkshire England. . . . To the delight of the town, three local girls, best friends from secondary school, have won prestigious scholarships to universities in London and Cambridge. But before they depart, they must survive the summer. While Hetty struggles to escape from her battle-scarred father and possessive mother by reading books, Una haltingly asserts her emerging womanhood with a young man from the wrong side of the tracks and of a decidedly leftist political bent. Meanwhile, Liselotte, a Jewish refugee living with a Quaker family since her arrival in 1939 via the Kindertransport, is whisked off to California to meet her last surviving relative." Libr J
Gardam "has thrown out the usual too-sensitive-for-you boilerplate of the coming-of-age novel, for which we can be thankful. Luckily, the generational conflict that remains is usually all the better for her wry indirection." N Y Times Book Rev

Old Filth. Europa 2006 289p pa $14.95
ISBN 1-933372-13-3   LC 2005-36039
First published 2004 in the United Kingdom
This "novel examines the life of Sir Edward Feathers, a desiccated barrister known to colleagues and friends as Old Filth (the nickname stands for 'Failed in London Try Hong Kong'). After a lucrative career in Asia, Filth settles into retirement in Dorset. With anatomical precision, Gardam reveals that, contrary to appearances, Sir Edward's life is seething with incident: a 'raj orphan,' whose mother died when he was born and whose father took no notice of him, he was shipped from Malaysia to Wales (cheaper than England) and entrusted to a foster mother who was cruel to him. What happened in the years before he settled into school, and was casually adopted by his best friend's kindly English country family, haunts, corrodes, and quickens Filth's heart; Gardam's prose is so economical that no moment she describes is either gratuitous or wasted." New Yorker

The people on Privilege Hill and other stories. Europa Editions 2008 196p $15.95
ISBN 978-1-933372-56-3

Contents: People on Privilege Hill; Pangbourne; Babette; Latter day of Mr. Jones; Flight path; Milly Ming; Hair of the dog; Dangers; Waiting for a stranger; Learning to fly; Virgins of Bruges; Fledglings; Snap; Last reunion

"The 14 stories in Gardam's marvelously titled new collection, The People on Privilege Hill, focus to a large extent on members of her generation (she was born July 11, 1928, soon to turn 80) or that of her parents. These generally feisty individuals recall sometimes troubling events from their prime while they cope with the affronts of aging in a changing world. Not all the stories are winners, but even the slightest offer the pleasures of Gardam's brisk, sharp sensibility. The title story brings back the splendid character Filth from her last novel. He's approaching 90, a widower who's retired to Dorset and misses the warm tropical rains of the Orient, where he practiced law for many years." Christ Sci Monit

The queen of the tambourine. St. Martin's Press 1995 226p
ISBN 0-312-13151-8   LC 95-15833
First published 1991 in the United Kingdom
This novel, constructed as a series of letters from Eliza Peabody to her neighbor, "examines what happens to a clever, imaginative, lively woman whose husband reaches the rank of senior civil servant and maroons her in a stodgy, semi-posh London suburb with no occupation but good works and no reliable company but the dog." Atl Mon
"With devilish wit, Ms. Gardam ushers Eliza into the ranks of heroines driven mad by splendid suburban isolation. . . . Yet Eliza's story takes on more and more sense as it emerges from her tragicomic vignettes." N Y Times Book Rev

Gardiner, John Rolfe

The Magellan House; stories; illustrations by Joan Gardiner. Counterpoint 2004 297p il $24
ISBN 1-582-43233-3   LC 2004-4932
Contents: The voyage out; Fugitive color; The doll house; The Ricus Adams; Morse operator; Leaving Port McHair; The head of Farnham Hall; The shape of the past; The Magellan House
"There is something tantalizingly sinister about Gardiner's short stories: a hint of intrigue and a soupcon of the illicit connect them all. This undercurrent of mystery and paranoia provides a thrilling tension that lurks just below the surface." Booklist

Gardiner, Meg

The Dirty Secrets Club. Dutton 2008 355p $24.95
ISBN 978-0-525-95066-0; 0-525-95066-4
          LC 2007-46757
"As a forensic psychiatrist, Jo Beckett determines whether murder or suicide has been committed in questionable deaths. The San Francisco Police Department needs her services after a string of suspicious suicides. The cops are concerned that more suicides are imminent,

Gardiner, Meg—*Continued*

and they're right-bodies start piling up, and the pressure is on Beckett to figure out what's going on and how to stop it." Libr J

"As Beckett gets in touch with her inner Rambo, Ericksen's acid-tinged delivery suddenly works just fine." Publ Wkly

Gardner, Lisa

Alone. Bantam Books 2005 324p $24

ISBN 0-553-80253-4 LC 2004-57577

The protagonist of this thriller is "Massachusetts police sniper Bobby Dodge. He meets his match in Catherine Gagnon, who as a girl was snatched, raped and nearly murdered. Now she's the wife of erratic, rich Jimmy Gagnon and mother of perpetually ill four-year-old Nathan. When Bobby kills Jimmy during a hostage situation at the Gagnons, he does it to save Catherine and Nathan. But was it a righteous shoot, or did Catherine engineer the killing? Judge James Gagnon and his wife, Maryanne, think Bobby murdered their son out of lust for Catherine. As other people start dying, very messily, and the DA and cops come down hard on Bobby, Gardner keeps the tension high and the pace fast." Publ Wkly

Garigliano, Jeff

Dogface; a novel. MacAdam/Cage 2008 360p pa $14

ISBN 978-1-59692-259-4; 1-59692-259-1

LC 2007-15666

"Loren is a 14-year-old Green Beret wannabe; when he acts out, he's shipped off to Camp Ascend!. Purportedly rehab for delinquent teens, the facility turns out to be a moneymaking scheme run by a con man and his family. Loren sniffs this out, and decides to rally his fellow detainees (a motley bunch, for sure) and break out." Entertainment Wkly

"With its bizarre characters, frank dialogue and violence, it belongs somewhere between Louis Sachar's Holes and a Carl Hiaasen comic thriller. . . . Despite the clichés, the novel never loses its freshness." Dallas Morning News

Garner, Helen, 1942-

The spare room; a novel. Henry Holt 2009 175p $22

ISBN 978-0-8050-8888-5; 0-8050-8888-1

LC 2008-10107

First published 2008 in Australia

"Helen prepares a room in her Melbourne home for Nicola, an old friend who travels from Sydney to begin a course of alternative treatment for bowel cancer. The central conflict of the story centers around these treatments: Helen fears they may be doing more harm than good, while Nicola has undying faith in the unorthodox practices of the Theodore Institute (these revolve around vitamin C injections), leading Helen to question her ability to care for someone so deep in denial." Publ Wkly

"Humour is not just an occasional relief in The Spare Room, it's actually the lifeblood of the book. The old cliché that 'you've got to laugh' in the face of tragedy is given new meaning by Garner. For all the sickness and suffering and thankless service involved in the story,

it's only an acute sense of the absurdity of the situation that keeps the heroine . . . sane. Garner's dealings with terminal illness are truly refreshing. Instead of focusing on the sufferer, Nicola, she delves inwards, exploring the impact on the carer. And she dares to express the unspeakable thoughts we often think when confronted by another's illness." PopMatters

Garry, Jane

(ed) Trial and error. See Trial and error

Garwood, Julie

The bride. Atria Books 2002 346p

ISBN 0-7434-5292-5 LC 2002-511767

First published 1989 in paperback by Pocket Books

By edict of the king, the mighty Scottish laird Alec Kincaid must take an English bride. His choice was Jamie, youngest daughter of Baron Jamison. While living in the Highlands, Jamie and Alec learn much about each other and about themselves. All the while, someone is out to put a stop to the love that is growing between them.

Gash, Joe *See* Granger, Bill

Gash, Jonathan, 1933-

Prey dancing; a Dr. Clare Burtonall mystery. Viking 1998 272p

ISBN 0-670-87764-6 LC 98-2830

"The unlikely team of cardiologist Clare Burtonall and her lover, male prostitute Bonn, risk murder when they attempt to carry out an AIDS patient's last request." Libr J

"Brilliantly written, mysterious, menacing, and filled with unforgettable characters." Booklist

A rag, a bone, and a hank of hair; the twenty-first Lovejoy novel. Viking 2000 344p

ISBN 0-670-88598-3 LC 99-52654

First published 1999 in the United Kingdom

"Pursued from East Anglia by the usual creditors and angry husbands, Lovejoy descends on London with a private commission to find out who is flooding the trade with bogus gemstones, a quest that takes him from trendy galleries on Chelsea's King's Road to the jumbled stalls of outdoor markets in Bermondsey, Camden Passage and Portobello Road." N Y Times Book Rev

The rich and the profane; a Lovejoy novel. Viking 1999 344p

ISBN 0-670-88346-8 LC 98-38951

First published 1998 in the United Kingdom

Lovejoy "takes on yet another persona when he impersonates a pop music impresario and produces a splashy variety show on the English Channel island of Guernsey—clever cover for an ingenious art fraud that draws the suckers like flies." N Y Times Book Rev

"With this dervish of comic activity and a romp that ends in a circuslike venue, Gash is in top form." Publ Wkly

Gaskell, Elizabeth Cleghorn, 1810-1865

Cranford; [by] Elizabeth Gaskell. Oxford University Press 1998 xxxii, 194p (Oxford world classics) pa $9.95 o.p.

ISBN 0-19-283209-3

* LC 98-204713

First published 1853

This novel "centres on the formidable Miss Deborah Jenkyns and her gentle sister Miss Matty, daughters of the former rector. Moments of drama are provided by the death of the genial Captain Brown, run over by a train when saving the life of a child; by the panic caused in the village by rumours of burglars; by the surprising marriage of the widowed Lady Glenmire with the vulgar Mr. Hoggins, the village surgeon; by the failure of a bank which ruins Miss Matty, and her rescue by the fortunate return from India of her long-lost brother Peter. But the greatest charm of 'Cranford,' which has kept it unfailingly popular, is its amused but loving portrayal of the old-fashioned customs and 'elegant economy' of a delicately observed group of middle-aged figures in a landscape." Oxford Companion to Engl Lit. 5th edition

Gatewood, Robert, 1974-

The sound of the trees; a novel. Holt & Co. 2002 289p $25

ISBN 0-8050-6802-3

LC 2001-51703

This novel "begins on horse back in Depression-era New Mexico with Trude Mason, a taciturn 18-year-old, and his mother fleeing their impoverished family ranch in predawn desperation to escape the escalating brutality of the young man's father. Enroute to Colorado, Trude's steadfastness of purpose is tested by personal tragedy and sharpened by the treachery of man. His fate becomes entwined with that of a girl whom fortune has placed in the hands of scoundrels. . . . Gatewood has created a richly textured tableau threaded with mysticism and sustained by pitch-perfect dialogue laced with quiet dignity." SLJ

Gautreaux, Tim, 1947-

The missing. Alfred A. Knopf 2009 375p $25.95

ISBN 978-0-307-27015-3; 0-307-27015-7

LC 2008-46739

"As the floorwalker in New Orleans' best department store in 1921, Sam Simoneaux knows the policy is to lock the store doors when a lost child is not found in 15 minutes. When he fails to implement that policy, kidnappers make off with three-year-old Lily, the pretty and talented daughter of riverboat performers Elsie and Ted Weller. Fired from his job, Sam—who understands the Wellers' grief, having lost a young son to illness—hires on at the riverboat and taps railroad stationmasters for information to find the kidnappers. His initial error is compounded when he finds Lily and makes a moral judgment he has no right to make. But Sam, the victim of a horrendous crime as an infant, goes to great lengths to right his own wrongs without seeking vengeance for wrongs against himself, even in the face of pure evil. Gautreaux . . . displays fluent prose, accomplished storytelling, and strong characterizations in this paean to the indefatigability of the human spirit. An exceptional novel." Booklist

Gay, William

I hate to see that evening sun go down; collected stories. Free Press 2002 303p $24

ISBN 0-7432-4088-X

LC 2002-73945

Contents: I hate to see that evening sun go down; A death in the woods; Bonedaddy, Quincy Nell, and the fifteen thousand BTU electric chair; The paperhanger; The man who knew Dylan; Those Deep Elm Brown's Ferry Blues; Crossroads Blues; Closure and roadkill on the life's highway; Sugarbaby; Standing by peaceful waters; Good 'til now; The lightpainter; My hand is just fine where it is

"Gay is richly gifted: a seemingly effortless storyteller, a writer of prose that's fiercely wrought, pungent in detail, yet poetic in the most welcome sense." N Y Times Book Rev

Twilight; a novel. MacAdam/Cage 2006 224p $25

ISBN 978-1-59692-058-3; 1-59692-058-0

LC 2006-19865

A "story set in rural Tennessee in 1951. Teenage Kenneth Tyler is on the run from Granville Sutter, a monstrously evil but wickedly efficient hit man who has been hired to retrieve some incriminating photos the boy has stolen from the local mortician, who has a penchant for doing unspeakable things to and with the corpses in his professional care." Booklist

The "absence of a soothing depth—of motive, reasons, understanding—is one of the great achievements of the novel. It sets up a central tension for the reader, who deaires to know more, while the writer resolutely adheres to the truth of his universe—that such comforts aren't available and that the quiverings of the individual consciousness aren't substantial enough in the face of life's darkly malevolent forces." Paste

Gear, Kathleen O'Neal

People of the masks; [by] Kathleen O'Neal Gear & W. Michael Gear. Forge 1998 416p

ISBN 0-312-85857-4

LC 98-8695

"A Tom Doherty Associates book"

"Great trouble begins for two tribes in what is now northeastern North America when Jumping Badger, a sadistic war leader, raids and destroys Paint Rock village and kidnaps the dwarf child Rumbler, whose power in the spirit world is legendary. Blue Raven, Jumping Badger's cousin, believes that the tribes need to work together to survive attacks from fiercer enemies. But as warriors begin to die, Rumbler is accused of casting evil spells, and Blue Raven can no longer protect him." Libr J

People of the mist; [by] Kathleen O'Neal Gear and W. Michael Gear. Forge 1997 432p maps

ISBN 0-312-85854-X

LC 97-14682

"A Tom Doherty Associates book"

"Red Knot has been betrothed to Copper Thunder in order to forge an alliance that will protect both their tribes. When she is murdered on the day of her wedding, it threatens to throw the tribal villages along the Chesapeake into a bloody war. Suspicion for the crime falls on Sun Conch, who had a relationship with the girl before she was promised away. Old Panther, a recluse, and possibly a powerful witch, is asked to look into the situation

Gear, Kathleen O'Neal—*Continued*

before it explodes." Booklist

"Simple prose brightened by atmospheric detail sweeps this fluid, suspenseful mix of anthropological research and character-driven mystery to a solid, satisfying resolution." Publ Wkly

People of the owl; a novel of prehistoric North America; [by] Kathleen O'Neal Gear and W. Michael Gear. Forge 2003 560p il maps $25.95

ISBN 0-312-87741-2   LC 2003-40019

"A Tom Doherty Associates book"

An "account of six prehistoric Native American clans living in the Lower Mississippi Valley. Salamander, the protagonist, is an unlikely leader of the Owl clan and struggles to maintain peace among the fractious clans. Even though many of his family, friends, and enemies believe him to be a naive young fool, a certain mystique surrounds him when his shamanistic visions empower him to keep violence at bay." Libr J

"Propelled by the Gears' spry storytelling, this sturdy epic skillfully navigates the ancient swamplands of Louisiana, with their lapping brown waters, hanging vines and brooding skies." Publ Wkly

(jt. auth) Gear, W. M. People of the thunder

Gear, W. Michael

Coyote summer. Forge 1997 427p

ISBN 0-312-86330-6   LC 97-5762

"A Tom Doherty Associates book"

Sequel to The morning river (1996)

"Richard Hamilton, the hero of this . . . western, rues the day when his father sent him west. Robbed and sold into indentured servitude on a keelboat, this young student of philosophy is forced to forsake his genteel Bostonian manners and breeding. In the harsh Upper Missouri country of the 1820s, it's kill or be killed. Dick learns that early, when he kills a Pawnee to save the life of an Indian woman, Heals Like the Willow. After a raiding party of Crows steals his company's horses, Dick is almost slaughtered himself when he accompanies brutal hunter Travis on a relentless pursuit of the thieves. Gear skillfully intercuts Dick's story with that of Willow." Publ Wkly

People of the thunder; [by] W. Michael Gear and Kathleen O'Neal Gear. Forge 2009 383p $25.95

ISBN 978-0-7653-1439-0; 0-7653-1439-8

LC 2008-38017

"A Tom Doherty Associates book"

"Set in the 1300s largely in what is now Alabama and Mississippi, this complex novel tracks three wanderers' quest to create peace in violent times. The Sky Hand people control their territory from Split Sky City (Moundville, Ala.), ruled by scheming chief Flying Hawk and his ruthless nephew, war chief Smoke Shield. While they plot to suppress the enslaved Albaamaha people and to conquer their neighbors, three people pursue a mission to restore peace. Old White is a prophet and 'the most dangerous man alive'; Trader is a man with blood on his hands and a stunning secret; Two Petals is a shaman woman who says and does everything backwards. Together this curious trio must bring down Flying Hawk and Smoke Shield. The story is loaded with early Native

American lore, spirituality, economics, government and daily life; however, it is not for the squeamish, as it also contains plenty of blood and gore, hideous torture, rape and chilling cruelty. . . . A terrific tale." Publ Wkly

(jt. auth) Gear, K. O. People of the masks

(jt. auth) Gear, K. O. People of the mist

(jt. auth) Gear, K. O. People of the owl

Gebert, Lizabeth Paravisini- *See* Paravisini-Gebert, Lizabeth

Geddes, Tom

(tr) Lindgren, T. Hash

Gee, Sophie, 1974-

The scandal of the season. Scribner 2007 335p $25

ISBN 978-1-4165-4056-4; 1-4165-4056-3

LC 2006-35556

"Written by Alexander Pope at the request of his friend John Caryll, 'The Rape of the Lock' clinched Pope's fame and assured his success. . . [This novel] provides the poem's backstory, portraying not only the beau and belle of the poem (Lord Robert Petre and Arabella Fermor) but also Pope's own coming to terms with his life: his relationship to longtime friends Teresa and Martha Blount, his attraction to and scorn for the fashionable world, and his uncomfortable social position as a cripple and a Catholic." Libr J

"Gee writes with scholarly confidence, underpinning the racy intrigue of her account with a real understanding of the characters and their world." New Yorker

Genazino, Wilhelm, 1943-

The shoe tester of Frankfurt; a novel; translated from the German by Philip Boehm. New Directions 2006 132p pa $14.95

ISBN 978-0-8112-1583-1; 0-8112-1583-0

LC 2006-9105

Original German edition, 2001

"Employed by a high-end shoe manufacturer to test new products, the narrator spends his days wandering through his native city, encountering faces from his past (primarily female) and experiencing anew the many manifestations of the mystery of life. In the grand tradition of literary flâneurs, he takes note of his surroundings, from the significant to the mundane, and assembles them into a sort of mental collage that is at once self-portrait and cityscape." Publisher's note

"Filled with the hypersensitive observations of a man who claims that he 'hardly thinks at all anymore—I only look round and about,' the novel shows the transformation of this character from someone who willfully closes his eyes to the world to one who looks around and begins to recognize his connections with the rest of the humanity. The author's tongue-in-cheek humor keeps the novel from imploding under its own weight, while the conclusion offers hope for the future. Slow to start, the novel evolves into a delightful exploration of one man's memories and his halting steps toward a new life." Mostlyfiction.com

George, Elizabeth

Careless in red; a novel. Harper 2008 626p $27.95

ISBN 978-0-06-116087-5; 0-06-116087-3

LC 2007-44629

"Thomas Lynley, grief-stricken in the wake of the death of his wife and unborn child, sets off walking around the southwest coast of England. On the 43rd day of his walk, Lynley comes upon the body of a young climber who has fallen to his death. When police discover that the equipment of the fallen climber has been tampered with, Lynley gets caught up in a murder investigation. New Scotland Yard sends Lynley's old friend and foil Barbara Havers to help with the case (and to keep an eye on Lynley)." Libr J

"As with George's other books, the reader is soon plunged into a vast back story of relationships and psychologically complex characters. It's a level of literary sophistication readers have come to expect from George." Seattle Times

(ed) A moment on the edge. See A moment on the edge

A traitor to memory. Bantam Bks. 2001 422p

ISBN 0-553-80127-9

LC 2001-25488

"Violin virtuoso and former child prodigy Gideon Davies suddenly loses his ability to play. As he works with a psychiatrist to regain his gift, Gideon begins to dredge up memories from his childhood. Suddenly, people involved in an incident from his past, beginning with his mother, are being run over by a big black car. Detective Inspector Thomas Lynley and constables Barbara Havers and Winston Nkata are asked to investigate the hit-and-run murders and, like Gideon, must reconstruct the past in order to understand what is happening in the present." Libr J

What came before he shot her. HarperCollins 2006 548p $26.95

ISBN 0-06-054562-3

LC 2006-43520

"Twelve-year-old Joel Campbell's father was gunned down by thugs, and his mother is confined to a mental institution. Joel and his siblings live with an unwelcoming aunt in a dangerous part of London. His 15-year-old sister, Vanessa, is trading sexual favors for drugs, and his eight-year-old brother, Toby, spends much of his time in an imaginary world called Sose. To gain protection for his vulnerable little brother, Joel gets involved with the Blade, a vicious neighborhood drug dealer. Joel is the boy who, at the end of George's last novel, With No One as Witness [2005], was arrested in the shooting death of Det. Peter Lynley's wife, Helen. This is an unusual sequel in that, rather than taking up where the last book left off, with the expected cast of characters—Barbara Havers, Winston Nkata, and Peter Lynley—it veers off to tell Joel's story." Libr J

"This is crime writing at its finest, with an almost painfully sharp view of the world and evil." Rocky Mountain News

George, Margaret

Helen of Troy. Viking 2006 611p $27.95

ISBN 0-670-03778-8

LC 2005-58473

"Helen's noble Spartan parents try to defy the fates when a seer foretells the tragedy Helen and her legendary beauty will cause, but, as the myth of Helen demonstrates, destiny cannot be altered. Helen's years of seclusion in Sparta lead to a frigid marriage to Menelaus before she connects with Paris, the Trojan prince with whom she forges an inextricable bond. Barely into her 20s, Helen escapes with Paris to Troy, but finds the Trojan royals welcome her with less than open arms." Publ Wkly

George's "characters are precisely crafted, and the lovely Helen, clear-eyed and intelligent, is a sympathetic narrator. Despite the novel's length, the pages practically turn themselves. An absorbing retelling of the classic Trojan War myth, and a sobering look at the utter futility of trying to change one's fate." Booklist

The memoirs of Cleopatra; a novel. St. Martin's Press 1997 964p

ISBN 0-312-15430-5

LC 96-51071

"Beginning with a memory at age three of witnessing her mother's death and ending with her own suicide, Cleopatra tells her story." Libr J

George "renders her myriad settings, whether in Athens, Syria, Actium or elsewhere, palpably real. The smell of the Alexandrian harbor, the taste of pomegranates, the visual grandeur of the pyramids and the clash of swords all come alive in her hands. Battles physical and political—Caesar's North African campaign, the Alexandrian War, the ill-fated struggle between Antony and Octavian for control of the world—are evoked with skill and passion, as are more domestic conflicts." Publ Wkly

Gerritsen, Tess

The apprentice; a novel. Ballantine Bks. 2002 344p $24.95

ISBN 0-345-44785-9

LC 2002-23185

Boston "detective Jane Rizzoli is called to a crime scene out of her jurisdiction. The victim is a wealthy doctor, found with his throat slashed, sitting on the floor of his living room in his pajamas, with a teacup in his lap. His wife is missing, but her nightgown is found folded neatly on a chair in the bedroom. There are unmistakable similarities to the work of serial killer Warren Hoyt, nicknamed 'the Surgeon,' but he is in prison, which leads Rizzoli to suspect a copcat killer." Libr J

Body double. Ballantine Bks. 2004 339p $24.95

ISBN 0-375-43374-0

LC 2004-49807

"Medical examiner Dr. Maura Isles has just returned from a trip to France to encounter a grisly discovery. A woman has been found shot to death in front of her home, and the woman is a dead ringer for Maura. The woman, whose name is Anna Leoni, turns out to be Maura's twin; both were given up for adoption 40 years ago. The mystery deepens when Officer Rick Ballard shows up and tells Maura and Detective Jane Rizzoli that Anna was on the run from an abusive boyfriend and under police protection. But that still doesn't answer the question of what led Anna to Maura's door, and that question leads Maura to trace her sister's steps to an old house in Maine." Booklist

"An electric series of startling twists, the revelation of ghoulishly practical motives and a nail-biting finale make this Gerritsen's best to date." Publ Wkly

The sinner. Ballantine Bks. 2003 342p $24.95

ISBN 0-345-45891-5

LC 2003-59151

Gerritsen, Tess—*Continued*

"When two Boston nuns are found brutally beaten—one fatally and one with a scintilla of life left in her—it's up to homicide detective Jane Rizzoli to find the perpetrator. Medical examiner Dr. Maura Isles, nicknamed the Queen of the Dead, has the unlucky fortune to discover that the murdered nun, a young woman about to make her final vows, hid untold secrets from the rest of the aging convent. . . . Woven within the horror of this gruesome story is the old allegory of good versus evil, but relating it through these two fascinating individuals, Gerritsen avoids cliches." Booklist

The surgeon. Ballantine Bks. 2001 359p
ISBN 0-345-44783-2   LC 2001-35901
Dr. Catherine Cordell "thought she had shot and killed her rapist and would-be murderer two years earlier in steamy Savannah, where he was a surgery intern at her hospital. Now, in Boston, as another hot summer begins, he appears to have miraculously returned and embarked once again on his grisly mission: he rapes women, then surgically removes their wombs. As two intrepid detectives—Thomas Moore and Jane Rizzoli—investigate, Cordell begins to doubt her own memories (or lack of) and discovers that not even her OR is safe." Publ Wkly
"A fascinating story with a gripping plot and believably human characters." Booklist

Gessel, Van C.

(tr) Endō, S. Deep river

Gessen, Keith

All the sad young literary men. Viking 2008 242p il $24.95
ISBN 978-0-670-01855-0; 0-670-01855-4
                            LC 2007-21009
"The book focuses on Sam, Mark, and Keith, young 'literary men' with ambitious plans to change the world. Unfortunately, these plans are often derailed by their difficulties in dealing with young adulthood. Mark is not so diligently working on a dissertation about the Mensheviks in dreary Syracuse, NY, while reeling from a recent divorce. Sam plans to write a great Zionist novel despite never having been to Israel. And Keith, the son of Russian immigrants and the most thoughtful of the three, struggles with family issues and alienation. Though the three never meet, their lives intertwine as they arrive at their own forms of adulthood." Libr J
"Gessen's humor is persistently Seinfeldian, avoiding the excesses of savage comedy or satire, or anything like raging spiritual despair, for All the Sad Young Literary Men is a post-postmodernist work of fiction in which spiritual impotence is the great subtextual theme, even as sexual promiscuity is the norm." N Y Rev Books

Ghosh, Amitav

The glass palace; a novel. Random House 2001 474p $25.95
ISBN 0-375-50148-7   LC 00-41477
This narrative "stretches from the British invasion of Burma, in 1885, through the country's independence, to the uneasy military rule of the present day. The novel is presided over by the Indian-born Rajkumar, a poor or-phan, who falls for Dolly, a servant of the exiled queen. Ghosh renders the polite imprisonment of the Burmese royal family in India and the lush, dangerous atmosphere of teak camps in the Burmese forest with fine detail—a perfect balance for the broad stroke of romance and serendipity that drive the story forward." New Yorker

Sea of poppies. Farrar, Straus and Giroux 2008 515p map $26
ISBN 978-0-374-17422-4; 0-374-17422-9
                            LC 2008-30854
"An adventure story set in nineteenth-century Calcutta against the backdrop of the Opium Wars. On the Ibis, a ship engaged in transporting opium across the Bay of Bengal, varied life stories converge. A fallen raja, a half-Chinese convict, a plucky American sailor, a widowed opium farmer, a transgendered religious visionary are all united by the 'smoky paradise' of the opium seed. Ghosh writes with impeccable control, and with a vivid and sometimes surprising imagination." New Yorker

Gibb, Camilla

Sweetness in the belly. Penguin Press 2006 c2005 338p $23.95
ISBN 1-59420-084-X   LC 2005-53451
First published 2005 in Canada
"Called farenji—foreigner—in Ethiopia and subsequently nurse at London's Lambeth Hospital, Lilly is a devout white Muslim woman who doesn't really belong to one culture. When she was eight, her wandering parents left her in the care of the Great Abdal—and never returned owing to a fatal car accident. Soon after, the local saint became Lilly's guardian and taught her the Qur'an. In 1969, when political upheaval comes to Morocco, she makes a pilgrimage to the ancient city of Harar in Ethiopia. Here she begins to teach the Qur'an to local children and falls in love with a young doctor who leaves an indelible mark on her life. In 1974, she is again forced to flee, this time to London." Libr J
"Utterly convincing and authentic . . . a novel that will take you to a place so far from yourself that you may wonder, from time to time, whether you are ever coming back." San Francisco Chronicle

Gibbons, Kaye, 1960-

Charms for the easy life. Putnam 1992 254p
ISBN 0-399-13791-2   LC 92-40690
This novel "concerns three generations of strong Southern women: a grandmother who heals with herbs and native wisdom, a mother passionately in love with the wrong man, and the daughter who narrates this tale." Libr J
"A touching picture of female bonding and solidarity. Related with the simple, tart economy of a folktale, the narrative brims with wisdom and superstition, with Southern manners and insights into human nature." Publ Wkly

Divining women. G. P. Putnam's Sons 2004 205p $23.95
ISBN 0-399-15160-5   LC 2003-60661
In this "tale of marital strife and female resilience, Gibbons considers conflicts between blacks and whites and men and women within the context of the First World War and the Spanish influenza epidemic. Martha

Gibbons, Kaye, 1960-—*Continued*

has sent her intelligent daughter, Mary, to North Carolina to help Martha's half-brother, Troop, and his expectant wife, Maureen, and Mary is amazed to find herself in a household as miserable as it is opulent. Troop is a cold-hearted, possibly insane despot; lovely and muddled Maureen is his prisoner; and Zollie and Mamie, their kind African American employees, are treated with appalling indifference. The hate, lies, and machinations at work in this psychotic hothouse rival that of the most gothic of southern melodramas, a tradition Gibbons shrewdly subverts as she divines the true nature of feminine power and points the way toward justice in this gorgeously moody and piquant fairy tale." Booklist

Ellen Foster; a novel. Algonquin Bks. 1987 146p $16.95

ISBN 1-56512-205-4

* LC 86-22136

A "novel narrated by an adolescent girl, Ellen, who relates the day-to-day experiences she endured as a child in a troubled family. Ellen's mother died young, her father was abusive, her other relatives were equally bad; it wasn't until she was taken into a foster home that she found the sort of peace and freedom to be innocent that most normal childhoods afford." Booklist

"What might have been grim, melodramatic material in the hands of a less talented author is instead filled with lively humor, . . . compassion and intimacy. This short novel focuses on Ellen's strengths rather than her victimization, presenting a memorable heroine who rescues herself." N Y Times Book Rev

Followed by The life all around me by Ellen Foster (2006)

The life all around me by Ellen Foster. Harcourt 2006 218p $23

ISBN 0-15-101204-0   LC 2005-14552

Sequel to Ellen Foster (1987)

In this sequel, "Ellen is now 15 and driven to succeed. She and her foster mother, Laura, scrape together enough money to send her to an academic enrichment weekend program at Johns Hopkins University, and she composes an ambitious letter to a professor at Harvard asking him to consider her for admission despite her youth. Yet as she writes poetry to finance her trip to Baltimore, Ellen still clings to her hometown and friends." Libr J

"This book lacks the strong story arc of its predecessor, which may make some readers impatient. But Ellen is still a remarkable creation, and her narrative voice, while it has matured and grown more sophisticated, remains compelling and unique." Booklist

On the occasion of my last afternoon. Putnam 1998 273p

ISBN 0-399-14299-1   LC 98-12947

"Now 70 and near death, Emma Garnet Tate begins her account by recalling her youth as a bookish, observant 12-year-old in 1842, living on a Virginia plantation in a highly dysfunctional family dominated by her foul-mouthed father, a veritable monster of parental tyranny and racial prejudice. Emma's long-suffering mother, of genteel background and gentle ways, is angelic and forgiving; her five siblings' lives are ruined by her father's cruelty; and all are discreetly cared for by Clarice, the clever, formidable black woman who is the only person Samuel Tate respects. . . . At 17, Emma marries one of

the Boston Lowells, a surgeon, and spends the war years laboring beside him in a Raleigh hospital." Publ Wkly

"Gibbons is unsparing in her depiction of the gruesome reality of the carnage, and unflinching in her effort to convey the madness of that time and the havoc it wreaked on people's souls." Booklist

Sights unseen. Putnam 1995 209p $19.95

ISBN 0-399-13986-9   LC 95-9781

"In flashback, Hattie describes the summer and fall of 1967, when she was 12 and living in Bend of the River, N.C., and when her beautiful, psychotically volatile mother, Maggie, was temporarily committed to the psychiatric ward at Duke University. A near-miracle occurs: for the first time in nearly two decades, Maggie becomes stabilized on medication. And, for the first time in her life, Hattie experiences a mother who relates to, touches and cares for her." Publ Wkly

"Gibbons has her quietly heroic narrator relate one wild and poignant incident after another, holding us rapt with wonder and empathy for Maggie and her loving, self-sacrificing family. This is a novel that deserves unwavering attention from start to finish." Booklist

Gibson, William, 1948-

Neuromancer; with a new introduction by the author; with an afterword by Jack Womack. 20th anniversary ed. Ace Books 2004 371p $25

ISBN 0-441-01203-5

* LC 2004-48718

First published 1984

"In a highly urbanized future dominated by cybernetics and bioengineering, anti-hero Case is rescued from wretchedness and given back the ability to send his persona into the cyberspace of the world's computer networks, where he must carry out a hazardous mission for an enigmatic employer. An adventure story much enlivened by elaborate technical jargon and sleazy, streetwise characters—the pioneering 'cyberpunk' novel and arguably the most influential SF novel of the 1980s." Anatomy of Wonder 5

Pattern recognition. Putnam 2003 356p $25.95

ISBN 0-399-14986-4

* LC 2002-67955

"Cayce Pollard is a brand consultant whose father disappeared on September 11th. She becomes fascinated by mysterious scraps of film footage—seemingly random scenes, luminously shot—that are disseminated on the Web and have spawned cults of viewers. Gibson wisely avoids addressing the import of 9/11 head on, but he somehow establishes a powerful correlative for it in Cayce's strange quest—through the Tokyo red-light district and the Moscow underworld—to find the anonymous filmmaker. In Gibson's eerie vision of our time, the future has come crashing upon us, fragmentary and undecipherable." New Yorker

Spook country. G.P. Putnam's Sons 2007 371p $25.95

ISBN 978-0-399-15430-0; 0-399-15430-2

LC 2007-3138

This novel portrays a "post-9/11 America, which, in thrall to ubiquitous media and vague threats of annihilation, has 'developed Stockholm syndrome toward its own government.' The convoluted and politically insistent plot

Gibson, William, 1948-—*Continued*

involves a missing shipping container, a former rock star, a Cuban-Chinese crime-facilitating family, and an Ativan addict coerced into domestic espionage. Fanciful touches include the creation of virtual art in public spaces using satellite mapping and Wi-Fi; texting in Volapuk, a Cyrillic-Latin amalgam; encrypting data within songs on an iPod; and the C.I.A.'s recruitment of sea pirates in the war on terrorism. (All but the last are verifiably real.) If Gibson's vision has got bleaker, his eye for the eerie in the everyday still lends events an otherworldly sheen." New Yorker

Gide, André, 1869-1951

The counterfeiters (Les faux-monnayeurs); translated from the French of André Gide by Dorothy Bussy. Knopf 1927 365p o.p.

　　　　　　　　　　　　　　　　　　　*

Original French edition, 1925
"The novelist Edouard keeps a journal of events in order to write a novel about the nature of reality. The intrigues of a gang of counterfeiters symbolize the 'counterfeit' personalities with which people disguise themselves to conform hypocritically to convention or to deceive themselves. The adolescent boys Bernard Profitendieu and Olivier Molinier, having left home in order to be free to find and develop their true selves, encounter many varieties of hyprocrisy and self-deception in human relationships and barely escape falling into such poses themselves. Both begin by seeking a close emotional tie with Edouard. Each, however, comes to recognize that Edouard is inadequate as an ideal for emulation, particularly when the novelist cannot recognize the psychological reality of the schoolboy Boris' useless suicide, which is an indirect result of the counterfeiters' machinations." Reader's Ency. 4th edition

The immoralist; translated by Richard Howard. Modern Lib. 1984 c1970 171p
　ISBN 0-394-60500-4
　　　　　　　　　　　　　　　* LC 83-42856
Original French edition, 1902. First United States edition, translated by Dorothy Bussy, published 1930 by Knopf; this translation first published 1970 by Knopf
"Michel takes his bride, Marceline, to North Africa, where he develops tuberculosis and becomes hyperconscious of physical sensations, particularly of his attraction to young Arab boys. Back on his French estate after being cured, he is encouraged by his friend Ménalque to rise above conventional good and evil and give free rein to all his passions. When Marceline falls ill with the tuberculosis she caught while nursing him, he takes her south. He neglects her demands on him more and more, however, in order to keep himself free, since his new doctrine demands that the weak be suppressed if necessary for the preservation of the strong. She dies, and he, guilt-ridden and debilitated by his excesses, tries to justify his conduct to a group of friends." Reader's Ency. 4th edition

Gien, Pamela

The syringa tree; a novel. Random House 2006 262p $24.95
　ISBN 0-375-50755-8　　　　　LC 2006-41054

"Gien's novel of apartheid is adapted from her one-woman play. . . . [The novel portrays the] imposition of apartheid in South Africa through the eyes and impressions of a young white girl. Lizzy Grace is 6 years old in 1963, when the story begins." N Y Times Book Rev
"As the meaning of apartheid unfolds, Lizzy struggles to understand racial laws that force her nanny to carry work papers and hide from the police. Through her eyes, readers see South African townships and experience the indignities that provoked underground resistance movements. Although the protagonist is occasionally cloying, this is part of the book's charm." Libr J

Gifford, Barry, 1946-

The stars above Veracruz. Thunder's Mouth Press 2006 262p $24
　ISBN 1-56025-807-1　　　　　LC 2006-282377
Contents: The ropedancer; The law of affection; After hours at La Chinta; What happened in Japan; Almost oriental; The god of birds; Dancing with Fidel; The sculptor's son; Wanted man; Murder at the Swordfish Club; The bearded lady of Rutgers Street; My catechism; This coulda happened anywhere; One leg; The stars above Veracruz; The ropedancer's recurring dream
"While the stories take place in cities from berlin to Havana to San Francisco and involve characters as disparate as a prizefighter, a schoolboy, and a one-legged ex-Legionnaire, each concerns the naked bravery of characters stepping into maturity. Gifford's great talent is capturing defining moments with the casual grace of anecdote. Each of these 16 stunning tales makes the anecdotal monumental." San Francisco Magazine

Gilb, Dagoberto, 1950-

The flowers. Grove Press 2008 250p $24
　ISBN 978-0-8021-1859-2; 0-8021-1859-3
"Sixteen-year-old Sonny lives with his single mother, Silvia, who attracts an array of colorful and dangerous boyfriends. Left alone, Sonny develops a habit of breaking into people's homes just to see how they live. We get the sense he longs for the warmth of a stable and happy family. His wish is partially fulfilled when Silvia moves in with her boyfriend, Cloyd Longpre, a 'hillbilly' with a silver tooth and fake blue suit. Cloyd owns an apartment complex called "Los Flores"(sic), where Sonny becomes the handyman — sweeping, cleaning window screens, painting. In the process, he meets the tenants: Cindy, a 19-year-old white girl who seduces him; Pinkie, an albino who sells cars to blacks and defends their civil rights; Bud, a racist construction worker; Josef, a Spaniard whose wife dies; Gina, who suspects Sonny is stealing her husband's pornographic magazines; and Nica, a Mexican immigrant who baby-sits her infant brother. Nica is young and innocent, and Sonny falls in love with her." Houston Chron
"A tightly woven narrative about a boy coming of age in a community bubbling with racial tension. It's beautifully rendered in part because Mr. Gilb nails the voice of 15-year-old narrator Sonny Bravo with pinpoint accuracy." Dallas Morning News

Gilbert, R. A.

(comp) The Oxford book of English ghost stories. See The Oxford book of English ghost stories

Gilchrist, Ellen, 1935-

The age of miracles; stories. Little, Brown 1995
260p o.p.   LC 94-37441
Contents: Among the mourners; The blue house; Death
comes to a hero; The divorce; Going to join the poets;
Joyce; Love at the Center; Love of my life; Madison at
69th, a fable; Paris; The Raintree Street Bar and
Washerteria; A statue of Aphrodite; The stucco house;
Too much rain; The uninsured; A wedding in Jackson
In several of the stories in this collection, the author
recounts the adventures of her recurring heroine Rhoda
Manning. "Elegant, independent, and successful, Rhoda
is approaching 60 with unwavering nerve, delighted with
the freedom age brings." Booklist

The cabal and other stories. Little, Brown 2000
272p $35
ISBN 0-316-31491-9   LC 99-36893
Contents: The cabal [novella]; The sanguine blood of
men; Hearts of Dixie; The survival of the fittest; Bare
ruined choirs, where late the sweet birds sang; The big
cleanup
The cabal "takes place in Jackson, Mississippi, upon
Caroline Jones' arrival in town to begin a college teaching job. It just so happens that Caroline's arrival coincides with the mental breakdown of the psychiatrist who
tends to the wellbeing of the town's artistic elite, a group
called 'the Cabal,' all of whom are subsequently threatened with the public revelation of their deep, dark secrets." Booklist

Ellen Gilchrist: collected stories. Little, Brown
2000 563p $38
ISBN 0-316-29948-0

*

Contents: The famous poll at Jody's Bar; Revenge;
There's a Garden of Eden; In the land of dreamy
dreams; 1944; Summer, an elegy; Victory over Japan;
Music; Jade Buddhas, red bridges, fruits of love; Miss
Crystal's maid name Traceleen, she's talking, she's telling everything she knows; Traceleen, she's still talking;
Drunk with love; The young man; Traceleen at dawn;
Anna, part 1; Some blue hills at sundown; The Starlight
Express; Light can be both wave and particle; Traceleen
turns east; Mexico; A statue of Aphrodite; Among the
mourners; The stucco house; The uninsured; Perhaps a
miracle; Lunch at the best restaurant in the world; You
must change your life; The brown cape; Fort Smith; A
prologue; A tree to be desired; Witness to the crucifixion; A lady with pearls; The Southwest Experimental
Fast Oxide Reactor
"Gilchrist is an important voice in contemporary
Southern fiction, and this book belongs in every library."
Libr J

Flights of angels; stories. Little, Brown 1998
327p $34 o.p.
ISBN 0-316-31486-2   LC 98-21420
Contents: A tree to be desired; While we waited for
you to be born; The carnival of the stoned children; Mississippi; Miss Crystal confronts the past; A sordid tale;
or, Traceleen continues talking; Phyladda; or, The
mind/body problem; Battle; The triumph of reason; Have
a *wonderful* nice walk; Witness to the crucifixion;
Ocean Springs; Excitement at Drake Field; A lady with
pearls; Excitement at Audubon Park; Free pull; Down at

the dollhouse; The Southwest Experimental Fast Oxide
Reactor
This collection "features some of Gilchrist's familiar,
endearingly eccentric narrators. . . . There are also some
new, young and engaging characters and, throughout the
book, a convincing evocation of the changing South."
Publ Wkly

Gill, Bartholomew, 1943-2002

Death in Dublin; a novel of suspense. Morrow
2003 294p $24.95
ISBN 0-06-000849-0   LC 2002-32582
"Gill's final novel pits Police Chief Peter McGarr
against a thief and murderer: a night watchman at Dublin's Trinity College has been killed and the irreplaceable
Book of Kells stolen. McGarr suspects an infamous and
most dangerous band of IRA zealots. Excellent work
from a tried-and-true hand." Libr J

The death of an Irish lover; a Peter McGarr
mystery. Avon Bks. 2000 265p $23
ISBN 0-380-97797-4   LC 99-58663
"McGarr of the Dublin Police, who is the chief homicide cop in Ireland, is summoned to the village of
Leixleap on the River Shannon to solve a double murder.
Two local fisheries officers, known as the 'eel police' for
their efforts to control the lucrative trade of eel poaching,
are discovered dead at the local upscale inn. The older
man and young woman apparently have been killed by
a single bullet. The fact that the room was locked at the
time of the murders is the least puzzling aspect of this
case." Booklist
"The contradictions Gill manages to unearth in one
small, placid patch of Irish ground are simply astonishing." N Y Times Book Rev

The death of an Irish sea wolf; a Peter McGarr
mystery. Morrow 1996 296p o.p.
                                            LC 96-15680
This novel is "part swashbuckling adventure . . . and
part modern detective story about the disappearance of
an old man with a dark past. Peter McGarr, head of the
Serious Crimes Unit of the Garda Siochana, applies muscle to break through the sullen reserve of the islanders,
an inbred lot who glare coldly at all outsiders. Mr. Gill
gives a rough tongue to these crusty salts; but when he
puts the town behind him and looks out to sea, there's
poetry in his voice." N Y Times Book Rev

Death on a cold, wild river; a Peter McGarr
mystery. Morrow 1993 251p o.p.   LC 93-7729
"In the opening scene Nellie Millar, 'the best fisher
bar none in all of Ireland,' meets her picturesque death
while casting for trophy salmon in the swollen floodwaters of the Owenea River. Peter McGarr, the chief of
Dublin's murder squad and Nellie's former lover, carries
his grief to the village in Donegal where she is being
waked, only to discover that the drowning was no accident." N Y Times Book Rev
"Gill writes well, setting the tone for introspective passages with evocations of Ireland's wild coastal landscape
on one page, while amusing us with witty pub banter on
another. . . . Unpredictable, philosophical, funny, and
ever so satisfying." Booklist

LIST OF FICTIONAL WORKS

Gilman, Charlotte Perkins, 1860-1935

The Charlotte Perkins Gilman reader; "The yellow wallpaper" and other fiction; edited and introduced by Ann J. Lane. Pantheon Bks. 1980 208p o.p.   LC 80-7711

Contents: The yellow wallpaper; When I was a witch; If I were a man; The girl in the pink hat; The cottagette; The unnatural mother; Making a change; An honest woman; Turned; The widow's might; Mr. Peebles' heart; The crux; What Diantha did; Benigna Machiavelli; Unpunished; Moving the mountain; Herland; With her in Ourland

The editor "has selected representative pieces by the early-twentieth-century American feminist socialist, including her best known (and best) quasi-autobiographical story, 'The Yellow Wallpaper,' plus excerpts from four novels and three writings about utopias." Booklist

Charlotte Perkins Gilman's Utopian novels; edited and with an introduction by Minna Doskow. Fairleigh Dickinson Univ. Press 1999 389p

ISBN 0-8386-3761-2   LC 98-23510

Contents: Moving the mountain (1911); Herland; With her in Ourland

In Moving the mountain, an explorer, lost in Tibet for thirty years, returns to the United States in 1940 and finds a society totally transformed by women

Herland; with an introduction by Ann J. Lane. Pantheon Bks. 1979 xxiv, 147p o.p.

"Written in 1915, Herland was serialized in Gilman's monthly magazine, 'The Forerunner.'" Introduction

"On the eve of World War I, three American male explorers stumble onto an all-female society somewhere in the distant reaches of the earth. Unable to believe their eyes, they promptly set out to find the men of the society, convinced that, since 'this is a "civilized" country . . . there must be men.' . . . [The novel examines] what is masculine and what is feminine, what is culturally learned and what is biologically determined in our society." Publisher's note

also in Gilman, C. P. The Charlotte Perkins Gilman reader

also in Gilman, C. P. Charlotte Perkins Gilman's Utopian novels p150-269

Moving the mountain

In Gilman, C. P. The Charlotte Perkins Gilman reader

In Gilman, C. P. Charlotte Perkins Gilman's Utopian novels p37-149

With her in Ourland; sequel to Herland; edited by Mary Jo Deegan and Michael R. Hill; with an introduction by Mary Jo Deegan. Greenwood Press 1997 200p $100.95

ISBN 0-313-27614-5   LC 96-51135

"Contributions in women's studies"

Written in 1916, With her in Ourland was serialized in Gilman's magazine, The Forerunner

"He's a brash American adventurer; she's an independent, albeit sheltered, sociologist from Herland, a 2000-year-old, all-female society. Not surprisingly, when Vandyck (Van) and Ellador marry, most everything becomes a point of negotiation, if not contention: sexual relations, family obligations and attitudes about race, class and the welfare state." Publ Wkly

also in Gilman, C. P. The Charlotte Perkins Gilman reader

also in Gilman, C. P. Charlotte Perkins Gilman's Utopian novels p270-387

Gilman, Dorothy, 1923-

The amazing Mrs. Pollifax. Doubleday 1970 234p o.p.

Mrs. Emily Pollifax, widow and grandmother, combats international espionage at the request of the C.I.A. in this spy adventure. The scene is Istanbul where Mrs. Pollifax must help a double agent escape. That she does, outwitting the enemy with her own special brand of logic

The elusive Mrs. Pollifax. Doubleday 1971 240p o.p.

Mrs. Pollifax "the genteel grandmother-heroine swings into action for the CIA by transporting in her hat some forged passports to the Bulgarian underground which turns out to be a group of five amateurs. In her travels Mrs. Pollifax meets some young Americans, one of whom is ostensibly imprisoned for espionage but actually held for ransom, and Mrs. Pollifax involves the underground and a paid informer in a daring rescue plan. Amusing spy adventure with more appeal for readers of light fiction than for espionage buffs." Booklist

Kaleidoscope; a Countess Karitska novel. Ballantine Bks. 2002 244p $21

ISBN 0-345-44820-0   LC 2002-277874

"Madame Karitska's trade as a fortune teller attracts a strange array of clients, including an artistic woman whose husband abandons her to join a religious cult and an Italian immigrant with a 'cursed' child. Karitska also helps her good friend, Detective-Lieutenant Pruden, solve the hit-and-run death of a young violinist and the murder of a local philanthropist. Her most troubling case, however, occurs when a subway incident leaves her with an attaché case full of diamonds. This [is a] well-written episodic adventure." Libr J

Mrs. Pollifax and the whirling dervish. Doubleday 1990 196p o.p.   LC 89-25796

"Mrs. Pollifax's present assignment is to pose as the aunt of a C.I.A. agent while the two, in the guise of tourists, verify the bona fides of the informants, matching faces to photographs. To find the seven, Mrs. Pollifax and her escort are expected to spend a week traversing the desert and mountain areas that lie between Fez and the Algerian border. No sooner do they begin their mission than the first informant is murdered—and Mrs. Pollifax herself is in danger of becoming the killer's next victim." N Y Times Book Rev

"The countryside is depicted in great detail, and so are the native people. Gilman's eye for background matches her marvelous sense of adventure." Booklist

Mrs. Pollifax, innocent tourist. Fawcett Columbine 1997 203p o.p.   LC 96-47715

Mrs. Pollifax is on "a trip to the Middle East with her CIA friend Farrell to retrieve a manuscript written by a murdered dissident. The manuscript, thinly disguised as fiction, provides provocative details of Saddam Hussein's

Gilman, Dorothy, 1923-—*Continued*
reign of terror. The pickup, arranged through an interme-
diary, proves much more difficult than Farrell or Mrs.
Pollifax anticipated, what with smugglers disguised as
businessmen, attacks by knife-wielding sheikhs, car
chases, and rides on berserk camels. . . . Fun and entertaining, this one is sure to be a hit with the legion of
Mrs. Pollifax fans." Booklist

Mrs. Pollifax pursued. Fawcett Columbine 1995
198p o.p.   LC 94-27625
Mrs. Pollifax "discovers a young woman in her hall
closet hiding from some men in a white van. Eager as
always, she elicits the girl's story, eludes the villains,
and enables the CIA to resolve the situation, which involves kidnapping, shady investments, attempted murder,
and the grandson of Ubangiba's last king. Agents actually consult reference books for essential background information, and a few literary allusions build character or relate to earlier Pollifax appearances. This fast-moving tale
sports a lively, energetic style." Libr J

A palm for Mrs. Pollifax. Doubleday 1973 226p
ISBN 0-385-09134-6
Emily Pollifax "registers as a guest at a posh resort-
clinic in Switzerland where the C.I.A. thinks some stolen
plutonium has been hidden. In the course of her investigation Mrs. Pollifax discovers the murdered body of her
Interpol contact, meets a charming jewel thief who becomes her ally, befriends a frightened little boy who is
the son of a leader in a Middle East nation, and escapes
through a latrine chute from a mountain top castle where
she and the boy are hiding from the killers who intend
to use the plutonium to upset the balance of power in the
Middle East." Booklist

Thale's Folly. Ballantine Pub. Group 1999 199p
ISBN 0-449-00364-7   LC 98-27657
"When New York City novelist Andrew Thale checks
on some neglected family property in Massachusetts, he
discovers four weird squatters—and subsequent mystery."
Libr J
"At first, it seems Gilman is rounding up the usual literary suspects, but her genial and well-paced writing,
vivid landscapes, and quirky characters are greater than
the sum of the clichés." Booklist

The unexpected Mrs. Pollifax. Doubleday 1966
216p o.p.
"Published for the Crime Club"
A "tale of espionage with the chase in Mexico and
through the mountains of Albania. Emily Pollifax, a widow of 63, was startled by her doctor's suggestion that the
cure for her depression was a job. The only career that
inspired Emily was spying, and despite her lack of quali-
fications, off she went to CIA headquarters in Langly,
Virginia, to apply. How she became a routine courier,
and why unexpected developments brought into play every scrap of skill and knowledge she had acquired in her
former secure life, is an exciting discovery for the reader." Libr J

Gilman, Keith

Father's Day. Minotaur Books 2009 259p
$24.95
ISBN 978-0-312-38365-7; 0-312-38365-7
                                              LC 2009-08003

"Lou Klein, an ex-Philadelphia cop-turned-PI, returns
to his old neighborhood and moves into his deceased
mother's house. He has been asked to find the missing
daughter of one of his oldest friends. Complications arise
when Lou's own daughter comes to stay and bodies begin springing up all over Philadelphia with possible connections to his case. Narrated in a wise-old-guy tone that
is matched by Lou's knack for getting under people's
skin, this debut takes us on a roller-coaster ride of surprises." Libr J

Gilmore, Jennifer, 1970-

Golden country; a novel. Scribner 2006 315p
$25
ISBN 978-0-7432-8863-7; 0-7432-8863-7
                                             LC 2005-57586
"Spanning the first half of the twentieth century, Golden Country . . . [tells] the intertwining stories of three
Jewish immigrants seeking their fortunes—the handsome
and ambitious Seymour, a salesman-turned-gangster-
turned-Broadway producer; the gentle and pragmatic Joseph, a door-to-door salesman; . . . and the irresistible
Frances Gold, who grows up in Brooklyn, stars in Seymour's first show, and marries the man who invents television. Their three families, though inextricably connected for years, are brought together for the first time by
the engagement of Seymour's son and Joseph's daughter." Publisher's note
"An ingeniously plotted family yarn. Gilmore's careful
planning results in a satisfying blend of story lines, and
her refusal to settle on one simple perspective enlivens
the myth of the American Dream." N Y Times Book
Rev

Gingrich, Newt

Gettysburg; a novel of the Civil War; {by}
Newt Gingrich and William Forstchen; and Albert
S. Hanser, contributing editor. St. Martin's Press
2003 463p il $24.95
ISBN 0-312-30935-X   LC 2003-41381
"On July 1, 1863, the Army of Virginia, under the
command of Gen. Robert E. Lee, and the Army of the
Potomac, under Gen. George G. Meade, clashed in deadly combat near Gettysburg, PA. Of course, Union forces
won, but Gingrich and Forstchen imagine a different outcome in which Confederate forces do a surprise march
around Union lines to flank and cut off the Union troops
from their supply and information routes. In the course
of their narrative, the authors depict the gallantry and
heroism of Lee, Longstreet, Chamberlain, Hancock,
Hunt, and many other officers and enlisted men on both
sides of the conflict." Libr J

Grant comes east; a novel of the Civil War; [by]
Newt Gingrich, William R. Forstchen and Albert
S. Hanser, contributing editor. 1st ed. Thomas
Dunne Books\St. Martin's Press 2004 404p il map
$24.95
ISBN 0-312-30937-6   LC 2004-43894
This alternate-history sequel to the author's Gettysburg
"centers on the Union government's bringing General
Grant eastward from his recent victory in Vicksburg; of
course, the immediate ramification of Lee's win at Get-
tysburg . . . is the threatened safety of Washington,

Gingrich, Newt—*Continued*

D.C.–and further down the line, the possibility of actual and official recognition of the Confederacy by the European powers. Gingrich and Forstchen's readjustments to history are notably original." Booklist

Gino, Carol, 1941-

(jt. auth) Puzo, M. The family

Ginsberg, Debra, 1962-

The grift; a novel. Shaye Areheart Books 2008 337p $23.95

ISBN 978-0-307-38272-6; 0-307-38272-9

LC 2008-947

"In The Grift, charlatan psychic Marina Marks relocates to an elite Southern California beach town, where she plans to fleece the local glitterati. But after accurately predicting a murder, Marina realizes her power of second sight is real — and she tries to hunt down the killer." Entertainment Wkly

"Leaving aside any question of tingling paranormal subtext, The Grift presents a lifelike, multishaded rendering of San Diego's blend of cultures, classes, ancestries and motivations. Ms. Ginsberg folds Marina into the lives and complicated romances of the locals like a stripe of colored sand in a painted-desert souvenir bottleSThe Grift is a gift with no strings attached, no dark outcome to dread, a satisfyingly voyeuristic vision of a mysterious stranger's supernaturally charged fortune." N Y Times Book Rev

Giroux, E. X.

A death for a dancer. St. Martin's Press 1985 198p o.p. LC 85-10896

"Barrister Robert Forsythe and his vigilant secretary, Miss Sanderson, are pressed by another barrister into examining a case involving a body found inconveniently in a miniature Chinese Temple on one of England's most sumptuous estates. The victim is con artist Katherine St. Croix, whose demise throws the family of Sir Amyas Dancer into giddy paroxysms of speculation that can only be relieved, claims Dancer, by a private investigator. Enter Forsythe and Sanderson and exit normalcy as the Dancer family surrounds them with their bizarrely eccentric demeanor." Booklist

Girzone, Joseph F.

Joshua and the city. Doubleday 1995 242p

ISBN 0-385-47420-2 LC 94-41941

In this inspirational novel set in late 20th century New York "a mysterious stranger named Joshua appears, bringing with him a vision for healing the city's numerous social ills. As he walks the city streets, Joshua enters the lives of a number of people who are trapped in the downward spiral of their society, offering them love and strong hope for a brighter future. Joshua reaches out to both rich and poor as he tries to build God's kingdom on Earth." Libr J

Joshua, the homecoming. Doubleday 1999 259p $19.95

ISBN 0-385-49509-9 LC 99-33129

In this inspirational novel set in 20th century America, the solitary carpenter Joshua returns to the small town of Auburn after a 20 year absence. Finding fear and spiritual insecurity among the new generation due to the coming Apocalypse, he calms the people with reminders of God's love

The shepherd. Macmillan 1990 246p o.p.

LC 90-2351

"On the eve of David Campbell's consecration as a Catholic bishop, he has an all-night vision that changes him from a strict observer of church law to a radical reformer." Libr J

"Girzone's story is a neat picture of where many American Catholics wish their church would head, but it may be far too unrealistically drawn to have an impact on real lives." Booklist

Glass, Julia

I see you everywhere. Pantheon Books 2008 287p $24.95

ISBN 978-0-375-42275-1; 0-375-42275-7

LC 2008-00212

"Sisters Clement (Clem) and Louisa Jardine alternate recounting their lives from 1980 to 2005, literally traversing the globe in pursuit of fulfillment and, sometimes, love. Clem, four years the younger, is a biologist and wildlife specialist who protects various forms of endangered species, herself included. Louisa is a potter-turned-art magazine writer who feels overshadowed by her daredevil sibling." Libr J

"Mourning, a dish that never grows cold, is the subtext of I See You Everywhere, but it is only part of the feast. Rich, intricate and alive with emotion, the book reconstructs the complicated bonds between Louisa and Clem, making neither sister a villain, neither a hero." N Y Times Book Rev

Three Junes. Pantheon Bks. 2002 353p

ISBN 0-375-42144-0

* LC 2001-55448

A "narrative of the McLeod family during three vital summers. . . . Paul McLeod, the reticent Scots widower introduced in the first section, is the father of Fenno, the central character of the middle section, who is a reserved, self-protective gay bookstore owner in Manhattan; both have dealings with the third section's searching young artist, Fern Olitsky, whose guilt in the wake of her husband's death leaves her longing for—and fearful of—beginning anew." Publ Wkly

"Free of gimmickry, 'Three Junes' brilliantly rescues, then refurbishes, the traditional plot-driven novel." N Y Times Book Rev

The whole world over. Pantheon Books 2006 506p $25.95

ISBN 0-375-42274-9 LC 2005-54043

"Greenie Duquette has a small bakery in Manhattan's West Village that supplies pastries to restaurants, including that of her genial gay friend Walter. When Walter recommends Greenie to the governor of New Mexico, she seizes the chance to become the Southwesterner's pastry chef and to take a break from her marriage to Alan Glazier, a psychiatrist with hidden issues. Taking their four-year-old son, George, with her, Greenie leaves for New Mexico, while figures from her and Alan's pasts

Glass, Julia—*Continued*

challenge their already strained marriage." Publ Wkly

"Glass is too capable to need recipes and four-legged friends to make her fiction a pleasure. It's a tribute to this unassuming but conspicuously talented novelist that even with far too many of them, The Whole World Over so often manages to sing." N Y Times Book Rev

Glavinic, Thomas, 1972-

Night work; translated from the German by John Brownjohn. Canongate 2008 375p pa $15

ISBN 978-1-84767-184-4; 1-84767-184-5

Original German edition, 2006

"The premise is incredibly simple. Jonas is a young Viennese man with an undemanding and unfulfilling job as an adviser on interior design, and a girlfriend, Marie, who has gone to visit her sister in Scotland for a few days. On July 4 he wakes up, and is surprised by how quiet the streets are. He can't get Marie on her mobile. The television is only showing static snow, on every channel. As he ventures out, he finds that the world is deserted. Every single living being has vanished. Something apocalyptic has happened, and for some reason Jonas has survived it. . . . Night Work is quite self-consciously philosophical. . . . The solitude makes Jonas prone to musing – about God, identity, love, death and memory. None of this jars or seems superfluous to the narrative." Scotsman

Gledson, John, 1945-

(tr) Hatoum, M. The brothers

Gloss, Molly

The hearts of horses. Houghton Mifflin Co. 2007 289p $24

ISBN 978-0-618-79990-9; 0-618-79990-7

LC 2007-8521

This novel "features a wandering taciturn tomboy who finds her place in rural Oregon while the men are away at war. After she leaves home in 1917, 19-year-old Martha Lessen plans to travel from farm to farm in Elwha County, Oregon, breaking horses left behind by owners away fighting. She winds up in small town Shelby, where farmers George and Louise Bliss convince her to stay the winter with them after she domesticates their broncos with soft words and songs instead of lariats and hobbles. While breaking the town's horses, Martha meets a slovenly drunk, a clan of Western European immigrants and two unmarried sisters running a ranch with the help of an awkward, secretive teenager." Publ Wkly

Gloss bases her novel on "historical accounts of cowgirls in the American West. With obvious appeal for horse lovers, it has a homespun quality, and varies in action between a gentle canter and energetic gallop." Libr J

Goddard, Robert

Beyond recall; a novel. Holt & Co. 1998 310p

ISBN 0-8050-5110-4   LC 97-28895

First published 1997 in the United Kingdom

When Chris Napier returns to Cornwall for "his niece's wedding, he is shocked to be confronted by childhood friend Nick Lanyon. Lanyon's father was hanged for the murder of Chris' great-uncle, an adventurer responsible for the Napier family fortune—money that would have gone to the Lanyons if there had been no murder. A mentally disturbed Nick promptly hangs himself after challenging Chris to find out the truth about the murder—that Lanyon's father was not the killer at all. Chris, feeling guilty about Nick's death, sets out to do just that." Booklist

"There's an elegant arc to Goddard's fluid style, which gracefully orchestrates the story over its broad time span and through the ambiguous testimony of its complex characters." N Y Times Book Rev

Into the blue. Poseidon Press 1990 415p

ISBN 0-671-70482-6   LC 90-42481

"When Heather Mallender, English schoolteacher, disappears while sightseeing in Greece with Harry Barnett, Barnett must discover whether she disappeared voluntarily or was a victim of malice. In Hitchcockian tradition, the hero finds himself trapped in a web of intrigue that threatens not only his reputation, but also his life. Barnett's quest leads him from Greece to England and back, followed everywhere he goes, encountering suspicion and resistance at every turn." Libr J

"During this quest, Harry's courage is tested as well as his judgment of people—all of whom turn out to be totally and depressingly human. An everyman's hero, against all mental and emotional odds, Harry finds Heather and renewed self-respect. A very satisfying novel in every way." Booklist

Never go back. Delta Trade Paperbacks 2007 336p pa $12

ISBN 978-0-385-34063-2; 038534063X

LC 2007-6336

First published 2006 in the United Kingdom

"In 1955, Harry Barnett and a group of fellow Royal Air Force servicemen participated in a teaching experiment in a castle on the outskirts of Aberdeen, Scotland. (Each agreed to be a guinea pig in lieu of punishment for bad behavior.) Now, 50 years later, surviving RAF alumni are invited to a reunion at the same royal locale. Though Barnett, now 70, is reluctant to be away from his wife and young daughter in Vancouver, British Columbia, he decides to go. Tragedy strikes when one of the retired servicemen jumps from the train en route from London (or was he pushed?). In the midst of the reunion, a suspicious automobile accident kills another, and suddenly this get-together doesn't seem like such a good plan. Police soon name Harry and former business partner Barry, whose shady financial dealings once landed him in prison, as prime suspects. Certain the violence is linked to the experiments carried out half a century ago, the two men launch an investigation of their own. Goddard's latest offering marks the return of unlikely hero Harry Barnett, star of Into the Blue (1990) and Out of the Sun (1997). It's a crackling good read, with clipped prose, complex characters, and a smart, sinuous plot." Booklist

Godden, Rumer, 1907-1998

The battle of the Villa Fiorita. Viking 1963 312p o.p.

A "novel about the immediate effects of their parent's divorce on two English children who run off to Italy to persuade their mother to return home. She is enjoying a

Godden, Rumer, 1907-1998—*Continued*

premarital honeymoon, days filled with sun, golden light, quiet and love, with an English film director. The two children crash into this peaceful pattern and the battle lines are drawn, children against adults." Publ Wkly

Godden's "characters live and linger in the mind, and the very feel of golden Italy counterpoints the sharp battle in which both sides so tragically lose." Libr J

Black Narcissus. Little, Brown 1939 294p o.p.
*

A "story of a small group of Anglican nuns newly settled in a convent, formerly a general's pleasure palace, on a high ledge facing Himalayan winds and snows. How the strange pagan environment and unusual experiences affect each of the Sisters, and how a year's effort to teach and heal the natives come to naught is related in a portrayal impressive for its beauty, poignancy and insight." Bookmark

The greengage summer; a novel. Viking 1958 218p o.p.
*

"The story tells of the summer adventures of a group of English children, in somewhat shadowed circumstances, at a second-rate hotel on the Marne, near the forest of Compiègne. . . . Their mother is taken seriously ill as they are enroute to the hotel Les Oeillets, at Vieux-Moutiers. Upon arrival, she is rushed to the hospital for a long stay. The disconcerted children are stranded at the hotel where neither the proprietress, Mademoiselle Zizi, nor her henchwoman, Mme. Corbet, want them. It is the somewhat mysterious Englishman, Eliot, apparently romantically involved with Mlle. Zizi, who takes them under his wing and casually superintends their stay." N Y Times Book Rev

"There is real evil in Miss Godden's novel as well as real good: sex and theft and even murder intrude upon her dewy world as baldly as on the daily papers. But even violence she handles with consummate delicacy. If she allows a moral to creep in, it is that we lose something valuable in gaining maturity." N Y Her Trib Books

Pippa passes. Morrow 1994 171p
ISBN 0-688-13397-5   LC 94-18336

"Pippa Fane, is the youngest member of the Midlands City Ballet. Chosen to go with the company on its Italian tour, she becomes fascinated with Venice, confused by romantic overtures from admirers of both sexes, and challenged by the demands of her dancing troupe." Libr J

"In less able hands, these highly romantic goings-on would seem contrived, but Godden's graceful storytelling keeps readers enthralled, with gorgeous Venice and the nitty-gritty of the dance troupe's routine providing a convincing backdrop for her winsome ingenue." Publ Wkly

Godey, John, 1912-2006

The taking of Pelham one two three. Putnam 1973 316p o.p.   LC 72-92306

A suspense novel about a "New York subway train that is hijacked by four desperate men who threaten to murder sixteen passengers unless the mayor pays $1 million ransom. . . . Ryder, the brain behind the caper, is an amoral, asexual fatalist who killed for country in Vietnam and for profit as a mercenary in the Congo and

Biafra. Longman, bitter at being sacked from his subway-motorman job, is willing to exploit his intimate knowledge of the transit system. Steever is a . . . hood who follows orders and Welcome is a surly Mafia reject who doesn't." Newsweek

"Brutally realistic and coarse in its details and language, but will be popular with suspense story readers." Booklist

Godwin, Gail, 1937-

Evensong. Ballantine Bks. 1999 405p
ISBN 0-345-37244-1   LC 98-15861
Sequel to Father Melancholy's daughter

Margaret Bonner (née Gower) "is now the pastor at All Saints High Balsam, a parish set in a conservative little resort community high in the Smokies in West North Carolina. She married the much older Adrian Bonner, who is struggling as headmaster of a local boys' school. . . . Into their lives, as they approach the millennium (the book is set a year from now, at Advent 1999) comes Tony, a strange old man with dyed hair who represents himself as a monk on the move; Grace Munger, a local woman with a grim past who has set up as an evangelical revivalist and seeks Margaret's participation in an end-time parade to bring salvation and healing to the mountains; and Chase Zorn, a bright but self-destructive orphaned youngster who is a student at Adrian's school." Publ Wkly

Godwin "has created a character who has enough flaws to satisfy contemporary skeptics but who also struggles convincingly with the old-fashioned task of being a good person. For all its leisurely pace, Evensong turns out, near the end, to have wasted few words." Time

The finishing school. Viking 1985 322p
ISBN 0-670-31494-3
* LC 84-40069

"Fourteen, yearning to grow up, and grieving for the world of Southern gentility she left behind when her widowed mother moved them up north to live with a determinedly middle-class aunt, Justin Stokes 'falls in love' that first summer in rural New York. Ursula DeVane, who shares the neighboring old mansion with her reclusive pianist brother, is 44, a sophisticated bohemian who dazzles . . . Justin with her worldliness and her attentions. A cabin in the woods becomes Justin's 'finishing school' as the . . . tale of Ursula's mysterious past unfolds. . . . [This story is] told from the point of view of a grown-up Justin, nearly 30 years later." Libr J

"'The Finishing School' is a strikingly accurate examination of the affinity between adolescence and middle age." N Y Times Book Rev

The good husband. Ballantine Bks. 1994 468p o.p.   LC 94-5651

Death "is the metaphorical 'good husband' whom brilliant professor Magda Danvers invokes as she lies dying, a process in which she participates with the same intellectual zest she has brought to her scholarship. While her body wastes away from cancer, she is devotedly tended by her own 'good husband,' Francis Lake, a former seminarian 12 years her junior. They are an unlikely pair: self-effacing Francis is content in his role as house husband and general factotum to flamboyant, iconoclastic Magda. In contrast, the union of Alice and Hugo Henry should constitute marital serenity. Hugo is a 50ish South-

Godwin, Gail, 1937-—*Continued*

ern novelist temporarily occupying a chair at Aurelia College; Alice is the empathetic editor who shepherded to publication the work on which his celebrity rests. Yet an icy chill has descended between them after the loss, at birth, of their son. And Hugo's prickly abrasiveness has been exacerbated by writer's block." Publ Wkly

"Godwin's intensely drawn characters are vividly portrayed during the most intimate times of love, marriage, and death." Libr J

A mother and two daughters. Viking 1982 564p
ISBN 0-670-49021-0   LC 81-65286
"Suddenly widowed Nell Strickland and her two daughters, reunited in grief, are all on the verge of change as the story begins. Bohemian Cate is twice divorced, almost 40, out of a teaching job and threatened by losses, while younger Lydia, who just left her husband, is winning: a college degree, a new lover, and fame as a TV personality. Ambivalent about accommodation and possibility but 'hospitable . . . to whatever came next,' each has created herself anew by the end. The North Carolina setting is as precisely evoked as [are] the many unusual, amusing characters." Libr J

Queen of the underworld; a novel. Random House 2006 336p $24.95
ISBN 0-345-48318-9   LC 2005-48592
"Emma Gant, Godwin's alter ego, is an eager young reporter just out of college, who lands at a Miami paper in 1959 and makes her way through a landscape populated by scheming journalists, Jewish mobsters, Cuban exiles, a schmalzy ex-beauty queen, and the former madam of an 'elite island whorehouse.'" New Yorker

"A master stylist with a dozen novels to her credit, Godwin has never written more voluptuously, nor had as much fun with a character or setting." Booklist

Goethe, Johann Wolfgang von, 1749-1832

Novella
  In Goethe, J. W. v. The sorrows of young
    Werther, and Novella p169-201

The sorrows of young Werther
  In Goethe, J. W. v. The sorrows of young
    Werther, and Novella p1-167

The sorrows of young Werther, and Novella; translated by Elizabeth Mayer and Louise Brogan; poems translated by W. H. Auden; foreword by W. H. Auden. Modern Lib. 1993 c1971 xx, 201p
ISBN 0-679-60064-7
                              * LC 93-5007
A translation of two of Goethe's works, originally published 1774 and 1828 respectively; this is a reissue of the 1971 edition published by Random House

"Werther is a sensitive artist, ill at ease in society and hopelessly in love with Charlotte, who is engaged to someone else. This novel, with the eventual suicide of the hero, caused a sensation throughout Europe." Oxford Companion to Engl Lit

Novella, is an example of a specific literary genre, the idyll. A tame tiger which escapes during a fire pursues a princess and is killed. The animal trainer and his family, lamenting its death, persuade the prince, who has been out hunting a lion, to let them tame that animal

rather than kill it. According to W. H. Auden it is "a parable about the relation between wild nature and human craft"

Goff, Annabel Davis- *See* Davis-Goff, Annabel

Gogol´, Nikolaï Vasil´evich, 1809-1852

The collected tales of Nikolai Gogol; translated and annotated by Richard Pevear and Larissa Volokhonsky. Pantheon Bks. 1998 xxii, 435p
ISBN 0-679-43023-7   LC 97-37228
Contents: St. John's Eve; The night before Christmas; The terrible vengeance; Ivan Fyodorovich Shponka and his aunt; Old world landowners; Viy; The story of how Ivan Ivanovich quarreled with Ivan Nikiforovich; Nevsky Prospect; The diary of a madman; The nose; The carriage; The portrait; The overcoat

Dead souls; [by] Nikolai Gogol; translated and annotated by Richard Pevear and Larissa Volokhonsky. Pantheon Bks. 1996 xxiv, 402p
ISBN 0-679-43022-9
                              * LC 95-24357
Original Russian edition, 1842
"Considered one of the world's finest satires, this picaresque work traces the adventures of the social-climbing Pavel Ivanovich Chichikov, a dismissed civil servant out to seek his fortune. It is admired not only for its enduring comic portraits but also for its sense of moral purpose." Merriam-Webster's Ency of Lit

The overcoat, and other tales of good and evil; [by] Nikolai V. Gogol; translated with an introduction by David Magarshack. Norton 1965 c1957 271p o.p.
This collection was first published 1957 in paperback by Doubleday with title: Tales of good and evil
Contents: The terrible vengeance; Ivan Fyodorovich Shponka and his aunt; The portrait; Nevsky Avenue; The nose; The overcoat

Gold, Glen David, 1964-

Sunnyside. Alfred A. Knopf 2009 559p $26.95
ISBN 978-0-307-27068-9; 0-307-27068-8
                              LC 2009-03804
This novel "novel tells the story of early Chaplin, the beginning of Hollywood as we know it and a young America getting ready to flex its muscles. Sunnyside starts shortly before America's involvement in World War I, on a day when Chaplin is simultaneously spied in hundreds of places around the country. It is told by a young Chaplin, already a star but not yet a legend; an Adonis-like lighthouse keeper; and an overeducated ne'erdowell. While the latter two do cross paths with Chaplin, their story is the story of a war fought by dregs and managed by idiots. . . . Chaplin does not go to war. Instead he tours with archrival Mary Pickford and friend Douglas Fairbanks, raising money for the cause. We travel with Chaplin, underneath that hat with his thoughts as he blunders his way past self-doubt and contempt and into greatness." BookPage

Goldberg, Myla

Bee season; a novel. Doubleday 2000 275p hardcover o.p. pa $13.95

ISBN 0-385-49879-9; 0-385-49880-2 (pa)
LC 99-47933

This novel concerns an eleven-year-old girl, Eliza Naumann, who wins the National Spelling Bee. "Eliza's supernatural gift for spelling thrills her father, Saul, a self-styled Jewish scholar who now believes he can train his daughter to literally talk to God. Unfortunately, that means shunting aside Eliza's older brother, Aaron, who joins a religious cult, and her scarily remote mother, Miriam, who begins breaking into houses in search of missing pieces of herself." Newsweek

"Some of the events that unfold . . . seem a little contrived. But Goldberg engenders considerable suspense around both Eliza's string of spelling successes and the fates of the other Naumanns." Time

Wickett's remedy. Doubleday 2005 326p $24.95
ISBN 0-385-51324-0   LC 2005-48103

This novel is "about a young Irish-American woman facing down tragedy during the Great Flu epidemic of 1918". Publisher's note

"In the margins of each page are voices from the dead commenting on or clarifying plot points. . . . There's a lot going on here, some of which is underdeveloped. Other parts are just plain distracting, particularly the notes from beyond, which are more often hokey than profound. But Goldberg is a skillful, smooth writer who has clearly done her research, and readers who can tune out the noise will be rewarded." Time

Goldblatt, Howard, 1939-

(tr) Mo Yan. Life and death are wearing me out

Golden, Arthur

Memoirs of a geisha; a novel. Knopf 1997 434p il $26.95; pa $7.99

ISBN 0-375-40011-7; 1-4000-9689-8 (pa)
* LC 97-74747

"How nine-year-old Chiyo, sold with her sister into slavery by their father after their mother's death, becomes Sayuri, the beautiful geisha accomplished in the art of entertaining men, is the focus of this . . . novel. Narrating her life story from her elegant suite in the Waldorf Astoria, Sayuri tells of her traumatic arrival at the *Nitta okiya* (a geisha house), where she endures harsh treatment from Granny and Mother, the greedy owners, and from Hatsumomo, the sadistically cruel head geisha. But Sayuri's chance meeting with the Chairman, who shows her kindness, makes her determined to become a geisha. Under the tutelage of the renowned Mameha, she becomes a leading geisha of the 1930s and 1940s." Libr J

"Rarely has a world so closed and foreign been evoked with such natural assurance, from the aesthetics of the Kyoto geisha's 'art'—to the fetishized sexuality of Gion in the thirties and forties, at once delicate and crude, repressed and flagrant." New Yorker

Golding, William, 1911-1993

Close quarters. Farrar, Straus & Giroux 1987 281p o.p.

* LC 87-5351

This second volume of the trilogy begun with Rites of passage is a "tale of the tragic misadventures befalling an 18th century fighting ship now converted to transporting cargo and passengers on the treacherous voyage from England to Australia. The novel is cast as a journal written by Edmund FitzHenry Talbot, a well-meaning, somewhat uncertain, slightly pompous officer and gentleman enroute to Sydney and a career in His Majesty's service. As a result of a green sailor's blunder, the ship's masts shatter, and it founders. Golding's principal achievement is the vivid, detailed depiction of a disintegrating vessel in the tropical seas, its progressive decay, and the wretchedness and despair of its passengers." Publ Wkly

Followed by Fire down below

Darkness visible. Farrar, Straus & Giroux 1979 265p o.p.

* LC 79-19206

"A child hideously maimed in the bombing of London during World War II grows up to inspire the messianic fantasies of the people with whom he comes in contact. In Golding's dark world the horrors of the physically deformed are mirrored in—but are no match for—the spiritual monsters who inhabit the novel's strange vision of contemporary life. A powerful contemplation of the evil at the root of human behavior." Booklist

Fire down below. Farrar, Straus & Giroux 1989 313p o.p.

* LC 88-18079

This is the concluding volume of the trilogy begun in Rites of Passage and continued in Close Quarters. "Narrated by young Edmund FitzHenry Talbot, the trilogy recounts his voyage from England to Australia on a former man-of-war during the Napoleonic era. The last of the three novels takes the badly damaged ship through several storms, an encounter with a gigantic iceberg (actually the continent of Antarctica, but the crew doesn't know it) and finally to the safe shelter of Sydney Harbor." N Y Times Book Rev

Golding is "translucent and economical. In his writing, allegorical motifs are revealed fleetingly in the everyday and in the ordinary. He is at once a complex and highly readable novelist." Economist

The inheritors. Harcourt 1962 c1955 233p o.p.
First published 1955 in the United Kingdom

A narrative "inhabiting the near-animal consciousness of Lok, a Neanderthal man, and describing in his clumsy terms and with great pathos the casual destruction of his species by *Homo sapiens*. The reader is shown his ancestors, already armed, arrogant, murderous, and corrupt—not superior to the Neanderthalers, only more clever and more evil." Wakeman. World Authors, 1950-1970

Lord of the flies; introduction by E. M. Forster; with a biographical and critical note by E. L. Epstein; illustrated by Ben Gibson. 50th anniversary ed. Berkley 2003 315p $23.95; pa $13

ISBN 0-399-52920-9; 0-399-50148-7 (pa)
* LC 2003-54825

Golding, William, 1911-1993—*Continued*

"A Perigee book"

First published 1954 in the United Kingdom; first United States edition, 1955, by Coward-McCann

"Stranded on an island, a group of English schoolboys leave innocence behind in a struggle for survival. A political structure modeled after English government is set up and a hierarchy develops, but forces of anarchy and aggression surface. The boys' existence begins to degenerate into a savage one. They are rescued from their microcosmic society to return to an adult, stylized milieu filled with the same psychological tensions and moral voids. Adventure and allegory are brilliantly combined in this novel." Shapiro. Fic for Youth. 3d edition

Rites of passage. Farrar, Straus & Giroux 1980 278p o.p.

* LC 80-16809

In this first volume of a trilogy the author "is fascinated by what might have occurred on a long sea voyage to the Antipodes (Australia) in the Napoleonic era. The passengers are a motley lot out of Britain; the crew, officers and men, and a tough-minded captain who hates the clergy, find their scapegoat in a pitiable parson who has no idea of his own latent homosexuality. Told partly from the viewpoint of an aristocratic dilettante aboard and then in the words set down by the tormented victim in a journal meant for his sister but becoming almost a confession to God." Publ Wkly

"In a sense the novel seems highly artificial, not only in its careful, detailed recreation of the period, but also in the elaborate system of correspondences and parallels—some clear, some obscure—which underpins the narration. Yet at the same time it is an extremely lively, enjoyable piece of work. Readers who know only the early Golding will be surprised by its humor." Times Lit Suppl

Followed by Close quarters

Goldman, William, 1931-

Marathon man. Delacorte Press 1974 309p o.p.

*

"'Babe' Levy, a graduate student, spends his free time running, and dreams of being a great marathon runner. The death of his brother in Babe's apartment starts a chain of mysterious and terrifying events. Pursued by government agents and ex-Nazis, Babe struggles to escape being assassinated. The torture scenes may make this suspenseful story an ordeal for some readers." Shapiro. Fic for Youth. 3d edition

Goldsborough, Robert

The missing chapter; a Nero Wolfe mystery. Bantam Bks. 1993 229p o.p.   LC 93-13714

A publisher hires Nero Wolfe and Archie Goodwin "to investigate the death, labeled a suicide, of Charles Childress, an ill-tempered author who had recently angered several people, including his agent, his editor and the possibly corrupt reviewer who had lambasted the latest Childress novel." Publ Wkly

"The publishing details ring true, and . . . Goldsborough does a masterly job with the Wolfe legacy." Booklist

Goldsmith, Olivia

The First Wives Club. Poseidon Press 1992 480p

ISBN 0-671-74693-6   LC 91-30959

"Annie, Elise, and Brenda are all good wives who have helped their husbands achieve success. Now that their men are at the pinnacle, they find themselves dumped for younger, sleeker 'trophy wives.' So they band together to form the 'First Wives Club' for the purpose of seeing justice done." Libr J

"This empowering romp will delight and invigorate nearly any woman who's ever stewed over a bad break-up." Publ Wkly

Pen pals. Dutton 2002 359p

ISBN 0-525-94644-6   LC 2001-47418

Protagonist Jennifer Spencer is "a rising star on Wall Street who is working at a prestigious firm and engaged to a brilliant lawyer. To help protect her trusted mentor-boss from exposure, Jennifer agrees to be the point person in an SEC investigation. After everything goes awry, Jennifer finds herself shackled in Jennings, a women's prison not at all like the country club, white-collar crime camp she envisioned. . . . The path from the despair of prison life to female conquest is glorious and satisfying without being man-hating; the cast of characters perfectly blends women from all walks of life, joined by their common goal." Booklist

Young wives; a novel. HarperCollins Pubs. 2000 512p $25

ISBN 0-06-017553-2   LC 99-48167

This novel features three protagonists: "sweet, innocent Angie, whose uptight but good-looking Boston lawyer husband is two-timing with his best friend; Jada, an African-American heroine who is at once a bank manager, churchgoer and devoted mother . . . and whose husband is a ne'er-do-well lazybones; and houseproud Michelle Russo, whose dream-boat Italian mate is . . . a high-level drug dealer on the side. All three women are put through purgatory by their husbands, crooked lawyers and a bent legal system until . . . they fight back in all-for-one, one-for-all style." Publ Wkly

Goldstein, Ann

(tr) Ferrante, E. The lost daughter

González Echevarría, Roberto

(ed) The Oxford book of Latin American short stories. See The Oxford book of Latin American short stories

Goodis, David, 1917-1967

Down there
    In Crime novels: American noir of the 1950s

Nightfall; a novel; with a new introduction by Bill Pronzini. Millipede Press 2007 213p $40; pa $14

ISBN   978-1-933618-18-0;   1-933618-18-3; 9781933618173 (pa); 1933618175 (pa)

Goodis, David, 1917-1967—*Continued*
First published 1947 by Messner
"Jim Vanning, a commercial artist living in Manhattan, is being hunted by a group of bank robbers who believe he ran off with $300,000 of their ill-gotten money. He's also being watched by a detective who's trying to suss out what Vanning did with the satchel of cash. Vanning denies stealing the money, but the money hardly matters—the satchel is just a MacGuffin. Nightfall's real story is about Vanning's despair about how to behave rationally when he knows he's being watched and the detective's self-questioning about whether a man can ever act with integrity without falling under suspicion. It's a relatively big theme for a noir, but Goodis keeps the story earthbound, rooting it in cynical observations designed to keep the mood of paranoia going." Washington City Paper

Goodman, Allegra

Intuition; a novel. Dial Press 2006 344p $25; pa $13
ISBN 0-385-33612-8; 0-385-33610-1 (pa)
LC 2005-51940
"Sandy Glass, a charismatic, publicity-seeking oncologist, and Marion Mendelssohn, a pure, exacting scientist, are codirectors of a lab at the Philpott Institute dedicated to cancer research and desperately in need of a grant. Both mentors and supervisors of their young postdoctoral proteges, Glass and Mendelssohn demand dedication and obedience in a competitive environment where funding is scarce and results elusive. So when the experiments of Cliff Bannaker, a young postdoc in a rut, begin to work, the entire lab becomes giddy with new-found expectations. But Cliff's rigorous colleague–and girlfriend–Robin Decker suspects the unthinkable: that his findings are fraudulent." Publisher's note
"With subtle but uncanny effectiveness, Goodman illuminates the inner lives of each character, depicting events from one point of view until another section suddenly throws that perspective into doubt. The result is an episodically paced but extremely engaging novel that reflects the stops and starts of the scientific process, as well as its dependence on the complicated individuals who do the work." Publ Wkly

Paradise park; a novel. Dial Press (NY) 2001 360p
ISBN 0-385-33416-8
LC 00-49376
This novel's heroine-narrator Sharon Spiegelman "is on a lifelong tear through the world in search of God. . . . Abandoned in a fleabag hotel in Waikiki sometime in the mid-1970's by her folk-dancing partner, with little more than a macramé bikini to her name, she throws herself into a chaotic, all-consuming quest for human and divine love." N Y Times Book Rev
"Like Saul Bellow and Philip Roth before her, Goodman has achieved a breakthrough book by discovering and recording a thoroughly uninhibited narrative voice." Time

Goodman, Carol

The drowning tree. Ballantine Books 2004 339p
ISBN 0-345-46211-4
LC 2004-47638

"Juno McKay is a glass artist, caught up with running a business and raising a teenaged daughter. A college reunion, which she reluctantly attends, brings up issues from the past and creates new problems when a close friend dies under mysterious circumstances. . . . Filled with descriptions of beautiful Hudson River scenery and references to mythology and art, this gripping novel will hold the reader's attention until the very last page." Libr J

The night villa; a novel. Ballantine Books 2008 413p pa $14
ISBN 978-0-345-47960-0; 0-345-47960-2
LC 2008-8519
"Classics professor Sophie Chase, after barely surviving a gunman with ties to a sinister cult, joins an expedition to Capri. A donor has funded both the exact reconstruction of a Roman villa destroyed when Mount Vesuvius buried nearby Herculaneum in A.D. 79, and a computer system that can decipher the charred scrolls being excavated from the villa's ruins. Sophie's hopes for a recuperative idyll fade after her old boyfriend, who disappeared years before into the same cult as the campus gunman, appears in the area, implicating the cult in a criminal conspiracy." Publ Wkly
"The pleasure of a Carol Goodman novel is in her enviable command of the classical canon–and the deft way she [writes] a book that's light enough for a weekend on the beach but literary enough for a weekend in the Hamptons." Chicago Tribune

The seduction of water. Ballantine Bks. 2003 357p
ISBN 0-345-45090-6
LC 2002-34463
This "is the story of Iris Greenfeder, a teacher who would rather be a writer, and the secrets her mother kept and her search for the truth about her mother's death." Libr J
"Mystery, folklore, a thoroughly modern romance, a strong sense of place and a winning combination of erudition and accessibility make this . . . novel a treat." Publ Wkly

Goolrick, Robert, 1948-

A reliable wife; a novel. Algonquin Books of Chapel Hill 2009 291p $23.95
ISBN 978-1-56512-596-4; 1-56512-596-7
LC 2008-49700
"In 1907, in a small Wisconsin town that bears his name, Ralph Truitt, the wealthy owner of an iron foundry, waits on the cusp of a looming blizzard for the train carrying Catherine Land, his mail-order bride from Chicago. From their first encounter, these desperate characters are plunged into a maelstrom of conflict." BookPage
"Goolrick is a ticky, mannered writer with an unusual love of clauses that can sometimes give you comma whiplash. This, combined with the graphic problems 'they' are having throughout the novel may be enough to turn some readers off. And that would be a shame, because in the middle of this book a secret is revealed that pushes the plot forward. Freed into clearer storytelling, A Reliable Wife relaxes into an entertaining novel full of all kinds of juicy things—deception, betrayal, murder, sex, and even love." PopMatters

Goonan, Kathleen Ann

In war times. Tor 2007 348p $25.95
ISBN 978-0-7653-1355-3; 0-7653-1355-3
LC 2007-5165

This is "the story of Sam Dance, who, while studying mathematics and electronics for the Army just before WW II, is seduced by a mysterious female physicist teaching one of his classes. Dr. Hadntz has plans for a device that might end war forever, by changing humanity's seeming need for conflict. From this premise, Goonan weaves a remarkable tale of quantum physics, human nature and jazz." SF Signal

Light music. HarperCollins Pubs. 2002 406p $25.95
ISBN 0-380-97712-5
LC 2001-55602

Sequel to Crescent city rhapsody

In this concluding volume of the Nanotech Quartet "the microscopic machines of the 22nd century have gone beyond creating sentient cities and controlling all communications on Earth—they are themselves evolving. When mysterious lights point to an alien presence and disappearing people arouse stark fear, three human survivors, including Argentine refugee Angelina, set out to solve the mystery and measure the threat to humanity. A lot of picaresque adventures ensue. . . . This classic novel of ideas, with state-of-the-art technology as its subject, remains the work of a powerful imagination with a superior command of language." Publ Wkly

Gopaleen, Myles Na *See* O'Brien, Flann, 1911-1966

Gopaleen, Myles *See* O'Brien, Flann, 1911-1966

Gordimer, Nadine, 1923-

Beethoven was one-sixteenth black; and other stories. Farrar, Straus and Giroux 2007 177p $21
ISBN 978-0-374-10982-0; 0-374-10982-6
LC 2007-33474

Contents: Beethoven was one-sixteenth black; Tape measure; Dreaming of the dead; A frivolous woman; Gregor; Safety procedures; Mother tongue; Allesverloren; History; A beneficiary; Alternative endings: the first sense; Alternative endings: the second sense; Alternative endings: the third sense

"A story narrated by a tapeworm. A vignette about a parrot unhappy at losing his usual cafe perch. A tale about a cockroach trapped inside a Kafka fan's typewriter . . . South African Nobel laureate Nadine Gordimer has come up with some true curiosities in her new short-story collection. . . . At its best, the book offers compelling psychosexual journeys, probing at marital tensions and the hazardous play of memory in the bereaved (Gordimer's husband, Reinhold Cassirer, to whom the book is dedicated, died in 2001). Some tales also afford glancing, revealing takes on life in post-apartheid South Africa." Seattle Times

The conservationist. Viking 1975 c1974 252p o.p.

First published 1974 in the United Kingdom

The author probes "the way of life that exists in South Africa today, and some aspects of the tensions that exist among English and Afrikaaners, Blacks, coloreds, Indian shopkeepers. . . . Mehring is rich, white, bored. His farm is a weekend pleasure place to which he once brought the mistress whose flirtations with left wing causes have now exiled her forever. His teenage son won't even come home for the holidays and wants out of all that South Africa stands for. Mehring is kind enough to his blacks, keeps them in their place, avoids his Boer neighbors with whom he has nothing in common. A loner, living for himself, deliberately isolated from any unpleasantness that might intrude, only gradually does he begin to perceive that there are forces at work in nature, in the closeness between the blacks and the land by which some day his way of life will be forever changed." Publ Wkly

Get a life. Farrar, Straus & Giroux 2005 187p $21
ISBN 0-14303-792-7
LC 2005-07199

"Paul Bannerman, a 35-year-old white ecologist in an unnamed city in South Africa, has just started treatment for cancer of the thyroid gland. The therapy sounds exotic to Paul's ears: following surgery, he must take radioactive iodine, which will accumulate in the remnants of his thyroid and, if he's lucky, destroy any residual tumor. During the treatment he will himself become radioactive for ''about 16 days,' as will anything he touches, apparently. His parents have offered to let Paul live with them during this time, to reduce his young family's exposure to hazard." N Y Times Book Rev

"Gordimer confronts the reader with questions of conservation, social welfare, and emotional ecosystems. The austere Gordimer's mastery of her craft means she never needs to point at herself, thus highlighting the difference between art and performance." Harper's

A guest of honor. Viking 1970 504p o.p.

The hero of this novel, James "Bray is a 54-year-old former administrator for one of Her Majesty's former African colonies. . . . He was cashiered for showing too much sympathy for the local independence movement. After independence, Bray accepts an invitation to return as an educational consultant to Miss Gordimer's nameless, composite, new African nation. His professional commitment to the excruciating process of Third World nation building is complicated because the country's opposing political factions—one moderate, the other revolutionary—are led by two of his former protégés." Time

July's people. Viking 1981 160p
ISBN 0-670-41048-9

* LC 80-24877

"When revolution breaks out against the whites in South Africa, Bamford and Maureen Smales are forced to flee. Their black servant July, loyal to them for fifteen years, takes them away to his people in a bush village. His role changes slowly to one not only of savior but also overseer. The change in their manner of living from the good, clean, well-regulated life of 'the ruling class' to that of the customs of July's people raises havoc within both the white and black families and in the delicate tissue of understanding between the Smales and their servant. There is much to be learned from this powerful story written by an author who lives in South Africa and who writes with authority on a subject that has import for any society where race relations or colonial conditions are fragile and explosive." Shapiro. Fic for Youth. 3d edition

Gordimer, Nadine, 1923-—*Continued*

Jump and other stories. Farrar, Straus & Giroux 1991 256p

ISBN 0-374-18055-5   LC 91-2687

Contents: Jump; Once upon a time; The ultimate safari; A find; My father leaves home; Some are born to sweet delight; Comrades; Teraloyna; The moment before the gun went off; Home; A journey; Spoils; Safe houses; What were you dreaming?; Keeping fit; Amnesty

This "collection of tales features an insider's intensity about people caught in the savage particulars of southern Africa today; at the same time, the surprise of the stories and the slash of their endings make the words resonate with the revelations of an ever-widening universe." Booklist

Loot, and other stories. Farrar, Straus & Giroux 2003 240p $23

ISBN 0-374-19090-9   LC 2002-42601

Includes the novellas Karma and Mission statement and the following short stories: Loot; Visiting George; The generation gap; L,U,C,I,E.; Look-alikes; The diamond mine; Homage; An emissary

In Karma a deceased insurance executive's spirit makes successive returns to earth in various guises. Mission statement is about a middle-aged Englishwomanwho has a sexual relationship with a native while working for an international aid agency in an impoverished African country

"This compelling collection presents a bleak view of human existence in general and of Africa's colonial past in particular. Written with a sharp sense of irony, it should be a part of every fiction collection." Libr J

My son's story. Penguin Books 1991 277p pa $9.95

ISBN 0-14-015975-4

* LC 91-17273

First published 1990 by Farrar, Straus & Giroux

"Sonny is a teacher of mixed race. He and his wife are . . . sympathetic to the plight of the 'real blacks,' yet ambitious that they may someday be accepted by the whites. Sonny's political education begins when he's fired for helping black children demonstrate in their township. Jailed for promoting boycotts and participating in illegal gatherings, Sonny meets and falls in love with a blond, blue-eyed woman who works for a human-rights organization. Sonny's adolescent son, Will, tells the story of his father's political and erotic development, the resentments and betrayals that ensue." Newsweek

This is a "thoughtful, poised, quietly poignant novel that not only recognizes the value and cost of political commitment, but also takes account of recent developments in South Africa and Eastern Europe in a way that Gordimer's previous work did not." Christ Sci Monit

None to accompany me. Farrar, Straus & Giroux 1994 324p

ISBN 0-374-22297-5   LC 94-7553

"In the final days of the old regime in South Africa, antiapartheid activists are released from prison or return home afters years of exile. Vera Stark, a white legal aid attorney representing the black community, recognizes many familiar faces from her youth, but she is shocked to see that they appear to have aged overnight. This unnerving experience causes her to reexamine her life.

Known around her law firm as someone impervious to con games, Vera is ruthless in exposing her own lies and deceptions. She faces unpleasant truths about her marriages, her affairs, and the effect her actions may have had on her children. But rather than cling to the security of a flawed life, Vera finds that the rapidly changing political situation encourages radical personal change." Libr J

"A novel that raises more questions than it answers, 'None to Accompany Me' is an unflinching and perceptive exploration of people living on the brink of changes—political and personal—with little but their own sense of self-reliance to guide them." Christ Sci Monitor

The pickup. Farrar, Straus & Giroux 2001 270p $23

ISBN 0-374-23210-5   LC 2001-23041

To South African "Julie Summer, rebellious daughter of a rich white investment banker, the black mechanic she meets at a garage is initially merely an interesting person to add to her circle of bohemian friends. But as their relationship swiftly escalates, Julie comes to understand her lover's perilous tightrope attempts to find a country that will shelter him. Abdu, as he calls himself (it's not his real name), is an illegal immigrant from an abysmally poor Arab country. Now on the verge of deportation from South Africa, he's forced to return to his ancestral village. Julie insists on marrying him and going with him." Publ Wkly

"Gordimer writes so tenderly and so searchingly about Julie's gradual transcendence of her western self that she manages to hold sceptism at bay." Women's Review of Books

Gordon, Emily Fox, 1948-

It will come to me. Spiegel & Grau 2009 267p $24.95

ISBN 978-0-385-52587-9; 0-385-52587-7

LC 2008-29338

"In this campus satire, Ben and Ruth Blau have settled into what appears to be a comfortable routine at their Southern university campus. Ruth, mourning her inability to follow up on an acclaimed early trilogy of novels, drinks a little too much; Ben, working on a manuscript about altruism, shirks bureaucratic duties in the philosophy department. Their lives are disrupted by two arrivals: a new president determined to shake up the staid faculty habits and a popular memoirist and self-help author who prods Ruth to begin writing again." New Yorker

Gordon, Mary, 1949-

The company of women. Knopf 1981 c1980 291p o.p.

* LC 80-5284

In this novel "Felicitas is nurtured by a large circle of Catholic women. After attending only parochial schools, Felicitas goes to Columbia University, where she becomes sexually involved with a married professor, gives up her studies, and becomes pregnant. She returns to the company of women, gives birth to her baby, and later marries only to provide a father for her child." Merriam-Webster's Ency of Lit

"Given its scope, depth, and the perfection of its lyri-

Gordon, Mary, 1949——*Continued*

cal passages (which are the more impressive because of Gordon's natural inclination toward the austere), it is fair to call this a brilliant novel." Saturday Rev

Final payments. Random House 1978 297p o.p.
* LC 77-90259

"Isabel Moore spends 11 years almost totally absorbed in caring for her invalid father, who suffered a paralyzing stroke after discovering his daughter in a compromising situation with one of his students. When she is thirty, her father dies; she is freed from responsibility for his welfare but not yet able to accept responsibility for her own life. Her involvement with two men adds complications as, guilt-ridden and filled with religious skepticism, Isabel searches for answers and begins to heal. Two childhood friends, Eleanor, an independent woman, and Liz, a tough married mother of two children, are instrumental in helping Isabel grow toward self-realization." Shapiro. Fic for Youth. 3d edition

Gordon, Neil, 1958-

The company you keep. Viking 2003 406p $24.95
ISBN 0-670-03218-2   LC 2002-44905

"When limousine-leftist lawyer and single dad Jim Grant is unmasked as Jason Sinai, an ex-Weather Underground militant wanted for a deadly bank robbery, he abandons his daughter and goes on the lam. As he evades a manhunt and seeks out old comrades, the author introduces a sprawling cast of drug dealers, bomb-planting radicals turned leftist academics, Vietnam vets, FBI agents and Republicans who collectively ponder the legacy of the '60s." Publ Wkly

"If the book has a political stance, it might be called the radical center, training equal skepticism, even humorous contempt, on the excesses of both left and right." N Y Times Book Rev

Gores, Joe

Cons, scams & grifts. Mysterious Press 2001 324p $24.95
ISBN 0-89296-594-0   LC 2001-30637

"Daniel Kearny Associates—San Francisco private investigators and auto-repossession specialists—have been hired by Cal-Cit Bank to repossess cars being sold by a dealer who hasn't paid off his loans. The bank has also employed the firm to protect some very valuable property on a remote estate. Meantime, Kearney's investigators are working for a very different client—a local gypsy clan trying to clear one of its own of a murder charge." Booklist

"Although this episodic caper looks like a free-for-all, [Gores'] brazen schemes require high levels of intelligence and the underlying design of his ploys is quite breathtaking." N Y Times Book Rev

Contract null & void. Mysterious Press 1996 309p o.p.
LC 96-12769

"Repo men of Daniel Kearny Associates scour the streets of San Francisco for luxury cars and electric guitars. When a flamboyant union leader is murdered, their searches lead them into corrupt backwaters." Libr J

"Master of surreal comedic style, Mr. Gores keeps finding outlandish assignments for his repo men. But in

the inspired ending, aptly called 'Walpurgisnacht,' the plot lines converge and all the insanity, believe it or not, makes perfect sense." N Y Times Book Rev

Gores, Joseph N. *See* Gores, Joe

Gorky, Maksim, 1868-1936

Selected short stories; [by] Maxim Gorky; with an introductory essay by Stefan Zweig. Ungar 1959 348p o.p.

Contents: Makar Chudra; Old Izergil; Chelkash; Afloat: an Easter story; Twenty-six men and a girl; Malva; Comrade; The ninth of January; Tales of Italy; The romancer; The Mordvinian girl; A man is born; The breakup; How a song was composed; The philanderer

Gorky, Maxim *See* Gorky, Maksim, 1868-1936

Gorman, Edward

Breaking up is hard to do; [by] Ed Gorman. Carroll & Graff Pubs. 2004 207p $24
ISBN 0-7867-1296-1

"In late October 1962, with Armageddon looming in the form of the Cuban missile crisis, life went on in Black River Falls, Iowa-except in the case of a young woman found murdered in gubernatorial candidate Ross Murdoch's under-construction bomb shelter. His political dreams dashed, Murdoch hopes to avoid the electric chair and hires young investigator-attorney Sam McCain to represent him. . . . Intelligent writing and great reading." Booklist

Fools rush in; a Sam McCain mystery; [by] Ed Gorman. Pegasus Books 2007 229p $25
ISBN 978-1-933548-32-3

"Black River Falls, Iowa, 1963: the violence of the civil-rights era lurks behind the double murder of a Peeping Tom photographer and a handsome black lothario, David Leeds, who was dating the daughter of a white Republican senator. Young Sam McCain, a lawyer and sometime private detective, is on the case. Motives are widespread. The senator was having an affair. Local bikers hated Leeds' success with a white woman to whom they could never aspire. The photographer was a blackmailer, and the white ex-boyfriend of the senator's daughter was a violent bully. . . . Readers unfamiliar with this fine series should hop onboard now and watch as an Iowa Mr. Marple starts to behave like a cornbelt Spenser." Booklist

Save the last dance for me; [by] Ed Gorman. Carroll & Graf Pubs. 2002 230p $24
ISBN 0-7867-0968-5
*

A mystery set in Black River Falls, Iowa in 1960. Sam McCain, "a part-time lawyer and part-time PI, gets hired by the town judge to investigate the murder of John Muldaur, a local fundamentalist preacher who used live rattlesnakes to test the 'purity' of his flock, after someone doses the preacher's bottle of Pepsi with strychnine. When he wasn't sleeping with the wife of one of his congregation, Muldaur was conducting a vigorous campaign to expose the conspiracy of Zionists and Roman Catholics to take over the world." Publ Wkly

Gorman, Edward—*Continued*

A "dead-on perfect journey to the underside of the late '50s and early '60s, exposing the anti-intellectualism and anti-Semitism that lurked beneath the era's placid surface." Booklist

Sleeping dogs; [by] Ed Gorman. Thomas Dunne Books/St. Martin's Minotaur 2008 238p $23.95

ISBN 978-0-312-36784-8; 0-312-36784-8

LC 2007-51733

"Unleashing a new series, Gorman gives us political speechwriter and sleuth-by-necessity Dev Conrad. He's just signed onto the unexpectedly troubled reelection campaign of a U.S. senator, and must deal with dirty tricks, campaign sabotage, a suicide and his increasing suspicions about the very man he's supposed to be helping stay in Congress." January

Gosling, Paula

The dead of winter. Mysterious Press 1996 c1995 328p o.p. LC 95-39099

First published 1995 in the United Kingdom

"After the discovery of a body in an ice-fishing hole nearly scares a tipsy man sober, Sheriff Matt Gabriel knows what to do. Because the victim has mob connections, Matt fears unrest in the usually peaceful Blackwater Bay. One of Jess Gibbons's high school students, meanwhile, disappears." Libr J

"This complicated puzzler, pivoting from cozy sewing circles to talk of mafia hit men and cocaine dens, comes to its brilliantly staged conclusion at the annual ice festival where Gosling dramatizes the point that smooth and shiny surfaces can hide a lot of treachery." Publ Wkly

A few dying words. Mysterious Press 1994 344p o.p. LC 94-18826

"A Blackwater Bay mystery novel"

"While bracing for the Blackwater Bay's annual Howl—a traditional Halloween celebration of carnival rides and pranks—Sheriff Matt Gabriel agrees to meet with clearly agitated retired pharmacist, Tom Finnegan. While driving to the sheriff's office, however, Finnegan is run off the road. Matt reaches the older man's side before he dies and hears him whisper 'not an accident.'" Publ Wkly

"Good writing, an inventive plot, and a nice balance of humor and horror make this an appealing mystery." Booklist

Gottlieb, Eli

Now you see him. William Morrow 2008 261p $22.95

ISBN 978-0-06-128464-9; 0-06-128464-5

"Nick Framingham is still reeling from the recent death of his childhood best friend, the writer Rob Castor, who committed suicide after killing his ex-girlfriend in Manhattan. Nick's own marriage to his college sweetheart, Lucy, begins to unravel as he struggles to understand what drove Rob to murder. Rekindling an old relationship with his first love, Belinda, Rob's volatile and beautiful sister, Nick begins to retrace not only Rob's last days but also their shared childhood, looking for clues to explain his friend's actions." Publ Wkly

This is a "haunting and affecting potrait not only of an unthinkable act of violence but also a deeply personal grief and the self-questioning that follows a psychologically scarring event." Vancouver Sun

Goudge, Eileen

Garden of lies. Viking 1989 528p

ISBN 0-670-82458-5 LC 88-40395

"Sylvia seizes the opportunity offered by a hospital fire to switch infants, taking a newborn whose appearance resembles her husband. Her true child, fathered by Sylvia's lover, is left to make her own way in the world. Rachel, raised in luxury as Sylvia's daughter, becomes a doctor. When her career is jeopardized, she is defended by Sylvia'a real daughter, who has overcome poverty to become a lawyer. The two women of course compete for the same man, as Sylvia herself tries to decide whether to marry Nikos, her former lover." Libr J

"The characters intrigue, the situations hold attention, and the sex scenes simmer near the boiling point." Booklist

Followed by Thorns of truth

One last dance. Viking 1999 384p $24.95

ISBN 0-670-88575-4 LC 98-54891

"The Seagrave sisters are emotionally unfulfilled despite their accomplishments: Daphne, a novelist married to a doctor, cannot forget her childhood sweetheart, while homespun cafe entrepreneur Kitty yearns to adopt a child, and newly divorced real estate agent Alex is drowning in mounting debt. When their mother shoots their father without explanation or apology, the daughters investigate the rumors and suspicions they have ignored all their lives to confront the truth about their philandering parent." Publ Wkly

"Ideal for readers looking for a fairy tale: lovely, talented women, handsome men who love them, and little permanent trauma from a violent death and the awful secrets it unleashes." Libr J

Stranger in paradise. Viking 2001 321p

ISBN 0-670-89987-9 LC 2001-17747

This first volume of a projected trilogy set in Carson Springs, California focuses on "48-year-old Samantha 'Sam' Kiley and her daughters, Alice and Laura. As the story opens, Alice is about to marry Wes Carpenter, a Ted Turneresque entertainment mogul nearly 30 years her senior. Then Wes's son, Ian, takes a shine to Sam and the two become romantically involved, alarming Sam's daughters and setting the gossipy town abuzz. Laura, divorced because she couldn't bear children, and given to taking in strays, gets a new lease on life when she provides shelter for 16-year-old female runaway Finch." Publ Wkly

Such devoted sisters. Viking 1992 562p o.p.

LC 91-29103

"In 1954, Dolly Drake mails a letter addressed to Senator Joseph McCarthy that contains damning information about her famous film star sister Eve Dearfield. After leaving small-town America for Hollywood, Dolly has had enough of Eve stealing the spotlight. And she can't tolerate Eve stealing her man, either. Ruining the offending sister's career and her life seems the only thing to do. Years later, of course, she's regretting her actions, but Dolly's far away in Manhattan, with her own chocolate store and a lot of money. And it just so happens that

Goudge, Eileen—*Continued*

Eve's two children, Annie and Laurel, have run away from home looking for Dolly, their long-lost aunt." Booklist

Thorns of truth. Viking 1998 398p

ISBN 0-670-87942-8   LC 97-53231

"Forty-six years after Sylvie Rosenthal abandoned Rose as a dark-haired newborn and stole blonde, blue-eyed baby Rachel to take her place, their lives are still intertwined, and Rachel still doesn't know the truth. Now Rose has problems of her own: her husband's death a year ago has left her with a law firm to manage; her stepdaughter is a drunk; and her eldest son, Drew, is planning to marry Rachel's mentally unstable daughter, Iris, against his mother's wishes. Rachel's life is starting to fray at the edges, too. Her job running a women's health clinic has caused a rift in her marriage to Brian, and, even medicated, Iris remains a constant worry." Publ Wkly

Trail of secrets. Viking 1996 443p

ISBN 0-670-86191-X   LC 95-39411

"In 1972, young Ellie's infant is stolen and privately offered to wealthy Kate and Will as an abandoned baby. Ellie's tragedy is heightened by her inability to conceive again, and her repeated attempts to adopt strain her marriage to Paul. Her daughter, Skyler, is now a lovely young woman, raised among love, money, and horses. She unexpectedly becomes pregnant by Tony, a policeman. Through a twist of events, she offers her baby to Ellie to adopt, not knowing that Ellie is her own mother and her unborn child's grandmother." Libr J

The author's "characters are sympathetic; her expressions of the fierce emotions of motherhood are immediate; and her crafty decision to reveal likely plot turns to her readers but not to her characters will keep all who love a secret riveted." Publ Wkly

Goudge, Elizabeth, 1900-1984

Green Dolphin Street; a novel. Coward-McCann 1944 502p o.p.

Published in the United Kingdom with title: Green Dolphin country

This novel is set on one of the English Channel Islands and in frontier New Zealand. "The principal characters are two sisters and the boy who had been their neighbor and companion in Green Dolphin Street on the island. The sisters are Marianne, stern and intellectual, and Marguerite, radiant and beautiful. It is Marguerite whom William loves, but when he writes the letter from New Zealand asking her father for her hand he unaccountably confuses the names and it is Marianne, who comes to be his wife." Wis Libr Bull

Gould, Judith

The best is yet to come. Dutton 2002 308p $24.95

ISBN 0-525-94659-4   LC 2002-23541

"After years of hard work, Carolina Mountcastle has finally made her flower shop the first choice of New York's most demanding hostesses. Factor in her storybook marriage to successful businessman Lyon, her 16-year-old son Richie and her great friends, and Carolina would appear to have it all. But when her husband suf-fers a fatal heart attack while traveling abroad for business and a mysterious woman and her daughter appear at the reading of his will, Carolina's world begins to unravel. . . . Gould's page-turning plot and deliciously evil villains distract artfully from some tone-deaf dialogue. . .and the flower descriptions are a delight." Publ Wkly

A moment in time. Dutton 2001 323p $24.95

ISBN 0-525-94607-1   LC 2001-25334

Valerie Rochelle has "found happiness, much to her society mother's bewilderment, working as a veterinarian in upstate New York. When Teddy, an old family friend, proposes, her mother is ecstatic, but Valerie is less than thrilled. Nonetheless, she accepts, but her reluctance is exacerbated when she pays a house call to the mysterious Stonelair estate to tend to an ailing horse. She and the estate's new owner, Wyn Conrad, connect on a level that she and Teddy never reach. . . . Gould's steamy tale about the lives of the rich and troubled is perfect for a read on the beach." Booklist

Gowdy, Barbara

Helpless; a novel. Metropolitan Books 2007 307p $24

ISBN 978-0-8050-8288-3   LC 2006-47348

This is the "tale of the stalking and kidnapping of a beautiful young mixed-race Canadian girl. . . . Celia, a single mom holding down two jobs to support her beloved daughter, nine-year-old Rachel . . ., is rushed into every parent's nightmare when the deeply creepy Ron, a small-appliance repairman, uses the cover of a Toronto summertime blackout to 'rescue' Rachel from what he sees as her unsavory poverty. With the help of his girlfriend, Nancy, an uneasy accomplice whose thwarted maternal instincts impel her to try to protect Rachel, Ron imprisons the girl in his basement apartment." Libr J

"There is a clean urgency to Gowdy's tale. We are helpless before her sure and beguiling hand because ultimately—and breathlessly—we are drawn in." Vancouver Sun

The romantic; a novel. Metropolitan Bks. 2003 305p $24

ISBN 0-8050-7190-3   LC 2002-29904

"At 10, a year after Louise's own mother left her and her father, the Richters, an older couple with an adopted son, move in next door. . . . Louise befriends Abel in order to get to Mrs. Richter, but her love soon transfers to the solitary, sensitive boy. The connection between the two flourishes, and Louise never stops thinking about Abel, even when he moves away. It is his return, when they meet at a high-school party, that marks the beginning of their adult relationship." Booklist

"Each of the characters, even minor ones, has a unique voice and a vivid, quirky personality. Louise's need to have Abel create the world for her resonates with unfulfilled passion." Publ Wkly

Grace, C. L.

For works written by this author under other names see Doherty, P. C.

Grady, James, 1949-

Six days of the condor. Norton 1974 192p o.p.
"When a branch of the CIA is mass murdered, Malcolm, the only survivor, becomes the object of an intense chase involving the Washington police, the CIA, the FBI, the NSC, and a host of other intelligence agencies. Trying to stay one jump ahead of his pursuers, Malcolm struggles to find out who within the agency has sold out his comrades." Libr J

Grafton, Sue

"A" is for alibi; a Kinsey Millhone mystery. Holt & Co. 1990 c1982 274p $27
ISBN 0-8050-1334-2

*

A reissue of the title first published 1982 by Holt, Rinehart & Winston
"California private eye, Kinsey Millhone, makes her debut in this story of a murder committed eight years before. Nikki Fife was convicted of killing her husband, but as soon as she's out of prison she hires Kinsey to find the true murderer." Libr J
"Kinsey Millhone is a cut above the usual woman private eye who flounces through fiction. Millhone is neither a sex bomb nor a detached cerebrum, but a believable, straightforward character." Booklist

"B" is for burglar. Holt & Co. 1985 229p $27
ISBN 0-8050-1632-5   LC 84-22378
When Kinsey Millhone "is hired to locate Elaine Boldt, a well-to-do widow, she sets the wheels of a routine missing-persons investigation in motion. The bizarre, outlandish behavior of Elaine's sister and brother-in-law leads Kinsey to suspect a murder has been committed, but in order to solve the crime, a corpse must be uncovered." Booklist
"Grafton's plot is solid p.i. procedural, but it is her sense of style that will truly delight readers. Her characters, from a punk dope pusher to a brave and resourceful eighty-eight-year-old woman, are completely convincing, and Grafton's ear for natural dialogue is among the best in the business." Wilson Libr Bull

"C" is for corpse; a Kinsey Millhone mystery. Holt & Co. 1986 243p $27
ISBN 0-8050-2818-8   LC 85-24797
Kinsey Millhone "meets a young man, Buddy Callahan, at the gym where she works out and agrees to take his case. He wants her to investigate an auto accident in which he was badly injured because he claims that it was a murder attempt. When a second attempt results in his death, Kinsey, although she no longer has him as a client, pursues the matter and, in a hair-raising finale that takes place in a morgue, she unmasks the murderer." Shapiro. Fic for Youth. 3d edition

"D" is for deadbeat; a Kinsey Millhone mystery. Holt & Co. 1987 229p $27
ISBN 0-8050-0248-0   LC 86-25843
"Ex-con and drunken bum John Daggett hires Millhone to deliver a check for $25,000 to a teenage boy whose family was killed in a violent car crash in which Daggett was the offending drunk driver. Daggett's retainer check bounces, and in trying to recoup her losses, Kinsey is swept up in a tangled web of hate, violence, and families

torn asunder." Booklist
"Social awareness and human weakness play a great part in the Millhone books, which always manage to finish with a heart-stopping climax." Libr J

"E" is for evidence; a Kinsey Millhone mystery. Holt & Co. 1988 227p $27
ISBN 0-8050-0459-9   LC 87-28100
"While private detective and former cop Kinsey Millhone is investigating a possible case of industrial arson involving a company owned by the family of a former schoolmate, someone tries to make it look as if she's on the take. A mysterious $5000 appears in her bank account. She sets out to clear herself, while two or possibly more cases of murder occur, including one by bombing." Publ Wkly
"The plot is just fine and does what a plot ought to in a good detective novel: it keeps us turning pages and serves as a vehicle for the really interesting stuff, an unveiling of the characters' foibles by the worldly-wise but uncorrupt private eye." NY Times Book Rev

"F" is for fugitive; a Kinsey Millhone mystery. Holt & Co. 1989 261p $27
ISBN 0-8050-0460-2   LC 88-27284
Kinsey Millhone "becomes involved in ugly doings in a California coastal town, where she attempts to prove a man's innocence on a 17-year-old murder rap. Floral Beach appears to be a cozy little place, but it's a hotbed of dirty secrets, most of them involving the long-dead Jean Timberlake, a confused yet apparently sexually quite precocious teenager. Kinsey's investigation opens closet doors, and some tawdry skeletons jump out." Booklist

"G" is for gumshoe; a Kinsey Millhone mystery. Holt & Co. 1990 261p o.p.   LC 89-24652
Private investigator Kinsey Millhone is hired to find and take "an elderly woman to a nursing home near her daughter. But the lady mysteriously disappears within hours of her arrival. Painfully aware of the fact that a contract has been arranged for her own murder, Kinsey unravels the events of the past." SLJ
"Millhone, whose background has made her believe that all families are dysfunctional, has unwittingly taken on another case of domestic violence. Grafton excels in this milieu. Never morally oblique, here she is slyly didactic about (among other things) attitudes toward the mentally ill." Newsweek

"H" is for homicide. Holt & Co. 1991 256p $27
ISBN 0-8050-1084-X   LC 90-25016
Detective Kinsey Millhone is "hired by California Fidelity to investigate a string of fraudulent automobile insurance claims filed by someone named Bibianna Diaz. To track down the elusive Bibianna, Kinsey adopts an undercover identity as Hannah Moore, a wisecracking, reckless vamp. As Hannah, she befriends Bibianna, a sexy young woman on the run. Both are quickly swept up in an evening of kidnapping and gunplay that ends with the two of them in jail. Through her relationship with Bibianna, Kinsey also stumbles onto a much bigger network of crime." N Y Times Book Rev

"I" is for innocent. Holt & Co. 1992 286p $27
ISBN 0-8050-1085-8   LC 91-45165

Grafton, Sue—*Continued*

Kinsey Millhone "lands the job of hunting up evidence for a wrongful-death suit against a high-living architect who couldn't be nailed in court for his wife's murder. It's a sobering case, weighted with the survivors' anger and suspicions and darkened by their sordid domestic affairs." N Y Times Book Rev

"J" is for judgment. Holt & Co. 1993 288p $27

ISBN 0-8050-1935-9   LC 92-35769

In this mystery, California P.I. Kinsey Millhone is "investigating a fraud case. Wendell Jaffe, a local businessman, set up a fraudulent Ponzi scheme and then disappeared, leaving his wife and business partner to deal with the creditors. His wife had Jaffe declared dead after five years and picked up a half-million-dollar life insurance settlement. Now Jaffe's supposedly been sighted in Mexico. If he's still alive, the insurance company wants its money back and hires Kinsey to find out what's what." Booklist

"Ms. Grafton writes a smart story and wraps it up with a wry twist; but she takes care to sweeten her tart characterizations with amused understanding and, in the case of Jaffe, even affection." N Y Times Book Rev

"K" is for killer. Holt & Co. 1994 284p $27

ISBN 0-8050-1936-7   LC 94-1242

"Grieving mother Janice Kepler asks Kinsey [Millhone] to investigate the nearly year-old death of her daughter Lorna. Janice believes Lorna was murdered, even though there were no signs of violence and the police concluded the young woman died of natural causes. Kinsey, always keen for a challenge, agrees to take the case and winds up working one of the oddest mysteries of her career." Booklist

"Despite an abrupt ending that has the reader frantically paging back for missed clues, the sturdily engineered plot drags Kinsey into the kind of joints that never seem to close: bars, nightclubs, diners, hospital emergency rooms. All this night crawling serves as an eye-opening experience for Kinsey, who is physically exhausted but mentally energized by her encounters with sad young prostitutes and other fascinating creatures of the night." N Y Times Book Rev

"L" is for lawless. Holt & Co. 1995 290p $27

ISBN 0-8050-1937-5   LC 95-12787

In this adventure "private investigator Kinsey Millhone is just doing a favor for a friend—checking the military status of a recently deceased neighbor—when she's sucked into a chase for the spoils of a 1941 bank heist. It's a lively outing with a couple of heart-pounding scenes, some interesting characters . . . and even a little detection. There are also hints of Kinsey's connecting with long-lost relatives, plus a romantic wedding of octogenarians." Libr J

"M" is for malice. Holt & Co. 1996 300p $27

ISBN 0-8050-3637-7   LC 96-30897

In this mystery set in Southern California, private eye Kinsey Millhone "looks for Guy Malek, the missing son and partial heir to a huge fortune. She finds him, but then he is murdered." SLJ

"This is a subtle and swiftly moving novel, pleasantly unpredictable, with an agreeable overlay of smoldering romance, as fellow PI and former lover Robert Dietz reenters Kinsey's life. Grafton's heroine—more introspec-

tive, yet still feisty and surefooted—leads this finely tuned and at times electrifying tale to a thoroughly satisfying conclusion." Publ Wkly

"N" is for noose. Holt & Co. 1998 289p $25

ISBN 0-8050-3650-4   LC 97-49320

"A Marian Wood book"

Kinsey Millhone "takes a case in tiny Nota Lake, Nevada, where deputy sheriff Tom Newquist has recently died of a heart attack. His grief-stricken widow, Selma, is convinced Tom died as a result of the terrible stress he was under during his last weeks, and she's determined to find out the source of that stress. . . . Apparently Tom was following up on a double homicide, and as Kinsey probes further into the bizarre details, she finds that he suspected the killer may have been one of his colleagues." Booklist

"Even when people are not nice to Kinsey, Grafton always deals fairly with them in this clean, well-constructed story about small-town insecurities." N Y Times Book Rev

"O" is for outlaw. Holt & Co. 1999 318p $26

ISBN 0-8050-5955-5   LC 99-14967

"A Marian Wood book"

"An unopened letter discovered in an abandoned storage locker is delivered, 15 years late, to P.I. Kinsey Millhone. It provides a possible alibi for Kinsey's first husband, Mickey, a cop who was accused of beating a man to death. The accusation ended Kinsey's marriage, and now guilt pangs lead her to reexamine her judgment of Mickey. When Mickey is shot with Kinsey's gun, Kinsey is only one step ahead of the police as she tries to solve the shooting and the crime attributed to Mickey." Libr J

"Everything that has always worked for this first class series works better here: the sturdy plotting, the animated characters, the breezy style and a heroine with foibles you can laugh at and faults you can forgive." N Y Times Book Rev

"P" is for peril. Putnam 2001 352p $26.95

ISBN 0-399-14719-5   LC 00-46024

"A Marian Wood book"

"Private investigator Kinsey Milhone is hired by Dr. Fiona Purcell to find her ex-husband, Dowan, a prominent physician who vanished with his passport and $30,000 in cash nine weeks earlier. Wondering what she can do that the Santa Rosa police haven't done already, Kinsey takes the case and quickly discovers that the nursing home Purcell administered is being investigated for Medicare fraud." Libr J

"Grafton gives us a truly complex heroine, marvelous depiction of Southern California architecture and interiors, and a writing style that can make a weed path interesting." Booklist

"Q" is for quarry. Putnam 2002 385p $26.95

ISBN 0-399-14915-5   LC 2002-68368

"A Marian Wood book"

"In the summer of 1969, the decomposed corpse of a young white female was discovered near a quarry off California's Highway 1. Her hands had been bound and her throat slashed. Despite months of investigation, 'Jane Doe' remained unidentified and the case unsolved. Now years later, Con Donlan and Stacey Oliphant, the police officers who had found her body, want Kinsey to help them to identify the girl and find her killer before they

Grafton, Sue—*Continued*

retire. At the same time, having learned that the body was found on a ranch owned by her estranged grandmother, Kinsey journeys into the past to retrace her own family history. Once again, an intriguing plot, fully drawn characters, and wry humor prove why Grafton's series is one of the best." Libr J

"R" is for ricochet; Sue Grafton. G.P. Putnam's Sons 2004 352p $26.95

ISBN 0-399-15228-8   LC 2004-44599

"Hired by dying millionaire Nord Lafferty to babysit his recently paroled daughter, Reba, Kinsey [Millhone] finds herself entangled in a complex money-laundering scheme when Reba decides to take revenge on the twotiming lover for whom she had gone to prison. Meanwhile, Kinsey's octogenarian landlord resigns himself to a loveless life after his interfering brothers sabotage a budding relationship with a lively widow. And the twice-divorced Kinsey has to decide whether to risk opening her heart to sexy cop Cheney Phillips. As demonstrated here, Grafton's series remains fresh and exciting, with complex plots and well-developed characters." Libr J

S is for Silence. Putnam 2005 374p $26.95

ISBN 0-399-15297-0   LC 2005-48923

"A Marian Wood book"

"On July 4, 1953, small-town wife and mother Violet Sullivan disappears without a trace. Did she leave her abusive husband and young daughter behind, never to contact them again, or did a secret (or not-so-secret) lover do her in? Fast-forward to the 1980s: Daisy, the missing woman's now grown daughter, enlists Kinsey Milhone . . . to resolve her mother's disappearance." Libr J

"Grafton uses the mystery of Violet's disappearance as a window into Serena Station, a sad little hamlet of boarded-up houses, abandoned oil rigs and rusting railroad tracks. Something vital went out of the place when Violet disappeared, and Kinsey's investigation forces the onetime neighbors of this lusty Jezebel to recall her unbridled sexual energy and reflect on their own joyless lives. By alternating Kinsey's brisk first-person narrative with dramatic flashbacks that catch the spirit of the town during its volatile postwar period, Grafton allows Violet to emerge as a dynamic but dangerous life force—irresistible to men, threatening to women and too reckless for her own good." N Y Times Book Rev

T is for trespass. G. P. Putnam's Sons 2007 387p

ISBN 9780399154485; 0-399-15448-5

LC 2007-29368

"Gus Vronsky, Kinsey's elderly next-door neighbor, suffers a fall and needs in-home care. A health-care nurse named Solana Rojas is hired, and Kinsey even does the background check, finding nothing out of order. As Gus's condition deteriorates and Solana limits access to her patient, Kinsey and her landlord, Henry, suspect that something is a little off with Solana-and 'little off' doesn't fully describe this identity thief and true sociopath. Digging around more carefully, Kinsey unearths horrifying details of Solana's past and must act quickly to save Gus. This is vintage Grafton, set in the 1980s but scarily current, carefully plotted, and fast paced." Libr J

Graham, James, 1929- *See* Higgins, Jack, 1929-

Graham, Jo, 1968-

Black ships; a novel. Orbit 2008 431p map pa $14.99

ISBN 978-0-316-06800-0; 0-316-06800-4

LC 2007-46166

"Born to a slave taken at the fall of Troy, the child named Gull is chosen by the oracle Pythia to succeed her in service to the Lady of Death because of her prophetic visions. When survivors of a later assault on Troy, called Wilusa by its inhabitants, free their enslaved people, Gull accompanies the captain of the seven black ships, the Trojan Prince Aeneas, as they search for a place to call home. Drawing her inspiration from Virgil's The Aeneid, debut author Graham recreates a vivid picture of the ancient world, a mysterious place in which gods and goddesses speak to their chosen." Libr J

Graham, Tom *See* Lewis, Sinclair, 1885-1951

Graham, Winston

Bella Poldark; a novel of Cornwall, 1818-1820. Macmillan 2002 530p $29.95

ISBN 0-333-98923-6

Earlier titles in the Poldark series: Ross Poldark (1945); Demelza (1946); Jeremy Poldark (1950); Warleggan 1953); Black moon (1973); The four swans (1976); The angry tide (1977); The stranger from the sea (1981); The miller's dance (1982); The loving cup (1984); The twisted sword (1990)

This is the twelfth and final novel of the Poldark series. "As the story opens, Valentine Warleggan's paternity still poisons the atmosphere, and his financial and marital trouble form a major narrative strand set firmly against the saga's familiar background of Cornwall. Meanwhile, Bella Poldark's desire for a musical career takes her to stages in London and France, where she is involved with rival suitors. Her widowed older sister, Clowance, must also choose between two men of vastly different backgrounds who propose marriage. A host of other characters and subplots, including a series of murders, keeps the action bubbling." Libr J

Granger, Bill

The el murders. Holt & Co. 1987 246p o.p.

LC 86-29399

This mystery features "Chicago homicide detective Terry Flynn and his lover, special investigator Karen Kovac. Flynn's case is the mugging-turned-murder of a gay man on an elevated-train platform. Kovac's case is a brutal rape that also takes place on an El platform. Flynn's key witness—the victim's lover—and Kovac's victim prove to be unacceptable witnesses, but neither Flynn nor Kovac retreats from the investigation." Booklist

"The two cases crisscross in this excellent police procedural filled with tough, streetwise characters and swift, rough action." Libr J

Grant, David, 1942-

For works written by this author under other names see Thomas, Craig, 1942-

Grant, Gavin J.

(ed) The Year's best fantasy and horror. See The Year's best fantasy and horror

Grant, John See Gash, Jonathan, 1933-

Grant, Michael, 1940-

Officer down. Doubleday 1993 437p

ISBN 0-385-41968-6   LC 92-37205

"First a bomb explodes at New York City's police headquarters, killing an officer, then a policewoman is executed. While it is clear that the police are targets of a highly organized group, the motive behind the attacks is kept secret. FBI agent Chris Liberti, DEA undercover agent Donal Castillo, and deputy inspector Dan Morgan form a special task force to identify the people behind the violence. They know a terrorist group known as *Punyo Blanco* has been formed by the Colombian drug cartels to force the United States to stop pressuring Colombia into action against the drug lords. . . . The plot is timely, the characters realistic, the motive plausible, and the pace electrifying." Libr J

Grant, Stephanie

Map of Ireland; a novel. Scribner 2008 197p $22

ISBN 978-1-416-55622-0; 1-416-55622-2

LC 2007-45912

"Ann's descriptions of life in Southie are so compelling that some readers may miss those passages, with their very specific, idiosyncratic details, when she steps out of this world she knows best into the wider world. But Grant emerges on the other side with her firm grip on originality, and ultimately, in spite of the wonderful epigraph by Heraclitus — 'Geography is fate' — Ann represents not so much her community, but herself. . . . Early on, she muses that 'the problem with the movies was that they made you think you had more experience than you actually did.' That, too, is the gift of a well-worded novel. 'Map of Ireland' is admirably ambitious, bold, and smart." Boston Globe

Grass, Günter, 1927-

The call of the toad; translated by Ralph Manheim. Harcourt Brace Jovanovich 1992 248p il o.p.   LC 92-20233

"A Helen and Kurt Wolff book"

The events recounted in this novel date from "November 2, 1989, only days before the Berlin Wall began to crumble. A chance encounter between a German art-historian, Alexander, and a Polish art-restorer, Alexandra, . . . [results in a plan to] found and develop a . . . Cemetery Association to enable exiles to opt for burial in their native Polish soil, uniting again those whom recent history has forced apart. . . . The plan snowballs out of control and into the hands of others more entrepreneurial and less naively idealistic than the quaint couple who had thought it all up." Times Lit Suppl

This book is a "skillful balancing act that juggles some very timely questions about the conflict between calls for ethnic self-determination and calls for international unity and cooperation." Christ Sci Monit

Cat and mouse; translated by Ralph Manheim. Harcourt, Brace & World 1963 189p o.p.

Original German edition, 1961

A novel about Mahlke, a teenager growing up in a Baltic port city during World War II who is set apart from his fellows by his huge Adam's apple. When a classmate attracts a cat to this 'mouse' he launches Mahlke on his career. Mahlke becomes an excellent swimmer and athlete, and later a hero to his nation. But the symbolic cat watching him is a society of petty men and Mahlke is eventually doomed

also in Grass, G. The Danzig trilogy

Crabwalk; translated from the German by Krishna Winston. Harcourt 2002 234p $25

ISBN 0-15-100764-0   LC 2002-13205

"The plot centers on the fate of the vessel Wilhelm Gustloff, which was built as a cruise ship in the Third Reich, was fitted out as a troop carrier in World War II and was turned into a refugee ship for German civilians fleeing the Russian Army. On Jan. 30, 1945, 12 years after the Nazis rose to power, it was torpedoed in the Baltic Sea by a Soviet submarine and, in what was apparently the biggest recorded disaster in maritime history, sank with the loss of some 9,000 souls." N Y Times Book Rev

"A writer who refuses to avert his eyes from unpleasant truths, Grass remains an eloquent explorer of his country's troubled 20th-century history." Publ Wkly

The Danzig trilogy; translated by Ralph Manheim. Harcourt Brace Jovanovich 1987 1030p

ISBN 0-15-123816-2   LC 87-8725

"A Helen and Kurt Wolff book"

Contents: The tin drum; Cat and mouse; Dog years

Dog years; translated by Ralph Manheim. Harcourt, Brace & World 1965 570p o.p.

"A Helen and Kurt Wolff book"

Original German edition, 1963

"A monumental parable on 'mass man,' materialism, and transcendence, written in the richly encrusted, playful, brutal, ironic, subtle, sensitive, surrealist, erudite, unique modern baroque. . . . [This novel tells] of Eduard Amsel, rumored to be half Jew, designer of fantastic scarecrows, endlessly ingenious and talented; of Walter Matern, athlete and compulsive tooth grinder, Amsel's blood brother, his defender, and helper until association with a Nazi S. A. group leads him to beat Amsel unmercifully; of Hitler's favorite dog Prinz of notable lineage and the howling dog days echoing down the centuries through World War II and aftermath. The cast is large; the canvas is chiefly Danzig and villages along the Vistula; and the scarecrow prevails as dominant symbol." Booklist

also in Grass, G. The Danzig trilogy

The flounder; translated by Ralph Manheim. Harcourt Brace Jovanovich 1978 547p o.p.

LC 78-53891

"A Helen and Kurt Wolff book"

Original German edition, 1977

"Grass's first-person narrator is the legendary fisherman who caught the magic fish and might have fared well had it not been for the foolishness of his wife Ilsebill. Grass uses the well-known fairy tale as a frame

Grass, Günter, 1927-——*Continued*

for his chronicler to relate his various lives' experiences (between the late Neolithic and [1970]) . . . to his pregnant wife Ilsebill in the course of nine months. While his story unfolds, the fish is on trial in a feminist courtroom after he has been caught again, this time by three women in West Berlin." Libr J

"It is perhaps best to take this fantasy . . . as a celebration of life in all its gross particularity, with Grass still telling the German people to beware of the abstractions that have too often made them flounder in a nordic mist." Times Lit Suppl

My century; translated by Michael Henry Heim. Harcourt Brace & Co. 1999 280p $31

ISBN 0-15-100496-X   LC 99-38690

"A Helen and Kurt Wolff book"

Original German edition, 1999

In this fictional collage of 20th century Germany "each year has a story, and each story is told by a first-person narrator. Sometimes that narrator is Grass himself. Ironically, the stories highlight and celebrate the individual in this century of mass destruction, mass coercion, and mass consumerism; however, taken altogether, the narratives are like an album of snapshots from a dusty attic." Booklist

"The best thing [this book] offers non-Germans, even if inadvertently, is the opportunity to hear, or to overhear, how Germans speak to one another about their history when the rest of us are not supposed to be listening." Natl Rev

The tin drum; translated from the German by Ralph Manheim; with an introduction by John Reddick. Knopf 1993 xxxvii, 551p

ISBN 0-679-42033-9

        * LC 92-54295

"Everyman's library"

Original German edition, 1959; this translation first published 1962 in the United Kingdom, 1963 in the United States by Pantheon Books

"Oskar Matzerath, born with an unusually sharp mind, describes the amoral conditions through which he has lived in twentieth-century Germany, both during and after the Hitler regime. This strange narrator stops growing when he is three years old and remains three feet tall until some time late, when he decides to grow a few inches more. After the war he escapes to West Germany, where he works in such capacities as an artist's model, a nightclub performer, and a black marketeer. Depicted as a freak (Oskar becomes a hunchback later in his life), this character symbolizes the deformed society of this century. It is through his tin drum, which he uses to stimulate recollections of his life, that Oskar describes his past while he is an inmate in a mental hospital." Shapiro. Fic for Youth. 3d edition

also in Grass, G. The Danzig trilogy

Too far afield; translated from the German by Krishna Winston. Harcourt 2000 658p $30

ISBN 0-15-100230-4   LC 00-29586

"A Helen and Kurt Wolff book"

Original German edition published 1995

The narrative's "focus is German reunification, in particular, the fate of the German Democratic Republic after the Wall came down in 1989. At the center of the novel are two characters, locked in a sort of political marriage:

Theo Wuttke, a former East German cultural figure and long-winded raconteur, and Ludwig Hoffstaller, a professional spy who served for years as Wuttke's shadow. They are both about to turn 70 in this new Germany and are now both employees of the agency responsible for privatizing state-held companies." Booklist

Grau, Shirley Ann, 1929-

The keepers of the house. Knopf 1964 309p o.p.

"This multigenerational novel deals with the twentieth-century heirs of a Southern dynasty, their relations to the past, and their involvement in the racial and political complexities of the present. The narrator is Abigail Mason Tolliver, granddaughter of William Howland, whose second wife had been a Freejack Negro. The townspeople have always assumed that she had been no more than William's mistress, but the truth of the legality of their marriage surfaces when Abigail's husband, John Tolliver, enters the race for governor. In addition to leading to Tolliver's defeat, the story of the marriage also incites a mob to burn down the old Howland house. Abigail saves the house but withdraws the economic support that the Howland family has always supplied the town, and lets it 'shrivel and shrink to its real size.'" Shapiro. Fic for Youth. 3d edition

Graver, Elizabeth

Awake. Holt & Co. 2004 288p $23

ISBN 0-8050-6540-7   LC 2003-55253

"Anna Simon has been living in the dark ever since she gave birth to Max, a child with a rare genetic disease for whom even an hour in sunlight could prove fatal. For years, Anna has homeschooled Max and structured her life around his schedule, despite the fact that her husband, Ian, favors mainstreaming and wants Max to attend school with his older brother. When Anna learns of a camp in upstate New York for children with light-sensitivity disorders, she sees room for a compromise between her own and Ian's approaches. . . . And so the summer that Max is nine, the family heads off to Camp Luna. At first, the place seems like the answer to their problems. But as Anna is drawn into life there and gets to know Hal, the camp's charismatic founder, freedom and safety soon prove to be complicated things." Publisher's note

"A beautifully constructed tribute to self-sacrificing parenting that segues into a clear-eyed anatomy of the inevitable destructive power of infidelity." Libr J

Graves, Robert, 1895-1985

Claudius, the god and his wife Messalina. H. Smith & R. Haas 1935 583p o.p.

"A vivid picture of profligate Rome during the years in which Claudius conquered Britain and instituted many reforms at home. A story complete in itself, though a continuation of 'I, Claudius.'" Booklist

Complete short stories; edited by Lucia Graves. St. Martin's Press 1996 331p

ISBN 0-312-16055-0   LC 96-5343

Contents: Honey and flowers; My new-bug's exam; Thames-side reverie; The shout; Avocado pears; Old Papa Johnson; Interview with a dead man; Está en su casa; Bins K to T; School life in Majorca 1955; Bulletin

Graves, Robert, 1895-1985—*Continued*
of the College of St Modesto of Bobbio; Treacle tart;
Week-end at Cwm Tatws; The full length; God grant
your honour many years; 6 valiant bulls 6; Flesh-
coloured net tights; Thy servant and God's; A man may
not marry his . . .; An appointment for candlemas; The
five godfathers; The white horse or 'The great southern
ghost story'; Epics are out of fashion; Earth to earth;
They say . . . they say; The abominable Mr Gunn; The
Whitaker negroes; Trin-Trin-Trin; Cambridge upstairs;
'Ha, Ha!' Chort-led Nig-ger; Ditching in a fishless sea;
Period piece; He went out to buy a rhine; Kill them! kill
them!; Harold Vesey at the Gates of Hell; Life of the
poet Gnaeus Robertulus Gravesa; Ever had a Guinea
worm?; A bicycle in Majorca; Evidence of affluence;
The French thing; A toast to Ava Gardner; The viscountess and the short-haired girl; She landed yesterday; The
lost Chinese; You win, Houdini!; The tenement: a vision
of Imperial Rome; The Myconian; Christmas truce; My
best Christmas; No, Mac, it just wouldn't work; Miss
Briton's lady-companion; My first amorous adventure
  "Graves is a master storyteller, and the stories collected here are both masterly and charming. Especially noteworthy are the sweetly humorous tales about school days
in Edwardian England and the breezy, gently witty stories about everyday life in Majorca, Graves's adopted
home." Libr J

I, Claudius; from the autobiography of Tiberius
Claudius, born B.C. 10, murdered and deified A.D.
54. H. Smith and R. Haas 1934 494p o.p.
                                                                *
  "Claudius is lame and a stammerer who seems unlikely
to carry on the family tradition of power in ancient
Rome. Immersing himself in scholarly pursuits, Claudius
observes and lives through the plots hatched by his
grandmother, Livia, political conspiracies, murders, and
corruption, and he survives a number of emperors. He
becomes emperor at last and is a just and well-liked ruler, in contrast to those who preceded him." Shapiro. Fic
for Youth. 3d edition
  Followed by Claudius, the god and his wife Messalina

Gray, Alasdair

  Poor things; episodes from the early life of Archibald McCandless M.D., Scottish public health
officer; edited by Alasdair Gray. Harcourt Brace
Jovanovich 1993 c1992 317p il
  ISBN 0-15-173076-8   LC 92-40018
  First published 1992 in the United Kingdom
  "Scottish public health physician McCandless's manuscript describes his adventures in late-19th-century Glasgow with a Frankenstein-like doctor and scientist, Godwin Baxter, and Baxter's protegee, Bella, who, thanks to
Baxter's surgical sorcery, has the body of a woman and
the brain of a child." Newsweek
  "Mr. Gray contrasts the political and moral bleakness
of contemporary Britain with the civic energy that characterized the best of Victorian values, now lost. He underlines the harm done to Scotland. 'Poor Things' is a
political book. It is also witty and delightfully written, if
at times two-dimensional. Attention to Victorian Glasgow
with its civic fountains, domestic interiors and medical
schools gives the book texture. It is the characters, and
strangely enough its phantasmagoria, that give it life." N
Y Times Book Rev

Great racing stories. See The Dick Francis treasury of great racing stories

Great stories of the American West; stories by
John Jakes [et al.]; edited by Martin H.
Greenberg. Fine, D.I. 1994 290p il o.p.
                                     LC 94-071113

  Contents: The bandit, by L. D. Estleman; At Yuma
crossing, by B. Garfield; The guns of William Longley,
by D. Hamilton; The debt of Hardy Buckelew, by E.
Kelton; Lost sister, by D. M. Johnson; The gift of Co-
chise, by L. L'Amour; The woman at Apache Wells, by
J. Jakes; Law of the hunted ones, by E. Leonard;
Snowblind, by E. Hunter; The corpse rides at dawn, by
J. D. MacDonald; The time of the wolves, by M. Muller;
Gamblin' man, by D. V. Swain; Vigilante, by H. A.
DeRosso; Markers, by B. Pronzini; In the silence, by P.
S. Curry; Wolf night, by B. Crider; Liberty, by A.
Sarrantonio; Hacendado, by J. M. Reasoner; Death
ground [novelette], by E. Gorman
  "This excellent collection of 19 short stories is a suit-
able introduction to western fiction or a marvelous way
to rekindle one's enthusiasm for the genre." Booklist

Greatest hits; original stories of assassins, hitmen,
and hired guns; edited by Robert J. Randisi.
Carroll & Graf 2005 318p $26
  ISBN 978-0-7867-1581-7; 0-78671-581-2
                                     LC 2006-297413

  Contents: Keller's karma, by L. Block; The catch, by
J. W. Hall; Quarry's luck, by M. A. Collins; A trip
home, by E. Gorman; Misdirection, by B. Seranella;
Snow, snow, snow, by J. Harvey; Upon my soul, by R.
J. Randisi; Karma hits dogma, by J. Abbott; The greatest
trick of all, by L. Child; Dr. Sullivan's library, by C.
Matthews; Retrospective, by K. Wignall; The right tool
for the job, by M. Pelegrimas; For sale by owner, by J.
Siler; The closers, by P. Guyot; Chapter and verse, by J.
Deaver
  Randisi "has gathered 15 memorable tales of contract
killers, antiheroes paid to carry out murders for a variety
of clients and motives. . . . While the moral code that
guides the actions of some of the murderers requires a
measure of suspension of disbelief, the taut language and
suspenseful plot twists that mark virtually all the stories
should draw in even non-hardboiled devotees." Publ
Wkly

Greeley, Andrew M., 1928-

  The bishop in the West Wing; a Blackie Ryan
story. Forge 2002 255p il
  ISBN 0-312-86873-1   LC 2001-58284
  "A Tom Doherty Associates book"
  "Bishop Blackie Ryan is summoned to Washington,
D.C., by the newly elected Democratic president to investigate a possible poltergeist. Shortly after his inauguration, President Jack Patrick McGurn, a South Side Chicago Irishman dubbed Machine Gun McGurn by a national media eager to discredit him, is plagued by a series of inexplicable psychic phenomena. . . . An entertaining romp through the West Wing." Booklist

Greeley, Andrew M., 1928-—*Continued*

The cardinal virtues. Warner Bks. 1990 449p
o.p.   LC 89-40463
"When Father Laurence ('Lar') McAuliffe, pastor of an
affluent suburban Roman Catholic church, acquires an
unconventional new assistant, reactionary elements within
the congregation of St. Finian's show their displeasure.
As Lar and young Father Jamie struggle to minister to
the disparate needs of their flock, archdiocesan conservatives attempt to undermine their unorthodox methods. In
addition to successfully challenging the ecclesiastical hierarchy, the dynamic spiritual duo also double as match-
makers, salvage disintegrating marriages, counsel spirited
teens, and, most impressively, vanquish a regressive secret society flourishing within the clergy. Greeley appears more comfortable in this reversion to his pastoral
roots than in his more sensationalistic fictional forays."
Booklist

Irish cream; a Nuala Anne McGrail novel; Andrew M. Greeley. Forge 2005 319p $24.95
ISBN 0-7653-0335-3   LC 2004-56322
Psychic Nuala McGrail and her husband, Dermot
Coyne "look into mysteries past and present: the first
chronicled in the diaries of Father Richard Lonigan, a
19th-century parish priest in Donegal, Ireland, the second
involving poor Damian 'Day' O'Sullivan, whom the couple hire to take care of their two Irish wolfhounds. Amid
the troubled political and religious environment in Donegal, where mostly poor Catholic villagers are overseen
by Protestant Lord Skeffington, Father Lonigan investigates two shootings while striving to prevent further violence. In present-day Chicago, Nuala and Dermot face
opposition to hiring Day O'Sullivan from the lad's father, since Day is not only a profound disappointment to
the O'Sullivan family but also a convicted felon." Publ
Wkly

Irish lace; a Nuala Anne McGrail novel. Forge
1996 303p o.p.   LC 96-24519
"A Tom Doherty Associates book"
This novel "finds the winsome 20-year-old recently
transplanted from Ireland to Chicago. Nuala is romantically involved with Dermot Coyne—just the backup she
requires, given her penchant for attracting dicey situations. Nuala's 'gift,' experiencing visions from the past,
allows the plot to career back to Camp Douglas, a Union
prison in Civil War-era Chicago. From thence the story
proceeds, . . . to envelop a contemporary art theft, Irish
terrorists, and corrupt city officials." Libr J
"Moving effortlessly between the (fictional) conspiracies of 1864 and 1995 Chicago, Greeley is at his top
page-turning form, throwing in a few stinging words
about racism and xenophobia and delivering a rousing
defense of the Bill of Rights." Publ Wkly

Irish stew!; a Nuala Anne McGrail story. TOR
Bks. 2002 303p
ISBN 0-312-87188-0   LC 2001-54805
"A Tom Doherty Associates book"
In this adventure, "set at an international music festival
in Milan, the McGrails really have their hands full. Not
only are there demands on Nuala professionally (in addition to sleuthing, she is an international singing star), they
must also solve the mystery surrounding one Seamus
Costelloe, whose sinister personage is doomed according
to Nuala's ESP. As usual with Greeley's fiction, there is

a Chicago connection; in addition to everything else going on, Dermot tries to solve the 100-year-old mystery of
who started the Haymarket riot. A light, entertaining
read." Booklist

Second spring; a love story. Forge 2003 347p
$24.95
ISBN 0-7653-0236-5   LC 2002-32549
"In this installation, Charles 'Chucky' O'Malley and
his spirited family face the 1970s. Here we find Chucky
approaching 50 and stuck in a vicious midlife and spiritual crisis. While O'Malley can count his blessings—an
adoring wife, an amazing sex life, a prestigious career,
and a large, happy family—he still feels unfulfilled. In
addition, he is no longer able to take comfort in his faith.
As a photographer of some importance, O'Malley travels
the world snapping historical photos and searching for
his own happiness." Booklist

September song. Forge 2001 317p
ISBN 0-312-87225-9   LC 2001-33552
"A Tom Doherty Associates book"
Fourth installment in the author's O'Malley Family
saga; previous titles A midwinter's tale (1998); Younger
than springtime; Christmas wedding (2000)
This installment "focuses on the spitfire Irish Chuck
O'Malley and his gorgeous wife, Rosemarie. Set against
the turbulent events of the 1960s following the Kennedy
assassination, the novel opens with Chuck handing in his
resignation as German ambassador to President Johnson.
On a first-name basis with all the major political figures
of the time, Chuck strongly opposes Lyndon's position
on the Vietnam War. He returns to Chicago with his
wife and five children, only to be notified by Bobby
(Kennedy, that is) of the historic civil rights march in
Selma, Ala. . . . Sprinkled with . . . silly endearments
and some chaste love-making scenes, the novel proceeds
along a predictable historic course, weaving a Forrest
Gump-like path through the '60s." Publ Wkly

White smoke; a novel about the next papal conclave. Forge 1996 384p o.p.   LC 96-1412
"A Tom Doherty Associates book"
Bishop John Blackwood "Blackie" Ryan is "in Rome
along with his boss, Sean, Cardinal Cronin of Chicago,
as the College of Cardinals meets to choose the next
pope. Covering the papal conclave is Dennis (Dinny)
Molloy, a Pulitzer Prize-winning reporter for the *New
York Times*, and his lovely ex-wife, Patricia McLaughlin,
a correspondent for CNN. There is serious dissension in
the ranks about whom should be the next spiritual leader
of the world's one billion Roman Catholics. . . . While
the clergy battle it out, sparks fly between Dinny and
Patty as they rediscover each other. The situation heats
up when Dinny unearths a new Vatican investment scandal and Cronin collapses." Libr J

Younger than springtime. Forge 1999 348p
ISBN 0-312-86572-4   LC 99-22198
"A Tom Doherty Associates book"
Sequel to A midwinter's tale (1998)
This novel about the O'Malley family of Chicago
"chronicles the romantic and spiritual fortunes of returned soldier Chuck O'Malley, who comes home in
1949, having been stationed for two years in postwar
Germany. . . . The central image, bookending the novel,
is a snapshot Chuck takes of beautiful Rosemarie Clancy,
the troubled alcoholic daughter of Chuck's father's best

Greeley, Andrew M., 1928-—*Continued*

friend. The photo of Rosemarie, in *déshabillé*, gets Chuck into trouble at Notre Dame and concatenates his search for spiritual meaning within the strict prohibitions of the Church. Chuck and Rosemarie's lifelong mutual attraction permeates the novel, with Greeley shifting focus in the middle of the book to Chuck's father, John. The elder O'Malley tells of how he met Chuck's mother, and the part Rosemarie's father, Jim Clancy, played in the eventual union. John O'Malley's story is deftly set in the center of Chuck's saga." Publ Wkly

Green, George Dawes

The juror. Warner Bks. 1995 420p o.p.

LC 94-18831

"Annie Laird is a single mother, a part-time data entry clerk, an aspiring sculptor, and a juror selected for the murder trial of a mob boss. When a suave, handsome art broker buys some of her work and then invites her to dinner, she thinks her luck may be changing. Her supposed admirer, a Wall Street financier and Taoist nicknamed 'The Teacher,' is actually the brains behind the jailed mobster. The Teacher is incredibly charming; he's also a vicious killer. He promises Annie the continued safety of her son and the assurance of a lucrative artistic career in exchange for help in acquitting the mobster. . . . [This novel] is less a courtroom drama than a gripping psychological cat-and-mouse game." Libr J

Ravens. Grand Central Pub. 2009 325p $24.99
ISBN 978-0-446-53896-1; 0-446-53896-5

LC 2008-48331

"When Shaw and Romeo pull up at a convenience store off I-95 in Georgia, their only thought is to fix a leaky tire and be on their way again to Florida—away from their dull Ohio tech-support jobs. But this happens to be the store from which a $318,000,000-million jackpot ticket has been sold. When a pretty clerk accidentally reveals to Shaw the identity of the winning family, he hatches a ferociously audacious scheme: he and Romeo will squeeze the family for half their prize." Publisher's note

"The stark good and evil imagery of Christianity stands in contrast to the ever-shifting quicksand of moral dilemmas, and what comes through in 'Ravens,' despite the coincidences needed to spur along the narrative, is how the naked need for money, power and love strips away the prospect of a cathartic journey to redemption, turning hope inside out and back upon itself." Los Angeles Times Book Rev

Green, Hannah *See* Greenberg, Joanne, 1932-

Green, Jane, 1968-

The beach house. Viking 2008 341p $24.95
ISBN 978-0-670-01885-7; 0-670-01885-6

LC 2008-15516

"Set on Nantucket, the novel follows a 65-year-old widow named Nan, who decides to rent rooms in her rambling oceanfront home after a series of bad investments leaves her close to broke. Soon, a disparate group of strangers — men and women — start moving into the beach house. Green shows us the formation of a new kind of family with Nan as its surrogate mother. The

book has a warm, bohemian flavor reminiscent of the 'Tales of the City' novels by Armistead Maupin." Connecticut Post

Green, Norman, 1954-

The angel of Montague Street. HarperCollins Pubs. 2003 293p $24.95
ISBN 0-06-018819-7   LC 2002-32885

Silvano Iurata "should never be in Brooklyn in the first place. It's 1973, the city is broke and mean, and he's ben bumming around since he got out of Vietnam, avoiding his Mafia-employed family and keeping clear of his loco cousin, Domenic, who wants to settle and old family quarrel by killing him with his bare hands. But Iurata is on some private redemptive mission, and he figures that if he can find out what happened to his sweet, mildly retarded brother, last seen in Brooklyn Heights, he might be able to give up the dead and rejoin the living. . . . Green writes about mobster families with a knowledge that is unnerving in its intimacy." N Y Times Book Rev

Shooting Dr. Jack; a novel. HarperCollins Pubs. 2001 288p $25
ISBN 0-06-018822-7   LC 2001-16841

This novel is "set in a Brooklyn junkyard. Fat Tommy Roselli, a k a Tommy Bagadonuts, the shady boss of the operation; his partner, the hopeless alcoholic Stoney; and their young, street-smart apprentice, Tuco, are a bunch of losers trying to get by at the junkyard on Troutman Street. . . . When the novel opens, Tuco discovers two dead teenagers in the lot and then learns that the company's accountant has been found dead of gunshot wounds in a Bronx motel. The murders bring the police, whose investigation could put a crimp in the junkyard's off-the-book business." N Y Times Book Rev

"The sharply drawn characters and the clever nicknames will invite comparisons to Elmore Leonard, but there's little of Leonard's flash and cockiness here, only a gritty realism, an attention to detail, and a resolute avoidance of clichés." Publ Wkly

Green, Tim

The letter of the law. Warner Bks. 2000 341p
ISBN 0-446-52299-6   LC 00-22285

Texan Casey Jordan "helps clear Eric Lipton, a law professor at the University of Texas, of the charge of disemboweling and murdering Marcia Sales. An instant before the jury foreman reads the verdict, Lipton whispers his guilt to Jordan. After the trial, suspicion rests on Donald Sales, the victim's father. Distraught with grief, hating Lipton, and humiliated by Jordan's trial accusation of incest, Sales abducts Jordan to teach her some of the pain his daughter suffered." Libr J

Green cane and juicy flotsam; short stories by Caribbean women; Carmen C. Esteves and Lizabeth Paravisini-Gebert, editors. Rutgers Univ. Press 1991 xxix, 273p
ISBN 0-8135-1737-0   LC 91-4788

Stories included are: Widow's walk, by O. P. Adisa; Little Cog-burt, by P. S. Allfrey; Cotton candy, by D. Alonso; See me in me Benz an t'ing, by H. D. Campbell; They called her Aurora, by A. Cartagena Portalatin;

Green cane and juicy flotsam—*Continued*

Columba, by M. Cliff; A pottage of lentils, by M. T. Colimon-Hall; Three women in Manhattan, by M. Condé; Hair, by H. Contreras; Piano-bar, by L. Dévieux; Barred: Trinidad 1987, by R. Espinet; The poisoned story, by R. Ferré; Cocuyo flower, by M. Garcia Ramis; How to gather the shadows of the flowers, by A. Hernández; Opéra Station. Six in the evening. For months . . ., by J. Hyvrard; Girl, by J. Kincaid; No dust is allowed in this house, by O. Nolla; Parable II, by V. Pollard; Red flower, by P. Poujol-Oriol; The day they burned the books, by J. Rhys; Lola; or, The song of spring, by A. Roemer; Bright Thursdays, by O. Senior; Tétiyette and the Devil; ADJ, Inc., by A. L. Vega; Of nuns and punishments, by B. Vianen; Passport to paradise, by M. Warner-Vieyra; Of natural causes, by M. Yañez

"Throughout, [this anthology] the race and class issues unique to Caribbean women are explored but in diverse ways and on a small scale, so that one comes away from the book with a uniquely personal sense of a much larger political phenomenon." Booklist

Greenberg, Joanne, 1932-

I never promised you a rose garden; a novel; [by] Hannah Green. Holt & Co. 1964 300p
  ISBN 0-8050-0872-1

Sixteen-year-old Deborah "is sick of rebelling against the lies she hears, the hatred she feels, and, at a summer camp, the antiSemitism she suffers. She is schizophrenic: she has invented for herself a mythical kingdom into which she retreats and only when her parents reluctantly commit her to an asylum does she begin with difficulty to face reality." Publ Wkly

"The hospital world and Deborah's fantasy world are strikingly portrayed, as is the girl's violent struggle between sickness and health, a struggle given added poignancy by youth, wit, and courage." Libr J

In this sign. Holt, Rinehart & Winston 1970 275p o.p.

"The life of deaf-mutes Abel and Janice Ryder is followed from their marriage to their old age. After they leave the cloistered world of the institution for those with their handicap, they are plunged, unprepared, into the terrifying world of the hearing. They are never fully assimilated into that society. When they have a daughter who can hear, they gain new perspectives, but poverty and personal tragedy—the death of a son—further separate them from others, even from other deaf people. Greenberg's insights into the lives of the deaf are sensitive and painful." Shapiro. Fic for Youth. 2d edition

Greenberg, Martin Harry

(ed) Great stories of the American West. See Great stories of the American West

Greene, Graham, 1904-1991

3: This gun for hire, The confidential agent, The ministry of fear. Viking 1952 3v in 1 o.p.

A one-volume edition of three suspense stories. The titles were first published 1936, 1939 and 1943, respectively

Brighton rock; an entertainment. Viking 1938 358p o.p.

"This novel presents the story of Pinkie Brown, a chilling, utterly evil 17-year-old gang leader who marries the plodding Rose in order to insure her silence about his crimes. Both Pinkie and Rose were reared as Roman Catholics, and that background continues to inform their thoughts, if not their actions. In the end Pinkie dies while attempting to kill Rose; later, a priest tells Rose that her love for Pinkie may have saved her, as the mercy of God may have saved Pinkie." Merriam-Webster's Ency of Lit

A burnt-out case. Viking 1961 c1960 248p o.p.

"The story opens as Querry, a European who has lost the ability to connect with emotion or spirituality, arrives at a leprosarium in the Belgian Congo. His spiritual aridity is likened to a medical burnt-out-case—a leper who is in remission but who has been eaten up by his disease. Querry is invigorated by his contact with the leprosarium and its inhabitants, and he begins to come to life. Parkinson, an opportunistic journalist, discovers that Querry is a distinguished architect with a lurid past and begins to write sensationalist newspaper articles about him. When Querry innocently consoles the wife of the manager of a local factory, he is shot dead by her husband." Merriam-Webster's Ency of Lit

The captain and the enemy. Viking 1988 188p o.p.
  LC 87-40664

"The novel takes the form of a memoir of a young man named Victor, who recounts how the mysterious 'Captain,' posing as a friend of his father, removed him from school one day and set him up in residence with Liza, a kind but equally inscrutable woman. Victor is renamed Jim, the Captain—an apparent thief, a liar, and prone to jaunts to the Continent—returns only occasionally to give Liza money and 'instruct' Jim on survival in the world, and the boy grows up bewildered but, in time, aware that his position in life has been that of a kind of gift to Liza, who, as his real father's paramour, once underwent an abortion unwillingly." Booklist

The author "wastes not a word in distilling the fictional preoccupations of a lifetime, omitting descriptive padding and elaborate transitions. But stripped down, the narrative runs fast and true across that bleak and poignant emotional landscape that is uniquely, immortally his." Time

Collected stories; including May we borrow your husband? A sense of reality [and] Twenty-one stories. Viking 1973 c1972 561p o.p.

Contents: May we borrow your husband?; Beauty; Chagrin in three parts; The over-night bag; Mortmain; Cheap in August; A shocking accident; The invisible Japanese gentlemen; Awful when you think of it; Doctor Crombie; The root of all evil; Two gentle people; Under the garden; A visit to Morin; The blessing; Church militant; Dear Dr. Falkenheim; Dream of a strange land; A discovery in the woods; The destructors; Special duties; The blue film; The hint of an explanation; When Greek meets Greek; Men at work; Alas, poor Maling; The case for the defence; A little place off the Edgware Road; Across the bridge; A drive in the country; The innocent; The basement room; A chance for Mr. Lever; Brother; Jubilee; A day saved; I spy; Proof positive; The second death; The end of the party

Greene, Graham, 1904-1991—*Continued*

The comedians. Viking 1966 309p o.p.

This "book concerns a back-slidden Catholic, a native of Monaco and owner of a rundown tourist hotel in Haiti; his affair with the German wife of a Latin American ambassador; and his involvement with a rascally British con man and an American Presidential candidate and his wife, in Haiti to propagate the cult of vegetarianism—most of them in varying degrees comedians on the stage of life, running a bluff, playing a role, substituting sham for sincerity." Libr J

The confidential agent

In Greene, G. 3: This gun for hire, The confidential agent, The ministry of fear

The end of the affair. Viking 1951 240p o.p.

*

"The novel is set in wartime London. The narrator Maurice Bendrix, a bitter, sardonic novelist, has a five-year affair with a married woman, Sarah Miles. When a V-1 bomb explodes in front of Bendrix's apartment and Sarah finds Bendrix pinned beneath the front door, she believes him dead. She promises a God in whom she does not believe that she will give Bendrix up if he is allowed to live. Just then, Bendrix walks into the room and Sarah begins her religious journey; she breaks off with Bendrix, railing against God even as she begins to take religious instruction. Gradually she comes to a profound religious faith." Merriam-Webster's Ency of Lit

The heart of the matter; introduction by James Wood. Deluxe ed. Penguin Books 2004 255p (Penguin classics) pa $15

ISBN 0-14243799-9

* LC 2004-275122

First published 1948

"Set in West Africa, it is a suspense story ingeniously made to hinge on religious faith. . . . The hero is Scobie, an English Roman Catholic who has vowed to make his devout wife happy though he no longer loves her. He borrows money from a local criminal to send her out of harm's way to South Africa; then he falls in love with a young woman from a group of castaways whose ship has been torpedoed. The return of his wife, the development of an adulterous affair, and blackmail drive Scobie deeper into deception and lies. Forced to betray someone, he betrays his god and himself, and finally commits suicide." Reader's Ency. 4th edition

The honorary consul. Simon & Schuster 1973 315p o.p.

This "novel relates the story of the politically motivated kidnapping of a minor British functionary near Argentina's Paraguayan border. The novel's major characters exemplify the kinds of personal sacrifices one must make in order to live in good conscience in a world where there is too much tyranny and injustice. A minor machismo novelist endures privation; a priest joins the radical underground movement; a physician gives up a lucrative Buenos Aires practice." Libr J

The human factor. Knopf 1992 c1978 xxviii, 338p $18

ISBN 0-679-40992-0

* LC 91-53189

"Everyman's library"

A reissue of the title first published 1978 by Simon & Schuster

"In the British Foreign Service 'the human factor' becomes a liability for employees and a conduit for suspense, intrigue, and tragedy. Maurice Castle, head of a division in which information seems to have been leaked, presents a very positive image that appears to assure his innocence, but Davis, directly responsible to him, is an object of speculation. For a secret agent, the normal relationships of love and family are fraught with danger. As is true of many of Greene's novels, there are questions in this book about the loyalty owed to a government whose activities are suspect." Shapiro. Fic For Youth. 3d edition

The last word and other stories. Reinhardt Bks. 1990 149p o.p.

LC 90-81665

Contents: The last word; The news in English; The moment of truth; The man who stole the Eiffel Tower; The lieutenant died last; A branch of the service; An old man's memory; The lottery ticket; The new house; Work not in progress; Murder for the wrong reason; An appointment with the General

"This modest volume gathers uncollected stories from the entire range of Greene's career. The earliest dates from 1923 (!) and the latest from 1989." Libr J

May we borrow your husband?

In Greene, G. Collected stories p1-161

The ministry of fear; an entertainment. Viking 1943 239p o.p.

"Probably the author's least remembered work, one showing the Buchan influence most clearly. A group of Fifth Column Englishmen attempt to corner and murder a neurotic fellow countryman who possesses a piece of military intelligence they want to pass on to Berlin." Smith. Cloak and Dagger Fic

also in Greene, G. 3: This gun for hire, The confidential agent, The ministry of fear

Monsignor Quixote. Simon & Schuster 1982 221p o.p.

LC 82-5937

"Father Quixote is a humble parish priest despised by his bishop. Through an accidental encounter with a stranded bishop, he is named Monsignor, much to his bishop's and his discomfort. He sets off on a journey with the communist ex-mayor of his town. The philosophy and thinking of the ex-mayor, Sancho, are diametrically opposed to that of the priest, and there is much provocative discussion between them as they follow paths similar to those taken by the priest's fictional forebear, Don Quixote. Some of their adventures bring the priest to some surprising places, such as an x-rated cinema and a church where religion is being commercialized and demeaned. There is much humor as well as theology to involve the reader in this delightful odyssey." Shapiro. Fic for Youth. 3d edition

Orient Express. Doubleday, Doran 1933 310p o.p.

First published 1932 in the United Kingdom with title: Stamboul train

This is the story of what happened to a number of people who board the Orient Express at Ostend to make the three-day journey across the continent to Constantinople

Greene, Graham, 1904-1991—*Continued*

Our man in Havana; an entertainment. Viking 1958 247p o.p.

"Set in Cuba before the communist revolution, the book is a comical spy story about a British vacuum-cleaner salesman's misadventures in the British Secret Intelligence Service. Although many critics found fault with the book's overly farcical style, it was also admired for its skillful rendering of the Cuban locale." Merriam-Webster's Ency of Lit

The power and the glory; introduction by John Updike. Viking 1990 295p hardcover o.p. pa $14
    ISBN 0-670-83536-6; 0-14-243730-1 (pa)
                                            LC 90-50052
First published 1940 with title: The labyrinthine ways
Set in Mexico, this novel "describes the desperate last wanderings of a whisky priest as outlaw in his own state, who, despite a sense of his own worthlessness (he drinks, and has fathered a bastard daughter), is determined to continue to function as priest until captured. . . . Like many of Greene's works, it combines a conspicuous Christian theme and symbolism with the elements of a thriller." Oxford Companion to Engl Lit

The quiet American. Modern Lib. 1992 c1955 247p
    ISBN 0-679-60014-0
                                          * LC 92-50219
First published 1955 in the United Kingdom; first United States edition published 1956 by Viking
"The novel is set in Vietnam during the French war against the Vietminh, and revolves around the death of Alden Pyle (the Quiet American), a naive and high-minded idealist who has arrived in the country as a member of the Economic Aid Mission. . . . The narrator, Thomas Fowler, is a middle-aged English journalist, cynical and detached. . . . Estranged from his wife in England, Fowler lives with an Annamite girl, Phuong. The story alternates between the period immediately after Pyle's murder and the events leading up to it." Camb Guide to Lit in Engl
"Mr. Greene has always been a master of suspense, and the particular excellence of 'The Quiet American' lies in the way in which he builds up the situation finally to explode the moral problem which for him lies at the heart of the matter." Times Lit Suppl

A sense of reality
    In Greene, G. Collected stories p164-323

The tenth man. Simon & Schuster 1985 157p o.p.
                                          LC 84-29830
"The Tenth Man is a long forgotten film treatment that Greene wrote for MGM in 1947. A prosperous French lawyer is held hostage during World War II by the Gestapo. He and his fellow prisoners must draw lots to see who must die. He draws the marked paper and, panic-stricken, offers everything he has to save his life. A consumptive young man accepts and leaves his new found estate to his mother and sister. The war ends and this lawyer, in disguise, returns to his chateau. It is occupied by the young man's senile mother, who awaits the return of her son, and the sister, who hatefully awaits the return of the man who bought her brother's life." West Coast Rev Books

"A fatal series of events follows, entwining narrative excitement with broader questions of identity, fate, and morality. As always with Greene, the basic plot is heightened by the novelist's compelling view of the human condition." Libr J

This gun for hire
    In Greene, G. 3: This gun for hire, The confidential agent, The ministry of fear

Travels with my aunt; a novel. Viking 1969 244p o.p.
"Aunt Augusta, in her late 70's, embroils her bachelor nephew, an utterly respectable, dahlia-growing retired bank manager, in a series of wild escapades. The action moves from London, across the European continent to Istanbul, and ends in Paraguay. Most of the characters are from Aunt Augusta's somewhat murky past, although there are contemporary figures such as a C.I.A. agent and his hippie daughter, and Wordsworth from Sierra Leone, who lives with Aunt Augusta as her 'valet.'" Libr J

"The book unmistakably turns its back on the Orphic preoccupations with the hereafter that characterized Greene's Catholic novels, and wholeheartedly embraces a Bacchic emphasis on the here and now." N Y Times Book Rev

Twenty-one stories
    In Greene, G. Collected stories p325-562

Greenleaf, Stephen

Blood type; the new John Marshall Tanner mystery. Morrow 1992 283p o.p.   LC 91-40057
San Francisco PI John Marshall Tanner "questions the supposed suicide of bar-buddy Tom, an ambulance driver whose beautiful, blues-singing wife has been dating a corporate raider of dubious integrity. Because he suspects murder, Tanner delves into Tom's background, tracks Tom's 'lost' schizophrenic brother, finds a motive, and uncovers a scheme involving San Francisco blood banks." Libr J
Greenleaf delivers "incisive social observations, compassionate characterizations and fine writing. . . . As befits an heir of Ross Macdonald, the author maintains his moral grip on what matters." N Y Times Book Rev

False conception; a John Marshall Tanner novel. Penzler Bks. 1994 273p
    ISBN 1-883402-87-5   LC 94-17371
"Stuart and Millicent Colbert can't conceive a child, but they have the resources to hire a surrogate mother. San Francisco private eye, Marsh Tanner is employed to investigate the surrogate, Greta Hammond. The catch: Hammond must never know the identity of the Colberts nor that she's being investigated. . . . Tanner novels are never just mysteries; Greenleaf always weaves in a larger human dilemma, and here he does it more successfully than ever before." Booklist

Flesh wounds. Scribner 1996 318p
    ISBN 0-684-81583-4   LC 95-24412
Private eye John Marshall Tanner "gives himself the masochistic pleasure of going to Seattle to do a job for an old flame. Although Tanner is still in love with this woman, he agrees to search for her fiancé's missing

Greenleaf, Stephen—*Continued*

daughter, a stunning figure model who has run afoul of an exploitative photographer described as 'a carnivore.'. . . He discovers the city's richer, darker colors when he traces the photographer's previous victims to the sex clubs and prostitutes' turf where they ended up after appearing in a pernicious new line of pornography using advanced digital technology." N Y Times Book Rev

"The Tanner series continues to be among the most emotionally and intellectually challenging in the genre." Booklist

Past tense; a John Marshall Tanner novel. Scribner 1997 282p

ISBN 0-684-83249-6 LC 96-35476

San Francisco investigator Tanner, "rushes to the aid of his best friend, a veteran homicide cop named Charley Sleet, who shoots a man dead in open court and refuses to offer any explanation or defense. Tanner is one of the best listeners in the business, and he gets an earful when he goes around interviewing people who knew either Charley or his victim, a creep whose daughter was suing him for sexual abuse. The characters met on these rounds are prime specimens, and their talk is choice." N Y Times Book Rev

Strawberry Sunday; a John Marshall Tanner novel. Scribner 1999 287p

ISBN 0-684-84954-2 LC 98-40955

"Tanner investigates the murder of a young woman who worked hard for labor reform among strawberry pickers in the Salinas Valley." Libr J

"The Tanner books often have been built around a specific social or political issue, and this one is no exception. Greenleaf takes a long, hard look at the miserable conditions in which many farmworkers live and toil, and builds a complex, absorbing plot around the topic." Publ Wkly

Greer, Andrew Sean

The path of minor planets. Picador 2001 273p $23

ISBN 0-312-27556-0 LC 2001-41818

"In 1965, several astronomers assemble on an island in the South China Sea to observe the comet Swift, but the event is marred by the accidental death of a young child. The tragedy seems to ignite a succession of relationship woes for two young scientists and their spouses. Like the galaxies they study, the progression of their lives and loves is updated as they reunite every six years to commemorate the anniversary of the comet's original appearance." Publ Wkly

"In this début novel, Greer pinpoints the 'tiny hidden madnesses in ordinary people' with unerring accuracy, and, in prose littered with sparks, makes palpable the longing for the celestial." New Yorker

The story of a marriage. Farrar, Straus & Giroux 2008 195p $22

ISBN 978-0-374-10866-3; 0-374-10866-8 LC 2007-46835

"A Frances Coady book"

"In San Francisco in 1953, narrator Pearlie relates the circumstances of her marriage to Holland Cook, her childhood sweetheart. Pearlie's sacrifices for Holland begin when they are teenagers and continue when the two reunite a few years later, marry and have an adored son. The reappearance in Holland's life of his former boss and lover, Buzz Drumer, propels them into a triangular relationship of agonizing decisions." Publ Wkly

"Greer's short novel feels admirably worked over like a long-simmered sauce. He near-brilliantly juxtaposes the nuances of love, sexual awakening and the sometimes suffocating sacrifices marriage demands against broader cultural observations about political turmoil, the physical and emotional effects of war, sexual repression and racism. His book is a perfect mix of what we seek from literature — captivating storytelling; a complex, finely tuned structure; stunning language; and astute observations about both the mundane intricacies of everyday relationships and society as a whole." Los Angeles Times Book Rev

Gregory, Daryl

Pandemonium. Del Rey 2008 288p pa $13

ISBN 978-0-345-50116-5; 0-345-50116-0 LC 2008-300445

"An ordinary day at Chicago's O'Hare airport takes a turn for the weird when one of the travelers is possessed by a demon. In Gregory's world, peopled by demons that seem to reflect archetypes from some collective unconscious, this event is inconvenient but not unusual. His present-day story is set in a world where demons have plagued humanity since their mysterious emergence in the 1950s. Del Pierce, who as a young boy was possessed by the entity known as the Hellion, witnesses this airport possession while struggling with the knowledge that something is drastically wrong with him—something connected to his own experience. To save his life, and the lives of countless others, Del will have to learn more about the origins and purposes of demons than any other person has dared." Voice Youth Advocates

"Gregory has produced a debut novel that combines suspense, philosophical conundrums, Jungian psychological theory, aspects of American pop culture, and a touch of neuroscience with skillful and ambitious storytelling." Strange Horizons

Gregory, Philippa, 1954-

The Boleyn Inheritance. Touchstone 2006 518p $25.95

ISBN 0-7432-7250-1; 978-0-7432-7250-6

"A Touchstone book"

An historical novel focusing on the family of Henry VIII. "Among the cast, who alternately narrate: Henry's fourth wife, Bavarian-born Anne of Cleves; his fifth wife, English teenager Katherine Howard; and Lady Rochford (Jane Boleyn), the jealous spouse whose testimony helped send her husband, Thomas, and sister-in-law Anne Boleyn to their execution. Attended by Lady Rochford, 24-year-old Anne of Cleves endures a disastrous first encounter with the twice-her-age king—an occasion where Henry takes notice of Katherine Howard. . . . Rich in intrigue and irony, this is a tale where readers will already know who was divorced, beheaded or survived, but will savor Gregory's sharp staging of how and why." Publ Wkly

Earthly joys. St. Martin's Press 1998 440p

ISBN 0-312-19262-2 LC 98-8771

Gregory, Philippa, 1954-—*Continued*

This story centers on "John Tradescant, gardener to several great lords and finally to the king himself during the darkest days of post-Elizabethan England. Tradescant is a loyal vassal of the old school. . . . The first great lord in Tradescant's life, Sir Robert Cecil, is a man of honor and intelligence, but none of his successors measure up. Under King James I and then his son, Charles I, the court sinks into corruption, decadence and greed, drawing Tradescant ever closer to its evil doings. His loyalty also leads him into a passionate and doomed affair with the most charming, favored and unscrupulous member of the court, the Duke of Buckingham. . . . This tale of forbidden love set against the turmoil of a country in chaos makes for both intelligent and satisfying reading." N Y Times Book Rev

Followed by Virgin earth

The other Boleyn girl; a novel. Scribner Paperback Fiction 2002 664p pa $16

ISBN 0-7432-2744-1   LC 2001-57646

"Before Henry VIII ever considered making Anne Boleyn his wife, her older sister, Mary, was his mistress. . . . [The author] uses the perspective of this 'other Boleyn girl' to reveal the rivalries and intrigues swirling through England." Libr J

This is "as much a tale of love and lust as it is a saga about an ambitious family who used their kin as negotiable assets. . . . Absorbing tale of a Renaissance family determined to climb as high as they can, whatever the cost." Kirkus

The queen's fool; a novel. Simon & Schuster 2004 504p pa $16

ISBN 0-7432-4607-1   LC 2003-67378

"A Touchstone book"

"It is winter, 1553. Pursued by the Inquisition, Hannah Green, a fourteen-year-old Jewish girl, is forced to flee Spain with her father. But Hannah is no ordinary refugee. Her gift of 'Sight,' the ability to foresee the future, is priceless in the troubled times of the Tudor court. Hannah is adopted by the glamorous Robert Dudley, the charismatic son of King Edward's protector, who brings her to court as a 'holy fool' for Queen Mary and, ultimately, Queen Elizabeth. Hired as a fool but working as a spy; promised in wedlock but in love with her master; endangered by the laws against heresy, treason, and witchcraft, Hannah must choose between the safe life of a commoner and the dangerous intrigues of the royal family that are inextricably bound up in her own yearnings and desires." Publisher's note

Virgin earth. St. Martin's Press 1999 576p

ISBN 0-312-20617-8   LC 99-48489

This sequel to Earthly joys "begins as John Tradescant the Younger, Charles I's gardener, sails to the New World in search of rarities for his gardens. Not only does he find exotic plants, but he also glimpses unimagined freedom. His father's death leads John to a marriage of convenience in England. Unwilling to fight for Charles I, he returns to Virginia, where he joins the Powhatan and finds a wife. But eventually John loses his place in the tribe because of his inability to kill settlers. Determined to maintain a commitment to his English family, he goes home to a country buffeted by civil war." Libr J

The wise woman. Pocket Bks. 1993 c1992 438p o.p.   LC 93-21824

First published 1992 in the United Kingdom

A novel of "passion and witchcraft in 16th-century England. Growing up as an ill-used apprentice to Morach, the much-feared wise woman of the moors, Alys finds respite by joining an order of Catholic nuns. When young Lord Hugo and his men burn the abbey to the ground during a drunken rampage, Alys is the only one to escape; she flees back to Morach. . . . Attracted to Hugo despite his murderous past, Alys begins to practice witchcraft in earnest to rid him of Catherine and become his wife." Publ Wkly

Grenville, Kate, 1950-

The idea of perfection. Viking 2002 401p $24.95

ISBN 0-670-03080-5   LC 2001-58133

First published 2000 in the United Kingdom

"Saving the picturesque Bent Bridge becomes both cause and catalyst for the most unlikely of love affairs when social outcasts Douglas Cheeseman and Harley Savage descend on a wayward village in the remote Australian outback." Booklist

"Grenville does her characters the honor of taking their pain seriously and is gracious enough to allow them their hard-earned pleasure. Her ability to move between these elements gives her novel a beautiful balance." N Y Times Book Rev

The lieutenant. Atlantic Monthly Presss 2009 307p $24

ISBN 978-0-8021-1916-2; 0-8021-1916-6

First published 2008 in Australia

"Grenville's novel, based on the true story of William Dawes, who was among the soldiers accompanying the first prisoners sent to Australia, concerns Daniel Rooke, a lonely, introverted sort whose skill as an astronomer earns him a privileged position in the first colonial mission sent to New South Wales, in 1787. Living apart from his regiment for the purpose of studying stars, Rooke befriends a young Aboriginal girl and begins to compile a vocabulary and grammar of her language. But as tensions between the two groups escalate he must choose between what he feels is right and what he considers his duty. Grenville's thematic relentlessness can be stultifying, but the honest beauty of her story wins out." New Yorker

The secret river. Canongate 2006 334p $24

ISBN 1-84195-682-4   LC 2006-365651

First published 2005 in Australia

"On his first night in New South Wales, in 1806, William Thornhill—Thames boatman, thief, banished convict—gazes despairingly into the forest outside his flimsy hut. A spear-wielding Aborigine appears before him, and his dejection turns to rage. All he has is his family—'those soft parcels of flesh,' sleeping behind him—and 'the dirt under his bare feet, his small grip on this unknown place,' and he is not about to give them up to a naked black stranger. The Aborigine responds with equal vehemence: 'Be off, be off!' The episode shows, in miniature, the project of Grenville's magnificent novel—an unflinching exploration of modern Australia's origins. Like the settlers, we instinctively turn away from the ugly truths behind every cleared riverbank and every

Grenville, Kate, 1950-—*Continued*

posted fence. But Grenville's psychological acuity, and the sheer gorgeousness of her descriptions of the territory being fought over, pulls us ever deeper into a time when one community's opportunity spelled another's doom." New Yorker

Gresham, William Lindsay, 1909-1962

Nightmare alley

In Crime novels: American noir of the 1930s and 40s

Grey, Zane, 1872-1939

Riders of the purple sage. Five Star 2005 368p $25.95

ISBN 1-59414-130-4

* LC 2004-60017

First published 1912 by Harper

"Well handled melodramatic story of hairbreadth escapes from Mormon vengeance in southwestern Utah in 1871." Booklist

West of the Pecos. Harper 1937 314p o.p.

"Romantic western which tells of Colonel Terrill, broken by the Civil War, and his tomboy daughter, their efforts to get a start in the new world of the west, the Colonel's brutal murder and Pecos Smith's ride to rescue the girl, left alone in a land of desperados." Wis Libr Bull

Woman of the frontier; a western story. Five Star 1998 320p $19.95

ISBN 0-7862-1156-3

LC 98-22717

"Five Star standard print western series"

"This tale, written in 1934, was rejected by magazines because of its vivid portrayal of the hardships of pioneer life, including the rape of Grey's heroine by a renegade Apache. A heavily edited version called 30,000 on the Hoof was finally published in 1940, a year after the author's death. This version, completely restored by Grey's son, Loren, recounts the trials and tribulations of Arizona rancher Logan Huett, his heroic wife, Lucinda, their three sons, and a girl named Barbara, who is abandoned by wagon-train travelers and raised by the Huetts." Booklist

Griesemer, John

Signal & noise. Picador 2003 593p $26

ISBN 0-312-30082-4

LC 2003-42938

"Brilliant engineer Chester Ludlow is soon transformed into a mesmerizing showman when he becomes involved in the laying of the trans-Atlantic cable. Attempting to raise the cash needed to launch the initiative, Ludlow travels with a musical 'Phantasmagorium Show,' which bowls over willing investors with its complex scene-shifting and inspiring narration. Soon the money is pouring in, and Chester becomes a celebrity and begins a passionate affair with the beautiful piano player. Meanwhile, his wife, Lily, still grieving the death of their child some years before, embarks on an intense spiritual quest in an attempt to communicate with her dead daughter." Booklist

Griesemer "has created some fine set pieces of disaster: the failed launch of the Great Eastern, two spectacular fires, a train crash that wrecks Ludlow's invention of

a great Civil War cannon and, best of all, a breathtaking storm at sea. At the other end of the scale, the detail that fleshes out the novel's world is equally convincing." N Y Times Book Rev

Griffin, Pauline

(jt. auth) Norton, A. Redline the stars

Griffin, W. E. B.

The aviators. Putnam 1988 409p (Brotherhood of war, bk8) o.p.

LC 88-12657

"Protaganist Johnny is a born soldier who distinguishes himself as a helicopter pilot in Vietnam and is promoted to aide-de-camp to the commanding officer of Fort Rucker. In his new post, he finds himself directly involved with the development of the Army's first Air Assault Division—a new force crucial to meet the challenge of guerrilla warfare in Vietnam. This is the story of Johnny's year of work and crisis, the making and breaking of rules, the development of friendships, and the awakening of love." Libr J

Blood and honor. Putnam 1996 553p o.p.

LC 96-19039

In this sequel to Honor bound "Marine pilot and OSS operative Cletus Frade is sent to Argentina, ostensibly as a military attaché to the U.S. ambassador. Actually, he is there to avenge his father's murder. An influential man in Argentine politics who was pro-Allies, Frade's father was killed by Nazi intelligence agents because they feared he might become president. Meanwhile, an SS intelligence officer arrives. Part of his mission is to help a German submarine infiltrate Argentine waters. The SS officer and Frade are soon playing cat and mouse, though they're hampered by Argentina's neutrality." Booklist

"There's no deep moral digging here as there is in, say, le Carré. But Griffin is a savvy old hand and here, working with an exotic setting and a complex plot, delivers the sort of sturdy entertainment his fans expect." Publ Wkly

Followed by Secret honor

By order of the President; W.E.B. Griffin. Putnam 2004 528p $26.95

ISBN 0-399-15207-5

LC 2004-53417

"This novel is about the effort to unravel and defeat a terrorist plot to crash a stolen 727 into the Liberty Bell in Philadelphia." N Y Times Book Rev

"Proving himself solidly in control of cutting-edge military material, Griffin bases his new series not on wars past but on today's murky exigencies of terrorism and international political intrigue. . . . In the end, there are a few bodies to account for, but it's the meticulous investigation that leaves readers standing on the tarmac waiting for Charley Castillo and his newly minted band of can-do compatriots to touch down and carry them away again on a new adventure." Publ Wkly

Close combat. Putnam 1993 383p (Corps, bk6) o.p.

LC 92-34677

Set in 1942 the sixth book in the series "revolves around a war bond tour featuring Marine heroes of the Guadacanal Campaign. Series fans will recognize the central characters, among them Marine general and presidential troubleshooter Fleming Pickering, his fighter pilot

Griffin, W. E. B.—*Continued*

son Pick, and movie mogul Homer Dillon, a Marine for the duration. Griffin has Marine Corps lore and trivia down pat, and he uses the bond-tour story line to convey the public-relations aspects of modern war." Publ Wkly

Followed by Behind the lines (1995)

Honor bound. Putnam 1994 c1993 474p o.p.

LC 93-36850

This "World War II novel pits U.S. Marine Captain Cletus Frade, late of Guadalcanal, against an ostensibly neutral ship in Buenos Aires in 1942. Naturally, the Nazis are angling for position in this vital South American port, and Clete's mission is to maintain Allied influence with the Argentine navy by destroying the German-controlled ship. Along the way, Clete encounters the father he's never met (now a top officer in the Argentine army), a sympathetic German Luftwaffe officer, and a beautiful Argentine 'virgin princess,' with whom he falls in love." Booklist

"Griffin's feel for the details of life in the military 50 years ago and the humanity of his characters on all sides of the covert war make this a superior war story in an interesting milieu." Libr J

Followed by Blood and honor

In danger's path. Putnam 1998 549p (Corps, bk8)

ISBN 0-399-14421-8 LC 98-18809

The hero of this novel is "Brigadier General Fleming Pickering, head of the OSS' Pacific operations during World War II. . . . Pickering is a can-do kind of guy, whose assignments include the rescue of some American ex-servicemen and their families who are fleeing the Japanese in the Gobi Desert, and the setting up of a weather station in the desert to aid in air attacks on the Japanese. As in Griffin's other novels, this one is packed with adventure." Booklist

The last heroes. Putnam 1997 c1985 342p

ISBN 0-399-14289-4 LC 96-39458

First published 1985 in paperback

First volume of the author's Men at War trilogy about the OSS during World War II

It is June 1941 and "no operation may be more critical than the one being conducted by hotshot pilot Richard Canidy and his half-German wild-card friend Eric Fulmar: to secure the rare ore that will power a top-secret weapon coveted on both sides of the Atlantic—the atomic bomb." Publisher's note

Followed by The secret warriors

Line of fire. Putnam 1992 414p (Corps, bk5) o.p.

LC 91-29971

Book five in the Marine Corps saga "is centered mainly on the World War II battle for Guadalcanal, from August through September of 1942. But not only Guadalcanal: in keeping with the form of preceding volumes, *Line of Fire* is vast in geographical scope, with action occurring in such diverse and far-flung locations as Australia; the Japanese-held island of Buka in the Solomon Sea; Parris Island, South Carolina; and Washington, D.C. The cast is appropriately large and liberally stocked with brave heroes, beautiful heroines, and assorted tough guys, and their adventures are rendered in the wry, salty narrative voice ex-soldiers like Griffin so often employ when they turn to writing." Booklist

Secret honor. Putnam 2000 497p

ISBN 0-399-14568-0 LC 99-35740

In this third novel in the Honor Bound series "a German general works toward the assassination of Adolf Hitler. In Buenos Aires, the general's son, codenamed Galahad, falls under suspicion by the SS after a Nazi operation suddenly goes bad. In the middle of it all is OSS agent Cletus Frade, who knows the identity of them both and what they will do next if they can survive that long. For not only are SS and Abwehr officers hot on their trails in both countries, but the OSS has branded Frade a rogue agent and is determined to shake the truth from him, at whatever cost." Publisher's note

The secret warriors. Putnam 1998 c1985 321p

ISBN 0-399-14381-5 LC 97-37485

First published 1985 in paperback

In this second volume of the Men at War trilogy the OSS drops agents into the Belgian Congo to locate and smuggle out uranium ore while avoiding German agents

Followed by The soldier spies

The soldier spies. Putnam 1999 c1986 352p $25.95

ISBN 0-399-14494-3 LC 98-33260

First published 1986 in paperback

"Secret agents Major Richard Caniday (who's really *not* a major) and Eric Fulmar, members of the fledging OSS, aim to smuggle out of Germany the scientist whose knowledge of metallurgy holds the key to the Third Reich's development of jet engines. . . . Cameos by such historical figures as William 'Wild Bill' Donovan, Joseph P. Kennedy Jr., David Niven and Peter Ustinov lend color." Publ Wkly

Special ops. Putnam 2001 665p (Brotherhood of war, bk9) $25.95

ISBN 0-399-14646-6 LC 00-62779

"In 1964, Cuba's Fidel Castro tried to export communism to Africa under the leadership of the legendary Che Guevara, and *Special Ops* details the efforts of the U.S. military and the CIA to stop him. With the world's attention focused on Vietnam and Europe, the deadly fighting in some of the world's most remote and primitive places went unnoticed. . . . This is an exciting, intriguing, and fast-paced novel about an often-ignored period in our recent history." Libr J

Under fire. Putnam 2002 576p

ISBN 0-399-14788-8 LC 2001-48245

In this novel "Captain Ken 'Killer' McCoy, a protege of ex-OSS officer Fleming Pickering, who knows a senator, who knows President Truman, has reported to General MacArthur that North Korea will be invaded. The report disappears, McCoy gets busted to the ranks . . . and the Communists start pouring across the thirty-eighth parallel. Truman, suspicious of MacArthur, gets wind of the report, and appoints Pickering and McCoy to the CIA. Boats, bullets, and carrier-launched avengers and corsairs make up the balance of this expansively told story." Booklist

Griffith, Bill *See* Granger, Bill

Grimes, Martha, 1931-

The Anodyne Necklace. Little, Brown 1983
250p o.p.

            * LC 83-880

"Sixteen-year-old Katie O'Brien, playing her violin in
an underground London station to make some money, is
mysteriously attacked. From that incident begins a mystery involving the theft of an emeral necklace, the murder of a young man whose fingers have been chopped
off, and still another murder. The characters in this absorbing tale include not only the residents of
Littlebourne, Katie's village, but some East End Londoners like the Cripps family, whose squalid home and bizarre behavior will not soon be forgotten by the reader.
Satirical humor enlivens the careful and patient unraveling done by the special detective featured in Grimes'
mysteries—the attractive Scotland Yard Superintendent
Richard Jury." Shapiro. Fic for Youth. 3d edition

Belle ruin. Viking 2005 346p $25.95
   ISBN 0-670-03461-4   LC 2005-42289

A mystery featuring "precocious 12-year-old Emma
Graham. . . . Basking in the glow of newfound fame after narrowly escaping a murder attempt, Emma has her
hands full reporting for the local newspaper, waitressing
in her mom's seedy hotel restaurant and performing in
her brother's low-budget production of 'Medea: The Musical.' She also creates havoc for the hotel's guests, hob-
nobs with the local sheriff and trades barbs with her
archenemy, Ree-Jane Davidow. Nonetheless, Emma's
never ending quest to discover the identity of a mysterious girl only she can see, as well as her passion for solving the 20-year-old mystery surrounding a baby kidnapped from the once famous Belle Rouen hotel are always her top priorities. Grimes' pungent prose and
catchy dialog breathe life into her charming young narrator and the novels' idiosyncratic cast of characters." Publ
wkly

Biting the moon; a mystery. Holt & Co. 1999
301p
   ISBN 0-8050-5621-1   LC 98-42823

Grimes "sends two brave girls on a hair raising road
trip from Santa Fe, N.M., to Salmon, Idaho, in pursuit of
a child molester and animal abuser. . . . At 14, smart,
shy Mary Dark Hope needs to come out of her shell,
which she does on this coming-of-age odyssey with the
big-eyed wonder of a true explorer. The young amnesiac
who calls herself Andi Olivier and feels an affinity with
the coyotes she frees from traps is more complicated.
Too wise for her years, she's a sober realist with a romantic imagination that makes reality bearable." N Y
Times Book Rev

The case has altered. Holt & Co. 1997 370p
   ISBN 0-8050-5620-3   LC 97-20791

A mystery featuring Scotland Yard CID Inspector
Richard Jury and aristocrat Melrose Plant. "Two murders
have taken place in the bleak Lincolnshire fens: two
weeks after glamorous actress Verna Dunn was found
shot to death, plain kitchen-maid Dorcas Reese turned
up, garroted and strangled. The local police have already
identified the prime suspect, Jury's longtime friend, Jenny Kennington. Although the motive is murky, Jenny
certainly had means and opportunity, and before long,
she's arrested for both murders. Jury is understandably

upset, and he and Plant determine to prove Jenny's innocence despite the steadily mounting evidence against
her." Booklist

"Psychologically complex and muted in tone, with the
characters' elliptical relationships reflecting the setting of
England's dreamlike fen country, the novel also boasts
Grimes's delicious wit." Publ Wkly

Cold Flat Junction. Viking 2001 390p
   ISBN 0-670-89491-5   LC 00-43992

"Emma Graham, the 12-year-old narrator of this . . .
coming-of-age mystery, related an earlier installment of
this story in 'Hotel Paradise,' named for the once grand
jewel of the decaying resort town where she lives. . . .
[Emma's] obsession with Mary-Evelyn Devereau, a 12-
year-old girl who drowned in Spirit Lake 40 years ago,
has not gone unnoticed by her good friend the sheriff,
who also suspects this observant child of poking into
more recent deaths in the Devereau family." N Y Times
Book Rev

"Listening to Emma grope for understanding in this
most tangled town is fascinating, and watching as the
seemingly unconnected bits come together is unnerving."
Booklist

Dakota; a novel. Viking 2008 414p $25.95
   ISBN 978-0-670-01869-7   LC 2007-41715

This novel, featuring the young woman who calls herself Andi Oliver [introduced in the author's Biting the
moon], "begins with Andi, who's still unaware of her
real name or her past, adrift in the Dakota badlands. After rescuing an abandoned donkey, Andi makes a temporary home for herself in the small town of Kingdom,
where she soon creates a stir by standing up to some local bullies. She really begins to shake things up in the
placid community, however, when she takes a job at a
pig farm to try to save the cruelly treated animals bred
there. . . . While one late plot development stretches
credibility, Grimes succeeds in sustaining suspense while
graphically portraying the ugliness of animal abuse."
Publ Wkly

The Deer Leap. Little, Brown 1985 236p o.p.
            LC 85-15916

This "novel is set in a Hampshire village and central-
ized in the quaint local pub of the title. Scotland Yard's
Jury is summoned to Ashdown Dean after local mystery
writer Polly Praed discovers a body in a telephone kiosk.
The murder ties in with a series of pet poisonings and
a controversy over blood sports. More murder follows
before the unflappable Jury can sort things out in this
satisfyingly cozy, old-fashioned tale that has the ele-
gant/macabre feel of Edward Gorey's drawings."
Booklist

The Dirty Duck. Little, Brown 1984 240p o.p.
            LC 83-25629

"When a group of tourists on holiday in Shakespeare
country are beset by brutal murder and kidnapping, with
the murderer leaving Elizabethan couplets as a calling
card, Superintendent Jury of Scotland Yard becomes
drawn into work on the case." Libr J

The author is an "elegant writer who has a strong
touch of poetry in her. Her prose flows limpidly, distinguished by its accurate dialogue, sophistication and quiet
humor. She also has a sympathetic understanding of human foibles." N Y Times Book Rev

Grimes, Martha, 1931-—*Continued*

The five bells and bladebone. Little, Brown 1987 299p o.p.   LC 87-3148

"Visiting his friend Melrose Plant in Plant's ancestral village, Jury is at the local antique shop when Simon Lean's body is found in a flaptop desk. The dealer has just bought the piece from Lady Summerston, mistress of the lush estate of Watermeadows where Simon had lived with his wife Hannah, the lady's granddaughter. Questioning the women, Jury sees the strong resemblance between the widow and Sadie Diver, who was murdered in London's notorious Limehouse district. . . . The splendid mystery has a tragic core, but the gloom is offset by the author's quiet humor." Publ Wkly

Foul matter. Viking 2003 372p $25.95

ISBN 0-670-03259-X   LC 2003-50153

"Best-selling author Paul Giverney will sign with publisher Mackenzie-Haack only if it drops literary author Ned Isaly and assigns Isaly's talented editor to Paul. Ambitious editor Clive Esterhaus wants Giverney for himself but isn't comfortable with the solution proposed by Bobby Mackenzie, owner of MackenzieHaack—hiring hit men." Libr J

"The serpentine plot is fun to follow, once Giverney realizes the extent of the mischief he has set in motion. But it's the nasty inside stuff—from the Dickensian names for authors and their publishing houses to the barbaric rituals of a power lunch—that incites rolling in the aisles." N Y Times Book Rev

Help the poor struggler. Little, Brown 1985 225p o.p.   LC 85-109

"An epidemic of child murders brings Jury and Chief Superintendent Macalvie, a local colleague, to reconsider the 20-year-old murder of a woman which had been witnessed by the victim's five-year-old daughter." Libr J

"This fine novel features a plot that startles, characters that convince, and an atmosphere that sparkles." Booklist

The Horse You Came In On. Knopf 1993 331p o.p.   LC 92-55069

"Scotland Yard superintendent Richard Jury joins his friend Melrose Plant in Baltimore, where they solve several seemingly unrelated mysteries and investigate the genealogy of a bunch of upstarts who claim to be descendants of Lord Baltimore." Libr J

"Notable for its themes of authorship and authenticity and for the cast of delightfully eccentric characters—who gather each day at a blue-collar bar called The Horse You Came In On—this mystery, with its feathery plot and fey, lighthearted tone, moves in quite a different direction than earlier Jury tales. Not bad, just different." Publ Wkly

Hotel Paradise. Knopf 1996 347p

ISBN 0-679-44187-5   LC 95-49356

Twelve-year-old "Emma Graham, who works as a salad girl at the decaying resort hotel where her mother cooks, loves investigating situations that stimulate her active imagination—like the mysterious death 40 years earlier of young Mary-Evelyn Devereau, who lived with three ugly aunts and drowned, silk-clad and sad, in nearby Spirit Lake. Emma pursues the Mary-Evelyn mystery with single-minded determination, and during the course of her investigation, finds answers to questions she didn't even know she wanted to ask." Booklist

"Emma's take on the colorful characters in her small-town world . . . makes this both a provocative study of lonely people and a delightful read." Publ Wkly

I am the only running footman. Little, Brown 1986 206p o.p.   LC 86-15305

"Scotland Yard's wise, kind Superintendent Richard Jury must determine if the case of Ivy Childess, strangled in London, is related to a similar crime in Devon. Ivy had left her sometime lover, David Marr, after a tiff in the Footman, so he heads the list of suspects. Jury's interrogation ends with Marr offering a strong alibi, backed by his prestigious family. Calling on the man's sister and other kin, the superintendent senses private fears behind a gracious facade. Jury is right, but his suspicions produce no evidence of collusion until a shocking truth sends him racing to save the killer's third intended victim. An artist at plotting, Grimes concludes this urbanely humorous, knife-edge thriller with a double twist." Publ Wkly

Jerusalem Inn. Little, Brown 1984 299p o.p.   LC 84-15495

Superintendent Richard Jury "taking a brief holiday a few days before Christmas, meets Helen Minton, a woman seeking answers about her past. Their acquaintanceship has no time to warm to love; Helen dies, of poisoning, it turns out. As Jury assists the local officials in the investigation, he chances upon a tangle of details that leads him to snowbound Spinney Abbey where occur a shot gun murder plus the apparent gradual poisoning of another woman." Best Sellers

The Lamorna wink; a Richard Jury mystery. Viking 1999 368p

ISBN 0-670-88870-2   LC 99-33525

This mystery "centers on Jury regular Melrose Plant/Lord Ardry, along with an intriguing, brilliant police friend of Jury's, Brian Macalvie, as they investigate the disappearance of one woman, the murder of another, and the horrific, four-year-old unsolved death of two children who lived in the Cornwall house Plant is renting. Ultimately, the events converge, and Jury appears to wrap things up." Libr J

The man with a load of mischief. Little, Brown 1981 263p il o.p.   LC 81-8251

"This book takes its intriguing title from the scene of one of several crimes perpetrated by a murderer with a macabre sense of humor and a penchant for depositing corpses in the vicinity or on the premises of English pubs. When a man is found strangled and deposited in a beer vat, likable but cunning Inspector Richard Jury spends his Christmas holidays in the 'picture postcard village' of Long Piddleton, determined to solve the growing number of crimes. Deft characterization and portrayal of English pub life add to the appeal of a cleverly contrived tale." Libr J

The Old Contemptibles. Little, Brown 1991 333p o.p.   LC 90-48647

Inspector "Jury is considering marriage to recently met widow Jane Holdsworth at the moment her teenaged son Alex finds her dead, apparently a suicide. Alex runs away, and Jury, required, as a suspect, to remain in London, sends old friend Melrose Plant up to the Lakes to

Grimes, Martha, 1931——*Continued*

learn what he can about the wealthy Holdsworth family, among whom Jane's death is the fourth suspicious one." Publ Wkly

The old fox deceiv'd. Little, Brown 1982 299p o.p. LC 82-7719

"The central mystery that confronts Inspector Richard Jury of Scotland Yard is not whounit, but to whom was it 'dun.' Was the young woman found mutilated with an ice-pick-like instrument Dillys March, the ward of Colonel Titus Crael who left home 15 years previously and recently returned to reclaim her inheritance? Or was the victim Gemma Temple, Dillys' look-alike, who tried to pass herself off as Dillys to gain the inheritance? The tiny English fishing village of Rackmoor is divided and tormented by this mystery, which threatens to rock its social structure." Booklist

The Old Silent. Little, Brown 1989 425p o.p.
* LC 89-31650

While vacationing in Yorkshire, at the inn of the title, Jury "observes a well-dressed, self-contained woman shoot her husband. With no question of who murdered whom, Jury is dogged by the whys. Officially off the case, he's irretrievably hooked when he learns that the victim's son, and the woman's stepson, is the musical prodigy presumed dead in a famous kidnapping case years before." Publ Wkly

"The calm moments in this moody mystery about parental ties and family schisms and relationships thicker than blood are as fine as anything Ms. Grimes has written." N Y Times Book Rev

The Old Wine Shades; a Richard Jury mystery. Viking 2006 352p $25.95

ISBN 0-670-03479-7 LC 2005-58460

In this Richard Jury "mystery, the Scotland Yard detective is on suspension because he decided to save lives rather than wait for a warrant in his previous outing . . . . With time on his hands, Jury is ensnared by the intriguing tale spun by Harry Johnson, a man who, apparently, just happens upon him in a London pub, the Old Wine Shades. Despite himself, Jury is drawn in by Johnson's account of the baffling disappearance of a mother, her autistic son and their dog–and the more baffling reappearance of the pet nine months later. The detective diligently follows every lead to determine the fate of the missing people, even as Johnson's digressions into the paradoxes of quantum physics lead Jury to question the truth of the man's narrative. The scheme Jury ultimately detects is ingeniously clever and sufficiently consistent with the personalities Grimes has created to overcome disbelief." Publ Wkly

Rainbow's end; a Richard Jury novel. Knopf 1995 383p

ISBN 0-679-44188-3 LC 94-48876

In this Richard Jury mystery, three women "die suddenly in public places: an aged textile restorer in Exeter Cathedral, a society matron in the Tate Gallery and an American tourist in the ruins of Old Sarum, near Salisbury. The deaths appear to be natural and unrelated, but the clever Brits come up with a connection: both Englishwomen had recently visited Santa Fe, N.M., where the American had a silver shop. Once in the Southwest, Jury follows his wispy lead to eye-catching

locations like a movie set in Santa Fe. . . . Meanwhile, back home, Jury's sidekick, Melrose Plant, pays nostalgic visits to people and places from previous novels, while mourning the passing of the grand old pubs." N Y Times Book Rev

The Stargazey; a Richard Jury mystery. Holt & Co. 1998 354p

ISBN 0-8050-5622-X LC 98-21214

"Jury is on the Fulham Road bus when he spots a beautiful blonde in a fur coat and feels compelled to follow her to the Fulham Palace grounds. Later she is found murdered on the palace grounds. But is it really she? Jury doubts it and follows a winding path to the truth." Libr J

Grimes "delivers a delightfully entertaining blend of irony, danger, and intrigue, liberally laced with wit and charm." Booklist

The train now departing
In Grimes, M. The train now departing: two novellas

The train now departing: two novellas. Viking 2000 185p

ISBN 0-670-89154-1 LC 99-53705

This volume "consists of a pair of atmospheric novellas. While both stories center on middle-aged, single women whose careful, well-ordered lives are gradually altered by meals they share with male acquaintances, these two novellas are quite distinct in their ambience and characterization. In 'The Train Now Departing,' Grimes eerily depicts a bright, analytical woman teetering into madness. 'When the Mousetrap Closes' is the story of Edith Parenger, a woman whose desperate loneliness is pitted against her keen powers of observation in an unflinching exploration of the power of illusion." Libr J

When the mousetrap closes
In Grimes, M. The train now departing: two novellas

The winds of change; a Richard Jury mystery. Viking 2004 407p $25.95

ISBN 0-670-03327-8 LC 2004-52636

This Richard Jury mystery involves "the murder of an anonymous five-year-old girl, shot in the back. . . . When he learns that the child was found near a house frequented by pedophiles, he's convinced there's a link. His suspicions grow stronger when the man supposedly behind the operation turns out to be the father of a child who mysteriously disappeared three years before from a country estate." Booklist

Grimsley, Jim, 1955-

The ordinary. Tor Bks. 2004 368p map $24.95

ISBN 0-7653-0528-3 LC 2003-71148

"Set in the same future world as Kirith Kirin (2000) . . ., Grimsley's latest SF novel intimately explores the conflicts between magic and science, subconscious and conscious action, the past and the future. The planet of the tech-using Hormling of Senal is connected to the land of Irion, home of the magic-believing Erejhen, via the mysterious Twil Gate, a portal of unknown origins in the ocean. Although traders on both sides enjoy brisk

Grimsley, Jim, 1955-—*Continued*

commerce through the gate, Hormling leaders look more and more to Irion as a means to provide land and resources for their expanding civilization. Translator Jedda Martele, member of a Senal diplomatic mission to Irion, is caught in the middle when the delegation's true purpose is revealed. . . . Grimsley's finely textured societies have a clockwork intricacy that fascinates even as it dispels surprise." Publ Wkly

Grippando, James

The abduction; a novel. HarperCollins Pubs. 1998 386p
ISBN 0-06-018262-8   LC 97-28153
"It's the year 2000, and U.S. Attorney General Allison Leahy is the country's first female presidential candidate. When opponent Lincoln Howe's granddaughter, Kristen, is kidnapped, Leahy—whose own daughter was abducted eight years earlier—is torn between her political advisors, who tell her to stay far away from the investigation, and her memories of her own tragedy. . . . This is a gripping (and frightening) story about the Machiavellian world of American politics." Booklist

Born to run; a novel of suspense. HarperCollins 2008 328p $25.99
ISBN 978-0-06-155611-1; 0-06-155611-4
LC 2008-23282
Miami attorney Jack Swyteck comes to the aid of his former governor father as he investigates the suspicious hunting death of the vice president.
"Grippando ratchets up the action to a breakneck pace in the last half of the novel, stopping to liberally sprinkle the proceedings with snarky dialogue, pointed satire, and some touching father-son moments." Booklist

Found money. HarperCollins Pubs. 1999 336p
ISBN 0-06-018263-6   LC 98-24310
"Just before Frank Duffy dies, he tells his physician son, Ryan, that there is $2 million hidden in the attic, and that Frank got the money through blackmail—albeit off someone who 'deserved it.' The level-headed Ryan considers both claims unbelievable—until he finds the money. . . . Meanwhile, Amy Parkins, while struggling to support her daughter and her grandmother and to put herself through law school, receives $200,000 from an anonymous benefactor, apparently Frank Duffy, whom she'd never met. . . . As Ryan and Amy search for the money's source and meaning, they uncover a conspiracy involving high-ranking government officials, multibillion-dollar corporations and a hidden crime committed on a hot summer night years ago. The final revelation is a real kicker." Publ Wkly

Hear no evil. HarperCollins Publishers 2004 310p $23.95
ISBN 0-06-056457-1   LC 2003-57138
This "Jack Swyteck mystery finds the Miami defense lawyer in unfamiliar territory. When a woman asks him to defend her against the charge of murdering her husband, Jack is initially reluctant: the victim is a U.S. naval officer; the crime took place at the naval base at Guantanamo Bay; and Jack has almost no experience with military courtroom procedures. But the woman has a very persuasive reason for Jack to take the case . . ., and soon Jack finds himself fighting for his client's life in an arena that is brand new to him." Booklist
"This character-driven, intricately plotted thriller will keep readers guessing up to the end." Publ Wkly

The informant. HarperCollins Pubs. 1996 360p o.p.   LC 96-16310
"There's a serial killer out there, but the locations are disparate and the victims seemingly unconnected. FBI agent Victoria Santos has developed a psychological profile of the killer, whose attention to detail results in a dearth of clues. Then *Miami Tribune* reporter Mike Posten receives calls from someone who claims he's not the killer, but he thinks so much like him he can predict the killer's next move. The caller will talk for cash, which the FBI supplies. The finale takes place on a cruise ship and pits the killer against Santos and Posten." Booklist
"Although his prose is stilted, Mr. Grippando, . . . has a nice flair for the grotesque. More to his credit, he has done his homework on F.B.I. forensics, criminal profiling and the internal protocol for backstabbing." N Y Times Book Rev

A king's ransom. HarperCollins Pubs. 2001 426p
ISBN 0-06-019241-0   LC 2001-16786
"When lawyer Nick Rey's father is kidnapped during a business trip to Colombia it's up to Nick to save him. The chain of events designed to make the task as difficult as possible queues up behind him—Nick must battle his own law firm, the insurance company, the outrageously unhelpful FBI, and a group of merciless guerillas who refuse to budge from their ransom demands." Libr J
Grippando's "research into the kidnapping industry currently thriving in Latin America adds a harrowing dose of realism to a taut, well-constructed page-turner." Publ Wkly

Lying with strangers. HarperCollins 2007 389p $24.95
ISBN 978-0-06-113838-6; 0-06-113838-X
LC 2006-50956
First published in slightly different form 2006 by Madison Park Press for Doubleday Entertainment's book clubs
"Peyton Shields, a doctor in her first year of residency at Children's Hospital in Boston, is driving home late one night when another car forces her off the road and into a pond. Rescued by a stranger who quickly disappears, Peyton is dismayed that neither the cops nor her husband, Kevin, believe her when she says the 'accident" was deliberate. Kevin, a struggling lawyer, has his own problems; he was in bed with another woman the night of the incident. Complicating matters is that his wife, suspicious of his actions, seeks solace from Gary, an old boyfriend and nurse in the hospital where she works. When Gary is killed, Peyton and Kevin find themselves on trial for murder, with a prosecutor intent on pitting one against the other." Libr J
"Grippando excels at the ordinary-person-in-extraordinary-circumstances story, and this one uses the premise expertly, building enough suspense to keep readers looking in dark corners and over their shoulders." Booklist

Grisham, John

The appeal. Doubleday 2008 358p $27.95

ISBN 978-0-385-51504-7; 0-385-51504-9

LC 2007-44905

This novel "begins with the shocking conclusion to a lawsuit filed against Krane Chemical by Jeannette Baker, a young woman who lost her son and husband to cancer within eight months. The $41 million settlement is unprecedented, and Krane isn't taking it lightly. Jeannette is only one of hundreds of people in fictional Bowmore, Miss., who have been affected by Krane's decades of dumping toxic waste in what has come to be known as Cancer County USA. If the chemical company doesn't get a reversal on appeal, future lawsuits on behalf of more than 160 cancer victims will drain its deep pockets, especially the gold-lined wallet of owner Carl Trudeau. He has vowed those 'ignorant people' won't get a dime of his money." USA Today

"It barely matters that the characters in The Appeal are essentially stick figures. What works for Mr. Grisham is his patient, lawyerly, inexorable way of dramatizing urgent moral issues." N Y Times (Late N Y Ed)

The brethren. Doubleday 2000 366p $30

ISBN 0-385-49746-6   LC 00-23841

This suspense novel revolves around two subplots. In the first three ex-judges, serving time in a federal prison in Florida, concoct a blackmail scheme that targets closeted gay men. The second storyline relates the CIA-backed presidential bid of a corrupt congressman

"Every personage in this novel lies, cheats, steals and/or kills, and while Grisham's fans may miss the stalwart lawyer-heroes and David vs. Goliath slant of his earlier work, all will be captivated by this clever thriller that presents as crisp a cast as he's yet devised, and as grippingly sardonic yet bitingly moral a scenario as he's ever imagined." Publ Wkly

The broker. Doubleday 2005 357p $27.95

ISBN 0-385-51045-4

"In his final hours in the Oval Office, the outgoing President grants a controversial last-minute pardon to Joel Backman, a notorious Washington power broker who has spent the last six years hidden away in a federal prison. What no one knows is that the President issues the pardon only after receiving enormous pressure from the CIA. It seems Backman, in his power broker heyday, may have obtained secrets that compromise the world's most sophisticated satellite surveillance system. Backman is quietly smuggled out of the country in a military cargo plane, given a new name, a new identity, and a new home in Italy. Eventually, after he has settled into his new life, the CIA will leak his whereabouts to the Israelis, the Russians, the Chinese, and the Saudis. Then the CIA will do what it does best: sit back and watch." Publisher's note

"If you will be satisfied with a workmanlike spy-cum-politics novel, with some first-rate cloak and dagger intrigue, an uplifting vignette of father-son redemption and a poignant pastiche of unrequited love, then 'The Broker' is the book for you." N Y Times Book Rev

The chamber. Doubleday 1994 486p

ISBN 0-385-42472-8   LC 94-11764

"The chamber in question is the gas chamber at the Mississippi State Penitentiary—and for 69-year-old Sam Crayhall, the road thence has been many years long. Sam

was twice tried and twice acquitted for murder after a 1967 Ku Klux Klan scare bombing accidentally killed the twin sons of the intended target; 14 years later he was tried a third time, convicted and sentenced to death row. Now, in 1990, a young Chicago lawyer, employed by the firm that represented Sam but which he has just unceremoniously dumped, wants Sam as a client. Adam Hall, the 26-year-old rookie, is Sam Crayhall's grandson. . . . Though the countdown to an execution is a well-worn plot device, it has seldom been as effective, especially in the novel's last 100 pages." Publ Wkly

The client. Doubleday 1993 422p $29.95; pa $7.99

ISBN 0-385-42471-X; 0-440-21352-5 (pa)

LC 92-39079

"While sneaking into the woods to smoke forbidden cigarettes, preteen brothers Mark and Ricky find a lawyer committing suicide in his car. Mark tries to save the man but is instead grabbed by him and told the location of the body of a murdered U.S. senator—a murder for which the lawyer's Mafia-connected client is accused. Witnessing the successful suicide sends Ricky into shock and Mark into a web of lies, half-truths, and finally into refusal to tell the confided secret to the police. Mark accidentally but fortuitously hires a lawyer, Reggie Love, who steers him through a maze of FBI agents, legal proceedings, judges, ambitious lawyers, and hit men. . . . This thriller is unique in its theme and in its suspense mixed with humor. A sure 'all-night' read." SLJ

The firm. Doubleday 1991 421p $30

ISBN 0-385-41634-2

* LC 90-3945

"Fresh out of Harvard Law School, Mitchell McDeere is recruited by an elite Memphis law firm. . . . {His colleagues} put in 19-hour days for their front-office clients, while beavering behind the scenes on money-laundering operations for the Mafia. . . . Mitch, in fear for his life, agrees to work undercover for the F.B.I." N Y Times Book Rev

"The aphorism 'between a rock and a hard place' aptly describes the dilemma of a young attorney pressed by the FBI to reveal crime-related secrets of his firm, while also hounded by his employers to simply take his huge salary and zip his lip. No aphorism, though, can convey the suspense, wit, and polished writing of this laser-sharp candidate for the best recent updating of the David and Goliath story." Libr J

The last juror. Doubleday 2004 355p $27.95

ISBN 0-385-51043-8

"In 1970, one of Mississippi's more colorful weekly newspapers, The Ford County Times, went bankrupt. To the surprise and dismay of many, ownership was assumed by a 23-year-old college dropout, named Willie Traynor. The future of the paper looked grim until a young mother was brutally raped and murdered by a member of the notorious Padgitt family. Willie Traynor reported all the gruesome details, and his newspaper began to prosper. The murderer, Danny Padgitt, was tried before a packed courthouse in Clanton, Mississippi. The trial came to a startling and dramatic end when the defendant threatened revenge against the jurors if they convicted him. Nevertheless, they found him guilty, and he was sentenced to life in prison. . . . Nine years later Danny Padgitt managed to get himself paroled. He re-

Grisham, John—*Continued*

turned to Ford County, and the retribution began." Publisher's note

"The novel will satisfy those with an appetite for legal thrillers and those who believe Grisham possesses more talent than those breathless page-turners sometimes reveal. It ranks among his best-written and most atmospheric novels." USA Today

A painted house; a novel. Doubleday 2001 388p il $27.95

ISBN 0-385-50120-X   LC 2001-266464

For "Lucas Chandler, the year 1952 is full of secrets—sweet, tragic, and mysterious. At 7, he still sleeps under the bed when he's scared and disappears behind his mother's skirts from time to time. But he's old enough to understand that prejudice, class rivalry (townies paint their houses; farmers don't), and violence are part of the fabric of his outwardly quiet farming community, and that he shouldn't be watching an unmarried teen give birth or pretty 17-year-old Tally bathing in the creek (even if she says it's okay). He also realizes that by confessing he's witnessed two vicious killings, he'll be threatening his family's livelihood and putting his loved ones in danger." Booklist

"Grisham is about as good a storyteller as we've got in the United States these days. . . . The plots and subplots twine. The pages turn. The characters take on their own lives." N Y Times Book Rev

The partner. Doubleday 1997 366p $30

ISBN 0-385-47295-1   LC 96-54702

"Money is essentially the principal character in [this novel]. It is a very large sum of it—$90 million, to be exact—that has motivated Gulf Coast lawyer Patrick Lanigan to concoct a scheme to disappear. . . . It is money that drove a crooked defense contractor to try to pry loose a huge sum from Washington, and got Patrick's greedy law firm involved in the first place. And it is varying sums of money that enable Patrick to bribe his way out of a collection of indictments against him a yard long—including one for first-degree murder—when he is eventually found in his Brazilian hide-away and brought back to the U.S. to face the music. . . . To call the plot of *The Partner* mechanical is at least partly a compliment: it is well-oiled, intricate and works smoothly." Publ Wkly

The pelican brief. Doubleday 1992 371p $30

ISBN 0-385-42198-2

                                    * LC 91-33235

"Set in the near future, the novel begins with an attention-getting double whammy, as two Supreme Court justices are assassinated within hours of each other. Brainy, self-possessed Tulane University law student Darby Shaw . . . proposes a theory about the murders in a brief that leaves chaos in its wake when it falls into the wrong hands." Publ Wkly

"Mr. Grisham has written a genuine page-turner. He has an ear for dialogue and is a skillful craftsman. Like a composer, he brings all his themes together at the crucial moment for a gripping, and logical, finale." NY Times Book Rev

Playing for pizza. Doubleday 2007 262p $21.95

ISBN 978-0-385-52500-8; 0-385-52500-1

                                    LC 2007-27656

"Third-string Cleveland Browns quarterback Rick Dockery becomes the greatest goat ever by throwing three interceptions in the closing minutes of the AFC championship game. Fleeing vengeful fans, he finds refuge in the grungiest corner of professional football, the Italian National Football League as quarterback of the inept but full-of-heart Parma Panthers. What ensues is a winsome football fable, replete with team bonding and character-building as the underdog Panthers challenge the powerhouse Bergamo Lions for a shot at the Italian Superbowl. The book is also the author's love letter to Italy." Publ Wkly

The rainmaker. Doubleday 1995 434p $29.95

ISBN 0-385-42473-6   LC 95-2291

"When the modestly sized law firm that contracted for his future services unexpectedly merges with a tony Ivy League firm, . . . {attorney Rudy Baylor} finds himself without a job and bankrupt. . . . To make a living, Rudy finds himself chasing ambulances for a racketeering shyster, leading to his becoming enthralled with a beautiful young woman hospitalized by her husband's murderous attack. When Rudy agrees to represent the parents of a dying 22-year-old denied insurance coverage for bone-marrow transplant, he finds that he is up against the firm that broke contract with him." Publ Wkly

The runaway jury. Doubleday 1996 401p $30

ISBN 0-385-47294-3   LC 96-13872

"In a Mississippi Gulf Coast town, the widow of a lifelong smoker who died prematurely of lung cancer is suing Big Tobacco. Enter Rankin Fitch, a dark genius of jury fixing, who has won many such trials for the tobacco companies and who foresees no special problems here. Enter also a mysterious juror, Nicholas Easter, whom Fitch's army of jury investigators and manipulators can't quite seem to track—and his equally mysterious girlfriend Marlee. . . . The details of jury selection are fascinating." Publ Wkly

The street lawyer. Doubleday 1998 348p $27.95

ISBN 0-385-49099-2   LC 97-47484

"Michael Brock, a slick antitrust lawyer in a blue-chip Washington legal factory, experiences a profound shock when he and other lawyers are held hostage by a deranged man with a legitimate beef—and a gun. Reordering his values, Michael leaves his high-pressure job and sterile marriage to become an advocate for the homeless. In his zeal for his new mission . . . he also steals a file and tries to sue his old firm on behalf of the people they illegally evicted from a valuable piece of real estate." NY Times Book Rev

"The cat-and-mouse between Michael and the firm is vintage Grisham, intricately plotted, but the emphasis in this smoothly told, baldly manipulative tale is less on action and suspense, which are moderate, than on Michael's change of heart and moving exploration of the world of the homeless." Publ Wkly

The summons. Doubleday 2002 341p $27.95

ISBN 0-385-50382-2   LC 2001-58185

Ray Atlee, a 43-year-old law professor in Virginia is summoned to his family's home in Mississippi by his dying father, a respected judge. Following his father's death Ray discovers over $3 million in cash in the study

This Summons "is a swift, no-nonsense story written in a highly effective, uncluttered fashion. . . . Mr.

Grisham, John—*Continued*

Grisham seems genuinely interested in the questions of conscience that snare Ray, and he makes them matter." N Y Times Book Rev

The testament. Doubleday 1998 435p $30

ISBN 0-385-49380-0   LC 99-186246

This novel "begins with the suicide of billionaire Troy Phelan, . . . who cuts his legitimate heirs out of his will and leaves his $11 billon to his illegitimate daughter, Rachel Lane, a missionary in Brazil. . . . [Nate Reilly's] firm dispatches him to the Brazilian back country to track down the heiress. . . . The physical journey turns into a spiritual quest for Nate midway through the novel." Newsweek

"Nate's search for redemption, which might have become hokey, is quite convincing. The big question—what will Rachel do upon learning she has inherited $11 billion—is nicely resolved." N Y Times Book Rev

A time to kill. Doubleday 1993 487p $30

ISBN 0-385-47081-9   LC 93-32545

A reissue of the title first published 1989 by Wynwood Press

In this novel, set in rural Mississippi, local criminal lawyer Jake Brigance defends a black man on trial for murdering the men who raped his daughter

Groff, Lauren

Delicate edible birds and other stories. Hyperion 2009 306p $23.95

ISBN 978-1-4013-4086-5   LC 2008-44002

Contents: Lucky Chow Fun; L. DeBard and Aliette; Majorette; Blythe; Wife of the dictator; Watershed; Sir fleeting; Fugue; Delicate edible birds

An "innovative and beautifully written collection that covers a wide swath of humanity, from east coast resort towns, to the early 20th century flu epidemic, to WWII Europe. . . . Even in the less successful stories, Groff's prose is lovely, and when she nails a story—like the title story about journalists fleeing Nazi-occupied Paris—the results are sublime." Publ Wkly

The monsters of Templeton; a novel. Voice/Hyperion 2008 364p il map $24.95

ISBN 978-1-4013-2225-0; 1-4013-2225-5

LC 2007-41360

"Left alone and pregnant after a failed relationship with her married prof, archaeology grad student Willie Upton returns to her quaint hometown in upstate New York. Templeton, however, is anything but serene. Not only has a mysterious creature appeared in a nearby lake, but Willie learns that her mother lied about the identity of her biological father. Soon, Willie discovers her town's pristine image conceals a villain more monstrous than its lake creature." Entertainment Wkly

"Forget the ghouls and cheap scares. What Groff is really digging at here is the enigma of the human spirit and how redemption and resilience shape our lives. The Monsters of Templeton is part mystery and part history, generating much of its appeal through the delightfully cranky, persistent Willie and a host of voices—maybe a few too many—from her tangled family tree." PopMatters

Grøndahl, Jens Christian, 1959-

Lucca; translated from the Danish by Anne Born. Harcourt 2003 c2002 332p $26

ISBN 0-15-100594-X   LC 2002-154301

Original Danish edition, 1998

"The title character is an actress who has renounced her career (for love) and then blinded herself in a drunken car crash after being dumped by her husband. Her doctor has become an emotional recluse since, or possibly before, being dumped by his wife. Over the course of many pages we get their back stories." N Y Times Book Rev

The author "proves himself to be master of the poetry of small moments that can lead to shattering discoveries." Libr J

Gross, Claudia, 1956-

Scholarium; Claudia Gross. Toby Press 2004 400p $19.95

ISBN 1-592-64056-7

"The scene is set with a pervasive cloud of impending evil hovering over the Cologne Scholarium. Master Casall's murderer sends perplexing riddles to the frustrated and suspicious faculty. Casall's widow and select students disappear, the prior stirs potions in a shack, and Master Lombardi hides a guilty secret. In the midst of the debate surrounding the murder, brilliantly timed accusations of witchcraft and sorcery emerge, and rumors fly about pagan sex rites on crumbling altars. . . . Gross weaves a fascinating tapestry depicting the birth of the schism between church and state and showing how the search for truth becomes a life-and-death quest for a group of determined scholars." Booklist

Grossman, Austin, 1969-

Soon I will be invincible. Pantheon Books 2007 287p $22.95

ISBN 978-0-375-42486-1; 0-375-42486-5

LC 2006-33296

"The story shifts between the perspectives of Doctor Impossible, a brilliant scientist turned world's greatest menace, and Fatale, a lonely cyborg and the newest addition to the venerable group of heroes known as the Champions. Though he's been out of commission for a while, Doctor Impossible hatches a scheme to knock the planet out of orbit . . . . Meanwhile, Champions leader Corefire goes missing, and Fatale has to learn the ropes of superherodom as the conventional climactic showdown (at Doctor Impossible's secret lair) draws near." Publ Wkly

"A heartbreaking genius of staggering evil, Doctor Impossible avenges lost love, a lonely adolescence, and a plethora of foiled doomsday devices. . . . Every comic-book cliché in this witty, stunning debut is lovingly embraced, then turned inside out." Wired

Grossman, David

Be my knife; translated by Vered Almog and Maya Gurantz. Farrar, Straus & Giroux 2002 307p

ISBN 0-374-29977-3   LC 2001-33645

Grossman, David—*Continued*

Original Hebrew edition, 1998

"When a thirty-three-year-old man named Yair catches a glimpse of Miriam at a class reunion, he senses a bond with her that goes beyond sexual attraction; because he is a practiced philanderer who is in search of something extraordinary, he implores her to enter a ruthlessly honest correspondence with him, on the understanding that they will never meet. . . . Most of the book is devoted to Yair's letters, and so we don't get to hear Miriam's responses until near the end. But it is Grossman's achievement that we understand from the start that Yair's vision of Miriam (and thus ours) is almost painfully incomplete." New Yorker

Someone to run with; translated by Vered Almog and Maya Gurantz. Farrar, Straus and Giroux 2004 343p $24

ISBN 0-374-26657-3

* LC 2002-29778

Original Hebrew edition, 2000

In Jerusalem, teenage Assaf "a shy misfit, embarks upon a quixotic journey with a lost dog to find its mistress. Tamar, a caustic fifteen-year-old who can sing Mozart and Leonard Cohen on demand, runs away from home to find the criminals who have ensnared her older brother. A young street musician, in the grip of a heroin habit as formidable as his talent, stumbles through his routines with death close behind. The resulting picaresque is a cross between 'Run Lola Run' and 'Oliver Twist,' and as the reader waits for these solitary odysseys to intersect, the urgency becomes almost unbearable. Grossman evokes teenage nobility and self-hatred in all its pimply particularity, while slyly suggesting that the arduous quest for connections should never be outgrown." New Yorker

Grossman, Edith

(tr) Fuentes, C. Happy families

(tr) Muñoz Molina, A. A manuscript of ashes

Grossman, Lev

The magicians; a novel. Viking 2009 402p $26.95

ISBN 978-0-670-02055-3; 0-670-02055-9

LC 2008-55900

"Quentin Coldwater is a geeky high-school senior in Brooklyn who is convinced that happiness and 'the life he should be living' are elsewhere—for example, in the series of nineteen-thirties British adventure novels that he was obsessed with as a child. When Quentin stumbles on a portal that takes him to a college for magicians in upstate New York, he learns that the world depicted in these novels, known as Fillory, is real, and he is forced to square his youthful ideas with the realities that exist there, too—boredom, regret, shame, and despair. Quentin's journey becomes an unexpectedly moving coming-of-age story in which he learns that magical worlds are much like the real one." New Yorker

Gruber, Michael

The book of air and shadows. William Morrow 2007 466p $24.95

ISBN 978-0-06-087446-9; 0-06-087446-5

LC 2006-46767

This thriller "centers on a hunt for an unknown autographed Shakespeare play. References to this play turn up in seemingly innocuous letters used as filler in the binding of an old book. Mishkin, an intellectual property attorney, comes into possession of some of these documents through his client, a Shakespearean scholar. Crosetti, who discovered the papers while working at a rare-book store, partners with Mishkin to find the play after the scholar's murder." Libr J

"Few thrillers will surpass [this book] when it comes to energetic writing, compellingly flawed characters, literary scholarship and mathematical conundrums." USA Today

The forgery of Venus; a novel. William Morrow 2008 318p $24.95

ISBN 978-0-06-087448-3; 0-06-087448-1

LC 2008-2363

This thriller "tells the story of Chaz Wilmot, a talented painter in the style of the Old Masters who is unable to make a living in the art world of today. His salvation comes when he is summoned to Italy to restore a ceiling painted by Tiepolo. Once there, he realizes that the job is not so much a restoration as it is a forgery. His work on the ceiling earns him the interest of a wealthy patron who hires him to paint other forgeries. Problems arise when Chaz begins to relive situations from his past and then travel back to the 17th century, where he becomes the Spanish artist Velázquez. Soon, he is no longer sure of even his own identity." Libr J

"Gruber writes passionately and knowledgeably about art and its history—and he writes brilliantly about the shadowy lines that blur reality and unreality. Fans of intelligent, literate thrillers will be well rewarded." Publ Wkly

Night of the jaguar. Morrow 2006 372p $24.95

ISBN 0-06-057768-1

LC 2005-40011

This "supernatural thriller completes the trilogy that began with Tropic of Night and Valley of Bones. All feature Miami cop Jimmy Paz, though the real star of this outing is the supposedly dull-witted Jenny Simpson, a gofer for the Forest Planet Alliance. When someone starts murdering Cuban-American businessmen in grisly fashion, suspicion falls on Moie, an Indian from a remote area of Colombia the victims had plans to develop. . . . Summoned out of retirement, Jimmy takes on the case, though he and his seven-year-old daughter, Amelia, are soon troubled by dreams of a jaguar with evil designs on Amelia. Every time Moie glides onto the page, the book shines, but it's Jenny, helping to shelter Moie, who steals the show . . . . Hotly spiced with hit men and guns, demon gods and piranhas, this one offers more social satire than its predecessors, mostly at the expense of do-gooder environmentalists." Publ Wkly

Valley of bones. William Morrow 2005 436p $24.95

ISBN 0-06-057766-5

Gruber, Michael—*Continued*

"When a Sudanese oil baron is thrown to his death from his hotel balcony, Miami detective Jimmy Paz finds a mysterious woman named Emmylou Dideroff vehemently praying at the scene of the crime; she quickly becomes the main suspect. The plot immediately thickens as Emmylou begins to write a lengthy confession about her disturbing childhood, how she reformed from a criminal to a woman of God, and what led her to the Miami hotel room that day. Is she crazy or does God really speak to her? Jimmy and criminal psychologist Lorna Wise investigate and are thrown into a whirlwind journey involving prostitution, white supremacists, the Sudanese civil war, and massive government cover-ups." Libr J

The author is "at least as eager to fathom the violent and the unknown as he is to exploit these things. Some books simply relish the darker sides of human nature. Mr. Gruber summons them with troubled inquisitiveness, with both brio and regret." N Y Times (Late N Y Ed)

Gruen, Sara

Water for elephants; a novel. Algonquin Books 2006 335p il $23.95

ISBN 1-565-12499-5   LC 2005-52700

"Life is good for Jacob Jankowski. He's about to graduate from veterinary school and about to bed the girl of his dreams. Then his parents are killed in a car crash, leaving him in the middle of the Great Depression with no home, no family, and no career. Almost by accident, Jacob joins the circus. There he falls in love with the beautiful performer Marlena, who is married to the circus' psychotic animal trainer. He also meets the other love of his life, Rosie the elephant. This lushly romantic novel travels back and forth in time between Jacob's present day in a nursing home and his adventures in the surprisingly harsh world of 1930s circuses. The ending of both stories is a little too cheerful to be believed, but just like a circus, the magic of the story and the writing convince you to suspend your disbelief. The book is partially based on real circus stories and illustrated with historical circus photographs." Booklist

Grumbach, Doris

The book of knowledge; a novel. Norton 1995 248p

ISBN 0-393-03770-3   LC 94-37901

This novel "follows the lives of four friends, each of whom departs from the sexual mores of the day in some way (homosexuality, incest, willful celibacy), from the summer of 1929—when, as prepubescent children, they first meet in an East Coast seaside town—through World War II and beyond." Libr J

"Grumbach's latest novel is grimly compelling in its portrayal of four lives filled with stifled desires, major depression, incest, self-sacrifice, and thwarted love. . . . Grumbach paints a glowing picture of warmth, security, and safety that is shattered by the Great Depression." Booklist

Grushin, Olga

The dream life of Sukhanov. G.P. Putnam's Sons 2005 354p $24.95

ISBN 0-399-15298-9   LC 2005-43175

"On one level, Grushin recounts the comfortable life of fiftysomething art critic and former artist Anatoly Sukhanov, who enjoys all the perks of a pre-Gorbachev existence, until the arrival of a mysterious cousin at his family's capacious Moscow apartment. As his secure life begins to fray and then unravel, Sukhanov, who had the potential of brilliance as a young artist but eventually joined the Soviet establishment, is forced to confront the loss of his beloved wife, his two children, his editorship at the country's leading art magazine, in a word, his identity. Though an absorbing chronicle of life at the end of the Soviet era, this is really much more–a meditation on society, art, truth, and life." Libr J

Guène, Faïza

Kiffe kiffe tomorrow; [translated from the French by Sarah Adams] Harcourt 2006 179p pa $13

ISBN 0-15-603048-9; 978-0-15-603048-9

LC 2005-30456

"A Harvest original"

Original French edition, 2004

"Fifteen-year-old Doria lives with her mother in Paradise Estates, a mostly Muslim housing project outside Paris. Her father has returned to greener pastures in his native Algeria and started a new family there, leaving Doria both furious and hurt. At the same time, she is a typical teenager, testing boundaries as she teeters toward independence. Doria is confounded by her changing body, as well as her burgeoning sexual and political interests, but she persistently struggles to figure things out." Libr J

"Think of Doria on the same adolescent raft as Huck Finn and Holden Caulfield. A cunning wonder." Harper's

Guest, Judith

Ordinary people. Viking 1976 263p hardcover o.p. pa $13

ISBN 0-670-52831-5; 0-14-006517-2 (pa)

*

"When his older brother drowns in a boating accident, seventeen-year-old Conrad Jarrett feels responsible and makes an unsuccessful attempt at suicide. After eight months in a mental institution, Conrad returns home to parents whose marriage is crumbling, friends who are wary of him, and a psychiatrist who works with him to help put the pieces together. The pain of adolescent anxiety and fragile family relationships are authentically depicted." Shapiro. Fic for Youth. 3d edition

Gulik, Robert Hans van, 1910-1967

The Chinese bell murders; three cases solved by Judge Dee; a Chinese detective story suggested by three original Chinese plots; with 15 plates drawn by the author in Chinese style. Harper 1959 c1958 262p il o.p.

First published 1958 in the United Kingdom

Judge Dee, a legendary magistrate and detective, who is based on a real 7th century Chinese person and was the subject of Chinese detective tales during the 17th and 18th centuries, made his American debut in this murder-rape case. The judge solves three interwoven crimes in

Gulik, Robert Hans van, 1910-1967—*Continued*
the provincial city of Pooyang. A postscript provides information on ancient Chinese detection and court procedure and on the Chinese sources of the story

The haunted monastery; a Chinese detective story; [by] Robert van Gulik; with eight illustrations drawn by the author in Chinese style. Scribner 1969 159p il o.p.

First published 1961 in Malaysia; first United States edition published 1963 in paperback

This mystery "finds Judge Dee and his family and retainers stranded because of a broken axle and a howling storm. He has to spend the night solving three murders and a problem of impersonation before he can proceed on his journey the following day." Ency of Mystery & Detection

The lacquer screen; a Chinese detective story; [by] Robert van Gulik; with ten illustrations drawn by the author in Chinese style. Scribner 1970 180p il o.p.

First published 1962 in Malaysia; first United States edition published 1963 in paperback

This tale is set in 7th century China. Magistrate detective Judge Dee and his lieutenant join the underworld in a district under the Judge's jurisdiction in order to solve three crimes. They share the life of the gangster-boss and his entourage while the underworld people unwittingly help them in their inquiries. The Judge eventually reveals the ugly secret hidden by the panels of a beautiful lacquer screen

The Red Pavilion; a Chinese detective story; [by] Robert van Gulik; with six illustrations drawn by the author in Chinese style. Scribner 1968 173p il o.p.

First published 1961 in Malaysia

Judge Dee, "solves more than one knotty criminal problem, all of them stemming out of the fact that he elects to stay in the infamous Red Pavilion on Paradise Island, not knowing it has been the scene of several mysterious deaths in the past. The Chinese atmosphere is suitably exotic and there is a lovely, mistreated courtesan for the judge to protect." Publ Wkly

The willow pattern; a Chinese detective story; by Robert van Gulik; with fifteen illustrations drawn by the author in Chinese style. Scribner 1965 183p il o.p.

"This adventure of the legendary Judge Dee, of Seventh Century China, is a strange, brooding tale of crime, cholera, and corruption. . . . The emperor and his court have fled the plague-ridden city and left the judge and his Colonels, Ma Joong and Chiao Tai, in charge of affairs. They quickly become involved in three murders: 'The Case of the Willow Pattern', 'The Case of the Steep Stairs', and 'The Case of the Murdered Bond-Maid.'" Libr J

Gunesekera, Romesh

The match; a novel. New Press 2008 308p $24.95

ISBN 978-1-59558-198-3; 1-59558-198-7

LC 2007-21883

First published 2006 in the United Kingdom

"As a teenager from Sri Lanka, Sunny is living the typical life of an expatriate in 1970s Manila—a privileged, carefree existence—until one day when the secret behind his mother's tragic death years earlier is accidentally revealed to him, turning Sunny's world upside down. His life takes a series of unexpected turns—first in England, where he falls in love with the luminous Clara, and later in Sri Lanka, where he returns during a brief lull in the country's brutal ethnic war." Publisher's note

"Many a novelist, drizzling throwaway contemporary references over the text, looks clumsy and laboured in the attempt. Here the forty-year narrative arc is traced across a sequence of precisely judged topical allusions, embracing everything from Skants underwear to Cherie Blair's late baby. Each emerges quite naturally from narrative and dialogue. Time never hangs too heavily on the story, but we are encouraged to value the experience of its passing. Few novelists have so skilfully underlined the beauty of patience as a redeeming virtue." Times Lit Suppl

Guo Xiaolu, 1973-

Twenty fragments of a ravenous youth. Nan A. Talese/Douleday 2008 204p il $21.95

ISBN 978-0-385-52592-3   LC 2008-1671

"Guo's début novel, first published eleven years ago in China and now reworked in English, distills the rush to modernization through the experience of Fenfang, a young peasant who leaves her village for Beijing. Part of the post-Cultural Revolution generation, Fenfang is untethered from history and profoundly alone, and Guo imbues her flailing efforts to establish herself with a raw, adolescent pain. Pirated books and DVDs provide an education, as Fenfang takes cues from 'Betty Blue,' 'Chungking Express,' Marguerite Duras, and Tennessee Williams, progressing from work as an extra in state film productions to a screenwriting career. Guo is a filmmaker herself, and, if her recurrent homages occasionally cloy, Fenfang's rage to express herself carries an unmistakable autobiographical intensity." New Yorker

A concise Chinese-English dictionary for lovers. Nan A. Talese/Doubleday 2007 283p $23.95

ISBN 978-0-385-52029-4; 0-385-52029-8

LC 2007-3118

The "tale of one young Chinese woman's attempt to learn a foreign language and assimilate into Western culture when she goes to London to study English. Zhuang's first lesson in the West is that no one can pronounce her name correctly, and she decides to call herself just "Z" in order to avoid awkward conversations about it. Every experience is new for Z, the daughter of factory owners in rural China, and she dutifully records each new word or idea in the journal she carries as religiously as her dictionary. Her confusion is compounded when she meets a man who quickly becomes her live-in lover." Libr J

The novel "cleverly courts our assumptions about the chasm between Chinese and Western cultures, only to upend them. It is an utterly captivating, and disorientating, journey both through language and through love." Independent (London)

Gurganus, Allan

Blessed assurance: a moral tale
In Gurganus, A. White people p192-252

He's one, too
In Gurganus, A. The practical heart

A hog loves its life: something about my grandfather
In Gurganus, A. White people p139-80

The oldest living Confederate widow tells all. Knopf 1989 718p
ISBN 0-394-54537-0
* LC 88-45870
"Ninety-nine year old Lucille Marsden, confined to a charity nursing home in North Carolina, is an American cousin of Joyce's Anna Livia Plurabelle. Lucy tells the story of her marriage to 'Captain' Will Marsden, ostensibly the Civil War's last survivor, whom she married when she was 15 and he was more than triple her age. She also tells about her husband's experiences in the war and after, the burning of her mother-in-law's plantation by Sherman's men, and the abduction from Africa of a former Marsden slave, midwife to Lucy's nine children as well as her best friend. But this novel is less about the War Between the States than about the war between the sexes." Libr J

"In a way, 'Oldest Living Confederate Widow Tells All' is as much about language and myth-making as it is about love and war. Whether one feels that it succeeds depends on how much leeway one is willing to give to this indomitable 'veteran of the veteran,' as Lucy describes herself." N Y Times Book Rev

The practical heart; four novellas. Knopf 2001 322p $25
ISBN 0-679-43763-0
LC 2001-32665
"In 'The Practical Heart,' the narrator recalls the proclivities of his great-aunt, daughter of a Scottish immigrant to Chicago. . . . 'Preservation News' is a fey portrait of a man who has just lost his battle with AIDS but who spent his last breath in the pursuit of the preservation of historic properties. . . . 'He's One, Too' offers an ironically sympathetic portrayal of a married man arrested for lewd acts with a younger man. And in the longest and most moving piece, 'Saint Monster,' a son remembers how the relationship between his ugly but kind father and his beautiful but faithless mother forced him into prematurely dealing with the rawer aspects of adulthood." Booklist

The practical heart [novelette]
In Gurganus, A. The practical heart

Preservation news
In Gurganus, A. The practical heart

Saint monster
In Gurganus, A. The practical heart

White people. Knopf 1991 c1990 252p
ISBN 0-394-58841-X
LC 90-52943
Contents: Minor heroism: something about my father; Condolences to every one of us; Art history; Nativity, Caucasian; Breathing room: something about my brother; America competes; Adult art; It had wings; A hog loves

its life: something about my grandfather {novella}; Reassurance; Blessed assurance: a moral tale {novella}

The novella A hog loves its life concerns a grandfather and his boyish grandson, the other novella Blessed assurance: a moral tale "is a funny, sad, confessional tale told by a man reflecting on his traumatic youth, when he collected funeral insurance premiums from poor blacks. Gurganus is a champion storyteller with particularly American roots, in the tradition of Mark Twain. This is a collection to be savored and reread." Publ Wkly

Gutcheon, Beth Richardson

Five fortunes; a novel; {by} Beth Gutcheon. Cliff St. Bks. 1998 398p
ISBN 0-06-017679-2
LC 97-48926
This is the "story of friendship and support among a group of five women who first meet on a week-long retreat at a health spa in Arizona. . . . During the following year, these strong, independent, and ambitious women face enormous challenges that bring them even closer: private detective Carter quits smoking and takes on drug dealers in L.A., the still vibrant Rae must face her husband's decline from Alzheimer's disease; Amy and her daughter, Jill, resolve old issues; and the recently widowed Laura declares her candidacy for the U.S. Senate." Booklist

More than you know; a novel; [by] Beth Gutcheon. Morrow 2000 269p
ISBN 0-688-17403-5
LC 99-45936
The novel opens "with an old woman named Hannah reminiscing about her youthful fling in the isolated, picturesque Maine coastal village of Dundee. . . . Hannah's romance is interwoven with a deadly love story, set 100 years earlier, that will in turn mysteriously haunt her. . . . The taut facility with which Gutcheon twines the two stories creates real suspense—both in the exact fates of the couples and the identity of the ghost, who grows viciously vengeful. While Gutcheon cannily evokes the ephemerality of passion, she also evinces, with stark and elemental resonance, the way love and hatred shape lives." N Y Times Book Rev

Saying grace; a novel; {by} Beth Gutcheon. HarperCollins Pubs. 1995 312p o.p.
LC 95-8677
"Rue Shaw is a wife, mother, and the dedicated headmistress of an elite California country day school. . . . When her daughter Georgia elects to drop out of Juilliard in favor of love and heavy metal, she sets off a chain of events that dramatically alters the lives of Rue, her husband, and her beloved school." Libr J

"As it follows Rue's trials, 'Saying Grace' provides a realistic portrait of both a good school and its gifted leader. Ms. Gutcheon knows private schools, and she knows her craft—and that's a winning combination." NY Times Book Rev

Guterson, David

East of the mountains. Harcourt Brace & Co. 1999 288p $25
ISBN 0-15-100229-0
LC 98-40512
This is the "story of one Ben Givens, a retired Seattle heart surgeon and widower who is dying of colon cancer. As the novel opens, Ben arises, depressed, after a sleep-

Guterson, David—*Continued*

less night. . . . Ben is so depressed that he has decided to kill himself, and he wants to make it appear accidental; he will die while bird hunting in the dry eastern Washington canyons of his youth. With a surgeon's meticulousness, he sets out early with his dogs in his Scout and a cup of steaming lemon tea in hand." N Y Times Book Rev

"Guterson draws compelling characters and creates a haunting sense of place and of humankind's paradoxical relationship with the natural world." Libr J

The other. Alfred A. Knopf 2008 255p $24.95
ISBN 978-0-307-26315-5; 0-307-26315-0
LC 2007-41098
This "novel contemplates the binding friendship between two boys who meet in their Seattle high school in 1972. Neil Countryman is a gifted lad from a working-class family who discovers an unlikely soul mate, John William Barry, a fortunate son who balks at his predictable future success. . . . Their story is poured forth in Countryman's confessional some 20 years after Barry's untimely death, describing how the paths of their lives diverge. After high school, Countryman meets a girl, settles down and becomes an English teacher with a secret ambition to finish a novel. Meanwhile, Barry exits civilized life to create a new, dangerous existence as what the media will later dub 'The Hermit of the Hoh.' Living in a cave in the remote wilderness of the Olympic Peninsula, Barry becomes more and more removed from reality." Rocky Mountain News

"With prose that's as careful and quiet as a mountain lion, The Other asks, and helps answer, two of life's most perplexing questions: How do we live in an imperfect world, and what are our obligations to those we love?" Outside

Our Lady of the Forest. Knopf 2003 323p $25.95
ISBN 0-375-41211-5
LC 2002-43322
"When Ann Holmes starts having visions of the Virgin Mary, the bedraggled teen runaway becomes the last hope for the inhabitants of a dank, economically depressed logging town and the hordes of miracle-seekers who descend on it. In this panoramic, psychologically dense novel, she also becomes a symbol of the intimate intertwining of the sacred and the profane in American life." Publ Wkly

Snow falling on cedars. Harcourt Brace & Co. 1994 345p $25
ISBN 0-15-100100-6
* LC 94-7535
"Japanese American Kabuo Miyomoto is arrested in 1954 for the murder of a fellow fisherman, Carl Heine. Miyomoto's trial, which provides a focal point to the novel, stirs memories of past relationships and events in the minds and hearts of the San Piedro Islanders. Through these memories, Guterson illuminates the grief of loss, the sting of prejudice triggered by World War II, and the imperatives of conscience. With mesmerizing clarity he conveys the voices of Kabuo's wife, Hatsue, and Ishmael Chambers, Hatsue's first love who, having suffered the loss of her love and the ravages of war, ages into a cynical journalist now covering Kabuo's trial." Libr J

Guterson, Mary

Gone to the dogs. St. Martin's Griffin 2009 278p pa $13.99
ISBN 978-0-312-54179-8; 0-312-54179-1
LC 2009-10691
"This irreverent novel inverts the romantic-farce convention of the hero as lovable loser. Here it's the heroine who's the ambitionless slob, a grad-school dropout treading water as a waitress and living in a pigsty of an apartment. When she's eighty-sixed by her jock fiancé for an Amazonian white-water-kayaking enthusiast, she's propelled into action: she kidnaps the new girlfriend's dog. With expert deadpan, Guterson keeps the premise from getting too cute." New Yorker

Guthrie, A. B. (Alfred Bertram), 1901-1991

The big sky; [by] A. B. Guthrie, Jr. Sloane 1947 386p o.p.
*
"After a quarrel and fight with his father, 17-year old Boone Caudill leaves his home in Kentucky headed for St. Louis and the west, where he hopes to hunt buffalo and shoot Indians. The story follows his adventurous course, by foot and horseback, to the Mississippi, then by keel boat to the land of the big sky at the headwaters of the Missouri, where for 13 years he leads the typical life of a mountain man for his period and in that short times sees the Indian degraded, the game killed off and the life he loved destroyed." Wis Libr Bull

The way West. Sloane 1949 340p o.p.
A story of an emigrant trek from Independence, Missouri, to Oregon in the 1840s. Dick Summers, one of the principal characters of the author's earlier novel, 'The Big Sky' reappears in this novel
"Where most writers of Western fiction concentrate on what their characters do, Mr. Guthrie concentrates on how they think and feel. It is this emphasis which gives his book depth and sense of reality." Christ Sci Monit

Guthrie, Alfred Bertram *See* Guthrie, A. B. (Alfred Bertram), 1901-1991

Gwyn, Richard, 1956-

The color of a dog running away. Doubleday 2007 c2005 305p $21.95
ISBN 978-0-385-51855-0; 0-385-51855-2
LC 2006-11900
First published 2005 in the United Kingdom
"At thirty-three, Lucas, a Welsh-born expatriate, has drifted into a modest but pleasurable life in Barcelona: occasional translation work, long nights in neighborhood bars, strong coffee in local cafés, and comical exchanges with an Andalusian neighbor who rears rabbits on their common roof. But when Lucas falls in love with a stunning woman he encounters at the Miró Foundation his life becomes the stuff of melodrama. . . . At once an absurdist riddle, a romantic quest, and a love letter to our antihero's chosen home, Gwyn's witty and assured first novel is as much about the different ways you can tell a story as it is about the story itself." New Yorker

H

Ha Jin, 1956-

The bridegroom; stories. Pantheon Bks. 2000 225p

ISBN 0-375-42067-3   LC 00-28405

Contents: Saboteur; Alive; In the kindergarten; A tiger-fighter is hard to find; Broken; The bridegroom; An entrepreneur's story; Flame; A bad joke; An official reply; The woman from New York; After Cowboy Chicken came to town

"In this dazzling collection of stories, set in provincial China in the fairly recent past, most of the protagonists are emerging from the numbing predictability of totalitarianism, realizing that they must abandon the passivity that has insured their survival in the past." New Yorker

The crazed. Pantheon Bks. 2002 323p

ISBN 0-375-42181-5   LC 2002-22427

This novel is "set in 1989 China in the wake of the Tiananmen Square massacre. As Jian Wan sits by the bedside of his professor and future father-in-law, who has been felled by a stroke, he begins to discover peculiar yet arresting secrets about the professor's past. The seemingly delirious Yang is given to outbursts of shouting, singing, and talking to individuals who are not there. Scared but intrigued, Jian decides to delve deeper into the catalyst for Yang's mysterious behavior." Libr J

"Writing with a searing restraint born of long-brewing grief over the Chinese government's surreal savageness, Ha Jin depicts a warped society in which everyone is driven mad by viciousness and injustice. But Ha Jin's dramatic indictment does not preclude love, or the ancient power of story to memorialize, awaken compassion, and shore up hope." Booklist

A free life. Pantheon Books 2007 660p $26

ISBN 978-0-375-42465-6; 0-375-42465-2

     LC 2007-6177

"Jin's main character, Nan Wu, is a graduate student in political science studying at Brandeis. He is married to a pretty, resourceful Chinese woman named Pingping. The Wus have a young son, Taotao, who has just been reunited with his parents after four years living with Nan's parents in China. . . . The Tiananmen riots mark a change in Nan's fortunes. Disillusioned about China's future, he drops out of school, determined to make a life in America any way he can. The events of 'A Free Life' move from Boston to New York, where Wu, frustrated in his literary pursuits, learns to be a chef the old-fashioned way by starting as a busboy; and then to the outskirts of Atlanta where Nan and Pingping become the new owners of a local Chinese restaurant named the Gold Wok. At each location Jin creates a rich community of characters — writers, artists, political dissidents, waiters, shopkeepers, even the Dalai Lama makes an appearance — that give this quiet story of modest triumph a universal dimension." Seattle Times

In the pond; a novel. Zoland Bks. 1998 176p

ISBN 0-944072-92-5   LC 98-33493

"When Shao Bin, in post-Cultural Revolution China, is not among the chosen few for new housing, his wife berates him for not bribing the powers that be. Instead, Bin, a factory worker with a talent for cartooning, takes aim against the bosses' corruption and gets his cartoons

published. Not surprisingly, the clownishly wicked bosses maintain an arsenal for zapping such gnats, and it seems that the war can have only the grimmest conclusion. But the author is as resourceful as his hero, and the simplicity of the narrative proves deceptive." New Yorker

Waiting. Pantheon Bks. 1999 308p $24

ISBN 0-375-40653-0   LC 99-21334

This novel focuses on Ling Kong, a Chinese "military doctor who agrees, as his mother is dying, to an arranged marriage. His bride, Shuyu, turns out to be a country woman who looks far older than her 26 years and who has, to Lin's great embarrassment, lotus (bound) feet. While Shuyu remains at Lin's family home in Goose Village, nursing first his mother and then his ailing father, and bearing Lin a daughter, Lin lives far away in an army hospital compound, visiting only once a year. Caught in a loveless marriage, Lin is attacted to a nurse, Manna Wu, an attachment forbidden by communist strictures." Publ Wkly

This novel "provides a dual education: a crash course in Chinese society during and since the Cultural Revolution, and more leisurely but nonetheless compelling exploration of the less exotic terrain that is the human heart." N Y Times Book Rev

War trash. Pantheon Books 2004 352p $25

ISBN 0-375-42276-5   LC 2004-43428

This is a "fictional memoir of a Chinese People's Volunteer, dispatched by his government to fight for the Communist cause in the Korean War. Yu Yuan describes his ordeal after capture, when P.O.W.s in the prison camp have to make a wrenching choice: return to the mainland as disgraced captives, or leave their families and begin new lives in Taiwan." New Yorker

"Written in the modest, uninflected prose of a soldier's letter home, Ha Jin's story, a mixture of authentic historical detail and realistic invention, is a powerful work of the imagination whose psychic territory is not the hunger and humiliation of the prison camp but the haunted past that was the old, lost China and the mysterious future that is in the process of becoming Mao Zedong's chimerical new China." Washington Post

Haasse, Hella S., 1918-

In a dark wood wandering; revised and edited by Anita Miller from an English translation from the Dutch by Lewis C. Kaplan. Academy Chicago 1989 574p

ISBN 0-89733-336-5   LC 89-17814

Original Dutch edition, 1949

This "book, whose action is set against the background of the Hundred Years War, deals with the internecine feuds among the French aristocracy and, in particular, with the life of the poet Charles d'Orléans, nephew of King Charles VI. When his father, the Duke of Orléans, is murdered by agents of Orléans's rival, Jean of Burgundy in 1407, the young, sensitive Charles promises his brokenhearted mother to avenge the deed. But Charles assumes his duties reluctantly; among these are his new conjugal responsibilities to an older cousin who soon dies in childbirth. He then allows himself to be married off to the daughter of Bernard d'Armagnac. . . . In this unlikely marriage Charles finds true love, but his happiness is short-lived. Captured in battle, he spends the bulk

Haasse, Hella S., 1918——*Continued*

of his adult life as a prisoner in England, where he pens his famous poems of love and longing for his wife and homeland." N Y Times Book Rev

"This novel exemplifies historical fiction at its best; the author's meticulous research and polished style bring the medieval world into vibrant focus." Libr J

Habila, Helon

Measuring time; a novel. W. W. Norton & Co. 2007 383p pa $13.95

ISBN 978-0-393-05251-0; 0-393-05251-6

LC 2006-30790

In a "story of contemporary Nigeria, twin brothers want to escape their village of Keti, and war seems the best way to fame and glory. But Mamo has sickle-cell disease, and he must stay home, reading his brother's letters about adventures across the border and, later, about the brutal wars in which he fights. The twins' wealthy politician father rejects the 'weak,' sickly son, but an uncle inspires Mamo to attend university, read widely, and teach; by the time the soldier returns many years later, Mamo has been offered work as palace biographer, but, instead of the expected hagiography, he writes a true history of his people." Booklist

"Habila's beautifully (and deceptively) simple style is matched by a story that is strong, clear and richly evocative." New Statesman (London, England: 1996)

Haddam, Jane, 1951-

Bleeding hearts. Bantam Bks. 1994 311p il o.p.

LC 93-14466

This mystery "focuses on Valentine's Day as it's celebrated on Philadelphia's Cavanaugh Street, home to retired FBI agent Demarkian and a host of fellow Armenian immigrants. Everyone in the neighborhood is surprised when homely Hanna Krekorian turns up with a new man in her life, but Demarkian is especially shocked when he finds that Hanna's friend is none other than Paul Hazzard, who was once suspected of violently murdering his wife. Hazzard may have some kind of twisted motive for courting Hanna—but what?" Booklist

"Never quite cozy and never quite tough, this tale combines the best of both styles to stunning effect." Publ Wkly

Cheating at solitaire; a Gregor Demarkian novel. St. Martin's Minotaur 2008 391p $24.95

ISBN 978-0-312-34308-8; 0-312-34308-6

LC 2007-49770

"When the outrageous behavior of a movie crew filming on Margaret's Harbor (a fictionalized Martha's Vineyard) results in the death of a crew member, the island's one-person police department requests the assistance of former FBI agent Gregor Demarkian. Moving slowly through the landscape of her story, Haddam turns the island and its ambiance into a vividly visual experience for readers. Brilliantly introspective, intellectual ruminations and multiple narrators—who fully convey the craziness of the paparazzi and the cutthroat attitudes of those with power—intersperse with Haddam's own unique and frequently unexpected conclusions." Libr J

Hardscrabble road. St. Martin's Minotaur 2006 309p $24.95

ISBN 0-312-35373-1

LC 2005-54793

"Arrested for driving under the influence and possession of drugs, ultraconservative radio-talk show commentator Drew Harrigan goes to rehab for 60 days. Then the homeless man accused of illegally procuring Harrigan's prescription drugs disappears. In this . . . novel featuring retired FBI agent Gregor Demarkian, it is bitter cold in Philadelphia, and Demarkian's longtime girlfriend is away on a book signing tour. Having nothing better to do, Demarkian reluctantly agrees to help find the missing man. His investigation leads him to a cloistered monastery of nuns who shelter the homeless and into the rarified atmosphere of the University of Pennsylvania, the Philadelphia radio business, and high-powered legal firms that deal with people of money and influence." Libr J

"Those new to Haddam will snap up her earlier work based on this captivating literate mystery, which shows how well a classic fair play whodunit can work in a contemporary setting." Publ Wkly

Somebody else's music. St. Martin's Minotaur 2002 328p $24.95

ISBN 0-312-27186-7

LC 2001-58899

"A famous woman writer with a rock-star lover returns to the hometown where as a nerdy teenager she was traumatized by a nearby, still unsolved murder. The rock star asks FBI Behavioral Sciences Unit chief Gregor Demarkian. . . to solve this case—and more." Libr J

"Haddam movingly explores what that means for our lives—past, present and future—and how that happens and why." Publ Wkly

True believers. St. Martin's Press 2001 328p

ISBN 0-312-20929-0

LC 00-51794

"Retired FBI agent Gregor Demarkian . . . investigates an unusual apparent murder/suicide in a Philadelphia church, for which police blame the husband. A nun believes otherwise, however, and so the plot thickens." Libr J

"Haddam's large cast pulses with petty jealousies, vanities and fears as they confront the mysteries of life and religion. This is an engrossingly complex mystery that should win further acclaim for its prolific and talented author." Publ Wkly

Haddon, Mark

The curious incident of the dog in the nighttime. Today Show Book Club ed. Doubleday 2003 226p il $24.95

ISBN 0-385-51210-4

Despite his overwhelming fear of interacting with people, Christopher, a mathematically-gifted, autistic fifteen-year-old boy, decides to investigate the murder of a neighbor's dog and uncovers secret information about his mother

"Unable to feel emotions himself, his story evokes emotions in readers—heartache and frustration for his well-meaning but clueless parents and deep empathy for the wonderfully honest, funny, and lovable protagonist. Readers will never view the behavior of an autistic person again without more compassion and understanding." SLJ

A spot of bother. Doubleday 2006 354p $24.95

ISBN 978-0-385-52051-5; 0-385-5205-1-4

LC 2006-16578

Haddon, Mark—*Continued*

"George Hall, retired and content with building his painting studio, discovers a lesion on his skin. Despite a diagnosis of eczema, he thinks he is dying of cancer, but no one in George's family notices his mental decline because of their own bit of trouble. Wife Jean is having a not-so-secret affair with David, one of George's old coworkers. Daughter Katie will soon marry someone unsuitable in the eyes of her family. Son Jamie feels 'he's landed on the wrong planet, in the wrong family,' as he copes with a breakup with his boyfriend." Libr J

This novel "pulls off the smart trick of delivering fully human characters whose flaws make them almost impossible to live with, then depicts their love for one another as completely convincing." Cleveland Plain Dealer

Hadley, Tessa

The master bedroom; a novel. Henry Holt and Co. 2007 339p $26

ISBN 978-0-8050-8076-6; 0-8050-8076-7

LC 2006-48781

This novel "chronicles the slow-burning midlife crisis of Kate Flynn. A cigarette-smoking, high-heel–wearing Russian lit. prof, Kate has given up frittering among the London intelligentsia to move back to Wales and care for her aging mother, Billie. Against the backdrop of wintry Cardiff, Kate contends with her rekindled desire for David Roberts, now a married public health doctor. She simultaneously attempts to ward off the infatuated advances of David's teenage son, Jamie." Publ Wkly

"Melancholy and starkly emotive, Hadley's enervating tale evokes the raw drama that lies at the emotional nexus between friends and lovers, husbands and wives, parents and children." Booklist

Sunstroke and other stories. Picador 2007 177p pa $13

ISBN 978-0-312-42599-9; 0-312-42599-6

LC 2007-13103

Contents: Sunstroke; Mother's son; Buckets of blood; Phosphorescence; The enemy; The surrogate; Exchanges; A card trick; The eggy stone; Matrilineal

"Deft and resonant, [these stories] encapsulate moments of hope and humiliation in a kind of shorthand of different lives lived. Hadley never fails to surprise, but her surprises are understated—not the 'aha' fakery of some gimmicky short fiction but the small shift in expectations or results that's deeply felt but doesn't show, like the twitch of a rudder that sets a boat gliding on a new course." N Y Times Book Rev

Hage, Rawi

De Niro's game. Steerforth Press 2007 277p $23.95

ISBN 978-1-58195-223-0; 1-58195-223-6

LC 2007-23905

First published 2006 in Canada

This novel tells the story of "two young men caught in Lebanon's civil war. Bassam and George are childhood best friends who have grown to adulthood in wartorn Beirut. Now they must choose their futures: to stay in the city and consolidate power through crime; or to go into exile abroad, alienated from the only existence they have known. Bassam chooses one path: obsessed

with leaving Beirut, he embarks on a series of petty crimes to finance his departure. Meanwhile, George builds his power in the underworld of the city and embraces a life of military service, crime for profit, killing, and drugs." Publisher's note

"This is a grim, flat book. Hage's flatness gives it the right tone of bruised emotion, disconnectedness, and violence; it's what makes this such an effective debut." Quill & Quire

Hagen, George

The Laments; a novel. Random House 2004 370p $24.95

ISBN 1-400-06221-7

LC 2003-66882

This novel "follows the lives of the Laments, a white South African family in the late 20th century. Howard is an engineer who marries the energetic and artistic Julia. In a twist of events, the Laments adopt Will, just delivered by a mother who has abducted their biological infant and is then tragically killed with the abducted child in an automobile accident. A few years later, Will's twin brothers, Marcus and Julius, are born as the Laments begin their nomadic flights from Rhodesia to the Persian Gulf, England, and, finally, the United States." Libr J

The author "has shaped an affectionate family portrait in which the characters come vividly to life, no matter how adrift they may be. The Lament parents are especially memorable, Julia for her sense of lost opportunity and Howard for his gradual way of losing heart. . . . Each of them sees new opportunity eternally on the horizon in ways that have the potential to make this a story of crushing disappointment. But Mr. Hagen somehow endows it with brightness and finds a universality here, too." N Y Times (Late N Y Ed)

Hager, Jean

The spirit caller. Mysterious Press 1997 257p o.p.

LC 96-42033

"Molly Bearpaw, major crimes investigator for the Cherokee nation, is drawn into the murder of her assistant's aunt, killed while trying to put a ghost to rest in the Tahlequah Native American Research Library." Libr J

"Hager offers readers a clever, well-written mystery that also provides an intimate and edifying look at Native Americans' beliefs, traditions, and lifestyle." Booklist

Haggard, H. Rider (Henry Rider), 1856-1925

King Solomon's mines; introduction by Alexandra Fuller; illustrations by Walter Paget; notes by James Danly. Modern Library 2002 xxv, 264p il pa $9.95

ISBN 0-8129-6629-5

* LC 2002-29519

First published 1885

"Highly coloured romance of adventure in the wilds of Central Africa in quest of King Solomon's Ophir; full of sensational fights, bloodcurdling perils and extraordinary escapes." Baker. Guide to the Best Fic

She; edited with an introduction and notes by Daniel Karlin. Oxford University Press 1998 xxxviii, 332p pa $9.95

ISBN 0-19-283550-5

*

Haggard, H. Rider (Henry Rider), 1856-1925—
Continued

First published 1885

"'She,' or Ayesha, is an African sorceress whom death apparently cannot touch. The young English hero, Leo Vincey, sets out to avenge the murder of his ancestor, an ancient priest of Isis. The setting of this weird romance is an extinct volcano." Univ Handbk for Readers and Writers

Haggard, Henry Rider *See* Haggard, H. Rider (Henry Rider), 1856-1925

Haig, Matt, 1975-

The dead fathers club. Viking 2007 328p $23.95
ISBN 0-670-03833-4   LC 2006-50108
First published 2006 in the United Kingdom

"Phillip Noble's father is killed in a car accident, and suddenly Uncle Alan is hanging around Phillip's mother. It isn't long before the ghost of Phillip's dad appears and tells the 11 year old that the death was no accident. The ghost also tells Phillip about the dead fathers club, whose members are doomed to an eternity of terrors because their murders were never avenged. The only solution is for Phillip to murder his uncle before his father's next birthday." Libr J

This novel is "clearly inspired by Shakespeare's Hamlet, and part of the fun for the reader is discovering the many droll and unforced parallels. But the real draw is the extraordinary voice that Haig has created for his first-person narrator. Given to panic attacks, Philip is a breathless storyteller who seldom stops for punctuation but whose honesty and innocence, which shine from every sentence, are utterly captivating and heartbreakingly poignant. The result is an absolutely irresistible read." Booklist

The Labrador Pact. Viking 2008 341p $23.95
ISBN 978-0-670-01852-9; 0-670-01852-X
                              LC 2007-19557
First published 2004 in the United Kingdom with title: The last family in England

The "tale of a noble dog's efforts to save his human family from ruin. Prince, the Lab narrator, begins his story on the day he says will be his last. Animals in this world are always talking to each other — and us, though we can't hear what they say. So they're forced to resort to barks and soulful looks. Labradors are bound by the rules of the titular pact, which requires the breed to make the safety of the human family paramount. For Prince, this means trying to keep his family, the Hunters, safe from the machinations of a seductive couple who clearly have designs on Adam and Kate Hunter, the weary parents of two teenagers." USA Today

"The animal perspective is fully adult—a puckish slant on the disillusionments of modern domestic life. . . . As Haig pushes beyond the usually somber boundaries of Urban Dysfunctional Fiction, maybe we should just enjoy his novel for what it is: a wry, serio-comic family tail, er, tale, for our serio-comic times." Washington Post Book World

The possession of Mr Cave. Viking 2009 c2008 244p $25.95
ISBN 978-0-670-02056-0; 0-670-02056-7

First published 2008 in the United Kingdom

The "study study of a father "bent on protecting his beautiful 15-year-old daughter, Byrony. Beset by tragedy-his wife was murdered and, later, Byrony's twin, Reuben, was accidentally killed by bullies-Terence focuses all his energy on Byrony, but when she begins sneaking out to meet boys, Terence's stepped-up efforts to thwart her behavior backfire, and soon she's seeing one of the boys involved in Reuben's death." Publ Wkly

"At times, the theme (which plays on the dual meanings of the word 'possession') can seem heavy-handed, but the near-compulsive emphasis on having, holding, keeping and protecting aptly reflects Cave's troubled state of mind. Haig effectively brings readers into Cave's unstable interior world, asking them to inhabit this closed-off, deeply unreliable space along with their narrator." Bookreporter.com

Haigh, Jennifer, 1968-

Baker towers; a novel. William Morrow 2005 334p $24.95
ISBN 0-06-050941-4   LC 2004-49073

This novel is "set in Bakerton, a mining town in post-World World II Pennsylvania. Haigh's focus is the Novak family, particularly the five children being raised by their Italian mother after their Polish father drops dead. All five make attempts to escape Bakerton at one point or another; some are successful, others are not. George, a veteran of WW II, neglects his Bakerton fiancee and marries a cold socialite. Dorothy goes to the nation's capital to work, but a nervous breakdown brings her home. Brilliant, cold Joyce thinks her future lies with the military, but she is sorely disappointed. Sandy is the golden son who escapes to dubious success. And Lucy is the youngest, who finds herself in college despite the nagging feeling that she never wanted to leave home in the first place. Haigh creates a real sense of a community and brings her mining town to life through a large cast of minor characters who pass in and out of the Novaks' lives." Booklist

The condition; a novel. HarperCollins 2008 390p $25.95
ISBN 978-0-06-075578-2; 0-06-075578-4

The "novel opens in 1976. Paulette McKotch arrives at her family's retreat in Cape Cod, with her three children in tow. The beautiful daughter of a prominent Massachusetts family, she treasures these vacations in the rambling old summer home. But the idyllic surroundings can't heal the fissures in her marriage to Frank, the charming scientist who chafes at the proprieties and traditions that Paulette honors. Instead, sun-bleached beaches are the stage for a parting of the ways that will set each member of the McKotch family on a very different path. The Condition is most obviously the chromosomal disorder, called Turner's syndrome, that afflicts Gwen, the youngest, who will forever be trapped in a child's body. It is during that Cape Cod trip that Frank realizes that something is very wrong with his 13-year-old daughter." USA Today

"The point of view in 'The Condition' shifts repeatedly, as each character replays the relevant scenes of his or her life. This structure adds dimension, but it slows momentum because time doesn't move forward in a linear fashion. Still, the inner lives of these people are so richly developed that they keep us engaged." Chicago Tribune

Haigh, Jennifer, 1968-—*Continued*

Mrs. Kimble. Morrow 2003 394p $24.95

ISBN 0-06-050939-2   LC 2002-70304

The title "refers to three women, each of whom marries an opportunist named Ken Kimble. The first wife, Birdie, is Ken's student at a small Christian college. With her, he has two children. Then he seduces another student and deserts his family, leaving Birdie to bring up the children alone. The second Mrs. Kimble is a successful career woman, reassessing her priorities in the wake of her mastectomy. Ken capitalizes on Joan's neediness and sweeps her off her feet. He also ingratiates himself with her uncle, a real estate tycoon. When Joan and Uncle Floyd die, Ken inherits from both. The third Mrs. Kimble had been the first Mrs. Kimble's babysitter. . . . Original and compelling." Libr J

Hailey, Arthur

Airport. Doubleday 1968 440p o.p.

"In the space of a single night at the . . . Lincoln International Airport nearly every imaginable man, machine or function goes wrong. One of the worst snowstorms in history has been raging over the airport for three days. The longest and widest runway is blocked by a mired Boeing 707. A traffic controller is suicidally depressed. And a Rome-bound flight lifts off with a man carrying a bomb in his briefcase. How Airport Manager Mel Bakersfield and a score of other characters cope provides the [plot of this novel]." Time

"Here are many minor conflicts—of love, sex, business, and psychological problems—all building up to the tremendously exciting scenes of a shattered transoceanic plane trying to make its way back to the airport, and a runway that can't, but must, be cleared." Publ Wkly

Detective; a novel. Crown 1997 400p o.p.

     LC 97-1204

The novel's "setting is the Miami Police Department, where Detective Sgt. Malcolm Ainslee, a former priest, hears the final confession of a killer he put on death row. Although Elroy Doil was tried for one horrible double murder, he's suspected of committing as many as seven others. His confession re-opens one of these cases, and Ainslee is soon following leads into powerful political circles." N Y Times Book Rev

"It's a measure of Hailey's skill as a storyteller that he gives up the killer way before the end but still manages to maintain the suspense." Publ Wkly

Hotel. Doubleday 1965 376p o.p.

This novel reveals the inner workings of a large hotel during a hectic week. "Among the many events, the hotel changes ownership, royalty staying at the hotel are involved in hit-and-run deaths, there is an attempted rape, there is a racial incident, and a thief makes off with sizable loot. This is also the story of Peter McDermott. As an honest and intelligent assistant general manager of the St. Gregory Hotel, he thinks quickly and effectively in handling the many problems that beset this gracious old hotel in New Orleans. Yet his personal record is blemished by a single event which may keep him from rising higher in hotel echelons." Libr J

Hailey, Elizabeth Forsythe, 1938-

A woman of independent means. Viking 1978 256p

ISBN 0-670-77795-1   LC 77-28414

This novel consists of letters tracing Bess Steed Garner's "life from childhood to old age, from the tranquility of Honey Grove, Texas, at the turn of the century to the turbulence of the late sixties. . . . Bess shares her triumphs and follies in love and marriage, in childbearing and child rearing, in travel, business, society." Publisher's note

The author "has succeeded in giving us a portrait of a woman, with all her frailties, strengths, failures and victories combining to prove that living a life is an accomplishment." Christ Sci Monit

Haldeman, Joe W., 1943-

The accidental time machine; [by] Joe Haldeman. Ace Books 2007 278p $23.95

ISBN 978-0-441-01499-6   LC 2007-6935

"Lowly MIT research assistant Matt Fuller toils away in a physics lab until one day he makes an odd discovery. A sensitive quantum calibrator keeps disappearing and reappearing moments later when he hits the reset button. With a little tinkering, Matt realizes that the device functions as a crude, forward-traveling time machine. With visions of Nobel Prizes dancing in his head, he latches it to a car and leaps into the future. The interesting wrinkle here is that each jump ahead is 12 times longer than the last. Matt's successive futures involve jail time, unwelcome celebrity, and assorted holocausts in the earth's climate. He begins to long for his native era. As usual, Haldeman's ingenuity delivers cutting-edge technological speculation and irresistibly compelling reading." Booklist

The coming; {by} Joe Haldeman. Ace Bks. 2000 216p

ISBN 0-441-00769-4   LC 00-29306

"On 1 October 2054, astronomy professor Rory Bell receives a message, 'We're coming,' from an Earthbound object way out in space that will arrive on New Year's Day. Soon Rory, her composer husband, her chief faculty protege, the university president, a mob shakedown artist, a Gainesville cop, the mayor, the governor of Florida, and, finally, the president and her cabinet are all conniving away in response to the momentous announcement. . . . Haldeman's fast-paced, cannily constructed yarn is ultimately most like that granddaddy of first-contact flicks, The Day the Earth Stood Still. Maybe better." Booklist

Forever free; [by] Joe Haldeman. Ace Bks. 1999 277p

ISBN 0-441-00697-3   LC 99-33231

This novel "reintroduces readers to William Mandella [featured in Forever War] who has been living peacefully on the planet called Middle Finger, a refuge for humans who refuse to become part of the group mind known as Man. But after decades of this peace, Mandella and others are tired of living like zoo animals. They're ready for a challenge, and they'd like to see Earth again. So they steal a starship—and embark upon a voyage that will forever change their understanding of the universe . . . and themselves." Publisher's note

Haldeman, Joe W., 1943—*Continued*

Forever peace; {by} Joe Haldeman. Ace Bks. 1997 326p
ISBN 0-441-00406-7   LC 96-52650

"It is 2043, and the U.S. and its allies are waging a seemingly endless war against a loose federation of Third World countries called Ngumi. Julian Class is a draftee, an infantryman, and part of a 'soldier-boy'—a mechanized, armor-plated, highly lethal unit run by a squad of men and women all of whom have been 'jacked' or linked together by surgical implantation. Add to the plot mix a plan to build a mammoth particle accelerator on Jupiter's moon, Io, and the rise of a fundamentalist, secretive religious sect, the Hammer of God, to the very highest military ranks." Booklist

The author "writes with uncommon intelligence and acuity about the terror of war and the horror of the human heritage in the middle of the next century." Publ Wkly

The forever war; [by] Joe Haldeman. St. Martin's Press 1975 c1974 236p o.p.

*

"Earth is battling the aliens from a planet in the constellation Taurus but in Haldeman's chronicle of the career of William Mandella from private to reluctant major, the war becomes an engrossing, poignant epic. Mandella was among the unlucky first recruits for a war that has been fought for 1,000 years." Booklist

"A naturalistic description of a war that lasts more than a thousand years, although the main characters age only a few years because of the relativistic effects of faster-than-light space travel. The situation of the soldiers fighting in this kind of war is complicated, however, by their alienation from their own societies by the time-dilation effect, and their growing disillusionment with the war." New Ency of Sci Fic

Marsbound; [by] Joe Haldeman. Ace Books 2008 296p $24.95
ISBN 978-0-441-01595-5; 0-441-01595-6
          LC 2008-19356

"As the story opens, Carmen Dula and her family have been chosen by lottery for a six-year trip to Mars. . . . Things don't go so well after Carmen arrives on Mars itself. The daily routine is dull, and the chief administrator on Mars, a woman named Dargo Solingen, takes an instant dislike to the girl. Stalking out in frustration, Carmen puts on her suit and goes for a walk on the planet's dry and dusty surface—where she promptly falls down a hole and is rescued by Red, the leader of another colony on Mars. A colony, as it happens, of aliens who came to Mars thousands of years before. Before long, Carmen is a key figure in an interplanetary struggle, the only liaison between the strangely powerful aliens and the human race they might destroy." Christianity Today

"Recalling Robert A. Heinlein's Red Planet and Podkayne of Mars, Haldeman updates the Martian setting while keeping faith in his characters' ability to respond to unexpected challenges." Publ Wkly

Hale, Edward Everett, 1822-1909

The man without a country. R. West 1977 106p il o.p.

*

First published 1863 in Atlantic Monthly; this is a reprint of the 1897 edition published by Roberts Bros.

"This long short-story concerns Philip Nolan, a young officer of the United States Army who is tried for the Aaron Burr conspiracy. During the courtmartial he exclaims, 'Damn the United States! I wish I may never hear of the United States again!' The court thereupon sentences him to live out his life on a naval vessel, and never hear news of the United States. The story recounts the mental torments of the countryless prisoner, who after fifty-seven years finally learns that his nation is thriving, and dies happy." Haydn. Thesaurus of Book Dig

Hale, Shannon

Austenland; a novel. Bloomsbury 2007 197p $19.95
ISBN 978-1-59691-285-4; 1-59691-285-5
          LC 2006-34165

"In 32-year-old singleton Jane Hayes's mind, no man in the world can measure up to Fitzwilliam Darcy—specifically the Fitzwilliam played by Colin Firth in the BBC adaptation of Pride and Prejudice. Jane is forced to confront her Austen obsession when her wealthy great-aunt Carolyn dies and leaves her an all-expenses-paid vacation to Pembrook Park, a British resort where guests live like the characters in Jane's beloved Austen novels." Publ Wkly

The author's "charming first book for adults is chick lit with soul. Though there's a laugh on nearly every page—Hale, like Austen, is adept at subtly skewering the ridiculous—there's also the more serious story of a woman learning the difference between fantasy and reality, and discovering that real life can be better than your dreams." Bookpage

Haley, Alex, 1921-1992

Mama Flora's family. Delta 1999 462p pa $23
ISBN 0-440-61409-0
First published 1998 by Scribner

In this multigenerational family saga, the "lives of Mama Flora and her family provide a whirlwind survey of the 20th-century black experience. As a young woman in a small Tennessee town, Flora bears a son and sees his father killed at the hands of white racists. She realizes that education is the only way out of poverty. Soon, her daughter becomes a social worker while her son dabbles in communism and enlists to fight in World War II. As Flora lays dying, she can look back on her family and their accomplishments with pride." Libr J

Halkin, Hillel, 1939-

(tr) Sholem Aleichem. Tevye the dairyman and The railroad stories

Hall, Adam, 1920-1995

Quiller Balalaika. Carroll & Graf/Otto Penzler 2003 242p $24
ISBN 0-7867-1265-1

Hall, Adam, 1920-1995—*Continued*

First published 1996 in the United Kingdom

"The detritus of the cold war in the former Soviet Union comprises self-serving bureaucracies, opportunistic ex-KGBers, and organized criminals who make their U.S. mafioso counterparts seem like mischievous delinquents. Into the mix drops pseudonymous Brit agent Quiller, with the intent of taking out a British national-Basil Seckes, aka Vasyl Sakkas-who is secretly heading up the burgeoning Russian criminal empire. To bring down Sakkas' empire, Quiller needs the help of one Marius Antonov, currently residing in a Gulag prison. Freeing Antonov entails Quiller making his way into the prison and then escaping with his target, no small feat because the prison is virtually escape proof. . . . The book is a typically atmospheric, exciting Quiller adventure." Booklist

The Quiller memorandum. Simon & Schuster 1965 224p o.p.

*

Published in the United Kingdom with title: The Berlin memorandum

"Quiller is a British 'Shadow executive', employed by 'the Bureau', a government agency assigned to carry out delicate tasks, and it is so secret it does not exist. As we follow Quiller's 'brain-think' sequences we learn that during the Second World War he was an infiltrator who arranged escapes from Nazi concentration camps. Quiller and others like him with specialised skills, do the jobs that M15 and M16 cannot do. Quiller is used only at the authorisation of the Prime Minister. In *The Quiller Memorandum* he exposes a large, well-organised neo-Nazi conspiracy in Berlin." McCormick and Fletcher. Spy Fic

Quiller Salamander. Penzler Bks. 1994 247p

ISBN 1-883402-40-9   LC 94-17372

British secret agent Quiller, "bored in London, takes on a rogue assignment—one the Bureau has not sanctioned but which is the private effort of one of the 'controls,' the enigmatic Flockhart. The mission: discover what Pol Pot is up to in his ongoing efforts to return the Khmer Rouge to power. Arriving in Phnom Penh, Quiller finds himself attracted to his first contact, a female French photographer who harbors an important secret, and suspicious of his field director. Following a narrow escape from a Khmer Rouge encampment, Quiller uncovers plans for yet another Cambodian bloodbath." Publ Wkly

"Mr. Hall, a master of intense prose and tense situations, has again come up with a story that wil not disappoint his admirers." N Y Times Book Rev

Quiller solitaire. Morrow 1992 286p

ISBN 0-688-10730-3   LC 91-31060

"When a fellow agent who has called upon him for protection is murdered before his eyes, an enraged and embarrassed Quiller pressures his superiors into giving him the dead man's assignment to investigate the murder of a British cultural attache in Berlin. The murder is apparently tied to former East German national Dieter Klaus, a madman who wants to gain attention for his terrorist splinter group." Publ Wkly

Hall, Albyn Leah, 1965-

The rhythm of the road. Thomas Dunne Books 2007 309p il $24.95

ISBN 978-0-312-35944-7; 0-312-35944-6

LC 2006-48680

"A truck driver's daughter who grows up in the front seat of her father's truck, Jo shares her father's love of country music, junk food, and the open highway. Jo's life is a perfect slice of Americana, except that their 'open road' is in England, and her father—the gentle, melancholy Bobby Pickering—is from Northern Ireland. The only truly American thing about Jo is her mother, whom she has never met. Jo is twelve when she and Bobby pick up hitchhiker Cosima Stewart, an American country singer whose band is touring England. They become dedicated fans, and Cosima, touched by the unlikely duo, comes to regard Jo with an indulgent, even sisterly, eye. But when Jo is sixteen, Bobby sinks into serious despair and Jo seeks refuge in Cosima and the band. When Bobby disappears, Jo's adoration becomes obsessive as she follows her idol all to the way to California." Publisher's note

"Hall's handling of details such as the formal arrival of puberty is remarkably delicate, and she's great at simultaneously making connections explicit while hiding them from Jo." PopMatters

Hall, Brian, 1959-

I should be extremely happy in your company; a novel of Lewis and Clark. Viking 2003 419p $25.95

ISBN 0-670-03189-5   LC 2002-66376

"Narrated in multiple distinct voices, this retelling of the story of Meriwether Lewis and William Clark's legendary expedition is less a historical blow-by-blow than an engaging character study of the two men. Hall focuses on a few significant episodes in the journey—such as the hunting accident that wounds Lewis and causes him to sink into his famous depression—as seen through the eyes of Lewis, Sacagawea, Clark and Toussaint Charbonneau, Sacagawea's French fur trader husband. The result is a memorable portrait of the expedition leaders." Publ Wkly

Hall, James Norman, 1887-1951

(jt. auth) Nordhoff, C. Botany Bay
(jt. auth) Nordhoff, C. The Bounty trilogy
(jt. auth) Nordhoff, C. Men against the sea
(jt. auth) Nordhoff, C. Mutiny on the Bounty
(jt. auth) Nordhoff, C. Pitcairn's Island

Hall, James W., 1947-

Blackwater sound; a novel. St. Martin's Minotaur 2002 339p $24.95

ISBN 0-312-20384-5   LC 2001-48594

"When a passenger plane crash-lands near Thorn's boat in the Florida coastal waters, Thorn finds himself thrust into a rescue operation that leads him deeper and deeper into the lunatic world of the Braswell family." Publ Wkly

"Hall's quiet studies of loners—the old man in his fog of memory, the marlin in the freedom of the deep—are truly haunting." N Y Times Book Rev

Hall, James W., 1947-—*Continued*

Buzz cut; by James W. Hall. Delacorte Press 1996 374p o.p.   LC 95-50425

In this mystery, "Thorn and Sugar take security detail on a luxury Caribbean cruiseship only to find that a brilliant madman named Butler Jack has hijacked the ship for reasons clear only to himself. Butler creates general havoc on board, altering the ship's course, causing near collisions, and randomly killing crew and passengers in spectacularly bloody fashion. Thorn and Sugar slowly unravel the twisted tale of greed and madness that drives the mind of the hijacker, finally reaching a very surprising truth." Libr J

"Butler Jack's love of words comes to him naturally, from an author who uses language with great delicacy, even when his characters are sticking knives into one another." N Y Times Book Rev

Off the chart; a novel. St. Martin's Minotaur 2003 337p $24.95

    ISBN 0-312-27178-6   LC 2002-191965

"Thorn's long-ago fling with a beautiful woman named Anne Joy comes back to haunt him years later when Anne's brother, Vic Joy, a modern-day pirate along the Gulf Coast, decides he needs to add Thorn's five-acre property to his ill-gotten business and real estate empire." Publ Wkly

"Yes, we like to imagine ourselves wearing Thorn's deck shoes, in a full-frontal assault on all those who endanger our world, but Hall, unlike most thriller writers, portrays the collateral damage wreaked when rugged individualists go into overdrive. This remains one of the best series in the genre." Booklist

Red sky at night; by James W. Hall. Delacorte Press 1997 326p

    ISBN 0-385-31638-0   LC 96-45621

"Ensconced in his Key Largo beach house, Thorn seems to have carved a lasting separate peace with the modern world until a senseless crime drives the other side of his personality to the fore, the side that says, 'There's something broken, and I have to fix it.' What's broken this time, though, is Thorn himself, mysteriously paralyzed from the waist down after attempting to confront an apparent prowler. The story begins with the slaughter of several dolphins-killed for their endorphins, the key ingredient in a miracle, pain-killing drug-and extends to Thorn's distant past and his relationship with his best childhood friend, who has been nursing a grudge against Thorn for decades. . . . Popular fiction at its absolute best." Booklist

Rough draft; a novel. St. Martin's Press 2000 335p

    ISBN 0-312-20383-7   LC 99-55532

In this suspense novel former Miami cop turned mystery writer Hannah Keller is trying to solve the murder of her parents when she finds a "copy of one of her books containing cryptic marginal notes that appear to be a message from the killer. Meanwhile, the FBI is tracking a psycho hit-man who dispatches his victims by crushing their hearts with his bare hands. The psycho is hunting the money launderer who may have killed Hannah's parents, and unbeknownst to her, she becomes the bait in the Bureau's elaborate sting operation. Hall weaves his contrapuntal plot strains beautifully, letting the reader know more than Hannah knows but never enough to be comfortable." Booklist

Hall, Radclyffe, 1886-1943

The well of loneliness; with a commentary by Havelock Ellis. Covici 1928 506p o.p.

This autobiographical novel traces "the life of the wealthy young woman Stephen Gordon from birth to her full realization that she is a 'congenital invert' (as she terms it), a lesbian by nature. . . . It is the first full, rich portrait of a lesbian in literature. At the time the publication was an act of outstanding bravery." British Women Writers

Hall, Sarah, 1974-

Daughters of the north; a novel. HarperPerennial 2007 209p pa $13.95

    ISBN 978-0-06-143036-7; 0-06-143036-6

Published in the United Kingdom with title: The Carhullan Army

In this novel, "a series of ecological and geopolitical disasters in Britain has caused all citizens to be herded into urban centers, where women are fitted with contraceptive coils. Hall's work covers familiar fictive ground in imagining a dystopia in which women's bodies have become the battleground for competing ideologies; what is new here, however, is the unflinching focus on physical control. This can make for squeamish reading, as bodies are continually being 'stretched and scoured' in the most vivid terms, but the result is a powerful argument that, when civil institutions, or the bodies of state, are compromised, so, too, is the integrity of the body. The book sometimes lacks suspense, owing, in part, to the limitations imposed by its framing device, a transcript of a prisoner's statement." New Yorker

Hall, Steffie *See* Evanovich, Janet

Hall, Steven

The raw shark texts. Canongate 2007 428p il $24

    ISBN 1-84195-902-2

In this novel, "Eric Sanderson wakes up in a place he doesn't recognise, unable to remember who he is. Attacked by a force he cannot see and confronted with memories he cannot ignore, Eric discovers he is being hunted by a psychic predator, a shark. This creature may exist only in his mind, but it soon starts making some very real appearances in his world. Loaded with letters from his past self, each signed 'With regret and also hope, The First Eric Sanderson', Eric embarks on a quest to recover his life." Publisher's note

"The novel's great virtue is its structure. Narrative tricks keep the reader surprised. Information is released in pieces, like time-release drugs in a capsule, their order derived from the progressive revelation of truths rather than the forward march of events. Only at the end do we accelerate towards a more conventional action-packed climax, though even that takes place in a sort of collective unconscious. In many ways, this is cyberfiction, a battle between archetypes in a virtual reality." Times Lit Suppl

Hallgrímur Helgason, 1959-

101 Reykjavik; a novel; translated by Brian FitzGibbon. Scribner 2003 339p $23

ISBN 0-7432-2514-7   LC 2002-29434

"Hlynur Björn is, by his own admission, a 33-year-old mommy's boy. He lives at home, spends his days watching porn and surfing the Web, and his nights at Reykjavik's nightclubs drinking and taking Ecstasy. He assigns every woman he encouonters a monetary value and refuses to commit to spending even a full night with his casual girlfriend, Hofy. When Hofy falls pregnant and his mother announces that her lesbian lover, Lolla, whom Hlynur slept with on New Year's Eve, is also pregnant, he must fight to protect his selfish and shallow way of life." Publ Wkly

"This novel uses caustic and irreverent humor to paint a vivid picture of Icelandic youth ideas and culture. . . . While the protagonist is confused, depressed, and futureless, the humor saves the book from being depressing." Libr J

Hallinan, Timothy

A nail through the heart. William Morrow 2007 328p $24.95

ISBN 978-0-06-125580-9; 0-06-125580-7

LC 2006-47085

In this thriller set in Bangkok, American Poke Rafferty, "author of a series of adventure guidebooks for young men, wants to adopt a street child named Miaow and marry Rose, a former bar girl. When Miaow runs into a former friend from the street named Superman, Rafferty gets roped into trying to track down several mysterious characters who may or may not have something in common. The unraveling of these connections occupies the main action of the novel. . . . In a refreshing deviation from the norm, Timothy Hallinan's real concern lies not with the crafting of a well-paced thriller (which he's done quite successfully), but with turning the classic hardboiled rugged individualist detective of American noir into a man whose greatest concern is the formation of a family. It's enough to make Raymond Chandler roll over in his grave." PopMatters

Halpern, Daniel, 1945-

(ed) The Art of the story. See The Art of the story

Halter, Marek

The book of Abraham; translated by Lowell Bair. Holt & Co. 1986 722p o.p.

LC 85-17582

Original French edition, 1983

The author "begins his tome in 70 A.D. in Jerusalem, when a scribe named Abraham flees the conquering Roman army. The author follows the dynasty of scribes descended from Abraham through the centuries, until he links them to his own real-life ancestors, a line of printers, one of whom worked with Gutenberg in Strasbourg. The book ends with death of Halter's grandfather, a printer, in the Warsaw ghetto, in 1943. The chronicle moves among dozens of cities in Asia and Europe, deftly encapsulating the historical events and social milieu of time and place, as each generation of this family hands

down the so-called Book of Abraham, a record of births and deaths that also symbolizes the continuity of the collective Jewish memory." Publ Wkly

Messiah; translated by Lauren Yoder. Toby 2008 487p $24.95

ISBN 978-1-59264-216-8; 1-59264-216-0

Original French edition, 1996

"In 1524, David Reubeni—a real-life prince and military envoy of a lost Jewish kingdom—traveled to Venice aiming to establish a Judeo-Christian alliance that would seize Jerusalem from Ottoman control. In Halter's remarkable imagining of David's travels, throngs of followers flock to David as he makes his way through the center of Christendom, mesmerized by the strange man's vast knowledge and regal charm. . . . But David's lofty goals also attract ruthless enemies and eager fanatics who mistake David for a messiah, all of whom jeopardize his mission. The harrowing adventure is satisfying in its ample twists and turns, but Halter's writing of David Reubeni into the historical fabric of premodern Europe—imagining David taking refreshment with Machiavelli, becoming the subject of a sculpture by Michelangelo and suggesting the creation of the College des Lecteurs Royaux to King Francis I—is the book's major pleasure." Publ Wkly

Sarah; a novel. Crown Publishers 2004 294p map $22

ISBN 1-400-05272-6   LC 2003-19648

Original French edition, 2003

"Sarah is the favorite daughter of a lord of Ur, a city-state of Sumeria. Raised in luxury and privilege, she defies her father on the day of her marriage and escapes into the lower city, where she meets Abraham of the nomadic mar.Tu people. Although soldiers take her home, she can't forget the young man who captured her heart and imagination. Owing to an injudicious use of infertility herbs in an effort to stave off marriage, Sarah renders herself sterile and is dedicated to the temple of Ishtar, where she serves as a revered Sacred Handmaid of the Blood for several years until she meets Abraham again. This time, she successfully escapes, and the two dedicate themselves to the one, true, invisible God and create a nation." Libr J

"Halter isn't afraid to present headstrong Sarah as bitter in her old age, and his complex portrait of the biblical matriarch gives this solid if predictable novel a dash of freshness." Publ Wkly

Hambly, Barbara

Days of the dead. Bantam Bks. 2003 314p il maps $23.95

ISBN 0-553-10954-5

* LC 2002-38571

"An extreme case of culture shock awaits Benjamin January. . .when he leaves cosmopolitan New Orleans, a city that loves life, for bellicose Mexico, a country that lives for its dead. Traveling with his bride, Rose, by overland coach in 1835, this Paris-trained surgeon (and former slave) encounters bloodthirsty bandits, fierce soldiers from Santa Anna's army, rebellious Yankees from uncivilized Texas and a hacienda teeming with feuding relatives on the country estate of the Spanish grandee Don Prospero's only son." N Y Times Book Rev

Hambly, Barbara—*Continued*

Dead water; Barbara Hambly. Bantam Books 2004 297p $25

    ISBN 0-553-10964-2   LC 2004-40766

This Benjamin January adventure "finds the amateur sleuth investigating a couple of mysteries. The bank that holds all his money has suddenly and suspiciously collapsed, and someone has apparently put a curse on a former student in the small school operated by January's wife, Rose. Just goes to show: New Orleans, circa 1836, is a wild and dangerous place. . . . Where many writers of historical mysteries get bogged down in exposition, or in cataloging details that most readers are not interested in, Hambly keeps things moving, always focused on her characters and her story, and not on showing off the quantity of research she's done." Booklist

A free man of color. Bantam Bks. 1997 311p hardcover o.p. pa $5.99

    ISBN 0-553-10258-3; 0-553-57526-0 (pa)

                          LC 96-44942

A romantic suspense novel set in 19th century New Orleans. "Benjamin January, a free Creole with dark brown skin, has returned to this society after living in Paris for more than a decade. He is trained as a surgeon, but in Louisiana, he makes his living playing the piano. Soon he is the main suspect in the death of a wealthy man's young mistress, found murdered at a ball. January spends the rest of the book gathering evidence in his defense." Libr J

"A few suspenseful moments not-withstanding, this isn't an action-packed or suspenseful whodunit. Rather, it's a richly detailed, telling portrait of an intricately structured racial hierarchy." Booklist

Graveyard dust. Bantam Bks. 1999 315p

    ISBN 0-553-10259-1   LC 98-43456

A historical mystery set in 19th-century New Orleans featuring physician Benjamin January, a free man of color. "The year is 1834, and January seeks to free his sister, who has been jailed for a voodoo-related murder. As he follows the trail, aided by his friend Hannibal, his own life is threatened by a monstrous fellow with the fateful name of Killdevil. While the city struggles to keep cholera in check, January stays one step ahead of his would-be-assassin, interviewing the family and friends of the victim and the accused." Libr J

"Hambly's plot, which revolves around evils confined to no race or class, is complex and often hard to track, but its emotional authenticity, varied cast and rich historical trappings give the novel power and depth." Publ Wkly

Patriot hearts; a novel of the founding mothers. Bantam Dell 2007 430p $25

    ISBN 978-0-553-80428-7; 0-553-80428-6

                          LC 2006-24174

This historical novel "opens with First Lady Dolley Madison waiting anxiously for husband 'Jemmy' and deciding what to save if they must flee the White House during the War of 1812. She is thus reminded of her predecessors Martha Washington and Abigail Adams, as well as Sally Hemings, and each of these women has her turn at personal narratives, which take place at critical points in the nation's early years and in their personal lives. The perspective offered is distinctly feminine and gives readers a sense of peeking backstage at a play they know well." Libr J

Sold down the river. Bantam Bks. 2000 317p $23.95

    ISBN 0-553-10257-5

                         * LC 99-54845

A historical mystery "featuring Benjamin January, a freed slave whose Paris education earns him a living in New Orleans and whose refined sense of justice puts him in peril wherever he goes. . . . Ben bends his back to the pain and humiliation of being a slave again when he goes undercover at a sugar cane plantation 20 miles up the river, were a rebellion may be brewing." N Y Times Book Rev

Those who hunt the night. Ballantine Bks. 1988 296p o.p.   LC 88-47803

"A Del Rey book"

"Someone is killing the vampires of London and James Asher, an Oxford professor and former British foreign service agent, has been recruited by one of the oldest vampires in London to locate the murderer." Voice Youth Advocates

"The characters are well drawn (in the case of the vampire Don Simon Ysidro, positively compelling) and plausibly motivated, and the historical setting is both well researched and well depicted." Booklist

Followed by Traveling with the dead

Traveling with the dead. Ballantine Bks. 1995 343p

    ISBN 0-345-38102-5   LC 95-30243

"A Del Rey book"

Sequel to Those who hunt the night

"Former British espionage agent James Asher is one of the few mortals aware of the existence of vampires. After he stumbles upon a meeting between an Austrian spy and the long-dead Earl of Ernchester, he embarks on a dangerous journey across Europe to prevent a catastrophic alliance beteen human governments and the inhumane society of the undead." Libr J

"From beginning to end, the book succeeds as both a classic vampire tale and a specimen of the relatively new genre, the historical thriller." Booklist

Die upon a kiss. Bantam Bks. 2001 333p

    ISBN 0-553-10924-3   LC 00-69666

In antebellum New Orleans "cultural war is declared between rival American and Creole opera houses when an Italian company attempts to open the season for the upstart Americans with an original and provocative version of 'Othello.' The composer is knifed in the alley, the lead soprano is poisoned, a prominent opera patron is murdered, and—oh, yes, the theater is torched. Benjamin January, a former slave and accomplished musician who plays in the orchestra, is well positioned for this backstage investigation." N Y Times Book Rev

Wet grave. Bantam Bks. 2002 288p

    ISBN 0-553-10935-9   LC 2001-43401

Benjamin January, "the former slave and Creole surgeon looks into the murder of a drunken whore whom no one seems to care about. Despite his education and musical and medical accomplishments, January is only a short, catastrophic step up from bottom in the oddly stratified society of 1830s New Orleans." Publ Wkly

"As with any good historical mystery, we are at least as captivated by the characters, dialogue, and environment as we are with the mystery itself." Booklist

Hamid, Mohsin, 1971-

The reluctant fundamentalist. Harcourt 2007 184p $22

ISBN 9780151013043; 0-15-101304-7

LC 2006-21732

In this post-9/11 novel, "a young Pakistani man, educated at Princeton and employed in a highly prestigious financial-analysis firm in New York, was about to start a brilliant career and had fallen for a young woman whose commitment to him, it must be admitted, was partial and elusive when the terrorist attacks occurred. Answering to his own conscience, he could not remain in the U.S. By the pull of his true personal identity, he must return to Pakistan, despite his reluctance to leave the enigmatic but beguiling young woman behind. From the perspective of a few years later, the young man relates his American experiences to an American man he meets in a cafe, whose visit to Lahore may or may not have to do with the young man's recent anti-American activities." Booklist

"This is a deeply provocative, excellent addition to the burgeoning sub-genre of September 11 novels. But it would be an understatement to call it merely that. Here is a novel rich in irony and intelligence. Hamid shows us the post-September 11 world from another angle. In doing so he offers up a mirror to the complex business of East-West encounters in these troubled times." Sydney Morning Herald

Hamill, Pete

Forever; a novel. Little, Brown 2002 613p $25.95

ISBN 0-316-34111-8

LC 2002-114241

"In 1740, an Irish Jew named Cormac O'Connor heads to New York in pursuit of the man who killed his father and gets tangled up in a rebellion against the English. Through a series of events involving an African slave with shamanistic powers, he is granted eternal life, provided that he never leaves Manhattan. There follows a tour of the city's history through Cormac's eyes: the political corruption and the poverty, but also the majestic growth of the metropolis through its culture, its buildings, and its people." New Yorker

Snow in August; a novel. Little, Brown 1997 327p hardcover o.p. pa $14

ISBN 0-316-34094-4; 0-446-67525-3 (pa)

* LC 96-36043

"In Brooklyn in 1947, Michael Devlin, an 11-year-old Irish kid who spends his days reading *Captain Marvel* and anticipating the arrival of Jackie Robinson, makes the acquaintance of a recently emigrated Orthodox rabbi. In exchange for lessons in English and baseball, Rabbi Hirsch teaches him Yiddish and tells him of Jewish life in old Prague and of the mysteries of the Kabbalah. Anti-Semitism soon rears its head in the form of a gang of young Irish toughs out to rule the neighborhood." Libr J

"Mr. Hamill is not a subtle writer, but his gift for sensual description and his tabloid muscularity . . . fit this page turner of a fable." N Y Times Book Rev

Hamilton, Clive *See* Lewis, C. S. (Clive Staples), 1898-1963

Hamilton, Jane, 1957-

Disobedience; a novel. Doubleday 2000 272p $24.95

ISBN 0-385-50117-X

LC 00-29504

"Henry Shaw is a high school senior when he intercepts e-mail messages between his mother, Beth, a musician and specialist in ancient music, and violin maker Richard Pollico. As he secretly eavesdrops on the liaison between 'Liza38' and 'Rpol,' Henry's emotions, ranging from horror to fear of abandonment to rage to deep sadness, take on a new dimension when he himself falls in love with a girl he meets in summer camp. Meanwhile, his generally bemused and patient father, Kevin, a high school history teacher, seems unaware of Beth's infidelity, since he spends much of his time coaching Henry's rebellious sister, Elvira, 13, who is obsessed with her desire to join a Civil War reenactment disguised as a boy." Publ Wkly

"Hamilton has written a novel so disturbing that no one will enjoy reading it. But 'Disobedience' is so provocative that you must." Christ Sci Monit

A map of the world. Doubleday 1994 389p

ISBN 0-385-47310-9

* LC 93-45723

"Alice Goodwin is caring for her best friend's children when two-year-old Lizzy Collins wanders to the pond on the Goodwin farm and drowns. The consequences of this tragedy reverberate through a small Wisconsin community, which never accepted Howard and Alice Goodwin. Theresa Collins, bereft at losing a child and a dear friend, draws on her Catholic religion and finds forgiveness. Alice, immobilized by guilt and grief and unable to function as a wife or mother to her own two daughters, is charged with abusing children in her part-time job as a school nurse." Libr J

This is "not an easy or light read; indeed, it takes on some of the toughest issues of modern life. But the writer's skill in describing a community and a way of life, as well as her insight into the hearts of her characters, render this story difficult to forget." Christ Sci Monit

The short history of a prince; a novel. Random House 1998 349p

ISBN 0-679-45755-0

LC 97-31627

This novel "alternates between two sections of narrative, set during two crucial years in [its protagonist's] life. The first introduces us to 15-year-old Walter in Illinois in 1972, coming to grips with his homosexuality, his lack of dancing skills and the fact that his confident, all-Amrican brother is dying of cancer. The second, which begins in September 1995, reveals 38-year-old Walter as a witty, warmhearted man full of regret for having spent his early adulthood pursuing 'The pleasures consigned to youth' in Manhattan's gay community—and full of determination to reorder his life by taking a job teaching high school English in a farm town near his family's summer home." N Y Times Book Rev

"Hamilton has an amazing way with the varieties of human pain. Her characters live with ordinary and sometimes extraordinary torment, yet her writing remains buoyant and her sensibility full of light." Newsweek

When Madeline was young; a novel. Doubleday 2006 273p $22.95

ISBN 0-385-51671-1

LC 2006-40238

Hamilton, Jane, 1957-—*Continued*

"When Aaron Maciver's beautiful young wife, Madeline, suffers brain damage in a bike accident, she is left with the intellectual powers of a seven-year-old. In the years that follow, Aaron and his second wife care for Madeline with deep tenderness and devotion as they raise two children of their own. Narrated by Aaron's son Mac, [the novel] chronicles the Maciver family through the decades, from Mac's childhood growing up in Wisconsin with Madeline and his cousin Buddy, through the Vietnam War, his years as a husband with children of his own, and his cousin's involvement in the subsequent Gulf Wars." Publisher's note

"Hamilton has never written more finely nuanced or beguiling prose, imagined more fascinating characters, or posed more provocative moral dilemmas. In each surprising permutation, Hamilton offers fresh perspectives on the puzzles of time, memory, and consciousness, and keenly gauges the many shades of guilt and audacity, grief and sacrifice, tenacity and goodness." Booklist

Hamilton, Masha

The camel bookmobile. Harper Collins 2007 308p $24.95

ISBN 978-0-06-117348-6; 0-06-117348-7

LC 2006-41316

"Languishing in a dead-end job in a Brooklyn library, Fiona Sweeney, 36, feels time is passing her by. So when the opportunity arises to travel to Africa to manage an unorthodox mobile library, Fi jumps at the chance to influence a culture of nomadic people whose existence is dependent upon more basic human requirements, such as water, food, and shelter. With everything from Seuss to Shakespeare, Fi's regular deliveries of books elate the village women and children but intimidate tribal elders, who fear change and anticipate the loss of their ancient ways. When the bookmobile's one intractable rule is broken, the village turns on the emotionally and physically scarred teenager whose act of rebellion jeopardizes everything Fi has worked for." Booklist

"Hamilton's portrayal of nomadic culture is lovingly and colorfully told. It's a painterly glimpse into a world that few Westerners will ever see." USA Today

Hamilton, Peter F., 1960-

The dreaming void. Del Rey/Ballantine Books 2007 630p $26.95

ISBN 978-0-345-49653-9; 0-345-49653-1

LC 2007-29244

"Humankind in the 34th century has effectively conquered mortality, but many humans are still searching for existential transcendence, and a growing number believe the answer can be found inside the Void at the galactic center. Once thought to be an enormous black hole, the Void, which supposedly contains an entire microuniverse inside an impenetrable event horizon, slowly devours stars to sustain itself. If left unchecked, it will eventually consume the entire galaxy. When the technologically augmented telepath Inigo begins experiencing revelatory dreams, his shared visions ignite a mass pilgrimage to the Void, which some believe will trigger the apocalypse." Publ Wkly

"There is a generous cast of characters and a handful of storylines involved here and it takes the overall story

a while to get going. But once it does, it feels like putting on a comfortable jacket; space opera is what Hamilton does and he does it well." SF Signal

Pandora's star. Del Rey\Ballantine Books 2004 758p $26.95

ISBN 0-345-46162-2

LC 2003-68753

"By the 24th century, the vast human Commonwealth has spread from Earth via artificial wormholes. Various benign or seemingly indifferent alien races have been encountered during exploration of new planets, but an astronomer sparks curiosity by announcing that a pair of stars is enclosed by a mysterious energy barrier. Unfortunately, a space expedition discovers that the shield was created to imprison an insatiably greedy mass mind that sees any other race as a mortal threat. When the barrier somehow is lowered, the alien immediately attacks the largely unprepared Commonwealth, while humans begin wondering if yet another inhuman power has manipulated events that unleashed this threat. The author deftly juggles many characters in multiple plot lines." Publ Wkly

Hamilton-Paterson, James

Gerontius. Soho Press 1991 264p

ISBN 0-939149-48-6

LC 91-6441

This is a novel based on an episode in the life of Sir Edward Elgar. "In 1923 Sir Edward Elgar, in his mid-60s and acknowledged as England's finest living composer, takes a cruise to the Amazon port city of Manaos. Rootless and dissatisfied, he repudiates his life's work as insignificant. . . . Elgar wants only to escape from himself, but in Manaos he meets a woman from his past." Libr J

Hammett, Dashiell, 1894-1961

Complete novels. Library of Am. 1999 967p $35

ISBN 1-88301-167-1

* LC 98-53911

Contents: Red harvest (1929); The Dain curse (1929); The Maltese falcon (1930); The glass key (1931); The thin man (1934); the last three titles are entered separately

In Red harvest the nameless operative for the Continental Detective Agency in San Francisco known as the Continental Op fights political corruption in the town of Personville, referred to by its citizens as "Poisonville." In The Dain curse Continental Op solves a jewel burglary, multiple murders, and deals with drug addiction and a family curse

Crime stories and other writings. Library of Am. 2001 934p $35

ISBN 1-931082-00-6

LC 00-54594

Includes the following short stories: Arson plus; Slippery fingers; Crooked souls; The tenth clew; Zigzags of treachery; The house in Turk Street; The girl with the silver eyes; Women, politics and murder; The Golden Horseshoe; Nightmare town; The Whosis Kid; The scorched face; Dead yellow women; The gutting of Couffignal; The assistant murderer; Creeping Siamese; The big knock-over; $106,000 blood money; The main death; This king business; Fly paper; The farewell murder; Woman in the dark; Two sharp knives

"The first great author in the hard-boiled detective

Hammett, Dashiell, 1894-1961—*Continued*

genre, Hammett remains one of the most entertaining, as demonstrated by this largest single gathering ever of his short fiction. This collection's main distinction is that editor Steven Marcus uses the original story texts from their appearance in *Black Mask* magazine." Publ Wkly

The Dain curse

In Hammett, D. Complete novels

The glass key. Knopf 1931 282p o.p.

Appointed special investigator in the district attorney's office to track down the murderer of a Senator's son, Ned Beaumont becomes involved with political bosses, bootlegging gangsters and romance

"One of the two best novels by the man who is generally regarded as the creator and still the acknowledged master of the 'hard-boiled' school of detective fiction. Brutal in its subject matter but excellently written." Howard Haycraft

also in Hammett, D. Complete novels

The Maltese falcon. Knopf 1930 276p o.p.

*

This novel "called the best American detective novel by some critics, opens with Space accepting a case from Brigid O'Shaughnessy, a statuesque redhead masquerading as a Miss Wonderly. Almost immediately, his partner, Miles Archer is killed. Spade hated him and has been having an affair with his wife, but feels duty-bound to find his killer. He becomes involved with an odd assortment of characters, each searching for a statue of a black bird, about a foot high, said to be worth a fortune." Ency of Mystery & Detection

also in Hammett, D. Complete novels

Nightmare town; stories; edited by Kirby McCauley, Martin H. Greenberg, and Ed Gorman. Knopf 1999 396p

ISBN 0-375-40111-3   LC 99-37237

Contents: Nightmare town; House dick; Ruffian's wife; The man who killed Dan Odams; Night shots; Zigzags of treachery; The assistant murderer; His brother's keeper; Death of Pine Street; The second-story angel; Afraid of a gun; Tom, Dick, or Harry; One hour; Who killed Bob Teal?; A man called Spade; Too many have lived; They only hang you once; A man named Thin; The first thin man; Two sharp knives

These "short stories feature enigmatic plots of devilish intricacy, rife with fisticuffs and pistol shots, and populated by stiffs, laconic coppers, lowlifes and droll, world-weary detectives. Sam Spade shows up several times, as does the Continental Op." Publ Wkly

Red harvest

In Hammett, D. Complete novels

The thin man. Knopf 1934 259p o.p.

*

"Nick Charles, a San Francisco detective, is the narrator. He and his amusing wife, Nora (on a visit to New York), take time out from drinking and dancing to solve the problem of what happened to an inventor whose disppearance coincided with the murder of his mistress-secretary. There is the right amount of underworld, and in lieu of the usual tough stuff we are treated to an adolescent (son of the disappeared—and deceased), who bat-

tens on the more lurid aspects of toxicology and pathology." Barzun. Cat of Crime. Rev and enl edition

"One of the first works to bring humor, and of a distinctly native brand, to the detective story in this country." Howard Haycraft

also in Hammett, D. Complete novels

Hammett, Samuel Dashiell *See* Hammett, Dashiell, 1894-1961

Hammond, Diane Coplin

Going to bend; a novel; [by] Diane Hammond. 1st ed. Doubleday 2004 293p $23.95

ISBN 0-385-50943-X   LC 2003-51945

"Feisty Petie Coolbaugh and serene Rose Bundy, both 31, have been best friends for years while living in the small fishing town of Hubbard, OR. Despite the intermittent help of Petie's husband and Rose's boyfriend, they must work to support their families. They begin making soups for Souperior's Caf, run by Los Angeles transplants Nadine and her twin brother, Gordon. This collaboration ignites undiscovered talents in both Rose and Petie. Set in the late 1980s, this first novel reverberates with a small cast of memorable, working-class characters." Libr J

Hamner, Earl, 1923-

The homecoming; a novel about Spencer's Mountain; [by] Earl Hamner, Jr. Random House 1970 115p o.p.

*

"Fifteen-year-old Clay-Boy of 'Spencer's Mountain' is again the protagonist in this short novel set in Virginia in the early 1930's. The story takes place one snowy Christmas Eve while the family of nine is anxiously waiting for the father to come home from his out-of-town job. It tells of Clay-Boy's trip to the woods for a Christmas tree, of his encounter with a fabled albino deer, and of his adventures with neighbors as he searches for his father, who is delayed by the storm. This picture of everyday happenings in a small mountain community and of close family relationships amid the hardships of the Depression years is painted with simplicity and charm." Libr J

Spencer's Mountain; [by] Earl Hamner, Jr. Dial Press (NY) 1961 247p o.p.

An "account of a boy's growing up in a large and impoverished family in the Blue Ridge Mountains of Virginia. . . . His chief problems are love and the fact that his father feels that a college education is a waste of money." Publ Wkly

"A novel filled with joie de vivre, frank simplicity, a little sinning, and much human goodness." Libr J

Han, Suyin

The enchantress. Bantam Bks. 1985 345p o.p.

LC 84-45185

"Set in the eighteenth century, in Switzerland, China, and Thailand, the tale concerns the exploits of Colin and his twin sister, Bea, free spirits whose Celtic roots have endowed them with a special ability to commune with nature. As a child in Switzerland, Colin learns from his

Han, Suyin—*Continued*

father how to make automatons, an early version of robots. After their parents' death, Colin and Bea travel to China, where craftspeople are needed to keep the automatons at the emperor's court in operating order. There, and subsequently in Thailand, they become embroiled in numerous affairs of the heart and state." Booklist

"This is an extremely well-told tale of life and love in the 18th Century. History comes alive, and there is a masterful blending of magic and science at a time when the division between the two were not so great." SLJ

Till morning comes; a novel. Bantam Bks. 1982 500p il o.p.   LC 81-19150

"This is a love story set in China during the period from World War II through the years of the Cultural Revolution. Stephanie Ryder, beautiful daughter of a rich Texan oilman, comes to China as a magazine correspondent and falls in love with Dr. Jen Yong, a physician from an upper class Chinese family who sympathizes with the Communist objectives. . . . Stephanie and Yong endure much censure, hardship and repression to sustain their relationship and marriage in the not very tolerant atmosphere of the Communist Revolution." Best Sellers

"Told with sensitivity, this is an engrossing story. Although her sympathies lie with the Communist uprising, Han does not spare that regime in depicting the purges." Libr J

Hand, Elizabeth, 1957-

Generation loss; a novel. Small Beer Press 2007 265p $24

ISBN 978-1-931520-21-8; 1-931520-21-6
                                    * LC 2006-102024

"Three decades ago, Cassandra Neary was an avantgarde photographer whose book, Dead Girls, was published to acclaim. But her hard-driving lifestyle, in concert with the rapid collapse of the counterculture, led to a downward spiral. Salvation appears in the form of an editor who offers her the chance to interview a reclusive photographer, Aphrodite Kamestos. But when Cass arrives at the photographer's private island, she finds that Kamestos had no idea she was coming. Rather than turn around and go home, Cass decides to use the opportunity to find out what she can about Kamestos, uncovering a few shocking secrets and one old mystery in the process." Booklist

This is a "crossover novel, difficult to classify, uncomfortable, spiky. Hand is one of those writers who has challenged the restrictions of genre writing. Here, she both fights with and against the conventions of the thriller genre to get at an evil deeper than its mere perpetrator. . . . So although Generation Loss moves like a thriller, it detonates with greater resound. It's a dark and beautiful novel that should not be read by anyone under the age of 30." Washington Post Book World

Mortal love. Morrow 2004 364p $24.95
ISBN 0-06-105170-5   LC 2003-62398

"In Victorian London, psychiatrist Dr. Learmont collects paintings by artists on the edge of insanity. Painter Radborne Comstock (think the Pre-Raphaelites) walks that edge, haunted by the image of a beautiful 'green woman.' Meanwhile, in present-day London, writer Daniel Rowlands, researching a book on the legend of Tristan and Iseult, meets the mysterious and mesmerizing Larkin Meade, becoming more and more feverishly obsessed with her. Parallels emerge between Comstock and Rowlands. Each has been seduced by a dangerous muse; to follow her will bring more trouble than inspiration." Libr J

"What lies behind the complex, even violent process that we call artistic inspiration? That is the final mystery evoked in Elizabeth Hand's ambitious and richly imagined novel. By tracing the turbulence and reverberations of that process back to its source, Mortal Love offers its readers the satisfactions of a detective thriller. Here, however, the mystery goes deeper than murder. Nothing, Hand convinces us, is quite as mysterious as art." Washington Post Book World

Handke, Peter, 1942-

Crossing the Sierra de Gredos; translated from the German by Krishna Winston. Farrar, Straus and Giroux 2007 472p $30

ISBN 978-0-374-28154-0; 0-374-28154-8
                                    LC 2006-31525

Original German edition, 2002

In this novel a "powerful female banker is traveling from her home in an unnamed northern European seaport. She has commissioned an author living in Spain's La Mancha region to write her life story, which the novel frames within her journey to the rather forbidden mountainous zone named in the novel's title." Los Angeles Times Book Rev

"The artistry of Peter Handke's language may well be unsurpassed among contemporary writers in German. His prose is at once serpentine and spare, dreamlike and exacting. . . . The translator, Krishna Winston, sensitively renders the mesmerizing beauty of his style. In this book, as in much of Handke's previous work, the most stirring passages disclose the inherent strangeness of the world." Bookforum

The left-handed woman; translated by Ralph Manheim. Farrar, Straus & Giroux 1978 87p o.p.
                                    LC 78-5568

Original German edition, 1976

"Marianne, 30, decides that Bruno, her well-to-do executive husband, will some day leave her, so she throws him out on the spot. She takes long walks through nearby woods, through an unnamed West German city and through the halls and rooms of her rented house. A friend asks her to join what seems to be a women's consciousness-raising group, but Marianne does not. She works at a translation of a French book about a woman trying to achieve independence; if there is a message here for Marianne, she does not get it. Friends, relatives and casual acquaintances gather round her and then disperse as aimlessly as they came. At the end, the woman is virtually catatonic." Time

"There are echoes of Beckett, Sartre, and Kafka in this chilly little novel. . . . Handke at his best handles that moribund trinity of modern themes—alienation, failure of communication and absurdity—with quirky originality." Newsweek

Repetition; translated by Ralph Manheim. Farrar, Straus & Giroux 1988 246p
ISBN 0-374-24934-2   LC 87-33065

Handke, Peter, 1942-—*Continued*

Original German edition, 1986

"In 1960, Filip Kobal, an alienated, 20-year-old, nascent Austrian writer of Slovenian descent, embarks on a quest to the land of his forebears. Ostensibly a retracing of his much older brother's last steps 20 years before (he was a Slovenian patriot, lover and revivifier of the language and tradition, and a doomed member of the Resistance), the journey is in fact an odyssey of self-discovery for Filip the man and the writer." Publ Wkly

"The author invests this process of self-discovery with such originality and marvelous psychological detail that Filip's journey becomes at one with the writer's and the reader's as well." Booklist

Handler, Daniel, 1970-

Adverbs. Ecco 2006 272p $23.95

ISBN 0-06-072441-2   LC 2005-52101

This novel is composed of "intertwining vignettes about love in all of its adverbial misery. Each piece, with an adverb for a title, focuses on young men and women negotiating the minefields of intimate relationships. People disappear, only to reappear in later stories skewering assumptions that were first developed in the earlier tales. . . . The stories feature two recurring images: that of the magpie picking up glittering pieces of material and depositing them in other stories, reflecting reality at different angles, and that of a catastrophic explosion–possibly natural, possibly human-made–that destroys everything and everyone in its wake." Libr J

Hanif, Muhammad

A case of exploding mangoes. Alfred A. Knopf 2008 323p $24

ISBN 978-0-307-26807-5; 0-307-26807-1

LC 2008-4150

"Benazir Bhutto called the mysterious 1988 plane crash that killed Pakistani dictator Mohammad Zia ul-Haq 'an act of God.' In this satirical reimagining of history, God gets help from a blind death-row inmate, a mango-crazy crow, and a Pakistani Air Force officer who suspects Zia's hand in his father's 'suicide.'" Entertainment Wkly

"There are many reasons to read this excellent novel, and one for which it should be celebrated: Hanif has found in Zia a veritable Homer Simpson of theocratic zealotry . . . . The inevitable comparison here is to Dr. Strangelove, and just as the Kubrick film crystallized the absurdities of nuclear escalation into an archetypal cast of idiots-who-run-the-world, Mangoes provides the necessary update." N Y Observer

Hannah, Kristin

On Mystic lake. Crown 1999 323p $19.95

ISBN 0-609-60249-7   LC 98-26448

Annie Colwater "finds herself abandoned after 20 years by a faithless husband and a college-bound daughter. Having no identity of her own after spending her life nurturing them, she returns to her native Mystic, a logging town in Washington State. There she finds her old high school beau in crisis after his wife's suicide. His depression prevents him from caring for his small daughter, Izzy, who is also emotionally troubled. Annie is able

to find meaning again through nurturing others." Libr J

"Never one to gush, [Hannah] is more than ever disciplined in her writing, and the result is a clean, deep thrust into the reader's heart." Publ Wkly

Hannah, Sophie

Little face. Soho Press 2007 310p $25

ISBN 978-1-56947-468-6; 1-56947-468-0

LC 2007-5185

First published 2006 in the United Kingdom

"Upon her return home from her first solo outing after giving birth, Alice Fancourt makes a horrifying discovery—her infant daughter has been replaced with another child, similar of feature to be sure, but not similar enough to deceive a new mother. Alice's husband, David, for his part, is convinced that Alice is delusional; her mother-inlaw, Vivienne, with whom the young couple lives, remains carefully neutral, but it soon becomes evident that she is pursuing her own agenda, at odds with Alice's. Things muddy up considerably when Alice disappears with the baby, calling into question once again the mysterious death of David's first wife. Two narrative voices move the story forward, Alice's and that of Detective Simon Waterhouse." BookPage

"A terrifying mystery of manipulation, counter-manipulation and, finally, astounding revelation. It's a haunting story told with bewitching skill." Scotsman

The wrong mother. Penguin Books 2009 c2008 415p pa $15

ISBN 978-0-14-311630-1; 0-14-311630-4

LC 2009-27521

First published 2008 in the United Kingdom with title: The point of rescue

"Sally Thorning, part-time environment rescuer and full-time mother, struggles to maintain her sanity and juggle the overwhelming demands of work and home. . . . During a week away from her husband and children, Sally has a brief affair. A year later a local headline tragedy—Sally's lover's wife appears to have murdered her six-year-old daughter then committed suicide—reveals that Sally's lover was not who he claimed to be and she needs to find out why." Publ Wkly

"Shockingly (and refreshingly) blunt riffs about the violent emotions of motherhood and the familial yearnings of men, along with chilling and darkly funny revelations about lust and loyalty, make this novel one of the season's most absorbing reads." O magazine

Hannan, Chris, 1958-

Missy. Farrar, Straus and Giroux 2008 304p map $24

ISBN 978-0-374-19983-8; 0-374-19983-3

LC 2007-37475

This novel "traverses the 19th-century American Southwest, a setting colorfully filled with opium smugglers, mule thieves, natives, and Civil War stragglers. Dropped in the center of the action is Dol McQueen, a brassy teenage prostitute struggling to hang on to a fortune in stolen opium. Hannan writes this character with impeccable style, crafting a vivid portrait whose emotional notes ring true. One cannot help but root for Dol as she withdraws onto the wagon trail, her pursuers ever near. This is a fantastic debut novel." Libr J

Hansen, Brooks, 1965-

The monsters of St. Helena. Farrar, Straus & Giroux 2002 306p $24

ISBN 0-374-27019-8   LC 2002-23433

This novel speculates on Napoleon's "second exile on the remote Atlantic island of St. Helena, where he spent his remaining years dictating his memoirs. Because his island residence is incomplete, the emperor-turned-prisoner stays with the Balcombe family, whose 14-year-old daughter Betsy befriends him. . . . As a contrast, the island's haunted history is revealed through its slaves, who all know the story of St. Helena's first exile, fallen nobleman Fernando Lopez, and his connection to the island." Libr J

"Hansen's characters, St. Helena aside, are obstinately alive, with their own plots, hopes and limits, especially with their own faith. The book's risky shape comes to seem almost as disciplined as a history—a matter of respect for the records Hansen has so precisely imagined." N Y Times Book Rev

Hansen, Erik Fosnes

Tales of protection; translated from the Norwegian by Nadia Christensen. Farrar, Straus & Giroux 2002 500p

ISBN 0-374-27240-9

Original Norwegian edition, 1998

"In present-day Norway, runaway Lea flees to her great-uncle Wilhelm's estate to escape a troubled past. . . . When Wilhelm dies, Lea finds herself entrusted to continue his vast business empire and lifework, which involves the connection between seemingly random events. From there, Hansen takes the reader on a journey to nineteenth-century Norway (where a lighthouse keeper's daughter battles illness) and to the escalating competition between two artists during the Italian Renaissance." Booklist

"Hansen favors the Russian doll approach to stories, in which one story is nested inside another. His 'serialism' is romantic in the deepest sense—allegories and narratives contain the deep structure of the world, while math and science are merely the mutable surface. The craft of 19th-century fiction and the complexity of 20th-century thought make this a gloriously rewarding novel." Publ Wkly

Hansen, Joseph

A country of old men; the last Dave Brandstetter mystery. Viking 1991 177p o.p.

* LC 90-50550

"While investigating the murder of a drug-dealing musician and the kidnapping of a little boy who witnessed the killing, the gay detective stubbornly ignores the conspicuously poor state of his own health. But even as he drags his creaky bones on an exhausting and dangerous hunt for the killer, his fine, strong mind keeps turning to thoughts of mortality. . . . A cool stylist who never loses control over his emotional voice, Mr. Hansen trusts his lifelike characters to earn our compassion." NY Times Book Rev

Early graves; a Dave Brandstetter mystery. Mysterious Press 1987 184p o.p.

* LC 87-15178

"Gay detective Dave Brandstetter tracks down a serial killer whose victims have all been young men dying of AIDS. Dave, in his 60s, has just returned to L.A. from a business trip, having been met at the airport by his young ex-lover, TV reporter Cecil, when he discovers the body of real-estate developer Drew Dodge on his porch steps. The man's death becomes linked to a string of stabbing murders, and it also becomes clear that he was killed first and then dropped at Dave's." Publ Wkly

Gravedigger; a Dave Brandstetter mystery. Holt, Rinehart & Winston 1982 183p o.p.

LC 81-6381

"A Rinehart suspense novel"

Insurance sleuth Dave Brandstetter "investigates the possible murder of a runaway teenage girl, who may have died by her own involvement with drugs, a strange cult, and the wrong kind of people. The missing girl's father, a corrupt lawyer engulfed by scandal, has run away, too, leaving Brandstetter with two cold trails and a lot of questions." Booklist

The little dog laughed; a Dave Brandstetter mystery. Holt & Co. 1986 184p o.p.

LC 86-12115

"A Rinehart suspense novel"

"Called in to investigate the death claims filed on the shooting demise of a globe-striding political journalist, insurance sleuth Brandstetter gets embroiled in international skulduggery. The writer was, of course, no suicide, and his death is linked to that of a young Latino sans green card who is from a Central American republic in turmoil." Booklist

Hansen, Ron

The assassination of Jesse James by the coward Robert Ford. Knopf 1983 304p

ISBN 0-394-51647-8

* LC 83-47851

This "book begins with Jesse at the height of his notoriety. Waiting to hold up a train with his brother, Frank, and their gang, he meets Robert Ford, the 19-year-old brother of one of the gang members; Ford idolizes Jesse and [eventually murders him]." N Y Times Book Rev

"Hansen's Jesse is in no way romanticized; his interest derives from the complexity of his psychopathology. The Jesse that emerges here is prematurely decrepit; he'll murder when he doesn't need to, but he reads his Bible and talks about God's peace. Canny, intuitive, he seems to welcome the disciple who will betray him, even gives him the pistol for the job. . . . The novel works not despite our knowledge of what will happen, but because of it a sense of fatality hangs over every scene." Newsweek

Atticus; a novel. HarperCollins Pubs. 1996 247p

ISBN 0-06-018217-2

* LC 95-38450

A novel "about Atticus Cody, a 67-year-old Colorado cattle man who goes to Mexico to retrieve the body of his younger son, an artist, alcoholic and, finally, a suicide. . . . A deeply grieving Atticus meets Scott's friends in the town of Resurrección and copes with the unknowns of a culture far removed from his ranch,

Hansen, Ron—*Continued*

where only recently 'carrots of ice were hanging from the roof's iron gutters.' As the Cody family history, which includes the death of Atticus's wife (mother of Scott, and his older, successful brother) in a car accident in which Scott was driving, is gradually revealed, Atticus comes to believe that Scott's death may have been at another's hand." Publ Wkly

"This is a didactic novel. It says that simplicity, purity and intelligence are good qualities to have. . . . It names great virtues and then looks at them glancingly, from all directions, finding them in unexpected forms. Mr. Hansen writes vigorously, and like an angel—so much so that 'Atticus' may end up giving didacticism a good name." N Y Times Book Rev

Exiles. Farrar, Straus and Giroux 2008 227p $23
ISBN 978-0-374-15097-6; 0-374-15097-4
LC 2007-46836
An historical novel "about 19th-century poet Gerard Manley Hopkins. . . . [It] zeroes in on one short period of Hopkins' life — circa 1875, when, as a Jesuit seminarian in Wales, he read about the death of five nuns in the sinking of a steamship and wrote what became a famous poem, 'The Wreck of the Deutschland.' Hansen conveys a man conflicted by his callings as both a spiritual vessel and a full-blooded artist." Entertainment Wkly

Hitler's niece; a novel. HarperFlamingo 1999 310p
ISBN 0-06-019419-7
LC 99-12656
"On September 18, 1931 Angelika (Geli) Raubal, the niece of Adolph Hitler, was found dead in her room in her uncle's flat, his pistol lying nearby. . . . Hansen's historically based novel offers one plausible scenario, that Hitler himself murdered her in a fit of anger over her attempts to escape his smothering jealousy. Using a variety of sources, including the memoirs and testimony of several of the principals involved, he attempts to dissect the nature of their relationship and show how such a conclusion is reasonable." Libr J

"Hansen's insightful, brilliantly interpretative, and frightening novel does more to illuminate the welter of evil that fueled Hitler than a dozen biographies." Booklist

Isn't it romantic?; an entertainment. HarperCollins Pubs. 2003 198p $17.95
ISBN 0-06-051766-2
LC 2002-69082
"Beautiful, self-possessed Parisian Natalie Clairvaux, a lover of all things American, decides to assuage her hurt feelings over her fiance's latest infidelity by taking a trip to the U.S. Appalled at Natalie's destination choice, the local travel agent grudgingly books her on a Greyhound See America tour. . . . When her fiance, Pierre, comes after her, they end up stranded by a flat tire in Seldom, Nebraska, and are lovingly embraced by the town's eccentric citizens." Booklist

"This is a preposterous plot, and at its best, 'Isnt It Romantic?' zips along like a Preston Sturges movie. Hansen slicks down his prose so the sentences are swift, and he punctuates them with a dry wit and some genuinely droll ripostes." N Y Times Book Rev

Mariette in ecstasy. Burlingame Bks. 1991 179p
ISBN 0-06-018214-8
LC 90-56362

This novel concerns "an early 19th-century monastery in upstate New York into which a beautiful young postulant comes in August 1906, only to be sent away in February 1907. The ostensible cause of neophyte Mariette's short-lived stay are her experiences of manifestations of the stigmata that begin four short months after her arrival and on the day of the death of her natural sister, who is 20 years her elder and also happens to be prioress of the monastery at the time." America

"The novel pulls its taut plot-thread smartly along from start to finish, weaving flash-forward patches of dialogue from the investigation of Mariette's 'case' into the unfolding action of her entry into the life of the convent. The finale is a stunner." N Y Times Book Rev

Harding, John Wesley, 1965-

By George; a novel; [by] Wesley Stace. Little, Brown 2007 383p
ISBN 978-0-316-83032-4; 0-316-83032-1
LC 2006-38194
"The multilinear and multigenerational tale begins with the last days of an elderly vaudeville ventriloquist, Echo Ender, whose onstage success with her dummy, Naughty Narcissus, ensures entry into the entertainment world for future generations of her family. First comes Echo's son, Joe, also a ventriloquist, who has a dummy named George; he's followed by his flamboyant daughter, Frankie, an actress; and then by her withdrawn son, also named George, who develops his own talent for throwing his voice at boarding school. The two Georges—one a boy, the other a dummy—are the joint narrators in this saga of the backstage failures behind one family's onstage success." Booklist

"Every novel is a ventriloquist act, in which the writer throws his or her voice into the mouths of characters and narrators. In some books you can see the author's lips move; in others the actual speaker seems to vanish altogether. Stace occasionally alerts the reader of his presence—he's something of a showoff. But these intrusions don't sour the spectacle. Some illusions delight even when you know how they're performed." Village Voice

Harding, Paul

For works written by this author under other names see Doherty, P. C.

Harding, Paul, 1967-

Tinkers. Bellevue Literary Press 2008 191p pa $14.95
ISBN 978-1-934137-12-3; 1-934137-12-X
LC 2008-39887
"This compact, adamantine début dips in and out of the consciousness of a New England patriarch named George Washington Crosby as he lies dying on a hospital bed in his living room. . . . The story traces Crosby's life back to his hardscrabble Maine childhood, where his father was a tinker and travelling salesman who suffered from epileptic seizures. Crosby's emotional life is dominated by his father's abandonment of the family on learning that his wife was planning to have him institutionalized, but the most memorable parts of Harding's novel may be his depiction of a nineteenth-century landscape complete with mule-drawn carts and 'frozen wood

Harding, Paul, 1967-—*Continued*
so brittle that it rang when you split it.' In Harding's
skillful evocation, Crosby's life, seen from its final moments, becomes a mosaic of memories." New Yorker

Hardwick, Mollie

The Duchess of Duke Street; a novel. Holt,
Rinehart & Winston 1977 c1976 303p
ISBN 0-03-018291-3
* LC 76-29903
First published 1976 in the United Kingdom in two
volumes with title The Duchess of Duke Street: Book 1:
The way up; Book 2: The golden years
An "adaptation of a BBC television series. . . . The
setting is 1900 London. Heroine Louisa Leyton sets out
to be the best cook in England and ends up running a
residential hotel and a catering service. The cast includes: Edward, Prince of Wales, whose interest in Luisa
goes beyond her culinary skills; Augustus Trotter, who
becomes Louisa's husband for propriety's sake and assists her as butler; and the Honorable Charles Tyrrel,
who befriends Louisa in her post-Edward days. Although
the episodic format is still evident in this novelization, it
does not impair readability. There is enough adventure
and humor here to entertain the reader willing to settle
for a light-hearted if slightly unbelievable story." Libr J

Malice domestic. St. Martin's Press 1986 218p
o.p.   LC 86-11376
This is the first novel featuring "Doran Fairweather, a
humorously perceptive antiques dealer, and her love, the
Reverend Chelmarsh, both of whom live in the isolated
village of Abbotsbourne, Kent. A wealthy bachelor takes
over the village's long-deserted great house. Events move
from cozy to chilling when a series of deaths ensues, including a teen suicide. Graceful writing embellishes this
stunning tale of evil." Booklist

Parson's pleasure. St. Martin's Press 1987 199p
o.p.   LC 87-4437
This novel takes Doran Fairweather "to Warwickshire
to track down the theft of priceless antiques from a rather eccentric elderly member of the aristocracy, Lady
Timberlake. What starts off as a working holiday with
her boyfriend, the prudish Rodney Chelmarsh, quickly
turns serious when one of the leads Fairweather is investigating, a gypsy antiques dealer, is brutally murdered.
Chelmarsh is the first to realize that Fairweather's own
life may be in jeopardy. Hardwick has managed to
breathe fresh life into this fairly conventional mystery.
Everything is vaguely familiar, from the cast of dotty
characters to the locale, but this only adds to the book's
charm." Publ Wkly

Hardy, Thomas, 1840-1928

Far from the madding crowd; with an etching
by H. Macbeth-Raeburn and a map of Wessex.
Knopf 1991 xxxiii, 243p $22
ISBN 0-679-40576-3
* LC 91-52978
"Everyman's library"
First published 1874
"Bathsheba Everdene is loved by Gabriel Oak, a young
farmer who becomes bailiff of the farm she inherits; by

William Boldwood, who owns a neighboring farm; and
by Sergeant Troy, a handsome inconsiderate young adventurer. She marries Troy, who mistreats her and squan-
ders her money. When he leaves her and is presumed
drowned at sea, Bathsheba becomes engaged to
Boldwood. Troy, however, reappears, and is murdered by
Boldwood, who goes mad as a result of his action and
is sent to a mental institution. Bathsheba then marries
Gabriel, the steadiest and most faithful of her three suitors." Reader's Ency. 4th edition

Jude the obscure. Knopf 1992 518p $20
ISBN 0-679-40993-9
* LC 92-52925
"Everyman's library"
First published 1895
"Jude Fawley, a poor villager, wants to enter the divinity school at Christminster (Oxford University). Side-
tracked by Arabella Donn, an earthy country girl who
pretends to be pregnant by him, Jude marries her and is
then deserted. He earns a living as a stonemason at
Christminster; there he falls in love with his independent-
minded cousin, Sue Bridehead. Out of a sense of obligation, Sue marries the schoolmaster Phillotson, who has
helped her. Unable to bear living with Phillotson, she returns to live with Jude and eventually bears his children
out of wedlock. Their poverty and the weight of society's disapproval begin to take a toll on Sue and Jude.
. . . The novel's sexual frankness shocked the public, as
did Hardy's criticisms of marriage, the university system,
and the church." Merriam-Webster's Ency of Lit

The Mayor of Casterbridge; with an introduction
by Craig Raine. Knopf 1993 362p map $18
ISBN 0-679-42035-5   LC 92-54297
"Everyman's library"
First published 1886. Variant title: The life and death
of the Mayor of Casterbridge
"Michael Henchard, a hay-trusser, gets drunk at a fair
and sells his wife and child for 5 guineas to a sailor,
Newson. When sober again he takes a solemn vow not
to touch alcohol for 20 years. By his energy and acumen
he becomes rich, respected, and eventually the mayor of
Casterbridge. After 18 years his wife returns, supposing
Newson dead, and is reunited with her husband. She
brings with her her daughter Elizabeth-Jane, and
Henchard is led to believe that she is his child, whereas
she is in fact Newson's. Through a combination of unhappy circumstances, and the impulsive obstinacy of
Henchard, troubles accumulate." Oxford Companion to
Engl Lit. 6th edition

The return of the native. Knopf 1992 xxxix,
497p map $22
ISBN 0-679-41730-3
* LC 92-52901
"Everyman's library"
First published 1878
"The novel is set on Egdon Heath, a barren moor in
the fictional Wessex in southwestern England. The native
of the title is Clym Yeobright, who has returned to the
area to become a schoolmaster after a successful but, in
his opinion, a shallow career as a jeweler in Paris. He
and his cousin Thomasin exemplify the traditional way
of life, while Thomasin's husband, Damon Wildeve, and
Clym's wife, Eustacia Vye, long for the excitement of
city life. Disappointed that Clym is content to remain on

Hardy, Thomas, 1840-1928—*Continued*

the heath, Eustacia, willful and passionate, rekindles her affair with the reckless Damon. After a series of coincidences Eustacia comes to believe that she is responsible for the death of Clym's mother. Convinced that fate has doomed her to cause others pain, Eustacia flees and is drowned (by accident or intent). Damon drowns trying to save her." Merriam-Webster's Ency of Lit

Tess of the D'Urbervilles; with an introduction by Patricia Ingham. Knopf 1991 xlviii, 472p map $22

ISBN 0-679-40586-0

* LC 91-52998

"Everyman's library"

First published in complete form 1891

"The tragic history of a woman betrayed. . . . Tess the author contends, is sinned against, but not a sinner; her tragedy is the work of tyrannical circumstances and of the evil deeds of others in the past and the present, and more particularly of two men's baseness, the seducer, and the well-meaning intellectual who married her. . . . The pastoral surroundings, the varying aspects of field, river, sky, serve to deepen the pathos of each stage in the heroine's calamities, or to add beauty and dignity to her tragic personality." Baker. Guide to the Best Fic

Under the greenwood tree; edited with an introduction and notes by Simon Gatrell. 2009 xxxiii, 218p pa $10.95

ISBN 9780199538515; 0199538514

LC 2009-290549

First published 1872

"The first of the Wessex novels proper, the common groundwork of which is a very vivid delineation of the people of Dorset and the neighbouring counties, and of the natural life and scenery. . . . An idyll of village life, in which the members of a carrier's family and the village life choir, a gathering of rustic oddities, furnish a sort of comic chorus to the love-affairs of a rustic boy and girl." Baker. Guide to the Best Fic

Wessex tales. Wordsworth 1995 189p map pa $7.95

ISBN 0-19-283558-0

First published 1888

Contents: Three strangers; Tradition of eighteen hundred and four; Melancholy Hussar; Withered arm; Fellow-townsmen; Interlopers at the knap; Distracted preacher

Harington, Donald

The pitcher shower. Toby Press 2005 202p $22.95

ISBN 1-59264-123-7   LC 2006-540298

This "tale of a late-blooming loner finds Harington circling back around the Ozarks town of Stay More, whose lives and times he's faithfully chronicled for a good many years now. Landon 'Hoppy' Boyd is a young projectionist–or 'pitcher shower,' as he calls himself–and Stay More is both hometown and hub on his circuit of the pre-television era sticks. He calls himself Hoppy because he only shows Hopalong Cassidy features, plus a childhood accident left him with a limp. . . . This ultimate outsider's life changes both for better and worse when he picks up a stowaway and then loses his movies

to a roving preacher. But this is a novel about the art of storytelling as much as it is about Hoppy himself." Booklist

With. Toby Press 2004 c2003 491p $19.95

ISBN 1-59264-050-8

In this novel, set in the Ozark town of Stay More, "a golden-haired seven-year-old girl is abducted and taken to a deserted house in the mountains by a retired cop. When he dies, she is left alone to fend for herself. Or almost alone: parts of the book dwell in the thoughts of a wise old dog who befriends her; others are narrated by the spirit of a young boy who had to leave Stay More when his parents moved to California, but who loved the place so much that part of him stuck around." New Yorker

"With is as whimsical as a paper-doll show while being deeply rooted in the earth; it gives the Garden of Eden myth a happy ending, and should find the wide readership that Harington so richly deserves." Washington Post Book World

Harkaway, Nick, 1972-

The gone-away world. Alfred A. Knopf 2008 497p $24.95

ISBN 978-0-307-26886-0; 0-307-26886-1

LC 2008-8701

This novel "is set in a dystopian future where humanity huddles in the shadow of the Jorgmund Pipe. The ragtag bunch of heroes are sent to put out a fire on the Pipe, a mission both dangerous and imperative, since the Pipe, like a vast futuristic Glade room-freshener, releases the only substance that keeps the psychic stinks and foul odours of this post-apocalyptic world at bay. On the way there, the unnamed narrator reminisces about his upbringing, college days, military service, the Go Away Bombs that created their surreal present, and above all his friend Gonzo, to whom he's always felt closer than a brother. Somehow their story brings in ninjas, first loves, pirate-kings, mime-artists, human monsters and, well, monster monsters. . . . The revelation of Gonzo's relationship to his nameless best friend (and the ways in which Harkaway keeps on teasing around us not knowing his name is one of the novel's joys) is both unexpected and obvious. The Gone-Away World is brakes-off fiction." Scotsman

Harlan, Thomas, 1929-

House of reeds. Tor Bks. 2004 414p map $25.95

ISBN 0-7653-0193-8   LC 2003-57060

"A Tom Doherty Associates book"

"Gretchen Anderssen and her team are shunted from long-overdue leave to the investigation of a rumored First Sun artifact on the obscure planet Jagan. There they land in the middle of a 'flowery war' arranged by the priests to improve the emperor's youngest son, Tezozomoc's, reputation. And Gretchen can't get a permit for the main site on Jagan, because of university politics and the archaeologist already working at it. But then she gets a tip about one city's oldest building, the House of Reeds. She befriends an aging member of the other species present, though also nonnative, on Jagan. He is a former gardener, and with him she enters the House of

Harlan, Thomas, 1929-—*Continued*

Reeds. . . . The mystery of the long-gone forerunners of the empire Gretchen knows develops grippingly." Booklist

Harper, Karen

The Poyson garden. Delacorte Press 1999 310p
ISBN 0-385-33283-1   LC 98-36420
"Elizabeth Tudor, daughter of Henry VIII and Anne Boleyn, bides her time as her half-sister, Queen Mary I, burns heretics and sickens in the year 1558. Elizabeth's time may be short, however: a murderer, possibly backed by Mary, is poisoning anyone related to the Boleyn family. . . . Closely guarded at Hatfield by Thomas Pope and his wife, Beatrice, Elizabeth nonetheless determines to uncover the mysterious veiled woman behind the poisonings." Publ Wkly

"Elizabeth's active role may strain credulity a bit, but this one is great fun all the same." Booklist

The queene's Christmas. Thomas Dunne Books 2003 287p map $24.95
ISBN 0-312-30175-8   LC 2003-46822
"It is the Christmas season of 1564, and Elizabeth wants her subjects to enjoy the holidays while she attempts to outwit her devious Catholic cousin, Mary Queen of Scots, who is plotting to steal the throne of England. Elizabeth has planned an elaborate holiday feast, but the preparations go awry when Master Hodge Thatcher, Dresser of the Queene's Privy Kitchen, is found hanging in his workroom adorned with the peacock feathers meant for decorating the roasted bird. Elizabeth must solve the crime before she becomes another victim. The wonderful historical detail mixed with intrigue and authentic Elizabethan recipes enliven this story." Booklist

The tidal poole; an Elizabeth I mystery. Delacorte Press 2000 290p
ISBN 0-385-33284-X   LC 99-43315
"During her coronation procession into the city of London, Elizabeth I finds herself in the midst of crime and political intrigue. The murders of a lady of the court and another victim may be part of a plot to overthrow her government. This mystery full of scheming Tudors, Seymours, and Dudleys is a page-turner based on historical sources." Booklist

Harrar, George, 1949-

The spinning man. Putnam 2003 341p $24.95
ISBN 0-399-14983-X   LC 2002-74532
This suspense novel "follows a philosophy professor under invesigation for the disappearance of a teenage cheerleader. Evan Birch gets pulled over by the police one evening on his way home from the supermarket with his 10-year-old twin sons. The police haul him in for interrogation, and he learns that a car much like his was spotted at the park where 16-year-old Joyce Bonner, a local high school student, was working the afternoon she disappeared. He's released after questioning, but damning circumstantial evidence continues to pile up." Publ Wkly

"A graceful and subtle writer, Harrar invites us to identify with the philosopher's struggles to maintain his mental equilibrium, even as the novel dangles the possibility that the mind might not always be in control of the body's behaviors." N Y Times Book Rev

Harries, Ann

Manly pursuits. Bloomsbury Pub. 1999 339p $24.95
ISBN 1-58234-019-6
"Cape Town, 1899, Cecil Rhodes, arch-imperialist and tycoon, believes he has only months to live, and that he can be saved only by hearing the sound of British birdsong. . . . Professor Francis Wills, a reclusive Oxford don, arrives in Cape Town with two hundred songbirds . . . on the eve of the Anglo-Boer war. But the birds, confused by the change of season and hemisphere, refuse to sing. In Rhodes' gloomy, male-dominated estate, suffused with erotic undercurrents, Wills is drawn into intrigue - romantic, political and ornithological." Publisher's note

"This is a fascinating look at the turn of the last century, the infancy of industrialization, and the decline of imperialism, with hints of the decadence of the sexually repressed Victorian era." Booklist

Harrigan, Stephen, 1948-

Challenger Park. Knopf 2006 397p $24.95
ISBN 0-375-41205-0   LC 2005-49403
This novel "centers on married astronauts Brian and Lucy Kincheloe, who struggle to balance the awesome prospects of space travel with the sobering realities of life on Earth. Handsome, hard-driving Brian is a former Gulf War pilot whose hubris on two previous missions has jeopardized his career. Brilliant, no-nonsense Lucy still eagerly awaits her first opportunity to conquer the great beyond. While their three-year-old daughter, Bethie, is healthy, older son Davis' bouts with asthma frequently land him in the ER. The Kincheloes' marriage grows more troubled over time, and when Lucy is chosen for a future mission, she finds herself drawn to Walt Womack, a stern but sensitive widower charged with training the shuttle crew." Booklist

"Harrigan makes his all-too-human characters—caring, needy, shortsighted, world-weary, salty-tongued—sympathetic without hiding the personal abysses into which they are drifting, and that is no small accomplishment." Fort Worth Star-Telegram

The gates of the Alamo; a novel. Knopf 2000 581p $25
ISBN 0-679-44717-2   LC 99-33437
This novel is set during the struggle between Texans and Mexicans for the Alamo in 1836. Harrigan concentrates "on fictional characters caught up in a struggle not of their own making—an American naturalist, a female innkeeper and her son, [and] Mexican soldiers." Newsweek

"Harrigan has crafted a compulsively readable historical drama on a grand scale, peopled with highly believable frontier personalities—Mexican as well as American—and suffused with period authenticity." Publ Wkly

Harris, Deborah Turner

(jt. auth) Kurtz, K. The temple and the stone

Harris, E. Lynn

And this too shall pass; a novel. Doubleday 1996 347p
ISBN 0-385-48030-X   LC 95-38844

Harris, E. Lynn—*Continued*

Among the African American characters featured in this novel are "Zurich Robinson, a gay pro-football quarterback; MamaCee, aka Miss Cora, his grandmother; Caliph Taylor, a Chicago cop who is devoted to his daughter; successful attorney Tamela Coleman; sports anchor Mia Miller; and gay sports reporter Sean Elliott. The major plot concerns Zurich's acceptance of his gayness and his developing relationship with Sean. Subplots involve Mia and Tamela, who both struggle with their careers, their relationships with men, and one another. . . . Ultimately both fun and moving, the book has something to impress nearly any reader." Booklist

If this world were mine; a novel. Doubleday 1997 318p

ISBN 0-385-48655-3   LC 97-18795

"Members of a monthly journal-writing group, four African American friends from college days who all live in the Chicago area, help each other through the dramas of their respective lives. They're all approaching 40 and looking for answers: Riley Woodson, a self-proclaimed Black Princess immured in a stultifying marriage; Yolanda Williams, a media consultant; gay psychiatrist Leland Thompson; and Dwight Scott, a computer engineer simmering with hatred for white people. . . . A supple raconteur, Harris explores the intimacies of friendship with a sensitive eye." Publ Wkly

Not a day goes by; a novel. Doubleday 2000 271p $19.95

ISBN 0-385-49824-1   LC 00-38368

"When John 'Basil' Henderson, ex-football player and sports agent on the rise, falls in love with haughty, ambitious Broadway star Yancey Harrington Braxton, it seems like a perfect match. But on the couple's wedding day, which opens the book, the extravagant nuptials are suddenly canceled. The narrative retraces the couple's rocky courtship. . . . Determined to mary, have children, and keep his homosexual proclivities a secret, Basil doesn't realize that Yancey has a few secrets of her own." Publ Wkly

Harris, Joanne

Chocolat; a novel. Viking 1999 242p

ISBN 0-670-88179-1   LC 98-21771

"When Vianne Rocher and her daughter arrive in the small French town of Lansquenet-sous-Tannes, they open a shop specializing in exquisite, voluptuous chocolates. This is the first breath of giddiness the town has ever felt. So isolated is the place, it still rigorously maintains Lenten abstinences, and the town priest takes umbrage at the effrontery of this *arriviste* scheduling a festival of chocolate for Easter Sunday. . . . Harris' writing conveys a multitude of images and captures the self-absorption of small town life in France." Booklist

Coastliners; a novel. Morrow 2002 350p

ISBN 0-06-019812-5   LC 2001-59045

A novel "set on the provincial French island of Le Devin. Madeleine Prasteau leaves her Paris apartment to return to the island village of Les Salants, where she discovers that her father, a widowed boat owner, is going downhill along with the village itself as the rival town of La Houssiniere grows and prospers. Despite her father's chilly greeting, Madeleine spruces up the family

home, and when she meets an attractive, mysterious stranger named Flynn she gets involved in a project to save Les Salants." Publ Wkly

Harris "expertly weaves her themes of family, community, and loyalty and shows how these values can be affected by money. Most impressively, she vividly depicts how a bleak, patchy strip of land can be synonymous with home." Booklist

Five quarters of the orange. Morrow 2001 307p $25

ISBN 0-06-019813-3   LC 00-48952

"Framboise Dartigen, a stoic widow, is almost 65 and living a shadow life in the small French farmhouse she and her family abandoned after a mysterious tragedy that took place during the German occupation in World War II. . . . Having returned as an old woman, no longer recognizable to the families in the village that last saw her at 9, Framboise opens up a restaurant, using her mother's recipes. All might be well, until Framboise begins to decode what happened so many years ago by reading the tortured scribblings of her mother, hidden in an album she bequeathed to her." N Y Times Book Rev

"Harris has constructed a multilayered plot, punctuated with scrumptious descriptons of French delicacies and telling depictions of the war's jolting effects on one fragile family. This intense work brims with sensuality and sensitivity." Publ Wkly

Gentlemen and players. William Morrow 2006 422p $24.95

ISBN 0-06-055914-4   LC 2005-47179

First published 2005 in the United Kingdom

"For generations, privileged young men have attended St. Oswald's Grammar School for Boys, groomed for success by the likes of Roy Straitley, the eccentric Classics teacher who has been a fixture there for more than thirty years. But this year the wind of unwelcome change is blowing. Suits, paperwork, and information technology are beginning to overshadow St. Oswald's tradition, and Straitley is finally, and reluctantly, contemplating retirement. He is joined this term by five new faculty members, including one who—unbeknownst to Straitley and everyone else—holds intimate and dangerous knowledge of St. Oswald's ways and secrets. Harboring dark ties to the school's past, this young teacher has arrived with one terrible goal: to destroy St. Oswald's." Publisher's note

"Constantly surprising and wickedly fun, this revenge tale is told by two narrators in alternating chapters. . . . Beyond the book's considerable entertainment value, Harris has written an unsettling reminder of how much our orderly lives depend on a fragile level of trust. Little grains of dishonesty and malice sprinkled in the gears of an organization are almost impossible to detect but can bring down the whole structure." Washington Post Book World

The girl with no shadow; a novel. William Morrow 2008 444p

ISBN 978-0-06-143162-3; 0-06-143162-1

    LC 2007-36447

"More than four years have passed since Vianne Rocher pitted her enchanted chocolate confections against the local clergy's interpretation of Lent in smalltown France; since then, Vianne has renounced magic, changed her name to Yanne Charbonneau and moved with her two daughters to Paris's Montmartre district.

Harris, Joanne—*Continued*

There, Yanne embraces conformity and safety, much to the dismay of her increasingly troubled older daughter, Anouk. When Anouk becomes entranced with Zozie de l'Alba, an exotic itinerant who happens upon a job at the new shop, and the relationship grows increasingly sinister, Yanne must call up all of Vianne's powers, culinary and mystical, to save her family." Publ Wkly

"The race against time gives the story intensity, and the three female characters come alive with Harris's trademark shifting narrations. Although it's a bit darker than Chocolat, readers will drink up this pleasurable tale of love." Libr J

Harris, Mark, 1922-2007

Bang the drum slowly; by Henry W. Wiggen; certain of his enthusiasms restrained by Mark Harris. Knopf 1956 243p o.p.

A baseball novel which centers on Bruce, a black catcher, who is slowly dying of Hodgkin's disease. The narrator tries to keep the matter a secret, but eventually it comes out. The rest of the book concerns the loyalty of Bruce's teammates to their doomed member

"Narrated by 'Author' in the raucous speech of the ball park, yet with an elegiac dignity." Booklist

Harris, Robert, 1957-

Archangel; a novel. Random House 1999 373p
ISBN 0-679-42888-7   LC 98-33655

This novel follows the "progress of Fluke Kelso, an academic who has dug up the diary of Stalin's last days. The failing dictator got a woman pregnant, the papers suggest, and she may have returned to Archangel, her home in the north." Time

"The sinewy plot never slackens, but what makes the book memorable are the vividly observed backgrounds. . . . No less authentic are the fragmented but undead relics of the old Soviet system." Natl Rev

Enigma. Random House 1995 320p o.p.
                                          * LC 95-11335

This thriller is set at "Bletchley Park, the remote, ultra-secret WW II British code-breaking center. In February 1943, having just cracked the key to the confoundingly complex Nazi code known as Shark, Thomas Jericho, an unworldly young academic, returns to his old digs at Cambridge to recuperate from nervous exhaustion and a broken heart. But Jericho has time to regain only a modicum of strength before he is pressed back into service to break the latest Nazi code—the putatively impregnable Enigma." Publ Wkly

"As one expects from a thriller-writer, Harris ensures the tension builds inexorably as the plot unfolds. Unlike some, however, he creates characters that linger in the mind, and he never bores his readers with gratuitous technical detail." New Sci

Fatherland. Random House 1992 338p o.p.
                                          * LC 91-51026

This thriller is "based on the premise that Hitler won the war and now rules a vast trans-European empire. On the eve of Hitler's 75th birthday, just when America's President Joseph P. Kennedy is expected in Berlin, the body of a once-important Nazi official washes up along the Rhine. Investigator Xavier March persists in checking out the case, despite orders to the contrary from the Gestapo itself, and soon he discovers a conspiracy whose roots date back to World War II." Libr J

"'Fatherland' is a bleak book. But what concerns the author is the indestructibility of the human spirit, as exemplified by Xavier March. If Hitler's Germany is hell, at least a few angels are floating around." N Y Times Book Rev

The ghost. Simon & Schuster 2007 335p $26
ISBN 978-1-4165-5181-2; 1-4165-5181-6
                                          LC 2007-29670

"Adam Lang was Britain's longest serving-and most controversial-prime minister of the last half century, whose career ended . . . after he sided with America in an unpopular war on terror. Now, after stepping down in disgrace, Lang is hiding out in . . . Martha's Vineyard to finish his much sought-after, potentially explosive memoir, for which he accepted one of history's largest cash advances. But the project runs aground when his ghostwriter suddenly and mysteriously disappears and later washes up, dead, on the island's deserted shore." Publ Wkly

"From the first paragraph, Harris' novel tugs the reader on through a thriller blessedly short on shoot'emup and long on character nuance, dead-on media satire and the damned-either-way consequences of wielding power in the murky wake of 9/11." Pittsburgh Post-Gazette

Imperium; a novel of ancient Rome. Simon & Schuster 2006 305p $26
ISBN 978-0-7432-6603-1; 0-7432-6603-X
                                          LC 2006-44393

"Tackling as his subject the brilliant orator and senator Marcus Cicero, Harris adopts the voice of Tiro, Cicero's faithful manservant and confidential secretary. Based on his real-life counterpart, Tiro, often credited as the inventor of shorthand and the author of a biography of Cicero tragically lost during the Middle Ages, narrates the story of his master's rise from relative obscurity to imperium, attainment of supreme power in the state. Thrusting himself upon the tumultuous Roman political scene at age 27, Cicero, an ambitious provincial lawyer, matches wits and wills with political and military heavyweights Caesar, Pompey, and Crassus. . . . A brilliant fictional biography of one of antiquity's most complex and triumphant characters." Booklist

Pompeii; a novel. Random House 2003 278p map hardcover o.p. pa $13.95
ISBN 0-679-42889-5; 0-8129-7461-1 (pa)
                                          LC 2003-58446

"An upstanding Roman engineer rushes to repair an aqueduct in the shadow of Mount Vesuvius, which, in A.D. 79, is getting ready to blow its top. . . . Lively writing, convincing but economical period details and plenty of intrigue keep the pace quick." Publ Wkly

Harris, Thomas, 1940-

Black Sunday. Dutton 2000 c1975 318p $26.95
ISBN 0-525-94555-5   LC 00-24649

A reissue of the title first published 1975 by Putnam

"In retaliation for American aid to Israel, an Arab terrorist group has determined to blow up the Super Bowl. Their prime weapon is Michael Lander, a former Navy pilot, whose own strange psyche, combined with his ex-

Harris, Thomas, 1940-—*Continued*

periences as prisoner of war in Vietnam, has driven him to seek revenge against a world he believes has savaged him. As the pilot of the Aldrich television blimp that floats above professional football games and a brilliant technician, Lander is uniquely qualified to carry out the act of madness that obsesses him." Publisher's note

"All is neck and neck, quite excitingly to the very end. . . . The action is . . . very violent (violent sexy episodes, too) and the plot is packed with business. Not a bit believable, but successful entertainment." Libr J

Hannibal. Delacorte Press 1999 486p $27.95
ISBN 0-385-29929-X   LC 99-29774
In this sequel to The silence of the lambs, "FBI agent Clarise Starling, is slated to take the fall for a botched arrest. Yet when a manipulative millionaire revives the FBI's interest in the still-at-large Lecter, Starling is reunited with her mentor, Jack Crawford, and sets to work on tracking the good doctor." Libr J

"Where Silence haunted and tantalized, Hannibal grosses out and gratifies. Yet there's still a basso ostinato of serious questions, and the answers are darker than in Silence." Nation

Hannibal rising; a novel. Delacorte Press 2006 323p $27.95
ISBN 978-0-385-33941-4; 0-385-33941-0
A prequel intended to explain the origins of Hannibal Lecter's evil. This novel begins as the Nazis invade Lithuania and drive the Lecters into hiding. It then recounts the "major trauma that transformed the young Lecter— the murder of his beloved younger sister, Mischa. . . . Lecter also has an unusual love interest, his uncle's Japanese wife, Lady Murasaki, but the bulk of the narrative focuses on Lecter's quest for revenge on those he holds responsible for Mischa's death." Publ Wkly

"There are images of morbid beauty here. . . . Harris' handling of the wartime violence is also impressive, as swift and vicious as the blitzkrieg itself." Los Angeles Times

Red Dragon. Dutton 2000 c1981 348p $26.95
ISBN 0-525-94556-3
                            * LC 00-22500
A reissue of the title first published 1981 by Putnam
This novel concerns "a psychopathic mass murderer with an intuitive FBI investigator on his trail. . . . [The ex-F.B.I. man] is Will Graham, whose acute perception gives him entree to murderers' minds. With two mass killers to his credit, he's lured from peaceful retirement and happy marriage to hunt the Red Dragon, slayer of two families within a month. A dedicated group of forensic experts and a dogged scandal sheet reporter also pursue the killer—born with a cleft palate, cruelly mistreated as a child, skewed by the sight of a powerful painting, and side-tracked by warm attention from a blind woman." Libr J

"This is a chilling, tautly written, and well-realized psychological thriller. . . . The suspense is sustained by deft characterizations, fascinating crime-lab details, a twisting plot, and understated prose." Saturday Rev

The silence of the lambs. St. Martin's Press 1988 338p $24.95
ISBN 0-312-02282-4
                            * LC 88-18203

"Agent Clarice Starling of the FBI's behavioral science section is assigned to conduct a psychological profile of Hannibal Lecter, a psychiatrist imprisoned for serial murder. Uncooperative at first, Lecter then says he can help identify a serial killer who has eluded authorities for months. Lecter's aid proves invaluable, and Starling soon finds herself using one madman to catch another." Libr J

"Harris places his clues with precision, and his characterizations . . . are superbly developed and richly complex." Booklist

Followed by Hannibal

Harrison, Colin, 1960-

Afterburn. Farrar, Straus & Giroux 1999 438p $25
ISBN 0-374-10205-8   LC 99-13660
"Powerful businessman Charlie Ravich, a former Vietnam POW, thrives on the hectic world of global commerce. Columbia dropout Christina Welles has been in prison for four years when she is mysteriously released. Her boyfriend, Rick, is desperate to find her, believing that mobster Tony V. arranged her release and wants her killed." Libr J

"Harrison writes extremely well, and sections of 'Afterburn' are as elegant as you'll hope to find in any novel." N Y Times Book Rev

The finder; a novel. Farrar, Straus and Giroux 2008 322p $25
ISBN 978-0-374-29949-1; 0-374-29949-8
                            LC 2007-36574
"Sarah Crichton books"
"A few pages into the story, a young Chinese woman, Jin Li, witnesses the grisly murder of two Mexican girls. The killers are really after Jin Li, who heads a cleaning company that handles document-shredding and other services for Manhattan firms. That role allows for all manner of discreet snooping – and fuels the illegal stock speculating ring led by her brother back in Shanghai. A forlorn firefighter who survived a nightmarish assignment inside the collapsed World Trade Center towers on 9/11 serves as the novel's hero. He's capable, brooding – and often lost in the maze of subplots. When he's on the stage, though, he grabs the reader's attention, as does Bill Martz, a conniving and captivating billionaire who's been burned by a mysterious plunging stock price engineered by You Know Who. Harrison mostly moves his pieces around the board in expert fashion and, Wolfean tics (exclamation points run amok!) aside, writes with a crisp authority. He's done his homework, too, as the detailed aside on sewage services will attest." Christ Sci Monit

The Havana room. Farrar, Straus and Giroux 2004 385p $24
ISBN 0-374-29986-2   LC 2003-9238
"What goes on in the by-invitation-only Havana Room of a midtown steakhouse is certainly bizarre—but no odder than what happens in a Long Island potato field when a Chilean wine maker decides to expand his empire. Caught in the middle are two most unlikely heroes: Bill Wyeth, a real estate lawyer whose career and marriage are destroyed by a terrible accident involving a child, and Jay Rainey, a hulking, strangely sympathetic con artist. Linking these two is a touching and compli-

Harrison, Colin, 1960-—*Continued*
cated woman, Allison Sparks, who manages the steakhouse but longs for more." Publ Wkly

"Most thrillers begin with a murder or a kidnapping or some other dread deed. 'The Havana Room' begins with a quote from Schopenhauer. The weighty epigraph signals an engagingly unconventional thriller, full of ruminations on the human condition. . . . Colin Harrison keeps the pages turning at a spanking clip." Economist

Harrison, Harry, 1925-

The Stainless Steel Rat joins the circus. TOR Bks. 1999 269p
ISBN 0-312-86934-7   LC 99-34005
"A Tom Doherty Associates book"

Following The Stainless Steel Rat goes to Hell (1996), the master criminal takes on a new assignment. "After taking a job infiltrating a suspicious circus on a four million credit a day retainer, DiGriz finds himself and his family bound up, literally at times, in a planet-wide swindle. Someone is robbing banks and other sources of wealth using The Rat's good name while he dutifully performs his magic act under the big top. Soon DiGriz is hunted by endless factions of the police, his son Bolivar is jailed, his wife Angelina kidnapped, his formerly benevolent employer is getting more sinister by the hour and worst of all, The Stainless Steel Rat is actually losing money!" Publ Wkly

The Stainless Steel Rat sings the blues. Bantam Bks. 1994 229p o.p.   LC 93-31809
"Caught in the act of robbing the new mint on the planet Paskonjak, master thief Jim DiGriz, a.k.a. the Stainless Steel Rat, is offered a deal by the Galactic League: discover a stolen artifact thought to be somewhere on the prison planet Liokukae within 30 days and go free—or die. In the same vein as previous adventures featuring Harrison's irrepressible antihero . . . this latest outing boasts fast-paced action, a hint of melodrama, and a sizable dose of satirical tweaks at modern culture." Libr J

Stainless steel visions; illustrated by Bryn Barnard. TOR Bks. 1993 254p il o.p.
                                        LC 92-43879
"A Tom Doherty Associates book"

Contents: The streets of Ashkelon; Toy shop; Not me, not Amos Cabot!; The mothballed spaceship; Commando raid; The repairman; Brave newer world; The secret of Stonehenge; Rescue operation; Portrait of the artist; Survival planet; Roommates; The golden years of The Stainless Steel Rat

"Thirteen of Harrison's robust, fast-paced tales. One is a new tale of his best-known hero, Slippery Jim DiGriz, the Stainless Steel Rat. Another is 'Roommates,' the basis for the movie *Soylent Green*. The other 11 range widely over Harrison's 40-year career and many interests (not to mention more than a few prejudices). All reflect Harrison's acknowledged status as heir to the pulp tradition of keeping the story moving forward at all costs." Booklist

Harrison, Jamie, 1960-

Blue Deer thaw; a mystery. Hyperion 2000 271p $22.95
ISBN 0-7868-6422-2   LC 99-27230

A mystery featuring Blue Deer, Montana sheriff Jules Clement, "a chronically depressed cop with a Ph.D. in archaeology and a history of drug abuse. Jules is moonlighting at the Sacajawea Hotel, taking inventory of Halsey Meriwether's fabulous, if eccentric, collection of art. . . . Halsey is a very rich man who has written a very dumb will that practically begs his heirs to murder him." N Y Times Book Rev

"Clement continues to be one of the most interesting and believable mystery heroes working the American turf, and Harrison demonstrates once again that she's among the most talented writers to grace the genre in recent years." Publ Wkly

An unfortunate prairie occurrence. Hyperion 1998 369p
ISBN 0-7868-6260-2   LC 97-24087

This "novel about Sheriff Clement and the residents of Blue Deer, Montana, opens with a crazy autumn crime wave—everything from serial rape to a divorced couple battling for custody of a dog. Then campers find a human skeleton, and an elderly rancher perishes in a truck fire—an apparent suicide. While keeping the lid on the mayhem, Clement and his deputies try to identify the skeleton and determine if the suicide is really murder." Booklist

The author allows "us to linger in Blue Deer long enough to learn its history, drink in the scenery and laugh at the kinks and quirks of its idiosyncratic residents. No wonder the world-weary Jules came running back home the first chance he got—the place is heaven." N Y Times Book Rev

Harrison, Jim, 1937-

The English major. Grove Press 2008 255p $24
ISBN 978-0-8021-1863-9; 0-8021-1863-1

"The protagonist of this wistfully comic novel is a sixty-year-old English teacher turned farmer, whose wife has left him for another man, and who takes to the road in the quixotic pursuit of renaming all the birds and all the states. Along the way, he picks up a neurotic, sex-hungry former student; despairs of road food; wanders into the desert without enough water; and muses on the ways life can suddenly turn upside down. . . . The premise is well-worn, but Harrison has created a character of such appeal and self-deprecating wisdom that even the more fantastical episodes—a nubile young woman cavorting in the nude for his pleasure—acquire a charmingly philosophical air." New Yorker

Returning to earth. Grove 2007 280p $24.95
ISBN 978-0-8021-1838-7; 0-8021-1838-0
                                        LC 2006-50802

"Slowly dying of Lou Gehrig's Disease, Donald, a middle-aged Chippewa-Finnish man, begins dictating family stories he has never shared with anyone, hoping to preserve history for his children." Publisher's note

"This could almost be Hemingway, in some of the Michigan stories, but it's even more stripped than Hemingway. . . . [The novel] is both familiar and strange, rooted and rootless, endlessly dark and occasionally hilarious." San Diego Union-Tribune

The road home. Atlantic Monthly Press 1998 446p $25
ISBN 0-87113-724-0
                                        * LC 98-8391

Harrison, Jim, 1937- —*Continued*

Sequel to Dalva (1988)

This novel "continues the multigenerational tale of Dalva's Northridge family, primarily Nebraska land baron John Northridge, his sons, his granddaughter Dalva, and Nelse, Dalva's son, who was taken from her at birth and is now trying to find her." Libr J

"This saga is as homespun as an old quilt. A woman and her grown son, whom she'd put up for adoption, are reunited. An old man makes his peace as he approaches death. Each family member stitches in a piece of the family history. They are such good company you forget they exist nowhere but in Harrison's imagination." Newsweek

Harrison, Kathryn

The binding chair; or, A visit from the Foot Emancipation Society: a novel. Random House 2000 312p

ISBN 0-679-45000-9   LC 99-34559

"Hobbled at the age of five by traditional foot-binding, Mai is also crippled by 19th-century gender rules that demand female subservience. After an arranged marriage turns abusive, Mai flees to Shanghai and becomes a prostitute, the only vocation open to women without familial support. A subsequent second marriage to do-gooder Arthur Cohen, and her integration into his extended family, are the vehicles through which Harrison delves into . . . questions about race, class, assimilation, and gender." Libr J

"Harrison's vision is bold and unsparing, portraying a world in which a woman's survival comes at a terrible cost. . . . The novel continually surprises. Its narrative turns and its tonal shifts—from the rhythms of the epic to those of the erotic, with pauses for comedy along the way—are as deft as they are unexpected." N Y Times Book Rev

The seal wife; a novel. Random House 2002 224p

ISBN 0-375-50629-2   LC 2001-48979

"In 1915, 26-year-old Bigelow Greene is sent to establish a U.S. weather station in Anchorage. . . . Bigelow is a single-minded man; he first becomes obsessed with the idea of building a huge kite to measure air temperature high in the atmosphere and thus enable long-range forecasting. But he's soon smitten with a woman the locals call the Aleut. She's mysterious, enigmatic, virtually mute—sex between she and Bigelow is wordless—and when he discovers that she's left Anchorage, Bigelow almost goes mad with longing." Publ Wkly

"Painterly in its pearlescent evocation of the Alaskan landscape, steeped in myth and the magic of science, this is a delectably moody, erotic, and provocative cross-cultural love story." Booklist

Harrison, M. John (Michael John), 1945-

Nova swing. Bantam Books 2007 252p pa $16

ISBN 978-0-553-38501-4; 0-553-38501-1

LC 2007-8288

"A Bantam Spectra book"

First published 2006 in the United Kingdom

In this "quasi-noir tale set in the universe of Light (2004), Harrison introduces Vic Serotonin, a ne'erdowell who makes his living running illegal tours of the Saudade event site, where hallucinatory and impossible experiences are the norm. When rich tourist Elizabeth Kielar hires him as a guide and then disappears in the area around the site, things get even stranger than usual. Police detective Lens Aschemann, who usually turns a blind eye to the tourism business, threatens dire consequences for Vic's sideline of event site artifact smuggling, while shady club owner Paulie DeRaad buys an artifact that begins to change him in bizarre ways." Publ Wkly

"The world Harrison has painted for us isn't pretty, and is often incomprehensible. But look around. It's that way already. Nova Swing is witty, mind-expanding, and entertaining. It's a book not to miss." scifidimensions.com

Harrison, Michael John *See* Harrison, M. John (Michael John), 1945-

Harrison, Sue

Brother Wind; a novel. Morrow 1994 494p o.p.

LC 94-14271

This volume completes the trilogy about "the harsh and dramatic adventures of Kiin, Samiq and other Aleutian Islanders of 9000 years ago. When her husband is killed by Raven (of the Walrus People tribe), Kiin, an accomplished carver, is forced to abandon both her own tribe of the First Men and one of her twin sons and return with the killer to his village. In revenge, Samiq, chief hunter of the First Men and brother of the murdered man, seeks Raven's death. . . . Informed by Native American legends, myths and traditions and replete with convincing recreations of trading practices, seal hunting and vision fasts, this novel offers an emotionally compelling conclusion to a monumental saga." Publ Wkly

Call down the stars. Morrow 2001 446p

ISBN 0-380-97372-3   LC 2001-30541

The concluding volume of the author's Storyteller trilogy set in prehistoric Alaska. This installment "features two storytellers: Yikaas, a young, handsome, and fiery-tempered member of the River People tribe; and Qumalix, a beautiful, clever, and high-spirited member of the Sea Hunters tribe. These two quick-witted characters spend their evenings sparring verbally and weaving tales of their historic ancestors for their gathered tribespeople. . . . Well-written and meticulously researched, Harrison's powerful yarn details the hardships and simplicity faced by prehistoric people while also emphasizing their humanity." Booklist

Cry of the wind. Avon Bks. 1998 448p

ISBN 0-380-97371-5   LC 98-8837

The second volume of the Storyteller saga continues the story "of K'os, who seeks revenge for rape and enslavement by the Near River people, and Chakliux, the Cousin River Village's respected storyteller and K'os's adopted son." Libr J

"Harrison's research is clearly reflected in her meticulous attention to details as disparate as the careful sewing of a parka and the rituals of a caribou hunt. Her characters are based on ancient Native American mythologies and storytelling traditions." Publ Wkly

Harrison, Sue—*Continued*

Mother earth, father sky. Doubleday 1990 313p
o.p.   LC 89-25656
This is "the story of an Aleutian woman living around
7000 B.C. When her village is destroyed by a hostile
tribe, Chagak flees to her grandfather in the Whale Hunter tribe. Along the way, she finds safety with old
Shuganan, but her trails do not end there. She endures
brutalization and childbirth. . . . Harrison's fine first
novel is based on thorough research into the lifestyle and
beliefs of ancient Aleutians; exquisite detail imparts great
viability to her characters." Booklist
Followed by My sister the moon

My sister the moon. Doubleday 1992 449p o.p.
                                        LC 91-29102
The second volume in the author's trilogy "picks up 16
years after 'Mother Earth Father Sky' leaves off. . . .
The beautiful Kiin is promised to Amgigh, but has been
in love with his brother Samiq for years. Violently
abused by her father, marriage is a relief for Kiin. But
her jealous younger brother brutally kidnaps and rapes
her and tries to sell her as a slave into a marriage far
from their homeland. The brutality and physical and sexual abuses are vividly portrayed, as well as the rigid
roles of men and women." Baya Book Rev
Followed by Brother Wind

Song of the river. Avon Bks. 1997 484p map
ISBN 0-380-97370-7   LC 97-18455
The first book of the Storyteller saga tells the story "of
poisonous revenge for the rape of a young woman, K'os,
by men from a neighboring village. Most of it transpires
several decades after that calamity, when K'os uses her
sexual prowess and manipulative abilities to stir up a war
with the offenders' village. . . . Complex and well imagined, the interlocking societies of Harrison's ancient
Aleutians make a compelling backdrop for this tale of romance and revenge." Booklist
Followed by Cry of the wind

Harrod-Eagles, Cynthia

Blood lines; an Inspector Bill Slider mystery.
Scribner 1996 281p
ISBN 0-684-80047-0   LC 96-8555
Inspector Slider investigates the "death of a prominent
music critic who comes to a violent end in the men's
room of a BBC recording studio. Each plot twist, including one devious turn that throws suspicion on a former
member of Slider's murder squad, hangs on the testimony of the complicated characters, who are among the author's finest stock." N Y Times Book Rev

Death to go. Scribner 1994 c1993 281p
ISBN 0-684-19650-6   LC 93-10374
First published 1993 in the United Kingdom with title:
Necrochip
"Detective Inspector Bill Slider is called on when a
teenager finds a human finger among the fried potatoes
she ordered at a London fish-and-chips shop. Body parts
continue to surface as events expand to include a sinister
business tycoon, a prostitutes' rooming house, three mysterious Asians, an odd mix of gay men and five murders." Publ Wkly
"Murder provides the foundation for this extraordinary
novel, but, it's finally an examination of love, love lost,
and ways in which people cope with both." Booklist

Death watch. Scribner 1993 c1992 280p o.p.
                                        LC 92-30924
First published 1992 in the United Kingdom
"Grim reality and intimations of immortality confront
London detectives Slider and Atherton when they respond to the arson murder of a womanizing salesman.
The victim, a deceptive man of failing business, marriage, and personal aspirations, serves as a foil to Slider
(himself unhappily married) and ladies' man Atherton,
who bounce theories off each other as they gather information and suspects." Libr J
"This is a fine example of the British procedural—a
simmering rather than boiling narrative, plenty of quick
wit, and a splash of romantic intrigue, all skillfully written and solidly plotted." Booklist

Game over; a Bill Slider mystery. Severn House
2008 234p $28.95
ISBN 978-0-7278-6615-8
In this "11th Bill Slider mystery . . . the detective inspector investigates the murder of civil servant Ed
Stonax, a former high-profile BBC correspondent, found
dead with his skull smashed on the floor of his West
London flat. . . . The various plot lines neatly intersect
at the highest levels of government by the end of this appealing English whodunit." Publ Wkly

Grave music; an Inspector Bill Slider mystery.
Scribner 1995 c1994 234p
ISBN 0-684-80046-2   LC 94-39222
First published 1994 in the United Kingdom with title:
Dead end
"Just as the Royal London Philharmonic is about to
start rehearsal, the famous conductor Sir Stefan Radek
drops dead on the podium, shot by a mysterious stranger.
Slider and his . . . partner Atherton get the case and
quickly discover that there is no lack of suspects due to
the widely held opinion that Sir Stefan was nasty, vindictive, and generally despicable—a view even shared by
his family." Booklist
"Though readers may guess the murderer early on in
this . . . [novel, Slider's] police cohorts, and his violinist
love, Joanna, are among the most appealing cast in recent memory. Their relationships, the music world setting, and the clever dialog . . . recommend this to all
collections." Libr J

Killing time; an Inspector Bill Slider mystery.
Scribner 1998 313p
ISBN 0-684-83776-5   LC 97-26290
First published 1996 in the United Kingdom
In this mystery London's Inspector Bill Slider's "attention is divided between solving the murder of a male
striptease dancer—a case that extends from seedy Soho
cabarets to the posh country homes of cabinet ministers—and sorting out the needs and demands of his estranged wife and new lover. . . . Many readers may
guess the killer early on, but that shouldn't interfere with
their appreciation for the rumpled, empathetic Slider,
whose ability to see the complexity in the people around
him is both his strength and his weakness." Booklist

Orchestrated death; a mystery introducing Inspector Bill Slider. Scribner 1992 c1991 266p
ISBN 0-684-19388-4   LC 91-29042

Harrod-Eagles, Cynthia—*Continued*
First published 1991 in the United Kingdom
"Detective Inspector Bill Slider [is] taken advantage of at work and pummeled verbally at home by his incompatible spouse. His own dissatisfaction leads Slider to become immersed in solving the murder of a beautiful young violin player. With the help of best friend Sergeant Atherton and the sympathetic ear of new-found true love Joanna, Slider uncovers a far-flung conspiracy." Libr J
A novel "remarkable for its rich, romantic tone, assured technique and perfect literary pitch." N Y Times Book Rev

Shallow grave; a Bill Slider mystery. Scribner 1999 312p $22
ISBN 0-684-83777-3   LC 99-21351
First published 1998 in the United Kingdom
"It isn't Inspector Bill Slider's passion for architectural oddities that brings him to the Mimpriss Estate, but the body on the terrace of the Old Rectory. . . . The way the neighbors tell it, the victim was 'an unprincipled slut,' the unfaithful wife of a local builder, a 'jealous beast' with means and motive to throttle his spouse. But Slider, whose own convulsive extramartial affairs in this refreshingly grown-up series have made him sensitive to the complexities of modern relationships, believes in looking beneath surfaces." N Y Times Book Rev

Harry Patterson, Martin Fallon, Huge Marlowe, James Graham *See* Higgins, Jack, 1929-

Harstad, Donald

Code sixty-one; a novel. Doubleday 2002 370p
ISBN 0-385-50118-8   LC 2001-52736
When Deputy Sheriff Carl Houseman, of Nation County Iowa, answers an attempted entry call he "pays little attention to the woman's charge that a vampire was peering in at her. That changes when two bodies are found in the next 48 hours, one across the river in Wisconsin, the other in Iowa, in a small-town mansion. Both victims have deep neck wounds, forcing Houseman to investigative the unthinkable. Initially, the other cops treat both the usually sensible Houseman and a professional vampire hunter who joins the hunt as nuts, but even they become more and more spooked as local Goths make their tastes known. A terrific read—by turns, funny, eerie, and insightful." Booklist

Hart, Carolyn G.

Death in paradise; a Henrie O mystery; {by} Carolyn Hart. Avon Bks. 1998 275p
ISBN 0-380-97414-2   LC 97-29701
"Journalist Richard Collins died in a tragic accident in Hawaii six years ago. Now his widow, Henrietta O'Dwyer 'Henrie O' Collins has received an anonymous message implying that Richard was murdered. Henrie O, who has played amateur sleuth before, knows she won't rest until she learns the truth." Booklist
Hart is at her "best as she tightens the suspense and keeps the killer's identity out of focus until the cliffhanging finale." Publ Wkly

Death walked in; a death on demand mystery; [by] Carolyn Hart. William Morrow 2008 293p $23.95
ISBN 978-0-06-072405-4; 0-06-072405-6
                              LC 2007-43589
A fortune in gold coins stolen from a house filled with visiting family members lies at the root of this Max and Annie Darling mystery.
"This tight, Agatha Christie-style puzzler will keep readers guessing to the end." Publ Wkly

Letter from home; {by} Carolyn Hart. Berkley Prime Crime 2003 262p $22.95
ISBN 0-425-19179-6   LC 2003-51953
"A letter from her Oklahoma hometown spirits famous journalist Gretchen Gilman back to 1944, when someone murdered Faye Tatum. People believed Faye's husband, jealous of her flirtations, did it and then disappeared. Gilman believed otherwise and set out for proof." Libr J
"Set in a small-town America that lives only in memory, this artfully narrated whodunit observes the residents of an unnamed Oklahoma hamlet over the hot and dusty summer of 1944 as they ration their food, count their war dead and turn on their neighbors." N Y Times Book Rev

Mint julep murder. Bantam Bks. 1995 277p
ISBN 0-553-09463-7   LC 94-34244
"While ensconced on Broward's Rock Island, South Carolina, mystery bookstore owner and amateur sleuth Annie Darling serves as author liaison for the Dixie Book Festival on Hilton Head. Problems arise when a self-serving, small-time publisher promises to write a scandalous roman à clef featuring Annie's five charges—all quite famous. After the would-be writer dies of poisoning, all evidence points to Annie." Libr J
"Hart combines genteel ambience, southern charm, a likable heroine, and some wonderfully nasty characters into a pleasantly entertaining mystery." Booklist

Murder walks the plank; a death on demand mystery; [by] Carolyn Hart. HarperCollins Publishers 2004 298p $23.95
ISBN 0-06-000474-6   LC 2003-51095
In this installment "mystery bookstore owner Annie Darling plans a mystery cruise as a benefit for the Island Literacy Council of Broward's Rock, South Carolina. Unfortunately, before the mystery is solved, one of the guests falls overboard. Or was she pushed? Annie believes she was pushed and becomes even more convinced when a suspicious death occurs soon after the cruise. Max and Acting Police Chief Cameron believe the two incidents are either accidents or suicides and are unconnected, leaving Annie, Emma Clyde (Broward's Rock's own mystery author), and mystery reader extraordinaire Henny Brawley no choice but to solve the crimes themselves." Booklist
This novel "can only reinforce Hart's high standing among the cozy mystery cognoscenti." Publ Wkly

Resort to murder; a Henrie O mystery; [by] Carolyn Hart. Morrow 2001 294p $24
ISBN 0-380-97773-7   LC 00-59446
"Recovering from pneumonia, Henrie O isn't sure she feels up to the task of dealing with the emotional maelstrom stewing around the Bermuda wedding of her son-in-law, Lloyd Drake, and beautiful Connor Bailey, a

Hart, Carolyn G.—*Continued*
wealthy widow. . . . The hotel where the party has gathered witnessed tragedy the year before, when Roddy Worrell, the manager's husband, plunged to his death from a tower. According to rumor, Roddy had been infatuated with Connor, who spurned his advances. When a ghost is sighted at the tower, word spreads that Roddy has come back to haunt Connor. The subsequent death of a hotel employee who knew more than he should about the apparition puts Henrie O on the murder scent once again." Publ Wkly

Scandal in Fair Haven. Bantam Bks. 1994 275p
o.p.   LC 93-40346
This Henrie O "adventure takes her to Fair Haven, Tennessee, where a local bookstore owner is accused of murdering his wealthy wife. . . . Hart offers a light and lively read with an appealing 'small-town America' ambience, a compelling plot, a potpourri of fascinating characters, and some revealing insights into what makes us humans tick." Booklist

Skulduggery. Five Star 2000 190p $22.95
ISBN 0-7862-2672-2   LC 00-30845
First published 1984 in the United Kingdom
"On a foggy San Francisco night, Jimmy Lee, a twentysomething Chinese man, comes to physical anthropologist Ellen Christie's Russian Hill apartment with the bones of Peking Man, which vanished in China in the chaos of World War II. Jimmy and Ellen quickly join forces, to protect the bones—and each other—from two, chillingly efficient hitmen. . . . The novel combines effective use of the San Francisco setting with solid characterizations and a 'McGuffin' as intriguing as Hammett's falcon." Booklist

Southern ghost. Bantam Bks. 1992 322p o.p.
                                        LC 92-2543
"According to the news story published in the *Chastain* (South Carolina) *Courier* at the time, leading citizen Judge Augustus Tarrant suffered a fatal heart attack on May 9, 1970, after learning of the accidental shooting death of his 21-year-old son, Ross. What has prompted young Courtney Kimball to hire Max Darling to investigate this family tragedy 22 years later? . . . Hart's southern-gothic mystery offers a wealth of suspects . . . a generous scattering of literary allusions and peripheral ghost stories, and a chain of intriguing flashbacks that will leave most readers puzzled to the end." Booklist

White elephant dead; {by} Carolyn Hart. Avon Twilight 1999 277p $23
ISBN 0-380-97530-0   LC 99-20833
"After demanding that leading citizens of Broward's Rock donate priceless objects to the annual White Elephant sale, a wicked blackmailer turns up dead. The leading suspect is a top customer at Annie Darling's Death on Demand bookstore, so Annie must get involved." Libr J
This "Death on Demand mystery, delivers charming characters, . . . a tantalizing mystery, and plenty of appealing descriptions of coastal landscapes." Booklist

Yankee Doodle dead; a death on demand mystery; {by} Carolyn Hart. Avon Bks. 1998 273p
ISBN 0-380-97529-7   LC 98-13565

Sleuth Annie Darling, "owner of an island resort mystery bookstore, witnesses the murder of a much-hated man during a Fourth of July fundraiser for the local library." Libr J

Hart, Harry *See* Frank, Pat, 1907-1964

Hart, John, 1965-

Down river. Thomas Dunne Books/St. Martin's 2007 325p $24.95
ISBN 978-0-312-35931-7; 0-312-35931-4
                                        LC 2007-21540
"A small North Carolina town is torn apart when a power company wants to buy up all the farmland on the river; some residents cling to their bucolic way of life, while others see only dollar signs. Adam Chase's family has owned the largest parcel in the area for centuries, and his father has no desire to sell. But tempers flare, and soon a young woman is severely beaten, a body is found on the Chase farm, and Adam is the chief suspect. Newly arrived after five years away, Adam is the town pariah. His stepmother had accused him of murdering a family friend, and while the court acquitted him, his family and friends did not. While time has softened some, others seem ready to unleash their stored-up anger. This work is reminiscent of Raymond Chandler's novels, hardboiled and rich with evocative metaphors." Libr J

The king of lies. St. Martin's Minotaur 2006 310p $22.95
ISBN 0-312-34161-X   LC 2005-49774
"Jackson Workman Pickens, whom most people call 'Work,' is a struggling North Carolina criminal defense attorney. Work has wrestled with inner demons for most of his life, especially after the death of his mother and the disappearance of his wealthy father, Ezra Pickens, a highly successful lawyer who took him into his practice. Trapped in a loveless marriage and haunted by poor emotional choices and his sister's psychological trauma, Work finds himself under suspicion when his father's corpse surfaces more than a year after Ezra was last seen alive." Publ Wkly
"More than anything else—more than a terrific whodunit, an unsentimental, clear-eyed story of love and forgiveness, and a gripping family saga—The King of Lies is a masterful piece of writing." Raleigh News & Observer

The last child. Minotaur Books 2009 373p $24.95
ISBN 978-0-312-35932-4; 0-312-35932-2
                                        LC 2008-45678
"A Thomas Dunne Book for Minotaur Books"
After his twin sister Alyssa disappears, thirteen year-old Johnny Merrimon is determined to find her. When a second girl disappears from his rural North Carolina town, Johnny makes a discovery that sends shock waves through the community.
The author has produced "a novel that is elegant, haunting, and memorable. His characters are given an emotional depth that genre characters seldom have, and the graceful, evocative prose lifts his stories right out of their genre and into the realm of capital-L literature. A must-read for every variety of fiction reader." Booklist

Hart, Josephine

Damage; a novel. Knopf 1991 195p
ISBN 0-679-40135-0

* LC 90-53393

The narrator of this novel, "an English paterfamilias and Tory M.P., leads a passionless existence until he meets his son's fiancée, with whom he becomes erotically enthralled." Newsweek

"Erotic obsession is a risky subject for fiction. No matter how besotted the victims of this malady may be, their behavior is likely to strike mere witnesses, i.e., readers, as distasteful, hilarious or both. This first novel . . . sidesteps such unintended responses, thanks to old-fashioned British reserve. . . . The understatement works wonders." Time

The reconstructionist. Overlook Press 2001 218p $26.95
ISBN 1-58567-170-3   LC 2001-33963

"Jack Harrington, a well-to-do London psychiatrist, immerses himself in the familial problems of his patients' pasts, while admirably repressing his own childhood trauma. His sister, Kate, a seductive writer of 'fluffy things,' is less able to cope with that trauma, and readers learn early on that Jack's good-natured protectiveness toward his sister belies a far more disturbing sort of sibling bond. . . . Hart has packed this little gem of a novel with sparkling aphoristic insights befitting Jack's profession, and her sketches of fragile, childlike characters masquerading as capable adults are deftly drawn." Publ Wkly

Sin; a novel. Knopf 1992 163p o.p.
LC 92-53853

This novel "focuses on the sin of envy, embodied here in the person of narrator Ruth, corrosively jealous of her orphaned cousin Elizabeth, raised and cherished by Ruth's parents as their own daughter. Ruth hates the good, generous, kind Elizabeth and waits for the moment when she will be able to break her rival and take everything." Libr J

"Hart has constructed an arch and streamlined melodrama inlaid with some undeniably shrewd and provocative observations about human nature." Booklist

The truth about love; a novel. Alfred A. Knopf 2009 205p $24
ISBN 978-0-307-27261-4   LC 2009-21375

This "novel explores the grief of the O'Hara family in an unnamed Irish town after the violent death of a teenage son. It is 1962, and the boy, who is also unnamed, is blown up in his own backyard while building a bomb. He was at the age when 'warriors' held a special fascination, his father explains, and the Christian Brothers at school had filled his head with stories of Irish heroes who had fought for independence against the British. . . . It is the second death in the O'Hara family. Shortly before the book opens, a young daughter has died after a long illness, and the loss of a second child is too great for Mrs. O'Hara, who collapses into a deep depression. . . . [This] is a serious, at times compelling, look at family and memory, despair and redemption." Wall Street J

Harte, Bret, 1836-1902

The best short stories of Bret Harte; edited, and with an introduction, by Robert N. Linscott. Modern Lib. 1947 517p o.p.

*

Contents: The Luck of Roaring Camp; The outcasts of Poker Flat; Tennessee's partner; Brown of Calaveras; Iliad of Sandy Bar; Poet of Sierra Flat; How Santa Claus came to Simpson's Bar; Passage in the life of Mr. John Oakhurst; Heiress of Red Dog; Ingénue of the Sierras; Chu Chu; Devotion of Enriquez; Yellow dog; Salomy Jane's kiss; Uncle Jim and Uncle Billy; Dick Spindler's family Christmas; Esmeralda of Rocky Cañon; Boom in the "Calaveras Clarion"; Youngest Miss Piper; Colonel Starbottle for the plaintiff; Lanty Foster's mistake; Four guardians of LaGrange; Ward of Colonel Starbottle's; Convalescence of Jack Hamlin; Gentleman of La Porte

The Luck of Roaring Camp, and other tales; with pictures of the author and his environment and illustrations of the setting of the book together with an introduction by Louis B. Salomon. Dodd, Mead 1961 309p il o.p.
"Great illustrated classics"

Contents: The Luck of Roaring Camp; The outcasts of Poker Flat; Miggles; Tennessee's partner; The idyl of Red Gulch; Brown of Calaveras; High-water mark; A lonely ride; The man of no account; Miss; The right eye of the Commander; Notes by flood and field; The mission Dolores; John Chinaman; From a back window; Boonder; How Santa Claus came to Simpson's Bar; Wan Lee, the pagan; Two Saints of the foothills; The fool of Five Forks; A ghost of the Sierras; My friend the tramp; The office-seeker

Hartog, Jan de See De Hartog, Jan, 1914-2002

Haruf, Kent, 1943-

Eventide. Knopf 2004 300p $24.95
ISBN 0-375-41158-5

* LC 2003-60480

This novel takes up where the author's Plainsong left off, "in the windy high-plains country in and around the tiny town of Holt, Colorado. Distress is general: out on their ranch, two stolid elderly brothers discover loneliness after the wayward girl they took in leaves for college; various troubles—illness, death, basic inability to cope—afflict the adults in town; and some young children are set adrift from disintegrating homes, with dangerous consequences. Every action in Holt casts a long shadow, and the gist of Haruf's story is what happens when those shadows touch. (The results are equal parts grace and calamity.) It's rare that such slow, deliberate prose is this highly charged, but Haruf's writing draws power from his sense of character—its limitations and its possibilities—and how it propels action." New Yorker

Plainsong. Knopf 1999 301p $27.50
ISBN 0-375-40618-2

* LC 99-15606

"Set in the plains of Colorado, east of Denver, the novel comprises several story lines that flow into one. Tom Guthrie, a high school history teacher, is having problems with his wife and with an unruly student at

Haruf, Kent, 1943-—*Continued*

school—problems that affect his young sons, Ike and Bob, as well. Meanwhile, the pregnant Victoria Roubideaux has been abandoned by her family. With the assistance of another teacher, Maggie Jones, she finds refuge with the McPheron brothers—who seem to know more about cows than people." Libr J

"From simple strands of language and cuttings of talk, from the look of the high Colorado plains east of Denver almost to the place where Nebraska and Kansas meet, Haruf has made a novel so foursquare, so delicate and lovely, that it has the power to exalt the reader." N Y Times Book Rev

Harvey, Caroline *See* Trollope, Joanna

Harvey, Jack *See* Rankin, Ian, 1960-

Harvey, John, 1938-

Cold in hand. Harcourt 2008 376p $26
ISBN 978-0-15-101462-0; 0-15-101462-0
LC 2008-5630
"An Otto Penzler book"
"Valentine's Day, and a dispute between rival gangs escalates into bloody violence. One teenage girl is left dead, another injured, and a police officer is caught in the crossfire. Resnick, nearing retirement, is hauled back to the front line to help deal with the fallout. But when the dead girl's father seeks to lay the blame on DI Lynn Kellogg, his colleague and partner, Resnick finds the line between personal and professional dangerously blurred." Publisher's note

"Resnick is now living with a much younger DI, Lynn Kellog, and their relationship is one of the best aspects of this fine crime novel, subtly described and convincing. . . . Cold in Hand reveals modern England in all its most depressing messiness while engaging the reader with characters whose warmth and humanity give real pleasure. There is no melodrama here; all the actions and motives that are eventually revealed are rooted in reality; and yet at the heart of the novel is an event so shocking in the context that it could rival anything in the most lurid thriller." Times Lit Suppl

Cold light. Holt & Co. 1994 370p
ISBN 0-8050-2046-2
LC 93-6263
This novel finds Charlie Resnick "and his fellow coppers in the industrial English city of Nottingham harried as usual, what with the customary run of Christmastime crimes. Matters take a decided turn for the worse, though, when a Social Services caseworker goes missing; messages from the kidnapper follow, indicating similarity to a previous case and suggesting that the perpetrator is very sick indeed." Booklist

"Nice men, murderers, child batterers, discarded lovers, grieving parents, weary probation officers, cynical cops—they all hurt, they all count and they all speak a kind of poetry in this writer's book." N Y Times Book Rev

Darkness and light. Harcourt 2006 350p
ISBN 978-0-15-101133-9; 0-15-101133-8
LC 2005-37771
In this procedural, retired policeman Frank Elder "grudgingly agrees to try to find Claire Meecham, the older, widowed sister of a friend of his ex-wife's. While

poking through the missing woman's Nottingham bungalow, Elder finds nothing untoward other than evidence that Claire was not quite so uninterested in sex, and possible new relationships, as her younger sister believed. Soon after, Elder is surprised when Claire turns up in her home dead, looking at peace, carefully dressed and laid out in the manner of a woman who met a similar fate years earlier—and whose killer was never caught." Publ Wkly

"A satisfying look at the twists and turns of police work, through a man who can't quite leave his former life behind." Arizona Republic

Easy meat. Holt & Co. 1996 388p o.p.
LC 96-7307
"A Marian Wood book"
"Inspector Charlie Resnick, now in his mid-forties, investigates the apparent suicide of a 14-year-old delinquent boy. Resnick knows the boy's mother, the boy's older brother is a suspect in other crimes, and his teenaged sister is headed for trouble, too." Libr J

"As Resnick's eyes are opened, Mr. Harvey writes with painful urgency about the kind of sexual and psychological abuse that no child can completely outgrow. If this is one of Mr. Harvey's darkest books, it is also one of his most enlightened." N Y Times Book Rev

Flesh and blood. Carroll & Graff Pubs. 2004 370p $25
ISBN 0-7867-1359-3
"After 30 years in the Nottinghamshire police, Frank Elder has retired to escape hassles and an unfaithful wife. Yet even fleeing to Land's End at the southwest tip of England can't prevent his being dogged by memories of the unsolved disappearance of a teenage girl. Soon Elder is drawn into helping the police investigate several violent crimes similar to those done by a man he helped catch 15 years ago. Past seems to merge with present, especially when Elder's own 16-year-old daughter is kidnapped." Libr J

"If anyone could make you feel sorry for a serial killer, it's John Harvey, who always writes with tender feeling about commonplace people killers among them damaged by criminal violence." N Y Times Book Rev

Gone to ground. Harcourt 2008 c2007 387p $25
ISBN 978-0-15-101363-0; 0-15-101363-2
LC 2006-37390
"An Otto Penzler Book"
First published 2007 in the United Kingdom
The author, "best known for his now-complete Charlie Resnick series, follows Cambridge police detectives Will Grayson and Helen Walker as they investigate the disfiguring murder of gay film professor Stephen Bryan. Initially focused on Bryan's love life, they soon sense secrets around a book he was writing on '50s movie queen Stella Leonard. Flashbacks from the star's last film add a noir chill to the tale. Bryan's sister, a journalist, uses her position to look into things on her own, with potentially dangerous results as Leonard's family grows fiercely protective. Harvey keeps the devastating secret at the center of the tale well hidden until the end." Rocky Mountain News

Last rites. Holt & Co. 1999 312p
ISBN 0-8050-4150-8
* LC 98-33766

Harvey, John, 1938-—*Continued*
"A Marian Wood book"
First published 1998 in the United Kingdom
This final Charlie Resnick mystery "finds Resnick and colleagues attempting to end a local drug war and track down an escaped killer. As always, Resnick slouches his way to understanding, recognizing eventually that the catalyst for much of the mayhem is a love story, as perverted as it is wrenchingly tender. Meanwhile, strands of stories left incomplete in earlier novels come together, some offering more snapshots of wasted lives, others providing glimmers of hope. Harvey ends his story, yes, but he avoids wrapping it all into too neat a package. The great strength of the Resnick series has always been Harvey's grasp of the mess and muddle of human life and his ability to find poetry in the midst of that mess." Booklist

Still waters. Holt & Co. 1997 311p
ISBN 0-8050-4149-4
* LC 97-12324
"A Marian Wood book"
"Charlie Resnick, the laconic British police investigator . . . is faced with the death of an abused woman, a friend of his lover, Hannah. At the same time, he tracks down the circumstances of an idiosyncratic art theft. This standard police procedural formula is given a bit of depth by passages detailing relationships, both business and personal, between the members of the Serious Crime Squad." Libr J

Wasted years. Holt & Co. 1993 339p o.p.
LC 93-247
Nottingham "Inspector Charlie Resnick's past comes back to mock him when a gang of armed robbers on a crime spree reminds him of a criminal who is up for parole. Ten years earlier Resnick put him away, under circumstances that cost the detective his marriage and made him a moody man. 'Boxing with shadows' is the police chief's opinion of Resnick's efforts to track his old enemy, resolve the old questions and maybe take back the lost years." N Y Times Book Rev
"By now Harvey's economy of prose is a given, as is his ability to pull together the many composite parts—the interlocking crimes, the boozing, infidelity and Resnick's very human bunch of underlings—that make a Charlie Resnick mystery such satisfying reading." Publ Wkly

Harvey, Kathryn, 1947-
See also Wood, Barbara, 1947-

Harvey, Michael T.

The Chicago way; [by] Michael Harvey. Knopf 2007 303p $23.95
ISBN 978-0-307-26686-6; 0-307-26686-9
LC 2007-7796
"When his old partner asks for help with an old rape case, Michael Kelly, former Chicago detective turned PI, finds himself in the middle of a massive coverup with links to a notorious serial killer on death row. With the help of his childhood friend, DNA analyst Nicole Andrews, feisty and sexy TV reporter Diane Lindsay and a handful of cops he hopes he can trust, Kelly must solve the original rape case while staying alive as the men who killed to keep a secret set their sights on him." Publ

Wkly
"Harvey's tightly plotted evocation of the Chicago underworld is set in the present but brings to mind the voices of Chandler and Hammett." New York

The Fifth Floor; [by] Michael Harvey. Alfred A. Knopf 2008 277p $23.95
ISBN 978-0-307-26687-3; 0-307-26687-7
LC 2008-1484
This Michael Kelly thriller "has the ex-Chicago cop taking on what he thinks is a simple domestic violence case. But when he tails Johnny Woods, a fixer for the city's powerful mayor, to what turns out to be a grisly murder scene, Kelly realizes he's stumbled onto a scandal that began with the great Chicago Fire of 1871. Digging deeper, Kelly unearths what was once considered an urban legend: two of Chicago's most eminent families conspiring to eradicate Irish immigrants by burning down the city's slums. As more bodies pile up and he becomes romantically involved with a judge with secrets of her own, Kelly vows to expose the conspiracy, even if that means putting himself on the wrong side of the city's most powerful men. Harvey's plot twists in all the right places, and his noir-inspired dialogue crackles without sounding showy. Marlowe and Spade would readily welcome Michael Kelly into their fold." Publ Wkly

Harwood, John, 1946-

The ghost writer. Harcourt 2004 369p $25
ISBN 0-15-101074-9
LC 2003-24918
"Gerard Freeman grows up on the windswept southern coast of Australia in the late 20th century with a controlling mother strangely silent about the details of her childhood in England. His only solace is steadfast English pen friend, Alice, to whom he confides everything. What was Gerard's mother, Phyllis, hoping to escape when she left England? The protagonist slowly pieces together his mother's past with the aid of short stories written by his great-grandmother, Viola. These cunning tales, filled with supernatural occurrences and séances, are seamlessly embedded in the main narrative, offering Gerard—and readers—enticing clues into his troubled family's history. After Phyllis's death, her newly liberated son travels to England, hoping to learn more and to pursue elusive Alice. As he searches through the country house his mother inhabited long ago, Gerard finds past and present fusing in horrifying fashion." Publ Wkly

Hašek, Jaroslav, 1883-1923

The good soldier Svejk; and his fortunes in the World War; translated and introduced by Cecil Parrott; illustrated by Josef Lada. Knopf 1993 800p $22
ISBN 0-679-42036-3
* LC 92-54304
"Everyman's library"
Original Czech edition published 1920-1923 in 4 volumes; this translation first published 1973 by Heinemann
"The novel reflected the pacifist, antimilitary sentiments of post-World War I Europe. The title character is classified as 'feeble-minded'; nevertheless, with the advent of World War I he is drafted into the service of Austria. Naive, instinctively honest, invariably incompetent, and guileless, Schweik is forever colliding with the

Hašek, Jaroslav, 1883-1923—*Continued*

clumsy, dehumanized military bureaucracy. Schweik's naiveté serves as a contrast to the self-importance and conniving natures of his superior officers and is the main vehicle for Hašek's mockery of authority." Merriam-Webster's Ency of Lit

Haskell, John, 1958-

American purgatorio. Farrar, Straus and Giroux 2005 239p $23

    ISBN 0-374-10432-8   LC 2004-20087

"After stopping for gas on his way to his mother–in–law's house, the narrator, Jack, emerges from a convenience store to find that his car and his wife, Anne, are nowhere to be found. After making his way back home, Jack discovers a U.S. map marked with an apparent route; imagining that this will lead him to his wife, he buys another car and sets off." Publ Wkly

"The novel becomes more visual and distinct the farther west Jack travels, and an undertow of regret begins to emerge, intimations of a marriage left unfulfilled. Gradually, Haskell creates a penetrating mood of loss. Turn the last page, and you'll realize that this strange, moving book has done just what a first novel should: it has left an impression." N Y Times Book Rev

Hassler, Jon, 1933-2008

The dean's list. Ballantine Bks. 1997 396p

    ISBN 0-345-41637-6   LC 97-10177

"In this sequel to Rookery Blues . . ., Hassler revisits Rookery State College in Minnesota some 30 years later. Leland Edwards, one of the faculty in the first book, is now dean of the college. In spite of growing older and more successful, however, he is still striving to understand his family and friends, tentatively exploring new relationship, and often simply trying to survive the follies of campus life in the 1990s." Libr J

Rookery blues. Ballantine Bks. 1995 484p

    ISBN 0-345-39356-2

                          * LC 95-2953

"Rookery is the name of a northern Minnesota state college where five faculty members get together to play the blues as well as endure them. The group—a beautiful singer, a tormented artist, a woebegone novelist, and two English teachers—includes a love triangle, and political strains arise as the members take different sides in a strike. Set in 1969, it feels like 1959—in large part because of its old-fashioned, four-square, apolitical humanism." New Yorker

Followed by The dean's list

The Staggerford flood. Viking 2002 199p $24.95

    ISBN 0-670-03125-9   LC 2001-56808

"A natural disaster threatens the unique rural charm of Hassler's Minnesota village in the latest installment in his ongoing series. . . . Agatha McGee is the 80-year-old sixth-grade teacher who is beginning to dread the onset of old age, so much so that a local radio personality suggests that she hold her own memorial party in advance to try to get a lift from the tribute. What invigorates Agatha instead is the threat of a flood, which distracts her from her preoccupation with local gossip and

causes her to offer shelter to several troubled residents, including a combative mother and daughter as well as several friends and acquaintances." Publ Wkly

Hatoum, Milton, 1952-

The brothers; translated from the Portuguese by John Gledson. Farrar, Straus & Giroux 2002 240p $23

    ISBN 0-374-14118-5   LC 2002-17054

    Original Portuguese edition, 2000

"Set in a Lebanese immigrant community in the Brazilian port town of Manaus, this is the story of identical twins, Yaqub and Omar, whose lives take radically different paths: one toward professional success in Brazil's metropolis São Paulo, the other to drunken dissipation in the lowly port of his birth. Set against the backdrop of a city whose very character is undergoing radical change, it is also the story of a family on the verge of conflagration from incestuous passion and riddled with secrets and guilt. . . . Hatoum suggests much while fully revealing little; he's content to unfold his lush narrative—replete with the dances, exotic sights, smells and fragrances of his luscious Brazil—one vivid bolt of cloth at a time." Publ Wkly

Havazelet, Ehud

Bearing the body; a novel. Farrar, Straus and Giroux 2007 296p $24

    ISBN 978-0-374-29972-9; 0-374-29972-2

                          LC 2007-09157

"Stoic and determined Holocaust survivor Sol Mirsky becomes a successful New York shoe manufacturer, but his two sons are plagued by despair and anger. Handsome and charming Daniel, a 1960s student activist, ends up in San Francisco addicted to heroin. After many fits and starts, his troubled brother, Nathan, is about to complete his medical training. Nathan and his widower father, now devoted to amassing information about Holocaust victims, have long been estranged from Daniel, which makes his violent death in 1994 confounding as well as shocking. Traumatized, they fly to San Francisco and are profoundly disoriented by what they discover." Booklist

"Havazelet's novel won't make you happier, unless it cheers you to admire a writer who doesn't merely describe but actually reproduces experiences that seem simultaneously universal and intimate. Reading about Sol and Nathan feels like being adopted into a family you might not want to have, precisely because (as with 'The Sopranos') you recognize the similarities it bears to your own." N Y Times Book Rev

Hawk, Alex *See* Kelton, Elmer, 1926-2009

Hawke, Ethan, 1970-

Ash Wednesday; a novel. Knopf 2002 221p

    ISBN 0-375-41326-X   LC 2002-20811

"When he discovers that his girlfriend is pregnant and well into the process of leaving him, Jimmy Heartsock resolves to win her back whatever the cost—in his case going AWOL from the Army and giving up his carousing, coke-snorting ways. Christy, whose flight by bus from upstate New York to her Texas home sets off this

Hawke, Ethan, 1970—_Continued_
interstate odyssey, is more leery about the shelf life of
passion but is willing to find out how far the domestic
kind of love will take them." N Y Times Book Rev

"Hawke's text at times reads raw, but the novel's conversational tone, dual first-person narration and, above
all, direct exploration of the simple truths of life and
love make this a worthwhile tale and an honest one."
Publ Wkly

Hawkes, John, 1925-1998

The blood oranges. New Directions 1971 271p
o.p.

"This novel focuses on an erotic quartet. Cyril and
Fiona and Hugh and Catherine, two married couples who
engage in mate swapping. . . . (Cyril) drifts into an affair with Catherine as easily as his wife does with Hugh.
. . . But even in liberal Cyril we begin to detect traces
of jealousy. Although trying to appear perfectly jolly and
casual about his wife's lover, he is actually quite disturbed. . . . Just how involved is Fiona?" Saturday Rev

"This highly rhapsodic, sensual novel suggests both in
title and substance the decline of vitality and enlightenment in the characters' lives as in each new day. Reminiscent of Lawrence in the concern with atmosphere and
lushness of description, the book is powerfully evocative
of a sometimes comic, sometimes hallucinatory sense of
timelessness, obsession, and escape from reality." Choice

Second skin; preface by Jeffrey Eugenides. New
Directions 2005 210p
ISBN 0-8112-1644-6
* LC 2005-21516

First published 1964

"Skipper, the narrator . . ., interweaves past and present–what he refers to as his 'naked history'–to tell the
story of a life marked by pitiful losses, as well as a more
elusive, but overwhelming, joy. The past: the suicides of
his father, wife, and daughter, the murder of his son-in-
law, a brutal rape and mutiny at sea. The present: caring
for his granddaughter, Pixie, on a 'northern' island where
he works as an artificial inseminator of cows and attempts to reclaim some of the innocence of his earlier
life." Publisher's note

"As with other contemporaries, such as Pynchon,
Barth, and Nabokov, and predecessors such as Faulkner,
Lautremont, and Blake, Hawkes has succeeded in creat-
ing a stylized, imagined world that doubles for the one
in which we live and read his novels." Reader's Ency of
Am Lit. 2d edition

Hawkins, Anthony Hope _See_ Hope, Anthony,
1863-1933

Hawthorne, Nathaniel, 1804-1864

The Blithedale romance; with an introduction by
Tony Tanner; and explanatory notes by John
Dugdale. Oxford University Press 2009 c1991 l,
256p (Oxford world's classics) pa $9.95
ISBN 978-0-19-955486-7; 0-19-955486-2

First published 1852

"Blithedale, a Utopian community, is modeled on
Brook Farm, the transcendentalist experiment at West
Roxbury, Massachusetts, in which Hawthorne had partici-

pated ten years before he wrote the novel. Miles Cover-
dale, the narrator, is a coldly inquisitive observer; in revealing his knowledge of the other members of the community, he reveals himself." Reader's Ency. 4th edition

also in Hawthorne, N. Collected novels

Collected novels. Literary Classics of the United
States 1983 1272p $39.50
ISBN 0-940450-08-9
* LC 82-18031

Contents: Fanshawe; The scarlet letter; The House of
the Seven Gables; The Blithedale romance; The marble
faun

In Fanshawe (1828), two students at Harley College—
one normal and outgoing, the other isolated and scholarly—both fall in love with a third student, Ellen Langdon.
When Ellen is kidnapped, the isolated Fanshawe rescues
her, only to turn down her marriage proposal afterward.
The scarlet letter, The House of the Seven Gables, The
Blithedale romance, and The marble faun are entered
separately.

Complete short stories of Nathaniel Hawthorne.
Hanover House 1959 615p o.p.

Contains the following stories: Gray champion; Wedding knell; Minister's black veil; Maypole of Merry
Mount; Gentle boy; Mr. Higginbotham's catastrophe;
Wakefield; Great carbuncle; Prophetic pictures; David
Swan; Hollow of the three hills; Vision of the fountain;
Fancy's show box; Dr Heidegger's experiment; Howe's
masquerade; Edward Randolph's portrait; Lady Eleanore's mantle; Old Esther Dudley; Village uncle; Ambi-
tious guest; The sister years; Seven vagabonds; White
old maid; Peter Goldthwaite's treasure; Shaker bridal;
Endicott and the Red Cross; Lily's quest; Edward Fane's
rosebud; Threefold destiny; The birthmark; Select party;
Young Goodman Brown; Rappaccini's daughter; Mrs.
Bullfrog; Monsieur du Miroir; Hall of fantasy; Celestial
railroad; Procession of life; Feathertop: a moralized legend; New Adam and Eve; Egotism; Christmas banquet;
Browne's wooden image; Intelligence office; Roger
Malvin's burial; P's correspondence; Earth's holocaust;
Passages from a relinquished work; Artist of the beauti-
ful virtuoso's collection; Snow-image: a childish miracle;
Great Stone Face; Ethan Brand; Sylph Etherege; Canter-
bury pilgrims; Man of Adamant; Devil in manuscript;
John Inglefield's Thanksgiving; Wives of the dead; Little
Daffydowndilly; My kinsman, Major Molineux; Antique
ring; Graves and goblins; Dr. Bullivant; Old woman's
tale; Alice Coane's appeal; Ghost of Doctor Harris;
Young provincial; Haunted quack; New England village;
My wife's novel; Bald Eagle

Doctor Grimshawe's secret; edited, with an introduction and notes, by Edward H. Davidson.
Harvard Univ. Press 1954 305p il o.p.

Written 1883

"In a New England town in the early 19th century
lives Dr. Grimshawe, an eccentric recluse, and two orphans, Ned and Elsie. The children are involved in a secret related to an estate in England, whence the doctor
originally came. This estate has lacked a direct heir since
the reign of Charles I, when the incumbent disappeared,
leaving a bloody footprint on the threshold. After their
guardian's death, the children are separated, but meet
again years later, in England. Ned, now Edward
Redclyffe, is injured while investigating the estate and is

Hawthorne, Nathaniel, 1804-1864—*Continued*
befriended by Colcord, his boyhood tutor. Lord
Braithwaite, the estate's present owner, invites Edward to
live at the Hall, where he meets Elsie, who warns him
of a presentiment of danger. He finds the hiding place of
an incredibly old man who 'haunts' the Hall, and recognizes him as the Sir Edward Redclyffe of the times of
the bloody footprint. When the old man dies, Colcord
produces a locket that proves Edward to be the heir."
Oxford Companion to Am Lit. 6th edition

Fanshawe
    In Hawthorne, N. Collected novels

The Hawthorne treasury; complete novels and
selected tales of Nathaniel Hawthorne; edited by
Norman Holmes Pearson. Modern Lib. 1999 1409p
    ISBN 0-679-60322-0   LC 98-47424
This volume includes the complete text of the following novels: Fanshawe, The scarlet letter, The House of
Seven Gables, The Blithedale romance, and The marble
faun. Also included are stories from twice-told tales,
Mosses from an old manse, and The snow-image and
other twice-told tales

The House of the Seven Gables; introduction by
Mary Oliver. Modern Library 2001 312p pa $8.75
    ISBN 0-375-75687-6
                                          * LC 00-64585
    First published 1851
"Follows the fortunes of a decayed New England family, consisting of four members—Hephzibah Pyncheon,
her brother Clifford, their cousin Judge Pyncheon, and
other cousin Phoebe, a country girl. At the time the story
opens Hephzibah is living in great poverty at the old
homestead, the House of the Seven Gables. With her is
[her brother] Clifford, just released from prison, where
he had served a term of thirty years for the supposed
murder of a rich uncle. Judge Pyncheon, who was influential in obtaining the innocent Clifford's arrest, that he
might hide his own wrongdoing, now seeks to confine
him in an asylum on the charge of insanity. Hephzibah's
pitiful efforts to shield this brother, to support him and
herself by keeping a scentshop, to circumvent the machinations of the judge, are described through the greater
portion of the novel. The sudden death of the malevolent
cousin frees them and makes them possessors of his
wealth." Keller. Reader's Dig of Books
    also in Hawthorne, N. Collected novels

The marble faun; or, The romance of Monte
Beni. Ohio State Univ. Press 1968 cxxxiii, 610p
$83.95
    ISBN 0-8142-0062-1
"Centenary edition of the works of Nathaniel Hawthorne"
    First published 1860
"The novel's central metaphor is a statue of a faun by
Praxiteles that Hawthorne had seen in Florence. In the
faun's fusing of animal and human characteristics he
finds an allegory of the fall of man from amoral innocence to the knowledge of good and evil. . . . The faun
of the novel is Donatello, a passionate young Italian who
makes the acquaintance of three American artists, Miriam, Kenyon, and Hilda, who are spending time in Rome.
When Donatello kills a man who has been shadowing

Miriam, he is wracked by guilt until he is arrested by the
police and imprisoned. Both of the women are tainted by
guilt." Merriam-Webster's Ency of Lit
    also in Hawthorne, N. Collected novels

Mosses from an old manse
    In Hawthorne, N. Tales and sketches,
        including Twice-told tales, Mosses from
        an old manse, and The snow-image; A
        wonder book for girls and boys;
        Tanglewood tales for girls and boys,
        being a second Wonder book

The scarlet letter; with an introduction by Alfred
Kazin. Knopf 1992 xxvii, 273p $18
    ISBN 0-679-41731-1
                                          * LC 92-52902
"Everyman's library"
"Set in 17th-century Salem, the novel is built around
three scaffold scenes, which occur at the beginning, the
middle, and the end. The story opens with the public
condemnation of Hester Prynne, and the exhortation that
she confess the name of the father of Pearl, her illegitimate child. Hester's husband, an old and scholarly physician, just arrived from England, assumes the name of
Roger Chillingworth in order to seek out Hester's lover
and revenge himself upon him. He attaches himself as
physician to a respected and seemingly holy minister,
Arthur Dimmesdale, suspecting that he is the father of
the child. The Scarlet Letter traces the effect of the actual and symbolic sin on all the characters." Benet's Reader's Ency of Am Lit
    also in Hawthorne, N. Collected novels

The snow-image
    In Hawthorne, N. Tales and sketches,
        including Twice-told tales, Mosses from
        an old manse, and The snow-image; A
        wonder book for girls and boys;
        Tanglewood tales for girls and boys,
        being a second Wonder book

Tales and sketches, including Twice-told tales,
Mosses from an old manse, and The snow-image;
A wonder book for girls and boys; Tanglewood
tales for girls and boys, being a second Wonder
book. Library of Am. 1982 1493p $39.50
    ISBN 0-940450-03-8   LC 81-20760
The stories in this collection have appeared in the five
books: Twice-told tales (1837); Mosses from an old
manse (1846); The snow-image (1852); A wonder book
for girls and boys (1851); Tanglewood tales for girls and
boys, being a second wonder book (1853)
    Contents: The hollow of the three hills; Sir William
Phips; Mrs. Hutchinson; An old woman's tale; Dr.
Bullivant; Sights from a steeple; The haunted quack; The
wives of the dead; My kinsman, Major Molineux; Roger
Malvin's burial; The gentle boy; The seven vagabonds;
The Canterbury pilgrims; Sir William Pepperell; Passages
from a relinquished work; Mr. Higginbotham's catastrophe; The haunted mind; Alice Doane's appeal; The village uncle; Little Annie's ramble; The gray champion;
My visit to Niagara; Old news; Young Goodman Brown;
Wakefield; The ambitious guest; A rill from the town-
pump; The white old maid; The vision of the fountain;

Hawthorne, Nathaniel, 1804-1864—*Continued*
The Devil in manuscript; Sketches from memory; The wedding-knell; The may-pole of Merry Mount; The minister's black veil; Old Ticonderoga; A visit to the clerk of the weather; Monsieur du Miroir; Mrs. Bullfrog; Sunday at home; The man of Adamant; David Swan; The great carbuncle; Fancy's show box; The prophetic pictures; Dr. Heidegger's experiment; A bell's biography; Fragments from the journal of a solitary man; Edward Fane's rosebud; The may-pole of Merry Mount; The minister's black veil; Old Ticonderoga; A visit to the clerk Peter Goldwaite's treasure; Endicott and the Red Cross; Night sketches; The Shaker bridal; Foot-prints on the seashore; Thomas Green Fessenden; Time's portraiture; Snow-flakes; The threefold destiny; Jonathan Cilley; Chippings with a chisel; Legends of the Province-House; The sister years; The lily's quest; John Inglefield's Thanksgiving; A virtuoso's collection; The old apple-dealer; The antique ring; The hall of fantasy; The new Adam and Eve; The birthmark; Egotism; or, The bosom-serpent; The procession of life; The celestial railroad; Buds and bird-voices; Little Daffydowndilly; Fire-worship; The Christmas banquet; A good man's miracles; The intelligence office; Earth's holocaust; The artist of the beautiful; Drowne's wooden image; A select party; A book of autographs; Rappaccini's daughter; P.'s correspondence; Main-street; Ethan Brand; The great stone face; The snow-image; Feathertop; The Gorgon's head; The Golden touch; The paradise of children; The three golden apples; The miraculous pitcher; The Chimaera; The Minotaur; The Pygmies; The dragon's teeth; Circe's palace; The pomegranate-seeds; The golden fleece
This volume contains all of Hawthorne's tales and sketches, which are arranged in order of their periodical publication

Twice-told tales; introduction by Rosemary Mahoney; notes by Gretchen Short. Modern Library 2001 xxiv, 404p pa $10.95
  ISBN 0-375-75788-0   LC 2001-31480
  First published 1837
  Contents: The Gray Champion; Sunday at home; The wedding-knell; The minister's black veil; The May-pole of Merry Mount; The gentle boy; Mr. Higginbotham's catastrophe; Little Annie's ramble; Wakefield; A rill from the town-pump; The Great Carbuncle; The prophetic pictures; David Swan; Sights from steeple; The hollow of the three hills; The toll-gatherer's day; The vision of the fountain; Fancy's show box; Dr. Heidegger's experiment; Howe's masquerade; Edward Randolph's portrait; Lady Eleanore's mantle; Old Esther Dudley; The haunted mind; The village uncle; The ambitious guest; The sister years; Snow-flakes; The seven vagabonds; The white old maid; Peter Goldthwaite's treasure; Chippings with a chisel; The Shaker bridal; Night sketches; Endicott and the Red Cross; The lily's quest; Footprints on the seashore; Edward Fane's rosebud; The threefold destiny
  also in Hawthorne, N. Tales and sketches, including Twice-told tales, Mosses from an old manse, and The snow-image; A wonder book for girls and boys; Tanglewood tales for girls and boys, being a second Wonder book

Hay, Elizabeth

Garbo laughs. Counterpoint 2003 294p $25
  ISBN 1-582-43291-0   LC 2003-11989

A novel set in Ottawa. "Harriet, the Garbo-like star of the book, is a novelist who has developed the curious habit of writing but not mailing confiding letters to her hero, the then still-living film critic Pauline Kael, and discussing, at length, such burning cinematic questions as who is sexier, Cary Grant or Sean Connery, with her sweetly precocious and equality movie-mad son and daughter. As Harriet indulges her grand obsession with movies, she struggles with her less than passionate feelings for her real-life leading man and forges a warm but risky friendship with a new neighbor, the earthy Dinah." Booklist
"This rich, lovely novel makes us think about the ambivalences and contradictions of relationships and the patience of love." Quill & Quire

Late nights on air; a novel. Counterpoint 2008 363p $24
  ISBN 978-1-58243-408-7; 1-582-43408-5
                                  LC 2007-43785
  First published 2007 in Canada
  A novel set during the "summer of 1975 in Yellowknife. A collection of lost souls find themselves at the local CBC radio station, resisting the network's plans to launch a TV station, caught in the timelessness of the midnight sun, and wondering if anyone is listening, knowing that likely no one is. Harry is the curmudgeonly, rumpled old pro, beaten down by failure in the south; Dido left the only man she knows she'll ever love; Gwen is crippled by shyness but is forced on air nonetheless. These broken souls are barely coping; they fall into the north and into each other. Gwen spends long nights on the radio, creating soundscapes and playing songs of longing; Harry tells stories of travelling deep within and never emerging, of loving strongly but unrequitedly." Quill & Quire
"The plot of this novel is a faint signal, a series of short moments, sometimes funny, sometimes poignant, often flecked with intimations of tragedy. Hay's writing is so alluring and her lost souls so endearing that you'll lean in to catch the story's delicate developments as these characters shuffle along through quiet desperation and yearning." Washington Post Book World

A student of weather. Counterpoint 2001 368p
  ISBN 1-58243-123-X   LC 00-64445
  This novel "begins circa 1930 on the drought-ravished prairies of Saskatchewan, the home of two motherless sisters. The elder, Lucinda, is fair and diligent, Norma Joyce dark and willful, and both fall for a handsome, rambling botanist from fabled Ottawa, Maurice Dove. . . . As the sisters embark on a tragic rivalry that will determine the course of their lives, their story becomes a fairy tale in which solitude, work, art, and desire acquire mystical significance as Hay adroitly weaves their passions into luminous descriptions of extreme weather and the grand cycle of the seasons." Booklist

Hayder, Mo, 1962-

Ritual. Atlantic Monthly Press 2008 410p $24
  ISBN 978-0-87113-992-4
  At the start of this crime novel featuring Det. Insp. Jack Caffery, "Sgt. Phoebe Flea Marley, a police diver, retrieves a severed hand from Bristol harbor. Without a corpse, the investigation stalls, until fingerprints identify the hand as belonging to Ian Mossy Mallows, a known

Hayder, Mo, 1962-—*Continued*

heroin junkie. While Caffery pursues the drug angle, Flea uncovers a possible connection to muti, a brand of African witchcraft and traditional medicine that incorporates body parts into its rituals. Digging deeper, Caffery and Flea discover that Mallows may still be alive and the men responsible may be using muti as a cover for even darker purposes. . . . Hayder vividly evokes torture and drug abuse, but the violence is never gratuitous. Readers looking for visceral thrills need look no further than this gritty English series." Publ Wkly

Haydon, Elizabeth

Destiny: child of the sky. TOR Bks. 2001 556p $27.95

ISBN 0-312-86750-6   LC 2001-27473

"A Tom Doherty Associates book"

Sequel to: Prophecy: child of earth

In this concluding volume of the first Rhapsody fantasy/romance trilogy "the harpist Rhapsody joins with the Firbolg king Achmed and his giant companion Grunthor to attempt to fight the powerful and elusive F'dor, a demon-born danger that threatens the fabric of existence." Libr J

"Though obviously inspired by music theory, Norse and Celtic folklore, and seemingly such authors as Tolkien, C.S. Lewis, Patricia A. McKillip, Anne McCaffrey and Palmer Brown (Cheerful), the author uses a fluid writing style to build a world uniquely and compellingly her own." Publ Wkly

Prophecy; child of earth. TOR Bks. 2000 480p $27.95

ISBN 0-312-86751-4   LC 00-26836

"A Tom Doherty Associates book"

Sequel to Rhapsody (1999)

"The skysinger Rhapsody and her two FirBolg companions seek to carve out a place for themselves in a new world even as their lives move inexorably toward the fulfillment of an ancient prophecy. As momentous events take shape around the three heroes, other forces work hard to undermine their hope and bring the powers of evil closer to victory. . . . Haydon's epic saga of the endless battle between light and darkness resounds with the richness of ancient myths reworked into new forms." Libr J

Requiem for the sun. TOR Bks. 2002 462p $27.95

ISBN 0-312-87884-2   LC 2002-28584

"A Tom Doherty Associates book"

First title in a second Rhapsody fantasy/romance trilogy

"Three years after she has helped bring peace and prosperity to the land of Navarne, Rhapsody, Lady Cymrian treasures her family and her people. When the death of the Dowager Empress at Sorbold leaves empty the line of succession, war threatens the fragile Cymrian Alliance—and an old and deadly foe of Rhapsody's rises up to threaten her and all she holds dear." Libr J

"Bears for neologisms may growl over words such as coronated and infrastructure, but even they will raise glasses to toast Haydon's generally high levels of achievement in characterization, world building through well-chosen detail, folkloric and musical expertise, and warmth of spirit." Booklist

Haymon, S. T.

A beautiful death. St. Martin's Press 1994 c1993 223p o.p.   LC 93-37005

First published 1993 in the United Kingdom

Inspector Ben Jurnet "plunges into his deepest fit of melancholia to date when his fiancée is blown to bits by a car bomb. . . . Racked with guilt for surviving the attack that was surely meant for him, the English copper stumbles through his grief, enduring the sympathy of his friends and the glee of his enemies, until he bolts for Ireland in pursuit of a neighborhood youth with terrorist clan connections in the old country. Ms. Haymon, an elegant and assured stylist whose esthetic juices are always stirred by a good, gloomy setting, finds the perfect lyric complement for Jurnet's dismal mood in the gray, misty drizzle of County Donegal in November." N Y Times Book Rev

Death of a hero. St. Martin's Press 1996 176p o.p.   LC 96-27968

"Posthumously published, Haymond's . . . final work details Detective Inspector Ben Jurnet's last case. Although still mourning the death of his fiancée, he investigates the murder of an idealistic protest leader in the local redlight district. A reliable police procedural." Libr J

Hays, Tommy

The pleasure was mine. St. Martin's Press 2005 255p $23.95

ISBN 0-312-33932-1   LC 2004-51311

This novel depicts the "transformation of a family in which an older man cares for his wife during her descent into Alzheimer's. The transformation begins when Prate Marshbanks, the remarkable, curmudgeonly protagonist, gets a visitor for the summer: his nine-year-old grandson, Jackson, whose mother died in a car accident several years before. But, despite Jackson's grieving presence, Marshbanks remains preoccupied with his own battle to ensure compassionate care for his wife, whom he has had to place in a nursing home. Hays's elegiac, penetrating description of Prate's marriage frames the landscape of this brilliant novel about love, loss, marriage and family. He offers a grim but hopeful treatment of a difficult subject, and his elegant writing and sharp, tender portraits of the Marshbanks make a potent combination." Publ Wkly

Hayter, Sparkle, 1958-

Bandit queen boogie. Three Rivers Press 2004 290p pa $13

ISBN 1-4000-4744-7 (pa)   LC 2003-25853

"Two childhood friends travel across Europe the summer after their college graduation. The trip was meant for Chloe and her boyfriend, but after he dumps her, Blackie agrees to go instead. Unfortunately, brokenhearted Chloe is not much fun to be around—until the two decide to start robbing the sleazy married men who proposition them. Chloe soon perks up, getting addicted to the thrill and the possibility of being caught. Although the story centers on Chloe and Blackie, numerous characters and story lines come together when they steal a statue of the Hindu god Ganesh that contains a valuable treasure belonging to an Indian crime boss. . . . The characters are vividly rendered, and Hayter deftly weaves together the varying story lines and settings." Libr J

Hazzard, Shirley, 1931-

The great fire. Farrar, Straus & Giroux 2003 278p $24

ISBN 0-374-16644-7

    * LC 2003-49189

"The time is 1947-48, and the place is, primarily, East Asia. . . . Our hero, and indeed he fills the requirements to be called one, is Aldred Leith, who is English and part of the occupation forces in Japan; his particular military task is damage survey. He has an interesting past, including, most recently, a two-year walk across civil-war-torn China to write a book. In the present. . .he meets the teenage daughter and younger son of a local Australian commander. And, as Helen is growing headlong into womanhood, this novel of war's aftermath becomes a story of love—or more to the point, of the restoration of the capacity for love once global and personal trauma have been shed." Booklist

The transit of Venus. Viking 1980 337p o.p.

    * LC 79-21754

This novel centers on "the lives and loves of two Australian sisters who emigrate to England and America in the mid-20th Century. . . . [Focus is on the sister Caro]. Caro's transit is circular: seduction and abandonment, marriage, widowhood, reunion with her betrayer and—at last and fatally—with the astronomer who loved her secretly all along." Libr J

This "is an exceedingly ambitious novel; a stunning and at times bewildering galaxy of ideas. From a literary and intellectual standpoint it is a challenge. . . . Miss Hazzard's greatest achievement in this novel is the suspense she creates from unfinished relationships. Instead of spinning off in different directions through space, these characters collide once again, drawn together by an ineluctable magnetism." Christ Sci Monit

Healy, J. F. (Jeremiah F.), 1948-

Invasion of privacy; a John Francis Cuddy mystery; [by] Jeremiah Healy. Pocket Bks. 1996 340p o.p.

    LC 96-1196

"Acting on behalf of successful bank employee Olga Evorova, Boston P.I. John Cuddy scopes out her secretive potential fiancé, a reclusive man of no apparent family or heritage. Cuddy's investigation stirs up trouble: representatives of the Milwaukee mob appear on the scene and apply pressure." Libr J

"The dialogue crackles, the plot is complex and clever, and Cuddy's relationship with his longtime lover faces a crisis in which machismo won't help." Booklist

Shallow graves; a John Cuddy mystery; [by] Jeremiah Healy. Pocket Bks. 1992 282p o.p.

    LC 91-44059

"On the verge of a big-time modeling career in New York, Boston model Mau Tim Dani is strangled in her apartment. It looks like a burglary gone bad, but her modeling agency, which carried a 'key employee' insurance policy on her with Empire Insurance, wants to know for sure. Boston private eye John Cuddy used to investigate claims for Empire, which is why he's taken aback when the firm hires him to investigate the death." Booklist

"Healy gives his readers an array of distinctive characters while engaging them in a deftly plotted and satisfying story." Publ Wkly

Spiral; a John Francis Cuddy mystery; {by} Jeremiah Healy. Pocket Bks. 1999 359p

ISBN 0-671-00955-9   LC 99-25769

"Boston private investigator John Cuddy is reeling from the death of his love, Nancy Meagher, in an airline disaster. He can barely cope with the present, and the future seems bleak when his past comes calling. A fellow Vietnam vet enlists Cuddy's investigative skills on behalf of their old commander, Nicolas Helides, whose 13-year-old granddaughter was murdered during a party at the Helides' Florida estate." Booklist

Healy, Jeremiah F. *See* Healy, J. F. (Jeremiah F.), 1948-

Hearon, Shelby, 1931-

Footprints. Knopf 1996 191p o.p.

    LC 95-42853

"Over 25 years, Nan Mayhall has made more than her share of compromises in return for a relatively stable marriage to Douglas, a successful academic. She finds the accompanying frustrations bearable until the shocking accidental death of Bethany, her adored daughter. Nan recoils from her husband's reaction to the tragedy: he becomes obsessed with the notion of part of Bethany living on through her transplanted heart. Douglas insists on establishing a relationship with the recipient, but he virtually ignores the grief experienced by his wife and their surviving child. Eventually, growing family divisions push Nan to seek a separate peace." Libr J

"Shelby Hearon takes a long, speculative look at the moment in the life of a family when a child departs. She has done a fine job of getting at this inevitable conflict between mother and child, between mother and father. She holds it to the light, turns and examines it with a caustic eye. We are the beneficiaries of a clear-eyed view that catches the humor and poignancy of the evolution of a woman's life." N Y Times Book Rev

Year of the dog; a novel. University of Texas Press 2007 227p (James A. Michener fiction series) $21

ISBN 978-0-292-71469-4; 0-292-71469-6

    LC 2006-22585

"Janey Daniels, 25, is taking a 'sabbatical' in Vermont from her job as a pharmacist in Peachland, S.C., after her high school sweetheart and husband of five years dumps her for an ex-girlfriend. In Vermont, with its brilliantly colored Octobers and frigid winters, Janey bonds with Beulah, a Labrador puppy she's raising to become a companion for a blind person. It's while walking Beulah that she meets James Maarten, a potential boyfriend who is secretive about his past." Publ Wkly

"This is not just a cute-sad book about loving and losing a dog but instead a complex and very real story of love and loss, changing perspectives, and making the best of what life gives you. In Hearon's more than capable hands, it is a pleasure." Booklist

Hedge, John *See* Buck, Pearl S. (Pearl Sydenstricker), 1892-1973

Heffernan, William, 1940-

The Dinosaur Club; a novel. Morrow 1997 303p

ISBN 0-688-14988-X   LC 96-46637

Heffernan, William, 1940-—*Continued*

"At age 49, Jack Fallon discovers that his life is plummeting out of control. In one fell swoop, his wife leaves him and corporate downsizing threatens his livelihood. Always the warrior, Jack organizes other fiftyish management employees to fight their ruthless corporate leaders, and the 'Dinosaur Club' is born. Working against formidable odds, the Dinosaurs engage in hilarious hijinks and serious espionage to foil their chief executives. What Jack does not count on is falling in love with Samantha Moore, legal counsel for the corporation. . . . Heffernan is masterly in examining the scruples of corporate downsizing with a discerning eye and blends levity in his cauldron of good and evil." Libr J

Red angel; a novel. Morrow 2000 273p $24
ISBN 0-688-16563-X   LC 99-36638
"New York City special investigative detective Paul Devlin leaves behind an apparent gang war to help Adrianna, his Cuban American lover, with a family problem in Cuba. Only after arriving do they discover the death of Adrianna's aunt—widely known in Cuba as a heroine of the Revolution—and learn that members of a voodoo cult have stolen her body. With the assistance of a local policeman and Devlin's New York partner, Devlin and Adrianna struggle against the machinations of the Cuban secret police and other to uncover the truth. Deeply involving, expertly detailed, and strategically plotted." Libr J

Hegarty, Frances *See* Fyfield, Frances, 1948-

Heggen, Thomas, 1919-1949

Mister Roberts; with an introduction by David P. Smith. Naval Inst. Press 1992 xxii, 200p $34.95
ISBN 1-55750-723-6   LC 92-9422
"Classics of naval literature series"
A reissue of the title first published 1946 by Houghton Mifflin
"Douglas Roberts, First Lieutenant on the *Reluctant*, a U.S. Navy supply ship in the Pacific, is the leading inspiration for the undeclared war between the crew and the unreasonable skipper. The dull life on ship is eased by humorous antics and the resulting rage of the commander. When Roberts is transferred to a destroyer, the crew is saddened by his departure." Shapiro. Fic for Youth. 3d edition
"The leisurely narrative is told in a very few incidents, all centering about an admirable young lieutenant miserably defeated in his desire to get into fighting. A quiet, credible story of the corroding effects of apathy and boredom on men who, in battle, might have been heroes." New Yorker

Hegi, Ursula

Stones from the river. Poseidon Press 1994 507p
ISBN 0-671-78075-1   LC 93-33533
"At the beginning of World War I, [this novel's narrator], Trudi Montag, a dwarf, is born to an unstable mother and a gentle father in a small Rheinish town. Through the Weimar Republic and the Third Reich into the era following World War II she first struggles with—and later draws strength and wisdom from—her inability to fit into a conformist and repressive society. As the town's

librarian and historian, Trudi keeps track of many secrets." Libr J
"This moving, elegiac novel commands our compassion and respect for the wisdom and courage to be found in unlikely places, in unlikely times." N Y Times Book Rev

The vision of Emma Blau. Simon & Schuster 2000 432p $25
ISBN 0-684-82997-5   LC 99-56392
This "novel follows three generations of family and its property. Stefan Blau, aged thirteen, ran away from a small German town in 1894, reached the United States, and would wind up as the proprietor of an elegant restaurant and the Wasserburg, . . . [an apartment house] on the shore of Lake Winnipesaukee, in New Hampshire. . . . His German-American family—one child by each of three wives—remained bicultural while splitting in various directions. Their affairs converge in a row over ownership of the now decaying Wasserburg." Atl Mon
"Hegi has created a milieu full of sexual energy—the book is often erotic—and has captured both the tension and love endemic to all tight-knit families. Compelling and absorbing, this old-fashioned saga is rife with passion, tragedy, and redemption." Libr J

The worst thing I've done; a novel. Simon and Schuster 2007 260p $25
ISBN 978-1-4165-4375-6; 1-416-54375-9
                                  LC 2006-101171
"Annie is addicted to talk radio, especially the dueling doctors who dispense psychological advice to the desperate. It makes her feel better about her own depressing circumstances, as she seeks to understand just how the special childhood friendship between herself, charismatic Mason, and steadfast Jake went so tragically wrong. When Annie's parents died on the day she married Mason, the three friends agreed to raise Annie's infant sister. But all their youthful optimism slowly begins to pall when the dynamics of their triangular relationship shift in disturbing directions." Booklist
"One of Hegi's most enchanting skills is her ability to recreate setting, here a Long Island coastal community. . . . A moving exploration of grief." Libr J

Heidish, Marcy

A woman called Moses; a novel based on the life of Harriet Tubman. Houghton Mifflin 1976 308p o.p.
This is a fictionalized account of "the life of Harriet Tubman, born in slavery on Maryland's Eastern Shore, who escaped North and spent her life in conducting hundreds of blacks to freedom along the Undergound Railroad prior to the Civil War." Libr J
"This fictional life story, told in the first person, is filled with incandescent raw materials, namely the cruelties of slavery, and the itineraries of escape." N Y Times Book Rev

Heilbrun, Carolyn G., 1926-2003
For works written by this author under other names see Cross, Amanda, 1926-2003

Heim, Michael Henry

(tr) Grass, G. My century

Heim, Michael Henry—*Continued*

(tr) Schlink, B. Homecoming

Hein, Christoph

Settlement; a novel; translated by Philip Boehm. H. Holt 2008 323p $27

ISBN 978-0-8050-7768-1; 0-8050-7768-5

LC 2008-09021

Original German edition, 2004

"The rags-to-riches life story of Bernhard Haber, a refugee living in a small East German town following World War II, is told in five segments, each narrated by someone who knew him: a school chum, his first girlfriend, a fellow rabble-rouser, a former lover, and a merchant colleague. As a child, Haber is tormented by townspeople who consider refugees filthy and lazy, and this cements his obsession with revenge in the form of power and wealth. The chillingly single-minded Haber remains fairly one-dimensional, but the side characters are fleshed with excruciating accuracy and detail." Booklist

Heinemann, Larry

Paco's story. Farrar, Straus & Giroux 1986 209p o.p.

LC 86-19527

"Lone survivor of a Viet Cong night attack that wipes out the 90-plus men of Alpha Company, Paco Sullivan returns to civilian life after much time spent in military hospitals. Narrated by a nameless dead soldier from Alpha Company, this . . . tale interweaves Paco's infantry days in Vietnam with his Valium- and Librium-soothed afterlife as a dishwasher in a smalltown cafe." Libr J

"Mr. Heinemann's carefully crafted, oblique narrative suggests that the right words are not going to be found in ever-more-graphic, frontal approaches to 'gruesome carnage.' Its horrors may be as forcefully conveyed by a haunting scene in a greasy spoon as by the tearing of human flesh." N Y Times Book Rev

Heinlein, Robert A. (Robert Anson), 1907-1988

Citizen of the galaxy. Scribner 1957 302p o.p.

*

"Although marketed as a juvenile novel, this work was serialized for adults in *Astounding*. The Horatio Alger hero is in an interstellar setting, except that his lad starts out closer to the edge than Horatio's bootblacks and newsboys: he is a slave on a far planet of a despotic empire. He escapes into space with a nomadic trading company and eventually gets back to Earth, where he assumes (by inheritance!) the headship of a giant financial corporation. This is a *bilungsroman,* except that the young hero never really grows up; but Heinlein's knack for creating sociologically plausible cultures is well displayed." Anatomy of Wonder 4

Friday. Holt, Rinehart & Winston 1982 368p il o.p.

LC 81-13221

"An artificially created superwoman, courier for a secret organization, has to fend for herself when the decline of the West reaches its climax; she ultimately finds a new raison d'être on the extraterrestrial frontier. Welcomed by Heinlein fans as action-adventure respite from his more introspective works." Anatomy of Wonder 4

Job: a comedy of justice. Ballantine Bks. 1984 376p o.p.

LC 84-3091

"A Del Rey book"

"Alexander Hergensheimer, a minister from an alternate-world America dominated by Bible Belt fundamentalism, is flipped from one alternate world to another in rapid succession, whereby his faith, his endurance, and his love for his Margrethe are supremely tested. There are occasional patches of discursive philosophical, religious, and ethical ramblings here, which will be familiar territory to most of Heinlein's readers. For the most part, however, this tightly written, provocative, and powerful book, with its large cast of intriguing characters and an irresistibly compelling love story, is eminently readable." Booklist

The moon is a harsh mistress. Putnam 1966 383p o.p.

*

"Colonists of the Moon declare independence from Earth, and contrive to win the ensuing battle with the aid of a sentient computer. Action-adventure with some exploration of new possibilities in social organization and fierce assertion of the motto 'There Ain't No Such Thing as a Free Lunch.'" Anatomy of Wonder 4

The puppet masters. Doubleday 1951 219p

ISBN 0-451-07339-8

"Heinlein's paranoia-laden tale of sluglike creatures, arrived in saucer-shaped craft to enslave humans by the particularly gruesome procedure of growing into each person's nervous system from a position on the upper back of the victim—making his or her profile humpbacked." Anatomy of Wonder. 3d edition

Starship troopers. Ace trade pbk. ed. Ace Books 2006 279p pa $15

ISBN 0-441-01410-0; 978-0-441-01410-1

LC 2006-40451

First published 1959 by Putnam

"Story about mobile infantrymen in an interplanetary war of thousands of years in the future. The tale is woven around the individual soldier's problems of courage, discipline, and loyalty, which presumably would be the same then as they are now and always have been." Springfield Repub

"Originally intended as a juvenile, although not published as such, this violent novel of interstellar 'war' won a 1960 Hugo but also gained RAH the reputation of being a militarist, even a 'fascist.'" Sci Fic Ency

Stranger in a strange land. Putnam 1961 408p pa $16.95 hardcover o.p.

ISBN 0-441-78838-6 (pa)

*

"The hero is a human born of space travelers from earth and raised by Martians. He is brought to the totalitarian post-World War III world that is in many ways depicted as a satire of the U.S. in the 1960s, marked by repressiveness in sexual morality and religion. The plot, which tells how the heroic stranger creates a Utopian society in which people preserve their individuality but share a brotherhood of community, made Heinlein and his novel cult objects for young people dedicated to a counterculture." Oxford Companion to Am Lit. 5th edition

Helgason, Hallgrímur *See* Hallgrímur Helgason, 1959-

Hellenga, Robert, 1941-

The Italian lover; a novel. Little, Brown 2007 343p $23.99

ISBN 978-0-316-11763-0; 0-316-11763-3

LC 2007-8716

"Hellenga reprises protagonist Margot Harrington from The Sixteen Pleasures (1995). . . . In the fall of 1990, book restorer and longtime American expat Margot is 53, living in her adopted Florence and awaiting the arrival of a film producer who wants to adapt her 1975 memoir for film. At the same time, Margot meets and falls in love with Alan 'Woody' Woodhull, an Illinois-bred guitarist who gigs at the Bebop Club and also teaches literature at the American Academy. Meanwhile, producer Esther Klein desperately wants to make the film The Italian Lover, her first solo production since her husband/production partner left her." Publ Wkly

"Hellenga smoothly merges past and present while injecting Margot's story with fresh talent. . . . This being Italy, there are affairs, fiery outbursts and lots of rich food. This being Hellenga, the story is just as rich." N Y Times Book Rev

Philosophy made simple; a novel. Little, Brown 2006 277p $23.95

ISBN 0-316-05826-2

LC 2005-10883

Featuring characters first introduced in The sixteen pleasures (1994), "Hellenga shifts perspective from father to daughter, detailing the former's postmarital adventures as he plans the latter's wedding. It's been seven years since the death of Rudy Harrington's beloved wife, Helen; his three daughters have flown the coop; and the time is ripe to sell his Chicago home of 30 years and buy an avocado grove in Texas. He's also been reading the college-level text Philosophy Made Simple by Siva Singh, his daughter Molly's fiancé's uncle, sparking a previously latent interest in life's big questions." Publ Wkly

"Hellenga possesses an exceptionally magnetic voice, enabling him to draw readers in with charm, then hand them profundity. Alone in his new digs, Rudy feels adrift in a strange and confounding world. A Christian radio station declares the Second Coming. An elephant named Norma Jean paints beautiful, brilliantly hued abstract compositions. . . . Supremely wily and compelling, Hellenga turns a human tale of reason versus feeling into a cosmic playoff between order and chaos." Booklist

Heller, Jane

Best enemies. St. Martin's Press 2004 341p $24.95

ISBN 0-312-28849-2

LC 2003-61063

"Amy Sherman and Tara Messer, lifelong best friends, are now all grown up and living in New York City. There has always been some friction in their relationship because Amy feels overshadowed by the extravagantly beautiful and elegant Tara (a lifestyle guru). When Amy catches her fiance, Stuart, in a passionate embrace with Tara two weeks before the wedding, she cuts both of them out of her life. The two eventually marry each other, while Amy focuses on her demanding job as publicity

director for a major publisher. Four years later, Amy and Tara are thrown together when Amy is assigned to promote Tara's new book. The two women weave a web of deception, with Tara pretending her life is perfect (even though Stuart is a serial womanizer) while Amy invents a rich, handsome boyfriend, whom she then has to produce." Booklist

Heller, Joseph

Catch-22; a novel. Simon & Schuster 1999 415p $26

ISBN 0-684-86513-0

* LC 00-265132

"A comic, satirical, surreal, and apocalyptic novel . . . which describes the ordeals and exploits of a group of American airmen based on a small Mediterranean island during the Italian campaign of the Second World War, and in particular the reactions of Captain Yossarian, the protagonist." Oxford Companion to Engl Lit. 6th edition

Followed by Closing time

Closing time; a novel. Simon & Schuster 1994 464p

ISBN 0-671-74604-9

LC 94-20604

"Just like the original *Catch-22*, this sequel opens with Yossarian in a hospital bed, flirting with the nurses. Now in his seventies, Yossarian is depressed by his perfect health: things can only get worse. He lives alone in a Manhattan apartment not far from most of his old war buddies, including Milo Minderbinder, a defense contractor straight out of *Dr. Strangelove*. Yossarian and company mourn the decline of New York City and American culture in general and look back longingly to the golden age of prewar Coney Island." Libr J

"Heller is richly paranoid about state paranoia, and his winning jokes are more vicious than anything even in Catch-22 itself. Besides which, although Closing Time is too often like an electricity grid in danger of fusing, there are many exchanges that display all the old verve." New Statesman Soc

Good as Gold. Simon & Schuster 1979 447p

ISBN 0-671-22923-0

LC 78-23894

"Dr. Bruce Gold, forty-eight-year-old professor (Jewish) of literature (English) and author of many seminal articles in small journals (unread), finds himself facing the prospect of becoming a high Washington official. The offer comes from Ralph Newsome (Protestant), a presidential aide. . . . [Gold accepts] and soon meets Andrea Conover, the tall, beautiful, gifted daughter (also Protestant) of a wealthy, retired career diplomat (anti-Semite), clearly the suitable mate for a man with a potential of becoming the country's (very first Jewish) Secretary of State." Publisher's note

Portrait of an artist, as an old man. Simon & Schuster 2000 233p $23

ISBN 0-7432-0200-7

LC 00-711802

"Eugene Pota, the hero, is an aging novelist whose imaginative powers have been in steady decline since his earlier, more successful works. The book is a record of Pota's attempts to cap off his career with another triumph, and consequently a collection of false starts: here a parody of 'The Metamorphosis,' there a Greek-myth burlesque set among lickerish gods. While these set pieces are almost uniformly unsatisfying (only a fantasia

Heller, Joseph—*Continued*

that anatomizes the melancholy of nineteenth-century authors really works), there is something bleakly bracing in Pota's obsession with his own literary desiccation." New Yorker

Something happened. Knopf 1974 569p
ISBN 0-394-46568-7

The protagonist of this novel "Bob Slocum, works for a large, nameless company that sells something. What, we never learn. Slocum has a wife without a name, a disgruntled 15-year-old daughter and adorable 9-year-old son, both also unnamed, and a retarded child, Derek, who has a name and nothing else. Slocum lives in terror at his office, where 'there are six people who are afraid of me, and one small secretary who is afraid of all of us. I have one other person working for me who is not afraid of anyone, not even me, and I would fire him quickly, but I'm afraid of him.' Slocum carries his anxieties home. . . . 'Only one member of the family is not afraid of any of the others, and that one is an idiot.' Between these dry equations Slocum circles and recircles the question of what went wrong with his life." Newsweek

Heller, Zoe

The believers; a novel. HarperCollins 2009 335p $25.99
ISBN 978-0-06-143020-6; 0-06-143020-X
LC 2008-24633

The "story of a severely dysfunctional New York family struggling to find its place in a quickly changing world. Joel Litvinoff, a famous civil rights lawyer, and his acerbic wife, Audrey, have spent their many years together as political protesters, raising their children with the same radical social consciousness. But when Joel suffers a stroke, the family, never a peaceful unit to begin with, loses what little cohesion it had. Eldest daughter Rosa, who had always mirrored her parents' views, decides to embrace Orthodox Judaism. Her meek and unattractive sister, Karla, a social worker married to a critical, arrogant union man, has an affair. Adopted son Lenny, an addict and ne'er-do-well, decides to sober up and get a job. Audrey remains in contention with all of them, angry that Rosa would stoop to religion, remorselessly picking on Karla's weight, and denigrating Lenny's efforts to remake his life apart from her." Libr J

Heller is an "extraordinarily entertaining writer, and this novel showcases her copious gifts, including a scathing, Waugh-like wit; an unerring ear for the absurdities of contemporary speech; and a native-born Brit's radar for class and status distinctions." N Y Times (Late N Y Ed)

What was she thinking?; notes on a scandal. Holt & Co. 2003 258p $23
ISBN 0-8050-7333-7
LC 2002-38809

"Barbara Covett, a sixtyish history teacher, is the kind of unmarried-woman-with-cat whose female friends sooner or later decide she is 'too intense.' Thus when a beautiful new pottery teacher, Sheba Hart. . .chooses Barbara as a confidante, she is deeply, even rather sinisterly, gratified. Sheba's secret is explosive: married with two kids, she is having an affair with a fifteen-year-old student.

. . .Equally adroit at satire and at psychological suspense, Heller charts the course of a predatory friendship and demonstrates the lengths to which some people go for human company." New Yorker

Helprin, Mark

Ellis Island
In Helprin, M. Ellis Island & other stories p128-96

Ellis Island & other stories. Delacorte Press 1981 196p o.p.
LC 80-18437

Contents: The Schreuderspitze; Letters from the Samantha; Martin Bayer; North light; A Vermont tale; White gardens; Palais de Justice; A room of frail dancers; La Volpaia; Ellis Island

This book "consists of a novella (the title story) and ten short stories whose variation in length, content, style, and theme attest to the remarkable versatility of the writer. . . . Written in the first person, 'Ellis Island' is a four-part story—the recollections of an enterprising Jewish immigrant who finds himself temporarily stranded on that famous stepping stone to the New World. His vulnerability to the arbitrary decisions of immigration functionaries, his efforts to keep from being deported, and his attempts to earn a living are adventures told with a whimsical humor by a raconteur with a zest for life." Best Sellers

The Pacific and other stories. Penguin Press 2004 366p $25.95
ISBN 1-594-20036-X
LC 2004-50505

Contents: Il colore ritrovato; Reconstruction; Monday; A billiant idea and his own; Vandevere's house; Prelude; Perfection; Sidney Balbion; Mar nueva; Rain; Passchendaele; Jacob Bayer and the telephone; Sail shining in white; Charlotte of the Utrechtseweg; Last tea with the armorers; The Pacific

This collection is "rich in big, life-shaping notions (love, honor, duty, regret) filtered through the language of longing and nostalgia in such a way that the world takes on a kind of fairy-tale luster." Washington Post

A soldier of the great war. Harcourt Brace Jovanovich 1991 792p $32
ISBN 0-15-183600-0
LC 90-45987

"In summer 1964, a distinguished-looking gentleman in his seventies dismounts on principle from a streetcar that was to carry him from Rome to a distant village, instead accompanying on foot a boy denied a fare. As they walk, he tells the boy the story of his life. A young aesthete from a privileged Roman family, Alessandro Giuliani found his charmed existence shattered by the coming of World War I. The war led to an onerous tour of duty, inadvertent desertion, near-execution, forced labor, service high in the Italian Alps that took advantage of his . . . skill at mountain climbing, capture by the enemy, and return home, dispossessed of most of his friends and family. Along the way, he gains, loses, and eventually rediscovers love." Libr J

"Helprin's big, rumbustious new novel is about four-fifths of a marvel. Helprin has simplified his language, though he still works up a good head of rhetorical steam, and he has moderated his enthusiasm for phantasmagoric set pieces. He has also picked themes—war and loss,

Helprin, Mark—*Continued*

youth and age—that suit a large, elaborate style. . . . For a very large chunk of the novel's center, Helprin writes with riotous energy and sustained brilliance." Time

Winter's tale. Harcourt Brace Jovanovich 1983 673p $35

ISBN 0-15-197203-6

* LC 83-273

This novel "opens in the years just preceding World War I. Peter Lake, a burglar and mechanic with unparalleled skills, attempts to rob the mansion of the wealthy Isaac Penn—and falls in love with Beverly, Isaac's beautiful but sickly daughter. They marry. She dies. He departs on an involuntary journey through time. One hundred years later, he reappears, and with the help of younger Penns and various hangers-on leads the city of New York through the horrible waning hours of the 20th century, into the justice of the third millenium." Christ Sci Monit

The author "describes the impossible with microscopic precision, and he summons the moods and myriad landscapes of the city with breathtaking poetry. . . . Again and again Helprin celebrates selfless love, a devotion to beauty, the desire to explore, and an acceptance of responsibility. . . . Helprin's freewheeling use of fantasy at times eclipses his essential seriousness, diminishing the novel as a whole. Yet there is unquestionable genius in the book's marvelous individual pieces." Saturday Rev

Hemingway, Ernest, 1899-1961

Across the river and into the trees. Scribner Classics 1998 272p $26

ISBN 0-684-84464-8   LC 98-159867

"This is the story of a peace-time army colonel, closely resembling the author, who comes to Venice on leave to go duck shooting, to see the young Italian countess he loves, and to make a significant pilgrimage to the place where he, Richard Cantwell (and Nick Adams, Frederic Henry, and the author himself), was wounded in World War I. . . . The novel is Hemingway's weakest. It points up sharply the importance of that war injury in the author's life and work, but in some of its postures and mannerisms it seems to read like a parody of his better fiction." Herzberg. Reader's Ency of Am Lit

A farewell to arms. Scribner Classics 1997 297p $27.50

ISBN 0-684-83788-9

* LC 96-53356

A reissue of the title first published 1929

This novel "deals with a love-affair conducted against the background of the war in Italy. Its excellence lies in the delicacy with which it conveys a sense of the impermanence of the best human feelings; the unobstrusive force of its symbolism of mountain and plain; above all the vast scope of its vision of war—the retreat from Caporetto is one of the great war-sequences of literature." Penguin Companion to Am Lit

The garden of Eden. Scribner 1986 247p

ISBN 0-684-18693-4   LC 86-3701

A novel Hemingway "began in 1946 and worked on intermittently in the last 15 years of his life and left unfinished." N Y Times Book Rev

This novel is "based on Hemingway's honeymoon with Pauline in May 1927 at Le Grau-du-Roi, a . . . fishing village in the Camargue. David and Catherine Bourne at first lead an idyllic existence—tasting the pleasures of board, bottle, beach, and bed. . . . After the Bournes meet a beautiful . . . young woman, Marita, Catherine sleeps with her, urges Marita to sleep with David, and then become jealous of David's passion for the blank and passive girl. The love triangle brings out the deep-rooted tensions in the Bournes' marriage." Natl Rev

"Whatever its problems, this version of 'The Garden of Eden' deserves publication for what it says about writing and for the short story which Hemingway shows us David writing." Newsweek

The Hemingway reader; selected with a foreword and twelve brief prefaces by Charles Poore. Scribner 1953 xx, 652p o.p.

Partially analyzed in Short story index

This one volume selection includes two complete novels: The sun also rises and The torrents of spring; excerpts from A farewell to arms; Death in the afternoon; Green hills of Africa; To have and have not; For whom the bell tolls; Over the river and into the trees; The old man and the sea; and eleven short stories

The stories included are: In our time; A way you'll never be; Fifty grand; A clean well-lighted place; Light of the world; After the storm; The short happy life of Francis Macomber; Capital of the world; The snows of Kilimanjaro; Old man at the bridge; Fable of the good lion

In our time; stories. Scribner 156p pa $10

ISBN 0-684-82276-8

First published 1930

Contents: On the quai at Smyrna; Indian camp; The doctor and the doctor's wife; The end of something; The three-day blow; The battler; A very short story; Soldier's home; The revolutionist; Mr. and Mrs. Elliot; Cat in the rain; Out of season; Cross-country snow; My old man; Big two-hearted river

Several of these "stories" picture episodes in the life of a growing boy in the timber country of the Middle West

"Of 'stories' in the commonly accepted sense of the word there are few. . . . Most of the others are psychological episodes, incidents, sketches . . . call them what you will. They are soundly and movingly done." Lit Rev

Islands in the stream. Scribner 1970 466p o.p.

This posthumous novel is divided into three parts: Bimini, Cuba and At Sea. "'Bimini' is Thomas Hudson in the 1930s entertaining the three sons of his two wrecked marriages; they fish; their love leaves him open to his loneliness, and then the death of two of them leaves him nothing but lonely. 'Cuba' is Thomas Hudson clandestinely war efforting in about 1942; his other son (the eldest) has been killed as a pilot; Thomas Hudson drinks; he meets his first wife who is all he has ever wanted. 'At Sea' is Thomas Hudson commanding the pursuit of some German U-boat survivors; the Germans die, and it may be that the wounded Thomas Hudson is about to too." N Y Rev Books

Men without women. Scribner 1927 232p o.p.

Contents: The undefeated; In another country; Hills like white elephants; The killers; Che ti dice la patria; Fifty grand; A simple enquiry; Ten Indians; A canary for one; An Alpine idyll; A pursuit race; Today is Friday; Banal story; Now I lay me

Hemingway, Ernest, 1899-1961—*Continued*

The Nick Adams stories. Scribner 268p pa $12
ISBN 0-684-16940-1
First published 1972
Contents: Three shots; Indian camp; The doctor and the doctor's wife; Ten Indians; The Indians moved away; The light of the world; The battler; The killers; The last good country; Crossing the Mississippi; Night before landing; Now I lay me; A way you'll never be; In another country; Big two-hearted river; The end of something; The three-day blow; Summer people; Wedding day; On writing; An Alpine idyll; Cross-country snow; Fathers and sons

Arranged chronologically, this collection of 24 tales contains all the semi-autobiographical Nick Adams stories

"The volume presents Nick as a child in the northern woods, as adolescent, as soldier, veteran, writer, husband and parent. The last Nick Adams story appeared in 1933, and what surprises here, in these . . . {stories} of varying length, quality and intent, is their freshness and immediacy." Publ Wkly

The old man and the sea; illustrations by C.F. Tunnicliffe and Raymond Sheppard. Scribner Classics 1996 93p il $20
ISBN 0-684-83049-3
  * LC 96-11419
A reissue of the title first published 1952
"The old fisherman Santiago had only one friend in the village, the boy Manolin. Everyone else thought he was unlucky because he had caught no fish in a long time. At noon on the 85th day of fishing, he hooked a large fish. He fought with the huge swordfish for three days and nights before he could harpoon it, but the battle came to nought when sharks destroyed the fish before Santiago could get back to the village." Shapiro. Fic for Youth. 3d edition

The short stories. Scribner Classics 1997 457p $30
ISBN 0-684-83786-2
  * LC 96-53349
Originally published 1938 in collection with the play The fifth column
Contents: The short happy life of Francis Macomber; The capital of the world; The snows of Kilimanjaro; Old man at the bridge; Up in Michigan; On the quai at Smyrna; Indian camp; The doctor and the doctor's wife; The end of something; The three-day blow; The battler; A very short story; Soldier's home; The revolutionist; Mr and Mrs Elliot; Cat in the rain; Out of season; Cross-country snow; My old man; Big two-hearted river; The undefeated; In another country; Hills like white elephants; The killers; Che ti dice la patria; Fifty grand; A simple enquiry; Ten Indians; A canary for one; An Alpine idyll; A pursuit race; Today is Friday; Banal story; Now I lay me; After the storm; A clean, well-lighted place; The light of the world; God rest you merry, gentlemen; The sea change; A way you'll never be; The mother of a queen; One reader writes; Homage to Switzerland; A day's wait; A natural history of the dead; Wine of Wyoming; The gambler, the nun, and the radio; Fathers and sons

The snows of Kilimanjaro and other stories. Scribner Classics 1995 143p $25
ISBN 0-684-86221-2
  LC 95-4764

A reissue of the title first published 1961
Contents: The snows of Kilimanjaro; A clean, well-lighted place; A day's wait; The gambler, the nun, and the radio; Fathers and sons; In another country; The killers; A way you'll never be; Fifty grand; The short happy life of Francis Macomber

The sun also rises. Scribner Classics 1996 222p $25
ISBN 0-684-83051-5
  * LC 96-11420
A reissue of the title first published 1926
"Set in the 1920s, the novel deals with a group of aimless expatriates in France and Spain. They are members of the cynical and disillusioned post-World War I Lost Generation, many of whom suffer psychological and physical wounds as a result of the war. Two of the novel's main characters, Lady Brett Ashley and Jake Barnes, typify this generation. Lady Brett drifts through a series of affairs despite her love for Jake, who has been rendered impotent by a war wound. Friendship, stoicism, and natural grace under pressure are offered as the values that matter in an otherwise amoral and often senseless world." Merriam-Webster's Ency of Lit

also in Hemingway, E. The Hemingway reader p89-289

To have and have not. Scribner Classics 1999 174p $25
ISBN 0-684-85923-8
  LC 00-266244
A reissue of the title first published 1937
This novel "deals with the effort of Harry Morgan, a native of Key West, to earn a living for himself and his family. He has operated a boat for rental to fishing parties, but, during the Depression of the 1930s, he is forced to turn to the smuggling of Chinese immigrants and illegal liquor. While assisting a gang of bank robbers to escape, he is shot and mortally wounded. He dies gasping, 'One man alone ain't got . . . no chance.'" Reader's Ency. 4th edition

The torrents of spring; a romantic novel in honor of the passing of a great race. Scribner 1926 143p o.p.
"A burlesque of 'Sherwood Anderson' and the 'Chicago school' of authors, this comic novel tells of Yogi Johnson and Scripps O'Neil, workers in a pump factory in Petosky, Mich.; of Scripp's amours with two waitresses in Brown's Beanery, and of Yogi's adventures with the Indians." Herzberg. Reader's Ency of Am Lit

also in Hemingway, E. The Hemingway reader p25-86

True at first light; edited with an introduction by Patrick Hemingway. Scribner 1999 319p $26
ISBN 0-684-84921-6
  LC 98-55510
This is a "'fictional memoir' of the first phase of the 54-year-old Hemingway's final visit to East Africa in 1953-54. . . . His second son, Patrick, has extrapolated it from the untitled first draft of a manuscript." Natl Rev
"The tension of lion and leopard executions is superbly conveyed, as are the joking and teasing among the men and that peculiar, depersonalized alertness that comes with total concentration on the surrounding environment." Atl Mon

Hemmings, Kaui Hart

The descendants; a novel. Random House 2007
283p $24.95

ISBN 978-1-4000-6633-9; 1-4000-6633-6

LC 2006-51098

The narrator this novel, "the scion of the last Hawaiian
landowning clan, has floated through his privileged life:
marriage to a model given to 'speedboats, motorcycles,
alcoholism'; children getting into trouble (cocaine, bullying) at élite schools; membership at a century-old beach
club that rejects those with 'unfavorable pedigrees.' But
when a catamaran accident leaves his wife in a coma he
must wake from his own 'prolonged unconsciousness,'
reacquaint himself with his neglected daughters, and
track down his wife's lover. Meanwhile, his cousins are
urging him to sell the family's vast landholdings for development—to relinquish, in his eyes, the final vestige of
their native Hawaiian ancestry. Hemmings channels the
voice of her befuddled middle-aged hero with virtuosity,
as he teeters between acerbic and sentimental, scoffing at
himself even as he grasps for redemption." New Yorker

Hemon, Aleksandar, 1964-

The Lazarus project; a novel; with photographs
by Velibor Bozovic and from the Chicago Historical Society. Riverhead Books 2008 304p il $24.95

ISBN 978-1-59448-988-4; 1-59448-988-2

LC 2008-6834

This novel "hangs upon two linked narratives — the
death of Lazarus Averbuch, a turn-of-the-century Jewish
immigrant to Chicago who is killed in a wash of bullets,
and a contemporary Bosnian immigrant to Chicago who
sets out to write Averbuch's tragic story. Together, the
two narratives paint a portrait of a world that is as funny
as it is terrible, characterized by violence and commerce,
populated almost entirely by haves and have-nots, the
quick and the dead. And the dead is the subject here.
You can push and bully and probe history, but dead is
dead. Nobody can bring back life. Not even one of our
most talented writers." Esquire

Love and obstacles; stories. Riverhead Books
2009 209p $25.95

ISBN 978-1-59448-864-1; 1-59448-864-9

LC 2008-50340

Contents: Stairway to heaven; Everything; The conductor; Good living; Szmura's room; The bees, part 1;
American commando; The noble truths of suffering

"The unnamed narrator who appears in each of these
eight stories is clearly another version of Hemon, and
readers of his earlier books will recognize his progress
from feckless Bosnian teenager to bewildered new immigrant to tentative celebrity writer. . . . Hemon shows us
the nobility and the absurdity of immigrant life, the cruelty and the openness of American character. He knows
both because he is both; and if this in-betweenness
makes Hemon a 'nowhere man,' his excellent work also
suggests that in between may be the best place for a
writer to live." Slate

Nowhere man; the Pronek fantasies. Doubleday
2002 242p $23.95

ISBN 0-385-49924-8

LC 2002-66208

This novel follows Joseph Pronek "from a peaceable
childhood in Sarajevo through a strange respite in Kiev
in 1991 to a series of often hilarious low-paid jobs in
Chicago, including an improbable but edifying stint as a
Greenpeace canvasser." NY Times Book Rev

"Pronek's constantly reconfiguring life makes the novel
a wild, twisty read, and Hemon's inimitable voice and
the wry urgency of his storytelling should cement his
reputation as a talented young writer." Publ Wkly

Hempel, Amy

The collected stories of Amy Hempel; with an
introduction by Rick Moody. Scribner 2006 409p
$27.50

ISBN 0-7432-8946-3

LC 2005-57608

Contents: In a tub; Tonight is a favor to Holly; Celia
is back; Nashville gone to ashes; San Francisco; In the
cemetery where Al Jolson is buried; Beg, sl tog, inc,
cont, rep; Going; Pool night; Three popes walk into a
bar; The man in Bogota; When it's human instead of
when it's dog; Why I'm here; Breathing Jesus; Today
will be a quiet day; Daylight come; The harvest; The
most girl part of you; Rapture of the deep; Du Jour;
Murder; The day I had everything; To those of you who
missed your connecting flights out of O'Hare; And lead
us not into Penn Station; In the animal shelter; At the
gates of the animal kingdom; The lady will have the
Slug Louie; Under no moon; The center; Tom-Rock
through the eels; The rest of God; Weekend; Church can-
cels cow; The children's party; Sportsman; Housewife;
The annex; The new lodger; Tumble home; Notes; Beach
town; Jesus is waiting; The uninvited; Reference
#3884758485; What were the white things?; The dog of
the marriage; The afterlife; Memoir; Offertory

"You could call Hempel part of a movement in the trajectory of the American short story, and Rick Moody, in
his intelligent introduction, places her alongside Alice
Munro, Grace Paley, Ann Beattie and others—women
writers who rise above what he sees as the 'rage' and
posturing of their male counterparts. But in the end such
comparisons don't matter. Amy Hempel is herself. You
read her stories and wonder, Why are they so wonderful?
The answer comes to you at the very end of this volume,
in a line toward the close of 'Offertory.' 'Because a human being made this.' That's all you need to know." N
Y Times Book Rev

Henderson, William Haywood

Augusta Locke. Viking 2006 419p $24.95

ISBN 0-670-03491-6

LC 2005-53165

"The hero of this century-spanning epic is a tough,
restless woman, Augusta 'Gussie' Locke. Born in 1903
in rural Minnesota to the beautiful Leota and the coarse,
handsome trapper Brud Tornig, Gussie proves a disappointing curiosity to her parents: homely, solitary and
given to running away. When Gussie catches her father
with another woman, she and Leota flee the state, landing in Greeley, Colo., where Leota marries the wealthy
Mr. Locke. On her first day as a Locke, the teenage
Gussie once again runs off, escaping civilized life to the
mountains of Wyoming. There, she finds work with the
oil and mineral crews in the Great Divide Basin and
cares for her daughter, Anne, conceived on the run from
Greeley. Anne's own trajectory echoes Gussie's, and be-

Henderson, William Haywood—*Continued*

fore long Gussie must face her mother's fate: abandoned by her only child." Publ Wkly

"As we move through Gussie's life, starting at the beginning of the 20th century, the landscape of the American west comes across as a living thing. Meanwhile, the characters who pass through her life are well-drawn, memorable, and not at all simple, whether minor players or major figures." Philadelphia Inquirer

Hendrie, Laura, 1954-

Remember me; a novel. Holt & Co. 1999 373p $24

ISBN 0-8050-6218-1   LC 99-13302

"Rose Devonic is not much liked in the little town of Quedero, NM, famed for its fine embroidery. . . . Rose's little brother and her uncle, regarded as a crazy dreamer/schemer, were killed along with her mother in an accident. Now Rose survives by embroidering for the tourist trade and living off-season for free in the Ten Tribes Motel, whose gruff but devoted proprietor, Birdie, taught her her stitches. But Birdie's sister Alice, who bought the motel for Birdie with the insurance money she got after her sister died in the same accident that felled Rose's family, wants to sell it. Birdie has a stroke, Alice is clearly developing Alzheimer's and Rose ends up caring for them both." Libr J

"Hendrie's beautifully crafted and gutsy novel is animated by an unusual and vivid cast and charged with sharp and knowing humor." Booklist

Henkin, Joshua

Matrimony. Pantheon Books 2007 291p $23.95
ISBN 978-0-375-42435-9; 0-375-42435-9

LC 2006-103202

"Julian Wainwright is the WASPy son of Yalie Richard Wainwright III and Constance Wainwright, a Wellesley graduate. He loves his parents and doesn't mind being rich, but he is ready to escape. So in 1986 he heads off to Graymont College, a small liberal arts college in Massachusetts, where he can pursue his writing and leave his heritage behind for awhile. During the course of the year, he meets the lovely Mia Mendelsohn while doing laundry. They are both smitten and begin a love affair that lasts 20 years." Libr J

The author "writes with a winningly anachronistic absence of showiness. There are no big themes or symbols in Matrimony. The idea of matrimony is not treated as a metaphor, nor is it burdened with the weight of heightened realism. This is just a lifelike, likable book populated by three-dimensional characters who make themselves very much at home on the page. This style becomes humorous, not to mention heretical, with academia as the story's backdrop." N Y Times (Late N Y Ed)

Henley, Patricia, 1947-

Hummingbird house; a novel. MacMurray & Beck 1999 326p $22
ISBN 1-87844-887-0   LC 98-31274

"For more than 20 years, over half her life, nurse-midwife Kate Banner and her oldest friend, Maggie Byrne, have been living and working in Central America. . . . In the early 1980s, after a devastating death and the end of a love affair, Kate decides to leave Nicaragua for Guatemala, the first step on the road home to Indiana. There, in the face of the increased violence, she finds comfort in the love she feels for eight-year-old Marta, whose brother is one of the many 'disappeared' children, and Father Dixie Ryan, a radicalized Catholic priest who came to Guatemala to help the people in their struggles to survive tragedy and make a better life for themselves." Booklist

"The prismatic trajectory of the tale may be deliberate, for the author's message is double-edged; that trying for a better world is necessary, demanding work, but no one can save herself through saving the world." Publ Wkly

In the river sweet. Pantheon Bks. 2002 291p
ISBN 0-375-42127-0   LC 2002-22018

"The heroine, Ruth Anne Bond, is a woman of 50, living in Indiana; Johnny, her husband of nearly 30 years, is the proprietor of an upscale restaurant. Everything seems picture perfect until devoutly Catholic Ruth Anne learns that their only daughter, Laurel, is a lesbian. While she adjusts to this revelation. . .her own secret past catches up with her: she is contacted by Tin, the illegitimate son she conceived with a blind Vietnamese boy when she was a teenager working in a convent in Saigon. . .(The author) balances long, stream-of-consciousness passages with short, potent sentences to wonderful effect, tilling the familiar ground of sexuality and spirituality with originality and grace." Publ Wkly

Hennissart, Martha

For works written by this author in collaboration with Mary J. Latsis see Lathen, Emma

Henry, April

Learning to fly. St. Martin's Minotaur 2002 308p $23.95
ISBN 0-312-29052-7   LC 2001-58549

"A gruesome freeway pileup (52 vehicles, 14 deaths) has unexpected benefits for a young woman whose hippie parents named her Free: a new identity plus a bag containing $750,000 in drug money. When a passenger in her car, killed in the carnage, is mistakenly identified as Free, suddenly our pregnant, unemployed heroine has a way out of her problems and the money to finance it. She becomes Lydia, and assembles a new life in what she believes is the safe obscurity of another woman's persona. But then two dangerous men start to track her." Publ Wkly

Henry, O., 1862-1910

The best short stories of O. Henry; selected and with an introduction by Bennett A. Cerf, and Van H. Cartmell. Modern Lib. 1994 c1945 340p $22.95
ISBN 0-679-60122-8
First Modern Library edition published 1945
Contents: The gift of the Magi; A cosmopolite in a café; Man about the town; The cop and the anthem; The love-philtre of Ikey Schoenstein; Mammon and the archer; Springtime à la carte; From the cabby's seat; An unfinished story; The romance of a busy broker; The furnished room; Roads of destiny; The enchanted profile; The passing of Black Eagle; A retrieved reformation; The Renaissance at Charleroi; Shoes; Ships; The hiding

Henry, O., 1862-1910—*Continued*

of Black Bill; The duplicity of Hargraves; The ransom of Red Chief; The marry month of May; The whirligig of life; A blackjack bargainer; A lickpenny lover; The defeat of the city; Squaring the circle; Transients in Arcadia; The trimmed lamp; The pendulum; Two Thanksgiving Day gentlemen; The making of a New Yorker; The lost blend; A Harlem tragedy; A midsummer knight's dream; The last leaf; The count and the wedding guest; A municipal report

O. Henry "is best known for his observations on the diverse lives of everyday New Yorkers, 'the four million' neglected by other writers. He had a fine gift of humor and was adept at the ingenious depiction of ironic circumstances, in plots frequently dependent upon coincidence." Oxford Companion to Am Lit. 6th edition

Cabbages and kings
  In Henry, O. The complete works of O. Henry p551-679

The complete works of O. Henry; foreword by Harry Hansen. Doubleday 1953 1692p $15.95
  ISBN 0-385-00961-5
                                                             *
An omnibus volume of 13 short story collections: The four million (1906); Heart of the West (1907); The gentle grafter (1908); Roads of destiny (1909); Cabbages and kings (1904); Whirligigs (1910); Options (1909); Sixes and sevens (1911); Rolling stones (1912); The voice of the city (1908); The trimmed lamp (1907); Strictly business (1910); Waifs and strays (1917)

The four million
  In Henry, O. The complete works of O. Henry p1-108

The gentle grafter
  In Henry, O. The complete works of O. Henry p267-354

Heart of the West
  In Henry, O. The complete works of O. Henry p109-266

Options
  In Henry, O. The complete works of O. Henry p680-810

Roads of destiny
  In Henry, O. The complete works of O. Henry p355-550

Rolling stones
  In Henry, O. The complete works of O. Henry p941-1060

Sixes and sevens
  In Henry, O. The complete works of O. Henry p811-940

Strictly business
  In Henry, O. The complete works of O. Henry p1484-1631

The trimmed lamp
  In Henry, O. The complete works of O. Henry p1365-1483

The voice of the city
  In Henry, O. The complete works of O. Henry p1253-1364

Waifs and strays
  In Henry, O. The complete works of O. Henry p1632-92

Whirligigs
  In Henry, O. The complete works of O. Henry p1094-1252

Henry, Sue, 1940-

Cold company; an Alaska mystery. Morrow 2002 294p
  ISBN 0-380-97882-2   LC 2001-44860
Jessie Arnold's "discovery of an old skeleton beneath her home sets her on the years-old trail of an infamous serial killer. When another woman disappears, Jessie's hunt becomes critical." Libr J
"One of the hallmarks of Henry's series is the beautiful and rugged Alaskan landscape, and she has never used it more effectively than she does here, as spring sets in motion new discoveries." Publ Wkly

Dead north; an Alaska mystery. Morrow 2001 280p
  ISBN 0-380-97881-4   LC 00-48077
"While driving a friend's Winnebago to Alaska from Idaho, musher Jess Arnold . . . picks up a hitchhiking teenager trying to escape from the abusive stepfather who just murdered his mother. Friends, police, and the murderer all follow." Libr J
This "story offers a tough mystery, compelling characters, vivid scenery, endearing dogs, and a breakneck pace." Booklist

Death takes passage; an Alex Jensen mystery. Avon Bks. 1997 292p
  ISBN 0-380-97469-X   LC 97-4002
"Alaska state trooper Alex Jensen and girlfriend Jessie Arnold cruise down the Inside Passage as part of the 100th anniversary of the Klondike Gold Rush. When robbery and death strike the ship, Alex must investigate." Libr J
"Henry refreshingly blends classic mystery devices (a missing passenger, double identities, and locked rooms) with frontier and nautical history and the great beauty of Alaskan glaciers, mountains, night skies, and wildlife. In addition, Henry's enjoyable, well-paced novel displays little gratuitous violence and contains an intriguing mix of real and fictional characters." Booklist

Death trap; an Alaska mystery. Morrow 2003 273p $23.95
  ISBN 0-380-97883-0   LC 2002-33734
"Sidelined from sled-dog racing this season because of a knee injury, musher Jessie Arnold agrees to help out a friend by working the Iditarod booth at the Alaska State Fair. The fun of the fair ends abruptly for Jessie when a man is found dead in a pond on the grounds, and her beloved lead dog, Tank mysteriously disappears from the booth. . . . Interesting developments in Jessie's personal life will please fans of this long-running series." Booklist

Henry, Sue, 1940—*Continued*

Murder on the Iditarod Trail. Atlantic Monthly Press 1991 278p o.p.   LC 90-20925

"After three 'accidental' deaths early in the running of the torturous Iditarod Trail (from Anchorage to Nome) dog sled race, Alaskan police and race officials step up efforts to prevent further mayhem. State trooper Alex Jensen, single, brooding, handsome, and adept with physical evidence, falls upon the puzzling events with relish, comparing lists, visiting checkpoints, searching sled cargoes, etc. Consulting with race participant Jessie Arnold, he learns some of the inside facts, experiences delaying blizzards, and becomes emotionally attached." Libr J

"Henry provides suspense and excitement in this paean to a great sporting event and to the powerful Alaskan landscape." Publ Wkly

Murder on the Yukon Quest; an Alaska mystery. Avon Twilight 1999 291p

ISBN 0-380-97764-8   LC 99-21641

"Jessie Arnold has run the world-famous Iditarod dogsled race but is a rookie in the demanding Yukon Quest, which begins in Canada's Yukon Territory and extends over 1,000 dangerous miles to the finish line in Fairbanks. But Jessie has plenty of spirit and a fit, well-trained dog team. All of that hardly prepares her, however, for what happens when one of her fellow racers is kidnapped, and Jessie must deliver the ransom, rescue the victim, and capture the bad guys." Booklist

Hensher, Philip

The Mulberry empire; or, The two virtuous journeys of the Amir Dost Mohammed Khan. Knopf 2002 486p

ISBN 0-375-41488-6

"In 1839, about 50,000 British troops entered Afghanistan to replace the amir with someone more palatable to the Empire. In this fictionalized account, we meet Burnes, a British explorer who ventures into the capital city of Kabul and befriends the soon-to-be-ousted Amir Dost Mohammed Khan." Libr J

"Hensher captures the mood of Western Victorian inquiry—mapping, botanizing, writing it all down—that seemed, in its bustle and energy, in its production of information, to underpin the whole imperial ideal. . . . The novel's plotting is smooth, its observations acute, and the minor and major characters are all beautifully drawn." N Y Times Book Rev

Herbert, Brian

Dune: House Atreides; [by] Brian Herbert and Kevin J. Anderson. Bantam Bks. 1999 604p

ISBN 0-553-11061-6   LC 99-17726

Set several decades before the first novel in the Dune series, this describes the origins, feuds and schemes that lay the foundation to the saga. "As Emperor Elrood's son plots a subtle regicide, young Leto Atreides leaves for a year's education on the mechanized world of Ix; a planetologist named Pardot Kynes seeks the secrets of Arrakis; and the eight-year-old slave Duncan Idaho is hunted by his cruel masters in a terrifying game from which he vows escape and vengeance." Publisher's note

"Though the plot here is intricate, even readers new to the saga will be able to follow it easily." Publ Wkly

Dune: House Corrino; [by] Brian Herbert and Kevin J. Anderson. Bantam Bks. 2001 496p

ISBN 0-553-11084-5   LC 2001-25777

"As Emperor Shaddam IV seeks to consolidate his power as Emperor of a Million Worlds through the monopoly of the spice trade, other forces array themselves in opposition to his increasingly tyrannical rule. . . . Though dependent on the previous books, this complex and compelling tale of dynastic intrigue and high drama adds a significant chapter to the classic Dune saga." Libr J

Dune: House Harkonnen; [by] Brian Herbert & Kevin J. Anderson. Bantam Bks. 2000 620p

ISBN 0-553-11072-1   LC 00-39804

In the second prequel "the young Duke Leto Atreides seeks to live up to his late father's expectations, [while] his rivals plot to bring about the downfall of House Atreides. Plots and counterplots involving the debauched Baron Vladimir Harkonnen, his Bene Gesserit enemies, and the treacherous schemers of the enigmatic Bene Tleilax escalate the tension among factions of a fragile galactic empire. Though power seems to reside in the hands of the emperor and his elite armies, the fate of many worlds hinges on the destiny of a single planet—the desert world known as Arrakis, or Dune." Libr J

Dune: The Butlerian jihad; [by] Brian Herbert and Kevin J. Anderson. TOR Bks. 2002 621p $27.95

ISBN 0-7653-0157-1   LC 2002-28581

"A Tom Doherty Associates book"

The authors "continue their prehistory of Frank Herbert's 'Dune' series with a new trilogy opener set in the distant past of Herbert's galactic saga. The authors reveal the origins of the Spacing Guild and the Bene Gesserit, as well as the root of the ancient feud between Houses Atreides and Harkonnen. This compelling saga of men and women struggling for their freedom is required reading for Dune fans." Libr J

Paul of Dune; [by] Brian Herbert and Kevin J. Anderson. Tor 2008 512p $27.95

ISBN 978-0-7653-1294-5; 0-7653-1294-8

       LC 2008-30213

"A Tom Doherty Associates Book"

"Paul Muad'Dib and his army of Fremen desert warriors have succeeded in their overthrow of the Emperor Shaddam IV, but holding onto a universe of fractious planets proves a challenge even for a man revered by his followers as a god. Set in the years following the late Frank Herbert's classic *Dune* and its sequel, *Dune Messiah*, . . . [this book] fills in the missing years of empire building and looks into the formative years of Paul's childhood as well as the histories of those closest to him. . . . A priority purchase for libraries of all sizes." Libr J

Herbert, Frank, 1920-1986

Chapterhouse: Dune. Putnam 1985 464p (Dune) o.p.   LC 84-17979

The sixth Dune novel "is set on the planet Chapterhouse, where the Bene Gesserits have installed their headquarters. They have fled from the slaughtering Honored Matres (a corrupt version of the Bene Gesserits), with plans to transform Chapterhouse into an-

Herbert, Frank, 1920-1986—_Continued_

other desert planet on which the valuable melange spice can be produced. The high point of the book is not the climactic raid on and capture of a group of Honored Matres, but rather a chapter in which a former Honored Matre undergoes the ritual spice agony to become a Bene Gesserit Reverend Mother." SLJ

Children of Dune. Berkley Pub. Corp. 1976 444p (Dune) o.p.

This third volume in the saga of Dune "centers on the development of twins Leto and Ghanima and their decision to assume the mantle of political and religious leadership spurned by their father. Herbert expands on many of the questions raised in earlier books, especially prescience and the evolution of mankind." Booklist

Followed by God Emperor of Dune

Dune. Ace Bks. 1999 c1965 517p il $27.95 ISBN 0-441-00590-X

First published 1965 by Chilton

"Herbert combines several classic elements: a Machiavellian world of political intrigue worthy of fourteenth-century Italy, a huge cast of characters, and a detailed picture of a culture. Duke Leto Atreides and his family are coerced into exchanging their rich lands for a barren planet, Dune, which produces a unique drug. Duke's son, Paul, becomes the leader of a group that leads the Fremen of Dune against the enemy. This is a science fiction story with sociological and ecological import." Shapiro. Fic for Youth. 3d edition

Dune messiah. Putnam 1969 220p (Dune) o.p.

In this second volume of the Dune series "the Bene Gesserit, a mystic sisterhood, plot to overthrow the god/emperor Paul Atreides, whom they created by special breeding but whom they cannot now control. Presented here via the narrative and quotes from journals and legends of the people of Dune, the imperial intrigue is engineered by such diverse characters as Bene Gesserit Mother Superior, a Tleilaxu face dancer, a 'ghola' re-creation of Paul's dead friend, and the Princess Consort. Paul's eventual victory because of his future-vision makes fascinating reading." SLJ

Followed by Children of Dune

God Emperor of Dune. Putnam 1981 441p (Dune) o.p.   LC 80-25149

In the fourth title of the Dune saga "Leto II, the God Emperor, combines melange, a spice drug, with religion in order to control his people. The scene is the planet now called Arrakis, since only a remnant of the desert, Dune, remains. It is 3,500 years after the events of 'Children of Dune,' which ended while Leto was young. After sacrificing his human body to melange in exchange for an estimated four-thousand year rule, Leto is still alive. Gradually the body of Shi-Hulud the Sandworm God is developing in him, while Leto the Emperor lives in the bosom of God, or so his followers believe. . . . His plan for the survival of humanity is the Golden Path, an enforced tranquility overriding man's desire for chaos, especially war." Best Sellers

Followed by Heretics of Dune

Heretics of Dune. Putnam 1984 480p (Dune) o.p.   LC 83-16040

"The fifth installment of the 'Dune Cycle' follows the lives of the two children on different planets: On Gammu, a young Duncan Idaho trains relentlessly for the moment that will awaken the memories of his former lives; on Rakis, the fremen-child Sheeana discovers her ability to command the fearsome sandworms of the desert—and becomes an object of worship." Libr J

Followed by Chapterhouse: Dune

Herbert, Rosemary

(ed) The Oxford book of American detective stories. See The Oxford book of American detective stories

Hériz, Enrique de, 1964-

Lies; translated from Spanish by John Cullen. Doubleday 2007 415p $26
ISBN 978-0-385-51794-2; 0-385-51794-7

Original Spanish edition, 2004

"After a boating accident in a Guatemalan backwater, Isabel, a Spanish anthropologist researching indigenous funeral rites, finds that one of the victims has been misidentified as her. She is strangely reluctant to return to her grieving children and husband in Barcelona, and her subterfuge turns out to be only the most recent instance of a family penchant for self-invention. De Hériz's chapters cut between Isabel's hallucinatory diary entries and her daughter's account of how she and her two brothers go about the business of mourning. The vivid, deadpan pacing recalls the films of Pedro Almodóvar." New Yorker

Herlihy, James Leo, 1927-1993

Midnight cowboy; [by] James L. Herlihy. Simon & Schuster 1965 253p o.p.

"The story of Joe Buck, a backward 27-year-old out of Albuquerque, who comes to New York to become a professional stud. In his fancy cowboy rig, Joe feels that he should be able to make his fortune. . . . He teams up with a handicapped pickpocket named Ratso Rizzo, who is just about as ineffectual a ponce as Joe is a hustler. . . . Living in an abandoned building with Ratso, he develops the strongest kinship with a human being since grandmother Sally Buck fell off a horse and died. He cares for Ratso when he is sick, steals for him, and tries to take him by bus to Florida, which he fancies as a land of greater opportunity. Eventually, Ratso breathes his last outside of Daytona—and once more Joe is left to face the world alone." N Y Times Book Rev

"An appalling story, told with great skill and important because Joe Buck is a characteristic product of the way we live and yet he cannot be adequately discussed outside of a novel." Saturday Rev

Hermans, Willem Frederik, 1921-

Beyond sleep; translated from the Dutch by Ina Rilke. Overlook Press 2007 c2006 311p $27.95
ISBN 978-1-58567-538-8; 1-58567-583-0
LC 2006-48743

Hermans, Willem Frederik, 1921-—*Continued*

Original Dutch edition, 1967; this translation first published 2006 in the United Kingdom

"Alfred Issendorf is a PhD candidate aiming to guarantee a cum laude degree by proving his mentor professor's pet theory about meteorite impacts in Norway's Finnmark region. Inadequately prepared, Alfred is disappointed by his professor's Norwegian contacts (this is mordant high-comic material), antipathetic to his companion field researchers except for the maudlin Arne, and maddeningly full of himself though he lacks all self-confidence. Stubborn, to boot, he badly bruises a leg in a fall due to his own inattention, and later he willfully takes off in the wrong direction and gets lost. He meets no tragic end, and when he finds one, he is minimally affected. He is also supremely unlovable, tolerable only because he's young and hence may outgrow his self-absorption. He's unpleasant, and so are the other characters. Finally, they're wryly funny, and in that lies the novel's brilliance." Booklist

Hernández, Felisberto, 1902-1964

Around the time of Clemente Colling
In Hernández, F. and Allen, E. Lands of memory

Lands of memory; translated by Ester Allen. New Directions 2002 190p $24.95
ISBN 0-8112-1483-4
* LC 2001-42589
Includes two novellas: Around the time of Clemente Colling and Lands of memory, and the following short stories: My first concert in Montevideo; Mistaken hands; The crocodile; The new house

The Lands of memory is an uncoventional fictional autobiography and Around the time of Clemente Colling is a bildungsroman about a one-eyed blind piano teacher and his pupil

"Hernandez revels in images that are simple and repetitive: arms, light and shadow, the houses of the wealthy and their odd contents. The stories acquire a luxurious sheen from the ease with which they navigate memories, taking pleasure in recounting them with no intention other than tracking the mind's twists and turns." Publ Wkly

Lands of memory [novelette]
In Hernández, F. and Allen, E. Lands of memory

Herron, Mick

Reconstruction. Soho Press 2008 352p $24.95
ISBN 978-1-56947-504-1; 1-56947-504-0
LC 2007-38618
"When young Jaime Segura slips into the South Oxford Nursery School and waves a gun at the teacher, cleaning lady, parent and two little boys he takes hostage, unpleasant things are bound to happen, and they do — but not until Herron has finished surprising us. First off, Jaime is no mad gunman but a fugitive on the run from British intelligence agents who would rather kill him than question him. But if Jaime's role is a bit ambiguous, so is that of certain of his hostages — not to mention all the men outside, armed to the teeth and about to storm the school. In Herrons book, there's no hiding under the desk." N Y Times Book Rev

Hersey, John, 1914-1993

A bell for Adano. Knopf 1944 269p o.p.
*

"The town bell of Adano is transformed into material for a cannon, and its loss symbolizes a moral loss to the very life of the people. When the town falls into the hands of the Americans and the Fascist forces are in retreat, Major Joppolo, a Brooklyn-born Italian, becomes a favorite of the townspeople because of the concern he has for them. Not only does he help Tina find her missing sweetheart, but he finds a replacement for the bell, retrieving it from a U.S. ship named after an Italian-American hero of World War I. To the town's dismay, Major Joppolo is relieved of his command by an American general whose unreasonable orders he ignores." Shapiro. Fic for Youth. 3d edition

Key West tales. Knopf 1994 227p
ISBN 0-679-42992-1
LC 93-11094
Contents: God's hint; Get up, sweet slug-a-bed; Did you ever have such sport?; The two lives of Consuela Castanon; They're signaling!; A game of anagrams; Cuba libre!; Fantasy fest; Just like you and me; Page two; Amends; Piped over the side; To end the American dream; The wedding dress; A little paperwork

"In this final collection of stories, Hersey focuses on his theme of ordinary people facing momentous events in their lives: death by AIDS, the death of a friend from AIDS, loss of innocence and virginity, meeting the son one had given up for adoption two decades before, or retirement from military service. As interludes, Hersey presents brief, italicized vignettes of the famous or powerful people who have lived in or visited Key West." Libr J

A single pebble. Knopf 1956 181p o.p.
"An American engineer's trip by junk up the Yangtze to locate a dam site, as he relates it years later in retrospect, symbolizes the contrast between the Western idea of progress and tempo of living and the passive resignation of China's ancient culture and traditions. With mounting tension, the story brings into focus the subtle relationship between the young engineer and the owner of the junk, his wife, and the head tracker, Old Pebble, in a drama heightened by the physical grandeur of the Great River." Booklist

The wall. Knopf 1950 632p pa $17.95 hardcover o.p.
ISBN 0-394-75696-7 (pa)
*

"This novel is presented as a journal kept by a diarist during World War II. It tells of life in the Warsaw Ghetto, depicting Jewish interdependence in a struggle for survival. The writer's observations enrich our understanding of Jewish culture. Although the diarist dies of pneumonia in 1944, his escape from the enclosure within which the Germans confined the Jews is a testament to hope and courage." Shapiro. Fic for Youth. 3d edition

Hershon, Joanna

The German bride; a novel. Ballantine Books 2008 304p $25
ISBN 978-0-345-46845-1; 0-345-46845-7
LC 2007-32842

Hershon, Joanna—*Continued*

"Eva Frank is a young Jewish girl living in 1860s Berlin who has an illicit affair, and the ensuing consequences are devastating. Driven by guilt over the affair, Eva feels compelled to marry and soon finds herself wedded to Abraham, a man whose dream is to move to the American Southwest. Living and adjusting to married life in America brings with it a multitude of problems, most of which are made worse by Abraham being what we now think of as a compulsive gambler and womanizer." Libr J

"Though sometimes stilted, the novel, with its colorful cast, setting and redemptive conclusion, eventually wins the reader over." Publ Wkly

Hervey, Evelyn *See* Keating, H. R. F. (Henry Reymond Fitzwalter), 1926-

Hess, Joan

Busy bodies. Dutton 1995 246p o.p.

LC 94-46120

"A Claire Malloy mystery"

In this Claire Malloy mystery, "painter Zeno Gorgias, who has recently moved to the small Arkansas town's historic neighborhood, is staging performance pieces, starring a nearly naked young woman with a rubber snake, on his front lawn. Not only are Claire's hyperbolic teenage daughter and her friend involved, but Claire's policeman lover has his hands full with crowd control. Zeno's estranged wife arrives and threatens to have him institutionalized for incompetence; she is found murdered, her body recovered from charred ashes of Zeno's house after it—and half a million dollars' worth of his paintings—are burned." Publ Wkly

A conventional corpse; a Claire Malloy mystery. St. Martin's Press 2000 275p

ISBN 0-312-24662-5   LC 00-29686

"Arkansas bookseller/sleuth Claire Malloy organizes a mystery convention at Farber College that goes awry. Five major writers and attendant quirks create problems, as does the appearance/disappearance of a hated mystery editor and the suspicious death of an attendee." Libr J

"Offering a teasingly intricate puzzle along with some zinging satire of current publishing trends, Hess has produced another first-rate mystery." Publ Wkly

Death by the light of the moon. St. Martin's Press 1992 227p o.p.

* LC 91-37884

"A Claire Malloy mystery"

"Bookstore owner/sleuth Claire Malloy . . . finds little but trouble when she and teenage daughter Caron attend the 80th birthday celebration of Miss Justicia, mother of Claire's late husband, at the family manor in the Louisiana bayous. Feuding relatives, mysterious hints about inheritances and terrible food begin a ghastly first night that will also include the drowning of the matriarch after she is seen careening drunkenly about the garden in her powered wheelchair." Publ Wkly

"Ms. Hess handles the complicated plot logistics with a deft touch, and although her overblown caricatures lack the affection she lavishes on the characters in her 'Maggody' series, she has a warm spot for teen-agers, whose insufferable ways elicit her funniest and kindest satirical swipes." N Y Times Book Rev

A holly, jolly murder. Dutton 1997 265p

ISBN 0-525-94240-8   LC 97-12895

"Small-town bookstore owner Claire Malloy lets curiosity get the best of her: she attends a Druid winter solstice festival. When the would-be celebrants discover their wealthy benefactor murdered, the Arch Druid (a feisty old lady) asks Claire's help." Libr J

Madness in Maggody. St. Martin's Press 1991 231p o.p.

LC 90-49306

"Chief of police Arly Hanks, lately of New York City, takes an offhand attitude toward crime or the lack of it in Maggody, Arkansas, until the tamales hit the fan during the grand opening of a supermarket that none of the other merchants in town wants to see succeed. Now Arly's got one death, and reams of rumors to unravel. Although the situation is loaded with humor and small-town high jinks, the solution to the murder shocks Arly so much she promises herself that in the future she will take her job more seriously." Booklist

Maggody and the moonbeams; an Arly Hanks mystery. Simon & Schuster 2001 254p

ISBN 0-7432-0229-5   LC 2001-20208

Police chief Arly Hanks, "to her extreme horror, gets railroaded by Mrs. Jim Bob Buchanon into acting as chaperone for a church youth group at Camp Pearly Gates in nearby Dunkicker. Unbeknownst to all, the camp is also the home of a weird commune, the Daughters of the Moon, which is made up of a group of women (known locally as 'Beamers') who sport shaved heads, magenta lipstick, and white robes. The typical Maggody madness and mayhem begins when one of the campers stumbles over the body of a Beamer whose head has been pulverized." Booklist

Mischief in Maggody; an Ozarks murder mystery. St. Martin's Press 1988 202p o.p.

LC 88-1867

"Maggody, a little Ozark town where nothing ever happens, has problems. Its first female police chief, Arly Hanks, . . . comes back from vacation to find the community in an uproar . . . local prostitute and moonshiner Robin Buchanon has disappeared, leaving behind five hungry children. . . . Arly manages to foist them onto Mrs. Jim Bob while she goes hunting for the mother, whom she finds with her head blown off in the middle of a marijuana patch. . . . Another death and the public humiliation of two of the town's most righteous citizens take place before peace comes to Maggody once again. Hess writes an engaging tale, although the raunchy characters impart a certain vulgarity to the text." Publ Wkly

Misery loves Maggody; an Arly Hanks mystery. Simon & Schuster 1999 285p $22

ISBN 0-684-84562-8   LC 98-28728

Maggody, Arkansas police chief Arly Hanks "investigates after out-of-town police arrest the mayor of Maggody in connection with the death of a riverboat showgirl." Libr J

Mummy dearest; a Claire Malloy mystery. St. Martin's Minotaur 2008 309p $24.95

ISBN 978-0-312-36360-4; 0-312-36360-5

LC 2007-51831

Hess, Joan—*Continued*

On a honeymoon trip to Luxor, Egypt, with her new husband, Lt. Peter Rosen, teenage daughter Caron, and Caron's best friend Inez, Arkansas bookseller Claire Malloy suddenly finds her honeymoon turned upside down when the two girls are chased through back alleys by unknown pursuers and a blonde college student is kidnapped by two young men on horseback.

"Humor, quirky characters, a rich mother-daughter relationship, and the fresh setting all add to this satisfying addition to Hess' long-running series." Booklist

Murder@maggody.com. Simon & Schuster 2000 253p

ISBN 0-684-84563-6   LC 99-46821

"It's a new headache for Arly Hanks, chief of police . . . when funding is provided for a community computer lab, and everyone in the sleepy backwoods Arkansas town of Maggody is standing on line to get on-line. Everyone is already in a stew provoked by the newest resident, the fetching Gwynnie, who, in the opinion of Maggody's women, caught the eye of too many of their men. When Gwynnie turns up murdered, a trace of her e-mails suggests someone in town could have done her in." Publisher's note

"Maggody's eccentric inhabitants and Hess's comic touch infuse this cozy with a refreshing dose of spunk, resulting in another triumph for both small-town America and Hess." Publ Wkly

Out on a limb; a Claire Malloy mystery. St. Martin's Minotaur 2002 306p

ISBN 0-312-26680-4   LC 2002-69939

"When a local developer tries to level a bunch of trees, a protester chains herself to one of them—while the developer's daughter apparently abandons her baby on bookseller-sleuth Claire Molloy's doorstep. By the time Claire tracks her down, the woman has been charged with murdering her father." Libr J

"The author deftly juggles the various plot strands, letting the local news reporter fill in the action in which Claire is uninvolved. The surprising denouement comes off with éclat." Publ Wkly

Hesse, Hermann, 1877-1962

Demian. Boni & Liveright 1923 215p o.p.

Original German edition, 1919

A novel "featuring young Emil Sinclair. Largely through the crude aggression of a school bully, Sinclair becomes troubled by the realization that life consists of conflicting, opposite forces. His confusion is both cleared and compounded by the appearance of a mysterious older boy named Max Demian. Both Demian and his mother become central influences in Sinclair's life, although their encounters are sporadic. In a letter, Demian tells Sinclair of the devil-god Abraxas, who is the embodiment of a fusion of all good and evil, of destruction and creation. When he is wounded in the war, Sinclair has a vision of Demian, in which his death is implied. From that time on, Sinclair feels himself to be the possessor of the wisdom and understanding he had attributed to Demian. The novel is one of Hesse's most poignant statements of the terrors and torments of adolescence." Reader's Ency. 4th edition

The fairy tales of Hermann Hesse; translated and with an introduction by Jack Zipes; woodcut illustrations by David Frampton. Bantam Bks. 1995 xxxi, 266p il pa $14.95 hardcover o.p.

ISBN 0-553-37776-0 (pa)   LC 94-49166

Contents: The dwarf; Shadow play; A man by the name of Ziegler; The city; Dr. Knoegle's end; The beautiful dream; The three linden trees; Augustus; The poet; Flute dream; A dream about the gods; Strange news from another planet; Faldum; A dream sequence; The forest dweller; The difficult path; If the war continues; The European; The empire; The painter; The fairy tale about the wicker chair; Iris

"Quirky and evocative, Hesse's fairy tales stand alone, but also amplify the ideas and utopian longings of such counterculture avatars as *Siddhartha* and *Steppenwolf.*" Publ Wkly

Gertrude; translated by Hilda Rosner. Rev. translation. Boni & Liveright 1969 237p o.p.

Original German edition, 1910; this translation first published in the United Kingdom

"The story has three major characters: Herr Kuhn, Herr Muoth, and Fräulein Gertrude Imthor, later Frau Muoth. Narrated by the aging Kuhn, the novel recounts his travails as a youth, his success as a composer, his frustrated love for Gertrude Imthor, and his strange friendship with Heinrich Muoth. . . . As a young man Kuhn had his leg crippled in an accident. The physical disability which prevents him from achieving happiness in life, especially with women, measurably accounts as well for his creativity." Saturday Rev

The glass bead game (Magister Ludi); translated from the German by Richard and Clara Winston; with a foreword by Theodore Ziolkowski. Holt, Rinehart & Winston 1969 558p o.p.

Original German edition, 1943; first published 1949 in the United States with title: Magister Ludi

This "novel follows the intellectual and spiritual odyssey of Josef Knecht, who lives in a utopian society in the 23rd century. The culture is dominated by a glass-bead game, practiced in its highest form (in which beads are not even used) by an intellectual elite. The game represents a balanced fusion of the active and contemplative disciplines; it is a combination of music and mathematics (art and science) but includes elements from virtually every cultural endeavor. Knecht becomes master of the game (Lat, *Magister Ludi*) but has doubts about the virtues of pure intellect. He renounces his order and departs to the outer world, where he eventually dies, the tragic result of a life dedicated entirely to the world of the spirit." Reader's Ency. 4th edition

Narcissus and Goldmund; translated by Ursule Molinaro. Farrar, Straus & Giroux 1968 315p o.p.

Original German edition, 1930; English translation published 1932 with title: Death and the lover; also 1959 in the United Kingdom, with title: Goldmund

"The setting is Germany in the late Middle Ages— dark forests, wandering scholars, sheltered monasteries, flourishing imperial cities, the plague. The problem is the conflict of the intellectual and the sensual, the scholar and the artist. The device is the biographical novel, half picaresque, half philosophical." Choice

"Hesse's prose, ranging from lyricism to allegory, and

Hesse, Hermann, 1877-1962—*Continued*

from unabashed sentimentality to an intellectuality of a high order, is not easily rendered into another language. . . . The present version . . . is close to perfection." Saturday Rev

Siddhartha; translated by Hilda Rosner. New Directions 1951 153p $16.95; pa $6.95

ISBN 0-8112-0292-5; 0-8112-0068-X (pa)

    *

Original German edition, 1923

"The young Indian Siddhartha endures many experiences in his search for the ultimate answer to the question, what is humankind's role on earth? He is also looking for the solution to loneliness and discontent, and he seeks that solution in the way of a wanderer, the company of a courtesan, and the high position of a successful businessman. His final relationship is with a humble but wise ferryman. This is an allegory that examines love, wealth, and freedom while the protagonist struggles toward self-knowledge." Shapiro. Fic for Youth. 3d edition

Steppenwolf; translated from the German by Basil Creighton. Holt & Co. 1929 309p pa $14 hardcover o.p.

ISBN 0-312-27867-5 (pa)

    *

Original German edition, 1927

"The hero, Harry Haller . . . is torn between his own frustrated artistic idealism and the inhuman nature of modern reality, which, in his eyes, is characterized entirely by philistinism and technology. It is his inability to be a part of the world and the resulting loneliness and desolation of his existence that cause him to think of himself as a 'Steppenwolf' (wolf of the Steppes). The novel, which is rich in surrealistic imagery throughout, ends in what is called the magic theater, a kind of allegorical sideshow. Here, Haller learns that in order to relate successfully to humanity and reality without sacrificing his ideals, he must overcome his own social and sexual inhibitions." Reader's Ency. 4th edition

Stories of five decades; edited and with an introduction by Theodore Ziolkowski; translated by Ralph Manheim. With two stories translated by Denver Lindley. Farrar, Straus & Giroux 1973 c1972 xx, 328p o.p.

Contents: The island dream; Incipit vita nova; To Frau Gertrud; November night; The marble works; The Latin scholar; The wolf; Walter Kompff; The field devil; Chagrin d'amour; A man by the name of Ziegler; The homecoming; The city; Robert Aghion; The cyclone; From the childhood of Saint Francis of Assisi; Inside and outside; Tragic; Dream journeys; Harry, the Steppenwolf; An evening with Dr. Faust; Edmund; The interrupted class

Hewson, David

The garden of evil. Delacorte Press 2008 470p $24

ISBN 978-0-385-33957-5; 0-385-33957-7

    LC 2007-45762

Roman detective Nic Costa and "his team are just starting to process a crime scene in an artist's shabby studio, where two corpses lie sprawled before a painting of a rapturous female nude redolent of Caravaggio, when they flush out a hooded gunman. The gunman escapes in the ensuing chase, but not before shooting dead Costa's wife of three months, former FBI agent Emily Deacon. While Costa is taken off the case, his rule-bending boss finds a way for him to help on the sly, assisting the unusual art expert—young Sister Agata Graziano—called in to investigate whether the canvas could really be a Caravaggio and what light it might shed on the murders." Publ Wkly

"A thought-provoking blend of art history and mystery, The Garden of Evil is . . . a treat for readers who like their entertainment literate." Richmond Times-Dispatch

Lucifer's shadow. Delacorte Press 2004 369p $21.95

ISBN 0-385-33794-9

"In 1733, a wealthy patron of the arts supplies a lovely and talented Jewish woman with a Guarneri violin and the venue for her debut as a concert soloist in a world hostile to both women and Jews. In modern Venice, a young scholar is manipulated into selling a stolen antique violin and pretending authorship of a brilliant concerto recently unearthed in his employer's basement. Both stories follow naive young men who fall in love with gifted and troubled women musicians, then become involved in tracking killers who leave behind only traces of their female victims. The pungent canals of beautiful Venice carry readers on a metaphorical journey, tracing the spread of evil through ghetto, church, concert hall, and even the mansions of the elite." Booklist

A season for the dead. Delacorte Press 2004 386p $21.95

ISBN 0-385-33722-1   LC 2003-62522

This mystery "introduces Nic Costa, a 27-year-old Rome Questura detective, Caravaggio aficionado, and son of a prominent Italian Communist. Initially on pickpocket detail around Saint Peter's, Costa and his partner become involved in an incident on Vatican turf that reveals the complex relationship between the sovereign Vatican state and surrounding Rome. By responding to a situation at the Vatican Library, the pair begins the hunt for a serial killer who uses his victims to create tableaux of famous martyr portraits." Libr J

"Outsized, eccentric characters, a complex story and an abundance of historical detail make this engrossing book more than just another cookie-cutter, religious-nut serial killer thriller." Publ Wkly

Heyer, Georgette, 1902-1974

Black sheep. Sourcebooks 2008 279p pa $13.95

ISBN 978-1-4022-1078-5; 1-4022-1078-7

    * LC 2007-50205

First published 1966 in the United Kingdom

"A lovely young spinster is both charmed and infuriated by the wealthy, unconventional black sheep uncle of the fortune hunter on whom her young niece has her heart set. This character-driven novel . . . is considered one of Heyer's best." Libr J

Frederica. Sourcebooks Casablanca 2008 437p pa $13.95

ISBN 978-1-4022-1476-9   LC 2008-43093

First published 1965 by Dutton

"A 37-year-old bachelor, wealthy, imperious, much the man-about-Regency-London, falls irresistibly for a pretty

Heyer, Georgette, 1902-1974—*Continued*

but not beautiful young woman who, at 24, considers herself put on the shelf and wants only to find a good husband for her younger sister. The girl's two impetuous young brothers and their large friendly dog add hilarious complications." Publ Wkly

The grand Sophy. Putnam 1950 307p o.p.

"On the Continent, where she had grown up and knew everyone in military, court, and diplomatic circles, Sophy was famous for her delightfully unexpected behavior, and for her irrepressible habit of managing less energetic people for their own good. When she returned to England, Regency London was also amused and startled by her antics, and her Rivenhall cousins, who offered her hospitality, were subjected to a reorganization of their lives. Sophy had learned the value of surprise attack from the Duke of Wellington, and applied it with shock tactics of her own to untangling the eldest Rivenhall cousins from unsuitable engagements, incidentally winning a husband for herself." Booklist

Penhallow. Doubleday, Doran 1943 309p o.p.

A "story about a family of terrorizing and oversexed males, embroiled with one or two victimized females, halfwits, illegitimate boot boys, and others. Very British, rural, and somewhat artificially 'tense.' . . . Here technique is equal to all improbabilities." Barzun. Cat of Crime. Rev and enl edition

Hiaasen, Carl, 1953-

Basket case. Knopf 2002 317p

ISBN 0-375-41107-0   LC 2001-38317

"In laying out the tale of Jack Tagger, a maladjusted, middle-aged Florida obituary writer who stumbles across a hot news story in the supposed scuba-diving death of Jimmy Stoma, former lead singer for a band called Jimmy and the Slut Puppies, Hiaasen skewers both corporate media operations and the world of pop stardom." N Y Times Book Rev

Lucky you; a novel. Knopf 1997 353p

ISBN 0-679-45444-6   LC 97-36885

"Sharing $28 million worth of lottery money with the holder of one other winning ticket wouldn't seem to be much of a burden to bear, but it is for Bodean Gazzer and his pal Chub, who crave all the cash to launch their own personal hate group, the White Clarion Aryans. The other winner, a black woman named JoLayne Lucks, plans to use her money to save a patch of Florida swamp, but that's before the Aryans assault her and steal the ticket. With the help of maverick journalist Tom Krome, JoLayne attempts to steal it back." Booklist

"Hiaasen writes witty dialogue that crackles, and his characters are eccentrically colorful." N Y Times Book Rev

Native tongue. Knopf 1991 325p

ISBN 0-394-58796-0

                           * LC 91-52713

This novel is set in the Florida keys. "There, just a few hundred miles south of Disney World, Francis X. Kingsbury, a k a Frankie King, a one time racketeer now enrolled in the Federal witness relocation program, has assembled a giant parcel of Florida real estate. . . . Kingsbury turns some of the property into an amusement park, the Amazing Kingdom of Thrills, and sets about

developing the rest into a turf of condominiums, villas and golf links. Trouble is, the ecologically minded grow enraged. . . . [They] set out to destroy Kingsbury and his developments." N Y Times Book Rev

"Hiaasen writes to a formula with brilliant success. His books are addictive. . . . One may miss the sour bite of bleaker comedy, found in the best crime stories of a more realistic kind, but for entertainment few can match him." London Rev Books

Nature girl. Alfred A. Knopf 2006 305p $25.95

ISBN 978-0-307-26299-8; 0-307-26299-5

                           LC 2006-49360

The author's "cast includes Boyd Shreave, a semicompetent telemarketer; Shreave's mistress and coworker, Eugenie Fonda; Honey Santana, a mercurial gadfly who ends up on the other end of one of Shreave's pitches for Florida real estate; and Sammy Tigertail, half Seminole, who at novel's start must figure out what to do with the body of a tourist who dies of a heart attack on Sammy's airboat after being struck by a harmless water snake. When Santana cooks up an elaborate scheme to punish Shreave for nasty comments he made during his solicitation call, she ends up involving her 12-year-old son, Fry, and her ex-husband in a frantic chase that enmeshes Tigertail and the young coed Sammy accidentally has taken hostage." Publ Wkly

"As usual, Hiaasen throws his colorful characters into an increasingly frenetic mix, and the fun lies in watching how, or if, they'll manage to extricate themselves. One reason Nature Girl works so well is the fact that much of the action is confined to a single island, allowing the characters to intermingle and weave in and out of view." San Francisco Chronicle

Sick puppy; a novel. Knopf 2000 341p

ISBN 0-679-45445-4   LC 99-33435

"Twilly Spree, an independently wealthy, psychologically unstable pseudo-ecologist, spends his time on a one-man crusade to preserve Florida's wildlife and natural beauty. When Twilly sees Palmer Stoat toss a Burger King wrapper from a car window, he vows to teach the litterbug a lesson. Twilly hits paydirt when he realizes that Palmer is a legislative lobbyist working for a land developer intent on building a mall, golf course, and condos on one of Florida's few undeveloped offshore islands. In a wild plot to get Palmer's attention, Twilly kidnaps Palmer's Labrador retriever but ends up with his wife as well." Libr J

"While there may be nothing laughable about unchecked environmental exploitation, Hiaasen has refined his knack for using this gloomy but persistent state of affairs as a prime mover for scams of all sorts. In *Sick Puppy*, he shows himself to be a comic writer at the peak of his powers." Publ Wkly

Skin tight. Putnam 1989 319p

ISBN 0-399-13489-1   LC 89-31580

"When Mick Stranahan, a retired investigator, is the attempted victim of murder, he becomes a little curious to find out who wants him dead. He trails the killer to a quack plastic surgeon who was a suspect in a murder case Stranahan investigated four years before. Someone is about to blab that the surgeon had a more than passing interest in the old case and Stranahan gets back in the harness to investigate." West Coast Rev Books

Hiaasen, Carl, 1953——*Continued*

Skinny dip; a novel. Alfred A. Knopf 2004 355p $24.95

ISBN 0-375-41108-9   LC 2004-44106

"Joey Perrone and her husband, Chaz, are taking a cruise to celebrate their wedding anniversary. One night, as the rain pours down, Chaz throws Joey overboard. He then proceeds to convince the authorities that he has no idea what happened to her. Unfortunately for him, Joey is rescued and begins to plot her ultimate revenge against her soon-to-be-patsy of a husband. The squirm-inducing mayhem that follows in this sometimes sidesplitting novel almost makes you feel sorry for Chaz. It has rarely been this much fun to read about the act of revenge. All of the trademark characters and Florida locales are used to maximum effect." Libr J

Stormy weather; a novel. Knopf 1995 335p

ISBN 0-679-41982-9   LC 95-78487

A Florida hurricane "puts on a collision course a demented cast of tourists, scam artists and eccentrics: New York ad exec Max Lamb, who decides to spice up his Orlando honeymoon by taking his bride and his camcorder into the teeth of the storm; Skink, the swamp-dwelling former Florida governor . . . who kidnaps Max in an effort to teach him to respect the land; Edie March, a seductive drifter who hatches a half-baked personal-injury scam with the help of Snapper, a sadistic ex-con; and Augustine, the altruistic son of a jailed drug smuggler, who juggles skulls to relax." Publ Wkly

"The crimes plotted are minor aspects of a fiction that explores the intersection of the grotesque and the human." Libr J

Strip tease; a novel. Knopf 1993 353p

ISBN 0-679-41981-0

     * LC 93-12358

"At the Eager Beaver, a topless bar in Fort Lauderdale, former FBI clerk Erin Grant dances nightly to pay for legal fees in her custody fight for her young daughter. There David Dilbeck, a poorly disguised, somewhat kinky and imbecilic U.S. Congressman owned by the state's sugar interests, is recognized by a sharp-eyed regular who, infatuated with Erin, initiates a blackmail plan meant to influence her court case. The resulting mayhem, occuring in an election year, involves machinations up to the highest state level." Publ Wkly

In among Hiaasen's "freaks and obsessives, his corrupters and corrupted, his brain-dead and his frenetically active, the author has dropped a real honest-to-God human being, an appealing young woman named Erin Grant. Her presence, her history and goals, make the cartoon nastiness around her less cartoony and more nasty than in previous Hiaasen novels." N Y Times Book Rev

Hickam, Homer H.

The keeper's son; a novel; [by] Homer Hickam. 1st ed. Thomas Dunne Books 2003 353p $24.95

ISBN 0-312-30189-8   LC 2003-54964

"This is the first novel of a planned series about rough and tumble Coast Guard Lt. Josh Thurlow and his unusual patrol boat crew during WWII. Josh, 31, is a career officer assigned to Killakeet Island, along North Carolina's treacherous Outer Banks. Both he and his father-the keeper of the Killakeet Lighthouse-are haunted by the loss at sea and presumed death of Josh's two-year-old baby brother 17 years earlier. Shaken from his brooding by the appearance of German U-boats, Josh must try to protect the merchant ships torpedoed every night offshore. . . . Well-crafted characters, gripping naval warfare and colorful island life come together in this dynamic and exciting tale." Publ Wkly

Higgins, George V., 1939-1999

At end of day; a novel. Harcourt Brace & Co. 2000 383p $30

ISBN 0-15-100358-0   LC 99-46414

This novel explores the "underworld of south Boston. Much of the story drills into the domain of two gangsters, Nick Cistaro and Arthur McKeath, and their unusual relationship with the city's top FBI men, tough veteran Jack Farrier and bumbling sycophant Darren Stoat. Both sides meet regularly for a civilized dinner, slipping each other just enough information so they can succeed at their respective pursuits." Publ Wkly

"The last novel of the late George V. Higgins shows no hint of failing skill or mellowing temper. The dialogue is as raffishly elegant as ever, the action as disconcerting to the lawfully minded, and the author's underlying attitude what it has regularly been—a plague on all your houses. . . . Questions of law and justice, as discussed by the characters, become almost equally unnerving. Higgins was a brilliantly clever, savagely bitter observer of society." Atl Mon

Bomber's law; a novel. Holt & Co. 1993 296p

ISBN 0-8050-2329-1   LC 93-26006

"A John Macrae book"

"A young detective, Harry Dell'Appa, discovers that his fellow detective and nemesis, Bob Brennan, has become curiously lax in his efforts to nail Short Joey Mossi, an aging Mafia hit man. Dell'Appa, who has been assigned to take over the Mossi case, begins to suspect that Brennan has gotten to know his subject a little too well—or rather, that he sympathizes too fully with Mossi. As the cops sit together in a cold car, waiting for Mossi to appear, Brennan talks on and on, digressing into stories about other criminals and about his own life. Dell'Appa listens fitfully." Commonweal

"A whiz of a stylist with a black belt in dialogue, Higgins lets his characters' conversation carry the story. This is our language as it is spoken, full of false stops and loony poetry." Newsweek

A change of gravity. Holt & Co. 1997 456p

ISBN 0-8050-4815-4   LC 97-6892

"A John Macrae book"

This novel "begins as two old-style, bent but not crooked Massachusetts pols discover that the Feds are about to indict one of them. The charges against former state representative Dan Hilliard are ultimately bogus yet grounded in fact, leaving Hilliard and his loyal campaign manager, Ambrose Merrion, in a major pickle." Booklist

"The story unfolds in a nonlinear way; it does so almost entirely through superb dialogue that reveals character in a far more complex and interesting way than does an omniscient author. . . . Characters often speak continuously for several pages, but convey such nuances about the mores and social strata of their time that we welcome their loquaciousness." N Y Times Book Rev

Higgins, George V., 1939-1999—*Continued*

The friends of Eddie Coyle. Knopf 1972 c1971
183p

ISBN 0-394-47327-2

                                   *

The action of the story "involves a series of bank robberies. Eddie Coyle is a small-time [Boston] crook who
is trying to crash the big time by providing the armament
for the robbers. His 'friends' use him, are used by him,
and ultimately there is double-crossing all the way along
the line." Publ Wkly

"Written entirely in riveting dialogue, this novel is a
compelling study of motive." Oxford Companion to Am
Lit. 6th edition

The Mandeville talent. Holt & Co. 1991 278p

ISBN 0-8050-1412-8   LC 91-9232

"A John Macrae book"

This book is about "a 23-year-old unsolved murder in
Goshen, Mass. When the granddaughter of murder victim
James Mandeville is offered a teaching post at Mount
Holyoke, her husband, Joe, a young lawyer in a big
Manhattan firm, grabs the chance to resign from the cor-
porate rat race, solve the old murder case and set up pri-
vate practice in the Berkshires. The local law can't help
(for diverse reasons) and sends him to retired Defense
Department investigator Baldad ('Baldo') Ianucci, who is
bored and looking for something to do." Publ Wkly

"The drama in this book comes simply from watching
the protagonists' minds work. Higgins makes us believe
that the paper trail of contemporary life actually leads
not to obfuscation but to clarity." Booklist

Higgins, Jack, 1929-

Bad company. Putnam 2003 287p $25.95

ISBN 0-399-14970-8   LC 2003-41365

"As the war is drawing to a close in 1945, Hitler gives
his diary to an aide for safekeeping. The diary contains
an account of a meeting between representatives of Hitler
and President Roosevelt at which they discussed ways to
negotiate a peace treaty and then to attack Russia. The
aide, Max von Berger, is now (in 2003) a billionaire industrialist and a silent partner with an international crime
family. Seeking revenge for a killing, Berger vows to reveal the diary's secret that would destroy the current
U.S. president. It's up to an American and a British
agent to get the diary before it falls into the hands of the
president's enemies." Booklist

Cold Harbour. Simon & Schuster 1990 318p
o.p.   LC 89-26198

A "tale of deception set in World War II Europe. Cold
Harbour, a tiny village on the English Channel in Cornwall, is being used by the Special Operations Executive
. . . as a base for running secret agents into and out of
occupied France. To safeguard that operation,
Englishmen masquerading as Germans patrol the Channel
in a captured German vessel and fly planes bearing
Luftwaffe insignia. But these deceptions are just the beginning. At a French chateau occupied by the German
High Command, the resident family—now reduced to an
elderly countess and her young niece, AnneMarie—pretend to be collaborators." N Y Times Book Rev

Confessional. Stein & Day 1985 278p

ISBN 0-8128-3025-3   LC 884-40777

"The hero of this spy-thriller is three people—a KGB
agent, an ordained Catholic priest and an IRA terrorist,
which means that he goes through a lot of cloak-and-
dagger changes as he slips from role to role. In 1958 the
Russians set up a mock Irish village in the Ukraine to
train future KGB agents so that they could more easily
blend into the Irish landscape and go about their nefarious activities of destabilizing English-Irish relations by
working through the IRA. Mikhail Kelly was a first-rate
candidate because his Irish father had been hung by the
British as an IRA activist and he had been raised by his
Russian mother in Ireland." Best Sellers

This novel is "tense. It is riveting. It is what a thriller
should be. If Mr. Higgins's prose is dull and his understanding of humanity shallow, it may only be because
good prose and a deeper understanding would inhibit the
race to the plot's final twist." N Y Times Book Rev

Day of judgment. Holt, Rinehart & Winston
1979 263p o.p.   LC 78-15043

"The time of the story is Spring 1963, just prior to
President Kennedy's planned visit to Berlin. To discredit
his good-will tour, members of the East German Intelligence have kidnapped a [Jesuit] Catholic priest known to
be a foe of Communism and a member of an organization that has been smuggling refugees from the East into
the West. They imprison him in a castle just fifty miles
inside the East German border, to try to break his will
and make him reveal certain facts that could prove an
embarrassment to the Free World, through brainwashing.
But they reckon without dedicated people, including
members of the Catholic Church and the members of a
non-Catholic monastery in the town where they are holding the priest. The rescuers also have the help of a Jesuit
father, a woman doctor and a British Intelligence Officer." West Coast Rev Books

The author "has used an episode in history to write a
finely crafted thriller with excellent characterization."
Booklist

Day of reckoning. Putnam 2000 295p $25.95

ISBN 0-399-14585-0   LC 99-34847

The journalist wife of Sean Dillon's "old comrade
Blake Johnson is killed in Brooklyn on orders of her latest object of investigation, Jack Fox, heir apparent to the
powerful Solazzo crime family. The law can't touch Fox,
but Blake and Dillon can and will. Aided by Dillon's
black-ops boss Brigadier Charles Ferguson, and his crew,
plus a father/son team of British gangsters, Blake and
Dillon strike again and again at Fox's wallet: shutting
down his London gambling den; sinking a boat laden
with his gold; destroying a cache of his weapons in Ireland; foiling his plans for a major robbery in London.
. . . The action is sleek and intensely absorbing." Publ
Wkly

Drink with the Devil. Putnam 1996 311p

ISBN 0-399-14154-5   LC 96-3821

This Sean Dillon adventure "finds the former terrorist
involved with a group of Irish Protestant paramilitaries in
1985 as they hijack a truck carrying £100 million in gold
bullion. Ten years later, Sean is working for British Intelligence when he is ordered to go after the gold again.
Now he is to prevent the bullion from disrupting the
peace between the Catholics and Protestants. Dillon, boss
Brigadier Ferguson, and partner Hannah Bernstein must
also deal with the Mafia. They ask 85-year-old Liam

Higgins, Jack, 1929-—*Continued*
Devlin for help, and the IRA legend of past Higgins books is only too pleased to participate. The excitement never lags as each side double-crosses the others." Libr J

The eagle has flown; a novel. Simon & Schuster 1991 335p o.p.   LC 91-4368
In this sequel to The eagle has landed, "Devlin is asked by the Germans to parachute into England and free Steiner from St. Mary's Priory, where he has been taken after being held captive in the Tower of London. This [adventure also] involves a plot to thwart the assassination of Hitler in order to prevent the nation's takeover by Himmler and the SS." Booklist
"Mr. Higgins is an expert storyteller, and he goes about 'The Eagle Has Flown' with typical gusto. Everything is carefully arranged, little pieces fitting into other little pieces to form an action-packed mosaic." NY Times Book Rev

The eagle has landed. Simon & Schuster 1991 399p o.p.
                                   * LC 90-44042
A revised edition containing the full text of the title first published 1975 by Holt, Rinehart & Winston
"After intense training a small force of German paratroopers lands on the Norfolk coast in November 1943, with the aim of capturing Churchill, who is spending the weekend at a neighbouring country house." Times Lit Suppl
"There are elements of heroism, duplicity, and heavy irony, plus considerable bloodshed, in this action-oriented yarn." Christ Sci Monit
Followed by The eagle has flown

Edge of danger. Putnam 2001 273p $25.95
ISBN 0-399-14701-2   LC 00-40268
"Pitting returning antihero Sean Dillon, once of the IRA, now with British intelligence, against an aristocratic English-Arab family bent on vengeance that threatens world order, the story whips along. From London to the Middle East, from Ireland to the White House, it swirls with intrigue and snaps with violence." Publ Wkly

Eye of the storm. Putnam 1992 320p o.p.
                                   LC 91-46736
"Early in 1991, while the Gulf war is in full bloom, operatives of Saddam Hussein hire legendary terrorist Sean Dillon to take the war to the enemy. A master of disguise and subterfuge, Dillon began his career with the IRA, earning the enmity of Liam Devlin—the unforgettable antihero of *The Eagle Has Landed*, who makes a featured appearance here—and of Martin Brosnan, an American Special Forces hero and IRA member turned college professor. After Dillon's attempt to assassinate former Prime Minster Margaret Thatcher during a visit to France fails, he decides to go after her successor John Major. . . . Although readers can be sure that Dillon's scheme will be foiled, fun remains in the how and why." Publ Wkly
Followed by Thunder point (1993)

Flight of eagles. Putnam 1998 328p
ISBN 0-399-14376-9   LC 97-37582
The author traces the exploits of twins Max and Harry Kelso "from 1917, when their wealthy American father marries a German baroness, through 1944. . . . Upon her

husband's death in 1930, the baroness returns to Germany with Max in tow, leaving Harry in the care of his American grandfather. By the early 1940s Max is Germany's premier flying ace–he eventually downs more than 300 Allied planes–and is famed as the Black Baron. Harry, meanwhile, has enlisted with the RAF and distinguished himself equally in the Battle of Britain and beyond. The narrative cuts briskly from one twin's adventures to the other's as the dashing, daring young men intersect with historical greats including Hitler, Himmler, Goring, FDR and Eisenhower." Publ Wkly

Luciano's luck. Stein & Day 1981 238p o.p.
                                   LC 881-40330
"It is 1943 and the Allied invasion of Sicily is imminent. General Eisenhower plans to enlist Sicilian Mafia support for the invasion by sending two emissaries into Sicily to sway Luca, the Sicilian 'capo di tutti capi.' Logically, perhaps, one emissary is the chief U.S. capo, Lucky Luciano (who is in prison); the second is Luca's alienated granddaughter. The commando expedition to effect a meeting between these three in German-occupied Sicily forms the basis for a fast-paced, action-crammed plot, suspenseful to the last page. The fictionalized Luciano is sympathetically portrayed, and although the romanticizing of the Mafia figures jars a little, the historical premises are acceptably plausible." Libr J

Midnight runner. Putnam 2002 289p
ISBN 0-399-14833-7   LC 2001-48124
This suspense novel finds "former IRA enforcer Sean Dillon and his present boss, Gen. Charles Ferguson, . . . responding to various revenge gambits by the beautiful and fabulously wealthy half-bedu, half-English Lady Kate Rashid, countess of Loch Dhu and head of the Rashid Bedu tribe of Hazar, whose three brothers were killed by Dillon and his comrades . . . after, among other acts of infamy, a Rashid assassination attempt on U.S. President Jack Cazalet." Publ Wkly

Night of the fox. Simon & Schuster 1986 316p o.p.   LC 86-29662
"Taking the form of a continuous flashback, 'Night of the Fox' begins with the aftermath of a U-boat attack off the coast of German-occupied Jersey, which results in the wounded body of an American soldier being washed ashore. For the Allies, Hugh Kelso is a dangerous liability; if the Germans learn what he knows about the proposed Normandy invasion, disaster would be inevitable. British agents Harry Martinique and Sarah Drayton secretly enter Jersey, posing as an SS officer and his mistress. Another form of deception is also taking place, as a gifted Jewish actor arrives on the island, impersonating Field Marshall Rommel and covering for the real 'Desert Fox,' who is in France on secret talks. The three imposters join forces in a daring and dangerous mission." Booklist
"Higgins combines powerful narrative with documentary detail in an exceptional tale that relies upon the interweaving histories of the various characters." Libr J

The president's daughter. Putnam 1997 278p
ISBN 0-399-14239-8   LC 96-48654
In this suspense novel, Sean Dillon, "now with British Intelligence, finds himself working on behalf of the U.S. president. . . . Dillon, Brigadier Charles Ferguson and Chief Inspector Hannah Bernstein are on the track of a Jewish extremist who calls himself Judas Maccabeus and

Higgins, Jack, 1929——*Continued*

is pressing President Jake Cazalet to sign off on a thorough bombing attack on Iraq, Iran and Syria. If Cazalet doesn't authorize the strikes, Judas will kill Contesse Marie de Brissac, Cazalet's illegitimate daughter, who was conceived in 1969 in Vietnam when Cazalet, then a Special Forces lieutenant, bedded Marie's mother." Publ Wkly

"Higgins offers the usual cast of characters—beautiful women and tough guys—and exotic locales, including London, Corfu, Sicily, Ireland, France, and the eastern Mediterranean. . . . [This] is another 'race against the clock' thriller, and Higgins' fans won't be disappointed." Booklist

Rough justice. G.P. Putnam's Sons 2008 326p $25.95

ISBN 978-0-399-15513-0; 0-399-15513-9
LC 2008-8905

This entry in the Sean Dillon thriller series "finds aging, arthritic ex-gangster Harry Salter retired from active operations, leaving Dillon, once the IRA's most feared enforcer, as the real leader of the loose gang of stalwart lads who covertly battle the foes of Western civilization. A newcomer to the team, Maj. Harry Miller, on the surface a mild-mannered MP who's in reality the British prime minister's secret hit man, hooks up with series regular Blake Johnson in Kosovo, where the Russians, intent on reclaiming old glory, are stirring up trouble. Meanwhile, Islamic fundamentalists are intent on bringing Britain to its knees. The action moves swiftly amid a variety of foreign locales, including Moscow, London and Beirut, to a climax that will leave readers asking themselves, evidence to the contrary, whether the great game is really over." Publ Wkly

Storm warning; a novel. Holt, Rinehart & Winston 1976 311p il o.p.

"Late in the Second World War, a German sailing ship disguised as a Swedish vessel sets out from Belém, Brazil, for Kiel, Germany—5,000 miles across the Atlantic—taking home a crew and group of passengers wishing to return to their collapsing fatherland. The trip is arduous, ending when the ship strikes a reef in the Outer Hebrides Islands off the coast of Scotland." Booklist

"What does work, exceedingly well, are the action at sea scenes, building up to the climax. . . . Basically what we have are decent people on both sides of the war, some of whom survive, some of whom do not, who come together in a desperate attempt to save the lives of the Germans aboard the ship who have fought so bravely to make it home." Publ Wkly

Touch the devil. Stein & Day 1982 251p o.p.
LC 82-40080

"Charles Ferguson of British intelligence persuades Devlin [featured in the Eagle novels] to join forces with Martin Brosnan, former comrade in the fight for Irish independence, to find and stop (by killing if necessary) another onetime rebel, Frank Barry, now in the pay of the Soviets. Barry, a cold assassin and thief of NATO secret weapons, is a match in cunning for Devlin and Brosnan, and he learns about the plot against him from a mole in Ferguson's office. He knows that Devlin and Brosnan's lover, Anne-Marie Audin, get help from the British to spirit Brosnan from a French prison, as grim as Devil's Island, where his revolutionary activities have landed

him. Anne-Marie takes the two men to her secluded farm house in southern France, where Barry and his hirelings lurk in ambush." Publ Wkly

The White House connection. Putnam 1999 323p $25.95

ISBN 0-399-14489-7
LC 98-42577

"Sean Dillon, a former IRA gunman, now works for the British prime minister; Blake Johnson heads a secret office for the U.S. president. Both have their various talents severely tested while trying to stop a vengeful 66-year-old woman who is assassinating members of the Sons of Erin, including a senator, thereby threatening both governments." Libr J

"When it comes to thrillers, Jack Higgins wrote the book. In fact, he wrote lots of them, and this is one of the best." Booklist

Highet, Helen MacInnes *See* MacInnes, Helen, 1907-1985

Highsmith, Patricia, 1921-1995

The boy who followed Ripley. Lippincott & Crowell 1980 291p o.p.
LC 79-29678

In this novel "two people meet casually, but their fates become inextricably, and dangerously, joined. Tom Ripley is an American expatriate living on the outskirts of Paris; he meets a 16-year-old American runaway, who turns out to be the son of a recently deceased food products tycoon. The boy is haunted by guilt over his father's death and pursued through Europe by kidnappers. Engrossing and shiver packed." Booklist

Ripley under ground

In Highsmith, P. The talented Mr. Ripley; Ripley under ground; Ripley's game

Ripley's game. Knopf 1974 267p o.p.

"Tom [Ripley], an American married to a lovely French woman and living in luxury in country France, is a diabolically clever killer and con artist. What he begins here starts as a fairly vicious practical joke to worry an Englishman who has snubbed Tom. Before the last ploy has been played out, several murders have taken place, the Mafia has embarked on ruthless revenge against Tom and the Englishman, the latter's happy marriage has been hopelessly damaged and Tom has survived as only someone as totally amoral as he can succeed in doing." Publ Wkly

"Highsmith uses a matter-of-fact, almost reportorial, tone to effect her measured, driving pace and to construct her tightly woven web. The second half of this literate and imaginative thriller is especially brilliant—all the way to the dazzling last page." Libr J

also in Highsmith, P. The talented Mr. Ripley; Ripley under ground; Ripley's game

The selected stories of Patricia Highsmith; with a foreword by Graham Greene. Norton 2001 724p $27.95

ISBN 0-393-02031-2
LC 2001-30878

Contents: Chorus girl's absolutely final performance; Djemal's revenge; There I was, stuck with Bubsy; Ming's biggest prey; In the dead of truffle season; The

Highsmith, Patricia, 1921-1995—*Continued*

bravest rat in Venice; Engine horse; The day of reckoning; Notes from a respectable cockroach; Eddie and the monkey robberies; Hamsters vs. Websters; Harry: a ferret; Goat ride; The hand; Oona, the jolly cave woman; The coquette; The female novelist; The dancer; The invalid; or, The bedridden; The artist; The middle-class housewife; The fully licensed whore; or, The wife; The breeder; The mobile bed-object; The perfect little lady; The silent mother-in-law; The prude; The victim; The evangelist; The perfectionist; The man who wrote books in his head; The network; The pond; Something you have to live with; Slowly, slowly in the wind; Those awful dawns; Woodrow Wilson's necktie; One for the islands; A curious suicide; The baby spoon; Broken glass; Please don't shoot the trees; Something the cat dragged in; Not one of us; The terrors of basket-weaving; Under a dark angel's eye; I despise your life; The dream of the Emma C; Old folks at home; When in Rome; Blow it; The kite; The black house; Mermaids on the golf course; The button; Where the action is; Chris's last party; A clock ticks at Christmas; A shot from nowhere; The stuff of madness; Not in this life, maybe the next; I am not as efficient as other people; The cruelest month; The romantic

The talented Mr. Ripley

In Crime novels: American noir of the 1950s

In Highsmith, P. The talented Mr. Ripley; Ripley under ground; Ripley's game

The talented Mr. Ripley; Ripley under ground; Ripley's game. Knopf 1999 877p $26

ISBN 0-375-40792-8

         * LC 99-38147

"Everyman's library"

Contents: The talented Mr. Ripley (1955); Ripley under ground (1970); Ripley's game (1974)

In the talented Mr. Ripley "Tom Ripley is hired by the wealthy Herbert Greenleaf to help him find his son, Dickie. Ripley travels to Europe and catches up to Dickie in Italy, meanwhile corresponding with Greenleaf through the mail. Later, after he has assumed Dickie's identity himself, he keeps up the imposture by writing to Dickie's friends and avoiding personal contact. He continues, however, to be 'Tom Ripley' when the occasion demands. Highsmith takes us into the mind of a repellent character but, through the sheer force of her communication of his personality, compels a sympathetic fascination on the part of the reader." Murphy. Ency of Murder and Mystery

In Ripley under ground Tom impersonates a dead artist and is drawn into murder when his deception is about to be discovered

Hijuelos, Oscar

Empress of the splendid season; a novel. HarperFlamingo 1999 342p

ISBN 0-06-017570-2   LC 98-34798

Once called the "'Professor of Cuba' by her father, Lydia is a long way from Havana in this novel, set in New York City from the 1950s to the mid-1980s. Disowned by her family, Lydia moves to New York and finds work as a seamstress. She marries and has two children, but her hopes of becoming a housewife come

to an end when her husband suffers the first of many heart attacks. Lydia goes to work cleaning homes for wealthy New Yorkers." Libr J

The author "tells his story without condescension or false sentimentality, in the tone of a neighborhood gossip. The literary device of the cleaning lady also provides a new and unexpected angle of vision on Manhattan's old money. . . . Hijuelos reaffirms his place in the front rank of American novelists and forces the Hispanic immigrant experience closer to the center of our cultural consciousness." Natl Rev

The fourteen sisters of Emilio Montez O'Brien; a novel. Farrar, Straus & Giroux 1993 484p

ISBN 0-374-15815-0   LC 92-41935

This novel "tells the story of the family of Nelson O'Brien, an Irish immigrant to the U.S. who travels to Cuba as a photographer during the Spanish-American War. There he falls passionately in love and marries the young and beautiful Mariela Montez. After the couple returns to the farm O'Brien owns in a small Pennsylvania town, he works as the local photographer and operates the community's movie theater, while she keeps busy bearing and rearing their 14 daughters and, finally, one son, Emilio Montez O'Brien." Time

"The sprawling narrative is sustained by the author's leniency in enforcing whatever conventions he adopts. Its pace speeds up and slows down, depending as much, it seems, on Mr. Hijuelos's mood as his material. . . . The changing degree of connectedness discernible among the characters and plot lines mirrors nothing so much as family life the way it is actually lived, by both great broods and small." N Y Times Book Rev

The Mambo Kings play songs of love; a novel. Farrar, Straus & Giroux 1989 407p o.p.

         * LC 89-1248

"The Mambo Kings are two brothers, Cesar and Nestor Castillo, Cuban-born musicians who emigrate to New York City in 1949. They form a band and enjoy modest success, playing dance halls, nightclubs and *quince* parties in New York's Latin neighborhoods. Their popularity peaks in 1956 with a guest appearance on the *I Love Lucy* show, playing Ricky Ricardo's Cuban cousins and performing their only hit song in a bittersweet event that both frames the novel and serves as its emblematic heart." Publ Wkly

"The novel alternates crisp narrative with opulent musings—the language of everyday and the language of longing. When Mr. Hijuelos falters, as from time to time he does, it's through an excess of self-consciousness: he strives too hard for all-encompassing description or grows distant and dutiful in an effort to get period details just right." N Y Times Book Rev

A simple Habana melody: from when the world was good; a novel. HarperCollins Pubs. 2002 342p

ISBN 0-06-017569-9   LC 2002-512611

"The story begins in 1947, when the 58-year-old Israel Levis returns to his native Habana after spending most of the 1930s in Paris and then enduring two years in Buchenwald (Levis, a Catholic, was assumed by the Nazis to be a Jew because of his name). Hijuelos jumps. . .between past and present, lingering on Levis' early years in Cuba, when he emerged as a musician and composer." Booklist

"While there is a faintly contrived air about Levis's

Hijuelos, Oscar—*Continued*

experience of the Holocaust. Hijuelos triumphs in capturing the sights and sounds of Habana at the edge of modernity." Publ Wkly

Hill, Joe

20th century ghosts; introduction by Christopher Golden. William Morrow 2007 316p $24.95

ISBN 978-0-06-114797-5; 0-06-114797-4

First published 2005 in the United Kingdom

Contents: Best new horror; 20th century ghost; Pop art; You will hear the locust sing; Abraham's boys; Better than home; The black phone; In the rundown; The cape; Last breath; Dead-wood; The widow's breakfast; Bobby Conroy comes back from the dead; My father's mask; Voluntary committal

"Hill's subject matter is steeped in the pop culture and tabloid detritus of the past 50 years: serial killers, abducted children, families living on the fault lines between divorce and poverty, horror movies and supernatural fiction. Yet his real focus is an almost obsessively nuanced exploration of the nature of American manhood. The presiding spirits of 20th Century Ghosts are lost boys and damaged men, running for their lives across a blighted, often surreal modern landscape. . . . Hill captures the heartbreaking longing for connection between men whose intelligence and decency aren't always enough to save them from the dark." Houston Chron

Heart-shaped box. William Morrow 2007 376p $24.95

ISBN 978-0-06-114793-7; 0-06-114793-1

LC 2006-46548

"Middle-aged rock star Judas Coyne collects morbid curios for fun, so doesn't think twice about buying a suit advertised at an online auction site as haunted by its dead owner's ghost. Only after it arrives does Judas discover that the suit belonged to Craddock McDermott, the stepfather of one of Coyne's discarded groupies, and that the old man's ghost is a malignant spirit determined to kill Judas in revenge for his stepdaughter's suicide." Publ Wkly

The author has created a "wild, mesmerizing, perversely witty tale of horror. In a book much too smart to sound like the work of a neophyte, he builds character invitingly and plants an otherworldly surprise around every corner." N Y Times (Late N Y Ed)

Hill, John *See* Koontz, Dean R., 1945-

Hill, Lawrence, 1957-

Someone knows my name; a novel. W.W. Norton & Co. 2007 486p $24.95

ISBN 978-0-393-06578-7; 0-393-06578-2

LC 2007-8035

"Around 1745, young Aminata Diallo is abducted from her West African home and sold into slavery in South Carolina. An observant and highly intelligent child, she quickly learns not only how to speak English but also how to read and write. On a trip to New York City with her master, Aminata escapes during chaotic anti-British demonstrations. She helps the embattled British compile The Book of Negroes, a list of thousands of black Loyalists, and these slaves are transported to Nova Scotia and

granted their freedom. Later some of them are sent to Sierra Leone as part of an abolitionist social experiment, and Aminata finally realizes her long-held dream of returning home." Libr J

What makes this novel "extraordinary is Hill's ability to transcend the facts—to make something magical out of them. Despite the unpalatable subject matter, he compels our attention and manages to delight. His Aminata is a heroic figure, a little larger than life, residing within and outside of history. You can never forget this character. She embeds herself in your heart." Toronto Star

Hill, Reginald, 1936-

Arms and the women; an elliad. Delacorte Press 1999 408p $23.95

ISBN 0-385-33279-3   LC 99-35873

"Andy Dalziel and Peter Pascoe, the ranking Yorkshire police officers in this series, marshal the troops when Pascoe's wife, Ellie and their little girl narrowly escape being abducted in broad daylight from their home. Suspicion naturally falls on any number of criminals with deep grudges against Pascoe; but once these obvious bad guys are eliminated, it begins to look as if Ellie has acquired an enemy of her own, perhaps within the circle of strong-minded political activists in her women's rights group." N Y Times Book Rev

Bones and silence. Delacorte Press 1990 332p o.p.   LC 89-48836

"Set in a cathedral city which will host a contemporary enactment of medieval mystery plays, Hill's narrative features the police duo Andrew Dalziel and Peter Pascoe looking into a series of related murders and disappearances tied to a builder who is coincidentally constructing garages for the police station. Meanwhile, the galvanizing director of the mystery plays, Eileen Chung, has cast Dalziel as God and the builder in question as Lucifer." Publ Wkly

"A complex, challenging and diverting novel, from one of the most cogent of detective writers." Times Lit Suppl

Child's play. Macmillan 1987 296p o.p.   LC 86-8712

"A Dalziel-Pascoe murder mystery"

This novel "has two plots. One concerns the will of a dotty, wealthy old woman who leaves her money to a son missing in action since 1944 and presumed dead. Hungry, greedy, angry relatives gather to see what can be done about breaking the will. . . . The other side of the story has to do with a tough cop who lives a secret life as a homosexual. Mr. Hill handles this aspect with grace; there also is a good deal of humor in the way Dalziel goes into action when, on orders from above, he has to track down the homosexual. He takes care of things in his own inimitable manner. Mr. Hill, as always, has a fine time jousting against hypocrisy and the hollow men of the bureaucracy." N Y Times Book Rev

Death comes for the Fat Man. HarperCollins 2007 404p $24.95

ISBN 978-0-06-082082-4; 0-06-082082-9

LC 2006-48655

"Detective Peter Pascoe is on the trail of the Knights Templar, an antiterrorist vigilante group that bombed a video store and left Peter's mentor, Andy 'Fat Man' Dalziel, in a coma. . . . Without the help of the indomi-

Hill, Reginald, 1936-—*Continued*
table Fat Man, he sets out to track down those responsible for the bombing." Libr J

"Hill delivers his usual bundle of literary treats, from a single fragrant reference to Voltaire to the voluptuous visions of earthly delights Dalziel clings to as he hovers near death. Characters major and minor march boldly through the dense plot, confident of being remembered for their singular personalities and inexhaustible verbal resources, while Pascoe, who catches himself trying to keep his boss alive by assuming his 'blunt and brutish' ways, fears he's losing his own identity." N Y Times Book Rev

Dream of darkness; {by} Patrick Ruell. Countryman Press 1991 204p o.p.

LC 90-38677

"A Foul Play Press book"

"In London 18-year-old Sairey Ellis suffers from a recurring, debilitating nightmare that shows the young Sairey viewing the open coffin of her mother in Uganda years ago. That did not happen, say her retired British security officer father, Nigel, and his sister, who raised Sairey after her mother's death. Sairey's analysis-prompted returning memory of the brief time with her mother in Uganda holds the key to her nightmare and seems to threaten family and friend—as does Nigel, who is writing his African memoirs." Libr J

"The story of Sairey's haunted nights and days alternates with selections from her father's memoirs, which detail his diplomatic career in Uganda during the Amin years. Ruell effectively uses these parallel narratives to slowly unravel the mystery of Sairey's mother's death. A gem of a book with a startling finale." Booklist

Good morning, midnight. HarperCollins 2004 433p $24.95

ISBN 0-06-052807-9   LC 2003-67603

Detectives Andy Dalziel and Peter Pascoe investigate "a locked-room suicide. . . . The case seems as closed as the room in which the local businessman's body was found until Hill and Pascoe discover that this suicide was committed 10 years to the day after the victim's father committed suicide in the same way and that the new suicide has left a very damning cassette tape. A cut-and-dried case morphs into a cold-case scenario in this wickedly clever, classic Brit-mystery puzzle, loaded with Yorkshire atmosphere and mordant wit." Booklist

Killing the lawyers. St. Martin's Press 1997 287p

ISBN 0-312-16877-2   LC 97-16249

"A Thomas Dunne book"

Joe Sixsmith is a "black PI in the not especially famous English town of Luton. He solves crimes less by detection than by his own brand of scrupulous honesty, which creates a kind of white light in which the bad guys invariably stand out. After Joe's insurance company undervalues his wrecked and beloved old car, he seeks the counsel of a rude and fancy lawyer. The visit ends in shouting—and becomes a case when the lawyer is murdered. Another lawyer in the dead man's firm is killed, and Joe, after being cleared as a suspect, is hired to investigate by a remaining partner in the firm." Publ Wkly

Pictures of perfection; a Dalziel/Pascoe mystery in five volumes. Delacorte Press 1994 307p o.p.

LC 93-47449

"The intrepid trio of Sergeant Wield and detectives Dalziel and Pascoe are called to the tiny hamlet of Enscombe to investigate the mysterious disappearance of a rookie constable. When they arrive, however, they find there are more problems than just a missing copper; skulduggery, thievery, forgery, lust, lechery, libel, and passion all lie in wait for the three unwitting chaps. This is an intelligent, stylish, scintillating, witty mystery that transcends its cozy trappings." Booklist

Recalled to life. Delacorte Press 1992 359p o.p.

LC 92-1380

A mystery set in England and the U.S. "As Inspector Dalziel and partner Pascoe work unofficially to refute new evidence concerning a 1963 case, they threaten to unearth various nasty political secrets." Libr J

"Though Hill relies too much on coincidence, the complex plot here sustains interest. The novel's chief rewards, however, are those of character: Dalziel is a brilliant, bearish delight and the supporting players, including a brash black woman CIA agent, provide a constant parade of pleasures." Publ Wkly

Singing the sadness; a private eye Joe Sixsmith mystery. Thomas Dunne Bks. 1999 251p

ISBN 0-312-24238-7   LC 99-16864

Black private eye Joe Sixsmith "a member of the local choir, is traveling with his fellow singers to the Llanffugiol Choral Festival when the bus passes a burning cottage; without thinking, Joe rushes into the inferno and rescues a woman from the flames. He is pronouced a hero, but there's a mystery brewing: the cottage was supposed to be empty, so who is the woman Joe rescued?" Booklist

The Stranger House. HarperCollins 2005 480p $24.95

ISBN 0-06-082081-0   LC 2005-40274

"Twentysomething Aussie math whiz Samantha Flood has fiery red hair and a fierce determination to learn the truth about her paternal grandmother, an orphan shipped from her native England to Australia under suspicious circumstances. Sober Spaniard Miguel Madero, who experiences ghostly visions and painful sensations in his feet and hands, has abandoned pursuit of the priesthood to engage in research about English Catholics during the Reformation. The paths of Samantha and Miguel (known to all as 'Mig') cross in the tiny English village of Illthwaite, home to the Stranger House, an inn that has hosted weary travelers for more than 500 years. Samantha and Mig, an unlikely duo, are drawn to one another as each discovers secrets simmering beneath the surface of Illthwaite's deceptively serene facade." Booklist

The wood beyond. Delacorte Press 1996 358p o.p.

* LC 95-32319

"Chief Inspector Andy Dalziel and Peter Pascoe investigate the discovery of some old bones near a large pharmaceutical research laboratory in Yorkshire. As the case progresses, Pascoe unearths surprising facts about his own grandfather, a World War I soldier." Libr J

Hill, Reginald, 1936-—*Continued*

"The theme of personal honor in a dishonorable world gives passion to the characters and urgency to their individual causes and obsessions." N Y Times Book Rev

Hill, Robert

When all is said and done. Graywolf Press 2006 220p $20

ISBN 1-55597-442-2   LC 2005-926374

This is a "portrait of an unusual early 1960s American marriage. Myrmy is a stylish and successful Madison Avenue advertising copywriter, wife, and mother. Her hunky and loving husband, Dan, is a war veteran turned tie salesman. Overriding anti-Semitic obstacles, Myrmy has moved her family out of the city into a suburb, where she remains a dynamo while Dan is plagued by strange maladies. Could his troubles be the result of a little radiation experiment conducted by the military? It's hard to find time for a diagnosis with three young boys to care for. Every aspect of this agile, intoxicating, hilarious, and poignant novel is compelling, but what elevates it is the exuberant language. Hill writes with velocity, rhythm, and wit, conveying a world of subtle emotions and social nuance in brilliantly syncopated inner monologues and staccato dialogue, creating a bravura and resounding performance." Booklist

Hill, Ruth Beebe

Hanta yo. Doubleday 1979 834p o.p.
          LC 77-74792

"The story is a fictional elaboration upon the chronological record kept on a tanned hide by a member of the Mahto band of the Teton Sioux. Hill follows the tribe from 1794 to 1835 in the seasonal moves across the plains. She unfolds . . . the tale of two families, and in particular, the . . . friendship between Ahbleza and Tonweya, the son of a warrior-leader and the son of a hunter." New Repub

"The practice of using the multi-generational family story to reflect changing times and/or historical events is almost a genre unto itself. This is such a novel. . . . The historical accuracy, linguistic acrobatics, and ethnological acuity do not limit the book's appeal. A superb style transcends the few minor flaws, and despite the scholarly impression given by the introduction, chronology notes, and glossaries, this book is first and foremost a well-written story." Libr J

Hill, Susan, 1942-

Mrs. de Winter; a novel. Morrow 1993 349p o.p.
          LC 93-5347

"What happened to Maxim de Winter and his second wife after Manderley burned? This suspenseful 'completion' of Daphne du Maurier's *Rebecca* begins with the couple's return to England, following a ten-year, self-imposed exile, for the funeral of Maxim's sister Beatrice. In a voice true to the original story, Hill's Mrs. de Winter chronicles Rebecca's continuing shadow on their life; a mysterious wreath bearing a card with the initial 'R' is discovered near Beatrice's grave, and unwelcome visitors include Jack Favell, who has visions of blackmail, and Mrs. Danvers, who seeks revenge." Libr J

The pure in heart; a Simon Serrailler crime novel. Overlook Press 2007 c2005 370p $24.95

ISBN 978-1-58567-928-7; 1-58567-928-3

First published 2005 in the United Kingdom

"A nine-year-old boy is kidnapped in broad daylight while waiting for his school ride outside his home in the British cathedral town of Lafferton, and the case falls squarely in the lap of Detective Chief Inspector Serrailler. It's a copper's worst nightmare—broken and grieving parents, intense media interest, and extreme pressure from the top police brass to solve the case "yesterday." But there are few leads and no apparent motive, and as the days go by and the child isn't found, hope drains away. Although the case hits Simon and his team exceptionally hard, he has other problems to deal with. . . . This is realistic, gritty, and gut-wrenching crime fiction, but it's also a poignant and thoughtful character study." Booklist

The various haunts of men; a Simon Serrailler crime novel. Overlook Press 2007 437p $24.95

ISBN 978-1-58567-876-1; 1-58567-876-7
          LC 2006-51546

"Lafferton, an idyllic village just far enough from the madness of London, is a paragon of tranquility and peace, with a lovely cathedral and a stand of ancient stones on 'the Hill.' But then a woman goes missing from there, and then another, and another. Young policewoman Freya Graffham is assigned to investigate the suspected serial killings. Recently transferred from London, she is young, bright, inquisitive, dedicated, and smitten with Detective Chief Inspector Simon Serrailler. . . . As their relationship and the investigation unfold, the killer is revealed in a series of eerie first-person passages. . . . Readers will be instantly drawn to her likable characters and beautiful landscape and will be carried along by the plot, right up to the shocking final twist." Libr J

Hill, Tobias, 1970-

The love of stones. Picador 2002 396p

ISBN 0-312-28773-9   LC 2001-50038

"Obsessed with finding a legendary stone set called 'The Three Brethren,' [jewel dealer Katharine] Sterne starts her search in Turkey, where she must first locate a rich, eccentric British woman who teases her with a lead about the whereabouts of the gems. As Sterne's quest continues, Hill introduces a parallel historical subplot dealing with the provenance of the stones." Publ Wkly

"Stories of jewels are often detective fictions. They involve a certain amount of theft, betrayal, royalty, beautiful women and hard travelling. Hill's novel contains all these things. The story takes us from Turkey to London via Baghdad, then heads east, from Tokyo to the remote coast of Japan. The quest also travels through time. Queen Victoria has a delightful cameo role." New Statesman (1913)

Hillerman, Tony

(ed) The Best American mystery stories of the century. See The Best American mystery stories of the century

Hillerman, Tony—*Continued*

The blessing way. Harper & Row 1970 201p o.p.

"A Joan Kahn-Harper novel of suspense"

"When Bergen McKee, a disillusioned anthropologist, goes to the reservation to continue his research on Navajo witchcraft, he finds himself involved in murder, intrigue, adventure, and, worst of all, what appears to be genuine witchcraft. . . . Investigating the crime is Lt. Joe Leaphorn of the Navajo Law and Order Division." Libr J

"Here's suspense enough for anyone, but what makes the first mystery by Tony Hillerman outstanding is the wealth of detail about the Navajo Indian—customs, rites, way of life—with which he has crammed his pages." Saturday Rev

also in Hillerman, T. The Joe Leaphorn mysteries

Coyote waits. Harper & Row 1990 292p o.p.
* LC 89-46098

Lieutenant Joe Leaphorn of the Navaho Tribal Police is investigating the murder of "his fellow policeman Delbert Nez. Meanwhile, {Jim} Chee, the erstwhile medicine man and Tribal Police officer, is also on the trail of Nez's murderer and believes he has already arrested the culprit in the person of a fellow Navajo, the old shaman Ashie Pinto." N Y Times Book Rev

"The story line has more twists, turns, and bumps than one of the many back-country roads on the Navajo reservation. . . . Hillerman's characters are not just there to provide dialogue for a story that dances along to a clever ending. Leaphorn and Chee each have a past they remember, a present they puzzle over, and a future they anticipate with mixed feelings." Christ Sci Monit

Dance hall of the dead. Harper & Row 1973 166p o.p.
*

"A Joan Kahn-Harper novel of suspense"

Navajo police lieutenant Joe Leaphorn faces a "mystery and possible murder in the disappearance of a Zuni youth and his Navajo best friend shortly before an important annual Zuni religious ceremony." Booklist

"While Leaphorn discovers the real truth, the white men concoct another 'truth' that satisfies their preconceptions. The lack of trust in and respect for the independence of the Native Americans by the white authority is forcefully brought home." Murphy. Ency of Murder and Mystery

also in Hillerman, T. The Joe Leaphorn mysteries

The dark wind. Harper & Row 1982 214p o.p.
LC 81-47793

"Jim Chee of the Navajo Tribal Police is drawn into the mystique of the Hopi tribal ways, which are very different from his own, as he follows a trail that leads him to a father seeking revenge for his son's death, a corrupt lawman and a fortune in cocaine." Publ Wkly

"Fascinating background and atmosphere makes something special out of an otherwise ordinary story." Libr J

also in Hillerman, T. The Jim Chee mysteries

The fallen man. HarperCollins Pubs. 1996 294p o.p.
LC 96-29469

"A skeleton is found on a high ledge of Ship Rock mountain, a place sacred to the Navahos. Tribal Police Lieutenant Chee and the now retired Leaphorn suspect correctly that it belongs to a wealthy rancher missing for 11 years, and Chee tries to discover if it is murder or an accidental death. Meanwhile, Leaphorn is hired by a lawyer to look into the investigation for the rancher's Eastern family, who want to own his land legally so they can accept a lucrative bid for the mining rights." SLJ

"In dealing with the pragmatic older cop and his dreamy young protege. Mr. Hillerman has always kept the frictions carefully contained. Here he gives his heroes more room to rub each other the wrong way. The personal tensions add another facet to the story, which continues the author's fascination with the savagery that men do to themselves and to the land they claim to hold sacred." N Y Times Book Rev

The first eagle; a novel. HarperCollins Pubs. 1998 278p
ISBN 0-06-017581-8
LC 98-6955

"Joe Leaphorn didn't believe in coincidences when he was a police officer, and he doesn't believe in them now that he's retired and working as a private investigator. So he's suspicious when his inquiry into the disappearance of a 'flea catcher,' a young woman working for the Arizona Health Department, leads him to the vicinity of the murder of a member of the Navajo Tribal Police. Acting Tribal Police Lieutenant Jim Chee isn't convinced there's a connection, but he knows there's something amiss about the story told by the accused cop killer, Robert Jano." Booklist

"Surrendering to Hillerman's strong narrative voice and supple storytelling techniques, we come to see that ancient cultures and modern sciences are simply different mythologies for the same reality." N Y Times Book Rev

The ghostway. Harper & Row 1985 c1984 213p o.p.
LC 84-48165

"A Harper novel of suspense"

Originally published 1984 in a limited edition by Dennis McMillan Publications

"The story concerns Navaho tribal detective Jim Chee's pursuit of the men who killed three Navaho of the Turkey clan. Chee solves the murders through his knowledge of the Indian way of life, which is gradually being eroded by white culture. As Navaho rituals help to solve Chee's murders, they also reinforce his doubts about the Indian in him. In an entertaining and fact-filled narrative, Hillerman offers a good look at the plight of contemporary Indians in the West. It is an engrossing and intelligent book for mystery fans and armchair anthropologists alike." Booklist

also in Hillerman, T. The Jim Chee mysteries

Hunting badger. HarperCollins Pubs. 1999 275p
ISBN 0-06-019289-5
LC 99-47906

This "mystery opens with the robbery of the Ute casino. The head of security is killed; a Navajo police officer working off-duty as a rent-a-cop is wounded; and the perpetrators flee into canyon country. Back from vacation, Jim Chee is reluctantly drawn into the hunt for the three men. . . . Retired Lt. Joe Leaphorn gets involved when a rancher gives him the names of the perpetrators." Libr J

Hillerman, Tony—*Continued*

This offers "several new insights into the mysteries of Navajo culture and a story with enough twists and surprises to make readers glad they checked in." Publ Wkly

The Jim Chee mysteries. HarperCollins Pubs. 1990 566p $26.95

ISBN 0-06-016478-6

Contents: People of darkness; The dark wind; The ghostway

The Joe Leaphorn mysteries; three classic Hillerman mysteries featuring Lt. Joe Leaphorn. Harper & Row 1989 499p o.p.   LC 89-45079

Contents: The blessing way; Dance hall of the dead; Listening woman

Listening woman. Harper & Row 1978 200p o.p.   LC 77-11788

"A Joan Kahn-Harper novel of suspense"

In this novel detective "Joe Leaphorn of the Navajo Tribal Police . . . {is} tracking down the murderer of a harmless old man and searching for a missing helicopter used for the getaway in a Brinks-style robbery pulled off by a militant Indian-rights group called the Buffalo Society. The desecration of some ritual sand paintings and the rumor of a sacred cave lead Leaphorn into a violent confrontation with the fanatical Buffalo Society. The terrorists are plotting to avenge the victims of a long-forgotten atrocity by recreating it—with white children as the pawns—in a vicious kidnapping/mass-murder scheme." N Y Times Book Rev

also in Hillerman, T. The Joe Leaphorn mysteries

(ed) The Mysterious West. See The Mysterious West

(ed) The Oxford book of American detective stories. See The Oxford book of American detective stories

People of Darkness. Harper & Row 1980 202p o.p.   LC 80-7605

"A Joan Kahn book"

"Navajo Tribal Police Detective Jim Chee, constantly confronted by the split between the ways of the Indian and those of the white man, is led into an investigation that challenges and torments him. A wealthy woman asks Chee to find a stolen box of keepsakes, which contains the key to a mysterious Navajo cult called 'The People of Darkness,' a buried Indian, peyote abuse, and danger. Hillerman has written an absorbing mystery and a fascinating cultural study." Booklist

also in Hillerman, T. The Jim Chee mysteries

Sacred clowns. HarperCollins Pubs. 1993 305p o.p.   LC 91-50470

"Lt. Joe Leaphorn and Officer Jim Chee of the Navajo police resolve personal issues as they investigate the murders of a tribal dancer and a white schoolteacher." Publ Wkly

"The author skillfully employs the elements of detection and routine police work while providing readers with an intriguing glimpse of Navajo culture. The relationships between the officers and between the other well-defined characters give depth to the story, which is spiced with both men's romantic interests." SLJ

The shape shifter. HarperCollins 2006 276p $26.95

ISBN 0-06-056345-1   LC 2005-52602

"Sgt. Jim Chee and his new wife, Bernie, have just returned from their honeymoon and thus have only a peripheral role here. Lt. Joe Leaphorn, recently retired from the Navajo police force, is front and center in the action, which begins when he receives a letter from an old acquaintance questioning the conclusions they reached years ago in the case of a burned-out trading post. The titular shape shifter refers to the many identities the bad guy has assumed and gives Leaphorn chances to relate Navajo tales of evil and witchcraft." Libr J

"Only Hillerman could so masterfully connect such disparate elements as an ancient cursed weaving, two stolen buckets of piñon sap and the Vietnam War. The conclusion is sure to startle longtime fans of this acclaimed mystery series." Publ Wkly

The sinister pig. HarperCollins Pubs. 2003 228p $25.95

ISBN 0-06-019443-X   LC 2003-42316

"A barren desert landscape is quickly filled with Navajo tribal police, customs patrol officers, and the FBI when a dumped, unidentified body is discovered on the Navajo Reservation. The gathering of experts gives Hillerman the chance to bring back both Lieutenant Joe Leaphorn, whom he retired but can't bear to live without, and Officer Bernie Manuelito, now reassigned to the customs patrol and still ambivalent about her on-again, off-again romance with Sergeant Jim Chee." Booklist

"With his usual up-front approach to issues concerning Native Americans such as endlessly overlapping jurisdictions, Hillerman delivers a masterful tale that both entertains and educates." Publ Wkly

Skinwalkers. Harper & Row 1987 216p hardcover o.p. pa $7.99

ISBN 0-06-015695-3; 0-06-100017-5 (pa)

In this mystery "Leaphorn has three unsolved murders to contend with, and then an attempt is made on Chee's life. Much to Leaphorn's dismay bone head figures are the sole clues found, indicating the work of a skinwalker or witch. Hillerman's Leaphorn and Chee novels convey the Navaho culture with all its intricacies set forth in a meaningful way." Libr J

Talking God. Harper & Row 1989 239p o.p.   LC 88-45914

This "complex tale hinges on the mysterious murder of a man in shiny old shoes who was apparently killed on his way to an ancient tribal ceremony. Leaphorn and Chee's investigation reveals a conflict over ceremonial masks, which in turn takes them from their familiar New Mexico haunts to Washington, D.C., where they must foil an assassination attempt. As in his previous works, Hillerman combines P. D. James' taut, precise narrative style with a consistently sensitive portrayal of the native American experience. The rural landscapes shimmer with realism, while the plot is crafted with skill and passion, like the masks that figure so strongly in the action." Booklist

A thief of time; a novel. Harper & Row 1988 209p o.p.   LC 87-46147

In this novel "Lieut. Joe Leaphorn and Officer Jim Chee of the Navajo Tribal Police . . . combine forces . . . in the search for a missing archeologist, Prof. Elea-

Hillerman, Tony—*Continued*

nor Friedman-Bernal. A specialist in Anasazi pots, she's on the verge of a major breakthrough—the identification of a specific artist, dead a thousand years—when, beneath a full desert moon, she seems simply to vanish." N Y Times Book Rev

"It is the complex relationship between Leaphorn and Chee and the rich view of Navaho culture that give the book its depth and resonance." Booklist

The wailing wind. HarperCollins Pubs. 2002 232p

ISBN 0-06-019444-8

* LC 2001-51734

"Sergeant Jim Chee lures his old boss, Lieutenant Joe Leaphorn, out of retirement with news of a murder that reaches back to an unsolved mystery that has long haunted both Chee and Leaphorn." Booklist

"Hillerman is never better than when he is circling a puzzle from various angles, playing with the perceptions of his detectives as well as the reader's." N Y Times Book Rev

Hilton, James, 1900-1954

Good-bye Mr. Chips; illustrated by H.M. Brock. Little, Brown 1962 c1934 132p il $22

ISBN 0-316-36420-7

*

"An Atlantic Monthly Press book"

First published 1934

"In 1870 Mr. Chipping begins a career teaching the classics at Brookfield Boys' Boarding School in England. After teaching three generations of Brookfield boys, Mr. Chips, as he is fondly called, retires to the boarding house directly across the street from the school. He continues to keep a close watch over the new group of boys and host afternoon teas as a way of sharing his reminiscences. This is a warm testimonial to a caring teacher." Shapiro. Fic for Youth. 3d edition

Lost horizon; a novel. Morrow 1995 c1933 262p hardcover o.p. pa $12.95

ISBN 0-688-14656-2; 0-06-059452-7 (pa)

* LC 96-160022

A reissue of the title first published 1933

"Hugh Conway is a British consul at Baskul when trouble erupts in 1931 and all civilians are evacuated. He and three others board a plane lent by a Maharajah. After they are airborne for several hours, they realize that they are headed in the wrong direction. When the pilot finally lands, the passengers find themselves in Shangri-La, a utopian lamasery whose inhabitants know the secret of attaining long life. Believing that war is going to destroy all civilization, the High Lama summons the newcomers to form the nucleus of a new civilization." Shapiro. Fic for youth. 3d edition

Random harvest. Little, Brown 1941 326p o.p.

"An Atlantic Monthly Press book"

"Charles Rainier, wealthy business man and M.P., for nearly twenty years unable to recall that period of his life between his World War injury and 1919 suddenly has his memory restored. The dramatic suspense is great as Rainier faces his two pasts, passionately resolved to find the Paula of his lost years, at whatever cost to his

present marriage and position. . . . Part of the story is related in the first person by Rainier's secretary and confidante who is interested in psychology." Libr J

Himes, Chester, 1909-1984

The collected stories of Chester Himes; foreword by Calvin Hernton. Thunder's Mouth Press 1991 429p o.p.

LC 90-25682

Contents: Headwaiter; Lunching at the Ritzmore; All God's chillun got pride; A nigger; Let me at the enemyan' George Brown; With malice toward none; A penny for your thoughts; Two soldiers; So softly smiling; Heaven has changed; Looking down the street; The song says 'Keep on smiling'; Her whole existence; He seen it in the stars; Make with the shape; Dirty deceivers; A modern marriage; Black laughter; A night of new roses; The night's for cryin'; Face in the moonlight; Strictly business; Prison mass; Money don't spend in the stir; I don't want to die; The meanest cop in the world; On dreams and reality; The way of flesh; The visiting hour; The things you do; There ain't no justice; Every opportunity; I'm not trying to hurt you; Pork chop paradise; Friends; To what red hell; His last day; In the rain; The ghost of Rufus Jones; Whose little baby are you?; Mama's missionary money; My but the rats are terrible; The snake; In the night; All he needs is feet; Christmas gift; The revelation; Daydream; Da-da-dee; Marihuana and a pistol; One more way to die; Naturally, the Negro; Winter coming on; Spanish gin; The something in a colored man; Tang; One night in New Jersey; A modern fable; Prediction; Life everlasting

Cotton comes to Harlem. Vintage Books 1988 c1965 159p pa $11.95

ISBN 0-394-75999-0

* LC 88-40045

First published 1965 by Putnam

In this mystery featuring "Coffin" Ed Johnson and "Grave Digger" Jones " which, revolves around a cotton bale filled with $87,000, [the author] parodies Marcus Garvey's back to Africa movement. Himes treats the black community with humor and respect, but does not hesitate to show blacks victimizing each other." Murphy. Ency of Murder and mystery

The real cool killers

In Crime novels: American noir of the 1950s

Yesterday will make you cry. Norton 1998 363p

ISBN 0-393-04577-3

LC 97-40364

Written in 1937; first published in different form 1953 with title: Cast the first stone

"This edition restores the work to its original form and chronicles the directionless life of Jimmy Monroe, a smart loser born poor white and rural, who bounces self-destructively through life until sentenced to 20 years in prison for robbery." Publ Wkly

"Is Himes's unexpurgated work anything more than a literary footnote? Some phrases still come off as pulp hardball, but the novel's emotional core continues to smolder. Rage tempered with compassion is the backbone of this story—and what makes it eminently worth reading." N Y Times Book Rev

Hiraoka, Kimitake *See* Mishima, Yukio, 1925-1970

Hirshberg, Glen, 1966-

The Snowman's children. Carroll & Graf Pubs. 2002 324p $24

ISBN 0-7867-1082-9

"Troubled 29-year-old Mattie Rhodes returns to Detroit in search of hs childhood friend Theresa, a brilliant, strange, and mysterious girl who, even now, haunts him. For a few magical months in 1977, Mattie, Theresa, and their friend, Spencer, the lone black boy bused to their school as part of Detroits' desegregation mandate, form a special bond, united by their outsider status. At the same time, a serial killer called the Snowman has been preying on children, snatching them in broad daylight. . . . As Mattie and Spencer begin to sense that Theresa is in danger of slipping away from them and descending into mental illness, they concoct a desperate plan to save her and instead condemn their families to the nightmare of media publicity." Booklist

Hoag, Tami

Dark horse. Bantam Bks. 2002 435p

ISBN 0-553-80192-9   LC 2002-74583

"Elena Estes is a former cop whose bravado on the force resulted in a colleague's death; it also cost her her job and her self-esteem. . . .She's been keeping a low profile at a friend's Florida ranch, but her world is disrupted when 12-year-old Molly Seabright, wise beyond her years, attempts to hire Elena to find her older sister, Erin, who has been missing for two days." Publ Wkly

"A tangled web of deceit and double-dealing makes for a fascinating look into the wealthy world of horses juxtaposed with the realistic introspection of one very troubled ex-cop." Booklist

Dust to dust. Bantam Bks. 2000 354p

ISBN 0-553-10634-1   LC 00-39786

"Minneapolis detective Sam Kovac and his young female partner, Nikki Liska, find themselves hot on the trail of some bad cops. It all starts when they are called to the scene of a homicide, where they find the nude, hanging body of a young Internal Affairs officer, the son of a department hero. Department brass want to declare the case a suicide and close it quickly. But after nosing around a bit, Kovac and Liska begin to suspect something much more sinister. . . . A classic whodunit with many twists and turns and a surprise ending." Booklist

Guilty as sin. Bantam Bks. 1996 470p

ISBN 0-553-09959-0   LC 95-38214

Sequel to Night sins

This suspense novel opens "with an accused kidnapper and child molester sitting in jail awaiting trial. But is the suspect—a respected and beloved college professor—really the author of a devilishly sick scheme to terrorize the families of idyllic Deer Lake, Minn.? Ellen North is the tough county prosecutor, armed with evidence and anger; Tony Costello is the flashy big-town lawyer intent on winning fame and fortune with a headline case; and Jay Butler Brooks is the reporter, a self-centered firebrand who appears to derive pleasure from the suffering of others. . . . As the criminal's clever plot unravels and North and her team come closer to the truth, the tangled relationships that lie just beneath the surface of Deer Lake are tantalizingly revealed." N Y Times Book Rev

Kill the messenger. Bantam Bks. 2004 419p $26

ISBN 0-553-80195-3   LC 2004-47612

Nineteen-year-old L. A. Bike messenger Jace Damon "picks up a package from a shady lawyer, but when he gets to the delivery address, he finds an empty lot; suddenly, someone attacks him and tries to grab the package. The bike messenger takes off, but the attacker pursues him, nearly runs him over with a car, and takes a couple of shots at him. Injured and frightened, Jace returns to Lowell's office only to find the place swarming with cops and the attorney murdered. The plot thickens as Jace attempts to elude both homicide detective Ken Parker, who wants some answers, and a menacing, shadowy figure, who is trying to get that package." Booklist

"A link to Hollywood provides a burst of fresh energy in the later chapters of this character-driven, solidly constructed thriller." Publ Wkly

Night sins. Bantam Bks. 1995 483p

ISBN 0-553-09961-2   LC 94-23910

The "community of Deer Lake, Minn., takes a turn toward Stephen King territory when the local lady doctor's son is snatched by a fiend who leaves enigmatic notes. Attempting to crack the case, feisty feminist Megan O'Malley—who hopes to become the first female field agent for the male-dominated Minnesota Bureau of Criminal Apprehension—finds herself paired with Mitch Holt, the town's love-scarred sheriff (and recovering alcoholic) who is facing assorted personal demons." Publ Wkly

Hoban, Russell

Angelica's Grotto; a novel. Carroll & Graf Pubs. 2001 271p $25

ISBN 0-7867-0878-6   LC 2001-35121

First published 1999 in the United Kingdom

To Harold Klein, 72-year-old art historian, "sexuality is an unavoidable element of art. But from these rarified artistic heights, Klein descends to a more prurient level when he clicks onto a Net sex site called Angelica's Grotto. Klein is already going through a crisis, having suffered a puzzling psychological breakdown similar to Tourette's syndrome. . . . In her cyber-grotto, Angelica (real name, Melissa) is eliciting responses from male viewers for a thesis on sexuality she is writing, and chooses Klein as a chat partner. Eventually, they meet in person (after the near-rape of Klein by one of Melissa's associates) and act out their fantasies in a sadomasochistic, May/December affair." Publ Wkly

"Harold's esoteric musings on art, sex, philosophy, sailing, and everything in between will not appeal to everyone, but those willing to follow his meandering thoughts will be rewarded by an intelligently bizarre novel." Booklist

Her name was Lola. Arcade Pub. 2003 207p $24

ISBN 1-559-70726-7   LC 2003-20375

"Max, a writer struggling with his next novel and meanwhile paying the bills with his children's books starring hedgehog Charlotte Prickles, is torn between two lovers. First, he met Lola, an aristocrat from a British family, and proclaimed her his destiny woman. A few days later, as he and Lola are exploring the National Gallery, he meets Lula Mae, a Texan transplant working in London for a technology company. Suffering from writer's block and the guilt of romancing two women at once, Max argues with himself about the best course of action. Inevitably, he is found out. Lola cannot believe

Hoban, Russell—*Continued*

he has been two-timing her and leaves in a hurry. Soon after, Lula Mae, who is pregnant with Max's child, takes off for the States, saying she doesn't need him." Libr J

"Hoban apparently wants to see how much outrageous artifice and wilful exposure of literary technique he can get away with while still working his magic on the reader. The answer is plenty. Far from being an arid exercise, the novel has great charm and grace." New Statesman

Linger awhile. David R. Godine 2007 132p pa $15.95

ISBN 0-7475-7984-9   LC 2007-123

First published 2006 in the United Kingdom

"Irving Goodman, an elderly and lecherous widower, believes he has fallen in love with a film star, Justine Trimble, the star of 1950s black-and-white cowboy movies. The only hitch is that Justine has been dead for 47 years. Obsessed with her womanly perfection, Irving calls on a hi-tech friend who manages to isolate Justine's 'particles' and, using a customised 'suspension of disbelief', converts the celluloid star into flesh and blood. To the unsuspecting reader, incredulity may interfere at this early stage. Press on, however, and Hoban's world becomes more thought-provoking than absurd. . . . This is, perhaps fortunately, essentially a comic novel. The characters slave to create their impossible dream only to find that their creation (quite literally) is sucking the lifeblood out of them — Hoban is laughing at himself as much as at the rest of us." London Times

Riddley Walker; afterword, notes, and glossary by Russell Hoban. Expanded ed. Indiana Univ. Press 1998 235p il

ISBN 0-253-33448-9

* LC 98-14996

A reissue of the title first published 1980 by Summit Bks.

"About 2,000 years before this novel begins, civilization was shattered by a great barm [bomb]—a flash of light followed by centuries of darkness and ignorance. Riddley [the narrator and interpreter] having reached manhood at 12 and having witnessed the crushing of his father during the unearthing of an ancient machine, sets off on foot across the ruined landscape of Inland [England]. Riddley's quest involves the reader in learning a new language based on English . . . a written language in which spelling is a rusty approximation of sounds handed down orally during the dark centuries." Newsweek

"No review can do more than suggest the range and effect of this extraordinary book. It is 'sui generis,' its inspirations both particular and diverse, its references legion, its craft remarkable—contributing to a whole that is vivid, compelling and certainly unforgettable." Encounter

Hobb, Robin

Assassin's apprentice. Bantam Books 1995 356p map

ISBN 0-553-37445-1   LC 94-28942

"As a royal bastard in the household of King Shrewd, a boy called 'Fitz' spends his early years in the king's stables. When the magic in his blood marks him for destiny, he begins receiving secret instruction, by order of the king, in the art of assassination, a calling that places

him in the midst of a nest of intrigue and arcane maneuverings. Firmly grounded in the trappings of high fantasy, Hobb's first novel features a protagonist whose coming of age revolves around the discovery of the meaning of loyalty and trust. [A] gracefully written fantasy." Libr J

Followed by: Royal assassin (1996) and Assassin's quest (1997)

The mad ship. Bantam Bks. 1999 647p

ISBN 0-553-10333-4   LC 98-51188

In the second volume of the Liveship trilogy "Althea Vestrit is now a seasoned sailor, and with the aid of her family, her lover Brashen Tell, and the curious woodcarver Amber, she restores the abandoned, blind liveship Paragon, the 'mad ship' of the title. Aboard him (Paragon is male), they set out on a bold quest to find and recover the Vestrit family's liveship Vivacia." Booklist

Followed by Ship of destiny

Ship of destiny. Bantam Bks. 2000 581p map

ISBN 0-553-10323-7   LC 00-37839

This is the final volume of the Liveship trilogy. "Unaware of the war that threatens the trading families of Bingtown, Althea Vestrit searches the sea lanes for her stolen liveship—only to discover the truth behind the origin of the sentient vessels. Hobb combines a unique fantasy vision with themes of devotion and selflessness to produce a powerful conclusion to an innovative saga." Libr J

Ship of magic. Bantam Bks. 1998 685p o.p.

LC 97-32216

First book in the author's Liveship traders trilogy

"The untimely death of Old Trader Ephron Vestrit deprives his daughter Althea of her inheritance and places her ambitious brother-in-law Kyle in command of the live ship *Viveca* and the family fortunes. . . . [This novels is] set in a world of sentient ships, merchant traders, ruthless pirates, dangerous treasures, seagoing dragons, and a mysterious elder race. Hobb excels in depicting complex characters; even her villains command respect, if not sympathy, for their actions." Libr J

Followed by The mad ship

Hobson, Laura Keane Zametkin, 1900-1986

Gentleman's agreement; a novel; by Laura Z. Hobson. Simon & Schuster 1947 275p o.p.

"Phil Green, a member of the editorial staff of 'Smith's Weekly,' is assigned to write a series of airiticles about anti-Semitism in America. He decides to pose as a Jew for six months, and he has some extraordinary experiences." Benet's Reader's Ency of Am Lit

Hobson, Will

(tr) Paasilinna, A. The howling miller

Hockensmith, Steve, 1968-

Holmes on the range. St. Martin's Minotaur 2006 294p $22.95

ISBN 978-0-312-34780-2; 0-312-34780-4

LC 2005-50406

Hockensmith, Steve, 1968——*Continued*

This western mystery "features Montana cowboys and brothers Gustav and Otto Amlingmeyer (better known as Old Red and Big Red, respectively). One night in 1892, Old Red becomes smitten with Sherlock Holmes on hearing his brother read 'The Red-Headed League' around the campfire during a cattle drive. Determined to follow in his hero's footsteps, Old Red gets the chance to apply the master's methods after some unsavory characters hire the pair to work at a ranch, whose general manager is soon found dead after a stampede. Another man turns up dead, apparently a suicide, just before the British aristocrats who own the ranch arrive to inspect their property." Publ Wkly

"This is a great reworking of the Holmes conceit, and one suspects Hockensmith will have a steady readership as long as the Amlingmeyers are on the case." Booklist

On the wrong track. St. Martin's Minotaur 2007 292p $23.95

ISBN 978-0-312-34781-9; 0-312-34781-2

LC 2007-5176

"Cowboy detectives Big Red and Old Red Amlingmeyer are back. . . . This time, they are railroad cops assigned to protect a train from the Give 'em Hell Boys." Libr J

"As a lively Holmes takeoff, as an inventive melding of mystery and western genres, and as a new source of damn good reading, this series demands attention." Booklist

Hodgins, Eric, 1899-1971

Mr. Blandings builds his dream house; illustrated by William Steig. Simon & Schuster 1946 237p il o.p.

"Expanded from a 'Fortune' short story, this book is an amusing tale of a New York advertiser who found his apartment much too small and bought 50 acres and a farmhouse in the country. Mr. Blandings' trials and tribulations from the time when the architect, after spending a great deal of time and money, decided that the farmhouse should be torn down instead of remodelled until the new home was finished at a cost of $45,000 more than they expected make hilarious reading." Ont Libr Rev

Høeg, Peter, 1957-

Borderliners; translated by Barbara Haveland. Farrar, Straus & Giroux 1994 277p

ISBN 0-374-11554-0   LC 94-18892

Original Danish edition, 1993

"Hoeg portrays the closed world of Biehl's, a Danish private school where a bizarre social experiment is underway. The narrator, Peter, is now a student at Biehl's after spending all of his life in children's homes and reform schools. He is a borderline case, along with Katarina, whose parents both died in the past year, and August, severely disturbed after killing his abusive parents. Although allowed no social interaction, the children conspire to conduct their own experiment to discover what plan is being carried out at Biehl's." Libr J

"The author avoids simple storytelling, preferring instead to explore the nature of time. 'What is time?' are the book's opening words, and later Mr. Hoeg actually provides brief historical passages on the development of theories of time. In a related device, the novel employs a dreamy, associative narrative, moving back and forth through the years, including flash-forwards to the adult Peter's family life. . . . 'Borderliners' is written from the heart, and its portrait of the embittered survivor Peter is moving." N Y Times Book Rev

The history of Danish dreams; translated by Barbara Haveland. Farrar, Straus & Giroux 1995 356p

ISBN 0-374-17138-6   LC 95-18355

Original Danish edition, 1988

A satiric family saga set in Denmark. "Introduced in the first section are four characters born around the turn of the century: Carl Laurids, whose ambitions lead him beyond his estate, where, in the 16th century, the resident count had banned the keeping of time; Amalie Teader, a girl whose delusion that she has been 'chosen' springs from a wealthy and powerful grandmother, who writes a newspaper that predicts the future; Anna Bak, a pastor's innocent child who is deemed worthy of bearing 'the new Messiah'; and Adonis Jensen, the son of roving thieves, who refuses to learn how to steal because of 'his compassion for mankind.' In Part II, which ends at 1939, these four become couples: Carl and Amalie have a golden child, Carsten, for a son, while Anna and Adonis produce rebellious Maria; in the final section, Carsten and Maria marry and have children of their own." Publ Wkly

"If *Dreams* is regarded not as a novel, but as a marvelous trunkful of loosely related funny bits, . . . it is a great success." Time

The quiet girl; translated from the Danish by Nadia Christensen. Farrar, Straus and Giroux 2007 408p map $26

ISBN 978-0-374-26369-0; 0-374-26369-8

LC 2007-8187

Original Danish edition, 2006

"The hero here is a world-famous circus clown and violinist, Kaspar Krone, who possesses a mystical ability to identify an individual's personality in terms of the sounds and musical keys that emanate from them. His special talent brings him in contact with a group of children who also possess mystical powers—perhaps even the ability to alter physical reality. One of those children, the 'quiet girl' of the title, has disappeared, and Krone is compelled to rescue her from the madman who seems determined to use the children to create panic in Copenhagen's financial institutions. Or possibly it is the quiet girl who is doing the manipulating." Booklist

"In the end, The Quiet Girl seems like two different novels—one a philosophical treatise, the other an adrenaline-laced thriller—that don't easily meet on common ground. It is a story wrapped in enigmas that build to a screeching pitch and leave you dizzy and stunned. But it's the melancholy wit of Hoeg's writing that keeps you engaged, and hoping Kasper finally does comes to terms with his place in the world." Chicago Sun-Times

Smilla's sense of snow; translated by Tiina Nunnally. Farrar Straus Giroux 1993 453p

ISBN 0-374-26644-1

* LC 93-17742

Høeg, Peter, 1957-—*Continued*

Original Danish edition, 1992; published in the United Kingdom with title: Miss Smilla's feeling for snow

This novel "is set in Copenhagen and features Smilla Qaavigaaq, a 37-year-old, part-Eskimo, part-Danish heroine who is investigating the death of Isaiah, her young neighbor. Although police officially rule Isaiah's death an accident, Smilla is convinced that he has been pushed off the roof of her apartment building. Discouraged by Danish officials, the tough, persistent, and resourceful Smilla follows Isaiah's trail to a ship that is docked off the coast of Greenland with a crew that is involved in drug trafficking and mysterious scientific experiments." Libr J

"Selfishness, menace and systematic corruption form the fabric of this mysterious novel. Relationships are all based on suspicion, and love has to be 'like a military operation.'. . . Peter Høeg has a remarkable feeling for sinister surprises." Times Lit Suppl

Tales of the night; translated by Barbara Haveland. Farrar, Straus & Giroux 1998 278p $23

ISBN 0-374-27254-9 LC 97-26664

Original Danish edition, 1990

Contents: Journey into a dark heart; Hommage à Bournonville; The verdict on the Right Honorable Ignatio Landstad Rasker, Lord Chief Justice; An experiment on the constancy of love; Portrait of the avant-garde; Pity for the children of Varden Town; Story of a marriage; Reflection of a young man in balance

These "stories take us to eight separate corners of the world on the night of March 19, 1929. . . . The deep despair and foreboding of well-intentioned Europeans victimized by the very culture that was supposed to educate them is often painfully credible. Potent but problematic, this collection lays bare the difficulties of love, even if it must make do without the dazzling lucidity of Hoeg's more recent works." Publ Wkly

The woman and the ape; translated by Barbara Haveland. Farrar, Straus & Giroux 1997 261p

ISBN 0-374-29203-5 LC 96-27289

"Madelene Burden is a 30-year-old Danish woman, a closet tippler trapped in a loveless marriage with Adam, a famous British zoologist. One day, Adam's horrid sister, Andrea, turns up with a wounded ape named Erasmus, who has escaped from some smugglers. The ape, we are initially led to believe, may be a member of a previously unknown species; receiving credit for this amazing discovery would win Adam the most important zoological post in Europe, perhaps the world. So the ape is spirited off to the conservatory behind Adam and Madelene's London mansion. But then strange things start happening. . . . Bored by her status as a trophy wife, she decides to discover precisely what's going on in that conservatory. Along the way, she develops a genuine affection for her 'irreplaceable playmate,' ultimately helping it to escape. But Erasmus is no ordinary ape. Erasmus is an ape that can talk." N Y Times Book Rev

This novel is "too fresh in its writing and its perceptions to fall into the sentimentality one might expect. An air of freedom surrounds Madelene's eventual abduction by the ape, and though their sexual involvement may seem over the top to some readers, you can't help but be carried along by Hoeg's convictions." Libr J

Hoffman, Alice, 1952-

At risk. Putnam 1988 219p o.p.

    LC 87-33240

"The Farrells are your typical New England upper middle class family. Ivan, the father, is an astronomer, and Polly, the mother, is a free lance photographer. Amanda is a typical 11-year old girl with a passion for gymnastics, and Charles is an 8-year old budding biologist, interested in specimens of frogs and insects and books on dinosaurs. Their comfortable lifestyle is shattered when Amanda is diagnosed as having AIDS. The family goes through stages of disbelief, denial, anger, despair, and finally numbing acceptance as Amanda withers away and is hospitalized at the end presumably with death close at hand." West Coast Rev Books

"Such is Ms. Hoffman's tenderness and perceptiveness that we come to care about her creations despite their imperfections the way we would care about those we love despite theirs." N Y Times Book Rev

Blackbird house. Doubleday 2004 225p

ISBN 0-385-50761-5 LC 2004-07958

Contents: The edge of the world; The witch of Truro; The token; Insulting the angels; Black is the color of my true love's hair; Lionheart; The conjurer's handbook; The wedding of snow and ice; India; The pear tree; The summer kitchen; Wish you were here

"The relationship of the characters to their surroundings is seen as a kind of magical bond, expressed in language that is both eerie and beautiful. The house of the title is one in which, from story to story, we glimpse various families over the course of two centuries. . . . Hoffman lets Blackbird House stand as an emblem for the transforming power of any long-established home, while reveling in the haunting quality of her own distinctive literary style." N Y Times Book Rev

Blue diary. Putnam 2001 303p hardcover o.p. pa $14

ISBN 0-399-14802-7; 0-425-18494-3 (pa)

    LC 2001-19517

Ethan Ford is "suddenly arrested on suspicion of the rape and murder of teenager Rachel Morris 15 years earlier in Maryland. Ethan confesses to the crime, but says that he is now 'a different man,' who has redeemed himself through exemplary behavior. What this revelation means to his beautiful wife of 13 years, Jorie [and] his 12-year-old son, Collie . . . allows the novel to investigate the themes of devotion, betrayal, guilt and forgiveness in trenchantly effective ways." Publ Wkly

Here on Earth. Putnam 1997 293p

ISBN 0-399-14313-0 LC 97-5382

"Set in Jenkintown, a seemingly isolated village within easy driving distance of Boston, [this novel] tells the story of the obsessive love between March Murray, a successful jeweler who lives in California with her professor husband and their 15-year-old daughter, and March's onetime teen-age heartthrob, the malevolent Hollis." N Y Times Book Rev

The novel "is a surprisingly successful recasting of Wuthering Heights. Like that book, it is charged with passion, but unlike their prototypes, the modern-day lovers indulge their lust to their demise. . . . [Hoffman] not only covers the much-furrowed ground of renewing old romances with startling energy, she evokes the tricky relationship between mother and teenage daughter with bitter-sweet insight." Times Lit Suppl

Hoffman, Alice, 1952——*Continued*

The ice queen; a novel. Little, Brown 2005
224p $23.95

ISBN 0-316-05859-9   LC 2004-26610

"Ever since she was eight years old, Hoffman's narrator, a devoted reference librarian, has believed that her temper tantrum caused her mother's death. Her guilt turned her solitary, stoic, and somewhat misanthropic, and she envisions herself as an ice queen. Even after she is struck by lightning. As her damaged narrator reluctantly joins a lightning-strike-survivor support group, Hoffman dramatizes the bizarre effects experienced by real-life lightning strike survivors, and orchestrates a highly erotic and risky romance between the ice queen and a fellow survivor known as Lazarus, whose breath ignites paper. As Hoffman's spellbinding and wonderfully insightful tale unfurls, she pays charming tribute to librarians, revels in metaphors of hot and cold, and poetically explores the meaning of trust, the chemistry of healing, and the reach of love." Booklist

Illumination night. Putnam 1987 224p o.p.

LC 86-30472

"A young couple's marriage has survived struggles and poverty in a countercultural transplant to the off-season isolation of Martha's Vineyard only to face a more unlikely and dangerous threat. A teen-age girl, who has moved next door to care for her sick grandmother, develops an erotic fixation on the husband. Hoffman probes the mythic connotations of the situation as she supplies convincing portraits of the man and woman and of the young girl who is determined to come between them. . . . All of this is delineated with both depth and clarity in a novel that encapsulates and transforms the characters' experiences into broader symbols of yearning and passion." Booklist

Local girls. Putnam 1999 197p $22.95

ISBN 0-399-14507-9   LC 98-50632

Contents: Dear diary; Rose Red; Flight; Gretel; Tell the truth; How to talk to the dead; Fate; Bake at 350°; True confession; The rest of your life; The boy who wrestled with angels; Examining the evidence; Devotion; Still among the living; Local girls

A collection of "interlinked stories about a Jewish Long Island family locked in a downward spiral after the parents' divorce. Most of the stories are told from the viewpoint of Gretel Samuelson as she moves from high-school years to young adulthood. . . . Hoffman doesn't sentimentalize her characters' lives: the tragedies they suffer are ordinary, after all. She has a light touch and a poet's knack for making diffuse elements fall into place with seeming effortlessness." Publ Wkly

Practical magic. Putnam 1995 244p

ISBN 0-399-14055-7   LC 94-47013

This novel is set in Massachusetts. "A family of women notorious for their witchcraft is at the book's center: the Owens sisters and the nieces they're raising, Sally and Gillian. The aunts are famous for dispensing potions to the lovelorn, but the old women are pariahs, too; so when Sally and Gillian grow up, they escape to what they hope will be normality, Sally becomes a perfect homemaker and Gillian a wild thing, but their inheritance can't be dismissed." Newsweek

"The tale of the Owenses' struggle is charmingly told, and a good deal of fun. Dark comedy and a light touch carry the story along to a truly Gothic climax." N Y Times Book Rev

The probable future. Doubleday 2003 322p hardcover o.p. pa $13.95

ISBN 0-385-50760-7; 0-345-45591-8 (pa)

LC 2003-40960

"In a New England family in which generations of women have magical powers, young Stella foresees a murder, a crime that her father is then accused of committing." SLJ

"Filled with vivid (if sometimes sketchy) characters and cinematic descriptions of New England landscapes, this book will be a hit wherever Hoffman is in demand." Libr J

The river king. Putnam 2000 324p

ISBN 0-399-14599-0   LC 00-23870

A novel set in the "small Massachusetts town of Haddan, where the locals resent the snotty denizens of a posh prep school. But not all of Haddan's students are privileged and arrogant. Poor, beautiful, and smart, Carlin is attending Haddan on a swimming scholarship and finds most of her peers callow at best. Gus is also smart, self-possessed, and defiant, and he cannot believe his good luck in befriending a girl as amazing as Carlin. But the boys in his dorm despise and torment him, and no one comprehends the severity of his situation. When his body is pulled from the river, Haddan's legacy of suicide is reexamined, but neither Carlin nor Abe, a maverick policeman, believe that Gus killed himself." Booklist

"It can be hard to find an example of good old-fashioned storytelling these days, but storytelling, refreshingly, is Alice Hoffman's strength." N Y Times Book Rev

Second nature. Putnam 1994 254p o.p.

* LC 93-11595

"Robin Moore rescues a wild, unspeaking young man—called the Wolf Man because he was found, injured, in a wolf trap—from impending transfer to a mental hospital. In the process of teaching Stephen how to live in 'civilized' suburban society, she falls in love with him. Meanwhile, neighborhood animals are found with their throats slit, and a teenage girl is murdered; the Wolf Man is naturally a suspect." Libr J

"In the end, Ms. Hoffman suggests that it is love in all its wondrous forms, from a parent's love for a child to the most consuming sexual passion that truly delineates mankind. Her abiding vision of this ineluctable and uniquely human power informs 'Second Nature' with grace and beauty, making it at once her richest and wisest, as well as her boldest, novel to date." N Y Times Book Rev

Seventh heaven. Putnam 1990 256p o.p.

* LC 89-28737

"The setting is a Long Island, N.Y., housing development from 1959 to 1960, a place of conforming, happy families where husbands mow the lawns of the tract houses and wives meet for coffee, where 'safety hung over the neighborhood like a net.' The arrival of Nora Silk, a brassy divorcée with two young children, is the catalyst for disturbing changes and events, some of them violent. Plucky, impetuous, innocently seductive and a messy housekeeper, Nora is anathema to the subdivision

Hoffman, Alice, 1952-—*Continued*

wives, who ostracize her and whose children torment her eight-year-old clairvoyant son, Billy. But as Nora's presence disturbs the community, it is slowly revealed that behind the identical facades of the houses are secret lives of turmoil, restlessness and longing." Publ Wkly

This is "one of those rare novels so abundant with life it seems to overflow its own pages, these aren't the sort of fictional characters who are all used up by the end of the book; on the contrary, they seem ready to leap straight into another volume." Newsweek

Skylight confessions. Little, Brown and Co. 2007 262p $24.99

ISBN 978-0-316-05878-0; 0-316-05878-5

LC 2006-01391

"On the day of her father's funeral, 17-year-old Arlyn Singer decides the first man who walks down the street will be her one love. That night, Yale senior John Moody stops to ask directions, and Arlyn and John take the first passionate steps toward what will become a marriage of heartache and mutual betrayal. After John's architect father dies, the couple moves into his Connecticut home, a glass house called the Glass Slipper, and Arlyn has an affair with a local laborer. She dies while her second child is still young, and the story forks to follow the divergent paths taken by the Moody children." Publ Wkly

This novel, "about the magic of love and the perils of fate, may be the saddest book [Hoffman's] ever written, but it is also one of her very best. . . . [Arlie's] ephemeral self is what fuels the tale—she is a fairy-tale creature, to be sure, and yet she is also obviously a flesh-and-blood woman with deep and compelling desires." Baltimore Sun

The story sisters; a novel. Shaye Areheart Books 2009 325p $25

ISBN 978-0-307-39386-9; 0-307-39386-0

LC 2008-51054

"The Story sisters, Elv, Meg, and Claire, are dark-haired beauties clustered in the attic of their old Long Island house, while their lonely mother broods below. Their all-female household, a sly variation on Little Women, is under a grim fairy-tale spell, and not even sojourns with their fairy-godmother-like grandmother in Paris can protect them. . . . Meg is practical, while Elv and Claire share a tragic secret, and Elv channels her anguish into elaborate, demon-haunted tales of an imaginary parallel world until she discovers more effective means of self-punishment." Booklist

The third angel; a novel. Shaye Areheart Books 2008 278p $25

ISBN 978-0-307-39385-2; 0-307-39385-2

LC 2007-28071

This is the "tale of three women, all terribly in love with the wrong men. The novel is . . . constructed in three sections, narrated in three different time periods. The women in each section stay on the seventh floor of the haunted Lion Park Hotel in London. The first woman, Maddy Heller, stays at the Lion Park in 1999 for her sister's wedding. Her story is compelling in that she is secretly and tragically in love with her sister's fiance. In 1966, the second woman, Frieda Lewis, falls in love with a guest at the hotel: an American rock star and drug addict who happens to be engaged to someone else. And

in 1952, the third woman, Bryn Evans, betrays her fiance at the Lion Park, to disastrous results. At the very end of the novel, Hoffman reveals the tragedy of the Lion Park ghost, the suspenseful event that connects all the women in powerful and mystical ways." Rocky Mountain News

Turtle Moon. Putnam 1992 255p

ISBN 0-399-13720-3   LC 91-37222

"Julian Cash, policeman, and Lucy Rosen, obit writer, both with hardened shells covering events that shattered their younger selves, are thrown together when they try to solve a murder that endangers Lucy's son and the murdered woman's child. In the ensuing days they gradually draw solace from each other and revisit their pasts in search of the solution to the murder; Lucy to Great Neck, New York where she lived after her parents died when she was 16; Julian to the foster mother who raised him and the gumbo-limbo tree where an imprisoned angel waits, the cousin Julian killed in a car accident 20 years earlier." Libr J

"Hoffman handles romance, suspense, and the healing properties of love and understanding with aplomb and a dash of magic." Booklist

Hoffman, Eva

Appassionata. Other Press 2009 265p $25

ISBN 978-1-59051-319-4   LC 2008-42015

First published 2008 in the United Kingdom with title: Illuminations

"Isabel is an accomplished pianist, and on one of her many tours abroad, she encounters the mysterious Chechen rebel Anzor. At first, she is drawn to him and feels sympathy for his cause, and soon enough she enters into an affair with him. They meet clandestinely in various European cities, but as she comes to learn more about his mysterious undertakings and witnesses at close range the havoc they can create, she comes to question her own values and her fragmented, unsettled way of life." Libr J

"Hoffman's prose is reliably gorgeous, and while the narrative lends itself nicely to sharp commentary and observations on politics, power and the role of the United States in a changing world, what's memorable is the way Hoffman maps the intersection of art, history and man's striving for meaning." Publ Wkly

The secret; a novel. PublicAffairs 2002 265p $25

ISBN 1-58648-150-9   LC 2002-73433

"The time is 2022, the place is Chicago, and Iris Surrey has an unusually close relationship with her chilly mother, Elizabeth. At 17, Iris is wearying of the odd stares she triggers in others, especially when her look-alike mother is with her. Iris wants to learn the identity of her father, which, alas, is not possible; the reader will figure out before Iris does that she is the product of genetic engineering. When Iris uncovers the truth, she goes on an emotional rampage, intent on tracking down any blood relatives in the hope that they will make her feel more authentic." Libr J

This work "is compelling throughout for Hoffman's prose, for her insights on identity, for her reflections on history." N Y Times Book Rev

Hoffman, Jilliane, 1967-

Retribution. G.P. Putnam's Sons 2004 420p $24.95

ISBN 0-399-15127-3   LC 2003-46502

"In the late 1980s, law student Chloe Larson was brutally raped and left for dead in her New York apartment. Fast-forward 12 years; Chloe, now known as C.J. Townsend, is one of the top prosecutors in Miami. It is in this capacity that she finds herself face to face with the man who terrorized her." Libr J

"The twists and turns are a suspense lover's dream the climax is chillingly good. An absolutely remarkable first outing." Rendezvous Magazine

Hoffman, Nina Kiriki

Catalyst. Tachyon Publications 2006 171p pa $14.95

ISBN 1-892391-38-4

"Soon after just-barely-adolescent Kaslin and his family join the human colony on the planet Chuudoku, Kaslin falls into the clutches of an alien tribe. Kaslin's life has had little to recommend it—his father's a deadbeat, his mother's a workaholic and he's frequently beaten up, poisoned and mocked by Histly, the physically augmented daughter of one of the richest men on the planet—so he throws himself into living his dream of first contact. The aliens are endlessly curious about human bodies, leading Kaslin to bizarre erotic couplings first with his captors and then with Histly." Publ Wkly

"Kaslin—and Histly, for that matter—are vibrant creations, their psychology utterly credible for smart adolescents. That the book ends with everything but Kaslin and Histly's relationship up in the air may indicate merely that Hoffman knew when she had achieved perfection." Booklist

Hofmann, Gert

Lichtenberg and the little flower girl; translated and with an afterword by Michael Hofmann. New Directions 2004 245p $19.95

ISBN 0-8112-1568-7

     * LC 2003-28140

Original German edition, 1994

"Georg Christoph Lichtenberg, an eighteenth-century Göttingen mathematician, physicist, and astronomer, is remembered for the satiric aphorisms he wrote in his spare time, which have been celebrated by luminaries from Nietzsche to Einstein. He was also a dwarf and a hunchback, attributes crucial to this lively fictionalization of his life by the late German novelist, which charts Lichtenberg's love affair with the progress of civilization and, in parallel, his failure to find a wife. Hofmann gives the scientist a delirious, childish glee at the universe's workings, and a sweetness of character that, true to Lichtenberg's biography, eventually wins him the love of a thirteen-year-old beauty. The author shares with his hero a gift for the epigram, which makes the book seem at first a rather weightless affair. But a mass of loneliness and longing just beneath the comedy keeps it from floating away." New Yorker

Luck; translated from the German by Michael Hofmann. New Directions 2002 266p $23.95

ISBN 0-8112-1502-4

     * LC 2002-3556

Original German edition, 1992

This novel "chronicles the bitter end of a marriage, capturing. . .the relationship's final day as experienced by father, mother, son and daughter. The son serves as the novel's nameless narrator, and in many ways the story itself, as well as the act of its telling, marks the end of his adolescence." N Y Times Book Rev

"Stripped, spare prose creates the impression that the boy is merely a detached witness to his parents' separation, but subtle clues belie his neutrality. . . .While Hofmann's desolate emotional landsapes and darkly comic observations are not for those seeking a literary lark, readers will appreciate his deft handling of the minimalist plot and his authentic rendering of a precociously perceptive boy baffled by his elders." Publ Wkly

Hofmann, Michael, 1957-

(tr) Roth, J. The collected stories of Joseph Roth

(tr) Stamm, P. On a day like this

(tr) Wander, F. The seventh well

Holden, Craig

The jazz bird. Simon & Schuster 2002 314p $25

ISBN 0-7432-1296-7   LC 2001-32259

"Charlie Taft is a prosecutor in late 1920s Cincinnati. . . . When bootlegger George Remus turns himself in, in October 1927, for shooting his society wife, Imogene, Charlie thinks he's been handed a career maker. But all is not as simple as it seems." Publ Wkly

This novel "is based on an actual murder that place in Cincinnati in 1927. In addition to its exploration of the Remus murder case, the book offers a portrait of a now-lost Cincinnati, with its jazz clubs, its great Roebling suspension bridge and its neighborhoods with names like Over the Rhine and Eden Park." N Y Times Book Rev

Holland, Cecelia, 1943-

The angel and the sword. Forge 2000 304p $23.95

ISBN 0-312-86890-1   LC 00-30668

"A Tom Doherty Associates book"

Set in "ninth-century Paris, the novel centers on King Charles the Bald's fight to save the city when the continued demands of the Vikings can no longer be met. To his aid comes the young, intensely spiritual Lord Roderick. Roderick is in fact the Princess Ragny, who fled her native Spain and incestuous father by disguising herself as a man. As Roderick, Ragny struggles with her sin of deception, her personal identity, womanhood, and the privileges and restrictions of manhood. She also manages to become a hero in battle. . . . A wonderful story of faith, love, hope, and justice." Libr J

The firedrake. Atheneum Pubs. 1966 c1965 243p o.p.

A "picaresque tale set in 11th century Germany, Flanders, Normandy and England. The Irish hero, named Laeghaire, the Gaelic spelling of Lear, is a brave, hard-fighting mercenary in the forces of William of Normandy. He is impetuous, brawling, very proud, with a plain and cutting tongue. Laeghaire kills men in battle with no

Holland, Cecelia, 1943-—*Continued*

hesitation, but he is haunted with nightmares about an ugly future. He is a restless adventurer, he is briefly a man in love, he is a violent man of action. This vital central character is placed against a colorful medieval background of castles and wild countryside and in the middle of one fight after another." Publ Wkly

Jerusalem. Forge 1996 318p o.p.
LC 95-38814
"A Tom Doherty Associates book"
This historical novel "takes place in the Holy Land, during the 12th century, in the years before Crusader Jerusalem fell to the Muslims—a time when the Christian leaders fought among themselves whenever Saladin gave them respite. . . . [Holland centers] her story on the Knights Templar, ferocious warriors who took vows of chastity and attempted to live like monks." N Y Times Book Rev
"The narrative structure may be simple, but Holland's masterful layering of subplots, historical detail and multiple perspectives makes for a great read." Publ Wkly

An ordinary woman; a dramatized biography of Nancy Kelsey. Forge 1999 223p
ISBN 0-312-86528-7
LC 98-48929
"A Tom Doherty Associates book"
A "fictionalized biography of Nancy Kelsey, the first American woman to reach California. Traveling by horse and on foot, 17-year-old Nancy leaves Missouri with a baby on her hip in search of California's holy grail. Part of the 1841 Bidwell-Bartleson party, Nancy and her husband, Ben, decide against the meandering Santa Fe Trail in order to take a more—direct and uncharted—course directly across the continent: traversing the Great Plains, the Rockies, the desert and the Sierra Nevadas. . . . The thorough research lends authority to a vivid and engaging narrative that suffers only a little from Holland's evident fervent admiration for her heroine." Publ Wkly

Pacific Street. Houghton Mifflin 1992 260p o.p.
LC 91-27314
"A Peter Davison book"
This novel creates a "montage of San Francisco in its wild beginnings. The aptly named Frances Hardheart, an escaped slave with a quick wit, a sharp tongue and a knack for using people, has found the Shining Light, a haven for non-whites. With her protégée, the beautiful and white Daisy Duncan, she sets up a stage show and bar, enlisting the aid of such likable characters as good-natured, white Gil Marcus and taciturn, Indian Mitya. Frances, aka Mammy, soon extends her influence to the city's rising political and social elite." Publ Wkly
"The plot's credibility runs a little thin at times, but Holland captures the lawlessness of early San Francisco with style and imagination and tells a story both engaging and romantic." Libr J

Pillar of the Sky; a novel. Knopf 1985 534p o.p.
LC 84-48659
The novel is set in prehistoric England, the "central character is Moloquin, who has lived as a wild child since his mother, Ael, was banished from her village by her brother Ladon, the ruler of the People. When Moloquin is adopted by Karella, the clan's storyteller, he joins the tribe, eventually overthrowing Ladon and becoming the People's new chief. Discovering the dark se-

cret of his father's true identity, the demon-possessed Moloquin buries his shame by overseeing the construction of Stonehenge in the Pillar of the Sky, an ancient burial ground." N Y Times Book Rev
"Part Christ figure and part avenger, [Moloquin] is companionable with women, but also amazingly brutal. The tale is full of subtleties and contradictions and depicts a long struggle between the forces of change and those favoring stability. . . . This is more a story of power and customs than of Stonehenge and the early Britons." Libr J

Valley of the Kings; a novel of Tutankhamun. Forge 1997 231p o.p.
LC 97-5499
"A Tom Doherty Associates book"
First published 1977 by Dutton under the pseudonym Elizabeth Eliot Carter
The first half of the "novel is narrated by a fictionalized Howard Carter, the Englishman who discovered Tut's tomb in 1922. Holland does an excellent job of rendering Carter's strained relationship with his upper-crust patron, Lord Carnarvon, while surrounded by obtuse British bureaucrats, archeologists more interested in treasure than history and a culture that Carter loves despite its otherness. . . . The second half of the book flashes back to the ancient Egypt of Tut and concerns three common Egyptians—a mason, a beggar and a maid—who are variously damaged and nurtured by the royals, who have their own problems." Publ Wkly

Holland, Isabelle

A death at St. Anselm's. Doubleday 1984 229p o.p.
LC 83-11668
"An Episcopal church is rocked by the brutal murder of the parish's business manager, Dick Grism. Grism's helplessness as a paraplegic underscores the savagery of the crime, leading New York City police to search for suspects among the drug addicts and mentally unbalanced who frequent St. Anselm's—including the disturbed, anorexic daughter of the female pastor." Booklist
"Holland remains one of the best of modern romantic suspense writers. Her characters (except for her maniacal murderer) are believable, and her settings (in this case, a modern urban church) are uncommon without being wildly exotic." Wilson Libr Bull

Holland, Travis

The archivist's story. Dial Press 2007 239p $23
ISBN 978-0-385-33995-7; 0-385-33995-X
LC 2006-31932
This "novel tracks the plight of disgraced literature teacher and reluctant archivist Pavel Dubrov, whose job, mainly, in 1939 Moscow, is to destroy books at Lubyanka prison, a dank, morbid depository for political prisoners where the boilers rarely work. When an unsigned story is discovered in a prison file, Pavel is ordered to authenticate its author, believed to be Isaac Babel, who is locked up at the prison. Haunted by his conversations with Babel and his love of Babel's work, Pavel steals the manuscript and hides it behind the crumbling bricks of his apartment's basement. (Later, he smuggles out a second manuscript.) He has little to lose: his young wife was killed in a train accident, his mentor is waiting to be carted off to prison for his unwillingness to walk the Party line, and his mother is succumbing to

Holland, Travis—*Continued*

a brain tumor." Publ Wkly

"There is a quiet authenticity about Holland's writing that draws you in, and soon you will find yourself sitting on the edge of your seat, silently cheering for his characters." Libr J

Hollingshead, Greg, 1947-

Bedlam. Thomas Dunne Books 2006 312p $24.95

ISBN 978-0-312-35474-9; 0-312-35474-6

LC 2006-44416

First published 2004 in Canada

This novel "begins in 1797 with a jolt: in the bedroom of a real (if minor) historical woman surprised by the unexpected arrival of her naked husband, James Tilly Matthews, an escapee from a London madhouse who is soon back within its walls. After this wrenching, lunatic scene, the novel details, in three different narrative voices, a prolonged struggle both to release him and to discover the possibly political reason for his incarceration. Interspersed are the emotional letters husband and wife write to each other and one touching note from their son. . . . 'Bedlam' has no end of gorgeous writing. Ostentatious language is always a danger when using narrators from the distant past, but Hollingshead's descriptions stand tastefully back from such overexuberance." N Y Times Book Rev

Holt, Victoria, 1906-1993

For works written by this author under other names see Plaidy, Jean, 1906-1993

The black opal. Doubleday 1993 275p o.p.

LC 92-33830

In this "romantic mystery, Dr. Marline and his ailing wife adopt young Carmel March after she is found wandering among the azaleas on their estate, Commonwood House. Soon she is on her way to a new life in Australia. When Carmel finally returns as a young woman, she realizes that she was hustled away to shield her from a mysterious murder at Commonwood House, and she is convinced that the wrong man has been convicted for the crime." Libr J

Bride of Pendorric. Doubleday 1963 288p o.p.

Favel Farrington is a young bride, married to handsome Roc Pendorric. She is fearful that he has chosen her for her money and that she will become another of the legendary brides of Pendorric Castle to die young and tragically

The Judas kiss. Doubleday 1981 400p o.p.

LC 81-43138

"Pippa Ewing discovers that her beloved older sister Francine has been murdered as she lay in bed with her husband Baron Rudolph. As evidence accumulates to show that Francine had not married him after all, Pippa is launched on a quest to solve her sister's murder and vindicate her name, a journey that takes her to the duchy of Bruxenstein; a job as a governess; and another encounter with Nordic, handsome Conrad, who had caused Pippa to 'fall down the slippery slope' one romantic evening. Mysteries pile up as two similar midnight fires take the lives of a pious and cruel grandfather and a young countess. . . . Plenty of romance, an agreeable amount

of sex, lots of danger and suspense in Gothic and exotic settings ensure that this will please Holt fans." Publ Wkly

Mistress of Mellyn. Doubleday 1960 334p o.p.

In this romantic novel set in late 19th century England, the heroine is an attractive, young English governess. "She takes charge of the motherless child of a handsome, arrogant gentleman who lives in a large creepy mansion in Cornwall. The plot is lively and complicated. Eventually, our bright heroine discovers that her little pupil's mother was murdered and she narrowly escapes being murdered herself." Publ Wkly

My enemy the Queen. Doubleday 1978 348p o.p.

LC 77-11366

This novel of the Elizabethan era is narrated by Lettice Knollys, cousin of the queen and wife of the Earl of Essex. "Aware that Robert Dudley is the favorite of Elizabeth I and of dark rumors about the death of his wife, Lettice becomes one of Dudley's closet strumpets anyhow. When her husband dies, the Countess dares the axe by marrying Robert, but then betrays him by carrying on with a young man who becomes her third husband when Dudley dies. All the events of a momentous age are colored by Lettice's vanity, even the beheading of her own son, the second Essex, who supplants his stepfather in the affections of the queen." Publ Wkly

Secret for a nightingale. Doubleday 1986 371p o.p.

LC 86-2206

"In this Victorian romance, Susanna Pleydell loses her husband to drugs and her dearly loved child to her husband's neglect. She develops an obsessive hatred for Damien Adair, the physician she holds responsible for both tragedies. She tries to forget by taking up a nursing career, eventually going to the Crimea. There, working beside Dr. Adair, she finds herself attracted to him despite her hatred. . . . This is one of the better Holt novels, with a well-drawn historical background." Libr J

Holthe, Tess Uriza

When the elephants dance; a novel. Crown 2002 368p il

ISBN 0-609-60952-1

A novel set "in the final days of the battle for the Philippines. During MacArthur's assault on Manila, a group of neighbors seek shelter in the cellar of an abandoned house. Cramped, starving and terrified, they begin to tell each other stories in order 'to stay alive when you have died inside'. . . . Full of weird, fantastic twists and folkloric wisdom, the stories become both a touchstone to and a respite from the horrific events unfolding outside." N Y Times Book Rev

Homes, A. M.

This book will save your life. Viking 2006 372p $24.95

ISBN 0-670-03493-2

LC 2005-54697

"Richard Novak's day-trading fortune has given him the good life in the hills above 21st-century Los Angeles, but a heart-attack scare exposes his isolation, and a rapidly expanding sinkhole in his front yard forces him to move to a Malibu rental. These crises throw Richard into the paths of such diverse characters as a donut shop

Homes, A. M.—*Continued*

owner, a runaway housewife, and a reclusive, iconic author. His eventual return to humanity culminates in a confrontational and emotional visit with teenage son Ben. . . . Overall, this is an engaging and timely tale told with a balanced mix of dark humor and sympathy for individuals enduring the foibles of everyday living." Libr J

Hood, Ann, 1956-

The knitting circle. W. W. Norton 2007 346p
ISBN 978-0-393-05901-4; 0-393-05901-4

          LC 2006-32223

"After the sudden death of her five-year-old daughter, Stella, Mary Baxter is advised by her mother that learning to knit will take her mind off her grief. When she joins the local knitting circle, she learns that all of its members have a tragic story as well. As she starts knitting and develops a group of friends who understand the depths of loss, Mary's grief begins to heal, allowing her to return to work, repair her marriage, and learn a terrible secret from her mother." Libr J

This novel was "written after Hood's own tragic loss, the death of her young daughter, and it is not hard to imagine the ways in which writing this novel must have been both painful and therapeutic. It is a wondrously simple book about something complicated: the nearly unendurable process of enduring after a great loss. The novel, like knitting, seems to make itself up as it goes along, the threads bound and gathered into a whole. In the end, there is something where there once was nothing." Washington Post Book World

An ornithologist's guide to life. W.W. Norton 2004 237p $23.95
ISBN 0-393-05900-6   LC 2004-6112

Contents: Total cave darkness; The rightness of things; The language of sorrow; After Zane; Joelle's mother; Escapes; Lost parts; Dropping bombs; Inside Gorbachev's head; New people; An ornithologist's guide to life

"Hood is a seductive storyteller, given her emotionally reckless and nonconformist characters, sensuous detail, precise dialogue, and keen rendition of the inner monologue that so often contradicts what we say and do. She also engineers just the sort of painful and inexplicable familial and romantic predicaments friends spend hours attempting to decipher." Booklist

Places to stay the night. Doubleday 1993 275p
ISBN 0-385-42556-2   LC 92-10526

"Small-town life in Holly, Massachusetts, serves as the backdrop for two family crisis. The lives of former high school classmates Tom and Libby Harper and Renata Handy intersect when beautiful but unhappy Libby decides to leave Tom and their children and Renata the outsider returns. While Libby seeks fulfillment, Renata only wants to give her fatally ill daughter a moment of normalcy. Despite their own confusion and anger, Tom and his teenage children provide a temporary refuge for Renata." Libr J

"Hood, an accomplished scene setter and dialogist, works out the consequences of the characters' confusion of dream with fantasy and their groping return to truth with a wonderful frankness that illuminates the lessons of paradox and our belief in romance. An exceptionally fluent tale about the unending process of growing up." Booklist

Hooker, Richard

MASH. Morrow 1968 219p pa $13 hardcover o.p.
ISBN 0-688-14955-3 (pa)

          * LC 68-29610

"Captains Hawkeye Pierce, Duke Forrest, and 'Trapper' John McIntyre, all M.D.'s, are stationed in Korea with the 4077th MASH (Mobile Army Surgical Hospital). The reader is soon involved in many operations and medical jargon. It is, however, the off-duty activities of these three that engages one's attention and laughter. Full of martinis, or bored, or tired, or all three, the men soon start raising hell. . . . Hilarious, occasionally very serious, full of warm, appealing eccentric characters, one could enjoy a very pleasant evening with this sMASHing novel." Libr J

Hooper, Chloe, 1973-

A child's book of true crime. Scribner 2002 238p $23
ISBN 0-7432-2512-0

"Kate Byrne, a primary-school teacher in Tasmania, is having an affair with the father of one of her students. But even as she obligingly plays the part of the slutty young mistress, she waits, like a child, to be punished; her lover's wife has just written a highly colored account of a local sex crime, and Kate is convinced that the older woman means to harm her. Hooper's first novel is at once suspenseful and self-conscious; crammed with fragments of animal fables, erotic fantasies, deaths remembered and foretold, it becomes a witty and unsettling meditation on innocence and experience." New Yorker

Hooper, Kay

Blood sins. Bantam Books 2009 296p $25
ISBN 978-0-553-80485-0; 0-553-80485-5

          LC 2008-34883

In this "paranormal thriller, the second in a trilogy (after Blood Dreams) . . ., Noah Bishop, of the FBI's Special Crimes Unit, and Haven, a civilian investigative organization, take on the fanatical Rev. Adam Deacon Samuel. At age 10, Samuel murdered his abusive prostitute mother by using psychic powers, which a few years later increased after lightning struck him during a tent revival. Noah and his colleagues suspect Samuel, the leader of the Church of the Everlasting Sin, of killing at least eight people via supernatural means and of abusing young girls to enhance his powers. Tessa Gray, a Haven operative posing as a recent widow, reluctantly infiltrates Samuel's compound in the small town of Grace, N.C., near where the body of a fellow Haven operative surfaced in a river. Hooper pulls out all the stops in depicting the unholy preacher's apocalyptic breakdown as Noah's elite team tackles one of their nastiest assignments yet." Publ Wkly

Finding Laura. Bantam Bks. 1997 322p il o.p.

          LC 97-10116

At the Kilbourne estate auction in Atlanta "striking redhead Laura Sutherland is delighted to acquire a beautiful 200-year-old mirror for her collection. But she's no longer convinced her purchase is a bargain when magnetic Peter Kilbourne turns up dead only hours after attempting to buy back the mirror, and the police immedi-

Hooper, Kay—*Continued*

ately consider her a suspect. . . . Hooper keeps the intrigue pleasurably complicated, with gothic touches of suspense and a statifying resolution." Publ Wkly

Haunting Rachel. Bantam Bks. 1998 346p

ISBN 0-553-09950-7 LC 98-607160

"Rachel Grant's fiancé, Thomas, was lost in the jungles of South America ten years ago, just before their wedding, and she has never found another man to replace him. After her parents die in a plane crash, Rachel begins to catch glimpses of a man who looks very much like Thomas, always right before suspicious accidents threaten her life. As the threats become more deadly and Rachel comes to know the mysterious stranger who resembles her dead lover, messages that seem to come from beyond the grave warn her away." Libr J

"The book keeps you on your toes with plenty of suspects and motives to choose from as well as a ghostly intervention or two." Booklist

Stealing shadows. Bantam Books 2000 356p pa $7.99

ISBN 0-553-57553-8 LC 2003-576744

"The first in a . . . 'thrill-ogy' of suspense novels, this is a serial killer tale charged with deeply felt dread and romance that will steal readers' hearts. Cassie Neill has inherited a psychic gift from her mother that is a mixed blessing at best because it enables her to enter the minds of serial rapists and killers. From her aunt, she inherits a house tucked away in a corner of quiet little Ryan's Bluff, North Carolina, where she takes refuge, hoping to distance herself from the grueling work she's done for the Los Angeles Police Department. But, just as there's no rest for the weary, there's no rest for the wicked either, and visions of a deranged man's plans to kill prompt Cassie to visit Ben Ryan, the small town's prosecuting attorney. Skeptical but interested, Ben finds himself drawn toward the oddly bewitching Cassie, just as she is pulled ever further into the psychotic soul of evil." Booklist

Followed by Hiding in the shadows (2000) and Out of the shadows (2000)

Hope, Anthony, 1863-1933

The prisoner of Zenda; being the history of three months in the life of an English gentleman. Holt & Co. 1894 226p o.p.

"Rudolf Rassendyll, an Englishman, makes a three month's visit to the kingdom of Ruritania. He arrives on the eve of the coronation of King Rudolf. The king has an enemy in his brother, Duke Michael, who aspires to the throne himself. During the festivities at Zenda Castle, the Duke drugs King Rudolf so that he is unable to attend his own coronation. Later, Rassendyll, . . . succeeds in impersonating the King and is crowned in his stead. In the meantime, Princess Flavia, the king's betrothed, falls in love with Rassendyll, who in turn loves her. After many dramatic and dangerous escapades, duels, and intrigues King Rudolf is rescued from Zenda Castle where he is held prisoner by Duke Michael. Rassendyll and Princess Flavia renounce each other when the King is restored, and Rassendyll returns to England." Haydn. Thesaurus of Book Dig

Hopley, George, 1903-1968

For works written by this author under other names see Woolrich, Cornell, 1903-1968

Hopley-Woolrich, Cornell George *See* Woolrich, Cornell, 1903-1968

Horan, Nancy

Loving Frank. Ballantine Books 2007 362p $23.95

ISBN 978-0-345-49499-3; 0-345-49499-7

LC 2007-14810

"In 1904, Frank Lloyd Wright started work on a house for an Oak Park couple, Edwin and Mamah Cheney, and, before long, he and Mamah had begun a scandalous affair. In her first novel, Horan, viewing the relationship from Mamah's perspective, does well to avoid serving up a bodice-ripper for the smart set. If anything, she cleaves too faithfully to the sources, occasionally giving her story the feel of a dissertation masquerading as a novel, she succeeds in conveying the emotional center of her protagonist, whom she paints as a proto-feminist, an educated woman fettered by the role of bourgeois matriarch. Horan best evokes Mamah's troubled personality by means of delicately rendered reflections on the power of the natural world, from which her lover drew inspiration." New Yorker

Horn, Dara

All other nights; a novel. W.W. Norton & Co. 2009 363p $24.95

ISBN 978-0-393-06492-6 LC 2008-53412

"Jacob Rappaport, a Jewish soldier in the Union army during the Civil War is ordered to murder his own uncle in New Orleans, who is plotting to assassinate President Lincoln. After this harrowing mission, Jacob is recruited to pursue another enemy agent, the daughter of a Virginia family friend. But this time, his assignment isn't to murder the spy, but to marry her." Publisher's note

The author "both unearths a fascinating, relatively unexplored aspect of American history—the role of Jewish Americans in the Civil War—and delivers a novel rich in human emotion and ambiguity. A triumph." Booklist

The world to come; a novel. W.W. Norton & Co. 2006 314p $24.95

ISBN 0-393-05107-2 LC 2005-14586

"An actual art heist inspired this fictional tale of former child prodigy and television quiz-show writer Benjamin Ziskind, who steals a Chagall sketch from a New York museum during a singles cocktail hour–he's convinced the painting, titled Over Vitebsk, belongs to his family. The provenance of the piece is revealed layer by layer in Horn's . . . novel, which takes readers from a 1920s Soviet orphanage (at which the real-life Chagall taught art to young Jewish boys) to the battlefields of Vietnam, where Benjamin's father lost one of his legs. With the help of his twin sister, Sara, a talented painter, Benjamin hopes to outsmart the comely museum representative who's pegged him for the crime." Booklist

There is "much to be said for this novel. Dara Horn is skillful with words. She is serious about writing 'Jewish literature,' and she knows her Jewish sources and treats them sensitively. Good at describing people and

Horn, Dara—*Continued*

places, she is also good at dialogue. And she has the ability to construct a complex story from a large number of components and to build an utterly coherent whole out of them. The World to Come is architecturally complicated, but as architecture it 'works' beautifully." Commentary

Hornberger, H. Richard, 1924-1997

For works written by this author in collaboration with W. E. Butterworth see Hooker, Richard

Hornby, Nick

About a boy. Riverhead Bks. 1998 307p
ISBN 1-57322-087-6   LC 97-46499
The protagonist of this satire set in London is 36-year-old underachieving bachelor Will Lightman. "Targeting single mothers, he joins a single parents' group under false pretenses and is soon drawn into the lives of depressed Fiona and her bright 12-year-old son, Marcus. Suddenly, his life is messy and complicated. . . . [Hornby] has an uncanny ability for homing in on wholly contemporary, often serious topics and serving them up in truly hilarious fashion." Booklist

High fidelity. Riverhead Bks. 1995 323p
ISBN 1-57322-016-7   LC 95-8469
"Owner of a small London record shop and musical snob of a high degree, [thirty-five-year-old protagonist Rob Fleming] . . . finds his life thrown into turmoil when live-in girlfriend Laura suddenly leaves. He embarks on a journey through the past, tracking down old lovers while finding solace with Marie, an American folk/country singer living in London, even as he yearns for Laura's return." Libr J
"Happily, Hornby does not rely on pop-cultural allusion to limn his characters' inner lives, but uses it instead to create a rich, wry backdrop for them." Time

How to be good. Riverhead Bks. 2001 305p
ISBN 1-57322-193-7   LC 2001-19395
"'I'm not a bad person. I'm a doctor,' says Katie Carr, liberal 1990s North London mother of two. This is her hollow mantra, the only comfort that she can feign while her 20-year marriage to surly David falls to pieces. Just when she is about to be kicked out of the house after confessing to an affair, David returns from a visit with an ecstasy-dropping club kid-turned-faith healer named DJ GoodNews a changed—a *good*—man." Libr J
This novel "hits the funny bone but bruises the conscience. . . . Hornby draws the curtain aside and drags our ethics onto center stage where we can watch them squirm." Christ Sci Mount

Juliet, naked. Riverhead Books 2009 406p
$25.95
ISBN 978-1-59448-887-0; 1-59448-887-8
                            LC 2009-23773
"Duncan is a middle-aged Brit living in the dreary seaside town of Gooleness. He's unhealthily obsessed with Tucker Crowe, a mostly obscure American singer-songwriter who hasn't put out an album since the 1980s. Annie is Duncan's girlfriend of 15 years. . . . Annie tolerates Duncan's musical obsession, but when she disagrees with his fawning review of a new Crowe outtakes album, she realizes her boyfriend is a bit of a wanker.

She leaves him. Soon, she serendipitously strikes up an email correspondence with Crowe himself, who's been living out of the public eye on a farm in Pennsylvania. Like Annie, he feels like he's wasted the last 15 years of his life. . . . [Hornby] shows how obsessing over music isn't the road to love and self-actualization. It's the road to heartbreak." N Y Post

A long way down. Riverhead Books 2005 333p
$24.95
ISBN 1-57322-302-6   LC 2004-58837
"Hornby follows four depressed people from their aborted suicide attempts on New Years Eve through the surprising developments that occur over the following three months. Middle-aged Maureen has been caring for her profoundly disabled son for decades; Martin is a celebrity-turned-has-been after sleeping with a 15-year-old girl; teenage Jess, trash-talker extraordinaire, is still haunted by the mysterious disappearance of her older sister years before; and JJ is upset by the collapse of his band and his breakup with his longtime girlfriend." Booklist
"Whatever limited consolations the book's survivors find in each other, Hornby resists melodramatic resolutions or glorious moments of redemption, and he doesn't smuggle away or refute all the reasons his characters took with them to the rooftop where they met, the ones that urged them toward the edge rather than down to the ground the slow way, back into the world." N Y Times Book Rev

Horowitz, James *See* Salter, James

Hospital, Janette Turner, 1942-

Due preparations for the plague. Norton 2003 401p $24.95
ISBN 0-393-05764-X   LC 2002-156598
"Lowell is a single father whose mother died when terrorists hijacked an Air France plane she was on in 1987. That event continues to haunt him and the other children of the victims, one of whom, Samantha, is convinced that the whole story of the hijacking has never been told and wants Lowell's help in unearthing it. When Lowell's father, a CIA agent, dies suspiciously and leaves his son incriminating evidence about the U.S.' role in Air France 64, Lowell reluctantly joins forces with Sam." Booklist
"Using the form of a politico-literary thriller, Janette Turner Hospital has attempted a meta-physical novel of evil. . . . 'Due preparations for the Plague'—the title and the frequent quotes from Camus indicate the author's larger intentions—is a descent through Dantean circles of governmental conspiracy and betrayal." N Y Times Book Rev

North of nowhere, south of loss. Norton 2004 c2003 286p $24.95
ISBN 0-393-05991-X   LC 2004-54723
Contents: The ocean of Brisbane; North of nowhere; For Mr. Voss or occupant; Unperformed experiments have no results; Our own little Kakadu; Cape Tribulation; Flight; Frames and wonders; Nativity; Credit repair; South of loss; Night train; Litany for the homeland; The end-of-the-line end-of-the-road disco
"Hospital's strength lies in capturing her character's interior lives with a poet's grace and precision. . . . The

Hospital, Janette Turner, 1942-—_Continued_
collection is thematically linked: each story explores the
geographies and memories that define and bind us even
as they change shape over time. How we embroider past
events or alter and manipulate memories from actual occurrences are key elements in many of the tales."
Booklist

Orpheus lost; a novel. W. W. Norton 2007 358p
$24.95

ISBN 978-0-393-06552-7; 0-393-06552-9
LC 2007-24023
"Leela is a mathematician who has escaped her Southern hometown to study in Boston. She meets an Australian musician, Mishka, and from the moment she first
hears him play his music grips her; they quickly become
lovers. Then one day Leela is picked up off the street
and taken to an interrogation center somewhere outside
the city. There has been an explosion in the subway; terrorism is suspected. The interrogator-an old childhood
friend-now reveals to her that Mishka may not be all he
seems." Publisher's note
"Hospital is relentless in her musical and mythological
references, even as the novel shifts halfway through from
romance to suspense when Mishka goes missing. While
the book could be tagged a literary thriller, Hospital
chooses to depict not clinical gore but hallucinatory pain.
. . . She is fascinated by religious and political fundamentalism, psychological and physical terror—and who
succumbs or resists." PopMatters

Oyster. Norton 1998 c1996 400p
ISBN 0-393-04618-4
LC 97-34071
First published 1996 in the United Kingdom
"In a part of the Australian Outback so remote it is literally off the charts, a tiny opal-mining and ranching
community faces the end of its world. A place of closed
minds and closely held secrets, Outer Maroo has become
dangerous since the arrival and departure of the fascinating, sinister spiritual leader calling himself Oyster. Since
Oyster's coming, certain areas of conversation are taboo,
minds are unhinged, and reality seems hard to define.
Outsiders are met with distrust, dislike, and worse, while
a seemingly endless drought heightens tension unbearably. When two particularly stubborn strangers demand
information about their lost children, disciples of Oyster,
they initiate Armageddon for Outer Maroo" Libr J
"With language that slips between the surreal and the
all-too-real, the sign of the beast and the meteorological
formation of a rain cloud [Hospital] delivers a world that
is at once our own and a place from another time, from
the old West, the Bible." N Y Times Book Rev

Hosseini, Khaled

The kite runner. Riverhead Bks. 2003 324p
$24.95; pa $14
ISBN 1-57322-245-3; 1-59448-000-1 (pa)
* LC 2003-43106
"Amir, the son of a well-to-do Kabul merchant, is the
first-person narrator, who marries, moves to California
and becomes a successful novelist. But he remains haunted by a childhood incident in which he betrayed the trust
of his best friend, a Hazara boy named Hassan, who receives a brutal beating from some local bullies. After establishing himself in America, Amir learns that the
Taliban have murdered Hassan and his wife, raising

questions about the fate of his son, Sohrab. Spurred on
by childhood guilt, Amir makes the difficult journey to
Kabul, only to learn the boy has been enslaved by a former childhood bully who has become a prominent
Taliban official." Publ Wkly
"Khaled Hosseini gives us a vivid and engaging story
that reminds us how long his people have been struggling to triumph over the forces of violence." N Y Times
Book Rev

A thousand splendid suns. Riverhead Books
2007 372p $25.95
ISBN 978-1-59448-950-1; 1-59448-950-5
LC 2007-8679
"Born a generation apart and with very different ideas
about love and family, Mariam and Laila are two women
brought jarringly together by war, by loss and by fate.
As they endure the ever escalating dangers around
them—in their home as well as in the streets of Kabul—
they . . . form a bond that makes them both sisters and
mother-daughter to each other." Publisher's note
"The texture of these characters' journey around the
craters of their country is no doubt well known to readers of international news. Rendered as fiction . . ., however, it devastates in a new way." Minneapolis Star Tribune

Houellebecq, Michel

The possibility of an island; translated from the
French by Gavin Bowd. Alfred A. Knopf 2006
337p $24.95
ISBN 0-307-26349-0
LC 2005-54527
Original French edition, 2005
The protagonist of this novel is "40-year-old Daniel, a
caustic comedian and filmmaker whose celebrity status
earns him access to Elohim, a cult of sexually promiscuous health fanatics who achieve immortality through
cloning. The narrative alternates between the original
Daniel (plagued by a succession of failed love affairs,
with affection remaining only for his Welsh corgi) and
his subsequent 'neohuman' incarnations." Booklist
The power of the novel is "limited by its utter nihilism, and its refusal to countenance the possibility of any
enduring good in human life. . . . Houellebecq's novel
wants to be both a contemporary satire of empty satisfactions and a dystopic fantasy about their unchecked prolif-
erations, provocative in its moral alarums and blasé
about the whole business. It's a book fit for an age done
in by wanting too musch for itself." Walrus

Hough, Robert

The stowaway. Arcade Pub. 2004 232p $24
ISBN 0-679-31146-7
LC 2004-9347
Based on an actual incident, this novel "relates how
two stowaways are discovered on a container ship bound
for North America. The stowaways, who speak only Romanian, are set adrift and soon drown. Several crew
members agonize over this, with Rodolfo, the bosun, particularly afflicted, since he notified the captain of the
stowaways' existence, assuming that they would be integrated into the work of the ship. Later, when two more
stowaways are discovered, Rodolfo and the rest of the
crew must decide whether to obey orders or to follow
their conscience." Libr J

Hough, Robert—_Continued_

"This is a moving, haunting novel, full of deeply sympathetic portraits of common people being uncommonly brave." Publ Wkly

House, Silas, 1971-

A parchment of leaves; a novel. Algonquin Bks. 2002 278p $23.95

ISBN 1-565-12367-0   LC 2002-66570

"In 1917 rural Kentucky, a young Cherokee woman named Vine, rumored to cast spells on unsuspecting men, falls in love with local Irishman Saul Sullivan, whom she eventually marries. . . (This novel) tells the story of Vine and Saul's tender relationship and the prejudice they face and eventually overcome." Libr J

"This is a moving love story set against a stunningly beautiful background, and House seems to capture it all—the deep emotion, the love of land, the customs of mountain people—in quietly eloquent prose." Booklist

House, Tom

The beginning of calamities; a novel. Bridge Works 2005 288p $24.95

ISBN 1-88259-369-3   LC 2002-152049

This novel is "set in the mid-1970s in a blue-collar Long Island town. Shy, awkward, 11-year-old Danny recreates the Passion of Christ as a school play to be performed for his fellow parochial school students during Holy Week. Impressed by his initiative, Danny's young teacher, Liz Kaigh, gets caught up in producing and directing the piece, whose troupe of players is eventually composed of the class misfits. The author effectively depicts Danny's constant personal angst and spiritual longings within the context of religious suffering but also manages to add a note of dark humor." Libr J

Houston, James D.

Bird of another heaven; a novel. Alfred A. Knopf 2007 337p $25.95

ISBN 978-1-4000-4202-9; 1-4000-4202-X
         LC 2006-48726

"Like a bolt from the blue, a San Francisco-area radio-show host receives a call from a woman insisting she is his grandmother. Primarily through a multivolume diary kept by her mother, two worlds, two cultures open up to his astonished and absorbent awareness: the final years of the reign of Hawaiian king David Kalakau and a California Indian tribe's shrinking as the nineteenth century comes to a close." Booklist

"Houston gives us an engaging historical detective story, but his novel succeeds most as a richly delineated portrait of 19th-century Hawaii and California populated with characters of real vigor . . . . He keeps his eye on the essential task: making the filaments that link the past to the present and the fiction to the history visible and strong." San Jose Mercury News

Houston, Pam

Cowboys are my weakness; stories. Norton 1992 171p o.p.

         LC 91-12920

Contents: How to talk to a hunter; Selway; Highwater; For Bo; What Shock heard; Dall; Cowboys are my weakness; Jackson is only one of my dogs; A blizzard under

blue sky; Sometimes you talk about Idaho; Symphony; In my next life

"Short stories, mostly first-person, told with verve and perfect pitch by women entangled with wild men in a cruel world." N Y Times Book Rev

Waltzing the cat. Norton 1998 288p

ISBN 0-393-02749-X   LC 98-10562

Contents: The best girlfriend you never had; Cataract; Waltzing the cat; Three lessons in Amazonian biology; The moon is a woman's first husband; Moving from one body of water to another; Like goodness under your feet; Then you get up and have breakfast; The kind of people you trust with your life; The whole weight of me

This collection "is far from perfect, but Houston's vigorous voice and lively take on what it's like to be a woman both physically bold and hopelessly romantic are to be cherished nonetheless." N Y Times Book Rev

Howard, Linda

Cry no more. Ballantine Books 2003 368p

ISBN 0-345-45341-7   LC 2003-45140

"Milla is a woman with a mission: 10 years after her baby son, Justin, was snatched from her arms, she still hunts for him every day. Her dedicated passion led her to start Finders, an agency set up to help others like her find taken loved ones. Although she has learned some sketchy details about Justin's abductors, they never led anywhere; all she has to go on is a name, Diaz. An anonymous tip about Diaz's location leads to a sighting of the one-eyed man who snatched Justin. When one of Finders' generous grantors offers a tip on finding Diaz, alleged to be a dangerous assassin, Milla takes it upon herself to seek Diaz out, only to learn that he is not tied to the abduction but can help find out who is. . . . At once heart-wrenching and thrilling." Booklist

Howard, Maureen, 1930-

Big as life; three tales for spring. Viking 2001 225p il $23.95

ISBN 0-670-89978-X   LC 2001-17904

"In 'Children with Matches,' a history professor unexpectedly inherits her family's dilapidated estate, while her lover, a famous economist, fears for his life in war-warped Africa. A young Irish woman's beauty brings her nothing but grief until she finds her calling as an army nurse in World War II, in 'The Magdalene.' And Audubon and his longsuffering wife are the subjects of the title story." Booklist

"Although Howard's style can be too elliptical for its own good (a fault that sometimes extends to her dialogue and that produces the odd longueur), it just as often succeeds in gorgeously evoking the movement of lives and minds and emotions. . . . This is a quiet and contemplative book of subtlety and grace, passion and commitment." Atl Mon

Natural history; a novel. Norton 1992 393p il o.p.

         * LC 92-7041

This novel "relates the tortured history of the Brays, an Irish-American family living in Bridgeport, Connecticut, at the close of World War II. As adults, James and Catherine leave home but cannot come to terms with their lives, for they are trapped in the shadow of their bigger-

Howard, Maureen, 1930——*Continued*

than-life father. . . . [One section of the book] juxtaposes the storyline with facts and myths about Bridgeport notables, among them P.T. Barnum, Robert Mitchum, and Walt Kelly of Pogo fame." Libr J

This is a "novel always in the midst of breaking free of itself, its pages filled with brilliant variations on the screenplay, the encyclopedia, the diary, and, of course, the history book." New Repub

Howard, Ravi

Like trees, walking; a novel. Amistad 2007 258p $24.95

ISBN 978-0-06-052959-8; 0-06-052959-8

LC 2006-48442

"The first day of spring, 1981, Mobile woke to find a badly beaten black teenager hanging from a tree just a few yards off the city's major thoroughfare. A Klan cross burned not far from the lynching. A quarter century after that horror, which went unsolved for years, Howard explores ways Michael Donald's murder changed the black community left behind. Working in a muted prose style, somber and hushed as the family funeral home where Roy, his teen narrator, watches and dreams, Howard tells the story of a community shocked out of normalcy forever, of lives eclipsed and lost as the ripples of a hate crime spread out across Mobile Bay and into the broader world." Paste

Howatch, Susan

Absolute truths; a novel. Knopf 1995 559p o.p.

LC 94-27510

Sixth in the Church of England series, this novel "is set during the mid-1960s, the period during which the Church of England . . . was rocked by widespread challenges to tradition. Again representing tradition is narrator Charles Ashworth, The Anglican Bishop of Starbridge. . . . Ashworth's archenemy—and doppelgänger—is Neville Aysgarth, the Dean of the Cathedral who is, according to Ashworth, unorthodoxly open to using the trappings of a capitalistic marketplace to benefit the financially deteriorating church building. To make matters worse, Aysgarth is an alleged dipsomaniac and womanizer, who once made a pass at Ashworth's beloved wife, Lyle. When Lyle dies suddenly, the bereaved widower strays dangerously from the fold." Publ Wkly

Cashelmara. Simon & Schuster 1974 702p o.p.

Divided into six sections, each narrated by a different character, this novel charts "the lives of three generations of the Anglo-Irish de Salis family between 1859 and 1891. They move between London homes, a Warwickshire estate, New York and Boston—where two Lords de Salis find their wives—but end always at the great white house on their Irish estate, Cashelmara. In the background are the simmering troubles between starving Irish tenants and callous English landlords." Christ Sci Monit

"With a copiousness of detail studded with adventure, rape, depravity, intrigue, and murder, the story plays out with clarity and brilliance." Best Sellers

Glamorous powers. Knopf 1988 403p o.p.

LC 88-45347

This "novel, the second in the Church of England series that began with 'Glittering Images,' weaves an intriguing and wholly involving story out of the otherwise

sober subject of Christian mysticism in the 20th-century Church of England. Howatch's chief characters are a clerical odd couple, rivals since their Cambridge days: Jonathan Darrow, a 60-year-old Anglo-Catholic monk with 'glamorous' psychic powers, and his Abbot-General, Francis Ingram, a practical, eloquent, urbane man with sophisticated insight into modern psychology. . . . The wisdom of 'Glamorous Powers' lies in the deft way it aligns psychological and spiritual truths to bring about healing in the broadest sense." N Y Times Book Rev

Followed by Ultimate prizes

Glittering images. Knopf 1987 399p

ISBN 0-394-56206-2

* LC 87-45130

This, the first in the Church of England series, "takes place in pre-World War II England, just after Edward VIII abdicated to marry the divorced Wallis Simpson. The event is emblematic, for this novel is about marriage and divorce and proper behavior within a religious context. . . . The narrator is a young intellectual cleric, Charles Ashworth, who is sent by the Archbishop of Canterbury to spy on Alex Jardine, the charismatic, liberal Bishop of Starbridge. Ashworth uncovers evidence in Jardine's household—which includes a depressive wife and her pretty female companion—of sexual scandal and a highly irregular interpretation of Anglican dogma. The revelation of the mystery of Starbridge sends Ashworth into a personal crisis of faith." N Y Times Book Rev

"An ambitious and lifelike work of uncommon depth." Booklist

Followed by Glamorous powers

The heartbreaker. Knopf 2004 c2003 483p $25

ISBN 1-4000-4147-3   LC 2003-62493

This title "in Howatch's series of novels investigating the juncture of the sacred and the profane in contemporary British life is set a little more than a decade ago in London's financial center, known as the City. Carta Graham, a former lawyer, had come somewhat unglued upon the death of her husband, and the good people at St. Benet's Church helped her through this life crisis. In turn, she now works for the church as its chief fundraiser. An old friend announces his intention to donate a large sum of money and the fact that he is besotted by a person he's been seeing outside his marriage. When he dies soon after these proclamations, Carta discovers that the person he had been head over heels in love with is a male prostitute, Gavin by name." Booklist

"Plot improbabilities and long sections of spiritual musing are redeemed by Howatch's strongly drawn characters: if Carta can come across as brittle and prudish, Gavin's self-absorbed cant is continually entertaining." Publ Wkly

The high flyer; a novel. Knopf 2000 500p

ISBN 0-375-41057-0   LC 99-58953

First published 1999 in the United Kingdom

In this novel "success-driven London lawyer Carter Graham is suddenly confronted with phenomena that test the coping abilities of her liberated, modern mind. The quintessential 'high flyer,' Carter has broken through the glass ceiling and become a partner in the prestigious law firm of Curtis, Towers. Recently married to Kim Betz, a handsome banker almost 15 years her senior, Carter lives in the 'right' apartment complex, drives a Porsche and is thinking of having a baby. However, Kim's hidden past

Howatch, Susan—*Continued*

(involvement with Nazis, the occult, group sex and an unsavory psychic healer named Mrs. Mayfield) threatens Carter's carefully orchestrated life plan." Publ Wkly

"A suspense novel mixed with Gothic overtones and spiritual dimensions, this story works on almost every level." Libr J

Mystical paths; a novel. Knopf 1992 433p o.p.
LC 91-58557

This novel is fifth in the Church of England series. "At 25, Nicholas Darrow, scion of eminent churchman Jonathan Darrow [featured in Glamorous powers] has inherited his father's psychic gifts, but overconfidence in his abilities and a dangerously frayed relationship with his father lead him close to the edge of an emotional abyss. Asked by the widow of his friend Christian Aysgarth to investigate her husband's death—Christian was drowned when swept overboard while sailing, but she fears that he committed suicide—Nick embarks on a quest that uncovers dark secrets in the linked lives of his friends and family." Publ Wkly

"Although this is all rather formulaic, Howatch has discovered that the Christian story is essentially a romance, and she has exploited this with considerable intelligence." Booklist

Followed by Absolute truths

Penmarric. Simon & Schuster 1971 735p o.p.

Set against the landscape of Cornwall, this novel relates the "life and amours of brutally selfish Mark Castallack through the end of the Victorian era and . . . the lives and amours of his children, legitimate and illegitimate and their progeny." America

"Throughout the story, the author keeps the reader aware of the great historical precedent and parallel for her fiction; the love of Henry II and Eleanor of Aquitaine; preceding each chapter are two pertinent quotations about that royal couple and the king's progeny. It is a neat and useful device, adding piquancy and historical flavor to an interesting tale." Best Sellers

Scandalous risks. Knopf 1990 385p o.p.
LC 90-53076

This novel, fourth in the Church of England series, is "narrated by Venetia Flaxton, a young woman of intellect and means but no direction, and centers around her strange affair in 1963 with 61-year-old Neville Aysgarth, dean of Starbridge Cathedral. Related mainly through their letters and conversations, the progress—and explosive dissolution—of their relationship is set in the context of a real-life theological precedent in England crystallized by the publication of *Honest to God*, a bestselling, situational-ethics view of God's relevance to modern man." Publ Wkly

"With sculptor's hands fashioning rich, lustrous three-dimensional characters, Howatch brilliantly shows how and why the situation between Venetia and her 'Mr. Dean' arose, flourished, then died away." Booklist

Followed by Mystical paths

Ultimate prizes. Knopf 1989 387p o.p.
LC 89-45303

This, third novel in the Church of England series, "is narrated by Neville Aysgarth, an ambitious archdeacon in the fictional English diocese of Starbridge. A brilliant administrator with a firm, practical faith in God and the Church of England, Neville has steadily moved up in life by 'chasing the prizes,' overcoming his humble birth and troubled youth to win for himself a perfect wife, a flock of delightful children and a powerful position, all before age 40. During his climb to success he has kept his mind as tidy as his diocese by relentlessly 'ringing down the curtain'—a mental curtain, that is—on disturbing memories and desires. But alas for Neville, his curtain is shortly to be twitched off its rod, first by an infatuation with a young society girl, then by a death in his family." N Y Times Book Rev

Followed by Scandalous risks

The wheel of fortune. Simon & Schuster 1984 973p o.p.
LC 84-5357

This "saga, based loosely upon the tragedies that beset Edward of Woodstock (the Black Prince) and his descendants, is 'a recreation in a modern dimension.' A cycle of tragedy plagues the descendants of a lecherous Robert Godwin, who allows the glittering family manor, Oxmoon, to disintegrate into rat fodder until his heirs take decisive action. The treasured Welsh estate is restored to its former grandeur, but a legacy of enormous guilt and a pattern of adultery and murder haunt further inheritors of Oxmoon." Booklist

This "absorbing novel convincingly demonstrates that a family saga can be more than the mere 'show and tell' of one generation following another. By using six different narrators to recount five generations of a 20th-century Welsh family, the author deftly supplies multiple viewpoints of events." Libr J

The wonder-worker. Knopf 1997 529p
ISBN 0-375-40102-4
LC 97-36886

"The narrative examines the self-delusions to which priests are susceptible as they deal with their own humanity. Nicholas Darrow, 45, first met in *Mystical Paths* is a gifted healer whose pre-conversion past is filled with hobgoblins and parlor tricks. He is sexually alluring but seems capable of keeping his responsibilities wisely in balance. Everyone is just waiting for him to show himself as fallible. And it happens, with disastrous consequences for the people within his orbit: Lewis, an older priest; a homely cook named Alice; a younger priest, Stacy; and Darrow's wife, Rosalind." Publ Wkly

"The setting is St. Benet's, a London parish church, and while every character displays a level of eccentricity verging on the gothic, Howatch's good-humored tone keeps the whole—just—from collapsing." New Yorker

Howe, Katherine

The physick book of Deliverance Dane; a novel. Hyperion 2009 371p $25.99
ISBN 978-1-4013-4090-2; 1-4013-4090-3
LC 2008-51627

"A Harvard doctoral candidate, Connie learns that 'Physick' is the 17th-century word for an herbal remedy, and that Deliverance Dane was a Massachusetts woman who knew this medicinal craft and kept her recipes—which she called receipts—in an almanac. Connie must discover the hidden location of this old volume of spells (there's no better word for what they are), but she discovers so much more along the way: great personal danger, unanticipated self-knowledge and love, in both its natural and preternatural aspects. The Salem witch trials of 1692 epitomize a moment when a society felt threatened by the notion of women's uncanny power. At stra-

Howe, Katherine—*Continued*

tegic points in the novel, Howe recreates, with harrowing vividness, intimate scenes from that historical crisis." BookPage

Howells, William Dean, 1837-1920

Annie Kilburn
   In Howells, W. D. Novels, 1886-1888

April hopes
   In Howells, W. D. Novels, 1886-1888

A foregone conclusion
   In Howells, W. D. Novels, 1875-1886

Indian summer
   In Howells, W. D. Novels, 1875-1886

The minister's charge
   In Howells, W. D. Novels, 1886-1888

A modern instance
   In Howells, W. D. Novels, 1875-1886

Novels, 1875-1886. Literary Classics of the U.S. 1983 1217p $40
   ISBN 0-940450-04-6
   * LC 82-112
Contents: A foregone conclusion; A modern instance; Indian summer; The rise of Silas Lapham

A foregone conclusion (1875) describes the love triangle between American expatriate Florida Vervain, American painter Henry Ferris, and lapsed priest Don Ippolito. In A modern instance (1882), Bartley Hubbard, an unscrupulous and philandering journalist is divorced by his wife and subsequently murdered by one of the individuals scandalized in his newspaper. In Indian summer (1886), Theodore Coville, a middle-aged American vacationing in Florence meets an old acquaintance and one of her young friends, eventually sparking relationships with each of them. The rise of Silas Lapham is entered separately.

Novels, 1886-1888. Library of America 1989 881p $35
   ISBN 0-940450-51-8
   LC 88-82728
Contents: The Minister's charge; April hopes; Annie Kilburn

"In The Minister's Charge (1886), Lemuel Barker leaves his impoverished farm and comes to Boston hoping to become a published poet. Proud, innocent, and implacably honest, he is quickly plunged into the humiliating depths of urban homelessness. His plight weighs on the conscience of David Sewell, a minister who could not bear to tell Barker how bad his poetry was. . . . In April Hopes (1887) Alice Pasmer is the only daughter of parents whose dwindling investments have forced their return from Europe to New England. When Alice meets Dan Mavering, the easygoing son of a wealthy wallpaper manufacturer, her mother begins a careful campaign to bring about their marriage. . . . The heroine of Annie Kilburn (1888) returns to her Hatboro', Massachusetts, home after eleven years abroad and finds a once-quiet village rapidly turning into a sprawling factory town with paved streets, electric lights, and a department store. Unmarried at thirty-one, the daughter of a prominent 'old' family, she renews ties with old friends and begins a life devoted to good deeds." Publisher's note

The rise of Silas Lapham; with an introduction by Kermit Vanderbilt. Penguin Books 1986 xxxi, 368p pa $12
   ISBN 0-14-039030-8
First published 1885

"Silas is a crude, uneducated man who makes his fortune by methods not above criticism, but manly and capable of better things when his conscience is awakened—a compendium of human virtues and vices, drawn with insight, tenderness and humor. The efforts of the prosperous Laphams to get into Boston society, with their mistakes and disillusionments, the sentimental tragicomedy of the two daughters, in love with the same young man; and Lapham's business troubles, are more or less neatly woven in to make the plot." Baker. Guide to the Best Fic

   also in Howells, W. D. Novels, 1875-1886

Hrabal, Bohumil, 1914-1997

I served the King of England; [translated by Paul Wilson] Harcourt Brace Jovanovich 1989 243p
   ISBN 0-15-145745-X
   LC 88-16482
This novel "is a picaresque allegory of 20th-century Czechoslovak history as lived and narrated by a short hotel waiter by the name of Ditie, meaning child. Rising from one hotel to another, each a stage of his country's history, he marries a Nazi during the war, and in the postwar years at last realizes his dream of becoming a millionaire, only to see his wealth vanish under Communism." N Y Times Book Rev

This novel "is a flood of meandering garrulous narration, with dreamlike, filmlike sequences, hyperbolic, grotesque and farcical analogues of familiar historical fact. No sober account, this, of how it might actually have been, yet still it projects through its debunking prism the shallowness, absurdity and cruelty of how it indeed was." Times Lit Suppl

Too loud a solitude; translated from the Czech by Michael Henry Heim. Harcourt Brace Jovanovich 1990 98p
   ISBN 0-15-190491-X
   LC 90-4313
"In this novella, written in 1976, . . . [the narrator] Hanta meditates on the 35 years he has spent at a hydraulic press in a dark cellar, compacting waste paper and books proscribed by various regimes. Though he no longer weeps or protests when rare treasures appear in his press, the books that he must destroy become his whole life, his only companions. When he is to be replaced by young workers with a more productive machine, Hanta dreams of a gigantic press that destroys not only himself but the entire city, with its traditions and culture." Libr J

"This is indeed Franz Kafka's Prague. . . . The book is funny, in its desperate, knockabout way. Along with Hant'a's incessant reading goes excessive swilling of beer, and the tone throughout is at once strident and woozy, so that the reader has the impression of being trapped in that basement room as the press grinds and the drunken operator rummages through the tatters of a ruined culture." N Y Rev Books

Hubbard, Susan, 1951-

The Society of S. Simon & Schuster 2007 304p $25

ISBN 978-1-4165-3457-0; 1-4165-3457-1

LC 2006-51265

"Ariella Montero's mother vanished the day she was born, leaving her to the care of her overprotective scientist father, who homeschools her and limits her contact with the outside world. Only when she reaches adolescence does Ari discover that her special diet and insular home life set her apart from her peers. Her father's confession that he was vampirized shortly before marriage, and that Ari can choose whether to be undead like him or mortal like mom, set her off on a road trip that eventually brings her to her mother." Publ Wkly

"Hubbard has created a literary mystery that will appeal to the fans of Diane Setterfield's The Thirteenth Tale or Elizabeth Kostava's The Historian. Well written and full of intriguing characters, the novel moves apace as the reader becomes engaged in the hunt for the truth about Ariella and her family." Libr J

Huddle, David, 1942-

La Tour dreams of the wolf girl. Houghton Mifflin 2002 196p $24

ISBN 0-618-08173-9   LC 2001-16915

"Shifting between two narratives—one concerning an unhappy wife in present-day Vermont, the other involving the 17th-century French painter Georges de La Tour and a 15-year-old model—the novel's premise sounds like a prescription for historical, escapist entertainment. But anyone looking for easy distraction or predictable romance will be disappointed; Huddle's book offers more complex pleasures. A study of the relation between art and life, the novel has an honesty and psychological depth that are at times painfully real and quietly moving." N Y Times Book Rev

Hudgens, Dallas, 1964-

Season of Gene; a novel. Scribner 2007 211p $24

ISBN 978-1-4165-4148-6; 1-4165-4148-9

LC 2007-11578

"Gruff, conscientious Joe owns a Washington, D.C., car-detailing service and ticket brokerage, while best friend Gene Dellorso manages a local limo service. Joe's the manager and catcher for the Vicodin-and-beer-fueled Whip Spa Yankees, for which Gene also plays. When Gene, 35, collapses dead at a game, his pre-game confessions of an unsalvageable marriage and a desire to flee for Las Vegas aren't the only secrets he's been hiding: a cavalcade of thugs come crawling out of the woodwork all wanting to claim a 1932 vintage bat used by Babe Ruth that's now worth a cool three million." Publ Wkly

Hudgens has "given readers an engaging, knowing glimpse of an odd, but no doubt real, world of arrested development. And he knows his baseball." Booklist

Hudson, Jeffery See Crichton, Michael, 1942-2008

Hudson, W. H. (William Henry), 1841-1922

Green mansions; a romance of the tropical forest. Putnam 1904 315p o.p.

"The hero, Mr. Abel, tells the tragic story of his love for the bird girl, Rima, an ethereal maiden whose jungle upbringing has brought her close to the powers and beauty of nature. Abel has just succeeded in awakening the human emotion of love in the half-wild girl when she is killed by a band of savages." Reader's Ency. 3d edition

Hudson, William Henry See Hudson, W. H. (William Henry), 1841-1922

Hueffer, Ford Madox See Ford, Ford Madox, 1873-1939

Hughes, Declan, 1963-

The price of blood; an Irish novel of suspense. William Morrow 2008 312p $24.95

ISBN 978-0-06-082551-5; 0-06-082551-0

LC 2007-40667

This Dublin thriller "featuring P.I. Ed Loy portrays the downside of the booming Irish economy. The real estate bubble has many young Dubliners in over their heads, days away from foreclosure and being forced to move into seedy subdivisions teeming with family gangs. His own dwindling bank balance finds Ed taking more domestic disturbance cases than he'd like, stuck doing surveillance in the same seedy subdivisions. When Father Vincent Tyrrell summons him to help with a very different kind of family matter, the change sounds appealing: he's to track down a missing member of the legendary Tyrrell horse racing dynasty. The case seems surprisingly simple after he finds a phone number linked to the missing Tyrrell in the pocket of a corpse while pursuing another matter. But Ed suddenly discovers himself caught in a web of drugs, race fixing, gambling, incest, and serial murder among the rich and famous." Libr J

"The dialogue is spare and edgy, the pacing crisp; Hughes' sense of local color, and particularly his ability to impart it to his readers, is absolutely spot on." BookPage

Hughes, Langston, 1902-1967

Laughing to keep from crying. Holt & Co. 1952 206p o.p.

Contents: Who's passing for who?; Something in common; African morning; Pushcart man; Why, you reckon; Saratoga rain; Spanish blood; Heaven to hell; Sailor ashore; Slice him down; Tain't so; One Friday morning; Professor; Name in the papers; Powder-white faces; Rouge high; On the way home; Mysterious Madame Shanghai; Never room with a couple; Little old spy; Tragedy at the Baths; Trouble with the angels; On the road; Big meeting

Not without laughter. Knopf 1930 324p o.p.

This novel portrays the lives of a poor black family in a small Kansas town

"A sympathetic portrayal, unmarred by bitterness or sentimentality, of a people to whom life, no matter how hard, was not without laughter." Booklist

Hughes, Langston, 1902-1967—*Continued*

Short stories of Langston Hughes; edited by Akiba Sullivan Harper; with an introduction by Arnold Rampersad. Hill & Wang 1996 299p pa $16 hardcover o.p.

ISBN 0-8090-1603-6

* LC 95-19554

Contents: Bodies in the moonlight; The young glory of him; The little virgin; Luani of the jungles; Slave on the block; Cora unashamed; The blues I'm playing; Why, you reckon?; Little old spy; Spanish blood; On the road; Gumption; Professor; Big meeting; Trouble with the angels; Tragedy at the baths; Slice him down; African morning; 'Tain't so; One Friday morning; Heaven to hell; Breakfast in Virginia; Saratoga rain; Who's passing for who?; On the way home; Name in the papers; Sailor ashore; Something in common; Mysterious Madame Shaghai; Never room with a couple; Powder-white faces; Pushcart man; Rouge high; Patron of the arts; Thank you, m'am'; Sorrow for a midget; Blessed assurance; Early autumn; Fine accommodations; The gun; His last affair; No place to make love; Rock, church; Mary Winosky; Those who have no turkey; Seventy-five dollars; The childhood of Jimmy

"Dating from 1919 to 1963, these pieces vary in theme, covering life at sea, the trials and tribulations of a young pianist and her elderly white patron, a visiting writer's experience in Cuba, a young girl's winning an art scholarship but losing it when it's learned she is black, and an ambitious black preacher trying to gain fame by being nailed to a cross. If you crave good reading don't pass up this gem." Libr J

Simple speaks his mind. Simon & Schuster 1950 231p o.p.

*

The central figure, is a Harlem black who expresses his views on many subjects, but always from the point of view of his own race. He dislikes whites, and makes no bones of it. Some of his favorite topics are women, landladies especially, parties, and beer

"Simple is completely frank in his opinions about white people; he dislikes them intensely. The race problem is never absent, but the flow of the book is light-hearted and easy." N Y Times Book Rev

Simple stakes a claim. Rinehart 1957 191p o.p.

In this book Simple, of Harlem, speaks his mind on a variety of subjects, ranging from housing conditions, to sex magazines

Simple takes a wife. Simon & Schuster 1953 240p o.p.

"Before Mr. Jesse B. Semple, the untutored philosopher of the Harlem rooming-house set, can divorce his wife and espouse the morally impeccable Joyce, he has to run the gauntlet of many problems. He discourses on them in Harlem bars over beers he has cadged from his sympathetic and more literate listener. Under the folklike humor of 'Simple's' monologs runs a bitter undercurrent of racial consciousness." Booklist

Simple's Uncle Sam. Hill & Wang 1965 180p o.p.

Contents: Census; Swinging high; Contest; Empty houses; The blues; God's other side; Color problems; The moon; Domesticated; Bomb shelters; Gospel singers;

Nothing but a dog; Roots and trees; For President; Atomic dream; Lost wife; Self-protection; Haircuts and Paris; Adventure; Minnie's hype; Yachts; Ladyhood; Coffee break; Lynn Clarisse; Interview; Simply Simple; Golden Gate; Junkies; Dog days; Pose-outs; Soul food; Flay or pray; Not colored; Cracker prayer; Rude awakening; Miss Boss; Dr. Sidesaddle; Wigs for freedom; Concernment; Statutes and statues; American dilemma; Promulgations; How old is old; Weight in god; Sympathy; Uncle Sam

Hughes, Richard Arthur Warren, 1900-1976

A high wind in Jamaica; [by] Richard Hughes; introduction by Francine Prose. New York Review Books 1999 c1929 279p pa $12.95 hardcover o.p. paperback available $7.95

ISBN 0-940322-15-3

* LC 99-14565

First published 1929 by Harper with title: The innocent voyage

"A family of children living in Jamaica in the 19th century are sent to England after a hurricane has partly destroyed their home. Amiable pirates capture them by mistake, and the children bring about the pirates' ruin; one girl becomes a murderess. The irrational, amoral world of children is powerfully conveyed." Reader's Ency. 4th edition

Hugo, Victor, 1802-1885

The hunchback of Notre Dame; revised translation and notes by Catherine Liu; introduction by Elizabeth McCracken. Modern Library 2002 xxviii, 483p pa $11.95

ISBN 0-679-64257-9

* LC 2002-18917

Original French edition, 1930. Variant title: Notre Dame de Paris

The hidden force of fate is symbolized by the superhuman grandeur and multitudinous imageries of the cathedral. "The first part . . . is a panorama of medieval life—religious, civic, popular, and criminal—drawn with immense learning and an amazing command of spectacular effect. These elements are then set in motion in a fantastic and grandiose drama, of which the personages are romantic sublimations of human virtues and passions—Quasimodo the hunchback, faithful unto death; Esmeralda, incarnation of innocence and steadfastness; Claude Frolla, Faust-like type of the antagonism between religion and appetite. Splendors and absurdities, the sublime and the grotesque are inextricably mingled in this strange romance. The date is fixed at the year 1482." Baker. Guide to the Best Fic

Les misérables; translated from the French by Charles E. Wilbour; with an introduction by Peter Washington. Knopf 1997 xxxvii, 1432p $27

ISBN 0-375-40317-5

* LC 98-156450

"Everyman's library"

Original French edition, 1862

"A panorama of French life in the first half of the [nineteenth] century, aiming to exhibit the fabric of civilization in all its details, and to reveal the cruelty of its pressure on the poor, the outcast, and the criminal. Jean

Hugo, Victor, 1802-1885—*Continued*

Valjean, a man intrinsically noble, thru the tyranny of society becomes a criminal. His conscience is reawakened by the ministrations of the saintly Bishop Myriel . . . and Valjean, reformed and prosperous, follows in the good bishop's footsteps as an apostle of benevolence, only to be doomed again by the law to slavery and shame. The 'demimondaine' Fantine, another victim of society; her daughter Cosette one of those whom suffering makes sublime; Marius, an ideal of youth and love; Myriel, the incarnation of Christian charity, are the leading characters of this huge morality, which is thronged with representatives of the good in man and the cruelty of society. Magnificent description . . . scenes invested with terror, awe, repulsion, alternate with tedious rhapsodies. Realism mingles with the incredible." Baker. Guide to the Best Fic

The **Hugo** winners; edited by Isaac Asimov. Doubleday 1962-1986 5v

v1 Novelettes are: The darfsteller, by W. M. MIller; Exploration team, by M. Leinster; The big front yard, by C. D. Simak; Flowers for Algernon, by D. Keyes; The longest voyage, by P. Anderson. Short stories are: Allamagoosa, by E. F. Russell; The star, by A. C. Clarke; Or all seas with oysters, by A. Davidson; The hellbound train, by R. Bloch

v2 Novelettes are: The last castle, by J. Vance; Weyrsearch, by A. McCaffrey; Riders of the purple wage, by P. J. Farmer; Gonna roll the bones, by F. Leiber; Nightwings, by R. Silverberg; The sharing of flesh, by P. Anderson. Short stories are: The dragon masters, by J. Vance; No truce with kings, by P. Anderson; Soldier, ask not, by G. R. Dickson; "Repent, Harlequin!", said the Ticktock-man, by H. Ellison; Neutron star, by L. Niven; I have no mouth, and I must scream, by H. Ellison; The beast that shouted love at the heart of the world, by H. Ellison; Time considered as a helix of semi-precious stones, by S. R. Delany

v3 Novelettes are: Ship of shadows, by F. Leiber; III met in Lankhmar, by F. Leiber; The Queen of Air and Darkness, P. Anderson; The word for world is forest, by U. K. LeGuin; Goat song, by P. Anderson. Short stories are: Slow sculpture, by T. Sturgeon; Inconstant moon, by L. Niven; The meeting, by F. Pohl; Eurema's dam, by R. Lafferty; The girl who was plugged in, by J. Tiptree; The deathbird, by H. Ellison; The ones who walk away from Omelas, by U. K. LeGuin; A song for Lya, by G. R. R. Martin; Adrift just off the islets of Langerhans: lattitude 38° 54' N, longitude 77° 00' 13" W, by H. Ellison; The hole man, by L. Niven

v4 Novelettes are: Home is the hangman, by R. Zelazny; By any other name, by S. Robinson; Houston, Houston, do you read? by J. Triptree; The Bicentennial Man, by I. Asimov; Stardance, by S. Robinson; The persistence of vision, by J. Varley; Hunter's moon, by P. Anderson. Short stories are: The borderland of Sol, by L. Niven; Catch that Zeppelin, by F. Leiber; Tricentennial, by J. Haldeman; Eyes of amber, by J. D. Vinge; Jefftyis five, by H. Ellison; Cassandra, by C. J. Cherryh

v5 Novelettes are: Enemy mine, by B. B. Longyear; Sandkings, by G. R. R. Martin; Lost Dorsai, by G. R. Dickson; The cloak and the staff, by G. R. Dickson; The Saturn game, by P. Anderson. Short stories are: The way of cross and dragon, by G. R. R. Martin; Grotto of the dancing deer, by C. D. Simak; Unicorn variations, by R.

Zelazny; The pusher, by J. Varley

The stories and novelettes included in these volumes won the Hugo Awards from 1939-1982

Hulme, Juliet *See* Perry, Anne, 1938-

Hulme, Kathryn, 1900-1981

The nun's story. Little, Brown 1956 339p o.p.
*

"Convent life, with its rigors and its compensations, has seldom been as fairly depicted as in this biographical account. An unhappy love affair was one of the reasons why 'Gabrielle Van der Mal' [fictitious name] entered a convent in Belgium, but her love of God and desire to serve her fellow men were also important influences. For 17 years she tried diligently to discipline her analytical and independent mind through prayer and hard work as a nurse, first in a hospital for the insane, then in a Congo mission, and finally in a TB sanatorium in occupied Holland. Ultimately, she faced the bitter truth that the religious life, with its inflexible authority, was not for her, and she was released from her vows." Libr J

Hulme, Keri

The bone people; a novel. Louisiana State Univ. Press 1985 c1983 450p
ISBN 0-8071-1284-4
* LC 85-12937
First published 1984 in New Zealand

"Hulme's novel tells the story of three people in rural New Zealand, Kerewin, a part-Maori woman; Joe, a Maori man; and Simon, Pakeba (European) child whom Joe finds washed up on the shore during a storm. Joe alternately loves the child passionately and thrashes him brutally. Although they are 'different and difficult people,' isolated from those around them, they are drawn into an intense relationship." Choice

"This novel is unforgettably rich and pungent. . . . Set on the harsh South Island beaches of New Zealand, bound in Maori myth and entwined with Christian symbols, Miss Hulme's provocative novel summons power with words, as in a conjurer's spell." N Y Times Book Rev

Hulse, Michael

(tr) Sebald, W. G. Vertigo

Humphreys, Helen, 1961-

Afterimage; a novel. Metropolitan Bks. 2001 240p $23
ISBN 0-8050-6666-7
LC 00-46907
First published 2000 in Canada

"It's 1865, in England, and both Isabelle Dashell and her husband, Eldon, are making pictures. She's intent on mastering a new medium, photography, and he's seeking renown as a cartographer. When Annie Phelan, a sober beauty orphaned by the Irish famine, answers their ad for a housemaid, she becomes Isabelle's muse and Eldon's confidante, and finds herself pressed into the service of art. Inspired by the work of Julia Margaret Cameron, this urgent, well-made novel charts the boundaries where light becomes shadow, and the known can suddenly appear awful and astonishing." New Yorker

Humphreys, Helen, 1961-—*Continued*

Coventry. W.W. Norton & Co. 2009 c2008 192p $23.95

ISBN 978-0-393-06720-0; 0-393-06720-3

LC 2008-37349

First published 2008 in Canada

"During the Second World War, on the night of the devastating Coventry blitz of November 14, 1940, widow Harriet Marsh finds herself navigating the streets of the town as German bombs explode around her. Alone, and still in mourning for the husband she lost in 1914, Harriet finds comfort amid chaos in the close companionship of a young man half her age, helping him search frantically through the burning streets for his mother. Through her use of actual historical records of the bombing, Humphreys evokes the wartime atmosphere of fear and dislocation with great poignancy, but her novel also emphasizes – especially through Harriet's stoicism and resourcefulness – the resilience of the common individual during times of exceptional challenge. . . . Humphreys' poetic language and imagery, though at times seemingly at odds with the narrative, frequently bring to vivid life the brutality and violence of that night in 1940." Quill Quire

The lost garden. Norton 2002 183p $23.95

ISBN 0-393-05183-8   LC 2002-26308

In this novel, set in the English countryside of 1941, "Gwen Davis, a desperately lonely botanist employed by the Royal Horticultural Society to investigate canker in parsnips, has signed up to direct young women agricultural volunteers on an estate requisitioned for the war effort. Humphreys is a metaphysical novelist; for her, intricate emotional content finds specific analogues in the made world—an astonishing photograph or, as here, an overgrown garden that, once cleared, reveals its consoling secrets." New Yorker

Humphreys, Josephine

The fireman's fair. Viking 1991 263p

ISBN 0-670-83907-8   LC 90-50575

"Rob Wyatt, unmarried at 32, has quit his job as a lawyer, moved out of a luxury apartment to poor housing, sold his Alfa for a cheap used car, and is looking for a new kind of life. Hurricane Hugo almost devastates the southern town in which he lives and also seems to have swept an uprooting storm through his personal life. His unceasing love for Louise, now married to wealthy Frank Camden, becomes not so firm when Billy Poe, 18 years old and naively innocent (or precociously wise) comes into Rob's life. She is a healer in her innocent wisdom and the novel has an ending especially welcome as a change from many violent and depressing contemporary novels." Shapiro. Fic for Youth. 3d edition

Nowhere else on earth. Viking 2000 341p

ISBN 0-670-89176-2   LC 00-36666

"In 1864, Rhoda Strong is a teenager of mixed ancestry in Scuffletown, an Indian settlement on the Lumbee River, in North Carolina. As the town's inhabitants find themselves caught between marauding Union soldiers and Confederates attempting to conscript their children for labor, Rhoda falls in love with a local outlaw who is fighting to protect the community. Humphreys has always been a master of telling a larger story through a deceptively intimate narrative, and Rhoda's tale, with its clear, distinct voice, is no exception." New Yorker

Huneven, Michelle, 1953-

Blame. Sarah Crichton Books 2009 291p $25

ISBN 978-0-374-11430-5; 0-374-11430-7

LC 2008-54299

"Patsy MacLemoore, a boozy history professor, is helping her boyfriend, Brice, take care of his niece, Joey, whose mother is undergoing cancer treatment. But when Patsy goes on a bender and emerges from a drunken blackout in jail, she learns she's accused of having run down a mother and daughter in her driveway. After her conviction, Patsy transforms from free spirit into a convict. . . . In a prison AA group, Patsy seeks redemption and meaning; she also develops a relationship with the man whose wife and daughter she killed and helps put his son through school, stays the course after her release and maintains a friendship with Brice and Joey." Publ Wkly

"Huneven makes Patsy's story unfold like a thriller, creating a sense of urgency and mystery even about everyday matters. . . . Huneven's prose moves like a hummingbird, in small bursts that are improbably fast and graceful." N Y Times Book Rev

Hunt, Laird

The exquisite; a novel. Coffee House Press 2006 246p pa $14.95

ISBN 978-1-56689-187-5; 1-56689-187-6

LC 2006-11901

A tale "set in post-9/11 New York City. Henry has lost his girlfriend, his cats, and his apartment. A beautiful woman he calls Tulip sends him to Aris Kindt, an eccentric old gent fond of herring and esoteric subjects who may be the mastermind behind a mock murder service—people pay strangers to pretend to kill them. But Henry may actually be a murderer. Perhaps he's a patient in a mental ward. Aris Kindt just so happens to be the name of the thief whose body is the subject of Rembrandt's famous autopsy painting, The Anatomy Lesson. Hunt cites W. G. Sebald as the inspiration for what he calls ghost noir, although Paul Auster seems more apt. . . . The result is an edgy and labyrinthine tale of longing, madness, and death." Booklist

Hunt, Samantha

The invention of everything else. Houghton Mifflin Co. 2007 257p $24

ISBN 978-0-618-80112-1; 0-618-80112-X

LC 2007-9416

"Set in New York City in 1943, the book focuses on Nikola Tesla, the underappreciated Serbian inventor. . . . Hunt's story unfolds over the last week of Tesla's life: He is 86 years old, destitute, and maybe a little crazy. He is also, of course, a genius. Tesla is an ideal person to bring back to life through fiction; technically, he's famous, but he's also largely unfamiliar. Because his actual story is so incredible (he was pals with Mark Twain, he fell in love with a bird, he tried to invent a 'death ray'), it's tricky to separate the pieces of Hunt's account that are drawn from fact from those that she's invented. Tesla is well balanced by the entirely fictional character of Louisa, a sensible, inquisitive young chambermaid who works at the hotel and befriends the inventor after he catches her snooping through his things. A classic sort of heroine, she treats the fading man like an oracle as she juggles her own daily dramas." Village Voice

Hunter, Adriana

(tr) Dai Sijie. Once on a moonless night

Hunter, Evan, 1926-2005

For works written by this author under other names see McBain, Ed, 1926-2005

The blackboard jungle. Simon & Schuster 1954 309p o.p.

*

A story "of an idealistic young man, facing the bitter realities of being a teacher in the frighteningly brutal world of a big city vocational high school. A near-rape, student sluggings, a knifing—all these plus a strong indictment of the inadequacies of routine teachers college preparation in helping teachers to learn how to discipline near-morons and prospective or actual delinquents." Libr J

"The author has not used his shocking material merely to appall. With a superb ear for conversation, with competence as a storyteller, and with a tolerant and tough-minded sympathy for his subject, he has built an extremely good novel." N Y Her Trib Books

Candyland; a novel in two parts; [by] Evan Hunter and Ed McBain. Simon & Schuster 2001 301p $25

ISBN 0-7432-1316-5   LC 00-49684

This novel "is written in two parts. The first half, attributed to Hunter, probes the psyche of Benjamin Thorpe, a sexually obsessed Los Angeles architect on the prowl in New York. The second half, attributed to McBain, is a police procedural in which a detective, Emma Boyle, investigates the murder of a prostitute and identifies the architect as a prime suspect. The novel is a gimmick, and it is a surprise that it works at all. That it works so superbly is a tribute to the skills of this great storyteller." N Y Times Book Rev

The Chisholms; a novel of the journey West. Harper & Row 1976 208p o.p.

This novel about the early nineteenth-century pioneer experience "tracks Hadley Chisholm and family, leaving their unproductive Virginia homeland to find a better life in California; the journey [which is followed up to their departure from Fort Laramie in Wyoming] is arduous, to say the least, for every member of the household." Booklist

"An affectingly spare, closely seen recreation of the pioneer spirit and what the search for new opportunity signified." Publ Wkly

Lizzie. Arbor House 1984 430p o.p.

LC 83-15642

"By legend, Lizzie Borden, a New England spinster, axed her father and stepmother to death one summer day in 1892. Writing fictionally about Lizzie and those horrible crimes, popular novelist Hunter uses actual inquest and trial material, but counterpoints the attempted resolution of the murders in that small Massachusetts town with invented events during a European trip that Lizzie took a couple of years previous. It is this trip wherein lie the seeds for the slaying of Mr. and Mrs. Borden, for Lizzie's latent lesbianism surfaces in Europe and leads her to desperate acts when she returns home." Booklist

"The portrait of Lizzie that emerges is fascinating, ultimately sympathetic: a murderess yes, but the victim of the repression and sexual exploitation of her time." Libr J

The moment she was gone; a novel. Simon & Schuster 2002 208p $25

ISBN 0-7432-0269-4   LC 2002-70532

"Andrew Gulliver is the first-person narrator, a New York teacher who learns that his flighty, erratic sister, Annie, has disappeared, leaving her family with no clue as to her destination or whereabouts." Publ Wkly

Hunter "is a masterfully adept storyteller and a very shrewd observer of human behavior. . . . Powerful reading." Booklist

"Carella and Meyer must team up on a murder investigation with Fat Ollie Weeks of the 88th because the lion habitat at the Isola Zoo straddles the boundary between the two precincts and one of the lions dragged part of a victim's body onto the 88th's turf. The body in the lion's den leads the detectives to several things: to a burglary, or at least the burglar; to some strange doings by the Secret Service; to some pretty big local drug dealers; and, finally, to some big-time dealers who don't mind leaving bodies strewn about." Libr J

Privileged conversation. Warner Bks. 1996 326p o.p.

LC 95-11148

"Psychiatrist David Chapman intervenes as Kate Duggan is mugged in Central Park on a beautiful summer day. While his wife vacations with their daughters, Chapman finds himself drawn into a passionate affair with Duggan. The novel, told from Chapman's point of view, moves back and forth from his sessions with patients to his deepening involvement with Duggan. Chapman sneaks back into New York City during his annual August vacation to spend time with Duggan, just as she begins getting letters and veiled threats from a stalker." Booklist

"Mr. Hunter is smart enough to poke fun at the book's echoes of 'Fatal Attraction.' Even better, he has a good feel for Dr. Chapman's midlife crisis and for the petty annoyances of New York social life." N Y Times Book Rev

Hunter, Stephen, 1946-

The 47th samurai; a Bob Lee Swagger novel. Simon & Schuster 2007 372p $26

ISBN 978-0-7432-3809-0; 0-7432-3809-5

LC 2007-6627

This Bob Lee Swagger adventure "begins in the closing days of World War II, when Bob Lee's father, Earl (Havana), earns the Medal of Honor on Iwo Jima and takes a Japanese officer's samurai sword as a souvenir. Decades later, Bob returns the sword to the dead officer's son and family. But the sword turns out to be historically and politically important, and the Japanese family is slaughtered to get it. This horror causes Bob Lee to obsess about both avenging the family and retrieving the sword. In effect, he becomes a samurai, and his confrontations with the murderers are extremely bloody. Although heavy on both the explanations of Japanese customs and the sordid world of incredibly savage Japanese criminals, this work is compelling, exciting, and satisfying, a dark adventure that will appeal to thriller fans." Libr J

Hunter, Stephen, 1946-—_Continued_

Black light. Doubleday 1996 463p o.p.

LC 95-43079

This suspense "novel pairs Russ, the son of State Trooper Bud Pewtie from _Dirty White Boys_ and sharpshooter Bob Lee Swagger (_Point of Impact_, 1993) as they dig into a decades-old cover-up that has the entire Arkansas power structure in a lather trying to keep buried. In a parallel story, Bob Lee's father, Earl, is trying to solve a mysterious abduction and murder that crosses the strictly divided racial lines of the time and place while trying to bring down an escaped convict he swore to reform in a battlefield oath." Libr J

"Mr. Hunter, who is a powerful and disturbing writer, tells this unholy story in a heroic style that gives mythic sweep to the generational waves of violence that seem to have had no beginning and threaten to have no end." N Y Times Book Rev

Dirty white boys; a novel. Random House 1994 436p o.p.

* LC 94-15359

"After killing a black inmate, the brutal Lamar Pye breaks out of the Oklahoma State Penitentiary along with his retarded cousin, Odell, and a hapless artist-turned-felon named Richard. They embark on a desperate run across Oklahoma and Texas, pursued by state troopers. The escapees hide out with a convict groupie who has lived alone since murdering her parents as an adolescent. In a parody of domesticity, Lamar embraces these losers as the family he never knew." Libr J

"The blood-soaked packaging of Mr. Hunter's big, mythic theme is thrilling, in the manner of the ancient storytellers, with battles fierce enough for a war and characters crazy enough to fight them to the death. There is no place to run for cover from this author's prose—no glades of pretty writing to cool his vision of a land of lost children, forgotten values and total desolation." NY Times Book Rev

Havana; an Earl Swagger novel. Simon & Schuster 2003 403p $24.95

ISBN 0-7432-3808-7   LC 2003-54461

"Fifty years ago the mob was enjoying huge profits from its extensive Cuban enterprises. The only cause for concern is a young lawyer named Fidel Castro. Under the auspices of the CIA, an assassination plot is advanced and an unsuspecting Earl Swagger, a Medal of Honor winner and legendary tough guy, is brought in as the shooter. The Communists are also interested in Fidel, and Speshnev, a KGB operator, is brought in to protect their investment. Earl and Speshnev soon discover their efforts are better directed at neutralizing the mob, the corrupt government, and their respective spy agencies." Libr J

"Havana's story line bobs and weaves like a prizefighter, taking the reader in many directions, from barely exciting scenes to intense ones." USA Today

Hot Springs; a novel. Simon & Schuster 2000 478p $25

ISBN 0-684-86360-X   LC 99-88530

Earl Swagger is "a no-nonsense marine who was awarded the Medal of Honor for heroism on Iwo Jima. After the war, Earl works as a foreman in a sawmill. But when he is offered a job training a group of young lawmen whose mandate is to rid Hot Springs, Ark., of its mob-run gambling houses, he eagerly accepts. . . . As Earl's deputies attempt to clean up Hot Springs, Earl's fearlessness makes his boss think he has a death wish. When he hires an investigator to look into Earl's background, the pious myths that surround Earl's father, a respected Arkansas sheriff, are shattered." N Y Times Book Rev

"Once upon a time, _hard-boiled_ implied more than a style; Hunter shows us what the real thing was all about." Booklist

Night of thunder; a Bob Lee Swagger novel. Simon & Schuster 2008 290p $26

ISBN 978-1-4165-6511-6; 1-4165-6511-6

LC 2008-17856

Sixty-three-year-old marksman Bob Lee Swagger is "back on the Montana farm that provides a haven for him and his family. But then he learns that his elder daughter, 24-year-old journalist Nikki, has been left in a coma after a hit-and-run near Bristol, Tenn. While local police are chalking up the accident to some teen, high on meth or NASCAR, Swagger fears that his daughter may be paying the price for his own violent past 87 kills at last count. And so it's off to the mountains of Tennessee and into the heart of the NASCAR Nation. . . . Perhaps few thriller writers out there can match Hunter's skill when it comes to writing about guns — not just in precise listings of caliber, range and impact, but in prose both lyrical and reverent. . . . Hunter succeeds as well in touching on the tragedies of the methamphetamine craze in rural America and later in capturing the throb and hum of the Bristol Motor Speedway." Washington Post Book World

Pale horse coming; a novel. Simon & Schuster 2001 491p

ISBN 0-684-86361-8   LC 2001-47386

In this sequel to Hot Springs, "Hunter continues the story of Arkansas state cop Earl Swagger. It's 1951, and Swagger is once again called on to clean up an evil empire. Deep in the swamps of Thebes, Mississippi, a prison for black criminals run by a gang of redneck thugs harbors a sinister conspiracy. After rescuing his friend Sam Vincent from Thebes and narrowly escaping from the prison himself, Earl gathers a team of legendary gunfighters . . . and sets out to liberate Thebes the only way he knows how—violently. . . . The character of Earl Swagger, equal parts gristle and determination, remains compelling, both as archetype and as complex human being." Booklist

Time to hunt; a novel. Doubleday 1998 467p

ISBN 0-385-48043-1   LC 97-46985

This novel featuring Bob Lee Swagger "begins in the early 1970s in Washington, when Marine Corporal Donny Fenn gets himself sent back to Vietnam for refusing to betray a fellow platoon member suspected of collaborating with student dissidents. Once in Southeast Asia, Fenn finds himself working as a spotter for the inimitable Swagger, and the two manage to save a pinned-down battalion before Fenn is killed by a Russian adversary who has been sent to Vietnam to hunt down the dynamic duo. After Fenn's death, Swagger leaves the Marine Corps to marry Fenn's widow, Julie, and start a family, but his Russian rival remains intent on finishing the job." Publ Wkly

"Swagger is a near-mythic character without peer in

Hunter, Stephen, 1946-—*Continued*

mystery fiction. He was born to soldier but longs to stop. As we revel in his adventures and triumphs, we also experience his pain." Booklist

Hurston, Zora Neale, 1891-1960

The complete stories; introduction by Henry Louis Gates, Jr. and Sieglinde Lemke. HarperCollins Pubs. 1995 xxiii, 305p pa $14 hardcover o.p.

ISBN 0-06-092171-4 (pa) LC 91-50438
Contents: John Redding goes to sea; Drenched in light; Spunk; Magnolia Flower; Muttsy; 'Possum or pig?; The Eatonville anthology; Sweat; The gilded six-bits; Mother Catherine; Uncle Monday; The fire and the cloud; Cock Robin Beale Street; Story in Harlem slang; High John de Conquer; Hurricane; The conscience of the court; Escape from Pharaoh; The tablets of the law; Black death; The bone of contention; Book of Harlem; Harlem slanguage; Now you cookin' with gas; The seventh veil; The woman in Gaul
This collection of Hurston's short fiction contains nineteen stories originally published between 1921 and 1951, arranged in the order in which they were published, and seven previously unpublished stories.

Jonah's gourd vine
In Hurston, Z. N. Novels and stories p1-171

Moses, man of the mountain
In Hurston, Z. N. Novels and stories p335-595

Novels and stories. Library of Am. 1995 1041p $35

ISBN 0-940450-83-6
    * LC 94-25757
Companion volume to Folklore, memoirs, and other writings
Contents: Short stories included are: John Redding goes to sea; Drenched in light; Spunk; Sweat; The bones of contention; Book of Harlem; The gilded six-bits; The fire and the cloud; Story in Harlem slang
This collection contains Hurston's four novels: Jonah's gourd vine, Their eyes were watching God, Moses, man of the mountain, and Seraph on the Suwanee. Also included are nine short stories
"Libraries without a complete set of Hurston's fiction will find this volume a necessary and easy purchase to fill that unfortunate gap." Booklist

Seraph on the Suwanee
In Hurston, Z. N. Novels and stories p597-920

Their eyes were watching God; with a foreword by Edwidge Danticat. HarperCollins Pubs. 2000 xxii, 231p $22; pa $15.95

ISBN 0-06-019949-0; 0-06-112006-0 (pa)
    * LC 00-58186
First published 1937 by Lippincott
This novel "treats social problems from a racial and feminist perspective. Janie Crawford, raised by her grandmother in rural poverty, flees her old and dictatorial husband with Joe Starks, an ambitious man who becomes the mayor of Florida's first town run by African Ameri-

cans. When Joe dies, Janie falls in love with the younger Teacake and follows him to the truck farming area of the Florida swamps. In the floods following a hurricane, he is bitten by a rabid dog and, crazed, attacks Janie. She shoots him, is charged with murder, and finally exonerated. When she returns to the town she and Joe built, she tells her story to a friend." HarperCollins Reader's Ency of Am Lit

also in Hurston, Z. N. Novels and stories p173-333

Hurwitz, Gregg, 1973-

The crime writer. Viking 2007 301p $24.95
ISBN 978-0-670-06321-5; 0-670-06321-5
    LC 2006-52822
"Successful crime-novelist Drew Danner has gained true tabloid fame-as the murderer of his ex-fiance. Found by the police in the midst of a brain-tumor-induced grand mal seizure, with her blood covering his hands and his fingerprints on the murder weapon, Danner seems to be the only person in L.A. who isn't sure he is a killer. Emergency surgery after his arrest removes the tumor, and a temporary insanity defense frees him, but his comfortable life is shattered. He can't live without knowing if he killed a woman he once loved. His only choice is to become a character in a story he hasn't written. Danner's anguish is compellingly described, and the plot has more twists and turns than Mulholland Drive." Booklist

Huston, Charlie

Already dead. Ballantine Books 2005 268p map pa $14
ISBN 0-345-47824-X LC 2004-62323
This is the first book in the author's series featuring Joe Pitt. "Manhattan is teeming with the undead, the island divided into often-warring vampire clans such as the Society, the Hood and the Enclave. . . . Rogue PI Joe Pitt (aka Simon), who like all vampires is infected with a virus that requires him to drink blood regularly, is hired by Marilee Horde, a prominent New York socialite, to locate her runaway teenage daughter, Amanda, who may be slumming with homeless goth kids in the East Village. Meanwhile, a 'carrier' is on the loose, infecting its victims with a bacterium that turns them into brain-eating zombies." Publ Wkly
"Huston's intricate, fast-paced, Chandleresque vampire-crime story has plenty of action, violence, and raw language. An excellent story but not for the squeamish in public libraries." Libr J

Caught stealing. Ballantine Books 2004 240p
ISBN 0-345-46477-X LC 2004-299530
"Having fled California for New York City after an injury cut short his promising baseball career, Hank Thompson settles into an aimless life as an alcoholic bartender. Still, Hank prides himself on making Manhattan a bit more hospitable by helping his friends, so how can he refuse when a neighbor asks him to cat-sit? One lost kidney later, Hank realizes that an Elmore Leonardesque collection of Russian mobsters, short-fused cons, and renegade cops will snuff out all 10 lives he and the cat share between them if that's what it takes to find the not-so-good neighbor. . . . [This book] definitely be-

Huston, Charlie—*Continued*

longs on every Elmore Leonard fan's to-read list. One note of caution: Lovers of mystery-solving felines should place paws over eyes during the hair-raising cat torture scene." Booklist

Every last drop; a novel. Del Rey 2008 252p il pa $14

ISBN 978-0-345-49588-4; 0-345-49588-8

LC 2008-26441

New York vampire PI Joe Pitt "has been exiled to the South Bronx. He's doing his best to keep a low profile and eke out enough of a living to keep him in blood, bullets and smokes. It's not easy. He's there on sufferance — despite the tolerance and interest of local boss Esperanza — and he's down to his last three bullets. Staying out of trouble doesn't come naturally to him either. So when Dexter Predo of the Coalition offers him a chance to go back to Manhattan, Joe takes it. Sure, Predo wants him dead but it's not like he's the only one. Joe is sent to spy on Manhattan's new vampire clan: the Cure. They were set up by Amanda Horde a broken, brilliant, teenage millionaire with a soft spot for Pitt — and are dedicated to finding a cure for Vyrus, the cause and carrier of vampirism. Some vampires consider the Cure to be heretics, others, like the Coalition, consider them a threat to the status quo. Dexter Predo wants to know what they are doing and what they have planned for the future. . . . [Huston] has crafted a riveting and enjoyable story." SF Site

Half the blood of Brooklyn; a novel. Del Rey/Ballantine Books 2008 223p map pa $13.95

ISBN 978-0-345-49587-7   LC 2007-28330

"Huston's third Joe Pitt vampire novel . . . takes his Manhattan-based hardboiled hero on a dangerous trip into the undead communities across the bridge in Brooklyn. The various vampire clans in New York are on the brink of conflict. Leadership has fallen apart, and to make things worse, a 'Van Helsing' is running amok and has recently murdered a longtime supplier of contraband blood. Worst of all, Pitt's AIDS-stricken girlfriend, Evie, is in the hospital failing fast. . . . Huston's formidable writing chops are on full display: his action scenes are unparalleled in crime fiction and his dialogue is so hip and dead-on that Elmore Leonard should be getting nervous." Publ Wkly

The mystic arts of erasing all signs of death. Ballantine Books 2009 319p $25

ISBN 978-0-345-50111-0; 0-345-50111-X

LC 2008-35293

"Web Goodhue, a thirtyish Hollywood elementary school teacher traumatized by the violent death of a student, quits his job and retreats into an emotional shell. Helping an acquaintance clean up crime scenes gets Web involved with a young woman whose father died in a very messy suicide. She and her maniacal brother entangle Web in stolen almonds, human smuggling, murderous criminals, and her own kidnapping." Libr J

"Oddly, given the willfully grisly subject matter and the rocket-like propulsive quality of Huston's short sentences (a paragraph with more than five lines in it comes to seem almost Proustian), this is a book with something tender and almost mushy at its core. The real subjects here are grief and the quest for friendship and family. . . . The dialogue is terrific . . . and Huston is excellent

too on Los Angeles. He doesn't so much evoke the city as allow a sense of it to sink into his prose like blood into a carpet." Los Angeles Times Book Rev

The shotgun rule; a novel. Ballantine Books 2007 248p $21.95

ISBN 978-0-345-48135-1; 0-345-48135-6

LC 2007-20511

"In the summer of 1983, four teenage boys (a brainiac, a punk rocker, an army wannabe, and an ex-drug-runner) reclaim their stolen bicycle. They also find a crystal-meth lab and rip-off a half a kilo to sell and perhaps buy their dream car with. The dope-pimp Arroyo brothers—led by obese stoner-hippie, Geezer—kick off a vengeful search. Mayhem, much of it over-the-top and delivered in gruesome detail—rocks the California suburb, and dysfunctional parents deal with their own demons while the boys prove surprisingly clever in a tough spot. From a sharp pitch, staccato dialogue and volatile action, durable characters and an intricate plot emerge, demonstrating Huston can still deliver the expected thriller goods." Paste

Hustvedt, Siri

The sorrows of an American; a novel. Henry Holt and Co. 2008 306p $25

ISBN 978-0-8050-7908-1; 0-8050-7908-4

LC 2007-31046

"The novel opens with narrator Erik Davidsen, a psychiatrist, and his sister Inga, an academic, flying from New York City home to Minnesota, where the pair begins the painful process of sorting through the study of their deceased father, Lars. . . . [This] is a novel of secrets and ghosts: Lars' ghosts, which follow him back to Minnesota after his service in World War II; Erik, divorced, lonely, plagued by a patient's suicide; the widowed Inga, who learns her husband, famous writer Max Blaustein, led a secret life during their tumultuous marriage. Even Sonia, Inga's 18-year-old daughter, carries painful burdens, including what she saw from her schoolroom window on September 11, 2001. . . . In a lesser writer's hands, this glut of thematic material could wind a novel into a hopeless knot. Hustvedt's facility is such that instead, we are lead through the inseparable interactions of mind and body as her characters move through the story. The effect is exhilarating rather than jarring, as events urge us forward, each secret offering up a truth that in turn unlocks another door." PopMatters

What I loved; a novel. Holt & Co. 2003 370p $25

ISBN 0-8050-7170-9   LC 2002-27358

The author "co-opts New York's competitive and faddish art world for its symbol-laden milieu. Leo Hertzberg, a thoughtful art historian, narrates a measured and mesmerizing tale of passion and tragedy that spans 20 years and involves his wife, Erica, a literary scholar, his close friendship with highly provocative painter Bill Wechsler; and his hidden infatuation with Bill's sexy muse and second wife, Violet, an expert in psychotic disorders associated with women's body images." Booklist

"The imprint of Henry James turns out to have reference not to the novel's prose style, which is cleanly colloquial, but to a tragic vision in which surface decorum hides subterranean upheaval. 'What I Loved' is a rare

Hustvedt, Siri—_Continued_

thing, a page turner written at full intellectual stretch, serious but witty, large-minded and morally engaged." N Y Times Book Rev

Huxley, Aldous, 1894-1963

Brave new world; a novel. Doubleday, Doran & Co. 1932 311p o.p.

*

"The ironic title, which Huxley has taken from Shakespeare's _The Tempest_, describes a world in which science has taken control over morality and humaneness. In this utopia humans emerge from test tubes, families are obsolete, and even pleasure is regulated. When a so-called savage who believes in spirituality is found and is imported to the community, he cannot accommodate himself to this world and ends his life." Shapiro. Fic for Youth. 3d edition

Collected short stories. Harper & Row 1957 397p o.p.

Contents: Happily ever after; Eupompus gave splendour to art by numbers; Cynthia; The bookshop; The death of Lully; Sir Hercules; The Gioconda smile; The Tillotson banquet; Green tunnels; Nuns at luncheon; Little Mexican; Hubert and Mimmie; Fard; The portrait; Young Archimedes; Half holiday; The monocle; Fairy godmother; Chawdron; The rest cure; The Claxtons

Point counter point. Doubleday, Doran & Co. 1928 432p o.p.

*

The book "presents a satiric picture of London intellectuals and members of English upper-class society during the 1920's. Frequent allusions to literature, painting, music, and contemporary British politics occur throughout the book, and much scientific information is embodied in its background. The story is long and involved, with many characters; it concerns a series of broken marriages and love affairs, and a political assassination. The construction is elaborate, supposedly based on Bach's 'Suite No. 2 in B Minor.' It is also a novel within a novel. Philip Quarles a leading character . . . is himself planning a novel, which echoes or 'counterpoints' the events going on around him." Reader's Ency. 4th edition

Huyler, Frank, 1964-

The laws of invisible things. H. Holt 2004 320p $25

ISBN 0-8050-7330-2   LC 2003-51116

This novel "focuses on Michael Grant, a newly divorced doctor who has just moved to North Carolina and joined the practice of widower Ronald Gass, a much older physician. Grant's lonely personal life is soon in turmoil as it intersects with the black Williams family. Soon after his arrival, Grant treats the granddaughter of Rev. Thomas Williams; the little girl dies, probably due to an oversight by Grant. As a favor to the minister, Grant agrees to see his son Jonas, the girl's father, who has bizarre symptoms that Grant thinks may indicate a previously unknown disease; Gass is skeptical, almost scornful of this idea. Within days, Gass dies of natural causes, Jonas is dead from the disease, and Grant himself is hospitalized with the same symptoms." Libr J

"Although the story elements are melodramatic, the intimate tone of Huyler's elegiac voice invites us to rise above our disgust and think again about the things we think we know." N Y Times Book Rev

Hyland, M. J., 1968-

Carry me down. Canongate 2006 334p $23

ISBN 1-84195-740-2

"At 11, John Egan is nearly six feet tall with a deep voice, and he feels like a freak, especially after he wets himself in class. John believes he is a gifted human lie detector, and he himself is a great liar; his obsession is to be famous and have his gift recognized in the Guinness Book of World Records. But why is Dad lying? The child's naive first-person, present-tense narrative brings achingly close his helplessness in a powerful adult world. He may be a giant, but he has no control. Why suddenly is the family moving? Where to? What is wrong? When they land up in the public-housing projects in Dublin, the scary threat seems to be from a brutal street gang, but the real terror turns out to be in the intimacy of his home. Focused on small things, the quiet plain scenes of daily life lead to the surprising and unforgettable climax." Booklist

Hynes, James

Kings of infinite space. St. Martin's Press 2004 341p $24.95

ISBN 0-312-45645-X   LC 2003-58563

"According to Paul Trilby, there's something weird going on at the Texas Department of General Services, where he slaves away as the lowliest-of-lowly corporate workers, the office temp. . . . Divorced, destitute, and driving a rattletrap clunker amidst a sea of sleek SUVs, Paul's down-and-out existence is a far cry from his former glory days as an up-and-coming university professor. Confronted by his smarmy coworkers (who are not above selling their souls for a better gig), Paul is introduced to a mysterious world of former employees, equally downtrodden middlemen downsized in state budget cuts. The only difference is—they're dead." Booklist

This "is social satire that slides smoothly and surreally into horror, and if it loses a little of its emotional heft in the process, you don't really miss it. The glee with which Hynes choreographs an in-office zombie-vs.-stapler fight scene is compensation enough." Time

The lecturer's tale. Picador 2001 388p $25

ISBN 0-312-20332-2

* LC 00-47836

"The protagonist is Nelson Humboldt, a once bright star in the English department at Midwest University but now reduced to teaching composition classes. Never one to publish much, Nelson's academic career is on the verge of perishing. That is until he realizes he has accidentally (in the literal sense) acquired a magic power over people that allows him to bend them to his will." Booklist

"The culture wars of the ivory tower may be well-charted waters, but Hynes wades in with Swiftian glee." Am Book Rev

I

Iagnemma, Karl

The expeditions; a novel. Dial Press 2008 322p $24

ISBN 978-0-385-33595-9; 0-385-33595-4

LC 2007-18324

This is "the tale of Elisha Stone, a sixteen-year-old runaway and amateur naturalist who, in 1844, wins a place on an expedition to Michigan's Upper Peninsula. The party's leader, a wealthy surveyor, is interested only in locating deposits of iron ore ('Fortunes are built from gold. But nations are built from iron'). He finds an antagonist in an idealistic professor desperate to discover artifacts to prove his theory of the single origin of all races. They are trailed by Elisha's father, a flawed minister, on the point of succumbing to a 'wet and thready' consumptive cough, who is determined to tell him of his mother's death." New Yorker

"Emotionally powerful and beautifully wrought. . . . One of this novel's many and considerable strengths is the way in which the author refuses to stack the decks for or against either of his protagonists or their prospective ideas—the man of faith and the man of science. Each has his flaws and each his admirable strengths." Los Angeles Times Book Rev

On the nature of human romantic interaction. Dial Press (NY) 2003 212cmp il $22.95

ISBN 0-385-33593-8

LC 2003-40953

Contents: On the nature of human romantic interaction; The phrenologist's dream; Zilkowski's theorem; The confessional approach; The Indian agent; Kingdom, order, species; The ore miner's wife; Children of hunger

"The meticulousness of science and mathematics is applied to the mysteries of love in Iagnemma's debut collection, which features eight complex, multilayered stories in which protagonists try to balance the demands of the heart against their need for rational, orderly thinking." Publ Wkly

Ignatius, David, 1950-

Body of lies; a novel. W.W. Norton & Co. 2007 349p $24.95

ISBN 978-0-393-06503-9; 0-393-06503-0

LC 2006-102362

This is the "story of idealistic CIA agent Roger Ferris, newly stationed in Jordan after being wounded in Iraq. After a failed initiative to flush out a terrorist mastermind known as Suleiman, Ferris, who's dedicated to forestalling further al-Qaeda attacks, develops an intricate scheme modeled after a British plan used successfully against the Nazis." Publ Wkly

"Unlike most of the folks writing fiction about the CIA these days, [Ignatius] understands the gestalt of the place and the internal and external pressure under which the agency's denizens operate." Washington Times

A firing offense. Random House 1997 333p o.p.

LC 96-29518

In this "espionage thriller, an up-and-coming journalist finds he has made a Faustian bargain when he takes information from the CIA. New York Mirror foreign correspondent Eric Truell's exposé of French governmental corruption leads him to probe the dynamics of power behind a pending French-Chinese communications contract—a deal that could mean the loss of billions for American businesses. Truell's CIA sources use their information to lure the ambitious but naive reporter into playing their own dangerous game in the murky new world order, where real power resides not with governments but with private enterprise." Libr J

"Thanks to great writing and an all-too-human protagonist, the preaching is kept to a minimum, but the sermon—about good journalism and bad, truth and lies—is there in bold letters." Publ Wkly

The increment; a novel. W.W. Norton & Co. 2009 390p $26.95

ISBN 978-0-393-06504-6

LC 2008-53857

"When Harry Pappas, the new CIA chief of the Iran Operations Division, receives an unsolicited e-mail from an alleged Tehran scientist who calls himself 'Dr. Ali' that implies Iran has in fact continued with its nuclear weapons program and is 'an imminent threat to global peace,' he shares the information with his superiors only to find an administration bent on warmongering. Having vowed never again to play a role in a senseless conflict that could potentially kill thousands of innocents, Pappas, whose only son was killed while serving in the second Iraq War, must somehow identify Dr. Ali, get him out of Iran and mine his knowledge before the U.S. blunders into another unnecessary war." Publ Wkly

The author "immerses readers in a totally believable universe. Jargon, geography and detail all ring true as his meticulously crafted, tightly woven tale moves from Washington to London and Iran. The plot grabs everything in its path like a snowball rolling down a hill." Kirkus

The Sun King; a novel. Random House 1999 305p

ISBN 0-679-44861-6

LC 99-13490

"Publishing mogul Sandy Galvin, a.k.a. the Sun King, arrives in Washington, DC, one day with plans to revive a dying newspaper. He hires David Cantor, a cynical lifestyle writer with a profound appreciation for fluff journalism, and Candace Ridgway, a former flame and scrupulous foreign affairs writer also known as The Mistress of Fact. Shortly, both men are deeply involved with the Mistress, and the threesome spend the rest of the book sparring about love and journalistic ethics." SLJ

"A thoroughly involving narrative with a sharp, satiric edge, Ignatius's contemporary take on the tragic confluence of love, power and ambition is a sophisticated look at the media mystique and the movers and shakers in our nation's capitol. His stylish, fluent prose, anchored with fine atmospheric detail, gives the story texture and momentum." Publ Wkly

Iles, Greg

Black cross. Dutton 1995 516p o.p.

LC 94-34642

This novel "tells the story of a physician from Georgia and a German Jew who manage to forestall Hitler's use of poison nerve gas during World War II by destroying a secret laboratory hidden in a Nazi death camp. The rash plan for infiltrating the camp and destroying the laboratory has been developed by the Allies and led by Winston Churchill and will require nerves of steel, physi-

Iles, Greg—*Continued*

cal and emotional stamina, unparalleled bravery, and incredible luck. If it works, millions of lives will be saved. But there is a horrible price to pay for the larger victory—hundreds of Jewish prisoners interred in the camp may also die. From the very first page, Iles takes his readers on an emotional roller-coaster ride, juxtaposing tension-filled action scenes, horrifying depictions of savage cruelty, and heart-stopping descriptions of sacrifice and bravery." Booklist

The devil's punchbowl. Scribner 2009 580p $26.99

ISBN 978-0-7432-9251-1; 0-7432-9251-0

LC 2008-49551

Penn Cage, "a former prosecuting attorney-turned-novelist, is now mayor of Natchez, MS, his hometown. But all is not well, for the promises he made as a candidate seem all but impossible to achieve as a working mayor. When one of his childhood friends is murdered a day after contacting him with information concerning dog fighting, prostitution, drugs, and money laundering presided over by the manager of a Natchez gambling casino, Cage takes on an investigation that makes him the target of organized crime, endangers the lives of his family and closest friends, and draws the wrath of the Justice Department and Homeland Security. . . . Provides a thrill a minute." Libr J

The footprints of God. Scribner 2003 459p $25.95

ISBN 0-7432-3469-3

LC 2003-45733

As the novel opens Dr. David Tenant is "contemplating his life after friend and mentor Andrew Fielding is found dead in his lab. A stroke is the suspected cause, but David knows better because both men were part of an ultra-top-secret project known as Project Trinity, a quantum leap in the future of supercomputing and artificial intelligence. Both men had warned their managers about the experiment's dangers, and now David believes that he is next on the hit list." Libr J

"Readers interested in the exploration of religious themes without the usual New Age blather or window-dressed dogma will snap up this novel of cutting-edge science." Publ Wkly

Mortal fear. Dutton 1997 564p o.p.

LC 97-194514

"When futures trader Harper Cole, who moonlights as the systems operator of an erotic online services called EROS, contacts the New Orleans police with information about the murder of celebrated author—and EROS subscriber—Karin Wheat, he immediately becomes the prime suspect in six other murders of EROS subscribers across the country." Publ Wkly

"Despite the artifice of the characters operating it, the technology involved in their ingenious computer chase—which gives new meaning to the term 'network'—is fascinating." N Y Times Book Rev

Third degree. Scribner 2007 385p $25.95

ISBN 978-0-7432-9250-4; 0-7432-9250-2

LC 2007-48097

"When Laurel Shields, a 35-year-old mother of two, discovers she's pregnant, she can't be sure her physician husband, Warren, is the father. Meanwhile, Warren is in trouble with the IRS. Laurel believes his obsessive

search for a document in their Athens Point, Miss., home is related to a federal Medicaid fraud investigation focusing on his medical partner, Kyle Auster. As the Feds prepare to swoop down on Warren and Kyle's office to collect the evidence of false billings and bribes to patients without any actual illnesses, Warren takes Laurel and their two children hostage. Iles squeezes every drop of suspense out of the prolonged standoff between the doctor and the police." Publ Wkly

Turning angel. Scribner 2005 501p $25.95

ISBN 0-7432-3471-5

LC 2005-54469

"Drew Elliott is a small town doctor with a stellar reputation. Penn Cage is a lawyer who returned to his hometown to raise his daughter after his wife's death. When the body of seventeen-year-old Kate Townsend is found near the Mississippi River, Drew confides to Penn that he was sexually involved with the girl. She was twenty years his junior, not to mention a patient. Drew swears he is innocent of Kate's death and begs Penn for legal counsel. Penn feels compelled to investigate Kate's murder himself, but he must turn to Mia Burke, his daughter's babysitter and a classmate of the dead girl, for help." Publisher's note

"All this is lurid in the extreme and, in Iles's hands, entirely gripping, but there is more to Turning Angel than sex and scandal. Iles offers an insider's heartfelt picture of a Southern town that is dying because of lousy schools, a failing economy and racial tensions–and, again, there is no reason to think Natchez is unique. Iles populates this town with characters who are all too real and makes clear that its privileged young people no longer live isolated lives. . . . This is a powerful piece of popular fiction." Washington Post Book World

Inman, Robert, 1943-

Captain Saturday; a novel. Little, Brown 2002 455p $24.95

ISBN 0-316-41502-2

LC 2001-23529

"Will Baggett has settled into a comfortable existence: he's a fixture of the Raleigh community as its most popular TV weatherman; his beatiful wife, Clarice, is a successful real estate broker; and his son, Palmer, is a medical student at UNC-Chapel Hill. Yet Will's seemingly perfect facade is destroyed when his news station is bought out and he is abruptly fired. This upset to his routine has a ripple effect; Clarice announces she wants a divorce, his relationship with Palmer is proven to be not as solid as he once believed, and Will finds himself accidentally embroiled in legal problems." Booklist

"Peopled with vivid, endearlingly quixotic characters and filled with dead-on insights into a shallow New South that defines itself by club memberships and designer labels, this richly textured epic is paean to the vagaries of the human heart." Publ Wkly

Innes, Hammond, 1913-1998

The wreck of the Mary Deare. Knopf 1956 296p o.p.

*

"When narrator John Sands first sights the freighter 'Mary Deare' from the deck of his salvage boat, she appears to be a ghostly derelict drifting toward the Channel reefs. Boarding her, however, he encounters her specter-

Innes, Hammond, 1913-1998—*Continued*

ridden captain, Gideon Patch, and becomes dangerously involved in the suspect seaman's desperate attempt to expose the conspiracy behind her last voyage." Booklist

Inness-Brown, Elizabeth, 1954-

Burning Marguerite. Knopf 2002 237p $23

ISBN 0-375-41196-8   LC 2001-29860

"When James Jack finds his 94-year-old Tante Marguerite frozen in the snow outside their house on a remote New England island, he sets out to give her the very private funeral she desired. . . . The narrative jumps from James Jack's point of view to Marguerite's, as gradually we learn the tragedy of her young life, which led to a period of exile in New Orleans and finally to her return to the isolated island, where she raised James Jack after the sudden death of his parents. This is a remarkably quiet novel, one that draws its power and beauty as much from silence as from human interaction." Booklist

Irish, William, 1903-1968

For works written by this author under other names see Woolrich, Cornell, 1903-1968

Irving, John, 1942-

3 by Irving. Random House 1980 718p o.p.

LC 79-5536

Contents: Setting free the bears (1969); The water-method man (1972); The 158-pound marriage (1974)

The first of these novels "involves a madcap scheme to liberate zoo animals, the second chronicles the misadventures of a bungling graduate student, and the third features a ménage-à-quatre in academe. . . . Irving's early fictions are noteworthy not only as forerunners to the remarkable *Garp* but also on their own merits. Possessing much of the same narrative inventiveness, zany wit, and sheer verve that so distinguish Irving's best-seller, they also maintain a *Garp*-like balance between the humorous and the macabre." Choice

The 158-pound marriage

In Irving, J. 3 by Irving p561-718

The cider house rules; a novel. Modern Library 1999 571p $24.95

ISBN 978-0-679-60335-1; 0-679-60335-2

LC 99-30034

First published 1985 by Morrow

"Homer Wells wants to be neither an orphan nor an abortionist. But he has little choice in either matter; failing to be adopted, he is fated to always return to Maine's Saint Cloud's Orphanage and his surrogate father, Dr. Larch, head administrator and resident abortionist. Although still in his teens, Homer learns 'perfect obstetrical procedure' while assisting Larch, but his unwillingness to perform abortions eventually leads him away from Saint Cloud's and into a head-on collision with life." Libr J

"The Cider House Rules is filled with people to love and to feel for. . . . The characters in John Irving's novel break all the rules, and yet they remain noble and free-spirited. Victims of tragedy, violence, and injustice, their lives seem more interesting and full of thought-provoking dilemmas than the lives of many real people." Houston Post

The fourth hand; a novel. Random House 2001 316p

ISBN 0-375-50627-6   LC 2001-18155

This novel's hero, "Patrick Wallingford, is a television reporter whose left hand is eaten by a lion while he is covering a story about the circus in India. Patrick eventually receives a transplanted hand from a man named Otto Clausen, who accidentally shot himself. . . . Otto's widow, Doris, who has chosen Patrick to be the hand recipient, not only declares that she has visiting rights with her late husband's hand, but also sexually assaults Patrick in order to become pregnant with his child." N Y Times

"Irving's set pieces are on that high level of American gothic comedy he has made uniquely his own." Publ Wkly

The Hotel New Hampshire. Dutton 1981 401p o.p.   LC 81-2610

"A Henry Robbins book"

This is "a family chronicle—a tale of generations of parents coping with children and siblings coping with each other. The chief parents are Win and Mary Berry of Dairy, New Hampshire, a couple brought together after high school at a seaside resort where, on summer jobs, they catch a glimpse of a joyous vocation (innkeeping). The Berry union produces five spirited and amusing children. . . . The story covers a quarter-century, beginning round about 1940, and the principal action takes place in three hotels, each called . . . The Hotel New Hampshire. (The hotels are situated in New Hampshire, Austria, and Maine.)" Atlantic

The author "keeps us moving, sacrificing rhetoric to pace, as in the most primitive narrative forms, the fable and the fairy tale. In fiction like this, meaning lies near the surface of the story and in the voice of the storyteller." New Repub

Last night in Twisted River; a novel. Random House 2009 554p $28

ISBN 978-1-4000-6384-0; 1-4000-6384-1

LC 2009-14449

"The story, told over five decades starting in 1954, centers on Dominic Baciagalupo, a logging-camp cook; his son, Daniel, who eventually becomes a writer with the pen name Danny Angel; and Dominic's best friend, Ketchum, a tough and loyal logger. Last Night's sentimental tone is established early — the logging industry is struggling, and Dominic is a single father whose wife died in a tragic accident. The logging camp is idyllic in a rustic way — until an incident featuring an eight-inch skillet, a bear, and a philandering sous-chef drives father and son on the lam. Their flight never ends, really — the vengeful force that sends them running is implacable, and wherever Dominic and Daniel run, they can never truly settle. . . . The real story is that Irving, defying the precepts of critics once again, has created another sprawling, sentimental, emotional tale, the kind that readers crave, however snooty or pedestrian their tastes." Entertainment Wkly

A prayer for Owen Meany; a novel. Modern Library 2002 xxiv, 641p $24.95

ISBN 0-679-64259-5

* LC 2002-26479

First published 1989 by Morrow

This novel is set in New Hampshire in the 1950s and 1960s. Owen Meany is a short boy with a squeaky voice,

Irving, John, 1942-—*Continued*

who foresees his own death and sees himself as an instrument of God. He hits a baseball that kills the mother of John Wheelwright, the novel's narrator. Because of Owen, John becomes a Christian

"Despite its theological proppings, A Prayer for Owen Meany is a fable of political predestination. As usual, Irving delivers a boisterous cast, a spirited story line and a quality of prose that is frequently underestimated even by his admirers. On the other hand, the novel invites trespass by symbol hunters. . . . To get lost in critical rummage would be to miss the point. Irving's litany of error and folly may strike some as too righteous; but it is effective." Time

Setting free the bears
In Irving, J. 3 by Irving p1-284

A son of the circus. Random House 1994 633p
o.p.   LC 93-44750
"At center stage is Farrokh Daruwalla, an alienated, middle-aged, Bombay-born doctor who returns to his birthplace to study circus dwarfs. Farrokh becomes entangled in a case involving a serial murderer who carves the image of a winking elephant on his victims' torsos. This storyline bounces around like the proverbial three-ring circus and features a cast of eunuchs, hippies, movie stars, transsexuals, and clergymen." Libr J

Irving "is at the peak of his powers in this new novel. He plunges the reader into one sensual or grotesque scene after another with cheerful vigour and a madcap tenderness for life. . . . The author knows what he is doing from first to last, and handles the dozens of strands of his plot with exuberant ease." Economist

Until I find you; a novel. Random House 2005 824p $27.95
ISBN 1-400-06383-3
This novel "recounts the life of an actor as he tries to find the father who abandoned him and to come to terms with the traumas of his youth: a mother who was an itinerant tattoo artist and occasional prostitute, schooling at an all-girls academy where he was tormented by older classmates, sexual molestation at the hands of a woman who had been a kind of nanny." New Yorker

"The fatal difference between Irving and his master is that in a Dickens novel the smallest components are thematically and even poetically tied to the central idea, rather than unnecessary and irrelevant. Still, Irving is a skillful, powerful writer, and his novels are nearly always worth the considerable time they demand. His latest, Until I Find You, is in many ways characteristic: generous, sprawling, vivid, and, as with all his work, quintessentially masculine." New Leader

The water-method man
In Irving, J. 3 by Irving p285-560

A widow for one year; a novel. Random House 1998 537p
ISBN 0-375-50137-1   LC 97-49166
The first half of this novel "tells the story of Eddie O'Hare, a prep school student with literary aspirations who lands a job as a personal assistant to noted children's author Ted Cole in the summer of 1958. O'Hare spends most of the time in bed with Cole's wife, Marion. The second half of the book describes O'Hare's ac-

quaintance, decades later, with Ruth Cole, Ted's daughter, who is also a successful writer. While researching her latest novel, Ruth witnesses the murder of an Amsterdam window prostitute." Libr J

"It is clearly not the outline of the plot that makes the book obstinately memorable. Rather, it is Irving's special gift for farcical incident . . . his piercing sense of the wonderful and terrible vulnerability of children, his poetic evocation of the ravages of time." Publ Wkly

The world according to Garp. Dutton 1978 437p o.p.
                                   * LC 77-15564
"A Henry Robbins book"
"Jenny Fields is the black sheep daughter of an aristocratic New England family; she becomes, almost by accident, a feminist leader ahead of her time. Her son, T. S. Garp (named for a father he never saw), has high ambitions for his artistic career, but he has an even higher, obsessive devotion to his wife and children. Surrounding Garp and Jenny are a wide assortment of people: school-teachers and whores, wrestlers and radicals, editors and assassins, transsexuals and rapists, and husbands and wives." Publisher's note

This "is a long family novel, spanning four generations and two continents, crammed with incidents, characters, feelings and craft. The components of black comedy and melodrama, pathos and tragedy, mesh effortlessly in a tale that can also be read as a commentary on art and the imagination." Time

Irving, Washington, 1783-1859

The complete tales of Washington Irving. Doubleday 1975 xxxvii, 798p o.p.
                                              *
Contents: Rip Van Winkle; The spectre bridegroom; The legend of Sleepy Hollow; The stout gentleman; The student of Salamanca; Annette Delarbe; Dolph Heylinger; The hunting-dinner; The adventure of my uncle; The adventure of my aunt; The bold dragoon; Adventure of the German student; Adventure of the mysterious picture; Adventure of the mysterious stranger; The story of the young Italian; Literary life; A literary dinner; The club of queer fellows; The poor-devil author; Notoriety; A practical philosopher; Buckthorne; Grave reflections of a disappointed man; The booby squire; The strolling manager; The inn at Terracina; Adventure of the little antiquary; The belated travellers; Adventure of the Popkins family; The painter's adventure; The story of the bandit chieftain; The story of the young robber; The adventure of the Englishman; Hell gate; Kidd the pirate; The devil and Tom Walker; Wolfert Webber; Adventure of the black fisherman; The adventure of the mason; Legend of the Arabian astrologer; Legend of Prince Ahmed al Kamel; Legend of the Moor's legacy; Legend of the three beautiful princesses; Legend of the rose of the Alhambra; The governor and the notary; Governor Manco and the soldier; Legend of the two discreet statues; Spanish romances; The legend of the enchanted soldier; Wolfert's roost; The Creole village; Mountjoy; The widow's ordeal; The grand prior of Minorca; A contented man; Guests from Gibbet Island; The early experiences of Ralph Ringwood; The Count Van Horn; Don Juan: a spectral research; Legend of the engulphed convent; The phantom island

Isaacs, Susan, 1943-

After all these years. HarperCollins Pubs. 1993
343p o.p.   LC 92-56200

"Rose Meyers was just an ordinary Jew from Queens
who married her sweetheart, became a teacher, moved to
the suburbs, and had two kids. Then her husband's business made him a millionaire. Suddenly, Rose and Richie
have a Long Island mansion, a fleet of BMWs, and invitations to all the soirees. Rose is in for a shock, though,
when Richie announces he's leaving her for a younger
woman. The divorce papers aren't even signed when
Rose, stricken with insomnia, goes downstairs one night
for a glass of milk and trips over Richie's corpse. The
cops immediately peg Rose as the prime suspect, but she
knows she didn't kill her husband, and she's determined
to find out who did." Booklist

Isaacs "has a field day lampooning upper-class mores
. . . but also weaves into this thoroughly diverting caper
unexpected moments of genuine tenderness and sly social
commentary." Publ Wkly

Almost paradise. Harper & Row 1984 483p o.p.
                                   LC 83-48357

"Nicholas is the scion of a wealthy family, although
Jane's bloodline is anything but aristocratic. They marry
after Jane convinces Nick that his true talent lies with
acting rather than law. In no time Nick is the rage of
Broadway and Hollywood. The marriage remains idyllic
until Jane develops a fear of crowds so great she is unable to walk to her own mailbox. But she continues to
make their Connecticut farmhouse the ideal place for her
husband to entertain his many guests. The arrangement
works for twenty years, as Nick resists the attempts of
countless women to seduce him. Nick finally succumbs
to a timid film student and Jane takes up with her
shrink." West Coast Rev Books

Close relations. Lippincott 1980 270p o.p.
                                   LC 80-7858

"David Hoffman would appear to be everything a girl
could want—and he appears in Marcia Green's life when
the politician she writes speeches for is lagging in the
gubernatorial primary and her lover Jerry Morrissey is
stubbornly resisting the longterm commitment she longs
for. But here's one big strike against David: Marcia's
family approves of him. Flashbacks to her childhood, her
first marriage, her unhappy promiscuity show the reasons
for her rebellion. Ultimately, she and David decide they
need each other enough to be happy despite the past."
Libr J

"Besides being simultaneously romantic, feminist, and
political, the novel is also a satire: of Jewish mothers and
success-orientation, late-marrying Irishmen, American political campaigns, WASP mores, and human relations."
Best Sellers

Compromising positions. Times Bks. 1978 248p
o.p.
                                 * LC 77-13896

"Judith Singer is a nice, average Jewish housewife—on
the surface—but beneath that placid exterior lurks a secret longing for high adventure. . . . When a local den-
tist-Lothario is murdered in his office and a neighbor
who was his last patient is a suspect, Judith cannot resist
getting into the act. Meddling, gossiping, she turns detective, and when she learns that the elegant late Dr.

Fleckstein was not only bedding virtually every woman
in town but getting them to pose for exceedingly porno
photos, there's no stopping her. Enter detective Nelson
Sharpe, much more attractive than Judith's stodgy husband. The two make a wild pair of sleuths as Sharpe
tracks down the murderer and an accomplice and exposes
smug suburban hypocrisy." Publ Wkly

Lily White; a novel. HarperCollins Pubs. 1996
459p o.p.   LC 96-17399

"Told in chapters alternating between her personal life
and her work, this is the story of Lily White, a funny,
ambitious, criminal-defense attorney. Lily becomes
overinvolved in the case of her current client, Norman
Torkelson, a con man who woos and then bilks desperate, lonely women. Something went terribly wrong in his
last con, and the mark ended up dead. . . . As Lily pulls
out all the stops in trying to determine what really happened, she also reveals her painful personal life—her increasing distance from her blue-blooded, ne'er-do-well
husband, his startling revelation that he is in love with
her sister, and her subsequent efforts to build a makeshift
family with her best friend and mentor, an elegant gay
black man." Booklist

"Susan Isaac's real subject here isn't murder or legal
thrills, of course, but the drama and suspense of middle-
class women's lives. In her rendition, it's white-knuckle
stuff." N Y Times Book Rev

Magic hour. HarperCollins Pubs. 1991 412p o.p.
                                   LC 90-55570

Isaacs' setting, "the various sections of Long Island's
Hamptons (N.Y.), allows her to depict the tension between the hardworking locals, many of whom live on the
edge of poverty, and the snooty summer people, phony
Manhattan culture hounds and social climbers. Movie
producer Sy Spencer is clearly among the latter, and
when he is shot by the side of his glitzy Southampton
swimming pool, homicide detective Steve Brady is not
surprised to discover plentiful evidence of widespread resentment and hatred of Spencer." Publ Wkly

"Best of all . . . is the subplot, an old-fashioned love
story (think 1940s movie) in which Brady falls hard for
his leading suspect, the dead producer's first wife.
There's no good reason why we should buy into this romance—it rests on a totally improbable premise—but
Isaacs sets the hook and reels us in anyway." Booklist

Red, white and blue; a novel. HarperCollins
Pubs. 1998 402p
   ISBN 0-06-017608-3   LC 98-34568

"Investigation of a radical Wyoming militia group
brings together two unlikely people—Charlie Blair, an
FBI agent and Wyoming native, and Lauren Miller, a
New York reporter. Before focusing on the investigation
and the developing relationship between Charlie and
Lauren, Isaacs tells the story of their Jewish immigrant
ancestors, showing how two such different individuals
can be descended from the same roots." Libr J

"It is no easy task to hold a reader's attention when a
novel's outcome is obvious from the very first page. But
Susan Isaacs has such a knack for entertaining her reader
with the details of American pop culture . . . that it's
easy to be distracted from the predictability of her plot."
N Y Times Book Rev

Shining through. Harper & Row 1988 402p
   ISBN 0-06-015979-0   LC 87-45630

Isaacs, Susan, 1943-—*Continued*

"Linda Voss is a 31-year-old secretary to the dreamiest looking man on Wall Street, international lawyer John Berringer, with whom she is secretly and hopelessly in love: she is a poor girl from Queens, and he boasts an Ivy League background along with his perfect profile. When circumstances lead to their unlikely marriage, however, sexual fireworks keep them together. As World War II engulfs Europe, the Berringers move to Washington, where both become involved in undercover work for the COI, soon to become the OSS. Heartbreak, plus a feeling of kinship for the victims of Nazism, leads Linda, whose childhood was spent in a German-speaking household, to volunteer for a dangerous mission in Berlin." Publ Wkly

"Whether completely believable or not, Isaacs' tale of bravery and romance makes exciting, entertaining reading." Booklist

Isegawa, Moses, 1963-

Snakepit. Knopf 2004 259p $24

ISBN 0-375-41454-1   LC 2003-60479

This novel is "set in Uganda in the 1970s. . . . Bat Kaanga is a Ugandan just returned to his homeland after two years in Britain. While he completed a postgraduate degree at Cambridge, he watched from afar as 'flag independence [gave] way to economic independence' in Uganda, his chances to make a fortune there increasing with each 'reform' imposed by Idi Amin. Now, when Bat lands a job as Bureaucrat Two in the Ministry of Power and Communications, he feels himself entering the top echelons of government." Publisher's note

"This is a headlong and blurry novel filled with violence and sex, deceit and revenge-a messy, captivating portrait of a desperate time and place." Publ Wkly

Isherwood, Christopher, 1904-1986

The Berlin stories; The last of Mr. Norris; Goodbye to Berlin; with a preface by the author. New Directions 1954 2v in 1 o.p.

*

The two titles included in this combined edition were originally published separately; the first in 1935 in the United Kingdom with title: Mr. Norris changes trains and the latter in 1939 by Random House, which is analyzed in Short story index

The last of Mr. Norris, set in Berlin during Hitler's rise to power, "is the story of the narrator's innocent friendship with odd, corrupt Mr. Norris. While pretending to be a sincere Communist, Mr. Norris is actually selling information to fascists and foreigners. Mr. Norris's masochistic sexual aberrations add to the impression that he is a symbol of the whole corrupt, disintegrating society." Reader's Ency. 4th edition

Goodbye to Berlin contains six short stories or sketches of life in Berlin in the last years before Hitler came to power. Though written in first person by one calling himself Christopher Isherwood, according to the author's statement, the material is not to be regarded as autobiographical. The sketches are entitled: A Berlin diary (Autumn 1930); Sally Bowles; On Ruegan Island (Summer 1931); The Nowaks; The Landauers; A Berlin diary (Winter 1932-3)

Goodbye to Berlin
In Isherwood, C. The Berlin stories

The last of Mr. Norris
In Isherwood, C. The Berlin stories

Ishiguro, Kazuo, 1954-

An artist of the floating world. Putnam 1986 206p

ISBN 0-399-13119-1   LC 85-25759

"Like figures on a Japanese screen, the painter Masuji Ono and his daughters Setsuko and Noriko are fixed in the formal attitudes that even their private conversations reflect. In the postwar 1940s, the father is a relic of traditional Japan, of teahouses, geishas and patterned gardens not yet destroyed by industry and Westernized thinking. He is unable to communicate with his daughters, unsure of the propriety of his wartime nationalism yet unwilling to exchange it for what seem to him doubtful modern values." Publ Wkly

"The tensions stay tight. And this is what makes Mr. Ishiguro not only a good writer but also a wonderful novelist." N Y Times Book Rev

Never let me go. Knopf 2005 288p $24

ISBN 1-4000-4339-5   LC 2004-48966

"Kathy, Ruth and Tommy were pupils at Hailsham—an idyllic establishment situated deep in the English countryside. The children there were tenderly sheltered from the outside world, brought up to believe they were special, and that their personal welfare was crucial. But for what reason were they really there? It is only years later that Kathy, now aged 31, finally allows herself to yield to the pull of memory. What unfolds is the . . . story of how Kathy, Ruth and Tommy slowly come to face the truth about their seemingly happy childhoods—and about their futures." Publisher's note

"Ishiguro serves up the saddest, most persuasive science fiction you'll read. Set in 'England, late 1990s,' the novel posits a technological breakthrough whose effect is to condemn the children of Hailsham to a fate that was, until this novel, unthinkable. Ishiguro's imagining of the children's misshapen little world is profoundly thoughtful, and their hesitant progression into knowledge of their plight is an extreme and heartbreaking version of the exodus of all children from the innocence in which the benevolent but fraudulent adult world conspires to place them." Atlantic Monthly

The remains of the day. Knopf 1989 245p o.p.
* LC 89-80445

"Mr. Stevens is a butler of high quality now employed by the American owner of Darlington Hall. His position as butler was quite different when Lord Darlington was his employer. Then there was a large staff, including Miss Kenton, whose friendly overtures to Stevens were met only by his inability to unbend or find some humor as an outlet offsetting his customary snobbish personality. As Stevens reflects on the past the reader gains insight into Lord Darlington's political connections after World War I with important government officials including Ribbentrop, representive of Germany's movement toward a dictatorship. Questions regarding an employee's unquestioning loyalty toward his employer and awareness of the political situation in the period just before Hitler's rise to power make this a thought-provoking novel." Shapiro. Fic for Youth. 3d edition

The unconsoled. Knopf 1995 544p

ISBN 0-679-40425-2   LC 95-15829

Ishiguro, Kazuo, 1954-—*Continued*

In this novel, "prominent concert pianist Ryder is at odds with his surroundings. Ryder arrives in an unidentified European city at a bit of a loss. Everyone he meets seems to assume that he knows more than he knows, that he is well acquainted with the city and its obscure cultural crisis. A young woman he kindly consents to advise seems to have been an old lover and her son quite possibly his own; he vaguely recalls past conversations. The world he has entered is a surreal, Alice-in-Wonderland place where a door in a cafe can lead back to a hotel miles away. The result is at once dreamy, disorienting, and absolutely compelling; Ishiguro's paragraphs, though Proust-like, are completely lucid and quite addictive to read." Libr J

When we were orphans. Knopf 2000 335p $25
ISBN 0-375-41054-6 LC 00-26120
"Christopher Banks is an Englishman born in early 20th-century Shanghai whose parents disappear mysteriously when he is nine. He is escorted to England, grows up to be a famed detective, and returns to Shanghai, convinced that his parents are still alive and that he must find them." Libr J

"For all its ellipses and evasions, When We Were Orphans, will linger in the mind as an often fascinating, imaginative work of surpassing intelligence and taste." Times Lit Suppl

Itani, Frances, 1942-

Deafening. Atlantic Monthly Press 2003 378p $24
ISBN 0-87113-902-2 LC 2003-45108
"Grania O'Neill has been deaf since an early childhod fever. . . . Leaving her intimate Canadian hometown for the Ontario School for the Deaf, she learns sign language and finds Jim, who expresses his love for her by describing beautiful sounds. Unfortunately for their marriage, Jim is off to the trenches of World War I, where the sounds (and sights) are horrifying indeed." Booklist

"This novel is not only a beautifully crafted love story but also an exploration of the possibilities of language and the eloquence of silence." Libr J

Remembering the bones. Atlantic Monthly Press 2007 282p $24
ISBN 978-0-87113-977-1; 0-87113-977-4
"On the way to a party for Queen Elizabeth II, Georgie Witley, an Anglophile Canadian born the same day, crashes and is thrown from the driver's seat of her car. Lying on her back, like a beetle, at the bottom of a ravine, Georgie dutifully recites a passage from her grandfather's volume of 'Gray's Anatomy': 'Femur, tibia, fibula. Radius, ulna.' The litany of bones anchors Georgie in her broken body, and also helps her to coax eight decades of memories from their hiding places. She reflects on a life given shape by marriage, motherhood, and world war, milestones that she and the Queen have in common. In unpretentious, quietly penetrating prose, Itani exposes the richness and depth beneath the surface of one ordinary life." New Yorker

Iyer, Pico

Abandon; a romance. Knopf 2003 353p $24
ISBN 0-375-41505-X LC 2002-70059

"John Macmillan is a student at a Santa Barbara, Calif., university trying to finish his thesis on the lesser works of Sufi master Rumi. John begins searching the globe for a secret Islamic manuscript, reputedly smuggled out of Iran after the Shah's downfall, that may contain lost poems by Rumi. He travels through Syria, Iran, Spain and India; though the search is mostly fruitless, along the way he finds himself drawn into a romance with the flighty, fragile, slightly New Agey Camilla Jensen." Publ Wkly

"Iyer's writing is often poetic, and in presenting the Persian diaspora in Southern California, he has an intriguing way of peeling back familiar landscapes to reveal hidden sights." Booklist

J

Jaber, Diana Abu- *See* Abu-Jaber, Diana

Jackson, Charles, 1903-1968

The lost weekend. Rinehart 1944 244p o.p.
Psychological study of a drunkard. The actual time covered is five days, but in those five days the story of a man's life is told. Don Biram, a sensitive, charming and well-read man, left alone for a few days by his brother, struggles with his overwhelming desire for alcohol, succumbs to it, and in the resulting prolonged agony, goes over much of his life up to and including the long weekend

"It's written with complete lack of literary pretensions; yet Jackson's sheer ability to lick the problems of flashback, stream of consciousness, mind wandering, twisted recollection and alcoholic delirium is spectacular. . . . Its frankness is sometimes shocking but never aimed to shock. The aim, and it is unerring, is always for accuracy and the complete truth" Book Week

Jackson, Jon A.

No man's dog; a Detective Sergeant Mulheisen mystery. Atlantic Monthly Press 2004 355p $24
ISBN 0-87113-920-0 LC 2003-69500
Detective Sergeant Fang Mulheisen retired from the force "to nurse his mother after she was injured in an apparent terrorist bombing of a suburban Detroit courthouse. That bombing has the curious effect of making partners of former antagonists Service and Mulheisen. Joining forces for different reasons to track down the bombers, these strange bedfellows-two of the most appealing, well-grounded characters in the genre-traipse about in the woods near Traverse City, sparring with a local militia roughneck. Jackson tackles the whole Patriot Act mess from an engaging everyman point of view." Booklist

Jackson, Joshilyn

Between, Georgia. Warner 2006 294p $22.99
ISBN 0-446-52442-5 LC 2005-23748
"The biological daughter of poor, scared teenager Hazel Crabtree, Nonny Frett was left at birth with the wealthy, respectable Frett clan—a secret that doesn't keep long in a rural Georgia town of 90 people. Growing

LIST OF FICTIONAL WORKS

Jackson, Joshilyn—*Continued*

up at the center of a Crabtree-Frett feud begun by her birth, Nonny is caught between her biological family and her adopted one, between contempt for her philandering husband and the comfort of marriage, between an apartment in Athens, Ga., and her childhood home, Between. When a Doberman belonging to Nonny's biological grandmother Ona Crabtree attacks Nonny's adopted mom, deaf and blind Stacia Frett, and Stacia's twin sister, Genny, the families' dormant 'war' awakens." Publ Wkly

"Underneath all the pyrotechnics, Joshilyn Jackson is cleverly exploring the nature of family and belonging. . . . Jackson loads her novel with eccentrics straight from Southern Gothic central casting, but her writing brims with enough humor to make it compulsively readable." Christ Sci Monit

Jackson, Sheneska

Caught up in the rapture. Simon & Schuster 1996 270p

ISBN 0-684-81487-0   LC 95-47337

In this novel, "two young African Americans hoping for pop-music stardom become lovers—and pawns in a record-company power struggle. . . . Jazmine Deems, a 26-year-old UCLA student anxious to escape her father's strict household, envies the freedom enjoyed by her best friend, Dakota, who introduces her to popular music, current fashion and sexy guys. Life hasn't been as smooth for Xavier Honor, aka X-Man, whose 'family' consists of two street buddies and who hopes to rap his way out of the 'hood. X-Man and Jazmine meet at a party thrown by Black Tie Records." Publ Wkly

"This first novel is vivid, realistic, and strong, with perfectly fleshed-out characters. Readers will be bound by each word as they watch Jazmine struggle with life and the pursuit of happiness." Libr J

Jackson, Shirley, 1919-1965

Come along with me; part of a novel, sixteen stories, and three lectures; edited by Stanley Edgar Hyman. Viking 1968 243p o.p.

Contents: Short stories included are: Janice; Tootie in peonage; A cauliflower in her hair; I know who I love; The beautiful stranger; The summer people; Island; A visit; The rock; A day in the jungle; Pajama party; Louisa, please come home; The little house; The bus; The night we all had grippe; The lottery

The haunting of Hill House. Viking 1959 246p pa $14 hardcover o.p.

ISBN 0-14-303998-9 (pa)

                                                    *

"Dr. John Montague, an anthropologist, is interested in the analysis of supernatural manifestations. He rents Hill House, which is reported to be haunted, and plans to spend the summer there with research assistants. Eleanor Vance, one of the researchers, is at first repelled by the house but soon adjusts. Other people come and signs of psychic activity are rampant, many of them centered on Eleanor. When Dr. Montague insists that she leave to insure her safety, the house does not release her." Shapiro. Fic for Youth. 3d edition

Just an ordinary day. Bantam Bks. 1997 388p o.p.   LC 96-23871

This collection includes unpublished and uncollected stories

Contents: The smoking room; I don't kiss strangers; Summer afternoon; Indians live in tents; The very hot sun in Bermuda; Nightmare; Dinner for a gentleman; Party of boys; Jack the Ripper; The honeymoon of Mrs. Smith (versions I and II); The sister; Arch-criminal; Mrs. Anderson; Come to the fair; Portrait; Gnarly the King of the Jungle; The good wife; Devil of a tale; The mouse; My grandmother and the world of cats; Maybe it was the car; Lovers meeting; My recollections of S. B. Fairchild; Deck the halls; Lord of the castle; What a thought; When Barry was seven; Before Autumn; The story we used to tell; My uncle in the garden; On the house; Little old lady in great need; When things get dark; Whistler's grandmother; Family magician; The wishing dime; About two nice people; Mrs. Melville makes a purchase; Journey with a lady; The most womderful thing; The friends; Alone in a den of cubs; The order of Charlotte's going; One ordinary day, with peanuts; The missing girl; The omen; The very strange house next door; A great voice stilled; All she said was yes; Home; I.O.U.; The possibility of evil; Fame

The lottery and other stories; introduction by Patrick McGrath. Modern Lib. 2000 292p

ISBN 0-679-64039-8

                        * LC 00-36064

A reissue of The lottery; or, The adventures of James Harris, published 1949 by Farrar, Straus

Contents: The intoxicated; The daemon lover; Like mother used to make; Trial by combat; The villager; My life with R. H. Macy; The witch; The renegade; After you, my dear Alphonse; Charles; Afternoon in linen; Flower garden; Dorothy and my grandmother and the sailors; Colloquy; Elizabeth; A fine old firm; The dummy; Seven types of ambiguity; Come dance with me in Ireland; Of course; Pillar of salt; Men with their big shoes; The tooth; Got a letter from Jimmy; The lottery

We have always lived in a castle. Viking 1962 214p pa $14 hardcover o.p.

ISBN 0-14-303997-0 (pa)

"Since the time that Constance Blackwood was tried and acquitted of the murder of four members of her family, she has lived with her sister Mary Catherine and her Uncle Julian in the family mansion. Mary Catherine takes care of family chores and Uncle Julian is busy with the writing of a detailed account of the six-year-old murders. Cousin Charles's arrival on the scene disrupts the quiet peace of the family, and Mary Catherine's efforts to get rid of him unloose a chain of events that bring everything down in ruins." Shapiro. Fic for Youth. 3d edition

Jacobson, Dan, 1929-

All for love; a novel. Metropolitan Books 2006 272p $24

ISBN 978-0-8050-8103-9; 0-8050-8103-8

                         LC 2006-43363

First published 2005 in the United Kingdom

"Jacobson presents the story of an affair, set deeply within a rich historical setting: pre-World War I Europe and a social sphere accustomed to palaces and luxurious

Jacobson, Dan, 1929-—*Continued*

hotels. The liaison partners are actual historical figures—Princess Louise, daughter of the king of Belgium, who married into a distinguished family high in court circles surrounding the emperor of Austria, and a more-or-less no-account lieutenant in the Austrian army, Geza Mattachich. Louise and Geza breach protocol by the carelessness of their affair. The result is banishment from Vienna, being viewed as social pariahs, and enduring critical financial hardship as they roam homeless over the continent." Booklist

"What makes this so gripping is its prose, sparkling and pungently suggestive. Jacobson's drama of transgression and repression is a compulsive page-turner." Sunday Times (London)

Jacobson, Howard, 1942-

Kalooki nights. Simon & Schuster 2007 c2006 450p $26

ISBN 978-1-4165-4342-8; 1-4165-4342-2

LC 2006-50183

First published 2006 in the United Kingdom

"Cartoonist Max Glickman's Jewishness, never far from mind, is his continuing subject. Raised in a nonobservant household outside Manchester, England, in the 1950s-where his atheist father sought to make Jewishness less of a burden and his mother played kalooki, a rummylike game favored by Jews-he was educated on the Holocaust by childhood friends. It was meek Manny Washinsky who first shared the Scourge of the Swastica, leading the two of them to develop the comic-book-history Five Thousand Years of Bitterness, later published by Max. And it was Manny who would murder his parents, gassing them in their beds, a deed that Max at midlife seeks to understand, initially in the interest of making a film." Booklist

"Jacobson spins a loose yarn around Max's inquiry into his old friend's crime, leaving plenty of opportunities for caustic insights and hilarious detours, as when the teen-aged Max, on his first double date, embarrasses himself in front of Isaiah Berlin." New Yorker

Jaffe, Rona

Class reunion; a novel. Delacorte Press 1979 338p o.p.

LC 78-25838

"In the Fifties, when rules were rules, college campuses were husband-hunting grounds, and 'going all the way' could ruin a girl's reputation, four Radcliffe students pursue the dream of Mr. Right, Marriage, and Living Happily Ever After. Jaffe builds this book around their 20th reunion, using alternate chapters to flash back through the tales of beautiful Annabel, witty Chris, golden girl Daphne, and insecure Emily. [The author focuses on these women's lives] from college romances to crises which rock them—loveless marriage, divorce, adultery both homosexual and heterosexual, murder, nervous breakdown, birth of a mongoloid child." Libr J

The room-mating season. Dutton 2003 326p $24.95

ISBN 0-525-94713-2

LC 2002-73855

"The year is 1963, and college friends Leigh and Cady are determined to begin their adult lives amid the cosmopolitan social whirl of New York City. An ad for room-mates brings two more young women into the circle: Vanessa, a sophisticated airline stewardess, and awkward, needy misfit Susan. . . . Jaffe traces the lives of her characters over the next four decades with wit and poignancy." Booklist

Jakeman, Jane

In the Kingdom of mists. Berley Prime Crime 2004 c2002 355p $23.95

ISBN 0-425-19512-0

LC 2003-62800

A novel about Claude Monet, "murder, and London in the year 1900. Oliver Cranston is trying to get out from under the thumb of his overbearing father by working for the Foreign Office. Oliver's job brings him to the Savoy, where the French painter Monet tries to capture the light and mist he sees on the Thames every morning and where an entire floor is devoted to the care of officer victims of the Boer War. It is Oliver's unlucky fate to see a woman's body wash up from the Thames, brutally and surgically murdered; he is luckier to make the acquaintance of the painter's son, Michel." Booklist

"The novel tells a dramatic story about crime and perception, art and reality through the eyes of the famous painter, the policeman and a young diplomat. Multilayered and voiced, this is a fascinating attempt to add an extra dimension to this historical crime novel." Guardian

Jakes, John, 1932-

American dreams. Dutton 1998 495p

ISBN 0-525-94437-0

LC 97-49163

In the second volume of the "Crown family chronicles," Jakes portrays American during the turbulent period from 1906 to 1917. Once again, the story centers on the family of German-American patriarch and Chicago beer baron Joe Crown, whose headstrong daughter Fritzi defies her father to pursue a dreadfully unsuccessful New York stage career. In desperation, she surrenders to the lure of performing in moving pictures, which takes her to 'empty, rural, and uncivilized' Hollywood, where she falls in love and achieves a measure of fame as a comic actress. Meanwhile, her brother Carl gets tossed out of Princeton, goes to work for eccentric car manufacturer Henry Ford, becomes a race-car driver with Barney Oldfield, 'Speed King of the World', and flies as an ace pilot during WWI. Their cousin Paul is a professional news cameraman driven to record the horrors of war." Publ Wkly

The best western stories of John Jakes; edited by Bill Pronzini and Martin H. Greenberg. Ohio Univ. Press 1991 275p o.p.

LC 90-49427

Contents: Shootout at White Pass; The woman at Apache Wells; Hell on the high iron; A duel of magicians; Death rides here!; The winning of Poker Alice; To the last bullet; Little Phil and the daughter of joy; The tinhorn fills his hand; The naked gun; Dutchman

"This collection combines new material with several of Jakes's better efforts published earlier in the pulp magazines of the 1950s." Libr J

California gold; a novel. Random House 1989 658p o.p.

LC 89-3779

"Driven by his father's failed California dream, young Mack sets out from an Appalachian coal mine and lands eventually on Nob Hill, becoming a maverick real estate

Jakes, John, 1932——_Continued_

and business tycoon who sets out to challenge the San Francisco establishment. As he's faced with mounting adversity, his affairs begin to crumble, and so, in 1906, does a large chunk of the city. 'California Gold' is the story of one man, one state and three women." N Y Times Book Rev

"The novel potently conveys the raw, irrepressible vitality of California, but the historical backdrop (especially the 1906 earthquake) outshines the conventional rags-to-riches plot. Jake's impressive research . . . enriches the story considerably." Publ Wkly

(ed) A Century of great Western stories. See A Century of great Western stories

Charleston; a novel. Dutton 2002 506p
ISBN 0-525-94650-0   LC 2002-21251
This novel "details the shifting fortunes of several generations of a powerful southern dynasty, the Bell family, set against the dramatic and fiery backdrop of the American Revolution and the Civil War. Told in three parts, the story follows the lives, loves, and changing fortunes of the Bells and the Charleston aristocracy to which they belonged. Never one to gloss over details, the author manages to show the bleak horrors of slavery, war, and greed while also confirming the essential goodness of American ideals. Jakes is in tiptop shape here." Booklist

Heaven and hell. Harcourt Brace Jovanovich 1987 700p o.p.
LC 87-17652
The concluding volume of the North and South trilogy "centers on Charles, Orry Main's cousin, a Southerner totally devastated by the Civil War. Displaced and just having lost his beloved Augusta, Charles heads West with his infant son hoping to make a new life. With Charles as the focal point, the narrative continually shifts to all the other family members, including . . . a madman bent on destroying both families." Libr J

"Mr. Jakes sets this fictional action against a meticulously detailed historical backdrop. Although his characters are not as vivid as his storytelling, his portrait of a divided, demoralized nation, inflamed with hatred, still emerges as an enjoyable work of popular historical fiction." N Y Times Book Rev

Love and war. Harcourt Brace Jovanovich 1984 1019p o.p.
LC 84-12895
This sequel to North and South "carries forward the entwined sagas of the Hazards of Pennsylvania, industrialists, and the Mains of South Carolina, plantation owners. . . . The story moves from action on the battlefield to the corridors of Washington to the shipyards of Liverpool. It encompasses deeds heroic and dastardly; passions licit and illicit; spying, assassination plotting and cynical profiteering; and the trying out of new military interventions." Publ Wkly

Followed by Heaven and hell

North and South. Harcourt Brace Jovanovich 1982 740p o.p.
* LC 81-47898
In this first novel of a trilogy the author "introduces two families: The Main family of South Carolina, and the Hazard family of Pennsylvania. The families are basically different. The Mains from the South grow rice and represent the old ways while the Hazards of the North produce iron and are examples of the Industrial

Revolution. Their paths converge however, when Orry Main meets George Hazard as the two are entering West Point in 1842. Their friendship is immediate and strong. Orry's family owns slaves, and George, while loving his friend, cannot understand it. As the years pass each grows more entrenched in his beliefs. . . . George's sister Virgilia, an avowed abolitionist, seeks to pry the friendship apart and nearly succeeds. George and Orry's struggles are representative of that which plague the nation." West Coast Rev Books

Followed by Love and war

On secret service; a novel. Dutton 2000 448p
ISBN 0-525-94544-X   LC 99-47951
"In 1861, Washington was located on the frontier between the Union and Confederacy; despite being the Union capital, it was a hotbed of Confederate sympathizers, some of whom were actual spies and even involved in the conspiracy to assassinate President Lincoln. . . . Jakes follows, throughout the four-year war period, a handful of individuals with intertwined allegiances as they worked both aboveboard and below for their various causes." Booklist

"Numerous historical figures are represented accurately and plausibly, and lesser-known events like the horrific Draft Riots in New York are vividly portrayed." Libr J

Savannah; or, A gift for Mr. Lincoln. Dutton 2004 288p il $23.95
ISBN 0-525-94803-1   LC 2004-49417
This "historical novel recounts the taking of Savannah by Gen. William Tecumseh Sherman's Union Army during Christmas 1864. Fundamentally, it is the story of Sara Lester and her precocious 12-year-old daughter, Hattie, who has an aversion to General Sherman until she finds herself in need of his help. The novel includes a rich cast of characters who, as Union forces move north, are ultimately left to their own devices. The narrative offers adventure, romance, humor, and crime along with the trials of an American city living under what is, to its citizens, occupation by a foreign army." Libr J

James, Henry, 1843-1916

The ambassadors; edited with an introduction by Harry Levin. Penguin Books 1986 517p pa $7
ISBN 0-14-043233-7   LC 87-29773
First published 1903 by Harper

"The central character and first 'ambassador,' Lambert Strether, is sent to Paris by Mrs. Newsome, a wealthy widow whom he plans to marry, in order to persuade her son Chad to come home. Chad is deeply involved with a charming French woman, Madame de Vionnet, and the novel deals chiefly with Strether's gradual conversion to the idea that life may hold more real meaning for Chad in Paris than in Woollett, Massachusetts. Strether comes to this conclusion in spite of his discovery that Chad and Mme de Vionnet are, in fact, more than just good friends. After the arrival of a second ambassador, Chad's sister Sarah, Strether decides to return to Woollett, urging Chad to remain in Paris. The essence of the novel is in Strether's remark, 'Live all you can; it's a mistake not to.'" Reader's Ency. 4th edition

The American; edited with an introduction and notes by Adrian Poole. Oxford University Press 1999 xxxiv, 400p pa $10.95
ISBN 0-19-283322-7   LC 98-42570

James, Henry, 1843-1916—*Continued*

First published 1877 by J. R. Osgood and Company

"A self-made American goes to Europe to enjoy his 'pile,' and becomes engaged to a French widow of noble family. The match is a good one for both parties, but at length the powers that rule this exclusive social world deliver their verdict: the engagement must be annulled. The American's pluck and good nature are happily contrasted with the colossal pride and essential meanness of the old noblesse." Baker. Guide to the Best Fic

"With much humour and delicacy of perception, the author depicts the reaction of different American types to the European environment." Oxford Companion to Engl Lit

The Aspern papers

In James, H. Complete stories, 1884-1891

In James, H. The complete tales of Henry James

In James, H. The Henry James reader p165-254

In James, H. Short novels of Henry James p257-354

The author of "Beltraffio"

In James, H. Complete stories, 1874-1884

In James, H. The complete tales of Henry James

In James, H. The Henry James reader

The beast in the jungle

In James, H. Complete stories, 1898-1910

In James, H. The complete tales of Henry James

In James, H. The Henry James reader p357-400

The Bostonians. Knopf 1992 394p

ISBN 0-679-41750-8

* LC 92-52889

"Everyman's library"

First published 1886 by Macmillan

In this satirical novel, "Basil Ransom, a Mississippi lawyer, comes to Boston to seek his fortune, and becomes acquainted with his cousins, the flirtatious widow, Mrs. Luna, and her neurotic sister, Olive Chancellor. He is taken by Olive, a radical feminist, to a suffragette meeting. . . . They hear an address by beautiful young Verena Tarrant, whose gift of persuasion interests Olive as an instrument for her own use. Olive removes the girl to her own luxurious home, converts her to the feminist cause, and even urges her to vow that she will never marry. Fleeing the attentions of Mrs. Luna, Ransom attempts to win Verena to his belief that her proper sphere is a home and a drawing room, not a career as lecturer for a preposterous political movement." Oxford Companion to Am Lit. 6th edition

This was "one of the first American novels to deal more or less explicitly with lesbianism." Reader's Ency. 4th edition

Complete stories, 1864-1874. Library of Am. 1999 972p $40

ISBN 1-883011-70-1   LC 98-53919

Contents: A tragedy of error; The story of a year; A landscape painter; A day of days; My friend Bingham; Poor Richard; The story of a masterpiece; The romance of certain old clothes; A most extraordinary case; A problem; De Grey: a romance; Osborne's revenge; A light man; Gabrielle de Bergerac; Travelling companions; A passionate pilgrim; At Isella; Master Eustace; Guest's confession; The madonna of the future; The sweetheart of M. Briseux; The last Valerii; Madame de Mauves [novelette]; Adina

Complete stories, 1874-1884. Library of Am. 1999 941p $35

ISBN 1-883011-63-9   LC 98-19252

Contents: Professor Fargo; Eugene Pickering; Benvolio Crawford's consistency; The ghostly rental; Four meetings; Rose-Agathe; Daisy Miller: a study [novelette]; Longstaff's marriage; An international episode [novelette]; The pension beaurepas; The diary of a man of fifty; A bundle of letters; The point of view; The siege of London [novelette]; The impressions of a cousin; Lady Barberina [novelette]; Pandora; The author of "Beltraffio" [novelette]

Complete stories, 1884-1891. Library of Am. 1999 904p $35

ISBN 1-883011-64-7   LC 98-19250

Contents: Georgina's reasons; A New England winter; The path of duty; Mrs. Temperly; Louisa Pallant; The Aspern papers [novelette]; The liar; The modern warning; A London life; The lesson of the master; The Patagonia; The solution; The pupil [novelette]; Brooksmith; The marriages; The chaperon; Sir Edmund Orme

Complete stories, 1892-1898. Library of Am. 1996 948p

ISBN 1-883011-09-4   LC 95-23463

Contents: Nona Vincent; The real thing; The private life; Lord Beaupré; The visits; Sir Dominick Ferrand; Greville Fane; Collaboration; Owen Wingrave; The wheel of time; The middle years; The death of the lion; The Coxon Fund; The altar of the dead; The next time; Glasses; The figure in the carpet; The way it came; The turn of the screw [novelette]; Covering end; In the cage [novelette]

Complete stories, 1898-1910. Library of Am. 1996 946p $35

ISBN 1-883011-10-8   LC 95-23462

Contents: John Delavoy; The given case; "Europe"; The great condition; The real right thing; Paste; The great good place; Maud-Evelyn; Miss Gunton of Poughkeepsie; The tree of knowledge; The abasement of the Northmores; The third person; The special type; The tone of time; Broken wings; The two faces; Mrs. Medwin; The Beldonald Holbein; The story in it; Flickerbridge; The birthplace; The beast in the jungle [novelette]; The papers; Fordham Castle; Julia Bride; The jolly corner; "The Velvet Glove"; Mora Montravers; Crapy Cornelia; The bench of desolation; A round of visits

The complete tales of Henry James; edited with an introduction by Leon Edel. Lippincott 1962-1965 12v o.p.

Contents: v1: 1864-1868: A tragedy of errors; The story of a year; A landscape painter; A day of days; My friend Bingham; Poor Richard; The story of a master-

James, Henry, 1843-1916—*Continued*
piece; The romance of certain old clothes; A most extraordinary case; A problem; De Grey: a romance

v2: 1868-1872: Osborne's revenge; A light man; Gabrielle de Bergerac; Travelling companions; A passionate pilgrim; At Isella; Master Eustace; Guest's confession

v3: 1873-1875: The Madonna of the future; The sweetheart of M. Briseux; The last of the Valerii; Madame de Mauves [novelette]; Adina; Professor Fargo; Eugene Pickering; Benvolio

v4: 1876-1882: Crawford's consistency; The ghostly rental; Four meetings; Rose-Agathe; Daisy Miller: a study [novelette]; Longstaff's marriage; An international episode [novelette]; The pension Beaurepas; The diary of a man of fifty; A bundle of letters; The point of view

v5: 1883-1884: The siege of London [novelette]; The impressions of a cousin; Lady Barberina [novelette]; The author of "Beltraffio" [novelette]; Pandora

v6: 1884-1888: Georgina's reasons; A New England winter; The path of duty; Mrs. Temperly; Louisa Panant; The Aspern papers [novelette]; The liar

v7: 1888-1891: The modern warning; A London life; The lesson of the master; The Patagonia; The solution; The pupil [novelette]

v8: 1891-1892: Brooksmith; The marriages; The chaperon; Sir Edmund Orme; Nona Vincent; The private life; The real thing; Lord Beaupré; The visits; Sir Dominick Ferrand; Collaboration; Greville Fane; The wheel of time

v9: 1892-1898: Owen Wingrave; The middle years; The death of the lion; The Coxon Fund; The next time; The altar of the dead; The figure in the carpet; Glasses; The way it came (The friends of the friends); John Delavoy

v10: 1898-1899: The turn of the screw [novelette]; In the cage [novelette]; Covering end; The given case; The great condition; "Europe"; Paste; The real right thing

v11: 1900-1903: The great good place; Maud-Evelyn; Miss Gunton of Poughkeepsie; The tree of knowledge; The abasement of the Northmores; The third person; The special type; The tone of time; Broken wings; The two faces; Mrs. Medwin; The Beldonald Holbein; The story in it; Flickerbridge; The beast in the jungle [novelette]; The birthplace

v12: 1903-1910: The papers; Fordham Castle; Julia Bride; The jolly corner; The Velvet Glove; Mora Montravers; Crapy Cornelia; The bench of desolation; A round of visits

Daisy Miller; introduction by Elizabeth Hardwick; notes by James Danly. Modern Library 2002 xxiv, 80p pa $14.50
  ISBN 0-375-75966-2   LC 2001-44626
  First published 1878
"The book's title character is a young American woman traveling in Europe with her mother. There she is courted by Frederick Forsyth Winterbourne, an American living abroad. In her innocence, Daisy is compromised by her friendship with an Italian man. Her behavior shocks Winterbourne and the other Americans living in Italy, and they shun her. Only after she dies does Winterbourne recognize that her actions reflected her spontaneous, genuine, and unaffected nature and that his suspicions of her were unwarranted." Merriam-Webster's Ency of Lit

    also in James, H. Complete stories, 1874-1884

    also in James, H. The complete tales of Henry James

    also in James, H. The Henry James reader p403-61

    also in James, H. Short novels of Henry James p1-58

The Europeans; a sketch; edited with an introduction and notes by Ian Campbell Ross. Oxford University Press 2000 pa $14.50
  ISBN 0-19-283500-9
                       * LC 00-703219
  First published 1878
"Two expatriates, the Baroness Muenster and her brother Felix Young, come to Boston to visit some relatives they have never seen. The baroness futilely tries to make a wealthy marriage, and Felix seeks to paint portraits of the Bostonians he meets. A contrast is drawn between the sophistication of the pair and the strict New Englanders. Felix marries one of his kinswomen, who is eager to escape from her bleak environment." Benet's Reader's Ency of Am Lit

The golden bowl. Knopf 1992 596p $22
  ISBN 0-679-41733-8   LC 92-52927
  "Everyman's library"
  First published 1904 by Scribner
Maggie Verver, daughter of an American millionaire living in London, marries an indigent "Italian prince who has had a love affair with Maggie's closest friend, Charlotte Stant. Charlotte visits the pair and continues her intimacy. Then she marries Maggie's father. Everybody tries to keep secret from the others that he or she knows all that has happened or is happening. The complications are solved when Maggie's father goes back to America with Charlotte. James depicts with all the subtlety of his late style the cultural and moral involvements that follow on international marriage and irregular sex relationships." Benet's Reader's Ency of Am Lit

The Henry James reader; selected with a foreword and headnotes by Leon Edel. Scribner 1965 626p o.p.
  Analyzed in Short story index
  Contains the short novels: Washington Square (1881); The Aspern papers (1888); The turn of the screw (1898); The beast in the jungle (1903); Daisy Miller (1878); The author of Beltraffio (1884); also the following short stories: Pandora; Owen Wingrave; The real thing; The two faces

In the cage
  In James, H. Complete stories, 1892-1898
  In James, H. The complete tales of Henry James
  In James, H. What Maisie knew, In the cage, The pupil

An international episode
  In James, H. Complete stories, 1874-1884
  In James, H. The complete tales of Henry James

Lady Barberina
  In James, H. Complete stories, 1874-1884
  In James, H. The complete tales of Henry James

James, Henry, 1843-1916—*Continued*

Madame de Mauves

In James, H. Complete stories, 1864-1874

In James, H. The complete tales of Henry James

The portrait of a lady. Knopf 1991 xxv, 626p $20

ISBN 0-679-40562-3

* LC 91-52999

"Everyman's library"

First published 1881 by Houghton

"This is one of the best James's early works, in which he presents various types of American character transplanted into a European environment. The story centres in Isabel Archer, the 'Lady,' an attractive American girl. Around her we have the placid old American banker, Mr. Touchett; his hard repellent wife; his ugly, invalid, witty, charming son Ralph, whom England has thoroughly assimilated; and the outspoken, brilliant, indomitable American journalist Henrietta Stackpole. Isabel refuses the offer of marriage of a typical English peer, the excellent Lord Warburton, and of a bulldog-like New Englander, Casper Goodwood, to fall a victim, under the influence of the slightly sinister Madame Merle (another cosmopolitan American), to a worthless and spiteful dilettante, Gilbert Osmond, who marries her for her fortune and ruins her life; but to whom she remains loyal in spite of her realization of his vileness." Oxford Companion to Engl Lit. 6th edition

The pupil

In James, H. Complete stories, 1884-1891

In James, H. The complete tales of Henry James

In James, H. Short novels of Henry James p355-405

In James, H. What Maisie knew, In the cage, The pupil

Roderick Hudson; edited with an introduction by Geoffrey Moore and notes by Patricia Crick. Penguin Books 1986 397p pa $12

ISBN 0-14-043264-7

First published serially 1875 in The Atlantic Monthly; in book form 1876 by J. R. Osgood and Company

"The titular hero is a talented young American sculptor who goes to study in Rome at the insistance of a wealthy benefactor and becomes gradually disillusioned about his art and utterly demoralized by his experience. He neglects his New England fiancée; becomes involved in a love affair with Christina Light and finally leaps over a cliff." Univ Handbk for Readers and Writers

Short novels of Henry James; with eight full-page illustrations; introduction by E. Hudson Long. Harcourt Brace Jovanovich 1961 530p il o.p.

"Great illustrated classics"

Contents: Daisy Miller (1878); Washington Square (1881); The Aspern papers (1888); The pupil (1892); The turn of the screw (1898)

The first, second and the last titles are entered separately. The pupil is entered in a combined edition with: What Maisie knew, In the cage and The pupil. "In 'The Aspern Papers,' an unnamed American editor rents a room in Venice in the home of Juliana Bordereau, the elderly mistress of Jeffrey Aspern, a deceased Romantic poet, in order to procure from her the poet's papers." Merriam-Webster's Ency of Lit

The short stories of Henry James; selected and edited with an introduction by Clifton Fadiman. Dodd, Mead 1945 xx, 644p o.p.

Contents: Four meetings; A bundle of letters; Louisa Pallant; The liar; The real thing; The pupil [novelette]: Booksmith; The middle years; The altar of the dead; "Europe"; The great good place; The tree of knowledge; The tone of time; Mrs. Medwin; The birthplace; The beast in the jungle [novelette]; The jolly corner

The siege of London

In James, H. Complete stories, 1874-1884

In James, H. The complete tales of Henry James

The spoils of Poynton; edited with an introduction by David Lodge and notes by Patricia Crick. Penguin Books 1987 247p pa $13

ISBN 0-14-043288-4

First published 1896 by Houghton

"Owen Gareth, heir to the great house at Poynton, spurns his mother's favorite, Fleda Vetch, to marry Mona Brigstock. Old Mrs. Gareth thereupon removes her art treasures from Poynton. Owen was in fact in love with Fleda, and offers her any object she may desire at Poynton, but suddenly the house is ruined by an accidental fire, which ruins the spoils that have warped so many lives." Haydn. Thesaurus of Book Dig

The turn of the screw; edited by Allan Lloyd Smith. J.M. Dent 1993 xxxii, 139p pa $8.95

ISBN 0-460-87299-0

LC 94-125860

First published 1898

This novella "is told from the viewpoint of the leading character, a governess in love with her employer, who goes to an isolated English estate to take charge of Miles and Flora, two attractive and precocious children. She gradually realizes that her young charges are under the evil influence of two ghosts, Peter Quint, the ex-steward, and Miss Jessel, their former governess. At the climax of the story, she enters into open conflict with the children, as a result of which Flora is alienated and Miles dies of fright." Reader's Ency. 4th edition

also in James, H. Complete stories, 1892-1898

also in James, H. The complete tales of Henry James

also in James, H. The Henry James reader p255-356

also in James, H. Short novels of Henry James p407-530

Washington Square. Modern Lib. 1997 248p

ISBN 0-679-60276-3

LC 97-25219

First published 1881 by Harper

"The novel concerns Catherine Sloper, the shy and stolid daughter of wealthy, urbane, sardonic Dr. Austin Sloper. When young Morris Townsend, who is courting Catherine for her money, learns that her father will disinherit her if she marries him, he leaves her. Renewing his courtship after Dr. Sloper dies and leaves Catherine a

James, Henry, 1843-1916—*Continued*

small fortune, Morris is rejected sadly but firmly by Catherine, who lives on at Washington Square and is by then a spinster. Thus Catherine, plain and unintelligent, nevertheless withstands the world's assaults." Benet's Reader's Ency of Am Lit

> *also in* James, H. The Henry James reader
> p1-163

> *also in* James, H. Short novels of Henry
> James p59-256

What Maisie knew
> *In* James, H. What Maisie knew, In the cage,
> The pupil

What Maisie knew, In the cage, The pupil. Kelley 1936 xxi, 576p $45
> ISBN 0-678-02811-7

"The Novels and tales of Henry James. New York edition v11"

A combined edition of one novel and two novelettes first published 1897, 1898 and 1891 respectively

What Maisie knew, concerns a twelve-year-old girl whose parents have divorced and remarried. Living alternately with each parent she learns that her stepmother and stepfather are having an adulterous affair, just as she had learned of her parents' earlier infidelities. She decides to go to live with her old governess rather than with either parent. In the cage concerns a young woman who works as a telegram dispatcher in a London grocery store. She experiences vicarious enjoyment by imagining details in the lives of her well-to-do customers and even puts off marriage to her working-class fiance while she tries to aid in the affairs of an aristocratic lady and her lover. But when she learns the unsavory truth about the couple from an outside source she decides to proceed with her marriage at once. The pupil deals with an American student who becomes a tutor for the sickly son of a shabby American family traveling about in Europe, develops a strong attachment to the boy, and tries to help him leave his despicable family—with tragic results

The wings of the dove. Modern Lib. 1993 711p
> ISBN 0-679-60067-1

> * LC 93-15338

First published 1902 by Scribner

"The story is set in London and Venice. Kate Croy is a Londoner who encourages her secret fiancé, Merton Densher, to woo and marry Milly Theale, a wealthy young American who is dying of a mysterious malady. This, Kate reasons, although Milly will die soon, she will at least be happily in love, Merton will inherit her fortune, and Kate and Merton can marry and be rich. Shortly after Milly learns of Merton's and Kate's motives, she dies, leaving Merton a legacy that he is too guilt-ridden to accept. Kate is unwilling to forgo the inheritance, and she and Merton part forever, their relationship destroyed by Milly's unwittingly prescient gift." Merriam-Webster's Ency of Lit

James, Marlon, 1970-

The book of night women. Riverhead Books 2009 417p $26.95
> ISBN 978-1-59448-857-3; 1-59448-857-6

> LC 2008-46309

"Lilith, the central character in James's story of slave life in 19th-century Jamaica, is a green-eyed beauty who kills the first slave driver who tries to rape her. This catches the attention of the Night Women, a secret society planning to burn down the plantation and murder its white owners. But in Jamaica it is never simply a question of black against white. There are deep ethnic tensions among the different African tribes, and black overseers known as Johnny-jumpers enforce white control throughout the island. No one can be trusted. There is almost palpable sexual tension as well, and in a broader sense the rebellious Night Women also include the British wives." Libr J

This novel "is both beautifully written and devastating. While the gruesome history of slavery in the Americas is a story we may dare to think we already know, every page of 'The Book of Night Women' reminds us that we don't know nearly enough. . . . While his cast includes sadistic plantation owners and vicious overseers, 'house Negroes' and field slaves, James deftly avoids the clichéd melodrama such characters all too often inspire." N Y Times Book Rev

James, P. D.

The black tower. Scribner 1975 271p o.p.

"Adam Dalgliesh, convalescing after a severe illness, arrives at Toynton Grange (Dorset coast), the rest home for the young disabled, just too late to find out why his old friend Father Baddeley had sent for him. The monk-robed Wilfred Anstey and his staff are an odd lot, as are the few patients, all in wheelchairs. There's already been a suspicious suicide, and Dalgliesh is not satisfied that the old priest's death was caused by myocarditis alone. Handicapped by poor health, he finally manages to unearth the secret of the grange." Barzun. Cat of Crime. Rev and enl edition

A certain justice. Knopf 1997 364p $25
> ISBN 0-375-40109-1 LC 97-36889

"Called in to investigate the murder of barrister Venetia Aldridge in Temple Court, Scotland Yard Commander/poet Adam Dalgliesh and his team find that the death is merely the centerpiece around which swirl other crimes and the dirty little secrets of Aldridge's fellow barristers." Libr J

"In obedience to the classic crime-writing genre, James finally offers up the guilty party, resolving a complicated plot with impeccable logic. But there the symmetry ends, for the moral and emotional questions she asks do not admit of such neatness." N Y Times Book Rev

Death in holy orders. Knopf 2001 415p
> ISBN 0-375-41255-7 LC 2001-88108

In this mystery "almost everything happens behind the closed doors of St. Anselm's, a small Anglican theological college set on a windy cliff abutting the sea. Commander Adam Dalgliesh, as always both wistful and stern, returns to St. Anselm's, where he spent a few blissful boyhood summers, to investigate the death of a student, but the case quickly expands as bodies begin to fall like so many dominoes. It's a pleasure to read James at the top of her form, as she often is here." New Yorker

James, P. D.—*Continued*

Death of an expert witness. Scribner 1977 322p
o.p.

* LC 77-21530

The setting of this novel is "a forensic-science laboratory in a small East Anglia village. One of the senior biologists is found murdered in his triple-locked and delicately alarm-wired office, and Commander Adam Dalgliesh of Scotland Yard . . . is assigned to the case." New Yorker

"Basically James is a novelist who happens to put her character into mystery stories. She is just as much interested in people and their relationships as she is in conventions of the genre. And being the perceptive and sensitive writer she is, she constructs books that can be read on several levels." N Y Times Book Rev

Devices and desires. Knopf 1990 c1989 433p
o.p.   LC 89-45305

First published 1989 in the United Kingdom

"Commander Adam Dalgliesh, travels to the coastal Norfolk community of Larksoken to settle up the estate of his recently deceased aunt. Inevitably, Dalgliesh becomes embroiled in the affairs of the locals, many of them connected with the Larksoken nuclear power plant, which has brought a new economy to the area but has also stirred the juices of antinuclear protestors. Meanwhile, a mad killer called the Whistler is aprowl, savaging women with a bizarre modus operandi." Booklist

"As always with P. D. James, the whodunit element is the lagniappe, so interesting are her characters, so absorbing her depiction of time and place, so rich the texture of the tale she tells." N Y Times Book Rev

Innocent blood. Scribner 1980 311p o.p.

LC 79-28699

"What starts things moving in the tale is a young (adopted) woman's determination to find her real parents. This headstrong wish is gratified, creating social difficulties, deep changes in personal relations, the plotting of a murder, the experience of jail, and miscellaneous sexual activity. The diverse characters are admirably drawn and the author's fingerwork in tying and untying threads is as deft as her touches of sordid life and as nimble as her prose." Barzun. Cat of Crime. Rev and enl edition

The lighthouse. Knopf 2005 335p $25.95
ISBN 0-307-26291-X   LC 2005-51039

"Combe Island, off the Cornish coast of England, was once a pirates' enclave but is now used as a retreat for powerful people who need time to recharge their batteries, making it all the more shocking when one of the guests is found murdered. Commander Adam Dalgliesh is called to the politically sensitive scene to investigate." Booklist

This novel "is too rooted in genre conventions to count originality as its strong suit. But it has deviousness to burn, and it also offers other enticements. It's the kind of book that boasts a wryly humorous Scrabble scene, not to mention a Scrabble-lover's vocabulary." N Y Times Book Rev

Original sin. Knopf 1995 c1994 416p o.p.

LC 94-26094

First published 1994 in the United Kingdom

A mystery featuring Commander Adam Dalgliesh of Scotland Yard. "Innocent House, a nineteenth-century pile on the Thames that accommodates the Peverell Press, presides over this novel of revenge. After Gerard Etienne, the new chairman of the press, announces his plan to sell the house, he ends up dead, with the head of a toy snake stuffed in his mouth. In this elaborate novel, the author . . . does what she does best: shows that guilt and blame have no single address." New Yorker

The private patient. Alfred A. Knopf 2008 416p $25.95
ISBN 978-0-307-27077-1; 0-307-27077-7

LC 2008-27137

"The book begins by introducing investigative journalist Rhoda Gradwyn, whose face is marked by a disfiguring scar. She chooses prominent plastic surgeon George Chandler-Powell to remove it at his private clinic in Cheverell Manor. . . . It's a place where the comfortably situated can have their cosmetic work done in privacy — and not everyone welcomes the arrival of a professional snoop. The evening after her surgery, Gradwyn is murdered. Dalgliesh and his team are called in to solve the mystery, then have to deal with a second murder. . . . The investigation disrupts lives and disturbs secrets far beyond the little group at the manor. James is in excellent form in 'Patient.' She engages the brain as she entertains with apt descriptions and wry asides, and sets the reader to thinking beyond the obvious." St. Louis Post-Dispatch

The skull beneath the skin. Scribner 1982 328p
o.p.   LC 82-5981

"Fading actress Clarissa Lisle has been receiving frightening notes and is terrified of failing in her comeback performance, a revival of 'The Duchess of Malfi', held on a small private island off Dorset. Her husband hires detective Cordelia Gray to stop the notes. Once on the island, Cordelia discovers that nearly everyone there has a good reason to hate Clarissa, who is soon found gruesomely battered to death. The isolated group of suspects, hidden clues, and macabre atmosphere of an island castle complete with skulls and underground passageways make a pleasant traditional mystery. But James is never superficial, and her in-depth characterizations and excellent writing reveal complex relationships, motives, and human frailties." Libr J

A taste for death. Knopf 1986 459p o.p.

LC 86-45273

Sir Paul Berowne, a minister of the Crown, is found with his throat cut in the vestry of St. Matthew's church in London. A tramp has also been killed. Dalgliesh and his assistant Kate Miskin seek the solution to the mystery in the victims' past. All the family members and witnesses have something to conceal

This "book is about murder and the way murder changes everything. . . . It is also about the human condition in London today, enlarged by a sense of the British past that stretches back like a rich and barely dwindling perspective." N Y Times Book Rev

An unsuitable job for a woman. Scribner 1973 c1972 216p o.p.

*

First published 1972 in the United Kingdom

"In this book James's usual investigator, Chief Superintendent Dalgliesh, plays only a minor part. It is

James, P. D.—*Continued*

Cordelia Gray, the young, intelligent, and clear-thinking owner of an unsuccessful detective agency, who solves the case. She is hired by Sir Ronald Callender to investigate the death by suicide of his son, Mark. Miss Gray's meticulous research leads her to suspect that Mark was murdered and makes her a prime target for murder. There are suspenseful moments, close calls, and a very surprising encounter, at last, between Cordelia and Supt. Dalgliesh." Shapiro. Fic for Youth. 3d edition

Jance, Judith A., 1944-

Birds of prey; a novel of suspense; [by] J.A. Lance. Morrow 2001 390p

ISBN 0-380-97407-X   LC 00-59445

"Retired Seattle cop J. P. Beaumont accompanies his newlywed, eightysomething grandmother and her crusty hubby, Lars Jenssen, on an Alaskan cruise to act as a chaperone of sorts. The jaded protagonist is inadvertently forced to masquerade as an FBI agent when Dr. Harrison Featherman's shrill blonde wife Margaret is tossed overboard, and the crime is captured on ship security cameras." Libr J

Breach of duty; a J.P. Beaumont mystery; [by] J.A. Jance. Avon Bks. 1999 343p

ISBN 0-380-97406-1   LC 98-42112

In this J.P. Beaumont "mystery, the sensitive Seattle police detective, a recovering alcoholic, juggles several mysteries, including the arson-induced death of an older woman and a series of crimes related to the stolen bones of a Native American shaman. Meanwhile, partner Sue Danielson is hounded by her ex-husband, and all three 'cases' move to violent conclusions almost simultaneously." Libr J

Dead to rights; a Joanna Brady mystery; [by] J. A. Jance. Avon Bks. 1996 373p o.p.

LC 96-24634

"When veterinarian Amos Buckwalter is murdered, all fingers point to Hal Morgan, the angry husband of a woman the drunken vet killed in a car accident the previous year. When she alone thinks he's innocent, Brady, herself a bereaved widow, is unsure if her personal feelings are getting in the way of her professional judgment. More deaths follow as the emotionally fragile Brady attempts to juggle her own family problems . . . with the trials of her job and a potential new love interest." Booklist

"Jance skillfully ties the mystery to the southeastern Arizona landscape, its historic mining towns and their modern problems." Publ Wkly

Devil's claw; a Joanna Brady mystery; [by] J.A. Jance. Morrow 2000 374p

ISBN 0-380-97501-7   LC 00-25805

Set "in Cochise County, Arizona. This time County Sheriff Joanna Brady is working two cases in the weeks before her wedding to Butch Dixon. The first involves the death of her octogenarian handyman, friend, and neighbor, Clayton Rhodes. . . . The other case involves the murder of a woman freshly released from prison after serving eight years for murdering her husband." Booklist

"The Arizona desert, as usual in Jance's mysteries, plays an unforgettable part in this atmospheric tale." Publ Wkly

Hand of evil; a novel of suspense; [by] J.A. Jance. Simon & Schuster 2007 368p $25.95

ISBN 978-0-4165-3753-3; 1-4165-3753-8

LC 2007-16986

Ali Reynolds "is a strong-minded woman who has fled L.A. in the wake of double disaster: wrongful dismissal from her TV-journalist job and the bizarre murder of her almost-ex-husband. Now carving out a new life in Sedona, she writes a popular blog, an activity that puts her in touch with a variety of people. In Sedona, meanwhile, Ali's allies include her grown son, Chris, and her pal Dave, a homicide detective and possible love interest. The main story among "Hand of Evil's" busy plots involves the elderly matriarch of a prominent family. An unexpected scholarship from this family once allowed a young Ali to attend college. Ali can hardly refuse, therefore, when the elderly lady summons Ali. The matriarch says she was a victim of incest and wants to demonstrate it by having Ali turn her diary into a memoir." Seattle Times

"Jance crowds the book with subplots, and her characters air a lot of opinions about sexual abuse and health care. But sparks between Ali and Dave and an upbeat ending keep this latest Ali outing on track." Publ Wkly

Kiss of the bees; [by] J. A. Jance. Avon Bks. 2000 389p

ISBN 0-380-97747-8   LC 99-35465

"In Tucson, twenty years ago, a psychopath named Andrew Carlisle brought blood and terror into the home of Diana Ladd Walker and her family [Hour of the hunter]. When Carlisle died in prison, Diana and her husband, ex-county sheriff Brandon Walker, believed their long nightmare was finally over. They were wrong. Their beloved adopted daughter Lani has vanished—a beautiful Native American teenager destined, according to Tohono O'othham legend, to become a woman of great spiritual power. A serial killer is dead, but his malevolence lives on in another—and now the fiend holds Lani's innocent life in his eager hands." Publisher's note

Lying in wait; a J.P. Beaumont mystery; by J.A. Jance. Morrow 1994 303p o.p.   LC 94-15565

Police detective J.P. Beaumont "tackles a case with its origins in the Nazi death camps of World War II. When not one but two grisly torture-murder victims are discovered in the Seattle area, Beau and his new partner, Sue Danielson, are called in to investigate. Much to Beau's surprise, he finds that one of the victims was married to a former high school classmate, Else Didricksen." Booklist

"Beau and Sue probe Else's high school romance, the missing accident victim and the Nazi connection before they come up with the killer in this red hot, fast-paced story." Publ Wkly

Skeleton canyon; a Joanna Brady mystery; [by] J. A. Jance. Avon Bks. 1997 373p o.p.

LC 97-3217

"When high-school valedictorian Bree O'Brien is found dead in the southeastern Arizona mountains, suspicion falls on her boyfriend, Ignacio Ybarra, who refuses to explain his fresh cuts and bruises. But the case isn't that simple, as Coshise County Sheriff Joanna Brady learns. . . . Jance's regional knowledge runs deep, whether she writes about troubled Anglo-Hispanic relations along the border or the surprising power of Arizona thunderstorms." Publ Wkly

Jen, Gish

The love wife. Knopf 2004 379p $24.95

ISBN 1-400-04213-5   LC 2004-40917

"A meddlesome Chinese-American mother bequeaths a Chinese nanny to her ambivalent son and his big blonde wife in this darkly comic fairy tale about cultural assimilation, biological destiny and domestic warfare." Publ Wkly

"In a story told from multiple points of view, Jen turns stereotypes upside down by giving each character an issue, label or characteristic you might not expect." USA Today

Mona in the promised land. Knopf 1996 303p o.p.   LC 95-44447

This continues the story of the Chang family which began in Typical American. "This time, the focus is on Ralph and Helen's brash teenager, Mona. The success of their pancake restaurant has enabled the Changs to move to 'the promised land': Scarshill, New York, circa 1968. Drawn by the good schools and the majestic landscaping, the Changs are unprepared to deal with their daughter's attempts to assimilate into the community, namely, her decision to convert to Judaism. As Mona takes instruction from an unconventional rabbi, participates in rap sessions with her fellow temple-goers, and has her first sexual encounter with a smart, politically active college dropout, the Changs are at first bemused and then thunderstruck by their daughter's un-Chinese-like behavior." Booklist

This work "has a wide-ranging exuberance that's unusual in what is still—to its credit—a realistic novel. Ms. Jen doesn't sacrifice her characters to satire. And her story can take the broad view even while it focuses on smaller, more personal matters because she works in so many voices and because she includes so many perfectly timed set pieces." N Y Times Book Rev

Typical American. Plume 1992 296p (Plume contemporary fiction) pa $13.95

ISBN 0-452-26774-9   LC 91-33814

First published 1991 by Houghton Mifflin

"Yefing Chang becomes Ralph Chang in America and begins a hard struggle to achieve the American dream—a career, a family and a home of his own. In poverty, he succeeds finally to win a doctoral degree, a college position, a happy marriage to Helen, two delightful daughters and a close reunion with his older sister, Theresa. The dream becomes a nightmare when he meets Grover Ding whose corrupt influence over Ralph and Helen begins to unravel all that the Changs have managed to achieve. This is an honest novel that does not promise happy endings and recognizes the human weaknesses that can destroy a family's stability." Shapiro. Fic for Youth. 3d edition

Followed by Mona in the promised land (1996)

Who's Irish?; stories. Knopf 1999 207p $22

ISBN 0-375-40621-2   LC 98-42801

Contents: Who's Irish?; Birthmates; The water faucet vision; Duncan in China; Just wait; Chin; In the American society; House, House. Home

"Jen's characters, Chinese immigrants and their American-born children, find themselves commuting between two cultures, between familial expectations and their own yearnings for self-definition, between remembered traditions and shiny, new dreams." N Y Times Book Rev

Jenkins, Will F., 1896-1975

Exploration team

In The Hugo winners p95-142

Jennings, Gary

Aztec. Atheneum Pubs. 1980 754p o.p.   LC 80-55608

"Mixtli (Dark Cloud), the book's hero, is a Mexicatl who is born on the outskirts of the capital city of Tenochtitlan a half-century before the arrival of Cortés. He becomes, in turn, a student, a scribe, a soldier, a merchant, a cultural anthropologist, an adviser to noble rulers, and finally an involuntary chronicler of his people's past for the victorious Spaniards. The book is presented as the verbatim transcript of the reminiscences of this 'elderly male Indian,' recorded at the command of Emperor Charles I, who is eager to learn more about his recently acquired colony of New Spain." N Y Times Book Rev

Aztec blood. Forge 2001 525p

ISBN 0-312-86251-2   LC 2001-40130

"A Tom Doherty Associates book"

An adventure tale set in "17th-century Mexico as seen through the eyes of a teenage boy. . . . Cristo is a *lepero*, a scorned *mestizo* beggar who lives by his wits, conniving and scheming merely to stay alive. He is taught to read, write, and converse in foreign tongues by Fray Antonio, a Catholic friar. When the friar is murdered, Cristo must flee for his life, although he doesn't know why. On the way to discovering the truth about himself, he encounters many colorful characters and adventures." Libr J

"Injustice has seldom been so keenly sketched nor valor so compellingly portrayed as in this swashbuckling adventure." Publ Wkly

Raptor. Doubleday 1992 980p o.p.   LC 92-9433

In this "historical novel about the Gothic conquest of the Roman Empire, Thorn, the hermaphrodite hero/heroine, is seduced first by a monk and then by a nun. Evicted from a monastery and a convent, Thorn is then schooled in the ways of the world by the grumpy, blasphemous woodsman Wyrd. Rugged yet sensitive, usually dressed as a man, Thorn is raptorial (i.e., predatory) in his thirst for lovers, male and female, and for adventure. He serves as field marshal, sidekick and spy for bloody Theodoric (A.D. 454-526), king of the Ostrogoths, depicted here as a benevolent despot." Publ Wkly

"Like Michener, Jennings fills his boldly sketched historical canvas with lively action and dense, well-researched detail; in the works of both, a strong plot and interesting characters often camouflage an absence of style. But readers will enjoy this trip to an exotic world." Booklist

Jensen, Mrs. Oliver *See* Stafford, Jean, 1915-1979

Jewett, Sarah Orne, 1849-1909

The best stories of Sarah Orne Jewett; selected and arranged with a preface by Willa Cather. Houghton Mifflin 1925 2v o.p.
"The Mayflower edition"
Contents: v1 Return; Mrs. Todd; Schoolhouse; At the schoolhouse window; Captain Littlepage; Waiting place; Outer island; Green island; William; Where penny-royal grew; Old singers; Strange sail; Poor Joanna; Hermitage; On Shellheap island; Great expedition; Country road; Bowden reunion; Feast's end; Along shore; Dunnett shepherdess; Queen's twin; William's wedding; Backward view
v2 A white heron; The flight of Betsy Lane; The Dulham ladies; Going to Shrewsbury; The only rose; Miss Tempy's watchers; Martha's lady; The guests of Mrs. Timms; The town poor; The Hilton's holiday; Aunt Cynthy Dallett

The country of the pointed firs. Houghton Mifflin 1896 213p o.p.

 *

"Highly regarded for its sympathetic yet unsentimental portrayal of the town of Dunnet Landing and its residents, this episodic book is narrated by a nameless summer visitor who relates the life stories of various inhabitants, capturing the idiomatic language, customs, mannerisms, and humor peculiar to Down-Easters." Merriam-Webster's Ency of Lit

   also in Jewett, S. O. The best stories of Sarah Orne Jewett

   also in Jewett, S. O. The country of the pointed firs and other stories p1-139

The country of the pointed firs and other stories. Modern Lib. 1995 247p
ISBN 0-679-60173-2   LC 95-2831
In addition to the title story, this volume also includes the following: The queen's twin; A Dunnet shepherdess; The foreigner; William's wedding

Jhabvala, Ruth Prawer

East into Upper East; plain tales from New York and New Delhi. Counterpoint 1998 314p
ISBN 1-88717-850-3   LC 98-34881
Contents: Expiation; Farid and Farida; Independence; Development and progress; A New Delhi romance; Husband and son; The temptress; A summer by the sea; Great expectations; Parasites; Fidelity; Bobby; Broken promises; Two muses
"Jhabvala is a connoisseur of divided souls, conceiving characters whose inner longings are at odds with their outer protective coloration—Indians who covet and achieve more tidy, 'modernized' existences, then feel as if someone had stolen their life force; Westerners who eagerly hand themselves over to India's chaotic bliss, then find it too rigorous to endure." N Y Times Book Rev

Heat and dust. Harper & Row 1976 c1975 181p o.p.

 *

"A Joan Kahn book"
First published 1975 in the United Kingdom
"The juxtaposition of past and present India is ex-plored in this novel. The 1923 storyline tells of Olivia, who, though married to a British officer stationed in India, falls madly in love with an Indian prince. It is also about Olivia's husband's granddaughter by a second marriage, who has come to India to discover the details of Olivia's life but finds that, although India and women have become modernized, she must face many of the same choices as Olivia. The intrusion of British culture on India's own traditions and values is a second theme in the novel." Shapiro. Fic for Youth. 3d edition

My nine lives. Shoemaker & Hoard 2004 277p $25
ISBN 1-59376-028-0
In this autobiographical novel the author turns the lens "upon herself in a series of self-described invented memories. Each of the nine chapters presents a possible past for its first-person narrator. The familial relationships depicted vary as much as the locales, spanning relations between parents, siblings, lovers, or husbands in settings as far-reaching as England, India, and the United States." Libr J
"Jhabvala name-drops Chekhov, and this is no pretension given the grace of her spiraling plots, the depth of her psychology, the elegance of her humor, the subtly of her eroticism, and her masterfully concise descriptions of imperiled households, eccentric personalities, sexual enthrallment, unexpected alliances, and transcendent love." Booklist

Out of India; selected stories. Morrow 1986 288p o.p.   LC 85-25961
Contents: My first marriage; The widow; The interview; A spiritual call; Passion; The man with the dog; An experience of India; The housewife; Rose petals; Two more under the Indian sun; Bombay; On bail; In the mountains; How I became a holy mother; Desecration
"Out of a web of subtle but not precious ironies, couched in a limpid style, arises a sense of the author's obvious love-hate attitude toward this land that is so difficult to live in, for foreigner and native alike. Jhabvala sensitively explores the tense juncture between Western and Indian cultures; plots and characters glow with realism and energy." Booklist

Shards of memory. Doubleday 1995 221p o.p.
      LC 94-45311
This novel chronicles "four generations of a family who, in varying degrees, follow a charismatic leader known as the Master. Told in the form of remembrances of people who were involved with the Master, as collected by Henry, his possible successor, the story becomes intensely personal because of the way it weaves its multiple memories. . . . Every member of the family is touched by the Master in a unique way. Elsa, the tempestuous woman who becomes his devoted follower, is the mother of Baby, who is able to experience the guru as more than master. Baby's lackluster daughter, Renata, comes to the Master's teachings late, but she is never sure whether he has given her a more profound gift than enlightenment—her son, Henry." Booklist
"Jhabvala's understanding of character is shrewd, and her language is controlled and lucid. . . . [Her] technical fluency and poise are admirable; combined with Jhabvala's sensitivity, and her understanding of characters, they make the novel feel startlingly realistic, so that

Jhabvala, Ruth Prawer—*Continued*
the vagueness of the central themes, and the sometimes slow development of plot seem almost irrelevant." Times Lit Suppl

Jiang Rong, 1946-

Wolf totem; a novel; translated by Howard Goldblatt. Penguin Press 2008 527p $26.95
ISBN 978-1-59420-156-1; 1-59420-156-0
LC 2007-37554
Original Chinese edition, 2004
"The book chronicles a few years in the life of young Beijing university student Chen Zhen, part of a group sent to work on a commune on the outer edge of Inner Mongolia. In the idyllic desolation of the grasslands of the Olonbulag, the young man works and lives with Mongolian herders, the last of a dying breed. It is here that Chen is first introduced to the Mongolian wolf as well as the forces out to exterminate it. As the story goes on, Chen becomes increasingly enchanted by the wolf and its relation to the herdsmen, enough so that he snatches a wolf cub to raise on his own." Los Angeles Times Book Rev
"The novel's literary claims are shaky; and Jiang Rong's apparent wish to transform China's national character through a benign conservationism is compromised by his boy-scoutish arguments for toughness. Yet few books about today's China can match Wolf Totem as a guide to the troubled self-images of so many of its people as they stumble, grappling with some inconvenient truths of their own, into modernity." N Y Times Book Rev

Jiles, Paulette, 1943-

The color of lightning; a novel. William Morrow 2009 349p $25.99
ISBN 978-0-06-169044-0; 0-06-169044-9
LC 2008-46339
"It is 1863, and Britt Johnson saddles up with a few other men from his North Texas settlement to ride to a nearby town for supplies. Johnson, a free African American, has brought his beautiful wife and three small children to this desolate, dangerous country to build a life he hopes will be freer of racism than it would have been in Kentucky. While he is gone, a war party of 700 Comanche and Kiowa descend into the valley, killing the men and kidnapping women and children. His wife and two younger children are taken as captives. . . . Based on the true story of an African American who was legendary for his ability to bargain with Native Americans for the return of captives, the novel also tells the fictional tale of a well-meaning, but naive young Quaker from Philadelphia, Samuel Hammond, who is sent to run a regional Bureau of Indian Affairs. The contrast between Johnson, a pragmatic man of action, and Hammond, an idealist who struggles with the ambiguities of reality, echoes the history of a period when government programs and westward expansion collided, ruinously, with Native cultures. Jiles' spare and melancholy prose is the perfect language for this tale in which survival necessitates brutality." Seattle Times

Enemy women. Morrow 2002 321p
ISBN 0-06-621444-0
LC 2001-40200

"For Adair Randolph Colley, at 18 the eldest daughter of a widowed Missouri Ozarks schoolmaster and justice of the peace, the Civil War becomes personal when her father, who has remained neutral in the conflict, is arrested by the Union militia, their home is nearly burned and their possessions stolen. At the start of this . . . novel, Adair and her two younger sisters try to follow their father's captors, but Adair is falsely denounced as a Confederate spy. At the prison in St. Louis, upright commandant Maj. William Neumann is . . . touched by Adair's beauty and spirit and asks her to give him some information so she can be released. Instead, she writes the story of her life, augmented by folk tales and fables, and he finds himself falling in love. When he gets his reassignment orders, he proposes marriage and asks her to escape, promising to find her after the war. Thus begins a long and terrible journey for each of them." Publ Wkly

Jin, Ha *See* Ha Jin, 1956-

Joe, Yolanda

My fine lady. Dutton 2004 221p $23.95
ISBN 0-525-94808-2
LC 2003-17788
"Imani Holland has a voice like 'velvet on fire,' and she raps the lyrics her boyfriend, Taz, writes; together they're gonna make it big. At an unofficial competition at the local college campus, Imani catches the attention of Orenthal Hopson, a gifted young musician and academic. Hopson's been butting heads with department chair Perkins over his theory of music's transformative powers, and Imani's raw talent makes her the perfect test—Perkins will give Hopson three months to make Imani into a jazz diva." Publ Wkly
"A fantastic update of Pygmalion and hip Americanization of My Fair Lady . . ., Joe's compelling tale about one woman's coming into her own and the dichotomy between educated African Americans and those living in poverty may well become a popular classic in its own right." Booklist

Johansen, Iris

And then you die—. Bantam Bks. 1998 344p
ISBN 0-553-10616-3
LC 97-40073
"When photojournalist Bess Grady is sent on assignment to a small town in Mexico, she unwittingly finds herself in the midst of a horrific nightmare. Every citizen of the town has died of anthrax poisoning as a result of a terrorist germ-warfare attack. Because she survived, Bess is sought by both the terrorists and a hard-hearted CIA man. The plot is filled with clever detours that twist and turn and cast suspicion on all of the main players until Bess doesn't know who to trust." Booklist

Blind alley. Bantam Books 2004 344p $25
ISBN 0-553-80341-7
LC 2004-54410
In this thriller featuring "Atlanta detective Joe Quinn and the love of his life, forensic sculptor Eve Duncan, Joe gives Eve a skull to reconstruct. Eerily enough, the face resembles 17-year-old Jane MacGuire, who has been offered sanctuary by Eve and Joe after surviving a rough-and-tumble life on the streets. . . . Several look-alikes have already been killed in Europe, and Scotland Yard sends in hunky Mark Trevor to help. Eve mistrusts

Johansen, Iris—*Continued*

him, but Jane, who has had recurring nightmares related to the killings, believes that he's there to help her. Eve and Joe want to protect Jane, but the intrepid teenager knows that unless she confronts the killer, she will live the rest of her life in fear. Johansen has become adept at mixing supernatural elements with intriguing suspense." Booklist

The face of deception. Bantam Bks. 1998 354p
ISBN 0-553-10623-6   LC 98-24713
Forensic sculptor Eve Duncan "is swept into a maelstrom of murder, deception, and political intrigue when she is coerced into rebuilding the face of an adult whose remains consist of a burned skull. Obsessed with establishing the identities of the skeletal remains of murdered children ever since her daughter was killed and the body was never found. Eve resists the request of billionaire John Logan to work on this mysterious case until her lab is destroyed and her mother threatened." Booklist
"With the help of well-timed, steady disclosures and surprising revelations, the book's twists and turns manage to hold the reader hostage until the denouement." Publ Wkly

Final target. Bantam Bks. 2001 340p $24.95
ISBN 0-553-80094-9   LC 00-65124
At the center of this thriller "is the Wind Dancer, a priceless gold statue of the winged horse Pegasus. The statue has been in the Andreas family since the fall of Troy and now, centuries later, U.S. President Jonathan Andreas is in Paris to lend the family heirloom to a museum. On the night of the ceremony, his daughter, seven-year-old Cassie, is awakened at the family's farmhouse in the south of France by masked men who murder her nanny and her nurse, intent on kidnapping Cassie and ransoming her in exchange for the Wind Dancer. Cassie is saved in the nick of time by the arrival of Michael Travis, international underworld information dealer, but eight months later, the child is being treated in the Virginia home of psychiatrist Dr. Jessica Riley and Jessica's psychically extrasensitive sister, Melissa, for severe catatonic trauma. . . . Michael Travis then reappears and lures Cassie and the Riley sisters into a web of intrigue." Publ Wkly

The killing game. Bantam Bks. 1999 355p
ISBN 0-553-10624-4   LC 99-20999
Following the abduction and murder of her daughter in The face of deception, forensic sculptor Eve Duncan "has abandoned the day-to-day world for life on a Tahitian island. Eve's tropical exile is interrupted, however, when Joe [Quinn] shows up to tell her that a pile of bodies has been discovered in the Georgia woods, including that of a young girl he believes may be Eve's daughter. Determined to reconstruct the skull and hoping to lay her daughter to rest, Eve returns to the U.S. Her arrival draws the attention of Dom, the psychotic serial killer responsible for the Georgia murders. Random attacks on social outcasts don't produce the rush they once did for Dom, and now he needs to up the ante, by stalking and murdering more prominent people and interacting with his victims before he attacks. Eve, whose story he has long followed in newspaper accounts, becomes his next target." Publ Wkly
"Johansen's novel of psychological suspense features a hair-raising plot, a fiendish killer, a brave heroine, and dozens of heartstopping plot twists." Booklist

Long after midnight. Bantam Bks. 1997 371p
o.p.   LC 96-24957
"Genetic research and industrial espionage are at the center of this story about Kate Denby, a research scientist working on a new way for medicine to be delivered to the human cell. Another researcher, who owns his own company, wants Kate to work for him. He needs what she's working on because it dovetails with the project he's working on: a powerful new drug that will strengthen the immune system beyond anything currently available. But there's somebody out there who doesn't want Kate to succeed." Booklist
"Johansen knows how to take the formula and run with it, and readers will be won over by her flesh-and-blood characters, crackling dialogue and lean, suspenseful plotting." Publ Wkly

The ugly duckling. Bantam Bks. 1996 378p o.p.
LC 95-36175
"Nell Carter is plain and plump—and, for some mysterious reason, the target of a drug cartel hit that maims her but wipes out her husband and young daughter. Her world destroyed, Nell wills herself to die, until a stranger gives her a purpose to live: revenge. The mysterious Nicholas Tanek, once master of his own criminal network, will do anything and use anyone to destroy the drug cartel that, he tells Nell, murdered a 'very close' friend. . . . Given a new face and identity, Nell throws herself into guerrilla and martial arts training with Nicholas." Publ Wkly
"A forceful, enigmatic hero with a dangerous past and a mission of his own; a focused, determined, and refreshingly creative heroine who develops quite nicely; and a few interesting secondary characters join forces in a well-executed story that deftly provides chilling suspense without sacrificing a warm romance." Libr J

Johnson, Adam

Parasites like us; a novel. Viking 2003 341p $24.95
ISBN 0-670-03240-9   LC 2002-41181
"Anthropology professor Hank Hannah studies the Clovis people, a prehistoric tribe of hunter-gatherers. His theory is that their hunting habits helped kill off 35 species of large mammals. The discovery of a Clovis arrowhead helps substantiate his claim, but disaster strikes when Hannah and two graduate students, publicity hound Brent Eggers and formidable Trudy Labelle, try to dig up the remains of a Clovis male. The police appear and Hannah is arrested for assaulting the officer who defiles the grave site. His stint at a luxury low-security prison, Club Fed, is interrupted by the outbreak of a deadly epidemic, transmitted from pigs to humans and triggered when Eggers and Labelle use the Clovis arrowhead to kill a pig." Publ Wkly
"Johnson relates all of this with great ingenuity and bravado—as well as a good deal of unfocused energy. . . . The most daring element in this heterogeneous mix, however, may well be the vein of earnest solemnity that Johnson adds to it. Unlike most satirists, he's not afraid to let the mask of irony fall occasionally." N Y Times Book Rev

Johnson, B. S. (Bryan Stanley), 1933-1973

The unfortunates; [with an introduction by Jonathan Coe] New Directions Pub. 2007 [134]p $24.95

ISBN 978-0-8112-1743-9; 0-8112-1743-4

LC 2007-23007

First published 1969; this edition 1999, in the United Kingdom

This is "a 'novel' published in the form of 26 sections [and an introduction] collected in a box. One section is labeled 'First' and another 'Last' the reader shuffles the rest in any order he or she might wish. In the story, Johnson travels to a provincial English city to write a freelance sports article (reproduced on the inside of the box). 'The Unfortunates' follows him from the moment he gets off the train and starts thinking about a deceased friend who lived there and died of cancer." Los Angeles Times Book Rev

"Johnson insisted that his randomly sorted sections were better at 'conveying the mind's randomness' than any other technique. But this novelty provides little in the way of mimesis, it only draws attention to itself. And yet it proves to be a great deal of fun. . . . For its honest depiction of how young men deal with cancer, 'The Unfortunates' can be widely recommended. . . Johnson's own dogged seriousness, and his concomitant boyishness, make a fascinating medium for his occasional bursts of pity and shy friendliness." N Y Sun

Johnson, Bryan Stanley See Johnson, B. S. (Bryan Stanley), 1933-1973

Johnson, Charles Richard, 1948-

Dr. King's refrigerator and other bedtime stories; [by] Charles Johnson. Scribner 2005 123p $20

ISBN 0-7432-6453-3   LC 2004-56642

Contents: Sweet dreams; Cultural relativity; Dr. King's refrigerator; The gift of the Osuo; Executive decision; Better than counting sheep; The queen and the philosopher; Kwoon

"Johnson is once again at the ready with his quirky, professorial writing style and his melange of Buddhism, Western philosophy and African magic realism." N Y Times Book Rev

Dreamer; a novel; [by] Charles Johnson. Scribner 1998 236p

ISBN 0-684-81224-X   LC 98-10201

"Chaym Smith doesn't have much going for him, except for his uncanny resemblance to Civil Rights leader Martin Luther King Jr. After a tour of duty in Korea, where he was severely wounded, Smith drifted around the East for several years. . . . Now, in the late 1960s, this modern-day Cain hopes to redeem himself by acting as a decoy for Dr. King at his increasingly dangerous public appearances. He quickly accepted into King's inner circle, where he learns to dress and speak like his hero. But as their partnership grows, King seems to take on some of Smith's characteristics. There are sinister hints that this mysterious doppelganger may be working for the FBI." Libr J

"It's a joy to read fiction in which there is a cultivated vision at work. Among the accomplishments of 'Dreamer' is an overarching argument that the Truth is an amalgamation, a messy mosaic full of contradictions . . . and that the best way to get at it is to include a lot." N Y Times Book Rev

Middle passage; [by] Charles Johnson. Atheneum Pubs. 1990 209p o.p.

* LC 90-32713

The protagonist of this novel, set in 1830, "is Rutherford Calhoun, a newly freed slave leading a dissolute life in New Orleans. Rutherford finds himself forced into marriage with Isadora Bailey, a proper yet severe Boston schoolteacher, and, to quickly escape both wedlock and his Louisiana debts, he stows away on the first available ship. To his shock and horror, Rutherford learns that the vessel, the Republic, is a slave ship bound for Africa. Its captain is the American soldier of fortune, Ebenezer Falcon, a buccaneer and empire-builder. . . . The Republic's mission is to transport the last survivors of a nearly legendary tribe, the Allmuseri, from their devastated homeland to the New World." Publisher's note

"Johnson's exciting sea narrative provides an unusual historical look at the horrifying Middle Passage experience. . . . Like Moby-Dick's Ahab, the captain of the Republic is on his own special quest (in this case, the capture of the African trickster god). . . . Above all, the book is valuable in offering a rare perspective of the shocking experience of the slave trade and the consequences of that event for American blacks." Choice

Johnson, Craig, 1961-

The dark horse. Viking 2009 318p $24.95

ISBN 978-0-670-02087-4; 0-670-02087-7

LC 2008-54093

In this outing, "Sheriff Walt Longmire goes undercover to prove that Mary Barsad, confessed murderer, did not kill her husband after he shot her horses and set the barn on fire. Walt finds that there is a lot more going on in Wyoming's remote Powder River area, as he meets a cast of characters with much to hide. . . . Johnson's deft, twisty storytelling immediately grips the reader. His latest has a heart as big as a Wyoming sky." Libr J

Johnson, Denis, 1949-

Jesus' son; stories. Farrar, Straus & Giroux 1992 160p $19 o.p.

ISBN 0-374-17892-5   LC 92-16880

Contents: Car crash while hitchhiking; Two men; Out on bail; Dundun; Work; Emergency; Dirty wedding; The other man; Happy hour; Steady hands at Seattle General; Beverly Home

In this is "masterfully bleak sequence of short stories narrated by a young heartland lowlife, brutality is unpredictable and unremarkable: shootings, stabbings, guns held to heads, heroin overdoses, gruesome car wrecks—and confrontations that don't turn violent only because the antagonists can't stay focused. . . . As grunge sociology, 'Jesus' Son' is claustrophobic; as art, it's exhilarating." Newsweek

Nobody move; a novel. Farrar, Straus and Giroux 2009 196p $23

ISBN 978-0-374-22290-1; 0-374-22290-8

LC 2008-43420

Johnson, Denis, 1949-—*Continued*

Originally serialized, in slightly different form, in Playboy

This noir novel revolves around "gambling addict Jimmy Luntz, on the run from kingpin Juarez, Juarez's bumbling strongman Gambol and the alcoholic karaoke aficionado, Anna Desilvera, who has the FBI on her tail." Publ Wkly

"Johnson's sympathies seem to be with Gambol, a bad man who isn't so much seeking redemption as having redemption thrust on him. When offered an exit out of this seedy underworld, he takes it with Mary, a 'heavyset blonde' and former Army medic who brings him back to health. Gambol may deal in death, and sometimes even take pleasure in it, but he is distinguished by a lack of human hatred for others and himself. In the brutal world of Nobody Move, that makes all the difference." Pittsburgh City Paper

Tree of smoke. Farrar, Straus & Giroux 2007 614p $27

ISBN 978-0-374-27912-7; 0-374-27912-8

LC 2007-06562

"Set mainly in southeast Asia, with a few stateside chapters thrown in, the novel takes place between 1963 and 1983. . . . William 'Skip' Sands, a U.S. spy working in Psychological Operations, has 'come to war to see abstractions become realities. Instead, he's seen the reverse. Everything was abstract now.' Skip's job is to win over the hearts and minds of the Vietnamese people even though he can't be certain where his own sympathies lie. He's working with a double agent and making enemies on both sides. Skip's primary loyalty is to his uncle, an infamous colonel with CIA connections. The Colonel isn't known for playing by the military's rules. He has his own ways of doing things, and they're not usually popular with the higher-ups." Miami Herald

"Mr. Johnson not only succeeds in conjuring the anomalous, hallucinatory aura of the Vietnam War as authoritatively as Stephen Wright or Francis Ford Coppola, but he also shows its fallout on his characters with harrowing emotional precision. He has written a flawed but deeply resonant novel that is bound to become one of the classic works of literature produced by that tragic and uncannily familiar war." N Y Times (Late N Y Ed)

Johnson, Diane, 1934-

Le divorce. Dutton 1997 309p o.p.

LC 96-9644

"A William Abrahams book"

"Film-school dropout Isabel Walker arrives in Paris intending to baby-sit for her sister Roxeanne and figure out her next move. Unfortunately, Roxeanne's French husband, Charles-Henri Persand, has abandoned her for another woman, and the pregnant Roxeanne seems suicidal. As the divorce proceedings heat up, the rights to an extremely valuable painting that Roxeanne has had since childhood are suddenly in dispute. Meanwhile, Isabel has become the mistress of a famous 70-year-old Persand relative, much to the Persands' distress, and as Isabel and Roxy's family descend on Paris, the American and French families face off." Booklist

"The author pokes fun at the Americans for moralizing, and at the French for being amoral; and she manages to be even-handed because she displays admiration for French elegance of behavior, and affection for American earnest good will." N Y Rev Books

L'affaire. Dutton 2003 340p $24.95

ISBN 0-525-94740-X

LC 2003-13725

"Amy Hawkins, a beautiful, naive, suddenly very rich Califonian dot-com entrepreneur, comes to a posh ski resort in the French Alps as part of her plan for cultural self-improvement. When she generously pays for transporting the dying Adrian Venn, a publisher crushed in a landslide, back to his native England, her humanitarian gesture backfires with exquisite irony. Venn's two grown English children, his illegitimate French daughter, his new much younger American wife and their toddler son become embroiled in a classic scenario of quarreling heirs, each seething with expectations at the expense of the others." Publ Wkly

"Much of the wit comes from Johnson's shrewd view of her characters' cultural assumptions, which are both simplistic and devilishly on target." N Y Times Book Rev

Lulu in Marrakech. Dutton 2008 307p $25.95

ISBN 978-0-525-95037-0

LC 2008-07700

The eponymous narrator is "an unlikely spy for the CIA who accepts an undercover posting to Morocco. What is pretty thirtysomething Lulu Sawyer's job exactly? To collect 'human intelligence' on Muslim terrorist networks by infiltrating the affluent expat culture and listening to gossip over cocktail-laden alfresco lunches. . . . Conveniently, Lulu just happens to have a rich, handsome British boyfriend already living in Morocco when her plane touches down." Entertainment Wkly

"The love story fizzles and pops and then seems to fizzle out, but as with any great mystery, the answers are not always what they seem, and Johnson rivets the story with romantic intrigue no matter how Lulu's luck is going." N Y Post

Le mariage; a novel. Dutton 2000 322p $23.95

ISBN 0-525-94518-0

LC 99-89849

This companion to Le divorce is "set again in Paris with a few overlapping characters, the plot revolves around two couples—Tim Nolinger, a Belgian American journalist engaged to the very French Anne-Sophie, a dealer in equine collectibles; and the very beautiful American Clara, a former actress married to the reclusive film director Serge Clay. Thrown into the entertaining mix is a stolen illuminated manuscript, a murdered flea market dealer, Y2K cults, an adulterous liaison, and of course Johnson's perceptive and witty insights on love, marriage, and Anglo-French relations." Libr J

Johnson, Stephanie, 1961-

The sailmaker's daughter. St. Martin's Press 2003 255p il map $23.95

ISBN 0-312-30693-8

LC 2003-40639

First published 1996 in the United Kingdom with title: The heart's wild surf

"The book follows 12-year-old Olive McNab during the month she is sent to her aunt and uncle's plantation while her mother is dying of influenza. Olive is haunted by ghosts of the family dead, appalled by her uncle's coarse brutality, fascinated by two free-spirited British lady travelers who are passing through, and, most of all,

Johnson, Stephanie, 1961---*Continued*
anguished by her mother's approaching death. In Johnson's poetic hands Olive and her eccentric family come to life." Libr J

Johnson, Wayne

The devil you know; a novel. Shaye Areheart Books 2004 381p $23
  ISBN 0-609-60964-5   LC 2003-11616
  "Set in Minnesota in the 1970s, this . . . is at once a coming-of-age tale and a survival story. Fifteen-year-old David Geist is the product of a troubled family. His father, Max, physically abused him before abandoning the family. A budding track star, David is now being bullied by a lunkish football player at school. When his estranged father returns, he proposes that David and his younger sister, Janie, take a trip to the north woods with him as a way of healing old wounds. Once there, the family runs afoul of a group of smalltime criminals. After David wards off a brutal attack on their campsite, he has to find a way to get his injured father and sister to safety while being pursued by the remaining thugs." Libr J

  "Johnson surrounds a mythic, Deliverance-like confrontation with evil . . . with a subtly realsitic coming-of-age story about a teenager's conflict with his abusive father. Rising above cliché at every seemily predictable turn, the novel works on both levels: a literary thriller with an abundance of heart." Booklist

Johnston, Terry C., 1947-2001

Dance on the wind. Bantam Bks. 1995 517p o.p.
                                   LC 95-7558
  "Johnston here reprises Titus Bass, the central character in several of his earlier novels. In this story of Bass's coming of age, the itchy-footed adolescent runs away from the sameness of his father's Kentucky farm in 1810. Teaming with flatboaters floating supplies down the Ohio and Mississippi rivers to New Orleans, he experiences the dangers and earthly pleasures of that breed of adventurer. But he finds river life unsatisfying and soon settles down at a blacksmith's forge in St. Louis—until a mountain man resurrects his restless desire to move West." Libr J
  The author "is a deservedly popular western author whose appeal lies not so much in the adventures he dramatizes as in the depth of his characters. They love, grieve, laugh, and feel guilt, anger, and jealousy. They're real people, not just providers of vicarious thrills." Booklist

Lay the mountains low; the flight of the Nez Perce from Idaho and the Battle of the Big Hole, August 9-10, 1877. St. Martin's Press 2000 xxii, 495p il
  ISBN 0-312-26189-6   LC 00-24201
  "In this tale of five Nez Perce tribal leaders who choose to resist the encroaching white settlers and who refuse to make treaties with the U.S. government, Johnston provides gripping, authentic details of historically accurate events; readers see the Nez Perce wars through the eyes of those involved and read actual letters and newspaper clippings of the day. Besides the historical details, the novel presents a compelling, action-packed story." Libr J

Wind walker. Bantam Bks. 2001 461p map $24.95
  ISBN 0-553-09090-9   LC 00-48570
  This final installment in the Titus Bass series "covers six years (1847-1853) and sees the scarred, aging, one-eyed mountain man struggling to find peace and sanctuary in a changing world. The fur trade is finished, free mountain men are few and white immigrants are flooding the pristine and untamed wilderness. Bass knows his independent way of life is over, so he takes his Indian family north, hoping to settle with his wife's Crow relatives. Bass's final journey, however, will not be easy. . . . Titus Bass is a believable, enduring character, a solitary man who lives by his wits, believes in mountain justice and is willing to use rifle or tomahawk to settle a score when he knows right is on his side." Publ Wkly

Johnston, Wayne

The colony of unrequited dreams. Anchor Bks. (NY) 1999 562p
  ISBN 0-385-49542-0   LC 99-19144
  This is the "fictional biography of Joe Smallwood, one of Newfoundland's most controversial political figures, and focuses on his early years and arduous rise to power: union organizer, newspaperman, socialist turned liberal, and Newfoundland's first premier after confederation with Canada in 1949. . . . [In] counterpoint are the views of Smallwood's lifelong friend, Sheilagh Fielding, as set forth in her acerbic newspaper columns, personal journals, and irreverently entertaining *Condensed History of Newfoundland.*" Booklist
  "The very human story of Smallwood and Fielding and its historical counterpoint may both appear inauspicious, even contrived, at first, but as the book proceeds they and their pairing gather momentum to achieve a mesmerizing inevitability." N Y Times Book Rev

The custodian of paradise. W. W. Norton & Co. 2007 510p $25.95
  ISBN 978-0-393-06491-9; 0-393-06491-3
                              LC 2006-102234
  First published 2006 in Canada
  The protagonist of this novel, set against the backdrop of WWII, first appeared in the author's The colony of unrequited dreams. "An only child haunted since age six by her mother's abandonment, Sheilagh Fielding was raised in the city of St. John's by her physician father, a man still devastated by his wife's departure and tormented by the suspicion that Sheilagh is not his offspring. Further anguish occurs when, at age 16, Sheilagh becomes pregnant and is sent to stay with her estranged mother, now remarried and living in New York City. Eventually, Sheilagh returns to St. John's and lives an eccentric life that includes writing a satiric newspaper column and drinking heavily." Libr J
  "If, as critics have suggested, Fielding is like Newfoundland itself—huge, beautiful, with an unknown heart (and an alcohol problem)—the trope here extends to her ancestry, which is irregular and also larger than life. In the manner of Lawrence Durrell's Alexandria Quartet, events in this book don't necessarily line up with those in the first. . . . By the book's end, many mysteries have been laid to rest, only to be replaced with new ones. This raises the happy possibility that Johnston intends to return to the scene again." Quill & Quire

Johnston, Wayne—*Continued*

The navigator of New York; a novel. Doubleday 2002 483p $27.95

ISBN 0-385-50767-4   LC 2002-71418

"Devlin Stead is the orphaned protagonist raised by his aunt and uncle in Newfoundland after his physician father dies in a polar expedition under the aegis of Robert Edwin Peary and Dr. Frederick Cook. The boy's sheltered existence is shattered when he receives a series of letters from Cook that reveal the explorer—who had committed an indiscretion with Devlin's mother—to be the boy's real father. Cook invites Devlin to New York, where he takes him under his wing and makes him an assistant." Publ Wkly

"Polar exploration—with its incredible hardships, its months of freezing isolation, darkness and despair—makes an irresistible metaphor for a lonely and uncertain childhood. The story itself is told through Devlin's deliberately understated narration and Cook's long expository letters and monologues, which can be tedious at times but which echo the straightforward humble-heroic tone of a Victorian explorer." N Y Times Book Rev

Jolliffe, June, 1920-1994 *See* Braybrooke, June, 1920-1994

Jones, Diana Wynne

A sudden wild magic. Morrow 1992 412p o.p.

LC 92-10860

"Computer expert Mark Lister, incidentally the only male member of the Inner Ring of witches in Great Britain, unexpectedly comes across evidence that Earth is being manipulated by a distant planet called Arth. This pirate world, an all-male society sworn to celibacy, is sending wars, plagues, and environmental disasters (notably global warming) to Earth and then observing and appropriating Earth's leaders' solutions. In defense, the witches' council decides to transport some attractive female recruits to Arth to sabotage the inhabitants' oaths and restore the balance of power." Booklist

"Jones's sly sense of humor and her accurate, affectionate depiction of relations between women and men give an extra kick to this effervescent tale." Publ Wkly

Jones, Douglas C., 1924-1998

Arrest Sitting Bull. Scribner 1977 249p o.p.

LC 77-7645

In this second volume of a western historical trilogy, the author tells it "as it really *did* happen when the order went out: 'Arrest Sitting Bull.' We begin with the Ghost Dance, when that confusion of Indian mythology and missionary-brought Christianity has fired the Plain Indians to a belief in the coming of an Indian Messiah. Sitting Bull, already the conqueror of Custer, the veteran of Buffalo Bill's Wild West Show, is back on the reservation, but at the center of a growing revolt against the white man. . . . Jones makes us understand the torment of a minority of decent white men and women who really cared about the Indians and of the Indians, trapped between a fight to the death (the novel closes with Wounded Knee three days off), and a willingness to try to assimilate themselves to the white man's ways." Publ Wkly

Followed by A creek called Wounded Knee

The court-martial of George Armstrong Custer. Scribner 1976 291p o.p.

In this novel, the first of a trilogy, history is reshuffled. "Custer survives the Little Big Horn, leaving behind 260 dead comrades. Professionally scandalized, the army under William Sherman charges Custer with insubordination although the man is a folk hero often puffed up in the papers. Marshalling evidence for the government falls to Judge Advocate General Asa Gardiner. A determined idealist, he senses that superiors deem Custer a menace, a 'Golden Cavalier' with dubious ambitions. The defense ostensibly rests on a breakdown in communication and bad field intelligence; actually the implications cut deeper: Custer knows enough to have his Civil War cronies (Schofield, Miles, Sheridan) put in the stockade." Publ Wkly

"Slowly building the cases for the prosecution and defense, Jones does well by mixing the drama of courtroom proceedings with the color of a controversial incident." Booklist

Followed by Arrest Sitting Bull

A creek called Wounded Knee. Scribner 1978 236p o.p.   LC 78-16660

In the concluding volume of the trilogy, the author "tells the story of the Wounded Knee tragedy through the eyes of the principals: the Indians, the Federal troops, and the Press. Each chapter of the novel begins with a verbatim lead from an 1890 newspaper that if not finding the war inevitable at least found it irresistible. The Press did much to make the day." Best Sellers

"We all know what will happen here, and Jones vividly dramatizes it, but, perhaps more important, he dramatizes how it had to happen. For him people create history, and their actions, beliefs, foibles, aspirations, and apprehensions combine to make his 'Wounded Knee' not a historical pageant but a very human tragedy." Libr J

Jones, Edward P.

All Aunt Hagar's children. Amistad 2006 399p $25.95

ISBN 978-0-06-055756-0; 0-06-055756-7

LC 2006-42746

Contents: In the blink of God's eye; Spanish in the morning; Resurrecting Methuselah; Old boys, old girls; All Aunt Hagar's children; A poor Guatemalan dreams of a downtown in Peru; Root worker; Common law; Adam Robinson acquires grandparents and a little sister; The devil swims across the Anacostia River; Blindsided; A rich man; Bad neighbors; Tapestry

"In 14 short stories, Jones . . . demonstrates his skill at drawing complex and nuanced characters and predicaments. Washington, D.C., is the setting for this collection of stories in assorted time frames with assorted characters, most of whom come from the rural South, and all of whom are coping with the transformation of their lives and their adjustments to a new way of life. . . . Jones' stories are rich in detail and emotions as he plumbs the intricacies of people's relationships with one another and with spiritual forces at work in urban as well as natural environments." Booklist

The known world. Amistad 2003 388p $24.95

ISBN 0-06-055754-0   LC 2003-40389

Jones, Edward P.—*Continued*

"Henry Townsend, born a slave, is purchased and freed by his father, yet he remains attached to his former owner, even taking lessons in slave owning when he eventually buys his own slaves. Townsend is part of a small enclave of free blacks who own slaves, thus offering another angle on the complexities of slavery and social relations in a Virginia town just before the Civil War." Booklist

"There are few certified villains in the novel, white or black, because slavery poisons moral judgements at the root. . . . The freshness of this story lies in its very incongruity and strangeness." N Y Times Book Rev

Jones, James, 1921-1977

From here to eternity. Scribner 1951 861p o.p.
*

A story of Army life in Hawaii in the last months before Pearl Harbor. The chief characters are two soldiers—Pfc Robert Prewitt and First Sergeant Milton Warden—and the women they loved

"Mr. Jones has grappled with a variety of materials and handles some of them less successfully than others. There is a good deal of weak stuff in the two love affairs and the characterizations of the women, and the sorties into the field of general ideas are unimpressive. The book as a whole, however, is a spectacular achievement; it has tremendous vitality and driving power and graphic authenticity." Atlantic

The thin red line. Scribner 1962 495p o.p.
*

"The Thin Red Line is a kind of companion piece [to From here to eternity] which describes the Guadalcanal campaign. . . . Company C-for-Charlie is the 'hero' of this novel which has no hero—except the collective behavior of a wide and varied cross-section of American military men. . . . From the abstract strategy of the Guadalcanal campaign and the Big Brass who have come to watch the show, down to the fighting men who carry out the battle plans without knowing or caring about them, [it] is a many-leveled chronicle of the whole amphibious military operation." N Y Times Book Rev

"This novel will surely offend some readers, lavishly bespattered as it is with Anglo-Saxon words and physiological detail. Nevertheless, it bears the Jones stamp of authenticity and is a major combat novel of World War II." Ont Libr Rev
Followed by Whistle

Whistle. Delacorte Press 1978 457p o.p.
LC 77-11980

This is the final installment of Jones' war trilogy, which also includes From here to eternity and The thin red line. This book begins in 1943, when "four soldiers from an infantry company in the Pacific are sent by boat and train to an army hospital in Tennessee. . . . These men, who have known no security except what the company provided, are quickly unhinged by faithless wives and intolerable families, by their rage and despair at the human condition. . . . To stave off disintegration, these out-of-work warriors resort to . . . drink and brawls, politics and sex. . . . The outline for the conclusion of the book . . . has been pieced together [following his death] from Jones's notes and conversations by his friend and fellow writer Willie Morris." Newsweek

Jones, Lloyd, 1955-

Mister Pip. Dial Press 2007 256p $20
ISBN 978-0-385-34106-6; 0-385-34106-7
LC 2007-5224

First published 2006 in Australia

"Thirteen-year-old Matilda is at a loss to understand the violence that has torn apart her tropical island. Her village, caught in the cross fire of the conflict between government troops and local armed rebels, has lost its teachers. The only white man to stay behind, the eccentric Mr. Watts, married to a local woman who is generally thought to be mad, takes over the post as teacher and begins to read to the class from his favorite novel, Charles Dickens' Great Expectations. Initially flummoxed by the meanings of such alien words as frost and moors, Matilda and her classmates soon become entirely riveted by the story and identify so heavily with the orphan Pip that Victorian England becomes more real to them than their own hometown." Booklist

"The novel is a paean to the transformative power of literature, particularly its ability to occlude an unpleasant reality with a fictional alternative and to expand an individual's sense of possibility." N Y Sun

Jones, Sadie

Outcast. Harper 2008 347p $24.95
ISBN 978-0-06-137403-6; 0-06-137403-2

"An explosive drama, fuelled by the repression of 1950s Britain. Troubled 19-year-old Lewis Aldridge has never recovered from the death of his mother. After a stint in prison, he heads home and attempts to convince his father of his worth. But his good intentions crumble in the face of his father's disapproval, and Lewis reveals the horrifying realities that lie under the seemingly sedate rural community. Devastatingly good." Marie Claire

Jong, Erica

Fear of flying; a novel. Holt, Rinehart & Winston 1973 340p o.p.
*

Isadora Wing, the heroine "is twice-married, Barnard-educated, under thirty, and . . . fiercely restless. . . . In Vienna with her psychiatrist husband, she meets an English Laingian who . . . exhorts her to cast off marital ties and live by his self-proclaimed existentialist nonrules. . . . After two weeks of roaring about the Continent in a Triumph, coupling with each other and with strangers met in roadside camps, they split: it's time for the English existentialist to rejoin his wife and kids. Spirits intact, Isadora hunts up her husband's holiday digs; finding him away when she calls, she awaits his return (on the closing page) in his tub." Atlantic

"At times, Jong gets caught in clichés about women, men, sex, and Jewish mothers, all [of] which she could do without. However, when she takes herself more seriously, the language is penetrating, paying tribute to her worth as a poet." Libr J

Followed by How to save your own life (1977) and Parachutes and kisses (1984 paper only)

Sappho's leap; a novel. Norton 2003 316p $24.95
ISBN 0-393-05761-5
LC 2002-155113

Jong, Erica—*Continued*

A "interpretation of the life of the first known woman poet, Sappho, who lived on the island of Lesbos 2,600 years ago and wrote and performed poems of indelible candor and eroticism. Jong envisions Sappho as an ardent and adventurous soul who, while still in her teens, meet the love of her life (the rebel poet Alcaeus), reveals her poetic talents, and is forced into exile and marriage to a wealthy old drunk." Booklist

Jong's "effort to bring to life an ancient writer engrossed in politics, family and the creation of poety is a relief from the relentlessly everyday sincerity of much current 'women-oriented' writing." N Y Times Book Rev

Jönsson, Reidar, 1944-

My life as a dog; translated by Eivor Martinus. Farrar, Straus & Giroux 1990 219p o.p.

LC 89-46390

Original Swedish edition, 1983; this translation first published 1989 in the United Kingdom

"This novel focuses on "the thirteenth and fourteenth years of a Swedish boy named Ingemar Johansson. Ingemar's mother is dying of tuberculosis, and his absentee father is away at sea. Somehow Ingemar repeatedly falls into exploits, scrapes, and disasters that, he thinks, make his mother's condition worse. Ingemar is . . . sent away to live with his uncle. . . . [His dog Sickan] is put to sleep because no one can spare the time and attention to care for it." Horn Book

"The novel's anecdotal style accommodates a boy's confabulation. Occasionally wayward and a bit too long in their descriptions, his comedic exploits cast Ingemar as schlemiel, underdog and, yes, dog. . . . It is Sickan's fate that finally helps Ingemar come to terms with his dead mother." N Y Times Book Rev

Jordan, Hillary, 1963-

Mudbound; a novel. Algonquin Books of Chapel Hill 2008 328p $22.95

ISBN 978-1-56512-569-8; 1-56512-569-X

LC 2007-44471

"In 1946, Laura McAllan, a college-educated Memphis schoolteacher, becomes a reluctant farmer's wife when her husband, Henry, buys a farm on the Mississippi Delta, a farm she aptly nicknames Mudbound. Laura has difficulty adjusting to life without electricity, indoor plumbing, readily accessible medical care for her two children and, worst of all, life with her live-in misogynous, racist, father-inlaw. Her days become easier after Florence, the wife of Hap Jackson, one of their black tenants, becomes more important to Laura as companion than as hired help. Catastrophe is inevitable when two young WWII veterans, Henry's brother, Jamie, and the Jacksons' son, Ronsel, arrive, both battling nightmares from horrors they've seen, and both unable to bow to Mississippi rules after eye-opening years in Europe." Publ Wkly

"With authentic, earthy prose . . . Jordan picks at the scabs of racial inequality that will perhaps never fully heal and brings just enough heartbreak to this intimate, universal tale, just enough suspense, to leave us contemplating how the lives and motives of these vivid characters might have been different." San Antonio Express-News

Jordan, Laura *See* Brown, Sandra, 1948-

Jordan, Laura, 1948-

For works written by this author under other names see Brown, Sandra, 1948-

Josipovici, Gabriel, 1940-

(ed) Kafka, F. Collected stories

Joss, Morag

The night following. Delacorte Press 2008 354p $22

ISBN 978-0-385-34118-9; 0-385-34118-0

LC 2007034711

"While shopping for groceries, a middle-aged woman discovers her husband's infidelity — there's a condom wrapper in the glove compartment of their car. Driving home minutes later, she strikes and kills a bicyclist, then leaves the body by the side of the road. In The Night Following, a bleak, exquisitely written novel, Morag Joss braids together three stories of shattering loneliness that intersect in surprising, haunting ways." Entertainment Wkly

Joyce, Graham

The limits of enchantment. Atria 2005 263p $22

ISBN 0-575-07231-8

"Although it's 1966, Mammy Cullen, a beloved midwife in rural Hallaton, still dispenses a kind of herbal medicine that women have practiced since time immemorial. But times are changing and prejudices are building. When one of her remedies appears to kill a patient, the locals turn on Mammy. Her practice falls to Fern, her adopted daughter and apprentice, who soon finds herself confronting contemporary reality in several forms: Arthur, an amorous biker with marriage on his mind; an intrusive commune of feckless hippies who settle next door; and a devious landlord who schemes to evict her from her cottage." Publ Wkly

"Generally the prose is economical, hurrying along a plot which engages as a whole, despite the weight of Fern's introspection." Times Lit Suppl

Joyce, James, 1882-1941

Dubliners. Knopf 1991 lxvii, 287p $19

ISBN 0-679-40574-7

* LC 91-53001

First published 1914 in the United Kingdom; first United States edition published 1916 by Huebsch

Contents: The sisters; An encounter; Araby; Eveline; After the race; Two gallants; The boarding house; A little cloud; Counterparts; Clay; A painful case; Ivy day in the committee room; A mother; Grace; The dead

"This collection of 15 stories provides an introduction to the style and motifs found in Joyce's writing. The stories stand alone as individual scenes of Dublin society and are intertwined by the use of autobiography and symbolism." Shapiro. Fic for Youth. 3d edition

Finnegans wake. Viking 1939 628p o.p.

*

This novel is "written in a unique and extremely difficult style, making use of puns and portmanteau words, (using at least 40 languages besides English) and a very

Joyce, James, 1882-1941—*Continued*

wide range of allusion. The central theme of the work is a cyclical pattern of history, of fall and resurrection inspired by Vico's Scienza nuova. This is presented in the story of Humphrey Chimpden Earwicker, a Dublin tavern-keeper, and the book is apparently a dream-sequence representing the stream of his unconscious mind through the course of one night. Other characters are his wife Anna Livia Plurabelle, their sons Shem and Shaun, and their daughter Isabel." Oxford Companion to Engl Lit. 6th edition

A portrait of the artist as a young man; with an introduction by Richard Brown. Knopf 1991 xli, 318p $18

ISBN 0-679-40575-5

                      * LC 91-52979

"Everyman's library"

First appeared serially, 1914-1915 in the United Kingdom; first United States edition published 1916 by Huebsch

This autobiographical novel "portrays the childhood, school days, adolescence, and early manhood of Stephen Dedalus, later one of the leading characters in Ulysses. Stephen's growing self-awareness as an artist forces him to reject the whole narrow world in which he has been brought up, including family ties, nationalism, and the Catholic religion. The novel ends when, having decided to become a writer, he is about to leave Dublin for Paris. Rather than following a clear narrative progression, the book revolves around experiences that are crucial to Stephen's development as an artist; at the end of each chapter Stephen makes some assertion of identity. Through his use of the stream-of-consciousness technique, Joyce reveals the actual materials of his hero's world, the components of his thought processes." Reader's Ency. 4th edition

Ulysses; with an introduction by Craig Raine. Knopf 1997 xlv, 1076p $25

ISBN 0-679-45513-2

                                   *

"Everyman's library"

First published 1922

"The novel is constructed as a modern parallel to Homer's Odyssey. All of the action of the novel takes place in Dublin on a single day (June 16, 1904). The three central characters—Stephen Dedalus (the hero of Joyce's earlier Portrait of the Artist as a Young Man), Leopold Bloom, a Jewish advertising canvasser, and his wife Molly Bloom—are intended to be modern counterparts of Telemachus, Ulysses, and Penelope, and the events of the novel parallel the major events in Odysseus' journey home. The main stream of *Ulysses* lies in its depth of character portrayal and its breadth of humor." Merriam-Webster's Ency of Lit

Judd, Alan

Legacy. Knopf 2002 245p $24

ISBN 0-375-41484-3   LC 2002-16262

First published 2001 in the United Kingdom

This "spy thriller, set in the 1970s, begins when fledgling British agent Charles Thoroughgood receives an assignment: he is to persuade his former Oxford classmate, Viktor Koslov, now a liaison at the Soviet Embassy and apparently an undercover operative, to defect. But before

he can do it, Koslov stuns him with the revelation that Thoroughgood's late father, an engineer who also had a military career, was working as a KGB agent." Publ Wkly

"Comparisons with John le Carre are inevitable, but Judd's style is more straightforward and his worldview far more benign. While fans of explosive action may find it slow going, this elegant and understated literary thriller is a worthy addition to the growing genre of historical espionage fiction." Libr J

Julavits, Heidi

The uses of enchantment; a novel. Doubleday 2006 356p $24.95

ISBN 0-385-51323-2   LC 2006-45434

"A spooky coming-of-age tale set in West Salem, Massachusetts, a town whose witch-hanging history both captivates and circumscribes the lives of the teenage girls who reside there. One afternoon in 1985, sixteen-year-old Mary Veal disappears from field-hockey practice at the austere Semmering Academy; she reappears a few weeks later claiming to have been abducted. The truth of what happened is only hinted at in Mary's sexually charged experiences with her supposed captor and in her provocative exchanges with the therapist assigned to her case. He decides that Mary is lying—aspects of her story seem taken from a previous student's faked abduction, itself inspired by a centuries-old fable involving a kidnapped girl and witchcraft—but, it turns out, he is not without his own agenda. Julavits expertly keeps the reader baffled until the end, but beneath the mystery is a sophisticated meditation on truth and bias." New Yorker

July, Miranda

No one belongs here more than you; stories. Scribner 2007 205p $23

ISBN 978-0-7432-9939-8; 0-7432-9939-6

                              LC 2006-51156

Contents: The shared patio; The swim team; Majesty; The man on the stairs; The sister; This person; It was romance; Something that needs nothing; I kiss a door; The boy from Lam Kien; Making love in 2003; Ten true things; The moves; Mon plaisir; Birthmark; How to tell stories to children

"July writes about desire — to be understood, to be part of another person. . . . The engine that drives these stories is July's voice — the book is full of wistful, wonderful observations about the limits of connection, about the hopes and disappointments of intimacy." Los Angeles Times

Jungstedt, Mari, 1962-

The inner circle; English translation by Tiina Nunnally. St. Martin's Minotaur 2008 280p map $24.95

ISBN 978-0-312-36378-9; 0-312-36378-8

                              LC 2008-24761

Original Swedish edition, 2005

"In summer the Baltic island of Gotland, Beowulf's old stomping ground, offers stunning scenery for tourists and white nights for love and lust, all of which shape the backdrop of Det. Supt. Anders Knutas's investigation into one horrifying crime after another. . . . . The decapi-

Jungstedt, Mari, 1962-——*Continued*

tation of a harmless pony is followed by the 'threefold' Viking ritual murder of a female archeology student, who's been carrying on a torrid affair with a secret lover, then two more grisly executions, all punctuated by chilling glimpses into a psychopathic mind. The fluid translation evokes the stark economy of the ancient sagas, where all that mattered was how one fought and died. A little of that old warrior spirit still inhabits Jungstedt's tired, frustrated Swedish policemen and journalists, facing monsters within and without and, like Beowulf, never giving in." Publ Wkly

Just, Ward S.

Exiles in the garden; [by] Ward Just. Houghton Mifflin Harcourt 2009 279p $25

ISBN 978-0-547-19558-2; 0-547-19558-3

LC 2008-49572

"Born and bred to the political arena, Alec Malone, son of a powerhouse U.S. senator, becomes an outsider twice removed, first by choosing photography as his profession and then by turning down an assignment in Vietnam. Content with his wife Lucia, the daughter of a Czech refugee, Alec dislikes the neighborhood cocktail parties, where a cosmopolitan mix of émigrés and exiles makes Lucia aware of the cultural chasm running through her marriage. Alec is devastated when she leaves him and bemused when, much later, his daughter follows in Senator Malone's footsteps, though it's the sudden appearance of Lucia's long-lost father that provokes Alec to question the meaning of an existence that has avoided the barricades." Publ Wkly

"Wars and their consequences make exiles of all involved. The commando, the senator and Alec the observer form an triangle, but not an equilateral triangle. Ward Just is too astute for that. And he leaves us pondering that ageless question of where the personal becomes the political or if it is possible to maintain a distinction at all." Miami Herald

Forgetfulness; [by] Ward Just. Houghton Mifflin Co. 2006 258p $25

ISBN 978-0-618-63463-7; 0-618-63463-0

LC 2006-13906

"Thomas Railles, an American expatriate and former 'oddjobber' for the CIA, is a respected painter living with his beloved wife, Florette, in the south of France. On an ordinary autumn day, Florette goes for a walk in the hills and is killed by unknown assailants. Her death devastates Thomas, and in the weeks and months that follow he struggles to make sense of a world that seems defined by violence and pain. Each night Thomas tracks the war in Iraq on the evening news while Florette's killers remain at large. When French officials detain four Moroccan terrorists and charge them with Florette's murder, Thomas is invited to witness the interrogation." Publisher's note

"Just makes no easy declarations in this often arduously analytical novel. . . . Thomas knows that forgetfulness is not a reasonable response to assault, either personal or national. But he also knows the utter futility of vengeance. This is the paradox that wrenches him in this mature meditation on the personal, private grief that's cultivated in a global war on terror, the search for subtle moral truths in a climate of slogans and curses." Washington Post Book World

An unfinished season; [by] Ward Just. Houghton Mifflin 2004 256p $24

ISBN 0-618-03669-5

* LC 2004-42722

"Set in 1950's Chicago during a single summer, this novel recounts the story of the owner of a printing company, the narrator's father, who is on the management side of a vicious union dispute and begins to carry a gun. Wilson Raven, his son, takes a summer job at a scandal rag, where no amount of ink on his sleeves lives down the day he arrives at work wearing his bowed dancing shoes from debutante balls on the ritzy North Shore." Economist

"Even if the setting of Just's . . . novel is the Midwest instead of Washington, Saigon or Paris, the territory is familiar: it's the world of memory tinged with regret. It's the early 1950s, the dawn of the cold war and the Red scare. . . This is vintage Just: elegant writing that captures the wounded spirit of the times." Newsweek

The weather in Berlin; [by] Ward Just. Houghton Mifflin 2002 305p $24

ISBN 0-618-03668-7

LC 2001-51885

This novel "follows a burned-out American movie director on a three-month stay at an artists-and-intellectuals institute in the capital of the new Germany. At 64, Dix Greenwood is remembered for a film made decades ago, an art-house favorite set in a German lake village just after World War I. . . . Ailing physically, tantalized by a fading memory of artistic inspiration, resenting his actress wife for her still-active career, Greenwood repairs to the city Willy Brandt once called Germany's Schicksalstadt, city of destiny. Berlin is experiencing a rebirth; perhaps Dix will too." N Y Times Book Rev

K

Kadare, Ismail

Agamemnon's daughter; a novella and stories; translated from the French of Tedi Papavrami and Jusuf Vrioni by David Bellos. Arcade Publishing 2006 226p $24

ISBN 9781559707886; 1-55970-788-7

LC 2006-18639

"This miscellany contains the title novella, finished in 1985 and published here in English for the first time, and two stories. The novella, a companion to Kadare's The Successor, follows one day in the life of a young, unnamed journalist about to attend a celebratory May Day parade. . . . His 'half-girl, half-woman' lover, Suzana, whose father's political star is on the rise, has just left the journalist in a sort of political sacrifice (the journalist is 'practically engaged to someone else' and it looks bad). Through a wry and compelling set of ruminations on the grandstand, the journalist finds that a government that would deny young love denies humanity, and seeks the isolation of every citizen—which in turn pits neighbor against neighbor in a fever of paranoid denunciation. That simple but powerful insight also lies behind the two shorter, more allegorical works in the collection, 'The Blinding Order' and 'The Great Wall,' which were completed in 1984 and 1993 respectively." Publ Wkly

Kadare, Ismail—*Continued*

Agamemnon's daughter [novella]

In Kadare, I. Agamemnon's daughter

The general of the dead army; a novel; [translated from the French of Jusuf Vrioni by Derek Coltman] Arcade Pub. 2008 264p $24.95

ISBN 978-1-55970-790-9   LC 2008-06946

Original Albanian edition, 1963; this translation first published 1971 in the United Kingdom and 1991 in the United States by New Amsterdam Books

"The book's protagonist is an Italian army officer who has come to Albania to recover the bodies of soldiers who died twenty years earlier in World War II. The General and his team carry crudely drawn maps and directions to burial sites supplied by aging war veterans. At first, the General fantasizes about returning home in triumph with his army of dead soldiers, but his optimism quickly fades. Rain and cold weather make recovery difficult, and the sullen Albanians continue to treat the Italians as invaders. . . . Before long, the General is haunted by terrifying dreams and hallucinations. He starts to see living people as skeletal remains and, fatally, begins to feel sympathy for the Albanians. This gloomy but powerful antiwar novel provides an excellent introduction to Albania's best-known author." Libr J

Spring flowers, spring frost; a novel; translated from the French of Jusuf Vrioni by David Belos. Arcade Pub. 2002 182p $23.95

ISBN 1-55970-635-X   LC 2002-20877

Original Albanian edition 2000

"Mark Gurabardhi, an artist in his late twenties, experiences the unfamiliarity of life after Communism in the provincial Albanian town where he was posted by the former regime. It feels almost like a loss not to be spied on, and he and his girlfriend thrill to words like 'heist,' so modern and Western do they seem. The couple discover, however, that dictatorship is replaced not so much by modernity as by old, crippling superstitions and family feuds. Throughout the book, images of icebergs, the Titanic, and enchanted snakes recur. . . . The result is like a dream-seemingly full of stirring meanings whose interpretations remain tantalizingly out of reach." New Yorker

The Successor; a novel; translated from the French of Tedi Papavrami by David Bellos. Arcade Publishing 2005 207p $24

ISBN 1-55970-773-9   LC 2005-10311

Original Albanian edition, 2003

This novel "depicts an Albania governed by the whim and vanity of the aging Guide when the Successor, second in command, is found dead in his bedroom. The international intelligence community and the citizens of Albania contemplate the questions of how the Successor fell from grace and whether he died through murder or suicide. From day to day, the official word varies as the Guide decides whether the Successor is an enemy of the state or a martyr for the party. Drawing on real events–Mehmet Shehu was poised to succeed Albanian dictator Enver Hoxha in 1981 when he mysteriously died–Kadare successfully builds suspense by portraying multiple suspects with the motivation to commit murder; all believe they are guilty of the crime in some small or large way." Libr J

The three-arched bridge; translated from the Albanian by John Hodgson. Arcade Pub. 1997 184p

ISBN 1-55970-368-7

* LC 96-41236

Originally written 1976-1978; published in French translation 1993

In this "matter-of-fact parable, a fourteenth-century Albanian monk attempts to 'record the lie we saw and the truth we did not see' about the building of a stone bridge that is a threatening wonder to the local people. The lie is the myths and legends exploited by the foreign builders to destroy their competitors; the truth is the mercenary nature of their crime. Kadare manages to appeal to a sense of outrage and hunger for evidence even as he suggests the outlines of today's Balkans." New Yorker

Kafka, Franz, 1883-1924

Amerika; the man who disappeared; translated and with an introduction by Michael Hofmann. New Directions 2002 216p $23.95

ISBN 0-8118-1513-X

*

Original German edition, 1927; this translation first published 1996 in the United Kingdom

The narrative of this unfinished novel "concerns the efforts of young Karl Rossmann, newly arrived in America, to find his place in an enigmatic and hostile society."

"Kafka left six completed chapters and a number of additional scenes, two of which appear in English for the first time in this new translation. . . . Anything by Kafka is worth reading again, especially in the hands of such a gifted translator as Hofmann." N Y Times Book Rev

The castle. Knopf 1992 xxxviii, 378p $17

ISBN 0-679-41735-4

* LC 92-52904

"Everyman's library"

Original German edition, 1926; this translation first published 1930

In this unfinished novel, the hero, "known only as K., is constantly frustrated in his efforts to gain entrance into a mysterious castle to which he believes he has been summoned to work as a land surveyor. The castle is administered by an extraordinarily complicated and incompetent bureaucratic hierarchy that refuses to either recognize or reject K.'s claim. He is put to work instead as a school janitor and is denied his right to practice his craft. According to Brod, Kafka intended K., an ailing man throughout the novel, to die of exhaustion at the end of the novel." Reader's Ency. 4th edition

Collected stories; edited and introduced by Gabriel Josipvici. Knopf 1993 lv, 503p $21

ISBN 0-679-42303-6

* LC 93-1858

"Everyman's library"

Contents: Children on a country road; Unmasking a confidence trickster; The sudden walk; Resolutions; Excursion into the mountains; Bachelor's ill luck; The tradesman; Absent-minded window-gazing; The way home; Passers-by; On the tram; Clothes; Rejection; Reflections for gentlemen-jockeys; The street window; The wish to be a red Indian; The trees; Unhappiness; The judgment; The stoker; The metamorphosis; In the penal colony; The new advocate; A country doctor; Up in the gallery; An old manuscript; Before the law; Jackals and

Kafka, Franz, 1883-1924—*Continued*

Arabs; A visit to a mine; The next village; An imperial message; The cares of a family man; Eleven sons; A fratricide; A dream; A report to an Academy; The bucket rider; First sorrow; A little woman; A hunger artist; Josephine the singer; Description of a struggle; Wedding preparations in the country; The student; The angel; The village schoolmaster {the giant mole}; Blumfeld, an elderly bachelor; The Hunter Gracchus; The proclamation; The bridge; The Great Wall of China; The knock at the manor gate; An ancient sword; New lamps; My neighbor; A crossbreed {a sport}; A splendid beast; The watchman; A common confusion; The truth about Sancho Panza; The silence of the sirens; Prometheus; The city coat of arms; Poseidon; Fellowship; At night; The problem of our laws; The conscription of troops; The test; The vulture; The helmsman; The top; Hands; A little fable; Isabella; Home-coming; A Chinese puzzle; The departure; Advocates; Investigations of a dog; The married couple; Give it up!; On parables; The burrow

The complete stories; edited by Nahum N. Glatzer; with a new foreword by John Updike. Centennial ed. Schocken Bks. 1983 xxi, 486p il o.p. LC 83-3233

First published 1971

Contents: Description of a struggle; Wedding preparations in the country; The judgment; The metamorphosis; In the penal colony; The village schoolmaster; Blumfeld, an elderly bachelor; The warden of the tomb; A country doctor; The Hunter Gracchus; The Hunter Gracchus: a fragment; The Great Wall of China; A report to an Academy; A report to an Academy: two fragments; The refusal; A hunger artist; Investigations of a dog; A little woman; The burrow; Josephine the Singer; or, The mouse folk; Children on a country road; The tradesman; Unhappiness; Unmasking a confidence trickster; A dream; A fratricide; A visit to a mine; Jackals and Arabs; The bucket rider; An old manuscript; The knock at the manor gate; Eleven sons; My neighbor; A crossbreed; The cares of a family man; The silence of the sirens; The city coat of arms; The problem of our laws; The conscription of troops; First sorrow; Advocates; The married couple

"All of Kafka's writing, with the exception of his three novels, is collected here and includes a number of fairly long stories followed by a group of shorter pieces varying in length from several pages to a single paragraph." Booklist

Metamorphosis. Vanguard Press 1945 98p il o.p.

Written in 1915 this is "often regarded as Kafka's most perfectly finished work. 'The Metamorphosis' begins as its hero, Gregor Samsa, awakens one morning to find himself changed into a huge insect; the story proceeds to develop the effects of this change upon Samsa's business and family life and ends with his death. It has been read as everything from a religious allegory to a psychoanalytic case history; it is notable for its clarity of depiction and attention to significant detail, which give its completely fantastic occurrences an aura of indisputable truth, so that no allegorical interpretation is necessary to demonstrate its greatness." Reader's Ency. 4th edition

also in Kafka, F. Collected stories p73-128

also in Kafka, F. The complete stories

also in Kafka, F. The metamorphosis and other stories p117-92

also in Kafka, F. The penal colony: stories and short pieces

also in Kafka, F. Selected short stories of Franz Kafka

The metamorphosis and other stories; translated by Joachim Neugroschel. Scribner 1993 xxiii, 227p pa $13 hardcover o.p.

ISBN 0-684-80070-5 LC 92-43912

The longer stories included are: Conversation with the worshiper; Conversation with the drunk; Children on the highway; Exposing a city slicker; The businessman; Unhappiness; The judgment; The stoker; The metamorphosis; An ancient manuscript; Jackals and Arabs; A fratricide; A dream; A report for an Academy

This is a collection of thirty stories, some of which are quite short. The stories are arranged in order of their original publication dates.

The penal colony: stories and short pieces; translated by Willa and Edwin Muir. Schocken Bks. 1948 320p il o.p.

Stories included are: The judgment; The metamorphosis; A country doctor; In the penal colony; A hunger artist

Selected short stories of Franz Kafka; translated by Willa and Edwin Muir; introduction by Philip Rahv. Modern Lib. 1993 xxv, 346p

ISBN 0-679-60061-2 LC 93-14747

First Modern Library edition published 1952

Contents: The judgment; The metamorphosis; In the penal colony; The Great Wall of China; The country doctor; Common confusion; New advocate; Old manuscripts; A fratricide; Report to an Academy; Hunter Gracchus; A hunger artist; Investigations of a dog; The burrow; Josephine the singer

The trial; translated from the German by Willa and Edwin Muir; revised, with additional notes, by E. M. Butler. Knopf 1992 299p $19

ISBN 0-679-40994-7

"Everyman's library"

Original edition 1924; first Everyman's Library edition, 1922

"Joseph K., a respected bank assessor, is arrested and spends his remaining years fighting charges about which he has no knowledge. The helplessness of an insignificant individual within a mysterious bureaucracy where answers are never accessible is described in this provocative and disturbing book." Shapiro. Fic for Youth. 3d edition

Kafka, Kimberly

Miranda's vines. Dutton 2004 258p $23.95

ISBN 0-525-94763-9

"Since college, Miranda and Bridie's relationship has been that of sisters, surpassing any friendship by the depth of their commitment. It was Bridie Miranda relied upon when her husband died before their son could be born, and it was Bridie Miranda called again when her father died, bequeathing her the struggling Oregon vine-

Kafka, Kimberly—*Continued*

yard to which he'd devoted his life. Now it's Miranda's turn. When Bridie, a champion Idatarod sledder, is critically injured, legs paralyzed and dangerously depressed, Miranda brings Bridie back to the vineyard she is reluctantly calling home again. In this lustrous tale of loyalty and devotion, Kafka limns the depths of intimacy and explores the nature of relationships, from mother to son, father to daughter, neighbor to stranger, and friend to friend." Booklist

Kalfus, Ken

The commissariat of enlightenment; a novel. Ecco Press 2003 295p $24.95

ISBN 0-06-050136-7   LC 2002-69308

"For Comrad Astapov of the Agitprop Section of the Commissariat of Enlightenment, the filmmaker protagonist of this début novel, 'life's struggle was not to control events, but the way in which they were remembered.' His story begins in 1910, at the press-besieged deathbed of Tolstoy, where his talent for manipulating film to satisfy events earns the notice of Stalin. Astapov's distortions are the perfect metaphor for Kalfus's own special effects: Stalin, of course, wasn't there when Tolstoy died. Preoccupied with truth, media, history, and politics, this novel shows its mechanisms proudly." New Yorker

A disorder peculiar to the country; a novel. Ecco 2006 237p $24.95

ISBN 978-0-06-050140-2   LC 2005-52697

"Like their country, Marshall and Joyce Harriman, a Brooklyn Heights couple, are at war. They are one year into an impossibly bitter divorce, and their hatred for one another has 'acquired the intensity of something historic, tribal, and ethnic.' When Joyce watches the destruction of the World Trade Center she is seized by a 'great gladness,' because Marshall works on the eighty-sixth floor of the south tower. But he escapes to fight another day in the apartment that neither will relinquish, home to their two young children—'their divorce's civilian casualties.' Kalfus skewers the pieties surrounding 9/11, but having set his black comedy in the shadow of that national trauma, he reverently charts the powerful sway that world events briefly held over the lives of individual Americans." New Yorker

Kallos, Stephanie

Broken for you. Grove Press 2004 371p $24

ISBN 0-8021-1779-1   LC 2004-40631

"Margaret Hughes lives alone in a Seattle mansion, divorced from her husband after the death of their son. She talks to her father's priceless antique porcelain collection and spends her days dusting. Wanda Schultz, abandoned as a child by her parents, cannot accept the rejection of her lover, Peter, whose solitary postcard brings her across the country in search of him. When cancer sends Margaret a wakeup call, she opens her home and her heart: first to Wanda and then to a flood of other new 'family' members as she learns to interact with people and eventually to atone for a past crime she only gradually understands." Booklist

"The novel itself is a mosaic of eccentric characters and their interlocking storylines, which sometimes border

on the fantastic. . . . So lovely is the world Kallos has created that it seems more reparative to curl up on the couch with this book and suspend belief than to deconstruct the plot." Washington Post Book World

Sing them home. Atlantic Monthly Press 2009 542p $25

ISBN 978-0-87113-963-4

"The Jones family would seem to have no luck. Aneira Hope Jones, already terminally ill, was swept away by a tornado in 1978. Now her husband has been felled by lightning, and his longtime mistress, Viney—best friend to his wife and virtually the stepmother of his three children—must rally alientated, overweight art scholar Larken; sex-obsessed Gaelen, a famed weatherman mostly because of his family history; and their slightly nutty little sister, Bonnie. The Jones siblings have had far from perfect lives. But they're also rooted in the warm and sensible little town of Emlyn, NE, proud of its Welsh heritage, and this fresh, invigorating novel fingers carefully through their pain." Libr J

Kamensky, Jane

Blindspot; by a gentleman in exile and a lady in disguise; [by] Jane Kamensky and Jill Lepore. Spiegel & Grau 2008 500p $24.95

ISBN 978-0-385-52619-7; 0-385-52619-9

LC 2008-3111

"Set in 1760s Boston, Blindspot evokes the rollicking bawdiness, humor, and wit of that turbulent era. The story concerns Stewart Jameson, a Scottish portrait painter who flees to Boston to escape debts at home. Seeking an apprentice, he takes on Fanny Easton, a disowned daughter from a prominent Boston family who is masquerading as a boy — a ruse that makes for some hilarious scenes. The narrative is propelled forward by a budding romance and a murder mystery, which plays out as the first stirrings of the looming revolution grip colonial Boston." Chron of Higher Educ

Kaminsky, Stuart M.

The big silence; an Abe Lieberman mystery. Forge 2000 268p $23.95

ISBN 0-312-86926-6

*   LC 00-31811

"A Tom Doherty Associates book"

Chicago cop Lieberman and "his morose partner, Bill Hanrahan, find themselves backed into a corner by a blackmailer who kills a mob informant's ex-wife, kidnaps his 17-year-old son and threatens to do away with the boy unless the informer pledges ultimate silence—by committing suicide. And that's only the first labor of the day for this herculean cop. Heaping one calamity on top of another, Kaminsky piles up a whole stack of woe to try his hero's soul." N Y Times Book Rev

Blood and rubles; a Porfiry Petrovich Rostnikov novel. Fawcett Columbine 1996 257p

ISBN 0-449-90949-2   LC 95-23885

"Rubles are scarce in Moscow, but Chief Inspector Porfiry Rostnikov and his subordinates are up to their shoe tops in blood: a shootout apparently involving a Mafia scheme to sell fissionable material to the highest bidder; three nearly feral small boys who kill passerbys for whatever they carry; and the kidnapping of a wealthy

Kaminsky, Stuart M.—*Continued*

businessman that turns into multiple murders. . . . It's hard not to feel compassion for the cops and the Moscovites in general, and Kaminsky is deft at creating this feeling with small, telling details of ordinary life." Booklist

A cold red sunrise; an Inspector Porfiry Rostnikov mystery. Scribner 1988 210p o.p.

LC 88-15359

"Inspector Porfiry Rostnikov of the Moscow police . . . is assigned to Tumsk in deepest Siberia. . . . Two people have died mysteriously—the young and beautiful daughter of a famed dissident father who is scheduled, in the new climate of 'glasnost,' to depart for the West, and the police Commisar from Moscow who was sent to Tumsk to investigate her death. With him on this mission is his trusted associate, Emil Karpo." West Coast Rev Books

"The author has fine-tuned Porfiry and Karpo into a delightful sleuthing team and a fascinating study in odd contrasts." Booklist

Dancing in the dark. Mysterious Press 1996 228p o.p.

LC 95-13095

"In 1943, Arthur Forbes is a respected California businessman, but not too many years earlier he lived in Detroit and was known as Fingers Intaglia because he liked to remove the fingers of his victims. Luna, his mistress, wants to learn to dance, and she wants Fred Astaire to teach her. . . . To get Luna and her lover off his back, Astaire hires Toby Peters, private eye to the stars. When Luna drops dead at Toby's feet, Fingers is ready to resume his former profession but doesn't want a scandal. A deal is cut: If Toby can find the killer, he can live." Booklist

The author "effortlessly choreographs Hollywood history, colorful cast and dirty doings." Publ Wkly

Death of a Russian priest. Fawcett Columbine 1992 223p o.p.

LC 91-58638

In this Inspector Porfiry Rostnikov mystery "two crimes need solving: the disappearance of a Syrian diplomat's daughter and the ax murder of a prominently outspoken priest. The missing girl becomes the preoccupation of Rostnikov's emotionally messed-up young assistant Sasha, while Rostnikov himself, working with the vampiric Karpo, uncovers the priest's secret life, hindered by silent friends who seem to be dying for their loyalty." Booklist

The dog who bit a policeman. Mysterious Press 1998 275p

ISBN 0-89296-667-X

* LC 98-13385

This Inspector Rostnikov novel "interweaves three crimes, all set amidst corrupt, Mafia-ridden contemporary Moscow: the disappearance of a politician, the serial murder of members of two rival gangs, and an illegal, big-money dogfight ring." Libr J

"Kaminsky takes care not to rob the beleaguered cops of their human core—a courtesy he also extends to Moscow, which comes across as a character in its own right: rough and dangerous and somehow tragic." N Y Times Book Rev

A fatal glass of beer. Mysterious Press 1997 246p o.p.

LC 96-49494

Hollywood private investigator Toby Peters "and W.C. Fields cross the country (chauffeured by a Swiss midget) in search of Lester O. Hipnoodle, the villian who has somehow gained access to Field's numerous hidden bank accounts." Libr J

The author "balances one-liners from Fields with headlines about the war effort in this amiable adventure that delivers a nicely twisted plot with fully dimensioned characters, including the usually caricatured misanthropic comedian." Publ Wkly

Hard currency. Fawcett Columbine 1995 247p o.p.

LC 94-28273

This Inspector Porfiry Rostnikov mystery takes the "Moscow detective to Havana, where he investigates the murder of a Cuban woman who was apparently killed by a minor intelligence officer in the Russian embassy. . . . Meanwhile, back in Moscow, Rostnikov's associate Emil Karpo is tracking down a vicious serial killer whose single-minded precision chillingly matches Karpo's own thought processes. Kaminsky, one of the genre's finest storytellers, is at the peak of his powers here." Booklist

Lieberman's choice; [by] Stuart Kaminsky. St. Martin's Press 1993 216p o.p.   LC 92-40797

"A Thomas Dunne book"

Abe Lieberman is "an aging Jewish Chicago cop who's comfortable and at ease on the street but troubled by his domestic life. He can handle the perpetrators but is puzzled by the paths that end in violence. The case here involves a cop who kills his wife and her lover and then barricades himself atop an apartment building. Political expediency clashes repeatedly with prudence as Abe struggles with the situation." Booklist

"Abe's conversation—whether with his old Jewish buddies, some small-time cons or his family—is pure pleasure, with never a false, extraneous note." Publ Wkly

Lieberman's day; [by] Stuart Kaminsky. Holt & Co. 1994 260p

ISBN 0-8050-2575-8   LC 93-22910

Chicago homicide detective Abe Lieberman's "nephew, David, and David's pregnant wife are shot in a late night mugging. David dies; his wife and unborn child survive, barely. Lieberman gets the case and in the following 24 hours deals with the grief of his brother and sister-in-law, the aftereffects of the collapse of his daughter's marriage, the desperate deal he cuts with a violent drug-dealer called El Perro to catch the killers and the busting of two con artists." Publ Wkly

The author is "extraordinarily attuned to the domestic minutiae of his detectives' lives." N Y Times Book Rev

Lieberman's folly; [by] Stuart Kaminsky. St. Martin's Press 1991 216p o.p.   LC 90-49309

"A Thomas Dunne book"

This mystery "features the partnership of Chicago cops Abe 'Rabbi' Lieberman and Bill 'Father Murphy' Hanrahan. When prostitute Estralda Valdez, a past informer, asks the pair for protection, tippler Hanrahan agrees to watch her apartment from a Chinese restaurant across the street. After Valdez is murdered during Hanrahan's watch, he and Lieberman investigate her death, despite the objections of their captain, who is unhappy about negative publicity." Publ Wkly

Kaminsky, Stuart M.—*Continued*

Lieberman's thief; [by] Stuart Kaminsky. Holt & Co. 1995 238p
ISBN 0-8050-2576-6　　　　　LC 94-27304

"George Patniks is a professional burglar and a good one. Unfortunately, the day he has chosen to burgle the Rozier home turns out to be the same day Mr. Rozier has chosen to kill Mrs. Rozier. . . . Chicago homicide detective Abe Lieberman and his partner Bill Hanrahan immediately suspect Rozier, but they have nothing on which to build a case. Kaminsky captures the sights and sounds of his Chicago setting most convincingly." Booklist

The man who walked like a bear; an Inspector Porfiry Rostnikov novel. Scribner 1990 261p o.p.
　　　　　LC 89-29082

"Beset by the usual demons (including the plumbing in his apartment), visited by a few new ones, and still a thorn in the side of the Soviet bureaucracy, Rostnikov must deal with a host of problems: . . . a plot to kill a Politburo member, shady deals in a Moscow shoe factory, and several demented nationalists who mastermind a scheme to destroy Lenin's tomb. Then there's the inspector's sick wife to visit in the hospital and the matter of getting his son out of the military." Booklist

"Kaminsky masterfully balances stories of family life, humorous anecdotes and riveting suspense involving his distinctive characters." Publ Wkly

Murder on the Trans-Siberian Express. Mysterious Press 2001 277p
ISBN 0-89296-747-1　　　　　LC 2001-26218

"The action reaches back to Siberia in 1894, when one man in a band of starving, disease-ridden convicts, sentenced to work on constructing the great rail line from Moscow to Vladivostok, buries his treasure—a leather pouch containing a tiny gold box with a letter inside. More than a century later, Inspector Porfiry of the Moscow Police is sent on the 6,000-mile rail line to find this box. Porfiry leaves behind two other investigations: the kidnapping of a skinhead rock star and a series of murders in the Moscow Metro. How Kaminsky weaves these tangled plot lines into a taut suspense fabric, while providing fascinating, sad-funny commentary on his characters and the tensions inherent in the new Russian social order, is a matter of wonder." Booklist

Not quite kosher; an Abe Lieberman mystery. Forge 2002 254p $23.95
ISBN 0-312-87453-7

This installment "finds Lieberman trying to cope with a jewelry heist gone bad, a potential gang war, two corpses washed up from Lake Michigan and his grandson's bar mitzvah." N Y Times Book Rev

"Although Kaminsky can plot with the best of them, his characters are the real delights of the book." Publ Wkly

Retribution; a Lew Fonesca novel. Forge 2001 272p
ISBN 0-312-87452-9　　　　　LC 2001-40483
"A Tom Doherty Associates book"

Lew Fonesca "rescued a teenage prostitute named Adele in 'Vengeance' and left her in the care of a rich and vulgar (but really sweet and lonely) widow who promised to put the girl through high school. Adele is in trouble again . . . and Lew has been charged with finding out why she skipped town with a cache of manuscripts, the unpublished life's work of the reclusive, Salingeresque author who was tutoring her." N Y Times Book Rev

Rostnikov's vacation; an Inspector Porfiry Rostnikov novel. Scribner 1991 244p o.p.
　　　　　LC 91-13874

"While on forced vacation in Yalta, Rostnikov chances upon the murder of an acquaintance from military intelligence. He also befriends an American policeman, who points out the man tailing Rostnikov. Back in Moscow, meanwhile, Rostnikov's subordinates track a beautiful young woman and two accomplices connected with the murder of a German businessman. Kaminsky solidly and ably controls all these complications, but not without offering certain political vagaries, a cold-blooded atmosphere, and a certain dry humor." Libr J

Terror town; an Abe Lieberman mystery. Forge 2006 256p $23.95
ISBN 0-765-31164-X　　　　　LC 2005-15690
"A Tom Doherty Associates book"

In this procedural featuring Chicago cops Abe Lieberman and Bill Hanrahan, "the focus is on sudden downfall: a former Cubs player is derailed by a blow to the head, making him depressed and fearful; a young woman whom Lieberman saved from a theft charge in another novel is slain on a city sidewalk; Hanrahan's hard-won happiness is jeopardized by a stalker." Booklist

Kaminsky "plots well and plays fair, while Lieberman keeps chaos at bay, holding his neighborhood together through the sheer force of his goodness." N Y Times Book Rev

To catch a spy; a Toby Peters mystery. Carroll & Graf Pubs. 2002 230p $24
ISBN 0-7867-1023-3　　　　　LC 2002-67254
"An Otto Penzler book"

In this installment the author supposes Cary Grant "to have been a British intelligence agent, his job to detect the activities of Nazi sympathizers in Hollywood. Married to Woolworth heiress Barbara Hutton at the time, he finds more pro-Nazis among his wife's rich friends than among the acting community. Grant hires Toby, who packs a .38 with which he's unable to hit the broad side of a sound stage, to deliver a satchel of money in the dark of night to a man who'll give him an envelope in return." Publ Wkly

Tomorrow is another day. Mysterious Press 1995 201p o.p.
　　　　　LC 94-18987

"Set during World War II, when Hollywood was at its most glamorous, the plot involves the mysterious stabbing death of an extra on the set of Selznick International's *Gone with the Wind*. Five years after the murder, the debonair Clark Gable approaches Toby [Peters] to ask for help—seems Gable's been receiving bizarre death threats in the form of poems. . . . Nostalgic readers with a yen for the good old days—when men were men and movies were *movies*—will find Kaminsky's story entertaining, clever, eminently readable, and chock-full of snippets from Hollywood's Golden Age." Booklist

Vengeance; a Lew Fonesca mystery. Forge 1999 328p
ISBN 0-312-86927-4　　　　　LC 99-38393

Kaminsky, Stuart M.—*Continued*

"A Tom Doherty Associates book"

"Fonesca is a middle-aged, widowed process server, a transplanted Chicagoan who has made a new home in Sarasota, Fla. . . . Occasionally he uses the investigative skills he developed while employed by the state attorney's office in Chicago to do a little ad hoc sleuthing. In [this novel] his skills and fortitude get stretched to the limit as he tries to locate two missing persons: a teenage girl whose sexually abusive and violent father has lured her away from her poverty-stricken mother, and a woman who has run away from her wealthy husband." Publ Wkly

Kanon, Joseph

The good German; a novel. Holt & Co. 2001 482p

ISBN 0-8050-6422-2   LC 2001-16968

"Jake Geismar, a U.S. reporter assigned to cover the Potsdam Conference for *Collier's* magazine, stumbles upon a story that is intertwined with his own life. Though he has returned to Berlin primarily to reunite with his prewar lover, Geismar confronts a Germany he no longer recognizes. Further, he is compelled to solve the murder of an American soldier found with a money belt stuffed with black market cash." Libr J

"Kanon hits every note just right, from the wide-angle descriptions of Berlin's pockmarked moonscape to the tellingly detailed portraits of the city's shellshocked survivors. Superb popular fiction, combining propulsive narrative drive with a subtle grasp of character and a fine sense of moral ambiguity." Booklist

Los Alamos; a novel. Broadway Bks. 1997 403p o.p.

LC 96-44055

This book's plot involves the murder of a security officer of the Manhattan Project, which developed the atomic bomb. "Michael Connolly, a civilian intelligence expert called to New Mexico to investigate the murder, soon finds himself entangled in the insular, secretive world of Los Alamos: first he falls in love with one of the scientist's wives, and then he comes under the . . . spell of Oppenheimer himself." Booklist

"'Los Alamos,' besides being a terrific mystery, wonderfully evokes the Southwest in the '40s, reminding us in a dozen subtle ways that life goes on even while history is being made." Newsweek

Kantner, Seth, 1965-

Ordinary wolves; Seth Kantner. 1st ed. Milkweed Editions 2004 324p $22

ISBN 1-571-31044-4   LC 2003-24025

"Growing up in the unforgiving wilderness with his back-to-the-land artist father and siblings, Cutuk learns all the traditional skills necessary for living off the tundra and develops an abiding love for wolves. But Cutuk is white, and although he reveres traditional native Alaskan ways and wants to be a great hunter, he remains an outsider. Then when the 1970s bring radical change even to this distant realm and his indigenous neighbors trade in their dogsleds for snowmobiles, he becomes even more of an anachronism. So he tries his luck in Anchorage, discovers an alien form of wilderness, and hastily acquires a whole new set of survival skills. At every turn, Kantner fearlessly orchestrates dramatic communions between humans and the wild, hilarious incidents of culture shock." Booklist

Kantor, MacKinlay, 1904-1977

Andersonville. World Pub. 1955 767p il o.p.

*

"After twenty-five years of research Kantor wrote this novel, which realistically portrays the atrocities of Andersonville Prison, home of many Yankee soldiers during the Civil War. Ira Claffey, Georgia planter and owner of the property on which Andersonville is built, serves as a humane central character whose sorrows and frustrations serve to point up the brutality of war. The primitive, indeed horrible, existence of the prisoners is described in detail." Shapiro. Fic for Youth. 3d edition

Kanwar, Asha

(ed) The Unforgetting heart: an anthology of short stories by African American women (1859-1993). See The Unforgetting heart: an anthology of short stories by African American women (1859-1993)

Kao, Hsing-chien *See* Gao Xingjian, 1940-

Kaplow, Robert

Me and Orson Welles; a novel. MacAdam/Cage Pub. 2003 269p $18.50

ISBN 1-931561-49-4   LC 2003-14982

"A comic coming-of-age novel set against the background of the twenty-two-year-old Orson Welles's debut production at the Mercury Theatre on Broadway. Richard Samuels is the stage struck seventeen-year-old from New Jersey who wanders onto the set one day and gets a small role in Welles's Julius Caesar. His life will never be the same." Publisher's note

"A delightful escape into a prewar coming-of-age, and coming-of-stage, story-perfect for a quick and totally entertaining read." Booklist

Karbo, Karen

Motherhood made a man out of me. Bloomsbury Pub. 2000 212p $23.95

ISBN 1-58234-083-8

This novel "contains two plots that are intertwined and equally weighted. There's the story of Brooke, the new mother of baby Stella, and her husband, Lyle—a mildly annoying, mildly dim would-be artist who can't understand why the fact that he looked after Stella for one evening a few weeks ago doesn't prove he's a good father. Then there's the story of Brooke's best friend, Mary Rose, a pregnant gardener who's engaged to marry Brooke's cousin Ward—a mildly annoying, mildly dim director of 'high-profile commercials' who forgot to tell Mary Rose that he's still married." N Y Times Book Rev

"Karbo writes about the intricacies of human nature and relationships with insight and humor, and her characters are realistic yet wonderfully over-the-top. The result is a fast-paced and delightful novel." Publ Wkly

Karinthy, Ferenc, 1921-1992

Metropole; translated from the Hungarian by George Szirtes. Telegram 2008 236p pa $14.95

ISBN 978-1-84659-034-4; 1-84659-034-5

Original Hungarian edition, 1970

"Budai, a linguist en route to a conference, steps off of a plane and finds himself not in Helsinki but in a land with an impenetrable language and a massive population swarming the streets and sidewalks. Every morning, he sets out to find his way home, or at least to find some-one who speaks Hungarian, and every night, he finds himself back at the hotel with his dwindling supply of money, bewildered by the world in which he is trapped. Karinthy's story is anxious and claustrophobic, but it's shot through with humor and surprising believability. Budai is relentless and resourceful, and Karinthy is a skilled enough writer that his protagonist's failed at-tempts to make headway never become monotonous. Metropole invites comparisons to Kafka, and manages to live up to them." NPR

Karnezis, Panos, 1967-

The maze. Farrar, Straus and Giroux 2004 376p $24

ISBN 0-374-20480-2   LC 2003-60261

"This novel is set in the 1920s, while Turkey was fighting for independence from Greece. The characters are either soldiers in the retreating Greek army, or Greek residents of a sleepy, doomed town where Christians used to live well. . . . The brigadier is addicted to mor-phine, his chief of staff is a secret communist and the padre, Father Simeon, is a hopeless kleptomaniac. In the town, the mayor and the schoolmaster compete for the attentions of the local courtesan, a Frenchwoman who is nurturing her own guilty secrets." Economist

"As with many an imperial expedition, the soldiers seem to be lost without honor; they massacre civilians on their fool's errand undertaken for worthless ends. Karnezis dramatizes their plight with remorseless clarity and dry humor." N Y Times Book Rev

Karon, Jan, 1937-

A common life; the wedding story. Viking 2001 186p il $24.95

ISBN 0-670-89437-0   LC 00-31984

This novel in the author's Mitford series focuses "on a key event in the life of Father Tim Kavanaugh—his marriage. The book begins with Father Tim's proposal to next-door-neighbor Cynthia and ends with their honey-moon at the bishop's summer cottage in Maine. In be-tween, Mitford's various residents prepare for the big day, each in his or her own way." Booklist

In this mountain. Viking 2002 382p $24.95

ISBN 0-670-03104-6   LC 2002-16877

In this Mitford novel "three years have passed since Father Tim Kavanagh and his wife, Cynthia, returned to Mitford from Whitecap Island, and depression and dis-content are gnawing away at the good cleric as he faces the big '7-0.' As Cynthia's career reaches new heights, Father Tim makes some personal decisions that lead to tragedy. . . . Homespun dialogue, fresh and lively de-scriptions, laugh-out-loud moments and poignant scenes mark the heartfelt book, which is a happy reunion form Mitford devotees." Publ Wkly

A new song. Viking 1999 400p $24.95

ISBN 0-670-87810-3   LC 98-55141

In this episode in the Mitford series "Father Tim Kavanagh heads for the islands to serve as an interim priest. Although most of the book takes place in his new parish, fans of Mitford's eccentric citizens are not left bereft. Frequent bulletins keep Father Tim up-to-date as well as worried about his former flock. While juggling news of mysterious thefts, the arrest of his adopted son, Dooley, and fights over historic properties, he also must deal with congregational squabbles, being a foster parent to an active three-year-old, surviving a terrible storm, and bringing a lonely man out of decades of solitude." Libr J

Out to Canaan. Viking 1997 342p $23.95

ISBN 0-670-87485-X   LC 97-5867

"Racing from one good deed to another, Father Timo-thy takes in stray sick folk, finds an abandoned child, and helps his favorite baker write a winning jingle. A mayoral race pitting the long-time mayor Esther Cun-ningham against the possibly corrupt Mack Stroupe makes for some colorful sparring. Father Timothy applies his own unique, time-honored method of intuition, prayer, or dietary indulgence to a multitude of problems big and small. His late-in-life marriage to Cynthia con-tinues to be a blessing readers will feel privileged to share." Libr J

Kasischke, Laura, 1961-

The life before her eyes. Harcourt 2002 273p $24

ISBN 0-15-100888-4   LC 2001-24311

"Diana and her best friend are confronted by a school-mate killer, but only Diana is spared. Fast-forward 20 years: Diana, now middle-aged and still beautiful, is a housewife and artist living in the same idyllic university town with a handsome professor-husband and a young daughter. She has seemingly repressed her memory of the event as well as her survivor's guilt, but her perfect world and her grip on reality are both starting to crack." Libr J

This novel "evokes terror and redemption, shadows and light. Kasischke treads a delicate line with the preci-sion and confidence of a tightrope walker." N Y Times Book Rev

Katkov, Norman

Blood & orchids. St. Martin's Press 1983 503p o.p.   LC 83-2889

"Set in Hawaii in the early '30s, [this] crime novel is based on an actual case. The story begins when a quartet of beach boys play Good Samaritan and end up accused of beating and raping the U.S. naval officer's wife they rescued, Hester Murdock. The trial brings to a boil the simmering racial tensions in the islands, and when it ends in a hung jury, vigilante justice takes over. Three of the boys are kidnapped and flogged by sailors, while the other is shot to death. A flamboyant trial lawyer named Bergman is imported from the States to defend the accused: Hester's husband, Gerald; Doris Ashby, her mother; and a hapless gob who was in the wrong place at the wrong time. As Honolulu detective Curt Maddox digs deeper into the matter, the situation is revealed to

Katkov, Norman—*Continued*

be even more sordid and scandalous than originally supposed. Studded with vivid characterizations, the story rolls inexorably to an awesome, tragic conclusion." Publ Wkly

Katzenbach, John

The analyst. Ballantine Bks. 2002 424p

ISBN 0-345-42626-6   LC 2001-43841

"On his 53rd birthday, a stodgy Manhattan psychoanalyst named Frederick Starks is given a life-or-death challenge by a cunning psychopath calling himself Rumplestiltskin. Starks has 15 days to identify his tormentor and the source of his grievance, or else commit suicide—unless he is willing to have some blameless relative die in his stead." N Y Times Book Rev

The author has "potently chronicled a long journey of revenge and redemption. Some of his psychological plot points . . . are a stretch, but the novel's fine sense of pacing, sudden switchbacks and chilling characterizations far overshadow its minor faults." Publ Wkly

Hart's war; a novel. Ballantine Pub. Group 1999 490p

ISBN 0-345-42624-X   LC 98-29890

"In 1942, Tommy Hart's B-25 is shot down over German territory. Prison life in Stalag Luft Thirteen is disrupted by the arrival of a young Tuskegee airman named Lincoln Scott. Capt. Vincent Bedford, a popular officer, is found murdered, and Scott is accused of the crime. Hart, formerly a Harvard law student, is assigned the nearly impossible task of defending a man who is presumed guilty because of his race and the preponderance of evidence pointing to him." Libr J

"Katzenbach's setting is flawlessly grim, and his characters chillingly reveal the divisive bigotry of soldiers ostensibly fighting for the same values, as well as some unexpected sources of redemption." Publ Wkly

Just cause. Putnam 1992 431p

ISBN 0-399-13626-6   LC 91-15135

"Matthew Cowart is at the top of his profession—a member of the editorial page staff of a major Miami newspaper. Cowart thinks his days as a crime reporter are behind him until he receives a letter from death row inmate Robert Ferguson, who not only proclaims his innocence, but also to have learned the identity of the real murderer. Cowart, his personal life a mess, takes the bait, hits the crime beat again, and writes a series of articles that lead to Ferguson's release and win the journalist a Pulitzer Prize. But Cowart has opened a Pandora's box of events which leads him to a showdown with the killer." Libr J

"Despite some extraneous subplots, the story generally proceeds at a breakneck pace, enhanced by ear-perfect dialogue and complex characterization." Publ Wkly

. The madman's tale. Ballantine Bks. 2004 438p $24.95

ISBN 0-345-46481-8

"When Francis Petrel, a former inmate of the Western State Hospital, returns for a commemoration, he begins to remember events surrounding the brutal rape and murder of a young nurse 20 years before. At the same time, prosecutor Lucy Jones has arrived to determine whether the nurse's death could be related to several recent kill-

ings. Despite the lack of help from hospital authorities, Lucy puts together a team made up of Francis, another inmate, and two orderlies. As his long-suppressed recollections become clearer, Francis goes off his medications and begins hearing voices and maybe having hallucinations. Poised between sanity and madness, he is able to empathize with others, much like a profiler, and begins to understand the killer, placing Lucy and her team in great danger." Libr J

The author "delivers an uplifting story of justice, friendship, mystery and, above all, the courage of certain men and women who rise up, no matter the circumstances, to defeat evil, no matter the consequences." Publ Wkly

State of mind. Ballantine Bks. 1997 409p

ISBN 0-345-38631-0   LC 97-1415

"The U.S. has become more horrible than anyone could imagine; crime is rampant, and all citizens carry semiautomatic or even automatic weapons. When a teenage girl is found dead in a supposedly crime-free area controlled by the government, called the Fifty-first State, the murder appears to be one of a series that began a number of years prior. The Fifty-first authorities turn to criminal-mind expert Jeffrey Clayton, who has little choice but to help out, even though it means he will meet with personal demons he didn't want to resurrect." Booklist

"Katzenbach is a master at creating believable people caught up in horrific situations." Libr J

The wrong man; a novel. Ballantine Books 2006 461p $25.95

ISBN 978-0-345-46483-5; 0-345-46483-4

      LC 2006-48254

"The one-night stand that Ashley Freeman, a Boston art history grad student, has with Michael O'Connell, a determined psychopath, leads to dire consequences. O'Connell quickly moves to obsessively control every aspect of Ashley's life, coupling a relentless will with ingenuity and computer skills that soon ensnare Ashley's loved ones as they seek to protect her from him. When their feeble attempts to buy or scare off O'Connell fail, Ashley's divorced parents, as well as her mother's lesbian partner, embark on a convoluted but ingenious plot of their own." Publ Wkly

"This haunting story will linger in your mind. . . . Katzenbach's wonderful, tense narrative flows effortlessly, drawing you deeper and deeper into a chilling atmosphere of evil, darkness, and shadows." Miami Herald

Kaufman, Bel

Up the down staircase. Prentice-Hall 1964 340p il o.p.

                   *

"Fresh from graduate study in English and crammed with pedagogy courses, young Sylvia Barrett begins her first year as a teacher in Calvin Coolidge High School. The experiences of this first year teacher, determined to remain true to her ideals despite the administrative confusion and organizational chaos of a New York City high school, form the core of Up the Down Staircase. . . . It tells its story through a series of letters, administrative memoranda, student compositions, suggestion box contributions, and intraschool communications." Best Sellers

Kaufman, Millard, 1917-2009

Bowl of cherries; a novel. McSweeney's Books 2007 326p $22

ISBN 9781932416831; 1-932416-83-8

"Judd Breslau is a child prodigy who leaves Yale at the age of 14 at his doctoral adviser's urging, only to fall in with Phillip Chatterton, a retired Egyptologist with poor hygiene who is working on his opus in a dilapidated mansion. Soon, Judd falls in love with Chatterton's daughter, develops a deep hatred for her boyfriend, befriends an international student, and eventually ends up arrested in Iraq, awaiting his own execution. These events, however unrelated they seem, are tied together by Kaufman's narration following no set time line, with the narrative alternating between the jail cell and the events leading Judd there." Libr J

"Kaufman's rapier-sharp prose and keen instinct for finding the absurd in everyday life makes this a social satire of the first order." LA Wkly

Kaufman, Sue

Diary of a mad housewife. Random House 1967 311p o.p.

*

"Bettina Balser, in her mid-thirties, with a husband, two daughters ages nine and seven, and a bright apartment on Central Park West, (New York City), has arrived at a point in her life where she has completely lost her way, her purpose, her identity. She is literally terrified of so many things . . . that she is also afraid she is losing her mind. She decides to write out the things that so alarm her, as a form of therapy." Best Sellers

Kavanagh, Paul *See* Block, Lawrence, 1938-

Kavenna, Joanna

Inglorious; a novel. Metropolitan Books 2007 286p $25

ISBN 978-0-8050-8189-3; 0-8050-8189-5

LC 2006-46868

The moment thirtysomething London journalist Rosa Lane quits her job "her life starts to fall apart. Her longtime boyfriend tells her to move out, her newly widowed father berates her, and the once-friendly bank manager can no longer tolerate her rising debt. Various friends only reluctantly allow her to stay in their flats. Rosa, it seems, is suffering more than a midlife crisis; she is wallowing in existential dread." Booklist

"Kavenna pursues the causes and trajectory of a nervous breakdown with a relentlessness that comes close to overwhelming the minimal plot; still, her understanding of the complexity of depression and her evocation of her heroine's bewilderment are precise, and Rosa, for all her misery, has an appealing and often funny voice." New Yorker

Kawabata, Yasunari, 1899-1972

Snow country

In Kawabata, Y. Snow country, and Thousand cranes p1-175

Snow country, and Thousand cranes; the Nobel Prize edition of two novels; translated from the Japanese by Edward G. Seidensticker. Knopf 1969 2v in 1 o.p.

First United States editions published 1957 and 1959, respectively

Snow country "describes the three visits of Shimamura, a rich Tokyo dilettante, to a hotspring in the west of Japan, the snowiest region in the world. Here a young geisha, Komako, becomes his mistress and falls in love with him. . . . Komako's sparkling freshness stirs him, and he is touched by the 'irresistible sadness' she makes him feel, a sense of beauty going to waste and of immanent decay. But he cannot return her love; and their strange relationship, to which she gives so much, is doomed from the start." Atlantic

The sound of the mountain; translated from the Japanese by Edward M. Seidensticker. Knopf 1970 276p o.p.

"This translation of the 1954 novel . . . is set in post-occupation Tokyo and Kamakura. An elderly businessman, nearing retirement, attempts to come to grips with the practical problems of the failing marriages of both his children and the psychological problems resulting from deaths of close friends and abortions completed or desired by his daughter-in-law and his son's mistress. Behind all is the nagging suspicion that his affection for his daughter-in-law is greater than that he has for his own daughter because the daughter-in-law resembles his early lost love, his wife's sister." Libr J

"The language is delicate, allusive, intensely Japanese; and, since plot and character development count for little, the style is all-important. We are fortunate that it should have been a writer with Mr. Seidensticker's gifts who ventured to convey [Kawabata's] rarefied novels into English." N Y Times Book Rev

Thousand cranes; translated by Edward G. Seidensticker. Knopf 1959 c1958 147p o.p.

*

Original Japanese edition, 1949

"This melancholy tale uses the classical tea ceremony as a background for the story of a young man's relationships to two women, his father's former mistress and her daughter. Although it has been praised for the beauty of its spare and elegant style, the novel has also been criticized for its coldness and its suggestion of nihilism." Merriam-Webster's Ency of Lit

also in Kawabata, Y. Snow country, and Thousand cranes p3-147

Kay, Guy Gavriel

The last light of the sun. Roc 2004 504p $24.95

ISBN 0-451-45965-2

A novel set during the "times when Vikings roamed the Anglo-Saxon and Welsh shores. . . . At the centre of the story is a young, self-exiled Viking who joins a Viking mercenary band. Set against the band are rival Welsh clans and their relations with Anglo-Saxon royalty. A fantastic element {in the novel concerns} . . . a faerie queen who claims the soul of a fallen prince." Publisher's note

"Kay's novel is an ambitious entertainment that transcends the historical record, offering cogent observations

Kay, Guy Gavriel—*Continued*

on fathers and sons, on the power of grief, on faith, courage, loyalty and the inevitability of change." Quill Quire

The summer tree. ROC 2001 383p map (The Fionavar tapestry) pa $16

ISBN 0-451-45822-2   LC 00-45803

First published 1984 in Canada

In this first book in the Fionavar tapestry series, "five university students embark on a journey of self-discovery when they enter a realm of wizards and warriors, gods and mythical creatures—and good and evil." Publisher's note

Followed by The wandering fire (1986) and The darkest road (1986)

Tigana. Penguin Bks. 1990 687p il map

ISBN 0-670-83333-9   LC 90-34423

"In a desperate attempt to revive the memory of a land banished from existence and to restore freedom to a battered world, a wandering musician and his small band of compatriots traverse a countryside bowed under the weight of its sorcerer-conquerors. . . . Memorable characters and cultures add depth to a gracefully plotted story." Libr J

Ysabel. Roc 2007 421p

ISBN 978-0-451-46129-2; 0-451-46129-0

     * LC 2006-28326

This novel is set in "Aix-en-Provence. Fifteen-year-old Ned is staying with his father, a renowned photographer, who is working on a book. While exploring the Saint-Sauveur Cathedral, he meets Kate, an exchange student from New York, and together they encounter a mysterious man rising from a grate in the baptistry." Quill Quire

"The author's historical detail, evocative writing and fascinating characters—both ancient and modern—will enthrall mainstream as well as fantasy readers." Publ Wkly

Kay, Terry

The runaway. Morrow 1997 406p

ISBN 0-688-15033-0   LC 97-16737

"Naively defying the mores of their small Georgia hometown, 12-year-olds Tom Winter, white, and Son Jesus Martin, black, have been friends their whole lives. But their twelfth summer brings change. Their accidental discovery of a human bone buried in a sawdust pile at an abandoned mill they pass while running away from home and the vicious rape of Son Jesus' sister by the family's white landlord set in motion events that forever change the boys' relationship and the way they see the world." Booklist

"The dialog is authentic and the storytelling has a homespun Southern texture." Libr J

Shadow song. Pocket Bks. 1994 388p o.p.

     LC 94-15369

"Naive and gentlemanly Madison Lee ('Bobo') Murphy is 17 when, in 1955, he leaves rural Georgia to work at a resort in the Catskills, where he experiences instant culture shock among the inn's Jewish clientele. He comes under the influence of Avrum Feldman, an elderly eccentric who has devoted his life to the memory of Amelita Galli-Curci, the legendary soprano. . . . Avrum encourages Bobo when he falls chastely in love with

Amy Lourie, a rich Jewish girl from New York visiting the resort with her protective parents. . . . Now, 38 years later, Bobo has returned to the Catskills to bury Avrum—and discovers that Amy is there too." Publ Wkly

"An absolutely enchanted and lyrical testimonial to the indomitable spirit of friendship and the tenacity of true love." Booklist

Kaye, M. M. (Mary Margaret), 1908-2004

The far pavilions. St. Martin's Press 1978 957p o.p.   LC 78-3975

This historical novel of India between the Mutiny of 1857 and the second Afghan war focuses on "the early life, loves, and military career of Ashton Pelham-Martyn, an impetuous Englishman born in mid-Victorian India, reared by a Hindu serving-woman, and educated in the stuffiest of British schools. Considered an odd duck by his fellow Englishmen for his liberal view on race, and held at arm's length by his Indian friends, Pelham-Martyn resolves undivided loyalties by serving as a secret agent for the British Guides. . . . A romantic subplot concerns his quest for an Indian princess he has loved all his life, and lost to a Rajah." Libr J

"It's a leisurely, panoramic, enjoyable tale, convincing and varied in characterization, rich in adventure, heroism, cruelty and love, rich in India." Publ Wkly

Shadow of the moon. St. Martin's Press 1979 614p o.p.   LC 79-5033

First published 1957 in the United Kingdom; an abridged version of this novel was published 1957, in the United States by Messner

The historical background of this novel "deals with the events leading up to and encompassing the Indian Mutiny of 1857, a rather haphazard rebellion by the Indian soldiers (Sepoys) against cruel and scornful British officers. . . . The novel tells the story of lovely Winter de Ballesteros, her premature engagement and marriage to the British Commissioner of Lunjore, her love for Captain Alex Randall, and her life and adventures in India. The book culminates in the bloody rebellion against the English which forces Alex and Winter, with two others, to flee into the shelter of the jungle." Best Sellers

The author exhibits "an intimate knowledge of Indian history, a deep feel for the land, unflagging vitality and an unfailing instinct for suspense. These qualities make her story delightfully readable." Publ Wkly

Kaye, Mary Margaret *See* Kaye, M. M. (Mary Margaret), 1908-2004

Kazantzakis, Nikos, 1883-1957

The last temptation of Christ; translated from the Greek by P. A. Bien. Simon & Schuster 1960 506p o.p.

"This novel is a retelling of the life story of Jesus of Nazareth as Kazantzakis imagined it might actually have happened, the human events from which the worshipful Gospel account was derived and their meaning to the people who experienced them." Atlantic

"The Christ created here by Kazantzakis is definitely not the Christ of the Gospels. . . . Far from it. Kazantzakis has composed a fictional biography of Jesus that is

Kazantzakis, Nikos, 1883-1957—*Continued*
written with passion, a colorful, lyric testimony of his,
Kazantzakis' own anguished search for God." Best Sellers

Zorba the Greek; translated by Carl Wildman.
Simon & Schuster 1952 311p o.p.

"The spirit of Zorba, full of energy and peasant philosophy, is contrasted with that of the narrator, a learned but staid Englishman who comes to Crete for adventure. The relationship between the two men deepens despite Zorba's mismanagement of the narrator's mining business, and despite Zorba's attempts to change his friend's behavior to a more zestful one. Kazantzakis creates in Zorba a character that represents the vitality sapped by the inhibitions civilization has created." Shapiro. Fic for Youth. 3d edition

Keating, H. R. F. (Henry Reymond Fitzwalter), 1926-

The bad detective. St. Martin's Minotaur 1999 279p
ISBN 0-312-24371-5   LC 99-33531
First published 1996 in the United Kingdom
"British copper Jack Stallworthy isn't a bad detective, exactly, but occasionally the opportunity has arisen for him to suppress evidence and, in the process, stash away a few pounds in his secret retirement fund. Jack's wife has decided on Ko Samui, a remote island paradise, as the perfect retirement spot, but Jack knows that his pension—even with the secret stash—won't be enough. So when a local entrepreneur asks Jack to steal a file from police headquarters in exchange for the deed to a hotel in Ko Samui, Jack can hardly believe his 'good luck.'" Booklist
"Keating's low-key sense of humor and his dexterity at making a crooked protagonist sympathetic are firmly in place, as is the story's satirical edge, which explores the disparity between the financial rewards received by criminals and police and the symbiotic relationship between cops and robbers." Publ Wkly

Bribery, corruption also. St. Martin's Press 1999 282p $23.95
ISBN 0-312-20502-3   LC 99-15494
"A Thomas Dunne book"
"Inspector Ghote, of the Bombay police, accompanies his wife to Calcutta in order to take possession of an inherited house. The hassles they encounter reveal corruption, conspiracy, and more." Libr J

Cheating death. Mysterious Press 1994 172p o.p.
    LC 94-9502
This "Inspector Ghote novel finds the lovable Indian detective embroiled in an academic cheating scandal, under pressure from his superiors and vexed by pressing domestic business. When a final exam paper is circulated throughout Bombay's Oceanic College prior to the test, Ghote is sent to investigate, only to find his prime suspect in a coma, having tried to commit suicide (Or was it a murder attempt?)." Publ Wkly

Doing wrong; an Inspector Ghote novel. Penzler Bks. 1994 218p o.p.   LC 94-9287
"From Bombay, the exquisitely courteous, ever persistent police detective, Inspector Ghote, travels to the holy city of Banaras to find the murderer of the much loved Mrs. Popatkar, 'veteran freedom fighter, former Minister, upholder of a hundred good causes'. . . . In spite of a leisurely pace befitting a country where foot-sore pilgrims, sacred cattle and auto rickshaws clog the roads, this is an absorbing tale and an illuminating tour of Banaras." Publ Wkly

The good detective; a mystery. Scribner 1995 199p o.p.   LC 95-9078
"Detective Ned French is smooth talking, ambitious, talented, and sure to move up quickly in the Norchester police. . . . Trouble is, Ned's so obsessed with keeping Norchester free of crime that he completely loses his good judgment. First, there's an illicit and ill-advised affair with attractive barrister Deborah Brooke, and then he foolishly covers up a damning incident from his past. Finally Ned makes his biggest mistake—a unilateral and extremely unwise decision about how to deal with a gang of 'London thugs' who are threatening Norchester. Deeply affecting and superbly written, this is an outstanding police procedural and a moving human drama." Booklist

Inspector Ghote trusts the heart. Doubleday 1973 c1972 201p o.p.

"Published for the Crime Club"
First published 1972 in the United Kingdom
In this mystery "Inspector Ghote is the go-between in a kidnapping case. The child of a rich man is snatched. A mixup follows, and it is a poor man's son who is taken. The kidnappers still hold the rich man up for ransom, posing him with a terrible dilemma." N Y Times Book Rev
The author "writes with wonderful ease and energy—his understanding of the individuality of human beings is profound." New Yorker

The soft detective. St. Martin's Press 1998 268p
ISBN 0-312-19335-1   LC 98-8817
First published 1997 in the United Kingdom
"When Detective Chief Inspector Phil Benholme begins investigating the murder of a Nobel Prize-winning physiologist, he can scarcely believe what he discovers: his own teenage son may be involved. Keating's latest is a gripping examination of one of a police officer's worst nightmares—a portrait of a man faced with the choice between defending his son and helping to prove he's a killer." Booklist

Keating, Henry Reymond Fitzwalter *See* Keating, H. R. F. (Henry Reymond Fitzwalter), 1926-

Keegan, Nicola

Swimming. Alfred A. Knopf 2009 305p $25.95
ISBN 978-0-307-26997-3   LC 2009-14051
"Philomena 'Pip' Ash's natural element is water. The moment her feet hit the pool in an aqua baby class, she knows joy and security. As her family careens from loss to loss—her older sister dies of cancer, her father is

Keegan, Nicola—Continued

killed in a plane crash, and her mother succumbs to a series of nervous breakdowns—swimming becomes Pip's haven, allowing her to shut out pain and emotions. But no escape works perfectly; throughout all the training for competitions, making the Olympic team, and winning medals, she is accompanied by the ghosts of her father and sister." Libr J

"Keegan's energy jumps off the page. . . . Swimming is a wonderful coming-of-age story, a richly detailed account of a young woman channeling her rage, grief and insecurity into a passion to win. The voice Keegan has invented for Pip is sarcastic, thoughtful, elegant, irreverent." Boston Globe

Keeland, Reg

(tr) Larsson, S. The girl with the dragon tattoo

Kehlmann, Daniel, 1975-

Measuring the world; translated from the German by Carol Brown Janeway. Pantheon Books 2006 259p $23

ISBN 0-375-42446-6   LC 2006-40480

Original German edition, 2005

A novel "loosely based on the lives of 19th-century explorer Alexander von Humboldt and a contemporary, mathematician Carl Friedrich Gauss. . . . Humboldt voyages to South America to map the Orinoco River, climb the Chimborazo peak in Ecuador and measure 'every river, every mountain and every lake in his path.' Gauss is the hedgehog to Humboldt's fox, leaping out of bed on his wedding night to jot down a formula and rarely leaving his hometown of Göttingen. The two meet at a scientific congress in 1828, when Germany is in turmoil after the fall of Napoleon. Other luminaries appear throughout the novel, including a senile Immanuel Kant, Louis Daguerre and Thomas Jefferson." Publ Wkly

The "author plays his fiction game with great refinement and sparkling wit. The plot is strong and its dialogue totally hilarious." Frankfurter Rundschau

Keillor, Garrison

Happy to be here. Atheneum Pubs. 1982 210p o.p.   LC 81-66033

Contents: Jack Schmidt, Arts Administrator; Don: the true story of a young person; My North Dakota railroad days; WLT (The Edgar era); The Slim Graves Show; Friendly neighbor; Attitude; Around the Horne; The new baseball; How are the legs, Sam?; U.S. still on top, says rest of world; Congress in crisis: the proximity bill; Re the tower project; How it was in America a week ago Tuesday; Shy rights: why not pretty soon; Mission to Mandalla; Nana hami ba reba; Plainfolks; The people's shopper; Your wedding and you; The lowliest bush a purple sage would be; Local family keeps son happy; Oya life these days; Your transit commission; Be careful; Ten stories for Mr. Richard Brautigan, and other stories; The drunkard's Sunday; Happy to be here; Drowning 1954

Lake Wobegon days. Viking 1985 337p

ISBN 0-670-80514-9   LC 85-40029

This book is the author's "history and season-by-season chronicle of his imaginary hometown, [Lake Wobegon]. . . . It's a town 'where nobody locks the doors or knows where the keys are,' where wearing black tennis shoes marks a boy for life and where it's thought that newfangled contraptions like dishwashers lead to degeneracy." Newsweek

"Much of this is satirical, but Keillor's subtle humor is gentle, rather than biting or mocking, as he exposes the foibles and faults of Lake Wobegonians with affection and sympathy." Publ Wkly

Lake Wobegon summer 1956. Viking 2001 291p

ISBN 0-670-03003-1   LC 2001-26312

"It is summer, and as the denizens of Lake Wobegon sit on their front porches, listening to the radio and to the swish of sprinklers on their lawns, 14-year-old Gary struggles to find his own place within the community. . . . Gary has, by his own admission, been a good boy, but he is now exploring what it means to be bad-as 'bad' is defined in 1950s Lake Wobegon. Keillor's wry vignettes of Gary's summer of change and turmoil are laced with his trademark self-deprecating humor." Libr J

Leaving home. Viking 1987 xxiii, 244p o.p.

     LC 87-40219

Contents: A trip to Grand Rapids; A ten-dollar bill; Easter; Corinne; A glass of Wendy; The speeding ticket; Seeds; Chicken; How the crab apple grew; Truckstop; Dale; High rise; Collection; Life is good; Lyle's roof; Pontoon boat; State Fair; David and Agnes, a romance; The killer; Eloise; The royal family; Homecoming; Brethren; Thanksgiving; Darlene makes a move; Christmas dinner; Exiles; New Year's; Where did it go wrong?; Post office; Out in the cold; Hawaii; Hansel; Du, du liegst mir im herzen; Aprille; Goodbye to the lake

"These radio monologues [from A Prairie Home Companion] read easily, and listeners to the weekly radio show will find the flow of Keillor's distinctive flat rendition ringing in their ears." Wilson Libr Bull

Love me. Viking 2003 272p $24.95

ISBN 0-670-03246-8   LC 2003-52540

This novel is "about fame, seduction and downfall as experienced by a Midwestern writer named Larry Wyler, whose common sense is hijacked by best-sellerdom. When his first novel, a prairie potboiler called 'Spacious Skies,' improbably takes off, so does Wyler. He abandons ho-hum St. Paul and his wife, Iris, for the diamond glitter of Manhattan, where he gets an apartment on Central Park, an office at The New Yorker and a killer case of creative constipation." N Y Times Book Rev

The author "blends humor and compassion with just a touch of cynicism, cooking up a funny, insightful, and touching story of ambition, sacrifice, and love." Booklist

WLT; a radio romance. Viking 1991 401p

ISBN 0-670-81857-7   LC 91-50160

This novel "chronicles the story of the birth (in 1926), ripening and decline of a Minneapolis radio station, the brainchild of the brothers Ray and Roy Soderbjerg. Its characters are WLT's principal staffers, both those on the mike and those behind it." N Y Times Book Rev

"Garrison Keillor's mythical America, unlike the faded and inoffensive Midwest of Sandburg, is dreamed with an unblinking eye. His characters are idiosyncratic. They

Keillor, Garrison—*Continued*

are culled from who knows where—from our collective past, certainly, but also from the demotic oral tradition of a rich and very real community that is gone and now exists only in recollection." Nation

Kellerman, Faye

Day of atonement; a Peter Decker/Rina Lazarus mystery. Morrow 1991 359p o.p.

LC 90-22682

"When Los Angeles detective Peter Decker and new wife Rina Lazarus visit her Jewish kinfolks in Brooklyn, startling events disturb their honeymoon. Quite unexpectedly and with great antipathy, Decker—an adoptee—recognizes his natural mother at a holiday gathering. Before he can confront her, though, her troubled 14-year-old grandson goes missing and Decker, fortuitously on hand, begins the search. . . . Hard-hitting details, vignettes of Jewish life, and uncomfortably close glimpses of a cold-hearted psycho make this an entrancing page turner." Libr J

The forgotten. Morrow 2001 374p
ISBN 0-688-15614-2

In this mystery Kellerman "balances Rina Lazarus's consuming Orthodox Judaism with the broader societal issues faced by her husband, L.A. homicide detective Peter Decker. Here they intertwine when the vicious defacement of their synagogue reverberates in a widening circle of murders. Ernesto Golding, a troubled, spoiled youth and acquaintance of Rina's son, Jacob, confesses to the crime, but several months later Ernesto and his therapists, Mervin and Dee Baldwin, are murdered." Publ Wkly

"The depiction of how teens and parents push and pull at one another's emotions is dead on." Booklist

Grievous sin; a Peter Decker/Rina Lazarus mystery. Morrow 1993 368p o.p.   LC 93-12344

"Complications in the delivery room lead to major surgery for Rina Decker, who, when last seen in *False Prophet*, [1992] was pregnant with her and husband Peter Decker's first child. She is barely out of danger when an infant vanishes from the hospital's understaffed nursery, and proud father Peter, an LAPD detective sergeant, declares . . . 'I *owe* it to that little baby girl to find her.'" Publ Wkly

"While the plot comes dangerously close to being overly saccharine and annoyingly artificial, Kellerman does know how to hook her readers. First, she tantalizes them with ambiguous clues and ominous glimpses of an unbalanced villain's psyche, then she teases them with a blend of pulse-quickening suspense and heartwarming family tableaux. Only then does she deliver the shocking climax." Booklist

Jupiter's bones; a novel. Morrow 1999 375p
ISBN 0-688-15612-6   LC 99-33356

"When Emil Euler Ganz, a brilliant former astrophysicist turned cult leader, is found dead with an empty fifth of vodka under his bed, it looks like suicide. But LAPD lieutenant Peter Decker is suspicious and begins to ask questions about the man who disappeared 25 years ago only to turn up ten years later as Father Jupiter, the charismatic leader of the Order of the Rings of God." Libr J

"Kellerman has pulled together elements of suspense, violence, humor, pathos, and love and wrapped them into a potent plot certain to captivate genre fans." Booklist

Justice. Morrow 1995 388p o.p.
* LC 95-14268

"A Peter Decker/Rina Lazarus novel"

In this mystery "a high school prom queen is strangled to death after a wild night of drugs, drink and boisterous group sex. Peter Decker, a Los Angeles homicide detective, who lies awake nights worrying about his own children, coaxes a confession from the dead girl's date. 'He's cold, he's calculating, he's eerie,' Decker says of this preternaturally self-contained youth, the nephew of a Mafia crime boss. . . . Rina Lazarus, Decker's wife and helpmate in this series, is uncharacteristically subdued here, which gives this sympathetic cop a rare chance to work independently on a case that raises touchy issues like ethnic stereotyping and religious prejudice." N Y Times Book Rev

Milk and honey; a novel. Morrow 1990 384p o.p.   LC 89-39592

"On a summer night in a housing development near Los Angeles, police sergeant Peter Decker finds a winsome two-year-old girl playing on a swing set—and wearing blood-soaked pajamas. Unclaimed, 'Sally' is placed in a foster home while Decker and partner Marge Dunn try to learn her identity. Bee stings on her arms lead them days later to the scene of a bloody multiple murder at a honey farm. While piecing together a bizarre puzzle of betrayal and revenge . . . Peter is also investigating rape and assualt charges brought against an old army buddy from Vietnam. The pressures of the murder case and doubts about his friend's innocence compound Peter's anxiety as he waits for young Orthodox Jewish widow Rina Lazarus to decide if she will marry him." Publ Wkly

Moon music; a novel. Morrow 1998 424p o.p.
LC 98-6735

Las Vegas homicide cop Romulus Poe finds himself "in charge of investigating the gruesome death of a showgirl turned hooker. The case reminds Poe of a brutal, unsolved murder 25 years in his own past and brings up his unresolved feelings for his partner's troubled wife. When a second, similarly mutilated body is found, Poe and his team must uncover the truth, even if it involves confronting a powerful, corrupt casino owner. Kellerman's characters have complex interrelationships that often seem more important than the murder investigation itself." Libr J

Prayers for the dead. Morrow 1996 406p o.p.
LC 96-7494

"A Peter Decker/Rina Lazarus novel"

This "mystery begins with the brutal murder and mutilation of renowned heart surgeon, researcher and fundamentalist Christian Azor Sparks. LAPD Lieutenant Decker gets the call. He also gets an abundance of suspects. . . . Religion and morality are integral to Kellerman's mysteries—built on the bedrock of the Deckers' orthodox Judaism. Here she deftly casts her net around the commanding victim, whose shadow lay equally over family and colleagues, and his son, the theologian Father Abram, whose past connection with Rina may force Decker off the case." Publ Wkly

Kellerman, Faye—*Continued*

The quality of mercy; a novel. Morrow 1989 607p o.p.   LC 88-29275

"Rebecca Lopez and William Shakespeare first encounter each other in a London graveyard where she is burying her betrothed and he his mentor and best friend. Their paths cross again as they seek to avenge these untimely deaths, she joining in her family's mission to rescue fellow Jews from the Spanish Inquisition, he searching for the murderer among London's criminals. Shakespeare offers excitement and intellectual stimulation to the brilliant, adventurous Rebecca, stifled by the restricted life of an Elizabethan woman, but political and religious events overtake them and doom the relationship." Libr J

"Deft characterization and dazzling prose evoke the ambiance of the period. More than just a mystery, the novel is a spectacular epic—romantic, bawdy, witty and abounding with adventure." Publ Wkly

Sanctuary; a Peter Decker/Rina Lazarus mystery. Morrow 1994 396p o.p.   LC 94-11350

"L.A.P.D. sergeant Pete Decker and his Orthodox Jewish wife, Rina Lazarus, the parents of a baby daughter, are caught up in a case involving Rina's old school chum, Honey Klein, who comes to stay with the Deckers after leaving her diamond-merchant husband. When Honey and her children mysteriously disappear, Rina is first puzzled and then alarmed, especially considering that Pete is working on a double homicide involving another Jewish diamond merchant and his family. To solve the case, the Deckers travel to Israel and find themselves risking their lives to track down the disturbing truth." Booklist

Serpent's tooth; a Peter Decker/Rina Lazarus novel. Morrow 1997 400p

ISBN 0-688-14368-7   LC 97-10685

"LAPD detective Pete Decker's latest case is a shocker. Estelle's, the watering hole favored by L.A.'s rich and famous, is the scene of a mass shooting that leaves a dozen dead and scores wounded. There is no need to look for the murderer, who shot himself following his killing spree, but Pete does have to figure out the killer's motive, wrap up loose ends, and make the LAPD come out looking good." Booklist

"The scope of the investigation is broad and the moralizing is kept to a minimum, giving Decker a rare chance to do some solid police work." N Y Times Book Rev

Stone kiss; a Peter Decker/Rina Lazarus novel. Warner Bks. 2002 390p $25.95

ISBN 0-446-53038-7   LC 2002-16886

In this mystery LAPD detective Decker and his wife Rina "come to New York to investigate the homicide of a distant relative in Decker's family. Natural grief and shame aside, there is something profoundly unpleasant about the rigidly closed-minded family of Hasidic Jews that rebuffs Decker's efforts to find out who murdered a rabbi's bookish son in a seedy Manhattan hotel room—and what become of the 15-year-old niece who was in his care." N Y Times Book Rev

"Whether Kellerman is depicting the ultra-Orthodox Jewish community or a pornographer's studio she is utterly convincing. Amid the wreckage of lives taken or thrown away, Kellerman's heroes find glimmers of hope and enough moral ambiguity to make even her most evil villain look less than totally black." Publ Wkly

Street dreams. Warner Bks. 2003 420p $25.95

ISBN 0-446-53131-6   LC 2003-45079

"Cindy, a rookie cop and Peter's 28-year-old daughter by his first marriage, takes center stage here. Both her rocky history with the department and with her dad come to the fore as she digs into the case of a developmentally disabled teenager who abandoned her baby, insists she was raped, and may have witnessed a murder. Following the strangely coincidental hit-and-run of another disabled teen from the same area, the case blossoms into a mystery that requires help from Peter." Booklist

Kellerman, Jesse

The genius. G.P. Putnam's Sons 2008 374p $24.95

ISBN 978-0-399-15459-1; 0-399-15459-0
                LC 2008-5810

"When Manhattan art dealer Ethan Muller is shown a dingy rent-controlled apartment bursting with fabulous work, he jumps on it, soon mounting a show — even though the artist, Victor Cracke, has vanished. Who was Cracke, and why do some of the faces in his drawings look like young boys murdered years ago, the crimes unsolved? Prodded by a retired cop, Ethan begins to investigate — first unwillingly, then compulsively — and it becomes clear that Cracke's story is intertwined with that of Ethan's own family. Despite some cumbersome flashbacks, Jesse Kellerman's The Genius boasts a masterful plot and dead-on pacing." Entertainment Wkly

Sunstroke; a novel. G.P. Putnam's Sons 2006 370p $24.95

ISBN 0-399-15330-6   LC 2005-51459

"L.A. novelty-company secretary Gloria Mendez, in love with her boss, is heartbroken when he dies while on vacation in Mexico. No family comes forward, so she heads south to claim the body. In sun-bleached Aguas Vivas, a dead town whose only industry is its graveyard, she finds ashes and a suspicious-acting cop. As Kellerman teasingly plays pieces of the puzzle, Gloria soon learns that nearly everything about the man she longed for has been a mirage—and she learns a few things about herself, too. This tightly focused thriller features expertly drawn characters, vivid scenes, and simmering tension." Booklist

Kellerman, Jonathan

Bad love. Bantam Bks. 1994 386p o.p.
                LC 93-26678

Child "psychologist Alex Delaware receives a terrifying audiotape full of bloodcurdling screams and a disjointed voice chanting, 'Bad love, bad love.' Alex can't connect the tape with anything, but when he begins to get threatening phone calls, and someone brutally harpoons one of his beloved koi fish, he realizes he could be in danger. With the help of his friend, Detective Milo Sturgis, Delaware begins to unravel the complex, multilayered plot that seems to be linked to a conference he chaired 20 years ago. Delaware finally discovers he's being pursued by a tormented, relentless, deranged killer." Booklist

The author "spins a tight, complicated plot and is careful to balance his grisly murder scenes with substantive shoptalk about childhood trauma and the devastating effects of authoritarian discipline." N Y Times Book Rev

Kellerman, Jonathan—*Continued*

Billy Straight; a novel. Random House 1999 467p

ISBN 0-679-45959-6   LC 98-19583

Hollywood homicide detective Petra Connor "frantically scours the city in search of a runaway 12-year-old boy who witnessed the vicious stabbing of a woman in Griffith Park. This case quickly draws the media carrion crows when it comes out that the victim was recently divorced from the popular star of a television series. Like Connor, the investigation is competent but strictly by the book—and not the reason you're turning the pages so fast. That distinction goes to the winsome title character and frequent narrator, a self-taught street kid with an artless affection for books." N Y Times Book Rev

Bones; an Alex Delaware novel. Ballantine Books 2008 353p $27

ISBN 978-0-345-49513-6; 0-345-49513-6
    LC 2008-35125

In this mystery featuring L.A. consulting psychologist Alex Delaware, "high school miscreant Chance Brandt has been assigned to perform community service at the Bird Marsh, a nature sanctuary near Marina del Rey. After Chance dismisses as a prank an anonymous phone call warning him that there's a corpse buried in the marsh, Lt. Milo Sturgis, now 'Special Case Investigator' for the LAPD, and Sturgis's team find four bodies there, all women missing their right hand." Publ Wkly

"Kellerman's strength is that he can set up an intriguing situation and keep things moving at a breakneck pace. He can also, when he wants to, write well. He's good at short, vivid descriptions. . . . I don't think the plot of "Bones" will withstand scrutiny, but most readers probably won't care. The story sweeps them along, offering plenty of snappy dialogue and cheap thrills, plus a fair amount of suspense that is relieved by the final unveiling of the killer." Washington Post Book World

The clinic. Bantam Bks. 1997 370p o.p.
    LC 96-24626

Alex Delaware conducts "an investigation into the savage stabbing murder of Hope Devane, a psychology professor and celebrity author. The LAPD, unable to solve the case after three months, reassigns it to Lieutenant Milo Sturgis. Milo calls on his friend Alex, a compassionate, astute psychologist, for insight into the victim, who had a seemingly routine academic career and marriage until writing a pop-psych relationship book." Publ Wkly

The author "has crafted another masterly, darkly psychological tale, drawing upon timely issues ranging from abortion to organ harvesting." Libr J

Devil's waltz. Bantam Bks. 1993 416p o.p.
    LC 92-18089

"Alex Delaware, the child psychologist and amateur sleuth . . . returns to the beleaguered Los Angeles pediatrics hospital where he was trained. Called in to consult on the baffling case of a 2-year-old girl with phantom ailments, Alex performs his clinical chores with his customary tenderness, while bearing the details of the child's extraordinary medical history. Despite Mr. Kellerman's overelaborate approach, he maintains the harrowing suspense of a medical mystery too horrid to be anything but real." N Y Times Book Rev

Dr. Death; a novel. Random House 2000 352p

ISBN 0-679-45961-8   LC 00-29065

In this mystery Dr. Alex Delaware works "with old LAPD buddy Detective Milo Sturgis on a particularly gruesome murder. Dr. Eldon Mate, a Kervokian-like 'Dr. Death,' is found vivisected in the back of an Econoline van, hooked up to his 'humanitron' suicide machine. A crass farewell note is stapled to his chest. It's obviously the work of an extremely intelligent and bold killer, and suspects abound." Libr J

"A heady blend of criminal profiling and police procedural." Booklist

Gone; an Alex Delaware novel. Ballantine Books 2006 365p $26.95

ISBN 0-345-45261-5   LC 2006-296289

"The abduction of two art students turns out to have been faked, but the murder that follows is very real. Alex Delaware tries to figure it all out." Libr J

"Delaware joins forces with his sometimes official partner in crime, LAPD detective Milo Sturgis, and together they pursue an investigative trail littered with corpses leading to an unconventional acting school and the family of the eccentric woman who runs it. While the murderer's identity may not be that surprising, the author's ability to convey the unrelenting sadness of his characters' lives and his deep psychological insights will satisfy those looking for more than mere thrills." Publ Wkly

Monster; a novel. Random House 1999 396p

ISBN 0-679-45960-X   LC 99-20098

"A handsome young actor is found murdered and mutilated, a female psychologist meets a similar fate, and twin brothers are gruesomely dispatched—all in separate events, on the same evening. The murders, though different, seem to be the work of the same killer. As Dr. Alex Delaware, psychologist and consultant to the LAPD, and detective Milo Sturgis unravel the mystery of the killer's identity, it becomes clear that Ardis Peake (a.k.a. 'Monster'), incarcerated in a psychiatric hospital for the criminally insane for the past 16 years, is somehow involved." Libr J

The murder book. Ballantine Bks. 2002 408p

ISBN 0-345-45253-4   LC 2002-74733

In this "caper starring Delaware and his mentor in police work, homicide detective Milo Sturgis, Delaware receives a package in the mail. It contains an official police case file, known as a 'murder book,' filled with stark crime scene photos and terse reports of some 40 cases. What Delaware finds most shocking, however, is the horrified reaction his hard-bitten detective pal Milo has upon seeing one particular scene. Kellerman departs from his standard focus on Delaware to a telling of Sturgis' story, going back to his struggles as a young black, gay cop and showing how his first victim, the girl depicted in the murder book, still haunts him." Booklist

Private eyes. Bantam Bks. 1992 475p o.p.
    LC 91-17314

"Harvard-bound, 18-year-old heiress Melissa Dickinson, whom child psychologist Alex Delaware had successfully treated for anxiety 10 years earlier, calls him with concerns about leaving her wealthy mother, an agoraphobe. Years before Melissa's birth, Gina Dickinson Ramp had been disfigured by acid thrown for never-revealed reasons by a former lover, now out of prison

Kellerman, Jonathan—*Continued*

and back in town. Widowed for many years, recently re-married and making progress in her own intensive thera-py with a noted husband-and-wife team of behavioral psychologists, Gina is still fragile. When she disappears, Melissa enlists Delaware's help and that of his friend, Milo Sturgis, on leave from the LAPD. . . . Kellerman deftly handles the strings of his plot." Publ Wkly

Self-defense. Bantam Bks. 1995 390p o.p.

LC 94-26175

Psychologist Alex Delaware "is treating 25-year-old Lucy Lowell for a recurring nightmare that she has been having ever since serving on the hanging jury that con-victed a serial killer. . . . When Lucy's terrifying dream is complicated by incidents of sleepwalking, bed-wetting, narcolepsy and a possible suicide attempt, Alex suspects a repressed childhood memory. After putting his patient through hypnotic regression, he is convinced that she witnessed a murder and he sets out to prove it. . . . An exciting story that is loaded with tension and packed with titillating insights into abnormal psychology." N Y Times Book Rev

Survival of the fittest; a novel. Bantam Bks. 1998 401p o.p.

LC 97-3182

In this mystery, psychologist Alex Delaware, "helps his friend, detective Milo Sturgis, solve a cold case: a deaf and mildly retarded Israeli girl, the daughter of a diplomat, is strangled in a park, and letters 'D-V-L-L' are found on a scrap of paper in her pocket. Authorities have failed to come up with a suspect or any leads, so the victim's father brings in a detective of his own, the great Daniel Sharavi." Libr J

"Kellerman has things down to a science now, know-ing instinctively what his fans want: suspense, adventure, romance, and a leading man to die for." Booklist

Therapy. Ballantine Bks. 2004 387p $26.95
ISBN 0-345-45259-3

*

"To help solve a young couple's murder, Alex Dela-ware needs to dig secrets out of a testy celebrity psy-chologist." Libr J

The author "manages to take the story of a lovers' lane double murder near Mulholland Drive to the point where it involves human rights atrocities in Rwanda. Along the way Mr. Kellerman packs in the descriptive detail that is one of his hallmarks and one of the incidental attractions in his fiction." N Y Times (Late N Y Ed)

Time bomb; a novel. Bantam Bks. 1990 468p o.p.

LC 90-349

This novel featuring "child psychologist and private detective Alex Delaware begins when Delaware is called upon to deal with the potential trauma to elementary-school children of a sniper killed in their midst during lunch recess. He quickly learns that the sniper's target may not have been the children at all, but either a right-wing politician holding a news conference at the school or his liberal counterpart, a publicity-hungry, former 1960's radical who had appeared unexpectedly for an im-promptu debate and whose bodyguard shot the sniper to death." N Y Times Book Rev

The web. Bantam Bks. 1996 342p o.p.

LC 95-32161

Child psychologist Alex Delaware "and his paramour Robin land on Aruk, a tiny Micronesian island, and un-wittingly begin the vacation from hell. Alex has been in-vited by Dr. Moreland, the island's richest and most in-fluential resident, to collaborate on a writing project. The eccentric Moreland, who keeps a zoo of large, creepy in-sects, seems literally to vanish after sunset, leaving Alex written clues based on the works of great thinkers." Libr J

"An intriguing, keep-'em-guessing plot, Kellerman's usual mix of psychologically fascinating characters, a megadose of suspense, and that always reliable heart-throb, Dr. Alex Delaware, make this one a must-have for all mystery collections." Booklist

When the bough breaks. Atheneum Pubs. 1985 293p o.p.

LC 81-16805

Psychologist Alex Delaware "turns detective when he is called upon to interview a young girl who is the only living witness to a brutal dual murder. Whatever the girl may have seen, the actual crime veils an even more hor-rible contemporary phenomenon: a ring of child molest-ers at a school in Southern California. The psychologist is soon out of his professional depth in pursuing clues and leads, but he plods onward to solve the case, nearly at the expense of the girl's and his own life. Kellerman's story is long on sensational descriptions and short on be-lievable disclosures—too many of the good turns of for-tune seem coincidentally opportune—but as a suspenseful drama, the novel does rack up its points." Booklist

Kellogg, Marjorie

Tell me that you love me, Junie Moon. Farrar, Straus & Giroux 1968 216p o.p.

*

"Junie Moon, in a rehabilitation center after a crazy boyfriend threw acid in her face, meets Warren, a para-plegic who has been shot in the spine on a hunting trip, and Arthur, who is slowly dying of a degenerative nerve disease. Amid the protests of the hospital staff the three decide to leave the center to set up a household. The re-action of their new neighbors is anything but encourag-ing, but one of them, an Italian fish merchant, befriends them and sends them on a vacation in his truck. It is a wonderful interlude until Arthur, recognizing that he is in the last stages of his illness, asks to be taken home to die." Shapiro. Fic for Youth. 3d edition

Kelly, James Patrick

(ed) Feeling very strange. See Feeling very strange

The wreck of the Godspeed; with a foreword by Bob Eggleton. Golden Gryphon Press 2008 358p $24.95

ISBN 978-1-930846-51-7   LC 2007-48662

Contents: The wreck of the Godspeed; The best Christ-mas ever; Men are trouble; Luck; The dark side of town; The Leila Torn show; Mother; Dividing the sustain; The edge of nowhere; The ice is singing; Serpent; Bernardo's house; Burn

"Thirteen stories, all originally published between 2002 and 2007, examine the struggle for human survival and

Kelly, James Patrick—*Continued*

identity in strange places." Publ Wkly

"Kelly's stories depend on future technologies based on physics, information theory, genetics, and other au courant disciplines, but they're about love, friendship, and loyalty." Booklist

Kelly, Jim, 1957-

The coldest blood. St. Martin's Minotaur 2007 341p $24.95

ISBN 978-0-312-36478-6; 0-312-36478-4

LC 2006-52203

"Elderly people are dying in one of Cambridgeshire's bitterest winters in memory, and newspaper reporter Philip Dryden . . . suspects that something is amiss. As he peels away the outer trappings of their lives, he finds that the victims may be connected to an ongoing criminal investigation of an orphanage. At the same time, he tends to his wife, who is slowly recovering from a coma." Libr J

"This is another winner in what has become one of the best British crime series on the market. Kelly should be read as much for his Dickensian atmosphere (his descriptions of the abandoned orphanage and the Victorian workhouse-turned-hospital are achingly bleak) and his full-throttle characterizations as for his masterful plotting." Booklist

Kelly, Thomas, 1961-

Empire rising. Farrar, Straus and Giroux 2005 390p $25

ISBN 0-374-14781-7   LC 2004-8580

"It is 1930, and ground has just been broken for the building dubbed 'the Eighth Wonder of the World.' One of the thousands of men working high above the city is Michael Briody, an Irish immigrant torn between his desire to make a new life in America and his pledge to gather money and arms for the Irish republican cause. When he meets Grace Masterson, an alluring artist who is depicting the great skyscraper's rise from her houseboat on the East River, Briody's life turns exhilarating and dangerous, for Grace is also a paramour of Johnny Farrell, Mayor Jimmy Walker's liaison with Tammany Hall and the New York underworld." Publisher's note

"The canvas is epic in scale, peopled with numerous arresting characters, recognizable in both senses: 'real' persons like Jimmy Walker, Babe Ruth, Primo Camera, the famously 'missing' Judge Crater and the many engaging but no less real inventions of his own. [Kelly's] special gift as a novelist is his ability to maintain a galloping tilt of narrative suspense, despite countless shifts in plot development, without overwhelming or confusing the reader. Unusual in an epic, to say the least, this novel is a page-turner; there is no plot-padding or authorial longueurs slackening the pace." America

Kelman, James

How late it was, how late. Norton 1995 373p

ISBN 0-393-03817-3

"Sammy, the novel's central figure, is an ex-convict who wakes on a Glasgow street after a two-day binge. . . . He gets himself into a fight with some soldiers. They beat him up, and then he is arrested and beaten some more by the police. The beatings cause him to lose his sight. He's released, blind, into the Glasgow streets, and must try to find his way home." N Y Times Book Rev

The novel "is a tour de force, both in its convincingly claustrophobic rendering of what it's like to be newly sightless and in its rhythmic prose." Newsweek

Kieron Smith, boy. Harcourt 2008 422p $26

ISBN 978-0-15-101348-7; 0-15-101348-9

The author's "books tend to be written in a Scottish working-class vernacular, and part of the pleasure is untangling some of the thornier brambles out loud. Kieron Smith, boy is crafted with a gentler tongue, so readers should have no fear of taking it on the subway. Kelman excels at serving up the psyches of marginalized people, and young Kieron's narrative of being ignored by his parents and punished by his older brother and moving away from the grandparents who love him is heartwarming without being cheesy. The writing is also piercing and observant without feeling inauthentically wise. By the time you follow Kieron from snakes, snails and puppy dog tails to the first fluttering of his adolescence, the boy will feel like part of the family." NPR

Kelman, Judith

Summer of storms. Putnam 2001 288p $24.95

ISBN 0-399-14674-1   LC 00-45728

This thriller "chronicles the rekindling of a long-dormant murder investigation and the return of a ruthless killer. Thirty years after her young sister's death, Anna Jameson is haunted by memories of what was dubbed the Sleeping Beauty Murder. On a stormy summer night, five-year-old Julie Jameson was killed in her bedroom while her family slept. . . . Fast-forward to Anna, now 33 and an aspiring photographer, who returns to New York to work as a photojournalist for a high-powered media conglomerate and to confront family demons." Publ Wkly

Kelton, Elmer, 1926-2009

After the bugles

In Kelton, E. Texas sunrise

Badger boy. Forge 2001 286p

ISBN 0-312-87319-0   LC 00-48457

"A Tom Doherty Associates book"

Sequel to The buckskin line

As the Texas Rangers disband, Badger Boy, a white boy whose parents were murdered by Comanches and who was himself captured and raised by a Comanche warrior, falls prisoner to David "Rusty" Shannon

Massacre at Goliad

In Kelton, E. Texas sunrise

The rebels; sons of Texas. Forge 2007 302p $24.95

ISBN 978-0-7653-1526-7; 0-7653-1526-2

LC 2007-28850

First published 1990 under the pseudonym Tom Early with title: Sons of Texas: the rebels

Kelton "concludes the Sons of Texas trilogy [previous titles: Sons of Texas and The raiders] with the strongest entry, set in the mid 1830s. The Lewis family—brothers

Kelton, Elmer, 1926-2009—*Continued*

Andrew, Michael and James, and sister Annie—are foreigners in a strange land, raising their families and farming while Mexican and American cultures, politics, racism and tempers simmer over the possibilities of rebellion and independence from Mexico. During these years, the Lewises must deal with outlaws, the Mexican army, troublemaking American politicians, a slick smuggler and their continuing feud with the thieving and back-shooting Blackwood brothers. When war does come, the Lewis boys and one Blackwood go off to fight in bloody battles at Velasco, the Alamo and San Jacinto, and not all come home. Historical figures—Sam Houston, General Santa Anna, Jim Bowie and Davy Crockett—have cameos and add depth and color to this superb saga of the Lone Star State." Publ Wkly

Slaughter. Doubleday 1992 369p o.p.

LC 92-10317

"Set on the Great Plains shortly after the end of the Civil War, the story focuses on the intertwining lives of a half dozen characters. Among them are Jeff Layne, a bitter, middle-aged Confederate veteran; Crow Feather, a proud Comanche warrior; Sully, a recently freed slave; and Arletta Browder, a displaced easterner who takes over her dead father's buffalo-hunting business. It is buffalo that throw them all together, the whites hoping to slaughter the great beasts for profit, the Indians hoping to preserve a way of life that requires the buffalo's survival." Booklist

"Well written and fast-paced, this powerful, moving novel proceeds inexorably toward the extinction of the great herds and of the indigenous peoples' way of life" Publ Wkly

Followed by The far canyon (1994)

Texas sunrise; two novels of the Texas Republic. Forge 2008 363p $24.95

ISBN 978-0-7653-2064-3; 0-7653-2064-9

LC 2008-34735

"A Tom Doherty Associates book"

"Two novels, both concerning the Texas revolution against Mexico as witnessed by two young brothers, Joshua and Thomas Buckalew. In the first book, 'Massacre at Goliad,' the Buckalews' dream of adventure and free land is dispelled by the harsh reality of the West: hard work, Indians, bandits and the simmering cultural, racial and political animosity between Americans and Mexicans. When violence finally breaks out, the boys miss the slaughter at the Alamo only to be caught up in the massacre of Texan prisoners at Goliad. Only one brother survives, going on to avenge Goliad at the Battle of San Jacinto. In 'After the Bugles,' the surviving brother returns home to rebuild his ranch and his life, but must contend with cheating opportunists, murderous outlaws and deadly Comanche attacks, as well as growing Texan racism against his Mexican friends and neighbors. As with all of Kelton's westerns, characters are colorful and well drawn, the action is fast and bloody, and the plotting carefully thought out." Publ Wkly

Texas vendetta. Forge 2004 301p $24.95

ISBN 0-7653-0572-0   LC 2003-17352

Texas Ranger "privates Andy Pickard, the onetime Comanche captive called Badger Boy, and the war-anguished Farley Brackett, are assigned to deliver a prisoner to the sheriff of a county some distance from the ranger camp on the San Saba River. The prisoner, Jayce Landon, has recently killed a man named Ned Hopper and is to stand trial for murder. The rangers quickly learn that the Landon and Hopper families are involved in a blood feud and that Jayce Landon is the target of both clans." Publisher's note

"Within the exciting context of a western adventure, [Kelton] explores paternal relationships-good and bad-and the crippling consequences of hanging on too tightly to a painful past." Booklist

The way of the coyote. Forge 2001 283p

ISBN 0-312-87318-2

* LC 2001-40482

"A Tom Doherty Associates book"

"Rusty Shannon, who was kidnapped by the Comanche as a child, rescues 10-year-old Andy Pinkard from the same fate. Andy's memories are all Comanche, and he struggles to adjust to the white life. Meanwhile, the young son of a woman Rusty once loved is kidnapped by the Comanche, and two rivals from Rusty's Texas Ranger days arrive as representatives from the corrupt state government and twist the law to confiscate Rusty's ranch." Booklist

"Kelton covers a wide swath of history with aplomb, illuminating a little-known period in Western history. California is still Mexican, Indians are a real threat and outlaws rule the land in this rough-riding adventure tale." Publ Wkly

Kemelman, Harry

The day the rabbi resigned. Fawcett Columbine 1992 273p o.p.   LC 91-72891

"Twenty-five years after coming to the Boston suburb of Barnard's Crossing, Rabbi David Small is considering retirement. But before he can get so much as one foot out of the pulpit, a local college professor dies in a car accident and the weary clergyman finds himself once again drawn from his own everyday concerns into more serious matters." Publ Wkly

"Mr. Kemelman's fans will be mollified by his clever resolution of Rabbi Small's career crisis, which is woven into a deft murder mystery involving several characters of different faiths." N Y Times Book Rev

Friday the rabbi slept late. Crown 1964 224p o.p.

"Rabbi Small, an unstylish young scholar, is up for contract renewal in a fashionable New England community, when a young girl's murdered body is found on the Temple grounds. Her purse is in his car. Because of his character, he is not a leading suspect and works with the Catholic police chief to find the killer." Book Week

"Here are conflict and suspense, understanding and conversation, and a remarkable Biblical explanation of the differences between priests, ministers and rabbis." Libr J

Monday the rabbi took off. Putnam 1972 316p o.p.

"The rabbi and his family set out for Israel. The action alternates between Massachusetts, where Rabbi Small may or may not be losing his congregation to the rabbi substituting for him, and Jerusalem, where he soon becomes embroiled in troubles involving a TV commentator, the commentator's son, and plotting Arab militants."

Kemelman, Harry—*Continued*
Saturday Rev

"This is not so much a novel of mystery and detection as it is a beautifully conceived and executed novel of conditions in Israel and a rabbi's dilemma." Best Sellers

One fine day the rabbi bought a cross. Morrow 1987 234p o.p.   LC 86-23571

"Central to the plot is a Palestine Liberation Organization arms cache that Druse fighters would dearly love to steal. An American professor unwittingly delivers a letter with a map of the cache to a Druse agent in Jerusalem. The American is promptly murdered. Rabbi Small is in Jerusalem and solves the case." N Y Times Book Rev

Saturday the rabbi went hungry. Crown 1966 249p o.p.

"The absent-minded knowledgeable young Rabbi, leader of a Conservative congregation, collaborates with his friend the Irish Catholic police chief in solving a mystery, this time deciding whether a death is murder or suicide and, if it is murder, who did it. The story is a good mixture of Jewish folk wisdom with modern community problems and with a murder mystery all nicely seasoned with humor." Publ Wkly

Sunday the rabbi stayed home. Putnam 1969 253p o.p.

"After six years at the Temple in Barnard's Crossing, Rabbi David Small is a little weary of the politics, dissention and factionalism of his congregation, and slightly disconcerted by the idea of a 'swinging Passover Service.' The weekend visit to Massachusetts College doesn't provide the release he expects, but neither does it prepare him for dealing with the rash of modern urban problems that confront him on Sunday when the body of Moose Carter is found in the empty house on the beach after a college student cookout." Libr J

Thursday the rabbi walked out. Morrow 1978 250p o.p.   LC 78-8466

"Kemelman's famous town, Barnard's Crossing, is in a turmoil after the murder of mean, anti-Semitic Ellsworth Jordan. Again Police Chief Lanigan asks Rabbi Small for help with the case, complicated by too many suspects. Those with motive and opportunity include members of Small's flock. Maltzman, president of the Temple, is one. So are the head of the local bank and his secretary as well as the dead man's illegitimate son by a Jewish mother." Publ Wkly

Wednesday the rabbi got wet. Morrow 1976 312p o.p.

In this story Rabbi Small "champions a young hippie, Akiva, suspected of causing a death. He has filled two prescriptions at his father's pharmacy. On the wet Wednesday, a wheeler-dealer member of Small's congregation, Safferstein, picks up the pills—a vial for his ailing wife and one for crotchety old Kestler. Kestler dies. His prescription is not what the doctor ordered. Dissension within the Temple's membership, with Small at odds with powerful men among them, adds to the excitement as the Rabbi applies Talmudic 'pilpul' (logical reasoning) to solve the problem of the switched dosage and exonerate the boy." Publ Wkly

Kemprecos, Paul
(jt. auth) Cussler, C. Fire ice

(jt. auth) Cussler, C. White death

Keneally, Thomas, 1935-

A family madness. Simon & Schuster 1986 336p o.p.   LC 85-26121

"Approximately half of the chapters of 'A Family Madness' are set in the present and concern a young working-class Australian, Terry Delaney, who becomes involved with a family of Byelorussian origin, the Kabbels (originally Kabbelski), who immigrated to Sydney in the late 1940's. The other half deals with the terrible modern history of that family, a history reaching back to the early days of World War II." N Y Times Book Rev

"Keneally brilliantly combines three diverse narrative techniques, and while the book is not light or easy reading, it is enormously rewarding." Publ Wkly

Flying hero class. Warner Bks. 1991 289p
ISBN 0-446-51582-5   LC 90-50524

"A troupe of Australian aboriginal dancers is flying from New York to Frankfurt on the last leg of a world tour when their jetliner is hijacked by Palestinian terrorists, and Frank McCloud their manager is identified as an enemy of the people and sentenced to death. In . . . [an] account of the next 48 hours Keneally relates blow-by-blow the hijackers' plot to intimidate, demoralize, and manipulate the minds of a plane load of people." Libr J

This is "despite some problems, a good book. Unlike many suspense novels, it never deadens our sensibilities with predictable characters, simpleminded politics or slick prose. Mr. Keneally's people are always fascinating, and so are the ideas his plot generates, making the hijacking a metaphor for the complex relationship between the West and third world peoples deprived of land and dignity." N Y Times Book Rev

Office of innocence. Doubleday 2003 319p $25
ISBN 0-385-50763-1   LC 2002-73653

A novel "about one young priest's crisis of faith in Sydney during World War II. Father Frank Darragh already feels conflicted about being out of the fighting when his regular duties as a soft-hearted confessor at St. Margaret's begin to put him in touch with war widows and American GIs. He is especially intrigued by Kate Heggarty, who seeks spiritual guidance when she's tempted to cheat on her P.O.W. husband. The monsignor objects to Father Frank's becoming so involved in her case, which explodes in the young priest's face when Kate turns up strangled." Libr J

Keneally moves his "protagonist, as confessor, from the banal to the transcendent: from insipid negotiations with schoolchildren to a primal reckoning in a war-ravaged landscape; from an innocence barely aware of its own spiritual vanity to a disillusioned acceptance of the ubiquity of sin and the stubborn mystery of fate." N Y Times Book Rev

River town. Talese 1995 324p o.p.
                                                 LC 94-48664

This is the "turn-of-the-century story of Tim Shea, an Irish storekeeper struggling with his own and society's demons to make a life for his family in New South Wales. Deaths frame the novel: Tim is haunted by the image of a nameless young woman, dead from an abortion, whose severed head is trotted around in a jar by the

Keneally, Thomas, 1935-—*Continued*

local constable in an effort to identify her; and after attending to a farmer killed in a gory buggy accident, Tim feels obliged to support the farmer's elder child, Lucy. First regarded as a hero for his quick action after the cart accident, then excoriated publicly for his anti-Boer War sentiments, Tim fears losing his business. A final quarantine after exposure to the black plague ends Tim's tribulations." Libr J

"There are times when Keneally's lapsed-Catholic sensibility and his not-at-all-lapsed Irish sensibility turn mawkish. . . . Nevertheless, Keneally's lapses are redeemed and overshadowed by his meticulous attention to psychological details which have nothing to do with his political agendas and which in fact subvert them." London Rev Books

Schindler's list. Simon & Schuster 1982 400p $25; pa $14

ISBN 0-671-51688-4; 0-671-88031-4 (pa)
* LC 82-10489

"An actual occurrence during the Nazi regime in Germany forms the basis for this story. Oskar Schindler, a Catholic German industrialist, chose to act differently from those Germans who closed their eyes to what was happening to the Jews. By spending enormous sums on bribes to the SS and on food and drugs for the Jewish prisoners whom he housed in his own camp-factory in Cracow, he succeeded in sheltering thousands of Jews, finally transferring them to a safe place in Czechoslovakia. Fifty Schindler survivors from seven nations helped the author with information." Shapiro. Fic for Youth. 3d edition

To Asmara. Warner Bks. 1989 290p o.p.
LC 89-40035

"An Australian journalist named Darcy disappears in the remote Ethiopian province of Eritrea, where rebels are fighting a savage war of independence against the ruling Marxist regime. His legacy: a number of cassette tapes and notebooks, in which he has recorded the details of his mysteriously aborted journey. From these sources we learn that Darcy had gone to Eritrea to investigate reports of rebel attacks on UN food shipments to that famine-oppressed region. In his company were an American aide seeking the rescue of his imprisoned Somali lover, an aging English feminist bent on putting an end to the ritualized mutilation of females, and a young French girl searching for her missing photojournalist father. After touring rebel-controlled territory and surviving many close scrapes with Ethiopian forces, Darcy learns that many of his basic assumptions about the famine are in error. Spurred on by this knowledge, he commits himself to a course of action that may or may not have claimed his life." Booklist

This novel "is a rare entity in contemporary fiction, a work of advocacy and engagement that unhesitatingly takes sides in one of the world's longest-running and least understood wars." N Y Times Book Rev

The tyrant's novel. Nan A. Talese 2004 235p $25

ISBN 0-385-51146-9   LC 2003-59670

The protagonist of this "novel is a successful author in a country that bears more than a passing resemblance to Iraq. One day, he is ordered to write a novel to be published under the name of the country's dictator—and given only a month for the task. As luck would have it, he has recently completed a novel that, with slight modification, will fit the bill. However, he has buried the novel with his late wife. Can he bear to disinter the manuscript in order to save himself? Though concerned with current events, Keneally takes care to give his tale wider resonance. The Middle Eastern characters go by English names, a technique that makes them less foreign to the reader and draws parallels between the subtle self-censorship of Western commercialism and the blunter kind practiced by the arts community in a dictatorship." New Yorker

Woman of the inner sea. Doubleday 1993 c1992 277p o.p.
* LC 92-28554

First published 1992 in the United Kingdom

"In the Australian state of New South Wales, Kate Gaffney-Kozinski, in her early thirties, has a marriage that's unworkable, despite all outward appearances of its success. Not ordinarily the kind of person who would do so, Kate nonetheless is pushed to the limit and flees—to the outback, where she hides her identity yet, tested again, comes into her own as a person." Booklist

This novel "succeeds on many fronts. It is a picaresque and often hilarious adventure story, recounting one woman's unforgettable if improbable travels. It is a series of love stories, as Kate meets the man who is appropriate for her at each stage of her life, and it is a mystery story as well. But the novel is also very much an exploration of ethics." N Y Times Book Rev

Kennedy, Douglas, 1955-

The big picture. Hyperion 1997 374p

ISBN 0-7868-6298-X   LC 96-44446

"Ben and Beth Bradford, who once dreamed of being hippie artists, bought into the American dream instead. Ben is a successful lawyer pulling down a six-figure salary, and Beth is a bored surburban housewife with everything Ben's money can buy. But the Bradford's are miserable, imprisoned in a loveless marriage, and tied to a lifestyle they hate. To relieve her tedium, Beth takes a lover, an aging hippie who, unlike Ben, hasn't given in to the almighty dollar. Naturally, Ben finds out about Beth's affair. The worst happens, and in a moment, the Bradfords' lives change forever." Booklist

"The book is more than just a compelling read: it also has poignant and moving things to say about lost opportunities and wasted lives in America, the cynical quality of sudden fame, the awfulness of willed seperation from deeply loved children." Publ Wkly

Kennedy, William, 1928-

Ironweed. Viking 1983 227p pa $14 hardcover o.p.

ISBN 0-14-007020-0 (pa)
* LC 82-40370

With this "tale of skid-row life in the Depression, Kennedy adds another chapter to his 'Albany cycle'—a group of novels set in the Albany, New York, underworld from the 1920s onward. Following 'Legs' and 'Billy Phelan's Greatest Game,' 'Ironweed' tells the story of Francis Phelan, a 58-year-old bum with muscatel on his breath and hallucinations on his mind. Chief among the latter is a vision of his infant son, who died after

Kennedy, William, 1928—_Continued_

falling out of Francis' arms. It is the desire to reconcile himself to the memory of his dead son that brings Francis home to Albany, ultimately opening the door to a possible reconciliation with his family." Booklist

Roscoe. Viking 2002 291p $24.95
ISBN 0-670-03029-5   LC 2001-33237

"Roscoe Owen Conway, fifty-five, fat, and in failing health, is the brains who protects and preserves Albany's Democratic Party, and, as Kennedy's seventh 'Albany Cycle' novel opens, Roscoe has plenty of protecting and preserving to do. It's V-J Day, 1945, and though the war in the Pacific is over, the war at home has just begun: the Democratic machine is facing a stiff challenge from the state's Republican governor. . . . When Elisha Fitzgibbon, the city's major Democratic funder and one of Roscoe's oldest friends, commits suicide, it looks as if the city's entire political tapestry might unravel." New Yorker

"As in all of Kennedy's Albany novels, the town is rendered with a hallucinatory, three-dimensional density. . . . This is an engrossing, comic vision of the dark side of politics." Publ Wkly

Very old bones. Viking 1992 292p o.p.
LC 91-40723

The protagonist and narrator in this installment of The Albany cycle is "Orson Purcell, the bastard son of artist Peter Phelan. . . . Building his tale around a family gathering in 1958, Purcell relates his own life story as well as episodes in the history of each family member, both living and dead, who struggle to overcome their collective and individual pasts." Libr J

"Orson is wounded, pompous, a bit pedantic in his initial attempt at family history. What transpires in [the book] is the growth and increasing authenticity of his voice. . . . Beneath the mete and just end of this closely worked novel lie bitter bones of estrangement, of love hidden or misplaced, lives wasted by jealousy and fear." N Y Times Book Rev

Kent, Alexander
  See also Reeman, Douglas

Kent, Kathleen, 1944-

The heretic's daughter; a novel. Little, Brown and Co. 2008 332p $24.99
ISBN 978-0-316-02448-8; 0-316-02448-1
LC 2008-01887

"After a bout of smallpox, 10-year-old Sarah Carrier resumes life with her mother on their family farm in Andover, Mass., dimly aware of a festering dispute between her mother, Martha, and her uncle about the plot of land where they live. The fight takes on a terrifying dimension when reports of supernatural activity in nearby Salem give way to mass hysteria, and Sarah's uncle is the first person to point the finger at Martha. Soon, neighbors struggling to eke out a living and a former indentured servant step forward to name Martha as the source of their woes. Sarah is forced to shoulder an even heavier burden as her mother and brothers are taken to prison to face a jury of young women who claim to have felt their bewitching presence. Sarah's front-row view of the trials and the mayhem that sweeps the close-knit community provides a fresh, bracing and unconventional take on a much-covered episode." Publ Wkly

Kerley, Jack

The hundredth man. Dutton 2004 307p $23.95
ISBN 0-525-94821-X   LC 2004-696

"A serial killer who leaves behind headless corpses is on the loose in Mobile, AL. Detectives Carson Ryder and Harry Nautilus are first assigned to the case but are later removed when their clues to the murderer lead them too close to the law enforcement community. Carson's older brother, a twisted serial killer who is serving a life sentence, understands enough to give them a disturbing insight into the killer's identity." Libr J

"Kerley jacks up the tension effectively with nicely placed jumps between Carson's narration and the tortured thoughts of the killer, building to an all-stops-out climax involving a raging river and a supremely horrific home movie." Booklist

Kerouac, Jack, 1922-1969

And the hippos were boiled in their tanks; [by] William S. Burroughs and Jack Kerouac. Grove Press 2008 214p $24
ISBN 978-0-8021-1876-9; 0-8021-1876-3

This novel "was co-written in 1945 by the Beat writers William S. Burroughs and Kerouac, when the two were just beginning their friendship in New York, as mentor and acolyte respectively, and years before Kerouac had even coined the term Beat Generation. Based on a real murder in 1944 involving two early members of the proto-Beat gang, Lucien Carr and David Kammerer, 'Hippos' recounts the so-called 'honor slaying' of the older, homosexual Kammerer by the young, blond and incredibly handsome Columbia University student Carr dubbed Rimbaud by Kerouac and their other Beat friend, Allen Ginsberg. . . . 'Hippos,' which by Kerouac's own account was 'hidden under the floorboards' for decades, is an essential document of the Beat Generation filled with precise details and precisely recorded dialogue from a place and period, pre-Atomic Age America, now almost irretrievably lost to us." San Francisco Chron

The Dharma bums. Viking 1958 244p o.p.

"This novel deals with Zen Buddhism. It's about two young men who are seeking to find themselves through meditation, voluntary poverty, separation from society, and intimate contact with nature, especially the Western mountains. . . . Sometimes Kerouac seems a little foolish, often he is extreme, but he is genuine, he is alive, and he is native." Libr J

also in Kerouac, J. Road novels 1957-1960

On the road. Viking 1957 310p o.p.

"Sal Paradise (a self-portrait of Kerouac), a struggling author in his mid-twenties, tells of his meeting Dean Moriarty (based on Neal Cassady), a fast-living teenager just out of a New Mexico reform school, whose soul is 'wrapped up in a fast car, a coast to reach, and a woman at the end of the road.' During the next five years they travel coast to coast, either with each other or to each other. Five trips are described." Oxford Companion to Am Lit. 6th edition

also in Kerouac, J. Road novels 1957-1960

Kerouac, Jack, 1922-1969—*Continued*

On the road: the original scroll; edited by Howard Cunnell; introductions by Howard Cunnell, Penny Vlagopoulos, George Mouratidis, and Joshua Kupetz. Viking 2007 408p $25.95

ISBN 978-0-670-06355-0; 0-670-06355-X

LC 2007-5306

"The biggest immediate difference between the first draft and the finished product . . . is that while we know On the Road as a novel—the great novel of the Beat Generation—the scroll is essentially nonfiction, a memoir that uses real names and is far less self-consciously literary. It is a dazzling piece of writing for all of its rough edges, and, stripped of affectations that in the novel can sometimes verge on bathos, as well as of gratuitous punctuation supplied by editors more devoted to rules than to music, it seems much more immediate and even contemporary. The scroll clarifies the book's connection to the past—to Mark Twain and tramp narratives and Woody Guthrie and cowboy sagas—and underlines the features it shares with its nearest contemporaneous cultural relative, Robert Frank's great photographic road book The Americans." N Y Times Book Rev

Road novels 1957-1960; [edited by Douglas Brinkley] Library of America 2007 864p $35

ISBN 978-1-59853-012-4

* LC 2007-924522

Contents: On the road; The dharma bums; The subterraneans; Tristessa; Lonesome Traveler [travel essays]; From the journals 1949-1954

On the road (1957) portrays "the fervent relationship between the writer Sal Paradise and his outrageous, exasperating, and inimitable friend Dean Moriarty. . . . The Dharma Bums (1958), at once an exploration of Buddhist spirituality and an account of the Bay Area poetry scene, is notable for its thinly veiled portraits of Kerouac's acquaintances, including Ginsberg, Gary Snyder, and Kenneth Rexroth. The Subterraneans (1958) recounts a love affair set amid the bars and bohemian haunts of San Francisco. Tristessa (1960) is a melancholy novella describing a relationship with a prostitute in Mexico City." Publisher's note

Kerouac's work "marked the articulation of a new voice far more interesting for what the author had to say and the way in which he said it than for the technical breakthroughs that it was heralded—and scorned—for at the time." San Francisco Chron

The subterraneans

In Kerouac, J. Road novels 1957-1960

Tristessa

In Kerouac, J. Road novels 1957-1960

Kerouac, Jean *See* Kerouac, Jack, 1922-1969

Kerouac, Jeanlouis *See* Kerouac, Jack, 1922-1969

Kerr, Katharine

Snare; a novel of the far future. TOR Bks. 2003 591p $27.95

ISBN 0-312-89045-1

LC 2002-40947

"A Tom Doherty Associates book"

"Three very different groups of human settlers go, not all willingly, to the planet Snare: a band of Islamic fundamentalists, a group of horse tribes and the pragmatic Cantons people. All descend on Snare's indigenous repitilian species the ChaMeech, and eight centuries of territorial and social turmoil follow." Publ Wkly

"Compelling male and female characters and a thoughtful premise make this epic adventure a strong addition to most sf collections." Libr J

Kerr, Philip

Dark matter; the private life of Sir Isaac Newton. Crown 2002 345p

ISBN 0-609-60981-5

LC 2002-24155

"One of the seventeenth century's greatest minds, Isaac Newton, is appointed warden of the Royal Mint during England's Great Recoinage. Aided by educated yet slow-witted sidekick and narrator Christopher Ellis, Newton employs the scientific method and logical deduction to thwart a high-reaching conspiracy to murder thousands of Catholics, pass counterfeit guineas, and reignite the war with France." Booklist

"Plot devices such as secret coded documents, the pseudoscience of alchemy, and a string of strange murders make for an exciting read. Using as backdrop the Tower of London, the Royal Mint, Bedlam madhouse, and Newgate Prison. . . [The author] weaves a rich tapestry of interesting characters and period details." Libr J

A quiet flame; a Bernie Gunther novel. G. P. Putnam's Sons 2009 389p $26.95

ISBN 978-0-399-15530-7; 0-399-15530-7

LC 2008-033847

"A Marian Wood book"

"A Berlin homicide cop conscripted into the SS during the course of the novels known as the Berlin Noir Trilogy, Bernie [Gunther] resurfaces in 1950 — on the same boat as Adolf Eichmann — in Buenos Aires, a vibrant city as depraved and dangerous as the one he left behind. Unlike other fugitive Nazi officers Juan Perón welcomed into Argentina, Bernie isn't allowed to slip into some anonymous job. Instead, he's pressed to solve the grisly mutilation murders of young girls, cases so similar to those he had to leave unsolved in Berlin when Hitler came to power that he suspects the same killer may now be on the loose in Argentina. Pursuing that lead, Bernie builds up contempt for government mendacity, expressing his reckless views in the wisecracking idiom of the hardboiled detective, rather than the suave tones of the undercover agent the Peronists would like him to be. But while his attitude is fashionably cynical, he cares too much about the future of civilized societies to pass himself off as a pessimist." N Y Times Book Rev

Kertész, Imre, 1929-

Detective story; translated from the Hungarian by Tim Wilkinson. Alfred A. Knopf 2008 112p $21

ISBN 978-0-307-26644-6; 0-307-26644-3

LC 2007-40216

Original Hungarian edition, 1977

"Now in prison, Antonio Martens is a torturer for the secret police of a recently defunct dictatorship. He re-

Kertész, Imre, 1929-—*Continued*

quests and is given writing materials in his cell, and what he has to recount is his involvement in the surveillance, torture, and assassination of Federigo and Enrique Salinas, a prominent father and son whose principled but passive opposition to the regime left them vulnerable to the secret police." Publisher's note

"The story is constructed with a delicate, scientific objectivity. . . . Physical description is kept to a minimum, but the feel for characters' psychology, even or perhaps especially those of the policemen, is acute. Much happens between the lines, increasing a sense of claustrophobic intensity." Los Angeles Times Book Rev

Kesey, Ken

One flew over the cuckoo's nest; a novel. Viking 1962 311p hardcover o.p. pa $7.99
ISBN 0-670-03058-9; 0-451-16396-6 (pa)
*

"Life in a mental institution is predictable and suffocating under the iron rule of Nurse Ratched, who tolerates no disruption of routine on her all-male ward. Half-Indian Chief Bromden, almost invisible on the ward because he is thought to be deaf and dumb, describes the arrival of rowdy Randle Patrick McMurphy. McMurphy takes on the nurse as an adversary in his attempt to organize his fellow inmates and breathe some self-esteem and joy into their lives. The battle is vicious on the part of the nurse, who is relentless in her efforts to break McMurphy, but a spark of human will brings an element of hope to counter the despotic institutional power." Shapiro. Fic for Youth. 3d edition

Sailor song. Viking 1992 535p o.p.
LC 92-5406

"The story, set some 30 years hence, involves Ike Sallas, a once-famous ecoterrorist now living in an Alaskan fishing village. Ike's carefully cultivated disengagement is threatened first by the arrival of a Hollywood film company, there to make a movie based on a children's book, and then by his thawing relations with Alice Carmody, a fisherman's wife whose marriage is on the rocks. When Ike discovers that the film company has a sinister motive, he tries to rally the town, yet defeat seems imminent until an environmental apocalypse throws a monkey wrench into everyone's plans." Libr J

The author "includes a great deal of purposeful foolery, flooding the narrative with farcical incongruities, crude asides, wacky in-jokes, and countless allusions to literary classics and popular culture. . . . In sum, Sailor Song is vintage Ken Kesey: not for the faint-hearted, perhaps, but certainly instructive, and never boring." New Leader

Sometimes a great notion. Viking 1964 628p o.p.
*

"This novel focuses on the person of Hank Stamper, raw and aggressive scion of an Oregon lumber empire. The struggle is . . . with a society unwilling to accommodate a strong individualist, but the issues are deepened and complicated by the fact that Hank's principal antagonist turns out to be his cerebral, introspective half-brother, Lee, and by Kesey's development of Lee as an equally appealing character, Kesey manipulates the clash of fraternal egos to a powerful climax, before reconciling the brothers to a tragic understanding of their own vulnerability to an indifferent fate and to a group of townspeople who have been made intolerably uncomfortable by the sight of the Stampers' strength." Ency of World Lit in the 20th Century

Kessel, John

The Baum plan for financial independence and other stories. Small Beer Press 2008 315p $24; pa $16
ISBN 978-1-931520-51-5; 1-931520-51-8; 978-1-931520-50-8 (pa); 1-931520-50-X (pa)
LC 2007-52319

Contents: The Baum plan for financial independence; Every angel is; Terrifying; The invisible empire; Powerless; It's all true; The red phone; Downtown; The last American; The snake girl; The juniper tree; Stories for men; Under the lunchbox tree; Sunlight or rock; Pride and Prometheus

"What makes Kessel the sort of writer we should pay more attention to is not a particular quality of style. Like many fine writers he adapts his style to the story he has to tell. Nor is it that he is an especially innovative writer. You do find fresh ideas in his work, but rarely of the kind or scale that blow you away. Kessel is not a writer you turn to if you are looking for the old fashioned astonishments of science fiction. No, what makes John Kessel so interesting is that he is one of the most reflexive, one of the most self-aware writers around. He is acutely conscious of the fictionality of the genre, and plays with it." SF Site

(ed) Feeling very strange. See Feeling very strange

Keyes, Daniel, 1927-

Flowers for Algernon. Harcourt Brace Jovanovich 1966 274p o.p.
*

"Charlie Gordon, aged thirty-two, is mentally retarded and enrolls in a class to 'become smart.' He keeps a journal of his progress after an experimental operation that increases his I.Q. Although Charlie becomes brilliant, he is unhappy because he cannot shed his former personality and is tormented by his memories. In the end he begins to lose the mental powers he has gained." Shapiro. Fic for Youth. 3d edition

Flowers for Algernon [novelette]
In The Hugo winners p245-73

Keyes, Marian

Last Chance Saloon. Morrow 2001 c1999 370p $25
ISBN 0-688-18072-8
LC 00-67891
First published 1999 in the United Kingdom

This novel's "protagonists are two London women who grew up together in the small, repressive Irish town of Knockavoy. Tara, a computer analyst, lives with Thomas, a bitter and miserly high school geography teacher. . . . Katherine Casey, an accountant for an advertising agency, wears boring suits, has a hyperorganized underwear drawer and brushes off all advances, including those of attractive advertising account

Keyes, Marian—*Continued*

executive Joe Roth. As they turn 31, each woman is full of suggestions for improving the other's life and full of excuses for doing nothing about her own. That begins to change when Fintan O'Grady, their gay pal and fellow Knockavoy refugee, falls ill with a mysterious disease." Publ Wkly

The other side of the story. W. Morrow 2004 516p $24.95

ISBN 0-06-052051-5   LC 2003-64939

This novel "follows the lives of three dynamic women-jilted Gemma Hogan; literary agent Jojo Harvey; and bestselling English author Lily Wright, who 'stole' Gemma's boyfriend Anton. Gemma, hurt and betrayed by her best friend's actions, must put her emotions on hold to care for her mam after her dad takes off with a younger woman." Publ Wkly

"Packing every page with her trademark one-liners, the insightful Keyes has the ability to examine life, love, and work issues with great wit and aplomb." Booklist

Keys, Angela

(tr) Ts̆ypkin, L. Summer in Baden-Baden

Keys, Roger

(tr) Ts̆ypkin, L. Summer in Baden-Baden

Khadra, Yasmina *See* Moulessehoul, Mohammed, 1955-

Khemir, Sabiha, 1959-

The blue manuscript. Verso 2008 307p $24.95

ISBN 978-1-84467-308-7; 1-84467-308-1

LC 2009-275213

"Set in Wadi Hassoun, a small village outside of Cairo, the novel tracks the work of an international team of archaeologists who've been commissioned by wealthy London financiers to unearth a holy Islamic text called the Blue Manuscript." Libr J

The "account of the dig, and the truths excavated for the archeologists and the villagers, is interspersed with scenes from the court of the Fatimid Caliph al-Muizz as he conquers Egypt and marches to Cairo in 972, and as his calligrapher Ibn al-Warraq produces the beautiful blue manuscript for the Caliph's mother. Al Khemir seduces readers with the manuscript's mythical beauty and the philosophy of its art form. . . . Her cast of archeologists is led by the avaricious Mark, accompanied by Zohra, their Tunisian-English translator. Their intrigues dominate the novel: thwarted professional aspirations, comic and complicated romantic geometries, and their interactions with villagers like their go-betweens Mustapha and Rayyed Ahmed, the cheeky little boy Mahmoud, the beautiful Zinab, and the blind sage Amm Gaber." Independent

Khoury, Elias

Gate of the sun; translated from the Arabic by Humphrey Davies. Archipelago Books 2006 539p (Rainmaker translations) $26

ISBN 0-976395-02-9   LC 2005-21036

Original Arabic edition, 1998

"At a makeshift hospital in the Shatila refugee camp on the outskirts of Beirut, Dr. Khalil sits by the bed of his gravely ill, unconscious friend and patient, Yunes, a Palestinian fighter, and reminisces about their lives in an attempt to bring him back to consciousness." Publ Wkly

"This is a challenging novel that demands from us an imagination potent enough to link its many loose threads. The good news is that Khoury's language is derived from everyday colloquial Arabic, rather than the formal language of intellectuals and the media. Humphrey Davies's translation is masterful, allowing us to appreciate Gate of the Sun's short, clear sentences and crisp metaphors afresh." New Statesman

Kidd, Sue Monk

The mermaid chair. Viking 2005 352p $24.95

ISBN 0-670-03394-4

"Forty-three-year old Jessie Sullivan is pulled out of her staid life in Atlanta with her husband and daughter, back to her childhood home on Egret Island after her mother, Nelle, cuts off one of her own fingers. Jessie has been uneasy with the island since her beloved father died when she was nine in a boating accident, a tragedy Jessie has always felt partially responsible for. At the behest of her mother's best friend, Jessie journeys back to the island to try to reconnect with the mother she's never been close to. Jessie wants to know what drove her obviously disturbed mother to sever her finger, and she thinks Father Dominic, one of the Benedictine monks who resides in a nearby monastery, might know more about her mother's state of mind. But it is another monk who claims Jessie's attention—handsome Brother Thomas, who ignites in Jessie a passion so intense it overwhelms her, leading her to question her marriage and rediscover her artistic drive." Booklist

This is an "emotionally rich novel, full of sultry, magical descriptions of life in the South." Publ Wkly

The secret life of bees. Viking 2002 301p $24.95; pa $14

ISBN 0-670-89460-5; 0-14-200174-0 (pa)

* LC 2001-26310

This is the "tale of a 14-year-old white girl named Lily Owen who is raised by the elderly African American Rosaleen after the accidental death of Lily's mother. Following a racial brawl in 1960s Tiburon, S.C, Lily and Rosaleen find shelter in a distant town with three black bee-keeping sisters." Libr J

"Lily is a wonderfully petulant and self-absorbed adolescent, and Kidd deftly portrays her sense of injustice as it expands to accommodate broader social evils." N Y Times Book Rev

Kienzle, William X., 1928-2002

Assault with intent. Andrews & McMeel 1982 273p o.p.

* LC 82-1628

"The action takes place in a seminary in Detroit and it involves an apparent plot to kill some or all of the priests in seminaries. It is a perfect setting for one of the instructors at the seminary, Father Koesler, a priest-detective. . . . The attempts at murdering the priests are continuously foiled either by circumstances or the ineptitude of the assailant. We are led from one seminary to

Kienzle, William X., 1928-2002—*Continued*

the other as the would-be murderers change their targets. The plot attracts such media attention that a TV movie is filmed at the major seminary to document the plot against the priests. In the process of the investigation attention is focused on a group of ultraconservative Catholics and their leader, Roman Kirkus." Best Sellers

Body count. Andrews & McMeel 1992 266p o.p. LC 92-3266

This mystery involves Father Koesler, "Detroit detective-priest in conflicts between old and new Catholic theology. Hitman Guido Vespa loudly confesses to Koesler that he has bumped off Father Keating, the spiritual leader of a nearby parish, and buried the body in the grave of the long-dead, much beloved Monsignor Kern. Overhearing the confession, exuberant new resident priest Nick Dunn is delighted: one of the reasons he came to St. Joseph's was to be near its sleuthing pastor. Nick's enthusiasm increases when the police ask Koesler for help with Keating's disappearance." Publ Wkly

The gathering. Andrews McMeel Pub. 2002 280p $22.95
ISBN 0-7407-2229-8 LC 2001-55969

Father Koesler "reaches back in time and memory to clarify the ambiguous details surrounding the death of an old friend and fellow priest. Father Stan Benson is declared accidentally dead by carbon monoxide poisoning. Nursing his own doubts, Koesler convenes a reunion with the five remaining members of a close-knit group of friends who all initially chose religious vocations as a way of life. . . . Koesler's natural flair for detection is surpassed only by his deep and abiding compassion for the human condition." Booklist

The greatest evil. Andrews McMeel Pub. 1998 278p o.p. LC 97-37738

"Father Robert Koesler is excited at the prospect of having Father Zachary Tully join his parish. Unfortunately, Bishop Vincent Delvecchio has misgivings about Tully's appointment. As Koesler and Tully discuss the matter, Koesler discovers a long-hidden mystery, which takes a back seat to numerous discussions that give fascinating insight into the working of the Catholic Church before Vatican II." Libr J

The man who loved God. Andrews & McMeel 1997 274p o.p. LC 96-34604

"Father Bob Koesler, the popular amateur sleuth and Detroit priest, takes a vacation literally and figuratively away from the action. Taking his place is Father Zachary Tully, who comes to Detroit (from Dallas) to present an award to banker and philanthropist Thomas A. Adams. Father Tully is also eager to meet the half-brother he never knew he had, Detroit police lieutenant Alonzo 'Zoo' Tully. When one of Adam's vice-presidents is murdered just after being named to head a new inner-city bank branch, Father Tully and his brother find themselves working together." Publ Wkly

The rosary murders. Andrews & McMeel 1979 257p o.p. LC 78-31833

"From Ash Wednesday, when the murderer first struck Detroit's Catholic community, the police seemed helpless to solve the string of senseless murders. The weeks that followed became a nightmare for the crack homicide team of investigators headed by Lieutenant Walter Koznicki, until Father Koesler broke the madman's code." Publisher's note

Kiernan, Caitlín R.

The red tree. Roc 2009 385p pa $16
ISBN 978-0-451-46276-3; 0-451-46276-9 LC 2009-15105

"Author Sarah Crowe leaves Atlanta after her girlfriend commits suicide, settling at a homestead in rural Rhode Island in order to finish her latest book, which is well past deadline. There's something sinister about the house, and Sarah quickly learns that the previous tenant, a professor and folklorist named Charles Harvey, killed himself while researching a book about the supernatural folklore of New England. Exploring the basement, Sarah discovers Harvey's manuscript, and she quickly finds herself in the middle of a living nightmare centered on a mysterious red oak tree in the house's yard. . . . [An] intelligent blend of folklore, horror, and dark fantasy." Libr J

Kijewski, Karen

Alley Kat blues. Doubleday 1995 342p o.p. LC 94-35200

In this mystery, Kat Colorado, "investigator and girlfriend of Las Vegas cop Hank Parker, becomes embroiled in a family controversy and murder investigation when she discovers a young girl's mangled body, an apparent hit-and-run victim. The girl's mother begs Kat to look into her daughter's death but her religious husband refuses to cooperate. To add to Kat's problem, Hank is involved with a murder investigation of his own." SLJ

The author "has written a solid narrative in a snappy style that fits Kat's clear-eyed intelligence and unpretentious methods of dealing with difficult people." N Y Times Book Rev

Copy Kat. Doubleday 1992 261p o.p. LC 92-14482

"A Perfect crime book"

"Hard-boiled female private eye Kat Colorado . . . takes on a new identity as Kate, the dyed-blonde bartender, to try to discover who murdered Diedre Durkin, the local bartender's wife. As she investigates motives, suspects, and alibis, Kat encounters blackmail and infidelity, a deep-seated and dangerous sibling rivalry, twisted family jealousies, and a web of bitter deceit and hatred." Booklist

Honky tonk Kat. Putnam 1996 323p o.p. LC 95-49335

"Country-western singing star Dakota Jones, a friend of Kat's since childhood, is worried. Like most stars, she has enemies, but someone has been sending her unusually unnerving letters and really nasty gifts. Dakota, afraid that her one out-of-control fan might do something stupid, asks Kat to join her entourage and find out who's up to what." Booklist

The author "captures the sweaty thrills of road life while taking a clear-eyed view of the boozy dives and greasy food and the scary adoration of desperate fans." N Y Times Book Rev

Kijewski, Karen—*Continued*

Kat scratch fever. Putnam 1997 323p o.p.

LC 96-51141

In this mystery Sacramento PI Kat Colorado "exposes embezzlement and extortion at Hope for Kids, a charity that aids crippled and disfigured children." Publ Wkly

"Taking the direct approach here, Kat marches up to the charity's most generous givers and demands to know if they were being blackmailed. When that doesn't work, she tries bullying, wheedling, groveling and breaking and entering. And when all her muscle and charm run out, she uses her brain." N Y Times Book Rev

Kat's cradle. Doubleday 1992 244p o.p.

LC 91-32218

"A Perfect crime book"

"Narrator Kat Colorado, a socially conscious Sacramento private investigator with a Las Vegas policeman lover, accepts the challenge of finding the birth parents of an 'orphan' whose autocratic-but-rich grandmother has just died. Paige Morrell and scruffy boyfriend Paul may be more interested in proving her right to inherit; however, Kat thinks she has a right to know about her folks." Libr J

"Outstanding among today's female detectives, PI Kat Colorado exhibits conscience and compassion, muscle and wisecracking savvy in an appealing and believable combination." Publ Wkly

Stray Kat waltz. Putnam 1998 311p

ISBN 0-399-14368-8

* LC 97-46986

Sacramento P.I. Kat Colorado is recovering from the murder of her fiancé Hank Parker. "Although the heartache that makes Kat weep into her pillow sensitizes her to the plight of a battered wife who comes to her for help, it also blunts the P.I.'s normally sharp instincts for deceit and danger. Sara Bernard might well be the stalking victim she claims to be. Her husband might also be the model-cop-gone-nuts she says he is. But both their stories seem fishy, and Kat's judgment is too clouded by emotional cobwebs for her to think clearly. She perks up, though, for some undercover scenes at a fancy rehab clinic, where the pretentiousness is enough to restore her mental equilibrium, not to mention her sense of humor." N Y Times Book Rev

Kim, Suki, 1970-

The interpreter. Farrar, Straus & Giroux 2003 294p $24

ISBN 0-374-17713-9   LC 2002-72120

This novel introduces Korean American "Suzy Park, a 29-year-old interpreter whose work involves her in a bevy of agencies throughout the five boroughs, from the Immigration and Naturalization Service to the criminal courts. Park is blasé about her occupation until a routine translating job reveals that her greengrocer parents were not murdered by random violence, as the police had indicated, but instead had been shot by political enemies. These data provide fodder for Park, and the novel tracks her investigation into what really happened." Libr J

"This is an intriguing, tortured portrait of a second-generation Korean-American by a promising young writer." Publ Wkly

Kimmel, Haven, 1965-

Iodine; a novel. Free Press 2008 223p $24

ISBN 978-1-4165-7284-8; 1-4165-7284-8

LC 2007-49565

"Brilliant college senior Trace Pennington lives under the radar, silently managing the distance between her constrictive Indiana roots and the intellectual refuge that she craves. Trace's present is ever so carefully constructed, and her past follows her like a lost dog. Then in one impulsive instant, she completely deconstructs her life and hands it over to a man, a father figure who remakes her into an idealized image. When an old friend comes to stay and brings along with him an outsider's viewpoint, that delicate line between insanity and reality simply cannot hold." Libr J

"The writing in 'Iodine' is genius. Comic renderings of parties — pretentious college kids demonstrating their love and obnoxiousness and equally pretentious professors demonstrating their civility and tedium — are downright hilarious. . . . As Trace's memories come and go, so does the book's sophistication of language and insight. Whether in Trace's voice, her dream journal voice or the narrator's voice, the writing in 'Iodine' is, at turns, fraught and hectic, and translucent and shimmering in its stillness." News & Observer

Something rising (light and swift). Free Press 2004 273p $24

ISBN 0-7432-4775-2   LC 2003-49114

This tale is set in a "small town in Indiana. Cassie Claiborne, the most grounded person in her family, longs for her feckless father to return home but in the meantime, she grows into a young woman and shoulders the burden herself. On one of his increasingly rare visits, her father takes her to a pool hall, and she watches him play. When she takes her turn with the cue, it becomes clear that Cassie has an innate talent for the game. She starts playing for money and routinely beats arrogant men who think they can easily best a young girl. Her skill ultimately leads her to a match with her father, but even pool playing can't make up for his abandonment of her, or the fact that Cassie's destiny might lie beyond Roseville." Booklist

"Kimmel's idea of a plot is not very linear. It's more like a net that hauls in great scenes. But while things may look superficially languid, this is one author who will not waste your time." Newsweek

The used world; a novel. Free Press 2007 308p $25

ISBN 978-0-7432-4778-8; 0-7432-4778-7

LC 2006-53172

This final entry in the trilogy that began with The solace of leaving early (2002) and Something rising (light and swift) (2004), "revolves around three extraordinary women from fictional Jonah, Indiana. All work at the Used World Emporium, a sprawling store crammed floor to ceiling with the stuff of people's lives. Fortysomething Claudia, mannish and a staggering 6 foot 5, desperately tries to cope with the reality of her beloved mother's death; red-haired Rebekah escapes the clutches of her family's religious zealotry only to find herself pregnant with no place to go; 65-year-old Hazel, armed with her belief in astrology, runs the emporium and serves as a mother hen of sorts to the two younger women. Kimmel's take on spirituality is intriguing, though her more

Kimmel, Haven, 1965—*Continued*

detailed passages about religion slow an otherwise swift plot. . . . . [She] covers an encyclopedic range of emotions in this tale of love, loss, and the irrevocable acts that define us." Booklist

Kincaid, Jamaica

Annie John. Farrar, Straus & Giroux 1985 148p hardcover o.p. pa $12

ISBN 0-374-10521-9; 0-374-52510-2 (pa)

*

"Episodes from the young life of Annie John, aged 10 to 17, as she grows up on the Caribbean island of Antigua. This is a magical coming-of-age tale, ripe with the special ambience of its tropical setting and sustained by Annie's far from naive awareness of the world around her. Death, illness, and poverty intrude on the narrator's perceptive sensibility from time to time, but even these experiences instruct her and expand her understanding of life and its shifting reality. . . . A poetic and intensely moving work." Booklist

Autobiography of my mother. Farrar, Straus & Giroux 1995 228p

ISBN 0-374-10731-9   LC 94-24580

The narrator of this novel is Xuela Claudette Richardson. "Raised without love and self-defined by her mother's death at the moment of her birth, Xuela regards life in her Dominican villages with disturbing disinterest and keen penetration. . . . Haunted by her mother's absence, Xuela ensures her own barrenness, endures a loveless affair with and marriage to the English doctor Philip, who loves her, and rejoices with stevedore Roland, whom she loves—or claims to." Libr J

In Kincaid's "poised and crystalline prose, precise and serene as a knife drawn through water, she now gives us this starkly memorable 'self-portrait' of a calm, thoughtful, utterly alienated woman who has learned to lead a life devoid of love, but not devoid of dignity." Christ Sci Monit

Lucy. Farrar, Straus & Giroux 1990 163p o.p.

* LC 90-83987

The narrator, Lucy Potter, a nineteen year old from Antigua, tells of her experiences as an *au pair* for a wealthy family in a large North American city

"The great motifs of Western literature, like goodness and evil, innocence and experience, resonate in Kincaid's novel in a completely updated and unselfconscious way. In other hands, this story of a West Indian *au pair* would just be sociology. In Kincaid's recasting, it is both art and argument." Christ Sci Monit

Mr. Potter. Farrar, Straus & Giroux 2002 195p $20

ISBN 0-374-21494-8

"Mr. Potter is a man without qualities, an illiterate taxi driver on Kincaid's native island of Antigua, whose life, though full of loss and suffering, is essentially uneventful. His illegitimate daughter, Elaine Cynthia, returns to the island after his death to write his story—in fact, to narrate this novel." N Y Times Book Rev

"Kincaid has exquisite control over her narrator's deep-seated rage, which drives the story but never overpowers it and is tempered by a clear-eyed sympathy. Her prose here is more incantatory and hypnotic than ever." Publ Wkly

Kincaid, Nanci

Verbena; a novel. Algonquin Bks. 2002 338p $24.95

ISBN 1-56512-348-4   LC 2001-56531

"A Shannon Ravenel book"

Sixth-grade teacher Verbena Eckerd "was happily married to Bob, or so she thought, until he died in a car accident with another woman at his side. She thinks she has raised her five children well, until her two oldest daughters run off with no-account men, her third moves away with Bena's arch rival, and her eldest son chooses the one woman in the world whose very name causes Bena anguish. She can't believe that good-natured mailman Lucky McKale really loves her, since he is married to Sue Cox, the most beautiful and richest woman in Baxter County, Ala. But after Sue Cox herself agrees to a divorce and blesses their union, Bena finally feels she can accept Lucky's proposal. A new kind of domestic unit is formed, with exes and stepchildren integrated into one colorful family. Then disaster strikes—Lucky disappears. Kincaid is both warmhearted and clear-eyed about the compromises people make to find happiness." Publ Wkly

Kinder, Chuck

Honeymooners; a cautionary tale. Farrar, Straus & Giroux 2001 357p $24

ISBN 0-374-17258-7   LC 00-63616

"Chronicle of two writers who share a 'stupendous dream' of fame and freedom in the Bay Area in the 1970s, the heyday of drugs, booze and indiscriminate sex. Aspiring writer Ralph Crawford (based loosely on Raymond Carver); Jim Stark, his sidekick in friendship, ambition and general fecklessness; and the two writers' mistresses and wives never quite recover from their adolescent pranks, cheerful amorality and determined debauchery, despite Crawford's rise to fame." Publ Wkly

"Both wives emerge as major characters, reflecting the humor and anguish of living with men who, despite their successes, seem headed for rock bottom. Kinder's speedy, wry prose transports the reader to a time when drug use and personal freedom were unquestioned." Libr J

Kinder, R. M. (Rose Marie)

An absolute gentleman; a novel. Counterpoint 2007 288p pa $14

ISBN 978-1-58243-388-2; 1-58243-388-7

LC 2007-17932

"Taciturn English professor Arthur Blume launches his narrative by boldly stating that he is believed to have murdered as many as 17 women. Yet what most outrages him, now that he has been incarcerated, is that journalists are depicting him as a monster. He pens a memoir to correct this impression. In it, he describes in lavish detail the outfitting of his newly rented rooms in the small university town of Mason, Missouri; demurs over particulars of his illicit love affair with a fellow professor; and shares self-deprecating anecdotes about his gallant championing of a maligned colleague. Tucked among these decorous tidbits, however, are tantalizing clues to the demon within, one Kinder allows to emerge as stealthily as a cobra sliding from its bamboo basket. The addition of

Kinder, R. M. (Rose Marie)—*Continued*

a self-explanatory epilogue regarding her personal experience detracts only slightly from Kinder's otherwise spellbinding debut novel, a pitch-perfect rendition of the cunning malevolence that can lie hidden beneath the guise of refined civility." Booklist

King, Dave, 1955-

The ha-ha; a novel. Little, Brown and Co 2005 340p $23.95

ISBN 0-316-15610-8   LC 2004-7398

"First-person narrator Howard Kapostash is unable to read or to speak coherently, the result of injuries suffered in Vietnam. Now middle-aged and living a low-key life in a large house he inherited from his parents, Howard is still friends with his former high school sweetheart, Sylvia. Before entering a drug rehab program, she entrusts Howard with her nine-year-old son, Ryan, completely upending Howard's lonely, disorganized existence. Also sharing his house are a Texas-raised Vietnamese woman, who runs a catering business, and two freewheeling young house painters. This unlikely family—heretofore all but strangers to one another—becomes a thriving parental unit centered on young Ryan. Everything begins to deteriorate, however, as the mother signals her return, and Howard fights in the only way he knows how to retain ties with Ryan." Libr J

"With Howard as a guide, a potentially corny situation develops into a complex exploration of loss and loneliness that packs a potently bittersweet punch." Washington Post Book World

King, Joseph Hillstrom *See* Hill, Joe

King, Laurie R.

The beekeeper's apprentice, or, On the segregation of the queen. Bantam Books 2002 xxi, 341p pa $12

ISBN 0-553-38152-0   LC 2001-43926

First published 1994 by St. Martin's Press

"In the early years of WWI, 15-year-old American Mary Russell encounters Holmes, retired in Sussex Downs where Conan Doyle left him raising bees. Mary, an orphan rebelling against her guardian aunt's strictures, impresses the sleuth with her intelligence and acumen. Holmes initiates her into the mysteries of detection, allowing her to participate in a few cases when she comes home from her studies at Oxford. The collaboration is ignited by the kidnapping in Wales of Jessica Simpson, daughter of an American senator." Publ Wkly

"A wonderfully original and entertaining story that is funny, heartwarming, and full of intrigue. . . . Holmes fans, history buffs, lovers of humor and adventure, and mystery devotees will all find King's book absorbing from beginning to end." Booklist

A darker place. Bantam Bks. 1999 384p

ISBN 0-553-10711-9   LC 98-29835

For 18 years, Professor Anne Waverly "has divided her time between teaching theology and working as an undercover operative for the FBI. This novel takes Anne inside a religious community called Change for what she vows will be her last investigative assignment. At its Arizona outpost she confronts not only the distorted goals and values of the community but the phantoms that lurk in her own past." Libr J

"King's solid research into alternative religious sects makes the desert commune feel like a real place, while her taut pacing insures that an air of menace hangs over the strange rituals that go on there. But the strongest appeal of the story lies in its superb characters, especially the children who become Anne's charges." N Y Times Book Rev

The game; a Mary Russell novel. Bantam Books 2004 368p map $23.95

ISBN 0-553-80194-5

                 * LC 2003-55684

"Mycroft Holmes sends his brother, Sherlock, and Sherlock's wife, Mary Russell, to India to investigate the disappearance of master spy Kimball O'Hara, the legendary 'Kim' made famous by Rudyard Kipling." Libr J

"Whatever this grueling land journey lacks in urgency, it repays in scenes of vibrant local color, described by Russell in the droll tongue of a woman with the wit to realize that, while she may be dirty and tired and in constant danger, she is having the time of her life." N Y Times Book Rev

Justice Hall; a Mary Russell novel. Bantam Bks. 2002 331p

ISBN 0-553-11113-2   LC 2001-37945

"Mary Russell is Sherlock Holmes' partner and wife. In the England of the 1920s, the pair find themselves shocked by the appearance of Ali and Mahmoud Hazr, their mysterious Arab associates from *O Jerusalem.* Ali is Alistair, and Mahmoud is Maurice (called Marsh). Who would have divined that this pair of cousins is actually British, and Marsh is about to be named duke to his family's ancestral manse, the Hall of the title? King breaks most of the rules of mystery narrative with voluptuous abandon, and we don't care." Booklist

Keeping watch. Bantam Bks. 2003 383p $23.95

ISBN 0-553-80191-0   LC 2002-34266

"At its simplest, this is the story of a man who helps rescue women and/or children from dangerously abusive men. King's lengthy, brilliantly executed backstory of Allen Carmichael's experiences in Vietnam, his disastrously unhappy return home and his eventual discovery of his 'calling' showcase some of her finest writing. Now in his early 50s, Allen is ready to retire from his dangerous vocation, to settle on his remote island and perhaps serve as a consultant to those who continue the struggle. But his last rescue, that of a 12-year-old boy trapped in a horrible situation, continues to haunt him." Publ Wkly

A letter of Mary; a Mary Russell novel. St. Martin's Press 1996 276p o.p.   LC 96-22424

"A Thomas Dunne book"

In this mystery "featuring Mary Russell, Oxford scholar, detective, and wife of Sherlock Holmes, Russell and Holmes are visited by Palestinian archaeologist Dorothy Ruskin, who leaves the pair an ancient parchment that is purportedly a letter from Mary Magdalene in which Mary calls herself an apostle of Jesus. Soon after, Ruskin is killed by a hit-and-run driver, and the Holmes' house is ransacked, presumably by people who want the document." Booklist

"For all the disparity of their investigative techniques, the ultra-perceptive Holmes and the super-scholarly Rus-

King, Laurie R.—*Continued*

sell make an engaging pair of sleuths. Their quick minds and quirky personalities insure a lively adventure in the very best of intellectual company." N Y Times Book Rev

Locked rooms; a Mary Russell novel. Bantam Books 2005 402p $24

ISBN 0-553-80197-X

"Tormented by recurring nightmares, Mary Russell . . . returns to San Francisco after a ten-year absence. She swears to husband Sherlock Holmes that she wasn't in the city during the 1906 fire, but events soon prove her wrong. What memories is she hiding from herself? Holmes suspects they are connected somehow to the terrible car crash that claimed the lives of Russell's father, mother, and younger brother in 1915. With his normally capable wife distracted by her emotions, it is up to Holmes to recruit new Irregulars and uncover the truth behind the 'locked rooms' that Russell dreams about." Libr J

"In alternating sections, told in first person for Mary and third for Holmes, the unraveling of long-buried and terrifying memories also unwinds a skein of wonderful historical texture: the place of Chinese immigrants and the use of feng shui; the nightlife of a city during the age of jazz, Prohibition, and flappers; and the presence of Dash Hammett, who plays a fascinating role as a very different sort of Irregular." Booklist

The moor; a Mary Russell novel. St. Martin's Press 1998 307p il

ISBN 0-312-16934-5   LC 97-31886

"A Thomas Dunne book"

Mary Russell "drops everything to join husband Sherlock Holmes in Devonshire, where the pair investigate an ancient family curse near the scene of *The Hound of the Baskervilles*—published some 20 years earlier. The forbidding moor nearby provides them both danger and inspiration." Libr J

"Sherlockians have their choice of being amused or affronted by these artful embellishments on the Holmes canon, and few will appreciate the curiously wan characterization of the great detective. But there's no resisting the appeal of King's thrillingly moody scenes of Dartmoor and her lovely evocation of its legends." N Y Times Book Rev

O Jerusalem. Bantam Bks. 1999 367p

ISBN 0-553-11093-4   LC 98-56124

In 1918, Sherlock Holmes and Mary Russell, "the 19-year-old Oxford student whom he takes under his wing as an apprentice and partner, are sent on a mission to Palestine by Mycroft, Sherlock's powerful older brother. When Russell and Holmes are deposited, under cover of darkness, on the shores of Palestine, the British, under General Allenby, have just wrested control of the area from the Turks. . . . Eventually they encounter Joshua, a British agent, and Allenby himself." Publ Wkly

"With the feminist heroine chronicling events and the cerebral detective stirring the pot, readers can't lose." Booklist

King, Rachael, 1970-

The sound of butterflies; a novel. William Morrow 2007 338p

ISBN 978-0-06-135764-0; 0-06-135764-2

LC 2007-37442

"In May of 1904, when Thomas Edgar returns to England from his butterfly-collecting expedition to Brazil, his young wife Sophie expects that their happy life together will resume its familiar contented course. Instead, she is faced with a different man altogether, one whose eyes are colder, and who hardly acknowledges her. . . . Thomas' almost sacred quest for a particularly beautiful and elusive butterfly sets up an unforgettably bittersweet story, with its elliptical search for meaning in a world where one kills the thing one loves, and the victim is silent. King's jungle descriptions are masterful. . . . Her rippling prose builds to a wave of intrigue and danger as the narrative unfolds long-hidden revelations of steamy encounters and power plays 'in this godforsaken place' of de facto slavery and disease." BookPage

King, Roger, 1947-

A girl from Zanzibar. Books & Co./Helen Marx Bks. 2002 307p $14.95

ISBN 1-885586-60-4 (pa)   LC 2002-105487

A picaresque novel about a young East African woman's adventures and loves across a dozen years and three continents.

"Marcella is the author's mouthpiece, his stage manager, theorizing, summing up the action, signaling transitions, and at times these extra roles blur her outline. But the minor characters are just themselves, seen whole with tragic clarity." N Y Times Book Rev

King, Ross, 1962-

Domino. Walker & Co. 2002 435p $26

ISBN 0-8027-3378-6   LC 2002-29620

"When a talented young artist, Sir George Cautley, goes to London from Shropshire in 1780 to make something of himself, he meets a glamorous, mystifying woman named Lady Petronella Beauclair. As he paints her portrait, she tells him the labyrinthine story of an old man named Tristano, one of Europe's most renowned castrati from decades ago, who is a dormant social presence in London. As Cautley begins studies with Sir Endymion Starker, a famous artist he meets while gambling, he also makes the acquaintance of Starker's mistress, Eleanora, who has her own sad tale to tell." Publ Wkly

"Replete with mystery and suspense and immersed in vivid historical details, this work is also a sharp, philosophical musing on the disguises of the world and the search for the truth that lies beneath." Libr J

King, Stephen, 1947-

Apt pupil

In King, S. Different seasons p103-296

The Bachman books: four early novels by Stephen King. New Am. Lib. 1985 692p o.p.

LC 85-11411

An omnibus edition of four novels first published in paperback under the author's pseudonym Richard Bachman

King, Stephen, 1947-——_Continued_

Contents: Rage (1977); The long walk (1979); Roadwork (1981); The running man (1982)

"In _Rage_, a high-school student goes berserk in the classroom, killing the teacher and holding the class hostage. Set in a militaristic ultra-conservative America, _The Long Walk_ pits 100 teenagers against each other in a grueling 450-mile marathon walk in which the penalty is death. _Roadwork_ is a novel of societal conflict, man vs. progress. The first three thrillers, while entertaining and gripping, occasionally suffer from unfocused and uneven writing. Unresolved questions cause the books to be somewhat unsatisfying. However the fourth novel, _The Running Man_ . . . is an action-packed futuristic romp. Protagonist Ben Richards bets his life on a TV show in order to win the money to save the life of his deathly ill daughter. The story combines social commentary, adventure and science fiction, set against the backdrop of a decaying society." SLJ

Bag of bones. Scribner 1998 529p

ISBN 0-684-85350-7   LC 98-23801

Suspense writer Mike Noonan is "mourning the untimely death of his wife. Plagued by vivid nightmares, writer's block, and ghostly visitations, Noonan nonetheless becomes willingly involved in a bitter custody dispute between a beautiful young woman and a wealthy computer magnate. All is not as it seems, however, and Noonan soon finds himself and his charges pawns of forces seeking revenge for an unspeakable, century-old crime." Libr J

"The big surprise here is the emotional wallop the story packs, particularly in the scenes where Noonan grieves for his dead wife. These are among the most disconsolate moments King has ever created." Newsweek

Black house; a novel; [by] Stephen King [and] Peter Straub. Random House 2001 624p

ISBN 0-375-50439-7   LC 2001-31657

Sequel to The talisman (1984)

"In French Landing, Wis., a serial killer called the Fisherman is doing unspeakable things to local children. But a retired Los Angeles homicide detective named Jack Sawyer, who has done a mighty job of repressing his boyhood trials in an alternate world called the Territories, knows that there's more to these crimes than mere banal human cruelty. . . . What elevates 'Black House' beyond ordinary horror novels is the richness of its cast, from a bunch of philosophy-reading bikers to a sleazy journalist to a grieving mother on the brink of madness." N Y Times Book Rev

Blaze; a novel; [by] Richard Bachman ; foreword by Stephen King. Scribner 2007 285p $25

ISBN 978-1-4165-5484-4; 1-4165-5484-X

LC 2007-15354

A novel originally written 1973 by Stephen King writing as Richard Bachman. "The protagonist is Clayton Blaisdell Jr., a lonely, brain-damaged outcast blessed (or perhaps cursed) with unusual physical strength. His life has been a series of heartbreaking calamities. Standing 6 foot 7 and weighing almost 300 pounds, Clayton is a man-child left 'soft in the head' after being twice thrown down a flight of stairs as a child by his abusive father. Bounced around foster homes and institutions for much of his childhood, Clayton eventually finds himself running with George, a know-it-all criminal who becomes

his constant companion and adviser, who continues to counsel Clayton from beyond the grave. Alternating between Clayton's past and the present, in which Clayton has kidnapped the infant son of wealthy parents and is holding him for ransom, Blaze is a suspenseful crime yarn as well as a moving, sympathetic portrait of a man yearning to find a place in a world that seems to have callously rejected him." PopMatters

The body

_In_ King, S. Different seasons p299-451

The breathing method

_In_ King, S. Different seasons p453-518

Carrie. Doubleday 1974 199p $32.50

ISBN 0-385-08695-4
                                                          *

"Carrie is 16, lonely, the butt of all her Maine classmates' tricks and jokes, an object of scorn even to her own mother, who is fanatically religious and believes anything remotely sexual is from the devil. Then one girl becomes ashamed of the cruelty being vented on Carrie and plans an act of kindness that will give her the first happiness in her young life. The only trouble is the act backfires horribly and Carrie is worse off than ever before. It is at this point, at the senior prom, that Carrie begins to put into effect her awesome telekinetic powers, powers with which she has only toyed before." Publ Wkly

"A terrifying treat for both horror and parapsychology fans." SLJ

Cell; a novel. Scribner 2006 355p $26.95

ISBN 0-743-29233-2   LC 2005-57531

"Clayton Riddell is in Boston to meet with publishers in hopes of selling his graphic novel series. Portfolio in hand, success within reach, Clay stops to watch the people flocking around a Mister Softee truck. Within moments the world is changed as a mysterious signal reaches cell phone users, turning them into zombies. Clay, who is cell-less . . ., soon teams up with others who have eluded the evil transmission. They embark on a quest to save themselves from the violence and destruction wrought by the changed beings who once owned cell phones." Libr J

"The zombies evolve in interesting ways. Midway through the book, Mr. King takes the story to a private school that has become a post-Pulse campground and reveals the telepathic patterns that have begun to shape collective behavior. It is the author's little joke that these messages are delivered via the worst easy-listening songs he can name, to the point where Lawrence Welk and 'You Light Up My Life' become part of the apocalypse." N Y Times (Late N Y Ed)

Christine. Viking 1983 526p $35

ISBN 0-670-22026-4   LC 82-20105

"Arnie Cunningham—a teenager who has never fit in—buys a dilapidated 1958 Plymouth Fury from an equally broken-down Army veteran, Roland LeBay. But Christine—and the soon-dead LeBay—have mysterious regenerative powers; Christine's odometer runs backwards and the car repairs itself. Arnie becomes obsessed by the car and possessed by its previous owner, losing his girlfriend and his best friend as they work together to save him from Christine's clutches." Publ Wkly

"As always, there is the sense of descriptive detail that

King, Stephen, 1947-—_Continued_

is the author's trademark. Yet the strength of King's prose is best seen here in the remarkable accuracy of language and attitude that captures the spirit of the teenage characters." Libr J

Cujo. Viking 1981 319p

ISBN 0-670-45193-2   LC 81-50265

"A Saint Bernard gone berserk, Cujo is the 200-pound family pet who is bitten by a rabid bat one very hot summer in Castle Rock, Maine. Victims of his violence are two families—that of his owner, backwoods auto mechanic Joe Cambers, and of Vic Trenton, an ad man struggling to keep an important account while 'dealing with his wife's infidelity and his four year old's fears.' Counterpoint to the ad campaign's folksy slogan and the writer's lush reveries are . . . vigils in stalled Pintos where one awaits deadly assault." SLJ

"Carefully plotted, the novel throbs with the malignant evil that permeates all of King's fiction." Saturday Rev

The dark half. Viking 1989 431p o.p.

LC 88-40628

The protagonist of this novel "is literary novelist Thad Beaumont, whose greatest success has come with three gory thrillers written under the pseudonym George Stark. . . . When a blackmailer threatens to reveal Stark's identity . . . Beaumont and his literary agent decide to foil the plan and capitalize on Stark's 'demise.' But Stark, who of course was never alive, will not stay dead either. Beaumont's alter ego . . . seeks revenge against all those involved in killing him off." Publ Wkly

The author is "a very good storyteller. 'The Dark Half' mostly succeeds, as both parable and chiller, in spite of occasional clichés of thought and expression and bits of sophomoric humor." N Y Times Book Rev

The dead zone. Viking 1979 426p

ISBN 0-670-26077-0

* LC 79-12785

"Following a car accident, New England high school English teacher Johnny Smith is unconscious for five years only to wake a bewildered psychic in post-Watergate America. He quickly runs afoul of a national scandal sheet that wants to exploit his power to see the future. He also catches a sex murderer and eventually takes an interest in presidential politics. In the end he turns assassin to save the country from a Hitler-like congressman with White House aspirations." Libr J

Desperation. Viking 1996 690p

ISBN 0-670-86836-1   LC 96-17259

This horror tale shares character's with The regulators, entered below. An "alien force is loose in Desperation, Nevada, and, having occupied the bodies of a succession of citizens . . . has gruesomely slaughtered everyone else in town. Now in the body of a patrolling cop, it is picking up people motoring by on U.S. 50. Foremost among those are burned-out novelist Johnny Marinville and 11-year-old David Carver, who barely a year ago underwent a serious religious conversion and occasionally hears the voice of God. It is God—the God of the Christian Bible, both Testaments—who eventually saves Johnny, David, and the rest of those who survive Desperation, but saves them only by means of their own free will and their own heroic and gory exertions. If King wants to show how to inject religion honestly and effectively into the normally crass horror genre, he succeeds beautifully." Booklist

Different seasons. Viking 1982 527p $37.95; pa $7.99

ISBN 0-670-27266-3; 0-451-16753-8 (pa)

LC 82-70145

Contents: Rita Hayworth and Shawshank redemption; Apt pupil; The body; The breathing method

This "is a collection of four novellas. . . . The first tale is about how one self-contained individual coped with life in a Maine jail. The second is not so much about Nazism today as it is about how victim and victimizer can develop a symbiotic relationship. In the third a search by 12-year-olds for a body in the woods has implications for their innocence. The last is a good old-fashioned horror story." Libr J

Dolores Claiborne. Viking 1993 305p

ISBN 0-670-84452-7

* LC 92-15467

This novel unfolds in the form of a monologue "by the title character, who is suspected of murdering her loutish, insensitive husband and the difficult, rich, and senile woman for whom she has kept house for many years. As Dolores tells her story to the local authorities, the details of a life of drudgery and marital unhappiness emerge, along with the ironic truth behind the deaths." Libr J

"What drives Dolores Claiborne is a powerful characterization of the title figure, a cranky old Maine islander who takes no guff from life or death. . . . King's mimicry is startlingly good." Time

Dreamcatcher; a novel. Scribner 2001 620p $28

ISBN 0-7432-1138-3   LC 00-67990

"One November afternoon in the Maine woods, four men, friends since childhood are on their annual hunting trip that has become as much a time for catching up on one another's lives as it is a time for drinking beer and pursuing game. But this congenial respite ends quickly for Pete, Beaver, Henry, and Jonesy when a dazed and disheveled stranger wanders into their campsite. The hours and days that follow are filled with spaceships, evil gray aliens, a toxic parasite called byrus, and a military search-and-destroy mission. . . . {King} serves up a powerful work that examines the interconnections between memory and imagination and studies the influence of friendship on the human condition." Libr J

Duma Key. Scribner 2008 611p $28

ISBN 978-1-416-55251-2; 1-416-55251-0

LC 2007-38941

"A construction crane crushes Minnesota self-made millionaire Edgar Freemantle in his pickup truck, costing him his right arm. He endures a torturous rehabilitation and terrorizes his wife with his uncontrollable rage until she files for divorce. Figuring that the only hope of regaining his sanity is a drastic change of scenery, Freemantle rents a beach house in the Florida Keys and settles in to pursue his newfound and highly unlikely passion, painting. . . . [In Florida] Freemantle wrestles with a talent he doesn't comprehend and familiarizes himself with his new neighbors, elderly heiress Elizabeth Eastlake and her caretaker, Jerome Wireman. All three harbor secrets, and as they size each other up, they all sense that occult forces have been set in motion around them. Edgar's freaky paintings seem to contain portents of future tragedies, while Eastlake's descent into Alzheimer's masks the origin of the evil that lurks on the key's deserted shore." San Francisco Chron

King, Stephen, 1947- —*Continued*

"King is at the height of his powers with Duma Key, allowing him to exploit such themes as family conflict, the mixed blessing of artistic talent, the nature of masculine friendship and loyalty, and the possibility of redemption for even those most broken in body and spirit. . . . That all this comes in a rousing reinvention of the ghost story diminishes King's achievement not a bit." Houston Chron

Everything's eventual: 14 dark tales. Scribner 2002 459p $28

ISBN 0-7432-3515-0   LC 2002-17738

Contents: Autopsy room four; The man in the black suit; All that you love will be carried away; The death of Jack Hamilton; In the deathroom; The Little Sisters of Eluria; Everything's eventual; L.T.'s theory of pets; The road virus heads north; Lunch at the Gotham Café; That feeling, you can only say what it is in French; 1408; Riding the Bullet; Luckey quarter

"Fourteen stories, most of them gems, featuring an array of literary approaches, plus an opinionated intro from King about the '(Almost) Lost Art' of the short story." Publ Wkly

Firestarter. Viking 1980 428p hardcover o.p. pa $7.99

ISBN 0-670-31541-9; 0-451-16780-5 (pa)

LC 80-14793

"Two college students sign up as paid guinea pigs for a secret and unknowingly dangerous government experiment in telekinesis. . . . When the subjects marry and have a baby, however, their child develops not only telekinesis but pyrokinesis as well; in short, the tot can not only push things with her mind, but set them ablaze as well. The government's plan to use the girl as a human weapon set [the author's] plot into action, and an extended chase ensues with expected havoc wreaked in vivid detail." Booklist

"This is your advanced post-Watergate cynical American thriller with some eerie parapsychological twists, and it's been done so distinctively well that we'd better talk about genius rather than genre." Quill Quire

Four past midnight. Viking 1990 763p pa $7.99 hardcover o.p.

ISBN 0-451-17038-5 (pa)   LC 90-50046

Contents: The Langoliers; Secret window, secret garden; The library policeman; The sun dog

This volume contains four novellas: The Langoliers; Secret window, secret garden; The library policeman; The sun dog.

This book "is hard to put down, truly chilling, and sure to be enjoyed by YA horror afficionados everywhere." SLJ

From a Buick 8; a novel. Scribner 2002 356p $28

ISBN 0-7432-1137-5

* LC 2001-55118

"In 1979, an odd man drives what at first glance looks like a 1954 mint-quality Buick Roadmaster up to a service station in rural Pennsylvania, then vanishes, leaving behind the car. The state police of Troop D deposit the vehicle in a shed near their barracks, where, up to the present, it remains a secret from all but cop colleagues— for the car isn't exactly a car; it may be alive, and it certainly serves as a doorway between our world and. . . . what? Another dimension? Another galaxy?" Publ Wkly

This is a "horror novel, but it's one that gnaws away at the very premises of the horror novel. It knows what you want and expect from it, but it deftly gives you something else instead, something equally worth having and all the more pleasing for being a surprise." N Y Times Book Rev

Gerald's game. Viking 1992 332p o.p.

LC 91-47628

"Jessie and Gerald Burlingame have been married for 20 years. Kinky sex is Gerald's game; lately he has taken to handcuffing his wife to the bedposts. During one such session, via a series of bizarre circumstances, Jessie accidentally kills her husband, and for the next 28 hours she is trapped." Publ Wkly

Even after escaping, Jessie "still has to deal with the corpse-like figure she thinks invaded the cabin just as she freed herself and that pursued her to her car and has haunted her during her convalescence. Was—is—it real? Somewhat like King's earlier naturalistic shocker, *Misery*, this book is grim and nasty. Unlike *Misery*, it's not semiconsciously misogynistic. Quite the reverse: it seems to say that virtually no man and no men's institution can treat a woman decently. A very disturbing stylistic tour de force, this may be King's darkest book." Booklist

The girl who loved Tom Gordon; a novel. Scribner 1999 224p $16.95

ISBN 0-684-86762-1

* LC 99-13109

"Nine-year-old Trisha McFarland is hopelessly lost in the woods. Out for a morning hike with her bickering mother and brother, she runs off to relieve herself and discovers she can't find her way back to the path. . . . Trisha wanders for a week in the mosquito-infested forest with nothing but her wits, her Walkman and the pitching prowess of her hero, the dreamy Red Sox reliever Tom Gordon, to guide her. As Trisha fights to stay alive, King demonstrates his empathy for the inner lives of children and an outdoorsman's knowledge of the edible wild flora of Maine." N Y Times Book Rev

Hearts in Atlantis. Scribner 1999 523p $28

ISBN 0-684-85351-5   LC 99-23889

Five interconnected fictions follow three friends from their sixth-grade year, 1960, to 1999. The war in Vietnam serves as a unifying theme

"The characters are compelling and well drawn, the action is ingeniously interwoven from story to story, and the feel of the 60s, and the baggage carried into later decades, is vivid, harsh, and absolutely true." SLJ

Insomnia. Viking 1994 787p

ISBN 0-670-85503-0   LC 94-784

"On one of the long, exhausting walks old Ralph Roberts starts taking as a brain tumor slowly kills his wife, he witnesses a friendly young neighbor, Ed Deepneau, behaving totally out of character—indeed, like someone possessed. About a year later and after his wife's death, Ralph begins waking early and then earlier and earlier. He also starts seeing things—intense colors streaming off people and animals. Meanwhile, Ed has turned into an antiabortion fanatic and wife-beater. Ralph intervenes to help Helen Deepneau escape from Ed, for which Ed threatens him. Or is it Ed? Ralph senses that someone or something else is in control of the troubled man. Ralph's

King, Stephen, 1947-—*Continued*

right, of course. Ed has been involuntarily recruited on one side, and, it develops, Ralph and his also-widowed neighbor, Lois Chasse, on the other, of a supercosmic struggle the import of which King reveals with deliciously tantalizing gradualness." Booklist

It. Viking 1986 1138p
ISBN 0-670-81302-8   LC 85-41062
"Six adults, living separately in a blessed fog of forgetfulness, are summoned back to their hometown to complete the destruction of a horrific, shape-changing entity who breakfasts on the city's children. This same group first encountered the menace more than a quarter century before, as schoolchildren in the 1950s. Their quest breeds some riveting chase scenes as adults and children alike flee from an assortment of menacing humans and slavering monsters—most of which are manifestations of an evil so vile its true nature can never be known. King's considerable talent for grounding this supernatural stuff in the minutiae of everyday life is evident." Booklist

Just after sunset; stories. Scribner 2008 367p $28
ISBN 978-1-4165-8408-7; 1-4165-8408-0
                                       LC 2008-13683
Contents: Willa; The gingerbread girl; Harvey's dream; Rest stop; Stationary bike; The things they left behind; Graduation afternoon; N.; The cat from hell; The New York Times at special bargain rates; Mute; Ayana; A vert tight place
King "presents 14 tales that range from the philosophically themed, to one in which the author gleefully admits to playing with the gross-out factor ('A Very Tight Place'), to 'The Cat from Hell,' which makes its hardcover debut some 30 years after its original publication as part of a contest in Cavalier, one of the gentleman's magazines that put food on the table in King's early years as a writer. In his introduction, King cites his recent stint as guest editor for the 2007 edition of Best American Short Stories as an impetus to return to the form in his own writing." Libr J
"Many of Sunset's stories have the aura of classic Twilight Zone episodes. And no matter your taste in frightful fantasies, there's something here for everybody." USA Today

Lisey's story; a novel. Scribner 2006 513p $28
ISBN 0-7432-8941-2   LC 2006-44382
This "story set in rural Maine. Lisey's husband, Pulitzer Prizewinning author Scott Landon, has been dead for two years at the book's start, but his presence is felt on every page. Lisey hears him so often in her head that when her catatonic sister, Amanda, begins speaking to her with Scott's voice, she finds it not so much unbelievable as inevitable. Soon she's following a trail of clues that lead her to Scott's horrifying childhood and the eerie world called Boo'ya Moon, all while trying to help Amanda and avoid a murderous stalker." Publ Wkly
"What King does that is so exceptional here is to get out of his comfort zone and dig deep into the skin of his main character until he's conjured up on the page a living, breathing human such as is rarely found in his pulpier creations. Lisey's narrative is an all-too-recognizable inner loop of private jokes and obsessive memories that moves the book forward only in fits and

starts. She doesn't just mourn Scott, she repeatedly conjures him without even trying, using all his dumb slang and repeating his awful jokes for no reason other than that, after a quarter-century of connected lives, his ghost is imbedded so deep within her that she couldn't exorcise him with a priest and a gallon of holy water. He's there to stay, as is the sadness of his being gone, and it's that inescapable reality that proves particularly terrifying here." PopMatters

The long walk
    In King, S. The Bachman books: four early novels by Stephen King

Misery. Viking 1987 310p o.p.
                                    * LC 86-40504
"Paul Sheldon is a serious novelist plagued by the commercial success of his 'Misery Chastain' romance series. He fictionally kills off his irritating heroine and finally writes his great American novel, celebrating with a drunken drive through a rural Colorado blizzard; but he learns what real misery means when he wrecks his car and awakens as the crippled prisoner/patient of a psychotic ex-nurse named Annie Wilkes—Misery's biggest, and angriest, fan. In a graphically gruesome story, Paul must bring Misery back to life just for Annie; but will this new novel buy his freedom, or is he only prolonging his physical and mental torture?" Libr J
"Even if 'Misery' is less terrifying than his usual work—no demons, no witchcraft, no nether-world horrors—it creates strengths out of its realities. Its excitements are more subtle. And, as such, it is an intriguing work." N Y Times Book Rev

Needful things. Viking 1991 690p
ISBN 0-670-83953-1   LC 91-50148
A mysterious entrepreneur named Leland Gaunt arrives in Castle Rock, Maine, and sets up an old curiosity shop. Calling his shop "Needful Things", Gaunt "sells objects that revive his customers' deepest and most selfish desires—things they must have at any cost. As part of the bargain, he requires that his purchasers carry out various 'pranks' on each other. One thing leads to another and an eventual bloodbath." Times Lit Suppl
"As the dreams of each strikingly memorable character, major and minor, inexorably turn to nightmare, individuals and soon the community are overwhelmed, while the precise nature of Gaunt's evil thrillingly stays just out of focus. King, like Leland Gaunt, knows just what his customers want." Publ Wkly

Night shift. Doubleday 1978 xxii, 336p $35
ISBN 0-385-12991-2   LC 77-75146
Contents: Jerusalem's Lot; Graveyard shift; Night surf; I am the doorway; The mangler; The boogeyman; Gray matter; Battleground; Trucks; Sometimes they come back; Strawberry spring; The ledge; The lawnmower man; Quitters, Inc.; I know what you need; Children of the corn; The last rung of the ladder; The man who loved flowers; One for the road; The woman in the room
The stories "all begin in our normal world, where everything is safe and warm. But in almost every instance, something slips, and we find ourselves in the nightmare world of the not-quite-real. . . . Such stories require a willing suspension of disbelief, of course, but they also require an author who is an expert manipulator. . . . King is an expert." Best Sellers

King, Stephen, 1947-—*Continued*

Nightmares & dreamscapes. Viking 1993 816p
o.p.
                    LC 92-46881
Includes the following stories: Dolan's Cadillac; The
end of the whole mess; Suffer the little children; The
Night Flier; Popsy; It grows on you; Chattery teeth; Dedication; The moving finger; Sneakers; You know they
got a hell of a band; Home delivery; Rainy season; My
pretty pony; The ten o'clock people; Crouch End; The
house on Maple Street; The fifth quarter; The doctor's
case; Umney's last case
"There's certainly nothing skimpy about this collection
of large, leisurely short stories. . . . Fans of Mr. King's
work will find here his usual menu: wild conspiracies;
repellent, zestful monsters; scenes speckled and splashed
with gore." N Y Times Book Rev

Pet sematary. Doubleday 1983 373p
  ISBN 0-385-18244-9   LC 82-45360
"For Dr. Louis Creed and his family, their new house
is perfection, with a fairyland forest within walking distance. But the woods contain a bizarre pet cemetery
tended by local children, and eventually the Creeds discover its secret—an ancient burial ground with the power
to raise the dead." Libr J
"King's characters are so solid and next-door neighborly that we are drawn quite naturally and trustingly into
their lives. And then, a single note at a time, the eerie
music begins and we are entranced." Best Sellers

Rage
  In King, S. The Bachman books: four early
    novels by Stephen King

The regulators; [by] Richard Bachman. Dutton
1996 466p
  ISBN 0-525-94190-8   LC 96-8931
This novel is "set in an idyllic Ohio suburb where a
group of residents are treated to a day-long horror show
courtesy of an autistic child who is serving as host to an
alien intelligence." Libr J
"The premise owes a big unacknowledged debt to the
classic *Twilight Zone* episode 'It's a Good Life'; echoes
of earlier Kings resound often as well. . . . But King
makes hay in this story in which anything can happen,
and does, including the warping of space-time and the
savage deaths of much of his large cast. The narrative itself warps fantastically, from prose set in classic typeface
to handwritten journals to drawings to typewritten
playscript and so on." Publ Wkly

Rita Hayworth and Shawshank redemption
  In King, S. Different seasons p1-101

Roadwork
  In King, S. The Bachman books: four early
    novels by Stephen King

Rose Madder. Viking 1995 420p
  ISBN 0-670-85869-2   LC 95-14376
"In the book's first scene, having beaten his cowed,
pregnant wife badly enough to induce a miscarriage,
Norman blithely makes himself a sandwich while waiting
for the ambulance to arrive. And when Rose suddenly
flees, after 14 years of abuse, Norman calmly begins
trolling for her, leaving in his wake a string of mutilated
corpses. Rose doesn't leave Norman because she's afraid

he'll kill her—she's driven to escape by the fear that he
won't, that his cruel torments will simply go on and on.
Her despair, her gradual creation of a new life in a Midwestern city, her hesitant romance with a wry, gentle
pawnbroker, are all convincingly rendered." N Y Times
Book Rev

The running man
  In King, S. The Bachman books: four early
    novels by Stephen King

Salem's Lot. Doubleday 1975 439p $35
  ISBN 0-385-00751-5
                                *
"The small Maine town of Jerusalem's Lot, or Salem's
Lot as the natives call it, has become what appears to be
a ghost town. Its streets, however, are deserted only in
the daylight hours, for the villagers have turned into
vampires." Booklist
"It is to Stephen King's credit as a stylist that he has
charmed us into such familiar territory. Sparing the endless atmospheric creaks and cobwebs and cupolas of this
New England landscape, he thrusts us into the private
terror of his characters." Best Sellers

The shining. Doubleday 1977 447p $35
  ISBN 0-385-12167-9
                         * LC 76-24212
"The Overlook Hotel, high in the mountains of Colorado, has in the past played host to a colorful selection of
visitors, from gangsters to presidents. But a few even
more extraordinary guests are in residence when Jack
Torrance comes to the Overlook with his wife, Wendy,
and son, Danny, to be winter caretaker. Danny is precognitive and telepathic, a condition that allows him to out-
maneuver the hotel's spirits of the dead that attempt to
lay claim to the entire Torrance family." Booklist
"In a fast-paced and gory denouement, the terror
comes to a violent end. King is a masterful technician of
suspense whose readers as well as characters are the victims of his relentless heightening of horror." Libr J

Skeleton crew. Putnam 1985 512p pa $7.99
hardcover o.p.
  ISBN 0-451-16861-5 (pa)   LC 84-15947
Contents: The mist; Here there be tygers; The monkey;
Cain rose up; Mrs. Todd's shortcut; The jaunt; The wedding gig; Paranoid: A chant; The raft; Word processor of
the gods; The man who would not shake hands;
Beachworld; The reaper's image; Nona; For Owen; Survivor type; Uncle Otto's truck; Morning deliveries (Milkman #1); Big wheels: a tale of the laundry game (Milkman #2); Gramma; The ballad of the flexible bullet; The
reach
This "collection of King's shorter work is a hefty sam-
pler from all stages of his career, and demonstrates the
range of his abilities. . . . There are several stories here
that must rank among King's best." Publ Wkly

The stand. Doubleday 1978 823p o.p.
                            LC 77-16928
"A flu-like plague escapes from an experimental lab.
Within days it devastates the country, leaving only a few
thousand immune people. Besides their immunity, the
survivors have in common a terrible dream pitting a
faceless man of evil against a woman of goodness. The
survivors make their choices and head west, gathering
for the confrontation between the satanic Randall Flagg

King, Stephen, 1947-—*Continued*
and the God-anointed Mother Abigail." Libr J

"Stephen King takes liberties permitted in science fiction and thrillers (the good guys share clairvoyant powers, and the plot often turns on lucky coincidences), but he grounds his apocalyptic fantasy in a detailed vision of the blighted American vista, and he avoids the formulas of less talented popular novelists." New Yorker

Thinner; [by] Richard Bachman. New Am. Lib. 1984 309p o.p.   LC 84-11462

"While driving, Billy Halleck is distracted by his wife and accidentally strikes and kills an old gypsy woman. After he's acquitted through the aid of two influential friends, all three are cursed by the gypsy leader. Halleck begins to lose weight rapidly, and must race with death to try to have the curse removed." Libr J

"Bachman blends extraordinary events so cleanly and credibly into the fabric of his characters' lives that we are compelled to read on to the story's chilling conclusion. A superbly crafted drama." Booklist

King, Tabitha, 1949-

Survivor. Dutton 1997 433p
ISBN 0-525-94241-6   LC 96-26347
"A William Abrahams book"

Maine college student Kissy Mellors "is the driver who stopped in time to avoid killing two young women—but the drunk who passed her did not. One woman dies, and the other goes into a coma that lasts for years. Kissy's life is changed forever by this event and by the relationships she forms because of it—with the comatose victim and her family, with the dead girl's boyfriend (a hockey player Kissy later marries), with the investigating officer, even with the drunk driver." Libr J

"King's brutally frank 'warts and all' writing style and bizarre dissection of ordinary events lend a chilling, vaguely eerie element to this suspenseful, enjoyable novel." Booklist

Kingsolver, Barbara

Animal dreams; a novel. HarperCollins Pubs. 1990 342p o.p.   LC 89-46571

This novel is set in Grace, Arizona. The narrator is Cosima (Codi) Noline, who returns home after abandoning a career in medicine. Codi looks after her aging father, the local doctor, and teaches high school biology. Her sister Halimeda (Hallie) is an agronomist helping the Sandinistas in Nicaragua. In Grace, Codi becomes involved with a former boyfriend, Loyd Peregrina, a Native American. She struggles to come to terms with her past and works to save the town from an impending ecological disaster

"Like all good novels, Animal Dreams is a web of interlacing news. It is dense and vivid, and makes ever tighter circles around the question of what it means to be alive." Nation

The bean trees; a novel. 10th anniversary ed. HarperFlamingo 1997 261p $19.95; pa $7.99
ISBN 0-06-017579-6; 0-06-109731-4 (pa)
                                     * LC 97-2691

A reissue of the title first published 1988

In this novel, "Taylor Greer, a poor, young woman, flees her Kentucky home and heads west. . . . While passing through Oklahoma, she becomes responsible for a two-year-old Cherokee girl. The two continue on the road. When they roll off the highway in Tucson, Taylor and the child, whom she has named Turtle, . . . meet Mattie, a widow who runs Jesus Is Lord Used Tires and is active in the sanctuary movement on the side." Ms

This book "gives readers something that's increasingly hard to find today—a character to believe in and laugh with and admire." Christ Sci Monit

Followed by Pigs in heaven (1993)

Pigs in heaven; a novel. HarperCollins Pubs. 1993 343p o.p.   LC 92-54739

In this sequel to The bean trees, Taylor Greer and her adopted Cherokee Indian daughter Turtle "are on a trip to the Hoover Dam, where Turtle is the only person to see a man fall over the side. . . . The rescue makes Turtle a heroine. But becoming a heroine, which culminates in an appearance on 'Oprah,' engenders a new disaster. Annawake Fourkiller, an Indian-rights lawyer, sees the white mother with her Cherokee daughter on TV and decides the child must be returned to the Cherokee Nation. . . . But Taylor isn't about to let go of the little girl. . . . They pack up and run." Newsweek

"Possessed of an extravagantly gifted narrative voice, {Kingsolver} blends a fierce and abiding moral vision with benevolent, concise humor." N Y Times Book Rev

The poisonwood Bible; a novel. HarperFlamingo 1998 546p $26; pa $15
ISBN 0-06-017540-0; 0-06-093053-5 (pa)
                                     * LC 98-19901

"In 1959, evangelical preacher Nathan Price moves his wife and four daughters from Georgia to a village in the Belgian Congo, later Zaire. Their dysfunction and cultural arrogance proves disastrous as the family is nearly destroyed by war, Nathan's tyranny, and Africa itself. Told in the voices of the mother and daughters, the novel spans 30 years as the women seek to understand each other and the continent that tore them apart." Libr J

"Buttressing her suspenseful chronicle with authentic background detail, Kingsolver's narrative is at once a compelling family saga and an astute look at Western imperialism in Africa." Publ Wkly

Prodigal summer; a novel. HarperCollins Pubs. 2000 444p $26
ISBN 0-06-019965-2   LC 00-61361

"A corner of southern Appalachia serves as the setting for the stories of three intertwined lives. . . . In the chapters called 'Predator,' forest ranger Deanna Wolfe is a 40-plus wildlife biologist and staunch defender of coyotes, which have recently extended their range into Appalachia. . . . Meanwhile, in the chapters called 'Moth Love,' newly married entomologist Lusa Maluf Landowski is left a widow on her husband's farm with five envious sisters-in-law, crushing debts—and a desperate and brilliant idea. Crusty old farmer Garnett Walker ('Old Chestnuts') learns to respect his archenemy, who crusades for organic farming and opposes Garnett's use of pesticides." Publ Wkly

The novel is full of "tenderness, humor, and earthy spirituality. . . . As usual, Kingsolver's dialogue is absolutely natural, often funny, and sometimes heartbreaking." Chris Sci Monit

Kipling, Rudyard, 1865-1936

Collected stories; selected and introduced by Robert Gottlieb. Knopf 1994 xxxvii, 911p $25

ISBN 0-679-43592-1

* LC 94-5854

"Everyman's library"

Contents: In the house of Suddhoo; Beyond the pale; A bank fraud; Pig; On Greenhow Hill; "Love-o'-women"; The drums of the fore and aft; Dray wara yow dee; "The City of Dreadful Night"; Without benefit of clergy; The head of the district; Jews in Shushan; The man who would be king; "The finest story in the world"; The mark of the beast; The strange ride of Morrowbie Jukes; The disturber of traffic; Mrs. Hauksbee sits out {play}; A wayside comedy; Baa baa, black sheep; The bridge-builders; The maltese cat; "In ambush"; A sahibs' war; "Wireless"; Mrs. Bathurst; "Swept and garnished"; Mary Postgate; "Dymchurch flit"; With the night mail; The house surgeon; The wish house; The Janeites; The bull that thought; A madonna of the trenches; The eye of Allah; The gardener; Dayspring mishandled; The church that was at Antioch; The manner of men

"There is an enormous range of subject matter, genre, styles, and tones in Kipling's prose work. . . . [He] is undoubtedly one of the great short-story writers in English and the subtlety of his early narrative technique has led some to claim him as a proto-Modernist." Oxford Companion to 20th Cent Lit in Engl

Kirshenbaum, Binnie

An almost perfect moment. Ecco 2004 321p $23.95

ISBN 0-06-052086-8   LC 2003-54961

The protagonist of this novel is Valentine Kessler. "A nice Jewish girl growing up in late-1970s Brooklyn, she becomes infatuated with her Polish American math teacher and with the Virgin Mary, for she mysteriously resembles the vision of Mary seen by Bernadette of Lourdes. Valentine's father left when she was a baby, and ever since her mother, Miriam, indulges her beautiful, newly withdrawn daughter while eating herself into obesity and playing mah-jongg every afternoon with her buddies. The so-called Girls are like a Greek chorus, commenting on life around them and wondering at Valentine's inspired silence. . . . Bursting with hyperbole, this is a hilarious and uncanny snapshot of a bygone era." Libr J

Kirst, Hans Hellmut, 1914-1989

Forward, Gunner Asch!; translated from the German by Robert Kee. Little, Brown 1956 368p o.p.

Sequel to The revolt of Gunner Asch

Original German edition, 1954; published in the United Kingdom as part two of the trilogy: Zero eight fifteen, with title: Gunner Asch goes to war

"The action of the book alternates between a sector of the Russian front in late winter of 1941-2, and a base depot somewhere in Germany. Gunner Asch and his companions, whom we met in the first volume training at home, have now gone to war. . . . The characters move like Breughel peasants against a bleak winter landscape; unshaven, filthy, swaddled in greatcoats and sacking, their minds set only on self-preservation, food, and, where possible, women." New Statesman (1913)

Followed by The return of Gunner Asch

The return of Gunner Asch; translated from the German by Robert Kee. Little, Brown 1957 310p o.p.

Sequel to Forward, Gunner Asch!

Original German edition, 1955; published in the United Kingdom as third part of the trilogy: Zero eight fifteen

The third volume in the author's series about the adventures of a German army sergeant in World War II describes "the disintegration of the front-line units of the German Army as the Allies advanced in the closing days of combat in Europe in 1945. Asch becomes involved in an effort to track down two officers who left their men to needless slaughter to catch up with a black-market cache." Booklist

Followed by What became of Gunner Asch (1964)

The revolt of Gunner Asch; translated from the German by Robert Kee. Little, Brown 1955 311p o.p.

First in a series of four novels about Gunner Asch; Original German edition, 1954; published in the United Kingdom as part of the trilogy Zero eight fifteen, with title: The strange mutiny of Gunner Asch

This is "a German novel poking fun at the more idiotic aspects of Army discipline. Set in a garrison town just before the last war, it tells of a one-man battle fought by Gunner Asch, a nice young man with a capacity for indignation, against the bullying N.C.O.'s of his company." Manchester Guardian

"A tale in which elements of drama and suspense are skillfully fused with high comedy—a tale which the author brings to a startling and altogether delightful conclusion. . . . Kirst has succeeded in distilling robust fun out of brutal realities without ever suggesting that the realities were other than brutal." Atlantic

Followed by Forward, Gunner Asch!

Kittredge, William

The Willow Field. Knopf 2006 342p $25.95

ISBN 1-4000-4097-3   LC 2006-45157

This "multigenerational saga begins with a stunning set piece—a classic horse drive, more than 200 head, from Nevada to Calgary. Rossie, a veteran ranch hand but still barely 20, signs on for the drive as a way of breaking ties with a girl and winds up forging even stronger ties with another girl, Eliza Stevenson, the unmarried but pregnant daughter of a rancher in Montana's Bitterroot Mountains. 'We could be it, entirely it,' Eliza says shortly after she meets Rossie, and as we watch their lives unfold, from the Depression through World War II and on into the 1960s, we realize that this strong-willed woman was both right and wrong. . . . Rossie and Eliza are 'entirely it,' but—fiery individuals both—they are also in perpetual conflict, cherishing their union just as they struggle not to be consumed by the other. This transcendent love story is at the heart of Kittredge's novel, but it is set against not one but two imposing landscapes—the Bitterroot and the Nevada desert, both of which demand their own allegiance from the characters' minds and hearts." Booklist

Klavan, Andrew

Empire of lies. Harcourt 2008 383p $25
ISBN 978-0-15-101223-7; 0-15-101223-7
LC 2007-33052
"An Otto Penzler book"
"A wickedly satiric thriller with political overtones. Jason Harrow was cynically immoral before he found God and became a conservative Midwestern family man. Now his former lover summons him back to New York City with the news that his teenage daughter (one he never knew about) is in trouble, mixed up with terrorists who are plotting a major atrocity. To save his daughter and thousands of others, Jason must confront the buried fear that he's inherited his mother's insanity and can't control his own dark urges. As Jason's insecurity intensifies, so does the novel's nightmarish mood. Disgusted by the excesses of the liberal media, Jason discovers that he's not just paranoid, he really is a persecuted outsider. The action builds to an explosive climax at the screening of a 3D movie at a Manhattan theater." Publ Wkly

Klein, Joe, 1946-

Primary colors; a novel of politics; [by] Anonymous. Random House 1996 366p
ISBN 0-679-44859-4
LC 95-39823
This is a "romance à clef about the 1992 Democratic Presidential primary campaign, featuring an ambitious . . . Southern governor named Jack Stanton seen through the eyes of [Henry Burton], a disillusioned aide." London Rev Books
"This is, in short, a quite outstanding novel of political process and motive that reads like a slightly hipper version of Gore Vidal." New Statesman (1913)

Klein, Matthew, 1968-

Con ed. Warner Books 2007 285p $23.99
ISBN 978-0-446-57955-1; 0-446-57955-6
LC 2006-18438
"Once-rich con-man Kip Largo is going straight, living small, and making $10 per hour in a dry-cleaning store after doing eight years for wire fraud. Life is dull, but Kip wants it that way, until his son Toby shows up, on the run from the Russian Mob. Kip needs a big score to save Toby, and a timely proposal from the stunning young wife of a dangerous Las Vegas casino owner provides him with a target for a grand scam. Con Ed is a brisk, clever, and charming page-turner." Booklist

Klein, Rachel, 1953-

The moth diaries; a novel. Counterpoint 2002 249p $24
ISBN 1-58243-205-8
LC 2001-7226
"The unnamed narrator of Klein's first novel is a studious, thoughtful 16-year-old at an elite boarding school in the late '60s. Her closest friend is her sweet, friendly roommate, Lucy, who navigates the school's social system with ease. The arrival of quiet, mysterious Ernessa upsets the balance between the friends when Ernessa befriends and seemingly takes Lucy away from the narrator. . . . Thanks to reading LeFanu's vampire story 'Carmilla' and other tales, and to Ernessa's odd behavior and Lucy's mysterious wasting illness, the narrator begins to suspect that Ernessa is a vampire. . . . The diary format of Klein's story gives it immediacy, and a menacing atmosphere permeates it." Booklist

Klíma, Ivan

No saints or angels; translated by Gerald Turner. Grove Press 2001 267p $24
ISBN 0-8021-1695-7
LC 2001-33994
Original Czech edition, 1999
"Kristýna, a divorced mother in her 40s, works as a dentist in Prague. Burdened with responsibilities, she is the sole caregiver for her aging, widowed mother; her terminally ill ex-husband; and her 15-year-old daughter, Jana, who may or may not be using hard drugs. Lonely and starved for affection, Kristýna begins dating Jan, a former student of her ex-husband and her junior by 15 years. While she tries to use the romance and morning glasses of wine to erase mounting concerns, Kristýna is unable to overcome her own unsentimental perceptions." Publ Wkly
"In Klima's world bureaucracy is a metaphor for the human condition: our dearest allies now are those who gassed our grandmothers, the young of the past had more purpose under interrogation than those of today have on the Internet, and we long for a God grown wholly inadequate to his creatures in the 21st century. Against this cosmic mismatch, frail, flawed human beings play out their volatile longings and their inglorious heroisms." N Y Times Book Rev

Klosterman, Chuck, 1972-

Downtown owl; a novel. Scribner 2008 275p $24
ISBN 978-1-4165-4418-0; 1-4165-4418-6
LC 2007-47088
This novel focuses on the lives of "the football-playing teenager Mitch, the 20-something Julia, and the elderly Horace. The three have little in common—they all live in the small town of Owl, North Dakota, but otherwise have little interaction—but by weaving their three stories around each other, Klosterman constructs a touching, incisive, and (of course) funny snapshot of small-town America circa 1984. And if the story occasionally falters or takes off on tangents, who cares? It's all tremendously fun to read." PopMatters

Kneale, Matthew, 1960-

When we were Romans; a novel. Nan A. Talese 2008 224p $23.95
ISBN 978-0-385-52625-8; 0-385-52625-3
* LC 2007-45523
First published 2007 in the United Kingdom
"Nine-year-old Lawrence is the man in his family. He carefully watches over his willful little sister, Jemima, and his mother, Hannah. When Hannah becomes convinced that their estranged father is stalking them, the family flees London and heads for Rome, where Hannah lived happily as a young woman. For Lawrence, fascinated by stories of popes and emperors, Rome is an adventure. Though they are short of money, and move from home to home, staying with his mother's old friends, little by little their new life seems to be taking shape. But the trouble that brought them to Italy will not quite leave

Kneale, Matthew, 1960-—Continued

them in peace." Publisher's note

"We, the adult readers of 'When We Were Romans,' learn to peer through the screen of Lawrence's limited point of view to see what's really going on even as our narrator begins to guess at what lies behind his mother's version of events and even to catch a glimpse of the mysteries of his own heart. In life as well as in books, there are some truths that it's much better to sneak up on." Salon.com

Knebel, Fletcher, 1911-1993

Seven days in May; by Fletcher Knebel and Charles W. Bailey II. Harper & Row 1962 341p o.p.

"The story set against a . . . political Washington background, is about a military plot to take over the government. Its hero is a President of the U.S. in the 1970's, who with six men he trusts, sets out to prove the plot exists and to foil it." Publ Wkly

Knight, Damon Francis, 1922-2002

The best of Damon Knight; with an introduction by Barry N. Malzberg. Taplinger 1978 c1976 307p o.p.

First published 1976 in paperback by Pocket Books

Contents: Not with a bang; To serve man; Cabin boy; The analogues; Babel II; Special delivery; Thing of beauty; Anachron; Extempore; Backward, O time; The last word; Man in the jar; The enemy; Eripmav; A likely story; Time enough; Mary; The handler; The big pat boom; Semper fi; Masks; Down there

"A writer of estimable talent, as these twenty-two stories from 1948-73 prove. Knight's motifs are common—time travel, after-the-holocaust, cyborgs, alien visitors to earth—but the wit, penetrating social satire, and quick narrative twists are distinctly his own." Booklist

Knight, Michael, 1969-

Goodnight, nobody. Atlantic Monthly Press 2002 160p $23

ISBN 0-87113-867-0   LC 2002-27944

Contents: Birdland; Feeling lucky; Killing Stonewall Jackson; The end of everything; The mesmerist; Keeper of secrets, teller of lies; Mitchell's girls; Ellen's book; Blackout

"Stylistically, Knight slaloms through old-fashioned noir and snarky postmodernism, and from Barthelmean set pieces to a riff on Stonewall Jackson that evokes one of Barry Hannah's Civil War fever dreams." N Y Times Book Rev

Knode, Helen

The ticket out. Harcourt 2003 340p $24

ISBN 0-15-100184-7   LC 2002-7804

The morning after a party, film critic Ann Whitehead "discovers aspiring moviemaker Greta Stenholm in the bathtub, dead from knife wounds. Even though the knife used to kill Greta belongs to her, Ann's primary concern is using the story as her ticket out of the movie-reviewing business and into feature writing. Even as she patiently answers taciturn Detective Doug Lockwood's

questions about the murder scene, she's busily hiding evidence. . . . Her increasingly intimate relationship with the complicated Lockwood is the high point in this very entertaining novel." Booklist

Knopf, Chris, 1951-

Hard stop. Permanent Press 2009 263p $28

ISBN 978-1-57962-183-4; 1-57962-183-X

LC 2008-51795

In this outing "corporate dropout-turned-carpenter/PI Sam Acquillo is forced to look for the missing girlfriend of his former boss, George Donovan. As Sam traces the successful young businesswoman to a house on Long Island shared with a bunch of Gen-Xers from Manhattan, he uncovers what looks like dirty business dealings. Knopf is very much a contemporary crime writer, revealing the dangers of the world of big deals, commercial espionage, and the barracudas hanging out for all they can get. For readers who enjoy hardboiled mysteries in the tradition of Raymond Chandler and Robert Parker." Libr J

Head wounds. Permanent Press 2008 310p $28

ISBN 978-1-57962-165-0   LC 2008-2517

"Ex-boxer and former corporate exec Sam Acquillo, now a hard-drinking carpenter living in a rundown cottage on the shores of the Little Peconic Bay in Southampton, N.Y., becomes the prime suspect in the murder of local builder Robbie Milhouser. . . . With the evidence against him almost overwhelming, Acquillo enlists a misfit group of supporters to help him uncover the real killer's identity. As he digs into the dead man's troubled past, Acquillo discovers a disturbing link between Milhouser and Acquillo's current girlfriend, Amanda Battiston. Knopf excels in describing the rustic underpinnings of Long Island's east end, especially its vast array of eccentric characters." Publ Wkly

The last refuge. Permanent Press 2005 287p $26

ISBN 1-57962-118-X   LC 2004-65314

Sam Acquillo is the "very epitome of the dropout. An ex-corporation man, divorced from his wife and estranged from his daughter, he lives in his parents' run-down cottage in Southampton, Long Island, and seems content to drink himself into oblivion. Then one day he finds the black and swollen body of his elderly neighbor, Regina Broadhurst, who has apparently drowned in her bathtub. Is it an accident or murder?" Publ Wkly

"While [Sam's] low-key investigation is only minimally suspenseful, the characters he chats up are such original oddballs and their conversation so bracing that you want to kick off your shoes and spend some time on the porch with them, just taking in the view and enjoying the talk." N Y Times Book Rev

Two time. Permanent Press 2006 261p $28; pa $18

ISBN 1-57962-129-5; 1-57962-164-3 (pa)

LC 2005-56564

At the start of this mystery, ex-boxer and retired engineer Sam Acquillo is "enjoying a drink with a lady friend at an East Hampton restaurant when a nearby car and its driver are firebombed out of existence. In the aftermath, Sam, assisted by his old buddy, retired cop Joe Sullivan, looks into who might had it in for the victim, wealthy consultant Jonathan Eldridge. After talking

Knopf, Chris, 1951——Continued
to Eldridge's agoraphobic widow and suspicious-acting lawyer, Sam continues to investigate—and the more he pokes around the more data he turns up suggesting a complex deception involving financial transfers, angry clients who may or may not be Mafia-connected, the murdered man's estranged artist brother and out-of-it mother. A sly depiction of the east end of Long Island and the Hamptons as they really are, combined with strong plotting, solid characters and hardboiled dialogue worthy of Elmore Leonard or John D. MacDonald." Publ Wkly

Knopf, Marcy, 1969-

(ed) The Sleeper wakes. See The Sleeper wakes

Knowall, George *See* O'Brien, Flann, 1911-1966

Knowles, John, 1926-2001

Peace breaks out. Holt, Rinehart & Winston 1981 193p
ISBN 0-03-056908-7   LC 80-19678
Set in the Devon School in New Hampshire, scene of A separate peace, this novel takes place during the 1945-46 term. "Pete Hallam—Class of '37—returning . . . as a teacher, hopes to recover there from wartime traumas. But the boys in the class of '46 are an edgy bunch, frustrated and guilty because they won't be graduating from the prep school to the armed forces like the classes before them. There's a simmering air of violence among them during the long winter as Pete in his low-keyed way tries to help them across the threshold to adulthood." Publ Wkly

A separate peace; a novel. Macmillan 1960 c1959 186p
ISBN 0-02-564850-0
                                                      *
First published 1959 in the United Kingdom
"Gene Forrester looks back on his school days, spent in a New England town just before World War II. He both admires and envies his close friend and roommate, Finny, who is a natural athlete, in contrast to Gene's special competence as a scholar. When Finny suffers a crippling accident, Gene must face his own involvement in it." Shapiro. Fic for Youth. 3d edition

Knox, Elizabeth, 1959-

Billie's kiss. Ballantine Bks. 2002 343p $24
ISBN 0-345-45052-3
A "romantic mystery set in 1903. Billie Paxton, an uneducated but perspicacious young woman, thinks the worst is over after a rough voyage on the *Gustav Edda,* a Swedish steamer that has taken her to the outer Scottish island of Kissack and Skilling, along with her pregnant sister, Edith, and her brother-in-law, Henry Maslen, a tutor who has accepted a position with the local squire, Lord Hallowhulme, at Kiss Castle. But just as the *Gustav Edda* is docking in port, an explosion shatters the hull, leaving Edith dead and Henry injured. An excellent swimmer, Billie immediately jumps off the stricken ship and scrambles to shore." Publ Wkly
Knox's "characters are unique and yet somehow familiar, in the sense that they are reminiscent of famous characters in Victorian literature." Booklist

Daylight. Ballantine Bks. 2003 356p map $23.95
ISBN 0-345-45795-1   LC 2003-544868
"Saint or vampire? The identity of the Blessed Martine Raimondi, a French nun murdered by the Nazis in 1944 for her part in the daring cave escape of rebel partisans, is only one question answered in this illuminating tour-de-force set in the south of France. . . . Brian 'Bad' Phelan, a New South Wales bomb tech and expert 'caver' on paid injury leave, helps retrieve Martine's blistered corpse outside a cave near the Italian border and discovers she bears a shocking resemblance to a woman he'd encountered years before in another flooded cave. He's further struck by Martine's resemblance to Eve Moskelute, the subject of a painting by Jean Ares, her Picasso-esque deceased husband. The author constructs an impressive mystery that dissects the meaning of miracles while putting a fresh spin on the vampire archetype." Publ Wkly

Koen, Karleen

Dark angels; a novel. Crown 2006 530p $25.95
ISBN 0-307-33991-2   LC 2005-30734
In this prequel to Through a glass darkly, the "central character is Alice Verney, former lady-in-waiting to Charles II's consort, Queen Catherine, then to the king's sister, Henrietta, married to the brother of France's Louis XIV. Upon Henrietta's mysterious death, Alice returns to England and begins her adventures, making certain not only to remain afloat but also to triumph in the commotion and excitement of the English royal court." Booklist
This "is the best kind of historical fiction: very accurate, highly dramatic and thoroughly entertaining." Washington Post Book World

Through a glass darkly. Random House 1986 743p o.p.   LC 86-422
Set in early eighteenth century England and France, this novel "tells the story of Barbara Alderley, who is fifteen when the story begins, and about to be bartered in marriage to the middle-aged but gorgeous Roger Montgeoffry. The barterer is her own mother, [Diana]. . . . Barbara is in love with Roger, Roger is in love with Bentwoodes, the family seat that is to be her dowry, and Diana is in love with money and power." N Y Times Book Rev
"Expertly paced, the novel blends quaint historical romance with a sharp-edged, contemporary psychodramatic style. Its characters are memorable and full-bodied, maturing through a series of rapidly escalating tragedies that bring the sweetly naive heroine into full womanhood and force her to make a decision that will forever change her life. A sophisticated, atmospheric work." Booklist

Koestler, Arthur, 1905-1983

Darkness at noon; translated by Daphne Hardy. Macmillan 1987 267p
ISBN 0-02-565210-9
                                          * LC 86-31273
First published 1940 in the United Kingdom; this is a reissue of the 1941 edition
This novel "deals with the arrest, imprisonment, trial, and execution of N. S. Rubashov in an unnamed dictatorship over which 'No. 1' presides. Koestler describes

Koestler, Arthur, 1905-1983—*Continued*
Rubashov as 'a synthesis of the lives of a number of men who were victims of the so-called Moscow trials,' and the novel did much to draw attention to the nature of Stalin's regime." Oxford Companion to Engl Lit. 6th edition

Koontz, Dean R., 1945-

The bad place. Putnam 1990 382p o.p.
LC 89-10861
"Married detectives Julie and Bobby Dakota agree to help frightened amnesiac Frank Pollard figure out what he does when he's asleep. . . . In due course, Frank and the Dakotas join forces against murderer Candy Pollard and his weird sisters, who want to kill Frank—evidently the sole human in the monstrous family. Candy extends psychic feelers toward potential victims, emanations that are sensed by Julie's younger brother Thomas. A Down's syndrome child, Thomas is telepathically gifted and able to warn Bobby of the demons who threaten Julie." Publ Wkly

Brother Odd; [by] Dean Koontz. Bantam Books 2006 364p $27
ISBN 978-0-553-80480-5; 0-553-80480-4
LC 2006-32253
"Odd Thomas, who narrates, is odd indeed: only 20, he works contentedly as a fry cook in a small fictional California town, despite a talent for writing. The reason for his lack of ambition? A much rarer talent: Odd sees and converses with ghosts, the lingering dead who have yet to pass on, a secret he has kept from nearly everyone but his girlfriend, an eccentric author friend and the local police chief, whom he occasionally helps solve terrible crimes. Odd also has the ability to see bodachs, malevolent spirits that feast on pain and whose presence signifies a likelihood of imminent violence. The proximity of bodachs to a weird-looking stranger in town, whom Odd dubs 'Fungus Man,' alerts Odd that trouble is brewing." Publ Wkly
"Odd is the kind of instantly and persistently likable narrator that Fredric Brown used in such detective classics as the Ed and Am mysteries . . . though the pace of a Brown novel is relaxed in comparison. Also like Brown, Koontz employs dry, goofy humor, often in daring counterpoint to the story's spikes in tension and horror. Koontz also waxes as honorably sentimental as Ray Bradbury, and writes in breathy, two-line paragraphs, recalling the punchy manner of Robert Bloch. Obviously, then, this is a book worthy of any of the great three Bs of pop fiction." Booklist

By the light of the moon; [by] Dean Koontz. Bantam Bks. 2002 431p $26.95
ISBN 0-553-80143-0
LC 2002-29902
The author "introduces readers to a twentysomething trio consisting of artist Dylan O'Conner, his autistic younger brother, Shep; and a stand-up comedienne named Jilly Jackson. One momentous evening, these threeunexpectedly find themselves coping with the bizarre effects of mysterious injections forced upon them by mad scientist Lincoln Proctor in an Arizona motel. With a generous helping of dark humor, Koontz quickly charges his characters with the task of harnessing their paranormal abilities as weapons against real-world violence and evil in a setting littered with present-day totems ranging from fast-food restaurants to sensation-mongering radio personalities." Libr J

Dark rivers of the heart; a novel; [by] Dean Koontz. Knopf 1994 487p o.p.
LC 94-12090
"Spencer Grant is on the run from a nameless, violent government agency. His goal is to keep away from his pursuers long enough to find the woman he met the night before, who appears to be their real target. Spencer has no idea why they want to kill Valerie Keene, but his brief acquaintance with her has convinced him that the killers have no good reason for wanting her dead. With his . . . dog, Rocky, Spencer leads the killers on a frustrating chase." Libr J
"Koontz has succeeded where many genre writers have failed: he has switched gears, put the zombies and creepy crawlers aside, and written a believable high-tech thriller." N Y Times Book Rev

The darkest evening of the year; [by] Dean Koontz. Bantam Books 2007 354p $27
ISBN 978-0-55380-482-9; 0-55380-482-0
LC 2007-40255
"Amy Redwing, the survivor of a horrifying marriage, establishes Golden Heart to rescue golden retrievers. . . . A supernatural chain of events ensues after Amy and her architect boyfriend, Brian McCarthy, rescue Nickie during a violent intervention in a family dispute. Soon the pair are on a mission that leads to a transformative confrontation with a number of ugly characters—Gunther Schloss, a frustrated aspiring novelist turned killer-for-hire; Moonglow, a psychobitch in the Mommie Dearest league; and Moonglow's lover, Harrow, a self-obsessed sicko. This is the perfect book for thriller addicts who know the darkest hour is just before dawn and for canine lovers who remember 'dog' spelled backwards is 'god.'" Publ Wkly

The face; [by] Dean Koontz. Bantam Bks. 2003 608p $26.95
ISBN 0-553-80248-8
LC 2003-40354
"The eponymous Face is the world's biggest movie star; he doesn't appear in the novel, but his smart, geeky 10-year-old-son, Fric, takes center stage, as does Ethan Truman, cop-turned-security chief of the Face's elaborate estate and Fric's main human protector when one Corky Laputa, who's dedicated his life to anarchy, decides to sow further disorderby kidnapping this progeny of the world's idol. . . . Koontz's characters are memorable and his unique mix of suspense and humor absorbing." Publ Wkly

False memory; [by] Dean Koontz. Bantam Bks. 2000 627p
ISBN 0-553-10666-X
LC 99-54782
"The heroes are Southern Californians Dusty and Martie Rhodes, he a housepainting contractor, she a computer game designer. . . . As Martie shepherds her terrified, agoraphobic friend, Susan, on a visit to Susan's shrink (Ahriman), Dusty deals with his drug-addled stepbrother/employee, Skeet, about to jump to his death from the roof of Dusty's latest project. Skeet leaps, taking Dusty with him, but both survive; as Dusty checks Skeet into rehab, Martie suffers her first of several horrific phobic episodes, in which she imagines mutilating Dusty with household items. Seeking help, she and Dusty turn

Koontz, Dean R., 1945-—*Continued*

to Ahriman, who, it's eventually revealed first to the reader, then to the couple, is responsible for all the trouble. . . . An expertly crafted, ornate suspenser." Publ Wkly

Fear nothing; by Dean Koontz. Bantam Bks. 1998 391p o.p. LC 97-41129

"Tale of one night in the California coastal town of Moonlight Bay as experienced by Chris Snow. Saddled with a genetic defect that makes direct sunlight toxic to him, Snow is a nocturnal creature whose father has just died. When he discovers that his father's corpse has been stolen, he begins pursuit. Koontz expertly illuminates Snow's nocturnal world and friends, and incrementally, cleverly, the crises erupting in Moonlight Bay take shape. The plot is wonderfully unpredictable, and though the surfer slang wears thin after a while, the narrative remains taut." Libr J

Followed by Seize the night

From the corner of his eye; [by] Dean Koontz. Bantam Bks. 2001 622p
ISBN 0-553-80134-1 LC 00-48619

This novel "chronicles the lives of three unique individuals. Bartholomew Lampion, born under miraculous yet tragic circumstances, has the most unusual and mesmerizing eyes ever seen. As he grows, he begins to exhibit abilities that defy physics. Angel, born in another city at the same time as Bartholomew, is also a miracle child; as she grows, she demonstrates the ability to see the world as it really exists. At the time of their births, ruthless and cunning Junior dreams that someone named Bartholomew will lead to his downfall. While attempting to find the nemesis he knows only by name, Junior is relentlessly pursued by a police detective." Libr J

"The large cast of characters, particularly the fully developed main players, is richly imagined. The plot is suspenseful and complex. Informing the novel throughout is a fascinating theory that involves quantum mechanics, faith, and human relationships." Voice Youth Advocates

The husband; [by] Dean Koontz. Bantam Books 2006 400p $27.95
ISBN 978-0-553-80479-9; 0-553-80479-0 LC 2006-42696

"One morning, Southern California gardener Mitchell Rafferty gets a call on his cellphone from a stranger saying that Mitch's beloved wife, Holly, has been kidnapped and that he has less than three days to come up with $2 million in cash. Of course, he's warned not to involve the police. While Mitch is still on the phone, the kidnapper proves his seriousness by directing Mitch's attention to a man walking a dog across the street. A moment later the man is shot dead. Mitch must walk a fine line—cooperating with the police inquiry into this murder without revealing Holly's plight." Publ Wkly

"Koontz focuses relentlessly on Mitch and, in chapters scattered judiciously throughout the latter 230 pages, Holly. Not for him the flirtation with evil thinking that an Elmore Leonard does so well or the temptation to sympathize with evildoers that an Alfred Hitchcock offers. And yet Koontz is no less an artist for his championing of the good and his determination to have readers identify with it, as this hair-raising thriller attests." Booklist

Intensity; a novel; by Dean Koontz. Knopf 1995 307p
ISBN 0-679-42525-X
* LC 95-33591

Chyna Shepherd, 26, child of a woman who "exposed the girl to plenty of mayhem until she fled Mom at age 16, goes for a pleasant Napa Valley weekend visiting the vintner parents of her best college friend, only to become the covert witness to the family's murder at the hands of thrill-addicted serial (and mass) murderer Edgler Foreman Vess. Hardened by her childhood . . . Chyna determines to keep on the killer's trail until she can bring him to justice or exact it herself." Booklist

"The velocity of the plot is the book's true pleasure; the story does not move so much as rocket up the portentously gloomy highway with the reader in violent pursuit." N Y Times Book Rev

Lightning. Putnam 1988 351p o.p.
LC 87-21649

"On the night of Laura Shane's birth, a stranger appears from the lightning to prevent her delivery's being botched by an alcoholic physician. Throughout Laura's childhood the stranger reappears at times of danger. He protects rather than threatens, yet menace seems to follow him. Thirty years later another storm flashes and the stranger collapses, shot, at Laura's door. Now Laura protects her erst-while guardian from mysterious hunters. He reveals that he and the hunters are time travelers. Laura, quick-witted and brave, leads the way to a bloody showdown." Libr J

The author "quickly grabs the reader's attention. But then he kicks in with his usual stop-start suspense rhythm, giving rise to a certain impatience with the heroine's roller-coaster perils. Nonetheless, there are enough imaginative twists here, along with likable characters . . . to win him new fans and please old ones." N Y Times Book Rev

One door away from heaven; [by] Dean Koontz. Bantam Bks. 2001 606p
ISBN 0-553-80137-6 LC 2001-49952

The "story coalesces from two converging subplots steeped in the weirdness of fringe ufology: in one, loser Michelina Bellsong struggles to save crippled nine-year-old Leilani Klonk from an evil stepdad planning to pass off her imminent disposal as a benevolent alien abduction; in the other, a strange boy who goes by the alias Curtis Hammond is the quarry of two cross-country manhunts, one led by the FBI and the other by mass murderers who, like the messianic Curtis, may not be what they seem. En route to a pyrotechnic finale in rural Idaho, Koontz shoots bull'seyes at target issues that shape his theme, including assisted suicide, substance abuse, the irresponsibility of the counterculture and the goofiness of true-believer ET enthusiasts." Publ Wkly

Relentless; a novel; [by] Dean Koontz. Bantam Books 2009 356p $27
ISBN 978-0-553-80714-1; 0-553-80714-5 LC 2009-09866

"'Cubby' Greenwich is a bestselling novelist with a new book out and reviews hitting the stands. When he's eviscerated by renowned critic Shearman Waxx in a review full of errors, he can't help but wonder at the man behind the critique, the inaccuracies, and the poor syntax. Following one relatively harmless run-in at a local res-

Koontz, Dean R., 1945-—*Continued*

taurant, Cubby and his family (wife and fellow author Penny, six-year-old son and off-the-charts genius son 'Spooky' Milo, and similarly spooky dog Lassie) are exposed to terrors beyond metaphorical slaying. Shearman Waxx is a man bent on destroying not merely Cubby's book sales but the man and his family. . . . This is an exquisite crafting of the thrilling, the unexplainable, and the personal." Libr J

Seize the night; by Dean Koontz. Bantam Bks. 1999 401p
ISBN 0-553-10665-1 LC 98-31410

In this second novel featuring Christopher Snow, "the horrifying tale of Chris's hometown, Moonlight Bay, continues to unfold. Chris and his tight band of friends take up the search for four missing children in this town, where experiments with a genetically engineered retrovirus have begun to turn several local residents into creatures that are less than human. Koontz successfully blends his special brand of suspense from generous measures of mystery, horror, sf, and the techno-thriller genre. But his greatest triumph in this series is the creation of Christopher Snow, a thought-provoking narrator with a facility for surfer-lingo and dark humor who, despite his extreme situation, is an undeniably believable character." Libr J

Strangers. Putnam 1986 526p o.p.
LC 85-25677

"Eight characters—all strangers to each other—form the core of the novel. Each is plagued by suspiciously similar fears and anxieties. Ernie Block, who runs a Nevada motel, fears the dark. Ginger Weiss, a Boston cardiology resident, suffers from panic attacks. Southern California horror novelist Dom Corvaisis is vexed with somnambulism. These and other seemingly disparate characters share only one link aside from their bewildering array of related symptoms—all had spent three days during the previous July at Block's motel, not far from a secret military depository." Booklist

The taking; [by] Dean Koontz. Bantam Bks. 2004 388p $27
ISBN 0-553-80250-X

"In a small California town, Molly and Neil Sloan wake in the night to find the world experiencing the communication breakdown and extreme weather phenomena that will presage an extraterrestrial annexation of Earth. Along with the assistance of some intelligent and intuitive dogs . . ., Molly and Neil try to save as many children as they can from being 'taken' or killed outright. In The Taking, Koontz continues his ongoing exploration of the capacity of human nature for hope, goodness, and innocence in the face of evil." Libr J

Velocity; [by] Dean Koontz. Bantam Books 2005 400p $27
ISBN 0-55380-415-4

"Billy Wiles, a 30-something bartender and former writer, is content with his solitary Napa County existence listening to 'beer-based psychoanalysis' from tavern regulars; visiting his hospitalized, comatose fiancée, Barbara; and carving wood sculptures. But the simple life gets mighty complicated when he finds a note with a deadly, time-sensitive ultimatum: he must choose between the death of a young schoolteacher or an elderly humanitari-

an in six hours. Reluctant local sheriff Lanny Olsen dismisses it as a joke until a comely teacher is found strangled and another threatening note appears—offering even less time for Billy to decide the fate of two more people. Who would have guessed that one of those people would be Olsen? After his friend's murder, Billy finds that the cunning killer has gained access to every aspect of his life as the ultimatums grow increasingly more personal. . . . Graphic, fast-paced action, well-developed characters and relentless, nail-biting scenes show Koontz at the top of his game." Publ Wkly

Watchers. Putnam 1987 352p hardcover o.p. pa $7.99
ISBN 0-399-13263-5; 0-425-18880-9 (pa)
LC 86-22687

"When the Russians sabotage a genetic research project in California, two mutated creatures escape from the lab. One is a golden retriever with high enough intelligence to think and communicate with humans; the other is the Outsider, a vicious monster created from a baboon and bred to kill. Both the man who befriends and adopts the dog and his new bride find themselves stalked by government agents anxious to find the dog, a particularly repulsive Mafia hit man intent on stealing him, and the Outsider, with whom the dog is linked telepathically." Libr J

Korda, Michael, 1933-

Curtain; a novel. Summit Bks. 1991 378p o.p.
LC 90-23198

"Robert Vance is a superb Shakespearean actor. He falls in love with an actress, Felicia Lisle, whose fastidious beauty conceals fierce passion. Unable to escape their marriages, they become Britain's favorite adulterous celebrity couple, playing the role of lovers both on stage and in private. Korda opens this page-turner with a prologue set 40 years in the future and hinting at dark, long-hidden secrets. He then flashes back to the 1940s when Vance and Felicia are stranded in Hollywood, broke after a disastrous attempt at taking *Romeo and Juliet* on the road in the U.S. Felicia, drinking and pill-popping, is on the verge of a breakdown, and Robby is anxious to return to London and serve in the RAF. . . . Having set his novel on stage, Korda can pull out all the stops—nothing is too theatrical. And it's a hit." Booklist

The fortune. Summit Bks. 1989 481p o.p.
LC 88-37980

"The wealthy, snobbish Bannerman family is a fictional hybrid of the Rockefellers and the Binghams. It's bad enough that Arthur Bannerman has the poor taste to die in the bed of an attractive young woman. But when she declares herself his widow and delivers a will giving her control of the family fortune, his son Robert and the redoubtable matriarch Eleanor haul out the heavy artillery. Korda has a wonderful ear for bitchy, brittle society chatter, and he takes satirical swipes in every direction." Publ Wkly

The immortals; a novel. Poseidon Press 1992 559p
ISBN 0-671-74526-3 LC 92-22265

A "novel about the love affair between John F. Kennedy and Marilyn Monroe. The theme it rests on is this: as JFK's star ascended, MM's descended, and as their stars

Korda, Michael, 1933-—*Continued*

crossed, heat was definitely generated. Korda understands politics as well as fatal attraction, so his fiction is several notches above your basic steamy romance." Booklist

Worldly goods. Random House 1982 353p o.p.
LC 81-40213

A saga about a "Hungarian family torn apart by various fortunes, a terrible betrayal back in Nazi days (there are flashbacks to Hitler, Himmler, and the Holocaust), and insatiable lust for money, power, and vengeance now. Paul Foster (née Grunwald) survived Auschwitz and has at last amassed the worldy wherewithal to avenge his father, all unbeknownst to his betraying uncle and cousin. Foster is a cold fish (though there's a heroine to adhere to him), but he only wants to take enough fortune away from his uncle to make him cry 'uncle.'" Saturday Rev

"At once a Holocaust novel from a new point of view, and a look at love, hate, power, and sex in the stratosphere of the modern corporation, this book is tightly constructed." Libr J

Kornbluth, C. M. (Cyril M.), 1923-1958

(jt. auth) Pohl, F. The space merchants

Kornbluth, Cyril M. *See* Kornbluth, C. M. (Cyril M.), 1923-1958

Koryta, Michael

The silent hour. Minotaur Books 2009 311p $24.95
ISBN 978-0-312-36157-0; 0-312-36157-2
LC 2009-10485

"A Thomas Dunne book for Minotaur Books"

When Cleveland, Ohio, PI Lincoln Perry "starts receiving letters from convicted murder Parker Harrison, he ignores them until the man shows up in his office. Twelve years earlier, the then recently paroled Harrison worked for Alexandra and Joshua Cantrell, a couple who ran a rehabilitation program for violent offenders. Then they disappeared, and Harrison wants Perry's help in tracking down Alexandra. Suspicious why Harrison waited so long, Perry discovers that Joshua's bones were recently unearthed in Pennsylvania. Ken Merriman, a Pittsburgh PI, soon arrives in Cleveland, asking Perry for help finding out who killed Joshua." Publ Wkly

"Koryta writes with maturity and grace, delivering clipped, crisp prose and crackling suspense." Booklist

Tonight I said goodbye; Michael Koryta. 1st ed. Thomas Dunne Books\St. Martin's Minotaur 2004 290p $21.95
ISBN 0-312-33245-9   LC 2004-46781

"The Cleveland police would charge private investigator Wayne Weston with murdering his wife and daughter except that their bodies can't be found and he's dead, apparently a suicide. Weston's father isn't buying it, however, and he hires private investigators Lincoln Perry and Joe Pritchard to clear his son's name and find his family. Perry is a former cop whose cheating ex-fiancée set him off on a bender that cost him his job. Pritchard, his old partner, is ready to retire and become what all retired cops become, a P.I. The hardboiled cliché works beautifully here as these two men find themselves chasing Rus-

sian Mafiya, a real estate mogul, and an ex-Marine while dodging bullets, cops, and the FBI. The Cleveland setting is a nice change from the usual East Coast/West Coast locales." Libr J

Kosinski, Jerzy N., 1933-1991

Being there; [by] Jerzy Kosinski. Harcourt Brace Jovanovich 1971 c1970 142p
ISBN 0-15-111700-4

*

"An illiterate gardener, Chance, knows the world only through his gardening and by watching television, to which he is addicted. Without education or any identifiable background, he is evicted into the outside world when his employer dies. He makes horticultural analogies to current events, which give him a reputation for wisdom that he really does not have, and which catapult him into national prominence. Chance's simple statements are interpreted by his listeners to be profound observations, and we see him being considered for positions of great importance. This is a satire on human behavior in the worlds of power, government, and the media." Shapiro. Fic for Youth. 3d edition

The devil tree; [by] Jerzy Kosinski. Harcourt Brace Jovanovich 1973 208p o.p.

This novel "confronts the disintegration of the American dream as seen through the eyes of Jonathan James Whalen, the man-who-has-everything. For Whalen and many of the people who surround him, the American dream has become the American nightmare. Their efforts to escape their roots become a frenetic search to find their roots, until, like the devil tree, they get turned upside down and confirm the fact of their own extinction. Jonathan Whalen is as empty as the life he leads, although on the surface he is a man who can be and do anything he wants." Publ Wkly

The painted bird; [by] Jerzy Kosinski. 2nd Modern Library ed. Modern Lib. 1983 c1965 234p
ISBN 0-394-60433-4
* LC 82-42869

First published 1965 by Houghton Mifflin

"In Eastern Europe during World War II a ten-year-old boy is separated from his parents and struggles to survive in primitive villages where he is viewed as an unwanted outsider. Dark-haired and dark-eyed, he is unlike the Polish villagers among whom he tries to find refuge. He is the gypsy, the 'painted bird,' and savage abuse is heaped upon him time after time. He has, nevertheless, the will to transcend the sadism and superstition of these ignorant people." Shapiro. Fic for Youth. 3d edition

Kostova, Elizabeth

The historian; a novel. Little, Brown and Co 2005 642p $25.95
ISBN 0-316-01177-0
* LC 2004-22563

"In the early 20th century, Paul, a young graduate student, learns from his advisor, Professor Rossi, that Prince Dracula is still alive as one of the undead. When the professor disappears one terrifying night, Paul goes in search of his mentor, whom he knows to be in Dracula's clutches. His search takes him to secret archives and libraries of ancient monasteries throughout Eastern Europe;

Kostova, Elizabeth—*Continued*

he is joined by his daughter, his wife, and friends, all historians and scholars themselves." Libr J

"Kostova's vampire is no campy Lugosi knockoff but a blend of the cunning, powerful count who debuts in Bram Stoker's 1897 classic novel and the actual Dracula, Vlad the Impaler, a 15th-century Romanian prince who was both a nationalist hero and a sadistic torturer. Blending history and myth, Kostova has fashioned a version so fresh that when a stake is finally driven through a heart, it inspires the tragic shock of something happening for the very first time." Newsweek

Kotzwinkle, William, 1938-

The bear went over the mountain. Doubleday 1996 306p

ISBN 0-385-48428-3   LC 96-2296

"Kotzwinkle has imagined a disconsolate Maine professor, Arthur Bramhall, who sets out to write a bestseller, only to have a bear steal it, thinking it's something to eat. This is no ordinary bear, however; he has aspirations to becoming a person. . . . What better way to establish an identity than by becoming a celebrity novelist? Soon, the bear has found a pseudonym, Hal Jam, an agent and a publisher. With his distinctively masculine presence, and a monosyllabic way of talking that reminds many of Hemingway, he's on his way to stardom with a novel that everyone agrees has its roots deep in the natural world." Publ Wkly

"This genuine parable for our time is as full of truth as it is of humor." Nation

E.T.; the extra-terrestrial; a novel. Putnam 1982 246p o.p.   LC 82-9078

"A ten million year old alien botanist is accidentally marooned on Earth. He is befriended by three children and in particular by Elliott, whose bedroom closet becomes his hideout. With their help he learns something of our planet's bewildering ways, puts together a beacon to call for rescue and thrives on a diet of M&Ms, Oreos and, even more important, the children's love. Of course, the government suspects his presence and is hunting him, but after he is captured Elliott helps him escape in time to rendezvous with his ship." Publ Wkly

"Kotzwinkle's many gifts, particularly for realistic detail and black humor, make this a book capable of standing on its own merits apart from the motion picture." Booklist

Krantz, Judith

Mistral's daughter. Crown 1983 c1982 531p

ISBN 0-517-54906-9   LC 82-17966

"Three generations of Lunel women are intimately involved with Julien Mistral, France's greatest artist. Maggy is his model, the inspiration for a series of remarkable nude paintings in 1925, and he is her first lover. Years later Teddy, star of her mother Maggy's New York modeling agency, meets Mistral on assignment and lightening strikes; she becomes his mistress and the mother of Fauve. And Mistral's daughter Fauve, though an 'enfante adulterine,' has some of his talent and brightens his life before their estrangement." Libr J

The author "possesses an undeniable talent for plot-weaving and descriptive detail." Best Sellers

Kraus, Nicola

(jt. auth) McLaughlin, E. The nanny diaries

Krauss, Nicole

The history of love. Norton 2005 252p $23.95

ISBN 0-393-06034-9   LC 2005-00936

"A boy in Poland falls in love and writes a book when World War II arrives, and both the love and the book are lost. Leo Gursky, now in his eighties and living in New York City, struggles to be noticed each day so that people will know he has not yet died. Meanwhile, 14-year-old Alma Singer wants her brother to be normal and her mother to be happy again after the death of Alma's father. In a quest for the story behind her name, Alma and Leo find each other, and Leo learns that the book he wrote so long ago has not been lost." Libr J

"Beyond the vigorous whiplash that keeps Ms. Krauss's [book] moving (and keeps its reader off-balance until a stunning finale), this novel is tightly packed with ingenious asides. They range from parodying various publications' characteristic obituaries of a very famous writer, a man who was best known for a single, ecstatic five-page paragraph (Ms. Krauss perfectly mimics the syntax of both The Times and The New Republic) to skewering the kind of editor whom all writers dread." N Y Times (Late N Y Ed)

Man walks into a room. Talese 2002 248p

ISBN 0-385-50399-7   LC 2001-53699

"When a tumor in his brain is discovered and removed, Samson Greene, an English professor in his thirties, finds himself afflicted by a peculiar kind of amnesia: he cannot remember anything that happened after he was twelve. Even as he struggles to connect with his wife, Anna, he thinks that he might prefer the blankness of his new life. Samson's loss takes place against a backdrop of secret experiments on human memory and the social implications of atomic testing, but it is his shadow-filled scrutiny of intimacy—as he wonders why he might have married this beautiful stranger, and whether he can love her—that is the book's real strength." New Yorker

Krentz, Jayne Ann, 1948-

For works written by this author under other names see Quick, Amanda, 1948-

Lost and found. Putnam 2001 341p

ISBN 0-399-14669-5   LC 00-44563

"Cady Briggs, a Santa Barbara-based art consultant specializing in decorative arts and antiques, has been doing some work for Mack Easton, who runs a company called Lost and Found that tracks the movement of art and antiquities. When her eccentric aunt Vesta, an excellent swimmer, drowns, Cady has a hunch that something isn't right, especially since Vesta left controlling shares of Chatelaine, her tony art gallery, to her instead of to cousin Sylvia, Chatelaine's much more business-oriented CEO. . . . Cady enlists Mack to help uncover the truth." Booklist

"This is romantic suspense at its most enjoyable, enhanced by Krentz's . . . trademark humor and quirky characters." Libr J

Krentz, Jayne Ann, 1948-—*Continued*

Running hot. G.P. Putnam's Sons 2008 337p
$25.95

ISBN 978-0-399-15521-5; 0-399-15521-X

LC 2008-28340

Reluctantly paired for a murder investigation by the paranormal Arcane Society, former cop Luther Malone and aura-reading librarian Grace Renquist find their mutual disgust dissolving into a powerful attraction, during a case that is further complicated by operatives for a ruthless underground psychic group.

"This arresting tale combines witty humor with clever plotting to weave an exceptionally memorable romance." Libr J

Smoke in mirrors. Putnam 2002 320p $23.95

ISBN 0-399-14792-6   LC 2001-19361

"The news of Meredith Spooner's death comes as no surprise to her half-sister, Leonora Hutton; after all, Meredith was a con artist who was adept at making enemies. But when Thomas Walker, a victim of Meredith's most recent scam, confronts Leonora, demanding that she help him find the $1.5 million that Meredith filched from the Bethany Walker memorial fund and intimating that Meredith may have been murdered, Leonora drops her reference desk position in California to do some amateur sleuthing in Wing Cove, Wash." Publ Wkly

"The politics of academe, eerie antique mirrors, secret passages, and psychic contact contribute a haunting quality to Krentz's enticing blend of suspense and top-notch romance." Booklist

Kress, Nancy, 1948-

Beggars & choosers. TOR Bks. 1994 315p

ISBN 0-312-85749-7   LC 94-21753

"A Tom Doherty Associates book"

Sequel to Beggars in Spain

"As a byproduct of their genetic mental enhancements, the Sleepless neither sleep nor age. For those reasons, they are reviled by the unmodified majority of humans. Yet in a world of overpopulation, chronic joblessness, environmental depletion, and uncontrolled plagues of nanotechnological origin, the Sleepless may hold the key to humanity's salvation—if only they can be persuaded to come out of their self-imposed hiding." Libr J

"Kress's work remains strongly character driven, an approach that in her hands raises social-speculation sf to about as high a level as one can reasonably expect." Booklist

Followed by Beggars ride

Beggars in Spain. Morrow 1993 438p o.p.

LC 92-25070

"An AvoNova book"

Based on a novella of the same title

In this novel, "genetic enhancements have placed Leisha Camden and a few other individuals in a category of their own. Smarter and healthier than normal humans, born without the need to sleep, the 'Sleepless'—as they are called—grow up in a world that turns increasingly hostile toward the super-achievers in their midst." Libr J

"This book is an intellectual roller-coaster ride, supplying no simple conclusions about right and wrong, and racing along with its brisk prose, stimulating ideas, and a variety of challenging characters." SLJ

Followed by Beggars & choosers

Beggars ride. TOR Bks. 1996 304p

ISBN 0-312-85817-5   LC 96-19956

"A Tom Doherty Associates book"

In this concluding volume of the Beggars trilogy, "the near-utopia that the genetically altered Sleepless finally realized is . . . well on the way to crumbling under the onslaught of warfare waged with tailored viruses. Society is devolving into a host of subgroups, some of which are virtually abandoning technology and surviving or failing as much through luck as through resistance to the viruses. Gradually, communication among tribes is restored, lost knowledge regained, disused knowledge again put to use, and the survival of the race assured." Booklist

"The scale of Kress's vision is large as she lays out a drama that-convincingly if unsurprisingly-argues that moral quandaries can't be addressed by technology." Publ Wkly

Dogs; a novel. Tachyon Publications 2008 280p
pa $14.95

ISBN 978-1-892391-78-0; 1-892391-78-3

"Tired of being passed over for promotion and suspecting that her recently deceased Tunisian husband is the cause, Tessa Sanderson leaves the FBI and relocates to the small town of Tyler, MD. Trouble follows her, however, in the form of a mysterious and sudden canine plague that heightens the aggression of its victims, causing them to attack anyone in their path-even their beloved owners. A series of threatening emails implicating Tessa in a terrorist plot connected with the plague causes her to turn fugitive in order to track down the perpetrators of the illness and restore the good name of both herself and her husband." Libr J

"The best scenes . . . have a straight-ahead, disaster novel feel to them, full of suspense and creepy details." San Francisco Chron

Probability moon. TOR Bks. 2000 334p $23.95

ISBN 0-312-87406-5   LC 00-27117

"A Tom Doherty Associates book"

"In this novel set in the distant future, humans explore the universe through tunnels that propel them to the far reaches of space. The most recent expedition takes an anthropological team to World, a planet with a peaceful sentient civilization. Anthropological answers are not all that humans seek on World. A covert military operation accompanies the team to study a strange moon that might have military significance." Voice Youth Advocates

"The climax of the book is a four-way conflict among the scientists, the two alien races, and the scientists' military superiors, each charging from a different corner, so to speak. Kress' characterizations are as sound as ever, but many will be agreeably surprised at her proficiency with military hardware and action scenes. Very impressive." Booklist

Probability sun. TOR Bks. 2001 348p $24.95

ISBN 0-312-87407-3   LC 2001-27119

"A Tom Doherty Associates book"

This sequel to Probability moon "continues humanity's war against the alien Fallers, a war humanity is losing. It again shows scientists and the military at odds if not in outright conflict while portraying the strengths and limitations of both with admirable even-handedness. A shipload of scientists has come to study the alien artifact discovered on the planet World, and the ship's military crew is holding the only Faller POW as a secret captive." Booklist

Kress, Nancy, 1948-—*Continued*

Steal across the sky. Tor 2009 317p il $25.95

ISBN 978-0-7653-1986-9; 0-7653-1986-1

LC 2008-46432

"A Tom Doherty Associates book"

"Aliens calling themselves the Atoners have confessed to committing crimes against the human race thousands of years ago and have recruited a few individuals to travel to select worlds to 'Witness' what they have done. Kress . . . . once again demonstrates her absolute mastery of alien-human encounters, fleshing out her characters as believable individuals while at the same time managing surprising plot twists and philosophical conundrums at every turn." Libr J

Kreyling, Michael, 1948-

(ed) Welty, E. Stories, essays & memoir

Kring, Sandra

Thank you for all things. Bantam Books 2008 432p pa $12

ISBN 978-0-385-34120-2   LC 2008-6979

"A Bantam discovery"

"Lucy McGowan is a 12-year-old genius with a photographic memory, an even more brilliant brother, Milo (IQ: 180), and a single mother, Tess, living in Chicago. What Lucy has that her brother doesn't is curiosity and people smarts, a quality that propels her to unearth the hidden relationships and buried secrets of her family. An imaginative and headstrong girl, Lucy finds herself on a grim family visit to her sickly, estranged grandfather in Timber Falls, Wis. Witnessing her mom's unshakable hatred for her dying father, Lucy begins to investigate her family's past; her love for the sick old patriarch she knows is challenged repeatedly by what she finds out about the angry, abusive man he used to be." Publ Wkly

The author's "delightful and nuanced take on Midwestern America . . . feels real and moving—perhaps because it is so unpretentious." Salon.com

Krist, Gary

Chaos theory; a novel. Random House 2000 347p

ISBN 0-375-50080-4   LC 99-13411

"On a whim, two middle-class high-school boys, one African American, the other white, venture into one of Washington, D.C.'s less savory neighborhoods to buy drugs. . . . A wacko with a gun greets them in an alley, and they break his arm in the course of escaping. Imagine their surprise when police question them regarding a dead undercover cop found in the same alley. A caring teacher enlists the aid of an FBI agent, who steps in to uncover a scam involving corruption at the highest level of city government." Booklist

"Spinning a plausible situation into an extraordinary story while training a marksman's eye on character, Krist has conceived a sleek and thoughtful thriller." Publ Wkly

Krüger, Michael, 1943-

The cello player; translated from the German by Andrew Shields. Harcourt 2004 200p $23

ISBN 0-15-100591-5   LC 2003-13369

The narrator of this novel is a "middle-aged German composer who writes serious avant-garde music, but makes a living writing theme music for television. When Judit, an ambitious young cello player from Budapest (whose mother was once the composer's lover and who may or may not be his daughter), shows up on his doorstep, he agrees to take her in while she studies at the conservatory in Munich." Publisher's notes

"Packed into this small, powerful novel is a dazzling array of well-chiseled, colorful characters, extracted from the grand tableau of history and from the author's imagination." New York Times Book Rev

Kundera, Milan

The book of laughter and forgetting; translated from the Czech by Michael Henry Heim. Knopf 1980 228p o.p.

* LC 80-7657

First published 1979 in France

"The novel is written in seven parts with an interwoven structure that the author likened to polyphonic music. The repetition of incidents, characters, and themes provides *The Book of Laughter and Forgetting* with its formal shape. Memories, which the characters want to keep or to forget, are a recurring subject, as is laughter, which is as often ironic as joyous." Merriam-Webster's Ency of Lit

Identity; a novel; translated from the French by Linda Asher. HarperFlamingo 1998 168p

ISBN 0-06-017564-8   LC 97-31907

"Recently divorced ad executive Chantal, on a vacation with her younger boyfriend, Jean-Marc, believes that she is too old to be considered attractive by other men. For Chantal, identity is defined by the perceptions of strangers. . . . When she returns from her vacation, she begins to receive letters from an anonymous admirer. She suspects each new man she encounters to be the mysterious scribe and fantasizes how each might perceive her. Gradually, these letters, along with a few dreams, affect how Chantal views herself and her relationship with Jean-Marc, until her feelings and identity become unrecognizable both to her lover and to herself." Publ Wkly

Ignorance; a novel; translated from the French by Linda Asher. HarperCollins Pubs. 2002 195p

ISBN 0-06-000209-3

"After nearly 20 years in Paris and after the fall of Czech communism, Irena considers moving back to her country and returns for a visit. In the airport, she meets Josef, also an immigrant, with whom she shared a single evening years ago in Prague. Irena remembers their initial meeting with detailed intensity and has always regretted its abrupt, chaste conclusion. Josef doesn't even recognize Irena, but he lies and a passionate climax follows." Booklist

"Kundera knows how to keep us turning the pages. He cuts his scenes skillfully, withholding essential information. . . . His characters may not linger on in the mind. But he is able in Ignorance to turn his house of ideas into a believable and moving edifice." New Leader

Kundera, Milan—*Continued*

Immortality; translated from the Czech by Peter Kussi. Grove Weidenfeld 1991 345p o.p.

* LC 90-28628

"Kundera, himself a prominent character in the circular narrative, here contrasts the troubled, comic relationships among Goethe; his wife, Christiane; and Goethe's much younger friend Bettina von Arnim to the modern-day triangle of three imaginary Parisians: Paul; his wife, Agnes; and Agnes's sister Laura." Publ Wkly

"Immortality swings easily, almost imperceptibly, from narrative to rumination and back again, collapsing the distinction between action and concepts. . . . Out of a story about contemporary neuroses, Kundera has fabricated a context in which everything, literally, can be claimed to matter. What is more, the author indulges this obsessiveness without ever droning or turning out a dull page. In its inventiveness and its dazzling display of what written words can convey, Immortality gives fiction back its good name." Time

The joke. definitive version, fully revised by the author. HarperCollins Pubs. 1992 317p o.p.

LC 91-58349

Original Czech edition, 1967; first English translation published 1969 by Coward, McCann

In this novel "a young communist intellectual, Ludvik, is imprisoned, then stigmatized for life for having written an irreverent postcard to a girlfriend ('Optimism is the opium of the people! . . . Long live Trotsky!'). Years later he seeks revenge in another 'joke'; he will cold-bloodedly seduce the wife, Helena, of the party leader who denounced him." Newsweek

"Kundera's brilliance resides in his ability to strip away the lies and disguises which Ludvik and the others need to survive, and which their society has institutionalized and sanctified." New Repub

Laughable loves; translated from the Czech by Suzanne Rappaport. Knopf 1974 242p o.p.

Original Czech edition, 1970

Contents: The hitchhiking game; Let the old dead make room for the young dead; Nobody will laugh; The golden apple of eternal desire; Symposium; Dr. Havel after ten years; Edward and God

"The stories in [this volume] are buoyantly energetic and virtuosic. . . . The politics here is sexual: male dominance and impotence, role-playing and fantasizing detonate with startling effect." Newsweek

Slowness; translated from the French by Linda Asher. HarperCollins Pubs. 1996 156p

ISBN 0-06-017369-6　　　　　　　　　LC 96-6253

"The narrator (the writer himself, 'Milanku) and his wife decide to vacation at a château, and en route he immediately begins meditating on slowness versus speed when they find themselves impeding the progress of the driver behind them. Before the end, Kundera has converted his philosophical ruminations into a . . . fictional piece in which the action takes place at the château. The writer sets up parallel stories of seduction; one set in the eighteenth century, the other contemporary." Booklist

"Mr. Kundera comes closer to polemic here than in his other fiction, but he is fiercely defending the 'spirit of complexity' that the novel embodies. . . . So it seems almost churlish to point out shortcomings in a writer of his spirit of play, breadth of reach and perspicacity—all admirably at work once again in 'Slowness.'" N Y Times Book Rev

The unbearable lightness of being; translated from the Czech by Michael Henry Heim. Harper & Row 1984 314p o.p.

* LC 83-48363

"Set against the background of Czechoslovakia in the 1960s, the novel concerns a young Czech physician who substitutes a series of erotic adventures over which he thinks he can maintain control for becoming involved in his country's politics, where he feels he can have no power or freedom. Inevitably, he is drawn into Czechoslovakia's political unrest. In a parallel vein, he is forced to choose among the women with whom he is involved." Merriam-Webster's Ency of Lit

Kunetka, James W., 1944-

(jt. auth) Strieber, W. Warday

Kunkel, Benjamin

Indecision; a novel. Random House 2005 241p $21.95

ISBN 1-4000-6345-0　　　　　　　　LC 2004-62894

"Twentysomething Manhattanite Dwight Wilmerding suffers from a fictional condition called abulia–the inability to make up his mind. Paralyzed by indecisiveness about his tech-support job, his complicated love life (there's Dutch bombshell Natasha who lives in Ecuador and coy Vaneetha in New York), and a distressing attraction to his psychiatrist sister, Dwight signs up for the trial drug Abulinix, which claims to tackle tentativeness with a little blue-and-white pill. Dwight travels to South America, only to discover that even the most potent pharmaceuticals are virtually powerless against the forces of fate." Booklist

"Ever the clever chef, Kunkel reduces the sprawling, indigestible postmodern novel to an amiable pop confection that goes down like a milkshake. The result is a stylistic triumph of sorts. The half-serious pastiche is the ideal vehicle for bright apercus, capers, riffs, and dreamy ruminations." New Leader

Kunzru, Hari

The impressionist. Dutton 2002 383p

ISBN 0-525-94642-X　　　　　　　　LC 2001-47137

"Until 1918, his 15th year, spoiled Pran Nath believes that he is the son of a wealthy Kashmiri merchant and a disturbed woman, Amrita, who died giving birth to him. When the housekeeper reveals that he is actually an Englishman's child, and thus a despised half-breed, he's thrown out on the street. After an involuntary stay in a brothel, a stint as a servant in the depraved household of the Nawab of Fatehpur, and a sojourn at a Bombay missionary's home, he moves on to England, where he pretends to be an orphaned heir, Jonathan Bridgeman." Publ Wkly

This novel "includes a multitude of richly imagined characters. A bold, unfashionably omniscient voice narrates the story as it tackles such subjects as race, class, colonialism, and the roots of personal identity" New Leader

Kunzru, Hari—*Continued*

My revolutions. Dutton 2008 c2007 280p $25.95
ISBN 978-0-525-94932-9; 0-525-94932-1
LC 2007-39459
First published 2007 in the United Kingdom

"Mike Frame, on the eve of his 50th-birthday bash, is a man with a problem. For starters, Mike Frame isn't his real name. For years he's been living a lie with his vaguely alternative but respectable live-in girlfriend (a Body-shop-type entrepreneur) and her grownup daughter. But, in the past few months, his far from respectable past has come racing up to join him. The whole pack of cards threatens to come crashing down. This is the setup of Hari Kunzru's My Revolutions, which shuffles between present, past and an uncertain future. Frame's secret . . . is that in his former life, in the 1970s, he was a left-wing terrorist. This makes up the most substantial narrative in the novel – how Chris Carver (the real Frame) underwent a transition from left-wing bohemia to Red Army faction-style bombs and guns." London Times

This novel "is, as Virginia Woolf said of George Eliot's Middlemarch, a book for grownup people (although that shouldn't imply it is at all ponderous or worthy) and it is very much a book about the process of growing up. My Revolutions is impassioned, intelligent and profoundly serious literature." Sydney Morning Herald

Transmission. Dutton 2004 276p $24.95
ISBN 0-525-94760-4
LC 2004-3295

"This novel introduces a daydreaming Indian computer geek whose luxurious fantasies about life in America are shaken when he accepts a California job offer. Lonely and naive, Arjun Mehta bides his time as a lowly assistant virus tester, pining away for his free-spirited colleague Christine. Despite building digital creatures in a feeble attempt to enhance his job security, Arjun gets laid-off like so many of his Silicon Valley peers. In an act of desperation to keep his job, he releases a mischievous but destructive virus around the globe that has major unintended consequences." Publisher's note

"Transmission is a tragicomedy, a subtle exploration of the relations between feeling, fiction and technology. . . . Martin Amis is a clear influence on Kunzru. His characters have the same foam-rubber resilience, his women are devastatingly sexy, his baddies grotesquely bad. This, together with a romping plot, makes Transmission enormous fun. It is also a thoughtful, and thought-provoking novel, which engages with important questions about twenty-first-century life." Times Lit Suppl

Kureishi, Hanif

The Buddha of suburbia. Viking 1990 284p
ISBN 0-670-83342-8
LC 90-168346

This novel deals with "father-son relations, punk rock, bisexuality, and class and racial prejudices in England. The story is told through the eyes of Karim Amir, 'an Englishman born and bred, almost.'" Libr J

"Resembling a modern-day Tom Jones, this is an astonishing book, full of intelligence and elan." Publ Wkly

Something to tell you; a novel. Scribner 2008 375p $26
ISBN 978-1-4165-7210-7; 1-4165-7210-4
LC 2008-13755

"Jamal, an English-born Pakistani psychoanalyst of some renown, tells the story of his life, moving at will between his present as an affluent professional living in the less-than-posh London neighborhood of Shepherd's Green and his past as a sometimes delinquent student. . . . Recently separated from his wife, he contentedly fist-bumps with his son, and eventually tells him, in a moment of fatherly largesse, that divorce will be his destiny, too. . . . An outspoken Freudian when he appears on TV, he believes that pleasure is the basic human good. His other main concern is the intense new relationship between his sister, Miriam, and his longtime best friend, Henry." N Y Sun

This is "the kind of book in which people do seriously bad things — murder, incest, copious sex — and then sit around talking about it. The work owes as much of a debt to Pedro Almodóvar as it does to Oscar Wilde. Yet melodrama aside, the best thing about Something to Tell You is that it reminds readers that there used to be a place for intelligent conversation. The anecdotes are brief and well sculpted. The jokes, subtle and sad." Esquire

Kurtz, Katherine

The harrowing of Gwynedd. Ballantine Bks. 1989 384p (Heirs of Saint Camber, v1) o.p.
LC 88-7414
"A Del Rey book"

This is the first volume of The heirs of Saint Camber trilogy; other titles are: King Javan's year (1992) and The bastard prince (1994).

This is a "tale of the events immediately after Saint Camber's death. The persecution of the Deryni is widespread and brutal, their own leadership is beginning to descend from the high culture of Camber's time to the petty politics of a later era, and Camber's daughter must face death to continue her father's work. Kurtz also manages to be sufficiently graphic about the violence without being gratuitous, and in short has added another well-told tale to the Deryni canon." Booklist

King Kelson's bride. Ace Bks. 2000 387p il (Histories of King Kelson, v4)
ISBN 0-441-00732-5
LC 99-48047

A fantasy "set in a land analogous to medieval Wales and featuring the Deryni, a human minority with magical powers. It also resolves the longstanding question of when King Kelson Haldane of Gwynedd is going to get married. He has missed two opportunities, one due to a lady's death and the other to family treachery." Publ Wkly

The quest for Saint Camber. Ballantine Bks. 1986 xxvi, 435p (Histories of King Kelson, v3) o.p.
LC 86-8249
"A Del Rey book"

Earlier titles in the King Kelson series are The bishop's heir (1984) and The King's justice (1985)

"The reported death of King Kelson on a quest for the tomb of the Deryni Saint Camber throws the Kingdom of Gwynedd into turmoil. As Kelson's friends set out to search for the truth, a power struggle at court brings deceit and murder in its wake. [This installment in the author's] Deryni series . . . skillfully combines magic with the medieval in a novel that will appeal to fantasy readers and medievalists alike." Libr J

Kurtz, Katherine—*Continued*

St. Patrick's gargoyle. Ace Bks. 2001 233p $21.95

ISBN 0-441-00725-2   LC 00-36275

"When Dublin's St. Patrick's Cathedral becomes the target of an act of vandalism, the gargoyle guardian of the building enlists the aid of an aging Knight of Malta to assist him in his pursuit of the vandals. Combining an interest in Irish history with snatches of Templar lore, the author. . . creates a story of angelic powers and demonic forces locked in an eternal struggle." Libr J

The temple and the stone; [by] Katherine Kurtz and Deborah Turner Harris. Warner Bks. 1998 456p

ISBN 0-446-52260-0   LC 98-14344

"Following a vision that foretells the formation of a new Temple of Solomon in Scotland, Brother Arnault de Saint Clair, a member of a secret magical order within the Order of the Knights Templar, becomes involved in the struggle for Scottish independence. The authors . . . vividly recreate one of Scottish history's most compelling periods, as Robert the Bruce and William Wallace share the limelight with fictional, but no less credible, characters." Libr J

Two crowns for America. Bantam Bks. 1996 375p o.p.

LC 95-32372

This novel presents an "alternate American Revolution driven by the occult machinations of an age-old Master as well as destiny and Masonic solidarity. . . . The Wallace family—Jacobite Andrew; his son Simon; Simon's wife, Arabella; and Arabella's brother, Justin Carmichael—provide viewpoints for most of the important action." Publ Wkly

"Vivid portrayals of Washington and Charles Edward Stuart ('Bonnie Prince Charlie') are at the core of the book, which is otherwise well up to Kurtz's historically well-informed standards." Booklist

Kurzweil, Allen

The grand complication. Hyperion 2001 359p

ISBN 0-7868-6603-9   LC 2001-16811

"Henry James Jesson III, the kind of wealthy eccentric who seems to exist only to send other men on wildgoose chases, hires Alexander Short, a down-on-his-luck librarian, to help solve the mystery of an eighteenth-century cabinet of wonders that is missing one of its objects. Eager to escape his problems with his wife, a French artist and pop-up-book designer, Short discovers that the missing item is a fantastically precise timepiece that allegedly belonged to Marie Antoinette, and he is soon consumed by the quest for the watch. Kurzweil's intricately constructed novel has no shortage of esoterica, and the author's fondness for sexual comedy supplies a welcome counterpart." New Yorker

Kushner, Anna

(tr) Rosales, G. The halfway house

Kushner, Rachel

Telex from Cuba; a novel. Scribner 2008 336p $25

ISBN 978-1-41656-103-3; 1-41656-103-X

LC 2007-42893

A "novel set in the American community in Cuba during the years leading up to Castro's revolution. . . . Young Everly Lederer and K.C. Stites come of age in Oriente Province, where the Americans tend their own fiefdom—three hundred thousand acres of United Fruit Company sugarcane that surround their gated enclave. . . . In Havana, a thousand kilometers and a world away from the American colony, a caberet dancer meets a French agitator named Christian de La Mazière, whose seductive demeanor can't mask his shameful past. Together they become enmeshed in the brewing political underground. When Fidel and Raúl Castro lead a revolt from the mountains above the cane platation, torching the sugar and kidnapping a boat full of 'yanqui' revelers, K.C. and Everly begin to discover the brutality that keeps the colony humming." Publisher's note

Kushner's novel is a "work of great care and research, directed at recreating a place that history has erased from the map. . . . With impressive fluency, [she] speaks in the voices of a series of latter-day colonialists." Bookforum

Kuznetsov, Anatoliĭ Vasil´evich *See* Anatoli, A., 1929-1979

Kyle, Aryn

The god of animals; a novel. Scribner 2007 305p $25

ISBN 978-1-4165-3324-5; 1-4165-3324-9

LC 2006-50605

A "novel about Alice Winston, a 12-year-old loner with family troubles in Desert Valley, Colo. Her mother hasn't left her bed since Alice was a baby; her father struggles to keep their horse ranch solvent; and her beautiful older sister, Nona, has eloped with a rodeo cowboy. Alice resists befriending the rich girl who takes riding lessons from her father, becomes obsessed with a classmate who drowns in a nearby canal and entangles herself with adults whose motives are suspect." Publ Wkly

This "turns out to be smarter than most [coming-of-age novels], as it moves through sexual stirrings, family disillusionment, issues of separation and deception. . . . Kyle can be overripe, but most of her prose is a joy, fluid on the page." Cleveland Plain Dealer

L

La Farge, Oliver, 1901-1963

Laughing Boy. Houghton Mifflin 1929 302p o.p.

"This novel takes place in the early years of the twentieth century in Navajo country in the American Southwest. It is the story of the ill-fated love of Laughing Boy, worker in silver and maker of songs, and Slim Girl, whose education in American schools has embittered her. The reader is immersed in their tender romance but also learns a great deal about the culture and philosophical outlook of the Native American." Shapiro. Fic for Youth. 3d edition

La Plante, Lynda

Cold blood. Random House 1997 402p o.p.

LC 98-107026

First published 1996 in the United Kingdom

"One night during the Mardi Gras in New Orleans, 18-year-old Anna Louise Caley vanishes. Eleven months later, when all other efforts have failed, the girl's mother (aging film star Elizabeth Caley) hires an ex-cop and recovering alcoholic named Lorrain Page and offers her a $1 million bonus if she finds Anna Louise, dead or alive. The investigation leads Lorraine and her team into a world of drugs, booze, adultery, suicide, voodoo, and murder." Libr J

"The mystery of what happened to Anna Louise is interesting, but the real suspense concerns whether Page—who finds herself drinking again and in bed with the missing girl's father—will fall apart." Publ Wkly

Labiner, Norah, 1967-

Miniatures. Coffee House Press 2002 381p $23

ISBN 1-566-89136-1   LC 2002-71283

"Fern Jacobi, the restless 29-year-old narrator of this eccentric novel . . . recounts an unhappy two months spent as a housekeeper in the home of two expatriate writers from America named Owen and Brigid Lieb. Owen is nearly three decades older than Brigid. The house where the Liebs live in Ireland carries the memory of Owen's first wife, Franny, a novelist who died of either suicide or murder when she was electrocuted in a bathtub." (NY Times Book NY Times Book

"This is a haunting novel, written in the first person and switching from past to present, from Fern's life to the other characters' lives. It slowly and achingly reveals secrets, evokes literary figures from the Bronte sisters to Marcel Proust, and explores biography as a literary form." Booklist

Lackey, Mercedes

The fairy godmother. Harlequin 2004 432p $24.95

ISBN 0-373-80202-1

This fantasy is "set in a world where The Tradition tries its magical—and surreptitiously-best to force the characters into their 'legendary' roles. But things sometimes go awry, and when Elena is denied her predestined Cinderella role because her kingdom's prince is too young, she is chosen as an apprentice by the local Fairy Godmother and ends up creating a legend of her own. A spirited, resourceful, though somewhat impulsive heroine, a prince who needs to learn a lesson in manners, humility, and compassion, and a host of magical creatures—including some delightful house elves and besotted unicorns—result in a lively, humorous fantasy romance." Libr J

Firebird. TOR Bks. 1996 352p o.p.

LC 96-23841

"A Tom Doherty Associates book"

In this coming-of-age fantasy, "the author transports readers to a medieval Russian world based on the folktale of 'The Firebird.' Ilya Ivanovitch is beaten and teased by his ruffian brothers and ignored by his father, a *boyar* or Russian prince, whose singular concern is his stolen cherries. While trying to catch the thief, Ilya

Ivanovitch is unknowingly cursed just by glimpsing at the Firebird, which is half maiden and half bird. During his brother's prewedding boar hunt, the young man gets lost, but becomes much wiser as the enchanting adventures unfold." SLJ

Joust. DAW Bks. 2003 373p il $24.95; pa $7.99

ISBN 0-7564-0122-4; 0-7564-0153-4 (pa)

LC 2003-544990

Vetch, an Altan serf, must learn the secret of the Tian jousters and their dragons in order to save his people

"This uplifting tale, which contains a valuable lesson or two on the virtues of hard work, is a must-read for dragon lovers in particular and for fantasy fans in general." Publ Wkly

The serpent's shadow. DAW Bks. 2001 343p $24.95; pa $7.99

ISBN 0-88677-915-4; 0-7564-0061-9 (pa)

LC 2002-265143

"To an alternative Victorian London Dr. Maya Witherspoon, {daughter} of a Brahmin lady and an English physician, comes to practice. Besides standard Western medicine, Maya knows the magic of India, where she grew up. Maya's aunt Shivani has also come to England, but as a devotee of Kali, she hates her sister's marriage and is determined to wreak havoc on the English. Maya must seek the aid of British magical masters before the powers of Kali devastate London." Booklist

Winds of fate. DAW Bks. 1991 385p il (Mage winds, bk1)

ISBN 0-88677-489-6

This first volume of a trilogy is set in the "imperiled land of Valdemar, encountered earlier in Lackey's Heralds of Valdemar series. The heir to the throne, Herald Elspeth, sets out with Gwena, her Companion (a Guardian Spirit embodied as a horse), to find an Adept who can teach her people both to use and to deflect the power of magic. . . . Lackey's delightful world of magic is inhabited by strong and believable men, women and creatures." Publ Wkly

Followed by Winds of change (1992)

Winds of fury. DAW Bks. 1993 387p il (Mage winds, bk3)

ISBN 0-88677-562-0   LC 93-219013

"In this concluding book of the Mage Winds trilogy . . . Elspeth returns home via the Forest of Sorrows where the manifest spirit of Vanyel and his lover, the bard Stefan, pull her from her intended destination to explain the now diminished shields against magic and the interlocking mind-web he once placed on Valdemar and how Elspeth must prepare to fight the evil and voracious Ancar of Hardorn." Voice Youth Advocates

(jt. auth) Norton, A. The elvenbane

(jt. auth) Norton, A. Elvenblood

Lagerkvist, Pär, 1891-1974

Barabbas; translated by Alan Blair; with a preface by Lucien Maury and a letter by André Gide. Random House 1951 180p o.p.

Original Swedish edition, 1950

This "is a psychological study of the spiritual journey of Barabbas, the criminal in the New Testament who was

Lagerkvist, Pär, 1891-1974—*Continued*

offered to the mob in place of Jesus but was spared from execution. The widely translated work was noted for its economical writing style, and it brought Lagerkvist international fame." Merriam-Webster's Ency of Lit

Lahiri, Jhumpa

Interpreter of maladies; stories. Houghton Mifflin 1999 198p $23

ISBN 0-618-10136-5   LC 98-50895

First published in paperback

Contents: A temporary matter; When Mr. Pirzada came to dine; Interpreter of maladies; A real durwan; Sexy; Mrs. Sen's; This blessed house; The treatment of Bibi Haldar; The third and final continent

"The rituals of traditional Indian domesticity—curry-making, hair-vermilioning—both buttress the characters of Lahiri's elegant first collection and mark the measure of these fragile people's dissolution. . . . Lahiri's touch in these nine tales is delicate, but her observations remain damningly accurate, and her bittersweet stories are unhampered by nostalgia." Publ Wkly

The namesake. Houghton Mifflin 2003 291p $24; pa $14

ISBN 0-395-92721-8; 0-618-48522-8 (pa)

LC 2003-41718

"A novel about assimilation and generational differences. Gogol is so named because his father believes that sitting up in a sleeping car reading Nikolai Gogol's 'The Overcoat' saved him when the train he was on derailed and most passengers perished. After his arranged marriage, the man and his wife leave India for America, where he eventually becomes a professor. They adopt American ways, yet all of their friends are Bengalis. But for young Gogol and his sister, Boston is home, and trips to Calcutta to visit relatives are voyages to a foreign land." SLJ

"Its incorrigible mildness and its ungilded lilies aside, Lahiri's novel is unfailingly lovely in its treatment of Gogol's relationship with his father. This is the classic American parent-child bond." N Y Times Book Rev

Unaccustomed earth. Alfred A. Knopf 2008 333p $25

ISBN 978-0-307-26573-9; 978-0-676-97934-3

LC 2007-17612

Contents: Unaccustomed earth; Hell-heaven; A coice of accomodations; Only goodness; Nobody's business; Once in a lifetime; Year's end; Going ashore

"In a collection of stories as limpid yet complex as her Pulitzer Prize-winning debut, Interpreter of Maladies (1999), [Lahiri] returns to familiar terrain—most of her Indians are highly educated, upper-middle-class suburbanites on the Boston-New York corridor—and to her well-honed role. Lahiri is an unillusioned anatomist of the greatest immigrant success story in the United States. But this time, she has captured more clearly than ever before a restless feeling of uprootedness that is as representative of America now, in the post-9/11 era, as the credo of wide-eyed openness ever was." Slate

Laird, Nick, 1975-

Utterly monkey. Harper Perennial 2006 344p pa $13.95

ISBN 0-060-82836-6   LC 2005-44784

First published 2005 in the United Kingdom

"Danny Williams didn't mean to be a lawyer, but somehow he is–and for up to eighteen hours a day. He's well paid, home owning, and twenty-seven but is also overworked, lonely, and frequently stoned. The plan was to leave the troubles of a small town in Northern Ireland for the big city in England, but one evening an old school friend, Geordie, bursts into Danny's shiny new life. On the run from a Loyalist militia, Geordie brings everything Danny thought he had left behind and dumps it on his doorstep." Publisher's note

"Part caper movie, part coming-of-age story, part urban satire, Monkey introduces a writer with a wonderfully original and limber voice – a writer who seems able to jump genres as easily as he shifts narrative gears. . . . Along the way, Mr. Laird also gives us a memorable and kinetic portrait of London as a city of dreamers and immigrants." N Y Times (Late N Y Ed)

Lake, Jay

Escapement. Tor 2008 383p $25.95

ISBN 978-0-7653-1709-4; 0-7653-1709-5

LC 2008-5263

"A Tom Doherty Associates book"

Sequel to: Mainspring

"Paolina Barthes is a teenage scientific prodigy born in a small Portuguese fishing village at the base of the massive equatorial gear-wall. Determined to learn from English engineering 'wizards' and understand the work of the great gears and wheels that move the universe, Paolina creates a homebrew chronometer, or 'gleam,' and sets off toward London. When she discovers the gleam has astonishing magical properties that only she can evoke, she becomes a target of various political and philosophical factions. . . . Lake effectively anneals steampunk with geo-mechanical magic in an allegorical matrix of empire building and Victorian natural science." Publ Wkly

Mainspring. Tor 2007 320p $25.95

ISBN 978-0-7653-1708-7; 0-7653-1708-7

LC 2007-7313

"A Tom Doherty Associates book"

"The world is a giant clockwork mechanism powered by hidden gears and moving along a track through the sky. When the Archangel Gabriel visits apprentice clockmaker Hethor, instructing him to take the Key Perilous and use it to rewind the Mainspring of the Earth lest the world come to an end, Hethor embarks on a journey that takes him to unexplored lands and sets him against many in high places who believe him to be deluded or heretical." Libr J

This is a "breathlessly exciting tale that takes the best old-school storytelling and the most vivid contemporary world-building sensibilities and spot-welds them together. Think Edgar Rice Burroughs or Philip José Farmer meets China Miéville or Ian R. MacLeod, by way of religious allegory. I'd call the book perfect were it not for Lake's regrettable tendency to activate the cheat codes whenever the going gets a little rough. Still, Mainspring is always gripping and often dazzling in its vision." SF Reviews.Net

Laken, Valerie

Dream house; a novel. HarperCollins Publishers 2008 336p $24.99
ISBN 978-0-06-084092-1; 0-06-084092-7
LC 2008-32946
"Kate and her husband, Stuart, have been living a student lifestyle—complete with all-night parties and a run-down apartment—since leaving college seven years before. When Kate's parents help them buy their own home, they don't know that the handyman special was the site of a murder nearly 20 years earlier. Nor do they expect that the fixer-upper will be the wedge that drives them further apart. When Stuart walks away from their gutted home in the middle of Kate's ambitious remodeling, Kate forms new relationships with two men who have ties to the murder and the house." Publ Wkly

"Laken has written the perfect haunted house story for these unnerving times. While the ghosts that come with this property don't rattle chains or shake the bed at night, they manifest themselves in subtler and crueler ways, by reminding us that the homes we love may not love us back." N Y Times Book Rev

Laker, Rosalind, 1925-

Banners of silk. Doubleday 1981 469p o.p.
LC 80-1453
"A historical romance portraying the rags-to-riches climb of two likable and hard-working couturiers in the nineteenth-century Parisian fashion world. Fate brings Charles Worth and Louise Vernet together when they are young and poor. Although they separate and lose touch, they again meet as colleagues after both have gained reputations as innovative dress designers." Booklist

The golden tulip. Doubleday 1991 585p o.p.
LC 90-27591
This novel "follows the exploits of Francesca Visser and her family during late seventeenth-century Holland, as they move in the circles of Rembrandt, Vermeer, and William of Orange. Francesca's dream to become a master artist threatens to be thwarted by the devious Ludolf van Deventer, who manipulates her heavily indebted father into signing a marriage contract for her. Only her own determination and the constant support of Pieter van Doorne—the tulip grower who loves her selflessly—and her sisters guide Francesca toward her goal." Booklist

"The suspense rarely slackens, for Francesca's spirited younger sisters, Aletta and Sybylla, enter into highly entertaining and surprising romances of their own. Laker's . . . tightly woven novel, swift-moving and filled with lusty characters, is weakened only by a convoluted, lengthy cloak-and-dagger finale." Publ Wkly

To dance with kings. Doubleday 1988 564p o.p.
LC 88-3698
"Set during the reigns of Louis XIV and Louis XVI, the sweeping saga takes place mainly in the Chateau of Versailles and the surrounding town from which the magnificent edifice took its name. . . . Spanning four generations, the protagonists are the women of one family, named, in turn, Marguerite, Jasmin, Violette and Rose, all of whose destinies are entwined with those of their monarchs as well as the dashing men who bring them love and heartache." Publ Wkly

Lamb, Wally

I know this much is true. HarperCollins Pubs. 1998 901p $27.50
ISBN 0-06-039016-6
LC 98-167337
"Lamb's narrator, Dominick Birdsey, has lost his mother, his wife, his infant daughter, his career. His identical twin brother, the gentle Thomas has lost his mind. A paranoid schizophrenic . . . Thomas goes into the public library one morning during the early rumblings of Desert Storm and cuts off his hand in a biblically inspired protest against the impending war. What follows is the 40-year-old Dominick's meltdown. In his struggle to do right by Thomas, the brother he loves, resents and envies in equal measure, he is forced to face not just his own demons but the entire cavalcade of nightmares that have bedeviled the Birdsey clan." N Y Times Book Rev

"The novel explores the subjects of mental illness, dysfunctional families and domestic abuse, but it also rings with humor and tenderness." Publ Wkly

Lambdin, Dewey

King's captain; an Alan Lewrie naval adventure. St. Martin's Press 2000 358p
ISBN 0-312-26885-8
LC 00-31764
Fresh from a stunning victory against the formidable Spanish Armada in the Battle of St. Vincent's Cape, Lewrie is promoted and rewarded with the command of an enviable new warship. Shortly after being installed as the captain of the H.M.S. Proteus, he must contend with a treasonable mass mutiny, a bitter enemy bent on revenge, and several rather complicated romantic entanglements. A rip-roaring sea yarn brimming with riveting action and lusty diversions." Booklist

Lambrecht, Patricia See Tracy, P. J.

Lambrecht, Traci See Tracy, P. J.

Lamott, Anne

Blue shoe. Riverhead Bks. 2002 291p
ISBN 1-57322-226-7
LC 2002-22824
This novel "tracks the efforts of Mattie Ryder to cope with her divorce, find a new man, deal with her mother's aging and restore the emotional equilibrium of her two young children." Publ Wkly

"The acceptence of one's imperfections is a pillar of wisdom in Lamott's New Age Christianity. Mattie is an embodiment of that philosophy, but she's better written than that makes her sound. She and her family are hilariously specific." NY Times Book Rev

L'Amour, Louis, 1908-1988

Bendigo Shafter. Dutton 1979 324p o.p.
* LC 78-15280
"This book's hero is 18-year-old Bendigo Shafter. He is part of a small band of migrants that breaks off its westward trek and builds a small community. The group increases with the coming of other members. It has to fight off the dangers of the frontier both within and outside its confines. Among the main influences on Ben's life are the Widow Macken, who inspires him to read

L'Amour, Louis, 1908-1988—*Continued*

Locke, Rousseau, and Blackstone; Uruwishi, an old Indian brave; and Ethan Sackett, woodsman nonpareil. There are heroes and villains, both white and red, and shooting from the hip in old Western style as Ben demonstrates all the traditional values of courage, honesty, loyalty, and stamina." Shapiro. Fic for Youth. 3d edition

Beyond the Great Snow Mountains. Bantam Bks. 1999 282p

ISBN 0-553-10963-4   LC 99-11757

The stories in this collection were written in the 1940s and 1950s

Contents: By the waters of San Tadeo; Meeting at Falmouth; Roundup in Texas; Sideshow champion; Crash landing; Under the hanging wall; Coast patrol; The gravel pit; The money punch; Beyond the Great Snow Mountains

The Californios. Saturday Review Press 1974 188p o.p.

"Eileen Mulkerin is about to lose her ranch because of debts but an ancient Indian, survivor of the Old Ones, leads her to a hidden cache of gold while her son fights off the killers sent to do them in." Booklist

"An expert blend of the fascinating settling of California in the 1840's; strong, self-reliant characters . . . and a plot of evil doings but triumphant good. The theme of mysticism and the legends of The Old Ones is what lifts this book above the typical western. Intriguing even for those who aren't westerns fans." Libr J

The Cherokee Trail. Bantam Bks. 1982 179p o.p.   LC 82-90288

"The leading character [of this novel] is a woman, Southern born and bred, who is left a widow with a small girl in Colorado of the 1860's. She is a tough lady who believes anything a man can do, she can do, and does. As the only woman operator of a station on the Cherokee Trail, Mary Breydon battles enemies with her guns, brains, and supportive friends, male and female. . . . As always, L'Amour respects the history and nature of the West: His characters and language are representative; his details of life on a station are accurate." Libr J

The daybreakers

In L'Amour, L. The Sacketts: beginnings of a dynasty

End of the drive. Bantam Bks. 1997 257p o.p.   LC 96-36872

Contents: Caprock rancher; Elisha comes to Red Horse; Desperate men; The courting of Griselda; End of the drive; The lonesome gods; Rustler roundup; The skull and the arrow

The haunted mesa. Bantam Bks. 1987 357p o.p.   LC 86-47576

This novel is a "combination of western and occult adventure, with the former given a decided edge. Mike Raglan, the hero, is an investigator of occult phenomena, but he is also a tough loner who knows how to use a six-gun. When he travels to a remote Southwest mesa to investigate the mystery of the Anasazi—a race of vanished cliff-dwellers—he manages to cross over to the Other Side, a fourth dimension that turns out to be very much another western frontier, replete with hidden gold, treacherous landscapes and plenty of Indians to shoot down." N Y Times Book Rev

"Although L'Amour's didactic approach and his needless repetition of details get in the way, this curious hybrid should satisfy fans of both genres." Booklist

Jubal Sackett. Bantam Bks. 1985 375p o.p.   LC 84-91724

This installment of the Sackett saga "features Jubal Sackett, a wily, homespun seventeenth-century hero who sets off to traverse the vast, unexplored North American hinterland. As he ranges through and beyond the mountains, Jubal befriends Keokotah, a fiercely proud Kickapoo brave, and together they help shield an astonishingly beautiful Natchez princess from a vengeful renegade Indian and an unscrupulous Spanish soldier." Booklist

"An absorbing story filled with adventure, romance, a hint of the occult, and information about Indian tribes and life in the mountains in the 17th century." Libr J

Lando

In L'Amour, L. The Sacketts: beginnings of a dynasty

Last of the breed. Bantam Bks. 1986 358p o.p.   * LC 86-3622

The setting "is modern-day Siberia; the main character [is] Maj. Joe Makatozi, a part Sioux, part Cheyenne Air Force pilot who has been forced down over the Soviet Union and imprisoned in a desolate region roughly equidistant from Moscow and the western tip of Alaska. . . . The athletically inclined 'Joe Mack' slips out of his cell, pole-vaults over the wall and begins heading east with the Russians, and most particularly a hulking Yakut named Alekhin, in hot pursuit." Newsweek

"Joe Mack is a classic American hero, thrown back into the wilderness and forced to rely on his wits and his ancestral skills to survive the deadly cold and elude his Soviet pursuers, including his nemesis, a Siberian tracker. L'Amour brings the same colorful realism to this sweeping adventure that has made his Westerns so beloved." Publ Wkly

The lonesome gods. Bantam Bks. 1983 450p o.p.   LC 82-45945

"In the early 1840s six-year-old Johannes Verne survives abandonment in the desert to spend his growing years dreaming of vengeance for the murder of his father and defending himself against enemies, including his grandfather, who are determined to kill him. The pace is almost leisurely, and the book is filled with splendid descriptions of the desert country, historical facts, and nature lore. An absorbing story of the early years of California with plenty of action, gun play, heroes, and villains." Libr J

May there be a road. Bantam Bks. 2001 276p

ISBN 0-553-80213-5   LC 2001-18127

Contents: Friend of a hero; May there be a road; Fighter's fiasco; The Cactus Kid; Making it the hard way; The hand of Kuan-yin; Red Butte showdown; The ghost fighter; Wings over Brazil; The vanished blonde

In this collection of 10 previously uncollected stories with settings ranging from the coasts of Brazil to the border of Tibet to the very heartland of America . . . [the author] takes us into those sudden moments when lives and futures are altered forever, when men and women face a deadly enemy, meet a kindred spirit, or confront their own mortality." Publisher's note

L'Amour, Louis, 1908-1988—*Continued*

Rustler roundup
In L'Amour, L. End of the drive p93-239

Sackett
In L'Amour, L. The Sacketts: beginnings of
a dynasty

The Sacketts: beginnings of a dynasty. Saturday
Review Press 1976 3v in 1 o.p.
Contains The daybreakers, Sackett, and Lando, originally published by Bantam Books in 1960, 1961 and
1962 respectively. The three novels included in this omnibus edition all concern members of the Sackett family
during the great frontier heyday of the 1850s and 1860s
"The first tale takes Tyrel and Orrin from the Tennessee hills to Santa Fe. The second adventure is told by
William Tell Sackett, the third by Lando. All are well-
drawn portraits of a unique period, unmistakably
L'Amour, unmistakably among his best." Booklist
Other titles about the Sacketts are: Mojave crossing
(1964); Sackett brand (1965); Mustang man (1966); The
lonely man (1966); The sky-liners (1967); Galloway
(1970); Treasure Mountain (1972); Ride the dark trail
(1972); Sackett's land; To the far blue mountains; The
warrior's path (1980); Lonely on the mountain (1980);
Ride the river (1983); and Jubal Sackett

To the far blue mountains. Saturday Review
Press 1976 287p o.p.
In this Sackett novel Barnabas returns from America
with a cargo of goods. He "is in Lincolnshire on business when he learns that there is a queen's warrant out
for him because he is suspected of stealing the crown
jewels. He is thrown in prison but manages to escape
and make his way to Bristol and a ship back to Raleigh's
Land. In Virginia, he recruits a band of brave settlers
and strong women and they take boats up the James River in the direction of the blue mountains until they find
rich land to farm. There Barnabas's children are born
and the community flourishes even though there is ever-
present danger from hostile Indians. This tale is much
more leisurely and nonviolent than the usual L'Amour
story, but it has its share of suspense and gives us a different kind of look at colonial America." Publ Wkly

The trail to Seven Pines; a Hopalong Cassidy
novel. Bantam Bks. 1992 244p o.p.
LC 91-43760
First published 1951 with title: Hopalong Cassidy and
the trail to Seven Pines, by the author writing as Tex
Burns
"Hopalong was headed northeast toward open country
when he crossed the path of six suspicious-looking men
wearing silver-plated Colts. By the time he heard the
gunshots, he was too far up the trail to do anything—riding back in time to find a robbed stagecoach and two
bodies lying sprawled and bloody in the dust. The shipment of gold was the fourth to be hijacked in only three
months, and appeared to be connected to the range war
exploding around the Rocking R Ranch in the nearby
town of Seven Pines. Hiring on at the Rocking R,
Hopalong organizes a rough and ragtag outfit to save the
ranch, only to find himself accused of murder and the
target of a ruthless gunman." Publisher's note

The walking drum. Bantam Bks. 1984 423p o.p.
LC 83-25703
"In 12th century Brittany, young Mathurin
Kerbouchard, escaping from the evil baron who has slain
Mathurin's mother and plundered their estate, is forced
into galley slavery. He gains control of the boat and
lands in Moorish Spain, where he quickly makes powerful friends and enemies. Mathurin's quest is to rescue his
corsair father, prisoner in the Persian stronghold of the
Assassins. On the way the youth becomes a famed scholar . . . warrior, merchant, doctor and lover." Publ Wkly

Lanchester, John

The debt to pleasure; a novel. Holt & Co. 1996
251p il
ISBN 0-8050-4388-8   LC 95-34658
The author "has written a novel masquerading as an
essay masquerading as a cookbook, and it somehow
manages to combine the virtues of all three. The narrator,
Tarquin Winot, is the brother of a famous sculptor, but
his own talent—as emerges in the course of his endlessly
digressive, enormously erudite disquisitions on food—is
for the art of murder. Tarquin's marvellously perverse intelligence never falters, and, fortunately, neither do his
lapidary sentences." New Yorker

Fragrant Harbor. Putnam 2002 342p
ISBN 0-399-14866-3   LC 2001-57876
"A Marian Wood book"
"In 1935, young Englishman Tom Stewart sails to
Hong Kong in search of adventure. During the six-week
voyage, he is taught Cantonese by a young Chinese mis-
sionary nun, Sister Maria. Upon his arrival in Hong
Kong, his proficiency in the language leads to a career
as a hotel manager. When the Japanese invade, Sister
Maria urges him to flee with her, but he's given his
word that he'll work as an undercover agent for the
British. After the war, which Tom spends mostly in the
notorious Stanley prison, his life and Sister Maria's continue to entwine." Publ Wkly
This "is not an enormous novel, but it feels like one—
it is bursting with ideas. Lanchester takes on almost every major theme and succeeds with most of them: race,
class, love, war, the fall of rulers and the rise of the
ruled." N Y Times Book Rev

Land, Brad, 1976-

Pilgrims upon the earth; a novel. Random House
2007 227p $23.95
ISBN 978-1-4000-6380-2; 1-4000-6380-9
LC 2006-49264
Fifteen-year-old Terry Webber's "mom is gone, his
millworker dad moves town to town, and his high-school
existence is pure ennui. . . . Alice Washington, a classmate on her own lost highway, plots with Terry to escape to her sister's commune in Colorado. Only hours
into the getaway journey, Alice dies in a car crash. The
second half of this . . .novel recounts Terry's grief-
stricken wobble through a high-school labyrinth of cigarettes, drugs, fistfights, petty crime and—just maybe—
back to hope again. . . . Land owns a spot-on gift for
rendering what it's like to be young and, all too frequently, absurdly miserable." Paste

Landers, Scott, 1952-

Coswell's guide to Tambralinga; a novel; Scott Landers. Farrar, Straus and Giroux 2004 338p $24

ISBN 0-374-13021-3   LC 2003-21116

A novel set on a fictional Southeast Asian island. "At the center is Conrad, a meek computer systems analyst on a desperate second honeymoon with Lucy, who's furious at him for losing her all-important guidebook. Fearing 'that he was missing it, that better half of existence, the throbbing center of what it meant to be alive,' Conrad heads to a brothel on another island, while Lucy finds the guidebook and embarks on her own adventure." Publ Wkly

"In this offbeat first novel, Landers puts a wry spin on the theme of self-discovery, suggesting that jealousy, hardship, and disillusionment are good for the soul." Booklist

Lange, John See Crichton, Michael, 1942-2008

Langton, Jane

Dead as a dodo; a Homer Kelly mystery. Viking 1996 339p il

ISBN 0-670-86221-5

* LC 96-6724

In this adventure "Homer takes a leave from Harvard to lecture at the Oxford University Museum. Exposed to the natural history scholarship at this seat of learning, he discovers Charles Darwin and is 'flabbergasted' by 'The Origin of Species.' . . . Homer is floored by a number of other things, including the theft of a 17th-century painting of a dodo, the discovery of some long-lost crustacean specimens collected by Darwin and two suspicious deaths. Adopting the style of a famous Oxonian, Charles Dodgson, Ms. Langton makes a Mad Tea Party of Homer's investigation of these curious events, which strike him as a Jabberwockian version of natural selection." N Y Times Book Rev

The deserter; murder at Gettysburg. St. Martin's Minotaur 2003 322p il $23.95

ISBN 0-312-30186-3   LC 2002-191961

"Homer Kelly's wife, Mary, wants to clear the name of her Civil War ancestor, purported to have been a deserter. As the narrative alternates between past and present, the Kellys find evidence of false identity and murder." Libr J

"The suspense builds as the author adroitly shifts between past and present. Period photos, an 1860 playbill for the Hasty Pudding show, quotations from Walt Whitman and loads of Harvard lore add historical weight." Publ Wkly

Emily Dickinson is dead; a novel of suspense; illustrations by the author. St. Martin's Press 1984 247p il o.p.

LC 83-24451

"A Joan Kahn book"

"In a mystery that pokes fun at the behavior of professors in the academic world, a famous poet is chosen as a theme for a literary conference. Stemming from a photograph that an undistinguished professor from a small midwestern college claims is an authentic photo of Emily Dickinson, the faculty of an elite university begin to fight among themselves—sometimes even physically—

about who will star at the conference. Entangled in that is Winifred Gaw, an overweight graduate student, and the professor whom she worships, as well as beautiful Allison Groves who becomes the object of Winifred's jealousy and hatred. Emily Dickinson, quietly dead for so many years, becomes a motivation for arson, forgery, and murder." Shapiro. Fic for Youth. 3d edition

The Escher twist; a Homer Kelly mystery. Viking 2002 240p il

ISBN 0-670-03067-8   LC 2001-26806

This "Homer Kelly book follows crystallographer Leonard Sheldrake as he pursues the enigmatic Frieda, who disappears after they meet at an Escher exhibition at a Cambridge, Mass., art gallery. The mystery here is less about the murders that crop up occasionally in this whimsical narrative than about identity." Publ Wkly

The face on the wall. Viking 1998 291p il

ISBN 0-670-87674-7   LC 98-2832

"Amateur sleuth Homer Kelly goes to the aid of his wife's niece, a book illustrator whose dream house has become the scene of murder." Libr J

"Overlaying her mythic design with a trim narrative of modern-day wickedness, [Langton] steps back to let us marvel at the patterns of evil that she traces from Mother Goose to the murderer next door." N Y Times Book Rev

Murder at Monticello; a Homer Kelly mystery; illustrations by the author. Viking 2001 256p il $22.95

ISBN 0-670-89462-1   LC 00-43369

"It's the bicentennial of Jefferson's election to the presidency, and Homer and his wife, Mary, are invited to a Fourth of July celebration at Monticello, Jefferson's Virginia home, where, incidentally, a serial killer has been murdering young women. Like the previous Kelly novels, this one features a smart mystery, delightful characters, and vastly entertaining dialogue." Booklist

The thief of Venice. Viking 1999 247p il

ISBN 0-670-88210-0   LC 98-54894

"A Homer Kelly mystery"

Homer Kelly, "a policeman-turned-scholar, and his professor wife, Mary, have ventured to Venice to attend a scholarly conference on rare books. Homer is intoxicated by the riches afforded in the Biblioteca Marciana, while Mary prowls the streets of the Italian city, camera in hand. An expatriate English doctor, Richard Henchard, seeking an apartment for his demanding mistress, stumbles upon a cache of golden artifacts. He kills twice to protect his secret, and his path soon intersects Mary's. . . . With a master hand, Langton develops the various subplots into a sophisticated, elegantly constructed thriller." Publ Wkly

Lankford, Terrill

Earthquake weather. Ballantine Bks. 2004 293p $24.95

ISBN 0-345-46777-9   LC 2004-41068

This novel starts with the "L.A. earthquake of 1994. Suffering from post-quake shell shock, Mark Hayes, D-Boy (or script reader) for schlocky producer Dexter Morton, finds his career in tatters, just like his quake-damaged apartment in the Valley. Then he finds a body floating in Dexter's pool and becomes a murder suspect.

Lankford, Terrill—*Continued*

Along with a motley crew of similarly dysfunctional cronies, including a washed-up writer who spouts cliches about 'killing creativity for a paycheck,' Mark slouches toward Armageddon or a jail cell, whichever comes first. Lankford nails the updated noir mood, and he fills the tale with juicy insider stuff about the 'industry'." Booklist

Lansdale, Joe R., 1951-

The bottoms. Mysterious Press 2000 328p $30

ISBN 0-89296-704-8

* LC 00-32886

A tale of "race violence and serial murder in a small East Texas town during the Depression. The aged narrator, Harry Collins, is lying in a rest home and letting his mind drift back to the events that changed his life in 1933 . . . when he and his little sister find the mangled body of a black prostitute in the deep bottom lands along the Sabine River. Harry's father, the town barber and constable, does his best; but when the killer claims a white victim, he can't stop his Klan neighbors from lynching an old black man for the crimes." N Y Times Book Rev

"An emotionally charged tale very reminiscent of *To Kill a Mockingbird*. Effectively combining mystery and family history, it offers a vivid, multifaceted glimpse back to a simpler, but not necessarily better, time." Booklist

A fine dark line. Mysterious Press 2003 307p $24.95

ISBN 0-89296-729-3   LC 2002-71387

A regional mystery "which harks back to 1958. Thirteen-year-old Stanley Mitchel, Jr., has enough on his hands just growing up in Dewmont, Tex., when he literally stumbles on a buried cache of love letters. Stanley pursues the identity of the two lovers with help from the projectionist at his family's drive-in, an aged black man who quotes Sherlock Holmes and doesn't mince words about the world's injustices. As the truth of a gruesome 20-year-old double murder comes to light in the sleepy town, so do the facts of life, death, men, women and race for young Stanley." Publ Wkly

"Stanley doesn't unravel everything, but race and power, and what people do to each other in the name of desire and religion, coalesce to a mighty climax." Booklist

Leather maiden. Alfred A. Knopf 2008 287p $23.95

ISBN 978-0-375-41452-7; 0-375-41452-5

LC 2007-51854

"Cason Statler, a Pulitzer Prize–nominated journalist with a checkered past, returns to his small hometown of Camp Rapture, Tex., to work as a columnist for the local newspaper. . . . On the hunt for spicy material, Statler latches onto the story of a missing college student who disappeared under strange circumstances a year earlier. Almost immediately, Statler connects the case to a recent string of kinky, unsettling crimes throughout east Texas. What's more, his brother, a college history professor, appears to be caught in the swirl of events as a victim or possibly even a suspect." Publ Wkly

"At the beginning of David Lynch's film 'Blue Velvet,' you may remember that the camera presents a typical American neighborhood and then moves closer, right

through the sod and down into the ground as a metaphor for the nasty secrets hiding behind the veil of societal correctness. Lansdale's novel is a trip into that same hidden shame. You may not enjoy the exposure, but you'll definitely enjoy the ride." Los Angeles Times Book Rev

Sunset and sawdust. Alfred A. Knopf 2004 321p $22

ISBN 0-375-41453-3

* LC 2003-60478

This novel is set in Depression-era East Texas. "After shooting her spouse during conjugal rape, spunky redhead Sunset Jones winds up with his job as constable of the roughhewn lumber town of Camp Rapture, thanks to the influence of a mother-in-law whose own marital woes are brought to an abrupt and gory end when her man lies down on the job at the sawmill. Already unpopular for thwarting a lynching, Sunset and her deputies— a devilishly handsome vagabond and his mulish rival— get in over their heads in a stew of greed and brutality when the oil-covered corpses of a mother and her newborn are plowed up in a black farmer's field." Libr J

"The mystery is only mildly engrossing here; the great pleasure of Lansdale's work lies in his pitch-perfect vernacular prose. . . . The book opens with a cyclone, ends with a plague of grasshoppers and in between there's insanity, extreme violence, sex, grotesques aplenty and an excellent dog. What's not to like?" Publ Wkly

Vanilla Ride. Alfred A. Knopf 2009 243p $24.95

ISBN 978-0-307-27097-9; 0-307-27097-1

LC 2009-08821

In this "outing, the unlikely partners—Hap's a white, horny heterosexual good ol' boy, and Leonard's a black homosexual Vietnam vet—rescue a friend's daughter from the clutches of drug dealers. Unbeknownst to our heroes, the dealers are part of the Dixie Mafia, which proceeds to send waves of assassins in retaliation, each worse than the last. Joking as they go, Hap and Leonard dispose of each with their usual brand of brutality. Then, the mafia sends its weapon of last resort, Vanilla Ride, a beautiful hit woman. . . . Lansdale's storytelling skills are as sharp as ever." Publ Wkly

Lansens, Lori

The girls; a novel. Little, Brown 2006 c2005 345p $23.95; pa $13.99

ISBN 978-0-316-06903-8; 0-316-06903-5; 978-0-316-06634-1 (pa); 0-316-06634-6 (pa)

LC 2005-24510

First published 2005 in Canada

This "novel is told from two viewpoints: that of Rose and that of Ruby Darlen, 29-year-old conjoined twins. Rose and Ruby are about to go down in history as the oldest surviving twins to be joined at the head. A recent medical diagnosis has spurred Rose to write her autobiography, and she encourages Ruby to do the same. Between the two sections, the story of their lives is revealed, beginning with their birth to an unwed teen mother and their adoption by Lovey Darlen, the nurse who was with their mother when she was in labor, and her strong, silent husband, Stash. The girls grow up on the Darlens' farm in rural Ontario, where Lovey refuses to accept the word of skeptical doctors who doubt the girls will ever be able to walk on their own." Booklist

Lansens, Lori—*Continued*

"Through their alternating narratives, Lansens captures a contradictory longing for independence and togetherness that transcends the book's enormous conceit." Publ Wkly

Lardner, Ring, 1885-1933

The best short stories of Ring Lardner. Scribner 1976 c1957 346p
ISBN 0-684-14743-2
"Hudson River editions"
A reprint of the 1957 edition
Contents: The Maysville minstrel; I can't breathe; Haircut; Alibi Ike; Liberty Hall; Zone of quiet; Mr. Frisbie; Hurry Kane; Champion; A day with Conrad Green; Old folks' Christmas; Harmony; The love nest; Ex parte; The golden honeymoon; Horseshoes; There are smiles; Anniversary; Reunion; Travelogue; Who dealt?; My roomy; Some like them cold; A caddy's diary; Mr. and Mrs. Fix-it

"A selection of twenty-five stories by one of the most original figures in American literature, the colorful personality who was noted as a sports writer, humorist and columnist, as well as short-story writer." N Y Her Trib Books

Ring around the bases; the complete baseball stories of Ring Lardner; edited and with an introduction by Matthew J. Bruccoli; foreword by Ring Lardner, Jr. Scribner 1992 609p il $35
ISBN 0-684-19374-4   LC 91-38363
Short stories included are: A busher's letters home; The busher comes back; The busher's honeymoon; A new busher breaks in; The busher's kid; The busher beats it hence; Call for Mr. Keefe; The busher reënlists; The battle of Texas; Along came Ruth; The busher pulls a Mays; My roomy; Sick 'em; Horseshoes; Back to Baltimore; Alibi Ike; Harmony; The poor simp; Where do you get that noise?; Good for the soul; The crook; The hold-out; The yellow kid; The bull pen; Women; Hurry Kane; One hit, one error, one left; When the moon comes over the mountain; Lose with a smile; Meet me in St. Louie; Holycaust; The ides of June; Take a walk

"This volume collects all [of Lardner's baseball] tales, including the famous Jack Keefe epistolary stories that made up the well-known volume *You Know Me Al* (1914), plus some prime journalistic pieces. . . They all display the writer's excellence in capturing the idiom and nuances of baseball talk." Libr J

You know me, Al
In Lardner, R. Ring around the bases

Larminie, Margaret Beda *See* Yorke, Margaret

Larsen, Deborah

The white; a novel. Knopf 2002 219p $22
ISBN 0-375-41359-6   LC 2001-53977
A reinterpretation of the "life of Mary Jemison, a white woman who was captured in 1758 by a Shawnee raiding party at her home in Gettysburg, Pa., while the rest of her family was murdered and scalped. . . . Mary is eventually adopted by another tribe, the Seneca. Learning their language and culture, marrying and bearing six children, Mary ultimately finds herself at home with them and no longer feels the compulsion to escape or return to white society at all." Publ Wkly

This novel "has escaped many of the dangers that ensnare fiction with this sort of subject. It is neither epic nor sentimental, nor does it bang any political or anthropological drum. Beneath the smooth beauty of its descriptive language, there is some terrific concision and lightness." N Y Times Book Rev

Larsen, Jeanne

Silk road; a novel of 8th century China. Holt & Co. 1989 434p il o.p.   LC 88-27286
The author has "several ideas going in this novel set in eighth-century China and seen through the eyes of a young girl transformed into a beautiful woman and eventually a wandering warrior. First, there's a romantic tale of how a heroine, snatched as a child from her parents, is sold into slavery and trained as a concubine. Second, there's a story of mystical revenge, with the girl seeking justice for the mother she barely knew. Superimposed on these stories are the details of Chinese history and culture." Booklist

This novel "maintains a wonderfully mellow tone, perhaps so even a tone as to subvert intensity. But it accommodates much merriment, and moments of sadness and joy, as this feminist fable of mother- and sister-bonding draws together." N Y Times Book Rev

Larsen, Nella

Passing; introduction by Ntozake Shange; critical foreword and notes by Mae Henderson. Modern Lib. 2002 lxxxv, 206p (Modern Library classics) pa $10.95
ISBN 0-375-75813-5   LC 2001-45037
First published 1929 by Knopf
"Irene Redfield, the novel's protagonist, is a woman with an enviable life. She and her husband, Brian, a prominent physician, share a comfortable Harlem town house with their sons. . . . Her hold on this world begins to slip the day she encounters Clare Kendry, a childhood friend with whom she had lost touch. Clare—light-skinned, beautiful, and charming—tells Irene how, after her father's death, she left behind the black neighborhood of her adolescence and began passing for white, hiding her true identity from everyone, including her racist husband." Publisher's note

This "is a shrewdly conceived and finely executed novella that raises questions not only of racial identity in a realistically rendered middle and upper-middle-class Negro society (in Harlem and Chicago, 1927) but of the murderous rage one woman might feel for another who has 'passed' beyond her." N Y Rev Books

Larsen, Reif

The selected works of T. S. Spivet. Penguin Press 2009 374p il map $27.95
ISBN 978-1-59420-217-9; 1-59420-217-6
                              LC 2009-06277
"T.S. is a 12-year-old cartographer-artist, a prodigy who lives on a Montana farm. But in other ways he's just a boy with a preoccupied scientist mother; a distant, cowboy father; an adolescent sister, Gracie; and a youn-

Larsen, Reif—*Continued*

ger brother, Layton, who recently shot himself to death in the barn during one of T.S.'s experiments. T.S. doesn't only map places. He tries to map everything. . . . T.S.'s more conventional maps and illustrations have been published in Science magazine and displayed at the Smithsonian, and as the story opens, T.S. receives a phone call from the institution, telling him he has won a prestigious award and inviting him to Washington, D.C., to give a speech. The catch is that no one at the Smithsonian is aware that he's a child, and T.S.'s family doesn't know he publishes his work. In the middle of the night, with a few dollars in his pocket and a package of food, he hops a train to get his prize." Boston Globe

"Only at the end does Larsen lose control of the already outlandish plot, but that's to be forgiven. His debut is oddly affecting, and T.S. Spivet is a character to root for." Dallas Morning News

Larson, Charles R.

(ed) Under African skies. See Under African skies

Larsson, Stieg, 1954-2004

The girl who played with fire; translated from the Swedish by Reg Keeland. Alfred A. Knopf 2009 503p $25.95

ISBN 978-0-307-26998-0; 0-307-26998-1

LC 2009-14053

Original Swedish edition, 2006

"Lisbeth Salander, the antisocial but brilliant computer hacker who helped journalist Mikael Blomkvist uncover a serial killer on a remote Swedish island in Larsson's . . . The Girl with the Dragon Tattoo, takes center stage in this second volume of his 'Millenium' trilogy. Opening 18 months after the events of the first book, the novel finds our heroine lounging by the pool at a Caribbean hotel, reading a math textbook, and watching a woman who may be a victim of domestic abuse, while in Sweden, Blomkvist, bewildered by Salander's abrupt disappearance from his life, is set to publish a magazine exposé on the sex trade. . . . The main plot takes off with the murders of Salander's legal guardian and the two writers of the article, and her fingerprints are found on the gun used in the killings." Libr J

"For all the complications of the melodramatic story, which advances at a brisk, violently cinematic clip in Reg Keeland's translation, it's clear where Larsson's strongest interests lie—in his heroine and the ill-concealed attitudes she brings out in men." N Y Times Book Rev

The girl with the dragon tattoo; translated from the Swedish by Reg Keeland. Alfred A. Knopf 2008 532p $24.95

ISBN 978-0-307-26975-1; 0-307-26975-2

LC 2008-411003

Origina Swedish edition, 2005

First title in the author's Millennium trilogy. "Convicted of libeling a prominent businessman and awaiting imprisonment, financial journalist Mikael Blomkvist agrees to industrialist Henrik Vanger's request to investigate the 40-year-old disappearance of Vanger's 16-year-old niece, Harriet. In return, Vanger will help Blomkvist dig up dirt on the corrupt businessman. Assisting in Blomkvist's investigation is 24-year-old Lisbeth Salander, a brilliant but enigmatic computer hacker." Libr J

"An intelligent, ingeniously plotted, utterly engrossing thriller that is variously a serial-killer saga, a search for a missing person and an informed glimpse into the worlds of journalism and business. . . . One must struggle with bewildering Swedish names, but that's a small price to pay. The story starts off at a leisurely pace, but the reader soon surrenders to Larsson's skillful narrative." Washington Post Book World

Lasdun, James

The horned man. Norton 2002 193p $24.95

ISBN 0-393-00336-1

LC 2002-539

"Brit Lawrence Miller, a professor of gender studies at Arthur Clay College, becomes convinced that a stranger is camping out nightly in his office. Though preoccupied by his wife's recent decampment and his membership on the college's sexual harassment committee, Lawrence fixates on the illustrious Professor Trumilcik, an Eastern European womanizer and ex-board member, who went mad on campus one afternoon and never returned." Publ Wkly

"This arch, assured satire is a psychological thriller, too, and it races cleanly and hungrily to unexpected (and expected) revelations; the academic and sexual politics that ground it are familiar, but this almost doesn't matter, since Lasdun is interested in the inevitability of error when we mistake trendiness for truth." New Yorker

It's beginning to hurt. Farrar, Straus and Giroux 2009 227p $23

ISBN 978-0-374-29902-6; 0-374-29902-1

LC 2008-54251

Contents: An anxious man; The natural order; The incalculable life gesture; The half sister; The old man; Annals of the honorary secretary; Cleanness; The woman at the window; A bourgeois story; Oh death; Cranley meadows; Totty; Peter Khan's third wife; Lime pickle; It's beginning to hurt; Caterpillars

"Reading Lasdun is like reading a sly collaboration between Kafka and Updike: elegant, acutely observed and utterly unflinching . . . . This is a collection that examines the most inward mechanisms of rage, fear and desire with astonishing skill and strangely lyric power." Times (London)

Lashner, William

A killer's kiss. William Morrow 2007 327p $24.95

ISBN 978-0-06-114346-5; 0-06-114346-4

LC 2007-61202

In this crime thriller featuring Philadelphia DA Victor Carl, "two police detectives pay Carl a late-night call to inform him that Dr. Wren Denniston, the husband of Carl's former fiancée, Julia, was found shot to death in his Chestnut Hill mansion earlier that evening. Since Carl, known for his malleable ethics, had been entertaining Julia at his apartment shortly before the detectives' arrival in an effort to revive their relationship, he becomes a prime suspect in the doctor's murder. Unsure whether his lover is setting him up, Carl must dodge a rogue's gallery of villains who had their own reasons for wanting Denniston out of the way before he can uncover

Lashner, William—*Continued*
the real culprit and figure out Julia's true feelings for him. Chandler and Hammett fans looking for a fix will be well rewarded." Publ Wkly

Kockroach; [by] Tyler Knox. William Morrow 2007 356p il $23.95
ISBN 978-0-06-114333-5; 0-06-114333-2
LC 2006-48138
"It is the mid-1950s, and in a fleabag hotel off Times Square, Kockroach, perfectly content with life as an insect, awakens to discover that somehow he's become, of all things, a human." Publisher's note
"Literary fiction is not often this wildly funny. . . . Knox shifts voices and perspective, from hard-boiled to modern-hip, dropping allusions to people as varied as Richard Nixon and the Ramones. You can tell when an author is having a good time, and Knox has a ball." Seattle Times

Laskas, Gretchen Moran

The midwife's tale. Dial Press (NY) 2003 243p $23.95
ISBN 0-385-33551-2
LC 2002-41010
"Set in pre-World War I West Virginia, this novel flows along like the tributaries that feed the book's Appalachian foothills, as narrator Elizabeth Whitely traces the arc of four generations of midwives in her family, she being the last of the line. Poverty, lack of clean water, unemployment, an influenza epidemic, and severe weather also figure in this often melancholy tale. Laskas has injected many period details into her first book and a lot of verve into her characters to make them come alive." Libr J

Laskowski, Tim, 1957-

Every good boy does fine; a novel. Southern Methodist Univ. Press 2003 176p $23.95
ISBN 0-87074-477-1
LC 2003-40726
"Robert was a recent college graduate with a promising future as a pianist when he fell in a mountain-climbing accident. After weeks in a coma and years in a nursing home, he is placed in a rehabilitation program. At the novel's beginning, he is accepted into an accelerated program that might prepare him for relatively independent living—if he can adapt." Libr J
"Laskowski keeps the focus on Robert's daily struggles in the early going, but as the book progresses he begins to pose wrenching questions about the nature of illness and sanity. The book closes with an elegiac recovery fantasy that serves as a poignant reminder of the strength of the human spirit in the face of devastating disability." Publ Wkly

Latham, Aaron

Code of the West. Simon & Schuster 2001 494p $26
ISBN 0-7432-0117-5
LC 00-51618
"Set in Texas during the 1860's, Aaron Latham's . . . novel transplants the Arthurian legend into the Wild West, where his hero—a cowboy named Jimmy Goodnight—employs a Colt revolver rather than Excalibur. Stolen as a child by Commanches who killed his family, Goodnight is an outsider who returns to white society when he coaxes an ax from a stone. He then collects a band of ruffians and establishes his own dusty Camelot in an immense canyon, successfully woos his Guinevere and befriends Jack Loving, a handsome, sharpshooting drifter who becomes his Lancelot." N Y Times Book Rev
"Latham is booth a lyrical and an economical writer, and his ability to bring Jimmy Goodnight fully to life even in the stolen chain mail of a much larger figure transforms this compulsively readable novel from a farce into a good western." Booklist

Lathen, Emma

Brewing up a storm; a John Thatcher mystery. St. Martin's Press 1996 248p o.p.
LC 96-22116
"A Thomas Dunne book"
In this novel "a protest organization sues a local brewery, claiming that the firm's new nonalcoholic beer contributed to the alcohol-related death of a teenager. When someone murders the protest leader, the brewery calls on series sleuth John Thatcher, a Wall Street banker." Libr J

Double, double, oil and trouble. Simon & Schuster 1978 255p o.p.
LC 78-5151
"A negotiation vital to construction in the North Sea oil fields is interrupted when an executive is kidnapped. A large ransom is paid and the British government awards the contract to the victim's firm, unfairly in the view of the competition. Matters become complicated when the victim is killed in a car bombing in Houston, and personal rather than business considerations become paramount." Libr J
"The scene shifts from London to Istanbul and Houston to Switzerland, in a story that wouldn't work in the hands of a less skilled writer. Lathen knows how to keep her novels from becoming bogged down by excess verbiage and unnecessary violence." Booklist

East is east. Simon & Schuster 1991 268p o.p.
* LC 91-32789
This John Putnam Thatcher adventure "takes the senior banking executive from the Sloan Guaranty Trust building in Manhattan on evenly paced travels to Japan, Alaska and England. Lackawanna Electric Industries, rebounding from bankruptcy under the forceful leadership of Carl Kruger, is about to pull off a distribution coup with Yonezawa Trading, one of Japan's largest corporations. Thatcher is present at the Tokyo signing, which is delayed by the discovery of a murdered accountant in Japan's Ministry of International Trade and Investment and a note suggesting a $1-million bribe." Publ Wkly
Ms. Lathen "has a wonderful knack for turning the driest, most complicated corporate maneuvers into high drama, and occasionally burlesque." N Y Times Book Rev

Going for the gold. Simon & Schuster 1981 251p o.p.
"Unprecedented banking demands in Lake Placid during the Winter Olympics have caused the Sloan to open a branch. But the man in charge is not what he seems and his doings are followed by two murders and a blizzard. Thatcher and Co. have 48 hours to straighten out

Lathen, Emma—*Continued*
the mess. As usual, the background—here athletic—is worked into the plot without seeming forced or padded." Barzun. Cat of Crime. Rev and enl edition

Right on the money; a John Putnam Thatcher mystery. Simon & Schuster 1993 256p o.p.

LC 92-35673

A "Wall Street mystery featuring banker John Thatcher of Sloan Guaranty Trust. When a Princeton manufacturing firm represented by a sister bank targets a Sloan family-owned business client for takeover, Thatcher monitors the ensuing negotiations. Friction erupts into fracas, however, when rumors fly, financial records burn, and possible industrial sabotage culminates in murder." Libr J

A shark out of water; a John Thatcher mystery. St. Martin's Press 1997 293p

ISBN 0-312-17018-1   LC 97-23036

"A Thomas Dunne book"

"Wall Street's Sloan Guaranty Trust sends banker John Thatcher to Poland to research possible investment in a scheme to modernize the Kiel Canal, the link between the North and Baltic seas. While there, of course, he becomes involved in hidden problems, personal agendas, and murder." Libr J

"Without ruffling his fabled composure, Thatcher manages to clarify the intricacies of international finance for the Polish police officer investigating the crime, and for the rapt reader too." N Y Times Book Rev

Something in the air. Simon & Schuster 1988 270p o.p.

LC 88-4491

This mystery featuring "John Thatcher of New York's Sloan Guaranty Trust is set mainly in Boston, headquarters of the commuter airline Sparrow Flyways. A product of airline deregulation, Sparrow is a nonunion operation surviving on horizontal management and project development teams. Mitchell Scovil, CEO and guiding figure of the founders, dreams of expansion, but a group of lower-level employees (and shareholders) is worried about their investment. When their arrogant spokesperson is murdered, the Sloan, holding 20% of unsalable Sparrow stock in a trust, becomes involved." Publ Wkly

Latour, José

The Havana World Series; José Latour. 1st ed. Grove Press 2003 320p $23

ISBN 0-8021-1754-6   LC 2003-60716

The author "tells the story of a gang of Cuban crooks, funded by New York Mob boss Joe Bonanno, who sets out to rob Meyer Lansky's Capri casino on the last day of the 1958 World Series (when the coffers are overflowing). The portraits of Lansky, Bonnano, and the other gangsters are full-bodied, but it's the fictional blue-collar crooks, led by mastermind Ox Contreras, who give the novel its appeal and afford the best view of Cuban life. Although the documentary style occasionally seems flat, it contrasts nicely with the richness of detail and quirkiness of character." Booklist

Latsis, Mary J., 1927-1997
For works written by this author in collaboration with Martha Hennissart see Lathen, Emma

LaValle, Victor D., 1972-

Big machine; a novel; [by] Victor LaValle. Spiegel & Grau 2009 352p $25

ISBN 978-0-385-52798-9; 0-385-52798-5

LC 2009-00381

"Ricky Rice is a down-on-his-luck former heroin addict who works as a janitor at a bus depot and focuses on just getting by. But this quickly changes when he receives a one-way bus ticket to Vermont from an unknown source in the mail, along with a note that enigmatically tells him the time has come to honor a secret promise he once made. Summoning all of his courage and going along for the ride, Ricky finds himself part of a ragtag band of investigators, tasked with finding and following a divine Voice in modern-day America." BookPage

"Despite its steady pulse of dark humor, its supernatural Voice and the presence of some creepy entities known as the Devils of the Marsh, Big Machine is a novel about faith and the ways in which religion can create monsters far more terrifying than anything dreamed up by H.P. Lovecraft." Washington Post Book World

The ecstatic; or, Homunculus; [by] Victor Lavalle. Crown 2002 272p $22.95

ISBN 0-609-61014-7   LC 2002-6766

The protagonist of this novel is "Anthony James, a 318-pound, 23-year-old, Cornell-educated schizophrenic. In order to keep a semblance of order in his unstable mind, he narrates his family's slow road to destruction. Stops along the way include a small-town beauty pageant in Virginia, a weight-loss clinic, and a McDonald's beseiged by protesting college students. Throughout, Anthony remains sarcastic, intelligent, and conscious of his condition, though control of it increasingly eludes him. His experience is brought to life by Lavelle's acute sensory details and hyperbolic wordplay." Libr J

Lawhead, Stephen R. *See* Lawhead, Steve, 1950-

Lawhead, Steve, 1950-

Avalon; the return of King Arthur; by Stephen R. Lawhead. Avon Eos 1999 442p $25

ISBN 0-380-97702-8   LC 99-25048

"In a near-future Britain, the death of King Edward IX throws the succession into disarray until a young man named James Arthur Stewart discovers his identity as the reborn King Arthur and claims his rightful throne." Libr J

"In revisiting nearly every romantic Arthurian cliché and playing off snappy contemporary derring-do against the powerful shining glimpses of the historical Arthur he created, Lawhead pulls off a genuinely moving parable of good and evil." Publ Wkly

Lawless, Anthony *See* MacDonald, Philip, 1899-1981

Lawrence, D. H. (David Herbert), 1885-1930

Collected stories; with an introduction by Craig Raine. Knopf 1994 xxxv, 1397p o.p.

LC 94-2493

"Everyman's library"

Contents: A modern lover; The old Adam; Her turn; Strike-pay; The witch à la mode; New Eve and old Adam; A prelude; Love among the haystacks; A chapel and a hay hut among the mountains; Once; A fly in the ointment; Lessford's rabbits; A lesson on a tortoise; The Prussian officer; The thorn in the flesh; Daughters of the vicar; A fragment of stained glass; The shades of spring; Second best; The shadow in the rose garden; Goose fair; The white stocking; A sick collier; The christening; Odour of chrysanthemums; England, my England; Tickets, please; The blind man; Monkey nuts; Wintry peacock; You touched me; Samson and Delilah; The thimble; The mortal coil; The primrose path; The horse dealer's daughter; Delilah and Mr. Bircumshaw; Fanny and Annie; The ladybird; The fox; The captain's doll; St. Mawr; The princess; Two blue birds; Sun; The woman who rode away; Smile; The border line; Jimmy and the desperate woman; The last laugh; In love; Glad ghosts; None of that; The man who loved islands; The lovely lady; Rawdon's roof; The rocking-horse winner; Mother and daughter; The blue moccasins; Things; The virgin and the gipsy; The man who died

Lady Chatterley's lover; the historic unexpurgated Grove Press edition; with Archibald MacLeish's letter to Barney Rosset, an introduction by Mark Schorer, and Judge Bryan's decision in the obscenity case. Modern Lib. 1993 liii, 491p

ISBN 0-679-60065-5

* LC 93-15337

First published 1928 in a limited edition in Florence

A novel "presenting the author's mystical theories of sex in the story of Constance, or Connie, the wife of an English aristocrat, who runs away with her gamekeeper. Her husband, Sir Clifford, has been rendered impotent by a war wound and is also an emotional cripple. The gamekeeper, Mellors, is a forthright individualistic man, uncontaminated by industrial society." Reader's Ency. 4th edition

The rainbow; with an introduction by Barbara Hardy. Knopf 1993 xxxv, 460p $20

ISBN 0-679-42305-2

LC 93-1860

"Everyman's library"

First published 1915

"The story line traces three generations of the Brangwen family in the Midlands of England from 1840 to 1905. The marriage of farmer Tom Brangwen and foreigner Lydia Lensky eventually breaks down. Likewise, the marriage of Lydia's daughter Anna to Tom's nephew Will gradually fails. The novel is largely devoted to Will and Anna's oldest child, the schoolteacher Ursula, who stops short of marriage when she is unsatisfied by her love affair with the conventional soldier Anton Skrebensky. The appearance of a rainbow at the end of the novel is a sign of hope for Ursula, whose story is continued in Lawrence's *Women in Love*." Merriam-Webster's Ency of Lit

Followed by Women in love

Sons and lovers. Knopf 1991 xxvii, 403p $17

ISBN 0-679-40572-0

* LC 91-53002

"Everyman's library"

First published 1913

"Paul Morel, adored youngest son of a middle-class mother who feels that her coal-miner husband was unworthy of her, has difficulty in breaking away from her. Mrs. Morel has given her son all her warmth and love for so long a time that Paul finds it impossible to establish a relationship with another women. Miriam is supportive and understanding of his artistic nature but appeals mainly to his higher nature; Clara Dawes becomes his mistress but she is married and will not divorce her husband. After the death of his mother, Paul arranges a reconciliation between Clara and her husband and, after months of grieving for his mother, at last finds the strength to strike out on his own." Shapiro. Fic For Youth. 3d edition

Women in love. Knopf 1992 475p

ISBN 0-679-40995-5

* LC 91-53191

"Everyman's library"

Sequel to The rainbow

First published 1920

This novel "examines the ill effects of industrialization on the human psyche, resolving that individual and collective rebirth is possible only through human intensity and passion. *Women in Love* contrasts the love affair of Rupert Birkin and Ursula Brangwen with that of Gudrun, Ursula's artistic sister, and Gerald Crich, a domineering industrialist. Birkin, an introspective misanthrope, struggles to reconcile his metaphysical drive for self-fulfillment with Ursula's practical view of sentimental passion. Their love affair and eventual marriage are set as a positive antithesis to the destructive relationship of Gudrun and Crich." Merriam-Webster's Ency of Lit

Lawrence, David, 1947-

The dead sit round in a ring. Thomas Dunne Books 2004 435p $24.95

ISBN 0-312-32710-2   LC 2004-41878

"Three of the four bodies sitting in a ring in a London flat are identified as elderly siblings in a suicide pact. The fourth turns out to be Jimmy Stone, a gofer for the notorious Tanner family, runner of drugs, guns, and girls. So begins Det. Sgt. Sheila Mooney's bedevilment. Dogged in her investigation of the murder, she disrupts a neighboring undercover operation and turns over another stone: the sexual exploitation of women lured from Eastern Europe by promises of visas and jobs. Nearing the breaking point at work, Sheila also has to wrestle with personal issues." Libr J

This mystery offers a "perspective on London that is darker and grittier than in conventional treatments. But the writing is the thing. Whether he's describing a bizarre death scene . . . or observing a group of streetwalkers plying their night trade . . . Lawrence, a published poet, writes with a delicacy and restraint rare in the genre." N Y Times Book Rev

Lawrence, David Herbert See Lawrence, D. H. (David Herbert), 1885-1930

Lawrence, Margaret K.

The burning bride; [by] Margaret Lawrence. Avon Bks. 1998 387p

ISBN 0-380-97620-X   LC 98-4491

This novel finds eighteenth-century midwife Hannah Trevor hesitating on the brink of marriage. Her tormented lover, town militia commander Daniel Josselyn, father of her daughter, Jennet, and of the child Hannah now carries, is finally free to wed. But will Daniel insist that she give up her fierce independence and assume the duties of a gentleman's lady? Before she has a chance to find out, a man is murdered and violence erupts in the small Maine community, testing both Hannah and Daniel's loyalties and opening a Pandora's box of dark secrets." Booklist

Hearts and bones; [by] Margaret Lawrence. Avon Bks. 1996 307p il o.p.   LC 96-2394

"The year is 1786; the place a rural community in Maine. Hannah Trevor, a midwife, healer, and Enlightenment thinker, finds Nan Emory apparently raped and murdered in her bed. A damaging letter in which Nan accuses her attackers is left behind. All evidence seems to point to Hannah's former lover, Daniel Josselyn. Daniel's invalid wife, Charlotte, turns to Hannah, who is convinced that Daniel was framed by an enemy, explores the evidence, and discovers the real murderer." Libr J

"Through a combination of diary entries, trial records, autopsy reports, and engrossing narrative, Lawrence reveals the story of a witness and a participant in a brutal war crime and their decade-long silence." Booklist

Lawrence, Starling

The lightning keeper; a novel. HarperCollins 2006 414p il $25.95

ISBN 0-06-082524-3   LC 2006-280882

"In a small Connecticut town in early 20th-century America, at a time when electricity is still a newfangled invention, Harriet Bigelow struggles with the decline of both her father's mental health and the family ironworks business, for which she has an aptitude. Then Balkan immigrant Toma Pekocevic (seen in . . . Lawrence's previous novel, Montenegro) gets involved in the business, and his genius for invention and passion for Harriet combine to create a tension and suspense that carry the reader to the novel's end. Adding to the tension is wealthy Senator Truscott, whose own interest in Harriet and the Bigelow Iron Company forces Harriet to make some difficult decisions." Libr J

"Beautifully written and richly detailed, Lawrence's story brings to life a colorful period in American history and provides a timely reminder that every generation expects too much from its modern marvels." Baltimore Sun

Lawson, Mary, 1910-1941

Crow Lake. Dial Press (NY) 2002 291p hardcover o.p. pa $14

ISBN 0-385-33611-X; 0-385-33763-9 (pa)
                                      LC 2001-53779

In this novel "four children living in northern Ontario struggle to stay together after their parents die in an auto accident. . . . Kate Morrison narrates the tale in flashback mode, starting with the fatal car accident that leaves seven-year-old Kate; her toddler sister, Bo; 19-year-old Luke; and 17-year-old Matt to fend for themselves." Publ Wkly

"Lawson achieves a breathless anticipatory quality in her surprisingly adept first novel, in which a child tells the story, but tells it very well indeed." Booklist

Lawton, John, 1949-

Old flames. Atlantic Monthly Press 2003 416p $24

ISBN 0-87113-864-6   LC 2002-28025

"April 1956, Nikita Krushchev is in London on a diplomatic errand. Chief Inspector Frederick Troy of Scotland Yard is assigned as a bodyguard to the Russsian leader. But he has a secret mission, too: Troy, fluent in Russian, is to spy on Khrushchev (who doesn't know the British cop speaks his language) by evesdropping on private conversations and reporting back to his superiors. It's a tough assignment, with a handful of tricky moral qualms, and it gets a heck of a lot tougher when a Royal Navy diver turns up dead." Booklist

"Lawton has created an effective genre-bending novel that is at once a cerebral thriller and an uproarious, deliciously English spoof." Publ Wkly

Lax, Andromeda Romano- See Romano-Lax, Andromeda, 1971-

Lazar, Zachary

Sway; a novel. Little, Brown and Co. 2008 255p $23.99

ISBN 978-0-316-11309-0; 0-316-11309-3
                                 * LC 2007-9920

This novel depicts "the early days of the Rolling Stones, including the romantic triangle of Brian Jones, Anita Pallenberg, and Keith Richards; the life of avantgarde filmmaker Kenneth Anger; and the community of Charles Manson and his followers. . . . Connecting all the stories in this novel is Bobby Beausoleil, a beautiful California boy who appeared in an Anger film and eventually joined the Manson 'family.'" Publisher's note

"It is not the now-historic acts of violence that make Sway so riveting, but its vivid character portraits and decadent, muzzy atmosphere, all rendered with the heightened sensory awareness associated with drugs and paranoia. The near miniaturist precision with which he describes Keith Richards's attempts to master his guitar, Brian Jones's acid trips and Anger's obsessive desire for Beausoleil bring this large-scale tableau into stunning relief." Time Out N Y

Le, Thi Diem Thuy, 1972-

The gangster we are all looking for. Knopf 2003 160p $18

ISBN 0-375-40018-4   LC 2002-33999

"The nameless first-person narrator is born in Vietnam, carried across the ocean by her father and 'washed to shore' in Linda Vista, a section of San Diego. Her 'Ba' finds work as a house painter, a welder and finally a gardener. It is two years before her mother joins them and her parents' tempestuous marriage moves to center stage, but the father is always a haunted, brooding presence in this drama of the narrator's coming-of-age." N Y Times Book Rev

Le, Thi Diem Thuy, 1972-—*Continued*

"The story opens slowly but gathers strength, and though it remains somewhat muted, Le's lyrical writing and skill with the telling vigette will reward patient readers." Libr J

Le Carré, John, 1931-

Absolute friends. Little, Brown 2004 455p $26.95

ISBN 0-316-00064-7   LC 2003-61196

"The central characters in this novel are Ted Mundy, an old-school Englishman, the misfit son of a disgraced British Army major and once a spy but now a tour guide at one of Mad King Ludwig's Bavarian castles; and Sasha, a 1960's German radical. . . . Sasha, whose father was a Lutheran minister with Nazi ties, is a double and possibly a triple agent. . . . Their lives as friends, secret agents and idealists have been intertwined for more than 40 years." N Y Times (Late N Y Ed)

"If le Carre's symbols are a little obvious and his rhetoric a little heated, his technical skill is pure joy." New Leader

The constant gardener; a novel. Scribner 2001 492p

ISBN 0-7432-1505-2

* LC 00-53340

"Tessa Quayle, a beautiful young lawyer, is posted to Nairobi as the wife of British diplomat Justin Quayle. In the course of the voluntary work in which she becomes involved, she uncovers a trail of intentional malfeasance by the vast pharmaceutical multinational KVH, which is fast-tracking a new TB drug using Africans as guinea pigs. She first calls on the British government to intervene and then decides to take her evidence to Richard Leakey. Le Carre's latest novel opens with Tessa's being murdered on her way to Leakey. Tessa was accompanied by her friend Arnold Bluhm, whom the official investigation finds guilty of her murder. But Tessa's husband begins his own probe, following her trail of contacts around the world." Libr J

"Globalization in its uglier aspects . . . has replaced the Cold War as the moral backdrop in Le Carre's work. His Cold War novels did not spare the conscience even of citizens on the 'right' side, confronting them with crimes committed in their names, and the globalization novels do not spare the stockholder." Atl Mon

The honourable schoolboy. Knopf 1977 533p o.p.

* LC 77-75001

Jerry Westerby is the honorable schoolboy of the title. He works with George Smiley of the British Secret Service, described by the author as The Circus, to discover why the Russian Secret Service is paying $25,000 a month into the bank account of the prosperous Hong Kong business man, Drake Ko. The action takes place in London and Southeast Asia. The story opens in the Hong Kong press club

This "is superbly well-organized, combining a grandiose sweep with an intricate pattern. It has hard-edged reality instead of fuzzy near-fantasy, a host of sharply etched characters instead of a few eccentric caricatures, and a style which, subtle and flexible . . . never obtrudes, yet never goes unnoticed." Times Lit Suppl

The little drummer girl. Knopf 1983 429p o.p.

LC 82-48733

"A series of bomb-attacks upon Israeli officials throughout Europe is investigated by Kurtz and his assistant Litvak . . . who plan not merely to track down the terrorists but to infiltrate the core of the illicit Palestinian organisation and explode it from within. Charlie, a footloose actress with radical affinities, is taken up by a . . . stranger who gradually introduces her into a network of political altruism. She is schooled to succumb to the charms of a Palestinian guerrilla yet at a deeper level to be still working for the Israelis." New Statesman (1913)

"Mr. le Carré's novel is certainly the most mature, inventive and powerful book about terrorists-come-to-life this reader has experienced. It transcends the genre." NY Times Book Rev

The looking glass war. Coward-McCann 1965 320p o.p.

This spy story "concerns a former military espionage department in London (small, left over from the . . . days of World War II) and its struggle to train one of its former agents for a mission into East Germany." NY Times Book Rev

"A bitter, cruel, dispassionate—yet passionate—study of an unimportant piece of espionage and the unimportant little men who are involved in it." Book Week

The mission song. Little, Brown 2006 339p $26.99

ISBN 0-316-01674-8   LC 2006-20099

This is the "tale of an idealistic and naïve British interpreter, Bruno 'Salvo' Salvador. The 29-year-old Congo native's mixed parentage puts him in a tentative position in society, despite his being married to an attractive upper-class white Englishwoman, who's a celebrity journalist. Salvo's genius with languages has led to steady work from a variety of employers, including covert assignments from shadowy government entities. One such job enmeshes the interpreter in an ambitious scheme to finally bring stability to the much victimized Congo, and Salvo's personal stake in the outcome tests his professionalism and ethics." Publ Wkly

The "novel's resolutions, romantic and political, are achieved at an emotional distance, behind a thick protective layer of thriller-awareness and thriller expectations. Le Carré has researched his chosen venue diligently . . . and delivered an entertainment whose foremost passion is a commendable indignation over the sufferings of a large African population at the hands of berserk militias, corrupt if not altogether absent government, and, from the West, cold corporate greed. 'The Mission Song' illuminates with animated personifications a portion of the globe's daily misery that tends to be, in American news, at least, murky and abstract." New Yorker

A most wanted man; a novel. Scribner 2008 323p $28

ISBN 978-1-4165-9488-8; 1-4165-9488-4

LC 2008-30704

Set in Hamburg, this novel "stars Issa Karpov, a Chechen refugee smuggled into town in strikingly murky circumstances. He is the illegitimate son of Grigory Karpov, a former Soviet soldier who laundered tainted money through Brue Frères, a failing Hamburg bank run by Tommy Brue, a middle-aged man whose marriage is falling apart. Tommy's father, Edward, set up accounts

Le Carré, John, 1931—*Continued*

called Lipizzaners, dedicated to laundering money such as Karpov's. Annabel Richter, a lawyer who works for Sanctuary North, an agency dedicated to asylum seekers and stateless persons, represents Issa . . . in his dealings with Brue. Also figuring in the plot: British, German, and American spies competing to see who can score the most points against the war on terror." Christ Sci Monit

"Le Carré's dialogue has snap, rhythm and wit, particularly in those passages where intelligence chiefs maneuver to gain an edge on each other. Too, his immaculate timing helps him fold in different plot lines without smudging narrative pace and tone. Ever the spymaster, he also differentiates the challenges faced by spies today from those of their Cold War counterparts." St. Louis Post-Dispatch

The night manager; a novel. Knopf 1993 429p o.p. LC 92-55070

"Jonathan Pine, hotel night manager and volunteer spy, [sets] out to avenge the death of Sophie, a high-class Egyptian prostitute whom he loved and betrayed. . . . With the help of a maverick branch of British Intelligence determined to wrest operational control from the latter-day cold warriors, Pine sets out to trap Dicky Roper, the man responsible for Sophie's death, a world-class arms dealer about to embark on a massive drugs-for-guns deal." Booklist

Le Carré "brings to the world of the drug wars the same skilled characterization, perceptive detail, and dramatic storytelling that made him the undisputed master of the Cold War spy novel. This novel is precisely what we have come to expect from him: a work of high literary merit that's also great entertainment." Libr J

Our game; a novel. Knopf 1995 301p
ISBN 0-679-44181-6　　　　　LC 95-2666
The "narrator is Tim Cranmer, former secret agent turned winemaker in rural Somerset. Tim's great espionage success was the recruiting of brilliant gadfly Larry Pettifer, who ended up not only stealing Tim's beautiful mistress, the enigmatic Emma, but also disappearing, apparently with a fortune lifted from Russian banks to aid the rebels through shady arms deals. Now the police are looking for Larry, the 'Office' is convinced Cranmer must be in on his schemes, and, using all his old spycraft, he sets out to find Larry and Emma." Publ Wkly

"This is classic le Carré, spun out beautifully: the ex-spy treated shabbily by his two-bit successors, then besting them by virtue of his superior spycraft. Delicious. But as the plot grows more complex, both politically and psychologically, it becomes clear that even after 14 novels, le Carré has no intention of repeating himself." Newsweek

A perfect spy. Knopf 1986 475p o.p.
　　　　　LC 85-45587
"The protagonist of the story, Magnus Pym, aged 53, is . . . a senior partner in 'the firm' of British intelligence, working out of the British Embassy in Vienna. He is a man respected and admired for his intelligence and common sense. He is also a man of mystery . . . [His disappearance] sets the plot in motion. Friends, colleagues, and family haven't a clue to his whereabouts. His superiors fear that 'the perfect spy' has defected and that British agents in Czechoslovakia, a group supervised

by Pym, may be targeted. Jack Brotherhood, Pym's agency superior, begins an investigation." West Coast Rev Books

"Not a spy novel in the usual sense . . . but a skillfully manipulated, complex, and probingly written study spiced with lively anecdotes. To be savored." Libr J

The Russia house. Knopf 1989 353p o.p.
　　　　　LC 88-46159
"A mysterious manuscript purporting to prove the Soviet defense system is unworkable is smuggled out of Moscow. It was intended for a flaky English publisher, a womanizing saxophone-playing boozer, but the smuggler has turned it over to British intelligence. In order to prove its authenticity, they recruit the publisher as an amateur spy and send him to Moscow to reestablish contact with the author. But the 'truth' Barley Blair finds there is love and a purpose for his shambles of a life." Libr J

"With scarcely an intimation of sex, no violence and not a side arm visible, Le Carre has again managed to construct a plot of commanding suspense. . . . The Russia House is both afire and thought provoking, a thriller that demands a second reading as a treatise on our time." Time

The secret pilgrim. Knopf 1990 335p o.p.
　　　　　LC 90-52944
This novel "takes the form of a reverie-memoir, a series of reflections on a long life in the espionage business recalled by a surnameless man called Ned. . . . Now on the verge of retirement, Ned is running Sarratt, the training school for new recruits to British intelligence. He invites the legendary George Smiley to address the impending graduates and, after dinner, the night is whiled away as the next generation of spies picks the brains of a past master. As Smiley responds to their questions, allusions and remarks that he makes trigger Ned's recollections about his own past." N Y Times Book Rev

"There's always been a didatic quality to le Carré's work that has been part of his novels' charm, but in no other book has he said so much about the ravages that the spying profession works upon the agent." Newsweek

Single & Single; a novel. Scribner 1999 345p $26
ISBN 0-684-85926-2　　　　　LC 98-47174
This book's title "is the name of a London family firm whose members seem to be investment bankers, but of a very peculiar and contemporary sort. In fact, they work with the kind of people—Russian gangsters, Swiss lawyers, creators of dummy corporations around the world—that specialize in making big money out of drugs and arms, and laundering the proceeds. The firm is run by Tiger Single, a modern buccaneer who wants his son, Oliver, to move up in the business." Publ Wkly

Le Carré "provides a fascinating journey through the new landscape of corruption. . . . The power of [this novel] stems from the author's portrait of a world in which individuals are no match for the organized mania of greed." Time

Smiley's people. Knopf 1980 c1979 374p o.p.
　　　　　LC 79-2299
First published 1979 in the United Kingdom
"George Smiley, who retired as master of the British secret service known as the Circus when the Cold War

Le Carré, John, 1931-—*Continued*

was supplanted by détente, is . . . recalled to duty when one of his former 'people,' a brilliant anti-Soviet Estonian emigré called the General, is murdered on Hampstead Heath. The General, as Smiley patiently works it out, had been trying to reach him with what was understood to be documentary evidence that could destroy the infamous Russian spymaster Karla." New Yorker

This novel "is a complete winner, exciting, well-paced, and convincing. . . . There is a lot of the Le Carré gloom, but now it seems almost elegiac and touching. Absolutely not to be missed." Libr J

The spy who came in from the cold. Walker & Company 2005 223p $19

ISBN 0-8027-1454-4

First published 1963 in the United kingdom; first United States edition published 1964 by Coward-McCann

"The story of Alec Leamas, 50-year-old professional secret agent who has grown stale in espionage, who longs to 'come in from the cold' and how he undertakes one last assignment before that hoped-for retirement. Over the years Leamas has grown unsure where his workday carapace ends and his real self begins. . . . Recalled from Berlin after the death of his last East German contact at the Wall, Leamas lets himself be seduced into a pretended defection-thereby providing the East Germans with data from which they can deduce that the head of their own spy apparatus is a double agent." N Y Times Book Rev

The tailor of Panama. Knopf 1996 331p

ISBN 0-679-45446-2   LC 96-34802

This is an "account of a British tailor in Panama whose manufactured universe collides tragically with reality. . . . Harry Pendel is pressured into becoming a spy by an amoral British agent. Desperate to avoid exposure as an ex-con, Harry fabricates a network of sources and plies the giddy Brits with tales of a coming Panamanian revolution." Booklist

Le Carré "reveals in the contortions of British diplomats, aghast at the *arriviste* spy masters whom they pretend to accept, all the while struggling to extricate themselves from absurd but inevitable catastrophe. Readers who wonder whether Graham Greene was not here 40 years ago are right, and Mr le Carré acknowledges his debt to 'Our Man in Havana'. This tale, told with wit and ingenuity, is a splendid homage from one master of political thrillers to another." Economist

Tinker, tailor, soldier, spy. Knopf 1974 355p o.p.

The novel's protagonist, British agent George Smiley, "is asked to come out of retirement and root out as unobtrusively as possible the 'mole,' or Russian agent, that has burrowed his way to the center of England's secret intelligence organization, the Circus. Smiley is feeling glum. His wife has left him and his retirement was forced upon him the year before when power was reshuffled at the Circus. It is clear, too, that the mole must be one of Smiley's old colleagues." Newsweek

Smiley "instinctively realises from the outset who the traitor is but refuses to confront the embarrassing truth. A perceptive reader will sense the secret too, but one goes on reading entranced not so much by the ramifica-

tions of the plot, beautifully engineered though it is, as by concern for the characters, a rare thing in thrillers." New Statesman (1913)

Le Guin, Ursula K., 1929-

The beginning place. Harper & Row 1980 183p o.p.   LC 79-2653

"For Hugh, on the run from the demands of his domineering mother and from the dullness of his job as a checkout boy at a local market . . . and for Irene, fearful of sexual harrassment at the hands of her stepfather and other men, [a fantastical] world becomes a refuge. Then an unknown evil begins to pervade their paradise and they are chosen to face the 'fear.' Irene, jealous of newcomer Hugh's acceptance into the world she has been visiting for so long, reluctantly acts as guide for Hugh who, as sword-wielder, is to be the savior. Having finally slain a monster, Irene and Hugh seek to escape Eden turned nightmare." SLJ

"The style is fluent, concise and elegant, and the story that is told is easily understood by anyone who has ever found himself at a loss to deal with the realities of modern life." Best Sellers

Betrayals

In Le Guin, U. K. Four ways to forgiveness p1-34

The birthday of the world and other stories. HarperCollins Pubs. 2002 362p $24.95

ISBN 0-06-621253-7   LC 2001-39508

Contents: Coming of age in Karhide; The matter of Seggri; Unchosen love; Mountain ways; Solitude; Old music and the slave women; The birthday of the world; Paradises lost

"Le Guin appears to have the most fun with her investigations of sex and gender . . . but the costs of revolution, religious bliss, and technology are also provicatively explored, and one returns to the current headlines with a fresh awareness of the exotic providional nature of human arrangements." New Yorker

The dispossessed; an ambiguous Utopia. Harper & Row 1974 341p il o.p.

"Shevek, a brilliant physicist, is caught between the prejudices and hatreds of two worlds. His quest to bridge the gap between Ararres, an anarchist, egalitarian society, and Varas, a structured, capitalistic world, unleashes a storm of intrigue and drama. The two distinct cultures provide insights into the role of women in society, the issue of free will versus obligation to the state, human rights, and ecomonic systems." Shapiro. Fic for Youth. 3d edition

Forgiveness day

In Le Guin, U. K. Four ways to forgiveness p35-92

Four ways to forgiveness. HarperPrism 1995 228p o.p.   LC 95-11459

Contents: Betrayals; Forgiveness day; A man of the people; A woman's liberation

"Four interrelated novellas deal with the Hainish culture on the twin planets of Werel and Yeowe and examine the relationship between love, freedom and forgiveness." Publ Wkly

Le Guin, Ursula K., 1929——_Continued_

The lathe of heaven. Scribner 1971 184p o.p.
"A psychiatrist sets out to use a patient whose dreams can alter reality to create utopia, but in usurping this power he is gradually delivered into madness." Anatomy of Wonder 4
"The author has done some profound research in psychology, cerebro-physiology and biochemistry. . . . In addition, her perceptions of such matters as geopolitics, race, socialized medicine and the patient/shrink relationship are razor-sharp and more than a little cutting." Natl Rev

The left hand of darkness; with a new afterword and appendixes by the author. 25th Anniversary ed. Walker & Co. 1994 345p
ISBN 0-8027-1302-5
* LC 94-27147
A reissue of the title first published 1969 by Walker & Company
"This is a tale of political intrigue and danger on the world of Gethen, the Winter planet. Genly Ai, high official of the Eukeman—the commonwealth of worlds—is on Gethen to convince the royalty to join the Federation. He soon becomes a pawn in Gethen's power struggles, set against the elaborate mores of the Gethenians, a unisex hermaphroditic people whose intricate sexual physiology plays a key role in the conflict. Allied with Estraven, fallen lord, Genly is forced to cross the savage and impassable Gobrin Ice." Shapiro. Fic for Youth. 3d edition

A man of the people
_In_ Le Guin, U. K. Four ways to forgiveness p93-144

(ed) The Norton book of science fiction. See The Norton book of science fiction

Orsinian tales. Harper & Row 1976 179p o.p.
Contents: The fountains; The barrow; Ile Forest; Conversations at night; The road east; Brothers and sisters; A week in the country; An die Musik; The house; The lady of Moge; Imaginary countries
This is a cycle of interrelated short stories. "Set in a vaguely Middle-European country, Le Guin's tales deal with love, freedom, and tyranny in a society which over a series of historical periods appears to be perpetually in the last stages preceding cataclysm." Booklist

The other wind. Harcourt 2001 246p
ISBN 0-15-100684-9   LC 2001-24632
"Alder, the man who unwittingly initiates the transformation of Earthsea, is a humble sorcerer who specializes in fixing broken pots and repairing fence lines, but when his beloved wife, Lily, dies, he is inconsolable. He begins to dream of the land of the dead and sees both Lily and other shades reaching out to him across the low stone wall that separates them from the land of the living. Soon, more general signs and portents begin to disturb Earthsea." Publ Wkly
"The Earthsea saga, begun in 1968 as a young adults' series, has evolved into one of Le Guin's, and modern science fiction's, signature achievements." N Y Times Book Rev

The telling. Harcourt 2000 264p
ISBN 0-15-100567-2   LC 00-29574

A title in the authors Hainish cycle. "As a member of the Ekumen's embassy on the planet Aka, Sutty undertakes a delicate mission that leads her to a mountain village reported to contain the last remnants of a dying culture. Following a trail of subtle clues concealed in stories and folk sayings, Sutty discovers the suppressed history of a planet willing to abandon its old ways in the name of progress. . . . This parable of the modern world's headlong rush toward monocultural sterility exemplifies the author's elegant simplicity and keen insight." Libr J

A woman's liberation
_In_ Le Guin, U. K. Four ways to forgiveness p145-208

The word for world is forest
_In_ The Hugo winners p225-327

Lear, Peter _See_ Lovesey, Peter

Leavitt, David, 1961-

The Indian clerk; a novel. Bloomsbury 2007 485p $24.95
ISBN 978-1-59691-040-9; 1-59691-040-2
LC 2007-9061
"Eventually becoming one of the greatest mathematicians of his era, Srinvasa Ramanujan was only a 23-year-old bank clerk in the Indian city of Madras when, in 1913, he wrote a letter to the highly esteemed British mathematician G. H. Hardy, who was seated at Cambridge. The letter suggests to Hardy that the writer is a math genius, and Hardy embarks on a campaign to bring him from India to England. Once there, the relatively bland Ramanujan nevertheless stood at the center of many people's personal and professional lives for a brief time before his untimely death." Booklist
"Mathematics and its paradoxes provide a deep vein of metaphor that Leavitt uses to superb effect, demonstrating how the most meaningful relationships can defy both logic and imagination." New Yorker

The lost language of cranes. Knopf 1986 319p
ISBN 0-394-53873-0
* LC 86-45277
"The story focuses on Philip Benjamin, a 25-year-old New Yorker, . . . gay, who is involved in his first 'serious' romance. This situation is complicated by the struggle of Philip's father to deal more openly with his own long-standing, but thus far closeted, homosexual inclinations. With Philip's coming out, father is thrown into even greater turmoil, mother begins to realize the complete truth, and all are forced to reexamine the ties that bind them." Libr J
"Mr Leavitt's sense of pacing, his graceful sentences and his storytelling ability dovetail nicely. On the other hand, the book feels young—experientially thin, intellectually timid, contrived, erratic and, understandably, not yet wise. . . . 'The Lost Language of Cranes' lingers in the mind, greater than the sum of its problematic parts." N Y Times Book Rev

Martin Bauman; or, A sure thing. Houghton Mifflin 2000 387p $26
ISBN 0-395-90243-6   LC 00-27589

Leavitt, David, 1961——*Continued*

"Martin Bauman, the gay writer protagonist of Leavitt's self-referential novel, has not even come out to himself let alone his parents or friends when he enters college in 1980. Happiest in the company of lesbians and seemingly immune to lust or love, he assiduously cultivates his literary ambitions under the brutal tutelage of professor Stanley Flint, who warns him that his need for approval and preference for 'a sure thing' could turn him into a mere hack. Flint continues to be his nemesis even after Martin achieves instant fame by disclosing his homosexuality in the first 'gay' short story ever published in *the* New York literary magazine, and Martin, analyzing himself two decades later, acknowledges Flint's prescience as he relates, in detail both mesmerizing and maddening, the story of his early success and rapid comeuppance." Booklist

(ed) Penguin book of gay short fiction. See Penguin book of gay short fiction

While England sleeps. Viking 1993 304p o.p.
LC 92-45878

This novel is narrated by "English public school boy Brian Botsford. During a promiscuous post-university period in the 1930s, Brian dallies with both leftist political interests and the affections of a working-class Underground ticket taker, Edward Phelan, in a highly charged sexual affair. He also convinces himself that he is in love with a young woman of his own class, Philippa Archibald, with whom he has a sexual liaison. Having discovered Brian's affair with Philippa, Edward flees to Spain to join the International Brigade. Risking prison, he later deserts, and Brian rushes to Spain to help." Libr J

"A narrative that for the most part rings true, though in a curiously mannered way. The reader ends up with a feeling of respect for the assiduous research that has been undertaken, rather than with any sense of deep involvement with the characters." N Y Times Book Rev

Lebbon, Tim, 1969-

Fallen. Bantam Spectra 2008 413p il pa $12
ISBN 978-0-553-38467-3; 0-553-38467-8
LC 2008-10401

"Some 4,000 years before the events of Dusk (2006), the people of Noreela are just beginning an era of expansion, with explorers going constantly further into unknown territory for profit and glory. Blocking the voyagers' southward journeys, however, is the Great Divide, a cliff that reaches into the clouds. Ramus Rheel, an aging explorer battling cancer, and Nomi Hyden, whose wealth has not diminished her craving for adventure, are friendly enemies who set out to scale the Divide and earn recognition as the greatest voyagers of all. When they find the lair of one of the ancient Sleeping Gods, they get considerably more excitement—and terror—than they bargained for. Lebbon creates vivid and convincing major and minor characters, places and creatures, blending wonder and nightmare in this dark and memorable novel." Publ Wkly

Lebrecht, Norman, 1948-

The song of names. Anchor Bks. 2004 c2002 311p pa $14
ISBN 1-4000-3489-2 (pa)
LC 2003-67451

In this novel, "two men who became friends as children in London during WWII are reunited after 40 years. In 1939, nine-year-old Martin Simmonds meets Dovidl Rapoport, a violin prodigy the same age. Martin's father is a music impresario, and when Dovidl is sent by his Polish parents to study in England, he offers the boy lodging in his own home. Dovidl and Martin quickly become best friends. Dovidl's parents perish in the Holocaust; then, in 1951, Dovidl-his name changed to the more palatable Eli-is about to embark on a career as a concert virtuoso when he disappears on the day of his debut. Martin becomes obsessed with his friend's disappearance, and after decades of searching finally finds him in a dreary town in the north of England." Publ Wkly

"Lebrecht's story delves into the horrors of the Holocaust and the Blitz, as well as the quiet communities of Hasidic Judaism that developed in Britain after the flight of so many refugees. What emerges is a vivid and outstanding story that sings about artistry, genius, music, love, envy, friendship, and revenge." Booklist

Lee, C. Y., 1917-

The flower drum song. Farrar, Straus & Cudahy 1957 244p o.p.

A story of family life in San Francisco's Chinatown. The principal characters are the elderly Mr. Wang and his oldest son, Wang Ta, torn between Chinese tradition and western custom

"A first novel that is always fascinating, and by turns amusing and pathetic—a novel written with grace and decorum in the even, unimpassioned narrative style that is characteristic of classical Chinese fiction." Chicago Sunday Trib

Lee, Chang-Rae

Aloft. Riverhead Books 2004 343p $24.95
ISBN 1-573-22263-1
LC 2003-58630

"Set on affluent Long Island, [this novel] follows the life of a suburban, upper-middle-class man during a time of family crisis. Jerry Battle's favorite diversion is to fly his small plane over the neighboring towns and villages. When his daughter and her fiance arrive from Oregon to announce their marriage plans, he looks back on his life and faces his disengagement with it . . . and the people he loves." Publisher's note

The author "creates a pointillist portrait of three generations of a family as it has motored its way from blue collar immigrant hopes to bourgeois respectability to new money indulgence, and in doing so he gently nudges Jerry and his relatives into holding up a mirror to the American Dream in all its glittering and treacherous promise." N Y Times (Late N Y Ed)

A gesture life. Riverhead Bks. 1999 356p
ISBN 1-573-22146-5
LC 99-28382

"Doc Hata lives an exemplary American small-town life, but . . . his decorum conceals an immigrant's tragic past. Born to poor ethnic Koreans but raised by wealthy Japanese, Hata falls in love with a comfort woman during the war. Haunted by her dire fate, he adopts a Korean girl, but, unable to express his love, he nearly loses her, too." Booklist

"This is a wise, humane, fully rounded story, deeply but unsentimentally moving, and permeated with insights about the nature of human relationships." Publ Wkly

Lee, Don, 1959-

Country of origin. W.W. Norton & Co 2004 315p $24.95

ISBN 0-393-05812-3   LC 2004-4722

"Set in Tokyo in 1980, the book centers on the disappearance of Lisa Countryman, a half-Japanese, half-black Berkeley graduate student who goes to Japan to research the 'sad, brutal reign of conformity' for her dissertation and, perhaps more importantly, embark on an identity quest. . . . When she vanishes, it is first brought to the attention of Tom Hurley, a vain and careless junior diplomat at the U.S. Embassy who tells people he's Hawaiian, though he's really half-Korean and half-white. The case is turned over to Kenzo Ota, a glum, divorced police inspector, who spent three hard years of his adolescence in Missouri." Publ Wkly

"Issues of race, class, and national identity drive this clear-eyed story of closure, redemption, and carving out a place in the world." Booklist

Lee, Gentry

(jt. auth) Clarke, A. C. The Garden of Rama
(jt. auth) Clarke, A. C. Rama II
(jt. auth) Clarke, A. C. Rama revealed

Lee, Gus

China boy; a novel. Dutton 1991 322p hardcover o.p. pa $14

ISBN 0-525-24994-X; 0-452-27158-4 (pa)

LC 90-21687

"The rough-and-tumble tale of Kai Ting, the only son of an aristocratic Shanghai couple whose escape from the Communists landed them in San Francisco's tough, predominantly black, Panhandle district. When Kai Ting's mother dies, his father marries a white woman who tries to eradicate her stepchildren's Chinese heritage. She sends the skinny, sheltered, and bewildered boy out into the neighborhood, where he becomes everyone's favorite punching bag." Am Libr

"Based on events in his own childhood, Mr. Lee's depiction of Kai's efforts to reconcile his Chinese heritage with the several equally bewildering worlds of American culture he is simultaneously exposed to . . . is vivid and moving." N Y Times Book Rev

Followed by Honor & duty (1994)

Lee, Harper, 1926-

To kill a mockingbird. 40th anniversary ed. HarperCollins Pubs. 1999 323p $19.95

ISBN 0-06-019499-5

          *

A reissue of the title first published 1960 by Lippincott

"Scout, as Jean Louise is called, is a precocious child. She relates her impressions of the time when her lawyer father, Atticus Finch, is defending a black man accused of raping a white woman in a small Alabama town during the 1930's. Atticus's courageous act brings the violence and injustice that exists in their world sharply into focus as it intrudes into the lighthearted life that Scout and her brother Jem have enjoyed until that time." Shapiro. Fic for Youth. 3d edition

Lee, Janice Y. K.

The piano teacher. Viking 2009 336p $25.95

ISBN 978-0-670-02048-5   LC 2008-27449

"This cinematic tale of two love affairs in mid-century Hong Kong shows colonial pretensions tainted by wartime truths. Will Truesdale, a rootless, handsome Briton, arrives in the colony in 1941, and is swept up by Trudy Liang, the blithe and glamorous daughter of a Shanghai millionaire and a Portuguese beauty. They quickly become inseparable, their days spent in a whirl of parties and champagne, but when the Japanese invade, Will is interned and Trudy resorts to increasingly Faustian methods to survive. After the war, Claire Pendleton, the naïve wife of a British civil servant, arrives. She begins giving piano lessons to the daughter of a rich Chinese couple, and falls in love with their wounded and inscrutable driver: Will. Lee unfolds each story, and flits between them, with the brisk grace and discretion of the society she describes—a world in which horrors are adumbrated but seldom told." New Yorker

Lee, Manfred, 1905-1971

For works written by this author in collaboration with Frederic Dannay see Queen, Ellery

Lee, Mark, 1950-

The canal house. Algonquin Bks. 2003 353p $23.95

ISBN 1-56512-379-4   LC 2003-40401

This is the "story of the life and death of war correspondent Daniel McFarland, who after a brush with death in Uganda develops a new sense of mission and responsibility toward those whose wracked lives he is covering. He is drawn into an affair with Julia Cadel, an English doctor who idealistically ministers to the suffering in war zones, and the book's title refers to a brief idyll they share in London before setting out again on dangerous missions. Their new one is in East Timor." Publ Wkly

"Lee is a foreign correspondent who creates a powerful aura of realism that will forever alter your perception of the news." Booklist

Lee, Tanith

White as snow. TOR Bks. 2000 319p

ISBN 0-312-86993-2   LC 00-41160

"A Tom Doherty Associates book"

In this reworking of Snow White "evil queen, Arpazia, first appears as an innocent princess of 14, who is terrified when Draco, a rising new leader, conquers her father's castle and rapes her. Soon after he has her sister, Lilca, hanged because Lilca betrayed the castle. Draco forces Arpazia to travel with him and his barbaric army. She later bears him a girl, Candacis, whom she immediately shuns as an incarnation of evil, mumbling death spells as the infant tries to suckle her." Publ Wkly

"Incorporating many traditional fairy-tale elements, Lee's Gothic story is set in a medieval world filled with castles, wars, dwarves, pagan lore, and Christian ritual." Libr J

Leebron, Fred G.

In the middle of all this. Harcourt 2002 251p $30

ISBN 0-15-100834-5   LC 2001-5955

"Martin Kreutzel teaches college in a small Pennsylvania town, where his house is leaking, his children seem to be normal, and his colleagues are facing such vicissitudes as a spouse's substance abuse and a student's suicide. His main concern at the moment is his London-based sister, Elizabeth, a vigorous woman who is dying of cancer. When Elizabeth's husband disappears for a few days, Martin rushes to London to be with her. After Martin returns home, Elizabeth herself disappears, presumably to make her own peace with her foreshortened future." Libr J

"Leebron's exceptional skills as a storyteller and observer of humanity produce a novel both tremendously enjoyable and grandly poignant, a novel almost anthropological in its keen examination of man's fate." Publ Wkly

Legal fictions; short stories about lawyers and the law; edited by Jay Wishingrad. Overlook Press 1992 402p o.p.   LC 91-46664

Contents: The tender offer, by L. Auchincloss; About Boston, by W. Just; The balloon of William Fuerst, by L. B. Komie; The contract, by H. Jacobs; Still life, by M. Thurm; After you've gone, by A. Adams; Weight, by M. Atwood; Puttermesser: her work history, her ancestry, her afterlife, by C. Ozick; Centaurs, by J. S. Marcus; Discipline, by L. Brown; Witness, by M. S. Bell; Earthly justice, by E. S. Goldman; The most outrageous consequences, by J. R. Parker; The colonel's foundation, by L. Auchincloss; Justice is blind, by T. Wolfe; Triumph of justice, by I. Shaw; The paradise of bachelors, by H. Melville; The web of circumstance, by C. W. Chesnutt; Bartleby, the scrivener, by H. Melville; Congress in crisis: the proximity bill, by G. Keillor; Szyrk v. Village of Tatamount et al., in the United States District Court, Southern District of Virginia, No. 105-87, by W. Gaddis; Coyote v. Acme, by I. Frazier; Before the law, by F. Kafka; The litigants, by I. B. Singer; Crimes of conscience, by N. Gordimer; A few selected sentences, by B. S. Johnson; Heart of a judge, by R. S. Easmon; Joy and the law, by G. Di Lampedusa; The condemned man's last night, by B. Peret; Legal aid, by F. O'Connor; General bellomo, by P. West; The Clairvoyant, by K. Čapek; The case for the defence, by G. Greene; Rumpole for the prosecution, by J. Mortimer; The judge's wife, by I. Allende

LeGuin, Ursula *See* Le Guin, Ursula K., 1929-

Lehane, Dennis

The given day; a novel. William Morrow 2008 704p $27.95

ISBN 978-0-688-16318-1; 0-688-16318-1
   LC 2008-35137

This novel is set at the "end of the First World War, as waves of immigration, uneasy race relations, and agitation over labor issues culminate in a police strike in Boston. Danny, a patrolman and the son of a powerful

captain, pursues a pair of anarchists determined to create chaos but also finds himself drawn to the growing police union; Luther, a talented black baseball player, flees to Boston after killing a drug lord in Tulsa. Lehane laces his narrative with melodrama—two brothers in love with the same woman, who harbors a secret past; a viciously racist cop out to destroy Luther and frame the burgeoning N.A.A.C.P.—and a subplot, involving Babe Ruth, feels stale and unnecessary. But he brings vividly to life the struggles that the working classes faced in pursuit of decent working conditions and a fair wage." New Yorker

Mystic river. Morrow 2001 401p il $25
ISBN 0-688-16316-5
            * LC 2001-273012

"Lehane identifies that turning point in the life and spiritual death of a working-class Boston neighborhood as the day in 1975 when 11-year-old Dave Boyle climbed into a car with two strange men—and his best friends, Sean Devine and Jimmy Marcus, did not. A quarter-century later, when the murder of Jimmy's 19-year-old daughter forces the three of them into a heart-scorching reunion, they still carry the scars of that childhood trauma. 'Maybe they *had* gotten in that car. All three of them,' Sean thinks. 'And what they now thought of as their life was just a dream state.' Lehane spares nothing in his wrenching descriptions of how a crime in the neighborhood kills the neighborhood, taking it down house by house, family by family." N Y Times Book Rev

Prayers for rain; a novel. Morrow 1999 337p $25

ISBN 0-688-15333-X   LC 99-22048

"In what he thinks is an open-and-shut case, Boston private investigator Patrick Kenzie and his sidekick Bubba Rowgoski convince Cody Falk, a stalker with a nasty record of rape and sexual assault, to cease his harassment of Patrick's client, Karen Nichols. But six months later, a naked Karen leaps to her death off the observation deck of the Custom House tower. . . . Aided by Bubba and ex-partner/ex-lover Angie Gennaro, Patrick decides to investigate Karen's death. . . . Lehane's love of Boston, its neighborhoods, and its people shines through his hard-edged prose." Libr J

Sacred. Morrow 1997 288p
ISBN 0-688-14381-4   LC 96-53115

"When detectives Patrick Kenzie and Angela Gennaro are kidnapped by dying billionaire Trevor Stone and forced to find his lost daughter, they become entwined in a vicious whodunit in which 'up is down and north is south.' The case takes them to Grief Release Inc., a Boston-area church/cult whose members purge their sins, secrets, and financial records; then, accompanied by Stone's henchmen, to Tampa, Florida, where a top-of-the-line sports car and all the money they can spend are put at their disposal. . . . When the detectives finally find their prize, the perfecto, leggy Desiree Stone, she turns out to be much more than they bargained for." Libr J

Shutter Island. Morrow 2003 325p $25.95
ISBN 0-688-16317-3   LC 2003-48744

"From the 1993 perspective of the prologue, Shutter Island is one of those unpopulated islands in Boston's outer harbor that always look so mysterious from a distance and so scruffy up close. But in 1954, when the United

Lehane, Dennis—*Continued*

States marshall Teddy Daniels and his partner, Chuck Aule, alight on its rocky shores to hunt for an escaped murderess, this bleak spot is home to Ashecliffe Hospital, a maximum-security institution for the criminally insane. . . . The atmosphere is properly dark and moody, and so long as Teddy and Chuck stick to the manhunt and their investigation of Ashecliffe's creepy medical staff, they play their roles with muscle and grace." N Y Times Book Rev

Lehrer, Jim

Purple dots; a novel. Random House 1998 262p $23.95

ISBN 0-679-45237-0   LC 98-12962

This novel, set in Washington, D.C., is a "tale of a stalled presidential nomination. One senator objects to promoting Joshua Bennett from DCI to director of the Central Intelligence Agency, and someone within the agency is passing information to the senator's aide. When Bennett can't figure out what's going on, a group of ex-spooks who support him take on the assignment." Booklist

"The bad guys in this comedy of errors are uniformly inept and arrogant. The good guys behave like overgrown kids. Lehrer . . . has produced a very funny novel of Washington politics, broad and subtle by turns, and sly throughout." Libr J

The special prisoner; a novel. Random House 2000 227p

ISBN 0-375-50371-4   LC 00-701284

"A chance airport encounter sends retired Methodist bishop John Quincy Watson to San Diego, following a man whose too-familiar eyes drag Watson 50 years into the past, to a Japanese prisoner of war camp, where the then youthful, red-haired B29 pilot became a 'special prisoner' when captured after parachuting from his dying plane. His pursuit of the interrogator he knew as Tashimoto, the Hyena, alternates with the minister's memories of the horrors of Camp Sengei 4." Booklist

Leiber, Fritz, 1910-1992

Gonna roll the bones
In The Hugo winners p460-83

Ill met in Lankhmar
In The Hugo winners p55-115

Ship of shadows
In The Hugo winners p5-50

The Wanderer. Walker & Co. 1970 c1964 318p o.p.

First published 1964 in paperback by Ballantine Books

A "novel telling of the havoc caused by the arrival of a strange planet in the Solar System. Its mosaic narrative technique, through which events are observed through a multiplicity of viewpoints, foreshadowed the profusion of such novels and films in the 1970s." Ency of Sci Fic

Leimbach, Marti

Daniel isn't talking. Nan A. Talese 2006 275p $22.95

ISBN 0-385-51751-3   LC 2005-52890

"Melanie Marsh has what seems to be the perfect life: an American woman living abroad in London, she and her husband, Stephen, have two beautiful children. But when a doctor tells her that her three-year-old son, Daniel, who isn't developing normally, is autistic, Melanie resists Stephen's increasingly insistent suggestions that Daniel needs to be placed in a special school for autistic children. Determined that her son speak, Melanie turns to Andy O'Connor, who believes with patience and attention he can get autistic children to speak and play. Melanie believes Daniel will speak, but what she doesn't anticipate is that her marriage is in real danger or that she'll be deeply attracted to the charismatic Andy." Booklist

"Watching a handicapped child rend the fragile seams of a woman's personality and her marriage exposes us to some of the more honest and guilty realities of being a parent, and with it a mother's very human pursuit of a livable, if not perfect, ending." N Y Times Book Rev

Leinster, Murray *See* Jenkins, Will F., 1896-1975

Leithauser, Brad, 1953-

A few corrections; a novel. Knopf 2001 273p $24

ISBN 0-375-41149-6   LC 00-62010

"At first, this exploration of a small-town Midwestern Lothario's life is like something out of Dreiser: Wesley Sultan—Rotarian, Episcopalian, and aspiring businessman—seems emphatically ordinary. The relevant characters, however, are Wesley's second wife, the brilliant, self-deprecating Sally, in France, who speaks in the style of the novels that fuel her mental life; and his brother Conrad, in Miami, riddled with disease and quite definitely raging against the dying of the light. The novel is formally constructed, each chapter offering a correction to the obituary of Wesley that appears on the first page, and this sobriety of design contrasts with the inventiveness of Leithauser's portraits." New Yorker

Lelchuk, Alan

Ziff; a life? : a novel. Carroll & Graf Pubs. 2003 408p $25

ISBN 0-7867-1115-9   LC 2002-191184

"Dimming literary light Danny Levitan takes a last shot at glory by penning a biography of his onetime mentor and sometime friend, Arthur Ziff, a great American writer whom many Jews consider a traitor, and whose sex-charged novels have been overlooked by the Pulitzer and Nobel committees. What gives this story frisson is author Lelchuk's similar relationship with Philip Roth." Booklist

Lem, Stanisław

Eden; translated by Marc E. Heine. Harcourt Brace Jovanovich 1989 262p o.p.

* LC 89-1963

"A Helen and Kurt Wolff book"

This novel "details the adventures of the crew of a crash-landed spaceship on an alien planet. The crew, composed of Captain, Engineer, Physicist, Cyberneticist, Doctor and Chemist, and remaining mostly nameless . . . sets about repairing the ship and exploring the beau-

Lem, Stanisław—Continued

tiful, unmapped planet. They encounter increasingly exotic creatures and phenomena which they assume they understand, but all-too-human errors lead them to misinterpret nearly everything. Finally, when a communication of sorts is initiated with one of the planet's natives, the crew learns the full extent of their illusions." Publ Wkly

"No one writes sf more intellectually challenging or of greater literary distinction than Lem." Booklist

Fiasco; translated from the Polish by Michael Kandel. Harcourt Brace Jovanovich 1987 322p o.p.
           * LC 86-31816

"A Helen and Kurt Wolff book"

Original Polish edition, 1986

The author "imagines a time when Earth has found evidence of life on the planet Quinta and has sent a spaceship, the Hermes, to open communications with its inhabitants. For reasons impossible to know, Quinta is a silent planet; the goal of the expedition is to make it speak. The Hermes is manned with specialists in logic, game theory and 'exobiology,' as well as a Dominican monk called Arago (after the 19th-century French physicist) and a master computer whimsically named DEUS." N Y Times Book Rev

"The crew's dense, challenging discussions—of physics, philosophy, military tactics, morality, cybernetics, psychology, game theory, etc.—are punctuated by bursts of action whose initial release only serves to increase the tension, as new data disproves old theses and one fiasco follows another. Brilliant and demanding, this is one of Lem's best novels, putting the reader through an intellectual and emotional wringer." Publ Wkly

His Master's Voice; translated from the Polish by Michael Kandel. Harcourt Brace Jovanovich 1983 c1968 199p o.p.
           LC 82-15765

"A Helen and Kurt Wolff book"

Original Polish edition, 1968

"A stream of 'signals' from outer space is the subject of various attempted decodings and an excuse for all kinds of wild hypotheses about who might have sent the message and why, in which are reflected various human hopes and fears. Good satire." Anatomy of Wonder 4

Memoirs of a space traveler; further reminiscences of Ijon Tichy; drawings by the author; translated by Joel Stern and Maria Swiecicka-Zirmionek. Harcourt Brace Jovanovich 1982 153p il o.p.
           LC 81-47310

"A Helen and Kurt Wolff book"

Contents: The eighteenth voyage; The twenty-fourth voyage; Further reminiscences of Ijon Tichy; Doctor Diagoras; Let us save the universe

"These stories of Ijon Tichy appeared in the original 1971 Polish edition of 'The Star Diaries' but were omitted from the English language editions of 1976. Some of these space age tall tales are funny, some are serious, but all are pointed. The targets range from SF itself to politics and commercialism." Publ Wkly

Solaris; translated from the French by Joanna Kilmartin and Steve Cox; afterword by Darko Suvin. Walker & Co. 1970 216p o.p.
   ISSN 0-8027-5526-7
           * LC 75-123267

Original Polish edition, 1962

"This novel combines profound philosophic speculation with the structure of action-adventure SF, embodied in a clear, vivid writing style that somehow survived two translations. A planet under study by Earth scientists is swathed in a world-girdling ocean, which the scientists conclude is sentient. For unknown reasons, the ocean 'reads' the deepest memories of the four men and sends each a double of a woman in his past. The mysterious world-ocean, constantly flinging up strange shapes that defy the savants' efforts at classification, may be the first, infantile phase of an emerging 'imperfect God.' A major work by any measure." Anatomy of Wonder 5

Lemann, Nancy

Malaise; a novel. Scribner 2002 253p $23
   ISBN 0-7432-1548-6   LC 2002-17584

"Fleming Ford is the sometimes outrageous narrator, former belle from Alabama who finds herself pregnant and stranded in Southern California as her husband, the endearingly oafish Mac MacMoreland, works on a project to discover underground water that can be piped to Mexico for an enormous profit. Fleming has little interest in her husband's efforts and she seems mildly terrorized by the prospect of caring for her two toddler daughters, so she turns her attention to Mr. Lieberman, the reserved widower who once signed her paychecks when she worked for his New York newspaper." Publ Wkly

Lemann's "novel is full of her customary antic charm, but here she has come up with something more: a beautifully nuanced anti-'Lolita,' in which the object of desire, wandering around L.A. in a brocade dressing gown and alligator slippers, is the now vanished twentieth century." New Yorker

L'Engle, Madeleine, 1918-2007

Certain women. Farrar, Straus & Giroux 1992 351p
   ISBN 0-374-12025-0   LC 91-34048

In this novel, "terminally ill David Wheaton, a prominent and much-married American actor, obsessively recalls an unfinished play about King David, a role he coveted. L'Engle explores Christian faith, love, and the nature of God by framing the delayed-maturation story of Emma, Wheaton's daughter, within three subplots: the Wheaton family saga, the story of King David, and the history of the play's development. The characterizations of both Davids are compelling, but the primary interest here is the community of women which surrounds each man. L'Engle describes complex truths very simply. . . . Because she also details the emotional cost of discovering and accepting such concepts, many readers will find these observations memorable but never simplistic." Libr J

A live coal in the sea. Farrar, Straus & Giroux 1996 323p o.p.
           LC 96-4909

This "is a family drama centered around astronomy professor Camilla Dickinson. In . . . present and flashback story lines, we learn all about the skeletons in the family closet. When 18-year-old granddaughter Raffi asks Camilla why her father—Camilla's son Taxi, a soap opera star—claims she's not really her grandmother, the complicated true story starts to spill out. Camilla's young, pretty mother, Rose, cheated on her husband. Ca-

L'Engle, Madeleine, 1918-2007—*Continued*

milla's husband, Macarios Wanthakos, an Episcopal priest and son of a bishop, had his own dark family stories." Libr J

"The story is not always pretty; it involves desertion, infidelity, miscarriages, untimely death, a four-year-old torn from his parents, and an eight-year-old seeing his father sodomized. But neither is it explicit. In fact, in L'Engle's hands it is infused with the warmth of love and mercy. A complex, modern saga that is most of all genteel." Booklist

The love letters. Farrar, Straus & Giroux 1966 365p o.p.

A "counterpoint tale of two young women, three centuries apart in time, tormented by their experience of love, each needing to understand love in its deepest sense for her salvation. One is Mariana, long-ago Portuguese nun, won from her vow and soon deserted by a French soldier. The other is Charlotte Napier whose disintegrating marriage, built on an emotionally insecure childhood, has sent her in flight to Beja, Portugal. Learning about Mariana, lingering over her published letters, and pondering her fate, Charlotte comes to understand what love demands of her." Booklist

The other side of the sun. Farrar, Straus & Giroux 1971 344p o.p.

"Set in the post-bellum era, [this Gothic novel] chronicles the experiences of a 19-year-old English girl, Stella, who shortly after her marriage is sent alone to the South while her husband embarks on a secret . . . mission to Africa. . . . Through a brace of aging, eccentric relatives and some violent encounters with the blacks who inhabit the nearby scrub, she comes to know something of the Renier family. Her curiosity grows until it plunges her into a cauldron of racial strife. . . . [Woven into the plot are] richly drawn characters, the scars and guilt of the Civil War, and scattered bits of brilliant insight into the human condition." Libr J

A severed wasp. Farrar, Straus & Giroux 1982 388p o.p.   LC 82-15694

In this sequel to The small rain, "international pianist Katherine Vigneras settles into her comfortable brownstone on Greenwich Village's 10th Street . . . [expecting] a music-dominated retirement, peaceful and restorative. Instead, she becomes involved, through friendship with one of her tenents, a Jewish doctor stationed at nearby St. Vincent's Hospital, with the Episcopal community of the great Cathedral of St. John the Divine. . . . At the cathedral she finds connections with her own tortuous past through her music, her friendship with a retired bishop and with the young family of the cathedral's present dean." Publ Wkly

Lennon, J. Robert, 1970-

Castle; a novel. Graywolf Press 2009 229p $22
ISBN 978-1-55597-522-7; 1-55597-522-4
LC 2008-935603

"Eric Loesch returns to his hometown of Gerrysburg in upstate New York and sets out to renovate a secluded farmhouse. A strange bird, Eric is unpleasant and obviously burdened with secrets that, though unknown to the reader, seem to be known by the townsfolk. Childhood flashbacks fill in the gaps, and as the terrifying details of

his past coalesce, Eric remains loathe to face the truth about some horrific events." Publ Wkly

"Like two other powerful novels of recent years—James Lasdun's Horned Man and Peter Cameron's Andorra—Castle is told by an egomaniacal, unlikable man with a precarious grasp on reality, especially his own. . . . Castle tells a terrific story, dire and confusing and convincing." N Y Times Book Rev

Lennon, John Robert *See* Lennon, J. Robert, 1970-

Lent, Jeffrey

Lost nation. Atlantic Monthly Press 2002 370p $25
ISBN 0-87113-843-3   LC 2001-56495

"In 1838, a man called Blood opens a tavern and one-girl brothel in an ungoverned area on the New Hampshire—Canada border. His prostitute, Sally, is a teenager he won in a game of cards. While the territory is already home to a number of society's escapees, Blood's presence introduces a new volatility. Blood and Sally's relationship grows in unpredictable ways, the law threatens to descend, and Blood's secret past returns in a surprising manner. . . . The author has tremendous literary gifts: a fine ear for speech, a keen eye for period detail, the ability to craft a well-turned phrase and create rich interior lives for his characters." Booklist

Leon, Donna

About face. Atlantic Monthly Press 2009 278p $24
ISBN 978-0-8021-1896-7; 0-8021-1896-8
LC 2009-12211

This Commissario Brunetti mystery "delves deeply into Venice's (literal and figurative) pollution, navigating the choked canals as he tries to solve the murder of a truck driver." Publ Wkly

"It would be easy to punch holes in a contrived subplot, thick with symbolism, about a beautiful young woman whose face was ruined by cosmetic surgery. But who would want to, when Leon is being so generous with the humanizing details that make this series special? There are long walks in Brunetti's warm company and lively talks with his clever wife and even more engaging father-inlaw. . . . As detective work goes, it's a tiny masterpiece of analysis." N Y Times Book Rev

Doctored evidence; Donna Leon. Atlantic Monthly Press 2004 245p $22
ISBN 0-87113-918-5   LC 2003-63941

"The crime at first seems an open-and-shut case: a Romanian housekeeper, accused of brutally murdering her miserly, elderly Venetian employer, is killed while fleeing the police. But when a neighbor steps forward to clear the housekeeper's name, Commissario Guido Brunetti seeks to find the real killer, especially when he learns that the original officer on the case is his enemy, the malevolent Lieutenant Scarpa." Libr J

"The detective's humane police work is disarming, and his ambles through the city are a delight; but it is this peculiar insistence on turning every case into a morality tale that gives Leon's fiction its subtlety and substance and makes us follow Brunetti wherever we must even into the sea." N Y Times Book Rev

Leon, Donna—*Continued*

The girl of his dreams. Atlantic Monthly Press 2008 276p $24

ISBN 978-0-87113-980-1; 0-87113-980-4

"Political reality prevails over justice, and a child's death goes unpunished despite the best efforts of Commissario Guido Brunetti in Leon's . . . Venetian mystery. When 11-year-old Ariana Rocich drowns in a canal and goes unidentified for days, she begins to haunt Brunetti's dreams. But Ariana is a Rom, or gypsy, found with stolen jewelry items secreted in and on her person, a discovery that makes Brunetti's investigation particularly sensitive in the face of new departmental directives regarding multicultural issues. The book opens with the funeral of Brunetti's mother before segueing into a subplot about a religious charlatan; so religion, as well as politics, becomes a topic around the family table for Brunetti, wife Paola, daughter Chiara, and son Raffi." Libr J

Uniform justice. Atlantic Monthly Press 2003 259p $24

ISBN 0-87113-903-0   LC 2003-44326

In this Guido Brunetti mystery "the Venetian police detective and family man is summoned to the exclusive San Martino Military Academy, where Cadet Ernesto Moro has been found dead, hanging in the lavatory." Publ Wkly

"As a thinking man, Brunetti reads Cicero for moral direction, looks to his wife for doses of cynical realism and humbly consults his secretary, the terrifyingly efficient Signorina Elettra, on practical matters. But it is as a man of sensibility that this endearing detective most engages us." N Y Times Book Rev

Leonard, Elmore, 1925-

Bandits. Arbor House 1987 345p o.p.

LC 86-14104

"Ex-con Jack Delaney, a former hotel burglar turned mortician's assistant, finds his 'window of opportunity' in the form of a Calvin Klein-clad ex-nun, Lucy Nichols, who enlists his help in a plot to steal five million dollars from Colonel Dagoberto Godoy, a Nicaraguan contra visiting New Orleans to raise money. Jack, Lucy, and two other ex-cons form a motley crew of bandits, each with a different set of motives and illusions." Booklist

"At its heart, the novel is about taking sides, the politically charged background of Contra aid used as one more tool to pull the reader in and out of the moral quicksand. Leonard is no Graham Greene, but the ethical issues called into play here give the novel depth and immediacy. This, then, is not just another gritty adventure novel; it's a top-notch thriller with a real moral resonance." Publ Wkly

Be cool. Delacorte Press 1999 292p

ISBN 0-385-33391-9

* LC 98-36601

Sequel to Get Shorty

"Ex-loan-shark-turned-movie-producer Chili Palmer needs a new hit. *Get Lost*, the sequel to his successful first film *Get Leo*, tanked at the box office. . . . Despite being pursued by several assassins (he promises one a screen test), the always unflappable Chili uses his own life to develop his movie, manipulating the people he meets and staging events to see how they would fit in a screenplay." Libr J

"Aside from the wit, the fun and the colorful figures that populate Elmore Leonard's novels, the real magic of his work is in the language. . . . This is Elmore Leonard at his best, the sweeping synaptic prose effortlessly echoing the argot of the gutter." N Y Times Book Rev

Cat chaser. Arbor House 1982 283p

ISBN 0-87795-398-8   LC 81-71687

"Ex-Marine George Moran intends to lead a quiet life at his Florida motel, but then he falls in love with the American wife of exiled Dominican General Andres de Boya. After a visit to the Dominican Republic, he's pestered by con men and private eyes, getting caught in the crossfire between them and de Boya, and it's hard to tell which is more dangerous." Libr J

This "is a tidy little thriller with sufficient twists and turns (not to mention sex and violence) to keep you intrigued and entertained. The characters are well drawn, the plotting is complicated but clear, and the suspense is strong without being too painful." Best Sellers

The complete Western stories of Elmore Leonard. William Morrow 2004 528p $27.95

ISBN 0-06-072425-0

* LC 2004-55969

Contents: Trail of the Apache; Apache medicine; You never see Apaches . . .; Red hell hits Canyon Diablo; The colonel's lady; Law of the hunted ones; Calvary boots; Under the friar's ledge; The rustlers; Three-ten to Yuma; The big hunt; Long night; The boy who smiled; The hard way; The last shot; Blood money; Trouble at Rindo's station; Saint with a six-gun; The captives; No man's guns; The rancher's lady; Jugged; Moment of vengeance; Man with the iron arm; The longest day of his life; The nagual; The kid; Only good ones; The Tonto woman; "Hurrah for Captain Early!"

Elmore Leonard's Dutch treat: 3 novels; introduction by George F. Will. Arbor House 1985 568p o.p.

LC 85-11246

An omnibus edition of three of the author's mid-1970s novels

Contents: Mr. Majestyk (1974); Swag (1976); The hunted (1977)

In "*Mr. Majestyk*, a California melon grower, is set upon by professional killers but manages to turn his predators into prey. In *Swag*, originally called *Ryan's Rules*, two small-time Detroit thieves prosper until they go for bigger loot. Riveting though these two tales are, they will strike readers as mere curtain raisers for *The Hunted*. Set in Israel, it focuses on the perilous state of Al Rosen, an American who receives large sums of money regularly from his lawyer in Detroit. When news of Rosen's whereabouts gets back to his home city, a gang of paid hoods jets to Tel Aviv and goes gunning for him. Sgt. Davis of the U.S. Marines, perceiving their lethal intentions, drives Rosen to a desolate spot in hopes of getting the drop on the pursuers. The climax to this story is a stunning, unforgettable surprise." Publ Wkly

Freaky Deaky. Arbor House 1988 341p o.p.

LC 87-19466

"Soon after Chris Mankowski—lately transferred from the bomb squad to sex crimes—visits rich, mindless alcoholic Woody Ricks on a rape complaint, someone

Leonard, Elmore, 1925-—*Continued*

blows up Woody's limousine—along with Woody's brother Mark. Ghosts from their student activist past have returned to haunt them. One ex-Panther even now takes care of Woody, and two ex-demonstrators hope to extort cash." Libr J

Leonard "excels here with his trademark menace and his deadpan, throwaway humor. His superlative ear for the vernacular makes all the characters spring to life; Woody, 'always in low with his dims on,' is a brilliant creation." Publ Wkly

Get Shorty. Delacorte Press 1990 292p o.p.
* LC 89-25816

When Chili Palmer, a Miami extortionist, "agrees to help a fellow mobster track down a movie producer trying to evade his Las Vagas debts, a new world of opportunities opens up before him." Quill Quire

"Leonard's strongest books make you stand up and sit down a lot during their tight moments, but 'Get Shorty,' despite its occasional white-knuckle passages, belongs to that vast vinegary canon known as the Hollywood novel. . . . Best of all is the portrait Leonard gives us of a seven-million-dollar-a-picture star named Michael Weir." New Yorker

Followed by Be cool

Glitz. Arbor House 1985 228p o.p.
LC 84-16794

This novel is "set in the high-roller world of casino gambling, alternating between Puerto Rico and Atlantic City. Miami cop Vincent Mora is on medical leave in San Juan when two seemingly unrelated events conspire to end his vacation: a paroled rapist who Mora arrested turns up bent on revenge, and a Puerto Rican girl employed by an Atlantic City casino owner turns up dead." Booklist

"There is a steady flow of intrigue and action set just outside the law in a world both dirty and glamorous. Several characters develop into complex personalities, but Mora is never quite clear." Libr J

The hot kid. William Morrow 2005 312p $25.95
ISBN 00-6072422-6

"The Hot Kid is part-Cuban, part-Indian Carlos Webster, who inadvertently gets his start in law enforcement at age 15 when he shoots a cattle thief. The investigating U.S. marshal thinks Carlos has potential and tells the kid to give him a call in five or six years. Carlos does and becomes Carl, though the next guy he shoots is a bank robber who once called him a 'greaser.' Carl Webster thrills the public with his soon-to-be signature line, 'If I have to pull my weapon I'll shoot to kill.' He's so cool he doesn't even know he's saying it—or does he? This Dust Bowl-era Okie ambler captures the era of Pretty Boy Floyd, Bonnie and Clyde, and John Dillinger with a slow-simmering feud between Webster and Jack Belmont, a pea-brained oil scion who wants to be a most-wanted outlaw. Trailing them both is Tony Antonelli, a journalist with a knack for turning gunfights into heroic battles." Booklist

"Where so much of Leonard's recent fiction has a sharp, almost hyperrealistic quality, 'The Hot Kid' is noirish and even a little pulpy at times, in the fashion of 30's movies and detective magazines. . . . Tony Antonelli isn't a portrait of the artist as young man, exactly, but rather a fond wink at the tradition of potboilers

and genre writing that gave rise to Leonard himself and from which, for all his success, he has never cut himself off." N Y Times Book Rev

The hunted
In Leonard, E. Elmore Leonard's Dutch treat: 3 novels

Killshot. Arbor House 1989 287p o.p.
* LC 88-31532

"When a professional hit man gets in on a shakedown planned by a psychotic killer, the luck that's kept him alive for 50 years starts running out. Trying to make the score, they run into not the realtor they'd targeted, but Carmen Colson and her ironworker husband, Wayne, who rough them up and run them off. The thugs decide to kill the couple, but that's not easily done. Electing protection by the Federal Witness Security Program, the Colsons have no picnic, either. The cops treat them like dirt, the home they're given by the program is a dump, and the deputy marshal guarding them puts the make on Carmen." Booklist

"Mr. Leonard has either done his homework or he's been there—up on the high beams in Detroit, on the Mississippi towing barges from Baton Rouge to Hickman, Ky., looking into the flat stare of an irritated cop, and somehow, improbably, inside the head of a woman who has had it with being treated like 'the wife.' 'Killshot' is pure, distilled, vintage Leonard." N Y Times Book Rev

LaBrava. Arbor House 1983 283p
ISBN 0-87795-527-1   LC 83-72676

"The time is now; the scene, Miami's South Beach area. Joe LaBrava is a former Secret Service agent turned freelance photographer. A friend of his has been taking care of Jean Shaw, a middle-aged beauty who was once a movie actress. LaBrava fell in love with Jean's image when he was 12. She played the spider-woman role: she enticed second leads to their deaths and never married the hero. Now in real life the predator may be cast as the victim: a psychotic extortionist and his creepy Cuban sidekick are looking for her. Jean receives a crudely typed note demanding that she pay $600,000 for the privilege of remaining alive." Newsweek

"What makes the author's work memorable is his uncompromisingly direct prose, his affectionately crafted yet very real characters, and, of course, the fact that Leonard knows that providing entertainment is the novelist's first commandment. Nobody brings the illogic of crime and criminals to life better." Christ Sci Monit

Maximum Bob. Delacorte Press 1991 295p
ISBN 0-385-30142-1   LC 91-6539

"Maximum Bob is a Florida judge famous for his tough sentencing and, among women who have to work with him, as a fairly crude lecher. Parole officer Kathy Diaz Baker is the book's protagonist, though. For a slight violation, her parolee Dale Crowe Junior gets one of Bob's stiff sentences, by which he's not too pleased. Moreover, Dale's uncle Elvin, just out after doing 10 years from Bob on a murder conviction, conceivably could be nursing a grudge. What's more, Elvin hooks up with rich Dr. Tommy Vasco, who's under house arrest for illegal drugs—a sentence given him by guess who. When a live and lively alligator shows up in the judge's backyard, swallowing his wife's dog and scaring its owner clean out of town, and then when shots are fired

Leonard, Elmore, 1925-—*Continued*
through hizzoner's windows, Kathy gets suspicious and suspiciouser. Leonard's trademark toughness, grit, and sleaze are on every page." Booklist

Mr. Majestyk

In Leonard, E. Elmore Leonard's Dutch treat: 3 novels

Mr. Paradise. Morrow 2004 291p $25.95
ISBN 0-06-008395-6   LC 2003-64867
"Roommates Kelly and Chloe are enjoying their lives and their downtown Detroit loft just fine. Kelly is a Victoria Secret catalog model. Chloe is an escort, until she decides to ditch her varied clientele in favor of a steady gig as girlfriend to eighty-four-year-old retired lawyer Tony Paradiso, a.k.a. Mr. Paradise. Evenings at Mr. Paradise's house, there's always an old Michigan football game on TV. And when Chloe's around, there's a cheerleader, too, complete with pleated skirt and blue-and-gold pompoms. One night Chloe convinces Kelly to join in the fun, along with Montez Taylor, Tony's smooth-talking right-hand man. But things go awry." Publisher's note
"Leonard addresses those who think they hear the same music he does, but who are open to questioning the familiar, to listening carefully and seeing when something has a different emphasis. . . . 'Mr. Paradise' is about deception. People deceive through false identity (appropriating, dissembling), just as they, themselves, have been deceived whether by the implied promise of collapsed dot-coms or by positive, false assumptions about family." N Y Times Book Rev

Out of sight. Delacorte Press 1996 296p o.p.
                              LC 96-8030
"U.S. Marshall Karen Sisco, 29, wearing a $3500 Chanel suit, meets escaping con, bank robber Jack Foley, 47, and can't get him out of her mind. The attraction is mutual, and as their paths diverge and converge, the Leonard-ian plot predictably gets more convoluted and the characters more bizarre. Foley and Co.'s hit on the house of an ex-junk bond trader who reportedly has a million stashed away there brings the star-crossed lovers together once more." Libr J
"A few stitches in the plot don't quite mesh, like the big part played by Foley's ex-wife, a magician's assistant. But even the finest silk suit can develop an errant thread, and this one, as sexy and well-tapered as Leonard's two new principals, will fit the author's fans just right." Publ Wkly

Pagan babies. Delacorte Press 2000 263p
ISBN 0-385-33392-7   LC 00-29506
"Father Terry Dunn, an American priest working in Rwanda, is forced to return to the United States after exacting penance from a group of local Hutu murderers. Upon returning to Detroit, ostensibly to raise money for African orphans, he becomes involved with Debbie, a recently released ex-convict hoping to strike it rich as a stand-up comedian. A plan for both Terry and Debbie to attain the riches they desire soon gives way to a mix of deceit and false loyalties." Libr J
This "is one of Mr. Leonard's funniest books, with a typically colourful cast of oddballs. The dialogue, too, is snappy. . . . Mr. Leonard steers the reader effortlessly through a maze of plots and counterplots, then brings the whole thing in with a bravura flourish and stops on a dime." Economist

Pronto. Delacorte Press 1993 265p
ISBN 0-385-30846-9   LC 93-2999
This novel "tracks the misadventures of Harry Arno, a small-time operator who runs a sports book for the Miami syndicate. Federal investigators try to pressure him to rat on his boss, Jimmy Cap, by planting a rumor that he is skimming. As, of course, he is. Squeezed by both sides, Harry takes his nest egg and flees to Rapallo, a harbor town on the Italian Riviera." N Y Times Book Rev
"Leonard's spare language and propulsive plotting still leave room for expositions of Sicilian slang, gamblers' lingo and Ezra Pound's private life. His colorful characters work together splendidly." Publ Wkly

Riding the rap. Delacorte Press 1995 294p
ISBN 0-385-30847-7   LC 94-38211
Two characters from Leonard's novel, Pronto, appear in this story set in Florida's Palm Beach. They are Harry Arno, a mob-connected bookie, and US Marshal Raylan Givens. As the book opens, Harry is "drinking too much Absolut vodka and making the mistake of hiring Puerto Rican tough guy Bobby Deo to collect 16.5K from a deadbeat who hasn't paid his sports bets. When the deadbeat and his cronie, a Bahamanian con man named Louis Lewis, join forces with Bobby Deo to abduct Harry, . . . Raylan gives chase with the help of a slightly bent fortune teller." Booklist
"Leonard's brilliance consists in having matched his style to his subject perfectly. These are not characters who would bloom into life in the hands of a more sophisticated writer. They are complete, because they are shallow." Commonweal

Road dogs. William Morrow 2009 262p $26.99
ISBN 0-06-173314-8; 978-0-06-173314-7
                              LC 2008-39607
"Road dogs are prison buddies who watch each other's backs. Jack Foley and Cundo Rey are trying to maintain that loyalty after they get out and start anew in Venice, CA, where Rey's girl Dawn Navarro awaits. Leonard . . . . brings back old favorites Foley and Rey, Dawn, and Karen Sisco—smart, sexy women and clever con artists, a mix the author knows well. Foley is being dogged by a rogue FBI agent who's convinced the infamous gentleman bank robber will strike again, and Rey's financial partner, Little Jimmy, is secretly in love with Dawn. The grifters' game of moving parts is quietly intriguing." Libr J

Rum punch. Delacorte Press 1992 297p
ISBN 0-385-30143-X   LC 91-38738
"A combination of coincidence and choice connects the fates of Jackie Burke, a 44-year-old, thrice-married stewardess, bail bondsman Max Cherry, overweight and in his 50s, and brash young gun dealer Ordell Robbie, in Miami. When Jackie is caught bringing cash into the U.S. from the Bahamas for Ordell, she agrees to cooperate with federal and state agents to catch him in a sting operation. Max, who has posted Jackie's bond and is drawn to her, becomes her sounding board as she contemplates a sting of her own." Publ Wkly
"Mr. Leonard never tells you; he shows you. The story is all action, a scam within a scam. . . . His style is the absence of style, stripped of fancy baggage . . . the absence, as far as it's possible, of an authorial ego." NY Times Book Rev

Leonard, Elmore, 1925——*Continued*

Split images. Arbor House 1982 282p o.p.

LC 81-67524

"When millionaire Robbie Daniels hires a trigger-happy cop as bodyguard, reporter Angela Nolan, who's been doing a story on Daniels, becomes worried. Daniels has killed people—supposedly by accident and in self-defense— and seems to be getting a taste for it. She and policeman Bryan Hurd find themselves in a deadly race to thwart Daniels' plans, which include video taping his killings. This is a fast-paced suspense novel with interesting characters and a warm-hearted romance between Hurd and Nolan." Libr J

Stick. Arbor House 1983 304p

ISBN 0-87795-436-4   LC 82-72073

"After seven years in a Michigan prison for armed robbery, Ernest Stickley, Jr. heads for Florida and gets together with a friend who served a three-four year sentence at the same prison for possession with intent to deliver. Stick is soon in the center of Miami's underworld of big money and illegal drugs. He barely escapes from the scene of a slaying, which is more of a human sacrifice than a murder. Soon a couple of drug-pushing czars and their goons are on his trail. But Stick is not exactly hiding, and his trail leads across yachts, through mansions, and to a country club gala." Best Sellers

"Despite his violence, Stick is likeable, and the scam he pulls on the drug dealers has the reader firmly on his side. Escapist but not shallow." Libr J

Swag

In Leonard, E. Elmore Leonard's Dutch treat: 3 novels

Tishomingo blues; a novel. Morrow 2002 308p

ISBN 0-06-000872-5   LC 2001-44405

Dennis Lenahan, an itinerant high diver setting up for a Mississippi casino show, watches a Dixie drug-ring murder from his eighty-foot diving platform. Various factions-a smooth-talking Detroit con man, a mob-backed explosives expert, redneck crank dealers, local police on either side of the law-try to badger or buy his silence or cooperation, but Lenahan stays cool and uncommitted, until a 'Shane'-like showdown at a local Civil War re-enactment. Lenahan's composure and his easy acrobatics feel like a stand-in for the author's; both seem to play it by ear even after the guns start firing. And the hurtling plot twists keep coming, right up to the perfect rip of a finish." New Yorker

Touch. Arbor House 1987 245p o.p.

LC 87-12624

"Charlie Lawson once served as Brother Juvenal in a Catholic order; now he cares for alcoholics in a Detroit hospice. Charlie/Juvenal cures those he touches through miracles manifested by the Stigmata, the wounds of Christ that appear on Charlie's body. The phenomenon lures a flashy promoter, Bill Hill, aiming to get rich by exploiting the reclusive, gentle man who is also the intended prey of rabid right-winger August Murray." Publ Wkly

"The hard-as-nails-and-twice-as-real dialogue and sharp characterizations make this weird nonviolent thriller . . . as absorbing as Leonard's usual, more menacing fare." Booklist

Up in Honey's room. William Morrow 2007 292p $25.95

ISBN 978-0-06-072424-5; 0-06-072424-2

LC 2006-47080

The protagonist of this novel is Carl Webster, "the mythic marshal who starred in The Hot Kid (2005). It's the waning months of World War II, and Carl, no longer on the trail of Dust Bowl bank robbers, is tracking down a couple of escaped German POWs. The trail leads to Detroit, where it appears the POWs, Jurgen and Otto, are being hidden by a German-born butcher, Walter Shoen, who just happens to look exactly like Heinrich Himmler. Also involved are Walter's ex-wife, Honey Deal, who has no time for a bunch of Nazis who don't laugh at her jokes, and Vera Mezwa, a real-life German spy with a taste for the finer things, including her houseboy, the faux transvestite Bohdan." Booklist

"There's violence eventually—nicely done, of course—but while it's crucial, it's not central. The pleasure of the tale comes from the telling of it. Leonard would probably think the comparison pretentious, but the way in which the voices of the characters and the threads of narrative are introduced and interwoven reminds one of nothing so much as a well-crafted fugue with its subject, countersubject, episodes, false entries, and stretto (where everything can seem to be happening at once). Most of the story unfolds in dialogue, but even the third-person narrative has a pungent drawl to it, which makes the transition from one to another seamless." PopMatters

When the women come out to dance, and other stories. Morrow 2003 228p $24.95

ISBN 0-06-008397-2   LC 2002-26426

Contents: Sparks; Hanging out at the Buena Vista; Chickasaw Charlie Hoke; When the woman come out to dance; Fire in the hole; Karen makes out; Hurrah for Capt. Early; The Tonto woman; Tenkiller

"Reading the clipped, unfailingly accurate dialogue that comes out of the mouths of Leonard's characters can make you feel as if you're in the presence of a writer who is both ventriloquist and psychic. It's not just that Leonard captures the cadences and elisions of each character's speech, it's that he has an uncanny sense of knowing what each will say next." N Y Times Book Rev

Lepore, Jill, 1966-

(jt. auth) Kamensky, J. Blindspot

Leroy, Margaret

Postcards from Berlin; a novel. Little, Brown 2003 391p $22.95

ISBN 0-316-73813-1   LC 2003-40069

"On the surface, Catriona (Cat) Lydgate enjoys a contented, middle-class life with a devoted husband, two lovely daughters, an elegant home, and a room to call her own: an attic where she dabbles at art. Things begin to unwind when Daisy, her younger daughter, comes down with the flu, which develops into a mysterious, malingering illness that causes her to stop eating and leaves her lethargic and achy. As specialist after specialist can find no physical explanation for the illness, they begin to suspect psychological causes." Libr J

"The resolution of Leroy's novel has a fairy-tale aspect, but fairy tales can nevertheless be very absorbing.

Leroy, Margaret—*Continued*

Despite the occasional straining of her plot, Leroy succeeded in making me care about these characters; even at my most incredulous." N Y Times Book Rev

Lescroart, John T.

The first law; a novel; by John Lescroart. Dutton 2003 403p $25.95

ISBN 0-525-94705-1   LC 2002-37902

"The popular lawyer-cop team of Dismas 'Diz' Hardy (lawyer) and Abe Glitzky (cop) returns for another episode of legal maneuvering on the streets of San Francisco. The bullet wound sustained by Abe in Lescroart's last adventure. . . confines him to a desk job, so he's no help to Diz when he goes up against the Patrol Special, a private-enterprise neighborhood security system supervised by the SFPD. It seems that Diz's good friend, John Holliday, a bar owner in one of the patrolled areas, is fingered as a murder suspect; however, John contends the corrupt beat 'cops' framed him. . . . Lescroart's expert crafting turns this legal thriller into quite a wild ride." Booklist

Guilt; [by] John Lescroart. Delacorte Press 1997 462p

ISBN 0-385-31655-0   LC 96-43756

"Mark Dooher, head of a high-powered San Francisco law firm, pushing 50 and tired of his alcoholic wife, is smitten with beautiful law student Christina Carrera. He begins a subtle campaign to woo her, revealing himself to readers . . . as manipulative, but believably so. When Dooher's wife is murdered in an apparent burglary, SFPD detective Abe Glitsky finds enough odd clues to press for a murder charge against Dooher. With Dooher's best friend, Wes Farrell, leading the defense (with Christina as second chair), the cold-blooded attorney takes on the police, the court and various hostile witnesses." Publ Wkly

"Lescroart effectively dramatizes the many moral dilemmas that emerge in this case, not the least of which is posed by the role of the Catholic Church." Booklist

The hearing; [by] John Lescroart. Dutton 2001 451p $25.95

ISBN 0-525-94575-X   LC 00-34119

In this legal thriller "attorney Dismas Hardy not only defends confessed murderer Cole Burgess but is forced to confront the fallibility of his friend, Abe Glitsky, chief of the San Francis Police Department's homicide division. Burgess, a heroin addict, is found near the lifeless body of a prominent female attorney, unable to remember the events that brought him there. Lescroart tantalizes readers with a tightly constructed plot in which Hardy and Glitsky track crime and political corruption to an unexpected source." Libr J

The mercy rule; a novel; by John Lescroart. Delacorte Press 1998 466p

ISBN 0-385-31658-5   LC 98-16726

In this "legal thriller, attorney Dismas Hardy agrees to defend his friend Graham Russo, accused of murdering his own father. Sal Russo, suffering from Alzheimer's disease and an inoperable brain tumor, is losing his capacity to take care of himself and is beginning to experience severe pain, making no secret of his plan to inject himself with morphine and eventually use the drug to

end his suffering. When Sal is found dead of an overdose, his apartment in disarray, and $50,000 missing, the police suspect that his death was not a suicide." Libr J

"Lescroart has the technical clues of the plot perfectly arranged, locking in the attention of mystery mavens until the connections are revealed, but it's his credible characters who cement this entertaining front-rank whodunit." Booklist

Nothing but the truth; [by] John Lescroart. Delacorte Press 1999 435p

ISBN 0-385-33353-6   LC 99-32584

"San Francisco lawyer Dismas Hardy has 72 hours to solve a murder that happened three weeks ago. Time is crucial because his wife, Frannie, has been jailed for contempt after refusing to reveal a secret (confided to her by her friend Ron Beaumont) to the grand jury investigating the murder of Beaumont's wife, Bree." Publ Wkly

"Lescroart orchestrates a cadre of multidimensional characters through a plot full of political subterfuge and action without losing track of the subtlety of modern personal relationships." Libr J

The oath; [by] John Lescroart. Dutton 2002 408p

ISBN 0-525-94576-8   LC 2001-47055

San Franciso attorney Dismas Hardy "finds himself representing Dr. Eric Kensing, who stands accused of murdering his boss, Tim Markham, the CEO of the Parnassus Medical Group, a struggling HMO providing health services to all the city's employees. An autopsy shows that Markham, hospitalized in critical condition following a hit-and-run, died not of his injuries but of a potassium overdose. . . . The author wisely steers clear of taking cheap shots at the HMO industry, yet manages to direct a sharp beam into some of its darker crevices." Publ Wkly

The second chair; [by] John Lescroart. Dutton 2004 390p $25.95

ISBN 0-525-94775-2   LC 2003-19782

An installment in the "San Francisco legal/detective series featuring lawyer Dismas Hardy and police detective Abe Glitzky. Amy Wu, a young attorney in the law firm now headed by Dismas, has a high-profile client in Andrew Bartlett, a high school student accused of shooting his girlfriend and drama coach. The evidence against Andrew is extremely damning, and Amy arranges a plea-bargain whereby Andrew would agree to admit guilt in exchange for the case remaining in the juvenile justice system. She's forced to antagonize the court and the district attorney, however, by reneging on the deal when Andrew continues to claim his innocence. Dismas appoints himself to the case as 'second chair' to salvage the reputation of his firm, just as it seems that Andrew might not be guilty after all." Libr J

Leshem, Ron

Beaufort; translated from the Hebrew by Evan Fallenberg. Delacorte Press 2008 360p $24

ISBN 978-0-553-80682-3   LC 2007-30292

Original Hebrew edition, 2006

"In order to limit Hezbollah's attacks on Israeli settlements, Israel maintained a security force in southern Lebanon for close to 20 years. Leshem's . . . novel chronicles the lives of the last group of Israeli soldiers

Leshem, Ron—_Continued_

to man the outpost at Beaufort, a crusader-castle ruin of questionable military significance. Written as the diary of Liraz 'Erez' Liberti, the hotheaded twentysomething leader of a 13-man commando unit stationed in an outpost prior to the Israeli withdrawal in 2000, the novel brings to life the situation of very young men on a dangerous mission. This is a picture of war from a soldier's point of view. Its language is crude, the body count rises, and yet the tenderness of the bonds among the men is extraordinary." Libr J

Lessing, Doris May, 1919-

African stories; [by] Doris Lessing. Simon & Schuster 1965 636p o.p.
Contents: The black Madonna; The trinket box; The pig; Traitors; The old Chief Mshlanga; A sunrise on the veld; No witchcraft for sale; The second hut; The nuisance; The De Wets come to Kloof Grange; Little Tembi; Old John's place; "Leopard" George; Winter in July; A home for the highland cattle; Eldorado; The antheap; Hunger; The words he said; Lucy Grange; A mild attack of locusts; Flavours of exile; Getting off the altitude; A road to the big city; Flight; Plants and girls; The sun between their feet; A letter from home; The new man; The story of two dogs
A collection of "tales which taken together reflect myriad aspects of African existence. Vivid personality delineation, narrative integrity, and artistry dominate each story whatever its subject or theme." Booklist

Ben, in the world; the sequel to The fifth child; [by] Doris Lessing. HarperCollins Pubs. 2000 178p
ISBN 0-06-019628-9   LC 99-89804
Ben Lovatt's "abnormal appearance and strength distinguishes him from other people. Rejected by his older siblings, he is now homeless in London. He has been fed and sheltered by the sickly Mrs. Biggs, but when she enters the hospital, Ben ends up staying with a prostitute named Rita. Rita's boyfriend enlists Ben's unknowing assistance to transport drugs to Paris, where he meets Alex and is taken to Brazil to make a movie. There, Ben meets a scientist who wants to run genetic tests on him. Ben is treated inhumanely but is excited when he hears that he may meet more people like himself." Libr J
"Lessing's unsentimental yet excruciating moral fable forces us to accept the Lovatts' dilemma as our own." New Yorker

Children of violence; [by] Doris Lessing. v1-5 o.p.
v1-4 published by Simon & Schuster; v5 published 1969 by Knopf with title: The four-gated city
Contents: v1 Martha Quest (1964; United Kingdom edition 1952); v2 A proper marriage (1964; United Kingdom edition 1954); v3 A ripple from the storm (1966; United Kingdom edition 1958); v4 Landlocked (1966; United Kingdom edition 1965); v5 The four-gated city (1969)
This "is an account of the life of Martha Quest and of her search for self-definition, which for her is to be achieved through total commitment to a person or a cause. We follow her from her beginnings as a wayward but intelligent child on a Rhodesian farm, through two unsuccessful marriages and active involvement in the Communist party in Salisbury during World War II. Af-

ter the war Martha goes to London and becomes an increasingly disenchanted observer of London life and behavior in the 1950s; the last volume of the sequence anticipates an apocalyptic, science-fiction future, as Martha dies in a devastated, radioactive world at the end of the twentieth century." Wakeman. World Authors, 1950-1970

The fifth child; [by] Doris Lessing. Knopf 1988 133p
ISBN 0-394-57105-3
                                              * LC 88-2680
"Mildly eccentric English couple Harriet and David Lovatt are the contented parents of four healthy children. Suddenly, their peace is forever shattered by their fifth child, Ben, a fiercely malevolent goblin-child with a penchant for violence. . . . Only Harriet tries to civilize the boy, and he gradually learns to function on a primitive level and even collects a band of similar outcasts about him. Unwanted, they leave their homes to wander England." Libr J
"Acting as a social moralist, Lessing exposes the division between the warm and comfortable domestic scene and the harsh reality of the outside world, piercing the boundary between the two as human desires clash with a more brutal vision of existence. A psychologically probing and emotionally powerful performance." Booklist
Followed by Ben, in the world

The four-gated city
_In_ Lessing, D. M. Children of violence

The golden notebook; [by] Doris Lessing. Simon & Schuster 1962 567p o.p.
                                                          *
"Regarded as one of the key texts of the Women's movement of the 1960s, it opens in London in 1957 with a section ironically entitled 'Free Women', a realistic account of a conversation between two old friends, writer Anna Wulf, mother of Janet, and Molly, divorced from Richard, and mother of disturbed son Tommy, who will later attempt suicide. The novel then fragments into the four sections of Anna's 'Notebooks.' . . . This pattern of five non chronological overlapping sections is repeated four times, as it tracks both the past and the present, and although one of Lessing's concerns is to expose the dangers of fragmentation, she also builds up through pastiche and parody, and through many refractions and mergings, a remarkably coherent and detailed account of her protagonists and the world they inhabit." Oxford Companion to Engl Lit. 6th edition

The good terrorist; {by} Doris Lessing. Knopf 1985 375p o.p.   LC 85-40214
"Alice Mellings is the 'good' terrorist, a sort of house mother for a group of London radicals who take over an abandoned and badly vandalized house as communal home and headquarters. Picketing with trade unionists and spray-painting bridges with slogans protesting vivisection, chemicals in food, Trident, and sexism, these smalltime revolutionaries get involved in something big, and very dangerous, as the story progresses. Alice, whose contempt for her mother's middle-class values informs her rebellion, winds up just like her mother, decorating the squatters' squalid home and cooking for her comrades. [This is] a novel about home, family, and revolt." Libr J
"Unsparingly, fiercely, often satirically, Lessing is

Lessing, Doris May, 1919——*Continued*
writing a narrative about death: the death of the heart when ideology tyrannizes over just, kindly human relations, abstractions over common sense." Ms

The grass is singing; [by]Doris Lessing. Crowell 1950 245p o.p.
The novel begins with the newspaper notice of the death of Mary Turner, wife of an unsuccessful South African farmer. There seems to be some reluctance among the other whites about discussing the case. The author then turns back to the story of Mary Turner's life, showing her gradual disintegration as a person, and ending with her murder by a Kaffir houseboy
This novel "besides being very well-written is an extremely mature psychological study. It is full of those terrifying touches of truth, seldom mentioned but instantly recognized. By any standards, this book shows remarkable powers and imagination." New Statesman (1913)

Landlocked
In Lessing, D. M. Children of violence

Love, again; a novel; {by} Doris Lessing. HarperCollins Pubs. 1996 352p o.p.
LC 95-53317
"Sarah Durham was widowed young; now in her mid-60s, she is manager of and playwright for a London fringe theater group. A production of a play based on the journals and music of a 19th-century quadroon from Martinique, Julie Vairon, inflames Sarah's dormant sexual impulses. And she is not the only one: all of the actors, the director and a rich patron, Stephen Ellington-Smith, are also sublimely seduced by Julie's words, music and the few portraits of her that survive. . . . Although the book is long and rambling, asking much of a reader's patience and willingness to spend so much time inside Sarah's head, Lessing, wields a formidable analytic intelligence that makes this work provocative and often astonishingly beautiful." Publ Wkly

Mara and Dann; an adventure; [by] Doris Lessing. HarperFlamingo 1999 407p
ISBN 0-06-018294-6   LC 98-30782
"In this futuristic novel, in Ifrik, a land savaged by war and environmental disaster, seven-year-old Mara and her little brother Dann are snatched from their home and severed from their pasts. The children grow up literally on the run, made to fight for their enemies one moment and left to starve the next. But their love for each other remains as fierce as their surroundings are terrifying, and it transfigures their brutal trials. On the surface a grand adventure, this novel at its heart makes a fascinating argument for the force of affection and the power of the questioning mind." New Yorker

Martha Quest
In Lessing, D. M. Children of violence

The memoirs of a survivor; [by] Doris Lessing. Knopf 1975 c1974 213p o.p.
*
First published 1974 in the United Kingdom
This "novel is a projection into the near future when technological structures have broken down and society is forging new patterns among the chaos. [The] speaker, never named, lives through progressive disorientation in an English city, (also never named) where bands of children terrorize those people who haven't left yet. As her everyday life becomes more and more survival-bound, she fashions an imaginary world beyond her living room wall. When [Emily], a young girl, comes into her care, she is forced to see her emerging strength and womanhood as the hope of an uncertain future." Libr J
This is "an extraordinary and compelling meditation about the enduring need for loyalty, love and responsibility in an unprecedented time that places unbearable demands upon people." Time

The other woman
In Lessing, D. M. Stories p157-211

A proper marriage
In Lessing, D. M. Children of violence

A ripple from the storm
In Lessing, D. M. Children of violence

Shikasta; re: colonised planet 5; personal, psychological, historical documents relating to visit by Johor (George Sherban) emissary (grade 9) 87th of the period of the last days; [by] Doris Lessing. Knopf 1979 364p (Canopus in Argos: archives) o.p.
* LC 79-11295
"First of the Canopus in Argos: Archives five-volume series. Shikasta is Earth, whose history—extending over millions of years—is here put into the cosmic perspective, observed by Canopeans who seem to be in charge of galactic history although responsible to some higher, impersonal authority. The sequels follow the exploits of various human cultures whose affairs are subtly influenced by the Canopeans; all share the remotely detached perspective that transforms the way in which individual endeavors are seen. Thoughtful and painstaking." Anatomy of Wonder 4
Followed by The marriages between zones three, four, and five (1980); The Sirian experiments (1981); The making of the representative for Planet 8 (1982); Documents relating to the sentimental agents in the Volyen Empire (1983)

Stories; [by] Doris Lessing. Knopf 1978 625p o.p.   LC 77-20709
Contents: The habit of loving; The woman; Through the tunnel; Pleasure; The witness; The day Stalin died; Wine; He; The eye of God in Paradise; The other woman; One off the short list; A woman on a roof; How I finally lost my heart; A man and two women; A room; England versus England; Two potters; Between men; Our friend Judith; Each other; Homage for Isaac Babel; Outside the ministry; Dialogue; Notes for a case history; To room nineteen; An old woman and her cat; Side benefits of an honourable profession; A year in Regent's Park; Report on the threatened city; Mrs. Fortescue; An unposted love letter; Lions, leaves, roses; Not a very nice story; The other garden; The temptation of Jack Orkney
"All of Lessing's non-African stories are brought together from three of her previous collections: 'The habit of Loving,' 'A Man and Two Women,' and 'The Temptation of Jack Orkney and other Stories'. In addition, 'The Other Woman,' a short novel, previously published only in Great Britain, is also included." Booklist

Lessing, Doris May, 1919-—*Continued*

The sweetest dream; [by] Doris Lessing. HarperCollins Pubs. 2002 478p hardcover o.p. pa $13.95

ISBN 0-06-621334-7; 0-06-093755-6 (pa)

LC 2002-279950

The epicenter of this novel "is a grand old house in London, the holdfast of the seemingly impervious widow Julia. It's the early 1960s and when her selfish and feckless communist son, Johnny, callously abandons his wife, Frances, and their two young sons, Julia persuades her resilient daughter-inlaw to move in with her. Soon Frances, a self-possessed yet endlessly empathic and accommodating earth mother, is presiding over a contentious commune of moody teenage 'waifs and strays.'" Booklist

"Lessing's understanding of relationships-both personal and political-has always been keen; now . . . it is unparalleled. This novel is warm and heartfelt, old-fashioned and ambitious in its historical sweep." New Statesman

Lester, Julius

Do Lord remember me; a novel. Holt & Co. 1985 c1984 210p o.p.

* LC 84-3845

"The final day of Rev. Joshua Smith's earthly existence is a reminiscence: of his turn-of-the-century boyhood in a hardscrabble county in Mississippi as the son of sharecroppers; of his gift as the 'singing preacher' for churches all over the segregated South; of his disappointment at never leading a big church in Detroit or Chicago; of his love for his fair-skinned wife and the trouble her appearance caused them." Publ Wkly

"Smith's memories link with those of older people in his past, whose stories take him back to slavery times. What emerges is a picture of black experience covering more than 150 years, with memory and storytelling providing continuity between present and past. A rich and moving reading experience." Booklist

Lethem, Jonathan

Chronic city. Doubleday 2009 467p $27.95

ISBN 978-0-385-51863-5; 0-385-51863-3

LC 2009-07587

"Set in Manhattan, the story focuses on an unusual friendship between Perkus [Tooth], a wayward cultural critic with a penchant for marijuana and conspiracies, and former child actor Chase Insteadman. Holed up in Perkus's clapboard apartment, the duo try to weave together the chaotic events occurring in the city by way of virtual worlds, ghostwriters, and Marlon Brando." Libr J

"Lethem's vision of New York can approach the Swiftian. It is impressively observant in its detail and scourging in its mocking satire." Boston Globe

The fortress of solitude; a novel. Doubleday 2003 511p $26

ISBN 0-385-50069-6

LC 2003-43535

"Dylan Ebdus is a white kid on a black-and-brown street. As he struggles through public school in 1970s Brooklyn, he is 'yoked'-put in a headlock-and frisked for change on a daily basis. Testing into a good Manhattan school, he steps into a long-lasting role: vulnerable among street kids, he's street-smart compared to his new,

privileged pals, and loathes himself as a poseur with both crowds. When he finds a ring that grants the power of flight, he's afraid to use it, but his black friend, Mingus, is not." Booklist

"The plot manages to encompass pop music from punk rock to rap, avant-garde art, graffiti, drug use, gentrification, the New York prison system-and to sing a vibrant, sometimes heartbreaking ballad of Brooklyn throughout. Lethem seems to have devoured the '70s, '80s, and '90sinhaled them whole-and he reproduces them faithfully on the page, in prose as supple as silk and as bright, explosive and illuminating as fireworks." Publ Wkly

Motherless Brooklyn. Doubleday 1999 311p

ISBN 0-385-49183-2

LC 99-18194

"The short and shady life of Frank Minna ends in murder, shocking the four young men employed by his dysfunctional Brooklyn detective agency/limo service. The 'Minna Men' have centered their lives around Frank. . . . Tourette's-afflicted Lionel has found security as a Minna Man and is shattered by Frank's death. Lionel determines to become a genuine sleuth and find the killer. The ensuing plot twists are marked by clever wordplay, fast-paced dialog, and nonstop irony." Libr J

You don't love me yet. Doubleday 2007 223p $24.95

ISBN 978-0-385-51218-3; 0-385-51218-X

LC 2006-11768

"A struggling L.A. alternative rock band with no name has yet to play a gig. Matthew, the lead singer, works in the zoo and brings home a kangaroo he thinks needs better care. Denise, the drummer, works in a sex shop. Lyricist Bedwin is a genius who can't even remember to eat. Lucinda, who plays bass, answers a complaint line for a performance artist whose theatrical piece consists of a fake office with actors as the workers who answer real phone lines. One of the callers, Carl, is attracted to Lucinda, and they eventually become lovers. She begins jotting down his ramblings, which Bedwin, inspired by Carl's ingenious phrasing, turns into the band's breakout songs. However, Carl, who is a professional phrase writer, wants to be compensated for his contribution—by becoming a member of the band." Libr J

"There's quite a bit of surface in this novel, but there's also a sweet truthfulness in its investigation of how the songs we love express something we can never fully articulate. Lethem understands this paradox, even if his characters don't." Paste

Letts, Billie, 1938-

Shoot the moon; Billie Letts. Warner Books 2004 333p $24

ISBN 0-446-52900-1

LC 2004-3447

"No one in sleepy DeClare, Oklahoma, has forgotten the 1972 murder of pretty Cherokee Gaylene Harjo and the abduction of her infant son, Nicky Jack. Hard-nosed deputy sheriff Oliver 'O Boy' Daniels pinned the blame on local preacher Joe Dawson, but few in town believed the kindly Joe was capable of such an act. Powerful emotions resurface 30 years later, when Nicky Jack, adopted and raised by a rich couple in Beverly Hills, mysteriously reappears, determined to learn about his mother and the circumstances surrounding her death. . . . Letts peppers her prose with a cast of quirky characters." Booklist

Leung, Brian, 1967-

World famous love acts; stories. Sarabande Books 2004 202p $14.95

ISBN 1-88933-016-7   LC 2003-11923

"Winner of the 2002 Mary McCarthy Prize in Short Fiction, selected by Chris Offutt"

Contents: Six ways to jump off a bridge; Executing Dexter; Leases; White hand; Dog sleep; Fire walk; Who knew her best; Desdimona's ruins; Drawings by Andrew Warhol; After; World famous love acts

"As diverse as they are similar, Leung's characters and their conditions run the gamut from elderly widower to precocious youngsters, porn star to AIDS victim, serial killer to estranged sisters, and all are lucidly portrayed in prose that is achingly lyrical and elegantly refined." Booklist

Levenkron, Steven, 1941-

The best little girl in the world. Contemporary Bks. 1978 196p o.p.   LC 78-9063

"Francesca is 15, an excellent student, a docile girl at home in her affluent parents' Manhattan apartment. But Francesca sets about killing her 'fat' self to become imaginary Kessa—slim and firm. Within weeks she starves herself, so that she drops from 98 to an alarming 84 pounds and is hospitalized, another young victim of anorexia nervosa. The reader is drawn into the arena where dedicated professionals battle to save Francesca's life and the lives of others like her. This book, fiction in name only, proves what an impassioned and skillful author can do to make a novel more powerful than dry facts." Publ Wkly

Levenson, J. C. (Jacob Claver), 1922-

(ed) Crane, S. Prose and poetry

Levenson, Jacob Claver See Levenson, J. C. (Jacob Claver), 1922-

Leventhal, Alice Walker See Walker, Alice, 1944-

Levi, Primo, 1919-1987

If not now, when?; translated from the Italian by William Weaver; introduction by Irving Howe. Summit Bks. 1985 c1982 349p o.p.   LC 85-2526

Original Italian edition, 1982

"The author, himself a victim of Nazi atrocities, has based his novel on true events. A band of Jewish partisans makes its way from Russia to Italy waging their personal war against the Nazis. They blow up trains, rescue concentration camp inmates, and face incredible dangers in their efforts to strike back against a ruthless, seemingly invincible enemy. The story is a testament to human endurance and courage." Shapiro. Fic for Youth. 3d edition

The monkey's wrench; translated from the Italian by William Weaver. Summit Bks. 1986 171p o.p.   LC 86-5803

Original Italian edition, 1978

"In this tale of two lonely and quite different men, a steel rigger entertains a chemist with memories of his world travels." Booklist

"Among other things, The Monkey's Wrench is a model of the interplay between storytellers and listeners. For their part, readers can envy Levi's sixth sense about building bridges between what can be seen and what must be imagined." Time

The sixth day, and other tales; translated by Raymond Rosenthal. Summit Bks. 1990 222p o.p.   LC 90-9734

Contents: The mnemogogues; Angelic butterfly; Order on the cheap; Man's friend; Some applications of the Mimer; Versamina; The sleeping beauty in the fridge: a winter's tale; The measure of beauty; Full employment; The sixth day; Retirement fund; Westward; Seen from afar; The hard-sellers; Small red lights; For a good purpose; Psychophant; Recuenco: the nurse; Recuenco: the rafter; His own blacksmith: to Italo Calvino; The servant; Mutiny: to Mario Rigoni Stern; Excellent is the water

"These bizarre stories from master storyteller Levi are full of shadowed meanings, conveying truths about our technological society and how our scientific appetites have outstripped our moral capacities." Libr J

Levien, David

City of the sun; a novel. Doubleday 2008 310p $24.95

ISBN 978-0-385-52366-0; 0-385-52366-1

     LC 2007-28002

"Jamie Gabriel lives in a community where boys still have paper routes; that is, until he and his bike vanish while delivering papers early one morning. His parents, Paul and Carol, report his disappearance to the police, but after a brief search leads nowhere, the authorities move on to other cases. More than a year later, on the advice of one of the deputies, the parents hire private investigator and former cop Frank Behr. . . . Tormented by the strain of having a missing child, Paul and Carol each try to cope in their own way, and their marriage suffers for it. Eventually, Paul starts working with Behr, and despite the cold trail, their quest leads them to some very troubling answers." Libr J

"While it deals with the practical mechanics of how a private detective tracks down a boy who has been missing for more than a year, this relentless novel is really about how parents suffer the loss of a child. As such, the story conveys a piercing sense of honesty, even when the investigation itself seems implausibly free of complications." N Y Times Book Rev

Levin, Ira, 1929-2007

The boys from Brazil; a novel. Random House 1976 312p o.p.   *

"Ninety-four potential Hitlers are created through the technique of cloning by Dr. Mengele, infamous doctor of Auschwitz. Striving to re-create the early environment of the original Hitler, Mengele plots the murder of the fa-

Levin, Ira, 1929-2007—*Continued*

thers of these ninety-four children. Yakov Liebermann, a pursuer of Nazis, tries to stop the murders at the cost of great, almost mortal, danger to himself." Shapiro. Fic for Youth. 3d edition

A kiss before dying. Simon & Schuster 1953 244p o.p.

"An Inner sanctum mystery"

"The plot has to do with a remarkably ingenious, subtle, and relentless murderer, who does away with a pregnant college girl, goes on from there to kill her sister and a more or less innocent bystander, and is cheated of the fortune that has driven him to these desperate measures only by a couple of tiny oversights that might easily have escaped Sherlock Holmes. The book is a succession of solid and quite legitimate surprises, the suspense is admirably sustained, the detail is thorough and convincing, and the writing is considerably above the level usually associated with fictional crime and passion." New Yorker

Rosemary's baby; a novel. Random House 1967 245p o.p.

"Guy and Rosemary Woodhouse dismiss the warnings of friends and move into a luxurious Manhattan apartment building where, supposedly, rites of witchcraft and suicides have occurred. Rosemary's instincts warn her to beware of their neighbors, the Castevets, but her husband is not convinced and they become a dominant influence on Guy when Rosemary becomes pregnant. She is alone in her fear and becomes a helpless victim." Shapiro. Fic for Youth. 3d edition

Followed by: Son of Rosemary (1998)

The Stepford wives. Random House 1972 145p
ISBN 0-394-48199-2

"Attractive, talented Joanna moves with her husband and kids to a suburb, where she comes to suspect that the village housewives have all been murdered and replaced by robots, the suspected villain being a chauvinistic Men's Association . . . and so Joanna begins to fear for her life." Libr J

"There is a broad current of humor beneath the horrific surface of this little ambush of Women's Lib, life and the pursuit of happiness." N Y Times Book Rev

Levin, Meyer, 1905-1981

Compulsion. Simon & Schuster 1956 495p o.p.

Using fictionalized names and probing deeply into the psychological aspects of the crime, this is a retelling of the Loeb-Leopold murder case

"The writing shows the hand of a master. Despite the fact that the reader who is familiar with the history of the case knows the outcome, Mr. Levin manages to fill this book with sustained suspense." N Y Times Book Rev

Levitt, Paul M.

Come with me to Babylon. University of New Mexico Press 2008 232p $24.95
ISBN 978-0-8263-4178-5; 0-8263-4178-0
LC 2007-39410

This historical novel "follows the Cohen family from their village in Russia to the United States, led by strong-willed Esther Cohen. Under the auspices of the Baron de Hirsch Fund, an agency focused on emigration, the Cohens are supposed to become farmers in rural New Jersey. But the bucolic occupation doesn't interest her husband, the gently raised Meyer Cohen. . . . All too soon, the Cohens have become a tenement family. Daughter Fanny is disabled in the Triangle Shirtwaist Co. fire, which killed more than 100 garment workers in a locked building. Son Ben begins dating a whore and running errands for a strikebreaking criminal. . . . Levitt hooks and plays his readers well. One influential character never appears directly: Jacob, Meyer and Esther's estranged son. The story of how he left the family, and how it grieves both parents, is a subtle but unmistakable undercurrent to Babylon." Rocky Mountain News

Levy, Andrea

Fruit of the lemon. Picador 2007 352p pa $15
ISBN 978-0-312-42664-4; 0-312-42664-X
LC 2006-52481

First published 1999 in the United Kingdom

This novel depicts the lives of London-born children of Jamaican immigrants "circa 1970, who grapple with the knowledge that they are often still considered outsiders. Faith, working as a dresser for children's television, is a somewhat heedless young woman whose assumption that she lives in a colorblind world is quickly demolished. At work, she finds that the only actors she's allowed to touch are dolls; soon afterward, she helps a black woman who has been attacked by three youths. Her concerned parents send her to Jamaica, where she slowly recovers a sense of balance and uncovers her family's past. Faith's initial obliviousness to prejudice makes the first half of the book feel implausible; but, once the narrative moves to Jamaica, Levy's remarkable ability to weave a complex, engrossing family history takes over." New Yorker

Small island. Picador 2005 c2004 441p pa $14
ISBN 0-312-42467-1
LC 2005-298527

First published 2004 in the United Kingdom

"In the shabby remnants of post-blitz London, three near-strangers find themselves in a single house. Queenie Bligh is a spirited Yorkshirewoman waiting for her husband to return from the war and taking in tenants to make ends meet. Gilbert Joseph, a Jamaican R.A.F. veteran, is struggling to establish himself in England, a country that he'd been taught was his motherland but which regards him as an interloper; his bride, Hortense, has just arrived in London and is bewildered that her education and class can't transcend the color of her skin. The narrative voice jumps between the characters, a technique that embeds familiar cultural observations in closely observed and surprising lives. If the plot sometimes verges on the operatic, Levy's writing deftly illuminates the complex and contradictory motives behind each character's behavior." New Yorker

Lewin, Michael Z.

Oh Joe. Five Star 2008 237p $25.95
ISBN 978-1-59414-667-1; 1-59414-667-5
LC 2008-016795

Lewin, Michael Z.—*Continued*

"Joe Prince drives a truck, loves his girlfriend, Kelly, and their infant son, Little Joe. But that isn't enough to keep him from straying, and when Kelly catches him in the act, she leaves him. As a form of self-imposed house arrest, he agrees to house-sit shady old pal George Wayne's permanently anchored houseboat in the middle of a large Indianapolis reservoir. But the loneliness wears on Joe. He jumps ship and swims for shore. A day or so later Joe finds himself under arrest for Wayne's murder. Steph Steponski, the lead detective assigned to the case, is sure of Joe's guilt—until she learns that Joe was played for a patsy and may now be at risk himself. . . . [Lewin] is as gently humorous and ironic as ever, and readers will find a kindred soul in Joe, as likeably flawed as any recent protagonist in mystery fiction." Booklist

Lewis, C. S. (Clive Staples), 1898-1963

The dark tower and other stories; edited by Walter Hooper. Harcourt Brace Jovanovich 1977 158p o.p.

Contents: The dark tower; The man born blind; The shoddy lands; Ministering angels; Forms of things unknown; After ten years

Out of the silent planet. Scribner Classics 1996 158p $22; pa $13

ISBN 0-684-83364-6; 0-7432-3490-1 (pa)

* LC 96-30110

A reissue of the title first published 1938 in the United Kingdom; first United States edition published 1943 by Macmillan

"The trilogy can be read on two levels: first for its exciting plot and second as a theological allegory, although Lewis denied this interpretation. The stories are about temptation. They concern the classic battle between good, as represented by Ransom, the philologist, and evil, as represented by Weston, the physicist. The battle is played out on the planets of Malacondra (Mars), Perelandra (Venus), and Earth." Shapiro. Fic for Youth. 3d edition

Followed by Perelandra (1943) and That hideous strength (1945)

Perelandra; a novel. Scribner Classics 1996 190p $22

ISBN 0-684-83365-4   LC 96-20724

A reissue of the title first published 1944 by Macmillan

In the second volume of the fantasy trilogy Dr. Ransom "is ordered to Perelandra (Venus) by the supreme being and finds there a paradise threatened by the villainous scientist Weston, who becomes the devil incarnate." Booklist

Followed by That hideous strength

That hideous strength; a modern fairy-tale for grown-ups. Scribner Classics 1996 380p $23

ISBN 0-684-83367-0   LC 96-20722

A reissue of the title first published 1946 by Macmillan

In the final volume of the fantasy trilogy Ransom and Weston again represent the struggle between good and evil, this time in a college community on Earth. Mark Studdock learns the error of his attempts to play faculty politics, and his wife discovers the footlessness of modern theories of love and life

Till we have faces; a myth retold. Harcourt Brace & Co. 1957 c1956 313p il o.p.

First published 1956 in the United Kingdom

"Introducing his own version of the myth of Psyche and Cupid the author weaves it into a fantasy in which he gives expression to some of his persisting ideas on the forces at work in the soul of man. Orual, queen of a fictional kingdom of the Near East in ancient times, tells the story." Booklist

"The religious allegory is plain to read. In Mr. Lewis's sensitive hands the ancient myth retains its fascination, while being endowed with new meanings, new depths, new terrors." Saturday Rev

Lewis, Clive Staples *See* Lewis, C. S. (Clive Staples), 1898-1963

Lewis, Jim, 1963-

The king is dead. Knopf 2003 259p $24

ISBN 0-375-41417-7   LC 2002-43288

Walter Selbly "was born in 1925 and became a World War II hero, lawyer, and indispensable aide to the governor of Tennessee. His life seemed complete when he married beautiful Nicole Lattimore, whom he adored, and they had a son, Frank, and a daughter, Gail. Then, on a single day, Walter's professional and personal lives were destroyed, and his young children were left without parents. Thirty-five years later Frank Cartwright (with his adoptive parents' name), an attractive, womanizing actor whose career is languishing, is provoked by a film proposal from a fabled dowager to find his roots. . . . Even if the parts of this novel outshine the whole, Lewis' language often soars." Booklist

Lewis, M. G. (Matthew Gregory), 1775-1818

The monk; by Matthew Lewis, with an introduction by Stephen King. Oxford Univ. Press 2002 442p (Oxford world's classics) $20

ISBN 0-19-515136-4

* LC 2002-25111

First published 1796 in the United Kingdom

"Ambrosio, the worthy superior of the Capuchins of Madrid, falls to the temptations of Matilda, a fiend-inspired wanton who, disguised as a boy, has entered his monastery as a novice. Now utterly depraved, Ambrosio falls in love with one of his penitents, pursues the girl with the help of magic and murder, and finally kills her in and effort to escape detection. But he is discovered, tortured by the Inquisition, and sentenced to death, finally compounding with the devil for escape from burning, only to be hurled by him to destruction and damnation. Although extravagant in its mixture of the supernatural, the terrible, and the indecent, the book contains scenes of great effect. It enjoyed a considerable contemporary vogue." Oxford Companion to Engl Lit. 6th edition

Lewis, Matthew Gregory *See* Lewis, M. G. (Matthew Gregory), 1775-1818

Lewis, Monk *See* Lewis, M. G. (Matthew Gregory), 1775-1818

Lewis, Sinclair, 1885-1951

Arrowsmith. Harcourt Brace & Co. 1925 448p
ISBN 0-15-108216-2

*

"Although he is most interested in bacteriology and research, Martin Arrowsmith turns from that area to general medicine and then to public health. He is unable, however, to deal with the political aspects of the public health field and returns to laboratory work and research. Martin develops an antitoxin that he believes will be effective against bubonic plague, but when he gets the chance to test the serum during an epidemic in the West Indies, he invalidates the results by not adhering to a control situation. Returning to the States, he feels that he is a failure and refuses the offer of a prestigious position in order to join an old friend at a rural laboratory in a search for a cure for pneumonia." Shapiro. Fic for Youth. 3d edition

also in Lewis, S. Arrowsmith; Elmer Gantry; Dodsworth

Arrowsmith; Elmer Gantry; Dodsworth. Library of America, Distributed to the trade in the U.S. by Penguin Putnam 2002 1346p $40
ISBN 1-931082-08-1   LC 2002-19451
Contents: Arrowsmith; Elmer Gantry; Dodsworth

Babbitt; with an introduction and notes by James M. Hutchisson. Penguin Books 1996 xxxii, 365p il pa $9.95
ISBN 0-14-018902-5
* LC 95-36188
First published 1922 by Harcourt, Brace
Satire on American middle-class life in a good-sized city. George F. Babbitt is a successful real estate man, a regular fellow, booster, Rotarian, Elk, Republican, who uses all the current catchwords, molds his opinions on those of the Zenith Advocate-Times and believes in "a sound business administration in Washington"
"The novel's scathing indictment of middle-class American values made Babbittry a synonym for adherence to a conformist, materialistic, anti-intellectual way of life." Merriam-Webster's Ency of Lit

also in Lewis, S. Main Street & Babbitt

Dodsworth; a novel. Harcourt Brace & Co. 1929 377p o.p.
"The book's protagonist, Sam Dodsworth, is an American automobile manufacturer who sells his company and takes an extended European vacation with his wife, Fran. *Dodsworth* recounts their reactions to Europeans and European values, their various relationships with others, their estrangement, and their brief reconciliation." Merriam-Webster's Ency of Lit

also in Lewis, S. Arrowsmith; Elmer Gantry; Dodsworth

Elmer Gantry. Harcourt Brace 1927 432p o.p.

*

This novel "deals with a brazen ex-football player who enters the ministry and, through his half-plagiarized sermons, his physical attractiveness, and his unerring instinct for promotion, becomes a successful evangelist and later the leader of a large Middle Western church. Carefully researched, the novel was realistic enough to shock both the faithful and unfaithful." Reader's Ency. 3d edition

also in Lewis, S. Arrowsmith; Elmer Gantry; Dodsworth

It can't happen here; a novel. Doubleday, Doran 1935 458p o.p.
"Doremus Jessup, editor of a small New England newspaper, follows the rise to the presidency of the United States of a fascist demagogue, Berzelius Windrip. Doremus and his friends publish an underground newspaper that tells the truth about what is happening. Doremus is imprisoned, escapes to Canada, and joins the underground movement, which is headed by the man who had opposed Windrip in the election. The novel inveighs against some aspects of capitalism as well as fascism, and communists come in for their share of criticism also." Shapiro. Fic for Youth. 3d edition

Main Street. Harcourt, Brace 1920 451p o.p.

*

"Carol Milford, a girl of quick intelligence but no particular talent, after graduation from college meets and marries Will Kennicott, a sober, kindly, unimaginative physician of Gopher Prairie, Minn., who tells her that the town needs her abilities. She finds the village to be a smug, intolerant, unimaginatively standardized place, where the people will not accept her efforts to create more sightly homes, organize a dramatic association, and otherwise improve the village life." Oxford Companion to Am Lit. 6th edition

also in Lewis, S. Main Street & Babbitt

Main Street & Babbitt. Library of Am. 1992 898p $40
ISBN 0-940450-61-5   LC 91-58224
In addition to Main Street, this book also features Babbitt (1922), a satire on American middle-class conventions. Set in the Midwest, it focuses on the life of George Babbitt, a prosperous and self-satisfied real estate man.

Lewycka, Marina

A short history of tractors in Ukrainian. Penguin Press 2005 294p
ISBN 1-59420-044-0   LC 2004-56542
"When their recently widowed father announces that he plans to remarry, sisters Vera and Nadezhda realize that they must learn to put aside a lifetime of bitter rivalry in order to save him. The new woman in his life is [Valentina], a voluptuous gold digger from Ukraine, fifty years his junior." Publisher's note
"The author's imaginary world lets her explore the sort of problems that other east European emigres in Britain often fear but seldom confront: chiefly, what to do with people we are supposed to like but don't trust or understand. Her dialogue, conducted between educated people who lack a common language, is a comic feast." Economist

Li Yiyun

A thousand years of good prayers; stories. Random House 2005 205p $21.95
ISBN 1-4000-6312-4   LC 2004-62891
Contents: Extra; After a life; Immortality; The princess of Nebraska; Love in the marketplace; Son; The arrangement; Death is not a bad joke if told the right way; Per-

Li Yiyun—*Continued*

simmons; A thousand years of good prayers

This collection is a "reminder that, at its best, the short story is the most elegant of literary forms. Each tale has a keen poignancy of its own, and assembled in a collection they give an impressively coherent sense of modern China. All melancholy, the stories are by turns angry and whimsical, and each bears the ugly imprint of Mao's China." Times Lit Suppl

The vagrants; a novel. Random House 2009 337p $25

ISBN 978-1-4000-6313-0; 1-4000-6313-2

LC 2008-23467

This novel "begins and ends with an execution, in 1979, in a small city in China, where democratic reform movements are beginning to ripple through the nation. Gu Shan is a former Red Guard leader turned counter-revolutionary, whose execution, at the age of twenty-eight, devastates her parents and entwines their lives with those of a crippled twelve-year-old girl, the feckless nineteen-year-old son of a Communist hero, an elderly street-cleaning couple, and a radio announcer who comes to question her role in the spread of government propaganda. Li offers both a bleak view of a historical moment when 'people were the most dangerous animals in the world' and a meditation on the act of martyrdom, which is presented both as a duty and as a 'luxury that few could afford.'" New Yorker

Liebmann-Smith, Richard, 1942-

The James boys; a novel account of four desperate brothers. Random House 2008 261p $25

ISBN 978-0-345-47078-2; 0-345-47078-8

LC 2007-38423

"In his first novel, The James Boys, humorist Richard Liebmann-Smith posits what life would have been like if real-life brothers Henry and William James (the novelist and the philosopher) had been the brothers of Frank and Jesse James (the outlaws)." NPR

The author "includes enough plot, to keep this single-joke, creatively imagined biography chugging along." Publ Wkly

Lightman, Alan P., 1948-

The diagnosis; [by] Alan Lightman. Pantheon Bks. 2000 369p

ISBN 0-679-43615-4

LC 00-24543

"Bill Chalmers is an executive at an 'information company' in Boston who on his way to work one day forgets completely who he is, what he does or where he is supposed to be going. After a number of nightmarish experiences, in which he rapidly becomes a homeless bum, he awakens in a hospital, more or less his old self—except that his body is beginning to turn numb." Publ Wkly

"A work of vivid sensuousness, sparkling intelligence, and poignant beauty, Lightman's gripping tale contrasts the needs of the body and spirit with the acquisitiveness of the mind and ponders the potential lethality of ideologies, be they cultural or technological." Booklist

Einstein's dreams; [by] Alan Lightman. Pantheon Bks. 1993 179p il o.p.

* LC 92-50465

"In 1905, while working as an examiner at the Swiss Patent Office in Bern, Einstein published three important papers in Annals of Physics. Here Lightman re-creates the dreams that allegedly culminated in the famous essay on the relativity of time." Libr J

"Lightman starts out with commonplaces, neurological conditions or abstractions of our personal experience of time. Then, with one or two exceptions, he embodies the concept in brilliant, folkloric tales with extraordinary assurance." New Statesman Soc

Ghost; [by] Alan Lightman. Pantheon Books 2007 243p $23

ISBN 978-0-375-42169-3; 0-375-42169-6

LC 2007-05298

This novel "tells the story of a divorced and childless forty-two-year-old man whose primary ambition has been to 'understand the world,' rather than change it. Believing that logic holds life together, he struggles to be content with his limited lot, but also admits to 'searching for something' beyond himself. . . . When he is let go from a mid-level banking position, he finds work in a mortuary, where, one day, he sees something he can only describe as a 'vapor' apparently emanating from, or getting sucked into, a corpse. In the ensuing frenzy—a local paper gets wind of the story—he is forced to wrestle with fundamental beliefs about human existence." New Yorker

"Satirical and compassionate, Lightman's brilliantly orchestrated and gripping tale dramatizes our marshaling of fear, fantasy, and faith as we confront the unknown and the inevitable. At base, all we can truly trust, Lightman suggests, is wonder and kindness." Booklist

Reunion; [by] Alan Lightman. Pantheon Bks. 2003 231p $23

ISBN 0-375-42167-X

LC 2002-34575

"Charles, a 'small-college professor' in his early 50's, more or less amicably settled into domestic banality in a leafy suburb, decides to attend his 30th college reunion. Once back at his unnamed alma mater . . . he is struck with eidetic force by recollections of his first passionate love affair, with an aspiring ballerina, Juliana. A narrative of this love affair and reflections upon it form the bulk of the novel." N Y Times Book Rev

"Lightman infuses even the simplest scenes with quiet menace as he explores the cataclysmic power of both erotic love and shocking betrayal." Booklist

Lin Yutang, 1895-1976

Moment in Peking; a novel of contemporary Chinese life. Day 1939 815p o.p.

A story of family life among the upper middle class of China, covering forty years from the time of the Boxer Rebellion to the Japanese invasion

"There are many scenes and passages of great beauty in the book, excerpts from the classics, poetry and philosophy. There are also incidents of humor, delicate and subtle. Equally skillful is the author in depicting scenes of dramatic intensity, stark tragedy of war and acts of heroism" Springfield Repub

Lindgren, Torgny, 1938-

Hash; a novel; translated from the Swedish by Tom Geddes. Overlook Press 2004 236p $23.95

    ISBN 1-585-67408-7   LC 2003-63976

    Original Swedish edition, 2002

"In December 1947, for the newspaper to which he corresponds from northern Sweden, a middle-aged man is writing about two newcomers to the village of Avaback: a schoolteacher, just released as cured from the tuberculosis sanitarium in which he spent his youth, and a middle-aged clothing peddler, who the writer believes is missing Nazi leader Martin Bormann. Then a messenger arrives with a termination letter from the newspaper editor, who has researched the places the writer reports on, only to be told that they don't exist. The writer stops writing, for 53 years, resuming at age 107, only after he has outlived old age and is regaining lost powers and attributes." Booklist

"Lindgren delivers a story that's a clever sendup of the conceits of storytellers and a bittersweet meditation on life and the pleasures that bind us to it." N Y Times Book Rev

Lindsay, Jeff *See* Lindsay, Jeffry P., 1952-

Lindsay, Jeffry P., 1952-

Darkly dreaming Dexter. Doubleday 2004 288p $22.95

    ISBN 0-385-51123-X   LC 2004-45460

Dexter Morgan is a "Miami police-department blood-spatter analyst with a weakness for bowling shirts and batidos, who, when the moon is full, carves up villains in a careful ritual, keeping a single drop of blood on a slide as a souvenir. (He's collected thirty-six so far.) When other victims start popping up, dispatched with the same creativity as Dexter's, he pursues the copycat murderer with acute professional self-interest. Like other charismatic killers—Hannibal Lecter, say, or Tom Ripley—Dexter has a set of motives that are tough to untangle. But his quest proves weirdly convincing as he ponders whether to turn his doppelgänger over to the cops or take care of the problem himself." New Yorker

Dearly devoted Dexter; [by] Jeff Lindsay. Doubleday 2005 292p

    ISBN 0-385-51124-8

This is the second book in the Dexter series. "Dexter Morgan, a Miami P.D. blood splatter analyst and ethical serial killer, is in a funk: his police department archnemesis, Captain Doakes, who rightly believes that Dexter is guilty of illegal behavior, is shadowing him. . . . So when a new serial killer with Doakes on his list arrives in Miami, Dexter is excited. Not only does he get to hunt a fellow hunter, but he also sees the opportunity to be rid of Doakes. The only thing worrying him is the involvement of his sister, since she's the only person for whom Dexter has feelings. . . . There's plenty of graphic violence and dark humor, but Lindsay manages to retain a light edge." Libr J

Dexter in the dark; a novel; [by] Jeff Lindsay. Doubleday 2007 302p $23.95

    ISBN 978-0-385-51833-8; 0-385-51833-1

          LC 2007-20277

Dexter Morgan is a serial killer who works as a blood-splatter expert for the Miami police department. In this installment "Dexter is shocked, while working a crime scene, to discover that his Dark Passenger, the evil thing that makes him who he is, has abruptly vanished. Soon after that, and still reeling from the unfamiliar sense of solitude, he learns that he's being stalked by someone more evil than anyone he's encountered in the past." Booklist

"Lindsay gives Dexter a great voice and provides the reader with several laugh-out-loud scenes." Libr J

Lindsey, David L.

The color of night; [by] David Lindsey. Warner Bks. 1999 480p $32

    ISBN 0-446-52361-5   LC 98-30770

"Harry Strand, a retired U.S. intelligence officer, thinks he's finally put his life back together after the tragic death of his wife. He has become a successful art dealer, and he's fallen in love with Mara Song, a beautiful collector. But everything changes abruptly when Harry discovers a tape in Mara's VCR that clearly shows his wife being murdered. Finding out who is responsible for her death proves to be far more complicated than this former spy can imagine. This is a fast-paced and exciting thriller." Booklist

The rules of silence; [by] David Lindsey. Warner Bks. 2003 405p $24.95

    ISBN 0-446-53163-4   LC 2002-33059

"Multimillionaire Titus Cain is approached with a strange proposition: if he doesn't give a certain man $64 million, this same man will kill off some (or perhaps all) of Cain's friends and loved ones. The money has to be given to the extortionist in such a way that no one suspects anything is going on . . . and if Cain even tries to seek help, the killings will start instantly. . . . Lindsey's novels sometimes suffer from lethargy, as though he's just sort of wandering through his story, but this one moves swiftly to its rousing finale." Booklist

Lindsey, Johanna

Gentle rogue. Avon Books 1990 426p (Avon historical romance) pa $7.99

    ISBN 978-0-380-75302-4   LC 90-93175

"Heartsick and desperate to return home to America, Georgina Anderson boards the *Maiden Anne* disguised as a cabin boy, never dreaming she'll be forced into intimate servitude at the whim of the ship's irrepressible captain, James Mallory." Publisher's note

Lindskold, Jane M.

(jt. auth) Zelazny, R. Donnerjack

Linington, Elizabeth, 1921-

For works written by this author under other names see Shannon, Dell, 1921-

Link, Kelly

Magic for beginners; illustrated by Shelley Jackson. Small Beer Press 2005 272p il $24

    ISBN 978-1-931520-15-7; 1-931520-15-1

          LC 2005-5394

Link, Kelly—*Continued*

Contents: The faery handbag; The hortlak; The cannon; Stone animals; Catskin; Some zombie contingency plans; The great divorce; Magic for beginners; Lull

"Link's second collection has a McSweeney's-like tendency to digress, but does so without irony. Whether describing witches filled with ants that carry pieces of time, or an orange-juice-colored corduroy couch that looks as if it 'has just escaped from a maximum security prison for criminally insane furniture,' these stories examine American middle and lower-middle-class life from unexpected angles that mix fairy tale, science fiction, and zaniness. . . . Reading Link, one has a sense that sometimes a person needs to wander off for a better perspective, and sometimes a person simply needs to wander off." New Yorker

(ed) The Year's best fantasy and horror. See The Year's best fantasy and horror

Linscott, Gillian

Blood on the wood; a Nell Bray mystery; Gillian Linscott. 1st St. Martin's Minotaur ed. St. Martin's Minotaur 2004 311p $24.95

ISBN 0-312-33148-7   LC 2003-69721

"After Edwardian British suffragette Bray discovers that a valuable painting bequeathed to the suffragettes is fake, she breaks into the owner's house to substitute the fake for the real. When she does, she chances upon murder." Libr J

"Readers will soak up fascinating detail about the Fabians, the Scipians, and the Arts and Crafts Movement while following the action in this delightful romp through England at the turn of the century." Booklist

Lipman, Elinor

The dearly departed; a novel. Random House 2001 269p $23.95

ISBN 0-679-46312-7   LC 00-67368

The author sets her "novel in King George, N.H., a small town where the sudden accidental deaths of a secretly engaged couple summon their two grown-up children to sort out the conundrum of their relation to each other. Both the dead woman's stoical daughter, Sunny Batten, and the man's cranky son, Fletcher Finn, possess an identical corona of satiny gray hair; both are 31; and neither has ever met the other, although their parents has been on-and-off lovers for years." Publ Wkly

The novel "entertains the reader with quirky details and amusing dialogue, but most nourishing is its picture of small-town life, in which everyone knows everyone else's business but they love one another just the same." Atl Mon

The family man. Houghton Mifflin Harcourt 2009 305p $25

ISBN 978-0-618-64466-7; 0-618-64466-0

LC 2008-46222

"When the comfortably wealthy and homosexual Henry Archer's recently widowed ex-wife, Denise Krouch, reappears after 24 years, his ordered life is turned upside down. The unwelcome reunion with the brash and socially inept Denise brings with it a silver lining: his reacquaintance with Denise's estranged daughter, Thalia, and a blind date with Todd. Henry soon finds himself in the midst of Denise's familial drama and struggling actress Thalia's doomed-to-fail publicity stunt with a horror film star. He also finds himself happily in love with both his daughter and Todd." Libr J

"Hilarious, literate and unnervingly accurate in its observations of the quirks of human nature, 'The Family Man' proclaims that whatever bizarre sort of family you have, you're better off with it than without it." PopMatters

The Inn at Lake Devine. Random House 1998 253p

ISBN 0-679-45693-7   LC 97-1307

"Casting her eye on the social mores of the 1960s and '70s, [Lipman] focuses most notably on the not-so-dainty dance that pulled Jews and WASPs into an assimilationist détente. Natalie Marx of Newton, Mass., is 13 in 1962 when she learns that the Inn at Lake Devine in Gilbert, Vt., strongly suggests to Jewish would-be guests that they would be more comfortable elsewhere. Her crank calls and letters to owner Ingrid Berry have no impact; only when she wangles an invitation from summer-camp friend Robin Fife does Natalie succeed in insinuating herself into this gentile enclave. When she and Robin meet again years later, Natalie finds herself re-entangled in the fate of the Inn." Publ Wkly

"Skillfully interweaving the bittersweet narrative with threads of both tragedy and comedy, Lipman displays a healthy amount of empathy and affection for her flawed and slightly eccentric cast of characters." Booklist

The ladies' man; a novel. Random House 1999 260p

ISBN 0-679-45694-5   LC 98-56450

"The basic premise of the book is that Nash Harvey, né Harvey Nash, has a crisis of conscience over an engagement he walked out on 30 years ago. He returns to Boston to see Adele Dobbin, his spurned fiancée. Nash's visit teaches Adele and her two unmarried sisters a new lesson 'about dignity being less important than love.' Nash is a shallow smooth talker, seemingly addicted to lust and unfamiliar with love." Libr J

"'The Ladies' Man' never suggests that all men are like Nash Harvey. . . . This book isn't even angry with its villain; it just shakes its head in amused amazement and, a little wiser, walks away." N Y Times Book Rev

My latest grievance. Houghton Mifflin 2006 243p $24

ISBN 0-618-64465-2   LC 2005-22576

"In the late 1970s, Frederica Hatch is the enchantingly outspoken daughter of brilliant college professors at a minor all-girls college in Massachusetts. Her temperate, mildly eccentric, and lovely parents, also union activists for the faculty of Dewing College, serve as houseparents at one of the dorms, where Frederica has lived her whole life. Wise beyond her years, Frederica takes it in stride when she discovers that her father was married once before and that Laura Lee French, the smashingly solipsistic first wife of Dr. David Hatch, has just been hired as housemother of one of the other dorms. Within hours of her arrival, French seduces the new president of Dewing in a flagrant affair that provides rich fuel for Frederica's hilariously dry wit and searing analysis of adult foibles." Libr J

The pursuit of Alice Thrift; a novel. Random House 2003 269p $23.95

ISBN 0-679-46313-5   LC 2002-31864

Lipman, Elinor—*Continued*

"The eponymous Alice is a sleep-deprived surgical intern at a Boston hospital. A graduate of MIT and Harvard and a congenital workaholic, she's also devoid of social skills, a sense of humor or elementary tact. Though miserably unequipped with self-esteem, Alice is an intelligent, well-brought-up offspring of upper-middle-class parents. Why, then, does she fall prey to the romantic blandishments of Ray Russo, a vulgar loudmouth and con artist who—it turns out—lies every time he opens his mouth? That Lipman can make this story plausible, and tell it with humor, pschological insight and rising suspense, is a triumph." Publ Wkly

Lippman, Laura

Hardly knew her; stories. William Morrow 2008 292p $23.95

ISBN 978-0-06-158499-2; 0-06-158499-1

Contents: The crack cocaine diet; What he needed; Dear Penthouse Forum (a first draft); The babysitter's code; Hardly knew her; Femme fatale; One true love; Pony girl; ARM and the woman; Honor bar; A good fuck spoiled; Easy as A-B-C; Black-eyed Susan; Ropa vieja; The shoeshine man's regrets; The accidental detective; Scratch a woman

Lippman "clearly agrees with Kipling that the female of the species is deadlier than the male. Women's victims here include a female friend, boyfriends (both current and ex), a husband, and one-night stands and strangers; their murders are all the more chilling. The novella 'Scratch A Woman,' featuring a single suburban Maryland soccer mom who works as a prostitute, and one of several stories featuring Tess [Monaghan] are the only entries not published previously. But those that have been published are scattered in a variety of anthologies over the last seven years, including Baltimore Noir. Here are nearly all of the short stories Lippman has ever written in one volume; read them fast, like a glutton, or slowly to savor each one. Either way, this is a treasure." Libr J

No good deeds. William Morrow 2006 343p $24.95

ISBN 978-0-06-057072-9; 0-06-057072-5

LC 2005-58358

In this Tess Monaghan "outing, an impulse to do good leads to murder. When Crow Ransome, Tess' live-in boyfriend, catches 16-year-old Lloyd Jupiter running a tire scam on his car, he takes him home to ensure he has a place to sleep for the night. By accident, Tess discovers their reluctant guest has some intriguing information about the high-profile murder of a federal prosecutor. When Tess turns the information over to the papers, she's assured her source will be anonymous; not so Tess herself, however, and it isn't long before an aggressive assistant U.S. district attorney and two burly federal cops are knocking on her door." Booklist

"Lippman has pulled off the near-impossible: writing a conventional procedural that still feels fresh. It's impossible not to like the complex, all-too-real Monaghan, a strong, wry detective prone to 'derailing my own gravy train.'" Washington Post Book World

Scratch a woman

In Lippman, L. Hardly knew her

What the dead know. William Morrow 2007 376p $24.95

ISBN 978-0-06-112885-1; 0-06-112885-6

LC 2006-52495

"A driver who flees a car accident on a Maryland highway breathes new life into a 30-year-old mystery—the disappearance of the young Bethany sisters at a shopping mall—after she later tells the police she's one of the missing girls. As soon as the mystery woman drops that bombshell, she clams up, placing the new lead detective, Kevin Infante, in a bind, as he struggles to gain her trust while exploring the odd holes in her story." Publ Wkly

"As artful as she is at interweaving disarming scenes of two spirited girls on the day they vanished with painful moments in the lives of their parents—maintaining all the while a thread of continuity in the current-day police investigation—Lippman pulls off something more ambitious than a high-wire act of technical virtuosity. With great thought and compassion, she uses her fractured narrative style to delve into the ways in which every serious crime tears to shreds the lives of its victims." N Y Times Book Rev

Lipsyte, Sam

Home land; a novel. Picador 2005 c2004 229p pa $13

ISBN 0-312-42418-3

LC 2004-57318

First published 2004 in the United Kingdom

"The hero of this comic novel, Lewis Miner, a.k.a. Teabag, was a high-school stoner, and now makes it his mission to write extremely candid letters to the alumni newsletter. His life, as he writes, 'did not pan out.' He works as a dishwasher in his father's cheesy catering business and spends his free time moping with his friend Gary, who sued his parents for molestation and then sued the shrink who conjured up these false memories. Teabag's letters detail his sexual fantasies (most of which involve the leg warmers of the school's jazz-dancing squad), his stalled ambition, and the misshapen pearls of wisdom he's garnered from his bottomed-out life. The story ends in an improbable shootout, but Lipsyte transfigures Teabag's self-loathing into a sensibility that is both hilarious and noble." New Yorker

Liss, David

The ethical assassin. Ballantine Books 2006 327p $24.95

ISBN 1-4000-6421-X

LC 2005-46446

An "ecoterrorist romp shot through with elements of the absurd. It begins with a 17-year-old Jewish encyclopedia salesman working door to door in a South Florida trailer park. . . . Lem Altick is saving money for college by tricking poor people into buying supermarket encyclopedias, but he gets more than he bargained for when an assassin with 'Warholishy' hair saunters into a trailer where Lem is about to close a deal and efficiently kills the two would-be encyclopedia readers and then engages Lem in a chat about his favorite Shakespeare play (Lem is partial to Twelfth Night). It only gets weirder from there, as Lem finds himself a sort of comrade-in-arms with the ethical assassin, whose real purpose seems to be raising havoc with some distinctly unethical pig farmers.

Liss, David—*Continued*

There's also a sicko small-town sheriff lurking in the wings, having apparently wandered into the action straight out of Jim Thompson's Pop. 1280." Booklist

A spectacle of corruption. Random House 2004 381p $24.95

ISBN 0-375-50855-4   LC 2003-54806

"Moments after his conviction for a murder he did not commit, at a trial presided over by a judge determined to find him guilty, Benjamin Weaver is accosted by a stranger who cunningly slips a lockpick and a file into his hands. In an instant he understands two things: Someone had gone to a great deal of trouble to see him condemned to hang and another equally mysterious agent is determined to see him free. . . . After a daring escape from eighteenth-century London's most notorious prison, Weaver must face another challenge: how to prove himself innocent of a crime when the corrupt courts have already shown they want only to see him hang." Publisher's note

Weaver "turns out to be the hard-outside, soft-inside private investigator of the noir thrillers inserted into 1720s London: Philip Marlowe done up in a wig and buckles." Washington Post Book World

The whiskey rebels; a novel. Random House 2008 525p $26

ISBN 978-1-4000-6420-5; 1-4000-6420-1

LC 2008-00075

"Set in and around Philadelphia, Pittsburgh and New York City in the years after the Revolutionary War, this . . . [thriller] follows the adventures of Ethan Saunders, once a valiant spy for General Washington, who's fallen on hard times by war's end. Suspected of treason, Ethan has lost the love of his life, Cynthia, who's married the fiendish Jacob Pearson, an entrepreneur who managed to prosper during the British occupation of Philadelphia. At Cynthia's urging, Ethan agrees to go looking for the missing Jacob, prompted in large part by a desire to redeem his reputation. Meanwhile, the so-called whiskey rebels on the western frontier are trying to bring down the hated Alexander Hamilton and his Bank of the United States." Publ Wkly

The author "delivers a portrait of postcolonial Philadelphia and New York, as well as the western frontier, that is convincing and acutely detailed." Houston Chron

Littell, Jonathan 1967-

The kindly ones; a novel; translated by Charlotte Mandell. Harper 2009 992p $29.99

ISBN 978-0-06-135345-1; 0-06-135345-0

LC 2008-30788

Original French edition, 2006

This novel recounts "one individual's moral struggle over his execution of hundreds of Jews during Hitler's reign. Now living the life of a cultured gentleman in France, Dr. Maximillian Aue has decided to write his memoir both to pass the time and to see whether he can still feel anything. In the course of his directionless meanderings, he recounts his numerous acts of murder, and he appears Zelig-like at the sides of Himmler, Eichmann, and even Hitler." Libr J

Littell "eagerly displays vast amounts of research. We are treated to several pages on the languages of the Caucasus as well as a remarkable description of Jawizowitz,

a subcamp of Auschwitz about which virtually no one who didn't survive its lethal mines would know. . . . Throughout Aue's morbidly picaresque travels, the tone is leering. A phenomenon that can only be called death porn saturates 'The Kindly Ones.' Despite its many, potent set pieces that vividly render the misery and insanity of war, the effect is voyeuristic as Aue, Littell and the unfortunate reader rubberneck at the innumerable bodies—gassed, shot, hanged, strangled, burnt, bombed, eyes gouged, intestines unwound, limbs severed, brains spattered—heaped in piles by history's roadside." Washington Post Book World

Littell, Robert, 1935-

The company; a novel of the CIA. Overlook Press 2002 894p $27.95

ISBN 1-58567-197-5

* LC 2001-51383

"Mixing real events and real people with the story of four fictional spies, Littell presents the history of the CIA, from post-war Berlin to the present. As we follow the intersecting careers of three Company agents and one KGB operative, we see the major events and personalities of the cold war from the inside." Booklist

"There is plenty here to amuse anyone with even a network news interest in current events—and a gold mine for true conspiracy theorists." N Y Times Book Rev

The Stalin epigram; a novel. Simon & Schuster 2009 366p $26

ISBN 978-1-4165-9864-0; 1-4165-9864-2

LC 2008-52277

"In 1934, real-life poet Osip Mandelstam struggles to get published in the totalitarian state. A battered idealist who has witnessed his share of Stalin-orchestrated horrors, Mandelstam feels writers have 'an abiding responsibility to be truth tellers in this wasteland of lies.' Much to the despair of his fellow poets, Osip writes an epigram likening Stalin to a ruthless killer, leading to Osip's arrest, brutal interrogation and exile. The . . . narrative employs an array of narrators, including Osip's devoted wife, Nadezhda; his disloyal lover, actress Zinaida Zaitseva-Antonova; and Stalin's personal bodyguard, Nikolai Vlasik." Publ Wkly

"This is a timeless story of courage and truth confronting the madness of absolute power. It's a brilliant work, always readable, sometimes funny and often heartbreaking. There are many books about Stalin's terror, but there cannot be many that bring its truths more vividly, painfully to life." Washington Post Book World

Vicious circle; a novel of complicity. Overlook 2006 300p $24.95

ISBN 1-58567-855-4

This novel "takes place in the volatile Holy Land of the near future. When the Arab leader of a terrorist faction kidnaps a rabbi who heads an ultraconservative settlers' group, Israeli security services go on red alert. In adding a smart-alecky American reporter to the mix, Littell . . . ratchets up the action to a heart-bursting sprint that stops only for big gulps of violence and torture. What makes this book unforgettable is the extraordinary relationship between kidnapper and victim. Extremists both, they joust with vehement hatred yet are

Littell, Robert, 1935-—*Continued*
strangely drawn together. Littell's acute portrayal of their inflamed psychological states illuminates an understanding that goes far beyond the day's headlines." Libr J

Walking back the cat. Overlook Press 1997
220p
   ISBN 0-87951-764-6   LC 96-49507
In this thriller, "'Parsifal,' a Soviet mole, discovers that he no longer carries out his 'wet work' (contract killing) for the KGB but for an unknown party who is using a New Mexico casino run by 'all that's left on earth of the Suma Apaches, the smallest Indian tribe in America, living on the smallest Indian reservation in America' to launder money. Parsifal joins forces with his final intended victim, a Gulf War dropout named Finn. Together they 'walk back the cat,' retracing the chain of command between Parsifal and the hidden executive who ordered Finn's execution." Libr J
"Sinister deeds and playful characterizations ricochet the reader through a complex plot, replacing the genre's usual hightech gizmos with the strengths and skills of lone-wolf heroes." Publ Wkly

Litvinov, Ivy, 1889-1977

(tr) Turgenev, I. S. The torrents of spring

Litwos *See* Sienkiewicz, Henryk, 1846-1916

Lively, Penelope, 1933-

Cleopatra's sister. HarperCollins Pubs. 1993
281p o.p.   LC 92-54424
In alternating chapters, the author "depicts the lives of paleontologist Howard Beamish and crusading journalist Lucy Faulkner, both successful in their careers but unfulfilled because they have not established enduring relationships. They meet when the plane they are taking to Cairo makes a forced landing in Callimbia, a fictional country in the throes of a bloody revolution led by a lunatic dictator. Lively's . . . construction of Callimbia's history ranges from its establishment by Cleopatra's sister Berenice through the rise of the 'moral renegade' who orders the plane's British passengers taken hostage. Through the eyes of Howard and Lucy, and in counterpoint to their growing love for each other, Lively depicts the passengers' responses to their plight." Publ Wkly

Consequences. Viking 2007 258p $24.95
   ISBN 978-0-670-03856-5; 0-670-03856-3
                      LC 2007-297882
This novel "begins in the 1930s as Londoners Lorna and Matt meet, marry, and move into a rural English cottage, where daughter Molly is born. When Matt dies in battle during World War II, the shattered Lorna moves back to London to live with Lucas, Matt's business partner and friend. When subsequent loss occurs, the narrative shifts to Molly, now a smart, independent young woman looking out for her younger brother and stepfather while making her way in the working world. Later, as Molly negotiates midlife, the narrative shifts again, settling on Molly's daughter, Ruth, a journalist who is married with two children and yet yearns for happiness." Libr J
"A keen perception of the meanings of time and space joins the three generations of women . . . . as much as their shared blood does; it also allows author Penelope Lively to observe the worlds of change that occur during their lifetimes. She remains a heartbreakingly human and elegant writer." BookPage

Heat wave; a novel. HarperCollins Pubs. 1996
214p o.p.   LC 96-19893
The novel's heroine, Pauline "is a freelance copy-editor. She is spending the summer in her [English] country cottage, working on the typescript of an epic novel about knights and maidens. Her daughter, Teresa, is staying next door with her husband, Maurice, and their infant son. From her cool, 'slightly opportunistic life of the unattached,' Pauline gradually becomes aware of the emotional shifts in her daughter's marriage." Times Lit Suppl
"Outwardly, the mother herself seems cool, but she is still seething over her own husband's infidelities, many years earlier. Wisdom tends to substitute for drama here, yet you don't want to part company with these characters, who, time and again, elicit a sensation of intense familiarity." New Yorker

Moon tiger. Grove Press 1988 c1987 208p
   ISBN 0-8021-3533-1
                    * LC 87-23798
First published 1987 in the United Kingdom
"The heroine is Claudia Hampton, an unconventional historian and former war correspondent who lies in a hospital bed dying of cancer. Forced inward, Claudia moves randomly across time and place to reconstruct the strata of her life." Libr J
"Moon Tiger is an extremely accomplished novel which tells an interesting story with an impressive variety of fictional techniques." Quill Quire

Pack of cards and other stories. Grove Press 1989 c1986 323p o.p.   LC 89-1851
First published 1986 in the United Kingdom with title: Pack of cards: stories, 1978-1986
Contents: Nothing missing but the samovar; The voice of God in Adelaide Terrace; Interpreting the past; Servants talk about people: gentlefolk discuss things; Help; Miss Carlton and the pop concert; Revenant as typewriter; Next term, we'll mash you; At the Pitt-Rivers; Nice people; A world of her own; Presents of fish and game; A clean death; Party; Corruption; Venice, now and then; Grow old along with me, the best is yet to be; The darkness out there; The pill-box; Customers; Yellow trains; The ghost of a flea; The art of biography; What the eye doesn't see; The emasculation of Ted Roper; A long night at Abu Simbel; Bus-stop; Clara's day; The French exchange; The dream merchant; Pack of cards; The Crimean hotel; A dream of fair women; Black dog
"These witty, profoundly civilized stories display Lively's compassion, intelligence, and versatility." Libr J

Passing on. Grove Weidenfeld 1990 c1989 210p
   ISBN 0-8021-1155-6
                    * LC 89-7459
First published 1989 in the United Kingdom
This novel describes the reactions of Helen and Edward Glover to the death of their mother Dorothy. "Long years in Greystones, the family nest in a pleasant Cotswold village, have all but atrophied their desire to make lives of their own, free of their widowed mother's commanding presence; both have remained unmarried. . . .

Lively, Penelope, 1933----_Continued_

Opening the novel with Dorothy's funeral, Lively traces the events of the months that follow and poses the question whether real change is possible in the lives of such repressed and gentle characters." Times Lit Suppl

"Penelope Lively is blessed with the gift of being able to render matters of great import with a breath, a barely audible sigh, a touch. The result is wonderful writing, and a marvelous book." N Y Times Book Rev

The photograph. Viking 2003 231p $24.95

ISBN 0-670-03205-0   LC 2002-32420

Widower "Glyn Peters, a famous British archeologist, discovers a compromising photograph of his wife, Katherine Targett, sealed in an envelope in a closet at home. Peters specializes in excavating the long defunct gardens, buried fields and covered-over roads of the British landscape. Reverting to professional habits, he treats Kath's infidelity as a sort of archeological dig. The photo depicts Kath and Nick Hammond, the husband of Kath's sister, Elaine, surreptitiously holding hands on some outing, with Elaine and Mary Parkard, Kath's best friend, in the background. Glyn decides to interview this cloud of witnesses, beginning with Elaine." Publ Wkly

"Lively's characters are shallow, their efforts at introspection often hilarious, but they are all obliged to confront their complicity in the premature death of a woman they each claim to have loved." N Y Times Book Rev

The road to Lichfield. Grove Weidenfeld 1991 215p o.p.   LC 90-47673

First published 1977 in the United Kingdom

This novel "centers around British housewife Anne, whose father is dying in a nursing home. Anne goes to see him, in Lichfield, and in the process of cleaning out his house discovers that her father was someone she hadn't known well at all. 'I knew my father in one dimension only,' she realizes. Her relationships with her husband, brother, and lover might be similarly described. Lively's prose is clean and readable." Libr J

Spiderweb; a novel. HarperFlamingo 1999 218p

ISBN 0-06-019233-X   LC 98-45696

First published 1998 in the United Kingdom

Anthropologist Stella Brentwood "is about to retire, so she buys a cottage in Somerset, England, and sets about learning to live the country life. Of course, Stella is _still_ an anthropologist, observing the strange customs of her neighbors. . . . In the process, Stella gets reacquainted with the husband of her oldest friend, now dead, whose life was decidedly more domestic. . . . Stella also has occasion to encounter her neighbors, a family that seems far more uncivilized and violent than any Stella may have encountered during her work. Stella's new life is . . . shattered by a terrible incident involving this family." Libr J

"Though the leisurely pace and purposefully digressive narrative are somewhat slow to build suspense, Lively's perceptive vision about the insularity of modern life rings true." Publ Wkly

Livesey, Margot

Banishing Verona; a novel. Henry Holt 2004 321p $24

ISBN 0-8050-7462-7   LC 2004-52383

The author relates the "love story of Zeke, a 29-year-old painter and carpenter . . ., and 37-year-old Verona, a pregnant radio host. In the 17 hours they spend together, they fall in love-only to be separated and put through impossible and unbearably stressful situations." Libr J

"Both Zeke and Verona have just enough quirks to be endearing without being implausible; the supporting characters are similarly well realized. As Livesey . . . probes the depths of longing, betrayal and forgiveness, her gift for creating sublimely unexpected sentences is abundantly on display." Publ Wkly

Criminals; a novel. Knopf 1996 271p

ISBN 0-679-44487-4   LC 95-31512

"On his way to see his sister in rural Scotland, Ewan, a dour, middle-aged investment banker, finds an abandoned baby in the washroom of a roadside bus stop. As he emerges with the baby, the bus carrying his belongings roars into motion, forcing him back on board with the intention of turning the baby over to the proper authorities when he arrives at his sister's. Mollie, his sister, recently separated from her long-time lover, is on emotionally shaky ground and views the arrival of a baby on her doorstep as providential. Conspiring to keep the baby, Mollie plunges herself and Ewan into morally murky waters." Libr J

The reader becomes "enmeshed in the complex windings of Ms. Livesey's plot, a web of criminal circumstance and moral consequence that conveys the awful randomness of life even as it offers the abiding pleasures of artfully constructed fiction." N Y Times Book Rev

Eva moves the furniture. Holt & Co. 2001 232p

ISBN 0-8050-6801-5   LC 00-143895

"Eva McEwen grows up engulfed by a vast and hopeful loneliness. She lives in a small Scottish town with her father and an overprotective aunt, her mother having died of the flu at her birth, in 1920. After Eva turns six, her solitary play is interrupted at unpredictable moments by a girl and a woman who, more than once, come to her aid. Only when she starts school does she realize that these two are invisible to everyone else-and, moreover, jealous of new acquaintances. At eighteen, Eva is desperate to escape the emotional tyrannies of her upbringing, but she eventually comes to feel the fullness of her love for both the real and the imaginary companions of her childhood. Livesey has written a ghost story, of sorts, minus the theremin musiclike 'Our Town,' with its speakers from the grave-and, if it moves you, the end will send you back to the beginning again." New Yorker

The house on Fortune Street. Harper 2008 311p $24.95

ISBN 978-0-06-145152-2; 0-06-145152-5

LC 2007-29611

"Dara, a therapist at a women's center, lives in the downstairs flat of her friend Abigail's London home. A workaholic actress and theatrical producer, Abigail lives upstairs with her boyfriend, Sean, a struggling Keats scholar and writer. Although Dara and Abigail were best friends in college, their lives are so busy there is not much time for getting together. Sean is financially strapped and agrees to coauthor a book on euthanasia. He suspects Abigail is having an affair. Dara is involved with a married man she is perennially sure will leave his wife. And although she is often able to help her clients with their problems, Dara has never resolved issues re-

Livesey, Margot—*Continued*

volving around her parents' divorce. Her father, Cameron, has never been able to tell her he struggled with attractions to young girls, whom he photographed obsessively." Libr J

"That people with the closest of bonds — lovers, family members, best friends — can be strangers to one another is a familiar literary motif, but it has seldom been more affectingly dramatized than in this extraordinary book." Entertainment Wkly

The missing world; a novel. Knopf 2000 325p
ISBN 0-375-40581-X   LC 99-35785

"Hazel loses three years of her past when a traffic accident wipes out her memory. She doesn't remember that she and Jonathan quarreled, and she moved out of their apartment. All she knows is that he has dropped everything to care for her. But she becomes a virtual prisoner when Jonathan decides he can't let her out of his sight for fear someone will 'remind' Hazel of what really happened." Booklist

"Adroitly paced, meticulously plotted and increasingly suspenseful, the novel transcends its genre as psychological thriller." Publ Wkly

The **living** dead; edited by John Joseph Adams. Night Shade Books 2008 487p pa $15.95
ISBN 978-1-59780-143-0; 1-59780-143-7

Contents: This year's class picture, by D. Simmons; Some zombie contingency plans, by K. Link; Death and suffrage, by D. Bailey; Ghost dance, by S. Alexie; Blossom, by D. J. Schow; The third dead body, by N. Kiriki Hoffman; The dead, by M. Swanwick; The dead kid, by D. Schweitzer; Malthusian's zombie, by J. Ford; Beautiful stuff, by S. Palwick; Sex, death, and starshine, by C. Barker; Stockholm syndrome, by D. Tallerman; Bobby Conroy comes back from the dead, by J. Hill; Those who seek forgiveness, by L. K. Hamilton; In beauty, like the night, by N. Partridge; Prairie, by B. Evenson; Everything is better with zombies, by H. W. Bowen; Home delivery, by S. King; Less than zombie, by D. E. Winter; Sparks fly upward, by L. Morton; Meathouse man, by G. R. R. Martin; Deadman's road, by J. R. Lansdale; The skull-faced boy, by D. B. Kirtley; The age of sorrow, by N. Kilpatrick; Bitter grounds, by N. Gaiman; She's taking her tits to the grave, by C. Cheek; Dead like me, A.-T. Castro; Zora and the zombie, A. Duncan; Calcutta, lord of nerves, by P. Z. Brite; Followed, by W. McIntosh; The song the zombie sang, by H. Ellison and R. Silverberg; Passion play, by N. Holder; Almost the last story by almost the last man, by S. Edelman; How the day runs down, by J. Langan

"These stories range from the truly disgusting (Poppy Z. Brite's 'Calcutta: Lord of Nerves') to the nearly wistful ('Followed' by Will McIntosh) and even one with no supernatural elements at all (Joe Hill's 'Bobby Conroy Comes Back from the Dead'). Included are pieces by big names in horror like Stephen King and Clive Barker but also contributions by less obvious suspects like Harlan Ellison, Sherman Alexie, and George R.R. Martin. The final treat is John Langan's 'How the Day Runs Down,' a nasty little play best described as Our Town with zombies. Highly recommended for all horror fiction collections." Libr J

Llewellyn, Richard, 1906-1983

How green was my valley. Macmillan 1940 495p o.p.

*

In this "novel of the Welsh mining country the story is told by Huw Morgan, youngest son of a miner's family. In his boyhood, in the '80's, the valley was green and beautiful, the people were prosperous and law abiding; gradually the countryside was changed to a place of desolation as slag-heaps of mine refuse covered the mountain slopes; hard times, with strikes and layoffs, brought suffering, and a wholesome way of life was destroyed." Booklist

"A remarkably beautiful novel of Wales. And although it follows stirringly in the romantic traditions, there is the resonance of a profound and noble realism in its evocation, its intensity and reach of truth." N Y Times Book Rev

Llosa, Mario Vargas *See* Vargas Llosa, Mario, 1936-

Llywelyn, Morgan

1916. Forge 1998 447p
ISBN 0-312-86101-X   LC 97-29838
"A Tom Doherty Associates book"

"A novel set in Ireland at the time of the Easter Rebellion. Llywelyn tells the tale of 15-year-old Ned Halloran, a young *Titanic* survivor who lost both of his parents in that disaster. Upon his return to his native Ireland, he becomes embroiled in its rapidly changing political scene. The headmaster of his school is a renowned scholar and also a rebel and patriot for the Irish cause. Ned acts as a courier for the rebels, becoming more and more supportive of their struggle." SLJ

"Battle scenes are both accurate and compelling. The betrayals, slaughters and passions of the day are all splendidly depicted as Llywelyn delivers a blow-by-blow account of the rebellion and its immediate aftermath. The novel's abundant footnotes should satisfy history buffs; its easy, gripping style will enthrall casual readers." Publ Wkly

1921. Forge 2001 445p $25.95
ISBN 0-312-86754-9   LC 00-49021
"A Tom Doherty Associates book"
Sequel to 1916

"Incessantly haunted by the rather passive role he played in the doomed Easter Rebellion, Henry Mooney, a journalist struggling for objectivity in the midst of controversy and mayhem, reevaluates his own convictions and commitment to the cause of a free Ireland. When Henry falls in love with an Anglo-Irish woman, simmering tensions wrought by centuries of domination and repression are reflected in a microcosm of passion and agony. The lucid narrative and the compelling subject matter will enthrall both Irish history buffs and fans of sweeping historical fiction." Booklist

1949; a novel of the Irish Free State. Forge 2003 414p $25.95
ISBN 0-312-86753-0   LC 2002-32525
"A Tom Doherty Associates Book"
Sequel to: 1921

"The story focuses on the indomitable Ursula Halloran

Llywelyn, Morgan—*Continued*

. . . a young woman who first works for the Irish radio service and later the League of Nations. The unwed Ursula discovers how oppressive the new Catholic state can be when she becomes pregnant and must flee the country. Eventually, Ursula must choose between the two men in her life, one an Irish civil servant, the other an English pilot." Publ Wkly

"Llywelyn's great strength is her ability to communicate sweeping historical events through the eyes of both passive bystanders and active participants." Booklist

1972; a novel of Ireland's unfinished revolution.
Forge 2005 365p $24.95

   ISBN 0-312-87857-5   LC 2004-51246
Sequel to 1949

The author "tells the story of Ireland from 1950-1972 as seen through the eyes of young Barry Halloran, son and grandson of Irish revolutionaries. Northern Ireland has become a running sore, poisoning life on both sides of the Irish border. Following family tradition, at eighteen Barry joins the Irish Republican Army to help complete what he sees as 'the unfinished revolution.'" Publisher's note

Druids. Morrow 1991 456p o.p.

                   LC 90-44292

"Caesar's Gallic Wars are recounted from the viewpoint of the losers in this . . . evocation of the culture of the European Celts. Ainvar of the Carnutes, a young orphan druid-in-training, receives instruction for the 'manmaking' rituals with prince Vercingetorix of the Arverni, forging a bond that will later unite them in an effort to free Celtic Gaul from Roman domination." Publ Wkly

"Llywelyn's skill at making ancient history come alive for a modern audience without sacrificing authenticity of fact or detail is nothing short of brilliant. A richly atmospheric tale filled with subtle flashes of humor, perceptive characterizations, and heart-stopping suspense." Booklist

The elementals. TOR Bks. 1993 303p o.p.

                   LC 93-12760

"Remnants of humanity escape the great flood and make their way to safety in prehistoric Ireland. A singer and his companions survive the volcanic eruption that destroys the palace of Minos in Crete. A farmer's wife in 19th-century New Hampshire discovers the secrets of a sacred stone, and in the 21st century, George Burning Feather seeks the wisdom of the past to combat the ultimate natural disaster—the death of the air. . . . Though the connections among the four stories comprising this volume emerge only in the final story, each tale bears its own compelling message." Libr J

The horse goddess. Houghton Mifflin 1982 417p
o.p.

                   LC 82-6234

"The Celts of 700 B.C. were a variety of tribes spread over Central Europe. Epona, a teenage Celt has just been initiated into womanhood when four strange horsemen visit her community. She is drawn to the leader, Kazhak, and leaves with the Scythians to escape the lecherous Druid priest. Epona's affinity for animals is held in awe by her new tribe, as is her boldness in a world where women are seen in veils only and never heard. Epona is eventually forced to flee the Russian steppes and returns

to her old home, where her acquired wisdom helps her become the new Druid priestess." Libr J

"The author emphasizes the independent status of Celtic women, a proto-feminist characteristic that should heighten the appeal of the book." Publ Wkly

The last prince of Ireland. Morrow 1992 368p
o.p.

                   LC 91-42516

Published in the United Kingdom with title: O'Sullivan's march

This "novel takes place in 17th-century Ireland as Queen Elizabeth I of England seeks to obliterate 2000 years of Celtic tradition and religion. It begins on December 30, 1602, soon after the Battle of Kinsale sounded the death knell for Irish independence. Fugitive nobleman Donal Cam O'Sullivan, the 'prince' of the title, denounces the queen and seeks to march 1000 followers to safety across wintry, dangerous terrain. Death, desertion, and near-constant fighting with the enemy, both English and Irish, reduce his band to a starving and exhausted group of 35 survivors." Libr J

"This tale of courage, love, cruelty and treachery, one of the great legends of Ireland, receives vivid, evocative treatment here." Publ Wkly

Pride of lions. Forge 1996 351p il o.p.

                   LC 95-42566

"A Tom Doherty Associates book"

"The perils of royal succession and a choice between love and glory form the dominant themes of Llywelyn's . . . sequel to *Lion of Ireland* (1979). That novel described the rise of High King Brian Boru, who became known as the 'Charlemagne of Ireland' after he managed to briefly unite the tribes of the Emerald Isle at the end of the 10th century. Here it's Brian's 15-year-old son, Donough, who aspires to the throne, made ambitious by a brief initial success in battle against the Vikings at Contarf, where Brian has met his death. But Donough's brother Teigue also claims the crown. . . . Llywelyn tells a strong story distinguished by its psychological depth and by his knowledge of ancient Irish history." Publ Wkly

Red Branch. Morrow 1989 558p o.p.

                   LC 88-13508

In this novel the author has created a legendary world "based on disparate tales of Ireland's mythical warrior-hero Cuchulain. . . . The story begins with a boy, Setanta, born in mysterious circumstances to Dectera, the King's half sister. Either Dectera's husband, the King, or a god is Setanta's father. But the truth is concealed from him, and in a land where status and privilege derive from birthright, his uncertain paternity is a painful mark of difference. Though still a youth, Setanta's ferocity while in combat with a monstrous wolfhound owned by a blacksmith, Cullen, earns him the name Cuchulain, or hound of Cullen. Soon after, he enters a warrior clan, the 'Red Branch' of the book's title." NY Times Book Rev

"Llywelyn works a massive canvas, peopling it with larger-than-life characters, yet shaping them with intimate insights." Publ Wkly

Silverlight; [by] Morgan Llywelyn, Michael Scott. Baen Pub. Enterprises 1996 406p

   ISBN 0-671-87728-3   LC 96-7635
Sequel to Silverhand

Caeled "possesses two magical artifacts that allow him to affect events but cause him to age with every use.

Llywelyn, Morgan—*Continued*

Joined by three companions who hate the despotic twins who rule the world, Caeled seeks the remaining two Arcana artifacts that he will use to restore order to the world. A morality tale about how much power one can have and whether to use it that belongs in most fantasy collections." Libr J

Lockridge, Ross, 1914-1948

Raintree County. Houghton Mifflin 1948 1066p il o.p.

                                           *

An epic novel describing a day, the Fourth of July of 1892, in the life of school teacher Johnny Shawnessy in which he participates in the holiday ceremonies of his small Indiana town and meets two old boyhood friends. These events set off a series of flashbacks in his mind and he relives his schooldays, his Civil war experiences, his brief political life, his two marriages, and a love affair that ends badly

"The book is full-blooded, it has gusto, ribaldry, vision, beauty, and narrative skill. It is also repetitious, overly 'organized,' reminiscent of a variety of predecessors, 'literary' in the wrong sense, and too dependent upon source material. But the breath of life sweeps through its voluminous pages." Saturday Rev

Lodge, David, 1935-

Deaf sentence. Viking 2008 294p $25.95
ISBN 978-0-670-01992-2; 0-670-01992-5
                                LC 2008-1772
"Sexagenarian Desmond Bates wears a hearing aid after being diagnosed some 20 years earlier with 'acquired deafness' and consistently misinterprets people's words (which Lodge milks to maximum comic effect). Bates longs for activities after his retirement from teaching applied linguistics, other than contemplating e-mail spam about erectile dysfunction and watching his wife, Winifred, enjoy her success as an interior designer. The novel takes the form of his newly begun daily diary. At a gallery event, Bates mistakenly agrees to help shapely, enigmatic American student Alex Loom with her Ph.D. thesis on suicide notes." Publ Wkly

"This is a brave novel, which puts a brave face on everything we'd rather not know about ageing, without ducking the atrocity of it all." London Rev Books

Nice work. Viking 1989 277p
ISBN 0-670-82806-8
                                LC 88-40480
A satirical look at "Thatcher's England. Two representatives from different worlds–the groves of academe and the dark satanic mills–meet and fall in (a semblance of) love as they aim to satisfy their physical passions and also open their emotions to new experiences. The academic is a young female professor of literature, and her industrial counterpart is a middle-aged factory manager. Their initial meeting does set off sparks but only to fan the flames of mutual antagonism before an attraction of sorts takes place." Booklist

"Lodge spoofs in a nonjudgmental way both the pretensions of academia and the materialism of the upper-middle business class. While lacking in stylistic elegance, this is a well-told tale full of gentle humor." Libr J

Paradise news; a novel. Viking 1992 293p
ISBN 0-670-84228-1
                                LC 91-32128

First published 1991 in the United Kingdom

"Bernard Walsh is planning a quiet visit to his sick aunt in Hawaii. A cynical ex-priest in search of a well-needed vacation, he is unprepared for this zany package tour from Hell populated with all the 'types': dueling newlyweds, boring salesmen, video happy seniors, romance starved spinsters, and a sexy native girl on a collision course with fate (or at least Walsh's father)." Libr J

"Mr. Lodge is a serious author who bravely uses coincidence and contrivance to tie up loose ends. And just under the surface of the spirited and often comic adventures of his travelers he runs an undercurrent of understanding about their longings for the perfection of paradise. This comes to us in graceful and disciplined prose that offers vivid glimpses of what lies beyond the tourist hotels of Waikiki–the natural and imperfect world." N Y Times Book Rev

Therapy; a novel. Viking 1995 320p
ISBN 0-670-86358-0
                                LC 95-16337
"Laurence 'Tubby' Passmore is a successful British TV sitcom writer. He has plenty of money, homes in London and Rummidge, a fast car, and all the therapists his calendar will hold. Yet Tubby is chronically unhappy. In fact, he is so wrapped up in dismal self-contemplation that he does not notice when his daughter's pregnancy is announced or his wife of 30 years demands a divorce. He discovers and obsesses about Kierkegaard, seeing many similarities between his own life and that of the philosopher. When his world begins to crumble around him, Tubby sets off on a pilgrimage to find Maureen Kavanaugh, his first girlfriend." Libr J

"The novel is almost Victorian in its earnest goodness, which shines through its humor straight to the enormously moving and exultant ending." New Yorker

Thinks—; a novel. Viking 2001 341p
ISBN 0-670-89984-4
                                LC 2001-17555
"At a grim and insular provincial university, Ralph, a married scientist who runs an artifical-intelligence program, is drawn to the newly arrived Helen, a novelist and a recent widow. In Lodgian fashion, adultery quickly becomes their chief preoccupation, as the narrative unfolds in shifting points of view (Ralph dictating into a tape recorder, Helen adding to a diary), with occasional third-person authorial assistance." New Yorker

"This is the first Lodge novel set in the world of science, and it paints an utterly persuasive portrait of it. The story is a cracking tale, but read it, too, for the ideas. It's obvious that Lodge has become fascinated by the science of thought. Reading this is, so will you." New Sci

Lofts, Norah, 1904-1983

Gad's Hall. Doubleday 1978 c1977 282p o.p.
                                LC 77-92220
First published 1977 in the United Kingdom

"Dismissing Mrs. Spender's claims that Gad's Hall is haunted, her son Bob and daughter-in-law Jill buy the grand English country estate. . . . With this setup, Lofts deserts her modern family to describe the lives of the Thorleys who founded Gad's Hall in the 1800s. The widowed Mrs. Thorley of that era exerts firm control over the affairs of her children and stepchildren. When unwed Lavinia becomes pregnant, Mrs. Thorley hides the girl

Lofts, Norah, 1904-1983—*Continued*

until the baby is born. The tragedy that results creates the ghosts that haunt the manor, to affect the Spenders, more than 100 years later." Publ Wkly

Followed by The haunting of Gad's Hall

Logan, Chuck, 1942-

South of Shiloh; a thriller. HarperCollins Publishers 2008 402p $24.95

ISBN 978-0-06-113669-6; 0-06-113669-7

LC 2007-25672

"When Minnesotan Paul Edin is killed during a re-enactment of the battle of Kirby Creek near Corinth, Miss., local law enforcement quickly declares his death a tragic accident. But when Paul's widow, Jenny, learns that the bullet may have been meant for deputy Kenny Beeman, she's determined to uncover the truth. Reconnecting with John Rane—her ex-lover and the biological father of the child she raised with Paul—Jenny persuades John to go to Corinth and investigate. A photographer and former cop known for taking risks, John joins forces with Kenny in Mississippi and attempts to unravel a complex web of family feuds. John soon realizes that the upcoming re-enactment of the battle of Shiloh could end up as bloody as the original. Despite a few plot holes, Logan skillfully immerses the reader in the traditions and eccentricities of the men who meticulously recreate every aspect of the Civil War." Publ Wkly

Loh, Vyvyane

Breaking the tongue; a novel. W.W. Norton 2004 407p map $24.95

ISBN 0-393-05792-5   LC 2003-15870

"On the eve of World War II, Claude Lim, a Chinese youth, uncertain of himself and his nationality, is being raised in a family that strongly identifies with the British colonists in Singapore. The family neither speaks nor understands Chinese and is proud of that fact. Their placid lives are disturbed by the hodgepodge of Asians, Eurasians, and British expatriates shifting in their roles and political sensibilities as the threat of invasion approaches. Prickly, pretentious Claude slowly metamorphoses into a young man with a budding Chinese identity and a wisdom wrought from the tortures and tragedies of war." Booklist

The author "explores such concepts as loyalty to one's family and country, the place of language in culture, and the roles of race, racism and ethnicity in how we perceive ourselves and others. In doing so, she has skillfully touched on questions at the very heart of politics, culture and global relations today." Washington Post Book World

London, Jack, 1876-1916

The call of the wild; pictures by Wendell Minor. Atheneum Books for Young Readers 1999 112p il $24; pa $4.95

ISBN 0-689-81836-X; 1-416-50019-7 (pa)

* LC 97-45019

First published 1903 by Macmillan

"Buck, half-St. Bernard, half-Scottish sheepdog, is stolen from his comfortable home in California and pressed into service as a sledge dog in the Klondike. At first he is abused by both man and dog, but he learns to fight ruthlessly. He becomes lead dog on a sledge team, after bettering Spitz, the vicious old leader, in a brutal fight to the death. In John Thornton, he finally finds a master whom he can respect and love. When Thornton is killed by Indians, Buck breaks away to the wilds and becomes the leader of a wolf pack, returning each year to the site of Thornton's death." Reader's Ency. 4th edition

also in London, J. Novels & stories

The complete short stories of Jack London; edited by Earle Labor, Robert C. Leitz, III, and I. Milo Shepard. Stanford Univ. Press 1993 3v $195

ISBN 0-8047-2058-4   LC 92-44856

"The London scholar and enthusiast will find this collection of Jack London's short fiction invaluable for the 5 previously unpublished stories it contains and for the 28 others it collects for the first time since their original publication in magazines." Choice

Martin Eden. Macmillan 1909 411p o.p.

A semi-autobiographical novel. "Eden has had a knock-about life as a sailor, and falling in love with a girl used to middle-class refinement and luxuries, tries to write. He is rejected by editors, and the girl jilts him. The abysmal contrast between the genius of this man, his vital ideals and the big realities of life, and on the other hand, the narrow, unintelligent mediocrity of the 'cultured classes' is brought out with characteristic force." Baker. Guide to Hist Fic

Novels & stories; Jack London. Literary Classics of the United States, Distributed to the trade by Viking Press 1982 1020p $35

ISBN 0-940450-05-4

* LC 82-249

Contents: The call of the wild; White fang; The sea-wolf; Short stories

The Sea-Wolf; with illustrations by W.J. Aylward. Macmillan 1904 366p o.p.

"Wolf Larsen, ruthless captain of the tramp steamer 'Ghost,' receives an unexpected passenger on the high seas, Humphrey Van Weyden, a wealthy ne'er-do-well. In spite of his selfish brutality, Larsen becomes an instrument for good. The treatment he gives to the dilettante Van Weyden teaches the latter to stand on his own legs. He and the poet Maude Brewster, whom the 'Sea-Wolf' loves also, escape to an island as the 'Ghost' sinks and Larsen, mortally sick, is deserted. The lovers later return to civilization." Haydn. Thesaurus of Book Dig

also in London, J. Novels & stories

Short stories of Jack London; authorized one-volume edition; edited by Earle Labor, Robert C. Leitz III, I. Milo Shepard. Macmillan 1990 xli, 738p o.p.   LC 90-6175

Contents: Story of a typhoon off the coast of Japan; The white silence; To the man on trail; In a far country; An odyssey of the north; Semper idem; The law of life; A relic of the pliocene; Nam-Bok the unveracious; The one thousand dozen; To build a fire (1902); Moon-face; Bâtard; The story of Jees Uck; The league of the old men; Love of life; The sun-dog trail; All gold canyon; A day's lodging; The apostate; The wit of Porportuk; The unparalleled invasion; To build a fire (1908); The

London, Jack, 1876-1916—*Continued*
house of pride; The house of Mapuhi; The Chinago; Lost face; Koolau the leper; Chun Ah Chun; The heathen; Mauki; The strength of the strong; South of the Slot; Samuel; A piece of steak; The madness of John Harned; The night-born; War; Told in the drooling ward; The Mexican; The pearls of Parlay; Wonder of woman; The red one; On the Makaloa mat; The tears of Ah Kim; Shin bones; When Alice told her soul; Like Argus of the ancient times; The princess; The water baby

South Sea tales. Macmillan 1911 327p o.p.
Contents: The house of Mapuki; The whale tooth; Mauki; "Yah! Yah! Yah"; The heathen; The terrible Solomons; The inevitable white man; The seed of McCoy

The star rover. Macmillan 1915 329p o.p.
In this science fiction novel about transmigration of the soul, Darrell Standing is condemned to solitary confinement in a corrupt prison. He discovers how to free his soul from his body and escapes through time and space to relive the experiences of his past lives, which include being a caveman, a Danish soldier in the Roman legions, a French swordsman, and an American pioneer boy

White Fang; pictures by Ed Young. Atheneum Books for Young Readers 2000 260p il hardcover o.p. pa $5.99
ISBN 0-689-82431-9; 1-416-91414-5 (pa)
* LC 98-19241
First published 1906
White Fang "is about a dog, a cross-breed, sold to Beauty Smith. This owner tortures the dog to increase his ferocity and value as a fighter. A new owner Weedom Scott, brings the dog to California, and, by kind treatment, domesticates him. White Fang later sacrifices his life to save Scott." Haydn. Thesaurus of Book Dig

also in London, J. Novels & stories
also in London, J. White Fang, and other stories p1-230

White Fang, and other stories; with photographs of the author and his environment as well as illustrations from early editions, together with an introduction by A.K. Adams. Dodd, Mead 1963 308p il o.p.
"Great illlustrated classics"
Short stories included are: The one thousand dozen; All Gold Canyon; The son of the wolf; In a far country
The title novel (entered separately) and short stories are about dogs in Canada's Yukon Territory

London, Joan, 1948-

The good parents. Black Cat 2009 349p pa $14.95
ISBN 978-0-8021-7057-6; 0-8021-7057-9
"A girl from the Australian outback heads to Melbourne and, in thrall to the idea of having a secret, grownup life, runs off with her older, married boss, a shady businessman who, she recognizes, has little genuine feeling for her. This is just an overture to the novel's central story, in which the girl's parents, in the wake of their daughter's disappearance, confront their own youthful rebellions—the mother's early romance with a gangster, the father's hippie wanderings—and the inchoate

ideals that led them to bury themselves in a rural backwater. The author comes at her characters from every angle, laying bare their compromises and delusions." New Yorker

Long, David, 1948-

The inhabited world. Houghton 2006 277p $23
ISBN 0-618-54335-X   LC 2005-20061
"Evan Molloy—a son, husband, and stepfather—fatally shot himself but doesn't know why. He is stuck in a state of purgatory in the house in Washington State where he lived and died. The woman who now lives there, Maureen Keniston, is in her late thirties and is trying to restart her life after breaking off a long affair with a married man. The novel . . . moves back and forth between the story of Evan's troubled life and Maureen's efforts to emerge from her own purgatory." Publisher's note
This is a "tale of everyday, getting-by existence in America, where joys can be sudden and painfully intense, and sorrows can be, too, and the trick is not to let the blues get the better of you. . . . This is a terrific novel, and you can't help thinking, from time to time, that in a better world David Long would be a famous writer. But, as the book makes pretty clear, there is no better world; just this one. And when the words are right, even this world is sweet enough." N Y Times Book Rev

Long, Jeff

The reckoning. Atria Books 2004 278p $25
ISBN 0-7434-6300-5   LC 2004-43657
A "journey into the dark past-and present-of Cambodia's former killing fields. Molly Drake, a would-be photojournalist, accompanies a U.S. Army-led search for the bones of a pilot shot down during the war. She meets Duncan O'Brian, an archeologist at a local dig, and John Kleat, who has come back to the country repeatedly, seeking his brother's remains. When bones unexpectedly turn up, Molly photographs them, breaking her agreement with the army not to take pictures of bodies. The captain in charge dismisses her along with O'Brian and Kleat, and the trio make their way to an ancient, fog-enshrouded Angkor-like city where they have evidence an army patrol went missing years ago. . . . Long's considerable knowledge of Cambodian folklore and history is put to good use as he superbly depicts the war-scarred country, its people and its beautiful, hazardous landscape." Publ Wkly

Longyear, Barry B.

Enemy mine
In The Hugo winners p5-67

Lopez, Barry Holstun, 1945-

Resistance; [by] Barry Lopez. Alfred A. Knopf 2004 163p il $18
ISBN 1-400-04220-8   LC 2003-65986
This novel is comprised of "nine fictional testimonials that chronicle a group of activists who have been called before the 'Office of Inland Security' for the crime of 'terrorizing the imaginations of our fellow citizens.'

Lopez, Barry Holstun, 1945-—*Continued*

These narrators—who come from various backgrounds (e.g., veteran, linguist, artisan) and parts of the world—focus on the transformative moment in their lives that led them to discover the injustices of the world." Libr J

"If it's true the author's erudite, well-meaning characters all sound very much alike, it's also true that one of his goals is to underscore the responsibility of artists to speak as one when speaking truth to power. To his credit, Lopez never sacrifices craft to politics." N Y Times Book Rev

Lord, Bette Bao

The middle heart; a novel. Knopf 1996 370p $25

ISBN 0-394-53432-8   LC 95-36165

The story begins in early 1930s China, "when three young people forge an unlikely alliance that survives five decades of loss and love. There's Steele Hope, the second son of the head of the once noble and powerful Li family; Mountain Pine, his 'bookmate' and retainer; and a destitute girl posing as a boy named Firecrackers. The novel's early sections sparkle with hope and joy as the three devoted friends romp and grow, but personal tragedy and war soon intrude." Booklist

Lordan, Beth

But come ye back; a novel in stories. Morrow 2004 278p $23.95

ISBN 0-06-053036-7   LC 2003-56217

This is the "story of Mary Curtin, an Irish nanny, and Lyle Sullivan, an American accountant, who fall in love, marry, and raise their two sons. When Lyle retires, Mary persuades him to relocate to her native Galway. She wants to live among her remaining family again and assures Lyle that he will love Ireland. Predictably, as in their earlier life together, there are joys and complications that stretch the ties that bind them, yet their marriage endures. Lyle reluctantly adapts to the idiosyncrasies of their small Irish community, and each spouse rediscovers the other in their new surroundings." Libr J

"Lordan's muted prose and fluting Irishisms ('Right, so,' 'Grand') are pleasant if rather selfconscious, and her characters are human, breathing people, forthrightly crafted. The novel-in-stories structure produces some inconsistencies and redundancies, but this is a quietly engaging effort." Publ Wkly

Lott, Bret

Ancient highway; a novel. Random House 2008 241p $25

ISBN 978-1-4000-6374-1; 1-4000-6374-4   LC 2007-38760

This novel "shows how one man's aspirations to become a famous Hollywood actor reverberate over three generations. In 1927, handsome Earl Holmes runs away from his Texas home at age 14 to Southern California. Some years later, after he has married budding, talented songstress Saralee Kennedy, his schemes to make it in the entertainment industry affect his young daughter, Joan. Years pass again, and Joan's twentysomething son, Brad, fresh off the boat after six years in the navy in Southeast Asia, arrives at Earl and Saralee's Southern California home to try to find direction in his life." Libr J

"Lott's language is poetic in its rhythm and rich in detail, lending equal humanity to a real-life Hollywood character and an imagined flea market vendor." San Francisco Chron

Lourie, Richard, 1940-

A hatred for tulips. Thomas Dunne Books 2007 182p $22.95

ISBN 978-0-312-34933-2; 0-312-34933-5   LC 2006-48862

"The novel opens in present-day Amsterdam with an elderly man known as Joop having just confessed a childhood secret he has kept for more than 60 years—a secret that involves Anne Frank. Joop recounts the ugly German takeover of Amsterdam, what it did to his family, and the choices he made to survive." Libr J

"Lourie's novel is more than a mystery: at its heart is not only Anne Frank's history, but all of Holland's. Joop derides the Dutch for indulging what, until recently, was a very real Anne Frank amnesia. . . . Ironically, the book is best where it has little to say about Anne Frank. The connection allows Lourie to pose interesting questions about collaboration and guilt during the war, but it rings truest as a story about a boy, in a difficult family, in a difficult time, and the unintended consequences of trying to do what looks like the right thing." Christ Sci Monit

Lovecraft, H. P. (Howard Phillips), 1890-1937

At the mountains of madness, and other novels; selected by August Derleth; with texts edited by S.T. Joshi and introduction by James Turner. Arkham House Pubs. 1985 c1964 458p

ISBN 0-87054-038-6   LC 85-1254

A reissue of the title first published 1964 and analyzed in Short story index

Contents: At the mountains of madness; The case of Charles Dexter Ward; The shunned house; The dreams in the witchhouse; The statement of Randolph Carter; The dream-quest of unknown Kadath; The silver key; Through the gates of the silver key

The Dunwich horror, and others; selected by August Derleth, with texts edited by S.T. Joshi and an introduction by Robert Block. Arkham House Pubs. 1985 c1963 433p

ISBN 0-87054-037-8

A reissue of the title first published 1963 and analyzed in Short story index

Contents: In the vault; Pickman's model; The rats in the walls; The outsider; The colour out of space; The music of Erich Zann; The haunter of the dark; The picture in the house; The call of Cthulhu; The Dunwich horror; Cool air; The whisper in darkness; The terrible old man; The thing on the doorstep; The shadow over Innsmouth; The shadow out of time

H. P. Lovecraft; tales; edited by Peter Straub. Library of America 2005 838p $35

ISBN 1-93108-272-3

     * LC 2004-48979

Lovecraft, H. P. (Howard Phillips), 1890-1937— *Continued*

Contents: The statement of Randolph Carter; The outsider; The music of Erich Zann; Herbert West—animator; The lurking fear; The rats in the walls; The shunned house; The horror at Red Hook; He; Cool air; The call of Cthulhu; Pickman's model; The case of Charles Dexter Ward; The colour out of space; The Dunwich horror; The whisperer in darkness; At the mountains of madness; The shadow over Innsmouth; The dreams in the witch house; The thing on the doorstep; The shadow out of time; The haunter of the dark

"If you spend enough time in Lovecraft's lonely landscapes, fear really does develop: not the fear that you will come across unearthly creatures, but the fear that you will come across little else. And what first seems horridly overdone accumulates a creepy minimalism. Taken as a whole, Lovecraft's work exhibits a hopeless isolation not unlike that of Samuel Beckett: lonely man after lonely man, wandering aimlessly through a shadowy city or holing up in rural emptiness, pursuing unspeakable secrets or being pursued by secret unspeakables, all to little avail and to no comfort. There is something funny about this—in small doses. But by the end of this collection, one does not hear giggling so much as the echoes of those giggles as they vanish into the ether lonely, desperate and, yes, very, very scary." N Y Times Book Rev

The horror in the museum, and other revisions; with texts edited by S. T. Joshi, and an introduction by August Derleth. Arkham House Pubs. 1989 450p o.p.   LC 88-7921

Contents: The green meadow; The crawling chaos; The last test; The electric executioner; The curse of Yig; The mound [novelette]; Medusa's coil; The man of stone; The horror in the museum; Winged death; Out of the aeons; The horror in the burying-ground; The diary of Alonzo Typer; The horror at Martin's Beach; Ashes; The ghost-eater; The loved dead; Deaf, dumb, and blind; Two black bottles; The trap; The tree on the hill; The disinterment; 'Till a' the seas'; The night ocean

"The volume is divided into 'Primary Revisions,' those stories that are all Lovecraft but for an idea, and 'Secondary Revisions,' clients' manuscripts heavily edited and revised." Publ Wkly

The mound

In Lovecraft, H. P. The horror in the museum, and other revisions p96-163

Tales of H.P. Lovecraft; major works selected and introduced by Joyce Carol Oates. Ecco Press 1997 328p

ISBN 0-88001-541-1   LC 96-47196

Contents: The outsider; The music of Erich Zann; The rats in the walls; The shunned house; The call of Cthulhu; The colour out of space; The Dunwich horror; At the mountains of madness; The shadow over Innsmouth; The shadow out of time

Lovecraft, Howard Phillips *See* Lovecraft, H. P. (Howard Phillips), 1890-1937

Lovesey, Peter

Bertie and the seven bodies. Mysterious Press 1990 196p o.p.   LC 89-12405

In this mystery "Albert Edward, the Prince of Wales—Bertie to the ladies—sallies forth on an elaborate hunt in Buckinghamshire and bags a murderer along with the other game." N Y Times Book Rev

"Narrated by Bertie himself, the voice here is perfectly accurate; Lovesey gives his main character just the right tone of sophistication, charm, anti-intellectualism, and savoir faire—mixed in with ennui. A wonderfully put together puzzle." Booklist

Bloodhounds. Warner Bks. 1996 359p o.p.
                    LC 96-22244

In this takeoff on the traditional "locked room" mystery "Lovesey's wise but beleaguered hero Peter Diamond confronts a homicide case as perplexing as any he's faced. The perpetrator appears to be both brilliant and devious, composing a series of riddles designed to offer clues to upcoming crimes while effectively throwing the police off the scent, then stealing a priceless postage stamp while the coppers' collective backs are turned." Booklist

Lovesey "skillfully pays homage to the old style whodunit in this thoroughly modern mystery." Publ Wkly

The detective wore silk drawers. Dodd, Mead 1971 188p o.p.

"A Red badge novel of suspense"

"Three London detectives of the 1880s, all boxing fans, uncover a clandestine center of the sport while investigating several headless corpses." Booklist

"Although the mystery is nothing special, it suffices, and the kicks come from the 19th century atmosphere of Victorian sex and mild sadism." Publ Wkly

Diamond dust. Soho Press 2002 343p $24
ISBN 1-56947-291-2

* LC 2002-17567

This "mystery, starring Peter Diamond, head of the murder squad in Bath, England, has the avuncular copper off the murder beat and assigned to an investigation of Bath's Mafia family. News of a murder in the city's Victorian formal gardens sends Diamond's spirits soaring, confident he will be returned to his home turf. As he draws back the plastic sheet over the woman's body, however, he discovers that the victim is his own wife." Booklist

"In a bold display of virtuosity, Lovesey takes his hero to emotional places he's never been before while constructing a plot of infernal ingenuity." N Y Times Book Rev

Diamond solitaire. Mysterious Press 1993 c1992 343p

ISBN 0-89296-535-5   LC 92-50660

First published 1992 in the United Kingdom

"Peter Diamond is plagued by bad karma. Formerly detective superintendent of police in Bath, he's sunk to being a security guard at Harrod's—until a small Asian child is found in the area of the store Peter patrols. Out of a job once again (security breaches are no laughing matter at terrorist-obsessed Harrod's), Diamond becomes intrigued by the Asian child, who is autistic and who remains unclaimed despite massive publicity. What starts out as a kindly effort to restore the child to her parents

Lovesey, Peter—*Continued*

turns into an international adventure as Diamond travels from London to New York to Japan and confronts millionaire sumo wrestlers, unethical drug researchers, and corrupt businessmen." Booklist

The house sitter. Soho Press 2003 346p $25

ISBN 1-56947-326-9 LC 2002-42626

"Initially brought in as an auxilliary police consultant, Bath's Inspector Peter Diamond soon proves himself indispensable to a missing person case turned murder investigation. A woman from Bath discovered dead on a Sussex beach turns out to have been strangled—apparently right there in the midst of a crowd. The main witnesses, a family of three, seem to be hiding something. The victim was a psychological offender profiler, apparently working on the case of a serial murderer." Libr J

"The identity of the killer, when finally revealed, is genuinely startling, and not because of authorial obfuscation. The writing is as smooth as polished steel." Publ Wkly

The last detective. Doubleday 1991 331p o.p.

LC 91-11859

"A Perfect crime book"

"Irascible, corpulent, cynical Chief Superintendent Peter Diamond of the Avon and Somerset murder squad attributes Britain's decline as a world power to the abolition of capital punishment in 1964. Spurning computer gadgetry, he sticks to common sense, index cards and gumshoeing: 'Knocking on doors. That's how we get results.' The almost clueless case of the naked woman's body found floating in Chew Valley Lake poses a supreme challenge for the detective, who is anxious to clear his name of recent charges of brutality." Publ Wkly

"An intricate, many-tiered examination of police work, especially modern forensic technology, complete with computers and genetic fingerprinting. Everything meshes perfectly in this airtight tale." Booklist

On the edge. Mysterious Press 1989 204p o.p.

LC 88-13549

"Set in Britain immediately after World War II, this is a novel that balances wit and wickedness, ambitions and just desserts. Rosie married badly—to a penniless philanderer. Antonia married well—to a wealthy man—but her lover is going to the U.S. and she wants to join him there. Rosie and Antonia meet by chance, talk, and a plan is gradually hatched. With a helpful shove from Antonia, Rosie's hubby comes to a bad end beneath a tube train. The second half of the deal becomes more convoluted, as Antonia's past (she having murdered her husband's first wife) and several secret agendas throw a wrench in the works." Booklist

"Told mostly in racy, ear-perfect dialogue that magnifies the impact of events, the story dodges from one unguessable outcome to the next." Publ Wkly

Rough cider. Mysterious Press 1986 216p o.p.

LC 86-18212

"A tightly knit tale that has its roots in the hanging for murder in England of an American G.I. Twenty years later his daughter, who lives in the U.S., attempts to exonerate his name by enlisting the aid of an English professor whose childhood was marked by the crime. Readers incidentally learn about cider making and discover some grisly evidence of murder and guilt in the course of the demonstration." Barzun. Cat of Crime. Rev and enl edition

Skeleton Hill. Soho Press 2009 326p $24

ISBN 978-1-56947-598-0; 1-56947-598-9

LC 2009-11128

"At a reenactment of a major battle of the English Civil War, two participants discover the headless skeleton of a young woman. When one of the participants is later found murdered on Lansdown Hill, Bath Inspector Peter Diamond . . . must coordinate a coinvestigation with the Bristol police." Libr J

Another of Lovesey's "convoluted plots, layered with historical lore and teeming with comic characters up to their necks in no good. Diamond is a classic—better catch him while you can." N Y Times Book Rev

Upon a dark night. Mysterious Press 1998 374p o.p. LC 97-48922

First published 1997 in the United Kingdom

Peter Diamond, "head of the murder squad in Bath, England, annoys his peers by poking around in two seemingly clear-cut suicides—an unknown woman who leaped to her death and a farmer who blew his head off with a shotgun. His poking soon uncovers murder, and eventually the two deaths become linked to the disappearance of an amnesia victim." Booklist

A "triumph of plotting from this master of the classic puzzle form." N Y Times Book Rev

The vault. Soho Press 2000 331p $23

ISBN 1-56947-208-4 LC 00-41010

First published 1999 in the United Kingdom

This mystery "relies on Peter Diamond, a British copper of eclectic cultural tastes, to unravel the complexities of a story that begins when a human hand is disinterred from a burial vault beneath the now-vanished house in Bath where Mary Shelley finished the classic horror story she famously started on a dark and stormy night at Lake Geneva." N Y Times Book Rev

"A wealth of good things fills this novel: Lovesey's deft plotting, his hilarious send-ups of the Brits through the perspective of the American professor, and his intriguing allusions to the architecture and literary history of Bath." Booklist

Waxwork. Pantheon Bks. 1978 239p o.p.

LC 77-90420

"There is certainly enough here to warrant the praise given this tale by more than one highly regarded colleague in crime. Set in the London and Kew of 1888, a case of KCN poisoning following upon blackmail taxes the abilities of the police, but in the end Sgt. Cribb really does distinguish himself. The title alludes to Tussaud's Waxwork Exhibition." Barzun. Cat of Crime. Rev and enl edition

Lovric, Michelle

The floating book; a novel. Regan Bks. 2004 480p $25.95

ISBN 0-06-057856-4 LC 2003-58400

A novel set in Venice in 1486. "Sosia Simeon, married to a Jewish doctor who is repulsed by her, finds comfort in the arms of many other men. German-born Wendelin von Speyer comes to Venice to capitalize on the invention of the printing press. Sosia bewitches handsome young Bruno, Wendelin's editor, but it is the cold, disinterested Felice, his scribe, who captivates her. Wendelin falls in love with Lussieta, the beautiful daughter of a

Lovric, Michelle—*Continued*

bookseller, and marries her. All of them are drawn in by the amorous poems of the Latin poet Catullus, which Wendelin intends to print. . . . Meticulous historical detail and a splendid, complex story make this portrait of Venice and its denizens memorable and moving." Booklist

Lowell, Elizabeth

Die in plain sight. Morrow 2003 385p $24.95
ISBN 0-06-050412-9   LC 2003-40606
"Art buyer and struggling southern California artist Lacey Quinn shows a few of her grandfather's paintings to renowned artist Susa Donovan, in the area for a charity event. The paintings are mostly landscapes, but also include a few samples from his dark later work, including detailed depictions of murder and death by fire and drowning. Believing that the landcapes are really the work of famous California plein air painter Lewis Marten, Susa asks Lacey to have them professionally appraised. Lacey resists Susa's pleas, fearing that her grandfather may have been guilty of forgery, but she discovers something far more complicated and horrifying. The murders her grandfather depicted actually took place." Publ Wkly

Pearl Cove. Avon Bks. 1999 376p
ISBN 0-380-97404-5   LC 99-21639
This is the author's "third book featuring the Donovan clan. . . . Archer, the oldest son, is plunged into the past with a call for help from the only woman he has ever loved, Hannah McGarry, his half-brother Len's wife. After an injury paralyzes Len, he focuses on developing a unique strain of black pearls and mentally torturing his wife. When a cyclone hits their Australian pearl farm, Hannah finds her husband dead and the pearls missing. Archer comes to protect her and avenge Len's death. . . . This is a riveting mix of suspense and romance." Booklist

Lowenthal, Michael

Charity girl. Houghton Mifflin 2007 323p $24
ISBN 978-0-618-54629-9; 0-618-54629-4
          LC 2005-37775
A "fictional account of the U.S. government's forced quarantine of thousands of young women who were found near military bases and suspected of having venereal disease during World War I. Seventeen-year-old Frieda Mintz, who has fled her family's home, works as a shop girl by day and often dances in the Boston ballrooms at night. It is when Frieda meets and spends the night with a young soldier, Felix Morse, with whom she becomes smitten, that the trouble begins. While trying to visit him at his military camp, Frieda is picked up and sent to a detention home, where she tests positive for VD. Quarantined and placed under treatment, Frieda hopes Felix will come to her aid." Libr J

"Lowenthal's narrative style is perfect for a heroine who suffers but remains a survivor, striking just the right mix of dark and light, worldly and innocent. Providing Frieda with flickers of humor and joy, he guarantees her our sympathy." N Y Times Book Rev

Lowry, Malcolm, 1909-1957

Under the volcano. Reynal & Hitchcock 1947 375p o.p.
          *

This novel "presents in detail the events of [a] single day in a single place—the Day of the Dead in a town in Mexico, with Popocatepetl and Ixtaccihuatl looking down. It is the last day on earth of the British Consul, Geoffrey Firmin, and he is dying of alcoholism. Like any tragic hero, he is fully aware of the choice he has made: he clings to his sloth, he needs salvation through love but will not utter the word which will bring it, he lets his morbid lust for drink drag him from bar to bar. In other words, he has made a deliberate choice of damnation. . . . We don't despise or even dislike Firmin, despite his weaknesses and his self-destructive urge. As with all tragic heroes (and this novel is a genuine tragedy) he sums up the flaws which are latent or actual in all of us." Burgess. 99 Novels

Lu Jiamin *See* Jiang Rong, 1946-

Ludlum, Robert, 1927-2001

The apocalypse watch. Bantam Bks. 1995 645p o.p.
          LC 95-1860
"Brilliant deep-cover American agent Harry Latham is captured and implanted with a mind-control microchip after he penetrates the secret Austrian headquarters of a contemporary movement to restore the Nazis to world domination. Programmed with false information incriminating legions of high-level officials around the free world, Harry is allowed to escape. Debriefed by the CIA in London, he contacts his brother Drew, also a secret agent for American Consular Operation in Paris. After revealing the name of one Nazi, Harry is assassinated by the sinister Brotherhood of the Watch, prompting Drew—aided by Karin de Vries, the beautiful and mysterious widow of Harry's former partner—to assume his identity." Publ Wkly

"A powerful, exploding novel that, frightening as it sounds, may not be so far reaching, for it touches on the issues of hate, ethnic cleansing, and racism that we read about every day." Booklist

The Aquitaine progression. Random House 1984 647p o.p.
          LC 83-19078
This novel "features five present or former generals from five different countries who mean to take over the world. They have decided to put an end to the quagmire of Western politics and set up a super-fascist state with themselves in control. The hub of this enterprise is Gen. George Marcus Delavane, a fanatic who makes Genghis Khan look like a Peace Corps volunteer. Joel Converse, an international lawyer, has reason to know and hate Delavane. It was Delavane who insisted on an Air Force mission in Vietnam that resulted in Converse's capture and subsequent agonies at the hands of the enemy. While in Geneva working on a case for his New York law firm, Converse is contacted by one A. Preston Halliday, who gives him information he finds hard to believe. But there follows a series of entanglements and murders that clearly prove Halliday's assertions." N Y Times Book Rev

Ludlum, Robert, 1927-2001—*Continued*

The Bourne identity. Marek, R. 1980 523p o.p.
* LC 79-23638

"Jason Bourne is shot and left for dead. He survives, but without a memory. Slowly, painstakingly, he retraces his past, only to find himself hunted by assassins of several governments, including his own. He fights against seemingly insurmountable odds—especially his very limited knowledge of his past—to discover his identity and stop his enemies before it is too late." Libr J

Followed by The Bourne supremacy

The Bourne supremacy. Random House 1986 597p o.p.
LC 85-18318

"In this sequel to The Bourne Identity David Webb, still suffering flashbacks to his Jason Bourne persona, is forced to undertake a final, possibly fatal mission after his wife is kidnapped. He must find and capture an assassin who is posing as Bourne in Hong Kong. By so doing he'll foil a plot that could plunge the Far East and then the world into war." Libr J

"Every chapter ends with a cliff-hanger; the story brims with assassination, torture, hand-to-hand combat, sudden surprise and intrigue within intrigue. It's a surefire bestseller." Publ Wkly

Followed by The Bourne ultimatum

The Bourne ultimatum. Random House 1990 611p o.p.
LC 89-43201

"When the international terrorist known as Carlos the Jackal penetrates his civilian identity, Webb must again assume the Bourne persona to protect his wife and small children. In their renewed struggle, the two master assassins uncover the revived existence of Medusa, the sinister alliance that originally led to the establishment of the Bourne identity." Publ Wkly

The Gemini contenders. Dial Press (NY) 1976 402p o.p.

"The twin sons of a former Italian government official search for a mysterious document he was forced to leave behind when fleeing his fascist-dominated homeland in 1939." Smith. Cloak and Dagger Fic

Ludlum is "at the top of his form here as he tells a suspenseful story that gives fresh slants to old themes." Publ Wkly

The Holcroft covenant. Marek, R. 1978 542p o.p.
LC 77-95295

"Thirty years after Hitler, Noel Holcroft sees an astounding document, drawn up by three supposedly contrite Nazis (all now dead), one of them his own father. If he signs it and collects signatures from the sons of the other two men, the Holocaust victims' heirs should become the beneficiaries of a gigantic fund. The fund's 'real' purpose is to establish the Fourth Reich, not atone for the Third, but Holcroft doesn't realize this as he flings around the world in search of those signatures, precipitating . . . ruthless clashes between secret Nazi and anti-Nazi organizations." Publ Wkly

The Janson directive. St. Martin's Press 2002 547p $27.95
ISBN 0-312-25348-6
LC 2002-5136

"The hero is Paul Janson, a private security consultant who retired a few years ago after a notorious career as the U.S. government's go-to guy for nasty jobs no one else was willing to take. Against his better judgment, Janson accepts an assignment to rescue Peter Novak, a Nobel Peace Prize-winning philanthropist and international troubleshooter held captive by Islamic extremists on an island in the Indian Ocean. . . . Extremely engaging and agonizingly suspenseful, Ludlum's plot bolts from scene to scene and locale to locale—Hungary, Amsterdam, London, New York City—never settling for one bombshell when it can drop four or five." Publ Wkly

The Matarese Circle. Marek, R. 1979 601p o.p.
LC 78-31673

This novel of international intrigue "features the world's top secret agents: Scofield, American, and Taleniekov, Russian. They have sworn to kill each other—Scofield was responsible for the death of Taleniekov's brother, Taleniekov for that of Scofield's wife—yet they have much in common besides their brilliance: both are semiretired, held in suspicion by their respective governments and encumbered (occasionally) by the humane streak in their characters. And now they are drawn into cooperation, as the only men capable of destroying an international circle of killers, The Matarese, originally Corsican, which is dedicated to reducing the world to chaos via assassination and terror." Publ Wkly

The Matlock paper. Dial Press (NY) 1973 312p o.p.

"James Matlock, instructor in Elizabethan literature at Carlyle University in Connecticut, formerly an Army officer in Vietnam, is drawn into the most personally dangerous and violent struggle of his life when he is requested to cooperate with a government narcotic agent in exploring Carlyle's connection with the expanding drug traffic in New England." Publ Wkly

The Parsifal mosaic. Random House 1982 630p o.p.
LC 84-8925

The novel "centers around the background figure of superstar Secretary of State Anthony Matthias, whose unhinged brilliance nearly leads to nuclear disaster. In the foreground is accomplished and durable U.S. deep-cover agent Michael Havelock (nee Mikhail Havlíček), protégé and surrogate son of fellow Czech Matthias. Forced to order the execution of the woman he loves, believing her to be an agent of the Soviet terrorist group VKR, Havelock leaves espionage service. But when he spots her alive in Rome he's back in, on a convoluted trial of international intrigue that leads to the highest levels of government." Libr J

"The tale has all the hallmarks of vintage Ludlum: non-stop action, precisely timed curtain-raisers, the darksome deeds of agent and double agent, a deadly secret ultimately revealed and an underlying theme of the whole world jeopardized by a few fanatics." Publ Wkly

The Prometheus deception. St. Martin's Press 2000 509p
ISBN 0-312-25346-X
LC 00-62585

"Nick Bryson works for an ultrasecret intelligence organization; after making a mistake during a mission, he's put out to pasture. Later, he's brought back into the game by a different intelligence group, and he learns that everything he believed about his former bosses was a lie-until, that is, he discovers that everything the second organization has told him is also a lie. Bryson winds up trying singlehandedly to save the world from a shadowy

Ludlum, Robert, 1927-2001—*Continued*

terrorist group, while simultaneously trying to figure out which of the various 'good guys' he should believe. . . . The pace is fast, the action plentiful, and the story confusing enough to keep us turning the pages." Booklist

The Rhinemann exchange. Dial Press (NY) 1974 460p o.p.

"A World War II espionage novel detailing an attempted treasonous exchange between the Germans and the Americans—the technological secret of a gyroscopic guidance system in return for industrial diamonds. This is to be brought off by a disenfranchised German Jew in Buenos Aires, tracked by an American agent not quite in the know and thus in jeopardy." Booklist

The Scarlatti inheritance; a novel. World Pub. 1970 358p o.p.

"An American agent becomes concerned about the decline in his family's fortune and looking into the matter finds that his relative, Ulster Scarlatti, is using the money to bankroll Hitler's World War II effort." Smith. Cloak and Dagger Fic

The scorpio illusion. Bantam Bks. 1993 534p o.p. LC 93-9272

In this thriller, "the beautiful, anarchistic Basque terrorist Amaya Bajaratt . . . modestly sets out to eliminate the leaders of the United States, Britain, France and Israel. The only person able to stop her and thus save civilization as we know it is Tyrell Nathaniel Hawthorne 3d, a disillusioned former United States Naval Intelligence officer, now going to seed in the Caribbean. The two adversaries circle warily, each desperate to eliminate the other, neither able to strike the fatal blow." N Y Times Book Rev

The Sigma protocol. St. Martin's Press 2001 535p

ISBN 0-312-27688-5 LC 2001-48240

"Anna Navarro, a U.S. homicide specialist for the enigmatic Internal Compliance Unit is sent to look into a spate of mysterious deaths around the world. All the victims are very old wealthy men, and all are connected to the secretive corporation Sigma A.G., founded in Switzerland during WWII. When her only living lead is murdered moments before Anna lands in Switzerland, she crosses paths with Ben Hartman, a New York financier who is dodging the killer who murdered his twin brother, Peter, when Peter discovered that their father, Max, was part of Sigma." Publ Wkly

"Ludlum keeps things moving with plenty of gunplay and running about. Uncharacteristically, he also lets things slow down from time to time, long enough for us to get to know the players in this complicated story." Booklist

Lupica, Mike

Wild pitch. Putnam 2002 352p

ISBN 0-399-14927-9 LC 2002-21952

An "account of the comeback of Showtime Charlie Stoddard, a pitching phenom for the New York Mets forced into early retirement by a ruined arm. Five years after his final sorry major league appearance, Charlie encounters a mysterious therapist named Chang, whose treatments make his tortured arm feel so good he dreams

of pitching again. . . . How Charlie ends up pitching for the Red Sox as they try to hold off the Yankees in a tight pennant race and just possibly shake off the collective curses of the Bambino, Bill Buckner and Bucky Dent, is fast and funny and occasionally brings a tear to the eye." Publ Wkly

Lurie, Alison

Foreign affairs. Random House 1984 291p o.p. LC 84-42657

This novel follows "the actions and reactions of two English professors, both Americans, both from the same university, who are on leave in London to do research: Virginia Miner, 54, unmarried, happy to be back in the city she adores, and Fred Turner, 28, separated from his wife and depressed over being more or less in exile. Both Vinnie and Fred indulge in, while there, affairs with unlikely persons, with the result that they learn more about themselves from the experiences." Booklist

"Lurie portrays these entanglements with her customary astute wit and deft characterization, but also with unexpected warmth and generosity. A wry, wonderful book." Libr J

The last resort; a novel. Holt & Co. 1998 321p

ISBN 0-8050-5866-4 LC 97-42985

In this novel a "forbearing New England wife puts up with an overbearing nature-writer husband; he's twenty-four years her senior, famous, and secretly thinks he's dying. During a sojourn in the Florida Keys, opportunities for mixing and rematching abound: she is coveted by a celebrated poet and by a lush lesbian, while he is worshipped by a would-be savior of manatees. Lurie sets this gavotte in a Key West whose pastels take on a tasty acidity, and the novel goes down like Key-lime pie." New Yorker

The nowhere city. Coward-McCann 1966 c1965 276p o.p.

First published 1965 in the United Kingdom

"Paul Cattleman, a young Harvard historian, goes West to spend a year writing the history of the Nutting Electronics Corporation; he is unwillingly followed by his wife Katherine. . . . He takes to transplantation . . . [but] his wife doesn't until she falls in with an ex-Mittel-Europa analyst." New Statesman (1913)

The author describes the Los Angeles "scene with such a cool and penetrating eye, such total disbelief in its existence, that she is able to portray it with a pristine freshness. . . . Transformed by her wicked wit, the most exhausted clichés come alive, galvanized into original revelation." Newsweek

Only children. Random House 1979 259p

ISBN 0-394-50471-2 LC 78-21994

"The novel spans the Fourth of July weekend [of 1935]. Bill and Honey Hubbard and their eight-year-old daughter Mary Ann, and Dan and Celia Zimmern and their daughter Lolly (and Dan's sullen adolescent son from a previous marriage) abandon New York City and its suburb, Larchmont, for the Catskill farm owned by Anna King, headmistress of the progressive school the two girls attend. This innocent outing doesn't turn out to be a relaxing weekend. . . . Instead the grownups start romping in an unseemly way and end up fighting while the two little girls look on, bewildered." New Repub

Lurie, Alison—*Continued*

"Lurie has a sharp, ironic eye for the man-woman game and a dramatic deftness for setting the scene. Her rendering of the children is particularly effective." Libr J

(ed) The Oxford book of modern fairy tales. See The Oxford book of modern fairy tales

The war between the Tates. Random House 1974 372p o.p.

The setting of the novel is the community of Corinth, New York during late 1969 and early 1970. "Brian Tate, a university professor, complete with neuroses, approaching 50, and not nearly so successful as he had hoped to be, becomes entangled with Wendy Gahaghan, a graduate student, who, unlike Erica Tate, gives of herself so freely that Brian consents to attempt to alleviate her infatuation. Wendy slowly moves into what little there is of the Tate's family life so that she can tell Erica everything. The personality and sexual problems of these characters, compounded by the rebelliousness of the obnoxious and beautifully drawn Tate children, are intriguingly set off against recurring metaphors which are tied to the Vietnamese war." Choice

"An outline of the plot does scant justice to the substance and wit of Lurie's novel. What makes the lines sing is her skill in catching the idiosyncracies of the mind and the tongue, the twists and turns of sophisticated sensibilities trapped in absurd situations." America

Women and ghosts. Talese 1994 179p o.p.
LC 93-46332

Contents: Ilse's house; The pool people; The highboy; Counting sheep; In the shadow; Waiting for baby; Fat people; Another Halloween; The double poet

"In each tale Lurie pits a female protagonist against an apparition of varied, often comical, spectral persuasions. . . . These entertaining and enchanting tales deliver far more than one might bargain for, with afterimages that reverberate long after the initial delight with Lurie's dexterous prose has worn off." Booklist

Lustbader, Eric Van, 1946-

Black Blade; [by] Eric Lustbader. Fawcett Columbine 1993 518p o.p.
LC 91-72890

New York homicide cop "Wolf Matheson is assigned to investigate a chain of murders perpetrated by the furtive Black Blade Society. That's a nationalistic, militaristic, but intellectual cabal that, for centries, has been nurturing the 'Oracle,' an enhanced mental state in which practitioners are able to predict the future and attain long lifespans. Alas, the Black Blade is bent on world domination and has been maneuvering events in both the U.S. and Japan toward world war. Wolf, with his sexy-but-clairvoyant Japanese girl friend, Chika, at his side, is equal to the task of saving the world, but he wouldn't be if it weren't for his Shoshone childhood, where shamans knew the same kind of stuff the Black Blade know." Booklist

Dark homecoming; [by] Eric Lustbader. Pocket Bks. 1997 353p
ISBN 0-671-00329-1   LC 96-48909

"Seeking refuge from his former life as a cop, Lew Croaker finds his reverie on his fishing boat in Miami cut short when his estranged sister, Matty, reappears.

Matty begs him to find a kidney donor for her daughter, Rachel, whose self-abusive lifestyle has left her near death. Suddenly, Croaker is catapulted into the nefarious world of the feral Bonita twins, who murder people to harvest their organs. In a race against time to save Rachel, he agrees to murder a Latin American drug lord in exchange for a kidney; and then his friends become his enemies." Libr J

"An accomplished crime novel from a writer whose work has grown in depth without sacrificing thrills." Booklist

Floating city; a Nicholas Linnear novel; by Eric Lustbader. Pocket Bks. 1994 404p o.p.
LC 93-49360

"Nicholas Linnear and his private-eye buddy, Lew Croaker, dash around the globe attempting to thwart the murder of the Yakuza boss of bosses and stop the development of a terrible new weapon and a supercartel bent on world domination." Booklist

Mistress of the pearl. Tor Bks. 2004 588p map $27.95
ISBN 0-312-87237-2   LC 2003-60698

"As Riane, the prophesied Dar-Sala-at destined to deliver the people of Kundala from their V'ornn conquerors, continues her search for the legendary Pearl believed to hold the key to deliverance for her people, other forces for change are at work within the world. A Resistance movement unites Kundalans with sympathetic V'ornns even as a group of V'ornn scientists conduct ruthless experiments to master a rare radioactive substance." Libr J

This novel "builds powerfully upon its predecessors, thanks to characters of uncommon depth and complexity, lots of perplexing dilemmas for them to wrestle with, and plenty of exciting swordplay and gore." Booklist

Second skin; a Nicholas Linnear novel. Pocket Bks. 1995 454p o.p.   LC 95-14365

In this adventure Nicholas Linnear "heads a computer firm on the verge of a mega-breakthrough that here is threatened by: a crazed Nietzsche-spouting American gangster who is Nicholas's doppelganger; the gangster's equally crazed, California-based brother, who's trying to take over the Eastern U.S Mafia family run by a middle-aged suburban matron; an unholy mix of Japanese tycoons, pols and Yakuza; and a creepy, untrustworthy aide to Nicholas's ailing mentor." Publ Wkly

Lutz, John, 1939-

Burn. Holt & Co. 1995 278p
ISBN 0-8050-3480-3   LC 94-32187

Florida private eye "Fred Carver's new client, an attractive, widowed housing developer with the 'guileless blue eyes' of a serial killer, claims he is being persecuted by a woman who has accused him of stalking her. Keeping an open mind, Carver sets out to determine whether the frantic businessman is your 'typical compulsive male sexual psychopath' or a much-maligned guy." N Y Times Book Rev

This mystery, "in which the motive isn't greed or passion but rather grief and loss, is one of the best in a fine series." Booklist

LIST OF FICTIONAL WORKS

Lutz, John, 1939-—*Continued*

Dancing with the dead. St. Martin's Press 1992
208p o.p.
LC 92-2997
"A Thomas Dunne book"
"St. Louis realtor Mary Arlington, whose mother is alcoholic and whose lover is physically abusive, lives for her mambo, cha-cha and tango lessons with Mel Holt at the Romance Studio. After kicking her lover out of her life and checking her mother into a detox center, Mary agrees to dance with Mel in the Ohio Star Ball, a major competition. Meanwhile in Seattle and New Orleans, women dancers resembling Mary are murdered. Rene Verlane, the husband of the New Orleans victim, insists the crime is related to his wife's dancing. Mary follows the case on TV and one night calls Verlane to offer her help in finding the killer." Publ Wkly

Death by jury. St. Martin's Press 1995 291p o.p.
LC 95-11363
"A Thomas Dunne book"
St. Louis detective Alo Nudger "is hired by Lawrence Fleck, an odious and permanently small-time attorney, to investigate his client, banker Roger Dupont, who is about to stand trial for the murder of his wife. The twist is that Fleck wants Nudger to find incriminating evidence because he wants his client to accept a plea bargain. Lutz is a master storyteller, and this plot is an intricate masterpiece." Booklist

Final seconds; by John Lutz and David August. Kensington Bks. 1998 316p
ISBN 1-57566-259-0
LC 97-75929
"Will Harper, a member of the NYPD bomb squad, lost part of a hand in an explosion at a city high school. While Harper is in Florida visiting his former partner, Jimmy Fahey, who works for a Tom Clancy-like writer, a letter bomb arrives at the author's compound. The explosion kills Fahey and two colleagues. Loyalty to his dead partner prompts Harper to investigate." Booklist
"The most welcome realism in the book comes from the authors' resistance to the far-fetched elements that creep into many thrillers. Their seamless collaboration is notable for the efficiency of the plotting and for the unusual credibility of the story, its characters and the methodical way they do their work." Publ Wkly

Lightning. Holt & Co. 1996 296p
ISBN 0-8050-4379-9
LC 95-43273
"This time out, crime strikes very close to private detective Fred Carver's home. His significant other, journalist Beth Jackson, is pregnant with their child. Carver is delighted when she changes her mind about having an abortion—until she goes to the clinic to cancel her appointment. As she enters, a bomb explodes, killing two clinic workers. Beth loses the baby. Local police and the FBI very quickly arrest a likely suspect, but driven by loss and anger, Carver begins to investigate other possibilities." Booklist
"Behind the intransigent and hackneyed rhetoric of both sides, Carver finds venality aplenty as he and Beth attempt to come to terms with their loss. Veteran novelist Lutz ties some nifty twists into his plot, which moves quickly towards a final deadly confrontation." Publ Wkly

Oops!; a Nudger mystery. St. Martin's Press 1998 278p
ISBN 0-312-18152-3
LC 97-36529

"A Thomas Dunne book"
"St. Louis private investigator Alo Nudger doesn't usually accept referrals from other PI's, but this time Lacey Tumulty does the referring. Her friendship and his dwindling bank account induce Nudger to attempt to find out if Betty Almer's death was an accident, as the police believe, or something else, as her father contends." Booklist
"Nudger's novice partner Lacey . . . provides sometimes humorous complications." Libr J

Lutz, Lisa, 1970-

Curse of the Spellmans. Simon & Schuster 2008 409p $25
ISBN 978-1-4165-3241-5; 1-4165-3241-2
LC 2007-21152
"Licensed P.I. Isabel 'Izzy' Spellman has been arrested for the fourth time in two months, and no one from her oddball family of fellow investigators will bail her out. Her sister, Rae, has run over Izzy's 'fiancé,' Inspector Henry Stone, during a driving lesson. The senior Spellmans have staged a 'disappearance,' their term for a vacation where no one can reach them. To complicate Izzy's life further, a man with the suspiciously ordinary name of John Brown has moved next door, and she's absolutely positive he's up to no good. . . . Once again, Lutz treats readers to a madcap roller-coaster ride." Libr J

Revenge of the Spellmans. Simon & Schuster 2009 375p $25
ISBN 978-1-4165-9338-6
LC 2009-2281
This "third installment of Lutz's series . . . opens with series protagonist Isabel 'Izzy' Spellman, the single, snarky middle Spellman child, in court-ordered therapy, where she spends her time avoiding personal questions. Despite her parents' desperate attempts to win her back, Izzy has sworn off investigating—but she's bored. Snooping and prying is a dominant family trait, and before long Izzy is lured away from her bartending job by a seemingly easy case of a possibly straying wife. But when her older brother, the straight-living David, goes missing, her instincts really kick in." Kirkus
"Those in the market for mayhem and mirth will revel in Lutz's irresistible blend of suspense, irony, and wit." Booklist

The Spellman files; a novel. Simon & Schuster 2007 352p $25
ISBN 978-1-4165-3239-2; 1-4165-3239-0
LC 2006-49161
"Isabel 'Izzy' Spellman, a San Francisco PI who began working for Spellman Investigations at age 12, could easily pass as Buffy or Veronica Mars's wiser but funnier older sister. Izzy digs TV, too, especially Get Smart (an ex-boyfriend's ownership of the complete bootlegged DVD set is his major selling point). Now 28, Izzy thinks she wants out, but elects to take on a cold case while dealing with 14-year-old sister Rae, a nightmarish Nancy Drew, and parents who have no qualms about bugging their children's bedrooms. At times the dialogue-heavy text reads like a script and the action flags, but these are quibbles. When Rae suddenly disappears, Izzy and her family must learn some serious lessons in order to find her." Publ Wkly

Lychack, William

The wasp eater. Houghton Mifflin 2004 164p $21

ISBN 0-618-30244-1 LC 2004-42728

In this "novel, 10-year-old Daniel tries to reunite his parents after his father, Bob . . . is kicked out of the house for having an affair with a waitress. On one of Bob's fleeting visits home, Daniel is given a pawnshop receipt for his mother's engagement ring. Thinking the ring might be the key to reconciliation, Daniel takes a bus from New England to New York to buy it back, but he runs into trouble and his father has to come and get him. Rather than return home, father and son set off on a road trip." Publ Wkly

"Just when the dysfunctional family drama seems entirely wrung out, along comes a book so freshly original that it seems to have invented the genre. What's so remarkable here is the understatedness, the quietly intense writing carefully containing more emotion than many louder novels have to show. Original, too, is the impulse to heal rather than break away-however mixed the outcome." Libr J

Lynch, Jim, 1961-

Border songs. Alfred A. Knopf 2009 291p $25.95

ISBN 978-0-307-27117-4; 0-307-27117-X

      LC 2008-53514

"The plot is episodic, and the ending. . . well, judge for yourself. Still, 'Border Songs' is worth the ride. Lynch is a former reporter, and while it's fashionable to be skeptical of journalists who turn to fiction, this ex-journalist brings a depth of knowledge and an attention to detail that should be the envy of more ivory-tower writers. Read 'Border Songs' in support of an author who has gotten off the beaten path . . . and brought us an off-the-grid world we'd otherwise be doomed to miss." Seattle Times

Lynch, Scott, 1978-

The lies of Locke Lamora. Bantam 2006 499p map $23

ISBN 0-553-80467-7; 978-0-553-80467-6

      LC 2006-42653

"A Bantam spectra book"

This is a "picaresque fantasy that chronicles the career of Locke Lamora orphan, thief and leader of the Gentlemen Bastards from the time the Thiefmaker sells Locke to the faking Eyeless Priest up to Locke's latest con of the nobility of the land of Camorr. As in any good caper novel, the plot is littered with obvious and not-so-obvious obstacles, including the secret police of Camorr's legendary Spider and the mysterious assassinations of gang leaders by the newly arrived Gray King. Locke's resilience and wit give the book the tragicomic air of a traditional picaresque, rubbery ethics and all." Publ Wkly

Lynn, Allison

Now you see it; a novel. Touchstone 2004 281p $13

ISBN 0-7432-5026-5 (pa) LC 2003-70450

In this "novel, a Manhattan couple decides to infuse their lives with meaning by having a child. David hangs out in the middle of the masthead at a middlebrow magazine while Jessica teaches school, but after several failed fertility treatments, they focus on clearing hurdles in the adoption process. And then one day, Jessica vanishes, her keys left on the counter, a bedroom window ajar. . . . So without evidence of a crime, the detached David and Jessica's increasingly desperate mother must come to grips with the jarring disappearance in their own way and time. David does so by revisiting the story of a U.S. businessman gone missing in Peru—the one real scoop of his career, which he landed on his honeymoon. Although Jessica is more plot device than compelling character, Lynn deftly employs David's journey to explore how someone might rediscover his internal compass when he no longer has any reason to lie to himself." Booklist

Lytton, Edward Bulwer Lytton, Baron, 1803-1873

The last days of Pompeii. Harper 1834 2v o.p.

The setting is Pompeii just before and during the famous eruption of Vesuvius, A.D. 79. "The simple story relates principally to two young people of Grecian origin, Glaucus and Ione, who are deeply attached to each other. The former is a handsome young Athenian, impetuous, high-minded, and brilliant, while Ione is a pure and lofty-minded woman. Arbaces, her guardian, the villain of the story, under a cloak of sanctity and religion, indulges in low and criminal designs. His character is strongly drawn; and his passion for Ione, and the struggle between him and Glaucus, form the chief part of the plot. . . . The book, full of learning and spirit, is not only a charming novel, but contains many minute and interesting descriptions of ancient customs; among which, those relating to the gladiatorial combat, the banquet, the bath, are most noteworthy." Keller. Reader's Dig of Books

M

Ma Jian, 1953-

Beijing coma; translated from the Chinese by Flora Drew. Farrar, Straus & Giroux 2008 586p $27.50

ISBN 978-0-374-11017-8; 0-374-11017-4

      LC 2008-925628

Awakening after a decade in a coma, former Tiananmen Square protester Dai Wei learns that his mother had sold one of his kidneys to finance his care, and that the China he knew has undergone radical change.

"A valuable work. Ma's writing can be lively, and his use of dialogue that embraces everyday chitchat gives the book a sense of reality. The idealism of youth is ably captured. Indeed, the students' frequently lofty and at times naive emotions are touching." New Leader

Stick out your tongue; translated from the Chinese by Flora Drew. Farrar, Straus and Giroux 2006 93p $16

ISBN 0-374-26988-2 LC 2006-4282

Ma Jian, 1953——*Continued*

Original Chinese edition, 1998

Contents: The woman and the blue sky; The smile of Lake Drolmula; The eight-fanged roach; The golden crown; The final initiation

In these five loosely connected stories "a Chinese writer whose marriage has fallen apart travels to Tibet. As he wanders through the countryside, he witnesses the sky burial of a Tibetan woman who died during childbirth, shares a tent with a nomad who is walking to a sacred mountain to seek forgiveness for sleeping with his daughter, meets a silversmith who has hung the wind-dried corpse of his lover on the wall of his cave, and hears the story of a young female incarnate lama who died during a Buddhist initiation rite. In the thin air of the high plateau, the divide between dream and reality becomes confused." Publisher's note

"In an afterword, the author notes that his work is controversial among both Tibetans and Chinese. Given their dark and explicitly disturbing nature, these stories will not be appreciated by all readers. But those who have read Xinran's Sky Burial will recognize the irony of hardship placed upon the human spirit set against the striking beauty offered by the Tibetan landscape." Libr J

Maalouf, Amin

Balthasar's odyssey; a novel; translated from the French by Barbara Bray. Arcade Pub. 2002 391p $25.95

ISBN 1-55970-666-X   LC 2002-74630

Original French editon, 2000

The author "sets this historical novel mostly in the Mediterranean of the mid-1600s. Balthasar Embriaco, an exiled Italian merchant, becomes fixated on retrieving a mysterious religious text called The Hundreth Name that he mistakenly sold to a traveler who stopped in his shop in the Levant. He thus sets out on a long journey, accompanied by his two nearly grown nephews, his man-servant, and a woman seeking her estranged husband." Libr J

"Maalouf has considerable success using cultural details to create an authentic atmosphere, and the novel effectively captures the flavor and spirit of 17th-century Europe." Publ Wkly

Leo Africanus; translated by Peter Sluglett. New Amsterdam 1992 360p pa $16.95

ISBN 1-561-31022-0   LC 91-36145

Original French edition, 1986; this translation first published 1988 in England with title: Leo the African

This "historical novel recreates the era when the Moors were expelled from Spain, and much of North Africa and southern Europe was in turmoil. Hassan al-Wazzan was just a child the year Columbus sailed to the New World. . . . The gradual exile of Hassan's family from Spain is developed through recollections of his proud, erring father, his badly treated mother and her diplomat brother. As a merchant and emissary, Hassan travels from Fez to Cairo to Mecca and—by misadventure—to Rome and the Vatican, where he is later renamed Leo Africanus." Publ Wkly

"Chronicling the loves and adventures of his wandering protagonist, the author deftly weaves into Hassan's account a score of the traveler's more famous contemporaries, including Columbus, the Medicis, Martin Luther, and Suleiman the Magnificent. Enjoyable reading for general readers." Libr J

Maazel, Fiona, 1975-

Last last chance. Farrar, Straus and Giroux 2008 337p $25

ISBN 978-0-374-18385-1; 0-374-18385-6

LC 2007-19428

This novel "follows the tribulations of Lucy, a young drug addict who works at a New York City kosher chicken plant. Lucy's father was a Centers for Disease Control bigwig who's recently committed suicide, presumably due to fallout from his perceived role in an outbreak of plague that is spreading across America. Her mother, Isifrid, is a crack-addled gazillionaire, while grandmother Agneth talks incessantly of reincarnation, and younger half-sister Hannah harbors a huge obsession with disease. As the novel opens, Lucy sets off with her alcoholic, over-50 coworker, Stanley, to attend the wedding of her best friend, Kam—who is marrying Eric, whom Lucy met first and fell in love with. After some hijinks, Lucy heads to a rehab facility in Texas." Publ Wkly

This is "one strange, beautiful novel. It's the most shattering fictionalization of addiction and recovery since David Foster Wallace's Infinite Jest—yet the narrator's story is set against the outbreak of a global superplague that threatens to decimate humanity. . . . [It] is overflowing with a gallow's humor that makes the impending end of the world almost palatable. Few modern novels have brought together brainy introspection and pure nail-biting entertainment so well." Anthem

MacAdam, Alfred J., 1941-

(tr) Fuentes, C. The years with Laura Diaz

MacAlister, Katie

A girl's guide to vampires. Love Spell 2003 374p pa $7.99

ISBN 0-505-52530-5

"All Joy Randall wants is a little old-fashioned romance, but when she participates in a 'Goddess evoking' ceremony with her friend, Roxy, Joy finds out her future true love is a man with the potential to put her immortal soul in danger. At first the ever-practical Joy is ready to dismiss her vision as a product of too much gin and too many vampire romances, but while traveling through the Czech Republic with Roxy, Joy begins to have some second thoughts about her mystery lover because she is suddenly plagued by visions of a lethally handsome stranger. . . . With its superb characterization and writing that manages to be both sexy and humorous, this contemporary paranormal love story is an absolute delight." Booklist

MacBride, Stuart

Flesh house. St. Martin's Minotaur 2008 467p il $24.95

ISBN 978-0-312-38263-6; 0-312-38263-4

LC 2008-23605

Det. Sgt. Logan McRae "is on the hunt for a serial killer called the Flesher who butchers his victims and then feeds their meat to their family members. The first murders occurred 20 years ago, and Ken Wiseman was convicted but later released on a technicality. Now the

MacBride, Stuart—*Continued*

Flesher is again terrorizing Aberdeen, and McRae is working to find Wiseman and stop the murders. To add to the pressure, a BBC documentary on the Grampian police force is being filmed during the investigation, so every move the officers make is being recorded. McRae, a very human hero, is juggling the investigation along with his superior officers' eccentricities and a breakup with his girlfriend, even as he ferries around a visiting police chief who was involved in the investigation of the first murders." Libr J

MacDonald, Ann-Marie

Fall on your knees; a novel. Simon & Schuster 1997 508p il

ISBN 0-684-83320-4   LC 96-34186

In this novel "James Piper and his Lebanese child bride raise their four daughters on Cape Breton Island in the early 1900s. Gorgeous, talented, and aloof, Kathleen finds her way to New York City, studying opera by day and sneaking into the smoky world of Harlem jazz by night. Her sister Mercedes, cursed with imperfect religious fervor, tries to keep the two youngest sisters safe from the dark forces that threaten the family left behind. Frances, with her own destructive secrets, seeks solace in sleazy back alleys and raunchy speakeasies. And little Lily, damaged by polio, whose ethereal innocence protects her from nothing, proves toughest of all." Libr J

The author "skillfully shifts the story backward and forward in time, giving it a mythic quality that allows dark, half-buried secrets to be gracefully and chillingly revealed." N Y Times Book Rev

The way the crow flies; a novel. HarperCollins Publishers 2003 722p $26.95

ISBN 0-06-057895-5   LC 2003-61076

This novel is "set during the early sixties on a suburblike Canadian air force base. . . . Madeleine is an exuberant eight-year-old still attached to her stuffed Bugs Bunny. When her creepy new teacher begins keeping her and other girls after school for 'exercises,' which gradually morph into full-blown sexual abuse, she feels she cannot talk about it because it is so alien to the sunny, wholesome world of her family. Meanwhile, her straight-arrow father, Jack, has been recruited by his revered former flying instructor, who now works for intelligence, to babysit an ex-Nazi scientist; Jack is soon faced with a moral dilemma tinged with the cynical overtones of realpolitik." Booklist

This is "a brilliant portrayal of child abuse and its consequences, but it is much more than that. It is a fiercely intelligent look at childhood, marriage, families, the 1960s, the Cold War and the fear and isolation that are part of the human condition." Washington Post Book World

Macdonald, Filip *See* MacDonald, Philip, 1899-1981

MacDonald, John D. (John Dann), 1916-1986

Cinnamon skin; the twentieth adventure of Travis McGee. Harper & Row 1982 275p o.p.

LC 81-48159

"Travis McGee and his friend Meyer search for Meyer's niece's new husband, who has killed his wife and faked his own death in an explosion. The search is plod-ding and long, but MacDonald makes it interesting through the diverse and lively characters involved. The showdown, on Mexico's Yucatán Peninsula, is a bit slow but colorful and original." Libr J

A deadly shade of gold. Lippincott 1974 c1965 336p o.p.

"The Travis McGee series"

First published 1965 in paperback by Fawcett Books

An old friend of Travis McGee's is found dead, and an Aztec idol worth more than its weight in gold disappears. McGee's search for the perpetrator (or perpetrators) leads him to Florida, New York, California and Mexico

The deep blue good-by. Lippincott 1975 c1964 200p o.p.

"The Travis McGee series"

First published 1964 in paperback by Fawcett Books

"Travis McGee, as usual helping out a damsel in distress, encounters a psycho ladykiller who makes most of the women he fancies soon wish they were dead. Plenty of action on the 'Busted Flush,' McGee's houseboat and on the deep seas off the Florida coast, but the deep blue of the title is that of a stolen sapphire. McGee's probings go back to the fly-boys of World War II, including some who came home from the China run with more gold than good conduct medals." Booklist

The dreadful lemon sky. Lippincott 1975 c1974 228p o.p.

"The Travis McGee series"

"After successfully smuggling a huge quantity of Jamaican marijuana into Florida in a plane and boat operation, a team of felons fall victim to greed and treachery among themselves. A member of the team, a girl who had once been Travis's lover, entrusts him with her share of the loot for safekeeping (not specifying its origin, of course). Then she's murdered. As Travis investigates this death, with the aid of his philosophical friend Meyer, he finds himself investigating a whole series of related deaths, none of them accidental." Publ Wkly

Dress her in indigo. Lippincott 1971 c1969 255p o.p.

"The Travis McGee series"

First published 1969 in a paperback edition

"Travis McGee and friend Meyer [go] to the Mexican village of Oaxaca, among the gay, the depraved, [the drug addicted] and the violent, to find out about the kind of life Bix Bowie led there before her tragic death." Libr J

Free fall in crimson. Harper & Row 1981 246p o.p.

LC 80-7871

"The Travis McGee series"

"A jig-saw trail takes Trav to a small Iowa town where Peter Kesner is making 'Free Fall' a movie about balloon racing he hopes will salvage his career after several flops. Financing the current flick is Josie Laurant, Kesner's lover. She has inherited a fortune from her former husband and daughter, both victims of unsolved murders McGee is investigating. Adding to the bank roll are porn flicks made by Desmin Grizzel, a real-life biker Kesner had featured in a film about motorcycle gangs. Grizzel has seduced local minors and forced them to take part in the scabrous movies, outraging the citizens. A mob attacks the film crew and a pitched battle leaves scores dead and injured." Publ Wkly

MacDonald, John D. (John Dann), 1916-1986—
Continued

The green ripper. Lippincott 1979 221p o.p.
LC 79-12063
"Gretel, Trav's fiancée, mentions the suspicious, secret visit of a leader in the Church of Apocrypha to a posh local resort. Soon after, Gretel dies, supposedly of a mysterious virus. But Trav's grief is increased by instincts that tell him his love was murdered. He leaves Florida on the trail of the cult members." Publ Wkly

"MacDonald is unsurpassed at showing the American brand of loneliness. He catches foibles in a phrase and gives us many-sided, wounded but courageous, characters." Booklist

The lonely silver rain. Knopf 1985 c1984 232p o.p.
* LC 84-23373
"The Travis McGee series"
"Travis McGee is growing older, and here he has good reason to feel his age. Besides combating a drug-smuggling potentate out to kill him, he finds himself the father of a young woman, all of which make the sleuth-philosopher reflect even more somberly on his life, his friends, his lonely job. One of the last MacDonald stories, it is also one of the best." Barzun. Cat of Crime. Rev and enl edition

The long lavender look. Lippincott 1972 c1970 264p o.p.
"The Travis McGee series"
First published in paperback 1970 by Fawcett Books
When McGee avoids running his Rolls Royce into a young girl, he finds himself embroiled in intrigue

One fearful yellow eye. Lippincott 1978 c1966 286p o.p.
LC 77-24165
"The Travis McGee series"
First published 1966 in paperback by Fawcett Books
Travis McGee "answers an SOS from Glory Geis. She tells him that her late husband had secretly disposed of a fortune in cash before his death, money Geis's other heirs accuse the widow of stealing. Smelling blackmail, McGee digs into the dead man's past and finds evidence of a venomous plot. A gang of Nazi criminals, passing for respectable citizens, had extorted Geis's money by threatening the lives of his wife and children." Publ Wkly

One more Sunday. Knopf 1984 311p o.p.
LC 83-48858
"John Tinker Meadows and his sister Mary Margaret head the Eternal Church of the Believer, a fundamentalist sect headquartered in the South. From a small country church, ECB has grown into a huge conglomerate, exuding power and wealth, masking a variety of sins—lust, greed, corruption, and murder." Libr J

The author "is far too wise to fall into any simplistic traps, nor does he dismiss all of the religious work as worthless. His descriptions of the church's organization and its power over ordinary mortals are brilliantly done, and the questions of conscience come vividly to life." NY Times Book Rev

A purple place for dying. Lippincott 1976 c1964 204p o.p.
"The Travis McGee series"
First published 1964 in paperback by Fawcett Books
"Travis McGee is pondering whether to take on the beautiful Mona Yeoman as a client when someone decides for him by shooting her in the back and hiding the body. Mona's husband soon dies of poison, and the killers might have been in the clear if they had not tried to add McGee (and one of those lovely women he always attracts) to their list. The usual literate and fast-paced stuff expected from MacDonald." Booklist

The scarlet ruse. Lippincott 1980 c1973 262p o.p.
LC 79-24843
"The Travis McGee series"
First published 1973 in paperback by Fawcett Books
Private detective Travis McGee, "who lives on a houseboat, is told that the owner is planning on cleaning up the waterfront so he's going to lose his mooring place. McGee is bothered by this but to take his mind off this impending disaster, he takes on a case wherein a dealer of rare stamps is being made the victim of a stamp collector who is substituting 'junk' stamps—worthless stamps for valuable one-of-a-kind stamps. MacDonald keeps the pot boiling as McGee conducts his investigation and, as tradition would have it, runs into all kinds of unforeseen difficulties in settling this case, up to and including murder." West Coast Rev Books

The turquoise lament. Lippincott 1973 287p o.p.
"The Travis McGee series"
McGee goes to the rescue of the daughter of a man who saved his life
"One of the best McGee adventures." Publ Wkly

Macdonald, Malcolm *See* Ross-Macdonald, Malcolm

Macdonald, Malcolm Ross- *See* Ross-Macdonald, Malcolm

MacDonald, Philip, 1899-1981

The list of Adrian Messenger. Doubleday 1959 224p o.p.
"Published for the Crime Club"
"A piece of paper listing ten men, six of them died 'accidentally,' sends Anthony Gethryn on a desperate man hunt for a diabolical killer." Publ Wkly

"If some readers find Mr. MacDonald's style a bit stiff and old-fashioned, they will also find that he provides such other old-fashioned elements as honest clues, characters who stick in the mind from page to page, an original idea, and, in Anthony Gethryn, a detective who inspires utter confidence." New Yorker

Macdonald, Ross, 1915-1983

Archer in Hollywood; with a foreword by the author. Knopf 1967 528p o.p.
An omnibus edition of three mysteries featuring Lew Archer: The moving target (1949); The way some people die (1951); The barbarous coast (1956)

Macdonald, Ross, 1915-1983—*Continued*

Archer in jeopardy; with a foreword by the author. Knopf 1979 757p o.p.　　　　LC 79-63807

An omnibus volume of three titles published separately 1958, 1962 and 1968 respectively

Contents: The doomsters; The zebra-striped hearse; The instant enemy

Three mysteries featuring Lew Archer. In The doomsters the activities of an unscrupulous doctor occupy the sleuth; in The zebra-striped hearse the detective becomes involved in an ice pick murder, and in The instant enemy it is the high school runaway that is the focus of Archer's attention

"Three classic Lew Archer mysteries. . . . This stunning trilogy is a must for all mystery enthusiasts." Booklist

The barbarous coast
In Macdonald, R. Archer in Hollywood
　　p171-346

The doomsters
In Macdonald, R. Archer in jeopardy

The drowning pool. Knopf 1950 244p o.p.
　　　　　　　　　　　　　　　　　*

"Admirers of the later Ross Macdonald will detect in this early book the capacities subsequently so well exploited. Lew Archer started as he continued: tough and straight; clever and informed, but not omniscient; full of love and hostility toward Southern California. This story, of a woman who has made a bad marriage to a mother-dominated husband of ambivalent sexual character, has a bit too much violence, but the character-drawing shows a sure hand, and the tangle is so capably manipulated that it does not annoy." Barzun. Cat of Crime. Rev and enl edition

The far side of the dollar. Vintage Books 1996 247p pa $12
　ISBN 0-679-76865-3
　　　　　　　　　　　　　* LC 97-120671

First published 1965 by Knopf

This mystery "begins with Lew Archer's visit to a school for troubled boys, in search of a lead on Tommy Hillman, who has just escaped. . . . It turns out that Hillman had borrowed and wrecked a neighbor's car, and was put in the school by his father to teach him a lesson. Next, Archer learns that a ransom of $25,000 has been demanded for the return of Tommy Hillman. The Hillmans are a typically horrifying wealthy couple whose life has become unmoored through too much lying. The investigation of their past at one point brings up a connection to Archer's, showing that he has more in common with these people than he at first supposed." Murphy. Ency of Murder and Mystery

The Galton case. Vintage Books 1996 242p pa $12
　ISBN 0-679-76864-5
　　　　　　　　　　　　　* LC 97-118474

First published 1959 by Knopf

"Archer is hired by Lawyer Gordon Sable on a hopeless case: to search for the elderly Mrs. Galton's son and heir, Anthony Galton. What he quickly turns up is a decapitated corpse buried on the spot where Anthony had lived twenty years before, and a young man working in a gas station who looks exactly like Anthony and may be his son. . . . The Galton trail leads to a bleak provincial town in Canada, and Macdonald's wry and funny glance at the beatnik poetry scene in San Francisco enriches the early part of the novel, putting on display the strength and flexibility of Macdonald's mature style. With The Galton case, Macdonald had 'arrived' precisely by finding a mythical form for his own beginnings." Murphy. Ency of Murder and Mystery

The goodbye look. Knopf 1969 243p o.p.

Private detective Lew Archer is brought "into the affairs of the Chalmers family because their lawyer thinks they are worried about a theft from their safe. But the Chalmers have other problems, and Lew becomes involved with murders old and new." Libr J

The instant enemy
In Macdonald, R. Archer in jeopardy

The moving target
In Macdonald, R. Archer in Hollywood
　　p3-169

Sleeping beauty. Knopf 1973 271p o.p.

The scene "is California and the concern is with what power and money can do to wreck a family. Lew [Archer] befriends a lost lady who is running away from fears and responsibilities and from her young husband. Before very long word comes that the girl has been kidnapped and a ransom is demanded of her oil rich family. Bit by bit, as Archer probes deeper into the family relationships, he begins to see that nothing is what it seems and the key to the present lies deep in the past." Publ Wkly

The underground man. Knopf 1971 272p o.p.
　　　　　　　　　　　　　　　　　*

"With his customary skill and economy of means, the author gets us, through Archer, into a tangle of passions about runaway spouses, disaffected and drug-taking children, amateur blackmail, and, of course, murder." Barzun. Cat of Crime. Rev and enl edition

The way some people die
In Macdonald, R. Archer in Hollywood
　　p347-528

The zebra-striped hearse
In Macdonald, R. Archer in jeopardy

MacInnes, Helen, 1907-1985

Above suspicion. Harcourt Brace & Co. 1954 333p
　ISBN 0-15-102707-2

A reprint of the title first published 1941 by Little, Brown

"An Oxford don and his pretty wife are chosen to perform a secret mission to Germany in late 1939. While using their vacation as a cover, they are to locate the whereabouts of an anti-Nazi agent. The plan seems foolproof—until someone betrays it and them." Smith. Cloak and Dagger Fic

Prelude to terror. Harcourt Brace Jovanovich 1978 368p o.p.

"Colin Grant, art consultant, is asked by a wealthy art collector to purchase a specific seventeenth-century painting at an art auction in Vienna. The owner of the paint-

MacInnes, Helen, 1907-1985—*Continued*

ing needs money to escape from Hungary, and the transaction must be kept secret. When Colin arrives in Vienna, he finds that the auction conceals a conspiracy for laundering money that is used to buy weapons for terrorist groups. In spite of great personal danger Colin searches for the key piece of information that will stop this source of financing." Shapiro. Fic for Youth. 2d edition

Ride a pale horse. Harcourt Brace Jovanovich 1984 355p o.p.   LC 84-9037

"Karen Cornell, journalist for an American world affairs magazine, is about to leave a peace convention in Prague disgruntled by her treatment and the lack of material when she is approached by a Czech intelligence officer who is about to defect. The papers he gives her to relay to a CIA expert on 'disinformation' start her on a harrowing course from Prague to Vienna, Rome, and Washington." Libr J

"The device of dual protagonists moves the plot along smartly, and the demonstration of the insidious uses of disinformation could hardly be more timely." Booklist

The Venetian affair. Harcourt, Brace & World 1963 405p o.p.

This "suspense novel is set in Paris and Venice in 1961. An American newspaperman on vacation picks up the wrong raincoat on arrival at Orly airport, and finds himself involved in a communist plot to assassinate De Gaulle and implicate the United States. American agents enlist his help to thwart the plotters and to unmask the mysterious and ruthless spymaster." Publ Wkly

Mackey, Nathaniel, 1947-

Bass cathedral; with a preface by Wilson Harris. New Directions 2007 c2008 183p il pa $16.95

ISBN 978-0-8112-1720-0; 0-8112-1720-5

LC 2007-34666

This is the fourth volume of From a broken bottle traces of perfume still emanate, the author's ongoing novel with no beginning or end

"Los Angeles, October 1982: Molimo m'Atet, formerly known as the The Mystic Horn Society, is preparing to release its new album Orphic Bend. The members of the jazz ensemble—Aunt Nancy, Djamilaa, Drennette, Lambert, N., and Penguin—are witness to a strange occurrence: while listening to their test pressing, the moment Aunt Nancy's bass solo begins a balloon emerges from the vinyl, bearing a mysterious message: I dreamt you were gone.... Through letters N. writes to a figure called Angel of Dust, the ever-mutating story unfolds." Publisher's note

"Plot serves as a platform from which Mackey launches a volley of poetic and philosophical concerns. . . . That these idiosyncratic yet rigorously applied thought processes never become overly cerebral is testament to Mackey's tremendous musicality. Such is the exquisitely rhythmic lyricism of the novel that not once does the conceptual language dampen the sound of the music inhabiting the prose. With [this work], Mackey writes in being a fiction worthy of the songs he interrogates." Bookforum

Mackin, Edward, 1929-

For works written by this author under other names see McInerny, Ralph M., 1929-

Mackintosh, Elizabeth *See* Tey, Josephine, 1896-1952

MacLean, Alistair, 1922-1987

Floodgate. Doubleday 1984 c1983 369p

ISBN 0-385-18263-5   LC 83-45013

First published 1983 in the United Kingdom

"The novel is set in and around Amsterdam, where a band of canny, sophisticated terrorists are threatening to flood the Netherlands by blowing up dikes and exploding offshore nuclear devices. The terrorists demand that Holland must negotiate with Great Britain for the withdrawal of all British troops from Northern Ireland. Peter van Effen, senior detective and explosives expert, eventually saves the nation, a task he carries out with cool, dispassionate efficiency." Booklist

"Readers accustomed to thrillers of a more lurid hue may well appreciate MacLean's stylistic restraint, neat plotting and attention to characterization." Publ Wkly

Force 10 from Navarone. Doubleday 1968 274p o.p.

The three heroes of The guns of Navarone, Mallory, Miller and Stavros are assigned a new mission during World War II. "They are dropped into Yugoslavia to join the Partisans, prevent a German attack, blow up a dam, and provide a diversion to draw German troops out of Italy." Publ Wkly

The guns of Navarone. Doubleday 1957 320p o.p.

"World War II is being fought, and the Germans control the island that guards the approaches to the eastern Mediterranean with big guns. After all other attempts have failed, a five-man British army team is chosen to silence the guns of Navarone. They land on the island, elude the Nazis, and scale a seemingly unclimbable cliff." Shapiro. Fic for Youth. 3d edition

Followed by Force 10 from Navarone

Ice Station Zebra. Doubleday 1963 276p o.p.

A novel of suspense and intrigue that begins on "a bitter-cold morning in Holy Loch, Scotland, when a British doctor with top-level endorsements from the American and British military forces seeks admission to an American nuclear submarine. The submarine is slated for a perilous trip to rescue the starving, freezing British crew of a meteorological station situated on an ice floe in the Arctic." Publ Wkly

Night without end. Doubleday 1960 287p o.p.

"An airliner crash lands on the Greenland icecap near a small I.G.Y. observation station. It soon becomes clear that the landing was planned and certain of the passengers and crew murdered for reasons unknown, while at least eight of the 10 survivors were drugged into insensibility—the other two of course, being the killers. But which two? . . . A sometimes barely credible, but always absorbing, thriller that combines elements of the espionage story and murder mystery with those of the 'castaway' adventure tale." Libr J

When eight bells toll. Doubleday 1966 288p o.p.

"Sure and deadly with guns and knives, an expert at underwater work, Philip Calvert, British secret service agent, polishes his skills to a high gloss in this tense ad-

MacLean, Alistair, 1922-1987—*Continued*
venture story set in the western Scottish Highlands. Calvert and his friends oppose a gang of killers who operate at sea and in harbors. What the killers are doing, why they are busy in this cold, rainy, windy part of Scotland, and whether Calvert will survive his fight against them are questions that provide suspense." Publ Wkly

Where eagles dare. Doubleday 1967 312p o.p.
"Secrecy and stealth are essential to the mission of an assorted crew from MI 6 who must rescue an American general, the coordinator of Overlord, from Schloss Adler, a castle built by a mad Bavarian prince, which is the combined HQ of the German Secret Service and the Gestapo of South Germany in the bitter winter of 1943-44. And if that isn't enough, there is Major Smith's second assignment to bring out the pyrotechnic display of excitement and suspense." Libr J

MacLeod, Alistair

Island; the complete stories. Norton 2001 434p
$25.95
ISBN 0-393-05035-1   LC 00-51524
Contents: The boat; The vastness of the dark; The golden gift of grey; The return; In the fall; The lost salt gift of blood; The road to Rankin's Point; The closing down of summer; To every thing there is a season; Second spring; Winter dog; The tuning of perfection; As birds bring forth the sun; Vision; Island; Clearances
"The author, an expatriate from Cape Breton, Nova Scotia, writes about his homeland and its dying traditions, in tales that marry the elemental themes of Gaelic song (loneliness, sorrow, work, death) with a simple but deceptively modern narrative style. In the course of the sixteen stories (presented in order of publication, from 1968 to 1999), MacLeod's spare style grows more artful, but the ache of loss is constant as he captures the direct eloquence of the islanders-the coal miners, lobstermen, farmers, and lighthouse keepers who know they are the last of their kind." New Yorker

MacLeod, Charlotte

Exit the milkman. Mysterious Press 1996 311p
o.p.   LC 96-18337
In this mystery Balacava Agricultural College's "Peter Shandy is the last person to see fellow professor Jim Feldster—a man who welcomes any excuse to get away from his wife—before he disappears. When Feldster's wife accuses the Shandys of hiding her husband, they begin sleuthing. Another series charmer." Libr J

The Gladstone bag. Mysterious Press 1990 218p
o.p.   LC 89-43143
"Six feisty and contentious characters with inventive names surround aging-but-active Emma Kelling during her stay at a friend's Maine retreat. Strange events, attempted theft, and a sodden body propel her to consult niece and nephew-in-law/detectives Sarah and Max Bittersohn . . ., as well as cousin-in-law Theonie. Tongue-in-cheek eccentricities, the usual casual but astute deductions, and a certain luxuriousness of language make this a most welcome addition to the MacLeod canon." Libr J

Rest you merry. Doubleday 1978 182p o.p.
     LC 77-27713
"Published for the Crime Club"
"Christmas time at Balaclava Agricultural College is the background for this academic mystery tale. Professor Peter Shandy capitulates to the badgering of a resident busy-body Jemima Ames and shows his Christmas spirit—by decorating his house with plastic reindeer, flashing lights, and leering Santas. . . . He then flees, but driven back by his conscience, he returns to find the body of Jemima in his living room. Helen Marsh, the new librarian, joins the professor in the investigation of the murder." Publisher's note

Vane pursuit; a Peter Shandy mystery.
Mysterious Press 1989 185p o.p.
     LC 88-25595
"Detective Peter Shandy, and his redoubtable wife, Helen the librarian, are swept up in the diabolical theft of antique weather vanes by crooks who use arson as their *mode d'accomplis.* . . . Endless puns punctuate MacLeod's delightfully absurd tale, which, beneath all the frivolity, is masterfully executed." Booklist

The withdrawing room. Doubleday 1980 186p
o.p.
"Published for the Crime Club"
"Widowed Sarah Kelling takes boarders into her stately home on Boston's Beacon Hill to pay the heavy mortgage, a move that means trouble. Mr. Quiffen, who settles into the former 'withdrawing room,' is killed and so is Mr. Hartler, who rents the vacated premises. Sarah appeals to her brainy, attractive friend Max Bittersohn for help but begins to investigate her guests personally, afraid that one may be the murderer." Publ Wkly

MacNeil, Duncan *See* McCutchan, Philip, 1920-

MacNeil, Robert, 1931-

Breaking news; a novel. Doubleday 1998 371p
$24.95
ISBN 0-385-42020-X   LC 98-19562
"Network anchor, Grant Munro, opens the book with a speech to the Radio and Television News Directors dinner comparing the media's Monica Lewinsky feeding frenzy to the behavior of the Bible's Gadarene swine. . . . Munro is under pressure: he is close to 60; ratings are dropping; and he is surrounded by kids (reporters, producers, etc.) who think sensation and sentimentality have much more appeal than what's happening in Washington or Kosovo." Booklist
"By the novel's end, MacNeil has delivered some extremely disheartening news about the state of our national news media wrapped neatly in a shiny literary package: Jim Lehrer's loss is fiction's gain." N Y Times Book Rev

Burden of desire. Doubleday 1992 466p o.p.
     LC 91-28919
"The story begins with a bang—literally, as a munitions ship blows up in Halifax, Nova Scotia, in 1917 in what will be the biggest, most destructive man-made explosion until the atomic bomb. Picking up the pieces in the well-evoked ruined city are young parson Peter Wentworth, an ambitious man in an unhappy marriage, and Stewart MacPherson, a psychiatrist just beginning to

MacNeil, Robert, 1931-—*Continued*

treat shell-shocked returning soldiers. The two read a diary accidentally lost in the wreckage, belonging to Julia Robertson, a young, unconventional woman whose beauty and self-acknowledged sensuality ensnares each of them in turn." Publ Wkly

This novel "is at once a wonderful romance involving one of the more appealing triangles in recent fiction and a thoughtful dissection of the glacial pace of social change." N Y Times Book Rev

Maguire, Gregory

Confessions of an ugly stepsister; illustrations by Bill Sanderson. ReganBooks 1999 368p il $25.95

ISBN 0-06-039282-7   LC 00-59085

Based loosely on the Cinderella story, this novel is set in 17th-century Holland. "The tale begins with the arrival of a recent widow from England, returned to her native Haarlem with her apparently retarded older daughter and a younger one who is unattractive but sharp and quickly develops an interest in painting. The three become housekeepers to the family of a tulip merchant; when his wife dies, leaving his own young daughter motherless, merchant and widow marry, and their daughters become stepsisters." Libr J

"Adult and sophisticated, . . . [the author's] musings on beauty, ugliness, magic, reality, and imagination explore how our past follows us always and shapes our self-perception." Chicago Trib

A lion among men; with illustrations by Douglas Smith. William Morrow 2008 312p il $26.95

ISBN 978-0-06-054892-6   LC 2008-16694

This third part of the author's "Wicked Years series, a revisionist chronicle of L. Frank Baum's classic *The Wonderful Wizard of Oz*, examines the tragically misunderstood life of the Cowardly Lion before and after his adventures with Dorothy and company. As all-out war looms between the Munchkinland guerrillas and the emperor of Oz's Emerald City soldiers, Brrr the lion, now working as an imperial spy, must somehow glean invaluable information from a crone named Yackle before she dies. But during his interrogation of the irritable oracle, Brrr, the proverbial loner and outsider, uncovers insights into his own mysterious past—and finally begins to understand what it feels like to belong." Publ Wkly

"Most of this is superbly entertaining, but Maguire has bitten off more complex interactions than he can chew, and his story's seams frequently show. No matter. Brrr and his acquaintances are irresistible company, and issues of legitimate and responsible rule are herein really rather subtly grafted onto the venerable free will vs. predestination conundrum. . . . Maguire's inspired world-building strides from strength to strength." Kirkus

Mirror mirror; a novel. Regan Books 2003 280p $24.99

ISBN 0-06-039384-X   LC 2003-46774

This novel sets the Snow White story in Renaissance Italy. Bianca de Nevada "is born on a farm in Tuscany in 1495, and when she is seven, her father is ordered by the duplicitous Cesare Borgia to go on a quest to reclaim the relic of the original Tree of Knowledge, a branch bearing three living apples that are thousands of years old. Bianca is left in the care of her father's farm staff

and the beautiful and madly vain Lucrecia Borgia, Cesare's sister. But Lucrecia becomes jealous of her lecherous brother's interest in the growing child and plots a dire fate for Bianca in the woods below the farm. There Bianca finds herself in the home of seven dwarves—the creators of the magic mirror who await the return of their brother, the eighth dwarf, long gone on a quest of his own." Publisher's note

This novel "unearths our buried fascination with the primal fears and truths fairy tales contain. Through this forest of wry, sometimes bawdy humor, Maguire leaves a trail of profound reflections on the nature of identity, the persistence of love, the self-destruction of evil." Christ Sci Monit

Son of a witch; a novel. ReganBooks 2005 337p il $26.95

ISBN 0-06-054893-2   LC 2005-46232

"This sequel to the adult fairy tale Wicked (1995) . . . begins ten years after the destruction of Elphaba, a.k.a. the Wicked Witch of the West. In Maguire's dark version of the Land of Oz, there's not much to ring the bells for in the Emerald City, despite the tyrannical Wizard's departure. Corruption is rife, political factions compete for power, and radicals proclaim 'Elphaba lives!' Elsewhere, a horribly injured young man called Liir wakes in the religious House of Saint Glinda to many puzzles. . . . Above all, was Elphaba his mother? These and other questions drive a tale that adroitly mixes drama, humor, and political satire into a well-knit examination of good and evil-and leaves several doors open for future journeys over the rainbow into this cleverly constructed dystopia." Libr J

Wicked; the life and times of the wicked witch of the West; illustrations by Douglas Smith. ReganBooks 1995 406p il $26.95

ISBN 0-06-039144-8

* LC 95-669

"Born with green skin and huge teeth, like a dragon, the free-spirited Elphaba grows up to be an anti-totalitarian agitator, an animal-rights activist, a nun, then a nurse who tends the dying—and, ultimately, the headstrong Wicked Witch of the West in the land of Oz. Maguire's strange and imaginative postmodernist fable uses L. Frank Baum's *Wonderful Wizard of Oz* as a springboard to create a tense realm inhabited by humans, talking animals (a rhino librarian, a goat physician), Munchkinlanders, dwarves and various tribes." Publ Wkly

Mahfouz, Naguib *See* Maḥfūẓ, Najīb, 1911-2006

Maḥfūẓ, Najīb, 1911-2006

Children of the alley; by Naguib Mahfouz; translated by Peter Theroux. Doubleday 1996 448p o.p.

LC 95-15510

Original Arabic version serialized 1959 in Cairo newspaper; previous English translation with title: Children of Gebelaawi, published 1981 in paperback by Three Continents Press

"Gabalawi's mansion sits at the desert's edge, surrounded by high-walled gardens. His sons, however, quarrel over his estate, and the omnipotent gangster banishes them from his earthly paradise. Their descendants

Maḥfūẓ, Najīb, 1911-2006—*Continued*
settle outside the wall, desperately poor but always praying to Gabalawi for salvation. As each succeeding generation spawns its messiah, the people rise up against the ruling gangsters, seizing their portion of the estate, but greed and ignorance prove their ultimate undoing, poverty and suffering their inescapable fate." Libr J

Theroux "skillfully conveys Mahfouz's fierce egalitarian message while capturing his gift for masterly storytelling. Mahfouz combines the universal appeal of archetypal dramatic conflicts—brother murders brother; wife betrays husband into the hands of his enemies; father expels defiant son—with the originality of his own inventive narrative structures." Publ Wkly

Midaq Alley; [by] Naguib Mahfouz; translated by Trevor Le Gassick. Anchor Bks. (NY) 1992 286p o.p.
                                    LC 91-27459
"Written in the 1940s, this novel . . . deals with the plight of impoverished classes in an old quarter of Cairo. The lives and situations depicted create an atmosphere of sadness and tragic realism. Indeed, few of the characters are happy or successful. Protagonist Hamida, an orphan raised by a foster mother, is drawn into prostitution. Kirsha, the owner of a café in the alley, is a drug addict and a lustful homosexual. Zaita makes a living by disfiguring people so that they can become successful beggars. Transcending time and place, the social issues treated here are relevant to many Arab countries today." Libr J

Palace of desire; translated by William M. Hutchins and Olive E. Kenny. Doubleday 1991 422p o.p.
                                    * LC 90-3753
Original Arabic edition, 1957
"Al-Sayyid Ahmad is mellowing as he leaves middle age. As this second novel of 'The Cairo Trilogy' opens, he is ending his self-imposed abstention from liquor and women, begun five years earlier upon the death of his son, Fahmy. . . . Meanwhile, his children are struggling with life beyond their father's domination. Yasin is twice divorced and incapable of resisting any woman. The two married daughters are split by an open feud. And Kamal, the intellectual center of this novel, enters college [and grapples with] . . . religion, science, and romance." Libr J

"Mr. Mahfouz excels at fusing deep emotion and soap opera. Fortunately, the translators . . . are equal to the task of animating rather than embalming Mr. Mahfouz's elegant and often explosive text." N Y Times Book Rev
Followed by Sugar Street

Palace walk; translated from the Arabic by William M. Hutchins with Olive E. Kenny. Doubleday 1990 c1989 498p o.p.
                                    * LC 89-23348
Originally published in Arabic
This is the first volume in the author's trilogy "dealing with three generations of a Cairo family in the first half of the twentieth century. The emotional and physical struggles of these middle-class people are depicted with a great deal of sympathy and honesty, from the torments of adolescent love through the banked passions of an established marriage. The novel begins with a series of domestic scenes featuring the five children of a merchant and his wife; later, the setting shifts to Cairo nightclubs, coffee shops, and stores as Mahfouz re-creates the every-

day existence of his characters in almost Dickensian detail." Booklist
Followed by Palace of desire

Sugar Street; translated by William Maynard Hutchins and Angele Botros Samaan. Doubleday 1992 308p o.p.
                                    * LC 91-12938
Original Arabic edition, 1957
This is the concluding volume of the author's Cairo trilogy. "The novel opens in 1935 as Egypt smolders under British occupation, and it extends through the war. Kamal, son of the gaunt, wasted patriarch, is a grade-school teacher and philosopher who veers between lusty debauches and reading Spinoza. One of his nephews, Abd Al-Muni'm, becomes a Muslim fundamentalist; another nephew, Ahmad, takes Marx as his prophet. These two diametrically opposed brothers will share the same fate—a jail cell. The inadvertent cause of their undoing may be another scion of the patriarch, young Ridwan, a closet homosexual whose liaison with a prominent politician apparently backfires." Publ Wkly

"The ordinary nature of Mr. Mahfouz's world, with its willingness to confront the complexities of human intentions, makes it an extraordinary exception in a marketplace of manufactured ideas and is, for that, all the more admirable." N Y Times Book Rev

Mailer, Norman, 1923-2007

Ancient evenings. Little, Brown 1983 709p o.p.
                                    LC 82-22839
"Set in the span between the reigns of Ramses II and Ramses IX, Mailer's . . . novel is narrated by the remnant spirits of Menenhetet I and his great-grandson as they join mutuality to survive the land of the Dead and to ascend to Ra. The story is largely the account of Menenhetet's first life (he has had four) as he rises from peasant stock to become first charioteer to Ramses II, then general, then overseer of the harem." Libr J

"This novel is perhaps the best reconstruction of the far past since Flaubert's 'Salammbo,' but Mailer's eye is on the modern age, especially the psychic problems of America. These problems may find a solution through an understanding of the repressed areas of human sexuality, with the reality of magic. Our own rationality has failed. Here, he seems to say, is a complex civilization of high achievement based on the irrational, on the radial power of magic whose centre is both decay and resurrection. This is a different book, on whose writing and research Mailer spent over ten years, but it is not only about magic, it is magical in itself." Burgess. 99 Novels

The castle in the forest; a novel. Random House 2007 477p $27.95
    ISBN 978-0-394-53649-1; 0-394-53649-5
                                    LC 2006-49389
A fictional "psychobiography of young Adolf Hitler or, more accurately, of Hitler's dysfunctional family. Mailer's unreliable narrator, one of Heinrich Himmler's SS investigators, painstakingly documents the family curse of incest and concludes that Hitler's father, a womanizing customs official, married his own illegitimate daughter. But as the book unfolds, the narrator also reveals that he is really a devil working directly for the Evil One." Libr J

"Over the course of the novel a complex demonology

Mailer, Norman, 1923-2007—*Continued*

is posited, clearly based on Dante and medieval scholasticism, and the narrator's chatty tone and Jesuitical logic are strangely reminiscent of C.S. Lewis' persuasive devil, Screwtape. All of this takes Hitler's life out of the realm of moral choice and into that of the supernatural, making it irrelevant to the novel's stated theme-unless one is an Augustinian Catholic, which as everyone knows the author is not. . . . . Occasionally a real insight slips in, almost by accident." New Leader

The executioner's song. Modern Lib. 1993 1002p

ISBN 0-679-42471-7

* LC 92-51066

A reissue of the title first published 1979 by Little, Brown

A "documentary narrative of 'the activities of Gary Gilmore and the men and women associated with him' between his release from prison in April 1976 and his execution for murder in early 1977. . . . The first half of the book, called 'Western Voices,' is the story of Gilmore's . . . attempt to fit in between the time he is released from prison and the time he is arrested, tried, and found guilty of two murders on two successive nights. But the second half, 'Eastern Voices,' is really the story of the marketing of Gilmore as he awaits—and demands—death in the Utah state prison." New Repub

"In this study of a condemned murderer Mailer not only vividly portrays the character in a real-life drama but also invokes the whole history of westward migration of the Mormons of Utah." Reader's Ency. 3d edition

The Gospel according to the Son. Random House 1997 242p o.p.
LC 96-48018

This is a "novel that purports to be a first-person memoir written by Jesus." Time

Mailer's "gospel is written in a direct, rather relaxed English that yet has an eerie, neo-Biblical dignity." New Yorker

Harlot's ghost. Random House 1991 1310p
ISBN 0-394-58832-0
LC 90-53152

"Harry Hubbard is a bright young man whose father and whose mentor, Hugh Montague (also known as Harlot), are both senior CIA figures and induct him into the Agency. Most of the book . . . is one long flashback, Harry's autobiographical account of his early career—partly in his own words, partly in an exchange of letters with Harlot's beautiful, brilliant wife, Kittredge, whom Harry admires from afar and will one day steal." Publ Wkly

"An immensely long but never laborious book, one where Mailer works compelling variations on his quintessential themes." Libr J

The naked and the dead. Holt & Co. 1948 721p o.p.

*

"In 1944 an American platoon takes part in the invasion and occupation of a Japanese-held island. The action is divided into three parts: the landing on the island, the counter-attack by night, and a daring patrol by the platoon behind enemy lines. The style is simple realism and therefore the language is rough, in keeping with the army setting." Shapiro. Fic for Youth. 3d edition

"The book is encyclopedic yet particular, both realistic

and symbolic. It is one of the best novels by an American about World War II." Benet's Reader's Ency of Am Lit

Tough guys don't dance. Random House 1984 229p o.p.
LC 84-42514

"Tim Madden is a writer who lives in Provincetown, where the action takes place one dreary November. . . . After a night of monumental drinking, Madden awakens with a mysterious tattoo on his arm, blood all over the passenger seat of his Porsche, and no memory of his actions. Later he discovers one, then another decapitated head buried with his stash of marijuana. Madden is obviously the prime suspect in the murders, and his task is to find which of the many unsavory characters of his acquaintance is responsible." Publ Wkly

"This genre is not exactly Mailer's forte, but the no-nonsense prose and the hard-as-nails style . . . may attract readers." Booklist

Maillard, Keith, 1942-

The clarinet polka. Thomas Dunne Bks. 2003 406p $24.95
ISBN 0-312-30889-2
LC 2002-32511

"Jimmy Koprowski returns from his stint in the Air Force in 1969 consigned to his boyhood attic bedroom and a minimun-wage job at a TV repair shop. He drifts into an alcohol-fueled, sexually charged affair with a doctor's wife and engages in ongoing arguments about his 'life plan' with his hard-working dad. . . . Then his ethnomusicologist sister decides to start an all-girl polka band, and that's when he meets singer Janice Dluwiecki." Booklist

"Jimmy is a wry, down-to-earth, irresistable narrator, and Maillard draws all the characters in the working-class community with compassion and obvious affection. This moving, well-drawn story of sin and redemption in a fading industry town may remind readers of Richard Russo." Publ Wkly

Maine, David, 1963-

The book of Samson. St. Martin's Press 2006 229p $23.95
ISBN 978-0-312-35339-1; 0-312-35339-1
LC 2006-45803

A "first-person account of the life of Samson, the Israelite judge remembered for his voluminous hair, Herculean strength and ill-advised relationship with Delilah. Samson delivers his monologue from the Philistine temple of Dagon where, shorn and shackled and awaiting execution, he reflects upon a life of 'frustration and pain plus a fair bit of sex and lots of killing and broken bones.' Hatred of the Philistines is the narrative's central theme, and Samson delights in recalling his violent exploits." Publ Wkly

"Here is a beguiling, original writer who is determined to reinterpret the Bible's humanity in ways that make sense in the modern world." N Y Times (Late N Y Ed)

Fallen. St. Martin's Press 2005 244p $23.95
ISBN 0-312-32849-4
LC 2005-46588

"The first recorded murder takes barely 26 lines in Genesis. What Maine does with those few facts is masterfully creative. The story is told in reverse, beginning with Cain as an old man waiting to die and mourning the

Maine, David, 1963—*Continued*

fact that the ghost of his murdered brother has left him. It deftly moves backward to the murder and God's punishment, where the point of view shifts to Abel just a few days before the murder. Finally, the point of view is shared by Adam and Eve alternately as they deal with aging and their burgeoning family, back to their first moments outside of the garden. Maine's explanations of Cain's hatred, God's dismissal of his sacrifice, and the real forbidden fruit are fascinating and often wildly funny. Once again he has turned his focus on the family dynamics and come away with a divinely passionate tale." Booklist

The preservationist. St. Martin's Press 2004 230p $24.95

    ISBN 0-312-32847-8

                          * LC 2003-70881

"Noah's family (or Noe as he's called here) his wife, sons, and daughters-inlaw tell what it's like to live with a man touched by God, while struggling against events that cannot be controlled or explained. When Noe orders his sons to build an ark, he can't tell them where the wood will come from. When he sends his daughters-inlaw out to gather animals, he can offer no directions, money, or protection. And once the rain starts, they all realize that the true test of their faith is just beginning." Publisher's note

This is an "elegant, inventive book and in no way a cynical one, despite the author's keen appreciation of the incongruous. . . . The book resounds with the gravity of Noe's mission even as it invents the quotidian details of his story." N Y Times Book Rev

Major, Clarence

(ed) Calling the wind. See Calling the wind

Makine, Andreï, 1957-

Dreams of my Russian summers. Arcade Pub. 1997 241p

    ISBN 1-55970-383-0

                          * LC 97-2720

Original French edition, 1995

This is the story "of Charlotte Lemonnier, born in France at the turn of the century, who as a child moved to Russia, where her father practiced medicine. Traveling back and forth over the years, she found herself in France on the eve of World War I, only to return to Russia with a Red Cross mission during the Revolution. There she remained to see the horrors of civil war and famine, and later witnessed the Stalinist purges, the war with Germany, the dehumanizing industrialization of the country and ultimately the fall of Communism's idols. By the time her grandson, the novel's narrator, begins visiting her for his summer holidays, she has been long settled in the sleepy Siberian town where her Russian husband lies buried." N Y Times Book Rev

"At first, the narrator's lyrical and poetic memoir is so Proustian that it seems almost a pastiche, but insidiously it brings home the surreal and heartbreaking wonder of this woman's life." New Yorker

Music of a life; translated from the French by Geoffrey Strachan. Arcade Pub. 2002 109p $21.95

    ISBN 1-55970-637-6   LC 2002-25854

Original French edition, 2001. Published in the United Kingdom with title: A life's music

"It is 1941, and Alexei, a budding concert pianist, is returning to his Moscow apartment two days before his first public recital when a neighbor warns his off: his parents are being arrested. Knowing that he will be sent to the Gulag, too, Alexei flees to the home of relatives in the countryside. Then the Germans invade, decimating his family's village but providing a plethora of bodies from which he can pillage an identity. . . . Stalin's atrocities are made visceral in this wisp of a book." New Yorker

The woman who waited; translated from the French by Geoffrey Strachan. Arcade Publishing 2006 182p $24

    ISBN 1-559-70774-7   LC 2005-10314

Original French edition, 2004

This novel "takes place in the mid-1970s in a rural town called Mirnoe near the White Sea. Our narrator, a 26-year-old folklorist from Leningrad who is documenting local songs and ceremonies, meets an intriguing older woman named Vera who has been waiting for 30 years for her lover, Boris, to return home from the battlefields of World War II. Boris was reported dead in the final days of the war, but Vera forsook her linguistics doctorate and a more cosmopolitan life to await his return in this isolated village, teaching and caring for the elderly in the meantime. Soon she begins a relationship with the folklorist, who has made several erroneous assumptions about Vera and her life." Libr J

"The Woman Who Waited quite deliberately avoids breaking your heart. It just comes very, very close. Vera is perceived only through the eyes of the narrator, but she is clearly more than just the woman who waits: only a fool would fail to understand that she's also the kind of woman worth waiting for, and far kinder and wiser than any romantic fiction." Washington Post Book World

Malamud, Bernard, 1914-1986

The assistant; a novel. Farrar, Straus & Giroux 1957 246p pa $13 hardcover o.p.

    ISBN 0-374-50484-9 (pa)

                                   *

This novel is "set in the prison of a failing grocery store, where Morris Bober, its elderly, long-suffering Jewish owner, teaches his assistant, Frankie Alpine, what it means to be a Jew, and what it means to be a man. After decades in which Jewish protagonists struggled to assimilate to the non-Jewish world around them, *The Assistant* is a tale about reverse assimilation, one in which Frankie takes over the store on Morris's death and undergoes a painful conversion to Judaism." Benet's Reader's Ency of Am Lit

    also in Malamud, B. A Malamud reader p75-305

The complete stories; introduction by Robert Giroux. Farrar, Straus & Giroux 1997 634p hardcover o.p. pa $18

    ISBN 0-374-12639-9; 0-374-52575-7 (pa)

                          * LC 97-12394

Contents: Armistice; Spring rain; The grocery store; Benefit performance; The place is different now; Steady customer; The literary life of Laban Goldman; The cost

Malamud, Bernard, 1914-1986—*Continued*
of living; The prison; The first seven years; The death of me; The bill; The loan; A confession of murder; Riding pants; The girl of my dreams; The magic barrel; The mourners; Angel Levine; A summer's reading; Take pity; The elevator; An apology; The last Mohican; The lady of the lake; Behold the key; The maid's shoes; Idiots first; Still life; Suppose a wedding; Life is better than death; The Jewbird; Black is my favorite color; Naked nude; The German refugee; A choice of profession; A pimp's revenge; Man in the drawer; My son the murderer; Pictures of the artist; An exorcism; Glass blower of Venice; God's wrath; Talking horse; The letter; The silver crown; Notes from a lady at a dinner party; In retirement; Rembrandt's hat; A wig; The model; A lost grave; Zora's noise; In Kew Gardens; Alma redeemed

"Whether, stark, comic or fanciful, Malamud's stories give us immigrant Jews and their descendants pondering moral questions and experiencing moments of magical intervention while enduring life's ridiculous situations. Yet the stories transcend their ethnic settings and achieve a universal resonance." Publ Wkly

The fixer. Farrar, Straus & Giroux 1966 355p pa $14 hardcover o.p.
  ISBN 0-374-52938-8 (pa)
                                                           *
"Yakov Bok, a handyman, is arrested and charged with the killing of a Christian boy. Innocent of the crime, he is only guilty of being a Jew in Czarist Russia. In jail he is mentally and physically tortured as a scapegoat for a crime he insists he did not commit. Although his suffering and degradation are unrelenting, Bok emerges a hero as he maintains his innocence. Malamud has fashioned a powerful story of injustice and endurance based on a true incident." Shapiro. Fic for Youth. 3d edition

A Malamud reader. Farrar, Straus & Giroux 1967 528p o.p.
  Short stories included: The mourners; Idiots first; The first seven years; Take pity; The maid's shoes; Black is my favorite color; The Jewbird; The magic barrel; The German refugee; The last Mohican

The natural. Harcourt Brace & Co. 1952 237p o.p.
                                                           *
"The fanaticism and seriousness of baseball to both players and fans are vividly pictured in this novel about a man whose sole ambition was to be 'the greatest ever.' Roy Hobbs, who has made his own bat, Wonderboy, starts off at nineteen years of age to a possible spot on a big team. That promising beginning is blasted when he has an encounter with an erratic, seductive woman. When we next meet Roy fifteen years later, he is trying again to realize his dream as the best baseball player. His wrong-headed decisions and the exciting descriptions of the games played by his team, The Knights, make this a tense story up to the last out." Shapiro. Fic for Youth. 3d edition

The tenants. Farrar, Straus & Giroux 1971 230p
  ISBN 0-374-27290-5   LC 71-165400
A novel "about Harry Lesser, a Jewish writer whose third novel is not completed after nearly ten years of incessant work. Lesser lives alone, the last occupant of an apartment building located in a dying neighborhood. The clash between Lesser and Willie Spearmint, an aspiring but as yet unpublished black writer who takes over one of the empty apartments, serves as the focus of the novel." Libr J
"A magnificent story is told with grieving insight into some of life's more damaging conflicts and betrayals." Saturday Rev

Mallinson, Allan

A close run thing; a novel of Wellington's army of 1815. Bantam Bks. 1999 306p
  ISBN 0-553-11114-0   LC 98-52512
First volume is a projected "series featuring Cornet Matthew Hervey, a young cavalry officer in Wellington's army of 1815." Publisher's note
"Hervey's story begins in 1814, with Napoleon's defeat. Hervey narrowly escapes a court martial for impetuous, albeit brave, action in the Peninsular Campaign against the French, and is invited to purchase his lieutenancy. He returns to Britain, rekindles his affections for his childhood sweetheart, and is posted to Ireland: there he explores the country's religious strife, rides horses and reads Pride and Prejudice. But when Bonaparte escapes from Elba and raises a new army for a rematch with Wellington, Hervey's dragoons must return to war." Publ Wkly
"An exciting historical adventure steeped in authentic military detail." Booklist

Mallon, Thomas, 1951-

Bandbox. Pantheon Books 2004 305p $24.95
  ISBN 0-375-42116-5   LC 2003-54861
"Bandbox is a hugely successful magazine, a glamorous monthly cocktail of 1920s obsessions from the stock market to radio to gangland murder. Edited by the bombastic Jehoshaphat 'Joe' Harris, the magazine has a masthead that includes, among many others, a grisly, alliterative crime writer; a shy but murderously determined copyboy; and a burned-out vaudeville correspondent. . . . As the novel opens, the defection of Harris's most ambitious protege has plunged Bandbox into a death struggle with a new competitor on the newsstand." Publisher's note
"Mallon, in his other books, has gravitated toward previous eras out of an affinity for something like reticence. 'Bandbox,' then, is a real departure: antic, stylized, and up-tempo. The dialogue has a Kaufman-and-Hart crackle, and the story boasts more lotharios, floozies, mobsters, and wised-up dames than an MG-M double feature." New Yorker

Dewey defeats Truman; a novel. Pantheon Bks. 1997 355p
  ISBN 0-679-44425-4
                                            * LC 96-26812
"Owosso, Michigan, was Dewey's birthplace, and in the summer and fall of 1948 the townspeople are basking in the national attention that brushes the town. Anne Macmurray, a bookstore clerk and aspiring novelist, is being courted by two men, one a U.A.W. organizer, the other a smug Republican lawyer running for state senator. That romantic rivalry is shaped not only by the political passions of 1948 but also by the skeletons buried (and in one case unburied) in the pasts of other Owossoans. This work is so tightly constructed that it

Mallon, Thomas, 1951-—*Continued*

sometimes feels contrived, but Mallon's gift for the telling detail, whether of place or of character, quickly banishes such reservations." New Yorker

Fellow travelers. Pantheon Books 2007 353p $25

ISBN 978-0-375-42348-2; 0-375-42348-6

LC 2006-24586

In this novel set in McCarthy-era Washington, D.C., "the young ladies in the secretary pool are agog over dapper bureaucrat Hawkins Fuller, though his attentions covertly focus on newly minted Fordham graduate and good Catholic Tim Laughlin. Hawkins helps Tim land a job and, after feeling out the impressionable young man, makes a place in his bed for him. Mary Johnson, a friend to both closeted men, watches with rising alarm as Tim and Hawkins carry on their affair and Washington seethes in paranoia over Communists and 'sexual deviation.'" Publ Wkly

"The author keeps his own political convictions to himself. . . . Mallon is not an ideologically driven writer; political issues are his springboard for questions of individual integrity. We might take Mary, the novel's most adult character, as his stand-in. She quietly uses her affluent father's connections to help a State Department coworker fired for "lavender" inclinations and works behind the scenes in Congress to stymie McCarthyite legislation. . . . . Rueful maturity and large-minded sympathy are not qualities that help you navigate a city gripped by political hysteria. They are, however, among the salient qualities of 'Fellow Travelers,' a work of art that tempers judgment with compassion." Los Angeles Times Book Rev

Two moons; a novel. Pantheon Bks. 2000 303p

ISBN 0-375-40025-7

LC 99-34235

This novel is "set in post-Civil War Washington, DC, where 35-year-old war widow Cynthia May lives on her own. Jobs for women are scarce, but Cynthia is a mathematical prodigy, and she finds employment as a 'computer' at the Naval Observatory, inauspiciously located in Foggy Bottom. Here she falls in love with a much younger astronomer, who is already exhibiting symptoms of the dreaded 'miasma,' or malaria. Like the newly discovered Martian moons, Cynthia and her lover orbit around a powerful 'War God,' lecherous Republican party boss Roscoe Conkling, who controls the observatory's budget." Libr J

"Mallon refracts questions of war, woman's rights, and the ordering of the cosmos through the perfect prism of her heroine's mind, adeptly mixing keen social commentary with sheer entertainment." Booklist

Malouf, David, 1934-

The complete stories. Pantheon Books 2007 508p $27.50

ISBN 978-0-375-42497-7; 0-375-42497-0

LC 2006-37694

Contents: The Valley of Lagoons; Every move you make; War baby; Towards midnight; Elsewhere; Mrs. Porter and the rock; The domestic cantata; At Schindler's; Closer; Dream stuff; Night training; Sally's story; Jacko's reach; Lone Pine; Blacksoil country; Great Day; Southern skies; A trip to the Grundelsee; The empty lunch-tin; Sorrows and secrets; That antic Jezebel; The

only speaker of his tongue; Out of the stream; The sun in winter; Bad blood; A change of scene; In trust; A traveller's tale; A medium; Eustace; The prowler

"Malouf is a master of the art of the short story in its most elusive, Chekhovian form, and he uses the genre, it seems to me, for three delicate purposes in particular: the exploration of the ordinary; the evocation of moments of change, often seemingly slight; and the interrogation of loss." Slate

Remembering Babylon. Pantheon Bks. 1993 200p o.p.

* LC 93-7888

This novel tells the story of Gemmy Fairley, "an English cabin-boy washed up on the Queensland coast in the 1840s, who is found there by Aboriginals. . . . [Sixteen years later] he is 'found' by some white children. . . . The book tells of the reactions to him of the particular family who take him in, . . . and of those of the school teacher, the minister, and the others he has joined. Amid this, Malouf recalls, in separate chapters, something of the past lives of each of the main characters, in Scotland or England, including that of the white 'native' himself." Times Lit Suppl

"The book is more reflective than polemic. Without excusing the actions of the townsfolk, . . . Malouf shows how difficult original thought is for members of a community that perceives itself as surrounded by danger. The book is a joy to read: richly layered, complex, and dense." Christ Sci Monit

Maloy, Kate, 1944-

Every last cuckoo; a novel. Algonquin Books of Chapel Hill 2008 277p $22.95

ISBN 978-1-56512-541-4; 1-56512-541-X

LC 2007-16641

"When 75-year-old Sarah Lucas's husband, Charles, succumbs to an injury at the peak of a particularly brutal Vermont winter, her worst later-life fears of physical mishap are realized. In grief, Sarah's memories take her back to the Great Depression, when her parents generously opened their home to countless friends and relatives, and to her own regretted missteps as a parent. The chance to recreate the one experience and rectify the other arrives uninvited when a variety of lost souls-Sarah's own teenage granddaughter; an Israeli pacifist; a devastated young mother and child-seek shelter and solace in Sarah's too-empty home." Publ Wkly

Maloy "has created a truly engrossing novel, with situations at times both joyful and horribly sad and an entirely likable protagonist surrounded by an eclectic cast of friends and family. An excellent book club selection." Libr J

Malraux, André, 1901-1976

Man's fate (La condition humaine); translated by Haakon M. Chevalier. Smith & Hass 1934 360p o.p.

*

Original French edition, 1933; published in the United Kingdom with title: Storm in Shanghai

"The time is 1927, during the unsuccessful Communist uprising in China. The author focuses on three types of revolutionaries. Ch'en, a Chinese terrorist, believes that

Malraux, André, 1901-1976—*Continued*

Chiang Kai-shek must be killed to start a revolution and is willing to sacrifice himself to bring this about. Kyo, half-French, half-Japanese, is drawn to the revolution because of his belief in human dignity. He finds it difficult to reconcile the idealistic theories of Marx with the political realities of the revolution. Katov, a Russian who has had experience in the revolution in his own country, feels there is strength in the solidarity of his comrades. Though his attempts at revolution fail, each man dies feeling he has given meaning to his life trying to bring change to China." Shapiro. Fic for Youth. 3d edition

Man's hope; translated from the French by Stuart Gilbert and Alastair Macdonald. Random House 1938 511p o.p.

Original French edition, 1937; published in the United Kingdom with title: Days of hope

The story of the first eight months of the Civil War in Spain based on the author's experiences as commander of the Loyalist government's international air force

"Vividly realistic as it is, the book is remarkably free from the senseless dwelling upon physical injuries which often weakens the effect of war novels. M. Malraux has concentrated upon the essential rather than the incidental horrors of war, of civil war in particular." Manchester Guardian

Malraux, Georges André *See* Malraux, André, 1901-1976

Manheim, Ralph, 1907-1992

(tr) Grass, G. The tin drum

(tr) Remarque, E. M. The night in Lisbon

Manicka, Rani

The rice mother. Viking 2003 432p $24.95

ISBN 0-670-03192-5   LC 2002-32421

"When 14-year-old Lakshmi marries a widower of 37, she believes that she is leaving her Sri Lankan village for a life of luxury in Malaysia. Instead, she endures hardship and poverty, giving birth to six children in the years before the Japanese invasion of World War II. In this gripping multigenerational saga, the tumultuous history of Malaysia becomes the backdrop for Lakshmi's indomitable spirit. The barbarity of the Japanese, postwar prosperity, the bursting of the Southeast Asian financial bubble, the vice trades of opium, gambling, and sex—all take their toll on Lakshmi's children and grandchildren." Libr J

Mankell, Henning, 1948-

Before the frost; translated by Ebba Segerberg. New Press 2004 375p $24.95

ISBN 1-565-84835-7   LC 2004-55197

Original Swedish edition, 2002

In this "Wallander mystery, the generational torch passes from father Kurt to his equally stubborn daughter, Linda, who recently finished her police training and is anxiously awaiting her first day on the job. But a seemingly random series of events jump-starts her career and enmeshes her and her father, along with Stefan Lindman . . . in a case with global ramifications" Publ Wkly

"Linda has a future in this series; but it takes a seasoned philosopher like Wallander to make sense of the horrors that men do to honor their gods. " N Y Times Book Rev

Dogs of Riga; a Kurt Wallander mystery; translated by Laurie Thompson. Norton 2003 326p $24.95

ISBN 1-56584-787-2   LC 2002-30503

Original Swedish edition, 1992

"Set against the chaotic backdrop of eastern Europe after the fall of the Berlin Wall, Mankell's intense, accomplished mystery, the last in his Kurt Wallander series. . . explores one man's struggle to find truth and justice in a society increasingly bereft of either. Here the provincial Swedish detective takes on a probably fruitless task: investigating the murders of two unidentified men washed up on the Swedish coast in an inflatable dinghy." Publ Wkly

The eye of the leopard; translated from the Swedish by Steven T. Murray. New Press 2008 315p $26.95

ISBN 978-1-59558-077-1; 1-59558-077-8

          LC 2008-299522

Original Swedish edition, 1990

"The story revolves around a young Swede, Hans Olofson, who flies to Zambia in the 1970s in search of himself and to fulfil the quest of a dead friend. For lack of anything better to do, Olofson finds himself taking over the running of an upcountry egg farm. Intending to stay weeks, 20 years pass before he finally manages to extricate himself. . . . Where his white farmer neighbours only speak to blacks when giving orders, he tries to befriend them, provides materials to improve their homes, builds a school, takes a woman called Joyce and her daughters under his care and tries a number of other ways to break down the barriers that stand between himself and the people around him. But in a tense tale whose violence and uneasiness contrast to great effect with Olofson's deadpan narrative tone and Mankell's spare prose, it is made clear that there are no easy fixes, no quick ways to remedy the situation. Olofson escapes the gruesome fate of his neighbours, whose butchered corpses he finds, but he cannot escape his own despair." Spectator

Firewall; translated by Ebba Segerberg. New Press (NY) 2002 405p $25.95

ISBN 1-56584-767-9   LC 2002-25543

Original Swedish editon, 1998

A mystery featuring Swedish police inspector Kurt Wallander. A "criminal mastermind is about to press the button and send the global financial network into free fall when his partner is murdered, giving Wallander a window of opportunity to scotch this mischief and let us use our A.T.M.'s again. Although things get pretty tense at the end in Ebba Segerberg's well-paced translation, this a thinking man's thriller bearing the messsage that no infernal machine is a match for a decent man with a sense of good and evil." N Y Times Book Rev

Mankell, Henning, 1948——*Continued*

The man who smiled; a Kurt Wallander mystery; translated from the Swedish by Laurie Thompson. New Press 2006 325p $24.95

ISBN 978-1-56584-993-8; 1-56584-993-0

LC 2006-21925

Original Swedish edition, 1994; this translation first published 2005 in the United Kingdom

"Detective Chief Inspector Kurt Wallander, on sick leave for more than a year after killing a man in self-defense, is drinking too much and contemplating resigning. Then a lawyer friend, questioning whether his father's death was accidental, appeals to Wallander for help. When this friend is murdered just days later, Wallander's investigative juices get flowing, and he's back on the job, zeroing in on title character Alfred Harderberger, a wealthy businessman." Libr J

"When the bleak landscapes of Henning Mankell's Swedish police procedurals start to look like home, it's time to head for the hills. Either that, or confront the grim truths about modern society that give weight to this author's absorbing but disquieting existential mysteries." N Y Times Book Rev

One step behind; translated by Ebba Segerberg. New Press (NY) 2002 408p $24.95

ISBN 1-56584-652-4

* LC 2001-34254

Original Swedish edition, 1997

This mystery, featuring chief Inspector Kurt Wallander of the Ystad, Sweden police turns on the "meticulously staged homicide of three friends who costumed themselves as 18th-century bacchants and went into the woods on Midsummer's Eve to party. When a murdered police officer is implicated in the widening investigation, Wallander suspects internal corruption. . . . The sweep and complexity of Mankell's plot are reason enough for tackling this dense book, thoughtfully translated by Ebba Segerberg. But his meditations on surprising subjects like time travel and 'man's relationship to monsters' make him something special." N Y Times Book Rev

The return of the dancing master; translated by Laurie Thompson. New Press 2004 391p $24.95

ISBN 1-56584-860-8

*

Original Swedish edition, 2000

Swedish policeman Stefan Lindman "faces a host of personal demons, not the least of which is his recent diagnosis of mouth cancer. On leave and unwilling to face up to his illness, he decides to travel to the small village of Sveg, where a retired colleague, Herbert Molin, has been murdered. Helping to investigate the crime, Lindman is shocked to discover that Molin was a life-long Nazi. Suddenly, Lindman's alternative 'therapy' has landed him in the middle of an international ring of neo-Nazis." Booklist

"With its expansive time frame and meticulous procedural details, the story (as translated by Laurie Thompson) has a density that demands–and rewards–intellectual involvement." N Y Times Book Rev

Mann, Erica *See* Jong, Erica

Mann, Thomas, 1875-1955

The black swan; translated from the German by Willard R. Trask. Knopf 1954 141p o.p.

LC 90-38617

Original German edition, 1953; this is a reissue of the 1954 Knopf edition

Tragic psychological tale of a middle-aged German widow's passion for the young American tutor of her son

In this novelette Mann "returns to the compact dimensions and to the subject matter of Death in Venice (transposed into heterosexual terms)—the infatuation of an aging person for a young one. The current novella—though it is not nearly as memorable a piece of storytelling as the masterpiece of 1913—is a provocative addition to Mann's writings." Atlantic

Buddenbrooks; the decline of a family; translated from the German by John E. Woods. Knopf 1993 648p

ISBN 0-679-41994-2

* LC 92-18990

Original German edition, 1901. First United States edition translated by H. T. Lowe-Potter published 1924 in two volumes

"Mann's first novel, it expressed the ambivalence of his feelings about the value of the life of the artist as opposed to ordinary, bourgeois life. The novel is the saga of the fall of the Buddenbrooks, a family of merchants, from the pinnacle of their material wealth in 1835 to their extinction in 1877." Merriam-Webster's Ency of Lit

Confessions of Felix Krull, confidence man; the early years; translated from the German by Denver Lindley. Knopf 1955 384p o.p.

Originally written as a short story in 1921; this novel was first published 1954 in Germany

"Krull, a charming young man with absolutely no moral awareness, avoids military service and takes a job in a hotel. This begins a series of erotic and criminal escapades that eventually lead the young man to prison, from where he purportedly writes his confessions. Like many of Mann's characters, Krull represents the artist, and his profession indicates the symbolic connection in Mann's mind between the artist and the actor, or charlatan." Reader's Ency. 3d edition

Death in Venice; translated from the German by Kenneth Burke. Knopf 1965 118p o.p.

*

Original German edition, 1913; this translation first published 1925 as the title novella of a collection

"Gustav von Aschenbach, the hero, is a successful author, proud of the self-discipline with which he has ordered his life and work. On a trip to Venice, however, he becomes aware of mysterious decadent potentialities in himself, and he finally succumbs to a consuming love for a frail but beautiful Polish boy named Tadzio. Though he learns that there is danger of a cholera epidemic in Venice, he finds he cannot leave the city, and eventually dies of the disease. The story is permeated by a rich and varied symbolism with frequent overtones from Greek literature and mythology." Reader's Ency. 4th edition

also in Mann, T. Death in Venice and other tales

also in Mann, T. Stories of three decades

Mann, Thomas, 1875-1955—*Continued*

Death in Venice and other tales; translated from German by Joachim Neugroschel. Viking 1998 366p

    ISBN 0-670-87424-8   LC 98-2803

    Contents: The will for happiness; Little Herr Friedemann; Tobias Mindernickel; Little Lizzy; Gladius Dei; Tristan; The starvelings: a study; Tonio Kroger; The wunderkind; Harsh hour; The blood of the Walsungs; Death in Venice

Doctor Faustus; translated from the German by John E. Woods. Knopf 1997 534p

    ISBN 0-375-40054-0   LC 97-2818

    A new translation of the novel originally published 1947 in German; first English translation by H. T. Lowe-Parker published 1948

    In this novel "the intense and tragic career of the hero Adrian Leverkühn, a composer, is made to parallel the collapse of Germany in World War II. To achieve this end, Mann employs the device of having another character, Serenus Zeitblom, narrate Leverkühn's story from memory, while the war is going on, and intersperse his narrative with remarks about the present situation. In this way, it is implied that it is the same demonic and always potentially destructive energy inherent in Leverkühn's music that is also, on a larger scale, behind the outburst of Nazism. Mann thus suggests that the violent 'Faustian' drive, when it is not diverted into art, or when there is no single artistic genius to harness it into creative process, will be perverted and result in grossly sub-human degradation." Reader's Ency. 4th edition

Joseph and his brothers; translated from the German by H. T. Lowe-Porter; with a new introduction by the author. Knopf 1948 xxi, 1207p $65

    ISBN 0-394-43132-4

    An omnibus edition of the author's tetralogy based on the Biblical story of Joseph

    Contents: The tales of Jacob; Young Joseph; Joseph in Egypt; Joseph the provider

    The tales of Jacob (1933; first United States edition 1934 with title: Joseph and his brothers) is mainly the story of Jacob. It describes his long service with Laban, the deception by which Leah was palmed off on Jacob in place of Rachel, the birth of Leah's sons, and of Rachel's death in childbirth

    Young Joseph (1934: first United States edition 1935) centers on adolescent Joseph, his father's favorite and the object of his brother's mounting jealousy. After he describes his arrogant dreams and flaunts his beautiful "picture robe," his brothers sell him to an Ishmaelite trader

    In Joseph in Egypt (1936: first United States edition 1938 in 2 volumes) Joseph is now owned by Potiphar and eventually becomes the household steward. He rejects the advances by Potiphar's wife who throws him into prison for revenge

    Joseph the provider (1943: first United States edition 1944) describes Joseph's imprisonment, rise to power, life in Pharaoh's court, reunion with his brothers and father, settlement in Egypt and death

    In these tales Mann has expanded upon "the original story tremendously, but most of the added episodes contribute not so much to the tale itself as to the characters' depth and symbolic significance. In its overall attitude, the 'Joseph' tetralogy is neither ambiguous like 'The Magic Mountain' nor tragic like 'Doktor Faustus,' but unqualifiedly redemptive." Reader's Ency. 4th edition

Joseph in Egypt

    In Mann, T. Joseph and his brothers p447-840

Joseph the provider

    In Mann, T. Joseph and his brothers p843-1207

The magic mountain; a novel; translated from the German by John E. Woods. Knopf 1995 706p

    ISBN 0-679-44183-2

                       * LC 94-42885

    Original German edition, 1924

    This novel "tells the story of Hans Castorp, a young German engineer, who goes to visit a cousin in a tuberculosis sanatorium in the mountains of Davos, Switz. Castorp discovers that he has symptoms of the disease and remains at the sanatorium for seven years, until the outbreak of World War I. During this time, he abandons his normal life to submit to the rich seductions of disease, introspection, and death. Through talking with other patients, he gradually becomes aware of and absorbs the predominant political, cultural, and scientific ideas of 20th-century Europe. The sanatorium comes to be the spiritual reflection of the possibilities and dangers of the actual world away from the magic mountain" Merriam-Webster's Ency of Lit

Six early stories; translated from the German with a note by Peter Constantine; edited with an introduction by Burton Pike. Sun & Moon Press 1997 128p

    ISBN 1-55713-298-4

    Contents: A vision "Prose sketch"; Fallen; The will to happiness; Death; Avenged, "Study for a novella"; Anecdote

    "These newly translated stories give insight into the still-forming mind of the Nobel laureate, revealing his philosophical and literary influences as well as demonstrating the uninhibited experimentation of a young, romantic writer." Publ Wkly

Stories of three decades; translated from the German by H. T. Lowe-Porter. Knopf 1936 567p o.p.

    Short stories included are: Little Herr Friedemann; Disillusionment; Dilettante; Tobias Mindernickel; Little Lizzy; Wardrobe; Way to the churchyard; Hungry; Infant prodigy; Gladius Dei; Fiorenza; Gleam; At the prophet's; Weary hour; Blood of the Walsungs; Railway accident; Fight between Jappe and Do Escobar; Felix Krull; Man and his dog; Disorder and early sorrow; Mario and the magician

    The novellas are psychological studies. Tonio Kröger is concerned with the struggle between the artist and normal citizen. Tristan's concern deals with music's irrational and frequently destructive powers. Death in Venice is entered separately

The tales of Jacob

    In Mann, T. Joseph and his brothers p3-258

Tonio Kröger

    In Mann, T. Stories of three decades

Mann, Thomas, 1875-1955—*Continued*

Tristan

In Mann, T. Stories of three decades

Young Joseph

In Mann, T. Joseph and his brothers p261-444

Mansbach, Adam, 1976-

The end of the Jews; a novel. Spiegel & Grau 2008 310p $23.95

ISBN 978-0-385-52044-7; 0-385-52044-1

LC 2007-19465

The author "takes on three generations of the Brodsky family in this epic of American life from the mid-1930s to the end of the 1990s. Tristan Brodsky, who grows up playing stickball in the Jewish Bronx, is constantly at odds with his family. At Queens College, he comes under the influence of a literature professor and is thrown into the world of black jazz musicians. Eventually, Tristan becomes a writer—his first book, The Angel of the Shtetel, portrays his atheist anger about the woes of immigrant life and the sad plight of the Jews—and he strongly influences American culture. His wife, a poet with a different agenda, tends to his needs. Their grandson Tris, aka RISK, a revolutionary, graffiti writer, and hip-hop aficionado, follows in his grandfather's footsteps and becomes a writer, but the angst he expresses reflects the end of the 20th century. Tris also hooks up with Nina Hricek, a teenage Czech refugee and photographer who has come to America with a black jazz band." Libr J

"Mansbach narrates in a syncopated style, moving back and forth among Tristan, Nina and Tris until the three stories finally merge at the novel's conclusion. His writing is adjective-happy and sometimes ungainly, but it charms with an almost goofy persistence." N Y Times Book Rev

Shackling water. Doubleday 2002 232p

ISBN 0-385-50205-2

LC 2001-47398

This novel "about an aspiring saxophonist in Harlem . . . introduces us to Latif James-Pearson, an 18-year-old from Boston who moves to New York to hone his chops and, ultimately, to meet his idol, the jazz aristocrat Albert Van Horn. Along the way, Latif faces a series of tests through a relationship with an older white woman, a jazz-club job dealing drugs and eventually an addiction to them; he loses touch with both his music and himself before a tragedy shocks him back to life." N Y Times Book Rev

"This bold, resonant portrait of the artist as a young man isn't flawless, but Mansbach's eloquence and energy are unwavering." Booklist

Manseau, Peter, 1974-

Songs for the butcher's daughter; a novel. Free Press 2008 370p $25

ISBN 978-1-4165-3870-7; 1-4165-3870-4

LC 2007-49787

This is "the story of fictional Yiddish poet Itsik Malpesh, born in the Moldovan city of Kishinev in 1903. Itsik's story is told through his Yiddish memoirs, which he helps a young American Catholic . . . translate. Inspired by the image of Sasha, the brave butcher's daugh-

ter who was present at his birth, Itsik reaches America in young adulthood through haphazard luck, a taste for troublemaking and the inventiveness of a printer. Sasha continually inspires and confounds Itsik throughout his life, becoming an apt symbol for Yiddish humor, sorrow and idealism. As Itsik's darkly picaresque immigrant narrative unfolds, it competes with the translator's modern romance and with insights into the art of translation and the history of Yiddish. Occasional narrative missteps are not enough to undercut this rich, often ironic homage to Yiddish culture and language." Publ Wkly

Mansfield, Katherine, 1888-1923

The garden party and other stories. Knopf 1991 xxxv, 267p o.p.

LC 91-53004

"Everyman's library"

Contents: The tiredness of Rosabel; Frau Brechenmacher attends a wedding; The swing of the pendulum; A birthday; Millie; The woman at the store; Bains Turcs; An indiscreet journey; The little governess; Prelude; Bliss; A married man's story; Carnation; This flower; The man without a temperament; The daughters of the late colonel; Her first ball; The voyage; At the bay; The garden party; Honeymoon

The short stories of Katherine Mansfield. Knopf 1937 688p $22.95

ISBN 0-394-44532-5

*

Contents: The tiredness of Rosabel; How Pearl Button was kidnapped; The journey to Bruges; A truthful adventure; New dresses; Germans at meat; The Baron; The sister of the Baroness; Frau Fischer; Frau Brechenmacher attends a wedding; The modern soul; At Lehmann's; The Luft bad; A birthday; The child-who-was-tired; The advanced lady; The swing of the pendulum; A blaze; The woman at the store; Ole Underwood; The little girl; Millie; Pension Séguin; Violet; Bains turcs; Something childish but very natural; An indiscreet journey; Spring pictures; The little governess; The wind blows; Prelude; At the bay; Late at night; Two tuppeny ones, please!; The black cap; A suburban fairy tale; Psychology; Carnation; Feuille d'album; A dill pickle; Bliss; Je ne parle pas Français; Sun and moon; Mr. Reginald Peacock's day; Pictures; See-saw; This flower; The wrong house; The man without a temperament; Revelations; The escape; Bank holiday; The young girl; The stranger; The lady's maid; The daughters of the late colonel; Life of Ma Parker; The singing lesson; Mr. and Mrs. Dove; An ideal family; Her first ball; Sixpence; The voyage; The garden-party; Miss Brill; Marriage à la mode; Poison; The doll's house; Honeymoon; A cup of tea; Taking the veil; The fly; The canary; A married man's story; The doves' nest; Six years after; Daphne; Father and the girls; All serene; A bad idea; A man and his dog; Such a sweet old lady; Honesty; Susannah; Second violin; Mr. and Mrs. Williams; Weakheart; Widowed

"In this comprehensive edition Katherine Mansfield's stories are arranged approximately in chronological order." Introduction

Mansfield, Kathleen Beauchamp *See* Mansfield, Katherine, 1888-1923

Mantel, Hilary

Beyond black. Henry Holt & Co. 2005 365p
$26

ISBN 0-00-715775-4   LC 2004-63589

"A John Macrae book"

"A paragon of efficiency, well-schooled in the mundane tasks of an average existence, Colette took the next natural step after finishing secretarial school–marrying a man who would do just fine. After a sobering do-it-yourself divorce, Colette, for the first time, is at a loss as to what to do next. Convinced that she deserves a life-affirming revelation, she strays into the world of psychics and clairvoyants. . . . At a psychic fair in Windsor she sneaks into Alison's show. Alison, beleaguered by spirits since early childhood, lives in a different kind of solitude. She can never escape the dead who speak to her, and the physical pain of their broken bodies–least of all the constance presence of Morris, her low-life spiritual guide." Publisher's note

"This is, I think, a great comic novel. Hilary Mantel's humor, like Flannery O'Connor's, is so far beyond black it becomes a kind of light." N Y Times Book Rev

Wolf Hall; a novel. Henry Holt and Co. 2009 532p $27

ISBN 978-0-8050-8068-1; 0-8050-8068-6
          LC 2009-19912

"A John Macrae book"

"Set in 16th-century Tudor England, Wolf Hall thrusts the reader into Henry VIII's seething court, where the players include Anne Boleyn, her sister Mary, Cardinal Wolsey, Thomas More and Jane Seymour. At the book's center: Thomas Cromwell, the ruthless blacksmith's son who rose to power under Henry VIII because of his intelligence, cunning and work ethic. . . . Mantel's novel is less about Henry's sex life and more about power: how to get it, wield it, keep it, particularly if you — like the lowborn Cromwell — lived in a merciless world ruled by the rich and titled. Cromwell usually is presented as a bully utterly lacking scruples, but Mantel's Cromwell is a sympathetic character modern readers will understand." USA Today

Mapson, Jo-Ann

Bad Girl Creek; a novel. Simon & Schuster 2001 381p

ISBN 0-7432-0256-2   LC 2001-27006

"Phoebe DeThomas has lived carefully all her life. Thirty-eight years old and in a wheelchair because of a bad heart, she's always felt dwarfed by her flamboyant aunt Sadie and her successful brother James. Now Sadie has died, bequeathing her a flower farm on California's Central Coast. In order to make a go of it, Phoebe takes in three women as boarder/farmhands. Each of the three is 'homeless,' having recently undergone traumatic life changes: Ness, a black cowgirl with a horse and a secret fear that she has AIDS, has lost her job; Nance, a down-on-her-luck Southern belle, has broken up with ber boyfriend; and Beryl, a former kindergarten aide with a prison record, has been evicted from her apartment. . . . Mapson combines poignancy with the good-natured banter of girlfriends in her tale of women in transition, waiting to be reborn." Publ Wkly

Loving Chloe; a novel. HarperCollins Pubs. 1998 347p

ISBN 0-06-017217-7   LC 97-20578

In this sequel to Hank and Chloe "refined college professor Hank is thrilled when the tough-talking horse-trainer Chloe reenters his life and tells him she is pregnant with his child. Chloe knows that Hanks is a good man, but she cannot fully commit herself to him, having put up her emotional defenses a long time ago, when she was shuttled from one foster home to another as a child. When she goes into labor unexpectedly, local Navajo legend Junior Whitebear delivers her child. Neither Chloe nor Junior is prepared for the intensity of the bond they forge during the delivery, and Chloe is left feeling torn between Hank and Junior." Booklist

"Mapson knows her territory intimately, and she populates it with memorable characters who readily engage our emotions. Her dialogue is earthy and funny, her setting evocative, her portrayal of good people facing difficult choices compassionate." N Y Times Book Rev

Marcantel, Pamela

An army of angels; a novel of Joan of Arc. St. Martin's Press 1997 578p

ISBN 0-312-15030-X   LC 96-31791

"In this historical novel, Marcantel resurrects the mysterious Jehanne, the Maid of Orleans, whose devotion to God led her to be burned at the stake for witchcraft before she is 20. Jehanne's visions and voices influenced her at an early age to leave her village and fulfill God's will. Guided to the future King of France, Charles VII, the peasant Jehanne persuades him to give her an army to recapture French lands from Henry VI's England." Libr J

"Rather than portraying Joan as a pious saint, Marcantel characterizes her as a flawed and vulnerable human being often plagued by both doubt and fear. An impassioned chronicle of an unparalleled heroine." Booklist

March, William, 1893-1954

The bad seed. Rinehart 1954 247p o.p.

"Rhoda Penmark at 8 years of age had a mind of her own and a will to match. Aged people doted on her splendid manners, but rogues knew her as one of themselves while older children were afraid of her. Christine, her mother suddenly discovers her daughter's horrible tendencies and also finds out that she is the murderess of two people who stood in her way. Christine resolves to check back and finds that she had been adopted and that the mother she had never known had also been a successful killer. Christine tries to stop the pattern in her daughter, but in the process dies herself." Libr J

Margolin, Phillip

After dark. Doubleday 1995 340p

ISBN 0-385-47548-9   LC 94-41997

In this novel, lawyer "Tracy Cavenaugh is shaken when she finds Oregon Supreme Court Justice Robert Griffen's clerk, Laura Rizatti, murdered in her office. Tracy thinks that she can put the murder behind her when she goes to work for Matthew Reynolds, a prominent attorney who specializes in death penalty cases—

Margolin, Phillip—_Continued_

that is, until Justice Griffen also ends up dead a month later." Libr J

"The reversals and revelations are many and diabolically clever. . . . No legal-triller fan, once hooked, will wiggle free of the story line of this hammy but exciting yarn before reaching its utterly surprising, and surprisingly dark, conclusion." Publ Wkly

The burning man. Doubleday 1996 344p

ISBN 0-385-48053-9   LC 96-12093

This novel "is set in Eastern Oregon, where a mildly retarded man is charged with the brutal slaying of a young woman. His lawyer, having never tried a capital crime case before, fumbles badly, but a glimmer of native wit gets him back on track. Working the genre with a discipline some popular authors have begun to ignore, Margolin relies on a few crafty stereotypes to keep up the pace and simplify the action. The dialogs in the jailhouse and the interrogation scenes, though, are intense and fierce. The moral zigzags of desperate people are laid out to contrast with the lawyer and his client as they feint and weave to avoid the ultimate penalty." Libr J

Fugitive; a novel. HarperCollins 2009 344p
$26.99

ISBN 978-0-06-123623-5; 0-06-123623-3

       LC 2008-50713

"When the editor-in-chief of World News magazine offers Amanda Jaffe a $500,000 retainer to defend Charlie Marsh, an ex-con turned bestselling spiritual guru, in . . . [this] fourth thriller to feature the Portland, Ore., lawyer . . . ., Amanda can't say no. Marsh, who fled the country in 1997 after being accused of murdering Congressman Arnold Pope Jr., has spent the 12 years since in the African country of Batanga 'under the protection of its benevolent ruler,' Jean-Claude Baptiste, whose threat to kill Marsh for sleeping with his favorite wife has prompted Marsh to return to the U.S. to stand trial." Publ Wkly

"The pages fly in this violent, twisty tale of one man's journey through the legal system." Libr J

Wild justice. HarperCollins Pubs. 2000 332p

ISBN 0-06-019624-6   LC 00-24351

"The plot is straightforward enough: a serial killer is torturing and murdering people seemingly at random, and investigators scramble to stop the psychopath. . . . There are not one but two prime suspects—Dr. Vincent Cardoni, a prominent surgeon, and Dr. Justine Castle, Cardoni's estranged wife. Each accuses the other of a frame-up, and Amanda Jaffe, a rather inexperienced young attorney, has to figure out which of her clients may be a murderer. A very clever thriller indeed." Booklist

Marías, Javier, 1951-

All souls; translated by Margaret Jull Costa. New Directions 2000 210p pa $14.95

ISBN 978-0-8112-1453-7; 0-8112-1453-2

       LC 00-55026

Original Spanish edition, 1989; this translation first published 1992 by HarperCollins

"'Oxford is, without a doubt, one of the cities of the world where the least work gets done.' So opens this arch portrait of a university town, marked by languid en-

nui and gossipy, semifossilized dons. The point of view is that of an unnamed visiting Spaniard scholar, whose memory flits among several eccentric people and events. Thus the recollection doesn't unfold chronologically. The reader learns early on that the Spaniard carried on a desultory affair with a don's wife, whom he met at 'High Table,' a stylized Oxfordian dinner that Marias spoofs to good effect. The personality of that wife, Clare, emerges in a discrete fashion, with dots of conversations and digressions of personal revelations that say, verily, this will not be an affair to remember. The Spaniard seems better acquainted with Cromer-Blake, a sickly professor, closet gay, and guide to Oxford's picayune atmosphere of bored superiority. Though nothing eventful occurs, Marias' refined prose achieves an appealing characterization of place." Booklist

Dark back of time; translated from the Spanish by Esther Allen. New Directions 2001 336p il map $27.95; pa $16.95

ISBN   978-0-8112-1466-7;   0-8112-1466-4; 978-0-8112-1570-1 (pa); 0-8112-1570-9 (pa)

       LC 00-69565

Original Spanish edition, 1998

Marias's "Dark Back of Time begins with the tale of the odd effects of publishing All Souls, his 1989 Oxford novel. All Souls, narrated by a visiting Spanish lecturer, is a book that swears to be fiction, but which its 'characters'—the real-life dons and professors and bookshop owners who have 'recognized themselves'—fiercely maintain to be a roman a clef." Publisher's note

This is "by far the brainiest, most emblematic book by Marias, as well as the most demanding. . . . I'm inclined to describe the book as a meditative essay. But to pigeonhole it seems preposterous anyway, for its strength lies precisely in its amphibious, if not anarchistic, structure. This, after all, is a nonlinear opera aperta that functions as a circuitous rendezvous through the realms of knowledge and imagination. It mixes autobiography with fiction, truth with lies, so as to show the extent to which an author—Javier Marias himself—is enriched and also cursed by his oeuvre." Nation

A heart so white; translated from the Spanish by Margaret Jull Costa. New Directions 2000 278p $24.95; pa $14.95

ISBN   978-0-8112-1505-9;   0-8112-1452-4; 978-0-8112-1505-3 (pa); 0-8112-1505-9 (pa)

       LC 00-55021

Original Spanish edition, 1992; this translation first published 1995 in the United Kingdom

"Narrator Juan's twice-widowed, secretive father, Ranz, is a mystery to his 34-year-old son. Before marrying Juan's mother, Ranz had wed her sister, who later killed herself. While Juan is afraid to ask his father about the incident, his own young bride, Luisa, draws the old man out, and the complicated truth slowly emerges. On his Havana honeymoon with Luisa and on his travels as a translator, Juan sees, overhears and stumbles upon scenes that increasingly remind him of what he is slowly learning about his father's world." Publ Wkly

Marias is "the most subtle and gifted writer in contemporary Spanish literature." Boston Globe

Marías, Javier, 1951-—_Continued_

The man of feeling; translated from the Spanish by Margaret Jull Costa. New Directions 2003 182p $22.95

ISBN 0-8112-1531-8

* LC 2002-153935

Original Spanish edition, 1986

"While in Madrid to perform the role of Cassio in Verdi's 'Otello,' a Spanish tenor meets a man whose job is to amuse the neglected wife of a powerful Brussels banker. The paid companion invites the singer on his outings with the woman, setting the stage for an affair. . . . (This). . . would seem to offer little more than banal melodrama. Everything depends, however, on how the plot unfolds. Marias avoids a straightforward delivery in favor of a digressive narrative that moves back and forth in time. . . . This suggestive indirection perfectly suits Marias's preoccupation: the erotic imagination." N Y Times Book Rev

Voyage along the horizon; translated from the Spanish by Kristina Cordero. Believer Books 2006 c1972 182p pa $16

ISBN 1-9324164-0-4

Original Spanish edition, 1988

"An unnamed narrator ruminates on the intentions of a man (variously called Holden Branshaw and Hordern Bragshawe) who decides not to publish a novel written by an unnamed author who died penniless pursuing the life of that novel's subject: Victor Arledge, an author who died a recluse at age 38. The plot is pure Borges; the elongated sentences reflect nested perspectives in a manner that recalls Conrad's Heart of Darkness. The bulk of the book is devoted to the reading aloud of the novel, titled Voyage Along the Horizon; it's set around 1900 and concerns a voyage of French and English writers, Arledge among them, to Antarctica headed by an American patrician and former steamboat captain named Kerrigan. The goal—a collaborative work based on their travels—gets derailed by a variety of stock fictive plot points. The reserved 19th-century diction is flawlessly translated throughout, and Marías's joy in folly is everywhere evident." Publ Wkly

Your face tomorrow: volume one: Fever and spear; translated from the Spanish by Margaret Jull Costa. New Directions 2005 387p $24.95

ISBN 0-8112-1612-8

LC 2005-992

Original Spanish edition, 2002

"Jaime Deza, separated from his wife in Madrid, is at loose ends in London when his old friend Sir Peter Wheeler, a retired Oxford don, introduces him to the head of a secret government bureau of elite analysts with the ability to see past people's facades and predict their future behavior. A cocktail party test proves Deza to be one of the elect, and he goes to work clandestinely observing all sorts of people, from South American generals to pop stars. Deza also brings his finely tuned mind to bear on Wheeler's mysterious past and on his own family history, both of which are shadowed by the Spanish Civil War." Publisher's Wkly

The book uses "spy novel elements in order to frame certain far-ranging meditations on history, memory, and identity. The resultant effect is reminiscent of the cerebral play of Borges, the dark humor of Pynchon, and the meditative lyricism of Proust." Review of Contemporary Fiction

Your face tomorrow: volume two: Dance and dream; translated from the Spanish by Margaret Jull Costa. New Directions 341p $24.95

ISBN 0-8112-1656-x

LC 2006-15589

Oiginal Spanish edition, 2004

The second volume of a trilogy "narrated by Jacques (or Jaime) Deza, a Spanish expat in London and former Oxford instructor working as an analyst for the intelligence service MI5. Deza's inscrutable, nihilistic handler, Bertram Tupra, doesn't clarify Deza's mission when he brings him to a nightclub to accompany the wife of a contact. There, Tupra terrorizes and beats a man for hitting on the wrong woman." Publ Wkly

"Marias's is a style of thinking more than writing. In 'Your Face Tomorrow' it is faithfully rendered by Margaret Jull Costa, his principal English translator, who achieves a rare feat: presence and near invisibility." N Y Times Book Rev

Marillier, Juliet

Daughter of the forest. TOR Bks. 2000 400p (Sevenwaters trilogy) hardcover o.p. pa $15.95

ISBN 0-312-84879-X; 0-312-87530-4 (pa)

LC 00-25216

"A Tom Doherty Associates book"

"As the only daughter and youngest child of Lord Colum of Sevenwaters, Sorcha grows up protected and pampered by her six older brothers. When a sorceress's evil magic ensorcels Colum's sons, transforming them into swans, only Sorcha's efforts can break the curse. . . . The author's keen understanding of Celtic paganism and early Irish Christianity adds texture to a rich and vibrant novel that belongs in most fantasy collections." Libr J

Foxmask. Tor Bks. 2004 2003 464p $27.95

ISBN 0-7653-0674-3

LC 2003-71154

"The Norseman Eyvind becomes a Wolfskin a Viking dedicated to Thor and travels to the mystical Orkney Islands, where he meets the Princess Nessa, a seer who becomes his soul mate. As Vikings and Orkney residents work out a peace, a new generation arises to forge strong ties. A question of paternity throws the delicate balance between the two peoples in jeopardy, and some young folk set out on a journey to discover the truth. The author . . . continues her exploration of the fusion of two cultures with strong family ties and great trust in powers beyond the merely human." Libr J

Marinick, Richard, 1951-

Boyos; a novel. Kate's Mystery Books 2004 274p $24.95

ISBN 1-932112-32-4

LC 2004-54843

"Set in and around 'Southie,' the South Boston working-class Irish-American enclave . . ., the story focuses on Jack 'Wacko' Curran, a rising young player in the criminal underworld. Local 'boyos' like Curran resent the steady influx of young working professionals, who are gentrifying the area and pricing the old-time residents out. Curran and his coked-out brother, Kevin, work for mob boss Marty Fallon, wholesaling drugs to a network of area dealers. Tired of giving Fallon a cut of every score, Jack dreams of replacing Fallon and figures that the bankroll from the armored-car heist he's planning will put him on his way." Publ Wkly

Marinick, Richard, 1951——*Continued*

"The writing is gritty and serious, the action intense, and the characters well drawn and compelling despite their imperfections." Libr J

Markandaya, Kamala, 1924-2004

Nectar in a sieve; with a new introduction by Indira Ganesan. Signet Classic 2002 190p pa $6.95

ISBN 0-451-52823-9   LC 2001-49544

First published 1954 in the United Kingdom; first United States edition published 1955 by Day

"This realistic novel of peasant life in a southern Indian village portrays the struggle that Nathan and Rukmani must make to survive. Their first child is a daughter, Irawaddy, and there follow five other children, all sons, after an interval of seven years. Hardships are innumerable and insurmountable, whether they are disasters of nature such as drought, or such manmade catastrophes as the coming of a tannery to their village and a subsequent labor conflict. After many crises, Nathan and Rukmani come to the city to seek help from one of their sons, but he has disappeared. Nathan, finally destroyed by privation, dies, believing to the end that his life with Rukmani has been a happy one." Shapiro. Fic for Youth. 3d edition

Marks, John, 1963-

Fangland. Penguin Press 2007 385p $25.95

ISBN 978-1-59420-117-2; 1-59420-117-X

LC 2006-49809

This novel's "protagonist, Evangeline Harker, a young producer for the TV news show The Hour, reluctantly accepts an assignment into the wilds of Romania to explore doing a segment on a legendary criminal figure, Ion Torgu. Evangeline soon finds herself at the very outskirts of civilization, and after hearing a missionary's account of a supernatural plague that affected a whole community in Africa, she's accosted by Torgu himself, doing an excellent impersonation of the vampire count." Publ Wkly

Marks has "written an electrifying modern tale of horror that pays homage to Bram Stoker's Dracula. He goes much further, however, creating a hideous vampire more horrifying than anything that ever came from Stoker's imagination." Libr J

Marks, Laurie J.

Fire logic. Tor Bks. 2002 335p $25.95

ISBN 0-312-87887-7   LC 2001-58352

"A Tom Doherty Associates book"

"The land of Shaftal, occupied by the nasty Sainnites, has just lost its Earth witch ruler and, in doing so, has seemingly lost the magic that the witch held. What follows is bitter guerilla warfare. Into this war comes Zanja na 'Tarwein, speaker for the people of the Ashawala'i, a woman who holds the power of elemental fire. What was not her war suddenly becomes personal when the Sainnites turn on her people and obliterate them in one night's battle. As sole survivor, Zanja becomes a resistance fighter." Publ Wkly

"Marks is an absolute master of fantasy in this book. Her characters are beautifully drawn, showing tremendous emotional depth and strength as they endure the unendurable and strive always to do the right thing." Booklist

Markson, David

The last novel. Shoemaker & Hoard 2007 190p pa $15

ISBN 978-1-59376-143-1; 1-59376-143-0

LC 2006-38793

"Constructed out of hundreds of anecdotes about and quotes by artists, composers, writers and other people of fame or infamy, the novel essentially follows a single character, Novelist, who is alone and at work on his last novel." Artvoice

"Just when one had started mourning the demise of avant-garde and postmodern fiction, buried under the avalanche of historical novels, chick lit and just plain old traditional stories, here comes David Markson's latest 'novel,' 'The Last Novel,' which is anything but a novel in any conventional sense of the term. Yet it manages to keep us enthralled during the length of its short 190-page span, and even moved to tears at the end. And what a thrill it is to witness the performance, a real tour de force." N Y Times Book Rev

Vanishing point; a novel. Shoemaker & Hoard 2004 191p pa $15

ISBN 1-59376-010-8 (pa)

"The premise is that 'The Author' as the narrator refers to himself, is assembling a box of note cards full of information he has gathered over the years with the hope of forging a novel. Life then imitates art as Markson literally accomplishes what his narrator hopes to: he creates a novel out of fragments of ideas and information. Vanishing Point feels a little like a literary Trivial Pursuit, or the associative stream of consciousness produced by a surrealist party game, and it's just as entertaining." Booklist

Wittgenstein's mistress. Dalkey Archive Press 1988 240p

ISBN 0-916583-25-2   LC 87-73068

"In this unsettling, shimmering novel, the reader is immediately drawn into the world of a woman who has gone mad because she is the last surviving creature on earth. Sitting at a typewriter in a beach house day after uncharted day—she keeps no calendar or clocks—she pours out her thoughts on music, art and ancient Greek legends, and remembrances of her travels across the globe in abandoned cars, looking for other living beings. But after a while, some discrepancies creep into her rambling, compelling monologue. . . . By the end of this seamless stream of consciousness, there is no distinction between fantasy and reality, past and present." Publ Wkly

Marlette, Doug, 1949-2007

Magic time. Farrar, Straus and Giroux 2006 480p $25

ISBN 978-0-374-20001-5; 0-374-20001-7

LC 2005-36396

"Sarah Crichton books"

In this novel, "investigative journalist Carter Ransom returns to his deceptively quiet hometown of Troy, MS, after a mental breakdown only to face ghosts from the Sixties. At that time, local Klansmen had burned a church, killing both worshipers and civil rights activists. One hit man was sent to prison by Carter's father, Judge Mitchell Ransom, but now, decades later, he has been

Marlette, Doug, 1949-2007—*Continued*

paroled and after a change of heart turns states' evidence to convict others at the top. The trial for the accused, Sam Bohanon, a local businessman and former imperial wizard, opens old wounds and puts Troy in the media spotlight. Carter fears that his father covered up the real killers' identity to protect an old family friend, and he even suspects his father was being blackmailed over his affair with one of the Klansmen's wives." Libr J

"Magic Time presents a realistic portrait of the collective amnesia of the South and the generational tensions that the civil rights movement stirred up, then and now. It's a real Mississippi story, not merely a faded imitation." Washington Post Book World

Marlowe, Hugh, 1929- *See* Higgins, Jack, 1929-

Marlowe, Ralph *See* Manheim, Ralph, 1907-1992

Maron, Margaret

Bootlegger's daughter. Mysterious Press 1992 261p o.p.   LC 91-58021

This mystery takes place in "Cotton Grove, N.C., a close-knit rural community on the outskirts of Raleigh, and introduces savvy Deborah Knott, a lawyer whose singular upbringing as a child of a bootlegging power broker has prepared her well for the county race for district court judge. But just as she begins her campaign . . . Deborah is asked to turn over the dead leaves of an 18-year-old murder case. It seems that the daughter of an old flame can't start her life until she finds out who killed her mother as she watched with uncomprehending infant eyes." N Y Times Book Rev

Fugitive colors. Mysterious Press 1995 260p o.p.   LC 95-1703

This mystery features "Lt. Sigrid Harald of the NYPD. The deaths of a fellow officer and of her artist lover throw Sigrid into decline—until her lover's legacy of valuable paintings leads to the murder of a greedy art dealer." Libr J

"Maron adeptly establishes a coolly thematic and deceptive link among the deaths as she constructs her affecting mystery out of distinctive blend of art-world politics, past crimes and present grief." Publ Wkly

High country fall. Mysterious Press 2004 303p $24

ISBN 0-89296-808-7

* LC 2004-1953

Judge Deborah Knott's "engagement to Deputy Sheriff Dwight has stirred a furor in her extended family, so she trades noise at home for the supposed quiet of court in the Blue Ridge Mountains. There . . . she becomes embroiled in a murder case with a wrongfully accused suspect." Libr J

"Deborah's narrative voice, with its engaging tone of amusement at the human foibles she witnesses in her travels, is just the ticket for this dramatic view of the spectacular Blue Ridge Mountains." N Y Times Book Rev

Home fires burning. Mysterious Press 1998 243p $32

ISBN 0-89296-655-6   LC 98-6632

North Carolina Circuit Court Judge Deborah Knott, "who narrates, is at the start of a reelection campaign when a nephew is arrested, with two friends, for desecrating a cemetery. When the same spraypainted graffiti appears at an African American church that's been torched, the young men are suspected of arson. Two more black churches are burned and two bodies uncovered before Deborah fingers the culprit." Publ Wkly

Killer market. Mysterious Press 1997 273p $21.50

ISBN 0-89296-654-8   LC 97-20835

"North Carolina district court judge Deborah Knott unintentionally 'crashes' several manufacturer's receptions at the internationally known Southeastern Furniture Market in High Point, where she becomes involved in murder. Initially befriended by a mysterious and elusive woman with bogus name tags, series protagonist Knott soon runs into an old woman friend from law school as well as a hunky ex-beau now in the furniture business. When Deborah later discovers the man dead, she and police begin investigating." Libr J

Shooting at loons. Mysterious Press 1994 229p o.p.   LC 93-47141

"District Court Judge Deborah Knott, a native North Carolinian, looks forward to filling in for a sick colleague at the Harker's Island courthouse. But on her first fishing trip after arriving on the island, she discovers the body of an old fisherman known to her since childhood. . . . The down-home prose flows well, spiced by Judge Knott's wit, charm, and extended family as well as by references to the local food and drink." Libr J

Slow dollar. Mysterious Press 2002 276p

ISBN 0-89296-764-1   LC 2002-20098

"It's opening night at Dobbs' Annual Harvest Festival, and Deborah, along with half of Colleton County North Carolina, is intent on riding the Ferris wheel, eating elephant ears, and, finally, throwing quarters at the Dozer game. When Deborah runs out of change, she steps into the interior of the game wagon, where she finds the proprietor dead on the floor, his mouth overflowing with quarters. . . . As always, the mystery takes a backseat to the engaging characters and the charming southern setting." Booklist

Southern discomfort. Mysterious Press 1993 241p o.p.   LC 92-56770

Newly appointed judge Deborah Knott, "threads her way through the intricacies of district court in a small North Carolina town where familial connections abound. Murder rears its ugly head only after shared family stories and relationships establish a stylistic context. Employing her intimate knowledge of the place, Knott discovers who assaulted her teenaged niece and killed a randy building inspector inside an unfinished WomenAid house." Libr J

"Maron's written a thriller that simply oozes southern charm and atmosphere. The clever plot is full of surprises—a good blend of menace, poignancy, and humor. But perhaps Maron's real strength is her refreshing heroine, who doesn't mind admitting she wears a size fourteen dress and who approaches life with humor, determination, and good sense." Booklist

Storm track. Mysterious Press 2000 260p $28

ISBN 0-89296-656-4   LC 99-51761

Maron, Margaret—_Continued_

"The residents of Colleton County, North Carolina, must contend with dual threats: Hurricane Fran, gearing up offshore, and the presence of a nasty murderer in their midst. Lynn Bullock, known as a tramp by all except, perhaps, her husband, is strangled in a local motel, dressed for a tryst, and Deborah's cousin Reid is a top suspect. More bodies turn up as the hurricane arrives to wreak another kind of destruction on the locals." Booklist

"Deborah Knott, the district court judge who presides over this enchanting regional series, guides us through these crises with her customary good sense. . . . Deborah is the voice of sanity and the soul of wit." N Y Times Book Rev

Uncommon clay. Warner Bks. 2001 288p $28

ISBN 0-89296-720-X   LC 00-66266

"The famous Nordan family, who live in an area of North Carolina known for its pottery, is being torn apart by a traumatic and bitter divorce. Judge Deborah Knotts . . . oversees distribution of the marital property, but her work is interrupted by a tragic death in the family—reminiscent of a terrible suicide two years earlier." Libr J

This mystery "does more than honor local folk art and the generations of artisans who carry on the regional heritage. It shows us how deeply these homespun crafts are rooted in the collective artistry of individual families—and what a devastating loss it is when these families die out." N Y Times Book Rev

Up jumps the Devil. Mysterious Press 1996 278p o.p.   LC 96-7715

"As the pecan trees of the beautiful North Carolina countryside give way to tract housing, land values are escalating rapidly, and all over Colleton County, longtime neighbors and family members are engaged in acrimonious disputes over whether to sell their family land. In this . . . entry in the Deborah Knott series, the straight-talking, down-to-earth district court judge is drawn into two murders tied to greed over land-development money." Booklist

"The droll characters and their lilting regional humor seem ever more endearing because we sense their days are numbered." N Y Times Book Rev

Márquez, Gabriel García _See_ García Márquez, Gabriel, 1928-

Marsh, Dame Ngaio, 1899-1982

Dead water. Little, Brown 1963 244p o.p.

Scotland Yard's Superintendent "Roderick Alleyn finds himself involved unofficially in magic and faith healing when his former French teacher, now a formidable lady of 80, inherits an island off the coast of Cornwall which has, as its chief claim to fame and source of income, a Pixie Well supposed to cure warts, asthma and other ills. . . . Skillful writing, convincing atmosphere, and sharply etched characterization will please Ngaio Marsh fans, but the plot is less complex than some of her others." Publ Wkly

False scent. Little, Brown 1959 273p o.p.

This mystery "takes place in the opulent London home of a famous—and temperamental—actress on her 50th birthday anniversary. The flamboyant people surrounding

Mary Bellamy are properly subdued only when the polished Roderick Alleyn of Scotland Yard and his capable assistant, Inspector Fox, enter the scene and uncover the ugly secrets that led to murder." Libr J

Grave mistake. Little, Brown 1978 252p o.p.   LC 78-16910

"When a rich eccentric old lady in a rest home suddenly dies, friends and the police suspect murder. [Inspector] Alleyn's trail leads him to the old lady's daughter, her fiance, his father, a close friend, and a few assorted others including a Scots gardener—named Gardener! When a will turns up leaving all her money to the doctor who runs the rest home, the supposed case of suicide really becomes murder." West Coast Rev Books

Last ditch. Little, Brown 1977 265p o.p.   LC 76-52287

The novel takes place on one of the Channel Islands, to which Ricky, Superintendent Roderick Alleyn's son, "has come during the Easter vacation to write a novel. Here he meets Jasper and Julia Pharamond, friends of his parents, and falls in love with the magnolia-skinned Julia. . . . A riding expedition ends in a fatal accident, attended by suspicious circumstances; at the same time Ricky stumbles, he thinks, across the tracks of a gang of drug smugglers. But Scotland Yard's attention has already been called to the island, and Chief Superintendent Alleyn and Inspector Fox are soon on their way there." Times Lit Suppl

Light thickens. Little, Brown 1982 232p o.p.   LC 82-13085

"A production of _Macbeth_, directed by Peregrine Jay at the Dolphin Theatre, is beset with macabre incidents. During rehearsals, realistic-looking dummy heads turn up in dark corners and on banquet trays, and a rat's head is found in the witch's effects. But the incidents cease, and reviews call the production 'the flawless _Macbeth_'—until the night when the actor playing Macbeth is decapitated during the play. Roderick Alleyn is, of course, in the audience." Libr J

When in Rome. Little, Brown 1971 260p o.p.

First published "1970 in the United Kingdom

Set in Italy, "much of the action takes place in an ancient church which reproduces three levels of civilization. . . . The mystery centers on a sinister blackmailing tour entrepreneur who gathers together a motley group of people, some innocent, some with good reason to want him out of the way. Drugs, sex orgies, even more delicate scandals are all grist to his mill and when he meets a very nasty demise the field of suspects is wide open. Not the least of the pleasures here is a charming love affair, and the slightly comic opera encounters between English Inspector Roderick Alleyn and the Rome police." Publ Wkly

Marshall, Catherine, 1914-1983

Christy. Avon Books 2006 576p pa $6.99

ISBN 0-380-00141-1   *

A reissue of the title first published 1967 by McGraw-Hill

"A spirited young woman leaves the security of her home to become a teacher in Cutter Gap, Kentucky. It is 1912 and the needs of the Appalachian people are

Marshall, Catherine, 1914-1983—*Continued*

great. Christy learns much from the poverty and superstition of the mountain folk. Marshall's Christian faith and ideals are intertwined in the plot, which includes a love story." Shapiro. Fic for Youth. 3d edition

Marshall, Paule, 1929-

Brown girl, brownstones; with a foreword by Edwidge Danticat; afterword by Mary Helen Washington. 2nd Feminist Press ed. Feminist Press at the City University of New York 2006 319p pa $16.95

ISBN 1-55861-498-2; 978-1-55861-498-7

LC 2005-29191

First published 1959 by Random House

"Set in Depression-era Brooklyn, NY, this 1959 coming-of-age novel finds Selina Boyce caught in the middle of her immigrant parents. Mom wants Selina to get an American education, while dad dreams of returning to Barbados. Along with her parental woes, our heroine must deal with the poverty and racism that surrounds her." Libr J

The fisher king; a novel. Scribner 2000 222p $23

ISBN 0-684-87283-8

LC 00-28470

"Story of a family in turmoil over the memory of Sonny-Rett Payne, a jazz pianist who fled the racism of New York for Paris in 1949. The action is set in the present, as Sonny's brother, Edgar, now a successful businessman in Brooklyn, organizes a memorial concert for his brother and lures Hattie Carmichael, Sonny's former lover, who lives in Paris with Sonny's grandchild, back to the States for the event. The narrative jumps from the present, as Edgar subtly attempts to gain custody of young Sonny, and the past, as Hattie remembers Sonny-Rett, his music, his wife, and their unconventional life in Paris." Booklist

"Marshall's prose is full of expert dialogue, mellifluous rhythms and sharply drawn portraits of Sonny-Rett's loved ones." N Y Times Book Rev

Praisesong for the widow. Putnam 1983 256p o.p.

LC 82-13215

This novel "tells of a sixtyish widow, Avey Johnson, refined, well-to-do, and complacent. Troubled by strange dreams and symptoms, she cuts short her annual Caribbean cruise and disembarks on a small island. An old man recognizes her as one of the 'people who can't call their nation,' and persuades her to join him and others on their yearly ritual visit to a neighboring island they call home. There, purged of her old self, Avey rediscovers her roots." Libr J

Marshall, Sarah Catherine Wood *See* Marshall, Catherine, 1914-1983

Marsten, Richard, 1926-2005

For works written by this author under other names see Hunter, Evan, 1926-2005; McBain, Ed, 1926-2005

Marston, Edward

The Bawdy basket. St. Martin's Minotaur 2002 262p

ISBN 0-312-28501-9

LC 2002-2510944

An Elizabethan mystery featuring "Nicholas Bracewell, stage manager of Lord Westfield's Men. . . . When a young actor's father is tried, convicted, and hung for a brutal murder he claims he did not commit, his sins are unfortunately visited upon his loyal son. Nicholas agrees to investigate the matter in an effort to clear the unlucky man's name and to restore a promising young thespian to the ranks of his beloved theater company." Booklist

The Devil's apprentice; a novel. St. Martin's Minotaur; distributed by 8 2001 273p

ISBN 0-312-26574-3

LC 2001-19259

Elizabethan stage manager Nicholas Bracewell "fends off accusations of witchcraft and worse after the troupe performs at a manor house in Essex. A new apprentice taken on there seems to be at the root of the trouble. Lively and entertaining: for fans of Elizabethan historicals." Libr J

The roaring boy; a novel. St. Martin's Press 1995 260p o.p.

LC 95-8568

"Elizabethan stage manager Nicholas Bracewell presents a new kind of play based on a sensational murder case. But the play leads to trouble for his actors, unless he can solve the actual murder." Libr J

"Marston's colorful (and convincing) characterizations shine as Nicholas chases the secrets of the murder in order to save the company. The plot, except for one transparently finagled episode, is expertly wrought, with the suspense building steadily to breathtaking climax and some surprises saved for the very end." Publ Wkly

The stallions of Woodstock. St. Martin's Press 1999 275p

ISBN 0-312-20021-8

LC 98-50733

First published 1997 in the United Kingdom

In this installment in the author's Domesday series "Gervase Bret and Ralph Delchard, commissioners to King William the Conqueror, are sent to Oxford, England, to settle a land dispute and soon find themselves embroiled in a murder investigation." Publ Wkly

The vagabond clown. St. Martin's Minotaur 2003 292p $24.95

ISBN 0-312-30789-6

LC 2002-191950

"Lord Westfield's Men, the actors' troupe for which Bracewell works as stage manager, are forced to leave their theater after a violent act of sabotage trashes the place. Worse, someone has killed one of Westfield's friends during the melee. Bracewell struggles to save the troupe and its reputation. An outstanding historical." Libr J

The wanton angel; a novel. St. Martin's Press 1999 279p

ISBN 0-312-20391-8

LC 99-22062

This mystery, set in Elizabethan England, finds Nicholas Bracewell's "acting troupe ejected from its theater at the Queen's Head when one of the actors impregnates the landlord's daughter and is then murdered." N Y Times Book Rev

Marston, Edward—*Continued*

The wildcats of Exeter; volume VIII of the Doomesday Books. St. Martin's Minotaur 2001 275p il

ISBN 0-312-25355-9

First published 1998 in the United Kingdom

In this installment tax collectors Gervase Bret and Ralph Delchard travel to Exeter in Devon. "A land dispute, already complicated by many claimants, grows ever more so when the current owner, one Nicolas Picard, meets a grisly death. He's clawed by a wildcat but also has his throat cut. The wildcats of the title also refer to several women wronged by Nicolas, all of whom have claims to his property. Monks peevish and saintly, a jester wise in his foolery, another murder, and some marital mayhem complete the entertaining picture." Booklist

Martel, Yann, 1963-

Life of Pi; a novel. Harcourt 2001 319p $25

ISBN 0-15-100811-6

* LC 2001-39737

"Pi Patel, a young man from India, tells how he was shipwrecked and stranded in a lifeboat with a Bengal tiger for 227 days." Booklist

"An impassioned defense of zoos, a death-defying trans-Pacific sea adventure à la 'Kon-Tiki,' and a hilarious shaggy-dog story starring a four-hundred-and-fifty-pound Bengal tiger named Richard Parker: this audacious novel manages to be all of these. . . . This breezily aphoristic, unapologetically twee saga of man and cat is a convincing hands-on, how-to guide for dealing with what Pi calls, with typically understated brio, 'major lifeboat pests.'" New Yorker

Martin, Charles, 1969-

Where the river ends. Broadway Books 2008 375p $19.95

ISBN 978-0-7679-2698-0; 0-7679-2698-6

LC 2007-42819

"Doss Michaels, a fishing guide and part-time artist in Charleston, SC, is willing to face possible kidnapping and other serious charges generated by his disapproving father-inlaw to fulfill his wife Abbie's last wishes for one more adventure together—a 130-mile trip down the St. Mary's River." Libr J

"This tale is a pleasure to read because it eloquently pictures unquestioning, steadfast love." Fayetteville Observer

Martin, Clancy W., 1967-

How to sell; [by] Clancy Martin. Farrar, Straus & Giroux 2009 296p $24

ISBN 978-0-374-17335-7; 0-374-17335-4

LC 2008-55450

"Bobby Clark is just sixteen when he drops out of school to follow his big brother, Jim, into the jewelry business. Bobby idolizes Jim and is in awe of Jim's girlfriend, Lisa, the best saleswoman at the Fort Worth Deluxe Diamond Exchange. What follows is the story of a young man's education in two of the oldest human passions, love and money." Publisher's note

This novel is, "with memorably dark comedy, a virtual handbook on fraud. The world the Clark boys build for

themselves and teeter precariously upon . . . is a compelling setting for Martin's propulsive storytelling. His narration feels cinematic, the sets and scenery popping off the page. With remarkable skill as the story spools out, Martin omits just enough exposition and interior insights to keep his characters shrouded in mystery, as if constantly reminding us that we'll always be the customer, never the insider." Elle

Martin, George R. R.

A clash of kings. Bantam Bks. 1999 761p (Song of ice and fire) $26.95

ISBN 0-553-10803-4

LC 98-37954

In the second title of the fantasy saga which began with A game of thrones, "a war for succession as king of the realm pits brother against brother in a battle of armies and politics. Caught in the struggle are seven noble families whose fortunes and lives depend on how well they play the game of intrigue, blackmail, kidnapping, treachery, and magic." Libr J

"The novel is notable particularly for the lived-in quality of its world, created through abundant detail that dramatically increases narrative length even as it aids suspension of disbelief; for the comparatively modest role of magic . . . and for its magnificent action-filled climax." Publ Wkly

A feast for crows. Bantam Books 2005 753p maps (Song of ice and fire) $30

ISBN 0-553-80150-3

LC 2005-53034

"A Bantam Spectra book"

This fantasy novel, the fourth in a series, is set in the Seven Kingdoms, an unstable aliance of states. "After centuries of bitter strife and fatal treachery, the seven powers dividing the land have decimated one another into an uneasy truce. Or so it appears. With the death of the monstrous King Joffrey, Cersei is ruling as regent in King's Landing. . . . Few legitimate claims to the once desperately sought Iron Throne still exist—or they are held in hands too weak or too distant to wield them effectively. . . . Daring new plots and dangerous new alliances are formed." Publisher's note

The author introduces "plot twists and characters that continue to flesh out one of the genre's most detailed and intriguing worlds. A must-purchase for libraries owning the series, this panoramic fantasy adventure is highly recommended." Libr J

A game of thrones. Bantam Bks. 1996 694p il (Song of ice and fire) o.p.

* LC 95-43936

The first volume in A Song of Ice and Fire saga, "combines intrigue, action, romance, and mystery in a family saga. The family is the Starks of Winterfell, a society in crisis due to climatic change that has created decades-long seasons, and a society almost without magic but with human perversity abundant and active. Martin reaches a new plateau in terms of narrative technique, action scenes, and integrating . . . his political views into the story." Booklist

Followed by A clash of kings

Hunter's run; [by] George R.R. Martin, Gardner Dozois, and Daniel Abraham. Eos 2008 303p $25.95

ISBN 978-0-06-137329-9; 0-06-137329-X

LC 2007-29817

Martin, George R. R.—*Continued*

"Ramon Espejo wakes in darkness, without clothes, without memories, until, little by little, his past returns. He is a prospector on the colony planet of Sao Paolo, ruled by the alien Enye. He also remembers a bloody knife, a corpse, and flight from the law-and gradually realizes that he is both hunter and hunted." Libr J

"The first item of business to get out of the way is the tripartite authorship of this book. At first it seems a rather circuslike distraction that, however, has actually resulted in a superb fusion of talents. . . . The book reads like the work of one melded intelligence, seamless and organic. In Ramón, the authors have created an appallingly attractive antihero straight out of Leigh Brackett's canon. His rough-and-tumble progress from unknowingness to self-awareness is handled deftly all the way." SciFi Wkly

Sandkings
In The Hugo winners p70-132

A song for Lya
In The Hugo winners p483-544

Martin, Malachi

Vatican; a novel. Harper & Row 1986 657p
ISBN 0-06-015478-0   LC 85-42645
The author "compresses the history of the modern Roman Catholic church into . . . the 40 years since World War II. Its focus is the highly secret inner workings of the Vatican State in Rome, a religious and political bureaucracy that affects not only its members but also individuals and events around the world. The novel opens with the arrival in Rome of Richard Lansing, who at age 24 is the youngest ranking monsignor in the powerful archdiocese of Chicago. We watch as he develops from a politically naive but dedicated religious into a papal emissary and eventually into the highest ranking leader of the Catholic church. . . . This authentic depiction of the world's richest, most powerful religion will stun readers with its revelations and intrigue them with its multitextured plot." Booklist

Windswept House; a Vatican novel. Doubleday 1996 646p o.p.   LC 95-26716
This novel about the Catholic Church in crisis focuses on the "conflict between two American brothers—one a priest, one a lawyer, both heirs to a fortune and to the family manse of Windswept House. . . . [As he develops his plot] . . . Martin's concern is what he sees as the erosion of the Church's moral authority, both from within and without. Here, a Slavic pope who's obviously John Paul II is being maneuvered into approving the Resignation Protocol, which, if enacted, will force him to resign in the name of Church unity. Martin attributes this erosion to a global conspiracy among world powers both East and West, fueled by Satanic influence and by the failure of John Paul XXIII to act upon the Third Prophecy of the Fatima Letter in 1960. The narrative is richly detailed with Church lore." Publ Wkly

Martin, Peter *See* Melville, James, 1931-

Martin, Roy Peter *See* Melville, James, 1931-

Martin, Steve, 1945-

The pleasure of my company; a novella. Hyperion 2003 163p $19.95
ISBN 0-7868-6921-6   LC 2003-49954
This work features "one of the odder yet more charming protagonists in recent fiction, Daniel Pecan Cambridge, a gentle soul suffering from a mild mix of autism and obsessive-compulsive disorder. Daniel, 33, lives in a rundown Santa Monica apartment, his life constricted by an armor of defensive habit. . . his dull days punctuated only by imagined romances and visits by his student social worker, lovely and kind Clarissa. Daniel's ways (a product of child abuse, Martin shows with subtlety) are challenged when Clarissa and her infant son, Teddy, move in to escape an abusive husband. . . . This novella is a delight, embodying a satisfying story arc, a jeweler's eye for detail, intelligent pacing and a clean, sturdy prose style." Publ Wkly

Shopgirl; a novella. Hyperion 2000 130p
ISBN 0-7868-6658-6
                                     * LC 00-38874
The main characters in this novella are Mirabelle Butterfield, "a 28-year-old woman behind the glove counter at the Neiman Marcus department store in Beverly Hills . . . and Ray Porter, the fiftysomething man Mirabelle admits into her solitary life." Time

There is "an impressive gravity about 'Shopgirl.' Its glints of comedy are sharp and dry. . . . The novella has an edge to it, and a deep, unassuageable loneliness." N Y Times Book Rev

Martin, Valerie

The confessions of Edward Day; a novel. Nan A. Talese 2009 286p $25
ISBN 978-0-385-52584-8; 0-385-52584-2
                                     LC 2008-44965
This novel recreates "the New York theater world of the 1970s and '80s. What seems quaint now — onstage nudity — was brand-new then, and the group of acting students in the novel is smack dab in the middle of the whole scene, which includes favorite bars and escapes to the Jersey Shore. On one such escapee, Edward, a young actor fresh from a successful seduction of the lovely Madeleine, goes for a late-night walk and falls into the sea. Guy Margate, a fellow actor, rescues him, setting up an everlasting debt which Edward can hardly repay. . . . After his dramatic rescue of Edward, Guy uses every opportunity to wrest payment from him, sometimes by asking for money, sometimes by appropriating Madeleine's wandering affections. She is the weakest link in the novel, having little will of her own. Guy and Edward pass her back and forth until matters escalate to a horrific and very theatrical climax." Seattle Times

Italian fever; a novel. Knopf 1999 259p $22
ISBN 0-375-40542-9   LC 98-31824
"When Lucy Stark's employer falls inelegantly down a well in Tuscany, Lucy must travel there to see that he's given a decent burial. Not surprisingly, within a day she has contracted the kind of gruesome fever that makes you revel in your own health, and she has encountered the kind of Italian lover that makes you book the next flight over. What lingers in the mind, though, is the nov-

Martin, Valerie—*Continued*

el's final touching twist, which slyly dismantles its own satire and casts a long and mysterious shadow over everything that has come before." New Yorker

Mary Reilly. Doubleday 1990 263p o.p.

* LC 89-38313

In this retelling of Robert Louis Stevenson's Dr. Jekyll and Mr. Hyde, "Mary Reilly, a loyal, trusted servant in the household of Dr. Jekyll records in her diary the mysterious circumstances which lead to her Master's tragic fate." Libr J

"Whereas the atmosphere of Robert Louis Stevenson's tale was all foggy nights and sinister uncertainties, Mary Reilly weaves a somewhat more ambiguous but equally gripping web of mystery around the same riveting events. In both cases the end product is a fascinating story." Quill Quire

Property. Talese 2003 196p $23.95

ISBN 0-385-50408-X   LC 2002-66846

This work "presents itself as a novel about the abuse of power within the loveless marriage between an antebellum plantation owner and his wife, their private suffering amplified by the social context of slavery. Bondage and its invitation to brutality are not unexplored terrain, but embedded within what might be mistaken as a morality play is a more subtle and compelling story—a contest of wills between two women, Manon Gaudet and Sarah, the slave she received from her aunt as a wedding gift." N Y Times Book Rev

Trespass; a novel. Nan A. Talese/Doubleday 2007 288p $25

ISBN 978-0-385-51545-0; 0-385-51545-6

LC 2006-101676

"Chloe Dales's life is in good order. Her only child, Toby, has started his junior year at New York University; her husband, an academic on sabbatical, is working at home on his book about the Crusades; and Chloe is busy creating illustrations for a special edition of Emily Brontë's Wuthering Heights. Yet Chloe is disturbed—by the aggression of her government's foreign policy, by the poacher who roams the land behind her studio, punctuating her solitude with rifle fire, and finally, by Toby's new girlfriend, a Croatian refugee named Salome Drago. . . . Chloe distrusts her on sight, and as Toby's obsession with Salome grows, Chloe's mistrust deepens, alienating her from her tolerant husband and besotted son." Publisher's note

The novel "provides a searing commentary on the human desire to set boundary lines against threats, perceived and real. It's a testament to Martin's skill as both storyteller and writer that her complex characters defy separation into two camps those who accept and those who judge. Nothing in 'Trespass' is quite as it seems, and that is precisely the point." San Francisco Chronicle

Martin, William, 1950-

Annapolis. Warner Bks. 1996 685p o.p.

LC 96-1021

This novel follows the fortunes of two families. "Each generation of Staffords has sent at least one son to sea since the Revolutionary War; the Parrishes, on the wrong side of the war, lost their Annapolis house to the Staffords and are still trying to get it back. Now, a distant cousin seeks to make a documentary film about the Staffords, aided by a black sheep Stafford who has been writing the family history. That history is interspersed with present-day squabbling over the property. But the predominant story is of the naval battles that the Stafford men fought, from skirmishes with pirates in Tripoli to Midway Island to the Tonkin Gulf." Libr J

"A storyteller whose smoothness equals his ambition, Martin has written a panoramic entertainment that brings to vivid life the history of the American struggle to control the high seas." Publ Wkly

Cape Cod. Warner Bks. 1991 652p o.p.

LC 90-50534

In this historical saga the author "follows two intertwined yet bitterly antagonistic families from their Pilgrim origins to the present day." Publ Wkly

"Martin embraces the entire sweep of American history with unflagging relish for authentic detail and private moments. He creates generation after generation of feisty Hilyards and cruel Bigelows, pitting them against one another in religious and political skirmishes and joining them in risky love. They endure hardships and shipwrecks, scandal and imprisonment, shame and anger, and contribute their bit to the making of America." Booklist

Harvard Yard. Warner Bks. 2003 580p map $25.95

ISBN 0-446-53084-0   LC 2003-12329

"When antiquarian bookseller Peter Fallon follows the clues he hopes will lead him to recover a lost Shakespeare play written in the bard's own hand, he himself becomes the target of both underworld thugs and unscrupulous academics. The most compelling action takes place in the past as he traces the utterly fascinating evolution of Harvard University by interweaving it with the intimate history of one of New England's first families. . . . The unexpected twists and turns through history will keep readers guessing and the pages turning." Booklist

Martinez, A. Lee, 1973-

The automatic detective. Tor 2008 317p pa $14.95

ISBN 978-0-7653-1834-3; 0-7653-1834-2

LC 2007-37645

"A Tom Doherty Associates book"

"Mack Megaton drives a cab in the mutant-infested 'technotopia' of Empire City. It's a step down for a massive killing machine created for world domination, but kindhearted Megaton has bucked his programming, and when his secretive neighbors, the Bleakers, go missing, he begins a search. Young Holt Bleaker has something in his mutant blood that makes him valuable to aliens poised to invade Empire City, and only a giant robot-a robot like Mack Megaton-can break him out of the fortress where he's held prisoner. Soon plans go awry when sinister psychic Grey subverts Megaton's programming, but he finds an unlikely ally in Lucia Napier, an outrageously beautiful and talented media star and roboticist" Publ Wkly

This is "a hardboiled, hardwired, hard-riveted, hard-hitting blend of classic detective stories and science fiction, giving off a distinctly retro-futuristic vibe as it plays up the conventions of old school science fiction and mystery." SF Site

Martínez, Nina Marie

¡Caramba!; a tale told in turns of the card. Knopf, distributed by Random House 2004 359p il $24.95

ISBN 0-375-41375-8   LC 2003-56192

This "novel, about the wacky goings-on in small Lava Landing, CA, is written in the form of la loteria, a Mexican version of bingo. Each chapter represents a turn of the cards, in which characters play out their destinies against the backdrop of a dormant volcano. Among them are Javier, a born-again Christian mariachi; his mother, Lulabell, a practicing witch; Lucha, Javier's beloved, who wants to sell her former lover's several kilos of cocaine; and True-Dee, the transvestite beautician. Central to the narrative are Natalie and Consuelo (Nat and Sway), best friends since second grade." Libr J

"At times, ¡Caramba! transcends kitschiness and absurdity to evoke something more authentic. Natalie and Consuelo's relationship, for instance, conveys genuine intimacy, particularly in their unique brand of shorthand-speak." Washington Post Book World

Martini, Steven Paul

The attorney; [by] Steve Martini. Putnam 2000 429p $25.95

ISBN 0-399-14536-2   LC 99-44260

In this suspense novel featuring San Diego attorney Paul Madriani "lottery winner Jonah Hale's drug-addicted daughter demands a big payoff when he won't relinquish the granddaughter she left in his care, then accuses him of sexual abuse when he refuses to deliver. A famed feminist activist helps spirit away mother and daughter and then gets bumped off." Libr J

"Tense courtroom drama, plenty of action, and a deviously twisted plot." Booklist

Compelling evidence; [by] Steve Martini. Putnam 1992 379p o.p.   LC 91-30253

"Ben Potter, successful lawyer and possible U.S. Supreme Court nominee, is found dead in his office—suicide or murder? All of the police evidence points to foul play, and his beautiful young wife, Talia, stands trial for a crime she claims she didn't commit—or did she? Paul Madriani defends Talia, but, in doing so, exposes a part of his own life that he would like to forget." SLJ

"Besides giving us the scoop on ballistics analysis and post-mortem blood distribution, the author answers just about every cynical question you've ever had about the games lawyers play." N Y Times Book Rev

Critical mass; [by] Steve Martini. Putnam 1998 436p

ISBN 0-399-14362-9   LC 98-24327

"Lawyer Jocelyn 'Joss' Cole sees a big retainer when she's hired by Dean Belden to handle his company's incorporation filings. But after Belden gets a federal subpoena, Joss sees him die in a fiery seaplane explosion. Now she's the only visible link to Belden's company (which was on the receiving end of two decaying nuclear weapons smuggled into the U.S. out of Russia), and that brings her to the attention of arms inspector Gideon van Ry, of the Institute Against Mass Destruction. After the feds determine that the militia has possession of the weapons, Gideon and Joss join the race to try to avert nuclear disaster." Publ Wkly

"A first-rate, post-Cold War espionage thriller that touches on many hot-button themes from today's headlines: distrust of the government, public apathy, high-tech crime, and antigovernment militias." Booklist

The judge; [by] Steve Martini. Putnam 1996 389p o.p.   LC 95-41835

"Judge Armando Acosta has been summarily dismissed from the bench after being arrested on what he maintains is a trumped-up charge of soliciting a prostitute. When the key witness in the case against Acosta is found murdered and all the evidence points to Acosta as the killer, the former judge suddenly finds himself in desperate need of a tough, savvy lawyer to handle his case. An ironic set of circumstances eventually leads him to his longtime enemy Paul Madriani." Booklist

"Legal thrillers don't get much better than this." Publ Wkly

The jury; [by] Steve Martini. Putnam 2001 291p

ISBN 0-399-14672-5   LC 2001-19834

Madriani, "still struggling to establish his law practice in San Diego, is defending Dr. David Crone, a brilliant genetic researcher accused of killing colleague Kalista Jordan: her strangled and dismembered body was found washed up on a beach. Not only does all the evidence point to Crone, but his lies and deceptions are starting to test the patience of Madriani and his partner, the quick-tempered Harry Hinds. . . .[Martini] takes the moving parts of a standard plot and spins them for maximum effect." Publ Wkly

The list; [by] Steve Martini. Putnam 1997 438p o.p.   LC 96-46410

A novel about "attorney-turned-novelist Abby Chandlis, who stretches the practice of ghost-writing to an extreme and perilous level. Fearful that glamour instead of grammar sells books in today's shallow publishing industry, Chandlis creates Gable Cooper, a strong, handsome, but definitely fictitious alter ego who as 'author' of her new novel should assure its success. Possessed of these qualities, rugged Jack Jermaine seems ideal for the role. However, his spooky past and dangerous tendencies soon cause Abby to regret the entire scheme." Libr J

The author "clearly had a good time writing this fanciful book, in which he manages to incorporate multiple settings, invent gossamer disguises for important publishing personalities and skewer the machinery that produces blockbuster books." Publ Wkly

Prime witness; [by] Steve Martini. Putnam 1993 384p o.p.   LC 93-16908

"When attorney Paul Madriani offers to assist a friend—the county's ailing district attorney, who subsequently dies—in investigating six brutal killings, he becomes entangled in a series of machinations that threaten his career and even his private life." Publ Wkly

"The novel effectively relays the great demands of being a district attorney and also depicts the behind-the-scenes maneuverings of a trial." Booklist

Undue influence; [by] Steve Martini. Putnam 1994 462p o.p.   LC 94-10144

"Recently widowered lawyer Paul Madriani has problems with his sister-in-law Laurel. She is involved in a nasty custody trial, and then she is arrested for the murder of her ex-husband's new wife. After Paul agrees to

Martini, Steven Paul—*Continued*
represent her, he gets sucked into a vipers' tangle involving Laurel, her two children, her ex-husband, a beautiful attorney, a bombing, and mistaken identities." Libr J

"The action builds to a rousing climax through a brilliant series of trial scenes with several surprises. The characters are sharply drawn, the facts of the case are presented simply and the courtroom psychology is laid out vividly." Publ Wkly

Marusek, David

Counting heads. Tor 2005 336p $24.95
ISBN 0-7653-1267-0   LC 2005-05316
"A Tom Doherty Associates book"

"Life on Earth in 2134 ought to be perfect: nanotechnology can manufacture anything humans need; medical science can control the human body's shape or age; and AIs, robots and contented clones do most of the work. If only there were a way to get rid of the surplus people. When Eleanor Starke, one of the major power brokers, is assassinated, her daughter's cryogenically frozen head becomes the object of a quest by representatives of several factions, including Eleanor's aged and outcast husband, a dense zealot for interstellar colonization, a decades-old little boy and husband and wife clones who are straining at the limitations of their natures. Marusek's writing is ferociously smart, simultaneously horrific and funny, as he forces readers to stretch their imaginations and sympathies." Publ Wkly

Followed by: Mind over ship (2008)

Marut, Ret *See* Traven, B.

Mason, Bobbie Ann

Feather crowns. HarperCollins Pubs. 1993 454p
ISBN 0-06-016780-7   LC 92-56227
This novel "tells the story of Chrissie Wheeler, a tobacco farmer's wife in Hopewell, Kentucky, who, in 1900, gives birth to America's first recorded quintuplets. Curiosity seekers pass in a steady stream through the Wheeler's small farmhouse. When the babies take ill and die, Chrissie and her husband are persuaded to go on tour, displaying the grotesquely painted bodies of the dead infants to the idly curious." Libr J

"Mason's triumph here is to make her uneducated, bewildered heroine as vivid as the country life she describes." Publ Wkly

In country; a novel. Harper & Row 1985 247p
hardcover o.p. pa $13.95
ISBN 0-06-015469-1; 0-06-083517-0 (pa)
LC 85-42579
"Sam, 17, is obsessed with the Vietnam War and the effect it has had on her life—losing a father she never knew and now living with Uncle Emmett, who seems to be suffering from the effects of Agent Orange. In her own forthright way, she tries to sort out why and how Vietnam has altered the lives of the vets of Hopewell, Kentucky. . . . A harshly realistic, well-written look at the Vietnam War as well as the story of a young woman maturing." SLJ

Love life; stories. Harper & Row 1989 241p
o.p.   LC 88-45535
Contents: Love life; Midnight magic; Hunktown; Marita; The secret of the Pyramids; Piano fingers; Bumblebees; Big Bertha stories; State champions; Private lies; Coyotes; Airwaves; Sorghum; Memphis; Wish

"Moments of insight emerge in Mason's stories as her Kentuckian characters encounter life's twists and turns. . . . The immediacy of these stories comes not just from Mason's frequent use of the present tense, or her often-criticized references to Wal-Mart and MTV, but, most of all, from her impressive ability to cut to the innermost emotions of a wide range of characters." SLJ

Midnight magic; selected stories of Bobbie Ann Mason; selected & introduced by the author. Ecco Press 1998 301p
ISBN 0-88001-595-0   LC 97-36369
Contents: Midnight magic; Bumblebees; The retreat; Love life; Big Bertha stories; Shiloh; Offerings; Drawing names; Coyotes; Residents and transients; Sorghum; Nancy Culpepper; Graveyard day; A new-wave format; Third Monday; Wish; Memphis

This "is a selection of 17 stories drawn from 'Shiloh and Other Stories,' the 1982 debut collection . . . and it's 1989 successor, 'Love life.' The book's characters live in the brave new world of strip malls and franchised food that is the New—or, rather, the New New—South. Most of them are Baptists, and they take the old strictures seriously, even though they're hardly able to live by them." N Y Times Book Rev

Nancy Culpepper; stories. Random House 2006
224p
ISBN 0-375-50718-3   LC 2005-541241
In addition to the novella Spence + Lila, this collection includes the following short stories: Nancy Culpepper; Blue country; Lying doggo; Proper Gypsies; The heirs; The prelude

This volume "collects all of Mason's fiction about its title character, but a single novella takes up almost half the book. 'Spence + Lila,' published on its own in 1988, showcases Nancy's return home after her mother, Lila, is hospitalized for a mastectomy. . . . Even in its lighter moments, Mason's fiction can inspire a yearning for something lost — whether it's a person, a place or a moment. That ache animates Nancy in the later stories as she moves through her middle years, always feeling slightly out of place, always searching for connections that just barely elude her." N Y Times Book Rev

Shiloh and other stories; with a foreword by George Ella Lyon. University Press of Ky. 1995
247p $19.95
ISBN 0-8131-1948-0   LC 95-16581
A reissue of the title first published 1982 by Harper & Row
Contents: Shiloh; The rookers; Detroit Skyline, 1949; Offerings; Still life with watermelon; Old things; Drawing names; The climber; Residents and transients; The retreat; The ocean; Graveyard day; Nancy Culpepper; Lying doggo; A new-wave format; Third Monday

"Capturing in vivid detail the emotional frustrations of her characters and the unsettling ambience of her small-town Kentucky settings, Mason portrays the uneasy feelings of people who don't know what they want out of life but who do know that what they have isn't it." Booklist

Mason, Bobbie Ann—*Continued*

Spence + Lila

In Mason, B. A. Nancy Culpepper

Zigzagging down a wild trail; stories. Random House 2001 209p $22.95

ISBN 0-679-44924-8   LC 00-66480

Contents: With jazz; Tobrah; Tunica; Thunder snow; Rolling into Atlanta; Three-wheeler; The funeral side; Window lights; Proper gypsies; Night flight; Charger

The author's terrain is "the Kentucky she's famous for writing about, but she has succeeded in making rural America seem exotic, strange, and mysterious, a looking-glass world. This lends a shimmering aura to each expertly rendered, boldly open-ended tale." Booklist

Mason, Daniel

A far country. Alfred A. Knopf 2007 267p $24

ISBN 978-0-375-41466-4; 0-375-41466-5

LC 2006-46530

"Raised in a remote village on the edge of a sugarcane plantation, fourteen-year-old Isabel was born with the gift and curse of 'seeing farther.' When drought and war grip the backlands, her brother Isaias joins a great exodus to a teeming city in the south. Soon Isabel must follow, forsaking the only home she's ever known, her sole consolation the thought of being with her brother again. But when she arrives, she discovers that Isaias has disappeared." Publisher's note

The author "doesn't try to make things easy-once Isabel makes it to the city, the plot gets so vague that readers may struggle to retain a purchase. But those who persevere will be rewarded by the climax, when Isabel at last discovers what has become of Isaias. While the novel doesn't attain the level of modern myth one senses Mason was striving for, it does achieve a certain power as an imperfectly realized, yet moving, fable." Christ Sci Monit

The piano tuner. Knopf 2002 317p $24

ISBN 0-375-41465-7   LC 2002-19069

In this novel, set in 1886, the author "sends piano tuner Edgar Drake deep into Burma. The British War Office, in an attempt to placate one of their key people, has requested the services of Drake to repair a grand piano. Army Sergeant-Major Anthony Carroll has a unique approach to keeping the peace in the southern Shan States—he uses poetry, music, and medicine to establish diplomatic connections with the community and their rulers. . . . Drake is drawn into Carroll's political scheme." Booklist

"Mason proves himself equally adept at scenes of wry humor and moments of rapture; most remarkable, he has written a profound adventure story with an unexpected climax, as the mild piano tuner finally becomes the hero of his own life." New Yorker

Massey, Sujata

The pearl diver. HarperCollins 2004 335p $23.95

ISBN 0-06-621296-0   LC 2003-67614

Japanese American antiques dealer Rei Shimura's "assignment to furnish a new Japanese restaurant in Washington yields wonderful detail about Asian cuisines and the multicultural kitchen workers who prepare them. The narrative dovetails nicely with a moving subplot about a war bride who in her native Japan had been an ama-san, a female shellfish diver, until both stories are swamped by blow-by-blow updates on the heroine's personal life and a smelly red herring about Washington politics. There are still lessons to be learned from the uncluttered and serene lines of Japanese art." N Y Times Book Rev

Massie, Allan, 1938-

Caesar. Carroll & Graf Pubs. 1994 c1993 228p o.p.   LC 94-26430

One of the author's novels set in ancient Rome; previous titles Let the emperor speak (1987) and Tiberius (1993)

First published 1993 in the United Kingdom

"Decimus Junius Brutus, a Roman general and one of Julius Caesar's closest friends, was one of the conspirators who killed Caesar on the Ides of March in 44 B.C. In this fictional memoir written while awaiting his death in Gaul, Brutus (cousin to the better known Marcus Junius Brutus) attempts to justify the murder by recounting Caesar's ever-growing lust for total power and his unbecoming desire to outshine Alexander the Great. Brutus and his friends believe that Caesar's megalomania has led him to betray the Roman Senate and destroy the Republic." Libr J

This work "offers an evocative portrait of ancient Rome as well as a gripping and suspenseful analysis of the most intriguing conspiracy of all time. Superb historical fiction." Booklist

Massotty, Susan

(tr) Nooteboom, C. All souls' day

Master's choice [v1]-2: mystery stories by today's top writers and the masters who inspired them; edited by Lawrence Block. Berkley Prime Crime 1999 2v v1 $21.95; pa $5.99; v2 pa $7.50

ISBN 0-425-17031-4 (v1); 0-425-17803-X (v1 pa); 0-425-18225-8 (v2 pa)   LC 99-30270

These volumes pair stories chosen as personal favorites by some of the genre's top crime-fiction writers with a story of their own. Among the authors represented are Joe Gores, Sharyn McCrumb, Stuart Kaminsky, Stanley Ellin, and Joyce Carrol Oates

Matar, Hisham, 1970-

In the country of men. Dial Press 2007 246p $22

ISBN 978-0-385-34042-7; 0-385-34042-7

*   LC 2006-50649

First published 2006 in the United Kingdom

This "novel tracks the effects of Libyan strongman Khadafy's 1969 September revolution on the el-Dawani family, as seen by nine-year-old Suleiman, who narrates as an adult. Living in Tripoli 10 years after the revolution with his parents and spending lazy summer days with his best friend, Kareem, Suleiman has his world turned upside down when the secret police-like Revolutionary Committee puts the family in its sights-though

Matar, Hisham, 1970——*Continued*

Suleiman does not know it, his father has spoken against the regime and is a clandestine agitator-along with families in the neighborhood. When Kareem's father is arrested as a traitor, Suleiman's own father appears to be next." Publ Wkly

"A remarkably perceptive and affecting portrait of a young boy's premature political awakening. . . . [Matar] expertly builds an atmosphere of palpable tension, and though this novel never delves directly into politics, the menacing pall cast by political tyranny looms over the proceedings." Miami Herald

Matas, Enrique Vila- *See* Vila-Matas, Enrique, 1948-

Matheson, Richard, 1926-

Hunted past reason. Forge 2002 335p $24.95

ISBN 0-7653-0271-3　　　　　LC 2001-50768

"A Tom Doherty Associates book"

"Two old friends, Bob (a novelist) and Doug (an actor), head off into the woods for a short hiking trip. Bob wants some hands-on experience for a novel he's working on; Doug is an expert in woodsmanship. From the get-go, there is tension between them: Doug seems excessively demanding; Bob reacts a little too sharply to his friend's criticisms of his stamina and abilities. Soon the mood turns dark, transforming the story into a psychological thriller." Booklist

I am legend. Tom Doherty Associates 2007 317p pa $14.95

ISBN 0-7653-1874-1; 978-0-7653-1874-9

　　　　　　　　　　　　　　　　　　　*

"A Tor book"

First published 1954

Contents: I am legend; Buried talents; The near departed; Prey; Witch war; Dance of the dead; Dress of white silk; Mad house; The funeral; From shadowed places; Person to person

A novella, and ten short stories, introduce us to the last man on earth; a man planning a funeral for his unsuspecting wife; and a man whose telephone rings inside his head—with calls from his dead father.

Mathews, Francine

Death in a cold hard light. Bantam Bks. 1998 323p o.p.

　　　　　　　　　　　　　　　　　LC 97-44253

"While visiting her future in-laws, Nantucket police detective Meredith ('Merry') Folger gets an urgent call from John Folger, her father and Nantucket chief of police. He needs help investigating the apparent drowning of Jay Santorski, a young scalloper. Santorski's death sets off a nor'easter of emotion and crime. . . . Mathews sustains a nail-biting pace to the finale, which takes place in a mansion on a stormy December night. Dialogue crackles, and most of the characters are well rounded." Booklist

Death in a mood indigo. Bantam Bks. 1997 294p o.p.

　　　　　　　　　　　　　　　　　LC 96-48324

"Detective Meredith Folger of the Nantucket police relishes the thought of solving an eight-year-old murder, especially since the initial missing person's investigation

was flubbed by an incompetent. Meredith feels that she 'owes' the dead woman, a prominent female psychiatrist, some kind of resolution, regardless of their impact on her children." Libr J

Mathews, Harry

My life in CIA; a chronicle of 1973. Dalkey Archive Press 2005 203p pa $13.95

ISBN 1-56478-392-8　　　　　LC 2004-63478

"Novelist Mathews, an American living in Paris circa 1973, can't convince his French artistic friends he is not a CIA agent, so he resolves to fake the part—it beats soaking up idle time by learning ancient Greek, he thinks. Knowing a spy needs cover, Mathews sets up as 'international travel counsel,' and the audience attending his seminar yields several recruiting prospects. 'Patrick,' also in the consultancy 'business,' develops into Mathews' boon companion to whom he confides his charade. A second prospect from that seminar (a Russian) becomes the plot's vehicle for eliding Mathews from a world of fantasy espionage into something more real, and menacing. Strangers contact him; he accepts a courier mission; Patrick vanishes; the Soviet embassy summons him, as does French counterintelligence, which warns Mathews a Stasi assassin is pursuing him. Evolving in mood from ludicrous to serious, the yarn's inventive literary elements elegantly mesh into a stylish amusement." Booklist

Matthiessen, Peter

Bone by bone. Random House 1999 410p $26.95

ISBN 0-375-50102-9　　　　　LC 98-46180

In this final volume in the trilogy about E.J. Watson, "Matthiessen has given us Watson's own story in Watson's own words. . . . That story goes right back to Civil War days in South Carolina, and the terrible childhood E.J. endured at the hands of his drunken, brutal and rascally father and his remote and vindictive mother. Thus were laid the seeds of the later outbursts of violence and rage that so frequently punctuated what should have been a promising life. For Watson, as he portrays himself, is ambitious, hardworking and ever ingenious at figuring ways to make the remote Florida Everglades shores yield riches—a true pioneer spirit." Publ Wkly

Far Tortuga. Random House 1975 408p il o.p.

　　　　　　　　　　　　　　　　　　　*

"Far Tortuga is the name given by West Indian turtle-fishing men to a remote inlet south of Cuba that is not found on modern charts. . . . To hunt the last turtles of the season Capt. Raib Avers sails from Grand Cayman island with a ragged crew in an even more ragged boat, the [Lillias] Eden. . . . The boat tacks about the cays and reefs off the coast of Nicaragua. It is too late to find more than a few turtles. As discord and desperation mount, the crew talks about better days: the folklore of hurricanes and pirate captains, of shipwrecks, ghosts and 'wild niggers' smuggled into Florida. . . . Avers, as a last gamble, strikes out for Far Tortuga." Newsweek

"Almost casually, we have been given a full measure of suspense, adventure, and first-rate descriptive writing; and along with and underneath these things, a group of characters who come fully alive with a complexity and even depth that the usual, traditional story of men at sea never gives us." Choice

Matthiessen, Peter—*Continued*

Killing Mister Watson. Random House 1990
372p o.p.

* LC 89-43424

This historical novel "traces the growth of the legend
of Edgar J. Watson, a famed outlaw in the Florida Everglades of a hundred years ago." Voice Lit Suppl

"By the time he was murdered, Watson was one of the
most successful sugar-cane farmers between Tampa and
Key West. Everyone liked and admired him, but no one
trusted him. Proof was always scant but people wound
up dead when Watson was around. . . . Matthiessen tells
his story through the voice of Watson's family and
neighbors in a series of oral histories, diary entries and
old newspaper accounts, all of it fiction. By turns droll,
rambunctious, foolish and wise, this collective narration
mounts into a carefully orchestrated cacophony of contradictory testimony in which suspicion and mistrust are
gradually revealed as the base elements of mystery."
Newsweek

Followed by Lost Man's River

Lost Man's River. Random House 1997 539p
ISBN 0-679-40377-9   LC 97-10124

In this sequel to Killing Mister Watson, "Lucius Watson, who has spent most of his life on the move, returns
home to try to separate the truths from the myths of his
father's killing, forty years earlier. A good part of
Matthiessen's sprawling, uneven, novel comes straight
from the characters' own mouths, but his ample skills as
a naturalist and a journalist are in evidence, too. The
Watson story is bound up in the landscape and the
bloody history of the region, where gator poaching has
given way to gunrunning, and where, nearly a hundred
years after Reconstruction, racism is still as firmly rooted
and as common as mangroves." New Yorker

Followed by Bone by bone

On the river Styx and other stories. Random
House 1989 208p o.p.   LC 86-3206

Six of the stories included in this collection originally
appeared in book form in Midnight turning gray, published 1984 in paperback by Ampersand Press

Contents: Sadie; The fifth day; The centerpiece; Late
in the season; Travelin man; The wolves of Aguila;
Horse latitudes; Midnight turning gray; On the River
Styx; Lumumba lives

Matthiessen's "stories delve into brutal facets of humankind and show the often hapless responses of well-
intentioned individuals. Bitter scenes of racism are portrayed in several stories, including the title piece, in
which a white couple on an innocuous fishing vacation
sparks a violent racial backlash." Booklist

Shadow country; a new rendering of the Watson
legend. Modern Library 2008 892p $40; pa $16
ISBN   978-0-679-64019-6;   0-679-64019-3;
978-0-8129-8062-2 (pa); 0-8129-8062-X (pa)

* LC 2007-25117

A reworking of Matthiessen's Watson trilogy. "With
the publication of Killing Mister Watson, Lost Man's
River and Bone by Bone, he felt, 'after twenty years of
toil . . . frustrated and dissatisfied.' So after 'six or sev-
en' years of 'recreation'—rewriting many passages, com-
pressing the timeline, shortening the work by some 400
pages and fleshing out supporting cast members (notably

black farmhand Henry Short)—the three books are in one
volume for the first time. . . . Florida sugarcane farmer
and infamous murderer—the latter bit according to legend, of course—Edgar J. Watson is brought to life
through . . . eyewitness accounts and journal entries
from friends, family and enemies alike." Publ Wkly

"Matthiessen is meticulous in creating characters, lyrical in describing landscapes, and resolute in dissecting
the values and costs that accompanied the development
of this nation." Seattle Times

Mattison, Alice

The wedding of the two-headed woman.
Morrow 2004 275p $23.95
ISBN 0-06-621378-9

"Fifty-something Daisy Andalusia sorts and organizes
the clutter of her New Haven, Conn., neighbors for a living, a profession that perfectly complements her affinity
for secrets. Married to a man she's not sure she loves,
she becomes romantically involved with a client entirely
unlike her husband. A tabloid headline she reads while
at work, "Two-Headed Woman Weds Two Men," accounts for the title of the book, inspires a community
theater production that establishes new and unexpected
bonds among its participants and illustrates Daisy's dual
role as wife and lover." Publ Wkly

"Mattison's voice is intelligent, spare and without pretense. She lays out Daisy's story in a way that makes it
seem as if not much is happening, while quietly weaving
in four or five intriguing subplots, including a murder
mystery, a rent strike and, toward the end, Sept. 11. All
these stories press in on Daisy in some meaningful way,
each playing a role in her quest to come to terms with
herself." Washington Post

Maturin, Charles Robert, 1782-1824

Melmoth the wanderer; edited with and introduction and notes by Victor Sage. Penguin Books
2000 xxxi, 659p pa $12
ISBN 0-14-044761-x

* LC 2001-265474

First published 1820 in the United Kingdom

This novel "was in effect the last, and also one of the
most effective, of the 'Gothic' school. The tale rushes
energetically through every kind of horror and iniquity,
and has moments of genuine power. Melmoth, who has
sold his soul for the promise of prolonged life, offers relief from suffering to each of the characters, whose terrible stories succeed one another, if they will take over his
bargain with the Devil. But Stanton, imprisoned in the
cell of a raving lunatic; Moncada in the hands of the Inquisition; Walberg, who sees his children dying of hunger; and many other sufferers, all reject the proposed
bargain." Oxford Companion to Engl Lit. 6th edition

Maugham, Somerset *See* Maugham, W. Somerset (William Somerset), 1874-1965

Maugham, W. Somerset (William Somerset), 1874-1965

The best short stories of W. Somerset Maugham; selected, and with an introduction by John Beecroft. Modern Lib. 1957 489p o.p.

Contents: The letter; The verger; The vessel of wrath; The hairless Mexican; Mr. Harrington's washing; Red; Mr. Know-All; The alien corn; The bookbag; The round dozen; The voice of the turtle; The facts of life; Lord Mountdrago; The colonel's lady; The treasure; Rain; P. & O.

Cakes and ale; or, The skeleton in the cupboard. Doubleday, Doran 1930 308p o.p.

This novel, Maugham's "most genial book, is a comedy about the good-natured Rosie Driffield, the wife of a Grand Old Man of Letters; whom most took to be based on Hardy; Alroy Kear, a self-promoting writer, was recognized as Hugh Walpole." Oxford Companion to Engl Lit. 5th edition

Complete short stories. Doubleday 1952 2v o.p.
*

Contents: v 1: Rain; Fall of Edward Barnard; Mackintosh; Red; Honolulu; The pool; The letter; Before the party; Force of circumstance; The outstation; Yellow streak; P. & O.; Jane Round dozen; Creative impulse; Miss King; Hairless Mexican; Giulia Lazzari; The traitor; His Excellency; Mr. Harrington's washing; Footprints in the jungle; Human element; Virtue; Alien corn; The book-bag; Vessel of wrath; Door of opportunity; Back of beyond; Neil MacAdam

v2: Woman of fifty; Man with the scar; The bum; Closed shop; Official position; Man with a conscience; French Joe; German Harry; Four Dutchmen; End of the flight; Flotsam and Jetsam; Casual affair; Mr. Know-All; Straight flush; Portrait of a gentleman; Raw material; Friend in need; The dream; The taipan; The consul; Mirage; Mabel Masterson; Marriage of convenience; Princess September; In a strange land; Lotus eater; Salvatore; Washtub; Mayhew; Happy man; Point of honour; The mother; Romantic young lady; The poet; Man from Glasgow; Lion's skin, Three fat women of Antibes; Happy couple; Voice of the turtle; Facts of life; Gigolo and gigolette; Appearance and reality; The luncheon; The unconquered; Ant and the grasshopper; Home; The escape; Judgment seat; Sanatorium; Louise; Lord Mountdrago; String of beads; The promise; The verger; Social sense; Colonel's lady; Episode; The kite; The treasure; Winter cruise

East and West
In Maugham, W. S. Complete short stories

The moon and sixpence. Doran, G.H. 1919 314p o.p.

"Based closely on the life of Paul Gauguin it tells of Charles Strickland, a conventional London stockbroker, who in middle life suddenly decides to desert his wife, family, and business in order to become a painter. He goes to paint in Tahiti, where he takes a native mistress. Eventually Strickland dies of leprosy." Reader's Ency. 4th edition

Of human bondage; introduction by Gore Vidal. Modern Library 1999 xxxix, 611p pa $11.95
ISBN 0-375-75315-X
* LC 98-46169

First published 1915
This novel's "hero is Philip Carey, a sensitive, talented, club-footed orphan who is brought up by an unsympathetic aunt and uncle. It is a study of his struggle for independence, his intellectual development, and his attempt to become an artist. Philip gets entangled and obsessed by his love affair with Mildred, a waitress. After years of struggle as a medical student, he marries a nice woman, gives up his aspirations, and becomes a country doctor. The first part of the novel is partly autobiographical, and the book is regarded as Maugham's best work." Reader's Ency. 4th edition

The razor's edge. Doubleday 1944 343p pa $14 hardcover o.p.
ISBN 1-4000-3420-5 (pa)
*

"The novel is concerned in large part with the search for the meaning of life and with the dichotomy between materialism and spirituality. The main focus of the story is on Larry Darrell, who has returned from service as an aviator in World War I utterly rejecting his prewar values. He is concerned chiefly with discovering the meaning of human existence and eliminating evil in the world. To that end, he spends five years in India seeking—but not finding—answers." Merriam-Webster's Ency of Lit

World over
In Maugham, W. S. Complete short stories

Maugham, William Somerset *See* Maugham, W. Somerset (William Somerset), 1874-1965

Maupin, Armistead

Michael Tolliver lives. HarperCollins Publishers 2007 277p $25.95
ISBN 978-0-06-076135-6; 0-06-076135-0
LC 2006-52979

The title character first appeared in the author's Tales of the city series about gay life in 1980s San Francisco. "While other names and faces from 'Tales' appear, this story is about Michael, now in his mid-fifties (despite AIDS) and happy in his relationship, his house, and his job. . . . Michael is confronting mortality and seeing the age in himself and everyone around him. His mother's illness creates an opportunity for him to return to Florida and connect with his biological family, while his San Francisco family faces challenges of its own, including new additions and worries about the frailty of Anna Madrigal, now in her eighties." Libr J

This is a "novel only in the loosest sense of the term. The chapters are independent yet interdependent, flowing into one another gracefully while remaining very much singular entities. . . . The book is great fun to read. Maupin is a master at sustained and sustaining comic turns." N Y Times Book Rev

Maurois, André, 1885-1967

The collected stories of André Maurois; translated by Adrienne Foulke. Washington Sq. Press 1967 396p o.p.
*

Contents: Reality transposed; Darling, good evening; Lord of the shadows; Ariane, my sister . . . ; Home port; Myrrhine; Biography; Thanatos Palace Hotel;

Maurois, André, 1885-1967—*Continued*
Friends; Dinner under the chestnut trees; Bodies and souls; The curse of gold; For piano alone; The departure; The fault of M. Balzac; Love in exile; Wednesday's violets; A career; Ten years later; Tidal wave; Transference; Flowers in season; The will; The campaign; The life of man; The Corinthian porch; The Cathedral; The ants; The postcard; Poor Maman; The green belt; The Neuilly Fair; The birth of a master; Black masks; Irene; The letters; The cuckoo; The house

Mawer, Simon, 1948-

The fall; a novel. Little, Brown 2002 370p $24.95

ISBN 0-316-09780-2 LC 2002-73193

"The book takes as its starting point the horrible accident of its title, with James Matthewson, a renowned but now middle-aged mountain climber, tumbling from the face of a Welsh cliff that he should not have been attempting by himself. He dies almost instantly, leaving behind a widow, an estranged best friend and a number of mysteries, among them why he would be climbing such a difficult route without ropes or a helmet. Could the veteran climber have been trying to commit suicide? It's a question for which the bulk of the novel is designed to provide an answer" N Y Times Book Rev

"Intricately weaving time and place, from the bombed-out ruins of World War II London to isolated Alpine mountain peaks, Mawer crafts a sinuously devastating tale of foridden love and faithless betrayal. A haunting and mesmerizing novel from an expert storyteller." Booklist

Maxwell, Katie *See* MacAlister, Katie

Maxwell, Robin, 1948-

The Queen's bastard; a novel. Arcade Pub. 1999 436p $24.95

ISBN 1-55970-475-6 LC 98-50502

Sequel to The secret diary of Anne Boleyn

"The reader is asked to believe that Queen Elizabeth I gave birth secretly to a boy, Arthur, son of Robin Dudley, Earl of Leicester, and that loyal servants tricked these parents into thinking their baby was stillborn. To save the queen's honor, Arthur was spirited away and raised by a trusted country gentleman." Libr J

"Arthur's first person narration is cleverly juxtaposed with third-person dramatization of significant events in the queen's life. . . . Maxwell's research examines the biographical gaps in, and documented facts about, the queen's life, making this incredible tale plausible, and the author aptly embellishes her story with rich period details and the epic dramas of the late 16th century." Publ Wkly

The secret diary of Anne Boleyn. Arcade Pub. 1997 281p

ISBN 1-55970-375-X LC 96-49275

This "novel supposes that Anne Boleyn, second wife of King Henry VIII of England, kept a secret diary that was delivered to her daughter, Elizabeth, upon her succession to the throne. Elizabeth was only three when Anne was renounced by Henry, tried for treason, and sentenced to death. Now, despite her queenly schedule, juggling affairs of state and heart, Elizabeth finds time to read her mother's story avidly and learns lessons that will secure her reign." Libr J

"Painting vicious court intrigue, national and international politics and the role of the Reformation, Maxwell brings not only the two queens but all of bloody Tudor England vividly to life." Publ Wkly

Followed by The Queen's bastard

The wild Irish. William Morrow 2003 393p $24.95

ISBN 0-06-009142-8 LC 2003-42184

"When Grace O'Mally, passionate clan chieftain and legendary Irish pirate, visits the court of Elizabeth I to plead for the release of her imprisoned son, the two most extraordinary women of their time find they have much in common. As Grace relates her incredible life and times to Elizabeth, the aging Bess also revisits her own often tragic past. Caught between these two powerful and magnetic females, Elizabeth's favorite courtier and one-time lover, Robert Devereaux, earl of Essex, is inexorably drawn into the tangled web of the Irish rebellion. . . . Superbly crafted, this dynamic tale brings a host of historical characters vividly to life." Booklist

Maxwell, William, 1908-2000

All the days and nights; the collected stories of William Maxwell. Knopf 1995 415p o.p.

LC 94-27509

Contents: Over by the river; The Trojan women; The pilgrimage; The patterns of love; What every boy should know; A game of chess; The French scarecrow; Young Francis Whitehead; A final report; Haller's second home; The gardens of Mont-Saint-Michel; The value of money; The thistles in Sweden; The poor orphan girl; The lily-white boys; Billie Dyer; Love; The man in the moon; With reference to an incident at a bridge; My father's friends; The front and the back parts of the house; The holy terror; What he was like; A love story; The industrious tailor; The country where nobody ever grew old and died; The fisherman who had nobody to go out in his boat with him; The two women friends; The carpenter; The man who had no friends and didn't want any; A fable begotten of an echo of a line of verse by W.B. Yeats; The blue finch of Arabia; The sound of waves; The woman who never drew breath except to complain; The masks; The man who lost his father; The old woman whose house was beside a running stream; The pessimistic fortune-teller; The printing office; The lamplighter; The kingdom where straightforward, logical thinking was admired over every other kind; The old man at the railroad crossing; A mean and spiteful toad; All the days and nights

Bright center of heaven
In Maxwell, W. Early novels and stories

The chateau
In Maxwell, W. Later novels and stories

Early novels and stories; [edited by Christopher Carduff] Library of America 2008 997p

ISBN 978-1-59853-016-2; 1-59853-016-X

LC 2007-934857

Maxwell, William, 1908-2000—*Continued*

The bright corner of heaven (1934) is a comic novel set in an artist's colony, They came like swallows (1937) is an autobigraphical novel set in the Midwest. In it a devoted wife and mother succombs to the Spanish flu during the epidemic of 1918. The folded leaf (1846), set in Chicago and a Middle Western college, is the story of an intense friendship between two adolescent boys. In Time will darken it (1948), set in a straitlaced Illinois community of 1912, gossip ruins the lives of a respected married lawyer and an ambitious young woman.

"At last—at last!—The Library of America brings out the first in a pair of volumes devoted to the writings of the New Yorker editor who in his spare time produced some of America's most lyrical and poignant fiction." Arts J

The folded leaf
In Maxwell, W. Early novels and stories

Later novels and stories; [edited by Christopher Carduff] Library of America 2008 994p $35
ISBN 978-1-59853-026-1; 1-59853-026-7
The setting of The chateau (1961) "is France in 1948, the place and its people still recovering from the German occupation. A newlywed American couple spends two weeks in the Loire Valley at the château of Mme Viénnot, an impoverished aristocrat whose actions and motivations are inscrutable to her paying guests. . . . So Long, See You Tomorrow (1980) is an Old Testament tragedy played out on the Illinois prairie. It is told by a witness to this tragedy's devastation–an old man much like Maxwell who, some 60 years after the murderous events he describes, struggles to forgive his failure to reach out to the survivors. . . . [Among the short stories included are] 'Over by the River' and 'The Thistles in Sweden,' two classic evocations of New York City life, and the complete contents of Billie Dyer (1992), a companion volume to So Long, See You Tomorrow collecting seven fictionalized portraits of figures from Maxwell's youth. The volume concludes with 40 . . . 'improvisations'–fairy tales that Maxwell wrote mainly to entertain his wife." Publisher's note

So long, see you tomorrow
In Maxwell, W. Later novels and stories

They came like swallows
In Maxwell, W. Early novels and stories

Time will darken it
In Maxwell, W. Early novels and stories

May, Julian, 1931-

The adversary. Houghton Mifflin 1984 xxxviii, 470p il (Saga of Pliocene exile, v4)
ISBN 0-395-36516-3   LC 83-49065
"In this concluding volume of the quartet, King Aiken and the children of the telepathic rebels, exiled from the future Milieu, must fight against Marc Remillard and his allies, the Firvulag. This book will be barely intelligible to those unfamiliar with the rest of the saga—despite May's extensive synopsis—but it should keep the author's regular readers turning pages." Booklist

Intervention, a novel linking the Saga of Pliocene exile with the Galactic Milieu trilogy was published in 1987

Blood Trillium. Bantam Bks. 1992 391p (Trillium)
ISBN 0-553-08851-3   LC 92-2888
Second in a fantasy series that started with Black Trillium by Marion Zimmer Bradley, Julian May, and Andre Norton

"The kingdom of Laboruwenda finds itself on the verge of war as a sorcerer thought to be dead returns to reclaim the three talismans of power held by Queen Anigel and her sisters, Kadiya and Haramis." Libr J

"A superior tale, giving life, character and emotion to the three Petals of the Living Trillium as they continue their adventures." Publ Wkly

Followed by Golden Trillium by Andre Norton

Diamond mask; a novel. Knopf 1994 461p o.p.
                LC 93-37802
The second book in the Galactic Milieu trilogy is "set in the year 2113 and told through the memoirs of Rogatien Remillard, the story looks back on events that took place half a century earlier, when humanity became part of a vast galactic civilization. Remillard's family, virtually immortal and psychically gifted, has become Earth's most powerful force. On the death of the evil Victor Remillard in 2040, an insane metapsychic creature known as Fury comes into being." Publ Wkly

The author "maintains a personal focus on her luminary characters, opening their private lives to intense scrutiny while at the same time expanding the boundaries of an imaginative future world. Rich in intrigue and vibrating with creative energy, this is a superb addition to sf collections." Libr J

Followed by Magnificat

The golden torc. Houghton Mifflin 1982 xxv, 381p il (Saga of Pliocene exile, v2)
ISBN 0-395-31261-2   LC 81-4126
"In this second volume of the saga, May continues the story of the diverse group of time-exiles we met in the first book and shows how they help to bring about the overthrow of the Tanu and the closing of the time gate. . . . May develops her premises seriously and gives her large cast of characters a surprising amount of life." Publ Wkly

Followed by The nonborn king

Jack the bodiless; a novel. Knopf 1992 463p o.p.   LC 91-53176
This is the first volume of the Galactic Milieu trilogy describing events that precipitated the action of the author's Saga of Pliocene exile tetralogy. "As a consortium of five alien races stands ready to accept Earth as a full partner in the Galactic Milieu, the birth of a very special child heralds a new stage in human evolution. . . . May combines a compelling vision of humanity's future with the drama and political intrigue surrounding the Remillard family, whose metapsychic powers and personal ambitions shape the destiny of the world." Libr J

Followed by Diamond mask

Magnificat; a novel. Knopf 1996 427p o.p.
                LC 95-35088
Concluding volume of the author's Galactic Milieu trilogy. "As human rebellion against the unified mind of the Galactic Milieu intensifies, the psychically powerful Remillard family races against time to find and destroy

May, Julian, 1931----*Continued*

the murderous Fury. Fascinating characters enhance an intricate and thoughtfully executed plot. [A] satisfying end to a remarkable feat of the imagination." Libr J

The many-colored land. Houghton Mifflin 1981 415p (Saga of Pliocene exile, v1)

ISBN 0-395-30230-7

In this first volume of a four part saga "a one-way, fixed-focus time portal to Europe in the Pliocene epoch allows the prehistoric past to become a last frontier and a refuge for misfits fed up with the well-ordered world of the 22nd century. This novel follows the adventures of a group newly arrived in Exile. They are prepared for almost anything but what they actually find, a world ruled by humanoid aliens who can control them with artificially augmented psionic powers. The arrogant, beautiful Tanu are opposed, however, by the ugly, outcast Firvulag. Allied with them the humans may hope to overthrow the Tanu and win the freedom they came for. Deftly combining SF and the Celtic myths of the Tuatha de Danaan, Julian May has made a most enjoyable entertainment that will have readers eagerly turning pages." Publ Wkly

Followed by The golden torc

The nonborn king. Houghton Mifflin 1983 xli, 394p il (Saga of Pliocene exile, v3)

ISBN 0-395-32211-1   LC 82-11950

"There is a new balance of power among the 22nd century's voluntary exiles to the Europe of 6-million years ago and the two factions of aliens (Tanu and Firvulag) they found waiting for them there. The humans are no longer slaves, and one of them, a trickster upstart named Aiken Drum, becomes the Tanu king. A new element is introduced in the form of yet another group of (involuntary) exiles, the remnants of the Metapsychic Rebellion of 2083. Beams of mental force clash spectacularly as Aiken seeks their help against Felice, the mad psychic prodigy, and in defending his throne against Tanu traditionalists." Publ Wkly

Followed by The adversary

Mayle, Peter

Anything considered. Knopf 1996 303p $23

ISBN 0-679-44123-9   LC 96-5761

This novel's "protagonist is Bennett, a Brit expatriate on his uppers. Having lost his savings in an investment scam, he is intent on finding the means to reside in Saint-Martin in Provence. He advertises his services: 'Anything considered except marriage'—and is hired by Julian Poe, a stupendously wealthy fellow Brit, who needs help in evading the French income tax. Pretending to be Poe in the latter's Monaco apartment, Bennett becomes involved in the hijacking of a case containing the secret formula for the successful cultivation of the elusive black truffle." Publ Wkly

Mayle has "written an entertaining thriller that moves along apace, but his loyal readers need not worry. Much of his raw material is familiar: wonderful meals decribed in succulent detail; vintage wines, all named to stimulate fantasy; and a rich assortment of French 'characters.'" NY Times Book Rev

Chasing Cézanne. Knopf 1997 295p $23

ISBN 0-679-45511-6   LC 97-71925

"When the photographer Andre Kelly, fresh from a shoot in the south of France, stumbles across a handyman loading a Cézanne onto a plumber's van outside a villa in Cap Ferrat, he uncovers a plot that will nearly cost him his life. It will also lead him to discover true love—but before it does, he must deal with an obnoxious magazine editor, a ruthlessly conniving art trader and a bumbling hit man." N Y Times Book Rev

"The trail to the lost Cézanne becomes a comedy of errors. Along the way, there are vibrant descriptions of Paris, Provence, Cap Ferrat, and of course mouthwatering French meals and wine. Part travelog and part art mystery caper, this . . . is a thoroughly enjoyable romp through the international art world." Libr J

A good year. Knopf 2004 287p $24

ISBN 0-375-40591-7   LC 2003-65674

"On the very day his boss steals his biggest account and maneuvers him out of his job in London's financial district, Max Skinner learns that he's inherited his uncle's vineyard in Provence. Unfortunately, the place is rundown and—worse–the wine it produces is awful. But what about the small plot at the edge of the vineyard that his caretaker badmouths and the private-label 'garage wine' being sold oh-so-discreetly in Bordeaux for $40,000 a case? Then there's the unexpected visit of Californian Christie Roberts, who knows a thing or two about wine herself and may have a valid claim to the estate. Though his plot is predictable, Mayle juggles complications, chicanery, and romance with entertaining and informative tidbits about wine-and his Provence never fails to charm." Libr J

Hotel Pastis; a novel of Provence. Knopf 1993 389p o.p.   LC 93-14641

"Encouraged by a sprightly young Frenchwoman, burned-out advertising executive Simon Shaw buys the local gendarmerie in Luberon, France and turns it into a hotel. Unfortunately, the visitors who crowd the town once the hotel opens include an escaped thief intent on a bank robbery." Libr J

The author "displays his satiric eye for social foibles by skewering advertising execs in England and the U.S.; he is equally adept at evoking typical Provencal villagers. Wickedly sharp and sympathetic at the same time, his characterizations are accurate down to nuances of class differences, voice, accent and vocabulary." Publ Wkly

Maynard, Joyce, 1953-

Labor Day; a novel. William Morrow 2009 244p $24.99

ISBN 978-0-06-184340-2; 0-06-184340-7

LC 2009-13167

"During a trip to the local discount department store, 13-year-old Henry, worldly well beyond the limits of his New Hampshire town, meets the mysterious, middle-aged Frank. Bleeding and limping, Frank asks Henry's lonely, single mom, Adele, to take him to their house. She wordlessly assents. Soon, over coffee, Frank reveals the root of his injury: an escape from the state penitentiary. What follows is the tale of a mid-1980s weekend that's physically imprisoning (with Frank on the lam, the house becomes a hideout) but emotionally freeing, for everyone. Frank and Adele, both broken in multiple ways, find comfort in each other, and Adele and Henry quickly turn

Maynard, Joyce, 1953-—*Continued*
from Frank's captives to his confidants. . . . Maynard
writes from the point of view of the angsty adolescent,
and compellingly so." USA Today

The usual rules. St. Martin's Press 2003 390p
$24.95
    ISBN 0-312-24261-1   LC 2002-36754
"The novel is about a thirteen-year-old girl whose
mother dies in the World Trade Center on September 11.
. . . Not long after that, [her] ne'erdowell biological dad
(Peter Pan) shows up and whisks Wendy off with him to
California." Women's Rev Books
"Wendy is a real teen and her decisions are correct for
her and the young woman she is becoming. This well
paced novel looks forward positively rather than backward with anguish, and will reward those who pick it
up." SLJ

Mayo, Jim, 1908-1988
    *For works written by this author under other
names see* L'Amour, Louis, 1908-1988

Mayor, Archer

The catch; a Joe Gunther novel. St. Martin's
Minotaur 2008 274p $24.95
    ISBN 978-0-312-38191-2; 0-312-38191-3
                      LC 2008-23437
"The killing of a deputy sheriff in Vermont leads to
the death of a big-time drug dealer in Maine. When a
joint task force including the Vermont Bureau of Investigation (VBI) and Immigration and Customs Enforcement
(ICE) sends local, state, and federal agents to investigate,
the complicated trail leads VBI head Joe Gunther to information that he would rather not have discovered."
Libr J
"Archer Mayor doesn't do quaint. He might use poetic
imagery to describe the austere beauty of New England's
rugged mountains and snowbound villages, but as far as
their crime content is concerned, his police procedurals
are about as authentic as it gets." N Y Times Book Rev

Chat. Grand Central Pub. 2007 326p $24.99
    ISBN 978-0-446-58258-2; 0-446-58258-1
                      LC 2007-15310
"On the same night that an unidentified body of a man
is found floating in a lake near Brattleboro, VT, detective
Joe Gunther must leave his investigative team at the
scene and return to his hometown, where his mother and
brother have been seriously injured in an automobile accident. . . . [This case] is one of the hardest for Gunther
because it becomes apparent that someone is trying to
kill his loved ones. Torn between his loyalty to his
coworkers and his commitment to his family, he discovers that people rise to the occasion and offer help in unexpected ways. All the ingredients for a great mystery
are here: fast pacing, a believable plot, a plausible solution, and characters so real they walk off the pages.
Mayor's books just get better and better." Libr J

Occam's razor. Mysterious Press 1999 339p $30
    ISBN 0-89296-682-3
                    * LC 99-26221
In this novel Lieutenant Joe Gunther of Brattleboro,
Vermont, and his investigators "have to deal with the
murder of a man left unconscious on a railroad track, the

knifing death of a woman living on the fringes of the
law and a series of phone calls that implicate an ambitious politician in both crimes." Publ Wkly
"As a stylist, Mayor is one of those meticulous construction workers who are fascinated by the way things
function. He's the boss man on procedures, and he loves
to poke around in whatever complicated mechanism is
making all the wheels turn." N Y Times Book Rev

The sniper's wife. Mysterious Press 2002 312p
$23.95
    ISBN 0-89296-767-6
                    * LC 2002-67183
This mystery delves into the troubled past of "Detective Willy Kunkle, of Joe Gunther's Vermont Bureau of
Investigation. When Kunkle learns that his ex-wife Mary
overdosed on heroin in Manhattan, he hastens there to
identify her body. Suspecting murder, he convinces Ward
Ogfden, a high-ranking NYPD detective, to reopen the
case. In tracing Mary's life in New York, Kunkle revisits
his own Manhattan childhood, membership in the NYPD,
the trauma of Vietnam and strained relations with his
dysfunctional family. When he's arrested during a raid
on an illegal club, Joe and detective Sammie Martens,
Kunkle's lover, come to New York, and the two country
cops prove they're as astute as their city counterparts."
Publ Wkly
"Mayor writes a tough story for his tortured protagonist, and the unfamiliar setting brings out a new, edge-of-
the-knife side of his incisive descriptive powers." N Y
Times Book Rev

Mazor, Julian, 1929-

Friend of mankind and other stories. Paul Dry
Books 2004 279p $19.95
    ISBN 1-589-88016-1   LC 2003-26634
    Contents: Gray skies; The Munster final; The Lone
Star Kid; Skylark; Friend of mankind; On experience;
Storm; Durango; The lost cause; The modern age
The author, "possessed of a classic light touch, is the
sort of assured and lucid storyteller readers trust immediately as they sense his acuity and affection for humanity,
gravitas and humorous inclination. . . . As Mazor's piquant characters struggle against ambivalence and romantic notions and strive to do the right thing, Mazor subtly
reminds readers to cherish life in all its perplexity."
Booklist

McAllister, Bruce, 1946-

The girl who loved animals and other stories;
with an introduction by Harry Harrison and an
afterword by Barry N. Malzberg. Golden Gryphon
Press 2007 306p $24.95
    ISBN 978-1-930846-49-4; 1-930846-49-5
                      LC 2007-9623
    Contents: Dream baby; athe man inside; Kin; World of
the wars; Assassin; The boy in Zaquitos; The ark; Stu;
Moving on; The girl who loved animals; Southpaw;
Benji's pencil; Spell; The faces outside; Angels; Little
boy blue; Hero, the movie
"How far would a person go to protect a loved one?
That question is at the heart of many of the 17 stories
in McAllister's career-spanning collection. . . . [His]
haunting work will enthrall any reader who appreciates
thoughtful, evocative science fiction." Publ Wkly

McAuley, Paul J.

White devils. Tor Bks. 2004 464p $25.95

ISBN 0-7653-0761-8   LC 2003-57067

"The African continent suffers from plague, civil war, and unchecked genetic experimentation. Sent to investigate a particularly heinous crime in the Congo, Nicholas Hyde and his team come under attack by a group of apelike creatures and find themselves in the middle of a government conspiracy to hide its actions from the common people." Libr J

"Though more complex than necessary, this novel serves as a powerful warning about the sinister possibilities inherent in genetic engineering." Publ Wkly

McBain, Ed, 1926-2005

For works written by this author under other names see Hunter, Evan, 1926-2005

Alice in jeopardy. Simon & Schuster 2005 292p $25

ISBN 0-7432-6250-6   LC 2004-52478

"Alice Glendenning has been surviving, just barely. When her husband, Eddie, died in a boating accident nearly a year ago, she was left a widow with two very young children and a life insurance policy with a fly-by-night company that has delayed payment because the body was lost at sea. But things can always get worse, much worse. The ransom call comes not long after her two kids don't return home on the bus after school. The instructions are simple: the money from the insurance policy or the kids are dead–plus the standard 'Don't call the cops.' Alice doesn't call the cops, but the baby-sitter does, and soon Alice is mired in a jurisdictional jihad among local, state, and federal law-enforcement agencies of varying levels of competence." Booklist

This is a "skilled performance from a master of the genre, the pacing and tone just right to keep you tense, curious and amused at each step." Washington Post Book World

The big bad city; a novel of the 87th Precinct. Simon & Schuster 1999 271p

ISBN 0-684-85512-7   LC 98-40890

"A young woman is murdered in a city park across town from her home. She has no identification except a wedding ring with the inscription IHS. Detetctive Steve Carella of the NYPD's 87th Precinct recognizes the inscription from his Catholic schoolboy days as a Latin monogram for 'Jesus, Savior of Men.' Jane Doe is a nun, Sister Mary Vincent, once known as Kate Cochrane. . . . Meanwhile, the man who killed Carella's father and walked because of an incompetent prosecution, Samson Wilber 'Sonny' Cole, has revenge on his mind." Booklist

Eight black horses; an 87th Precinct novel. Arbor House 1985 250p il o.p.   LC 85-7348

"The Deaf Man, scourge of McBain's famed 87th precinct, returns to plot his biggest coup in this . . . thriller. While Carella, Hawes, Brown, Kling and the other detectives investigate the murder of a woman bank teller, their legendary adversary sends them clues to his operation. . . . By switching the narrative from activities at the precinct to a description of the psychotic's fail-safe plan, the author keeps the tension at white heat from the first word to the shattering conclusion of the drama." Publ Wkly

Fat Ollie's book; a novel of the 87th Precinct. Simon & Schuster 2002 271p $25

ISBN 0-7432-0270-8

     * LC 2002-75830

This installment features "Det. Oliver Wendell Weeks of the 88th Precinct. Fat Ollie, of the gross appetite and the even grosser ignorance of political correctness. . . . Two major crimes occur at almost the same time: the shooting of Councilman (and possible mayoral candidate) Lester Henderson as he is getting ready for a rally and the theft of the just completed manuscript of Ollie's first novel, Report to the Commissioner. Ollie enlists Carella's help (Henderson lived in the 87th) and pursues both the murderer and the thief." Publ Wkly

"In McBain's howlingly funny sendup, the novel is pure drivel; but Ollie loved it, and darned if we don't like him for that." N Y Times Book Rev

Fiddlers; a novel of the 87th Precinct. Harcourt 2005 259p $25

ISBN 0-15-101216-4   LC 2005-4255

"A blind violinist is shot in the alley behind the restaurant where he works. A sales rep is gunned down in her apartment while cooking dinner. They are both killed with the same gun. Detective Steve Carella and his 87th Precinct team investigate. The case grows more confusing when an elderly priest and an old woman walking her dog are also murdered with the same gun. The killer, a seemingly ordinary man, is on a last fling with a call girl, who doesn't understand the darkness residing within the man she hopes will pull her out of the life. . . . This one will have readers waking in the middle of the night wondering if they, too, have killers inside themselves." Booklist

The frumious Bandersnatch; a novel of the 87th Precinct. Simon & Schuster 2004 287p $25

ISBN 0-7432-5034-6   LC 2003-57258

"Tamar Valparaiso, a hot young singer on the verge of superstardom, is set to launch her debut CD and video Bandersnatch when she is kidnapped in the middle of a performance for a record industry party and the press. The whole episode is caught on camera, but the masked abductors flee, leaving behind few clues. Steve Carella and Cotton Hawes of the 87th Precinct are called in and are soon joined by a Joint Task Force and FBI agents. Detective Ollie Weeks, resident racist, homophobe, and misogynist, is also back on the scene, this time romancing a fellow officer. McBain displays his usual mastery of the police procedural along with an astute grasp of the music industry, the news media, and publicity, as well as political ramifications within the force." Libr J

Hark!; a novel of the 87th Precinct. Simon & Schuster 2004 293p il $24.95

ISBN 0-7432-5035-4   LC 2004-49102

"The Deaf Man is not a dead man. The brilliant criminal, double-crossed by his female partner . . . and left for dead, is back to make life miserable for the detectives of the 87th Precinct. The cops' frustration begins with the murder of the Deaf Man's former accomplice, a crime that leads the investigating officers down a dead end. But then come the notes, hand delivered to the precinct by a parade of junkies, prostitutes, and panhandlers, and containing combinations of Shakespearean quotes, encrypted anagrams, and palindromes. The Deaf Man is providing clues to the crime he is going to commit, if

McBain, Ed, 1926-2005—*Continued*

only the detectives are clever enough to decipher their meaning." Booklist

"Vintage McBain, complete with pitch-perfect dialogue, subplots that thrust various precinct cops into the spotlight, a pace that encourages the reader to forget about dinner or a good night's rest, and a plot that teases and tantalizes from start to finish." Publ Wkly

Heat; an 87th Precinct novel. Viking 1981 227p o.p. LC 81-65263

"Jeremiah Newman's death was almost definitely suicide, but certain details—for instance, the air conditioning was off on a 99 degree day—bother Detective Steve Carella. His partner, Bert Kling, has other problems—his wife may be cheating on him and someone's taking shots at him." Libr J

Ice; a major new novel about the world of the 87th Precinct. Arbor House 1983 317p o.p. LC 82-74061

"A dancer in a hit musical, a cocaine-pushing punk, and a middle-aged diamond merchant have all been 'iced' the same gruesome way, with the same weapon. Searching for the missing links, the cops fan out through a variety of urban enclaves, from the ghetto to the theater district, from high-rent high-rises to 'Ramsey University.'" Newsweek

A "vivid, often brutal, description of life in the ghetto with its subculture of hookers, pushers, addicts, burglars, muggers, rapists and even savage killers. Yet despite this, it is not without its moments of humor, tenderness, compassion and occasional optimism." Best Sellers

Kiss; a novel of the 87th Precinct. Morrow 1991 351p o.p. LC 91-15908

"Detective Steven Carella must investigate the attempted murder of beautiful Emma Bowles while his father's murderer is tried in the city's courts. Emma's wealthy, handsome stockbroker husband imports a bodyguard for her from Chicago, who stays on the job even after the man who twice tried to kill Emma is found shot *and* hung. Carella and partner Meyer Meyer know something's not right, and doggedly keep investigating. Stoically, Carella also sits in court wondering if his father's killer will be convicted." Booklist

"With its interwoven threads of violence, tenderness and world-weary ruminations on the breakdown of urban life, this is hardboiled mystery in the tradition of Chandler and Hammett. And the ending features the best kind of twist: it's both surprising and satisfying." Publ Wkly

The last dance; a novel of the 87th Precinct. Simon & Schuster 2000 269p il

ISBN 0-684-85513-5 LC 99-53534

"Detectives Meyer Meyer and Steve Carella are questioning Cynthia Keating, whose father lies lifeless in a nearby bed. Cynthia claims she hasn't touched Andrew Hale since she discovered his body, but the cops suspect she's lying: for one thing, the corpse's feet are blue from postmortem lividity, a sign of death by hanging." Publ Wkly

An "accomplished mix of police procedure, characterization, social commentary and tight plotting that has long distinguished this landmark series." Booklist

Learning to kill; stories. Harcourt 2006 478p

ISBN 978-0-15-101222-0; 0-15-101222-9 LC 2005-27059

"An Otto Penzler book"

Contents: First offense; Kid kill; See him die; The molested; Carrera's woman; Dummy; Good and dead; Death flight; Kiss me, Dudley; Small homicide; Still life; Accident report; Chinese puzzle; The big day; Runaway; Downpour; Eye witness; Every morning; The innocent one; Chalk; Association test; Bedbug; The merry merry Christmas; On the sidewalk, bleeding; The last spin

McBain "wrote short fiction, paid by the word, for 1950s pulp magazines such as Manhunt and Argosy under the names of Richard Marsten, Hunt Collins, and Evan Hunter. This collection presents 25 of those crime stories, published between 1952 and 1957 . . . . Grouped thematically under such headings as 'Women in Jeopardy,' 'Private Eyes,' and 'Cops and Robbers,' the stories are definitely of the period, long on hardboiled tone, short on subtlety. More interesting than the stories themselves are McBain's general introduction, which presents both comic details about his career and valuable insights into his writing, and the short prefaces he gives each section, which provide a window into the times and his own development as a writer." Booklist

Lightning; an 87th Precinct novel. Arbor House 1984 304p o.p. LC 84-3030

"A grotesque series of crimes confronts the officers of the 87th Precinct. First, two women college track stars are found hanging, lynch-mob style, from the lampposts of brilliantly lit city streets; and then a rapist who harbors wild psycho-sexual/religious hang-ups stalks an ever-increasing number of victims, torturing them through repeated attacks. A key role in catching the maniac is played by gutsy Eileen Burke, an undercover officer in Special Forces whose aggressive work puts her own life in peril. Filled with realistic police procedure, cop humor, and eerie action." Booklist

Lullaby; an 87th Precinct novel. Morrow 1989 350p o.p. LC 88-13709

"Returning from a party, a couple find their adopted baby and her teenaged sitter murdered. There are so many ramifications, including the later death of the biological mother, that the case seems hopelessly muddled. But Carella and Meyer, outraged by the crime, stick to the wearying routine and finally bring the guilty to book. . . . McBain's staccato dialogue and authentic characters, as always, make . . . [this] a page turner." Publ Wkly

Mischief; a novel of the 87th Precinct. Morrow 1993 346p o.p. LC 93-10404

"The Deaf Man, nemesis of the beleaguered 87th Precinct, is back, and he's scattering cryptic clues all over town, which only serves to multiply the frustrations of Detective Steve Carella and his coworkers. Not that their usual potpourri of crime doesn't offer its own fair share of frustration: graffiti writers are turning up dead in a series of seemingly random killings; mentally impaired senior citizens are being 'dumped' on local hospitals; and, in a city on the edge of racial violence, a free outdoor concert is expected to attract a quarter-million rap fans. . . . McBain tackles social issues . . . tells a good joke, reveals small details of his regular characters' personalities, and provides subplots that add depth and humanity to all the crime in the foreground." Booklist

McBain, Ed, 1926-2005—*Continued*

The mugger. Armchair Detective Lib. 1990 150p o.p. LC 90-32352

First published 1956 in paperback

In this 87th Precinct mystery the police "must contend with a plethora of eccentric criminals, including a guy who steals household cats and a mugger who attacks women, then bows debonairly and offers a polite fairwell. . . . McBain fans will instantly recognize the crisp dialogue that the series would soon become famous for: a hypnotic mix of terse truths, perpetual perplexities, and crude coptalk." Booklist

Nocturne. Warner Bks. 1997 291p o.p.
* LC 96-42030

In this 87th precinct novel "detectives Carella and Hawes catch the first call on the night shift: the shooting death of a destitute woman who was once a renowned concert pianist. . . . Right away we're hooked, because these cops not only know their procedures, they also value a human life. Before this long, dark night is through, Mr. McBain will make us care abot a 19-year-old hooker who is savagely killed in a gang rape, a pimp and a drug dealer who also die hard and 25 roosters torn up in a cockfight." N Y Times Book Rev

Poison; an 87th Precinct novel. Arbor House 1987 264p o.p. LC 86-17342

"Detectives Steve Carella and Hal Wallis interrogate beautiful, wealthy Marilyn Hollis when one of her swains dies of poison, possibly a suicide. Marilyn becomes a murder suspect later, as two more men she has been socially and sexually involved with are killed in a development that creates a serious problem for the investigators. Wallis is now the woman's lover, living with her despite Carella's protest. Both detectives continue to track Marilyn's former male companions, looking for a jealous killer. But Wallis, heartsick, begins to believe that Marilyn is guilty. The taut, gripping story closes with a knockout surprise." Publ Wkly

There was a little girl. Warner Bks. 1994 323p o.p. LC 94-29145

In this Matthew Hope novel "the hero spends most of his time in a semi-coma after being shot outside a bar on the seedy side of Calusa, Fla. . . . Meanwhile, Hope's PI pals Warren Chambers and Toots Kiley, as well as police detective Morris Bloom, try to reconstruct Hope's previous week, probings that are intercut with flashbacks to Hope's own investigation of the years-old suicide of a circus star. What emerges is an intricate, lurid tale of sex, blackmail and murder fueled by greed." Publ Wkly

Three blind mice; a novel. Arcade Pub. 1990 293p o.p.
* LC 89-18543

In this Matthew Hope mystery "the Calusa, Fla., lawyer takes on a 'hopeless case,' defending Stephen Leeds, arrested for murder. The victims were three Vietnamese tried but found not guilty of raping Leeds's wife, Jessie. Every bit of evidence ties the crimes to Leeds, who had publicly sworn to avenge his wife's abuse, but Hope believes in his client and works diligently to free him." Publ Wkly

"Mr. McBain's square-jawed dialogue and stout grip on detection procedures give his narrative the muscularity characteristic of the whole Hope series. But the real strength to flex those muscles comes from the perfectly constructed plot." N Y Times Book Rev

Tricks; an 87th Precinct novel. Arbor House 1987 247p o.p. LC 87-11350

This novel "begins on a Halloween eve, and with the most unlikely of events. Four kids, wearing costumes and garish masks, hold up a series of liquor stores and kill the proprietors before escaping with their plunder. Detectives Brown and Genero make a grisly discovery in a garbage can—a headless torso. A professional magician, Sebastian the Great, puts on a disappearing act that confounds his attractive wife. She appeals to the police for help. Meanwhile, Detective First Class Eileen Burke draws the unenviable assignment of playing a hooker at a notorious bar in hopes of engaging a serial killer who is heavily armed and has a fondness for ladies of the evening." West Coast Rev Books

Vespers; a novel of the 87th Precinct. Morrow 1990 331p o.p. LC 89-13124

"A priest is killed in his church, which is the scene of a standoff between a drug dealer and his assailants. Meanwhile, four blocks away, devil worshippers hold their own religious meetings. The men of the precinct must find the killer, extract the truth from myriad conflicting accounts, and explore the link with the demonic church." Booklist

Widows; a novel. Morrow 1991 332p o.p.
LC 90-49861

"On the same summer night that a young blond woman, the mistress of a wealthy, older, married man, is stabbed to death, detective Steve Carella's father is killed in his bakery by two thieves. Distracted by grief, Carella, with colleague Arthur Brown, investigates the woman's murder, which is followed by the wealthy man's death and those of his first and second wives." Publ Wkly

(jt. auth) Hunter, E. Candyland

McBride, James 1957-

Miracle at St. Anna. Riverhead Bks. 2002 271p
ISBN 1-573-22212-7 LC 2001-48778

This novel follows a "period in the life of four 'Buffalo Soldiers' from the Army's all-black 92nd Division. These soldiers are stranded for several days in late 1944 in the Italian town of Bornacchi. In this interval from fighting, as the four Americans become acquainted with the villagers and partisan Italian fighters battling the Germans, the personalities of the men emerge. . . . The book's final catastrophe is set in motion by the Army's Jim Crow-style racism and its 'unwritten law that no colored should ever be able to tell a white man what to do.'" N Y Times Book Rev

"Through his sharply drawn characters, McBride exposes racism, guilt, courage, revenge and forgiveness, with the soldiers confronting their own fear and rage in surprisingly personal ways at the decisive moment in their lives." Publ Wkly

Song yet sung. Riverhead Books 2008 359p $25.95
ISBN 978-1-59448-972-3; 1-59448-972-6
LC 2007-35969

McBride, James, 1957-—*Continued*

The author sets this novel on Maryland's eastern shore in 1850. "His heroine is Liz Spocott, a beautiful runaway slave who has the gift of being able to see the future. But first she has to survive the present as someone else's property. In the first few pages of the book, she is shot in the head and kills an attack dog with her bare hands before being nabbed by a feared trader named Patty Cannon, a rogue woman who steals and sells slaves. Liz then leads a violent escape of 14 slaves from Cannon's clutches into the swamps of Maryland, only 80 miles from the freedom line — so close but so far away." Pittsburgh Post-Gazette

"McBride borrows liberally from actual historical events and figures to fabricate this engrossing tale, and then emphasizes the implications of past actions by interspersing them with Liz's recurring nightmares of the future. . . . [His] characters evoke an extraordinary time that spawned ghosts that haunt us still." Seattle Times

McCabe, Eugene, 1930-

Heaven lies about us; stories. Bloomsbury 2004 309p $24.95

ISBN 1-582-34427-2   LC 2003-52367

Contents: Heaven lies about us; Truth; Victorian fields; Roma; Music at Annahullion; Cancer; Heritage; Victims; The orphan; The master; The landlord; The mother

"The heaven of Eugene McCabe's title is found in the more rural corners of the Irish border counties, with their centuries-old buildings and calcified layers of piety and tradition. But there isn't much paradise here; McCabe's characters tend to be miserable, improbably eloquent and never, ever dull." N Y Times Book Rev

McCabe, Patrick, 1955-

The butcher boy. Fromm Int. 1993 c1992 215p ISBN 0-88064-147-9

                              * LC 93-2831

First published 1992 in the United Kingdom

"Young Francie is a have-not—poor, ignorant, Catholic—in a small Irish town, but he is savvy enough to size up those who do enjoy privilege. His envy is turned up a notch after the deaths of his alcoholic father and emotionally disturbed mother. Francie then engages in increasingly desperate acts, leading to a harrowing depiction of events that are alluded to on the book's first page." Publ Wkly

"'The Butcher Boy' is the side of the murder story never revealed in the newspapers: a map of a murderer's mind, a revelation of a murderer's reason. It is the story of the heritage of madness and loneliness, a stunning picture of the desperation of the unloved." N Y Times Book Rev

Winterwood; a novel. Bloomsbury Pub. 2007 c2006 242p $23.95

ISBN 978-1-59691-163-5; 1-59691-163-8

                              LC 2006-15837

First published 2006 in the United Kingdom

"Beginning as a journalist who travels to a rural area to visit an old musician named Ned Strange, narrator Redmond Hatch soon starts telling the story of his idyllic marriage to Catherine and the birth and early years of their daughter, Imogen. Then the marriage collapses, daughter and mother abandon him for reasons only hinted at, and Redmond stages a fake suicide, reemerging as Dominic. As he begins stalking his estranged family, he is haunted by the stories of the old musician, who turns out to be a child molester and killer—a fate the new Dominic may be doomed to replicate in his confused and alcoholic state." Libr J

"This is grim stuff, but no grimmer than your average Stephen King novel. Like King, McCabe knows how to invest pop culture with a sinister bathos. . . . McCabe is also more intense than King (or just about anyone else), and his characters are so trapped inside their own skulls that his novels can feel hermetically sealed. In the past, he's balanced that with an appealing dark humor, but in Winterwood he settles for urgent, sustained apprehension." N Y Times Book Rev

McCaffrey, Anne

Acorna; the unicorn girl; [by] Anne McCaffrey and Margaret Ball. HarperPrism 1997 291p o.p.
                              * LC 97-11099

"Found in a survival pod in space by prospectors, the infant Acorna soon exhibits the ability to analyze deficiencies in plants by taste, purify water and air, and heal. Taken to the planet Kezdet to avoid scientists who want to study her, Acorna discovers barbaric child-labor practices and vows to rescue the children. McCaffrey and Ball have created a magical alien in this fantasy/science fiction story." Libr J

Followed by Acorna's quest

Acorna's people; [by] Anne McCaffrey and Elizabeth Ann Scarborough. HarperPrism 1999 314p

ISBN 0-06-105094-6   LC 99-12850

In the third title in the series "Acorna is at last among her own. The beautiful healing horn in the center of her forehead and the 'funny' feet and hands that once set her apart now make her one with the telepathic Linyaari who live on as lush agrarian planet where they pursue their peaceful dreams. Acorna's people welcome her with a lavish costume ball-and an already-chosen mate! But Acorna still has much to do before she can enjoy the peaceful home she is offered. The legendary resting place of the lost *Linyaari* ancestors has yet to be found. With the help of the rogue spacetrader Becker and his cat, RK (RoadKill), Acorna must strive to right an unspeakable wrong and defeat an enemy even more cruel than the Khleevi themselves." Publisher's note

Followed by Acorna's world

Acorna's quest; [by] Anne McCaffrey and Margaret Ball. HarperPrism 1998 292p

ISBN 0-06-105297-3   LC 97-51201

"Acorna has grown into a lovely adolescent humanoid whose physical appearance is reminiscent of the fabled unicorn. Her human protectors plan to help her seek her home world, but she and Calum leave prematurely and follow an unpredictable path on their mission to search the sector of space where her survival pod has launched from. Subsequent events intervene with her quest for home. . . . McCaffrey and Acorna fans will delight in this." Voice Youth Advocates

Acorna's rebels; [by] Anne McCaffrey and Elizabeth Ann Scarborough. Eos 2003 308p $24.95

ISBN 0-380-97899-7   LC 2002-73873

McCaffrey, Anne—*Continued*

In this sixth title in the series "Acorna continues to hunt for her beloved life-mate, Aari. . . . She travels aboard the starship Condor to the planet Makahomia, which she finds in the grip of a plague killing the sacred temple cats. Acorna fights a desperate reaerguard action against the plague with her horn's healing power, but the mystery clearly lies deeper." Publ Wkly Eos 2003 p. cmp

ISBN 0-380-97899-7; 0-380-81847-7 (alk. paper)

LC 2002-73873

Acorna's search; [by] Anne McCaffrey and Elizabeth Ann Scarborough. Eos 2001 292p

ISBN 0-380-97898-9   LC 2001-33562

In this fifth installment in the series "Acorna helps her people, the Linyaari, try to restore their beloved home world, which was literally laid waste by the vicious Khleevi. Aari, the young man so brutally tortured by the Khleevi, is now Acorna's life mate and at work on a survey team trying to locate mountains and rivers in all the rubble." Booklist

Acorna's triumph; [by] Anne McCaffrey and Elizabeth Ann Scarborough. 1st ed. Eos 2004 308p $24.95

ISBN 0-380-97900-4   LC 2003-59622

"The Linyaari home world of Vhiliinyar has been reclaimed, and Acorna, the unicorn-horned girl, has found her life-mate, Aari, who had once suffered at the hands of the Khleevi invaders. However, all is not right, since Aari has changed drastically, and Acorna discovers a new threat of an invasion by the Linyaari's ancient enemies. . . . [The authors] combine their talents in this conclusion to a series about a young woman's growth into maturity and her determined search for her missing people and her vanished mate." Libr J

Acorna's world; [by] Anne McCaffrey and Elizabeth Ann Scarborough. HarperCollins Pubs. 2000 320p

ISBN 0-06-105095-4   LC 00-28830

In the fourth installment in the series Acorna "finds herself unable to adjust to her native culture because of her upbringing by her human 'uncles' and her involvement in so many space adventures. So she ships out with the salvager Becker; his ship's cat, Roadkill; and Aari, a young man of Acorna's race whose torture at the hands of the vicious, buglike aliens, the Khleevi, has left him hornless and vulnerable." Booklist

All the Weyrs of Pern. Ballantine Bks. 1991 404p (Dragonriders of Pern) o.p.

LC 91-91910

"A Del Rey book"

"The dream of generations of Dragonriders draws within reach as, with the aid of an intelligent computer, the possibility of destroying the devastating phenomenon known as 'Thread' becomes a reality." Libr J

"This is an exciting, full-bodied, richly detailed . . . chapter in the Pern chronicle as the knowledge of the first settlers is united with the wisdom of the descendants. . . . Once again McCaffrey's narrative flows smoothly, maintaining the world and characters she has so lovingly created and setting new challenges for them to meet." Booklist

The chronicles of Pern; first fall. Ballantine Bks. 1993 306p o.p.   LC 93-10079

"A Del Rey book"

Includes the following stories: The survey: P.E.R.N.; The dolphins' bell; The ford of Red Hanrahan; The second weyr; Rescue run

"These five original stories . . . offer a glimpse into the early history of the world of 'thread' and Dragonriders. McCaffrey's unadorned prose allows characters and plot to take center stage." Libr J

The city who fought; [by] Anne McCaffrey, S.M. Stirling. Baen Pub. Enterprises 1993 435p

ISBN 0-671-72166-6   LC 93-2651

Previous titles in this series published in paperback are: The ship who sang (1969); Partnership (1992); and The ship who searched (1992)

"Space Station SSS-900C, a profitable but out-of-the-way trading and mining center, is attacked by Kolnari, pirates from a planet of sociopathic exiles. While awaiting the arrival of the Central Worlds' Navy, the inhabitants play for time with a major deception planned by Simeon, the shellperson operating the station." Publ Wkly

"Within the fabric of McCaffrey's universe, she and Stirling merge seamlessly, sporting wit, action galore, superior characterization, and plausible hardware." Booklist

Followed by The ship who won (1994)

Crystal line. Ballantine Bks. 1992 294p o.p.

LC 92-53219

"A Del Rey book"

Sequel to Killashandra

In this conclusion of the trilogy, "crystal singer of the Heptite Guild, Killashandra Ree enjoys the benefits of increased longevity and the status of an elite artisan at a terrible price: the slow erosion of her memory. When the Guild faces a crisis that could result in its demise, Killashandra faces a battle to overcome her own fears and learn to trust in someone other than herself." Libr J

Crystal singer. Ballantine Bks. 1982 311p o.p.

LC 82-4009

"A Del Rey book"

In this first volume of a trilogy "Killashandra Ree learns she has failed her final audition despite ten years of all-consuming preparation for a career as a vocal concert soloist. By coincidence that day she meets a vacationing crystal singer, joins him for the remainder of his holiday and becomes acquainted with the side effects and risks of crystal singing. . . . The story ends as she accomplishes a difficult job, cutting and placing black crystal on four remote planets so they may have instant interstellar communication." SLJ

"This is a well-constructed story with a strong-willed and courageous young heroine who finds her niche in the workplace." Voice Youth Advocates

Followed by Killashandra

Dragonflight; volume 1 of "The Dragonriders of Pern". Ballantine Bks. 1978 337p il (Dragonriders of Pern) hardcover o.p. pa $12.95

ISBN 0-345-27749-X; 0-345-48426-6 (pa)

* LC 78-16707

"A Del Rey book"

First published 1968 in paperback. Based on two award winning stories entitled: Weyr search and

McCaffrey, Anne—*Continued*
Dragonrider

The planet Pern, originally colonized from Earth but long out of contact with it, has been periodically threatened by the deadly silver Threads which fall from the wandering Red Star. To combat them a life form on the planet was developed into winged, fire-breathing dragons. Humans with a high degree of empathy and telepathic power are needed to train and preserve these creatures. As the story begins, Pern has fallen into decay, the threat of the Red Star has been forgotten, the Dragonriders and dragons are reduced in number and in disrepute, and the evil Lord Fax has begun conquering neighboring holds

Dragonquest; volume 2 of "The Dragonriders of Pern". Ballantine Bks. 1979 351p il o.p.
LC 78-19721

"A Del Rey book"
Sequel to Dragonflight
First published 1971 in paperback
The inhabitants of Pern begin to resent the attitudes of the oldtime Dragonriders who were brought forward in time to aid their modern counterparts in defeating the deadly Thread from the Red Star and now feel that their new world owes them a living. The Weyrleader F'lar and his consort Lessa try to mediate between the Dragonriders and the landbound people they had protected, but new forces upset Pern's delicate social structure and threaten to destroy not only the unique privileges of the Dragonriders, but their very reason for existence
Followed by The white dragon

Dragon's Kin; [by] Anne McCaffrey [and] Todd McCaffrey. Del Rey/Ballantine Bks. 2003 304p $24.95

ISBN 0-345-46198-3
The action in this Dragonriders of Pern tale "takes place during an unexplored period in the history of Pern, before the coming of the Thread. The watch-whers are already playing a prominent role, however, keeping watch at night at the holds and weyrs and helping in the mines. The protagonists are Kindin and Nuella, young people living in a mining camp. A cave-in wipes out Kindin's father and brothers as well as the old watch-wher, and Kindin moves in with camp Harper. There he learns the skills of being a Harper, including discretion and mediation. Eventually, he and Nuella learn the secret of how watch-whers see in the dark, and about their communication with dragons, which opens a wholly new range of capabilities for the dragon-riders." Booklist

Dragonsdawn. Ballantine Bks. 1988 431p (Dragonriders of Pern) o.p.
LC 88-9307
"A Del Rey book"
Chronologically the first novel in the Dragonriders of Pern series "it tells of the colonizing of the uninhabited planet Pern by a few thousand carefully selected humans, of the colonists' first encounter with the life-threatening spores known as Thread and of the creation (by genetic engineering) of the winged, telepathic, fire-breathing 'dragons' who become the colonists' first line of defense against the periodic falls of Thread." Booklist

Dragonseye. Ballantine Bks. 1997 353p (Dragonriders of Pern) o.p.
LC 96-44206
"A Del Rey book"
In this title, in the Dragonriders of Pern series "the Dragonriders finally get to protect their world from the danger they've been anticipating for 200 years. When signs appear that Thread, the deadly silver strands that devour everything organic, will soon make an appearance, Dragonrider Chalkin's failure to believe in the danger of Threadfall threatens to destroy the entire civilization." Libr J

The author "brings us another diverse cast of responsible, heroic good guys and dragons in a novel that's going to please fans old and new." Publ Wkly

Freedom's landing. Putnam 1995 342p o.p.
* LC 94-43820

In this first volume of a series "the Catteni, an alien race of slavers, are settling a habitable but dangerous planet with recalcitrant slaves from a variety of races, including the human; all must learn to cooperate with one another to survive. Among the conscripted colonists is an exiled Catteni noble, Zainal, who is resented by some other colonists because he is a member of the overlord race, and Kristin Bjornsen, a spirited young human who finds herself not only working closely with Zainal but drawn to him romantically." Booklist

"With her customary talent for imaginative storytelling, the author skillfully portrays the environmental and personal challenges faced by the new colonists." Libr J
Followed by Freedom's choice (1997) and Freedom's challenge (1998)

Freedom's ransom. Putnam 2002 288p $23.95
ISBN 0-399-14889-2
LC 2001-56669
"An Ace/Putnam book"
Fourth title in the author's Cattani/Freedom series. "In *Freedom's Challenge* (1998), the colonists on the planet Botany, who were initially dropped there as slaves, freed themselves from the Eosi-dominated Cattani overlords. Now it is time to reestablish contact with Earth and 'ransom' Earth's stolen technological materials, which are in warehouses on the Cattani planet Barevi. Zainal and Kris head an expedition to a decimated and devastated part of slowly recovering Earth to trade for items to use in bartering with shifty Barevi merchants." Booklist

"The visit to a bleak Manhattan after the Eosian looting is as disturbing, touching and humorous as the trading in the Barevian market." Publ Wkly

The girl who heard dragons. TOR Bks. 1994 352p il o.p.
LC 94-118
"A Tom Doherty Associates book"
Contents: The girl who heard dragons {novelette}; Velvet fields; Euterpe on a fling; Duty calls; A Sleeping Humpty Dumpty Beauty; The Mandalay cure; A flock of geese; The greatest love {novelette}; A quiet one; If Madam likes you; Zulei, Grace, Nimshi, and the damnyankees; Cinderella switch; Habit is an old horse; Lady-in-waiting; The bones do lie

This is a "diverse assortment of 15 short fiction pieces never before gathered in one volume. The heroine of the engaging title story, a new Pern novella and the only Pern tale in the collection, is somewhat akin to Menolly in *Dragonsong* in that she, too, eventually rises above her birthright to follow the destiny that her particular talent dictates. Perhaps the strongest inclusion here is 'The Greatest Love,' also a novella, which predicted in 1977 (when McCaffrey wrote it) the extrauterine fertilization of a human ovum to produce a healthy baby. . . . Other stories focus on everything from spaceship adventure, shifting time-storms, and the unwitting near-destruction

McCaffrey, Anne—_Continued_

of sentient life-forms by human colonists on a distant planet (and the fitting, if gruesome consequences)—to ghosts and romance." Booklist

The girl who heard dragons [novelette]
  _In_ McCaffrey, A. The girl who heard dragons p21-64

The greatest love [novelette]
  _In_ McCaffrey, A. The girl who heard dragons p169-225

Killashandra. Ballantine Bks. 1985 303p o.p.
LC 85-6193
"A Del Rey book"
In this second volume of the trilogy "crystal singer Killashandra Ree is desperate to get off the crystal-mining planet of Ballybran, so she takes what at first sounds like a routine assignment replacing a shattered crystal in the main Sensory Organ on planet Optheria. While she is there she is also to find out why Optherians never leave the planet. She is kidnapped and marooned on an isolated island, but escapes, only to encounter her handsome kidnapper Lars Dahl, with whom she eventually falls in love." SLJ
"This suspenseful and romantic story exhibits McCaffrey's usual verve in building convincing societies, developing vital characters, and sustaining mood." Booklist
Followed by Crystal line

The Masterharper of Pern. Ballantine Bks. 1998 431p (Dragonriders of Pern)
  ISBN 0-345-38823-2   LC 97-30896
"A Del Rey book"
This installment in the Dragonriders of Pern series "details the life, loves, and heartbreaks of Robinton, Pern's most beloved harper. Readers follow him through a childhood filled with rejection and neglect by his Mastercomposer father, the loss of his wife, the death of his best friend, to his becoming Masterharper of Pern. This is McCaffrey at her best, combining excellent writing with vivid settings and detailed, fully fleshed-out characters." SLJ

Pegasus in space. Ballantine Bks. 2000 373p
  ISBN 0-345-43466-8   LC 99-53225
"A Del Rey book"
"Following _To Ride Pegasus_ (1973) and _Pegasus in Flight_ (1990), this is a third prequel to the Rowan series. . . . Here, the first space station becomes a reality, and quadriplegic teenager Peter Reidinger, whose telekinetic Talent proved amazing in _Pegasus in Flight_, is the protagonist. Peter tests and hones his ability not only to move his body naturally but also to teleport large objects instantaneously through space. Peter helps other Talents, as such gifted youngsters are called, thwart a mutiny aboard the nearly finished space station." Booklist

The renegades of Pern. Ballantine Bks. 1989 384p il (Dragonriders of Pern) o.p.
LC 89-6694
"A Del Rey book"
This tale "begins during the time of _Dragonquest_ and continues beyond the closing of _The White Dragon_, focusing on some of the commoners, and how they cope

with the return of the life-consuming Thread. A number of lives intertwine, such as that of the trader boy Jayge Lilcamp, whose family is almost destroyed when his father refuses to believe the first Thread warning." Publ Wkly

The skies of Pern. Ballantine Pub. Group 2001 434p (Dragonriders of Pern)
  ISBN 0-345-43468-4   LC 00-51859
"A Del Rey book"
A Dragonriders of Pern novel. "With the discovery of Aivas, the artificial intelligence hidden for centuries in Pern's southern continent, the residents of the third planet of the sun called Rukbat have learned how to end the threat posed by the periodic fall of Thread from the erratic red star that orbits the planet. Despite the abundance of rediscovered knowledge, new dangers and old fears surface, forcing Dragonriders, Holders, and Craftmasters all to reconsider their purpose and functions in society." Libr J
"As all her Pern novels amply demonstrate, McCaffrey's sexy and cunning dragons carry the day—and the novel—with impeccable, irresistible panache." Publ Wkly

Wehr search
  _In_ The Hugo winners p329-87

The white dragon; volume 3 of "The Dragonriders of Pern". Ballantine Bks. 1978 497p il o.p.
LC 77-18913
"A Del Rey book"
Sequel to Dragonquest
"A prologue summarizes the first two volumes of the saga. . . . Young Jaxom and his white dragon Ruth (a male), previously encountered, mature, fight the deadly Threads from the Red Planet, help open the largely unexplored continent and discover in an ancient spaceship a map, key to major changes for Pern. Once all the necessary background is assimilated, it's a rousing adventure and colorful portrayal of a unique and carefully-worked-out culture." Publ Wkly

McCaffrey, Todd J.

(jt. auth) McCaffrey, A. Dragon's Kin

McCaig, Donald

Jacob's ladder; a story of Virginia during the war. Norton 1998 525p
  ISBN 0-393-04629-X   LC 97-31165
This historical novel "tells the interlocking story of three families, white and black, masters and slaves. The scion of one slave-owning family, Duncan Gatewood, has an affair with a mulatto slave, Maggie, and when Maggie gives birth to a son, she and the child are sold by Gatewood's angry father. A Gatewood slave, Jesse, is deeply in love with Maggie, and he tries to escape, again and again, to find her and the son he wants to claim for his own. Eventually, he succeeds and enlists in the Union Army and finally confronts his former masters." Libr J
"Delving into letters, diaries and memoirs for period detail, McCaig follows Jesse, Maggie and a large cast of characters through the battlefields, hospitals, prisons and slave wharves of the crumbling Confederacy. Throughout, he binds his narrative with a meticulous respect for authenticity." N Y Times Book Rev

McCall Smith, Alexander, 1948-

Blue shoes and happiness. Pantheon Books 2006
227p $21.95

ISBN 0-375-42272-2   LC 2005-52122

In this installment "Botswana detective Precious
Ramotswe faces one of her toughest challenges: losing
weight. Luckily, there are plenty of dilemmas to keep her
mind off her girth: a nearby village that seems under the
influence of witchcraft, a cook suspected of filching food
for her increasingly portly spouse, and a newspaper advice columnist who's doing more damage than good.
Readers become better acquainted with assistant detective
Mma Grace Makutsi, best known for earning a stellar 97
percent grade at the Botswana Secretarial College. . . .
McCall Smith renders brisk, seamless tales that are both
wry and profound. Amidst the mayhem (like the cobra
that slithers its way into the detective agency's headquarters) are eloquent descriptions of the serene African
country that holds a special place in his heart." Booklist

The comforts of a muddy Saturday. Pantheon
Books 2008 240p $23.95

ISBN 978-0-375-42513-4; 0-375-42513-6

        LC 2008-18573

Philosophical sleuth Isabel Dalhousie, "who's recently
assumed ownership of the obscure journal she's edited
for many years, the Review of Applied Ethics, applies
her deductive gifts to the case of a disgraced doctor.
When a patient dies after taking a new antibiotic that
Marcus Moncrieff deemed safe in clinical trials, the doctor's original report turns out to contain falsified data.
Did Moncrieff skew the data to please the drug manufac-
turers? Moncrieff's wife turns to Isabel for help in lifting
her husband out of his despondency. While the truth isn't
straightforward, the motives of the guilty party prove to
be both plausible and rational. The strengths of the book
. . . lie in its protagonist's determination to treat others
without judgment—and in the author's revealing
glimpses into the human soul." Publ Wkly

The good husband of Zebra Drive. Pantheon
Books 2007 213p (No. 1 Ladies Detective
Agency) $21.95

ISBN 978-0-375-42273-7; 0-375-42273-0

        LC 2006-39047

In this mystery, set in Botswana, "Dr. Cronje, who's
half Xhosa and half Afrikaner, consults . . . Precious
Ramotswe, because patients at his hospital who have occupied a particular bed have been dying mysteriously at
the same time of day. Meanwhile, Mma Ramotswe's recently engaged assistant, Grace Makutsi, threatens to
break their longstanding association. Mma Ramotswe
must adjust their relationship in order to retain Mma
Makutsi's services. The author's subtlety of touch and
humane portrayal of figures at all levels of society will
continue to win him new readers even as his deepening
of the ties binding the main figures will satisfy those
who have followed the lady detectives from their first recorded case." Publ Wkly

In the company of cheerful ladies. Pantheon
Books 2005 233p $19.95

ISBN 0-375-42271-4

        * LC 2004-56827

In this installment, "Botswana detective Precious
Ramotswe, the traditionally built-and newly married-
owner of the No. 1 Ladies' Detective Agency, is saddled
with a surfeit of challenging cases and personal crises.
There has been an intruder in her home (he managed to
escape, but left a telltale pair of trousers in his wake).
And the levelheaded sleuth is flustered by an encounter
with a man from her past. Meanwhile, Mma Ramotswe's
husband, master mechanic Mr. J.L.B. Matekoni, is neck-
deep in work after the resignation of one of his apprentices, who has become romantically entangled with a
married woman (Mma Ramotswe and assistant detective
Grace Makutsi slyly gather the scurrilous details). . . .
[The author] renders colorful characters with names that
trip off the tongue." Publ Wkly

The lost art of gratitude. Pantheon Books 2009
262p $23.95

ISBN 978-0-375-42514-1; 0-375-42514-4

        LC 2009-22618

A mystery featuring Scottish philosopher Isabel
Dalhousie. "Minty Auchterlonie, who once alerted Isabel
to some insider trading, fears someone is out to get her.
The tax authorities have suddenly investigated Minty,
and an unknown party has sent her a funeral wreath.
When Isabel looks into these provocative acts, she draws
on lessons learned from the journal she edits, the Review
of Applied Ethics, to arrive at the complex truth behind
them. Meanwhile, the father of Isabel's young son proposes marriage, and a defeated academic rival accuses
her of knowingly publishing plagiarism. Smith's trademark humor and telling observations about people
heighten the appeal." Publ Wkly

Love over Scotland. Anchor Books 2007 357p
pa $13.95

ISBN 978-0-307-27598-1   LC 2007-22072

First published 2006 in the United Kingdom; originally
serialized in The Scotsman

In this installment "anthropologist Domenica has flown
off to the Straits of Malacca to study modern-day pirates.
Back in Edinburgh, Pat moves from 44 Scotland Street
and develops a crush on fellow art student Wolf, whose
strange ways hint at a darker subplot that involves Pat's
flatmate. Pat moves in with gallery owner Matthew, who
struggles with both a sudden fortune and a yearning for
Pat. Meanwhile, child prodigy saxophonist Bertie becomes a reluctant member of the Edinburgh Teenage Orchestra at age six and later, on a trip to Paris, finds himself wonderfully unsupervised. Poet/portrait painter Angus is tormented by the theft of his beloved dog Cyrus.
The proceedings sparkle with McCall Smith's trademark
wit (It was not always fun being a child, just as it had
not always been fun being a medieval Scottish saint),
proving once again, he's a true treasure. Illustrations by
Iain McIntosh enliven the text." Publ Wkly

The world according to Bertie. Anchor Books
2008 c2007 343p il pa $13.95

ISBN 978-0-307-38706-6; 0-307-38706-2

        LC 2008-28140

First published 2007 in the United Kingdom

The newest resident of 44 Scotland Street "is 20-year-
old Pat, who rents a room from the slightly older and irresistibly handsome Bruce. Pat's eccentric neighbors include Dominica, an artsy and wise widow; Bertie, a five-
year-old saxophone player; and Bertie's overbearing

McCall Smith, Alexander, 1948——*Continued*
mother, Irene. In order to make ends meet, Pat takes a
job as a receptionist at a nearby art gallery. Her boss is
the ineffectual Matthew, whose father owns the gallery.
When Pat gets a hunch that one of the gallery's paintings
might be valuable, and then the piece of work goes missing, the action takes off." Libr J

"It is clear even to an outsider that someone who
knows Edinburgh would recognize many people and
places in '44 Scotland Street.' But an outsider can still
relish McCall Smith's depiction of this place 'of angled
streets and northern light,' and enjoy his tolerant, good-
humored company." N Y Times Book Rev

McCall Smith, R. A. *See* McCall Smith, Alexander, 1948-

McCammon, Robert R.

Boy's life. Pocket Bks. 1991 440p o.p.
* LC 91-2813
"In 1964, 12-year-old Cory Mackenson lives with his
parents in Zephyr, Alabama. It is a sleepy, comfortable
town. Cory is helping with his father's milk route one
morning when a car plunges into the lake before their
eyes. His father dives in after the car and finds a dead
man handcuffed to the steering wheel. Their world no
longer seems so innocent: a vicious killer hides among
apparently friendly neighbors." Libr J

"McCammon is both a precise and lush writer, and
thus the trail Cory takes to deciphering the puzzle the
dead man represents quickly firms up into a compelling,
even haunting yarn of adult demons being faced and
fathomed by the young. This look at life's blacker sides
is neither cloying nor jejune." Booklist

Gone south. Pocket Bks. 1992 359p
ISBN 0-671-74306-6   LC 92-28062
"Dan, dogged by depression and Agent Orange-
induced leukemia, has accidentally killed a man. On the
run, he meets Arden, a disfigured woman abandoned at
a truck stop. He reluctantly agrees to help her on her
journey to the Louisiana swamps where, she believes, the
legendary Bright Girl will heal her. Meanwhile, an unlikely pair of bounty hunters is on Dan's trail: Flint began life as a carnival freak, with his Siamese twin's tiny
arm and half-formed face protuding from his chest; he is
saddled with training Cecil, a self-deprecating and pathetically friendly Elvis impersonator. These four misfits collide and, finally, arrive where the Bright Girl may actually live." Libr J

"The plot flows well and quickly. The extreme characters only point up McCammon's theme: everybody has
a hidden deformity and can only become free and happy
by facing it. An engrossing read." Booklist

The Queen of Bedlam; [by] Robert McCammon.
Pocket Books 2007 645p pa $16
ISBN 978-1-416-55111-9; 1-416-55111-5
"Set in Manhattan in 1703, this . . . sequel to Speaks
the Nightbird (2002) . . . finds Matthew Corbett, a 23-
year-old magistrate's clerk, on the trail of the Masker, a
killer who stalks prominent businessmen. Matthew stumbles on the bodies of two of the Masker's victims, including pederast Eben Ausley, the headmaster of the orphanage Matthew once reluctantly called home. Plucky

Matthew, who becomes a junior associate of the New
York branch of a London problem-solving firm called
the Herrald Agency, discovers a possible link to the
crimes in the person of an elderly amnesiac patient in a
mental asylum who's known as the Queen of Bedlam.
Matthew and his cohorts later make a dangerous foray to
the headquarters that the villainous Professor Fell maintains for young-criminals-in-training. McCammon brilliantly captures colonial New York and closes with a tantalizing cliffhanger that suggests more exciting sleuthing
to come." Publ Wkly

McCann, Colum, 1965-

Dancer; a novel. Metropolitan Bks. 2003 336p
$26
ISBN 0-8050-6792-2   LC 2002-71879
"A fictionalized account of the life of Rudolph Nureyev—the Cold War danseur noble lauded as the world's
first 'pop star dancer'—as told by those who knew him.
Among the narrators are the irrepressible Yulia, the
daughter of Nureyev's first ballet teacher, Margot Fon-
teyn, Rudik's brilliant dance partner; Victor, a gay hustler from the Lower East Side with a penchant for blow;
bath houses, and back talk; and others." Libr J

"It's hard to tell what a reader unfamiliar with the outlines of Nureyev's life might make of 'Dancer.' Much,
deliberately, is left unsaid. Reduced to words, the dance
evaporates—only passion and the personal can make it
move again." N Y Times Book Rev

Let the great world spin; a novel. Random
House 2009 349p $25
ISBN 978-1-4000-6373-4; 1-4000-6373-6
                                            LC 2008-46963
This "begins on August 7, 1974, when New Yorkers
are stopped in their tracks by the sight of a man walking
between the towers of the World Trade Center. Yes, it's
Philippe Petit, the subject of the Academy Award–
winning documentary Man on Wire and one of
McCann's many intense and valiant characters. The cast
also includes two Irish brothers: Corrigan, a radical
monk, and Ciaran, who follows him to the blasted
Bronx, where he encounters resilient prostitute Tillie and
her spirited daughter Jazzlyn. Gloria lives in the same
housing project, and she befriends Claire of Park Avenue
as they mourn the deaths of their sons in Vietnam.
McCann's hallucinatory descriptions of a great city tattooed and besmirched with graffiti, blood, and drugs in
the midst of a financial freefall are eerie in their edgy
beauty, chilling reminders of how quickly civilization unravels. Here, too, are portals onto war, the justice system,
and the dawning of the cyber age." Booklist

Zoli; a novel. Random House 2007 c2006 333p
$24.95
ISBN 978-1-4000-6372-7; 1-400-06372-8
                                            LC 2006-42922
First published 2006 in the United Kingdom
This novel is "loosely based on the Romany poet
Papusza. . . . Zoli, a Communist, is first betrayed by the
Party—which, after initially exalting the Gypsies, burned
their wagons and forced them into housing projects—and
then cast out by her own people for allowing the gadze
to publish her work. In a frenzy of remorse, she attempts
to destroy her poems and outrun her past." New Yorker

"Zoli becomes a flash point for her tribe while raising

McCann, Colum, 1965-—*Continued*

an important question: In a world driven by conformity and (more lately) consumerism, how can the outsider survive? . . . . McCann's story feels like an important reminder of one dimension that has gladly been left behind: the soul-deadening totalitarianism that snuffs out dissent and difference with the force of its bureaucracy." Seattle Times

McCarry, Charles

Old boys. Overlook Press 2004 476p $25.95
ISBN 1-58567-545-8

* LC 2004-48320

"When Paul Christopher, the enigmatic hero of several earlier McCarry novels, disappears while on a quest for his nonagenarian mother, Lori, his black-sheep cousin, Horace Hubbard, convenes a discreet cadre of over-the-hill spies to find their confrere-and to save the world from Ib'n Awad, an aging Islamic terrorist in possession of 12 nuclear suitcase bombs. In a beguiling twist . . . ., all parties also seek a fabled ancient scroll that unmasks Jesus as an agent provocateur, handled by Judas for Roman spymaster Paul. The nonstop peregrinations of this league of extraordinary spooks take them to a score of exotic locales, pitting them against Chechen thugs, Chinese secret police, Nazi doctors, and a case of acute myocardial fibrillation. McCarry's commitment to this fanciful premise is absolute, and the resulting yarn combines the intrepid exploits of John Buchan, the cagey intrigue of Eric Ambler, and the clipped cadences of Dashiell Hammett. Tremendous fun." Booklist

McCarthy, Cormac, 1933-

All the pretty horses. Knopf 1992 301p $27.50; pa $14.95
ISBN 0-394-57474-5; 0-679-74439-8 (pa)

* LC 91-58560

In the spring of 1950, after the death of his grandfather, sixteen-year-old John Grady Cole "is evicted from the Texas ranch where he grew up. He and another boy Lacey Rawlins, head for Mexico on horseback, riding south until they finally turn up at a vast ranch in mountainous Coahuila, the Hacienda de la Purisima, where they sign on as vaqueros. . . . John Grady's unusual talent for breaking, training and understanding horses becomes crucial to the hacendado Don Hector's ambitious breeding program. For John Grady, La Purisima is a paradise, complete with its Eve, Don Hector's daughter, Alejandra." N Y Times Book Rev

"Though some readers may grow impatient with the wild prairie rhythms of McCarthy's language, others will find his voice completely transporting." Publ Wkly

Blood meridian; or, The evening redness in the West. Random House 1985 337p
ISBN 0-394-40027-5

*

"This book is set in the south-west borderland between the United States and Mexico, and follows the experiences of the (unnamed) kid, as he gets involved with a gang of mercenaries called the Glantons, and meets one of the most menacing figures in modern literature, Judge Holden, a huge, pale, manic individual who seems to know every aspect of human culture and to conduct a single-handed and satanic campaign to destroy it all. This is a savage book, full of rape and pillage, with more scalpings described in more detail–the Indians are just as savage as the whites–than (surely) in any other book. It is also beautifully written, a great poetic exploration of nature and the myth of the West." Good Fiction Guide

Cities of the plain. Knopf 1998 291p $27.50
ISBN 0-679-42390-7   LC 98-11583

The final volume of the Border trilogy finds John Grady and Billy Parkam working on a New Mexico cattle ranch in the early 1950s. John Grady "falls in love with an epileptic teenage prostitute across the border in Juarez and vows to rescue her, whatever the cost." Libr J

"McCarthy's language carries a brooding, evolutionary sense of time and labor—in his hands the changing of a tire on an old truck becomes a mythic deed. The weight of history rests on the shoulders of John Grady, too, and he's doomed to learn that 'when things are gone they're gone. They aint comin back.'" New Yorker

The crossing. Knopf 1994 425p
ISBN 0-394-57475-3   LC 94-4281

This second novel in McCarthy's "Border Trilogy" is the story of "Billy Parham, 16, and his kid brother, Boyd, growing up . . . on a high desert ranch in southern New Mexico. A vagabond Indian appears who warns the boys of dire events, and then a she-wolf begins pulling down the Parham cattle. Billy ingeniously traps the wolf but cannot bring himself to kill her; almost on a whim, he crosses the border to return her to the distant mountains she came from. When he comes home after months of wandering in the desert, he finds that his parents have been killed by Mexican horse thieves. He and Boyd go after their family's remuda. . . . Boyd is killed, and Billy returns to the U.S., a rootless, restless young man with an uncertain future." Booklist

The author "is a great and inventive storyteller, and he writes brilliantly and knowledgeably about animals and landscapes—but . . . the power and delight of the book derive from the fact that he seems incapable of writing a boring sentence. Reading him, one is very much in the hands of a stylist. . . . The style comes from Joyce and Hemingway out of Gertrude Stein. It is a matter of straight-on writing, a veering accumulation of compound sentences, stinginess with commas and a witching repetition of words." N Y Times Book Rev

No country for old men. Knopf 2005 309p $24.95
ISBN 0-37540-677-8

"Llewelyn Moss, hunting antelope near the Rio Grande, instead finds men shot dead, a load of heroin, and more than $2 million in cash. Packing the money out, he knows, will change everything. But only after two more men are murdered does a victim's burning car lead Sheriff Bell to the carnage out in the desert, and he soon realizes how desperately Moss and his young wife need protection. One party in the failed transaction hires an ex-Special Forces officer to defend his interests against a mesmerizing freelancer, while on either side are men accustomed to spectacular violence and mayhem." Publisher's note

"As devised and refined by James M. Cain, Jim Thompson and their gloomy paperback peers, the crime novel aimed its cheap handgun at the heart of America's most prized beliefs about its destiny: that the loot we've

McCarthy, Cormac, 1933-—*Continued*

scooped up will belong to us forever and that history allows clean getaways. Cormac McCarthy's 'No Country for Old Men' is as bracing a variation on these noir orthodoxies as any fan of the genre could expect." N Y Times Book Rev

The road. Knopf 2006 241p $24
ISBN 978-0-307-26543-2; 0-307-26543-9
LC 2006-23629

In this novel McCarthy "exchanges the bleak Western setting of previous works for an even bleaker post-apocalyptic one. As usual, lawless space engenders violence, but here a nuclear holocaust has reduced everything to ash, mummifying all but a few unlucky souls, who must kill or be killed (and eaten). The main characters are a father and his son, who was born a few nights after the bombs fell. 'We're still the good guys,' the man repeatedly assures the boy as they scavenge their way south for the winter, trying to avoid 'bad guy' survival techniques. Even by McCarthy's standards, the horrors here—an infant 'headless and gutted and blackening on the spit'—are extreme, and, deprived of historical context, his brutality can seem willful. But McCarthy's prose retains its ability to seduce—the deathscape is 'like the onset of some cold glaucoma dimming away the world'—and there are nods to the gentler aspects of the human spirit." New Yorker

McCarthy, Mary, 1912-1989

Birds of America. Harcourt Brace Jovanovich 1971 344p o.p.

*

The main character is "Peter Levi, a young American who spends his junior year at the Sorbonne at the time of the bombing of Hanoi and who is much preoccupied with Kant's categorical imperative and the Destruction of Art and the Death of Nature. The Death of Nature, in fact, is the central theme. . . . The final scene, in which Peter develops a near-fatal infection after a swan attack and is visited by Kant in a vision, powerfully resolves the author's theme." Libr J

"Miss McCarthy is astringent and sharp in all the right places, gentle where she should be. What she has written is an honest and appropriate love letter to an essentially decent young American." Publ Wkly

A charmed life. Harcourt Brace & Co. 1955 313p o.p.

"John and Martha Sinnott encounter an amazing assortment of would-be bohemians when, in the hope of gaining a new lease on their marriage, they move to the artistic community of New Leeds. They long for privacy but cocktail parties, drama groups, and Martha's first husband Miles keep breaking in. Even Martha's pregnancy brings unforeseen problems for due to one after-the-party interlude the question of fatherhood broadens to two possibilities: John or Miles. The author is at her brilliant best in this comic tragedy of modern man's dilemma: the fluctuation between belief and unbelief, courage and despair." Booklist

The group. Harcourt Brace & Co. 1963 378p o.p.

*

The Group is made of "eight Vassar girls of the class of '33 who had lived together during their upperclass years, in the South Tower of Main. We see them first at the wedding of Kay Strong to Harald Petersen a week after Commencement. . . . We see them last at Kay's funeral seven years later." N Y Times Book Rev

"It is perhaps as social history that the novel will chiefly be remembered; but over and above its sensitive observations it has a quality that one has not come to expect from this particular author, and that is compassion." Saturday Rev

The groves of Academe. Harcourt Brace & Co. 1952 302p o.p.

"An intelligent and satirical dissection of faculty life at Jocelyn, a small progressive college in Pennsylvania. The impending dismissal of self-styled liberal, Henry Mulcahy, Joycean scholar and instructor in literature, and the spring Poetry Conference are the main incidents in the narrative; but woven around them and even tying them together quite neatly is the probing, satirical and often deadly accurate account of college administration and personalities. A few of America's leading poets seem to appear pseudonymously during the conference." Libr J

McCarthy, Tom, 1969-

Remainder. Vintage Books 2007 308p pa $13.95
ISBN 978-0-307-27835-7; 0-307-27835-2
LC 2006-50565

First published 2005 in France

The nameless narrator is a "Londoner severely injured in an accident. Months later, he received an £8.5 million settlement on the condition that he never speak about the payout or the incident again—not a problem, since he doesn't remember it. Our hero then begins to wholly recreate and reenact portions of his old life with a salaried cast of extras, set designers, and stuntmen." Entertainment Wkly

"In a very subtle way, McCarthy is saying something about our attitude toward pleasure. Fleeting moments no longer count; we require the best all the time. Then we discover the pursuit of this goal turns fetishistic." Cleveland Plain Dealer

McCauley, Stephen

Alternatives to sex. Simon & Schuster 2006 289p $24
ISBN 978-0-7432-2473-4; 0-7432-2473-6
LC 2005-54121

This "novel lays bare the inner life and obsessive-compulsive behavior of William Collins, a gay 40-something Boston realtor who struggles to give up trolling the Internet for impersonal sexual liaisons. Taking stock of the year following 9/11, William attributes his promiscuity to 'posttraumatic self-indulgence' and unsuccessfully attempts to trade one addiction for another: cleaning house (not always his own). When affluent straight couple Charlotte O'Malley and Samuel Thompson arrive at his office, prowling for a new home, William hopes he can close the sale and wonders if he can

McCauley, Stephen—*Continued*

look to their marriage as inspiration for a long-term relationship. While McCauley entertains with a motley group of supporting characters, the novel pivots on William's close friendship with Edward, a flight attendant." Publ Wkly

"With his self-effacing wit and disarming compassion for even the most unlikely characters, McCauley proves once again that he's a master of the modern comedy of manners." USA Today

True enough. Simon & Schuster 2001 314p $24

ISBN 0-684-81054-9   LC 00-66177

"Jane Cody, producer of public TV shows of questionable merit in Boston, and Desmond Sullivan, gay New Yorker and biographer of mediocre artists, meet during Desmond's time in Boston as a visiting professor. Jane's new project, a series of televised biographies of the unfamous, may be just the spur he needs to finish his second book about a long-forgotten singer." Booklist

McCauley is "uncannily good at illuminating character through speech. . . . [He] wants nothing more than to entertain us, and if that's become an old-fashioned thing to do, it may be because few writers do it so well." N Y Times Book Rev

McClure, James, 1939-

The steam pig. Harper & Row 1972 c1971 247p o.p.

"A Joan Kahn-Harper novel of suspense"

First published 1971 in the United Kingdom

White Lieutenant Kramer and his Zulu sergeant Zondi investigate the grisly murder of a beautiful white girl in a small South African town

"An absolutely scathing look at contemporary South Africa is provided in [this] . . . novel that is uncanny in its multi-leveled perceptions. It is a grotesquely vivid picture of life under apartheid. But it is also a first-rate mystery with a solution that is a shocker." Saturday Rev

McConchie, Lyn

(jt. auth) Norton, A. Beast Master's ark

McCorkle, Jill, 1958-

Carolina moon; a novel. Algonquin Bks. 1996 260p $18.95

ISBN 1-56512-136-8   LC 96-16115

This novel is "set in the small town of Fulton, North Carolina, and revolves around big-hearted Quee Purdy. Quee is a sixtysomething entrepreneur who has just opened a no-smoking clinic . . . where smokers are loved and pampered right out of their addiction. Her clinic serves as the hub for many charming if wayward folks, including therapist Denny Parks, on the run from a bad marriage and a bad case of nerves, and handyman Tom Lowe, who daily paces off the boundaries of his sunken, underwater property, the sum total of his inheritance from his father." Booklist

"We sense that the author, like a modern-day phrenologist, has her hands on the head of Fulton to study its psychological profile. Seemingly plotless, the novel's final revelation shows how much of a craftswoman McCorkle really is." America

Ferris Beach; a novel. Algonquin Bks. 1990 343p

ISBN 0-945575-39-4

* LC 90-37089

The protagonist and narrator, Katie Burns, tells of growing up in a small town in the South during the 1960s and '70s. "Ferris Beach is where excitement and glamour start—at least that's what Kate thinks as she hears about her cousin Angela who lives there. Kate has had a humdrum, 'normal' childhood; her conservative mother and humorous father have brought her up 'properly,' while Angela has had freedom and romance. But even freedom has its dark side, as Kate finds out." SLJ

"The central metaphor is the place that gives the novel its name—a place associated with ideas of sex, freedom, and broken dreams. . . . Here, Katie will get a powerful dose of reality and suffering rendered so wistfully and obliquely, with multiple forewarnings designed to heighten the sense of foreboding, and a commendable balance of tragedy and mirth, that the full texture of a child's wonder and terror is preserved." Booklist

McCoy, Horace, 1897-1955

They shoot horses, don't they?

In Crime novels: American noir of the 1930s and 40s

McCracken, Elizabeth

The giant's house; a romance. Dial Press (NY) 1996 259p

ISBN 0-385-31433-7

* LC 95-52433

"The story begins in a small Cape Cod town in 1950, when a 6-foot-2-inch 11-year-old boy walks up to the 25-year-old librarian's desk, looking for books about magic. James Carlson Sweatt . . . quickly enchants the misanthropic Miss Cort. By the time of his death nine years later, the young giant (now 8 feet 7 inches and 415 pounds) has transformed the heart of the lonely spinster from a tabula rasa into a fully annotated book of love." N Y Times Book Rev

"The reader is mesmerized by this low-key narrative, first lured by Peggy's alternately acerbic and tender voice, then captivated by James's situation and intrigued by his family, later engulfed by pathos as James's body begins to fail and, finally, amazed by a turn of events that ends the novel with a major surprise. McCracken also invests the narrative with humor, sometimes through Peggy's astringent comments and more often through the use of minor characters who add vivid color and their own distinctive voices." Publ Wkly

Niagara Falls all over again. Dial Press (NY) 2001 308p

ISBN 0-385-31837-5   LC 2001-28314

This novel chronicles the ups and downs in the relationship between two vaudeville entertainers. It is narrated by an aging Moses Sharensky, who as Mose Sharp was the straight man to his more exuberant partner Rocky Carter

"McCracken understands the ambiguous relationship between comedy and tragedy as well as she understands the relationship between these two funny men. Even a fictional celebrity memoir risks being maudlin, but

McCracken, Elizabeth—*Continued*

McCracken knows when to pull back. . . . {She} has a wonderful ear for the way a line or a friendship breaks." Christ Sci Monit

McCrumb, Sharyn

The ballad of Frankie Silver. Dutton 1998 386p
ISBN 0-525-93969-5

* LC 97-24867

A mystery "set in the Appalachians. Sheriff Spencer Arrowood has been summoned to the execution of Fate Harkryder, a man Arrowood put in jail 20 years earlier for the brutal murder of two hikers. While reading over his notes of the case, Arrowood is drawn into researching the story of Frankie Silver, who in 1833 became the first woman to be hung in the state of Tennessee." Libr J

"By working in two time frames and alternating the narrative voice, McCrumb threads both stories into a single pattern, a dense and lovely but very dark design that illustrates the social hypocrisy of the legal system as much as the harshness of mountain justice—then and now." N Y Times Book Rev

Foggy Mountain breakdown and other stories. Ballantine Bks. 1997 326p
ISBN 0-345-41493-4   LC 97-18787

Contents: Precious jewel; Telling the bees; Love on first bounce; John Knox in paradise; Southern comfort; A snare as old as Solomon; The witness; Not all brides are beautiful; A shade of difference; A wee doch and doris; Remains to be seen; The luncheon; A predatory woman; Happiness is a dead poet; Nine lives to live; Gentle reader; The monster of Glamis; The matchmaker; Old rattler; Among my souvenirs; Typewriter man; Gerda's sense of snow; An autumn migration; Foggy Mountain breakdown

The author "has an uncanny knack for picking up the subtle nuances of dialogue, place, and personality that make her characters and settings sparkle with life. She can perfectly mimic the hillbilly twang of an Appalachian healer or the dulcet, pearshaped tones of an upperclass Briton; she can create the excitement of teenagers in lust, mirror the evil that lurks in a serial killer's heart, or convey the quiet desperation of a woman trapped in a miserable marriage. But most of all, McCrumb can make her readers believe what she writes." Booklist

The hangman's beautiful daughter. Scribner 1992 306p
ISBN 0-684-19407-4   LC 91-46057

"Revisiting some of the characters from *If Ever I Return, Pretty Peggy-O* . . . McCrumb weaves Appalachian folklore and death, in natural and unnatural forms, into a story that meanders like a mountain stream through the hills of east Tennessee. . . . Wake County Sheriff Spencer Arrowood asks Laura Bruce, wife of the local Baptist minister, who is now an Army chaplain stationed overseas, to comfort the bereaved at the scene of a bloody murder. Ret. Maj. Paul Underhill, his wife and two of his four children are dead, shot apparently by one of the sons, who took his own life after killing the others. Laura serves as advocate for the surviving children. . . . But when deputy Joe LeDonne discovers that the two have disinterred their father's body from its grave, he wants to know what really happened on the night of the shooting." Publ Wkly

If ever I return, pretty Peggy-O. Scribner 1990 312p
ISBN 0-684-19104-0

* LC 89-24337

"Two events cause palpitations for the gentle folk of Hamelin, Tennessee. A high school reunion is planned, fanning old jealousies, and Peggy Muryan, a famous 1960s folkie—whose one-time lover and singing partner was reported MIA 20 years before—arrives in town, fixing to stay. Soon threatening letters begin arriving, animals are ritualistically slaughtered, and a local girl bearing a striking similarity to the younger Peggy is pulled from a nearby river. Local policeman Spencer Arrowood must find the killer, deal with the upcoming reunion, and grapple with the volatile collapse of his marriage." Booklist

The author's "strongly individualized characters give serious and intelligent thought to the ghosts raised by the reunion—including the tangible spector of a murderer." N Y Times Book Rev

If I'd killed him when I met him; an Elizabeth MacPherson novel. Ballantine Bks. 1995 277p o.p.
LC 94-23701

"Elizabeth MacPherson, Southern sleuth and forensic anthropologist, investigates a pair of murders for her brother's Virginia law firm." Libr J

"Buoyed by intriguing characters, a wry—sometimes macabre—wit, and lush Virginia atmosphere, McCrumb's mystery spins merrily along on its own momentum, concluding that justice will triumph . . . but in surprising ways." Publ Wkly

MacPherson's lament; an Elizabeth MacPherson mystery. Ballantine Bks. 1992 260p o.p.
LC 92-52661

In this mystery Elizabeth MacPherson's "brother, Bill, a new lawyer, sets up shop in Danville, Va., with Amy Powell (A.P.) Hill, descendant of the southern general known by the same initials. The firm's first few cases aren't auspicious. . . . The pace picks up when the body of a young woman is found in the trunk of A.P.'s client's car and a wealthy businessman from New York wants to buy the house very quickly. Elizabeth, who has been represented in letters sent from Scotland, finally flies home to help the fledgling attorneys. Interspersed is the tale of Civil War soldier Gabriel Hawks, who with a friend confiscates a part of the Confederate treasury." Publ Wkly

A "witty story that will beguile both mystery buffs and Civil War enthusiasts." Booklist

Missing Susan; an Elizabeth MacPherson mystery. Ballantine Bks. 1991 295p o.p.
LC 91-91887

Elizabeth MacPherson, "an American forensic anthropologist with an interest in historical true-crime cases, takes a busman's holiday: an organized tour of England's most notorious murder sites. Looking forward to a little shoptalk . . . the quick-witted heroine is disappointed to find the obnoxiously eccentric tour guide, Rowan Rover, so guarded and, well, so very nervous about having a chat. Elizabeth attributes Rover's manner to 'a natural shyness on his part,' not knowing that, on an earlier tour of Jack the Ripper's killing ground, the financially strapped guide accepted a murder commission from an American tourist." N Y Times Book Rev

McCrumb, Sharyn—*Continued*

The author "spins the British cozy formula on its ear, slipping in the expected sly one-liner or two and driving her plot so far up a narrative one-way street that only a writer with her nerve and ever-ready wit would have a snowball's chance in hell of pulling the whole tricky caper off." Booklist

The rosewood casket. Dutton 1996 303p
ISBN 0-525-94011-1   LC 96-11135
"Old man Stargill is dying, and his four grown sons are called home to the small mountain town where they grew up to say good-bye and carry out their daddy's dying wish: that his 'boys' build him a rosewood casket. But a dying man's wishes aren't the only problems the splintered Stargills are forced to face." Booklist

"Ms. McCrumb spins out the Stargill family secret in the hypnotic tones of a storyteller who knows she has a warming fire at her back and rapt listeners at her feet. Longstanding conflicts and quarrels within this ornery clan give substance to the characters; and some anxiety, if not suspense, is built up when a predatory real estate speculator starts sniffing around the farm. But the author reserves her most persuasive voice for the old stories that she digs out of these ancient hills." N Y Times Book Rev

She walks these hills. Scribner 1994 336p
ISBN 0-684-19556-9   LC 94-9458
"In 1779, Katie Wyler, 18, was captured by the Shawnee in North Carolina. The story of her escape and arduous journey home through hundreds of miles of Appalachian wilderness is the topic of ethno-historian Jeremy Cobb's thesis. . . . As Cobb begins to retrace Katie's return journey, 63-year-old convicted murderer Hiram (Harm) Sorley escapes from a nearby prison. Suffering from Korsakoff's syndrome, he has no recent memory. . . . Hamelin, Tenn., police dispatcher Martha Ayers uses the opportunity to convince the sheriff to assign her as a deputy. . . . Deftly building suspense, McCrumb weaves these colorful elements into her satisfying conclusion." Publ Wkly

The songcatcher; a ballad novel. Dutton 2001 321p
ISBN 0-525-94488-5   LC 00-50831
"McCrumb follows a single ballad through seven generations of the McCourry family, beginning with Malcolm McCourry, kidnapped as a child from the Scottish Isle of Islay in 1751 and brought to the American frontier. The 'songcatcher' is Lark McCourry, a contemporary country-western singer, haunted by her memory of fragments of this ballad from her childhood. Past collides with present when Lark is called home to care for her dying father, from whom she has long been estranged. . . . Investing surprising suspense into Lark's search for the words to the ballad and for the tune of her own life, McCrumb gives the reader intriguing characters, great insight into the landscape and folkways of the South, and rich bits of comedy." Booklist

St. Dale. Kensington 2004 311p $25
ISBN 0-7582-0776-X
"A group of stock car racing fans embarks on a bus tour of Southern speedways—seven states in eight days—as a tribute to legendary NASCAR champion Dale Earnhardt in this meandering road novel modeled after the Canterbury Tales. Harley Claymore, a down-and-out race car driver who yearns to be reinstated, is a tour guide with an encyclopedic knowledge of spectacular races and risk-loving drivers. His 'Where are you folks from?' introduces a diverse group of tour participants: Karen and Shane plan to be married at the first stop, where the bride's Wiccan mother will be waiting, and the groom will try to come to terms with his grief over the death of his hero, Dale, in the 2001 Daytona 500; longtime fan Jim, married 47 years to Arlene, hopes her incipient Alzheimer's won't spoil their enjoyment of the tour; Bill Knight, an Episcopalian priest in smalltown Canterbury, N.H., is chaperone for a dying orphan who was selected for a Last Wish trip; Nebraska resident Ray has proudly plowed his alfalfa field with a giant three (Dale's racing number). Veteran McCrumb provides a lively illustration of the cult of celebrity and offers instructive speculation about the human need for heroes." Publ Wkly

The Windsor knot; an Elizabeth MacPherson mystery. Ballantine Bks. 1990 281p o.p.
            LC 90-34168
"Back in Chandler Grove for her nuptials, forensic anthropologist Elizabeth MacPherson finds herself involved in a local police investigation when she is called upon to identify some cremated remains." Booklist

"Elizabeth is less centrally involved in the crime and detection than usual, but this doesn't diminish the appeal of McCrumb's sparkling spoof." Publ Wkly

McCullers, Carson, 1917-1967

The ballad of the sad café [novelette]
 In McCullers, C. Collected stories p195-253
 In McCullers, C. Complete novels

Clock without hands
 In McCullers, C. Complete novels

Collected stories; including The member of the wedding and The ballad of the sad café; introduction by Virginia Spencer Carr. Houghton Mifflin 1987 392p o.p.
            LC 87-3944
Contents: Sucker; Court in the west eighties; Poldi; Breath from the sky; The orphanage; Instant of the hour after; Like that; Wunderkind; The aliens; Untitled piece; The jockey; Madame Zilensky and the King of Finland; Correspondence; A tree. A rock. A cloud; Art and Mr. Mahoney; The sojourner; A domestic dilemma; The haunted boy; Who has seen the wind?; The ballad of the sad café; The member of the wedding

"McCullers often wrote about grotesques, people afflicted physically and emotionally. Her themes include loneliness and the mental anguish that stems from love gone awry. Her style is unadorned, quietly rigorous. She's both charming and disquieting—an absorbing challenge to readers of serious fiction." Booklist

Complete novels. Library of America, Distributed to the trade in the United States by Penguin Putnam 2001 827p $35
ISBN 1-931082-03-0
          * LC 2001-29049
Contents: The heart is a lonely hunter; Reflections in a golden eye; The ballad of the sad café; The member of the wedding; Clock without hands

McCullers, Carson, 1917-1967—*Continued*
The heart is a lonely hunter. Modern Lib. 1993
430p $14.95
ISBN 0-679-42474-1   LC 92-51062
A reissue of the title first published 1940 by Houghton
Mifflin
"After his friend is committed to a hospital for the in-
sane, John Singer, a deaf mute, finds himself alone. He
becomes the pivotal figure in a strange circle of four oth-
er lonely individuals: Biff Brannon, the owner of a cafe;
Mick Kelly, a young girl; Jake Blount, a radical; and
Benedict Copeland, the town's black doctor. Although
Singer provides companionship for others, he remains
outside the warmth of close relationships." Shapiro. Fic
for Youth. 3d edition
   also in McCullers, C. Complete novels

The member of the wedding. Houghton Mifflin
1946 195p hardcover o.p. pa $7.95
ISBN 0-395-07981-0; 0-618-49239-9 (pa)
"Twelve-year-old Frankie is experiencing a boring
summer until news arrives that her older brother will
soon be returning to Georgia from his Alaska home in
order to marry. Plotting to accompany the newlyweds on
their honeymoon occupies much of Frankie's waking
hours, while at the same time she is coping with the
pressures of puberty and its effects on her body and
mind. Particularly revealing are her conversations with
her six-year-old cousin and the nurturing black family
cook, Bernice." Shapiro. Fic for Youth. 3d edition
   also in McCullers, C. Collected stories
     p255-392
   also in McCullers, C. Complete novels

Reflections in a golden eye. Houghton Mifflin
1941 182p o.p.
"Set in the 1930s on a Southern army base, the novel
concerns the relationships between self-destructive misfits
whose lives end in tragedy and murder. The cast of characters includes Captain Penderton, a sado-masochistic, latent homosexual officer; his wife, who is having an affair
with Major Langdon; the major's wife, who responds to
the trauma of her son's death with self-mutilation;
Anacleto, a homosexual servant who is befriended by the
major's wife, and an army private who engages in voyeurism." Merriam-Webster's Ency of Lit
   also in McCullers, C. Complete novels

McCullough, Colleen, 1937-

Caesar; let the dice fly. Morrow 1997 664p il
ISBN 0-688-09372-8   LC 97-24391
The fifth novel in the Masters of Rome series "opens
in 54 B.C., with Caesar civilizing and romanizing the
different tribes in Britannia and Gaul. After five years of
almost constant warfare, Caesar turns all his political
brilliance to defeating Pompey, his former son-in-law,
who wants to strip Caesar of his power." Libr J
"Caesar is essentially the same character one recalls
from his admittedly self-promoting memoirs—brilliant,
ambitious, ruthless and fascinating. The real tragic hero
here is Pompey, whose military triumphs are overshadowed by his rival's, whose political fortunes are undermined by Cato and the *boni*, and whose assassination
in Alexandria closes this thoroughly Romanized epic
novel." N Y Times Book Rev

Caesar's women. Morrow 1996 696p
ISBN 0-688-09371-X   LC 95-34498
The fourth novel in the author's series about the Roman Empire "details Caesar's rise to power from 68-58
B.C. Caesar repeatedly outmaneuvers his enemies, who
devise one scheme after another to bring about his political, economic, and social downfall. Eventually he allies
himself with Pompey and Crassus to create a formidable
triumvirate. Despite the book's title, women play minor
roles in the novel. Caesar consults his shrewd mother
about strategy and depends on her to manage his household. He adores his daughter and misses his dead mother. Nonetheless, he consistently subordinates personal affection to political ambition." Libr J
"With great brio, and ample attention to Roman customs and rites, as well as to the religious, sexual and social institutions of the day, including slavery,
McCullough captures the driven, passionate soul of ancient Rome." Publ Wkly
Followed by Caesar

The first man in Rome. Morrow 1990 896p il
o.p.
           * LC 90-37080
The first installment in the Masters of Rome series
"outlining the demise of the Roman republic and tracing
the origins of the Roman Empire, this volume commences in 110 B.C.E. and revolves around the smoldering political ambitions of two seemingly unsuitable
statesmen. Lacking the requisite patrician pedigree, stolid
and wealthy Gaius Marius, a brilliant general, acquires
respectability by marrying into the irreproachable Julian
dynasty. Deprived of his noble birthright by a dissolute
and profligate father, the impoverished and curiously
amoral Lucius Cornelius Sulla resorts to murder in order
to claim an inheritance and purchase his way into the
senate. Branded as outsiders, Marius and Sulla forge a
formidable alliance, culminating in a succession of
unparalled military and political triumphs." Booklist
Followed by The grass crown

Fortune's favorites. Morrow 1993 878p il o.p.
           LC 93-534
The third novel in the Ancient Rome series "begins in
the year 83 B.C. and runs through 69 B.C., a violent and
volatile era that brought the rise and bloody rule of the
maniacal, disease-ridden dictator Sulla; the career of the
cocky if dense 'Magnus' Pompey; and the youth and education of Julius Caesar." Booklist
"Painstakingly researched, McCullough's Roman saga
is like a trip through time. Her characters come to life
as do their surroundings. While giving us rollicking good
fiction, McCullough has also made clear the bribery and
chicanery that made up Roman politics. She has given us
clear insight into how Rome found itself changing from
a republic to an empire." Libr J
Followed by Caesar's women

The grass crown. Morrow 1991 894p il o.p.
           LC 91-17009
In the second novel in the author's series about the
Roman Empire "the action hinges on the rivalry between
arrogant, paunchy general Marius, eager to fulfill a
prophecy and become consul of Rome for a seventh
time, and Sulla, a monster who has turned to war-making
out of either sexual frustration or boredom. . . . In recreating the Social War between Rome and the rebellious

McCullough, Colleen, 1937-—*Continued*
Italian nations (90-88 B.C.), Sulla's crushing of King
Mithridates of Pontus and the ensuing bloody Roman
civil war, McCullough sustains a keen sense of urgency,
framing precarious personal lives against an empire in
flux. A quietly magnificent tour de force." Publ Wkly
Followed by Fortune's favorites

An indecent obsession. Harper & Row 1981
317p o.p.

* LC 81-47547

This novel is "set in the psychiatric ward of a small
military hospital in the South Pacific soon after the end
of the Second World War. A novel about duty (the 'indecent obsession'), it has the prescribed mix of best-
selling ingredients, romance, sex, violence and paranoia."
Oxford Companion to Australian Lit

Morgan's run. Simon & Schuster 2000 604p il
ISBN 0-684-85329-9   LC 00-41006
A historical saga about Richard Morgan, "a man who
falls afoul of villains and suffers the degradation of the
18th-century British penal system. But, as even he admits, he has great luck as a convict. His resourceful cousin, a druggist, fixes him up with survival necessities,
and wherever the beautiful, strong, educated Richard
goes—overcrowded jails or the hulks of convict transports, suffering the appalling conditions of passage to an
unknown continent—he becomes a leader of men. The
novel displays fine, informative period details." N Y
Times Book Rev

**The October horse; a novel about Caesar and
Cleopatra.** Simon & Schuster 2002 792p $28
ISBN 0-684-85331-0   LC 2002-32753
This sixth and final volume in the Masters of Rome
series "traces the last days of the Roman Republic, including the events leading up to the assassination of Julius Caesar and the aftermath of that famous murder.
Here, that most renowned of Romans, at the height of
his power, and Cleopatra, his illustrious mistress, are at
center stage." Booklist
"Though some readers may find the sheer wealth of
detail occasionally tedious, the book will find a niche
among those who can appreciate the scholarship and research that contributed to recreating Caesar's remarkable
career." Libr J

The song of Troy. Orion 2001 c1998 404p maps
ISBN 0-7528-1705-1   LC 98-215810
First published 1998 in the United Kingdom
"McCullough's version of the 10-year siege of Troy by
the armies of Greece unfolds slowly and dramatically,
with each chapter narrated by one of the conflict's major
players. . . . This vivid portrayal of the people and
events of the Trojan War is actually a rewritten version
of McCullough's first novel, which was never published." Booklist

The thorn birds. Harper & Row 1977 533p o.p.

*

"A multigenerational saga of life, love, and death on
an Australian sheep ranch." Reader's Ency. 3d edition
"The backdrop to this congested, sensational and often
bizarre plot, is the Australian outback, with its dramatic
landscapes, vast distances, isolation, bush camaraderie,
and natural hazards. The novel aroused lively literary
controversy. It was labelled by its critics as a 'potboiler':

crudely crafted, sensationally exaggerated, devised to cater to the florid expectations of the mass of undiscrimi-
nating readers of modern popular fiction. Its supporters
see it as a vigorously-written and racy narrative." Oxford
Companion to Australian Lit

McCutchan, Philip, 1920-

Apprentice to the sea. St. Martin's Press 1995
c1994 183p o.p.   LC 94-45091
First published 1994 in the United Kingdom with title:
Tom Chatto
This story of life at sea is set in the nineteenth century.
"Tom Chatto, 17, fresh from a country vicarage in the
West of Ireland, goes to the seaside offices of the Porter
Holt Shipping Company and signs aboard a vessel that
will carry cargo from Liverpool to South America. He
finds among the crew a savage first mate, a remote cap-
tain, and, as a fellow apprentice, a condescending fop."
SLJ
"McCutchan effectively and economically limns bus-
tling Liverpool, the daunting mission of beating around
the Horn and Victorian England's rigid caste system. Despite its sometimes excessive jargon . . . this spankingly
paced novel augurs well for Tom's further voyages."
Publ Wkly
Followed by The second mate

Cameron's crossing. St. Martin's Press 1993
171p o.p.   LC 93-24284
"Commander Cameron along with a small crew of enlisted men take passage on the escort carrier HMS
Charger, which is sailing from Belfast to Norfolk, Virginia, for an overhaul. On passage across the Atlantic
HMS *Charger* is beset by a severe North Atlantic storm
that not only damages her beyond recovery but reveals
the inadequacy of the commanding officer, Captain Ma-
son-Goodson. Cameron takes command in an effort to
save both ship and crew from a watery grave." Libr J
"As usual, the stolid, intrepid Cameron soldiers along
very ably, while McCutchan's spare prose smartly re-
creates the lore and real lives of the British navy." Publ
Wkly

The last farewell; a novel. St. Martin's Press
1991 308p o.p.   LC 90-49227
"McCutchan weaves a tapestry of stories about the
passengers and crew aboard the *Laurentia* as it makes its
final voyage from New York to England in 1915. Without a protective escort, Captain Pacey must guide his
ship through waters and times more treacherous than he
can possibly believe. The U-boat commander has his
problems, too, as the action moves from the liner to the
submarine to the offices of the British ministers, who, in
noncommittal ways, have sentenced the *Laurentia* to its
dismal fate. A mesmerizing tale of the sea and the men
who pit their lives against nature and politics." Booklist

The new lieutenant. St. Martin's Press 1997
181p
ISBN 0-312-15604-9   LC 97-10026
First published 1996 in the United Kingdom with title:
Tom Chatto, RNR
This "installment of the Tom Chatto military series
finds our hero out of the merchant marine and into the
Royal Navy Volunteer Reserve in the first year of WWI.
Chatto is navigator and third officer (and eventually mas-

McCutchan, Philip, 1920-—*Continued*

ter) of *Geelong,* an armed decoy battling German U-boats in the Mediterranean, and must face not only hostile submarines but also the personal problems of various shipmates. . . . Though the writing occasionally lapses into generic passages about war disillusionment, readers who have followed Tom Chatto will be interested in the challenges—both epic and personal—posed by The Great War." Publ Wkly

The second mate. St. Martin's Press 1996 c1995 186p o.p.   LC 96-1189

First published 1995 in the United Kingdom with title: Tom Chatto, second mate

"It is now some years after the events of *Apprentice, to the Sea* and Chatto is second mate of a liner on the South American run. After a trouble-plagued voyage, he plays a heroic role in trying to save a derelict sailing ship, with the unexpected help of Patience, the bucko mate from the *Pass of Drumochter.* . . . *Second Mate* is that rare thing today, a book that could easily have been twice as long without boring the sea-loving reader." Booklist

Followed by The new lieutenant

McDermid, Val

The distant echo. St. Martin's Minotaur 2003 404p $24.95

ISBN 0-312-30199-5   LC 2003-52902

"Winter of 1978, St Andrews University, Scotland. Four drunken young students on their way home from a party stumble upon local barmaid Rosie Duff, who has been raped, stabbed, and left to die. Unable to save her, the men become suspects in the case but are never formally charged. The stigma and shame of the experience follows these men into their adult lives. About 25 years later, two of the four men have been murdered. The remaining two, Alex Gilbery and the Rev. Tom Mackie must identify their friends' killer before they become the next victims of this revenge murder spree." Libr J

"Individually, the characters are sensitively drawn. Collectively, they present the inscrutable face of closed-off communities so terrified of change they would kill for peace." N Y Times Book Rev

Grave tattoo. St. Martin's Minotaur 2007 c2006 390p $24.95

ISBN 978-0-312-33921-0; 0-312-3392-6
                                          LC 2007-295846

First published 2006 in the United Kingdom

This "novel begins with the discovery in a Lake District bog of an old body bearing distinctive Polynesian tattoos from the 1800s. Jane Gresham, a William Wordsworth scholar who was raised near where the body is found, has always been intrigued by the local legend that Fletcher Christian wasn't killed on Pitcairn Island and wonders whether the body could be his. She knows that Christian and Wordsworth were schoolmates and has found a letter pointing to a secret manuscript Wordsworth may have written that she hypothesizes may tell the story of the mutiny on the Bounty from Christian's viewpoint. However, Jane is not the only one interested in the existence of the manuscript—and someone may be willing to kill for it." Libr J

Once all the "narrative balls are tossed in the air, McDermid provides enough violence to add real urgency

to her intriguing premise, which the late curator of the Wordsworth Trust declared 'improbable, but charmingly plausible.' Even without the melodramatic plot twists, the novel's scholarship is exciting on its own terms, and entirely appropriate for a district so wildly beautiful that it attracts both poets and pirates." N Y Times Book Rev

A place of execution. St. Martin's Minotaur 2000 403p

ISBN 0-312-26632-4   LC 00-59145

First published 1999 in the United Kingdom

"When a 13-year-old English schoolgirl goes missing from her Derbyshire village in the winter of 1963, George Bennett, the police inspector in charge of the case, quickly realizes that the secrets of the child's life and possible death are locked in the collective mind of Scardale, an isolated hamlet of inbred families united by their common surnames and their hostility to strangers. Through Bennett's exhaustive efforts, the likely villain is caught and hanged—or so it seems, until the story reaches 35 years into the future for its chilling resolution." N Y Times Book Rev

McDermott, Alice, 1953-

After this. Farrar, Straus and Giroux 2006 279p $24

ISBN 978-0-374-16809-4; 0-374-16809-1
                                          LC 2006-5598

An "examination of the modern Irish American Catholic experience. Through a series of linked vignettes, this quiet story highlights events in the Keane family of Long Island over several decades. John and Mary Keane's somewhat surprising engagement in the late 1940s (both are a little past the usual marrying age) brings about an enduring union. Together, they manage to meet the challenges of raising four children on a limited income, confronting the social and religious struggles of the mid-20th century, and—hardest of all—losing to the Vietnam War the son they had named for a long-dead World War II soldier." Libr J

McDermott's "easy authority with this material, combined with her clear-eyed sympathy for her characters, results in a moving, old-fashioned story about longing and loss and sorrow." N Y Times (Late N Y Ed)

At weddings and wakes. Farrar, Straus & Giroux 1992 213p o.p.   LC 91-42070

Set in Brooklyn during the sixties, this novel "tells the story of an extended Irish-American family observed primarily through the eyes of the children, son and two daughters. Time circles backwards and forwards around a variety of family rituals: holiday meals, vacations at the shore, the wedding of a favorite aunt. The poignant middle-aged romance that develops between the aunt, a former nun, and her suitor, a shy mailman, exacerbates already pronounced family tensions. As they listen to oft-repeated stories about poverty, disease, and early deaths, the children are solemn witnesses to the Irish immigrant experience in America." Libr J

Charming Billy; a novel. Farrar, Straus & Giroux 1998 280p

ISBN 0-374-12080-3
                                        * LC 97-77089

McDermott, Alice, 1953-—*Continued*

This "novel opens at the wake of the debonair Billy Lynch—gifted talker, abandoned suitor, faithful husband, devout Catholic, raging alcoholic. It then ranges back and forth through dozens of family theories and anecdotes to answer the question of what did or didn't make him who he was. At once a love story, a portrait of Irish Catholic Queens, and an ode to an edenic postwar East Hampton, this novel honors the consequences of everyday decisions, both sacred and profane, burnishing them in the retelling to a high shine." New Yorker

Child of my heart. Farrar, Straus & Giroux 2002 242p $23

ISBN 0-374-12123-0 LC 2002-69764

Fifteen-year-old "Theresa's Irish-American 'well-read but undereducated' parents have little money but plenty of foresight; when they see that their only daughter will be beautiful, they move to East Hampton, Long Island, summer playground of New York's richest, in the hopes that Theresa's beauty will eventually win her a wealthy husband." Publ Wkly

This is a "summer idyll in which a cat is hit by a car, a dog is shot, the heroine loses her virginity, and her fairy-like cousin succumbs to a fatal disease and want of parental love. All this loss—of innocence, of dearly loved creatures—and yet, there is not a word of sentimentality or taste of treacle. On the contrary, Child of My Heart is a golden and luminous memory retrieved by a narrator who has achieved a cool and slightly ironic distance from one of those summers in the late fifties or early sixties." Commonweal

That night. Farrar, Straus & Giroux 1987 183p $14.95

ISBN 0-374-27361-8

* LC 84-45765

The novel's "narrator reflects on an incident that shattered the serenity and naïveté of her suburban world of the early 1960s, when she was 10 years old. . . . An opening scene of violence played out under a 'bright navy sky' on a soft midsummer night 'when Venus was bright', captures the tone and focus of the novel, which recalls the doomed love affair of teenagers Sheryl and Rick." Publ Wkly

"In spite of its brevity, 'That Night' is a wonderfully unfettered, ample novel, one that celebrates voice, personality and feeling when so much fiction avoids those rewarding characteristics. Ms. McDermott has invested her novel with a strong sense of historical authority, rendering with sure clarity a time and place marked by both a cultural innocence and the premonition of its inevitable loss." N Y Times Book Rev

McDermott, J. M., 1979-

Last dragon. Wizards of the Coast Discoveries 2008 390p pa $14.95

ISBN 978-0-786948-57-4; 0-786948-57-4

LC 2007-18085

"A journey focused on revenge becomes an odyssey of self-discovery and of the founding of an empire in blood and sacrifice. As Zhan searches for her grandfather, a creature no longer human that has killed his entire village, she travels in the company of Seth, a fire-breathing shaman; Korinyes, a gypsy who is more than she seems; and Adel, a paladin present at the slaying of the last

dragon. McDermott's debut novel requires careful reading to piece together a story told in nonlinear form, as mercurial as memories and as visceral as death. This fantasy adventure belongs in libraries where literary fantasy in the tradition of Gene Wolf, A.A. Attanasio, and Gabriel García Márquez is popular." Libr J

McDevitt, Jack

Infinity beach. HarperCollins Pubs. 2000 435p $25

ISBN 0-06-105123-3 LC 99-40569

"On the colony world of Greenway, humans still search in vain for evidence of alien intelligence. When Kim Brandywine, fund-raiser for the Seabright Institute's Beacon Project, begins an investigation into the disappearance of her cloned sister Emily, also involved in the search for extraterrestrial life, she opens a door that leads her to her fondest dreams and darkest nightmares." Libr J

McDevitt "has created a future that is technologically sound and filled with hubristic, foolish people who make choices based more on how they will look to history than on what's best for it. Though his aliens are insubstantial . . . the mystery of what happened to Kim's sister and her fellow celestial seekers unfolds as precisely as an origami flower, and will hold readers in thrall." Publ Wkly

Mcdonald, Gregory, 1937-2008

Carioca Fletch
In Mcdonald, G. The Fletch chronicles

Confess, Fletch
In Mcdonald, G. The Fletch chronicles

Fletch. Bobbs-Merrill 1974 179p o.p.

*

"A rich young California industrialist, Stanwyck, who is apparently dying of cancer, offers someone he takes to be a beach bum a rich reward if he'll murder him on a particular date. The 'bum' chosen is Fletch, ace journalist, ace philanderer, who accepts the proposition. However, Fletch, who is already investigating the beach drug scene for his newspaper, now investigates Stanwyck—his marital and extramarital life, his relationship with his parents, his obsession with piloting experimental planes. The two strands of the story come together in one deft twist as Fletch . . . both gets the drop on the doublecrossing Stanwyck and uncovers the source of the beach's drugs." Publ Wkly

also in Mcdonald, G. The Fletch chronicles

Fletch and the man who
In Mcdonald, G. The Fletch chronicles

Fletch and the Widow Bradley
In Mcdonald, G. The Fletch chronicles

The Fletch chronicles. Hill & Co. Pubs. 1987-1988 3v o.p. LC 87-8742

"Rediscovery books"

Contents: one: Fletch won (c1985) entered separately; Fletch, too (c1986) entered separately; Fletch and the Widow Bradley (c1981)

[two]: Fletch (c1974) entered separately; Carioca

Mcdonald, Gregory, 1937-2008—*Continued*
Fletch (c1984); Confess, Fletch (c1976)
three: Fletch's fortune (c1978); Fletch's moxie (c1982); Fletch and the man who (c1983)

Fletch, too
also in Mcdonald, G. The Fletch chronicles

Fletch won
also in Mcdonald, G. The Fletch chronicles

Fletch's fortune
In Mcdonald, G. The Fletch chronicles

Fletch's moxie
In Mcdonald, G. The Fletch chronicles

Son of Fletch. Putnam 1993 236p o.p.
LC 93-684
"Good-natured hero Irwin Maurice ('Fletch') Fletcher discovers he has a heretofore unknown son from a friendly one-night stand 20 years earlier. Somehow son Jack has become involved with a bunch of neo-Nazi thugs fresh out of prison, but Fletch has trouble believing that the fruit of his loins could really be a bad guy at heart. . . . Good pacing, good humor, and good writing make Mcdonald's latest another fan pleaser in a predictable but comfortable series." Booklist

McDonald, Ian 1960-

River of gods. Pyr 2006 597p $25
ISBN 1-59102-436-6; 978-1-59102-436-1
* LC 2005-35110
"It's 2047, and the centennial of India's nationhood approaches. Amid the turmoil and vigor of a nation teeming with people and clogged with information, the lives of nine individuals, including a policeman, a journalist, a scientist, a politician, and a standup comic, intersect in an unanticipated union with the fate of their country at stake. . . . [The author] provides a kaleidoscopic, freewheeling encounter with the near future in one of the most exotic—and impoverished—parts of the world. . . . Every library should purchase this multitextured tale of future perils and possibilities in the land of a thousand gods." Libr J

Brasyl; a novel. Pyr 2007 357p $25
ISBN 978-1-59102-543-6; 1-59102-543-5
LC 2007-1563
"McDonald sets up three separate characters in different eras—a cynical contemporary reality-TV producer, a near-future bisexual entrepreneur and a tormented 18th-century Jesuit agent. He then slams them together with the revelation that their worlds are strands of an immense quantum multiverse, and each of them is threatened by the Order, a vast conspiracy devoted to maintaining the status quo until the end of time." Publ Wkly
"Much more often than not, McDonald's prose is a wonder, from a hundred vivid and witty details . . . to sustained passages of perfectly judged atmosphere. . . . McDonald finds the poetry and the energy of the outcast, the refuse of society." Strange Horizons

McDonald, Roger, 1941-

Mr. Darwin's shooter. Atlantic Monthly Press 1999 365p
ISBN 0-87113-733-X
LC 98-36819
This novel focuses on the life of a British sailor, Syms Covington. McDonald portrays him as Charles Darwin's aide-de-camp, a man "who, though he's barely mentioned in Darwin's writings, toiled at his side throughout his early career, bagging the vast array of specimens upon which Darwin founded his theory of natural selection." Time
"Mr. MacDonald is a generous, leisurely author who gives the reader a large cast of quirky characters, much peripheral detail, lively action, and a view of nineteenth-century social patterns. Covington, moreover, is no plaster saint, and the Beagle's long voyage offers opportunities for adventure. One need not be pro or anti either Darwin or Genesis to enjoy this well-written tale." Atl Mon

McDonell, Nick

An expensive education; a novel. Atlantic Monthly Press 2009 294p $24
ISBN 978-0-8021-1893-6; 0-8021-1893-3
"Michael Teak, an American spy freshly plucked from Harvard's hallowed halls, finds himself in the vortex of a geopolitical storm as he uncovers scandal in East Africa, involving everyone from a local guerilla fighter to a glamorous college professor, to some of his fellow chosen ones back home." Vanity Fair
"McDonell is stingy with the action sequences, but when they come, they're swift and hot, showing us how Teak strikes, kills and subdues with awesome precision. It would seem silly if McDonell didn't write with such disciplined restraint, and fortunately he's far more interested in showing Teak wrestling with his conscience than with his enemies." San Jose Mercury News

McElroy, Joseph

Actress in the house; a novel. Overlook Press 2003 432p $26.95
ISBN 1-58567-350-1
LC 2002-34555
The plot of this novel turns "literally on the impact of a single glimpsed action—an actor slapping an actress with unfeigned force during a performance of a play—as it registers in the mind of Bill Daley, a man in the audience. The fact of the slap then gathers implication and mystery as Daley returns to the theater after hours and meets the actress, Becca; and finally spirals outward as the two get involved and begin, as any couple might, to ask questions and tell their stories." N Y Times Book Rev
"McElroy's prose, especially his dialogue, is enigmatic and layered with meaning, and the mood he creates is both subtly threatening and achingly wistful. Over a 40-year career, McElroy has been compared to William Gaddis, Don DeLillo, and Thomas Pynchon. This absorbing and unsettling novel, his first in 14 years, may finally bring him the wider recognition he deserves." Booklist

McElroy, Lee *See* Kelton, Elmer, 1926-2009

McEwan, Ian

Amsterdam. Doubleday 1999 193p
ISBN 0-385-49423-8   LC 98-41401

"Two longtime friends meet at the cremation of the woman they shared, beautiful restaurant critic and photographer Molly Lane. Clive Linley, a celebrated composer, and Vernon Halliday, the editor of a financially troubled London tabloid, could never understand Molly's third liaison—with conservative Foreign Secretary Julian Garmony, who is angling to be prime minister, or her marriage to dour but rich publisher George Lane. . . . Immediately afterwards, both Clive and Vernon are enmeshed in a crisis: Clive must finish his commissioned Millennium Symphony so it can premiere in Amsterdam, and Vernon must grapple with the moral issue of publishing photos of Julian Garmony in drag that George has discovered with Molly's effects." Publ Wkly

McEwan "has written a tastily vicious tale in his usual polished prose." Libr J

Atonement; a novel. Doubleday 2002 351p $26
ISBN 0-385-50395-4   LC 2001-44291
First published 2001 in the United Kingdom

The major events of the novel "occur one day in the summer of 1935. Briony Tallis, a precocious 13-year-old with an overactive imagination, witnesses an incident between Cecilia, her older sister, and Robbie Turner, son of the Tallis family's charwoman. . . . It then becomes easy for her to believe that the shadowy figure who assaults her cousin Lola late that night is Robbie. Briony's testimony sends Robbie to prison and, through an early release, into the army on the eve of World War II. Gradually understanding what she has done, Briony seeks atonement first through a career in nursing and then through writing, with the novel itself framed as a literary confession it has taken her a lifetime to write." Libr J

This is a "work of astonishing depth and humanity. . . . The upper-class milieu, the sense of place and time, are rendered with an exactitude worthy of Elizabeth Bowen. . . . Mr McEwan has achieved the difficult task of combining literary sophistication with moral gravity." Economist

Black dogs. Putnam 1992 xxii, 149p o.p.
* LC 92-7418

"The narrator of this taut, questioning tale is an orphan relentlessly drawn to other people's parents. This habit of attraction and need takes full form when Jeremy becomes intrigued with his in-laws. June is spiritual, reclusive, and fatally ill; Bernard is active, pragmatic, and political. They fell in love during the grieving yet determined days following World War II, united by an ardent and idealistic faith in communism and a bold sexual passion. But their bliss was short-lived. The source of the philosophical chasm that quickly opened between them, June's epiphanic confrontation with two black dogs in rural France, is alluded to often but not fully explained until that last chapter." Booklist

This novel is "compassionate without resorting to sentimentality, clever without ever losing its honesty, an undisguised novel of ideas which is also Ian McEwan's most human work." Times Lit Suppl

The child in time. Houghton Mifflin 1987 263p
ISBN 0-395-42912-9   LC 87-8603

"On a balmy outing to a supermarket with his adored three-year-old daughter, Stephen Lewis, a writer of successful children's books, experiences the unthinkable. His daughter disappears. He searches frantically but can't find his Kate. Finally, despairingly, he must return home, must tell his wife, Julie, the terrible fact." West Coast Rev Books

"Many of the plot turns in the novel may seem improbable and even fanciful, but the feelings expressed by the characters and their sense of time (running up, running down and running out) are, without exception, genuine. . . . [This is an] astonishing book." Time

Enduring love; a novel. Talese 1998 252p
ISBN 0-385-49112-3   LC 97-23029
First published 1997 in the United Kingdom

As this novel opens, "several men struggle to hold down a hot air balloon that threatens to break free, carrying a small child with it. One by one they let go, until one man is left hanging and is carried off to drop shortly to his death. For [the] narrator, Joe, one of the men struggling to hold down the balloon, this is only the beginning of the nightmare. Another would-be rescuer, a devout Christian [named Jed] who happens to be gay, conceives a passion for Joe and begins stalking him relentlessly, both to convert him and to draw him away from his beloved Clarissa. In the meantime, a mystery grows up around the dead man, a dedicated doctor and family man whose presence in the field that fateful day needs explaining." Libr J

McEwan is a "maestro at creating suspense: the particular, sickening, see-sawing kind that demands a kind of physical courage from the reader to continue reading." New Statesman (1913)

The innocent. Doubleday 1990 270p o.p.
* LC 89-25669

"Basing his story on an actual (but little known) incident, McEwan tells of the secret tunnel under the Soviet sector which the British and Americans built in 1954 to gain access to the Russians' communication system. The protagonist, Leonard Marnham, is a 25-year-old, naive, unsophisticated English post office technician who is astonished and alarmed to find himself involved in a top-secret operation. At the same time that he loses his political innocence, Leonard experiences his sexual initiation in a clandestine affair with a German divorcée five years his senior. As his two secret worlds come together, events develop into a gruesome nightmare." Publ Wkly

"There is . . . a point to all this, which is to display the astonishing deeds that human beings can perpetrate and yet retain a measure of innocence. . . . In spite of what has happened, Leonard is able to live with himself. This is far and away Ian McEwan's most mature work." New Statesman Soc

On Chesil Beach. Nan A. Talese/Doubleday 2007 176p $22.95
ISBN 978-0-385-52240-3; 0-385-52240-1
LC 2006-100720

This novel "opens on the anxious Dorset Coast wedding suite dinner of Edward Mayhew and the former Florence Ponting, married in the summer of 1963 at 23 and 22 respectively; the looming dramatic crisis is the marriage's impending consummation, or lack of it. Edward is a roughhewn but sweet student of history, son of an Oxfordshire primary school headmaster and a mother

McEwan, Ian—*Continued*

who was brain damaged in an accident when Edward was five. Florence, daughter of a businessman and (a rarity then) a female Oxford philosophy professor, is intense but warm and has founded a string quartet. Their fears about sex and their inability to discuss them form the story's center." Publ Wkly

McEwan's brief novel is as "tautly constructed as anything he has written, though sprawling in imagination. It's emblematic of a generation, a semi-scornful elegy for a repressed age, sarcastic about mores and unrelentingly honest about psychological and sexual intimacy. It's a big book in a little space. You can feel the author at times wishing to burst the bounds of his limited span, to go crashing past these tightly constrained boundaries and begin sweeping up the host of other generational topics available to him. McEwan resists the urge, which is for the best, this is a book better suited for the sprint than the marathon." PopMatters

Saturday. Nan A. Talese/Doubleday 2005 289p $26

ISBN 0-385-51180-9

This novel is "set within a single day in February 2003. Henry Perowne is a contented man—a successful neurosurgeon, happily married to a newspaper lawyer, and enjoying good relations with his children. Henry wakes to the comfort of his large home in central London on this, his day off. . . . After an unusual sighting in the early morning sky, he makes his way to his regular squash game with his anaesthetist, trying to avoid the hundreds of thousands marchers filling the streets of London, protesting against the [Iraq] war. A minor accident in his car brings him into a confrontation with a smalltime thug. To Perowne's professional eye, something appears to be profoundly wrong with this young man, who in turn believes the surgeon has humiliated him." Publisher's note

"It's clear that with this volume, Mr. McEwan has not only produced one of the most powerful pieces of post-9/11 fiction yet published, but also fulfilled that very primal mission of the novel: to show how we—a privileged few of us, anyway—live today." NY Times (Late NY Ed)

McFadden, Bernice L.

Sugar; a novel. Dutton 2000 229p

ISBN 0-525-94531-8   LC 99-35589

"A small Arkansas town in the 1950s provides the setting for a story of redemption and forgiveness. Sugar, a dark, beautiful black woman with a bitter past and a life of prostitution, arrives in Bigelow and disrupts the social order. For her neighbor, Pearl, Sugar bears a disturbing resemblance to her daughter, who was sexually assaulted and killed 15 years earlier. Pearl, virtually withdrawn since her daughter's death, is slowly revived by the saucy, uninhibited Sugar." Booklist

"McFadden captures the full character of small-town life and the strengths and weaknesses of its people." Libr J

McFarland, Dennis

A face at the window. Doubleday 1997 309p o.p.   LC 96-31232

In this "ghost story, Cookson Selway flies to England with his wife, who will be sopping up atmosphere for her next mystery. But for Cook the mystery is more immediate; at the hotel, the hypersensitive Cook, who has had odd, out-of-time experiences in the past, hears music no one else hears and then has visitations from a ghostly little girl and her slovenly uncle, who died years ago in a fall from one of the building's window. . . . With the help of Pascal, the French clerk, and an Asian couple who frequent the hotel's dining room, Cook starts investigating his visitors. Soon he is so caught up in them that he leaves reality behind." Libr J

The author "has a most beguiling narrative style: he is sometimes funny and sometimes moving; in descriptions of the hauntings he is so exact that it is easy to suspend disbelief, and in his ulterior purposes he is persuasive. Behind the haunting of Cookson Selway by the ghosts of the hotel and the ghosts of his own past lurks the haunting of the author by the idea of the dysfunctional American family. The whole makes for a thoroughly satisfying novel." N Y Times Book Rev

Letter from Point Clear; a novel. Henry Holt and Company 2007 290p $25

ISBN 978-0-8050-7766-7; 0-8050-7766-9
                              LC 2006-52574

"Safely ensconced in their respective New England homes, siblings Ellen and Morris Owen learn of their younger sister's impetuous marriage to an evangelical minister actually named Pastor Vandorpe, and that the couple are now residing in the family mansion along the Alabama coast. Assuming that, like her drug abuse and failed acting career, this is yet another one of Bonnie's reckless forays into self-destruction, Ellen and Morris rush home to assess the situation for themselves. They find Bonnie calm, happy, and several months pregnant, but as the pastor spends more time with the brother-in-law he just found out is gay, his ministerial duty to correct the error of Morris' ways threatens to unravel his marriage, if not his psyche." Booklist

"With its finely evoked tableaus from Wellfleet to the Alabama coast, 'Letter From Point Clear' is a gratifying, emotionally resonant novel—its heart and longing steeped in the Old South, its sensibility years and miles beyond." Boston Globe

The music room. Broadway Bks. 1990 275p o.p.
                              * LC 89-71721

"Marty Lambert, a San Francisco record company executive, is facing an impending divorce when his younger brother Perry, a talented composer, commits suicide in New York. Mystified by his brother's death, Marty goes to New York to seek an explanation, following an elusive trail of clues that leads from his brother's friends to the troubled history of his wealthy Virginia family. In the end he learns as much about himself as Perry, coming to terms with a legacy of alcoholism." Libr J

"In one startling realistic scene after another, with evocative description and a fluid, natural language, 'The Music Room' itself builds to a comprehensive vision, remarkable from its beginning to its surprising, satisfying end." N Y Times Book Rev

McFarland, Dennis—*Continued*

School for the blind. Houghton Mifflin 1994 287p

ISBN 0-395-64497-6   LC 93-49831

This novel "chronicles the waning years of two elderly siblings, Francis and Muriel Brimm, as they reluctantly come to grips with the past and learn to accept their gradual decline. . . . Walking on the golf course near the Florida town where Muriel has spent her life and to which retired photojournalist Frank has returned, they discover the bones of two students from the nearby school for the blind. The search for the killer's identity forces Frank and Muriel to abandon their own willed 'blindness' and to retrieve memories of their childhood with a mean, alcoholic father and a stern, cold mother." Publ Wkly

"Readers of 'School for the Blind' may find their attention held less by the plot than by everything that supports it. This is an inversion of expectations, but not finally a disappointing one." N Y Times Book Rev

Singing boy; a novel. Holt & Co. 2001 309p $25

ISBN 0-8050-6608-X   LC 00-32051

"One night, Malcolm, husband of Sarah and father of eight-year-old Harry, is shot to death in front of his horrified family. . . . We soon realize that Sarah and Harry have no emotional support network. Sarah, unable to resume her work as a chemistry professor at a prestigious Boston university, turns to Malcolm's best friend, Deckard, a black Vietnam vet and recovered drug addict. But for Deckard, Malcolm's murder stirs up not only grief but also painful flashbacks of war and an abusive childhood. As Sarah and Deckard's friendship becomes strained, Harry suffers through nightmares on his own." Libr J

"The language here is always apt, and always in tune with the characters' thoughts. McFarland has a gift for selecting details, so that we see this novel's world with remarkable intimacy." N Y Times Book Rev

McGahan, Andrew

The white earth. Soho 2006 376p $25

ISBN 1-56947-417-6   LC 2005-50415

"Set in Australia's Queensland province, the novel begins with the blaze of 70 acres of wheat, a conflagration that consumes nine-year-old William's father and sends the boy and his mother packing to his great-uncle John McIvor's rotting mansion on the arid plains of what was once a vast sheep ranch. Chapters alternate between William settling into his new existence (action set in the early 1990s), and the story of John's youth on the ranch, where as the son of the ranch manager he nurtured ambitions to one day own the estate. John recruits William's help in organizing a rally for his right-wing group, which opposes the proposed Native Title laws that would return Aboriginal-claimed land to the original inhabitants. The novel's first half is a slow build, the second half, a well-wrought, meditative reflection on Australia's colonialist demons, brings the book's gothic intimations home to roost." Publ Wkly

McGahern, John, 1934-2006

By the lake; a novel. Knopf 2002 335p

ISBN 0-679-41914-4

     * LC 2001-50258

"The story is an old one: in search of a quieter way of life, Joe and Kate Ruttledge have traded their careers in London for a farm near a small Irish village, where they learn how to raise sheep and are steadily drawn into the lives of their neighbors. There's the Shah, a rich bachelor in search of an heir for his business; John Quinn, a weaselly sexual predator, and a danger to women throughout the county; and Jimmy Joe McKiernan, an I.R.A. leader whose exploits periodically stir up high feeling. McGahern is never sentimental, and the novel's greatest pleasures come from the unflinching probity of his observations." New Yorker

McGarrity, Mark, 1943-2002 *See* Gill, Bartholomew, 1943-2002

McGarrity, Michael

The big gamble; a Kevin Kerney novel. Dutton 2002 272p $23.95

ISBN 0-525-94656-X   LC 2002-20755

"When two murder victims turn up after a fire in an abandoned fruit stand on a rural highway, Kerney, now the police chief of Sante Fe, N. Mex., takes a personal interest in the case. One blackened corpse is a John Doe. The other remains belong to a 29-year-old college student, Anna Marie Montoya, who disappeared 11 years before. As it happens, Kerney was involved in the search for the missing Anna Marie. Investigating the John Doe is Kerney's estranged son, Clayton Istee, now a deputy sheriff for the Lincoln County (N. Mex.) police." Publ Wkly

Death song; a Kevin Kerney novel. Dutton 2008 293p $24.95

ISBN 978-0-525-95036-3   LC 2007-26642

"Written in the terse staccato of law enforcement, Death Song sets a police procedural with plenty of action in Albuquerque, Santa Fe and northern New Mexico. The double homicide of a Lincoln County sheriff's deputy and his wife bring together Santa Fe Police Chief Kevin Kerney and his Mescalero Apache son, a Lincoln County officer. Their investigation uncovers a major international drug ring, but the killers and the real reason for the crimes elude police as more murders ensue." Rocky Mountain News

Everyone dies; a Kevin Kerney novel. Dutton 2003 273p $23.95

ISBN 0-525-94761-2

     * LC 2003-9208

In this installment "an unidentified psycho has his sights set on Kerney, his family, and his soon-to-be-born child. . . . McGarrity contrasts the painstaking investigatory work that leads to identifying a suspect with the personal crisis Kerney and his wife, Sara, face. Uncertain about how a child will affect their relationship, the couple must now contend with a much more immediate threat to their lives." Booklist

"Michael McGarrity is one of those low-key pros who keep the genre honest with realistic crime stories and plain-talking cops who know the procedures." N Y Times Book Rev

The Judas judge; a Kevin Kerney novel. Dutton 2000 274p

ISBN 0-525-94547-4

     * LC 99-89181

McGarrity, Michael—*Continued*

Kevin Kerney "returns to his childhood home near Tularosa to investigate the murder of six people found at various campgrounds along one stretch of road in southern New Mexico. The trail leads to a retired judge and his disaffected children, all of whom have skeletons aplenty in their dysfunctional closets." Booklist

"McGarrity is no nature writer, and his sketches of dusty desert towns like Alamogordo and Ruidoso are as blunt as his unsentimental character studies. Still, his portrait of the region is a strong one, built on meticulously detailed intelligence gathered, sifted and analyzed for unspoken secrets and lies by the author's own deeply cunning mind." N Y Times Book Rev

Nothing but trouble; a Kevin Kerney novel. Dutton 2006 305p $24.95

ISBN 0-525-94916-X   LC 2005-25660

In this Kevin Kearney mystery "readers are treated to moviemaking in New Mexico and, in a real departure for the series, a venture to Ireland featuring the Santa Fe police chief's wife, Sara, an army officer. McGarrity dedicates a third of the book to Sara, homing in on her covert operation in Ireland as she tries to capture a fugitive whose schemes have ties to important U.S. government officials. Her operation upsets a superior officer who immediately deploys her to Iraq. Although Kevin and Sara are accustomed to a long-distance marriage, they now have just a few days to make arrangements for Kevin to assume the care of their five-year-old son. In the meantime, Kevin gets involved with the filming of a movie along the Mexican border, thus allowing McGarrity to once again exhibit his remarkable ability to make the landscape and people of the Southwest a vital character in his story." Libr J

Under the color of law; a Kevin Kearney novel. Dutton 2001 272p $23.95

ISBN 0-525-94604-7   LC 00-69406

Kevin Kerney "is settling into his new job as police chief of Santa Fe, N. Mex., and his new subordinates are of two minds whether they should trust him or not. They have ample opportunity to observe him in action, because as the book opens, Phyllis Terrell, the estranged wife of an ambassador and ex-military honcho, is found stabbed to death in the kitchen of her hilltop mansion, and Father Joseph Mitchell, an ex-soldier turned priest researching the government's covert operations, turns up dead in the Christian Brothers Residence at the College of Santa Fe." Publ Wkly

McGinniss, Joe, 1970-

The delivery man; [by] Joe McGinniss Jr. Black Cat 2008 276p pa $14

ISBN 978-0-8021-7042-2; 0-8021-7042-0

"After attending college in New York, Chase returns to [Las Vegas] and is drawn into the lucrative but dangerous world of a teenage call-girl service with his childhood friend Michele, a beautiful Salvadorean immigrant with whom he shares a tragic past." Publisher's note

"A harrowing journey set in the suburbs and exurbs of Las Vegas, this debut novel . . . provides a snapshot from hell of a contemporary youth culture in full cardiac arrest, children forced to become adults all too soon, compelled to absorb childhood traumas and adolescent catastrophes in a quiet and understated way until the whole bloody mess comes boiling to the surface in anarchic, antisocial behavior." PopMatters

McGowan, Heather

Duchess of nothing; a novel. Bloomsbury Pub. 2006 215p $23.95

ISBN 1-59691-066-6   LC 2005-18197

"After leaving her husband and their suffocating marriage for a new lover in Rome, the narrator of Duchess of Nothing has her freedom, but is still trapped by the routine of life and haunted by her past. Even worse, her lover, Edmund, is just as self-absorbed and remote as her former husband. Her one source of entertainment is Edmund's seven-year-old brother, a curious, precocious, and defiant child who becomes her responsibility during her lover's long absences." Publisher's note

McGowan reveals her "narrator's character slowly, with delicacy and precision. 'Duchess of Nothing' is the kind of book that relies entirely on the power of its voice. McGowan is no ironist, smirking at the world and going for cheap laughs. There's plenty of comedy here, but its function turns out to be solace." N Y Times Book Rev

Schooling. Doubleday 2001 314p $24.95

ISBN 0-385-50138-2   LC 00-47452

The "story of a young American girl, Catrine Evans, who is bewildered to find herself suddenly installed in an English boarding school after the death of her mother. The book takes in too the inner lives of three men: Catrine's Welsh father, whose old school, Monstead, she now attends, and two Monstead masters, the chemistry instructor and amateur painter, Mr. Gilbert, and the sad, frustrated, literary Mr. Betts." N Y Times Book Rev

"McGowan works in an experimental mode. At once lush and harsh, and inventive in form, the novel reads like an extended sensory exercise. Readers who prefer a straightforward narrative may be bemused, but those willing to accept the challenge will be rewarded with a beautifully written coming-of-age tale." Publ Wkly

McGowan, Kathleen

The expected one. Simon & Schuster 2006 449p (Magdalene line, book 1) $25.95

ISBN 978-0-7432-9942-8; 0-7432-9942-6

This novel "introduces readers to Maureen Pascal, a journalist unprepared for the visions that haunt her as she researches her new book on misunderstood heroines of the past. In France, Maureen uncovers a family secret and a document that many have died to protect (both linked to Mary Magdalene) and becomes entwined with two secret societies whose rivalry has extended over centuries. McGowan's ability to create dimensional characters while sustaining multiple, fast-paced story lines is sure to win her many readers. This work, based on 20 years of research, may prove to be . . . controversial . . ., as it addresses not only the possibility that Jesus and Mary Magdalene produced offspring but also that other biblical relationships may have differed from what the Catholic Church had ordained to be true." Libr J

McGown, Jill

Murder at the old vicarage. St. Martin's Press 1989 c1988 256p o.p.   LC 88-30603

"A Thomas Dunne book"

First published 1988 in the United Kingdom with title: Redemption

"While snow blankets the small village of Byford, the vicar, George Wheeler, is in a hopeless muddle. . . . He finds himself attracted to a young widow—a fact that has not escaped his wife's notice. In addition, his daughter has moved back to the vicarage in order to escape an abusive husband. When the husband is discovered dead, the three members of the Wheeler family are the prime suspects. What appears to be a simple case of domestic murder to Chief Inspector Lloyd and Sergeant Judy instead becomes a complicated plot to love and revenge." Booklist

"McGown's complex plot is masterful and her sleuths and their predicament are enthralling." Publ Wkly

Picture of innocence. Ballantine Pub. Group 1998 325p

ISBN 0-449-00250-0   LC 97-45816

"Inspectors Lloyd and Hill study a bizarre case of murder. Someone has finally killed the obnoxious, abusive man who ruined two marriages in his financially motivated quest to produce a male heir." Libr J

This "mystery possesses a wealth of psychological nuance and narrative depth, all the way through to the resolution, a masterpiece of controlled complexity." Publ Wkly

Plots and errors. Ballantine Bks. 1999 375p $22.95

ISBN 0-345-43313-0   LC 99-14226

First published 1998 in the United Kingdom

"When Andy Cope and his wife, Kathy, owners of a struggling detective agency, are found dead in their car . . . Detective Chief Inspector Lloyd rejects the majority opinion that they committed suicide. His theory, that the Copes were murdered, receives serious consideration when their one client, wealthy Mrs. Angela Esterbrook, is shot to death. Why would someone with her sort of money employ an untried agency to carry out an investigation? That's just one of many puzzles that Lloyd and his partner, Judy Hill, confront in a case that defies reason." Publisher's note

The stalking horse. St. Martin's Press 1988 186p o.p.   LC 88-15834

"A Thomas Dunne book"

"Businessman Bill Holt fails to convince anyone that he did not commit the two murders of which he is accused: that of his lifelong friend, Alison Bryant, and of a private detective he never even met, Michael Allsopp, who had been assigned to trail Alison. Holt spends 16 years in prison pondering the link between the crimes and becomes obsessed with discovering the identity of the murderer, belatedly realizing that it had to be one of his acquaintances. When he is paroled, he returns home to the English countryside in quest of the truth and the person who framed him." Publ Wkly

"McGown has constructed a taut, enthralling mystery, borrowing from the hard-boiled and the British procedural styles to write in a way all her own." Booklist

Verdict unsafe. Fawcett Columbine 1997 327p o.p.   LC 97-4949

"In an English Midlands town, Colin Drummond, known as 'the stealth bomber,' is in prison for rape. Forty-year-old Detective Inspector Judy Hill took his confession. Now, after three years in prison, Drummond has been released to be tried again. He harasses Hill with phone calls and threats, and she fears that he will add to his total of four rapes. Judy's lover, Detective Chief Inspector Lloyd . . . is also involved in the case." Libr J

"The pace is methodical and the cast cheerless, but McGown wraps her grim tale in a complex, satisfying solution." Publ Wkly

McGrath, Patrick, 1950-

Asylum. Random House 1997 254p

ISBN 0-679-45228-1   LC 96-24849

This novel is set in an insane asylum and narrated by Dr. Peter Cleave. It is 1959. "Stella Raphael is a psychiatrist's wife. She is a dissatisfied beauty on the verge of middle age who falls madly in love . . . with Edgar Stark, sculptor, lover, psychopath, killer and inmate of the asylum where her dull husband is the ambitious deputy superintendent. Stella and Edgar embark on a disastrous affair. . . . He escapes from the asylum. And so, a little later, does she." Times Lit Suppl

"It is part of McGrath's bemusing artfulness in Asylum that he can make the reader suffer the fate of all his characters. Everyone in the novel, that is to say, is deranged by their own, and other people's, plausibility. When anyone speaks in Asylum–and McGrath has an extraordinary ear for the hollows in conversation, for the lurking soliloquies–we seem to see through them in the full knowledge that they never see through themselves." London Rev Books

The grotesque. Poseidon Press 1989 186p

ISBN 0-671-66509-X   LC 89-3486

"The setup is macabre: a distinguished paleontologist is brain-damaged and slowly turning into a vegetable. He cannot speak, but narrates an interior monologue of all he sees and hears: a lot of sexual shenanigans and a particularly grisly murder, all centered around 'Fledge,' the butler, who has ambitions." Publ Wkly

"Part of the fun of reading 'The Grotesque' is recognizing the literary allusions and watching as one after another the subgenres of murder mystery, Gothic horror, social satire, black comedy and stories of the double are invoked and skillfully woven together." N Y Times Book Rev

Martha Peake; a novel of the Revolution. Random House 2000 367p

ISBN 0-375-50081-2   LC 00-29064

"A Young man named Ambrose is summoned by his dying Uncle William to an ancient pile called Drogo Hall, there to hear the story that the uncle, with the last of his strength, is driven to tell. It is the story of Harry Peake—smuggler, poet, freak, madman, tormented soul—and of his splendid red-haired daughter, Martha, who emigrates to America and becomes an early martyr of the Revolution. But Uncle William is erratic in his delivery and wandering in his mind. . . . So it is Ambrose who by means of sympathy, imagination, intuition, must fashion a coherent account." N Y Times Book Rev

"McGrath is a vivid writer, and his detailed evocations

McGrath, Patrick, 1950—— *Continued*
of the atmosphere and settings of its various times and places are among the pleasures of the book." Times Lit Suppl

Spider. Poseidon Press 1990 221p
ISBN 0-671-66510-3   LC 90-7492
The novel is the "purported journal of Dennis 'Spider' Cleg, a frail, deranged Londoner. . . . After many years away, Spider returns to his old neighborhood in London's East End slums. Ensconced in a small drab room in a grubby boarding house, he keeps a written record in which he reconstructs and grapples with the mysterious events in his childhood that caused his long sojourn in Canada." N Y Times Book Rev
"Despite a less pungent second half, Spider confirms McGrath's mastery of the terrain he's staked out for himself: a twisted place where the most rank, hideous experiences are conveyed in a prose so tight, assured, and essentially self-mocking that he maintains a fine balance between high gothic horror and fussy stylization." Voice Lit Suppl

Trauma. Alfred A. Knopf 2008 209p $24.95
ISBN 978-1-4000-4166-4; 1-4000-4166-X
                                      LC 2007-31071
This "tale concerns Charlie, a psychiatrist, and his dysfunctional life and family. A distant father and alcoholic mother have left their marks on him, his rivalry with older brother Walter has festered unabated for years, and Charlie gamely maintains on-again, off-again relationships with his ex-wife, Agnes, and his sometime lover, Nora. Agnes's brother committed suicide while Charlie was treating him for posttraumatic stress disorder, one of the many ghosts haunting the cobwebby mansion of Charlie's mind. Frequent references to Manhattan's East Sixties, the Son of Sam case, and passing glimpses of the World Trade Center make this very much a New York novel." Libr J
"Beautifully crafted and paced, Trauma can be viewed as either a superb psychological thriller or as a masterly evocation of modern alienation and despair—assuming, of course, there is any difference. The contemporary novel of terror typically focuses on the breakdown of personality, the return of the repressed, the untimely mixing of memory and desire. Happily for us wimps, McGrath eschews splatter or gruesomeness, instead relating Charlie Weir's story in clear, quick-flowing prose, as if Dick Francis had rewritten Ford Madox Ford's The Good Soldier. . . . Trauma is, in short, a terrific literary entertainment." Washington Post Book World

McGregor, Elizabeth

The ice child. Dutton 2001 372p
ISBN 0-525-94567-9   LC 00-67703
This novel "centers around three journeys: that of the doomed 1845 Arctic expedition headed by Sir John Franklin; a present-day trek undertaken by a polar bear and her dying cub; and the search, by a journalist named Jo Harper—whose fiancé, a Franklin devotee named Doug Marshall, dies when he is hit by a car—for bone marrow that will save their dying 2-year-old son, Sam." N Y Times Book Rev
"McGregor introduces perhaps one dramatic twist too many, but her novel otherwise artfully mixes historical background, up-to-date medical information about a rare

disease, a bit of pop psychologizing and some upbeat lessons about the survival of the human spirit." Publ Wkly

McGuane, Thomas, 1939-

The cadence of grass. Knopf 2002 238p
ISBN 0-679-44674-5
                                      * LC 2001-50623
"Sunny Jim Whitelaw is dead, but he continues to cast a shadow over his family's life. His will requires that his daughter Evelyn patch up her relationship with her no-good husband, Paul—if she doesn't, the ownership and profits of Sunny Jim's Montana bottling plant will be lost." Publ Wkly
"The real engine of the book is not plot . . . but language: McGuane's sentences are like no one else's, crisp and spare, yet some how baroque, and he perpetually balances the picaresque against the sublime." New Yorker

Gallatin Canyon; stories. Knopf 2006 220p $24
ISBN 1-4000-4156-2   LC 2005-44680
Contents: Vicious circle; Cowboy; Ice; Old friends; North coast; The zombie; Miracle boy; Aliens; The refugee; Gallatin Canyon
"McGuane has become our poet-philosopher of the arm's length, of the prudently aborted intimacy that keeps both isolation and commitment equally at bay." N Y Times Book Rev

Keep the change. Houghton Mifflin 1989 230p
ISBN 0-395-48887-7; 0-7710-5517-X
                                      LC 89-30996
"Joe Starling leaves his family's Montana ranch as a teenager, attending Yale and later becoming a successful painter in New York. Now in a state of emotional and spiritual disarray, he returns, hoping to lay claim to the rundown ranch and 'find a restored coordination for his life' in the old values of hard work and closeness to the land. But his romantic notions run aground on the realities of the modern West: He ultimately loses the ranch to his mad Uncle Smitty's scheming and discovers the duplicity of the seemingly innocent Ellen, the ranch owner's daughter he romanced one summer and now longs to return to." Libr J
"Thomas McGuane is the pool shark of our prose. His sentences click with imperious precision. Masse and carom and draw shots follow each other with elan. McGuane puts English on his English so the words swerve with fatal charm. . . . What singles out this novel is the honesty with which McGuane has tested his version of Huck Finn. The final pages have overwhelming authority." Christ Sci Monit

Ninety-two in the shade. Farrar Straus and Giroux 1973 197p
ISBN 0-374-22259-2
                                      * LC 73-76222
This novel concerns Thomas Skelton, who, "having rejected the straight life and become a fishing guide near Key West, Florida, is the victim of an extravagant practical joke designed to drive him out of the guiding business. When Skelton blows up the joker's skiff in retaliation, the joker [Nichol Dance] wanting to establish his 'credence' in his opponent's eyes, promises to kill him should he guide again, Skelton does guide again and the

McGuane, Thomas, 1939—*Continued*

joker kills him." Libr J

Despite "unexpected, complex ironies, the relation of Skelton and Dance is too laconic and abstract to achieve quite the classic fatality McGuane aims for. . . .What keeps [the novel] exciting to read is McGuane's feeling for the rambunctious oddities, forlorn vulgarity and green beauty of Key West. . . . [This] is, with its faults, a very fine book." Newsweek

Nobody's angel. Random House 1981 227p

ISBN 0-394-52264-8   LC 81-13885

At 36 melancholy, ex-juvenile delinquent, ex-prep school student, ex-Army captain, Patrick Fitzpatrick "returns to his family's Montana ranch . . . tends his grandfather, a dotty cowpoke, and his loony sister [Mary], and feels exhausted, depleted, bewildered. . . . At a party he meets Claire, a young Oklahoma woman who's beautiful, oil-rich and married. The action moves between Patrick's attempts to keep his family and ranch shipshape and his struggle to . . . woo and conquer Claire." Newsweek

"What stamps this as a McGuane novel are the bizarre episodes he invents for his character and the wit with which he reports them; what is new . . . is a depth of feeling." N Y Times Book Rev

Nothing but blue skies. Houghton Mifflin 1992 349p

ISBN 0-395-54540-4   LC 92-23623

"Frank Copenhaver is a mix of modern businessman and old-style rancher. . . . As the novel begins, his wife, Gracie, leaves him, and his domestic upheaval signals a succession of setbacks in his business life. Copenhaver's downward spiral gathers speed as he engages in a series of fleeting sexual liaisons, lands in jail after a bar fight, demolishes the pick-up truck of a fling's jealous cowboy boyfriend, and almost destroys his Montana business empire." Times Lit Suppl

"The author's underlying theme is the unimportance of money by comparison with love, an old point that he makes with novel means and without sentimental sugar." Christ Sci Monit

Panama. Farrar Straus and Giroux 1978 175p

ISBN 0-374-22942-2   LC 78-12344

"The plot finds drugged-out and washed-up rock star Chet Pomeroy trying to get his act together in wild and wonderful Key West, Florida." Libr J

"Thomas McGuane is the pool shark of our prose. His sentences click with imperious precision. . . . The words swerve with fatal charm." Christ Sci Monit

McHugh, Maureen F.

Nekropolis. Eos 2001 257p

ISBN 0-380-97457-6   LC 2001-33525

"As a 'jessed' or bonded servant, Hariba possesses a chemically induced sense of loyalty to her master until her growing affection for an artificial construct drives her to an act of desperation and changes her life forever. . . . This luminous tale of forbidden love in a near-future Morocco explores the evolution of human nature in a world where technology has redefined the meaning of the word *human*." Libr J

McInerney, Jay, 1955-

Bright lights, big city; a novel. Vintage Bks. 1984 182p pa $15

ISBN 0-394-72641-3   LC 84-40074

"A Vintage original"

"A would-be writer drifts between clubs and [cocaine], dissatisfied with his work as a verifier of facts for a prestigious magazine and racked by the desertion of his wife. . . . Finally, after fighting his brother, the nameless narrator faces the . . . vacuousness of New York life and comes to some kind of terms with his mother's death." Libr J

This "is a very funny, oddly touching book, and something of a tour de force as well. McInerney employs an unusual and challenging narrative device; he tells his tale through the second person in the historical present tense and fashions a coherent and engaging voice with it, one that is totally believable at almost every moment in the novel." New Repub

The good life. Knopf 2006 353p $25

ISBN 0-375-41140-2   LC 2005-44370

This is a novel "about 9/11's effects on four privileged Manhattanites: a retired corporate raider, a would-be screenwriter, a former model, and a book editor. . . . This is really the story of two of the above, part of a cast meaningfully reassembled from Brightness Falls (1992), who meet as volunteers at a soup kitchen for rescue workers at Ground Zero. Both of them are in miserable marriages, and they're left shaken when the nation's worst day leads to the best days of their lives. McInerney probes the human response to tragedy, and the complexity of human desire, with both precision and empathy." Booklist

How it ended; new and collected stories. Alfred A. Knopf 2009 331p $25.95

ISBN 978-0-307-26805-1; 0-307-26805-5

     LC 2008-53518

Contents: It's six a.m. Do you know where you are?; Smoke; Invisible fences; The madonna of turkey season; Third party; In the NorthWest Frontier Province; My public service; The waiter; The queen and I; The debutante's return; Simple gifts; Story of my life; Con doctor; Getting in touch with Lonnie; Summary judgment; How it ended; Philomena; I love you, honey; Sleeping with pigs; Everything is lost; Reunion; Putting Daisy down; The business; Penelope on the pond; The march; The last bachelor

"Mr. McInerney was a callow, facile and extremely entertaining writer from the very first. He had a smart student's command of technical virtues and an eagerness to show them off. He also had such a tiresome infatuation with 1980s-style decadence that it lingers sentimentally even now. But his stories have grown more elegant, subtle, shapely and reflective over time, to the point where some of the recent works are perfect specimens. He has quietly achieved the literary stature to which he once so noisily laid claim." N Y Times (Late N Y Ed)

McInerney, Monica

Upside down, inside out; a novel. Ballantine Books 2008 419p pa $14

ISBN 978-0-345-50624-5; 0-345-50624-3

     LC 2008-274694

McInerney, Monica—*Continued*

First published 2002 in Australia

"Set in Ireland, England and Australia, this is the . . . story of two people whose lives are about to turn upside down and inside out. Eva is off to Australia on a break from her job in a Dublin delicatessen, hoping to forget a fizzled romance and find inspiration for a new career. Joseph is taking a holiday from his stressful London job. Each is on a search for some answers about life. Then something quite unexpected happens. They meet each other." Publisher's note

"There is a huge 'aaahh' factor in Monica McInerney's second novel. . . The book is great fun (but) laughter aside, there's also a serious aspect regarding communication, truth and honesty and how vital these are in close relationships." Irish Examiner

McInerny, Ralph M., 1929-

Bishop as pawn; a Father Dowling mystery; [by] Ralph McInerny. Vanguard Press 1978 219p o.p.
LC 78-54978

"Father Dowling's housekeeper's husband returns after a desertion of 15 years, only to be killed. Involved in this odd collection of bits and pieces is a good Catholic girl who wants to marry an irreligous man, leading to a singularly bleak affair, a young undogmatic and fundamentalist priest much disliked by Father Dowling, and an incomprehensible kidnapping of the remarkably smooth bishop." Libr J

Body and soil; an Andrew Broom mystery; {by} Ralph McInerny. Atheneum Pubs. 1989 245p o.p.
LC 88-38209

In this mystery Indiana attorney Andrew Broom, "represents some very unpopular clients, including a strange young man who has confessed to the murder of a local boy. In the midst of that trial, the town's wealthiest couple brawls in public, loudly insists on a divorce, and hires Broom and his partner/nephew as opposing attorneys. Then murder interrupts the proceedings. In a departure from the traditional whodunit, McInerny offers readers front-row seats to observe the villain's activities." Booklist

The book of kills; a mystery set at the University of Notre Dame; [by] Ralph McInerny. St. Martin's Minotaur 2000 275p $23.95
ISBN 0-312-20346-2   LC 00-40257

"A series of pranks, including the kidnapping of the chancellor, has alarmed the Notre Dame administration, and the Knight brothers get the call to investigate. The various shenanigans seem somehow related to the claim by a group of Native Americans that the land on which the famed university stands was stolen from them and should be returned. . . . Another deft and mordantly witty excursion into the rarefied atmosphere of Notre Dame." Publ Wkly

A cardinal offense; [by] Ralph McInerny. St. Martin's Press 1994 372p o.p.   LC 94-3481

"A Father Dowling mystery"

"A man, pursuing an annulment, and his wife, who is opposed, meet separately with Fr. Dowling in St. Hilary's rectory on the same day that the priest receives two surprise tickets to the next Notre Dame-Southern California football game. The husband says his wife was never really a Catholic; she insists that the 30-year marriage and the couple's grown children remain valid. After the man is murdered, Dowling and his cop friend Phil Keegan consider possible suspects." Publ Wkly

Celt and pepper; [by] Ralph McInerny. St. Martin's Minotaur 2002 210p $22.95
ISBN 0-312-29117-5   LC 2002-69938

"After a young Notre Dame professor/Poet dies unexpectedly, Professor Roger Knight. . . suspects murder. His erudition, coupled with assistance from his brother Philip, a private investigator, ultimately leads to a killer. Solid plotting from a practiced hand." Libr J

Grave undertakings; a Father Dowling mystery; [by] Ralph McInerny. St. Martin's Minotaur 2000 374p
ISBN 0-312-20309-8
* LC 99-54817

"Mimi O'Toole is hoping for a miracle when she asks Father Dowling in the hospital for absolution for her dying husband, a shooting victim. Vincent O'Toole was known to be an associate of the Pianone crime family, and his funeral draws every notable in the local underworld to St. Hilary's church in Fox River, Ill. The cops don't seem all that anxious to find O'Toole's killer, until someone tries to dig up his grave on Halloween and his casket is later discovered to be empty. In his effort to figure out what happened to O'Toole both before and after death, Father Dowling remains the calm center in a swirl of events." Publ Wkly

Irish coffee; [by] Ralph McInerny. St. Martin's Minotaur 2003 247p $23.95
ISBN 0-312-30901-5   LC 2003-50620

"Everybody likes Fred Neville, who works in Notre Dame's sports information office. Everybody but one person-the person who killed him. A different side of unassuming Fred surfaces when two women arrive at his funeral, each claiming Fred as their fiance. Because South Bend, home of Notre Dame, is always deferential to the university, the locals have no objection when the Knight brothers become unofficial consultants on the case. Phillip Knight is a streetwise PI, and his immensely rotund brother, Roger, is an amateur sleuth and a revered professor of Catholic studies. . . . A fine effort by a deservedly respected genre veteran." Booklist

Irish tenure; a mystery set at the University of Notre Dame; [by] Ralph McInerny. St. Martin's Minotaur 1999 246p
ISBN 0-312-20345-4
* LC 99-16992

"Two young philosophy professors, Amanda Pick and Hans Wiener, are vying for the single tenured spot open in their department. . . . Pick has become the object of obsession of a Chesterton expert on the English faculty, Prof. Sean Pottery. So when her body is found in a lake on campus, Pottery seems like a good suspect. . . . A second murder clouds the issue momentarily, but sleuth Roger Knight, a mountain of a man who holds a chair in Catholic Studies at Notre Dame, uncovers the truth." Publ Wkly

McInerny, Ralph M., 1929-—*Continued*

Judas Priest; a Father Dowling mystery; [by] Ralph McInerny. St. Martin's Press 1991 184p o.p.

LC 91-21819

"A seminary friend of Dowling's, former priest Chris Bourke, and his ex-nun wife now promote sexual liberation as televangelists of Enlightened Hedonism (EH). Meeting Dowling one day after Mass, Bourke asks the parish priest to talk about the hard facts of religious life with his daughter, Sonya, who wants to enter the convent. Before Dowling can do that, Sonya is reported kidnapped and then found stabbed to death. . . . Dowling, worldly-wise and armed with ready references to St. Paul and other Church fathers, is at his vintage best." Publ Wkly

Last things; a Father Dowling mystery; [by] Ralph McInerny. St. Martin's Minotaur 2003 307p $24.95

ISBN 0-312-30899-X   LC 2003-40641

"Father Dowling first becomes involved with the Bernardo family when Eleanor Wygant asks him to try to persuade her niece, Jessica Bernardo, to stop writing a novel based on the Bernardo family. Eleanor is afraid of the resultant scandal if her long-buried secret is revealed. . . . There is a murder for Father Dowling to solve, of course, but this time McInerny seems more interested in exploring the motivations and entwined family relationships of his characters. There's also plenty of the Catholic minutiae that Father Dowling fans enjoy." Booklist

Requiem for a realtor; a Father Dowling mystery; [by] Ralph McInerny. St. Martin's Minotaur 2004 263p $23.95

ISBN 0-312-32417-0   LC 2004-41858

"Stanley Collins is Fox River's most notorious philandering realtor. His wife, Phyllis, wants to divorce him but is afraid to lose her claim on an impending inheritance. She is stringing along her dentist, love-struck Dave Jameson, who's also a devout Catholic. Jameson is a prominent member of St. Hilary's parish and, as an emissary for Phyllis Collins, asks Father Dowling's advice regarding a divorce and her standing in the church. Circumstances change when Stanley Collins is run down by his own car a couple of blocks from the apartment of a local nightclub torch singer, with whom he is having an affair. Dowling closely watches as the investigation–directed by his closest friend, Phil Keegan, of the Fox River PD–unfolds. . . . McInerny adds a moral catch-22 for Dowling as he struggles to choose between helping solve a murder and betraying the sanctity of a parishioner's confidences." Booklist

Second vespers; a Father Dowling mystery; [by] Ralph McInerny. Vanguard Press 1980 224p o.p.

LC 79-56379

Father Dowling "moves in on the criminals uncovering their various attempts to cheat collectors of O'Rourke memorabilia. Among the characters are two people who have a bookshop located in the old O'Rourke mansion, the local librarian who has a collection of letters, and another who is trying to get his hands on all the available O'Rourke papers. When a body is discovered, it throws doubt on the state of the 'estate' and also on the murder of O'Rourke." West Coast Rev Books

Still life; a novel; [by] Ralph McInerny. Five Star 2000 255p $21.95

ISBN 0-7862-2895-4   LC 00-61724

This mystery features "Captain Egidio Manfredi of the Fort Elbow, Ohio, police force. Manfredi is staring at mandatory retirement when he and his young assistant are ordered to reopen a 30-year-old case involving the disappearance of the poet-wife of a now-retired professor." Booklist

"Clever repartee, hidden alliances both present and past, false claims of guilt, pointed observations on aging, and surprising marriage plans underscore the author's talents." Libr J

Thicker than water; a Father Dowling mystery; [by] Ralph McInerny. Vanguard Press 1981 255p o.p.

LC 81-10432

This "Father Dowling mystery takes off from a couple of petty crimes . . . to a series of bizarre murders. Father Dowling . . . discovers a dead body in a pickup truck parked in front of the rectory. Murders start piling up around the quiet little town." Booklist

McIntyre, Vonda N.

Dreamsnake. Houghton Mifflin 1978 313p o.p.

LC 77-18891

"This is based on McIntyre's Nebula Award-winning novelette, 'Of Mist, and Grass, and Sand,' which is also the first chapter of the book. Snake, the healer, and her three healing serpents attend a young boy ill with a tumor. His fearful parents kill Grass, the dreamsnake, who can ease the dying by removing their pain. Without Grass, Snake is incomplete as a healer, and since the dreamsnakes come from off-world, she cannot get a replacement. To atone for her carelessness in losing Grass, Snake sets off for the city where off-worlders trade, hoping to get more dreamsnakes. She has many heart-stopping adventures, and the reader is engrossed every step of the way." Libr J

McKillip, Patricia A., 1948-

Alphabet of thorn. Ace Books 2004 314p $22.95

ISBN 0-441-01130-6   LC 2003-62912

"The day that the new queen of Raine is crowned, a translator working in the palace receives a book written in a strange language of thornlike characters. As Nepenthe, the translator, unlocks the language's secret, she learns of a legend from the ancient past that involves her and the queen in an intrigue that threatens the kingdom itself. McKillip . . . creates the atmosphere of a fairy tale with her elegantly lyrical prose and attention to nuance. Her characters are at once intimately personal and larger than life." Libr J

The sorceress and the Cygnet. Ace Bks. 1991 231p o.p.

LC 90-44103

"More than 1000 years ago the Gold King, Dancer, Blind Lady and Warlock fought the Cygnet, lost and were banished. Commoners put their story in the constellations to remember it. Ro Holding has the sign of the Cygnet and rules the other Holds, which have the other signs. But now the Gold King, seeing a way to reestablish the alliance, sets up an elaborate plot to trick Nyx

McKillip, Patricia A., 1948-—*Continued*
Ro, daughter of the ruling family and a powerful Sorceress, and Corleu, a peasant of the Wayfolk, into releasing the vanquished and helping them find the Heart of the Cygnet." Publ Wkly

This fantasy "features imaginative worldbuilding, strong male and female characters, and an intense (though sometimes esoteric) style." Libr J

Followed by The Cygnet and the firebird (1993)

McKinney-Whetstone, Diane

Blues dancing; a novel. Morrow 1999 307p
ISBN 0-688-14995-2
"This love story is set in Philadelphia. Verdi is the naive, pampered only child of a prominent Southern preacher who has come north for college, while black student leader Johnson is brash, energetic, and sometimes angry. . . . Caught between the desire for success and the fast life of the streets, Johnson experiments with drugs, ultimately becoming addicted to heroin and getting Verdi addicted as well. Upright, conservative professor Rowe, who believes that it is his duty to guide Verdi in the right direction, falls in love with her and eventually leaves his wife for her. They live together comfortably for 20 years, until Johnson returns and forces Verdi to make a decision that will change her life forever. A captivating read." Libr J

Leaving Cecil Street; a novel; Diane McKinney-Whetstone. 1st ed. Morrow 2004 297p $24.95
ISBN 0-688-16385-8   LC 2003-55845
"Cecil Street is a quiet, tree-lined haven in West Philadelphia, a place where everyone knows everyone else, a place removed from the turmoil and violence of the late 1960s. Yet the residents of Cecil Street have their problems. Joe and Louise's marriage is strained; Johnetta's sexy niece has arrived, ripe for trouble; and teenaged Shay tries to help best friend Neet deal with an unwanted pregnancy. When Neet's abortion goes tragically wrong, everyone on the street must rally around her, while Joe, Louise, and Neet's mother, Alberta, discover how their pasts have now drawn them together. McKinney-Whetstone's portrayal of African American family life is sensitive and compassionate, with characters who love, work, live, and die without veering into soap opera." Libr J

Tempest rising; a novel. Morrow 1998 280p o.p.
LC 97-40942
This "novel is set in Philadephia during the sixties. Three sisters, Bliss, Victoria, and Shern, are raised as privileged middle-class children until tragedy unravels their lives. . . . The death of the family's 'rock' causes the mother to suffer a nervous breakdown, and the girls are removed from her care. The novel focuses on the attention they receive and the relationship that develops between each girl and their caregivers, Mae and Ramona. Mae is a politically connected foster-care provider, but she shows little concern for her own daughter, Ramona. Ramona struggles to accept her role as secondary child-care provider, yet she resents the children and her mother's abuse. Each character is unforgettable." Booklist

McKinzie, Clinton

Crossing the line; Clinton McKinzie. Delacorte Press 2004 373p $23
ISBN 0-385-33637-3   LC 2003-64602
"Antonio Burns is a cop, not a saint. Having earned the scornful nickname "QuickDraw" for a shooting that went very wrong, the Wyoming narcotics agent is fighting for redemption and holding on to his family with all the strength he possesses. His brother, Roberto, is another story. His quicksilver heart, hair-trigger temper, and unquenchable hunger for adrenaline rushes have landed him in prison and make him the right person for an FBI agent with a plan. Agent Mary Chang cool, collected, and always under control wants to take down Jesus Hidalgo, a murderous drug lord who has moved his methamphetamine operation from Mexico to a remote Wyoming canyon. In Roberto, Chang has found someone who can penetrate Hidalgo's heavily guarded crime ranch." Publisher's note

"When the Burns brothers are high up on a rock face or hunting down evil banditos, the pace and intensity shoot skyward. Readers will find themselves hanging on by their fingernails as they wait to see who will fall and who will live to climb again." Publ Wkly

McLaglen, John J., 1938-
For works written by this author under other names see Harvey, John, 1938-

McLarty, Ron

Art in America. Viking 2008 366p $25.95
ISBN 978-0-670-01895-6; 0-670-01895-3
LC 2007-40454
"In Creedemore, Colo., a land-rights dispute pitches locals against one another and attracts national media attention. Into the fray arrives Steven Kearney, a prolific New York author of unpublished novels, poems and plays, who has been invited by the Creedemore Historical Society to write and direct a play dramatizing the town's history. Steven's relocation sparks a colorful fish-out-of-water story populated with cowboys, environmental activists, hordes of reporters, performance artists, ecoterrorists and bona fide outlaws. Keeping the peace is sheriff Petey Myers, whose recollections of (and occasional conversations with) his slain partner provide some of the novel's finest moments." Publ Wkly

Traveler. Viking 2007 280p $24.95
ISBN 978-0-670-03474-1; 0-670-03474-6
LC 2006-46763
"When Jono Riley, an aging NYC actor and bartender, receives word that his first love, Marie D'Agostino, has died, he immediately returns to his hometown of East Providence, Rhode Island. Marie died when a bullet, lodged in her back some 40 years ago, traveled, causing her heart to stop. Jono was present on the winter day in 1961 when the shooting occurred, but the shock of Marie's death has caused him to remember the event in more detail. He seeks the aid of a retired cop who is still bothered that he never solved the case. McLarty gives us a real sense of place here, evoking both East Providence's past as an immigrant enclave for dockworkers and its newly gentrified present." Booklist

McLaughlin, Emma

The nanny diaries; a novel; [by] Emma McLaughlin and Nicola Kraus. St. Martin's Press 2002 305p

ISBN 0-312-27858-6   LC 2001-48652

This is a novel "about a Park Avenue family and the college student who is hired to babysit. . . . [Mrs. X is a] spoiled, imperious, spa-trotting matron. . . . [Mr. X] supports the household in extravagant style but is almost never around. Cheating on Mrs. X makes it hard for him to make family vacations to Aspen, Nantucket, Lyford Cay and other stops on their social circuit." N Y Times (Late N Y Ed)

This is "a diabolically funny New York story. . . . [Nanny] is a vastly entertaining narrator and impromptu social critic. . . . Not surprisingly, 'The Nanny Diaries' fades slightly when the X's are out of sight, despite the boyfriend and family matters that are meant to fill out Nanny's story. The heart of the matter remains perfectly pitched social satire. . . . This book is saved from self-righteousness not only by the authors' cleverness but also by their compassion. For oblivious parents, lonely offspring and overworked, underpaid employees alike, they're out to fix something that's broken." N Y Times (Late N Y Ed)

McMahon, Thomas A., 1943-1999

Ira Foxglove. Brook Street Press 2004 169p $21.95

ISBN 0-9724295-3-0   LC 2003-21792

This novel is about "a talented scientist whose . . . heart has been broken physically and spiritually. In an odyssey to repair both Ira ventures on a fantastical journey by blimp to try and recover his fractured family. Along the way he also works on an unorthodox creation of a prosthetic heart." Publisher's note

This is a "darkly genial novella discovered among McMahon's papers a year or so after his death. . . . This may be an early work, set aside for who knows what reason, but it has the same loopy charm and rueful insight as McMahon's previously published fiction." N Y Times Book Rev

Principles of American nuclear chemistry; a novel. University of Chicago Press 2003 c1970 246p (Phoenix fiction) pa $15

ISBN 0-226-56110-0

* LC 2003-48355

First published 1970 by Little, Brown

"What was life like for the scientists working at Los Alamos? Thomas McMahon imagines this life through the wide eyes of young Tim McLaurin, the thirteen-year-old son of an MIT physicist who, inspired by a young woman named Maryann, worked on the project." Publisher's note

"One of the rewarding things about [this] novel . . . is the total absence of any predictable generation-gap bitterness. Beyond lost innocence the book is about a problem that troubles the age–a sense of having pursued wrong priorities too hotly, an awareness of the neglect of life and love that results." Time

McMillan, Rosalyn

Blue collar blues. Warner Bks. 1998 359p $30

ISBN 0-446-52243-0   LC 98-19553

"Thyme Tyler is an African American plant manager for Champion Motors (a hybrid of Ford, GM and Chrysler) who has hit the glass ceiling even though she holds a Ph.D. Khan Davis is a handsomely paid factory worker who faces the threat of layoff and daily struggles for overtime in the plant. The two women maintain a . . . friendship despite their class differences and despite Khan's refusal to forgive Thyme's marriage to a sterotypically lily-white Champion exec." Publ Wkly

McMillan, Terry, 1951-

A day late and a dollar short. Viking 2001 448p

ISBN 0-670-89676-4   LC 00-46232

Viola Price "and her estranged husband, Cecil, both live in Las Vegas, and their four grown children, while scattered across the country, lead the kind of complicated lives that make Viola sick with worry." N Y Times Book Rev

McMillan "takes a multiperspective view of dysfunctional families with each member of the Price clan giving his or her own version of how screwed up they all are. . . . Their heavy load—incest, substance abuse, poverty, infidelity, death—makes this a soap opera, but it is leavened with a big dollop of sass." Time

Disappearing acts. Viking 1989 384p

ISBN 0-670-82461-5   LC 88-40412

"Franklin is an on-again off-again construction worker trying to get his life on a firmer foundation. Zora is a music teacher and would-be singer. They meet and start a relationship that initially seems ideal. Soon, however, problems emerge. Franklin's ego has never recovered from his destructive mother's abuse, and the repeated blows the oppressive white society dishes out make him increasingly depressed and hostile. The relationship begins to fall apart. Zora and Franklin have to grow a long way alone before they can come back together." Libr J

"What raises this work above a mere sentimental love story is the finely tuned humor, which McMillan uses effectively to subtly alter the meaning of a scene or to draw the reader into her circle of characters." Booklist

How Stella got her groove back. Viking 1996 368p o.p.

* LC 96-15374

"Stella Payne is a successful 42-year-old investment analyst and divorced mother of an 11-year-old son, Quincy. But Stella has begun to feel that her life needs some 'groove.' On the spur of the moment, she plans a trip to Jamaica to relax and escape from her routine. She meets a man, half her age, whose honesty and physical charm challenge her perceptions of what is acceptable and force her to rethink and re-prioritize her image of herself and her life." Booklist

"Readers who have been yearning for a Judith Krantz of the black bourgeoisie—albeit one with a dirty mouth and a more ebullient spirit—will be pleased with this fantasy of sexual fulfillment." Publ Wkly

The interruption of everything. Viking 2005 365p $25.95

ISBN 0-670-03144-5   LC 2005-42207

"Marilyn Grimes, wife and mother of three, has made a career of deferring her dreams to build a suburban California home and lifestyle with her workaholic husband, Leon. She also troubleshoots for her grown kids, cares

McMillan, Terry, 1951-—*Continued*

for her live-in mother-in-law (and elderly poodle, Snuffy), keeps tabs on her girlfriends Paulette and Bunny and her own aging mother and foster sister—and holds down a part-time job. But at forty-four, Marilyn's got too much on her plate and nothing to feed her passion. She feels like she's about ready to jump. She's just not sure where." Publisher's note

"With twists on familiar themes, irreverent humor, and a heroine who has more backbone than we initially thought, . . . [this book] brings it all back home. This is life-affirming women's fiction delivered by one of the best in the field." Libr J

Waiting to exhale. Viking 1992 409p $22.95
ISBN 0-670-83980-9
* LC 91-46564

This novel "tells the stories of four 30ish black women bound together in warm, supportive friendship and in their dwindling hopes of finding Mr. Right. Savannah, Bernadine, Robin and Gloria are successful professionals or self-employed women living in Phoenix. All are independent, upwardly mobile and 'waiting to exhale'—to stop holding their breaths waiting for the proper mate to come along." Publ Wkly

"Terry McMillan's heroines are so well drawn that by the end of the novel, the reader is completely at home with the four of them. They observe men—and contemporary America—with bawdy humor, occasional melancholy and great affection. But the novel is about more than four lives; the bonds among the women are so alive and so appealing they almost seem a character in their own right." N Y Times Book Rev

McMullen, Sean, 1948-

Glass dragons. Tor Bks. 2004 495p map $27.95
ISBN 0-7653-0797-9
LC 2003-60677

In this sequel to Voyage of the Shadowmoon (2002), "the honorable vampire Laren, the priestess Terikel, and the voluptuous Lady Velander continue their journey aboard the exploratory ship Shadowmoon. Their search for a doomsday weapon known as the Dragonwall leads them to an encounter with a fugitive bard, a runaway sailor, and a widowed princess. Australian author McMullen depicts a world filled with intrigue and strange magic, where the borders between the living and the dead are thin and where mystical weapons have the power to destroy the world. His sometimes whimsical, always literate style brings a gentle touch of wry humor to a tale of courage and cowardice, love and death, mystery and magic." Libr J

Souls in the great machine. Tor Bks. 1999 448p
ISBN 0-312-87055-8
LC 99-21934

"A Tom Doherty Associates book"

"In the fortieth century, librarians rule the world. Through a byzantine system of political favor, mathematical expertise, civil service testing, and dueling, the librarians strive for power in the 'mayoralty' of Rochester, the most powerful of several Australian fiefdoms that emerged long ago from a nuclear winter. The highliber is the scheming yet honorable Zarvora. She has ruthlessly assembled scores of mathematicians, who make the Calculor, a bizarre flesh-and-machine supercomputer that Zarvora needs to unify this quasi-medieval world and

save it from the impending doom implicit in the Call. . . . Decidedly original, sometimes whimsical, and captivating, this is a genuine tour de force." Booklist

McMurtry, Larry

Anything for Billy. Simon & Schuster 1988 382p o.p.
* LC 88-22732

This novel is based on the legend of Billy the Kid (William Bonney), here named Billy Bone. The story is "told by Ben Sippy, a dime novelist from Philadelphia who went west in 1878 in search of the real life he'd made up stories about. There he befriended a likable, bucktoothed 17-year-old who already had a reputation as a killer, and he later wrote a novelette about Billy Bone that gave him his legendary name. . . . The 'real story' is . . . recounted by Sippy in old age." Newsweek

"McMurtry's prose is as readable as ever, served up in short, episodic chapters that effectively capture time and place, conjure up authentic images of pathetic heroes and villains, and yet pull the reins in on action. The tale's strength lies in Sippy's commanding first-person delivery and the less-than-admirable profile of the title character." Booklist

Boone's Lick; a novel. Simon & Schuster 2000 287p
ISBN 0-684-86886-5
LC 00-56342

This "novel concerns itself with a trek made by the Cecil clan—the tough-minded matriarch, Mary Margaret; her dissembling brother-in-law, Seth; her children, Shay, G. T., Neva and baby Marcy; and Grandpa Crackenthorpe—from Boone's Lick, Mo., to Fort Phil Kearney, in what would later become the state of Wyoming, shortly after the Civil War." N Y Times Book Rev

"McMurtry's historical novel, told with humor and candor from the perspective of Mary Margaret's oldest son, Shay, is highly recommended for adults and adolescents alike." Libr J

Buffalo girls; a novel. Simon & Schuster 1990 351p o.p.
LC 90-42486

"This is a nostalgic, funny, and sad novel about the Old West when cowboys and Buffalo girls whooped it up. Their behavior was amoral rather than immoral, and they lived by their own special code of behavior. Friendship was often life-saving as well as comforting, and the women of the bawdy houses called their clients 'sweethearts' even if their encounter was only for one night. Jim Ragg and Bartle Bone had become almost a dying breed and Custer, in their opinion, was a stupid old man at Little Big Horn to think that he could fight 3,000 Indians with 200 of his men. Highlights of the book are Bill Cody's (Buffalo Bill's) Wild West show and Calamity Jane's (whose drunkenness was calamitous) letters to a daughter. Fact and fiction are entwined in an enjoyable story that is mythic and memorable." Shapiro. Fic for Youth. 3d edition

By sorrow's river; a novel. Simon & Schuster 2003 347p (Berrybender narratives, Book 3) $26
ISBN 0-7432-3304-2
LC 2003-53892

"In this third volume of McMurtry's Berrybender Narratives, Lord Berrybender and his obnoxious, sniveling brood are, surprisingly, still alive on the dangerous Great Plains of Wyoming and Colorado. The wry story of

McMurtry, Larry—*Continued*

mountainman adventure and European stupidity, set in the 1830s, is just as wacky and gruesome as its predecessors." Publ Wkly

Cadillac Jack; a novel. Simon & Schuster 1982 395p

ISBN 0-671-45445-5   LC 82-5962

"Jack was a rodeo bulldogger before he graduated to roaming America 'in a pearl-colored Cadillac with peach velour interior,' scouting for antiques he can resell to collectors. . . . But now Jack is undergoing a midlife crisis, juggling old wives and new girl friends as he flounders in the amiable venality and lechery of Washington, D.C." Libr J

"The sheer exuberance of McMurtry's imagination makes this book well worth reading." West Coast Rev Books

Comanche moon; a novel. Simon & Schuster 1997 752p

ISBN 0-684-80754-8   LC 97-29609

This novel "follows Woodrow Call and Augustus McCrae through their years as Texas Rangers as they create legends for themselves fighting the Comanche to open west Texas for settlement." Libr J

"McMurtry has created a sprawling, picaresque novel that, like the history of the West itself, leaves more than a few loose ends. . . . The characters are the novel's strength. McMurtry's rangers are heroic because of their vulnerabilities, not despite them." N Y Times Book Rev

Dead man's walk; a novel. Simon & Schuster 1995 477p

ISBN 0-684-80753-X   LC 95-21011

"We meet Woodrow Call and Gus McCrae when they're novice Texas Rangers not yet 20 years old. They are part of a pack of Rangers bound for new frontiers in the Wild West. Traveling with the team is Mathilda, a heavyset whore who provides both comfort and wisdom. When the group gets word that the town of Santa Fe—full of gold and silver and prosperity—is primed to be captured, they head out for a long, dangerous, and ill-fated journey." Booklist

"If Dead Man's Walk were not a prequel, it would be worth only glancing notice. As things are, it is a satisfactory foothill, with the grand old mountain in view. There are no heroics, though there is plenty of calamity. . . . McMurty has a fine time with youthful damnfoolishness, and so does the reader." Time

The desert rose; a novel. Simon & Schuster 1983 254p o.p.   LC 83-4687

"A topless dancer in a casino, Harmony 'had been said by some to have the best legs in Las Vegas and maybe the best bust too.' But now Harmony is approaching her 39th birthday, and her teenage daughter Pepper has become a contender for those honors. . . . [The] novel charts good-natured Harmony's sudden decline and Pepper's . . . well, peppery rise." Libr J

Duane's depressed; a novel. Simon & Schuster 1999 431p

ISBN 0-684-85497-X   LC 98-45712

In this novel, Duane Moore, rich and bored, surprises a Texas town "by ditching his pickup truck and walking everywhere." Time

"Duane is no intellectual, but he isn't stupid. Abandoning the ordinary ways of making do, he moves to a crude cabin on the prairie and starts trying to figure out where his life stalled. Before long he is seeing a psychiatrist, who has him reading Proust as part of his therapy. Novelistically, some of this seems too, um, made up, but Duane himself is always achingly affecting and real. . . . He is one of McMurtry's greatest characters." Newsweek

The evening star. Simon & Schuster 1992 637p o.p.   LC 92-2596

Sequel to Terms of endearment

Aurora Greenway's "aging boyfriend, the general, has lost some of his zest, and her new lover is the psychoanalyst she's gone to with her troubles. Those troubles include her grandchildren—Tommy, who's in jail for shooting his girlfriend; brilliant Teddy, who met *his* girlfriend on a visit to *his* therapist; and pregnant, overweight Melanie, who has picked up yet another hapless boyfriend and is heading for California." Libr J

"The success of a book like this one depends on the tone the author manages to muster up. Mr. McMurtry's is sentimentality laced with comic irony, and it works very well. . . . And if, in the end, Aurora Greenway and her extended and highly dysfunctional family turn out to be more entertaining than genuinely moving, it's reassuring to know that they—and the reader—are in the hands of a real pro." N Y Times Book Rev

Folly and glory. Simon & Schuster 2004 236p (Berrybender narratives, Book 4) $25

ISBN 0-7432-3305-0   LC 2003-64173

"This is the fourth and concluding volume of the Berrybender Narratives. . . . Once again, the heart of the story is the evolving relationship between Tasmin Berrybender and her enigmatic, primitive husband, Jim Snow. Both have changed. Tasmin has learned to cope with the physical demands of a nomadic life and the emotional demands and trauma of motherhood and death. Jim, still capable of savage violence, seems more tender and vulnerable here. As they and their familiar entourage journey eastward from Santa Fe, they encounter various historical personages, including William Clark, Charles Bent, and Davy Crockett. They also endure searing landscapes, cholera, and the constant threat of horrific brutality at the hands of Apaches, Kiowas, Commanches, and slave traders." Booklist

"While McMurtry doesn't stint on frantic action, violence or seemingly round-the-clock gropings, Folly and Glory marks a somber and satisfying end to a long, rambunctious trip." N Y Times Book Rev

Lonesome dove; a novel. Simon & Schuster 1985 843p hardcover o.p. pa $17

ISBN 0-671-50420-7; 0-684-85752-9 (pa)

               * LC 85-2192

"Two former Texas Rangers have been running a ramshackle stock operation near the Mexican border with a lot of work and not much success. When they hear rumors of freewheeling opportunities in the newly opened territory, they decide to break camp, pull up stakes, and head north. Their dusty trek is filled with troubles, violence, and unfulfilled yearning." Booklist

"'Lonesome Dove' shows, early on, just about every symptom of American Epic except pretentiousness. McMurtry has laconic Texas talk and leathery, slim-

McMurtry, Larry—*Continued*

hipped machismo down pat, and he's able to refresh heroic clichés with exact observations about cowboy prudery, ignorance and fear of losing face." Newsweek

Loop group. Simon & Schuster 2004 242p $25
ISBN 0-7432-5079-6   LC 2004-52216
"Maggie is divorced, nearing 60, and still gainfully self-employed on the fringes of the Los Angeles movie industry. Following a hysterectomy, she finds herself feeling low and disengaged from her former self and others. This particularly infuriates her three married daughters, who have always been able to count on Maggie's connection to them and her generosity to their families. . . . Maggie teams up with her sexy but aging friend Connie, and they light out on a cross-country trip to Texas. They fling caution to the wind, rail against growing older, and decry the loss of their wild, gallivanting, man-cruising days." Libr J

"Clearly, more sincere praise of the mature woman is overdue. And McMurtry's adulation is more than sincere, it's heated. He doesn't shy away from the pleasures of sexagenarian flesh." N Y Times Book Rev

Rhino Ranch; a novel. Simon & Schuster 2009 278p $26
ISBN 978-1-4391-5639-1; 1-4391-5639-5
LC 2009-19648
With this novel "McMurtry ends the west Texas saga of Duane Moore, begun in 1966 with The Last Picture Show. . . . Duane, now in his late 60s, is a prosperous and retired widower, lonely in his hometown of Thalia, Tex. Then billionaire heiress K.K. Slater moves in and opens the Rhino Ranch, a sanctuary intended to rescue the nearly extinct African black rhinoceros. Slater is a strong-willed, independent woman whose mere presence upsets parochial Thalia, and Duane can't quite figure her out. His two best buddies, Boyd Cotton and Bobby Lee Baxter, both work for Slater, and the three friends schmooze with the rich, talk about geezer sex, rat out local meth heads and try to keep track of a herd of rhinos." Publ Wkly

"In Rhino Ranch, McMurtry gets back to what he does best: the dead-on depiction of this small Texas town and its quirky inhabitants who immediately engage the reader in their less than perfect lives." BookPage

Sin killer. Simon & Schuster 2002 300p (Berrybender narratives, Book 1) $25
ISBN 0-7432-3302-6   LC 2002-17616
"The first of four tales of the Berrybender family. It's 1832, and Lord and Lady Berrybender—wealthy Brits incongruously venturing into the Wild West—make their way up the Missouri River. . . . Among those in the sizable entourage are 6 of the 14 Berrybender children, including Tasmin, a gutsy, industrious young woman who generally takes charge of the hapless group. . . . But Tasmin's independence brings strife, too, especially when she hooks up with frontiersman Jim Snow, an Indian fighter and wanna-be preacher." Booklist

"McMurtry's prose is plain and exact, exhibiting the kind of clarity that appears simple yet is anything but." N Y Times Book Rev

Streets of Laredo; a novel. Simon & Schuster 1993 589p o.p.
* LC 93-19279
This sequel to Lonesome Dove "takes place 20 years after the death of Gus McCrae. In this novel, Captain Woodrow Call, McCrae's old partner, tracks a young Mexican train robber, Joe Garza, with the help of a railroad accountant named Brookshire, a Texas deputy named Ted Plunkett and Pea Eye Parker, who is trying to build a family life with his wife Lorena and their children. Across the Texas Panhandle and into northern Mexico, Call pursues his prey." America

"As in some great 19th-century saga, the story has more than its share of improbable coincidences—but these seem only mild contrivances to shape a story packed with action, terror, humor and pathos. *Laredo* is a fitting conclusion to a remarkable feat of reconstruction and sheer storytelling genius." Publ Wkly

Telegraph days; a novel. Simon & Schuster 2006 289p $25
ISBN 978-0-7432-5078-8; 0-7432-5078-8
LC 2005-57458
"Once considered minor gentry in Virginia, 22-year-old Nellie Courtright and her brother, Jackson, are now all that remain of their family after an ill-fated journey out West. A dusty town on the plains called Rita Blanca becomes the Courtrights' new home. Nellie takes a job as a lickety-split telegraph operator, and her brother becomes the sheriff's deputy. When he singlehandedly takes down the notorious Yazee gang, Nellie scribbles a booklet about the gunfight, becoming an author. Soon she meets Buffalo Bill Cody, and because Nellie strikes him as organized, he offers her a job overseeing his many businesses while he runs around the country producing his Wild West Show." Libr J

"Few male writers can match McMurtry for his ability to understand and conjure strong female characters. . . . Some of the novel's most entertaining moments involve Nellie's long-running relationship with Cody, a restless publicity hound and entrepreneur. . . . The wistful closing chapters—which center on Cody's death and Nellie's affluent decades in southern California at the dawn of the movie age—speak to McMurtry's fascination with Christ Sci Monit

Terms of endearment; a novel. Simon & Schuster 1975 410p o.p.
*
"Houstonian Aurora Greenway, a transplanted New Englander, is a well-to-do widow trying to settle her own life and at the same time to dominate and control the lives of those around her—Emma, her married daughter; Rosie, her long-suffering maid; an array of suitors that includes a retired Patton-style general, an aging yachtsman, a broken-down opera singer, a bank vice president and a truly eccentric Texas millionaire. . . . Aurora alternately delights and infuriates those around her." Libr J

"Suddenly, just when we are enjoying ourselves the most, McMurtry changes his style, and we are plunged into a moving but agonizing realistic account of daughter Emma's death from cancer at 37 and the way in which her family and old friends react. . . . The shift of pace may throw some readers off stride badly. McMurtry certainly remains, however, one of our most exciting novelists." Publ Wkly

Followed by The evening star

McMurtry, Larry—*Continued*

Texasville; a novel. Simon & Schuster 1987 542p

ISBN 0-671-62533-0 LC 86-31520

"McMurtry returns to the town of Thalia, Texas, site of the 'The last picture show' (1966). The backwater town of the 1950s has experienced the oil boom and is now enduring the oil glut. Although some of the characters from the previous novel make appearances, McMurtry focuses on oilman Duane Moore—dynamic, yearning, caught up in the maelstrom of times. Duane is struggling with a twelve-million-dollar debt and is further bewildered by the manic behavior of his wife, his children, and other citizens of Thalia, all of whom seem to be reacting to hard times by going slightly berserk." Booklist

"What's funniest, and most lifelike, about McMurtry's . . . book is that his people, having enjoyed a brief but exhilarating run of American abundance (both financial and sexual), don't mind indulging in a little harmless romanticizing of their frontier history, but they're not about to give up what they've got and go back to their arid, windswept beginnings without some kicking and screaming. . . . In its affable, offhand way, McMurtry's novel, which ends with a joke about repetition . . . really is about history, at least as Americans live it." New Yorker

Followed by Duane's depressed

The wandering hill; a novel. Simon & Schuster 2003 302p (Berrybender narratives, Book 2) $26

ISBN 0-7432-3303-4 LC 2002-30595

"In the second installment of 'The Berrybender Narratives,' a tetralogy that opened with Sin Killer, McMurtry continues the saga of the aristocratic Lord Berrybender and his entourage. Having abandoned the luxury steamer on which they traveled up the Missouri River because it was stuck in the ice, the party of 17 family members, servants, and numerous hangers-on waits out the winter at a trading post on the Yellowstone before moving on." Libr J

"The landscape is stunningly beautiful, but the beauty is often disrupted by spasmodic, gruesome violence. Nonetheless, this novel is an engrossing, exciting, and sometimes heart-rending saga of the American West that shows McMurtry at his best." Booklist

Zeke and Ned; a novel; by Larry McMurtry and Diana Ossana. Simon & Schuster 1997 478p o.p.

LC 96-44906

"In the years just after the Civil War, life in the Indian Territory west of Arkansas—Cherokee land since the Trail of Tears—is more than a bit rugged, particularly for the Indians. Guns blaze with minimal provocation. Women are at the mercy of wandering marauders. And when the white man's justice does come, it's usually meted out by thugs from Arkansas, temporarily deputized as Federal marshals. Against this backdrop, a Cherokee named Zeke Proctor accidentally shoots the woman he had planned to bring home as his second wife—a killing that sets in motion a chain of events that destroys several families, nearly leads to war and concludes with a mountaintop standoff between Federal marshals and Zeke's friend and son-in-law, Ned Christie." N Y Times Book Rev

"What gives this well-wrought tale its depth is how McMurtry and Ossana convey the era's various moral shades of gray." Publ Wkly

McNamer, Deirdre

Red rover; a novel. Viking 2007 264p $24.95

ISBN 978-0-670-06350-5 LC 2006-36075

"Brothers Neil and Aidan Tierney grow up on the prairies of pre–WWII Montana, and after Pearl Harbor Neil becomes a B-29 pilot in the Pacific, and Aidan joins the FBI and is assigned to covert duty in Argentina. Upon their return in 1946, Neil establishes a life, but Aiden is dying of a mysterious disease and embittered by what he saw and did during the war. His threats to go public with bureau business call back to his life Roland Taliaferro, also an FBI agent, whose alcoholism has put his career on the rocks. In short order, Aiden is found dead, an apparent suicide by shotgun. Neil suspects a coverup, but he has no way of disproving the official report." Booklist

"McNamer depends on a complex web of coincidence to tell her story, and some readers may resist threads that connect so neatly. Arranging for so many people to be assembled in the same room 75 years down the road might be a difficult assignment even for hale survivors on the high plains of Montana. Nevertheless, it would be hard to argue against the wholly satisfying ending this reunion produces. We can be grateful that, in McNamer's world, it is never too late for a redemptive act; never too late for a life to matter." Houston Chron

McNaught, Judith

Paradise. Pocket Bks. 1991 489p

ISBN 0-671-60129-6 LC 91-12897

"Heiress to a famous department store fortune, Meredith Bancroft chafes under the strict supervision of her interfering father. When she meets ambitious, handsome steelworker Matt Farrell, Meredith is ripe for the picking, and trouble brews on both sides of the tracks when she becomes pregnant at 18. Mcnaught's skillful treatment of Meredith, the self-styled ugly duckling and poor little rich girl, will pique readers' interest and engage their sympathy." Libr J

McNicholl, Damian

A son called Gabriel. CDC Books 2004 343p $22.95

ISBN 1-59315-018-0

"A coming-of-age story set in Northern Ireland during the years 1964-78 . . . . Catholic schoolboy Gabriel Harkin faces formidable obstacles to fitting into his family and community. In the background lurks the threat of religious prejudice; in the foreground is his increasing awareness that he may be homosexual. Subjected to brutal hazing by his more athletic classmates, Gabriel feigns an interest in football and seeks to repress his sexuality. He becomes almost hyperaware of all the characteristics that mark him as different and channels his energy into studying for the exams that will become his ticket out of his insular, increasingly violent hometown. A secret involving his uncle, a conflicted priest, also haunts the family. Perhaps the most poignant aspect of this novel, though, is the way his parents and siblings, although severely limited in their knowledge of how to help him, seek to comfort him in his struggle to conform." Booklist

McPhee, Jenny

A man of no moon; a novel. Counterpoint Books 2007 271p $24

ISBN 978-1-58243-375-2; 1-58243-375-5

LC 2007017929

"In post-World War II Italy, Dante Sabato, the country's most famous living poet, is alternately planning his suicide and his next sexual encounter. At a star-studded party, he meets the Godfrey sisters, Gladys and Prudence, B-level American actresses who have found film work in Italy. Captivated by their alluring scents, their brashness, and their mystery, Dante embarks on a perverse sexual affair with Gladys and falls obsessively in love with Prudence. . . . Focusing primarily on the film world, McPhee . . . expertly depicts 1940s movie glamour; in fact, the beginning of the novel reads like a film noir." Libr J

No ordinary matter; a novel. Free Press 2004 259p $23

ISBN 0-7432-6072-4

LC 2004-43246

"For more than a decade, thirtysomething sisters Lillian and Veronica have met at a Manhattan Hungarian bakery the first Monday of the month. Stunningly beautiful but ice-cold Lillian is a brilliant neurologist. Her lovely younger sister, warmhearted, insecure Veronica, is a scriptwriter for the wildly popular soap opera Ordinary Matters. Veronica has spent a lifetime worshiping her older sister, who unfailingly swats back at Veronica's overtures. In a series of coincidences that would give Victor Hugo pause, the sisters' already complicated and deeply entwined lives become even more so. A dysfunctional childhood (a dead father and a neglectful mother), a pregnancy, a new lover, a psychiatrist with Tourette's syndrome, several independent private investigations into secret second families, a long-lost brother, and other delicious surprises draw the reader in for the fun." Libr J

McPhee, Martha

Gorgeous lies. Harcourt 2002 326p $31

ISBN 0-15-100613-X

LC 2002-7213

Sequel to Bright angel time (1997)

"In 20 years, many things have changed in the lives of the large Furey-Cooper clan. Once the members were widely known as exemplars of a new kind of blended family, living out the utopian visions of patriarch Anton. Now Anton lies virtually helpless, dying slowly with many dreams unrealized and his magnum opus on human sexuality unwritten. The siblings gather at the family farm, linked painfully not only by grief but also by longtime resentments, disappointments, and misunderstandings that fester as Anton's end approaches." Libr J

"As the novel unfolds, Anton's unlikely past is revealed: his Texas childhood, his early stint in a Jesuit seminary and his grand passion for the communal haven of Chardin. His insatiable need for connection—particularly with women—can be repellant (as when he pursues one of his stepdaughters), but it is his infectious zest for life that drives this invigorating of convoluted novel." Publ Wkly

L'America. Harcourt 2006 294p $25

ISBN 0-15-101171-1

LC 2005-20986

"Beth's parents fall in love during the Vietnam era; then, after Beth's mother dies, mourning becomes her father's raison d'etre. He founds a Pennsylvania commune in his wife's memory and never leaves. Beth, whose passion for the culinary arts dawns early, escapes his isolated holdfast, secures an ally in her Manhattan grandmother, and finds her spiritual home in Italy, where she falls in love with the country and with Cesare, heir to a traditional banking family. Over the years, the footloose American and the entrenched Italian cause each other as much agony as ecstasy." Booklist

McPhee "is a brilliant stylist, and here she creates characters so palpably real, they seem to ache on the page. . . . L'America is dizzyingly hypnotic, roaming back and forth across time, telling the story through Cesare, Beth and, later, through Beth's grown daughter, Valeria. The shadow of 9/11 is subtly referenced throughout the story, and its power becomes almost unbearable." Washington Post Book World

McPherson, Jessamyn West See West, Jessamyn, 1902-1984

Mda, Zakes, 1948-

The Madonna of Excelsior. Farrar, Straus and Giroux 2004 258p $23

ISBN 0-374-20008-4

* LC 2003-54728

"In 1971, nineteen citizens of Excelsior, a farming community in South Africa's rural Free States, were charged with breaking apartheid's Immorality Act, which forbade sexual relations between blacks and whites on the pretext of avoiding miscegenation. The women were jailed as they awaited trial and their white counterparts were released on bail. In the end, the state withdrew the charges, but the accused women's lives, already complicated, became harder than ever. Mda tells the story of a family at the heart of the scandal." Publisher's note

"The voice that emerges suggests not just a writer who can seduce us through beautiful language and unfailing humor. We also encounter a writer who has the power to shock and frighten us, to astound and anger and unsettle us. The Madonna of Excelsior suggests, in short, that his is a voice for which one should feel not only affection but admiration." N Y Times Book Rev

The whale caller. Farrar, Straus and Giroux 2005 230p $23

ISBN 0-374-28785-6

LC 2005-14196

A "love story set in postapartheid South Africa. A man known only as the Whale Caller stands on the shores of the real-life village of Hermanus, blowing his kelp horn to woo a spirited female whale named Sharisha. There he catches the eye of Saluni, a fiery, red-haired recovering alcoholic obsessed with a pair of twin teenage girls whose angelic voices induce euphoria. The Whale Caller and Saluni form an uneasy romantic alliance, each envious of the other's obsessions." Booklist

"Despite the lighthearted and often hilarious antics, this love triangle, like so many others, is tragically unsustainable. Perhaps this is where The Whale Caller defies expectation: If it is a morality play, these are unusually funny, richly developed characters. If it is a quirky, romantic comedy, it's dispensed with a heaping helping of human frailty, tragic behavior and self-

Mda, Zakes, 1948——_Continued_

destruction. With an offhanded mastery of lyrical language, this gifted storyteller's prose shimmers without extravagance." Washington Post Book World

Means, David

The secret goldfish; stories. Fourth Estate 2004 211p

ISBN 0-00-716489-0   LC 2004-50617

Contents: Lightning man; Sault Ste. Marie; It counts as seeing; Blown from the bridge; A visit from Jesus; Petrouchka [with omissions]; Elyria man; The project; Hunger; Counterparts; Dustman appearances to date; Carnie; The nest; Michigan death trip; The secret goldfish

"With stunning simplicity, Means offers 15 stirring portraits of tragedy, loss, and love." Esquire

Medlicott, Joan A.

Gardens of Covington; a novel; [by] Joan Medlicott. Thomas Dunne Bks. 2001 326p $23.95

ISBN 0-312-27555-2   LC 2001-19149

Sequel to The ladies of Covington send their love

"Amelia, Grace and Hannah are now happily ensconced in their beautiful old farmhouse in the foothills of North Carolina, but when developers threaten to turn their Eden into a condo haven, Hannah at least is up in arms. Grace and her lover, Bob, are busy preparing to open a tearoom and Amelia's photography talent continues to bloom. She falls for a man she meets in a fender-bender, but the new romance isn't all sweetness and light." Publ Wkly

The ladies of Covington send their love; [by] Joan Medlicott. St. Martin's Press 2000 326p

ISBN 0-312-25329-X   LC 99-89922

"A Thomas Dunne book"

"Grace, Hannah, and Amelia are about as different as any three women can be, but the petty miseries of their dismal retirement boarding house near Philadelphia have forged an iron bond of friendship. When Amelia unexpectedly inherits a dilapidated farmhouse in North Carolina, the women screw up their collective courage and decide to renovate the house." Booklist

"The women grow in self-confidence until one publishes a book, one finds love, and one runs a physically demanding business. The ending is pure fantasy, but readers will enjoy the ride." Libr J

Meek, James

The people's act of love. Canongate 2005 391p $24

ISBN 1-841-95706-2   LC 2005-363497

"Thrown together in a remote Siberian village during the civil war that followed the Russian Revolution, the leader of a sect of Christian castrates and an escaped convict who aspires to be a terrorist revolutionary play out the fatal logic of, respectively, religious and political extremism. Meek expertly renders each man's devotion to the task of securing paradise on earth, and exposes the unsettling affinity between the devout servant of God and the cold, calculating murderer. The higher purpose assumed by Meek's tormented believers is mocked by the

novel's subsidiary characters, a lusty village woman and the Jewish lieutenant of an occupying Czech legion." New Yorker

We are now beginning our descent. Canongate Books 2008 295p $24

ISBN 978-1-84195-988-7; 1-84195-988-X

"The world around journalist and would-be novelist Adam Kellas is cracking. As a war correspondent in the Afghan mountains during post-9/11 operations, Kellas reports on prescheduled surgical strikes with a nagging sense of complicity. At dinner parties in chic North London, he uneasily joins the debate of the wars from the comfort of their immaculate dinner tables. Divorced, unstable, spurned by his lover and publishing houses from Paris to New York, Kellas embarks on a strange and difficult journey that will lead him to a tiny rural town near the Chesapeake Bay. There, the elusive American reporter Astrid, with whom Kellas shared one passionate night, waits for him, holding a glimmer of hope for Kellas' life but also an unsettling secret." Publisher's note

"Meek, himself a former war correspondent, writes with authority about the physical and psychological landscapes of war, especially wars that unfold through the reporting of modern media. . . . He fills We Are Now Beginning Our Descent to the brim with ideas. And while the plot slackens and occasionally staggers under the weight of its concepts, Meek holds onto our attention by writing some of the most breathtaking and provocative sentences in contemporary English." BookPage

Mehta, Gita

Raj; a novel. Simon & Schuster 1989 479p o.p.

LC 88-38504

An "historical novel that traces the life of an Indian princess from her birth during the year of Queen Victoria's Diamond Jubilee in 1897 until India wins its independence from the empire in the mid-twentieth century. Princess Jaya treads a path that leads from the ancient traditions of the maharajas—in which the woman was subjugated to the man—through the days in which India was held and exploited as a British possession; she becomes in the end a woman who has achieved her own independence and identity along with her country." Booklist

"Grounded in details of ancient royal tradition and Hindu ritual, Jaya's story counterpoints a vanished way of life against the complex political realities involved in the passing of the Raj and the birth of the modern nations of India and Pakistan." Publ Wkly

A river Sutra. Doubleday 1993 291p o.p.

LC 92-35779

"The narrator has left his high-ranking government job and the bustling life of the city for the tranquility of the country. He manages a rest house along the banks of the sacred Narmada River, devoting quiet hours to contemplation of the river's might, mystery, and beauty. But this seemingly peaceful realm is actually electric with the passion and tragedy of human existence as pilgrims from all walks of life make their way to the holy river. As our innkeeper converses with these troubled travelers, he becomes immersed in their startling stories." Booklist

"This is an idealized India, free of political and religious violence. 'A River Sutra' takes place in a fabled land of the romantic imagination, drawing on timeless

Mehta, Gita—*Continued*

literary traditions. Told with skill and sensitivity, Gita Mehta's tales are a delight to read, bringing to Western readers the mystery and drama of a rich cultural heritage." N Y Times Book Rev

Melman, Peter Charles, 1971-

Landsman; a novel. Counterpoint Press 2006 323p $24.95

ISBN 978-1-58243-367-7; 1-58243-367-4

LC 2006-33305

"A barely literate hard-bitten gambler and petty criminal, Elias Abrams, the 20-year-old cardsharp hero of Melman's . . . debut, flees hometown New Orleans (and a bogus murder charge), joins the Confederate Army and realizes "every circumstance of his life now conspires to kill him." He survives the infantry as he had the city—using his wiles, card skills and fists—until his colonel hands over an envelope containing a charming missive from Nora Bloom, a young New Orleans maiden who wrote a support-the-troops letter at the urging of her rabbi. Unexpectedly stirred, Elias begins a correspondence and finds himself obsessively fantasizing about her. A battlefield injury leads to a furlough during which he returns to the city to meet both Nora (he falls in love) and cronies from his seedy past, who use his new flame as leverage to draw him into a sinister plot." Publ Wkly

"At times ribald and always real, Melman creates a rich and authentic story." Booklist

Melnyczuk, Askold

The house of widows; an oral history. Graywolf Press 2008 255p pa $16

ISBN 978-1-55597-491-6 (pa); 1-55597-491-0 (pa)

"James Pak is a divorced, brooding 40-year-old 'trapped, like so many, in the weather of the past,' on a mission to sort through the details surrounding his father Andrew's suicide. It's 2006 16 years to the week since Andrew's death and James walks the streets of Vienna, where he lives, recalling that before his father killed himself, he gave his only son a letter 'in a language he knew I couldn't read.' The remaining sum of James' inheritance is his father's British military ID card and a cracked glass jar. An expatriate historian who works by day at the U.S. Embassy, James is obsessed by his family's Ukrainian roots, a story filled with lacunas and layers of deceit." Los Angeles Times Book Rev

"A superbly written tale of intrigue, contemporary history, mystery and illicit international trade. . . . Literary, cerebral, elegant, almost every sentence perfect." Milwaukee Journal Sentinel

Meloy, Maile

A family daughter; a novel. Scribner 2006 325p $24

ISBN 0-7432-7766-X

LC 2005-51574

"Continuing the family saga of her first novel, 'Liars and Saints.' Meloy's second follows Abby Collins from the age of seven, when her feckless mother and sober father separate, to her success as a young novelist. The kernel of the story is a melodrama involving her uncle Jamie, who rescues her first from the boredom of her childhood illness and then, later, from grief after the sudden death of her father. When a mutual sexual attraction develops, though, Abby must learn to rescue herself, which she does mainly by recasting the dilemmas of her extended family as a work of fiction. All this might easily come off as soap opera were Meloy not a wise and astonishing conjurer of convincing realities." New Yorker

Liars and saints; a novel. Scribner 2003 260p $24

ISBN 0-7432-4435-4

LC 2002-30852

"The Santerres, starting with lovely Yvette and uptight Teddy, a World War II marine, are hardly a typical Catholic family. When their eldest daughter gets pregnant in high school, Yvette concocts an elaborate ruse and convinces Teddy that the baby is theirs. Similar secret begettings, concealed identities, and hidden anguish occur in each subsequent generation as Yvette becomes increasingly religious and Teddy struggles to love his rule-breaking progeny." Booklist

"Meloy's unerring mastery of narrative is remarkable. The disciplined economy and resonant clarity of her prose allow her to present a complex story in swift, lean chapters. The alternating points of view of eight main characters shine with authenticity and illuminate the moral complexities felt by each generation." Publ Wkly

Meltzer, Brad

The book of lies. Grand Central Pub. 2008 336p il $25.99

ISBN 978-0-446-57788-5; 0-446-57788-X

LC 2008-13692

A "conspiracy mystery inspired by the Biblical tale of Cain and Abel and real-life story of comics scribe Jerry Siegel, who co-created Superman with artist Joe Shuster in 1932. In his book — which concerns a Florida activist with a family secret linked to Siegel and a centuries-spanning conspiracy involving Nazis, secret societies, and a cryptic tome called The Book of Lies Meltzer advances the theory that the death of Siegel's father (who may or may not have been murdered in a robbery gone wrong) inspired his son to make the ultimate wish fulfillment fantasy of 20th-century pop culture." Entertainment Wkly

Dead even. Weisbach Bks. 1998 401p

ISBN 0-688-15090-X

LC 98-5935

New Yorkers "Sara Tate and Jared Lynch are married to each other and to their legal careers: he's a rising star for the defense in a big firm; she's just starting as an assistant district attorney after six months of job seeking. On her first day, Sara hears that a budget cut could put her back on the unemployment lines, so she swipes a burglary case earmarked for a top man in the pecking order. But this is more than a routine burglary, and a powerful villain named Oscar Rafferty wants it to go away. He hires Jared to defend the accused, a sadistic monster called Tony Kozlow, telling him that unless Kozlow walks, Sara dies." Publ Wkly

The author "gives the reader well-rounded characters; demonizing neither prosecution nor defense, he shows both as human beings doing a job." Libr J

The first counsel. Warner Bks. 2001 479p $25.95

ISBN 0-446-52728-9

LC 00-28963

Meltzer, Brad—*Continued*

"Michel Young, an idealistic lawyer in the White House counsel's office, is on a date with Nora, the very sexy, intriguing, enigmatic daughter of the president, when they see the chief counsel in a compromising position. Nora's questionable behavior quickly throws them into the middle of a plot that involves blackmail and murder." Booklist

Meltzer "relies on some heavy-handed techniques to generate suspense . . . and the plot has a familiar Hollywood ring to it. But Meltzer's relentless narrative finally digs its hooks in, and even skeptical readers will want to continue through the twists and turns, if only to confirm their own predictions." Publ Wkly

The tenth justice. Morrow 1997 389p
ISBN 0-688-15089-6   LC 96-44815

"Hotshot young lawyer Ben Addison is on top of the world. Just out of Yale Law School, he's already landed the highly desirable top job of clerk to a Supreme Court justice, experiences instant chemistry with his new co-clerk Lisa, and shares an apartment with three lifelong friends. Then a misplaced trust leads Ben to reveal a confidential court decision, and his world begins to crash. With Ben's career in jeopardy and a blackmailer on his trail, his friends use their job connections at the State Department, a Washington newspaper, and a senator's office to aid Ben and Lisa in a plot to apprehend Ben's blackmailer." Libr J

"Meltzer moves the story along at a crisp pace, spicing the action and legalese with lively banter and intriguing D.C. arcana." Publ Wkly

The zero game. Warner Bks. 2004 460p $25.95
ISBN 0-446-53098-0   LC 2003-15157

"Bored congressional staffer Harris Sandler plays something called the zero game with his coworkers, but it turns deadly when a vote concerning an abandoned gold mine in South Dakota is brought to the floor. Together with a 16-year-old Senate page named Viv Parker, Harris finds himself being chased by a ruthless killer in the halls of the Capitol as well as in the bowels of the mine." Libr J

This thriller is "packed with plenty of backroom D.C. ambience and lots of action." Booklist

Melville, Herman, 1819-1891

Billy Budd, sailor; supplementary material written by Kathleen Helal. Pocket Books 2006 xxi, 166p pa $4.99
ISBN 978-1-416-52372-7; 1-416-52372-3
                                * LC 2006-299200

Written in 1891 but in a still "unfinished" manuscript stage when Melville died. First publication 1924 in the United Kingdom, as part of the Standard edition of Melville's complete works

"Narrates the hatred of petty officer Claggart by Billy, handsome Spanish sailor. Billy strikes and kills Claggart, and is condemned by Captain Vere even though the latter senses Billy's spiritual innocence." Haydn. Thesaurus of Book Dig

also in Melville, H. The complete shorter fiction

also in Melville, H. Pierre; or, The ambiquities, Israel Potter: his fifty years of exile, The piazza tales, The confidence-man: his masquerade, Uncollected prose, Billy Budd, Sailor: (an inside narrative)

The complete shorter fiction; with an introduction by John Updike. Knopf 1997 478p $20
ISBN 0-375-40068-0
"Everyman's library"

Contents: The piazza; Bartleby, the scrivener; Benito Cereno; The lightning-rod man; The encantadas; or, Enchanted isles; The bell-tower; Fragments from a writing desk; Authentic anecdotes of "Old Zack"; Hawthorne and his mosses; The happy failure; The fiddler; Cock-a-doodle-doo!; Poor man's pudding; Rich man's crumbs; The two temples: Temple second; The paradise of bachelors; The tartarus of maids; Jimmy Rose; The 'gees; I and my chimney; The apple-tree table; Billy Budd, sailor; The two temples: Temple first

The confidence-man: his masquerade; edited, with an introduction and notes by John Bryant. Modern Library 2003 xlix, 331p pa $11.95
ISBN 0-375-75802-X   LC 2003-44561
First published 1857

"The scene is a Mississippi River boat, ironically named the 'Fidele.' A plotless satire taking place on April Fool's Day, the book is filled with characters difficult to distinguish from one another; most of them are different manifestations of the confidence man. A sign hanging on the door of the 'Fidele's' barbershop expresses the theme: 'No Trust.' The confidence man, king of a world without principle, succeeds in gulling men by capitalizing on false hopes and offering false pity. At the end of the book, the flickering light hanging above the table where an old man reads the Bible goes out completely." Reader's Ency. 4th edition

also in Melville, H. Pierre; or, The ambiquities, Israel Potter: his fifty years of exile, The piazza tales, The confidence-man: his masquerade, Uncollected prose, Billy Budd, Sailor: (an inside narrative)

Israel Potter
In Melville, H. Pierre; or, The ambiquities, Israel Potter: his fifty years of exile, The piazza tales, The confidence-man: his masquerade, Uncollected prose, Billy Budd, Sailor: (an inside narrative)

Mardi: and a voyager thither
In Melville, H. Typee: a peep at Polynesian life; Omoo: a narrative of adventures in the South Seas; Mardi: and a voyager thither

Moby-Dick; or, The whale; illustrated by Rockwell Kent. Modern Library 1992 xxxv, 822p il $21
ISBN 0-679-60010-8
                                * LC 92-50222

Melville, Herman, 1819-1891—*Continued*
First published 1851

"Moby Dick is a ferocious white whale, who was known to whalers as Mocha Dick. He is pursued in a fury of revenge by Captain Ahab, whose leg he has bitten off; and under Melville's handling the chase takes on a significance beyond mere externals. Moby Dick becomes a symbol of the terrific forces of the natural universe, and Captain Ahab is doomed to disaster, even though Moby Dick is killed at last." Univ Handbook for Readers and Writers

"'Moby-Dick' had some initial critical appreciation, particularly in Britain, but only since the 1920s has it been recognized as a masterpiece, an epic tragedy of tremendous dramatic power and narrative drive." Oxford Companion to Engl Lit. 5th edition

> *also in* Melville, H. Redburn, his first voyage; White-jacket, or, The world in a man-of-war; Moby-Dick, or, The whale

Omoo: a narrative of adventures in the South Seas; edited by Harrison Hayford, Hershel Parker, G. Thomas Tanselle. Northwestern University Press 1999 316p pa $16.95

ISBN 0-8101-1765-7

* LC 99-41391

First published 1847 by Harper

"Based on Melville's own experiences in the South Pacific, this episodic novel, in a more comical vein than that of *Typee*, tells of the narrator's participation in a mutiny on a whale ship and his subsequent wanderings in Tahiti with the former doctor of the ship." Merriam-Webster's Ency of Lit

> *also in* Melville, H. Typee: a peep at Polynesian life; Omoo: a narrative of adventures in the South Seas; Mardi: and a voyager thither

The piazza tales

> *In* Melville, H. Pierre; or, The ambiguities, Israel Potter: his fifty years of exile, The piazza tales, The confidence-man: his masquerade, Uncollected prose, Billy Budd, Sailor: (an inside narrative)

Pierre

> *In* Melville, H. Pierre; or, The ambiguities, Israel Potter: his fifty years of exile, The piazza tales, The confidence-man: his masquerade, Uncollected prose, Billy Budd, Sailor: (an inside narrative)

Pierre; or, The ambiguities, Israel Potter: his fifty years of exile, The piazza tales, The confidence-man: his masquerade, Uncollected prose, Billy Budd, Sailor: (an inside narrative). Library of America 1984 1478p $45

ISBN 0-940450-24-0

LC 84-11249

Pierre; or, The Ambiguities (1852) "moves between the idyllic Berkshire countryside and the nightmare landscape of early New York City. Its hero, a young American patrician trying to redeem the secret sins of his father, elopes to the city, discovers Bohemian life, attempts a literary epic, and struggles his way through incest, murder, and madness. . . . Israel Potter [1855, is] the story

of a veteran of the Revolution, victim of a thousand mischances, and a long-suffering exile in England. . . . The Piazza Tales [1856, is a collection of six stories], including 'The Encantadas,' about nature's two faces—enchanting and horrific; the famous 'Bartleby the Scrivener,' about a Wall Street copyist who 'would prefer not to'; and the enigmatic 'Benito Cereno,' about a credulous Yankee sea captain who stumbles into an intricately plotted mutiny aboard a disabled slave ship. The Confidence-Man [1857], Melville's last published novel, is in many ways a forerunner of modernist American fiction. . . . Many pieces never before collected are also included. . . . Finally, there is the posthumously published masterpiece Billy Budd, Sailor, the haunting story of a beautiful, innocent sailor who is pressed into naval service, slandered, provoked to murder, and sacrificed to military justice." Publisher's note

Redburn, his first voyage

> *In* Melville, H. Redburn, his first voyage; White-jacket, or, The world in a man-of-war; Moby-Dick, or, The whale

Redburn, his first voyage; White-jacket, or, The world in a man-of-war; Moby-Dick, or, The whale. Literary Classics of the United States, Inc, Distributed to the trade by the Viking Press 1983 1437p $35

ISBN 0-940450-09-7

LC 82-18677

Redburn (1849) is a semiautobiographical novel about a young man's ill-fortuned trip across the Atlantic. White-jacket (1850), another semiautobiographical novel, centers around a young sailor nicknamed for the white jacket that he buys in Peru and wears throughout the novel. It also features an appearance by Jack Chase, a character who appears in several of Melville's works and who is here the first captain of the top, and a vivid description of the floggings and other punishments suffered by the crew for often minor infractions. Moby-Dick is entered separately.

Typee: a peep at Polynesian life. Northwestern Univ. Press 1968 374p il $75

ISBN 0-8101-0161-0

"The Writings of Herman Melville"

First published 1846

"Based on Melville's own experiences, the story tells of the hero and his friend Toby, who jump ship in the Marquesas Islands and wander mistakenly into the valley of Typee, which is inhabited by cannibals. The Typees become their benevolent captors, refusing to allow them to leave. Toby escapes, while the hero, suffering from a leg wound, remains to be nursed by the lovely Fayaway. Tempted to enjoy a somnolent, vegetative existence, the moral American chooses, with regret, to return to civilization." Reader's Ency. 4th edition

> *also in* Melville, H. Typee: a peep at Polynesian life; Omoo: a narrative of adventures in the South Seas; Mardi: and a voyager thither

Typee: a peep at Polynesian life; Omoo: a narrative of adventures in the South Seas; Mardi: and a voyager thither. Library of Am. 1982 1333p $40

ISBN 0-940450-00-3

* LC 81-18600

Melville, Herman, 1819-1891—*Continued*

Omnibus edition of the author's first three novels. The first two titles are entered separately. In Mardi, first published 1849, Melville "entertained questions of ethics and metaphysics, politics and culture, sin and guilt, innocence and experience. The complexity of the novel's content, in fact, destroys all pretensions to literary form. Originally a narrative of adventure, 'Mardi' became an allegory of mind." Benet's Reader's Ency of Am Lit

White-jacket: or, The world in a man-of-war
In Melville, H. Redburn, his first voyage; White-jacket, or, The world in a man-of-war; Moby-Dick, or, The whale

Melville, James, 1931-

The chrysanthemum chain. St. Martin's Press 1982 181p o.p.   LC 82-5546
"An English subject living in Japan is murdered and the British consul and the local police want to know why. David Murrow was a distinguished educator but he moved in a rather peculiar, though prominent, circle of friends, which included many political luminaries. There is great concern among them about the case and its possible effect on the out-come of an impending election. . . . Although Melville keeps the action moving in this fast paced novel, he still pays close attention to characterization and background." Best Sellers

Melville, Jennie
See also Butler, Gwendoline

Mendelson, Cheryl

Morningside Heights; a novel. Random House 2003 326p $24.95
ISBN 0-375-50836-8   LC 2002-31760
The first title of a projected trilogy. The "intersecting lives of a group of Manhattanites living in the staid but rapidly changing Upper West Side neighborhood of Morningside Heights near Columbia University are the focus of this [novel]. . . . Opera singer Charles Braithwaite; his wife, Anne, a pianist; and their three (soon to be four) childen are the novel's ostensible protagonists. The books's real hero, however, is their beloved neighborhood, which they fear they will soon have to leave, unable to afford their cramped apartment." Publ Wkly
"With her motley cast, Mendelson paints an accurate, often comical portrait of the Upper West Side." N Y Times Book Rev

Menendez, Ana

The last war; a novel. HarperCollins 2009 225p $24.99
ISBN 978-0-06-172476-3; 0-06-172476-9
LC 2008-40919
The author focuses on "life in Istanbul, Afghanistan, and Iraq in a novel narrated by a freelance photographer known as 'Flash.' Her husband, Brando, a journalist reporting from the war in Baghdad, waits for her to join him there; Flash, however, chooses to remain in Istanbul, their base for several years. The reasons for this consume most of Menendez's impressionistic and introspective

tale, as Flash grapples with a vague feeling that 'something essential' is giving way in their marriage—a feeling compounded by an anonymous letter alluding to Brando's ongoing affair. . . . Flash is weary of their constant migration from one war zone to the next, while Brando seems slavishly devoted to war for his very existence. Menendez offers astute and perceptive commentary on both the hidden and obvious effects of war and its aftermath." Booklist

Mengestu, Dinaw, 1978-

The beautiful things that heaven bears. Riverhead Books 2006 228p $22.95
ISBN 978-1-59448-940-2; 1-59448-940-8
LC 2006-25058
"In his rundown store in a gentrifying neighborhood of Washington, D.C., Ethiopian immigrant Stepha Stephanos regularly meets with fellow African immigrants Ken the Kenyan and Joe from the Congo. Their favorite game is matching African nations to coups and dictators, as they consider how their new immigrant expectations measure up to the reality of life in America after 17 years. . . . When Judith, a white woman, and Naomi, her mixed-race daughter, move into the neighborhood, Stephanos finds tentative prospects for friendship beyond his African compatriots." Booklist
"A tender, thoughtful novel that quietly takes on serious themes: the meaning of home and family, of nationality and exile, of isolation and connection." People

Meno, Joe

Bluebirds used to croon in the choir. Northwestern University Press 2005 180p $21.95; pa $12.95
ISBN 0-8101-5167-7; 0-8101-2424-6 (pa)
LC 2005-19766
Contents: The use of medicine; Our neck of the woods; A trip to Greek mythology camp; Happiness will be yours; Be a good citizen; In the arms of someone you love; The moll; Tijuana women; Hold on to your hat; I'll be your sailor; Midway; Mr. Song; A strange episode of Aqua Voyage; How to say good night; Women I have made cry; A town of night; Astronaut of the year
"In Meno's offbeat universe, a horse predicts the future by crying into a bucket, and the Astronaut of the Year gets memorialized on ceramic garlic holders. The author . . . narrates his tales of awkward interpersonal relationships unfolding amid semisurreal situations in a cool, half-adolescent deadpan. . . . Though these stories don't always end as well as they begin, they're edgy and interesting, with a fine blend of the dark and the absurd." Publ Wkly

The boy detective fails. Akashic 2006 320p pa $14.95
ISBN 1-933354-10-0   LC 2006-923114
"In their youth, Billy Argo, his kid sister Caroline, and their friend Fenton solved a series of puzzling crimes with only a cheap detective kit and their imaginations. After Billy goes to college to study criminology, Caroline commits suicide and guilt-ridden Billy attempts it, ending up heavily sedated in a mental hospital. Ten years later, he connects with two other outcast, nerdy sorts to help solve the mysteries going on in their lives and in

Meno, Joe—*Continued*
that of a kleptomaniac widow who is as fragile and traumatized as he is. The one mystery he can't solve is Caroline's death. This is postmodern fiction with a head and
a heart, addressing such depressing issues as suicide,
death, loneliness, failure, anomie, and guilt with compassion, humor, and even whimsy." Libr J

The great perhaps; a novel. W. W. Norton &
Company 2009 414p $24.95
  ISBN 978-0-393-06796-5; 0-393-06796-3
                                       LC 2008-54280
This novel "novel chronicles a family of five tortured
souls on the verge of total dissolution. Scientist Jonathan,
who gets epileptic fits from seeing clouds, has had his
life's work scooped by a bitter rival, social scientist
Madeline has lost him to his research while hers suffers,
daughters Amelia and Thisbe are outcasts struggling to
find their place in the world, and grandfather Henry desires only to escape his hellish nursing-home existence."
Libr J
"Meno's plain style is set off nicely by his taste for
modernist formal daring: the novel makes room for
drawings, long transcripts of old radio serials, declassi-
fied government documents and several chapters consisting of exactly 26 short sections, each headed by a letter
of the alphabet. There is an occasional streak of fancy to
events as well." N Y Times Book Rev

Meredith, George, 1828-1909

The ordeal of Richard Feverel; a history of father and son; edited with an introduction and notes
by Edward Mendelson. Penguin Books 1998 xxxi,
522p (Penguin classics)
  ISBN 978-0-14-043483-5; 0-14-043483-6
                                       * LC 99-461805
First published 1859
This novel is representative of Meredith's "best work,
full of allusion and metaphor, lyrical prose and witty dialogue, with a deep exploration of the psychology of motive and rationalization. The novel's subject is the relationship between a cruelly manipulative father and a son
who loves a girl of a lower social class. Both men are
self-deluded and proud, and the story's ending is tragic."
Merriam-Webster's Ency of Lit

Mérimée, Prosper, 1803-1870

Carmen; translated from the French and illustrated by Edmund H. Garrett, with a memoir of the
author by Louise Imogen Guiney. Little, Brown
1896 xxx, 117p il o.p.
                                                    *
Original French edition, 1845
"Georges Bizet's opera *Carmen* is based on the story.
As a hot-blooded young corporal in the Spanish cavalry
stationed near Seville, Don José is ordered to arrest Carmen, a young, flirtatious Gypsy woman, for assaulting a
coworker. Greatly charmed by her, José allows her to escape. He deserts the army, kills two men on Carmen's
account, and takes up a life as a robber and smuggler.
He is insanely jealous of Carmen, who is unfaithful to
him, and when she refuses to change on his behalf, he
kills her and surrenders himself to the authorities."
Merriam-Webster's Ency of Lit

Mertz, Barbara, 1927-
*For works written by this author under other
names see* Michaels, Barbara, 1927-; Peters, Elizabeth, 1927-

Merullo, Roland, 1953-

Breakfast with Buddha; a novel. Algonquin
Books of Chapel Hill 2007 323p $23.95
  ISBN 978-1-56512-552-0; 1-56512-552-5
                                       LC 2007-7978
"Otto Ringling, a successful New York editor and contented family man, has been in a slump ever since his
parents were killed in an automobile accident. To settle
the estate, he and his loopy sister, Cecilia, must drive to
the family homestead in North Dakota. Then Cecilia tells
him she's giving him half of the farm to her guru, the
maroon-robed Volya Rinpoche, and that she wants Otto
to drive him there. A grumbling Otto reluctantly agrees,
mapping out a route that will take them along some of
the Midwest's most charming backroads, and treating the
rotund monk to a taste of American fun, including a tour
of the Hershey chocolate factory and a round of miniature golf." Booklist
"Somewhere between bowling and yoga class,
Rinpoche teaches Otto to examine himself, and readers
will be rooting for the success of this unlikely pair.
Merullo's clear writing ensures that readers will master
Rinpoche's sometimes cryptic reflections as well."
BookPage

Messud, Claire, 1966-

The emperor's children. Alfred A. Knopf 2006
431p $25
  ISBN 0-307-26419-X   LC 2005-57783
"A comedy of manners set in the months immediately
before and after the September 11th 2001 attacks and involving three bright young things who work in the media
in New York." Economist
The author "writes with the archness of a Muriel
Spark, only more subtly and sympathetically wielded.
. . . Ultimately, most impressive is the way Messud relates 9/11 to her characters' lives: The public tragedy
doesn't eclipse but rather seeps into and amplifies their
private sorrows." Nation

The hunters; two short novels. Harcourt 2001
181p $29
  ISBN 0-15-100588-5   LC 00-50571
Contents: A simple tale; The hunters
"These novellas both have displaced protagonists who
cannot decide whether to seek a deathlike stillness or to
embrace life's mess. In the first, a Toronto cleaning
woman finds that the ritualized relationship she enjoys
with a long-term employer has provided more continuity
than anything else in her life, which has included famine
in rural Ukraine, slave labor in Germany, love in a dis-
placed-persons camp, emigration, and a cozy family existence. In widowhood, however, her sense of order is in
danger of taking over and annihilating all that is left. Being almost too fastidious to live is also the dilemma of
the narrator of the second tale, an American academic in
London who loathes the friendly woman who lives
downstairs. The tone is Jamesian, but the ending holds
a beast in the jungle only for the hapless fellow-tenant."
New Yorker

Messud, Claire, 1966-—*Continued*

The hunters [novelette]
In Messud, C. The hunters

A simple tale
In Messud, C. The hunters

Mestre-Reed, Ernesto, 1964-

The second death of Única Aveyano; a novel.
Vintage Contemporaries 2004 259p $13
ISBN 1-400-03316-0 (pa)   LC 2003-52544
"A Miami nursing home is no place for Unica
Aveyano, as she vociferously reminds her daughter-inlaw
at every opportunity. Although she is ill with terminal
cancer and terribly frail, she cannot bear the thought of
spending one more night wandering the halls or sitting
by the cracked windows. Miraculously, she finds her way
out the door, across a four-lane highway, and into the
ocean. When she is rescued by her male nurse, she
gravely tells him that she was led there by a pack of
wild angels. Her past is suddenly more alive to her than
the present, and she spends hours immersed in memories
of her Cuban childhood, her marriage, and her son, a bisexual artist who refused to emigrate with them. She has
no time for her mournful husband, who is sick at the
thought of being left behind. Mestre-Reed . . . is a lyric
novelist of uncommon power, creating a memorable portrait of a woman wracked by longing and memory yet
fearlessly embracing her impending death." Booklist

Mewshaw, Michael, 1943-

Shelter from the storm; a novel. Putnam 2003
280p $23.95
ISBN 0-399-14988-0   LC 2002-74640
In this thriller "a feral child from the steppes of Central Asia becomes the bargaining chip in a hostage negotiation. Scarred hero Zack McClintock, a private-sector
intelligence agent, travels to ex-Soviet territory in search
of his kidnapped son-in-law and finds plenty of people
with plenty to hide. . . .This is the sort of intelligent and
morally ambitious thriller—like those of Craig Nova or
Paul Watkins—that offers a welcome change from typical fare." Libr J

Meyer, Carolyn

Brown eyes blue; a novel. Bridge Works 2003
228p $23.95
ISBN 1-88259-368-5   LC 2002-12674
"Daughter Dorcas' return home is prompted by a call
from a friend who tells her about the scandal caused by
her mom's latest art exhibit. Instead of the pastoral
Amish scenes for which she is know, Lavinia's latest
show consists of brilliantly executed, graphic nudes. Dorcas, too, feels reckless and buys an old mansion to convert into an inn, and in the process remakes her own life.
Then granddaughter Sasha shows up pregnant and with
a lesbian partner." Booklist
"Little do these women guess how much they have in
common—shared passions, losses and secrets that lead
them to question the choices they have made in their
lives. Meyer weaves the story of three generations of
women who, with their distinctive voices, will endear
themselves to readers." Publ Wkly

Meyer, Deon

Devil's peak; a novel; translated by K.L. Seegers. Little, Brown 2008 409p $24.99
ISBN 978-0-316-01785-5; 0-316-01785-X
LC 2007-30129
Original Afrikaans edition, 2004; this translation first
published 2007 in the United Kingdom
"Former mercenary Thobela Mpayipheli is trying to
live a peaceful life, but these plans are shattered when
his eight-year-old son, Pakamile, is shot dead. The two
gunmen responsible escape before sentencing, and the
grieving father decides to take matters into his own
hands. As he pursues his son's killers, Mpayipheli begins
to target pedophiles and other perpetrators of violence
against children, meting out justice with a Xhosa tribal
sword called an assegai. Dubbed 'Artemis' by the papers
as the killings increase, Mpayipheli becomes a kind of
folk hero to the people of Capetown. Insp. Benny
Griessel, an aging alcoholic whose struggles with the
bottle have all but cost him his family and his life,
works the case with a desperate intensity." Publ Wkly

Heart of the hunter; translated by K. L. Seegers.
Little, Brown 2004 c2003 374p $23.95
ISBN 0-316-93549-2   LC 2003-25683
"Thobela Mpayipheli has settled into a sedate but rewarding life with the woman he loves. He works as a
gofer at a South African motorcycle shop and readies his
partner's young son for life on a farm-until an ex-boss
asks him to perform a dangerous favor. His Xhosa warrior's heart racing, Thobela soon finds himself driving
hard toward Nigeria with a hard drive full of secrets the
unified government wishes to file away for good."
Booklist
"Despite the complexity of its tightly woven plot-
skillfully revealed through newspaper articles and intelligence reports-Meyer's U.S. debut moves at a breathtaking pace that will carry readers away. A sympathetic protagonist and the landscape of South Africa add color to
the story." Libr J

Meyer, Nicholas

The seven-per-cent solution; being a reprint
from the reminiscences of John H. Watson, M.D.,
as edited by Nicholas Meyer. Dutton 1974 253p
o.p.
*
"In this final memoir, dictated from a nursing home in
1939, Watson [the biographer of the famous detective
Sherlock Holmes] confesses that the events he recounted
in 'The Final Problem' are a total fabrication. . . . Watson observes that Holmes's agitation over Moriarty's evil
doings occurs only when he has been taking cocaine.
Fearing that Holmes is destroying himself, Watson tricks
him into a trip to Vienna, where he turns him over to
Sigmund Freud. . . . Freud cures Holmes of his addiction, and Holmes lingers on to observe that the schizophrenia of one of Freud's patients results from a criminal
conspiracy as yet unsuspected by anyone." Newsweek
"In a field replete with pastiche Meyer succeeds because of a superior ear for Conan Doyle's style, a gentle
sense of fun, and a talent for plot that few of the imita-
tors have possessed." Libr J

Meyer, Nicholas—*Continued*

The West End horror; a posthumous memoir of John H. Watson, M.D., as edited by Nicholas Meyer. Dutton 1976 222p o.p.

This novel "is set in London's theatre district in 1895. A much disliked theatre critic has been murdered, and Sherlock Holmes is engaged to find the murderer. His client is another critic of the day whose years of fame are ahead of him: George Bernard Shaw. Inspector Lestrade, Holmes's old foil, is on the scene, but, as always, his efforts are misdirected and before long he has managed to incarcerate an obvious innocent. Clues abound and so too do real but suspicious characters." Best Sellers

Meyer, Philipp, 1974-

American rust. Spiegel & Grau 2009 368p $24.95

ISBN 978-0-385-52751-4; 0-385-52751-9

LC 2008-22461

"Meyer offers up a character-driven near-noir set in Buell, a dying Pennsylvania steel town, where aimless friends Billy Poe and Isaac English are trapped by economic and personal circumstance. Just before their half-hearted escape to California, Isaac accidentally kills a transient who tries to rob Poe. The boys return to the crime scene the next day with plans to cover up the crime, setting the plot in motion. Poe is soon under suspicion, and Isaac, distraught after discovering Poe has been carrying on a relationship with Isaac's sister, Lee, sets off for California alone. Meanwhile, Poe's mother, Grace, mourns her own lost opportunities, broods over her son and pines for her on-again-off-again love, the local sheriff." Publ Wkly

The author "conjures up this blue-collar Rust Belt town with the same sort of social detail and emotional verisimilitude that Richard Russo has brought to his depictions of upstate New York and Russell Banks has brought to downstate New Hampshire. He writes about his characters' lives in Buell with sympathy and unsentimental clarity." N Y Times (Late N Y Ed)

Meyer, Stephenie, 1973-

The host; a novel. Little, Brown and Co. 2008 619p $25.99

ISBN 978-0-316-06804-8; 0-316-06804-7

LC 2007-33060

This novel "is set in some vague future, when the Earth (all of it, apparently) has been invaded by a species whose members call themselves 'souls' ('parasites' the renegade bands of humans call them) that take over human bodies. Existing apart from their host creatures as feathery silver ribbons, souls are inserted into the host body via a small slit in the back of the neck made by alien doctors called Healers. . . . The central character is a soul named Wanderer, renowned among her species for having lived on eight previous planets, as a spider, a bear, a dolphin. Unlike other souls who have settled into one species on one planet, she seeks knowledge, growth and adventure, so she is chosen for insertion into a particularly resistant host named Melanie Stryder. The problem for Wanderer, and the premise of the novel, is that Melanie's consciousness won't be obliterated. She hangs out in this jointly tenanted mind, having conversations with Wanderer, showing her memories and urging her own agenda." Pittsburgh Post-Gazette

"While the straightforward narrative is short on detail about the invasion and its stunning aftermath, it shines with romantic intrigue, especially when a love triangle (or quadrangle?!) develops for Wanda/Melanie." Publ Wkly

Meyers, Kent

The work of wolves. Harcourt 2004 416p $24

ISBN 0-15-101057-9   LC 2003-26365

In this novel, set in South Dakota, "several different lives intersect on the edge of the Sioux reservation when a group of mistreated horses is discovered. Carson Fielding, a horse trainer who lives on a farm that has been in his family for several generations, is hired by wealthy landowner Magnus Yarborough to train said horses and teach Rebecca, his young wife, to ride. When Yarborough suspects that the lessons have led to something more, he takes out his anger on Carson through the horses, setting in motion a series of events that draws together Carson; Earl Walks Alone, a Lakota teenager who discovers the half-starved horses in a secluded pen; and Willi, a German exchange student with a troubled past." Libr J

Meyer's "spare dialogue is brilliantly and often comically expressive, and Carson, his taciturn, rational hero, is an original and compelling character. Strong themes of generational responsibility and family history add resonance to this gratifying, very American novel." Publ Wkly

Michael, Judith

Acts of love. Crown 1997 376p

ISBN 0-517-70324-2

In this novel "theater director Lucas Cameron discovers a box of letters left behind by his deceased grandmother, the famous stage actress Constance Bernhardt. The letters were written by her protégée Jessica Fontaine, who disappeared from the stage years before. Even in the midst of his busy world . . . Luke finds himself returning again and again to the letters, recognizing in them a deeply passionate young woman discovering herself and the magic of the theater. Luke begins to realize that he has fallen in love with the woman who wrote them. Finally he can bear it no longer—and tracks down the elusive Jessica Fontaine. But when he travels to her hideaway on Lopez Island off the coast of Washington, nothing is as he expected it." Publisher's note

A certain smile. Crown 1999 301p

ISBN 0-517-70325-4   LC 98-52333

"Miranda Grant, a 40-year-old widow with two adolescent children, travels from her home in Boulder, Colo., to Beijing. . . . The story focuses on Miranda's relationship with Yuan Li, a successful builder/construction engineer. The son of a Chinese mother and an American soldier, he becomes her soulful guide to China, romance and personal growth. Danger intrudes after Miranda innocently acts as courier for a letter from a former dissident, now in America; the authorities put Miranda and Yuan Li under round-the-clock surveillance." Publ Wkly

Deceptions. Pocket Bks. 1982 472p o.p.

"A Poseidon Press book"

"When twin sisters, who have been mistaken for each other all their lives, are on vacation together in China,

Michael, Judith—*Continued*

they decide on a whim to switch roles for a week, thus beginning a deception that has far-reaching effects. The aristocratic Lady Sabrina, assuming the suburban housewife's duties of her sister Stephanie Anderson, is surprised to find she scarcely misses her former high life, reveling instead in the acceptance and security of being part of a family. Stephanie, leaving her humdrum life behind to assume Sabrina's jet-set life of partying and dealing in antiques, so much enjoys her liberation that she is reluctant to come home. Sabrina has fallen in love with Stephanie's husband; she postpones ending the deception until a freak accident leaves her unsure of her identity at all." Publ Wkly

Followed by A tangled web

Sleeping beauty; a novel. Poseidon Press 1991 539p o.p.   LC 91-31298

"The wealthy, influential Chatham family, founders of a Chicago-based realty empire, present a wholesome image to the outside world. But 30-year-old financial whiz Vince Chatham has raped his 13-year-old niece, Anne, and continues to abuse her sexually. When Anne overcomes her fear and guilt to accuse Vince at a family gathering, she is met with skepticism from her relatives and denial from Vince. After Anne runs away from home, however, Vince is stripped of his position at the corporation; enraged, he vows to destroy the rest of the Chatham clan." Publ Wkly

"Michael does this sort of thing much better than most of the competition: the characters, naturally larger than life, are still believable." Booklist

Michaels, Anne, 1958-

Fugitive pieces. Knopf 1997 294p
ISBN 0-679-45439-X

        * LC 96-36678

First publishd 1996 in Canada

This "tale revolves around the life of a young Polish Jew, Jakob Beer, who, after witnessing the murder of his parents, is miraculously rescued by Athos, a Greek geologist. A man of heroic intellect and spirituality, Athos risks his life to bring Jakob to Greece only to find that the tide of evil has even reached those hallowed shores. They immigrate to Canada, and their mentor-disciple relationship deepens as each studious year passes." Booklist

Michaels "offers a richly imagined portrait of Jakob's slow progress from reticence to poetic eloquence and of the complex blend of memories, feelings, insights, and experiences that makes him the man he becomes. She even tackles the perpetually troubling question of how so many seemingly ordinary, 'civilized' people could have eagerly committed such monstrous crimes against defenseless children and civilians." Christ Sci Monit

Michaels, Barbara, 1927-

For works written by this author under other names see Peters, Elizabeth, 1927-

The dancing floor. HarperCollins Pubs. 1997 326p o.p.   LC 96-39331

"Frumpy but spunky American tourist Heather Tradescant's vacation in Britain is blighted by her parents' recent death. Hoping to fulfill her late father's dream, she tries to visit the 17th-century garden of Troytan House, home of businessman Frank Karim and his taciturn son, Jordan. Rebuffed, Heather finds a hidden entrance to the estate, but as she wanders through a bramble-thickened maze, she falls at the feet of the Karims enjoying an al fresco breakfast. At first hostile, the Karims soon prove more than hospitable, begging her to stay because they believe she's an horticultural expert. . . . An unlikely object of desire, Heather attracts the men around her through her strong personality, lively wit and huge appetite. She and other well-delineated characters make this tale everything a romance reader can ask for." Publ Wkly

Houses of stone. Simon & Schuster 1993 334p o.p.   LC 93-27926

"Michaels sets her heroine, Professor Karen Holloway, to the task of discovering the provenance of a remnant from an old manuscript. Holloway is convinced that it is a thinly disguised autobiographical novel by an obscure feminist poet whose verses have already helped Holloway carve a niche in the cutthroat business of academia. The professor's archenemies, two fellow literature experts, are equally convinced of the work's value and attempt desperate measures to gain access of the manuscript. Michaels has composed a mystery that is brimming with suspense yet revolves around authorial research rather than money and multiple murders." Booklist

Shattered silk. Atheneum Pubs. 1986 369p
ISBN 0-689-11620-9   LC 86-47658

Karen Nevitt "begins a new life in Georgetown after her unhappy marriage crumbles. She plans to open an antique-clothing shop with the encouragement of old and new friends. But a series of seemingly unrelated yet terrifying events begins to unfold, and Karen is caught up in a web of deadly suspense." Libr J

Stitches in time. HarperCollins Pubs. 1995 307p
ISBN 0-06-017763-2   LC 95-4286

A "mystery based on a haunted quilt. Rachel Grant is a doctoral student working on her thesis—an investigation of women's garments designed for important rites of passage—when she takes a part-time job at a chic vintage clothing shop run by two women, Kara and her sister-in-law Cheryl. When Cheryl's police officer husband is shot, Rachel is drawn into the family because she moves into Cheryl's home, which is connected to the shop. Meanwhile, the message from the quilt lures Rachel into dangerous misdeeds. The unraveling of the mystery proves fascinating." Booklist

Michaels, Fern

Celebration. Kensington Pub. Corp. 1999 358p
ISBN 1-57566-402-X   LC 98-67474

"When her husband retires and disappears with their savings, Kristine's whole family structure disintegrates as her children express their disgust with her continuing faith in a man they've known for years as a self-centered womanizer. With the help of friends and, eventually, a new love interest, Kristine focuses on work and rebuilds her family's toy business but keeps her new love at arm's length." Booklist

Finders keepers. Kensington Bks. 1998 396p
ISBN 1-57566-323-6

Michaels, Fern—*Continued*

"Adorable toddler Hannah Larson, only child of poor but decent Grace and Ben, is sitting in her stroller outside a Tennessee gas station when baby-starved Thea and Barnes Roland pull in for a cream soda. Thea snatches the child, Barnes puts pedal to metal and Hannah becomes 'adopted' Jessie, doomed to a life of smothering love and material overabundance in Charleston, S.C., while her birth parents suffer and hope. On her way to NYU . . . Jessie detours through Washington and talks herself into a job as secretary to powerful Texas Senator Angus Kingsley, who has an icy wife, Alexis; a dying mistress, Irene; and a gorgeous son, Tanner. Jessie, of course, marries Tanner, and the trouble really begins." Publ Wkly

Michaels, Leonard, 1933-2003

The collected stories. Farrar, Straus and Giroux 2007 403p $26

ISBN 978-0-374-12654-4; 0-374-12654-2

* LC 2006-102556

Contents: Manikin; City boy; Crossbones; Sticks and stones; The deal; Intimations; Making changes; Mildred; Fingers and toes; Isaac; A green thought; Finn; Going places; Murderers; Eating out; Getting lucky; Storytellers, liars, and bores; In the fifties; Reflections of a wild kid; Downers; Trotsky's garden; Annabella's hat; I would have saved them if I could; Hello Jack; Some laughed; The captain; Journal; Honeymoon; A girl with a monkey; Tell me everything; Viva la Tropicana; Nachman; Nachman from Los Angeles; Nachman at the races; The penultimate conjecture; Nachman burning; Of mystery there is no end; Cryptology

"Michaels never stopped reflecting on the condition of being Jewish. Now that he is gone, it is easier to place him in a broader context, as part of that astonishing flowering of American Jewish writing that included Bellow, Malamud, Mailer and Roth, toward which he can be seen as both filial heir and mischievous critic." Nation

Michener, James A., 1907-1997

Alaska. Random House 1988 868p o.p.

LC 87-43232

This novel begins with the prehistory of Alaska before concentrating on the history of the region since the 18th century

"Besides multiple heroes and heroines, there are knaves and opportunists who have depleted Alaska's resources and contributed to the high rates of alcoholism and suicide. One of Michener's favorite words is *noble*, but after mushing through his Arctic saga of persistence and greed, one is not surprised that he uses it mainly to describe grizzly bears, salmon and whales." Time

The bridges at Toko-ri. Random House 1953 146p o.p.

*

"In this hard-hitting novel of the Korean conflict, Admiral George Tarrant commands the Naval Task Force, whose carrier-based jets are to knock out strategic points throughout Korea. The focal point of the novel is Harry Brubaker, a lawyer who goes reluctantly to war after being called up as a jet pilot. The reader will remember also Beer Barrel, the landing officer who can get the jets back on the carrier's decks, no matter how rough the seas; and Mike Forney, helicopter rescue pilot who gets pilots out of the freezing waters if they are downed." Shapiro. Fic for Youth. 3d edition

Caravans; a novel. Random House 1963 341p o.p.

The story, set in Afghanistan in the year 1946, "focuses on Ellen Jasper, an American bored with her native land, who flees to Afghanistan to become the second wife of a man named Nazrullah. Her parents haven't heard from her in 13 months and Mark Miller, of the U.S. Embassy in that country, is sent to investigate. The search takes Miller into unknown territory. He joins a nomad tribe and experiences a love affair of rare beauty with Mira, daughter of the Great Zulfiqar, chieftain of all the nomadic peoples scattered around Afghanistan. [The novel describes] Ellen's degeneration into a sensualist, [and] the encounter of Miller (a Jew) with an ex-Nazi who tortured Jews." America

Caribbean. Random House 1989 672p o.p.

LC 89-42785

A novel about the "Caribbean islands from the days when the peace-loving Arawak Indians were overpowered by cannibalistic Caribs, to a ship's tour of today's still lush, but troubled, paradise. Sir Francis Drake, pirate Henry Morgan, Horatio Nelson, Haitian General Toussaint L'Ouverture, Fidel Castro march across the pages, and while the pace is sometimes achingly slow, the dialogue stilted and the characterization skimpy, Michener laces the whole with fiery Caribbean drama." Publ Wkly

Centennial. Random House 1974 909p o.p.

*

"Written to celebrate the United States centennial, the book centers on a fictional town in Colorado. It begins with an examination of the geological formation of the land and a discussion of the first animals to live there. It continues with the arrival of the Indians, the coming of the first settlers, the traders, the search for gold, the building of the railroads, and the start of cattle ranching—virtually all the activities that made this country develop as it did. The conclusion brings us to the social and ecological problems of the 1970s." Shapiro. Fic for Youth. 3d edition

Chesapeake. Random House 1978 865p o.p.

LC 78-2892

"Through the interwoven stories of three families and the Indians, Blacks, and Irish immigrants with whom they interact, Michener chronicles four centuries of life on Maryland's Eastern Shore. . . . Michener elaborates . . . variations on his themes of personal accountability for social change, man's self-expulsion from paradise, and the interrelated ecological network of all things." Libr J

The covenant. Random House 1980 887p o.p.

LC 80-5315

This novel spans 500 years of South African history. Three families mingle "with the outstanding historic figures of their times. They are the Nxumalos, the Van Doorns, and the Saltwoods, representing respectively the African, Afrikaans, and English. . . . Over several hundred years their descendants make contact, and thrive through the contact, only to become adversaries as con-

Michener, James A., 1907-1997—*Continued*

tact subsequently gives way to conflict. Finally they find themselves irretrievably stuck in the hard concrete of South Africa's racial policies." Christ Sci Monit

Creatures of the kingdom; stories of animals and nature; illustrations by Karen Jacobsen. Random House 1993 281p il o.p.   LC 92-46075

Contents: From the boundless deep; The birth of the Rockies; Diplodocus, the dinosaur; A miracle of evolution; The mastodon; Matriarch, the woolly mammoth; Portrait of Rufous; The beaver; The eagle and the snake; The hyena; Nerka the salmon; Onk-or; The invaders; Jimmy the crab; Lucifer and Hey-You; The Colonel and Genghis Khan

"Gathered in this delightful 'anthology' . . . are sections from Michener's novels that deal with animals and other less animate aspects of the natural world. . . . These selections represent nature writing as its most fluid and involving." Booklist

The drifters; a novel. Random House 1971 751p o.p.

This novel, "narrated by a 60-year-old American financier who roams Europe and Africa in search of good investments, follows six young adults as they travel in search of something else. . . . Each young person has a special set of circumstances with which to contend." NY Times Book Rev

"The Drifters is something of a guidebook loosely dressed up as fiction; a guide to quaint and colorful places, especially on the Iberian peninsula, and to the life-styles of the rebellious young." Saturday Rev

Hawaii. Random House 1959 937p o.p.
                                                            *

A "novel in which the racial origins of Hawaii are traced through several narrative strands that merge in contemporary history. The original Tahitian colonizers welcome the white missionaries who bring in Chinese and Japanese laborers, and all together make up the present-day 'golden' Hawaiian." Wis Libr Bull

"High-domed, long-haired *littérateurs* may argue that Michener's characters are often as paper-thin as the colored image in which Hawaii is held by mainland tourists, but 'Hawaii,' is still a masterful job of research, an absorbing performance of storytelling, and a monumental account of the islands from geologic birth to sociological emergence as the newest, and perhaps the most interesting of the United States." Saturday Rev

Mexico. Random House 1992 625p o.p.
                                          LC 92-50151

In this novel set in Mexico City, "Mexico-born Norman Clay, a journalist for a New York publication, returns to his natal city to report on the bullfights that highlight its annual festival. This year two matadors are joined in a rivalry that could end in death." Libr J

"There are splendid and authentic scenes in the *plaza de toros* that are as dramatic as any written by Ernest Hemingway or Barnaby Conrad, and one chapter, where the bulls' horns are shaved by the father of a torero, is James Michener the storyteller and parabolist at his finest." N Y Times Book Rev

The novel. Random House 1991 446p
ISBN 0-679-40133-4   LC 90-53489

"'The novel' is divided into four parts, each told from a different point of view. The first is that of the novelist, Lukas, a plain, clean-living but big-bucks author in his late 60's whose most recent work, 'Stone Walls,' is the final work in the Grenzler Octet, an opus set in the Pennsylvania Dutch country, where he was born and raised. The second voice is that of Yvonne Marmelle, née Shirley Marmelstein, his editor. The third is that of the literary critic Karl Streibert, Lukas's fellow Pennsylvania Dutchman. And the fourth is that of a reader, Jane Garland, grand dame and philanthropist who is also Lukas's friend." N Y Times Book Rev

"To his credit, Michener tries to be fair to both sides of the literary vs. popular fiction debate. The elitist Streibert is presented as an honest, well-intentioned man who genuinely loves literature and worries about the dangers of commercialism. The position Michener seems to be advocating in 'The Novel' is that experimental, elitist fiction and old-fashioned storytelling are both legitimate forms for the novel." Christ Sci Monit

Poland. Random House 1983 556p o.p.
                                          LC 83-4477

"Centering on the fictional village of Bukowo on the Vistula River, the novel's action occurs as a series of vignettes of Polish life from the 1200s to the 1980s. Each chapter tells the story of a different generation of three families of Bukowo—the wealthy magnate counts Lubonski, the minor nobles Bukowski, and peasants Buk." Libr J

"The author's description of the devastating invasions of Poland by Tartars, Germans, Swedes, Turks, Russians and Soviets is historically accurate as well as highly vivid. . . . But the most unforgettable and deeply moving pages of the book are those in which Michener narrates the horrid experiences of the inmates of the Polish concentration camp of Majdanek, where 140,000 Jewish and 220,000 Christian prisoners died. . . . Michener's Poland is an engrossing and fast moving novel by a superb storyteller." America

Recessional. Random House 1994 484p
ISBN 0-679-43612-X   LC 94-17414

"Opening with obstetrician Andy Zorn taking a job as manager of one of the nation's poshest retirement and final-care facilities, the novel weaves through the challenges Zorn faces and the experiences of many of the residents of the Palms in Florida. . . . The fine line between euthanasia and the excessive use of mechanical life supports is drawn with poignant scenes of aging and AIDS patients. Despite the dreary subject, this novel is full of life and romance." Booklist

Sayonara. Random House 1954 243p o.p.

The love story of an American Air Corps major and a beautiful Japanese girl. When Major Gruver sets up housekeeping with Hanaogi there is consternation among the Americans, for Gruver is engaged to an American general's daughter. Contrary to the course of Madam Butterfly, in this instance it is the Japanese girl who says Sayonara (farewell) to the American

Space. Random House 1982 622p o.p.
                                          LC 82-40127

This novel "begins at the time of World War II and features characters who eventually find themselves, in one capacity or another, involved with the space program. Some are engineers; some are politicians; some are

Michener, James A., 1907-1997—*Continued*

astronauts." Libr J

"Michener has caught the essence of what motivated and then enfeebled our space program. . . . As usual, Michener has done his homework, this time with affection and excitement as well—his pro-space enthusiasm is the book's driving force, and he has deftly woven an incredible amount of information into the tale." Natl Rev

Texas. Random House 1985 1096p o.p.

LC 85-8248

This novel covers Texas history from 1527 to the present. "Texas then and now is, in a sense, all here: the Spanish missions; the early settlers; fights with the Comanches and Apaches; the Battle of the Alamo, won by the flamboyant and wily Mexican general Santa Anna . . . Sam Houston's heroic victory at San Jacinto; the birth of the Lone Star Republic—and so on." Publ Wkly

"As a novel, this book is remarkably good. . . . Michener, however, has given us here something even more: a marvelous and sympathetic analysis of historical and social relations." Best Sellers

Miéville, China, 1972-

The city & the city. Del Rey Ballantine Books 2009 312p $26

ISBN 978-0-345-49751-2; 0-345-49751-1

LC 2009-13775

"A murder mystery set in two cities, Ul Qoma and Beszel, one rich and one poor, where residents have been trained to 'unsee' each other in order to coexist. . . . The story takes the form of a police procedural as the protagonist, Inspector Tyador Borlú of the Extreme Crime Squad, tries to crack the murder case. There are no elves or UFOs. Instead, the story focuses on the lengths to which people will go to enforce borders and maintain separate cultural identities. Evoking such writers as Franz Kafka and Mikhail Bulgakov, Mr. Miéville asks readers to make conceptual leaps and not to simply take flights of fancy." Wall Street J

Iron council. Del Rey/Ballantine Books 2004 564p $24.95

ISBN 0-345-46402-8   LC 2004-49394

"As the city of New Crobuzon carries on an interminable war against the wizards of Tesh, life becomes more and more repressive for the many humans, near humans, nonhumans, and "the Remade"people subjected to magical body reconstruction as a form of punishment. Cutter, a member of the Caucus, an organization of various factions of rebels, sets off on a journey to locate the legendary Iron Council." Libr J

"In myriad ways, China Miéville's New Crobuzon is an unweeded garden of unearthly delights, and Iron Council a work of both passionate conviction and the highest artistry." Washington Post Book World

Perdido Street Station. Del Rey 2001 710p map pa $18.95

ISBN 0-345-44302-0   LC 00-67474

"Scientist Isaac Dan der Grimnebulin and his lover, an insectlike creature named Lin, discover the risks of meddling in the affairs of mobsters, renegades, and revolutionaries when they fall afoul of the powers that rule the sprawling city of New Crobuzon. The author . . . delivers a powerful tale about the power of love and the will

to survive in a dystopian universe that combines Victorian elements with a fantasy version of cyberpunk." Libr J

The scar. Ballantine Books 2002 638p pa $18.95

ISBN 0-345-44438-8

"A Del Ray book"

This book is "set in the alternate world of Bas-Lag, where linguist Bellis Coldwine is fleeing the city of New Crobuzon. On her journey, pirates capture her ship, and she and the slaves onboard are taken to the floating city of Armada, ruled by the twisted Lovers. The Lovers have a plan that will change the lives of more than the inhabitants of Armada forever, and the quest to find the mysterious reality-shifting place called the Scar begins." SLJ

"This complicated fantasy seemingly could go in any number of directions and doesn't end up in quite the places a reader expects it to. Armada, a vibrant creation, with the uncertainties of its press-ganged residents and the machinations of its politics, makes this compelling reading." Booklist

Miles, Jonathan

Dear American Airlines. Houghton Mifflin 2008 180p $22

ISBN 978-0-54705-401-8; 0-54705-401-7

LC 2007-52150

In this novel, "Benny Ford, a 53-year-old recovering alcoholic and failed poet, has been stranded at Chicago's O'Hare International Airport for most of a day. He is about to miss his long-lost daughter's wedding. While he waits, Benny decides to give the airline a piece of his mind in writing. The letter he writes turns into his life story. Rage and a rambling self-narrative is a brutal barroom combination, best avoided on the page, too. But Miles is such a clever, amusing writer that he turns what should be a shtick into a terrifically fun read." Boston Globe

Millar, Kenneth *See* Macdonald, Ross, 1915-1983

Miller, Alyce L.

Water; nine stories. Sarabande Books 2007 217p $15.95

ISBN 978-1-932511-56-7   LC 2007-10152

Contents: Ice; Swimming; Getting to know the world; Aftershock; Hawaii; Dimitry Gurov's dowdy wife; My summer of love; Cleaning house; Friends: an elegy

"These stories, which feature interracial relationships in small-town Ohio and Oakland, CA, mirror the ebb and flow of personal struggles and project the reader, believably, into a future that makes sense for the characters we come to know. Miller's skill at manipulating point of view is admirable. The relaxed fluidity of these stories makes their dénouements all the more surprising." Libr J

Miller, Andrew, 1960-

Oxygen. Harcourt 2002 323p $30

ISBN 0-15-100721-7   LC 2001-51459

Miller, Andrew, 1960-—*Continued*

First published 2001 in the United Kingdom

This novel "tells of Alec Valentine, a translator who leaves his bland life in London to care for his dying mother in the West Country. His golden-boy brother, Larry, is a former tennis champion and now an actor in California whose career and marriage are heading south. When Larry joins his brother in England as their mother lies dying, both of their seemingly failing lives come into focus as their mother's impending death forces them to grapple with their own inadequacies. Interspersed in this family tale is the story of playwright László Lázár, a Hungarian exile living in Paris, whose play Alec is translating." Booklist

"Written in elegant, resonant prose, this book breathes with compassion and honesty, and with the rare quality called hope." Publ Wkly

Miller, Arthur, 1915-2005

Homely girl, a life, and other stories. Viking 1995 115p o.p.   LC 95-14267

These three stories "evoke the pre- and postwar New York City of the author's best-known plays. After being dominated for years by her Communist first husband, the homely girl of the title story finds happiness and fulfillment with a blind musician. In 'Fame,' a newly acclaimed playwright fears he won't be able to write another play. And in 'Fitter's Night,' a cynical Italian metalworker risks his life on a freezing January evening to repair a destroyer headed out to protect a World War II convoy. . . . The ability to sum up in clear, unequivocal prose the essence of an emotion, a situation, a theme—characteristic of Mr. Miller's best writing—makes the reader wish that these stories were longer, and that there were more of them." N Y Times Book Rev

Miller, Henry, 1891-1980

Tropic of Cancer. Grove Press 1961 318p o.p.
                                                                         *

First published 1934 in France

"An autobiographical first novel recounting the experiences, sensations, thoughts of Miller, a penniless American in the Paris of the early thirties. It is not so much a novel as an intense journal, written daily about what was happening to him daily . . . as he scrounged for food, devoured books, conversed volubly, and flung himself into numerous beds." New Repub

Miller "uses themes—cadging for food, shelter, and sex; attacks on such bourgeois values as work and marriage; denunciations of traditional art and literature—and imagery—wild, exuberant, often shockingly frank—that together represent a savage, nihilistic (and at times enormously funny) revulsion against a world of stupidity and ugliness." Ency of World Lit in the 20th Century

Followed by Tropic of Capricorn

Tropic of Capricorn. Grove Press 1962 c1961 348p o.p.
                                                                         *

First published 1939 in France

"In a form like that of *Tropic of Cancer* the autobiographical account describes the writer's boyhood in Brooklyn, his quest to discover himself by sexual experiences and by other means, and his fury at the faults he finds in many of the values and ways of life in the U.S." Oxford Companion to Am Lit. 6th edition

Miller, Rebecca, 1962-

The private lives of Pippa Lee. Farrar, Straus and Giroux 2008 239p $23

ISBN 978-0-374-23742-4; 0-374-23742-5
                                                                LC 2007-47321

This novel "probes the life of housewife Pippa Lee. Fifty-year-old Pippa lives a contented life with her older husband, Herb. However, everything changes when Herb announces that they are leaving Manhattan for a retirement community. Unsettled in her new home, Pippa begins sleepwalking through life—literally. She catches herself on a security camera cooking and eating while unconscious, then finds evidence that her somnambulist self has taken up smoking. In light of her erratic behavior, Pippa reconsiders the life she has built for herself and the example she is setting for her two grown children." Publ Wkly

"This is a book about do-overs and, as suggested by the title, about the different possibilities contained in each human life span. It's a beautifully written novel, choppy and delicate and true, as unique as Pippa herself. Miller shows that the sum of a person's life is not what she has accomplished but what she has experienced, not her legacy but her memories." San Francisco Chron

Miller, Risa

Welcome to Heavenly Heights. St. Martin's Press 2003 230p $23.95

ISBN 0-312-30180-4   LC 2002-31876

This novel follows a group of American Jews who have settled in the West Bank. "Tova struggles with flashes of homesickness and worries about the changes this new life has wrought in her daughter. Nathan and Sandy argue over how to discipline their boisterous and impulsive son, Yossi. Mr. Stanetsky, a Holocaust survivor, carries a dog-eared photograph of his parents and sister with him as he collects rent from his tenants. In the backgrouond, the threat of violence and political upheaval are a constant rumble." Booklist

The author "has peered inside Tova's life to show us the search for joy that lies at the heart of her religious ritual and the beauty of people like her who devote themselves to that search. And then Miller has broken our hearts—with Tova's—byshowing us how horrible it is when the poetic liturgical metaphors of Judaism become the terrible realities of nationalism, when holiness tries to reconcile itself with the inevitable human corruption of statehood." N Y Times Book Rev

Miller, Sue

The distinguished guest. HarperCollins Pubs. 1995 282p o.p.   LC 95-2951

"The guest of the title is a woman who in her seventies wrote a celebrated memoir about being the wife of the radical minister of an integrated church in Chicago, and who eventually split with her husband over issues of black separatism and militancy. Now in her Parkinson's-afflicted eighties, she is visiting her architect son, whose view of his mother is necessarily different from her public image. This novel, as full of rich domestic detail as Miller's previous books, is, like them, a work of consolation informed by a psychotherapeutic perspective—very literal, yet also highly readable." New Yorker

Miller, Sue—*Continued*

Family pictures; a novel. Harper & Row 1990
389p o.p.
LC 89-46109

This novel chronicles "forty years in the lives of the
Eberhardts, a Chicago family. David and Lainey's third
child, Randall, is autistic. 'According to the experts of
the '50s, the fault is Lainey's for unconsciously rejecting
her infant son; David—himself a psychiatrist—agrees
with them. A few decades later science will absolve her,
but the shock and pain of her husband's betrayal throw
a curse on their relationship that is never quite dispelled." Newsweek

"'Family Pictures' is a novel that might have intrigued
and startled Woolf—profoundly honest, shapely, ambitious, engrossing, original and true, an important example
of a new American tradition that explores what it means,
not to light out for the territories but to make a home,
live at home and learn what home is." N Y Times Book
Rev

For love. HarperCollins Pubs. 1993 301p o.p.
LC 92-54422

"Fortyish freelance writer Lottie leaves her new husband in Chicago to spend part of the summer in Cambridge, Massachusetts, getting the family house ready to
sell now that her brother Cameron has placed their alcoholic mother in a nursing home. While she and her son
Ryan paint and clean, Lottie examines the concept of
love in an article she is writing, studying her own troubled marriage and Cameron's resumption of a love affair
with childhood sweetheart Elizabeth. For Elizabeth, who
is staying with her mother after leaving her philandering
husband, this romance is just a fling. But Cameron's obsessive love for the golden girl of his youth leads to [an
accident]." Libr J

Miller "maps emotional terrain carefully, precisely,
graphically, with a grit and grace that at first invite the
reader's appreciation—and then, before we know it, have
us involved." N Y Times Book Rev

The good mother. Harper & Row 1986 310p
o.p.
* LC 85-45475

In this novel "Anna Dunlap, newly divorced, is shaping a life centered around her three-year-old daughter,
Molly. Then Leo Cutter sparks a sexual responsiveness
new to Anna . . . Molly and Leo like each other, too,
and Anna sees them as a loving family unit—until her
ex-husband sues for custody, citing sexual activities that
put his child at risk. The love affair is irrevocably
changed, as Anna opens her life to a court-appointed
psychiatrist and bends the truth to her lawyer's strategy."
Libr J

"The fulcrum on which the novel's plot pivots is the
allegation by Anna's ex-husband that Anna's lover has
molested Molly, and the ensuing custody trial. Miller's
treatment of this high point of tension in the novel is
dramatic, discreet, compassionate. Each development in
the legal process increases the tension. The drama
heightens, the suspense builds, character is further developed, and the latitude for choice logically narrowed. Like
a final judgment, the custody decision breaks over reader
and character alike." Christ Sci Monit

Inventing the Abbotts and other stories. Harper
& Row 1987 180p o.p.
LC 86-46089

Contents: Inventing the Abbotts; Tyler and Brina; Appropriate affect; Slides; What Ernest says; Travel; Leaving home; Calling; Expensive gifts; The birds and the
bees; The quality of life

"These stories report from a frontier, from the discontented and guilty world of divorce and the single parent,
of marriage as a threatened institution, and if the landscape is a bleak and dispiriting one, that is not the author's fault; she is merely giving evidence. As stories
they vary—some effective, others less so—but as testi-
monies of our times they seem highly apposite." NY
Times Book Rev

Lost in the forest. Knopf 2005 247p $24.95
ISBN 1-400-04226-7
LC 2004-48963

"Eva, the divorced and happily remarried mother of
three, has finally put the disaster of her first marriage behind her and has even become good friends with her ex.
Then her second husband is killed in a tragic accident,
and the peace Eva has worked so hard to attain is instantly shattered as she succumbs to an overwhelming
grief. Her middle child, Daisy, was extremely close to
her stepfather and is emotionally paralyzed by the sudden
turn of events, unable to process or even speak of her
grief. While her older sister, Emily, pretty and popular,
is able to reach outside the family for support, and her
brother, Theo, is too young to understand what happened, Daisy feels utterly trapped by her own misery and
abruptly embarks on an ill-advised affair with a much
older, married man." Booklist

"Miller has always been adept at rendering the complexities of family life, the way even well-intentioned,
decent people can't walk across a room without wounding at least one person they love. But while some of her
plots . . . can be cluttered and occasionally clumsy, Lost
in the Forest has a seemingly effortless grace; Miller
quickly captures and never loses our attention." N Y
Times Book Rev

The senator's wife. Alfred A. Knopf 2008 306p
$24.95
ISBN 978-0-307-26420-6
LC 2007-14659

"Meri, short for Meribeth, is going through some major changes: she just got married, moved to another state,
and bought a new home. When she and her husband, Nathan, move into their New England townhouse, they
learn that their neighbor, Delia Naughton, is the wife of
the vaunted Sen. Tom Naughton. Delia is at the other
end of the spectrum from Meri: her children are grown,
and, for her, life is slowing down. Yet the two women
hit it off and quickly become friends. Having their first
child together teaches Meri and Nathan the nuances of
married life; Meri, meanwhile, uncovers the mysteries of
Delia and Tom's relationship. An intervening tragedy
then causes a savage rift between Meri and Delia." Libr
J

"No one captures the domestic landscape with language as lush as Miller's. She is the Martha Stewart of
fictional space. From peeling an orange to laying out
Christmas dinner to arranging lilies on a table, her prose
is almost erotic. Moreover, her writerly gift extends beyond graceful imagery. She describes sexual encounters
with graphic intensity and brings to Meri's labor and delivery a verisimilitude that will flatten you." Houston
Chron

Miller, Sue—*Continued*

While I was gone. Knopf 1999 265p

ISBN 0-375-40112-1   LC 98-14211

In this novel, Joey Becker, a veterinarian married to a minister, "is just beginning to feel dissatisfied with her predictable life when Eli Mayhew, a housemate from her hippie past, moves to town. His presence both reawaken's questions about an old, unsolved murder and kindles in Joey what she has been hungering for: a youthful 'sense of a surprise, that heady feeling of not knowing' what life will bring." Time

"Miller's narrative is a beautifully textured picture of the psychological tug of war between finding integrity as an individual and satisfying the demands of spouse, children and community." Publ Wkly

The world below; a novel. Knopf 2001 275p $25

ISBN 0-375-41094-5   LC 2001-33731

In this novel, two women are "at the center of the narrative: Catherine Hubbard, twice divorced mother of three, the first-person voice of life in the present, and her grandmother, Georgia Rice Holbrooke, the voice of a past time who, after Catherine's discovery of the dead woman's journals, becomes a living presence in her granddaughter's imagination." N Y Times Book Rev

"As Catherine sorts through her grandmother's life, she also sorts through her own: her mother's death, her two marriages, her boyfriends and her children. . . . As readers have come to expect, Miller limns contemporary life in deft, sure strokes, with an unerring ear for the way parents and children talk; no one can parse a modern marriage as well as she can. But in this novel Miller's special gift to readers is her rendering of Georgia's life, particularly the two love stories that mark it." Publ Wkly

Miller, Walter M., 1923-1996

A canticle for Leibowitz; a novel; by Walter M. Miller, Jr. Lippincott 1960 c1959 320p pa $13.95 hardcover o.p.

ISBN 0-06-089299-4

         *

"Here is science fiction of the highest literary excellence and thematic intelligence. A monastery founded by the scientist Leibowitz is discovered decades after an atomic war. In the first part of the book a young novice in the monastery is the protagonist; in the second part we see scholars in a new period of enlightenment; and in the final section we observe man's proclivity for repeating mistakes and the apparent inevitability of history's repeating itself." Shapiro. Fic for Youth. 3d edition

The darfsteller

In The Hugo winners p5-71

Millet, Lydia, 1968-

How the dead dream; a novel. Counterpoint 2008 244p $24

ISBN 978-1-59376-184-4; 1-59376-184-8

      LC 2007-35242

"T. has always accumulated wealth. As a child, it was through paper routes and bogus charity drives; as a college student, it was through stock-market investments; and as an adult, it is by buying land and developing planned communities. He has never let anyone close enough to derail him from his commitment to accumulate. But the vagaries of love unhinge him: his mother's mental degeneration and subsequent indifference to him, the feelings he has for a dog he rescues from the pound, the love-at-first-sight experience with a woman he meets at a party, and the grief at her sudden loss-all these things affect T. in a powerful and bizarre way. He becomes obsessed with endangered species and routinely breaks into zoos at night to sleep in wolves' and elephants' paddocks." Libr J

"For the reader, T.'s adventures with animals carry more emotional impact than any of the human encounters. They prompt the serious, sometimes convoluted but always moving meditations that are the spine if this strange, lovely novel." Chicago Sun-Times

Millhauser, Steven

An adventure of Don Juan

In Millhauser, S. The king in the tree: three novellas

Dangerous laughter; thirteen stories. Alfred A. Knopf 2008 244p $24

ISBN 978-0-307-26756-6; 0-307-26756-3

      * LC 2007-22929

Contents: Cat 'n' mouse; The disappearance of Elaine Coleman; The room in the attic; Dangerous laughter; History of a disturbance; The dome; In the reign of Harad IV; The other town; The tower; Here at the Historical Society; A change in fashion; A precursor of the cinema; The Wizard of West Orange

"While most short-story writers in the past three decades joined the realist rebellion against the fabulism of the '70s, Steven Millhauser has stayed true to the fantastic tradition that extends from Scheherazade to Poe, to Kafka and Barth. He rejects the ordinary world of the merely real, and playfully and powerfully explores the incredible world of purely aesthetic creation. . . . Millhauser's stories are not mere ingenuity, although they are devilishly clever. Millhauser is motivated by the desire to see a world in a grain of sand, to affirm that the road of excess leads to the palace of wisdom. He is our most brilliant practicing romantic, for whom surface reality is merely an uninteresting illusion." San Francisco Chron

The king in the tree

In Millhauser, S. The king in the tree: three novellas

The king in the tree: three novellas. Knopf 2003 241p $23

ISBN 0-375-41540-8

      * LC 2002-72956

"An excitable widow leads the reader on a tour of her house—apparently being offered for sale—in the harrowing 'Revenge'. . . . 'An adventure of Don Juan' finds the famous philanderer, bored with a lifetime of easy conquests, leaving the Continent for a change of scenery on his friend's English estate, where he will experience unrequited desire for the first time. Millhauser retells the tragedy of Tristan and Isolde in the title story. . . . Millhauser's precision, coupled with his brave imagination, makes these stories as smart and fresh as they are grim." Publ Wkly

Millhauser, Steven—*Continued*

The knife thrower and other stories. Crown 1998 256p

ISBN 0-609-60070-2   LC 97-45796

Contents: The knife thrower; A visit; The sisterhood of night; The way out; Flying carpets; The new automaton theater; Clair de Lune; The dream of the consortium; Balloon flight, 1870; Paradise Park; Kaspar Hauser speaks; Beneath the cellars of our town

"In these darkly magical stories, Millhauser turns town squares, backyards, and department stores into strange and luminous realms." New Yorker

Martin Dressler; the tale of an American dreamer. Crown 1996 294p

ISBN 0-517-70319-X

* LC 96-683

The author "again examines the American imagination in terms of cosmology. This time, his world-creator is young Martin Dressler, an entrepreneurial wunderkind who starts out at his father's cigar store. What ensues is an expertly woven fable of Victorian Manhattan, as Martin transforms his hunger for 'something else' into a series of colossal hotels. Martin's sights are firmly set on tomorrow, but he's cursed to be forever premodern: the skyscraper always seems to lurk around the next turn of the page, but he can envision only period eclecticism. As the new century dawns, Martin's crowning achievement, the Grand Cosmo, begins to look like the ultimate castle in the air, and he ponders—without regret—the consequences of having 'dreamed the wrong dream.'" New Yorker

Revenge

In Millhauser, S. The king in the tree: three novellas

Milligan, J.

Jack Fish; a novel. Soho Press 2005 217p il $23

ISBN 1-569-47382-X   LC 2004-48190

This "novel features a man from Atlantis, a spy to be precise, sent into New York to find and assassinate a rogue agent. Along the way, he has to deal with an assortment of problems, mostly connected with making the adjustment to breathing air and passing as a Topworlder." Booklist

"Moving from Brooklyn diner to Midtown architecture firm to New Jersey theme park, the novel has the stealthy and web-toed Jack tangling with New York demimondaines and corporate wonks as he dodges a violent gang called the Maltese. The book brims throughout with hyperspecific detail and hipster patois; it's like a Mark Leyner novel, but with a plot, and harpoons." N Y Times Book Rev

Mills, Mark

Amagansett; Mark Mills. Putnam 2004 394p $24.95

ISBN 0-399-15184-2   LC 2004-44394

"In the small town of Amagansett, perched on Long Island's windswept coast, generations have followed the same calling as their forefathers, fishing the dangerous Atlantic waters. Little has changed in the three centuries since white settlers drove the Montaukett Indians from the land. But for Conrad Labarde, a second-generation Basque immigrant recently returned from the Second World War, and his fellow fisherman Rollo Kemp, this stability is shattered when a beautiful New York socialite turns up dead in their nets." Publisher's note

"The novel combines a touching love story, told in flashback, with a nicely detailed procedural starring an unlikely investigative duo: the taciturn Basque and the Amagansett assistant police chief, who hopes to resurrect his career in the wake of scandal. . . . This is a novel to savor, both for its portrait of roughhewn individuals finding selfhood beyond the breakers and for its snapshot of the postwar world not yet locked in the death grip of modernity." Booklist

Milton, Giles, 1966-

Edward Trencom's nose; a novel of history, dark intrigue, and cheese. Thomas Dunne Books/St. Martin's Press 2007 310p $23.95

ISBN 978-0-312-36217-1; 0-312-36217-X

LC 2006102652

"The eponymous Trencom owns the finest cheese shop in London, one that has been in the possession of his family since the 17th century. He also owns the finest nose in generations, one that can distinguish the provenance of a cheese down to the cow from which it originated. . . . When the story opens in 1969, he appears to have never questioned the strange fates that befell his ancestors—particularly odd since most of them met grisly ends. . . . So when Edward Trencom is warned by a mysterious stranger that he is being watched, his first reaction is to be completely baffled. After all, the world of cheese isn't exactly the world of high espionage and Trencom is no 007. So his second reaction is that of the mild-mannered introvert—to start researching his family history, from which he uncovers many surprises. . . . What it all adds up to is a highly entertaining novel." PopMatters

Min, Anchee, 1957-

Becoming Madame Mao. Houghton Mifflin 2000 337p $25

ISBN 0-618-00407-6   LC 99-58520

A novel about "Jiang Qing, the late wife of Chairman Mao Zedong. . . . In the late 1970s, she went from being one of the most powerful figures in her counry to a convict who would live the rest of her days in prison, reviled by the Chinese people." N Y Times Book Rev

"Min reveals the complexities of love, betrayal, and ambition in this lyrical and thrilling depiction of a once-powerless woman in the jaws of power, giving us an all-too-rare glimpse into the life of a woman within the machine." Ms

Empress Orchid. Hougton Mifflin 2004 336p $24

ISBN 0-618-06887-2   LC 2003-56891

This historical novel portrays the life and times of the nineteenth-century Chinese Empress Dowager Tzu Hsi. In the novel "she is called Orchid by her family and intimates. . . . Min traces Orchid's transformation from a girl determined to maintain some control over her destiny to a young woman wavering in her commitment to a life constructed by empty ritual and burdened by political in-

Min, Anchee, 1957——Continued
trigue." Women's Rev Books

The author "has done a prodigious amount of on-site research to capture the glorious, hopeless last days of the Ching dynasty. . . . Readers will be enthralled by the gorgeously woven cultural tapestry and the psychologically astute portrait of the empress a talented girl from the provinces who married (way) up." Publ Wkly

The last empress. Houghton Mifflin 2007 308p
$25
    ISBN 978-0-618-53146-2; 0-618-53146-7
                                                LC 2006-030466
A sequel to Empress Orchid about the life of Lady Yehonala, a.k.a. the Dowager Empress, or the last empress of China. The author "picks up Orchid's story from the time of her mother's death and takes readers through the empress's own death in 1908. Departing from the stereotype of Orchid as the 'dragon lady' empress, Min uses first-person narration to portray her as a caring mother to Emperor Tung Chih and her nephew, Emperor Guang-hsu. The softness of Orchid's persona is revealed in her relations with her eunuchs, Ante-hai and Li-Lien-ying, while her strength is played out in the politics of the period and in her ability to survive the hardships of the Boxer Rebellion." Libr J

Mina, Denise

The dead hour; a novel. Little, Brown and Co. 2006 341p $24.99
    ISBN 978-0-316-73594-0; 0-316-73594-9
                                                LC 2006-01610
"On her rounds as a crime reporter for the Scottish Daily News, Paddy Meehan visits the scene of a disturbance at a home in Beardsden, a wealthy suburb of Glasgow. There she finds an attractive couple who appear to be in the midst of a domestic dispute. The police give the couple a warning and, as they are leaving, the man presses a 50-pound note into Paddy's hand and asks her to keep the matter out of the paper. The next morning Paddy reads in the paper that the woman, a lawyer and political activist, has been murdered. The man was not her husband. Suddenly, Paddy has to confront the class prejudices that allowed her to leave another woman in a dangerous situation and decide what to do about the money she accepted from the murderer." Libr J

"Surely Paddy Meehan is the most unlikely, and most relistic, investigator in recent crime fiction. . . . The Dead Hour is some kind of magnificent." Wall Street Journal

Deception; a novel. Little, Brown 2004 c2003 311p $23.95
    ISBN 0-316-73592-2   LC 2003-65861
"A 30-year-old forensic psychiatrist newly sacked from Sunnyfields State Mental Hospital, Susan Harriot is convicted of murdering her former patient, serial killer Andrew Gow, in the same manner in which he mutilated his victims. Convinced of her innocence, her husband, Lachlan, searches Susie's secret study for evidence for her appeal." Libr J

"Mina's novel is a smart example of the crime novel as postmodern puzzle, a work that coolly offers to match wits with the unwary reader and is not likely to lose the game." Washington Post Book World

Slip of the knife; a novel. Little, Brown and Co. 2008 340p $24.99
    ISBN 978-0-316-01558-5; 0-316-01558-X
                                                LC 2007-42881
First published 2007 in the United Kingdom

In this third title of a planned quartet, it's 1990, and Paddy Meehan's "life has improved greatly since her days as a copy editor. Now one of Scotland's leading newspaper columnists, she is living contently as a single mother—until one night when she finds out that her former lover, Terry, has been murdered, possibly by the IRA. She is even more stunned to discover that he left her his country cottage and private notebooks. As Paddy starts connecting the dots in his murder that nobody else seems to see, she becomes embroiled in dangerous secrets." Bookmarks

"Mina excels at this kind of writing, the back-and-forth of competitors and colleagues, the way tension and love bind people uneasily. She's a leisurely writer; although Terry's murder opens the book, the action plays out slowly, and she lets us soak up the abundant ambience and personality." Boston Globe

Minot, Eliza

The Brambles. Knopf 2006 243p $23.95
    ISBN 1-4000-4269-0   LC 2005-44421
This "novel follows three siblings as they cope with their father's impending death from cancer, not long after their mother was killed in an airplane accident. The siblings' main preoccupations, though, are more individual. Margaret, a harried mother of three, has difficulty accepting that her children are growing up. Max can't bring himself to tell his wife that he quit his job in a moment of frustration, and he resents the burden that she and their baby son represent. The youngest, Edie, has fewer responsibilities, but is the most adrift, deeply lonely and plagued by an eating disorder. These quotidian problems sometimes seem overwrought, and the book's end brings an unnecessary plot twist, but the precision of Minot's descriptions succeeds in making her characters seem real and sympathetic." New Yorker

Minot, Susan

Evening. Knopf 1998 264p
    ISBN 0-375-40037-0
                                                * LC 98-15437
"Ann Lord's life has been shaped by the men who have married her. As she lies on her deathbed, trying to make some sense of that life, a rediscovered balsam pillow evokes a Maine wedding, in 1954, where she fell in love for the first—and perhaps the last—time. This almost crude conceit produces a narrative of considerable ambition and complexity. . . . For heroine and reader alike, death's painful confusions are tempered by the spirited directness of Ann's younger self, as yet unscathed by time and experience." New Yorker

Folly. Houghton Mifflin 1992 278p
    ISBN 0-395-60339-0   LC 92-21035
This novel opens in the aftermath of America's entry into the First World War. "Lilian Eliot is the product of Brahmin Boston, whose traditions and socially correct attitudes have been instilled in her. She has been cast in the mold. Yet at times she longs to break free, to be someone different. Lilian sees that her choice of a hus-

Minot, Susan—*Continued*

band will determine her future, but she finds herself most comfortable with what is familiar and marries accordingly. Later in life she is again faced with the choice—to break free or stay. In making her choice, Lilian finally discovers herself." Libr J

The author's "carefully thought out depiction of Lilian's inner world and of the difficulty of finding an accommodation between desire and reality, silence and self-expression, has a universal resonance." Christ Sci Monit

Lust & other stories. Houghton Mifflin 1989 147p o.p.
LC 89-1677
Contents: Lust; Sparks; Blow; City night; Lunch with Harry; The break-up; The swan in the garden; The feather in the toque; The knot; A thrilling life; Ile Sèche; The man who would not go away

"Men remain emotionally distant and unwilling to commit throughout these 12 short stories, while women attempt to hold back. Alas, love insinuates itself and the man disappears. Minot's writing is sparse and poetic, painfully close to the surface." Libr J

Monkeys. Dutton 1986 159p
ISBN 0-525-24342-9
* LC 85-30775
Interconnected episodes "trace the fortunes of a large boisterous New England family. Arranged into rough chronological order, the stories dramatize the growing up of the seven Vincent siblings. Their everyday world of family gatherings, teenage parties, and vacations seems frivolous on the surface but is underlaid with tension and ultimately leads to tragedy. The episodic nature of the book leaves a few questions unanswered about the engaging clan, while occasionally some events are reiterated. Yet there is a wonderful sense of slipping into the private, important moments of the Vincents, sharing their fun and their sadness." Booklist

Rapture. Knopf 2002 115p $18
ISBN 0-375-41327-8
LC 2001-38377
"This novella takes place during a single act of oral sex. . . . Benjamin is a handsome and hapless film director with a moneyed and supportive fiancée; Kay is his former production designer, with whom he had a fling on a shoot in Mexico. After three years of agonized liaisons and enforced partings, Benjamin and Kay fall into bed once more, but they seem to bring the rest of their lives along with them, and Minot's saucy conceit evolves into a disconcerting examination of love and war between the sexes." New Yorker

Mirvis, Tova

The outside world. Alfred A. Knopf 2004 283p $24
ISBN 1-400-04161-9
LC 2003-58923
In this novel " 22-year-old Orthodox Tzippy, born and bred in Jewish Brooklyn and insulated from secular society but secretly curious and eager to experience it, is barraged with meddlesome questions and with a slew of seemingly endless carbon-copy dates intended to facilitate her marriage to a reputable yeshiva boy before she turns into a spinster. Meanwhile, not too far away, Naomi and Joel, Modern Orthodox Jews, are straining to knock some sense into their suddenly ultrareligious son,

Bryan. . . . When these two formerly separate worlds collide, parents, siblings and spouses must reflect on what their faith means to them and what to do when their beliefs unexpectedly diverge from those of loved ones." Publ Wkly

"Beneath the women's wigs and the men's black fedoras, Mirvis finds reservoirs of belief, doubt, ambition, folly, lust and the rest of the human equation." Washington Post Book World

Mishima, Yukio, 1925-1970

The decay of the angel; translated from the Japanese by Edward G. Seidensticker. Knopf 1974 236p (Sea of fertility)
ISBN 0-394-46613-6
*
Original Japanese edition, 1971
This final novel in the series "treats the themes of purity, beauty, evil and death. . . . [Judge Honda] is now near death, while that spirit of tragic purity which in the earlier stories was respectively incarnate in Kiyoaki, Isao and Ying Chan is found here in Toru, an evil teenaged orphan, Toru is employed, symbolically enough, as a ship watcher when Honda, seeing him as both evil like himself and marked for an early death, adopts him as his son in order to thwart that destiny. Over several years Honda proves no more of a match for Toru than does the bride he chooses for him, but neither man is to escape an eerie doom." Publ Wkly

"The novel concludes with a superbly written scene that casts doubt on the reality of the events described in the four volumes. In the end we discover that the 'sea of fertility' may be as arid as the region of that name on the moon, although it seems to suggest infinite richness." Ency of World Lit in the 20th Century

Runaway horses; translated from the Japanese by Michael Gallagher. Knopf 1973 421p (Sea of fertility)
ISBN 0-394-46618-7
Original Japanese edition, 1969
In the second volume of the Sea of fertility cycle "the political and economic upheaval of the 1930's is seen primarily through the eyes of a young zealot intent upon an imperial restoration through assassination of key industrialists and then his own ritual suicide. The secondary strand involves a middle-aged judge whose carefully constructed rational and legalistic life crumbles when exposed to the younger man's idealism." Choice

"Mishima uses the same literary artistry in this novel as in the first but changes the gently romantic tone to one of martial ideology with a weirdly beautiful emphasis on ritual suicide. In the interplay of entanglements between the two novels, each self-contained, the author experiments with the Buddhist doctrine of reincarnation." Booklist

Followed by The Temple of Dawn

The sound of waves; translated by Meredith Weatherby; drawings by Yoshinori Kinoshita. Knopf 1956 182p il o.p.
"Returning to his village after a day on the fishing boats, Shinji, 18 years old, comes upon a beautiful stranger, Hatsue, who is the daughter of the wealthiest man in the village. After several unplanned encounters

Mishima, Yukio, 1925-1970—*Continued*

the two realize that they are in love, but many obstacles must be overcome before they can be married." Shapiro. Fic for Youth. 3d edition

Spring snow; translated from the Japanese by Michael Gallagher. Knopf 1972 389p (Sea of fertility)
ISBN 0-394-44239-3

                                                                    *

"UNESCO collection of representative works: Japanese series"

Original Japanese edition, 1968

"Kiyoaki Matsugae, a young Japanese, comes from a wealthy family whose attention to the most formal aspects of Japanese life has changed because of their attraction to Western culture. His best friend, Shigekuna Honda, is not so handsome or affluent but is a more serious scholar. The story emphasizes the difference in the character of the two young men as the plot describes the passionate, although ambivalent, love that Kiyoaki feels for the beautiful Satoko. When she concludes that Kiyoaki does not return her love, despite the fact that their affair has been serious and intimate, she allows herself to be betrothed to someone else. As always, what is forbidden becomes more desirable and Kiyoaki tries desperately to regain his loved one. Japanese customs and rituals intervene to bring a tragic ending to this love story." Shapiro. Fic for Youth. 3d edition

Followed by Runaway horses

The Temple of Dawn; translated from the Japanese by E. Dale Saunders and Cecilia Segawa Seigle. Knopf 1973 334p (Sea of fertility)
ISBN 0-394-46614-4

                                                                    *

Original Japanese edition, 1970

The third volume in the Sea of fertility series is "divided into two parts: the first is set in southeast Asia, where we first see the Thai princess who is the reincarnation of Isao; the second takes place in Japan after World War II, when the old values of society have been corrupted." Ency of World Lit in the 20th Century

Followed by The decay of the angel

The temple of the golden pavilion; translated by Ivan Morris; introduction by Nancy Wilson Ross; drawings by Fumi Komatsu. Knopf 1959 262p il o.p.

"Based on an actual incident in 1950, when a Zen Buddhist acolyte burned down a temple which was a national shrine. Like the real arsonist, the fictional Mizoguchi is ugly and a pathological stutterer, and long before his hostility becomes overt, has developed a compulsion to destroy whatever is morally or physically beautiful. As told by the young acolyte, this is a masterly description of the growth of an obsession and an acute interpretation of the deliberate symbolism underlying Mizoguchi's irrational, perverse behavior." Booklist

Miss Read *See* Read, Miss, 1913-

Mistry, Rohinton, 1952-

Family matters. Knopf 2002 431p
ISBN 0-375-40373-6

First published 2001 in the United Kingdom

The setting is the "city of Bombay during a 1990s wave of violent religious extremism, and the focus is on and extended Parsi family suffering the long-term consequences of a Juliet and Romeo-like tragedy. Septuagenarian widower Nariman survived the catastrophic love affair, but Parkinson's disease is now eroding his health and autonomy, forcing him to confront his guilt over capitulating to his family's vehement objections to the non-Parsi love of his life and entering into an unhappy arranged marriage with a Parsi widow with two children." Booklist

"Mistry is not just a fiction writer; he's a philosopher who finds meaning—indeed, perhaps a divine plan—in small human interactions. This beautifully paced, elegantly expressed novel is notable for the breadth of its vision as well as its immensely appealing characters and enticing plot." Publ Wkly

A fine balance; a novel. Knopf 1996 603p
ISBN 0-679-44608-7   LC 95-49317

This novel has four main characters. "Dina is a Parsi widow in her early 40s who runs a small apartment building in Bombay; Maneck is a student from the mountains who takes a room with her; and Ishvar and Om are two village tailors, uncle and nephew, who long to pull themselves up from their Untouchable status. All four . . . find their lives intertwined when Indira Gandhi announces her State of Emergency—her absolute rule—in 1975." Time

"It is impossible not to seethe at the injustices of the police state, and impossible not to take these characters passionately to heart: this is a novel that can stand with the best of Dickens." New Yorker

Mitcham, Judson

Sabbath Creek; a novel. University of Georgia Press 2004 169p $22.95
ISBN 0-8203-2577-5

                                                * LC 2003-15704

In this novel "14-year-old Lewis Pope is caught in the middle of a dangerous family crisis. While attempting to run away from his abusive father, Lewis and his frightened mother drive aimlessly for days through southern Georgia, unsure where to go or what to do. Their car breaks down in the sleepy backwater of Sabbath Creek, and they end up stranded at a ramshackle hotel owned by a 93-year-old black man named Truman Stroud." Libr J

"Lewis observes everything with the alertness of someone who does not yet take common experiences, such as kissing and drunkenness, for granted; he never resorts to shorthand to convey them, but describes them with a scrupulous fidelity to his own perceptions." N Y Times Book Rev

Mitchard, Jacquelyn

The deep end of the ocean. Viking 1996 434p
ISBN 0-670-86579-6

                                                * LC 95-26234

"When 3-year-old Ben Cappadora disappears from a hotel lobby in Chicago, a presumed kidnap victim, nothing positive ever comes from his loss. The family he leaves behind is ruined. Ben's father, Pat, a kindly restaurateur, develops cardiac problems—the victim of a lit-

Mitchard, Jacquelyn—*Continued*

eral broken heart. His mother, Beth, becomes an emotional zombie. Vincent, the 7-year-old who was watching Ben when he disappeared, grows into a high-I.Q. juvenile delinquent. Baby Kerry has lived in a mournful, hostile house for so long she thinks it's normal." N Y Times Book Rev

"One of the most remarkable things about this rich, moving and altogether stunning first novel is Mitchard's assured command of narrative structure and stylistic resources. Her story about a child's kidnapping and its enduring effects upon his parents, siblings, and extended family is a blockbuster read." Publ Wkly

No time to wave goodbye; a novel. Random House 2009 228p $25
ISBN 978-1-4000-6774-9; 1-4000-6774-X
LC 2009-12905
"In this sequel to The Deep End of the Ocean, Mitchard returns to the Cappadora family. It's been 13 years since Ben was returned to his family after being abducted at age three. Now, the family is gathered to watch the premiere of oldest son Vincent's documentary about abducted children. As they watch the film, his parents are hurled back into their troubled past. As much as they would like to leave all the turmoil behind, the family is thrust once again into the spotlight as the documentary earns an Oscar nomination. And then another child is abducted." Libr J

"Mitchard charts a tormented family dynamic with shocking ease. This action-packed and emotionally rich drama is every bit as satisfying as its predecessor." Publ Wkly

Still summer. Warner Books 2007 307p $24.99
ISBN 978-0-446-57876-9; 0-446-57876-2
LC 2006-33941
"Friends since childhood, Tracy, Holly, and Olivia charter a private yacht for some girl-time R & R, bringing along Tracy's 19-year-old daughter, Cammie. Manning the vessel are two Virgin Island residents: Lenny, the captain, and Michel, his mate. Just as some mounting mother-daughter tension between Tracy and Cammie begins to dissipate amid the tropical setting, Cammie and Michel commence a flirtation that seems at first innocent but progresses too quickly for Tracy. The youngsters' courtship becomes secondary, however, as bad weather separates the women and the boat from the crew, and Tracy takes the lead by default. Diminishing food supply, piqued anxiety, and increasing desperation conspire to undo the group, revealing one of them to be vindictive and conniving—and possibly vicious when survival is at stake." Booklist

"This fast-paced novel borrows qualities from several genres—suspense, survival epic, coming-of-age—and mostly succeeds in melding the better aspects of each, though Mitchard has a surer hand in creating women characters than men." Publ Wkly

A theory of relativity. HarperCollins Pubs. 2001 351p $26
ISBN 0-06-621023-2
LC 00-54261
"Keefer Nye, only a year old when her parents die in a car crash near Madison, Wis., is the focal point of a bitter, protracted and precedent-setting custody battle. Keefer's bachelor uncle, 24-year-old science teacher Gordon McKenna, seems the most appropriate custodian for

his tiny niece, since he helped his elderly parents care for Keefer while his sister (Keefer's mother, Georgia) battled cancer. Challenging his claim, the affluent Nye grandparents, country-club Floridians, believe that their niece and her husband, born-again Christians, should get custody. Mitchard's nuanced character portrayals are her strong suit; no one is without frailties." Publ Wkly

Twelve times blessed. HarperCollins Pubs. 2003 532p $25.95
ISBN 0-06-621475-0
LC 2002-31781
"True Dickinson has everything: a loving 10-year-old son, Guy; a successsful business; and a cadre of friends who mostly fill the empty places in her life—until she falls for Hank Bannister, a restaurateur 10 years her junior." Booklist

"Mitchard infuses the courtship and domestic life with gentle humor." Publ Wkly

Mitchell, Breon

(tr) Timm, U. Morenga

Mitchell, David

Black swan green; a novel. Random House 2006 294p $23.95; pa $13.95
ISBN 1-400-06379-5; 978-1-4000-6379-6; 0-8129-7401-8 (pa); 978-0-8129-7401-0 (pa)
LC 2005-52914
This is a "portrait of a thirteen-year-old boy, growing up in Worcestershire in 1982, who is afflicted with a stammer, unhappy parents, and a snide older sister. Mitchell hasn't abandoned his fascination with the chapter: his meditation on being thirteen has thirteen sections, each featuring a self-contained story. This time, however, his approach has the subtlety of a watermark. . . . By settling into a single narrative voice, and skipping the pyrotechnics, Mitchell has come by something that eluded him before: a sense of earned emotion." New Yorker

Cloud atlas; a novel. Random House Trade Paperbacks 2004 509p pa $14.95
ISBN 0-375-50725-6 (pa)
* LC 2003-69314
The author "presents six narratives that evoke an array of genres, from Melvillean high-seas drama to California noir and dystopian fantasy. There is a naïve clerk on a nineteenth-century Polynesian voyage; an aspiring composer who insinuates himself into the home of a syphilitic genius; a journalist investigating a nuclear plant; a publisher with a dangerous bestseller on his hands; and a cloned human being created for slave labor. These five stories are bisected and arranged around a sixth, the oral history of a post-apocalyptic island, which forms the heart of the novel. Only after this do the second halves of the stories fall into place, pulling the novel's themes into focus: the ease with which one group enslaves another, and the constant rewriting of the past by those who control the present. Against such forces, Mitchell's characters reveal a quiet tenacity." New Yorker

Number9dream; a novel. Random House 2002 400p
ISBN 0-375-50726-4
LC 2001-41910

Mitchell, David—*Continued*

First published 2001 in the United Kingdom

"Eiji Miyake, the young protagonist, leaves his rural Japanese home and travels to Tokyo to find the father who abandoned him years before. What begins as a fairly straightforward filial quest soon devolves into a kaleidoscopic adventure filled with Japanese mobsters and increasingly baroque futuristic scenarios. What is even more alarming, Eiji does not always maintain a firm grasp on reality. Mitchell's pyrotechnics are never less than interesting." New Yorker

Mitchell, James C., 1942-

Lovers crossing. St. Martin's Minotaur 2003 294p $23.95

ISBN 0-312-31530-9   LC 2003-41350

"Roscoe Brinker, a Tuscon-based private detective and former INS agent, left the service after being shot in the line of duty by, he suspects, a fellow agent. A local business mogul, Mo Crain, hires him to look into the murder of Crain's wife, Sandra, who worked along the border as a nurse helping abandoned and battered children. Sandra seems to have had few enemies, but as Brinker's investigation proceeds, it seems that her death might be linked to a smuggling operation, and to Henry Sanchez, the corrupt INS agent that Brinker believes shot him." Publ Wkly

"The instantly likable Brinker is full of surprises, and the secondary characters who surround him also have great depth." Booklist

Mitchell, Margaret, 1900-1949

Gone with the wind; with a new preface by Pat Conroy and an introduction by James A. Michener. 60th Anniversary ed. Scribner 1996 959p il

ISBN 0-684-82625-9

* LC 95-52609

A reissue of the title first published 1936 by Macmillan

This novel "shows both considerable literary skill and social insight. The heroine, Scarlett O'Hara, is an embodiment of the indomitable spirit of the South. She wants to marry Ashley Wilkes, but he marries Melanie Hamilton instead, and in a pique Scarlett marries Charles Hamilton. Later she marries another man for his money, and then finally marries Rhett Butler, a dashing and outspoken Byronic hero. Around her surges the tumult of the Civil War, the despair of Reconstruction days, and the collapse of the old social order. Scarlett's dogged determination to restore Tara, the family estate, after Sherman destroys Atlanta, attains its goal, but the cost of the realization that she has sacrificed everything else for money and security." Benet's Reader's Ency of Am Lit

Mitchell, Mark

(ed) Penguin book of gay short fiction. See Penguin book of gay short fiction

Mitford, Nancy, 1904-1973

Love in a cold climate

In Mitford, N. The pursuit of love & Love in a cold climate p285-617

The pursuit of love

In Mitford, N. The pursuit of love & Love in a cold climate p{1}-283

The pursuit of love & Love in a cold climate; two novels. Modern Lib. 1994 617p $19.95

ISBN 0-679-60090-6

* LC 93-43632

A combined edition of two titles about the Radlett family originally published 1945 and 1949 respectively. Subsequent works about the family and its associates are The blessing (1951) and Don't tell Alfred (1960)

These quasi-autobiographical novels take a satiric look at the various social and amatory trials and triumphs of an eccentric upper-class English family following World War I

Miyamoto, Teru, 1947-

Kinshu: Autumn brocade. New Directions 2005 196p $22.95

ISBN 0-8112-1633-0   LC 2005-20111

Original Japanese edition, 1982

This novel "features letters exchanged over the course of about a year between Aki Katsunuma and her ex-husband, Yasuaki Arima. Aki's initial letter stems from a chance encounter with Yasuaki over a decade after their divorce. Through their correspondence, readers discover Aki's grief in having to raise her eight-year-old mentally challenged son with her unfaithful second husband, Soichiro Katsunuma. Aki herself learns the true motives behind the suicide/murder that Yasuaki's then lover attempted, which, in an ironic twist of fate, ends her life only to save his. After Yasuaki recovers from his attack, his life is no picnic either as he learns to confront his own share of demons while striving to forge ahead. As the story progresses, the former husband and wife come to realize the cathartic properties of their letters; by learning to forgive and respect each other, they bring about a sense of closure to their relationship once and for all. Though brief, this novel features a distinctly compelling narrative; credit Thomas's effective translation." Libr J

Mizner, David

Political animal; a novel. Soho Press 2004 293p $24

ISBN 1-569-47386-2   LC 2004-11250

"Arnie Schecter ("Shecter the Protector") is running for the New York senate with the help of Director of Communications Ben Bergin. As dedicated as Bergin is to Schecter's liberal causes, he's even more zealous in his pursuit of fellow staffer Calliope Berkowitz. His concern with winning Calli's affection vastly outweighs his zeal for winning the election, and Ben idolizes Calli with a sweetly bumbling fervor that exhibits all the angst of a prepubescent youth. Not since Bridget Jones has a character parsed contemporary dating rituals with such a fine degree of anxiety and self-doubt, as Mizner uproariously captures the incipient insanity inherent in both courting and campaigning. An endearing and irreverent love story." Booklist

Mo, Yen *See* Mo Yan, 1956-

Mo Yan, 1956-

Life and death are wearing me out; translated from the Chinese by Howard Goldblatt. Arcade Pub. 2008 540p $29.95

ISBN 978-1-55970-853-1; 1-55970-853-0

LC 2007-22843

Original Chinese edition, 2006

"Yan's hero and chief narrator, Ximen Nao, is a former rich landowner who falls victim to Mao Zedong's Land Reform Movement. Although known as a fair and decent man, Nao loses both his land and his life to the Communist regime. Relegated to Hell, Nao is forced by Lord Yama, King of the Underworld, to be reborn, again and again, until his anger with his perceived injustice is purged from his soul. First, he reenters the world as a donkey, then, in succession, as an ox, pig, dog, and monkey, until he finally returns as a human. From the unique vantage point as an animal with some lingering human thoughts, Nao relates the life of his peasant village and its people through 50 years of economic and personal struggle. Inventing a large cast of believable people is one thing. (Yan's list of principle characters numbers 17.) To bring them vividly to mind while simultaneously fashioning a counter world of animal intelligence — the smells, sights, fears and violence implicit in the daily life of creatures — is a spectacular achievement." Seattle Times

Moberg, Carl Artur Vilhelm *See* Moberg, Vilhelm, 1898-1973

Moberg, Vilhelm, 1898-1973

The emigrants; a novel; translated from the Swedish by Gustaf Lannestock. Simon & Schuster 1951 366p o.p.

*

Original Swedish edition, 1949

This is the first volume of a cycle which tells the story of a band of Swedish emigrants to the United States. This volume tells the story in particular of one family, Karl Oskar Nilsson, his wife and children, and his young brother Robert; of their life in Sweden; and of the long, arduous journey across the Atlantic in the summer of 1850

"A novel of peasant life, drawn to the last homely and superstitious detail. It is a story of poverty and heartbreak over which human faith has its will. And it is filled with an earthly humor, the unpredictable flash of human malice and emotion which bring Mr. Moberg's characters sharply into focus." N Y Times Book Rev

Followed by Unto a good land

The last letter home; a novel; translated from the Swedish by Gustaf Lannestock. Simon & Schuster 1961 383p o.p.

Originally published in Sweden 1956 and 1959. Parts 3 and 4 of the author's cycle, the first of which is The emigrants and the second, Unto a good land

"It is solemn, rather slow and quietly moving. Mr. Moberg is at least as much concerned with the thoughts and emotions of his stolid characters as with the historical events of their time." Publ Wkly

Unto a good land; a novel; translated from the Swedish by Gustaf Lannestock. Simon & Schuster 1954 371p o.p.

Sequel to The emigrants

Original Swedish edition, 1952

The book "tells how farmer Karl Oskar Nilsson, his wife and children, and ten other peasants from his own parish in the province of Smaland, sailed in the brig Charlotta in the spring of 1850 to North America, landing ten weeks later at the East River Pier in New York on a sweltering June day and how, by river-boat and steam-wagon, on foot and in an ox-drawn cart, Karl Oskar and his family reach at last the shore of the Minnesota lake where out of the great trees he finds there he hews himself a home." N Y Her Trib Books

Followed by The last letter home

Modesitt, L. E., Jr.

Archform; beauty. TOR Bks. 2002 330p $25.95

ISBN 0-7653-0433-3

LC 2001-59655

"A Tom Doherty Associates book"

"Four hundred years from now, nanotechnology protects the elite and provides clean, safe production for most material needs. But it doesn't eliminate normal human perversity, in either individuals or group relations. When a series of mysterious deaths begins, Modesitt has us see it from the steadily converging viewpoints of a music teacher, a news researcher, a politician (complete with constituents), and an ambitious, ruthless dynastic businessman." Booklist

"Set against a background of biological terrorism, Modesitt's tale explores social issues . . . sure to resonate with many readers. This brilliant novel is as thought provoking as it is entertaining." Publ Wkly

Viewpoints critical; selected stories; [by] L.E. Modesitt, Jr. Tor 2008 350p $25.95

ISBN 978-0-7653-1857-2; 0-7653-1857-1

LC 2007-42148

"A Tom Doherty Associates book"

Contents: The great American economy; Second coming; Rule of law; Iron man, plastic ships; Power to . . . ?; Precision set; Fallen angel; Black ordermage; Understanding; News clips recovered from the NYC ruins; Beyond the obvious wind; Always outside the lines: four battles; The pilots; The dock to heaven; Ghost mission; Spec-ops; Sisters of Sarronnyn, sisters of Westwind; The difference; The swan pilot

This "collection of reprints dating back to 1973 and a handful of new stories displays Modesitt's breadth of experience and knowledge to great effect. . . . As in Modesitt's novels, eloquent prose and skilled characterization are evident, only slightly diminished by occasional outbreaks of slow pacing. Readers will find this an excellent showcase of a very fine writer's highest quality work." Publ Wkly

Mofina, Rick

Every fear. Pinnacle Books/Kensington Pub. 2006 381p $6.99

ISBN 0-7860-1746-5 (pa)

This novel begins with a "baby's kidnapping and his mother's near-fatal hit-and-run. . . . Seattle Mirror reporter Jason Wade is on the story—pressured by an un-

Mofina, Rick—*Continued*

scrupulous editor to get the story, even embellish it, if necessary. . . . Despite his digging, Jason can't find out why the hardworking, nice couple who were high school sweethearts were targeted. As the case becomes more bizarre, Jason draws on all his journalistic skills. An unusual break comes from his father, with whom Jason hasn't always had the best relationship. A recovering alcoholic and a former cop, his father also is trying to reinvent himself as a private detective. Mofina shows his strength at creating gripping plots enhanced by realistic characters and social awareness." PopMatters

Moggach, Deborah

Tulip fever. Delacorte Press 2000 281p
ISBN 0-385-33489-3   LC 99-42048
First published 1999 in the United Kingdom

A novel set in 17th-century Amsterdam. "Moggach introduces us to the elderly Cornelis Sandvoort; his beautiful young bride, Sophia, . . . her lover, Jan, who is hired to paint the Sandvoorts' portrait; and Sophia's maid, Maria. As 'Tulip Fever' unfolds, Sophia's tentative romance with Jan gradually becomes so reckless that it is analogous to Amsterdam's obsession with tulips. Made ruthless by love, the couple plan to escape the city. . . . Moggach's book reads like a thriller: it's a novel that ponders what it means to push things too far, and keenly examines what the consequences might be." N Y Times Book Rev

Molina, Antonio Muñoz *See* Muñoz Molina, Antonio, 1956-

Moloney, Susie

The dwelling; a novel. Atria Bks. 2003 408p $25
ISBN 0-7434-5662-9   LC 2003-276274

In this tale of a haunted house, "Moloney attempts to depict 362 Belisle as a being with a mind of its own, beckoning realtor Glenn Darnley throughout the multiple showings of the house, and claiming or rejecting its inhabitants. The tenants seem quite ordinary until mysterious events begin to occur, each episode terminating at a horrifying moment before Moloney launches into the next inhabitant's story. Newly widowed Glenn's travails connect the sagas of her three buyers, as her thoughts of her dead husband fill the gaps between stories." Publ Wkly

The house "is a character in its own right, but Moloney . . . has thankfully peopled the narrative with other well-developed characters as well, ones with such recognizable strengths and weaknesses that the reader actually cares about their outcomes. The ending is horrible but poignant and exactly fitting." Libr J

Momaday, N. Scott

The ancient child; a novel. Doubleday 1989 313p o.p.
LC 89-31304

"Locke Setman, a highly successful Bay Area painter, fears that he has lost touch with his 'inner child' in the process of making it big. Then, during a brief trip to Oklahoma, he meets a beautiful American Indian woman named Grey who dresses in beaded buckskin, speaks Kiowa and Nanajo like one of the elders, and has elaborate visionary conversations with the ghost of Billy the Kid. Armed with a medicine bundle and a bag of peyote buttons, Grey slowly draws Setman into a magical world of ritual that both revitalizes and transforms him. . . . A fascinating and hypnotically beautiful book that belongs in every collection of Western Americana." Libr J

House made of dawn. Harper & Row 1968 212p o.p.

"Abel, a young American Indian, lives with his grandfather, observing Indian customs, until he is drafted into the army. The story covers the years 1945 to 1952, during which time Abel seems unable to find his place either in the white world, where he is driven to violence, or on the Indian reservation where he was born. The pain of being caught between two cultures is keenly felt and can be comprehended as a problem that has affected other ethnic groups." Shapiro. Fic for Youth. 3d edition

A **moment** on the edge; 100 years of crime stories by women; edited by Elizabeth George. HarperCollins 2004 540p $24.95
ISBN 0-06-058821-7   LC 2003-67608

Contents: A jury of her peers, by Glaspell, S.; The man who knew how, by Sayers, D. L.; I can find my way out, by Marsh, N.; The summer, by Jackson, S.; St. Patrick's Day in the morning, by Armstrong, C.; The purple is everything, by Davis, D. S.; Money to burn, by Allingham, M.; A nice place to stay, by Tyre, N.; Clever and quick, by Brand, C.; Country lovers, by Gordimer, N.; The irony of hate, by Rendell, R.; Sweet baby Jenny, by Harrington, J.; Wild mustard, by Muller, M.; Jemima Shore at the sunny grave, by, Fraser, A.; The case of the Pietro Andromache, by Paretsky, S.; Afraid all the time, by Pickard, N.; The young shall see visions, and the old dream dreams, by Rusch, K. K.; A predatory woman, by McCrumb, S.; Jack be quick, by Paul, B.; Ghost station, by Wheat, C.; New moon and rattlesnakes, by Hornsby, W.; Death of a snowbird, by Jance, J. A.; The river mouth, by Matera, L.; A scandal in winter, by Linscott, G.; Murder-two, by Oates, J. C.; English autumn—American fall, by Walters, M.

"George here collects short mysteries by women, bracketing the 26 entries with two tales about the death of abusive husbands, written more than 80 years apart. Between them springs an entertaining assortment of locked-room murders, theatrical whodunits, white-collar-crime and detective stories, and psychological puzzlers, each headed by revealing author notes." Booklist

Monaghan, Nicola

The killing jar; a novel. Scribner 2007 288p $24
ISBN 978-0-7432-9968-8; 0-7432-9968-X
LC 2006-48679
First published 2006 in the United Kingdom

"The narrator, Kerrie-Ann, nicknamed 'Kez,' lives in Nottingham public housing with her heroin-addicted mother. By the age of 10, Kez is working as a drug courier for her mother's dealer boyfriend. By 13, she's had an abortion and is dropping Ecstasy; when her mother leaves, she's making enough money on her own to take care of her younger brother, Jon, and to save money for a better life. In the meantime, she shacks up with another

Monaghan, Nicola—*Continued*

dealer, Mark, whose tenderness transforms into violent possessiveness as his heroin addiction gets the better of him." Publ Wkly

"The violence of The Killing Jar is often difficult, the inhumanity often unbearable, but the book rewards a reader who wants an unsparing-really, really unsparing-account of a disastrous childhood, an account that is nonetheless sensitively rendered and deceptively simple." City Paper (Baltimore)

Monette, Paul

Afterlife. Crown 1990 278p o.p.

LC 89-48754

In this novel about AIDS "three men whose lovers all died in the same hospital during the same week decide how to live as they await their own illnesses." Booklist

"Despite its comic flourishes, this is a tough, painful book about gay sex and love, pursued in the valley of the shadow of AIDS. And its unrelenting descriptions of the ravages of the disease, along with its sexual details and 'talking dirty,' are surely going to make some readers uncomfortable." N Y Times Book Rev

Monfredo, Miriam Grace

Blackwater spirits. St. Martin's Press 1995 328p o.p.   LC 94-40980

"A Thomas Dunne book"

A "historical mystery featuring Glynis Tryon, librarian in Seneca Falls, N.Y., in the mid-18th century. Glynis and the newly arrived doctor, a young Jewish woman from New York City, overhear a farmer voice fears for his life to Constable Cullen Stuart. Soon the farmer is fatally poisoned, and Cullen enlists Glynis's aid in talking to the farmer's angry widow, who suggests her husband's murder will be followed by others." Publ Wkly

The stalking horse. Berkley Prime Crime 1998 340p

ISBN 0-425-15783-0   LC 97-21547

This historical mystery is "set just after Lincoln's presidential election. The Southern states are calling for secession and there is talk of war. Bronwyn Llyr, the niece of Seneca Falls, NY, librarian Glynis Tryon, has left school and taken a job as an operative with the Pinkerton Detective Agency. Her first assignment is to accompany a railroad owner to Alabama and learn about possible plans to confiscate the train line. Bronwyn accidentally overhears a conversation about a secret plan called Equus, which she correctly fears is an assassination plot." SLJ

The author "ably mixes real-life figures with her own creations into an engaging brew that combines solid historical research with a fast-moving plot." Publ Wkly

Moning, Karen Marie

The immortal highlander. Delacorte Press 2004 267p $15

ISBN 0-385-33825-2   LC 2004-40764

"For eons Adam Black has aided humanity and meddled in its affairs, much to the chagrin of the queen of the Seelie Court. He has finally pushed her too far and finds himself, a once powerful Fae, invisible and very human. But he is still as resourceful as ever, and finds a way to reach the queen and plea to have his curse lifted with the help of a young lawyer, Gabrielle O'Callaghan, a human born with the ability to see his kind. As old enemies yearn to take advantage of his weakened state, threatening his life and all existence, Adam discovers that Gabrielle threatens a heart he never thought he had." Booklist

Monninger, Joseph

(jt. auth) Rice, L. The letters

Monsarrat, Nicholas, 1910-1979

The cruel sea. Knopf 1951 509p o.p.

*

"The *Compass Rose* is a British corvette commissioned to convoy duty and to the hunting of German U-boats during World War II. First Mate Lockhart and Skipper Erikson develop a close relationship. When their ship is sunk and few of the crew survive, Lockhart and Erikson team up again on a new ship, undaunted by the experiences visited upon them by the cruel sea." Shapiro. Fic for Youth. 3d edition

Montero, Mayra, 1952-

Dancing to "Almendra"; translated by Edith Grossman. Farrar, Straus and Giroux 2007 264p $25

ISBN 978-0-374-10277-7; 0-374-10277-5

LC 2006-12552

Original Spanish edition, 2005

"Montero's novel is narrated by a man named Joaquin Porrata, a 22-year-old reporter living in Havana during the last days of Batista, who shows up for work one morning and finds he's been assigned the story of a hippopotamus that has escaped from the zoo and been shot to death. As it happens, that same night the mafia capo Umberto Anastasia was murdered in a hotel barber's shop in New York City, and from a . . . zookeeper named Juan Bulgado, . . . Porrata discovers that the two killings are related." N Y Times Book Rev

"Montero probes [the] depths of inner ruin with the gelid calm and lucid exactitude that belies her characters' tortured passions and the story's tropical settings . . . [Her] sentences, planed to a soothing smoothness by Spanish translator extraordinaire Edith Grossman, slide up against each other, inexorably building to a truly tragic—and truly disturbing—ending. [Montero is] a worthy peer for the likes of Mario Vargas Llosa." San Francisco Chronicle

Moody, Bill, 1941-

Looking for Chet Baker; an Evan Horne mystery. Walker & Co. 2002 253p $23.95

ISBN 0-8027-3368-9   LC 2001-56772

In London, jazz pianist and amateur sleuth Evan Horne "meets an old friend, Ace Buffington. An English professor who needs to publish one more book to achieve tenure, Ace wants Horne to help him research real-life jazz great Chet Baker. . . . Horne has no interest in more detective work, but when he gets to Amsterdam, he discovers that Ace has disappeared. Since the police express little interest in finding the missing professor, Horne is

Moody, Bill, 1941-—*Continued*
obliged to go looking for his buddy himself. Ace's trail
parallels that of Chet Baker's last days, so Horne has to
learn a lot more about Baker, his legendary talent, his
tragic addiction to drugs. Moody does a wonderful job of
re-creating the man and his times." Publ Wkly

Moody, David 1970-

Hater. Thomas Dunne Books 2009 281p $21.95
ISBN 978-0-312-38483-8; 0-312-38483-1
LC 2008-36519
First published 2006 in the United Kingdom
"Danny McCoyne, an employee of the Parking Fine
Processing office in an unnamed, possibly British city,
barely manages to support his wife and children. Things
get a lot worse after incidents of random violence escalate to a condition that threatens the social fabric of the
country. Those afflicted with the violent impulse are
dubbed Haters. The rapid onset of the disorder, exacerbated by the frighteningly inadequate government response, leaves Danny and his family virtual prisoners in
their own home." Publ Wkly
"The novel moves at a deliberate, relentless pace, feeding readers just enough information to keep them perplexed and paranoid, and the depiction of a society being
rent at the seams by violence rings true. Moody creates
some truly chilling scenes, but there are also flashes of
black comedy. At times savagely brutal—the moments of
outrageous violence may be considered over-the-top by
some readers—but engrossing and effective." Kirkus

Moody, Rick

The Albertine notes
In Moody, R. Right livelihoods

K&K
In Moody, R. Right livelihoods

The Omega Force
In Moody, R. Right livelihoods

Right livelihoods; three novellas. Little, Brown
2007 223p $23.99
ISBN 978-0-316-16634-8; 0-316-16634-0
LC 2006-26937
"In 'The Omega Force,' a tale rife with satirical meaning, the patriotic doctor defending the security of his domain against people who are 'dark-complected' turns out
to be a lunatic. Paranoia is also evident in 'K&K' as an
office manager finds some dissident messages in the
company's suggestion box and suspects a conspiracy. The
third, 'The Albertine Notes,' introduces an amateur
journalist who, while researching the drug issue for a
porno magazine, falls victim to drug culture and suffers
from hallucinations that New York City is being obliterated. The unreliable and eccentric characters that so often
populate Moody's novels again effectively remind us of
the nation's collective hysteria. His convoluted narrative
may challenge the patience of some readers, but those
who persist will find it rewarding." Libr J

Moon, Elizabeth

Moon flights; with an introduction by Anne
McCaffrey. Night Shade Books 2007 272p $24.95
ISBN 978-1-59780-109-6; 978-1-59780-108-9

Contents: If nudity offends you; Gifts; Politics; And ladies of the club; Accidents don't just happen-they're
caused; New world symphony; No pain, no gain; Hand
to hand; Tradition; Fool's gold; Judgment; Gravesite revisited; Sweet charity; Welcome to Wheel Days; Say
cheese
"Fans of the Chicks in Chainmail anthology series will
enjoy 'And Ladies of the Club' and three other tales of
the intrepid females of the Ladies' Aid and Armor Society. . . . The heart of the collection is 'Politics,' a story
of young soldiers serving a questionable authority; it
sums up many of Moon's themes, from honor and family
to being true to oneself. Readers who only know Moon's
novels will be thrilled to learn that her short stories are
equally entertaining and thoughtful." Publ Wkly

Once a hero. Baen Pub. Enterprises 1997 400p
ISBN 0-671-87769-0
LC 96-48176
In this novel, "Lt. Esmay Suiza faces a military court
hearing following her emergency captaining of a patrol
ship during battle after the captain turned out to be a
traitor. Tormented by nightmares from repressed memories of sexual assault, Esmay determinedly recaptures her
self-esteem and the military's trust." Libr J
"Moon's mastery of contemporary science fiction is
evident in every line. The characters spring to life on the
page, the intricacies of societies are astutely explored,
and the pace never flags." Booklist

The speed of dark. Del Rey Bks. 2002 340p
$23.95
ISBN 0-345-44755-7
LC 2002-20771
Set in the near future, this novel "depicts an autistic
adult struggling with a momemtous decision. Lou
Arrendal functions on a fairly high level: he has a job
with a pharmaceutical company and leads a quiet, independent life. . . . When an experimental treatment offers
Lou a chance to reverse his autism, he must choose between remaining himself or possibly becoming a different person." Libr J
"Moon is effective at putting the reader inside Lou's
mind, and it is both fascinating and painful to see the behavior and qualities of so-called normals through his
eyes." Booklist

Moorcock, Michael, 1939-

An alien heat; volume one of a trilogy "The
dancers at the end of time". Harper & Row 1973
c1972 158p (Dancers at the end of time) o.p.
First published 1972 in the United Kingdom
This novel "is set near the end of the world, when
Earth is populated by hedonistic immortals who
restructure continents and their own bodies at whim. A
young man named Jherek becomes unfashionably obsessed with Mrs. Amelia Underwood, a time traveler
from the 19th century, his favorite period. He follows her
to London of 1896, where he is tried for murder and
hanged, which somehow returns him to the future, sans
Amelia but with insights into love and the true human
condition. This tale could be called an Art Nouveau morality play or a science fiction comedy of manners. The
humor is genuine, the style lush but controlled." Libr J
Followed by The hollow lands

Moorcock, Michael, 1939-—*Continued*

The best of Michael Moorcock; edited by John Davey with Ann & Jeff VanderMeer. Tachyon Publications 2009 403p pa $14.95

ISBN 978-1-892391-86-5; 1-892391-86-4

Contents: A portrait in ivory; The visible men; A dead singer; Lunching with the Antichrist; The opium general; Behold the man; A winter admiral; London bone; Colour; Going to Canada; Leaving Pasadena; Crossing into Cambodia; Doves in the circle; The deep fix; The birds of the moon; The Cairene Purse; A slow Saturday night at the Surrealist Sporting Club

"One of the progenitors of the sword-and-sorcery genre as well as the New Wave literary sf movement, Moorcock crosses genres, bends boundaries, and breaks rules as only a master storyteller can. This important contribution to the author's oeuvre contains variant versions and some previously uncollected stories." Libr J

The dreamthief's daughter; a tale of the albino. Warner Bks. 2001 343p $35

ISBN 0-446-52618-5   LC 00-43836

"In this latest installment in his multivolume saga of the Eternal Champion, Moorcock . . . teams his favorite hero, the melancholy albino swordsman Elric of Melniboné, with Count Ulric von Bek, the last in a line of German noblemen. . . . War is in the offing, and Hitler, having learned that the von Bek family may own both an enchanted sword and the Holy Grail itself, sends SS Major Gaynor von Minct to take possession of these mystical relics so they may be used to further the cause of the Third Reich. Von Bek and Gaynor, however, are merely the current earthly avatars of the Eternal Champion and one of his greatest foes; they are knights fighting in the causes, respectively, of Chaos and Law, in innumerable, gorgeously described, alternate realities." Publ Wkly

The end of all songs; volume three of a trilogy "The dancers at the end of time". Harper & Row 1976 271p (Dancers at the end of time) o.p.

"Moorcock wraps up his Dancers at the End of Time trilogy with a volume that . . . brings together the two central characters—Jhereck Carnelian, one of the hedonistic immortals who dwell at the End of Time, and Mrs. Amelia Underwood, a reluctant time traveler from Victorian England. Although their reunion is a cause for celebration, the fabric of time has been ruptured, threatening to plunge all into disordered chronological gulfs. Even the inhabitants at the End of Time—an amoral, whimsical, all-but-thoughtless, utterly powerful, and thoroughly likable lot—know concern for the first time in their immortal lives." Booklist

The hollow lands; volume two of a trilogy "The dancers at the end of time". Harper & Row 1974 182p o.p.

In this volume "jaded Jhereck Carnelian is back in his futuristic world after narrowly escaping being hanged in 1896 London while on a time trip with Mrs. Amelia Underwood. He's bored with his life of instant gratification and wants to return to his Victorian lady, but he can't find a working time machine anywhere. Until he falls into a pit full of never-aging children and a robot nurse shoots him back to 1896. Lost in London, he luckily stumbles on Frank Harris and H. G. Wells at the Cafe Royale, and they help reunite him with Amelia." Publ Wkly

Followed by The end of all songs

The skrayling tree; the albino in America. Warner Bks. 2003 330p $24.95

ISBN 0-446-53104-9   LC 2002-27247

"In the sequel to The Dreamthief's Daughter, Oona, protagonist of the earlier book, has married Ulric von Bek, last of his line of Grail Defenders. On vacation in Canada, Ulric is abducted, allegedly to fight a wind demon leading an army bent on destroying a golden city that possesses the Skrayling Tree, a key support of the Multiverse of Moorcock's Eternal Champion yarns. Meanwhile, Oona is in a Native American universe, enlisted by the shaman White Crow to fight pygmies who threaten a golden city. In another universe, Oona's father, Elric, seeking those who forged his black sword, ends up in Vinland's City of Gold, asked to help pygmies there, whose gold has been stolen by an evil giant named . . . White Crow." Booklist

"The tale's power stems largely from the astounding lyricism of the author's prose, the only flaw being the sometimes stilted and overly expository dialogue about the nature of the Multiverse." Publ Wkly

Moore, Brian, 1921-1999

Black robe; a novel. Dutton 1985 246p o.p.

* LC 84-21222

"A William Abrahams book"

This is a novel about a French priest in Canada in the 17th century, "Father Laforgue, who must journey from Quebec to a remote village to find out what happened to two other priests. Through snowstorms and along rivers, amid the majestic grandeur of the forests and brushes with sex and death, Laforgue comes to doubt the depth and meaning of his faith." Libr J

"Each culture is seen whole, with intelligence and sympathy, and considering the clichés that prevail about both Indians and priests, that alone makes 'Black Robe' special." N Y Times Book Rev

Cold heaven; a novel. Holt, Rinehart & Winston 1983 265p o.p.

* LC 82-18720

"A William Abrahams book"

"Alex and Marie, two Americans on vacation, are pedal-boating in the Baie-des-Anges. Alex dives into the water to swim alongside the little boat. He is hit by an out-of-control motor boat and pronounced dead. But at the hospital, his corpse disappears. Later, returning to their hotel room, Marie finds Alex's wallet, flight tickets and travel checks missing. Throughout, Marie has the feeling that an omnipotent power is controlling her life. She is haunted by a miraculous vision." Libr J

"What begins as an extravagant thriller becomes a metaphysical story of a woman's struggle to regain control of her life. . . . The religious view that Moore expresses here is rarely found in fiction; it has the same kind of freshness that Alaric brought to Rome. 'Cold Heaven's' spell derives from its author's skill at preparing a most meticulously realistic field in which he plants two uncanny seeds—just to see what the effect will be." Newsweek

Moore, Brian, 1921-1999—*Continued*

The lonely passion of Judith Hearne. Little, Brown 1956 c1955 223p o.p.

*

"An Atlantic Monthly Press book"

First published 1955 in the United Kingdom with title: Judith Hearne

"Judith Hearne is a middle-aged spinster whose plain looks and loneliness make her depressed and increasingly isolated from any social contact. The other renters in her Belfast boarding house disdain her. Only Mrs. O'Neill, an old school friend, treats her kindly. When her landlady's brother, Jim Madden, returns from America, he pays some attention to Judith, thinking she has money. Jim's bad character is revealed in many ways, including a sexual attack on a young housemaid, and Judith finds more and more solace in drinking. Her pathetic world falls apart completely when even her religious faith deserts her. This sad novel presents a portrait of despair that is almost unbearable." Shapiro. Fic for Youth. 3d edition

The statement. Dutton 1996 250p

ISBN 0-525-94128-2   LC 95-43885

"A William Abrahams book"

This "novel dramatizes the narrow escapes and glaring self-deceptions of a 70-year-old Catholic Frenchman, Pierre Brossard, who is being newly pursued for his participation, while a member of the Vichy-affiliated Milici during World War II, in the execution of Jews. Brossard was offically pardoned in 1971 by the French president, but soon afterwards he was condemned internationally for 'crimes against humanity.' He has remained a fugitive ever since, receiving asylum at various sympathetic Catholic monasteries and abbeys in France." Booklist

"'The Statement' is a book to be read in one sitting. A straightforward shocker, a psychological thriller, a chase and travelogue through France, a religio-political conundrum—any way you take it, this is first-class fare." N Y Times Book Rev

Moore, Christopher, 1957-

A dirty job; a novel. Morrow 2006 387p il $24.95

ISBN 0-06-059027-0   LC 2005-57501

This satirical fantasy is set in "San Francisco, where ridiculously apprehensive brand-new father Charlie Asher runs a secondhand shop. Charlie obsesses that little Sophie won't draw her next breath. Instead, his wife Rachel doesn't, and Charlie blames the seven-foot guy in the mint-green suit whom he intercepts in Rachel's room. Would it were that simple. Charlie eventually learns he has joined a tiny band, to which the tall intruder already belongs, whose members must collect soul vessels—objects in which the souls of the just-deceased are lodged–and keep them until their proper, necessarily soulless, next human receptacles come along. Unfortunately, four hideous demons or deities of death want the soul vessels, too, for sustenance as they prepare to conquer the world. The book unfolds as a struggle between Charlie, who thinks he's supposed to be the new big cheese of death, and the demons." Booklist

"Much of the pleasure of Moore's tale resides not only in the ingeniously unpredictable events but also in the prickly vitality of his language. Striking figures of speech . . . and aphorisms grace the text." Washington Post Book World

Fluke; or, I know why the winged whale sings. Morrow 2003 321p $23.95; pa $13.95

ISBN 0-380-97841-5; 0-06-056668-X (pa)

LC 2002-43231

"Nate Quinn spends his time in the waters off Maui researching whales. . . . One day, when photographing the tail of one particular whale to determine its size, Nate spies foot-high letters on the underside spelling out, 'Bite Me.' . . . When Nate finds the group's offices plundered and all of the data either stolen or ruined, the scientists are thrown into the beginning of a bizarre plot complete with . . . scientific explanations, potential alien conspiracies, and well-rounded, hilarious characters." Voice Youth Advocates

You suck; a love story. Morrow 2007 208p $21.95

ISBN 978-0-06-059029-1; 0-06-059029-7

This sequel to Bloodsucking friends (1995), "features Tommy and Jody trying to make an undeath for themselves after Jody kills her lover/food source, Tommy, and turns him into a vampire. They have a few problems—like finding a new food source (Chet the giant cat might not have been a good idea), recruiting minions to help them when the sun is up, and dealing with a homicidal elder vampire." Libr J

Moore "manages, despite figures like a blue-painted prostitute who prompts visions of sex with a Smurf, to keep the book's eccentricity in check and its screwball antics from becoming insufferable. As with his best work, there's a fundamental sweetness beneath the antics." N Y Times (Late N Y Ed)

Moore, Lorrie

Birds of America. Knopf 1998 291p

ISBN 0-679-44597-8   LC 98-6144

Contents: Willing; Which is more than I can say about some people; Dance in America; Community life; Agnes of Iowa; Charades; Four calling birds, three French hens; Beautiful grade; What you want to do fine; Real estate; People like that are the only people here: canonical babbling in peed onk; Terrific mother

"These stories chart the intersection of the ridiculous and the tragic. . . . Moore peers into America's loneliest perches, but her delicate touch turns absurdity into a warming vitality." New Yorker

A gate at the stairs; a novel. Alfred A. Knopf 2009 321p $25.95

ISBN 978-0-375-40928-8; 0-375-40928-9

LC 2009-03091

"Just months after 9/11, college student Tassie Keltjin, the brilliant daughter of a Midwestern farmer, becomes a part-time nanny for an older white couple who have adopted an African American baby. Enjoying her delightful young charge and reveling in her love affair with her Brazilian boyfriend, Tassie has a growing suspicion that her employers are somehow off. When their identities, as well as her boyfriend's, are blown, Tassie heads home, only to be hit with another, more devastating shock." Libr J

"The novel concludes in a tone of wan hope, with Tassie wiser and stronger, though forever sadder. . . . This book is—not above all, but in the service of all—funny. Moore is not shy about the bad joke, and never

Moore, Lorrie—*Continued*

pushes a great one too far. Her humor, always pointed at insight and elaboration, strikes the perfect balance between taste and feeling." PopMatters

Moore, Susanna

The big girls. Alfred A. Knopf 2007 224p $24
ISBN 978-1-4000-4190-9; 1-4000-4190-2
LC 2006-48819

"Set in a women's prison on the Hudson River, Moore's sixth novel chronicles the aftermath of a highly publicized murder and its impact on four intertwined lives. The story is told in the alternating voices of Helen, who has long suffered terrifying schizophrenic hallucinations and is serving a life sentence for killing her two small children; Helen's psychiatrist, a single mother who came to work at the prison out of guilt over a patient's suicide; a corrections officer who becomes involved with the psychiatrist; and an ambitious Hollywood star whom Helen believes to be her sister. Moore gradually probes Helen's psychosis to its horrifying origins, while also delivering a nuanced and devastating account of the fights, rapes, and alliances built from necessity that constitute prison life." New Yorker

Moravia, Alberto, 1907-1990

Two women; translated from the Italian by Angus Davidson. Farrar, Straus & Giroux 1958 339p o.p.

"The disintegrating effects of war upon the personalities of an Italian mother and her 17-year-old daughter who are evacuated to the country in 1943. Cesira and Rosetta struggle to resist the corruption and dishonor which surround their countrymen but they are defeated by lust and by greed." Publ Wkly

"Through his description of the brutal, dehumanizing forces of war we see Moravia's belief that man is man because he suffers most cogently illustrated. This novel is also probably the most poignant expression of Moravia's view of the human condition." Ency of World Lit in the 20th century

Moreton, Andrew *See* Defoe, Daniel, 1661?-1731

Morgan, Richard K.

Altered carbon. Del Rey Bks. 2003 375p pa $13.95
ISBN 0-345-45768-4
LC 2002-31165

First published 2002 in the United Kingdom

"In the 25th century, it's difficult to die a final death. Humans are issued a cortical stack, implanted into their bodies, into which consciousness is 'digitized' and from which—unless the stack is hopelessly damaged—their consciousness can be downloaded ('resleeved') with its memory intact, into a new body. While the Vatican is trying to make resleeving (at least of Catholics) illegal, centuries-old aristocrat Laurens Bancroft brings Takeshi Kovacs (an Envoy, a specially trained soldier used to being resleeved and trained to soak up clues from new environments) to Earth, where Kovacs is resleeved into a cop's body to investigate Bancroft's first mysterious,

stack-damaging death." Publ Wkly

A "seamless marriage of hardcore cyberpunk and hardboiled detective tale." Times (London, England)

Broken angels. Del Rey Bks. 2004 c2003 366p pa $14.95
ISBN 0-345-45771-4 (pa)
LC 2003-62515

"In the far future, UN Envoy and special operative Takeshi Kovacs travels to the planet Sanction V to crush a revolution. When he joins a secret team assigned to recover an archaeological find, he becomes involved in a deadly conspiracy that threatens the existence of the human race-and war seems an easy ride in comparison." Libr J

This novel "is clearly the work of a gifted, ambitious storyteller. Morgan's prose is clean and direct, his characters almost uniformly hard-edged, his future convincing, well conceived and decked out with an almost limitless array of technological marvels." Washington Post Book World

Thirteen. Del Rey 2007 544p $24.95
ISBN 978-0-345-48525-0; 0-345-48525-4
LC 2007-10617

Published in the United Kingdom with title: Black man

"Carl Marsalis, a genetically engineered soldier (a 'variant thirteen'), is busted out of jail to help track down a serial murderer who escaped from the Mars colony and crash-landed a spaceship into the ocean—but not before killing and eating everyone onboard. Now the psychopath is on a rampage, slaughtering seemingly unconnected innocents with no apparent reason or pattern. Partnered up with a female Colony Initiative investigator, Carl soon learns that finding his prey will take him to places he would rather not visit and will teach him things about his own past that he would rather not know." Booklist

"For all that Morgan steps outside some of the usual conventions he is still recognisably working in the format and [Thirteen] comes with some of its bad habits. . . . Morgan's approach is problematic but at the same time it is so utterly different to anything else ou there that it is almost impossible not to admire it." Strange Horizons

Moriarty, Laura

The center of everything. Hyperion 2003 291p $22.95; pa $14
ISBN 1-401-30031-6; 0-7868-8845-8 (pa)
LC 2002-32898

"Any map clearly shows that Kansas is the center of everything. Ten-year-old Evelyn Bucknow notices it on every map that she sees and truly believes that is where she belongs—in the center. Unfortunately, Evelyn is forced to parent her mother, a flighty, unrealistically romantic woman who is having an affair with her married boss. . . . Fortunately, Evelyn takes the events of her life and her mother's life and learns her lessons, with a few glitches along the way. Young people will find Evelyn appealing and real despite the book's setting in the age of Ronald Reagan and big hair, and they will respond positively to her determination." VOYA

Morley, Isla

Come Sunday. Sarah Crichton Books/Farrar, Straus and Giroux 2008 322p $25

ISBN 978-0-374-12687-2; 0-374-12687-9

LC 2008-38829

This novel "begins with a sense of foreboding and a dark secret tied to the protagonist's family farm in South Africa. . . . Abbe Deighton has since fled her homeland and now lives with her husband and young daughter in Hawaii. She chafes in her role as minister's wife and suburban mother and is unhappy without really being able to pin down why. When her daughter's accidental death tears her life apart, Abbe must return to South Africa in order to discover the truth about her own mother and to begin healing." Libr J

"Although true resolution is far from sure, Come Sunday, organized by portions of the liturgical year, ends with Ascension Day. It's a hopeful note that promises redemption." Christianity Today

Morrell, David, 1943-

The brotherhood of the rose; a novel. St. Martin's Press 1984 353p o.p.   LC 83-21324

"Agent-assassins Chris and Saul are orphans who were raised as brothers by enigmatic Eliot, a veteran C.I.A. operative . . . Eliot trained the two to become master killers, and when he mysteriously turns against them, they band together to destroy him." N Y Times Book Rev

"Though Morrell's tale is thoroughly incredible, its engaging protagonists, whirlwind pace, and heartstopping action scenes make it an adventure of great cinematic appeal." Booklist

Scavenger. Vanguard Press 2007 349p $24.95

ISBN 978-1-593154-41-7; 1-593154-41-0

LC 2006-37662

This thriller features ex-cop Frank Balenger, who was first introduced in Creepers (2005). Frank and his lover Amanda, "the only survivors of an incident at the Paragon Hotel, are swept into a deadly situation by a devious video game designer. Amanda is kidnapped, and while Frank searches for her, she is forced to search for a geocached time capsule in a Roanoke-like town in Wyoming. Told in near real time, the novel is fraught with tension and ever-ratcheting suspense." Libr J

Morris, Keith Lee, 1963-

The dart league king. Tin House Books 2008 270p pa $14.95

ISBN 978-0-9794198-8-1; 0-9794198-8-3

LC 2008-20391

This novel "follows five characters through a handful of hours culminating in a dart contest on a Thursday night in Garnet Lake, Idaho: Russell Harmon, who lives for the dart league and his cocaine habit; teammate Tristan Mackey, who is haunted by having not prevented the drowning of a classmate; Kelly Ashton, who wants desperately for someone to rescue her and her young daughter from this small town; Russell's darts rival Brice Habersham, a DEA agent posing as the owner of a gas station; and drug dealer Vince Thompson, who, tonight, is carrying a 9mm Beretta to his meeting with Russell." Publ Wkly

"A dark and deeply involving novel with a haunting moment on just about every page. Suspenseful, gritty, great." McSweeney's

Morris, Mary McGarry

A dangerous woman. Viking 1991 358p

ISBN 0-670-83699-0   LC 90-50405

"Martha Horgan, the emotionally disabled protagonist, was gang-raped as a teenager; now, 15 years later, her life is finally flowing smoothly. She has moved away from her cold, domineering aunt and has a job at the cleaners, a room in a boarding house, even a worshipful admirer in Wesley Mount, the town mortician. But someone has been stealing from the till and 'Marthorgan' as her taunters call her, gets canned. Back at her aunt's place she is seduced by the caretaker, a frustrated, manipulative writer, and then must suffer through his affair with her aunt." Libr J

"Morris performs one of the most difficult writing tasks, creating a character crazy enough to be interesting but sane enough to describe her own dilemma." Time

Fiona Range. Viking 2000 418p

ISBN 0-670-89156-8   LC 99-87724

"Fiona is a love child. Her mother gave birth to her out of wedlock and shortly afterward disappeared. Fiona was brought up alongside three cousins by her aunt and uncle, Arlene and Charles Hollis, leading citizens in their small New England town. . . . When the novel opens, Fiona is running out of patience with her circumstances. Haltingly, she embarks upon a quest: to discover her real family, to find a place where she belongs, to redeem herself. Her progress is often painful." N Y Times Book Rev

"The characters have weirdly varying powers of perception, and that keeps the juggled plots in the air, but it doesn't matter if you guess the gothic family secrets: this author is the literary equivalent of Spanish fly." New Yorker

The lost mother. Viking 2005 274p $23.95

ISBN 0-670-03389-8   LC 2004-57170

This novel tells the "story of 12-year-old Thomas and eight-year-old Margaret. . . . Reduced to living in a tent in Vermont during the Depression, the children and their father, Henry Talcott, a butcher who must travel daily seeking work, are barely surviving their abandonment by the children's reluctant mother. The shattered family aches with the desire to bring home beautiful, troubled Irene while Henry crumbles into a 'whipped man... worn down and grim,' and Thomas takes on the role of caretaker. Henry's longtime friend Gladys shows the family rare kindness, but a longstanding animosity between her crotchety father and Henry makes it impossible for the Talcotts to accept her charity. In typical Morris fashion, the author paints a brutal landscape and authentic characters with delicacy and precision: from the chaotic household of Irene's alcoholic sister to the creepy relationship between a sick boy and his doting mother, who wants to adopt Thomas and Margaret." Publ Wkly

Songs in ordinary time. Viking 1995 740p

ISBN 0-670-87907-X   LC 94-44071

A novel set in a small Vermont town during the summer of 1960. "With no support from her alcoholic ex-husband Sam, Marie Fermoyle has struggled for eight

Morris, Mary McGarry—*Continued*

years to raise her three children. She is sharp-tongued, bitter, resentful and driven nearly to distraction by unending money worries and her own shame at being a poor divorcée in a staunchly Catholic town. The arrival of mysterious Omar Duvall with his con man's spiel of sudden riches brings Marie hope that she can change her dead-end existence." Publ Wkly

"The novel is frequently perceptive about the bitter pathos bred by the feeling that you've always lived on someone else's leftovers. . . . The novel is also insightful and frightening on the unshakable resilience of family grudges." N Y Times Book Rev

Morris, R. N., 1960-

The gentle axe. Penguin 2007 305p $24.95
ISBN 978-1-594-20112-7; 1-594-20112-9
LC 2006-49543

This historical crime novel "opens in 1866 with a gruesome scene in St. Petersburg's Petrovsky Park: a man's corpse hangs from a tree, and the dead body of a dwarf lies nearby, his skull split in two. An autopsy determines that the dwarf has been poisoned, raising suspicions about the presumed murder-suicide. The case is assigned to Porfiry Petrovich, Raskolnikov's prosecutor in Crime and Punishment." Libr J

The author's "use of a generic form does not dilute the idea of human suffering that Dostoyevsky wished to explore. Morris' twist is investigating the suffering of the investigator, not the criminal. In identifying with the killers he chases, Petrovich bears the terrible weight of suffering in the world. His profession forces him to perpetually wander the Siberia of his own soul. Morris' novel is a book not about the metaphysics of murder, but rather the metaphysics of the investigation of murders." PopMatters

Morris, Roger N. *See* Morris, R. N., 1960-

Morris, Willie

Taps; a novel. Houghton Mifflin 2001 340p $26
ISBN 0-618-09859-3
* LC 00-68250

"Set in the small Mississippi Delta town of Fisk's Landing in the 1950's, 'Taps' covers a year in the life of 16-year-old Swayze Barksdale, the only son of a widowed mother." Christ Sci Monit

"Over the course of a year, in intervals framed by a dozen graveside ceremonies for men shipped back from Korea to the summer-baked or winter-frozen cemetery outside town, Swayze tells the story of a passing Southern world and his own troubled growing up. . . . Funerals are its talismans and 'Taps' is at it strongest when it describes them." N Y Times Book Rev

Morris, Wright, 1910-1998

Collected stories, 1948-1986. Harper & Row 1986 274p o.p.
* LC 86-45334

Contents: The ram in the thicket; The sound tape; The character of the lover; The safe place; The cat in the picture; Since when do they charge admission?; Drrdla; Green grass, blue sky, white house; A fight between a white boy and a black boy in the dusk of a fall afternoon in Omaha, Nebraska; Fiona; Magic; Here is Einbaum; In another country; Real losses, imaginary gains; The cat's meow; The lover and the beloved; The customs of the country; Victrola; Glimpse into another country; Going into exile; To Calabria; Fellow creatures; Wishing you and your loved ones every happiness; Country music; Things that matter; The origin of sadness

"Spanning close to 40 years of Morris's work and ranging in settings throughout the U.S. and in many cities abroad, this collection deals with wartime experiences, race relations in the South and displacement, both cultural and temporal. Through his eyes we glimpse the mysteries of life and the small epiphanies that render them a little more comprehensible." Publ Wkly

Morrison, Toni, 1931-

The bluest eye; with a new afterword by the author. Knopf 1993 215p
ISBN 0-679-43373-2
* LC 93-43124

A reissue of the title first published 1970 by Holt, Rinehart & Winston

"This tragic study of a black adolescent girl's struggle to achieve white ideals of beauty and her consequent descent into madness was acclaimed as an eloquent indictment of some of the more subtle forms of racism in American society. Pecola Breedlove longs to have 'the bluest eye' and thus to be acceptable to her family, schoolmates, and neighbors, all of whom have convinced her that she is ugly." Merriam-Webster's Ency of Lit

Jazz. Knopf 1992 229p $26.95
ISBN 0-679-41167-4
LC 91-58555

This novel "tells the story of Violet and Joe Trace, married for over 20 years, residents of Harlem in 1926. . . . Violet works as an unlicensed hairdresser, doing ladies hair in their own homes, and Joe sells Cleopatra cosmetics door to door. . . . When the novel opens, Joe has shot his 18-year-old lover, Dorcas, and Violet has disfigured the dead girl's body at her funeral in a fit of rage. Joe, who was not caught, is in mourning, crying all day in his darkened apartment, and Violet has taken on the task of finding out whatever she can about Dorcas." Voice Lit Suppl

"As the story unfolds, we come to understand, if not excuse, what happened. The characters themselves cannot excuse their own behavior, which baffles them. Violet is obsessed by the memory of the dead girl whose face she slashed: What was it about her that Joe found so special? She is driven to visit the girl's aunt Alice, who is understandably frightened. . . . Some of the most interesting scenes in the book are the subsequent meetings of these two very different women who come to respect each other, even before they learn to understand each other." Christ Sci Monit

Love. Knopf 2003 201p $23.95
ISBN 0-375-40944-0
LC 2003-52737

"There were days, back in the 1940s and 1950s, when the Cosey Hotel and Resort was the place for blacks to vacation, dance, and dine. Bill Cosey, a charismatic figure greatly attractive to woman, ran the resort. But now Bill is dead, and the story is, as we see, not only a pean to past good times but also a portrait of Bill Cosey's power. . . . Now, in his absence, the women in his life

Morrison, Toni, 1931-—*Continued*
jockey for their own power in the vacuum he left behind; their world now revolves around his will, scribbled many years ago on a dirty menu." Booklist

"Like all of Morrison's best fiction, this is a village novel. Race and racism, ancillary concerns in 'Love' for the most part, throw the small groups she writes about upon one another, steeping their passions. Even when the setting is contemporary, Morrison's books feel old fashioned, set in a world where the perpetual distraction of the media hasn't diluted people's fascination with their neighbors." N Y Times Book Rev

A mercy; a novel. Knopf 2008 167p $23.95

ISBN 978-0-307-26423-7; 0-307-26423-8

LC 2008-21067

"The fate of a slave child abandoned by her mother animates this allusive novel — part Faulknerian puzzle, part dream-song — about orphaned women who form an eccentric household in late-17th-century America. Morrison's farmers and rum traders, masters and slaves, indentured whites and captive Native Americans live side by side, often in violent conflict, in a lawless, ripe American Eden that is both a haven and a prison — an emerging nation whose identity is rooted equally in Old World superstitions and New World appetites and fears." N Y Times Book Rev

Paradise. Knopf 1998 318p $25

ISBN 0-679-43374-0

LC 97-80913

"In 1950, a core group of nine old families leaves the increasingly corrupted African American community of Haven, Okla., to found in that same state a new, purer community they call Ruby. But in the early 1970s, the outside world begins to intrude on Ruby's isolation, forcing a tragic confrontation. It's about this time, too, that the first of five damaged women finds solace in a decrepit former convent near Ruby. . . . The individual stories of both the women and the townspeople reveal Morrison at her best." Publ Wkly

Song of Solomon. Knopf 1977 337p $27.50

ISBN 0-394-49784-8

* LC 77-874

"Chaos marked the world into which Macon (known as Milkman) Dead was born. Each member of his family was haunted by some wild obsession—his father's desire for money, land, and social status, his mother's need for love, his sisters' silence, and his Aunt Pilate's madness. To these was added Macon's desire to unearth the family's buried past. This is a novel of mystery and revelation as it unfolds the lives of four generations of blacks in America." Shapiro. Fic for Youth. 3d edition

Sula. Knopf 1974 c1973 174p $26

ISBN 0-394-48044-9

This "is the story of two black women friends and of their community of Medallion, Ohio. The community has been stunted and turned inward by the racism of the larger society. The rage and disordered lives of the townspeople are seen as a reaction to their stifled hopes. The novel follows the lives of Sula and Nel from childhood to maturity to death." Merriam-Webster's Ency of Lit

Tar baby. Knopf 1981 305p $26.95

ISBN 0-394-42329-1

* LC 80-22821

"Retired on the Isle des Chevaliers in the Caribbean, rich Philadelphia businessman Valerian Street and his wife Margaret await the arrival of their estranged son for Christmas; and an already restless household is sharply disrupted when Margaret discovers a primitive black man hiding in her closet. The intruder, called Son, is a fugitive American on the run whose presence alters the lives of the Streets; their devoted black retainers Sydney and Ondine; the Sydney's niece Jade, an educated Paris model with whom Son falls in love." Libr J

"Each of the characters in Toni Morrison's Tar Baby comes with a history, quite a complete history that is given to us in a series of stunning performances." New Repub

Morrow, James, 1947-

The last witchfinder; a novel. William Morrow 2006 526p il $25.95

ISBN 0-06-082179-5

LC 2005-47177

The protagonist of Morrow's "novel is a self-confident young woman named Jennet Stearne, whose father is a witchfinder in late 17th-century England; upon his death, her brother picks up their father's mantle to scourge Satan in Salem, MA. When Jennet's bluestocking aunt, Isobel, is burned at the stake for witchcraft, Jennet determines that her one goal in life will be to bring down the Parliamentary Witchcraft Act of 1604. She moves to the Colonies, where, after many adventures, she takes a young Ben Franklin as lover. She fakes being a witch to gain a forum for her Newtonian views on the absurdity of witchcraft; her brother prosecutes her, and the Baron de Montesquieu, one of the greatest political philosophers of the era, defends her at her trial." Libr J

"Although steeped in period language and scholarship, the narrative never falters. Morrow's panoramic vision of the Enlightenment encompasses the ideology of that turbulent, transformative era, and his wry commentary–related through the sprightly voice of Newton's Principia Mathematica, speaking for itself–lightens the novel's tone without softening its message. This impeccably researched, highly ambitious novel. . . is a triumph of historical fiction." Booklist

The philosopher's apprentice. William Morrow 2008 411p $25.95

ISBN 978-0-06-135144-0; 0-06-135144-X

LC 2007-29815

This novel " begins with Mason Ambrose walking out on his Ph.D. defense, disgusted by what he perceives as the innate hypocrisy in the process. He stumbles into a job for which he seems ideal. Edwina Sabacthani, world-renowned geneticist, hires him to teach her 17-year-old daughter, Londa, about morality. According to Edwina, Londa suffered an accident that caused not only profound amnesia but a complete loss of her moral sense. . . . A satirist of the first water, Morrow gives us a novel by turns poignant, piquant and potent. From his initial premise — part 'Frankenstein,' part 'Emile,' with a dash of 'The Island of Dr. Moreau' thrown in — he backs away from none of the implications of the technology or the ideologies of the main characters, taking us down a rabbit hole that is both haunting and exhilarating. He confronts the reader with the ramifications of choice and action, offering a harrowing tour of cause and consequence." St. Louis Post-Dispatch

Mortimer, John, 1923-2009

Felix in the underworld. Viking 1997 246p o.p.

LC 97-16562

This is a novel about a British writer "who suddenly finds himself floundering about in the messy real world. Felix Morsom, once dubbed the Chekhov of Coldsands-on-Sea, is in a bit of rut: his latest novel isn't selling, and his attraction to his publicist has remained drearily unconsummated. Everything changes when a paternity suit arrives in the mail, followed closely by the murder of a man linked to the woman doing the suing." Booklist

"This novel is actually about the characters of literary and legal London, and we soon realize that the point is not just to allow these people to circulate in the pages of narrative but, more importantly, to turn character into caricature. . . . John Mortimer's writing is fluent, gently humorous, and possesses the comic's virtue, tact." Times Lit Suppl

Paradise postponed. Viking 1986 c1985 373p

ISBN 0-670-80094-5

* LC 85-40712

First published 1985 in the United Kingdom

"A realistic novel of manners in the grand nineteenth-century British tradition, this sweeping look at postwar England focuses on a group of villagers from the London suburb of Rapstone Fanner. From the upwardly mobile conservative politician through the activist vicar to the jazz-playing country doctor, these characters reflect the comic follies of the modern age as they try to come to grips with an overwhelming sense of expectations unfulfilled." Am Libr

Quite honestly. Viking 2006 206p $24.95

ISBN 0-670-03483-5   LC 2005-53157

First published 2005 in the United Kingdom

"Life couldn't be better for Lucinda Purefoy. She's got a steady boyfriend, a degree in social sciences from Manchester University, and the offer of a high-powered job in advertising. With all this good fortune, isn't it appropriate for her to give something back to society? With her newly minted membership in Social Carers, Reformers, and Praeceptors (SCRAP for short), an organization that recruits women to become the guides, philosophers, and friends to ex-convicts coming out of prison, Lucy finds herself standing outside the gates of Wormwood Scrubs waiting to greet a career burglar called Terry Keegan." Publisher's note

"Good intentions pave Lucy Purefoy's way into all kinds of misadventures in this engaging satire. . . . Mortimer clearly enjoys poking fun at middle-class do-gooders-especially Lucy's dad, a bishop so tolerant that he probably puts a 'pretty please' at the end of the Sixth Commandment. The end result is a tad slight, but fine for readers who enjoy light satire with a little larceny on the side." Christ Sci Monit

Rumpole à la carte. Viking 1990 245p o.p.

LC 91-161338

Contents: Rumpole à la carte; Rumpole and the summer of discontent; Rumpole and the right to silence; Rumpole at sea; Rumpole and the quacks; Rumpole for the prosecution

Rumpole and the angel of death. Viking 1996 260p o.p.   LC 95-41851

Contents: Rumpole and the model prisoner; Rumpole and the way through the woods; Hilda's story; Rumpole and the little boy lost; Rumpole and the rights of man; Rumpole and the angel of death

Rumpole and the golden thread

In Mortimer, J. The second Rumpole omnibus p193-442

Rumpole for the defence

In Mortimer, J. The second Rumpole omnibus p11-192

Rumpole misbehaves. Viking 2007 196p $23.95

ISBN 978-0-670-01830-7; 0-670-01830-9

LC 2007-37323

Published in the United Kingdom with title: The anti-social behaviour of Horace Rumpole

In this installment, "the quirky English barrister agrees to defend 12-year-old Peter Timson, who's been served with an 'Antisocial Behaviour Order' (ASBO) for playing soccer in the streets of a posh London neighborhood. Later, Rumpole takes on a more serious case: a shy civil servant, Graham Wetherby, stands accused of murdering a prostitute, an illegal Russian immigrant." Publ Wkly

"Rumpole has for many volumes now . . . remained fixed in our imaginations at about age 70. Perhaps it's because of the author's age, but this novel, which is rather intricately plotted and propulsively rich in incident for so short a narrative, has the feeling of a summation. Over its course, the incorrigible Horace will meet and surmount not only a variety of novel challenges — political correctness and human trafficking, for example — but also old temptations, particularly the pressure to sacrifice his generally undeserving clients on the expedient altar of long unrealized ambition." Los Angeles Times Book Rev

Rumpole on trial. Viking 1992 243p o.p.

Contents: Rumpole and the children of the devil; Rumpole and the eternal triangle; Rumpole and the miscarriage of justice; Rumpole and the family pride; Rumpole and the soothsayer; Rumpole and the reform of Joby Jonson; Rumpole on trial

Rumpole rests his case. Viking 2002 210p $24.95

ISBN 0-670-03139-9   LC 2002-19046

Contents: Rumpole and the old familiar faces; Rumpole and the remembrance of things past; Rumpole and the asylum seekers; Rumpole and the Camberwell carrot; Rumpole and the actor Laddie; Rumpole and the teenage werewolf; Rumpole rests his case

"With Mortimer's greatly felicitous style and careful plotting, these stories are sheer, absolute reading pleasure." Booklist

Rumpole's last case

In Mortimer, J. The second Rumpole omnibus p443-667

Rumpole's return. Armchair Detective Lib. 1992 c1980 159p o.p.   LC 91-29415

First published 1980 in paperback in the United Kingdom

"After losing in Judge Bullingham's court for the tenth

Mortimer, John, 1923-2009—*Continued*

straight time, Rumpole finds the beaches of Florida a welcome change from the dampness of home. Basking in the sun, he comes across an account of the Notting Hill Gate murder in a back copy of *The Times* which sparks a nerve. This is the sort of case he enjoyed. The evidence is stacked against the accused. . . . Rumpole's uncanny assessment of the situation is that the facts are out of synch." Publisher's note

The second Rumpole omnibus. Viking 1987 667p o.p.

Companion volume to The first Rumpole omnibus (1983)

Contents: Rumpole for the defence (c1981) {variant title: Regina v. Rumpole}; Rumpole and the golden thread (c1983); Rumpole's last case (c1987)

Rumpole for the defence: Rumpole and the confession of guilt; Rumpole and the gentle art of blackmail; Rumpole and the dear departed; Rumpole and the rotten apple; Rumpole and the expert witness; Rumpole and the spirit of Christmas; Rumpole and the boat people

Rumpole and the golden thread: Rumpole and the genuine article; Rumpole and the golden thread; Rumpole and the old boy net; Rumpole and the female of the species; Rumpole and the sporting life; Rumpole and the last resort

Rumpole's last case: Rumpole and the blind tasting; Rumpole and the old, old story; Rumpole and the official secret; Rumpole and the judge's elbow; Rumpole and the bright seraphim; Rumpole and the winter break; Rumpole's last case

The sound of trumpets. Viking 1999 272p
ISBN 0-670-87861-8　　　　LC 98-38968
First published 1998 in the United Kingdom
This novel "chronicles the bewildering career of the young Labour candidate Terry Flitton, who madly accepts Titmuss's offer of aid when the local Conservative M.P. is found face down in a swimming pool and the seat Flitton covets becomes vacant." New Yorker

Summer's lease. Viking 1988 288p o.p.
"The advertisement that Molly Pargenter answered made the Tuscany villa to let sound like the ideal place—suspiciously too ideal—for her family to spend its summer vacation. Arriving in Italy with her husband, three daughters, and father, she finds an unusual assortment of locals and English expatriates for neighbors, as well as detailed notes on the proper use of the house left by her absentee landlord, one S. Kettering. Molly's obsession with learning as much as possible about the Kettering household leads her to some ominous conclusions." Libr J
"Mortimer puts in a graceful performance as he untangles a whole bundle of liaisons and portrays a whole array of human emotions with skill and subtlety." Booklist

Titmuss regained. Viking 1990 280p
ISBN 0-670-82333-3　　　　LC 89-40801
This sequel to Paradise postponed "is the story of how Titmuss . . . attempts to go green. He does so as an expedient to protect his newly acquired country manor, threatened by a new town, and to conserve the votes of the green-welly brigade." Economist
"Mortimer's touch remains as light as ever, and the novel is full of beautifully-poised social comedy–but there can be no denying the bitterness with which he views contemporary Britain." New Statesman Soc

Mortman, Doris

The lucky ones. Kensington Bks. 1997 407p
ISBN 1-57566-204-3　　　　LC 96-80069
"When rising politician Benjamin Knight gets married on a perfect summer day, the four women watching don't realize how prophetic the best man's toast for success is. And over the next 20 years, the women all forge their own ambitious careers: Zoë becomes a foreign affairs analyst, a career choice made in order to get as far from Ben as possible; Celia, Ben's sister-in-law, uses her beauty and talent to build a career in national television; Georgie, Ben's childhood friend, becomes a congresswoman; and Kate, Ben's college classmate, founds a national child protection organization following the murder of her daughter. When a dangerous hostage situation arises overseas in an election year, the current president announces he will not run again. A heated political race erupts, and Ben throws his hat in the ring." Booklist
"In the midst of a well-paced thriller, Mortman takes a bubbly peek into the drawing rooms and back rooms where history is brokered." Publ Wkly

True colors; a novel. Crown 1995 c1994 553p
o.p.　　　　LC 94-13068
"The internationally renowned artist Isabelle de Luna, born into the aristocracy of Barcelona, Spain, lost a life of privilege when her mother was brutally raped and murdered. For Isabelle's protection she is sent to New Mexico to live with the Durans, friends of the family who raise her together with their adopted daughter, Nina. As adults, the two young women become successful but lose their bonds of sisterhood." Libr J
"Mortman sets out quite a feast: alluring and sophisticated characters, steamy sex, and a captivating plot involving murder, great wealth and power, international intrigue, art, ambition, and redemption." Booklist

Morton, Kate, 1976-

The house at Riverton; a novel. Atria Books 2008 473p $24.95
ISBN 978-1-4165-5051-8; 1-4165-5051-8
　　　　LC 2008-7023
First published 2006 in Australia with title: The shifting fog
"For decades, Grace Reeves has kept secret the truth of a poet's violent death by the lake at Riverton House in Oxfordshire. Now at the end of her life, 98-year-old Grace's memory is swept back, after interviews for a film about the tragic incident, to those years of her service for the Hartford family. At 15, Grace begins her adult life as a housemaid in the grand Riverton House, quickly learning her place in the servant hierarchy. Her loyalty and attachment to Hannah and Emmeline Hartford grow over the years, as the Hartford family is affected by war, death, financial failings, and illicit love. . . . . A suspenseful and beautifully atmospheric novel capturing the transitional time from the end of the Edwardian era through World War I into the Roaring Twenties." Libr J

Moser, Benjamin

(tr) García-Roza, L. A. Alone in the crowd

Moses, Kate

Wintering; a novel of Sylvia Plath. St. Martin's Press 2003 292p $23.95

ISBN 0-312-28375-X   LC 2002-36753

"A fictionalization of the grueling months following the dissolution of Plath's marriage to Ted Hughes and leading up to her suicide at the age of 30 in 1963. 'Wintering' is beautiful and moving. The narrative voice is a distillation of Plath's diaries, letters and poems; with lyrical dexterity and great economy, Moses portrays a demanding, pitiless woman struggling against the stark fact of her husband's infidelity and her own inner demons." N Y Times Book Rev

Mosher, Howard Frank

On Kingdom Mountain. Houghton Mifflin Co. 2007 276p $24

ISBN 978-0-618-19723-1; 0-618-19723-0

     LC 2006-23568

"Jane Hubbell Kinneson is the sole owner and last resident of Kingdom Mountain, Vermont, a wild and unspoiled place on the U.S.–Canadian border in 1930. Outside forces led by her cousin Eben are trying to get the Connector, a new highway that will run through the mountain, pushed through. Miss Jane says, 'Over my dead body,' and means it. On her fiftieth birthday, stunt pilot and rainmaker Henry Satterfield crashes his biplane on her lake. Miss Jane offers him shelter and Henry joins her fight against the Connector. Henry is in Vermont to solve the riddle his Confederate grandfather left him about the location of stolen federal gold." Booklist

"Mosher's passionate geographical hyperbole is both justifiable and charming, producing a wonderfully intriguing sense of place." Washington Post Book World

Mosley, Walter

Always outnumbered, always outgunned. Norton 1997 208p

ISBN 0-393-04539-0   LC 96-54870

Contents: Crimson shadow; Midnight meeting; The thief; Double standard; Equal opportunity; Marvane Street; Man gone; The wanderer; Lessons; Letter to Theresa; History; Firebug; Black dog; Last rites

"In these interconnected short stories about an aging black man, Socrates Fortlow, living in a makeshift two-room apartment in an abandoned Watts building, Mosley turns on its head the fundamental fantasy of the detective story. . . . These are often difficult stories to read; never sentimental, they are finally, one and all, about pain and how we live with it. Perhaps that's why those brief moments when Socrates eases someone else's pain deliver such a powerful sense of catharsis." Booklist

Bad Boy Brawly Brown. Little, Brown 2002 311p

ISBN 0-316-07301-6   LC 2002-16232

Los Angeles "teenager Brawly Brown has left home and is running with the radical Urban Revolutionary Party. Easy quickly find the boy, but he is just as quickly caught up in the murder of one of the party's leaders." Booklist

"As Easy persists in his investigation, he is dismissed by black radicals and rousted by racist cops. . . . So he can't really be blamed for spending more time than he should in places like Sam's Hambones soul food diner, engaging in invigorating of often aimless conversations with characters who have little to offer on Brawly's whereabouts but lots to say about whatever is on their minds. Aside from their appealing hero, Mosley's crime novels take their vitality from the racy language and boisterous humanity of his characters, so these neighborhood encounters provide their own joy." N Y Times Book Rev

Black Betty. Norton 1994 255p

ISBN 0-393-03644-8   LC 94-6839

"Mosley's distinctive black investigator, Easy Rawlins, has moved from Watts to West L.A. with his two adopted children, but trouble still follows him. Hired to locate a sultry female acquaintance from his early days in Houston, Easy searches for her gambler brother and questions her Beverly Hills employer, unwittingly provoking racist police harassment. Meanwhile, friend Raymond ('Mouse') has been released from prison and vows revenge on the snitch who put him there." Libr J

"Mosley gives us a recognizable moment in American history viewed through the eyes of a single black man. This perspective, rare in crime fiction, vivifies not only the black experience but the larger event as well. Here we feel the hot winds that would eventually ignite the Watts riots not as abstract issues in race relations, but as emotions in the hearts of individuals we have come to know and care about." Booklist

Cinnamon kiss. Little Brown 2005 312p $24.95

ISBN 0-316-07302-4   LC 2005-5739

"Easy Rawlins needs some easy money-his daughter is in for some expensive medical treatment-so he agrees to find a missing attorney who seems to be more trouble than he's worth." Libr J

"As ever, Mosley is able to capture the era–hippies, Watts, communes–in brief strokes that provide a brilliant background to Easy's search for solutions to both a convoluted mystery and complex personal problems." Publ Wkly

Devil in a blue dress. Norton 1990 219p $19.95

ISBN 0-393-02854-2

     * LC 89-25503

In this novel "Ezekiel 'Easy' Rawlins, a young, tough black veteran living in 1948 Los Angeles, only wants respect and enough money to pay his mortgage. When fired from his factory job, however, he undertakes some paid errands for a shady white mobster who wishes to locate a light-haired, blue-eyed beauty. As Easy plumbs his usual hangouts for clues, he relays information to the mobster, runs afoul of the police, meets the mysterious woman, discovers a murder, then investigates in self-defense." Libr J

"Mosley's prose is a little stiff and his plot is far too complicated. But he has a keen eye for period details. . . . And his lowdown humor never deserts him." Newsweek

Fear itself; a mystery. Little, Brown 2003 316p $24.95

ISBN 0-316-59112-2   LC 2003-46092

Mosley, Walter—*Continued*

"Set in 1955 Los Angeles, this . . . thriller finds Fearless and compatriot Paris Minton, the story's narrator, searching for a friend's missing husband. That seemingly simple task rapidly escalates into a case of multiple murders, blackmail, and a quest for a priceless heirloom that makes this Mosley's answer to the Maltese Falcon." Libr J

"It's a tossup which gives more pleasure in Mosley's vibrant views of neighborhood life, the high-stepping, free-talking who bob and weave their way through this convoluted plot, or the colorful local haunts like Henrietta's Gumbo House where they do their shuckin' and jivin'." N Y Times Book Rev

Fear of the dark. Little, Brown and Co. 2006 308p $25.99

ISBN 978-0-316-73458-5; 0316734586

LC 2006-12741

A mystery featuring bookseller Paris Minton set in Watts, 1956. "Trouble comes to Paris's door in the form of his cousin Ulysses 'Useless' S. Grant IV, who needs help after getting mixed up in a scheme that has gotten totally out of hand. Despite refusing to even let Useless cross his threshold, Paris is drawn, violently, into the fray." Publ Wkly

This is a "funny, funky novel, but like all of Mosley's work, it's troubling, too that's clearly what he intends, and he does his work well." Washington Post Book World

Fearless Jones; a novel. Little, Brown 2001 312p

ISBN 0-316-59238-2

* LC 00-53502

This "mystery is narrated by Paris Minton, a black man who sells used books in nineteen-fifties L.A. Paris's life is perfect—he reads all day without interruption—until a bewitching young woman named Elana Love walks through his door. She's looking for a religious group called the Messenger of the Divine, but the thug who bursts in after her is looking for a bond worth thousands of dollars. Mayhem and seduction ensue, and when Paris's bookstore is burned to the ground, he knows it's time to seek the aid of the incomparable Fearless Jones. The unlikely friendship of these men—Fearless is all fists and testosterone, Paris is a gun-shy truth-seeker—is the source of the novel's humor, and propels the reader through the plot's knottier moments." New Yorker

Fortunate son. Little, Brown and Co. 2006 313p $23.95

ISBN 978-0-316-11471-4; 0-316-11471-5

LC 2005-24477

"Tommy was born out of wedlock with a hole in his heart; he's also lame and black. Eric, on the other hand, glows with health; he is so beautiful that people want to touch him–and he's white. For a few years, the boys live together after Tommy's mother and Eric's widowed doctor father fall in love after meeting in the hospital ward. Then Tommy's mother dies, and Tommy is wrested from the only family he's known. Eric grows up leading a life that appears blessed, but with Tommy gone, he's lost all that is important to him. Tommy, meanwhile, ends up on the street but feels lucky simply to be alive. In their twenties, the two still dream of each other when they are reunited by accident, and the bond between them is renewed." Libr J

"With the lightest, slyest of touches, Mosley shows how a certain kind of inarticulate, carnal, involuntary affection transcends just about anything. It's not love, it's fate, and it's breathtaking." Publ Wkly

Gone fishin'; an Easy Rawlins novel. Black Classic Press 1997 244p o.p.   LC 97-124077

This novel marks the first appearance of Mosley's detective-hero, Easy Rawlins. "Written before the other Rawlins novels but never published, it takes Easy and his lethal friend Mouse back to Texas before World War II and their subsequent move to Los Angeles. The 19-year-old Easy . . . knows little of the larger world. His journey to awareness begins with a soul-changing road trip to the bayous of Pariah, Texas, where Mouse hopes to settle a score with his hated stepfather." Booklist

This is "in some respects, the best of Mosley's novels. . . . It firmly establishes Mosley as a writer whose work transcends the thriller category and qualifies as serious literature." Time

A little yellow dog; an Easy Rawlins mystery. Norton 1996 300p

ISBN 0-393-03924-2   LC 96-4231

This mystery, set in the early 1960s, finds Easy Rawlins "working in a high school as head custodian for the Board of Education two years after giving up drinking and the 'street life.' When a corpse turns up on school grounds, Easy finds himself reluctantly caught up in the investigation—between the rock and the hard place of the cops and the killers. Mosley writes in the grand tradition of the American hard-boiled private investigator. His dialog is sharp and his characters vivid—the reader can almost feel the mean L.A. streets." Libr J

The long fall. Riverhead Books 2009 305p $25.95

ISBN 978-1-59448-858-0; 1-59448-858-4

LC 2008-46238

In this initial installment, Mosley introduces Leonid McGill, an African American private detective in New York City. "McGill, a 53-year-old former boxer who's still a fighter, finds out that putting his past life behind him isn't easy when someone like Tony 'The Suit' Towers expects you to do a job; when an Albany PI hires you to track down four men known only by their youthful street names; and when your 16-year-old son, Twill, is getting in over his head with a suicidal girl." Publ Wkly

The novel "accomplishes most of what an inaugural installment of a mystery series should. The three major plot strands are solidly developed and neatly resolved. McGill's quest for redemption, however, is far from over, but it will be interesting to watch it play out across a number of subsequent volumes. If 'The Long Fall' is overstuffed with incidental characters whose importance may not be obvious until later installments, that's a minor flaw. Having retired Easy Rawlins, Mosley has devised a worthy successor in Leonid McGill." San Francisco Chron

The man in my basement; a novel. Little, Brown 2004 249p $22.95

ISBN 0-316-57082-6   LC 2003-56317

Mosley, Walter—*Continued*

"Charles Blakey is an unemployed black man, deep in debt, who drinks too much, has few friends, is awkward with women, and lives alone in a large house where the basement is filled with artifacts of his family's rich history. . . . Anniston Bennett, a wealthy white man with mysterious motives, wants to rent Blakey's sizable basement. . . . Bennet wants Blakey to hold him prisoner for 65 days, his way of atoning for 'crimes against humanity'. Blakey is extremely reluctant, but the 'rent' is considerable and his options are dwindling, so he agrees. At first, he's afraid of his voluntary prisoner, but the balance of power begins shifting unpredictably as the two men engage in heated question-and-answer sessions." Booklist

"In this successful and intriguing departure from his usual work, Mr. Mosley creates a substantial subplot about heritage and history. . . . In the end this audacious novel is about facing up to such brutal realities. But it is also about seeking refuge." N Y Times (Late N Y Ed)

A red death. Norton 1991 284p
ISBN 0-393-02998-0   LC 90-23660
"In this second installment in the series, the calendar has moved ahead to the early 1950s, and the good-natured (and aptly named) Easy is in a pickle. The IRS is after him for hiding income from the apartment buildings he secretly owns; a Red-hating FBI agent strong-arms him into investigating a labor agitator; and the local police suspect him in two murders." Booklist

RL's dream. Norton 1995 267p
ISBN 0-393-03802-5   LC 95-8695
As this novel opens, "Atwater 'Soupspoon' Wise, an aging bluesman in New York City, is evicted from his apartment. Kiki Waters, a young white woman, takes him in, nursing him back to health and forging the necessary health insurance information to get him treated for cancer. The two form a strange friendship; both are from the South, and both have left behind pasts that demand to be dealt with. Soupspoon knew the legendary Robert 'RL' Johnson in his youth and is haunted by the desire to learn the secret of Johnson's music; Kiki was abused by her father and ran away in her early teens." Libr J

"A mesmerizing and redemptive tale of friendship, love, and forgiveness. . . . [This] is, without doubt, the author's finest achievement to date, a rich literary gumbo with blue-stinged rhythms that make it a joy to read and a book to remember." San Francisco Rev Books

Six easy pieces. Atria Bks. 2003 278p $24
ISBN 0-7434-4252-0
Contents: Smoke; Crimson stain; Silver lining; Gator green; Gray-eyed death; Amber gate
"Mosley is as fine as ever, offering compelling commentary on black-white relations in 1964, writing in a style so simple that it deceives us into thinking wwriting great fiction is as easy as putting one foot in front of the other. It's not, but turning these pages is." Booklist

Walkin' the dog. Little, Brown 1999 260p $35
ISBN 0-316-96620-7   LC 99-16407
Contents: Blue lightning; Promise; Shift, shift, shift; What would you do?; A day in the park; The mugger; That smell; Walkin' the dog; Mookie Kid; Moving on; Rascals in the cane; Rogue
In this "volume of interconnected short stories, Mosley gives his hero, 59-year-old ex-con Socrates Fortlow, a

new job, a new home, and a new commitment to ridding his Watts neighborhood of a rogue cop. Overtly political fiction is difficult to pull off, but Mosley makes it work by grounding his issues in the felt life of his characters." Booklist

White butterfly. Norton 1992 272p $19.95
ISBN 0-393-03366-X   LC 91-44700
"Black detective Easy Rawlins aids his dangerous-but-loyal friend Mouse, accused of killing several bar girls in 1958 Los Angeles." Libr J

"Standard stuff, to be sure—the makings of your typical made-for-television movie. But what elevates it is the character. It is not just that Rawlins is such an engaging fellow. He is a man who both ages and evolves." N Y Times Book Rev

Mosse, Kate, 1961-

Labyrinth. G. P. Putnam's Sons 2006 c2005 515p $25.95
ISBN 0-399-15344-6   LC 2005-50985
First published 2005 in the United Kingdom
"In 2005, Alice Tanner stumbles into a hidden cave while on an archeological dig in southwest France. Her discovery—two skeletons and a labyrinth pattern engraved on the wall and on a ring—triggers visions of the past and propels her into a dangerous race against those who want the mystery of the cave for themselves. Alais, in the year 1209, is a plucky 17-year-old living in the French city of Carcassone, an outpost of the tolerant Cathar Christian sect that has been declared heretical by the Catholic Church. As Carcassonne comes under siege by the Crusaders, Alais's father, Bertrand Pelletier, entrusts her with a book that is part of a sacred trilogy connected to the Holy Grail." Publ Wkly

"Medieval life in the Languedoc region is brought vividly to life, and Mosse manages to integrate her research smoothly into the tale. Fans of fantasy and historical romance are the most likely to enjoy the tale, which relies on reincarnation, ancient spells, and other genre conventions." Christ Sci Monit

Moulessehoul, Mohammed, 1955-

The swallows of Kabul; translated from the French by John Cullen. Nan A. Talese\Doubleday 2004 195p $18.95
ISBN 0-385-51001-2   LC 2003-50769
"Before the destruction wrought by the Soviet war and Taliban rule, Mohsen was an affluent merchant; now he wanders the streets while his beautiful wife is confined to home and burka. Atiq, a volatile ex-mujahideen, guards the prisoners awaiting public execution. One day, Mohsen stops to observe the public stoning of a prostitute, one of Atiq's charges. Caught up in the frenzy, he joins in, initiating a series of tragic events." New Yorker

The author is "intimately familiar with the consequences that war and religious extremism have on people's daily lives, and in this book he gives the reader a tactile sense of what life under the Taliban might have been like." N Y Times (Late N Y Ed)

Mowat, Farley

The Snow Walker. Little, Brown 1975 222p o.p.
*

"An Atlantic Monthly Press book"
Stories included are: The blinding of André Maloche; Stranger in Taransay; The iron men; Two who were one; The blood in their veins; The woman and the wolf; The Snow Walker; Walk well, my brother; The white canoe; Dark odyssey of Soosie

The stories range "from the ancient to the overwhelmingly modern. . . . There are tales of starvation, cannibalism out of love, the giving of one body to another with the poignancy of the Eucharist. There are tales so simple and strong you read them again to make sure you haven't been tricked into feeling a story in your stomach for a change." N Y Times Book Rev

Mrazek, Robert J.

Unholy fire; a novel of the Civil War. Thomas Dunne Bks. 2003 299p $24.95

ISBN 0-312-30673-3   LC 2002-32512

"After being critically wounded in a Union battle fiasco, Lieutenant McKitredge is sent to a makeshift hospital on the outskirts of Washington, D. C. to die. Believing he has no chance of survival, well-meaning doctors continually dose him with laudanum. Defying the odds, kit survives, one of the many Civil War heroes to be rewarded with a serious opium addiction. Dispatched to the office of the provost marshal, he is assigned to investigate the cases of thieves, murderers, and deserters. Caught up in a murder case that seems to implicate General Joseph Hooker, he must unravel a perplexing mystery and foil a plot to assassinate the president." Booklist

"Mrazek's portrayal of Civil War battle is stark, graphic, bloody and exciting, and is only exceeded by his memorable description of Washington, D. C. as a Gomorrah on the Potomac." Publ Wkly

Mueenuddin, Daniyal

In other rooms, other wonders. W. W. Norton & Company 2009 247p $23.95

ISBN 978-0-393-06800-9; 0-393-06800-5
                              LC 2008-40632

Contents: Nawabdin electrician; Saleema; Provide, provide; About a burning girl; In other rooms, other wonders; Our Lady of Paris; Lily; A spoiled man

"In eight beautifully crafted, interconnected stories, Mueenuddin explores the cutthroat feudal society in which a rich Lahore landowner is entrenched. . . . An elegant stylist with a light touch, Mueenuddin invites the reader to a richly human, wondrous experience." Publ Wkly

Mullen, Thomas

The last town on earth; a novel. Random House 2006 394p $23.95

ISBN 1-4000-6520-8   LC 2005-46687

The setting of this novel is a "mill town called Commonwealth in the remote northern forests of Washington, founded on progressive, even socialist ideals. But such ideals are hard to sustain in the autumn of 1918 when the deadly Spanish influenza sweeps across the globe in the last months of World War I. To protect itself against infection, the town has voted an absolute and unforgiving quarantine: no one is allowed to come in; no one who leaves is allowed to return." N Y Times Book Rev

The author "patiently unfolds the plot, using historical facts as a springboard. His long and absorbing novel is a timely and sobering look back at a nation during a deadly war involving a human enemy far away, a disease at home, fear, and political and cultural forces." Libr J

Muller, Marcia

Both ends of the night. Mysterious Press 1997 353p o.p.   LC 97-10129

Sharon McCone "sets out to help a friend and former flying instructor find her missing lover, but soon the friend has been murdered, and a missing-persons case has been transformed into a grudge match. With the help of her own lover and fellow flyer Hy Ripinsky, McCone ventures into the depths of the federal witness protection program, finding first the missing lover and then the killer in the wilds of Minnesota. There's plenty of nicely paced action here, and the flying lore provides effective ballast. Best of all, though, there is McCone at work, both as day-to-day professional detective and as aggrieved friend out for justice." Booklist

The broken promise land. Mysterious Press 1996 388p o.p.   LC 95-52187

San Francisco private eye Sharon McCone investigates "a series of threatening letters sent to her brother-in-law, country singer Ricky Savage. . . . Suspects range from higher-ups at the singer's former record label, who resent Savage for starting his own record company, to a former lover, who holds him accountable for alleged promises never kept." Booklist

"Leading Sharon into the rocky psychological terrain of families, Muller gives her meticulously plotted story, with its absorbing picture of the music industry, a commanding emotional authenticity." Publ Wkly

Burn out. Grand Central Pub. 2008 309p $24.99

ISBN 978-0-446-58107-3; 0-446-58107-0
                              LC 2008-4500

"Traumatized by a recent life-or-death investigation, Sharon McCone flees to her ranch in California's high desert country to contemplate her future. Deep depression shadows her days and nights, and a chance encounter with a troubled, highly secretive Native American woman begins to haunt her dreams. Even though she is determined not to investigate anything during her stay—and perhaps not ever again—McCone is drawn into the plight of the young woman and her dysfunctional family." Publisher's note

"By the upbeat ending, McCone has learned that with judicious use of both her investigative and executive skills she can reshape her life." Publ Wkly

Cyanide Wells. Mysterious Press 2003 292p map $24.95

ISBN 0-89296-781-1   LC 2002-45516

"Matt Lindstrom leaves the life he has rebuilt in British Columbia to search for his ex-wife, Gwen. After she vanished from their California home, innuendo that he had murdered her ruined him, forcing his relocation. He discovers that she's in a Soledad County town called Cyanide Wells, living with a lesbian lover and an adopt-

Muller, Marcia—*Continued*

ed child. When he goes there—For revenge? for solace?—he discovers she has taken off again, this time with the child. He and Carly McGuire, publisher of the county newspaper and Gwen's partner, perform an uneasy dance as they try to bring her back." Booklist

The dangerous hour. Mysterious Press 2004 290p $25

ISBN 0-89296-804-4   LC 2003-24625

"The arrest of her newest operative for credit-card theft jeopardizes the apparently rosy future of McCone's Investigations, but Sharon McCone musters the best legal help available. Operative Julia Rafael has overcome a background that includes a juvenile record; however, a recent case she handled for an ambitious Latino city supervisor backfired. Sharon investigates immediately and finds that the supervisor is not all that he appears to be." Libr J

"Muller's plotting isn't quite as tidy as usual . . ., but once again she gives us a solid slice of a San Francisco community and a protagonist with character. Fans of the sturdy, ongoing series will be especially pleased with the final scene, which opens the way for a new chapter in McCone's personal life." Booklist

Dead midnight. Mysterious Press 2002 289p

ISBN 0-89296-765-X

* LC 2002-20097

This mystery has Sharon McCone "gathering evidence for a wrongful-death suit brought by the family of a sensitive young man driven to kill himself by the deplorable working conditions at a trendy online magazine. But events never advance in a straight line in Muller's complicated narratives, and the job that McCone took on because she thought it would help her come to grips with her own brother's suicide turns into a lethal game of industrial sabotage." N Y Times Book Rev

Listen to the silence. Mysterious Press 2000 289p $28

ISBN 0-89296-689-0   LC 99-87734

"When Detective Sharon McCone's father dies suddenly, she is startled to learn that he has requested that she, not her four siblings, go through his personal effects. In a box marked 'Legal Papers,' Sharon discovers a long-secret document that shatters her very identity and threatens to tear her family apart. As she begins to investigate, a Shoshone lawyer who may be the key to the mystery is nearly killed, and Sharon becomes tangled in a land dispute between Native Americans and white developers that involves greed, environmental corruption, racism, and a 40-year-old murder." Libr J

Muller "delivers an emotion-packed tale that adds new depth to her heroine." Publ Wkly

Pennies on a dead woman's eyes; a Sharon McCone mystery. Mysterious Press 1992 297p o.p.

LC 91-58025

Sharon McCone is "repelled by the gruesome details of a 1956 murder case that her San Francisco law firm plans to argue in a mock trial before the city's Historical Tribunal. 'There's too much emotion swirling around' for her liking, and no new evidence to vindicate the woman, recently released from prison, who was convicted of killing her husband's young mistress. Sharon, who acknowledges herself to be 'a demonic researcher,' overcomes

her revulsion when she finds some loopholes in the prosecution's case." N Y Times Book Rev

"Muller is perhaps the least showy crime author around. Her protagonist, driven always into dangerous and emotional culs-de-sac, emerges as a pleasing composite of toughness and vulnerability without seeming to be either overstated or overwritten." Booklist

The shape of dread. Mysterious Press 1989 218p o.p.

LC 89-42606

Sharon McCone "is on the long cold trail of a missing comedian, presumed dead. A young parking valet at the club has been convicted of the 'no-body' crime, and his appeal falls into the sensitive lap of the legal co-op that offers low-paid employment to the spirited McCone." Booklist

"Solid plots, sound procedures and enlightening views of San Francisco's diversified neighborhoods are characteristic of the author's sensible style, which makes up in technical skill what it lacks in esthetics." N Y Times Book Rev

There's something in a Sunday; a Sharon McCone mystery. Mysterious Press 1989 213p o.p.

LC 88-22005

"San Francisco investigator Sharon McCone is hired to watch a man on his day off as he drives from flower garden to flower shop. Then the shirtmaker who has employed her is murdered, the man she follows disappears, a Mission District bum goes into hiding . . . and dark deeds are uncovered at the ranch where the missing man works." Booklist

"This is a provocative work, infused with compassion and sensitivity, that explores the complexities of human relationships and the plight of the homeless." Publ Wkly

Till the butchers cut him down; a Sharon McCone mystery. Mysterious Press 1994 339p o.p.

LC 93-42306

Sharon "McCone has just left the All-Souls Legal Cooperative and opened her own business when an eccentric friend from her UC-Berkeley days, who now specializes in rescuing failing corporations, asks her to find out who is sabotaging his efforts to save a San Francisco shipping firm and threatening his life." Publ Wkly

Trophies and dead things. Mysterious Press 1990 266p o.p.   LC 90-33448

"San Francisco detective Sharon McCone . . . uncovers murderous passions still simmering from the Vietnam anti-war movement when she undertakes an investigation into why a sniper victim changed his will to disinherit his children and leave more than $1 million to four strangers." Publ Wkly

"Like her heroine, Ms. Muller works in a style more admirable for its clarity and efficiency than for boldness or brilliance. Her dense plots are models of construction, and if her characters lack spark, they are observed in a manner both sensible and rational." N Y Times Book Rev

A walk through the fire. Mysterious Press 1999 293p $23

ISBN 0-89296-688-2   LC 98-51314

In this adventure, "Sharon McCone is seduced by the legends of Hawaii and nearly by one particular Hawaiian. Brought to Kauai initially to investigate 'accidents'

Muller, Marcia—*Continued*

on the set of her filmmaker friend's documentary, McCone finds herself dealing with murder, Hawaiian militants, and drug dealers." Libr J

Where echoes live. Mysterious Press 1991 326p o.p.   LC 90-84898

"Private eye Sharon McCone is on the ecological beat, as a renovated gold mine that could lead to environment destruction also leads to several deaths. A good mystery as fresh as today's headlines." Booklist

While other people sleep. Mysterious Press 1998 344p

ISBN 0-89296-650-5   LC 98-13394

"The renowned Sharon McCone finds life and livelihood threatened by a malicious look-alike. When police detain Sharon for a crime committed by the imposter, anger spurs her to find her double." Libr J

"Muller's straightforward, no-nonsense writing and fully dimensioned characterizations lend credibility and color to her deftly plotted tale." Publ Wkly

A wild and lonely place. Mysterious Press 1995 386p o.p.   LC 94-48255

Sharon McCone's "precious Mission District is looking mean and dirty, and colleagues at her legal collective have turned into greedy bureaucrats. Tossing caution over her shoulder, McCone signs on with a secret security agency to go after the Diplo-bomber, a terrorist who attacks embassies and consulates. The mission takes McCone to a heavily guarded hideaway in the Leeward Islands, where she executes a daring ocean swim in the dead of night to rescue an Arab diplomat's granddaughter from kidnappers." N Y Times Book Rev

"A mellow, engaging and determined Sharon here heads a diverse and intriguing supporting cast." Publ Wkly

Wolf in the shadows. Mysterious Press 1993 356p o.p.   LC 92-50536

"San Francisco private eye Sharon McCone is understandably concerned about the disappearance of her mysterious lover, Hy Ripinsky. When she finds out that he had gone to Mexico to deliver $2 million in ransom, she *really* gets worried." Libr J

Muñoz Molina, Antonio, 1956-

In her absence; translated by Esther Allen. Other Press 2007 c2006 134p $13.95

ISBN 978-1-59051-253-1; 1-59051-253-7 (pa)   LC 2006-38139

Original Spanish edition, 2001

This "account of the unraveling of a strained marriage follows Mario, a Spanish civil servant who thrives on routine, after he becomes convinced his wife, Blanca, has deserted him and left in her place an impostor. Mario blames himself for not paying closer attention to his beloved in happier times, but his more pointed regret centers around Lluís Onésimo, a 'villainous multimedia artist' whose arrival in their small city of Jaén, Mario believes, doomed his marriage. Blanca, a longtime art lover, became fixated on Lluís and his art, the latest in a long line of Blanca's artists du jour." Publ Wkly

"Mario's limited yet intensely focused world does not let the reader take a breath for even a paragraph. Perhaps

that is why the novel is so short. Neither the writer nor the reader could sustain such a pitch of living inside the head of an increasingly disturbed human being. But how can a short novel, a mere 134 pages, with little action and a mystery left unsolved, take hold of the reader in this way? The power is in the writing—preserved masterfully in Esther Allen's translation—the ability to slice away the exterior of a character like Mario and to offer a simple, naked view of his small joys and great sufferings." Washington Post Book World

A manuscript of ashes; translated from the Spanish by Edith Grossman. Harcourt 2008 305p $25

ISBN 978-0-15-101410-1; 0-15-101410-8   LC 2007-36557

Original Spanish edition, 1986

"Minaya, a university student in Madrid, returns to his uncle's home in the mythical town of Mágina to write a dissertation on the late forgotten poet Jacinto Solana. With the maid's help 32 years after the fact, Minaya uncovers the identity of his uncle's wife's murderer. Furthermore, as it turns out, Solana is not only very much alive, but Minaya also plays an important role in this work's creation. Using memory as a narrative device, Muñoz Molina guides readers to the surprise ending through a sequence of events that flit back and forth between the Spanish civil war era and the postbellum period." LIbr J

"The most piercing moments arrive as the narrative edges toward Minaya's own voice. It may be that the author was still discovering how to experiment with the limitations and possibilities of third-person narration. Regardless, the release of this first novel not only provides insight into Munoz Molina's development as a writer but also ably introduces readers to one of his favorite themes: that the essence of a story lies in the mechanics of its telling." Bookforum

Munro, Alice

Carried away; a selection of stories; with an introduction by Margaret Atwood. Alfred A. Knopf 2006 xxxv, 559p (Everyman's library) $25

ISBN 0-307-26486-6   LC 2006-43585

Contents: Royal beatings; The beggar maid; The turkey season; The moons of Jupiter; The progress of love; Miles city, Montana; Friend of my youth; Meneseteung; Differently; Carried away; The Albanian virgin; A wilderness station; Vandals; Hateship, friendship, courtship, loveship, marriage; Save the reaper; Runaway; The bear came over the mountain

"Munro's stories are composed with a clarity and economy that make novel-writing look downright superfluous and self-indulgent." N Y Times Book Rev

Friend of my youth; stories. Knopf 1990 273p o.p.   LC 89-43295

Contents: Friend of my youth; Five points; Meneseteung; Hold me fast, don't let me pass; Oranges and apples; Pictures of the ice; Goodness and mercy; Oh, what avails; Differently; Wigtime

"Ms. Munro, who has deepened the channels of realism, is a writer of extraordinarily rich texture; her imagery stuns or wounds and her sentences stick to the rough surfaces of our world." N Y Times Book Rev

Munro, Alice—*Continued*

Hateship, friendship, courtship, loveship, marriage; stories. Knopf 2001 320p

ISBN 0-375-41300-6 LC 2001-29870

Contents: Hateship, friendship, courtship, loveship, marriage; Floating bridge; Family furnishings; Comfort; Nettles; Post and beam; What is remembered; Queenie; The bear came over the mountain

"Opulent in their beauty and gem-bright psychology, the extraordinary stories in {this} collection span the spectrum from romance to tales of manners to deep meditations on love and mortality, and all evince Munro's profound understanding of the power of memories and the stories we tell ourselves." Booklist

Lives of girls & women. McGraw-Hill 1971 250p

ISBN 0-07-044043-3

"Although the locale is Canada, Del Jordan's story could take place in the United States as well. She lives among hard-working, lower-middle-class people in a family that includes her parents and a brother, Owen. The mother seeks independence from the traditional role of women and even goes 'out on the road,' as her disapproving sisters-in-law term it, to sell encyclopedias. For Del's mother the pursuit of knowledge is an ideal. For Del and her best friend Naomi more interest lies in their maturing and curiosity about sex as a vital part of growing up. There is humor and recognizable adolescent self-questioning. While sexual scenes are explicit, they are also sensitive and real and avoid both vulgarity and titillation. In spite of the experiences that Naomi and Del have, it becomes clear that the paths they will follow will diverge greatly." Shapiro. Fic for Youth. 3d edition

The love of a good woman; stories. Knopf 1998 339p

ISBN 0-375-40395-7 LC 98-36721

Contents:The love of a good woman; Jakarta; Cortes Island; Save the reaper; The children stay; Rich as stink; Before the change; My mother's dream

"Munro knows her characters intimately, yet she is at peace with the fact that their lives will, and should, retain a fundamental mysterious quality. This paradox, which originates in a knowledge of life, is not often so knowledgeably conveyed in fiction." Yale Rev

The moons of Jupiter; stories. Knopf 1983 c1982 233p o.p.

LC 82-48734

First published 1982 in Canada

Contents: Chaddeleys and Flemings: I Connection; Chaddeleys and Flemings: II The stone in the field; Dulse; The turkey season; Accident; Bardon bus; Prue; Labor Day dinner; Mrs. Cross and Mrs. Kidd; Hard-luck stories; Visitors; The moons of Jupiter

"These stories expose the conundrums of love and mortality. At the least they are engaging, and at their luminous best, reveal precision as the highest wisdom." Saturday Rev

Open secrets; stories. Knopf 1994 293p

ISBN 0-679-43575-1 LC 94-2099

Contents: Carried away; A real life; The Albanian virgin; Open secrets; The Jack Randa Hotel; A wilderness station; Spaceships have landed; Vandals

The author "peoples these exquisite tales with sad, lonely eccentrics leading lives of quiet self-deception.

Her heroines are often troubled souls with the unforgiving task of fitting into the rigorously confining community that spawned them. . . . Munro expertly captures the vagaries of history and geography in this satisfying and immensely pleasurable collection." Booklist

Runaway; stories. Knopf 2004 337p $25

ISBN 1-400-04281-X LC 2004-46539

Contents: Runaway; Chance; Soon; Silence; Passion; Trespasses; Tricks; Powers

"Munro's spare style belies the psychological depth of the stories, which feature characters running away from someone or something (often representative of the past) or telling a lie by commission or omission (another form of running away)." Libr J

Selected stories. Knopf 1996 545p $30

ISBN 0-679-44627-3 LC 96-4145

Contents: Walker Brothers cowboy; Dance of the happy shades; Postcard; Images; Something I've been meaning to tell you; The Ottawa Valley; Material; Royal beatings; Wild swans; The beggars maid; Simon's luck; Chaddeleys and Flemings; Dulse; The turkey season; Labor Day dinner; The moons of Jupiter; The progress of love; Lichen; Miles City, Montana; White dump; Fits; Friends of my youth; Meneseteung; Differently; Carried away; The Albanian virgin; A wilderness station; Vandals

"Little gems from one of Canada's best writers, drawn from seven collections." Libr J

The view from Castle Rock; stories. Knopf 2006 349p

ISBN 1-4000-4282-8 LC 2006-45261

Contents: No advantages; The view from Castle Rock; Illinois; The wilds of Morris Township; Working for a living; Fathers; Lying under the apple tree; Hired girl; The ticket; Home; What do you want to know for?; Messenger

This collection differs from Munro's "usual examinations of women in rural Canada leaving home to remake their possibilities. She draws instead on family documents, historical records, and what feels like memoir to piece together, in 12 parts, a fictionalized chronicle of how her tough-minded clan got from the Ettrick Valley near Edinburgh, Scotland, to America. The book shows how much can be done in a simple short story but breaks every rule ever taught in a writing seminar, setting up a writing master class along the way." Time

Munro, H. H. *See* Saki, 1870-1916

Murakami, Haruki, 1949-

After dark; translated from the Japanese by Jay Rubin. Knopf 2007 191p $22.95

ISBN 978-0-307-26583-8; 0-307-26583-8

LC 2007-4828

The author "paints a portrait of Tokyo through its night people: fashion model Eri and her studious sister, Mari; a jazz trombonist; a Chinese prostitute; and more." Libr J

"The narrative flows like a jazz ballad, excruciatingly slow yet hypnotically entrancing . . . . Each character is unique in his or her form of loneliness, yet each possesses a capacity for momentary empathy that is both sweet

Murakami, Haruki, 1949-—*Continued*

and heartbreaking. Murakami's genius, on both large and small canvases, is to create worlds both utterly alien and disconcertingly familiar." Booklist

After the earthquake; stories; translated from the Japanese by Jay Rubin. Knopf 2002 181p $22

ISBN 0-375-41390-1   LC 2001-38829

Original Japanese edition, 2000

Contents: UFO in Kushiro; Landscape with flatiron; All god's children can dance; Thailand; Super-frog saves Tokyo; Honey pie

"These six stories, all loosely connected to the disastrous 1995 earthquake in Kobe, are Murakami. . . at his best. The writer, who returned to live in Japan after the Kobe earthquake, measures his country's suffering and finds reassurance in the inevitability that love will surmount tragedy, mustering his casually elegant prose and keen sense of the absurd in the service of healing." Publ Wkly

Blind willow, sleeping woman; twenty-four stories; translated from the Japanese by Philip Gabriel and Jay Rubin. Knopf 2006 333p

ISBN 1-4000-4461-8   LC 2005-44544

"Murakami's first collection of short stories in more than a decade again demonstrates his fabulous talent for transporting readers and making 'the world fade away' with a few short strokes of his pen. . . . Murakami's characters are as alienated as any in Albert Camus, and as lost as any in J.D. Salinger. . . . What shines in all of [the stories] is Murakami's love for the open-ended mystery at the core of existence and his willingness to give himself up 'to the flow' in order to capture some of the magic in the mundane." Christ Sci Monit

Kafka on the shore; translated from the Japanese by Philip Gabriel. Knopf 2005 436p $25.95

ISBN 1-400-04366-2   LC 2004-48907

Original Japanese edition, 2002

In this novel, "15-year-old Kafka Tamura runs away from home, both to escape his father's oedipal prophecy and to find his long-lost mother and sister. As Kafka flees, so too does Nakata, an elderly simpleton whose quiet life has been upset by a gruesome murder. . . . What follows is a kind of double odyssey, as Kafka and Nakata are drawn inexorably along their separate but somehow linked paths, groping to understand the roles fate has in store for them." Publ Wkly

"Like his characters' quests, Murakami's expeditions off the worn path of literature can be both rewarding and terrifying. Finishing 'Kafka on the Shore' is like waking from a great dream. Nothing has changed, but everything about the world looks different." Newsweek

South of the border, west of the sun; translated from the Japanese by Philip Gabriel. Knopf 1999 213p

ISBN 0-375-40251-9   LC 97-49459

"Two only children who were schoolmates and best friends meet again after a 25-year separation. Hajime is now married, the father of two little girls and a successful owner of two jazz clubs. Shimamoto has also changed; she has become a very beautiful woman. She is always immaculately and expensively dressed, but she will not talk about her life or anything that has happened to her. Nevertheless, Hajime believes that he loves her

more than life itself; he is convinced that he could leave his family and his business to be with her. After they spend a night together, a night filled with raw passion, she vanishes." Libr J

"The narrative unfolds as an introspective ghost story in which Hajime must exorcise his past in the person of the enigmatic Shimamoto before he can affirm the new direction of his life. The ending, at once tender and hopeful, shows Murakami in a more mellow aspect than his work has exhibited before." Publ Wkly

The wind-up bird chronicle; translated from the Japanese by Jay Rubin. Knopf 1997 610p

ISBN 0-679-44669-9

                 * LC 97-2813

Original Japanese edition, 1995

"After his wife disappears, unemployed 30-year-old paralegal Toru Okada gets embroiled in a surreal, sprawling drama. . . . As Okada searches for his wife (in an abandoned lot near his home, and in a city park), he encounters characters who are dream-like projections of his own muted fears and desires—among them, a precocious, death-obsessed, 16-year-old neighbor and Okada's brother-in-law, a sinister politician. Peculiar events and strange coincidences abound." Publ Wkly

Murakami's "protagonist is a harmless fellow who merely wants to recover his cat and his wife. The troubles, real and delusional, that he encounters can be seen as extravagant metaphors for every ill from personal isolation to mass murder. The novel is a deliberately confusing, illogical image of a confusing, illogical world. It is not easy reading, but it is never less than absorbing." Atl Mon

Murakami, Ryu, 1952-

In the miso soup; translated by Ralph McCarthy. Kodansha International 2004 180p $22.95

ISBN 4-7700-2957-8

Original Japanese edition, 1997

The novel is "told from the point of view of Xenji, who is twenty years old and self-employed as a tour guide for foreigner wishing to explore Tokyo's sex industry. A few days before New Year's, he is hired by an American, Frank, who Kenji grows to suspect is a serial killer." Am Book Rev

"Beyond one terribly shocking scene, Miso is a thoughtful novel about loneliness, lack of identity and cultural and moral corruption. Through simple yet chilling language, Murakami doesn't condemn his characters. Instead he takes aim at rampant consumerism and the dumbing-down of Japanese and American culture. No one, Murakami seems to say, is completely guilty because we are shaped by the world around us." USA Today

Murasaki Shikibu, b. 978?

The tale of Genji; a novel in six parts; [by] Lady Murasaki; translated from the Japanese by Arthur Waley. Modern Lib. 1960 1135p o.p.

"A Japanese romance of the Heian period (794-1185). . . . This vast chronicle, often considered the world's first novel for its psychological depth, centers on the career of Prince Genji, his progeny, and the women with whom they associate. While delineating the elaborate rit-

Murasaki Shikibu, b. 978?—*Continued*

uals of courtly life, this work reflects the melancholy beauty of a world in constant flux and the vulnerability of women dependent upon the instability of human affection. Rich in poetry and elaborate wordplay, this work has had tremendous impact on the subsequent literary tradition." Reader's Ency. 4th edition

Murdoch, Iris

An accidental man. Viking 1971 442p
ISBN 0-670-10208-3

*

"The central figure of this novel is one of those accident-prone figures whose . . . misfortune becomes a substitute source of strength. . . . Ever since his brother injured his hand in a childhood incident, the world owes Austin a blank cheque to cover subsequent reverses—which do not fail to arrive. But someone is always sorry for him, always getting him out of trouble even at the price of their own. His self-pity destroys others in accordance with what Miss Murdoch . . . calls 'whatever deep mythological forces control the destinies of men.'" New Statesman (1913)

The bell; a novel. Viking 1958 342p o.p.
"The setting is an Anglican lay community attached to an abbey on one of the great estates of England. . . . The members of this community and its temporary residents are on the whole an odd, and certainly an oddly assorted, bunch. And their high-minded leader is a homosexual who was once involved in a scandal that ended his plans for entering the church. The story concerns itself with the relationships between various members of this hothouse world, with the arrival of a new bell for the abbey and the simultaneous discovery in the lake of the lost fourteenth-century bell about which there is a sinister legend. The climax is an eruption of scandal and disaster." Atlantic

The book and the brotherhood. Viking 1988 c1987 607p o.p.   LC 87-40294
First published 1987 in the United Kingdom
This novel is set in England in the 1980s. "A group of idealistic men and women, who met as students [at Oxford], later formed a society to support one of their number, a brilliant radical named David Crimond, in his efforts to write a major work tackling the big questions of history, politics, philosophy, art, and ethics. As the story opens, the group members, now middle-aged, are having qualms about Crimond and the enterprise they once agreed to fund." Christ Sci Monit
"Despite its excessive length and passages that can seem almost as self-indulgent as the characters they represent, The Book and The Brotherhood demonstrates again and again that Iris Murdoch is among the most gifted descriptive and narrative writers in English—and certainly one of the most consistently entertaining." NY Rev Books

A fairly honourable defeat. Viking 1970 436p o.p.
This is a "treatment of a homosexual menage which, when the chips are down, turns out to be more stable and durable than the happy heterosexual marriage which is subject to the same malicious interference by a cruel manipulator." Publ Wkly

"As is usual with a Murdoch novel, the action in summary seems preposterous. But given her inventiveness, her Gothic imagination, her gift for melodrama and suspense, she creates a world that becomes an effective vehicle for her moral vision." Choice

The good apprentice. Viking 1986 522p o.p.
LC 85-40635
This "novel is organized thematically around sets of opposing characters and structurally around a dramatic string of reversals. Harry Cuno is a monster of will, 'a disappointed spoilt child.' His son Stuart is a monster of will-lessness. Stuart avoids life's complications, while his stepbrother Edward, having precipitated a friend's suicide, is agonizingly caught up in them. Edward seeks absolution from his 'real' father Jesse, a legendary painter and Lear-like figure imprisoned in a decaying 'enchanter's palace' by the sea." Libr J
"The esthetic puzzle is whether the comic story and the spiritual kernel can be held together by Miss Murdoch's archaic stance as an authorial will. And yet no other contemporary British novelist seems to me of her eminence." N Y Times Book Rev

The green knight. Viking 1994 c1993 472p o.p.
* LC 93-30618
First published 1993 in the United Kingdom
"Peter Mir, the 'Green Knight' of [this novel's] title, is nearly killed when he intervenes to protect Clement Graffe from being murdered by Graffe's half-brother, Lucas. Mir mysteriously reappears and demands reparation from Lucas, provoking various responses from the two brothers and their circle of friends: Harvey Blacket; Bellamy Jones; the three Anderson sisters, Aleph, Sefton, and Moy; and their mother, Louise." Libr J
"That a cold, dark, evil act should open up a gap through which warmth and light can flood into the world is a paradox characteristic of Iris Murdoch's deeply meditated insight into the nature of the good." London Rev Books

Jackson's dilemma. Viking 1996 249p o.p.
LC 95-39986
First published 1995 in the United Kingdom
"The friends and relatives of Edward Lannion and Marian Fox are gathered at Hatting Hall in readiness for their wedding. On the night before the ceremony is to take place, however, Edward receives word that Marian cannot go through with it. Thus begins a search for the missing Marian that will significantly change the course of events. . . . There is a mysterious figure hovering at the periphery, quietly affecting the lives of all the players. In this case, it is a manservant called Jackson, who has insinuated himself into the lives of the main characters and who, while attending to their needs, has made himself indispensable." Libr J
"The peripheries of 'Jackson's Dilemma' are lush with anecdotal material; Murdoch has a way, with her minor or even offstage characters, of suggesting a wealth of motivation, a repletion of interior life." N Y Times Book Rev

The nice and the good. Viking 1968 378p o.p.
The action "begins with a violent death in the chambers of Whitehall faintly suggestive of a Le Carré thriller. . . . At times hilariously funny, slightly shivery (intimations of blackmail, suicide, dabblings in black magic) 'The Nice and the Good' is first and foremost a delight-

Murdoch, Iris—*Continued*

ful love story. The friends, relatives, hanger-ons, whose lives revolve around the happily married Octavian and Kate Gray are all seeking after love in their own ways. They find it, too, and sometimes in the most amazing places. The characterizations are superb, the mood that of a happy fairy tale crossed with highly sophisticated sexual comedy." Publ Wkly

Nuns and soldiers. Viking 1981 c1980 505p o.p.

LC 80-16935

First published 1980 in the United Kingdom

This novel explores the tangled lives of recently widowed Gertrude; Tim, a painter; Anne, a former nun; and "Count" Peter who is in love with Gertrude

"The glory of Iris Murdoch at her best—as she almost always is in Nuns and Soldiers—is that she can convey with total respect the awareness, readjusting and hunger, and at the same time 'place' it, with a severe but not savage irony, in a world which hints at quite different forces and priorities." New Statesman (1913)

The philosopher's pupil. Viking 1983 576p o.p.

* LC 82-45901

At the heart of this novel are "aging philosopher John Robert Rozanov and his former (and rejected) pupil George McCaffrey. The scene is English spa Ennistone, George's home and Rozanov's birthplace. While the desperately bitter George hopes that Rozanov's unexpected reappearance in Ennistone heralds a reconciliation, it becomes apparent that Rozanov has returned instead to settle the future of his orphaned granddaughter. This he accomplishes, setting in motion a chain of events both farcical and tragic." Libr J

This "collaboration between Murdoch and her imagination is both challenging and irresistible: a combination of gossip and profundity, modern times and ancient edicts." Time

The sea, the sea. Viking 1978 502p o.p.

LC 78-13516

The narrator of this "novel is Charles Arrowby, a former actor and director who has retired from the theater to take up solitary residence in a remote house on a northern coast. His tale begins as a mixture of diary and memoir: alternately he records his first impressions of his new home and reviews his past life as though the better to understand the man he has become. . . . His recollections largely concern a succession of love-affairs with actresses; but before all these, and dwarfing them in its importance to his development, was an unconsummated but passionate childhood relationship with a girl named Hartley, who disappeared abruptly and woundingly from his life before he was twenty and married another man." Times Lit Suppl

Something special; a story; illustrated by Michael McCurdy. Norton 2000 55p $15.95

ISBN 0-393-05007-6   LC 00-40212

First published in Winter's Tale, no.3, 1957

Set in the 1950's this story "concerns one epiphanic evening in the life of Yvonne Geary, a spirited Dublin shopgirl who seeks to flee her oppressive life. Though 24, she still shares a bed with her mother and can only dream of escape on the mail boat to England, the place where 'every Irish person with a soul in them' wants to travel. Even the arrival of a suitor fails to provide re-

lease—Sam may be a responsible, doting man, but he is still 'nothing special.' Pressure from her mother persuades Yvonne to go out with him anyway. . . . Murdoch's story can be subtle and heartfelt, most notably as it charts the melancholy, meandering voyage the young couple take toward compromised lives." N Y Times Book Rev

Murphy, Margaret, 1959-

Darkness falls. St. Martin's Minotaur 2004 c2002 355p $24.95

ISBN 0-312-32851-6   LC 2003-70098

This thriller "opens with a cheerfully frantic domestic scene of Clara Pascal prosecuting counsel, wife, mother, and seemingly typical thirtysomething career-home juggler-trying to get to chambers on time while answering the demands of her daughter, excited and clingy on her ninth birthday. Two chapters later, Counsel Pascal is chained to a wall in a stranger's pitch-dark cellar. She is anything but a passive victim, however, as she uses her formidable argumentation skills to keep herself alive." Booklist

"The critical task, as sleekly presented in the form of a police procedural, is to identify the kidnapper and trace him through his underworld associates. Meanwhile, in alternating chapters written in the skin-chilling style of a thriller, Murphy places the reader in the cellar where Clara has been blindfolded, beaten and shackled to the wall by a man who challenges her to defend her values and plead for her life. The objective is still to identify the stranger and determine his motive. But in Murphy's bold treatment, the victim is made to acknowledge her own intimate acquaintance with evil." N Y Times Book Rev

Murphy, Yannick

Signed, Mata Hari; a novel. Little, Brown 2007 278p $23.99

ISBN 978-0-316-11264-2; 0-316-11264-X

LC 2006-102966

"Weaving back and forth in time between Mata Hari's prison cell in Paris and her prior life in its many manifestations, the seductive narrative spins an irresistible tale of a woman whose legendary exploits are still a matter of historical debate. Was she or was she not a victim of time and circumstance? Did she really deserve to be executed as a spy? In the end, it doesn't really matter, but what does matter is that Murphy has fashioned a mesmerizing novel that creatively reimagines the life of one of the most notorious, and perhaps overvilified, women of all time." Booklist

Murr, Naeem

The perfect man; a novel. Random House Trade Paperbacks 2007 451p pa $13.95

ISBN 978-0-8129-7701-1; 0-8129-7701-7

* LC 2006-43088

"Abandoned by his white father and his absent Indian mother, rejected by his intolerant London relatives, Rajiv Travers, 12 years old in 1954, is sent to stay with his father's other brother, Oliver, who has recently followed the love of his life, romance novelist Ruth, from New York City to tiny Pisgah, Mo. In short order, Oliver

Murr, Naeem—*Continued*

commits suicide, and Ruth becomes an uneasy guardian to this curious young boy, who shields himself from pain and prejudice with his quick wit and shrewd impersonations. Peerwise, Raj is quickly taken under the wing of Annie Celli, already a striking beauty, joining a group that also includes Annie's soul mate, the delicate and emotionally fragile Lewis. As the friends grow into young men and women, Annie finds herself torn between her devotion to the increasingly unstable Lewis (who witnessed his younger brother's murder) and her undeniable feelings for Raj." Publ Wkly

This novel "succeeds in recreating an entire world with a full spectrum of human emotions in a small Missouri town, as Faulkner did in the imaginary Yoknapatawpha County in Mississippi." Times Lit Suppl

Murray, Sabina

Forgery. Grove Press 2007 248p $24
ISBN 978-0-8021-1844-8; 0-8021-1844-5
LC 2006-52645

"In the summer of 1963, American Rupert Brigg travels to Greece to collect classical pieces for his Uncle William's art collection. . . . Journeying to the secluded island of Aspros, among a circle of artists and aristocrats each with their own secrets, Rupert finds the very pieces he's searching for, but can he escape the tragedy that ended his brief marriage? As beautiful as Rupert's discoveries are, beneath the surface lurk rumors of insurrection, fabrication, and even murder." Publisher's note

The author "juxtaposes the subject of fake antiquities with both fake and real portraits of characters. Lacking rhythm, the restrained prose does not effectively create flowing dialog, but with just a few words Murray conjures images that stay with the reader for days." Libr J

Murray, Steven T.

(tr) Larsson, S. The girl who played with fire

(tr) Mankell, H. The eye of the leopard

Musil, Robert, 1880-1942

The man without qualities; translated from the German by Sophie Wilkins. Knopf 1995 2v 1774p
ISBN 0-394-51052-6
* LC 92-37943

"The first two volumes of this monumental work were published in 1930 and 1932; a fragmentary third was published posthumously in 1942, and in 1952 the novel appeared, with additional chapters, in one volume. Apart from providing a brilliant, existential portrait of Ulrich, the scholarly, purposeless 'man without qualities' the book is a vivid depiction of Austrian decadence before the outbreak of World War I. This single remarkable work established Musil as one of the most influential German-language novelists in the first half of the 20th century." Reader's Ency. 4th edition

My mistress's sparrow is dead; great love stories, from Chekhov to Munro; edited by Jeffrey Eugenides. HarperCollins 2008 587p $24.95; pa $15.99
ISBN 978-0-06-124037-9; 0-06-124037-0; 978-0-06-124038-6 (pa); 0-06-124038-9 (pa)
LC 2007-35989

Contents: First love and other sorrows, H. Brodkey; The lady with the little dog, by A. Chekhov; Love, by G. Paley; A rose for Emily, by W. Faulkner; The dead, by J. Joyce; Dirty wedding, by D. Johnson; Natasha, by D. Bezmozgis; Some other, better Otto, by D. Eisenberg; The hitchhiking game, M. Kundera; Lovers of their time, by W. Trevor; Mouche, by G. de Maupassant; The moon in its flight, by G. Sorrentino; Spring in Fialta, by V. Nabokov; How to be an other woman, by L. Moore; Yours, by M. Robison; The bad thing, by D. Gates; First love, by I. Babel; Tonka, by R. Musil; Jon, by G. Saunders; Red rose, white rose, by E. Chang; Fireworks, by R. Ford; We didn't, by S. Dybek; Something that needs nothing, by M. July; The magic barrel, by B. Malamud; What we talk about when we talk about love, by R. Carver; Innocence, by H. Brodkey; The bear came over the mountain, by A. Munro

Eugenides "has assembled something quite extraordinary here: a fascinating, consistently compelling, and superbly edited collection of short stories about romantic love. Part of the collection's appeal is its range and depth: at 600 pages, it offers gems and new discoveries at every turn." Libr J

Myles, Symon, 1949-

For works written by this author under other names see Follett, Ken, 1949-

The **Mysterious** West; edited by Tony Hillerman. HarperCollins Pubs. 1994 392p o.p.
LC 94-25842

Includes the following stories: Forbidden things, by M. Muller; New moon and rattlesnakes, by W. Hornsby; Coyote peyote, by C. N. Douglas; Nooses give, by D. Stabenow; Who killed Cock Rogers? by B. Crider; Caring for Uncle Henry, by R. W. Campbell; Death of a snowbird, by J. A. Jance; With flowers in her hair, by M. D. Lake; The lost boys, by W. J. Reynolds; Tule fog, by K. Kijewski; The river mouth, by L. Matera; No better than her father, by L. Grant; Dust Devil, by R. Burns; A woman's place, by D. R. Meredith; Postage due, by S. Dunlap; The beast in the woods, by E. Gorman; Blowout in Little Man Flats, by S. M. Kaminsky; Small town murder, by H. Adams; Bingo, by J. Lutz; Engines, by B. Pronzini

"This stunning collection . . . offers readers some wonderful choices in fiction. Each story is strikingly different in tempo, plot, and setting, yet each is part of and contributes to the diversified world of the mysterious West." SLJ

N

Na gCopaleen, Myles *See* O'Brien, Flann, 1911-1966

Na Gopaleen, Myles *See* O'Brien, Flann, 1911-1966

Nabb, Magdalen, 1947-2007

Some bitter taste. Soho Press 2002 247p $24
ISBN 1-569-47317-X   LC 2002-70579
"Marshal Guarnaccia of the Florentine police has at last lined up a case against a man accused of importing and exploiting Albanian prostitutes. But he is distracted when a seemingly paranoid old woman who had complained to him about people entering her apartment winds up murdered. Though not strictly a detective, the marshal begins to reconstruct the life of the victim, an early refugee from the Nazis." Libr J

The author "has Simenon's knack of unlocking the deeper mysteries of ordinary people's pedestrian lives. . . . In Nabb's world, nothing is simple and no life, after all, is ordinary." N Y Times Book Rev

Nabokov, Vladimir Vladimirovich, 1899-1977

Ada; or, Ardor: a family chronicle; [by] Vladimir Nabokov. McGraw-Hill 1969 589p o.p.

*

"In its prodigious length and with the family tree on its frontispiece the book recalls the great 19th-century novels of the author's native Russia, but *Ada* boldly turns its predecessors on their heads. For his rich, sweeping saga of the Veen-Durmanov clan, Nabokov invented an incestuous pair of 'cousins' (actually siblings, Van and Ada), a hybrid country (Amerussia), a familiar but strange planet (Antiterra), and a dimension of malleable time. The novel follows the lovers from their childhood idylls through impassioned estrangements and reunions to a tenderly shared old age. The work's rich narrative style incorporates untranslated foreign phrases, esoteric data, and countless literary allusions." Merriam-Webster's Ency of Lit

also in Nabokov, V. V. Novels, 1969-1974

Bend sinister
In Nabokov, V. V. Novels and memoirs, 1941-1951

King, queen, knave; a novel; [by] Vladimir Nabokov; translated by Dmitri Nabokov in collaboration with the author. McGraw-Hill 1968 272p o.p.

*

Original Russian edition, 1928
"The image of a deck of playing cards is used throughout the novel. Franz, an unsophisticated young man, works in the department store of his rich uncle Dreyer. Out of boredom Martha, the uncle's young wife, seduces Franz. The lovers subsequently plot to drown Dreyer and marry each other. Martha changes her mind abruptly when she learns that an invention by Dreyer stands to increase his wealth, but she then dies suddenly from pneumonia. Her husband never discovers his wife's duplicity." Merriam-Webster's Ency of Lit

Lolita; [by] Vladimir Nabokov. Knopf 1992 c1955 335p $19
ISBN 0-679-41043-0
*   * LC 92-52931

"Everyman's library"
First published 1955 in France
"Humbert Humbert is a middle-aged intellectual who has a passion for girls between the ages of nine and fourteen. He falls in love with the twelve-year-old Dolores Haze, whom he calls Lolita. In his plot to seduce her, he marries Dolores's mother, whose accidental death then allows Lolita and Humbert to take off on an odyssey across the U.S. Humbert is surprised when, contrary to his schemes, Lolita seduces him and again when she leaves him for Clare Quilty, whom Humbert later murders. Lolita eventually marries Richard F. Schiller. The book presents a quest for eternal innocence, albeit in satirical terms. . . . It combines parody, fanciful imaginative flights, literary puzzles, and a brilliant satirical overview of American culture." Reader's Ency. 4th edition

also in Nabokov, V. V. Novels, 1955-1962

Look at the harlequins!; [by] Vladimir Nabokov. McGraw-Hill 1974 253p o.p.

In this pseudo-autobiographical novel, the narrator, a Russian émigré novelist and college professor who has lived in London, Paris and the United States, recalls his life, loves (including four marriages) and work in a manner which often parodies Nabokov's own life and writings

This is a book "to enchant Nabokov fans and irritate everybody else. . . . [It] is part roman a clef, part fantasy, a tale of 'wives and books interlaced monogrammatically.' It is full of erudite allusions, Russian words in various stages of translation and absurd mistranslation, puns, anagrams, acronyms. Also opinions. . . . Comic, polished, international, [Nabokov] offers sophisticated entertainment, a concoction of romantic and literary matters." Christ Sci Monit

also in Nabokov, V. V. Novels, 1969-1974

Novels, 1955-1962. Library of Am. 1996 904p $35
ISBN 1-883011-19-1   LC 96-15256
Contents: Lolita; Pnin; Pale fire; Lolita, a screenplay

Novels, 1969-1974. Library of Am. 1996 824p il $35
ISBN 1-883011-20-5   LC 96-15255
Contents: Ada; Transparent things; Look at the harlequins!
Transparent things (1972) is a novella about a rootless American who murders his wife

Novels and memoirs, 1941-1951; . Literary Classics of the U.S. 1996 710p il (Library of America, 87) $35
ISBN 1-883011-18-3   LC 96-15257
Contents: The real life of Sebastian Knight; Bend sinister; Speak, memory: an autobiography revisited
The real life of Sebastian Knight (1941) is about a Russian living in Paris who learns about his half-brother, a famous English novelist, by writing his biography. Bend sinister (1947) is about a professor's attempts to maintain his integrity in a totalitarian state.

Nabokov, Vladimir Vladimirovich, 1899-1977—
Continued

Pale fire; a novel; [by] Vladimir Nabokov.
Putnam 1962 315p o.p.

*

This novel is "both pedantry and a satire on pedantry.
The core of the novel is a 999-line poem by an American author, John Shade—a sort of Robert Frost—which
consists mainly of a rather moving meditation on the
tragic end of the poet's daughter. After Shade's death, a
foolish scholar named Kinbote—an exile from the mythical country of Zembla and a visiting professor of
Zemblan at Wordsmith College, New Wye, Appalachia—
edits this work, providing a preface and a detailed corpus
of notes. But Kinbote has an 'idée fixe'—the history of
his own country—and he believes that Shade's poem is
an allegory of this history, with Kinbote himself—fanta-
sized into the deposed King Charles Xavier II—as the
hero. The humour—and Nabokov's humour is subtle as
well as occasionally brutal—lies in the disparity between
the simple truth of the poem and the gross self-exalting
hallucinations of its editor." Burgess. 99 Novels

also in Nabokov, V. V. Novels, 1955-1962

Pnin; [by] Vladimir Nabokov. Doubleday 1957
191p o.p.
"Not a novel, not really a collection of short stories,
but rather a series of sketches, all of them dealing with
Timofey Pnin, professor of Russian in a small American
university. Each one finds Pnin valiantly trying to cope
with the daily crises of American society—Pnin on the
wrong train, Pnin learning to drive, Pnin giving a party,
Pnin and the washing machine. They are all gently amusing, affectionate portraits of a Russian expatriate of the
old school caught up in the inexplicable complexities of
daily life." Libr J

also in Nabokov, V. V. Novels, 1955-1962

The real life of Sebastian Knight
In Nabokov, V. V. Novels and memoirs,
1941-1951

The stories of Vladimir Nabokov. Knopf 1996
{i.e. 1995} 659p
ISBN 0-394-58615-8   LC 95-23466
For this chronologically-arranged collection, "Nabokov's son Dmitri has assembled the 52 stories published
in English before Nabokov died in 1977, and translated
another 13 written in Russian between 1920 or '21 and
1924." Newsweek
Contents: The wood-sprite; Russian spoken here;
Sounds; Wingstroke; Gods; A matter of chance; The seaport; Revenge; Beneficence; Details of a sunset; The
thunderstorm; La Veneziana; Bachmann; The dragon;
Christmas; A letter that never reached Russia; The fight;
The return of Chorb; A guide to Berlin; A nursery tale;
Terror; Razor; The passenger; The doorbell; An affair of
honor; The Christmas story; The Potato Elf; The aure-
lian; A dashing fellow; A bad day; The visit to the mu-
seum; A busy man; Terra incognita; The reunion; Lips
to lips; Orache; Music; Perfection; The admiralty spire;
The Leonardo; In memory of L. I. Shigaev; The circle;
A Russian beauty; Breaking the news; Torpid smoke;
Recruiting; A slice of life; Spring in Fialta; Cloud, castle,
lake; Tyrants destroyed; Lik; Mademoiselle O; Vasiliy
Shishkov; Ultima thule; Solus rex; The assistant produc-

er; "That in Aleppo once . . ."; A forgotten poet; Time
and ebb; Conversation piece, 1945; Signs and symbols;
First love; Scenes from the life of a double monster; The
Vane sisters; Lance

Transparent things
In Nabokov, V. V. Novels, 1969-1974

Naipaul, V. S. (Vidiadhar Surajprasad), 1932-

A bend in the river. Knopf 1979 278p o.p.
                                    * LC 78-21591
"Salim, an East African of East Indian descent . . .
buys a general store in a large town in the interior of an
unnamed African country. A man without any 'home
ground' to stand on, Salim builds his business out of the
rubble left by one post-independence revolution. He discovers a great deal about his own mundane existence and
about that of his circle of bewildered young Africans, bedraggled European ex-patriates, and displaced East Indians, as the town (and the country) lurches toward yet another cataclysmic revolt." Saturday Rev
"This is a beautifully composed book, with an almost
Conradian power of description. Aesthetically most satisfying, it is also profoundly depressing. But depression is
sometimes a stone on the road to literary exaltation."
Burgess. 99 Novels

Guerrillas. Knopf 1975 248p o.p.

*

The action of this novel "takes place on a troubled Caribbean island, inhabited by Asians, Africans, Americans
and British colonials. Corruption and poverty are everywhere. . . . The homes of the well-to-do lie hidden in
the hills. The poor are angry, the rich are panicked. . . .
At the center of the brewing storm are Peter Roche, a
white South African and lapsed revolutionary working
for an island business; Jane, his British mistress, in confused search of adventure and challenge; and Jimmy Ahmed, a half-Chinese, half-black politician who has set up
an agricultural commune that may be giving shelter to
the guerrillas. Roche, cynical and self-absorbed, is employed by his firm to control Jimmy. Jimmy is obsessed
with visions of personal glory, rape and mystical manhood. Jane, careless and quixotic, becomes the mistress
of both men." Newsweek
"This is a novel without a villain, and there is not a
character for whom the reader does not at some point
feel deep sympathy and keen understanding, no matter
how villainous or futile he may seem." N Y Times Book
Rev

Half a life. Knopf 2001 211p $24
ISBN 0-375-40737-5   LC 2001-33730
"Willie Chandran, the central figure here, is born in India in the 1930s, the son of a bitter mixed caste marriage
between a Brahmin and a 'backwards' person, or untouchable. . . . Going to London on a scholarship, Willie
mixes in immigrant and bohemian circles, and even publishes a book. . . . Willie meets Ana, a woman of mixed
African descent, when she writes him a fan letter about
his novel. They become lovers. Willie goes back with
Ana to her large outback estate in the 'half and half'
world of a Portuguese colony like Mozambique, where
he remains for 18 years." Publ Wkly
"In the book's last moments a narrative that has
seemed to meander pulls suddenly tight, giving 'Half a

Naipaul, V. S. (Vidiadhar Surajprasad), 1932-—
Continued

Life' an interest that lies beyond its relation to Naipaul's other work. . . . The very fissures in its structure, its change from voice to voice, transform 'Half a Life' into a meditation on the difficulties of building a coherent self." N Y Times Book Rev

A house for Mr. Biswas; with an introduction by Karl Miller. Knopf 1995 xxi, 564p $20
ISBN 0-679-44458-0

*

"Everyman's library"
A reissue of the title first published 1961 by McGraw-Hill
"Trinidad, West Indies, is the setting for the story of lonely Mr. Mohun Biswas, a Hindu of high caste but low economic status. Throughout the book he longs for independence from his wife's large family and a house of his own. In a portrait that is both funny and compassionate, West Indian life is vividly described, especially the relationships among members of Mr. Biswas's family." Shapiro. Fic for Youth. 3d edition

Magic seeds. Knopf 2004 280p $25
ISBN 0-375-40736-7   LC 2004-48964
At the beginning of this "novel, Willie is in Berlin with his bossy sister, Sarojini. It is 18 years later. Revolution has uprooted Willie's African existence. Sarojini hooks him up with a guerrilla group in India, and Willie, always ready to be molded to some cause, returns to India. The guerrillas, Willie soon learns, are 'absolute maniacs.' But caught up, as ever, in the energy of others, Willie stays with them for seven years. He then surrenders and is tossed into the relative comfort of jail. When an old London friend (a lawyer named Roger) gets Willie's book of short stories republished, Willie's imprisonment becomes an embarrassment to the authorities. He is now seen as a forerunner of 'postcolonial writing.' He returns to London, where he alternates between making love to Perdita, Roger's wife, and looking for a job." Publ Wkly
The author "has written a calculated polemic. . . . Naipaul is suggesting that our racial and ethnic fate is sealed; we can never escape who we are, and must learn to live with our unchosen identities whether we like them or not. It's not a consoling vision; neither is it despairing. It simply is." N Y Times Book Rev

A way in the world; a novel. Knopf 1994 380p
ISBN 0-394-56478-2   LC 93-44680
In this autobiographical fiction, Naipaul examines "feelings of rootlessness, the realities of the colonial experience, the impact of cultural displacement, and our need to belong. He does so through a series of linked historical narratives. Among them is an imagined vision of Raleigh's desperate but futile search for El Dorado. We are also introduced to Francisco de Miranda, one of the precursors to Bolivar's revolution. We are witness to the irony inherent in the life of Lebrun, a Trinidadian/Panamanian Communist of the 1930s. And then there is Blair, a former co-worker of the narrator in Trinidad, whose African roots prove no help when he becomes an adviser to an East African despot. These are tales of lost souls desperate to find a place at the table but who never quite succeed, leaving them doomed to remain on the fringes of history." Libr J

Naipaul, Vidiadhar Surajprasad *See* Naipaul, V. S. (Vidiadhar Surajprasad), 1932-

Nance, John J.

Fire flight. Simon & Schuster 2003 353p map $25
ISBN 0-7432-5050-8   LC 2003-59095
"Fires are raging out of control in Yellowstone National Park, and planes from the aging fleet of water tankers are crashing. Veteran pilot Clark Maxwell has returned from retirement to help out—not only in his official capacity but also as an investigator in light of the recurring crashes. Where have the planes been over the preceding winter instead of having lifesaving maintenance performed on them? Maxwell suspects a major cover-up. Despite a rushed and contrived ending, Nance has crafted an exciting and compelling story." Libr J

The last hostage. Doubleday 1998 373p
ISBN 0-385-49055-0   LC 97-44861
"Airbridge Airlines pilot Ken Wolfe fakes engine trouble to force a landing; then, having tricked his co-pilot off the plane, he takes off. His plan: to extort a confession from a surprise passenger, U.S. Attorney General nominee Rudolph Bostitch. It seems that, as a Connecticut DA, Bostitch covered up for the man who Wolfe believes tortured and killed his 11-year-old daughter. Wolfe rolls the plane to convince the crew that a hijacker with a bomb shares the cockpit, a Flitephone call alerts the FBI and novice female negotiator Kat Bronsky is put on the case." Publ Wkly
"Nance is a master of suspense, and his fast-moving plot has more twists than a corkscrew." Libr J

Medusa's child. Doubleday 1997 388p o.p.
LC 96-27656
"For his livelihood, pilot and small businessman Scott McKay leases a converted Boeing 727 and ferries cargo across the country, much like a truck driver. On one particular flight, however, he comes to realize that his cargo hold contains a thermonuclear bomb: a modern instrument of destruction dubbed the Medusa device and capable of an incredible act of terrorism—destroying every computer chip within a very wide radius. The effort to incapacitate the bomb before it can detonate is the warp and woof of an exciting plot that offers hours of pure diversion." Booklist

Pandora's clock. Doubleday 1995 357p o.p.
LC 95-8409
"Shortly after Quantum Airlines Flight 66 departs Frankfurt, Germany, for New York, one of the passengers succumbs to an apparent heart attack. It may be, however, that Professor Ernest Helms was exposed to a doomsday virus just before boarding his flight; if so, more than 200 passengers and crew members could be dead within a matter of hours. Word of this imminent disaster leaks to governments and media organizations around the world, of course, and the jumbo jet is refused landing clearance everywhere." Publ Wkly
"A uniquely suspenseful and terrifying story." Booklist

Narayan, R. K., 1906-2001

The bachelor of arts
In Narayan, R. K. Swami and friends, The bachelor of arts, The dark room, The English teacher

The dark room
In Narayan, R. K. Swami and friends, The bachelor of arts, The dark room, The English teacher

The English teacher
In Narayan, R. K. Swami and friends, The bachelor of arts, The dark room, The English teacher

The financial expert
In Narayan, R. K. Mr. Sampath—the printer of Malgudi, The financial expert, Waiting for the Mahatma

The grandmother's tale and selected stories. Viking 1994 312p o.p.   LC 94-4581
Contents: The grandmother's tale; Guru; Salt and sawdust; Judge; Emden; An astrologer's day; The blind dog; Second opinion; A horse and two goats; Annamalai; Lawley Road; A breath of Lucifer; Under the banyan tree; Another community; The shelter; Seventh house; Cat within; The edge; Uncle
Set in India these stories "emphasize perceptively drawn characters and situations rather than their colorful foreign backdrops. All the tales display a wry, gentle humor." Publ Wkly

Malgudi days. Viking 1982 246p o.p.
                                    * LC 81-52204
Contents: An astrologer's day; The missing mail; The doctor's word; Gateman's gift; The blind dog; Fellow-feeling; The tiger's claw; Iswaran; Such perfection; Father's help; The snake-song; Engine trouble; Forty-five a month; Out of business; Attila; The axe; Lawley Road; Trail of the green blazer; The martyr's corner; Wife's holiday; A shadow; A willing slave; Leela's friend; Mother and son; Naga; Selvi; Second opinion; Cat within; The edge; God and the cobbler; Hungry child; Emden
"This selection distills, magically, Malgudi's vibrancy, its mythological-animistic throb, the large and small corruptions of its citizens—from bureaucrats to back-street people—and the reassuring backdrop of its cyclical rhythms. Distinguished writing; rewarding reading." Booklist

Mr. Sampath—the printer of Malgudi
In Narayan, R. K. Mr. Sampath—the printer of Malgudi, The financial expert, Waiting for the Mahatma

Mr. Sampath—the printer of Malgudi, The financial expert, Waiting for the Mahatma; with an introduction by Alexander McCall Smith. Everyman's Library 2006 xxxviii, 578p $25
ISBN 0-4000-4477-4   LC 2006-279228
An omnibus edition of three novels first published 1949, 1952 and 1955, respectively
"Mr. Sampath—The Printer of Malgudi is the story of a businessman who adapts to the collapse of his weekly newspaper by shifting to screenplays, only to have the glamour of it all go to his head. In The Financial Expert, a man of many hopes but few resources spends his time under a banyan tree dispensing financial advice to those willing to pay for his knowledge. In Waiting for the Mahatma, a young drifter meets the most beautiful girl he has ever seen—an adherent of Mahatma Gandhi—and commits himself to Gandhi's Quit India campaign, a decision that will test the integrity of his ideals against the strength of his passions." Publisher's note

Swami and friends
In Narayan, R. K. Swami and friends, The bachelor of arts, The dark room, The English teacher

Swami and friends, The bachelor of arts, The dark room, The English teacher; with an introduction by Alexander McCall Smith. Everyman's Library 2006 xxxvii, 609p $25
ISBN 1-4000-4476-6   LC 2006-279229
An omnibus edition of four titles first published 1935, 1937, 1938 and 1945, respectively
"Swami and Friends introduces us to Narayan's beloved fictional town of Malgudi, where ten-year-old Swaminathan's excitement about his country's initial stirrings for independence competes with his ardor for cricket and all other things British. The Bachelor of Arts is a poignant coming-of-age novel about a young man flush with first love, but whose freedom to pursue it is hindered by the fixed ideas of his traditional Hindu family. In The Dark Room, Narayan's portrait of aggrieved domesticity, the docile and obedient Savitri, like many Malgudi women, is torn between submitting to her husband's humiliations and trying to escape them. The title character in The English Teacher, Narayan's most autobiographical novel, searches for meaning when the death of his young wife deprives him of his greatest source of happiness." Publisher's note

Under the banyan tree and other stories. Viking 1985 193p o.p.   LC 85-3234
"An Elisabeth Sifton book"
Contents: Nitya; House opposite; A horse and two goats; The Roman image; The watchman; A career; Old man of the temple; A hero; Dodu; Another community; Like the sun; Chippy; Uncle's letters; All avoidable talk; A snake in the grass; The evening gift; A breath of Lucifer; Annamalai; The shelter; The mute companions; At the portal; Four rupees; Flavour of coconut; Fruition at forty; Crime and punishment; Half a rupee worth; The antidote; Under the banyan tree
"Narayan's clarity, his mastery of technique, his respect for the spectrum of human predicament, his absence of malice and his freedom from a single philosophy that explains everything away put him in the unique position of being able to turn a teeming cultural life into lucid and enjoyable stories." New Statesman

Waiting for the Mahatma
In Narayan, R. K. Mr. Sampath—the printer of Malgudi, The financial expert, Waiting for the Mahatma

Nasaw, Jonathan Lewis, 1947-

Twenty-seven bones; a thriller; [by] Jonathan Nasaw. Atria Books 2004 360p $25

ISBN 0-7434-4653-4　　　　　LC 2003-69637

"Former FBI agent E.L. Pender heads to St. Luke, one of the Virgin Islands, to help hunt for a murderer whose modus operandi is to torture his victims, cut off their right hands, and leave them to bleed slowly to death. The authorities, fearful of bad publicity, want to keep the killer's existence quiet. Pender, clearly from the mainland and unaccustomed to the speech patterns and social customs of the island, is at a disadvantage as he tries to familiarize himself with the community and its inhabitants. . . . Although the reader knows who is behind the killings, tension arises from not knowing whether Pender will figure it out in time to save other people while putting himself at grave risk." Libr J

Naslund, Sena Jeter

Abundance; a novel of Marie Antoinette. William Morrow 2006 545p $26.95

ISBN 978-0-06-082539-3; 0-06-082539-1

LC 2006-43817

"The life of Marie Antoinette from her 'birth as a citizen of France' at age 14 to her execution, told from her own point of view." Booklist

"With vivid detail and exquisite narrative technique, Naslund exemplifies the best of historical fiction, finding the woman beneath the pose, a queen facing history as it rises up against her." Publ Wkly

Ahab's wife; or, The star-gazer; a novel. Morrow 1999 668p $28

ISBN 0-688-17187-7　　　　　LC 99-22135

"At age 12, Una escapes her religiously obsessed father in rural Kentucky to live with relatives in a lighthouse off New Bedford, Mass. When she is 16—disguised as a boy—she runs off to sea aboard a whaler, which sinks after being rammed by its quarry. Una and two young men who love her are the only survivors of a group set adrift in an open boat, but the dark secret of their cannibalism will leave its mark. Rescued, Una is wed to one of the young men by the captain of the *Pequod*, handsome, commanding Ahab, who has not as yet met the white whale that will be his destiny. . . . Una's later marriage to Ahab—a passionate and intellectually satisfying relationship—the loss of her mother and her newborn son in one night, and her life as a rich woman in Nantucket are further developments in a plot teeming with arresting events and provocative ideas." Publ Wkly

Four spirits; a novel. Morrow 2003 524p $26.95

ISBN 0-06-621238-3　　　　　LC 2003-51170

"During the civil rights conflict, Birmingham, Ala. was notorious for the ferocity of its racial bigotry: peaceful demonstrators attacked with fire hoses and dogs by police chief Bull Connor; the Klan-set explosion at a black church that killed four little girls. The four victims are only background figures in Naslund's . . . evocation of the city and the era, but they appear to several characters in the form of spirits who promise the reconciliation to come. The novel is constructed as a series of vignettes that follow a dozen or so characters whose lives finally intersect." Publ Wkly

"Naslund has done something unusually fine—she's written a drifting collective portrait of a city in distress. The characters of 'Four Spirits' are deeply entwined, sometimes without knowing it." N Y Times Book Rev

Nathan, Robert, 1894-1985

Portrait of Jennie. Knopf 1940 c1939 212p o.p.

"Eban Adams, a struggling artist who is unable to sell his art work, meets an unusual child named Jennie in the park and immediately begins to prosper. He knows little about her except that she belongs in the past and that every few months, when their paths cross, she has aged by years. His finest painting is a portrait of her, a token of his love, which ends in predestined tragedy." Shapiro. Fic for Youth. 3d edition

Nathanson, E. M., 1928-

The dirty dozen. Random House 1965 498p o.p.

"Project Amnesty was a plan to drop 12 viciously trained American soldier-prisoners (murderers, rapists, thieves, all doomed to either execution or lengthy prison terms) behind the German lines in France just before D-Day. Their trainer-warden, 30-year-old Captain John Reisman resents the assignment." Book Week

This "is not an ordinary war book. The fight here is not so much against the Wehrmacht as it is against self, society, and 'the system.' . . . If the situation seems impossible, if Reisman seems a superman, no matter, for the insights into good and evil are richly rewarding in this exciting and highly compelling novel." Libr J

Naylor, Gloria

Bailey's Café. Harcourt Brace Jovanovich 1992 229p o.p.　　　　　LC 91-42089

Bailey's Cafe is the setting in which the book's characters "tell stories from their lives. . . . Bailey's and the nearby boarding house (which some call a bordello) offer respite for those who have been battered in the outside world." Libr J

The author "takes us many keys down, and sometimes back up, in this virtuoso orchestration of survival, suffering, courage and humor, sounding through the stories of these lives." N Y Times Book Rev

Linden Hills. Ticknor & Fields 1985 304p o.p.

LC 84-16222

The author "sketches the development of the community of Linden Hills through its founder, Luther Nedeed, and successive generations of Nedeeds, showing in the decline of the family the corrosive effect of ambition, arrogance and the abuse of power. The residents of Linden Hills are similarly subverted by the accommodations, sacrifices and perversions of soul blacks must endure to live in an affluent community, even, as in this case, an all-black one." Publ Wkly

"Its flaws notwithstanding, the novel's ominous atmosphere and inspired set pieces—such as the minister's drunken fundamentalist sermon before an incredulous Hills congregation—make it a fascinating departure for Miss Naylor, as well as a provocative, iconoclastic novel about a seldom-addressed subject." N Y Times Book Rev

Naylor, Gloria—*Continued*

Mama Day. Ticknor & Fields 1988 311p o.p.
* LC 87-18157

"Willow Springs is a sparsely populated sea island just off America's southeast coast whose small black community is dominated by the elderly matriarch, Miranda 'Mama' Day. When Mama Day's greatniece, Cocoa, marries, she returns to Willow Springs with her husband for an extended visit. Once there, strange forces—both natural and supernatural—work to separate the couple." Libr J

"When she is not didactically fostering our spiritual instruction, Gloria Naylor serves another worthy purpose beautifully: she invites us to imagine the lives of complex characters at work and play, and gives us a faithfully rendered community in all its seasons." Ms

The men of Brewster Place. Hyperion 1998 173p

ISBN 0-7868-6421-4   LC 97-45987

"Ben, a neighborhood janitor (and chorus) resurrected from the previous Brewster Place novel, narrates seven tales of neighborhood men and the women who love them. Their travails feature the familiar ills of the inner city, yet Naylor lends these archetypal situations complexity and depth: Basil yearns to be the kind of father he never had but chooses a path that leads to heartbreak; Eugene's restlessness in his marriage and friendship with a transsexual force him to face a difficult fact about himself; Reverend Moreland T. Woods rehearses his political aspirations with maneuvers on his church's board; and C.C. Baker, involved in local drug trafficking, keeps a startling truth from the police." Publ Wkly

The women of Brewster Place. Viking 1982 192p o.p.   LC 81-69969

This "novel is set, as the title indicates, in Brewster Place, a block-long dead-end street of run-down apartment buildings in a northern city. In an interrelated series of vignettes, Naylor focuses on seven black women, residents of Brewster Place. She is concerned with the distance between their dreams and realities, problems and solutions; these women are of different ages, come from different backgrounds, react differently to their blackness and to men, and have different notions of personal accomplishment, but all are burdened by being both black and female. Naylor is not angry; she writes with conviction and beautiful language, but spares the reader any bitterness. Characters are not puppets but exist and function as well-rounded personalities." Booklist

Naylor, Phyllis Reynolds, 1933-

After; Phyllis Reynolds Naylor. Soho Press 2003 371p $25

ISBN 1-569-47354-4   LC 2003-50695

"Naylor's novel about 56-year-old Harry Gill's first year as a widower deals in the minutiae of daily life, focusing on the common but incontrovertibly human emotions surrounding death, marriage and family ties. Harry runs a garden shop in a Washington, D.C., suburb. When his wife dies of ovarian cancer, he grieves, but his grief is tempered with bouts of anger, exasperation and longing for other women. This longing is reciprocated. Neighbors, friends and even colleagues hurl themselves at Harry, who, although likable enough, seems to attract them simply because of his new status as an unattached man." Publ Wkly

"Especially in its early sections, the novel will remind many readers of Anne Tyler, with its slightly off-center characters and its sympathetic but wry and somewhat distanced point of view...After is popular fiction for intelligent readers, something always in short supply and always welcome." Washington Post

Nebula Awards showcase [date]; the year's best sf and fantasy chosen by the Science Fiction and Fantasy Writers of America. Roc

ISSN 0741-5567

First volume in this series, edited by Damon Knight, was published by Doubleday in 1965. Editors and publishers vary. Variant titles: Nebula Award stories; Nebula winners

Included in this annual collection of award-winning stories and runners-up are genre essays and tributes to seminal authors as well as lists of nominees and winners in various categories

Neel, Janet, 1940-

To die for. St. Martin's Press 1999 240p

ISBN 0-312-20598-8   LC 99-18077

A mystery featuring Chief Superintendent John McLeish and his wife Francesca. "The investors in Judith Delves's London cafe, including her co-owner, want to sell, but Judith is obstinately against the transaction. Shortly after her friend and partner, Selina, comes around to her way of thinking, Selina's body is found stuffed into an unused freezer." Publ Wkly

Neely, Barbara

Blanche cleans up. Viking 1998 258p

ISBN 0-670-87626-7   LC 97-39834

Boston cleaning lady Blanche White "takes over her cousin Charlotte's best friend Inez's job as cook at the home of snobbish, phony Allister Brindle, who aspires to be Massachusetts's next governor. Blanche is good at listening at doors and does not like Brindle's fawning over black leaders no one follows; in fact, she does not like any of the comings and goings at the Brindle residence, especially when they lead to murders." Libr J

"Blanche's caustic comments, streetwise attitude and lusty approach to life cast an illuminating light on both ends of the social spectrum and add sparks to an already sizzling mystery." Publ Wkly

Nelscott, Kris

Stone cribs. St. Martin's Minotaur 2004 323p $24.95

ISBN 0-312-28784-4   LC 2003-50604

"One year after the assassination of Martin Luther King Jr., Smokey Dalton has moved from Memphis to Chicago with an 11-year-old witness to the shooting. There, he investigates rental housing owned by white girlfriend Laura Hathaway. Adding to the unsettled political climate is the fight for the right to abortion, crystallized by Smokey and Laura's involvement in saving a young black woman, pregnant as the result of rape, from death-by-botched-abortion. Smokey subsequently hunts down the rapist, as well as the clumsy abortionist. . . . Nelscott skillfully recreates a troubled 1960s Chicago,

Nelscott, Kris—*Continued*

complete with sympathetic protagonists who fight its racial inequalities, widespread ignorance, and political ineptness." Libr J

Némirovsky, Irène, 1903-1942

Fire in the blood; translated by Sandra Smith. Alfred A. Knopf 2007 137p $22

ISBN 978-0-307-26748-1; 0-307-26748-2

LC 2007-28730

"Found among papers that Némirovsky left with her editor in early 1942 before she went on the run from the Nazis, 'Fire in the Blood' first appeared in France earlier this year. . . . Set deep in the French countryside, it might be described as a pastoral — except that it's far more gritty than Arcadian in content. Narrator Silvio is a 'prodigal son' who fled his native village and sowed his wild oats in Africa, Canada and Tahiti, only to come home feeling he's accomplished nothing. By going away, he has lost much of his local status (not to mention land and fortune). Now, in late middle age, he's a cranky loner, regarded by his extended family with a certain fondness and, perhaps, a certain wariness." Seattle Times

"In a book fuelled with images of fire and embers, Némirovsky brilliantly depicts a closed-in, inward-looking community, then gives what happens in it universal resonance by exhibiting not only what people do to each other but what the passing of time does to us all." London Times

Suite Francaise. Knopf 2006 401p $25

ISBN 1-4000-4473-1   LC 2006-3461

Original French edition, 2004

"Nemirovsky, a young Russian Jewish emigre, became a celebrated novelist in Paris at age 26 in 1929. She wrote eight more novels; then, even though she was certain that she wouldn't survive Germany's occupation of France, she embarked on a . . . work about France's collaboration with the Nazis. She completed two of five planned movements before she was sent to Auschwitz, a heart-wrenching story meticulously documented in a supplemental section. As for Nemirovsky's masterpiece, it begins with the tumultuous 'Storm in June,' in which diverse Parisians frantically evacuate Paris during the June 1940 German invasion. Nemirovsky's gift for combining the panoramic with the intimate, high emotion with stinging wit, is reminiscent of Turgenev, Babel, and Berberova. Acutely sensitive to class differences, and mordantly scornful of hypocrisy, she orchestrates a veritable carnival of cowardice, lies, larceny, and murder as a panicked populace drops all pretense of civilization. The second movement, 'Dolce,' evokes the eye of the storm in the village of Bussy, where German officers are billeted in French homes, and life and love resume. Suite Francaise is a magnificent novel of the insidious devastation of occupation, and Nemirovsky is brilliant and heroic, summoning up profound empathy for all, including regretful German soldiers." Booklist

Nersesian, Arthur

The swing voter of Staten Island; a novel. Akashic Books 2007 271p $22.95

ISBN 978-1-933354-34-7; 1-933354-34-8

LC 2007-926051

"All Uli knows is that he's supposed to shoot Dropt outside Cooper Union, then get back to Kennedy to catch the next flight out. As he makes his way to Cooper Union, however, his memory starts coming back to him, and he realizes he's not in New York City, but Rescue City of New York, NV. Nersesian . . . an alternative world circa 1981, in which Nixon served out his term, the Vietnam War still rages, and Rescue City-built to house refugees and dissidents-is playing host to a political battle." Libr J

"Though sometimes uncomfortably similar to the B-movie classic Escape From New York, Swing Voter aspires to be more than just a genre thriller. This isn't always a good thing: The central mystery is solved on the last page, as though it were an afterthought; for long stretches, Nersesian ditches the plot and focuses on the Armenian genocide. But the book succeeds as a teasing love letter to the dirtier city of yesteryear—downtown stalwarts like P.S.122, Tompkins Square Park, and CBGB appear in disguise. La MaMa materializes, rendered as Mamasita's Blah Blah Theater. Of course, in Nersesian's world, it's a place for both political drama and a gruesome double murder by means of sharpened broomstick. That's entertainment." Village Voice

Nesbø, Jo, 1960-

The redbreast; translated from the Norwegian by Don Bartlett. HarperCollins 2007 521p $24.95

ISBN 978-0-06-113399-2; 0-06-113399-X

Original Norwegian edition, 2006

The protagonist is "police detective Harry Hole, a borderline alcoholic who lands the assignment of assisting the U. S. Secret Service during a presidential visit to Oslo. It all goes hopelessly wrong, and Hole winds up shooting a secret service agent. Normally that would spell the end of a career, but with true Murphy's Law precision, Hole gets a promotion. It will catapult him into the strangest case of his career, a modern-day murder mystery with tendrils reaching back to World War II, when Norway forged an uneasy alliance with the Axis powers." BookPage

"This is a fine novel, ambitious in concept, skillful in execution and grownup in its view of people and events. In important ways it's also a political novel, one concerned with the threat of fascism, in Norway and by implication everywhere. All in all, The Redbreast certainly ranks with the best of current American crime fiction." Washington Post Book World

Neugeboren, Jay, 1938-

1940; a novel. Two Dollar Radio 2008 274p pa $15

ISBN 978-0-9763895-6-9

* LC 2008-900720

"Dr. Eduard Bloch, an Austrian doctor who achieved notoriety for being Adolf Hitler's childhood physician, accepts favors 'granted to no other Jew' and finds himself at the beginning of WWII living out his twilight years in the Bronx. Inspired by a visit from the striking Elisabeth Rofman, an inquisitive medical illustrator, Dr. Bloch decides to write his recollections of the Hitler family. He soon finds himself in the middle of a spat between Elisabeth and her pompous ex-husband over the proposed castration of Daniel, their institutionalized men-

Neugeboren, Jay, 1938-—*Continued*

tally ill son. In the midst of this dispute, Elisabeth's father disappears, and Daniel arrives at Dr. Bloch's apartment, seeking shelter. Through Dr. Bloch's diary entries, he charts the inevitable convergence of his romance with an increasingly unhinged Elisabeth, the unstable yearnings of Daniel and his own surreal remembrances of the teenage Hitler." Publ Wkly

"Neugeboren traverses the Hitlerian tightrope with all the skill and formal daring that have made him one of our most honored writers of literary fiction and masterful nonfiction. This new book is, at once, a beautifully realized work of imagined history, a rich and varied character study and a subtly layered novel of ideas, all wrapped in a propulsively readable story." Los Angeles Times Book Rev

Neville, Katherine, 1945-

The eight; a novel. Ballantine Bks. 1989 c1988 550p o.p.
LC 87-91363

This "novel is in and of itself a complex conundrum featuring two completely interdependent plots. As the action races back and forth between the era of the French Revolution and contemporary America and Algeria, both the historical and modern characters serve as pawns in an intricately executed game of chess. Players compete to unravel the sinister secret and curse of the mythical Montglane Service, an ornate chess set custom designed for Charlemagne, possessing certain mystical powers and endowed with an almost unlimited capacity for good or evil." Booklist

"Involving Napoleon, Talleyrand, Casanova, Voltaire, Rousseau, Robespierre and Catherine the Great in the quest, Neville has great fun rewriting history and making it all ring true." Publ Wkly

The fire; a novel. Ballantine Books 2008 451p il $26
ISBN 978-0-345-50067-0; 0-345-50067-9
LC 2008-26624

"Alexandra Solarin, child chess prodigy now grown, finds herself immersed in the Game, searching for a legendary chess set, the Montglane Service, which when assembled spells out the formula for the secret of immortality. The quest for the set ranges from the harem of Ali Pasha in 19th-century Albania to present-day Baghdad and Washington, D.C., and involves such historic figures as Charlemagne, Isaac Newton, Lord Byron and Napoleon. Despite the staggering amount and quality of the research, nothing feels shoehorned or extraneous. The story's relentless pace is matched by characters both sympathetic and real." Publ Wkly

The **new** space opera; edited by Gardner Dozois and Jonathan Strahan. Eos 2007 517p pa $15.95
ISBN 978-0-06-084675-6; 0-06-084675-5
Contents: Saving Tiamaat, by G. Jones; Verthandi's ring, by I. McDonald; Hatch, by R. Reed; Winning peace, by P. J. McAuley; Glory, by G. Egan; Maelstrom, by K. Baker; Blessed by an angel, by P. F. Hamilton; Who's afraid of wolf 359?, by K. Macleod; Valley of the gardens, by T. Daniel; Dividing the sustain, by J. P. Kelly; Minla's flowers, by A. Reynolds; Splinters of glass, by M. Rosenblum; Remembrance, by S. Baxter; Emperor and the maula, by R. Silverberg; Worm turns, by G.

Benford; Send them flowers, by W. J. Williams; Art of war, by N. Kress; Muse of fire, by D. Simmons

"An exceedingly fine set of stories written specifically for this collection by some of the best sf authors writing today. These 18 tales run the gamut from technologically centered hard science (think exploding comets and artificial intelligence) to character-driven soft science (settling on new worlds). Alien perspectives are balanced by humanistic introspection. Many of the stories mine the genre's favorite nuggets by exploring political and ethical questions from varied and unusual points of view." Libr J

New stories from the South: the year's best [date]; edited by Shannon Ravenel. Algonquin Books of Chapel Hill
ISSN 0879-9073
Annual. First published 1986

An annual collection of short stories culled from a wide variety of magazines. Among the authors represented are Frederick Barthelme, George Singleton, Chris Offutt, Tony Earley, Janice Daugharty, and Elizabeth Spencer

The **New** treasury of great racing stories; Dick Francis and John Welcome, editors. Norton 1992 211p $42
ISBN 0-393-03102-0
LC 92-9647

First published 1991 in the United Kingdom with title: Classic lines: more great racing stories

Contents: Spring fever, by D. Francis; My first winner, by J. Welcome; Man who shot the 'Favourite', by E. Wallace; Pick the winner, by D. Runyon; Night at the Old Bergen County Racetrack, by G. Grand; Blister, by J. T. Foote; Dead cert, by J.C. Squire; Inside view, by C.C.L. Browne; Tale of the gypsy horse, by D. Byrne; Pullinstown, by M. Keane; Occasional licences, by Somerville & Ross; Good thing, by C. Davy; Losers, by M. Gee; Oracle, by A.B. (Banjo) Paterson

Newman, Denise

(tr) Christensen, I. Azorno

Newman, Janis Cooke

Mary; a novel. MacAdam/Cage Pub. 2006 707p $26
ISBN 978-1-93156-163-1; 1-93156-163-X
LC 2006-15591

A "portrait of Mary Todd Lincoln. Writing in her journal while confined to Bellvue asylum, Mary alternates between recalling her past life as First Lady and detailing her current experiences in that institution. The first-person narrative and liberal use of descriptive details, perfected perhaps by Newman's extensive experience writing nonfiction, enlist the reader's sympathy for the mentally unstable Mrs. Lincoln. At the same time, we can become dismayed at her seeming lack of common sense. Her obsessions are chronicled, from compulsive shopping and fears for the safety of her loved ones, to her sexual needs. Mary's hopes, dreams, feelings, and thoughts are conveyed with depth and subtlety." Libr J

Newman, Sharan

Strong as death. Forge 1996 384p o.p.

LC 96-1410

"A Tom Doherty Associates book"

A "medieval mystery featuring the indefatigable Catherine Le Vendeur. En route to Santiago de Compostela, Spain, in order to petition for a child at the holy shrine of the apostle Saint James, Catherine and her beloved husband, Edgar, join forces with a curious band of pilgrims. Their fellow wayfarers include four aging knights, a couple of wandering musicians, an imperious gentlewoman, a bitter prostitute, and two zealous monks. As their journey progresses, a series of fatal misfortunes plagues various members of their company, prompting Catherine and Edgar to undertake a quiet investigation." Booklist

"Colorful characters and thoroughly researched culture add up to wonderful historical fiction." Libr J

Newton, Charlie

Calumet City. Touchstone/Simon & Schuster 2008 388p pa $14

ISBN 978-1-4165-3322-1; 1-4165-3322-2

LC 2007-16112

"Confrontational and uncompromising Patti Black, Chicago's most decorated cop, gets caught in a web of murder and betrayal. . . . When several unrelated cases threaten to reveal her horrific childhood as an abused runaway and teenage rape victim, Patti defies everybody to find Roland Ganz, her bête noir, who she suspects is behind the crimes; she must also locate the son she put up for adoption whom she thinks Roland is seeking. Accompanied by her sometime friend and rugby teammate, newspaper reporter Tracy Moens, she frantically follows a trail from Chicago to nearby Calumet City, the Arizona desert and back." Publ Wkly

"An atmospheric shocker. . . . Newton certainly has all the hallmarks and above all the classic noir tone — urban and nocturnal, stealthy and smoky, grim determination doing its two-step with gallows humor." Chicago Sun Times

Nexø, Martin Andersen See Andersen Nexø, Martin, 1869-1954

Ng, Fae Myenne, 1956-

Bone. Hyperion 1993 193p

ISBN 1-56282-944-0

LC 92-6028

The novel concerns "two generations of Chinese Americans in San Francisco's Chinatown. Mah, who has worked hard all her life in garment sweatshops, finally is able to own her baby-clothing store. Her husband, Leon, who used to be a merchant seaman, worked two shifts in ships' laundry rooms to provide for his family. Nevertheless, the family is torn apart after Ona, the middle daughter, jumps from the tallest building in Chinatown. . . . Nina, the youngest daughter, leaves Chinatown for New York City and then Leila, the oldest, marries and moves out to the suburbs. Leon, the 'paper son' to old Leung, fails to keep his promise to take Leung's bones back to China." Libr J

"Ng is a master storyteller. Her gift for observation and language make Bone truly extraordinary." Women's Rev Books

Nicholls, David, 1966-

A question of attraction. Villard Books 2004 c2003 338p $23.95; pa $13.95

ISBN 1-400-06181-4; 0-8129-7140-X (pa)

LC 2003-59627

"The year is 1985. Brian Jackson, a working-class kid on full scholarship, has started his first term at university. The usual freshman anxiety over fitting in is compounded by the gap between his own humble origins and the privileged backgrounds of his better-off classmates. Brian also has a dark secret–a long-held, burning ambition (stoked by his late father) to appear on the wildly popular TV quiz show University Challenge–and now, finally, it seems the dream is about to become reality." Publisher's note

The author "has a talent for droll dialogue and a wonderful sense of the ridiculous. He marries the agony of adolescence with ironic humor, producing a union of subtlety and slapstick that's not to be missed." USA Today

Nichols, John Treadwell, 1940-

The Milagro beanfield war; by John Nichols; illus. by Rini Templeton. Holt, Rinehart & Winston 1974 445p o.p.

*

"Joe Mondragon, a very small time troublemaker in the sleepy Chicano town of Milagro, irrigates a little field he owns in order to grow some beans. He is violating the local water laws but the rich and powerful are afraid to take action for fear of arousing Joe's friends and neighbors. (There's a big-money, Milagro-exploiting land development in the offing; they don't want to make waves.) Actually Joe's neighbors are generally resentful of his troublemaking, or are afraid to support him. But they eventually rally to the cause, having been pushed around too long, and the resulting interaction is touching and hilarious by turns." Publ Wkly

"Nichols has written a bawdy, slangy, modern proletarian novel that is—if finally perhaps excessively sentimental—still a consistently entertaining film scenario while at the same time it manages to make funny-serious sense out of a contemporary situation enduring injustice and imminent violence." Choice

The sterile cuckoo; by John Nichols. McKay, D. 1965 210p o.p.

When the heroine, Pookie Adams "first stumbles on the hero, Jerry Payne, waiting at a cross-country bus stop, he sees only a skinny, scrubby-haired girl, balancing a toothpick on her tongue. Then she bursts into speech and Jerry . . . remains bewitched until the last syllable. Her pursuit of Jerry is launched with . . . determination. . . . When fate places the couple at neighboring Eastern colleges, Jerry succumbs to his first frantic affair. . . . As their romance plunges into its second year, they make a final attempt to slow to a more normal pace, but on a New York weekend, somewhat the worse for an over indulgence in Tiki Puka Pukas, their affair staggers to a close." Publisher's note

Nichols, Leigh, 1945-

For works written by this author under other names see Koontz, Dean R., 1945-

Nichols, Peter, 1950-

Voyage to the North Star; a novel. Carroll & Graf Pubs. 1999 342p $24

ISBN 0-7867-0664-3

This novel's "protagonist is Will Boden, a skilled seaman down on his luck in depression-era New York. In a moment of ill judgment, he once abandoned the ship he was captaining, and is now reduced to scraping a living, literally, on the waterfront. Along comes Carl Schenck, a wealthy industrialist who wants to ape his idol, Teddy Roosevelt, as a big game hunter, but fears it's all been done. He hits upon the notion to take the beautiful luxury yacht he has just acquired up into the Arctic to hunt for seal, bear, whatever he can find, and among the motley crew he assembles, including a skipper who is a fake British naval officer, is poor Will." Publ Wkly

"A gripping novel of blood lust, human folly, and desperate hope in the tradition of Melville, Conrad, and Jack London." Libr J

Nicholson, Christopher, 1956-

The elephant keeper. William Morrow 2009 298p $24.99

ISBN 978-0-06-165160-1; 0-06-165160-5

LC 2009-00852

"Tom Page is the plain-spoken narrator who begins his working life as a stable boy to Mr. John Harrington, sugar merchant of Bristol, and who later finds his vocation as the elephant keeper to Lord Bidborough of Sussex. In 1773, Tom's master, in the cause of science, instructs Tom to write a full description of the elephant in his care. The elephant's story, as related by Tom, is of course his own story. In Nicholson's hands, however, it is also a lively portrait of 18th-century manners and ideas." Boston Globe

Nicholson, Margaret Beda See Yorke, Margaret

Niffenegger, Audrey

Her fearful symmetry; a novel. Scribner 2009 406p il $26.99

ISBN 978-1-4391-6539-3; 1-4391-6539-4

LC 2009018771

"The endurance of love animates this gothic story set in and around Highgate Cemetery, in London. When Elspeth Noblin dies of cancer, she leaves her estate, including an apartment overlooking the graveyard, to the twin daughters of her twin sister, from whom she has been estranged for twenty years. When Valentina and Julia show up to claim their inheritance, they soon discover that Elspeth is still in residence, in ghostly form." New Yorker

The novel is "at its best in its early pages, when Niffenegger gives herself room to present her cast of characters; there are some charming descriptions, particularly of these odd, wan mirror twins. The author's love for and deep research into Highgate is also apparent. . . . Not a deep meditation, the novel requires its readers to thoroughly suspend their disbelief and to go along for the haunted ride." Chicago Trib

The time traveler's wife; a novel. MacAdam\Cage 2003 518p $25

ISBN 1-931561-64-8   LC 2003-10159

"Young lovers often believe themselves crossed by fate or by time, but those in Niffenegger's spirited first novel have more reason than most. Henry suffers from Chrono-Impairment—a quasi-medical condition that catapults him, unwillingly, from one random point in time to another. Clare first meets him in 1977, when she is six and he materializes near her parents' garden as a thirty-six-year-old from 2000; he returns regularly throughout her childhood from different times in their shared future. At last, when Clare is twenty and Henry twenty-eight, they meet in his present, and the relationship begins in earnest. But romance proves even trickier than usual when one person keeps vanishing to distant, and occasionally dangerous, times." New Yorker

Niffenegger "writes with the unflinching yet detached clarity of a war correspondent standing at the sidelines of an unfolding battle. She possesses a historian's eye for contextual detail. This is no romantic idyll." USA Today

(jt. auth) Niffenegger, A. Her fearful symmetry

Nin, Anaïs, 1903-1977

Children of the albatross

In Nin, A. Cities of the interior p128-238

Cities of the interior; introduction by Sharon Spencer. Swallow Press 1974 xx, 589p o.p.

First one-volume version published 1959 by the author. Although intended as a connected work exploring the lives of women, it was originally published as five separate novelettes. This edition contains the expanded and retitled version of the fifth novelette

In Ladders to fire (1946), which concerns a largely American group of characters in Paris, Lillian's hunger for life and love leave her unsatisfied with her seemingly changeless marriage to Larry. She develops an increasingly possessive relationship with Djuna, whose inner clarity and control, concealed beneath a delicate feminine exterior, offer a comforting contrast to her own emotional turbulence. Lillian's love affair with the painter Jay is complicated by the love-hate relationship which they both establish with Sabina

Children of the albatross (1947) focuses on Djuna, who achieved a sense of liberation through dancing after an unhappy childhood in an orphan asylum. It deals with her youthful love for Michael, who fled to a homosexual lover after his jealousy drove them apart, her relationship with the joyful painter Lawrence and the youth Paul who seeks shelter and love from her after fleeing his parent's stifling home, and the relationships of Jay to her, Lillian and Sabina

In The four-chambered heart (1950), Djuna and the Guatemalan guitarist Rango become lovers and Djuna takes up residence on a houseboat in the Seine. Rango's supposedly invalid wife pretends to accept and even welcome the situation, but her feigning of illness and increasingly apparent insanity nearly wreck Djuna's life

In A spy in the house of love (1954), set in and around New York City, Sabina acts out relationships with her husband and lovers who include the opera singer Philip, the African drummer Mambo, and the painter Jay. She explores who longing for freedom and guilty feelings about the lies her many loves seem to make necessary

In Seduction of the Minotaur (1961; an expanded version of the Solar barque), Lillian seeks a liberating es-

Nin, Anaïs, 1903-1977—*Continued*
cape from her past in a Mexican town. Discovering that
she is reenacting old relationships with her new acquaintances, she realizes she can transcend her past only by
understanding rather than evading it and that her quest
for freedom cannot take place apart from her husband,
whose changelessness is a necessary complement to her
own mutability

The four-chambered heart
In Nin, A. Cities of the interior p239-358

Ladders to fire
In Nin, A. Cities of the interior p1-127

Seduction of the Minotaur
In Nin, A. Cities of the interior p463-589

A spy in the house of love
In Nin, A. Cities of the interior p360-462

Niven, Larry

The burning city; {by} Larry Niven & Jerry
Pournelle. Pocket Bks. 2000 486p
  ISBN 0-671-03660-2   LC 99-57479
"In a world where magic is dying and the gods are
slowly becoming myth, Whandall Placehold passes from
boyhood to manhood in a city beset by devastating Burnings. To save his family and his home from the ravages
of the dying god Yangin-Atep, Whandall leaves his familiar surroundings and embarks on a journey of self-
discovery that leads to a greater destiny. Set in the world
first described in Niven's classic *The Magic Goes Away*,
the latest effort by coauthors Niven and Pournelle blends
the grim background of a post-apocalyptic world with the
mystic intensity of a vision quest." Libr J

Lucifer's hammer; by Larry Niven & Jerry
Pournelle. Playboy Press 1977 494p o.p.
                   LC 77-8074
"The hammer of the title is an eons-old comet that
strikes earth with devastating physical and psychological
consequences that are meticulously dramatized in the
lives of dozens of major and minor characters. The second and more powerful part details the immense task of
rebuilding civilization or preserving what remains of it.
The authors excel in their suspenseful and thought-
provoking hypothesis about the nature of civilized man
and the ethics of survival when the future of their fragile
community is at stake." Booklist

The Mote in God's Eye; by Larry Niven & Jerry Pournelle. Simon & Schuster 1974 537p pa
$7.99 hardcover o.p.
  ISBN 0-671-74192-6
                            *
"Superior space opera in which Earth's interstellar
navy contacts and does battle with an enormously hostile
alien race. The scenes of space warfare are well handled,
and the alien Moties are fascinating." Anatomy of Wonder 4

Ringworld. Ballantine Bks. 1970 342p pa $7.99
  ISBN 0-345-33392-6
                            *

"The Ringworld, a world shaped like a wheel so huge
that it surrounds a sun, is almost too fantastic to conceive of. With a radius of 90 million miles and a length
of 600 million miles, the Ringworld's mystery is compounded by the discovery that it is artificial. What phenomenal intelligence can be behind such a creation? Four
unlikely explorers, two humans and two aliens, set out
for the Ringworld, bound by mutual distrust and unsure
of each other's motives." Shapiro. Fic for Youth. 3d edition

The Ringworld engineers. Holt & Co. 1980
"Twenty-three years after their original journey, Louis
Wu and Speaker-to-Animals once more find themselves
kidnapped companions of a mad Puppeteer who returns
with them to Ringworld to steal a transmutation device.
The Puppeteer encounters unexpected obstacles to this
goal, however: Louis has become a wirehead addicted to
the electric current fed almost constantly to his brain;
Speaker-to-Animals is now a kzinti Patriarch and resents
his enforced participation in the venture; the Ringworld
has developed an unstable orbit and is about to
desintegrate into its sun." SLJ
"This is a good example of the kind of novel where
the basic idea—the Ringworld itself—is the true 'hero.'"
Booklist
Followed by The Ringworld throne

The Ringworld throne. Ballantine Bks. 1996
424p o.p.   LC 95-47882
"A Del Rey book"
The third title in the author's Ringworld series "offers
two stories crowded into one. A motley array of hominid
inhabitants are seeking to defeat a plague of vampires.
Meanwhile, returning hero Louis Wu is battling what effectively is a plague of Protectors . . . whose rivalries
threaten Ringworld's existence. The battle against the
vampires is the more exciting of the two stories, filled
with action, scenes of the Ringworld and explorations of
ritualistic interspecies sex. Wu's pursuit of the Protectors
displays Niven's deft hand at portraying aliens." Publ
Wkly

Ringworld's children. Tor Bks. 2004 $24.95
  ISBN 0-7653-0167-9   LC 2003-26581
In this fourth title in the series, "the Ringworld, an artificially engineered realm resembling a ribbon or ring
that is home to over a trillion people of wildly different
species, faces threats from outsider ships from the inhabited worlds and its own aging superstructure. Newly restored in mind and body, Louis Wu, a member of the
first expedition to Ringworld, joins three individuals of
different species to prevent the destruction of
Ringworld." Libr J
"Action and clever world building should captivate
newcomers to Ringworld, while returners will appreciate
picking up loose ends from previous Ringworld volumes." Booklist

Saturn's race; [by] Larry Niven & Steven
Barnes. TOR Bks. 2000 317p
  ISBN 0-312-86726-3   LC 00-28646
"A Tom Doherty Associates book"
In this futuristic thriller a council led by Saturn, a vir-
tual creation, "attempts to control population growth by
causing a whole generation of sterile women. Japanese
American computer expert Chaz Kato is actually the
grandfather of the young man who, thanks to massive

Niven, Larry—*Continued*

surgery and medication, he appears to be. With his two lovers, American Lenore Myles and Indonesian Clarise Maibang, he discovers an increasingly bloody trail leading to the contraceptive conspiracy, which finally erupts in global war." Booklist

"Brilliantly weaving high-tech internets, augmentation technologies and social issues into a fast-paced cloak-and-dagger action adventure, this novel effortlessly moves from the depths of the ocean to the heights of VR to create a dazzling, seamless whole." Publ Wkly

Noel, Katharine

Halfway house. Atlantic Monthly Press 2006 367p $23

ISBN 0-871-13934-0   LC 2005-53636

"When bright and athletic Angie Voorster experiences a sudden mental breakdown at age 17, she goes from the hospital to a "farm" for five months. She repeats her senior year, rejoins the swim team, and applies to college. From outside the Voorster home, things appear to be back to normal; in reality, Angie's mother, Jordana, is having an affair, her brother Luke is slipping out each night and not returning until dawn, and Angie is barely keeping herself together. She makes it through seven months at Middlebury College, then overdoses on lithium and ends up in a halfway house." Booklist

"There are moments when the author could have allowed feel-good plot turns to transform the story into a sentimental domestic drama, but instead she tenaciously adheres to the realistic trajectory of mental illness. While reading [the novel], a reader can't help considering the classic protagonist of this literary genre: Esther Greenwood in 'The Bell Jar,' by Sylvia Plath. . . . Thankfully, Ms. Noel doesn't attempt to reinvent Plath's masterpiece; she steers clear of the first-person voice and instead relies on her third-person tapestry. That said, Ms. Noel offers her own contemporary, insightful chronicle of a young woman trying to define herself through the miasma of mental illness." N Y Times (Late N Y Ed)

Noon, Jeff

Vurt. Crown 1995 342p o.p.   LC 94-25544

First published 1993 in the United Kingdom

This novel of the future is set in Manchester "Vurt is a type of virtual reality (but without computers), and a kind of drug. You put a coloured feather in your mouth and you're in a dream-world—or a nightmare. Scribble is searching for [Desdemona,] his kid sister (and lover) who went into a Vurt world with him and never came back. He roams the backstreets with a gang of friends, trying to find a dealer who will supply him with a Curious Yellow feather, so he can go back to the same world to find her." New Statesman Soc

This "fluorescent and phantasmagorical novel . . . isn't quite the equal of Anthony Burgess's A Clockwork Orange, with which it is being compared, but in some ways it comes close. It's good enough in its first 50 or 60 pages of atmosphere setting, all smoke machines and flashing strobes, that the reader blinks, shakes his head and wonders whether Noon can sustain the weirdness." Time

Nooteboom, Cees, 1933-

All souls' day; translated from the Dutch by Susan Massotty. Harcourt 2001 338p $31

ISBN 0-15-100566-4

     * LC 2001-24310

Original Dutch editions, 1998

In this novel, set in Berlin, "protagonists Arthur and Elik are haunted by personal calamities. Arthur, philosophical and quiet, is a documentary filmmaker attempting to recover from the loss of his wife and child in a plane accident. Elik, impulsive and mysterious, is a graduate student who is still deeply troubled by a traumatic childhood incident." Libr J

"Not the least of the novel's satisfactions is the deftness with which Nooteboom incorporates signposts of Western high culture into his densely observant narrative." New Yorker

Lost paradise; translated from the Dutch by Susan Massotty. Grove Press 2007 151p $23

ISBN 978-0-8021-1855-4; 0-8021-1855-0

     *

Original Dutch edition, 2004

"After surviving a gang rape in São Paulo, a young, affluent Brazilian woman, Alma, takes off for Australia with her best friend, Almut: the two plan to train as masseuses. Nooteboom then cuts to an embittered middle-aged critic, Erik Zondag, who is cast out of his home in Amsterdam by his fed-up younger girlfriend and sent to an Alpine spa in order to dry out and become a different man. The first part of the novel tracks the two Brazilians as they travel though Australia with hope of stopping at the legendary Aboriginal Sickness Dreaming Place. Their Australian adventures take a turn involving the Angel Project, a multisite piece of participatory art in Perth. For the second part, Eric endures a punishingly ascetic stay at the Alpine spa, where he recognizes his masseuse." Publ Wkly

"Calling a novel Lost Paradise invites a daunting comparison, but Cees Nooteboom has the reputation and the chutzpah to lay down a few gauntlets of this sort. He includes himself in a list of Dutch 'literary giants' reeled off by one character, and remarks in the epilogue that the author of Lost Paradise 'knew what he was doing'. This self-reference could be irritating, but it's tempered by a sense of playfulness and justified by the book's content." New Statesman

Nordan, Lewis

Wolf whistle; a novel. Algonquin Bks. 1993 290p

ISBN 1-56512-028-0

     * LC 93-1011

"The wolf whistle of the title comes from Bobo, a black teenager from Chicago visiting in Arrow Catcher, Mississippi. Directed at the wife of the town's most prominent white resident, this whistle soon leads to Bobo's murder. Based on the Emmett Till lynching, . . . [this novel] examines the intertwined fates of blacks and poor whites in the Mississippi delta." Libr J

"Propelled by Nordan's musical prose, much of this narrative soars above the commonplace into the realm of myth." Publ Wkly

Nordhoff, Charles, 1887-1947

Botany Bay; by Charles Nordhoff and James Norman Hall. Little, Brown 1941 374p o.p.

"The story of the Australian penal colony at Botany Bay, and especially of Hugh Tallant, an American, who had been stranded in England, turned highwayman, and was one of the first criminals shipped to Botany Bay, where life was bitterly hard and adventurous." Ont Libr Rev

The Bounty trilogy; by Charles Nordhoff and James Norman Hall; illustrated by N. C. Wyeth. Little, Brown 1982 691p il o.p.

"An Atlantic Monthly Press book"

A reissue of the combined volume first published 1936

Based on actual events stemming from a mutiny on a British war vessel in 1787, "this great trilogy begins with the story of the men who mutinied against the now famous Captain Bligh—'Mutiny on the Bounty.' In 'Men Against the Sea' Bligh and his supporters, set adrift in a small boat, made an incredible journey to safety. 'Pitcairn's Island' is the story of the mutineers who found refuge on a remote Pacific island." Books for you

Men against the sea; by Charles Nordhoff and James Norman Hall. Little, Brown 1934 251p o.p.

Sequel to Mutiny on the Bounty

This volume tells the story of Captain Bligh and the eighteen loyal men, who under his leadership sailed in an open boat thirty-six hundred miles from the Friendly Islands in the South Pacific to the Dutch colony of Timor in the East Indies. The story is told as if by Ledward, the surgeon, but the events, the wind and the weather of the narrative are those recorded in Captain Bligh's log

Followed by Pitcairn's Island

also in Nordhoff, C. and Hall, J. N. The Bounty trilogy

Mutiny on the Bounty; by Charles Nordhoff and James Norman Hall. Little, Brown 1932 396p hardcover o.p. pa $13.95

ISBN 0-316-61157-3; 0-316-61168-9 (pa)

This narrative is "based on the famous mutiny that members of the crew of the 'Bounty', a British war vessel, carried out in 1787 against their cruel commander, Captain William Bligh. The authors kept the actual historical characters and background, using as narrator an elderly man, Captain Roger Byam, who had been a midshipman on the 'Bounty.' The story tells how the mate of the ship, Fletcher Christian, and a number of the crew rebel and set Captain Bligh adrift in an open boat with the loyal members of the crew." Reader's Ency. 4th edition

also in Nordhoff, C. and Hall, J. N. The Bounty trilogy

Pitcairn's Island; by Charles Nordhoff and James Norman Hall. Little, Brown 1934 333p o.p.

Sequel to Men against the sea

"This final volume {of the trilogy} is the history of those mutineers who, with eighteen Polynesian men and women, reached Pitcairn's Island and there destroyed the 'Bounty.' Unvisited for eighteen years, the community fought over women and possession, and all but one of the men died violent deaths. A blood-curdling story, not for the squeamish reader." Booklist

also in Nordhoff, C. and Hall, J. N. The Bounty trilogy

Norman, Howard

The bird artist. Farrar, Straus & Giroux 1994 289p o.p.

* LC 94-70542

"Fabian, son of Alaric and Orkney Vas, has spent his entire life in remote Witless Bay, Newfoundland. Looking back on his life, he decides that he has distinguished himself in only two ways: as a modestly successful artist whose illustrations graced the covers of *Bird Lore* magazine and as the murderer of the local lighthouse keeper, Botho August. The murder was the result of excessive coffee consumption combined with the stress brought on by his parents' plan to force him into an arranged marriage with a cousin he had never seen; this in turn would keep him from his hard-drinking girlfriend." Libr J

This work evokes "a way of life, a distinctive community and a fatalistic view of human behavior. The novel sings with tension and sparkles with antic humor." Publ Wkly

The haunting of L. Farrar, Straus & Giroux 2002 326p $24

ISBN 0-374-16825-3   LC 2001-51120

"In 1926, Peter Duvett meets and sleeps with Kala Murie on her wedding day in Churchill, an isolated village on the shores of the Hudson Bay. Kala's husband is Vienna Linn, the photographer Peter has come to assist. He has traveled from Halifax, escaping painful memories of his mother's suicide—or, as he is convinced, her murder. Soon Peter becomes the repository of the emotions and secrets of Kala and Vienna's hazardous partnership." Publ Wkly

"This is a mesmerizing melodrama rendered magical thanks to lyrical evocations of fog and storm, sexual bliss and fear, a conflation of atmospheric conditions and states of mind that makes of the human heart a realm as treacherous and exquisite as the Arctic." Booklist

The museum guard; a novel. Farrar, Straus & Giroux 1998 310p

ISBN 0-374-21649-5   LC 98-8413

"An orphan whose parents died in a dirigible crash when he was eight, DeFoe is raised in a Halifax hotel by his incorrigibly alcoholic and amorous Uncle Edward, a guard in the town's art museum. High-school dropout DeFoe becomes a guard there, too, and he goes stoically through his days caring for his perennially derelict and self-destructive uncle. DeFoe also tries to nourish his failing relationship with Imogen Linny, the caretaker at the Jewish cemetery, whose debilitating headaches have increased since she's become obsessed with a painting on loan to the museum." Publ Wkly

The author "fills this enigmatic novel with elements of fable and fairy tale blended with memorable characterizations and subtle narrative probings into the nature of self and the consequences of actions." Libr J

Norman, Diana *See* Franklin, Ariana

Norris, Benjamin Franklin *See* Norris, Frank, 1870-1902

Norris, Frank, 1870-1902

McTeague; a story of San Francisco; edited with an introduction by Kevin Starr. Penguin Books 1994 xlviii, 442p pa $10.95

ISBN 0-14-018769-3

First published 1899 by Doubleday

"A prime example of the American naturalistic novel, *McTeague* treats the gradual degeneration of a stupid, but initially harmless, giant of a man whose instincts are nearer brute than human. McTeague practices dentistry without a license in a poor section of San Francisco's Polk Street and marries Trina, who has just won $5,000 in a lottery. He soon loses his job and takes to drink. Trina becomes a miser, and McTeague murders her in a fit of rage and steals her money but is tracked down and killed by her cousin." Benet's Reader's Ency of Am Lit

also in Norris, F. Novels and essays

Novels and essays. Library of America 1986 1232p $40

ISBN 0-940450-40-2

Contents: Vandover and the brute; McTeague; The octopus; Essays

Vandover and the brute (1914) depicts the degeneration of a once affable and talented young man after he is afflicted with the psychological condition lycanthropy. McTeague and The octopus are entered separately.

The octopus; a story of California. Doubleday 1901 652p o.p.

First volume of an unfinished trilogy The epic of wheat

"The battle waged between the wheat growers and the railroad men in California is the theme of this novel. Concerned with social injustice, man's inhumanity to man, and the relentlessness of power struggles, Norris is able to combine these themes with a love interest." Shapiro. Fic for Youth. 3d edition

Followed by The pit

also in Norris, F. Novels and essays

The pit; a story of Chicago. Doubleday 1903 o.p.

The second volume of the author's unfinished The epic of wheat trilogy "is a story of manipulations in the Chicago Exchange. Curtis Jadwin, a stock speculator, is so absorbed in making money that he neglects his emotionally starved wife Laura. Into this situation steps Sheldon Corthell, dilettante artist, to console her. Laura loves her husband, and postpones for awhile going away with the aesthete. Meanwhile, Jadwin engages in a struggle with the Crookes gang of speculators. He beats them, but is crushed by fluctuations in wheat production. He and Laura effect a reconciliation." Haydn. Thesaurus of Book Dig

Vandover and the brute
In Norris, F. Novels and essays

North, Andrew *See* Norton, Andre, 1912-2005

North, Anthony *See* Koontz, Dean R., 1945-

Norton, Alice Mary *See* Norton, Andre, 1912-2005

Norton, Andre, 1912-2005

Beast Master's ark; [by] Andre Norton and Lyn McConchie. TOR Bks. 2002 318p

ISBN 0-7653-0041-9   LC 2002-67249

Third volume in the author's Beast Master series begun with the Beast Master (1959) and Lord of Thunder (1962)

"A mysterious killer, referred to as 'Death-which-come-in-the-night' by the planet Arzor's indigenous inhabitants, threatens to eradicate sentient life on the desertlike world. Beast Master Storm Hosteen discovers that the only chance of saving his adopted home lies with a young woman name Tani, who has learned to deny her own Beast Master heritage." Libr J

The elvenbane; an epic high fantasy of the Halfblood chronicles; [by] Andre Norton, Mercedes Lackey. Doherty Assocs. 1991 390p (Halfblood chronicles) o.p.   LC 91-21177

"A TOR book"

"In a world ruled by some of the most brutal and tyrannical elves ever encountered, the most persecuted are the part-human, part-elven halfbloods. After her human mother is cast into the desert, [Shana] the bastard daughter of the powerful Lord Dyran survives and is raised by dragons to seek her destiny as the Elvenbane." Booklist

Followed by Elvenblood

Elvenblood; an epic high fantasy; [by] Andre Norton and Mercedes Lackey. Doherty Assocs. 1995 348p (Halfblood chronicles, bk2) o.p.

LC 95-5797

"A TOR book"

"Following rumors of the existence of a tribe of humans immune to the enslaving magics of the land's elven overlords, halfelven rebel Shana and her dragon companion encounter unexpected complications in their struggle for freedom. The talents of collaborators Norton and Lackey blend seamlessly as they expand the background to their epic fantasy to include an exotic desert culture, which provides a rich contrast to the stifling atmosphere of elven society." Libr J

Golden Trillium. Bantam Bks. 1993 296p (Trillium)

ISBN 0-553-09507-2   LC 92-43875

Third in the fantasy series that includes Black Trillium by Marion Zimmer Bradley, Julian May, and Andre Norton, and Blood Trillium by Julian May

"Having aided her sisters in establishing peace in the land of Ruwenda, the warrior-maiden Kadiya journeys through the swamps to return the Three-Orbed Sword to the place of its origin only to find that her fight against evil is not yet done. The grande dame of sf and fantasy returns to a favorite theme—the discovery of an ancient and highly advanced lost civilization—in this heroic adventure." Libr J

Redline the stars; [by] Andre Norton, P.M. Griffin. Tor Bks. 1993 304p o.p.   LC 92-43708

"A Tom Doherty Associates book"

The authors "recreate the flavor of Norton's four *Solar Queen* books . . . while updating some concepts and

Norton, Andre, 1912-2005—*Continued*
quite a bit of technology. The crew of the Free Trader vessel *Solar Queen*, flying under Capt. Miceál Jellico, has mixed reactions to new crewmate Rael Cofort, who is plying the space lanes as a jack-of-all-trades despite her position as a physician and status as sister of the successful rival Free Trader, Teague Cofort. Upon arriving at Canuche of Halio, the most advanced planet of the sector, the *Queen's* crew is endangered when Rael picks up the odor of man-eating rodents used in a gruesome gem-stealing scheme." Publ Wkly

The **Norton** book of science fiction; North American science fiction, 1960-1990; edited by Ursula K. Le Guin and Brian Attebery; Karen Joy Fowler, consultant. Norton 1993 869p pa $38.13 hardcover o.p.

ISBN 0-393-97241-0 (pa)   LC 93-16130

Damon Knight, Robert Silverberg, Connie Willis and Harlan Ellison are among the authors represented in this anthology of more than 60 stories.
A "compilation of intelligent and entertaining sf that belongs in virtually every fiction collection." Booklist

Norway, Nevil Shute *See* Shute, Nevil, 1899-1960

Nothing but you; love stories from The New Yorker; edited by Roger Angell. Random House 1997 471p

ISBN 0-679-45701-1   LC 96-43079

Contents: The diver, by V. S. Pritchett; A country wedding, by L. Colwin; Blackbird pie, by R. Carver; The nice restaurant, by M. Gaitskill; Goodbye Marcus goodbye Rose, by J. Rhys; How to give the wrong impression, by K. Heiny; Marito in Città, by J. Cheever; The Jack Randa Hotel, by A. Munro; Hey, Joe, by B. Neihart; Here come the Maples, by J. Updike; Yours, by M. Robison; Roses, rhododendron, by A. Adams; Influenza, by D. Menaker; How old, how young, by J. O'Hara; Eyes of a blue dog, by G. Garcia Márquez; We, by M. Grimm; The dark stage, by D. Plante; Song of Roland, by J. Kincaid; The man in the moon, by W. Maxwell; The Kugelmass episode, by W. Allen; The Cinderella waltz, by A. Beattie; Experiment, by J. Barnes; Scarves, beads, sandals, by M. Gallant; Ten miles west of Venus, by J. Troy; The circle, by V. Nabokov; The Profumo affair, by E. Carroll; Elka and Meir, by I. B. Singer; Sculpture 1, by A. Patrinos; Dating your mom, by I. Frazier; The man with the dog, by R. P. Jhabvala; The plan, by E. O'Brien; Spring fugue, by H. Brodkey; In the gloaming, by A. E. Dark; Attraction, by D. Long; Ocean Avenue, by M. Chabon; Love life, by B. A. Mason; After rain, by W. Trevor; Overnight to many distant cities, by D. Barthelme

Nothomb, Amélie

Tokyo fiancee; translated from the French by Alison Anderson. Europa Editions 2009 152p pa $15

ISBN 978-1-933372-64-8; 1-933372-64-8

Original French edition, 2007
A "story of first love set in late 1980s and early '90s Tokyo. Amélie is a 21-year-old Belgian student studying Japanese in Tokyo when she begins tutoring Rinri, a sweet, shy and wealthy 20-year-old, in French. The relationship quickly evolves into a friendship and, soon after that, into romance. Rinri is a young soul who is easily swept up in his love for Amélie, and his charm is undeniable as he courts her, but Amélie wrestles with the classic situation: she loves spending time with Rinri, but she doesn't love him, and she cannot deny her need for independence." Publ Wkly
"Nothomb exoticizes Japanese culture without succumbing to Orientalist stereotypes. The situations she refreshingly depicts reveal Amelie's education in the Japanese art of living. . . . [A] spare, elegant novel." N Y Times Book Rev

Novak, Joseph *See* Kosinski, Jerzy N., 1933-1991

Novakovich, Josip

April Fool's Day; a novel. HarperCollins Publishers 2004 226p map $23.95

ISBN 0-06-058397-5; 0-06-058398-3
          LC 2003-67656
"Politics turn personal for Ivan Dolinar, born April 1, 1948, in Croatia, as the ricocheting course of his life reflects the tumult of his home country. His medical studies are cut short when he's imprisoned after a classmate jokes about assassinating Tito, who-along with Indira Gandhi-visits the labor camp and offers Ivan a Cuban cigar and a longer sentence. Released but barred from medicine, Ivan is drafted into the Yugoslav army just before the Croats organize their own defense force, putting him into an absurd and horrific war with his own countrymen. Finding his captain raping his former classmate Selma, Ivan rescues and later marries her, raising her daughter as his own. But marriage, fatherhood, hypochondria, and adultery fail to bring the peace Ivan finds in life after death." Booklist
"A heartfelt novel about the war-torn Balkans that's actually quite funny. . .and touching." GQ

Novik, Naomi, 1973-

His majesty's dragon. Del Rey 2006 356p (Temeraire series, v1) pa $7.50

ISBN 0-345-48128-3   LC 2005-46342
Published in Great Britain with title: Temeraire
In this novel, the opening salvo of the Temeraire series, Novik "blends fantasy into the history of the Napoleonic wars. Here be dragons, beasts that can speak and reason, bred for strength and speed and used for aerial support in battle. Each nation has its own breeds, but none are so jealously guarded as the mysterious dragons of China. Veteran Capt. Will Laurence of the British Navy is therefore taken aback after his crew captures an egg from a French ship and it hatches a Chinese dragon, which Laurence names Temeraire. When Temeraire bonds with the captain, the two leave the navy to sign on with His Majesty's sadly understaffed Aerial Corps." Publ Wkly
"A completely authentic tale, brimming with all the detail and richness one looks for in military yarns as well as the impossible wonder of gilded fantasy." Entertain-

Novik, Naomi, 1973——*Continued*
ment Wkly
Followed by: Throne of jade (2006), Black powder
wars (2006), Empire of ivory (2007), Victory of eagles
(2009)

Nunez, Elizabeth

Anna in-between. Akashic Books 2009 347p
$22.95
ISBN 978-1-933354-84-2; 1-933354-84-4
LC 2009-922936
"Traveling back to her Caribbean island home on vacation from her high-pressure job as a book editor in Manhattan, Anna Sinclair is predisposed to be at odds with
the vast dichotomy between her two worlds. Not only
does the languid pace of tropical life take some adjustment but Anna is perennially frustrated by the fractious
relationship with her mother, taking quick umbrage at the
hypercritical woman's subtle faultfinding. So it goes until
the day when her normally proper and reserved mother
swallows her pride and reveals the hideous lump that has
deformed her breast. Shocked by her mother's life-
threatening condition, appalled by her father's seeming
indifference to his wife's deteriorating health, Anna
struggles to convince her parents to return with her to
New York, where her mother can receive proper care."
Booklist
"The title of her latest novel suggests a sitcom, or the
upbeat identity lit marketed to teenagers. But Elizabeth
Nunez layers Anna In-Between, a psychologically and
emotionally astute family portrait, with dark themes like
racism, cancer and the bittersweet longing of the immigrant. Foremost, she explores the late innings of a successful marriage, in which husband and wife cling together in the shadow of mortality." N Y Times Book
Rev

Grace. Ballantine Bks. 2003 294p $23.95
ISBN 0-345-45533-9
LC 2002-26260
"Trinidad-born Justin Peters seemingly has it all: a
beautiful, accomplished wife named Sally; a precocious
four-year-old daughter; a fabulous brownstone in the hip
Fort Greene section of Brooklyn; and a professorship at
a public university. Everything is picture perfect until his
mate blindsides him by confessing that she is unhappy
and planning to move out, taking their child with her."
Libr J
"This is a tender, graceful novel of personal amd material struggle that also explores the power of literature and
poetry in everyday life." Booklist

Nunez, Sigrid

The last of her kind. Farrar, Straus and Giroux
2006 375p $25
ISBN 0-374-18381-3
LC 2005-40098
This "portrait of countercultural America in the sixties
and seventies opens in 1968, when two girls meet as
roommates at Barnard College. Ann is rich and white
and wants to be neither, confiding, 'I wish I had been
born poor'; Georgette has no illusions about poverty,
having just escaped her depressed home town, where
'whole families drank themselves to disgrace.' Georgette
finds Ann at once despicable and mesmerizing, and she's
stunned—if not entirely surprised—when, years after the

end of their friendship, Ann is arrested for killing a cop.
In previous works, Nunez has proved herself a master of
psychological acuity. Here her ambitions are grander, and
the result is a remarkable and disconcerting vision of a
troubled time in American history, and of its repercussions for national and individual identity." New Yorker

Nunnally, Tiina

(tr) Jungstedt, M. The inner circle

Nye, Robert, 1939-

The late Mr. Shakespeare; a novel. Arcade Pub.
1999 398p $25.95
ISBN 1-55970-469-1
LC 98-50763
First published 1998 in the United Kingdom
The narrator of this novel is Pickleherring, "who at age
thirteen was recruited into the theater by Mr. Shakespeare himself. The playwright was in need of a lad to
play the little prince in King John. Pickleherring stayed
with the company all the way to The Tempest. Now ancient, he is holed up in the attic of a London brothel and
writing the life of his adored patron." Atl Mon
"Nye brilliantly weaves together almost all the known
facts about Shakespeare, a great many of the spurious
anecdotes which have been attached to his life, and a tissue of rare inventions of his own." Times Lit Suppl

O

Oates, Joyce Carol, 1938-

American appetites. Dutton 1989 340p o.p.
LC 88-18904
"A William Abrahams book"
"Ian McCullough, 50 years old, is editor of a prestigious journal and a research fellow. His wife, Glynnis,
writes cookbooks. Their marriage is not perfect but far
from unfulfilling. Then an incident from the past—Ian
loaned money to a friend of Glynnis' for an abortion—
resurfaces and provokes a horrible row between husband
and wife. Glynnis ends up falling through a pane of glass
and being killed." Booklist
"A zippy story about successful lives dramatically altered by one sudden and inexplicable lapse of judgment."
Publ Wkly

Because it is bitter, and because it is my heart.
Dutton 1990 405p o.p.
* LC 89-25965
"A William Abrahams book"
This novel "is set in a small town in western New
York from the early 1950s to the early 1960s, and fol-
lows the . . . fortunes of two families, one white (the
Courtneys) and one black (the Fairchilds). When Jinx
Fairchild, at 16, gets in a fight with a white kid who has
menaced Iris Courtney, 14, and ends up killing him, the
secret they share is . . . both a bond and a barrier be-
tween the two." Nation
"At its best, the novel awakens the reader to something
like the unexpected new comprehensions of the universe
that Iris experiences." N Y Rev Books

Bellefleur. Dutton 1980 558p
ISBN 0-525-06302-1
* LC 79-28193

Oates, Joyce Carol, 1938—*Continued*

"A Henry Robbins book"

"In this Gothic novel, Oates weaves a shimmering tapestry made of odd and contradictory threads: a hermaphroditic birth, a vulture that devours an infant, a dwarf with 'powers,' a vampire, a cannibal, religious mystics and clairvoyants. Such are the Gothic trappings of this epic about the Bellefleurs, an old and powerful American family whose estate is located in the Adirondacks and whose history is an interpretation of American history from pioneer days to the present." Benet's Reader's Ency of Am Lit

Black girl/White girl. Ecco 2006 272p $25.95

ISBN 0-06-112564-4   LC 2006-48306

"On entering tony Schuyler College in the mid-1970s, Genna, a liberal and well-meaning prep-school grad, is looking forward to rooming with devoutly religious African American scholarship student Minette Swift. But the girls have little in common, other than an uncomfortable shyness with each other and uneasy relationships with adored but flawed fathers—Minette's dad is a charismatic minister, while Genna's dad is an attorney notorious for defending anti-Vietnam War radicals. The girls' tentative moves toward friendship and loyalty are undermined by the stresses of their first year of college and a series of hateful encounters that ends in tragedy and grief." Libr J

"Oates has never been shy about peering into the darkest corners of American culture. Her best books . . . showcase her fascination with violence, her almost vampiric ability to tap into the subconscious of her troubled characters and her taste for appropriating real-life tragedy. Oates's latest offering is no exception." N Y Times Book Rev

Black water. Dutton 1992 154p o.p.

LC 91-40463

"A William Abrahams book"

"A 26-year-old woman drowns when a senator's car goes off a bridge; but the point of view in this . . . novel belongs to the victim." N Y Times Book Rev

"Those who remember Chappaquiddick can predict Kelly's ultimate fate, but certainly not the horrors she must have suffered strapped to the seat of a car that would become an aqueous death chamber. Immense courage shines through the tangled streams of her thoughts, memories, and hallucinations. As witnesses to her plight, we can only keep vigil as she drifts in and out of consciousness, waiting for the reprieve that surely must be hers. Oates brilliantly redefines the meanings of guilt and innocence, vengeance and reward in this thought-provoking allegory of our life and times." Libr J

Blonde. Ecco Press 2000 738p

ISBN 0-06-019607-6

"In a five-part narrative corresponding to the stages of [Marilyn] Monroe's life, Oates renders the squalid circumstances of Norma Jeane's upbringing: the damage inflicted by a psychotic mother and the absence of an unknown (and perpetually yearned for) father, and the desolation of four years in a orphanage and betrayal in a foster home. She reviews the young Monroe's rocky road to stardom, involving sexual favors to studio chiefs who thought her sluttish, untalented and stupid, while they reaped millions from her movies, she conveys the essence of Monroe's three marriages and . . . establishes Monroe's insatiable need for security and love." Publ Wkly

"Joyce Carol Oates takes the boldest path to comprehending 'the riddle, the curse of Monroe' by proceeding directly and frankly to fiction. Her novel 'Blonde' is fat, messy and fierce. It's part Gothic, part kaleidoscopic novel of ideas, part lurid celebrity potboiler, and it is seldom less than engrossing." N Y Times Book Rev

A Bloodsmoor romance. Dutton 1982 615p o.p.

LC 82-2416

The novel "details the bizarre goings-on in a 19th-century inventor's family. One daughter becomes a medium, another an actress and Mark Twain's mistress, a third runs away on her wedding night. Even Octavia, the perfect wife, is secretly subversive. . . . The narrator misunderstands and misinterprets much that happens; the reader, therefore, enters into collusion with the characters who use the period's conventions to subvert prescribed female roles." Libr J

Broke heart blues. Dutton 1999 369p $24.95

ISBN 0-525-94451-6   LC 98-51570

A novel "about bad-boy John Reddy Heart, who, in the little upstate New York town of Willowsville, was tried for murder and sent to a detention center. The murder, John Reddy's flight from justice, and his dramatic capture sent a tidal wave of publicity across not only the community but also the country. After he did his time, John Reddy came back to Willowsville, and because his family left town, he lived by himself while resuming his high school education. But he is now a legend, and his legend casts a shadow over the town for years to come." Booklist

Oates "dramatizes how wanting and memory compete. It's about how lonely, unhappy people mythologize their adolescence. . . . This is not a bashful or subtle book. It doesn't woo you so much as run you down." N Y Times Book Rev

The collector of hearts; new tales of the grotesque. Dutton 1998 321p

ISBN 0-525-94445-1   LC 98-17508

"A William Abrahams book"

Contents: The sky blue ball; Death mother; The hand-puppet; Schroeder's stepfather; The sepulchre; The hands; Labor Day; The collector of hearts; Demon; Elvis is dead: why are you alive?; Posthumous; The omen; The sons of Angus MacElster; The affliction; Scars; An urban paradox; Unprintable; Intensive; Valentine; Death astride bicycle; The dream-catcher; Fever blisters; The crossing; Shadows of the evening; The temple; The journey

Dear husband,. Ecco 2009 326p $24.99

ISBN 978-0-06-170431-4; 0-06-170431-8

Contents: Panic; Special; Blind man's sighted daughters; Magda Maria; Princeton idyll; Cutty Sark; Landfill; Vigilante; Heart sutra; Dear Joyce Carol,; Suicide by fitness center; Glazers; Mistrial; Dear husband,

"Oates' characters are masterfully rendered, but she is particularly gifted at creating a certain type: The appallingly egocentric, sometimes to the point of (usually) unwitting hostility. . . . Oates' characters are all self-absorbed to some extent. They all regard themselves as more real than their bystanders, with needs that always take precedence. They appear to exist for their own benefit, certainly not the reader's. While it may seem obvi-

Oates, Joyce Carol, 1938-——*Continued*

ous that any worthwhile fiction will feature such characters, some authors are more skilled at delivering them than others. In this regard, Oates is one of the best." Idaho Statesman

Faithless; tales of transgression. Ecco Press 2001 386p

ISBN 0-06-018525-2   LC 00-60007

Contents: Au Sable; Ugly; Lover; Summer sweat; Questions; Physical; Gunlove; Faithless; The scarf; What then, my life?; Secret, silent; A Manhattan romance; Murder-two; The vigil; We were worried about you; The stalker; The vampire; Tusk; The high school sweetheart: a mystery; Deathwatch; In Copland

"As the subtitle suggests, the book's preoccupation is sin, but otherwise the stories are richly various. They range from quiet, intimate tales-such as the chilling opening effort, 'Au Sable,' about a man let in on a suicide he cannot prevent—to the satiric fantasia on TV journalism and police brutality that closes the volume." Publ Wkly

The falls; a novel. Ecco 2004 481p $26.95

ISBN 0-06-072228-2

       * LC 2004-43310

"A man climbs over the railings and plunges into Niagara Falls. A newlywed, he has left behind his wife, Ariah Erskine, in the honeymoon suite the morning after their wedding. 'The Widow Bride of the Falls,' as Ariah comes to be known, begins a restless, seven-day vigil in the mist, waiting for his body to be found. At her side throughout, confirmed bachelor and pillar of the community Dirk Burnaby is unexpectedly transfixed by the strange, otherworldly gaze of this plain, strange woman." Publisher's note

"Set around Niagara, the story reflects all the romance, mystery, and terror of that spectacular waterfall. It's a great confluence of tones-grotesque and domestic, tragic and comic. The currents of various styles and points of view blend together in a way that can't possibly work, but does." Christ Sci Monit

Foxfire; confessions of a girl gang. Dutton 1993 328p

ISBN 0-525-93632-7   LC 92-43858

"The leader of Foxfire, a flamboyant girl gang, is Legs Sadovsky, a tall, angular blond with enough attitude to turn her upstate New York hometown on its ear. It's 1955 and Legs, Lana, Rita, Goldie, and Maddy, the gentle narrator, are almost 16 and most certainly not sweet. These gals live on the wrong side of the tracks; their parents are deceased or alcoholic, their home lives depressing and loveless. They form Foxfire for the same reason kids always form gangs: for mutual support and protection, to demand respect, and acquire power." Booklist

"Legs Sadovsky is a brilliant creation—wholly heroic, wholly convincing, racing for her tragic consummation impelled by a finer sensibility and a more thoughtful daring than is usually granted to the tragic male outlaws we love and need. . . . 'Foxfire' burns brightly; it is completely assured and occasionally exhilarating." N Y Times Book Rev

A garden of earthly delights. Vanguard Press 1967 440p o.p.

The book describes the early life of Clara Walpole, the daughter of a migrant farm worker; her life after she leaves her father; her romance with a rum-runner; and her marriage to a rich man, whom she convinces is the father of her illegitimate baby. The final part of the novel deals with the childhood and adolescence of Swan, the son

"The book has much to say of society's indifference to the plight of the disadvantaged, and of the shallowness of a way of life based entirely on getting and spending." Libr J

The gravedigger's daughter; a novel. Ecco 2007 582p $26.95

ISBN 978-0-06-123682-2; 0-061-23682-9

       LC 2006-48546

"The Schwarts flee Nazi Germany in 1936 and settle in upstate New York, where the only job available to Rebecca's father is gravedigger. For Rebecca, being the gravedigger's daughter is only one stigma she has to bear: her two older brothers create problems, her father's frustration turns into paranoia, her mother slips into isolation, and she has trouble finding friends. After the death of both parents, Rebecca eventually marries and has a son, but her husband is often on the road and can become violent when he returns home. Rebecca disappears with son Zach, changing her name and moving regularly until she meets Chet Gallagher, a failed piano prodigy who takes an interest in her and the gifted Zach." Libr J

"This is neither a depressing story nor an uplifting one. Oates succeeds here, as she often does, in making such judgments feel simpleminded. What it all seems is true and therefore moving and somewhat terrible, but in an exhilarating way. Every aspect of the ungainly plot feels right, including its ungainliness." Washington Post Book World

Haunted; tales of the grotesque. Dutton 1994 310p o.p.   LC 93-25223

"A William Abrahams book"

Contents: Haunted; The doll; The bingo master; The white cat; The model [novella]; Extenuating circumstances; Don't you trust me?; The guilty party; The premonition; Phase change; Poor Bibi; Thanksgiving; Blind; The radio astronomer; Accursed inhabitants of the House of Bly; Martyrdom

"All the pieces here have a redeeming literary bent, although some are transparent in their motives. Undoubtedly a master of this form, Oates plies her craft like a skilled seducer, setting the mood and moving in for the conquest night after night after night." Publ Wkly

Heat, and other stories. Dutton 1991 397p o.p.

       LC 91-8007

"A William Abrahams book"

Contents: House hunting; The knife; The hair; Shopping; The boyfriend; Passion; Morning; Naked; Heat; The buck; Yarrow; Sundays in summer; Leila Lee; The swimmers; Getting to know all about you; Capital punishment; Hostage; Craps; Death valley; White trash; Twins; The crying baby; Why don't you come live with me it's time; Ladies and gentlemen; Family

Oates, Joyce Carol, 1938-—*Continued*

High lonesome; new & selected stories, 1966-2006. Ecco 2006 664p $34.95

ISBN 0-06-050119-7; 978-0-06-050119-8

LC 2005-51147

Contents: Spider Boy; The fish factory; The cousins; Soft-core; The gathering squall; The lost brother; In hot May; High lonesome; *BD*11 1 87; Fat man my love; Objects in mirror are closer than they appear; Upon the sweeping flood; At the seminary; In the region of ice; Where are you going, where have you been?; How I contemplated the world from the Detroit House of Corrections, and began my life over again; Four summers; Small avalanches; Concerning the case of Bobby T.; The tryst; The lady with the pet dog; The dead; Last days; My Warszawa: 1980; Our wall; Raven's wing; Golden gloves; Manslaughter; Nairobi; Heat; The knife; The hair; The swimmers; Will you always love me?; Life after high school; Mark of Satan

This "collection, which includes classic stories like "In the Region of Ice," which won the O. Henry prize in 1967, and the much anthologized "Where Are You Going, Where Have You Been?" as well as 11 new stories, spans Oates's career and gives a remarkably coherent picture of her work." N Y Times Book Rev

I am no one you know; stories. Ecco 2004 290p $24.95

ISBN 0-06-059288-5

LC 2003-61283

Contents: Curly Red; In hiding;I'm not your son, I am no one you know; Abiding and abetting; Fugitive; Me & Wolfie, 1979; The girl with the blackened eye; Cumberland breakdown; Upholstery; Wolf's Head Lake; Happiness; Fire; The instructor; The skull: a love story; The deaths: an elegy; Jorie (& Jamie): a deposition; Mrs. Halifax and Rickie Swann: a ballad; Three girls; The mutants

"Oates is vitally concerned, even obsessed, with the most primal and disturbing encounters between females and males, and her new searing short stories explore the malevolent aspects of human sexuality with unflinching authenticity and a cathartic fascination." Booklist

I lock my door upon myself. Ecco Press 1990 98p

ISBN 0-88001-260-9

* LC 90-31878

"In turn-of-the-century rural America, willful and elusive Calla, muzzled by an enforced marriage, church, and kin she no longer cares about, chooses a life of inertia and indifference until the arrival of roving black water dowser Tyrell Thompson." Libr J

Is this "all a parable of the artist's position as an observer and interpreter of society? Is it an illustration of how a writer constructs a coherent story out of disjointed events? Either way, it provokes thought." Atlantic

Little bird of heaven; a novel. Ecco Press 2009 442p $25.99

ISBN 978-0-06-182983-3; 0-06-182983-8

The narrators of this novel, set in upstate New York, are "an angry young man whose mother is murdered and a shy, introspective young woman whose father is a suspect. But the character who leaps most off the page is the victim, Zoe Kruller. . . . She abandons her son, Aaron, and her husband, Delray. She has an affair with Eddy Diehl, whose daughter Krista finds life in their small town of Sparta almost impossible to bear. And singing with her band, the Black River Breakdown, she wears spangly outfits, enchants the townspeople and belts out the song that gives the novel its title. . . . Krista and Aaron meet as teenagers. He's a gruff, rough, half-Indian guy with tattoos and little use for school. She is a blond waif, trying to tough it out on the basketball court to win the affection of her daddy and the respect of her peers. But it is her longing for Aaron that rules her life, particularly after Zoe Kruller is found murdered. Her death seals their connection forever, even though they rarely speak and, when they are together, the conditions are as far from romantic as you can get. . . . Oates deftly merges the personalities of Zoe, Eddy, Krista and Aaron into what is essentially a mystery." St. Louis Post-Dispatch

Marriages and infidelities; short stories. Vanguard Press 1972 497p o.p.

Contents: The sacred marriage; Puzzle; Love and death; 29 inventions; Problems of adjustment in survivors of natural/unnatural disasters; By the river; Extraordinary popular delusions; Stalking; Scenes of passion and despair; Plot; The children; Happy onion; Normal love; Stray children; Wednesday's child; Loving, losing, loving a man; Did you ever slip on red blood?; The metamorphosis; Where I lived, and what I lived for; The lady with the pet dog; The spiral; The turn of the screw; The dead; Nightmusic

Marya; a life. Dutton 1986 310p o.p.

LC 85-16283

"A William Abrahams book"

In this novel, which begins in "a mining town near the Erie Canal, eight-year-old Marya Knauer's father is bludgeoned to death. Her mother walks away from Marya and her infant brothers. Raised by her uncle's family, and sexually abused by her cousin, Marya develops a shell: she's quick-witted, sarcastic and . . . friendless because she's so hard, so bright. She discovers that her reputation for brilliance serves as 'a sort of glass barrier that would keep other people at a distance.' Driven by work, Marya presses through graduate school, becomes a tenured professor at a college much like Dartmouth, then quits to become a lioness in the New York literary world." Newsweek

"Marya's development and her innermost fears and insecurities are revealed in a very personal, almost autobiographical manner. A major work by an important writer." Libr J

Middle age; a romance. Ecco Press 2001 464p

ISBN 0-06-620946-3

LC 2001-23062

"Adam Berendt, an eccentric sculptor, goes sailing on the Hudson River one Fourth of July. A nearby boat capsizes, and Adam leaps in to save a drowning child. He gets to her in time, but is struck by a heart attack as he holds her afloat, and dies. Adam's death is the engendering mistake, the accidental firecracker that sets off the rest of the book. In 'Middle Age,' the people affected are those left behind: Adam Berendt's neighbors in Salthill-on-Hudson." N Y Times Book Rev

"So often dark and malicious, Oates is oddly lighthearted in this gawky but mordant novel about people caught in that awkward transitional stage between youth and old age." Christ Sci Monit

Missing mom. Ecco 2005 434p $25.95

ISBN 0-06-081621-X

LC 2005-40002

Oates, Joyce Carol, 1938-—*Continued*

"Nicole, 31, is living an extended adolescence, still in rebellion against her parents' suburban middle-class, do-the-right-thing lifestyle. Her father has recently died; her older, domestic diva sister is prone to histrionics. Nicole herself is involved with a married man and does not have a clue how her actions may impact other people. Everything changes in an instant when Nicole's mother, Gwen, dies in a violent assault. After the ensuing investigations and memorials, everyone is surprised when Nicole steps into her mother's shoes and gradually begins to adopt aspects of Gwen's personality. Within this transformative process, hidden details of Gwen's life come to light." Libr J

"Oates's grip on crime, violence and the long-buried is sure, but Missing Mom is actually more disturbing in its relentless, dead-on accretion of small-time, small-town, middle-class details. Oates piles them on with pitiless virtuosity." N Y Times Book Rev

The model

In Oates, J. C. Haunted p99-144

(ed) The Oxford book of American short stories. See The Oxford book of American short stories

Rape; a love story. Carroll & Graf 2004 154p $16

ISBN 0-7867-1294-5

A novel "about the nearly fatal beating and gang rape of Teena MacGuire on the Fourth of July in the small town of Niagara Falls. Teena and her 12-year-old daughter, Bethel, are walking home from a party when the vicious attack takes place, and Bethel only narrowly escapes her mother's terrible fate. Terrorized but valiant, Bethel identifies their assailants and is determined to testify, but the townspeople close ranks behind the indicted brutes, their sons and brothers, and Teena is assaulted all over again in court. But there is one man on the case who possesses a clear and unshakable sense of justice, and his empathic connection with Bethel is at the heart of this lean and potent tale." Booklist

Them; introduction by Greg Johnson; afterword by the author. 2000 Modern Library ed. Modern Lib. 2000 xxiv, 546p $21.95

ISBN 0-679-64025-8   LC 99-54471

A reissue of the title first published 1969 by Vanguard Press

"Violent and explosive in both incident and tone, the work is set in urban Detroit from 1937 to 1967 and chronicles the efforts of the Wendell family to break away from their destructive, crime-ridden background. Critics praised the novel for its detailed social observation and its bitter indictment of American society." Merriam-Webster's Ency of Lit

We were the Mulvaneys. Dutton 1996 454p

ISBN 0-525-94223-8   LC 96-17267

"A William Abrahams book"

An upstate New York "family, loving parents and four children, are destroyed when one daughter is raped by a high-school classmate. Wealthy, churchgoing and optimistic in their hubristic heyday, the Mulvaneys are not prepared for the psychological dysfunction that follows the act of violence." Publ Wkly

"Oates has written an uncharacteristically cathartic book with a provocatively happy ending. . . . Oates elo-

quently employs daily details, cataloguing Corinne's antiques, mapping Patrick's Ithaca jogging route, calculating the number of paint gallons required to spruce up High Point Farm. She is a vivid storyteller, and the occupations, names and places are rich in allusive imagery. . . . Oates is fascinated by the markings of kinship. Particularly impressive is her shaping of siblings' passions, allegiances and resentments." Nation

Where are you going, where have you been?; selected early stories. Ontario Review Press 1993 522p o.p.   LC 92-44899

Contents: Edge of the world; The fine white mist of winter; First views of the enemy; At the seminary; What death with love should have to do; Upon the sweeping flood; In the region of ice; Where are you going, where have you been?; Unmailed, unwritten letters; Accomplished desires; How I contemplated the world from the Detroit House of Correction and began my life over again; Four summers; Love and death; By the river; Did you ever slip on red blood?; The lady with the pet dog; The turn of the screw; The dead; Concerning the case of Bobby T.; In the warehouse; Small avalanches; The widows; The translation; Bloodstains; Daisy; The molesters; Silkie

Where is here?; stories. Ecco Press 1992 193p o.p.   LC 92-3634

Contents: Lethal; Area man found crucified; Imperial presidency; Bare legs; Turquoise; Biopsy; The date; Angry; The ice pick; The mother; Sweet!; Forgive me!; Transfigured night; Actress; The false mirror; From the life of. . .; The heir; "Shot"; Letter, lover; My madman; Cuckold; The escape; Murder; Insomnia; Love, forever; Old dog; The artist; The wig; The maker of parables; Embrace; Beauty salon; Abandoned; Running; Pain; Where is here?

Wild nights!; stories about the last days of Poe, Dickinson, Twain, James, and Hemingway. Ecco 2008 238p $24.95

ISBN 978-0-06-143479-2; 0-06-143479-5

LC 2008-273051

Contents: Poe posthumous; or, The light-house; EDickinsonRepliLuxe; Grandpa Clemens & angelfish, 1906; The master at St. Bartholomew's Hospital, 1914-1916; Papa at Ketchum, 1961

"The classic authors who appear as fictionalized characters in 'Wild Nights!' aren't the ones most of us met in Intro to American Literature. Edgar Allan Poe copulating with a one-eyed amphibian? Mark Twain pursuing pubescent girls? Henry James clubbing a cat to death? Joyce Carol Oates may cause a few elderly professors to keel over, but the rest of us can take perverse delight in her five surreal tales. In each, Oates imagines the final days of a famous author, drawing from biographical fact but freely embroidering with Gothic excess." Buffalo News

Will you always love me? and other stories. Dutton 1996 326p o.p.   LC 94-43865

"A William Abrahams book"

Contents: Act of solitude; You petted me, and I followed you home; Good to know you; The revenge of the foot, 1970; Politics; The missing person; Will you always love me?; Life after high school; The goose-girl; American, abroad; The track; The handclasp; The girl

Oates, Joyce Carol, 1938---_Continued_

who was to die; June birthing; The undesirable table; Is laughter contagious?; The brothers; The lost child; Christmas night 1962; The passion of Rydcie Mather; The vision; Mark of Satan

"Joyce Carol Oates's readers have come to expect from her a sensationalistic terrain of accident, suicide, rape, murder and madness, all of which are well represented in this collection, which includes none of the small, too-precious moments that can vitiate the short story." N Y Times Book Rev

O'Brian, Patrick

Blue at the mizzen. Norton 1999 261p il $24

ISBN 0-393-04844-6   LC 99-42043

"With Bonaparte finally through troubling the nations of Europe, Jack Aubrey and Stephen Maturin . . . are on a hydrographic and diplomatic journey to Chile. There Aubrey's crew aboard H.M.S. Surprise lends its support to the Chilean independence movement and the forces of Bernardo O'Higgins." New Yorker

"There is nothing in this century that rivals Patrick O'Brian's achievement in his chosen genre. His novels embrace with loving clarity the full richness of the 18th-century world." N Y Times Book Rev

The commodore. Norton 1995 281p $22.50

ISBN 0-393-03760-6

* LC 95-2653

First published 1994 in the United Kingdom

Another "novel in O'Brian's series following Captain (now Commodore) Jack Aubrey and his surgeon friend, Stephen Maturin, through the naval side of the Napoleonic Wars. Although O'Brian is ingenious at devising new adventures, it is the richness of his characters which justifies his readers' continuing enthusiasm. The most arresting moments in this installment come not in battle but in dramas of parenthood and marriage far from the sea. O'Brian acknowledges Jane Austen as one of his inspirations, and she need not be ashamed of the affiliation." New Yorker

The golden ocean; a novel. Day, J. 1957 c1956 316p il o.p.

First published 1956 in the United Kingdom

"This novel is based on the exploits of Commodore George Anson, who set out in 1740 with five men-of-war to circle the globe and returned four years later with one ship and a small but very wealthy crew. The expedition is seen through the eyes of Peter Palafox, a young midshipman who blossoms into an able-bodied seaman. . . . As always, the author's erudition and humor are on display. . . . The attention to period speech and detail is uncompromising, and while the cascades of nautical lore can be dizzying, both aficionados and newcomers will be swept up by the richness of Mr. O'Brian's prodigious imagination." N Y Times Book Rev

The hundred days. Norton 1998 280p $24

ISBN 0-393-04674-5   LC 98-35866

"The title refers to Napoleon's escape from Elba and brief return to power. Capt. Jack Aubrey must stop a Moorish galley, loaded with gold for Napoleon's mercenaries, from making its delivery. . . . We're quickly reacquainted with the two heroes: handsome sea dog Jack Aubrey, by now a national hero, and Dr. Stephen

Maturin, Basque-Irish ship's doctor, naturalist, English spy and hopelessly incompetent seaman." Publ Wkly

"Battles there are aplenty, and O'Brian matches Forester in the excitement, detail and bloody realism of his reconstructions. But these naval tales are blended into a larger panorama of Georgian society and politics, science, medicine, botany and the whole conspectus of contemporary Enlightenment knowledge about the natural world." N Y Times Book Rev

The unknown shore. Norton 1995 313p $23

ISBN 0-393-03859-9   LC 95-32887

First published 1959 in the United Kingdom

"Based on British Commodore Anson's 1740 circumnavigation of the world . . . this is the story of HMS _Wager,_ a ship separated from Anson's squadron while sailing around Cape Horn. The _Wager_ is shipwrecked off Patagonia, and the largest part of the narrative details the hardships of the diminishing band of survivors on that inhospitable shore. . . . Though this novel isn't quite as polished or stylish as the author's later work, it's a most honorable ancestor." Publ Wkly

The wine-dark sea. Norton 1993 261p $22.50

ISBN 0-393-03558-1

* LC 93-1521

One of a series of novels set during the Napoleonic Wars and featuring Jack Aubrey, a "Royal Navy captain, and his friend Stephen Maturin, who sails with him as ship's surgeon and undercover intelligence agent. . . . On this occasion, duty takes them to the South Pacific. Here, Aubrey is to harry enemy shipping and—the true purpose of the voyage—to land Maturin in Peru to foment the independence movement against Spain." Times Lit Suppl

"The naval actions are bang-on and bang-up—fast, furious and bloody—and the Andean milieu is as vivid as the shipboard scenes." Publ Wkly

The yellow admiral. Norton 1996 261p $24

ISBN 0-393-04044-5   LC 96-24149

"As their careers have advanced and their children have grown, Captain Jack Aubrey and Stephen Maturin have battered Napoleon's ships and thwarted his spies, but here, at last, the Emperor is Elba-bound, and our heroes are left high and dry. Aubrey, ashore at half pay and with scant hope of promotion, prays that peace may not last long—a sentiment doubtless shared by O'Brian's readers. Still, Elba is not St. Helena, so war will surely return, if only for a short finale." New Yorker

O'Brien, Dan, 1947-

The contract surgeon; a novel. Lyons Press 1999 316p $24.95

ISBN 1-55821-932-3   LC 99-35243

This novel is "based on the true story of the unusual friendship between Crazy Horse and Dr. Valentine McGillicuddy, a civilian surgeon contracted to serve with the army during the Indian wars on the Great Plains. McGillicuddy relates the tale as an old man. . . . He faces his greatest moral test when Crazy Horse is bayoneted in the back by a soldier, and McGillicuddy is pressured by the army to keep the famous warrior alive, because his death would spur on the Indians to renewed battle. . . . This powerful story is a thinking man's western, in which action is secondary to O'Brien's nuanced exploration of character and the tragic dimensions of a morally fraught conflict." Publ Wkly

O'Brien, Edna

The country girls

In O'Brien, E. The country girls trilogy and epilogue p3-175

The country girls trilogy and epilogue. Farrar, Straus & Giroux 1986 531p o.p.

                 * LC 85-32113

Omnibus edition of three titles originally published separately in 1960, 1962 and 1964 respectively, with an epilogue added by the author

Contents: The country girls (c1960); The lonely girl (c1962) {variant title: Girl with the green eyes (1964)}; Girls in their married bliss (c1964; first United States edition 1968)

The country girls portrays two friends, Kate and Baba, growing up in Ireland. They are sent to a convent school they despise and they contrive to get expelled and move to Dublin. In The lonely girl, Kate, now 21, becomes involved first with an older married man, then with a filmmaker. Eugene encourages and pampers her, but she is unresponsive. The relationship disintegrates and she moves to London. In Girls in their married bliss, Kate has married Eugene and has a son, but the marriage is destroyed when Eugene's indifference pushes Kate into a love affair. Meanwhile, Baba settles into marriage and financial security with an architect, and pulls through the crisis of a pregnancy brought on by a one-night stand. The Epilogue contains Baba's reflections, twenty years later

"O'Brien's particular appeal is that she can be tender yet merciless, romantic yet grittily sexual. She resides admirably where quality and popular writing intersect." Booklist

A fanatic heart; selected stories of Edna O'Brien. Farrar, Straus & Giroux 1984 461p o.p.

              LC 84-13762

Contents: The Connor girls; My mother's mother; Tough men; The doll; The bachelor; Savages; Courtship; Ghosts; Sister Imelda; The love object; The mouth of the cave; Irish revel; The rug; Paradise; A scandalous woman; Over; The creature; The house of my dreams; Number 10; Baby blue; The small-town lovers; Christmas roses; Ways; A rose in the heart of New York; Mrs. Reinhardt; Violets; The call; The plan; The return

"Each story is superbly written and, despite the overall seriousness, graced by humor." Publ Wkly

Girls in their married bliss

In O'Brien, E. The country girls trilogy and epilogue p381-508

House of splendid isolation. Farrar, Straus & Giroux 1994 232p $21

  ISBN 0-374-17309-5   LC 93-42602

"The story centers on a tormented encounter between young IRA fugitive/killer McGreevy and his hostage—rich, reclusive, middle-aged Josie O'Meara. Both have been widowed by the protracted 'troubles.' Josie, a former barmaid, who once did a stint as a domestic in Brooklyn, reminisces before and during her 'captivity' on her advantageous but flawed marriage." Publ Wkly

The author "manages to sum up a century of Irish sorrow in this taut, lyrical novel, filled with scenes so vividly rendered they seem captured in a flash of lightning."

Not the least of O'Brien's accomplishments is her ability to present both sides of the Irish problem in all their complexity without settling heavily on either side." Libr J

In the forest. Houghton Mifflin 2002 262p $24

  ISBN 0-618-19730-3   LC 2001-51883

From an early age, Michen O'Kane "displays spontaneous unsociability, for which he is punished with unremitting cruelty, first by his wife-beating father, then by the villagers of Cloosh, his small Irish village, and then by the Irish juvenile detention system, where he is sodomized and psychologically tortured. O'Kane comes back to Cloosh a ticking bomb, hearing voices in his head. After he sets up a camp in the woods, he sets his sights on a relative stranger in the village, a free spirit named Eily Ryan who, with her son, Maddie, is living a modern, single mother's lifestyle obscurely disapproved of by the conservative villagers. One morning O'Kane kidnaps her and the boy. She's forced to drive O'Kane to his woods, passing through the village in full view of several frightened bystanders, who do nothing to help her. After murdering his two victims, O'Kane kidnaps a priest and repeats the act." Publ Wkly

A novel about "how a community can be collectively paralyzed by fear. The result is a brilliant illumination of human nature." Booklist

Lantern slides; stories. Farrar, Straus & Giroux 1990 223p

  ISBN 0-374-18332-5   LC 90-33594

Contents: "Oft in the stilly night"; Brother; The widow; Epitaph; What a sky; Storm; Another time; A demon; Dramas; Long distance; A little holiday; Lantern slides

"O'Brien's short stories expand on the anguish and brutality endemic to modern Irish lives, and her characters have more than their own secret problems to brood and moon about. . . . O'Brien mines her home territory to splendid effect with her glinting looks at what the Irish have made of their struggle and what Ireland has made of their unhappy lives." Booklist

The lonely girl

In O'Brien, E. The country girls trilogy and epilogue p179-377

Time and tide. Farrar, Straus & Giroux 1992 325p o.p.

                 * LC 92-3962

"Nell is a devoted young wife, but she is also a rebel against tyranny, be it from husband or parents. Inevitably, her two sons, Paddy and Tristan, become pawns in the lengthy . . . battle that her separation from her husband involves. Nell adores her sons, yet at the same time she is . . . searching for love and adventure. Her restlessness, her dabbling with drugs and bohemia, take her to the brink and back, but not before she has lost house and home." Publisher's note

This novel is O'Brien's "harshest yet most beautiful work. She has a touchy, rich theme: the sexuality of the bond between mothers and sons. . . . O'Brien brings together the earthy and the delicately poetic: she has the soul of Molly Bloom and the skills of Virginia Woolf." Newsweek

Wild Decembers. Houghton Mifflin 2000 259p $24

  ISBN 0-618-04567-8   LC 99-56110

O'Brien, Edna—*Continued*

First published 1999 in the United Kingdom

This novel is set in "the tiny western Irish village of Cloontha. . . . Michael Bugler has arrived fresh from a sheep farm in Australia to claim the land left to him by a deceased uncle, and the newcomer's presence stirs up the villagers. Especially agitated is Joseph Brennan, whose ancestral farm borders Bugler's property. . . . Relations between the two men skid into a series of affronts, real or perceived, while Breege, Brennan's younger sister, looks on with mounting dread." Time

"The novel is a dirge that keens and lulls by turns. The entrancing rhythms and refrains, the density and chant-like, drumming fragmentation work on the reader like magic. . . . O'Brien combines this lyricism with a masterly storytelling instinct, so that [the novel] reads at once like an intricate poem and a taut, suspenseful page-turner." Commonweal

O'Brien, Flann, 1911-1966

At swim-two-birds
  In O'Brien, F. The complete novels

The complete novels; with an introduction by Keith Donohue. Everyman's Library 2007 xxxiii, 787p $25
  ISBN 978-0-307-26749-8; 0-307-26749-0
                                              *

Contents: At swim-two-birds (1939); The third policeman (1967); The poor mouth (first published in Gaelic as An béal bocht in 1941, and in English translation by Patrick C. Power in 1973); The hard life (1961); The Dalkey archive (1964)

The narrator of At swim-two-birds is "writing a novel about another man writing a novel, in a Celtic knot of interlocking stories. . . . The narrator of The Third Policeman, who has forgotten his name, is a student of philosophy who has committed murder and wanders into a surreal hell where he encounters such oddities as the ghost of his victim, three policeman who experiment with space and time, and his own soul. . . . The Poor Mouth, a bleakly hilarious portrait of peasants in a village dominated by pigs, potatoes, and endless rain, is a giddy parody aimed at those who would romanticize Gaelic culture. A naïve young orphan narrates the deadpan farce The Hard Life, and The Dalkey Archive is an outrageous satiric fantasy featuring a mad scientist who uses relativity to age his whiskey, a policeman who believes men can turn into bicycles, and an elderly, bartending James Joyce." Publisher's note

"Truth is an odd number, even numerals are the province of the devil class, and there is safety in a triad. These are some of the essential wisdoms in the world of Flann O'Brien, the Irish writer who is often said to form, along with Samuel Beckett and James Joyce, 'the holy trinity of modern Irish literature.' . . . There may be safety in a triad, but to lump O'Brien with Joyce and Beckett is to miss the playfulness, black humor, and deranged whimsy that characterize his style." Slate

The Dalkey archive
  In O'Brien, F. The complete novels

The hard life
  In O'Brien, F. The complete novels

The poor mouth
  In O'Brien, F. The complete novels

The third policeman
  In O'Brien, F. The complete novels

O'Brien, Tim, 1946-

Going after Cacciato; a novel. Lawrence, S. 1978 338p o.p. pa $14.95
  ISBN 0-440-02948-1; 0-7679-0442-7 (pa)
                                    * LC 77-11723

"Paul Berlin's squad is sent to retrieve Cacciato, a young deserter from the Vietnam War. Fantasy colors the progress of the squad as a dream of peace and the possibility of forsaking war follow them through many adventures. The horror and destruction of war is vividly conveyed and the language is rough, as would be expected. Cacciato becomes a kind of symbol for resisting bureaucratic militarism and an enviable model for Berlin himself." Shapiro. Fic for Youth. 3d edition

In the Lake of the Woods. Houghton Mifflin 1994 306p
  ISBN 0-395-48889-3   LC 94-5395
The protagonist of this novel "is a politician whose promising career has been destroyed by the revelation of his misconduct in Vietnam. His wife, well aware that Vietnam torments his dreams, had known nothing of the [My Lai] murder and massacre underlying the nightmares. The husband is equally ignorant of her opinions on several important matters. When the two retreat to a cabin in the wilds of Minnesota to recover from the shock of a disastrous election, their partnership explodes." Atl Mon

"What O'Brien really offers is a portrait of one man and woman at the most critical juncture of their relationship. It's a dark portrait, taking issue with a stock notion of commercial fiction: that after suffering comes redemption. Maybe not. Maybe there's only oblivion. A beautifully written, haunting novel that evokes lives in deep crisis." Booklist

The things they carried; a work of fiction. Houghton Mifflin 1990 273p o.p.
                                    * LC 89-39871
Contents: The things they carried; Love; Spin; On the rainy river; Enemies; Friends; How to tell a true war story; The dentist; Sweetheart of the Song Tra Bong; Stockings; Church; The man I killed; Ambush; Style; Speaking of courage; Notes; In the field; Good form; Field trip; The ghost soldiers; Night life; The lives of the dead

This is a collection of stories about American soldiers in Vietnam. . . . All of the stories "deal with a single platoon, one of whose members is a character named Tim O'Brien." N Y Times Book Rev

"This book may be self-conscious . . . but through its determination to treat these men with dignity and decency it proves immensely affecting." Newsweek

O'Connell, Carol

Crime school. Putnam 2002 352p
  ISBN 0-399-14928-7   LC 2002-22860
Detective Kathy Mallory, "of the Special Crimes Unit, comes face to face with her past when she and her partner are called to a crime scene in which a call girl has

O'Connell, Carol—*Continued*

been ritualistically murdered. The call girl, Sparrow, offered Mallory protection when she was a child but later betrayed her. Before Mallory has time to call up her knowledge of Sparrow's past in finding the killer, she and her partner are thrown into a morass of spree killings on the streets of New York. O'Connell's crime-scene investigations techniques ring true, her plotting is breathtaking, and her psychology acute. Searing suspense." Booklist

Judas child. Putnam 1998 340p $24.95

ISBN 0-399-14380-7   LC 97-46504

"When two remarkable fifth-grade girls—Gwen Hubble, the beautiful daughter of the lieutenant governor, and Sadie Green, an imaginative and plucky child obsessed with horror comics and movies—are kidnapped from the St. Ursula's Academy, two adults afflicted by their own tragedies are drawn into the investigation. Forensic psychologist Ali Cray draws stares both for her slit skirts and for a disfiguring facial scar, the result of a secret childhood trauma. Policeman Rouge Kendall is haunted by the memory of his twin sister's murder 15 years earlier. The killer was supposedly caught, but similarities between the old murder and the current case make Cray begin to doubt." Publ Wkly

"O'Connell thoughtfully tackles material that in other hands would be merely sensational. Dark in tone, gripping suspense, and tempered with the hope of redemption, this is highly recommended." Libr J

Killing critics. Putnam 1996 308p o.p.

LC 95-43894

"NYPD detective Kathleen Mallory revisits a 12-year-old double murder case first investigated by her beloved adoptive father. . . . The murder of a second-rate performance artist in mid-performance has many associations to the earlier, grisly and still unsolved homicides, which also touched the art world." Publ Wkly

"As mesmerizing as the murder case is, it's heartless, soulless Mallory herself—computer genius, street fighter, provocative waif, peerless investigator, manipulative beauty—who's absolutely the star of this brilliant thriller." Booklist

Mallory's oracle. Putnam 1994 286p o.p.

LC 94-2234

"The investigation of a series of murders of wealthy, elderly women from the Gramercy Park area intensifies when Louis Markowitz, the head of the NYPD Special Crimes Section, is found dead with the third victim. Kathleen Mallory, his adopted daughter and a policewoman assigned to office duty, is beautiful, intelligent, fiercely independent, and obsessed with finding the killer. Mallory's computer skills supplement the street-survival savvy she learned before her adoption and the 'wall' of clues and case details left by Markowitz." Libr J

The author's "writing is stunning in its luminosity, originality, simplicity, and power. Her plot is ingenious, inventive, and enigmatic, and her characters sparkle with originality and charm." Booklist

The man who cast two shadows. Putnam 1995 278p o.p.   LC 94-43797

This mystery features New York cop Kathleen Mallory. "Taken off suspension to cover the murder of a woman at first identified as Mallory herself, she pits

her uncanny intelligence and formidable computer skills against a compulsive and evasive adversary. Moments of wry humor invade the author's incisive prose, tempering an admirable female protagonist sure to gather a following." Libr J

Stone angel. Putnam 1997 341p o.p.

LC 96-44504

Computer whiz and New York cop Kathleen Mallory "leaves the Big Apple to return to her enigmatic Southern beginnings. Seventeen years earlier, in the hamlet of Dayborn, La., the murder of a young woman, Cass Shelley, set off events that transformed her six-year-old daughter, Kathy, into the thief who, four years later, would be rescued from the New York streets by the cop who became her adoptive father. Returning to Dayborn like an avenging angel, Mallory is soon arrested for the murder of a local evangelist near her old house." Publ Wkly

How the author "manages to imbue what's basically a who-was-that-masked-man tall tale of revenge with Molierian elegance is as great a mystery as who killed Mallory's mother nearly two decades ago." New Yorker

O'Connell, Jack, 1959-

The resurrectionist; a novel. Algonquin Books Of Chapel Hill 2008 304p $24.95

ISBN 978-1-56512-576-6   LC 2007-49423

"In the first storyline, Sweeney appears at the Peck Clinic, a monstrosity of a family-run hospital for coma patients, hoping that they'll take better care of his comatose young boy, Danny. . . . While Sweeney just seems to want the best for Danny, there are demons chasing him, and apparently a whole batch of new ones waiting at the Clinic, which seems to have plans for Danny that don't involve making him better. In the second storyline, O'Connell inserts installments from the epic, tragic story of a band of traveling circus freaks in Old Bohemia (an invented Balkan/Eastern Europe country from earlier O'Connell novels); this turns out to actually be stories from the comic Limbo, a hugely popular series Danny had loved and which Sweeney still reads to him as often as possible. The story of Limbo seems shockingly gothic for a hit comic (with requisite film, TV, and merchandise spin-offs, of course), but given that the supposedly real storyline quickly involves biker gangs, a nurse with witchlike powers, and a salamander who just might be magic, the line does seem to be a thin one." PopMatters

O'Connor, Edwin, 1918-1968

All in the family. Little, Brown 1966 434p o.p.

"An Atlantic Monthly Press book"

"The Kinsellas are a wealthy, Irish Massachusetts family, dominated—at first—by the father, who insists that his sons enter politics to clean up a thoroughly corrupt political situation. One son is elected Governor, but political power subtly affects him, ethical problems evoke sharp differences and cause the eventual breakup of the family." Libr J

"The plot though rather melodramatic is outweighed by the felicitous childhood recollections of Jack, the authenticity of dialog, and the skillful establishment of political atmosphere." Booklist

O'Connor, Edwin, 1918-1968—*Continued*

The last hurrah. Little, Brown 1956 427p o.p.

＊

"Typical of the old style political boss Frank Skeffington had kept his power as mayor of a large eastern U.S. city for almost 40 years. During the course of his last campaign . . . he is seen not only as the corrupt grafter ruthless with his enemies but also as a man of infinite charm who truly loved his city." Booklist

"A revealing study of a benevolent dictator at work. More, it is a genuine portrait of all the ebullience and rascality, loyalty and duplicity that enliven the typical Irish-American community." Christ Sci Monit

O'Connor, Flannery

Collected works. Library of Am. 1988 1281p $35

ISBN 0-940450-37-2

＊ LC 87-37829

Contents: Wise blood; A good man is hard to find; The violent bear it away; Everything that rises must converge; Stories and occasional prose; Letters

The complete stories. Farrar, Straus & Giroux 1971 555p pa $17 hardcover o.p.

ISBN 0-374-51536-0

Contents: The geranium; The barber; Wildcat; The crop; The turkey; The train; The peeler; The heart of the park; A stroke of good fortune; Enoch and the gorilla; A good man is hard to find; A late encounter with the enemy; The life you save may be your own; The river; A circle in the fire; The displaced person; A Temple of the Holy Ghost; The artificial nigger; Good country people; You can't be any poorer than dead; Greenleaf; A view of the woods; The enduring chill; The comforts of home; Everything that rises must converge; The Partridge festival; The lame shall enter first; Why do the heathen rage?; Revelation; Parker's back; Judgement Day

This collection is "arranged in chronological order from the story she wrote for her master's thesis at the University of Iowa to 'Judgement Day.' . . . The stories here include the original openings and other chapters of her two novels 'Wise Blood' and 'The Violent Bear It Away.'" N Y Times Book Rev

Everything that rises must converge. Farrar, Straus & Giroux 1965 xxxiv, 269p o.p.

Contents: Everything that rises must converge; Greenleaf; A view of the woods; The enduring chill; The comforts of home; The lame shall enter first; Revelation; Parker's back; Judgement Day

A good man is hard to find and other stories. Harcourt Brace & Co. 1955 251p o.p.

Contents: A good man is hard to find; The river; The life you save may be your own; A stroke of good fortune; A temple of the Holy Ghost; The artificial nigger; A circle in the fire; A late encounter with the enemy; Good country people; The displaced person

The violent bear it away. Farrar, Straus & Cudahy 1960 243p o.p.

"A macabre tale set in the backwoods of Georgia and presenting the fanatical mission of a boy intent on baptizing a still younger boy." Oxford Companion to Am Lit. 6th edition

Wise blood. Harcourt Brace & Co. 1952 232p o.p.

This novel "centers on Hazel Motes, a discharged serviceman who abandons his fundamentalist faith to become a preacher of anti-religion in a Tennessee city, establishing the 'Church Without Christ.' Motes is a ludicrous and tragic hero who meets a collection of equally grotesque characters. One of his young followers, Enoch Emery, worships a museum mummy. Hoover Shoats is a competing evangelist who creates the 'Holy Church of Christ Without Christ.' Asa Hawks is an itinerant preacher who pretends to have blinded himself to show his faith in redemption." Merriam-Webster's Ency of Lit

O'Connor, Frank, 1903-1966

Collected stories; introduction by Richard Ellmann. Knopf 1981 701p hardcover o.p. paperback available $20

ISBN 0-394-51602-8

LC 81-1253

Contents: Guests of the nation; The late Henry Conran; The bridal night; The Grand Vizier's daughters; Song without words; The shepherds; The long road to Ummera; The cheapjack; The Luceys; Uprooted; The mad Lomasneys; News for the church; Judas; The babes in the wood; The frying-pan; The miracle; Don Juan's temptation; First confession; The man of the house; The drunkard; Christmas morning; My first Protestant; Legal aid; The masculine principle; The sentry; The lady of the sagas; Darcy in the Land of Youth; My Oedipus complex; The pretender; Freedom; Peasants; The majesty of the law; Eternal triangle; Masculine protest; The sorcerer's apprentice; The little mother; A sense of responsibility; Counsel for Oedipus; The old faith; Unapproved route; The study of history; Expectation of life; The ugly duckling; Fish for Friday; A set of variations on a borrowed theme; The American wife; The impossible marriage; The cheat; The weeping children; An out-and-out free gift; The Corkerys; A story by Maupassant; A great man; Androcles and the army; Public opinion; Achilles' heel; The wreath; The teacher's Mass; The martyr; Requiem; An act of charity; The Mass island; There is a lone house; The story teller; Last post; The cornet player who betrayed Ireland; Ghosts

The author "grew up with 'the troubles,' but the Ireland he evokes in these 72 stories . . . is the provincial life of his Cork boyhood." Libr J

O'Connor, Mary Flannery *See* O'Connor, Flannery

O'Connor, Robert, 1959-

Buffalo soldiers. Knopf 1993 323p o.p.

LC 92-54278

"The hero of this novel is Ray Elwood, a soldier stationed at a United States Army base in present-day Germany. Elwood is a battalion clerk, a wily factotum to a buffoonish colonel whose vanity and ineptitude provide Elwood with the opportunity—and the cover—to pursue his real vocations, which are to deal drugs to his fellow G.I.'s, to get high and to survive." N Y Times Book Rev

"O'Connor writes bitter, funny prose and creates bureaucratic snafus of the first order. Alternating scenes of Army idiocy and clinically realistic drug addiction are far more compelling than O'Connor's attempt to attribute his

O'Connor, Robert, 1959-—*Continued*
hero's bracing nihilism to his tragic past. Toward its end
the book falters, as Elwood flirts with maudlin self-pity.
But O'Connor misfires now and then only because he
aims high." Publ Wkly

O'Dell, Tawni

Back roads. Viking 1999 338p $24.95
ISBN 0-670-88760-9   LC 99-20649
In this novel, set in a small Pennsylvania coal town,
19-year-old Harley Altmyer is saddled with the "custody
of three younger siblings—a responsibility inherited
when his mother killed his abusive father and went to
prison for life. While he works two dead-end jobs to
support his sisters, Harley lusts after a married neighbor,
Callie Mercer. When Callie indicates that she's attracted
to him, too, the resulting sexual fireworks set off a series
of events with tragic consequences." Libr J
"Harley's first-person account of the deterioration of
his family and his own slow-motion meltdown is harrowing. O'Dell, a native of western Pennsylvania, renders
finely detailed characters and settings in a desperate and
failed mining town. This is a riveting first novel of violence, incest, murder, and madness." Booklist

Coal Run. Viking 2004 354p $24.95
ISBN 0-670-89995-X   LC 2003-62645
"After more than 15 years living in Florida, Ivan
Zoschenko returns to his home in western Pennsylvania,
his arrival coinciding with the release from prison of his
highschool alter ego, Reese Raynor. Ivan is not thrilled
to return home: he had gladly left behind memories of
the explosion at the mine that killed his father and nearly
100 other miners when he was six, and he doesn't look
forward to hearing the locals' reaction to the bizarre injury that brought his career as a pro football player to an
abrupt end. But here he is, sleeping on his sister's couch
and working temporarily as deputy for the sheriff's office. The novel takes place over the course of only one
week, yet O'Dell manages to give the story an epic dimension through masterful intercutting of past and present. Reese's pending release drives the plot, and as the
day nears, Ivan confronts his own demons and secrets
with true-to-life reluctance." Booklist

Sister mine; a novel. Shaye Areheart Books
2007 416p $23
ISBN 978-0-307-35126-5; 0-307-35126-2
                              LC 2006-15355
"At 40, Shae-Lynn Penrose has overcome a mostly
motherless, abusive childhood and a teenage pregnancy
to finish college, work for the D.C. Capitol Police, raise
her son alone, and return to her coal-mining hometown
of Jolly Mount, Pennsylvania. Here she runs a one-
vehicle cab company; her father died in a mine; her best
friend, E. J., was one of the Jolly Mount 5, whose survival after a mine explosion made headlines; and her
son, Clay, is a deputy for Sheriff Ivan Zoschenko . . . .
Then Shannon, the younger sister Shae-Lynn thought
long dead, shows up and reveals an unorthodox means of
making money that's causing a ruckus. Dealing with a
burgeoning love affair and revelation of parentage, plus
the surviving miners' intent to sue the coal company,
O'Dell also examines such issues as abuse, betrayal,
abandonment, perseverance, and reconciliation, with love
at the heart of it all, in crisp, insightful prose that sweeps
the reader along. A knockout." Booklist

Odom, Mel, 1950-

The destruction of the books. Tor 2004 381p
$25.95
ISBN 0-7653-0723-5   LC 2003-27368
"Almost 100 years after the events of The Rover
(2002), Edgewick Lamplighter is grandmagister at the
Vault of All Known Knowledge, a secret repository of
books rescued from destruction by the dreaded goblinkin.
This time the protagonist is Jugh, another halfling, whom
Wick rescued from goblin slavers and made his apprentice. Feeling an outsider on the island, Jugh ships out as
a crew member on one of the ships that service and help
protect the island. But when he discovers that a book is
aboard a goblin ship, he manages with great difficulty
and danger to retrieve it and take it back to the island.
The book turns out to be designed to open a path for
dark forces to invade the island and destroy the library."
Booklist
"The narrative moves along at a snappy pace, with
much good humor, zest and color." Publ Wkly

O'Donnell, Lillian

Blue death. Putnam 1998 215p $22.95
ISBN 0-399-14367-X   LC 97-47589
"The proud mother of an adopted toddler as well as
the head of her own homicide division, NYPD Lieutenant Norah Mulcahaney learns how difficult it is to balance home life and work. . . . Just when her live-in sitter suddenly quits, she's confronted with a case that has
left some NYPD higher-ups a little nervous. It seems
there's a rash of suicides among police officers.
. . . A clever, low-key puzzler, this is a nice break from
the usual violent, high-octane police procedural."
Booklist

Pushover. Putnam 1992 239p o.p.
                              LC 91-30205
Norah Mulcahaney "is called in to investigate the murder of an aging screen star, only to find, in addition, that
the woman's grandson is missing. While sorting through
suspects and evidence for a kidnapping charge, Norah is
also asked to assist the New York City transit authority
police in finding the 'perp' who pushes young women to
their deaths from subway platforms. O'Donnell's snappy
style sets the pace here, as Mulcahaney races to solve the
mysteries before another death occurs." Booklist

The raggedy man. Putnam 1995 232p o.p.
                              LC 95-3925
"When NYPD sergeant Ray Dixon nudges PI Gwenn
Ramadge into hiring a suspended rookie detective for
help in an investigation, the Brooklyn investigator . . .
is drawn into a bitter—but for readers, delicious—brew
of murder and police corruption." Publ Wkly

O'Donovan, Michael *See* O'Connor, Frank, 1903-
1966

Ōe, Kenzaburō

An echo of heaven; translated by Margaret
Mitsutani. Kodansha Am. 1996 204p $25
ISBN 4-7700-1986-6
                                        *

Ōe, Kenzaburō—*Continued*

Original Japanese edition, 1989

"K., the author's double, has been asked to write the story of an acquaintance of his, Marie Kuraki, a woman of great charm and intellect whose life is torn apart after her two disabled sons throw themselves into the sea. . . . Marie goes on a quest for meaning, searching for an alternative to her grim reality. She joins a radical cult that eventually moves to California. When this group dissolves, she hesitantly takes up the offer to become a symbol of fortitude and saintliness in a small Mexican farming village." Publ Wkly

"This profound novel is . . . as concerned with common humanity as with art and ideas. Indeed, it constitutes an argument that art is greatest when it is concerned with the essentially human, with death, suffering, fellowship, and sex—each of which figures prominently in it." Booklist

Nip the buds, shoot the kids; translated and introduced by Paul St. John Mackintosh and Maki Sugiyama. Boyars, M. 1995 189p $22.95

ISBN 0-7145-2997-4   LC 94-40897

Original Japanese edition, 1958

"In the waning days of WW II, a group of Japanese reformschool boys are evacuated to a remote village in a densely wooded valley. The villagers treat the teenagers horribly, making them bury a mountain of animal corpses, locking them into a shed for the night and feeding them raw potatoes. The unnamed narrator—one of the group's leaders—discovers that a plague is ravaging the valley. When a couple of people are infected by the disease, the villagers panic. Believing the boys to be infected, the villagers remove themselves to the other side of the valley and block the only road out of town. At first, the boys can think only of escape, but then . . . they start to make the village their own. . . . But each pleasant turn, every apparently liberating step away from unremitting brutality, serves to make the characters' inevitable future suffering even more painful." Publ Wkly

The pinch runner memorandum; translated by Michiko N. Wilson and Michael K. Wilson. Sharpe, M.E. 1994 251p $59.95

ISBN 1-56324-183-8   LC 93-26114

"An East Gate book"

Original Japanese edition, 1976

"Based on the metaphor of a sandlot baseball pinch runner, the novel centers around the exchange of identities of a father and a son who venture out together to confront the kingpin of the political underworld. Ōe unfolds the adventure through the complex narrative structure of the protagonist's words, which sometimes resonate and sometimes clash with the narrative voice of his ghost-writer, who initiates the tale. These two layers of the text are further enriched by a third voice, that of the idiot son Mori who speaks to his 'switch*ed*-over' father through the conduit of their clasped hands. Simultaneously, the reader is treated to a smorgasbord of satire, black humor, *manga*-like slapstick, Mikhail Bakhtin's grotesque realism, and various socio-political phenomena such as marginalization, factionalism, and terrorism." Introduction

A quiet life; translated from the Japanese by Kunioki Yanagishita with William Wetherall. Grove Press 1996 240p o.p.

* LC 96-25795

Original Japanese edition, 1990

"A famous Japanese writer whose first name begins with K takes off with his wife for a year to become writer in residence at 'one of the several campuses of the University of Carolina,' leaving their almost equally famous son, an idiot savant who is a remarkable composer, in the care of their daughter, Ma-chan. It is Ma-chan, a conscientious young woman acutely aware of the responsibility that devolves on her during her parents' absence, who tells the story related in Kenzaburo Oe's novel 'A Quiet Life,' and the translators, Kunioki Yanagishita and William Wetherall, admirably succeed in conveying a certian archness of style that infuses the work with Ma-chan's personality." N Y Times Book Rev

Somersault; a novel; translated from the Japanese by Philip Gabriel. Grove Press 2003 570p $29.95

ISBN 0-8021-1738-4   LC 2002-29746

Original Japanese edition, 1999

This novel "takes place against the background of a religious cult's terrorist plan (even more drastic than Aum Shinrikyo's 1995 gas attack on the Tokyo subway), which is thwarted when the cult's leaders appear on television to renounce their creed-the 'somersault' of the title. Now, ten years later, the cult's charismatic guru is planning to reestablish his church. . . . Through the believers' motivations for joining the cult, Oe explores the struggle of contemporary Japanese to situate themselves between a traditional culture and the bullet-train pace of the boom years." New Yorker

O'Faoláin, Seán, 1900-1991

The collected stories of Seán O'Faoláin. Little, Brown 1983 1304p il o.p.

* LC 83-205346

"An Atlantic Monthly Press book"

Contents: Midsummer night madness and other stories: Midsummer night madness; Lilliput; Fugue; The small lady; The bombshop; The death of Stevey Long; The patriot

A purse of coppers: A broken world; The old master; Sinners; Admiring the scenery; Egotists; Kitty the wren; My son Austin; A born genius; Sullivan's trousers; A meeting; Discord; The confessional; Mother Matilda's book; There's a birdie in the cage

Teresa and other stories: Teresa; The man who invented sin; Unholy living and half dying; The silence of the valley; Innocence; The trout; Shades of the prison house; The end of a good man; Passion; A letter; Vive la France; The woman who married Clark Gable; Lady Lucifer

From the finest stories of Sean O'Faolain: Childybawn; Lovers of the lake; The fur coat; Up the bare stairs; One true friend; Persecution mania; The Judas touch; The end of the record; Lord and master; An enduring friendship

I remember! I remember!: I remember! I remember!; The sugawn chain; A shadow, silent as a cloud; A touch of autumn in the air; The younger generation; Love's young dream; Two of a kind; Angels and ministers of grace; One night in Turin; Miracles don't happen twice;

O'Faoláin, Seán, 1900-1991—*Continued*

No country for old men

The heat of the sun: In the bosom of the country; Dividends; The heat of the sun; The human thing; One man, one boat, one girl; Charlie's Greek; Billy Billee; Before the daystar; £1000 for Rosebud; A sweet colleen

The talking trees and other stories: The planets of the years; A dead cert; Hymeneal; The talking trees; The time of their lives; Feed my lambs; Our fearful innocence; Brainsy; Thieves; Of sanctity and whiskey; The kitchen

Foreign affairs and other stories: The faithless wife; Something, everything, anything, nothing; An inside outside complex; Murder at Cobbler's Hulk; Foreign affairs; Falling rocks, narrowing road, cul-de-sac stop; How to write a short story; Liberty

Unpublished stories: Marmalade; From Huesca with love and kisses; The wings of the dove—a modern sequel; The unlit lamp; One fair daughter and no more; A present from Clonmacnois

Foreign affairs and other stories
In O'Faoláin, S. The collected stories of Seán O'Faoláin p1061-1226

The heat of the sun
In O'Faoláin, S. The collected stories of Seán O'Faoláin p700-886

I remember! I remember!
In O'Faoláin, S. The collected stories of Seán O'Faoláin p544-699

Midsummer night madness and other stories
In O'Faoláin, S. The collected stories of Seán O'Faoláin p9-162

A purse of coppers
In O'Faoláin, S. The collected stories of Seán O'Faoláin p163-319

The talking trees and other stories
In O'Faoláin, S. The collected stories of Seán O'Faoláin p889-1060

Teresa and other stories
In O'Faoláin, S. The collected stories of Seán O'Faoláin p320-445

O'Farrell, Maggie, 1972-

The vanishing act of Esme Lennox. Harcourt 2007 c2006 245p $23
ISBN 978-0-15-101411-8; 0-15-101411-6
LC 2007-6079
First published 2006 in the United Kingdom
"Iris Lockhart leads a solitary if spicy life, managing her clothing shop in Edinburgh and dallying with her married lover. But when Iris learns that she has a great-aunt Esme waiting to be released from Cauldstone Hospital, where she has been locked away for 60 years, it is as if a bomb has dropped. The hospital is closing, and someone must collect Esme, who upon inspection seems frail, quiet, and a little quirky but hardly mentally ill. As far as Iris knew, her grandmother Kitty had no siblings; Kitty is still alive but suffering from Alzheimer's. The secret of Esme's existence is only the first of many family secrets revealed in a tale told through shifting viewpoints, among them Kitty's fragmented recollections." Libr J

"At the heart of this fantastic new novel is a mystery you want to solve until you start to suspect the truth, and then you read on in a panic, horrified that you may be right." Washington Post Book World

Ogawa, Yoko, 1962-

The housekeeper and the professor; translated by Stephen Snyder. Picador 2009 180p pa $14
ISBN 978-0-312-42780-1 (pa); 0-312-42780-8 (pa)
LC 2006-41568
"This is the intimate story of a young housekeeper and her ten-year-old son who come to care for an aging math professor with a peculiar problem: he lives with only eighty minutes of short-term memory." Asian Pages

"A mysterious, suspenseful, and radiant fable. . . . The smart and resourceful housekeeper, the single mother of a baseball-crazy 10-year-old boy the Professor adores, falls under the spell of the beautiful mathematical phenomena the Professor elucidates, as will the reader, and the three create an indivisible formula for love." Booklist

Ogilvie, Elisabeth, 1917-2006

When the music stopped. McGraw-Hill 1989 326p
ISBN 0-07-047792-2
LC 88-28636
"Author Eden Winters, finds herself in the midst of local scandal and terrifying deaths. Set in a small town along the Maine coast, the plot turns on the return to town of two aging sisters who had left on the wings of scandal decades earlier. While there are plenty of people with reason to despise the returning ladies—who audaciously take up residence in the area's most elegant house—there are just as many people, such as Eden and her family, who are delighted to see them. When the women are found brutally murdered, suspects abound, including a stranger who alternately captures Eden's suspicions and heart. Well-crafted fiction that holds the reader's attention and avoids contrivance." Booklist

O'Hagan, Andrew, 1968-

Be near me. Harcourt, Inc. 2007 c2006 305p $24
ISBN 978-0-15-101303-6; 0-15-101303-9
LC 2006-30402
First published 2006 in the United Kingdom
This novel "features Father David Anderton, a proud descendant of Lancashire's Catholic martyrs, who undergoes his own ordeal when he transfers to the deprived parish of Dalgarnock. Though born in Edinburgh, he is perceived as an Englishman among Scots, an Oxford-educated wine sipper amid the ale-drinking unemployed, and a Catholic priest in an angrily Protestant town. . . . Aware of all this yet politically naïve, Father David alienates locals with his insistence on high culture and tentative support for the Iraq war. When he falls into an uneasy friendship with two teenage hoodlums—whose bracing portrayal make them recognizable to any teacher—the plot takes a predictable turn toward priests behaving badly and the ensuing small-town witch trial." Libr J

O'Hagan, Andrew, 1968—*Continued*

"A distinctive voice resonates clearly through the first-person narrative, clerically portentous at times, a shade trite or unabashedly sentimental at others, yet in all its registers convincing. What it tells us is a story compounded from passion and resurrection as opposed to professional failure or spiritual collapse." Times Lit Suppl

O'Hara, John, 1905-1970

Appointment in Samarra. Modern Lib. 1994 c1934 xxi, 269p $14.95

ISBN 0-679-60110-4

* LC 94-4340

A reissue of the title first published 1934 by Harcourt Brace & Co.

"Julian English is not a bad man, only a very weak one. He is popular with the country-club set, has the right connections with the local bootlegger, and has an attractive wife. He succeeds in offending the man who holds the mortgage on his car dealership and the bootlegger whose girl he pays too much attention to when he has again had too much to drink. When his wife announces her intention to divorce him, Julian feels that there is nothing left for him in life." Shapiro. Fic for Youth. 3d edition

"The novel is written episodically, but achieves integration by its hard-boiled theme of the destructive effects of fast living." Haydn. Thesaurus of Book Dig

Butterfield 8; a novel. Harcourt Brace & Co. 1935 310p o.p.

*

"A novelization of the sensational lives of the nightclub set involved in an actual New York murder case. Young Gloria Wandrous is found drowned on a beach near New York. The problem is to find the murderer and his motive. The investigation, described in machine-gun reportage, reveals that Gloria had had a good education, but owing to an adolescent sexual experience had become a 'party girl' in the unsavory life of New York speakeasies and luxurious Long Island clubs. Under the sleekness of Park Avenue sophistication, O'Hara reveals New York's hard soullessness." Haydn. Thesaurus of Book Dig

Collected stories of John O'Hara; selected and with an introduction by Frank MacShane. Random House 1984 414p o.p. LC 84-42661

Contents: The doctor's son; It must have been spring; Over the river and through the woods; Price's always open; Are we leaving tomorrow; Pal Joey; The gentleman in the tan suit; Good-by, Herman; Olive; Do you like it here; Now we know; Free; Too young; Bread alone; Graven image; Common-sense should tell you; Drawing room B; The pretty daughters; The moccasins; Imagine kissing Pete; The girl from California; In the silence; Exactly eight thousand dollars exactly; Winter dance; The flatted saxophone; The friends of Miss Julia; How can I tell you?; Ninety minutes away; Our friend the sea; Can I stay here?; The hardware man; The pig; Zero; Fatimas and kisses; Natica Jackson; We'll have fun

From the terrace; a novel. Random House 1958 897p o.p.

"Alfred Eaton, the younger son of Samuel Eaton, steel magnate of Port Johnson, Pennsylvania, had a tolerably happy childhood until the death of his older brother William, when Alfred was twelve. After the death of his favorite son, Samuel Eaton retreated into an obsessive grief. Alfred's mother, neglected, turned elsewhere for affection and Alfred was left to grow up as best as he could, closer to the servants than to his parents. The rest of his life though rewarded with business success and filled with a variety of amorous adventures, was basically barren and loveless." Booklist

The novel describes "the ways of Social Register families on the Pennsylvania-New York axis—especially in sexual encounters and marriage—in what may be described as morbidly fascinating detail. Indeed the novel's central achievement is surely the impression it conveys of the morality—or amorality, of immorality—of this class." N Y Her Trib Books

Ten North Frederick. Random House 1955 408p o.p.

A character study of one of the 'first citizens' of a Pennsylvania town, Gibbsville. "In the first quarter of a crowded, eventful narrative, Joe Chapin is seen only through the eyes of some of those at [his] funeral. Then [O'Hara] . . . switches back to Joe's parents, who established the home at Ten North Frederick Street, where Joe lived all his life. He tells Joe's story from the beginning, and the stories of those whose lives have touched Joe's at some significant point." N Y Times Book Rev

Okuizumi, Hikaru, 1956-

The stones cry out; translated from the Japanese by James Westerhoven. Harcourt Brace & Co. 1999 138p $20

ISBN 0-15-100365-3 LC 98-14434

Original Japanese edition, 1993

This "novel features Tsuyoshi Manase, the owner of a successful bookstore who is also a husband, the father of two sons, and a self-taught geologist. . . . Troubled by memories of World War II, Manase must deal with an alcoholic wife, an eventual divorce, and the untimely death of his two children." Libr J

"A monstrous tale, *The Stones Cry Out* is written with a lyrical beauty that only underscores the horror Manase's life becomes. As Okuizumi elegantly plays Manase's nightmare out, Manase is compelled to reenact the real atrocities he has tried so desperately to forget." Booklist

Ólafsson, Bragi *See* Bragi Ólafsson, 1962-

Ólafur Jóhann Ólafsson

The journey home; [by] Olaf Olafsson. Pantheon Bks. 2000 296p $24

ISBN 0-375-42061-4

* LC 00-39186

Original Icelandic edition, 1999

"Disa leads a serene life in England as the co-owner of a small hotel, where she shares a passion for cooking and nature with her partner, Anthony. When Disa is diagnosed with a fatal illness, she travels back to Iceland,

Ólafur Jóhann Ólafsson—*Continued*

revealing an unsettled past. The daughter of a doctor, she left her small village to be educated in Reykjavik. Disa soon alienated her mother by choosing a career as a chef and falling in love with Jacob, a German Jew. Disa and Jacob share a passionate, bohemian life in the English countryside until he returns to Germany to help his parents escape the Holocaust. Waiting for Jacob, Disa works in the house of an influential family and is swept into painful and startling events." Libr J

"This is not a morose novel, but one lifted by love, friendship and cooking, an art Disa has spent much of her life perfecting at an English country inn. Hers is a hard, unflinching life, and one skillfully revealed in a steady stream of memories that accompanies Disa on a last migration back to her Arctic nest." Time

Oliver, Chad, 1928-1993

From other shores; an omnibus. NESFA Press 2007 403p $26

ISBN 978-1-886778-66-3; 1-886778-66-5

Contents: Shadows in thee sun (1954); Unearthly neighbors (1960); The shores of another sea (1971)

In Shadows in the sun, Paul Ellery discovers a colony of aliens while making an anthropological study of a small Texas town. Subsequently, he must decide whether he wants to be educated to take his place in the alien society. In Unearthly neighbors, investigators from a future Earth undertake an anthropological study of planet Sirius Nine's humanoid civilization. In The shores of another sea, an anthropologist makes first contact with aliens while conducting a study of baboons in Kenya.

Oliver was "a pioneer in the application of competent anthropological thought to sf themes. . . . He is a careful author whose speculative thought deserves to be more widely known and appreciated." Clute and Nicholls. Ency of Sci Fi

Shadows in the sun
In Oliver, C. From other shores

The shores of another sea
In Oliver, C. From other shores

Unearthly neighbors
In Oliver, C. From other shores

Oliver, Symmes Chadwick *See* Oliver, Chad, 1928-1993

Olmstead, Robert

Coal black horse. Algonquin Books of Chapel Hill 2007 218p $23.95

ISBN 978-1-56512-521-6; 1-56512-521-5

* LC 2006-42914

A "Civil War tale that tracks a boy's search for his father on the battlefield at Gettysburg. At 14, Robey Childs is on the cusp of manhood when he sets off from the family farm at his mother's behest to find his soldier father and bring him home. A sympathetic farmer loans Robey an uncommonly beautiful and sturdy black horse. On the road, Robey passes carts carrying the maimed and dead, and bands of Native Americans and runaway slaves. A chain of horrific trials begins for Robey when a man dressed as a woman shoots him and steals the horse. He's taken prisoner as a suspected spy, witnesses a girl's rape and is caught up in a carnage-drenched raid. However, he survives the attack, is reunited with the stolen horse and sets out again, days later finding his father on the battlefield, mortally wounded." Publ Wkly

This novel "is mostly memorable as an exquisite corpse, a fictive vision of war so vivid and gruesome that it remains in the memory—grotesque, stiff and gape-mouthed—after every other detail of Olmstead's tale fades away." Paste

Olsen, Tillie

Tell me a riddle; a collection. Lippincott 1961 156p o.p.

Contents: I stand here ironing; Hey sailor, what ship; O yes; Tell me a riddle

"In writing which is individualized but not eccentric, experimental but not obscure, Mrs. Olsen has created imagined experience which has the authenticity of autobiography or memoir. With a faultless accuracy, her stories treat the very young, the mature, the dying—poor people without the means to buy or invent lies about their situations—and yet her writing never succumbs to mere naturalism." Commonweal

Olsson, Linda

Astrid & Veronika. Penguin Books 2007 259p pa $14

ISBN 978-0-14-303807-8; 0-14-303807-9

LC 2006-50660

First published 2005 in New Zealand with title: Let me sing you gentle songs

"Veronika, a 30-year-old Swedish writer, rents a home in a remote village to finish work on her second novel. Her only neighbor for miles is Astrid, a reclusive octogenarian who has earned a reputation (perhaps undeserved) as the village witch. Veronika and Astrid gradually become friends, taking long walks and sipping wine made from the wild strawberries in Astrid's garden. Each shares painful secrets along the way." Booklist

"Unlike the voice of the novel's omniscient narrator, [Veronika and Astrid's] are natural and vivid, utterly convincing. And unlike the nove's flatly depicted present, the physical world of the past, in which their stories take place, generously opens to admit us." N Y Times Book Rev

O'Nan, Stewart, 1961-

The good wife. Farrar, Straus and Giroux 2005 312p $24

ISBN 0-374-28139-4

LC 2004-53247

"One night Patty Dickerson wakes up to a phone call from her husband, Tommy, who has been arrested for an unspecified crime. He is soon charged with murder, cannot afford a decent lawyer and is sentenced to 25 years to life. Patty, 27 and pregnant, understands she will now make her living, raise her child and spend her nights alone." N Y Times Book Rev

"From the trial, through the various appeals process, the visits to the prison, the waiting, the hoping, the struggle to make ends meet, and the gradual resilience and

O'Nan, Stewart, 1961—*Continued*

self-sufficiency, O'Nan, with seldom a false beat, perceptively and compassionately depicts the bureaucratic insanities of the penal system and the hardships, fears, and frustrations of those left behind." Booklist

Last night at the Lobster; a novel. Viking 2007 146p $19.95

ISBN 978-0-670-01827-7; 0-670-01827-9

LC 2006-102825

"It's December 20, closing day for the New Britain, CT, Red Lobster restaurant, abandoned by headquarters owing to mediocre sales. Manager Manny De Leo had to let most of his employees go—only five can transfer with him to the Olive Garden—and is counting on the good will of a few to run the place. . . . Manny will miss it; it's his shop, and he takes pride in it. He'll also miss Jacquie, the waitress with whom he had a brief, intense affair. As snow falls, Manny handles the regulars, Christmas parties, the mall crowd, and his small crew with aplomb, constantly aware of his losses." Libr J

"O'Nan's empathy for his characters is one of his great gifts as a novelist, and it is an impressive achievement that Manny's misplaced affection for Red Lobster is not risible, but tragic." N Y Times Book Rev

The names of the dead. Doubleday 1996 399p o.p.

* LC 95-36745

"As an army medic in Vietnam in 1969, Larry Markham had the job of keeping the wounded alive. But first aid never seemed to help, and the men died anyway. Now, 13 years later, Larry has a dead-end job delivering snack cakes in Ithaca, New York. His marriage is on the rocks, his father is showing signs of Alzheimer's disease, and an ex-CIA assassin from his veterans' support group is stalking him. Feelings of stress and helplessness bring on flashbacks of the war." Libr J

"O'Nan's language is powerfully restrained; his word pictures of the war and its effect on the men who fought there are fresh and vivid. He rightfully refuses to pander to our desire for easy answers and happy endings." Booklist

The night country; or, The darkness on the edge of town. Farrar, Straus & Giroux 2003 229p $23

ISBN 0-374-22215-0   LC 2002-44765

"The aftermath of a Halloween tragedy haunts a New England town on the one-year anniversary of a typical teen joyride that ended with a car wrapped around a tree. Toe, Marco, and Danielle were instantly killed. Kyle lives on, sort of; a severe brain injury obliterates the rebel in him, the accident leaving him with the mind of a child. Tim, 'the lucky one' in the backseat, his arms around Danielle, survived but now has a death wish. Officer Brooks, the first on the scene, was terribly alterered by the event, and his life in shambles." Booklist

"O'Nan is wonderful at describing teenage ritual, the simultaneous desire for the comforting familiarity of friends and the lust for speed and novelty and excitement that will lift teenagers out of the confines of their suburban town, the routine of school, out of their own restless bodies." N Y Times Book Rev

Snow angels. Doubleday 1994 305p

ISBN 0-385-47574-8   LC 94-12037

This novel "follows the disintegration of two households in a small western Pennsylvania town in the dead of winter. One is Arthur Parkinson's. Arthur, small yet wise for his 15 years, is coping with his parents' divorce and the loss of their home. While he picks his way through the emotional land mine his parents have created, Arthur falls in love, learns to drive, and, strangely enough, gets drawn into the wreck of his former babysitter's life. As a child, Arthur adored Annie for her long red hair and joshing indulgences. Now he can't believe the sickening irony of having to be the one person out of dozens of searchers who finds the body of her drowned three-year-old daughter. Arthur's narrative alternates with the sad tale of Annie's busted marriage, the mental breakdown of her estranged husband, and her [murder]." Booklist

The author "weaves together these seemingly disparate small-town tragedies—one narrated in the first person, the other in the third—with consummate skill, seamlessly shifting the focus among characters he wishes to make the reader care about." Libr J

Songs for the missing. Viking 2008 287p $25.95

ISBN 978-0-670-02032-4; 0-670-02032-X

LC 2008-22274

"The novel starts with the bright and self-confident Kim Larsen savoring the landmark summer after her highschool graduation, as she hangs out with friends and works at a gas station before going away to college. Then Kim suddenly vanishes, entering a void somewhere between driving from her home to her job. And 'Songs for the Missing' becomes a chorus of varied viewpoints — with alternating chapters written from the perspective of Kim's anxious father, Ed, a real-estate agent, and her mother, Fran, a hospital clerk, as well as Kim's boyfriend, her younger sister Lindsay and her two closest female pals." Seattle Times

The author's "greatest literary talent lies with his characters. It's as if he has lived each of the lives he creates, and nothing is too mundane nor too overblown. . . . O'Nan has honed his ability to tap into the most basic components of small town life and ordinary people. His latest is both an intriguing page-turner and a sometimes agonizing look at human emotion in the face of inexplicable loss." Rocky Mountain News

Ondaatje, Michael, 1943-

Anil's ghost. Knopf 2000 307p $25

ISBN 0-375-41053-8   LC 99-59208

In this novel "Anil Tissera, 33, a forensic anthropologist, returns to the Sri Lanka she left at age 18 as one member of a U.N. team allowed into the country by the government to investigate alleged human rights violations, i.e. death squad murders. Her assigned partner . . . is a Sri Lankan archaeologist named Sarath Diyasena, 49, who is, by virtue of his position, a government employee. Anil immediately wonders whether her co-worker will be helping her or reporting on her. . . . Before long, they turn up a suspiciously fresh skeleton in a government-protected archaeological site." Time

"Anil comes with Western-bred investigative passion: the certainty that facts are there to be unearthed and that truth is to be constructed out of them. Sarath, a polymorphous spirit and the book's most memorable figure, cautions that the real truth of his country is ambiguous and

Ondaatje, Michael, 1943-—_Continued_
unobtainable. . . . It is Ondaatje's extraordinary achievement to use magic in order to make the blood of his own country real." N Y Times Book Rev

The English patient; a novel. Knopf 1992 307p $25

ISBN 0-679-41678-1
* LC 92-53089

"Four diverse people who suffer from the physical and emotional damages of WW II meet in a deserted Tuscan villa. The badly burned English patient will die without revealing his identity, his young nurse will begin to recover her will to live, the maimed thief will watch over her and the Anglo-Indian bomb-defusing specialist will learn to exist in the atomic age." Publ Wkly

"This is a poetic and solemn narrative of the horrible process of war, the discipline, displacement, loss, and sudden, desperate love. Ondaatje seems to whisper, even confess each scene to his readers, handling them gingerly like shards of shattered glass." Booklist

In the skin of a lion; a novel. Knopf 1987 243p o.p.
LC 87-45340

The main character in this novel "is Patrick Lewis, who grows up in Canadian logging country and in 1923, at the age of twenty-one, arrives in Toronto 'as if it were land after years at sea'. He becomes one of an army of searchers for Ambrose Small, millionaire personification of 'bare-knuckle capitalism', who has vanished. Lewis's success in the search brings him into contact with Small's lover Clara Dickens and then into a deepening relationship with Clara's intimate friend Alice Gull, an actress and political activist." Times Lit Suppl

Ondaatje is a "beautiful writer. What he writes about most beautifully is _work_. Mr. Ondaatje is passionate about process, the way work, particularly construction of all kinds, is done and how it feels to do it. This is, of course, a rarity in fiction at any time, and one can only be grateful for a man who is not focused on the classroom, the bedroom and the bar." N Y Times Book Rev

O'Neal, Kathleen M.
See also Gear, Kathleen O'Neal

O'Neill, Anthony

The lamplighter; a novel. Scribner 2003 308p 308

ISBN 0-7432-4349-8
LC 2002-36453

"It is 1886. Although the new electric lamp has conquered Paris and London, it has yet to make its way to Edinburgh, whose medieval streets and modern boulevards are still illuminated at dusk by the 'leeries,' the traditional lamplighters. But someone—or something—is also coming out in the evenings, leaving a trail of horribly mutilated bodies: those of a professor, a lighthouse keeper, and a shady businessman. Assigned to the case is acting Chief Inspector Carus Groves." Libr J

O'Neill, Egan, 1921-
For works written by this author under other names see Shannon, Dell, 1921-

O'Neill, Jamie

At swim, two boys; a novel. Scribner 2002 572p $27

ISBN 0-7432-2294-6
LC 2001-57694

First published 2001 in the United Kingdom

This is the "story of two boys—scholarly, reticent James and cocksure, poverty-stricken Doyle—and their tragic involvement in the 1916 Easter Uprising. . . . James and Doyle strike up a friendship at Forty Foot, a local beach, and make plans to swim to Muglins Rock far out in Dublin Bay on Easter Sunday a year hence. As the two draw closer and eventually fall in love, they must contend with disapproval of their relationship from peers and from the church and the jealousy of upper-class Anthony MacMurrough, who has served time in jail for sexual misconduct." Booklist

"In this novel the cause of Ireland and the cause of gay people fuse with a complete lack of apology or embarrassment. . . . O'Neill is not, however, being patly outrageous; the closeness and exactness of his vision prove that." N Y Times Book Rev

Kilbrack; or, Who is Nancy Valentine? Scribner 2004 305p pa $14

ISBN 0-7432-5595-X (pa)
LC 2003-65911

"O'Leary Montague, a facially scarred amnesiac as the result of a car accident, travels to the Irish village of Kilbrack because it is the setting of his favorite novel, Ill Fares the Land, by Nancy Valentine. The small-town residents prove to be deeply eccentric, with habits ranging from button hoarding to cocaine addiction, so O'Leary, a veritable bundle of nervous tics and obsessions, fits right in. His desire to write a biography of the revered Nancy Valentine leads him to a hapless meeting with reclusive Valentine Brack, a still raffish if aging member of the landed gentry who harbors a terrible secret. O'Neill sends up the rural Irish to a fare-thee-well, devoting paragraph after paragraph to the hidebound villagers' convoluted conversations, so cryptic in tone that they inevitably lead to absurdly comic misunderstandings." Booklist

O'Neill, Joseph, 1964-

Netherland. Pantheon Books 2008 256p $23.95

ISBN 978-0-307-37704-3; 0-307-37704-0
LC 2007033711

This novel is "narrated by a Dutch financier whose privileged Manhattan existence is upended by the events of Sept. 11, 2001. When his wife departs for London with their small son, he stays behind, finding camaraderie in the unexpectedly buoyant world of immigrant cricket players, most of them West Indians and South Asians, including an entrepreneur with Gatsby-size aspirations." N Y Times Book Rev

O'Nolan, Brian _See_ O'Brien, Flann, 1911-1966

Orczy, Emmuska, Baroness, 1865-1947

Adventures of the Scarlet Pimpernel. Doubleday, Doran 1929 302p o.p.

Further "exploits of the Scarlet Pimpernel, Sir Percy Blakeney, the daring Englishman, who, with his loyal friends and helpers, rescues aristocrats from the guillotine during the French Revolution. Each chapter records a separate adventure." Cleveland Public Libr

Orczy, Emmuska, Baroness, 1865-1947—*Continued*

The elusive Pimpernel. Dodd, Mead 1908 344p
o.p.

Another chapter in the adventurous life of The Scarlet
Pimpernel, that thorn in the side of the terrorists of the
French Revolution, and a delivering angel to condemned
aristocrats. In an increasingly tense situation, this languid, Englishman deliberately enters the French trap in
an attempt to rescue his wife, the beautiful Marguerite
Blakeney

The Scarlet Pimpernel; [by] Baroness Orczy.
Alfred A. Knopf 1999 299p (Everyman's library
children's classics) $14.95
ISBN 0-375-40658-1

* LC 2001-272396

First published 1905 by Putnam

"An adventure story of the French Revolution. The apparently foppish young Englishman, Sir Percy Blakeney,
is found to be the daring Scarlet Pimpernel, rescuer of
distressed aristocrats." Reader's Ency. 4th edition

Orwell, George, 1903-1950

Animal farm; with an introduction by Julian Symons. Knopf 1993 xl, 113p $16
ISBN 0-679-42039-8

* LC 92-54299

"Everyman's library"

First published 1945 in the United Kingdom; first
United States edition 1946

"The animals on Farmer Jones's farm revolt in a move
led by the pigs, and drive out the humans. The pigs become the leaders, in spite of the fact that their government was meant to be 'classless.' The other animals soon
find that they are suffering varying degrees of slavery. A
totalitarian state slowly evolves in which 'all animals are
equal but some animals are more equal than others.' This
is a biting satire aimed at communism." Shapiro. Fic for
Youth. 3d edition

Nineteen eighty-four; with an introduction by
Julian Symonds. Knopf 1992 xlii, 325p $19
ISBN 0-679-41739-7

* LC 92-52906

First published 1949 by Harcourt, Brace

Ä dictatorship called Big Brother rules the people in a
collectivist society where Winston Smith works in the
Ministry of Truth. The Thought Police persuade the people that ignorance is strength and war is peace. Winston
becomes involved in a forbidden love affair and joins the
underground to resist this mind control." Shapiro. Fic for
Youth. 3d edition

O'Shaughnessy, Mary

*For works written by this author in collabora-
tion with Pamela O'Shaughnessy see
O'Shaughnessy, Perri*

O'Shaughnessy, Pamela

*For works written by this author in collabora-
tion with Mary O'Shaughnessy see O'Shaughnessy,
Perri*

O'Shaughnessy, Perri

Breach of promise. Delacorte Press 1998 435p
$23.95
ISBN 0-385-31872-3   LC 98-5519

Lake Tahoe's "Nina Reilly, struggling in her legal
practice, accepts the impossible-to-win case of Lindy
Markov, a woman who wants just desserts after the
wealthy man she lived with for 20 years, never legally
married, left her for a younger woman." Libr J

"O'Shaughnessy offers up a gripping courtroom drama,
throws in pithy ethical and moral dilemmas and some
surprising plot twists, and adds plenty of heart-stopping
action." Booklist

Invasion of privacy. Delacorte Press 1996 419p
o.p.   LC 96-1251

"Tahoe-area attorney Nina Reilly was shot at the end
of Motion to Suppress. As the increasingly alarming
facts of her latest case pile up, she is haunted by memories of that wounding. No less haunting are certain details of her personal past, which Nina's new client, Terry
London, an energetically spiteful documentary filmmaker,
seems to know as much about as Nina does. Out of that
past and into Tahoe comes Kurt Scott, the father of
Nina's son, Bob. Almost immediately, Terry is murdered,
Kurt is accused of the crime and Nina must assemble his
murder defense. . . . Fans of the genre will luxuriate in
this deft, multileveled tale of legal and criminal treachery, whose pleasures include elegant courtroom sleight-
of-hand and the eerily wintry backdrop of Lake Tahoe."
Publ Wkly

Motion to suppress. Delacorte Press 1995 420p
o.p.   LC 95-5615

"When attorney Nina Reilly agrees to represent Tahoe
barmaid Misty Patterson in a divorce suit, she gets more
than she bargained for. Within days, Misty is accused of
the murder of her husband, and Nina, still bruised from
the collapse of her own marriage, undertakes the defense." Libr J

"Although the characterizations are a bit uncertain (the
luscious Misty is unbelievably prim and proper), the plot
is a real puzzler, with twists diabolical enough to take to
court." N Y Times Book Rev

Obstruction of justice. Delacorte Press 1997
392p o.p.   LC 96-48585

In this thriller, attorney Nina Reilly is "a witness to
the death by lightning of a construction mogul in the Tahoe
Mountains. When his father returns from a business trip,
he wants Nina to have the body exhumed and autopsied
for signs of murder, setting off a family furor. Suddenly,
the grave is empty, the bodies of both father and son
turn up in a smoldering mountain cabin, and the grandson is charged with murder. Nina is then asked to clear
the grandson amid an increasingly complex series of interrelationships involving the D.A., his dead wife, a not-
so-grieving widow, and, of course, the gardener. . . . A
compelling story with some great courtroom drama and
a likable heroine." Libr J

Unlucky in law. Delacorte Press 2004 376p $25
ISBN 0-385-33646-2   LC 2004-47840

In this legal thriller California lawyer Nina Reilly has
"moved herself and 14-year-old son Bob from their usual
Tahoe turf to the Monterey Peninsula to spend time with
her lover, PI Paul van Wagoner. Paul has asked Nina to

O'Shaughnessy, Perri—*Continued*

marry him, offering a big diamond to seal the deal. Nina puts him off while she prepares for a big trial: she's newly employed at Pohlmann, Cunningham, and Turk, and her first case, working with Klaus Pohlmann, is defending 28-year-old Stefan Wyatt, charged with murder and grave robbing. O'Shaughnessy has been accused of sloppy plotting in the past, but not so here." Publ Wkly

Writ of execution. Delacorte Press 2001 403p
ISBN 0-385-33483-4   LC 2001-28468

"Jessie Potter, trying to dodge an alleged stalker, slides up to a dollar slot machine and tries to look like a regular gambler. Unlike most gamblers, however, she hits the jackpot, winning a prize of more then $7 million. Down-on-his-luck Silicon techie Kenny Leung witnesses the jackpot and is dazzled by the woman and her money. To keep her win discreet, Jessie enlists Kenny's help and hires popular Lake Tahoe attorney Nina Reilly to protect her interests." Booklist

"Readers will relish the myriad plot details and the procedural drama, and enjoy the cast of offbeat characters." Publ Wkly

Ossana, Diana

(jt. auth) McMurtry, L. Zeke and Ned

Oster, Christian

My big apartment; translated and with an introduction by Jordan Stump. University of Neb. Press 2002 155p pa $20
ISBN 0-8032-3567-4; 0-8032-8612-0 (pa)
                                        LC 2002-17977

Original French edition published, 1999

"In a nutshell, [this is] the story of a man who loses his keys and finds a life, sort of, maybe. That's all that really happens—well, that and a few laps in a pool and a driving lesson and an episiotomy. The specifics don't much matter anyway. This is simply the course the man, a Parisian called Gavarine, follows, and he has no more control over his fate than the leaf in the stream has over the eddy." N Y Times Book Rev

Othmer, James P.

The futurist; a novel. Doubleday 2006 257p $23.95
ISBN 0-385-51722-X   LC 2005-51871

As this "novel opens, famed pop pundit J.P. Yates, having emptied his hotel minibar, experiences an epiphany: he's a fake. After years of peddling insights to any group willing to pay him well—one week he assures a Bible college's graduates that God has a future, the next he assures adult video distributors that porn has a future—he stuns attendees at a Futureworld conference in South Africa by declaring himself 'founding father of the Coalition of the Clueless.' Ironically, his career takes off: he's more in demand than ever and is even recruited to travel the world asking why everyone hates the U.S." Publ Wkly

The author's "voice echoes other, well-established ones: Max Barry's for outrageously deft business satire, Christopher Buckley's for geopolitical comedy of errors, Bruce Wagner's for free-floating malice. That he can even dimly be equated with any of them makes 'The Futurist' an impressive foray into satirical fiction." N Y Times (Late N Y Ed)

Otsuka, Julie, 1962-

When the emperor was divine; a novel. Knopf 2002 141p hardcover o.p. pa $10.95
ISBN 0-375-41429-0; 0-385-72181-1 (pa)
                                        LC 2002-20814

This novel traces the "fortunes of a Japanese-American family from the spring of 1942—when President Roosevelt's evacuation order came through—to the spring of 1946. In four brief chapters, we follow a mother, daughter and son from their comfortable home in Berkeley through their five months in a temporary 'assembly center' (a converted stable at a racetrack south of San Francisco) to an internment camp in Topaz, Utah, where they spend three years." N Y Times Book Rev

Otsuka "demonstrates a breathtaking restraint and delicacy throughout this supple and devastating first novel." Booklist

Otto, Whitney

How to make an American quilt. Villard Bks. 1991 179p $20
ISBN 0-679-40070-2   LC 90-48233

This novel "set in the small central California town of Grasse, chronicles the local quilting circle and its eight members. The stories of these women's lives are framed by a ninth one, that of the narrator, Finn Bennett-Dodd (granddaughter of one of the members), an about-to-be-married eavesdropper who is collecting advice. As she prepares for her own adult life, Finn has a wide array of stories and lessons to sort through." N Y Times Book Rev

"Otto has tremendous insight and compassion, understanding the rareness of a perfect marriage, the anger of thwarted lives, and the vagaries of love and motherhood." Booklist

Øvstedal, Barbara, 1925-

For works written by this author under other names see Laker, Rosalind, 1925-

Owen, John Pickard *See* Butler, Samuel, 1835-1902

The **Oxford** book of American detective stories; edited by Tony Hillerman, Rosemary Herbert. Oxford Univ. Press 1996 686p $35; pa $18.95
ISBN 0-19-508581-7; 0-19-511792-1 (pa)
                                        LC 95-4504

This collection includes stories by B. Pronzini, E. A. Poe, E. S. Gardner, E. Queen and M. Muller

The **Oxford** book of American short stories; edited by Joyce Carol Oates. Oxford Univ. Press 1992 768p $40; pa $18.95
ISBN 0-19-507065-8; 0-19-509262-7 (pa)
                                        LC 92-1353

"Fifty-six short stories showcase this ever-vital and challenging art form's suppleness and power from Washington Irving's classic, 'Rip Van Winkle,' to the work of Sandra Cisneros. While Oates couldn't resist master-

The Oxford book of American short stories—
Continued

pieces such as Ernest Hemingway's 'A Clean, Well-Lighted Place,' her goal was 'familiar names, unfamiliar titles,' and her intention was to call our attention to works by the likes of Edgar Allan Poe, Harriet Beecher Stowe, Henry James, Kate Chopin, William Carlos Williams, and Saul Bellow that aren't anthologized to death. . . . Her standards of excellence are consistent throughout." Booklist

The Oxford book of English ghost stories; chosen by Michael Cox and R. A. Gilbert. Oxford Univ. Press 1987 c1986 504p o.p.

LC 86-8690

First published 1986 in the United Kingdom
Arranged chronologically, the forty-two stories gathered here "date from the 1820s . . . to the 1980s. . . . In addition to featuring those writers one would expect to find here—Sheridan Le Fanu, M. R. James, and Walter de la Mare, for example—there is also a bounty of wonderful authors with whom U.S. audiences may not be familiar." Booklist

The Oxford book of English love stories; edited by John Sutherland. Oxford Univ. Press 1997 452p $30

ISBN 0-19-214237-2   LC 96-38252

Contents: The adventure of the Black Lady, by A. Behn; The picture, by W. Hazlitt; The trial of love, by M. Shelley; The heart of John Middleton, by E. Gaskell; Dennis Haggarty's wife, by W. M. Thackeray; The Parson's daughter of Oxney Colne, by A. Trollope; To Esther, by A. Ritchie; Enter a dragoon, by T. Hardy; Olive's lover, by C. C. K. Gonner; The wish house, by R. Kipling; Miss Winchelsea's heart, by H. G. Wells; A long-ago affair, by J. Galsworthy; Claribel, by A. Bennett; Episode, by W. S. Maugham; Fifty pounds, by A. E. Coppard; The legacy, by V. Woolf; Samson and Delilah, by D. H. Lawrence; The tunnel, by J. Cary; Something childish but very natural, by K. Mansfield; Love and money, by P. Bentley; Hubert and Minnie, by A. Huxley; A love story, by E. Bowen; Blind love, by V. S. Pritchett; The blue film, by G. Greene; Stone boy with dolphin, by S. Plath; An English unofficial rose, by P. Theroux; The loneliness of the long-distance runner, by S. Maitland; A small spade, by A. Mars-Jones

The Oxford book of English short stories; edited by A.S. Byatt. Oxford Univ. Press 1998 xxx, 439p hardcover o.p. pa $19.95

ISBN 0-19-214238-0; 0-19-280376-X (pa)

LC 97-44998

In this anthology Byatt "includes necessary masters—Rudyard Kipling, Saki, D. H. Lawrence, and V. S. Pritchett, to name a few. But . . . she draws into the fold the work of several extremely talented writers of which few readers on this side of the Atlantic will have heard. Falling into this category are such writers as Malachi Whitaker, H. E. Bates, Sylvia Townsend Warner, and Charlotte Mew." Booklist

The Oxford book of gothic tales; edited by Chris Baldick. Oxford Univ. Press 1992 xxiii, 533p pa $19.95 hardcover o.p.

ISBN 0-19-286219-7 (pa)   LC 91-27290

This chronologically arranged anthology contains thirty-seven stories dating from the 18th to 20th century. Among the authors are Hawthorne, Poe, Stevenson, Hardy, Faulkner, Welty, Borges, Angela Carter and Isabel Allende.

The Oxford book of Irish short stories; edited by William Trevor. Oxford Univ. Press 1989 567p $40; pa $17.95

ISBN 0-19-214180-5; 0-19-280193-7 (pa)

LC 88-28147

"The great Irish writers—from Oliver Goldsmith and Oscar Wilde to James Joyce and Edna O'Brien—are represented in a collection for older advanced readers." Booklist

The Oxford book of Jewish stories; edited by Ilan Stavans. Oxford Univ. Press 1998 493p $30

ISBN 0-19-511019-6   LC 98-16631

Contents: The rabbi's son, by Rabbi Nakhman of Bratzlav; The calf, by S. J. Abramovitsh; If not higher . . ., by I. L. Peretz; A Yom Kippur scandal, by Sholem Aleichem; The mother, by I. Svevo; Tug of love, by I. Zangwill; The kiss, by L. Shapiro; America and I, by A. Yezierska; Holy land, by L. Lewisohn; Before the law, by F. Kafka; At night, by D. Bergelson; The fool and the forest demon, by Der Nister; Camacho's wedding feast, by A. Gerchunoff; A whole loaf, by S. Y. Agnon; The street of crocodiles, by B. Schulz; The story of my dovecot, by I. Babel; The Spinoza of Market Street, by I. B. Singer; The sacrifice of the prisoner, by E. Canetti; Prophet in our midst: a story for Passover, by A. M. Klein; In dreams begin responsibilities, by D. Schwartz; Angel Levine, by B. Malamud; Looking for Mr. Green, by S. Bellow; House at the sea, by N. Ginzburg; The hand that fed me, by I. Rosenfeld; The mirror maker, by P. Levi; The key game, by I. Fink; Midrash on happiness, by G. Paley; Letter from his father, by N. Gordimer; Family ties, by C. Lispector; The shawl, by C. Ozick; The true waiting, by E. Wiesel; The Zulu and the Zeide, by D. Jacobson; Criers and kibitzers, kibitzers and criers, by S. Elkin; Playing ball on Hampstead Heath, by M. Richler; Bertha, by A. Appelfeld; The conversion of the Jews, by P. Roth; Dogs and books, by D. Kiš; The Yatir evening express, by A. B. Yehoshua; In the name of his name, by A. Muñiz-Huberman; The ballad of the false messiah, by M. Scliar; Nomad and viper, by A. Oz; The conversion, by I. Goldemberg; Useful ceremonies, by F. Prose; Lazar Malkin enters heaven, by S. Stern; The legacy of Raizel Kaidish, by R. Goldstein; Postscript to a dead language, by M. J. Bukiet; Bottles, by A. L. Domecq; Elvis, Axl, and Me, by J. Eidus; Cherries in the icebox, by D. Grossman; Three nightmares, by I. Stavans; Endless visibility, by J. Rosen; The art biz, by A. Goodman

The **Oxford** book of Latin American short stories; edited by Roberto González Echevarria. Oxford Univ. Press 1997 481p o.p.   LC 97-5395

Contents: The slaughter house, by E. Echeverria; He who listens may hear—to his regret: confidence of a confidence, by J. M. Gorriti; Fray Gomez's scorpion, by R. Palma; Where and how the Devil lost his poncho, by R. Palma; Midnight mass, by Machado de Assis; The death of the Empress of China, by R. Dario; Yzur, by L. Lugones; The decapitated chicken, by H. Quiroga; The baby in pink buckram, by J. do Rio; The man who resembled a horse, by R. Arevalo Martinez; The braider, by R. Guiraldes; The man who knew Javanese, by A. H. de Lima Barreto; Peace on high, by R. Gallegos; The Christmas turkey, by M. de Andrade; The Daisy dolls, by F. Hernandez; The photograph, by E. Amorim; The clearing, by L. M. Levinson; The garden of forking paths, by J. L. Borges; Journey back to the source, by A. Carpentier; The tree, by M. L. Bombal; The legend of "El Cadejo", by M. A. Asturias; Encarnacion Mendoza's Christmas eve, by J. Bosch; The third bank of the river, by J. G. Rosa; The image of misfortune, by J. C. Onetti; Tell them not to kill me!, by J. Rulfo; Hahn's pentagon, by O. Lins; The switchman, by J. J. Arreola; The featherless buzzards, by J. R. Ribeyro; Meat, by V. Pinera; Unborn, by A. A. Roa Bastos; The night face up, by J. Cortazar; Cooking lesson, by R. Castellanos; The doll queen, by C. Fuentes; The walk, J. Donoso; Balthazar's marvelous afternoon, by G. Garcia Marquez; The challenge, by M. Vargas Llosa; The crime of the mathematics professor, by C. Lispector; Buried statues, by A. Benitez-Rojo; A woman's back, by J. Balza; The warmth of things, by N. Pinon; The threshold, by C. Peri Rossi; The parade ends, by R. Arenas; When women love men, by R. Ferre; Penelope, by D. Trevisan

The **Oxford** book of modern fairy tales; edited by Alison Lurie. Oxford Univ. Press 1993 455p $30; pa $14.95
ISBN 0-19-214218-6; 0-19-282385-X (pa)
            LC 92-28007

This volume is "full of old favorites and some priceless new gems, with a wonderful chronological arrangement that allows readers to absorb information on literary developments and trends, or simply to enjoy the welltold tales. . . . The whole collection is first rate and demonstrates beautifully that modern fairy tales are not just for kids." SLJ

The **Oxford** book of science fiction stories; edited by Tom Shippey. Oxford Univ. Press 1992 xxvi, 587p o.p.   LC 92-9512

Contents: The land ironclads, by H. G. Wells; Finis, by F. L. Pollack; As easy as ABC, by R. Kipling; The metal man, by J. Williamson; A Martian odyssey, by S. G. Weinbaum; Night, by J. W. Campbell; Desertion, by C. D. Simak; The piper's son, by L. Padgett; The monster, by A. E. van Vogt; The second night of summer, by J. H. Schmitz; Second dawn, by A. C. Clarke; Crucifixus etiam, by W. M. Miller; The tunnel under the world, by F. Pohl; Who can replace a man?, by B. Aldiss;

Billennium, by J. G. Ballard; The ballad of lost C'mell, by C. Smith; Semley's necklace, by U. K. Le Guin; How beautiful with banners, by J. Blish; A criminal act, by H. Harrison; Problems of creativeness, by T. M. Disch; How the whip came back, by G. Wolfe; Cloak of anarchy, by L. Niven; A thing of beauty, by N. Spinrad; The screwfly solution, by R. Sheldon; The way of cross and dragon, by G. R. R. Martin; Swarm, by B. Sterling; Burning chrome, by W. Gibson; Silicon muse, by H. Schenck; Karl and the ogre, by P. J. McAuley, Piecework, by D. Brin

The **Oxford** book of short stories; chosen by V.S. Pritchett. Oxford Univ. Press 1981 547p $35; pa $16.95
ISBN 0-19-214116-3; 0-19-282113-X (pa)
            LC 81-156872

In addition to one of his own short stories, Pritchett has selected 40 others, written in English during the 19th and 20th centuries. Most of the authors are English, Irish or American and include Somerset Maugham, D. H. Lawrence, Faulkner, Twain, and Eudora Welty.

The **Oxford** book of spy stories; edited by Michael Cox. Oxford Univ. Press 1996 356p $30
ISBN 0-19-214242-9   LC 95-15519

Includes the following stories: Parker Adderson, philosopher, by A. Bierce; The red carnation, by E. Orczy; The rider in the dawn, by A. T. Quiller-Couch; The Brass Butterfly, by W. Le Queux; Peiffer, by A. E. W. Mason; Mr. Collingrey, MP, by E. Wallace; The lit chamber, by J. Buchan; The reckoning with Otto Schreed, by E. P. Oppenheim; Giulia Lazzari, by W. S. Maugham; Judith, by C. E. Montague; The pigeon man, by V. Williams; Jumbo's wife, by F. O'Connor; Affaire de coeur, by W. E. Johns; Flood on the Goodwins, by A. D. Divine; How Ryan got out of Russia, by E. J. M. D. P. Dunsany; A patriot, by J. Galsworthy; A double double-cross, by P. Cheyney; The army of the shadows, by E. Ambler; Citizen in space, by R. Sheckley; Risico, by I. Fleming; Keep walking, by G. Household; Paper casualty, by L. Deighton; Signal Tresham, by M. Gilbert; Final demand, by J. Wainwright; The rocking-horse spy, by T. Allbeury; The great divide, by W. Haggard; A branch of the service, by G. Greene; Waiting for Mrs. Ryder, by D. Hoch

The **Oxford** book of travel stories; edited by Patricia Craig. Oxford Univ. Press 1996 441p $35
ISBN 0-19-288031-4   LC 96-51543

Contents: The holly-tree, by C. Dickens; The lazy tour of two idle apprentices, by C. Dickens; A ride across Palestine, by A. Trollope; From Miltzow to Lauterbach, by E. Von Arnim; A Journey, by E. Wharton; Human habitation, by E. Bowen; Cruise, by E. Waugh; Travelogue, by R. Lardner; Show Mr. and Mrs. F. to number-, by F. S. Fitzgerald; Local colour, by W. Plomer; Gliding gulls and going people, by W. Sansom; Deliverance, by R. West; A good man is hard to find, by F. O'Connor;

The Oxford book of travel stories—*Continued*

Request stop, by D. Jacobson; Big trip to Europe, by J. Kerouac; Brimmer, by J. Cheever; A journey to the seven streams, by B. Kiely; Scholar and gypsy, by A. Desai; The lady from Guatemala, by V. S. Pritchett; Loser wins, by P. Theroux; Death in Jerusalem, by W. Trevor; Siegfried on the Rhine, by S. T. Warner; The faithful, by E. Hardwick; The bridge at Arta, by J. I. M. Stewart; Greyhound people, by A. Adams; The compartment, by R. Carver; A long night at Abu Simbel, by P. Lively; The man who blew away, by B. Bainbridge; Chinese funeral, by J. Gardam; The kyogle line, by D. Malouf; Cuckoo clock, by D. Johnson; Somewhere else, by R. Ingalls; Questions of travel, by E. Bishop

The **Oxford** book of twentieth-century ghost stories; edited by Michael Cox. Oxford Univ. Press 1996 425p o.p.   LC 96-4913

Contents: In the dark, by E. Nesbit; Rooum, by O. Onions; The shadowy third, by E. Glasgow; The diary of Mr. Poynter, by M. R. James; Mrs. Porter and Miss Allen, by H. Walpole; The nature of the evidence, by M. Sinclair; Night-fears, by L. P. Hartley; Bewitched, by E. Wharton; A short trip home, by F. Scott Fitzgerald; Blind man's buff, by H. R. Wakefield; The blackmailers, by A. Blackwood; Yesterday street, by T. Burke; Smoke ghost, by F. Leiber; The cheery soul, by E. Bowen; All but empty, by G. Greene; Three miles up, by E. J. Howard; Close behind him, by J. Wyndham; The quincunx, by W. De la Mare; The tower, by M. Laski; Poor girl, by E. Taylor; I kiss your shadow, by R. Bloch; A woman seldom found, by W. Sansom; The Portobello road, by M. Spark; Ringing the changes, by R. Aickman; On terms, by C. Brooke-Rose; The only story, by W. Trevor; The loves of lady purple, by A. Carter; Revenant as typewriter, by P. Lively; The little dirty girl, by J. Russ; Watching me, watching you, by F. Weldon; The July ghost, by A. S. Byatt; The highboy, by A. Lurie; The meeting house, by J. Gardam

Oyeyemi, Helen, 1984-

The opposite house. Nan A. Talese/Doubleday 2007 257p $23.95

ISBN 978-0-385-51384-5; 0-385-51384-4
                                LC 2006-36812

The protagonist of this novel is "Maja, a 24-year-old black Cuban woman whose family fled Castro's revolution for London when she was seven. Maja has recently moved in with her boyfriend, Aaron, and discovers she is pregnant with the child she's wanted since she was five years old. And though adjusted to life in London, she begins to wonder about the country her family left behind. Coloring her search for a sense of belonging are the gods and goddesses of Santeria. . . . Interwoven is the story of Aya, a goddess of Santeria who lives in the 'somewherehouse,' which has one door that opens onto Lagos and one onto London." Publ Wkly

The novel is "insightful, urgently and sometimes painfully so. What Oyeyemi shows us about cultural alienation, about what makes and marks a migrant, needs to be seen. . . . At times, it's true, Maja's skin feels thin, stretched, raw. We can feel Oyeyemi writing through her character. But those times are rare; on most of the pages in this novel Maja lives, and it matters that she lives. This is her life." Strange Horizons

Oz, Amos

Don't call it night; translated from the Hebrew by Nicholas de Lange. Harcourt Brace & Co. 1996 199p o.p.   LC 96-14587

Original Hebrew edition, 1994

This novel is set in Tel Kedar, an Israeli town in the Negev Desert. "The human beings who relate the place to us—speaking alternate chapters through most of the book—are Theo, a sixty-year-old semi-retired planner, and [his lover] Noa, a forty-five-year-old teacher of literature." Times Lit Suppl

"This novel is a piece of sweet but melancholy chamber music—light but not necessarily insubstantial. It belongs to a genre of restful novel that is ruled by an esthetic of peace and a yearning for peace. If one is looking for politics, there is that—clearly, if quietly." N Y Times Book Rev

Fima; translated from the Hebrew by Nicholas de Lange. Harcourt Brace & Co. 1993 322p o.p.
                                * LC 92-44200

"A Helen and Kurt Wolff book"
Original Hebrew edition, 1991

"Efraim 'Fima' Nisan, sometime poet, sometime journalist, full-time dreamer, polemicist, philosopher and receptionist at a Jerusalem gynecological clinic, has made a mess of what was once a promising life. Twice divorced, supported mainly by gifts from his loving father, he bumbles through his days in an absentminded fog interrupted by long interior monologues and obsessive verbal diatribes in which he rails against the corruption of Israeli values." Publ Wkly

"Not only does Mr. Oz strive toward a Chekhovian compassion for his characters, but his novel depends . . . on making us believe in the possibility of last-minute grace. When tragedy strikes, we watch Fima rise to the occasion and begin to tap his own resources of generosity, humility, common sense, and his sense of purpose." N Y Times Book Rev

Panther in the basement; translated from the Hebrew by Nicholas de Lange. Harcourt Brace & Co. 1997 147p $21

ISBN 0-15-100287-8   LC 97-20577
Original Hebrew edition, 1995

"It is Jerusalem in 1947, during the final days of the British mandate in Palestine, and Proffy, a twelve-and-a-quarter-year-old Jewish boy, is leading a double life. In his parents' eyes, Proffy (short for Professor) is a word savant. By his own definition, he is second-in-command of the underground organization F. O. D. (Freedom or Death), for whose noble cause he scatters bent nails and composes war slogans like 'Perfidious Albion, hands off Zion!' Proffy's identity as an eloquent militant is threatened, however, when his compatriots charge him with treason for befriending a British policeman, and he is forced to reevaluate the implications of word 'enemy.'" New Yorker

The same sea; translated from the Hebrew by Nicholas de Lange in collaboration with the author. Harcourt 2001 201p $30

ISBN 0-15-100572-9   LC 2001-24121
Original Hebrew edition, 1999

This novel depicts "the lives of four people brought together by death: Albert, an aging tax lawyer whose wife

Oz, Amos—*Continued*

recently died of ovarian cancer; his son Enrico, who flees to Tibet; Enrico's girlfriend, Dita, a voluptuous screenwriter; and Bettine, a widowed accountant who is drawn into an uncomfortable intimacy with Albert." New Yorker

"Never has the author's writing been more controlled and polished. . . . His depictions of his characters' lives are tableaux vivants, succint and visual." Times Lit Suppl

Ozick, Cynthia

Dictation; a quartet. Houghton Mifflin 2008 179p $24

ISBN 978-0-547-05400-1; 0-547-05400-9

LC 2007-52331

Contents: Dictation [novella]; Actors; At Fumicaro; What happened to the baby?

"In the wonderfully witty and biting opening novella, 'Dictation,' Miss Bosanquet and Miss Hallowes, the respective amanuenses of Henry James and Jospeh Conrad at the height of their careers, concoct a marvelous scheme to write themselves into posterity. . . . 'Actors' follows the fortunes of Matt Sorley as he searches for work in New York and eventually is tapped to play Lear in an adaptation of the play that features Lear as a Jewish emigrant. Sorley's production is interrupted by a real Lear—an elderly and quite mad Jewish actor who had performed this role originally many years ago. In 'At Fumicaro,' an art critic attempts to marry his Italian maid only to realize that she has strung him along to rob him. Finally, in 'What Happened to the Baby?' a young girl rehearses the story of her uncle's infidelity and her aunt's Medea-like revenge. Ozick is at the top of her form in these splendid stories." Libr J

Dictation [novelette]

In Ozick, C. Dictation

Heir to the glimmering world. Houghton Mifflin 2004 310p $24

ISBN 0-618-47049-2

* LC 2004-42723

"In 1933, the Mitwissers, a family of German Jews, arrive in America after a narrow and eccentric escape from Berlin. . . . After landing somewhat haphazardly in New York, they place an ad for help in a local paper. The only applicant for the job is an eighteen-year-old orphan, Rose Meadows, who narrates the story, and who observes the Mitwissers with the dry neutrality of an invisible servant. Her duties are vaguely defined—part nanny, part secretary—and her salary comes intermittently, the family's sole source of income being the whimsy of a troubled benefactor. Ozick portrays this ramshackle household to dazzling effect, as it adjusts to its many states of exile—from a sense of security, from cherished ideas, and from the consolations of each other." New Yorker

The Messiah of Stockholm; a novel. Knopf 1987 141p $15.95

ISBN 0-394-54701-2

LC 86-46014

"The protagonist, Lars Andemening, a book reviewer for a Stockholm newspaper, is obsessed with Bruno Schulz, a Polish Jewish writer murdered by the Nazis. Lars, an orphan, believes that he is Schulz's son. His dream is to find his father's lost manuscript, 'The Messiah.' When a manuscript bearing that name turns up, Lars's determination to know the truth about its provenance leads him to increasingly dark waters." Christ Sci Monit

This "novel is a complex and fascinating meditation on the nature of writing and the responsibilities of those who choose to create—or judge—tales. Yet on a purely realistic level, it manages to capture the atmosphere of Stockholm and to be, at times, very funny indeed about the daily operations of one of the city's newspapers and Lars's peculiar detachment from everyday work and life." N Y Times Book Rev

The Puttermesser papers. Knopf 1997 235p $23

ISBN 0-679-45476-4

* LC 96-39155

This book presents "five previously published episodes from the imagined life of Ruth Puttermesser. . . . The first paper, 'Puttermesser: Her Work History, Her Ancestry, Her Afterlife,' introduces the protagonist, age 34, as a New York Jew who has quit the 'blue-blood Wall Street' law firm where she was going nowhere fast. She is now working in the Department of Receipts and Disbursements of the City of New York, where she is going nowhere even faster." N Y Times Book Rev

"This entertaining fable is a social commentary as well as a comic tour de force, and it bristles with Ozick's formidable intelligence and wit." Publ Wkly

Rosa

In Ozick, C. The shawl

The shawl. Knopf 1989 69p $12.95

ISBN 0-394-57976-3

LC 89-2652

"This volume comprises a five-page short story entitled 'The Shawl' and a novella entitled 'Rosa.' Both first appeared in The New Yorker, the first in 1981, the second in 1984. 'The Shawl' focuses on an . . . incident in a Nazi concentration camp where Rosa Lubin, Polish Jew, has hidden her fifteen-month-old baby, Magda, in a shawl. . . . Rosa's fourteen-year-old niece, Stella, steals the shawl; subsequently, in the search for it, Magda is killed by a camp guard, who flings the baby against an electrified fence. . . . 'Rosa' opens three decades later in Miami, where Rosa, now a fifty-eight-year old, resides in the 'dark hole' of a single room at a hotel for elderly retirees. . . . She is being begrudgingly subsidized by her forty-nine-year-old niece, Stella, who appeared in 'The Shawl.'" Commonweal

"Rosa is brilliantly realized. Her dark night of the soul is lit by flashes of insight about memory, culture, old age, a welcome meditation on the euphemistic inadequacy of the word 'survivor.'" N Y Times Book Rev

P

Paasilinna, Arto

The howling miller; translated by Will Hobson from the French of Anne Colin de Terrail. Canongate 2007 284p pa $14

ISBN 978-1-84767-181-3; 1-84767-181-0

Paasilinna, Arto—*Continued*

Original Finnish edition, 1981

"Gunnar Huttunen buys an abandoned flour mill in a small village in northern Finland after World War II and is soon labeled eccentric when the villagers witness him imitating animals and howling at night. His behavior becomes intolerable after he goes on a rampage in the general store, and the local doctor gets Gunnar committed to a mental asylum. After a short time there, he escapes and hides in the forest, evading capture with the help of a few friends—the drunken postman, a sympathetic police constable, and Sanelma Känyränmö, the horticulture adviser who has fallen in love with him. Finally, the police track him down and shackle him to his constable friend, Portimo. They escape into the woods, where they are supposedly transformed into a wolf and a dog." Libr J

"Paasilinna describes the frenetic inner workings of his characters' minds with an expert touch. . . . It is Paasilinna's gift in this gem of a novel (in Will Hobson's pellucid translation from the French of Anne Colin du Terrail) to wring humor from the most desperate of circumstances." N Y Times Book Rev

Packer, Ann

The dive from Clausen's pier; a novel. Knopf 2002 369p hardcover o.p. pa $14

ISBN 0-375-41282-4; 0-375-72713-2 (pa)

* LC 2001-42522

"A reckless attempt to impress Carrie, Mike's dive off Clausen's Pier rendered him paralyzed. Now Carrie finds herself torn between the loyalty she's expected to feel toward Mike and her need to transform herself. She takes a dive of her own—into adulthood—when she escapes to New York." Booklist

Songs without words. Knopf 2007 321p $24.95

ISBN 978-0-375-41281-3   LC 2006-100512

This "novel examines the bonds of female friendship and how the connections formed by a childhood tragedy develop with age. Liz, married to a Bay Area technology executive and the mother of two teenagers, is preoccupied with yoga and creating a pleasurable environment for her children. Sarabeth, who was absorbed into Liz's family when her mother committed suicide, lives a makeshift existence in Berkeley. When Liz's daughter attempts to kill herself, a rift opens between the two women. . . . [Packer] shows a deft touch in framing emotional dilemmas, such as whether it is the duty of those who have been raised with affection to compensate those who have gone without." New Yorker

Packer, ZZ, 1973-

Drinking coffee elsewhere. Riverhead Bks. 2003 238p hardcover o.p. pa $14

ISBN 1-57322-234-8; 1-57322-378-6 (pa)

LC 2002-73971

Contents: Brownies; Every tongue shall confess; Our Lady of Peace; The ant of the self; Drinking coffee elsewhere; Speaking in tongues; Geese; Doris is coming

"The predominantly African American characters in Packer's first collection of short fiction struggle to maintain their sense of self while they confront unexpected life events." Booklist

Paddock, Jennifer

A secret word; a novel; Jennifer Paddock. Simon & Schuster 2004 206p $13

ISBN 0-7432-4707-8 (pa)   LC 2003-57343

This is the "story of three girls from Fort Smith, Ark., linked for life by a high school tragedy. In 1986, tennis and country club pals Sarah and Chandler hitch a ride to lunch from the less privileged Leigh; they're pursued by footballer Trey, who crashes his car and dies. Flash forward to 1990: Chandler and Sarah have gone to college; Leigh stays behind to work at a dry cleaner's. But their paths continue to intersect, and Paddock follows her characters through 15 years as they peel apart and reunite, capturing each of the young women in separate first-person chapters." Publ Wkly

"Filled with many moving and sometimes devastating moments and observations, Paddock's first novel is three coming-of-age stories for the price of one." Booklist

Page, Katherine Hall

The body in the Big Apple. Morrow 1999 239p $22

ISBN 0-688-15748-3   LC 99-33511

This prequel to the Faith Fairchild series "catches the amateur sleuth at the start of her career. . . . It's winter in Manhattan and 23-year-old Faith is darting from one holiday party to the next, bearing hearty comfort foods to a chic clientele of East Side socialites and yuppies. . . . At one of these soirees Faith runs into an old school chum, now married to an up-and-coming politician, who confides that she is being blackmailed." N Y Times Book Rev

The body in the bog. Morrow 1996 276p o.p.

LC 96-3468

"Sleuth Faith Fairchild occupies her time in small-town Massachusetts with her husband, Tom, a preacher; their two small children; Have Faith, her catering business; and an occasional murder. When wetlands are converted into a chi-chi housing development, poison pen letters fly, one of the houses burns, and police discover murder. Faith's persistent quest for clues exposes many secrets, but the ultimate confrontation occurs in Have Faith's kitchen. Well-delineated action and characters mix easily with Faith's attendant domesticity." Libr J

The body in the bookcase. Morrow 1998 244p $22

ISBN 0-688-15747-5   LC 98-36708

A mystery featuring Faith Fairchild, "the Aleford, Mass., caterer, wife and mother of two. Faith, like everybody else in town, is appalled when 80-year-old Sarah Winslow is found dead after her house is burglarized. After her own home is broken into, Faith decides to solve the crimes. . . . Page's tale is tightly written, with strong characterizations and delightful descriptions of its New England setting." Publ Wkly

The body in the vestibule. St. Martin's Press 1992 211p o.p.

LC 92-18455

"A Thomas Dunne book"

This Faith Fairchild mystery is "set in Lyons, France. Faith, four months pregnant, her husband Tom, a minister who is finishing research for his dissertation, and their three-year-old Ben live in a huge fifth-floor apart-

Page, Katherine Hall—*Continued*

ment. Taking out the garbage one evening, Faith finds the body of a homeless man from the neighborhood in the trash bin. When the police arrive, however, the body is gone and Faith's credibility is in question. At a party she meets Chief Inspector Michel Ravier, who asks about the body and tells her to call if she witnesses anything else unusual. . . . With beautifully detailed descriptions of Lyons added to Faith's intelligent observations, Page . . . continues to hit the mark with this charming series." Publ Wkly

Palahniuk, Chuck

Diary; a novel. Doubleday 2003 260p $24.95
ISBN 0-385-50947-2   LC 2003-43900
This "is the story of a lonely artist named Misty Marie Wilmot and the spooky community of blue-blood islanders she's married into. . . . Her story takes the form of a diary written to her husband, Peter, who lies contorted and comatose in the hospital after a suicide attempt. On Waytansea Island, the Wilmot ancestral home, Misty struggles to take care of their daughter, Tabbi, and Peter's mother, Grace, while making ends meet as a maid at the island hotel." N Y Times Book Rev
"Catchy, jarring prose, cryptic pronouncements and baroque flights of imagination are instantly recognizable, and [the author's] sharp, bizarre meditations on the artistic process make this twisted tale one of his most memorable works to date." Publ Wkly

Lullaby; a novel. Doubleday 2002 260p
ISBN 0-385-50447-0   LC 2001-52979
"Middle-aged journalist Carl Streator discovers that all children who died of SIDS are read the same poem the night before their deaths. . . Once he discovers that simply reciting the poem in someone's direction is invariably fatal, Streator can't stop murdering. Then he finds out that Helen Hoover Boyle, a real-estate agent who sells the same haunted houses over and over again, knows the secret, too. They set out on a grand literary road trip to destroy all extant copies of the song." Booklist
"This is vintage Palahniuk: weird, creepy, twisted, upsetting, and ultimately a great read for anyone who wants to be scared for pleasure." Libr J

Rant; an oral biography of Buster Casey. Doubleday 2007 320p $24.95
ISBN 978-0-385-51787-4; 0-385-51787-4
                              LC 2006-28918
"Buster Casey, destined to live fast, die young and murder as many people as he can, is the rotten seed at the core of [this novel]. . . . Set in a future where urbanites are segregated by strict curfews into Daytimers and Nighttimers, the narrative unfolds as an oral history comprising contradictory accounts from people who knew Buster. These include childhood friends horrified by the boy's macabre behavior (getting snakes, scorpions and spiders to bite him and induce instant erections; repeatedly infecting himself with rabies), policemen and doctors who had dealings with the rabies 'superspreader'; and Party Crashers, thrill-seeking Nighttimers who turn city streets into demolition derby arenas." Publ Wkly
"In telling this utterly bizarre tale, a story that only gets heavier as it goes on, Rant's friends and family give their recollections of the twisted things he did as a kid

and young adult before his violent death, stories as improbable as the all-American tall tale, only really gross. Gross, but fiercely smart, and in Palahniuk's signature way of raging against the deadening sterility of modern life." PopMatters

Paley, Grace

The collected stories. Farrar, Straus & Giroux 1994 386p $27.50
ISBN 0-374-12636-4
                              * LC 93-42230
This volume includes stories from three previously published collections
Contents: The little disturbances of man: Goodbye and good luck; A woman, young and old; The pale pink roast; The loudest voice; The contest; An interest in life; An irrevocable diameter; The used-boy raisers; A subject of childhood; In time which made a monkey of us all; The floating truth
Enormous changes at the last minute: Wants; Debts; Distance; Faith in the afternoon; Gloomy tune; Living; Come on, ye sons of art; Faith in a tree; Samuel; The burdened man; Enormous changes at the last minute; Politics; Northeast playground; The little girl; A conversation with my father; The immigrant story; The long-distance runner
Later the same day: Love; Dreamer in a dead language; In the garden; Somewhere else; Lavinia: an old story; Friends; At that time; Anxiety; In this country, but in another language, my aunt refuses to marry the men everyone wants her to; Mother; Ruthy and Edie; A man told me the story of his life; The story hearer; This is a story about my friend George, the toy inventor; Zagrowsky tells; The expensvie moment; Listening

Palliser, Charles

The quincunx. Ballantine Bks. 1990 c1989 788p o.p.
                              * LC 89-91787
"Set in England during the 1820s and '30s, the novel is chiefly narrated by a character who first appears as a young boy named John Mellamphy. He lives with his mother in a small village; he has no knowledge of his father, nor does he realize that Mellamphy is not his real surname. Gradually, he comes to understand that his mother possesses something that a number of other people desperately want. It is the codicil to an old, disputed will concerning the immense Huffam estate. The present holder of that property, Sir Perceval Mompesson, wants to obtain the codicil so he can destroy it." Time
"This is not an ironic parody à la Barth, not an echo of Eco, but a genuine reproduction of a full-bodied 19th-century page-turner of a novel, set in late Regency England, thick with characters of all classes, with plots, counterplots, fore-bodings, reversals and interpolated tales. . . . Mr. Palliser's re-creation of this period is absolutely convincing, his dialogue never jars, his command of details never falters." N Y Times Book Rev

The unburied. Farrar, Straus & Giroux 1999 403p $25
ISBN 0-374-28035-5   LC 99-14740

Palliser, Charles—*Continued*

"On a visit to an old school friend in Thurchester, England, professional historian Courtine looks forward to doing research in the cathedral library and renewing ties; he does not expect to become embroiled in a controversy surrounding a centuries-old mystery, nor does he anticipate being a major witness to a gruesome murder." Libr J

"All the murders are puzzles, and Palliser constructs his plot like a maze and lures his readers into it. The book's ruthless consistency of style and the somewhat bleak view of humankind set it apart from the usual thriller." New Yorker

Palmer, Michael, 1942-

The fifth vial. St. Martin's Press 2007 372p $25.95

ISBN 978-0-312-34351-4; 0-312-34351-5

LC 2006-50971

"What do three very different people—Harvard medical student Natalie Reyes, Chicago PI Ben Callahan and scientific genius Joe Anson—have in common? Natalie, in Brazil for a conference, is attacked, hospitalized and loses a lung; Ben gets hired to discover how a mutilated anonymous body died; Joe, the inventor of an untested medical breakthrough, is forced into an operation for his life-threatening pulmonary fibrosis. All three seek answers connected to the Whitestone Foundation, a conglomerate that's a front for the Guardians, a secret cabal of medical specialists." Publ Wkly

"Palmer is adept at tapping into people's natural fear of disease, doctors, and hospitals and converting that fear into unnerving suspense. In this . . . medical thriller, Palmer plays with the phenomenon of organ donation, forcing the reader to ask nervously, 'Where do donated organs come from?' The answer comes slowly, in the best medical-thriller tradition." Booklist

Miracle cure. Bantam Bks. 1998 399p $23.95

ISBN 0-553-10523-X   LC 98-4884

A medical thriller revolving around a new drug "called Vasclear, a heart medication being developed at the Boston Heart Institute by Newbury Pharmaceuticals. The FDA is being pressured by a Massachusetts senator (who, it turns out, is secretly taking Vasclear himself) to approve the release of the drug. And Vasclear may be the magic wand that can save the life of Jack 'Coach' Holbrook, whose health is declining after a quintuple bypass. Coach's son, Brian . . . not only faces the ethical dilemma of stealing the drug if he can't place his father as a test patient but also finds evidence of potentially dangerous side effects—evidence that could derail the drug's release to the public." Publ Wkly

The patient. Bantam Bks. 2000 324p $24.95

ISBN 0-553-10983-9   LC 99-57838

This medical thriller features "Dr. Jessie Copeland, a neurosurgeon in her 40s with a combined under-graduate degree in biology and mechanical engineering. Now working under egomaniacal chief surgeon Carl Gilbride at a top Boston hospital, Jessie gets to try out ARTIE (Assisted Robotic Tissue Incision and Extraction) on cadavers, while Gilbride coaxes foundations to cough up millions for the revolutionary new procedure. Attracted by the media attention, . . . shadowy terrorist Claude Malloche, known as 'the Mist,' who also has a brain tu-

mor, comes to the hospital for treatment—and winds up holding patients and staff hostage in case the operation fails. It's finally up to Jessie and a rogue CIA agent to keep everyone healthy." Publ Wkly

The society. Bantam Bks. 2004 351p $25

ISBN 0-553-90057-9   LC 2004-303038

This thriller begins "with the murder of several loathsome CEOs of HMOs in Massachusetts. Dr. Will Grant is a talented and caring physician in the Boston area who works long hours and hates the unfair and obstructive practices of the big insurance companies. Patty Moriarity is a rookie state cop whose first big case is investigating the deaths of the health care vultures. After some early research, Patty suspects Will, but soon enough that's all straightened out and they're smooching on the couch. After Will is drugged and collapses during a delicate operation, things get rough: he's kicked out of his hospital for drug abuse and sued. Next he's being tortured, while Patty, shot after attempting to save the boorish chauvinist detective who has taken over her case, lies in a coma. The action is a bit preachy in the beginning, but once Palmer gets all his characters in place, the suspense builds." Publ Wkly

Palwick, Susan

Shelter. Tor 2007 576p pa $15.95

ISBN 978-0-312-86602-0; 0-312-86602-X

LC 2007-7316

"Meredith Walford has spent most of her life avoiding her omnipresent father, multibillionaire Preston Walford, the first human to have his personality posthumously translated into an online presence. When the threads of her life once more become entangled with those of a homeless man whose memory has been legally erased, a young woman whose caring for a damaged student cost her her freedom, and a 'smart house' whose personality seems strangely familiar, Meredith finally learns to confront the monsters that have haunted her past. [The novel is] set in a precarious near-future in which environmental storms make shelter even more of a necessity, where altruism is considered a mental disease and 'brainwiping' a desirable cure for antisocial behavior." Libr J

"Palwick has built a rich and complex possible future, complete with political and religious systems, rapid and extraordinary technological advancement, and all the moral polarization that naturally follows such developments." Strange Horizons

Pamuk, Orhan, 1952-

The museum of innocence; translated from the Turkish by Maureen Freely. Alfred A. Knopf 2009 535p il map $28.95

ISBN 978-0-307-26676-7; 0-307-26676-1

LC 2009-19475

Original Turkish edition, 2008

Readers "view Istanbul in the tumultuous 1970s and '80s through the lens of a doomed love affair. Kemal is happily engaged to a beautiful, intelligent woman of his own social class, Sibel—and yet, he falls deeply, irrevocably in love with a poor, distant relation, Füsun. When Kemal refuses to leave Sibel, Füsun disappears. Inconsolable, he returns almost daily to the scene of their love-making, cradling the objects she once touched as though they still contain some trace of her. He descends deeper

Pamuk, Orhan, 1952--—*Continued*

into despair, alienating everyone around him except Sibel, now bound to him as much by love as by the shame that she will face should they break off their engagement. But Kemal cannot forget Füsun, and will dedicate his life to possessing her—or at least, the objects that remind him of her—even to the point of destroying himself, and those he loves most." BookPage

"Pamuk is brilliant at the human parade, and especially at humiliation in its masculine forms, frequently played out in Istanbul along East-West tensions." Cleveland Plain Dealer

My name is Red; translated from the Turkish by Erdağ Göknar. Knopf 2001 417p
  ISBN 0-375-40695-6
  * LC 2001-29866

Original Turkish edition, 1998
"In 16th-century Istanbul master miniaturist and illuminator of books Enishte Effendi is commissioned to illustrate a book celebrating the sultan. Soon he lies dead at the bottom of a well, and how he got there is the crux of this novel. A number of narrators give testimony to what they know about the circumstances surrounding the murder." Libr J

"The Ottoman Istanbul, which Mr. Pahmuk depicts with skill and linguistic energy, is a rich, cruel and claustrophobic world where art leads, through dark alleyways to murder. The novel is also about the conflicts of Turkishness, about . . . a society caught between religious zealotry and an authoritarian state—themes as relevant to Turkey now as they were 400 years ago." Economist

Snow; translated by Maureen Freely. Knopf 2004 426p $26
  ISBN 0-375-40697-2
  *

Original Turkish edition, 2002
"Upon returning to his home in secular Turkey, a poet named Ka discovers two things that will change his life: Ipek, the girl he loved as a child, still lives in the city of Kars, and the community has been stunned by a rash of suicides of zealously religious girls who refused to remove their head scarves while in public. With an investigator's eye, Ka seeks out information about the tragedies from all sources, eventually leading to the man at the eye of the storm, Blue, a charismatic Islamite who will not let the message that these girls carried be silenced." Libr J

"Pamuk's sometimes exhaustive conversations and descriptions create a stark picture of a too-little-known part of the world, where politics, religion and even happiness can seem alternately all-consuming and irrelevant. A detached tone and some dogmatic abstractions make for tough reading, but Ka's rediscovery of God and poetry in a desolate place makes the novel's sadness profound and moving." Publ Wkly

Pancake, Ann

Strange as this weather has been; a novel. Shoemaker & Hoard 2007 360p pa $15.95
  ISBN 978-1-59376-166-0; 1-59376-166-X
  LC 2007-11838

"With her beloved West Virginia hollows and valleys under constant onslaught by a savage coal-mining industry whose raping of the land threatens her home with devastating floods, Lace Ricker finds herself battling callous forces both without and within her own family. As thunderous blasts weaken their home's foundation and poisoned wastewater infiltrates their well, Lace and her daughter, Bant, secretly become more determined to find a way to stop the mines, while Lace's husband pragmatically refuses to fight the union bosses, and her sons tentatively, then calamitously, accept the challenges and adventure of life lived in the shadow of imminent danger. By tracing the devastating impact of coal mining through the eyes of Lace and her four children, Pancake's powerful debut novel evinces a poetic pathos and authentic respect for the land and the people who love it." Booklist

Paravisini-Gebert, Lizabeth

(ed) Green cane and juicy flotsam. See Green cane and juicy flotsam

Paretsky, Sara

Bitter medicine. Morrow 1987 321p o.p.
  LC 86-33238

"A young Hispanic woman and her premature infant die in a wealthy suburban hospital. Her doctor is found beaten to death the next day. As a favor to Lottie Herschel, her long-time friend and mentor, Chicago private investigator and lawyer V. I. Warshawski agrees to look into the case. Abortion and medical ethics are the backdrop for this powerful and moving novel." Libr J

Blacklist; a V.I. Warshawski novel. Putnam 2003 415p $24.95
  ISBN 0-399-15085-4
  LC 2003-43157

"A dead reporter, a missing Egyptian boy wanted in connection with terrorist activities, and an elderly woman convinced that an intruder is in her family manse are all elements of Paretsky's . . . novel featuring Chicago private investigator V. I. Warshawski. As V. I. looks into these peoples' lives, she discovers connections among them. She uncovers a story of betrayal and secrets that spans several generations and involves Chicago's wealthiest families, the Red Scare, and the House Un-American Activities Committee hearings of the 1950s. As always, V. I.'s determined pursuit of the truth ensures at least a few heart-stopping moments." Libr J

Bleeding Kansas. G.P. Putnam's Sons 2008 431p $25.95; pa $9.99
  ISBN 978-0-399-15405-8; 978-0-451-22448-4 (pa)
  LC 2007-35962

"Set in the rural Kaw River Valley, where the author grew up, and sparked by a feud between two families that pioneered this farm region during the 1850s, the multigenerational narrative bristles with the kind of prickly social issues that give substance to Paretsky's detective stories. . . . The blood-boiling issue in Bleeding Kansas is religious intolerance. Bigotry comes naturally to the members of the Schapen clan, who worship at the Salvation Through the Blood of Jesus Full Bible Church and become apoplectic when Gina Haring, a New York lesbian and New Age Wiccan, moves into an old farmhouse and attempts to practice her beliefs. . . . Any inclination on the part of the reader to sympathize with the

Paretsky, Sara—*Continued*

Schapens (for being born and bred stupid) in this barn-yard feud are wiped out when Chip Grellier, who joins the Army after being suspended from school for a fight started by his Schapen tormentors, is killed in Iraq. But the Schapens do provide much black humor by breeding the 'perfect red heifer' referred to in the Old Testament, creating an international storm that ensnares both funda-mentalist Christians and ultraorthodox Jews." N Y Times Book Rev

Blood shot; a novel. Delacorte Press 1988 328p o.p. LC 88-3861

"Blood Shot takes [the detective-heroine V.I. Warshawski] back to the working-class Chicago neighbourhoods of her youth, where a callous industrial-ist lurks at the centre of a deadly web of violence and intrigue." Quill Quire

Burn marks. Delacorte Press 1990 340p o.p. * LC 89-23418

This "adventure of Chicago private eye Victoria Iphenigia Warshawski begins with arson and proceeds to homicide as the intrepid V.I. contends with ambitious politicians, a construction-business scam, a corrupt cop and the best intentions of her closest family friends." Publ Wkly

"The 'whydunit' in Ms. Paretsky's books is often em-bedded in the fabric of problems that confront us all—the poisoned environment, for example, or urban blight. This extra dimension adds an immediacy to 'Burn Marks' that is not found in many private-eye novels." N Y Times Book Rev

Fire sale. Putnam 2005 402p $25.95
ISBN 0-399-15279-2 LC 2005-47601

This entry draws V. I. Warshawski "back to her South Chicago roots when she reluctantly agrees to coach the girls basketball team at her former high school, which is struggling with poverty, teen pregnancy, a lack of equip-ment, and gang influence. The old neighborhood has de-clined, too, and when a small local factory is sabotaged, V.I. is persuaded to investigate. Meanwhile, she hopes to gain financial support for the basketball team from By-Smart, a megadiscount chain whose founder also grew up in South Chicago. In a series of events that includes an explosion at the local factory, a horrifying murder, and the disappearance of a basketball player, V.I. is drawn into a deadly conflict between By-Smart and South Chicago's residents. Fast-paced and as entertain-ing." Libr J

Ghost country. Delacorte Press 1998 386p $24.95
ISBN 0-385-29933-8 LC 98-12294

Chicagoans "Harriet and Mara Stonds have been raised in luxury by their grandfather, famous neurosurgeon Abraham Stonds. Harriet is the apple of her grandfather's eye—tall, blond, successful at everything she does, al-ways the good girl. Mara plays the role of ugly stepsis-ter, at least to her grandfather, who has told her for years that she's lazy, stupid, and ungrateful. But things are about to change for the Stonds family. A drunken opera singer, a softhearted psychotherapist, a group of home-less women, and a mysterious visitor who performs mira-cles will each play a key role in opening the eyes of Harriet and Mara to a world they've never imagined. This book is rich, astonishing, and affecting." Booklist

Guardian angel. Delacorte Press 1992 370p o.p. LC 91-24976

While investigating a local manufacturer Chicago pri-vate eye V.I. Warshawski uncovers a bond-parking scheme that reaches into her ex-husband's law firm and ties into the bizarre behavior of her neighbors

"The plot serves nicely to bring V.I. into contact with tough, down-and-out types, whom Ms. Paretsky draws extremely well. . . . Bits and pieces of V.I.'s back-ground are worked into the narrative unobtrusively, so that we come to know her as the story progresses, the way we come to know people in real life." N Y Times Book Rev

Hard time; a V.I. Warshawski novel. Delacorte Press 1999 384p $24.95
ISBN 0-385-31363-2 LC 99-22214

When V. I. Warshawski "swerves to avoid a body ly-ing in the middle of the road, she never imagines that her search for the reasons behind the vicious beating death of Nicola Aguinaldo will take her from the upper classes of Chicago society to a long stint behind bars at a private women's prison overrun with sadistic guards and almost equally threatening inmates." Libr J

Indemnity only; a novel. Dial Press (NY) 1982 244p o.p. LC 81-5452

"Chicago private eye V. I. Warshawski is hired to lo-cate a young woman and instead comes across the body of her boyfriend, a crooked union, and an insurance scam. Thugs beat V. I. up, and another man is murdered. This is all standard hard-boiled detective stuff, except that V. I. is a woman—tough, independent, good look-ing, and believable. Paretsky has done an excellent job of presenting a real female private eye, without falling into parody." Libr J

Total recall; a V.I. Warshawski novel. Delacorte Press 2001 414p
ISBN 0-385-31366-7 * LC 2001-28801

"At a Chicago conference on Jews and Christians, an unassuming man calling himself Paul Radbuka makes some startling assertions. Claiming that a recovered memory therapist has recently helped him to regain memories of a childhood destroyed by the Holocaust, he seeks to find his true family. Before she knows it, pri-vate detective V.I. Warshawski is drawn into the turmoil unleashed by these claims and watches helplessly as her dearest friend and mentor, Lotty Hershel, is consumed by a past she wishes to forget." Libr J

This mystery "is written with the stylistic verve and in-tellectual energy of a writer just coming into her own." N Y Times Book Rev

Tunnel vision. Delacorte Press 1994 432p o.p. LC 94-6050

Chicago private detective V.I. Warshawski uncovers a "cynical swindle when she tries to help a wretched fami-ly she finds living in the basement of her office building. After getting the bum's rush from an advocacy group for the homeless and from feminist friends protecting their own grants, V.I. sticks out her jaw and goes it alone on this dirty, complicated fraud case. Mustn't feel sorry for V.I., though, because her outrage gives her the strength to take on the whole corrupt establishment. This princi-

Paretsky, Sara—*Continued*

pled private eye intimidates people because she doesn't know the meaning of compromise and won't tolerate moral slackers." N Y Times Book Rev

Windy City blues; V. I. Warshawski stories. Delacorte Press 1995 258p o.p.   LC 95-8302

Contents: Grace notes; The Pietro Andromache; Strung out; At the old swimming hole; The Maltese cat; Settled score; Skin deep; Three-dot po; The Takamoku joseki

"Although V.I.'s just as feisty and tough-talking as ever, she presents a somewhat softer side in this series of stories that gives a nostalgic nod to Vic's friends, family, and past." Booklist

(ed) A Woman's eye. See A Woman's eye

Pargeter, Edith, 1913-1995

For works written by this author under other names see Peters, Ellis, 1913-1995

Parini, Jay

The apprentice lover; a novel. HarperCollins Pubs. 2002 307p $24.95

ISBN 0-06-621071-2   LC 2001-39675

"Derailed by his brother's death in Vietnam, Alex Massolini, Parini's immensely likable, jejune hero, has dropped out of Columbia and secured the position of secretary for the renowned Scots writer Rupert Grant, currently ensconced in a villa on Capri with his astute yet longsuffering wife and two lovely and worshipful 'research assistants.' . . . Parini's lucent and sensuous tale nimbly dissects the confluence of ego and art and ponders the unending wounds of war, ultimately affirming the consoling power of literature, however disappointing writers themselves may be. Wittily drawn cameos of W. H. Auden, Graham Greene, and Gore Vidal add to the deep pleasures of this smart, graceful novel." Booklist

Park, Ed, 1970-

Personal days; a novel. Random House Trade Paperbacks 2008 241p pa $13

ISBN 978-0-8129-7857-5; 0-8129-7857-9
          LC 2007-40834

This novel is "narrated by a collective 'we' of youngish Manhattan office grunts who watch in helpless horror as their company keeps shrinking, taking their private world of in-jokes and nicknames along with it. . . . As office survivors Lizzie, Jonah, Pru, Crease, Lars and Jason II try to figure out who's next to get the axe, mysterious clues point to a conspiracy that may involve one or more of the survivors." Publ Wkly

"What at first appears to be a Dilbert-esque story soon twists into a dizzying, surreal tale in which even the card-key readers conceal sinister purposes." Details

Parker, Barbara, 1947-

Blood relations. Dutton 1996 374p o.p.
          LC 95-32085

"Prosecutor Sam Hagen is known for being a straight arrow, so he's the perfect choice to investigate a potentially explosive case and dismiss it for lack of evidence. Or so think both his boss, the Miami DA, who has his eye on national office and doesn't want controversy, and

the city manager, who's courting the tourist industry. The plaintiff is a young model who claims that several men, including a well-connected local businessman and a football player turned actor, raped her. Hagen believes the girl and, despite political pressure, pursues the case." Publ Wkly

"Stylish writing, glamorous characters, a glitzy setting, and an intricately constructed plot—there's a formula for success in any genre of popular fiction." Booklist

Criminal justice. Dutton 1997 304p o.p.
          LC 96-44143

"Dan Galindo was a Boy Scout among the Federal prosecutors in Miami. Because he refused to put a flawed and sleazy witness on the stand, a drug kingpin walked. His virtue was rewarded by the loss of his job, forcing him to take up private legal scut work. Now, defending a beautiful but scary rock musician on a minor criminal charge, Dan finds himself in a web of money launderers, suspected bigtime drug lords, informants and ruthless narcs who may even have murdered to cover their tracks." N Y Times Book Rev

The author "has written a brutal commentary on the Miami music scene, offering unforgettable characters and some hilarious potshots at suburbia." Libr J

Suspicion of betrayal; a novel. Dutton 1999 347p $23.95

ISBN 0-525-94468-0   LC 98-52080

This suspense novel features Miami "attorney Gail Connon, whose love affair with high-powered defense attorney Anthony Quintana is going full-speed ahead. Gail's plate is way too full as she tries to save her struggling solo practice while addressing a custody dispute with her ex over their 10-year-old daughter, Karen. Just when Gail thinks everything's under control, the bottom falls out when Karen starts receiving anonymous death threats." Booklist

Suspicion of deceit. Dutton 1998 358p $23.95

ISBN 0-525-94401-X   LC 97-38429

A novel featuring attorneys Gail Connor and Anthony Quintana. "To build business for her new solo practice, Gail takes on the Miami Opera as a client, only to learn of a pending crisis: the rising young bass-baritone scheduled to play Don Giovanni in Mozart's opera sang recently in Castro's Cuba. The singer may be in danger, as may several of Gail's opera contacts who have ties to puzzling aspects of Anthony's past, ties that lead back to Nicaragua in the late 1970s." Booklist

"The narrative triumphs, . . . thanks to Parker's rich mix of tropical politics, edgy romance and secrets from the past." Publ Wkly

Suspicion of vengeance. Dutton 2001 359p $23.95

ISBN 0-525-94601-2   LC 2001-33521

Gail Connor "is asked to take on the case of an old family friend's grandson, Kenny Ray Clark, who was convicted of the stabbing death of a housewife over a decade earlier, indirectly causing the death of her infant son. Now, after 11 years on death row, his appeals are about to run out. Anthony, Gail's on-again, off-again fiancé, himself a high-powered Florida attorney, warns her of the futility of trying to save Clark. But Gail digs into the records and finds, among other things, a drunk defense attorney, a bogus confession and a witness who would have provided an alibi but was threatened by police." Publ Wkly

Parker, Dorothy, 1893-1967

Here lies; the collected stories of Dorothy Parker. Viking 1939 362p o.p.

         *

Contents: Arrangement in black and white; Sexes; Wonderful old gentleman; Telephone call; Here we are; Lady with a lamp; Too bad; Mr. Durant; Just a little one; Horsie; Clothe the naked; Waltz; Little Curtis; Little hours; Big blonde; From the diary of a New York lady; Soldiers of the republic; Dusk before fireworks; New York to Detroit; Glory in the daytime; Last tea; Sentiment; You were perfectly fine; Custard heart

Parker, K. J. (Kenneth John)

The company. Orbit 2008 419p $24.99

ISBN 978-0-316-03853-9; 0-316-03853-9

         LC 2008-35282

The author "blends gritty military fantasy with the 18th-century 'island story' tradition. Seven years after the end of a war between unnamed countries, four friends who fought together have settled back into civilian life. Then their former leader, Kunessin, now a celebrated and embittered general, turns up and reminds them of their old pledge to retire together to a peaceful island. Better yet, he's found a suitable place and will fund the venture. A local matchmaker finds women smart and desperate enough to be colonists, and they marry the ex-soldiers in a group wedding that sets the tone of the book: humorous, grim and utterly unromantic. The would-be republicans soon reach the island and settle in, but the discovery of gold in a stream changes everything." Publ Wkly

Devices and desires. Little, Brown 2007 635p (Engineer trilogy, book 1) pa $12.99

ISBN 978-0-316-00338-4; 0-316-00338-7

         LC 2007-9926

First published 2005 in the United Kingdom

"When engineer Ziani Vaatzes is sentenced to death for building a device that differs from the official standards, he manages to flee from his home in the Guild-controlled Republic of Mezentia and find refuge in the enemy country of Eremia. To ensure his safety, he offers to teach Mezentine engineering techniques to the technologically ignorant Eremians, so that they can build weapons equal to those of their Mezentine enemies. Eremia's Duke Orsea reluctantly gives his approval, unwittingly laying himself and those he loves open to the machinations of a man out for vengeance against the country that condemned his work as well as the enemy who gave him succor. . . . [A] richly textured and emotionally complex fantasy." Libr J

Parker, Kenneth John *See* Parker, K. J. (Kenneth John)

Parker, Robert B., 1932-

Appaloosa. Putnam 2005 276p $24.95

ISBN 0-399-15277-6

         * LC 2004-58745

In this western, "deputy Everett Hitch recounts the struggle between lawman Virgil Cole and outlaw rancher Randall Bragg for control of the little town of Appaloosa. Modeled on Wyatt Earp, Cole is the kind of man who never loses a fight, and he comes close to taking down the murderous Bragg with ease, until Bragg's hired guns rescue him by abducting Cole's romantic interest and using her as a hostage. This precipitates a long chase, a struggle with wandering Kiowa, and a gunfight reminiscent of the OK Corral. The story gallops along to a surprise ending, but beneath the trappings of this gunfighter novel, Parker really has something to say about the nature of men and women in the Old West." Libr J

Back story. Putnam 2003 291p $24.95

ISBN 0-399-14977-5   LC 2002-36901

"As the title implies, the story is full of references to the past, starting with an unsolved 1974 robbery in which a young California mother visiting her sister was shot dead when she went to cash some traveler's checks at the old Shawmut Bank in Boston. Spenser takes the case to give the victim's daughter peace of mind, only to discover that he has disturbed a cover-up involving the F.B.I., an organized crime figure and the remnants of a gang of counterculture revolutionaries." N Y Times Book Rev

"The repartee between Spenser and Hawk is fast and funny; the sentiment between Spenser and Susan and the musings about Spenser's code are only occasionally cloying; and there's a scattering of remarkable action scenes including a tense shootout in Harvard Stadium." Publ Wkly

Brimstone. G.P. Putnam's Sons 2009 293p $25.95

ISBN 978-0-399-15571-0; 0-399-15571-6

         LC 2009-08107

"Parker's gunslinging saddle pals Virgil Cole and Everett Hitch return for their third adventure. . . . Here, Virgil and Everett rescue Allie French, Virgil's former sweetie who ran off to become a prostitute, and head to Brimstone, where the two gunmen sign on as deputy sheriffs. Brimstone, however, doesn't exactly provide a quiet respite for this trio. Virgil and Allie have a hard time getting over his hurt and her shame, a mysterious Indian is killing local folks and leaving taunting messages, and brutal saloon owner Pike and corrupt preacher Brother Percival are headed for a showdown. . . . The result is classic Parker—exciting, suspenseful, fast-moving and entertaining." Publ Wkly

A Catskill eagle; a Spenser novel. Delacorte Press/Seymour Lawrence 1985 311p o.p.

         LC 84-28617

After Spenser "receives a plea for help from true love Susan Silverman (who is being restrained by the son of a shadowy armaments manufacturer), Spenser travels from Boston to California to Chicago to Connecticut to Idaho, taking Hawk, his favorite colleague, with him on the rescue quest. All this is mainly an excuse for derring-do and violence. At one point the FBI and CIA contract with Spenser to kill the armaments manufacturer. The plot may be ridiculous, but the dialogue is snappy as usual, and the characters are fascinating." Libr J

Chance. Putnam 1996 307p o.p.

         LC 95-49950

"A second-echelon hoodlum, Julius Ventura, hires Spenser and his partner/sidekick Hawk to find his daughter's missing husband, a middle-management criminal named Anthony Meeker, who, it turns out, had money-

Parker, Robert B., 1932-—*Continued*
handling responsibilities. Speedily determining that Meeker liked to gamble, Spenser and his lover, psychiatrist Susan Silverman, and Hawk depart for Las Vegas." Publ Wkly

"Parker's stouthearted hero proves that he is still as tough and manly as they come, and more principled than ever in this punchy private-eye caper." N Y Times Book Rev

Cold service. Putnam 2005 305p $24.95
ISBN 0-399-15240-7   LC 2004-56608
"As the tale begins, the heretofore-indestructible Hawk is recovering from a near-death experience: shot in the back while protecting a bookie from the upstart Ukrainian Mob. It's payback time, of course, but not before Hawk nurses himself back to psychic and physical health. Meanwhile, Spenser does a bit of sleuthing on his own, determining that Hawk's assailants are the tip of a Ukrainian iceberg that has stuck its tentacles deep into Boston's underworld. Payback, Hawk style, requires eliminating not just the shooters but also the entire Mob. The action comes in a rush near the end, but the satisfying part here is watching Parker dig deeply into the remarkable friendship between two tough guys constitutionally averse to the whole touchy-feely side of life." Booklist

Crimson joy. Delacorte Press 1988 211p o.p.
                                      LC 87-33043
"When Police Lieutenant Marty Quirk is faced with an insane serial killer, who threatens to ignite all of Boston into a racial bonfire, he turns to Spenser for help. There aren't many clues to point the way, until the killer makes it personal by first going after Spenser and then his lady, psychologist Susan Silverman. Never one to take such an affront lightly, Spenser and his pal Hawk set out to put an end to these brutal murders." West Coast Rev Books

"Parker skillfully weaves Susan's objective theorizing, Spenser's *mot juste* narrative, and the killer's subjective emotions into fascinating psychological interplay." Libr J

Death in paradise. Putnam 2001 294p
ISBN 0-399-14779-9   LC 2001-31874
Jesse Stone, "erstwhile drunk and now sheriff of small-town Paradise, Mass., tackles two criminal and two personal mysteries here: the murder of a teenage girl found shot dead in a local lake, and the chronic beating of a local wife by her husband; the conundrum of Jesse's attraction to alcohol, and the mess of his love life, shaped by his dependence upon his estranged wife but encompassing a highly sexed affair with a school principal." Publ Wkly

"Given his raw nerves, bursts of violence and unhealthy devotion to his ex-wife, Jesse is still unpredictable and a little scary. Let's trust Parker to keep him on the edge." N Y Times Book Rev

Double Deuce. Putnam 1992 224p o.p.
                                      LC 91-29594
In this novel Spenser "finds himself, at the behest of his pal Hawk, defending the residents of a gang-terrorized Boston housing project known as Double Deuce. The drive-by shooting of a teenage mother and her child brings the duo into a confrontation with gangleader Major Johnson and his posse." Publ Wkly

Double play. Putnam 2004 288p $24.95
ISBN 0-399-15188-5   LC 2004-40029

"In this standalone historical from Parker, it is 1947, and the Brooklyn Dodgers have signed Jackie Robinson at first base. While a young Bobby Parker (that is, the author) avidly follows the national pastime, Joseph Burke, a shell-shocked World War II veteran, is working as a bodyguard in New York City. Emotionally stunted, Joseph lives in a world devoid of feeling-until he becomes Robinson's bodyguard." Libr J

"Parker pretty much defies category altogether in this deeply felt and intimately told memory tale, which takes place during the historic baseball season of 1947, when Jackie Robinson broke the color bar in major-league baseball by playing first base for the Brooklyn Dodgers. Fusing this chapter of sports history with a hardboiled gangster plot and haunting recollections of his own Boston boyhood, Parker fashions a hugely entertaining fiction that also serves as a blueprint for the themes that preoccupy him as a writer and the code of values that sustains his work." N Y Times Book Rev

Family honor. Putnam 1999 322p $22.95
ISBN 0-399-14566-4   LC 99-27488
Private detective Sunny Randall "is hired by a powerful family to find their runaway daughter, Millicent, who, it transpires, is hooking and needs rescuing. . . . Millicent, it happens, witnessed a conspiracy to murder arising from her cold, ambitious parents—her father aims to be governor—and the Italian mobsters who control them. The mobsters now want her dead, and Sunny, too, if need be. . . . The high suspense is equaled by the emotional power of Sunny's bonding with the damaged girl. A bravura performance." Publ Wkly

Gunman's rhapsody. Putnam 2001 289p
ISBN 0-399-14762-4   LC 00-53327
This western details the time Wyatt Earp "and his brothers spend in Tombstone, culminating in the shootout at the O.K. Corral." Publ Wkly

The novel "shows surprising fidelity to most of the known facts without letting them get in the way of a good story. Parker's strengths here, as in his crime novels, are plot and dialogue." N Y Times Book Rev

Hugger mugger. Putnam 2000 307p
ISBN 0-399-14587-7   LC 99-56105
"Spenser has been hired by Walter Clive, a race horse owner in Lamarr, GA. to work with the local security firm in order to find out who killed three of his horses. Clive is particularly concerned about Hugger Mugger, believed to be the next Secretariat." Libr J

"Culture shock brings out a certain waggishness in Spenser, who is fascinated by the elaborately staged lives of the horsy set and more amused than appalled by the character flaws he uncovers beneath all the polite gentility. Without compromising his expert sleuthing techniques . . . he manages to pick up enough regional skills to communicate with the devious natives in their own idiom—and catch them at their own wicked games." N Y Times Book Rev

Hush money. Putnam 1999 309p $22.95
ISBN 0-399-14458-7   LC 98-37344
In this mystery Boston private eye Spenser "is thrown by the lethal combination of sex (straight, gay, kinky) and politics (racial, sexual, academic) that erupts at a certain university in Cambridge when an African-American professor is implicated in the suicide of a militantly gay graduate student. In a situation that adds to his

Parker, Robert B., 1932-—*Continued*

discomposure, Spenser finds himself being sexually hounded by a woman whom he has just rescued from the similarly unhealthy attentions of a former boyfriend." NY Times Book Rev

Melancholy baby. Putnam 2004 296p $24.95

ISBN 0-399-15218-0   LC 2004-50377

"Boston P.I. Sunny Randall is unhappy to learn that the ex-husband she still loves is getting married to someone else. Her life seemingly a mess, Sunny seeks the help of psychiatrist Susan Silverman. In between sessions that probe her relationship with her insufferable mother and beloved father, Sunny works on the case of Sarah Markham, a distraught 21-year-old woman who wants to track down her biological parents. The only trouble is that the couple who raised her claim she's theirs but refuse to take a DNA test to prove it. Sunny soon learns that Sarah's parents have lied about their past. . . . Parker, as always, leavens his story with sly wit while relying on dialog to advance the plot and develop character." Libr J

Night passage. Putnam 1997 322p $21.95

ISBN 0-399-14304-1   LC 97-6901

"Jesse Stone's career as an LAPD homicide detective is over, as is his marriage, thanks largely to booze. The good news is that Paradise, Massachusetts, needs a police chief. What Stone doesn't know is that city father Hasty Hathaway and acting chief Lou Burke are looking for a pushover to put in charge, and they figure a lush might do nicely. They pick the wrong lush." Booklist

This mystery features "complex, expertly shaded relationships, especially romantic, as Jesse flails and fails at loving both his ex-wife and his new girlfriend. The most powerful romance here, though, is between Parker and the written word." Publ Wkly

Now and then. G. P. Putnam's Sons 2007 296p $25.95

ISBN 978-0-399-15441-6; 0-399-15441-8

LC 2007-23056

In this "addition to the series, the troubled client is a husband who feels his wife has been behaving bizarrely. Spenser thinks she's probably having an affair, and through the magic of a planted listening device, he presents the worried husband with the damning evidence. The device has also picked up that the wife's lover is involved in a group called Last Hope, which turns out to be a kind of brokerage outlet for terrorists looking for equipment and other terrorists. The case has moved from the kind of private-eye work that Spenser finds sleazy to one with horrific ramifications. The story itself makes compelling reading on its own, but Parker, as usual, spikes it with caustic wit and the interplay between Spenser and his longtime love, Susan. And here he ups the ante by calling on Spenser to use all his brain and brawn to protect Susan. Terrific." Booklist

Paper doll. Putnam 1993 223p o.p.

LC 92-30528

In this novel, Spenser is hired by "Louden Tripp to investigate the murder of his wife. Olivia Tripp was bludgeoned to death, the apparent victim of random street crime. Tripp feels the Boston PD glossed over the case. Spenser . . . decides to check Olivia's background. That thread takes him to Alton, South Carolina." Booklist

"Mr. Parker has trimmed his language and characterizations right down to the knuckle to tell this poignant story about the false fronts that people put up to shield themselves from shame. There's no flab on Spenser, either." N Y Times Book Rev

Perchance to dream; Robert B. Parker's sequel to Raymond Chandler's The big sleep. Putnam 1991 271p o.p.   LC 90-47004

"Private eye Philip Marlowe spins a yarn of greed, madness and death with the cool-eyed cynicism (and good-guy core) that made him the classic hardboiled dick. The era is post-WWII . . . possibly early '50s . . . the L.A. dream beginning to sour. Psychotic Carmen Sternwood is missing from an expensive sanatorium. After sultry Vivian has enlisted suave gangster Eddie Mars to locate her sister, the family butler, Norris, hires Marlowe for the same purpose." Publ Wkly

"Parker plots with little more scope and linear logic than Chandler ever managed, and he fires off enough smart-ass one-liners to keep most readers happy. It's true, he never ventures near the subterranean emotional depths that Chandler would occasionally explore, but, after all, sequels—even when, they're written by the same person—rarely match the originals." Booklist

Potshot. Putnam 2001 294p

ISBN 0-399-14710-1   LC 00-68342

"Spenser takes on the job of clearing out a gang of 'mountain trash' who are intimidating the residents of Potshot, Arizona. Even the supremely resourceful Spenser needs a little help with this one, so he drafts six of his compadres from previous adventures." Booklist

"Rounding up this posse of urban gunslingers—all hard-bitten veterans of previous Spenser novels—was pure inspiration on Parker's part, because another shrewd way of keeping a sleuth in shape over the long haul is to guarantee that he has some fun." N Y Times Book Rev

Resolution. G.P. Putnam's Sons 2008 292p $25.95

ISBN 978-0-399-15504-8; 0-399-15504-X

LC 2008-6589

In this sequel to Appaloosa "narrator and hired gun Everitt Hitch takes a job as lookout in Amos Wolfson's Blackfoot Saloon and, in short order, guns down local upstart Koy Wickman and stands up for the town's beleaguered prostitutes. Without fully intending it, he creates a haven of orderliness amid the chaos of sheriffless Resolution. But larger forces are at work as Eamon O'Malley, competing with Wolfson for control of Resolution, hires freelance thugs Cato and Rose to replace Wickman. Lest Everitt end up outnumbered, his old friend Virgil Cole turns up just as Wolfson and O'Malley amass armies for a decisive battle. . . . Though the plot meanders its way to a too-fast climax, Parker's dialogue is snappy and his not-a-word-wasted scenes suit this Spartan western." Publ Wkly

Rough weather. G.P. Putnam's Sons 2008 294p $26.95

ISBN 978-0-399-15519-2; 0-399-15519-8

LC 2008-33702

"When Heidi Bradshaw hires Spenser to 'support' her at her daughter's wedding on Tashtego Island in Buzzards Bay, Mass., an old nemesis of Spenser's, the Gray

Parker, Robert B., 1932——*Continued*

Man, who almost killed Spenser in Small Vices (1977), also shows up on the island. Spenser is unable to prevent the kidnapping of the bride or the deaths that attend it. Assisted by a cadre of familiar players, Spenser persists in trying to find the missing bride in spite of warnings from the Gray Man." Publ Wkly

"The familiar elements here include the child in distress, the wealthy with their own agenda, the killer with a code of honour, and an almost interminable repetition of the Spenser-Susan-Hawk mutual self-appreciation society. I'm not sure if Parker figures he's got to reprise the psychology between this triangle, . . . but he does and they do at great length here, to the detriment of what is otherwise a pretty interestingly plotted book. . . . Parker remains the master of the easy-reading, compelling, thriller." Crime Time

School days. Putnam 2005 295p $24.95
  ISBN 0-399-15323-3   LC 2005-74690
"A wealthy grandmother hires Spenser to clear her 17-year-old grandson of being the coconspirator and co-killer in a school shooting at a private school that has left five students, a teacher, and an administrator dead. The boy's buddy has named him, and he has confessed to the crime. Everyone–police, school officials, the defense lawyer, and the immediate family–has given up on the kid, but Spenser has never seen a slammed door he didn't long to break down. Soon he's questioning everyone in the kid's circle, looking for the chink in that slammed door. Along the way, he rummages through all sorts of closets in the privileged world of the private school, turning up links to the underworld." Booklist

Sea change. Putnam 2006 295p $24.95
  ISBN 0-399-15267-9   LC 2004-43150
"The body of an unidentified woman is found in a cove off the Massachusetts village of Paradise, where Jesse Stone, former L.A. homicide detective, is now chief of police. With no clues and a bevy of nonlocals in town for the annual sailboat competition, Stone must use every resource at his disposal to find out who the woman was, what happened to her, and why no one has reported her missing. . . . Parker is a master at creating memorable characters and crime stories that are inevitably tied to social issues of some importance." Libr J

Shrink rap. Putnam 2002 304p $24.95
  ISBN 0-399-14930-9   LC 2002-24826
The Sunny Randall novel "has the Boston private eye on a national book tour with a best-selling author who is being stalked by her former husband, an unethical and possibly unhinged psychiatrist. The situation proves ideal for Parker's patented brand of knowing humor, yielding glossary snapshots of dithering book dealers, dollar-driven publishers and awe-struck fans." N Y Times Book Rev

Small vices. Putnam 1997 308p $21.95
  ISBN 0-399-14244-4   LC 96-9827
"Ellis Alves, a black man with sexual assaults on his record, was convicted easily when two witnesses said they saw him kidnap the victim. Former prosecutor Rita Fiore suspects a frame-up, however, and hires old pal Spenser to investigate. . . . Sure enough, reopening the case pits them against the victim's influential parents, her hostile tennis-star boyfriend and his wealthy family, and the state cop who arrested Alves. Four Boston thugs

can't force Spenser off the case, but an imported hit man pours several bullets into him." Publ Wkly

"Mr. Parker has written a powerful piece about the defeat and reclamation of a hero, but I wouldn't say that Spenser's dance with death teaches the old knight to act his age. . . . By virtue of his mythic death and rebirth, he has defied mortality altogether and become like some fertility god who lowers himself into the ground each winter and comes roaring back to life each spring." N Y Times Book Rev

Taming a sea-horse; a Spenser novel. Delacorte Press/Seymour Lawrence 1986 250p o.p.
                           * LC 85-29297
Spenser is "in grave danger on an all but unpaid quest to avenge the deaths of a prostitute he met briefly and a pimp he disliked. He confronts slick mob bosses, two-bit thugs and corrupt financiers, relying on his wits but not fearing to apply a little muscle." Time

Thin air. Putnam 1995 293p o.p.
                            LC 94-39046
Spenser's "friend and ultradeadly ally, Hawk, is off in Burma, leaving Spenser on his own when longtime pal Frank Belson of Boston Homicide needs help. Belson's beautiful young bride, Lisa St. Claire, has disappeared. When Belson is wounded in an ambush that may be related to Lisa's disappearance, Spenser undertakes the search." Booklist

Trouble in Paradise. Putnam 1998 324p $22.95
  ISBN 0-399-14433-1   LC 98-7354
This novel finds Jesse Stone, "the chief of police of modest Paradise, Mass., battling a ruthless gang of thieves even as he jousts with personal demons. Two parallel plotlines tell the story. One follows career criminal James Macklin and his moll, Faye, and their planning and subsequent execution of the heist of all the money and valuables on super-rich Stiles Island, which is connected by bridge to Paradise. Meanwhile, there's Stone, a cool customer who's not afraid to step on wealthy toes but who can't get his love life in order and can barely control his taste for booze. . . . Stone's romantic entanglements, particularly his troubled relationship with his ex-wife, add texture to the novel." Publ Wkly

Walking shadow. Putnam 1994 270p o.p.
                            LC 94-5127
Boston PI Spenser "encounters danger, venality and plenty of comic material in this . . . tale spanning the worlds of experimental theater and illegal immigration. While he'd rather be at work renovating the old farmhouse that he and his lover, psychiatrist Susan, have bought in nearby Concord, Spenser agrees to find out who is following the Artistic Director of the Port City Theater Company, on whose board of directors Susan sits." Publ Wkly

Widow's walk. Putnam 2002 294p
  ISBN 0-399-14845-0   LC 2001-48771
"Attorney Rita Fiore, who's worked with the Boston PI before, hires Spenser to find out if her new client, Mary Smith, . . . indeed shot to death her husband, banker and Mayflower descendant Nathan Smith, as the evidence indicates. . . . The writing is as clean as fresh ice, and from the opening sentence ('I think she's probably guilty,' Rita Fiore said to me), it's clear that readers are in the hands of a vet who knows what he's doing." Publ Wkly

Parker, T. Jefferson

Black water. Hyperion 2002 338p

ISBN 0-7868-6804-X   LC 2001-51903

"Merci Rayborn, homicide detective for the Orange County, California, sheriff's department, has a crime scene that's a puzzler. And it's going to be very high profile—it's in an upscale enclave of million-dollar estates, and one of the victims is a cop. Gwen Wildcraft is dead, and her husband, Archie, is unconscious with a severe head wound. Wildcraft is a patrol officer with the department, and his gun appears to be the murder weapon. Merci's superiors would prefer a quick call of murder-suicide, but her instincts tell her that's the wrong conclusion. . . . A thoughtful, multilayered tale in which crime is a catalyst rather than the centerpiece." Booklist

The blue hour. Hyperion 1999 359p $23.95

ISBN 0-7868-6288-2   LC 98-43135

This Orange County, California, police procedural pairs "retired expert cop Tim Hess with brash young detective Merci Rayborn. They're an unlikely team fighting a nasty serial killer who abducts wealthy, attractive women, eviscerates them, and then apparently saves their bodies." Libr J

"Solid police work, beefed up with some ingenious devices from Parker's bottomless bag of tricks, makes it all come out right—but not before the wondrously weird characters have taken this lurid plot to its outer limits." N Y Times Book Rev

California girl. Morrow 2004 370p $24.95

ISBN 0-060-56236-6

A mystery set in 1960s Southern California. "The Becker boys (Andy the homicide reporter, Nick the cop, and David the minister; Clay was killed in Vietnam) grew up near the Vonns, a troubled, abusive family burdened with more than its share of tragedy. When 19-year-old beauty queen Janell Vonn, the essence of a California girl, is found beheaded in the abandoned SunBlesst packing house, the Becker brothers begin their separate quests to find her killer, finally bringing him to justice while realizing redemption for themselves. But 40 years after a conviction, it becomes apparent that the Beckers were wrong, very wrong. Drenched in lust, love, betrayal, and unfulfilled promise, California Girl features masterly plotting, smart prose, and memorable characters." Libr J

Cold pursuit. Hyperion 2003 360p $23.95

ISBN 0-7868-6805-8   LC 2002-32940

"The murder of retired San Diego Port Commissioner and local politician Pete Braga falls in the lap of homicide detective Tom McMichael, whose family has a multigenerational feud going with the Bragas. Parker makes the most of a standard mystery device here—murder driven by a motive from the distant past—but the real joy of the novel is its remarkably evocative prose, which flows seamlessly from lyrical descriptions of rainy San Diego to crisp, no-nonsense dialogue." Booklist

The fallen; a novel. William Morrow 2006 323p $24.95

ISBN 0060562382   LC 2005047934

"When Garrett Asplundh's body is found under a San Diego bridge, Robbie Brownlaw and his partner, McKenzie Cortez, are called on to the case. After the tragic death of his child and the dissolution of his marriage, Garrett . . . left the SDPD to become an ethics investigator, looking into the activities of his former colleagues. At first his death . . . looks like suicide, but the clues Brownlaw and Cortez find just don't add up. With pressure mounting from the police and the city's politicians, Brownlaw fights to find the truth, all the while trying to hold on to his own crumbling marriage." Publisher's note

"This stand-alone classic police procedural, replete with its portrait of big-city crime and power-hungry politicians, follows a recognizable storyline. However, its lively writing, well-paced plot, rounded characters (from call girls to shady politicians), and twists stand out." Bookmarks Magazine

L.A. outlaws; a novel. Dutton 2008 372p $25.95

ISBN 978-0-525-95055-4; 0-525-95055-9

       LC 2007-33722

"By day, Allison is Suzanne Jones, an eighth-grade history teacher with three sons in Los Angeles; by night, she dons a mask, straps on her derringer and steals from the greedy. Beloved by the media, she never uses the gun; her victims are never sympathetic; and she gives part of her loot to charity. But while stealing diamonds belonging to a master criminal known as the Bull, she witnesses a gangland-style bloodbath at the hands of Lupercio, a ruthless assassin working for the Bull. As she's leaving the scene of the crime, L.A. sheriff's deputy Charles Hood stops her, and that's when the plot gets complicated." Publ Wkly

"Parker writes with an understanding of the West's essential character: in Outlaws, he casts Los Angeles as an eternally sprawling, brawling camp town, populated by bandits and bigots, the quick and the dead, where the poor who once rendered tallow now work the deep fryer at KFC. . . . His concise prose, at once low-key and lyrical, plays almost like cowboy poetry." Los Angeles Times

Laguna heat. St. Martin's Press 1985 342p o.p.

       LC 85-10055

"The hero is Tom Shephard, 'the new and sole member of the Laguna Beach Police Homicide Division.' Normally, one man would be all that is needed; there are not many homicides in Laguna Beach. But suddenly a sadistic murderer is loose, burning bodies after mutilating them. Shephard, an experienced cop, gets a lead very fast, is attacked and hurt, finds his home vandalized and goes through other harrowing experiences, many psychological." N Y Times Book Rev

"Parker's narrative is a bit heavy-handed, but his ultimately satisfying novel delivers deep and sensitive characterizations." Booklist

Little Saigon. St. Martin's Press 1988 354p o.p.

       LC 88-11586

"Chuck Frye, a surf bum who has recently failed at journalism, business and marriage, lives in the shadow of his war-hero brother Bennett, and their father, a wealthy real-estate tycoon. Bennett's Vietnamese wife is a singer whose protest music has made her a heroine among anticommunists and Asian expatriates. When she is kidnapped during a performance, Chuck joins the search for her, hoping to end his estrangement from the Frye clan. But the more he learns about the crime's motive—politics, gang warfare or revenge are all possibilities—the more intently his family tries to shut him out of the investigation." Publ Wkly

Parker, T. Jefferson—*Continued*

Pacific beat. St. Martin's Press 1991 364p o.p.

LC 90-27411

"John Weir, an ex-sheriff's department employee, and brother-in-law Raymond battle corrupt police, development-at-all-cost advocates, and a known sex offender when they try to find the murderer of John's beloved sister. Splayed against the coastal community of Newport Beach, California, where oldtime residents hope to elect a 'slow-growth' candidate, their investigation reveals ever-deeper layers of deception. This exciting, multidimensional plot should grab even the most demanding mystery reader." Libr J

Silent Joe. Hyperion 2001 341p

ISBN 0-7868-6728-0   LC 00-53938

"Joe Trona is a dutiful son, but horrible facial scars have made him an outcast. He lived in an orphanage until he was adopted at five by Will Trona, a powerful politician in Southern California's Orange County. As a hulking teenager and later as a young man, Joe became Will's right-hand man—running errands, extracting revenge on enemies, protecting his flank—all the while living a lonely life because of his disfigurement. One night, Joe drops his guard for a moment, and Will is gunned down. Despite aggressive investigations by the FBI and sheriff's department, Joe seeks his own vengeance." Publ Wkly

"A complex mix of seemingly unconnected plot lines, vivid characterization, and real mystery merge to form a truly satisfying thriller." Libr J

Storm runners. HarperCollins 2007 370p $25.95

ISBN 978-0-06-085423-2; 0-06-085423-2

"In Southern California, as San Diego weather lady Frankie Hatfield puts it, 'Rain is life!' Rain is also raw power in the land of avocadoes and sod farms. When Hatfield stumbles upon a family secret that allows her to control the rain, that discovery brings her unfathomable power with potentially deadly consequences. P.I. Matt Stromsoe is battling with his own demons—his wife and child have been murdered, and he's seeking redemption—and he willingly accepts an assignment to protect Hatfield. The case takes him from fragrant orange groves in the San Diego hills to the cold cement of Pelican Bay State Prison. Parker's trademark is the ability to create real characters—tangible, flawed, and heroic—and Stromsoe follows the tradition." Libr J

Where serpents lie. Hyperion 1998 432p $23.95

ISBN 0-7868-6287-4   LC 97-2633

A thriller set in "Orange County, California, where cop Terry Naughton, head of Crimes Against Youth, a division he helped create, is fiercely trying to track down a creepy pedophile who calls himself Horridus . . . before he kills one of the young girls that he has kidnapped. It seems that besides child pornography and rape, Horridus is also into snakes—really big, hungry snakes—and there's evidence that he has used these 'pets' to dispose of victims in the past. . . . This taut police procedural mixes high supense with believable characters; it's a real page-turner." Libr J

Parkhurst, Carolyn, 1971-

The dogs of Babel. Little, Brown 2003 264p $21.95

ISBN 0-316-16868-8

* LC 2002-43644

"When the book opens, Paul, a linguist who lives in suburban Virginia, has just learned that his wife, Lexy Ransome, has died in their backyard in a mysterious fall from an apple tree. Lorelei is the sole witness to this event, and Paul resolves to make her reveal what hapened. Never mind that she is a dog. He will each her to talk." N Y Times Book Rev

"As Paul slips into ever more desperate behavior, we hear an account of his and Lexy's courtship and marriage—the tender, tentative union of two damaged people. But then Paul contacts a man convicted of operating on dogs to install vocal chords, and what had been a poignant, affecting tale turns truly frightening . . . . Parkhurst delivers a remarkable debut in quiet, authoritative prose." Libr J

Lost and found. Little, Brown and Co. 2006 292p $23.95

ISBN 978-0-316-15638-7; 0-316-15638-8

LC 2005-029741

This "novel focuses on several characters competing on an Amazing Race-like reality show called Lost and Found, where teams of two travel from destination to destination following enigmatic clues and collecting various items in hopes of winning the game. Laura wants to connect with her sullen teenage daughter, Cassie, after a traumatic experience highlighted the distance between them. Justin and Abby believe they have cast off their homosexual urges in favor of a traditional Christian marriage, but the game offers unexpected tests for their resolution. Carl and Jeff are two middle-aged, recently divorced brothers looking for adventure. Juliet and Dallas are former child stars seeking to recapture fame and willing to do just about anything to achieve that end. Emotional confrontations, suppressed desires, and unexpected connections surprise the various contestants as they continue to play a game that is starting to disgust them." Booklist

"Satire so on-point, you'd swear you've already seen this series." Entertainment Wkly

Parkinson, Heather, 1974-

Across open ground; a novel. Bloomsbury Pub. 2002 248p $23.95

ISBN 1-58234-243-1   LC 2001-56527

"The book is set in 1917, and news of World War I reaches the Idaho high country like a faint trace of wood smoke. Parkinson weights her story equally between Walter Pascoe, a 17-year-old sheepherder, and the woman he falls in love with—a trapper named Trina Ivy. Their brief summer idyll ends when Walter departs to fight in the trenches of France. Pregnant and penniless, Trina must stay in Idaho and fend for herself." N Y Times Book Rev

"The narrative is often powerful, . . . with a concern for female characters and a tenderness generally absent from more conventional books about this era in the American West." Publ Wkly

Parks, Gordon, 1912-2006

The learning tree. Harper & Row 1963 303p
o.p.

*

"At 12 years of age Newt is awakening to the world
around him in his small town of Cherokee Flats, Kansas,
in the 1920s. There is the impact of a first sexual experience and a first love, and because he is a Negro, special
responsibility of behavior when one individual may represent an entire group in the eyes of the community."
Shapiro. Fic for Youth. 3d edition

Parks, Suzan-Lori

Getting mother's body; a novel; [by] Suzanne
Lori. Random House 2003 257p $23.95
ISBN 1-400-06022-2   LC 2002-31762
"Billy Beede is a girl with troubles. Unmarried, pregnant by a married man, and needing a lot of money fast,
Billy decides to travel from Texas to Arizona to retrieve
her dead mother's body, hoping to find a small fortune
in jewels presumably buried in the grave." Libr J
"Set in the summer of 1963, and recounted in a slow,
Southern drawl befitting the mood, the story unravels
from a myriad of viewpoints, including the no-good custom coffin salesman who's fathered Billy's unborn baby,
the one-legged neighbor in love with Billy, and her deceased mother's feisty lesbian lover." Publ Wkly

Parks, Tim

Cleaver; a novel. Arcade Publishing 2008 c2006
316p $25
ISBN 978-1-55970-855-5   LC 2007-22844
First published 2006 in the United Kingdom
"British journalist Harold Cleaver — egotist, incurable
philanderer, unapologetic gourmand — scores a career
high by humiliating the U.S. president in a televised interview. But his son has just published a scene-stealing
roman à clef. Retreating to an isolated cabin in the Alps
without TV or cell-phone reception, Cleaver engages his
son, the president, and a doll (yes, a doll) named Olga
in intense, imaginary debates. It's much saner than it
sounds, as Tim Parks draws a lively critique of modern
media out of Cleaver's soul-searching rants and a surprisingly affectionate portrait of self-reflection and forgiveness in Cleaver." Entertainment Wkly

Destiny. Arcade Pub. 2000 248p $24.95
ISBN 1-559-70517-5   LC 00-130423
First published 1999 in the United Kingdom
"The narrator, Christopher Burton, learns that Marco,
his schizophrenic son, has committed suicide by stabbing
himself with a screwdriver. His first reaction, however,
is not shock or grief; he thinks that now, at last, he can
leave his hateful wife. 'Destiny' examines how and why
he arrives at this grotesque response." N Y Times Book
Rev
"As Burton's stream of consciousness approaches disintegration, he finally admits truths about himself and his
behavior in what becomes a deeply affecting portrait of
a man in mental anguish." Publ Wkly

Rapids; a novel. Arcade Pub. 2006 c2005 246p
$24
ISBN 1-55970-811-5   LC 2005-29292

First published 2005 in the United Kingdom
"Set against the backdrop of nature, global warming,
and middle-age crises, 15 members of a kayaking club
from Britain descend upon the Italian Alps to test their
mettle on the white waters of the torrential River Aurino.
Clive, the strong and stoic leader of the expedition, along
with Michela, his Italian partner, are fresh from protesting globalism in Milan. Vince, a recently widowed banker–whose late wife was formerly active in the group–
along with his daughter, joins the group and immediately
must confront his own fears, insecurities, and shortcomings. . . . An infatuation with kayak-savvy but emotionally unstable Michela forces Vince to reappraise his marriage, his career, and his worldview." Booklist
"Parks is prolific, and his books are written with a
compelling urgency and energy. In Rapids this urgency—
and the varied cast—sometimes lead to narratorial
splashiness: big ideas and themes are introduced only for
some of them to be left underdeveloped. Yet the book
has great strengths. It is thrillingly paced. Vince is a
monumental character, difficult and rewarding. And
Parks is constantly alert to the nuances of everyday pat-
ter, a clever and magnanimous describer of ordinary people." London Rev Books

Parry, Richard

The winter wolf; Wyatt Earp in Alaska. Forge
1996 380p $24.95
ISBN 0-312-86017-X   LC 96-18269
"A Tom Doherty Associates book"
"It's 1897, and the days of the OK Corral are a memory, but notoriety is still a burden for hard-up Wyatt Earp.
He and his second wife, Josie, are heading north to Alaska to make their fortune in the gold rush. Circumstances
conspire against him, however, and he must settle for
law-related jobs. At every turn, he's wary that an old
nemesis may be coming up behind him, but the greatest
danger zeroing in on Earp is the son he didn't know he
had." Booklist
"The inevitable confrontation between father and son
packs geniune emotional wallop. Parry, who lives in
Alaska, skillfully evokes both era and place." Publ Wkly

Parsons, Julie

Mary, Mary; a novel. Simon & Schuster 1999
c1998 299p $22.50
ISBN 0-684-85324-8   LC 98-33753
First published 1998 in the United Kingdom
In this novel, a "middle-aged widow named Margaret
Mitchell returns to her native Ireland from New Zealand
to care for her dying mother. Concerned when her 20-
year-old daughter, Mary, fails to return from an evening
out with friends, Margaret is devastated when the girl's
raped and mutilated body is fished out of the river. In
her rage and grief, she spurns the compassion of the
homicide detective who loves her and takes her own revenge on the sadistic killer, who has slipped through the
courts on a technicality and is now stalking her." N Y
Times Book Rev
"Parsons writes short, quickly paced scenes that raise
the suspense level in taut increments, and her story is
full of genuine surprises and fresh plot twists. While
shocking, the novel's conclusion is powerful and convincing." Publ Wkly

Passos, John Dos *See* Dos Passos, John

Pasternak, Boris Leonidovich, 1890-1960

Doctor Zhivago; [by] Boris Pasternak. Pantheon Bks. 1958 558p o.p.

First published 1957 in Italy

"The account of the life of a Russian intellectual, Yurii Zhivago, a doctor and a poet, during the first three decades of the 20th c. A broad epic picture of Russia is developed as the background to Zhivago's family life, his creative ecstasies, his love for Lara (another man's wife), his emotional upheavals, wanderings, and moments of happiness. Though the novel ends with Zhivago's decline and death as a result of what the author saw as the dehumanization of life that prevailed in the postrevolution years, the epilogue is full of expectations of the freedom that is to come." Ency of World Lit in the 20th Century

Patchett, Ann

Bel canto; a novel. HarperCollins Pubs. 2001 318p $25

ISBN 0-06-018873-1   LC 00-53671

"An impoverished South American country hosts a birthday extravaganza for a Japanese industrialist in the hope of securing new foreign investment. The lure? An internationally renowned lyric soprano. Indeed, when Roxane Coss sings, even the ragtag terrorists who are about to flood through the air-conditioning vents and take the guests hostage hold their breath, transported by the beauty of her voice. Patchett's tragicomic novel—a fantasia of guns and Puccini and Red Cross negotiations—invokes the glorious, unreliable promises of art, politics, and love." New Yorker

Run. HarperCollins Publishers 2007 295p $25.95

ISBN 978-0-06-134063-5; 0-06-134063-4
          LC 2006-41297

"Boston lawyer and ex-politician Bernard Doyle has nurtured his three sons—Sullivan, 33, and African American Tip, 21, and Teddy, 20, brothers adopted 20 years earlier—since the death of his beloved wife, Bernadette, some 15 years ago. Then, one snowy evening, Tip, inattentive and annoyed at his father, is pushed out of the way of an oncoming vehicle by a woman, herself hit and badly injured, who turns out to be the boys' birth mother and who's been watching the boys for years, along with her 11-year-old daughter, Kenya." Booklist

"Ms. Patchett gives her readers much to contemplate when genetics, privilege, opportunity and nurture come into play. And to her credit she is neither vague nor reductive about any of these things; she creates a genuinely rich landscape of human possibility." N Y Times (Late N Y Ed)

Paterson, James Hamilton- *See* Hamilton-Paterson, James

Paton, Alan

Ah, but your land is beautiful. Scribner 1982 c1981 271p

ISBN 0-684-17336-0   LC 81-13547

First published 1981 in the United Kingdom

This novel on racial unrest in South Africa covers the years 1952 to 1958 "and charts the response of the newly formed Liberal Party to the Suppression of Communism Act, the dispossession of black farmers, the destruction of Sophiatown, the disenfranchisement of Coloured voters, the influence of the Broederbond within the Nationalist Party and the rise to power of their premier, 'Dr. Hendrik'. . . . The parts played by Trevor Huddleston, Patrick Duncan, Geoffrey Clayton, Helen Joseph and . . . other historic figures, living and dead, are interspersed with the imagined destinies of representatives from different sections of the community." New Statesman (1913)

"Alan Paton's considerable practical life in South Africa aside, his place in the literature of social protest has been secured by his steady devotion to the ideal of the empathetic imagination in fiction." N Y Times Book Rev

Cry, the beloved country. Scribner Classics 2003 316p $28; pa $15

ISBN 0-7432-6195-X; 0-7432-6217-4 (pa)

First published 1948

"Reverend Kumalo, a black South African preacher, is called to Johannesburg to rescue his sister. There he learns that his son Absalom has been accused of murdering a young white attorney whose interests and sympathies had been with the natives. Despite this, the attorney's father comes to the aid of the minister to help the natives in their struggle to survive a drought." Shapiro. Fic for Youth. 3d edition

Tales from a troubled land. Scribner 1961 128p o.p.

Contents: Life for a life; Sponono; Ha'penny; The wasteland; The worst thing of his life; The elephant shooter; Debbie go home; Death of a tsotsi; The divided house; A drink in the passage

"Most of the tales are told from the point of view of a compassionate white director of a boy's reformatory; however, one of the most moving concerns a native shepherd who, though innocent, becomes a victim when his employer is robbed." Booklist

Too late the phalarope. Scribner 1953 276p o.p.

"The story is basically that of a well loved white police lieutenant who in his need turns to a native girl. He is betrayed, reported and thus brings shame on himself and his family. The narrator of the story is an aunt who fills in the entire picture of family pride, righteous disdain, unbending adherence to an imposed restriction, and the falsity of many basic customs in parts of South Africa." Libr J

"The book is written with superb simplicity. It is cadenced but unaffected; it will inevitably be called Biblical and yet there is no conscious parodying of scriptual prose. It flows relentlessly to its crisis, and sometimes we cry out at its power. The people are all clear and real, the South African backgrounds are colorfully and deeply etched. The conflicts are diverse but they all contribute to the basic struggle; father and son, races, languages, prejudices." Christ Sci Monit

Paton Walsh, Jill, 1937-

(jt. auth) Sayers, D. L. Thrones, dominations

Patterson, Harry, 1929- *See* Higgins, Jack, 1929-

Patterson, Henry, 1929- *See* Higgins, Jack, 1929-

Patterson, James

1st to die; a novel. Little, Brown 2001 424p $32
ISBN 0-316-66600-9   LC 00-61123
"The story opens in San Francisco with the gruesome murder of a bride and groom on their wedding night. Detective Lindsay Boxer is called to the scene, just after learning she is suffering from a rare and potentially life-threatening blood disease. For help with the case, she calls on her best friend, Claire, a medical examiner, and, reluctantly at first, Cindy, a newspaper reporter who is covering the story. . . . Patterson keeps up the suspense until the very last page." Booklist

Along came a spider; a novel. Little, Brown 1993 435p
ISBN 0-316-69364-2
                              * LC 92-24581
"Alex Cross, a black Washington, D.C., police detective with a Ph.D. in psychology, and Jezzie Flanagan, a white motorcycling Secret Service agent, become lovers as they work together to apprehend a chilling psychopath who has kidnapped two children from a posh private school. . . . Patterson's storytelling talent is in top form in this grisly escapist yarn." Libr J

Cat & mouse; a novel. Little, Brown 1997 399p
ISBN 0-316-69329-4
                              * LC 97-20277
Black Washington, D.C. detective/psychologist Alex Cross' "old nemesis, psychopath Gary Soneji, is dead set on killing Alex in the ugliest, most terrifying way he can devise, but first, he's decided to play a game of cat and mouse with his intended victim. In Europe, a sadistic torturer dubbed 'Mr. Smith' is on the loose, and if Soneji is the king of cat and mouse, Mr. Smith is the grand high emperor. Elusive and terrifying, he performs autopsies on his living victims. FBI Agent Thomas Pierce has been assigned to the Smith case, but he's come back to America especially to help Alex track down Soneji." Booklist
"All story lines connect in this thriller, whose driving plot will distract you from thinking about its implausibilities and keep you turning pages to the last." Libr J

Cross. Little, Brown and Co. 2006 393p $27.99
ISBN 978-0-316-15979-1; 0-316-15979-4
                              LC 2006-12929
"Beginning with a flashback to the murder of Cross's wife, Maria, Patterson quickly introduces Michael Sullivan (aka the Butcher of Sligo). What follows is a frenetically paced series of brutal rapes and killings by Sullivan, once employed by the mob as a freelancer and now at war with them. Cross juggles being a single parent and being involved in the dangerous game of tracking serial killers until he finally decides to give it up for his family. Needless to say, he's drawn back into the game when it promises a chance of finding Maria's killer." Publ Wkly
"Even as the story whips by with incredible speed, Patterson manages to pack it full of suspense, emotion, and a resolution that, while perfectly satisfying, carries the author's trademark teaser hinting at the 'more' that surely will come." Booklist

Four blind mice; a novel. Little, Brown 2002 387p $27.95
ISBN 0-316-69300-6   LC 2002-67540
"Alex Cross is on the brink of retirement from the Washington Police Force when his best friend, John Sampson, comes to him with an urgent request. Sampson's friend, Sergeant Ellis Cooper, has just been convicted by a military court for the murders of three women. Cooper swears he's innocent, and Sampson believes him." Booklist
"The action leads, as is Patterson's custom, to a firecracker string of climaxes; the finale finds Cross handcuffed and stripped naked in deep woods, about to be killed. Throughout, Patterson expertly balances the conspiratorial action with intriguing developments in Cross's domestic life." Publ Wkly

Hide & seek; a novel. Little, Brown 1996 356p
o.p.   LC 95-35928
"Beautiful Maggie Bradford seems to have it all: a successful career as a singer/songwriter, fame, money, and two precious children. However, she killed her first husband in self-defense and now she's in jail awaiting trial for the murder of her second husband, Will Shepherd, a charming, psychotic professional soccer player. At first, Maggie's marriage seems fine, but soon Will begins to act irrationally. The increasing tension comes to a head when Maggie comes to believe that Will has been sexually abusing her daughter, the resulting confrontation ends in Will's death and Maggie's arrest. Climaxing in Maggie's celebrity trial, this page-turner delivers a solid punch, complete with a surprise ending." Libr J

Jack and Jill; a novel. Little, Brown 1996 432p
ISBN 0-316-69371-5   LC 96-8037
This novel features "African American psychologist-turned-detective Alex Cross. . . . Alex is troubled when a young child is murdered near the school his son attends and frightened when the murderer strikes again. On the other side of town, away from the scary inner-city D.C. streets, a pair of killers who call themselves Jack and Jill are terrorizing the movers and shakers by murdering a series of high-profile people. . . . A fast-paced, electric story that is utterly believable." Booklist

Kiss the girls; a novel. Little, Brown 1995 451p
ISBN 0-316-69370-7   LC 94-14177
"'Casanova' works the East Coast, 'The Gentleman Caller' works the West Coast, and these two serial killers might just be working together. Washed-up Washington, D.C., police detective Alex Cross gets involved when his niece is abducted." Libr J

London bridges; a novel. Little, Brown and Co 2004 391p $27.95
ISBN 0-316-71059-8   LC 2004-16752
"Terrorists have seized the worlds largest cities. London, Washington, DC, New York, and Frankfurt will be destroyed, unless their demands are met. . . . Heading up the investigation by the FBI, CIA, and Interpol, Alex Cross is stunned when surveillance photos show Geoffrey Shafer, the Weasel, near one of the bombing sites. He senses the presence of the Wolf as well, the most vicious predator he has ever battled." Publisher's note
"The book is a model of economy, delivering a full package of suspense, emotion and characterization in a minimum number of words." Publ Wkly

LIST OF FICTIONAL WORKS

Patterson, James—*Continued*

Pop! goes the weasel; a novel. Little, Brown 1999 423p $26.95

ISBN 0-316-69328-6   LC 99-21473

In this suspense novel Alex Cross "is working on a series of Jane Doe murders in southeast Washington. His hard-nosed boss doesn't want to waste precious resources investigating the deaths of a bunch of 'worthless prostitutes and druggies,' but Cross is convinced the women are the victims of a particularly deadly serial killer. He's right, of course, and he nearly meets his match in Geoffrey Shafer, respectable British Embassy staffer by day, homicidal maniac by night." Booklist

"If Shafer is almost too good to be true—another fictional psychopath with infinite resources—Patterson is shrewd enough to show him making mistakes . . . as he comes apart at the seams. The killer is caught in the middle of the narrative, setting the scene for a bold courtroom drama." Publ Wkly

Roses are red; a novel. Little, Brown 2000 400p

ISBN 0-316-69325-1   LC 00-28192

In this Alex Cross thriller set in Washington, D.C. a sociopath calling himself "the Mastermind" orchestrates a series of bank robberies, but he "isn't content to relieve the banks of their cash. He also has to torment the bankers by massacring their families when the mood strikes him. Having captured people's attention with these acts of cunning cruelty, the Mastermind pulls off a *coup de théâtre* when he hijacks a tour bus carrying the wives and children of insurance company executives and demands $30 million in ransom." N Y Times Book Rev

Suzanne's diary for Nicholas; a novel. Little, Brown 2001 266p $28

ISBN 0-316-96944-3   LC 00-50707

"The story alternates between diary entries, written by a young wife and mother named Suzanne to her newborn son, Nicholas, and the present, as the diary is read by Kate, who has just been abandoned by her new love—who happens to be Matthew, the young husband in the diary. . . . How Kate, Matthew, and Suzanne connect in the beginning of the novel and what happens by the pretty predictable ending will entertain and please most readers." Libr J

Patterson, Kevin, 1964-

Consumption; a novel. Nan A. Talese 2007 384p $25

ISBN 978-0-385-52074-4   LC 2006-36573

First published 2006 in Canada

"In the early sixties, the 'anachronistic malady' of tuberculosis haunts a small Inuit community in the Canadian Arctic. A child is taken from her family for treatment in Montreal and returns six years later, forever marked as unique by her hunger for the outside world and the scars of a brutal surgery. Meanwhile, an influx of white men—and modernity—has estranged the natives from the land and the traditions that enabled them to survive there. Sweeping in scale but microscopic in its portrait of dislocated lives, this début novel finds its most compelling voice in the rueful meditations of a blundering, morphine-addicted American doctor, marooned by his own volition at the edge of the world." New Yorker

Patterson, Richard North

Balance of power. Ballantine Bks. 2003 611p $27.95

ISBN 0-345-45017-5   LC 2003-51848

"Gun control and tort reform are the thorny issues tackled in this political drama, with Patterson hero Kerry Kilcannon ensconced in the White House and planning his marriage to former television journalist Lara Costello." Publ Wkly

"This complex novel has a fascinating debate at its heart. To his credit, Patterson has done his research, and though it's clear which side he's on, he does a good job of presenting all the arguments." Booklist

Conviction; a novel. Random House 2005 465p $25.95

ISBN 0-345-45019-1   LC 2004-51175

"Fifteen years ago, brothers Rennell and Payton Price were sentenced to death for the brutal murder of nine-year-old Thuy Sen. Now, as Rennell's scheduled execution approaches, pro bono lawyer Theresa Peralta Page (also seen in Eyes of a Child), along with her attorney husband and attorney stepson, takes his final appeal all the way to the Supreme Court. At the same time, Theresa deals with her troubled teenage daughter and her own guilt. While it is apparent that the author opposes the death penalty, Patterson nevertheless provides compelling evidence for both sides of the argument." Libr J

Dark lady; a novel. Knopf 1999 384p $25.95

ISBN 0-679-45043-2   LC 99-23565

"Stella Marz is the assistant county prosecutor in a struggling Midwestern city. Her boss is running for mayor, and Stella hopes to be elected to his job. First, however, she must investigate the deaths of two prominent men—the project manager for the construction of a new baseball stadium and the city's leading defender of drug cases." Libr J

"Patterson is familiar with the civic shenanigans that can destroy a community, and he draws wisely on the history and geography of Cleveland to portray a city struggling to escape its bondage to organized crime, racial conflict and the entrenched corruption of its elected officials." N Y Times Book Rev

Degree of guilt. Knopf 1993 547p o.p.

     * LC 92-54446

"TV journalist Mary Carelli shoots and kills famous writer Mark Ransom in his hotel room, claiming that Ransom tried to rape her. The man she asks to defend her is Christopher Paget, with whom she has had a complicated relationship: Paget is the father of Mary's son, who lives with Paget and whom Mary has not seen for eight years. Paget agrees to defend Mary to protect his son." Libr J

"For those not put off by the sudsy plotting and the People magazine cast, the legal machinations are satisfactorily intricate." Time

Eclipse; a novel. Henry Holt and Company 2009 369p $26

ISBN 978-0-8050-8772-7; 0-8050-8772-9

     LC 2008-17386

"Successful lawyer Damon Pierce had an unrequited love affair with Marissa Brand, but she was in love with a cause in the West African nation of Luandia (think Nigeria) and its leader, Bobby Okari. The divorcing Damon

Patterson, Richard North—*Continued*

receives a plea for help from Marissa, so he flies off to Africa and learns that the head of the government is tied into PetroGlobal, the American oil company making billions from West African oil. He also finds that the water supply has been repeatedly compromised by oil, there is no infrastructure, and the people are starving and disease-ridden while being brutalized by the government. Bobby had led a demonstration during the night of the eclipse, and then the government slaughtered everyone in his village and tortured and arrested him, accusing him of murder. Damon has his hands full trying to get a fair trial for Bobby, and because Marissa is an American, the world is watching." Libr J

"Eclipse aspires to be any number of books: a novel of political intrigue, an international conspiracy thriller, a courtroom drama, a romance, even a straightforward murder mystery. . . . To Patterson's credit, the novel succeeds on all counts." Washington Post Book World

Eyes of a child. Knopf 1995 593p o.p.

LC 94-28630

"The plot concerns the death of ne'er-do-well Ricardo Arias, who may or may not have committed suicide. Because of the widely publicized custody battle waged with Arias by his ex-wife and her lover, Christopher Paget (hero of *Degree of Guilt*), both are investigated and Paget indicted." Libr J

"Local San Francisco politics and an accusation of child molestation against Paget's teenage son contribute to this complex brew, in which . . . narrative skill and legal know-how take precedence over characterization and credibility." Publ Wkly

The final judgment. Knopf 1995 437p

ISBN 0-679-42989-1   LC 95-35083

"San Francisco lawyer Carolyn Masters, featured in *Eyes of a Child* returns as this story's central character, drawn back to her New England home on the eve of her presidential appointment to the Court of Appeals. Her young niece Brett is accused of brutally murdering the boy she loves, and Caroline comes to her defense. Caroline has had no contact with her family in years and now must confront the sister and father who fatally betrayed Caroline's own young love 20 years before." Libr J

"Filled with surprises, 'The Final Judgment' uses a backdrop of courtroom fireworks to tell a tightly wound story of loss and betrayal." N Y Times Book Rev

No safe place. Knopf 1998 497p o.p.

LC 98-14573

"The main character, Kerry Kilcannon, is an Irish Catholic U.S. senator, reminiscent of the Kennedy brothers. Embroiled in a close campaign with the vice president for the Democratic presidential nomination, Kilcannon struggles to maintain his honesty and upright values in a sleazy world where everything depends on image and the proper spin. At the same time, a militant right-to-lifer vows to kill Kilcannon for his pro-choice stance on abortion. Throughout the constant twists and turns of the plot, Patterson builds realistic supporting characters and brings to life the surrealistic world of a presidential campaign." Libr J

Protect and defend; a novel. Knopf 2000 549p il

ISBN 0-679-45044-0   LC 00-712975

"When the Chief Justice drops dead at the inauguration of Kerry Kilcannon, the charismatic new president appoints federal judge Caroline Masters to the high court and begins assembling a strategy to get her approved by a contentious Congress. Meanwhile, a pregnant teen with a damaged fetus goes to court to challenge her parents, who helped to pass a new parental-consent law that prevents her from having an abortion. The two events become intertwined. . . . Patterson skillfully juggles a large cast of characters and controversies." SLJ

Silent witness. Knopf 1997 493p

ISBN 0-679-45040-8   LC 96-36672

This novel "revolves around a friendship that begins on a high-school football field and is tested half a lifetime later in a Lake City, Ohio, courtroom. Tony Lord, a noted California criminal lawyer, returns to the home of his youth to defend his oldest friend, Sam Robb, against the charge of murdering his 16-year-old mistress. Lord takes the sordid case in part because his own life was nearly shattered when, as a teenager, he was suspected of murdering his own girlfriend." Publ Wkly

"*Silent Witness* is more than a typical legal thriller; it is a story about the growth of two men and how each one deals with and subsequently changes after experiencing the anguish and the introspection that come from being accused of murder." Booklist

Pattison, Eliot

The skull mantra. St. Martin's Minotaur 1999 403p $24.95

ISBN 0-312-20478-7   LC 99-23847

"Sentenced to penal servitude in Tibet, Shan, a disgraced prosecutor, is assigned instead to complete a pro forma investigation of the gruesome murder of a Chinese official. The party line is that dissident Tibetan monks are to blame, but Shan quickly realizes that the truth lies in other directions." Libr J

"Set against a background that is alternately bleak and blazingly beautiful, this is at once a topnotch thriller and a substantive look at Tibet under siege." Publ Wkly

Patton, Frances Gray, 1906-2000

Good morning, Miss Dove; illustrated by Garrett Price. Dodd, Mead 1954 218p o.p.

Miss Dove had taught geography in the same school for thirty-five years; some people in town thought that was too long. Miss Dove was a stern disciplinarian with old-fashioned ideas and ideals, but on the April day when she was stricken in the classroom the whole town came to realize how much Miss Dove had meant in their lives

"Leavened with wit and sound common sense, written with an unerring rightness of touch, the whole book rings with the truth about human nature in its nicer aspects." N Y Her Trib Books

Paul, Barbara, 1925-

For works written by this author under other names see Laker, Rosalind, 1925-

Paul, Jim, 1950-

Elsewhere in the land of parrots. Harcourt 2003 405p $24

ISBN 0-15-100495-1   LC 2003-7918

Paul, Jim, 1950——*Continued*

When reclusive poet David Huntington "receives an exotic parrot from his father, his preferred life of airless solitude is turned upside down, and in frustration David soon tosses it out his apartment window. Little does he know that through that open window his carefully controlled and spiritless existence has begun its exit as well. David's guilty search for the bird serendipitously leads him into an adventure outside his quiet apartment and all the way to the swamplands of Ecuador, where a young researcher named Fern happens to be studying the same type of parrot in its native habitat." Libr J

"Paul's story successfully weds an odd theme —the ethology of parrots—to the perennial fascinations of human courtship behavior." Publ Wkly

Pawel, Rebecca, 1977-

Death of a nationalist. Soho Press 2003 262p $24

ISBN 1-56947-304-8   LC 2002-26921

"Madrid in 1939 is filled with bomb craters, desecrated churches and nearly abandoned streets, while black markets are just about the only markets with anything to sell. The hatreds and atrocities shared by the Nationalists (supported by the Communists) still simmer and erupt in sporadic violence. The Guardia Civil has the responsibility to maintain authority—and their enthusiasm and ruthlessness for enforcing order terrorizes the citizens. The intertwined fates of Sergeant Tejada Alonzo Leon of the Guardia Civil and that of Gonzalo Llorente, a wounded Republican in hiding are handled with unusual skill and subtlety." Publ Wkly

Peace, David

Tokyo year zero. Alfred A. Knopf 2007 $24
ISBN 978-0-307-26374-2; 0-307-26374-6
          LC 2007-23813

This novel is based "on a real-life serial-killer case in post-WWII Japan. When the nude body of a young woman turns up in a local park, Inspector Minami of the Tokyo police and his squad of detectives investigate. At the crime scene, Minami finds another woman's body nearby and begins to suspect there will be more to come. Minami, married and a father of two, is smart, tenacious and experienced; he's also addicted to sedatives, keeps a mistress, is in the pocket of a local crime lord and not above sampling the wares of prostitutes he encounters while roaming the city at night. . . . Peace, whose complex style feels like a cross between Haruki Murakami and James Ellroy, delivers an expressionistic portrait of a harrowing, devastated time and place." Publ Wkly

Pearce, Mary Emily, 1932-

Apple tree lean down; [by] Mary E. Pearce. St. Martin's Press 1976 494p o.p.

This volume contains Apple tree lean down, Jack Mercybright and The sorrowing wind, originally published separately in the United Kingdom in 1973, 1974 and 1975 respectively

The combined stories provide a chronicle of three "earthy families inhabiting the rural Midlands during the late 18th and early 19th century. Beth Tewke forsakes easy living when she estranges her prosperous grandfather by marrying poor Jesse Izzard. Betony, their eldest child, is sharp and ambitious. In her teens she goes to London to establish a career as a teacher but becomes disillusioned with the hypocrisy and ill-treatment of the poor in the city. . . . Giving up the chances of an advantageous marriage, she devotes herself to the local school and to the care of invalid soldiers quartered nearby, to the general welfare of her community." Publ Wkly

"Many novels have depicted the upper classes of this era; few have delved so deeply into the lives of the common laborers and the lower middle class." Libr J

Followed by The land endures (1978) and Seedtime and harvest (1982)

Apple tree lean down [novel]
In Pearce, M. E. Apple tree lean down

Cast a long shadow; [by] Mary E. Pearce. St. Martin's Press 1983 c1977 246p o.p.

          LC 83-2953

First published 1977 in the United Kingdom

"The blissful early years of Richard Lancy and Ellen Wainwright's marriage in the small English village of Dingham are shattered after Richard is accidentally trapped in the cellar of a burned-out mill for 16 days. Richard's horrifying experience distorts his entire life and disrupts his family as well. After throwing his wife and son out of their house (and forcing them to find refuge with the compassionate village blacksmith), the disturbed Richard lurks about as a specter. His haunting presence torments Ellen and John and threatens the new lives they try to forge for themselves in this closed, watchful English village." Booklist

"Old-fashioned story-telling, people one cares about and low-key charm add up to solid reading pleasure." Publ Wkly

Jack Merrybright
In Pearce, M. E. Apple tree lean down p203-332

The sorrowing wind
In Pearce, M. E. Apple tree lean down p333-494

Pearl, Matthew

The Dante Club; a novel. Random House 2003 372p $24.95
ISBN 0-375-50529-6   LC 2002-17886

A literary thriller about a "serial murderer who draws gory inspiration from the torments of Dante's Inferno. . . . The author sets this novel in Boston in 1865, when Henry Wadsworth Longfellow, James Russell Lowell, and Oliver Wendell Holmes were translating Dante into English. As they work through the cantos, the Dante-inspired corpses arrive on cue, and the versifiers must turn detective." New Yorker

The last Dickens; a novel. Random House 2009 386p $25
ISBN 978-1-4000-6656-8; 1-4000-6656-5
          LC 2008-46962

"It is 1870, and Charles Dickens, wildly popular on both sides of the Atlantic, has just died, leaving his last book, 'The Mystery of Edwin Drood,' half-finished. His Boston publisher, James Osgood of Fields, Osgood &

Pearl, Matthew—*Continued*

Co., desperately needs to know the book's ending in order to stave off other publishers — notably, the unscrupulous Harper Brothers of New York — from publishing cheap, unauthorized copies. Osgood dispatches his young clerk to Boston's waterfront to retrieve the latest installment of the 'Drood' manuscript, shipped over from London. The clerk is pursued by book pirates called 'bookaneers' and by a mysterious stranger. He is mortally wounded and found with needle tracks on his arm. The pages are missing." Boston Globe

"Pearl is too smart to hinge his plot on mere publishing rights. Like Dickens, he finds compelling stories in every social stratum, viewing the downtrodden with sympathy and the upper crust with a gimlet eye." N Y Daily News

Pears, Iain

Death and restoration; a Jonathan Argyll mystery. Scribner 1998 223p $22

ISBN 0-684-81461-7   LC 97-39932

This mystery features "esthete-sleuth, Jonathan Argyll, and his companion, Flavia di Stefano, a senior, investigator for Italy's Art Theft Squad. Most of the legwork falls to Flavia when an icon is stolen from a rundown monastery in Rome and a French dealer is discovered floating in the Tiber. This frees up Jonathan to sprinkle his acidic wit on art experts and thieves like Dan Menzies, . . . who has been engaged by the monastery to apply his savage artistry to its dubious Caravaggio." N Y Times Book Rev

The dream of Scipio. Riverhead Bks. 2002 398p

ISBN 1-57322-202-X   LC 2001-58916

"Juggles three different historical periods, radically different but united by the presence of a siege—the fall of the Roman Empire in the fourth century, the spread of the plague in the fourteenth century, and World War II in the twentieth century. The setting in all three interlocking plots is Provence, and there is a love story at the center of each. The fabric that connects the characters and their stories across centuries is a neoPlatonic essay called 'The Dream of Scipio' written by Manlius Hippomanes at the point when Gaul was about to be overrun by barbarians." Booklist

"Pears builds a multilayered tale of moral choice, love, danger and loss. Like an archaeologist, he uncovers worlds beneath worlds in a few square miles of Provencal earth." N Y Times Book Rev

The immaculate deception. Scribner 2000 221p

ISBN 0-7432-1257-6   LC 2001-267391

In this Jonathan Argyll "mystery, set in Rome and Tuscany, the police investigator Flavia di Stefano is called in to find a painting that has been stolen by a radical performance artist; meanwhile, her husband, an art historian, is trying to track down the provenance of a beguiling little fifteenth-century Virgin that belongs to Flavia's former boss. Like those classic Nick and Nora whodunits, this book is really a comedy in disguise: the plot twists are finely turned, our heroes flirt harmlessly with danger, and in the end everyone gets what he may not have known he wanted all along." New Yorker

An instance of the fingerpost. Riverhead Bks. 1998 691p $27

ISBN 1-57322-082-5   LC 97-23899

First published 1997 in the United Kingdom

"Robert Boyle, the devout chemist, and John Thurloe, Cromwell's inscrutable spymaster, are among the historical characters who figure in this richly imagined mystery set in Oxford in the sixteen-sixties, after Charles II has been restored to the throne. A Fellow of New College is found dead, and a woman accused of whoring and witchcraft is sentenced to hang for the murder. Three narrators—all unreliable and all self-interested—tell their versions of the story, which unfolds in a turbulent atmosphere of scientific, political, and religious dissent. Not until a fourth, and final, narrator speaks are the mysteries, including the meaning of the book's title, revealed." New Yorker

The last judgment. Scribner 1996 c1993 224p

o.p.   LC 95-38120

First published 1993 in the United Kingdom

"Jonathan Argyll, British art dealer, and his amour, Flavia de Stefano, a member of Rome's art-theft squad, have decided to marry after happy months of living together. But first, there's business to tend to. On a buying trip to Paris, Jonathan is asked by a colleague to deliver a valuable painting to a client in Rome. He soon discovers that whoever is interested in this picture seems to wind up dead. . . . A sophisticated, adventurous, and gripping story that is sure to hold wide appeal." Booklist

Stone's fall; a novel. Spiegel & Grau 2009 594p $27.95

ISBN 978-0-385-52284-7; 0-385-52284-3

                                      LC 2009-00472

"An aging ex-reporter attends the funeral of an elderly widow. A solicitor approaches him and hands him a packet of papers that were to be delivered to him only after the woman's death. Reading them, he is transported back to events he has never forgotten. In 1909, industrialist-arms seller John Stone fell to his death from the window of his study. In his will, he left a bequest to an unknown daughter. His widow asked the young reporter to find the daughter, setting him on a search that transforms his life. Back through time the story goes—London 1909, Paris 1890, Venice 1867—with startling revelations at every step." Libr J

"Pears manages his complicated structure with a confidence and dexterity possible only to a master of the craft of fiction. It is a novel which frequently and daringly challenges credibility, skating on the thinnest of ice, and yet meets that challenge successfully every time." Scotsman

Pearson, Ridley

The angel maker; a novel. Delacorte Press 1993 341p o.p.   LC 92-36573

In this crime thriller someone is "running around with a scalpel removing a kidney here, a lung there, then selling the organs to desperate patients willing to pay upward of $15,000. This grisly brand of 'harvesting' comes to light in Seattle when victims begin turning up minus a part or two. It's the job of a police psychologist named Daphne Matthews, aided by her piano-playing ex-lover, Lou Boldt, to try to bring the perpetrator of these ghastly crimes to justice." N Y Times Book Rev

"Pearson's engaging forensic detail . . . and brisk prose will have readers racing to the cliffhanger climax." Publ Wkly

LIST OF FICTIONAL WORKS

Pearson, Ridley—*Continued*

The art of deception. Hyperion 2002 451p
ISBN 0-7868-6724-8   LC 2002-69055

This Lou Boldt-Daphne Matthews suspense novel "finds the Seattle police lieutenant and his forensic psychologist colleague investigating two cases that ultimately become one. Boldt is tracking a serial killer, and Matthews is investigating the death of a woman who was thrown from Seattle's Aurora Bridge. . . . Pearson makes particularly good use of his Seattle setting this time; the legendary Underground (created when the city was rebuilt after its great fire of 1889) has often appeared in mysteries, but Pearson's detail-rich treatment goes well beyond the typical clichés of dark passages and abandoned storefronts. On every level, this series remains one of the mystery genre's great pleasures." Booklist

Beyond recognition. Hyperion 1997 480p o.p.
                                    LC 96-21125

"A rag and a bone are literally all the Seattle PD has to work with after a violent fire consumes a home and its helpless female occupant, a divorced mother. When a second victim dies the same way, detective Lou Boldt and police psychologist Daphne Matthews begin the process of profiling a serial killer who uses rocket fuel to torch women because they resemble his mother. Elsewhere, a young boy named Ben, whose abusive stepfather has all but driven him into the street, has been befriended by a fraudulent 'psychic' named Emily Richland, who hires Ben to scout her clients' vehicles while they're meeting with her. This task leads, . . . to Ben witnessing an exchange of cash for rocket fuel, a sighting that in turn eventually takes the police to their killer." Publ Wkly

"Moving from one punchy scene to the next, this fuse-burning suspense tale is wonderful reading for a wide audience." Libr J

The body of David Hayes. Hyperion 2004 344p $23.95
ISBN 0-7868-6725-6

                                   * LC 2003-56575

In this "Detective Lou Boldt thriller, computer whiz David Hayes has embezzled $17 million from the bank where he worked and hidden it within the computer system. Now paroled for the crime, he wants to get the money and be free of all competing parties, including some utterly ruthless Russian Mafia types who will stop at nothing to get the loot. Years before, Hayes had an affair with Boldt's wife—now VP of systems at the bank—and he blackmails her into helping him recover the money. Though dedicated and skilled, Boldt and his team are human and fallible; Boldt must balance his jealousy as a husband with his professionalism as a detective. Pearson's novels are always well written, and he takes special care with richly drawn subordinate characters." Libr J

Chain of evidence. Hyperion 1995 348p o.p.
                                    LC 95-32320

"Police Lieutenant Joe 'Dart' Bartelli is called to one suicide after another of various psychopaths (a vicious child molester, a hard-core pornographer) in the Hartford, Connecticut, area. The deaths seem more like murders to Dart, who was well trained in police investigation by his mentor, former police sergeant Walter Zeller. Dart care-

fully, plausibly tracks down the killer with the help of former love, Ginny, fellow lieutenant Abby Lang, and various three-dimensional characters who add believably to his painstaking search. Bad guys, burnouts, and screwups—all the characters are well delineated." Libr J

The first victim. Hyperion 1999 381p $23.95
ISBN 0-7868-6440-0   LC 98-49992

"Inside a shipping container that has washed ashore near Seattle during a storm is heard the 'unmistakable cry of human voices.' From this dramatic opening springs . . . [this] Lou Boldt thriller, in which the Seattle Police Department goes head to head with the INS to bust an immigrant-smuggling ring run by Chinese gangs." Libr J

"Boldt's usual partner, forensic psychologist Daphne Matthews, plays a lesser role this time, but in her place Pearson substitutes television news anchor Stevie McNeal, who mounts her own investigation, thus introducing a meaty subplot involving media excesses. As always, Pearson builds suspense incrementally, brilliantly amassing details until his plot reaches critical mass at just the right moment." Booklist

Killer summer. G. P. Putnam's Sons 2009 367p $24.95
ISBN 978-0-399-15572-7; 0-399-15572-4
                                   LC 2009-12998

Sheriff Walt Fleming returns in this tale of "rich people at play in the affluent resort town of Sun Valley. At an exclusive wine festival, the star attractions are three old bottles allegedly presented to John Adams by Thomas Jefferson. Fleming is a good guy, but he has problems; a messy divorce is on the agenda, his kids and nephew need help, and he has a love-hate relationship with his domineering father. He's attracted to his crime photographer, who has problems of her own, and, oh yes, somebody wants to steal the rare wine, which may or may not be worth millions." Libr J

"Although his ending is a bit flat, seasoned thriller writer Pearson serves up steady suspense and a compelling setting in which members of society's underbelly prey on those living above it all." Booklist

Middle of nowhere; a novel. Hyperion 2000 375p
ISBN 0-7868-6563-6   LC 99-51670

"Seattle police lieutenant Boldt and forensic psychologist Matthews must contend not only with a string of robbery assaults—one victim of which is a fellow officer—but also with the effects of a 'blue flu' that has left the department seriously understaffed and riddled with internal conflict." Booklist

This thriller "boasts simmering suspense, a plot with a level of detail that comes only from painstaking research, and dynamic chemistry between Boldt and his colleagues and family." Publ Wkly

No witnesses; a novel. Hyperion 1994 365p o.p.
                                    LC 94-11158

"Wealthy food industry mogul Owen Adler receives a series of FAXes demanding that he liquidate his business and commit suicide within a month. The alternative is that consumers of Adler Foods will begin to die. After the deadline passes and two children are hospitalized with a mysterious infection, Adler lets his girlfriend, Seattle forensic psychologist Daphne Matthews, contact de-

Pearson, Ridley—*Continued*

tective Lou Boldt. Boldt's empathy for the rising number of victims compels him to put his life at risk as he coordinates an extended investigation while trying to prevent mass panic." Libr J

Undercurrents. St. Martin's Press 1988 386p o.p.

LC 88-1014

"A killer is on the loose—a brutal, terrifying murderer who was himself supposed to be dead. Seattle Police Sergeant Lou Boldt, haunted by the deaths of the man he believed to have been the Cross Killer (so called because of the crosses he slashes onto his victims) and of the real criminal's new victims, is in charge of the case and determined to solve it. . . . *Undercurrents* is not for the squeamish; it is grittily detailed and no punches pulled. But Pearson clearly understands what makes a good mystery move, and this one sprints breathlessly along, taking the reader with it to a surprising, and satisfying, conclusion." West Coast Rev Books

Pearson, T. R., 1956-

Blue Ridge. Viking 2000 243p $24.95

ISBN 0-670-89269-6   LC 00-25826

"Ray Tatum is the new sheriff's deputy in sleepy Hogarth, Va., where some hikers discover a human skeleton, its skull bashed in, on the Appalachian Trail. Investigating the case with the help of a brassy female African-American park ranger named Kit Carson, Ray is forced to come to terms with the collapse of his marriage, his somewhat arid life and the nature of the backwoods town he calls home. Meanwhile, Ray's cousin Paul, an actuary in Roanoke, is summoned to Manhattan to identify what may be the remains of a young man named Troy, the son he never really knew." Publ Wkly

"Pearson has never been timid about pushing form to its limits, and his splendid prose is also artifical, stunningly so—high-pitched, evocative, decorative and closer to the human heart than the rictus-grinned pseudo-realism of many modern mysteries." N Y Times Book Rev

Cry me a river; a novel. Holt & Co. 1993 258p

ISBN 0-8050-2200-7   LC 92-13860

"A police officer is found brutally murdered in a small southern town, his head so disfigured by bullet wounds that he can only be identified by the distinctive smell of his hair tonic. A fellow officer vows to find the killer. Accompanied by a whiskey-addled sidekick who functions as a backwoods Dr. Watson, the investigator assembles clues, interviews suspects, proposes and discards theories, and in the process paints the portrait of an entire community." Libr J

A short history of a small place; a novel. Linden Press/Simon & Schuster 1985 381p

ISBN 0-671-54352-0   LC 84-29720

"Narrated by young Louis Benfield [this] is the story of Miss Myra Angelique Pettigrew, sister of the late mayor of a small Southern town, who is elegant and beautiful and has gone quite mad. After many years of seclusion, she finally emerges from her home to jump to her death from the water tower. In the process of telling his tale, Louis offers vignettes about other residents of Neely, N.C., and their strange habits and activities." Publ Wkly

"Pearson handles the interlinked strands of these stories with a truly wonderful offhand comic style that doesn't dismiss the reality of his characters' lives." Booklist

Peck, Robert Newton, 1928-

A day no pigs would die. Knopf 1973 c1972 150p $25; pa $5.50

ISBN 0-394-48235-2; 0-679-85306-5 (pa)

*

"Rob lives a rigorous life on a Shaker farm in Vermont in the 1920s. Since farm life is earthy, this book is filled with Yankee humor and explicit descriptions of animals mating. A painful incident that involves the slaughter of Rob's beloved pet pig is instrumental in urging him toward adulthood. The death of his father completes the process of his accepting responsibility." Shapiro. Fic for Youth. 3d edition

Peden, Margaret Sayers

(tr) Fuentes, C. The old gringo

(tr) Pérez-Reverte, A. The painter of battles

Peebles, Frances de Pontes

The seamstress; a novel. HarperCollins 2008 646p map $25.95

ISBN 978-0-06-073887-7; 0-06-073887-1

This "historical saga of Brazil in the 1920s and 1930s follows sisters Emília and Luzia dos Santos from their impoverished childhoods as village seamstresses to their unimaginable futures: Emília marries the scion of an upper-class family in Recife, while Luzia marries The Hawk, an infamous bandit-cum-Robin Hood who terrorizes provincial landowners. Using as backdrop the populist revolt of 1930 and the push to develop Brazil's enormous resources at the expense of the subsistence farmers, Peebles creates a vast and diverse cast of characters. . . . However, the novel's true beauty is the exquisitely realized relationship between Emília and Luzia, two strong women who, despite the separate paths their lives take, remain connected and committed to each other." Libr J

Pekearo, Nicholas T., d. 2007

The wolfman; [by] Nicholas Pekearo. Tor 2008 286p $23.95

ISBN 978-0-7653-2026-1; 0-7653-2026-6

LC 2008-3984

"A Tom Doherty Associates book"

"At first glance, Marlowe Higgins seems like a typically flawed noir protagonist: He's an ill-tempered Vietnam War veteran who has drifted from job to job since returning to the U.S. a changed man. He has a propensity for razor-sharp sarcasm, jaw-dropping profanity, binge drinking and sudden outbursts of psychotic violence . . . . Although he has never had a lasting relationship (he's currently involved with a prostitute named Alice), Higgins is a diehard romantic with a heroic code of honor. He also happens to be a werewolf, and when transformed into the beast he is nothing short of 'the wrath of God.' Having slaughtered more than 300 people since returning from the war, and now settled down in the small town of Evelyn, Higgins, who retains the memories

Pekearo, Nicholas T., d. 2007—*Continued*

and mannerisms of all those he has killed, has vowed to use his torturous affliction for the greater good. Every full moon when he becomes a primeval 'boogeyman,' he tracks down criminals in the region with the help of information from Danny Pearce, a detective with the local police who is the closest thing Higgins has to a friend. . . . Crime-fiction, paranormal-fantasy and horror fans alike should cherish this outstanding debut." Cicago Tribune

Pelecanos, George P.

The big blowdown. St. Martin's Press 1996 313p

ISBN 0-312-14284-6

* LC 95-53148

"Set in Washington, D.C., from the 1930s to the 1950s, Pelecanos's . . . novel traces a group of boyhood friends as they make their way in the richly detailed Greek and Italian neighborhoods of the city. Peter Karras, a Greek, and his friend Joe Recevo, an Italian, grow up together, serve separately in World War II, and reunite for a time after the war as Joe becomes involved in organized crime in the city. Peter cannot stomach the practice of shaking down immigrants for loan vigorish and is brutally cast out by the gangsters, as Joe stands by. The two friends will inevitably cross paths again." Libr J

"Pelecanos lovingly recreates old Washington with small details about soft-drink brands, finned cars and cherished smokes. The ending is a haze of gunsmoke that drifts away to leave a mixed tableau of heroism and futility. With stylistic panache and forceful conviction, Pelecanos delivers a darkly powerful story of the American city." Publ Wkly

Drama city; a novel; [by] George Pelecanos. Little, Brown and Co 2005 291p $24.95

ISBN 0-316-60821-1   LC 2004-16757

"After serving eight years for a drug rap, Lorenzo Brown is trying to live a straight life. Working as a Humane Society officer in Washington, DC, doesn't provide the life of wealth that Lorenzo had enjoyed as part of the drug game, but he's doing okay. His parole officer, Rachel Lopez, is fighting her own battle against a tough past and reckless behavior. A violent act committed by a character from Lorenzo's old life places both Lorenzo and Rachel in jeopardy. Now, Lorenzo must decide whether to risk his second chance at a straight life for a shot at vengeance." Libr J

"There is a fierce inevitability to the way George Pelecanos's new book unfolds. Drama City is unleashed, not simply set in motion. In the tough, imperiled parts of Washington, where his earlier books have been set, Mr. Pelecanos puts the forces of good and evil on a collision course, igniting the kind of suspense that hinges on heartbreak. As this lean, stirring, knife-edged novel escalates, the question is not whether one of its principals will become a casualty. The question is when." N Y Times (Late N Y Ed)

Hard revolution; a novel; [by] George Pelecanos. Little, Brown 2004 376p $24.95

ISBN 0-316-60897-1   LC 2003-54501

This novel "tells the story of two brothers-one a rookie police officer, one a recently returned Vietnam veteran-caught up in the chaos that engulfed D.C. in 1968, when riots followed the assassination of the Reverend Martin Luther King, Jr. Derek Strange is his family's straight arrow, but his older brother Dennis has always had a harder time. Home from the war and in several varieties of trouble, Dennis is in danger of making one bad decision too many. While Derek tries to be there for Dennis, no amount of brotherly love can save Dennis from Alvin Jones, a local drug dealer who draws him into his web." Publisher's note

"Pelecanos's foray into Strange's past does not in the end diminish, but rather adds to, our sense of his complexity and humanity. In narrating Derek's buried crime story, Pelecanos has further tapped into an archetypal vein of family experience in the black community since the 1950's, as drugs, murder and prison cut a swath through three generations of young men." N Y Times Book Rev

Hell to pay; a novel. Little, Brown 2002 344p $24.95

ISBN 0-316-69506-8   LC 2001-38111

This mystery, set in Washington, D.C., features ex-cop detectives Derek Strange and Terry Quinn. "As a black man with plenty of miles behind him, Strange has access to neighborhoods where his Irish partner would be handed his head; but both of them take big chances when they cross Worldwide Wilson, a menacing pimp who breaks in teenage runaways, and then go after the wild street kids who shot the 9-year-old quarterback of the Petworth Panthers, the Pee-Wee team Strange coaches. Pelecanos's style is one of total-shock immersion in the sights, sounds and cultural codes of the dangerous world he roams." N Y Times Book Rev

The night gardener; a novel. Little, Brown 2006 377p $24.99

ISBN 978-0-316-15650-9; 0-316-15650-7

LC 2006-1286

"In 1985, the body of a 14-year-old girl turns up in a Washington, D.C., park, the latest in a series of murders by a killer the media dub 'The Night Gardener.' T.C. Cook, the aging detective on the case, works with a quiet, almost monomaniacal, focus. Also involved are two young uniformed cops, Gus Ramone, who's diligent, conscientious and unimpressed by heroics, and Dan 'Doc' Holiday, an adrenaline junkie who's decidedly less straight. Fast forward 20 years. Detective Ramone, now married with kids of his own, investigates the murder of one of his teenage son's friends. The homicide closely resembles the earlier unsolved Night Gardener murders. Holiday, now an alcoholic chauffeur and bodyguard, follows the case on his own and tracks down Cook, long retired but still obsessed with the original murders." Publ Wkly

A "disturbingly gritty excavation of racism and social politics in modern Washington." Christ Sci Monit

Right as rain; a novel. Little, Brown 2001 332p

ISBN 0-316-69526-2   LC 00-34886

This novel is set in Washington D.C. The hero is a "middle-aged black ex-cop named Derek Strange. Shortly after the book begins, Strange is hired by the mother of Chris Wilson, a black policeman who has been killed by a white colleague during a street altercation. The white

Pelecanos, George P.—*Continued*

cop, Terry Quinn, came upon Wilson holding another man at gunpoint. When it looked to Quinn as if Wilson was pointing his weapon at Quinn and his partner, Quinn fired, killing the man. Officially exonerated by his department, Quinn, . . . quit. He sees Strange's investigation as his means of clearing the suspicion that lingers around him." N Y Times Book Rev

"What is perhaps most remarkable about this outstanding novel . . . is the way his plot-rich, extremely violent stories parallel the turbulence of his characters' inner lives. We care about these characters passionately, and we savor their tentative moments of tranquility as we do our own." Booklist

Shame the devil; a novel. Little, Brown 2000 299p $24.95

ISBN 0-316-69523-8   LC 99-29854

This novel picks up the story of Marcus Clay and Dimitri Karras ten years after the events in The sweet forever, with the aging childhood friends "settling into the quiet pleasures of middle age. Then a restaurant robbery goes bad, the entire staff is murdered, the gunman's brother is killed, and Karras' toddler son, crossing the wrong street at the wrong time, is run over by the speeding getaway car. Three years later Karras is adrift, his marriage over, his only solace coming in weekly meetings with the families of the shooting victims. Into this simmering pot Pelecanos stirs the killer, Frank Farrow, returned to Washington and determined to avenge the death of his brother." Booklist

"Pelecanos is one of those dangerous writers who aren't afraid to take risks, so there's a merciless reality to his characters and a cold clarity about the way they talk, think and feel. Whatever their flaws, none of the people in this writer's world are ashamed to tell the truth." N Y Times Book Rev

Soul circus; a novel. Little, Brown 2003 341p $24.95

ISBN 0-316-60843-2   LC 2002-16207

"Strange and Quinn once again find themselves struggling to save even one not-yet-lost young soul from the ravages of drugs and violence, but this time their knightly pursuits are undermined by a growing sense of moral ambivalence." Booklist

"Pelecanos is fascinated with the way things work, and he takes apart the gun trade like an urban anthropologist, fitting the pieces into the drug business and the gang culture with an exactness that is breathtaking—and depressing. At the same time, he treats his criminals like human beings, talking their talk, driving their cars, listening to their music, getting into their world with something that can only be called sympathy." N Y Times Book Rev

The sweet forever; a novel. Little, Brown 1998 298p $23.95

ISBN 0-316-69109-7

* LC 97-41963

Sequel to King Suckerman (1997)

"Dirty cops, drug money, racism, violence, and sex all mar 1980s Washington, D.C. When a neighborhood drug dealer's collection man crashes and burns in front of Marcus Clay's record store, an opportunist makes off with the guy's sack of cash. The drug dealer and associates will try anything to get the money back, including threatening Clay and employees, one of whom, coke-happy Dimitri Karras . . . knows what happened to the cash." Libr J

"Pelecanos's kickback style works just as well when his characters put down their weapons to watch a ball game or to hit the music clubs on a Friday night. This may be a battleground, but it's also Pelecanos's home ground, and he knows the territory as well as any crime writer alive." N Y Times Book Rev

Followed by Shame the devil

The turnaround; a novel; [by] George Pelecanos. Little, Brown, and Co. 2008 294p $24.99

ISBN 978-0-316-15647-9; 0-316-15647-7

LC 2007-33276

In Washington, D. C. in "1972, three white teenagers drive into a solidly African American neighborhood bent on 'rais[ing] a little hell.' What follows is tragic: one boy is left dead, another scarred for life, and a young African American is in prison. Thirty years later, two survivors of that fated afternoon accidentally reconnect and explore accommodation. But a third party to these past events has more sinister plans." Libr J

"Pelecanos does what few, if any, American writers do: He tells the truth. Twain told the truth; Faulkner toyed with the truth; Hemingway told his version of the truth and Chandler certainly told a cold, cynical truth. Pelecanos' truth is from deep in the heart, from places where red blood cells know more than all the sweet, heady words truth usually hides behind." Chicago Sun-Times

The way home; a novel; [by] George Pelecanos. Little, Brown and Co. 2009 323p $24.99

ISBN 978-0-316-15649-3   LC 2008-54837

This novel "examines a generational battle between working-class Thomas Flynn, owner of a Washington, D.C., carpet business, and his son Chris, who is more concerned with the rules of the urban streets than with his future. . . . [Chris eventually lands] in the Pine Ridge facility for juveniles, where punishment, not redemption, is the order of the day. Chris survives the system, but the jailhouse code of standing tall, staring down authority and avenging wrongs dogs him as he tries to build a new, adult life in the face of temptation. In a sense, 'The Way Home' is a coming-of-age story, as Chris tries to find his place in the world. More fortunate than most of the boys who share his past, he can succeed, Pelecanos tells us — but not everybody is quite so lucky." PopMatters

Pelevin, Victor, 1962-

The sacred book of the werewolf; translated by Andrew Bromfield. Viking 2008 304p $25.95

ISBN 978-0-670-01988-5; 0-670-01988-7

Original Russian edition, 2004

"The heroine of Victor Pelevin's 'The Sacred Book of the Werewolf' is, in fact, a 20-century-old werefox named A Hu-Li (which in Chinese means 'the fox named A,' but in Russian is an unprintable insult). Bright-eyed and bushy-tailed, A Hu-Li disguises herself in a human body that makes Humbert Humberts go gaga. Werefoxes, she tells us, derive their nourishment by sapping the sexual energy of humans and by chicken hunting. But the one big thing for this 2,000-year-old virgin may just be the love of a super werewolf, himself disguised as a high official in Russia's successor to the KGB." Chicago Tri-

Pelevin, Victor, 1962-—_Continued_
bune

"It's a joy to read Pelevin's phantasmagoria so brilliantly translated by Andrew Bromfield, a crowning achievement of the pair's longtime association. Complex ideas are rendered simply and organically, never disturbing the narrative flow. Bromfield's English text is fleet and magical." N Y Times Book Rev

Penguin book of gay short fiction; edited by David Leavitt and Mark Mitchell; introduction by David Leavitt. Viking 1994 655p o.p.

LC 93-1390

Contents: A poem of friendship, by D. H. Lawrence; Arthur Snatchfold, by E. M. Forster; Sally Bowles, by C. Isherwood; Me and the girls, by N. Coward; My father and myself, by J. R. Ackerley; May we borrow your husband? by G. Greene; Hands, by S. Anderson; The teacher of American business English, by J. Kirkup; Falconer, by J. Cheever; The folded leaf, by W. Maxwell; Servants with torches, by D. Windham; Jimmy, by D. Hogan; Torridge, by W. Trevor; Some of these days, by J. Purdy; A glass of blessings, by B. Pym; Reprise, by E. White; Dramas, by E. O'Brien; "Mrs. Tefillin", by L. Kramer; Spunk, by P. Bailey; The times as it knows us, by A. Barnett; The princess from Africa, by D. Plante; Adult art, by A. Gurganus; The Cinderella waltz, by A. Beattie; Good with words, by S. Greco; Nothing to ask for, by D. McFarland; Ignorant armies, by M. Cunningham; Run, mourner, run, by R. Kenan; Six fables, by B. Cooper; Perrin and the fallen angel, by P. Wells; My mother's clothes: the school of beauty and shame, by R. McCann; A place I've never been, by D. Leavitt; Notes towards a performance of Jean Racine's tragedy Athalie, by N. Bartlett; Buried treasure, by G. Glickman; Self-portrait in twenty-three rounds, by D. Wojnarowicz; Jump or dive, by P. Cameron; Gentlemen can wash their hands in the gents', by C. Coe; The dancing lesson, by G. Albarelli; A real doll, by A. M. Homes; The whiz kids, by A. M. Homes

The **Penguin** book of lesbian short stories; edited by Margaret Reynolds. Viking 1994 c1993 429p o.p.

LC 93-34061

First published 1993 in the United Kingdom

Includes the following stories: Martha's lady, by S. O. Jewett; Prince Charming, by R. Vivien; Leves amores, by K. Mansfield; The wise Sappho, by H.D.; Miss Furr and Miss Skeene, by G. Stein; Ladies almanack, by D. Barnes; Miss Ogilvy finds herself, by R. Hall; Nuits blanches, by Colette; Olivia, by D. Strachey; The blank page, by I. Dinesen; Cities of the interior, by A. Nin; I am a woman, by A. Bannon; Les guérillès, by M. Wittig; These our mothers, by N. Brossard; Sweethearts, by J. A. Phillips; Esther's story, by J. Nestle; How to engage in courting rituals 1950s butch-style in the bar, by M. Mushroom; Bread, by R. Brown; His nor hers, by J. Rule; 5½ Charlotte Mews, by A. Livia; Lullaby for my dyke and her car, by S. Maitland; Don't explain, by J. Gomez; A lesbian appetite, by D. Allison; The vampire, by P. Califia; The secret of Sorrerby Rise, by F. Gapper; City of boys, by B. Nugent; Cold-blooded, by M.

Atwood; Words for things, by E. Donoghue; The language of the body, by K. Acker; The poetics of sex, by J. Winterson

Penman, Sharon Kay

Cruel as the grave; a medieval mystery. Holt & Co. 1998 242p $22

ISBN 0-8050-5608-4   LC 98-13085

"A Marian Wood book"

"Young Justin de Quincy, bastard son of a highly placed clergyman, toils as a special agent for Eleanor of Aquitaine. The dowager queen is attempting to hold the throne for her beloved son, Richard the Lionheart, held captive by the Holy Roman Emperor, against the machinations of her youngest son, John. A neighbor asks Justin to investigate the death of a young Welsh girl named Melangell." Publ Wkly

"Penman's clear prose and engrossing plot, the skill with which she brings the politics, people, and ambience of medieval England alive, and her engaging characters make this a must-read, must-have mystery." Booklist

Devil's brood. G. P. Putnam's Sons 2008 734p $28.95

ISBN 978-0-399-15526-0   LC 2008-29451

"A Marian Wood book"

Final volume in the author's trilogy based on the lives of Henry II and Eleanor of Aquitaine; earlier titles: When Christ and his saints slept; Time and chance

"As the novel opens, [Eleanor and Henry's] four sons are beginning to chafe under the heavy hand of their father, who has crowned the eldest, Hal, as a coregent but gives him little authority or power. Egged on by their mother, the young king and his brothers mount a decadelong crusade of rebellion and treachery against their father and each other as they vie for land, money, and power. The empathetic reader can't help but be both horrified by the machinations of this grievously dysfunctional family and filled with pity for the pain they inflict upon one another. Penman does a remarkable job of depicting passionate, dramatic characters and the perilous times in which they live. For those who like their historical fiction as complex and tightly woven as a medieval tapestry, this book cannot fail to please." Libr J

Dragon's lair; a medieval mystery; Sharon Kay Penman. G.P. Putnam's Sons 2003 322p $23.95

ISBN 0-399-15077-3   LC 2003-46745

In this mystery, "Justin de Quincy, tries to recover, quite literally, a king's ransom in coffers of precious metals and bales of wool, which are as valuable as gold, that have been stolen in northern Wales. It's 1193, and Queen Eleanor of Aquitaine fervently needs to ransom her eldest son, Richard Lionheart, from the Holy Roman Emperor before King Philippe of France can interfere and her younger son, John, can seize the crown. Justin proceeds into the thickets and wild forests of Wales, where he's deeply mistrusted both as an Englishman and an outsider. He must penetrate abundant Welsh intrigues and deceptions in order to discover the treasure as well as solve murders and comfort bereaved lovers. Despite a large cast of characters from every social class, Penman keeps them all clearly distinguishable." Publ Wkly

Penman, Sharon Kay—*Continued*

Falls the shadow. Holt & Co. 1988 580p o.p.
LC 87-32255

In this second volume of the trilogy begun with Here be dragons "Penman focuses on the mid-13th-century reign of England's Henry III and stories of those who opposed that inept king. A main detractor is French-born Simon de Montfort, Earl of Leicester, who leads the fight for parliamentary restrictions on the monarch, and later becomes Henry's brother-in-law through marriage to Eleanor, Countess of Pembroke. She emerges as a major figure, as does a distant relative by marriage, Llewelyn ap Gruffydd, who fights for supremacy in Wales." Libr J

Followed by The reckoning

Here be dragons. Holt, Rinehart & Winston 1985 704p o.p.
LC 84-23480

This first title in the author's historical trilogy about 13th century England "is the story of one man, a Welsh prince called Llewelyn the Great, who dares to dream of peace and who will spend a lifetime trying to wrest his country away from feudal England. Standing in his way is King John, who marries his daughter, Joanna, to Llewelyn in hopes of taming the rebellious prince. Penman focuses her novel on the tempestuous emotional and political battles that Joanna is forced to endure as both the daughter and wife of warring kings." Booklist

Followed by Falls the shadow

The queen's man; a medical mystery. Holt & Co. 1996 291p $20

ISBN 0-8050-3885-X
LC 96-15027

"A Marian Wood book"

"In the troubled time of King Richard, his mother, Eleanor of Aquitaine, commissions Justin de Quincey, the bastard son of the bishop of Chester, to find the murderer of a goldsmith in her employ. Thus dunked into the dangerous waters of royal conspiracy, Justin defies one treachrous current after another." Libr J

"Penman's authentic period details, larger-than-life characters, and fast-paced plot add up to great reading for both mystery fans and history buffs." Booklist

The reckoning. Holt & Co. 1991 592p o.p.
LC 90-27099

Set in 13th-century Wales and England, this concluding volume in the author's trilogy "continues the saga of three royal families, those of swashbuckling Llewelyn ap Gruffydd, prince of Wales, and his fractious, treasonous brothers; the children of heroic Lord Simon de Montfort . . . and the ruling house of England, now headed by wily Edward I." Publ Wkly

"The action involves religious and political intrigue, battles and plots. The players include well-researched historical personages and fictional characters. As with Penman's other historical novels, this one is both informative and enjoyable. Settings, events, and individuals are well drawn." Libr J

The sunne in splendour. Holt, Rinehart & Winston 1982 936p o.p.
LC 81-20149

"Today most historians agree that England's Richard III has been unjustly maligned. Penman's novel tells of a devoted brother who, as Duke of Gloucester, faithfully served his brother King Edward IV and earned a reputation for personal integrity. Richard's own tragedy begins

with the death of Edward, when political circumstances force him to claim the crown for himself and declare his brother's children illegitimate. Did Richard murder the young princes as Tudor chroniclers claim? No, says Penman, and she gives a plausible account as to what might have happened." Libr J

"The novel covers a great deal of ground, tracing the shifting alliances and the battles between the noble houses of York and Lancaster from 1459, when Richard was seven to 1492, seven years after his death on Bosworth Field. . . . A historical novel of the first rank." Publ Wkly

Time and chance. Putnam 2002 515p
ISBN 0-399-14785-3
LC 2001-48255

"A Marian Wood book"

Sequel to: When Christ and his saints slept

This second volume of the author's medieval trilogy "re-creates the drama, the intrigue, and the passion that distinguished the lives of Henry Plantagenet, Eleanor of Aquitaine, and Thomas Becket. Though the subject has been exhaustively chronicled in both history and literature, this fictionalized account of the trials and tribulations of this prominent trio of historical figures manages to breathe new life into a familiar story." Booklist

When Christ and his saints slept. Holt & Co. 1995 746p il o.p.
LC 94-22593

With this novel, "Penman inaugurates a trilogy focusing on the lives of King Henry II of England and his colorful consort, Eleanor of Aquitaine. This initial volume paints the background of Henry II's reign: the civil war that raged in England for two decades as the result of a dispute between his mother and her cousin over the succession to the throne. From the darkness of this quarrel, which left England completely wrung out, ultimately stepped Henry Plantagenet, whose ascension as Henry II brought the country back into the light." Booklist

The author "showcases her mastery of the historical novel in this long and thoroughly engrossing study of pragmatic politics, idealism, and the role of women during the 12th century. She brings to life a vast array of unforgettable characters, both historical and invented, all of whose loyalties are being constantly tested by the chaos of the times." Libr J

Penney, Stef

The tenderness of wolves; a novel. Simon & Schuster 2007 371p $25

ISBN 978-1-4165-4074-8; 1-4165-4074-1
LC 2006-100796

First published 2006 in the United Kingdom

A novel set on the 19th-century Canadian frontier. "Seventeen-year-old Francis Ross disappears the same day his mother discovers the scalped body of his friend, fur trader Laurent Jammet, in a neighboring cabin. The murder brings newcomers to the small settlement, from inexperienced Hudson Bay Company representative Donald Moody to elderly eccentric Thomas Sturrock, who arrives searching for a mysterious archeological fragment once in Jammet's possession. Other than Francis, no real suspects emerge until half-Indian trapper William Parker is caught searching the dead man's house. Parker escapes and joins with Francis's mother to track Francis north, a journey that produces a deep if unlikely bond between them." Publ Wkly

Penney, Stef—*Continued*

A "confident and complex portrait of 1860s Ontario. . . . Between twists and turns of plot, Penney evokes the land—its shades of light and changes of weather, its marshes and treacherous waters. Rarely has winter seemed so febrile." Books of Canada

Penny, Louise

The cruelest month; a Three Pines mystery. St. Martin's Minotaur 2008 311p $23.95

ISBN 978-0-312-35257-8; 0-312-35257-3

LC 2007-42422

Chief Inspector Armand Gamache of the Surete du Quebec is called to investigate the death of a villager at an Easter seance that was held at the Old Hadley House.

"Penny paints a vivid picture of the French-Canadian village, its inhabitants and a determined detective who will strike many Agatha Christie fans as a 21st-century version of Hercule Poirot." Publ Wkly

Still life. St. Martin's Minotaur 2006 312p $22.95

ISBN 978-0-312-35255-4; 0-312-35255-7

LC 2006-41992

First published 2005 in the United Kingdom

"The residents of a tiny Canadian village called Three Pines are shocked when the body of Miss Jane Neal is found in the woods. Miss Neal, the village's retired schoolteacher and a talented amateur artist, has been a good friend to most of the townsfolk, so her loss is keenly felt. At first, her death appears to be a tragic accident—it's deer-hunting season, and it looks a stray hunter's arrow killed her. But some folks are suspicious, and Chief Inspector Armand Gamache of the Montreal Surete is called in to investigate." Booklist

The author's "deceptively simple style masks the complex patterns of a well-devised plot rather like the subtle designs of Jane's 'primitive' pictures. Chief Inspector Armand Gamache of the Sûreté du Québec, who is as bemused as we are by life in Three Pines, has the wit and insight to look well beyond its idyllic surface." N Y Times Book Rev

Penzler, Otto, 1942-

(ed) Best American mystery stories [date] See Best American mystery stories [date]

(ed) The vicious circle. See The vicious circle

Percy, Walker, 1916-1990

Lancelot. Farrar, Straus & Giroux 1977 257p o.p.

*

This story is told as a monologue by its protagonist Lancelot Lamar who "discovers himself to be a cuckold. (He confirms his initial suspicions by spying with the help of a videotape machine.) One night he leaps upon the coupled bodies of wife and lover and attempts to bear-hug them to death. He fails, but he does manage to slit the lover's throat with a Bowie knife. The New Orleans mansion in which this action takes place has a wing . . . built atop a capped natural gas well. Lance . . . uses the residual methane to blow up the mansion. Others perish, but he is thrown clear by the blast, and sur-

vives to tell his tale from his madhouse cell." Atlantic

In this novel the author "knowledgeably fingers what he perceives as the rotting fabric of Southern aristocratic life, and describes it with vividness and a kind of affection, even as he starts to shred it." Christ Sci Monit

The last gentleman. Modern Lib. 1997 c1966 442p $18.50

ISBN 0-679-60272-0

* LC 97-15381

The hero, 25-year-old Williston Bibb Barrett, "returns to the South without identity, suffering from periodic amnesia and spells of 'déjà vu', with their telescoping of ancestral past and personal present. He hires on as tutor-companion to Jamie, a dying boy, son of 'Poppy' Vaught, a rich Alabama auto dealer, brother of Kitty, the displaced Southern belle Barrett loved at first sight—through his telescope up North in Central Park. . . . What Barrett seeks is some clue as to how to live." Newsweek

"The plot is less important than the delineation of character, the preoccupation with the way people speak and define themselves geographically and historically . . . and the rendering of a composite South." Burgess. 99 Novels

Followed by The second coming

Love in the ruins; the adventures of a bad Catholic at a time near the end of the world. Farrar, Straus & Giroux 1971 403p o.p.

"An extravaganza with a Southern setting is a satire on pseudoprofound novels and a sardonic commentary on the bogging down of religion, culture, and interracial, intergroup and interpersonal relationships in the not-too-distant future. The narrator is one Dr. More, descendant of Sir Thomas More, who believes he has invented a device that will analyze and cure the woes of society." Booklist

"A beautifully comic and humane work, the satirist's projection of a grotesque future world based on the realities of the present and stimulus to thought and evaluation and, hopefully, to improvement. Percy's style shows mastery of language." Choice

The moviegoer. Knopf 1961 241p $26

ISBN 0-394-43703-9

*

"A philosophical exploration of the problem of personal identity, the story is narrated by Binx Bolling, a successful but alienated businessman. Bolling undertakes a search for meaning in his life, first through an obsession with the movies and later through an affair." Merriam-Webster's Ency of Lit

The second coming. Farrar, Straus & Giroux 1980 359p

ISBN 0-374-25674-8

LC 80-12899

In this sequel to The last gentleman, Will Barrett "has become a widowed, middle-aged millionaire. He didn't marry Kitty, who he loved in the earlier book, but a crippled heiress. He has had an unforeseen success as a Wall Street lawyer, fathered a [daughter] . . . and now, retired, suffers undiagnosed fall-downs on the golf course. Released from the amnesia that used to afflict him, he remembers . . . his suicidal father's attempt to kill him before taking his own life. Will meets and falls in love with a schizophrenic girl escaped from an asylum, who

Percy, Walker, 1916-1990—*Continued*

speaks in rhymes and is gradually revealed to be Kitty's daughter." Newsweek

"A beautiful . . . exploration of Percy's recurrent theme—an individual man's search for the hand of God in the meaningless muddle of contemporary life." Booklist

Perdue, Lewis

Slatewiper. Forge 2003 367p $24.95

ISBN 0-7653-0111-3   LC 2002-45496

"A Tom Doherty Associates book"

"In Tokyo, a particularly violent and deadly plague has broken out. Inexplicably, it seems as if the virus only uses Koreans as its carrier. Enter Lara Blackwood, a genetic engineer recruited to fight this virus that somehow piggybacks itself on people with specific genetic characteristics. Ejected from her own company, Lara sees in this investigation her chance to get herself back in the research game, but she doesn't count on uncovering a genetic weapon of unimaginable power. . . . Perdue unflinchingly treads on Crichton's turf but emerges with a novel that feels fresh and original." Booklist

Perec, Georges, 1936-1982

Life; a user's manual; translated by David Bellos. Godine 1987 581p

ISBN 0-87923-700-7   LC 87-8782

Original French edition, 1978

The author of this novel set in a Paris apartment house on a single day describes the building's 100 rooms and the life stories of past and present occupants as a painting in progress, the work of one of the tenants

"The inextricable incoherence of things is presumably the basic theme of the late Georges Perec's work, but this pessimistic view of life is dramatized with inventiveness, audacity, and even humor." Atlantic

A void; translated by Gilbert Adair. HarperCollins Pubs. 1994 285p

ISBN 0-00-271119-2

*

Original French edition, 1969

This novel was written and translated without using the letter "e." The plot "concerns (probably) the disappearance of one Anton Vowl (A. Vowl) and the attempts of an irregular group of friends to discover what's what. The Sphinx is consulted, and the white whale, and clues start to glimmer dangerously: there are 26 cartons, but the fifth one is missing." N Y Times Book Rev

"Gilbert Adair has now shown quite brilliantly that a lipogrammatic text in one language can be more than adequately done into another, retaining not only the alphabetical constraint but much of the virtuosity of the original." London Rev Books

Pérez Galdós, Benito, 1843-1920

Doña Perfecta; translated by Mary J. Serrano; introduction by William Dean Howells. Harper & Row 1896 319p o.p.

Original Spanish edition, 1876

"The social problem which engrosses so much of the author's interest, the struggle between scientific and social enlightenment and the tyrannous obscurantism of the church, is here set forth in the domestic conflict of a group of characters and the political strife agitating a provincial town. Dona Perfecta is a devout lady whose daughter is sought by a promising young man, a representative of modernism. A wily priest is her chief ally, and eventually the rival intrigues drag in a host of forces on either side." Baker. Guide to the Best Fic

Torquemada; translated from the Spanish by Frances M. López-Morillas. Columbia Univ. Press 1986 569p o.p.   LC 85-19560

Omnibus edition of the author's Torquemada tetralogy portraying middle-class Madrid society, and focusing on the miserly Francisco de Torquemada from the time he is 50 years old to his deathbed ten years later. The novels were originally published separately in the late nineteenth century

Contents: Torquemada at the stake; Torquemada on the cross; Torquemada in Purgatory; Torquemada and Saint Peter

Torquemada and Saint Peter
   In Pérez Galdós, B. Torquemada p405-569

Torquemada at the stake
   In Pérez Galdós, B. Torquemada p1-60

Torquemada in Purgatory
   In Pérez Galdós, B. Torquemada p221-404

Torquemada on the cross
   In Pérez Galdós, B. Torquemada p61-220

Pérez-Reverte, Arturo

Captain Alatriste; translated from the Spanish by Margaret Sayers Peden. Putnam 2005 253p $23.95

ISBN 0-399-15275-X

* LC 2004-60210

"Captain Alatriste, a veteran of Spain's Flemish wars, deploys his sword for anyone who will pay, which inevitably leads him into some dicey situations; the one detailed here is a commission to assassinate, under the cover of darkness, two Englishmen on a visit to Madrid. At the last moment, Alatriste decides against running them through and spares their lives—which turns out to be fortunate on a diplomatic level, since his intended victims are revealed to be the Prince of Wales and the Duke of Buckingham, in Spain to attempt to arrange a marriage between the prince and the Spanish king's daughter." Booklist

"Equipped with a quick-witted, charismatic hero and much to provoke and goad him, Mr. Pérez-Reverte has the makings of a flamboyantly entertaining series. Captain Alatriste ends with a wicked flourish, an evil laugh and a strong likelihood that the best is yet to come." N Y Times (Late N Y Ed)

The Club Dumas; translated from the Spanish by Sonia Soto. Harcourt Brace & Co. 1996 362p il $23

ISBN 0-15-100182-0

* LC 96-11962

Original Spanish edition, 1993

"Corso, a tough-guy bibliophile living in Madrid, is hired by a wealthy client to track down a rare seven-

Pérez-Reverte, Arturo—*Continued*

teenth-century book on how to summon the Devil. He soon finds himself in noir metafiction in which he's been cast as D'Artagnan and is threatened by characters suspiciously like Richelieu's agents—a menacing man with a scar and a blonde with a fleur-de-lis tattoo. Even a reader armed with a Latin dictionary and a copy of 'The Three Musketeers' cannot anticipate the thrilling twists of this stylish, Escher-like mystery." New Yorker

The fencing master; translated from the Spanish by Margaret Jull Costa. Harcourt Brace & Co. 1999 245p $24

ISBN 0-15-100181-2   LC 98-35536
Original Spanish edition, 1988

This novel is set in the Spain of 1868. "All Madrid, with the exception of Don Jaime, is preoccupied with political plots and rumors of the Queen's abdication. Don Jaime is a fencing master devoted to honor and his art. He is an anachronism, which causes him serious difficulty with murders and stolen documents." Atl Mon

"In lieu of snappy pater, Pérez-Reverte provides artful, intricate conversation. Rather than send his characters on a relentless search, he provides them with an inexorable unfolding of revelation, increasingly ghastly. And instead of the clever puzzle that lies at the heart of many a lesser crime novel, he substitutes a subtle meditation on the deeper mysteries of fate and choice." N Y Times Book Rev

The nautical chart; translated from the Spanish by Margaret Sayers Peden. Harcourt 2001 466p

ISBN 0-15-100534-6   LC 2001-39446
Original Spanish edition, 2000

"This is the story of a down-and-out sailor ('We could call him Ishmael, but in truth his name is Coy') who washes up in modern-day Barcelona, where he is recruited to join in the treasure hunt for a cargo of emeralds . . . that went down with a merchant ship that sank off the Spanish coast in 1767." N Y Times Book Rev

"Adept as ever at mixing historical and contemporary material, Perez-Reverte takes his genrebending to another level this time by merging the swashbuckling spirit of the best sea adventures with an introspective, philosophical meditation on the idea of navigation." Booklist

The painter of battles; a novel; translated from the Spanish by Margaret Sayers Peden. Random House 2008 211p $25

ISBN 978-1-4000-6598-1; 1-4000-6598-4
          LC 2007-16997
Original Spanish edition, 2006

"The character of the title is Andrés Faulques, a hermit who spends his time painting a colossal battle scene on the interior of a watchtower. Faulques was once a war photographer, famed for his ability to capture in a single image horror, beauty and geometry. One day he has a visitor, the subject of one of Faulques's most celebrated shots: a weary Croatian soldier in the hour of dejected defeat. The photograph helped to change Faulques's life, winning an award. It also changed the soldier's: its publication and his identification as the husband of a young woman sheltering in a Serbian village saw her raped and then, along with his son, tortured and murdered. Now he has come to pay Faulques back. What follows is a game of mental chess, an excursion into art, history and imagi-

nation, and both men's lives as Faulques realises that only the continuation of their discourse, and his painting, is keeping him alive." London Times

Purity of blood; translated from the Spanish by Margaret Sayers Peden. G.P. Putnam's Sons 2006 267p $23.95

ISBN 0-399-15320-9   LC 2005-50984
Original Spanish edition, 1997

In this installment featuring the 17th-century swordsman, Alatriste "is contracted to help a man from a Jewish-turned-Catholic family rescue his daughter from behind the thick walls of a Madrid convent, which the chaplain 'has turned . . . into his private seraglio.' This novel is written in the mold of Dumas' musketeer novels and excitingly upholds the tradition." Booklist

Perlman, Elliot

Seven types of ambiguity. Riverhead Books 2004 628p $27.95

ISBN 0-571-20717-0   LC 2004-45348

This is a novel, "told from seven perspectives, about the effects of the brief abduction of six-year-old Sam Geraghty by Simon Heywood, his mother Anna's ex-boyfriend. Charismatic, unemployed Simon is still obsessed with Anna nine years after their breakup-to the dismay of his present lover, Angelique, a prostitute. Anna's stockbroker husband, Joe, is one of Angelique's regulars, which feeds Simon's flame. When Angelique turns Simon in to the cops, he claims he had permission to pick Sam up; his fate hinges on whether Anna will back up his lie. Most of the perspectives are linked to Simon's shrink, Alex Klima, who writes to Anna and counsels Simon, Angelique and Joe's coworker, Dennis." Publ Wkly

"This is an exciting gamble of a novel, one willing to lose its shirt in its bid to hold you. Be prepared to give it time. Be prepared to skim when you come to a particularly annoying digression. But most of all be prepared to stay with it for the long haul. It's worth it." N Y Times (Late N Y Ed)

Perrotta, Tom, 1961-

The abstinence teacher. St. Martin's Press 2007 358p $24.95

ISBN 978-0-312-35833-4; 0-312-35833-4
          * LC 2007-21961

"Ruth Ramsey, divorced, is the human sexuality teacher at the local high school; she believes in being honest with her students, telling them that some people 'enjoy oral sex.' She lands in hot water when an evangelical church, offended by her curriculum, forces the school board to include a section on abstinence. Tim Mason is the beloved soccer coach of Ruth's young daughter, Maggie. He is also a reformed stoner/loser and an entrenched member of the church that attacked Ruth. Things get interesting when Tim, in a moment of crisis, leads his team of girls in prayer, and Ruth publicly drags her daughter from the soccer field." Booklist

"Perrotta, an accomplished satirist who has made the suburbs his personal stomping ground, turns Stonewood Heights . . . into a battleground for the hearts and minds (and, need I add, souls) of his characters. While Perrotta does do more than give lip service to both sides, it's

Perrotta, Tom, 1961-—_Continued_
pretty clear where his allegiance lies. . . . What keeps
the book from getting too heavy-handed, besides the
sharply written humor, is the fact that Perrotta makes his
evangelical Christian protagonist less of a zealot than the
atheist." Christ Sci Monit

Joe College. St. Martin's Press 2000 306p
ISBN 0-312-26184-5   LC 00-31722
"Danny, a New Jersey working-class boy at Yale, circa
1980, finds himself both enchanted by a schoolmate and
dodging calls from a hometown girlfriend. Spring break,
and the inevitable crisis, loom." Newsweek
"Perrotta's genius is his ability to depict student culture with dead-on accuracy. His satiric touch is like a
light, but killing frost." Christ Sci Monit

Little children. St. Martin's Press 2004 355p
$24.95
ISBN 0-312-31571-6
                                  * LC 2003-15947
"The eponymous children in this satirical novel are actually adults who, chafing at the burdens of parenthood,
try to recreate their unencumbered youth. Sarah, an
overeducated young homemaker, likens her tantrum-
prone daughter to a 'brooding Russian epileptic' out of
Dostoevsky, and pines for lost college days of feminism
and bisexuality. While her husband orders used panties
online, she has furtive sex with a stay-at-home dad
whose repeated failure to pass the bar has earned him the
contempt of his gorgeous wife. The humor is sometimes
cruel, but Perrotta never betrays the complexity of his
characters." New Yorker

Perry, Anne, 1938-

Bedford Square. Fawcett Columbine 1999 330p
$24.95
ISBN 0-449-90633-7   LC 98-29854
"Through a campaign of 'whisper, suspicion and innuendo,' someone is slandering men of high position in
1891 London society, and it is up to Thomas Pitt, commander of the Bow Street police station, to scotch these
poisonous rumors of dishonorable behavior before reputations are destroyed and lives ruined. Through his discreet
investigations, the sympathetic Pitt exposes the subtle
cruelty of the anonymous letters that bring disgrace to
one man and death to another." N Y Times Book Rev

Belgrave Square. Fawcett Columbine 1992 361p
o.p.   LC 91-73144
"While investigating the murder of back-street usurer
William Weems, killed when one of his own gold coins
is fired from a gun [Inspector Thomas] Pitt learns that
the victim had been blackmailing members of London's
high social circles." Publ Wkly
The author "paints handsome portraits of . . . [Victori-
an] aristocratic society and provides luxurious details of
the gala balls and garden parties, the fashionable outings
at Covent Garden and the Royal Academy of Arts, where
they congregate to preen themselves. But it isn't all done
for show. The author has the eyes of a hawk for character nuance and her claws out for signs of the criminal injustices rampant among the privileged classes during this
gilded historical period." N Y Times Book Rev

Bluegate Fields. St. Martin's Press 1984 308p
o.p.   LC 84-11769
"Inspector Pitt and his splendid wife, Charlotte, pursue
[a] murder investigation that takes them from the squalor
of the slums to the hypocrisy of high-society drawing
rooms in Victorian London. Pitt is uncomfortable with a
case built against a humorless tutor by a zealous young
policeman who possesses a potentially obstructive reverence for the upper class. However the witnesses appear
irrefutable . . . and Pitt's superior is adamant about not
reopening so embarrassing a case—a teenager from a
wealthy family was murdered in a bathtub and shoved
down a London sewer. Charlotte, impelled by the tutor's
wife, launches her own campaign to prove that the
wrong man has been arrested." Booklist

A breach of promise. Fawcett Columbine 1998
374p $25
ISBN 0-449-90849-6   LC 98-21212
"Gifted architect Killian Melville begs barrister Sir Oliver Rathbone to defend him in what is certain to be an
ugly breach-of-promise suit. Melville claims he never
asked lovely young Zillah Lambert, the daughter of his
mentor and patron Barton Lambert, to marry him. Unfortunately, the young lady and her mother think otherwise.
. . . Days later, Melville is dead, an apparent suicide.
Rathbone can't get the unfortunate young man out of his
mind and determines to get to the bottom of the case."
Booklist
"Aside from the jarring coincidence that sets up the
resolution, the story is full of feeling and weighted with
intelligent thought about the status of women in mid-
Victorian society." N Y Times Book Rev

Buckingham Palace gardens; a novel. Ballantine
Books 2008 312p $26
ISBN 978-0-345-46931-1; 0-345-46931-3
                                LC 2007-42767
A mystery featuring Perry's 19th-century police inspector, Thomas Pitt. "Unlike so many detective series gliding on cruise control, this mature work provides a fine
introduction to Perry's alluring world of Victorian crime
and intrigue. Ever the master of her milieu, she delivers
sumptuous descriptions of life among the gentry when
England still basked in its imperial glory. And in an intricate plot about a murder at the palace while the Prince
and Princess of Wales are in residence, she also marshals
the series's major themes: the way crime reverberates
throughout the social classes; the precarious status of
women of every rank; and the need for honorable heroes
to preserve and protect the Empire, sometimes from itself." N Y Times Book Rev

Cain his brother. Fawcett Columbine 1995 390p
o.p.   LC 95-8680
Genevieve Stonefield comes to Victorian detective
William Monk "for help, believing that her missing husband, the upright Angus Stonefield, has been murdered
by his depraved twin brother, Caleb. When Monk finds
evidence of Angus's death, he also comes upon a makeshift typhoid hospital staffed by his two friends, Lady
Callandra Daviot and Hester Latterly." Publ Wkly
"This one deserves high marks for superb plotting, fine
writing, intriguing characters, and outstanding historical
detail." Booklist

Perry, Anne, 1938-—*Continued*

Cardington Crescent. St. Martin's Press 1987 314p o.p.

LC 86-27942

A Victorian "mystery featuring the stalwart Inspector Thomas Pitt of Scotland Yard and his inquisitive wife, Charlotte. When Charlotte's beloved sister is suspected of poisoning her philandering husband, the Pitts undertake the investigation of the unfortunate victim's seemingly irreproachable, upper-crust family. Amid the luxurious splendor of an elegant town house and the hideous squalor of a London slum, they uncover a scandalous web of depravity and corruption that has inevitably culminated in the murder. A detailed period puzzler suffused with atmosphere, emotion, and suspense." Booklist

A dangerous mourning. Fawcett Columbine 1991 330p o.p.

LC 91-70655

"Murder in an aristocratic London household pits Inspector William Monk . . . against the Victorian sense of propriety, a bootlicking superior officer and a family's fierce determination to protect its reputation. Octavia Haslett, widowed daughter of Sir Basil Moidore, is found stabbed to death in her bedroom dressed only in nightclothes; when Monk proves no outsider could have entered the house that night, the family and servants remain sole suspects. As tension mounts in the household and a handsome and disliked footman becomes a scapegoat, Monk covertly arranges to introduce Hester Latterly, who served with Florence Nightingale in the Crimea and has helped Monk before, as a nurse in the Moidore home." Publ Wkly

Death of a stranger. Ballantine Bks. 2002 337p

ISBN 0-345-44005-6

LC 2002-66735

This Monk mystery "opens with the murder of a wealthy railroad businessman in a brothel. Outraged by the crime, high society pressures the police into cracking down on prostitution. But a police presence is bad for business, and the pimps take out their frustration on the call girls. These battered women seek medical assistance at a Coldbath Square clinic rum by Monk's wife, Hester. . . . Meanwhile, a mysterious young socialite asks Monk to investigate her fiancé, a partner in a successful railroad company that, she fears, is involved in fraud and corruption." Libr J

Defend and betray. Fawcett Columbine 1992 385p o.p.

LC 92-52665

In Victorian London a "proud nurse and a brilliant lawyer team up with former policeman William Monk to defend a sympathetic upper-class woman who confesses to murdering her much-respected husband in a fit of jealousy." Libr J

"The climactic trial, and its ugly disclosures, are well wrought. . . . Throughout, the plight of the intelligent, educated woman who is not rich—her need for a meaningful independence, her culture's resistance to her fulfillment—is, while not deeply explored, frequently touched upon." N Y Times Book Rev

The face of a stranger. Fawcett Columbine 1990 328p o.p.

LC 90-34169

"William Monk, attached to the police in 1856 London, returns to work with amnesia after otherwise recovering from a nasty accident. Assigned to solve the murder of an aristocrat wounded in the Crimean War, he discovers, while hiding his memory loss from others, that

he abhors his own character." Libr J

The author "understands her amnesiac sleuth so intimately that she knows he can rediscover himself only in moments of inspiration along the trail of his quarry. This, and the fact that Monk has more to learn about himself even as the story concludes, are brilliant touches that effectively blend contemporary understanding of character with a Victorian sensibility." N Y Times Book Rev

Farriers' Lane. Fawcett Columbine 1993 374p o.p.

LC 92-54390

"In the wave of anti-Semitic hysteria in 1884 that follows the crucifixion of an English gentleman, a young Jewish actor is hastily tried and executed for the crime. Five years later, a justice of the appeals court is murdered when he attempts to reopen the sensational case. Only a man of discretion, intelligence and integrity—a man like Inspector Thomas Pitt of the Bow Street police division—can solve the devious affair of passion and political intrigue in Victorian London." N Y Times Book Rev

Funeral in blue. Ballantine Bks. 2001 344p

ISBN 0-345-44001-3

LC 2001-37481

A mystery featuring Hester and William Monk. "In the studio of a London artist, two women have been murdered, one of them the wife of Dr. Kristian Beck, a physician from Vienna with whom Hester's dear friend, Lady Callandra, is secretly in love. When Beck is charged with the murder, Callandra enlists the aid of Hester and William. . . . The author excels at re-creating the ambience of 1860s London streets." Publ Wkly

Half Moon Street. Ballantine Bks. 2000 312p

ISBN 0-449-00655-7

LC 99-55232

"Superintendent Pitt is summoned to the Thames when police discover the body of a young man dressed in a torn green velvet gown, manacled to a punt, 'in parody of ecstasy and death'. At first it seems the victim is Henri Bonnard, a functionary in the French embassy; eventually, Pitt and dour sidekick Sergeant Tellman identify the body as Delbert Cathcart, a gifted photographer. Was there a connection between Cathcart and lookalike Bonnard?" Publ Wkly

"Perry sinks inspector Pitt knee-deep in the morally suspect world of the theater and the completely subterranean culture of pornography. . . . Cameos from Oscar Wilde and W.B. Yeats add to the sense of artistic turmoil set against middle-class timidity." Booklist

Highgate rise. Fawcett Columbine 1991 330p o.p.

LC 90-85131

"Inspector Thomas Pitt, is appalled by the callousness of an arsonist who torches a physician's town house, burning his wife to death. Pitt's highborn wife, Charlotte, shares his horror when she learns that the dead woman was a quiet crusader on behalf of poor slum tenants. . . . Ms. Perry gives Pitt a breather from his customary gutter research by confining his investigation to the victim's upper-class social circle. Following her own conscience, Charlotte insinuates her way into elegant drawing rooms where the author's satirical wit is free to spread its rather showy skirts." N Y Times Book Rev

The Hyde Park headsman. Fawcett Columbine 1994 392p o.p.

LC 93-22124

Inspector Thomas Pitt "struggles to solve the brutal and confounding murder of Captain the Honorable Oakley Winthrop, R.N., who's been found beheaded in

Perry, Anne, 1938-—*Continued*

Hyde Park. Pitt suspects the victim knew his killer, but it's only after three more deadly murders take place that enough evidence can be mustered to accuse the real killer." Booklist

No graves as yet; a novel of World War I. Ballantine Bks. 2003 642p $25.95

ISBN 0-345-45652-1   LC 2003-52233

'This is the debut novel in Perry's projected five-book series about a British family during World War I. The family in question includes brothers Matthew and Joseph Reavley and sisters Judith and Hannah, whose parents are killed in a car accident when the book opens. Reavley pere had been on his way to deliver a document that purports to be of national importance. Matthew, a trusted employee in the Intelligence Service, can't quite believe that the document could really threaten Britain's honor. Meanwhile, Joseph, an ordained minister and teacher of classical languages at Cambridge, struggles with the senseless murder of his brilliant protege." Libr J

"Perry's melancholy evocation of the 'eternal afternoon' that would soon turn to night all over England is lovely." N Y Times Book Rev

Paragon Walk. St. Martin's Press 1981 204p o.p.

"A psychopathic killer stalks the fashionable London neighborhood called Paragon Walk—the rapist's atrocities are as incredible, and terrifying to the Paragon Walk aristocrats as a sudden outbreak of the bubonic plague. Inspector Pitt's investigation of one brutal slaying, that of 17-year-old Fanny Nash, leads him to his own family—and himself." Booklist

Pentecost Alley. Fawcett Columbine 1996 405p o.p.   LC 95-43557

"Two years after the short, bloody reign of Jack the Ripper, a wave of terror rips through Whitechapel . . . when a local prostitute is savagely murdered. Thomas Pitt, who heads the Bow Street police command, promises to bring the sadistic killer to justice." N Y Times Book Rev

"Perry has created a superbly plotted, grippingly suspenseful period piece filled with intriguing characters and fascinating descriptions of the manners and customs of Victorian London." Booklist

Resurrection row. St. Martin's Press 1981 204p o.p.   LC 81-8846

"For no discernible reason, someone digs up the corpses of recently buried citizens and sets them up in public places. With these crimes demanding Pitt's concentration, he also has to investigate the murder of Godolphin Jones—an artist, pornographer and blackmailer. The detective's efforts to gather evidence against Jones's clients, obvious suspects, are fruitless until (as always) his quick-witted wife Charlotte drops a startling hint." Publ Wkly

Seven dials. Ballantine Bks. 2003 345p $25.95

ISBN 0-345-44007-2   LC 2002-35605

"When the Egyptian mistress of a senior cabinet minister is discovered in her garden in the middle of the night, using a wheelbarrow to dispose of the body of a junior diplomat, the apparent crime of passion turns into an international incident. Thomas Pitt. . . chafes at the order

from Special Branch to extricate the government official, Saville Ryerson, from the affair; but he sees the gravity of the political situation. . . . Although the focus of the plot tends to drift, the visual panorama is voluptuous to behold." N Y Times Book Rev

Shoulder the sky. Ballantine Bks. 2004 338p $25.95

ISBN 0-345-45654-8

This sequel to No graves yet "follows the wartime careers of the Reavley siblings. Joseph, serving as a chaplain at the Western Front, strives to build morale among the troops amidst the harsh realities of World War I. He is also determined to find out who murdered Eldon Prentice, an abrasive, arrogant journalist, even though no one else cares. Judith finds meaning in her life by driving ambulances near Ypres and falling in love with the married general she chauffeurs. Back in London, Matthew secretly investigates the identity of the 'Peacemaker,' who would manipulate the British into surrendering. Matthew has a personal stake in stopping him, because the 'Peacemaker' orchestrated the deaths of the Reavley parents." Libr J

"Questions about the morality of war resonate throughout this harrowing novel, which Perry has constructed with hallmark attention to period detail and sense of place. Her vivid evocations of the battlefield . . . are unforgettable." Booklist

The silent cry. Fawcett Columbine 1997 361p $24.95

ISBN 0-449-90848-8   LC 97-16848

In this Victorian mystery "one man is found murdered and another on the edge of death in the notorious London slum called St. Giles. Although it looks as if they may have engaged in a mortal fight, they are in fact father and son from a well-to-do family. Later, links develop between these men and a series of violent rapes of prostitutes. Hester Latterly, nurse and protector of the surviving son, Rhys, counterbalances detective William Monk in their mutual pursuit of the truth." Libr J

"With her grimly detailed descriptions of the match factories, sweatshops, paupers hospitals and tenement 'rookeries' crowded into these slums, Perry brings a rank sense of reality to the wretched living conditions of the working poor." N Y Times Book Rev

The sins of the wolf. Fawcett Columbine 1994 374p o.p.   LC 94-12099

"Nurse Hester Latterly, who served courageously in the Crimean War and has assisted former policeman William Monk in many of his investigations . . . is charged with murdering a patient for personal gain. Hester hires on to accompany aging but lively Mary Farraline by train from Edinburgh to London and to administer the proper dose of heart medication. But Mary dies enroute—and her pearl brooch is discovered in Hester's bag. The dead woman's family, the police and most of Edinburgh are convinced that Hester killed her to obtain the pin. Coming to her aid are former policeman Monk, barrister Oliver Rathbone and Lady Callandra Daviot." Publ Wkly

Slaves of obsession. Ballantine Bks. 2000 344p

ISBN 0-345-43326-2   LC 00-40375

"William Monk, agent of enquiry, is employed to discover who is blackmailing respectable merchant and arms dealer Daniel Alberton. Monk soon finds himself

Perry, Anne, 1938-—*Continued*

investigating Alberton's murder, however, and looking for the murderer on the battlefield at Bull Run." Libr J

"Perry's images of the carnage and confusion of battle are relentless in their intensity, unflinching in their truth-telling detail." N Y Times Book Rev

Southampton Row. Ballantine Bks. 2002 326p
ISBN 0-345-44003-X

* LC 2001-52664

Thomas Pitt "ventures into the world of spiritualism when, on the eve of a critical parliamentary election, the wife of the Liberal candidate is implicated in the murder of a clairvoyant. As she has done increasingly in recent books, Perry links the crime to a secret political cabal known as the Inner Circle and draws everyone into its machinations. . . . Perry's proto-feminists have the kind of intellectual radiance that eludes their spouses." N Y Times Book Rev

Traitor's gate. Fawcett Columbine 1995 411p
o.p.

LC 94-27624

This mystery, set "in turn-of-the-century London, has Inspector Thomas Pitt and his wife, Charlotte, investigating the mysterious death of Thomas' mentor, Sir Arthur Desmond. The death has been ruled a suicide, but Sir Arthur's son is convinced his father was murdered for attempting to expose treason in the Colonial Office." Booklist

"In combination with her meticulous research, Ms. Perry's infallible feeling for the historical moment yields animated political debate over the colonization of Africa, glittering views of Victorian society at play and tantalizing glimpses of a confident, assertive creature known as the 'new woman.'" N Y Times Book Rev

The twisted root. Ballantine Bks. 1999 346p $25
ISBN 0-345-43325-4   LC 99-34689

"A beautiful widow named Miriam Gardiner has disappeared, leaving behind a distraught fiancé and a dead coachman. Monk is called in to find Gardiner and then must uncover the truth when she is charged with murdering the coachman." Libr J

Weighed in the balance. Fawcett Columbine 1996 355p o.p.

* LC 96-34824

William Monk "a Victorian-era 'agent of inquiry,' is still haunted by a baffling amnesia, and he feels that his associates—the rigidly proper barrister Sir Oliver Rathbone and the uncompromising and outspoken nurse Hester Latterly—have taken on more than they can handle when Sir Oliver decides to defend Countess Zorah Rostova against a slander charge. The patriotic Zorah has accused Princess Gisela of Felzburg of murdering her husband, Prince Friedrich, heir to the throne, who presumably had died as a result of a fall from a horse. Gisela is suing." Publ Wkly

"Monk, the dark and brooding hero who infuses this luxuriantly detailed series with its romantic soul, is not immune to the seductive appeal of this aristocratic crowd. . . . But he also comes to understand the human passions behind the political forces that transformed Europe in the mid-1800's." N Y Times Book Rev

The Whitechapel conspiracy. Ballantine Bks. 2001 341p
ISBN 0-345-43328-9   LC 00-64206

"When Pitt delivers the testimony that condemns a prominent man for murder, he is 'rewarded' by being shuffled off to the Special Branch, which operates in London's risky East End." Libr J

Perry's interpretation of the Jack the Ripper killings is "a beauty, brilliantly presented, ingeniously developed and packed with political implications that reverberate on every level of British society." N Y Times Book Rev

Perry, Thomas

Blood money; a novel. Random House 2000 351p $24.95
ISBN 0-679-45304-0   LC 99-18340

In this Jane Whitefield suspense novel "Bernie 'the Elephant' Lupus, who handled—in his head—the finances of 12 major mob families for 50 years, fakes his own murder and winds up in the hands of Jane, at first out to help only his maid. But soon the three of them, along with an accountant, are involved in a plot to steal over $14 billion of the mob's investments and then donate the funds to charity." Libr J

"Perry's inventive ways of keeping Jane and her charges one step ahead of the mob squad are downright dazzling—all the more so because they pass up coldblooded technology and go for good old human wit and ingenuity." N Y Times Book Rev

Dance for the dead. Random House 1996 324p
ISBN 0-679-44911-6   LC 95-32716

In this thriller, Native American private agent Jane Whitefield, "appoints herself the guardian angel of Timmy Phillips, a little boy with a big trust fund. The master criminal who had Timmy's foster parents murdered has an ingenious scheme for plundering his inheritance; but, since 'none of this works if the heir is alive,' Jane takes aggressive action to save his life." N Y Times Book Rev

Death benefits; a novel. Random House 2001 383p $24.95
ISBN 0-679-45305-9   LC 00-41476

San Francisco insurance data analyst John Walker is "sleepwalking through his young life when the boss assigns him to assist a private detective on an inside job involving Walker's ex-girlfriend, a claims adjuster who disappeared after being implicated in a $12 million scheme to defraud the company. Judicious applications of Perry's knowing wit energize the tutor-pupil dynamics between Walker and Max Stillman, the crafty and somewhat sinister P.I. who calls the shots on this case." N Y Times Book Rev

The face-changers; a novel. Random House 1998 372p $24
ISBN 0-679-45303-2   LC 97-34078

Seneca Indian guide Jane Whitefield "is asked by her surgeon husband to help his old mentor, Dr. Richard Dahlman, who has been accused of murdering his research partner. In her attempts to keep Dahlman out of the hands of the law and far away from the two men who want to kill him, she finds that someone is using her name to make people disappear permanently, and Dahlman has gotten caught in the backlash. . . . The plot is full of heart-stopping suspense, Native American lore, and engaging characters, but the real pull is how Jane will surmount adversity and still keep her honor and ethics intact." Libr J

Perry, Thomas—*Continued*

Fidelity. Harcourt 2008 357p $25

ISBN 978-0-15-101292-3; 0-15-101292-X

LC 2007-26507

"An Otto Penzler book"

In this thriller, "Emily Kramer tries to find out why her husband, Phil, was shot dead and discovers he'd been keeping secrets from her. Jerry Hobart completed his contract killing of Phil Kramer, but now his employer wants Phil's wife dead as well; Jerry decides he can instead make more money finding out what his employer is hiding. And rich, successful Ted Forrest likes young women-reallyyoung women. This predisposition got him into trouble once before, and he's not going to let it happen again." Libr J

Perry's "characters are uncannily good at sizing one another up and anticipating what the next moves will be. Though he briefly equates Hobart's tactics to the ways a coyote slinks through a neighborhood, Mr. Perry need not even articulate this. It's always built into his storytelling, and it's already on the page." N Y Times (Late N Y Ed)

Nightlife; a novel. Random House 2006 373p $24.95

ISBN 1-4000-6004-4   LC 2005-46449

"In contrast to most serial killers, Tanya Starling is a woman, and she has no signature MO except that most of her corpses are male. The victim of her mother's emotional abuse and men's abandonment, Tanya takes on and sheds identities and hair color willy-nilly as she moves from man to man, becoming stronger with each murder. Her nemesis is another relentless woman, Portland detective Catherine Hobbes, who tracks her to LA and back and nearly becomes a victim herself. The novel veers back and forth between Tanya and Catherine, with occasional side trips to Joe Pitt, a former police investigator, now private, who provides the romance in Catherine's dull personal life." Libr J

"This novel's intensity comes from the skillful way in which Perry lets readers in on the secrets of the serial killer: we see her change disguises and identities; we see her pick up and destroy men. We see more than the police and the private eye do, as they try to find the woman they suspect killed the Portland man, and as we see her leave that old identity far, far behind. Perry also offers a complex character in detective Catherine Hobbes as she races against the private eye to catch a protean killer." Booklist

Pursuit; a novel. Random House 2002 370p $24.95

ISBN 0-679-45306-7   LC 2001-40365

The key players in this thriller "are James Varney, a sociopathic hit man whose handiwork has left 13 people dead in a Louisville, Ky., restaurant, and Roy Prescott, the professional manhunter hired to track him down by the father of one of the victims. . . . Although Prescott initiates most of the fiendish maneuvers, he is checkmated at every turn by his opponent's ability to anticipate or recover from each trap. When this brilliant game is finally called, it isn't advanced weaponary or high-tech skills that determine the victor; it's one player's greater insights into the other's twisted mind—a mind very much like his own." N Y Times Book Rev

Runner. Houghton Mifflin Harcourt 2009 441p $26

ISBN 978-0-15-101528-3; 0-15-101528-7

LC 2008-7119

"An Otto Penzler book"

This episode finds Jane Whitefield, "a Native American 'guide' who helps people assume new identities, living quietly under an alias in western New York State, married to a local doctor. Shortly after pregnant Christine Monahan shows up at the hospital where Jane's husband works, desperately searching for Jane, a bomb explodes in the hospital. The two women wind up fleeing cross-country with a cadre of thugs hot on their trail. Jane learns that Christine is the girlfriend of an abusive real estate mogul in San Diego obsessed with finding her and their unborn child. By giving Christine and her baby new identities, Jane once again puts herself in mortal danger." Publ Wkly

"Never melodramatic and always masterful at creating conflicted characters . . ., Perry offers a highly enjoyable tale in which the roles of hunter and hunted are reversed with devastating effect." Libr J

Shadow woman. Random House 1997 350p $22

ISBN 0-679-45302-4

Native American private agent Jane Whitefield "engineers the 'disappearance' of Peter Hatcher from his old life at Pleasure, Inc., a gambling casino. But the casino's honchos think Peter knows too much about their expansion plans and hire a brutally vicious hit team to find, and assassinate, him." Libr J

"Although the frantic pace allows no time for sightseeing, Perry lingers long enough over Pete's amiable character to make him worth all this excruciating suspense." N Y Times Book Rev

Vanishing act. Random House 1995 289p

ISBN 0-679-43536-0   LC 94-17413

"Jane Whitefield is a Seneca Indian from upstate New York who has set herself up as a one-woman underground railroad to help worthy fugitives disappear. . . . A desperate man like John Felker is right up her alley. A burned-out cop who quit the job to become an accountant, Felker was set up on an embezzlement rap. But he grabbed the dough anyway, and now he has a contract on his head. Drawing on her clan contacts, Jane guides Felker on a trip into oblivion, via a rugged route across the Canadian border. This is all very satisfying and quite scenic—until certain deadly reversals tip off Jane that her operation has been compromised." N Y Times Book Rev

Pesci, David

Amistad; the thunder of freedom. Marlowe & Co. 1997 292p hardcover o.p. pa $12.95

ISBN 1-56924-748-X; 1-56924-703-X (pa)

LC 96-54050

"In August 1839, Singbe-Pleh, a Mende tribesman, led his fellow African captives aboard the Spanish ship Amistad in successful revolt. The Africans took over the ship but could not sail it back to Africa. They were captured and put on trial in Connecticut. . . . The case was politically charged, with proslavery President Van Buren's administration wanting to give the Africans to Spain, abolitionists rallying for their freedom, and former President John Quincy Adams eventually defending them before the Supreme Court. Pesci deftly blends the facts of this fascinating historical episode with story." SLJ

Peshkov, Alexei Maximovich *See* Gorky, Maksim, 1868-1936

Pessl, Marisha

Special topics in calamity physics. Viking 2006 514p il $25.95

ISBN 0-670-03777-X   LC 2005-58474

This coming-of-age tale is told through the "voice of its heroine, Blue van Meer. After a childhood moving from one academic outpost to another with her father (a man prone to aphorisms and meteoric affairs), Blue is clever, deadpan, and possessed of a vast lexicon of literary, political, philosophical, and scientific knowledge—and is quite the cineaste to boot. In her final year of high school at the elite (and unusual) St. Gallway School in Stockton, North Carolina, Blue falls in with a charismatic group of friends and their captivating teacher, Hannah Schneider. But when the drowning of one of Hannah's friends and the shocking death of Hannah herself lead to a confluence of mysteries, Blue is left to make sense of it all with only her gimlet-eyed instincts and cultural references to guide—or misguide—her." Publisher's note

"Even the physics equation on the book's back cover has outsized verve. And what begins as a dubious proposition, in a world wholly without need for additions to its Prep School Confidential bibliography, becomes a whirling, glittering, multifaceted marvel, delivered in an irrepressibly smart and flamboyant new voice." N Y Times (Late N Y Ed)

Peters, Elizabeth, 1927-

For works written by this author under other names see Michaels, Barbara, 1927-

Children of the storm. Morrow 2003 400p $25.95

ISBN 0-06-621476-9   LC 2002-41083

This installment, set in 1919, finds Amelia Peabody "back in Egypt, reunited with her extended brood of family and friends (a helpful preface sorts them all out) and anticipating an enriching season at the archaeological dig being excavated by her husband. In some respects, the story follows the formula of the 14 earlier books in this spirited series—precious tomb artifacts go missing and the logical suspect turns up dead, necessitating adventures filled with romance and fraught with peril." N Y Times Book Rev

The deeds of the disturber; an Amelia Peabody mystery. Atheneum Pubs. 1988 289p o.p.

LC 87-33457

"Determined Victorian feminist Peabody refuses to be intimidated by a phenomenon reported at the British Museum, where a *sem* priest is supposedly working a curse in revenge for the desecration of an ancient mummy. The priest's supernatural figure is momentarily glimpsed at the exhibit, before a murderer strikes. Disobeying Emerson, of course, Peabody lays her life on the line and unmasks the decidedly human villain." Publ Wkly

The golden one. Morrow 2002 429p

ISBN 0-380-97885-7   LC 2001-52169

"On arriving in Luxor for a season of archaeological investigation, Amelia {Peabody Emerson} and her family discover that war (it's 1917) has taken its toll on their beloved Egypt. Before too long, the conflict intrudes on their plans and embroils them in an adventure, complete with double agents, Turkish spies, derring-do, and the ever-puzzling Sethos. At the same time, they must reckon with tomb robbers, killers, and antiquities fraud." Booklist

Guardian of the horizon. Morrow 2004 416p $24.95

ISBN 0-06-621471-8

       * LC 2003-67665

"During 1907-08, an era unaccounted for in previous Amelia Peabody tales, the redoubtable detective must help Prince Tarek of the Lost Oasis keep his throne." Libr J

"Peters' writing works on several levels. She maintains a fast-paced mystery story, her characters are complex, and the fictional cast interacts with historical figures convincingly." Archaeology

He shall thunder in the sky; an Amelia Peabody mystery. Morrow 2000 400p

ISBN 0-380-97659-5   LC 00-25807

In this episode, set in 1915, Amelia Peabody's family's "annual excavations in Egypt are overshadowed by the specter of world war. An invasion of Egypt by the Turks seems imminent, the climate is ripe for spies, and it isn't long before the Emerson clan is up to its eyebrows in intrigue. Then there's Emerson's discovery of a beautiful gold statue: Has the ardent archvillain Sethos returned with more tricks? Peters works in drama galore, plus the usual shots of wry humor and local color." Booklist

The hippopotamus pool. Warner Bks. 1996 384p o.p.

LC 95-31886

In this mystery set in 19th century Egypt, Amelia Peabody "is celebrating the turn of the century at a New Year's Eve ball at Shepheard's Hotel in Cairo when she and her husband, the sexy Egyptologist Radcliffe Emerson, are approached by a mysterious stranger who hands over a scarab ring that he claims was recovered from the lost tomb of Queen Tetisheri. 'Oh, good Gad!' Emerson explodes. 'Are we to have another of these melodramatic distractions?' Indeed we are—and it's a dandy one too. Such romantic nonsense. Such fun." N Y Times Book Rev

The last camel died at noon. Warner Bks. 1991 352p il o.p.

LC 90-26759

In this mystery archaeologist Amelia Peabody, "her handsome, fearless husband, Radcliffe, and their precocious 11-year-old son, Ramses, are in the Sudan, searching for archeologist Willoughby Forth, who disappeared 14 years earlier with his new wife. Rescued in the desert after every camel in their caravan dies, the Emersons are taken to a lost city where ancient Egyptian customs have been carried into modern times. There, entangled in two half-brothers' battle for the throne, Amelia and family fight for the freedom of the slave class while ferreting out the fate of Forth and his bride." Publ Wkly

"The Emersons are decidedly unstodgy Victorians—feminist, democratic, egalitarian, respectful of other cultures—and charming, witty, entertaining sleuths." Booklist

Peters, Elizabeth, 1927-—*Continued*

Lion in the valley; an Amelia Peabody mystery. Atheneum Pubs. 1986 291p o.p.   LC 85-48126

"The stouthearted Victorian Englishwoman, Amelia Peabody Emerson, and her lusty, irascible husband are back in Egypt (with their precocious eight-year-old son, Ramses in tow). . . . The master criminal whom they thwarted but did not bring to justice in 'The Mummy Case' is once again up to nefarious deeds, which include kidnapping Amelia in order to woo her. Murder, mayhem . . . and a pair of distressed young lovers, not to mention a modicum of archaeological pursuits, round out a decided treat for fans of the indomitable duo—or, perhaps, with Ramses, it is now a trio." Booklist

The mummy case. Congdon & Weed 1985 313p o.p.   LC 84-21500

"Victorian Amelia Peabody with her virile husband Emerson and precocious son Ramses embarks on a . . . archaeological dig in Egypt—but not before the death of a dealer in stolen antiquities. A disappearing mummy case and missing Coptic Papyri are the clues in this slapstick comedy-mystery. The ample archaeological detail is vivid, albeit a bit confusing. The irresistible attraction of this story: the heroine's droll tone and intrepid spirit." Libr J

Night train to Memphis. Warner Bks. 1994 353p o.p.   LC 94-3967

Vicky Bliss, "a curator at Munich's National Museum, is asked to go undercover on a cruise down the Nile. Her mission: to spot who among her fellow passengers might be the master criminal about to carry out a major theft of valuable antiquities. Vicky has a sneaking suspicion that the thief the police are after is the mysterious man she knows as John, who's perfectly capable of illegal activities and who's been her sworn enemy and her sometime lover. When John shows up on the cruise and a crew member is murdered, Vicky begins to fear her suspicions are correct—but she doesn't have enough evidence to rule out the other passengers. This one is vintage Peters at her entertaining best." Booklist

Seeing a large cat. Warner Bks. 1997 386p il o.p.   LC 96-37998

"Amelia Peabody and family begin the 1903 'digging' season in Egypt with the usual anticipation. At least two pleas for help and a mysterious warning about a Valley of the Kings tomb, however, complicate life and lead to the expected dangerous adventure." Libr J

"Amelia's unquenchable *joie de l'aventure* continues to define the exuberant style of these mysteries, but Peters doesn't leave it at that. There are always grand views of Egyptian antiquities in her stories, as well as acidic caricatures of globe-trotting tourists and the endlessly entertaining spectacle of busy professional parents confounded by their own progeny." N Y Times Book Rev

The snake, the crocodile, and the dog. Warner Bks. 1992 340p o.p.   LC 92-54096

In this mystery novel, archaeologist Amelia Peabody Emerson and her husband leave their son Ramses in England to excavate in Egypt. "Amelia anticipates time alone with Emerson, but the Master Criminal devises otherwise: In his quest for directions to the . . . Lost Oasis, he attempts abduction, subterfuge, and espionage." Libr J

Trojan gold; a Vicky Bliss mystery. Atheneum Pubs. 1987 o.p.   LC 86-26486

Art historian Vicky Bliss "receives a photograph of a modern woman dressed in the gold jewelry that Schliemann discovered in his archaeological excavation of Troy. The gold has been missing since the night the Soviet Army marched into Munich in 1945. The usual assortment of male admirers gather round, all trying to outmaneuver Vicky; but she manages to side-step nicely and come out the winner in this scintillating, captivating tale." Libr J

Peters, Ellis, 1913-1995

The benediction of Brother Cadfael. Mysterious Press 1992 348p il maps o.p.   LC 91-50965

A combined edition of A morbid taste for bones and One corpse too many, both entered separately. This volume also includes a description of Cadfael country by Rob Talbot and Robin Whiteman

Brother Cadfael's penance; the twentieth chronicle of Brother Cadfael. Mysterious Press 1994 292p o.p.   LC 94-27140

This Brother Cadfael mystery "has the gentle monk leaving his cloister on a journey that will prove both dangerous and wrenching. In twelfth-century Britain, a rebellion has arisen, with factional fighting between the knights supporting Empress Maud and those swearing allegiance to her cousin Stephen. Philip FitzRobert, a traitor to the empress, has taken 30 hostages, among them a young man named Olivier de Bretagne, who is Cadfael's son from a chance encounter years earlier. Although Cadfael has lost tract of the boy's mother, he's never forgotten his son, and once he finds out that Olivier has been spirited away and imprisoned, nothing . . . can keep him from setting out to find the young man who has never known his true father." Booklist

Dead man's ransom; the ninth chronicle of Brother Cadfael. Morrow 1985 189p o.p.   LC 84-22668

First published 1984 in the United Kingdom

This "novel focuses on the brutality of civil war between England and Wales in the early twelfth century, as the Benedictine monk is pulled into a hostage drama that turns into a politically repercussive murder. A young Welshman is exchanged for the sheriff of Shropshire and taken to Cadfael's abbey, where he falls in love with the sheriff's daughter. The sheriff's subsequent murder leaves rampant speculation that the young lovers are the perpetrators of the crime. Cadfael, as ever, is patient and insightful. A wonderfully atmospheric whodunit." Booklist

Death to the landlords!. Morrow 1972 221p o.p.

The setting is "southern India, and the landlords are wealthy landholders who are the objectives of a terrorist murder gang. Dominic Felse . . . is at the center of the action, touring with a casual American acquaintance. The two young men meet up again and again with some of the same people as they travel India's Cape Comorin, among them a very intense English girl and a shy Indian nurse. Although the setting seems idyllic and the young people most attractive there is an undercurrent of brutal violence that hits home hard. The deaths are achieved by

Peters, Ellis, 1913-1995—*Continued*

bombing. . . . Most effective of all is the interesting, perceptive, intuitive portrait of . . . problem-ridden India that emerges." Publ Wkly

Fallen into the pit. Mysterious Press 1994 c1951 324p o.p.   LC 92-50656

First published 1951 in the United Kingdom

"This mystery launched Peters's Inspector Felse series. Set in Britain just after WW II, the main sleuth here is not actually George Felse but his 13-year-old son Dominic. He and his best friend, Pussy Hart, are playing when Dom finds the body of Helmut Schauffler, an ex-P.O.W. who had stayed on after the war in the Comerford area. An autopsy indicates that Schauffler's skull was fractured by blows that were 'precise, neat and of murderous intention.' Helmut, a loathsome blend of cruelty, cowardice and anti-Semitism, is hardly mourned, but his death so rends the village's social fabric that solving the case is imperative. In his first murder investigation, George has difficulty viewing his neighbors as suspects." Publ Wkly

The hermit of Eyton Forest. Mysterious Press 1988 224p o.p.

* LC 87-40398

"A 10-year-old boy in school at the abbey suddenly finds himself Lord of Eaton when his father dies. His grandmother has plans for him; she wants him to marry a neighboring heiress. The abbot refuses to let him go. The grandmother takes steps to get him back. During all this, a mysterious monk living as a hermit and an equally mysterious young man who runs errands for him make their presence strongly felt. A nobleman is murdered, and the sharp eyes of Brother Cadfael notice things that are not apparent to all." N Y Times Book Rev

The holy thief. Mysterious Press 1992 246p o.p.

LC 92-50451

"The Benedictine monks at the Abbey of St. Peter and Paul in Shrewsbury are devastated by the inexplicable disappearance of their holiest and most revered relic, the remains of their patroness and guardian, Saint Winifred. Much to Brother Cadfael's consternation, the theft of the sacred casket could lead to the exposure of his own benign transgression. Years earlier, in compliance with the saint's final wish, he secretly exhumed her bones and buried them in her native Wales. Now Cadfael must recover the reliquary and solve a murder in order to protect himself and to exonerate a young monk accused of the crime." Booklist

"Twelfth-century Shropshire comes vividly alive when peopled with Peter's aristocratic ladies, sturdy lawmen, eager squires and, above all, devout—and devious—monks." Publ Wkly

Monk's-hood; the third chronicle of Brother Cadfael. Morrow 1981 c1980 223p il o.p.

LC 80-26326

First published 1980 in United Kingdom

In this novel Brother "Cadfael investigates the murder by monkshood of Gervase Bonel, a wealthy man who was about to donate his lands to the monastery. Along the way, Cadfael becomes swept up in the monastery's internecine power plays. Peters' language has a full, rich cadence, and her story is wonderfully vivid." Booklist

A morbid taste for bones

also in Peters, E. The benediction of Brother Cadfael p3-129

One corpse too many

also in Peters, E. The benediction of Brother Cadfael p211-348

The pilgrim of hate; the tenth chronicle of Brother Cadfael. Morrow 1985 c1984 190p o.p.

LC 85-62509

First published 1984 in the United Kingdom

"It is A.D. 1141, a year that brings a tide of pilgrims to the Benedictine Abbey at Shrewsbury. The occasion is a joyous one—a celebration in honor of St. Winifred, whose sacred relics were transferred to the abbey from Wales four years earlier. . . . Meanwhile, far away in embattled Winchester, a knight, supporter of the Empress Maud (who is campaigning against Stephen for the throne of England), is mysteriously murdered. But this seemingly disparate event, Cadfael begins to suspect, may be connected to the arrival at the shrine of a pair of pilgrims." Publisher's note

The potter's field; the seventeenth chronicle of Brother Cadfael, of the Benedictine Abbey of Saint Peter and Saint Paul, at Shrewsbury. Mysterious Press 1990 230p o.p.   LC 90-6340

"After the body of a woman is found buried in a Benedictine Abbey field, Brother Cadfael tries to discover the woman's identity and locate the person responsible for her unlawful burial." Booklist

"In place of the pretty romances with which the author often lightens her historically plausible fictions, Ms. Peters provides darker characters and a more somber view of Shrewsbury life. More than the brilliant detection of a crime, the true subject of her wintry tale is human misery, as it extends from the meanest peasant cottage to the grandest manor house." N Y Times Book Rev

A rare Benedictine. Mysterious Press 1989 c1988 118p il $19.95

ISBN 0-89296-397-2   LC 89-42603

First published 1988 in the United Kingdom

Contents: A light on the road to Woodstock; The price of light; Eye witness

The author "reveals for the first time how her medieval sleuth, Brother Cadfael, came to his calling at Shrewsbury Abbey. . . . For all his spirituality, mild Brother Cadfael once again impresses us with his practical grasp of the criminal side of human nature." N Y Times Book Rev

The rose rent; the thirteenth chronicle of Brother Cadfael. Morrow 1986 190p o.p.   LC 87-5733

"When Judith Perle, a most generous benefactor of the abbey, vanishes without a trace, Cadfael immediately connects her disappearance with the vicious murder of a pious young monk and the seemingly senseless destruction of a rose bush. An accomplished whodunit meticulously wrought with a wealth of medieval detail." Booklist

Saint Peter's Fair; the fourth chronicle of Brother Cadfael. Morrow 1981 219p il o.p.

LC 81-11020

Brother Cadfael, "who led an adventurous life in the world before becoming a monk, is on the side of young love, honor and truth as he investigates deaths taking place while a local fair is in full swing. A well-respected merchant is found murdered, and his lovely daughter

Peters, Ellis, 1913-1995—*Continued*

takes it upon herself to keep secrets so she involves two young men, both of whom fancy her. Another death occurs. Peters has an authentic eye and ear for her 12th century way of life and death, and engages our interest all the way." Publ Wkly

The sanctuary sparrow; the seventh chronicle of Brother Cadfael. Morrow 1983 221p o.p.

LC 83-5389

Brother Cadfael "undertakes the problems of young Liliwin, a juggler and acrobat of Shrewsbury who stands accused of pilfering the valuables of one Master Walter Aurifaber, the townships's goldsmith, while Liliwin was amusing Aurifaber and the assembled patrons who were at the wedding feast of Aurifaber's son, Daniel." West Coast Rev Books

The summer of the Danes. Mysterious Press 1991 251p o.p.

LC 91-11621

In this novel Brother Cadfael "must pilgrimage deep into Wales on an errand of Church diplomacy. He is accompanied by young Brother Mark and the passionate Heledd, a young woman fleeing an arranged marriage. The three become pawns in the battle between two Welsh princes and the mercenary Danes whom one prince has hired to help vanquish his brother. There is a murder to be considered when Bledri ap Rhys—who has offended everyone from Heledd's father, Canon Meirion, to countless common soldiers—is found in his bed, stabbed through the heart." Publ Wkly

The virgin in the ice; the sixth chronicle of Brother Cadfael. Morrow 1983 c1982 220p il o.p.

LC 82-14500

First published 1982 in the United Kingdom

"The setting is England during the winter of 1139, A.D. Brother Cadfael, who has taken a vow against war and arms, finds himself in a country torn by civil war. Brother Elyas, a fellow monk of a nearby town, is sent to deliver two orphans, Ermina and Yves Hugonin, and their chaperone Sister Hilaria, to Laurence d'Angers, the childrens' uncle. During the journey Ermina sees her chance to escape and marry her lover. . . . Brother Elyas is attacked by a brutal band of marauders and left for dead. Brother Cadfael, sent on a medical errand to look after Brother Elyas, takes over his responsibility to bring the three safely to Laurence d'Angers. During his journey, Brother Cadfael discovers a murder and feels morally obliged to solve it." Best Sellers

Peterson, Paula W.

Women in the grove. Beacon Press 2004 205p $20

ISBN 0-8070-8352-6   LC 2003-14314

Contents: A miracle; Africa; Big brother; The woman in the long green coat; Cherry's ghost; Alfie and grace; The a's and the i's; In the grove; Song of Camille

"Each of the stories in this beautiful collection focuses on a woman living with HIV/AIDS. . . . [Peterson] clearly knows her subject, and she challenges the reader to put an individual face and story on the HIV/AIDS epidemic. Rich with emotion, this book is too good to be categorized as any one genre of fiction but should be celebrated and read widely." Libr J

Petry, Ann Lane

The street; [by] Ann Petry. Houghton Mifflin 1946 435p o.p.

*

"Set in Long Island, New York, in suburban Connecticut, and in Harlem, *The Street* is the story of intelligent, ambitious Lutie Johnson, who strives to make a better life for herself and her son despite a constant struggle with sexual brutality and racism." Merriam-Webster's Ency of Lit

Petterson, Per, 1952-

In the wake; translated from the Norwegian by Anne Born. Thomas Dunne Books 2006 202p $22.95

ISBN 0-312-34383-3   LC 2006-40196

Original Norwegian edition, 2002

"Arvid Jansson remembers April 7 the way many Americans remember September 11. It was the day his parents and two younger brothers were all killed in a horrific ferry accident. Even though it is now six years later, Arvid still suffers crippling grief. A divorced father of two girls whom he rarely sees, he is also estranged from his only remaining sibling, an older brother. . . . Yet he yearns for human contact and has stilted relationships with two neighbors, a Kurdish man who knows only three words of Norwegian and a woman who lives across the way." Booklist

This novel is, "among other things, a story about literature itself. . . . Arvid, amid his struggles, reads and rereads the works of favorite writers and poets. Ultimately, moving between literature, with its ability to confer meaning on life, and his growing willingness to reengage with life, Arvid cautiously rejoins the world. In 'In the Wake' Mr. Petterson demonstrates, through his own commanding art, the solace of the written word as well as the necessity of human connection. It is understandable why European readers have long admired his work." N Y Times Book Rev

Out stealing horses; translated by Anne Born. Graywolf Press 2007 258p (Lannen translation series selection) $22

ISBN 978-1-55597-470-1; 1-55597-470-8

* LC 2006-938263

Original Norwegian edition, 2003; this translation first published 2005 in the United Kingdom

In this "novel, Trond Sander, a widower nearing seventy, moves to a bare house in remote eastern Norway, seeking the life of quiet contemplation that he has always longed for. A chance encounter with a neighbor—the brother, as it happens, of his childhood friend Jon—causes him to ruminate on the summer of 1948, the last he spent with his adored father, who abandoned the family soon afterward. Trond's recollections center on a single afternoon, when he and Jon set out to take some horses from a nearby farm; what began as an exhilarating adventure ended abruptly and traumatically in an act of unexpected cruelty. Petterson's spare and deliberate prose has astonishing force, and the narrative gains further power from the artful interplay of Trond's childhood and adult perspectives." New Yorker

Pevear, Richard, 1943-

(tr) Chekhov, A. P. Complete short novels

Pevear, Richard, 1943——Continued

(tr) Dumas, A. The three musketeers

(tr) Tolstoy, L., graf. War and peace

Phillips, Arthur, 1969-

Prague; a novel. Random House 2002 367p
ISBN 0-375-50787-6   LC 2001-48975
A novel "about a group of young American (and on
Canadian) expatriates living in Budapest in 1990, just after the Communist empire has collapsed." Publ Wkly
"In Phillips's wry and skillful telling, a sexual tryst or
the renting of an apartment can become a tragicomic
pantomime about East and West. . . . As 'Prague' progresses, each of the five foreigners at the cafe table becomes less and less attractive, and the satiric edge to
Phillips's portrayal sharpens into something close to anger: at their solipsism, their savage cynicism, their detachment from their surrounding and from one another."
N Y Times Book Rev

The song is you; a novel. Random House 2009
254p $25
ISBN 978-1-4000-6646-9; 1-4000-6646-8
                                 LC 2008-28845
"Julian Donahue is a New York-based director of television commercials. Estranged from his wife, Rachel, after the death of their young son, he is sexually and emotionally incapacitated, more plugged in to his music player than into his work or relationships. . . . Ducking into
a Brooklyn bar one snowy night, he sees a performance
by Cait O'Dwyer, a singer-songwriter in her early 20s.
She is beautiful, blazing with talent, as fiery as he is frozen. A master of inducing longing (he is, after all, a
commercial director), Julian drunkenly scrawls a series of
professional tips to the young singer on a set of bar
coasters. Soon after, he hears some of his words incorporated as lyrics to one of her songs, and so their mating
ritual begins. He calls her on the phone when she is volunteering for an on-air fund-raising drive. They exchange
e-mails, voice mails, browser bookmarks, blog posts, forum comments, their digital dance becoming ever more
obsessive and charged." Boston Globe
This novel "takes on loneliness, alienation, middle age
and what it means to feel passé and weighted down by
your past. . . . Yet despite these sober concerns, Phillips' sparkling prose makes for a seriously fun read." San
Francisco Chron

Phillips, Caryl

Crossing the river. Knopf 1994 c1993 237p o.p.
                              * LC 93-35933
First published 1993 in the United Kingdom
This novel "begins in 18th-century Africa as three children—Nash, Martha and Travis—are sold into slavery.
What follows are 'their' life stories along with excerpts
from the logbook of the slave ship's captain. Nash returns to Africa as a Christian missionary in the 1830s.
Martha is a former slave whom we meet as she lays
dying in Denver, having failed to reach California and
find her only child, taken from her years before. Travis
is reincarnated as an American GI stationed in England
in 1943; his story is . . . told by the British woman he
marries." Libr J
"One of the values of fiction is that it can tell the story
anew, can go back and include a neglected truth. 'Crossing the River' does this and is therefore a book with an
agenda. Mr. Phillips proposes that the diaspora is permanent, and that blacks throughout the world who look to
Africa as a benevolent fatherland tell themselves a stunted story. They need not to trace but to put down roots.
The message, however, is neither simply nor stridently
conveyed." N Y Times Book Rev

Dancing in the dark. Knopf 2005 209p $23.95
ISBN 1-4000-4396-4   LC 2005-44106
"This novel centers on the life of Bert Williams, the
black vaudeville performer of the late 19th and early
20th centuries. He and his partner George Walker performed to wild acclaim on New York City and London
stages, with Williams often donning blackface." Libr J
"As subjects for historical novels go, Bert Williams is
an inspired choice; his strange career exemplified all the
ironies and paradoxes that confronted the African-
American performers of his time. . . . Dancing in the
Dark is riveting when it recreates mores and social conventions our culture has done its best to forget." N Y
Times Book Rev

A distant shore. Knopf 2003 277p $23.95
ISBN 1-400-04109-0
"Two lonely lives intertwine in this . . . novel set in
contemporary England. Dorothy has recently moved to a
new subdivision in a small village after a forced retirement leaves her desperate for a new life. Solomon, an illegal immigrant escaping a violent past in Africa, is the
night watchman at the subdivision. They form a cautious
friendship despite the distrust and isolation each is experiencing in new surroundings." Libr J
"This muted, sad novel breaks down the distinction between the placed and the displaced, dissolving our sense
of security, if we had one, about safely belonging in the
world, dispelling our illusion of being at home. We are
all adrift, Phillips says, whether we know it or not: a fact
not of race or nationality, but of the human condition."
N Y Times Book Rev

Foreigners. Alfred A. Knopf 2007 235p $24.95
ISBN 978-1-4000-4397-2   LC 2007-29219
In this triptych, Phillips "reclaims the lives of three
black men in England, deciphering the toxic social chemistry that first gave each man hope, and then destroyed
him. Francis Barber, brought to England from Jamaica at
age 10, became Dr. Johnson's most trusted companion
during the great literary genius' wretched last days, only
to fall into an abyss of poverty and prejudice. Randolph
Turpin, a mixed-race Englishman, astonished the world
in July 1951 by winning a match against Sugar Ray
Robinson, but Britain's first black champion boxer lost
his bout with a hostile world. David Oluwale, a bright
and ambitious Nigerian teenager, stowed away on a ship
to England, intent on becoming an engineer. Instead he
became the target of racist and sadistic policemen. A
lone freedom fighter, he stood up to his attackers, who
murdered him in 1969." Booklist
"With great empathy, and through a collage of voices,
Phillips has created three distinct portraits. All are superbly crafted and utterly absorbing . . . . As Phillips
suggests, Englishness, like foreignness, is a complex and
changeable thing. An important and sobering book, highly relevant today." Daily Mail

Phillips, Caryl—*Continued*

The nature of blood. Knopf 1997 212p $23

ISBN 0-679-45470-5   LC 96-49641

"The novel's primary voice belongs to Eva Stern, a young woman who has just been liberated by the English army from a German camp. Through a series of flashbacks and recollections, Eva remembers life with her family, and then her experience in the camp. Phillips intercuts Eva's story with two wildly discontinuous narratives: one a retelling of *Othello* in Othello's own voice; the other an account of the 15th-century persecution of the money-lending Jews of the Italian city Portobuffole, who were accused of murdering a Christian child." Publ Wkly

"Phillips's object in creating a work in which dialogue, description and characterization are of no real significance has been, laudably enough, to protect the universality of his themes." Times Lit Suppl

Phillips, Jayne Anne, 1952-

Lark and Termite; a novel. Alfred A. Knopf 2009 254p $24

ISBN 978-0-375-40195-4; 0-375-40195-4

      LC 2008-33453

"Central to the narrative are a remarkable pair of siblings orphaned by the Korean War. Born the day his soldier father perished in the notorious No Gun Ri massacre, the young boy called Termite possesses unusual perception unnoticed by most observers because of his severe disabilities. His prospects in tiny Winfield, WV, seem dismal, but teenage sister Lark, who adores her little brother, won't give up. She schemes to gain a happy mutual future even while she is pursued romantically by a much older man, threatened with Termite's removal by the state, and endangered by approaching floodwaters." Libr J

Phillips "has done in Lark and Termite what she did in previous novels such as Machine Dreams (1984) and Shelter (1994), which is to take a relatively simple, straightforward tale and twist it into something luminous and haunting and singular. This is Phillips' first novel in almost a decade, but it doesn't feel tardy or excessively fussed over. It feels fresh. It feels as if it has been taken straight from the griddle and is still too hot to touch. And because it deals with issues over which people have been arguing for centuries—family and war—the novel's raw immediacy is really quite spectacular." PopMatters

MotherKind; a novel. Knopf 2000 295p $24

ISBN 0-375-40194-6   LC 99-49256

"Over the course of a year, Kate, a resolutely independent poet and editor, becomes enmeshed in domesticity: she has a baby, acquires two stepchildren, and discovers that her mother is dying of cancer. Kate has always resisted her mother's desire to care for others perfectly, but she's now preoccupied with making crisp French fries, turning down beds, ironing out problems; frequently overwhelmed, she must also rely on nurses and efficient neighbors. Phillips, an abundantly talented writer, never lapses into sentimentality while describing this woman." New Yorker

Phillips, Marie, 1976-

Gods behaving badly; a novel. Little, Brown and Co. 2007 293p $23.99

ISBN 978-0-316-06762-1; 0-316-06762-8

      LC 2007-9919

"The Olympian gods have fallen on hard times. Their power is fading, and as a result they have been living in a house in London for the past 300 years, working at menial jobs and squabbling among themselves. Artemis hires a mortal woman named Alice to clean the house. Apollo falls in love with Alice, and when she rejects his advances, he tricks Zeus into killing her. Artemis takes Alice's boyfriend, Neil, through the portal to the underworld. First they have to get past Charon, conveyor of the dead, and Cerberus, the three-headed dog. This accomplished, they confront Hades, who gives Neil a choice—save the world or save the woman he loves." Libr J

This first novel, " hovers somewhere between Pride and Prejudice and an episode of 'Bewitched.' I'm not complaining; I have an unusually high regard for Elizabeth Montgomery's oeuvre. And Austen got off some good lines, too. . . . The tension doesn't ratchet too high; it's a romantic comedy, after all. The key is to fly through a book like this very fast—on Hermes' wings. But Phillips has an Olympian sense of absurdity, and there's enough ambrosial wit here to seduce most mortals for an afternoon or two on the divan." Washington Post Book World

Phillips, Susan Elizabeth

Ain't she sweet. Morrow 2004 383p $24.95

ISBN 0-06-621124-7   LC 2003-59297

"Fifteen years ago, Sugar Beth Carey reigned supreme over the small Mississippi town of Parrish, but now she's returning home a little bit shabby around the edges to claim a valuable painting left to her by her disapproving aunt. Fifteen years ago, Colin Byrne arrived in Parrish from England as a new teacher only to have his career destroyed by a spiteful young Sugar Beth. Fifteen years ago, Sugar Beth had everything Winnie Davis ever wanted, but because Winnie had the one thing Sugar Beth could never have, she turned Winnie's life into a perpetual hell. So now Colin, a bestselling author, and Winnie, Parrish's richest citizen, are determined to exact revenge for Sugar Beth's past sins, but much to their surprise, neither one finds revenge to taste quite as sweet as they expected once they get to know the new Sugar Beth." Booklist

This "light, contemporary, and enjoyable love story is filled with alluring plot lines." Libr J

It had to be you. Avon 2008 c1994 381p pa $12.95

ISBN 978-0-06-155581-7; 0-06-155581-9

First published 1994

"The Windy City isn't quite ready for Phoebe Somerville — the outrageous, curvaceous New York knockout who has just inherited the Chicago Stars football team. And Phoebe is definitely not prepared for the Stars' head coach Dan Celebow, a sexist jock taskmaster with a one-track mind. Celebow is everything Phoebe abhors. And the sexy new boss is everything Dan despises — a meddling bimbo who doesn't know a pigskin from a pitcher's mound." Publisher's note

Phillips, Susan Elizabeth—*Continued*

Natural born charmer. William Morrow 2007 394p $24.95

ISBN 978-0-06-073457-2; 0-06-073457-4

LC 2006-49173

"After her ex-boyfriend Monty insists that she is the only person he ever loved, Blue Bailey packs up everything she has (which isn't much) and moves from Seattle to Colorado to be with him. But once Blue arrives, she discovers Monty has found love again with a younger, blonder new girlfriend. With few job options and practically no money, Blue thought she might be stuck in Colorado for a long time, until Dean Robillard drives through on his way to Tennessee. The last person Blue wants to ask for a favor is a way-too-gorgeous-for-his-own-good stranger who annoys her to no end. And who turns out to be the quarterback for the Chicago Stars. But Dean is Blue's only ticket out, even if it means she is stuck with him all the way to Tennessee." Booklist

"While the verbal sparring in this textbook case of opposites attracting feels stagy at first, the rough edges come together in an alluring way." Publ Wkly

Piazza, Tom, 1955-

City of refuge; a novel. HarperCollins Publishers 2008 403p $24.95

ISBN 978-0-06-123861-1; 0-06-123861-9

LC 2008-13673

In New Orlean's "gritty Lower Ninth Ward, African-American Vietnam veteran, widower and carpenter S.J. Williams toils at his job and to keep his sister's family together. On the other side of town, white, Midwestern magazine editor Craig Donaldson savors every breath of air, every taste of cuisine and every other shard of sensory information that comprises the city's zeitgeist (even though his wife no longer does). When Katrina arrives, one family flees, one stays put, but both are hurled into the storm, and the bursting of the levees that sparked the destruction of a city, its people, and way of life." N Y Post

"Piazza describes the families' experience with a journalist's eye for detail and a New Orleanian's fury over the mismanagement that led to the breach of the levees and the government's lackadaisical approach to helping the survivors. . . . Righteous anger propels 'City of Refuge' forward, but occasionally it can overwhelm the story line." Christ Sci Monit

Pickard, Nancy

The 27 ingredient chili con carne murders. Delacorte Press 1993 296p o.p. LC 92-17498

The author completes a "story begun by Virginia Rich, a onetime food writer and, at the time of her death in 1984, the author of three . . . culinary mysteries." N Y Times Book Rev

"In her home in New England, the widowed Mrs. Potter receives a call from Ricardo Ortega, manager of her Arizona ranch, who hints at trouble. Alarmed, she flies out to find that Ricardo and his granddaughter have disappeared. As neighboring ranchers and friends conduct a search, Mrs. Potter tries to determine the cause of Ricardo's unease. . . . Suspense with dollops of romance and gossip makes this offering irresistible." Publ Wkly

Blue corn murders; a Eugenia Potter mystery. Delacorte Press 1998 257p $21.95

ISBN 0-385-31224-5 LC 98-11354

In this mystery based on Virginia Rich's notes, Pickard "continues the adventures of 64-year-old Arizona rancher Eugenia Potter, taking her to an archaeological hiking camp in Colorado. There, amid splendid scenery and mystical ancient cities, Eugenia encounters idiosyncratic characters, a camp management under stress, and savage murder. Among the suspects are a spiteful old woman on the camp's board of directors, a pair of selective teachers, and a spacey blonde Indian wannabe. Delightful plot, colorful surroundings, and solid prose makes this a winner." Libr J

Bum steer; a Jenny Cain mystery. Knopf 1990 240p o.p.

* LC 89-49198

This novel takes "Jenny Cain, director of the Port Frederick Civic Foundation, to Kansas City, where she hopes to discover why a dying millionaire has willed a vast cattle ranch to her little-known foundation. Thwarted upon arrival by the man's murder, she visits the ranch, fraternizes with two transplanted cowboys, searches out three ex-wives, and takes on a troubled teenager—all in hopes of finding the murderer." Libr J

"Although Jenny gets perkier, her companions more eccentric and their adventures more hair-raising as the hunt goes on, Ms. Pickard maintains her control over the derring-do and delivers an exciting climax." N Y Times Book Rev

But I wouldn't want to die there; a Jenny Cain mystery. Pocket Bks. 1993 243p o.p.

LC 93-15772

"When a colleague . . . in New York is stabbed to death in a street mugging, Jenny does the generous, if unlikely, thing: she moves into her friend's still-warm apartment, temporarily takes over her job and sets out to find her killer." NY Times Book Rev

"Pickard's in fine form here, combining a wonderfully acerbic, wickedly humorous commentary on the 'joys' of big-city life with a keep-'em-guessing plot and a smart, sexy, sensible . . . heroine." Booklist

Confession; a Jenny Cain mystery. Pocket Bks. 1994 307p o.p. LC 93-87794

"One steaming August day, Jenny, recently resigned as director of a foundation, and her police lieutenant husband, Geof Bushfield, are visited at home by angry 17-year-old David Mayer, who announces that he is Geof's illegitimate son by Judy Mayer, a high school classmate of Geof's. The winter before, Judy, an invalid, had been killed by her husband Ron, who then committed suicide. David, foulmouthed and hateful, demands that Geof reopen the case and prove the deaths were murders." Publ Wkly

"Fortunately, Geof and Jenny have a strong sense of humor, a sturdy marriage, plenty of common sense, and enough love to get them through one of the toughest tests they've faced together. Fine reading from an outstanding mystery writer." Booklist

Dead crazy; a Jenny Cain mystery. Pocket Bks. 1988 276p o.p. LC 88-15324

"As director of a charity foundation in a small Massachusetts town, Jenny runs into community opposition—and two nasty murders—when she tries to purchase an

Pickard, Nancy—*Continued*

abandoned church for restoration as a recreation center for the mentally disabled." N Y Times Book Rev

"Pickard nicely balances Jenny's wit and likability against her tough-minded, realistic examination of mental illness and its treatment. An outstanding mystery series." Booklist

Generous death. Scribner 1993 c1984 239p o.p.

First published 1984 in paperback

This is the "first Jenny Cain story that Pickard wrote and serves as an introduction to the attractive and vivacious director of the Port Frederick Civic Foundation as well as to other characters who figure prominently in the series. The plot concerns the murders of several wealthy donors to the foundation. If the nasty little poems left with each of the bodies are any indication, Jenny herself may be the next victim." Booklist

Marriage is murder; a Jenny Cain mystery. Dark Harvest 1987 210p o.p.   LC 87-4911

"Three homicides in two weeks: each victim the husband of a battered wife, each family beset by drinking problems, poverty, and too many children to feed. Either the wives are fighting back with a vengeance, or someone is doing their fighting for them. This is Pickard's fourth mystery starring wealthy young philanthropist Jenny Cain and her lover, policeman Geof Bushfield." Booklist

"An energetic array of Jenny's friends and co-workers keep this novel—a fine mix of romance, violence, and sleuthing—moving at a fast clip." Publ Wkly

No body; a Jenny Cain mystery. Scribner 1986 227p o.p.   LC 86-13118

Jenny Cain, "serving as the head of the Port Frederick Civic Foundation, relates events that stun the population in her New England town when a mud slide reveals the disappearance of 133 bodies, supposedly interred during the 19th century in the old cemetery. At the same time, the corpse of Sylvia Davis is found in the casket with John Rudolph just before he's due to be buried in the new cemetery. The next day, Rudolph's widow is murdered, and Jenny sets out to gather evidence on possible killers." Publ Wkly

The truth hurts. Simon & Schuster 2002 328p $24

ISBN 0-7434-1203-6   LC 2002-510452

In this Marie Lightfoot mystery, "the Florida-based true crime writer is working on a book about her parents, civil rights activists in Alabama who disappeared in 1963 when Lightfoot was a toddler. She's suddenly threatened by a mysterious fan, who signs his emails Paulie Barnes and demands that she collaborate with him on a book about her own murder, or he'll start killing her friends, including her lover, Franklin DeWeese." Publ Wkly

"The campaign of terror against Lightfoot, involving psychological torture through devices like e-mail and FedEX, is wickledly well constructed and convincing." Booklist

The whole truth. Pocket Bks. 2000 264p $22.95

ISBN 0-671-88795-5   LC 99-46816

A mystery "featuring true-crime writer Marie Lightfoot. Lightfoot's latest project is investigating Raymond Raintree, accused of kidnapping and brutally murdering six-year-old Natalie McCullen. At first the case

against Raintree seems straightforward. But when Lightfoot digs into Raintree's past to uncover the full story she discovers that he might be just as much of a victim as McCullen." Libr J

"By alternating chapters from Lightfoot's book about the case with coverage of the trial and the sleuth's search for information, Pickard effectively uses her character's work in progress as a narrative device." Booklist

Pickens, Cathy

Southern fried. St. Martin's Minotaur 2004 277p $23.95

ISBN 0-312-32492-8   LC 2003-58548

"After losing her job in Columbia, attorney Avery Andrews returns home to Dacus, SC, where everybody knows everybody else's business. She soon lands a corporate client, Garnet Mills, which is due for an inspection by government environmental authorities. Not surprisingly, the plant blows up, and vital documents are destroyed. Meanwhile, Avery becomes involved in a 15-year-old missing-persons case. Police have just recovered the body of the woman, a former Garnet employee, and are suspicious of her husband, who has just returned to town. Pickens's lively first mystery . . . features tidy plotting rounded out with gossipy humor, colorful characters, and Southern ethos." Libr J

Picoult, Jodi, 1966-

Change of heart; a novel. Atria Books 2008 447p $26.95; pa $16

ISBN 978-0-7434-9674-2; 0-7434-9674-4; 978-0-7434-9675-9 (pa); 0-7434-9675-2 (pa)
          LC 2007-35721

"Freelance carpenter Shay Bourne was sentenced to death for killing a little girl, Elizabeth Nealon, and her cop stepfather. Eleven years after the murders, Elizabeth's sister, Claire, needs a heart transplant, and Shay volunteers, which complicates the state's execution plans. Meanwhile, death row has been the scene of some odd events since Shay's arrival—an AIDS victim goes into remission, an inmate's pet bird dies and is brought back to life, wine flows from the water faucets. The author brings other compelling elements to an already complex plot line: the priest who serves as Shay's spiritual adviser was on the jury that sentenced him; Shay's ACLU representative, Maggie Bloom, balances her professional moxie with her negative self-image and difficult relationship with her mother. Picoult moves the story along with lively debates about prisoner rights and religion." Publ Wkly

Keeping Faith; a novel. Morrow 1999 422p $24

ISBN 0-688-16825-6   LC 98-43953

"When seven-year-old Faith White and her mother, Mariah, swing by the house on the way to ballet class, they find that Daddy is home and he's brought a playmate. This is not the first time he's been caught cheating. After the fuss and feathers have settled and Dad has moved out, Faith begins talking to an imaginary friend who, it seems, is God. And God is not male but female. Faith is able to effect miraculous cures and is also occasionally afflicted with stigmata. When the media gets wind of this, the circus begins. . . . If you can suspend disbelief on one or two points, this is an entrancing novel." Libr J

Picoult, Jodi, 1966-—*Continued*

My sister's keeper; a novel. Atria 2004 423p $25; pa $15

ISBN 0-7434-5452-9; 0-7434-5453-7 (pa)

LC 2004-300043

"Thirteen-year-old Anna Fitzgerald walks into the office of lawyer Campbell Alexander and announces she wants to sue her parents for the rights to her own body. Anna was conceived after her older sister, Kate, developed a rare form of leukemia at the age of two, and has donated bone marrow and blood to her sister. Now she has been asked to donate a kidney, and she intends to refuse. Campbell is a jaded young man who nevertheless decides to take her case pro bono. Anna's parents are shocked when they learn of her lawsuit, and her mother, a former civil defense attorney, decides to represent them. Anna refuses to budge on her position despite the fact that she clearly loves her sister and longs for her family's happiness. As the gripping court case builds, the story takes a shocking turn." Booklist

"Picoult's timely and compelling novel will appeal to anyone who has thought about the morality of medical decision making and any parent who must balance the needs of different children." Libr J

Nineteen minutes; a novel. Atria Books 2007 455p $26.95; pa $15

ISBN 978-0-7434-9672-8; 0-7434-9672-8; 978-0-7434-9673-5 (pa); 0-7434-9673-6 (pa)

LC 2006-49276

"Peter Houghton, an alienated teen who has been bullied for years by the popular crowd, brings weapons to his high school in Sterling, N.H., one day and opens fire, killing 10 people. Flashbacks reveal how bullying caused Peter to retreat into a world of violent computer games. Alex Cormier, the judge assigned to Peter's case, tries to maintain her objectivity as she struggles to understand her daughter, Josie, one of the surviving witnesses of the shooting." Publ Wkly

"Picoult's adept character development and intelligent plot twists make for a story that runs deeper than mere voyeurism of titillation. [The novel] is both a page turner and a thoughtful exploration of popularity, power, and the social ruts that can define us in ways we may not wish to be defined." Rocky Mountain News

Vanishing acts; a novel. Atria Books 2005 418p $25

ISBN 0-7434-5454-5

LC 2004-59454

"Delia Hopkins has led a charmed life. Raised in rural New Hampshire by her widowed father, Andrew, she now has a young daughter, a handsome fiance, and her own search-and-rescue bloodhound, which she uses to find missing persons. But as Delia plans her wedding, she is plagued by flashbacks of a life she can't recall. And then a policeman knocks on her door, revealing a secret that changes the world as she knows it." Publisher's note

"Picoult weaves together plot and characterization in a landscape that is fleshed out in rich, journalistic detail, so that readers will come away with intriguing questions rather than pat answers." Publ Wkly

Piercy, Marge

Braided lives; a novel. Summit Bks. 1982 443p

ISBN 0-671-43834-4

LC 81-16695

This novel concerns the lives of two women who were girls during the 1950's. Parents, friends, lovers appear as the story "follows its narrator-heroine, Jill Stuart, now 40 and an established writer who claims that her 'idea of hell is to be young again,' from her 1950's adolescence in working-class Detroit to the university in Ann Arbor, and on to New York. Jill writes, loves, suffers, commits herself to radical politics and reproductive rights, and survives. Throughout, her emotional anchor is her . . . friendship with Donna, her cousin and college roommate." Libr J

"As with most of Piercy's work, this is very political, and a major theme here is abortion—the dire need for safe, legal abortion. But while abortion is the visible theme, what lies beneath it is a rich, complex and thoroughly satisfying examination of life." Publ Wkly

Gone to soldiers; a novel. Summit Bks. 1987 703p o.p.

LC 86-30118

This is an "episodic story of World War II both at home and abroad. The turmoil of these years is shown through the lives of the numerous characters, from the female French Jewish Resistance fighter; to the Jewish factory worker/college student from Detroit and the U.S. ferry pilot, both women taking on men's roles, and the latter not wanting to give them up; to the cryptanalyst in Washington, D.C., escaping from the narrow life of his family; to the 'women's magazine' writer finally able to cover the war." Libr J

"In many male war novels character development is sacrificed; the 'woman's touch' here is excellent. The battlefront is not all blood and guts—there is also the grief of separation from family and the mitigating solace of friendship. On the home front there are race riots as well as ration books, and the heartbreak of shattered families." N Y Times Book Rev

The longings of women; a novel. Fawcett Columbine 1994 455p

ISBN 0-449-90907-7

LC 93-34125

"The three heroines are Leila, a middle-aged Boston college professor and writer; her long-suffering and secretly homeless 60-ish housekeeper Mary; and Becky, an ambitious young wife accused of murdering her husband and who is the subject of Leila's new book. All three face problems typical of women ill-used by men and by society." Publ Wkly

"As Piercy draws us into the alarming predicaments of each of these women, she traces the progress of their struggles to earn respect and love with unerring accuracy and discernment. Magnetic from start to finish." Booklist

Sex wars; a novel of the turbulent post-Civil War period. Morrow 2005 411p $24.95

ISBN 0-06-078983-3

LC 2005-41499

This novel, "set in post-Civil War New York stars a true-life cast of characters that includes Victoria Woodhull, the spiritualist turned first woman to run for the U.S. presidency; passionate suffragette Elizabeth Cady Stanton; the aged Cornelius Vanderbilt, who sits atop a $100-million fortune as he tries to make contact with his dead son; and Anthony Comstock, a crusading moralist who dedicates his life to outlawing pornography and 'obscene objects made of rubber.' . . . Most poignant among the invented characters is Freydeh Leibowitz, a young Russian-Jewish widow, who, far from the scandalous headlines and saloon gossip of the

Piercy, Marge—*Continued*

times, makes a living for herself and her adopted children, penny by penny, as a manufacturer of reliable condoms." Publ Wkly

This "is an enjoyable book—usually entertaining and, in its best sections, engrossing. In Woodhull and Freydeh, Piercy has created fascinating portraits of women determined to live on their own terms. As the freewheeling Gilded Age gives way to a growing conservatism that traps both women, observant readers will notice obvious parallels to our own time." Christ Sci Monit

Summer people; a novel. Summit Bks. 1989 380p o.p.   LC 89-30007

"After 11 years, the ménage à trois of Dinah Adler and Willie and Susan DeWitt is a strong family unit, accepted in its Cape Cod community. Dinah is a respected composer, devoted to her music, and Willie is a sculptor and carpenter happy with his life (and the envy of the local men). But Susan's growing discontent—with her work as a fabric designer and her role as unofficial gofer and hostess for summer people—ruptures the relationship and leads to tragedy. Libr J

"Piercy eschews sensationalism in portraying her unorthodox trio; her characterizations are solid and believable. Some readers may find the story's pace too deliberate, but those who like to ponder the ways in which character influences fate will welcome this solidly satisfying novel." Publ Wkly

Three women. Morrow 1999 309p $25
ISBN 0-688-17106-0   LC 99-13324
This novel centers on "Suzanne Blume, an idealistic but pragmatic law professor. Approaching 50 and the mother of two grown daughters, Suzanne is enjoying her busy and productive life when, nearly simultaneously, her stroke-weakened mother, Beverly, and her unsettled older daughter, Elena, arrive on her doorstep in need of expensive and time-consuming attention. Until her stroke, Beverly had been an old-style leftist who majored in men and minored in child-rearing. Elena is a lost soul who is still recovering from a violent episode in her teens. Suzanne must also deal with Jake, a man with whom a cozy on-line flirtation has suddenly become an in-the-flesh reality." N Y Times Book Rev

"Piercy keeps the plot humming with issues of motherhood, Judaism, generational tensions, sexuality, and independence. Her pacing is confident, as usual, and she interweaves the three narrative threads with aplomb. Apart from Jake, who remains an elusive sketch, Piercy's insight into her characters' emotional lives is an accurate reflection of intergenerational tensions." Publ Wkly

Vida. Summit Bks. 1979 412p
ISBN 0-671-40110-6
                                          * LC 79-19298
"Wanted for a 1970 bombing which stemmed from her radical antiwar activism, Vida has been a fugitive and underground revolutionary for nine years. Shifting the narrative back and forth between the present and the years from 1967 to 1974. Piercy traces the evolution of a political movement through Vida's perceptions and her relationships with a small band of fellow adherents." Libr J

This novel "is not 'simply' a novel but a political brief. I have my differences with 'Vida,' but I think they are substantive rather than literary. It is an interesting—

and challenging—book. . . . Marge Piercy has written about movement people before but never, I think, as lovingly as here." N Y Times Book Rev

Woman on the edge of time. Knopf 1976 369p o.p.
                                                       *

"A Hispanic-American mother undergoes experimental psychosurgery. She makes psychic contact with the 22nd-century world that has resulted from a feminist revolution whose success may depend on the subversion of the experiments in which she is involved. Outstanding for the elaborate description of the future utopia and the graphic representation of the inhumanity inherent in the way that contemporary people can and do treat one another." Anatomy of Wonder 4

Pilcher, Robin

A risk worth taking. Thomas Dunne Bks. 2004 308p $24.95
ISBN 0-312-27002-X   LC 2003-58564
"Dan Porter had it all: the nice house in suburban London, three children, a beautiful wife, and a great job in finance until the dot-com crash and 9/11 changed his outlook about life and making money. Dan lost a good friend in the tragedy, and is now content being a househusband focusing on his family, while his wife, Jackie, pursues her high-level job with a fashion designer, but changes in income have caused strife. His wife and daughters want their old life back, and Jackie perceives Dan and their son, Josh, as loafers because they seem content with less. Recognizing his wife's discontent, Dan takes action after reading an article in a women's magazine about a woman who started a clothing company in a remote area of Scotland and now wants to sell. Dan travels to Scotland with the hope of buying the company and expanding the business, but he finds something much more valuable. Pilcher offers a charming story about life in the new millennium and one man's pursuit of happiness." Booklist

Pilcher, Rosamunde, 1924-

Coming home. St. Martin's Press 1995 728p $25.95
ISBN 0-312-13451-7   LC 95-21656
"A Thomas Dunne book"

"The book's heroine is Judith Dunbar, who is a schoolgirl of 13 when the tale begins in 1935. Sent to boarding school in Cornwall because her parents are posted to Singapore, Judith becomes friends with Loveday Carey-Lewis, who introduces her to a family and an estate, Nancherrow, that is to influence her for the rest of her life. Pilcher does a marvelous job of describing life in England before World War II." Booklist

Flowers in the rain & other stories. St. Martin's Press 1991 277p o.p.   LC 91-18237
"A Thomas Dunne book"

Stories included are: The doll's house; Endings and beginnings; Flowers in the rain; Playing a round with love; Christabel; The blackberry day; The red dress; A girl I used to know; The watershed; Marigold garden; Weekend; A walk in the snow; Cousin Dorothy; Whistle for the wind; Last morning; Skates

"Throughout this collection of stories, Pilcher main-

Pilcher, Rosamunde, 1924-—*Continued*

tains a pervasive gentility along with an abiding wisdom. Filled with poignant scenes, romantic and bittersweet, these stories, many written earlier in the author's career, will appeal to readers of Pilcher's very successful novels." Booklist

September. St. Martin's Press 1990 536p
ISBN 0-312-04419-4   LC 89-70340
"A Thomas Dunne book"
"A lavish coming-out party for the daughter of one of the leading families of a town in the Scottish Highlands brings together characters whose lives change in various ways during the novel's four-month span. The Airds and the Balmerinos of Strathcroy and their friends and relatives in London, Majorca and the States are the focal point of the love affairs, domestic complications, estrangements, reconciliations and other gently momentous events." Publ Wkly
"Character is at the heart of a story, and this fine tale has plenty of that." N Y Times Book Rev

The shell seekers. St. Martin's Press 1987 530p o.p.

          * LC 87-28345
"A Thomas Dunne book"
"Set in England's Cotswolds, the novel begins with a crisis: the mother has signed herself out of the hospital against doctor's orders and is determined to resume her independent life. This introduces the two daughters and one son who must deal not only with their mother and with each other, but also with the relationships they have established for better or worse in their own lives." Booklist
"It is a measure of this story's strength and success that a reader can be carried for more than 500 pages in total involvement with Penelope, her children, her past and the painting that hangs in her country cottage. 'The Shell Seekers' is a deeply satisfying story, written with love and confidence." N Y Times Book Rev

Voices in summer. St. Martin's Press 1984 215p o.p.

          LC 83-22998
"Laura, married to Alec, an older divorcé, feels alienated from the people and events of her husband's past, especially his daughter and longtime friends. A recuperative stay with Alec's aunt and uncle in a lovely Cornwall mansion finally forces these and many other issues into the open." Booklist
The author "evokes the sense of contentment that flows from affection grounded in a comfortable lifestyle, all of which makes for gently entertaining reading." Publ Wkly

Winter solstice. Thomas Dunne Bks. 2000 454p $27.95
ISBN 0-312-24426-6   LC 00-31713
A novel set in "northern Scotland, where five vaguely connected people find themselves together at Christmas in a large Victorian house. . . . Elfrida, a lonely retired actress, befriends Oscar, who is barely surviving the grief of the deaths of his wife and daughter in a car crash. Carrie, bereft after an aborted love affair, takes over the holiday care of her 14-year-old niece, Lucy, who is unwanted by her mother, grandmother, and indifferent father, Sam, in town to take charge of the old woolen mill, is reeling because his wife left him for another man. What lifts this saga above melodrama is the author's skill at creating believable, multifaceted characters." Libr J

Pincherle, Alberto *See* Moravia, Alberto, 1907-1990

Pipkin, John

Woodsburner; a novel. Nan A. Talese 2009 365p $24.95
ISBN 978-0-385-52865-8; 0-385-52865-5
          LC 2008-33233
A novel "about an infamous moment in American literary history: Henry David Thoreau accidentally starting a massive fire that burned 300 acres of woods near Concord, MA, in 1844. . . . There are three other major characters in the novel—an orphaned Norwegian farmhand, a Puritan-style preacher, and a bookseller and aspiring playwright—and each ends up influencing Thoreau in some significant way as they fight the fire together." Libr J
"Pipkin doesn't underplay Thoreau's horror at what he's done (or overplay the inherent irony of the author of 'Walden' burning down the woods). Instead, he concentrates on the ability of a natural disaster to act as a catalyst in people's minds and lives. The result is, well, transcendent." Christ Sci Monit

Pirandello, Luigi, 1867-1936

The outcast; authorized translation from the Italian by Leo Ongley. Dutton 1925 334p o.p.
Condemned and cast out by husband and father for a crime she has not committed, Marta makes a brave attempt to build life over again. She goes with her mother and sister to a town where she is unknown and there supports them by teaching. After a time happiness comes back to the three. Then the man for whose sake Marta was persecuted comes to their village. He finds Marta lovelier and more desirable than ever. The result is inevitable. The outcry against her breaks forth afresh, and she is forced into the situation she has tried to escape. Too late her chastened husband sues for forgiveness. This drama of Italian life draws to a close in a moving scene of reconciliation
The novel is "significant thematically for its unconventional treatment of adultery and historically for its subtle undermining of the assumptions of naturalism on which it appears to be based." Ency of World Lit in the 20th Century

Short stories; selected, translated and introduced by Frederick May. Oxford Univ. Press 1965 xxxvi, 260p o.p.
"Oxford library of Italian classics"
Contents: The little hut; The cooper's cockerels; A dream of Christmas; Twelve letters; Fear; The best of friends; Bitter waters; The jar; The tragedy of a character; A call to duty; In the abyss; The black kid; Signora Frola and her son-in-law, Signor Ponza; The man with the flower in his mouth; Destruction of the man; Puberty; Cinci; All passion spent; The visit; The tortoise; A day goes by

Pirie, David

The patient's eyes; the dark beginnings of Sherlock Holmes. St. Martin's Minotaur 2002 244p il
ISBN 0-312-29095-0

Pirie, David—*Continued*

"A 'fictional' account of Arthur Conan Doyle's early life that relates how his association with Edinburgh physician Joseph Bell was the inspiration for his Holmes character. Pirie vividly evokes the dark ambience of Victorian England, his prose is elegant, and his gift for mimicking the slightly haughty tone of Doyle's writing is uncanny." Booklist

Plaidy, Jean, 1906-1993

For works written by this author under other names see Holt, Victoria, 1906-1993

The captive Queen of Scots. Putnam 1970 c1963 410p o.p.

Sequel to Royal road to Fotheringay (1968)

First published 1963 in the United Kingdom

"The story of the last 18 years of Queen Mary's life, during which she was first a prisoner of her Scottish enemies and later, after a dramatic escape and flight to England, the captive of her archenemy, Queen Elizabeth. Treated with at least some respect due a queen, Mary is pictured with her retinue of loyal friends and servants, living in varying degrees of discomfort and confinement as she moved from one castle to another at the whim of Elizabeth. She emerges as a generous, overly trustful, emotional victim, attractive even as she grew older though not wise, who met her tragic fate because she could not cope with the treachery and intrigue of both friends and enemies." Booklist

Murder most royal. Putnam 1972 542p o.p.

First published 1949 in the United Kingdom

"Concentrating on Anne Boleyn and her younger cousin Catherine Howard, the author follows the two from childhood to death on the block, with her usual thoroughness, sentimentality, and overdramatization, sparing the reader few details of torture, violence, intrigue, or thwarted love affairs." Booklist

The pleasures of love; the story of Catherine of Braganza. Putnam 1992 c1991 329p

ISBN 0-399-13731-9   LC 91-34593

First published 1991 in the United Kingdom

When Catherine, daughter of King John IV of Portugal, finally married Charles II her "happiness as the new Queen of England was short-lived. The Merry Monarch's notorious affairs amused the public but devastated Catherine, who longed for the love only a husband and children could provide. When it became clear that Catherine was barren, the people verged on rebellion and court intimates intrigued against her, hoping that Charles would divorce his queen, marry one of his mistresses, and beget an heir. But while Charles would never be faithful to Catherine, he loved her and was her fiercest protector. And in the end, their struggle against their enemies only drew the king and queen closer together." Publisher's note

William's wife. Putnam 1993 276p o.p.

LC 92-32588

In this historical novel about the "struggle for power between Catholic and Protestant, England's heir to the throne, the lovely and bright Princess Mary, is forced to marry William of Orange in order to prevent the kingdom from falling under Catholic rule. Despite Mary's attempts to win her husband's love, the dour, power-hungry William won't even feign affection for her; instead, he continues a blatant affair with Elizabeth Villiers. As the inevitable power struggle ensues between her husband and her father, James II, Mary finds herself torn between marital and filial loyalties. But with the crown of England the ultimate prize, Mary discovers that while she is James's daughter, she is first and foremost William's wife." Publisher's note

Plain, Belva

Blessings. Delacorte Press 1989 340p o.p.

LC 89-1565

"The entanglements of a teenage romance surface more than a decade later to disrupt the life of a successful attorney. Jennie Rakowski finally has her life together. She provides legal counsel for poor, battered women and is on the verge of marrying a charming, widowed corporate attorney with three small children. Suddenly, Jill, the daughter Jennie gave up for adoption 19 years earlier, appears at Jennie's door; even worse, Jill brings along the man who fathered her then disappeared from Jennie's life." Booklist

"The author stretches an awkward subplot concerning mob-connected real estate developers far too thin, but her mixture of romance, suspense, and deeply felt familial conflicts should leave her fans well entertained." Publ Wkly

Crescent City; a novel. Delacorte Press 1984 429p o.p.

LC 84-5045

A novel "set against the backdrop of America's South during the Civil War. At the story's center is Miriam Raphael, a European Jew transplanted as a child to New Orleans, the 'Crescent City' nestled at the mouth of the Mississippi. Both she and her older brother, David, must adjust to what seems a bright, promising new land filled with languid days and lavish feasts. But all too quickly their eyes are opened to the grimmer features of their landscape—the slaves whom David vows to set free and the southern tradition of youthful marriage, which Miriam, herself no better off than a slave, must gracefully endure." Booklist

Evergreen; a novel. Delacorte Press 1978 593p o.p.

LC 77-20778

"The young orphan Anna shows her spunk by leaving Poland to make a way for herself in the turn-of-the-century U.S.A. Opting for domestic service rather than the sweatshops of lower Manhattan, she becomes infatuated with the master's son, Paul Werner. His marriage to another woman puts a damper on Anna's longing, and she settles for poor but loyal Joseph Friedman. Joseph is hard working and has a vision of fulfilling the American Dream. He persuades his wife to borrow some money from the Werners, and Anna finds herself asking Paul for the money. He gladly obliges, but the old flame is fanned into heedless passion and Anna leaves with the money and a secret she will carry with her for the rest of her life." Best Sellers

"This warm and sympathetic family saga gives life and meaning to the commonplace events of unspectacular lives." Publ Wkly

Followed by The golden cup

Plain, Belva—*Continued*

The golden cup. Doubleday 1986 399p o.p.

LC 86-8851

Evergreen, "told the story of immigrant Anna Friedman and her love for Paul Werner. Here the focus shifts to Paul's aunt, Hennie DeRivera, from age 18 in 1891 through World War I. As a volunteer, Hennie teaches English at a settlement house where she meets Daniel Roth. Their relationship is frowned upon by her family, but they marry when she becomes pregnant. Her uncertainty over whether Dan would have married her otherwise is aggravated by his roving eye. The grown-up Paul, Hennie's son Fred, and Leah, an orphan she raises, are also featured." Libr J

The author "invests her story with dignity and historical relevance while insightfully depicting the class consciousness of Progressive Era Americans." Publ Wkly

Followed by Tapestry

Harvest. Delacorte Press 1990 409p o.p.

LC 90-34417

This novel continues the "saga of the Werners and their extended clan as they reaffirm their Jewish heritage during the stormy 1960s. Dark, sensitive Iris, daughter of the glowing, russet-haired Anna (by urbane banker Paul Werner—unbeknownst to Iris) is married to wealthy, improvident Dr. Theo Stern, whose European glamour excites other women. Iris's jealousy goads her to play at her own romance with a sinister partner. Her four children are growing up, but rebel Steve balks at his bar mitzvah, already anticipating the anarchist/bomb expert he will be at college, radicalized by cynical professor Tim Powers, whom he doesn't know is his distant cousin. When Paul's wife dies and his mistress leaves to fulfill her mission as a doctor in Israel, Paul hovers protectively over Iris's, troubled family." Publ Wkly

Looking back. Delacorte Press 2001 340p $25.95

ISBN 0-385-33471-0   LC 00-65691

A "story about three college roommates—brainy Norma, lovely Amanda, preppy Cecile. . . . When the three women graduate, Amanda, desperate to escape her lower-class background, marries Larry Balsan, Norma's brother, who is in the family real estate business. As Mrs. Balsan, she can shop to her heart's content, but she soon realizes she is not as happy as Cecile, who marries her college sweetheart, or even Norma, who is biding her time until she meets Mr. Right." Publ Wkly

Random winds. Delacorte Press 1980 496p o.p.

LC 79-26845

"Three generations of doctors in the Farrell family span the gamut from a dedicated general practitioner in the Adirondack Mountains of New York to a world-renowned but troubled brain surgeon and on to a budding feminist medical student with a career/marriage conflict. This is a dynamic record of domestic tragedies to be endured, bitter arguments to be fought, and agonizing choices to be made as the Farrells sort out lives, loves, and hopes and set forth to challenge medical traditions and forbidden passions." Booklist

The author "knows how to sweep from one dramatic scene to another, often evoking poignancy, and the irony underlying Martin's daughter's romance with Fern's stepson produces a bittersweet ending." Publ Wkly

Tapestry. Delacorte Press 1988 440p o.p.

LC 87-22346

"Paul Werner, the key figure of a powerful New York banking family, is the protagonist in this saga of one man's concerns with the impending doom of World War II and the plight of his German-Jewish relatives and friends. Paul is caught in a passionless, childless marriage, and he struggles for years with the memory and reality of his first love and subsequent affairs of the heart." Libr J

Followed by Harvest

Plath, Sylvia

The bell jar; with an introduction by Diane Wood Middlebrook. Knopf 1998 xxv, 229p $17

ISBN 0-375-40463-5

* LC 98-27309

"Everyman's library"

First published 1963 in the United Kingdom; first United States edition published 1971 by Harper & Row

"Esther Greenwood, having spent what should have been a glorious summer as guest editor for a young woman's magazine, came home from New York, had a nervous breakdown, and tried to commit suicide. Through months of therapy, Esther kept her rationality, if not her sanity. In telling the story of Esther, Plath thinly disguised her own experience with attempted suicide and time spent in an institution. Like Esther, she was rehabilitated and finished college. She went to London, married poet Ted Hughes, had three children and published some poetry and this novel. When she felt the world slipping away from her again, she did commit suicide." Shapiro. Fic for Youth. 3d edition

Poe, Edgar Allan, 1809-1849

The collected tales and poems of Edgar Allan Poe. Modern Lib. 1992 1026p $20

ISBN 0-679-60007-8   LC 92-50231

A reissue of The complete tales and poems of Edgar Allan Poe published 1938

Short stories included are: The unparalleled adventure of one Hans Pfaal; The gold-bug; The balloon-hoax; Von Kempelen and his discovery; Mesmeric revelation; The facts in the case of M. Valdemar; The thousand-and-second tale of Scheherazade; Ms. found in a bottle; A descent into the maelström; The murders in the Rue Morgue; The mystery of Marie Rogêt; The purloined letter; The black cat; The fall of the House of Usher; The pit and the pendulum; The premature burial; The masque of the Red Death; The cask of Amontillado; The imp of the perverse; The island of the fay; The oval portrait; The assignation; The tell-tale heart; The system of Doctor Tarr and Professor Fether; The literary life of Thingum Bob, Esq.; How to write a Blackwood article; A predicament; Mystification; X-ing a paragrab; Diddling; The angel of the odd; Mellonta Tauta; Loss of breath; The man that was used up; The business man; Maelzel's chess-player; The power of words; The colloquy of Monos and Una; The conversation of Eiros and Charmion; Shadow—a parable; Silence—a fable; A tale of Jerusalem; The sphinx; The man of the crowd; Never bet the Devil your head; "Thou art the man"; Hop-Frog; Four beasts in one: the homo-cameloparad; Why the little Frenchman wears his hand in a sling; Bon-bon; Some

Poe, Edgar Allan, 1809-1849—*Continued*
words with a mummy; Magazine-writing—Peter Snook;
the domain of Arnheim; Landor's cottage; William Wilson; Berenice; Eleonora; Ligeia; Morella; Metzengerstein;
A tale of the ragged mountains; The spectacles; The Duc
De L'Omelette; The oblong box; King Pest; Three Sundays in a week; The devil in the belfrey; Lionizing
This volume contains short stories, poems, and a sampling of Poe's essays, criticism and journalistic writings

Complete stories and poems of Edgar Allan Poe.
Doubleday 1966 819p $21.95
ISBN 0-385-07407-7

*

This volume contains five sections: Tales of mystery
and horror; Humor and satire; Flights and fantasies; The
narrative of A. Gordon Pym of Nantucket and The poems
Short stories included are: The murders in the Rue
Morgue; The mystery of Marie Rogèt; The black cat;
The gold-bug; Ligeia; A descent into the maelstrom; The
tell-tale heart; The purloined letter; The assignation; Ms.
found in a bottle; William Wilson; Berenice; The fall of
the House of Usher; The cask of Amontillado; The pit
and the pendulum; A tale of the ragged mountains; The
man of the crowd; Morella; "Thou art the man"; The oblong box; The conversation of Eiros and Charmion;
Metzengerstein; The masque of the Red Death; The premature burial; The imp of the perverse; The facts in the
case of M. Valdemar; Hop-Frog; The system of Doctor
Tarr and Professor Fether; The literary life of Thingum
Bob, Esq.; How to write a Blackwood article; A predicament; Mystification; Loss of breath; The man that was
used up; Diddling; The angel of the odd; Mellonta Tauta;
The thousand-and-second tale of Scheherazade; X-ing a
paragrab; The business man; A tale of Jerusalem; The
sphinx; Why the little Frenchman wears his hand in a
sling; Bon-bon; The Duc de l'Omelette; Three Sundays
in a week; The devil in the belfry; Lionizing; Some
words with a mummy; The spectacles; Four beasts in
one; Never bet the devil your head; The balloon-hoax;
Mesmeric revelation; Eleanora; The island of the fay;
The oval portrait; The domain of Arnheim; Landor's cottage; The power of words; The colloquy of Monos and
Una; Von Kempelen and his discovery

The imaginary voyages: The narrative of Arthur
Gordon Pym; The unparalleled adventure of one
Hans Pfaall; The journal of Julius Rodman.
Twayne Pubs. 1981 667p o.p.   LC 81-2915
"Collected writings of Edgar Allan Poe"
Omnibus edition of three titles, the first of which is
entered separately under variant form: The narrative of
Arthur Gordon Pym of Nantucket, The unparalleled adventure of one Hans Pfaall, first published 1835 describes a voyage to the moon and The journal of Julius
Rodman, an unfinished novel first published anonymously in 1840 deals with exploration of the Missouri River
Basin

The journal of Julius Rodman
    In Poe, E. A. The imaginary voyages: The
        narrative of Arthur Gordon Pym; The
        unparalleled adventure of one Hans
        Pfaall; The journal of Julius Rodman
        p508-653

Narrative of A. Gordon Pym
    also in Poe, E. A. The collected tales and
        poems of Edgar Allan Poe

The narrative of Arthur Gordon Pym of Nantucket. Harper 1838 201p o.p.
"A New England boy stows away on a whaler, surviving mutiny, savagery, cannibalism, and wild pursuit. At
the end of the story, the hero drifts toward the South
Pole in a canoe; before him, out of the mist, rises a great
white figure. There is some confusion in detail, because
Poe, serializing the story, often did not pick up the loose
ends. Based on the factual travels of J. N. Reynolds,
whose book Poe had reviewed." Reader's Ency. 4th edition
    also in Poe, E. A. Complete stories and
        poems of Edgar Allan Poe p617-736
    also in Poe, E. A. The imaginary voyages:
        The narrative of Arthur Gordon Pym;
        The unparalleled adventure of one Hans
        Pfaall; The journal of Julius Rodman
        p4-365

The unparalleled adventure of one Hans Pfaall
    In Poe, E. A. The collected tales and poems
        of Edgar Allan Poe p3-41
    In Poe, E. A. The imaginary voyages: The
        narrative of Arthur Gordon Pym; The
        unparalleled adventure of one Hans
        Pfaall; The journal of Julius Rodman
        p366-506

Poe's children; the new horror: an anthology;
[edited by] Peter Straub. Doubleday 2008 534p
$24.95
ISBN 978-0-385-52283-0; 0-385-52283-5
                                            LC 2008-3013

Contents: The bees, by D. Chaon; Cleopatra Brimstone, by E. Hand; The man on the ceiling, by S. Rasnic
Tem and M. Tem; The great god Pan, by M. J. Harrison;
The voice on the beach, by R. Campbell; Body, by B.
Evenson; Louise's ghost, by K. Link; The sadness of detail, by J. Carroll; Leda, by M. Rickert; In praise of folly, by T. Tessier; Plot twist, by D. J. Schow; The two
Sams, by G. Hirshberg; Notes on the writing of horror:
a story, by T. Ligotti; Unearthed, by B. Percy; Gardener
of heart, B. Morrow; Little red's tango, by P. Straub;
The ballad of the flexible bullet, by S. King; 20th century ghost, by J. Hill; The green glass sea, by E. Klages;
The kiss, by T. V. Travis; Black dust, by G. Joyce; October in the chair, by N. Gaiman; Missolonghi 1824, by
J. Crowley; Insect dreams, by R. P. Stevenson
"An impressive, highly personal assortment of perspectives and techniques. The result is a remarkably consistent, frequently unsettling book that does as much to blur
the artificial boundary between genre fiction and 'literature' as any anthology in living memory. . . . [The anthology] transcends genre labels and deserves to be recognized for what it is: first-rate fiction." Washington
Post Book World

Pohl, Frederik, 1919-

The annals of the Heechee. Ballantine Bks.
1987 388p o.p.　　　　　　　LC 86-26584
"A Del Rey book"

Sequel to Heechee rendezvous

In this episode "the human-Heechee cooperation that
first materialized in 'Heechee Rendezvous' has solidified
as the two races unite against a common enemy. Once
again Robinette Broadhead—alive after death as a ma-
chine-stored personality, compliments of Heechee technology—is called upon to face a dangerous challenge.
He is the only one able to meet eyeball to eyeball with
the deadly Foe, aliens determined to mold the universe
to their own needs. . . . The novel is gripping, both in
story line and in the colorful depiction of the alien
Heechee." Booklist

Beyond the blue event horizon. Ballantine Bks.
1980 327p o.p.　　　　　　　LC 79-21757
"A Del Rey book"

Sequel to Gateway

"Multimillionaire Robinette Broadhead, still mourning
the loss of his great love from the first book, backs an
expedition to investigate one of the alien Heechee's
'food factories.' Earth is overpopulated, and the ship's
resources are desperately needed to prevent mass starvation. The members of the expedition are all from the
same family: Lurvey, a veteran space pilot and her engineer husband; Lurvey's money hungry father, and her
precocious 14-year-old sister. Despite the tensions which
surface during their three and a half year voyage, the
family manages to successfully make contact with the
factory and its innocent, human occupant. They begin to
explore the marvels of the alien technology, but events
on Earth and the inhabitants of another Heechee spaceship threatens to end the expedition in disaster." Voice
Youth Advocates

Followed by Heechee rendezvous

The boy who would live forever; a novel of
Gateway. Tor Bks. 2004 380p $25.95
　ISBN 0-7653-1049-X　　　　　LC 2004-49579

A title set in the author's Heechee universe. "When recently orphaned Stan Avery inherits enough money to
buy a trip to Gateway, the alien Heechee waystation that
allows travel to all parts of space, he doesn't realize that
his voyage has effectively cut him off forever from the
world he left behind. Pohl's first Gateway novel in 15
years (the 1977 original Gateway won the Hugo and
Nebula Awards) revitalizes a favorite far-future setting as
it tells the tale of a young man's journey to self-
realization amid the stars." Libr J

Chernobyl; a novel. Bantam Bks. 1987 355p
　ISBN 0-553-05210-1　　　　　LC 86-47896

The author "re-creates in fiction the massive 1986
Ukrainian nuclear power plant disaster. The book opens
during normal days just before the accident; suspense
builds, as the reader expects the worst. Characters that
would actually have been on the scene are seen being
overwhelmed by berserk technology, their lives shattered.
The tale is gripping, and the locale well established."
Libr J

Gateway. St. Martin's Press 1977 313p o.p.
　　　　　　　　　　　　　　　　*

First volume in the author's Heechee saga

"The novel's protagonist, Robinette Broadhead, suffers
from tremendous feelings of guilt: for the death of his
parents, for his wealth (a stroke of luck he feels he does
not deserve), and for the living death of his girl friend
and fellow crew members. Gateway presents Broadhead's
story in chapters that alternately describe his life before
the novel opens and record present conversations between Broadhead and his computer psychiatrist, Sigfrid
von Shrink. With a sensitive mixture of humor and sympathy, Pohl explores Broadhead's condition and ends
with one of the finest affirmations of humanity in any
literary work." New Ency of Sci Fic

Followed by Beyond the blue event horizon

Heechee rendezvous; a novel. Ballantine Bks.
1984 311p o.p.　　　　　　　LC 83-15637
"A Del Rey book"

Sequel to Beyond the blue event horizon

In this novel "the elusive, benevolent aliens called
Heechee are forced to come out of hiding because the
future not only of humankind but of the universe itself
is at stake. Compelled by personal reasons, tycoon
Robinette Broadhead takes part in another dangerous
venture into space, moving inexorably toward his surprising yet fitting destiny." Booklist

Followed by The annals of the Heechee

Homegoing. Ballantine Bks. 1989 279p o.p.
　　　　　　　　　　　　　　　LC 88-7413
"A Del Rey book"

"An alien spaceship lands on Earth for a double purpose: to give the people of Earth the benefit of their advanced technology and to return to them a human rescued in infancy and raised by the kangaroo-like Hakh'hli
to be as 'human' as possible—under the circumstances.
Pohl's unerring gift for satire delivers a splendidly
skewed alien-eye-view of human culture while spinning
a touching, slightly quirky story of a young man's coming of age." Libr J

Man Plus. Random House 1976 215p o.p.
　　　　　　　　　　　　　　　　*

"The novel describes the transformation of a human
astronaut into a cyborg capable of living on Mars and
confronts the question of human dignity: as the central
character, Roger Torraway, becomes less 'human,' the
people who were once so important to him are unable to
cope with what he is, and Roger must also learn to handle the new thing he has become. Moreover, Roger's reflections on his growing inability to control his own life
parallel the thoughts of people throughout the country
who believe the world has gone out of control. The result is a remarkably readable novel that succeeds in presenting a fully rounded character in an SF setting." New
Ency of Sci Fic

Mars Plus; [by] Frederik Pohl, Thomas T.
Thomas. Baen Pub. Enterprises 1994 342p $20
　ISBN 0-671-87605-8　　　　　LC 93-44782

Fifty years after the events in Man Plus, "man is, or
seems to be, on Mars to stay, but things have become
. . . strange, even compared to the population of
cyborgs, half-cyborgs and just plain humans who now
occupy the Red Planet. The computer net on which all

Pohl, Frederik, 1919-—*Continued*

Martian life depends has long seemed to have 'a mind of its own,' and now that mind seems to be in a very bad mood." Publisher's note

The space merchants; by Frederik Pohl and C. M. Kornbluth. Ballantine Bks. 1953 179p o.p.

*

"Control of the Venus economy and market is the sought-after plum of mega-advertising agencies. Mitchell Courtenay must persuade colonists to go there, but he is thwarted by the despised conservationists. Sabotage, warfare, and the degradation of the life of a consumer pervade this attack on modern consumer society." Shapiro. Fic for Youth. 3d edition

"Kornbluth later stated that he and Pohl packed into this story everything they hated about advertising, and it came out with Swiftian savagery. One of the first novels by writers with primary roots in the pulps to make an impact in mainstream circles." Anatomy of Wonder 4

Followed by The merchants' war (1984)

The world at the end of time. Ballantine Bks. 1990 393p o.p.   LC 89-18462

"A Del Rey book"

"As vast intelligences play deadly power games using stars for pawns, the fledgling colonists on the planet Home fight to maintain their existence while 'unknown forces' wreak havoc with the laws of physics and the universe. Pohl's sparkling wit attaches itself to macro- and microcosmic themes in a novel which pits a luckless human hero against a childlike being of inordinate power and extraordinary paranoia. Grand in scope, poignant in delivery." Libr J

Polito, Robert, 1951-

(ed) Crime novels: American noir of the 1930s and 40s. See Crime novels: American noir of the 1930s and 40s

(ed) Crime novels: American noir of the 1950s. See Crime novels: American noir of the 1950s

Pollock, Donald Ray, 1954-

Knockemstiff. Doubleday 2008 206p

ISBN 978-0-385-52382-0   LC 2007-39806

Contents: Real life; Dynamite hole; Knockemstiff; Hair's fate; Pills; Giganthomachy; Schott's Bridge; Lard; Fish sticks; Bactine; Discipline; Assailants; Rainy Sunday; Holler; I start over; Blessed; Honolulu; The fights

"Knockemstiff — real name, real town — is full of the sorriest group of people imaginable, a bunch of damaged souls with crass manners, greasy hair, sour breath, addictions galore and savage tendencies. Some can sense the possibilities of a better life, but their longing for escape just might lead them to do something crazy. Others are simply rotting away, trapped by self-defeating habits impossible to shake. Pollock underscores their struggles with vivid imagery and, at times, a tender touch. . . . Pollock's writing has been compared to that of Flannery O'Connor, Raymond Carver and Cormac McCarthy. He draws his readers in slowly, tangling them in the mundane toil of small-town life, before smacking them upside the head with something unexpected and primal. Small moments yield big surprises." Oregonian

Popp, Walter

(jt. auth) Schlink, B. Self's punishment

Porlock, Martin *See* MacDonald, Philip, 1899-1981

Porter, Joseph Ashby, 1942-

All aboard; stories; [by] Joe Ashby Porter. Turtle Point Press 2008 187p pa $15.95

ISBN 978-1-933527-17-8; 1-933527-17-X

                                        * LC 2007-910440

Contents: Merrymount; Solstice; Pending; Reunion eve; Dream on; Forgotten coast

"Beyond disregarding literary fashion, Joe Ashby Porter seems to inhabit his own world, producing compelling short fiction exclusively on his own terms. His latest collection contains six valuable and unique studies of connection and detachment as mediated by age, sexuality, and proximity. Though more grounded in the familiar than his previous collection, Touch Wood, an initial strangeness, both of content and style, still threatens to alienate the casual reader. Consideration, however, is rewarded." Bookslut

The near future; [by] Joe Ashby Porter. Turtle Point Press 2006 248p pa $15.95

ISBN 1-88558-641-8   LC 2005-926845

"Denise and her boyfriend are on their way to Key West to put a pyramid scheme into action, but first they stop to visit her grandparents in Manatee, a Florida retirement village. Her grandfather, Vince, shows them around, and when the "Library" turns out to be a "cocoon of hologram screens," readers' suspicions that this is a speculative work are affirmed. Denise is also confronted with the unexpected: her grandparents have separated. Vince decides to join Denise and Tink on their risky quest, and brings along the delectably self-possessed Lola. The mismatched quartet finds quite a carnival in Key West, what with Hemingway and Gertrude Stein look-alikes, Deadheads, Trolls, steroid-pumped drug dealers, and the blue-spotted victims of the latest plague." Booklist

"Porter's narrative style is vaguely cubist, with words often turned at slight angles to one another. But what the occasional sentence loses in textbook syntax it gains in color and sheer playfulness. . . . 'The Near Future' is an exceedingly odd book yet also, despite the gunplay, a genuinely endearing one." N Y Times Book Rev

Porter, Katherine Anne, 1890-1980

Collected stories and other writings. Library of America 2008 1093p $40

ISBN 978-1-59853-029-2   LC 2008-927625

Contents: Maria Concepción; Virgin Violeta; The martyr; Magic; Rope; He; Theft; That tree; The jilting of Granny Weatherall; Flowering Judas; The cracked looking-glass; Hacienda; The source; The journey; The witness; The circus; The fig tree; The last leaf; The grave; The downward path to wisdom; A day's work; Holiday; The leaning tower; Old mortality; Noon wine; Pale horse, pale rider

In addition to short prose (reviews, criticism, essays, travel pieces, and more), this volume contains three col-

Porter, Katherine Anne, 1890-1980—*Continued*
lections of short stories: Flowering Judas and other stories (1935); Pale horse, pale rider: three short novels
(1939); The leaning tower and other stories (1944)

The collected stories of Katherine Anne Porter.
Harcourt Brace & World 1965 495p pa $16
hardcover o.p.
  ISBN 0-15-618876-7

                                      *

  Contains three collections of short stories: Flowering
Judas, and other stories (1935); The leaning tower, and
other stories (1944); Pale horse, pale rider (1939); and
four additional short stories: Virgin Violeta; The martyr;
The fig tree; and Holiday.
  "These are perfect examples of the short story and are
representative not only of the best American writing but
of the best in the world." SLJ

Flowering Judas and other stories. Harcourt
Brace Jovanovich 1935 285p o.p.
  First published 1930. This edition adds four additional
stories
  Contents: María Concepción; Magic; Rope; He; Theft;
That tree; The jilting of Granny Weatherall; Flowering
Judas; The cracked looking-glass; Hacienda
    In Porter, K. A. Collected stories and other
      writings

The leaning tower, and other stories. Harcourt
Brace & Co. 1944 246p o.p.
  Contents: The source; The witness; The circus; The old
order; The last leaf; The grave; The downward path to
wisdom; A day's work; The leaning tower
    In Porter, K. A. Collected stories and other
      writings

Noon wine
    In Porter, K. A. Collected stories and other
      writings
    In Porter, K. A. Pale horse, pale rider: three
      short novels

Old morality
    In Porter, K. A. Collected stories and other
      writings

Old mortality
    In Porter, K. A. Pale horse, pale rider: three
      short novels

Pale horse, pale rider [novelette]
    In Porter, K. A. Collected stories and other
      writings
    In Porter, K. A. Pale horse, pale rider: three
      short novels

Pale horse, pale rider: three short novels.
Modern Library ed. Modern Lib. 1998 205p
$18.95
  ISBN 0-679-60303-4

                          * LC 98-12008
  A reissue of the title first published 1939 by Harcourt,
Brace
  Contents: Old mortality; Noon wine; Pale horse, pale
rider

  In the title story "Miranda, a young journalist, is
caught in a personal dilemma. She must choose between
a career and a commitment to Adam, a soldier on leave
during World War I. Porter's simple tale becomes more
complex as Miranda's anxieties and fears about war,
death, and personal loss are revealed. She hovers close
to death during the terrbile flu epidemic of 1918.
Miranda survives and the war ends, but it brings her no
happiness because the epidemic has claimed Adam as a
victim." Shapiro. Fic for Youth. 3d edition
    In Porter, K. A. Collected stories and other
      writings
      also in Porter, K. A. The collected stories of
      Katherine Anne Porter p173-317

Ship of fools. Little, Brown 1962 497p o.p.
  "An Atlantic Monthly Press book"
  "A satire in which the world is likened to a ship
whose passengers, fools and deranged people all, are
sailing toward eternity. Porter's novel is set in 1931
aboard a German passenger ship returning to Bremerha-
ven, Germany, from Veracruz, Mexico. The ship carries
a microcosm of peoples, including Germans, Americans,
Spaniards, Gypsies, and Mexicans, Jews, anti-Semites,
political reactionaries, revolutionaries, and neutrals coexist aboard ship, at the same time that jeaolusy, cruelty
and duplicity pervade their lives." Merriam-Webster's
Ency of Lit

Porter, William Sydney *See* Henry, O., 1862-
  1910

Portes, Andrea

Hick. Unbridled Books 2007 245p pa $14.95
  ISBN 978-1-932961-32-4; 1-932961-32-1
                                LC 2007-105
  "The 13-year-old narrator of Hick is headed down the
wrong path in life, but it's not one she has chosen. . . .
After a particularly bad episode involving her drunken
father and estranged mother, Luli opts out, she leaves
Nebraska to begin anew in Vegas. . . . Luli's journey
begins as a series of rides. Her street smarts come in
handy immediately when goggle-eyed cowboy Eddie
picks her up. He's not a good guy, but tough Luli takes
care of herself—something she's been doing her whole
life. Her next ride comes from Glenda, a Patsy Cline fan
with smeared red lips and a cocaine habit. Luli immediately finds herself entranced by Glenda's straight-
shooting personality and seemingly glamorous life on the
road. A surreal quality emerges when Luli discovers that
Glenda knows Eddie. From here, Luli becomes inextricably linked to this particular group of societal outcasts.
Throughout her experiences with Glenda, including a
botched robbery job, it's easy to forget Luli is just 13.
She's the antithesis of the modern American teenager;
she has grit. Her story is especially interesting as it is
based on the real-life experiences of Hick's author,
Portes." PopMatters

Portis, Charles

The dog of the South. Knopf 1979 245p
  ISBN 0-394-4506146
                               * LC 78-65780

Portis, Charles—*Continued*

This novel "features Ray Midge, a bore with few interests and even less ambition whose major pastime is collecting old weapons. But when Ray's wife runs off with her first husband, the hated Guy Dupree, along with Ray's car and credit cards, the jilted husband takes to the road, driving from Arkansas to Honduras to reclaim all that he has lost." Book Magazine

"Simultaneously hilarious and heart breakingly odd. . . you find yourself laughing so hard in sections that tears run down your face." Baltimore Sun

Gringos; a novel. Simon & Schuster 1991 269p
ISBN 0-671-72457-6
* LC 90-42476

This novel "features Jimmy Burns, an idler from Louisiana transplanted to Mexico, where he ekes out a living finding missing persons and doing odd jobs. Equally odd are the other motley expatriates. Ninety-pound Louise Kurle, who's writing a book about benign space dwarfs, suspects her missing husband, Rudy, was abducted by UFOs. Big Dan, a paunchy ex-con guru/white supremacist/kidnapper, poses to his band of deranged hippies as El Mago, the wizard whom the Mayas predict will appear at the end of time. Murder, adventure and Indian lure animate a Mexico aswarm with New Age mystics, kooks, skinheads, graduate students, maverick archeologists and looters of shrines." Publ Wkly

"'Gringos,' by far, is Portis's most inward-turning book, a story of a grownup trying to grow up, to keep it together with some dignity. Watching him pull it off is one of the finest pleasures afforded by any novel in a long time." Newsweek

Masters of Atlantis; a novel. Knopf 1985 247p
ISBN 0-394-54683-0
* LC 85-40212

This novel "concerns the establishment of the order of Gnomons, a secret society purporting to teach the hidden knowledge of Atlantis. The action begins in 1917, when soldier Lamar is relieved of $200 by a fast-talking stranger in exchange for the key to Gnomonism. The plot spins dizzily along as sly Sydney Hen and antic Austin Popper are drawn into the society, engineer a farcical schism, and espouse assorted crackpot causes. . . . Those who enjoy deadpan comedy should get a good laugh here." Libr J

Norwood. Simon & Schuster 1966 190p o.p.
LC 66-21822

The hero of this book, Norwood Pratt, "an ex-Marine and would-be Country and Western singing star, covers a good stretch of the American highway on a series of fool's errands (picking up a wife along the way)." Book Week

"An artlessness and simplicity in style and plot skillfully projects Norwood and his problems quite convincingly. For those readers more interested in characterization than action." Libr J

True grit; a novel. Simon & Schuster 1968 215p o.p.

"Mattie Ross, a fourteen-year-old living in Yell County, Arkansas, is determined to get justice when her father is killed by a hired hand. She is joined in her quest by Rooster Cogburn, a U.S. marshal, and by a Texas Ranger. This strange trio faces a series of perilous encounters requiring true grit to confront them." Shapiro. Fic for Youth. 3d edition

Potok, Chaim, 1929-2002

The ark builder
In Potok, C. Old men at midnight

The chosen; a novel. Simon & Schuster 1967 284p o.p.
*

"Living only five blocks apart in the Williamsburg section of Brooklyn, New York, Danny and Reuven meet as opponents in a softball game. Out of this encounter evolves a strong bond of friendship between a brilliant Hasidic Jew and a scholar who is Orthodox in his religious thinking. During the course of their relationship Reuven becomes the means by which Danny's father, a rabbi, can communicate with his son, who has been reared under a code of silence." Shapiro. Fic for Youth. 2d edition

Followed by The promise

The gift of Asher Lev. Knopf 1990 369p o.p.
LC 89-43401

Sequel to My name is Asher Lev

"Following the death of his beloved uncle, Asher, who is now middle-aged and settled in France, finds he must return with his family to the Brooklyn Hasidic Jewish community from which he has been exiled 20 years. Greeted there with suspicion and anger by many who still insist that his art is anathema to Hasidim—a sentiment that continues to haunt his relationship with his father, a tireless, well-respected ambassador for the religious community's Rebbe—Asher finds himself struggling once again to balance art and faith, this time in a difficult emotional coming-to-terms that involves the future of his five-year-old son, Avrumel." Booklist

My name is Asher Lev. Knopf 1972 369p o.p.
*

"Young Asher Lev is an obedient son of strict Jewish parents. When his artistic endeavors are discovered, he is sent to a religious leader for consultation because artists are not viewed favorably by the Hasidim. Asher's struggle for fulfillment and his ultimate rejection by his parents are poignantly drawn." Shapiro. Fic for Youth. 3d edition

Followed by The gift of Asher Lev

Old men at midnight. Knopf 2001 273p $23
ISBN 0-375-41071-6
LC 2001-33861

"A collection of three novellas that share a character, Ilana Davita Dinn, and the theme of the effects of war on men's lives. In 'The Ark Builder,' which takes place the summer before she begins college, Ilana begins to teach English to a young boy, Noah, who has survived the Holocaust. . . . In the second story [The war doctor] Ilana is hardly present at all; a former KGB officer leaves her the story of his life in written form. . . . Finally, in 'The Troupe Teacher,' Ilana, now a writer, coaxes a disturbing story out of Benjamin Walter, a professor of warfare. A moving and powerful book." Booklist

The promise. Knopf 1969 358p o.p.
Sequel to The chosen

"Reuven Malter and Danny Saunders, two Jewish friends living in Brooklyn, choose to alter the destinies chosen for them by their fathers. Reuven, studying to be a rabbi, finds his vocation blocked by a challenge to his

Potok, Chaim, 1929-2002—*Continued*
scholarship and his father's book. Danny, who is studying clinical psychology, risks his career by a decision, based on intuition, that he feels can save a young boy's sanity." Shapiro. Fic for Youth. 3d edition

The troupe teacher
In Potok, C. Old men at midnight

The war doctor
In Potok, C. Old men at midnight

Pottinger, Stanley, 1940-

The fourth procedure. Ballantine Bks. 1995 550p
ISBN 0-345-38400-8   LC 94-34282
In this novel "corpses of antiabortionists keep turning up in Washington, D.C., in unlikely spots, but even more unlikely is their condition—all have fresh incisions and a toy doll with a message stuffed inside it. Drawn into this web of murder and mystery is a wide variety of characters whose seemingly random connections turn out to be not so random after all. Each one has a past that sheds light on the current abortion controversy." Libr J
"Pottinger handily proves the adage that politics makes strange bedfellows, adding ironic twists that skewer long-accepted assumptions." Publ Wkly

The last Nazi. St. Martin's Press 2003 324p $24.95
ISBN 0-312-27676-1   LC 2003-53852
"Melissa Gale, a lawyer and agent with an investigative unit of the FBI, is on the trail of the mysterious Adalwolf, a former assistant to Joseph Mengele, who aided in experiments on concentration camp prisoners. For Melissa it's not just a job, it's a personal mission because her grandmother died in a concentration camp. When she and her partner botch the swat team operation, their careers are put in jeopardy, and the elusive Nazi is emboldened to continue with his plot to develop a killer virus." Booklist
"Be prepared to feel horror for a villain who is not only the last Nazi but also one of the most terrifying." Libr J

Pouncey, Peter R., 1937-

Rules for old men waiting; a novel; [by] Peter Pouncey. Random House 2005 210p $21.95
ISBN 1-400-06370-1   LC 2004-54174
This novel "details the last days of historian, war veteran, and proud Scotsman Robert MacIver. Upon the death of his beloved wife, MacIver is at loose ends and in rapidly failing health. Rambling around his large old house on the Cape, he determines that he will meet his fate with dignity. Without a shred of self-pity, he formulates a set of rules to get by, including eating regular meals, keeping warm, and listening to music. He also sets about writing a fairly gripping story set during World War I about a group of conflicted soldiers. This story, in turn, acts as a conduit for his own memories—his experiences in combat, his great love affair with his wife, the death of their son in Vietnam, the rewards of their respective careers as a teacher and a painter." Booklist
"As MacIver's book-within-a-book takes shape,

Pouncey reminds us how the smallest choices can make a dramatic difference in the breadth and scope not just of a story but of a life." N Y Times Book Rev

Pournelle, Jerry, 1933-
(jt. auth) Niven, L. The burning city
(jt. auth) Niven, L. Lucifer's hammer
(jt. auth) Niven, L. The Mote in God's Eye

Powell, Anthony, 1905-2000

The acceptance world
In Powell, A. A dance to the music of time

At Lady Molly's
In Powell, A. A dance to the music of time

Books do furnish a room
In Powell, A. A dance to the music of time

A buyer's market
In Powell, A. A dance to the music of time

Casanova's Chinese restaurant
In Powell, A. A dance to the music of time

A dance to the music of time. University of Chicago Press 1995 12v in 4 pa set $72.80
ISBN 0-226-67719-2
             * LC 94-47228
An omnibus reissue of the twelve titles comprising The Music of time series, which were originally published separately
Contents: {v1} First movement: A question of upbringing (1951); A buyer's market (1952); The acceptance world (1955)
{v2} Second movement: At Lady Molly's (1957); Casanova's Chinese restaurant (1960); The kindly ones (1962)
{v3} Third movement: The valley of bones (1964); The soldier's art (1966); The military philosophers (1968)
{v4} Fourth movement: Books do furnish a room (1971); Temporary kings (1973); Hearing secret harmonies (1975)
"The novels, spanning a period of over fifty years, from the early 1920s, describe the school days, youth, and maturity of the narrator-hero, Nicholas Jenkins, and his upper-class cohorts, especially the egregious Widmerpool. Though primarily satiric in tone, they express an underlying melancholy about life and time reminiscent of Marcel Proust." Reader's Ency. 4th edition

Hearing secret harmonies
In Powell, A. A dance to the music of time

The kindly ones
In Powell, A. A dance to the music of time

The military philosophers
In Powell, A. A dance to the music of time

A question of upbringing
In Powell, A. A dance to the music of time

The soldier's art
In Powell, A. A dance to the music of time

Temporary kings
In Powell, A. A dance to the music of time

Powell, Anthony, 1905-2000—*Continued*

The valley of bones
In Powell, A. A dance to the music of time

Powell, Dawn

Angels on toast
In Powell, D. Novels, 1930-1942

Come back to Sorrento
In Powell, D. Novels, 1930-1942

Dance night
In Powell, D. Novels, 1930-1942

The golden spur
In Powell, D. Novels, 1944-1962

The locusts have no king
In Powell, D. Novels, 1944-1962

My home is far away
In Powell, D. Novels, 1944-1962

Novels, 1930-1942. Library of Am. 2001 1068p
$35
ISBN 1-931082-01-4   LC 00-54595
Contents: Dance night (1930); Come back to Sorrento
(1932); Turn, magic wheel (1936); Angels on toast
(1940); A time to be born (1942)
Dance night is about obsessive longing set in a 1920s
Ohio factory town. Come back to Sorrento depicts a
woman's friendship with a music teacher. Turn, magic
wheel is a satirical look at New York's literary world.
Angel on toast is a comic treatment of New York businessmen on the make. A time to be born portrays a monstrously egotistical woman just before America's entry
into World War II

Novels, 1944-1962. Library of Am. 2001 969p
$35
ISBN 1-931082-02-2   LC 00-54596
Contents: My home is far away (1944); The locusts
have no king (1948); The wicked pavilion (1954); The
golden spur (1962)
My home is far away is the fictionalized memoir of
Powell's life in small town Ohio. The locusts have no
king is a satirical look at a scholar's brush with celebrity.
The wicked pavilion portrays the habitués of a Greenwich Village cafe. The golden spur is a satirical look at
the Manhattan art world of the late 1950s

A time to be born
In Powell, D. Novels, 1930-1942

Turn, magic wheel
In Powell, D. Novels, 1930-1942

The wicked pavilion
In Powell, D. Novels, 1944-1962

Powell, Padgett

Edisto; a novel. Farrar, Straus & Giroux 1984
183p
ISBN 0-374-14651-9
* LC 83-25334

"His parents' separation is a difficult problem for 12-
year-old Simons. The 'Doctor' (his mother) says he
should be a writer. The 'Progenitor' (his father) says he
should play baseball. And Taurus (his mother's friend)
says the boy has enough on his mind just being 12. Cast
between these poles of adult influence, Simons gropes
his way into adolescence under the coastal sun of Edisto,
South Carolina." Libr J
This is "distinctly a tour de force. . . . Powell's ear is
acute: one of the pleasures of the book is his ability to
catch the nuances of Southern speech, whether it is the
malicious conversation of the Doctor's academic colleagues at a cocktail party or the genial banter of country
Negroes at the fishing pier." N Y Times Book Rev

Edisto revisited; a novel. Holt & Co. 1996 145p
ISBN 0-8050-4237-7   LC 95-34071
This sequel, set in South Carolina, "begins with Simons [Manigault] having a short but steamy affair with
first-cousin Patricia. . . . This proves too much for poor
recent college graduate Simons, who escapes for a series
of adventures deeper south. He tries his hand at fishing
in Corpus Christi, quits, and again flees, this time to visit
with Taurus, Simons's alcoholic mother's former lover,
who is a game warden in the deepest bayou in Louisiana.
All the while he debates accepting the responsibility concomitant with adulthood." Libr J
"'Edisto Revisited' is a puzzling work of high style, a
rendering of haplessness that seems to poeticize passivity. While his novel may make you wonder if it has much
of what is called meaning, Mr. Powell finally overpowers
such doubts with his countless quotable passages, his humor and his seductive evocation of the romance of giving up." N Y Times Book Rev

Powell, Sophie, 1980-

The Mushroom Man. Putnam 2003 196p $23.95
ISBN 0-399-14963-5   LC 2002-21355
At the heart of this novel is a "child's invented fairy
tale, set in a Welsh forest, about an amiable hermit who
fashions umbrellas from wild mushrooms to protect the
local fairy population from the rain. . . . Eleven-year-old
Amy—a triplet who lives on a farm in the Welsh countryside with her identical sisters; her older brother, Joseph; and her widowed mother, Beth—is the creator of
the tale. One night she tells it to her 6-year-old cousin,
Lily, who's so enchanted that she sets out to find the
mushroom man and goes missing in the process, thus
setting the novel's plot in motion. . . . The Welsh countryside has never seemed so alluring, or the existence of
simple magic, despite the nasty disappointments of adult
life, so probable." N Y Times Book Rev

Power, Susan, 1961-

The grass dancer. Putnam 1994 300p hardcover
o.p. pa $7.99
ISBN 0-399-13911-7; 0-425-14962-5 (pa)
LC 93-47199
"Set on a North Dakota reservation, 'The Grass Dancer' tells the story of Harley Wind Soldier, a young Sioux
trying to understand his place among people whose intertwined lives and shared heritage move backward in time
in the narrative from the 1980's to the middle of the last
century." N Y Times Book Rev

Power, Susan, 1961——*Continued*

This "is a passionate portrayal of universal human emotions and a vivid account of Native American history and culture." SLJ

Powers, J. F. (James Farl), 1917-1999

Morte d'Urban. Doubleday 1962 336p o.p.

          *

"Father Urban, member of a Catholic order that is financially impoverished, spends his time in two worlds, the religious and the secular. He must try to gain friends and funds for the Clementine order and yet make decisions that may cost him the friendship of his wealthy benefactors, among them eccentric and willful Billy Cosgrove and Mrs. Thwaites. The wide cast of characters within the church and the world outside makes for both a sad and amusing portrait." Shapiro. Fic for Youth. 3d edition

Wheat that springeth green. Knopf 1988 335p o.p.

          * LC 87-46104

This novel "illuminates the world of the Catholic parish. Set in the turbulent months of the late 1960s, it gently and satirically probes the inner mysteries of a younger and perhaps wiser Catholic Church. Its focus is Father Joe Hackett, a tenacious rebel of the faith in his mid-40s who has tested himself on women and drink in his youth and now seems on the verge of religious suicide." Libr J

"The beauty of Mr. Powers's writing lies in its art's being almost invisible. The craft and balance of the novel's literary achievement are discernible in every sentence, but only on second thought, so thoroughly has the author subordinated form to function." N Y Times Book Rev

Powers, James Farl *See* Powers, J. F. (James Farl), 1917-1999

Powers, John R.

Do black patent-leather shoes really reflect up?; a fictionalized memoir. Regnery Bks. 1975 227p o.p.

          *

Sequel to The last Catholic in America

Powers "reproduces the insulated milieu of the big-city Catholic school where harsh discipline and religious fervor molded students for an alternatively naive and cynical survival. The interludes of sentimentality don't detract as Powers' episodic structure and genuine affection carry the day." Booklist

The last Catholic in America; a fictionalized memoir. Saturday Review Press 1973 228p o.p.

          *

"Eddie Ryan, salesman, pauses during a business trip to visit the haunts of a South Side Chicago neighborhood where, in the 1950's, he spent his youth. The scene triggers . . . memories of his Catholic upbringing in St. Bastion's parish, where sin was clearly defined, and punishment and reward handily dispensed." Libr J

"Bittersweet variations on the familiar U.S. literary theme of growing up Catholic . . . strike funny, trite, sometimes overlong, and inevitably sensitive chords. The nostalgic entertainment, occasionally bordering on the mawkish, rings true with seriocomic overtones and honest dialog." Booklist

Followed by Do black patent-leather shoes really reflect up?

Powers, Kim

Capote in Kansas; a ghost story. Carroll & Graf 2007 254p $25

    ISBN 978-0-7867-2033-0; 0-7867-2033-6

In the last year of his life Truman Capote is "plagued by the ghosts of the people whose deaths he chronicled in his greatest book, In Cold Blood. The now-old Harper Lee, or Nelle as she calls herself, is the only one who has a shot at understanding Truman—his childhood friend, she served as companion and researcher on the trip to Kansas that produced In Cold Blood. But Nelle has her own ghosts to exorcise having to do with why she never wrote a second book. In Kansas, Powers speculates, Truman exposed Nelle to her own sexuality, which she continues to suppress. And at his famous 1966 Black and White Ball, green with envy over Nelle's having won the Pulitzer Prize for fiction, Truman spreads the rumor that it was he who wrote To Kill a Mockingbird, not she. Powers . . . succeeds brilliantly in blending fact and fiction to produce a sensitive portrait of two lost souls." Libr J

Powers, Richard, 1957-

The echo maker. Farrar, Straus and Giroux 2006 451p $25

    ISBN 978-0-374-14635-1   LC 2006-00093

"On a winter night on a remote Nebraska road, 27-year-old Mark Schluter flips his truck in a near-fatal accident. His older sister Karin, his only near kin, returns reluctantly to their hometown to nurse Mark back from a traumatic head injury. But when he emerges from a protracted coma, Mark believes that this woman-who looks, acts, and sounds just like his sister-is really an identical impostor. Shattered by her brother's refusal to recognize her, Karin contacts the cognitive neurologist Gerald Weber, famous for his case histories describing the infinitely bizarre worlds of brain disorder. Weber recognizes Mark as a rare case of Capgras Syndrome, a doubling delusion, and eagerly investigates." Publisher's note

This "novel—a kind of neuro-cosmological adventure—is an exhilarating narrative feat. The ease with which the author controls his frequently complex material is sometimes as thrilling to watch as the unfolding of the story itself." Washington Post Book World

Galatea 2.2. Farrar, Straus & Giroux 1995 329p

    ISBN 0-374-19948-5

          * LC 94-44319

In this novel, "protagonist Richard Powers is a humanist-in-residence at the Center for the Study of Advanced Science, where he uses his literary expertise to help Dr. Philip Lentz, a cognitive neurologist, win a bet that he can create a thinking machine capable of passing a comprehensive master's exam in English. As the computer, Helen, learns the fundamentals of language and literature, she develops a sense of her own identity and self-worth. Paralleling Powers' growing attachment to Helen is a

Powers, Richard, 1957——_Continued_

reassessment of the year he spent living in Holland writing his novels and the demise of his longtime relationship with a former student." Booklist

"Powers may be the last humanist with a scientific competence, an invaluable thing when the notion that humans may be just another variety of complex system haunts our sense of ourselves. In its strongest moments Galatea 2.2 realizes the possibilities of that position splendidly." Nation

Generosity; an enhancement. Farrar, Straus and Giroux 2009 296p $25

ISBN 978-0-374-16114-9; 0-374-16114-3

LC 2008-54249

"A Frances Coady book"

"Algerian refugee Thassadit Amzwar has witnessed a great deal of violence in her young life, yet she radiates joy. Now attending college in Chicago, she meets Russell Stone, writing instructor and all-around slump of a guy, who is fascinated by Thassadit's glowing countenance. After consulting with campus counselor (and eventual love interest) Candace Weld, Stone theorizes that Thassadit may be the carrier of a gene that produces happiness. Once the story makes its way to the media, all hell breaks loose." Libr J

"Depending on personal philosophy, readers will disagree as to whether Generosity has a happy ending. But few will fail to be moved by Thassadit's joyful vision of human life." Dallas Morning News

The gold bug variations. Morrow 1991 639p

ISBN 0-688-09891-6

LC 90-20267

The novel "jumps back and forth between the late '50s, when brilliant scientists Stuart Ressler is involved with an Illinois research team trying to break the mysteries of DNA coding, and the '80s, when librarian Jan O'Deigh and computer programmer Franklin Todd get to know Ressler, now holding an insignificant night job at a massive computer database operation in Brooklyn, N.Y., and try to figure what derailed his promising career." Publ Wkly

"Mr. Powers's page is Velcro. Every allusion possible is compulsory. His novel is a dense, symmetrical symphony in which no note goes unsounded." N Y Times Book Rev

Operation wandering soul; a novel. Morrow 1993 352p

ISBN 0-688-11548-9

LC 92-43860

"Set in the pediatric ward of a large metropolitan hospital, this novel is about the plight of the world's children in a time of cynicism, corruption and easy destruction of life. The only recognizable adults are surgical resident Richard Kraft, desperately weary of trying to patch up the shattered lives and bodies of innocents, and therapist Linda Espera, who tries to instill hope through storytelling and play-acting. The two are deeply involved with a band of patients led by a precociously wise but hopelessly crippled Thai girl and a cynical, commanding boy whose rare disease has withered his body into that of an old man." Publ Wkly

This novel is "filled with glorious examples of both high and low culture. Mr. Powers is a cerebral writer with a deep awareness of the material world. . . . But the culture on which his book draws most heavily is children's culture. The therapist's unconventional treatment for her patients requires her and the surgeon to spin tales about imperiled children throughout history. . . . The prose sprints in and out of these tales with verbal dexterity and great flashes of wit." N Y Times Book Rev

Plowing the dark. Farrar, Straus & Giroux 2000 415p $25

ISBN 0-374-23461-2

* LC 99-45084

"In Seattle, a woman painter joins a team of software engineers who are devising a virtual-reality module; at the same time, an American hostage, moldering in a bare cell in Beirut, tries to mentally reconstruct his Stateside existence. Powers's intellectual dexterity is dazzling, especially in the descriptions of virtual-realty programming, and he has plenty to say about the intersections of art, war, commerce, and literature." New Yorker

Prisoner's dilemma. Beech Tree Bks. 1988 348p

ISBN 0-688-07350-6

LC 87-31824

"The present of the novel is late 1978. Edward Hobson's recurring fainting spells have worsened, and two of his children–Artie, a 25-year-old law student, and Rachel, a 23-year-old actuary–have come home to DeKalb to see him, their mother, and two children still living at home, the just-divorced Lily and high school senior Eddie. During this weekend visit and a Christmas reunion in Chicago, the family tries to decide what to do about Edward's health." New Repub

"Prisoner's Dilemma is a paradigm for the nuclear game, the only door left ajar by Hobbes's enlightened self-preservation, the dictates of right reason. Or, is Artie's last oracular pronouncement on his father's legacy the hard answer: 'What we can't bring about in no way releases us from what we must.' We finish this novel, as we do all grand fiction, ready to figure on. Prisoner's Dilemma is magnificent." Nation

The time of our singing. Farrar, Straus & Giroux 2002 631p $28

ISBN 0-374-27782-6

* LC 2002-22397

"The book follows the mixed-race Strom family through much of the 20th century, from 1939—when German-Jewish physicist David Strom meets Delia Daley, a black, classically trained singer from Philadelphia—through the 1990s." Publ Wkly

"Powers's blending of unlikely tones in order to probe the problems of a society that continues to insist, all grays to the contrary, on seeing everything in terms of black and white is, more often than not, a fascinating, stimulating and moving artistic imagining of a harmony that continues to elude us in life." N Y Times Book Rev

Powers, Tim

Three days to never; a novel. William Morrow 2006 420p $25.95

ISBN 978-0-380-97653-9

LC 2006-41900

"Imagine a world where time travel is possible. Now imagine a world where the mummified head of an Einstein clone is helping a secret sect, led by a quasi-hermaphroditic ghost who speaks in iambic pentameter, track down and locate the time machine, an integral component of which is Charlie Chaplin's footprints in a cement slab, and you'll begin to get a grasp on just how bizarrely populated Powers' world is. Almost despite its

Powers, Tim—*Continued*

wonderful weirdness, this thriller maneuvers at a frantic clip as Frank Marrity, Einstein's great-grandson, must pit his wits against not only the malicious secret society bent on attaining immortality but also a specialized paranormal branch of Israel's Mossad, who'd like to use the time machine to avert the Six Days' War of 1967, a stunning psychic assassin who can only see out of other people's eyes, and none other than his own bitter, alcoholic future Frank Marrity self to save his daughter, Daphne, from not merely death but from never having been." Booklist

Poyer, David

Black storm. St. Martin's Press 2002 292p
ISBN 0-312-26969-2   LC 2001-58562
In this "Dan Lenson adventure, Poyer injects the special ops ace into the heart of Operation Desert Storm and confrontation with the menace of Iraqi biological warfare. Attached, along with Major Maddox, a female army doctor, to a marine recon team aiming to infiltrate Baghdad and target a suspected bioweapons site, Lenson survives claustrophobic rides in a milk truck's tank, mad SAS men, and capture and torture by the Iraqis. . . . The remarkably vivid portraits he draws of the variety of men and women drawn to serve their country merit high praise, too." Booklist

China Sea. St. Martin's Press 2000 337p il
ISBN 0-312-20287-3   LC 99-55067
A naval adventure featuring Lt. Commander Dan Lenson. "It is 1990-91, at the start of the Gulf War. The navy, ready to discard the *U.S.S. Gaddis*, has asked Lenson to ready the ship for a final voyage. Accompanied by a crew of misfits and brigrats, Lenson endures a journey filled with bungling allies, hurricanes, a chronic supply problem, and piracy. The crew is ready to mutiny—the vagueness of his orders and a disgruntled executive officer have undermined Lenson's authority. And to top it all off, Lenson soon realizes that one of his crew is committing murders in every port." Libr J
Lenson and his crew "engage the Chinese in a climactic battle that ranks high among single-ship actions in maritime fiction. Readers who can meet Poyer halfway with knowledge of modern seafaring stand to be especially richly rewarded." Booklist

The circle. St. Martin's Press 1992 432p o.p.
LC 92-2980
The author "gives us an ensign fresh out of Annapolis, assigned to a destroyer in the North Atlantic. His ship is an obsolete bucket of plates and bolts held together by mucilage. The ship is undermanned and has a resentful crew. The executive officer is a sadistic right-wing bully. Ship and crew battle furious storms. They are ordered to join the North Atlantic fleet for exercises, and something terrible occurs that results in a court-martial. The young ensign undergoes a trial by fire." NY Times Book Rev
"The individual events convincingly present the gritty details of life aboard a pre-computer-age destroyer, and Poyer provides a compelling sense of the Cold War Navy's operational dynamics." Publ Wkly

The command. St. Martin's Press 2004 386p map $24.95
ISBN 0-312-31836-7   LC 2003-28058

"After receiving the Congressional Medal of Honor for action in Iraq, Commander Daniel V. Lenson is given new orders: 'Take over as skipper of USS Thomas W. Horn.' His mission: Prepare the Tomahawk-equipped strike destroyer and her crew for the Red Sea, where she'll join an international task force searching for weapons of mass destruction." Publisher's note

A country of our own; a novel of the Civil War at sea. Simon & Schuster 2003 429p $24
ISBN 0-684-87134-3   LC 2003-45435
"Lt. Ker Claiborne has reluctantly relinquished his commission in the U.S. Navy and joined the Confederacy. He's an anomaly—a Virginian who opposes slavery. The plot follows Claiborne throughout the South and then across the Atlantic as captain of a highly successful and feared rebel commerce raider. There are enough spies, plots, battles, storms, and shipwrecks to satisfy any reader." Libr J

Down to a sunless sea; a Tiller Galloway thriller. St. Martin's Press 1996 306p
ISBN 0-312-14589-6   LC 96-3120
Ex-Navy SEAL Tiller Galloway's "troubles are unending. He's broke, his boat is destroyed, his partnership is dissolving, and the teenaged son he hasn't seen in years unexpectedly arrives in a stolen car. So when the wife of an old friend, Bud, calls with news of her husband's death and requests Tiller's help selling his cave-diving business, Tiller heads south with son in tow. And once in the murky darkness of Florida's submerged tunnels, Tiller soon discovers the dangers and thrills of cave diving, along with evidence that Bud's drowning was no accident, but part of a conspiracy involving drugs and water rights." Libr J
"The cave-diving scenes are riveting, claustrophobic, terrifying, and beautiful, and Tiller has grown into one of the most spectacularly flawed and failed characters ever to seek redemption in popular fiction." Booklist

Fire on the waters; a novel of the Civil War at sea. Simon & Schuster 2001 445p
ISBN 0-684-87133-5   LC 2001-20307
This novel "introduces naval officer Elisha Eaker. The pampered son of a successful shipping magnate, Eli enlists to take a stand for his country and against his overbearing father. Commissioned to protect the Union forces at Fort Sumter, Eli and Captain Parker Bucyrus Tresevant, a Southerner torn between allegiances, sail into the danger, intrigue, and indecision necessarily engendered by a nation at war with itself." Booklist
"An interesting character study of a young man's coming of age as well as an accurate historical novel." Libr J

The gulf. St. Martin's Press 1990 xx, 442p o.p.
LC 90-36140
"Dan Lenson, is the executive officer on a frigate in the Persian Gulf, assigned to convoy a succession of oil tankers through perilous waters. Lenson's shipmates include hard-living helicopter pilots, minor crooks, and idealistic young officers. Not far away, a group of divers, naval reservists, must battle the hostility of 'real' sailors as they undertake a dangerous mission of their own. Lenson's physical and mental courage are sorely tried in the climactic scenes, where he battles enemies and the ocean itself." Libr J

Poyer, David—*Continued*

Thunder on the mountain. Forge 1999 382p $25.95

ISBN 0-312-86494-9   LC 98-43454

"A Tom Doherty Associates book"

"A fiery accident at a Pennsylvania oil refinery in 1935 inspires the workers at Thunder Oil Company to strike. During a bitterly cold winter in the depths of the Depression, workers are desperate for decent food, better wages, warm housing, and fair treatment from management. When a ruthless professional strikebreaker and a CIO organizer with thinly veiled Communist sympathies join the dispute, the strike escalates to betrayal, sabotage, and murder." Libr J

Poyer's "pitch-perfect dialogue and explosive imagery capture both sides of the bloody battle that gave birth to the unions. This is a stunning period tale in which the oft-forgotten essence of the American dream is visible in every chapter." Publ Wkly

Pramoedya Ananta Toer *See* Toer, Pramoedya Ananta, 1925-2006

Pratchett, Terry

The color of magic; a novel of Discworld. Harper 2005 224p pa $13.95

ISBN 0-06-085592-4

     * LC 2005-46289

First published 1983 by St. Martin's Press with title: The colour of magic

This first book of Discworld features the tourist Twoflower, the wizard Rincewind, and several other unusual characters as they travel together on a flat planet.

The fifth elephant; a novel of Discworld. HarperPrism 2000 321p

ISBN 0-06-105157-8   LC 99-43960

"When news of a dispute over the dwarven succession reaches the city of Ankh-Morpork, Lord Vetinari dispatches an unlikely group of ambassadors—including a dwarf, a werewolf, a troll, and the intrepid Watch Commander Vines—to address the problem." Libr J

"Pratchett cheerfully takes readers on an exuberant tale of mystery and invention. . . . Along the way, he skewers everything from monarchy to fascism, as well as communism and capitalism, oil wealth and ethnic identities, Russian plays, immigration, condoms and evangelical Christianity—in short, most everything worth talking about." Publ Wkly

Going postal; a novel of Discworld. HarperCollins 2004 377p $24.95

ISBN 0-06-001313-3   LC 2004-47391

"When petty con man Moist von Lipwig is hung for his crimes . . . it appears to be the end. But this is Discworld after all, a world 'a lot like our own but different.' Moist awakes from the shock of his hanging to find that the city's Patrician, Lord Vetinari, has assigned him a government job (a fate worse than death?) restoring the defunct postal system. Of course, there is much more to restore than the flow of letters and packages. Justice as well as communication has been poorly served by a hostile takeover of the 'clacks' a unique messaging system that is part semaphore, part digital, and under the monopoly of the Grand Trunk Company. Before Moist can get very far into the job, he encounters ghosts, the voices of unsent letters, and a ruthless corporate conspiracy. . . . The author's inventiveness seems to know no end, his playful and irreverent use of language is a delight, and there is food for thought in his parody of fantasyland." SLJ

Monstrous regiment; a novel of Discworld. HarperCollins Pubs. 2003 353p $24.95

ISBN 0-06-001315-X   LC 2003-50800

"Polly Perks, an exuberantly determined Borogravian barmaid, decides to disguise herself as a man to infiltrate the Tenth Foot Light Infantry (aka the Ins-and-Outs) and find her missing soldier brother, Paul." Publ Wkly

"Pratchett revels in pricking pomp and assurance, but it isn't going too far to say that of late his real subject, like Wilfred Owen's, is the pit of war. Pratchett's approach may be less lyrical, but he can move from farce to sadness in seconds." N Y Times Book Rev

Thief of time; a novel of Discworld. HarperCollins Pubs. 2001 324p

ISBN 0-06-019956-3   LC 00-65347

"The cast includes Death; Miss Susan, Death's granddaughter; Jeremy Clockson, a clockmaker; Lobsang, a novice monk; and Lu-Tze, a sweeper at the temple of the History Monks. When a mysterious lady asks Jeremy to make a clock that is perfectly timed (even to the last tick), trouble begins—it seems that such a clock would have the power to stop time completely." Publ Wkly

"This is Discworld, an adolescent Oz in which far fewer folks are immortal, but long life doesn't entail decrepitude; magic works; and politics and culture are fluid, far off, and mostly for old guys. Spun out of words and wit, it is as light and curiously tasty as cotton candy." Booklist

Thud!; a novel of Discworld. HarperCollins 2005 384p $24.95

ISBN 0-06-081522-6   LC 2005-46271

"Commander Sam Vines of Ankh-Morpork's City Watch finds a 'perfect day' going downhill quickly. Not only is there a murderer loose in the city but Sam also faces pressure to add a vampire to a police force that already contains trolls and werewolves and an old rivalry that threatens to break out into overt warfare. It's all in a day's work for the City Watch in the latest novel set in the author's hilariously surreal Disc World." Libr J

The truth; a novel of Discworld. HarperCollins Pubs. 2000 324p il

ISBN 0-380-97895-4   LC 00-31928

"When he stumbles upon the dwarven secret of movable type, young scribe William de Word discovers a new career and starts a newspaper—the first of its kind in the city of Ankh-Morpork. Pratchett's . . . 'Discworld' novel takes on the press and investigative journalism in a hilarious romp that examines the fleeting nature of truth and lies." Libr J

(jt. auth) Gaiman, N. Good omens

Preston, Douglas

Blasphemy; [by] Douglas J. Preston. Forge Books 2008 c2007 414p il $25.95

ISBN 978-0-7653-1105-4; 0-7653-1105-4

     LC 2007-31811

Preston, Douglas—_Continued_

This suspense novel centers around "Isabella, a giant superconducting supercollider particle accelerator. . . . The ostensible goal of Isabella's creator, physicist Gregory North Hazelius, is to discover new forms of energy, but what he really wants is to talk to God. The project, located inside Red Mesa (a five-hundred-square-mile tableland on the Navajo Indian Reservation), is behind schedule, so presidential science adviser Stanton Lockwood hires ex-CIA man Wyman Ford to go to Red Mesa and find out what's causing the holdup. Meanwhile, a Navajo medicine man, a televangelist and a pastor who runs a failed mission on the reservation are gearing up to pull the plug on Isabella before she destroys the earth. Science has often tangled with religion in this genre, but Preston puts his own philosophical spin on the usual proceedings, and when he gets his irate villagers with their burning torches headed for the castle, the pages simply fly." Publ Wkly

Brimstone; [by] Douglas Preston and Lincoln Child. Warner Bks. 2004 497p $25.95

ISBN 0-446-53143-X   LC 2004-1968

A mystery featuring FBI agent Pendergast. "In an exotic mansion, Jeremy Grove's charred remains are discovered in an otherwise locked and barricaded room. The area smells of brimstone, and singed into the floorboard appears to be a cloven hoofprint. According to rumor, Jeremy made a Faustian pact with Satan in his youth. Did the Dark Lord finally demand payment? Pendergast can't resist a mystery, and he incorporates the help of police officers from the authors' previous novels. In addition, a major character appears courtesy of Wilkie Collins's The Woman in White." Libr J

"Erudite, swiftly paced, brimming (occasionally overbrimming) with memorable personae and tense set pieces, this is the perfect thriller." Publ Wkly

The cabinet of curiosities; {by} Douglas Preston and Lincoln Child. Warner Bks. 2002 466p

ISBN 0-446-53022-0   LC 2001-39580

"Construction of an apartment building in Manhattan is haltred when excavators discover the remains of 36 dismembered bodies, the apparent victims of a serial killer who operated more than a century ago. Archaeologist Nora Kelly and FBI agent Pendergast (both have appeared in the authors' previous books) team up to track down the identity of the long-dead killer." Booklist

This novel features "fabulous locales, colorful characters, pointed riffs on city and museum politics, cool forensic and paleontological speculation and several gripping set pieces including an extended white-knuckle climax." Publ Wkly

The codex. Forge 2004 396p $24.95

ISBN 0-7653-0700-6   LC 2003-49427

"A treasure hunter and tomb raider, Maxwell Broadbent is one of the wealthiest men on the planet owing to his extensive art collection. Dying of cancer, he decides to force his three estranged sons to work together for their inheritance. Leaving them a videotape of his plan, Max takes everything of value and buries himself and the goods somewhere in the world. To claim their inheritance, his sons have to find the tomb. Others are watching and rooting them on so that they can claim the rewards for themselves. One item of significance is a Mayan codex that contains the secret instructions to

create medicine from the native jungle plants. This discovery would revolutionize the pharmaceutical industry. Fascinating characters, exotic jungle scenery, and surprising twists make this nonstop thrill ride well worth deciphering." Libr J

Reliquary; [by] Douglas Preston, Lincoln Child. Forge 1997 382p $24.95

ISBN 0-312-86095-1   LC 96-53533

"A Tom Doherty Associates book"

In this sequel to Relic "Margo Green, the curator of the Natural History Museum in New York, rejoins police lieutenant Vincent D'Agosta, FBI agent Pendergast, and famed evolutionist Dr. Frock as they try to solve multiple cases of brutal murders. Their search focuses on the 'mole people' who live deep within the infinite mazes of underground tunnels lying beneath New York City." SLJ

"Although _Reliquary_ is a sequel, its exposition carries us easily into the new plot and excites interest in seeing what Preston and Child come up with next, after this yarn's all-loose-ends-tied finale." Booklist

Riptide; [by] Douglas Preston and Lincoln Child. Warner Bks. 1998 417p $25

ISBN 0-446-52336-4   LC 97-23907

"Dr. Malin Hatch is at first reluctant to let the Thalassa Group plunder his Ragged Island, off the coast of Maine, in yet another attempt to reclaim pirate Red Ned Ockham's 17th-century treasure. But its leaders assure him that they have the technology and skill to breach the deadly Water Pit that has claimed the lives of countless treasure hunters. They also have the encrypted diary of the Pit's designer, which, they claim, holds the key to the treasure's reclamation." Libr J

"Machine-gun pacing, startling plot twists and smart use of legend, scientific lore (including cyptanalysis) and the evocative setting carry the day." Publ Wkly

Still life with crows; [by] Douglas Preston and Lincoln Child. Warner Bks. 2003 435p $24.95

ISBN 0-446-53142-1   LC 2002-192401

FBI Agent Pendergast arrives "in tiny Medicine Creek, KS, just in time to investigate a series of gruesome murders. Life in rural Medicine Creek usually revolves around the local turkey-processing plant and growing corn, but all hell breaks loose when a female corpse is found in a clearing in a cornfield, surrounded by a ring of dead crows impaled on arrows." Libr J

Tyrannosaur Canyon. Forge 2005 368p $24.95

ISBN 0-765-31104-6   LC 2005-5171

"A prospector discovers the treasure of his lifetime and takes bullets in the back for his effort. With his dying breath, he gives a journal to innocent bystander Tom Broadbent (the hero of Preston's . . . The Codex) and asks Tom to deliver the information to his daughter. The prospector's killer, of course, wants the ledger, so now Tom and his wife are in mortal danger. Why is the journal so valuable? It contains information leading to the fossilized remains of a complete Tyrannosaurus rex, a scientific discovery worth millions and a lifetime of accolades to the finder. In addition, a mysterious black ops agency wants the skeleton to hide a deadly secret originally discovered on the moon over 30 years ago by the crew of Apollo 17. The truth will shake the foundation of paleontology to its core. Preston's exhilarating and absorbing science-based effort will thrill readers from the first page to the last." Libr J

Preston, Douglas—*Continued*

The wheel of darkness; [by] Douglas Preston &
Lincoln Child. Warner Books 2007 388p $25.99

ISBN 978-0-446-58028-1; 0-446-58028-7

LC 2007-20551

In this supernatural thriller, "FBI agent Aloysius
Pendergast and his ward, Constance Greene, seek peace
of mind at a remote Tibetan monastery, only to fall into
yet another perilous, potentially earthshaking assignment.
The monastery's abbot asks them to recover a stolen relic, the cryptic Agozyen, which could, in the wrong
hands, wipe out humanity. The pair follow the trail to a
luxury cruise ship, where a series of brutal murders suggests the relic's evil spirit might already have been invoked. . . . While not as frightening as others in the series, this entry still shows why the authors stand head
and shoulders above their rivals in this subgenre." Publ
Wkly

Preston, Richard

The Cobra event; a novel. Random House 1997
404p $25.95

ISBN 0-679-45714-3

LC 98-106915

"When two completely unrelated people die horrifically
in New York City, Alice Austen, a young doctor working for the Centers for Disease Control in Washington,
D.C., is called in to investigate. What Austen finds in
New York is like nothing she has ever seen; two victims
whose symptoms include self-cannibalism and brains that
have turned to mush. More victims follow, and soon she
realizes that the mystery illness was caused by a man-
made virus that spreads as easily as the common cold.
Drawing on her findings, a team of government scientists
is formed and set up on Governor's Island in the middle
of New York Harbor. Their job is to find the person behind the virus and to stop him before he causes a world-
wide outbreak." Libr J

"Preston marshals his narrative with sufficient precision to persuade and terrify readers." Publ Wkly

Price, Eugenia

Savannah. Doubleday 1983 595p o.p.

LC 82-45572

The first volume in the author's Savannah quartet; other titles To see your face again (1985); Before darkness
falls (1987) and Stranger in Savannah (1989)

This "novel tells the story of a handsome young Yankee, Mark Browning, who finds a secure place for himself in the gracious society of Savannah, Georgia, in the
early 19th century. Browning, befriended by a merchant
named Robert Mackay, is taken into the man's mercantile firm, and soon finds himself in love with Mackay's
virtuous wife. The situation is further complicated by
Mark's growing attraction to his first cousin, Caroline
Cameron, and his relationship with a blackguard uncle,
Osmund Kott, who may or may not be on the edge of
true repentance and conversion to Christianity." Publ
Wkly

Price, Nancy, 1925-

Night woman. Pocket Bks. 1992 314p

ISBN 0-671-74993-5

LC 92-50164

"Mary Eliot leads a puzzling double life: her interior
world of great creativity and strength somehow survives
the constant abuse of her exterior existence. Her husband
is insane, a professor of literature who poses as the family breadwinner and successful novelist while Mary is, in
fact, the actual author. When he dies, she feels gloriously
free until she finds herself overwhelmed by a second
possessive and abusive male with murderous intent."
Booklist

"Gritty, wry characterization, chilling images of insanity, and a long, ultimately satisfying tease which ends
with Mary at last getting her due will keep readers flipping pages." Publ Wkly

Sleeping with the enemy. Simon & Schuster
1987 c1986 332p o.p.   LC 86-29778

"Battered women don't usually have the courage of
Sara Burney. Desperate and bruised physically and emotionally, she evolves a plan to flee her obsessive husband. She knows he will come after her and kill her
eventually, so that mere flight will offer only temporary
reprieve. So she decides to 'get lost.' She assumes a new
identity, a new look, and seeks respite and a new life
hundreds of miles from their home in Massachusetts.
. . . Price has written an absorbing tale and her language
has a sensual quality that transports the reader into her
panoramas that affect all the senses." West Coast Rev
Books

Price, Reynolds, 1933-

Blue Calhoun. Atheneum Pubs. 1992 373p $23

ISBN 0-689-12146-6   LC 91-22877

This novel depicts circumstances in the life of "Blue
(short for Bluford) Calhoun, a 65-year-old salesman in a
music store in Raleigh. . . . The tale that Blue has to tell
takes the form of a lengthy epistle addressed to his teenage granddaughter, who blames him for failing to prevent the suicide of her father. In his attempt to win her
understanding and 'mercy,' Blue ranges over the main
events in his life since 1956, the year when, at the age
of 35, he falls in love with a 16-year-old girl named
Luna Absher." N Y Times Book Rev

"Price is in top form here, forcing us to wrestle with
Blue even as he wrestles with himself, portraying his anguish in painfully clear, clean prose that captures perfectly the rhythms of the South and of the human heart."
Libr J

The collected stories. Atheneum Pubs. 1993
625p $25

ISBN 0-689-12147-4

* LC 92-36807

Contents: Full day; The Warrior Princess Ozimba; The
enormous door; A told secret; Watching her die; Serious
need; The company of the dead; A sign of blood; Rapid
eye movements; Twice; Washed feet; Sleeping and wak-
ing; Morning places; Michael Egerton; The last news;
The anniversary; Invitation; My parents, winter 1926;
The knowledge of my mother's coming death; Life for
life; Design for a tomb; Endless mountains; Long night;
A new stretch of woods; The last of a long correspon-
dence; Deeds of light; Walking lessons; His final mother;
This wait; The happiness of others; A dog's death; Scars;
Waiting at Dachau; The golden child; Truth and lies;
Breath; Toward home; The names and faces of heroes;
Nine hours alone; Night and silence; Summer games; A

Price, Reynolds, 1933——*Continued*

chain of love; Two useful visits; A final account; Uncle Grant; Troubled sleep; Good night; An evening meal; Bess Waters; An early Christmas

"Many of the characters in these magical, quietly revelatory, death-obsessed tales are transformed by chance encounters, in settings that include Price's native south but also range throughout the world." Publ Wkly

The foreseeable future. Atheneum Pubs. 1991 253p $21.95

ISBN 0-689-12110-5   LC 90-45463

Contents: The fare to the moon; The foreseeable future; Back before day

"In his eloquent and distinctive voice, Price reveals in each of these stories how love and memory, loss and redemption, and essential human goodness 'prop' us up and allow us to move forward into an uncertain future." Libr J

The good priest's son. Scribner 2005 278p $26

ISBN 0-7432-5400-7

     * LC 2004-65383

"On September 11, 2001, Mabry Kincaid—a fiftyish art conservator—is flying home after a much-needed rest in Rome and Paris. Halfway across the Atlantic, his plane is diverted from New York to Nova Scotia. Two days later, when the United States has recovered sufficiently from the attack on the World Trade Center, Mabry discovers that his downtown New York loft is uninhabitable. He flies south to North Carolina instead to visit his aged father. A widowed Episcopalian priest, Tasker Kincaid has been injured in a recent fall and is cared for by live-in Audrey Thornton, an African-American divinity student at Duke University, and her grown son, Marcus, an ambitious painter." Publisher's note

This novel is "thematically rich—indeed, it is rather bowed by its meanings—and features many pleasing Southern voices, along with an impeccable depiction of the region's deep-rooted traditions." N Y Times Book Rev

Kate Vaiden. Atheneum Pubs. 1986 306p

ISBN 0-689-11787-6

     * LC 85-48143

In this novel, Kate Vaiden tells her own story "to justify herself to a son she abandoned as a baby and hasn't seen in 40 years. The decisive event in Kate's life occurred in 1938, when she was 11. Her father inexplicably murdered her mother and killed himself, leaving a letter that Kate doesn't read until many years later. . . . [Kate] is lovingly raised by a taciturn aunt and uncle with a secret sorrow she gradually learns: their homosexual son, Walter, ran off 12 years earlier with another local boy. When Walter comes home on a visit, he befriends Kate, who later runs off to live with him and has a child by his lover." Newsweek

"Mr. Price's successful creation of a female voice may be a tour de force, but it never feels like a showy ventriloquial act. Instead, Kate is a wholly convincing girl and a not improbable woman." N Y Times Book Rev

The promise of rest. Scribner 1995 353p

ISBN 0-684-80149-3   LC 94-48086

Conclusion of the author's Mayfield family trilogy begun with The surface of earth (1975) and The source of light (1981). "Wade Mayfield, great-grandson of the

woman whose runaway marriage in 1903 set the family's tragic 20th-century history in motion, is dying of AIDS. Long estranged from his parents (his black lover, Wyatt Bondurant, hated them as complicit beneficiaries of the South's racist past), Wade comes home to North Carolina in April 1993, after Wyatt's death. His mother, Ann, has left his father, Hutchins, claiming that her husband has shut her out of his life for years. Meanwhile, Hutchins's lifelong friend and onetime lover, Strawson Stuart, makes his own reproaches about Hutchins's inability to fully accept love. Extended family and friends gather around the dying Wade, grappling with matters as general as America's poisoned racial heritage and as intimate as the Mayfield legacy." Publ Wkly

Roxanna Slade. Scribner 1998 301p $25

ISBN 0-684-83292-5   LC 97-39167

This is the "story of a women's life, told in her own precise and feisty voice. Roxanna Slade has not led what would be considered an outwardly distinguished life, a life she clearly recalls now in her 90s. Certainly not in her dotage, for she is still as alert as ever, Roxanna recounts the contents of her long decades on earth." Booklist

"Many of the virtues that have endeared Price . . . to readers are present in this story of a North Carolina woman and several generations of her family. Price's musically cadenced, nostalgia-washed prose, plangent with portent and loss and vibrant with imagery, is as beguiling as ever. His picture of life in the South a century ago is imbued with candor about customs and attitudes—especially those concerning women and race." Publ Wkly

The tongues of angels. Atheneum Pubs. 1990 192p $17.95

ISBN 0-689-12093-1   LC 89-37427

This novel focuses on "Bridge Boatner, a famous painter who looks back at the summer of 1954, when he was a counselor at a camp in North Carolina; and Raphael Noren, a prematurely wise, otherworldly 14-year-old who was a camper there that summer. . . . [The two] had come to the camp to find a way to cope with the sudden death of a parent. . . . Boatner finds himself as an artist that summer, producing a painting that stands the test of time." Time

"As much prey to mutual irritation as to esteem, they worry and argue their way—the 14-year-old boy and the 21-year-old man—through the 10-week intimacy of the camp, cut of from so-called civilization and therefore free, in terms they hold in common, to aim beyond the commonplace: into myth, art, ritual and pain." N Y Times Book Rev

Price, Richard, 1949-

Clockers. Houghton Mifflin 1992 599p

ISBN 0-395-53761-4

     * LC 91-43318

The author "divides his narrative between two main characters: Strike (a k a Ronald Dunham), the black crew leader of a small-time group of cocaine dealers—the 'clockers' of the title—in the slums of northern New Jersey, and Rocco Klein, an experienced but disillusioned white homicide detective who's about to take early retirement. The stories of Rocco and Strike are pulled together when Strike's by-all-accounts paragon brother, Victor, confesses to an apparently routine drug murder

Price, Richard, 1949——*Continued*

and Rocco, refusing to believe Victor guilty, becomes convinced that he's taking the heat for his brother." N Y Times Book Rev

This is "an incredible course in urban street life, particularly the crack culture." Booklist

Freedomland. Broadway Bks. 1998 546p $25
ISBN 0-7679-0024-3   LC 98-10527

A novel set in an inner-city neighborhood in northern New Jersey. "Through a haze of shock and exhaustion, a young white woman manages to tell a disjointed story of being carjacked by a black man outside the Henry T. Armstrong housing projects; she claims her four-year-old son was asleep in the backseat. Asthmatic black policeman Lorenzo 'Big Daddy' Council catches the case and can sense the political firestorm brewing in the background. . . . As the frantic search for the boy ensues, the media, project residents, a neighboring majority white police district, black activists, and a zealous missing-children's group all converge on the scene, each with their own agendas." Booklist

"Price's characters are, as usual, dead-on, and his eye for unflinchingly capturing humans at their very best—and very worst—is unrivaled." Libr J

Lush life. Farrar, Straus & Giroux 2008 455p $26
ISBN 978-0-374-29925-5; 0-374-29925-0
      LC 2008-8437

This is "a tale set on the gentrifying-but-still-mean streets of the lower East Side. It's the era of 'Quality of Life' law enforcement, where trendy restaurants are opening alongside bodegas. . . . As the uptown up-and-comers line up outside the hot new restaurant managed by once-ambitious actor/screenwriter Eric Cash, the locals jam into a Yemenite family's bodega, forking over a dollar to glimpse the Virgin, whose image has mysteriously appeared in the condensation of the beer fridge. Shortly thereafter, Detective Matty Clark collars Cash for the shooting death of a co-worker, Ike Marcus, a young man who had bigger plans than winding up dead after a night out clubbing. The book's central focus then becomes the aftermath of the crime—starting with the fact that Cash is innocent. After a day in the 8th Precinct's interrogation room and a night in the tombs, the dead-end path Cash was on before now takes a more destructive turn." N Y Daily News

"Price has been around for what seems like forever, but there's a reason we still read him. Because every sentence is a pleasure. Because he never puts a foot wrong, and never lingers. He takes just enough time to make you care." Esquire

Samaritan. Knopf 2003 377p $25
ISBN 0-375-41115-1

"Ray Mitchell, an Emmy-nominated TV writer who returned to teach pro bono at his old high school amid the projects of Dempsy, New Jersey, has had his head bashed in. Nerese Ammons, a cop 10 weeks from retirement, takes the case personally because of a good turn Ray did her when they were children. But Ray, deteriorating in the hospital, doesn't want to tell her who attacked him." Booklist

"'Samaritan' is two books. One belongs to Ray, the other to Nerese, a division emphasized by the use of cuts and jumps. Chapters recounting Ray's return to Dempsy

are interspersed with scenes fo Nerese's investigation of the whos and whys of this return. The structure, though obtrusive, does its job, bringing stereoscopic depth to the events." N Y Times Book Rev

Priest, Cherie, 1975-

Boneshaker. Tor 2009 416p pa $15.99
ISBN 978-0-7653-1841-1   LC 2009-18700

"A Tom Doherty Associates book"

"The book's heroine, Briar Wilkes, having survived the zombie takeover that claimed most of Seattle, has dedicated her life life to providing for her teenage son Zeke. But when he vanishes over the wall into the zombie-infested center of Seattle, Briar has to take matters into her own hands and, reluctantly, start to make peace with the demons of her past in the process." Wired

"Intelligent, exceptionally well written and showcasing a phenomenal strong female protagonist who embodies the complexities inherent in motherhood, this yarn is a must-read for the discerning steampunk fan." Publ Wkly

Pritchett, V. S. (Victor Sawdon), 1900-1997

Complete collected stories. Random House 1991 c1990 1219p o.p.
      * LC 90-47478

First published 1990 in the United Kingdom

Contents: Sense of humour; A spring morning; Main road; The evils of Spain; Handsome is as handsome does; The aristocrat; The two brothers; X-ray; The scapegoat; Eleven o'clock; The upright man; Page and monarch; Miss Baker; You make your own life; The sailor; The lion's den; The saint; It may never happen; Pocock passes; The Oedipus complex; The voice; Aunt Gertrude; Many are disappointed; The chestnut tree; The ape; The clerk's tale; The fly in the ointment; The night worker; Double divan; The landlord; Passing the ball; A story of Don Juan; The ladder; The satisfactory; Things as they are; The sniff; The collection; The wheelbarrow; The fall; When my girl comes home; The necklace; Just a little more; The snag; On the scent; Citizen; The key to my heart; Noisy flushes the birds; Noisy in the doghouse; Blind love; The nest builder; A debt of honour; The cage birds; The skeleton; The speech; The liars; Our oldest friend; The honeymoon; The chain-smoker; The last throw; The Camberwell beauty; The diver; Did you invite me?; The rescue; The marvellous girl; The spree; Our wife; The lady from Guatemala; On the edge of the cliff; A family man; The Spanish bed; The wedding; The worshippers; The vice-consul; The accompanist; Tea with Mrs. Bittell; The fig tree; A careless widow; Cocky Olly; A trip to the seaside; Things; A change of policy; The image trade

(ed) The Oxford book of short stories. See The Oxford book of short stories

Pritchett, Victor Sawdon *See* Pritchett, V. S. (Victor Sawdon), 1900-1997

Pronzini, Bill

Blue lonesome. Walker & Co. 1995 207p o.p.
      LC 95-13049

"Two quotes that connect hell, the devil, and loneliness foreshadow the suicide of a woman known as Ms. Lonesome. The often-solitary James Messenger sets out in

Pronzini, Bill—*Continued*

search of the aloof woman's identity even though he spoke to her only once. He finds himself in Beulah, Nevada, a harsh countryside dominated by embittered people, violent murder, and mulish sensibilities. Pronzini skillfully handles Messenger's quest. He uses jazz to accompany changes in mood, but is not verbose." Libr J

Bones. St. Martin's Press 1985 196p o.p.
LC 85-1708
"The 'Nameless Detective' is hired by Michael Kiskadon to find out why his father, pulp writer Harmon Crane, committed suicide 35 years ago. This proves to be a locked room puzzle. The twisting plot eventually turns up three murders. This is a crisply written mystery with perfect pacing; new clues are cunningly placed so that reader interest is constantly piqued." Libr J

Crazybone; a "nameless detective" novel. Carroll & Graf Pubs. 2000 197p
ISBN 0-7867-0730-5
*
Pronzini's nameless detective "lumbers down the San Francisco Peninsula to a private enclave of wooded estates and walled country clubs to find out why a grieving widow has refused a $50,000 insurance settlement for the accidental death of her husband. The look of 'raw terror' on the woman's face when he confronts her . . . suggests that she might have something to hide, and the nameless hero does a good job of ferreting out her secret. But the real fun comes from watching the old war horse plod through a hostile social environment, observing the swells at their selfish pursuits and making them regret every condescending sneer they threw in his face." N Y Times Book Rev

The crimes of Jordan Wise. Walker & Co. 2006 233p $23.95
ISBN 0-8027-1493-5
LC 2006-46115
"In 1977, Jordan Wise, an accountant in a large San Francisco firm, falls in love with a woman who wants money and all that it can buy more than she wants Jordan. So he concocts a fool-proof scheme to embezzle $600,000 from his firm, and the couple flees to the Virgin Islands. Twenty-seven years later, Jordan recounts what happened following their escape to a man who recognizes him." Libr J
"Like an expert fisherman, Pronzini spins out his yarn to its inevitable conclusion; there's only one way to end the old story of a lovesick sap and a dame whose appetites can never be satisfied. The Crimes of Jordan Wise is a neat piece of writing: James M. Cain by way of Jimmy Buffett." Washington Post Book World

Fever; a Nameless Detective novel. Forge 2008 288p $24.95
ISBN 978-0-7653-1818-3; 0-7653-1818-0
LC 2008-5228
"A Tom Doherty Associates book"
"Mitchell Krochek, who's worried about the gambling addiction of his wife, Janice, hires Nameless to trace Janice, who's disappeared for the fourth time in four years. When Jake Runyon, Nameless's associate, traces Janice to an apartment hotel near their San Francisco office, Nameless and Jake decide to honor Janice's request not to reveal her location to her husband. Later, a battered Janice shows up at the detective agency's office, where

she agrees to go home, only to vanish again amid circumstances strongly indicating foul play. . . . This insightful novel will appeal to those who like the mean streets portrayed with understatement and subtlety rather than gory violence." Publ Wkly

Hardcase; a "Nameless Detective" mystery. Delacorte Press 1995 215p o.p.
LC 95-5723
This mystery "opens as the California PI, approaching 60, marries his longtime girlfriend, Kerry. After a civil ceremony marked by his nervous clumsiness, Nameless takes on a client who wants him to find her birthparents. Melanie Ann Aldrich has just discovered that she was adopted and is sure there's a reason her adoptive parents, who are deceased, kept this information from her. Nameless fairly quickly identifies the woman's birthparents, but that's just the beginning." Publ Wkly

Illusions; a "Nameless Detective" novel. Carroll & Graf Pubs. 1997 243p o.p.
LC 97-4274
"Shaken by the suicide of his former partner and one-time best friend, a pathetic figure whose life had shrunk to 'drinking, brooding, building his own private gallows day by day,' Nameless throws himself into a job for a Santa Fe businessman who wants to contact his former wife. The woman is easily found; but before the shamus can cash his check, a second suicide delivers another body blow to his code of ethics and deposits another load of guilt on his conscience. . . . The parallel investigations offer prime examples of Pronzini's ace plotting techniques . . . and if you can take the mood swings, Nameless is a good man to walk you through the noir landscape." N Y Times Book Rev

In an evil time. Walker & Co. 2001 266p $23.95
ISBN 0-8027-3353-0
LC 00-49996
"Jack Hollis, a family man and law-abiding citizen, is ready to cross the line. His daughter, Angela, is being stalked by her abusive second husband, David Rakubian, a successful personal-injury lawyer in San Francisco. In fact, it's Rakubian's knowledge of the law's limitations that makes him so dangerous to Angela and her toddler son. Jack has weighed the options and sees Rakubian's death as the only way out for his daughter. . . . [Pronzini] has fashioned a nail-biter out of the issue of domestic abuse and the law's inability to deal with it effectively." Booklist

Mourners; a nameless detective novel. Forge 2006 285p $24.95
ISBN 0-7653-0932-7
LC 2005-43510
"When Nameless made his assistant, Tamara, a partner in his detective agency and hired Jake, a new operative, he genuinely felt he was moving toward retirement. But business has increased, and Nameless finds himself reluctant to give up the work that has defined him for so long, even though he has recently become a husband and father. His current case involves a wealthy financial planner who attends the funerals of strangers, walks deserted beaches at night, and makes solitary visits to a secret rental apartment. His wife is worried and hires the firm to investigate. . . . Pronzini's series becomes more layered and complex with each entry. This time the primary characters are all in one stage or another of mourning, but the only one who recognizes it is the initial subject of the investigation. He is also the only one who understands the timeless omnipresence of grief. . . . A dark, foreboding entry in a classic series." Booklist

Pronzini, Bill—*Continued*

Nightcrawlers; a nameless detective novel. Forge 2005 301p $24.95

ISBN 0-7653-0931-9   LC 2004-56323

"A Tom Doherty Associates book"

"The 'Nameless' detective is doing his best to settle into semiretirement after making his longtime assistant, Tamara Corbin, a partner in the agency and adding Jake Runyon, a former cop, as a field operative. However, some cases require Nameless' attention. Thugs are roaming the streets of San Francisco's Castro district, attacking gay men. Runyon's son's lover is one of the thug's victims, prompting Runyon and Nameless to investigate. Meanwhile Tamara, on a routine surveillance of a credit deadbeat, sees her subject carry something into his house that raises the hair on the back of her neck. The long-running Nameless series continues to evolve. With the novels no longer exclusively first-person narratives by Nameless, parallel plotlines have been introduced from multiple points of view, giving readers a chance to view Nameless as others see him. And, as always, the novels are never just about crime." Booklist

The other side of silence; a novel of suspense. Walker and Co. 2008 216p $24

ISBN 978-0-8027-1713-9; 0-8027-1713-6

A "suspense novel set in Las Vegas and California's Mohave Desert. While camping in the desert, Rick Fallon, a corporate security officer whose marriage has finally crumbled in the wake of his son's accidental death, comes across Casey Dunbar, who's tried and failed to kill herself after months of fruitlessly searching for her young son, who's been abducted by her ex-husband. Fallon empathizes with the woman, and what follows is a good old-fashioned search-and-capture mission with all the usual Pronzini virtues: a simple yet disciplined prose style; a strong, multilayered central character; and a compelling plot that builds to a nice little closing twist." Publ Wkly

Quarry; a "Nameless Detective" mystery. Delacorte Press 1992 216p o.p.

* LC 91-15284

In this novel the "Nameless Detective hunts for a methodical, brutal stranger who is pursuing withdrawn Grady Haas, 31, daughter of rancher Arlo Haas, the detective's old friend. Secretive Grady won't tell why she has suddenly left her job as an insurance adjuster specializing in marine claims and returned to the Salinas Valley. Nameless finds that her San Francisco apartment has been thoroughly tossed. All he has to go on are the three claims Grady had been investigating and her ex-boyfriend's savage beating by a stranger seeking Grady's whereabouts." Publ Wkly

"Pronzini can get a shade overwrought . . . but his detective is a welcome journey into yesterday, where a shamus could bend the law and not have to agonize about it for too long afterwards." Booklist

Savages; a nameless detective novel. Forge 2007 300p $24.95

ISBN 978-7653-0933-4; 0-7653-0933-5

"San Francisco detective Nameless is asked by a former client to look into the death of her sister, who was trapped in an unhappy marriage. Althought the death had been ruled an accident, Nameless soon finds himself stymied by ethical questions and lack of evidence. Meanwhile, Jake Runyon, a partner in Nameless's agency, is trying to serve a subpoena and gets caught in a case of serial arson and murder. It is hard to find a better crime writer than Pronzini, and his understanding of feminine angst as well as male motivations has made this one of the best detective series ever." Libr J

Spook; a nameless detective novel. Carroll & Graf Pubs. 2003 233p $25

ISBN 0-7867-1086-1

"The case seems simple enough. Spook, a homeless street person, becomes a fixture at a local business; its employees provide assistance as needed for the obviously mentally disturbed individual. He is murdered in an especially heinous assault. His unofficial 'family' wants San Francisco private investigator 'Nameless' to learn his real identity. Nameless hands the case over to his newly hired field operative, Jake Runyon, a former Seattle cop. . . . A fascinating entry in a series that continues to redefine noir fiction even as it honors its roots." Booklist

Step to the graveyard easy. Walker & Co. 2002 165p $21.95 o.p.

ISBN 0-8027-3375-1

* LC 2001-55914

"Matt Cape is 35 and stuck in a rut: when his wife catches him in bed with another woman, he quits his job and takes to the road, leaving his old life (or lack thereof) behind. He heads south, then west, eventually landing in San Francisco, where he is fleeced in a card game by Boone Judson and his sidekick, Tanya. Cape gets his and the other players' money back, along with some mysterious photographs. He returns the money to its owners and follows the cardsharps to Lake Tahoe, where he also tracks down the people in the photos and warns them that they may be in danger." Publ Wkly

"Compelling modern noir with a thought-provoking conclusion." Booklist

A wasteland of strangers. Walker & Co. 1997 257p $22.95

ISBN 0-8027-3301-8   LC 96-50927

"Beneath the surface in the northern California resort community of Pomo swirls a viper's nest of desire, jealousy, loneliness, and crime. When a sexual assault occurs, the obvious suspect is an outsider, John Faith; after all, the sheriff doesn't like Faith's interest in a sexy local widow he fancies himself. Neither does a boozy reporter, who launches a yellow-journalism campaign against the outsider. When the widow is murdered, the town explodes." Booklist

"The story fairly tears along to the jolting climax. Even after everyone has his or her say in the epilogue, readers still don't know John Faith's secrets. But that mystery is more haunting than maddening. Pronzini's . . . story is a gem." Publ Wkly

Prose, Francine, 1947-

Blue angel; a novel. HarperCollins Pubs. 2000 314p $25

ISBN 0-06-019541-X

* LC 99-40564

This novel "charts the downward spiral of a creative writing professor caught up in a sexual harassment scandal. Ten years ago, Ted Swenson wrote a major novel

Prose, Francine, 1947-—*Continued*

about growing up with a crazy father who later killed himself. Now Swenson's blocked on a new novel with a contrived plot and hasn't written anything in years. An autobiographical writer in the throes of a mid-life crisis, he feels he's suffocating in his comfortable, boring job at a small New England college, stuck with a predictable wife, a sullen daughter, and a life that offers him nothing to write about. So he becomes entranced by his most talented student, Angela, a girl with numerous facial piercings who can spin a page-burning novel out of her imagination." Libr J

An "ironic gloss on Von Sternberg's tragedy of erotic abasement. . . . Prose's retelling focuses less on the ridiculous and self-destructive behavior of the professor . . . than on the far more laughable (and hazardous) rigidity of the politically correct behavior codes governing his tiny Vermont campus." New Yorker

A changed man; a novel; Francine Prose. HarperCollins Publishers 2005 421p $24.95

ISBN 0-06-019674-2   LC 2004-47448

A "satire of liberal pieties, the radical right and the fund-raising world. The 'changed man' of the title is Vincent Nolan, a 32-year-old tattooed ex-skinhead who appears one morning in the New York offices of World Brotherhood Watch, a foundation headed by Meyer Maslow, a Holocaust survivor. Vincent declares that he has had a personal conversion (never mind that it was triggered by a heavy dose of Ecstasy) and wants to work with the foundation to 'save guys like me from becoming guys like me.' Meyer takes Vincent on faith—and convinces Bonnie Kalen, the foundation's fundraiser, to put Vincent up in the suburban home she shares with her two sons, Max, 12, and Danny, 16. Prose tears into this unusual premise with the piercing wit that has become her trademark." Publ Wkly

Goldengrove; a novel. HarperCollins Publishers 2008 275p $24.95

ISBN 978-0-06-621411-5; 0-06-621411-4

LC 2008-02112

In this novel, "narrator Nico, 13, comes upon Gerard Manley Hopkins's 'Spring and Fall' (which opens 'Margaret, are you grieving/ Over Goldengrove unleaving?') in her father's upstate New York bookstore, also named Goldengrove. It's the summer after her adored older sister, Margaret—possessed of beauty, a lovely singing voice and a poetic nature—casually dove from a rowboat in a nearby lake and drowned. In emotive detail, Nico relates the subsequent events of that summer. Nico was a willing confidant and decoy in Margaret's clandestine romance with a high school classmate, Aaron, and Nico now finds that she and Aaron are drawn to each other in their mutual bereavement. Unhinged by grief, Nico's parents are distracted and careless in their oversight of Nico, and Nico is deep in perilous waters before she realizes that she is out of her depth." Publ Wkly

"Nico's introduction into adult situations is accelerated and scary, and Prose doesn't handle the topic with kid gloves. As Nico's relationship with Aaron progresses, her thoughts about physical intimacy run rampant. Prose expertly conveys the newfound sexual desires teenagers experience as they grow into adults." Deseret News

Household saints. St. Martin's Press 1981 227p o.p.   LC 80-29116

"When Joseph Santangelo, the sausagemaker, wins the bride, Catherine, in a pinochle game, he sets in motion a pattern of events laced with ancient Mediterranean customs, superstition and religion that affect the women in his life. In addition to Catherine, there is his mother, a nonstop oracle of doom, and his Americanized daughter who seeks and perhaps finds Jesus in obsessive domesticity. A skillful fabulist, [the author] . . . not only captures the domestic scenes and smells of Little Italy but allows her 'naifs' to unfold in recognizable earthiness and warmth as they confront life's mysteries." Publ Wkly

Hunters and gatherers. Farrar, Straus & Giroux 1995 247p o.p.   LC 95-3569

This novel's "protagonist, Martha, is a relentlessly literal-minded person (she's a fact checker at a chic women's magazine) whose emotional life is a mess, and who takes up, in the wake of a failed romance, with a group of zany women who have allied themselves with a contemporary Goddess cult. Their leader, Isis Moonwagon, is a sweepingly compassionate but accident-prone former academic who sees visions but has to fight hard to keep her often brutally cynical troops in line." Publ Wkly

This is a "delightful satire, . . . irreverent, funny, critical, compassionate. . . . Prose brilliantly captures the absurdities and hypocrisies inherent in such groups. The women obsess about wombs, menstrual periods and the glories of being female. Yet separatism does not remove the worst dynamics between women." Women's Rev Books

Primitive people. Farrar, Straus & Giroux 1992 227p

ISBN 0-374-23722-0

* LC 91-28692

"Simone is an illegal immigrant from Haiti, working as an au pair for a family in upstate New York. There, she learns about American life from the shallow, self-centered 'primitive people' around her: her employer Rosemary, who is camping out with her withdrawn children in the ancestral home of her estranged husband; Rosemary's brittle and caustic best friend Shelly, an interior decorator; and Shelly's narcissistic, sexually ambiguous boyfriend Kenny, who owns a children's hair salon." Libr J

This "comedy of manners has a serious purpose but it is never earnest and provides a lot of shrewd and malicious fun. . . . The author finds it hard to write a dull sentence. Her gargoyles are sometimes gruesome. They are also witty and she has a perfect ear for the chatter of this particular set of rich Americans." Economist

Proulx, Annie

Accordion crimes; [by] E. Annie Proulx. Scribner 1996 381p

ISBN 0-684-19548-8   LC 96-16299

"Following successive owners of an accordion—from its creator, an Italian immigrant, who was lynched in Louisiana in 1891, to some fatherless black children living on the edge of a noxious landfill in 1991—this twelve-car pileup of a book brims with the sort of disasters you read about on the inside pages of the paper." New Yorker

Proulx, Annie—*Continued*

Bad dirt; Wyoming stories 2. Scribner 2004
219p $25

ISBN 0-7432-5799-5   LC 2004-56530

Contents: The hellhole; The Indian wars refought; The
trickle down effect; What kind of furniture would Jesus
pick?; The old badger game; Man crawling out of trees;
The contest; The Wamsutter wolf; Summer of the hot
tubs; Dump junk; Florida rental

"This poignant and often humorous collection is
packed with well-drawn characters that linger in the
mind and heart. As expected, the Wyoming landscape is
the enduring character in each story, silently wielding its
magical and brutal power." Libr J

Close range; Wyoming stories; watercolors by
William Matthews. Scribner 1999 283p il $23.50

ISBN 0-684-85221-7   LC 98-56066

Contents: The half-skinned steer; The mud below; 55
miles to the gas pump; The bunchgrass edge of the
world; A lonely coast; Job history; Pair of spurs; People
in Hell just want a drink of water; The governors of Wyoming; The blood bay; Brokeback Mountain

"Geography, splendid and terrible, is a tutelary deity to
the characters in 'Close Range': hardpan ranchers, battered cowpokes and bull riders, bar girls and bar brawl-
ers. Their lives are a futile uphill struggle conducted as
a downhill, out-of-control tearaway. Proulx writes of
them in a prose that is violent and impacted and mas-
tered just at the point where, having gone all the way to
the edge, it is about to go over." N Y Times Book Rev

Fine just the way it is; Wyoming stories 3.
Scribner 2008 221p $25

ISBN 978-1-4165-7166-7; 1-4165-7166-3
                                      LC 2008-13682

Contents: Family man; I've always loved this place;
Them old cowboy songs; The sagebrush kid; Great divide; Deep-blood-greasy-bowl; Swamp mischief; Testimony of the donkey; Tits-up in a ditch

This "collection of Wyoming tales, continues
[Proulx's] Dickensian delight in memorable nomencla-
ture. So, prepare to meet: Duck Slaver, Harp Daft, the
Grainblewer twins, Wacky Lipe, Fenk Fipps, Tug
Diceheart and more. Like Dickens, Proulx has a keen eye
for the eccentricity of the individual, admitting that 'everyone in the sparsely settled country' is noted for a
'salty dog quirk or talent' that their names might suggest.
. . . Proulx's writing can be as fine as anything being
produced in America today." Times Lit Suppl

Postcards; by E. Annie Proulx. Scribner 1992
308p il

ISBN 0-684-18718-3   LC 91-25089

"Postcards are the only communication between Loyal
Blood and the poor, hardworking farm family he leaves
behind in Vermont. The secret Loyal carries with him—
the accidental killing of his girlfriend, Billy—is revealed
in the first pages, and, thereafter, as he prospects for uranium, traps coyotes, or digs for dinosaur bones, his messages continue to arrive home from across the U.S., long
after his father has died and his brother, sister, and mother have moved away." Booklist

"Ms. Proulx's expansion of the concept of postcards is
what transforms a rambling tale into a minimalist saga.
. . . Story makes this novel compelling; technique makes
it beautiful. What makes 'Postcards' significant is that

Ms. Proulx uses both story and technique to make real
the history of post-World War II America." N Y Times
Book Rev

The shipping news. Scribner 1993 337p o.p.
                                    * LC 92-30315

The author tells "the story of a washed-up newspaperman who decides to resettle in the Newfoundland town
of his ancestors—bringing with him an elderly aunt and
two young daughters." Libr J

The author "blends Newfoundland argot, savage history, impressively diverse characters, fine descriptions of
weather and scenery, and comic horseplay without ever
lessening the reader's interest in Quoyle's progress from
bumbling outsider to capable journalist." Atlantic

That old ace in the hole; a novel. Scribner 2002
361p $26

ISBN 0-684-81307-6   LC 2002-30462

This novel's "hero, Bob Dollar, a decent sort who was
abandoned at 8, is sent by his company to Woolybucket,
Tex., to scout locations for factory hog farms, but is
soon smitten with the high, flat country, the locals and
their tales of stubborn ranchers, plagues of locusts and
family farms undone by corporate greed." N Y Times
Book Rev

Proust, Marcel, 1871-1922

The captive

In Proust, M. The captive [and] The fugitive

In Proust, M. Remembrance of things past
        p1-422

The captive [and] The fugitive; translated by
C.K. Scott Moncrieff & Terence Kilmartin; revised
by D.J. Enright. Modern Lib. 1993 957p (In search
of lost time, v5) $24.95

ISBN 0-679-42477-6   LC 93-15168

Sequel to Sodom and Gomorrah

Original French edition, 1923

In The captive "Albertine is living in the narrator's Paris home, where he attempts to keep complete watch on
her activities. The Verdurins provoke a scandalous rupture between Morel and Charlus. Albertine suddenly
flees, just as the narrator is ready to dismiss her. [In the
fugitive] the narrator seeks the return of Albertine, but
after her death he observes the gradual encroachment of
oblivion on grief until, on a trip to Venice, he finds his
pain completely cured. Gilberte has become the social-
climbing Mlle de Forcheville; she marries Saint-Loup,
who is now Morel's lover." Merriam-Webster's Ency of
Lit

Followed by Time regained

Cities of the plain [variant title: Sodom and Go-
morrah]

In Proust, M. Remembrance of things past
        p623-1169

The complete short stories of Marcel Proust;
compiled and translated by Joachim Neugroschel;
foreword by Roger Shattuck. Cooper Sq. Pubs.
2001 201p $25.95

ISBN 0-8154-1136-7   LC 00-65739

Proust, Marcel, 1871-1922—*Continued*

Contents: The death of Baldassare Silvande, Viscount of Sylvania; Violante or high society; Fragments of commedia dell'Arte; Social ambitions and musical tastes of Bouvard and Pécuchet; The melancholy summer of Madame de Breyves; Portraits of painters and composers; A young girl's confession; A dinner in high society; Regrets, reveries the color of time; The end of jealousy; Norman things; Memory; Portrait of Madame X.; Before the night; Another memory; The indifferent man

This collection contains Proust's "first literary endeavor, 'Pleasures and Days,' translated into English for the first time in 50 years, along with six additional stories, never before seen in English. . . . Delicately translated by Neugroschel . . . these early musings are priceless, insightful venturing into the mind of a maturing virtuoso." Booklist

The fugitive [variant title: The sweet cheat gone]

> *In* Proust, M. The captive [and] The fugitive
>
> *In* Proust, M. Remembrance of things past p425-706

The Guermantes way; translated by C.K. Scott Moncrieff and Terence Kilmartin; revised by D.J. Enright. Modern Lib. 1993 834p (In search of lost time, v3) $23.95

> ISBN 0-679-60028-0   LC 92-33975
>
> Sequel to Within a budding grove
>
> Original French edition published 1920-1921
>
> "The narrator, whose family have been tenants in the large Guermantes home in Paris, conducts his laborious ascent to the summit of high society, finally attending the duchesse de Guermantes's reception. He also describes Saint-Loup's passion for the actress and prostitute Rachel, and the death of his own beloved grandmother." Reader's Ency. 4th edition
>
> Followed by Sodom and Gomorrah
>
> > *also in* Proust, M. Remembrance of things past p3-620

Remembrance of things past. Random House 1981 3v

> ISBN 0-394-50643-X (set)
>
>   * LC 79-5542
>
> Includes the seven volumes, published separately and entered in this catalog. Volume one and two translated by C. K. Scott Moncrieff and Terence Kilmartin; volume three by C. K. Scott Moncrieff, Terence Kilmartin and Andreas Mayor
>
> Contents: v1: Swann's way; Within a budding grove; v2: The Guermantes way; Cities of the plain; v3: The captive; The fugitive (variant title: The sweet cheat gone); Time regained (variant title: The past recaptured)
>
> This "is the first complete English version of Proust's masterpiece, translated from the definitive 1954 Pléiade edition. Terence Kilmartin has checked the Scott Moncrieff translation (which comprised the first 11 volumes of the English language version and was made from the uneven first French edition) against the impeccable Clarac-Ferre Pléiade edition. The 12th volume, Andreas Mayor's 1970 translation of 'Time Regained' was the only English translation based on the Pléiade edition prior to this one and has been incorporated into it with only minor changes." Libr J

Sodom and Gomorrah; translated by C.K. Scott Moncrieff and Terence Kilmartin; revised by D.J. Enright. Modern Lib. 1993 747p (In search of lost time, v4) $22.95

> ISBN 0-679-60029-9   LC 92-27272
>
> Sequel to The Guermantes way
>
> Original French edition published 1921-1922. Variant title: Cities of the plain
>
> "Marcel again meets Swann at a reception given by the Princesse de Guermantes, a cousin of the Duchesse. Swann is now suffering from a deadly ailment. He is an ardent adherent of Alfred Dreyfus. Swann urges Marcel to write to Gilberte, since she speaks of him frequently. But Gilberte, no longer has any enchantment for Marcel; Albertine again holds his affections. She offers herself to him, but distracted by physical attachments for other owmen, he desires her company only at intervals to titillate his jaded senses. Eventually he is drawn closer to her, but now his suspicion that she is a Lesbian causes him jealousy and endless torment." Haydn. Thesaurus of Book Dig
>
> Followed by The captive

Swann's way; translated by C.K. Scott Moncrieff and Terence Kilmartin; revised by D.J. Enright. Modern Lib. 1992 xx, 615p (In search of lost time, v1) $21.95

> ISBN 0-679-60005-1   LC 92-25657
>
> Original French edition, 1913
>
> The first volume of the In search of lost time series "describes in an involved parenthetical style, with a multitude of details, the brilliant society in which the author moved. The 'Marcel' of the story is Proust's own counterpart, and it is through his hypersensitive and critical eye that we examine the tastes, feelings, motives and actions of the characters, most of whom can be identified as real people." Enoch Pratt Free Libr
>
> Followed by Within a budding grove
>
> > *also in* Proust, M. Remembrance of things past p3-462

Time regained; translated by Andreas Mayor and Terence Kilmartin; revised by D.J. Enright. Modern Lib. 1993 749p (In search of lost time, v6) $24.95

> ISBN 0-679-42476-8   LC 93-3628
>
> Sequel to The fugitive
>
> Original French edition, 1927
>
> In this final volume of the series "World War I accelerates the kaleidoscopic changes in society. The narrator attends a reception of the new princesse de Guermantes, actually the former Mme Verdurin, and finds most of his acquaintances almost unrecognizable. He has enjoyed three 'privileged moments' of memory, and in contemplating them discovers that his vocation is to be the shaping of his experiences into a literary work of art." Reader's Ency. 4th edition

Time regained [variant title: The past recaptured]

> > *also in* Proust, M. Remembrance of things past p709-1107

Proust, Marcel, 1871-1922—*Continued*

Within a budding grove; translated by C.K. Scott Moncrieff and Terence Kilmartin; revised by D.J. Enright. Modern Lib. 1992 749p (In search of lost time, v2) $24

ISBN 0-679-60006-X   LC 92-25656

Sequel to Swann's way

Original French edition, 1918

"As he grows up, Marcel falls in love with Swann's daughter, Gilberte. It is a deep and poetic attachment, but she gradually tires of him; his ardent nature and his attentions begin to irritate her. Out of wounded pride he avoids her, although he continues his friendly relations with the Swanns. Two years later he feels he is thoroughly cured of his hopeless passion, when he becomes involved with Albertine, a beautiful brunette he meets in Balbec. But he eventually discovers that she is interested only in platonic relations with men, and so he suffers another disappointment." Haydn. Thesaurus of Book Dig

Followed by The Guermantes way

also in Proust, M. Remembrance of things past p465-1018

Puig, Manuel

Kiss of the spider woman; translated from the Spanish by Thomas Colchie. Knopf 1979 281p o.p.

     * LC 78-14307

Original Spanish edition, 1976

"Mostly consisting of dialogue between two men in an Argentine jail cell, the novel traces the development of their unlikely friendship. Molina is a middle-aged homosexual who passes the long hours in prison by acting out scenes from his favorite movies. Valentin is a young socialist revolutionary, who initially berates Molina for his effeminacy and his lack of political conviction. Sharing the hardships of a six-month prison term, the two eventually forge a strong relationship that becomes sexual. In an ironic role reversal at the end of the novel, Molina dies as a result of his involvement in politics while Valentin escapes the pain of torture by retreating into a dream world." Merriam-Webster's Ency of Lit

Purdy, James, 1914-2009

In a shallow grave. Arbor House 1975 140p

ISBN 0-87795-124-4

     * LC 75-30399

"Garnet Montrose is a man severely disfigured in the war, a modern leper, an often drugged prophet of the disintegration of values. Unwilling to hide in a veteran's hospital, Montrose returns to his home in Virginia. Obsessed with a childhood sweetheart, now the widow Georgina Rance, he devises an elaborate system of correspondence to woo her, depending on his 'applicants' to carry letters to the lady. The relationship with these applicants forms the basis of the book. Quintus Pearch is quiet and mysterious, a wraithlike character who reads to Montrose from abstract tomes and rubs his master's feet with cynical adoration. Potter Daventry is a wild young man with twisted values and a go-for-broke attitude. Daventry courts Georgina for Montrose, then for himself. He marries her and is carried away by a freak storm. The implications are biblical in proportion; Purdy utilizes ev-

ery subtlety and shading of language to enhance the demented howlings of these three lost souls. Purdy's skill consists of taking the familiar and distorting it; the results are often eerie." Independent Publisher

The nephew. Farrar Straus and Cudahy 1960 210p o.p.

     * LC 60-15672

This novel "tells of the revelations following the death in war of the nephew of a doting spinster, a retired schoolteacher, in a small Midwest town, who decides to write a memorial booklet. She thereby learns more than she wants to about him and about life as she discovers he was a homosexual." Oxford Companion to Am Lit. 6th edition

Pushkin, Aleksandr Sergeevich, 1799-1837

Alexander Pushkin: complete prose fiction; translated with an introduction and notes, by Paul Debreczeny; verse passages translated by Walter Arndt. Stanford Univ. Press 1983 545p $60

ISBN 0-8047-1142-9

     * LC 81-85450

Included in this volume are the following titles: The blackamoor of Peter the Great; A novel in letters; The tales of the late Ivan Petrovich Belkin; A history of the village of Goriukhino; Roslavlev; Dubrovskii; The Queen of Spades; Kirdzhali; Egyptian nights; and the novel: The captain's daughter

Also included are the following unfinished fictional fragments: The guests were arriving at the dacha; In the corner of a small square; A tale of Roman life; We were spending the evening at Princess D's dacha; Maria Schoning

This collection also contains the non-fictional History of Pugachev (which furnishes historical background for The captain's daughter) and Appendices which contain minor fictional fragments and outlines

"The translations are accurate and graceful and well supported by an ample array of footnotes." Libr J

The captain's daughter

In Pushkin, A. S. Alexander Pushkin: complete prose fiction p266-357

Putney, Mary Jo

A kiss of fate. Ballantine Bks. 2004 340p $23.95

ISBN 0-345-44916-9

"Born into a legendary family of mages known as the Guardians, Gwyneth Owens believes that she has little inherited power. She does, however, have a destiny to fulfill. When the Guardian elders seek to forestall a coming disaster by invoking her Guardian oath and asking her to marry Duncan Macrae, Lord Ballister, the most powerful weather mage in the realm, she cannot honorably refuse. Although they are already attracted to each other, Gwyneth can't forget the single kiss from him that sent alarming visions of destruction flaming through her mind—or the sword that he held in his hand. Intelligent, compelling characters that appeal to both heart and mind, a brilliant blending of history and fantasy, and a beautifully unfolding love relationship combine to produce a magical tale." Libr J

Puzo, Mario, 1920-1999

The family; a novel; completed by Carol Gino. ReganBooks 2001 373p il

ISBN 0-06-039445-5   LC 2001-31876

"In his final novel, 'The Family' Puzo died in 1999, and this book was completed by his companion, the novelist Carol Gino-he has dipped back into 15th-century Italy to tell the tale of the Borgia family, led by Cardinal Rodrigo Borgia, who became Pope Alexander VI." N Y Times Book Rev

"The saga is lush, full of detail, with characters who manage to be larger than life while seeming entirely realistic. The dialogue is slightly ornmented but never clumsy, and the plot is appropriately epic in scope, mixing fact and fiction seamlessly." Booklist

The godfather. Putnam 1969 446p $24.95

ISBN 0-399-10342-2

This novel focuses on "Vito (Don) Corleone, boss of an important New York City Mafia family. Names, places, crimes have been changed, but the Mafia world remains true to fact. Here is Cosa Nostra: the wars of the competing families; their changing 'business enterprises'; their struggle for power and money; their weapons—graft, guns, spies, violence, murder. A wide variety of characters are colorfully drawn. The Don comes though as a person you will remember." Libr J

The last Don. Random House 1996 482p o.p.

LC 96-3401

"The story opens in 1965, with Don Clericuzio, head of the most powerful Mafia family in the country, deciding to make his enterprises legit. He is looking ahead to his grandchildren's lives, wanting them to enjoy his largesse without the danger inherent in life in the criminal underworld. Zoom—we're transported to the present day and involved in how the don's plans for his family's future are playing out. Hollywood and Las Vegas provide venues for one grandson's attempts, at the expense of another grandson, to undermine the master plan." Booklist

"Mr. Puzo wraps up his intricate plot with the same ingenuity he exhibits throughout this satisfying novel." N Y Times Book Rev

The Sicilian. Linden Press 1984 410p o.p.

LC 84-17087

This novel "follows the wayward career of one handsome, charismatic renegade, Salvatore (Turi) Guilliano, who creates and works at enhancing his romantic hero image. While the peasants of postwar Sicily adore Turi, the Mafia leaders resent his territorial infringements. . . . After seven years of increasing difficulties, Turi can do no more: with the help of the exiled Michael Corleone (son of the Godfather), he attempts to escape to America." Libr J

"Perhaps only an American writer with deep Sicilian roots and passions could have succeeded as Mr. Puzo has in symbolizing a desperate society through the deeds of a desperado, and in revealing how thin is the line that often separates a freedom-fighter from a terrorist." N Y Times Book Rev

Pye, Michael, 1946-

The pieces from Berlin. Knopf 2002 335p $24

ISBN 0-375-41436-3   LC 2002-20524

This novel "examines the shady life of fictional Lucia Muller-Ross, who spirited vanloads of valuable antiques entrusted to her by their Jewish owners out of Berlin and into Switzerland at the end of WWII. Sixty years later, Lucia is the elderly, proud and respected owner of an antiques shop in Zurich, when Sarah Freeman, a Holocaust survivor, spies in the store's window a table she once owned. Sarah's anguished need for emotional restitution sparks a tragic upheaval in Lucia's family." Publ Wkly

"Pye writes well, and this is a mature novel. It must also be said that it is not an easy novel, in its themes or its structure. A lot of assembling and clue-tracking is required to make sense of the narrative. It's a page-turner, but often one is turning the pages backward to find some lost, or tenuous, connection. Yet this hard work seems appropriate, even necessary." N Y Times Book Rev

Pym, Barbara

Civil to strangers

In Pym, B. Civil to strangers and other writings p7-170

Civil to strangers and other writings. Dutton 1988 c1987 388p o.p.   LC 87-30341

First published 1987 in the United Kingdom

This is a volume of selections from Pym's unpublished writings. It contains a complete novel, Civil to strangers, written in 1936, sections of three others: Gervase and Flora, Home front novel, and So very secret, written between 1937 and 1941, four short stories (So, some tempestuous morn; Goodbye Balkan capital; The Christmas visit; Across a crowded room) and a radio talk

"We are not often given the chance to witness a writer's struggle to find a voice. But this 'last sheaf,' blemishes and all, shows us how very hard Barbara Pym worked for the voice she eventually found." N Y Times Book Rev

Excellent women. Dutton 1978 c1952 256p o.p.

LC 78-19877

First published 1952 in the United Kingdom

"Mildred Lathbury, 30ish, a spinster, a clergyman's daughter, is an excellent woman, one who, with no life of her own to speak of, finds herself somewhat unwillingly a part of the lives of others. Her days are made up of small things—church, flowers, dinner with the bachelor vicar and his sister, brief encounters with neighbors. . . . Pym's singular world is a lonely, bittersweet familiar place. She travels it with rueful wit, views the human landscape with a wise, sharp, compassionate eye." Publ Wkly

Jane and Prudence. Dutton 1981 222p o.p.

LC 81-68399

First published 1953 in the United Kingdom

"Jane is the somewhat scatterbrained wife of a country vicar; Prudence, once her student at Oxford, works at a 'vague cultural organization' in London, where she alternately revels in and despairs over her unrequited passion for the rather dreary little man who is her employer. As she goes about doing 'those tasks in the parish that seem within her powers,' Jane knows she really is unsuited to be a clergyman's wife—she somehow never seems to have the right money for the collection plate—but she does love Nicholas. And in her good-hearted, if usually

Pym, Barbara—*Continued*

ineffectual, way she tries to look after Prudence too, hoping to supply a suitable man for her younger friend." Libr J

Quartet in autumn. Dutton 1978 c1977 218p o.p.
LC 78-58498

First published 1977 in the United Kingdom

This novel "follows the lives and thoughts of four elderly single people on the verge of retirement, in a society that has no time for them but relegates them to the impersonal care of the Welfare State. Here Pym achieves something of a tour de force, showing, with wit and compassion, how ordinary quirky acts of impulsive kindness and human feeling make the difference between despair and hope." Libr J

The sweet dove died. Dutton 1979 c1978 208p o.p.
LC 78-74024

First published 1978 in the United Kingdom

"Leonora Eyre is single, beautiful, fastidious, slightly affected, more than slightly vain. Approaching 50, she attracts a widowed antique dealer, Humphrey, whom she decides to bypass for his 24-year-old nephew, James. . . . Leonora asks, she thinks, no more than the pleasure of James's company, but [then tries] . . . to eliminate her rivals, first a feckless young woman named Phoebe, then a more formidable foe, an American homosexual who plays power games more openly and ruthlessly than Leonora can." Newsweek

"Pym's extraordinary vision of an ordinary world wherein she details the intricacies of loneliness, the ditherings of hesitating souls, the comedies of errors, sexual and asexual makes this a little masterpiece." Publ Wkly

An unsuitable attachment. Dutton 1982 256p
ISBN 0-525-24117-5
* LC 82-70741

"The world of which Pym writes is the Anglican parish with its attractive young vicar; his wife, overly devoted to her cat; the unmarried sister-in-law and her garish dress; the veterinarian and his sister; the shy anthropologist. 'An unsuitable attachment' refers to that formed between John, a young, sometime actor, and Ianthe, an older librarian." Libr J

"The bygone mysteries of the Church of England and the lost snobberies of empire return as ghostly and gently comic echoes of themselves in the habits and pretensions of Barbara Pym's people, who, like the good antiques that furnish their rented bed-sitters . . . are no longer quite appropriate to the present day." N Y Times Book Rev

Pynchon, Thomas

Against the day. Penguin Press 2006 1085p $35
ISBN 1-59420-120-X
LC 2006-50714

"The improbable action begins onboard a hydrogen skyship, the Inconvenience, manned by the Chums of Chance, a fabled do-gooder aeronautics club on its way to Chicago for the 1893 World's Columbian Exposition. Aside from some Jules Verne-like voyages beneath the earth's surface, the bickering Chums provide an aerial view of the carnivalesque proceedings as this many-voiced saga modulates in tone from cliffhanger jocularity to metaphysical speculation, lyricism, and devilish satire. As Pynchon whirls his way through such milestones as

the invention of dynamite, harnessing of electricity, evolution of photography and movies, development of diabolical weapons, and the bloody turmoil in the Balkans and the Ottoman Empire leading up to World War I, his motley characters circle the globe on quests for enlightenment, profit, revenge, romance, and sanctuary." Booklist

"For all its brilliant passages, this is the book that makes you wonder whether even Pynchon knows what lies behind all those veils he's always urging us to part. But wouldn't you know it? Even when he jumps the shark, he does it with an agility that can take your breath away." Time

The crying of lot 49. Lippincott 1966 183p o.p.
*

"Oedipa Maas becomes a coexecutor of the estate of her former multi-millionaire lover, Pierce Inverarity. She becomes involved in tracking down the significance of a geometric symbol that appears to have some connection with the existence of an ancient, revolutionary mail service. In this search, she meets a strange assortment of characters, loses her husband, her psychiatrist (named Hilarious!), and her lover. The author aims his arrows at many of those phenomena that have turned people into things. Among his targets are rock 'n' roll (a group called 'The Paranoids'), right-wing extremists, and a strange group called Inamorati Anonymous." Shapiro. Fic for Youth. 3d edition

Gravity's rainbow. Viking 1973 760p
ISBN 0-670-34832-5
*

The antihero of this novel "is Tyrone Slothrop, an American lieutenant stationed in London during the Blitz. . . . The Lieutenant becomes the equipment of PISCES (Psychological Intelligence Schemes for Expediting Surrender) when his bizarre gift is discovered: Slothrop erections anticipate German rocket launchings. . . . In his desperate attempts to avoid being taken over as a pure instrument, Slothrop runs for it, from London to the Riviera to Berlin, pursued by Furles disguised as Baggy-pants comedians." Atlantic

"Fiction allows at last what was forbidden to the original suffering poets and novelists of 1914-18—the utmost in obscene description, the limit of masochistic pornography. If 'Gravity's Rainbow' is often nauseating it is in a good cause. This is the war book to end them all." Burgess. 99 Novels

Inherent vice. Penguin Press 2009 369p $27.95
ISBN 978-1-59420-224-7; 1-59420-224-9
LC 2009-07705

"An account of the adventures of a hippie private eye pursuing assorted nonlucrative commissions in a Southern California beach town around 1970, 'Inherent Vice' is a sun-struck, pot-addled shaggy dog story that fuses the sulky skepticism of Raymond Chandler with the good-natured scrappiness of 'The Big Lebowski.' It's an inspired formula; the mystery plot supplies the novel with a minimum of structure (as well as confidence that there's some point to the enterprise) and the genre provides ample cover for Pynchon's literary weaknesses." Salon

Mason & Dixon. Holt & Co. 1997 773p $27.50
ISBN 0-8050-3758-6
LC 97-6467

Pynchon, Thomas—_Continued_

"From historical odds and ends and the Field Journal they left behind, Pynchon re-imagines Mason and Dixon before, during and after the four-plus years, 1763-1767, they took to draw their 244-mile-long line through the American wilderness, dividing the proprietorships of the Penns of Pennsylvania and the Calverts of Maryland, ordaining our North and South. From his omnivorous reading, with his diabolical genius for mimicry, he also re-creates their tumultuous era." Nation

V.; a novel. Lippincott 1963 492p o.p.

*

This novel is a "parody of the 'Black Humor' techniques it employs. The multiple plots involve the _schlemiel_ Benny Profane, a hunter of alligators in New York's sewers, and Herbert Stencil, who becomes obsessed by his pursuit of V., an initial he found in his dead father's notebooks. V.'s various manifestations include a femme fatale, a spy, and a hag who happened to be present at every significant event in Europe from 1890 to World War II." Reader's Ency. 4th edition

Vineland. Little, Brown 1990 385p o.p.
LC 89-13025

"Vineland, a zone of blessed anarchy in northern California, is the last refuge of hippiedom, a culture devasted by the sobriety epidemic, Reaganomics, and the Tube. Here, in an Orwellian 1984, Zoyd Wheeler and his daughter Prairie search for Prairie's long-lost mother, a Sixties radical who ran off with a narc." Libr J

This is "manifestly the work of a man of quick intelligence and quirky invention. Many of its episodes flicker with an appealingly far-flung humor. And Pynchon displays throughout Vineland what might be called an internal loyalty: he keeps the faith with the generally feckless and almost invariably inarticulate misfits he assembles, tracking their looping thoughts and indecisive actions with a patience that seems grounded in affection." N Y Rev Books

Pyper, Andrew

The killing circle. St. Martin's Minotaur 2008 321p $24.95
ISBN 978-0-312-38476-0; 0-312-38476-9
LC 2008-20635

"Patrick Rush is a lonely widower, a wannabe novelist, and the father of a young son. He joins a writer's workshop or, as its leader refers to it, a 'circle.' The leader is a minor novelist from the seventies who disappeared from the Toronto literary scene after some scathing reviews and allegations of criminal sexual behavior. During the circle's weekly meetings, Patrick is mesmerized by the writing of a young girl whose unadorned yet ethereal prose reveals an intensely personal childhood story of abandonment, abuse, and stalking by the Sandman, a character who may be real, may be symbolic, and may have followed her to Toronto. Bodies are turning up in Patrick's neighborhood, and Patrick's concern for the safety of his son grows, even as the readings in the circle—and the behavior of its leader—become more ominous." Booklist

The novel is "gorgeously written and thoroughly unnerving. . . . Taken as either a classy ghost story or the chronicle of one man's mental breakdown, this is a terrific yarn." N Y Times Book Rev

Pywell, Sharon L.

What happened to Henry; [by] Sharon Pywell. G.P. Putnam's Sons 2004 292p $19.95
ISBN 0-399-15168-0
LC 2003-62239

The plot of this novel revolves around a "tightly knit family. Henry, Lauren, and Winston Cooper are 10, 7, and 5 in 1960, when their newborn sister dies of SIDS. Henry pulls his younger siblings through their grief while their mother is barely functioning and their father is lost in his work. But four years later, Henry begins to crack, becoming obsessed with a picture of a man near Hiroshima's firestorm. . . . A powerful novel full of surprises, unbreakable sibling bonds, and insightful reflection on the power of love to overcome grief." Booklist

Q

Qashu, Sayed, 1975-

Dancing Arabs; translated from the Hebrew by Miriam Shlesinger. Grove Press 2004 227p $24
ISBN 0-8021-4126-9
LC 2003-67765
Original Hebrew edition, 2002

"After solving a quiz-show riddle, the young Palestinian protagonist earns the rare opportunity to study at a Jewish university in Jerusalem. There is hope for him, so we suspect, and for his village and people. In Jerusalem, though, he feels the truth of his father's pessimism ('once an Arab, always an Arab, and you don't stand a chance') and finds and forfeits forbidden love with Naomi. Yet nationalism, optimism, and his family's hope that his intelligence will lead to the first Arab atom bomb fizzle out and leave a headachy and resentful middle-aged man, unhappily married to an Arab wife back in the borderlands." Booklist

Qiu Xiaolong, 1953-

Red mandarin dress. St. Martin's Minotaur 2007 320p
ISBN 978-0-312-37107-4; 0-312-37107-1
LC 2007-44109

In this mystery featuring Shanghai's Chief Inspector Chen, "young women, clad in torn, red mandarin dresses—hose with slits on the sides to show attractive legs—start turning up dead in public places. Chen is away, pursuing his love of literature, and the case bumps along, murder victim after murder victim, and the Shanghai police department looks incompetent in its duty of protecting the public. Then Chen becomes re-engaged halfway through the book, and the story takes off at a brisk pace. The suspense, and the way Qiu weaves in the human wreckage caused by Mao Zedong's Cultural Revolution, gives one of contemporary fiction's best pictures yet of the wrenching changes facing China as it struggles with its recent, wretched past." St. Louis Post-Dispatch

When red is black. Soho Press 2004 309p $25
ISBN 1-569-47369-2
LC 2003-23436

"When Yin Lige, the author of a banned book, is found murdered in her Shanghai apartment, detective Yu Guangming and his boss, Chief Inspector Chen Cao, must solve a case that may have far-reaching political and social implications." Publ Wkly

Qiu Xiaolong, 1953-—_Continued_

This mystry "offers a complex and riveting portrait of Shanghai, a city in transition from a proletarian dictatorship to a capitalist playground." Washington Post Book World

Queen, Ellery

The best of Ellery Queen; four decades of stories from The mystery masters; edited by Francis M. Nevins, Jr. and Martin H. Greenberg. Beaufort Bks. 1985 238p o.p.   LC 84-21572

Contents: The glass-domed clock; The bearded lady; The mad tea-party; Man bites dog; Mind over matter; The inner circle; The Dauphin's doll; The three widows; Snowball in July; My queer Dean!; GI story; Miracles do happen; Last man to die; Abraham Lincoln's clue; Wedding anniversary

A fine and private place. World Pub. 1971 214p o.p.

"The 'padrone,' Nino Importuna, heads a huge conglomerate. He catches one of his executives embezzling, and as the price of freedom, demands that he hand over his young daughter as the aging Nino's bride. Of course, this is the perfect setup for murder. First Nino's two brothers, who share in the conglomerate, die, then Nino himself. For the solution, Ellery Queen returns to his (their) original style of detection—a stream of bizarre clues that confuse the detective Queen no end." Publ Wkly

The Roman hat mystery; a problem in deduction. Stokes, F.A. 1929 325p o.p.

"Inspector Richard Queen and his son Ellery tackle a puzzling murder with immense thoroughness and almost fatiguing pertinacity. Though the egregious bonhomie of the Queens and Ellery's pseudo bookishness occasionally irritate, the neatness of the plot involving a missing hat in a theater murder cannot be denied. But the police procedure is not what it would be now, and the criminal's luck in carrying out his complex plan strains the believables." Barzun. Cat of Crime. Rev and enl edition

The tragedy of X
    _In_ Queen, E. The XYZ murders p7-216

The tragedy of Y
    _In_ Queen, E. The XYZ murders p217-419

The tragedy of Z
    _In_ Queen, E. The XYZ murders p421-575

The XYZ murders; three mysteries in one volume complete and unabridged: The tragedy of X; The tragedy of Y; The tragedy of Z. Lippincott 1961 575p o.p.

These books were originally published under the name of Barnaby Ross in 1932, 1932 and 1933 respectively

Drury Lane, retired Shakespearean actor and brilliant connoisseur of crime, helps New York City's District Attorney Bruno and Inspector Thumm solve the mysteries

Quick, Amanda, 1948-

For works written by this author under other names see Krentz, Jayne Ann, 1948-

I thee wed. Bantam Bks. 1999 341p $23.95
ISBN 0-553-10084-X   LC 98-37168

"Strong-willed, and with a redhead's combustible temper, paid companion Emma Greyson finds herself embroiled in a dangerous adventure with the dashing Edison Stokes. A wealthy member of Regency England's 'Polite World,' Stokes follows the clue in a dying man's last words to arrive at Ware Castle, where he suspects a dark plot is underway. At the castle he encounters Emma, who stands out among the era's decadent and depraved society as a woman of sharp intelligence. . . . Attractive protagonists, loose bodices, thwarted love and odds overcome prove themselves once again the ingredients for success in this genre." Publ Wkly

Late for the wedding. Bantam Bks. 2003 322p $24.95
ISBN 0-553-80271-2   LC 2002-34254

"The killer, an insider with easy access to the opulent homes of Regency England's elite, has left his calling card, a memento-mori ringa jeweled, coffin-topped band with a white skull inside. He's clever, but not nearly clever enough to fool the fearless team of Lavinia Lake and Tobias March." Booklist

"As this engaging effort demonstrates, Quick has the Regency-murder mystery mix down to a fine science." Publ Wkly

The paid companion. Putnam 2004 418p $24.95
ISBN 0-399-15174-5   LC 2003-62348

"Elenora Lodge is in quite a fix. Her stepfather lost her farm and all of her possessions in a mining venture, and her fiance dumps her faster than the proverbial hot potato. But Elenora is practical and pragmatic. So when Arthur Lancaster, earl of St. Merryn, offers her a position as a paid companion, she accepts. St. Merryn is in a bit of a fix himself. His favorite uncle has been murdered, and he's sworn vengeance on the killer, a mad alchemist intent on perfecting the ultimate weapon of mass destruction. Unfortunately, St. Merryn's fiancee has also dumped him, and his renewed status as one of London's most eligible bachelors is interfering with his quest for justice, hence his paying Elenora to pose as his new fiancee. . . . {Quick} mixes humor, suspense, and tantalizing historical detail with all the savory ingredients her fans have come to expect: a feisty, resourceful heroine; a hero with a decidedly dangerous edge; witty repartee; and strongly appealing secondary characters." Booklist

Slightly shady. Bantam Bks. 2001 343p
ISBN 0-553-80188-0   LC 00-58528

"Londoner Lavinia Lake had made a comfortable home for herself and her niece, running an antique store in Rome. Little did she know, however, that a band of thieves was using her quaint little shop for their illegal purposes. This bit of information was made perfectly clear to Lavinia when one Tobias March barged in and began tearing the antique shop—junk shop, to be more precise—apart, searching for incriminating evidence." Booklist

"Arch humor and the expert removal of bodices are Quick's stock in trade, and the old formula still works splendidly." Publ Wkly

Wicked widow. Bantam Bks. 2000 297p
ISBN 0-553-10087-4   LC 99-59194

"Regency-era historical romance features Madeline Deveridge, a misunderstood London widow with a reputation for murder, and the strapping Artemis Hunt, a secret owner of the Dream Pavilions, a popular pleasure

Quick, Amanda, 1948-—*Continued*

garden. When one of Madeline's maids is abducted outside the Dream Pavilions, she blackmails Artemis into helping her in the rescue. . . . A delicious combination of adventure and romance, this lively tale keeps the reader enthralled from start to finish." Booklist

Quill, Monica, 1929-

For works written by this author under other names see McInerny, Ralph M., 1929-

Quindlen, Anna

Black and blue. Random House 1998 293p $23
ISBN 0-679-43539-5   LC 97-25208
This novel's "protagonist is Frannie Benedetto, a 37-year-old Brooklyn housewife, mother and nurse who finally finds the courage to escape from her violent husband Bobby, a New York City cop. Under an assumed identity in a tacky central Florida town, Frannie and her 10-year-old son, Robert, attempt to build a new life, but there is a price to pay, and when it comes, it carries the heartstopping logic of inevitability and the irony of fate." Publ Wkly

"Following fault lines of power, dependence, and love, Quindlen takes her heroine to a bereaved country where there are no answers, only choices; in Brooklyn-born Frannie, she has created an utterly believable, flinty character." New Yorker

Blessings; a novel. Random House 2002 226p
ISBN 0-375-50223-8   LC 2002-24802
"The wealthy and reclusive 80-year-old Lydia Blessing lives in the eponymous 'Blessings,' the country estate to which she was banished by her family after the death of her husband in World War II. Two events conspire to change the remaining years of Lydia's life: she hires Skip Cuddy as a handyman, and a baby is abandoned on her doorstep. Skip, whose friendship with some local lowlifes led to a stint in jail, tries to hide the existence of the baby from his prickly and critical employer, to no avail. Both Skip and Lydia fall in love with the baby, whom they name Faith, and in spite of their misgivings come together as a makeshift family." Libr J

"Quindlen's fine-tuned ear for the class distinctions of speech results in convincing dialogue. Evoking a bygone patrician world, she endows Blessings with an almost magical aura. While it skirts sentimentality by a hairbreadth, the narrative is old-fashioned in a positive way." Publ Wkly

Object lessons. Random House 1991 262p
ISBN 0-394-56965-2   LC 90-48656
This novel describes a summer in the life of an Irish American family in suburban New York in the 1960s. The central figure is twelve-year-old Maggie, daughter of Tommy Scanlan and Connie, an Italian American whose father is a cemetery caretaker in the Bronx. Tommy's father John, who made a fortune in religious goods and construction, is dying after a stroke, but still seeks to control the lives of his children and grandchildren, especially Tommy, the rebel

"Quindlen's social antennae are acute: she conveys the fierce ethnic pride that distinguishes Irish and Italian communities, their rivalry and mutual disdain. Her character portrayal is empathetic and beautifully dimensional, not only of Maggie but of her mother, who experiences her own wrenching rite of passage." Publ Wkly

One true thing. Random House 1994 289p
ISBN 0-679-40712-X   LC 94-22238
This novel "follows the psychological travails of Ellen Gulden, who against all personal inclinations returns home to care for her dying mother, Kate, and eventually finds herself accused of mercy-killing. Ellen, an intelligent though not particularly warm person, has spent her life earning her professor father's approval. After achieving high school valedictorian and Harvard honors, she aspires to advance her New York career. At her father's insistence, however, she leaves her job and takes on the role of nurse and homemaker. Through long hours as companion to Kate, she discovers the real value of her mother's life." Libr J

"Quindlen's story sustains an emotional momentum, and she addresses difficult issues with compassion." Publ Wkly

Quinn, Spencer *See* Abrahams, Peter, 1947-

Quoirez, Françoise *See* Sagan, Françoise, 1935-2004

R

Raban, Jonathan

Surveillance. Pantheon Books 2007 257p $24
ISBN 978-0-375-42244-7; 0-375-42244-7
                                     LC 2006-50332
"In a near-future Seattle, a police state, replete with imagined disaster scenarios, spy cameras, and intelligence gathering, is in effect, and everyone is under a surveillance of some kind. Aspiring actor Tad Zachary performs in emergency drills while his friend Lucy Bengstrom, a freelance journalist and single mom, tries to support her 11-year-old daughter. Lucy hits pay dirt when GQ hires her to write about August Vanags, a reclusive author of a memoir describing his World War II childhood. But as she delves into his life, Lucy starts to suspect literary fraud," Bookmarks

"Raban is deadly serious in his portrayal of a country running scared, but he also has a taste for sly social comedy. His ear for idiom is well-nigh faultless, be it the ironic locutions of Seattle school kids or the braying tones of a haughty Englishwoman, and his character-sketching is precise and assured." Daily Telegraph

Waxwings; a novel. Pantheon Bks. 2003 281p
$24
ISBN 0-375-41008-2   LC 2003-42997
"Tom Janeway is a professor of writing, a novelist and a public radio commentator; his wife, Beth, works for GetaShack.Com, a startup providing virtual neighborhood tours for prospective house buyers. They have a four-year-old son named Finn, and they appear content. Behind the happy facade, though, Beth has grown deeply unhappy with her self-absorbed husband. . . . Unfolding in counterpoint to Raban's chronicle of the rather civilized collapse of their marriage is the story of a shady Chinese immigrant called Chick; he survives a horrific journey to America and becomes an off-the-books contractor who bullies Tom into employing him to renovate their gloomy old house after Beth moves out." Publ

Raban, Jonathan—*Continued*

Wkly

This novel "succeeds as a sharply observed satire of the Internet boom and as a bittersweet meditation the American dream." Libr J

Rabb, Jonathan

The book of Q; a novel. Crown 2001 375p

ISBN 0-609-60483-X   LC 00-47550

"Father Ian Pearse, a researcher at the Vatican Library, stumbles upon an ancient conspiracy that could destroy the Catholic Church. Long thought dead, a dangerous sect called the Manichaeans has resurfaced, and Pearse must decipher an enigmatic prayer if he is to stop their plan. His life in jeopardy, Pearse finds that the closer he gets to the truth, the closer he gets to the Pope himself." Libr J

"A solid, hard-edged tale set in a climate of Catholic intrigue and social controversy." Publ Wkly

Rabinovitch, Sholem *See* Sholem Aleichem, 1859-1916

Rabinowitz, Sholem Yakov *See* Sholem Aleichem, 1859-1916

Rabinowitz, Solomon *See* Sholem Aleichem, 1859-1916

Radcliffe, Ann Ward, 1764-1823

The mysteries of Udolpho; [by] Ann Radcliffe; edited with an introduction and notes by Jacqueline Howard. Penguin Books 2001 xxxix, 653p (Penguin classics) pa $13

ISBN 0-14-043759-2

              * LC 2001-277143

First published 1794 in the United Kingdom

"The orphaned Emily St Aubert is carried off by her aunt's villanous husband Montoni to a remote castle in the Apennines, where her life, honour, and fortune are threatened and she is surrounded by apparently supernatural terrors. These are later explained as due to human agency and Emily escapes, returns to France and, after further mysteries and misunderstandings, is reuinted with her lover Valancourt." Oxford Companion to Engl Lit. 6th edition

Rae, Hugh C., 1935-

See also Stirling, Jessica

Raffel, Burton

(tr) Stendhal. The red and the black

Rampling, Anne *See* Rice, Anne, 1941-

Ramsland, Morten, 1971-

Doghead; translated from the Danish by Tiina Nunnally. St. Martin's Press 2009 383p $24.95

ISBN 978-0-312-37654-3; 0-312-37654-5

              LC 2008-35410

Original Danish edition, 2005; this translation first published 2007 in the United Kingdom

This "quirky novel follows three generations of a Scandinavian family with enough dysfunction to make Augusten Burroughs squirm: There's Askild, the alcoholic grandfather who survived a Nazi concentration camp; Jug Ears, the father forced to wear an armor-plated corset as a youngster so that he'd stop touching his ears; and narrator Asger, who as a child felt a certain satisfaction in wrestling his obese, mentally challenged aunt. Sound bizarre? It is, but the absurd scenes are infused with enough playful emotion to make their outlandishness forgivable, and even enjoyable. Though intricate shifts in time make for a complex read, Doghead — which has plenty of bite — is definitely worth the effort." Entertainment Wkly

Rand, Ayn, 1905-1982

Anthem. 50th anniversary ed, with a new introduction and appendix by Leonard Peikoff. Dutton 1995 253p $23.95

ISBN 0-525-94015-4   LC 95-9854

First published 1946 by Pamphleteers

"A short novel about a heroic dissenter in a future monolithic and collectivized state." Oxford Companion to Am Lit. 6th edition

Atlas shrugged. Random House 1957 1168p o.p.

              *

"In a technological civilization Rand's characters remain insecure and look to the government for protection. In exchange they sacrifice their creativity and independence. The heroes, a copper tycoon and an inventor, reject this philosophy and fight for the individualist." Shapiro. Fic for Youth. 3d edition

The fountainhead. Macmillan 1943 754p o.p.

              *

First published by Bobbs-Merrill

This novel "celebrates the achievements of an architect (presumably suggested by Frank Lloyd Wright) who is fiercely independent in pursuing his own ideas of design and who is therefore an example of the author's concept of Objectivism, which lauds individualism and 'rational self-interest.'" Oxford Companion to Am Lit. 5th edition

We the living. Random House 1959 433p o.p.

Originally published in 1936 by Macmillan, this edition of Rand's first novel contains a foreword describing the plight of the individual in the Soviet Union since then. It is the story of post-revolutionary Russia, and of a woman torn between two men who love her, one a Communist, the other an aristocrat

Randall, Alice

The wind done gone. Houghton Mifflin 2001 210p $23

ISBN 0-618-10450-X   LC 00-46544

The premise of this parodic sequel to Gone with the Wind is "that Scarlett O'Hara was half sister to a slave, the illegitimate daughter of Scarlett's father and her beloved Mammy. Randall's book, which picks up about a month after 'Gone with the Wind' left off, is made up of the . . . diary of this overlooked woman, Cynara. Throughout, Randall lifts characters and plot lines direct-

Randall, Alice—*Continued*

ly from Mitchell's novel, though she tweaks the names."
N Y Times Book Rev

"Cynara's voice and character are, in fits and starts, inspired and inspiring. Newly emancipated and literate, she
acquires, by virtue of what she calls her 'crazy quilt' education, an arresting fictional presence." Time

Randisi, Robert J.

(ed) Greatest hits. See Greatest hits

Rankin, Ian, 1960-

Black and blue; an Inspector Rebus mystery. St.
Martin's Press 1997 394p o.p.

         * LC 97-25381
Edinburgh police detective John Rebus "has a lot on
his plate: an oil-rig worker has been sadistically murdered (or has he?), a television news series has prompted
an inquiry into one of Rebus' earlier cases, and—worst
of all—a serial killer is on the loose." Booklist

"Rankin has a point to make about the corrosive effects of human wickedness that, if left unchecked, seeps
into the bloodstream and poisons the national body—a
point well made in his blunt and bruising style." N Y
Times Book Rev

The black book; an Inspector Rebus novel.
Penzler Bks. 1994 c1993 278p o.p.

         LC 94-8929
Frist published 1993 in the United Kingdom
In this mystery novel, Inspector Rebus of Edinburgh
"has alienated his girlfriend, his ne'er-do-well brother has
deposited himself in Rebus' apartment with every appearance of staying for good, his promising new sergeant
has been mugged, and his most unfavorite colleague is
again out to discredit Rebus. But Rebus' personal troubles pale when a local butcher is stabbed, and the investigation leads Rebus to conclude that the attack is somehow connected to a years-old unsolved arson-homicide
case. . . . Rankin's compelling and original plot is *almost* as intriguing as the gruff, tough, rebellious Rebus,
whose rough exterior hides a charming, funny, tender-
hearted human being we'd all like to know." Booklist

Dead souls; an Inspector Rebus novel. St.
Martin's Minotaur 1999 406p $24.95
    ISBN 0-312-20293-8   LC 99-44276
In this novel "Inspector John Rebus, is in another of
his black moods. A colleague commits suicide; the
teenage son of his high school sweetheart goes missing;
a pedophile crawls onto his turf; and a mad-dog killer arrives from America to play a sadistic game of chicken
with him. An irreligious man who harbors a perverse
streak of spirituality, Rebus blames blind fate (or an
uncaring God) for conjoining these seemingly random
circumstances into a force field of evil so strong that it
sweeps aside his sense of decency and pulls him in." N
Y Times Book Rev

Exit music. Little, Brown and Co. 2008 421p
$24.99
    ISBN 978-0-316-05758-5; 0-316-05758-4
                     LC 2008-1888

First published 2007 in the United Kingdom
The "final novel in Rankin's Inspector Rebus series is
set during the Edinburgh detective's final week at work.
(He is nearing the mandatory retirement age of sixty.)
The novel begins with a dissident Russian poet beaten to
death, and expands to take in smalltime drug dealers,
cloak-wearing women who act in walking mystery tours
of the city, international oligarchs, and Scottish bank executives. A contemporary artist who makes sound instal-
lations may be in league with politicians agitating for
Scotland's independence. Rebus is as gruffly mischievous
as ever, and the novel ends in a cliffhanger scene with
his archenemy that will have readers gasping into the
blank space that follows. Rankin's work is crime fiction
at its most consuming, cerebral best." New Yorker

The falls; an Inspector Rebus novel. St. Martin's
Minotaur 2001 c2000 399p $24.95
    ISBN 0-312-20610-0   LC 2001-41946
First published 2000 in the United Kingdom
Inspector Rebus "needs all his interviewing skills to
get a handle on Philippa Balfour, a 20-year-old art student at the University of Edinburgh who has gone missing. It's like extracting molars to get information from
Philippa's father, mother, boyfriend or friends, who are
in turn too controlling, browbeaten, calculating or
clueless to be anything but obstructive. The plot opens
up when a nasty little doll in a creepy little coffin directs
Rebus to an interactive game that Philippa has been playing on the Internet." N Y Times Book Rev

Rankin combines "complicated multiple plot lines with
finely drawn characters and fascinating Scottish lore and
settings." Libr J

The naming of the dead; an Inspector Rebus
novel. Little, Brown and Co. 2007 c2006 425p
$24.99
    ISBN 978-0-316-05757-8; 0-316-05757-6
                     LC 2006-31495
First published 2006 in the United Kingdom
"It's July 2005, and Bush, Blair, and other international leaders are coming to Scotland for the G8 conference
to be held outside Edinburgh. Anything but a company
man, Detective Inspector Rebus finds himself relegated
to the sidelines until he takes a call that lands him smack
where he's not supposed to be: butting heads with conference organizers in an attempt to make sense of the apparent suicide of an attendee at a preconference dinner.
The plot mushrooms out from there, of course, encompassing an ongoing serial-killer investigation and personal crises in the lives of both Rebus and his partner and
protege, Siobhan Clarke." Booklist

"In his backhanded, reluctant way Rebus winds up
uniting all the book's loose ends, and seeing how he accomplishes this is a pleasure. Besides, 'The Naming of
the Dead' isn't really about its detective plot. It's about
Rebus's taking stock, not only of his own past but also
of the world around him." N Y Times (Late N Y Ed)

A question of blood; an Inspector Rebus novel.
Little, Brown and Co. 2004 406p $22.95
    ISBN 0-316-09564-8
                    * LC 2003-59549
First published 2003 in the United Kingdom
"Rebus finds himself in hot water again, this time liter-
ally, with severely scalded hands, the result of either too
hot dish or bathwater. After the stalker of a colleague

Rankin, Ian, 1960-—*Continued*

turns up dead-in a fire-suspicion naturally falls on Rebus, who is suspended for the duration of the investigation. Meanwhile, a school shooting reminiscent of the Dunblane massacre in 1996 leaves two students and the assailant dead, with a third wounded. It all seems elementary enough, until Rebus, with time on his bandaged hands, is called in as a consultant." Libr J

"This series's strength starts with Rebus himself, who . . . has emerged as the baddest of the bad boys of modern crime fiction. He is fiftyish, overweight, alcoholic, a chain smoker, surly, short-tempered, divorced, estranged from his family, a loner, a nut about obscure rock-and-roll groups, hostile to all authority and possibly psychotic. Needless to say, women love him—ladies love outlaws—and his police colleagues tolerate him because he's an ace detective." Washington Post Book World

Resurrection men; an Inspector Rebus novel. Little, Brown 2003 436p $23.95

ISBN 0-316-76684-4   LC 2002-16271

"It's the perfect cover. Edinburgh Detective Inspector John Rebus, the maverick's maverick, guilty of throwing a coffee cup at his superior officer, is sent to a remedial 'career counseling' course on being a better team player. But the fix is in; Rebus' real assignment is to investigate four Glasgow renegade coppers also forced to take the course." Booklist

"We are well and truly in Rankin country—a shady world where good and evil are relative terms and truth is an arbitrary concept." N Y Times Book Rev

Set in darkness. St. Martin's Press 2000 415p

ISBN 0-312-20609-7

"Rebus has been assigned to a bogus task force called the Policing of Parliament Liaison Committee. Things liven up, though, when a body is found inside a bricked-up fireplace in one of the buildings under construction for the new Scottish Parliament. That's a tantalizing enough mystery, but when a top politico is found dead at the construction site, Rebus has something he can sink his teeth into—a decades-old crime whose tentacles touch the present and lead to a new confrontation with Rebus' longtime nemesis, Edinburgh crime boss Big Ger Cafferty. . . . Nobody writes darker than Rankin." Booklist

Watchman. Little, Brown and Co. 2007 258p $24.99

ISBN 978-0-316-00913-3; 0-316-00913-X
          LC 2007-19761

First published 1988 in the United Kingdom; first American edition published 1991 for the Crime Club by Doubleday

This thriller "features British spy Miles Flint, a markedly different sort of agent than, say, James Bond. Flint is a watcher from behind darkened windows, a listener to tapped phone lines. When a lapse in judgment results in the death of a valued source, his shot at redemption comes in the form of a seemingly routine mission to Belfast. . . . The mission quickly turns deadly, and Flint realizes that he has been set up by someone in his organization. Watchman keeps the reader on pins and needles from page one." BookPage

Rash, Ron, 1953-

Saints at the river. Henry Holt 2004 239p $24

ISBN 0-8050-7487-2   LC 2003-67630

"When the 12-year-old daughter of a wealthy banker drowns in South Carolina's Tamassee River, her death sets off an emotionally charged battle between the grieving parents, who want to put up a dam to recover her body, and the local environmentalists, who will risk everything to defend the pristine state of their river. . . . The book is rich with nuance, mostly because Rash selects Maggie Glenn as his first-person narrator. A Tamassee native who now works as a news photographer in the state capital, Columbia, Maggie has deep ties to the town, but she's detached from the main fray. As a result, her news angles and her romantic attachments keep shifting. Maggie's rage against her father isn't sufficiently explored to carry the weight it bears in the plot, but Rash compensates for this weakness by creating detailed, highly particular characters." Publ Wkly

Serena; a novel. Ecco 2008 371p $24.95

ISBN 978-0-06-147085-1; 0-06-147085-6
          LC 2008-00712

"Set in 1929, in the rugged mountains of North Carolina, Rash's novel is a tightly knit tale of industrial development, greed, and betrayal. George Pemberton and his new bride, Serena, maintain a close watch over a burgeoning logging empire, dealing with their workers while fighting off the efforts of environmental activists to expand the country's network of national parks. As the title character—a Depression-era Lady Macbeth wholly comfortable in the wilderness—drives her husband to commit increasingly malevolent acts, he must also contend with the reemergence of a woman with whom he had an illegitimate child years earlier. Rash's evocative rendering of the blighted landscape and the tough characters who inhabit it recalls both John Steinbeck and Cormac McCarthy, while the malignant character of Serena, who projects a 'stark unflinching certainty' about her actions, propels his finely paced story." New Yorker

Rathbone, Julian, 1935-

The last English king. St. Martin's Press 1999 381p $24.95

ISBN 0-312-24213-1   LC 99-55913

"William the Conqueror defeated King Harold at the Battle of Hastings in 1066, and three years later Walt, one of Harold's personal guards, is wandering continental Europe as a broken man. He encounters Quint, an ex-monk, and together they decide to travel to the Holy Land. On their journey, Walt finally begins to heal by telling his story to Quint." Booklist

"Rathbone takes considerable historical liberties, writing in contemporary vernacular modern prose and painting King Edward as a man more interested in Harold's fetching brother Tostig than in the sister, whom he is slated to marry. However, Rathbone defends his decisions convincingly in an author's note, and his narrative presents an interesting interpretation of a tumultuous period in English history." Publ Wkly

Rattray, Simon, 1920-1995

For works written by this author under other names see Hall, Adam, 1920-1995

Raucher, Herman

Summer of '42. Putnam 1971 251p o.p.

This is a novel "describing with great accuracy what it was like to be a 15-year-old boy just entering the obsessed-with-sex stage of life in the wartime summer of 1942. Hermie and Oscy and Benji are three tough, foul-mouthed but innocent Brooklyn boys spending the summer on Packett Island off the coast of Maine. The central story revolves around Hermie's tender and believable relationship with a war widow who initiates him into sex at the end of the novel." Publ Wkly

"There is hilarity here and vulgarity, warmth and humanity—and so much detail and nostalgia that the work seems almost like a historical novel." Libr J

Ravenel, Shannon

(ed) New stories from the South: the year's best [date] See New stories from the South: the year's best [date]

Rawlings, Marjorie Kinnan, 1896-1953

Short stories; edited by Rodger L. Tarr. University Press of Fla. 1994 376p $49.95

ISBN 0-8130-1252-X   LC 93-30649

Contents: Cracker chidlings; Jacob's ladder; Lord Bill of the Suwannee River; A plumb clare conscience; A crop of beans; Gal young un; Alligators; Benny and the bird dogs; The pardon; Varmints; A mother in Mannville; Cocks must crow; Fish fry and fireworks; The pelican's shadow; The enemy; In the heart; Jessamine Springs; The provider; The shell; Black secret; Miriam's houses; Miss Moffatt steps out; The friendship

Raymond, Jonathan

The half-life; a novel. Bloomsbury 2004 355p $23.95

ISBN 1-582-34448-5   LC 2003-22602

"In the early nineteenth century, a half-starved band of fur trappers struggles through the Oregon woods. Their young, diffident cook is intimidated by the rougher members of the group. When another young man, fleeing from some vengeful Russians, stumbles into camp, a friendship blossoms. Move ahead to the Reagan era. A teenager is dragged by her mother to live in an Oregon commune. Lonely and resentful while living among slightly absurd, aging counterculturists, she is drawn to the only other young woman in the settlement, and as their bond grows, they work together on a film project. The discovery of a pair of skeletons buried on the commune provides the link between these pairs of friendships. Raymond, in his first novel, seamlessly links the two narratives with elegant and often haunting prose. The characters are finely drawn, and Raymond poses them against a seductively beautiful landscape." Booklist

Rayner, Richard

The cloud sketcher; a novel. HarperCollins Pubs. 2001 435p

ISBN 0-06-019634-3   LC 00-56695

This novel is "about a young Finn whose early contact with an elevator convinces him to construct buildings so high that they tickle the clouds. Surviving Finland's early brush with the Bolsheviks, he begins his architectural career, but soon the re-emergence of his first sweetheart drives him to New York City, where he meets other architects, gangsters, {and} capitalists." Libr J

The author "vividly captures details of Finnish culture, history and landscape and the developing architectural aesthetic of the age. This is an old-fashioned novel in the best sense: full of incident and passion, presenting a slice of history and relating a gripping story." Publ Wkly

Read, Miss, 1913-

Affairs at Thrush Green; illustrations by J. S. Goodall. Houghton Mifflin 1984 c1983 256p il o.p.   LC 84-6702

First published 1983 in the United Kingdom

"The catastrophic fire that destroyed Thrush Green rectory in *Gossip from Thrush Green*, has caused Charles Henstock and his wife, Dimity, to move into the luxurious, large rectory in Lulling, thus drawing the adventures of the residents of these two towns even closer. . . . Henstock tends to his new duties with gracious vigor despite his own doubts and those expressed by several parishioners." Booklist

At home in Thrush Green; illustrated by J.S. Goodall. Houghton Mifflin 1986 c1985 261p il o.p.   LC 86-20864

First published 1985 in the United Kingdom

The author describes "a year of bustling and visiting at Thrush Green. The creation of eight homes for elderly residents on the site of the old vicarage takes up much of the novel's action, absorbing the interests of the villagers as the recipients must be decided upon and settled in. School life under the stern Miss Watson and the more amiable Miss Fogarty also receives a share of attention. Readers familiar with Thrush Green's inhabitants will be delighted to note the changes in the lives of their favorite characters and will be pleased as always by the book's emphasis on familiar annual patterns." Booklist

Chronicles of Fairacre; comprising: Village school, Village diary and Storm in the village; illustrated by J. S. Goodall. Houghton Mifflin 1977 c1964 534p il o.p.

First published 1964 in the United Kingdom. A combined edition of three titles first published separately in 1956 (1955 in the United Kingdom), 1957, and 1959 (1958 in the United Kingdom) respectively

Village school describes one year in the life of an English schoolmistress in a two-room church-governed school in the rural English village of Fairacre. Through her eyes we see the whole of village life with its fetes, sales, outings, festivals, quarrels and friendships. Village diary continues the account of school and village life. When a retired male school teacher settles in the village, the villagers hope for a romance for their schoolmistress until a wife appears. In Storm in the village, the "storm" is caused by fear that the British Atomic Research Authority is going to take over Harold Miller's "Hundred Acre Field" to make room for a new housing development and that the village school will be closed

Read, Miss, 1913——Continued

Farewell to Fairacre; illustrations by John S. Goodall. Houghton Mifflin 1994 213p il o.p.

LC 94-25628

"With an influx of new students, Miss Read's worries about the future of her beloved school can finally be set aside. In their wake, however, come concerns about the head mistress' own health. Two small strokes spur her decision to retire, and she spends her final months in her usual busy fashion, tending to her students at Fairacre, fending off the surprising attentions of two suitors, and becoming ever more comfortable with thoughts of a new life ahead. Nostalgic without being sentimental, this is a fitting conclusion to a delightful series, recalling old friends and pleasant times in a tranquil English village." Booklist

Friends at Thrush Green; illustrations by John S. Goodall. Houghton Mifflin 1991 c1990 244p il o.p.

LC 91-10857

First published 1990 in the United Kingdom

In this novel "we meet a crazy-quilt collection of delightfully eccentric characters who eagerly await and gossip endlessly about their old friends' return visit. The town's attention is also riveted to the pending sale of the much-loved residence abutting the schoolhouse at Thrush Green, speculation about which gives rise to a cornucopia of interesting tales and rumors surrounding various townspeople. While some readers might deem Miss Read's novel sluggish for its seeming uneventfulness, many others will be drawn to this throwback to an easier, slower-paced life." Booklist

Mrs. Pringle; illustrations by John S. Goodall. Houghton Mifflin 1990 c1989 165p il o.p.

LC 90-4669

First published 1989 in the United Kingdom

This novel focuses on the exploits of Mrs. Pringle, the custodian of the school in the village of Fairacre

Return to Thrush Green; illustrated by J.S. Goodall. Houghton Mifflin 1979 255p il o.p.

LC 79-858

First published 1978 in the United Kingdom

In this chronicle of Thrush Green "Albert Piggott, the sexton, is his usual irascible self despite the efforts of his wandering wife and his loyal daughter. On the other hand, the return of Joan Young's ailing father works out much better than expected. Miss Fogarty handles the school crises capably and finds that some clouds do have silver linings. As flowers bloom and birds do nest, neighbors chat away as usual, and Dotty Harmer cares for her stray animals and offers acorn coffee to friends. Best of all is the village's newest romance, one that takes just about everyone by surprise." Publ Wkly

Storm in the village

In Read, Miss. Chronicles of Fairacre p361-534

Thrush Green; illustrated by J.S. Goodall. Houghton Mifflin 1960 c1959 226p il o.p.

First published 1959 in the United Kingdom

"Confined to the events of May 1, the day when Mrs. Curdle's traveling carnival brings its special magic to Thrush Green, the story tells what takes place in the lives of a small boy, a lonely girl, an elderly doctor and his young assistant, and various other people, including the redoubtable Mrs. Curdle herself." Booklist

Village diary

In Read, Miss. Chronicles of Fairacre p177-360

The village school

In Read, Miss. Chronicles of Fairacre p9-176

Read, Piers Paul, 1941-

Alice in exile. St. Martin's Press 2002 344p $24.95

ISBN 0-312-30398-X

"As striking in her beauty as she is shocking in her behavior, Alice Fry has an uninhibited sexuality that makes her attractive to two very different men. Pregnant with fiance Edward Cobb's child, Alice is abandoned by him when her father becomes embroiled in a sexual scandal that threatens Cobb's political ambition. With no one to turn to and nowher to go, Alice is rescued by Baron von Rettenberg, a womanizing Russian nobleman who hires her as his children's governess. . . .To read Read is to be caught up in an epic wonder of passion, scandal, adn international intrigue." Booklist

The professor's daughter. Lippincott 1971 276p o.p.

Henry Rutledge, "the professor is a middle-aged old-line liberal who has dabbled in politics behind the scenes in the Kennedy era. In . . . flashbacks we learn how and why he and his wife have become the kind of people they are, and what has gone wrong with their marriage. The professor's daughter is something else again, desperate, attempting suicide, all but destroyed sexually and every other way by traps she has drifted into without ever understanding what was happening to her. When father and daughter strike up an incongruous but ultimately quite believable alliance with a group of campus radical activists who believe assassination is a valid revolutionary tool, tension mounts to a keen pitch." Publ Wkly

A season in the West. Random House 1989 238p o.p.

LC 88-29682

"Defecting from Czechoslovakia, writer Josef Birek is taken under the wing of Laura Morton, the wife of a wealthy banker, who works part-time as a translator at a foundation for dissident émigrés. Shallow, discontented Laura sees her opportunity: she introduces the naive, idealistic Birek to her friends and literary contacts, invites him to move into her home and eventually begins an affair with the overwhelmed young man. Lionized by London's sophisticated social set, Birek finds himself financially and spiritually enslaved, while Laura becomes obsessed by the liaison." Publ Wkly

"Read engages his audience with biting pictures of British publishing and banking circles, while the romance is played up for all its blazing erotic qualities. Witty commentary on sedate lives moved by unruly passions." Booklist

Reasoner, James

Antietam. Cumberland House 2000 383p $22.95

ISBN 1-58182-084-4

LC 00-22578

Reasoner, James—*Continued*

This novel focuses on "the Brannon clan of Culpepper County, Virginia. As the hostilities move ever closer and finally threaten the security of the family farm in northern Virginia, each of the six Brannon siblings is faced with an inevitable crisis of either the heart or the conscience. . . . Fraught with passion, tension, and tenderness, this enthralling family saga will appeal to fans of epic well-researched historical fiction." Booklist

Rebeck, Theresa

Three girls and their brother; a novel. Shaye Areheart Books 2008 341p $23.95

ISBN 978-0-307-39414-9; 0-307-39414-X

LC 2007-036711

A "satire of celeb-obsessed NYC about flame-haired teenage sisters who get photographed for The New Yorker and soon become megastars. Rebeck relies on four narrators, cannily beginning with the girls' brother (who retains our sympathy even as he tosses barbs like 'I've been over here on the Planet of Total Morons, someplace you apparently own property'). If the ending strains believability, well, by then we'll buy anything — even supermodels scarfing burgers." Entertainment Wkly

Redfern, Elizabeth

Auriel rising. G.P. Putnam's Sons 2004 386p $24.95

ISBN 0-399-15105-2   LC 2003-58507

The "setting is London in 1609, and the city is rife with hostility between Catholics and Protestants. Two years after he was involved in the escape of a Catholic prisoner, young Ned Warriner has returned to London to find that he still has many enemies, one of them now married to the love of his life, Kate. Even worse, he has stumbled upon a mysterious letter that appears to contain the secret for making gold but in reality contains the seeds of a plot that reaches to the highest levels of British royalty. With not only personal survival but national security at stake, Ned must decipher the contents while navigating the dangerous relationships between some of the city's most powerful men." Booklist

"Redfern sets a blistering pace and never breaks stride or tone. Resisting the standard static historical tableau, she gives us a troubled city constantly reinventing itself, peopled by souls no less changeable." N Y Times Book Rev

Redfield, James

The celestine prophecy; an adventure. Warner Bks. 1994 246p $19.95

ISBN 0-446-51862-X   LC 93-61754

"The saga begins when the unnamed middle-aged male narrator whimsically quits his nondescript life to track down an ancient Peruvian manuscript (pretentiously called the Manuscript) containing nine Insights that supposedly prophesy the modern emergence of New Age spirituality. South of the border, he encounters resistance from the Peruvian government and church authorities, who believe the document will undermine traditional family values. While dodging evil soldiers, paranoid priests and pseudoscientific researchers, our hero sequentially discovers all nine Insights during a series of chance

encounters. Redfield has a real talent for page-turning action." Publ Wkly

Followed by The tenth insight (1996)

Redhill, Michael, 1966-

Consolation; a novel. Little, Brown and Co. 2007 c2006 340p $24.99

ISBN 978-0-316-73498-1; 0-316-73498-5

LC 2006-934104

First published 2006 in the Canada

In twin narratives, the author "contemplates the history of the prosperous metropolis of Toronto. The first story line, set in the mid-1850s, features Jem Hallam, a British apothecary who immigrates to Canada and forms a fortuitous friendship with a clever if somewhat eccentric photographer named Samuel Ennis. . . . The second plot, set a century and a half later, involves widower Marianne Hollis, whose husband uncovered clues to the whereabouts of the earliest photographs of Toronto, research cut short by his death from Lou Gehrig's disease. (The images, presumably taken by Hallam, were sealed in a strongbox on a ship that sank in the city's harbor more than 100 years before.) With the help of her daughter's fiance, grief-stricken Marianne honors her husband's memory by taking up his cause." Booklist

"A gentle but unfaltering cadence, a well-tempered voice, and a highly resolved sense of detail bring readers back and forth smoothly between these two eras." Quill & Quire

Reed, Barry, 1927-2002

The choice. Crown 1991 358p

ISBN 0-517-58124-8   LC 90-48217

"Frank Galvin is at the peak of his legal career with a blue-chip Boston law firm. As chronicled in The Verdict [1980] he has risen to the height of Boston's legal set through a brilliant performance in a highly publicized hospital case. When he is approached by a young and inexperienced attorney with evidence that a highly touted new wonder drug may cause birth defects, he sees it as an opportunity to exert his firm's sense of humanity. However, the firm is the principal legal counsel for the drug's manufacturer. What seems at first to be a simple matter of potential conflict of interest rapidly escalates into an intricate web of intrigue involving both U.S. and British law as well as medical ethics." Libr J

The indictment. Crown 1994 370p

ISBN 0-517-59433-1   LC 94-8346

This novel concerns "a possible grand jury indictment against a prominent doctor suspected of murdering a young woman. When Boston attorney Dan Sheridan agrees to defend Dr. Christopher Dillard, he pits himself against a DA with an eye on a U.S. Senate seat and a shady Irish kingmaker who wants the entire case buried. Sheridan also becomes an unwitting target of an FBI sting operation against local lawyers suspected of criminal ties, even as he becomes romantically involved with the agent who is working undercover as one of his secretaries." Publ Wkly

"Reed surrounds the mystery plot with an intriguing, behind-the-scenes look at the historically fascinating sociopolitical world of Boston, and he offers plenty of detail on the decision-making, strategy, and processes that go into preparing a criminal case." Booklist

Reed, Ernesto Mestre- *See* Mestre-Reed, Ernesto, 1964-

Reed, Ishmael, 1938-

Japanese by spring. Atheneum Pubs. 1993 225p o.p.

* LC 92-36280

A "satiric thrust at university life in America. Ambitious black professor Chappie Puttbutt wants to rise at predominantly white Jack London University, but he gets more than he bargained for when his serene tutor in Japanese—actually leader of a filthy-rich group of Asians—suddenly buys the university and threatens to take over the American West." Libr J

"Borrowing from vivid African-American slang and turning academic jargon inside out, Mr. Reed constructs brilliant verbal fusillades that reduce his targets to their most ridiculous components." N Y Times Book Rev

Reed, Kit, 1932-

The baby merchant. Tor 2006 334p $24.95

ISBN 978-0-7653-1550-2; 0-7653-1550-5

LC 2006-40385

"A Tom Doherty Associates book"

Set in a "future world with a falling birth rate, closed borders and lengthy adoption waiting lists, Reed's . . . novel explores the lengths desperate people will go to become parents. Jake Zorn and Maury Bayless, a childless couple in their 40s, approach Tom Starbird, a go-to man for high-end illicit 'adoptions,' but Jake, a newsman, isn't satisfied to just do business. If Starbird doesn't get them a baby, Jake threatens to not only ruin Starbird but also broadcast a shattering exposé about Starbird's mother, an unstable poet. Starbird, forced to agree, marks the baby of a pregnant artist, Sasha Egan, who lives in a home for unwed mothers. But Sasha flees the home and lays low, forcing Starbird to revise his plans. The inevitable clash among Sasha, Starbird and Jake forces each to rethink his or her motives." Publ Wlky

"In Reedland—the fantasy world where the author's characters live, breathe, and inevitably screw up—half the fun is viewing how surreal events send her anti-heroes bumping into each other like so many demented dominoes." Hartford Courant

Enclave. Tor 2009 366p $25.95

ISBN 978-0-7653-2161-9; 0-7653-2161-0

LC 2008-46433

"A Tom Doherty Associates book"

"An ex-Marine named Sargent Whitmore, scarred by three tours of combat in places like Iraq, seeks to atone for sins of war by establishing a place where children can be protected from technology, degenerate culture, their own depravity, and a pending socio-eco-techno apocalypse. Retrofitting a remote mountaintop monastery off the coast of Greece, he collects 100 children from the world's richest families, willing and able to pay astronomical sums to save and/or get rid of troubled progeny. He cuts off all contact with the world and begins the open-ended task of turning the spoiled, over-privileged offspring into decent human beings by way of education, military-style routine, and calming drugs slipped into their food. . . . Benedict, the lone remaining monk, now

the gardener, keeps perilous secrets. When a mysterious Christ-like young man appears, along with a plague and a computer virus, anarchy descends quickly." PopMatters.com

Reed's "characters may be flawed and immoral, but they are also fascinating and believable. The carefully crafted plot and multiple points of view engage readers immediately." Romantic Times

Reed, Lillian Craig *See* Reed, Kit, 1932-

Reeman, Douglas

A ship must die. Morrow 1979 284p o.p.

LC 79-66009

"In January 1944 Captain Richard Blake, Royal Navy, is preparing to hand over his battle-scarred cruiser 'Andromeda' to the Australian navy. Before he can do so, a German commerce raider appears in the Indian Ocean, and Blake is ordered to destroy him." Libr J

"Reeman gives dimension to his characters and imparts his usual sense of realism in vivid scenes of battle action." Booklist

Reich, Christopher

Rules of deception. Doubleday 2008 390p $24.95

ISBN 978-0-385-52406-3; 0-385-52406-4

LC 2007-36368

"Reich's everyman hero, Jonathan Ransom, is plunged into a world of intrigue when his wife dies in an accident. Growing questions about her true identity dig him deeper into trouble. Ransom is unaware that he is interrupting the endgame of an enormous and long-running conspiracy that he—and the Swiss cop tracking him—could derail. Reich . . . throws readers off the scent but never loses control of the plot. He skillfully handles the pacing, and this results in a suspenseful story balanced by cinematic action scenes. . . . Fans of early Ludlum will particularly enjoy it." Libr J

Reich, Tova

My Holocaust; a novel. HarperCollins 2007 326p $24.95

ISBN 978-0-06-117345-5; 0-06-117345-2

LC 2007-297195

In this satire, Reich "sketches a gallery of 'Holocaust hangers-on,' grotesques eager to hijack the Shoah for tawdry commercial and ideological purposes. Presiding over the strategic exploitation is Maurice Messer, a retired ladies' undergarment maker who has parlayed inflated claims of being an anti-Nazi partisan into the chairmanship of the United States Holocaust Memorial Museum; his feckless son, Norman, president of Holocaust Connections Inc., a brand consultancy with the motto 'Make Your Cause a Holocaust' (of which Maurice is board chairman); Norman's daughter, Nechama, who has embarrassingly run off to join the convent across the street from Auschwitz; and Maurice's right-hand man, Monty Pincus, who expertly deploys melancholy over the six million to seduce women." Publ Wkly

"Tova Reich is fearless, in the best possible way, and her take on the culture of victimization spares no captives in the gulag of self-anointed martyrdomS. Reich's gift for satire is impeccable, her ear for absurdity pitch perfect." Philadelphia Inquirer

Reichs, Kathleen J.

Bare bones; [by[Kathy Reichs. Scribner 2003 306p $23.95

ISBN 0-7432-3346-8

* LC 2003-40725

"Tempe, a forensic anthropologist, is back home in Charlotte, N.C., anticipating a nice, long vacation from the county medical examiner's office, when a series of unnatural disasters drags her back to the lab. . . . Whether she's examining the pulverized remains of the victims of a suspicious plane crash or reassembling the bones of an illegally slaughtered bear, Tempe is a pro's pro at her job, but also a compassionate woman who isn't afraid to show her outrage at the cruelty done to man and beast for the sake of a dirty dollar." N Y Times Book Rev

Break no bones; [by] Kathy Reichs. Scribner 2006 339p $25.95

ISBN 978-0-7432-3349-1; 0-7432-3349-2

LC 2006-45038

"While supervising a dig of Native American burial grounds in Charleston, S.C., Brennan finds more recent remains. Soon, her ex-husband, who's a lawyer, appears in town, pursuing leads in a missing persons case connected with a local church. Bodies start piling up at an alarming rate, and Brennan begins to suspect that the deaths are linked to each other—and her ex-husband's inquiry. Reichs's down-to-earth heroine is an appealing creation, who deftly juggles personal problems with professional challenges." Publ Wkly

Deadly décisions; [by] Kathy Reichs. Scribner 2000 333p $25

ISBN 0-684-85971-8

* LC 00-22220

Forensic anthropologist Temperance Brennan "is outraged at the death of a child in a war among bikers vying for the Quebec province drug trade, and she joins the investigation. Tension mounts as she becomes embroiled in the rivalries of outlaw motorcycle gangs, 'the mafia of the new millennium.' The case becomes more complex as another biker is killed and the death and dismemberment of a teenage girl years before in North Carolina are linked to the Quebec biker mayhem." Libr J

"The author doesn't dumb down the scientific stuff, delivering the full textbook version of subjects like hydrocephalus, blood-spatter analysis, ground-penetrating radar devices and the history of outlaw motorcycle clubs in North America." N Y Times Book Rev

Death du jour; {by} Kathy Reichs. Scribner 1999 379p $25

ISBN 0-684-84118-5

LC 98-48763

This mystery opens with forensic anthropologist Temperance Brennan "digging up the body of a nun buried more than a century ago in a convent graveyard in Quebec. While her job is to identify the corpse as a possible saint, Tempe's attention is drawn to the grisly killings of four-month-old twin boys and their parents. At the same time, Tempe's troubled sister Harry comes to Montreal to take a self-help workshop. Investigating these deaths leads Tempe back to the Carolinas, where more bodies are discovered on an island monkey preserve, and clues point to a mysterious cult." Libr J

"Well presented are Tempe's refreshing compassion in the face of relentless autopsies, her ability to describe a corpse with judiciously graphic detail and her penchant for revealing the art behind the science on such matters as the preservation of a corpse's teeth." Publ Wkly

Déjà dead; [by] Kathy Reichs. Scribner 1997 411p o.p.

LC 97-2990

"Dr. Tempe Brennan, a trowel-packing forensic anthropologist from North Carolina, works in Montreal's Laboratoire de Médecine Légale examining recovered bodies to help police solve missing-persons cases and murders. It's clear to Tempe that the remains of several women killed and savagely mutilated point to a sadistic serial killer, but she can't convince the police. Determined to prevent more brutal deaths, she sleuths solo, tracking her quarry through Montreal's seedy underworld of hookers, where her anthropologist friend Gabby, doing her own scary research, is being stalked by a creep. . . . Except for imparting an excess of lab information, Reichs, also a forensic anthropologist, drives the pace at a heady clip. A first-class writer, she dazzles readers with sensory imagery that is apt, fresh, and funny." Libr J

Grave secrets; [by] Kathy Reichs. Scribner 2002 317p $25

ISBN 0-684-85973-4

LC 2002-22695

"While in Guatemala to assist in the exhumation of an old mass grave, forensic specialist Temperance Brennan is called upon to determine whether a body found in a septic tank is that of the missing daughter of the Canadian ambassador to Guatemala. The gruesome search, vividly described, leaves even the toughened Tempe aghast." Booklist

Monday mourning; [by] Kathy Reichs. Scribner 2004 305p $25

ISBN 0-7432-3347-6

LC 2004-45263

This Temperance Brennan mystery "finds the forensic anthropologist in Montreal to testify in a murder case. Arriving a day early to prepare, she becomes caught up in a new investigation when three sets of human bones are discovered in the basement of a pizza parlor. Examining the remains, she discovers that the victims were Caucasian and female. Antique buttons found near the bodies lead Homicide Detective Claudel to believe that the remains are over a century old, but Tempe is not so convinced and investigates with the help of her friend Anne, who has come to visit while contemplating her marriage. Readers of the series will be pleased to see the relationship between Tempe and Detective Andrew Ryan develop further." Libr J

Reisman, Nancy

The first desire. Pantheon Books 2004 310p $24

ISBN 0-375-42308-7

LC 2004-44665

"The catalyst for this narrative about the hidden dramas of a Jewish family living in Buffalo from the late 1920s to 1950 occurs offstage. Rebecca Cohen, wife of jewelry store owner Abe, has died, leaving five adult children. Goldie, the eldest, on whom the responsibility for caring for her siblings has fallen, suddenly disappears without a word. Her departure leaves Sadie Cohen Feldstein, the only married sister, to cope with her tyrannical father and difficult siblings, who live together in the family home." Publ Wkly

Reisman, Nancy—*Continued*

"The novel is both lovely and heartbreaking in its vision of family ties at their most inevitable." N Y Times (Late N Y Ed)

Remarque, Erich Maria, 1898-1970

All quiet on the western front; translated from the German by A. W. Wheen. Little, Brown 1929 291p $24.95

ISBN 0-316-73992-8

*

"Four German youths are pulled abruptly from school to serve at the front as soldiers in World War I. Only Paul survives, and he contemplates the needless violation of the human body by weapons of war. No longer innocent or lighthearted, he is repelled by the slaughter of soldiers and questions the usefulness of war as a means of adjudication. Although the young men in this novel are German, the message is universal in its delineation of the feelings of the common soldier." Shapiro. Fic for Youth. 3d edition

Followed by The road back

Arch of triumph; translated from the German by Walter Sorell and Denver Lindley. Appleton-Century 1945 455p o.p.

"A story of Paris in the period preceding the [Second World] war. The central character is a German doctor who, having escaped from the Nazis, is living illegally in France, subject to deportation if the police discover his presence. Without a passport and identification papers he is not allowed to practice, but in secret performs difficult operations for a well-known society doctor. Other refugees, figures from the underworld, outcasts and derelicts are the characters in a book which pictures a society nearing its doom." Wis Libr Bull

The night in Lisbon; translated by Ralph Manheim. Harcourt, Brace & World 1964 244p o.p.

Original German edition, 1962

"One night in Lisbon in 1942 a German refugee offers passage to the U.S. and his passport to another refugee on condition that he be kept company through the night and that he be permitted to tell his story. The narration reveals the first refugee's flight from Germany in the 1930's, his hazardous return after five years to see his wife, his second escape in which his wife joins him, and their subsequent flight from place to place in Europe during which, in spite of dangers, they achieved moments of intense happiness because of their mutual love and understanding." Booklist

The road back; translated from the German by A. W. Wheen. Little, Brown 1931 343p o.p.

Sequel to All quiet on the western front

Containing some of the characters of All quiet on the western front, this story is about a "little group of war-weary, disillusioned German soldiers [who] return to their homes and find that adjustment to peace in a Fatherland which is a rioting, cynical republic is impossible." Cleveland Public Libr

"A profoundly moving, a painfully moving, document. Unlike tragedy, it has no katharsis, but, like a tragedy, it has to be looked at open-eyed, honestly, courageously." Spectator

A time to love and a time to die; translated from the German by Denver Lindley. Harcourt Brace & Co. 1954 378p o.p.

"Ernst, a young German soldier, gets a furlough in the closing days of World War II. He marries Elizabeth, a neighbor girl, who grew up while he was away. Their brief but touching honeymoon helps them to discover love and each other—a time to love. Upon his return from a furlough, Ernst is sent to guard four Russian prisoners. In a generous gesture, he releases them, but one of them, turns on him and kills him—a time to die." Wis Libr Bull

"The whole story is told with great restraint, with little sentimentality for those in misery and with little open rage at those who caused it." Chicago Sunday Trib

Renault, Mary, 1905-1983

The bull from the sea. Pantheon Bks. 1962 343p o.p.

*

"A sequel to *The King Must Die*, this mythological novel begins with Theseus, King of Athens, returning in triumph from Crete, where he has killed the Minotaur. On a subsequent adventure he captures and falls in love with the warrior princess, Hippolyta. Although married to Phaedra of Crete, Theseus continues his relationship with Hippolyta and both women bear him sons. Tragedy occurs when Phaedra is attracted to and spurned by Hippolyta's youthful son." Shapiro. Fic for Youth. 3d edition

Funeral games. Pantheon Bks. 1981 335p o.p.

LC 81-47273

This concludes the story of Alexander the Great that began in Fire from heaven and The Persian boy. "At 32 Alexander is dying in Babylon. The generals, two pregnant wives and a covey of conspirators keep a jackal-like vigil, anticipating the fight for possession of the empire, extending from Europe to India, that will break out when the godlike leader dies. At his death, the murderous power struggle ensues—Alexander's mother and his brain-injured half-brother, Philip, vie with the Regent and other extrafamilial seekers of the throne." Publ Wkly

"Miss Renault's main problem has been to make these monsters and monomaniacs believable, and this, at times with disconcerting insight, she does. . . . It might be argued that Funeral Games lacks a dominant central character. In fact the true center is the empty throne, and it is Alexander himself who, in death as in life, commands the scene absolutely." N Y Rev Books

The king must die. Pantheon Bks. 1958 338p pa $14 hardcover o.p.

ISBN 0-394-75104-3

"Retold by its hero, the legend of Theseus becomes a logical sequence of adventures that befell a slight, wiry, quick-witted youth impelled to prove his manhood in a semibarbaric society that put a premium on size and brawn. Although, at seventeen, he was already a king and a seasoned warrior, Theseus obeyed his patron god's prompting and voluntarily joined a company of young people conscripted for the bull-dances in Crete, became a renowned bull-leaper, and took advantage of an earthquake to overthrow the Cretan kingdom." Booklist

Followed by The bull from the sea (1962)

Renault, Mary, 1905-1983—*Continued*

The last of the wine. Pantheon Bks. 1956 389p
o.p.

           *

"This is a fictionalized account of Athens during the
years of the Peloponnesian War told by Alexias, a young
Athenian of good family background. We learn the details of daily life within the Greek city state, including
the literary, cultural, recreational, and political texture of
the time. One very memorable account is that of a wrestling match at the Isthmian Games." Shapiro. Fic for
Youth. 3d edition

The Persian boy. Pantheon Bks. 1972 432p o.p.
This sequel to Fire from heaven continues the "story
of Alexander the Great, focusing upon his momentous
expedition into Asia. This time we observe events
through the eyes of Bagoas, a beautiful Persian eunuch
who was loved by King Darius and then by Alexander
himself. The multiple facets of Renault's art, familiar to
a host of admirer's, are once again apparent: a particularly sensitive depiction of boyhood and youth; an astounding grasp of the facts and the spirit of the ancient world;
an unerring sense of the dramatic which, along with her
superb descriptive powers, brings to life a great historical
period." Libr J
Followed by Funeral games

Rendell, Ruth, 1930-
See also Vine, Barbara, 1930-

Adam and Eve and Pinch me; a novel. Crown
2002 356p pa $13.95
    ISBN 0-609-61025-2; 1-4000-3118-4 (pa)
                       LC 2001-32539
First published 2001 in the United Kingdom
This psychological thriller "concerns the wreckage
wrought on a variety of Londoners by a womanizing con
man who speaks in rhymes. . . . Araminta 'Minty'
Knox, the fragile center of the plot, is a 30-something
woman, alone and obsessed with hygiene, who works in
a dry-cleaning shop. All the world is a petri dish for
Minty, who sees germs everywhere, which she attacks
with Wright's Coal Tar Soap. She is equally tormented
by the ghosts she imagines, her domineering 'Auntie'
and the man who took her virginity." Publ Wkly
"Part ghost story, part serial-killer hunt, part excoriation of the wicked ways of Westminster and Fleet Street,
this tale tightens the noose of suspense through the build-
up of vivid domestic and social detail." Booklist

Blood lines; long and short stories. Crown 1996
215p o.p.
                       LC 96-852
  Contents: Blood lines; Lizzie's lover; Burning end;
The carer; The man who was the god of love; Expectations; Shreds and slivers; Clothes; Unacceptable levels;
In all honesty; The strawberry tree
"In this collection of short stories, Rendell is at her
best, using her own quixotic brand of dark humor and an
often heartwrenching poignancy to produce 11
minimasterpieces." Booklist

The bridesmaid. Mysterious Press 1989 259p
    ISBN 0-89296-388-3
                    * LC 88-43471

"Londoner Philip Wardman falls for a beautiful, enigmatic woman he meets at his sister's wedding. Wardman
abhors any depiction of violent death, but Senta believes
they should each kill someone to prove their love for
each other. He fantasizes a murder, while she, an actress
and perhaps just a little mad, tells a quite convincing story of murdering one of his enemies. What he discovers
about her tale leads to grief and horror." Libr J
"Ms. Rendell is a diabolically subtle writer. For much
of this claustrophobic study of mutual obsession, she has
us peering into Senta's mind through Philip's eyes, suspiciously analyzing her bizarre statements and mysterious
behavior. But, like a cunning old spider, the author has
caught two flies in her web; and in the end, Philip
proves the more interesting study, with his phobia about
violence and his fanaticism for propriety." N Y Times
Book Rev

Collected stories. Pantheon Bks. 1988 c1987
536p o.p.
                    * LC 87-35949
First published 1987 in the United Kingdom
The fallen curtain and other stories contains the following stories: The fallen curtain; People don't do such
things; A bad heart; You can't be too careful; The double; The venus fly trap; The clinging woman; The vine-
gar mother; The fall of a coin; Almost human; Divided
we stand
Means of evil contains the following stories: Means of
evil; Old wives' tales; Ginger and the Kingsmarkham
chalk circle; Achilles heel; When the wedding was over
The fever tree and other stories contains the following
stories: The fever tree; The dreadful day of judgement;
A glowing future; An outside interest; A case of coincidence; Thornapple; May and June; A needle for the devil; Front seat; Paintbox place; The wrong category
The new girl friend and other stories of suspense contains the following stories: The new girl friend; A dark
blue perfume; The orchard walls; Hare's house; Bribery
and corruption; The whistler; The convolvulus clock;
Loopy; Fen Hall; Father's Day; The green road to
Quephanda

The crocodile bird. Crown 1993 361p o.p.
                    * LC 93-14734
"After the police question her mother, Eve, about the
death of Jonathan Tobias, the owner of Shrove House,
16-year-old Liza runs away with Sean, the young garden
hand at the remote English manor. It is to him, over the
course of 101 nights, that Liza gradually reveals her
strange upbringing, living alone with Eve in the
gatehouse of the Tobias estate." Publ Wkly
"A kind of fairy-tale unreality informs this narrative,
for all its present-day accoutrements; it is written in careful, straightforward, almost childlike prose; and it keeps
you on tenterhooks, once you've surrendered to the atmosphere." Times Lit Suppl

The face of trespass. Doubleday 1974 184p o.p.
"Published for the Crime Club"
"Gray Lanceton, depressed, impoverished and struggling with a serious writing block, holes up in the 'hovel,' a shabby cottage deep in the English woods. He is
in flight from himself and the world. Gradually we learn
what has brought him to this pass—a feverish sexual obsession with a willful married woman who is always
promising to come away with him forever—if only her

Rendell, Ruth, 1930-—*Continued*

tiresome husband can be gotten out of the way." Publ Wkly

The author "conveys the derelict half-dream, half-nightmare life Gray is leading in an Essex hovel far better than a crime-writer need, and through this . . . makes credible the blindness that allows him to be led to total disaster." Times Lit Suppl

The fallen curtain and other stories
In Rendell, R. Collected stories p1-135

The fever tree and other stories
In Rendell, R. Collected stories p265-406

Going wrong. Mysterious Press 1990 260p o.p.
LC 90-40421

"Guy Curran—remarkably handsome, rich, the product of London's underworld, at once ill educated and quite bright—is obsessed with Leonora Chisholm, a childhood sweetheart who has drawn away from him, indeed plans to marry another man, but who oddly and somewhat irresolutely continues to have a rital lunch with Curran every Saturday. Curran repeatedly convinces himself that she is still in love with him but has been turned away by a college roommate, or her mother, stepfather or some other evil figure." N Y Times Book Rev

"Rendell is a master of depicting the long, slow slide into madness, making each tiny step toward the abyss resound with chilling logic." Publ Wkly

Harm done; an Inspector Wexford mystery. Crown 1999 346p $24
ISBN 0-609-60547-X
LC 99-20432

Three of the cases Wexford is involved in "have to do with the abuse of women or children. The crimes range from the ridiculous (a petulant university girl and a mentally challenged girl from a low-income housing project are each kidnapped to do housework and returned for ineptitude) to the monstrous (Wexford and his men must protect a child molester who was released from prison while a rich man tortures his wife in the comfort of his spacious home." Publ Wkly

Heartstones; illustrations by George Underwood. Harper & Row 1987 80p il o.p.
LC 86-46098

"The Harper short novel series"

"Adolescent Elvira is in intense spiritual communion with her father; she plans to devote all the rest of her life to him. Elvira's mother is dead, and her sister is outside the orbit that Elvira and her father have created for themselves. This arrangement works fine, as long as it lasts, but trouble arrives in the form of a woman Elvira's father wants to marry. Elvira is determined the marriage will not take place. And, alas, the fiancée dies—violently!" Booklist

"Such is Rendell's mastery of psychological suspense that throughout we remain unsure of the seriousness of Elvira's intentions." Libr J

A judgment in stone. Doubleday 1978 c1977 188p o.p.
* LC 77-76961

"Despite our knowing on p.2 who will die, and at whose hand, we are carried along by the powerful suspense of events in one upper-middle-class English family. The sense of impending doom amply takes the place of detective work, of which there is a little in the last

three short chapters. The depiction of the 'perfect servant' is masterly and the whole thing a tour de force." Barzun. Cat of Crime. Rev and enl edition

The keys to the street; a novel of suspense. Crown 1996 326p $24
ISBN 0-517-70685-7
LC 96-3114

A novel about the "homeless denizens who haunt Regent's Park in London. Residents of the exclusive neighborhoods abutting the park make a point of not even noticing wretches like Effie and Dill and Pharaoh and Roman. Only Mary Jago, a frail, sensitive young woman who has recently moved into the neighborhood as a housesitter, pays any attention to these street people—until someone starts killing them and impaling their bodies on the spiked railings that surround the park. . . . All the characters are drawn with psychological insight, but it takes a visionary author to see the bonds that connect them all." N Y Times Book Rev

Kissing the gunner's daughter. Mysterious Press 1992 378p o.p.
LC 91-50615

"Chief Inspector Reginald Wexford investigates his first case in four years, conducting us to stately Tancred House, where celebrity writer Davina Flory and her family have been murdered. The only survivor is granddaughter Daisy, who is pointedly contrasted with Wexford's own rebellious daughter." Libr J

This is an "intricate story that hinges on vanity and self-deception, a story in which the most minor and seemingly innocent relationships are charged with meaning and malice." N Y Times Book Rev

Live flesh. Pantheon Bks. 1986 272p o.p.
LC 86-4922

"The main character of [this novel] is a mentally disturbed young man. Driven by an uncontrollable panic, Victor Jenner has committed several rapes. He shoots a promising young police officer in the back, confining David Fleetwood to a wheelchair for the rest of his life. Victor is sent to prison for 14 years. After he is released he befriends David and his girlfriend Clare, with disastrous results." Christ Sci Monit

"The obvious way to write this novel would have been to tell it through the eyes of the crippled policeman; Rendell takes the bolder path of getting inside the mind of Jenner. . . . [This] is a frightening, resonant novel—an extraordinary achievement." New Statesman (1913)

Means of evil, five mystery stories
In Rendell, R. Collected stories p137-262

The new girl friend and other stories of suspense
In Rendell, R. Collected stories p409-536

Not in the flesh; a Wexford novel. Crown 2008 c2007 303p $25.95
ISBN 978-0-307-40681-1; 0-307-40681-4
LC 2007-40945

First published 2007 in the United Kingdom

In this Chief Inspector Wexford novel "a truffle-hunting suburbanite and his dog stumble across a long-buried body on a vacant property. Upon investigation, Wexford and his team uncover a second murder victim in the basement of the abandoned house on the property. The crimes were committed so long ago that the bodies themselves yield few clues, but the neighbors all seem to

Rendell, Ruth, 1930-—*Continued*

have reasons to be cast in a suspicious light." Libr J

"Rendell has been documenting change in her imaginary Kingsmarkham for 44 years; 'Not in the Flesh' continues to hold a mirror to British society. . . . [She] also weaves into the story Wexford's heartbreaking attempts to address the tradition of female genital mutilation within the Somali community of Kingsmarkham." Los Angeles Times Book Rev

Road rage. Crown 1997 344p o.p.

LC 97-1200

"Taking what he vows will be his last walk in the deep woods that border his Sussex village, Chief Inspector Reginald Wexford contemplates with dread the new superhighway that will soon plow it all under. . . . But whatever sympathy he feels for the militant conservationists who pitch camp in Framhurst Great Wood to protest the highway is lost when a radical splinter group calling itself Sacred Globe kidnaps five innocent people—including Wexford's wife—and threatens to kill them unless the road is stopped." N Y Times Book Rev

A sight for sore eyes. Crown 1999 327p $24

ISBN 0-609-60417-1   LC 98-27654

"Rendell charts a harrowing collision course for two preternaturally beautiful teen-agers: Teddy Brex, an unloved child who grows up to be a sociopath, and Francine Hill, an overprotected child who grows up to be his ideal victim. . . . Reaching back a generation to get more traction for her macabre love story, Rendell takes a ruthless probe to every person (from Teddy's emotionally arrested parents to the faceless stranger who murdered Francine's mother) who had a hand in shaping the psyches of this ill-met pair. Spare and unforgiving, these incisive character studies illuminate the darker corners of Teddy's and Francine's family histories without dimming the originality of their bizarre lives." N Y Times Book Rev

Simisola. Crown 1995 327p o.p.

LC 95-8428

This novel features Chief Inspector Reginald Wexford. A "Nigerian-born doctor in Kingsmarkham, England, reports his daughter, Melanie, as missing. Not long afterward, the body of a young black woman is found. She turns out not to be Melanie . . . and is conjectured rather to be an immigrant female, probably Nigerian, who was forced to work as a slave for one of the well-to-do local families. Another young woman, who may have spoken to the dead girl, is murdered." N Y Times Book Rev

"Rendell's long acquaintance with her characters has not diminished the freshness of her work, nor her consummate storytelling. Rather, in Simisola, she offers a finely tuned moral tale that raises questions as it solves crimes." Times Lit Suppl

A sleeping life. Doubleday 1978 180p o.p.

LC 77-27716

When Chief Inspector Wexford is "called in to investigate the murder of one Rhoda Comfrey he is baffled to be unable to learn anything at all about her private life, friends, or means of supporting herself. His only clue, an expensive leather wallet, leads him up and down blind alleys until a chance remark by his own daughter, whose marriage is in jeopardy, leads him to Webster's International Dictionary and a brilliant deduction about the motive of the murderer." Shapiro. Fic for Youth. 3d edition

Thirteen steps down; a novel. Crown 2005 c2004 340p $25

ISBN 1-4000-9842-4   LC 2005-750

First published 2004 in the United Kingdom

"Fitness-equipment repairman Mix Cellini lodges in a crumbling London mansion presided over by octogenarian Gwendolen Chawcer. Mix and Gwendolen have little in common except a lack of nurturing as children that has impaired their ability to develop meaningful relationships. The decay of the house mirrors the disintegration of Mix's personality as his obsessions with fame, murder, and beautiful model Nerissa Nash (a fellow lodger) eat his mind like a cancer. The creepiness of the mansion and its occupants is so pronounced that it is, at times, difficult to maintain interest in their fate. However, Rendell . . . veers away from the expected in her characters and in her plot, which saves the novel and makes for riveting reading." Libr J

The tree of hands. Pantheon Bks. 1985 c1984 271p o.p.

LC 84-19002

First published 1984 in the United Kingdom

"Benet, successful author and unwed mother, is visited by her mentally unstable mother, Mopsa. When the baby dies, Mopsa snatches another child to give to Benet. Substitute-baby Jason is the offspring of child abuser, larcenous Carol. The child's putative father is a gigolo intent on defrauding his current patroness. The story explores spectrum of parental feeling against a background of pervasive anxiety and impending doom. This is not a mystery, really, but rather an engrossing psychological thriller." Libr J

The water's lovely; a novel. Crown Publishers 2007 c2006 340p $25.95

ISBN 978-0-307-38136-1; 0-307-738136-6

LC 2006-29492

First published 2006 in the United Kingdom

"Ismay and Heather live with and care for their mother, who has been mentally unbalanced since finding her children's stepfather drowned in the bathtub. Ismay has always believed that her sister killed him, thinking that Heather was protecting her from his unwanted attentions. Keeping the dark secret seems to have tainted every area of their lives, as Ismay is emotionally unable to confront Heather and find out the truth about their stepfather's death." Libr J

"Rendell is in absolute top form here. The Water's Lovely is as suspenseful as any crime novel she has written, but it also has the generous humanity of her best Inspector Wexford cases. . . . Rendell provides the reader with many pleasures: her intelligence and humanity, her sculpted sentences, her jokeless wit, her refusal to join her colleagues in the torture-porn business to spice up her plots. Oh, yes—those plots. What a sneaky mind the woman has." Washington Post Book Rev

Resnick, Mike, 1942-

The return of Santiago. TOR Bks. 2003 464p $25.95

ISBN 0-7653-0224-1   LC 2002-75660

Sequel to: Santiago (1986)

"A century after the alleged demise of the legendary Santiago, the greatest outlaw of the Inner Frontier, a petty thief named Danny Briggs stumbles upon a lost collection of poems by Black Orpheus, the interstellar bard

Resnick, Mike, 1942-—*Continued*

whose verses immortalized Santiago. Inspired by his discovery, Briggs—now renamed Dante—sets off across the galaxy in search of someone to re-create the legend of Santiago and start a rebellion against the enemies of freedom." Libr J

"An eminently satisfying space western, with just the right mixture of fast-drawing gunmen and talented women to keep the action going." Booklist

Restrepo, Laura

Delirium; a novel; translated from the Spanish by Natasha Wimmer. Nan A. Talese/Doubleday 2007 320p $23.95

ISBN 978-0-385-51990-8; 0-385-51990-7

LC 2006-20282

Original Spanish edition, 2004

"Agustina's Bogota family is rich and troubled, and she is burdened by psychic powers. When her husband, a literature professor fallen on hard times, returns from a short trip, he finds Agustina in a hotel and out of her mind. As he struggles to piece together the events that precipitated her worst breakdown yet, Restrepo slowly unveils the baroque secrets of Agustina's German immigrant grandfather, her aunt Sofi's true role in the household, the plight of her gay brother, and shocking encounters with a gangster known as Midas." Booklist

"Restrepo—very ably translated here by Natasha Wimmer—manages her tricky, time-hopping, polyphonic structure with uncommon grace. Everything in 'Delirium' flows, like tributaries into a river. And where that mighty stream is meant to take us, I think, is back to that large body of passionate, history-obsessed literature that is, (or was) Latin American fiction. Restrepo's techniques in this novel recall the favored narrative methods of the so-called Boom years, invoking the spirits of Juan Rulfo, Jose Donoso, Manuel Puig and many others." N Y Times Book Rev

Reuland, Rob, 1963-

Semiautomatic; a novel. Random House 2004 242p $24.95

ISBN 0-375-50502-4

LC 2003-46806

"Brooklyn prosecutor Andrew Giobberti has been exiled to the Appeals Bureau for so long he's almost forgotten that putting away murderers is in his DNA. Almost. When he's pulled out of purgatory to rescue a politically sensitive homicide trial prepped by a green, painfully ethical prosecutor, Giobberti's soon ready for his courtroom comeback. But even as he shows his unwilling partner the ropes they'll use to encircle the defendant's neck, disturbing holes start appearing in the case" Booklist

This thriller is "notable not for violence but for subtle characterizations, moral ambiguities and exceptional writing." Washington Post Book World

Reuss, Frederick, 1960-

Henry of Atlantic City. MacMurray & Beck 1999 249p

ISBN 1-87844-889-7

LC 99-26946

This novel "begins in the modern-day casino town where Henry's father, a chief security officer at Caesar's Palace with mob connections, is on the run for embezzlement. The six-year-old Henry, being a precocious (he has a photographic memory) but lonely child, spends his time poring over The Coptic Gnostic Library and comes to think of himself as living the life of a saint in fifth-century Byzantium. And so the new and old worlds conflate into one seamless whole in young Henry's mind. . . . The rest of the story follows Henry as he winds through several cities, encountering thieves, prostitutes, and priests who baffle and are baffled by him." Booklist

"Reuss's manner—a spare third-person narrative, sticking largely to terms and phrases Henry knows—becomes a courageously concentrated show of authorial control and tonal fidelity." Publ Wkly

Horace afoot. MacMurray & Beck 1997 278p

ISBN 1-878448-79-X

* LC 97-21601

In this novel, "Quintus Horatius Flaccus, a man of wealth and mystery, moves to Oblivion, a small midwestern town. Horace, who changed his name from William Blake, is fleeing from the vagaries and dissonance of contemporary life. Horace's idiosyncrasies—no car, wandering the town at odd hours, a propensity for turning up in the wrong places at the wrong times and frequently without clothes, his random phone calls to engage Oblivionites in Socratic dialogues on topics such as what is love—do not endear him to the town's residents. Gradually, real life intrudes as Horace becomes friends with a dying librarian, rescues a rape victim, and becomes the target of a malicious adolescent." Booklist

This novel "combines two strands of plot: a sly satire of Midwestern life and a restrained account of how a closed heart comes to be unlocked. . . . combines two strands of plot: a sly satire of Midwestern life and a restrained account of how a closed heart comes to be unlocked." N Y Times Book Rev

Mohr; a novel. Unbridled Books 2006 312p il $25.95

ISBN 1-932961-17-8

LC 2005-37958

"On a trip to Germany, Reuss . . . came upon some photos of the family of distant relative Max Mohr, a Jewish playwright who left his gentile wife, Kä the, and his schoolgirl daughter, Eva, and immigrated to Shanghai during the Nazi era. Determined to piece together this family's story, Reuss constructed a novel around the photos . . . . In alternating chapters he describes the family's idyllic life in the Tegernsee valley and Mohr's life in wartorn Shanghai, where he works as a physician." Libr J

"Reuss's prose rarely if ever impresses through sheer imagery or wordplay or beauty, but it's concise and solidly-constructed, and it conveys his meaning well. The strength of Reuss's writing is more in his observations, the way he builds emotions out of little details like the objects in the clutter of a room or the way a certain person moves. The writing and the photographs play off of one another, illustrating each other. And the images seem to perfectly capture the mood of the story as it goes on." PopMatters

The wasties. Pantheon Bks. 2002 229p $23

ISBN 0-375-42071-1

LC 2001-55450

Reuss, Frederick, 1960-—*Continued*

"English professor Michael 'Caruso' Taylor has lost the ability to speak and embarks on a journey of infantilization that progressively strips him of his autonomy—a condition he labels 'the wasties.' He grows entirely dependent on others: his pregnant wife, Gina; his nurse, Theresa; and a host of health-care professionals who attempt to rein in his childish impulses. Taylor communicates via scribbled messages, IBM ThinkPad and hand gestures." Publ Wkly

"This should appeal to sophisticated readers who like darkly humorous, cerebral fiction." Booklist

Reverte, Arturo Pérez- *See* Pérez-Reverte, Arturo

Reyn, Irina

What happened to Anna K.; a novel. Simon & Schuster 2008 244p $24

ISBN 978-1-4165-5893-4; 1-4165-5893-4

LC 2007-39332

"A Touchstone book"

"Set among early 21st-century Russian Jewish immigrants in New York City, Reyn's debut . . . adapts Anna Karenina's social melodrama for a decidedly different set of Russians. Anna, 30-something with a string of bad relationships behind her and a restless, literarily inclined soul, is wooed into marriage by the financial stability and social appropriateness of Alex K., an older businessman with roots in her Rego Park, Queens, community. As Anna chafes at her unromantic life, trouble hits in the form of David, the hipster-writer boyfriend of her sweet, naïve cousin, Katia." Publ Wkly

"It takes a lot of self-confidence to suggest that your first novel is a modern-day retelling of Anna Karenina. But once you're finished marveling at Reyn's audacity, her formidable storytelling gift sweeps you along and keeps you turning the pages in rapt anticipation, even as you're aware that the sound in the distance is the rumble of that inevitable approaching train." N Y Times Book Rev

Reynolds, Alastair, 1966-

The prefect. Ace Books 2008 410p $25.95

ISBN 978-0-441-01591-7; 0-441-01591-3

LC 2008-60017

"As a prefect working for the Panoply, Tom Dreyfus enforces the law in the utopian society of the Glitter Band, a collection of space habitats that orbit the planet Yellowstone. When an attack on one of the habitats leaves nearly 1000 people dead, Dreyfus uncovers a plot that threatens the freedom of the entire Glitter Band. Reynolds . . . returns to the universe of Revelation Space as he demonstrates his powerful ability to blend futuristic suspense/intrigue with personal drama in a tale of one man's search for truth, however unpleasant or demanding it may be. . . . Action-packed hard sf." Libr J

Reynolds, Margaret

(ed) The Penguin book of lesbian short stories. See The Penguin book of lesbian short stories

Reynolds, Marjorie, 1921-1997

The Starlite Drive-in; a novel. Morrow 1997 282p $23

ISBN 0-688-15389-5

LC 97-728

"When developers find a body in a well at the old Starlite Drive-In, Callie Ann Benton knows whose body it is. It takes her back to when she was 12; her father ran the drive-in, and her mother, Teal, had become completely trapped inside her house by agoraphobia. It traps her father, too, forcing him to give up dreams, and his resentment comes out in nasty sniping, continuous putdowns that drain her—until a drifter named Charlie Memphis arrives, falls in love with Teal, and plans to take her and Callie away. This stunning novel is told by 12-year-old Callie, torn between her crush on Memphis, her love for her father, and her resentment of her mother's sexuality and personhood." Libr J

Reynolds, Sheri

A gracious plenty; a novel. Harmony Bks. 1997 205p $21

ISBN 0-609-60225-X

LC 97-21544

The narrator "is a deeply troubled woman growing up in a Southern fundamentalist culture. Hideously burned in an accident when she was only 4, Finch Nobles is shunned and persecuted. . . . Worse yet, she becomes the inspirational 'project' of the adult women's Sunday school class. Wishing she were already dead and buried, she dedicates herself to caring for the local cemetery, where she communes with the spirits of the departed." NY Times Book Rev

"Lyricism and the gentle voice of her heroine carry this poignant but redemptive story of an emotionally and physically scarred woman who finds her way out of the land of the dead and into the land of the living." Publ Wkly

Rhodes, David, 1946-

Driftless. Milkweed Editions 2008 429p $24

ISBN 978-1-57131-059-0; 1-57131-059-2

LC 2008-20881

"Set in a rural Wisconsin town, the book presents a series of portraits that resemble Edgar Lee Masters's 'Spoon River Anthology' in their vividness and in the cumulative picture they create of village life. There's a drifter trying to put down roots, a hardworking dairy farmer being taken advantage of by a corrupt milk coöperative, a female pastor who hears heavenly voices, and a cranky retiree who discovers a cougar living in his haymow." New Yorker

Rhodes, Jewell Parker

Voodoo dreams; a novel of Marie Laveau. St. Martin's Press 1993 436p o.p.   LC 93-24283

This novel is about "Marie Laveau, New Orleans' legendary nineteenth-century voodoo queen. Although few biographical facts are known about Marie, Rhodes has parlayed them into a character of vast dimension and feminine power. Like her grandmother and mother before her, Marie is a *voodooienne*, a woman visited and possessed by the African god Damballah, and the third Marie Laveau to suffer the consequences of this terrifying

Rhodes, Jewell Parker—*Continued*

blessing in a world poisoned by the sin of slavery. As Rhodes imagines Marie's strange and painful life, from her protected childhood deep in the bayou to her reign as healer in New Orleans, she evokes all the lust, tumult, and cruelty of that race-obsessed city." Booklist

Yellow moon. Atria Books 2008 293p $24
ISBN 978-1-4165-3710-6; 1-4165-3710-4
LC 2008-15221

This sequel to Voodoo season (2006) is the second title in the author's New Orleans trilogy

In this thriller, "a wazimamoto, or African vampire, stalks Dr. Marie Laveau, a 21st-century doctor, modern voodoo practitioner and descendant of the legendary Voodoo Queen of New Orleans. Haunted by the unquiet spirits of people killed by the wazimamoto, the young doctor vows to stop it with the help of new boyfriend NOPD Det. Daniel Parks; her Creole boss, Dr. Louis DuLac; and others devoted to Marie and her young adopted daughter, Marie-Claire. . . . Rhodes includes an informative author's note about the evolution of the African vampire as a 'response and a warning about racist brutality' and 'cultural vampirism,' giving some cultural weight to this hypnotic thriller." Publ Wkly

Rhys, Jean

The collected short stories; introduction by Diana Athill. Norton 1987 403p o.p.
LC 88-138678

Contents: Illusion; A spiritualist; From a French prison; In a café; Tout Montparnasse and a lady; Mannequin; In the Luxemburg Gardens; Tea with an artist; Trio; Mixing cocktails; Again the Antilles; Hunger; Discourse of a lady standing a dinner to a down-and-out friend; A night; In the Rue de l'Arrivée; Learning to be a mother; The blue bird; The grey day; The Sidi; At the Villa d'Or; La grosse Fifi; Vienne; Till September Petronella; The day they burned the books; Let them call it jazz; Tigers are better-looking; Outside the machine; The lotus; A solid house; The sound of the river; I spy a stranger; Temps perdi; Pioneers, oh, pioneers; Good-bye Marcus, good-bye Rose; The Bishop's feast; Heat; Fishy waters; Overture and beginners please; Before the deluge; On not shooting sitting birds; Kikimora; Night out 1925; The Chevalier of the Place Blanche; The insect world; Rapunzel, Rapunzel; Who knows what's up in the attic; Sleep it off lady; I used to live here once; Kismet; The whistling bird; Invitation to the dance

Quartet. Simon & Schuster 1929 228p o.p.

First published 1928 in the United Kingdom with title Postures

"The ingredients: an English girl in Paris, married to a Polish adventurer, who is imprisoned for theft and leaves her penniless, a stranger except for casual acquaintances in the foreign colony, to become the guest of an English couple, a man who desires her and can arouse her passion, and his wife, who keeps the girl in the home where she has her always under observation, always at a disadvantage, until she can finally crush her. The attitudes of the three are exposed with pitiless precision—the utter helplessness of the victim, the diabolic ingenuity of the wife, the social cowardice of the husband which makes a peculiarly disgusting setting for his lust.

The background of Paris, in its cold hostility, with its tedious round of mechanical pleasures, throws the episode into harsh relief." Bookman (NY)

Wide Sargasso Sea; introduction by Francis Wyndham. Norton 1967 c1966 189p o.p.
*

First published 1966 in the United Kingdom

This novel, "set in Dominica and Jamaica during the 1830s, presents the life of the mad Mrs. Rochester from 'Jane Eyre,' a Creole heiress here called Antoinette Cosway; in the brief last section she is imprisoned in the attic in Thornfield Hall." Oxford Companion to Engl Lit. 6th edition

Riboud, Barbara Chase- *See* Chase-Riboud, Barbara, 1939-

Rice, Anne, 1941-

Blackwood Farm. Knopf 2002 527p (Vampire chronicles) $26.95
ISBN 0-375-41199-2
LC 2003-272519

In this ninth volume in the author's vampire chronicles "fledgling vampire Quinn Blackwood makes a desperate appeal to the older, stronger Lestat to save his loved ones from Goblin, a doppelganger out to destroy them. Since Quinn entered the dark world of the undead, the once caring and protective Goblin has amassed tremendous strength and a ruthlessness that cannot be controlled. Lestat is intrigued but refuses to make a decision until Quinn tells his life story. Slowly, the dark, Gothic settings and eccentric characters that make Rice's fiction so fascinating emerge." Libr J

Blood and gold; or, The story of Marius. Knopf 2001 471p (Vampire chronicles) $26.95
ISBN 0-679-45449-7
LC 2001-94703

This eighth volume of the Vampire chronicles features Marius, a mentor to Lestat, the creator of Armand, and the lover of Pandora. "The intellectual and artistic 'Child of the Millennia' meets ice-age Thorne, another vampire, who's just waking up after a very long sleep and is eager to hear his history. Marius grants Thorne's wish, taking him and the reader on a rollicking vampire adventure through time." Booklist

Blood canticle. Knopf 2003 305p (Vampire chronicles) $25.95
ISBN 0-375-41200-X
LC 2002-192475

This tenth volume of the Vampire chronicles takes up where "Blackwood Farm ended, the now-doppelganger-free Quinn Blackwood and Lestat save Quinn's true love, the witch Mona Mayfair, from certain death by making her an immortal. In his effort to attain sainthood, Lestat must deal with a lot of metaphysical angst. The opulent Blackwood estate and its spooky swamps, as well as New Orleans and a Caribbean isle, provide the settings for many elegant costume changes as the exquisite vampiric triumvirate gleefully suck several deserving victims dry and lay waste to dozens of a drug lord's minions." Publ Wkly

Christ the Lord: out of Egypt. Knopf 2005 336p $25.95
ISBN 0-375-41201-8
LC 2005-44077

Rice, Anne, 1941---*Continued*

"Seven-year-old Jesus narrates the story of his extended family's trek from Alexandria, Egypt, to Nazareth. The novel opens with the death and resurrection of Eleazer, both of which young Jesus is responsible for. After an angry mob shows up on Joseph and Mary's doorstep, they decide to leave Egypt in favor of the Holy Land, despite the protests of Jesus' teacher and Philo, a nobleman who has taken an interest in the thoughtful boy. But Joseph will not be swayed, and the family sets sail, with aunts, uncles, and cousins in tow as well. The journey is not an easy one, and more hardship awaits them in Jerusalem, which is in turmoil after the death of corrupt King Herod, and in Nazareth, which is overrun with Roman soldiers." Booklist

"Rice is a first-rate writer. There are no purple patches in this narrative, and no attempts to sermonize. There is a story to tell, and since we know the story on which it is based, Rice adroitly forces us to think about how she is going to weave in the gospel stories without sounding contrived or forced." Commonweal

Christ the Lord: the road to Cana. Knopf 2008 242p $25.95

ISBN 978-1-4000-4352-1; 1-400-04352-2

The second title in the author's projected four-volume life of Christ "opens with Jesus, known as Yeshua, as a young man, now more than 30, living with his extended family in the village of Nazareth. He knows who he is, or rather what he is, to be sure, but the path of this book takes him through his 40 days in the desert to the first great miracle of his ministry, the changing of water into wine. The story of Christ is the most famous story in the world; what revelations are there for the novelist? One of the great achievements of Rice's undertaking, thus far, is to reveal Christ's Jewish roots in all their strength and complexity. . . . Rice has achieved a prose style that is much simpler, much more straightforward, than that of her earlier works. Yet, in moments of revelation, her old breathless rapture serves her well." New Orleans Times-Picayune

The Feast of All Saints. Simon & Schuster 1979 571p o.p.   LC 79-16680

"The world of the Free People of Color (the 'gens de couleur libre') in antebellum New Orleans (the old French city) is the background for this romantic historical novel that brings to life an era and a place. . . . Quadroon Marcel Ste. Maria and his lovely sister Marie, children of a white plantation owner, and the lovely Cecile, his dusky mistress, grow up in the demimonde, housed and supported and educated as gentility by their father, but destined to be separated from his world by virtue of their mixed blood. . . . [The story] pits passion and principle and love against the hard realities of class and color in old New Orleans." Publ Wkly

Interview with the vampire. Reset for anniversary ed. Knopf 1996 340p $27.95; pa $7.99

ISBN 0-394-49821-6; 0-345-33766-2 (pa)
                                              * LC 96-232882

First published 1976

"In contemporary New Orleans a young reporter listens as Louis, a vampire, unfolds his tale. His story spans several hundred years . . . of a Faustian search for some meaning to his life-in-death existence, an existence complicated by his relationship to three other vampires.

Lestat, the vampire who made him, is hated by Claudia, the five-year-old extraordinarily beautiful child-vampire Louis loves. . . . After Claudia attempts to kill Lestat she and Louis go to Europe in search of other vampires. In Paris they find Armand, Master Vampire, and he and Louis fall in love, remaining together for a time after Claudia's death in a state of meaningless immortality." Libr J

Followed by The vampire Lestat (1985); The queen of the damned (1988); The tale of the body thief (1992); Memnoch the Devil (1995); The vampire Armand (1998); Merrick (2000); Blood and gold; or, The story of Marius (2001)

Lasher; a novel. Knopf 1993 577p $30

ISBN 0-679-41295-6   LC 93-12246

"Returning to the Mayfair clan she introduced in *The Witching Hour* Rice offers another vast, transcontinental saga of witchcraft and demonism in the tradition of Gothic melodrama. . . . Embedded in this antique demonism is a contemporary tale of incest and family abuse that achieves resonance. It is maintained through the character of Lasher, both child and man at the same time, who manipulates his victims with his own pain. At their best, Rice's characters rise above the more wooden plot machinations with an ironic and modern complexity." Publ Wkly

Followed by Taltos

Memnoch the Devil. Knopf 1995 353p (Vampire chronicles) $25

ISBN 0-679-44101-8   LC 95-77866

The fifth volume of the Vampire chronicles "finds vampire Lestat de Lioncourt being courted by fallen archangel Memnoch, a.k.a. Satan, to be his lieutenant in Hell, but not for the purpose of pursuing evil. Memnoch instead desires Lestat's help in redeeming souls." Libr J

The author "boldly probes the significance of death, belief in the afterlife and other spiritual matters." Publ Wkly

Followed by The vampire Armand

Merrick; a novel. Knopf 2000 307p $26.95

ISBN 0-679-45448-9   LC 99-88556

The seventh volume of the Vampire chronicles. Narrated "by the fledgling David Talbot, the book introduces Merrick, a potent witch with the usual irresistible charms, who aids David in a request involving a desperate Louis—a request that climaxes in disaster and alters Louis profoundly." Libr J

"This volume merges several long-running plots. . . . Merrick must revisit the Guatemalan rainforest, where she traveled as a young girl, to locate a secret treasure trove of ominous ancient runes. Displaying her imaginative talents for atmosphere and suspense, Rice creates a riveting scene that shows Merrick's awesome magic at work." Publ Wkly

The queen of the damned; the third book in the vampire chronicles. Knopf 1988 448p (Vampire chronicles) $27.50

ISBN 0-394-55823-5
                                              * LC 88-45311

In this third volume in the Vampire chronicles "the plot revolves around an internecine struggle in vampiredom. On one side is 6000-year-old Akasha, who has concluded that the world would be a safer, more

Rice, Anne, 1941-—*Continued*

peaceful and equitable place if women ran it. Her plan is to set herself up as the reigning Goddess of Earth; then to kill off all human males except a few breeders, until such time when female values are firmly in place and males can be allowed to flourish again. Her opponents argue that you can't make a peaceful world through violence." Ms

"Don't let the title or the subject matter fool you; this is quality fiction written with care and intelligence. There are no false steps or wasted words in the multilayered plot, and the many characters each have a distinct voice. It's not absolutely necessary to have read the other 'Chronicles' to understand this one, but it would add greatly to the richness of the whole." Libr J

Followed by The tale of the body thief

The tale of the body thief. Knopf 1992 430p (Vampire chronicles) $30

    ISBN 0-679-40528-3   LC 92-53085

In this fourth novel in the Vampire chronicles Lestat encounters Raglan James, "a mortal con man whose extraordinary psychic powers let him cheat the vampire out of his demonic, enormously powerful body. . . . Lestat, in a male human body, charges about the world with his mortal friend David Talbot, trying to reclaim his vampire body." Time

"Readers who crave a happy ending, a justice and a moral coherence that transcend the muddle they really live in, may feel [the author] has broken faith with them. After all, isn't that what escapist fiction is supposed to provide? Grown-ups, on the other hand, will be intelligently entertained, and no more disquieted than usual." Newsweek

Followed by Memnoch the Devil

Taltos; lives of the Mayfair witches. Knopf 1994 467p $25

    ISBN 0-679-42573-X   LC 93-35693

"This third book in the Mayfair Witches series tells the story of Ash, a centuries-old Taltos who resides in New york City. The Taltos grow to a height of seven feet, carry an extra set of chromosomes, and have a superior intelligence that enables them to digest dictionaries and encyclopedias in moments. There is something rotten in the state of the Talamasca, an order of scholars who study the supernatural and keep records of the Mayfair witches. When one such scholar is murdered, Rowan Mayfair, the mother of the two late Taltos in *Lasher*, and husband Michael Curry investigate. . . . Although this novel is a suspenseful and sometimes thought-provoking page-turner, it does not stand on its own; the first two books in the series must be read first." Libr J

The vampire Armand. Knopf 1998 387p (Vampire chronicles) $26.95

    ISBN 0-679-45447-0   LC 98-14579

The sixth volume of the Vampire chronicles follows the vampire Armand "from his boyhood in Kiev Rus, a conquered city under the rule of the Mongols, to ancient Constantinople, where he is sold into slavery by vicious Tartars, to the palazzo in Renaissance Venice, where he meets the great vampire Marius, who gives him the gift of the vampire blood and shows him how to be an 'ethical' vampire. . . . As always, Rice paints a fascinating and dazzling historical tapestry, providing a beautifully written and incredibly absorbing tale." Booklist

The vampire Lestat; the second book in the chronicles of the vampires. Knopf 1985 481p (Vampire chronicles) $27.50

    ISBN 0-394-53443-3   LC 85-40123

In this second volume of the Vampire chronicles Lestat "isn't dead, but has been alive, well, and resting in his New Orleans crypt since 1929. The chance to become the lead singer with a satanic heavy metal rock band is just enough to wrest him from his unquiet grave, however, and Lestat's desires to become a celebrity and to set the world straight on vampires prompt him to recount his life." Booklist

This novel "is ornate and pungently witty. In the classic tradition of Gothic fiction, it teases and tantalizes us into accepting its kaleidoscopic world. Even when they annoy us or tell us more than we want to know, its undead characters are utterly alive. Their adventures and frustrations are funny, frightening and surprising at once." N Y Times Book Rev

Followed by The queen of the damned

Vittorio the vampire; new tales of the vampires. Knopf 1999 292p $19.95

    ISBN 0-375-40160-1   LC 98-14209

In this novel, "Vittorio tells of his human life and the dramatic events that led him to join the ranks of the undead. He is 16, living the privileged life of the nobility in Renaissance Italy, when a host of vampires savagely attacks his family. His parents, brother, and sister are ruthlessly murdered, but Vittorio has caught the eye of the beautiful vampiress Ursula and is spared. Eventually, Vittorio has his revenge on the demons who have destroyed his loved ones, but he pays a terrible price." Libr J

The witching hour; a novel. Knopf 1990 965p $29.95

    ISBN 0-394-58786-3

                  * LC 90-53103

Rice "tells the story of the prominent and wealthy Mayfair family who, for five centuries, has cavorted with a supernatural entity that has brought them both great bounty as well as abject misery. Neurosurgeon Rowan Mayfair inherits the family fortune, along with the sinister attentions of this entity. When Rowan saves the life of Michael Curry their fates become entwined, and together they seek to understand and destroy the terrible force that holds her family in its power. Helping them in this dangerous task is occult investigator Aaron Lightner. . . . Although a bit long-winded at times, this is still a compelling novel." Libr J

Followed by Lasher

Rice, Luanne

Blue moon. Viking 1993 305p o.p.

                  * LC 92-50732

This novel focuses on "four generations of a Rhode Island resort-town fishing family. The action focuses primarily on the grand-daughters of the family founders (and mainly on the youngest, Cass), who are helping their parents run the family's waterfront restaurant. . . . Dad is thinking of retiring and selling off the waterfront property to developers, Cass's teenage son can't believe how incredibly dense his parents are, and Billy, Cass's husband, is nearly lost at sea." Libr J

"Such a rare combination of realism and romance

Rice, Luanne—*Continued*

comes along well, once in a blue moon. You don't have to be a sucker for happy endings to love this book, but it helps." N Y Times Book Rev

The deep blue sea for beginners; a novel. Bantam Books 2009 302p $26

ISBN 978-0-553-80514-7; 0-553-80514-2

LC 2009-13277

This sequel to Geometry of sisters is "about a reunion of a mother and her two daughters who've been separated for 10 years due to a disturbing secret. Set on the picturesque isle of Capri, Rice's touching tale reflects on how families can survive and thrive despite tragedies. Lyra Nicholson is a lonely heiress living in Italy while her equally lonely daughters, 16-year-old Pell and Lucy, a 14-year-old math whiz, live in Newport, R.I. with their grandmother. Lucy's already tried to contact (via equations) the ghost of her dead father with Beck, her BFF and the sister of Pell's boyfriend, Travis. Pell travels to Italy, wanting Lyra, who abandoned her and Lucy, to finally take responsibility for them. . . . Rice gives Pell an old-beyond-her-years stability that Lyra lacks in this beguiling beach read." Publ Wkly

The geometry of sisters. Bantam Books 2009 319p $25

ISBN 978-0-553-80513-0; 0-553-80513-4

LC 2008-55703

"Maggie Shaw second-guesses herself all the way from Columbus, Ohio, to Newport, Rhode Island, after two tragedies threaten to tear her family apart. While on vacation, her husband drowned, and her oldest daughter Carrie ran away after surviving the accident. Maggie is uprooting her son Travis, the football star, and her fragile daughter Beck, who mourns the loss of her beloved sister, so she can support the family as a teacher at a unique private high school. Maggie's past is anchored to Newport, with her estranged sister and J. D., the man who drove a wedge between them, living nearby. . . . The always insightful and engaging Rice explores the mystical bond between sisters as she portrays families learning what it means to love and forgive." Booklist

Home fires. Bantam Bks. 1995 312p o.p.

LC 94-23911

In this novel, "privileged New Yorker Anne Davis returns to her New England island childhood home after the death of her four-year-old daughter and the breakup of her marriage. Seeking solitude from her sister, who has never left the island, she finds kinship—and love—with a scarred fireman who understands tragedy, having survived it himself. At the same time she reconnects with her teenaged niece, whose high school days are in danger of becoming a haze of alcohol and lust. . . . A strikingly real story of family feelings and grief." Libr J

Last kiss. Bantam Books 2008 339p $25

ISBN 978-0-553-80512-3; 0-553-80512-6

LC 2007-52179

"Rice makes a . . . return visit to the Hubbard's Point, Conn., setting of Beach Girls (2004). As the book opens, a year soaked in Wild Turkey has passed since singer/songwriter Sheridan Rosslare lost her son, Charlie, in a random New York mugging. While Sheridan drowns her sorrows, Charlie's girlfriend, Nell Kilvert, is more assiduous; she hires private investigator Gavin Dawson

to prove there was nothing random about Charlie's death. For his part, Hubbard's Point native Gavin, a New York transplant, had pretty much written off Hubbard's Point after Sheridan, once the love of his life, dumped him for his wild and reckless ways years before. Now, older and wiser, he's still in love with Sheridan and wants to start over, but Sheridan's grief soon proves a formidable obstacle. An element of supernatural whimsy, a dark secret involving a trust fund and a disturbing question related to Charlie's estranged father, Randy, add complexity, while cameos from other Beach Girls characters contribute an engaging, homey touch." Publ Wkly

The letters; [by] Luanne Rice & Joseph Monninger. Bantam Books 2008 199p $22

ISBN 978-0-553-80741-7; 0-553-80741-2

LC 2008-25627

"Sam West dogsleds across Alaska to the site of the plane crash that killed his only child, Paul, three years earlier. Meanwhile, Sam's wife, Hadley, rents a cabin off the coast of Maine to rekindle her passion for art. Paul had dropped out of Amherst College and was on his way to teach in a remote Inuit village when he died. His death signaled the last breath of the Wests' marriage as well. Or had it been dying long before their son's demise? Sam initiates the correspondence, but soon each spouse comes to view it as a means of being truly honest one last time before their divorce becomes final." Libr J

"With each character–and each author–providing vivid descriptions of his and her surroundings and intense emotions, it's hard for the reader to remember that she is reading fiction and not eavesdropping on personal correspondence saturated with sadness and love." Booklist

Safe harbor. Bantam Bks. 2002 337p

ISBN 0-553-80218-6   LC 2001-49954

A novel set in the seaside town of Black Hall, Connecticut. "Grief-stricken Dana Underhill returns home to care for her two nieces, Quinn and Allie, following the death of her sister, Lily, and Lily's husband, Mike, in a sailing accident. Dana, a professional painter, had intended to whisk her nieces back to France with her, but her plans are put on hold when she realizes that change may not be what's best for Quinn and Allie. Indeed, Quinn, a cigarette-smoking 12-year-old with a chip on her shoulder, is dead set against leaving, particularly since she's determined to uncover the circumstances surrounding her parents' deaths. . . . Dana's childhood acquaintance, oceanographer and Yale professor Sam Trevor, arrives to provide Dana with a shoulder to lean on and to help Quinn find the answers she seeks." Publ Wkly

Summer light. Bantam Bks. 2001 372p

ISBN 0-553-80122-8   LC 2001-25475

A novel about wedding planner May Taylor and her "daughter, Kylie, a special child who seems to feel things more deeply than others and who sees angels. It's Kylie who brings her mother and Bruins hockey star, Martin Cartier, together. For Martin, its love at first sight, but May is leery of relationships. She finally agrees to marriage, but life is complicated as their careers require that they live alternately in Connecticut, Canada, and Boston. . . . With her gift, Kylie tries to unite the family in the face of tragedy, and the prolific Rice skillfully blends romance with magic." Booklist

Rich, Nathaniel, 1980-

The mayor's tongue. Riverhead Books 2008 310p $24.95

ISBN 978-1-594-48990-7; 1-594-48990-4

LC 2008-06832

"Both Eugene Brentani and Mr. Schmitz are on quests to the enchanted hinterlands of Italy's mountainous North—one for his disappeared lady love, the other for his inexplicably deteriorating best friend. Their journeys are distinct but complementary, not overlapping so much as being similarly mired in a fantastical domain ruled by the words and rumored presence of Constance Eakins, a celebrated lothario, philosopher king and profligate poet. The novel's foremost delight is its measured, nearly imperceptible descent into the realm of fairy-tale. There is no rabbit hole to fall through—reality and fairy-tale coexist, sharing the same borders, the same characters, and the same heartbreak for jilted lovers." Paste

Rich, Virginia

The baked bean supper murders. Dutton 1983 267p o.p.

LC 83-70156

"Eugenia Potter arrives at her sometime home in Northcutt Harbor, Me., just in time for the annual baked-bean dinner. She is also just in time to see her dearest friends carried off, first by accident and then by natural causes. She begins to feel uneasy, and when her beloved weimaraner is electrocuted in an accident that saves her own life, she takes another look at the earlier deaths. While Mrs. Potter goes about discovering who is responsible for what she determines to be murder, we get to sample Maine cooking, complete with recipes." Publ Wkly

"Colorful and chatty, with a fleet of diverse, realistic characters, this novel presents the rich tapestry of small-town life." Libr J

The cooking school murders. Dutton 1982 207p o.p.

LC 81-22162

"Harrington, Iowa, has its own 'beautiful people' and 12 of them gather for the first session of a gourmet cooking class. James Redmond, chef 'extraordinaire,' instructs his students in the versatility of a thin, sharp boning knife. The next day, the enrollment is minus three. One lies dead, stabbed with a boning knife. One is an apparent suicide and murderer. One is drowned accidentally. Eugenia Potter, home on a visit, knows the town and suspects that not all is what it seems." Publ Wkly

The Nantucket diet murders. Delacorte Press 1985 276p o.p.

LC 84-21501

"It is the middle of winter in Nantucket, and a group of year-round residents, more or less well-to-do widows who call themselves 'Les Girls,' gather to welcome home an old friend, Eugenia Potter, an erstwhile member of the group who now resides in Arizona and Maine. Their latest subject for talk is the arrival of a charismatic diet doctor, the mysterious Count Tony Ferencz, who has Les Girls all in a flutter and looking better than they have in years. No sooner has Eugenia arrived however, than strange events begin to occur. . . . Eugenia finally manages to find the answers in a dangerous and suspense-filled conclusion. Fans of Nantucket and haute cuisine will find and enjoy both in this somewhat over-long, but well-written book." Publ Wkly

Richards, David Adams, 1950-

The bay of love and sorrows; a novel. Arcade Pub. 2003 307p $24.95

ISBN 1-55970-650-3

LC 2002-38348

"In the early Seventies, Michael Skid, the privileged son of a judge, returns to his hometown on the Oyster River in rural New Brunswick from his postgraduate wanders through India. He takes up with a dangerous crowd, including Everette Hutch, an ex-convict who makes a practice of surreptitiously taping his friends in order to blackmail them later, and his coterie of drug-using associates." Libr J

"Michael is as naive as the other downtrodden individuals Everette has chosen as pawns to carry out his darkly laid plans, and the tragic events that ensue will forever be ingrained in the minds of the townpeople residing in The Bay of Love and Sorrows. Richards' story falls into place with the ease of a domino rally, providing all of the elements for a riveting story." Booklist

Richardson, C. S.

The end of the alphabet. Doubleday 2007 119p $16.95

ISBN 978-0-385-52255-7; 0-385-52255-X

LC 2006-36823

"Ambrose Zephyr, a 50-ish man leading a boring, contented life, discovers at his annual medical exam that he has an unspecified illness with no cure, and only 30 days, give or take, to live. The news comes as a blow both to Ambrose and to his loving wife, Zipper. Attempting to come to terms with this loss of life and love, they try to satisfy Ambrose's previously unfulfilled desire to travel by racing from one place to the next, each geographical location corresponding with successive letters of the alphabet." PopMatters

"The surprise of this little book is not that it is poignant but that it is delightful: graceful, stylish, humorous, intelligent and lacking even the faintest whiff of sanctimony." Washington Post Book World

Richardson, Charles Scott See Richardson, C. S.

Richardson, Kat

Greywalker. Roc 2006 341p pa $14

ISBN 0-451-46107-X

LC 2006-11233

"Recovering from a brutal assault that had left her clinically dead for two minutes, private investigator Harper Blaine finds her perceptions have changed. Now she sees people that others can't and often struggles against a grayish mist that seems to permeate her world. A friendly couple with experience in the paranormal explain to her that she is a Greywalker, someone with the ability to cross between the living and the ghostly worlds. Suddenly, her life—and her business—grow a lot more interesting and much more dangerous. Richardson's first novel features a genuinely likable and independent heroine with a unique view of reality." Libr J

Richardson, Samuel, 1689-1761

Clarissa; or, The history of a young lady; edited with an introd. and notes by Angus Ross. Penguin Books 1985 1533p

ISBN 0-14-043215-9

Richardson, Samuel, 1689-1761—*Continued*
First published 1749
In this epistolary novel Clarissa Harlowe "has been coldly commanded by her tyrannical family to marry Mr. Solmes, a man she despises. She refuses, even though it pains her to defy her parents. Locked in her room, isolated from family and friends, Clarissa corresponds secretly with Robert Lovelace, a suitor disapproved of by her family; she finally throws herself upon his protection and flees with him. It soon becomes clear to her, however, that Lovelace's sole aim is to seduce her. Her virtue is so great that Lovelace becomes obsessively absorbed in breaking it down." Reader's Ency. 4th edition

Pamela; or, Virtue rewarded; edited with explanatory notes by Thomas Keymer and Alice Wakely; with an introduction by Thomas Keymer. 2008 c2001 xxlv, 546p (Oxford world's classics) pa $9.95
ISBN 978-0-19-953649-8; 0-19-953649-X

*

First published 1740-1741
"On the death of Pamela Andrews' mistress, her mistress's son, Mr. B, begins a series of mild stratagems designed to end in Pamela's seduction. These failing, he abducts her and renews his siege in earnest. Pamela spurns his advances, and halfway through the novel Mr. B offers marriage. In the second half of the novel, Pamela wins over those who had disapproved of the misalliance." Merriam-Webster's Ency of Lit

Richler, Mordecai, 1931-2001

Barney's version; a novel, with footnotes and an afterword by Michael Panofsky. Knopf 1997 355p $25
ISBN 0-679-40418-X

* LC 97-37033
At sixty-seven, Barney Panofsky, "has decided to set the record straight about his Bohemian days in Paris in the 1950s, his circle of famous and infamous acquaintances, his wildly successful career as a television producer, and his three wildly unsuccessful marriages. Mostly, though, he is writing his memoirs to clear his name of the murder of his once-cherished friend, the nearly important writer Bernard 'Boogie' Moscovitch." Quill Quire
"What entertains and affects us in 'Barney's Version' is the headlong, spendthrift passage of a life, redeemed from oblivion in the unbridled telling. The edge of the grave makes a lively point vantage." New Yorker

Solomon Gursky was here; a novel. Knopf 1990 413p o.p.

* LC 89-43393
This is a "reworking of Canadian history that chronicles the fortunes of the mythical Gursky family. . . . From patriarch Ephraim, a con man who arrived with a doomed British Arctic exploration team, through his bootlegger grandsons Bernard, Solomon, and Morrie, who parlayed prohibition into a distillery fortune, the Gurskys' penchant for grand and petty larceny is played off against upper-crust-Canadian and English society, torn between greed and anti-Semitism. Moses Berger, Solomon's appropriately alcoholic biographer, assembles the pieces of Gursky history in a hilarious narrative that jumps back and forth from Victorian England to modern Montreal and all points in between." Libr J
Richler is a "ringmaster, making his performers do dazzling backflips without missing a beat. At the same time he is a moralist, recoiling from those who would sentimentalize the Holocaust or make power a sacrament." Time

Richler, Nancy, 1957-

Your mouth is lovely; a novel. Ecco Press 2002 357p $25.95
ISBN 0-06-009677-2   LC 2002-23521
This "novel summons up the lost world of the Russian shtetls around the Pripet marshes in Ukraine, and shows how these communities were first changed and then annihilated by the events that led, ultimately, to the Russian Revolution. At the center of Richler's tale is Miriam Lev, whose mother drowned herself when she was a day old, and who at age six is taken in hand by her father's new wife, Tsila, a harsh, beautiful seamstress who teaches Miriam the alphabet and dreams of another life. After an ill-starred and and painful series of events, Miriam ends up, at nineteen, in Siberia, having shot an officer of the Tsar at point-blank range. Miriam's hegira is told here as a letter to her own daughter, whom she hasn't seen since she gave birth to her, in prison. Richler's work recalls the stories of Isaac Babel, in which the knowable is charged with mystery." New Yorker

Richmond, Michelle, 1970-

No one you know; a novel. Delacorte Press 2008 306p $23
ISBN 978-0-385-34013-7; 0-385-34013-3
          LC 2008-13508
"Twenty years ago, Ellie Enderlin's sister, Lila, a mathematical prodigy, was murdered, and Andrew Thorpe, Ellie's English professor and a friend, exploited the family's grief with a true-crime bestseller that claimed Peter McConnell, Lila's married lover and colleague, was the killer. On a coffee-buying trip to Nicaragua, Ellie encounters McConnell, whose life was destroyed by Thorpe's conjecture. Sparked by this meeting, Ellie traces her way back through Lila's life and work, pursuing leads that the manipulative Thorpe abandoned when they did not fit his literary ambitions." Publ Wkly
"As complex and beautiful as a mathematical proof, this gripping, thought-provoking novel will keep you thinking long after the last page has been turned." Family Circle

Richter, Conrad, 1890-1968

The awakening land. Knopf 1966 3v in 1 o.p.
          *
Contents: The trees; The fields; The town
This trilogy depicts " a pioneer family and settlement's slow evolution from virgin wilderness to an organized community." Reader's Ency. 4th edition

The fields
In Richter, C. The awakening land p169-329

The light in the forest. Knopf 1953 179p o.p.
          *
Companion volume to A country of strangers (1966)
"John Butler is kidnapped at the age of four and raised by Delaware Indians. Eleven years later, under a truce

Richter, Conrad, 1890-1968—*Continued*

agreement between the Indians and the colonials, he is forcibly returned to his family. Irrevocably divided in his heart, he escapes and goes back to the Indians but is sent away after the failure of an Indian ambush." Shapiro. Fic for Youth. 3d edition

The sea of grass. Knopf 1937 149p o.p.

*

"Set in New Mexico in the late 19th century, the novel concerns the often violent clashes between the pioneering ranchers, whose cattle range freely through the vast sea of grass, and the farmers, or 'nesters,' who build fences and turn the sod. Against this background is set the triangle of rancher Colonel Jim Brewton, his unstable Eastern wife Lutie, and the ambitious Brice Chamberlain. Richter casts the story in Homeric terms, with the children caught up in the conflicts of their parents." Merriam-Webster's Ency of Lit

The town
In Richter, C. The awakening land p331-630

The trees
In Richter, C. The awakening land p1-167

Rickards, John

Winter's end; John Rickards. 1st U.S. ed. Thomas Dunne Books 2003 297p $23.95

ISBN 0-312-31097-8   LC 2003-46874

"Sheriff Dale Townsend asks for an old friend's help in interrogating a very slippery and clever murder suspect in small-town Maine. Dale himself found the suspect standing over the victim clutching the alleged murder weapon, but the guy refuses to give his name or answer any questions. When Dale's PI friend Alex Rourke, an ex-FBI agent good at interrogation, appears, he bores a few chinks in the guy's armor. Strangely, the suspect knows about Alex and seemed to expect him. An attention-getting plot, riveting prose, calculated suspense, and tense, human-interest subplotting mark this noteworthy first novel." Libr J

Ricks, Thomas E.

A soldier's duty; a novel. Random House 2000 250p $24.95

ISBN 0-375-50544-X   LC 2001-18601

"When a peacekeeping mission in Afghanistan goes tragically wrong, officers led by Gen. B.Z. Ames form a treasonous group called the 'Sons of Liberty' to unravel American foreign policy and further General Ames's position. Army majors Cindy Sherman and Bud Lewis are newly assigned to the Pentagon, where they become involved in both sides of the developing problem." Libr J

"One would have to look far for a novel that touches so deftly on the complexities and challenges of leadership of military organizations at the highest levels." Parameters

Ridley, John, 1965-

A conversation with the Mann; a novel. Warner Bks. 2002 433p

ISBN 0-446-52836-6   LC 2001-52605

This "roman a clef is set against the backdrop of 19501960s Hollywood, Rat Pack Las Vegas and the Civil Rights movement, The fictional narrator is a mordant, world-weary Harlem-raised black comic, Jackie Mann, who irreverently recounts a journey from poverty to his symbol of success, an appearance on The Ed Sullivan Show, a path strewn with compromise and degradation. . . . Ridley vividly brings to life noirish panoramas of high-stakes show business, as well as the myriad humiliations endured by a black man trying to win fame in segregated America. The novel is a veritable 'who's who' of well-known showbiz personalities." Publ Wkly

Rigosi, Giampiero, 1962-

Night bus; translated from the Italian by Ann Goldstein. Bitter Lemon Press 2006 c2005 348p pa $14.95

ISBN 1-904738-11-7   LC 2006-386274
Original Italian edition, 2000

"Francesco is a gambling-addicted bus driver in Bologna, with a thuggish debt collector on his trail; Leila is a smart dame with a great pair of legs, who each night looks for a man to bed, drug, and rob. In perfect noir fashion, the two become uneasy allies, trying to escape a pair of vicious intelligence agents after Leila unknowingly swipes a mysterious document from a victim's apartment. Rigosi somewhat overdoes character quirks—one agent has a condition that leads him to constantly leak tears as he slices apart his victims—but an ever-expanding cast of creeps and criminals keeps the plot accelerating, and he describes the dripping of blood and the angle of a broken neck as lovingly as the preparation of a nice eggplant parmigiana." New Yorker

Rikki *See* Ducornet, Rikki

Riley, Judith Merkle

In pursuit of the green lion. Delacorte Press 1990 440p o.p.   LC 90-32498

"This novel continues the story of spunky Margaret [begun in A vision of light] widowed once again and married to acerbic scholar Gregory who rescues her from her former husband's rapacious relatives only to plunge her into the midst of his own family's greedy machination to control her wealth. The eternal wars of the 14th century beckon, however, and Gregory, now a knight in the Duke of Lancaster's forces in France, is captured. Margaret, accompanied by wise Mother Hilde and alchemist Brother Malachi journeys to the stronghold of the sinister Count of St. Medard, where once again her unusual powers and quick wit overcome the forces of evil." Libr J

"In this non-stop picaresque adventure quips fly as thickly as a barrage of arrows; a steady stream of drunken noblemen, corrupt priests, scheming ladies and truculent ghosts keep the action white-hot." Booklist

The serpent garden. Viking 1996 467p o.p.   LC 95-36067

"Susanna Dallet is determined to support herself after the untimely death of her spouse and turns to the art of miniature portraiture, a profession she learned from her enlightened father. After Susanna becomes enmeshed in the political intrigue of the court of Henry VIII, she is

Riley, Judith Merkle—*Continued*

sought after by a heretical religious sect, a minor demon, and a free-spririted archangel, all of whom believe she is the key to their success. Riley . . . creates a stunning period fantasy that combines historical detail with magical realism." Libr J

A vision of light. Delacorte Press 1989 442p o.p. LC 88-17514

"14th century Englishwoman Margaret of Ashbury heeds a 'voice' commanding her to compose her life story. Her kindly old husband Roger Kendall pays for her to dictate her memoirs to unfrocked Brother Gregory. . . . First married at 14 to a sadistic fur merchant—reputed to be the Devil—who leaves her for dead during the Plague, Margaret survives to become appricted to the herbalist Mother Hilde. In trances of divine light Margaret gains the healing gift, and envisions a forged, steel-fingered weapon for the soldierly work of midwifery. But these forceps and Margaret's powers stir the envy of priests and male doctors, and she is forced to clear herself of witchcraft." Publ Wkly

This "is a chronicle rich with the ambience and flavor of the Middle Ages, but it is a 14th-century story told with a 20th-century sensibility." N Y Times Book Rev

Followed by In pursuit of the green lion

Rinaldi, Nicholas

Between two rivers. HarperCollins 2004 448p $24.95

ISBN 0-06-057876-9

This novel "tells the intertwined stories of a dozen or so residents of a posh Manhattan apartment building. . . . At the centre of it is Farro Fescu, Echo Terrace's Romanian concierge. . . . [The residents] include Theo Tattafruge, an Egyptian-born plastic surgeon who specialises in sex-change operations, and Karl Vogel, a former Luftwaffe ace. There is Muhta Saad, a slimy Iraqi spice merchant, and, high up in the penthouse, Harry Falcon, a frozen-foods magnate dying of cancer." Economist

"Though the timeline of Between Two Rivers steers inevitably toward the horrors of 9/11, there is nothing overdetermined or reductive about the stories themselves. Rinaldi . . . indulges his characters in their untidy lives, and readers who do the same will find their patience rewarded." N Y Times Book Rev

Rinehart, Mary Roberts, 1876-1958

The circular staircase; with illustrations by Lester Ralph. Bobbs-Merrill 1908 362p il o.p.

Featuring the detective talents of Mr. Jamieson, this novel concerns a maiden aunt and her nephew and niece who take a country house for the summer and are plunged into a series of mysterious crimes

Haunted lady

In Rinehart, M. R. Miss Pinkerton: adventures of a nurse detective p249-403

Miss Pinkerton [novel]

In Rinehart, M. R. Miss Pinkerton: adventures of a nurse detective p95-245

Miss Pinkerton: adventures of a nurse detective. Rinehart 1959 403p o.p.

Contents: The buckled bag; Locked doors; Miss Pinkerton (1932); Haunted lady (1942)

Two short stories and two novels featuring the exploits of nurse Hilda Adams

Rinehart, Steven

Built in a day; a novel. Doubleday 2003 241p $23.95

ISBN 0-385-49855-1 LC 2003-41968

"Andrew, the antihero of this blackly humorous novel, is still in college in his 30s, has a job as a youth counselor that involves nothing more than hanging out with teens all day and is skilled at manipulating women. When his new wife dies, leaving him in charge of her teenaged sons and 16-year-old foster daughter, he finally has adult responsibility thrust upon him. He responds to his new role by taking his sexually precocious female charge to bed and making starry-eyed plans to marry her while also thinking about seducing her social worker." Publ Wkly

"The charm of the protagonist, clearly, is not the primary appeal of this novel. The charms of Rinehart's writing, however, more than countervail; though stripped-down and deadpan, his sentences pack a lot of raw, juicy comic power." N Y Times Book Rev

Riordan, Rick

Cold Springs. Bantam Bks. 2003 340p $23.95

ISBN 0-553-80236-4 LC 2003-40365

"Cold Springs is an east Texas wilderness boarding school for troubled teens. Haunted by his own unresolved guilt over his daughter's death from a heroin overdose nine years earlier, ex-teacher Chadwick now makes his living escorting children into this boot camp for losers, giving them a second chance whether they want it or not. When an ex-lover asks him to locate her self-destructive 15-year-old daughter and take her to Cold Springs, Chadwick finds himself involved in a case of blackmail, murder, and financial skullduggery." Libr J

Riordan's "voice is fresh yet sure, with insights so trenchant they nearly provoke tears. And Riordan's characters, even the minor ones, are achingly believable." Booklist

Robards, Karen

Ghost moon. Delacorte Press 2000 313p $24.95

ISBN 0-385-31972-X LC 99-47420

"Summoned home at the request of a dying stepaunt, single mom Olivia Morrison returns to LaAngelle Plantation in the steamy swamps of Louisiana with her eight-year-old daughter, Sara. . . . What she discovers is that her closest cousin, Seth, is also divorced and the father of an eight-year-old daughter, who suffers mightily from spoiled rich-kid syndrome. Meanwhile, alternate chapters detail the stalkings of a serial killer who preys on girls the same age as Sara. . . . As Olivia works toward reconciliation with her stepfamily, she is haunted by dreams of her mother's supposed suicide. She also finds herself romantically drawn to Seth." Booklist

Robards "has crafted a mossy modern gothic drenched

Robards, Karen—*Continued*

in gore. . . . [She] conveys the dusty heat of the Louisiana summer, and has an ear for the nuances of dialogue." Publ Wkly

To trust a stranger. Pocket Bks. 2001 341p

ISBN 0-671-78653-9　　　　　LC 2001-52056

"Julie Carlson, once a poor girl from the wrong side of the tracks but now the beautiful owner of a successful boutique in Charleston, S.C., seems to have it all. As the novel begins, however, a hit man circles her suburban mansion: Julie's rich husband, Sid, has hired thugs to kill her. Unaware of the danger she is in but convinced that Sid is cheating on her, Julie slips out of the house just in time and follows her husband to the red-light district, where she serendipitously—and literally—runs into private detective Mac McQuarry, dressed up in drag to spy on a client's husband. . . . Soon she and Mac are working together to get the goods on Julie's crooked husband." Publ Wkly

Robb, Candace M.

The cross-legged knight; an Owen Archer mystery; [by] Candace Robb. Mysterious Press 2003 321p $23.95

ISBN 0-89296-772-2　　　　　LC 2002-27248

"When William of Wykeman, bishop of Winchester, fears reprisal after being blamed for the death of a local knight by his irate family, Owen Archer. . . must protect him. In the meantime, Owen copes with wife Lucie's overwhelming sorrow upon losing the child she was carrying." Libr J

"Once again, Robb provides the reader with an evocative and suspenseful whodunit thoroughly bolstered by a wealth of authentic historical detail." Booklist

A gift of sanctuary; an Owen Archer mystery; [by] Candace Robb. St. Martin's Press 1998 195p $22.95

ISBN 0-312-19266-5　　　　　LC 98-41394

In this medieval mystery Owen Archer returns "to his native Wales to inspect the duke's Welsh fortifications and to recruit two companies of archers in anticipation of a threatened French invasion of the British Isles. Joined on his journey by poet and author Geoffrey Chaucer, the two must solve a perplexing murder and investigate a possible case of treason against the crown." Booklist

"Robb deftly interweaves a complex story of love, passion and murder into the troubled and tangled fabric of Welsh history, fashioning a rich and satisfying novel." Publ Wkly

The riddle of St. Leonard's; a medieval mystery; [by] Candace Robb. St. Martin's Press 1997 303p o.p.

　　　　　　　　　　　　　　LC 97-16231

"The plague is taking its toll in 14th-century York, and all the one-eyed former royal spy wants is to weather it without losing any family members. However, Owen is called to detective duty by the master of St. Leonard's Hospital when its pensioners start dying in rapid succession." Publ Wkly

"An evocative historical mystery steeped in authentically gritty period detail." Booklist

Robb, J. D., 1950-

Naked in death. G.P. Putnam's Sons 2004 294p

ISBN 0-399-15157-5　　　　　LC 2003-54813

This is the first volume in the author's futursitic police procedural At death series. Over thirty titles have followed

"Naked in Death features Lt. Eve Dallas of the NYPD as she searches for a serial killer of prostitutes. It hints at the isolation, neglect, and sexual abuse that Eve suffered as a child, memories that she tries to suppress. The adult Eve is slow to trust and awkward when faced with affection and kindness. Yet over the course of this series, she acquires a husband, Roark; a partner, Peabody; and a varied host of friends—hardboiled reporter Nadine, humanitarian doctor Louise, and worldly wise, bursting with life, rock star Mavis." Libr J

Robbins, David L., 1954-

The last citadel; a novel of the Battle of Kursk. Bantam Bks. 2003 421p $24.95

ISBN 0-553-80177-5　　　　　LC 2003-44304

"The battle for the Soviet city of Kursk in July 1943 during World War II involved two million soldiers. Code-named Citadel, it was Hitler's frenzied—and final—attempt to defeat Russia on the eastern front and was the largest buildup of German armed power of the war. Robbins re-creates the battle in this rousing novel: its characters being Hitler; his generals and advisers; Russian, German, and Spanish foot soldiers and tank drivers; fighter pilots (both men and women); partisans; and even elderly men and women digging trenches." Booklist

War of the rats; a novel. Bantam Bks. 1999 392p $23.95

ISBN 0-553-10817-4　　　　　LC 98-43918

"Inspired by actual events, this novel is set during the battle of Stalingrad during World War II. The plot centers around two crack snipers, one Russian, one German, who pursue each other to the death in a series of cat-and-mouse maneuvers." Libr J

"The final confrontation takes a while to play out, but once Robbins . . . gets to the heart of the matter, he presents a riveting account of a battle within a battle, and the sniper motif proves an ideal vehicle to analyze the strengths and weaknesses of both sides." Publ Wkly

Robbins, Harold, 1916-1997

Sin city. Forge 2002 383p $25.95

ISBN 0-7653-0001-X　　　　　LC 2002-69257

"A Tom Doherty Associates book"

"Jack 'Lucky' Riordan is the illegitimate and unwanted son of millionaire Howard Hughes, exiled from Las Vegas to face a hardscrabble existence. The tale begins in the 1960s when an adult Riordan returns to Vegas, seeking his fortune in the gaming industry. His street smarts stand him in good stead as he shrewdly acquires wealth and power." Booklist

"Though questions linger about just how much Robbins contributed to later books published under his name, this posthumous novel moves quickly and is great fun, a roman à clef reminiscent of his early bestselling bildungsroman." Publ Wkly

Robbins, Tom

Fierce invalids home from hot climates. Bantam Bks. 2000 415p

ISBN 0-553-10775-5   LC 99-51683

"Switters, the protagonist, is an errand boy for the CIA, a secret lover of Broadway show tunes and a pedophile. On assignment in Peru . . . Switters encounters a Kandakandero medicine man who gives him mind-altering drugs and wisdom, but in exchange inflicts a curse: if Switters's feet ever touch the ground, he will be struck dead instantly. So Switters spends the rest of the novel in a wheelchair, although this in no way slows him down. He returns to Seattle, chases after his 16-year-old stepsister and numerous art students, then embarks on a mission to Syria to sell gas masks to Kurds; there, he beds a nun who even so remains a virgin. In true Robbins style, the writing throughout is lush and sexy, containing a great deal of witty social and political commentary." Publ Wkly

Half asleep in frog pajamas. Bantam Bks. 1994 386p o.p.   LC 94-11549

In this novel "Gwen, an endangered stockbroker, is involved with straitlaced Belford and his born-again monkey. When she is attracted to Larry—who has cancer and is currently between trips to Timbuktu—she must choose among the American dream, the Timbuktu alternate, and something else." Libr J

"The yarn has a genuineness, a warmth, a humor, and an incredibly compelling plot, which hold our attention to the end." Booklist

Jitterbug perfume. Bantam Bks. 1984 342p o.p.
                                   LC 84-45233

"Priscilla Partido, a Seattle member of Daughters of the Daily Special (waitresses with college degrees), gets a beet tossed in her window; Madame Devalier and V'lu Jackson, New Orleans purveyors of fine perfume, get a beet too; so do the owners of LeFever Odeurs in Paris. What does it all mean? . . . The real theme here is immortality, in the person of Alobar, a 1000-year-old Nordic imp who sports across the globe (ending up as Einstein's janitor) with the secrets to olfactory wisdom and eternal life and love. Also at large is a Leary-esque philanderer, Wiggs Dannyboy, who as founder of an immortalist sect, the Last Laugh Foundation, accompanies Priscilla on her quest for happiness and the perfect (beet-based) scent. Robbins is still in top form, still mixing the lunatic and the thoughtful—or rather, doing a literary watusi up every page and jitterbugging back down." Publ Wkly

Skinny legs and all. Bantam Bks. 1990 422p il o.p.   LC 89-18309

"A painter's struggle with her art, a restaurant opened as an experiment in brotherhood, the journey of several inanimate objects to Jerusalem, a preacher's scheme to hasten Armageddon, and a performance of a legendary dance: these are the diverse elements around which Robbins has built this wild, controversial novel. Ellen Cherry Charles, one of the 'Daughters of the Daily Special' in *Jitterbug Perfume*, takes center stage. She has married Boomer Petway and moved to New York, hoping to make it as a painter. Instead, she winds up a waitress at the Isaac and Ishmael, a restaurant co-owned by an Arab and a Jew. . . . Few contemporary novelists mix tom-foolery and philosophy so well." Libr J

Still life with Woodpecker. Bantam Bks. 1980 277p o.p.
                                   * LC 81-103498

This novel "relates the meeting (at an ecological 'Care Fest') and subsequent love affair between Leigh-Cheri, an all-American princess of a deposed royal line, and Bernard Mickey Wrangle, alias The Woodpecker, an anarchistic bomber and self-styled 'outlaw.' He is captured and imprisoned; she . . . tries to remain close to him by mimicking his experience, living as a recluse in her parents' attic. When he rejects this as a futile gesture, she agrees to marry a fabulously wealthy oil-sheik and, having been introduced by her solitary incarceration with [a] packet of Camels to the mysteries of pyramid-power, demands a new, full-sized pyramid as a wedding gift. The story's climax is her reunion with Bernard in the inner sanctum of this pyramid." Times Lit Suppl

"The author's prose, as spasmodic as his heroine's sex life, is marbled with limping puns heavily splattered with recurrent motifs and a boyish zeal for the scatalogical." SLJ

Villa incognito. Bantam Bks. 2003 241p $27.50

ISBN 0-553-80332-8   LC 2003-40353

"The novel begins with the story of Tanuki, a badgerlike Asian creature with a reputation as a changeling and trickster and a fondness for sake. Also part of the cast is a beautiful young woman who may or may not have Tanuki's blood in her veins. . . and three American MIAs who have chosen to remain in Laos long after the Vietnam War. Events are set in motion when one of the MIAs, dressed as a priest, is arrested with a cache of heroin taped to his body. In vintage Robbins style, the plot whirls every which way, as the author, writing with unrestrained glee, takes potshots at societal pillars: the military, big business and religions of all ilks. The language is eccentric, electrifying and true to the mark." Publ Wkly

Roberts, Gillian

The bluest blood; an Amanda Pepper mystery. Ballantine Bks. 1998 230p $22

ISBN 0-345-40326-6   LC 97-26868

"Something isn't quite right with Philadelphia bluebloods Neddy and Tea Roederer, benefactors of the Philadelphia Prep School library. Philly Prep teacher and amateur sleuth Amanda Pepper sees the first signs in the Roederers' son's glum manner. Then a more urgent problem appears: the crusade of the Reverend Harvey Spiers' book-burning Moral Ecologists—the same Reverend Spiers whose stepson, Jake, is best friends with the Roederers' son. As Amanda talks with both boys, she realizes there are much deeper problems, and when the crusading Reverend Spiers is murdered, she knows things have spun out of control." Booklist

A "swift and intriguing spin through the sometimes murderous precincts of Philadelphia." Publ Wkly

Helen hath no fury; an Amanda Pepper mystery. Ballantine Bks. 2000 228p $23

ISBN 0-345-42933-8

                                   * LC 00-40360

"Schoolteacher Amanda Pepper seeks the person who killed a member of her book club the day after members discussed a fictional suicide. Amanda's probes, . . . bring her dangerously close to the villain." Libr J

Roberts, Gillian—*Continued*

"Roberts skillfully negotiates some rather tricky emotional waters in this . . . addition to a series notable for its smooth mix of traditional mystery conventions with the darker underpinnings of modern crime fiction." Publ Wkly

The mummers' curse; an Amanda Pepper mystery. Ballantine Bks. 1996 231p $21

ISBN 0-345-40323-1   LC 96-3472

"Philadelphia schoolteacher Amanda Pepper . . . witnesses the murder of a clown in the Mummer's Parade. When a fellow teacher (and principal suspect) falsely names Amanda as his alibi, she begins sleuthing. Fascinating plot and wit-filled prose." Libr J

Roberts, Kenneth Lewis, 1885-1957

Arundel; by Kenneth Roberts. Doubleday, Doran 1930 618p o.p.

An historical novel of the Revolutionary period, the setting of which is the garrison house at Arundel in southern Maine. Steven Nason, the hero of the story, goes with his friend Benedict Arnold on a hazardous expedition against Quebec. Young Nason has a very personal interest in the success of the enterprise, since Mary Mallinson, the girl he loves, has been taken by the Indians and is a captive in Quebec. Steven's recollections of the hardship and dangers of the expedition, and its blunders and failure in spite of individual acts of heroism, make up the bulk of the narrative

Followed by Rabble in arms

Lydia Bailey; by Kenneth Roberts. Doubleday 1947 488p o.p.

"A susceptible young Maine lawyer who has fallen in love with the portrait of a girl he believes to be in Haiti reaches the island just as Napoleon's attempt to take over the government sets off the bloody . . . uprising under Toussaint. The hero finds the girl, and from that point the extremely elaborate plot carries them through an encounter with Tobias Lear, the pig-headed evil genius of Jefferson's State Department; spirited engagements against the French; capture by Barbary pirates and slavery in Tripoli; and, finally, the Tripolitan War and its intrigues and political jealousies." New Yorker

Northwest Passage; by Kenneth Roberts. Doubleday, Doran 1937 709p o.p.

"This sprawling novel describes Major Robert Rogers' expedition in 1759 to destroy the Indian town of St. Francis and then his idea of finding an overland route to the Northwest. . . . In preparing his novel, Roberts made extensive research and unearthed documents that historians had believed were lost. The book is one of Roberts' best works." Benet's Reader's Ency of Am Lit

Oliver Wiswell; [by] Kenneth Roberts. Doubleday, Doran 1940 836p o.p.

"The American revolution as seen by Oliver Wiswell, a young American who remained loyal to the English government, and was therefore the victim of fanatics, bent not only on fighting for liberty but also on destroying the liberty of others. Hounded out of his home in Milton, he fled to Boston with his father and a constantly devoted friend. He experienced there the privations of war and observed the tactical stupidities of the English.

Then on to Halifax, England, France and finally back to America, where he fought with the Loyalists. The war over, Oliver found again his childhood sweetheart and turned with new hope to Nova Scotia." Booklist

Rabble in arms; a chronicle of Arundel and the Burgoyne invasion; by Kenneth Roberts. Doubleday, Doran 1933 870p o.p.

Sequel to Arundel

The principal villain of this realistic, unromantic tale of the American Revolution is the American Congress, the real hero is Benedict Arnold. The story relates the adventures of a group of men from Arundel, Maine, who fight with the American forces in the campaign ending with the battle of Saratoga. Men and events, politics and battles are seen through the eyes of one Peter Merrill, mariner, who tells the story

Followed by The Lively Lady (1931) and Captain Caution (1934)

Roberts, Michèle

Reader, I married him. Pegasus Books 2006 229p pa $13.95

ISBN 1-933648-02-3

First published 2004 in the United Kingdom

"To say that Aurora has been unlucky in love is an understatement. Husbands one, two, and three all met untimely deaths, but now Aurora is ready to move on with her life. A trip to the Italian countryside, ostensibly to scout out new tempting tidbits for her London delicatessen and visit with her old friend, the feisty feminist turned convent abbess Leonora, seems just the ticket, and would have been, had not Aurora's domineering stepmother, Maude, arrived along with her parish priest, the oh-so-attractive and oh-so-mysterious Father Michael. Unable to stay at the convent for more than one night, Aurora is offered lodging in the museum apartment owned by another old friend, Frederico, a man whose sexual orientation Aurora has evidently mistaken. As Aurora succumbs to her passion for the erstwhile priest, Frederico expresses more than just friendship for the vulnerable Aurora. Roberts whimsically indulges her passion for favored themes of religion, sex, and food in this riotous and ribald tale that packs a didn't-see-that-one-coming ending." Booklist

Roberts, Nora, 1950-

Angel's fall. G. P. Putnam's Sons 2006 439p $25.95

ISBN 0-399-15372-1   LC 2006-40902

"After suffering a horrific shock, Reece Gilmore is slowly starting to put her life back together. Leaving her home in Boston, Reece travels around the country, but when she arrives in Angel's Fist, Wyoming, her car refuses to go any further. Planning on staying only until she earns enough money to fix her car, Reece takes a job as a cook in the Angel Food Cafe. Then, as she gets to know her new boss, her coworkers, and the other residents of the little town, including Brody, an annoyingly stubborn yet mysteriously sexy writer, she starts to believe that for the first time in a very long time, she may have found a place she might actually want to call home. Reece's hard-won happiness and sense of security is threatened, however, when she becomes not only the sole

Roberts, Nora, 1950---—*Continued*

witness to a murder but also the next target of the killer, who is determined to drive her crazy. . . . Roberts deftly imbues a deliciously subtle sense of menace into a chilling and thrilling plot." Booklist

Honest illusions. Putnam 1992 383p

ISBN 0-399-13761-0   LC 92-277

"Max Nouvelle is the patriarch of a family of magicians and jewel thieves made up of Lily, his partner in love; Roxanne, his headstrong, beautiful daughter; and Luke, the abused runaway Max had taken in years ago, now a charming young man. They join Max in elaborate performances onstage and in equally elaborate robberies. For years Roxanne and Luke battle constantly, but as young adults they finally realize they are deeply in love. Luke, haunted by the fear that his past will hurt his adopted family, is the target of coldblooded Sam Wyatt, driven by a vow of revenge on the Nouvelles." Publ Wkly

Midnight Bayou. Putnam 2001 352p

ISBN 0-399-14824-8   LC 2001-41643

"When wealthy Boston attorney Declan Fitzgerald discovers that Manet Hall, a dilapidated mansion on the bayou just outside New Orleans, is for sale, he leaves his practice and moves in to renovate, restore, and redecorate. Independent and tough, bar owner Lena fascinates him from the minute he lays eyes on her. Believing that he's incapable of romance, he's amazed by how quickly and overwhelmingly he falls head over heels in love with her. But he worries about his own sanity when he experiences fugue states that leave him with memories of events and people who lived in the mansion more than 100 years earlier. . . . Roberts has cleverly crafted an enticing tangle of times and relationship." Booklist

River's end. Putnam 1999 420p $23.95

ISBN 0-399-14470-6   LC 98-36160

"One summer night in 1979, four-year-old Olivia Tanner finds her doped-up father, Sam, bloodied shears in hand, poised over the dead body of her movie-star mom. Haunted by the image of 'the monster' pursuing her, Olivia is sent to live with her grandparents in the Pacific Northwest, where she is sheltered from her memories by towering Douglas firs. Two decades later, the specter of the 'monster' returns. From prison, her father urges young investigative reporter Noah Brady—son of the police detective who discovered Olivia after the murder—to research the crime." Publ Wkly

Robertson, R. Garcia y *See* Garcia y Robertson, R.

Robinson, Elisabeth

The true and outstanding adventures of the Hunt sisters; a novel. Little, Brown 2004 327p $23.95

ISBN 0-316-73502-7   LC 2003-47713

"As a Hollywood producer, Olivia has suffered through her share of bad movies, but now her own life rivals the worst box office bomb. She has lost her job at Universal Pictures, is on the verge of being evicted, and has been dumped by her true love when she learns that her sister Maddie has leukemia." Libr J

"Over the course of about 200 letters (and a few e-mails), Robinson succinctly shows the full range of Oliv-

ia's emotions and relationships, from the optimism she tries to instill in her shocked family to the admiration she holds for Maddie's spouse. She poignantly portrays the frustration of trying to sustain a relationship while engaged in a consuming profession." USA Today

Robinson, Kim Stanley

Antarctica. Bantam Bks. 1998 511p $24.95

ISBN 0-553-10063-7

* LC 97-41701

"Antarctica in the 21st century serves as a site for scientific research, tourism, and industrial exploitation—until a terrorist attack by environmental extremists calls into question humanity's right to invade the earth's last unexplored continent." Libr J

This is "an exhilarating addition to a body of work distinguished by two elements all too rare in modern science fiction: a sense of character and a sense of place. Robinson brings the two together by writing about people who are in love with where they are." N Y Times Book Rev

Blue Mars. Bantam Bks. 1996 609p o.p.

LC 95-46700

In this concluding volume of the trilogy "colonists almost succeed in terraforming Mars. While they fight for independence from Earth and attempt to avert a civil war, they find their new civilization threatened by an ice age." Libr J

"Conceptually and stylistically, the Mars trilogy is mature science fiction, a landmark in the history of the genre. It requires close reading and amply rewards the effort." N Y Times Book Rev

Green Mars [novelette]

In Robinson, K. S. The Martians

The Martians. Bantam Bks. 1999 336p $24.95

ISBN 0-553-80117-1   LC 99-13115

Set in the universe of the author's Mars trilogy this volume includes vignettes, essays, fables, poems, and the following short stories: Michel in Antarctica; Exploring Fossil Canyon; Maya and Desmond; Four teleological trails; Coyote makes trouble; Michel in provence; Arthur Sternbach brings the curveball to Mars; Jackie on Zo; Keeping the flame; Big Man in love; Sexual dimorphism; What matters; Sax moments; A Martian romance; Purple Mars

"Also included is 'Green Mars,' a previously published novella about climbing Olympus Mons, the highest mountain in the solar system. . . . Some of the pieces here will be of interest only to those who have already read the trilogy, but the finest of the short fiction stands firmly on its own. As is the norm with Robinson's work, the stories are beautifully written, the characters are well developed and the author's passion for ecology manifests on every page." Publ Wkly

Red Mars. Bantam Books 1993 519p il hardcover o.p. pa $7.99

ISBN 0-553-09204-9; 0-553-56073-5 (pa)

* LC 92-21607

This novel, the first of a trilogy "concerns the first permanent settlement on Mars, a multinational band of 100 hardy experts, and their mission—to begin making Mars habitable for humans by releasing underground water and

Robinson, Kim Stanley—*Continued*

oxygen into the atmosphere. Unfortunately, they are divided over whether this is a desirable step in human evolution or an ecological crime." Booklist

"A novel fully inhabited both by detailed technical processes and by people whose careers those processes are; it is also a novel with a complex sense of political reality. . . . This is one of the finest works of American SF because it is one of the few that aspire to the dignity of the genuinely tragic." Times Lit Suppl

The years of rice and salt. Bantam Bks. 2002 658p
ISBN 0-553-10920-0

* LC 2001-43492

"The premise is that a mutating, hypervirulent strain of the fourteenth-century Black Death has wiped out nearly the entire population of Europe, and Islam has moved into Europe, China into North America, and South Asia holds the balance between them, thanks to high military skills and energy. All three parties compete for Africa." Booklist

"Because this alternate history is set in the same lawful universe as ours, its science must be the same. Because its people have the same basic human needs, their societies resemble ours. However, as events march toward the alternative year of 2002, some of his characters come to believe, despite much evidence to the contrary, that they can change the way they live. The reader is left to ponder whether this is an illusion." N Y Times Book Rev

Robinson, Lewis, 1971-

Water dogs; a novel. Random House 2009 244p $25
ISBN 978-1-4000-6217-1; 1-4000-6217-9
LC 2008-16564

"Bennie knows that the details of his life don't show well. A twenty-seven-year-old college dropout with stalled ambitions, he works at an animal shelter and lives with his bullheaded older brother, Littlefield, in their old family home on Meadow Island, Maine. . . When a massive blizzard hits the state one Saturday afternoon, Bennie, Littlefield, and a crew of roughneck war-game enthusiasts decide to play paintball at the local granite quarry. Bennie accidentally falls into a gully, landing in the hospital, and wonders if his life can get any worse. But when one of the players disappears during the storm and Littlefield becomes the main suspect in the disappearance, Bennie realizes that the game might have had much higher stakes. Then Littlefield takes off without a word of explanation, forcing Bennie to seriously question his loyalty to his enigmatic brother. With the guidance of his intrepid girlfriend, Helen, and his twin sister, Gwen, Bennie goes looking for answers. . . . Written in prose as arresting and spare as the novel's rural Maine setting, Lewis Robinson's Water Dogs is a marvel of modern fiction, a book rich in empathy that follows one man's path through the uncertainties of youth and loss toward self-discovery." Bookmarks

Robinson, Lynda Suzanne

Murder at the feast of rejoicing; a Lord Meren mystery; [by] Lynda S. Robinson. Walker & Co. 1996 229p $20.95
ISBN 0-8027-3274-7
LC 95-33190

This novel is set in "the sun-seared landscape of the Egyptian Nile in the days of Tutankhamun. One of the young Pharoah's close confidants, Lord Meren, visits his family estate for a brief rest but finds, instead, that his sister has invited a tedious group of friends and relatives for a family celebration. One of these unwelcome guests has the bad taste to be murdered." SLJ

"Good scholarship authenticates the historical setting; imagination provides the sense of danger and romance to make it come alive." N Y Times Book Rev

Murder at the God's gate; a Lord Meren mystery; [by] Lynda S. Robinson. Walker & Co. 1995 236p $19.95
ISBN 0-8027-3198-8
LC 94-28806

"Young King Tutankhamun's chief adviser/agent Lord Meren, known to some as the Falcon, investigates the murder of a priest in a temple dedicated to the teenaged Tut. Robinson . . . surrounds Meren with palace and temple intrigue, authentic details of daily life, and frequent mention of a wide assortment of indigenous animals." Libr J

Robinson, Marilynne

Gilead. Farrar, Straus and Giroux 2004 247p $23
ISBN 0-374-15389-2

* LC 2004-47063

This is an "epistolary autobiography written by the Rev. John Ames to his son in 1956; the father, dying of heart disease, is 77 and the boy is 6. A Congregationalist minister in fictional Gilead, Iowa, Ames is a bachelor until late in life and a loner even then. His grandfather was a gun-toting abolitionist who ran with John Brown. His father was a pacifist. Ames himself is . . . somewhat more equivocal than either. How to act, when to intercede, when to stand back-these are his abiding questions. When the prodigal son of another local minister comes home, Ames discovers that this young man harbors a secret. Ames tries to help, but his good intentions mire him in the same intractable problems of race-America's original sin-that ensnared his grandfather." Newsweek

"Gilead possesses the quiet ineluctable perfection of Flaubert's A Simple Heart as well as the moral and emotional complexity of Robert Frost's deepest poetry. There's nothing flashy in these pages, and yet one regularly pauses to reread sentences, sometimes for their beauty, sometimes for their truth." Washington Post Book World

Home. Farrar, Straus & Giroux 2008 325p $25
ISBN 978-0-374-29910-1; 0-374-29910-2
LC 2008-18301

This novel features characters who first appeared in the author's 2004 novel Gilead, set in a small Iowa town. "Glory Boughton, aged thirty-eight, has returned to Gilead to care for her dying father, [the Rev. Robert Boughton]. Soon her brother, Jack—the prodigal son of the family, gone for twenty years—comes home too, looking for refuge. . . . A bad boy from childhood, an alcoholic who cannot hold a job, he is perpetually at odds with his surroundings and with his traditionalist father, though he remains Boughton's most beloved child. Brilliant, lovable, and wayward, Jack forges an intense bond with Glory and engages painfully with [pastor John] Ames, his godfather." Publisher's note

Robinson, Marilynne—*Continued*

"There is almost no first-rate American fiction about what happens in a household where religion is the family business, but if you ever wondered what it's like to be a preacher's kid, you can't do better than 'Home.' Robinson's greatest achievement is that she manages to introduce the notions of belief and religious mystery without ever seeming vague. She never shies from uncomfortable truths." Newsweek

Robinson, Patrick, 1939-

Kilo class. HarperCollins Pubs. 1998 442p $25
ISBN 0-06-019129-5   LC 97-51172
In this sequel to Nimitz class, "the plot concerns 10 formidable Soviet-built Kilo Class patrol submarines, which can run submerged at speeds up to 17 knots without being detected, travel 6,000 miles before refueling, and fire nuclear-tipped torpedoes. An insolvent Russian military has agreed to sell them to China. With the subs, China could control the Taiwan Strait, blocking Western trade routes. The Chinese could then attack and conquer Taiwan. The U.S. Navy must stop delivery of the subs without starting World War III." Booklist

Nimitz class. HarperCollins Pubs. 1997 411p il
o.p.   LC 96-46872
"The Nimitz Class nuclear aircraft carrier USS *Thomas Jefferson* and its accompanying Carrier Battle Group is secretly attacked and destroyed. At first, the loss of the carrier and its 6000-person crew is deemed an accident, but Lieutenant Commander Bill Baldridge convinces the president that the ship was attacked by a diesel sub with a nuclear-tipped torpedo. The ensuing investigation takes him from Britain's top-flight submarine school to the depths of the Bosporus in pursuit of a rogue Iraqi sub captain and his commandeered Russian submarine." Libr J

"Military fiction fans will admire [the author's] authoritative exploitation of weaponry and tactics, however, and most readers will be engaged, despite some sluggish passages, by his persuasive cautionary tale about the perils of military downsizing at a time when rogue nations are amassing weapons of great and terrible destructiveness." Publ Wkly

Followed by Kilo class

Robinson, Peter, 1950-

Cold is the grave. Morrow 2000 369p
ISBN 0-380-97808-3   LC 00-37231
Yorkshire's Inspector Alan Banks "devoutly loathes his distant and chilly superior officer, Chief Constable Jimmy Riddle. But when Riddle spots his wayward 16-year-old daughter, Emily, posing nude on a pornographic Web site, Banks, who has a teenage daughter of his own, hasn't the heart to turn down the distraught father's plea to journey down to the fleshpots of London and rescue the girl." N Y Times Book Rev

"Banks discovers the precariousness of Emily's position in her new life and, more disturbingly, the grotesque truth behind a facade of perfect family life. A cunningly constructed plot, enhanced by Robinson's engaging descriptions and insights." Booklist

The first cut. Dark Alley 2004 310p $13.95
ISBN 0-06-073535-X (pa)   LC 2003-67660

"Recent university graduate Kirsten survives a brutal Jack the Ripper-style attack of which she has no memory. As Kirsten recovers, she becomes fixated on finding the man who nearly killed her. Miles away, Martha has come to the coastal town of Whitby, where she is doing research for a book. Or is she? Carefully surveying her surroundings, Martha grows more obsessed with the object of her trip. The women's stories are told in alternate chapters until the unsettling end. This atmospheric tale of suspense will keep readers wondering what's really going on." Libr J

Innocent grave; an Inspector Banks mystery.
Berkley Prime Crime 1996 346p o.p.
                               * LC 95-38218
This story finds "Inspector Alan Banks attempting to solve the murder of 16-year-old Deborah Harrison, who was found strangled to death in a graveyard. The victim was the daughter of a prominent businessman, who wants the killer apprehended posthaste. A suspect is identified, jailed, and sent to trial, only to be declared innocent." Booklist

"Although the story follows the classical form of a whodunit, the characters have complexity and the issues range broad and deep, raising interesting moral questions about bigotry, class privilege and the terrible crime of being different." N Y Times Book Rev

Piece of my heart. William Morrow 2006 336p
$24.95
ISBN 978-0-06-054435-5; 0-06-054435-X
                              LC 2005-58363
"As volunteers clean up after a huge outdoor rock festival in Yorkshire in 1969, they discover the body of a young woman wrapped in a sleeping bag. She has been brutally murdered. . . . It looks as if the victim was somehow associated with the up-and-coming psychedelic pastoral band the Mad Hatters. Thirty-five years later, Inspector Alan Banks is investigating the murder of a freelance music journalist who was working on a feature about the Mad Hatters for MOJO magazine. Aging rock superstars, the Mad Hatters have once again been brushed by tragedy. Banks finds he has to delve into the past to find out exactly what hornet's nest the journalist inadvertently stirred up." Publisher's note

The author "invokes the most disturbing aspects of the 60's—to the point at which even the Manson murders have repercussions in Yorkshire—to sustain the book's ominous mood. There is pathos too, as Banks winds up revisiting characters who were young and energetic in 1969 but are now tea-sipping retirees." N Y Times (Late N Y Ed)

Robinson, Roxana

Cost. Farrar, Straus & Giroux 2008 420p $25
ISBN 978-0-374-27187-9; 0-374-27187-9
                              LC 2007-47954
"Sarah Crichton books"
"New York art professor Julia is spending the summer in her ramshackle Maine home with her very elderly parents. Julia's older son, Steven, arrives for a visit and shatters the surface serenity with his suspicion that his younger brother, Jack, is a heroin addict spiraling out of control. When Steve's worst fears are confirmed, Julia's ex-husband, Wendell, brings Jack to Maine for an intervention, conducted by Ralph Carpenter, a tough ex-addict

Robinson, Roxana—*Continued*

who runs a Florida recovery program." Libr J

"It's a nice touch that no one much likes Carpenter, the bossy and authoritative purveyor of unwelcome information. One of Robinson's most impressive achievements is to show that even in extreme situations, individual personalities come into play, and people respond in characteristic ways. . . . Bleak though it undeniably is, 'Cost' is also a warmly human and deeply satisfying book, marking a new level of ambition and achievement for this talented author." Chicago Tribune

A perfect stranger; and other stories. Random House 2005 235p $23.95

ISBN 0-375-50918-6   LC 2004-59537

Contents: Family Christmas; The face-lift; Assistance; Choosing sides; At the beach; Blind man; The treatment; Assez; Intersection; Shame; The football game; Pilgrimage; A perfect stranger

Robinson's "finely tuned realism, as well as her settings and characters—New York, its bedroom communities, the Eastern seaboard and the comfortable upper-middle-class living there—recall Cheever and Updike. . . . The collection's most affecting stories touch on the chasm between parents and children, husbands and wives. Robinson's ear is wonderful, her graceful prose a real pleasure." Publ Wkly

Sweetwater; a novel. Random House 2003 319p $24.95

ISBN 0-375-50916-X   LC 2002-31830

"A widow for two years, 47-year-old Isabel Green marries her ardent suitor, Paul Simmons, hoping that her affection for him will turn into love. During a visit to Sweetwater Lodge, the Simmons family's lakeside compound in the Adirondacks, she meets Paul's cold disapproving parents, Douglas and Charlotte. . . and his bachelor brother, Whit, with whom Paul maintains a vicious sibling rivalry. Fundamental issues soon convince Isabel that her marriage is a dreadful mistake." Publ Wkly

"Robinson writes big solid scenes bubbling with tension, that hold the reader's interest. She has always shown her characters' flaws, and the dark emotions stirred up by divorce and parenthood; here she has reached farther to relate her characteristic predicaments to the larger world outside." N Y Times Book Rev

Robinson, Spider

By any other name
  In The Hugo winners p141-97

Callahan's con. Tor Bks. 2003 286p $23.95

ISBN 0-7653-0270-5   LC 2003-40285

"A Tom Doherty Associates book"

"When Jake Stonebender and his wife, Zoey, move to Florida and open up the Place, the latest incarnation of the unusual bar once known as Callahan's Place, he acquires a collection of strange friends, including a talking German shepherd, a merman, and a foul-mouthed parrot. An encounter with the Florida bureaucracy over the homeschooling of his hyperintelligent daughter, Erin, and the intrusion of the local Mafia result in a grand scheme to outwit both intrusions and rescue Jake's missing wife in the process. Robinson's latest entry in his Callahan series features more zaniness, good humor, and bad jokes." Libr J

Stardance [novelette]
  In The Hugo winners p327-88

Robison, Mary

One D.O.A., one on the way; a novel. Counterpoint 2009 166p $23

ISBN 978-1-58243-305-9; 1-58243-305-4
                                 LC 2008-35700

"Constructed of miniature, numbered packets of terse observations, darkly comic dialogues, lists dashed off in anger or despair, this novel by Mary Robison viscerally evokes the physical and emotional exhaustion of living in post-Katrina New Orleans, that erstwhile good-time city drowning in neglect. Decadence has always been the local specialty, and Robison evokes that as well in the monologue her frazzled narrator, Eve, unfolds in bits and pieces. Eve is married to Adam, a sardonic conceit, for what they are witnessing is clearly the destruction of something, not the creation. Eve has been struggling among the ruins to revive her business while attending with rather less determination to her husband. Afflicted with hepatitis and ennui, Adam has moved back in with his genteel parents and his drug-addicted twin brother. So tenuous is the marriage that Eve has trouble telling the two men apart. From time to time the narrative breaks the fourth wall of fictional illusion and bursts into a diatribe enumerating the woes of New Orleans, kicked to the curb like a used-up floozy. But the story has an appointment with destiny, and Robison makes sure it gets there." Boston Globe

Robson, Justina

Keeping it real. Pyr 2007 337p pa $15

ISBN 978-1-59102-539-9; 1-59102-539-7
                                 LC 2007-483

First title in the author's Quantam gravity series
First published 2006 in the United Kingdom

"The world changed in 2015, when the Quantum Bomb tore a hole in the fabric of reality and opened doors to other dimensions, including Alfheim, or Elfland. When undercover agent Lila Black, part human and part combat machine, is hired as a bodyguard for an elven rock star, she gets caught up in an elaborate game that affects not only relations between Otopia (the Earth) and Alfheim, but the other quantum realms as well." Libr J

"Life is anything but real in this entertaining fusion of SF and fantasy spiced with sex, rockin' elves and drunk faeries. . . . Deft prose helps the reader accept what in lesser hands would be merely absurd." Publ Wkly

Living next door to the god of love. Bantam Books 2006 453p pa $13

ISBN 0-553-58742-0   LC 2005-56271

"Francine is a runaway to Sankhara, a 'high interaction universe.' Arriving penniless and without any means of support, she resourcefully survives for a while under the auspices of the Love Foundation and eventually finds work with a scientist who is cataloging the many facets of the Stuffverse; that is, the world of the novel, in which anything that can be imagined is possible. Unity, the godlike entity that manipulates the stuff of the universe and can even create people, is hunting a splinter of itself. The destruction Unity leaves in its wake and the people who have been absorbed by it attract the attention

Robson, Justina—*Continued*

of SolarGov. Jalaeka, who is the splinter, flees the threat of being consumed by Unity, and Francine finds in him a boyfriend who has been a god of love, among other things." Booklist

Robson "handles her characters' voices with confidence and wit, weaving together multiple stories to produce an elaborate whole that's somehow, finally, compacted into a simple seed, a timeless myth of death and resurrection." Strange Horizons.com

Rock, Peter, 1967-

My abandonment. Houghton Mifflin Harcourt 2008 240p $22

ISBN 978-0-15-101414-9; 0-15-101414-0
LC 2007-44412

This novel is "is narrated by 13-year-old Caroline, who lives in a woodsy area near Portland, OR, with her father, not in a tidy suburban neighborhood but in a cave. They visit the city periodically, carefully dressed in city clothes so as not to attract attention, where Father picks up his government checks 'for being in a war.' It's up to Caroline to calm her father during his frequent nightmares about helicopters swarming and rattling the night. Their unconventional life changes suddenly when the authorities swoop in to take charge of Caroline and her father and send them to a farm where Father is put to work. Even though Caroline is content with the routine and their small but clean living quarters, Father still can't tolerate being confined, and they escape back into the woods only to meet tragedy again." Libr J

"The narrative unfolds as a meditative interior monologue, with some of the plot developing beyond Caroline's immature comprehension, leaving tantalizing gaps for the reader to fill. Gaps that may be filled with crime and sex. Yet bit by bit steady as water dripping on limestone reality carves a groove in Caroline's consciousness, turning her childhood trust into a sense of betrayal. . . . If this is a Bildungsroman, it's one for grownups. Caroline comes of age in circumstances so harsh yet so tender that her redemption will be tempered by loss and uncommon learning." Newsday

Rodriguez, Alisa Valdes- *See* Valdes-Rodriguez, Alisa

Roger Caras' Treasury of great cat stories. Dutton 1987 495p $19.95

ISBN 0-525-24398-4
LC 86-2200

"A Truman Talley book"
An anthology featuring feline tales by Kipling, Wodehouse, Saki, Gallico, Twain, and others

Roger Caras' Treasury of great dog stories. Dutton 1987 497p $19.95

ISBN 0-525-24399-2
LC 86-6264

"A Truman Talley book"
Among the authors represented in this collection are Turgenev, Narayan, Bradbury, Terhune and O. Henry

Rogers, Jane, 1952-

Mr. Wroe's virgins. Overlook Press 1999 276p
ISBN 0-87951-702-6
* LC 99-10232

First published 1992 in the United Kingdom

This novel, "based on historical events and set in Lancashire in 1830, begins when John Wroe, 'prophet' of a Judeo-Christian sect, claims that God has instructed him to comfort himself by taking seven virgins into his home. The story spans the nine months the women spend under Wroe's roof before he is ousted by his congregation following charges of indecency." Booklist

"Rogers's wry account of the Christian Israelite community's abbreviated tenure is alternately narrated by four of the chosen virgins. . . . The virgins' narratives read like four diaries spliced together to create a chronology of events, incidentally providing a forum of conflicting opinions and perspectives." N Y Times Book Rev

Rogers, Rob

Devil's Cape. Wizards of the Coast Discoveries 2008 409p il pa $14.95

ISBN 978-0-786949-01-4; 0-786949-01-5
LC 2007-21311

"Devil's Cape is a town in Louisiana, just a few miles away from New Orleans. The town was founded by pirates and, today, the bad guys rule in Devil's Cape. Pity any superhero who dares try to fight them. If they can't kill you, they'll kill your family. If you don't have a family, they'll find someone close to you to kill, whatever it takes for them to keep their power over you – and the city. Rogers creates a vivid and vibrant world from whole cloth which seems like it truly can exist right outside your window. And that is what makes this book so successful. Devil's Cape is a quick read in the best sense of the word. It is truly difficult to put down. It proudly deserves a place next to Tom Clancy and Stephen King as a sterling example of the best of genre fiction. Even if you don't like superheroes, you are bound to be captivated by Devil's Cape." PopMatters

Roiphe, Anne Richardson, 1935-

An imperfect lens; a novel; [by] Anne Roiphe. Shaye Areheart Books 2006 296p $25

ISBN 1-4000-8211-0
LC 2005-11250

"Commissioned by an aging Louis Pasteur to identify and isolate the cholera microbe and 'bring glory to France,' an eclectic band of young researchers arrive in plague-stricken Alexandria in 1883. Set loose in this exotic locale, these novice scientists face a daunting task as pestilence and disease ravage the city. In addition to racing against time and famed German scientist Dr. Robert Koch, the team members face multiple political, cultural, and romantic distractions. Roiphe does an incredible job of painting paradoxical portraits of collective fear and coolheaded reason as she painstakingly reconstructs the life cycle of a deadly epidemic. This authentically detailed blend of fact and fiction gift wraps the history of an astonishing medical and scientific breakthrough inside an irresistible love story, providing a little something for everyone across a wide spectrum of readers." Booklist

Roiphe, Anne Richardson, 1935-—_Continued_

Lovingkindness; a novel; by Anne Roiphe. Summit Bks. 1987 279p o.p.

* LC 87-6448

"Annie Johnson, widowed before the birth of her daughter Andrea, is a modern, successful, professional woman. Her relations with Andrea has been marked with alienation on her daughter's part, as she appears to be intent on destroying her life as a drop-out from schools, an abuser of drugs, and a young woman who has already experienced three abortions. Annie Johnson seeks psychiatric help for Andrea with no success. It is not until Andrea, finding herself a visitor in Israel, is taken into a yeshiva community that some change in her behavior comes about. The rigorous, although warm, Jewish orthodox discipline appears to change Andrea into a submissive young woman living a life completely foreign to anything her mother understands. The destruction inherent in some parent-child conflicts is painfully described here." Shapiro. Fic for Youth. 3d edition

Rølvaag, Ole Edvart, 1876-1931

Giants in the earth; a saga of the prairie; by O. E. Rölvaag; translated from the Norwegian. Harper 1927 465p o.p.

*

This novel "chronicles the struggles of Norwegian immigrant settlers in the Dakota territory in the 1870s. . . . The book's indomitable protagonist, Per Hansa, his wife Beret, their children, and three other Norwegian immigrant families settle at Spring Creek, living in makeshift sod huts. Surviving the winters' fierce blizzards, they see their crops destroyed by locusts in summer. They nonetheless persist; new settlers arrive, and the community grows." Merriam-Webster's Ency of Lit

Followed by Peder Victorious

Peder Victorious; a novel; by O. E. Rölvaag; translated from the Norwegian; English text by Nora O. Solum and the author. Harper 1929 350p o.p.

"Carries on the characters of 'Giants in the earth,' the interest centering in Peder Victorious and Beret, the boy's mother, against the background of a community no longer intensely struggling with the soil, but adapting itself to the ways of the new country, or resisting adaptation as Beret continues to do. The boy Peder, with his changing ideas and his ardent pursuit of girls is a foil for the character of Beret, perhaps the most finely conceived personality in the book." N Y Libr

Followed by Their father's God (1931)

Romano, Marc

(tr) Simenon, G. The man who watched trains go by

Romano, Tony, 1957-

When the world was young. HarperCollins 2007 309p $24.95

ISBN 978-0-06-085792-9; 0-06-085792-7

LC 2006-43312

A "novel about an immigrant family during the 1950s features Angela Rosa and Agostino Peccatori, who still long for the sight of the Apennine Hills ringing their Italian hometown. With five children, however, they have no time for self-indulgence. Angela Rosa is constantly cooking and cleaning, while Agostino puts in long hours running the family-owned corner tavern. Their oldest son, Santo, is longing for a girlfriend and a job that would give him some independence, while 16-year-old Victoria, feeling suffocated by her family's strict rules, has begun to smoke and flirt with bad-boy Eddie Milano. But when their baby brother, Benito, succumbs to a high fever, the entire family seems to come apart, each nurturing a private grief." Publ Wkly

"The complexities and mysteries of familial bonds are brought into sharp, agonizing focus. . . . Romano's tale emerges into surprising and satisfying territory." Chicago Sun-Times

Romano-Lax, Andromeda, 1971-

The Spanish bow. Harcourt 2007 554p $25

ISBN 978-0-15-101542-9; 0-15-101542-2

LC 2006-100937

This novel "traces the professional and personal evolution of a world-class cellist. As Feliu Delargo moves from prodigy to major talent, he travels from anarchist Barcelona to royalist Madrid. The volatile relationship between the idealistic Delargo and the pragmatic pianist Justo Al-Cerraz mirrors all the passion and turmoil of a Spain on the brink of civil war. Colleagues, friends, and rivals, the two take radically divergent paths when Franco assumes power, but are reunited in Paris on the eve of the Nazi invasion. Joining forces, they prepare for one last fateful concert in order to save Aviva, the Jewish violinist they both love." Booklist

"Expertly woven throughout the book are cameo appearances by Pablo Picasso, Adolf Hitler, Francisco Franco, Bertolt Brecht, and others, but it is the fictional Feliu, Justo, and Aviva who will keep you mesmerized to the last page." Christ Sci Monit

Roosevelt, Elliott, 1910-1990

The Hyde Park murder. St. Martin's Press 1985 231p o.p.

LC 85-1752

"A stock swindle threatens to keep two young lovers apart. Bob Hannah is the son of the indicted financier, and his fiancée's father wants no part of a family marked by scandal. Mrs. Roosevelt's matchmaking for the two sweethearts is further complicated when the elder Hannah dies in what is claimed to be a suicide. Bob Hannah and Eleanor suspect murder." Wilson Libr Bull

"The author's fascinating glimpses into history, into the Roosevelts at home, and into corrupt politics are delivered in a measured and surefooted manner." Booklist

Murder and the First Lady. St. Martin's Press 1984 227p o.p.

LC 83-24659

"This historical mystery is set just before World War II, when international tensions are at a peak. Philip Garber, a lowly bookkeeper and assistant to the chief usher at the White House, is found murdered. Eleanor Roosevelt turns sleuth when it's discovered that Garber was found dead in the room of her British secretary, Pamela Rush-Hodgeborne." Booklist

Roosevelt, Elliott, 1910-1990—*Continued*

Murder at midnight; an Eleanor Roosevelt mystery. St. Martin's Press 1997 216p $20.95

   ISBN 0-312-15596-4   LC 96-53530

"A Thomas Dunne book"

"Judge Horace Blackwell, friend and adviser to the president, is stabbed to death in his White House suite, and Sara Carter, a black maid, is arrested after finding the body. After promising the girl a fair hearing and gaining the confidence of lead investigator Lawrence Pickering, Eleanor takes an active role. Her doubts about Sara's guilt lead to some disturbing discoveries, not least of which is that the judge appears to have been a sadistic womanizer. . . . Peopled with famous lights of 1933, including Babe Ruth, William Faulkner and Gertrude Stein, Washington, D.C., is bought to life in the mirror of the White House." Publ Wkly

Murder at the palace. St. Martin's Press 1987 232p o.p.   LC 87-27961

"A Thomas Dunne book"

This novel "is set at Buckingham Palace in wartime London. On a visit to British and American troops (including son Elliott), Mrs. Roosevelt greets the king and queen, princesses Margaret and Elizabeth, and Sir Alan Burton. . . . When Burton becomes a suspect in a top-secret and terribly embarrassing murder case, Mrs. Roosevelt comes to his aid." Booklist

Murder in the Blue Room. St. Martin's Press 1990 215p o.p.   LC 89-77677

"A Thomas Dunne book"

"Set in 1942 during Soviet Foreign Minister Molotov's secret visit to FDR, [this] mystery . . . finds the author's mother, Eleanor Roosevelt, solving a double murder and combating racial discrimination in the armed forces. A droll, yet affectionate, portrait that is standard but intriguing fare." Booklist

Murder in the map room; an Eleanor Roosevelt mystery. St. Martin's Press 1998 251p il $21.95

   ISBN 0-312-18168-X   LC 97-37243

"A Thomas Dunne book"

"When Mrs. Roosevelt discovers a murder in the White House during the state visit of Madame Chiang Kai-shek in 1943, her investigation is hampered by both diplomatic protocol and the fact that the U.S. is deeply involved in a war raging on two fronts. . . . As usual, Elliot Roosevelt's respectfully playful portrayal of his down-to-earth mother as a clever sleuth is enough to keep the pages turning." Booklist

Murder in the Oval Office; an Eleanor Roosevelt mystery. St. Martin's Press 1989 247p o.p.

                        LC 88-18848

"A Thomas Dunne book"

"Her sense of justice (not to mention her curiosity) sparked by the murder of a Southern Congressman during a White House soiree, the resourceful First Lady shows spunk and wit, and also considerable charm, in her investigation of the locked room puzzle." N Y Times Book Rev

Murder in the Rose Garden. St. Martin's Press 1989 232p o.p.   LC 89-35326

"A Thomas Dunne book"

"During the summer of 1936, popular Washington hostess Vivian Taliafero is strangled in the White House

Rose Garden. . . . The First Lady helps the Secret Service and the D.C. police gather information about the murdered woman who was, it turns out, an extortionist. . . . Vivian's partner in blackmail, photographer Joe Bob Skaggs, is killed, as is one of their victims, while Mrs. Roosevelt strives to solve the mystery." Publ Wkly

The White House pantry murder; an Eleanor Roosevelt mystery. St. Martin's Press 1987 231p o.p.   LC 86-26249

"A Thomas Dunne book"

"It is December, 1941, and Winston Churchill is a guest at the White House. The body of an unidentified man is found in the White House freezer. When weapons are found in a storm sewer leading to the White House, espionage or an assassination attempt is suspected. Mrs. Roosevelt, ably assisted by Secret Service agent Deconcini and British Lieutenant-Commander Leach, must find the person responsible before something terrible happens." Libr J

Roosevelt, Kermit

In the shadow of the law. Farrar, Straus and Giroux 2005 370p $24

   ISBN 0-374-26187-3   LC 2004-24222

This novel "goes behind the scenes at Morgan Siler, one of Washington, D.C.'s most powerful K Street law firms, as several lawyers become embroiled in two difficult cases: a pro bono death penalty case in Virginia and a class action suit brought against a Texas chemical corporation after an explosion kills dozens of workers. . . . Though the novel features plenty of satisfying twists and turns, the book transcends the legal thriller genre. Roosevelt . . . offers a fascinating insider's look into the culture of a high-stakes firm, while also presenting a considered meditation on the law itself and its potential to compromise those driven to practice it." Publ Wkly

Roquelaure, A. N. *See* Rice, Anne, 1941-

Rosales, Guillermo, 1946-1993

The halfway house; introduction by Jose Manuel Prieto; translated by Anna Kushner. New Directions 2009 121p pa $14.95

   ISBN 978-0-8112-1802-3   LC 2009-05947

Written 1987; original Spanish edition, 2003

A "story set in a Miami home for the mentally ill. William Figueras, a 38-year-old [exiled schizophrenic Cuban writer] . . ., is deposited in a boarding house by his aunt, because nothing more can be done. His writing was deemed morose, pornographic, and also irrelevant by the Cuban government, and now he has grown as hopeless and abandoned as the other desperate outcasts who inhabit the shabby home owned by the miserly Mr. Curbelo and run by a beer-guzzling flunky named Arsenio. Figueras despises the other residents and clearly recognizes how they are being exploited by Mr. Curbelo and Arsenio, yet out of his own state of self-debasement, he joins in the cruelty. Briefly, hope inspires him in the form of a new female inmate, and together they plan an escape. However, life outside promises to be more treacherous than staying in the ward. It's a frightening, nihilistic cousin of One Flew Over the Cuckoo's Nest." Publ Wkly

Rose, Joel

Blackest bird; a novel of murder in nineteenth-century New York. W.W. Norton 2007 479p $24.95

    ISBN 978-0-393-06231-1; 0-393-06231-7

                       LC 2006-31703

"Sixty-nine-year-old High Constable Jacob Hays is facing a long, hot summer in 1841. The soaring temperatures are nothing compared to the heat being generated by the sensation-seeking newspapers and the vicious gangs that rule the New York neighborhoods known as the Five Points. When Mary Rogers, a pretty clerk at a tobacco shop, is found brutally murdered in the Hudson River, Hays is charged with the search for her killer. A long-respected lawman known for creating a new interrogation technique called the third degree, Hays is starting to feel the full weight of his position, caught between public outrage and political red tape. High on his list of suspects is the eccentric poet Edgar Allan Poe, who freely admits that he was in love with the 'cigar girl.'" Booklist

"Rose does a scrupulous and impressive job of mustering the pace and mood of the rapidly expanding city, its still pastoral fringes and its customs." PopMatters

Rosen, Jonathan, 1963-

Joy comes in the morning. Farrar, Straus and Giroux 2004 389p $25

    ISBN 0-374-18026-1   LC 2004-1742

"In her work as a hospital volunteer, Deborah Green, a Manhattan rabbi, encounters an ailing Holocaust survivor—recovering from a debilitating stroke and a suicide attempt—and his skeptical son. To complicate matters, she is beautiful and single, while the skeptical son is a shy bachelor; the romance causes crises of faith for both, as they negotiate their divergent attitudes toward their religion. As the story moves from wedding to funeral and back again, and Deborah officiates at the momentous changes in other people's lives, she increasingly finds her own life empty of the things that she has always counselled her congregation to treasure. Served with the merest teaspoon of schmaltz, Rosen's touching novel of Jewish manners thoughtfully addresses the question of whether piety can teach us faith." New Yorker

Rosenberg, Nancy Taylor

Abuse of power. Dutton 1997 326p $23.95

    ISBN 0-525-93768-4   LC 96-44141

In this novel, "policewoman Rachel Simmons takes on a corruption-riddled police force. Molested as a child, she is filled with a fiery purpose and uncompromising honesty. These scruples act against her when she witnesses an abuse of police authority and reports it. The duel between Rachel's conscience and her own family's safety forms the basis of the plot line. The novel moves rapidly to a powerful conclusion." Libr J

Buried evidence. Hyperion 2000 359p

    ISBN 0-7868-6619-5   LC 00-35073

Sequel to Mitigating circumstances

"Lily Forrester, formerly of the Ventura DA's office, is now DA in Santa Barbara. Her ex-husband, John Forrester, who has been living with their 18-year-old daughter, Shana, is losing his battle with the bottle and has been arrested for vehicular manslaughter. . . . John blackmails Lily into bailing him out of jail, bartering Lily's secret in an effort to escape prosecution. (Six years before, Shana was brutally raped while Lily was forced to look on, and Lily shot and killed the wrong man in retaliation.) The real rapist has recently been released on parole and is once again stalking the two women." Publ Wkly

First offense. Dutton 1994 338p o.p.

                       LC 94-550

"Probation officer Ann Carlisle's husband, a highway patrolman, disappeared mysteriously four years ago, and it's been tough for Ann and her 12-year-old son to put their lives back together. A new love interest plus a heavy caseload at work are just beginning to help heal Ann's wounds when she becomes involved in a narcotics trial that will unravel her life all over again." Booklist

"Just when readers will have figured all the angles, savvy Rosenberg unveils the villain and flips the plot into an exciting manhunt, with Ann as bait." Publ Wkly

Interest of justice; a novel. Dutton 1993 368p o.p.   LC 93-13005

"Lara Sanderstone, a California judge, finds her life turned upside down when her house is burglarized, her sister and brother-in-law are brutally murdered, and she's left with a sullen 14-year-old nephew to care for. With the help of police sergeant Ted Rickerson, Lara tries to determine if the crimes were the random work of some sicko or if one of the deadbeats she's sent to prison is out for revenge." Booklist

"Lara Sanderstone is such an intelligent, finely detailed character that even the unlikeliest plot twists work in this absorbing legal thriller." Publ Wkly

Mitigating circumstances. Dutton 1993 362p o.p.   LC 92-23035

In this novel "Lily Forrester, a district attorney in Southern California, is an ambitious woman with a deteriorating marriage. Her life becomes a nightmare when both she and her daughter are brutally attacked. Recognizing their attacker, but unwilling to submit her child to the abuse of the legal system, Forrester moves to deal out justice herself." Libr J

"For all the adrenaline that the author pumps into her story, her writing is far more persuasive when it isn't so feverish—during intimate mother-daughter exchanges, for example, and in the realistically mundane procedures of ordinary, hard-working cops and lawyers." N Y Times Book Rev

Sullivan's law. Kensington Bks. 2004 314p $24

    ISBN 0-7582-0618-6

Carolyn Sullivan is a "probation officer attending night school to become an attorney. Juggling her coursework and her job is hard enough, let alone having to worry about how she'll handle single parenthood with her preteen daughter and college-bound son. Carolyn's pressures only mount when one of her probationary charges, convicted killer and paranoid schizophrenic Daniel Metroix, is arrested for rape. . . . Rosenberg puts it all together here with another thoroughly believable heroine dealing with corruption, greed, deceit, and danger." Booklist

Rosenberg, Robert

This is not civilization. Houghton Mifflin 2004 293p $24

ISBN 0-618-38601-7

"In far-off Kyrgyzstan, Anarbek Tashtanaliev deals with stubborn daughter Nazira even as he tries to maintain the sham that his village's collective is still producing cheese; communism may have fallen, but the government keeps sending stipends. Flash forward to an Apache reservation, where well-meaning but hapless Jeff Hartig has failed in his attempt to establish a teen center, notwithstanding his friendship with Adam Dale, son of a tribal councilman. Jeff ends up as a Peace Corps volunteer in Anarbek's village, then reappears in Istanbul, where he works for the U.S. government processing refugees. For various reasons, Anarbek, Adam, and Nazira all converge on Jeff. And then the brutal 1999 earthquake hits." Libr J

"This is risky comedy that in less deft hands would clunk into condescension, but Rosenberg keeps it aloft with a sweet sense of appreciation. . . . What a generous, bighearted book this is, perceptive enough to catch the goodness in all these well-intentioned people." Christ Sci Monit

Rosenblatt, Roger

Lapham rising. Ecco 2006 243p $23.95

ISBN 0-06-083361-0   LC 2005-48835

"Harry March is a reclusive writer living on a small island separated by a creek from the 'mainland' of Long Island, in the posh area known collectively as the Hamptons. He's basically a misanthrope, separated from his wife and wondered about by his three grown children. And he has a dog he speaks to (and who talks back to him. . .). Across the creek, a rich businessman is constructing a monstrously outlandish new 'castle.' Harry is determined to undermine this awful example of bad-taste consumerism and environmental despoilation; however, his efforts only lead him to shoot himself in the foot." Booklist

"This is a zany tale. It is a comic novel perfectly conjugated, moving the reader with delight through a three-act plot featuring a hero who is slightly mad, not quite prevailing over the antagonist, who is slightly mad; all of this with appropriate commentary from Hector, a talking dog who is pious and insolent." National Rev

Rosenfeld, Lucinda

I'm so happy for you; a novel about best friends. Little, Brown 2009 268p pa $13.99

ISBN 978-0-316-04450-9 (pa); 0-316-04450-4 (pa)
          LC 2008-45124

"The hapless, too-eager-to-please heroine of Rosenfeld's new novel is an ill-paid editor at an obscure leftist journal who secretly resents her husband for abandoning his job to write a sci-fi screenplay and for failing to get her pregnant. No wonder she thrills to the travails of her best friend, a suicidal beauty who has always overshadowed her but is now languishing in a dead-end affair. Then, to her chagrin, her friend meets Mr. Right. The book's confectionery veneer belies a heart of poison, as Rosenfeld tartly dispels the cherished chick-lit notion that female friendship conquers all. Equally ruthless is

her sendup of overachieving New York women in feral pursuit of have-it-all motherhood without having first ascertained if they even like children." New Yorker

Rosenfelt, David

Don't tell a soul. St. Martin's Minotaur 2008 306p $24.95

ISBN 978-0-312-37395-5; 0-312-37395-3
          LC 2008-14777

"Unjustly suspected of killing his wife in a boating accident, Tim Wallace, co-owner of a construction company, is shadowed by Jonathon Novack, a relentless homicide detective who knows in his gut he's chasing a killer. Then, in a bar one New Year's Eve, Tim encounters a drunk who confesses to having murdered a woman three months earlier. When her death is linked to his wife's, the first of many surprises to come, Tim goes on the run, pursued by Detective Novack and the FBI." Libr J

"Rosenfelt keeps the plot hopping and popping as he reveals a complex frameup of major proportions with profound political ramifications both terrifying and enlightening." Publ Wkly

Ross, Ann B.

Miss Julia throws a wedding. Viking 2002 308p

ISBN 0-670-03105-4   LC 2001-56798

"The inimitable Miss Julia pushes an indecisive couple toward matrimong in this Southern comedy-of-manners, . . . which begins with the protagonist frustrated at the inability of her friend, Miss Hazel, to get her beau to propose. But another opportunity surfaces when Sheriff Coleman Bates proposes to his lawyer girlfriend Binkie Enloe. . . . Ross gets a bit carried away with wedding details, but her cheeky style works flawlessly once Miss Julia digs into the romantic intrigue and begins to ply her unique combination of common sense and old-fashioned, smalltown wisdom." Publ Wkly

Ross, Leonard Q. *See* Rosten, Leo, 1908-1997

Ross, Malcolm *See* Ross-Macdonald, Malcolm

Ross-Macdonald, Malcolm

For they shall inherit; a novel; [by] Malcolm Macdonald. St. Martin's Press 1985 c1984 591p o.p.
          LC 84-52352

First published 1984 in the United Kingdom with title: In love and war

This "novel is set in 19th century England and centers on a dynamic friendship, cemented in boyhood, between clever, ambitious, working-class Freddy and aristocratic Clive, son of the wealthy industrialist who is Freddy's first employer. The fireworks begin when they fall in love with the same woman and Freddy finds himself the legal father of his friend's child. Thereupon they embark on careers that feature exotic adventures in South Africa, South America, the Middle East and elsewhere, accompanied by Freddy's relentless rise to power and wealth, finally at Clive's expense, and the inextricable social and genetic intertwining of their two families." Publ Wkly

"MacDonald skillfully depicts the English class system and the struggles inherent in it. The characters are

Ross-Macdonald, Malcolm—*Continued*
multifaceted and solidly drawn, and the writing is smooth. An absorbing portrayal of human emotion and an individual's will to prevail." Libr J

The rich are with you always; [by] Malcolm Macdonald. Knopf 1976 483p o.p.
"In this sequel to 'The World From Rough Stones' Macdonald continues the interlocking family dramas of John and Nora Stevenson, born dirt poor, driving hard for money and power in Victorian England, and Walter and Arabella Thornton, aristocratic, unhappy, the Stevensons' opposites in every way. It is Nora and John who dominate this part of the saga in the fierce get-rich-quick era of railroad schemes and bonanzas and bankruptcies." Publ Wkly
Followed by Sons of fortune (1978)

Tamsin Harte; [by] Malcolm Macdonald. St. Martin's Press 2000 345p il $24.95
ISBN 0-312-20628-3   LC 99-88104
"Set in a Cornish fishing village at the turn of the last century. . . . Tamsin Harte and her mother, Harriet, fall from the upper echelon of society when Tamsin's father dies and his shipping firm goes bankrupt. They open a boarding house to get by. Energetic, enterprising and ambitious, Tamsin discovers that she has a mind suited to business enterprises. (Her secret ambition is to build 'the best hotel in Cornwall.') When it comes to romance, however, she is still bound by tradition." Publ Wkly

The Trevarton inheritance; [by] Malcolm Macdonald. St. Martin's Press 1996 395p $24.95
ISBN 0-312-14748-1   LC 96-20035
This novel's protagonist, Crissy Moore, "loses both parents and her grandfather within a few days. Determined to keep her orphaned family of six together, she puts herself at the mercy of the grandmother who years ago disowned Crissy's mother. The old woman offers Crissy the position of lady's maid while secretly arranging to break up the family by having all the other children placed in agencies throughout Cornwall. A secondary plot concerns the attempt of Crissy and Jim, the young man she eventually marries, to establish a business photographing tourists at the seaside." Libr J
"Macdonald always maintains a brisk narrative pace, and his sound social commentary adds to the reader's enjoyment." Publ Wkly

The world from rough stones; [by] Malcolm Macdonald. Knopf 1975 535p il o.p.
"Within a year, in the early 1840s, John Stevenson, with Nora at his side, rises from the ranks of railroad construction laborer to the position of a respected and influential contractor. Nora, the ragged and starving teenage girl who had come to John out of the night, becomes his wife. . . . The minor characters, Walter and Arabella Thornton, are middleclass English who are swept along by the tumultuous Stevensons. Walter driven by his sexual fantasies and urges, and Arabella, the pious and good but frigid wife." Best Sellers
"This saga of England in 1839-40 and the start of a great railroad building dynasty opens fast and never once lets up its pace and drama. Above all, its people are believable human beings, caught up in the tumultuous movement of beginning social change." Publ Wkly
Followed by The rich are with you always

Rossner, Judith, 1935-2005

August. Houghton Mifflin 1983 376p
ISBN 0-395-33970-7   LC 83-6191
"'August,' when analysts vacation, is the tale of an analysis, with parallel story-lines for patient and doctor. Teenaged golden girl Dawn Henley has a bizarre background: orphaned as an infant, she was raised by a beloved lesbian aunt and her lover, whose 'divorce' sent Dawn to an analyst. Fortyish Dr. Lulu Shinefeld is twice divorced with a grown daughter from whom she's estranged. So Dawn becomes Dr. Shinefeld's 'analytic daughter.'" Libr J
"Rossner writes about the technical side of analysis and simultaneously shows it at work. In spite of a few awkward passages that tell rather than show how analysis works and an unavoidable lack of completeness resulting from the nature of her topic, Rossner has written a fascinating study of the human mind growing." Best Sellers

Emmeline. Simon & Schuster 1980 331p o.p.
                               LC 80-15553
The novel concerns Emmeline Mosher who "was 13 years old in 1839 when she was sent from her family's farm in Maine to earn 55 cents a week in the cotton mills of Lowell, Mass. There she was seduced by an overseer, gave birth to a child at the home of an aunt before her fifteenth birthday and returned to her parents without telling them her secret. Her venture into the world had saved her family from destitution. In her 30s, having resigned herself to a single life, she made a happy marriage, which ended in calamity. She lived another 40 years as an outcast. . . . Her story is true, according to [the author]." Newsweek
The author "handles her material so meticulously that she inspires a renewed respect for the complexities of skillful story-telling. Instead of propagandizing, she evinces complete respect for the period and setting of her story." Books of the Times

Looking for Mr. Goodbar. Simon & Schuster 1975 284p o.p.
                                                        *

This novel opens with the police transcript of a murderer's confession. The novel "is based loosely on the actual case of Roseann Quinn, a quiet, rigidly brought-up Catholic schoolteacher, who was wholly unremarkable except that she sought out her sexual partners in New York singles bars. The last of them bashed in her skull on New Year's Day, 1973. The question the author asks as she tours the life of Theresa Dunn, the Roseann Quinn-like character of the book, is 'What's a nice girl like you doing in a place like this?'" N Y Times Book Rev
"The tale is stark, capably told, believable; Rossner's prose is a delight, and her sense of the inner life of her characters, all tortured, is deft and sure. This is a very good novel." Booklist

Perfidia; a novel. Talese 1997 308p o.p.
                               LC 97-10882
This is the "story of a model high-school student who kills her alcoholic, violently abusive mother in self-defense. . . . When she is five years old, narrator Maddy Stern is taken by her restless, amoral mother, Anita, from Hanover, N.H., where her father is a professor at Dartmouth, to Santa Fe, where Anita wholeheartedly enters into the 1970s drug and sex scene." Publ Wkly

Rossner, Judith, 1935-2005—*Continued*

"Rossner reveals a gritty new style, stripped down to the clean bones of feeling. 'Perfidia' is an unsparing close-up of the seductive attachment and growing repulsion of a mother and daughter who mean far too much to each other." N Y Times Book Rev

Rosten, Leo, 1908-1997

Captain Newman, M.D. Harper 1962 c1961 331p o.p.

First published 1961 in the United Kingdom

"Describes life in a hospital at an Air Force base in the Southwest during the war. Captain Newman, chief of the psychiatric ward, is a warm, kindly person, the antithesis of the military man, and it is around him that the story revolves. The action is made up of a series of episodes." Libr J

"A book of great insight, warmth and humor. . . . It is a tremendously impressive piece of verbal tight-rope walking. There are the expected flashes of GI humor, the much-documented war of rank, there are also moments of great tenderness and understanding in this chronicle of that most delicate of explorations, the exploration into the shattered minds that are the common responsibilities of all of us." N Y Her Trib Books

Roth, Henry, 1906-1995

Call it sleep. Ballou, R.O. 1934 599p o.p.

        *

"The years between the sixth and ninth birthdays of a young boy are described in this vivid, sensitive portrayal of a Jewish childhood in the ghettos of Brownsville, and the Lower East Side in New York. Because David's father is a violent and bitter man, the child always turns to his mother, with whom he is very close. Her love protects him from the terrors of street gangs, poverty, the sexual conflicts between his parents, and his own initiation into sex by a lame girl. A literary technique that distinguishes between the language used by members of this family when they are speaking their native tongue (Yiddish) and when they speak broken English they have learned as immigrants in the United States is an unusual feature in this remarkable book." Shapiro. Fic for Youth. 3d edition

A diving rock on the Hudson. St. Martin's Press 1995 418p (Mercy of a rude stream, v2)

ISBN 0-312-11777-9

This second volume of the author's autobiographical cycle "continues the saga of Ira Stigman, teenage son of Orthodox Jewish immigrant parents, as he struggles to find his way in the larger world. Narrated by the now elderly Ira, it effectively evokes both life in 1920s New York and the angst of adolescent existence. In Ira's case, this angst results not only from the growing distance that separates his and his parents' views of the world but from uncontrollable urges that drive him to violate one of society's strongest taboos."

"Simultaneously, we are inside the mind of a troubled adolescent and that of an aged but still mentally vital man, a man engaged with words, with concepts, obsessively reconsidering the role of the artist and in particular his own responsibility in portraying events truthfully." Booklist

Followed by From bondage

From bondage. St. Martin's Press 1996 397p (Mercy of a rude stream, v3) $25.95

ISBN 0-312-14341-9

This third volume of Roth's autobiographical cycle "continues the story of Ira Stigman, son of East European Jewish immigrant parents and now college aged, as he struggles to find his way in 1920s New York. But, like the previous volumes, it is also the story of Ira the octogenarian writer who, nearing the end of his life, is trying to come to terms with both the forces and the choices that shaped it. Paralleling Roth's own experience, this volume focuses on the beginnings of what was to become a decade-long affair between Ira and NYU professor Edith Welles." Libr J

Followed by Requiem for Harlem

Requiem for Harlem. St. Martin's Press 1997 291p il (Mercy of a rude stream, v4) $24.95

ISBN 0-312-16980-9   LC 97-17824

This concluding volume of Roth's autobiographical cycle picks up the story in 1927. "Still living in the Harlem slums with his parents and young sister, City College senior Ira Stigman is on fire with Milton's poetry and wracked by guilt over his sexual relations with his 16-year-old cousin Stella. Although the reader has known since volume three that Ira's eventual deliverer and muse will be his NYU English instructor (and the mistress of his best friend), Roth delays the inception of this affair until the novel's conclusion and meanwhile dwells on what seem red herrings: Stella's pregnancy scare and her grandfather's apparent discovery of her trysts with Ira." Publ Wkly

"Even as we see the older writer commenting ruefully on all that has come to pass, we see the young artist taking in every detail of the world. . . . And if it is hard to sympathize with either the egocentric youth or the rueful old man, taken together they meld into a living whole. This is Roth's achievement, this double vision of the artist as both young and old man, hungry and regretful, flawed and penitent." N Y Times Book Rev

A star shines over Mt. Morris Park. St. Martin's Press 1994 290p (Mercy of a rude stream, v1) o.p.

        * LC 93-37270

The first volume of Roth's autobiographical cycle. "Ira Stigman, the protagonist narrates both as a boy, in the past, and in the present, as a philosophical and pain-wracked octogenarian. Young Ira's tale begins in 1914, when he and his parents move from the East Side's cozy Jewish enclave to Harlem, then primarily Irish. This dislocation, which makes Ira despise his Jewishness, coincides with the arrival of his mother's parents and siblings, fresh off the boat from Austria-Hungary. As Ira copes with all these changes, he takes comfort in books. . . . As he navigates the rough course of his impoverished life from ages 8 to 15, he reports on the absurdities and abusiveness of family life, school, and various jobs as well as the shadow of war, the many hues of anti-Semitism and racism, and the shock of sexuality." Booklist

"Mr. Roth remains an admirable craftsman, and the scenes of immigrant life in the second decade of the century are evoked with persuasive concreteness." N Y Times Book Rev

Followed by A diving rock on the Hudson

Roth, Joseph, 1894-1939

The bust of the emperor

In Roth, J. The collected stories of Joseph Roth

The collected stories of Joseph Roth; translated with an introduction by Michael Hofmann. Norton 2002 400p $27.95

ISBN 0-393-04320-7

* LC 2001-44747

This collection includes three novellas: The triumph of beauty, The bust of the emperor and The leviathan, and the following short stories: The honors student; Barbara; Career; The place I want to tell you about. . .; Sick people; Rare and ever rarer in this world of empirical fact. . .; The Cartel; April the story of a love affair; The blind mirror; The grand house opposite; Strawberries; This morning, a letter arrived; Youth; Stationmaster Fallmerayer

The triumph of beauty explores the impact of a fickle hypochondriac on her husband. In the bust of the emperor an elderly nobleman continues to perform dutifully even after the state renders his commitment obsolete. The leviathan portrays a coral merchant preoccupied with the mystery of the exotic life forms that provide his livelihood

"Combining a shrewd reportorial eye with a taste for the fantastic and droll, Roth portrays characters living materially and spiritually impoverished lives in isolated Eastern European villages and those left homeless in their own homes in the tumultuous aftermath of World War I." Booklist

The leviathan

In Roth, J. The collected stories of Joseph Roth

The triumph of beauty

In Roth, J. The collected stories of Joseph Roth

Roth, Philip

American pastoral. Houghton Mifflin 1997 423p

ISBN 0-395-86021-0

* LC 96-49368

"Swede Levov's life has been charmed from the time he was an all-star athlete at Newark's Weequahic high school. . . . He successfully runs his father's glove factory, refusing to be cowed by the race riots that rock Newark, marries a shiksa beauty-pageant queen, who is smart and ambitious, buys a 100-acre farm in a classy suburb—the epitome of serene, innocent, pastoral existence—and dotes on his daughter, Merry. But when Merry becomes radicalized during the Vietnam War, plants a bomb that kills an innocent man and goes underground for five years, Swede endures a torment that becomes increasingly unbearable as he learns more about Merry's monstrous life." Publ Wkly

"This cultural horror story is deepened by Roth's genius for blending humor, pathos, sympathy and rage. . . . You will search the shelf of contemporary fiction long and hard to find a parental nightmare projected with the emotional force and verbal energy that Roth brings to American Pastoral." Time

The anatomy lesson. Farrar, Straus & Giroux 1983 291p o.p.

* LC 83-11645

"Roth's novelist/hero in The Ghost Writer and Zuckerman Unbound, Nathan Zuckerman at 40 can no longer write: he has lost his subject ('as a medium for his books he had ceased to be') and is losing his hair. Severely incapacitated by chronic pain . . . and addicted to painkillers, Zuckerman decides to become a doctor, one who deals not in words but in real 'stuff,' 'the lowest of genres—life itself.' He ends up in a hospital rather than medical school when a disastrously euphoric return to Chicago, scene of his first literary triumph, results in a drug-induced breakdown." Libr J

"A ferocious, heartfelt book. . . . One might venture to say that, like a goodly number of Roth's previous works, 'The Anatomy Lesson' revolves around the paradox of incarnation—the astonishing coexistence in one life of infantilism and intelligence, of selfishness and altruism, of sexual appetite and social conscience—and has the form and manner of a monologue conducted under psychoanalysis." New Yorker

also in Roth, P. Zuckerman bound

The breast

In Roth, P. Novels, 1967-1972

The counterlife

also in Roth, P. Novels and other narratives 1986-1991

Deception

In Roth, P. Novels and other narratives 1986-1991

The dying animal. Houghton Mifflin 2001 156p $22

ISBN 0-618-13587-1   LC 00-54225

David Kepesh, protagonist of Roth's The breast and The professor of desire, "is now an eminent 70-year-old cultural critic and lecturer at a New York college, recalling a devastating, all-consuming affair he had eight years before with voluptuous 24-years-old Consuela Castillo, a graduate student and daughter of a prosperous Cuban émigré family." Publ Wkly

"Like many works of modern literature, The Dying Animal ends on a note of radical ambiguity and indeterminacy. What is rather unusual about it is the way it challenges the reader at every point to define and defend his own ethical position toward the issues raised by the story. It is a small, disturbing masterpiece." N Y Rev Books

Everyman. Houghton Mifflin 2006 182p $24

ISBN 0-618-73516-X   LC 2005-31538

"Roth's everyman is a hero whose youthful sense of independence and confidence begins to be challenged when illness commences its attack in middle age. A successful commercial advertising artist, he is the father of two sons who despise him and a daughter who adores him. He is the brother of a good man whose physical well-being comes to arouse his bitter envy. He is the lonely ex-husband of three very different women with whom he has made a mess of marriage. Inevitably, he discovers that he has become what he does not want to be." Publisher's note

"From a distance, Everyman looks like a shaggy dog

LIST OF FICTIONAL WORKS

Roth, Philip—*Continued*
story—a long, quotidian story whose meaning resides in its final pointlessness. Up close, though, it is a parable that captures, as few works of fiction have, the pathos of Being, as it's manifested even in the favored precincts of affluent America." Washington Post Book World

Exit ghost. Houghton Mifflin 2007 292p $26
ISBN 978-0-618-91547-7; 0-618-91547-8
LC 2006-102467
"The ninth novel to feature famous writer Nathan Zuckerman finds Roth's close alter-ego in the 'winter' of his life: at age 71, suffering the depressing side effects of prostate surgery and living a hermit's existence in rural Massachusetts, in self-imposed exile from people and technology. This . . . novel has a relatively limited time frame: one week, when Zuckerman returns to New York City, his former home, for a surgical procedure, this event conspiring to make him believe he wants to regain society . . ., specifically to pursue feminine pulchritude anew, despite his impotence and incontinence." Booklist
"Mr. Roth has created a melancholy, if occasionally funny, meditation on aging, mortality, loneliness and the losses that come with the passage of time. . . . For fans of the Zuckerman books, it provides a poignant coda to Nathan's story, putting a punctuation point to his journey from youthful idealism and passion through midlife confusion and angst toward elderly renunciation." N Y Times (Late N Y Ed)

The ghost writer. Farrar, Straus & Giroux 1979 179p o.p. LC 79-13146
"A brief but intricate tale about a young writer [Nathan Zuckerman] who, when accused of travestying his fellow Jews, seeks counsel from a respected older Jewish author and finds this distinguished figure ambiguously involved with a girl whom the young writer fantasizes to be Anne Frank." Oxford Companion to Am Lit. 6th edition
Followed by Zuckerman unbound
also in Roth, P. Zuckerman bound

Goodbye, Columbus
In Roth, P. Novels & stories, 1959-1962

Goodbye, Columbus, and five short stories. Modern Lib. 1995 298p hardcover o.p. pa $14
ISBN 0-679-60159-7; 0-679-74826-1 (pa)
* LC 94-44528
A reissue of the title first published 1959 by Houghton Mifflin
Contents: Goodbye, Columbus; Conversion of the Jews; Defender of the faith; Epstein; You can't tell a man by the song he sings; Eli, the fanatic
"The title story in this collection is about a young Radcliffe girl and a Rutgers boy who learn that there is more to love than exuberance and passion. All of the stories dramatize the dilemma of modern American Jews, torn between two worlds." Publ Wkly

The great American novel. Holt, Rinehart & Winston 1973 382p
ISBN 0-8050-1734-8
"Sportswriter 'Word' Smith narrates the chaotic history of a forgotten ('suppressed,' he claims) third major league and its bungling nemeses the Ruppert Mundays, a team of neurotic misfit leftovers. In 1943, war has decimated the league; the Mundys are cast out from their stadium (which is needed for wartime priorities) on 'an endless road trip,' to wander the circuit and suffer." Libr J
This novel is "at once a burlesque and an allegory, its telling of the downfall of a great baseball team serving as a satirical parallel to contemporary American political and social events." Oxford Companion to Am Lit. 6th edition
also in Roth, P. Novels, 1973-1977

The human stain. Houghton Mifflin 2000 361p $26
ISBN 0-618-05945-8 LC 99-89867
"Coleman Silk, a brilliant classics professor at sleepy Athena College in western Massachusetts, is forced into early retirement by the zealots of political correctness when an African American student accuses him of using the word *spook* as a racial epithet. This groundless claim is supported by the department chair, a French feminist motivated by sexual jealousy. The irony is that Silk, who has always claimed to be Jewish, is in fact African American himself. Not even his wife and children know the truth. . . . Silk asks his neighbor Nathan Zuckerman to write a book about the affair, and *The Human Stain* is Zuckerman's final report, completed after Silk's untimely death." Libr J
"Roth is clearly enjoyed himself. The Human Stain is as fresh, as angry and as bitterly amused as his early fiction. It vibrates with mockery, disapproval, poetry, and a healthy dose of personal vindictiveness that one would be tempted to dismiss as unworthy if it weren't so funny." New Leader

The humbling. Houghton Mifflin Harcourt 2009 140p $26
ISBN 978-0-547-23969-9; 0-547-23969-6
LC 2009013742
Simon Axler "gives two dreadful and derided performances in Washington D.C. Suddenly, he feels, he has lost his acting magic. His wife leaves him. He has a stay in a psychiatric hospital. He emerges to live a depressed and solitary life in the country, resisting his agent's plea to return to the stage. The lesbian daughter of an old friend visits, cares for him, administers bouts of increasingly kinky sex, then suddenly leaves. His brief hopes extinguished—perhaps he could act again—he cradles a gun and wonders whether he has the guts to kill himself." Boston Globe
"In this searing novel, Roth adds dark shadings to the austere vision he has explored in recent works like Everyman and Exit Ghost; there are precious few shafts of light that break through his clinical examination of one man's catastrophic fall from grace. But in recounting with unrelenting precision the grim story of Simon—not a bad man, simply a tragically human one—Roth offers another unflinching assessment of the essence of our mortality." BookPage

I married a communist. Houghton Mifflin 1998 323p $26
ISBN 0-395-93346-3 LC 98-16797
"Roth's old alter ego, Nathan Zuckerman, narrates the story of Ira Ringold, aka Iron Rinn, a supremely idealistic political radical and celebrated radio star of the 1950s who is blacklisted and brought to ruin when his wife, Eva Frame (a self-hating Jewish actress born Chava Fromkin), writes an expose called *I Married A Commu-*

Roth, Philip—*Continued*

nist. The impetus for Eva's treacherous act is Ira's insistence that she evict her 24-year-old daughter from their house." Publ Wkly

"What Zuckerman/Roth does with this imagined material is constantly mesmerizing. Library shelves groan under the weight of books published about the witch hunts and blacklistings during the Truman and Eisenhower presidencies, but it would be hard to find one among them that presents as nuanced, as humanly complex an account of those years as I Married a Communist." Time

Indignation. Houghton Mifflin Company 2008 233p $26

ISBN 978-0-54705-484-1; 0-54705-484-X

LC 2008-11431

"We are back in nineteen-fifties Newark, and nineteen-year-old Marcus Messner, the son of a kosher butcher, attempts to escape his father's stifling influence by enrolling at a college in Ohio farm country. Messner is a scholarly type, while his new classmates are an unfriendly bunch of churchgoing, beer-swilling louts. Stubbornly disregarding overtures of friendship from members of the school's only Jewish fraternity, Messner devotes his attentions to a troubled Gentile named Olivia Hutton. There's something of Portnoy in the masturbation-filled high jinks that follow, but Messner, fearful that he might 'wind up a rifleman in Korea,' is a far darker creation." New Yorker

Letting go. Random House 1962 630p $12.50

ISBN 0-394-43305-X

Gabe Wallach is "a young university instructor who is literally unable to let go in his personal relationships. This is true with his father, a well-to-do Jewish dentist who suffers because his wife is dead and his only child lives in Chicago instead of New York; with Martha Reganhart, a divorcée, mother of two small children, a woman Gabe loves enough to make his mistress but not his wife; and with Paul and Libby Herz, a young couple suffering the difficulties arising from a mixed marriage, no money, inability to have children, and a host of other problems real and imagined." Libr J

also in Roth, P. Novels & stories, 1959-1962

My life as a man. Holt, Rinehart & Winston 1974 330p o.p.

The "novel consists of three stories: a long autobiographical narrative told by the novelist Peter Tarnopol, preceded by two of Peter's stories, 'useful fictions' in which elements of his 'true story' are metamorphosed. Peter's alter ego, Nathan Zuckerman, is, like his author, a highly self-conscious intellectual urban Jew, adept at eliciting astonishing sexual performances from teen-age girls, but fatally drawn into a disastrous marriage with an older, damaged woman who is incapable of sexual response." Newsweek

also in Roth, P. Novels, 1973-1977

Novels & stories, 1959-1962; Philip Roth. Library of America 2005 913p $35

ISBN 1-931082-79-0

* LC 2005-40916

Contents: Goodbye, Columbus; Five short stories; Letting go

Novels, 1967-1972. Library of America 2005 671p $35

ISBN 1-931082-80-4

* LC 2005-40917

Contents: When she was good; Portnoy's complaint; Our gang; The breast

When she was good and Portnoy's complaint are entered separately. Our gang (1971) is a satire of the Nixon administration, featuring a president named Trick E. Dixon. The breast (1972) is "a novella about a male professor of literature who suffers a Kafka-like transformation into a gigantic breast." Oxford Companion to Am Lit 6th edition

Novels, 1973-1977. Library of America 2006 912p $35

ISBN 978-1-931082-96-9; 1-931082-96-0

LC 2006-41030

In The Great American novel (1973), "Roth lifts the lid on the suppressed history of the homeless Ruppert Mundys of baseball's despised and vanquished third major league, turning the national pastime into unfettered picaresque farce. . . . My Life as a Man (1974) is Roth's . . . lurid account of the all-out battle waged between the young writer Peter Tarnopol and the wife who is his nemesis, his demon, and his muse. . . . The Professor of Desire (1977) charts the second sexual metamorphosis of David Kepesh, protagonist of The Breast. Roth follows Kepesh, an adventurous man of intelligence and feeling, into a vast wilderness of erotic possibility." Publisher's note

Novels and other narratives 1986-1991. Library of America 2008 767p

ISBN 978-1-598530-30-8

In addition to the novels The counterlife and Deception this volume also includes two nonfiction titles: The facts and Patrimony

The focus in The counterlife (1986) is how people enact "their dreams of renewal and escape, some going so far as to risk their lives to alter seemingly irreversible destinies. Illuminating these lives in transition is the skeptical, enveloping intelligence of the writer Nathan Zuckerman. . . . At the center of . . . Deception (1990), are a married American named Philip, living in London, and the married Englishwoman—trapped with a little child in a loveless upper-middle-class household—who eloquently and minutely reveals herself to her lover as they talk before and after making love." Publisher's note

Our gang
In Roth, P. Novels, 1967-1972

The plot against America. Houghton Mifflin 2004 391p $26

ISBN 0-618-50928-3

LC 2004-47490

"When the renowned aviation hero . . . Charles A. Lindbergh defeated Franklin Roosevelt by a landslide in the 1940 presidential election, fear invaded every Jewish household in America. Not only had Lindbergh, in a nationwide radio address, publicly blamed the Jews for selfishly pushing America toward a pointless war with Nazi Germany, he negotiated a cordial 'understanding' with Adolf Hitler, whose conquest of Europe and virulent antiSemitic policies he appeared to accept with difficulty. . . . [The protagonist Philip Roth] recounts what it was like for his Newark family . . . during the menac-

Roth, Philip—*Continued*
ing years of the Lindbergh presidency." Publisher's note
"Philip Roth has written a terrific political novel, though in a style his readers might never have predicted. . . . The novel is sinister, vivid, dreamlike, preposterous and, at the same time, creepily plausible." N Y Times Book Rev

Portnoy's complaint. Random House 1969 274p o.p.
*
"An irreverently funny account of a modern man torn between the repressive, traditional values embodied by his Jewish mother, his passion for WASP women, and his desperate desire to be released from the past to create himself as a human being out of his own nothingness." Reader's Ency. 4th edition
"Roth has the courage to wish to show things as he has experienced them, but the exaggerations of *Portnoy's Complaint* have a shrillness which could be considered unwholesome if the book were not so funny. It is very funny." Burgess. 99 Novels
also in Roth, P. Novels, 1967-1972

The Prague orgy
In Roth, P. Zuckerman bound

The professor of desire. Farrar, Straus & Giroux 1977 263p
ISBN 0-374-23756-5   LC 77-24032
This novel concerns "David Kepesh, professor of comparative literature. . . . Kepesh becomes involved with a series of women: the coeds at Syracuse University, whom he affronts with his outrageous candor; two Swedish girls in London, who join him, one with self-loathing and the other with zest, in various sexual adventures; a disorganized California beauty, with whom he takes up at the end of his graduate studies at Stanford University; and a well-organized New York beauty, who rescues him from the wreckage of his marriage to the Californian." New Yorker
"Like most writers who prove they have enough talent for the long haul of a career, Roth has found the story he will tell until either he or it is exhausted. It is a good story and, as The Professor of Desire proves, it gets better with each telling." Time
also in Roth, P. Novels, 1973-1977

Sabbath's theater. Houghton Mifflin 1995 451p
o.p.   LC 95-914
"Mickey Sabbath is an elderly relic of the diabolical young puppeteer who was once arrested for coaxing a young Columbia student's breast out of her blouse with the sheer effrontery of his insinuating performing fingers. Now, living in obscure poverty in New Hampshire with a wife who's in aggressive recovery from the alcoholism to which he has driven her, he is reviewing his life. . . . He has had a deliriously erotic relationship with Drenka, the concupiscent wife of a local Yugoslavian innkeeper, and her sudden death from cancer quite undoes him." Publ Wkly
"There is plenty of the nasty in this virtuoso performance by our best literary stand-up comic. . . . The verbal play is almost tactile, like slaps, as the narrative moves from third-person comic to first-person perverse confession, but there is a polemical energy that lifts it beyond verbal playfulness; at times the message is painful." N Y Times Book Rev

When she was good. Random House 1967 306p o.p.
This is "a story of a girl obsessed with her own criteria of what a man should be. Set in a Midwestern town the novel is concerned with Lucy Nelson, who disappointed with a feckless father, fights him and scorns her mother for her love of him. Having wreaked havoc in her parents' marriage, she applies the same steely demands to a husband who has been either the seduced or the seducer depending on whose view is accepted. She destroys the marriage and herself in a final abandonment to her compulsion." Booklist
"Roth knows exactly what he's doing. With unerring fidelity, he records the flat surface of provincial American life, the look and feel and sound of it—and then penetrates it to the cesspool of its invisible dynamisms. Beneath the 'good,' and impelling it, he says, lies the horrid." Newsweek
also in Roth, P. Novels, 1967-1972

Zuckerman bound; a trilogy and epilogue, 1979-1985. Library of America 645p $35
ISBN 978-1-59853-011-7; 1-59853-011-9
LC 2007-926533
"The Ghost Writer (1979) introduces Nathan Zuckerman in the 1950s, a budding writer infatuated with the Great Books, discovering the contradictory claims of literature and experience while an overnight guest in the secluded New England farmhouse of his literary idol, E. I. Lonoff. Zuckerman Unbound (1981) finds him far from Lonoff's domain—the scene is Manhattan as the sensationalizing 1960s are coming to an end. Zuckerman, in his mid-thirties, is suffering the immediate aftershock of literary celebrity. The high-minded protégé of E. I. Lonoff has become a notorious superstar. The Anatomy Lesson (1984) takes place largely in the hospital isolation ward that Zuckerman has made of his Upper East Side apartment. It is Watergate time, 1973, and to Zuckerman the only other American who seems to be in as much trouble as himself is Richard Nixon. Zuckerman, at forty, is beset with crippling and unexplained physical pain; he wonders if the cause might not be his own inflammatory work. In The Prague Orgy (1985), entries from Zuckerman's notebooks describing his 1976 sojourn among the outcast artists of Soviet-occupied Czechoslovakia." Publisher's note

Zuckerman unbound. Farrar, Straus & Giroux 1981 225p o.p.
* LC 81-4640
"After three marriages and a respected body of fiction, Nathan Zuckerman has suddenly struck free with the scandalous and subversive success of a book about a Portnoyish complainer called Carnovsky. The promising apprentice of The Ghost Writer who engaged in biographical fantasy, has himself become a creature of public fantasy who cannot cope comfortably even with material success. The consequences range from bizarre comedy (the plague of a ruined quiz show contestant who claims his life has been plagiarized) to the distortion of family relations." Libr J
Followed by The anatomy lesson
also in Roth, P. Zuckerman bound

Rothfuss, Pat

The name of the wind; the Kingkiller chronicle, day 01; by Patrick Rothfuss. DAW Books 2007 661p $24.95

ISBN 978-0-7564-0407-9; 0-7564-0407-X

The first title in a projected fantasy trilogy. "From his childhood as a member of a close-knit family of the nomadic Edema Ruh to his first heady days as a student of magic at a prestigious university, humble bartender Kvothe relates the tale of how a boy beset by fate became a hero, a bard, a magician, and a legend." Libr J

This is "quite simply the best fantasy novel of the past 10 years, although attaching a genre qualification threatens to damn it with faint praise. Say instead that The Name of the Wind is one of the best stories told in any medium in a decade." Onion

Roy, Arundhati

The god of small things. Random House 1997 321p o.p.   LC 96-39190

A novel "set in the tiny river town of Ayemenem in Kerala, India. The story revolves around a pair of twins, brother and sister, whose mother has left her violent husband to live with her blind mother and kind, if ineffectual, brother, Chacko. Chacko's ex-wife, an Englishwoman, has returned to Ayemenem after a long absence, bringing along her and Chacko's lovely young daughter. Their arrival not only unsettles the already tenuous balance of the divisive household, it also coincides with political unrest." Booklist

"If the symbolism is a trifle overdone, the lush local color and the incisive characterizations give the narrative power and drama." Publ Wkly

Roza, Luiz Alfredo García- *See* García-Roza, Luiz Alfredo, 1936-

Rozan, S. J.

Winter and night. St. Martin's Minotaur 2002 338p $24.95

ISBN 0-312-24555-6   LC 2001-48659

In this mystery featuring New York PIs Lydia Chin and Bill Smith it is "Smith's turn to tell the story, which here concerns his teenage nephew, Gary Russell, the athlete son of his estranged sister Helen. When Gary is arrested for pickpocketing in Manhattan, the boy asks for his uncle's help. Gary denies running away from his Warrenstown, N. J. home; he was doing something important. Then the boy vanishes, drawing Smith and Chin into a nightmarish case in which a small town's obsession with its high school football team overwhelms standards of justice and morality." Publ Wkly

Ruark, Robert

Uhuru; a novel of Africa today. McGraw-Hill 1962 555p o.p.

This novel "tells of the Kenya of 1960—eight years after the Mau-Mau rebellion—a Kenya where native Africans are heard in the House of Parliament and the UN, where modern-day sophistication is blended with ancient tribal customs to produce a new form of cannibalism, where one nauseating throat-cutting ceremony follows another nauseating betrayal of ethics and morals." Libr J

Rucker, Rudy von Bitter, 1946-

Mathematicians in love; [by] Rudy Rucker. Tor 2006 364p $24.95

ISBN 978-0-7653-1584-7; 0-7653-1584-X
                                                     * LC 2006-5725

"A Tom Doherty Associates book"

"Set in an alternate-universe Berkeley, California, dubbed Humelocke, the story revolves around a bizarre romantic triangle involving cerebral math majors Bela and Paul and their seesawing love interest, Alma. With the dubious patronage of their mentally unbalanced advisor, Professor Roland, Paul and Bela develop a proof for a radical new theorem that may facilitate prediction of future events with astounding accuracy. The roadblock to capitalizing on their discovery lies in creating a 'paracomputer' to spit out usable data. When the cockroach monsters Professor Roland claims to have seen begin appearing in Bela's mirror with a written solution, reality begins to take a decidedly surrealistic turn." Booklist

Rucker "is palpably and quiveringly tuned in to the zeitgeist and can offer cultural and scientific commentary and satire better than almost any other SF author practicing today. . . . But aside from all the glories of the speculative science and math and interdimensional jaunts . . ., what we have here is a rollicking, roisterous, (ir-)reverent campus novel." Sci Fi Wkly

Postsingular; [by] Rudy Rucker. Tor 2007 320p $25.95

ISBN 978-0-7653-1741-4; 0-7653-1741-9
                                                     LC 2007-20210

"In the very near future, two influential and maladjusted individuals initiate a radical transformation of the world through the use of sentient nanotechnology-only to have their plans foiled by Chu, the autistic son of two scientists engaged in nanotechnology research. The persistence of money and politics, however, creates a strange new world in which humans become telepaths and can travel to other worlds in the quantum universe; finally, gigantic visitors from another place entirely arrive to sort things out. Rucker . . . excels in mind-bending premises and thought-stretching stories peopled with appealingly flawed characters that resonate with familiarity despite their eccentricities." Libr J

Ruff, Matt

Bad monkeys. Harper Collins Publishers 2007 230p $20

ISBN 978-0-06-124041-6; 0-06-124041-9
                                                     LC 2006-52184

"In a holding cell in the psychiatric wing of a prison, a psychologist is interviewing inmate Jane Charlotte. She's been charged with homicide. Although she does not deny it, she weaves an outrageous story about the circumstances surrounding the murder. She claims to be working for a secret organization devoted to fighting evil with an array of fantastical weapons, including a gun that, depending on the setting, can induce a heart attack, a stroke, or a coma. Jane details her initial contact with the organization when she was a teenager, her 'lost years' as a homeless drug addict, and her eventual work for the division dubbed Bad Monkeys, which targets and eliminates 'irredeemable persons.'" Booklist

"At times the twists are enough to give the reader

Ruff, Matt—*Continued*

whiplash. Ruff's expert characterization of Jane and agile manipulation of layers of reality ground the novel and make it more than just a Philip K. Dick ripoff." Publ Wkly

Ruiz, Luis Manuel, 1973-

Only one thing missing; translated from the Spanish by Alfred Mac Adam. Grove Press 2003 308p $24

ISBN 0-8021-1730-9   LC 2002-29723

Original Spanish edition, 2000

"A distraught young woman living in Seville, Spain, Alicia has just lost her husband and only child in a horrible accident. She suffers from terrifying nightmares of wandering through a nameless city whose monuments and inhabitants begin appearing to her during waking moments. Carmen Barroso, the most sought-after psychotherapist in Seville. . . treats her with hynosis and medication but is strangely dismissive of her harrowing dreams. . . . Aided by her brother-in-law, Esteban, who loves her deeply, Alicia comes to realize that she is the victim of a sinister conspiracy with roots in devil worship." Libr J

"As translated by Adam, Ruiz's prose is ornate and word-drunk. Ruiz sometimes falls in love with the sound of his narrator's voice, but it is easy to forgive him." Booklist

Ruiz Zafón, Carlos, 1964-

The angel's game; translated into English by Lucia Graves. Doubleday 2009 531p $26.95

ISBN 978-0-385-52870-2; 0-385-52870-1

LC 2008-53650

A prequel to: The shadow of the wind

Original Spanish edition, 2008

"As the book opens in 1917, David Martín is 17, a down-on-his-luck Barcelona writer and budding journalist. An orphan since his father was murdered, David is forced by necessity to subvert his lofty literary ambitions in the service of writing a series of pulp novels in the macabre Grand Guignol tradition. Then a mysterious stranger named Andreas Corelli, a close relative of the stranger in Mark Twain's book of the same name and every other deal-with-the-devil tale you've ever read, presents a proposal to Martín — write a book that will create a perfect narrative for a religion. In essence, his assignment is to create a mythical story that will seduce the masses into belief. The mortal medical condition Martín suffers from goes into remission, and a fortune is placed in his bank account. And off we go. This novel operates on so many levels, a brief review can't quite do justice to its many layers." Seattle Times

The shadow of the wind; translated by Lucia Graves. Penguin Press 2004 486p $24.95

ISBN 1-59420-010-6   LC 2003-062376

Original Spanish edition, 2001

"In post-World War II Barcelona, young Daniel is taken by his bookseller father to the Cemetery of Forgotten Books, a massive sanctuary where books are guarded from oblivion. Told to choose one book to protect, he selects The Shadow of the Wind, by Julian Carax. He reads it, loves it, and soon learns it is both very valuable and very much in danger because someone is determinedly burning every copy of every book written by the obscure Carax. . . . Daniel's initiation into the mysteries of adulthood is given the same weight as the mystery of the book-burner. And the setting—Spain under Franco—injects an air of sobriety into some plot elements that might otherwise seem soap operatic. Part detective story, part boy's adventure, part romance, fantasy, and gothic horror, the intricate plot is urged on by extravagant foreshadowing and nail-nibbling tension." Booklist

Runcie, James, 1959-

Canvey Island; a novel. Other Press 2008 c2006 301p pa $13.95

ISBN 978-1-59051-293-7; 1-59051-293-6

LC 2007-52431

First published 2006 in the United Kingdom

"In 1953 Canvey Island, off the coast of Britain, suffered the ill effects of a storm surge, which flooded the island. In this fictionalized account of the tragedy, nine-year-old Martin and his mother, Lily, fight to stay above water, but Lily is unable to free herself from the debris, and she is swept under. Her death becomes the defining moment of Martin's life; he grows up obsessed with water and becomes an engineer, forever trying to figure out the best way to hold back the sea. He never quite forgives his father, Len, for failing to save his wife and for taking up with her sister, the flamboyant Violet. Martin himself gives up his free-spirited girlfriend, in part because he loves her too much, opting instead to marry Claire, a vicar's daughter with a rebellious streak. In highly readable chapters narrated by each family member, the book manages to address class and generational conflict as it travels through the decades." Booklist

Runyon, Alfred Damon *See* Runyon, Damon, 1884-1946

Runyon, Damon, 1884-1946

Blue plate special

In Runyon, D. Guys and dolls p345-505

Guys and dolls. Lippincott 1950 505p o.p.

An omnibus volume of three titles first published by F.A. Stokes in 1931, 1935 and 1934 respectively and analyzed in Short story index

Contents: Guys and dolls: Bloodhounds of Broadway; Social error; Lily of St. Pierre; Butch minds the baby; Lillian; Romance in the roaring forties; Very honorable guy; Madame La Gimp; Dark Dolores; "Gentlemen, the King!"; Hottest guy in the world; Brain goes home; Blood pressure

Money from home: Earthquake; Bred for battle; Breach of promise; Story goes with it; Sense of humor; Broadway financier; Broadway complex; It comes up mud; Nice price; Pick the winner; Undertaker song; Tobias the terrible

Blue plate special: Hold 'em Yale!; That ever-loving wife of Hymie's; What, no butler?; Brakeman's daughter; Snatching of Bookie Bob; Dream Street Rose; Little Miss Marker; Dancing Dan's Christmas; Old doll's house; Lemon drop kid; Three wise guys; Princess O'Hara; For a pal

Money from home

In Runyon, D. Guys and dolls p167-337

Rush, Norman

Mating. Knopf 1991 480p o.p.

* LC 90-25752

The author "relates the tale of an American female anthropologist in Africa, whose thesis research (on fertility) has already gone dead when she falls for a man who is in Africa running a utopian community for unfortunate women." Booklist

"Mr. Rush has created one of the wiser and wittier fictive meditations on the subject of mating. His novel illuminates why we yield when we don't have to. It seeks to illuminate the nature of true intimacy—how to define it, how to know when one has achieved it. And few books evoke so eloquently that state of love at its apogee." N Y Times Book Rev

Mortals; a novel. Knopf 2003 715p $26.95

ISBN 0-679-40622-0   LC 2002-43289

This "novel is about middle-class Americans in Botswana, Africa. . . . The protagonist is a minor secret CIA agent in the early 1990s with the region in turmoil as Mandela struggles to come to power across the border. Ray's not quite sure how he landed in his spy job, but he quite likes it. He's sure he's never been involved with anything really bad. What matters to him is his beautiful wife, Iris. After 17 years, he's still totally obsessed with every part of her body, every glance, every funny word. But is she having an affair with Morel, the black American doctor who believes the way to fix broken Africa is to get rid of Christianity? When Ray is sent on a bungled mission and lands up with the brutal apartheid paramilitary, Morel comes to the rescue, and the two bond in a prison cell." Booklist

"The richness of Rush's vision, and its stringent moral clarity, sweep the reader into his brilliantly observed world." Publ Wkly

Rushdie, Salman

East, west; stories. Pantheon Bks. 1995 c1994 214p o.p.   LC 94-28277

First publishd 1994 in the United Kingdom

Contents: Good advice is rarer than rubies; The free radio; The prophet's hair; At the auction of the ruby slippers; Christopher Columbus and Queen Isabella of Spain consummate their relationship (Santa Fé, AD 1492); The harmony of the spheres; Chekov and Zulu; The courter

"Rushdie's brilliant style reinforces his stories' marvelous combination of dignity and poignancy. Though these stories were originally published in such periodicals as the New Yorker and the Atlantic, the collection will serve for many readers as an introduction to Rushdie's talent in the short story form." Booklist

The enchantress of Florence; a novel. Random House 2008 355p $26

ISBN 978-0-375-50433-4; 0-375-50433-8

LC 2008-70

"A tall, yellow-haired, young European traveler calling himself 'Mogor dell'Amore,' the Mughal of Love, arrives at the court of the Emperor Akbar, lord of the great Mughal empire, with a tale to tell that begins to obsess the imperial capital, a tale about a mysterious woman, a great beauty believed to possess powers of enchantment and sorcery, and her impossible journey to the far-off city of Florence." Publisher's note

"A beguiling, incandescent tale of travel, treachery, and transformation set in the Renaissance Florence of Machiavelli and the Medicis and in India's Mughal Empire. . . . While Mogor's risky quest and fate are central . . . Rushdie ushers in a caravan of low, laughable characters in the service of his weighty and witty observations on religion, politics, sex, war, art, philosophy, and science in an East-West world of white mischief and black magic, of enigmatic nightmares and inscrutable dreams." Elle

The ground beneath her feet; a novel. Holt & Co. 1999 575p $26

ISBN 0-8050-5308-5   LC 98-42407

"Ormus Cama, a supernaturally gifted musician, and his beloved, Vina Apsara, a half-Indian woman with a soul-thrilling voice, meet in Bombay in the late '50s, discover rock and roll, and form a band that goes on to become the world's most popular musical act. Narrator Rai Merchant, their lifelong friend, is a world-famous photographer and Vina's 'backdoor man.' Rai tells the story of their great, abiding love . . . which thrives on obstacles. . . . Ultimately, Ormus and Vina reenact the Orpheus myth, not once but twice." Publ Wkly

"Vina and Ormus are icons, not fully formed characters. But that's the point. And Rai . . . is the most moving character Rushdie's ever created." Newsweek

Haroun and the sea of stories. Granta Books in association with Viking 1990 219p pa $14 hardcover o.p.

ISBN 0-14-015737-9 (pa)   LC 90-45496

"This delightful fantasy is filled with adventures, amusing characters with names like Iff and Butt, and villains to fight against and defeat. Rushdie's puns and rhymes will be enjoyed by young and old—the catchy tunes by the younger readers and the political allegory by the adults. Rashid is a professional story-teller whose son, Haroun, delights in hearing them. When Rashid's source of stories seems to have disappeared Haroun faces many dangerous opponents to help his father regain his Gift of Gab." Shapiro. Fic for Youth. 3d edition

Midnight's children; with an introduction by Anita Desai. Knopf 1995 xxxi, 589p $20

ISBN 0-679-44462-9

* LC 90-38447

"Everyman's library"

A reissue of the title first published 1980 in the United Kingdom; 1981 in the United States

"The novel is about Shiva and Saleem, two of the 1,001 babies born in the hour following independence at midnight on August 15, 1947. It is notable as much for its portrayal of contemporary politics in India as for the brilliance of its style and insights into human nature and mind." Reader's Ency. 4th edition

The Moor's last sigh. Pantheon Bks. 1996 c1995 435p o.p.   LC 95-24392

First published 1995 in the United Kingdom

"A picaresque recounting of the rise, decline and plunge to extinction of a Portuguese merchant family anciently established in southern India, focusing on the period from 1900 to the present. The hapless narrator, Moraes Zogoiby, . . . has composed these pages during exile and imprisonment in a replica of the Alhambra built and run by a madman (a former protégé of the family)

Rushdie, Salman—*Continued*

in rural Andalusia. Moraes, nicknamed the Moor, is the last living member of the da Gama-Zogoiby line." N Y Times Book Rev

This is a "marvellously inventive display of verbal dexterity; an exuberant, entertaining, zestful novel which proves, if proof were needed, that Mr Rushdie's spirit remains undiminshed." Economist

The satanic verses. Viking 1989 546p $27.95

ISBN 0-670-82537-9

* LC 88-40266

A "panoramic novel which moves with dizzying speed from the streets and film studios of Bombay to multicultural Britain, from Argentina to Mount Everest, as Rushdie questions illusion, reality, and the power of faith and tradition in a world of hijackers, religious pilgrimages and warfare, and celluloid fantasy." Oxford Companion to Engl Lit. 6th edition

Shalimar the clown. Random House 2005 398p $25.95

ISBN 0-679-46335-6   LC 2005-42796

"Los Angeles, 1991. Ambassador Maximilian Ophuls . . . is murdered in broad daylight on his illegitimate daughter India's doorstep, slaughtered by a knife wielded by his Kashmiri Muslim driver, a mysterious figure who calls himself Shalimar the clown. The dead man is a . . . charismatic World War II Resistance hero, a man of formidable intellectual ability, a former US ambassador to India and subsequently America's counter-terrorism chief. The murder looks at first like a political assassination, but turns out to be passionately personal. This is the story of Max Ophuls, his killer and his daughter–and of a fourth character, the woman who links them, whose story finally explains them all." Publisher's note

"Rushdie has written an intensely political novel, infused with recent events, but its emotional scope reaches so far beyond our current crisis and its vision into the vagaries of the heart is so perceptive that one can imagine Shalimar the Clown being read long after this age of sacred terror has faded into history." Washington Post Book World

Russell, Karen, 1981-

St. Lucy's home for girls raised by wolves. Knopf 2006 246p

ISBN 0-307-26398-3   LC 2006-45156

Contents: Ava wrestles the alligator; Haunting Olivia; Z.Z.'s sleep-away camp for disordered dreamers; The stargazer's log of summertime crime; Children's reminiscences of the westward migration; Lady Yeti and the palace of artificial snows; The city of shells; Out to sea; Accident brief, occurrence # 00/442; St. Lucy's home for girls raised by wolves

"A series of upbeat, sentimental fables, the 10 stories of Russell's debut are set in an enchanted version of North America and narrated by articulate, emotionally precocious children from dysfunctional households. Each merges the satirical spirit of George Saunders with the sophisticated whimsy of recent animated Hollywood film." Publ Wkly

Russell, Mary Doria, 1950-

Children of God; a novel. Villard Bks. 1998 438p $23.95

ISBN 0-679-45635-X   LC 97-42160

"Having returned from a disastrous, 21st-century expedition to the planet Rakhat, Jesuit Father Emilio Sandoz, the sole survivor of the mission, faces public rage over the order's part in the war between the gentle Runa and the predatory Jana'ata—fury more than matched by the priest's own self-hatred and religious disillusionment. . . . He is forced to return to Rakhat with a new expedition more interested in profits than prophets. When they discover the planet in turmoil and the Runa precariously in power, the temptation to interfere is more than they can withstand." Publ Wkly

"Russell succeeds in painting an alien culture with remarkably detailed verisimilitude." N Y Times Book Rev

Dreamers of the day; a novel. Random House 2008 251p il

ISBN 978-1-40006471-7; 1-400-06471-6

LC 2007-24665

"In her historical novel set primarily in the Middle East during the Cairo Peace Conference of 1919, Russell focuses on the life of Agnes Shanklin. The 40-year-old schoolteacher, who had been constantly demeaned by her mother, recently deceased, uses her inheritance for an adventure to Egypt. There she falls in with Winston Churchill, T.E. Lawrence, Gertrude Bell and other historical figures who are carving up the Middle East after the defeat of the Ottoman Empire in World War I. Amid the maneuverings and plotting at the Peace Conference over regional influence and oil, Agnes finds love with a sophisticated and mysterious European. The suave, caring lover uses their relationship and Agnes' friendship with Lawrence and Churchill to glean information about British plans for the conference." Rocky Mountain News

"Russell perfectly captures the political and social milieus of the 1920s, driving home how important it is to consider history when dealing with present-day issues. . . . The fact that Agnes is telling her story after she has—yes—already died does not come across as a literary conceit but as perfectly fitting for this perfectly enchanting tale." BookPage

The sparrow. Villard Bks. 1996 408p o.p.

* LC 96-11180

This novel about first contact with an extraterrestrial civilization features "Father Emilio Sandoz, a Jesuit linguist whose messianic virtues hide his occasional doubt about his calling. . . . The narrative ping-pongs between the years 2016, when Sandoz begins assembling the team that first detects signs of intelligent extraterrestrial life, and 2060, when a Vatican inquest is convened to coax an explanation from the physically mutilated and emotionally devastated priest." Publ Wkly

"An intriguing venture into the journey of faith by way of science fiction, anthropology and the Society of Jesus. . . . God is the silent character in this story." America

Followed by Children of God

A thread of grace; a novel; Mary Doria Russell. 1st ed. Random House 2005 430p $25.95

ISBN 0-375-50184-3   LC 2004-50942

Russell, Mary Doria, 1950-—*Continued*

"As the story opens, the mountainous region of north-west Italy has been relatively untouched by WWII, and even Jews have been safe. When Italy breaks with Germany in 1943 and pulls out of southern France, thousands of Jewish refugees cross the mountains in search of safety. But the German occupation of Italy poses a new threat." Booklist

"This is a morality play that at times uses black humor, and then shifts to solemn reflection or moving portraiture. A Thread of Grace is deft, sensate, ruthless in its moral incisiveness, and affirming in that even in the worst of times, the lamp of humanity cannot be completely extinguished." Hudson Rev

Russo, Richard, 1949-

Bridge of sighs. Alfred A. Knopf 2007 528p $26.95

ISBN 978-0-375-41495-4   LC 2007-27970

A novel set mostly in "an upstate New York town where a tannery creates the jobs and pollutes the waters. . . . The novel covers the past 50 years in the lives of three friends who are a romantic triangle of sorts. Two stay at home. One because he can't imagine living anywhere other than Thomaston, N.Y. He's content to take over and expand the family-run deli. His wife, a would-be artist, stays more reluctantly—out of love and duty, although she's haunted by a question, 'Which was more important: to love or be loved?' The third friend becomes a famous painter in Venice where he struggles with personal demons and his own past." USA Today

"Whatever the scale of their lives, Russo's characters—the stars and the walk-ons are gorgeously drawn. The writing is always in service of illuminating them—with one exception. The black characters speak in a corny-sounding dialect, which can make the reader stop to decode sentences. In this case, the reach for authenticity doesn't work. But everything else works brilliantly. . . . That Russo manages to juggle so many characters, themes, places, and time periods through 528 delicious pages is an astounding achievement. From its lovely beginning to its exquisite, perfect end, Russo has written a masterpiece." Boston Globe

Empire Falls. Knopf 2001 483p $29.95

ISBN 0-679-43247-7

* LC 2001-88568

"Miles Roby is a typical Russo hero: wry, unlucky in love and money; and just a little bit smarter than the people who populate his run-down industrial town. In this case, the town is Empire Falls, Maine, where Miles manages a restaurant that serves as a kind of meeting hall for the novel's large cast of characters. There's David, Miles's recovering-alcoholic brother; Walt, the health-club entrepreneur who has stolen Miles's estranged wife; Tick, Miles's precocious, befuddled teenage daughter; and Francine Whiting, the rich widow who runs everything. Russo is preoccupied with the death of a certain version of the American dream, but his belief in the power of comedy—sometimes low, sometimes high—rescues his work from bathos and elvates it into the realm of literature." New Yorker

Nobody's fool. Random House 1993 549p

ISBN 0-394-57778-7

* LC 92-56844

"Sixty-year-old Sully is *nobody's fool*, except maybe his own. Out of work (undeclared-income work is what he does, when he can), down to his last few bucks, hampered by an arthritic broken knee, Sully is worried that he's started on a run of bad luck. And he has. The banker son of his octogenarian landlady wants him evicted; Sully's estranged son comes home for Thanksgiving only to have his wife split; Sully's own high-strung ex-wife seems headed for a nervous breakdown; and his longtime lover is blaming him for her daughter's winding up in the hospital with a busted jaw. But Sully's biggest problem is the memory of his own abusive father." Libr J

"A grand read sparkling with witty dialogue and memorable characters, Russo's novel is a rollicking tale of a born loser on a downward slide. An economically depressed upper New York State community is the setting, and its lower-middle-class and blue-collar inhabitants are portrayed with empathy and a shrewd understanding of human nature." Publ Wkly

The risk pool. Random House 1988 479p

ISBN 0-394-56527-4   LC 88-42666

"A story on not-so-successful folk in a decaying town in New York as seen through the eyes of Ned Hall, better known as 'Sam's son.' Sam was once an average citizen who grew up, married, and went off to fight in World War II but returned a drifter. Leaving his wife and small son at home, he would haunt the bars and pool halls and hobnob with his cronies. Now and then he'd appear from nowhere to take Ned with him. When Ned's mother, Jenny, trips over the edge, Ned goes to live with Sam in a delapidated loft above the town's one department store and share his father's roguish life." Libr J

"A superbly original, maliciously funny book, peopled by characters that most of us would back away from plenty fast if they ever lurched toward our barstool. It is Mr. Russo's brilliant, deadpan writing that gives their wasted lives and miserable little town such haunting power and insidious charm." N Y Times Book Rev

The straight man. Random House 1997 391p

ISBN 0-679-43246-9   LC 96-48578

"Hank Devereaux was voted interim chair of the English department at a Pennsylvania college based on his loudly voiced contempt for bureaucratic procedures. Long mired in old grievances and thwarted ambitions, the contentious English faculty figure they can count on Hank to do absolutely nothing, thereby preserving the status quo. They figured wrong. Perpetual wise guy Hank has managed to stir things up on all fronts." Booklist

"The novel's greatest pleasures derive not from any blazing impatience to see what happens next, but from pitch-perfect dialogue, persuasive characterization and a rich progression of scenes, most of them crackling with an impudent, screwball energy reminiscent of Howard Hawks's movies." N Y Times Book Rev

That old Cape magic; a novel. Alfred A. Knopf 2009 261p $25.95

ISBN 978-0-375-41496-1; 0-375-41496-7

LC 2009-20311

"Joy and Jack Griffin head to Cape Cod to attend a friend's wedding, where their daughter Laura announces her own engagement. Sensing the malaise in their 30-year marriage, the Griffins decide to reconnect by visiting the B & B where they once honeymooned. Their arrival in separate vehicles seems symbolic of the discord

Russo, Richard, 1949-—*Continued*

in their hearts and minds. Jack, still coming to terms with his father's death and bristling at his mother's constant criticism, feels restless in his career as a college professor, wondering whether he should have left a lucrative screenwriting gig in L.A. Joy, chafing at Jack's implicit displeasure with her sunny disposition and maddening family, longs for an empathetic listener." Libr J

"Suffused with Russo's signature comic sensibility, and with insights, by turns tender and tough, about human frailty, forbearance, fortitude, and fervor." Boston Globe

The whore's child; and other stories. Knopf 2002 225p

ISBN 0-375-41168-2   LC 2002-19023

Contents: The whore's child; Monhegan light; The farther you go; Joy ride; Buoyancy; Poison; The mysteries of Linwood Hart

"Russo's rueful understanding of the twisted skein of human relationships is as sharp as ever, and the dialogue throughout is barbed, pointed and wryly humorous." Publ Wkly

Rutherfurd, Edward

The forest; a novel. Crown 2000 598p il

ISBN 0-609-60382-5   LC 00-22219

This historical saga focuses on "the New Forest, part of the southern coast of England bounded by the English Channel. Rutherfurd traces the lives of peasants, smugglers, churchmen, woodsmen, and upper-class families from the 11th to the 20th centuries. These assorted men and women take part in the events surrounding the death of King Rufus (William the Conqueror's son), the failure of the Spanish Armada, England's Civil War, and more." Libr J

London. Crown 1997 829p $25.95

ISBN 0-517-59181-2   LC 97-10176

First published 1995 in the United Kingdom

This "fictional history of London is told through the experiences of a group of diverse families who, over generations, meet, mingle, intermarry, and feud. Beginning with prehistory and continuing to the present, Rutherfurd combines geological details, historical events, real people, and his fictional characters to bring London to life." Libr J

The princes of Ireland; the Dublin saga. Doubleday 2004 776p $27.95

ISBN 0-385-50286-9

* LC 2003-70005

"Beginning in the tribal, pre-Christian times of the warrior kings at Tara, this first book in a two-part novelized history of Ireland sweeps readers through the early centuries of Druids, chieftains, monks, Vikings, noblemen, merchants, and mercenaries, ending with the disastrous invasion of England that tragically changed the course of Irish history. Through the eyes of the men and women who built the mighty city that became Dublin, the unfolding of a colorful and turbulent history is told with energy and a meticulous attention to historical detail." Libr J

The rebels of Ireland; the Dublin Saga. Doubleday 2006 xxv, 863p $28.95

ISBN 0-385-51289-9   LC 2006-273953

"Beginning with Elizabeth's ascendancy to the English throne and the 'plantation' period of the English conquest of Ireland and ending with the founding of the Irish republic in 1922, this sequel to Princes of Ireland vividly tells the history of Irish suppression through the lives of ordinary people on both sides of the turmoil. It is a story of bitter and tragic contrast. Rutherfurd casts the Irish, thought to be savages by England's Protestant elite, against a backdrop of a vibrant, intellectual Dublin, deeply divided by religion and politics yet aglow with the literary renaissance of Yeats, Shaw, and Joyce." Libr J

Russka; the novel of Russia. Crown 1991 760p

o.p.   LC 90-34457

"Tells the story of a Ukrainian village . . . and some of the families who lived there from A.D. 180 to the 1917 Revolution and, anecdotally, almost to the present." N Y Times Book Rev

The book "does provide a sweeping overview of the land whose very vastness and complexity make it overwhelming and fascinating." Christ Sci Monit

Sarum; the novel of England. Crown 1987 897p

o.p.   LC 87-6710

This novel, set in Salisbury, England, aims to trace English history from the last Ice Age to the present through the lives of five fictional families

"Rutherfurd is strong on the explication of trends and the narration of events. But he relies heavily on the repetition of character types. Nevertheless, 'Sarum' is fascinating and will appeal to Anglophiles, history buffs, and fans of epic-style novels." Christ Sci Monit

Ryan, Nigel

(tr) Simenon, G. My friend Maigret

Ryan, Rachel *See* Brown, Sandra, 1948-

Ryan, Rachel, 1948-

For works written by this author under other names see Brown, Sandra, 1948-

Ryder, Jonathan *See* Ludlum, Robert, 1927-2001

S

Saavedra, Miguel de Cervantes *See* Cervantes Saavedra, Miguel de, 1547-1616

Sabatini, Rafael, 1875-1950

Captain Blood; his odyssey. Houghton Mifflin 1922 356p o.p.

"Peter Blood was many things in his time—soldier, country doctor, slave, pirate, and finally Governor of Jamaica. Incidentally, he was an Irishman. Round his humorous-heroic figure Mr. Sabatini has written an exciting romance of the Spanish Main, the facts of which he alleges to have been found in the diary and log books of one Jeremiah Pitt, a follower of Monmouth in 1685 and Blood's faithful companion in adventure." Times Lit Suppl

Sabatini, Rafael, 1875-1950—*Continued*

Scaramouche; a romance of the French revolution. Houghton Mifflin 1921 392p o.p.

"The story, primarily of love and adventure, is woven around a hero who devoted himself to furthering the republican cause during the first years of the French Revolution (1788-1792). The title character, successively a lawyer, politician, swordsman, and buffoon, crosses paths repeatedly with his sworn enemy, in the end attaining love and happiness." Lenrow. Reader's Guide to Prose Fic

Followed by Scaramouche, the king-maker (1931)

Saberhagen, Fred, 1930-2007

Berserker fury. TOR Bks. 1997 383p $23.95
ISBN 0-312-85939-2   LC 97-1157
"A Tom Doherty Associates book"
This adventure "finds the intelligent, deadly Berserker machines infiltrating human colonies to destroy them. The humans have cracked the Berserkers' codes and plan a battle defense. Although it helps to be familiar with the series, this novel can stand alone." Libr J

Berserker's star. TOR Bks. 2003 368p $24.95
ISBN 0-7653-0423-6   LC 2003-41016
"A Tom Doherty Associates book"
"Wanted in parts of the galaxy for his theft of a powerful space cannon, pilot Harry Silver accepts a business proposition from a mysterious woman who claims she wants to rescue her husband from cultists on Maracanda, a pseudo-planet wedged between a black hole and a neutron star. En route, Silver discovers that his passenger's agenda is not quite what it seems and, after making planefall, he finds that Maracanda holds secrets and terrors beyond his worst fears. . . . Witty dialog, clever plot twists, and a likeably roguish protagonist make this a good selection for most sf collections." Libr J

The fifth book of lost swords: Coinspinner's story. Doherty Assocs. 1989 244p o.p.
LC 89-39878
"A TOR book"
"When the legendary sword Woundheale disappears from its resting place in the White Temple of Sarykam, investigations reveal that the Sword of Chance, Coinspinner, is once again loose in the world." Libr J

The first book of lost swords: Woundhealer's story. Doherty Assocs. 1986 281p o.p.
LC 86-50319
"A TOR book"
This book begins a new sequence in the author's fantasy series about mythical swords
"Hoping to find a cure for the mysterious illness that has cursed his son since birth, Prince Mark makes a pilgrimage to the shrine of the legendary sword Woundhealer only to find that his enemies have preceded him." Libr J
A "pleasant adventure that benefits greatly from Saberhagen's narrative gifts as the various strands leapfrog forward, keeping the reader off balance but constantly intrigued." Publ Wkly

The fourth book of lost swords: Farslayer's story. Doherty Assocs. 1989 252p o.p.
LC 89-11638
"A TOR book"
"Two rival families wage a war of attrition and vengeance for possession of 'Farslayer,' one of the 12 Lost Swords made by the gods and imbued with unearthly powers. A grim sense of fatality underlies the deceptive simplicity of the author's style." Libr J

The last book of swords: Shieldbreaker's story. TOR Bks. 1994 255p o.p.   LC 93-43232
"A Tom Doherty Associates book"
In this concluding book of the saga, "battle extends from palace to peasant hut—indeed, all the way to the moon—and is loaded with remnants of premagical technology as well as the secret of why the Old World fell and magic came to rule. Key to the battle against Vikata the Dark King is Prince Mark's second son, Prince Stephen, who turns out to be a formidable wielder of swords. By the time journeys and battles are done, the only one of the twelve swords that survives is Woundhealer, for even the terrifying Shieldbreaker has perished." Booklist

The second book of lost swords: Sightblinder's story. Doherty Assocs. 1987 248p o.p.
LC 87-50477
"A TOR book"
"The present story limits itself to a single locale, the island castle of the wizard Honan-Fu, where Prince Mark is imprisoned in ice alongside the wizard by the usurper called the Ancient One. Mark's friends find themselves the temporary allies of Honan-Fu's traitorous daughter, Ninazu, and of the magician emperor, currently incognito with a traveling show. . . . An entertainment of high order." Publ Wkly

The seventh book of lost swords: Wayfinder's story. TOR Bks. 1992 251p o.p.   LC 92-858
"A Tom Doherty Associates book"
"One of 12 magical swords forged by the Gods, Wayfinder has the power to guide its possessor to whatever the seeker wants. Chance brings Wayfinder to Ben of Purkinje, who uses it to find Woundhealer, the sword with powers to cure the injured wife of Prince Mar of Sarykam. The evil magician Wood also wants the swords; his attack on Ben brings Mark, and even more swords, into the fray. . . . Saberhagen keeps the plot moving, providing a pleasurable light reading experience." Publ Wkly

The sixth book of lost swords: Mindsword's story. TOR Bks. 1990 250p o.p.   LC 90-38899
"A Tom Doherty Associates book"
"Intended as a peace offering from Prince Murat to the Princess Kristin, the Mindsword—one of the legendary weapons used in the war that brought about the death of the gods—plunges two countries into near-war as the well-meaning Murat falls victim to the sword's seductive powers. Saberhagen treads a fine line between fantasy and moral fable in his latest addition to a popular series." Libr J

Saberhagen, Fred, 1930-2007—*Continued*

The third book of lost swords: Stonecutter's story. Doherty Assocs. 1988 247p o.p.

LC 87-51397

"A TOR book"

This novel "deals with the search of Prince al-Farabi and Magistrate Wen Chang for the lost sword Stonecutter. The book's virtues include a cast of well-drawn characters and some vividly realized societies, as well as Saberhagen's usual spare prose and sound narrative technique." Booklist

Sackville-West, V. (Victoria), 1892-1962

All passion spent. Doubleday, Doran 1931 294p o.p.

"When Lady Slane, after the death of her famous husband, shocks her family by going to live by herself in a little house in Hempstead, she is for the first time in her eighty-eight years asserting her right to live her own life. The year of quiet reminiscences there is not without exciting moments, for a man who has loved her silently for sixty years renews his friendship, tells her of his love, then suddenly dies, and leaves her his enormous fortune. What she does with this fortune is another instance of her self-assertion. Gentle, charming Lady Slane, her family, and her friends, drawn with wit and skill in this tale of graceful old age, create an impression of subtlety and beauty." Booklist

The Edwardians. Doubleday, Doran 1930 314p o.p.

The setting of this story of Edwardian England is the beautiful old manor-house of Chevron. The characters are grouped around Sebastian, the young heir to the dukedom, and his mother, a famous hostess of the day. Individuals count for less in the novel—a decadent but decorative society. The close of the story, marked by King George's coronation, finds the young duke breaking with the traditions that have bound him, not unwillingly, and starting a new era for himself

"'The Edwardians' is of undoubted excellence from two points of view. First, it is a magnificent portrait of a class and an era. Secondly, it is remarkable for its excellent prose style." Springfield Repub

Sackville-West, Victoria *See* Sackville-West, V. (Victoria), 1892-1962

Safire, William

Freedom. Doubleday 1987 xxl, 1,125p o.p.

LC 86-29254

This novel spans the first twenty months of the Civil War. It covers the period "between Lincoln's suspension of habeas corpus and his signing of the Emancipation Proclamation." Libr J

"The book is a triumph of historical imagination. . . . Safire uses the trained eye of a Washington insider to show us the characters' tentative political and military gropings based on limited information and sketchy precedents. . . . Our scribe tells this monumental and heartbreaking tale in a way one won't soon forget." Christ Sci Monit

Scandalmonger. Simon & Schuster 2000 496p il
ISBN 0-684-86719-2   LC 99-58831

This historical novel is set in the new American republic during the 1790s. The cast of characters includes Alexander Hamilton, Aaron Burr, Thomas Jefferson, and James Monroe, as well as two journalists. "William Cobbett is a pompous English import who bloviated in his Porcupine's Gazette on behalf of Hamilton and his law-and-order Federalists. His rival in vitriol is James Thomson Callender, wanted for sedition in his native Scotland. He was Jefferson's hit man who, when slighted, . . . spread informed innuendo about his arrangement with slave and lover Sally Hemings." Time

"Since his book is a work of fiction, . . . it cannot easily do what a work of history can—explain the larger social and cultural context for particular events. Nonetheless, Safire has a historian's feel for the period and uses history as fairly and as honestly as one could expect." NY Rev Books

Sagan, Carl, 1934-1996

Contact; a novel. Simon & Schuster 1985 432p o.p.   LC 85-14645

"Ellie Arroway, working with a huge array of radio telescopes in the New Mexico desert, discovers a signal from the star Vega. The message has several levels, one of which contains instructions for building a faster-than-light spacecraft. A debate ensues between scientists and religious leaders as to whether or not such a machine should be built; the scientists win, and finally the long-sought 'contact' is established." Booklist

"A serious blend of science fact and speculation with a fast-paced and well-crafted story . . . suggesting that Sagan is more interested in illustrating human relations and human response than depicting alien creatures. . . . Sagan has provided a novel of ideas, and finds drama in how people interact with them in a situation of challenge and discovery." Christ Sci Monit

Sagan, Françoise, 1935-2004

Bonjour tristesse; translated from the French by Irene Ash. Dutton 1955 128p o.p.

Original French edition, 1954

"The story of a jealous, sophisticated 17-year-old girl whose meddling in her father's impending remarriage leads to tragic consequences, it was written with 'classical' restraint and a tone of cynical disillusionment. The book showed the persistence of traditional form during a period of experimentation in French fiction." Merriam-Webster's Ency of Lit

Sainsbury, Geoffrey

(tr) Simenon, G. A man's head

(tr) Simenon, G. Strangers in the house

Saint, Dora Jessie *See* Read, Miss, 1913-

Saint, H. F. (Harry F.)

Memoirs of an invisible man. Atheneum Pubs. 1987 396p
ISBN 0-689-11735-3   LC 85-48144

Saint, H. F. (Harry F.)—Continued

"A clash between a scientist and an antinuclear demonstrator at a nuclear energy plant catalyzes an explosion that renders Nick Halloway, a securities analyst, invisible. Realizing that he will become a caged, scrutinized guinea pig if he surrenders to federal intelligence agents, Nick makes a run for his freedom. . . . Nick displays the distinct sensibilities of a fugitive and a Wall Street smart guy as he invisibly fends for himself in the jungles he knows best—the East Side of Manhattan and the trader's desk." Publ Wkly

"The CIA agents, always just one step behind, are deliciously funny Keystone Cops, ridiculous in their attempts to capture a non-entity. This delightful first novel updates a common childhood fantasy with the excitement of a spy story and a hilarious adult portrayal of life and love under the most peculiar conditions." Libr J

Saint, Harry F. See Saint, H. F. (Harry F.)

Saint-Aubin, Horace de See Balzac, Honoré de, 1799-1850

Saint-Exupéry, Antoine de, 1900-1944

The little prince; written and illustrated by Antoine de Saint-Exupery; translated from the French by Richard Howard. Harcourt 2000 83p il $18; pa $12

ISBN 0-15-202398-4; 0-15-601219-7 (pa)
* LC 99-50439

A new translation of the title first published 1943 by Reynal & Hitchcock

"This many-dimensional fable of an airplane pilot who has crashed in the desert is for readers of all ages. The pilot comes upon the little prince soon after the crash. The prince tells of his adventures on different planets and on Earth as he attempts to learn about the universe in order to live peacefully on his own small planet. A spiritual quality enhances the seemingly simple observations of the little prince." Shapiro. Fic for Youth. 3d edition

Night flight; preface by André Gide; translated by Stuart Gilbert. Century 1932 198p o.p.

"In a story that captures the adventures of early aviation, Rivière, chief of the airport at Buenos Aires, supervises the night flights of airmail in South America. He challenges his crew to meet any and all obstacles. When one of his three mail planes crashes over the Andes, he dispatches the European mail plane on schedule anyway." Shapiro. Fic for Youth. 3d edition

Sakamoto, Kerri

One hundred million hearts. Harcourt 2003 279p $23

ISBN 0-15-101037-4   LC 2003-57064

"Set in Toronto, the novel opens with 32-year-old Miyo narrating the story of her life with her Canadian-born Japanese father, Masao, who singlehandedly raised her. When he suddenly falls ill, Miyo is surprisingly reunited with Setsuko, her father's former live-in girlfriend. Miyo then learns that she has a half-sister, Hana, living in Japan. In the rest of the story, Sakamoto focuses on Miyo's emotional journey to Japan to meet her sister, which also leads to the unraveling of her father's past as a kamikaze pilot." Libr J

"Sakamoto is a gentle storyteller who never forces the point, but rather lets the details slowly surface." Booklist

Sakey, Marcus

The blade itself. St. Martin's Minotaur 2007 307p $22.95

ISBN 978-0-312-36031-3; 0-312-36031-2
LC 2006-50562

"After a job goes horribly wrong—a shop owner is shot—smalltime burglar Danny Carter leaves the crime business behind for good. He is now a well-paid, respected construction manager in Chicago with a great girlfriend and a comfortable life. Then his former partner in crime, Evan McGann, is released from prison with plans to resume their alliance. Danny isn't interested, but Evan threatens to expose Danny's past, including his presence when the shop owner was shot. . . . Trapped, Danny agrees to Evan's plan: kidnap the son of Danny's boss." Booklist

As the author "takes Danny apart and looks to see what the man is really worth, the novel delivers some implicit social commentary about the shaky foundation on which Danny's new life has been built. . . . Not until the very end of the story is it clear who Danny is or where he stands. His ability to churn these questions so vigorously will bring Mr. Sakey attention." N Y Times (Late N Y Ed)

Saki, 1870-1916

The short stories of Saki; with an introduction by Christopher Morley. Modern Lib. 1983 c1930 $12.95

ISBN 0-394-60428-8
* LC 83-5468

First published 1930 by Viking; first Modern Library edition 1951

Contents: Reginald; Reginald on Christmas presents; Reginald on the academy; Reginald at the theatre; Reginald's peace poem; Reginald's choir treat; Reginald on worries; Reginald on house-parties; Reginald at the Carlton; Reginald on besetting sins; Reginald's drama; Reginald on tariffs; Reginald's Christmas revel; Reginald's Rubaiyat; Innocence of Reginald; Reginald in Russia; Reticence of Lady Anne; Lost Sanjak; Sex that doesn't shop; Blood-feud of Toad-water; Young Turkish catastrophe; Judkin of the parcels; Gabriel-Ernest; Saint and the goblin; Soul of Laploshka; Bag; Strategist; Cross currents; Baker's dozen; Mouse; Esmé; Match-maker; Tobermory; Mrs. Packletide's tiger; Stampeding of Lady Bastable; Background; Hermann the Irascible—a story of the great weep; Unrest-cure; Jesting of Arlington Stringham; Sredni Vashtar; Adrian; Chaplet; Quest; Wratislav; Easter egg; Filboid Studge, the story of a mouse that helped; Music on the hill; Story of St. Vespaluus; Way to the dairy; Peace offering; Peace of Mowsle Barton; Talking-out of Tarrington; Hounds of fate; Recessional; Matter of sentiment; Secret sin of Septimus Brope; "Ministers of grace"; Remoulding of Groby Lington; She-wolf; Laura; Boar-pig; Brogue; Hen; Open window; Treasureship; Cobweb; Lull; Unkindest blow; Romancers; Schwartz-Metterklume method; Sev-

LIST OF FICTIONAL WORKS

Saki, 1870-1916—*Continued*

enth pullet; Blind spot; Dusk; Touch of realism; Cousin Teresa; Yarkand manner; Byzantine omelette; Feast of Nemesis; Dreamer; Quince tree; Forbidden buzzards; Stake; Clovis on parental responsibilities; Holiday task; Stalled ox; Storyteller; Defensive diamond; Elk; "Down pens"; Nameday; Lumberroom; Fur; Philanthropist and the happy cat; On approval; Toys of peace; Louise; Tea; Disappearance of Crispina Umberleigh; Wolves of Cernogratz; Louis; Guests; Penance; Phantom luncheon; Bread and butter miss; Bertie's Christmas; Forewarned; Interlopers; Quail seed; Canossa; Threat; Excepting Mrs. Pentherby; Mark; Hedgehog; Mappined life; Fate; Bull; Morivera; Shock tactics; Seven cream jugs; Occasional garden; Sheep; Oversight; Hyacinth; Image of the lost soul; Purple of the Balkan kings; Cupboard of the yesterdays; For the duration of the war; Square eggs; Birds on the western front; Gala programme; Infernal parliament; Achievement of the cat; Old town of Pskoff; Clovis on the alleged romance of business; Comments of Moung Ka

Salak, Kira, 1971-

The white Mary; a novel. Henry Holt and Co. 2008 351p $25
  ISBN 978-0-8050-8847-2; 0-8050-8847-4
                      LC 2008-7278
"Boston-based magazine writer Marika Vecera is taking time off from covering war in order to develop a relationship with Sebastian 'Seb' Gilman. She's also writing a biography of Pulitzer Prize-winning war correspondent Robert Lewis, who has committed suicide. But in the midst of her research, someone claims to have seen Lewis alive in Papua New Guinea. If he is dead, could his suicide be linked to the atrocities he has seen around the world? If he's alive, did he fake his own death, and why? Marika realizes that to get past the horrors she, too, has seen, she must find out what happened to Lewis. With a guide named Tobo, she sets off across Papua New Guinea in search of answers." Dallas Morning News

"Salak's descriptions of the jungle passage are compelling and dreamlike. Even stronger are flashbacks of Marika in Bodo and a wrenching, horrific account of Lewis's capture and torture in East Timor. Salak's own journalistic experiences—she covered the Rwandan genocide and the 2003 war in the Congo, among other conflicts—have armed her with heartfelt, if indelibly grim, insights into man's capacity for 'an endless stream of the worst, most inconceivable acts of inhumanity'. . . . In The White Mary, Salak shows the courage of facing down that darkness and the inescapable price it exacts upon one's soul." Washington Post Book World

Salinger, J. D. (Jerome David), 1919-

The catcher in the rye. Little, Brown 1951 277p $24.95; pa $5.99
  ISBN 0-316-76953-3; 0-316-76948-7 (pa)
                               *
"The story of adolescent Holden Caulfield who runs away from boarding-school in Pennsylvania to New York where he preserves his innocence despite various attempts to lose it. The colloquial, lively, first-person narration, with its attacks on the 'phoniness' of the adult

world and its clinging to family sentiment in the form of Holden's affection for his sister Phoebe, made the novel accessible to and popular with a wide readership, particularly with the young." Oxford Companion to Engl Lit. 5th edition

Franny & Zooey. Little, Brown 1961 201p $24.95; pa $5.99
  ISBN 0-316-76954-1; 0-316-76949-5 (pa)
                               *
"At 20, Franny Glass is experiencing desperate dissatisfaction with her life and seems to be looking for help via a religious awakening. Her brother Zooey tries to help her out of this depression. He recalls the influence on their growth and development of their appearance as young radio performers on a network program called 'It's a Wise Child.' An older brother, Buddy, is also an important component of the interrelationships in the Glass family." Shapiro. Fic for Youth. 3d edition

Nine stories. Little, Brown 1953 302p $24.95; pa $5.99
  ISBN 0-316-76956-8; 0-316-76950-9 (pa)
                               *
Contents: A perfect day for bananafish; Uncle Wiggily in Connecticut; Just before the war with the Eskimos; The laughing man; For Esmé—with love and squalor; Pretty mouth and green my eyes; De Daumier-Smith's blue period; Teddy; Down at the dinghy

This collection "introduced various members of the Glass family who would dominate the remainder of Salinger's work. Critical response divided itself between high praise and cult worship. Most of the stories deal with precocious, troubled children, whose religious yearnings—often tilting toward the East—are in vivid contrast to the materialistic and spiritually empty world of their parents. The result was a perfect literary formula for the 1950s." Benet's Reader's Ency of Am Lit

Raise high the roof beam, carpenters, and Seymour: an introduction. Little, Brown 1963 248p $24.95
  ISBN 0-316-76957-6
                               *
This volume "reprints stories from *The New Yorker* (1955, 1959), in which Buddy Glass tells, first, of his return to New York during the war to attend his brother Seymour's wedding and of Seymour's jilting of the bride and then of their later elopement; and, second, after Seymour's suicide, of Buddy's own brooding, to the point of breakdown, upon Seymour's virtues, human and literary." Oxford Companion to Am Lit. 6th edition

Seymour: an introduction
  In Salinger, J. D. Raise high the roof beam, carpenters, and Seymour: an introduction p1

Zooey
  In Salinger, J. D. Franny & Zooey

Salinger, Jerome David *See* Salinger, J. D. (Jerome David), 1919-

Sallis, James, 1944-

Cripple Creek; a novel. Walker & Co. 2006 193p $23

ISBN 978-0-8027-3382-5; 0-8027-3382-4

LC 2005-28095

"As this tale opens, Turner, ex-cop, ex-con, and ex-psychotherapist, remains on the lam in rural Cypress Grove, Tennessee, escaping the demons of past lives in Memphis, but he is starting to mend. There's a developing relationship with Val Bjorn, teacher and country musician; there's the appearance of his daughter from Seattle; and there's the fact that he has come out of hibernation to accept the job as deputy sheriff of Cypress Grove. Then his boss, the kindly sheriff, is assaulted by a gang of mobbed-up toughs in the act of breaking one of their own out of the small-town jail. Turner pursues the thugs to Memphis, confronting his past and giving vent to his suppressed blood lust. Every action prompts a reaction, however, and soon the thugs return to Cypress Grove looking for some blood of their own. Sallis tells the violent tale quietly, effectively using jump cuts, flashbacks, and flashforwards to generate both suspense and, simultaneously, a sense of inevitability. The stunning finale makes clear that Turner has a lot more healing to do." Booklist

Cypress Grove. Walker & Co. 2003 255p $24

ISBN 0-8027-3380-8

LC 2002-41480

"Turner ('just Turner'), a former Memphis cop who went to prison for something he'd like to forget, has dropped out of human circulation and buried himself in a cabin in the deep woods. Because Turner's communication skills are rusty, Sallis gives him a constrained narrative voice, the guarded speech of a man so wary of emotion that the very act of speaking seems to leave his throat raw. When the sheriff of this rural backwater asks for his help with a murdered drifter who was found with a wooden stake in his chest, Turner crawls out of hibernation." N Y Times Book Rev

Salt River; a novel. Walker & Company 2007 146p $21.95

ISBN 978-0-8027-1617-0; 0-8027-1617-2

In this mystery featuring John "Turner—Vietnam veteran, former cop, ex-con, retired psychiatrist, and interim sheriff of a rural county south of Memphis—Sallis's story meanders through a summer and fall, chronicling Turner's professional and private lives as they merge into one. Turner's tranquillity is shattered when the son of his predecessor drives what might be a stolen car through the front of the city hall, seriously injuring himself and launching a case that escalates into breaking and entering, elder abuse, kidnapping, and murder. Meanwhile, Turner deals with the return of a friend who is wanted by the police in Texas and a less-than-welcome report from his physician. Sallis has created a laid-back, small-town setting in which understanding motives sometimes takes precedence over punishing crimes." Libr J

Salter, James

Last night. Knopf 2005 132p $20

ISBN 1-4000-4312-3

LC 2004-57793

Contents: Comet; Eyes of the stars; My Lord you; Such fun; Give; Platinum; Palm Court; Bangkok; Arlington; Last night

"All of the stories in 'Last Night' are superb, but the title story is the tautest and most memorable. . . . This story about the consequences of adultery gives new meaning to the phrase 'the morning after.' Despite its shocking plot twist, the story maintains the exacting, calm narrative voice that has distinguished all of Salter's work. His characters may be haunted by death and disappointment, but Salter never judges them, never even pretends to have them neatly pegged. He lets them stay elliptical, in shadow." N Y Times Book Rev

Salvatore, R. A.

Immortalis. Ballantine Bks. 2003 487p il map $26.95

ISBN 0-345-44122-2

LC 2002-33046

"Jilseponie Wyndon is no longer Queen of Ursal. Her newly rediscovered, totally unscrupulous son, Aydrian, has usurped the throne. In alliance with the unscrupulous, perhaps even demon-possessed weretiger and Abellican priest Marcallo De'Unnero, Aydrian sets out to conquer the world, initially without any scruples as to who gets killed in the process. But the alliance begins to fray as De'Unnero realizes that his protégé is more magically potent and ruthless than he is." Booklist

"A satisfying tale of personal responsibility, forgiveness, and redemption, this conclusion to the second 'DemonWars' trilogy features strong, memorable characters and superb plotting and storytelling." Libr J

Salzman, Mark

Lying awake. Knopf 2000 181p $21

ISBN 0-375-40632-8

LC 99-89890

"It's 1997, and Sister John of the Cross, a Carmelite nun in a monastery just outside Los Angeles, seeks treatment for epilepsy, although the remedy threatens to diminish her formidable spiritual powers." Publ Wkly

"Salzman, who doesn't claim to be a believer, handles the religious setting amazingly well. His artistic intuition helps him avoid the sermonizing that might tempt a more religious (or antireligious) writer. He clearly loves his characters." Christ Century

Samarasan, Preeta

Evening is the whole day. Houghton Mifflin 2008 340p $24

ISBN 978-0-618-87447-7; 0-618-87447-X

LC 2008-4729

This "novel revolves around a wealthy Indian family living in modern-day Malaysia. What seems like a simple act—the firing of the servant girl—has greater implications for the family than it could ever have imagined, especially for six-year-old Aasha. Aasha has a secret, one that could devastate not only her family but also the entire community. Samarasan wisely withholds this secret and others, pulling readers in. Because the description of Malaysia and its diverse population is so achingly lyrical, readers will want to slow down to absorb each word; at other times, as when they get caught up in the family drama, they will want to quicken their pace." Libr J

Samjatin, Jewgenij See Zamiátin, Evgenii Ivanovich, 1884-1937

Sams, Ferrol, 1922-

Down town; the journal of James Aloysius Holcombe, Jr. for Ephraim Holcombe Mookinfoos. Mercer University Press 2007 309p $25

    ISBN 978-0-8814-6072-8; 0-8814-6072-9

                           LC 2007-12030

"For poetry-spouting bachelor lawyer James 'Buster' Aloysius Holcombe Jr., even the finest Southern woman is no competition for his beloved Georgia hometown. . . . [This novel is] crafted as a folksy journal tracing the paths of the good people of Fayette County, Georgia, from the Civil War right up to the prosperous present. . . . Despite Buster's penchant for quoting Edna St. Vincent Millay as a means of seduction, in advancing years he ambles on blissfully single. After all, who needs romance when the folks in your hometown are so utterly charming—the wise doctor, the wealthy and eccentrically frugal banker and his blithering albeit loveable wife all keep Buster plenty busy with their conceits and confidences. Like the best road trips, Down Town is not intent upon reaching any particular destination, but rather savoring the journey along the way." BookPage

Sanchez, Thomas, 1944-

King Bongo; a novel of Havana. Knopf 2003 309p $25

    ISBN 0-679-40696-4   LC 2002-40770

"The title character of Sanchez's latest novel is a Cuban American living in Havana in 1957, just before Castro's revolution. Ethnically and socially, Bongo is a man of two worlds, by day a mild-mannered insurance salesman, by night an acclaimed bongo drum virtuoso. Bongo's sister, a stunning exotic dancer known as the Panther, has not been seen since the night the Tropicana was bombed by terrorists. Bongo's desperate search for her takes him to every corner of the decadent city." Libr J

"The byzantine plot is neatly constructed and thoroughly involving but never an end in itself. Sanchez shows us a city and a people on the eve of revolution but filters it all through the emotions of a conflicted hero, sympathetic to the cause but loyal only to himself and those he loves. Havana is both setting and soul in this pulsing bolero of a novel." Booklist

Sand, George, 1804-1876

Lélia; translated, with an introduction by Maria Espinosa. Indiana Univ. Press 1978 xxi, 234p o.p.

                          * LC 77-23639

Original French edition, 1833

"Independent and sensual Lélia has had many lovers. Now repelled by physical passion, which represents the means by which men dominate women, Lélia tells her sister Pulchérie, a courtesan, that neither celibacy nor love affairs satisfy her. Pulchérie suggests that Lélia become a courtesan; she may find fulfillment by giving pleasure to others. Lélia tries to seduce Sténio, a young poet who is in love with her; she cannot continue, however, and sends Pulchérie in her stead. As a result of this betrayal, Sténio falls into utter debauchery, and despite attempts to rescue him, he comes to a tragic end." Merriam-Webster's Ency of Lit

Marianne. Carroll & Graf Pubs. 1988 171p o.p.

                            LC 88-7308

Original French edition, 1876

"Marianne Chevreuse, the 25-year-old heroine of this romantic tale set in 1825 . . . is independent yet intensely female, and she breaks many conventions of society while living by her own deeply held moral beliefs. Pierre André is an older man who has known her since her childhood. When asked to introduce her to a prospective suitor, he discovers his own love for Marianne. The plot twists and turns until the unsuitable Philippe Gaucher—who is indeed gauche—is sent packing and Pierre and Marianne are betrothed. While very much a period piece, this last scrap of Sand's tremendous oeuvre is a charming bit of entertainment." Publ Wkly

Sand, Jules *See* Sand, George, 1804-1876

Sandburg, Carl, 1878-1967

Remembrance Rock. Harcourt Brace & Co. 1948 1067p o.p.

"Sandburg's only novel, the work is a massive chronicle that uses historical facts and both historical and fictional characters to depict American history from 1607 to 1945 in a mythic, passionate tribute to the American people." Merriam-Webster's Ency of Lit

Sanders, Dori

Clover; a novel. Algonquin Bks. 1990 183p $17.95

    ISBN 0-945575-26-2

                          * LC 89-39072

After her father dies within hours of being married to a white woman, Clover Hill, a ten-year-old black girl, learns with her new stepmother to overcome grief and to adjust to a new place in their rural Black South Carolina community

The author "has staked out an impressive new territory here, replete with peach farmers, textile workers, drunks and crazy people, with the newly middle class as well as the terminally poor. As a specimen of the new realism in regional fiction, 'Clover' is very much the genuine item." N Y Times Book Rev

Sanders, Lawrence, 1920-1998

The first deadly sin. Putnam 1973 566p o.p.

                                  *

This novel "pits a psychopathic killer loose in New York against a tough, dedicated police officer who is not without his own hangups. Telling his story alternately from the psychopath's point of view and that of the detective, Mr. Sanders draws the two men closer and closer together on an inevitable collision course. Probing the dark side of the killer's mind, his sexual conflicts and involvement with a strange trio of brother, sister and valet who are as kinky as they come, he shows the man's accelerating descent into total madness. Meanwhile, Captain Edward X. Delaney, in whose upper East Side precinct a series of random murders is taking place, accepts an undercover assignment to track down the man responsible." Publ Wkly

Sanders, Lawrence, 1920-1998—*Continued*

The fourth deadly sin. Putnam 1985 380p o.p.

LC 84-24789

"When psychiatrist Dr. Ellerbee is beaten to death with a ball-peen hammer, retired detective Edward X. Delaney agrees to supplement the police investigation. The victim's beautiful wife provides a list of potentially violent patients for Delaney and his team to question." Libr J

"Delaney displays that combination of computerlike efficiency and human touch that make him such an appealing detective. It's a masterly performace, not only chilling, but thought-provoking and often touching." Publ Wkly

Guilty pleasures. Putnam 1998 310p $24.95

ISBN 0-399-14365-3   LC 97-32937

Scandal rocks a wealthy South Florida publishing family as brother and sister "battle for future control of the empire—never guessing that a trusted family friend with a hidden agenda is quietly manipulating them all." Publisher's note

McNally's dilemma. Putnam 1999 309p $24.95

ISBN 0-399-14490-0   LC 99-20988

"McNally is a Palm Beach gumshoe who, with his attorney father, makes up the firm of McNally and Son's Department of Discreet Inquiries. . . . This time, the action begins with a late-night call from wealthy Melva Ashton Manning Williams, who has just blown away her second husband, Geoff Williams, née Wolinsky, after finding him in the arms of another woman. Things quickly shift from murder to blackmail and puzzles within puzzles, all of which Archy sorts out in his usual stylish fashion." Booklist

McNally's gamble. Putnam 1997 307p $24.95

ISBN 0-399-14248-7

* LC 96-50369

A "comic whodunit featuring Archy McNally, the foppish but likable head of 'discreet inquiries' at his father's law firm in Palm Beach, Fla. This time Archy's task is to investigate the credentials of a suspicious investment adviser, Frederick Clemens, and his secretary, Felix Katz. . . . Mr. Sanders clearly delights in playing up the bumbling, spoof aspects of this detective yarn, especially during its climactic but unavoidably funny denouement." NY Times Book Rev

McNally's luck. Putnam 1992 319p o.p.

LC 92-1394

"Hot on the trail of a stolen cat on behalf of a client of his family's law firm, McNally and Son, Archy enters Palm Beach's seamy nether-world of psychics, charlatans, and thieves. His seemingly innocuous search for the missing cat leads him to the heart of a grisly and intricate plot. As the body count climbs, Archy must resolve the links between several violent local murders and the disappearance of the ill-tempered feline." Publisher's note

McNally's puzzle. Putnam 1996 311p o.p.

LC 95-45703

In this mystery, playboy/sleuth Archy McNally "must dig into the gruesome death of a millionaire parrot-shop owner named Hiram Gottschalk in an attempt to unravel the circumstances of his passing and the tangled mess of the family he leaves behind. . . . The real focus is on Archy's prancing and preening and so-called life of the mind as he tools around south Florida entertaining the millionaire's twin daughters, fencing with his housekeeper and tracking the bizarre activities—parrot smuggling is one, perhaps—of Gottschalk's troubled stepson." N Y Times Book Rev

McNally's secret. Putnam 1992 317p o.p.

LC 91-9803

"Four priceless U.S. airmail stamps issued in 1918 and known as 'inverted Jennies' have been stolen from a wealthy matron's mansion in Palm Beach. . . . McNally's task is to find the thief 'without the barest hint of scandal coming to light.' There are lots of suspects, a couple of deaths, and a fine romance." Booklist

McNally's trial. Putnam 1995 309p o.p.

LC 94-33943

Palm Beach's Archy McNally, "an occasional investigator for his stuffy lawyer father, here agrees to look into the sudden 'uptick' in business that is worrying a pretty exec at the exclusive Whitcomb Funeral Homes. Too many people are dying, observes the woman, and being shipped up north in coffins." Publ Wkly

The novel "boasts a delightful assembly of supporting characters, especially Archy's pal, the totally dissolute, utterly inept would-be detective Binky Watrous. A pleasant diversion." Booklist

The second deadly sin. Putnam 1977 412p o.p.

LC 77-3652

A "police procedural in which Edward X. Delaney, recently retired as Manhattan's chief of detectives, returns by invitation of the department to work on the mystery-murder of a thoroughly unlikable genius, painter Victor Maitland. Delaney, a curious mixture of force and sensitivity, is teamed with a young sergeant, whose drinking has brought him to the edge of dismissal. The two, with an accidentally added starter, Jason T. Jason (black, smart, and very big), by a combination of hard work, intuition, and some luck finally track down the killer." Booklist

The sixth commandment; a novel. Putnam 1979 350p

ISBN 0-399-12305-9   LC 78-13158

When the investigator for a philanthropic group arrives in a small upstate New York town to research the application for a grant made by a former Nobel laureate in medicine, "the town's leading citizen, no suspicions are aroused. Yet, a few interviews reveal that the town is shielding some damaging secret about the famous man. When the sleuth penetrates the screen he finds a sordid love affair, but also the shocking revelation that the doctor is using human subjects in his experiments to achieve immortality." Libr J

"This gloomy escapade about a hard-drinking, chain-smoking, world-pitying investigator . . . is brimful of juice and excitement, with some insight and much foolishness—a genuinely riveting diversion." New Yorker

Sullivan's sting. Putnam 1990 348p

ISBN 0-399-13542-1   LC 89-70046

This novel "profiles the slimy underbelly of south Florida, where con men posing as financial wizards bilk greedy, unsuspecting investors out of their money (aging widows are a prime mark). The main player here is sexy David Rathbone, a man who apparently could sell igloos to Eskimos. Equally sexy undercover cop Rita Angela

Sanders, Lawrence, 1920-1998—*Continued*

Sullivan is on a mission from the SEC to 'sting' Rathbone. She traps her prey, starts to play house, and moves in for the kill—then finds herself falling in love with the guy." Booklist

The tenth commandment; a novel. Putnam 1980 385p

ISBN 0-399-12500-6   LC 80-13002

Joshua Bigg, "chief investigator for a New York law firm, gets two tough assignments from his bosses. One is a missing person case: a crotchety professor whose family want an estate settlement. The other is an apparent suicide: an aging textile manufacturer whose merry young widow has suddenly become religiously attracted to a churchless clergyman. Bigg plows his way through mountains of clues, allies himself with a black police detective and unearths evidence to indicate that the suicide was murder and that the missing man is dead." Publ Wkly

The third deadly sin. Putnam 1981 444p o.p.

LC 80-26325

"Sergeant Boone of Manhattan's Homicide Squad persuades former Chief of Detectives Delaney to help find what police fear most, a random killer. The two men . . . begin the slow, almost hopeless, scrupulously painstaking chore of tracking down and piecing together the tiniest clues. The detecting account alternates with vivid, step-by-step descriptions of drab Zoe Kohler, who tarts herself up periodically and ritually murders men she picks up in convention-crowded hotels. In the telling, Sander's characters discuss facets of feminism and crime provocatively, and not at all simplistically, adding to the dimensions of a superior mystery." Publ Wkly

The Timothy files. Putnam 1987 380p o.p.

LC 86-25496

Three novella-length episodes "feature Timothy Cone, 'the Wall Street dick,' who works for an investigative agency. . . . The files deal respectively with a murderous real-estate conglomerate, a fertility clinic devoted to considerably more than 'original biotechnological research' and an investment house involved in drugs—though only detective work of the highest caliber can discover the seamy details." Publ Wkly

Timothy's game. Putnam 1988 382p o.p.

LC 87-29073

This novel is "set on Wall Street, where clever detective Timothy Cone dresses in Salvation Army chic, chain-smokes Camels, and drinks too much. Cone has a cat named Cleo who eats ham hocks, potato salad, and garlic salami, and a girlfriend named Samantha who sports long, auburn hair. Throw in a foul-mouthed woman who owns a garbage-hauling firm controlled by the mob, an insider-trading leak, murder, and a tong war in Chinatown, and you have the usual brand of Sanders' readable fiction." Booklist

Sanderson, Brandon, 1975-

Elantris. Tor 2005 492p il $27.95

ISBN 978-0-765-31177-1   LC 2004-63765

"A Tom Doherty Associates book"

"Ten years have passed since the benevolent, godlike beings who ruled Arelon from their city of Elantris suffered a sudden, catastrophic change that left them little

better than the walking dead and their glorious capital city little more than a slime-covered tomb. Now faced with the possibility of an invasion by the religious fanatics of neighboring Fjordell, the rulers of Arelon and the independent land of Teod plan a marriage between Arelon's Prince Raoden and Teod's Princess Sarene, a union meant to join their countries in mutual defense." Libr J

This fantasy is "refreshingly complete unto itself and free of the usual genre clichés, offers something for everyone: mystery, magic, romance, political wrangling, religious conflict, fights for equality, sharp writing and wonderful, robust characters." Publ Wkly

Mistborn: the final empire. Tor 2006 541p il $27.95

ISBN 978-0-765-31178-8; 0-765-31178-X

LC 2005-34496

"A Tom Doherty Associates book"

First volume of the author's epic fantasy trilogy

"The Sliver of Infinity, the Lord Ruler, is the locus of religious and temporal order in a world in which the skaa are slaves or worse. Half-skaa erstwhile thief Kelsior is the only person to survive and escape the Lord Ruler's most brutal prison, in which, however, he discovered he has the powers of the Mistborn, which are based on the internal 'burning' of certain metals, all of which the Mistborn can use, while most others can burn only one. Now Kelsior plans his most daring raid ever, into the center of the palace to discover the secret of the Lord Ruler's power. . . . Intrigue, politics, and conspiracies mesh complexly in a world Sanderson realizes in satisfying depth and peoples with impressive characters." Booklist

Followed by: The well of ascension (2007) and The hero of ages (2008)

Sandford, John, 1944-

Broken prey. Putnam 2005 390p $26.95

ISBN 0-399-15272-5   LC 2005-42981

Lucas Davenport, a "Minnesota State Bureau of Criminal Apprehension investigator, had lately been doing political fix-it jobs for the governor, but this time he's got a psychopathic serial killer on his hands. . . . The first victim, a young woman, was 'scourged' with a wire whip; number two, a young man, had his penis cut off. Evidence first points to recently released sex offender Charlie Pope. Though Charlie is pretty dumb and the killer is extremely smart, it takes Davenport and his series partner, Detective Sloan, a while to realize they're chasing the wrong guy. Sandford introduces some lighter moments, the most entertaining about Davenport's new iPod and his quest to compile a list of the 100 best rock songs ever recorded, which every cop on the force gives him suggestions for. These moments allow readers to catch their breath amid the otherwise nonstop tension." Publ Wkly

Certain prey. Putnam 1999 339p $24.95

ISBN 0-399-14496-X   LC 99-19048

"Trying to avoid facing his empty personal life, enigmatic Minneapolis Deputy Police Chief Lucus Davenport is jolted out of the doldrums by the handiwork of professional hitwoman Clara Rinker, in town to do what she does best. Adding to his problems is glamorous defense attorney Carmel Loan, a clever and intimidating lawyer.

Sandford, John, 1944-—*Continued*

When Davenport suspects an alliance between the two women, he soon faces two deadly enemies. Sandford keeps the level of suspense dizzyingly high as he shifts viewpoints between the women and Davenport." Booklist

Chosen prey. Putnam 2001 357p

ISBN 0-399-14728-4 LC 2001-18594

"Troubled by both city politics and his relationship with his fiancee, Minneapolis Deputy Police Chief Lucas Davenport finds the comfortable routines of a murder investigation as soothing as a worn pair of jeans. The discovery of a young woman's body, missing 18 months, leads to a local pornographic photography ring that posts its handiwork on the Internet." Booklist

Easy prey. Putnam 2000 407p

ISBN 0-399-14613-X LC 00-23962

"Minnesota-born supermodel Alie'e Maison is back in Minneapolis for a photo shoot. At the raucous wrap party, she turns up dead. Lucas Davenport, the millionaire homicide specialist who often corrals serial killers, is called to the scene." Booklist

"Although Lucas makes his own strong fashion statement . . . his smooth professional moves are the best feature of his style. A shrewd gamester who made his personal fortune designing computer games, he follows sound police procedures and devises one intricate ploy after another to draw out the killers." N Y Times Book Rev

Hidden prey. Putnam 2004 393p $26.95

ISBN 0-399-15180-X LC 2004-44351

"When a Russian man is found murdered on the shores of Lake Superior, Lucas Davenport must join forces with a cop from Moscow to track down the culprit." Libr J

"Readers will be pleased with this relaxed version of the moody Minneapolis investigator. In past novels, the womanizing Davenport would have romanced the good-looking Russian lady, but the new Davenport is content to play the part of friend and protector and go back to his cozy family with an unstained and remarkably contented soul." Publ Wkly

Mind prey. Putnam 1995 323p o.p.

LC 95-3790

"When psychiatrist Andi Manette and her two young daughters are kidnapped, [Davenport] must discover whether it's a ransom snatch, the work of one of Andi's ex-patients or the ruse of someone in her life who might benefit from her death. . . . Readers know the kidnapper is John Mail, a scary ex-patient who's entertained nasty dreams of Andi for years. . . . Sandford expertly ratchets up the suspense from beginning to the brutal finish." Publ Wkly

Mortal prey. Putnam 2002 354p

ISBN 0-399-14863-9 LC 2002-19051

Assassin Clara Rinker, an old nemesis of Lucas Davenport's "is now back on the prowl, looking for revenge against old enemies from Kansas City who killed her fiancé and shot her in the gut. The bullet spared her life, but not that of her baby. The FBI, knowing she's headed to Missouri, assembles a huge team of shirt-and-tie, laptop-carrying agents, but also taps Davenport to make the trip. . . . Longtime fans should take note that changes are ahead for Davenport. He's marrying his sweetie, Dr. Weather Karkinnen, and they're having a

kid. He's also about to leave the city police force, following his boss, Rose Marie Roux, to a job with the state police." Publ Wkly

Naked prey. Putnam 2003 359p $26.95

ISBN 0-399-15043-9

* LC 2003-41364

Lucas Davenport "is now Director of Regional Studies in the Minnesota Bureau of Criminal Apprehension, which is a fancy name for the job of investigating difficult crimes as quickly as possible and answering to the governor of the state. Known for his ability to solve the unsolvable, he goes to a remote area of the state to discover why a black man and a white woman were hanged in a groove of trees. . . . Fast paced and full of surprises, this may be Sandford's best novel yet." Libr J

Night prey. Putnam 1994 336p o.p.

LC 94-7564

"Minnesota deputy police chief Lucas Davenport is on the trail of a serial killer—this time a particularly nasty specimen with a yen for disemboweling his victims. Meagan Connell, an investigator from a state agency, plays the . . . role of Davenport's feisty, determined female assistant. Davenport is also peripherally involved in a case that appears to involve the Seeds, a loosely organized group of white supremacists." Booklist

"Despite its length, *Night Prey* is a tight, fast-moving thriller with appealing good guys and a suitably evil villain. Especially fascinating among the characters is Policewoman Connell." Libr J

Rules of prey. Putnam 1989 316p o.p.

LC 89-4040

"A killer who calls himself the 'maddog' has been murdering Minneapolis women, seemingly without pattern or motive. The crimes are linked only by their brutality and by the slayer's 'signature': at each scene, he leaves a written rule of crime, such as 'Never kill anyone you know,' or, 'Never carry a weapon after it has been used.' Into the case comes Lucas Davenport, a policeman with five kills in the line of duty, a surefire sense of how to handle the thirsty media and strong instincts about the killer's psyche." Publ Wkly

Silent prey. Putnam 1992 320p o.p.

LC 91-43696

"Mad pathologist Bekker's face is battered and broken after his encounter with unorthodox Minneapolis cop Lucas Davenport in *Eyes of Prey.* Now Bekker's on the loose again, having escaped during his trial and landed in New York City. Even more nutso than ever, he's determined to exact revenge on Lucas and to continue his evil experiments, in which he searches the eyes of his victims in the few, pain-creased seconds before death." Booklist

Sudden prey. Putnam 1996 360p o.p.

LC 96-4598

This Lucas Davenport adventure "opens with the Candy LaChaise gang's robbery of a Minnesota credit union. When Candy is ambushed and killed by Davenport and his men, Candy's husband, Dick LaChaise, swears vengeance on the spouses and families of all officers involved. A series of attacks ensue in which spouses are killed at work. With the lives of Davenport's own daughter and his fiancée threatened, he quickly metamorphoses into a hunting machine himself." Libr J

Sandford, John, 1944-—_Continued_

Winter prey. Putnam 1993 336p o.p.
* LC 92-42072

"In a rural area of northern Wisconsin, a family of three is savagely wiped out by the Iceman, who then torches their house. In pursuit of a damaging photograph—a snapshot of him in a sexual situation with a local boy—this fiend puts no value on human life. Enter Davenport, the laconic, slightly cynical ex-cop from Minneapolis, who uncovers several disturbing truths before determining the Iceman's identity." Publ Wkly

"Davenport, a cool, cynical man of action, is entirely in his element in this harsh terrain—so bitter that it turns animals against men, so brutal that it turns men into beasts." N Y Times Book Rev

Sansom, C. J.

Winter in Madrid. Viking 2008 537p $25.95
ISBN 978-0-670-01848-2; 0-670-01848-1
LC 2007-42552
First published 2006 in the United Kingdom
This novel is set in a "destitute Madrid that has been bled not only of people but also of color. To Harry Brett, reluctant spy for the British secret service, the city is as drab as wartime London and far murkier. His old school friend Sandy Forsyth is now a slick Madrid businessman with connections to Franco's regime, and Harry's mission is to rekindle the friendship and deliver Sandy let's not say how or why to his British handlers. Any tactic is fair game, in their view, if only Franco can be persuaded (or blackmailed) to enter the war against Germany. Matters are further complicated by the fact that Sandy is living with Barbara Clare, an old flame of Harry's who has a secret mission of her own: to rescue the love of her life, socialist Bernie Piper, who disappeared after the Battle of Jarama." Boston Globe

"Sansom deftly plots his politically charged tale for maximal suspense, all the way up to its stunning conclusion. . . . This moving opus leaves the reader mourning for the Spain that might have been—and the England that maybe never was." Publ Wkly

Sansom, Ian

The case of the missing books. HarperCollins 2006 336p pa $12.95
ISBN 978-0-06-082250-7; 0-06-082250-3
This title launches a "new series set in Tumdrum, Northern Ireland, the small village that transplanted Londoner Israel Armstrong reluctantly makes his home. The nebbishy Jewish vegetarian shows up at the Tumdrum and District Public Library eager to assume his post as the new librarian, only to find the place boarded up and that it's his job to steward the beat-up mobile library instead. When he finally gets inside the library building, he discovers its 15,000 books are missing. Less astute than the detective characters in the novels he has devoured, Israel blunders through an investigation, making startling discoveries while suffering some hard knocks along the way." Publ Wkly

Santmyer, Helen Hooven, 1895-1986

"—and ladies of the club". Ohio State Univ. Press 1982 1344p o.p.
LC 81-22401
"In 1868 in a small town in southwestern Ohio, a group of women form a literary club. Through the personal, political, and social upheavals of the next 64 years the club remains the one constant factor in the lives of these diverse women and their descendants." Libr J

The author's "perceptive saga is steeped not just in the changing political, religious, and social mores of the period covered, but also in the personal joys, sorrows, and scandals that beat the cadence of life in a midwestern town. This novel has an old-fashioned dignity and seriousness that will win some readers and lose others, and although its girth is perhaps its most notable quality, its literary scope and depth of feeling are equally impressive." Booklist

Saramago, José, 1922-

All the names; translated by Margaret Jull Costa. Harcourt 2000 238p $24
ISBN 0-15-100421-8
Original Portuguese edition 1997; this translation first published 1999 in the United Kingdom
"The title refers to the miles of archival records among which the protagonist toils at the Registry of Births, Marriages and Deaths in an unnamed small country whose inhabitants still live by ancient rules of hierarchical social classes. . . . A penurious, reclusive, lonely bachelor, Senhor José has only one secret passion: he collects clippings about famous people and surreptitiously copies their birth certificates, purloining them from the registry at night and returning them stealthily. Purely by accident, the index card of a 36-year-old woman unknown to him becomes entangled in the clippings he steals. Suddenly, he is stricken by a need to learn about this woman's life." Publ Wkly

"Modest, self-mocking, mildly ironic, yet magisterial, Saramago's gentle voice rings with the unmistakable authority of the true artist." Christ Sci Monit

Blindness; a novel; translated from the Portuguese by Giovanni Pontiero. Harcourt Brace & Co. 1998 294p $22
ISBN 0-15-100251-7
* LC 98-12009
Original Portuguese edition, 1995; this translation first published 1997 in the United Kingdom
"A man waiting in his car for a red light to turn green is the first of an entire city's population—with one exception—to be blinded by a 'milky sea' of dazzling whiteness. The inexplicably disabled victims grope and stumble their way through nightmarish landscapes—first an asylum where those initially afflicted are quarantined, and then the chaotic, squalid streets to which they return. Saramago's surreal allegory explores the ability of the human spirit to prevail in even the most absurdly unjust of conditions, yet he reinvents this familiar struggle with the stylistic eccentricity of a master." New Yorker

The cave; translated from the Portuguese by Margaret Jull Costa. Harcourt 2002 307p $25
ISBN 0-15-100414-5
* LC 2002-2355

Saramago, José, 1922--—*Continued*

Original Portuguese edition, 2000

"Widowed Cipriano Algor is a 64-year-old Portuguese potter who finds his business collapsing when the demand dries up for his elegant, handcrafted wares. His potential fate seems worse than poverty—to move with his daughter, Marta, and his son-in-law, Marçal Gacho, into a huge, arid complex known as 'The Center,' where Gacho works as a security guard. But Algor gets an order from the Center for hundreds of small ceramic figurines, a task that has Marta and Algor hustling to meet the delivery date." Publ Wkly

"As a further warning against the urge to seek safety on common ground—moving to the center, as it were—the writer highlights the menaces of cliche by parodying the worldly-wise narrative interventions of an earlier era. . . . Such deft manipulations in Saramago's style are brilliantly rendered in Margaret Jull Costa's agile English version of his Portuguese." N Y Times Book Rev

Death with interruptions; translated from the Portuguese by Margaret Jull Costa. Harcourt 2008 238p $24

ISBN 978-0-15-101274-9; 0-15-101274-1

LC 2008-10088

Original Portuguese edition, 2005

"Starting at the stroke of midnight on New Year's, in an unidentified country in an undetermined year, in Jose Saramago's new novel, death goes on strike. Nobody dies from illness or suicide or, Mr. Saramago writes, 'from a car accident, so frequent on festive occasions, when blithe irresponsibility and an excess of alcohol jockey for position on the roads to decide who will reach death first.' Thus the Saramago sentence: conversational but a conversation with oneself; portentous yet ludicrous, like a solemn address delivered by someone who has forgotten to wear pants. Thus too the Saramago plot: an impossible event like universal blindness, or Portugal's history altered because of a proofreader's error in a history book. Or, as here, death feeling unappreciated and refusing to oblige. . . . Mr. Saramago, one of the last of the old-line Communists, has written an atheist's religious parable; a story abounding in sentiment and purged of it." N Y Times (Late NY Ed)

The history of the siege of Lisbon; translated from the Portuguese by Giovanni Pontiero. Harcourt Brace & Co. 1997 c1996 314p o.p.

LC 96-46826

Original Portuguese edition 1989; this translation first published 1996 in the United Kingdom

"Raimundo Silva, proofreader for a Portuguese publishing house, violates the fundamental ethic of his profession by adding the word *not* to a sentence in a history textbook, so it reads that in 1147 the king of Portugal reconquered Lisbon from the Saracens with out any help from the Crusaders. Although the change is caught, and an errata slip added to the book, Silva's supervisor, rather than firing him, asks him to write an alternative history based on his emendation of the text." Booklist

"Although the novel's stream-of-consciousness technique, baroque prose and paragraphs that run on for pages may daunt some readers, this hypnotic tale is a great comic romp through history, language and the imagination." Publ Wkly

Seeing; translated from the Portuguese by Margaret Jull Costa. Harcourt 2006 307p $25

ISBN 0-15-101238-5　　　　　　　LC 2005-32688

Original Portuguese edition, 2004

This sequel to Blindness "begins with a postelection-day crisis involving the discovery that more than 70 percent of ballots counted in a city resembling Lisbon are blank. The government, terrified at the apparent mass protest, adopts increasingly severe measures to convince the people that government supervision is required." Harper's

"With run-on paragraphs and dialogue, the author challenges readers to pay close attention; the appreciators of literary fiction who do so will find a clever, even sly, but also sobering exploration of when governments do and when they do not have reason to be paranoid." Booklist

Sargent, Colin 1954-

Museum of human beings. McBooks Press 2008 337p map $23.95

ISBN 978-1-59013-167-1; 1-59013-167-3

LC 2008-37492

"Twenty-four-year-old Sacagawea, though married, becomes William Clark's lover while helping guide the Lewis and Clark Expedition; after she dies on the trail, Clark adopts her son, Baptiste. Soon, Clark establishes his home in St. Louis, as well as a garish museum dedicated to his expedition, and sets to educating his new son. Soon, Baptiste is traveling Europe under the protection of Duke Paul, a cruel man who, when he isn't exhibiting the boy to royal courts, repeatedly rapes young Baptiste. Six years later, Baptiste returns to America (astonishingly, still accompanied by Paul), where he confronts Clark over his mother's mysterious death; unsatisfied and restless, Baptiste heads west and finds work as a fur trapper, an Army scout and gold prospector." Publ Wkly

"Sargent sends the youthful Baptiste on a multi-leveled grand tour of discovery that never lets up or disappoints . . . With wit, humor, detailed understanding of the time, imagination and uncomplicated storytelling, Sargent opens a door on an era." Maine Sunday Telegram

Saroyan, William, 1908-1981

The human comedy. Rev by the author. Dell 1971 192p pa $7.50

ISBN 0-440-33933-2

First published 1944 by Harcourt, Brace and Company

"Homer, the narrator, identifies himself in this novel as a night messenger for the Postal Telegraph office. He creates a view of family life in the 1940s in a small town in California. His mother, Ma Macauley, presides over the family and takes care of four children after her husband dies. Besides Homer, there is Marcus, the oldest, who is in the army; Bess; and Ulysses, the youngest, who describes the world from his perspective as a solemn four-year-old." Shapiro. Fic for Youth. 3d edition

Sarton, May, 1912-1995

Anger; a novel. Norton 1982 223p

ISBN 0-393-01643-9　　　　　　　LC 82-7843

Sarton, May, 1912-1995—*Continued*

"Successful Boston banker Ned Fraser finds himself captivated by an unexpected encounter with mezzo-soprano Anna Lindstrom. He pursues the gifted, determined-to-be-famous performer without success until, at a chance meeting, he wins her—somewhat to the surprise of them both. They marry within a short time, no starry-eyed youngsters, but two mature adults. Both are settled in their emotional patterns: she given to outspoken and tempestuous outbursts of joy and despair, he to internalizing his feelings and maintaining the proper facade. This results in a lack of communication that threatens their marriage until Anna penetrates Ned's reserve. A romantic, yet realistic portrait." Libr J

As we are now; a novel. Norton 1973 133p $10.95

ISBN 0-393-08372-1

This book is "a novel in the form of a diary, written by a retired schoolteacher. Mentally tough but not quite physically able to care for herself, she is deposited by relatives in an old people's home. Subjected to subtle humiliations, petty and almost unthinking cruelties, deprived of all mental stimulus, she fights a tough battle to preserve first her dignity, then her sanity." Christ Sci Monit

"It is a bitter book, more a tract than a novel, and an utterly desolating experience, as it is meant to be. There are complexities that unwind themselves now and then, which preserve the concerns of the novel; but on the whole, the work is a piece of rhetoric, and very good rhetoric, too. . . . For the book satisfies in the way that cold anger can when it is pure, despairing, and written with no aim but the impulse to record the way things are." Saturday Rev/World

Kinds of love; a novel. Norton 1970 464p

ISBN 0-393-08620-8

The novel "is set in a small New Hampshire town much visited over the years by summer people. Christina and Cornelius Chapman, elderly and long-standing summer people, have retreated to Williard following Cornelius's partly crippling stroke and have resolved to winter there for the first time. Around them and around their house swirl the events of the story." N Y Times Book Rev

"The touching friendship of two elderly women, the love/hate relationship of the permanent residents and the summer people, and a young girl's discovery of the magic and the pain of love are some of the threads in this quiet tale." Booklist

A reckoning; a novel. Norton 1978 254p o.p.
* LC 78-9691

"Laura Spelman, genteel Boston widow, has just learned that she is dying of cancer. Determined to take a candid look at herself as a means of tying up loose ends, she is surprised to find her thoughts turning mostly to women. Confiding in strangers, avoiding her family, Laura speaks of discovering herself as a woman. In particular, she examines her relationships with her domineering mother and with a dearly loved friend, the two people who, she feels, have shaped her life most profoundly. Ironically, as her body becomes increasingly unfamiliar, her old, unexamined passions begin to resolve themselves." Atlantic

"Sarton incorporates . . . the issues of mother/daughter relationships, what it is to be a woman (and a man), and the conflict of art and life." Libr J

A small room; a novel. Norton 1961 249p o.p.

"Lucy Winter, professor and seeker of refuge in the kingdom of a progressive [New England] women's college, becomes involved when a top student is caught in a case of plagiarism, and peace dissolves. The faculty must face the guilt of having pushed for intellectual attainment with inadequate knowledge and consideration for emotional factors, i.e. the crime of not teaching 'the whole child.' Each person reacts to crisis differently—sometimes disastrously, but all can meet finally in the small room to evaluate the past and to agree on the college's proposed plan for the future." Libr J

Sarton "presents her cast of faculty types with scrupulous respect. There is no villain among them. . . . The essence of this novel is not so much in the conflict of characters as in the conflict in ideas—and ideas about teaching." N Y Her Trib Books

Sartre, Jean Paul, 1905-1980

The age of reason; translated from the French by Eric Sutton. Knopf 1947 397p (Roads to freedom, 1) o.p.
*

Original French edition, 1945

First of a series of three novels by the French philosopher, exponent of existentialism. The scene of this novel is Paris in 1938. A fourth title was never completed

"The central character is Mathieu, a professor of philosophy who writes one short story a year. . . . The problem that obsesses Mathieu, that of freedom, how to remain free, is worked out in the story and exemplified in the lives of the characters. . . . Mathieu differs from your ordinary character of fiction in that he is motivated by this abstract ethical ideal to keep his freedom. It is assailed as soon as the novel opens, for he learns that his mistress is pregnant; the action consists largely of his attempts to raise by borrowing—in the end, by stealing—the five thousand francs required to procure an abortion; unnecessarily, as it turns out, for Marcelle decides to marry someone else and have the child." Spectator

Followed by The reprieve

Intimacy, and other stories; translated by Lloyd Alexander. New Directions 1952 c1948 270p o.p.

First published 1948 in a limited edition with title: The wall, and other stories

Contents: The wall; The room; Erostratus; Intimacy; The childhood of a leader

"The most impressive thing about the book, rising from it like a stench, is a disgust for life, a sense of universal defilement. The insistence on the physical in the stories is indistinguishable from an aversion to it." New Repub

Nausea; translated from the French by Lloyd Alexander. New Directions 1949 238p o.p.
*

Original French edition, 1938

"*Nausea* is written in the form of a diary that narrates the recurring feelings of revulsion that overcome Roquentin, a young historian, as he comes to realize the banality and emptiness of existence. As the attacks of

Sartre, Jean Paul, 1905-1980—*Continued*

nausea occur more frequently, Roquentin abandons his research and loses his few friends. In an indifferent world, without work, love, or friendship to sustain him, he must discover value and meaning within himself." Merriam-Webster's Ency of Lit

The reprieve; translated from the French by Eric Sutton. Knopf 1947 445p (Roads to freedom, 2) o.p.

Original French edition, 1945

This sequel to The age of reason "confines itself to the eight frenetic days that led to the Munich Pact and the rape of Czechoslovakia. The original characters reappear merging now with many others as a shocked France mobilizes for war. Sartre, the leading exponent of Existentialism manages in this kaleidoscope novel to re-create the confusion, even the odor of the fear that gripped Europe in September, 1938." Libr J

Followed by Troubled sleep

Troubled sleep; translated from the French by Gerald Hopkins. Knopf 1950 421p (Roads to freedom, 3) o.p.

Sequel to The reprieve

Original French edition, 1949; published in the United Kingdom with title: Iron in the soul

"A story of the French people after the fall of Paris in World War II, of many individuals of different walks of life and their reactions to defeat." Publ Wkly

"No other book gives such insight into the anguished feelings of the French as they passed from apathy to consciousness of their dignity as men revolting against fate, accepting their solidarity with other men—wretched, but lucid and free fighters." Saturday Rev

Saul, John

Darkness. Bantam Bks. 1991 341p
ISBN 0-553-07373-7   LC 90-25842
This is the "tale of a little town in the Florida swamps where a lot of old guys are remarkably youthful and a lot of kids rather soulless. 'Dead in the eyes' is how folks see these children, a new one of whom, Kelly Anderson, has just come to town with her adoptive parents. She hooks up with another teenager, also an adoptee, Michael Sheffield. Together they find out about, and are irresistibly drawn to, a mysterious circle of children controlled by the Dark Man that meets deep in the swamp." Booklist

The homing. Fawcett Columbine 1994 389p $21.50
ISBN 0-449-90863-1   LC 93-50606
"Karen Spellman and her daughters Julie, 16, and Molly, 9, move from L.A. back to the bucolic community in which Karen grew up. For with the girls' father years dead, Karen has remet and decided to marry farmer Russell Owen. Things start going awry right away: at Karen and Russell's home wedding, Molly is stung by a bee, and although it's happened before with no untoward results, this time she nearly dies. More accidents with bees and other insects occur—not least to Julie—and while local entomologist Carl Henderson, who works for the agricultural branch of a huge chemical company, is able to provide seemingly effective antivenins when folks react badly to bites, he also occasionally behaves most peculiarly." Booklist

The author provides "splendidly creepy bug-infested house of horrors and a fitting revenge for the villain." Libr J

Midnight voices. Ballantine Bks. 2002 341p
ISBN 0-345-43331-9   LC 2002-283839
"Mother of two and widow of a murdered Central Park jogger, Caroline Evans thinks she has found the answer to her prayers in her new husband, Anthony Fleming. The family moves into his apartment in the Rockwell, a storied old Upper West Side building. Ryan and Laurie, the children, quickly begin to have nightmares in which they are haunted by menacing voices, while Ryan realizes that he doesn't like his creepy stepfather." Publ Wkly

"This is good, drafty atmospheric horror stuff unafraid to indulge in not-at-all subtle gory bits." Booklist

The presence. Fawcett Columbine 1997 338p $25
ISBN 0-449-91055-5   LC 97-14756
Anthropologist Katharine Sundquist has recently moved to Hawaii with her teenage son Michael. "Katharine has come to the islands to study anomalies of early human development found in the lava beds of Maui. She is quickly distracted from her work by Michael's suddenly worsening asthma attacks and by the inexplicable disappearance and death of several boys with whom he went on a secret nighttime scuba dive. It's only a matter of time before she discovers that her research and Michael's problems are interrelated through the Serinus Project, a covert scientific experiment funded by her employer for the purpose of investigating the genetic origins of human life. . . . Although he breaks no new ground, Saul distills familiar elements of horror, science fiction and the cyberthriller into a potent brew." Publ Wkly

The right hand of evil. Ballantine Bks. 1999 344p $25
ISBN 0-345-43316-5   LC 98-51980
In this psychological thriller a "family moves into an old house, intending to refurbish it as a hotel, but, soon, both the father and his son begin to act rather oddly. . . . Saul makes Ted, the father, a raving alcoholic who becomes, under the influence of whatever's possessing him, a model dad. In several places, the story seems to be going in one way, until Saul wrenches it in a different direction, keeping his readers on their toes. Although the novel is sometimes drastically overwritten . . . the author clearly succeeds in his primary mission: to give readers a serious case of the willies." Booklist

Second child. Bantam Bks. 1990 341p o.p.
LC 89-77149
Melissa "doesn't fit into the snooty social life of the exclusive East Coast beach community of Secret Cove, and her cruel mother hates her for this failing. The arrival of Melissa's beautiful half-sister, Teri, exacerbates the situation. Melissa escapes her mother's punishments by entering a trance state where her imaginary friend D'Arcy protects her. And who is D'Arcy? Apparently, the ghost of a spurned servant girl who returned an engagement ring still attached to her severed hand. Murderous Teri tries to manipulate Melissa's apparent psychosis, but D'Arcy intercedes. Mother and half-sister are evil incarnate." Booklist

Saul, John—*Continued*

Shadows. Bantam Bks. 1992 390p o.p.

LC 92-1317

"Ten-year-old genius Josh MacCallum is bored, lonely and almost always angry at his older, teasing classmates. After he attempts suicide, his frantic single mother jumps at the chance to enroll him in the Academy, a school for very gifted kids in Northern California. Run by aloof Dr. Engersol and matronly housemother Hildie, the school, which occupies an old mansion, offers Josh a friend in another genius, Amy Carlson. . . . Engersol and Hildie are revealed as nasty and the mad-scientist plot hurtles to a violent conclusion featuring dueling brains connected to a mainframe computer." Publ Wkly

Saunders, George

In persuasion nation; stories. Riverhead Books 2006 228p $23.95

ISBN 1-59448-922-X   LC 2005-57715

Contents: I CAN SPEAK!™; My flamboyant grandson; Jon; My amendment; The red bow; Christmas; Adams; 93990; Brad Carrigan, American; In persuasion nation; Bohemians; Commcomm

"The most unnerving fiction boldly envisions the dire consequences of our most hubristic tendencies: our bottomless greed, maniacal competitiveness, hypermaterialism, environmental obliviousness, spiritual callousness, and fear of being different. Following in the footsteps of Orwell, Bradbury, and Atwood, Saunders writes shrewd, off-the-charts speculative fiction. . . . In his third savagely imaginative collection, his most riveting to date, he considers various forms of diabolical persuasion in a techno-colonized world in which advertising governs every aspect of life." Booklist

Savage, Sam

The cry of the sloth; the mostly tragic story of Andrew Whittaker being his collected, final, and absolutely complete writings. Coffee House Press 2009 224p pa $14.95

ISBN 978-1-56689-231-5; 1-56689-231-7

LC 2009-20904

Protagonist Andrew Whittaker "is something of a literary lowlife. He's a writer who is a legend in his own mind, the vexing editor of a marginal literary journal, an incompetent slumlord, an increasingly tired and tiresome bore and boor, a man about to crash from his own imaginary space into a very unforgiving earth. This novel consists of everything he has written over four months: mostly letters but also remnants of his tortuous prose, shopping lists, and diary entries." Libr J

"Success, sex and sense all elude Whittaker as he half-heartedly tries to keep his life together . . . . Savage's sense of humor is true to his name, but The Cry of the Sloth reminds us of the great Russian satirist Ivan Goncharov, who also saw the tragedy in pretending to be productive." Time Out Chicago

Firmin; adventures of a metropolitan lowlife: a novel. Coffee House Press 2006 151p pa $14.95

ISBN 978-1-566-89181-3; 1-566-89181-7

LC 2005-35803

In this dark comedy, "the titular metropolitan lowlife is a rat, albeit one with lofty literary ambitions. The runt of 13 siblings spawned in the basement of a shambolic Boston bookshop, Firmin survives his lean first weeks by munching on the edges of books. He quickly develops a predilection for actually reading them, too. Soon he's perusing everything from Joyce to compendiums of dirty jokes and even developing a secret fondness for the bookshop's owner, Norman. Tutored by a sign-language book, Firmin tries to communicate with Norman and his human brethren with predictably disastrous results until an obscure science fiction author, who writes about rats and lives above the bookshop, takes him in as a pet. There Firmin enjoys a brief respite of security, writing odes in his head and dreaming of glory, until the wrecking ball threatens the decaying neighborhood. Blending philosophy and abundant literary references with originality, Savage crafts a small comic gem about the costs and rewards of literary illusions." Booklist

Savery, Constance

(jt. auth) Brontë, C. Emma

Sayers, Dorothy L. (Dorothy Leigh), 1893-1957

Busman's honeymoon; a love story with detective interruptions. Harper & Row 1986 c1937 381p $17.95

ISBN 0-06-055021-X

* LC 86-45139

First published 1937 by Harcourt, Brace

"Not near the top of her form, but remarkable as a treatment of the newly wedded and bedded pair of eccentrics, Peter Wimsey and Harriet Vane, with Bunter in the offing and three local characters, chiefly comic. Peter's mother-dowager duchess of Denver-Peter's sister, John Donne, a case of vintage port, and the handling of 'corroded sut' provide plenty of garnishing for an indifferent murder, even if we weren't also given an idea of Lord Peter's sexual tastes and powers under trying circumstances." Barzun. Cat of Crime. Rev and enl edition

Clouds of witnesses. Dial Press (NY) 1927 288p o.p.

Variant title: Clouds of witness

The unpleasant duty of clearing his brother, the Duke of Denver, of a murder charge devolves upon Lord Peter Wimsey. Even when his only sister is involved—the dead man was her unregretted fiancé—Lord Peter does not lose his head

The Dawson pedigree. Dial Press (NY) 1928 c1927 299p o.p.

First published 1927 in the United Kingdom; reissued 1987 by Harper & Row with title: Unnatural death

A chance remark overheard in a restaurant starts a long inquiry and an apparently natural death is proved to have been a murder. But Lord Peter Wimsey, aided by his friends, Parker from Headquarters, and that garrulous and delightful maiden lady, Miss Climpson, has a very difficult time to catch the murderer

Sayers, Dorothy L. (Dorothy Leigh), 1893-1957—Continued

The documents in the case; by Dorothy L. Sayers and Robert Eustace. Brewer & Warren 1930 304p o.p.

       *

A reissue of the title first published 1930 by Brewer & Warren

An "account, largely in letter form, of a case of poisoning by synthetic muscarine alkaloid made to look like mushroom poisoning. Evidence of optical activity and what it means beautifully handled, although the authors are said to have made a mistake in their choice of the particular mushroom to which the 'accidental' death should be attributed. Characters outstanding." Barzun. Cat of Crime. Rev and enl edition

The five red herrings; (Suspicious characters). Harper & Row 1958 c1931 306p il o.p.

       *

First published 1931. Variant title: Suspicious characters

Lord Peter Wimsey had always found himself welcome in the proud Scottish village of Kirkcudbright, although the villagers were not ordinarily tolerant of outsiders. But one day the body of an artist was found on the pointed rocks. The artist might have fallen, but there were too many suspicious elements in his death, especially when six suspects had wished him dead. Lord Peter uses all his ingenuity to unravel the tangles of this crime

"A work that grows on rereading and remains in the mind as one of the richest, most colorful of her group studies. The Scottish setting, the artists in the colony, the train-ticket puzzle, and the final chase place this triumph among the four or five chefs d'oeuvre from her hand." Barzun. Cat of Crime. Rev and enl edition

Gaudy Night. Harcourt Brace & Co. 1936 469p o.p.

First published 1935 in the United Kingdom

Harriet's return to Oxford for the Gaudy Dinner is welcomed by poison-pen letters and attempted blackmail. Lord Peter, of course, summons all his skill to detect the blackmailer and win Harriet

"Harriet Vance and the grown-up nephew of Lord Peter help give variety, and the college scene justifies good intellectual talk. The motive is magnificently orated on by the culprit, a scene that in itself is a unique bit of work. And though the don-esses are sometimes hard to keep apart, the architecture is very good." Barzun. Cat of Crime. Rev and enl edition

Hangman's holiday. Harper & Row 1987 c1961 191p $21.95

    ISBN 0-06-055033-3   LC 86-45691

A reissue of the title first published 1933 by Harcourt, Brace and analyzed in Short story index

Short stories included are: The image in the mirror; The incredible elopement of Lord Peter Wimsey; The queen's square; The necklace of pearls; The poisoned Dow '08; Sleuths on the scent; Murder in the morning; One too many; Murder at Pentecost; Maher-shalal-hashbaz; The man who knew how; The fountain plays

Have his carcase. Brewer, Warren & Putnam 1932 448p o.p.

Harriet Vane finds a body on the beach and Lord Peter Wimsey has a case to solve. Other ingredients of the mystery are an ivory-handled razor, three hundred pounds in gold coins and a coded message

"A great achievement, despite some critics' carping. The people, the motive, the cipher, and the detection are all topnotch. Here, too, is the first (and definitive) use of hemophilia as a misleading fact. And surely the son, the mother, and her self-deluded gigolo are definitive types." Barzun. Cat of Crime. Rev and enl edition

In the teeth of the evidence and other stories. Harcourt Brace & Co. 1940 311p o.p.

First published 1939 in the United Kingdom

Short stories included are: Absolutely elsewhere: a Lord Peter Wimsey story; Arrow o'er the house; Bitter almonds: a Montague Egg story; Blood sacrifice; My best thriller; Dilemma; Dirt cheap: a Montague Egg story; False weight: a Montague Egg story; In the teeth of the evidence; Inspiration of Mr. Budd; Leopard lady; The milk-bottles; Nebuchadnezzar; Professor's manuscript: a Montague Egg story; Scrawns; Shot at goal: a Montague Egg story; Suspicion

Lord Peter; a collection of all the Lord Peter Wimsey stories; compiled and with an introduction by James Sandoe; coda by Carolyn Heilburn; codetta by E.C. Bentley. Harper & Row 1972 464p o.p.

Analyzed in Short story index

Contents: The abominable history of the man with copper fingers; The entertaining episode problem of Uncle Meleager's will; The fantastic horror of the cat in the bag; The unprincipled affair of the practical joker; The undignified melodrama of the bone of contention; The vindictive story of the footsteps that ran; The bibulous business of a matter of taste; The learned adventure of the Dragon's Head; The piscatorial farce of the stolen stomach; The unsolved puzzle of the man with no face; The adventurous exploit of the cave of Ali Baba; The image in the mirror; The incredible elopement of Lord Peter Wimsey; The queen's square; The necklace of pearls; In the teeth of the evidence; Absolutely elsewhere; Striding folly; The haunted policeman

Murder must advertise; a detective story. Harcourt Brace & Co. 1933 344p o.p.

Lord Peter Wimsey, less whimsical and more interesting than usual, enters the advertising profession in order to solve the possible murder by catapult of an advertising copywriter

"A superb example of Sayers' ability to set a group of people going. The advertising agency is inimitable, and hence better than the De Momerie crowd that goes with it." Barzun. Cat of Crime. Rev and enl edition

The nine tailors. Harcourt Brace Jovanovich 1989 c1934 397p il $15.95

    ISBN 0-15-165897-8   LC 89-38102

"An HBJ modern classic"

A reissue of the title first published 1934

"One New Year's Eve, Lord Peter Wimsey, driving through a snowstorm, goes off the road near Fenchurch, St Paul, and is the chance guest of the rector. A providential visit all around, for Peter, acquainted with the an-

Sayers, Dorothy L. (Dorothy Leigh), 1893-1957—*Continued*

cient art of bellringing, acts that night as a substitute, but further than that, he finds use for his versatile mind later, upon the shocking discovery of a mutilated corpse in another man's grave. The unusual plot is developed with dexterity and ingenuity." N Y Libr

Strong poison. Brewer & Warren 1930 344p o.p.

Because Harriet Vane's lover died of arsenic poisoning, and because Harriet was writing a book on the subject of poisons, everybody—except Lord Peter Wimsey—was convinced of her guilt. Lord Peter, with the aid of the inimitable Miss Climpson, gets to work on the business of clearing Harriet

Thrones, dominations; [by] Dorothy L. Sayers and Jill Paton Walsh. St. Martin's Press 1998 312p $23.95

ISBN 0-312-18196-5   LC 97-42585

In 1936, Dorothy L. Sayers began a mystery novel featuring Lord Peter Wimsey and Harriet Vane. The "partial manuscript has now been completed . . . according to her outline by Jill Paton Walsh. . . . Sayers's story opens in 1936 at a restaurant in Paris, where Harriet and Peter are enjoying a brief respite between the execution of the murderer he brought to justice in Busman's Honeymoon and the demands of the Wimsey family and social position back home. At the restaurant they are introduced to Laurence and Rosamund Harwell, a rich Englishman and his beautiful young wife, and the lives of the two couples begin to intertwine—and, to take a dangerous turn." Publisher's note

Paton Walsh "has made a valiant and resourceful stab at mimicry. No devotee of Lord Peter and his novelist wife Harriet Vane will want to miss it." New Stateman (Engl)

The unpleasantness at the Bellona Club. Harper & Row 1986 c1928 345p $17.95

ISBN 0-06-055026-0   LC 86-45145

A reissue of the title first published 1928 by Payson & Clarke

Lord Peter Wimsey investigates the murder of an elderly member of a staid men's club

Whose body? Boni & Liveright 1923 278p o.p.

When a nude corpse, wearing a golden pince-nez only, is found in the bathtub of the flat of a timid little architect, and the discovery coincides with the disappearance of a wealthy financier, Sir Reuben Levy, whom the body resembled, Sir Peter's sporting blood is aroused. Together with a friend from Scotland Yard he unofficially, playfully, as it were, conducts a roundabout inquiry under the jealous eye of the bungling official Scotland Yard investigators and finally tracks down the murderer

Saylor, Steven, 1956-

The house of the Vestals; the investigations of Gordianus the Finder. St. Martin's Press 1997 260p $22.95

ISBN 0-312-15444-5   LC 97-7597

Contents: Death wears a mask; The tale of the treasure house; A will is a way; The lemures; Little Caesar and the pirates; The disappearance of the Saturnalia silver;

King Bee and honey; The Alexandrian cat; The house of the Vestals

"Saylor serves up a collection of short stories designed to fill in some of the gaps that have piqued the curiosity of devoted fans of his popular Roma Sub Rosa series. Set between the years 80 and 72 B.C., these nine tales document some of the early adventures of Gordianus the Finder. . . . While each brief mystery presented is a gem in and of itself, readers will delight in the informational overview provided by the collection as a whole. As usual, Saylor does a superb job of seamlessly incorporating the tumultuous history of the Roman Republic into the narrative flow." Booklist

The judgment of Caesar; a novel of Ancient Rome. St. Martin's Minotaur 2004 290p maps $24.95

ISBN 0-312-27119-0   LC 2003-69548

This "installment, set in Alexandria, once again features Caesar, now maneuvering between the two rivals for the Egyptian throne, Ptolemy and Cleopatra, in an effort to consolidate his own claim to rule Rome. Gordianus's reputation as an honest fact finder, and his familiarity with the centers of power, make him a valuable asset to all three leaders, even as he grapples with a bitter personal loss." Publ Wkly

"Readers will be equally absorbed by the bloody history unfolding (Saylor's description of the beheading of Pompey is both suspenseful and wrenching); by the historical figures depicted (Ptolemy listening to his flute player with the head of Pompey in a clay jar at his feet is a miniature study in royal pathology); and by the mysteries Gordianus must solve to keep his own head. Wonderful reading." Booklist

A mist of prophecies. St. Martin's Press 2002 270p

ISBN 0-312-27121-2   LC 2001-58901

A mystery set in "Rome during the Civil War. A beautiful young woman, given the street name Cassandra for her habit of delivering prophesies, is found murdered. Gordianus is disturbed that no one claims her body—even though, he reflects, someone cared enough to murder her. Yet, at Cassandra's funeral pyre, seven of the most powerful women in Rome, including the wives of Caesar, Cicero, and Marc Antony, attend. Gordianus sorts out the tangled motives of the women who watched Cassandra burn, believing one of them to be her murderer. Saylor brings a wealth of historical information lightly to bear on a chilling mystery." Booklist

Roma; the novel of ancient Rome. St. Martin's Press 2007 555p map $25.95

ISBN 978-0-312-32831-3; 0-312-32831-1

LC 2006-51179

This historical novel "uses two families to tell the history of Rome from its beginnings in 1000 B.C. as a stop on the salt trade route to the founding of the empire." USA Today

"Livy's Early History of Rome offers fertile material for a crime writer. The body count is high, and Saylor adds plenty more along the way. Even Livy smelt a 'whodunit' in the sudden apotheosis of Romulus in a thunderclap in the middle of a Senatorial meeting. Saylor illuminates the mystery in gory detail as, with unfailing efficiency, he unravels the enigmas. There is plenty of instruction here for students of classical civilization but

Saylor, Steven, 1956-—*Continued*

sometimes the period detail founders in bathos when characters explain to each other facts they must already know, for the reader's benefit. Sometimes, though, with the scalpel-like deftness of a Hollywood director, Saylor puts his finger on the very essence of Roman history." Times Lit Suppl

Rubicon; a novel of ancient Rome. St. Martin's Press 1999 276p $23.95

ISBN 0-312-20576-7   LC 99-18090

In this mystery "Gordianus the Finder attempts to solve the murder of Pompey's cousin Numerius. The civilized world of 49 B.C.E. is in turmoil at the onset of the Roman Civil War. Julius Caesar has crossed the Rubicon River into Italy with his hand-picked troops. Pompey, his chief rival for control of Rome, has fled Rome with his followers from the Senate, and all is chaos as the people leave the city. . . . This novel is an excellent blending of mystery and history." Libr J

The triumph of Caesar; a novel of ancient Rome. St. Martin's Minotaur 2008 311p $24.95

ISBN 978-0-312-35983-6; 0-312-35983-7

LC 2008-3668

"Julius Caesar, the dictator of Rome, and Cleopatra, the queen of Egypt, have followed the Gordianus clan back to Rome, and Caesar is planning to celebrate not one but four triumphs in recognition of his many military victories around the Mediterranean. Hieronymus, an old friend of Gordianus . . . has become a spy for Calpurnia, Caesar's wife, and gotten himself stabbed in the heart for his pains. Calpurnia is obsessed with the idea that Caesar's life is in danger, and Gordianus reluctantly agrees to investigate Hieronymus' death. . . . Saylor's vivid character sketches of historical figures are just as strong as always, with bright cameos by Arsinoë (Cleopatra's younger sister) and, for the first time in this series, the aloof, reserved Octavius (the future emperor Augustus). But Saylor's acute historical sensibility is aware that his readers already know how the story ends." January

Scalzi, John, 1969-

The android's dream. Tor 2006 396p $24.95

ISBN 978-0-765-30941-9; 0-765-30941-6

LC 2006-10480

"A Tom Doherty Associates book"

"When a human diplomat causes the death of an alien counterpart, the aliens threaten war unless Earth's government can present them with a particular kind of sheep used in their race's coronation ceremony. War hero and superhacker Harry Creek, along with his friend Brian Javna (now an artificial intelligence), tracks down the sheep, only to discover that it is, in fact, Robin Baker, a pet store owner whose DNA contains remnants of sheep genetic material. While Creek and Javna attempt to find a way around their dilemma, other forces are searching for Baker—and they don't care whether she's dead or alive. . . . . A tongue-in-cheek sf adventure that delivers serious action and intrigue as well as clever comedic barbs aimed at diplomatic airs, sf cults, and other foibles of the modern era." Libr J

The ghost brigades. Tor 2006 317p $23.95

ISBN 0-765-31502-5   LC 2005-27330

"A Tom Doherty Associates book"

The author's Old man's war (2005) "introduced readers to the Colonial Defense Forces (CDF), an Earth-based galactic army composed of senior citizens rejuvenated by high-tech wizardry into youthful warriors. In this . . . battle-driven sequel, the CDF's latest operation entails tracking down renegade scientist Charles Boutin, who is responsible for handing over deadly military secrets to humanity's extraterrestrial enemies. Fortunately, a computer-based replica of Boutin's consciousness is on file and ready for transfer into newly cloned special-forces soldier Jirad Dirac, who shares Boutin's DNA. When the consciousness transfer doesn't quite take, Dirac is handed off to a battalion for routine but closely monitored training. Just when Dirac is getting comfortable with his own identity, however, Boutin's memories kick in, and Dirac and his team are summarily dispatched to an enemy planet to capture Boutin and solve the mystery of his treason before humanity is destroyed." Booklist

"The premise of a schizophrenic soldier allows Scalzi to explore the essence of conciousness and the ways in which it is shaped and influenced by memory, experience, and the individual's intrinsic personality. Combine that with good battle scenes, clever storytelling, and the ability to juggle abstruse scientific principles without breaking a sweat, and it makes for an impressive piece of work." Philadelphia Inquirer

Old man's war. Tor 2005 316p

ISBN 0-765-30940-8   LC 2004-57953

"With his wife dead and buried, and life nearly over at 75, John Perry takes the only logical course of action left him: he joins the army. Now better known as the Colonial Defense Force (CDF), Perry's service-of-choice has extended its reach into interstellar space to pave the way for human colonization of other planets while fending off marauding aliens. The CDF has a trick up its sleeve that makes enlistment especially enticing for seniors: the promise of restoring youth. After bonding with a group of fellow recruits who dub their clique the Old Farts, Perry finds himself in a new body crafted from his original DNA and upgraded for battle, including fast-clotting 'smartblood' and a brain-implanted personal computer." Booklist

"The story obviously resembles such novels as Starship Trooper and Time Enough for Love, but Scalzi is not just recycling classic Heinlein. He's working out new twists, variations that startle even as they satisfy. The novel's tone is right on target, too—sentimentality balanced by hardheaded calculation, know-it-all smugness moderated by innocent wonder." Publ Wkly

Scarborough, Elizabeth Ann

(jt. auth) McCaffrey, A. Acorna's people
(jt. auth) McCaffrey, A. Acorna's rebels
(jt. auth) McCaffrey, A. Acorna's search
(jt. auth) McCaffrey, A. Acorna's triumph
(jt. auth) McCaffrey, A. Acorna's world

Schaefer, Jack Warner, 1907-1991

The collected stories of Jack Schaefer; with an introduction by Winfield Townley Scott. Houghton Mifflin 1966 520p o.p.

Contents: Major Burl; Miley Bennett; Emmet Dutrow; Sergeant Houck; Jeremy Rodock; Cooter James; Kittura Remsberg; General Pingley; Elvie Burdette; Josiah

Schaefer, Jack Warner, 1907-1991—*Continued*

Willett; Something lost; Leander Frailey; Jacob; My town; Old Anse; That Mark horse; Ghost town; Takes a real man; Out of the past; Hugo Kertchak, builder; Prudence by name; Harvey Kendall; Cat nipped; Stalemate; Nate Bartlett's store; Salt of the earth; One man's honor; The old man; The coup of Long Lance; Enos Carr; The fifth man; Stubby Pringle's Christmas

"The author's mastery of narrative technique, his excellent character development, and his consistently concise description combine in avoiding the unfortunate aspects of typical 'Western' fiction and melodrama." Libr J

Monte Walsh. Houghton Mifflin 1963 501p o.p.

This novel of the old West follows Monte from runaway boy to trail hand, to topnotch cowhand and bronc buster, to aging saddle bum and encompasses the rise, the peak and the eventual collapse of the open range

"His characters seem real, and, according to the author, the characters and the episodes are based upon historical accounts. This is not just another 'Western.' It is worthy of a place alongside the writing of Will James and Eugene Manlove Rhodes." Libr J

Shane; [by] Jack Schaefer; illustrated by John McCormack. Houghton Mifflin 1954 214p il $18

ISBN 0-395-07090-2

*

Illustrated edition of the title first published 1949

"Wyoming in 1889 is the scene of conflict between cattlemen and homesteaders when Shane mysteriously disappears. He works hard as a hired hand for the Starrett family, and young Bob Starrett grows to love him, unaware that he is a feared gunfighter escaping his past." Shapiro. Fic for Youth. 3d edition

Schickler, David

Sweet and vicious. Dial Press 2004 242p $23

ISBN 0-385-33568-7   LC 2004-47830

"Sexy and willful, Grace McGlone is saving herself for the right man. When Henry Dante pulls into the small Wisconsin town where she works at the car wash, she instantly knows he's the one. He knows it too. But when Grace discovers Henry has 'The Planets'—a stolen set of famous Spanish diamonds—stashed in the back seat of his truck, she's having none of it. She's 'trying for heaven,' and the ill-gotten jewels must go. And so they do, in a race across the American landscape from Chicago to Yellowstone, pursued by a savage gangster obsessed by the diamonds he thought were his." Publisher's note

"Schickler is a rare find; with straightforward and yet deeply insightful writing, he mixes love, violence, ardor, and humor in this funny and heartbreaking modern-day fable." Booklist

Schine, Cathleen

The love letter. Houghton Mifflin 1995 257p o.p.

LC 95-5202

"One summer morning in her 41st year, Helen MacFarquhar, the divorced owner of an audaciously pink bookstore in an exclusive Connecticut shore town, finds a mysterious letter in her mail. Addressed 'Dear Goat,' and signed 'As Ever, Ram,' it is a love letter of such intensity and passion that she becomes obsessed by its ur-

gently suggestive message. The effect of that letter on Helen's orderly life is the burden of this comedy of manners." Publ Wkly

"As light, and as risky, as a soufflé, The Love Letter indulges an enchanting fantasy, while invoking the powerful interplay of language and love. Literature, Schine suggests, can make booksellers glamorous, can ignite passion in the most unlikely of settings, and can even allow doomed love to live on." N Y Rev Books

The New Yorkers; with drawings by Leanne Shapton. Farrar, Straus and Giroux 2007 290p il $24

ISBN 978-0-374-22183-6; 0-374-22183-9

LC 2006-32711

"An ensemble novel centered on an Upper West Side street. Jody, a lonely 39-year-old musician/music teacher who's lived in the same rent-controlled studio since college, rescues a pit bull mix named Beatrice from the ASPCA. After eight months of blissful pet ownership, Jody bumps into divorced 50-year-old Everett while walking Beatrice and falls in love with the stranger after he shoots her a smile. George, a 28-year-old waiter, moves into the neighborhood when his younger sister, Polly, rents an apartment in Everett's building and acquires the puppy left behind by the last tenant. . . . Down the street live Simon, a reclusive social worker whose only joy in life is foxhunting, and Doris, an embittered, prep-school guidance counselor with no love lost for pooches. Orbits slowly begin to overlap as winter gives way to spring and then the summer of the 2003 blackout—an event that sends a few characters in unexpected directions." Publ Wkly

"A swift-moving, gently poignant romantic comedy of manners. . . . The breezy storytelling in The New Yorkers is deceptive: the novel offers more than a sweet story of puppy love. Schine strikes a rare, deeply personal, and very loving chord as she portrays the way these devoted pets elicit joy from the depressed (except once, when it's already too late) and humanity from the merciless, and inspire flirtations and encounters between the shy and monastic." Village Voice

Schlink, Bernhard

Homecoming; translated from the German by Michael Henry Heim. Pantheon Books 2008 260p $24; pa $14.95

ISBN 978-0-375-42091-7; 0-375-42091-6; 978-0-375-72557-9 (pa); 0-375-72557-1 (pa)

LC 2007-16121

Original German edition, 2006

"The novel opens with Peter Debauer's reminiscences of being sent alone to visit his paternal grandparents in Switzerland during his boyhood summer holidays. . . . Peter's grandparents edit a pulp fiction series called 'Novels for Your Reading Pleasure and Entertainment.' They send him home with bound galleys as scrap paper, making him promise not to read the stuff. Inevitably, he sneaks a peak. The first manuscript he reads is a homecoming story sprinkled with allusions to 'The Odyssey.' It's about a German soldier who escapes from a Russian POW camp and makes his way home to find his wife with a new husband and daughter. To Peter's frustration, the last pages of the novel are missing. The omission triggers an obsessive quest to discover who wrote this

Schlink, Bernhard—*Continued*
book set in the precise geography of his early childhood
and to learn what happens after the soldier rings his
wife's doorbell." Los Angeles Times Book Rev

This is "an exceedingly delicate meditation on the German past that refuses to moralize. Decent people can be
driven to do the devil's work, just as truly moral verdicts
can result in unimaginable collateral damage: Debauer
witnesses both of these." N Y Sun

The reader; translated from the German by Carol Brown Janeway. Pantheon Bks. 1997 218p $20
ISBN 0-679-44279-0

* LC 97-1511

Original German edition, 1995
"In post WW II Germany, a teenage boy is seduced by
a streetcar conductor twice his age who insists that he
read to her before they make love. Years later, when he
is a law student, she appears as a defendant on trial for
war crimes during the Nazi era. This novel raises provocative questions about guilt and responsibility, as well
as the power of literature to heal and bind." Publ Wkly

Self's punishment; [by] Bernhard Schlink and
Walter Popp; translated from the German by Rebecca Morrison. Vintage Books 2005 248p pa $14
ISBN 0-375-70907-X   LC 2004-57166
This mystery features former Nazi prosecutor turned
investigator Gerhard Self. "It's the early 1980s, and Self
has been hired by a boyhood friend to smoke out a hacker who's playing havoc with the computers at Rhineland
Chemical Works. But after Self springs a trap that gets
the troublemaker murdered, he gradually faces the guilt
he still carries for his youthful embrace of National Socialism. His simple refusal to let himself off the hook
and step back into his old public prosecutor's role after
the war doesn't seem like penance enough anymore. . . .
Self's unwitting participation in the new crime drives
him to pursue the path of justice wherever it may lead.
A fascinating exploration of how people often manage to
carve out normal lives even after being complicit in terrible acts." Booklist

Schmitz, Ettore *See* Svevo, Italo, 1861-1928

Scholz, Carter

The amount to carry; stories. Picador 2003 208p
$23
ISBN 0-312-26901-3   LC 2002-192667
Contents: The eve of the last Apollo; A catastrophe
machine; Blumfeld, an elderly bachelor; The menagerie
of Babel; A draft of Canto CI; Altamira; Travels; At the
shore; The nine billion names of God; Invisible ink;
Mengele's Jew; The amount to carry
"In each keenly meta-physical fable Scholz, a connoisseur of the imagination, parses the language of science,
literature, art, and music as he ponders the
quintessentially human habit of telling stories, a valiant
attempt to render sense out of the delirium of existence."
Booklist

Radiance. Picador 2002 388p $24
ISBN 0-312-26893-9

* LC 2001-56018

"It is the mid-1990s, and the press has just learned that
a recent demonstration of a missile interception system
was rigged. Leo Highet, the Machiavellian director of a
California defense lab, is forced from his position and replaced by his rival Philip Quine, a closet peacenik." Libr
J

"Wickedly satiric and eggheaded in its level of scientific detail, 'Radiance' is a serious, engrossing novel." N
Y Times Book Rev

Schulberg, Budd

Waterfront; a novel. Random House 1955 320p
o.p.

*

"The prize-winning screen play 'On the waterfront' has
been expanded into a novel which differs on several
counts from the film. It remains an angry indictment of
racketeering in the labor unions along the New Jersey
waterfront, but the happy ending of the screen play has
been supplanted by a tragic one, in which the hero Terry
Malloy is murdered by the henchmen of Johnny Friendly, the labor racketeer, and the terrorism along the waterfront continues. The more leisurely framework of the
novel form permits the author to document to the full the
abuses in longshoremen's unions, without sacrificing the
explosive force of the film." Booklist

What makes Sammy run? Modern Lib. 1941
303p o.p.

*

"The protagonist, Sammy Glick, is a tough New York
youth who works his way into a position of power in the
motion-picture industry, where his harshness and crude
manners are not out of place." Benet's Reader's Ency of
Am Lit

Schulze, Ingo, 1962-

New lives; the youth of Enrico Türmer in letters
and prose; edited and with commentary and foreword by Ingo Schulze; translated from the German
by John E. Woods. Alfred A. Knopf 2008 570p
$28.95
ISBN 978-0-307-26559-3; 0-307-26559-5
     LC 2008-19615
Original German edition, 2005
"All his life Türmer has wanted nothing so much as to
write a novel, to pour experience onto the page and
make it ripple. . . . But he never manages to create a
shaped and formed work. The only writing he produces
is a series of long letters about his agonies to his sister,
friends, and love interests. As it happens, all of Türmer's
letters are all composed in the first half of 1990, in the
months between the fall of the Berlin Wall and the reunification of East and West Germany – a strange era,
at once a kind of twilight and a dawn. Despite his failure
to write a novel, when Türmer rereads these letters, he
finds his literary aspirations renewed. . . . He believes
he now has the material for an epistolary novel in his
hands, a work that will 'essentially write itself.' It is
these letters, with their mixture of ambition and naiveté,
that are presented to us in 'New Lives' as collected and
annotated by a skeptical but fastidious literary scholar
named Ingo Schulze." Christ Sci Monit
"Throughout, Schulze captures something ephemeral
but critical about how the idealism that brought down the
Wall also brought down itself." Publ Wkly

Schupack, Deborah

The boy on the bus; a novel. Free Press 2003 215p $23

ISBN 0-7432-4220-3 LC 2002-32179

"One afternoon, Vermont housewife Meg discovers that the boy on the school bus outside her door is almost, but not quite, her eight-year-old son, Charlie. . . . Meg's panic recalls her aloof, restless husband from his job in Canada and her bratty, rebellious teenage daughter from boarding school, but neither they nor the local sheriff nor the family doctor can verify Charlie's authenticity." Publ Wkly

"Motherhood with all its contradictions has rarely been shown so nakedly. Schupack gives us Meg's view and everyone else's in overlapping layers. . . . From beginning to end in this novel, nothing is ordinary, while at the same time everything is." N Y Times Book Rev

Schwartz, John Burnham

The commoner; a novel. Nan A. Talese 2008 351p $24.95

ISBN 978-0-385-51571-9; 0-385-51571-5

LC 2007-15391

This "novel fictionalizes the life of Haruko, empress of Japan, who narrates a touching and complicated tale of breaking traditions and facing the reality of living as royalty. Raised in an upper-class family, Haruko attends private school and plays tennis at the nearby country club. In 1959, she is selected as the first nonaristocratic woman to marry into the Japanese monarchy, which she discovers to be an oppressive world of mysterious rules and regulations. The strains caused by constant breaches in protocol and betrayals by the royal family and the staff cause Haruko to suffer a nervous breakdown and lose her voice. But she soon recovers with a new view of her duties and responsibilities. Thirty years later, Haruko is now the empress, and she faces the duty of marrying her son to a young woman who is a rising star in the foreign ministry." Libr J

"An American taking on a fictional memoir about a living Japanese empress is a gutsy move, but Schwartz makes it work. . . . While the external details of life in the palace remain stunning, it's Schwartz's grasp of [Haruko's] internal struggle that resonates after the last page is turned." Denver Post

Reservation Road; a novel. Knopf 1998 292p o.p.

LC 98-14580

This novel focuses on "two unhappy Connecticut families linked by one violent moment. The Learners are the victims of tragedy: an ordinary stop at a country gas station turns to horror when their oldest child is killed by a hit-and-run driver in full view of his father, Ethan. As his wife and small daughter suffer through grief, depression, and guilt, Ethan is consumed by his compulsion to find and punish his son's murderer after the police give up. Nearby, . . . Dwight Arno tortures himself with his memories of speeding away from the accident." Libr J

"The story is told in the alternating voices of father, mother and murderer, which overlap and swell to a crescendo in an operatic chorus of pain." Economist

Schwartz, Leslie, 1962-

Angels Crest; a novel. Doubleday 2004 303p $23.95

ISBN 0-385-51185-X LC 2003-64635

"Ethan Denton is out for a drive with his three-year-old son, Nate, in the woods of Northern California, when he decides to stop to follow several bucks he spots just off the road. When he returns 15 minutes later, his son is gone, and his own personal hell, as well as that of the small town of Angels Crest, is just beginning. Ethan's alcoholic ex-wife, Cindy, who lost custody of Nate; his former best friend, Glick, who slept with Cindy; Rocksan and Jane, a settled lesbian couple; and Jack, a lonely judge from outside the town are among those who help Ethan search for his son. . . . This beautiful, moving novel works brilliantly as a study of a tragedy and the various characters' reactions to the tragedy itself, as well as how it causes them to reexamine their own lives." Booklist

Schwartz, Lynne Sharon

Disturbances in the field. Harper & Row 1983 371p o.p.

* LC 83-47555

"Lydia is a chamber musician . . . Victor is an artist, and their life in Manhattan is at last coming together. Lydia revels in the individual personalities of her four children and of her best women friends from college (Barnard) with whom, as in the old days, she argues philosophy in the most sincere, least highbrow manner possible. But her two youngest children are killed in a bus crash, a tragedy so profound she doesn't know how to react. . . . Then Victor moves out to live with another woman, although neither he nor Lydia can totally divorce themselves from all they have shared together." Publ Wkly

"There are weighty passages and themes here, not for the casual reader. However, the journey from resignation to a grudging reaffirmation of living, of returning to the field, disturbs the reader's own field with its unmistakable ring of truth." Libr J

The fatigue artist; a novel. Scribner 1995 320p il $23

ISBN 0-684-80247-3 LC 94-48009

"Laura, the protagonist narrator, is a Manhattan woman suffering from Chronic Fatigue Syndrome (CFS), the catch-all diagnosis for a patchwork quilt of vague symptoms including weakness, tiredness, malaise, and muscle aches. Laura endures her increasingly debilitating illness while trying to cope with the violent death of her husband, the demands of two lovers, her complicated relationship with her stepchildren, the pressures of social obligations, and the stress of her writing career." New Leader

"Like Laura, Schwartz is a writer's writer, indulging in lavish description, then subverting clichés with succinct turns of phrase. Her dialogue is arrestingly urbane." Women's Rev Books

In the family way; an urban comedy. Morrow 1999 325p $24

ISBN 0-688-17071-4 LC 99-22134

Schwartz, Lynne Sharon—*Continued*

"The story takes place in an apartment building on New York's Upper West Side and centers on Roy, a psychotherapist; his first wife, Bea, a caterer; and their quest to preserve family. Bea's mother is the landlady of the building, and the tenants include Bea's lesbian sister, Bea's Russian lover, the superintendent, and Roy's second and current wife. In an attempt to keep her four children and their father together, Bea convinces Roy and his new wife to reside in her mother's building." Libr J

"A fast-paced, hugely entertaining novel about a group of people unwilling to compromise on their hopes for happiness." Booklist

The writing on the wall; a novel. Counterpoint 2005 297p $24

ISBN 1-582-43299-6   LC 2004-24877

Renata, this novel's protagonist, "is a secretive individual-and solitary, until boyfriend Jack comes into her life. On the morning of September 11, 2001, she is walking to work across the Brooklyn Bridge when the World Trade Center is attacked. It becomes clear in the days ahead that Renata cannot keep memories of her buried past-of a twin sister, a betrayal, of family truths too ugly to acknowledge-at bay." Publisher's note

This novel "would have been excellent already without its 9/11 ballast. It is full of intuitive dread, as if Joan Didion had written Play It As It Lays in the same Brooklyn boarding house where Norman Mailer was writing Barbary Shore." Harper's

Schwarz, Christina

All is vanity; a novel. Doubleday 2002 368p $24.95

ISBN 0-385-49972-8   LC 2002-67583

"This novel concerns a Manhattan schoolteacher named Margaret who quits and tries her hand at writing about something . . . far afield: the ennui of a Vietnam vet. . . . [Later] Margaret ditches Vietnam, and secretly bases her novel on her friend Letty's life. Letty's husband has a falshy new job at a museum in California, and the couple's been spending crazy money trying to seem less nouveau and more riche. Margaret encourages Letty to spend without end." Newsweek

"Schwarz's portrait of the talentless, self-absorbed Margaret is surgically accurate. . . . Anyone who has ever tried to write and been blocked will howl with recognition at the indignities that befall the novelist. . . . The novel is both a page turner and a cautionary tale of consumerism run amok." N Y Times Book Rev

Drowning Ruth. Doubleday 2000 338p $23.95
ISBN 0-385-50253-2   LC 00-29523

"In 1919, while serving as a nurse in a Milwaukee hospital for severely wounded soldiers, Amanda Starkey . . . goes home to rest at her parents' farm in rural Wisconsin. . . . The only people living there now are Matilda Neumann, Amanda's younger sister, and Mattie's three-year-old daughter, Ruth. Carl Neumann, the husband and father, is still recovering in France from his wartime injuries. And then, suddenly, Mattie too is dead, having fallen through the ice on a nearby lake and drowned." Time

"The vivid realism of the novel's setting adds depth to an already gripping plot. . . . Schwarz maintains her mystery with an expert hand, arriving at far more than a simple determination of guilt." N Y Times Book Rev

Schwarz-Bart, André, 1928-

The last of the just; translated from the French by Stephen Becker. Atheneum Pubs. 1960 374p o.p.

Original French edition, 1959

This novel "traces the martyrdom of the Jews through thirty-six generations of the Levy family, culminating with the death of Ernie in the Auschwitz concentration camp." Reader's Ency. 4th edition

"The thread that runs through the narration is the ancient Jewish tradition of the Lamed-Vov, according to which the world reposes upon 36 Just Men, who often are not aware themselves of the position they hold. . . . Harrowing as the book is, it is a valuable addition to the titles on the Holocaust, lest we forget how inhumane man can be." Shapiro. Fic for Youth. 3d edition

Schwegel, Theresa

Person of interest. St. Martin's Minotaur 2007 372p $24.95

ISBN 978-0-312-36426-7; 0-312-36426-1
                                      LC 2007-33535

"Chicago PD detective Craig McHugh is deep into an undercover investigation of a deadly batch of heroin allegedly being peddled by the Fuxi Spiders, a powerful Chinese gang. Hoping to gain their trust, Craig burns through his department allowance and his own funds playing at a Fuxi card game. Meanwhile, Craig's sullen teenage daughter, Ivy, is dragged home from a party by his police colleagues after being caught with ecstasy. Unaware of her husband's undercover assignment, Craig's wife, Leslie, is convinced he's having an affair, and she soon begins flirting with Ivy's handsome jazz-playing boyfriend." Publ Wkly

Schwegel "creates a portrait of a family in crisis, and her vivid characterizations — stressed husband, yearning wife, floundering daughter — lift the thriller plot of Person of Interest to literary-novel status." Entertainment Wkly

Scoppettone, Sandra, 1936-

Everything you have is mine. Little, Brown 1991 261p o.p.   LC 90-48889

"Lauren Laurano, a bighearted, wisecracking lesbian who makes her debut here as a Manhattan private eye, brings cunning as well as caring to her investigation of the murder of a young rape victim who might have met her killer by hooking into a dating service on her personal computer." N Y Times Book Rev

Gonna take a homicidal journey. Little, Brown 1998 229p $22.95

ISBN 0-316-77665-3   LC 97-44247

"While helping her life partner and friends renovate a beach place in a small Long Island town, private investigator Lauren Laurano becomes sidetracked by murder. Hired by the old-money cousin of a supposed suicide, Lauren soon detects a pattern that may include the deaths of several women and children. Each suspect she questions withholds crucial information; meanwhile, the idea of a police conspiracy grows. The wide-ranging, all-encompassing case may seem shallow or far-fetched, but Scoppettone's tongue-in-cheek attitude makes the book work." Libr J

Scoppettone, Sandra, 1936-—*Continued*

My sweet untraceable you. Little, Brown 1994
275p o.p.
LC 93-47426
"NYC lesbian private eye Lauren Laurano agrees to
search for the truth about an ex-con's mother who has
been presumed dead for 38 years." Libr J

"Scoppettone is a highly entertaining writer with her
fingers on current political and commercial pulses. So
she ably transmits the modish urban-grit feel of
Laurano's encounters with Manhattan's winos, weirdos,
and wise guys as she counterpoints the complex case her
sleuth is solving with the deterioration from AIDS of the
brother of Laurano's lesbian partner of 14 years."
Booklist

Scott, Alicia *See* Gardner, Lisa

Scott, Anne

Calpurnia. Knopf 2003 293p $24
ISBN 0-375-41380-4
LC 2002-30096
"Elizabeth Oliver is overseeing the sale of an estate
called Calpurnia, a large Philadelphia mansion once
owned by Maribel Archibald Davies, painter and self-
appointed bohemian. As Elizabeth gathers, organizes, and
catalogs the items of the estate, she finds herself drawn
into the family's intimate relationships as well as the
mysterious circumstances surrounding Maribel's death."
Booklist

"Scott sets the book in the 1980's, before online antique auctions and the advent of dot-com billionaires who
might have competed fiercely to buy a flashy old pile
like Calpurnia. Her central theme, however, the impulse
to make and live with art, is timeless." N Y Times Book
Rev

Scott, Joanna

Everybody loves somebody; stories. Back Bay
Books/Little, Brown and Co. 2006 260p $13.99
ISBN 978-0-316-01345-1; 0-316-01345-5
LC 2006-12310
Contents: Heaven and hell; Stumble; Worry; Freeze-
out; Across from the Shannonso; The Queen of Sheba is
afraid of snow; Yip; Everybody loves somebody; Or else
(parts I-IV); The lucite cane
A "collection of 10 stories that stalk across the 20th
century to document love and its consequences. . . .
Scott's craft can be breathtaking—and her perceptions
uncanny." Publ Wkly

Follow me; a novel. Little, Brown and Company
2009 420p $24.99
ISBN 978-0-316-05165-1; 0-316-05165-9
LC 2008-42643
Scott "traces the meandering path of a runaway girl
from place to place, name to name, starting as 16-year-
old Sally Werner in 1947 rural Pennsylvania. Her saga
begins with an innocent motorcycle ride with an older
cousin at a church picnic, which results in a baby son
and rejection by her fundamentalist parents. She decides
her only option is escape, following the Tuskee River
that snakes across the Werners' back fields. . . . Over
the next four decades, she washes up in towns farther
along the Tuskee, surviving on the kindness of strangers.

. . . Her many reincarnations are pieced together years
later by her granddaughter and a man who believes he
is the infant that Sally abandoned. Scott . . . excels in
her stream-of-consciousness descriptions of the mysterious Tuskee that provides Sally's true north." Washington
Post Book World

Tourmaline; a novel. Little, Brown 2002 279p
$23.95
ISBN 0-316-77618-1
* LC 2002-67111
"In 1956, extravagant, debt-ridden Murray Murdoch
takes his wife and four young sons on a vacation to
Elba, where he becomes convinced that he can profit
from the island's abundant deposits of semiprecious
gems. When the summer comes to an end and Murray
still hasn't found the valuable tourmaline that he's looking for, the Murdochs decide to postpone their departure
indefinitely. Their idyllic existence is shattered when a
mysterious local girl goes missing and the community
begins to suspect that the 'investor from the United
States' is somehow involved. The story is told by Ollie,
the youngest of the four boys, who was five when the
family arrived on the island and is 50 now." Publ Wkly

"Book reviewers are fond of calling belletristic novels
'poetic.' 'Tourmaline' isn't poetic because of its pretty
writing but because of its sympathetic ordering and reordering of ideas, its philosophical probing." N Y Times
Book Rev

Scott, Michael, 1959-
(jt. auth) Llywelyn, M. Silverlight

Scott, Paul, 1920-1978

The day of the scorpion; a novel. Morrow 1968
483p o.p.
This second volume of the Raj quartet tells the lives
of Sarah and Susan Layton, Lady Manners and Parvati;
Kasim and his two sons and Captain Merrick, all caught
up in the violence and strife that engulfed India when the
Congress Party adopted a resolution calling for a nationwide insurrection
The author's "ability in characterization and in realization of the love-hate relationship of Indian and Englishman are again amply demonstrated in a poignant story
constantly interest-holding." Booklist
Followed by The towers of silence

also in Scott, P. The Raj quartet

A division of the spoils; a novel. Morrow 1975
597p o.p.
In this concluding volume of The Raj quartet, the end
of the British rule in India is viewed primarily through
the eyes of Guy Perron, a young historian serving as a
sergeant in an army intelligence unit. The novel "spans
the pivotal years 1945-1947 just before India and Pakistan gained independence. Central to the plot is Ronald
Merrick, wounded, enigmatic colonel of the police whose
interference in the lives of members of the British Raj
. . . leads to cruelties as well as to revelations of individual responsibilities." Booklist

"Scott makes nothing simple; thus his work bears a
disturbing resemblance to life. He mixes up lovers,
friends, enemies, families, servants, strangers, soldiers,
businessmen, murders, suicides, illnesses in five or six
interrelated stories. . . . And all have one focus: corrupted British morality in India." N Y Times Book Rev

Scott, Paul, 1920-1978—*Continued*

also in Scott, P. The Raj quartet

The jewel in the crown; a novel. Morrow 1966 462p o.p.

This is the first volume of The Raj quartet

"Around a central incident of the rape of a young Englishwoman in an Indian garden in August, 1942, the author has woven a . . . picture of India before independence. The two main threads of plot are the fate of the raped girl and the tragic end of an elderly English school-teacher who is a very brave woman. There are other stories within the story. . . . This is a masterly narrative, a leisurely and skillful depiction of a wide Indian landscape and a large canvas showing people who are made very real. It is also a dissection of Anglo-British animosities." Publ Wkly

Followed by The day of the scorpion

also in Scott, P. The Raj quartet

The Raj quartet; introduction by Hilary Spurling. Alfred A. Knopf 2007 2v 1032p ea $32.50

ISBN 978-0-307-26396-4 (v1); 0-307-26396-7 (v1); 978-0-307-26397-1 (v2); 0-307-26397-5 (v2)

LC 2007-277260

"Everyman's library"

Contents: v. 1 The jewel in the crown; The day of the scorpion v2 The towers of silence; A division of the spoils

Staying on; a novel. Morrow 1977 215p o.p.

* LC 77-1491

"After India succeeds in obtaining independence from Britain, Tusker and Lucy Smalley, part of the British colonial army, stay on in the country where almost all their married life has been spent. The book describes their relationships with the Indians who, at this point, constitute all of their daily and social contacts. . . . There is humor in the informative portrayals of the relationships between the British and the Indians, and the final scene is as simple and moving a description of loss as has ever been written." Shapiro. Fic for Youth. 3d edition

The towers of silence; a novel. Morrow 1972 c1971 392p o.p.

First published 1971 in the United Kingdom

In the third volume of the Raj quartet "attention focuses on Barbara Batchelor, the retired mission-school teacher, and many, but not all, of the events are seen through her eyes. This time the Manners case and Congress leader Mohammed Ali Kasim are relegated to the background, but the earlier reported activities of Mildred Layton and her daughters, Teddie Bingham, Captain Merrick, and others are repeated." Libr J

"This elegy on the decline and fall of the Indian empire sounds harsh notes, but is moving as well. Mr. Scott has the trick of being sympathetic without ever losing his clear sightedness." Times Lit Suppl

Followed by A division of the spoils

also in Scott, P. The Raj quartet

Scott, Sir Walter, 1771-1832

The bride of Lammermoor; edited by J.H. Alexander. Columbia Univ. Press 1995 398p $44.50

ISBN 0-231-10572-X   LC 96-143055

First published 1819

"The most tragic of Scott's romances, on which Donizetti's opera 'Lucia di Lammermoor' is based. The last scion of a ruined family and the daughter of his ancestral enemy in possession of the estates fall in love. For a while there is a glimpse of hope and happiness; but the ambitious mother opposes the match, prophecies and apparitions prognosticate tragedy, and the romance closes in death and sorrow. . . . Caleb Balderstone, the faithful retainer, is one of Scott's humorous creations, whose obstinate care for his unhappy master relieves the overpowering tragedy." Baker. Guide to the Best Fic

Ivanhoe; a romance. Modern Lib. 1997 xxxvii, 535p $16

ISBN 0-679-60263-1

* LC 96-48579

First published 1819

"The action occurs in the period following the Norman Conquest. The titular hero is Wilfred, knight of Ivanhoe, the son of Cedric the Saxon, in love with his father's ward Rowena. Cedric, however, wishes her to marry Athelstane, who is descended from the Saxon royal line and may restore the Saxon supremacy. The real heroine is Rebecca the Jewess, daughter of the wealthy Isaac of York, and a person of much more character and charm than the mild Rowena. Richard the Lion-Hearted in the guise of the Black Knight and Robin Hood as Locksley play prominent roles." Reader's Ency. 4th edition

Rob Roy; with an introduction by Eric Anderson. Knopf 1995 xliii, 494p $20

ISBN 0-679-44362-2

*

"Everyman's library"

First published 1817; first Everyman's library edition 1906

"Full of intrigue with political overtones, it is set in northern England just before the Jacobite rebellion of 1715, and it is considered one of the author's masterpieces. Francis Obaldistone, the novel's hero, contends with his jealous, unscrupulous cousin Rashleigh for the hand of the beautiful Diana Vernon. Aided by the Scottish outlaw Rob Roy (based on a historical Jacobite outlaw), Francis succeeds in exposing Rashleigh's villainy." Merriam-Webster's Ency of Lit

Scott, Warwick, 1920-1995

For works written by this author under other names see Hall, Adam, 1920-1995

Scottoline, Lisa

Dead ringer. HarperCollins Pubs. 2003 339p $25.95

ISBN 0-06-051493-0   LC 2002-191931

A "legal caper featuring the lady lawyers of series heroine Bennie Rosato's Philadelphia law firm Rosato and Associates. This time out it's Bennie playing the lead role, as she fights to save her financially sinking firm; mother her lovable partners, Mary DiNunzio and Judy Carrier; solve the murder of a valuable client; and battle her evil twin, Alice. . . . Bennie grows on you, and soon enough you're rooting for the home team and laughing at her corny jokes." Publ Wkly

Killer smile. HarperCollins 2004 358p $25.95

ISBN 0-06-051495-7   LC 2003-67650

Scottoline, Lisa—*Continued*

In this installment in the "series starring the all-female Philadelphia law firm of Rosato & Associates, young Mary DiNunzio takes center stage. Mary has taken on a pro bono case representing her 'peeps' an Italian American business group (the circolo) working on behalf of the estate of Amadeo Brandolini, who committed suicide while interned during World War II. The estate seeks reparations, and Mary feels drawn to the case, so much so that others fear she's obsessed with it. Under the guise of taking a vacation, Mary visits the site of the internment camp in Montana where Amadeo killed himself and finds herself with still more unanswered questions. Interesting author's notes at the end of this engaging drama disclose Scottoline's own discovery of her grandparents' internment, lending this unusual story a welcome authenticity." Booklist

Legal tender. HarperCollins Pubs. 1996 291p
o.p.   LC 96-7165

The protagonist of this legal thriller is Philadelphian Bennie Rosato "a ravishing six-foot blonde, one of two partners in a thriving law firm. In quick order, the foundations of her world come crashing down. Her partner and ex-lover, Mark, turns up murdered shortly after he tells Bennie that he is planning to dissolve the partnership. It's not surprising that she then becomes the cops' prime suspect. When the murder weapon is found in her apartment, Bennie goes underground. Then a drug company CEO is killed, and she is falsely accused of that death, too." Publ Wkly

Mistaken identity. HarperCollins Pubs. 1999 480p $24
  ISBN 0-06-018747-6   LC 98-43200

In this legal thriller "maverick lawyer Bennie Rosato must defend a woman claiming not only to have been framed for a murder by the Philadelphia police but also to be Bennie's long-lost identical twin sister. Rosato is shocked when she meets the woman, who turns out to look just like her; and as she unfolds the questionable and mysterious circumstances surrounding the case, Rosato reveals level after level of corruption." Booklist

Scottoline "succeeds in creating a brisk, multilayered thriller that plunges Rosato & Associates into a maelstrom of legal, ethical and familial conundrums, culminating in an intricate, dramatic and intense courtroom finale." Publ Wkly

Moment of truth. HarperCollins Pubs. 2000 358p
  ISBN 0-06-019609-2   LC 99-89325

"Lawyer Jack Newlin faces his most difficult assignment when he has to convince the police to accept his confession to a crime he didn't commit. Coming home to find his wife stabbed to death, Jack assumes the killer is their 16-year-old daughter, a super model who had recently announced her pregnancy. To insure his conviction, he hires novice lawyer Mary Di Nunzio to defend him. Not only does Mary develop a crush on him but she also is determined to prove him innocent." SLJ

"Sharp, funny characters, crafty plot twists, and a flavorful depiction of high- and lower-middle Philadelphia society will keep readers riveted to this tense, often mischievous page-turner." Publ Wkly

Rough justice. HarperCollins Pubs. 1997 344p
o.p.   LC 97-5810

"During the biggest snowstorm in the history of Philadelphia, the jury is out. The defense is confident of a verdict of not guilty, but then client Elliot Steere admits to his council that he is a murderer. Marta Richter does not take this revelation happily. In fact, she's so outraged that she wants her client's secret revealed no matter what it does to her career. Steere isn't about to let her blow his chances, and with powerful connections, money, and muscle, he works from his jail cell to silence Marta and her colleagues before the sequestered jury makes a decision." Libr J

"Scottoline deftly balances the varied personalities of the women and manages a large cast, including judge and jury, with precision. She skillfully depicts personal quirks that give her characters dimension." Publ Wkly

The vendetta defense. HarperCollins Pubs. 2001 390p
  ISBN 0-06-018507-4   LC 00-50556

A legal yarn featuring Judy Carrier of Philadelphia's all-female firm of Rosato & Associates. The plot "revolves around Anthony 'Pigeon Tony' Lucia, a lovable septuagenarian who killed his longtime rival, Angelo Coluzzi, who murdered Lucia's wife in their native Italy 60 years ago. Coluzzi, the wealthy, mob-connected owner of a big construction firm, always seems to get the upperhand-until Pigeon Tony breaks his neck during a showdown at the pigeon-racing club where they're both members. Pigeon Tony freely admits he killed Coluzzi, but maintains he was justified because of the longstanding Italian tradition of vendetta; Carrier knows it will be a big stretch to make that argument fly before a 21st-century American jury." Publ Wkly

Scudder, Bernard, 1954-2007

(tr) Arnaldur Indriðason. The draining lake

Searles, John

Boy still missing. Morrow 2001 292p
  ISBN 0-688-17570-8   LC 00-40758

"It is 1971, and one of 15-year-old Dominick Pindle's regular activities is a game of sorts—the game is less funny to his mother—that he calls Find-Father-First. The key is to spot his father's truck and then pull him out of whatever bar he's drinking in. Life has become increasingly difficult for this Massachusetts family; Dominick's father carries on with another woman, his mother becomes involved with a police officer, and a bizarre accidental death leads Dominick—through a series of twisted circumstances—to kidnap a child in Manhattan." N Y Times Book Rev

"Searles builds suspense and excitement with surprising turns of plot weaving back into one another, and while many of the secondary characters lack depth, Dominic Pindle will resonate with readers." Booklist

Sears, Michael *See* Stanley, Michael

Sebald, W. G. *See* Sebald, Winfried Georg, 1944-2001

Sebald, Winfried Georg, 1944-2001

Austerlitz; [by] W.G. Sebald; translated by Anthea Bell. Random House 2001 298p il $25.95

ISBN 0-375-50483-4

* LC 2001-19785

"The unnamed narrator met Austerlitz, an architectural historian, in Belgium in the '60s, then lost track of his friend in the '70s. When they accidentally run into each other in 1996, Austerlitz tells the story that occupies the rest of the book—the story of Austerlitz's life. For a long time, Austerlitz did not know his real mother and father were Prague Jews. . . . While exploring the Liverpool Street railroad station in London, Austerlitz experiences a flashback of himself as a four-year-old. Gradually, he tracks his history, from his birth in Prague to a cultivated couple through his flight to England, on the eve of WWII, on a train filled with refugee children." Publ Wkly

"As so often in Sebald's fiction, direct connections are never highlighted in the vast loops and sudden knottings of his rhetoric, but the reader cannot escape the inference that in the long sweep of history the Nazis were not alone, but that an inquirer searching for meaning is." NY Times Book Rev

The emigrants; [by] W.G. Sebald; translated by Michael Hulse. New Directions 1996 237p il $22.95

ISBN 0-8112-1338-2   LC 96-22223

Original German edition, 1995

The four fictional "accounts/reports/reminiscences tell of . . . people who left Germany in the 20th century. Three are about Jews who went to England or Switzerland—either in the 1930s or before WW I—die or commit suicide long after WW II, but who, nonetheless, are victims of the Holocaust. One is about the narrator's non-Jewish great uncle, who went to America at the turn of the century, led an adventuresome life, and died a horrible death in the 1950s." Choice

"A profound and original work . . . . W. G. Sebald has created an end-of-century meditation that explores the most delicate, most painful, most nervously repressed and carefully concealed lesions of the last hundred years. Illuminatingly engaged with the history and literature of the modern era, Mr. Sebald's book gains power through its poetic obsessions with the past." N Y Times Book Rev

Vertigo; [by] W.G. Sebald; translated by Michael Hulse. New Directions 2000 263p il $23.95

ISBN 0-8112-1430-3

* LC 99-58955

Original German edition published 1990; this translation first published 1999 in the United Kingdom

"The first-person narrator travels through Europe during the 1980s, spurred on by history's ghosts and his own melancholic yearning for adventure. Having left his base in England to explore Vienna, Venice and Verona, he concludes with a bittersweet pilgrimage to his hometown in southwestern Germany. In four nonlinear chapters, the narrator sustains himself along his journey by establishing parallels with places and personages throughout history." Publ Wkly

"W.G. Sebald is unusual for a literary star. He fuses genres (travelogue, biography, the novel, meditation, myth), confounding the categories most readers are used to. The narrator of 'Vertigo' offers a fair account of Mr. Sebald's intricate methods. . . . This is poetic or philosophical fiction for readers content to follow the path of a remarkable author's thoughts without the guard-rail of an overarching story." Economist

Sebold, Alice

The almost moon; a novel. Little, Brown and Co. 2007 291p $24.99

ISBN 978-0-316-67746-2; 0-316-67746-9

LC 2007-09917

"In a moment of panic, Helen Knightly kills her dementia-ridden mother. Appalled but not apologetic, Helen spends the next 24 hours pondering the chain of events that led her to this choice." Libr J

This novel is "brilliantly paced, it's brutally honest, and the Gordian knot at its core— an abusive mother and her traumatically attached daughter — is depicted with such generous intelligence that the fineness of the novel more than surpasses its own horror show of circumstance. Sebold has managed to give us a sympathetic protagonist who smothers her mother in the opening pages, and yet the decades that led up to this black moment are delivered without a shred of sentimentality or melodramatic overkill. It's a tightrope walk of character building." Boston Globe

The lovely bones. Little, Brown 2002 328p $21.95; pa $13.95

ISBN 0-316-66634-3; 0-316-16881-5 (pa)

* LC 2001-50622

Sebold's "heroine, 14-year-old Suzy Salmon, is murdered in the first chapter, on her way home from school. Suzy narrates the story from heaven, viewing the devastating effects of her murder on her family." Booklist

"As pleasant as Susie's heaven is, there's no God there, and certainly no Jesus. This is spirituality for an age that's ecumenical to a fault. But emotionally, it's faultless. Sebold never slips as she follows this family. The risks she walks are enough to give you vertigo." Christ Sci Monit

Sedia, Ekaterina

Alchemy of stone. Prime 301p pa $12.95

ISBN 978-0-8095-7284-7; 0-8095-7284-2

This "steampunk fable about the price of industrial development, follows Mattie, an emancipated automaton, as her home city is rent by conflict between alchemists and the mechanics whose clanking, steaming inventions are changing society. Though created by a leader of the mechanics, Mattie chose to join the alchemists, but her creator still holds the key that winds her up. When a terrorist bombing and an assassination touch off all-out war between the two factions, she discovers the ugly secrets and exploitation that keep the city supplied with food and coal. Sedia's exquisitely bleak vision deliberately skewers familiar ideas from know-it-all computers to talking statues desperate for souls." Publ Wkly

See, Carolyn

The handyman. Random House 1999 220p $22.95

ISBN 0-375-50155-X

* LC 98-21098

See, Carolyn—*Continued*

"Bob Hampton, a future great artist, leads a quintessentially California life as a freelance handyman before he answers his true calling; in the course of a hot Los Angeles summer, he worries about his lack of aesthetic sophistication, comforts lonely housewives in the time-honored way, and rescues a drowning child and an AIDS patient. Despite a confusing start, the novel quickly takes on the brightness of a sun-dazzled swimming pool and makes a case for shadowless living—a state its hero achieves through an unlikely combination of application and hedonism." New Yorker

There will never be another you; a novel. Random 2006 242p $24.95

ISBN 0-679-46317-8   LC 2005-44932

"Set in the UCLA Medical Center of the near future, [this novel] follows three generations of Californians as they struggle to live in a post-9/11 world amid the threat of bioterrorism. As the Los Angeles area weathers one medical crisis after another, the four protagonists of this . . . novel—a heartbroken widow, a poetry-loving gangbanger, an innocent coed, and a dermatologist recruited to a highly classified emergency response team—strive to define themselves within and outside the most significant relationships of their lives." Libr J

"Among the most potent and poignant new novels to address post-9/11 America. . . . It is potent because the sense of dread and unease that mark almost every moment in the book is palpable; it is poignant because See, who in previous books has proven eminently capable of skewering her characters when they misbehave, has such compassion for the largely villain-less ensemble that populates this tale." Washington Post Book World

See, Lisa

Dragon bones; a novel. Random House 2003 348p $24.95

ISBN 0-679-46320-8   LC 2002-24871

"The controversial construction of a massive dam on the Yangzi River is the backdrop for the latest adventures of Liu Hulan, inspector in the Ministry of Public Security in Beijing, and her husband, American lawyer David Stark." Publ Wkly

"Hulan and David must overcome their estrangement and work together to solve the crimes. In a land where bribery and corruption are the norm, there are many suspects. The novel flows beautifully, engaging readers in the mystery while gently introducing them to China's rich cultural history." Libr J

Peony in love; a novel. Random House 2007 284p $23.95

ISBN 978-1-4000-6466-3; 1-4000-6466-X   LC 2007-01623

"The sheltered daughter of a scholar in 17th-century China, Peony so loves the opera The Peony Pavilion that when she dies, she returns as a ghost to pursue her interest. She also manages to insinuate herself into her former fiance's new marriage." Libr J

This novel, "is—for the reader willing to venture a crucial suspension of disbelief—a complex period tapestry inscribed with the age-old tragedy of love and death and bordered round with vignettes from Chinese metaphysics, dynastic history and the intimate chamber tales of women's friendship and rivalry. . . . See is gifted with a lucid, graceful style and a solid command of her many motifs." N Y Times Book Rev

Shanghai girls; a novel. Random House 2009 314p $25

ISBN 978-1-4000-6711-4; 1-4000-6711-1   LC 2008-49245

"Pearl and May Chin are 'Beautiful Girls,' models in 1930s Shanghai whose images grace calendars and ads and who party with the young and restless in the Paris of Asia. But the party is soon over. . . . Their father sells them into arranged marriages with the sons of a Chinese family that emigrated to Los Angeles. The daughters rebel and literally miss the boat — until the Japanese attack on Shanghai in 1937 forces them on an Odyssean journey to America. In this moving historical novel, Lisa See explores her Chinese-American roots and those of the Chinese who headed to California in the early 20th century in hopes of a better life, only to find hardship and discrimination." USA Today

Segal, Erich, 1937-

Love story. Harper & Row 1970 131p o.p.

*

"Oliver is Harvard, rich, a big campus athlete. Jenny is a Radcliffe scholarship student in music from a poor Italian Catholic background. They meet, fall in love, and marry, even though the boy's father wants him to go to law school first. Jenny gives up a chance to study in Paris and works to put her young husband through law school—and they win out to the beginnings of a great life and promising career for him. Then tragedy steps in." Publ Wkly

"A very professionally crafted short first novel. The author makes no great claims of insight for his work. Indeed, the story is all on the surface. But it is funny and sad and generally recommended." Libr J

Followed by Oliver's story (1977)

Segal, Lore Groszmann

Shakespeare's kitchen; stories; [by] Lore Segal. The New Press 2007 225p $22.95

ISBN 978-1-59558-151-8; 1-59558-151-0   LC 2006-30107

Contents: Money, fame, and beautiful women; An absence of cousins; The talk in Eliza's kitchen; Garbage thief; At whom the dog barks; A gated community; Fatal wish; Other people's deaths; Reverse bug; Picnic; Mistral; Leslie's shoes; Yom Kippur card

"In Segal's world, a world where domestic tragedies occur against the backdrop of historic human cruelties, people tend to behave badly not out of a perverted sense of ambition or power but from a deep need for attachment and belonging. And so it's crucial that the book doesn't move in a straight line. The same people who are good are not good. The bad guys sometimes do decent things. The truth—surprise!—is nuanced, and so is the story, which doesn't end the way it seems to be heading." N Y Times Book Rev

Segerberg, Ebba

(tr) Mankell, H. One step behind

Seidensticker, Edward, 1921-2007

(tr) Mishima, Y. The decay of the angel

Seiffert, Rachel

Field study. Pantheon Books 2004 215p $19.95
ISBN 0-375-42259-5   LC 2003-66364
Contents: Field study; Reach; Tentsmuir sands; Dog
leg lane; Blue; Architect ; The late spring; The crossing;
Frances John Jones; Dimitroff; Second best
In this collection of stories, "all set primarily in Europe, we meet a variety of characters, among them an architect losing his grip on his profession and on reality,
a British soldier AWOL in World War II Italy, a
teenaged couple struggling with the reality of becoming
parents, and an American woman driving her elderly father-in-law to his former street in East Berlin. . . . This
is a fine collection from a young writer who displays a
modern Europe with its particular social and political issues amid universal human themes." Libr J

Self, Will

The Book of Dave; a revelation of the recent
past and the distant future. Bloomsbury Pub. 2006
495p $24.95
ISBN 0-670-91443-6   LC 2006-4750
"In this tale of an embittered taxi-driver whose psychotic rantings become the creed of a blighted people
hundreds of years after his death, Self unleashes his apparently boundless misanthropy on modern London, the
origins of religion, and the postapocalyptic future. Dave
Rudman, driven mad by divorce and ill-prescribed
antidepressants, thinks he is God and writes a vitriolic
screed, which he has printed on metal plates and buries
in a garden. Discovered by the survivors of a catastrophic flood and adopted as a gospel, it demands the complete separation of mothers and fathers (children to spend
exactly half the week with each). Switching between a
narrative of Dave's unlucky life and the phonetically rendered 'Mokni' speech of his wretched followers, Self
achieves an elaborate vision of vicious superstition and
hopeless struggle." New Yorker

Dorian; an imitation. Grove Press 2002 277p
$23
ISBN 0-8021-1729-5   LC 2002-29962
"In this retelling of Oscar Wilde's The Picture of Dorian Gray, most of the original's characters are cleverly
transmuted into their late-20th-century counterparts: dissolute Henry Wotton, now openly homosexual with a
nasty heroin habit; his protege, eager young video artist
'Baz' Hallward; and the title character, the quintessential
amoral narcissist. . . . Self uses Wilde's plot to examine
post-Stonewall gay life, from its drug-fueled hedonistic
excesses to the reckoning of the AIDs epidemic. The
novel skewers every layer of British society—street hus-
tlers, members of Parliament and the idle rich." Publ
Wkly

Selgin, Peter

Drowning lessons; stories. University of Georgia
Press 2008 235p (Flannery O'Connor Award for
Short Fiction) $24.95
ISBN 978-0-8203-3210-9; 0-8203-3210-0
LC 2008-20377

Contents: Swimming; The wolf house; Color of the
sea; Driving Picasso; Sawdust; Our cups are bottomless;
The girl in the story; The sea cure; Wednesday at the ba-
gel shop; El malécon; Boy B; The sinking ship man; My
search for red and gray wide-striped pajamas
"Whether as a force for life or one of destruction, water in all its forms is the unifying theme in writer and
artist Peter Selgin's powerful collection, Drowning Lessons. Selgin is never heavyhanded in his use of metaphor, and it's rewarding to trace the skill with which he
employs it in many of these 13 stories." BookPage

Seth, Vikram, 1952-

An equal music. Broadway Bks. 1999 380p $25
ISBN 0-7679-0291-2   LC 99-20421
As violinist Michael Holme "travels through Europe as
a member of a quartet, he reminisces about his lost love,
Julia McNicholl, a pianist. The former lovers are reunited, but the depth of their love and trust is put to the test
when Michael discovers that not only is Julia married
and the mother of a young son but that she is also going
deaf." Libr J
Seth's "writing is a throwback, freely romantic, wondrously out of date, totally unhedged. His book attempts
no cool, contains not a single pose. He can be playful
with language, though not distractingly so. . . . The
book is also stocked with humor, which appears when it
is most needed, as the story grows almost suffocatingly
sad." Natl Rev

A suitable boy; a novel. HarperCollins Pubs.
1993 1349p o.p.
* LC 92-54744
"Set in the post-colonial India of the 1950s, this
sprawling saga involves four families—the Mehras, the
Kapoors, the Chatterjis and the Khans—whose domestic
crises illuminate the historical and social events of the
era. Like an old-fashioned soap opera (or a Bombay talk-
ie), the multi-charactered plot pits mothers against daughters, fathers against sons, Hindus against Muslims and
small farmers against greedy landowners facing govern-
ment-ordered dispossession." Publ Wkly
This novel is, "at its heart an elegy as well as a comedy of manners, about a traditional society in a time of
change, and about a leisurely world of graces giving way
to a new, more democratic time." Times Lit Suppl

Seton, Anya, d. 1990

Avalon. Houghton Mifflin 1965 440p o.p.
"The romance is a deep lifelong attachment between a
wandering French prince, an idealistic, poetic man, and
a Cornish girl of peasant and Viking blood. The story
opens in a courtly, gentle mood which changes to fury,
lust and murderous greed when the scene shifts to the
English court, and to adventure and exploration when the
girl is captured by her father's people and the Vikings
take the center of the stage." Publ Wkly
"Late tenth- and early eleventh-century life in England
and in the lands colonized by the Norsemen [i.e. Iceland]
is re-created from early Anglo-Saxon chronicles, French
manuscripts, and secondary sources. . . . The action and
milieu are vivid and though the characterization is not
strong the psychological and historical motivations are
believable. An honest historical novel for enthusiasts of
the genre." Booklist

Seton, Anya, d. 1990—*Continued*

Dragonwyck. Houghton Mifflin 1944 336p o.p.

An American "Gothic" novel. The time is the 1830's and 1840's; the place, New York City and the great Van Ryn estate, Dragonwyck, on the Hudson. A young farm girl, a distant cousin of the Van Ryn's goes to live at Dragonwyck as governess to the Van Ryns' small daughter. At the death of the child's mother, Miranda becomes the second Mrs. Van Ryn. The story of Miranda's gradual horrified awakening follows

"For all its trappings and devices—and they are good, spine-chilling trappings, handled with considerable skill—the novel manages to have life and substance." NY Her Trib Books

Green darkness. Houghton Mifflin 1973 c1972 591p o.p.

First published 1972 in the United Kingdom

"Reincarnation is the theme of [this] . . . novel. A 16th-century Benedictine monk, Stephen Marsdon, falls prey to a consuming passion for alluring Celia de Bohun and forsakes his vows. The tragic end of the lovers, involving murder and suicide, brings, nearly 400 years later, madness and near death to their reincarnations, newlyweds Celia and Richard Marsdon. Fortunately, a Hindu doctor (himself a reincarnated Italian physician in Tudor England who longed for warmer climates) hovers nearby to monitor the proceedings and brings the souls to rest." Libr J

Katherine. Houghton Mifflin 1954 588p o.p.

Historical romance about the life of Katherine Swynford, sister-in-law of Geoffrey Chaucer, and mistress and later wife of John Gaunt

"It is a story that demands no intellectual or emotional effort from the reader. . . . But Miss Seton presents her facts accurately. Her research extends as far as visiting what remains of any of John of Gaunt's 30 castles and her zest for her subject communicates itself to the reader." San Francisco Chron

The Winthrop woman. Houghton Mifflin 1958 586p o.p.

In this biographical novel the author rallies to the defense of a maligned historical figure. "The young widow Elizabeth Winthrop was perhaps the most unwilling Puritan who ever came to New England, for she detested and feared Governor John Winthrop, who was her uncle as well as her father-in-law. A second marriage to Robert Feake, the governor's choice, dragged through years of Robert's increasing insanity; when he deserted her Elizabeth secured a divorce in New Amsterdam, contracted a common-law marriage with virile William Hallet, and found with him a love that was adequate recompense for exile and persecution." Booklist

"The novel is noteworthy for its insights into the Puritan 'Bible Commonwealth.'" Saturday Rev

Settle, Mary Lee

Charley Bland. Farrar, Straus & Giroux 1989 207p il

ISBN 0-374-12078-1   LC 89-207125

"Having fled the suffocating small-town environment of her West Virginia home and recreated herself as a writer in postwar Paris, the heroine of this condensed, lyric novel returns to discover that having dreams come true is sometimes disastrous. For there she again meets Charley Bland, the golden boy she worshiped as a child, now the town's most eligible–and elusive–bachelor. . . . The affair they begin quickly demolishes everything this woman had made of herself in the years she had been away." Libr J

This novel's "precision and emotional power urge one to listen ferociously for the hidden melodies that reveal the history underneath the social plottings, the story not just of people but of a world." N Y Times Book Rev

The killing ground. Farrar, Straus & Giroux 1982 385p

ISBN 0-374-18107-1

LC 82-2477

"In this novel, the last of the Beulah Quintet, Settle describes the various homecomings of Hannah McKarkle, a woman from an affluent West Virginia coal-mining family who has pursued a writing career in New York. In 1960, Hannah returns to find that her brother Johnny has been killed by a man who turns out to be a poor distant relative. The brother's death, the intricate interplay among classes in the closed rural society of West Virginia, and the inevitable pull of one's native home on the heart and soul are central to her subsequent visits in 1978 and 1980." Libr J

O Beulah Land; a novel. Viking 1956 368p o.p.

First published volume of the author's Beulah Quintet, set in rural West Virginia. Chronologically follows Prisons (1973). Subsequent titles in the series: Know nothing (1960); The scapegoat (1980) and The killing ground

Historical novel of the Virginia frontier from 1754 to 1775. "Jonathan Lacey is a strong man, as only a gentleman is strong. And he is a gentleman, by the standards of the Virginia wilderness country in the years preceding the American Revolution. After his service at the Battle of Little Meadows in 1775, Johnny scouts and surveys far into the mountains, and leads a heterogeneous group of early Americans westward with him, to claim and clear his bounty land in the undefended King's Part of the colony, beyond the Proclamation Line. It is on this land, called Beulah by Jeremiah the New Light preacher, that Johnny proves his strength." N Y Times Book Rev

Seymour, Gerald

The heart of danger. HarperCollins Pubs. 1995 358p

ISBN 0-06-100968-7   LC 95-4808

"Behind the lines in former Yugoslavia is a mass grave of victims of Serbian atrocities. The grave's excavation elicits a mystery: the body of Dorrie Mowat, a young British woman. What was Dorrie doing there, and why did she die? Britain's Security Service refers her anxious mother to ex-agent Bill Penn to investigate. As Penn draws closer to the truth, he enters the dangerous territory of Serbian warlord Milan Stankovic. Searching for evidence of war crimes, he puts life on the line by going into the war zone to try to bring Stankovic to justice." Libr J

"Using this wheels-within-wheels frame, Seymour con-

Seymour, Gerald—*Continued*

structs a harshly detailed novel about a dirty little war, peopled with a wide variety of deeply etched characters and suffused with a nearly palpable sense of despair and weariness." Publ Wkly

Killing ground. HarperCollins Pubs. 1997 390p o.p.   LC 96-51178

"Twenty-three-year-old Charlotte 'Charlie' Parsons is suffocating. Living at home with her parents in a small village in Cornwall, she sees no future except teaching snotty first-formers in the village primary. But excitement enters her life twice in one day. First, she receives a letter from Giuseppe and Angela Ruggerio, the Italian family Charlie worked for one wonderful summer. Will she come back to Italy and take care of the three Ruggerio children? To Charlie, it's a heaven-sent opportunity to escape. Later that day, she's visited by a coldly sinister American DEA agent named Axel Moen, who plans to use Charlie to reel in Mario Ruggerio, brother of Giuseppe and capo of the Sicilian Mafia. . . . A gripping thriller that leads to a shattering climax." Booklist

Rat run. Overlook Press 2007 240p $24.95
ISBN 978-1-58567-894-5; 1-58567-894-5
LC 2006-51533

"Malachy Kitchen loses his job with British intelligence and is reduced to living on the street, abandoned by family and friends, after an apparent act of cowardice during the current Iraq war. Rescued by a stranger who judges him worthy of another chance, Kitchen moves to a drug-wrecked, gang-infested London housing project. After failing to prevent the mugging of an elderly neighbor, Kitchen employs his professional expertise against the local gangs. Meanwhile, a local drug lord is directed by his Hamburg supplier to do something that will carry him into far more shadowy realms than the drug trade." Publ Wkly

"Seymour gives us two stories to follow: Malachy's pursuit of drug lord Ricky Capel and the saga of his gradual personal redemption. The pursuit story is intricate and suspenseful, as Seymour's many fans have come to expect; in the redemption story, he nimbly avoids most of the cliches associated with the type (it's probably not possible to avoid them all). A thriller with a human side." Booklist

Shaara, Jeff, 1952-

The glorious cause; a novel of the American Revolution. Ballantine Bks. 2003 638p $26.95
ISBN 0-345-42756-4   LC 2002-34240
Sequel to Rise to rebellion

This novel is "told from the perspectives of various historical players. George Washington is prominent, as are Benjamin Franklin, the under appreciated Nathanial Greene, and, intriguingly, Britain's Lord Cornwallis." Libr J

"This is vivid and compelling historical fiction, but also a primer on leadership and the arts of war and diplomacy. Shaara reaches new heights here, with a narrative that's impossible to put down." Publ Wkly

Gods and generals. Ballantine Bks. 1996 498p $25
ISBN 0-345-40492-0   LC 95-53360

This novel "focuses simultaneously on the lives of four men who played significant roles in the military side of the Civil War in battles leading up to the great one at Gettysburg. The novel follows Stonewall Jackson, Winfield Scott Hancock, Joshua Chamberlain, and Robert E. Lee from 1858 to 1863, giving the reader splendidly detailed witness to how the war drew them into commanding positions. As should be the case with good historical fiction, Shaara, in taking actual figures from the past, rekindles them; he uses the personal experiences of these four men to meaningfully explore the political and military issues of the day." Booklist

Gone for soldiers. Ballantine Bks. 2000 424p il
ISBN 0-345-42750-5   LC 00-22745

This novel of the Mexican-American War focuses on "then-Captain Robert E. Lee's induction into the mysteries of supreme command. The future rebel is first seen shelling the defenses of Vera Cruz in 1847. After the city falls, Lee bends an attentive ear to the leadership methods of his boss, General Winfield Scott. When not making mental notes of Scott's decision, Lee tends to think about duty, God, and country—but mostly duty." Booklist

"The book is simply wonderful, populated with eminently human heroes who are called upon to perform Herculean tasks in a war muddied beyond redemption by the ambitions of back-home and battlefield politicians." Libr J

The last full measure. Ballantine Bks. 1998 560p map $25
ISBN 0-345-40491-2   LC 97-49383

This volume follows "the course of the war in Virginia from Lee's retreat from Gettysburg to his surrender at Appomattox Court House. Ulysses S. Grant has come East to assume command of all Federal forces and to confront Lee, and the war they make is marked by such horrendous battles as The Wilderness and Spotsylvania. As characters, Grant and Lee dominate this book. . . . Civil War buffs will find Shaara nodding on some small details, but they generally will be delighted with this book." Libr J

Rise to rebellion. Ballantine Bks. 2001 492p $26.95
ISBN 0-345-42753-X   LC 2001-18448

"The first of two projected novels on the American Revolution, Rebellion takes the reader from the Boston Massacre to the signing of the Declaration of Independence." Libr J

"Making excellent use of a you-are-there approach, Shaara focuses on a handful of prominent historical figures, including Benjamin Franklin, George Washington, John and Abigail Adams, and British general Thomas Gage. . . . Shaara's novel gives historical figures flesh-and-blood viability." Booklist

The rising tide; a novel of the World War II. Ballantine Books 2006 xxxvi, 536p $27.95
ISBN 978-0-345-46141-4; 0-345-46141-X
LC 2006-42936

Shaara opens this first volume of a projected trilogy "in the deserts of North Africa, where Allied troops attempt to match wits and forces with the Desert Fox, wily German commander Field Marshall Erwin Rommel, and his formidable Afrika Korps. After Hitler overruns

Shaara, Jeff, 1952——*Continued*

France, solidifying his position in Western Europe, he turns his attention eastward toward the vast Russian expanse. With the German focus split, the Allies sense the time is right to launch a united second front in North Africa, setting their sights on an eventual invasion of southern Italy. As plans for Operation Torch become a reality, Shaara vividly recreates a cast of military and political heroes and villains, including General Dwight D. Eisenhower, General George Marshall, General George Patton, British general Bernard Montgomery, German field marshal Erwin Rommel, Adolf Hitler, Winston Churchill, and Franklin Roosevelt." Booklist

The steel wave; a novel of World War II. Ballantine Books 2008 xxvi, 493p map $28

ISBN 978-0-345-46142-1; 0-345-46142-8

LC 2008-4813

Sequel to The rising tide; this is the second volume of Shaara's World War II trilogy

This "epic-scale novel opens on January 25, 1944, with British commandos gathering soil samples on Omaha Beach to assess landing sites. Shaara gives the Americans, called the great waves of steel by the Germans, their due portion in the grisly, brutal Allied invasion, and the experiences of the grunt soldiers—most notably the indefatigable U.S. Army Sgt. Jesse Adams—offers a field-level view of D-Day and afterward, generating more suspenseful reading than the matter-of-fact accounts of the big-brass dealings of Eisenhower and Churchill. The Allied leaders' personalities emerge with agile clarity, while German Field Marshal Erwin Rommel embodies the good soldier laboring under a delusional Hitler and German High Command ensconced in cozy Berlin. Rommel's ambivalent complicity in the assassination plot on Hitler is convincingly rendered and paves the way for the final act. The muscular prose, deft sense of military drama and relentless pacing are well suited for this crackerjack saga." Publ Wkly

Shaara, Michael, 1929-1988

The killer angels; a novel. Random House 1993 374p il $24

ISBN 0-679-42541-1

* LC 92-38365

This is a fictionalized account of four days in July, 1863 at the Battle of Gettysburg. The point of view of the Southern forces is represented by Generals Robert E. Lee and James Longstreet, while Colonel Joshua Chamberlain and General John Buford are the focus for the North

"Shaara's version of private reflections and conversations are based on his reading of documents and letters. Although some of his judgments are not necessarily substantiated by historians, he demonstrates a knowledge of both the battle and the area. The writing is vivid and fast moving." Libr J

Shabtai, Yaakov

Uncle Peretz takes off; short stories; translated from the Hebrew by Dalya Bilu. Overlook Press 2004 239p $24.95

ISBN 1-585-67340-4

LC 2004-58316

Contents: Adoshem; Model; True tenderness; Uncle Shmuel; A marriage proposal; Past continuous; Cordoba; Twilight; The voyage to Mauritius; A private and very awesome leopard; Uncle Peretz takes off; The visit; Departure; The Czech tea service

"At their best, the stories in this collection . . . are masterful, ironically drawn character studies evoking the Israeli frontier spirit under the British mandate while capturing the shift from old world religiosity to new world secularism. Originally published in Hebrew in 1972, the collection is bookended by two linked stories chronicling the deaths of the narrator's grandparents and with them the loss of Jewish traditions." Publ Wkly

Shade, Eric, 1970-

Eyesores; stories. University of Ga. Press 2003 205p $24.95

ISBN 0-8203-2432-9

LC 2002-7151

Contents: Eyesores; Blood; The heart hankers; Superfly; A rage forever; Stability; Kaahumanu; A final reunion; Hoops and wires and plugs; The last night of the couonty fair; Souvenirs

A collection of stories set in a small Pennsylvania town. "Windfall, recently bypassed by a freeway, is losing its blue-collar jobs and shuddering toward new life as a destination for golfers. Residents are torn between the desire for and the fear of change. . . . Shade captures perfectly the way in which it's hard to leave your mistakes behind when you're surrounded by people who remember when you made them." Booklist

Shafak, Elif, 1971-

The bastard of Istanbul. Viking 2007 360p $24.95

ISBN 978-0-670-03834-3; 0-670-03834-2

LC 2006-42116

"The novel's ruling force is gorgeous Zeliha, the unapologetically sexy proprietor of an Istanbul tattoo parlor. An unwed mother at 19, she has raised her daughter, Asya (now 19 herself and obsessed with Johnny Cash), in a chaotic, food-centric household that includes her mother, grandmother, and three sisters: Banu, the pious clairvoyant; Cevriye, the high-strung history teacher; and Feride, the neurotic. The sisters haven't seen their Americanized brother, Mustafa, for almost 20 years, and are stunned when his 19-year-old stepdaughter, Armanoush, whose mother is from Kentucky and whose father is Armenian, arrives in Istanbul to search for her Armenian roots. As Asya and Armanoush forge a tentative friendship unaware of all that they actually share, others panic over the looming revelation of shocking secrets." Booklist

"Shafak's writing is seductive; each chapter of her novel is named for a food, and the warmth of the Turkish kitchen lies at the center of its wide-ranging plot. The Bastard of Istanbul portrays family as more than merely a function of genetics and fate, folding together history and fiction, the personal and the political into a thing of beauty." Elle

Shaffer, Mary Ann, 1934-2008

The Guernsey Literary and Potato Peel Pie Society; [by] Mary Ann Shaffer & Annie Barrows. The Dial Press 2008 277p $22

ISBN 978-0-385-34099-1; 0-385-34099-0

LC 2008-15477

The letters comprising this "novel begin in 1946, when single, 30-something author Juliet Ashton (nom de plume Izzy Bickerstaff) writes to her publisher to say she is tired of covering the sunny side of war and its aftermath. When Guernsey farmer Dawsey Adams finds Juliet's name in a used book and invites articulate—and not-so-articulate—neighbors to write Juliet with their stories, the book's epistolary circle widens, putting Juliet back in the path of war stories." Publ Wkly

"Juliet's ready wit is enchanting, as are the discussion of authors from Catullus to Shakespeare. . . . There is the occasional false note. . . . However, 'The Guernsey Literary and Potato Peel Pie Society' is a labor of love, and it shows on almost every page." Christ Sci Monit

Shakespeare, Nicholas, 1957-

Secrets of the sea. HarperPerennial 2008 c2007 402, 25p pa $14.95

ISBN 978-0-06-147470-5; 0-06-147470-3

LC 2007-41924

"An Ecco book"

First published 2007 in the United Kingdom

"Following the death of his parents in a car crash, eleven-year-old Alex Dove is torn from his life on a remote farm in Tasmania and sent to school in England. Twelve years on, he must return to Australia to deal with his inheritance. But the timeless beauty of the land and his encounter with a young woman, whose own life has been marked by tragedy, persuade him to stay. They marry, and he finds himself drawn into the eccentric, often hilarious dynamics of island life. Longing for children, the couple open their home to a disquieting guest, a teenage castaway, whose presence on the farm begins to unravel their tenuously forged happiness, while at the same time offering the prospect of a much greater fulfilment." Publisher's note

This is a "novel fundamentally interested in marriage that long-term investment in that capricious thing love. There will be gossip, there will be harvest, the weather will affect the bounty now and again, surprises will upset the whole enterprise and there will be the slog and beauty of routine, but, at bottom, the static commitment remains, and while reading 'Secrets of the Sea,' one wants to believe in it." San Francisco Chron

Snowleg. Harcourt 2004 386p $25

ISBN 0-15-101146-X

LC 2004-47543

"British student Peter Hithersay learns on his sixteenth birthday that his real father was an East German political prisoner, and his life is never the same. Developing an obsession with all things German, he opts to attend medical school in Hamburg. Lured to Leipzig by a theatrical troupe and his own desire to see the scene of his mother and father's brief tryst, he ends up falling in love with a willful, passionate young woman nicknamed Snowleg. But at a crucial moment in their relationship, he fails her. For the next 20 years, he struggles on all fronts, succumbing to drug addiction and a series of empty affairs. Shakespeare paints an especially chilling picture of the repressed lives of East Germans, one in which a young girl's straightforward declaration of love takes on near-heroic stature. A beautifully written, utterly compelling story of love and politics." Booklist

Shalev, Meir

A pigeon and a boy; translated from the Hebrew by Evan Fallenberg. Schocken Books 2007 311p $25

ISBN 978-0-8052-4251-5; 0-8052-4251-1

LC 2007-843

Original Hebrew edition, 2006

"Yair Mendelsohn, a middle-aged Israeli tour guide favored with bird watchers, learns that one of his new American clients fought in the Palmach, a clandestine military force in Israel's 1948 war of independence. The American recounts a day when a homing pigeon handler, nicknamed the Baby for his childlike features, was killed in that war and, in his final moments, sent off one last pigeon. Yair is familiar with the American's story and listens with wistfulness. As Yair slowly tells of his present and his past, Shalev patiently builds tension around the Baby's final dispatch, giving vivid detail on homing pigeons and conveying the unique relationship between the birds and their keepers—which echoes the touching care with which the Baby and his true love, the Girl, treat one another. The dark, stocky Yair, whose marriage is threatened by his burgeoning relationship with childhood friend Tirzah, makes a sympathetic protagonist. This gem of a story about the power of love, which won Israel's Brenner Prize, brims with luminous originality." Publ Wkly

Shalev, Tseruyah

Husband and wife; [by] Zeruya Shalev; translated from the Hebrew by Dalya Bilu. Grove Press 2002 311p $24

ISBN 0-8021-1718-X

LC 2001-58479

"Na'ama is a social worker who heals ailing young mothers and their children, though she is unable to turn an observant eye on the lives of her own husband and child, or herself. When her husband, Udi, a healthy hiking guide who periodically leaves the family for long, solitary jaunts into nature, wakes up one morning unable to move his legs, Na'ama begins an inner monologue, wrestling over whether to take him to a hospital. . . or whether to keep him at home, where she and their nine-year-old daughter Noga can finally have a constant relationship with him." Publ Wkly

Shalev, Zeruya *See* Shalev, Tseruyah

Shames, Laurence

Mangrove squeeze. Hyperion 1998 309p $22.95

ISBN 0-7868-6301-3

LC 97-35880

"The Russian mafia is alive and well in Key West, operating a string of T-shirt shops as a cover for their more nefarious activities. Selling advertising space for the local newspaper, Suki Sperakis meets Lazslo Kalynin, who in a fit of lust reveals too much about the real business he and his Russian cohorts are conducting. Because Suki knows too much Lazslo is ordered to kill her. On the other side of town, Suki has met Aaron Katz, a former

Shames, Laurence—*Continued*

New Yorker renovating a guest house while taking care of his aging father. . . . [Shames] has included his signature cast of geriatric zanies and organized-crime types doing what they do best—causing mayhem and hilarity in the seemingly calm, sun-drenched streets of Florida." Libr J

Virgin heat; a novel. Hyperion 1997 274p $21.95

ISBN 0-7868-6203-3   LC 96-26804

"Beautiful Angelina, the slightly strange daughter of a mobster just out of prison, runs away from home to find her true love, the now—Key West bartender who betrayed her father years earlier. Once in town, Angelina hooks up with simpatico gay Michael—also looking for love. Angelina's concerned favorite uncle soon arrives, as does a government agent keeping tabs on the bartender. And Angelina's vengeful father cannot be far behind." Libr J

"The plot of this slapstick caper, a gravity-defying structure of impossible coincidences, has been built for fun, not analysis. But into this raucous hilarity Mr. Shames sneaks some nice observations on fading mobsters." N Y Times Book Rev

Welcome to paradise; a novel. Villard Bks. 1999 220p $22.95

ISBN 0-375-50252-1   LC 98-50785

This "caper novel finds Big Al Marracotta, a low-level mobster, vacationing in Key West while his rival, an equally inept thug, plots to have him bumped off. Stumbling into the fray is a nerdy furniture salesman from New Jersey who happens to have the same 'Big Al' license plate as his mobster namesake. The hitmen naturally confuse their Als, and the chaos begins." Booklist

Shames "is both hilariously funny as well as insightful in his handling of his characters." Libr J

Shamsie, Kamila, 1973-

Kartography. Harcourt 2002 305p $24

ISBN 0-15-101010-2   LC 2003-4989

"Karachi, Pakistan's largest city, is a place under constant siege: ethnic, factional, sectarian and simply random acts of violence are the order of the day. This violence—and the lingering legacy of the civil war of 1971—is the backdrop for the story of Raheen and Karim, a girl and boy raised together in the 1970s and '80s, whose lives are shattered when a family secret is revealed. . . . This is a complex novel, deftly executed and rich in emotional coloratura and wordplay." Publ Wkly

Shan Sa, 1972-

The girl who played go; translated from the French by Adriana Hunter. Knopf 2003 312p $22.95

ISBN 0-4000-4025-6

Original French edition, 2001

"When a young Japanese soldier meets a lovely 16-year-old Chinese girl playing Go in the Square of a Thousand Winds, they form a silent bond, meeting daily to play the game. As a fragmented China battles for her dignity, the 1930 Japanese occupation of Manchuria is in full force. The girl and the soldier are opponents in more than just a game of Go; they are on opposite sides of a

deadly war in which their muted love receives a crushing blow." Booklist

"The alternating parallel tales add an extra spark of energy to this swift-moving novel, as Sa portrays tenderness and brutality with equal clarity." Publ Wkly

Shange, Ntozake

Betsey Brown; a novel. St. Martin's Press 1985 207p o.p.   LC 85-2663

The novelist presents "the life of a prosperous black family in St. Louis during 1957, the year of school desegregation. The story focuses on three generations of women, 13-year-old Betsey Brown and her mother and grandmother." Libr J

"Miss Shange is a superb storyteller who keeps her eye on what brings her characters together rather than what separates them: courage and love, innocence and the loss of it, home and homelessness. Miss Shange understands backyards, houses, schools and churches. [This novel] rejoices in—but never sentimentalizes—those places on earth where you are accepted, where you are comfortable with yourself." N Y Times Book Rev

Sassafrass, Cypress & Indigo; a novel. St. Martin's Press 1982 224p o.p.   LC 82-5565

This novel "tells of three sisters from Charleston, South Carolina. Indigo, the youngest, is full of magic and has trouble reconciling her inner worlds and reality. She bridges the gap with her poetry and her violin playing; both reveal an idiosyncratic style. Sassafrass, the oldest, writes and weaves, lives in Los Angeles with a man who seems a sometime thing, and tries to make sense of life, its connections and memories. Cypress is a dancer living in New York: 'when she danced, she was alive; when she danced, she was free.'" Publ Wkly

"Poetry, magical spells, recipes, and choreographs are woven into the narrative providing a vital interplay between the sisters and their creations. The setting of much of the story, Charleston, South Carolina, becomes a place of magic and joy for the reader." Libr J

Shannon, Dell, 1921-

Chaos of crime. Morrow 1985 190p o.p.   LC 84-22624

"A maniac is loose on the streets of Los Angeles, tying prostitutes to their beds, beheading them, disemboweling them, and then surgically dissecting them like laboratory animals. Detective Luis Mendoza and the Los Angeles Police Department are sufficiently stumped in trying to locate this madman who never leaves a clue—until finally the discovery of a rare French wristwatch helps to reveal a seemingly unlikely killer." Booklist

The Manson curse. Morrow 1990 262p o.p.   LC 90-36989

An American reporter based in London visits his novelist friend in Cornwall and becomes curious about the writer's obsession with the occult

Shannon, Doris

See also Giroux, E. X.

Shapiro, Dani

Black & white. Alfred A. Knopf 2007 255p $24

ISBN 978-0-375-41548-7; 0-375-41548-3

LC 2006-30424

"As the novel opens, Clara Brodeur returns to Manhattan to face her dying mother, Ruth Dunne, whom she has not seen in 14 years. Clara dropped out of high school, fled New York at 18 and finally made herself a home all the way up in Maine, on Mount Desert Island. . . . Clara had fled, all those years ago, because her mother's fame as a photographer arose out of the images she took of her daughter, images Clara has needed to leave behind." N Y Times Book Rev

"The novel reminds us that the stories of our past are just constructs of how we've chosen to remember them. . . . [Shapiro] writes with an economy that draws the reader into the dramatic fray of the scenes, without the curse of melodrama." Providence Journal

Shapiro, Fred R., 1954-

(ed) Trial and error. See Trial and error

Shapton, Leanne, 1973-

Important artifacts and personal property from the collection of Lenore Doolan and Harold Morris, including books, street fashion, and jewelry. Farrar, Straus & Giroux 2009 129p il pa $18

ISBN 978-0-374-17530-6; 0-374-17530-6

LC 2008-43417

"Sarah Crichton books"

This is a "faux auction catalog consisting of sediment — love letters, vintage clothes, paperbacks, etc. — left in the wake of a couple's breakup. As the highs and lows of Lenore and Harold's relationship (2002–06) slowly reveal themselves in Important Artifacts and Personal Property from the Collection of Lenore Doolan and Harold Morris, Including Books, Street Fashion, and Jewelry, you're likely to find yourself swooning and cursing along with the lovers. Of course, there's something suffocating about their privileged and meticulously curated lives — their cleverly inscribed first editions, vintage designer clothes, stationery from the Chateau Marmont, postcards of Nan Goldin photos, tastefully hip mix CDs — and so you may also find that you hate them." Entertainment Wkly

Sharfeddin, Heather

Mineral spirits; a novel. Bridge Works 2006 250p $21.95

ISBN 978-1-882593-98-9; 1-882593-98-7

LC 2006-762

"Freshly elected as the sheriff in a one-lawman town in Montana, Kip Edelson is immediately put to task when 10-year-old Gray Dausman discovers a rotting corpse down by the river. As Edelson attempts to discern the identity of the victim, he becomes increasingly convinced that it is none other than the boy's missing mother, and he reluctantly takes Gray under his wing even as his own marriage evaporates before him. When Edelson stumbles upon an illicit drug ring involving the local tavern owner and various other shady locals, the identity of the corpse takes on a new, unexpected significance."

Booklist

The author "blends Western and mystery genres into a fine, heady concoction." Libr J

Sharpe, Matthew, 1962-

The sleeping father; a novel. Soft Skull Press 2003 291p pa $14

ISBN 1-932360-00-X (pa)

LC 2003-13840

"Divorced, depressed Bernard Schwartz is taking Prozac, but the accidental ingestion of another antidepressant lands him in a coma. His adolescent children, the conflicted and caustically witty Chris, and the serious, earnestly spiritual Cathy, must muddle through their father's helplessness in this character-driven tale." Publ Wkly

"Sharpe's arch tone is charmingly at odds with the sprawling, inclusive structure of 'The Sleeping Father.' His raised-eyebrow formality suggests a host surveying unwanted guests, yet he keeps waving more and more characters in the front door. He's a rare find: an ironist who actually seems to like other people." N Y Times Book Rev

Shattuck, Jessica

Perfect life; a novel. W.W. Norton & Co. 2009 315p $24.95

ISBN 978-0-393-06950-1; 0-393-06950-8

LC 2009-15080

"Jenny, a former prom queen climbing the corporate ladder in the pharmaceutical industry, has gone to great lengths to keep her ex, the underachieving Neil, at a distance. When he returns to Boston after a long L.A. exile, however, he quickly draws in another old friend, the vulnerable Laura, just as the sharp-minded scientist Elise gets tangled in the ropes of familial obligation. The four main characters are pulled together and spun apart by various dramas (sperm-donor babies, corporate espionage) that could come off as soap-opera-ish in lesser hands, but Perfect is too nuanced to slide into broad archetypes or easy resolutions. With her elegant prose, Shattuck manages to make her characters' stories feel both engrossing and utterly real." Entertainment Wkly

Shaw, Irwin, 1913-1984

Beggarman, thief. Delacorte Press 1977 436p

ISBN 0-440-00673-2

LC 77-24523

Sequel to Rich man, poor man

"Wayward brother Tom Jordache has been murdered, leaving his son Wesley with a legacy of violence and revenge that is echoed in his nephew Billy, who becomes involved in a terrorist group in Brussels while serving in the U.S. Army. The story does not focus entirely on the second generation—the tangled lives of the older Jordaches are also featured. . . . Scenes from the earlier novel are interwoven allowing the unfamiliar reader to complete enjoyment and understanding." Booklist

Bread upon the waters. Delacorte Press 1981 438p

ISBN 0-440-00911-1

LC 81-3106

This novel "concerns the effects of misdirected philanthropy on a middle-class New York family—the Strands. Allen Strand is a history teacher at a public (state)

Shaw, Irwin, 1913-1984—*Continued*

school. His wife Leslie gives piano lessons to bring in extra money. Jimmy, their son, has ambitions to be a rock singer. The elder daughter, Eleanor, is an executive in a large corporation, and the younger daughter, Caroline is a sporty schoolgirl. One night Caroline . . . saves a millionaire called Russell Hazen from attack by a gang of muggers. She takes him home to have a wound dressed and Hazen is swiftly entranced by the warmth and harmony of the Strand family. His gratitude prompts him to set about making their dreams come true." Times Lit Suppl

Evening in Byzantium. Delacorte Press 1973 368p o.p.

The author writes of "a once-famous Hollywood producer, now 48, something of a has-been, who is reliving the past and preparing a final conquest of the future at the Cannes Film Festival. Jesse Craig is in trouble and he knows it. His marriage has been a failure, he is desperately fond of his daughter but cannot help her at a crisis moment in her own life, his attractive mistress is making demands he no longer cares to meet, and a shrewd, tough-minded young woman interviewer has him just where she wants him." Publ Wkly

Rich man, poor man. Delacorte Press 1970 723p o.p.

"A family chronicle which tells the story of the three children of Axel Jordache, a baker in a small town on the Hudson River. Thomas becomes a prizefighter, Rudolph a successful business man, and Gretchen eventually achieves a theatrical career after being seduced by the local mill-owner. . . . This is the dawn-to-dusk, 1940's-to-1970's, success-to-failure, poor-to-rich spectrum." N Y Times Book Rev

"Each member of the clan is doomed in one way or another. They fight, love, live hard and their fortunes are inevitably intertwined. Mr. Shaw has juxtaposed their rise and fall against a panoramic picture of the times. . . . This may not be great literature but it certainly has popular appeal." Publ Wkly

Followed by Beggarman, thief

Short stories: five decades. Delacorte Press 1978 756p o.p.   LC 78-16020

Contents: The eighty-yard run; Borough of cemeteries; Main currents of American thought; Second mortgage; Sailor off the Bremen; Strawberry ice cream soda; Welcome to the city; The girls in their summer dresses; Search through the streets of the city; The monument; I stand by Dempsey; God on Friday night; Return to Kansas City; Triumph of justice; No jury would convict; The lament of Madame Rechevsky; The deputy sheriff; Stop pushing, Rocky; "March, march on down the field"; Free conscience, void of offense; Weep in years to come; The city was in total darkness; Night, birth and opinion; Preach on the dusty roads; Hamlets of the world; Medal from Jerusalem; Walking wounded; Night in Algiers; Gunners' passage; Retreat; Act of faith; The man with one arm; The passion of Lance Corporal Hawkins; The dry rock; Noises in the city; The Indian in depth of night; Material witness; Little Henry Irving; The house of pain; A year to learn the language; The Greek general; The green nude; The climate of insomnia; Goldilocks at graveside; Mixed doubles; A wicked story; Age of

reason; Peter Two; The sunny banks of the river Lethe; The man who married a French wife; Voyage out, voyage home; Tip on a dead jockey; The inhabitants of Venus; In the French style; Then we were three; God was here but he left early; Love on a dark street; Small Saturday; Pattern of love; Whispers in bedlam; Where all things wise and fair descend; Full many a flower; Circle of light

The young lions. Random House 1948 689p o.p.

"World War II changes the lives of Christian, ex-Communist and Nazi; Michael, a Broadway stage manager; and Noah, an American Jew married to a Christian woman. We follow their lives during the years 1938 to 1945 as they experience frustrations, hardships, and the dangers of the war. The three fight, and two are killed." Shapiro. Fic for Youth. 3d edition

Shearn, Amy

How far is the ocean from here; a novel. Shaye Areheart Books 2008 307p $23

ISBN 978-0-307-40534-0   LC 2007-33956

"Susannah Prue is a surrogate mother on the run and ready to give birth. She has fled Chicago and the Forsythes, the baby's biological parents, in a car that makes it as far as a kitschy Southwestern motel. Her third-trimester panic has been brewing for some time, as she learns more about Kit and Julian Forsythe, wealthy, educated, yet often shallow and emotionally dysfunctional. The Thunder Lodge Motor Inn, inhabited by owners Marlon and Char Garland and their developmentally disabled teenaged son, Tim, is an unlikely oasis for Susannah. Other guests arrive, including Dicey and her hermaphrodite niece, Frankie. These unlikely inhabitants create a sort of impromptu family. . . . With Susannah's due date drawing near and her car still waiting for repairs, she makes a last-ditch attempt to reach the ocean, taking Frankie and Tim with her." Libr J

"Ms. Shearn's shifting points of view are a bit tricky. The book is told mostly through Susannah's eyes, but every now and then we're suddenly in Frankie's head or Tim's or Kit's for a paragraph or two. She also has a glorious way with description, conjuring vivid images with brevity and wit." Dallas News

Sheck, Laurie

A monster's notes. Alfred A. Knopf 2009 544p $30

ISBN 978-0-307-27105-1; 0-307-27105-6

LC 2008-55081

"The book's conceit is high-concept: that Shelley's literary monster was inspired by a mysterious being who visited her as a young girl during visits to her mother's grave. (That would be author and proto-feminist Mary Wollstonecraft, who died days after giving birth to Shelley.) But this 'real' creature, who has survived into the 21st century, is gripped by a profound identity crisis; his understanding of self is limited to the backstory Shelley devised. He attempts to glean further enlightenment by — and here's where this gets tricky — envisioning correspondence written by Shelley, her stepsisters, and Wollstonecraft, as well as (and here's where it gets really tricky) two fictional characters, Henry Clerval from Frankenstein and a leper dying in an Italian sanitarium. These letters are presented as part of the monster's journal,

Sheck, Laurie—*Continued*

which also contains articles on subjects — robotics, genetic privacy, the nature of time, John Zorn's experimental music, medieval philosophers — that speak to the creature's existential plight. Yep: This is a heady, hard read, at times repetitive and ponderous. Nonetheless, A Monster's Notes is a thrilling feat of literary scholarship, beautiful wordsmithing, and deep empathy." Entertainment Wkly

Sheehan, Aurelie, 1963-

The anxiety of everyday objects; a novel. Penguin Books 2004 278p pa $14

ISBN 0-14-200370-0 (pa)   LC 2003-49873

This novel is "set at the law firm of Grecko Mauster Crill, where Winona Bartlett toils as a secretary. She has the potential to be much more and, indeed, aspires to be a filmmaker. Her would-be film, entitled The Anxiety of Everyday Objects, centers on the theme of how people misreading something as simple as a street sign can gain significant insight into their lives. The only one who seems to see Winona's potential (other than Rex, the cute lawyer who has a crush on her) is the firm's new associate, Sandy Spires, who has been hired in conjunction with a case involving the beauty makeover consulting firm Lisa Box. Sandy–beautiful, glamorous, and blind–befriends Winona, treating her to a day at a spa and introducing her to a filmmaker. But as Winona becomes interested in Sandy as a subject for her film, she gradually realizes Sandy may be as manipulative as she is charming. A quirky, introspective novel about a creative woman finding her footing in a very corporate world." Booklist

Sheers, Owen, 1974-

Resistance; a novel. Nan A. Talese/Doubleday 2008 c2007 306p $23.95

ISBN 978-0-385-52210-6; 0-385-52210-X

LC 2007-15068

First published 2007 in the United Kingdom

The author "reimagines the events of World War II; it is late 1944, and the Germans, fresh from their victory against the Russians on the eastern front, have successfully invaded and occupied England. One morning, a group of women in a remote Welsh valley awake to find their husbands have left them to join the resistance. Soon, a German patrol arrives on a mysterious mission, and the two groups are forced together when a blizzard cuts the valley off from the outside world." Libr J

"Sheers is at his best describing the everyday rituals of rural life amid the rocky and unforgiving Welsh countryside, and in particular the tenderness exerted by the women in caring for their livestock in a strangely childless community. The novel's most memorable image is of an orphaned lamb sewn into the skin of a larger, dead lamb to lure the bereaved ewe into accepting the orphan as her own. That mixture of brutality and kindness—the bloody exigencies carried out not only in wartime, but in everyday rural life—is the great insight of Resistance." N Y Times Book Rev

Shelby, Philip

Days of drums; a novel. Simon & Schuster 1996 318p

ISBN 0-684-80177-9   LC 95-31045

"Rookie Secret Service agent Holland Tylo, daughter of the late Senator Beaumont, has a plum assignment in guarding Senator Westbourne during a meeting of Washington moguls at his estate. As she escorts the senator to his guest house for a late night tryst, he's suddenly shot dead, and her career with him. As the investigation progresses, more bodies fall while a professional assassin stalks Washington. Holland becomes both hunter and hunted as she fights to vindicate herself and sort out the good guys from the bad." Libr J

"Shelby delivers an edge-of-the-seat page-turner with a likable cool-headed heroine." Booklist

Gatekeeper. Simon & Schuster 1998 331p $25

ISBN 0-684-84260-2   LC 97-39934

"Hollis Fremont, a functionary at the American embassy in Paris, is duped by her superior and boyfriend, Paul McGann, into accompanying a man she believes to be a small-fry criminal back to the States for country-club prison incarceration. In fact, the rumpled expat turns out to be 'the Handyman,' a freelance assassin on a mission. At Kennedy Airport the Handyman bolts and disappears, and Hollis falls under the protective wing of Sam Crawford (the Gatekeeper of the title), who is an agent for the mysterious Omega group. While the Handyman stalks his quarry around the Statue of Liberty, Hollis and her 'friends' . . . try to track him down." Publ Wkly

"Well-defined characters, compelling intrigue, and a crisp-paced plot whisk the reader along. And Hollis Fremont is no wimpy damsel in distress." Libr J

Sheldon, Alice Hastings Bradley *See* Tiptree, James, 1916-1987

Sheldon, Raccoona, 1916-1987

See also Tiptree, James, 1916-1987

Sheldon, Sidney, 1917-2007

The doomsday conspiracy. Morrow 1991 412p $22

ISBN 0-688-08489-3   LC 91-12109

"Navy Commander Robert Bellamy is assigned to investigate the crash of a weather balloon in the Swiss Alps. All witnesses to the accident must be found and questioned. However, for Bellamy it is the beginning of a journey of terror into the incomprehensible. From Washington to London, Zurich, Rome, and Paris the story unfolds to reveal Bellamy's past—why the woman he loves most cannot return his love, why his friends become his deadly enemies, and why the world must never learn an incredible secret shielded by an unknown lethal force." Publisher's note

Master of the game. Morrow 1982 495p

ISBN 0-688-01365-1   LC 82-60920

"Kate Blackwell, born of a loveless marriage, striving through will, intelligence, and charm to control one of the richest conglomerates in the world, uses her power in wonderfully fiendish ways, which almost result in the destruction of those she loves most. The South African diamond mines provide vivid adventure; when the scene shifts to the United States, we encounter the more political maneuverings of business, but the pace never slackens." Libr J

Rage of angels. Morrow 1980 504p

ISBN 0-688-03687-2   LC 80-13328

Sheldon, Sidney, 1917-2007—*Continued*

"Young lawyer Jennifer Parker makes an incredible blunder in her first day as assistant D.A. Fired and in disgrace, she is reduced to serving writs to earn a living. Smart and stubborn, she perseveres, taking on unpromising clients. By inspired strategies of courtroom drama, she wins a few spectacular cases. Soon the world is taking notice, especially the Mafia. Their attractive offers are refused, but one day Parker must ask them for help in a desperate situation. In return, she becomes a Mafia mouthpiece, tempered somewhat by her love affair with the Mafioso." Libr J

Windmills of the gods. Morrow 1987 384p o.p.

LC 86-23593

The heroine of this novel is a "college lecturer from Kansas elevated to the politically volatile position of ambassador to Romania. Mary Ashley is plunged unaware into a cauldron of intrigue. Her surprise appointment, coming after the mysterious death of her husband, is the first stage in a newly elected president's plans to cement East-West relations. Up against Mary and the president are a secret alliance of political extremists and a ruthless international assassin known as Angel." Booklist

"The story speeds along and the epilogue is a chiller." Libr J

Shelley, Mary Wollstonecraft, 1797-1851

Frankenstein; or, The modern Prometheus; with an introduction by Wendy Lesser. Knopf 1992 xxxiii, 231p $15

ISBN 0-679-40999-8

* LC 91-53195

"Everyman's library"

First published 1818

"The tale relates the exploits of Frankenstein, an idealistic Genevan student of natural philosophy, who discovers at the university of Ingolstadt the secret of imparting life to inanimate matter. Collecting bones from charnel-houses, he constructs the semblance of a human being and gives it life. The creature, endowed with supernatural strength and size and terrible in appearance, inspires loathing in whoever sees it." Oxford Companion to Engl Lit. 5th edition

Maurice; or, The fisher's cot; a tale; edited with an introduction by Claire Tomalin. Knopf 1998 179p il $20

ISBN 0-375-40473-2

LC 98-88124

The manuscript of this previously unpublished story was discovered in Italy in 1997. It "is the tale of a lost child and opens with a small boy in tears following a coffin. It is set on the coast in Devonshire. . . . It was written in Pisa in 1820, about a year after Mary Shelley had lost her own child, little William Shelley, to a lethal fever. . . . The child in the story, Maurice, is befriended by a kindly old fisherman and is eventually found by his loving father." N Y Rev Books

Shepard, Jim

Like you'd understand, anyway; stories. Alfred A. Knopf 2007 211p $23

ISBN 978-0-307-26521-0

LC 2007-3639

Contents: The Zero Meter Diving Team; Proto-scorpions of the silurian; Hadrian's wall; Trample the dead, hurdle the weak; Ancestral legacies; Pleasure boating in Lituya Bay; The first South Central Australian Expedition; My Aeschylus; Eros 7; Courtesy for beginners; Sans farine

"Each of the 11 stories is presided over by a different narrator, and they're as diverse as can be: Chernobyl engineers, Roman centurions, high school football stars, Victorian Australian explorers, Russian cosmonauts and the chief executioner of Paris' age of terror all tell their tales, shoving the reader from continent to continent, and from past to present like a pinball. . . . Despite the variety of voices in these stories, they are sewn deftly together with a dark and ominous thread; in all their diversity, the characters share troubled fates, with many of the pieces ending either on the very edge of impending disaster or with a foreboding abruptness that hits the reader like a power outage." St. Louis Post-Dispatch

Shepard, Lucius

The best of Lucius Shepard. Subterranean Press 2008 623p $40

ISBN 978-1-59606-133-0; 1-59606-133-2

Contents: The man who painted the dragon griaule; Salvador; A Spanish lesson; The jaguar hunter; R & R; The arcevoalo; Shades; Delta Sly honey; Life of Buddha; White trains; Jack's decline; Beast of the heartland; Radiant green star; Only partly here; Jailwise; Hands up! who wants to die?; Dead money; Stars seen through stone

"Shepard is fantasy literature's Joseph Conrad or perhaps its Saul Bellow, a writer who never tires of staring directly into the abyss." Booklist

Softspoken. Night Shade Books 2007 179p $23.95

ISBN 978-1-59780-073-0; 1-59780-073-2

"A chilling and mysterious voice becomes audible to Sanie shortly after she and her husband Jackson move into the decaying antebellum mansion that is the Bullard ancestral home in rural South Carolina. At first, she wonders if the voice might be a prank played by Jackson's peyote-popping brother Will or his equally off-kilter sister Louise. But soon Sanie discovers that the ghostly voice is merely a single piece in the decadent, baroque puzzle that comprises the Bullard family history." Publisher's note

"Sanie's tale is, ultimately, after the final page is turned, a little slight. . . . But while you're immersed in its ectoplasmic toils, you get the full measure of domestic creepiness and occult horror." Sci Fi Wkly

Shepard, Sam, 1943-

Great dream of heaven; stories. Knopf 2002 142p $20

ISBN 0-375-40505-4

LC 2002-70054

Contents: The remedy man; Coalinga 1/2 way; Berlin Wall piece; Blinking eye; Betty's cats; The door to women; Foreigners; Living the sign; The company's interest; Concepción; It wasn't Proust; Convulsion; An unfair question; A frightening seizure; Tinnitus; The stout of heart; Great dream of heaven; All the trees are naked

"Each involving story is psychologically loaded, but

Shepard, Sam, 1943-—*Continued*

what lassoes the reader is the tension between Shephard's acuity and tenderness, his high regard for the recklessness of life." Booklist

Shepherd, Michael *See* Ludlum, Robert, 1927-2001

Sher, Ira

Gentlemen of space. Free Press 2003 291p $23
ISBN 0-7432-4218-1   LC 2002-192807

This "novel is told from the perspective of Georgie Finch, whose father, Jerry—a high school science teacher—wins a trip to the moon. Jerry's rise to celebrity status as an astronaut brings a crowd of media and the curious, who suddenly disrupt the lives of Georgie and his mother, Barbara, in the small community of Magnolia Court, Fl. While Jerry is on the moon, Barbara learns that he had an affair with Georgie's babysitter, who is now pregnant." Libr J

"Sher's affection for his characters is clear, and they shine with softly absurd humor . . . and a DeLillo-like nostalgia for Americana and belief. This is a beautiful, eloquent first novel." Booklist

Sherman, Jory

The Baron war. Forge 2002 318p
ISBN 0-7653-0255-1   LC 2001-54750

"A Tom Doherty Associates book"

"Set in the lawless Texas landscape, this latest installment in Sherman's Baron series . . . reaches a watershed on the eve of the Civil War. Grieving the shameful death of his wife, Caroline, estranged patriarch Martin Baron must mend fences with his son, Anson—the new owner of the family's Box B Ranch—in order to face a deadly threat from a fractious neighbor, Matteo Aguilar. . . . Strong female characters and plenty of romance could help this title bridge the western gender gap." Publ Wkly

Sherrill, Martha

My last movie star; a novel of Hollywood. Random House 2003 349p $23.95
ISBN 0-375-50769-8   LC 2002-69707

"Fed up with her manipulative editor, entertainment journalist Clementine James is packing up to move to her boyfriend's Virginia farm when Flame magazine asks her to write an in-depth profile of captivating actress Allegra Coleman. When their interview ends in a car crash, Clementine awakes to find herself a celebrity. Allegra has vanished, and Clementine was the last person to see her. Allegra's disappearance catapults her into instant superstardom." Booklist

"The novel is as much a celebration of screen legends (buffs will be drawn to Sherrill's filmography) as it is a cautionary tale." N Y Times Book Rev

Sherwood, Frances, 1940-

The book of splendor. Norton 2002 348p $25.95
ISBN 0-393-02138-6   LC 2002-520

"A young, illiterate Jewess of dubious birth, given to fanciful stories, Rochel is able to escape poverty through an arranged marriage to Zev, a widowed tailor. This do-

mestic scene is played out in the shadow of 17th-century imperial Prague alongside oppression and poverty during the reign of Habsburg Emperor Rudolph. . . . The characters include the famous Rabbi Loew, who fashions the man of mud, the Golom of Prague; astromomers Tycho Brahe and Johannes Kepler; the alchemists John Dee and Edward Kelley; and an assortment of spies, lepers, monks, and mountebanks." Libr J

This is a "provocative, gripping novel that's part farce, historical adventure, theological meditation, and bodice-ripping romance. Fans of magic realism will love this." Booklist

Night of sorrows. Norton 2006 425p map $24.95
ISBN 978-0-393-05825-3; 0-393-05825-5
                              LC 2006-420

"Following the death of her beloved and indulgent father, ten-year-old Malintzin, an Aztec princess, is sold into slavery by her mother. Over the next few years, she is passed from master to master, until she is given as tribute to the Spanish conquistador, Hernando Cortés, in spring 1519. . . . Malintzin quickly learns Spanish, falls in love with Cortés, and becomes the translator for the vastly outnumbered Spanish invaders as they make their way to Tenochitlán (Mexico City) and June 30, 1520—the Night of Sorrows—when the Aztecs almost succeeded in wiping out the Spaniards." Libr J

"An account of conquest and dehumanization, [this novel] is also a story of survival in the midst of a harsh cultural clash. The linguistic and narrative riches of the book enhance its moral complexity: Sherwood has refused to settle for the black-and-white thinking that so often mars this sort of historical fiction." N Y Times Book Rev

Shields, Carol

The republic of love. Viking 1992 366p o.p.
                              LC 91-16154

"Fay McLeod and Tom Avery are likable souls: kind to their parents, close to friends and co-workers, dedicated to their professions (she's a folklorist, he's a radio talk show host). But thus far both have been unlucky in love. Fay has never married; Tom has married and divorced rather too often. Participating on the periphery of lives of married friends has begun to pall. They finally meet, and it is a *coup de foudre* for both, but Fay is leaving that night for a month of mermaid research in Europe. Even when she returns, their affair is jeopardized by upheavals in others' lives." Libr J

"Not only are Fay and Tom exceptionally likable and capable of arresting insights, their worlds are complete and organic. Secondary characters are respectfully but economically drawn via short monologues, and the city of Winnipeg bustles in the background." Publ Wkly

The stone diaries. Viking 1994 361p il o.p.
                              * LC 93-30239

This "novel provides, glancingly, a panorama of 20th-century life in North America. Written in a diary format, it traces the life of one seemingly unremarkable woman: Daisy Goodwill Flett, who is born in 1905 and lives into the 1990's." N Y Times Book Rev

This book is a "miraculous meeting of intellectual rigour and imaginative flow. On the one hand, it's a sharp-as-tacks investigation into the limits of the autobiographi-

Shields, Carol—*Continued*

cal form; on the other, a novel of effortless pleasure and sensuality. Daisy Goodwill . . . attempts intermittently to tell the story of a life remarkable only in its large tracts of ordinariness." New Statesman (1913)

Unless; a novel. Fourth Estate/HarperCollins Pubs. 2002 213p

ISBN 0-00-714107-6   LC 2002-19923

Reta Winters-loving helpmate "to a doctor, mother of three cheerful daughters, and author of a successful comic novel—has always considered herself happy, even blessed. Then her eldest child, nineteen-year-old Norah, briefly disappears and resurfaces as a panhandling mute on a Toronto street corner, holding up a homemade placard that says 'Goodness.' Shields's ability to use Reta's darkest fears to reveal the order lurking in chaos, without ever losing her light touch . . . is nothing short of astonishing." New Yorker

Shields, David

Dead languages; a novel. Knopf 1989 245p o.p.
                                    * LC 88-13444

This "coming-of-age novel, set in California, tells the . . . story of Jeremy Zorn, whose 1960s childhood is centered on one problem: his stuttering. Jeremy's highly literate parents, both journalists, use language to earn their living: 'My family was living in language whereas I was dying in it.' Jeremy's goal is to rid himself of the prison that words have made for him. Many of his cures are amusing (learning Latin, no need to articulate) or sad (love affairs with insensitive and inappropriate girls)." Booklist

"As touching and funny a rendering of adolescence as *The Catcher in the Rye*. Those recently emerged from adolescence will readily see its truth; the well read will delight at Shields's ability with narrative. But *Dead Languages* speaks to everyone who has ever struggled to articulate an emotion and failed to find the words." Libr J

Shikibu, Murasaki *See* Murasaki Shikibu, b. 978?

Shippey, T. A. (Tom A.)

(ed) The Oxford book of science fiction stories. See The Oxford book of science fiction stories

Shippey, Tom A. *See* Shippey, T. A. (Tom A.)

Shirley, John, 1953-

Demons. Ballantine Pub. Group 2002 372p $25

ISBN 0-345-44647-X   LC 2001-43478

"A Del Rey book"

This "apocalyptic tale, redolent with the terror of inexplicable carnage, is two novels in one: a first-person account of an initial advent of demons in everyday reality, followed by the story of their later return. Ira, narrator of the first, plays a significant role in the second, and Shirley links the two episodes nearly seamlessly. Ira reports a world gone mad with demonic possession, its people clinging to normality for dear life." Booklist

Shlesinger, Miriam, 1947-

(tr) Qashu, S. Dancing Arabs

Shoemaker, Bill, 1931-

Stalking horse. Fawcett Columbine 1994 311p o.p.
                                    LC 93-22125

Ex-jockey Coley Killebrew is enlisted by Raymond Starbuck, "the man who ruined his career to help stop an underworld takeover of one of the nation's great tracks. The assignment takes him to Louisiana's Magnolia Park, where he insinuates himself into a milieu of fast horses, even faster women, and a dangerous array of unsavory characters presided over by corrupt aristocrat Remy Courville." Booklist

"The plot is big, complicated and thoroughbred-fast as Coley's hard-boiled, first-person chapters alternate with a third-person focus on Starbuck. Shoemaker's characters provide the most fun." Publ Wkly

Shoemaker, Willie *See* Shoemaker, Bill, 1931-2003

Sholem Aleichem, 1859-1916

The adventures of Menahem-Mendl; translated from the Yiddish by Tamara Kahana. Putnam 1969 222p o.p.

Original Yiddish edition published 1909 in Russia

This book "consists of an exchange of letters between the hero and his . . . wife Sheineh-Sheindl, whom he has left behind looking after the children in their . . . native town of Kasrilevka while he tries to make his fortune in the big city—first Odessa, then Kiev. Menahem-Mendl is . . . [an] over-optimistic schemer who somehow contrives to make a living out of thin air; at one moment he is a currency speculator . . . then next a dabbler in commodities, after that a would-be broker, a journalist, a matchmaker, an insurance agent." N Y Rev of Books

The adventures of Mottel, the cantor's son; translated by Tamara Kahana; illustrated by Ilya Schor. Abelard-Schuman 1953 342p il o.p.

"The lighthearted humor of young Mottel, the narrator, adds a touch of pathos to the stories of an impoverished Jewish family in a European village, its wanderings in Europe en route to America, and finally its arrival and settlement in the U.S." Booklist

The best of Sholom Aleichem; edited by Irving Howe and Ruth R. Wisse. New Republic Bks. 1979 276p o.p.

Contents: The haunted tailor; A Yom Kippur scandal; Eternal life; Station Baranovich; The pot; The clock that struck thirteen; Home for Passover; On account of a hat; Dreyfus in Kasrilevke; Two anti-semites; A Passover expropriation; If I were Rothschild; Tevye strikes it rich; The bubble bursts; Chava; Get thee out; From Mottel the cantor's son; Bandits; The guest; The Krushniker delegation; One in a million; Once there were four

The further adventures of Menachem-Mendl; New York—Warsaw—Vienna—Yehupetz; translated by Aliza Shevrin. Syracuse Univ. Press 2001 172p $26.95

ISBN 0-8156-0677-X   LC 00-55701

Sholem Aleichem, 1859-1916—*Continued*

"Written in Yiddish in 1913 and only now translated into English, it's a sequel to *The Adventures of Menachem-Mendl*, which was first translated and published in the U.S. in 1969. Loosely based on Aleichem's experience, the story is told in the form of letters between Menachem-Mendl (who now has a job as a writer on a Warsaw newspaper) and his wife, Sheyne-Sheyndl, left behind with the children in a Kasrilevka village, where she faces crushing poverty and persecution." Booklist

The nightingale; or, The Saga of Yosele Solovey the cantor; translated by Aliza Shevrin. Putnam 1985 240p o.p.   LC 85-12073

Originally written in Yiddish and copyrighted 1917

"The cantor's son, Yosele Solovey, has a voice so lovely that he is called 'The Nightingale.' He is a timid lad, living in a small town (shtetl) that is peopled with earthy as well as flighty types. Innocently, he is introduced to nefarious pursuits like gambling and womanizing by a famous cantor who is a wheeler-dealer and whose influence creates havoc in Yosele's life and in the shtetl's, as well." West Coast Rev Books

This "is more than a popular novel; it is a social document, a study of a failed artist and, in its way, an early feminist work." N Y Times Book Rev

Tevye the dairyman and The railroad stories; [by] Sholom Aleichem; translated from the Yiddish and with an introduction by Hillel Halkin. Schocken Bks. 1987 xli, 309p pa $15 hardcover o.p.

ISBN 0-8052-1069-5 (pa)   LC 86-24835

"Library of Yiddish classics"

Includes the following stories: Tevye strikes it rich; Tevye blows a small fortune; Today's children; Hodl; Chava; Shprintze; Tevye leaves for the land of Israel; Lekh-Lekho; To the reader; Competitors; The happiest man in all Kodny; Baranovich Station; Eighteen from Pereshchepena; The man from Buenos Aires; Elul; The slowpoke express; The miracle of Hoshana Rabbah; The wedding that came without its band; The tallis koton; A game of sixty-six; High school; The automatic exemption; It doesn't pay to be good; Burned out; Hard luck; Fated for misfortune; Go climb a tree if you don't like it; The tenth man; Third class

"In the first eight stories of this collection, Tevye, the Russian Jew so familiar from *Fiddler on the Roof*, bemoans his fate. In these as well as the following 21 tales, the author displays his splendid storytelling skills." Booklist

Tevye's daughters; translated by Frances Butwin. Crown 1949 302p o.p.

     *

Contents: Bubble bursts; If I were Rothschild; Modern children; Competitors; Another page from The Song of Songs; Hodel; Happiest man in Kodno; Wedding without musicians; What will become of me; Chava; Joys of parenthood; Littlest of kings; Man from Buenos Aires; May God have mercy; Schprintze; The merrymakers; Easy fast; Little pot; Two shalachmones; Tevye goes to Palestine; Gymana-sia; Purim feast; From Passover to Succos; Get thee out; Passover expropriation; The German; Third class

Translated from the Yiddish, many of these stories are

"about the seven daughters of Tevye the Dairyman and the life each chooses as she comes of age in Russia during the years preceding the first World War." Publ Wkly

Sholokhov, Mikhail Aleksandrovich, 1905-1984

And quiet flows the Don; [by] Mikhail Sholokhov; translated from the Russian by Stephen Garry. Knopf 1934 755p o.p.

     *

"Set in the Don River basin of southwestern Russia at the end of the czarist period, the novel traces the progress of the Cossack Gregor Melekhov from youthful lover to Red Army soldier and finally to Cossack nationalist. War—in the form of both international conflict and civil revolution—provides the epic backdrop for the narrative and determines its tone of moral ambiguity." Merriam-Webster's Ency of Lit

Followed by The Don flows home to the sea

The Don flows home to the sea; {by} Mikhail Sholokhov; translated from the Russian by Stephen Garry. Knopf 1941 777p o.p.

This translation first published 1940 in the United Kingdom

This sequel to And quiet flows the Don, covers the period following the Revolution of 1917 to the end of the civil war in 1921. The narrative traces the fortunes of a group of Cossacks as they fight alternately with the Reds and the Whites

"It is a tale of misfortunes multiplied, yet a broad and earthy humor and the hearty Cossack gaiety break continuously over the grim surface. At the end the Cossack, with his intense individualism, his passionate love of the land, and his primitive pride, stands revealed." Nation

Followed by Seeds of tomorrow (1959)

Sholom Aleichem *See* Sholem Aleichem, 1859-1916

Shonk, Katherine, 1968-

The red passport. Farrar, Straus & Giroux 2003 209p $22

ISBN 0-374-24847-8   LC 2003-7680

Contents: The death of Olga Vasilievna; Our American; The young people of Moscow; My mother's garden; Kitchen friends; The conversion; The wooden village of Kizhi; Honey month

In this "collection set primarily in post-Communist Russia, expatriates and natives alike endeavor to make their way in a new social and economic landscape, often sharing an intense desire for whatever the other possesses: money, freedom, love, family. . . . Shonk is at her best examining the lives of Americans whom the natives revere as potential saviors at the same time they dismiss them as frivolous tourists who could never hope to understand life in the former Soviet republic. That tension lends these stories an impressive vitality." Publ Wkly

Shreve, Anita, 1946-

All he ever wanted. Little, Brown 2003 310p $25.95

ISBN 0-316-78226-2

     * LC 2002-36847

LIST OF FICTIONAL WORKS

Shreve, Anita, 1946——*Continued*

"Escaping from a New Hampshire hotel fire at the turn of the 20th century, Prof. Nicholas Van Tassel catches sight of Etna Bliss and is instantly smitten. She does not reciprocate his feeling, for she has her own unrequited lust, for freedom and independence. That they marry guarantees tragedy. Nicholas tells the story in retrospect, writing feverishly on a train trip in 1933 to his sister's funeral in Florida." Publ Wkly

"Aside from an exchange of letters between his wife and his rival, everything is seen from the point of view of Nicholas, who grows increasingly jealous and pathetic, his motives couched in formal, self-justifying language that almost always sounds like a form of evasion. In the end, he admits, he's telling 'the story of a faintly ridiculous man,' but luckily it's a tale that also flirts with full-scale tragedy as well as the darkest kind of comedy." N Y Times Book Rev

Body surfing; a novel. Little, Brown and Co. 2007 295p $25.99

ISBN 978-0-316-05985-5; 0-316-05985-4

LC 2006-31133

"Already once divorced and now recently widowed, 29-year-old Sydney Sklar looks at a tutoring job at a New Hampshire beach house as the perfect escape from pain and grief. But the Edwardses offer more—and less—than she would have hoped for. . . . Helping 18-year-old Julie Edwards prepare for the SATs becomes a complex undertaking as Sydney realizes that Julie is slow and, as hard as she tries, will never be accepted at the prestigious colleges Mrs. Edwards prefers. Mr. Edwards loves his garden and his daughter, and he makes Sydney yearn to be part of a family. With the arrival of Julie's much older brothers, Ben and Jeff, the path for Sydney becomes as precarious as the shoreline where she revels in body surfing." Libr J

"Shreve's devastating depiction of the family's dissolution—the culmination of sublimated jealousies suddenly exploding into the open—is wrenching. Shreve's omniscience is asserted with such ease that it often feels like she's toying with her characters, but her control is masterful, particularly in the sure-handed and compassionate aftermath." Publ Wkly

Eden Close; a novel. Harcourt Brace Jovanovich 1989 265p $17.95

ISBN 0-15-127582-3

* LC 89-34712

"As next-door neighbors, 'best buddies,' and then awkward adolescents, Eden and Andy find solace in each other's company until a tragic event occurs as Andy prepares to leave their small home town and heads off to college. The awful accident drives them apart, but then inadvertently draws them together again some 15 years later. Their relationship is rekindled when Andy returns home to attend his mother's funeral." Libr J

"'Eden Close' is not a novel of suspense but one of sensibility. Its insights are keen, its language measured and haunting. In it, a sense of loss and then of rupture is everywhere." N Y Times Book Rev

Fortune's Rocks; a novel. Little, Brown 2000 453p $24.95

ISBN 0-316-78101-0

LC 99-42665

The protagonist is "15-year-old Olympia Biddeford, the only child of wealthy, cultured, and well-meaning parents. It's summer, and the Biddefords have moved for the season into their New Hampshire seaside cottage. . . . [As the novel begins] Olympia suddenly senses that she is no longer a child. Even her father, who has been home-schooling her, detects something different about his smart and beautiful daughter as he instructs her to read a book of socially conscious essays written by Dr. John Haskell, who, along with his wife and children, will be their dinner guest. Olympia evinces no interest until she and Haskell—41, handsome, and intense—come face-to-face and are shot through with that awful current that signals love-at-first-sight. Their reckless affair precipitates a scandal of immense proportions, resulting in a harrowing separation and pregnancy." Booklist

"The level of suspense never falters, but becomes breathtaking during a custody court battle. . . . The astounding denouement of cascading events will leave no reader unmoved." Publ Wkly

The last time they met; a novel. Little, Brown 2001 313p $28

ISBN 0-316-78114-2

* LC 00-53496

In this novel featuring Thomas Janes, first introduced in the author's The weight of water, "we learn the history of Thomas's great love with fellow poet Linda Fallon. The novel is told in reverse time, starting with the present, when Linda and Thomas, now in their fifties, reconnect at a literary festival. The middle section takes place in Africa, where the couple, then age 26, had a disastrous affair that horribly affected a number of loved ones and changed their own lives forever." Libr J

"Romantic regret is Anita Shreve's subject in this instantly captivating novel. . . . Fiction writers could go to school on Shreve's command of scene." Atl Mon

Light on snow; a novel. Little, Brown and Co 2004 305p $24.95

ISBN 0-316-78148-7

LC 2004-8907

"After retreating from a family tragedy to a house tucked away in the New Hampshire woods, 12-year-old Nicky and her father are thrust back into the world when one wintry afternoon they discover an abandoned newborn outdoors. How they deal with the reality of the baby's mother, who shows up at their house, and the detective who is hellbent on putting the pieces together is narrated by a now-adult Nicky looking back at her past." Libr J

"The story shifts brilliantly between childlike visions of a simple world and the growing realization of its cruel ambiguities. Aside from a few saccharine moments and a rather pat ending, Shreve does a skilled job of portraying grief, conflict and anger while leaving room for hope, redemption and renewal." Pub Wkly

The pilot's wife; a novel. Little, Brown 1998 293p $23.95

ISBN 0-316-78908-9

LC 97-51647

"Kathryn Lyons has just had the shock of her life. Roused from bed in the middle of the night, she has discovered that her husband, an airline pilot, has been killed in a crash. But Kathryn soon has a lot more to handle. A tape recovered from the plane suggests that husband Jack committed suicide, taking a planeload of people, with him, and the news is leaked to the press. As she

Shreve, Anita, 1946-—*Continued*

scrambles to deal with importuning reporters, oily investigators, and her grieving daughter, Kathryn starts uncovering unsettling little facts." Libr J

"The climax, less dramatic than meditative, may strike some readers as too muted: understatement is one of this novel's strengths. What haunts us is the way Jack's secret life gradually weakens its hold on Kathryn's imagination and ours." Publ Wkly

Resistance; a novel. Little, Brown 1995 222p o.p.

LC 94-39269

"In December 1943, an American fighter plane is downed near a small village in Belgium. The pilot, Lt. Ted Brice, is rescued by a member of the local resistance movement. As he is hidden in the small attic at the home of Claire Daussois, he becomes acutely aware of the danger to himself as well as his hostess and her husband. A bond develops between Claire and Ted during his 20-day stay that changes both of their lives forever." SLJ

The author "adds subtle gray shadings to a familiar morality tale of good and evil, bravery and betrayal. In her vivid story, . . . Ms. Shreve questions the very nature of courage." N Y Times Book Rev

Sea glass; a novel. Little, Brown 2002 378p

ISBN 0-316-78081-2   LC 2002-20897

"The year is 1929 and Honora Beecher and her husband, Sexton, are just settling into a new marriage and a cottage on the coast of New Hampshire. While Honora fixes up the derelict house and searches for bits of sea glass on the beach, Sexton risks everything they own to buy the house they both love. Along with millions of other Americans, he is blindsided by the stock market crash and finds himself penniless. The only work he can find is in a nearby mill, where a labor conflict is erupting into violence." Publisher's note

"Shreve does not use her characters frivolously. They reveal who they are through their actions, with the author—who writes with admirable economy—rarely having to point a finger or underline the obvious. The true power of her novel comes from the appalling social conditions she describes so vividly, the grim but heroic lives her characters live." N Y Times Book Rev

Strange fits of passion; a novel. Harcourt Brace Jovanovich 1991 336p

ISBN 0-15-185760-1   LC 90-23874

This novel opens "with oblique hints of a violent event—here a murder committed by a woman in response to domestic abuse—then segues to flashbacks that slowly reveal the circumstances leading up to it. A reporter who wrote a book about the crime shares her notes, presented in alternating versions and voices. Most affecting is the voice of the accused woman, who flees Manhattan with her six-month-old daughter to seek sanctuary in a coastal Maine village where she is protected by the clannish but sympathetic townspeople. She finds temporary solace in an affair with a sensitive lobsterman, but is betrayed to her husband by another man out of jealousy." Publ Wkly

Testimony; a novel. Little, Brown 2008 307p $25.99

ISBN 9780316059862; 0-316-05986-2

LC 2008-5027

"The first paragraph foreshadows a tragedy in which three marriages are destroyed, the lives of three students at a private school in Vermont are ruined, and death claims an innocent victim. The precipitating event is a sex tape involving three members of the boys' basketball team and a freshman girl. Beginning with an account of the debacle by the Avery School's then headmaster, and segueing to the voices of the participants in the orgy, plus their parents and others touched by the scandal, the narrative explores the widening consequences of a single event." Publ Wkly

"Shreve arrows in on many targets—underage drinking, instant exposure via the Internet, familial expectations, youthful insecurities, and peer pressure, among them—as she flawlessly weaves a tale that is mesmerizing, hypnotic, and compulsive." Libr J

The weight of water. Little, Brown 1997 246p $22.95

ISBN 0-316-78997-6   LC 96-21326

"In 1873, two women living on the Isles of Shoals, a lonely, windswept group of islands off the coast of New Hampshire, were brutally murdered. A third woman survived, cowering in a sea cave until dawn. More than a century later, Jean, a magazine photographer working on a photoessay about the murders, returns to the Isles with her husband, Thomas, and their five-year-old daughter, Billie, aboard a boat skippered by her brother-in-law, Rich, who has brought along his girlfriend, Adaline. As Jean becomes immersed in the details of the 19th-century murders, Thomas and Adaline find themselves drawn together—with potentially ruinous consequences." Publ Wkly

"Deftly moving among almost as many plot lines as there are islands and employing at least two distinct voices, Ms. Shreve unravels themes of adultery, jealousy, crimes of passion, incest, negligence, loss and guilt, and then manages somehow to knit them all together into an engrossing tale." N Y Times Book Rev

Where or when; a novel. Harcourt Brace & Co. 1993 240p o.p.

LC 92-39392

"When 44-year-old real estate insurance salesman Charles Callahan sees a photograph of poet Siän Richards, he recognizes her as the young woman he met three decades earlier at a Catholic camp for teenagers. Impulsively, he writes Siän, and sets in motion the love affair they were destined to have. Though both are married and have children, each is unfulfilled, craving true partnership." Publ Wkly

The "two main characters are not presented in isolation, enveloped by a cloud of concupiscence. Instead, they are placed against a richly drawn background that encompasses everything from the grim reality of a deteriorating economy to the thin black dirt of the Richards farm." N Y Times Book Rev

Shreve, Susan Richards

A country of strangers. Simon & Schuster 1989 239p

ISBN 0-671-64409-2

* LC 88-28735

"Outside of Washington, D.C., in the midst of World War II, Charley Fletcher strives to create a perfect community for himself and his family. He purchases a large rural estate, but, in doing so, has to confront the Bel-

Shreve, Susan Richards—*Continued*

lows, the black tenants who have moved into the empty residence from their shacks on the property. Fletcher's awkward, friendly overtures are met with bewilderment and hostility, though his step-daughter, Kate, finally finds some success when she forms a deep alliance with Prudential Bellows, 13 years old and awaiting the birth of a child." Booklist

This is an "ambitious novel that attempts to create a parable of how racial harmony may be achieved. And, because of their youthful exuberance and quirkiness, Prudential and Kate are finally memorable characters." N Y Times Book Rev

Daughters of the new world. Doubleday 1992 471p o.p.
LC 91-8146
This "novel chronicles the lives of a remarkable family of women. The story begins with passionate Anna, a servant who marries the master's son; scandal drives the couple west. Daughter Amanda grows up with the Chippewe Indians and then, disguising herself as a man, becomes a photographer in France during World War I. Her daughter Sara, Sara's youngest daughter Eleanor, and Eleanor's two young daughters bring the novel into the present." Libr J

"As the novel unfolds and daughters become mothers, mothers grandmothers, grandmothers great-grandmothers, Shreve explores the wonder of personalities and genetics, the astonishing accommodation and resiliency of women, the courage and dignity of true love, and the surge of change that has driven this unlikely century. An enveloping, rewarding, and heroic tale told with great skill and much heart." Booklist

Plum & Jaggers; a novel. Farrar, Straus & Giroux 2000 228p
ISBN 0-374-23462-0
* LC 99-47619
"Sam is the only one of the four McWilliams kids who can remember exactly what happened on the day their parents were killed in the terrorist bombing of a Rome-bound train. Their Scottish-born father and American mother had led the family on a carefree tour of the world, but after the tragedy, the kids–all under seven–are shipped off to their nice but vague grandparents in Grand Rapids. Years later, Sam turns his orphan family unit into a comedy team inspired by the missing parents, whose nicknames for each other were Plum and Jaggers. They are a big hit on late-night television." Booklist

Shreve "writes eloquently, painting a story of tragedy, obsession, love, and loss with a broad brush." Libr J

A student of living things. Viking 2006 246p $24.95
ISBN 0-670-03758-3
LC 2005-57473
"Her affinity for biology prompted her mother to call her a 'student of living things,' although Claire Frayn had no qualms about scrutinizing the dead. Not that this enables her to cope with her brother's death, especially since she was standing beside him on the library steps when he was shot. Claire and Steven had been living at home in a Washington, D.C., suburb while attending graduate school. Bombings and other terrorist acts have become commonplace in a grim near-future, and it is against this malevolent backdrop that the politically outspoken Steven is assassinated. The Frayns—an eccentric extended family of survivors of many atrocities and sor-

rows sensitively and charmingly portrayed—are unaware of the danger Claire is in as she is drawn to an enigmatic man who claims to have been Steven's friend. Shreve's novels are always elegant in their blend of restraint and intensity, and this is an exquisite hybrid, a poetic and resonant story of grief, family bonds, risk, and love that is as propulsive and unpredictable as a first-class thriller." Booklist

The visiting physician. Talese 1996 288p
ISBN 0-385-47701-5
LC 95-23877
"Twenty-odd years ago, Helen Fielding suffered severe trauma on a visit to her aunt in small-town Ohio when her toddler sister disappeared while in Helen's care. Now a doctor, Helen returns to Meridian as an outbreak of legionella threatens the town's children. One child is dead, another has disappeared, and so has the town doctor. Meridian itself has lost its collective innocence after being the subject of an unscrupulous TV director's documentary on the perfect small town. . . . A well-structured method of revealing the past adds to the story's appeal." Libr J

Shriver, Lionel

The post-birthday world. HarperCollins Publishers 2007 517p $25.95
ISBN 978-0-06-118784-1; 0-06-118784-4
LC 2006-49233
"Irina McGovern, a children's book illustrator in London, lives in comfortable familiarity with husband-in-everything-but-marriage-certificate Lawrence Trainer, and every summer the two have dinner with their friend, the professional snooker player Ramsey Acton, to celebrate Ramsey's birthday. One year, following Ramsey's divorce and while terrorism specialist 'think tank wonk' Lawrence is in Sarajevo on business, Irina and Ramsey have dinner, and after cocktails and a spot of hash, Irina is tempted to kiss Ramsey. From this near-smooch, Shriver leads readers on a two-pronged narrative: one consisting of what Irina imagines would have happened if she had given in to temptation, the other showing Irina staying with Lawrence while fantasizing about Ramsey." Publ Wkly

"Lawrence often verges on being a parody of a judgmental, snobbish prig, while Ramsey often verges on being a parody of a hard-living, irresponsible celebrity. . . . That we're able to overlook the flaws of Ramsey and Lawrence is, in the end, a testament to Ms. Shriver's ability to make Irina into a thoroughly compelling character, an idiosyncratic yet recognizable heroine about whom it's impossible not to care." N Y Times (Late N Y Ed)

We need to talk about Kevin. Counterpoint 2003 400p
ISBN 1-58243-267-8
LC 2002-152753
"This is the story, narrated in the form of letters to her estranged husband, of Eva Katchadourian, whose son has committed the most talked-about crime of the decade—a school shooting reminiscent of Columbine." Libr J

"It's a harrowing, psychologically astute, sometimes even darkly humorous novel, with a clear-eyed, hard-won ending and a tough-minded sense of the difficult, often painful human enterprise." Publ Wkly

Shteyngart, Gary

Absurdistan; a novel. Random House 2006 333p $24.95

ISBN 1-4000-6196-2   LC 2005-54308

"Set in Russia in the summer of 2001, this . . . stars one Misha Vainburg, the dissipated, American-educated, 325-pound son of Boris Vainburg, a Russian Jewish dissident-turned-oligarch after the fall of the Soviet Union and the '1,238th richest man in Russia.' After spending some time in St. Petersburg, Misha longs to return to America to join Rouenna, his streetwise New York girlfriend. Barred from getting a visa because his father killed an American businessman, Misha journeys to the Caspian republic of Absurdistan, from which he hopes to emigrate after getting Belgian citizenship. Upon his arrival, he faces a phony civil war, concocted to gain American economic support. With the borders closed, and stuck in the midst of a war that's increasingly real, Misha finds himself growing up in unexpected ways." Libr J

This is "a satire that is profoundly funny, genuinely moving and wholly lovable. . . . The same way Gatsby chased Daisy, Misha chases his imagined America–with perfect, pure good faith, going further and further out on a limb until he's the only true believer in sight. He is, of course, doomed to be disillusioned and heartbroken–the novel ends hopefully, but the dateline is early morning, Sept. 11, 2001. Still, there's no doubt that he will reillusion himself again, repeatedly, as many times as necessary." Time

The Russian debutante's handbook. Riverhead Bks. 2002 452p

ISBN 1-57322-213-5   LC 2001-47676

"Failurchka-Mother's Little Failure-is what Vladimir Girshkin's overweening Russian immigrant mother calls her 25-year-old son at the beginning of this picaresque . . . first novel. Vladimir is stuck in a dead-end job and saddled with girlfriend Challah, 'queen of everything musky and mammal-like.' Then through a series of chance encounters, he is catapulted to the eastern European city of 'Prava' to find himself welcomed into the fold of powerful Mafiosi." Libr J

"Shteyngart's playful, carnivalesque sensibility fits within a Russian satirical-fantastic tradition that stretches from Nikolai Gogol in the 19th century to Mikhail Bulgakov in the Stalin period and Vassily Aksyonov in the Soviet twilight. The sturdy conventions of the traditional novel . . . are blithely disregarded in favor of digressive, madcap inventiveness." N Y Times Book Rev

Shulman, Alix Kates

Memoirs of an ex-prom queen; a novel. Knopf 1972 274p o.p.

"In the third grade, tomboy Sasha realizes that 'there's only one thing worth bothering about: becoming beautiful,' and begins to apply herself to that end. At 15 she has succeeded: she is elected queen of the high school prom and loses her virginity the same evening, an occurrence not at all coincidental, since she measures beauty in terms of sex appeal. By her 25th birthday, she's had 25 lovers. Although she's intelligent (a Columbia Ph.D. candidate) and ambitious, she is unable to escape the trap she has set for herself. Her identity is determined only in terms of her femininity and her relationships with men. Her ideas and ambitions must be sacrificed to theirs, if necessary, and it always seems to 'be' necessary. Her decline from potential philosopher to typical housewife appears completed by the birth of her children, but age and fading looks finally prove to be her salvation." Publ Wkly

Shulman, Max, 1919-1988

The many loves of Dobie Gillis; eleven campus stories. Doubleday 1951 223p o.p.

Contents: Unlucky winner; She shall have music; Love is a fallacy; Sugar bowl; Everybody loves my baby; Love of two chemists; Face is familiar but—; Mock governor; Boy bites man; King's English; You think you got trouble

"Here are 11 short stories dealing with Dobie Gillis, of the crew cut set, and his adventures and misadventures on the Golden Gopher's campus. The stories appeared individually in the Saturday Evening Post, American Magazine and other periodicals. Most of the time Dobie is becoming infatuated or disinfatuated with one fair coed or another, and the woes and worries which these damsels bring with them supply obstacles for the nimble-witted freckled Casanova." San Francisco Chron

Rally round the flag, boys!. Doubleday 1957 278p o.p.

"The setting is a small Connecticut town where three ethnic groups struggle for dominance—the Commuters, the Italians, and the Yankee Natives. The establishment of a Nike base in the town leads to no end of hilarious complications." Libr J

"A bit of lusty fun at the expense of commuters, exurban manners and mores, teen-age cults, Army red tape, progressive education, and whatever else catches the author's satiric eye." Booklist

Shute, Nevil, 1899-1960

On the beach. Morrow 1957 320p o.p.

"A nuclear war annihilates the world's Northern Hemisphere, and as atomic wastes are spreading southward, residents of Australia try to come to grips with their mortality. In spite of the inevitability of death, these people face their end with courage and live from day to day. They even plant trees they may never see mature." Shapiro. Fic for Youth. 3d edition

Siddons, Anne Rivers

Heartbreak Hotel. Simon & Schuster 1976 252p

ISBN 0-671-22315-1

"Maggie Deloach, a Southern beauty of the 50s, seems well on the way to success Dixie-style. Sorority girl, well-born, a leader, she is pinned to Boots Claiborne, scion of an old land-owning Delta family. It would seem that marriage and a happy-ever-after life are ahead of her. But Randolph University exposes her to more that frat parties and frivolity. A professor, a reporter and a student from New Jersey sow the seeds of questions. A visit to Boot's family and an ugly incident there make Maggie's questions more insistent and, for her, unnerving since they not only challenge her carefully planned future, but reveal stirring in the South she had never anticipated." Publ Wkly

Siddons, Anne Rivers—*Continued*

Islands. HarperCollins 2004 374p $24.95
ISBN 0-06-621111-5   LC 2003-51139
"When Charleston protagonist Anny Butler marries Dr.
Lewis Aiken, she becomes a member of the 'Scrubs' a
longtime group of friends who all have medical connections. For years, they share their free time together at a
communal beach house. Then misfortune begins to
plague the group, resulting in three deaths. . . . Gaynelle
Toomer, a Harley-riding, freckle-faced, enormous-
breasted librarian, is hired to do odd jobs for the Scrubs.
She and her seven-year-old daughter, Britney, a beauty
pageant contestant regular, become constant companions
to Anny's frail friend, Camilla. Camilla, the stabilizing
force of this group, turns out to be not at all what she
appears, making the story's end a shocker." Libr J

Nora, Nora; a novel. HarperCollins Pubs. 2000
263p $25
ISBN 0-06-017613-X   LC 00-40996
"In 1961, Nora, an outrageous, exotic, outspoken woman who smokes cigarettes and drives a pink Thunderbird,
arrives in the sleepy, segregated town of Lytton, GA.
While some residents are ruffled by her 'unsouthern' behavior, the effect Nora has on her adolescent and impressionable cousin Peyton is electric, opening Peyton's
senses to the world around her." Libr J
"In addition to her impeccable re-creation of Southern
speech and atmosphere, Siddons captures the angst of adolescence with practiced skill." Publ Wkly

Outer banks; a novel. HarperCollins Pubs. 1991
400p
ISBN 0-06-016249-X   LC 90-56370
"Kate Abrams hasn't spoken to three of her sorority
sisters for 28 years. But now Ginger, the eager rich girl
who stole and married Kate's brilliant boyfriend, is hosting a reunion at her home in Nags Head, N.C. And
Cecie, the orphan whose wit and cynical reserve attracted
Kate, and Fig Newton, the unsightly and bumbling outcast, will both attend. . . . The narrative flows smoothly,
journeying seamlessly between places and eras. While
the pseudo-thriller ending seems pat, Siddons displays
real strength in her subtle characterizations and delineation of emotional nuances." Publ Wkly

Sweetwater Creek; a novel. HarperCollins 2005
356p $24.95
ISBN 0-06-621335-5   LC 2005-46279
"Twelve-year-old Emily Parmenter helps in the family
business of raising hunting spaniels at their Charleston
area plantation, Sweetwater Farm. Her only pals are her
own dog, Elvis, and her deceased older brother, Buddy
(who speaks to her from the grave). But her life is about
to change radically with the arrival of rich, sophisticated
20-year-old Lulu Foxworth. During her visit to the plantation, she falls in love with the dogs and Emily's family
before moving in. . . . Under Lulu's tutelage, Emily
leaves her child's world and enters one for which she's
not quite ready. As usual, Siddons never lets you forget
where you are–the essence of South Carolina's Low
Country is prominently featured and intricately . . . described." Libr J

Sidor, Steven

The mirror's edge. St. Martin's Minotaur 2008
287p $24.95
ISBN 978-0-312-35413-8; 0-312-35413-4
LC 2007-51830
"As the first anniversary of the kidnapping of two-
year-old twins Liam and Shane Boyle approaches . . .
Chicago freelance journalist Jase Deering decides to investigate with his partner and girlfriend, the blind Robyn
Matchfrost. Jase has his own demons: his 12-year-old
brother, Matthias, was abducted and murdered when they
were children. With the help of police detectives, Jase
traces the palindrome mirrorrorrim, which the twin's ab-
ductor carved into their nanny's living flesh, to cult leader Aubrey Hart Morick, who advocated human sacrifice.
Though Morick is long dead, Jase discovers that his son,
Graham, lives in the area and isn't as harmless as he first
appears. . . . Sidor is a master of the unsettling, and
each twist is more grisly and unexpected than the last."
Publ Wkly

Skin River. St. Martin's Minotaur 2004 241p
$23.95
ISBN 0-312-32949-0   LC 2004-46784
"When a psychotic almost kills the single-
mother/waitress who lives above his rural Wisconsin tavern, Buddy Bayes goes ballistic. Buddy recently found
the severed hand of a different victim, and because of his
own former criminal life in Chicago, he feels both attacks may be a message for him. So he secretly returns
to the Windy City to see if there's still a contract on
him, while back in Wisconsin the serial killer continues
to operate with chilling immunity. Deft descriptions,
slick prose, and growing tension mark this first novel."
Libr J

Siegel, James, 1954-

Deceit. Warner Books 2006 369p
ISBN 978-0-446-53186-3; 0-446-53186-3
LC 2006-08610
This novel's "flawed protagonist, Tom Valle, is a journalist in exile after writing more than 50 fake stories for
a major New York City newspaper, a scandal that led to
criminal charges for him and disgrace for the respected
editor blamed for not having caught his lies. Now, Valle
toils for a small California paper, covering mall openings
and the birthdays of elderly locals. One such fluff assignment, which entails a visit to a senior citizen home
whose oldest resident just turned 100, gives Valle a
chance at redemption when he suspects that the woman's
recollection of a recent visit from her long-dead son is
more than a senile delusion." Publ Wkly
Siegel's "inventive plotting and delicious humor are in
the forefront, while his fluid writing masks a multitude
of sins in characterization and dialogue, resulting in first-
rate entertainment." Booklist

Derailed. Warner Bks. 2003 339p $23.95
ISBN 0-446-53158-8   LC 2002-73572
Charles Schine "writes advertising copy and worries a
lot about his stressed-out wife and diabetic daughter.
Charles makes his fatal mistake one morning on the 9:05
commuter train from Babylon to Penn Station, when he
looks up from his newspaper. . . and makes eye contact
with a beautiful stockbroker named Lucinda. One thing

Siegel, James, 1954——*Continued*
leads to another, but their hotel tryst is interrupted by an armed intruder who rapes Lucinda, pistol-whips Charles and proceeds to blackmail them. Desperate, Charles resorts to criminal measures to stop this sadistic torment." N Y Times Book Rev

"With its clean prose, high-velocity plotting and just the right amount of emotional shading darkening its sharply drawn characters, this novel is the bomb." Publ Wkly

Siegel, Sheldon

Final verdict. Putnam 2003 391p $25.95
ISBN 0-399-15042-0   LC 2002-37189
This legal procedural features "law partners Mike Daley and ex-wife Rosie Fernandez working together in their San Francisco firm, Fernandez, Daley and O'Malley. . . . Skid row resident Leon Walker, successfully represented by Michael and Rosie in a murder case 10 years earlier, reappears and seeks legal help once again. Leon is charged with the murder of Tower Grayson, a Silicon Valley venture capitalist found stabbed to death in a Dumpster behind a liquor store. Publ Wkly

"An ending that's full of surprises—both professional and personal—provides the perfect finale to a supremely entertaining legal thriller." Booklist

Sienkiewicz, Henryk, 1846-1916

The deluge; in modern translation by W. S. Kuniczak. Copernicus Soc. of Am. 1991 2v o.p.
              LC 91-5047
Original Polish edition, 1886
In this second volume of the trilogy "a mere five years have passed since the knights of the Polish-Lithuanian Commonwealth threw back the Cossack invasion from the East, yet a new and far more dangerous threat appears: Swedish troops are pouring across the Northern border. . . . Central to the story is Andrei Kmita, a young Lithuanian noble whose ruthlessness obscures his military sagacity and bravery, branding him an outlaw. But for the love of the beautiful Olenka, he undertakes to reshape his character in the forge of battle, and in so doing helps save king, country, and church from the heretic invaders." Libr J
Followed by Fire in the steppe

Fire in the steppe; in modern translation by W. S. Kuniczak. Copernicus Soc. of Am.; distributed by Hippocrene Bks. 1992 717p $24.95
ISBN 0-7818-0025-0   LC 92-218600
Original Polish edition, 1887
"The Polish people's struggle against Cossacks, Tartars and Turks in the 1670s prefigures modern Poland's quest for nationhood in this [final] installment of the rousing epic of love, war, adventure and madness. Basia, the gutsy, bright, determind heroine, who chases bandits on horseback, riding a man's saddle, almost steals the show from her Hamlet-like husband, Col. Pan Volodyovski." Publ Wkly
This "is an unabashed, extravagant celebration of romance and patriotism, but with a difference: the novel ends with wrenching scenes of Polish nobility, courage and hope in the face of defeat—showing why Sienkiewicz's trilogy is so beloved in his native country." N Y Times Book Rev

Quo Vadis; a narrative of the time of Nero; translated from the Polish by Jeremiah Curtin. Little, Brown 1896 541p o.p.

A historical novel dealing with the "Rome of Nero and the early Christian martyrs. The Roman noble, Petronius, a worthy representative of the dying paganism, is perhaps the most interesting figure, and the struggle between Christianity and paganism supplies the central plot, but the canvas is large. A succession of characters and episodes and, above all, the richly colorful, decadent life of ancient Rome give the novel its chief interest. The beautiful Christian Lygia is the object of unwelcome attentions from Vinicius, one of the Emperor's guards, and when she refuses to yield to his importunities, she is denounced and thrown to the wild beasts of the arena. She escapes and eventually marries Vinicius, whom Peter and Paul have converted to Christianity." Reader's Ency. 4th edition

With fire and sword; in modern translation by W.S. Kuniczak; foreword by James A. Michener. Copernicus Soc. of Am. 1991 1135p o.p.
              LC 91-161
Original Polish edition, 1883
"The first book in a trilogy covering Polish history from 1648 to 1673. The novel's main stage is occupied by the Ukrainian cossacks' rebellion against the Poles. Yan Skshetuski, a Polish lieutenant dispatched to gather information about the rebellion, is taken prisoner by the cossacks. After numerous battles, retreats, and betrayals on both sides, the revolt culminates in the cossacks' siege of the city of Zbaraz." Booklist
This novel "should have taken place in the general literary repertory long ago, alongside the works of the elder Dumas, Walter Scott, Margaret Mitchell." N Y Times Book Rev
Followed by The deluge

Sigler, Scott

Contagious. Crown Publishers 2008 438p $24.95
ISBN 978-0-307-40631-6; 0-307-40631-8
              LC 2008-39985
Sequel to: Infected
"In the near future, U.S. president John Gutierrez goes straight from his inauguration to crisis management when his national security team informs him that he must focus his attention on Project Tangram, a secret government program to stave off an epidemic caused by alien parasites, which form itchy blue triangular patches on the skin. Victims eventually become paranoid and violent. As the infestation spreads, Gutierrez must decide whether the outbreak can be contained without the use of tactical nukes on American soil. Meanwhile, the creatures responsible for the parasites get a foothold in Michigan through a seven-year-old girl, who manifests possession by drawing blue triangles on her dolls. . . . This page-turner builds inexorably to an explosive ending." Publ Wkly

Infected; a novel. Crown Publishers 2008 342p il $24.95
ISBN 978-0-307-40610-1; 0-307-40610-5
              LC 2007-41037

Sigler, Scott—*Continued*

Originally released as a podcast in 2006

In this "horror thriller, alien seeds from outer space infect a number of unlucky humans, who develop some unusual symptoms—itchy, blue triangular growths on their skin—that eventually result in the carriers becoming screaming, homicidal maniacs. CIA agent Dew Phillips must find out why these formerly docile citizens are running amok, aided by Margaret Montoya, a Centers for Disease Control epidemiologist, who reported the first of the strange cases. One of the infected, former football player Perry Dawsey, doesn't take any crap from anybody, not even the aliens residing in his body. Sigler . . . leads the reader from one startling detail to the next . . . until even hardened genre fans will find themselves whimpering at each new revelation." Publ Wkly

Sigurðardóttir, Yrsa *See* Yrsa Sigurðardóttir

Silber, Joan

Ideas of heaven; a ring of stories. W.W. Norton 2004 250p $23.95

ISBN 0-393-05908-1   LC 2003-24324

Contents: My shape; The high road; Gaspara Stampa; Ashes of love; Ideas of heaven; The same ground

"Six elegantly connected stories explore, through first-person narratives, the conflicts and commonalities of love, faith and sex. A minor character in the first story becomes the narrator in the second, and so on, with each story building on its predecessor until they come full circle. . . . Silber uses the device of interwoven narratives beautifully; these lengthy stories can stand alone, but the subtle connections and emotional resonances help create a satisfying structural unity." Publ Wkly

The size of the world; a novel. W.W. Norton 2008 288p $23.95

ISBN 978-0-393-05909-0; 0-393-05909-X

LC 2008-01342

This "work of fiction consists of interlinked stories where minor or passing characters in one piece become the narrators of others, roaming from WWII Sicily to roaring '20s Siam, and from Vietnam-era Mexico to 9/11-era Bloomington, Ind. All six stories turn on the tensions between home, exile and otherness, but to follow any of the threads would be to give away the subtle connections among the characters, from a male Sicilian-American postcolonialist professor from Hoboken to a Florida woman named Kit who can sum up an old boyfriend as the sort of boy who seemed startled when having sex. At the time his awe and confusion were endearing. The frankness of Silber's characters is deliciously at odds with the delicacy of their observations as they absorb children, affairs, fractured and repaired families and early death in environments familiar and alien to them." Publ Wkly

Silko, Leslie, 1948-

Gardens in the dunes; a novel; [by] Leslie Marmon Silko. Simon & Schuster 1999 479p $25

ISBN 0-684-81154-5   LC 98-51987

Set in the 19th century this is the "tale of two sisters, the last remaining members of the ancient Sand Lizard tribe. Sister Salt, so called for her light skin, and her younger sister, Indigo, learn all about the hidden, life-sustaining plants of the desert from Grandma Fleet, who teaches them how to live happily with a minimum of material goods and a wealth of knowledge. Such self-sufficiency is essential if they are to stay free from the misery of reservation life, but even so their liberty is put at risk when they travel to the mean little town of Needles, Arizona, where hundreds of Indians gather to dance in anticipation of the arrival of the Messiah. In the chaotic aftermath of the miraculous visitation, the girls lose their mother and grandmother and then are cruelly separated by the authorities." Booklist

Sillitoe, Alan

The loneliness of the long-distance runner. Knopf 1960 c1959 176p o.p.

First published 1959 in the United Kingdom

Contents: The loneliness of the long-distance runner; Uncle Ernest; Mr. Raynor the schoolteacher; The fishing-boat picture; Noah's ark; On Saturday afternoon; The match; The disgrace of Jim Scarfedale; The decline and fall of Frankie Buller

"This collection of short stories portrays life from the point of view of the English working class. The unnamed narrator in the title story, which is probably the best known in the book, is a roguish young man who has been in trouble with authority all his life. He is told by the head of a Borstal institution where he is an inmate that he can reform himself by training to be a long-distance runner. He enters into training, and during practice runs, his thoughts go back to the circumstances that led to his detention. The climax of the story is in a track meet between his penal institution and a private school. The boy easily outruns his competitors but pulls up at the finish line and refuses to cross it, thus revenging himself against the head of the institution and spoiling the victory of the other school." Shapiro. Fic for Youth. 3d edition

Saturday night and Sunday morning. Knopf 1959 c1958 239p o.p.

First published 1958 in the United Kingdom

This novel's "protagonist, anarchic young Arthur Seaton, lathe operator in a Nottingham bicycle factory, provided a new prototype of the working class Angry Young Man; rebellious, contemptuous towards authority in the form of management, government, the army, and neighbourhood spies, he unleashes his energy on drink and women, with quieter interludes spent fishing in the canal. . . . A landmark in the development of the post-war novel." Oxford Companion to Engl Lit. 6th edition

Silone, Ignazio, 1900-1978

Bread and wine; a new version translated from the Italian by Harvey Fergusson II; with a new preface by the author. Atheneum Pubs. 1962 331p o.p.

First published 1937 in the United States by Harper

"Translated from the edition revised by the author to modify the political concepts of the original." Publ Wkly

"The hero, Pietro Spina, returns to his native Abruzzi

Silone, Ignazio, 1900-1978—*Continued*

after fifteen years of exile to continue his antifascist agitation. As he travels through the country, disguised as a priest, he sees the inroads made upon the Italian character by Mussolini's rule. Finding that the underground movement is in chaos and doubting the validity of his old revolutionary slogans, he eventually flees to avoid certain arrest." Reader's Ency. 4d edition

Followed by The seed beneath the snow (1942)

Silva, Daniel

The mark of the assassin; a novel. Villard Bks. 1998 465p $25

ISBN 0-679-45563-9   LC 98-5268

"When an airliner is shot down after taking off from New York's Kennedy Airport, an Islamic terrorist group called the Sword of Gaza is immediately blamed for the crime. But CIA operative Michael Osbourne suspects a different perpetrator, a lone assassin with the code name October who, years earlier, took the life of Osbourne's girlfriend in a London confrontation." Publ Wkly

"With concise, vivid character sketches, Silva weaves a swiftly paced, internationally tangled plot." Libr J

The messenger. Putnam 2006 388p $25.95

ISBN 0-399-15335-7   LC 2006-367534

A "thriller starring Israeli art restorer and spymaster Gabriel Allon. Ahmed bin Shafiq, a former chief of a clandestine Saudi intelligence unit, targets the Vatican for attack, in particular Pope Paul VII and his top aide, Monsignor Luigi Donati. . . . Shafiq, who now heads his own terrorist network, is allied with a militant Islamic Saudi businessman known as Zizi, a true believer committed to the destruction of all infidels. Gabriel's challenge is to infiltrate Zizi's organization, a task he assigns to a beautiful American art expert, Sarah Bancroft." Publ Wkly

"An engrossing and beautifully written contemporary spy thriller." Booklist

Moscow rules. G.P. Putnam's Sons 2008 433p $26.95

ISBN 978-0-399-15501-7; 0-399-15501-5

LC 2008-18318

"A Russian journalist dies and once more Gabriel Allon, the mysterious Israeli agent/fine picture restorer, ends up back in Moscow. . . . It seems a second Russian journalist wants to tell Allon and only Allon why the first journalist, his coworker, was killed. This meeting never takes place – the second journalist is killed right before Allon can get to him – and in short order, Allon has a full-fledged case on his hands. . . . Allon summons up an Israeli investigative team and he and his fellow agents eventually turn up the name of one Ivan Kharkov, a former KGB colonel. Kharkov has carried over his previous covert training into his new career as an international arms dealer, and one willing to sell to Al-Qaeda. To collect information on him, Allon must persuade Kharkov's wife to betray her husband. . . . Silva's latest is both fast-past thriller with all the appropriate twists and turns and a fascinating look at the inner workings of Russian society today." Houston Press

Prince of Fire. Putnam 2005 369p $25.95

ISBN 0-399-15243-1   LC 2004-60066

"Not long after an explosion in Rome destroys the Israeli embassy compound, a file linked to the terrorists behind the bombing surfaces; it contains a remarkably comprehensive account of the career of Gabriel Allon, including the date of his recruitment by the Israeli secret service. Living in Venice and about to embark upon the restoration of a priceless Rubens painting, Gabriel, a talented art restorer and a reluctant spy, must return to Israel and the auspices of the agency bureaucrats. He is assigned the task of identifying the bombers, which eventually results in a face-to-face meeting with Yassar Arafat, the man responsible for the death of Gabriel's child and the maiming of his wife some 10 years earlier. He suspects that Arafat is deeply connected to the Rome bomber, whom Gabriel believes is a third-generation terrorist who has been protected and schooled as a mastermind by Arafat himself. Along with the meticulously detailed plot, Silva . . . provides a clear-eyed chronicle of the endless warfare between the Israelis and the Palestinians." Booklist

The secret servant. G.P. Putnam's Sons 2007 385p $25.95

ISBN 978-0-399-15422-5; 0-399-15422-1

LC 2007-17548

"Gabriel Allon is back, investigating the murder of terrorism analyst Ephraim Rosner by a Muslim immigrant in Amsterdam. The plot thickens with the kidnapping of the U.S. ambassador's daughter in London." Libr J

"Daniel Silva is a craftsmanlike writer of international thrillers. He has a nice, no-nonsense style; he plots simply, directly and suspensefully; and in Gabriel Allon he has a reliable protagonist." Los Angeles Times Book Rev

Silver, Katherine, 1957-

(tr) Castellanos Moya, H. Senselessness

(tr) Skármeta, A. The dancer and the thief

Silver, Marisa

The god of war. Simon & Schuster 2008 271p $23

ISBN 978-1-4165-6316-7; 1-4165-6316-4

LC 2007-25424

"Twelve-year-old Ares Ramirez has a life as unique as his name. His mother, who has a taste for men who don't stick around, raises Ares and his mentally handicapped brother, Malcolm, on the shores of the isolated Salton Sea in the California desert. Ares is saddled with far too much responsibility while his mother flits through life as a free spirit, leaving him to watch over the brother Ares thinks he damaged by dropping him accidentally as a baby. Ares looks elsewhere for the attention and acceptance he's not getting at home, finally finding it in the kindly librarian who tutors Malcolm and her dangerous foster son, Kevin. Ares's new friend leads him on a path of destruction with a tragic end." Libr J

"Finely wrought characters and an illuminating portrait of the secret world of autism makes for a powerful, often tragic tale." Kirkus

Silverberg, Robert

The collected stories of Robert Silverberg. v1: Secret sharers. Bantam Bks. 1992 546p pa $25
ISBN 978-0-553-37068-3; 0-553-37068-5
LC 92-9958
Contents: Homefaring; Basileus; Dancers in the time-flux; Gate of horn, gate of ivory; Amanda and the alien; Snake and ocean, ocean and snake; Tourist trade; Multiples; Against Babylon; Symbiont; Sailing to Byzantium; Sunrise on Pluto; Hardware; Hannibal's elephants; The pardoner's tale; The iron star; The secret sharer; House of bones; The dead man's eyes; Chip runner; To the promised land; The Asenion solution; A sleep and a forgetting; Enter a soldier. Later: enter another
Followed by: v2 The secret sharer (1993); v3 Beyond the safe zone (1994); v4 Road to nightfall (1995); v5 Ringing the changes (1997); v6 Lion time in Timbuctoo (2000)

Downward to the Earth
In Silverberg, R. A Robert Silverberg omnibus

The longest way home. Eos 2002 294p $25.95
ISBN 0-380-97858-X
LC 2001-55601
"Joseph Master Keilloran, young heir to the great House Keilloran, is visiting relatives 10,000 miles from home when a rebellion of the serflike Folk turns his world—a planet conquered long ago by his ancestors—upside down. Joseph, who has never questioned the wealth and privilege to which he was born, barely escapes with his life. Cut off from all sources of comfort and support, he decides to walk home, across a huge continent he knows almost nothing about." N Y Times Book Rev
"While neither the protagonist of this bildungsroman nor his transformation is remarkable, the land that our young hero journeys through and the exotic creatures that inhabit it testify to the author's rich imagination." Publ Wkly

Lord Valentine's castle. Harper & Row 1980 449p o.p.
* LC 79-2658
"Majipoor is an enormous planet inhabited by intelligent beings and ruled by a benevolent lord. . . . The story begins as Valentine, a young amnesiac, wanders into the city of Pidruid in time for a festival celebrating a once-in-a-lifetime visit of another Valentine, Lord Valentine, the supreme ruler of the planet. Early in the book readers know what Valentine is slow to understand; he is the real Lord Valentine and the one in power is an imposter. On a coming-of-age journey to Lord Valentine's Castle, gathering friends, supporters, and ultimately troops en route, Valentine discovers his true identity and gains a better understanding of the people and place he is destined to rule. A good story, inventively told, which abounds with adventure and curious characters." SLJ
Followed by Majipoor chronicles

The man in the maze
In Silverberg, R. A Robert Silverberg omnibus

Nightwings [novelette]
In The Hugo winners p503-57

In Silverberg, R. A Robert Silverberg omnibus

A Robert Silverberg omnibus; The man in the maze; Nightwings; Downward to the Earth. Harper & Row 1981 544p o.p.
LC 80-8232
An omnibus edition of three titles first published separately 1969, 1969, and 1970 respectively
In the novel Nightwings Earth is taken over by aliens; the man in the maze dramatizes aspects of alienation and Downward to the Earth employs religious imagery in a story of repentence and rebirth
All three novels in this collection "feature strong but psychologically wounded male protagonists, descriptions of bizarre beings and far-away worlds and imaginative, if sometimes unrealistic plots. . . . For readers who appreciate swiftly-paced action." Voice Youth Advocates

Roma eterna. Eos 2003 396p $25.95
ISBN 0-380-97859-8
* LC 2002-35416
This is "a what-if history of the world, starting from the premise that the Roman Empire never fell. Spaning 1,500 years, the narrative unfolds in a world without Christianity. It seems that the failure of the ancient Hebrews to escape Pharaonic oppression prevented the rise of mystical religious cults in the province of Syria Palaestina, thereby guaranteeing the survival of Roman hegemony down to the beginning of space travel. Silverberg, who has written numerous popular works of history and archaeology, brings his alternate Rome to life by blending invention with a dazzling array of details borrowed from the annals of the real Rome." N Y Times Book Rev

Simak, Clifford D., 1904-1988

The big front yard
In The Hugo winners p171-226

Simenon, Georges, 1903-1989

Inspector Maigret and the killers; translated from the French by Louise Varèse. Doubleday 1954 187p o.p.
"Published for the Crime Club"
Original French edition, 1952. Variant title: Maigret and the gangsters
"Inspector Lognon, widely known as 'the most dismal man in the Paris police,' is always trying to solve some spectacular case that will land him with Maigret's Crime Squad on the Quai des Orfevres. Lognon's latest exploit involves a drug stakeout during which he sees a car pull up to the curb and a body dumped out on the pavement. By the time Lognon makes his call, another car has pulled up to retrieve the corpse. Maigret joins Lognon in finding the disappearing body, while events become more outlandish and dangerous. The witty pace featuring kidnappings and shootings, is effectively sustained throughout." Booklist

Maigret and the black sheep; translated from the French by Helen Thomson. Harcourt Brace Jovanovich 1976 158p o.p.
"A Helen and Kurt Wolff book"
Original French edition, 1972
"The victim is a retired carton manufacturer who has

Simenon, Georges, 1903-1989—*Continued*
been shot, without apparent motive, while sitting at home in his favorite armchair. To [Chief Inspector Maigret's] chagrin, he can find no crack or crevice in the utter respectability of the dead man's life. . . . The season is the end of summer. Parisians are drifting back to the city from their vacations, there is a nip in the air. . . . Maigret sips his beer in several cafés, confers with his faithful colleague Lapointe, and ponders the many facts of this . . . case." New Yorker

Maigret and the fortune-teller; translated by Geoffrey Sainsbury. Harcourt Brace Jovanovich 1989 140p o.p.   LC 88-16301
"A Helen and Kurt Wolff book"
Original French edition, 1944
Maigret "is forewarned of a murder but fails to prevent it. He tracks down the villain by exercising his famous 'capacity for putting himself in other people's shoes.' In this case, the shoes belong to a woebegone old man, apparently senile, who was found at the scene of the crime. Obviously more terrified of his wife and daughter than he is of the thunderous Maigret, the old man piques the policeman's interest and so leads him to the solution." Booklist

Maigret and the madwoman; translated from the French by Eileen Ellenbogen. Harcourt Brace Jovanovich 1972 176p o.p.
                                                                    *
"A Helen and Kurt Wolff book"
Original French edition, 1970
"Maigret exerts himself to make up for his failure to prevent the murder of a nice old lady who had told him of her fears. He goes to Toulon to interview a suspect and generally behaves as a chief superintendent should. Madame Maigret plays a larger part than usual." Barzun. Cat of Crime. Rev and enl edition

Maigret and the Saturday caller; translated by Tony White. Harcourt Brace Jovanovich 1991 124p o.p.   LC 90-46032
"A Helen and Kurt Wolff book"
Original French edition, 1962
"Maigret is visited by a harelipped man who confesses that he wants to murder his wife and her lover but hasn't yet done so. Needless to say, Maigret cannot dismiss the man's plans as the fantasy of a harmless lunatic and begins to probe around the edges, irritated by the handicaps imposed by the public prosecutor's recent restrictions on police powers." Booklist

Maigret and the toy village; translated by Eileen Ellenbogen. Harcourt Brace Jovanovich 1979 139p o.p.   LC 79-1843
"A Helen and Kurt Wolff book"
Original French edition, 1944
In this novel "Maigret, the solemn, slow-moving, yet brilliant Chief Superintendent of the Police Judiciare, is entangled in the most exasperating murder case of his career. A man is slain in a new suburban housing development (the 'toy village' of the title). The prime suspect is his housekeeper, a young woman who has the motive for murder (she stands to inherit the old man's money), plenty of opportunities to execute the crime, and a maddening propensity for keeping Maigret at bay." Booklist

Maigret and the wine merchants; translated from the French by Eileen Ellenbogen. Harcourt Brace Jovanovich 1971 187p o.p.
                                                                    *
"A Helen and Kurt Wolff book"
Original French edition, 1970
"A wealthy wine merchant [in Paris] is shot down. His wife takes the news with complete unsurprise and a shrug of the shoulders. His business associates discuss him as some sort of artifact coolly, unemotionally. His mistresses neither liked nor disliked him. Eventually the murderer comes into Maigret's sight." N Y Times Book Rev

Maigret bides his time; translated by Alastair Hamilton. Harcourt Brace Jovanovich 1985 c1966 165p o.p.   LC 84-25134
"A Helen and Kurt Wolff book"
Original French edition, 1965; this translation first published 1966 in the United Kingdom
This novel "combines a delight in the sensual world with an exploration of the horrors of human cruelty. The plot revolves around the murder of master jewel thief and gang leader Manuel Palmari, a criminal Maigret has known for many years and whose death he half-guiltily mourns. The chief suspect is Palmari's young mistress, though Maigret finds many more suspects and motives crowded into the deceased man's life. Maigret's investigation does not end until a welter of vice has been uncovered—and more murder is committed. Vintage Simenon." Booklist

Maigret goes home; translated by Robert Baldick. Harcourt Brace Jovanovich 1989 139p o.p.   LC 89-2011
"A Helen and Kurt Wolff book"
Original French edition, 1931; this translation first published 1940 in the United Kingdom
"The countess of the estate where Maigret grew up drops dead during early mass on All Souls' Day, shocked to death by a fake newspaper report falsely reporting the suicide of her son. Although the estate had been heavily mortgaged to pay for the son's debts and the countess' young lovers, the inheritance is still not inconsiderable, and, of course, there are at least three likely suspects." Booklist

Maigret in Holland; translated by Geoffrey Sainsbury. 2nd ed. Harcourt Brace & Co. 1993 165p o.p.   LC 92-30504
"A Helen and Kurt Wolff book"
Original French edition, 1931; first English translation with title Crime in Holland, published 1940 in the collection Maigret abroad
"Although Maigret speaks no Dutch, he is called to Holland to assist a compatriot, Jean Duclos. Unfortunately, Duclos was present when Conrad Popinga, a former captain in the merchant marine, was murdered, and the Dutch police think Duclos, along with Popinga's wife and sister-in-law, a young sailor, and a local farm girl, is a prime suspect. Once the capable but long-suffering Maigret arrives, he methodically reviews the evidence and questions suspects. . . . Readers will marvel at the inspector's brilliant logic." Booklist

Simenon, Georges, 1903-1989—*Continued*

Maigret's memoirs; translated from the French by Jean Stewart. Harcourt Brace Jovanovich 1985 c1963 134p o.p.   LC 85-8591

"A Helen and Kurt Wolff book"

Original French edition, 1951; this translation first published 1963 in the United Kingdom

"Inspector Maigret, upset by writer Georges Simenon's 'caricature' of him, decides to correct the world's misconception of his personality and his cases by writing his memoirs. . . . Maigret outlines a few criminal cases, digresses about the Parisian weather, explains his dislike for Simenon, and presents his views on the criminal mind and on life in general in this odd but marvelous 'autobiographical' account." Booklist

The man who watched trains go by; a new translation by Marc Romano, D. Thin; introduction by Luc Sante. New York Review Books 2005 203p (New York Review Books classics) pa $12.95

ISBN 978-1-59017-149-3; 1-59017-149-7
LC 2005-8102

Original French edition, 1938

"Kees Popinga is a solid Dutch burgher whose idea of a night on the town is a game of chess at his club. Or so it has always appeared. But one night this model husband and devoted father discovers his boss is bankrupt and that his own carefully tended life is in ruins. Before, he had looked on impassively as the trains to the outside world swept by; now he catches the first train he can to Amsterdam. Not long after that, he commits murder." Publisher's note

A man's head; translated by Geoffrey Sainsbury. Penguin Books 2006 170p pa $12

ISBN 0-14-303728-5; 978-0-14-303728-6
LC 2006-41670

"A Penguin mystery"

Original French edition, 1931; first United States edition published 1940 with title: The patience of Maigret. Also previously published under title: Maigret's war of nerves

Maigret is convinced that Heurtin, a condemned prisoner is innocent. The Inspector persuades officials to allow Heurtin to escape hoping that he will lead Maigret to the real killer.

My friend Maigret; [an Inspector Maigret mystery]; translated by Nigel Ryan. Penguin Books 2007 195p pa $13

ISBN 978-0-14-311284-6   LC 2007-25931

"A Penguin mystery"

Original French edition 1949

"This 1949 outing in Simenon's wonderful Inspector Maigret mystery series finds the sleuth leaving Paris to investigate the murder of a small-time crook who was talking loudly about him just before being killed." Libr J

Strangers in the house; ttanslated by Geoffrey Sainsbury; with revisions by David Watson & others; introduction by P.D. James. New York Review Books 2006 194p (New York Review Books classics) pa $14

ISBN 978-1-59017-194-3; 1-59017-194-2
LC 2005-36189

Original French edition, 1940; this translation first published 1951 in the United Kingdom

"Dirty, drunk, unloved, and unloving, Hector Loursat has been a bitter recluse for eighteen long years—ever since his wife abandoned him and their newborn child to run off with another man. Once a successful lawyer, Loursat now guzzles burgundy and buries himself in books, taking little notice of his teenage daughter or the odd things going on in his vast and evermore-dilapidated mansion. But one night the sound of a gunshot penetrates the padded walls of Loursat's study, and he is forced to investigate. What he stumbles on is a murder. Soon Loursat discovers that his daughter and her friends have been leading a dangerous secret life. He finds himself strangely drawn to this group of young people, and when one of them is accused of the murder, he astonishes the world by taking up the young man's defense." Publisher's note

Simmons, Dan

Drood; a novel. Little, Brown and Co. 2009 775p $26.99

ISBN 978-0-316-00702-3; 0-316-00702-1
LC 2008-24501

"In this creepy intertextual tale of professional jealousy and possible madness, Wilkie Collins tells of his friendship and rivalry with Charles Dickens, and of the mysterious phantasm named Edwin Drood, who pursues them both. Drood, cadaverous and pale, first appears at the scene of a railway accident in which Dickens was one of the few survivors; later, Dickens and Collins descend into London's sewer in search of his lair. Meanwhile, a retired police detective warns Collins that Drood is responsible for more than three hundred murders, and that he will destroy Dickens in his quest for immortality. Collins is peevish, vain, and cruel, and the most unreliable of narrators: an opium addict, prone to nightmarish visions. The narrative is overlong, with discarded subplots and red herrings, but Simmons, a master of otherworldly suspense, cleverly explores envy's corrosive effects." New Yorker

Endymion. Bantam Bks. 1996 486p o.p.
* LC 95-33191

"The protagonist, a good-hearted soldier named Raul Endymion, sets off on a quest with historic consequences: he must keep from harm a young girl who holds the key to a rebirth of human civilization. Arrayed against him is the power of the Pax, a militarized Catholic Church that offers its adherents a literal resurrection of the body. It is Mr. Simmons's inspiration to embody the Pax in the person of Father Captain Federico de Soya, a starship commander who pursues Endymion and the young girl from one exotic planet to the next." N Y Times Book Rev

Followed by The rise of Endymion (1997)

The fall of Hyperion. Doubleday 1990 517p

ISBN 0-385-24950-0   LC 89-37438

"A Foundation book"

"While the worlds of the Hegemony fight a desperate war in space against the Ouster rebels who threaten galactic unity, a group of seven pilgrims on the planet Hyperion wage their own war within the Tombs of Time, a mysterious artifact which conceals a hideous creature whose freedom means death for humanity. In this sequel

Simmons, Dan—*Continued*

to *Hyperion*, Simmons weaves together many strands of a complex plot with lucidity and poetic imagination." Libr J

Hyperion. Doubleday 1989 481p
ISBN 0-385-24949-7   LC 88-33407
"A Foundation book"

"On the world called Hyperion, beyond the law of the Hegemony of Man, there waits the creature called the Shrike. There are those who worship it. There are those who fear it. And there are those who have vowed to destroy it. In the Valley of the Time Tombs, where huge, brooding structures move backward through time, the Shrike waits for them all. On the eve of Armageddon, with the entire galaxy at war, seven pilgrims set forth on a final voyage to Hyperion seeking the answers to the unsolved riddles of their lives. Each carries a desperate hope-and a terrible secret. And one may hold the fate of humanity in his hands." Publisher's note

Followed by The fall of Hyperion

Ilium. Eos 2003 576p $25.95
ISBN 0-380-97893-8
                            * LC 2002-44791

"Restored to life by the 'gods,' a race of beings who dwell on the heights of Olympos, 20th-century scholar Thomas Hockenberry travels back in time to observe the events of the Trojan War, as chronicled in Homer's epic poem. There, one of the gods recruits him in a secret war against her brother and sister deities. Set in a far future in which the population of true humans is kept strictly regulated by extraplanetary forces and machine intelligences study Proust and Shakespeare as they perform their duties throughout the universe." Libr J

"For answers to the mysteries laid out in 'Ilium'— from the true identity of the Olympian gods to the fate of robots and humans and of the 'little green men' on Mars for whom communication means death—you will have to wait for the promised sequel. For now, matching wits with Simmons and his lively creations should be reward enough." N Y Times Book Rev

Followed by Olympos (2005)

Muse of fire. Subterranean Press 2008 c2007 105p $35
ISBN 978-1-59606-181-1; 1-59606-181-2

In the "far future, Earth is a mausoleum and the far-flung human race occupies the lowest level of a complex interstellar hierarchy. The Earth's Men travel to distant worlds and perform Shakespeare before human servants and slaves, bringing them some moments of pleasure and notions of Earth's lost glory. When aliens take an interest, the Earth's Men find themselves giving command performances of King Lear, Hamlet and 'the Scottish play' for a series of increasingly important alien species, with evidence that the fate of all humanity may rest on the quality of their work. This finely crafted novella is a perfect example of Simmons's many strengths." Publ Wkly

Olympos. HarperCollins 690p $25.95
ISBN 0-380-97894-6   LC 2005-40024
Sequel to Ilium (2003)

In this sequel to Ilium, "posthumans masquerading as the Greek gods and living on Mars travel back and forth through time and alternate universes to interfere in the real Trojan War, employing a resurrected late 20th-century classics professor, Thomas Hockenberry, as their tool. Meanwhile, the last remaining old-style human beings on a far-future Earth must struggle for survival against a variety of hostile forces. Superhuman entities with names like Prospero, Caliban and Ariel lay complex plots, using human beings as game pieces. From the outer solar system, an advanced race of semiorganic Artificial Intelligences, called moravecs, observe Earth and Mars in consternation, trying to make sense of the situation, hoping to shift the balance of power before out-of-control quantum forces destroy everything. This is powerful stuff, rich in both high-tech sense of wonder and literary allusions, but Simmons is in complete control of his material as half a dozen baroque plot lines smoothly converge on a rousing and highly satisfying conclusion." Publ Wkly

The rise of Endymion; a novel. Bantam Bks. 1997 579p o.p.
                            * LC 97-5658
Sequel to Endymion (1996)

In this concluding volume of the author's series about a far-future interstellar society, "most of the galaxy is populated by born-again Christians and ruled by the Catholic pope. Nonbelievers are persecuted and forced to accept the cruciform parasite, which allows people to be resurrected. The biggest threat to the establishment is Aenea, a young female architectural apprentice who teaches peace and the way to immense knowledge of the heart and mind. Aided by her lover, Raul Endymion, Aenea exposes organized religion as a parasite of the Core—the sentient evolution of the World Wide Web." Libr J

"For vastness of scope, clarity of detail and seriousness of purpose, Simmons's epic narrative is on a par with Isaac Asimov's Foundation series, Frank Herbert's 'Dune' books, Gene Wolfe's multipart 'Book of the New Sun'; and Brian Aldiss's Helliconia trilogy. No one in modern science fiction . . . has dealt more sensitively with the interface between religion and science." N Y Times Book Rev

The terror; a novel. Little, Brown and Co. 2007 769p $25.99
ISBN 978-0-316-01744-2; 0-316-01744-2
                            * LC 2006-14608

This historical suspense novel follows the "difficulties of the dwindling remains of Sir John Franklin's failed 1840s mission to find the Northwest Passage. However, in addition to scurvy, frostbite, botulism, snow-blindness, and threats of mutiny, the crews of HMS Terror and HMS Erebus are harried by some enormous Thing out on the ice. The story is told from the viewpoints of several members of the ships' crews, with emphasis on Terror captain Francis Crozier and Erebus surgeon Harry Goodsir." Libr J

"A deeply absorbing story that combines awe-inspiring myth, grinding horror and historically accurate adventure." Seattle Times

Simon, Claude, 1913-2005

The trolley; translated from the French by Richard Howard. New Press (NY) 2002 112p
ISBN 1-56584-734-2   LC 2002-19026

Simon, Claude, 1913-2005—*Continued*

Original French edition, 2001

"The structure of this novelette alternates between the recollections of the narrator during his youth (in particular the trolley that transported him to school every day) and the recounting of his experience in a hospital in old age." Libr J

This "slim but dense new novel is indebted to Proust in everything from its labyrinthine, parentheses-laden sentences to its meditations on memory and painstaking representations of a bygone time." N Y Times Book Rev

Simpson, Dorothy, 1933-

Dead and gone; an inspector Luke Thanet novel. Scribner 2000 247p

ISBN 0-684-86336-7   LC 99-39091

First published 1999 in the United Kingdom

"Inspector Thanet is the very model of the paternalistic English detective, offering comfort to the relatives of a woman who was pushed down a well to her death, while shrewdly picking apart every detail of their alibis until he lays bare every dirty little secret in this affluent, complacent household. Tactful and discreet, Thanet is also relentless as he guides the investigation backward in time. . . . A perfect puzzle, perfectly solved." N Y Times Book Rev

Dead by morning. Scribner 1989 277p o.p.

    LC 89-6270

"Inspector Thanet is faced with a murder at a luxurious English country inn and an overzealous superintendent who is busily reorganizing with all the annoying haste of the newly promoted." Booklist

Doomed to die. Scribner 1991 245p o.p.

    LC 91-4185

"Inspector Thanet's mother-in-law has had a heart attack; Sergeant Lineham's wife is clinically depressed; and Superintendent Draco has just learned that his beloved wife, Angharad, has leukemia. Among the civilian populace of this suddenly blighted Kentish town, a young nanny is stricken with a ruptured appendix, and the woman who takes her place, a tormented artist with an abusive husband and a dying mother, is found murdered." N Y Times Book Rev

"Confirmed clue-sniffers should be ready for a surprise here: both the solution and the sinner are shockers, though eminently fair ones." Booklist

Last seen alive; a Luke Thanet mystery. Scribner 1985 220p o.p.

    * LC 85-14530

The author "invites us to reflect on the murder by strangling of a lovely woman, widowed, who is spending one night only in a small Kentish village, ostensibly to hear a violin recital. What could possibly account for a killing under such conditions? The congenial pair of Thanet and Lineham uncovers several 'pasts,' 20 years distant, when all parties were teen-agers in school. Dramatic surprises punctuate a piece of detection in which the ratiocination is neither static nor obvious." Barzun. Cat of Crime. Rev and enl edition

No laughing matter. Scribner 1993 262p o.p.

    LC 93-19799

Scotland Yard's Inspector Luke Thanet investigates the murder of a "vintner who went through the laboratory window of his prosperous family-owned vineyard in the Kentish countryside." N Y Times Book Rev

"Simpson turns out her usual high-caliber tale and gives the reader more to ponder than a simple mystery. Her shrewd understanding of what makes humans tick results in a story that is both entertaining and thought-provoking." Booklist

Once too often; an Inspector Luke Thanet novel. Scribner 1998 223p o.p.   LC 97-32513

In this Thanet mystery, an "unlikable woman named Jessica Dander, a reporter for a newspaper in Kent, is found lying at the foot of the stairs in her home, her neck broken. Even though the death appears to be an accident, any number of people might have killed her: the husband she humiliated, the lover she annoyed, the teenage admirer she fascinated. With the exception of Thanet, a thoughtful man with a rich emotional history, the characters are well observed without being especially complex." N Y Times Book Rev

Simpson, Helen

In the driver's seat; stories. Alfred A. Knopf 2007 177p $22

ISBN 978-0-307-26522-7; 0-307-26522-6

    LC 2006-37215

Contents: Up at a villa; The door; The year's midnight; Every third thought; Early one morning; The tree; In the driver's seat; If I'm spared; The phlebotomist's love life; The green room; Constitutional

"Helen Simpson is mordantly funny and unafraid of life's big issues, such as love, aging, and war . . . . Vigorously written." Atlantic

Simpson, Mona

Anywhere but here. Knopf 1987 c1986 406p o.p.   LC 86-45282

The "novel opens with its two heroines, Adele and her daughter Ann, fleeing their provincial home-town in Wisconsin for a fresh start in California. . . . Adele is both protector and manipulator, encouraging Ann's success as a child star but also displaying her own unrealistic expectations and selfish motives. Ann tolerates her mother's lying and eccentricity, but she longs for a rootedness her mother cannot give her. The . . . flashbacks to stories told by Adele's Wisconsin relatives give us a sense of the home they have left behind, and the disparity between it and their new home." Libr J

"Any single episode could stand on its own, but Simpson keeps piling them on, building with strength and grace." Booklist

Off Keck Road. Knopf 2000 167p

ISBN 0-375-41010-4   LC 00-40569

"When Bea Maxwell returns to her small home town, in 1964, after college and a stint at a big-city ad agency, she wants to believe that this is not the end of her story—that the chapter including 'the startling redemption' is still to come. But what follows is less a story than a catalogue of fragile moments that never crystallize into actual events. Bea wrestles with the propriety of a woman telephoning a man, flirts awkwardly with a priest, and deflects a sexual advance from her married boss, to her regret. It's not easy to write a novel in which the central tragedy is that nothing happens, but the author uses the cumulative power of small details to convince us that Bea's stalled life is a life worth knowing." New Yorker

Sinclair, April

Coffee will make you black. Hyperion 1994 239p o.p.

LC 93-13271

This novel's protagonist "is Jean ('Stevie') Stevenson, a spunky 11-year-old when the story begins; a high-school student when it concludes. The setting is Chicago, circa 1965-70. . . . Raised by a strict, if well-meaning, mother and an affectionate, if vague, father, Stevie soon finds herself caught up in one of the many riddles of youth: to be cool or be square. . . . Meanwhile, she is listening to Dr. Martin Luther King and Malcolm X and liberating herself from the confines of her upbringing and her fear of being 'different.'" Booklist

"Sinclair gives a realistic portrayal of personal awakening during a politically tumultuous time." Publ Wkly

Sinclair, Upton, 1878-1968

The jungle; introduction by Jane Jacobs. Modern Library 2002 xx, 382p pa $9.95

ISBN 0-375-75950-6

* LC 2001-44823

First published 1906 by Doubleday, Page

"Jurgis Rudkus, an immigrant from Lithuania, arrives in Chicago with his father, his fiancée, and her family. He is determined to make a life for his bride in the new country. The deplorable conditions in the stockyards and the harrowing experiences of impoverished workers are vividly described by the author." Shapiro. Fic for Youth. 3d edition

Singer, Isaac Bashevis, 1904-1991

Collected stories: A friend of Kafka to Passions. Library of America 2004 856p $35

ISBN 1-931082-62-6

* LC 2003-66057

The sixty-five short stories in this volume have appeared in the three books: A friend of Kafka and other stories (1970); A crown of feathers and other stories (1973); Passions and other stories (1975).

Collected stories: Gimpel the fool to The letter writer; [Ilan Stavans is the editor of this volume] Library of America 2004 789p $35

ISBN 1-931082-61-8

* LC 2003-66055

The fifty-four short stories in this volume have appeared in the four books: Gimpel the fool & other stories (1955); The Spinoza of Market Street (1966); Short Friday & other stories (1964); and The séance & other stories (1968). Gimpel the fool & other stories is entered separately.

Collected stories: One night in Brazil to The death of Methuselah. Library of America 2004 899p $35

ISBN 1-931082-63-4

LC 2003-66081

Most of the short stories in this volume have appeared in the six books: Old love (1979); The collected stories of Isaac Bashevis Singer (1982); Image & other stories (1985); Gifts (1985); and The death of Methuselah & other stories (1988). Also included are thirteen uncollected stories at the end of the volume. The collected stories of Isaac Bashevis Singer and The death of Methuselah are entered separately.

A crown of feathers and other stories

In Singer, I. B. Collected stories: A friend of Kafka to Passions

Enemies, a love story. Farrar, Straus & Giroux 1972 280p

ISBN 0-374-14830-9

Originally written in Yiddish, 1966

This novel is "about a Polish Jew who, out of gratitude, marries the girl who helped him escape the Nazis after he believes his wife is dead, takes a mistress whom he bigamously weds when she becomes pregnant, and then discovers that his first wife has also escaped from Poland to New York." Oxford Companion to Am Lit. 6th edition

"The book has the surface gaiety, ribaldry and surprise of a medieval fabliau. Yet the New York subways, telephone calls, Bronx Zoo, bus trip to the Adirondacks are solidly, meticulously real. Herman's three women expand into mythic dimension. . . . Whether or not you accept its ending, [this] is a brilliant, unsettling novel." Newsweek

The estate. Farrar, Straus & Giroux 1969 374p o.p.

Sequel to The manor (1967)

This novel covers the last years of the nineteenth century. It explores the lives of a Polish Jewish family who have emerged from the ghettos to seek a new life in a country that is itself struggling to emerge from a feudal past.

"Even in their manner of dying, Singer's characters seem to be literally swept away by storms of passion. Indeed, the only thing that keeps the book from disintegrating into an anthology of melodramatic episodes is Singer's unfaltering stylistic control." N Y Times Book Rev

The family Moskat; translated from the Yiddish by A.H. Gross. Knopf 1950 611p o.p.

"Panoramic in sweep, the novel follows many characters and story lines in depicting Jewish life in Warsaw from 1911 to the late 1930s. Singer examines Hasidism, Orthodoxy, the rise of secularism, the breakdown of 19th-century traditions, assimilation, Marxism, and Zionism." Merriam-Webster's Ency of Lit

A friend of Kafka and other stories

In Singer, I. B. Collected stories: A friend of Kafka to Passions

Gimpel the fool and other stories

also in Singer, I. B. Collected stories: Gimpel the fool to The letter writer

The image and other stories

In Singer, I. B. Collected stories: One night in Brazil to The death of Methuselah

An Isaac Bashevis Singer reader. Farrar, Straus & Giroux 1971 560p o.p.

Contents: Gimpel the fool; The mirror; The unseen; The Spinoza of Market Street; The black wedding; The man who came back; Short Friday; Yentl the Yeshiva boy; Blood; The fast; The séance; The slaughterer; The lecture; Getzel the monkey; A friend of Kafka; My father's friend; Dreamers; A wedding; Had he been a Kohen

LIST OF FICTIONAL WORKS

Singer, Isaac Bashevis, 1904-1991—*Continued*

This anthology "contains among works previously published in journals and other collections, 15 short stories, a novel 'The magician of Lublin,' and four episodes not included in the English translation of 'In my father's court.'" Booklist

The magician of Lublin. Farrar, Straus & Giroux 246p o.p.

*

Originally serialized 1959 in Yiddish newspaper; first published in book form 1960 by Noonday

"The novel is set in late 19th-century Poland. It concerns Yasha Mazur, an itinerant professional conjurer, tightrope walker, and hypnotist. He loves five women, including his barren and pious wife. To support himself, his assorted women, and his future plans to escape to Italy, he attempts a robbery and fails. Yasha has a crisis of conscience and returns to his wife, becoming a recluse. People begin to refer to him as Jacob the Penitent, and they flock to him as if to a holy man." Merriam-Webster's Ency of Lit

> *also in* Singer, I. B. An Isaac Bashevis Singer reader p317-560

Old Love
> *In* Singer, I. B. Collected stories: One night in Brazil to The death of Methuselah

Passions and other stories
> *In* Singer, I. B. Collected stories: A friend of Kafka to Passions

The séance & other stories
> *In* Singer, I. B. Collected stories: Gimpel the fool to The letter writer

Shadows on the Hudson; translated by Joseph Sherman. Farrar, Straus & Giroux 1998 548p $28
ISBN 0-374-26186-5   LC 97-18677
Originally serialized 1957-1958 in Yiddish newspaper
A novel "about a postwar circle of emigres who gather for Sabbath dinners in the Upper West Side apartment of the wealthy Boris Makaver. The events are unceasingly tempestuous: Grein, an investor with a passionate streak, runs off to Miami with Anna, Makaver's daughter (both are married); Luria, whom Anna abandoned, begins to have visions of his first wife, Sonia, who died in the camps; Solomon, Makaver's oldest friend, re-establishes contact with his first wife, who left him for a Nazi; and so on. Nothing that happens, however, is so pressing that it cannot be interrupted for fierce argument—about sin, the dead, lost pieties, God's betrayals." New Yorker

Short Friday & other stories
> *In* Singer, I. B. Collected stories: Gimpel the fool to The letter writer

The Spinoza of Market Street
> *In* Singer, I. B. Collected stories: Gimpel the fool to The letter writer

Singer, Israel Joshua, 1893-1944

The brothers Ashkenazi; [by] I. J. Singer; translated from the Yiddish by Maurice Samuel. Knopf 1936 642p o.p.

*

"Deals with the rise and decay of the textile city of Lodz, Poland, and with the fortunes of the Polish-Jewish brothers, Max and Jacob Ashkenazi, whose personalities gradually come to dominate the life of the town. . . . What gives the book its significance is not the picture of nineteenth-century Jewish family life, and not the characterizations of the two brothers, but the clear exposition of the class struggle of which Max and Jacob form unconscious parts." New Yorker

Sinha, Indra

Animal's people. Simon & Schuster 2008 374p $25
ISBN 978-1-4165-7878-9; 1-4165-7878-1
* LC 2007-42118
"Animal is a teenage boy who lives on the streets of the Indian city of Khaufpur. He goes around on all fours since his spine is badly damaged; he cannot walk normally. As an infant, he was one of the thousands of victims of a poison gas leak at an American-owned company, here just called 'the Kampani.' Animal also lost his parents 'that night' (as the local people refer to the horrible event). Animal has a lively mind and a way with words, some of them angry and profane, some of them bitterly funny, as he gets caught up in the struggle of those in Khaufpur who seek long-delayed justice from the Kampani. Sinha . . . has clearly based his story on the human and environmental disaster at the Union Carbide factory in Bhopal in 1984. The result is a gripping novel that also reminds us of a continuing real-life tragedy." Libr J

Sinisalo, Johanna, 1958-

Troll; a love story; translated from the Finnish by Herbert Lomas. Grove Press 2004 278p pa $12
ISBN 0-8021-4129-3 (pa)   LC 2003-69113
Original French edition 2000; this translation first published 2003 in the United Kingdom with title: Not before sundown
"Thirtysomething Angel, on the way home from the bar one winter night, rescues a young troll from a gang of boys. Bleary and hungover the next morning, he thinks perhaps he dreamed the rescue—until he discovers the troll drinking from the toilet. Falling utterly under its spell, he names it, a male, Pessi, and frantically searches for information on its care and feeding. He discovers that trolls emit pheromones with powerful erotic effects on others nearby, which explains why things become bizarre for Angel. Keeping the essentially wild Pessi as a sort of pet eventually leads to disaster and an accidental killing. Angel escapes with Pessi to the forest, where he meets Pessi's older relations." Booklist
"Sinisalo handles all this mythic conflict in an admirably matter-of-fact way; her main innovations have to do with the novel's narrative structure. She has all the players drawn into Angel's dark fairy-tale intrigue relate their part in short first-person snippets, which are then intercut with reference materials, of both online and print vintage,

Sinisalo, Johanna, 1958- —*Continued*

recounting the Finnish history of troll-sightings and the symbolic significance of the forest creatures in the nation's myth and folklore." Washington Post Book World

Sittenfeld, Curtis

The man of my dreams; a novel. Random House 2006 272p $22.95

ISBN 1-400-06476-7　　　　　　LC 2005-52910

"Fourteen-year-old Hannah Gavener is abruptly shipped off from Philadelphia to live with her aunt in Pittsburgh when her mercurial, vindictive father breaks up his marriage and family, which includes Hannah's older sister, Allison, and their browbeaten mother. Sweet but insecure and passive, Hannah had 'been raised. . . not to be accommodated but to accommodate,' an upbringing that hobbles all her subsequent relationships. The novel follows Hannah through her teens and late 20s (from 1991 to 2005), as she searches for romantic fulfillment, navigates friendships (e.g., with her larger-than-life cousin Fig) and alternately tries to reconcile with her father and distance herself from him. But the most influential connection Hannah makes is with her psychiatrist, Dr. Lewin, whom she begins seeing her freshman year at Tufts." Publ Wkly

"The exciting thing about Sittenfeld, aside from her remarkably lucid, incisive prose is thet she has the potential to carve out a new place, based largely on the strength of that prose, for every woman who wants to write (or read) good fiction about growing up and messing up—just the way the boys do—without being issued a stigma and a cutesy cover." San Francisco Chronicle

Prep; a novel. Random House 2005 406p $21.95; pa $13.95

ISBN 1-400-06231-4; 0-812-97235-X

　　　　　　　　　　　　　　LC 2004-46858

"Lee Fiora, a scholarship student at the prestigious Ault School (not Ault Academy, as her parents embarrassingly refer to it), negotiates her days there in a blaze of self-consciousness that is, by turns, hilarious and excruciating: 'I believed then that if you had a good encounter with a person, it was best not to see them again for as long as possible.' And yet she becomes an expert on the rituals that govern the rarefied microenvironment in which she finds herself: the students' fondness for catchphrases like 'therein lies the paradox' and 'LMC' (lower middle class); the taboo against enthusiasm for anything other than sports; the fact that the school always sings 'God be with you till we meet again' at chapel before breaks. In the end, Lee's incisive vision of herself and others is her downfall but also—as this richly textured narrative suggests—her greatest gift." New Yorker

"This readable coming-of-age tale . . . [is] suitable for YA collections if mildly sexually explicit scenes are not objectionable." Libr J

Sjöwall, Maj, 1935-

Cop killer; the story of a crime; [by] Maj Sjöwall and Per Wahlöö; translated from the Swedish by Thomas Teal. Pantheon Bks. 1975 296p o.p.

Original Swedish edition, 1974

"A divorced woman is murdered, has 'disappeared,' but Martin Beck, Chief Detective Inspector, is called in from Stockholm to investigate. Prime suspect is a former convict who lived near the victim, Sigbrit; and her ex-husband, ex-ship captain, may also be guilty. It takes a midnight shoot-out between three cops and two teenagers to help speed the identification of the real killer." Best Sellers

The laughing policeman; [by] Maj Sjöwall and Per Wahlöö; translated from the Swedish by Alan Blair. Pantheon Bks. 1970 211p o.p.
　　　　　　　　　　　　　　　　　　　*

Original Swedish edition, 1968

In this Martin Beck mystery "a Stockholm city bus is found one rainy night with a cargo of bullet-riddled corpses. Nothing unites the passengers that could explain the mass murder, but one of the victims is a young colleague from the homicide division. . . . The gloomy weather of the Swedish winter, the commercialization of Christmas, Vietnam War protests, and the low morale of the much-criticized police leave Beck and his harassed colleagues with not much to laugh about. The atmosphere and ingenious plotting of the novel make it one of the best in the series." Murphy. Ency of Murder and Mystery

The locked room; [by] Maj Sjöwall and Per Wahlöö; translated from the Swedish by Paul Britten Austin. Pantheon Bks. 1973 311p o.p.

Original Swedish edition, 1972

"A man commits suicide or is murdered in a completely locked room [in Stockholm]. He is shot but there is no weapon. Martin Beck rises from his sick bed to handle this situation." Best Sellers

The man on the balcony; the story of a crime; [by] Maj Sjöwall and Per Wahlöö; translated from the Swedish by Alan Blair. Pantheon Bks. 1968 180p o.p.

Original Swedish edition, 1967

"The chief problem is child murder in Stockholm, and it is a macabre race with death when the only clues are disturbing and intangible for Beck and for the 75-man force assigned to help him." Libr J

Murder at the Savoy; [by] Maj Sjöwall and Per Wahlöö; translated from the Swedish by Amy and Ken Knoespel. Pantheon Bks. 1971 216p o.p.

Original Swedish edition, 1970

"In the dining room of the posh Savoy hotel in Malmö, Viktor Palmgren's address is interrupted when a killer guns him down, then escapes through a window. Was the wealthy industrialist murdered for personal reasons—or for political motives related to his arms shipments to Africa? Once again Chief Inspector Martin Beck of Swedish National Police goes into action." Saturday Rev

Skármeta, Antonio

The dancer and the thief; a novel; translated from the Spanish by Katherine Silver. W. W. Norton 2008 300p $24.95

ISBN 978-0-393-06494-0; 0-393-06494-8

　　　　　　　　　　　　　　LC 2007-33340

Original Spanish edition, 2003

A novel set in "contemporary Santiago, Chile, where the memory of Pinochet's reign and the disappearing of

Skármeta, Antonio—*Continued*

citizens still looms. Presidential amnesty has granted freedom to some nonviolent criminals, releasing 20-year-old Ángel Santiago, a passionate young man imprisoned for impulsively stealing a wealthy rancher's horse, and 60-year-old Nico Vergara Grey, a gentleman-thief who has repented his life of crime. Ángel plans a grand heist and some payback, but Ángel's heist is dependent on Nico, who wants only to be taken back by his estranged wife and son. Looming in the background is the warden who allowed inmates to rape and torture Ángel. Fearing (correctly) that Ángel will want revenge, the warden hires an assassin to kill him. Intertwined is Ángel's meeting with Victoria Ponce, a ballet student who wants to compose a dance to commemorate her dead father, a resistance member murdered by Pinochet's goons." Publ Wkly

"Though Skarmeta scarcely ranks at the very top of Latin America's remarkably distinguished and varied literary elite, he is a serious writer to whom the death and rebirth of democracy in his native Chile is an endlessly compelling subject. . . . Though the ending that Skarmeta gives his characters falls well short of happy, the Chile that he portrays herein is vibrant and strong." Washington Post Book World

Skinner, B. F. (Burrhus Frederic), 1904-1990

Walden two. Macmillan 1948 266p o.p.

*

"Unlike most post-World War II science fiction, which considered social control by psychological conditioning to be a form of hell on Earth, Skinner presented it grandly as utopian. The structure of the story (which, as a story, doesn't amount to much) is a debate between an advocate of human free choice and a champion of behavioral manipulation, which is offered as the answer to all of society's ills." Anatomy of Wonder 4

Skinner, Burrhus Frederic *See* Skinner, B. F. (Burrhus Frederic), 1904-1990

Škvorecký, Josef

When Eve was naked; stories of a life's journey. Farrar, Straus & Giroux 2002 352p

ISBN 0-374-14975-5 ($25)   LC 2002-20652

Contents: Why I lernt how to read; Eve was naked; Why do people have soft noses?; A remarkable chemical phenomenon; How my literary career began; My Uncle Kohn; My teacher, Mr. Katz; Dr. Strass; The cuckoo; Fragments about Rebecca; Feminine mystique; An insoluble problem of genetics; Three bachelors in a fiery furnace; The end of Bull Mácha; Spectator on a February night; Laws of the jungle; Filthy cruel world; Song of forgotten years; Pink champagne; The mysterious events at night; Wayne's hero; According to Poe; Jezebel from Forest Hill; A magic mountain and a willowy wench

"Like memory, the collection is kaleidoscopic, shifting perspectives, hurtling jerkily through time, filtering its narrative through the author's momentary preoccupations. Written over a period of 50 years, the stories read to some extent like a diary, capturing an emotional landscape in lucid detail." N Y Times Book Rev

Slattery, Brian Francis

Liberation; being the adventures of the Slick Six after the collapse of the United States of America. Tor 2008 299p pa $14.95

ISBN 978-0-7653-2046-9; 0-7653-2046-0

LC 2008-31020

"A Tom Doherty Associates Book"

A "fable of a near-future America fallen into economic and social chaos. Marco Angelo Oliveira breaks out of prison, determined to rejoin the Slick Six, his 'family' of supercriminals. He meets stiff opposition from the Aardvark, a mob boss who now runs New York City. Meanwhile, the nation has fragmented into squabbling regions, from the New Dominion of Virginia to the New Sioux of the plains; like Marco's gang, they see little reason to reunite." Publ Wkly

Slattery's novel "has many brilliant ideas, but its depiction of a 21st century revival of slavery is really what burns it into your memory. . . . It's a book that rewards attention, and you'll find yourself flipping back after you finish it to find the best parts of its off-kilter odyssey and piece together new connections between its huge and memorable cast of characters. It's also a book that gets even better on the second read." io9

Spaceman blues; a love song. Tor 2007 219p $22.95; pa $12.95

ISBN   978-0-7653-1610-3;   0-7653-1610-2; 978-0-7653-1614-1 (pa); 0-7653-1614-5 (pa)

LC 2007-9543

"Manuel González, a legendary New York City party animal, has disappeared and his apartment has exploded, leaving behind only the memories of his thousands of friends and enemies. His lover, Wendell Apogee, is determined to find out what happened. So are police inspectors Herman Trout and Lenny Salmon, who uncover a web of bizarre characters, from Lucas Henderson, former Lunar Temple cult member, and Arturo El Flaco Domínguez, González's worst enemy, to a washed-up '80s pop band the Marsupials. As Wendell tracks González through Darktown, the place where you find lost things, the prophecies of the apocalyptic Church of Panic begin coming true: aliens threaten to invade Earth, and Wendell must become superhero Captain Spaceman and save the planet." Publ Wkly

This novel is a "welcome Band-Aid for those still mourning the loss of Kurt Vonnegut and his uniquely wacky, satirical brand of sci-fi. There's also a touch of Paul Auster's flair for genre blending and New York mythologizing. . . . A strange and whimsical mash note to the city, Slattery's apocalyptome proves that this newcomer is as thoughtful and irreverent as doomsayers come." Time Out New York

Slaughter, Karin, 1971-

Beyond reach. Delacorte Press 2007 404p $25

ISBN 978-0-385-33947-6; 0-385-33947-X

LC 2007-9359

In this installment in the Grant County, Ga., crime series, "Dr. Sara Linton, the county's resident pediatrician and medical examiner, is mired in a devastating lawsuit, accused by grieving parents of indirectly causing the death of their terminally ill son. Then Sara and her husband, police chief Jeffrey Tolliver, must travel to rural Reese, Ga., where Lena Adams, Jeffrey's often reckless

Slaughter, Karin, 1971-—*Continued*

detective, has been injured in an explosion that killed a local woman. Lena's mysterious escape from the hospital plunges her, Sara and Jeffrey into a dangerous web of meth trafficking, white supremacy groups and long-buried family secrets." Publ Wkly

"Slaughter's latest page-turner offers both wrenching emotional highs and lows and a gripping plot, but what gives it emotional heft is its unwavering focus on the grim social ills of the rural South." Booklist

The **Sleeper** wakes; Harlem Renaissance stories by women; edited and with an introduction by Marcy Knopf; foreword by Nellie Y. McKay. Rutgers Univ. Press 1993 xxxix, 277p o.p.

LC 92-30446

Contents: The sleeper wakes; Double trouble [and] Mary Elizabeth, by J. R. Fauset; Wedding day, by G. Bennett; Free, by G. D. Johnson; Funeral; The typewriter [and] Prologue to a life, by D. West; One boy's story; Drab rambles [and] Nothing new, by M. Bonner; The closing door, by A. W. Grimké; Bathesda of Sinners Run, by M. I. Owens; The foolish and the wise: Sallie Runner is introduced to Socrates and Sanctum 777 N.S.D.C.O.U. meets Cleopatra, by L. A. Pendleton; Cross crossings cautiously [and] Three dogs and a rabbit, by A. S. Coleman; Blue aloes [and] To a wild rose, by O. B. Graham; His great career [and] Summer session, by A. Dunbar-Nelson; Masks [and] Mademoiselle 'Tasie, by E. B. Thompson; John Redding goes to sea [and] The bone of contention, by Z. N. Hurston; Sanctuary; The wrong man [and] Freedom, by N. Larsen

"This anthology rescues short stories written by the women writers of the Harlem Renaissance from archival obscurity. . . . While these writers share some common themes . . . each has her own distinctive voice, and none sacrifices the art of storytelling for polemics. A passionate, dynamic, and invaluable collection." Booklist

Slouka, Mark

God's fool. Knopf 2002 271p $24
ISBN 0-375-40216-0   LC 2001-53975

This novel about Siamese twins Chang and Eng Bunker is narrated by Chang "The story follows the twins across three continents, from a prosperity in Siam marred by the loss of their father and many siblings; to a life of exploitation in Europe; and finally to America, where the brothers eventually ditch Barnum and retire to North Carolina. There the family of Chang and Eng grows to include wives, children and even more loss." Booklist

"Slouka, a gifted stylist, eschews much of the freak-show energy that thrust Chang and Eng onto the stage of world history, in favor of an alluring balance between the elegiac and the ironic." Publ Wkly

The visible world. Houghton Mifflin 2007 242p $24
ISBN 978-0-618-75643-8; 0-618-75643-4
LC 2006-23705

"An unnamed American man from Queens, the son of Czech parents who emigrated after World War II, struggles to understand his mother's tragic past. . . . [In the first part], a series of reminiscences from his early years, he attempts to piece together her story and that of East-

ern Europe's wartime generation—a tale involving secret executions, SS leader Reinhard Heydrich's assassination, and a family friend's hidden history as a Nazi interpreter. As he travels through Czechoslovakia as an adult, he meets villagers who reveal startlingly insightful truths about how people conceal their pasts in order to survive. Ultimately finding no concrete answers, he decides to recreate his mother's story in fiction, a section that imagines her love affair with a member of the Resistance during 1942." Booklist

"It is a rare thing for a novel to split open the illusion of narrative . . . to reveal the underlying mechanics of creation, memory and desire. It is even rarer for a tricky book like this to hit you in the heart." Washington Post Book World

Smiley, Jane, 1949-

The age of grief; a novella and stories. Knopf 1987 213p o.p.   LC 87-45120

Contents: The pleasure of her company; Lily; Jeffrey, believe me; Long distance; Dynamite; The age of grief

"These short pieces are about male-female relations—the high points and the pitfalls (more of the latter than the former). Smiley knows her characters inside out and lets the reader in on everything she knows." Booklist

The age of grief [novelette]
In Smiley, J. The age of grief p119-213

Good faith. Knopf 2003 417p $26
ISBN 0-375-41217-4   LC 2002-73096

"Everyone trusts Joe Stratford, the affable Pennsylvania real-estate agent who narrates Smiley's ninth novel—his clients, his bankers, his boss, his boss's sexy married daughter, and even the irascible contractor who builds the most beautiful houses in the country. But when Marcus Burns, a charismatic I.R.S. agent turned developer, comes to town, Joe feels that no one else understands his potential the way Marcus does. With Joe as his partner, Marcus soon seduces half the county into investing in a development venture that he says will make everyone rich. It is hard to imagine a novelist better suited to taking on the S.& L. scandals of the nineteen-eighties than Smiley." New Yorker

The Greenlanders. Knopf 1988 555p o.p.
LC 88-2758

An "historical novel based on the tenth-century settlement of Greenland by Norseman Erik the Red and a band of Norse colonists. After flourishing in Greenland for centuries, the colonists disappeared, leaving behind only their buildings and artifacts." Booklist

"Vivid, even stunning descriptions of the land and customs of these 'lost settlements' are the book's strong points. Characterizations are less successful; many personalities remain wooden throughout the lengthy action. Nevertheless, the exotic subject matter will appeal to historical novel fans." Libr J

Horse heaven. Knopf 2000 561p
ISBN 0-375-40600-X   LC 99-52728

In this novel about thoroughbred horse racing Smiley introduces "new characters in nearly every chapter, from rich and troubled owners to eccentric and troubled trainers; nervous fillies and scampish stallions; a boy with the gift for picking winners; an articulate, horse-crazy 11

Smiley, Jane, 1949-—*Continued*

year-old girl; a gorgeous store clerk who catches the eye of a wealthy rap star then goes horse-crazy; horse-crazy Irish cousins; an animal communicator who can tune into a horse's stream of consciousness; a kind horse masseur; a calm and creative veterinarian; and a young mother trying valiantly to run her grandfather's stud farm." Booklist

"What's remarkable about Smiley's handling of horses as characters is that she manages to bring it off at all—and more, she does it brilliantly." N Y Times Book Rev

Moo. Knopf 1995 414p o.p.   LC 94-12840

"This metafiction, set in a sprawling Midwestern university known as Moo, concerns an economics professor who's cozy with corrupt Latin-American governments and rapacious corporations, a seven-hundred-pound hog named Earl Butz, many couples in and out of love, and a secretary who quietly runs the whole place. As usual, Smiley knows more than seems likely about everything from equine management and the niceties of butchering to—of course—the nuances of how people feel and behave toward animals of their own species." New Yorker

Ten days in the hills. Knopf 2007 449p $26
ISBN 978-1-4000-4061-2; 1-400-04061-2
    LC 2006-46579

In this satirical novel, Smiley makes "use of a literary antecedent, this time using as a template Boccaccio's Decameron. While Boccaccio's group of 10 women and men hope to escape the Black Death by sequestering themselves for 10 days in a villa outside Florence, Smiley quarantines her characters in a mansion high in the hills of Hollywood as the U.S. invades Iraq. Ensconced in luxury if plagued with moral quandaries, they sort out complex family and romantic relationships and argue over the war. Movie director Max, 58, has found contentment with Elena, 50, a charmingly commonsensical writer of unexpectedly intelligent how-to books, and the novel's ethical center. Then there's Elena's mischievous son; Max's socially conscious daughter; Max's ex, the supremely beautiful singer and actress Zoe; her imperial Jamaican mother; and Zoe's current lover, an annoyingly serene guru. A neighbor tells gossipy tales of old Hollywood, Max's agent pitches an unlikely project, and a friend from Max's boyhood irritates everyone." Booklist

"Each chapter is roughly half talk and half sex. The sexual descriptions set a new mark for explicitness in a work of non-pornographic intent. . . . The twists of libido are wound into a cultural exchange, and the anatomy of our inward hollows is illuminated to surprising and comic effect." New Yorker

A thousand acres. Knopf 1991 371p $25
ISBN 0-394-57773-6
    * LC 91-52720

The author "creates an idyllic world of family farm life in Iowa in 1979: the neat yard, freshly painted house, clean clothes on the line, and fertile, well-tended fields. The owner of these well-managed acres is Larry Cook, who abruptly decides to turn the farm over to his two eldest daughters and their husbands. Ginny and Ty are hard-working farmers who try to placate her ornery father, while sister Rose and hard-drinking Pete try to stand up to him. Dark secrets surface after the property transfer and the family's careful world unravels with a

grim inevitability." Libr J

"What makes this novel such a triumph is Smiley's brilliant twist on the Lear story: she tells it not from Larry's point of view but from his eldest daughter's. . . . In the end Smiley does what Shakespeare himself never did: she creates a female heroine who grows through her own anguish until she towers over the hero and conquers him." Newsweek

Smith, Alexander McCall *See* McCall Smith, Alexander, 1948-

Smith, Ali, 1962-

The accidental. Pantheon Bks. 2006 c2005 305p $22.95
ISBN 0-375-42225-0   LC 2005-51031
First published 2005 in the United Kingdom

At the opening of this "novel, a barefoot, thirtysomething stranger named Amber abandons her broken-down car and arrives at the doorstep of Eve and Michael Smart, who are summering in Norfolk, England, with Eve's children, 12-year-old Astrid and 17-year-old Magnus. Amber stays for dinner and quickly weaves her way into the Smarts' lives, befriending impressionable Astrid; seducing math-whiz Magnus (guilt-ridden over his unwitting role in the suicide of a fellow student); enchanting their haughty, adulterous stepfather, Michael; and swiftly sizing up their mother, Eve, a writer conflicted over the success of her hack novels. The novel is alternately narrated by each member of the Smart family." Booklist

Smith "is a wonderful ventriloquist, adept at throwing her voice into an astonishing array of characters. . . . [She] can do suicidal teenage angst and middle-aged ennui, a 12-year-old's sardonic innocence and an aging Lothario's randy daydreams with equal aplomb. And in riffing on the stream of consciousness form, pioneered by such highbrow litterateurs as Joyce and Woolf, she manages to make it as accessible and up to the minute (if vastly more entertaining) as talk radio or an Internet chat room." N Y Times (Late N Y Ed)

Smith, April, 1949-

Good morning, killer. Knopf 2003 356p $24
ISBN 0-375-41240-9   LC 2002-35917

"This kidapping thriller starts off like most kidnapping thrillers, with the abduction of a pampered teenager, 15-year-old Juliana Meyer-Murphy, that has the local cops running around in circles. But we know we're in uncharted territory here when Juliana returns home, raped, battered and deeply traumatized, and Ana Grey, the F.B.I. agent assigned to the case, is so distressed by the girl's condition that she ignores procedures and starts acting on impulse. . . . A risk taker herself, Smith writes in the forceful style of a true literary maverick, someone who has earned the right to break a few rules." N Y Times Book Rev

Judas horse; an FBI special agent Ana Grey mystery. Alfred A. Knopf 2008 318p $23.95
ISBN 978-1-4000-4205-0; 1-4000-4205-4
    LC 2007-42863

Smith, April, 1949-—Continued

"In this sequel to Good Morning, Killer, FBI Agent Ana Grey has just returned to the job from enforced time off when she is selected to go deep undercover to infiltrate a violent ecoterrorist group suspected of murdering a fellow agent." Libr J

Smith "writes too well to settle for the mindless shootouts of a plot geared to summon armed-to-the-teeth SWAT teams at the least provocation. With every dynamic scene, including a wild mustang roundup that thunders right off the page, the reader, like Ana, is reminded of the lost ideals and divided loyalties that make these mortal conflicts so bloody—and so sad." N Y Times Book Rev

North of Montana; a novel. Knopf 1994 295p $23

    ISBN 0-679-43197-7   LC 94-12311

As this mystery opens, "success-hungry L.A.-based FBI agent Ana Grey is just waiting for the case that will catapault her from the humdrum Bank Robbery Squad into the exalted Kidnapping and Extortion Division. The hoped-for promotion is Ana's first step to her ultimate goal: a plum job as Special Agent in Charge. But department politics, a jealous supervisor, and Ana's abrasive impatience detour her to a case that's a real hot potato. Glamorous movie star Jayne Mason, past her prime but still adored by her fans, claims a local M.D. hooked her on painkillers. She wants his head on a platter courtesy of the FBI, even though the doctor appears to be clean as a whistle." Booklist

This is "an LA novel in the tradition of some of the best writers of detective fiction. . . . There are swift, vivid portraits of scene and characters." Times Lit Suppl

Smith, B. J., 1957- See Smith, Brad, 1957-

Smith, Betty, 1896-1972

Joy in the morning. Harper & Row 1963 308p o.p.

                    * LC 62-14560

"When their families find out that Annie McGairy and Carl Brown have married, the two are cut off without a cent. Carl, a law student, takes a full-time job and goes to law school at night. Annie, who had dropped out of school to help her family, longs to be at college. She is given a chance to audit a course in literature because of her abiding interest in it. Her pregnancy, however, increases the pressure on their lives, and only their deep love sees them through their difficulties." Shapiro. Fic for Youth. 3d edition

A tree grows in Brooklyn; with a foreward by Anna Quindlen. HarperCollins Pubs. 2001 493p $23.95; pa $16.95

    ISBN 0-06-000194-1; 0-06-112007-3 (pa)

                    * LC 2001-39509

A reissue of the title first published 1943

"Life in the Williamsburg section of Brooklyn during the early 1900s is rough, but the childhood and youth of Francie Nolan is far from somber. Nurtured by a loving mother, Francie blossoms and reaches out for happiness despite poverty and the alcoholism of a father whose weakness is somewhat compensated for by his lovable disposition." Shapiro. Fic for Youth. 3d edition

Smith, Brad, 1957-

All hat; a novel. Holt & Co. 2003 308p $24

    ISBN 0-8050-7217-9   LC 2002-27307

"His attempt to live 'a half-ass normal life' doomed out of the starting gate, ex-con Ray Dokes hatches a plot to swap racehorses before a race. Set in rural Onario and featuring an ensemble cast of delightfully eccentric, even downright loopy, characters, this big-hearted caper novel mixes laugh-out-loud-comedy with streaks of country noir that call to mind Daniel Woodrell." Booklist

Smith, Caesar, 1920-1995

For works written by this author under other names see Hall, Adam, 1920-1995

Smith, Diane

Pictures from an expedition. Viking 2002 277p

    ISBN 0-670-03129-1

"Set in the Montana badlands a decade after the Civil War, the novel begins with fossil hunters stumbling upon the remains of possibly the largest dinosaur ever uncovered. Thrown in with a peripatetic crew of scientists and settlers, explorers and exploiters, Eleanor Peterson, a scientific illustrator hired to document their discoveries, recounts those daring days through her remembrances of the circumstances that inspired a series of paintings done by her traveling companion and mentor, Augustus Starwood, an eccentric artist." Booklist

Smith's "precise evocation of the stark western landscape matches her exacting portrayal of scientific debate and the assimilation of new theories." Publ Wkly

Smith, Dodie, 1896-1990

I capture the castle. Little, Brown 1948 343p il o.p.   LC 48-4880

"From its memorable opening line, 'I write this sitting in the kitchen sink', the 17-year-old narrator, Cassandra Mortmain, captivates the reader as she describes a life of penury in a gloomy Gothic castle with her oddball family. Wise beyond her years, romantic and lyrical, yet beadily perceptive . . ., Cassandra is wonderfully engaging and believable." Good Fiction Guide

Smith, Dominic

The beautiful miscellaneous; a novel. Atria Books 2007 329p $24

    ISBN 978-0-7432-7123-3; 0-7432-7123-8

                    LC 2007-297066

This novel "probes the fate of Nathan Nelson, who must suffer his quark-physicist father's efforts—whiz kid camps, science drills—to mold him into a prodigy. While Mrs. Nelson retreats into obsessive housewifery, the disappointed professor buries himself in work. . . . When a head injury gives Nathan synesthesia (an inexplicable cross-wiring of the senses), it also confers on him the genius denied at birth, and his father embraces the freakish gift as a second chance." Texas Monthly

"This unusual, gorgeously written novel is filled with pleasures: among them are richly imagined supporting characters. . . . Best of all, though, is the book's invitation to wonder—about the imponderables of life and death, the nature of intelligence, and the ultimately inexplicable relationships of fathers and sons." Booklist

Smith, Florence Margaret *See* Smith, Stevie, 1902-1971

Smith, Julie, 1944-

82 Desire; a Skip Langdon novel. Ballantine Pub. Group 1998 309p $24
ISBN 0-449-00060-5   LC 98-22259
"Russell Fortier, a prominent businessman, has vanished. His wife asks Langdon, a New Orleans detective, to look into his disappearance. Later, a private detective who was investigating Fortier turns up dead, and one of his employees, a poet and freelance computer expert, wants to know how Fortier's disappearance is connected with the murder. . . . The novel is intricately constructed, and while Smith keeps nothing important unfairly hidden from her readers, she manages to spring some nice little surprises." Booklist

Crescent city kill; a Skip Langdon novel. Fawcett Columbine 1997 326p $23.50
ISBN 0-449-91000-8   LC 97-22099
"New Orleans police detective Skip Langdon pits her skills against a vigilante group known as The Jury. Skip suspects her old nemesis, the con man and killer Errol Jacomine." Libr J
"The New Orleans ambiance is less pronounced than in most Skip Langdon mysteries, but Smith's colorful characterizations and the showdown with Jacomine make this an excellent addition to the series." Publ Wkly

House of blues; a Skip Langdon novel. Fawcett Columbine 1995 343p o.p.   LC 94-48823
"Arthur Hebert, a prominent restaurateur and domineering patriarch hated by his children, doesn't attend the opening of his restaurant in New Orleans' first casino—because he's been gunned down at home while enjoying his usual Monday evening meal of red beans and rice. Hebert's daughter, his son-in-law and his baby granddaughter have vanished. In the race to find the killer and the missing family, Skip calls on the denizens of the New Orleans underworld. . . . Smith carries off a tricky balancing act, rendering Skip heroic while imbuing her with a credibly textured emotional life. But the real star of this superb effort is New Orleans, which has never seemed more dangerous or alluring." Publ Wkly

Jazz funeral; a Skip Langdon novel. Fawcett Columbine 1993 365p o.p.
* LC 92-54997
This mystery featuring New Orleans cop Skip Langdon is "about the murder of a local jazz entrepreneur and the disappearance of his 16-year-old sister. . . . Even though she wears her badge like a piece of jewelry, Skip has the social skills to pump information from her uptown friends, and her amateur detection methods pay off with solid insights into an emotionally bankrupt family. Ms. Smith takes special pains to be gentle with a musically gifted teen-ager who runs away from the horrors of home to join a family band very much like the Neville Brothers. The kid is a bit of a brat, but the portrayal has such integrity that it makes up for Skip's lax procedures." N Y Times Book Rev

The kindness of strangers; a Skip Langdon novel. Fawcett Columbine 1996 338p $21
ISBN 0-449-90937-9   LC 95-52460

Langdon "takes on the Big Easy's corrupt political machine, as three 'pick the best of the worst' candidates line up for the mayoral race. New Orleans voters, tired of years of corruption and scandal, are leaning toward Errol Jacomine, a Christian right-winger who appears to have the right stuff. But Skip senses evil lurking behind Jacomine's jovial facade, and she figures to discredit him before he gains control of the city. . . . Smith serves up a gritty, gripping story along with a big helping of action and a pinch of humor." Booklist

Louisiana hotshot. Forge 2001 335p $24.95
ISBN 0-7653-0058-3   LC 2001-18958
"A Tom Doherty Associates book"
A mystery set in New Orleans featuring "Talba Wallis (aka Baroness de Pontalba), the black poet/computer expert and would-be investigator. . . . Answering an unlikely ad with her customary bravado lands her a job as assistant to aging PI Eddie Valentino. The young black female and 65-year-old Italian male have striking similarities that offset their obvious differences. Both are stubborn and strongly attached to, if somewhat alienated from, their families. Throw in a vulnerable young girl, Cassandra, being preyed on by a rap star's hanger-on identified only by the nickname 'Toes,' and you have a story that spans generations, races and lifestyles." Publ Wkly

Mean woman blues. Forge 2003 304p $24.95
ISBN 0-7653-0552-6   LC 2003-40018
"A Tom Doherty Associates book"
"The Formosan termites that infest new Orleans every May haunt police detective Skip Langdon's dreams, an apt image for the gnawing fear that her happiness will collapse. That happiness is based on the fact that her long distance lover, a documentary filmmaker, has moved to New Orleans. Her fear is that her enemy, an evangelical fanatic who aspires to the mind control of Jim Jones, is coming back to kill her, after a disappearance of two years." Booklist

New Orleans beat; a Skip Langdon novel. Fawcett Columbine 1994 359p o.p.
LC 93-46506
New Orleans detective Skip Langdon "investigates the suspicious death of a man who was involved with an electronic bulletin board community." Libr J
"Smith is a skilled writer who can evoke the steamy, mysterious ambience of New Orleans while simultaneously proving that computer jargon can be comprehensible even to the 'computer-challenged.' This is a humorous, suspenseful mystery." Booklist

Smith, Lee, 1944-

The devil's dream. Putnam 1992 315p o.p.
LC 92-1027
The author traces the history of country music "through several generations of the Bailey family of Grassy Springs, Virginia. Starting in 1833 with the marriage of Moses Bailey, a preacher's son who thinks fiddle music is the voice of the Devil laughing, to Kate Malone who comes from a fiddle-playing family, the Baileys are torn between their love of God and their love of music. Plain Baptist hymns and haunting Appalachian ballads shape the lives of the early generations. Grandsons R.C. and Durwood marry Lucie and Tampa, who,

Smith, Lee, 1944——*Continued*

as the Grassy Branch Girls, take part in the early 'hillbilly recordings' of the 1920s. Rose Annie and Blackjack Johnny Raines are the 'King and Queen of Country Music' in the Rockabilly 1950s until Rose Annie shoots Johnny after he's cheated on her once too often. Cousin Katie Crocker abandons the bland Nashville sound of the 1960s when she cuts a traditional record with her family at the Opryland Hotel." Libr J

"It is ultimately the writer's sensibility that gives 'The Devil's Dream' its charm and power. If there's weeping to be done, Ms. Smith allows her reader to weep, but she never descends to sentimentality." N Y Times Book Rev

Fair and tender ladies. Putnam 1988 316p
ISBN 0-399-13382-8

* LC 88-10915

This novel of life in the Appalachians "unfolds through a series of letters written by Ivy Rowe, a Virginia mountain girl. Ivy, born with the century, begins her letter writing when she is about 10 years old; the letters continue for nearly 65 years." N Y Times Book Rev

An "exquisite novel. . . . Through Ivy's curiously spelled and situated letters, we see the growth not only of her own family, but also of wider Appalachia." Christ Sci Monit

Family linen. Putnam 1985 272p
ISBN 0-399-13080-2   LC 85-3664

"The Hess clan gather in their hometown of Booker Creek, Virginia, upon the death of their matriarch, Miss Elizabeth. There are some serious skeletons in the family closet—sexual abuse, an illegitimate child, a murder. The family history is recounted in turn by relatives spanning four generations, and their narratives reveal both comical attempts to seek solace and bewilderment at the complexity of their lives." Booklist

"This is a companionable, chatty book populated by people who tell us about themselves in a rambling style and with good humor." N Y Times Book Rev

The last girls; a novel. Algonquin Bks. 2002 384p
ISBN 1-565-12363-8   LC 2002-18671
"A Shannon Ravenel book"

In this novel, a "group of former coeds, who once traveled down the Mississippi on a raft of their own construction, reunite to make the same trip on a fancy steamboat to scatter the ashes of one departed member. Along the way, we learn the stories of the unmarried Harriet, wealthy romance writer and once-poor West Virginia girl Anna, straying society wife Courtney, and Catherine and husband Russell." Libr J

Smith is "perhaps best known for her nuanced portraits of gritty, often dirt-poor Appalachian women. It's a pleasure to see her directing her talents to a different class of women with a different set of concerns." N Y Times Book Rev

On Agate Hill; a novel. Algonquin Books of Chapel Hill 2006 367p $24.95
ISBN 1-56512-452-9   LC 2006-45859
"A Shannon Ravenel book"

"Former beauty queen Tuscany Miller gave up her dissertation on 'Beauty Shop Culture in the South: Big Hair and Community' to get married. When her disastrous marriage ends, Tuscany discovers a young girl's diary in the attic of her father's bed-and-breakfast, a rundown postbellum plantation called Agate Hill. Tuscany's letters to her former doctoral advisor alternate with entries from this diary, kept by young Molly Petree, a Civil War orphan in North Carolina driven from her home, Agate Hill, by the Yankees and handed 'round from relatives to finishing schools until her 18th year. Molly's own diary and the diaries of her teachers and friends form a patchwork quilt of Molly's life from birth to death." Booklist

"Molly is like a grown-up, Southern version of Louisa May Alcott's Jo, only she is thrown into circumstances that test her essentially wholesome nature. For the most part, she battles back not with sass—which modern novels seem to think is universally charming—but pluck. As this is Smith's first historical novel, she deserves credit for understanding this subtle, but essential period point." Denver Post

Oral history. Putnam 1983 286p
ISBN 0-399-12794-1

* LC 82-18081

This "is the tale of the working out of a family curse, the revenge of a red-haired witch spurned by one Almarine Cantrell. Almarine (b.1876), is a subsistence farmer, the owner of all of Hoot Owl Holler in the western corner of Virginia, husband of two women, father of seven, stepfather of one, grandfather of at least five and a regional figure to reckon with. The story is told in a series of voices and includes mountain neighbors and citizens of nearby Tug and Black Rock." Nation

"Smith is excellent at making the separate voices distinctive. . . . Serious fiction readers will be interested in Smith's techniques and will appreciate her decision to utilize this 'oral history' format to best achieve her intentions." Booklist

Saving Grace. Putnam 1995 273p
ISBN 0-399-14050-6

* LC 94-43904

"Florida Grace is the daughter of Virgil Shepherd, a snake-handling self-appointed preacher who starves and sometimes abandons his many children. Of all these, Gracie is the 'contentious and ornery' one who will not embrace Jesus—though she does, along the way (between the ages of seven and thirty-eight), embrace a half brother, a kindly minister, and middle-class luxury. Grace narrates, in irresistible Southern mountain tones." New Yorker

Smith, Lillian Eugenia, 1897-1966

Strange fruit; a novel; [by] Lillian Smith. Reynal & Hitchcock 1944 371p o.p.
*

This novel, set in a small town in Georgia, is about the love of an educated black girl for a white man. The reaction to this affair results in murder and a lynching

This is a "regional novel, in the finest sense. As such, it offers a magnificently detailed picture of the small-town South, lashed by an urge for self-destruction as old as time. The author has suggested no cure for that urge: you will find no black messiahs here, no white devils." N Y Times Book Rev

Smith, Martin Cruz

December 6; a novel. Simon & Schuster 2002 339p

ISBN 0-684-87253-6   LC 2002-29437

This "thriller is set in Tokyo in the last days of 1941, just before the bombing of Pearl Harbor; its central character, the American Harry Niles, grew up in Japan, where his missionary parents were preaching the Word. Harry isn't very holy, however: he owns a night club called the Happy Paris, dabbles in assorted short cons, and spends much of his time with various mistresses. . . . As the rumors of war heat up, Harry finds that he has become too Japanese, and the Japanese suspect him of being a spy. Smith's plot is more than slightly reminiscent of 'Casablanca' and the spectre of the Second World War seems, at this distance, almost quaint, but the characters are so well drawn and the local color so colorful that these quibbles hardly interfere with the novel's pleasures." New Yorker

Gorky Park. Random House 1981 365p o.p.

     * LC 80-6022

"Chief Investigator Renko of the Moscow police is determined to solve the mystery of the three mutilated bodies in Gorky Park, despite obstruction by other officials. His main help comes from New York police Lt. William Kirwin, in Moscow to find his brother, who turns out to be one of the Gorky Park victims. Renko falls in love with Irina, the major witness in the affair, and is brought with her to New York by agents of both nations to defuse what's become a serious situation." Libr J

The author "has succeeded in rendering very believable, realistic, and gripping portrayals of certain segments of Soviet society and of one man's search for meaning." Christ Sci Monit

Havana Bay; a novel. Random House 1999 329p $25.95

ISBN 0-679-42662-0   LC 99-235977

Arkady Renko "has been summoned to Havana to identify the body of his old comrade, Russian embassy attaché Sergei Sergeevich Pribluda. The Cuban police maintain that Pribluda died of a heart attack while fishing from an inner tube in Havana Bay, but that unlikely scenario has Arkady wondering. Nevertheless, he is too consumed by his wife's recent death to investigate—until the embassy's interpreter comes at him with a knife." Publ Wkly

"His earnest unsentimentality and calm tenaciousness on the hunt are what make Renko one of the most interesting detectives in modern fiction. What a clever stroke for Smith to dispatch him to Havana, where sentimentality and passion are in rare abundance." N Y Times Book Rev

Polar Star. Random House 1989 386p il o.p.

     LC 88-43232

This mystery "finds former Moscow investigator Arkady Renko toiling as a second-class seaman on a Russian factory ship, the *Polar Star,* which is part of a joint U.S.-Soviet fishing venture in the Bering Sea. Labeled 'politically unreliable' after the events of *Gorky Park,* Renko has spent years dodging the KGB in Siberia—hence, his ignominious station on the ship's 'slime line,' gutting and chopping fish. Things change when the

body of a Russian girl, who worked in the ship's galley, turns up in a fish net. At first unwillingly, Renko becomes swept up in the investigation, which leads to cocaine trafficking, elaborate espionage plots, and a grisly climax on the ice-covered sea." Booklist

"Rich in humor, generous in spirit, endlessly entertaining and deeply serious, 'Polar Star' is not merely the work of our best writer of suspense, but of one of our best writers, period." N Y Times Book Rev

Red Square. Random House 1992 418p o.p.

     LC 92-50166

"Just prior to the 1991 attempted coup, [Arkady Renko] finds himself reestablished as an investigator with the Moscow police and struggling to contain a flourishing underworld in the newly democratic Soviet Union. . . . A seemingly straightforward murder investigation leads Arkady first to corruption in high places, then to official censure, and finally to Munich, where he is reunited with Irina, the lover who got him in . . . trouble back in the early 1980s." Booklist

Rose. Random House 1996 364p o.p.

     LC 95-37914

Until 1872, Jonathan Blair "was an avid explorer of Africa's Gold Coast, but now he has been exiled by his employer, Bishop Hannay, to the Lancashire mining town of Wigan. Blair's ostensible mission is to find John Rowland, the missing curate who was engaged to Hannay's daughter, but he quickly learns that he'll need all his bush survival skills just to stay alive in Wigan, where no one seems to want the curate found." Publ Wkly

"*Rose* has everthing a compelling novel needs: Blair is a fascinating protagonist, by turns a hero and a boor; other significant characters are complex and as multifaceted as a chunk of coal; the mystery is gripping. But it is the horrific, mesmerizing portrayal of the dark, hellish Wigan, the mines themselves, and the lives of miners that makes this novel much more than a good read." Booklist

Stalin's ghost; an Arkady Renko novel. Simon & Schuster 2007 333p $26.95

ISBN 978-0-07432-7672-6; 0-7432-7672-8

     LC 2006-100963

In this crime novel, Moscow-based Senior Investigator Arkady Renko, "investigates a murder-for-hire scheme that leads him to suspect two fellow police detectives, Nikolai Isakov and Marat Urman, both former members of Russia's elite Black Berets, who served in Chechnya. Isakov, a war hero, is now running for public office. Renko must also look into reports that the ghost of Stalin has begun appearing on subway platforms and why several bodies of Black Berets who served in Chechnya with Isakov have turned up in the morgue." Publ Wkly

"Every page reeks of Moscow: dirty snow, the stink of cigarette and vodka fumes, the cynicism and tasteless opulence of the mafia, the all-pervasive corruption. . . . Like the Red Army facing the Nazis, Renko refuses to give up, surrendering neither his investigation nor those he loves. In this subtle, moving book, he is an everyman, whose loyalty and courage speak to all of us." Economist

Stallion Gate. Random House 1986 321p o.p.

     * LC 85-24444

"In a New Mexico blizzard, four men cross a barbed-wire fence at Stallion Gate to select the test site for the first atomic weapon. They are Oppenheimer, the physi-

Smith, Martin Cruz—*Continued*

cist; Groves, the general; Fuchs, the spy. The fourth man is Sergeant Joe Peña, a hero, informer, fighter, musician, Indian. Oppenheimer and Groves have hidden Los Alamos on a mesa surrounded by vast Indian reservations. . . . To it come soldiers, roughnecks and scientists, including Anna Weiss, a mathematician and refugee from the Holocaust with whom Joe falls in love." Publisher's note

"Obviously Stallion Gate is not meant to be taken too literally. There is a touch of the folk hero about Peña as he moves across the New Mexican landscape. A conscious stylist, Smith relies strongly on emotional echoes and calibrated suspense." Time

Wolves eat dogs; a novel. Simon & Schuster 2004 337p $25.95

ISBN 0-684-87254-4   LC 2004-52585

Senior Investigator Arkady Renko "must determine whether the defenestration death of a Russian tycoon was suicide or murder. The discovery of radioactive salt in the dead man's apartment leads Renko to the abandoned Ukrainian towns of Chernobyl and Pripyat, still dangerously contaminated 18 years after the world's deadliest nuclear accident. There he finds a ghostly world inhabited by scavengers, elderly villagers, and a small group of Russian militia and scientists. As Renko pursues his investigation, he uncovers a greater crime, the sad legacy of Soviet ineptitude and corruption." Libr J

Smith, Mary-Ann Tirone *See* Tirone Smith, Mary-Ann, 1944-

Smith, Michael Marshall

The intruders; [by] Michael Marshall. William Morrow 2007 392p $24.95

ISBN 978-0-06-123502-3; 0-06-123502-4

LC 2006-47087

This novel "introduces readers to Jack Whalen, a former LAPD officer who wrote a book about crime scenes in Los Angeles. He and wife, Amy, now live in Washington State, where he's attempting to write another book while she pursues a successful career as an ad agency executive. Jack's feeling that something is not right in his marriage is confirmed when he tries to contact Amy at her hotel during a business trip and there is no sign that his wife has ever checked in. The same day, he gets a visit from an old high school friend who asks him to investigate a home invasion and murder in Seattle." Libr J

"Mr. Marshall recalls Stephen King's ability to set a story in the world of the commonplace, then suddenly jolt it into a more hellish realm. He also has some of Mr. King's ability to rivet attention with eerie surprises. It's not necessary to believe this book's spooky underlying premise to be caught up in the campfire-tale power of its action." N Y Times (Late N Y Ed)

Smith, R. A. McCall *See* McCall Smith, Alexander, 1948-

Smith, Richard Liebmann- *See* Liebmann-Smith, Richard, 1942-

Smith, Robert Kimmel, 1930-

Jane's house. Morrow 1982 344p o.p.

LC 82-2277

"This book is about how one family deals with the loss of a parent. Paul Klein's wife of 18 years, Jane, died suddenly, leaving him to raise their two children, Hilary and Bobby. The first part of the book deals with Paul's slow adjustment to single parenthood, emphasizing the day-to-day problems. Then he meets Ruth, a lively and intelligent advertising woman. They fall in love and marry. The second part of the story is seen mostly through Ruth's eyes, as she tries to gain the children's friendship." Libr J

Smith, Rosamond, 1938-
See also Oates, Joyce Carol, 1938-

Smith, Scott, 1965-

The ruins; a novel. Knopf 2006 319p $24.95

ISBN 1-400-04387-5   LC 2005-57782

"Two twentysomething American couples are vacationing in Cancun, where they befriend Mathias, an English-speaking German, and Pablo, an easygoing Greek. Amy is the worrier. Stacy, her best friend, is an impulsive airhead. Jeff is the ambitious can-do guy. Eric is laid-back and passive. All they intend to do is party, but when Mathias goes to look for his brother at an archaeological site near some Mayan ruins, the others go along. Naive and hubristic, the vacationers are soon entrapped by people they can't understand and besieged by a creepy, inexplicable power." Booklist

"One of the creepy pleasures of 'The Ruins' is the way it combines genre cliches with the verisimilitude that is Smith's great gift. . . . 'The Ruins' is superior horror literature, but it does not entirely overcome the pile-driving limitations of the genre; it might have been more effective as a short story. But its relentless bleakness—it is almost clinically bloody—played out at novel length is also what sets it apart from other books of this kind." N Y Times Book Rev

A simple plan; a novel. Knopf 1993 335p

ISBN 0-679-41985-3

* LC 92-42478

"When Hank Mitchell, his obese, feckless brother Jacob and Jacob's smarmy friend Lou accidentally find a wrecked small plane and its dead pilot in the woods near their small Ohio town, they decide not to tell the authorities about the $4.4 million stuffed into a duffel bag. Instead, they agree to hide the money and later divide it among themselves. The 'simple plan' sets in motion a spiral of blackmail, betrayal and multiple murder." Publ Wkly

This novel is so "cunningly imagined that for the most part Mr. Smith drags us willingly through what in less deft hands could be a morally repugnant story." N Y Times Book Rev

Smith, Stevie, 1902-1971

Novel on yellow paper; or, Work it out for yourself. New Directions 1994 252p il (A revived modern classic) pa $10.95

ISBN 0-8112-1239-4

* LC 93-49827

Smith, Stevie, 1902-1971—*Continued*
First published 1936 in the United Kingdom
This novel is "narrated in the first person by Pompey
Casmilus, who lives with her darling Auntie Lion, and is
an outpouring of her thoughts and feelings about the
world around her–about fear, love, death, marriage, religion, sex, anti-Semitism; about her friends and lovers
and her childhood. To list the topics cannot begin to capture the delicious flavour, which is whimsical, poetic,
self-deprecatingly (or at times, mercilessly) humorous,
and often absurd." Good Fiction Guide

Smith, Tom Rob

Child 44. Grand Central Pub. 2008 439p $24.99
ISBN 978-0-446-40238-5; 0-446-40238-9
LC 2007-28272
"In the workers' paradise of Stalin's Russia, crime cannot exist. Loyal, hardworking citizens will have all their
needs met by the state, making crime unnecessary. The
one exception is political crime, and MGB (State Security) officer Leo Demidov works long hours arresting people and delivering them to dreaded Lubyanka Prison.
Deeply patriotic, but covetous of the perks of his position, Leo knows that many of the people he arrests are
innocent, and he knows that he could suffer a similar
fate. He does, almost, when office politics, MGB style,
dictate his transfer to the lowly militia in a small city
hundreds of miles east of Moscow. There he discovers
that a serial killer is preying on children in cities along
the Trans-Siberian Railroad. Having lost almost everything, Leo seeks redemption by hunting the killer, but his
effort makes him a high-profile enemy of the state."
Booklist
"Smith captures the rhythm of day-today paranoia in
Stalinist Russia and the ways that personal jealousies can
balloon into ruthless vendettas. It's hard to fathom which
is more grisly, the descriptions of the serial murders or
the scenes of torture perpetrated by Leo's colleagues in
the MGB. Throughout, Smith's prose is propulsive but
plain; his real genius is his careful plotting." Entertainment Wkly

The secret speech. Grand Central Pub. 2009
407p $24.99
ISBN 978-0-446-40240-8; 0-446-40240-0
LC 2008-48329
"Former state security officer Leo Demidov, eyes now
wide open to Soviet excess, is struggling to forge a new
life. His heroism in 'Child 44' earned him a job in the
newly formed Moscow homicide bureau, but his efforts
to create a family with his wife Raisa and two orphaned
girls are a struggle, mainly because the elder, Zoya,
rightly blames Leo for her parents' deaths. Other things
have changed as well: Stalin is dead, and a widely distributed, once-secret letter denouncing his actions —
from his successor Khrushchev — acts as a catalyst for
those seeking revenge against Stalin's oppressors. Like
Leo. Based on real events, 'The Secret Speech' is jam-
packed with action — the near-sinking of a prison ship,
a violent takeover at a Kolyma gulag, and a rebellion in
Hungary — and Smith explores pertinent questions of revenge, morality and responsibility." PopMatters

Smith, Wilbur A.

Birds of prey; a novel; [by] Wilbur Smith. St.
Martin's Press 1997 554p o.p.   LC 97-8192
"In 1667, Sir Francis Courteney commands his ship off
the coast of Africa in England's war against the Dutch.
He has groomed his son Hal to succeed him as captain.
Birds of Prey chronicles Hal's swift and bloody passage
to manhood after his father's torture and death at the
hands of the Dutch. Escaping with the remaining crew,
Hal makes his way overland to claim his father's hidden
treasure and confront the treacherous English captain
who betrayed them." Libr J
"Smith's depiction of the African coast, and of life
aboard ship, is vivid and believable. He handles the action sequences well, opting for short, trenchant paragraphs to sustain momentum. . . . Smith knows what his
readers want, and once again he delivers the goods."
Publ Wkly
Followed by Monsoon

Golden fox; {by} Wilbur Smith. Random House
1991 c1990 433p
ISBN 0-394-58971-8   LC 90-39062
First published 1990 in the United Kingdom
This novel in the Courtney family series is set in 1969.
"Ramón de Santiago y Machado is a fallen Spanish mar-
ques working for the KGB and involved with Cuban
guerrillas fighting in Africa. He sets his sights on Isabella Courtney, daughter of South African industrialist
Shasa Courtney, woos her, and impregnates her, with the
hollow promise that he will make things legit as soon as
his divorce comes through. It's all a ruse, of course. Ramon's intentions are dastardly, and his superiors abduct
the child that is born and blackmail Isabella into helping
them sabotage the political and military plans of the
white South African government." Booklist
"Smith excels at creating finely drawn characters; descriptive settings in London, Europe, and Africa; and a
masterful development of an action-packed thriller that
gets better as each new predicament unfolds." SLJ

Monsoon; [by] Wilbur Smith. St. Martin's Press
1999 613p $26.95
ISBN 0-312-20339-X   LC 99-24554
"A Thomas Dunne book"
This sequel to Birds of Prey "finds Sir Hal Courtney
and his sons up to their bloody sword arms in piracy, intrigue, treachery and civil war in late 17th and early 18th
century East Africa and Arabia. . . . Wealthy English
landowner Sir Hal earned his fortune as a sea captain
with the East India Company. To protect his overseas investments, he becomes a privateer to combat Arab pirates attacking company ships from bases in Zanzibar
and Madagascar. Accompanied by three of his four sons,
Sir Hal embarks on a desperate voyage that will bring either glory and treasure or ruin. . . . Clever plot twists
and lavish historical detail attend the siblings' adventures." Publ Wkly

Power of the sword; [by] Wilbur Smith. Little,
Brown 1986 618p
ISBN 0-316-80171-2   LC 86-10279
"The central characters in this robust tale of politics,
adventure and romance set in South Africa are stepbrothers Manfred and Shasa, sons of Centaine Courtney
(from 'The Burning Shore'), owner of a diamond mine.

Smith, Wilbur A.—*Continued*

As representatives, respectively, of the Afrikaner cause and that of the more liberal, English-speaking whites, headed in the early days by Jan Smuts, they are, however, destined to be enemies. . . . What Smith may lack in subtlety, he makes up for in raw vigor." Publ Wkly

Followed by Rage

Rage; by Wilbur Smith. Little, Brown 1987 627p o.p.   LC 87-3078

This novel in the Courtney family saga is set in post-World War II South Africa. "Shasa Courtney is a wealthy United Party minister to the South African Parliament. A moderate of English heritage, he is often opposed to the Nationalist Party's Manfred De La Rey, an Afrikaner. Their mother, the matriarchal Centaine Courtney-Malcomess, is able to mediate their conflicts but not to control Shasa's wife, Tara, who . . . falls in love with the black Moses Gama, an advocate of violent opposition to apartheid." Publ Wkly

"The interlocking stories of these and many others, set against the authentic African historical and cultural background that Smith so effectively provides, produces both a compelling tale and some real insights into South Africa." Libr J

Followed by A time to die

River god; [by] Wilbur Smith. St. Martin's Press 1994 c1993 530p o.p.   LC 93-45249

"A Thomas Dunne book"

First published 1993 in the United Kingdom

This novel, set in Egypt ca.1780 B.C., "tells the story of Taita the eunuch, slave to a noble's daughter. Taita narrates the dramatic events of which he was either witness or participant as his mistress receives the dubious honor of marriage to the pharaoh. The brutality of life in ancient times is everywhere evident in Taita's tale, which involves fatal intrigue at every turn. It's clear Smith knows his subject: his graphic depiction of lust, bloodletting, politics, and, in Taita's case, honor is firmly grounded in rich details that evoke the period." Booklist

Followed by The seventh scroll

The seventh scroll; {by} Wilbur Smith. St. Martin's Press 1995 486p o.p.   LC 95-768

"A Thomas Dunne book"

This sequel to River god "pairs blueblood, devil-may-care Sir Nicholas Quenton-Harper, who recently has lost his wife and children in a tragic accident, and half-English, half-Egyptian archeologist Royan Al-Sima, herself recently bereaved, in a desperate race to unearth Pharaoh Mamose's fabulous treasures. Their rival in this quest is Gotthold von Schiller, an old, crazed, murderous German collector of antiquities whose mistress, a porno actress, dresses up as an ancient Egyptian queen to titillate him. The major clue is the eponymous seventh scroll, key to the tomb's location, written by ancient Egyptian scribe Taita." Publ Wkly

"Smith excels at action sequences, getting his attractive heroes and despicable villains into and out of hugely entertaining predicaments, all the while tossing off vivid descriptions, bits of historical detail, and classic low-key British banter." Booklist

A time to die; [by] Wilbur Smith. Random House 1990 c1989 448p

ISBN 0-394-58475-9   LC 89-27360

First published 1989 in the United Kingdom

This novel in the Courtney family saga, focuses on "Sean Courtney, Rhodesian African Rifles officer turned big-game hunter. Leading a safari on his licensed land in Africa, Courtney is lured over the Mozambique border in pursuit of a long-sought elephant trophy, for which his client promises him half a million dollars. Courtney turns into the quarry, however, when a Mozambiquan guerrilla leader kidnaps the client's daughter, Claudia, and forces Courtney into abetting the rebel cause. A few stolen American-made missiles and the devastation of a Soviet-equipped helicopter base later, Courtney and Claudia are fleeing for their lives through the African wilderness." Booklist

Followed by Golden fox

Smith, Zadie

The autograph man; a novel. Random House 2002 347p

ISBN 0-375-50186-X   LC 2002-69705

"Tells the story of a young half-Chinese, half-Jewish autograph trader named Alex-Li Tandem who achieves a trade-specific form of enlightenment by tracking down the reclusive aging actress Kitty Alexander, whose extremely rare signatures are the envy of collectors everywhere." Libr J

"Smith's pen portraits of the shabby, yobbish autograph trading circle are intermittently funny, but her prose is so busy being clever that the laughter never builds. This is disappointing but, even with its faults, the novel points to a literary talent of a high order." Publ Wkly

On beauty. Penguin Press 2005 445p $25.95

ISBN 1-59420-0637

"The Belsey family is multicultural as well as multinational. Howard is English, teaching art history at liberal Wellington College near Boston. His [African-American] wife, Kiki, is from Florida, and as practical as her husband is intellectual. Although they love each other dearly, Howard's waning career and wandering eye have caused a strain. Their children follow their own paths: Jerome is a Christian; Zora is a socially concerned intellectual; and Levi is trying to be a black man of the streets. When Jerome falls in love with the daughter of Howard's archrival, Monty Kipps, the two families are thrown together in a personal and cultural battle. Although the romance sours, Howard and Monty's rivalry kicks up a notch, while Kiki and Mrs. Kipps develop an unlikely bond." Booklist

"Ms Smith has her shortcomings. The novel's first half is under-edited; surely we do not need to meet every guest at an anniversary party. . . . Nevertheless, the book gathers momentum, and the second half gallops along." Economist

White teeth; a novel. Random House 2000 448p $24.95

ISBN 0-375-50185-1

                                            * LC 99-43658

"Hapless Archibald Jones fights alongside Bengali Muslim Samad Iqbal in the English army during WWII, and the two develop an unlikely bond that intensifies when Samad relocates to Archie's native London, Smith traces the trajectory of their friendship through marriage, parenthood and the shared disappointments of poverty

Smith, Zadie—*Continued*
and deflated dreams." Publ Wkly

"Hopscotching through several continents and 150 years of history, 'White Teeth' encompasses a teeming family saga, a sly inquiry into race and identity and a tender-hearted satire on religious antagonism and cultural bemusement. . . . Smith holds it all together with a raucous energy and confidence." N Y Times Book Rev

Smollett, Tobias George, 1721-1771

The expedition of Humphry Clinker; introduction and notes by Thomas R. Preston; the text edited by O M Brack, Jr. University of Georgia Press 1990 lx, 500p
   ISBN 0-8203-1203-7
                                          * LC 89-36020
   First published 1771

In this epistolary novel "the letters are written by Matthew Bramble, his sister Tabitha, their niece, their nephew, and their maid, Winifred Jenkins. Each correspondent has a highly individual style and caricatures himself unwittingly. The titular hero of this comic masterpiece, who plays a lesser role than the Brambles, is a workhouse lad who enters into their service by chance and who later becomes a Methodist preacher. He falls in love with Winifred, and is eventually found to be the natural son of Mr. Bramble. The 'expedition' of the title is a family tour through England and Scotland, during which the correspondents express surprisingly varied reactions to the same events. Of particular note is the picture of Hot Wells (a sobriquet for the city of Bath), a fashionable watering place." Reader's Ency. 4th edition

Snicket, Lemony, 1970-
   See also Handler, Daniel, 1970-

Snow, C. P. (Charles Percy), 1905-1980

The conscience of the rich. Scribner 1958 342p (Strangers and brothers) o.p.

"As a result of his friendship with Charles March, Lewis Eliot is taken into the private world of one of England's wealthiest and most influential Jewish families and through his eyes the March drama is slowly unfolded; the close bond between Charles, his father, and his sister, Charles's marriage to a gentle Communist, and the ensuing political scandal which estranges father and son, brother and sister. . . . Set in London during the late 1920's and the 1930's." Booklist

Corridors of power. Scribner 1964 403p (Strangers and brothers) o.p.

"The workings of inner power in the British government—with key administrators, politicians, and the wealthy manipulators, male and female—[are] traced in a novel of the period 1955-1958. . . . Since the power in this fictional case is concerned with the use of nuclear arms, the fate of the world can easily hang on the fate of one minister, Roger Quaife." Publ Wkly

"We see the corridors of political power illuminated with a fine and discriminating light." Libr J

Homecoming. Scribner 1956 399p (Strangers and brothers) o.p.

Published in the United Kingdom with title: Homecomings

"An introspective, subtly shaded novel which again

stars Lewis Eliot. . . . Eliot's unhappy marriage to a neurotic woman, her death, and his affair with an eventual marriage to a woman more worthy of his love comprise the chief incidents in a story that accents not the events themselves but their psychological effect upon the persons involved. Crisp, carefully fashioned prose; for the discriminating." Booklist

Last things. Scribner 1970 435p (Strangers and brothers) o.p.

"Student protest, Lewis Eliot's decision on whether or not to enter the Labor government's ministry, his serious eye operation during which a cardiac arrest brings him near to death—these are some of the essential plot elements [of this novel]." Publ Wkly

The light and the dark. Scribner 1961 c1947 406p (Strangers and brothers) o.p.
                                                              *

First published 1947 in the United Kingdom
Cambridge University is the scene of the greater part of this character study of a young Cambridge don. In an attempt to curb his dark moods Roy tries promiscuity, drink, concentration on his studies, and religion. With the out-break of the war he joins the RAF and is killed in action

"A painstaking and readable account of university life seen from high table." Times Lit Suppl

The masters. Macmillan 1951 374p (Strangers and brothers) o.p.

"Lewis Eliot, a Cambridge Fellow, tells about the election of a new Master of his college, and uses the rivalry and jealousy attendant on the election to illuminate the lives and hearts of the candidates and their friends and enemies. The book begins with notice of the impending death of the old Master, Vernon Royce, continues at a leisurely rate as Royce waits to die and finally dies, and ends with the election of the new Master." New Yorker

"For a quiet novel of subtle characterization this one contains a surprising element of suspense." Ont Libr Rev

The new men. Scribner 1954 311p (Strangers and brothers) o.p.
                                                              *

The novel describes a group of nuclear scientists and high government officials working together in England during the war. As usual Lewis Eliot is the narrator

The author "handles a fateful new theme with challenging insight and impressive moral sensitivity. . . . [This is a] novel which searchingly explores the moral dilemmas created by the atom bomb." Atlantic

Strangers and brothers. Scribner 1960 309p (Strangers and brothers) o.p.
                                                              *

First published 1940 in the United Kingdom
George Passant, a solicitor in an English provincial town, exerts a crucial influence on his group of young protegés, Lewis Eliot among them. An idealist, courageous and high-principled Passant seems destined for great things yet the story ends in his trial for fraud. The reasons for this are revealed

"Essentially the tragedy of a good man defeated by the mediocrity of his world, the story of George Passant is completed in the novel 'Homecoming.' . . . Like all the novels in the series, 'Strangers and Brothers' is distin-

Snow, C. P. (Charles Percy), 1905-1980—Continued
guished by virtue of its analysis of motive and character
and its anatomization of a world in which a smooth mediocrity is the greatest virtue." Libr J

Time of hope. Macmillan 1950 c1949 416p
(Strangers and brothers) o.p.
"Here, as in 'Light and the Dark' (1948) Lewis Eliot
is the main character that typifies middle class English
life, and as in the earlier work, Mr. Snow shows the impact of spiritual values on individuals. The 1930s are the
background here and the years are brilliantly drawn. Moral problems are vivid and the characters are varied in
their reactions." Libr J

Snow, Charles Percy *See* Snow, C. P. (Charles
Percy), 1905-1980

Snow, Lucy *See* Aubert, Rosemary, 1946-

Snow white, blood red; edited by Ellen Datlow &
Terri Windling. Morrow 1992 411p o.p.
LC 92-24899

"An AvoNova book"
Contents: Like a red, red rose, by S. Wade; The moon
is drowning while I sleep, by C. de Lint; The frog
prince, by G. Wilson; Stalking beans, by N. Kress;
Snow-drop, by T. Lee; Little red, by W. Wheeler; I shall
do thee mischief in the wood, by K. Koja; The root of
the matter, by G. Frost; The princess in the tower, by E.
A. Lynn; Persimmon, by H. Jacobs; Little Poucet, by S.
R. Tem; The changelings, by M. Tem; The Springfield
swans, by C. Stevermer; Troll bridge, by N. Gaiman; A
sound, like angels singing, by L. Rysdyk; Puss, by E. M.
Friesner; The glass casket, by J. Dann; Knives, by J.
Yolen; The snow queen, by P. A. McKillip;
Breadcrumbs and stones, by L. Goldstein
"The dark and shadowed aspects of well-known folk
stories and fairy tales are explored in updated retellings.
. . . Some of these tales are enchanting; some are horri-
fying; most, like the originals, offer insight into human
nature." Publ Wkly

Snyder, Don J.

Night crossing; a novel. Knopf 2001 277p $24
ISBN 0-375-40906-8   LC 00-62008
When Nora Andrews, 42 and pregnant, discovers her
husband is having an affair she "boards a plane to Ireland alone, where she promptly witnesses a terrorist
bombing. Having seen too much, she is drawn into a
British anti-IRA plot and is charged with the safekeeping
of a wounded British soldier." Booklist
"This competent—albeit derivative and inflammatory—
thriller delivers some exciting moments as well as insights into the mind of a woman who slowly realizes her
own complicity in the wreck of her marriage." Publ
Wkly

Sofer, Dalia, 1972-

The Septembers of Shiraz. Ecco/HarperCollins
Publishers 2007 340p $24.95
ISBN 978-0-06-113040-3; 0-06-113040-0
LC 2007-299587

In this "novel, Isaac Amin, a Jewish businessman in
Tehran, is imprisoned following the Iranian Revolution.
As Amin attempts to survive his brutal treatment and
convince his captors that he is not a Zionist spy, his
wife, young daughter, and son (a college student in New
York City) find various ways to cope with the radical
change in their way of life and the knowledge that they
may never see Amin again." Libr J
"Sofer paints a complicated picture of
postrevolutionary Iran: The Amins (and especially their
relatives) aren't entirely innocent, having shut their eyes
to brutality and corruption under the shah, but [the au-
thor] recoils from the idea of justice by 'collective retribution' voiced by Farnaz's formerly docile housekeeper.
While the dialogue can feel overly formal at times, the
impression the reader is left with at the end is that of a
powerful story honestly told." Christ Sci Monit

Sollosy, Judith

(tr) Esterházy, P. Celestial harmonies

Solomita, Stephen

Damaged goods. Scribner 1996 380p o.p.
LC 95-33277
"Jilly Sappone truly is 'damaged goods.' The gunshot
that wrecked his brain years before also made him into
a vicious killer. Released from prison by family connections, he takes revenge on everyone responsible for his
prison term. Beginning with his ex-wife, Ann, Jilly and
his brainless psychotic partner, Jackson-Davis, commence
a spree of kidnapping and violent murders. Ex-cop Stanley Moodrow is hired, as is detective cum-computer-whiz
Ginny Gadd, to track down Jilly." Libr J
"The pace is energetic, and with Ginny at his side to
blunt his cynicism, Moodrow seems less morose and
more alert than we've seen him in a long time." N Y
Times Book Rev

A good day to die. Penzler Bks. 1993 297p o.p.
LC 93-19400
"Roland Means, a chronic maverick in the NYPD, is
pulled from cop purgatory—ballistics duty—to go after
'King Thong,' the supposed serial killer responsible for
the murder of seven male prostitutes in New York City.
Vanessa Bouton, a black cop, hates Means's guts but
needs his streetwise methods to help prove her hunch
that only one killing was prompted by a motive, which
the other six are meant to mask." Publ Wkly
"As Means researches the profiled backgrounds of serial killers, he recognizes his own abused childhood; his
search for the killer becomes a search for himself. This
multiethnic thriller vividly depicts the gritty streets of the
city, the dark and feral forest, and the danger lurking in
both." Libr J

Last chance for glory. Penzler Bks. 1994 310p
o.p.   LC 93-38616
"Marty Blake, an out-of-work private investigator, is
hired to help clear the name of a slightly retarded young
man wrongly convicted of murder. To aid in the investigation, Marty contacts Sgt. Bela Kosinski, the original
arresting officer, who is now retired from the NYPD and
drinking himself to death. As this unlikely pair
reinvestigate the murder, they find it easy to prove the

Solomita, Stephen—*Continued*

young man's innocence, but they also discover a murder cover-up that extends into the highest echelons of the police force and New York City government." Libr J

"Blake and Kosinski initially form an uneasy alliance that inevitably turns to friendship, but it happens easily and believably. It's the old mismatched-partner plot, but seldom has it been handled better." Booklist

Solomon, Nina

Single wife; a novel. Algonquin Bks. 2003 307p $23.95

ISBN 1-56512-382-4   LC 2003-40406

"Most men who leave their wives have the courtesy to (at least) leave a note, but not journalist Laz Brookman. At the start of this. . . novel, he casually leaves his New York apartment one morning and never returns. . . . Anxious to save face and preserve the precarious normality of her life, and certain that he will soon return—mysterious several-day-long disappearing acts not being uncommon with her husband—Grace Brookman secretly begins living two lives, Laz's and her own." Publ Wkly

"Solomon tells a funny and bizarre story that is both hard to believe and hard to put down, with characters who are real, almost tangible. She captures the essence of the struggle for self." Libr J

Solzhenitsyn, Aleksandr, 1918-2008

Cancer ward; translated from the Russian by Nicholas Bethell and David Burg. Farrar, Straus & Giroux 1969 560p o.p.

         *

"Set mostly in a provincial cancer ward, the novel traces the ways in which a number of moribund patients come to terms with their death, centering on an investigation of the moral and psychological development of the exiled hero, Kostoglotov. This novel, in which the cancer ward has been widely interpreted as symbolizing the Soviet state, was typeset for publication in the Soviet Union but never published there until after Perestroika began." Reader's Ency. 4th edition

In the first circle; a novel; [by] Aleksandr I. Solzhenitsyn; translated by Harry T. Willetts. the restored text. Harper Perennial 2009 xxx,741p pa $18.99

ISBN 978-0-06-147901-4

         * LC 2008-39336

First English version, translated by Thomas P. Whitney, published 1968 by Harper & Row with title: The first circle

"Set in Moscow during a three-day period in December 1949, The First Circle is the story of the prisoner Gleb Nerzhin, a brilliant mathematician. At the age of thirty-one, Nerzhin has survived the war years on the German front and the postwar years in a succession of Russian prisons and labor camps. His story is interwoven with the stories of a dozen fellow prisoners." Publiisher's note

"It has taken a half-century for English-language readers to receive the definitive text of 'In the First Circle,' the best novel by one of the greatest authors of our time. Such is the fate of art created under a totalitarian regime. But now it is finally available in the West as the author

envisioned it. The English translator is Harry T. Willetts, renowned for combining fidelity to Aleksandr Solzhenitsyn's rich, complex Russian with supple equivalents in English prose and the only person Solzhenitsyn fully trusted to render his fiction into English." Wall Street J

One day in the life of Ivan Denisovich; translated from the Russian by H. T. Willets; with an introduction by John Bayley. Knopf 1995 xxvii, 159p $15

ISBN 0-679-44464-5

         *

"Everyman's library"

Original Russian edition, 1962; this is a reissue of the translation published 1991 by Farrar, Straus & Giroux

"Drawing on his own experiences, the author writes of one day, from reveille to lights-out, in the prison existence of Ivan Denisovich Shukhov. Innocent of any crime, he has been convicted of treason and sentenced to ten years in one of Stalin's notorious slave-labor compounds. The protagonist is a simple man trying to survive the brutality of a totalitarian system." Shapiro. Fic for Youth. 3d edition

Somers, Jane *See* Lessing, Doris May, 1919-

Somerville, Patrick, 1979-

The cradle; a novel. Little, Brown 2009 203p $23.99

ISBN 978-0-316-03612-2; 0-316-03612-9

         LC 2008-25148

"Matt enjoys the missions his pregnant wife, Marissa, sends him on until she remembers the cradle. It's a family heirloom, and she must have it. But Marissa does not know its whereabouts, because her mother disappeared when Marissa was a little girl. Still, Marissa expects Matt to take time off from his factory job and search for the cradle. This is a quest destined to inflame Matt's long-banked anger over his own painful childhood as a neglected and abused foster child. Matt struggles with searing memories while zigzagging across the Midwest, negotiating fairy-tale-strange encounters with deranged and dangerous individuals." Booklist

"Somerville's Midwesterners . . . must often be forced into honest selfSexamination, preferring to hide behind work and duty to prevent the ice-crusted layers of memory from melting into the present. . . . Matt finds the cradle. In fact, that happens more easily than he — or the reader — expects, and the detours and false leads he follows en route feel superfluous, even in this slim novel. The post-cradle journey — and what he discovers — becomes the life-rattling trip." N Y Times Book Rev

Somerville, Rowan, 1966-

The end of sleep. W. W. Norton & Co. 2008 246p $23.95

ISBN 978-0-393-06660-9; 0-393-06660-6

         LC 2008-18240

"In this madcap picaresque, we follow Fin, an Irish journalist, as he spends a day in the streets of Cairo pursuing a story of buried treasure that he believes will restore his floundering career at an English-language newspaper there. Fin seeks a 'pacy linear narrative with obvious and satisfying climaxes,' but Somerville leads us, in-

Somerville, Rowan, 1966—*Continued*

stead, down numerous back alleys and side streets, with frequent breaks for mint tea. The best moments are those of unbridled irreverence, such as when Fin, who is conversant only in 'gastronomical Arabic,' becomes 'inappropriately passionate' on the subject of the perfect kebab (the secret ingredient is thyme), or when we are told that the desert air is 'so pure you can smell the farts of the camels.' Fin's surreal experiences amid Cairo's chaos are a vivid reminder of the challenges inherent in encountering the foreign, and the rewards of 'not only learning to accept, but inhabit' difference." New Yorker

Somoza, José Carlos, 1959-

Zig Zag; a novel; translated from Spanish by Lisa Dillman. Rayo 2007 504p $24.95
ISBN 978-0-06-119371-2; 0-06-119371-2
LC 2006-50406

Original Spanish edition, 2006
"In 2015, Madrid physics teacher Elisa Robledo receives a phone call that plunges her back 10 years to a time when she worked with famous Spanish physicist David Blanes. Blanes theorizes that by using quantum physics and string theory he can build a machine that will enable researchers to see the past. Elisa joins Blanes and a small team of scientists on New Nelson, a mysterious island where they realize all of Blanes's theories. After intriguing glimpses of dinosaurs and Jerusalem during Jesus' lifetime, the project begins to go seriously awry." Booklist
This novel "could've been a bad Crichton tech-thriller knockoff, but José Carlos Somoza displays an unhurried style and a refreshing appreciation for advanced science." Entertainment Wkly

Sontag, Susan, 1933-2004

In America; a novel. Farrar, Straus & Giroux 2000 387p $26
ISBN 0-374-17540-3
* LC 99-54641

"In 1876, 35-year-old Maryna Zalewska, Poland's brilliant, revered actress, packs up her 14-person entourage, including husband, child, maid, and assorted relatives and admirers, and emigrates to Anaheim, CA, determined to shed her glittering life and disappear into the unglamorous anonymity borne of the radical, hardscrabble work of her commune. After a couple of years, with the failure of the farm looming, Maryna returns to the stage in a dazzling U.S. comeback that rockets her to renewed fame, fortune, and smashing success across the nation and overseas." Libr J
This novel "displays Sontag in a relaxed, pleasure-seeking mode, guiding her characters through a long travelogue in time, specifically the beginnings of the gilded age in the brave new world." Time

The volcano lover; a romance. Farrar, Straus & Giroux 1992 419p il $22
ISBN 0-374-28516-0
LC 92-71738

"The 'volcano lover' of the title is Sir William Hamilton, the British diplomat and antiquary who is best remembered as the complaisant husband of Emma Hamilton, notorious mistress of Admiral Nelson. The book is set for the most part in Naples, where, from 1764 until his recall under a cloud in 1800, Sir William was the British envoy to the court of the egregious Bourbon monarch Ferdinand IV, later to become Ferdinand I, King of the Two Sicilies. . . . The novel is a kind of triptych, divided among Hamilton, his wife and Lord Nelson." N Y Times Book Rev
Sontag's "narrative deftly blends the magnetism of personality and the suspense of event with shrewd commentary and sly mockery as she contrasts the habits of thought in that age with ours and reflects on the meaning of mercy and vengeance, self-invention and praise, love and obsession. In all, a memorable group portrait and a brilliant, fresh improvisation on classically grand themes." Booklist

Sorokin, Vladimir, 1955-

Ice; translated from the Russian by Jamey Gambrell. New York Review Books 2007 321p $23.95
ISBN 978-1-59017-195-0
LC 2006-21077

Original Russian edition, 2002
"The ice of the title is from a giant comet that landed in Tungus, Siberia, in 1908 and transformed 23,000 alien beings of light into human form, all blue-eyed blonds. Only a few are aware of their true selves, and they must locate the others to awaken their hearts by bashing them in the chest with axes made from the cosmic ice. For every new Brother or Sister of Light so transformed, many humans must die. Sorokin builds the suspense by incrementally telling the story from the perspectives of three beings in the process of reawakening, their spiritual leader, and a variety of beings who are transformed in their version of the Rapture. Ice succeeds brilliantly as both a thriller and a cautionary tale about totalitarianism, bigotry, elitism, and fundamentalism." Libr J

Sorrentino, Gilbert, 1929-2006

The moon in its flight; stories. Coffee House Press 2004 266p $16
ISBN 1-56689-152-3 (pa)
LC 2004-665

Contents: The moon in its flight; Decades; Land of cotton; The dignity of labor; The sea, caught in roses; A beehive arranged on human principles; Pastilles; Allegory of innocence; Sample writing sample; Times without number; Subway; Facts and their manifestations; It's time to call it a day; Life and letters; Perdido; Lost in the stars; Psychopathology of everyday life; Gorgias; In loveland; Things that have stopped moving
"A sort of grim nostalgia pervades his stories, many of the best of which are set in a perfectly evoked mid-20th century New York of shabby cocktail lounges and afternoon papers." N Y Times Book Rev

A strange commonplace. Coffee House Press 2006 154p pa $14.95
ISBN 1-56689-182-5
LC 2005-35804

This novel "portrays a circle of struggling New Yorkers living back in the sexist, alcohol-sodden, and hypocritical 1950s on into the egomaniacal present. Ugly sex, adultery, and vicious domestic battles make a misery of marriage and family life, and old age is nothing to aspire to. Memories fizzle and morph into fantasies, and one elderly fellow courts death with solitary card games. The book itself resembles a deck of cards, what with its 52

Sorrentino, Gilbert, 1929-2006—*Continued*

tales imprinted with repeating patterns and emblems, and sly Sorrentino shuffling the cards, cutting the deck, and dealing some tough hands." Booklist

Southgate, Martha

The fall of Rome; a novel. Scribner 2002 223p hardcover o.p. pa $13

ISBN 0-684-86500-9; 0-7432-2721-2 (pa)

LC 2001-34225

A "novel about a token black teacher at an élite New England boarding school. Jerome Washington is a classics scholar who, armed with a Harvard education and an accent purged of his Georgia-sharecropper roots, has spent his life trying to defeat racism through sheer decorum. But his hermetic existence is threatened by the arrival of a black student from a Brooklyn ghetto and a white female teacher who fancies herself a champion of the underprivileged." New Yorker

The author "delves deeply into the social and emotional elements that unite and divide us. Issues of race, identity, and integrity are intensely explored through a tragic human triangle." Booklist

Spanidou, Irini

Before. Alfred A. Knopf 2007 211p $23

ISBN 978-0-375-41381-0; 0-375-41381-2

LC 2007-5265

A novel set against "a backdrop of dissolute culture in 1970s New York. Twenty-five-year-old Beatrice is married to Ned, a painter, who is enraged by his obsessive love for her. Meanwhile, Beatrice's love for Ned has consumed her desire to finish her thesis and write poetry. While their tortured relationship sinks to levels of sexual humiliation, other characters with their own particular obsession for Beatrice come to the fore. Fellow tenant Colin is in love with her; Perkins, their recently paroled neighbor, is constantly staring at her; Chris, a heroin addict and prostitute, sees her as his salvation; childhood friend Faye's cruelty masks a deep passion; and Cyril fell for Beatrice at first sight." Libr J

"Spanidou's beautiful writing almost perfectly evokes the 1970s in New York, its fascinating characters, its low rents and withheld ambitions—her sentences have just the right measure of elegant lassitude, of quiet, humming sexiness, and of a singular devotion to seeing things deeply, no matter what the cost." Oprah Magazine

Spark, Muriel

The Abbess of Crewe. Viking 1974 116p o.p.

Set in the convent of Crewe in England, this novel traces the efforts of Sister Alexandra to win the elective position of abbess. "The problem is Sister Felicity, who has a following amongst the nuns. But Felicity has committed certain indiscretions, and Alexandra and her supporters are able to discredit her." Christ Sci Monit

"The Abbess of Crewe has the closely woven texture and the structural coherence of good poetry: it is executed with a subtlety and intelligence that safeguard against the tones of complacent moralizing that might very easily have spoiled the articulation of the book's themes." Saturday Rev/World

Aiding and abetting. Doubleday 2000 166p

ISBN 0-385-50153-6   LC 00-55559

"A tall, whitehaired man walks into the Paris consulting room of Hildegaard Woolf, a psychiatrist from Bavaria. Revealing himself as Lord Lucan, he threatens to unmask Dr. Wolf as Beate Pappenheim, a former student revolutionary. Tired of being poor, she had bilked credulous people by persuading them that the menstrual blood she smeared on herself was a sign of the stigmata." Economist

"The unsettling wit of 'Aiding and Abetting' hits the funny bone as hard it pricks the conscience. . . . It's kiln-dried wit that never cracks, with a smile that dares you to laugh. As always [Spark] is breathtakingly deft with the anxieties of well-bred people, people who know how to dress, where to eat, and how to commit the most heinous cruelty. If satire is your cup of tea, . . . [this is a] perfectly seeped book to be savored." Christ Sci Monit

The bachelors. New Directions 1999 186p pa $12.95

ISBN 0-8112-1424-9   LC 99-30688

First published 1960 in the United Kingdom; first published in the United States 1961 by Lippincott

This "novel follows a group of British bachelors whose cozy little world is shattered when they suddenly find themselves the target of blackmail, fraud, and other bits of nastiness courtesy of one of the lads. Spark is always a great read." Libr J

The ballad of Peckham Rye. Lippincott 1960 160p o.p.

"Young Dougal Douglas, the Devil in contemporary clothing, has quite an impact on an industrial town adjacent to London since, among other things, he is responsible for a groom leaving his bride-to-be at the altar and the nervous breakdown of a veteran employee in one of the local factories." Booklist

"A fresh comic style does not appear every day, and that is what Muriel Spark has developed in this expert fantasy. . . . The wackiness is cumulative, the style dead-pan and blow-by-blow, and above all no overt attempt is ever made to get a laugh." N Y Times Book Rev

also in Spark, M. A Muriel Spark trio p233-386

The comforters

In Spark, M. A Muriel Spark trio p13-228

The driver's seat. Knopf 1970 117p o.p.

Originally published in the New Yorker, this is the story of "Lise, a fascinatingly eccentric, pent-up creature whose vacation in the South of Europe turns into a macabre disaster, one she herself helps to bring about." Choice

"The author's perspective is cosmically cool and fantastic: she knows no more about her protagonist, Lise, than does the reader. . . . She follows this woman, another of her slightly bizarre lunatics, through a day's grotesque project, narrating only its circumstances, leaving all motive, all emotion, all inner plan to be inferred. The result is a long, elusive joke that casts as deep an irony on life's arbitrariness as do the more 'compassionate' ironies of, say, E. M. Forster." Nation

A far cry from Kensington. Houghton Mifflin 1988 189p

ISBN 0-395-47694-1

* LC 88-5904

Spark, Muriel—*Continued*

"The narrator, Mrs. Hawkins, remembers back to 1954 when she was a young war widow living in furnished rooms in a boarding house in South Kensington, London. Mrs. Hawkins was the unwitting confidante of her fellow boarders and coworkers—she was an editor but lost two jobs because of standing up against a writer she believed was a hack. This same man intruded into her private life as well." Booklist

"Spark balances devastatingly eccentric characters and funny situations with darker elements, even pathos. Her well-constructed novel has no loose ends and few contrived situations." Libr J

The finishing school; Muriel Spark. 1st ed. Doubleday 2004 181p $16.95

ISBN 0-385-51282-1   LC 2004-45533

This novel "takes place in a finishing school in Switzerland run by a young married couple. Theirs is not the old-fashioned type of finishing school, in which young ladies learn deportment; rather, it is one in which both male and female students, after high school and before college, take a wide range of courses about culture and civilization. The husband is blocked in performing what is of primary importance to him: his writing. Contributing to his burden is his great envy of the apparent ease and fluidity with which one of the male students seems to be composing his own novel." Booklist

The author "satirically assails, among other subjects, the culture of spectacle that has grown up around novel writing, particularly novel writing by attractive young people." Atl Mon (1993)

The girls of slender means. Knopf 1963 176p o.p.

*

"The novel, set primarily in London during World War II, focuses on the inhabitants of a residential club for unmarried women and on the friendship of several of them with a young man named Nicholas Farringdon. When tragedy strikes and 13 of the women are killed, Nicholas realizes that there is no safety anywhere, especially for those on whom fortune had once seemed to smile. This epiphany stimulates his conversion to Roman Catholicism. Years later, he dies in Haiti, where he has gone as a missionary." Merriam-Webster's Ency of Lit

Loitering with intent. Coward, McCann & Geoghegan 1981 217p

ISBN 0-698-11047-1   LC 80-26049

"Would-be novelist Fleur Talbot works for the snooty, irascible Sir Quentin Oliver at the Autobiographical Association, whose members are all at work on their memoirs. When her employer gets his hands on Fleur's novel-in-progress, mayhem ensues when its scenes begin coming true. Generating hilarious turns of phrase and larger-than-life characters (especially Sir Quentin's batty mother), Sparks's inimitable style make this literary joyride thoroughly appealing." Publ Wkly

The Mandelbaum Gate. Knopf 1965 369p o.p.

"The changing shape of any identity, be it of person or of situation, is the theme of this novel, typified by the Mandelbaum Gate of the title, 'hardly a gate at all, but a piece of street between Jerusalem and Jerusalem' . . . The narrative goes and returns piecemeal between the two parts of the Holy Land, focusing on two English characters–Barbara Vaughan, a spinster, half Jewish by birth and Roman Catholic by conviction, come to Israel to be near her archeologist fiance (and lover) in Jordan and to make a pilgrimage to the Holy sites; and Freddy Hamilton, proper foreign officer, moved by an unexpected impulse to change his personal pattern of responsibility and by kindness to keep Barbara from the danger of being apprehended by Jordan authorities because of her background." Libr J

"The novel deals compellingly with issues of religious and personal identity, and makes the story of its protagonist's quest for the reconciliation of the two cultural and religious traditions to which she belongs as exciting as any thriller." Oxford Companion to 20th-century Lit in Engl

Memento mori. Lippincott 1959 c1958 224p o.p.

*

"Several elderly London friends receive anonymous telephone calls with a single message: 'Remember you must die.' Each hears and interprets the words differently. Old rivalries and romances still color the friends' relations, and Spark makes clear that their personalities in old age are but a continuation of their earlier lives." Merriam-Webster's Ency of Lit

also in Spark, M. A Muriel Spark trio p393-608

A Muriel Spark trio; The comforters; The ballad of Peckham Rye; Memento mori. Lippincott 1962 608p o.p.

The three complete novels reprinted here were first published 1957, 1960 and 1959 respectively. The comforters is a novel in experimental form. It is a book within a book, in which many of the characters are neurotics or oddities of some sort. The most normal character is Louisa Jepp, aged seventy-eight, whose experiments with smuggling diamonds provide much of the action. The scene is England, and Roman Catholic life is part of the background

Open to the public; new & collected stories. New Directions 1997 376p $24.95

ISBN 0-8112-1367-6

* LC 97-20607

Contents: The Portobello Road; The curtain blown by the breeze; The black madonna; Bang-bang you're dead; The Seraph and the Zambesi; The twins; The Playhouse called Remarkable; The pawnbroker's wife; Miss Pinkerton's apocalypse; 'A sad tale's best for winter'; The leaf sweeper; Daisy Overend; You should have seen the mess; Come along, Marjorie; The ormolu clock; The dark glasses; A member of the family; The house of the famous poet; The fathers' daughters; Open to the public; Alice Long's dachshunds; The go-away bird; The first year of my life; The gentile Jewesses; The executor; The fortune-teller; Another pair of hands; The dragon; The girl I left behind me; Going up and coming down; The pearly shadow; Chimes; The thing about police stations; Harper and Wilton; Ladies and gentlemen; Lavishes ghost; The hanging judge

"With 10 tales new to American readers, *Open to the Public* brings Spark's stories up to date with the rest of her prolific output." Publ Wkly

Spark, Muriel—*Continued*

The prime of Miss Jean Brodie. Lippincott 1962 c1961 187p o.p.

                                               *

First published 1961 in the United Kingdom

"Miss Jean Brodie, teacher at the Marcia Blaine School for Girls in Edinburgh in the 1930s, gathers around herself a group of young girls who are set apart from other students as the Brodie set: Monica Douglas, who will be famous for her mathematical ability; Rose Stanley, who will be famous for her sex appeal; Eunice Gardiner, of great swimming and gymnastic ability; Sandy Stranger, of the small eyes and outstanding vowel sounds; and Mary MacGregor, who is considered a silent lump. Miss Brodie will make these girls the 'crème de la crème,' especially if they will follow her advice to recognize their prime. Her teaching is unorthodox and her relationship with the students most informal, so that they are privy to her affair with the school's music teacher. We get glimpses into the future of these young girls and are made aware that students are capable of treachery as well as teacher-worship." Shapiro. Fic for Youth. 3d edition

Reality and dreams. Houghton Mifflin 1997 160p

   ISBN 0-395-83811-8   LC 96-52913

First published 1996 in the United Kingdom

"A glimpse of a girl selling hamburgers at a French campground ignites film director Tom Richard's imagination, and around it he builds his latest movie. When the film is still in production, he suffers a serious accident and awakens to find his vision being threatened as others try to take over the story. He also awakens to disruptions in his 'real' life-many of those around him are losing their jobs, his daughters' marriages are in the process of breaking up, and long held resentments/jealousies, both personal and professional, are coming to the surface." Libr J

"Dame Muriel is as enigmatic in this novel, as distinct, as relentlessly observant of human habits and unguarded moments as she has ever been." N Y Times Book Rev

Sparks, Nicholas

A bend in the road. Warner Bks. 2001 341p

   ISBN 0-446-52778-5   LC 2001-26419

Deputy sheriff Miles Ryan's "high school sweetheart, Missy, was killed in an unsolved hit and run accident, leaving him to raise their son, Jonah, in New Bern, N.C. [Sarah Andrews'] politically ambitious husband, Michael, dumped her when her ovaries proved inactive, and she fled to New Bern to teach, and love, other people's kids. Miles and Sarah meet at a parent-teacher conference, and the sparks fly. But there's a fly in the ointment as well." Publ Wkly

"Sparks brings a powerful tale of true love to fruition, proving that love stories can be sweet without being cloying." Booklist

Dear John. Warner Books 2006 276p $24.99

   ISBN 978-0-446-52805-4; 0-446-52805-6

                               LC 2006-020714

"John Tyree is on the fast track to nowhere. At 20 he has no real relationship with his strange and dispassionate father, no attachments to anyone else, and no job, so after breaking up with his girlfriend, he decides to join the army. Military life does alter him, yet he remains disconnected. While home visiting his father in Wilmington, North Carolina, however, he meets Savannah Curtis, a college coed who is everything he is not. A warm, morally straight-ahead woman with a commitment to special education, she captures John's heart and he hers. In the short time they spend together, he opens up to Savannah and true love develops as they plan for a future. Then September 11 changes everything. John feels that it is his duty to renew his commitment to the army, while Savannah wants him home with her. The good soldier now lives in dread of receiving a 'Dear John' letter. Sparks . . . lives up to his reputation with his latest novel, a tribute to courageous and self-sacrificing soldiers." Booklist

The guardian. Warner Bks. 2003 384p $24.95

   ISBN 0-446-52779-3   LC 2002-192411

"On Christmas Eve, Julie Barenson, 25 years old and newly widowed, finds an unexpected present—a Great Dane pup that her late husband, Jim, had arranged for her to receive after she died from a brain tumor. . . . Julie's new dog, Singer, turns out to be a better judge of character than she, which is unfortunate because the dog nearly gives away the book's ending when he growls warily at Richard Franklin, the new man in Julie's life." Publ Wkly

Message in a bottle. Warner Bks. 1998 322p $20

   ISBN 0-446-52356-9   LC 97-39158

"Boston parenting columnist Theresa Osborne has lost faith in the dream of everlasting love. Three years after divorcing her cheating husband, the single mother is vacationing on Cape Cod when she finds a bottle washed up on the shore. Inside, a message begins: 'My Dearest Catherine, I miss you.' Subsequent publication of the poignant missive in her column turns up two more letters, found by others, from the same mysterious writer, Garrett Blake. Piqued by his epistolary constancy, Theresa follows the trail to North Carolina, where she discovers that Garrett has been mourning his late wife for three years; writing the seaborne messages is his only solace. Theresa also finds that Garrett just might be ready to love again . . . and that she might be the woman for him." Publ Wkly

Nights in Rodanthe. Warner Bks. 2002 212p

   ISBN 0-446-53133-2   LC 2002-66189

"Adrienne Wills is a 45-year-old mother of three whose husband recently abandoned her for a younger woman. When she visits the small coastal town of Rodanthe, North Carolina, seeking a bit of respite from her problems, she meets Paul Flanner, a 54-year-old doctor who has sold his thriving medical practice and come to Rodanthe to escape his own tortured past." Booklist

"Sparks builds a taut, plausible relationship between his protagonists." Publ Wkly

The notebook. Warner Bks. 1996 214p $16.95

   ISBN 0-446-52080-2

                             * LC 96-33815

"At 80, Noah Calhoun reads daily from a notebook containing the love story of Noah and Allie. We learn of the teenaged lovers, their 14-year separation and reunion in New Bern, North Carolina, just weeks before Allie is to marry another man. Back in the present, we learn that Noah and Allie did marry and were happy for more than 40 years. Now, they are residents of a nursing home,

Sparks, Nicholas—*Continued*

separated both by rooms and, more profoundly, by Allie's Alzheimer's. Noah's daily reading from the notebook is not to himself; he reads aloud to Allie, hoping that the power of their love story will reach her." Libr J

A walk to remember. Warner Bks. 1999 240p $19.95

ISBN 0-446-52553-7   LC 99-12079

In Beaufort, North Carolina in 1958, 17-year-old high school senior Landon Carter takes Jamie Sullivan, the minister's daughter, to the homecoming dance, stars with her in the Christmas play, and falls in love with her, only to discover her sad secret

The author "is a master at pulling heartstrings and bringing a tear to his readers' eyes. . . . Told in Landon's down-home voice, this bittersweet tale will enthrall Sparks' numerous fans." Booklist

Sparks, Timothy *See* Dickens, Charles, 1812-1870

Spencer, Elizabeth

Knights and dragons
In Spencer, E. The stories of Elizabeth Spencer p127-218

The light in the piazza
In Spencer, E. The southern woman p258-311

The southern woman; new and selected fiction. Modern Lib. 2001 448p $23.95

ISBN 0-679-64218-8
                                      * LC 00-54612

Contents: The little brown girl; The eclipse; First dark; A southern landscape; Ship island; The fishing lake; The adult holiday; Sharon; The finder; The Bufords; A Christian education; Indian summer; The girl who loved horses; The business venture; The white azalea; The visit; The cousins; The light in the piazza (novella); I, Maureen; Jack of diamonds; The skater; The legacy; The master of shongalo; The runaways; The weekend travelers; First child; Owl

"This collection offers selections from the Mississippi native's earlier short fiction together with several new stories. Best known of the earlier fiction is her stunning novella, *The Light in the Piazza* (1960), the deceptively simple tale of an American mother and daughter in Florence." Libr J

The stories of Elizabeth Spencer; with a foreword by Eudora Welty. Doubleday 1981 429p

ISBN 0-385-15697-9   LC 79-6601

The stories included in this collection were written between 1944 and 1977 and were originally published in various periodicals. The novelette Knights & dragons was published separately in 1965 by McGraw-Hill. It concerns an American divorcee living in Rome. Other stories in the collection are: The little brown child; The eclipse; First dark; A southern landscape; Moon rocket; The white azalea; The visit; Ship Island; The fishing lake; The adult holiday; The Pincian gate; The absence; The day before; The Bufords; Judith Kane; Wisteria; A bad cold; Presents; On the Gulf; Sharon; The finder; Instrument of destruction; Go South in the winter; A kiss

at the door; A Christian education; Mr. McMillan; I, Maureen; Prelude to a parking lot; Indian summer; The search; Port of embarkation: The girl who loved horses

Spencer, LaVyrle

Bitter sweet. Putnam 1990 382p

ISBN 0-399-13508-1   LC 89-38089

"The untimely death of her husband leaves Maggie Pearson wealthy but emotionally bereft. Two decades after she has left home, Maggie returns to Wisconsin to fortify her spirits and decides to open a bed-and-breakfast despite dire warnings from her tight-lipped mother and the hurt fury of her college-age daughter. Her first love, Eric Severson, is also back in town, running a family-owned charter fishing boat to the great displeasure of his beautiful, ambitious wife." Publ Wkly

"Readers who can accept the plausibility of Maggie's original separation from Eric will enjoy following her journey of self-discovery and reawakening." Booklist

Forgiving. Putnam 1991 382p o.p.

                                      LC 90-42821

"Sarah Merritt arrives in Deadwood, Dakota territory, in 1876 with her father's printing press and two ambitions—to find her sister Addie and to establish a local newspaper. In a town of mining bachelors, Sarah quickly becomes the center of attention in more ways than one, particularly when she knocks heads with marshal Noah Campbell, her soon-to-be romantic interest. Sarah finds Addie working in a local brothel and commences a long struggle to win back her affection and her soul." Publ Wkly

"Bowing to the formulaic demands of historical romance without descending into parody or cliché, Spencer gives us an interesting, titillating story peopled by intriguingly human characters." Booklist

Morning glory. Putnam 1989 384p

ISBN 0-399-13413-1   LC 88-28166

"Tall, dark and handsome Will Parker has served time for the killing of a Texas prostitute, but keeps losing jobs as his reputation becomes known. In the small town of Whitney, Ga., at the beginning of WW II, he answers the advertisement of a pregnant widow and mother of two, the abused and reclusive Eleanor Dinsmore, who is looking for a husband. Soon in love with ostensibly plain, bedraggled Ellie, Parker dotes on her two boys, and works to support the family. Fittingly for this sort of bucolic idyll, Will and Ellie, despite their rudimentary educations, love books and develop a special friendship with wise old Miss Beasley, the local librarian. Alas, brazen and rapacious Lula Peak, the town floozie, sets her sights on Will, waylaying him in the library; meantimes, Lula is blackmailing her lover, the cowardly Harley Overmire, who is no friend of Will. The clearly drawn characters fulfill their imperatives—including Will, who becomes a war hero—and all is neatly and pleasingly resolved." Publ Wkly

Small town girl. Putnam 1997 364p

ISBN 0-399-14249-5   LC 96-24317

"When small-town girl Tess McPhail followed the pull of Nashville's glittering lights, she placed her dreams on becoming a country singer. Eighteen years later, she is a megastar and is caught in a whirlwind of tours, recording sessions, and financial meetings—a whirlwind that

Spencer, LaVyrle—*Continued*

crashes to a stop when her sister demands her help in caring for their mother. Angered at her sister's orders, Tess breezes in to town for a month and crashes straight into the past in the form of Kenny Kronek, the boy-next-door 'dork' from high school who has been helping her mother." Booklist

That Camden summer. Putnam 1996 368p
ISBN 0-399-14120-0   LC 95-20055
In 1916, divorceé Roberta Jewett, "returns to her provincial hometown of Camden, Maine, in order to build a new life for herself and her three daughters. Braving adversaries such as her lecherous brother-in-law, condemning mother, and a community that considers a divorced woman little better than a prostitute, Roberta Jewett behaves 'scandalously,' securing a job as a country nurse to support her children, learning to drive, and buying a 'Model-T car.' Roberta is embittered by her humiliating marriage to an outrageous philanderer, but not surprisingly she 'finds love' with Gabriel Farley, the gruff yet inwardly sensitive widowered carpenter retained to renovate her home. Although predictable and somewhat belabored, Spencer's latest novel is overall an enjoyable read." Libr J

Spencer, Scott

Endless love. Knopf 1979 417p o.p.
                                    * LC 79-2089
"A 17-year-old boy, David Axelrod, forbidden to see his girl friend, Jade Butterfield, for 30 days because their love affair has become too intense, sets fire to the Butterfield house on an impulse. That act changes everyone's life: the Butterfield family is scattered, and David is sent to a mental institution and forbidden ever to contact them. This novel is a record of the subsequent ten years of David's life, and his one goal of being reunited with Jade." Libr J

The author "has achieved something quite remarkable in this unabashedly romantic and often harrowing novel. He has created an adolescent love that is believably endless. . . . Mr. Spencer has an acute grasp of character and situation. He gives us details that make these often tormented people uncommonly convincing." N Y Times Book Rev

Willing. Ecco 2008 244p $24.95
ISBN 978-0-06-076015-1; 0-06-076015-X
                                    LC 2007-28230
The protagonist of this novel is "Avery Janowsky, a 37-year-old New York City writer who—after being unceremoniously dumped by his 20-something girlfriend—is given an unusual gift by his flashy uncle: an all-expenses-paid ticket on an ultra-high-class sex tour through Iceland, Norway and Latvia. The tour is the brainchild of Lincoln Castle, who charges wealthy men $135,000 to spend time with women much too classy to be regarded as mere prostitutes." PopMatters

"Spencer's sumptuous prose adds much to the pleasure of this novel's provocative, and often disturbing, story. His elaborate and hilarious verbal riffs recall some of Philip Roth's writing at its best. Willing doesn't flinch in exposing one seamy corner of a world where everything can be bought and sold—for the right price." BookPage

Spencer-Fleming, Julia

All mortal flesh. St. Martin's 2006 336p $22.95
ISBN 0-312-31264-4
"When Millers Kill, NY, police chief Russ Van Alstyne tells his wife that he is in love with Clare Fergusson, the Episcopal priest for St. Albans Church, she throws him out. A few weeks later, her mutilated body is found in her kitchen, and suspicion falls upon Russ and Clare." Libr J

While the "setup might sound conventional, Spencer-Fleming's handling of it is far from mechanical. Her unusual heroine has brains and wit and the fearless spirit of an ex-Army chaplain and helicopter pilot who saw action in Kuwait. If anyone can clear Russ and find the real murderer, Clare can do it — if she can only escape from Elizabeth de Groot, the 'frighteningly competent deacon' who has been sent by the bishop to monitor her unorthodox behavior. In a story as unpredictable as its characters, the resolution takes this series in a direction that should give the good bishop heart palpitations." N Y Times Book Rev

In the bleak midwinter. Thomas Dunne Bks. 2002 308p $23.95
ISBN 0-312-28847-6   LC 2001-51303
A mystery set in the "upstate New York town of Millers Kill. As the new (and first female) priest of St. Alban's Episcopal Church, Clare [Fergusson] faces her first test when an infant is left on the rectory doorstep by an unwed teenage mother who is found frozen to death by the river. More crises follow in this freshly conceived and meticulously plotted whodunit when a police investigation raises suspicions about two parishioners who are frantic to adopt the child, and when Clare's own inquiries within her conservative flock turn up troubling evidence of domestic abuse." N Y Times Book Rev

Spiegelman, Ian, 1974-

Everyone's burning; a novel. Villard Bks. 2003 164p $18.95
ISBN 1-400-06056-7   LC 2002-33191
"A nightmarish tour of the drug-fueled subculture of Queens. Leon Koch, a recent high-school graduate, leads a streamlined existence: his goals are to avoid getting killed by any of the neighborhood psychopaths who might have any grievance (real or imagined) against him and to make sure he has enough cocaine and alcohol to cushion his bleak existence. He bounces from one dead-end job to another and seeks out sadomasochistic relationships with the equally damaged women who make up his world." Booklist

"Spiegelman's characters talk to one another like David Mamet's: in staccato bursts, with verve and irony." N Y Times Book Rev

Spiegelman, Peter

Black maps. Knopf 2003 285p $22.95
ISBN 1-4000-4075-2   LC 2003-273218
This mystery introduces John March, "a Manhattan P.I. who walks the mean streets of Beaver and Broad. As the rebel son in four generations of merchant bankers, who turned his back on the family business to become a cop . . . he's quick enough to grasp the byzantine forensic accounting procedures that fire up this technically accomplished financial mystery." N Y Times Book Rev

Spiegelman, Peter—*Continued*

Red cat. Alfred A. Knopf 2007 285p $22.95

ISBN 978-0-307-26316-2; 0-307-26316-9

LC 2006-49529

"Wall Street may be a rarefied world, but its inhabitants also can plumb the depths. John March is the black sheep of an investment banking family, formerly a cop and now a private investigator. When his very respectable older brother, David, comes to him for help, John quickly finds himself in a sordid world of perverse sex, dubious art, and, of course, murder." Libr J

"Spiegelman has a genuine understanding of what we are capable of doing for love and the cruel cost of settling for anything else. Mystery fans will love his nifty guess-again plot, fuel-injected prose and deeply complex characters, but what shines is the way the author makes the murky psychological secrets of relationships just as thrilling as the crime itself." People

Spillane, Frank Morrison *See* Spillane, Mickey, 1918-2006

Spillane, Mickey, 1918-2006

The big kill

In Spillane, M. The Mike Hammer collection [v2]

The Goliath bone; [by] Mickey Spillane with Max Allan Collins. Harcourt 2008 274p $23

ISBN 978-0-15-101454-5; 0-15-101454-X

LC 2008-10091

"An Otto Penzler book"

"During a Manhattan snowstorm, Spillane's legendary Mike Hammer . . . saves two Columbia University archaeology students from a violent mugging. It turns out the couple had uncovered what might be the greatest find since King Tut's tomb, the leg bone of Goliath, the biblical giant." Libr J

"Much of the jargon is vintage, as is the indomitable Hammer as he strives to protect the kids and prevent the Goliath bone from setting off the next big war. While not on a par with early Spillane classics, this is a fitting capstone to Hammer's career." Publ Wkly

I, the jury

In Spillane, M. The Mike Hammer collection [v1]

Kiss me, deadly

In Spillane, M. The Mike Hammer collection [v2]

The Mike Hammer collection [v1]; [introduction by Max Allan Collins] New Am. Lib. 2001 513p pa $16

ISBN 0-451-20352-6

* LC 00-52728

Omnibus edition of the author's first three Mike Hammer mysteries. Includes *I, the jury* (1947), *My gun is quick* (1950), and *Vengeance is mine* (1950). "Hammer is a foul-mouthed, violent vigilante and a sucker for beautiful damsels in distress, some of whom pull the wool over his eyes. With his trusty, sexy assistant Velda keeping him honest (sort of), he exacts revenge on racketeers, cheats and murderers." Publ Wkly

The Mike Hammer collection [v2]; [introduction by Lawrence Block] New Am. Lib. 2001 517p pa $17

ISBN 0-451-20425-5

*

Omnibus edition of three Mike Hammer mysteries. Includes *One lonely night* (1951), *The big kill* (1951), and *Kiss me, deadly* (1952).

My gun is quick

In Spillane, M. The Mike Hammer collection [v1]

One lonely night

In Spillane, M. The Mike Hammer collection [v2]

Vengeance is mine

In Spillane, M. The Mike Hammer collection [v1]

Spiotta, Dana, 1966-

Eat the document. Scribner 2006 291p $24

ISBN 0-7432-7298-6

LC 2005-54050

This novel is "about a fugitive radical from the 1970s who has lived in hiding for twenty-five years. . . . Bobby DeSoto and Mary Whittaker—passionate, idealistic and in love—design a series of radical protests against the Vietnam War. When one action goes wrong, the course of their lives is forever changed. The two must erase their past, forge new identities, and never see each other again. Now it is the 1990s. Mary lives in the suburbs with her fifteen-year-old son, who spends hours immersed in the music of his mother's generation. She has no idea where Bobby is, whether he is alive or dead." Publisher's note

"Spiotta has written a glorious sendup of contemporary social and ecological activists with all their preening idealism and absurdity—especially the intelligent—sounding nonsense people spew at one another, even as they rarely connect on any meaningful level." N Y Times Book Rev

Sprott, Duncan, 1952-

The Ptolemies. Knopf 2004 xxii, 462p map $25.95

ISBN 1-400-04154-6

LC 2004-5305

"Sprott chronicles the calamitous, ill-fated reign of the first Greek pharaoh of Egypt. . . . The initial chapters chart Ptolemy's ascension from soldier to leader in Egypt, where he becomes a satrap, keeping the body of the late Alexander the Great around as a good luck charm. After consolidating his power, Ptolemy agonizes over the decision to declare himself pharaoh while facing military challenges from a parade of enemies; he also must overcome emotional fallout from his exhausting relationship with his two wives, Berenike and Eurydice. . . . Sprott's scholarship and his command of the material is formidable and impressive, and structurally the novel hangs together despite the author's insistence on documenting much of the historical minutiae of Ptolemy's reign." Publ Wkly

St. Claire, Erin, 1948-

For works written by this author under other names see Brown, Sandra, 1948-

Stabenow, Dana

A deeper sleep. St. Martin's 2007 256p
ISBN 0-312-34322-1; 978-0-312-34322-4
LC 2006-52221
"Private investigator Kate Shugak is determined to find the evidence to convict Louis Deem, who has been arrested and tried for several serious crimes but never convicted. When a double homicide occurs after his latest acquittal, Kate investigates. A witness places Deem at the scene, but Kate wants additional evidence to convince the jury. Deem is a dangerous character who intimidates witnesses, and Kate and her family won't be safe until he is in jail." Booklist

A fine and bitter snow. St. Martin's Minotaur 2002 211p $24.95
ISBN 0-312-20548-1
LC 2002-22863
The "Alaskan P.I. finds herself in the middle of a volatile situation involving proposed drilling for oil in a wildlife preserve. A ranger there is fired for political reasons, and then an important conservationist is poisoned." Libr J

"Rich with details about life in this snowbound culture, the story moves at a steady pace to a classic ending." Publ Wkly

Hunter's moon; a Kate Shugak mystery. Putnam 1999 260p $23.95
ISBN 0-399-14468-4
* LC 98-33465
Aleut sleuth Kate Shugak "and her boyfriend sign on here as wilderness guides for the management team of a German software company whose arrogant C.E.O. fancies himself a big-game hunter. . . . His cowed employees would have been better advised to bone up on 'The Most Dangerous Game,' because the first big catch is one moose, a few salmon and two junior executives." NY Times Book Rev

Killing grounds. Putnam 1998 273p $22.95
ISBN 0-399-14356-4
LC 97-23900
"Alaskan private investigator Kate Shugak . . . who practically wallows in the surrounding wild beauty of nature, spars with an abusive, strikebreaking fisherman who later winds up dead. Kate's recently returned lover, enigmatic kin, and eccentric acquaintances make this a delightful read." Libr J

The singing of the dead. St. Martin's Minotaur 2001 254p map $23.95
ISBN 0-312-20957-6
LC 2001-19146
"Anne Gordaoff, candidate for the Alaska state senate, is receiving threatening letters. Though sharp, fiesty Aleutian PI Kate Shugak is still recovering from her last job, she allows herself to be talked into protecting Anne." Libr J
"With well-drawn characters, splendid scenery and an insider's knowledge of Alaskan history and politics, this fine novel ranks as one of Stabenow's best." Publ Wkly

So sure of death; a Liam Campbell mystery. Dutton 1999 275p $23.95
ISBN 0-525-94519-9
LC 99-25121
"Alaska state trooper Liam Campbell begins to investigate the murders of a family on a fishing boat and an archaeologist on a dig. Meanwhile, on a personal level, he entertains two very different visitors: his overbearing,

perfectionist father and his great love Wyanet Chouinard. Personal and professional come together when Wyanet helps with the investigations and when the murders appear to be linked to Liam's father." Booklist

Whisper to the blood. Minotaur Books 2009 354p map $24.95
ISBN 978-0-312-36974-3; 0-312-36974-3
LC 2008-33959
Between two suspicious murders and a series of attacks on snow mobilers up the Kanuyaq River, part-time P.I. and newly elected chairman of the Niniltna Native Association Kate Shugak has her hands full.
"A dynamite combination of atmosphere, action, and character." Booklist

Stace, Wesley Harding *See* Harding, John Wesley, 1965-

Stade, George

Love is war. Turtle Point Press 2006 300p pa $16.95
ISBN 1-885586-47-7
LC 2005-926846
This satirical novel "features an English professor who teaches at Columbia University. Acerbic George Lockhart channels his 'wiseassisms' into his literary criticism when he isn't directing them at his wife, Jane—their relationship seems to consist of one long argument about conservative radio host Dr. Lena and various lines-in-the-sand drawn over household chores. Deciding that he has felt sexually deprived for too long, he enters into a joyful affair with a married redheaded poet. Soon the two are reciting poetry to each other and plotting to murder their respective spouses. Stade leaves a few seams showing in stitching such disparate story lines together—the poignancy of Lockhart's quest for meaning at midlife doesn't quite mesh with his (not entirely credible) homicidal streak. Still, Stade offers a pleasing prose style, with many subtle literary allusions . . . and a nice touch of the absurd." Booklist

Stafford, Jean, 1915-1979

The collected stories of Jean Stafford. Farrar, Straus & Giroux 1969 463p o.p.
Contents: Maggie Meriwether's rich experience; The children's game; The echo and the nemesis; The maiden; A modest proposal; Caveat emptor; Life is no abyss; The hope chest; Polite conversation; A country love story; The bleeding heart; The lippia lawn; The interior castle; The healthiest girl in town; The tea time of stouthearted ladies; The mountain day; The darkening moon; Bad characters; In the zoo; The liberation; A reading problem; A summer day; The philosophy lesson; Children are bored on Sunday; Beatrice Trueblood's story; Between the porch and the altar; I love someone; Cops and robbers; The captain's gift; The end of a career

Stamm, Peter, 1963-

On a day like this; a novel; translated by Michael Hofmann. Other Press 2007 229p $23.95
ISBN 978-1-59051-279-1; 1-59051-279-0
LC 2007-35108

Stamm, Peter, 1963-—*Continued*

Original German edition, 2006

"Andreas is a forty-something German teacher in Paris whose life consists of monotonous routines and impersonal encounters. 'Emptiness was the normal state of things,' Stamm writes. Yet when he develops a bad cough he decides not to wait for his biopsy results; he quits his job and sells his apartment to seek out a girl from his youth, with whom he thinks he may still be in love. Stamm's affectless tone belies the richness of his psychological portraiture; in spite of attempts to shrug off connections ('He had always been careful not to be loved too much himself'), Andreas is driven to revisit primal scenes of loss and mourning." New Yorker

Standiford, Les

Black Mountain; a novel. Putnam 2000 320p

ISBN 0-399-14584-2　　　　　　LC 99-32943

This thriller's protagonist "is Richard Corrigan, a NYC transit cop who takes down a homeless man apparently threatening New York governor Fielding Dawson. In reward, Dawson invites Corrigan to join him and 15 others, including a film crew and pretty USA Magazine reporter Dara Wylie, on a highly publicized foray into the Absaroka. In Wyoming, meanwhile, a pair of hired killers, one man, one woman, are—for reasons revealed only at novel's end—plotting to wipe out the Dawson expedition." Publ Wkly

"Even the most contrived scenes . . . capture the treacherous beauty of the wilderness, defined here in the crisp lines and clear detail of an assured author's strong prose style." N Y Times Book Rev

Bone Key. Putnam 2002 319p

ISBN 0-399-14874-4　　　　　　LC 2002-19052

"This time out, Deal travels to Key West to talk over a prospective project. He finds trouble, . . . first in a bar, where the smoky-voiced singer turns out to be the unresolved love of his life. He next finds trouble on the side of the road, where he witnesses cops beating up a black kid. Both chanteuse and youth are tied in with the real-estate developer. Deal finds these ties lead to murder and a 60-year-old secret cache buried in the Keys." Booklist

"The labyrinthine plot, involving a case of rare wine worth $100,000, will delight oenophiles. Thriller buffs in general and readers of South Florida mysteries in particular should find this one well up to Standiford's standard." Publ Wkly

Deal on ice; a novel. HarperCollins Pubs. 1997 239p o.p.　　　　　　　　　　LC 96-8431

Miami sleuth John Deal "sets out to find the murderer of a bookstore-owning friend, who dies holding a religious tract. Deal finds himself struggling against dangerously ultraconservative preacher James Ray Willis, whose megalithic organization plots to control all area media. A solid crime novel." Libr J

Deal with the dead; a novel. Putnam 2001 302p

ISBN 0-399-14704-7　　　　　　LC 00-55938

In this John Deal novel, "the independent building contractor working in South Florida is still marinating in his guilt over how his wife was nearly killed during his last caper and his agony over the splintering apart of their marriage. A blast from Deal's late father's checkered past, in the form of a visit from one of Dad's cronies just after Deal has been awarded a lucrative waterfront project, theatens to annihiliate his carefully pieced together recovery. . . . The action is nonstop, the setting of volatile South Florida from the 1950s to the present is fascinating, and the characterization of a man forced to defend what he loves because of the greed of others is compelling." Booklist

Havana run. Putnam 2003 304p $24.95

ISBN 0-399-15059-5　　　　　　LC 2002-37021

John Deal "is rebuilding the failed Miami construction firm he inherited from his father, dead by suicide. Soon after moving to Key West to oversee a major construction contract, Deal is approached by Antonio Fuentes, a mysterious businessman, who attempts to hire him to oversee a huge rebuilding project in Havana, slated to begin once Castro has departed the scene. Deal has his suspicions, especially after Fuetes offers a check for a million dollars as a retainer." Publ Wkly

"Standiford does a superb job of setting up his complex plot, using the color-drenched, ever-threatening Havana landscape both to ratchet up the tension and to emphasize the otherworldly nature of this latest and most baffling call from the grave." Booklist

Stanišic, Saša, 1978-

How the soldier repairs the gramophone; translated from the German by Anthea Bell. Grove Press 2008 304p $24

ISBN 978-0-8021-1866-0; 0-8021-1866-6

"Through the eyes of the fourteen-year-old narrator, Aleksandar Krsmanovi, we witness a massacre perpetrated by Bosnian Serbs against their Muslim neighbors in the town of Višegrad in 1992. The outlines of the plot are autobiographical: The protagonist's escape to Germany from the attack on Višegrad parallels the author's own at the same age. But rather than rendering a direct account, Stanisic refracts these events through his young narrator's wildly imaginative storytelling. A hyperactive fabulist, Aleksandar embarks on madcap flights of invention and comic exaggeration, which clash movingly with the painfully real chronicle of terror, loss, and exile at the story's heart." Bookforum

Stanley, Michael

A carrion death; introducing Detective Kubu. HarperCollins 2008 467p map $23.95

ISBN 978-0-06-125240-2; 0-06-125240-9

　　　　　　　　　　　　　LC 2008-299326

"A skeleton is found in the Kalahari Desert in modern-day Africa. It is unclothed, one of its arms is missing, and its teeth have been knocked out, making identification difficult. It falls to Det. David Bengu (aka Kubu) of the Botswana police to figure out what happened; in the meantime, more deaths follow." Libr J

"Readers may be lured to Africa by the landscape, but it takes a great character like Kubu to win our loyalty." N Y Times Book Rev

Stansberry, Domenic

The ancient rain. St. Martin's Minotaur 2008 293p $24.95

ISBN 978-0-312-36453-3; 0-312-36453-9

　　　　　　　　　　　　　LC 2007-49768

Stansberry, Domenic—*Continued*

In this Dante Mancuso mystery "the former San Francisco cop becomes entangled in a cold case surrounding the unintentional shooting death of a woman during a bank robbery involving a group of militant political anarchists in 1976. In a paranoia-fueled post 9/11 America with new antiterror laws, a federal prosecutor with a deep-rooted grudge arrests Bill Owens, an acquaintance of Mancuso's who was the prime suspect in the 1976 murder. Hired to help exonerate Owens, Mancuso tracks down individuals linked to the original case. . . . Equal parts contemporary crime fiction and dark, existential poetry, this novel should win Stansberry new fans." Publ Wkly

Stark, Richard

For works written by this author under other names see Westlake, Donald E.

Ask the parrot. Mysterious Press 2006 279p $23.99

ISBN 0-89296-068-X   LC 2006-927625

"Parker is on the lam from the botched robbery in Nobody Runs Forever (2004) when he meets up with reclusive Tom Lindahl, who helps him escape a posse of Massachusetts lawmen and their pack of howling dogs. Tom rescues Parker because he has a scheme to rob a local racetrack where he was fired after blowing the whistle on illegal money laundering, and he needs the aid of a professional thief. Parker joins in not only because he knows a good heist when he hears it, but because Tom offers him a way out of a tight situation." Publ Wkly

"Unconscious in front of the TV is the fate awaiting most in this corner of purgatory, and Parker's assistance in helping Tom Lindahl escape its confines with a decent stash is the closest he's come to an act of mercy in his entire bullet-ridden career. As for what happens to the parrot—don't ask." N Y Times Book Rev

Breakout. Mysterious Press 2002 299p $23.95

ISBN 0-89296-779-X   LC 2002-23492

This is an "entry in the Parker series. After a pharmaceutical heist goes south, Stark's strong, silent antihero faces a dose of hard time. While awaiting arraignment in an overcrowded detention center, Parker formulates an escape with the help of two fellow prisoners, a crooked defense attorney, and sometime-partner-in-crime Ed Mackey. A series of breakouts follow, as Parker and company hit pothole after pothole on their crooked road to freedom." Booklist

"Richard Stark (the name that Donald E. Westlake uses when he lets Parker off the leash) writes with ruthless efficiency. His bad guys are polished pros who think hard, move fast and turn on a dime in moments of crisis. And because talk doesn't come cheap, every bit of dialogue counts." N Y Times Book Rev

Comeback. Mysterious Press 1997 292p o.p.

LC 97-7019

In this mystery, master thief Parker "teams up with two men and a woman to steal $400,000 in small bills from a sleazy televangelist's 'Christian Crusade.' The heist goes off perfectly—until one of the crew attempts to eliminate his partners to claim the whole score." Booklist

"The plot for this caper is a cunningly engineered sequence of catastrophes, each one set in motion by some seemingly minor miscalculation that escalates into disaster. Oiling the machinery is the author's biting irony toward characters who talk the big talk about love and trust and loyalty but ditch their Christian values for a hot babe or a cool buck. In a world of warped values, an honest crook like Parker is a true treasure." N Y Times Book Rev

Dirty money. Grand Central Pub. 2008 276p $23.99

ISBN 978-0-446-17858-7; 0-446-17858-6

LC 2007-931314

"Lots went wrong after Parker and two partners robbed an armored car in rural Massachusetts of $2.2 million in 2004's *Nobody Runs Forever*. The money was 'poisoned' (i.e., marked); one of his partners was captured before killing a marshal and escaping; and bounty-hunter Sandra Loscalzo wants to cut herself in on the take. The pragmatic, quick-thinking Parker must find a way to retrieve the stashed haul he and his confederates left in Massachusetts without getting caught by the law or nibbled to death by other crooks." Publ Wkly

The hunter. University of Chicago Press ed. University of Chicago Press 2008 198p pa $14

ISBN 978-0-226-77099-4; 0-226-77099-0

LC 2008-11226

First published 1963 by Pocket Bks.

In this first novel of the author's Parker series, "Parker roars into New York City, seeking revenge on the woman who betrayed him and on the man who took his money, stealing and scamming his way to redemption." Publisher's note

The jugger; with a new foreword by John Banville. The University of Chicago Press 2009 211p pa $14

ISBN 978-0-226-77102-1; 0-226-77102-4

LC 2008-42432

"A Parker novel"

First published 1965 by Pocket Bks.

This novel in the author's Parker series has the main character in Sagamore, Nebraska, at the request of Joe Sheer, a retired safe cracker who carries many of Parker's criminal secrets.

Starr, Jason, 1966-

Lights out. St. Martin's Minotaur 2006 296p $22.95

ISBN 978-0-312-35972-0; 0-312-35972-1

LC 2006-45057

"High school baseball stars Jake Thomas and Ryan Rossetti were destined to make it out of the mean streets of Brooklyn and into the major leagues, but a career-ending injury to Ryan's pitching arm sends him back to living with his parents and making $10 an hour as a house painter. Charmed Jake becomes one of the most promising young players, earning a $10 million signing bonus—and an ego to match. Jake returns home for a celebration weekend, mainly to announce his engagement to high school sweetheart Christina Mercado, not out of love but to negate the bad publicity from a sex scandal lurking in his past. Meanwhile, Christina has fallen in love with Ryan and must choose between living in Brooklyn with a house painter or a loveless future on Easy Street. . . . [This novel] sizzles with streetwise dialog and furious emotional energy." Libr J

Starr, Jason, 1966--—*Continued*

Panic attack. Minotaur Books 2009 324p $24.99

ISBN 978-0-312-38706-8; 0-312-38706-7

LC 2009-10486

"Carlos Sanchez wasn't expecting anyone to be home, much less have an entire clip emptied into him as he reached the top of the stairs of the brownstone he breaks into in Forest Hills Gardens, Queens. The gun-wielding psychologist, Adam Bloom, is almost equally surprised-instead of being hailed as a hero for defending his wife and daughter in his own home, the media vilify him as a crazed vigilante for using all 10 bullets. Even worse, the sociopathic Johnny Long, going along with his pal Carlos for an easy score, decides to make the Blooms pay in more blood for the incident after he escapes into the night." Publ Wkly

"Baleful and scorching. No one in the suspense field today does nasty as well as Starr." Kirkus

Stavans, Ilan

(ed) The Oxford book of Jewish stories. See The Oxford book of Jewish stories

Stead, Christina, 1902-1983

The man who loved children; with an introduction by Doris Lessing. Knopf 1995 xxxvii, 529p $22

ISBN 0-679-44364-9

*

"Everyman's library"

A reissue of the title first published 1940 by Simon & Schuster

"Unfolding a harrowing portrait of a disintegrating family, Stead examines the hostility between a husband and wife: Sam Pollit, revealed to be a tyrannical crank far removed from the civilized man he thinks he is, whose claim to love his children lends the ironic title; and Henny, who has become a bitter virago." Merriam-Webster's Ency of Lit

Steel, Danielle

Amazing grace. Delacorte Press 2007 324p $27

ISBN 978-0-385-34023-6

LC 2007-7523

"Sarah Sloane, 30-something wife of Seth, a wildly successful hedge fund entrepreneur, and mother of two, has planned to perfection a high-ticket charity auction. The only thing she hasn't counted on is the biggest seismic event to hit San Francisco since 1906 and the aftershocks it will cause in her marriage. Meanwhile, hot Grammy-winning 19-year-old singer Melanie Free, flown in to perform at the benefit, likewise finds her life overturned. . . . Sarah and Melanie face change with support from the 40-ish Sister Maggie Kent, a California nun whose good deeds draw the interest of recovering alcoholic and former AP photojournalist Everett Carson, who captures her in pictures. As marriage, faith and vows of chastity are tested, there's nothing complicated to spoil the romance. Steel delivers a sparkly story with an uplifting spiritual twist." Publ Wkly

The house on Hope Street. Delacorte Press 2000 231p $19.95

ISBN 0-385-33306-4

LC 00-25688

"Married legal team Liz and Jack Sutherland have a successful family law practice and a house on Hope Street near San Francisco, where they live with their five happy children (one with special needs). Liz and her children's lives are changed forever when Jack is murdered on Christmas Day. In the year following the murder, Liz struggles to come to terms with the loss of her husband, both personally and professionally, and is dealt another devastating blow when her eldest son has a near-fatal accident. Divorced doctor Bill Webster saves her son and becomes close to Liz, much to the chagrin of her daughters, who accuse her of betraying their dead father." Libr J

Johnny Angel. Delacorte Press 2002 181p $19.95

ISBN 0-385-33549-0

LC 2001-37188

"Killed in a car crash after his senior prom, 17-year-old Johnny Peterson is sent back to earth as an angel. His mission: to fix certain troubles left unresolved at the time of his death involving his girlfriend, Becky, her impoverished mother and his dysfunctional family. . . . Steele's heartfelt depiction of the central relationship between Johnny and his mother is touching, and few readers will get through the revelation of Johnny's final gift with dry eyes." Publ Wkly

Journey. Delacorte Press 2000 323p $26.95

ISBN 0-385-31687-9

LC 00-31512

"To the outside world, Washington, D.C., television coanchor Maddy Hunter appears to have an enviable life. . . . Yet Maddy—whose current husband saved her from a physically abusive former spouse—is trapped in another relationship that's as devastating and destructive as her first. Jack doesn't hit Maddy, but he subjects her to mind games, putdowns and constant undermining; it's obvious psychological abuse to observers, though not to Maddy. Using Maddy's participation in a commission on violence against women chaired by the nation's First Lady, Steel explicates the various forms of spousal abuse." Publ Wkly

The kiss. Delacorte Press 2001 347p $26.95

ISBN 0-385-33540-7

LC 00-66009

"Isabelle Forrester is the unhappy wife of a coldhearted and distant Parisian banker. . . . Unable to bear the strain of her lonely, unhappy life, Isabelle strikes up an innocent friendship—conversing mostly by phone or mail—with American Bill Robinson. A Washington power broker, Robinson is also trapped in an unhappy marriage. The pair's relationship intensifies steadily until they finally agree to meet in London for a few passionate days. There they are involved in a serious car accident, which leaves them both in a coma, fighting for their lives." Booklist

No greater love. Delacorte Press 1991 392p $23

ISBN 0-385-29909-5

LC 90-29106

As this novel "opens, the boisterous Winfield family is boarding the ill-fated ocean liner *Titanic* for their return to America from England. Kate Winfield, mistress of the perfect family, nobly stays behind with her beloved husband and thrusts her children into the lifeboats under the care of 20-year-old daughter Edwina. After the disaster, Edwina takes seriously her mother's entreaty to care for her five siblings, who range in age from 2 to 16. For the next 12 years, Edwina, aided by a substantial inheritance, dutifully cares for the kids, even to the point of pursuing

Steel, Danielle—*Continued*

her runaway teenage sister back to England (by boat) and wresting her out of the arms of a cad. Steel's tale eventually takes an interesting turn into the early days of Hollywood." Booklist

Sunset in St. Tropez. Delacorte Press 2002 230p $19.95

ISBN 0-385-33546-6   LC 2001-47517

Three pairs of friends in their 50s and 60s decide to vacation together in St. Tropez

"Shortly before the vacation begins, one of the women dies of a heart attack, and the other women are scandalized when her supposedly grieving husband brings along a hot, young movie star in his wife's stead. Another scandal soon unfolds as another husband is revealed to be having an affair with a much younger woman. In addition, the house the group has rented (sight unseen) turns out to be a dump and comes complete with two very strange caretakers, who lend a bit of comic relief to the high drama all around them." Booklist

Steele, Allen M.

Coyote; a novel of interstellar exploration. Ace Bks. 2002 390p $23.95

ISBN 0-441-00974-3   LC 2002-74517

"At first, this novel. . . looks like a fairly conventional tale of high-tech intrigue—in this case, rebels against a right-wing American dictatorship plot to steal the prototype interstellar spaceship built to immortalize the government's ideology by planting a colony of fanatics on another star's planet. However, once the freedom seekers arrive on the new world, Coyote, things get a lot more interesting. Coyote, is habitable but alien, full of flora and fauna that upset the colonists' easy preconceptions." Publ Wkly

"A much-foreshadowed 'surprise' ending is by far the least of the surprises in Steele's bag of tricks. But each page of this novel bears evidence of fresh thought about the opportunities inherent in science fiction to take the familiar and make it new." N Y Times Book Rev

Stefaniak, Mary Helen

The Turk and my mother; a novel. W.W. Norton 2004 316p $24.95

ISBN 0-393-05924-3   LC 2004-1102

This novel explores the "history of a Croatian-American family settled in Milwaukee after World War I. The book's Decameron-esque framework is set from the beginning as George, the first-generation American son of Josef and Agnes, is on his deathbed, surrounded by his adult children. The stories he tells about life in Milwaukee in the 1930s lead to stories-within-stories told by his grandmother Staramajka, the family matriarch, who steals the show. . . . Stefaniak's easy familiarity with the vernacular idioms of the old country and the new, and her zestful, respectful ear for different voices, create a world whose past, present and story-loving afterlife are at once magical and grounded in reality." Publ Wkly

Stegner, Wallace Earle, 1909-1993

All the little live things; [by] Wallace Stegner. Viking 1967 345p o.p.

"When Joseph Allston, 64, and his wife, Ruth, move West to their 'Prospero's island' (rural California, near San Francisco), the retirement days 'drip away like honey off a spoon.' They live quietly without involvement . . . hoping to erase scars caused by the death of their rebellious son. The press of life first intrudes on them when young Jim Peck, a bearded free-thinker, camps on their property. . . . Then a young married couple, Marian and John Caitlin, arrive in the neighborhood, and the Allstons find themselves exposed to a depth of emotional involvement with others they had not wanted to experience ever again." Publ Wkly

"Mr. Stegner's narrative skill and his talent for imaginative recreation is evident throughout the book. His choice of words, the turn of a phrase, evoking a scene, an emotion, or a personality are to be savored. His writing, leisurely as it may appear, can be dramatic and moving." Best Sellers

Followed by The spectator bird

Angle of repose; [by] Wallace Stegner. Doubleday 1971 569p o.p.

This novel "is set mainly in the West in the late 1800's; but the central characters cannot be confined to the West nor to the 19th Century. They have a healing effect on the narrator, their grandson and biographer. . . . The beautiful, talented, charming Susan and her inarticulate engineer husband Oliver Ward rough it in mining camps and desolate, unfinished irrigation project camps. Their lives are hard and their marriage is strained past redemption. Yet their suffering and their strength do redeem." Libr J

The Big Rock Candy Mountain; [by] Wallace Stegner. Duell, Sloan & Pearce 1943 515p o.p.

*

This novel is set in far western states and Saskatchewan from about 1906 to 1942. The "principal characters are Bo Mason, his wife Elsa, and their two boys. Life is an almost continuous moving day because the next town, county, or state persistently beckons to Bo as the place where he will make his fortune." Libr J

"A well-written study of the footloose family. . . . The life of the household is a misery of continual cruelty and often crushing poverty, alternating with occasional scenes of simple family happiness which stand out beautifully and unforgettably." New Yorker

Collected stories of Wallace Stegner. Random House 1990 525p o.p.

* LC 89-37342

Contents: The traveler; Buglesong; Beyond the glass mountain; The berry patch; The women on the wall; Balance his, swing yours; Saw gang; Goin' to town; The view from the balcony; Volcano; Two rivers; Hostage; In the twilight; Butcher bird; The double corner; The colt; The Chink; Chip off the old block; The sweetness of the twisted apples; The blue-winged teal; Pop goes the alley cat; Maiden in a tower; Impasse; The volunteer; A field guide to the western birds; Something spurious from the Mindanao deep; Genesis; The wolfer; Carrion spring; He who spits at the sky; The city of the living

"This retrospective . . . exhibits a mastery of the ef-

Stegner, Wallace Earle, 1909-1993—*Continued*

fortlessly beautiful metaphor, an abiding interest in the American West, and an ability to create quick but complete portraits and concise but fully engrossing narratives." Booklist

Crossing to safety; [by] Wallace Stegner. Random House 1987 277p o.p.

* LC 87-20482

"The Langs and the Morgans, young couples who meet when their husbands begin teaching at a Wisconsin university, forge bonds of wonderful, lasting friendship. Charity Lang and Sally Morgan are unlike in personality but see each other through devastating crises because of that friendship. Sid Lang is a frustrated poet whose life is over-directed by his wife; Larry Morgan, much less financially secure than Sid, realizes a slow but successful climb to a position of noted writer. This novel has no violence, explicit sex or ugliness. Instead it is a hymn to solid marriages and loyalty in friendship. The dramatic events are those that occur in the lives of ordinary people." Shapiro. Fic for Youth. 3d edition

Stein, Garth

The art of racing in the rain; a novel. Harper 2008 321p $23.95

ISBN 978-0-06-153793-6; 0-06-153793-4

LC 2007-33890

"Enzo narrates his life story, beginning with his impending death. Enzo's not afraid of dying, as he's seen a television documentary on the Mongolian belief that a good dog will reincarnate as a man. Yes, Enzo is a dog. And he belongs to Denny: husband, father, customer service technician. Denny's dream is to be a professional race-car driver, and Enzo recounts the triumphs and tragedies-medical, financial, and legal-they share in this quest, the dangers of the racetrack being the least of their obstacles. . . . [Stein] creates a patient, wise, and doggish narrator that is more than just fluff and collar." Libr J

Stein, Gertrude, 1874-1946

Three lives; stories of the good Anna, Melanctha, and the gentle Lena. Grafton Press 1909 279p o.p.

*

"Written in a clear and masterly style, free from any of its author's later stylistic mannerisms, this book consists of three character studies of women. 'The Good Anna' deals with a kindly but domineering German servingwoman; 'Melanctha' is concerned with an uneducated but sensitive black girl; and 'The Gentle Lena' is about a pathetically feebleminded young German maid." Reader's Ency. 4th edition

Steinbeck, John, 1902-1968

Burning bright

In Steinbeck, J. Travels with Charley and later novels, 1947-1962

Cannery Row. Viking 1945 208p o.p.

*

"In this episodic work Steinbeck returned to the manner of Tortilla Flat (1935) and produced a rambling account of the adventures and misadventures of workers in

a California cannery and their friends." Herzberg. Reader's Ency of Am Lit

Followed by Sweet Thursday (1954)

also in Steinbeck, J. Novels, 1942-1952

East of Eden. Viking 1952 602p o.p.

*

"The saga of more than half a century in the lives of two American families—the Trasks, a mixture of gentleness and brutality doled out in unequal measure and the Hamiltons, Steinbeck's own forebears, a well adjusted, lovable group who provide a tranquil background for the turbulent careers of the Trasks. The scene is chiefly Salinas, California from the turn of the century through the first World War, and thanks to a great wealth of fascinating detail woven through the plot, we are given a complete and unforgettable picture of country and small town life during the period." Libr J

Steinbeck's "most ambitious post-war novel is . . . a parable of the fall of man, of Cain and Abel, and of human possibility, showing many of the virtues of his best books, but touched with sentimentality, melodrama and intrusive commentary." Penguin Companion to Am Lit

also in Steinbeck, J. Novels, 1942-1952

The grapes of wrath. Viking 1939 619p o.p.

*

"In this moving book, Steinbeck wrote a classic novel of a family's battle with starvation and economic desperation. The story also tells in vivid terms the story of the westward movement and the frontier. The Joads, Steinbeck's central figures, are 'Okies,' farmers moving west from a land of drought and bankruptcy to seek work as migrant fruit-pickers in California. They are beset by the police, participate in strike violence, and are harried by death." Benet's Reader's Ency of Am Lit

In dubious battle. Covici-Friede 1936 349p o.p.

"One of the more important books to come out of the proletarian movement. This was Steinbeck's first successful novel. 'In Dubious Battle' deals with a fruit strike in a California valley and the attempts of the radical leaders to organize, lead, and provide for the striking pickers. Perhaps the most important, although not the central, character is Doc Burton, who helps the strikers and is concerned with seeing things as they exist, without labels of good and bad attached. The strike fails, and Jim, one of the two leaders, is senselessly killed." Benet's Reader's Ency of Am Lit

also in Steinbeck, J. Novels and stories, 1932-1937

The long valley. Viking 1938 304p o.p.

Contents: The chrysanthemums; The white quail; Flight; The snake; Breakfast; The raid; The harness; The vigilante; Johnny Bear; The murder; St. Katy the virgin; The red pony; The leader of the people

This volume "includes the four magnificent 'Red Pony' stories, and could serve as an admirable introduction to Steinbeck, showing his characteristic interests—the tensions of the town and country, of past and present, of labour and ownership, as well as the objectivity of biological observation and a sort of Lawrencean mystic concept of personal power." Penguin Companion to Am Lit

Steinbeck, John, 1902-1968—*Continued*

The moon is down; a novel. Viking 1942 188p o.p.

This novel describes the occupation of a small mining town, presumably in Norway, by an unidentified army, evidently German. The villagers resort to sabotage and completely ignore the invaders whenever possible. In the end the courageous village mayor is shot to bring the people to terms. The mayor goes to his death reciting Socrates's dying message, knowing full well that his people will understand his death, and will continue their resistance

also in Steinbeck, J. Novels, 1942-1952

Novels, 1942-1952. Library of America, Distributed to the trade in the United States by Penguin Putnam 2001 983p il $35

ISBN 1-931082-07-3   LC 2001-38119

Contents: The moon is down; Cannery Row; The pearl; East of Eden

Novels and stories, 1932-1937; John Steinbeck. Library of America, Distributed to the trade in the U.S. by Penguin Books USA 1994 909p $35

ISBN 1-88301-101-9   LC 94-2943

Contents: The pastures of heaven; To a god unknown; Tortilla Flat; In dubious battle; Of mice and men

The pastures of heaven (1932) is a linked collection of short stories, all of which deal with the inhabitants of the California farm community of the same name. To a god unknown (1933) tells the story of a California farmer who performs pagan fertility rites to ensure good crops. After a long drought, the farmer commits suicide at his own altar of worship. Tortilla Flat, In dubious battle, and Of mice and men are entered separately.

Of mice and men. Covici-Friede 1937 186p o.p.
*

"Two uneducated laborers dream of a time when they can share the ownership of a rabbit farm in California. George is a plotter and a schemer, while Lennie is a mentally deficient hulk of a man who has no concept of his physical strength. As a team they are not particularly successful, but their friendship is enduring." Shapiro. Fic for Youth. 3d edition

also in Steinbeck, J. Novels and stories, 1932-1937

The pastures of heaven
In Steinbeck, J. Novels and stories, 1932-1937

The pearl; with drawings by José Clemente Orozco. Viking 1947 122p il o.p.

"Kino, a poor pearl-fisher, lives a happy albeit spartan life with his wife and their child. When he finds a magnificent pearl, the Pearl of the World, he is besieged by dishonest pearl merchants and envious neighbors. Even a greedy doctor ties his professional treatment of their baby when it is bitten by a scorpion to the possible acquisition of the pearl. After a series of disasters, Kino throws the pearl away since it has brought him only unhappiness." Shapiro. Fic for Youth. 3d edition

also in Steinbeck, J. Novels, 1942-1952

The red pony
In Steinbeck, J. The long valley

The short reign of Pippin IV; a fabrication; drawings by William Péne du Bois. Viking 1957 188p il o.p.

A satire on French politics. Having run out of governments the French decide to revive the monarchy and settle on Pippin, a quiet amateur astronomer who happens to be a descendant of Charlemagne. Bored with the whole situation Pippin is instrumental in starting a revolution, and finally wanders off home

Sweet Thursday. Viking 1954 273p o.p.
Sequel to Cannery Row

After World War II the "Palace Flophouse passed into new hands, the Bear Flag Café got a new madam named Fauna (nee Flora), and Doc lost his old pleasure in women, liturgical music, and the Western Biological Laboratories. Then Suzy came to Cannery Row . . . [and] egged on by the others, she brought Doc back to his prewar contentment." Booklist

also in Steinbeck, J. Travels with Charley and later novels, 1947-1962

To a god unknown
In Steinbeck, J. Novels and stories, 1932-1937

Tortilla Flat; illustrated by Ruth Gannett. Covici-Friede 1935 316p o.p.

"This episodic tale concerns the poor but carefree 'paisano' Danny and his friends Pillon, Pablo, Big Joe Portagee, Jesus Maria Corcoran, and the old Pirate, all of whom gather in Danny's house, which Steinbeck tells us 'was not unlike the Round Table.' The novel (accepted after nine publishers had turned it down) contrasts the complexities of modern civilization with the simple life of the 'paisanos.'" Benet's Reader's Ency of Am Lit

also in Steinbeck, J. Novels and stories, 1932-1937

Travels with Charley and later novels, 1947-1962. Library of America 2007 990p $40

ISBN 978-1-59853-004-9; 1-59853-004-6
                            LC 2006-48757

In addition to the memoir Travels with Charley in search of America, this volume contains the following novels: The wayward bus, Burning bright, Sweet Thursday, and The winter of our discontent; all but Burning bright are entered separately

First published 1950, Burning bright, "an allegory set against shifting backgrounds (circus, sea, farm) and revolving around the fear of sterility and the desire for self-perpetuation, marks Steinbeck's involvement with the drama in its fusion of the forms of novel and play." Publisher's note

The wayward bus. Viking 1947 312p o.p.

"A novel in which the passengers on a stranded bus in California become a microcosm of contemporary American frustrations." Camb Guide to Lit in Engl

also in Steinbeck, J. Travels with Charley and later novels, 1947-1962

The winter of our discontent. Viking 1961 311p o.p.

Ethan Allen Hawley, the impoverished heir to an upright New England tradition is the focus of this story. Ethan, under pressure from his restless wife and discon-

Steinbeck, John, 1902-1968—*Continued*

tented children who want more of this world's goods than his grocery store job provides, decides to take a holiday from his scrupulous standards to achieve wealth and success. What happens as he compromises with his integrity makes up this story

In this novel Steinbeck "continues his exploration of the moral dilemmas involved in being fully human, this time in contemporary America, where choices between genteel poverty and corrupt comfort press in upon the protagonist with a force and reality that suggest no easy resolution." Ency of World Lit in the 20th Century

also in Steinbeck, J. Travels with Charley and later novels, 1947-1962

Steinbeck, Thomas

Down to a soundless sea. Ballantine Bks. 2002 283p

ISBN 0-345-45576-2

Includes the novella Sing Fat and the Imperial Duchess of Woo and the following short stories: The night guide; The wool gatherer; Blind luck; An unbecoming grace; The dark watcher; Blighted cargo

Sing Fat and the Imperial Duchess of Woo is "about a Chinese immigrant who meets the love of his life while studying medicine with an older Chinese apothecary." Publ Wkly

This "collection draws on folklore, historical research, and tales that Steinbeck (son of John) heard growing up. The stories celebrate the early lore of Monterey County, CA. . . . Set in the dusky past of horse trails, grizzly bears, and small fishing villages and ranging forward to the early 1930s, they portray humble people living in a beautiful but often unforgiving environment." Libr J

Steinhauer, Olen

The Bridge of Sighs. St. Martin's Minotaur 2003 278p $23.95

ISBN 0-312-30245-2   LC 2002-68127

"Set in 1948 in a small, unnamed Eastern European country devastated by WWII and still occupied by Russian troops, [this novel]. . . introduces 22-year-old homicide inspector Emil Brod of the People's Militia. Brod's police academy training has prepared him for neither the rude reception he receives from his homicide comrades nor the difficult and risky asignment handed him as his initiation." Publ Wkly

"This is an intelligent, finely polished debut, loaded with atmospheric detail that effortlessly re-creates the rubble-strewn streets of the postwar period in an Eastern state 'liberated' from German occupation by the Russians." Libr J

The tourist. Minotaur Books 2009 408p $24.95

ISBN 978-0-312-36972-9; 0-312-36972-7

LC 2008-33958

Steinhauer "offers an emotionally damaged protagonist who is an experienced spy or 'tourist' but now a family man and desk-bound agent of the post-9/11, scandal-ridden CIA. When Milo Weaver is called back to fieldwork and assigned to capture an international assassin, it sets off an investigation into one of Milo's colleagues." Libr J

"As rich and intriguing as the best of Le Carré,

Deighton or Graham Greene, Steinhauer's complex, moving spy novel is perfect for our uncertain, emotionally fraught times." Los Angeles Times Book Rev

Steinke, Rene

Holy skirts. Morrow 2005 360p $24.95

ISBN 0-688-17694-1   LC 2004-52783

This is a "fictionalized account of the true adventures of Baroness Elsa von Freytag-Loringhoven, a poet, artist's model and friend of Marcel Duchamp whose irrepressible life bordered on the fashionably sordid. Fleeing her burgher home in Swinemunde, Germany, at age 19 for the liberation–and poverty–of Berlin circa 1904, Elsa learns early to lie about her past and dress outrageously (often in male clothing), attracting numerous men who provide entrée to high society." Publ Wkly

"Steinke's writing is vivid and wonderful, and she can make even a sorrowful story entertaining because she never allows the character's melancholy to infect the prose. The baroness might have been sad, but not tragic. The heroism of her spirit is expressed in a way that transcends the shroud of misfortune." Hudson Rev

Stemple, Jane H. Yolen *See* Yolen, Jane

Stendhal, 1783-1842

The charterhouse of Parma; translated from the French by Richard Howard; illustrations by Robert Andrew Parker. Modern Lib. 1999 507p il maps $24.95

ISBN 0-679-60245-3

* LC 98-36417

Original French edition, 1839. Variant title: The chartreuse of Parma

"The scene is a little Italian Court, whither the young adventurer Fabrice has found his way, and in dramatic importance plays second fiddle to the fascinating Duchess Sanseverina and her jealous lover, the astute minister, Count Mosca. The book opens with a famous narrative of the battle of Waterloo. It is a novel that set a standard of flawless technique, of the lucid unfolding of character and motive, of accurate comprehension of the inherent disorder of life, that has rarely been approached in dramatic narration." Baker. Guide to the Best Fic

The red and the black; a chronicle of 1830; a new translation by Burton Raffel; introduction by Diane Johnson; notes by James Madden. Modern Library 2003 xxii, 524p

ISBN 0-679-64284-6

* LC 2002-40798

Original French edition, 1830; first United States edition published 1898 by G.H. Richmond

"The author's most celebrated work, it is equally acclaimed for its psychological study of its protagonist— the provincial young romantic Julien Sorel—and as a satiric analysis of the French social order under the Bourbon restoration. Its intensely dramatic plot is purposively romantic in nature, while Stendhal's careful portraiture of Sorel's inner states is the work of a master realist, foreshadowing new developments in the form of the novel." Reader's Ency. 4th edition

Stephens, Eve *See* Anthony, Evelyn, 1928-

Stephenson, Neal

Anathem. William Morrow 2008 937p $29.95
ISBN 978-0-06-147409-5; 0-06-147409-6
LC 2008-13175

"Set on an Earthlike planet called Arbre and narrated by Fraa Erasmus, a young scholar, the story begins within the walls of Saunt Edhar, a 3,400-year-old monastery. A home to cloistered philosophers, scientists and mathematicians, Edhar opens its gates to the 'saecular' world at Apert, a celebration that happens every one, ten, hundred or thousand years. This rite allows visitors to enter and residents to experience a taste of an 'extramuros' society steeped in religion, obsessed with technology and diverted by movies, shopping and legalized gambling. While he does provide a glossary and a timeline, Stephenson isn't interested in quickly explicating Arbre's history and language for the casual reader. . . . Readers who persevere, however, will be rewarded by a slight acceleration in the plot when Erasmus, along with some of his peers and teachers, is expelled from Saunt Edhar and sent on a mission in which the fate of the entire planet hangs in the balance." San Francisco Chron

Cryptonomicon. Avon Bks. 1999 918p $27.50
ISBN 0-380-97346-4
LC 99-11685

This novel's "dual plots include a World War II tale of codebreaking, espionage and Nazi gold; and a contemporary tale of a software startup trying to establish a Data Haven on a remote Pacific island." Newsweek

"This fast-paced, genre-transcending novel is full of absorbing action, witty dialogue and well-drawn characters. Amazingly, it is also, even at its tremendous length, only the first volume in what promises to be one of the most extravagant literary creations of the turn of the millennium—and beyond." Publ Wkly

The diamond age; or, Young lady's illustrated primer. Bantam Bks. 1995 455p
ISBN 0-553-09609-5
LC 94-30486

"A Bantam spectra book"

"In the 22nd century, nation-states have withered away, to be replaced by 'phyles,' groups of people united by self-defined interests. . . . The action in 'The Diamond Age' centers on the neo-victorians, who share an admiration for the social discipline of 19th-century England, and a group of Chinese who are trying to erect a neo-Confucian phyle in the power vacuum left by the collapse of the 'Mao Dynasty.' On his own initiative, a neo-Victorian Equity Lord orders a 'bespoke engineer' named John Percival Hackworth to fashion an interactive primer that will teach young people a genuinely subversive lesson: that only by questioning everything they are taught about their world can they hope to become truly useful members of their phyle. When the primer falls into the hands of Nell, a child of the despised underclass, the repercussions are global." N Y Times Book Rev

"With breathtaking vision and insight, Stephenson establishes himself as not only a major voice in contemporary sf but also a prophet of technology's future." Booklist

Steptoe, Lydia See Barnes, Djuna, 1892-1982

Sterling, Bruce

The caryatids. Del Rey/Ballantine Books 2009 295p $25
ISBN 978-0-345-46062-2; 0-345-46062-6
LC 2008-51828

"In a world suffering from extreme global warming, three cloned sisters, collectively known as the Caryatids, have the ability to sense patterns and propose solutions, some of which make use of technology not yet fully developed. Their only drawback: a mutual dislike for one another." Libr J

"Whether tackling ubiquitous computing, biotechnology, natural disasters, failed states, celebrity, or the social dynamics of family, Sterling unites astute powers of observation, sharp wit, and powerful imagination to astound the reader with infinite possibilities." Booklist

Holy fire; a novel. Viking 1996 326p o.p.
LC 96-15139

"Mia Ziemann so dreaded pain and death that at 93 she'd undergone all the miracles that science could offer to extend her life. In 2095 the world is so medically obsessed and globally hooked into the Net that Mia exists, more than lives, in a sterile environment. After the death of an old lover, she undergoes a radical medical procedure that rejuvenates her and propels her on a quest for the holy fire of love she lacks." Libr J

The author "understands that salvation in a posthuman world can only be a process, not a prize. He has written a book in praise of ambiguity that manages to find consoling moments of joy in the most unlikely places." N Y Times Book Rev

Schismatrix plus. Ace Books 1996 319p pa $16
ISBN 0-441-00370-2
LC 97-106127

Contents: Schismatrix; Swarm; Spider rose; Cicada queen; Sunken gardens; Twenty evocations

This compilation of short stories in the author's Shapers-Mechanists universe includes *Schismatrix* (1985), which focuses on the life and political struggles of Shaper-trained renegade Abélard Lindsay.

Stern, Steve, 1947-

The angel of forgetfulness. Viking 2005 403p $24.95
ISBN 0-670-03387-1
LC 2004-57155

Stern "combines three distinct but interlinked narratives. The first tells the story of Nathan Hart, a Jewish immigrant on the Lower East Side circa 1910 who woos young Jewish bohemian Keni by telling her the second narrative—a tale about an angel named Mocky and his half-human son, Nachman, both of them also living on the Lower East Side in self-imposed exile from heaven. The third narrative belongs to Keni's nephew Saul, a morose, lonely young man who embarks on an odyssey through the post-Vietnam sexual and psychedelic revolutions that takes him to a hippie commune and an avant-garde theater troupe before he settles down as a hermetic Jewish-studies scholar." Publ Wkly

The author "has little interest in reworking Yiddish literature's social realist strains, or in excavating the political events that helped shape the world he loves. What he offers instead is a rollicking compendium of myth and historical tidbits, of dybbuks, wonder-working rebbes and

Stern, Steve, 1947-—*Continued*

clandestine prayer houses where lapsed Talmud students meditate on the holy letters of God's name until they levitate." N Y Times Book Rev

Sterne, Laurence, 1713-1768

The life and opinions of Tristram Shandy, gentleman

In Sterne, L. The life and opinions of Tristram Shandy, gentleman and A sentimental journey through France and Italy p1-689

The life and opinions of Tristram Shandy, gentleman and A sentimental journey through France and Italy. Modern Lib. 1995 832p $19.50

ISBN 0-679-60091-4

A combined edition of two titles first published 1759-67 and 1768 respectively

The life and opinions of Tristram Shandy, gentleman is the "chaotic account by Tristram of his life from the time of his conception to the present. . . . In between are sandwiched his 'opinions,' long-winded and philosophical reflections on everything under the sun, including his novel, and accounts of the lives of 'Yorick'; his father, Walter Shandy; his mother; and his Uncle Toby. . . . The form of the book is in fact the character of Tristram himself, doomed by improbably fantastic fatalities to write a hodgepodge instead of a history." Reader's Ency. 4th edition

A sentimental journey is a "combination of autobiography, fiction, and observations made by Sterne on his own travels, chronicles the journey through France of a charming and sensitive young man named Yorick and his servant LaFleur. (Though the title mentions Italy, the book ends before they reach that country.)" Merriam-Webster's Ency of Lit

A sentimental journey through France and Italy

In Sterne, L. The life and opinions of Tristram Shandy, gentleman and A sentimental journey through France and Italy p691-832

Stevens, Marcus, 1959-

The curve of the world; a novel. Algonquin Bks. 2002 302p $23.95

ISBN 1-56512-336-0   LC 2001-56530

"Lewis Burke is aboard a plane forced to make an emergency landing in the Congo. Once on the ground, the passengers become the hostages of rebels. Lewis sees an opportunity to escape and plunges into the rain forest. Meanwhile, Lewis' wife, Helen, learns that his plane is down and departs immediately for Kinshasa with their seven-year-old son, blind since birth. The diffident Lewis lurches through the wilderness with no idea of how to survive, while the tenacious Helen defies U.S. diplomats and sets out for the rebel-held interior. Their stories are told in parallel." Booklist

Stevens summons the African "landscape and atmosphere with vividly descriptive detail, and captures the terror of a man reduced to life's essentials." Publ Wkly

Useful girl; a novel. Algonquin Books of Chapel Hill 2004 306p $24.95

ISBN 1-565-12366-2   LC 2003-70808

"When a construction crew uncovers the remains of a Cheyenne girl, the foreman, anxious about deadlines, orders his men to keep working. Charlie White Bird is not willing to overlook this breach in regulations, and he enlists the foreman's daughter, Erin Douglass, in his quest to rebury the remains in a sacred place. Erin, still grieving the recent death of her mother and unable to draw her reticent father into any meaningful conversation, finds in her passionate relationship with Charlie an outlet for her repressed emotions. In parallel with this contemporary love story, Stevens recreates the life of the young Cheyenne girl and the circumstances that led to her death." Booklist

"The descriptions of late 19th-century battles and living conditions are unsettling in their vivid and authentic detail, riveting even the least historically minded reader, and the account of Erin's plight is clear-eyed and uncompromising. Writing with compassion and grace, Stevens delivers a timeless story of brutality and forgiveness." Publ Wkly

Stevenson, Jane, 1959-

The shadow king. Houghton Mifflin 2003 304p $24

ISBN 0-618-14913-9   LC 2003-47899

This is the second volume of the author's historical trilogy. "Here the protagonist is Balthasar, the son of the queen of Bohemia (sister to Britain's late King Charles I) and the queen's secret husband, Pelagius, a prince of the West African nation of Oyo. Having completed his medical studies in Leiden, Balthasar returns to Zeeland to establish his practice. Circumstances involve him with Aphra Behn, the so-called first feminist writer. Unhappily married to a Dutchman, she is a spy for England; she steals the papers that certify Balthasar's royal birth. A decade later, after the plague has decimated Europe, Balthasar moves to Restoration England, where he marries a servant woman, Sibella. Her family roots are gentry, and her father has willed her property in Barbados, so the newlyweds settle in the Caribbean." Publ Wkly

"Stevenson has immersed herself in the literature of the period, and one can sense the heady zest with which she details Balthasar's medical treatments or spins off a line of dialogue." N Y Times Book Rev

The winter queen. Houghton Mifflin 2002 307p $25

ISBN 0-618-14912-0

First published 2001 in the United Kingdom with title: Astraea

This first volume of a projected trilogy is set during the 17th century "in the chilly capital of Protestant Holland. [Stevenson] rewrites the story of Othello in the love between Pelagius van Overmeer, a dispossessed African prince, and the Winter Queen, the exiled Elizabeth of Bohemia." New Statesman (Engl)

"Without apparent strain, Stevenson extends her reach to Calvinist doctrine, Yoruba divination, 17th-century European politics and the details of daily life in the Low Countries. In her hands, the clandestine love story is inseparable from the political and spiritual preoccupations of the time, making vivd a world no less complex and capricious than our own." N Y Times Book Rev

LIST OF FICTIONAL WORKS

Stevenson, Robert Louis, 1850-1894

The beach of Falesá
    In Stevenson, R. L. The complete short stories p307-71
    In Stevenson, R. L. The complete short stories of Robert Louis Stevenson
    In Stevenson, R. L. The strange case of Dr. Jekyll and Mr. Hyde, and other famous tales

The complete short stories; edited and introduced by Ian Bell. Holt & Co. 1994 2v set $50
    ISBN 0-8050-3203-7
                      * LC 93-79628
Contents: v1 The Plague-Cellar; When the devil was well; Edifying letters of the Rutherford family; An old song; A lodging for the night; Will o' the Mill; The Sire de Malétroit's door; The Suicide Club: Story of the young man with the cream tarts; Story of the physician and the Saratoga trunk; The adventure of the hansom cabs; The Rajah's diamond: Story of the bandbox; Story of the young man in holy orders; Story of the house with the green blinds; The adventure of Prince Florizel and a detective; Providence and the guitar; The pavilion on the links; The story of a lie {novelette}; Thrawn Janet; The body snatcher; The Merry Men {novelette}
v2 The treasure of Franchard; Diogenes; Zero's tale of the explosive bomb; Markheim; Dr Jekyll and Mr Hyde {novelette}; The misadventures of John Nicholson {novelette}; Olalla; The enchantress; The bottle imp; The beach of Falesá {novelette}; The Isle of Voices; The waif woman; Fables

The complete short stories of Robert Louis Stevenson; with a selection of the best novels; edited and with an introduction by Charles Neider. Viking 1969 xxx, 678p o.p.
Contents: A lodging for the night; Story of the young man with the cream tarts; Story of the physician and the Saratoga trunk; The adventure of the hansom cab; Story of the bandbox; Story of the young man in holy orders; Story of the house with green blinds; The adventure of Prince Florizel and a detective; Providence and the guitar; The Sire de Maletroit's door; Will o' the mill; The story of a lie [novelette]; Thrawn Janet; The merry men [novelette]; The body snatcher; Markheim; Strange case of Dr. Jekyll and Mr. Hyde [novelette]; The bottle imp; The beach of Falesá [novelette]; The isle of voices
The strange case of Dr. Jekyll and Mr. Hyde is entered separately. In The story of a lie (first published 1879 in New Quarterly magazine, 1882 in book form) Dick Naseby, a young Englishman, becomes estranged from his father due to a misunderstanding and from the girl he loves due to his concealment of the true character of her father—an untalented, parasitical but likable painter, whom the girl hasn't seen since childhood and romantically idolizes. The Merry Men (1887) is set on an island off the coast of Scotland. It deals with a man of dour religious temperament who kills the survivor of a shipwreck in a fit of drunken madness and is driven to death by his guilt after another shipwreck. The beach of Falesá (first published 1893 in Island nights' entertainments) concerns a trader on a South Seas island whose marriage to a native woman is promoted by a business rival who knows that she is the object of a native taboo which will pass on to her husband

Dr. Jekyll and Mr. Hyde [variant title: The strange case of Dr. Jekyll and Mr. Hyde]
    In Stevenson, R. L. The complete short stories p102-64

The Merry Men
    In Stevenson, R. L. The complete short stories p436-77
    In Stevenson, R. L. The complete short stories of Robert Louis Stevenson

The misadventures of John Nicholson
    In Stevenson, R. L. The complete short stories p165-222

The story of a lie
    In Stevenson, R. L. The complete short stories p361-408
    In Stevenson, R. L. The complete short stories of Robert Louis Stevenson

The strange case of Dr. Jekyll and Mr. Hyde; with an introduction by Joyce Carol Oates. Vintage Books 1991 97p pa $8.95
    ISBN 0-679-73476-7
                      * LC 90-50600
First published 1886. Variant title: Dr. Jekyll and Mr. Hyde
"The work is known for its vivid portrayal of the psychopathology of a 'split personality.' The calm, respectable Dr. Jekyll develops a potion that will allow him to separate his good and evil aspects for scientific study. At first Jekyll has no difficulty abandoning the drug induced persona of the repulsive Mr. Hyde, but as the experiments continue the evil personality wrests control from Jekyll and commits murder. Afraid of being discovered, he takes his life; Hyde's body is found, together with a confession written in Jekyll's hand." Merriam-Webster's Ency of Lit
    also in Stevenson, R. L. The complete short stories of Robert Louis Stevenson
    also in Stevenson, R. L. The strange case of Dr. Jekyll and Mr. Hyde, and other famous tales p1-69

The strange case of Dr. Jekyll and Mr. Hyde, and other famous tales; with photographs of the author and his environment as well as illustrations from early editions of the stories, together with an introduction by W. M. Hills. Dodd, Mead 1961 339p il o.p.
"Great illustrated classics"
Contents: The strange case of Dr. Jekyll and Mr. Hyde [novelette]; The pavilion on the links; A lodging for the night; Markheim; The Sire de Malétroit's door; The beach of Falesá [novelette]; The suicide club; Story of the young man with the cream tarts; Story of the physician and the Saratoga trunk; The adventures of the hansom cab
The title novelette is entered separately, and the novelette: The beach of Falesá is described under: The complete short stories of Robert Louis Stevenson. The three-part story: The suicide club, which originally appeared in The New Arabian Nights (1882) is a partly satirical fan-

Stevenson, Robert Louis, 1850-1894—*Continued*

tasy-adventure story about a sinister London club which exploits the nihilistic tendencies of its members, and the mysterious Prince Florizel who opposes it

Stewart, Edward, 1938-1996

Deadly rich. Bantam Bks. 1991 566p o.p.
LC 91-17638

A "thriller about a serial murderer who calls himself 'Society Son of Sam.' His first victim is a wealthy socialite found unpleasantly done in on a dressing room floor of an exclusive department store, and after a few more high society types are similarly dispatched, Lieutenant Vince Cardozo of the NYPD finds himself deeply involved in Yuppie scandal." Libr J

Stewart, Fred Mustard, 1932-2007

Ellis Island; a novel. Delacorte Press 1983 396p
ISBN 0-688-01622-7   LC 82-14301

"In 1907 five young immigrants arrive at the legendary Ellis Island, the gateway to the American Dream. There's Jacob Rubenstein, fortunate to escape the pogrom that destroyed his family; Tom Banicek, who fled conscription into the Austro-Hungarian Army; Marco Santorelli, possessed of magnificent looks and driving ambition; and the beautiful O'Donnell sisters, escaping the Irish troubles." Libr J

"Stewart is a wonderful storyteller, and his novel—sentimental and even corny in spots—is nevertheless thoroughly satisfying." Publ Wkly

Stewart, George Rippey, 1895-1980

Earth abides. Random House 1949 373p
LC 49-11267

"In a near future, a plague devastates humankind, leaving isolated pockets of survivors. . . . One group in the San Francisco Bay area subsists for some time on the bounties of civilization that have remained intact. But the subtler social fabric, formerly held together by the cooperation of large numbers of people, is too much for this handful to sustain. With a mournful backward look at the millions of now-doomed volumes in the University of California library, the protagonist teaches the new children how to make bows and arrows. He lives long enough to see society forming itself anew at the tribal level. He himself is fated to be misremembered as a legendary culture hero. A major work." Anatomy of Wonder. 5th edition

Stewart, Mary, 1916-

Airs above the ground. Mill, M.S. 1965 286p
o.p.

Vanessa, a young English veterinarian, "after inadvertently discovering that her husband is not just a traveling salesman but doubles as a secret agent, helps him solve a case involving the Lipizzan horses, a medieval Austrian castle, a circus, a murder, and a narcotics ring." Booklist

The crystal cave. Morrow 1970 521p o.p.
*

First title in the author's Merlin trilogy. "Presumed to be the offspring of the daughter of the King of Wales and the devil himself, Merlin spends a difficult childhood

in the court of the king. He learns much that is mystical under the tutelage of a learned wizard and gains a knowledge of several languages. Escaping to 'Less Britain,' Merlin becomes an important element in the struggle to unite all Britain. The book is rich in descriptions of fifth-century Britain and Brittany, the Druids and their fearful rites, and the superstitions surrounding pagan worship." Shapiro. Fic for Youth. 3d edition

Followed by The hollow hills

In Stewart, M. Mary Stewart's Merlin trilogy

The Gabriel hounds. Forge 1967 320p o.p.

"This story is freely based on the accounts of the life of the Lady Hester Stanhope." Author's note

"Traveling in the Middle East Christy Mansel runs into her second cousin Charles in Damascus and the pair decide to visit their great aunt, an eccentric recluse who lives in a crumbling palace in Lebanon. Odd even for their aunt's household the situation at the castle arouses the cousins' suspicions, and their investigation turns up a startling secret in the underground passages." Booklist

The hollow hills. Morrow 1973 499p o.p.
*

This second novel in the author's Merlin trilogy begins with "Merlin's dismissal by Uther, Arthur's father, who has nonetheless promised to deliver the babe, when born, to Merlin's care. The book traces Merlin's travels to the east, during which time he monitors, through his second sight, Arthur's growth in Brittany and in England. Merlin returns to finish Arthur's education, and the book concludes with Arthur being proclaimed king. With this Merlin epic Mary Stewart has rightly won an honorable place among the modern writers of Arthurian legend." Tymn. Fantasy Lit

Followed by The last enchantment

In Stewart, M. Mary Stewart's Merlin trilogy

The ivy tree. Mill, M.S. 1961 320p o.p.

A Canadian girl visiting England is mistaken for a missing and supposedly dead heiress to an estate "by handsome Connor Winslow, a cousin of the runaway, and now manager of Whitescar. Finally convinced that she is Mary Grey, he and his dour sister Lisa persuade her to masquerade as the long-gone Annabel, promising her the opportunity to claim the considerable legacy left to Annabel by her mother on condition that she surrender her share in Whitescar to Connor upon the death of Uncle Matthew. Reluctantly, Mary enters into the scheme, but soon repents but finds herself too deeply involved." Best Sellers

The last enchantment. Morrow 1979 538p o.p.
LC 79-12937

This is the concluding volume of a trilogy about "Merlin the Enchanter, set amidst the turbulent events of fifth-century Britain when Arthur became High King. . . . This novel tells of the early years of Arthur's reign: the battles with the Saxons, building of Camelot, marriages with two successive Guiniveres, and birth of Mordred" Libr J

In Stewart, M. Mary Stewart's Merlin trilogy

Mary Stewart's Merlin trilogy. Morrow 1980 919p maps $29.95
ISBN 0-688-00347-8   LC 80-21019

Stewart, Mary, 1916——*Continued*

An omnibus edition of: The crystal cave, The hollow hills and The last enchantment, first published 1970, 1973 and 1979 respectively

The first novel in this trilogy based on Arthurian legends concerns the difficult childhood and youth of the magician Merlin who grows up as a bastard at the court of the King of Wales where he is believed to be the offspring of the King's daughter and the devil. He gains much knowledge from a learned wizard and escapes to "Less Britain" where he becomes involved in efforts to unite all of Britain. The second novel tells of Merlin's involvement with the childhood of Arthur and Arthur's search for the magical sword, Caliburn. The last novel deals with Merlin's death and Arthur's turbulent reign.

The author's "skill in creating colorful characters, suspense, and a brooding atmosphere serves her well in portraying England's Dark Ages, where witches, sorcerers, and tragic kings moved heroically through an enchanted land. Though Arthur's rise to power is the subject, the true star and narrator of the tale is Merlin the magician." Husband. Sequels

The moon-spinners. Mill, M.S. 1963 c1962 303p o.p.

First published 1962 in the United Kingdom

"Nicola Ferris, an English girl on vacation in Crete, decides to walk the last mile over a rough track to the tiny village where she is expected the next day. She walks into a mystery. She stumbles upon a shepherd's hut guarded by a Greek who threatens to kill her if she makes a sound. Inside the hut, she finds a young Englishman seriously wounded and much upset by her intrusion. In her determination to help him, she is drawn into his dangerous situation." Horn Book

My brother Michael. Mill, M.S. 1960 313p o.p.

This suspense story has "a modern Greek setting enriched by classical antiquities and haunted by the shades of Hellenic tragedy. Camilla Haven, the heroine-narrator, is on her way to Delphi when she encounters Simon Lester, an English schoolmaster who has come to investigate the death of his brother Michael, supposedly killed fighting during World War II. A strange letter written just before his death leads Camilla, along with Simon, through a terrifying maze of danger and violence to an amazing discovery on the slopes of Mount Parnassus." Booklist

Nine coaches waiting. Mill, M.S. 1959 c1958 342p o.p.

First published 1958 in the United Kingdom

"Intelligent, spirited Linda Martin comes to Valmy, an isolated château in the French Alps, as English governess to nine-year-old Philippe, the orphaned Comte de Valmy. After several frightening 'accidents' Linda discovers that her pupil is the object of a murder plot which apparently involves his crippled uncle and the latter's handsome son Raoul, with whom she is in love." Booklist

The stormy petrel. Morrow 1991 189p o.p.
LC 91-14509

The title "refers to both a little seabird and a boat piloted by one of the two young men who intrude upon young professor Rose Fenemore's country-cottage holiday on one of the smaller Hebrides. Unfortunately, the Petrel pilot, although he's the handsomer, turns out to be a dicey character. It's the other gent, helming another boat, who's steadier, though plainer." Booklist

"The visitors are jumpy, evasive and mutually antagonistic, and Rose's suspicions are aroused. The mystery of their relationship and real purpose, never menacing, is quickly solved, and takes second place to Stewart's vivid rendering of Moila's lochs, glens and wild birds, especially the graceful stormy petrels who nest there." Publ Wkly

Thunder on the right. Mill, M.S. 1958 c1957 284p o.p.

First published 1957 in the United Kingdom

"Jennifer answers her cousin Gillian's plea to visit a French convent in the Pyrenees where Gillian hopes to become a nun. On her arrival from England, Jennifer discovers that her cousin has supposedly died after a mysterious auto accident. She does some sleuthing and unveils smuggling and murder. All the ingredients for a mystery-love story with authentic background." Libr J

Touch not the cat. Morrow 1976 336p o.p.

A "tale set on a family estate in England. Garbled words of warning uttered by her dying father lead Bryony Ashley into danger as she investigates the intricacies of past and present intrigues within the Ashley family. Bryony's inherited extrasensory abilities add to the suspenseful story." Booklist

The wicked day. Morrow 1983 453p o.p.
LC 83-12091

The author "returns to the Arthurian world she portrayed . . . in her Merlin trilogy. The principal character is Mordred, born of the incestuous liaison between Arthur the High King and his half-sister, the evil sorceress and northern queen Morgause. Mordred is summoned to Camelot by the formidable warrior king, along with Morgause and her four legitimate but ungovernable sons, and told of his true parentage. After growing to manhood in Arthur's court . . . Mordred is left in charge of the kingdom, and of Queen Guinevere, while Arthur is off fighting the Romans in Brittany. Reported dead, the king returns to Britain and there ensues the fulfillment of the 'wicked day' that has been prophesied by Merlin." Publ Wkly

Wildfire at midnight. Appleton-Century-Crofts 1956 214p o.p.

Gianetta Brooke comes to the Isle of Skye to forget the husband she has painfully divorced and finds herself in danger as a series of murders takes place

Stirling, Jessica

The island wife. St. Martin's Press 1998 c1997 410p $24.95
ISBN 0-312-19289-4   LC 98-35162

First published 1997 in the United Kingdom

This novel, first of a trilogy, "about a dysfunctional nineteenth-century family living on the rural Scottish island of Mull focuses on two sisters, Innis and Biddy Campbell, one modest, intelligent, and thoughtful; the other seductive, self-centered, and conniving. When both take an interest in Michael Tarrant, a handsome and mysterious shepherd, conflicts arise, and bitter emotions and dark family secrets are exposed." Booklist

"The characters are well drawn, with realistic motivations, and the atmosphere is 'like the island itself, two-

Stirling, Jessica—*Continued*
faced and moody.' Some of the Scottish words will be unfamiliar to Americans, but this does not detract from the enjoyment." Libr J
Followed by The wind from the hills

The marrying kind. St. Martin's Press 1996 c1995 359p o.p.   LC 96-1191
First published 1995 in the United Kingdom
Set in pre-WWII Glasgow, This sequel to the The penny wedding "coming-of-age novel centers around third-year medical student Alison Burnside as she struggles toward the realization that having it all is impossible. At the same time, all the characters, one way or another, illustrate just how naïve the world was on the eve of Hitler's reign of terror. . . . Exposing her characters to feminism, class conflict and the stormclouds of war, Stirling expertly guides them through the growing pains of the heart into genuine maturity." Publ Wkly

The penny wedding. St. Martin's Press 1995 c1994 394p o.p.   LC 95-1732
First published 1994 in the United Kingdom
"A working-class Scottish family strives to survive personal tragedy and financial devastation during the Great Depression. When her mother unexpectedly dies and her father loses his job, gifted and intelligent 17-year-old Alison Burnside expects to forgo her dreams of obtaining a medical degree in order to help support her struggling family. Before she has a chance to leave school, however, her favorite teacher and her four older brothers intervene on her behalf. . . . A bittersweet portrait of a realistically flawed family banding together out of a sense of love, loyalty, and necessity in a heartfelt effort to overcome poverty and misfortune." Booklist
Followed by The marrying kind

The piper's tune. St. Martin's Press 2002 486p $26.95
ISBN 0-312-28870-0   LC 2001-57854
"Eighteen-year-old Lindsay Franklin gets an unexpected jolt when her shipbuilding magnate grandfather gives her a share of the family business. At the same time, her all-too-charming Irish cousin, the womanizing Forbes McCulloch, comes to Glasgow to learn the family business from the bottom up and sets his sights on marrying Lindsay. The style and design of the cover give the impression that this is a historical romance, but the tale is much more than a formulaic love story. Stirling does a bang-up job of illustrating how character shapes a person's life." Publ Wkly

The wind from the hills. St. Martin's Press 1999 442p $25.95
ISBN 0-312-24433-9   LC 99-50171
First published 1998 in the United Kingdom
This novel, the second in the Isle of Mull trilogy begun with The island wife, finds Innis married to Michael Tarrant and Biddy a wealthy widow with few ties to her past

The workhouse girl. St. Martin's Press 1997 472p o.p.
LC 97-5500
First published 1996 in the United Kingdom
Set in Victorian Scotland, "Stirling's tale follows Cassie Armitage into an unfortunate marriage to the evil, deceitful, and abusive Reverend Robert Montague.

Cassie's servant, Nancy Winfield, is the workhouse girl of the book's title. Nancy shares the story's center stage and is as engaging and likable as her wealthy counterpart. But it is Nancy's station in life to carry the weight of an illegitimate child on her very capable and resourceful shoulders. . . . A thoroughly entertaining and satisfying read." Booklist

Stirling, S. M.
(jt. auth) McCaffrey, A. The city who fought

Stoker, Bram, 1847-1912

The Bram Stoker bedside companion; 10 stories by the author of Dracula; edited and with an introduction by Charles Osborne. Taplinger 1973 224p o.p.
Contents: The secret of the growing gold; Dracula's guest; The invisible giant; The Judge's House; The burial of the rats; A star trap; The squaw; Grooken sands; The combeen man (from The snake's pass); The Watter's Mou'

Dracula; edited with an introduction and notes by Maurice Hindle; preface by Christopher Frayling. Penguin Books 2003 xlvii, 454p pa $11
ISBN 0-14-143984-X
* LC 2003-269578
First published 1897
"Count Dracula, an 'undead' villain from Transylvania, uses his supernatural powers to lure and prey upon innocent victims from whom he gains the blood on which he lives. The novel is written chiefly in the form of journals kept by the principal characters—Jonathan Harker, who contacts the vampire in his Transylvanian castle; Harker's fiancee (later his wife), Mina, adored by the Count; the well-meaning Dr. Seward; and Lucy Westenra, a victim who herself becomes a vampire. The doctor and friends destroy Dracula in the end, but only after they drive a stake through Lucy's heart to save her soul." Merriam-Webster's Ency of Lit

Midnight tales; edited and with an introduction by Peter Haining. Owen, P.; distributed by Dufour Eds. 1990 182p il o.p.
Contents: The dream in the dead house; The spectre of doom; The dualitists; Death in the wings; The Gombeen man; The squaw; A deed of vengeance; The man from Shorrox'; The Red Stockade; Midnight tales; A criminal star; The bridal of death

Stone, Irving, 1903-1989

The agony and the ecstasy. New American Library 2004 776p pa $16
ISBN 0-451-21323-8
*
First published 1961 by Doubleday
"Michelangelo's career is traced from his promising boyhood apprenticeships to the painter Ghirlandajo and the sculptor Bertoldo thru all the many years of his flowering genius. . . . Florence and Rome are the principal cities which serve as background for the development of the artist's life and work." Chicago Sunday Trib
"Stone's Michelangelo is an idealized version, purged not only of ambisexuality, but of the egotism, faultfinding, harsh irony, and ill temper that we know were characteristic of Michelangelo." Saturday Rev

Stone, Irving, 1903-1989—*Continued*

Love is eternal; a novel about Mary Todd and Abraham Lincoln. Doubleday 1954 468p o.p.

This novel presents a sympathetic portrait of Mary Todd Lincoln. The author absolves her from the shrewishness with which many historians have clothed her and pictures her marriage to Abraham Lincoln as a great love story

"Recommended in spite of the controversial nature of its interpretation of Mary Todd Lincoln." Booklist

Lust for life; a novel of Vincent van Gogh; illustrated with 150 reproductions of Vincent van Gogh's pictures arranged by J. B. Neumann. Twentieth anniversary ed. Doubleday 1954 507p il o.p.

First published 1934 by Longmans, Green and Co.

"Vincent Van Gogh lived a turbulent life but throughout it he was loved and supported by his brother, Theo. Sons of a Dutch Protestant minister, Vincent and Theo were raised rather strictly, but Vincent's love of color and movement led him into the life of an artist. He always felt challenged to fill a blank canvas with light and color. Vincent's search for meaning and fulfillment in his life took him over Europe but only toward the end of his life did he meet other artists who shared his artistic views, and it was not until after his death that his work began to be appreciated." Shapiro. Fic for Youth. 3d edition

Stone, Katherine

Happy endings. Kensington Pub. Corp. 1994 362p o.p.

"Raven Winter is the best entertainment attorney in the business. She is handling the reclusive, best-selling author Holly, who fears that Jason Cole, an Academy Award-winning filmmaker, is going to change the happy ending in the film version of her book. Nick is introduced to this group when Raven distractedly jogs in front of his nursery truck. . . . Most romance readers expect a happy ending, but the pleasure comes in the journey to reach it, and Stone does not disappoint." Libr J

Stone, Nick, 1966-

The king of swords; a novel. Harper 2008 559p $25.99

ISBN 978-0-06-089731-4; 0-06-089731-7

LC 2008-33704

"A bizarre death in a Miami primate park sets the tone for [this] mystery. . . . What starts out as a standard murder investigation soon leads hardboiled detective Max Mingus and his partner, Joe, into the underworld of Haitian voodoo. Their probe brings the partners into contact with a pimp, his tarot card-reading mother, a corrupt cop whom they can't sniff out, and an almost-mythical Haitian crime lord named Solomon Boukman." Libr J

"The Miami of the early 1980s has become an almost mythical place, an era steeped in the lore of Miami Vice and Scarface and seen as the epicenter for drugs and the glamour of a new South Beach. Nick Stone captures that reality in his gritty, brutal and expertly plotted The King of Swords, offering an authentic vision of South Florida along with plenty of hardboiled action." Miami Herald

Stone, Robert, 1937-

Bay of souls. Houghton Mifflin 2003 249p $25

ISBN 0-395-96349-4

* LC 2002-192171

"Michael Ahearn is a respected professor of literature at a small college in the upper Midwest, with a lovely wife and 12-yer-old son, but a vague dissatisfaction gnaws at him, exacerbated by a frightening incident while deer hunting and the near-death of his son from exposure. When Michael meets a new professor, the beautiful and electrifying Lara Purcell, he falls under her spell and launches an affair, endangering his marriage and his relationship with his son. At Lara's prompting, Michael travels with her to her Caribbean island home of St. Trinity, a nation rife with political violence, where Lara hopes to repossess the soul she believes has been captured by a voodoo goddess." Publ Wkly

"Unusual (for Stone) in is brevity, this is a highly concentrated work, probably the least violent yet most unnerving of his novels. And the philosophical conflict dramatized in it ends surprisingly, in a way that provokes new questions about what Stone is up to in his writing." N Y Times Book Rev

Damascus Gate. Houghton Mifflin 1998 500p $26

ISBN 0-395-66569-8

LC 97-49615

"Chris Lucas, this novel's protagonist, an American journalist of mixed Catholic and Jewish background, is in Israel 'writing a book on the Jerusalem syndrome'— the phenomenon of religious pilgrims who believe that God has called them there for a special purpose. In his research, he encounters some of the city's . . . seekers, including Sonia Barnes, a nightclub singer and practicing Sufi, Adam De Kuff, a manic-depressive who has been manipulated into believing that he is the Messiah, and the House of the Galilean, a fundamentalist-Christian group plotting with ultra-Orthodox Jews to bomb the Temple Mount." Libr J

Stone "is so comprehending of Israel's convoluted workings and its bifurcated culture—where the Biblical fervor of Jerusalem coexists with the disco fever of Tel Aviv—that he makes other writers on the subject seem like the breeziest of literary tourists." New Yorker

Dog soldiers; a novel. Houghton Mifflin 1974 342p o.p.

This novel "chronicles the nightmarish misadventure of Converse, Marge, and Hicks, who smuggle a bundle of Vietnamese heroin into the U.S. only to be pursued and 'ripped off' by a corrupt narcotic agent." Libr J

"Part melodrama, part morality play, 'Dog Soldiers' offers a vision of a predatory, insensate society from which all moral authority has fled. It is a world in which innocence or vestigial remnants of decent behavior prove fatal to their owners; Hicks . . . is nearly violent enough to survive, but he is done in by his own loyalty to Marge. All of this corruption and vulnerability, this savagery and stoned withdrawal, this combination of passion and cynicism works convincingly, for Stone is a very good storyteller indeed." Newsweek

A flag for sunrise; a novel. Knopf 1981 439p

ISBN 0-394-40757-1

LC 81-47507

Stone, Robert, 1937——*Continued*

"A dramatic tale with political and philosophic views of a Latin American country undergoing revolution in the post-Vietnam era." Oxford Companion to Am Lit. 6th edition

This book is "at once a high-tension adventure tale, a densely plotted political novel and, at its heart, a meditation on the inavailability of God. Stone writes as if announcements of the death of the novel had not reached him: 'A Flag for Sunrise' shows narrative confidence, crisscrossed motives, a moral sense and sustained inventiveness of an amplitude we have almost given up expecting from fiction." Newsweek

Outerbridge Reach. Ticknor & Fields 1992 409p
o.p.
* LC 91-34875

This novel concerns Owen Browne, an ex-navy man who has become a successful sailboat salesperson. "Avid for honor and glory, he enters a highly publicized, round-the world, singlehanded sailboat race. As the loneliness and exertion of his voyage tests Browne, so the attention of a shallow filmmaker test Anne, Browne's wife. Both learn truths about themselves and one another which destroy one spouse but which compel the other to further trials of strength and will." Libr J

"Robert Stone's blend of heroic aspiration and mordantly deflationary irony results in something like tragicomedy. . . . But whatever you call it, 'Outerbridge Reach' seems to me a triumph—a beautifully and painstakingly composed piece of literary art." N Y Times Book Rev

Stone, Zachary, 1949-

For works written by this author under other names see Follett, Ken, 1949-

Stott, Rebecca

Ghostwalk; a novel. Spiegel & Grau 2007 304p
il $24.95
ISBN 978-0-385-52106-2; 0-385-52106-5
LC 2006-22326

"A Cambridge historian dies under suspicious circumstances, leaving behind the nearly completed manuscript of a book on the alchemical experiments of Isaac Newton. Her son, a research scientist, hires his former lover, Lydia, to finish the book. Meanwhile, a shadowy group of animal-rights activists escalate their violent attacks. As Lydia is drawn further into Newton's seventeenth-century world, she begins to believe that his ghost is haunting her and, perhaps, directing the murderous events of the present." New Yorker

"Stott brings a nervy intelligence to her work, skillfully linking the war on terror, quantum physics, alchemy, serial murder, ghosts, and thwarted romance." Miami Herald

Stout, Rex, 1886-1975

Black orchids; &, the silent speaker; introduction to Black orchids by Lawrence Block ; introduction to The silent speaker by Walter Mosley. Bantam Books 2009 various pagingp il pa $16
ISBN 978-0-553-38655-4; 0-553-38655-7
LC 2009-464755

Black orchids first published 1942 by Farrar & Reinhart; The silent speaker first published 1946 by Viking Press

Contains two titles in the author's Nero Wolfe series. In *The black orchids*, Wolfe goes to a flower show to see a rare black orchid; "unfortunately, the much-anticipated event is soon overshadowed by a murder as daring as it is sudden. . . . [In *The silent speaker*,] a government power broker scheduled to speak before an influential group of millionaires turns up dead. . . . Soon a second victim is discovered, a missing stenographer's tape causes a panic, and a dead man speaks, after a fashion." Publisher's note

The doorbell rang; a Nero Wolfe novel. Viking 1965 186p o.p.

"Nero Wolfe tangles with the FBI, on behalf of a wealthy woman who has sent as gifts to prominent people 10,000 copies of Fred Cook's book criticizing the FBI. . . . She is being shadowed and spied on by the FBI. To the surprise of Wolfe and of Archie Goodwin, they have the good will of the New York Police Department. The New York Police believe that FBI agents have murdered a magazine writer who was doing an article on the FBI. The police are powerless to prove anything or to prosecute. Clever and ingenious, this ranks among the best Rex Stout mysteries." Publ Wkly

Fer-de-lance; &, The league of frightened men; introduction to Fer-de-lance by Loren D. Estleman; introduction to The league of frightened men by Robert Goldsborough. Bantam Books 2008 285, 302p il pa $16
ISBN 978-0-553-38545-8; 0-553-38545-3
LC 2008-299738

Combined edition of two titles first published 1934 and 1935 respectively by Farrar & Rinehart

Contains two titles in the author's Nero Wolfe series. "The fer-de-lance is among the most deadly snakes known to man. When someone makes a present of one to Nero Wolfe, his partner, Archie Goodwin, suspects it means Wolfe is getting close to solving the devilishly clever murders of an immigrant and a college president. . . . [In *The league of frightened men*,] Paul Chapin's Harvard cronies never forgave themselves for the hazing prank that left their friend a cripple. Yet they believed that Paul himself had forgiven them—until a class reunion ends in death and a series of poems promising more of the same. Now this league of frightened men is desperate for Nero Wolfe's help." Publisher's note

Gambit; a Nero Wolfe novel. Viking 1962 188p
o.p.
*

"Nero Wolfe, with his usual witty, urbane, conversational approach, looks into a case of arsenic poisoning in a Manhattan chess club." Publ Wkly

"There is more detection in this story than in any other of the mulling-and-quizzing sort; here we really see N.W.'s thoughts whirring. Moreover, Archie is in excellent form, and although a chess tournament is a feature, the game itself is not. The great scene is that in which Nero reads and burns the pages of Webster's Dictionary, Third Edition." Barzun. Cat of Crime. Rev and enl edition

Stout, Rex, 1886-1975—*Continued*

The rubber band & The red box; introduction to The red box by Carolyn G. Hart. Bantam Books 2009 189, 257p pa $15

ISBN 978-0-553-38603-5; 0-553-38603-4

LC 2009-455172

Combined edition of two titles first published 1936 and 1937 respectively by Farrar & Rinehart

Contains two titles in the author's Nero Wolfe series. In *The rubber band*, "a forty-year-old pact, a five-thousand-mile search, and a million-dollar murder are all linked to an international scandal that could rebound on the great detective and his partner, Archie, with fatal abruptness. . . . [In *The red box*] a beautiful woman is poisoned after indulging in a box of candy." Publisher's note

Some buried Caesar & The golden spiders; introduction to Some Buried Caesar by Diane Mott Davidson; introduction to the Golden Spiders by Linda Barnes. Bantam Books 2008 206p pa $15

ISBN 978-0-553-38567-0   LC 2008-301309

Some buried Caesar first published 1939 by Farrar & Rinehart; The golden spiders first published 1953 by Viking Press

Contains two titles in the author's Nero Wolfe series. In *Some buried Caesar* "a prize bull destined for the barbecue is found pawing the corpse of a late restaurateur. Wolfe is certain that Hickory Caesar Grindon, the soon-to-be-beefsteak bull, isn't the murderer. But who among a veritable stampede of suspects—including a young woman who's caught Archie's eye—turned the tables on Hickory's would-be butcher? . . . [In *The golden spiders*] a twelve-year-old boy shows up at Wolfe's brownstone with an incredible story. Soon the great detective finds himself hired for the grand sum of $4.30 and faced with the question of why the last two people to hire him were murdered. To keep it from becoming three, Wolfe must discover the unlikely connection between a gray Cadillac, a mysterious woman, and a pair of earrings shaped like spiders dipped in gold." Publisher's note

Too many cooks; & champagne for one; introduction to Champagne for One by Lena Horne. Bantam Dell/Random House, Inc. 2009 179, 205p pa $15

ISBN 978-0-553-38629-5; 0-553-38629-8

LC 2009-464724

Too many cooks first published 1938 by Farrar & Rinehart; Champagne for one first published 1958 by Viking Press

Contains two titles in the author's Nero Wolfe series. *Too many cooks* involves a poisoning at a gathering of great chefs in which Wolfe is a guest of honor. In *Champagne for one*, "Faith Usher talked about taking her own life and even kept cyanide in her purse. So when she died from a lethal champagne cocktail in the middle of a high society dinner party, everyone called it suicide—including the police. But Nero Wolfe isn't convinced—and neither is Archie. Especially when Wolfe is warned by four men against taking the case." Publisher's note

Stowe, Harriet Beecher, 1811-1896

The minister's wooing

In Stowe, H. B. Uncle Tom's cabin: or, Life among the lowly; The minister's wooing; Oldtown folks p521-876

Oldtown folks

In Stowe, H. B. Uncle Tom's cabin: or, Life among the lowly; The minister's wooing; Oldtown folks p877-1468

Uncle Tom's cabin; with an introduction by Alfred Kazin. Knopf 1995 xxix, 494p $20

ISBN 0-679-44365-7

"Everyman's library"

"The book relates the trials, suffering, and human dignity of Uncle Tom, an old slave. Cruelly treated by a Yankee plantation owner, Simon Legree, Tom dies as the result of a beating. Uncle Tom is devoted to Little Eva, the daughter of his white owner, Augustine St. Clare. Other important characters are the mulatto girl Eliza; the impish black child Topsy; Miss Ophelia St. Clare, a New England spinster; and Marks, the slave catcher. The setting is Kentucky and Louisiana." Reader's Ency. 4th edition

also in Stowe, H. B. Uncle Tom's cabin: or, Life among the lowly; The minister's wooing; Oldtown folks p1-519

Uncle Tom's cabin: or, Life among the lowly; The minister's wooing; Oldtown folks. Library of Am. 1982 1477p il $47.50

ISBN 0-940450-01-1   LC 81-18629

Omnibus edition of three titles first published 1852, 1859 and 1869 respectively

In the minister's wooing, a young woman rejects her suitor because he has no religious faith. Oldtown folks concerns the everyday life of a small Massachusetts town

Stowe, Harriet Elizabeth *See* Stowe, Harriet Beecher, 1811-1896

Strahan, Jonathan

(ed) The new space opera. See The new space opera

Straight, Susan

The gettin place. Hyperion 1996 488p $22.95

ISBN 0-7868-6086-3   LC 95-50065

"The principal setting is Rio Seco, a fictional California city outside of L.A. The 'gettin place' of the title is a parcel of land along an old canal where the extended Thompson clan has its adobe homes and the family businesses—a garage and towing yard, a rib joint and a small olive orchard. When the bodies of two white women are found burned in a dilapidated car in the lot, and when the body of a man dressed in drag is discovered nearby, the Thompsons become the focus of law enforcement attentions." Publ Wkly

"Against the backdrop of the under-acknowledged race riots of 1920s Tulsa and the contrastingly media-saturated 1992 L.A. riots, Straight realizes the chillingly

Straight, Susan—*Continued*

natural, almost blithe cynicism and violence of teenagers, the profound weight of hard history on the old, and the bewilderment of those in-between. A lyrical and un-flinching stunner." Libr J

Highwire moon; a novel. Houghton Mifflin 2001 306p map $24

ISBN 0-618-05614-9   LC 00-53878

"The story of an illegal Mexican immigrant named Serafina, the novel chronicles the 12-year aftermath of an INS raid that separates her from her American daughter. Told in the alternating voices of parent and child, the novel explores numerous worlds: migrant workers are juxtaposed with amphetamine addicts; homeless teens with well-tended foster children; industrial laborers with indigenous farm workers." Libr J

"Susan Straight's Rio Seco is a microcosm of suspicious, segregated America, a place where racism often boils down to fear, ignorance and willful obliviousness." N Y Times Book Rev

I been in sorrow's kitchen and licked out all the pots; a novel. Hyperion 1992 355p

ISBN 1-56282-963-7   LC 92-3566

"Self-conscious and restless around people, Marietta is happiest alone in the woods behind her tiny coastal community of old slave cabins in South Carolina. Even though it's the late 1950s, life there has a distinctly antebellum flavor. Her father died before she drew breath, so when her mother dies, Marietta, only 15, takes off on her own to Charleston. Her size and blue-black skin amaze and intimidate people, but she finds work and works hard, ever-watchful and courageous. When she becomes pregnant, she goes home to have her twins, two strapping boys, and finds work on the abandoned plantation that is being restored to attract tourists. In a distressing sort of déjà vu, Marietta finds herself reenacting the lives of her ancestors, an impossible, even dangerous situation as the fight for civil rights ignites across the South." Booklist

"Time and place . . . are evoked with stirring accuracy. But it is Marietta's intricate constitution, and the Gullah rhythms streaming through her mind, that give the novel its special edge and distinction." N Y Times Book Rev

Followed by Blacker than a thousand midnights (1994)

A million nightingales. Pantheon Books 2006 340p $24.95

ISBN 0-375-42364-8   LC 2005-50052

"Moinette, a mulatto slave girl, lives on a plantation south of New Orleans in the early 1800s. She is a personal maid to the daughter of her owners, who are trying to prepare their daughter for her entrance into the social world and marriage. When the young woman suddenly dies, Moinette is abruptly sold and shipped off, torn from her mother and the only world she has ever known. The novel follows her as she begins life on another plantation; tries to escape; is brutally punished, raped, and impregnated; and is finally sold again to another slave owner under whose employ she saves her money in the hopes of one day buying her freedom and reuniting with her mother and child." Libr J

"Straight's book is a deep consideration of the servitude all women experienced then—and, in some ways and some places, continue to experience even now. . . . But her novel is, besides, a powerful and moving story,

written in language so beautiful you can almost believe the words themselves are capable of salving history's wounds." N Y Times Book Rev

Straub, Peter

(ed) American fantastic tales: terror and the uncanny from Poe to the pulps. See American fantastic tales: terror and the uncanny from Poe to the pulps

(ed) American fantastic tales: terror and the uncanny from the 1940s to now. See American fantastic tales: terror and the uncanny from the 1940s to now

Ghost story. Coward, McCann & Geoghegan 1979 483p

ISBN 0-698-10959-7

                            * LC 78-27120

"Set largely in a snow-bound village in present-day upstate New York, this . . . tale of supernatural menace pits two elderly lawyers, a novelist, and a teenager against a life-form that thrives on one's memories and with time on one's blood." Libr J

"With considerable technical skill, Peter Straub has constructed an extravagant entertainment which, though flawed, achieves in its second half some awesome effects." Newsweek

The Hellfire Club. Random House 1995 462p

o.p.   LC 95-21773

"A former nurse in Vietnam, Nora Chancel lives in Westerholm, Connecticut, with her ineffectual husband, Davey. While visiting the local police station to identify the most recent victim of a serial killer, Nora is kidnapped by the accused killer, the satirical villain Dick Dart. Intertwined with the kidnapping plot is an account of the terrifying events that followed the writing of a horror story at the Shorelands writers' colony in 1938. Fighting her own demons from Vietnam, Nora becomes stronger and braver as the story progresses. The climax brings the two stories together, as Dart and Nora visit Shorelands. Horror meets horror in this bizarre, enigmatic tale, which reveals itself in onion-like layers." Libr J

In the night room; a novel. Random House 2004 330p $21.95

ISBN 1-400-06252-7   LC 2004-51425

In this sequel to Lost boy lost girl, horror novelist Tim Underhill receives "an e-mail sent to him by the spirit of an ancient Byzantine, who explains that the daughter of one of the serial killers in Lost boy lost girl wasn't murdered by her father, as Tim supposed; that the exceedingly strange fan who cornered Tim in his local breakfast hangout is an embodiment of the wronged murderer's spirit; and that, yes, that was an angel Tim saw fly away over Manhattan while he walked home. Meanwhile, over in New Jersey, YA novelist Willy Patrick is about to marry mysterious Mitchell Faber when she comes upon evidence that he is responsible for her husband's violent, gangland-like killing. She flees Faber's estate, pursued by his minions, to New York and into a reading-signing appearance by Tim. There is a catch to this, for Willy's plot is that of the new novel Tim has been writing; that is, a character Tim created has emerged in his reality. As Tim and Willy repair to their hometown, Millhaven, Illinois, to slake the murderer's spirit, his real and her fic-

Straub, Peter—*Continued*

tive worlds converge toward an ending that promises, like that of Lost boy lost girl, the transcendent redemption of violated souls. Inventive and moving." Booklist

Lost boy lost girl; a novel. Farrar, Straus & Giroux 2003 281p $24.95

ISBN 1-4000-6092-3   LC 2003-046689

"A woman commits suicide for no apparent reason. A week later, her son—beautiful, troubled fifteen-year-old Mark Underhill—vanishes from the face of the earth. To his uncle, horror novelist Timothy Underhill, Mark's inexplicable absence feels like a second death. After his sister-in-law's funeral, Tim searches his hometown of Millhaven for clues that might help him unravel this mystery of death and disappearance." Publisher's note

"Inquisitive and open-minded as Tim is, he makes it easy for Mr. Straub to move from conventionally hair-raising effects . . . to the more happening teenage world of cyberscares. Strongly visual without resorting to secondhand cinematic imagery, the book is equally well equipped to play both kinds of tricks." N Y Times (Late N Y Ed)

(ed) Lovecraft, H. P. H. P. Lovecraft

Magic terror; seven tales. Random House 2000 335p

ISBN 0-375-50393-5   LC 99-53216

Includes the following stories: Ashputtle; Isn't it romantic?; The ghost village; Bunny is good bread; Pork pie hat; Hunger, an introduction; Mr. Clubb and Mr. Cuff

"Straub is not called a master of horror for nothing. In this collection of seven tales, ranging from the story of a grade school teacher with an evil secret to a Vietnam War grunt whose reality is @melting at the edges,' Straub shows that horror comes in numerous forms—many of which are not so much frightening as deeply disturbing." Libr J

Mr. X; a novel. Random House 1999 482p $25.95

ISBN 0-679-40138-5   LC 98-47688

"From childhood, Ned Dunstan has experienced precognitive visions. . . . Summoned home to Edgerton, Ill., by a premonition of his mother's death on the eve of his 35th birthday, Ned finds himself implicated in a tangle of felonies and murders, all of which point to someone strenuously manipulating events to frame him. Digging into local history, he finds reason to believe that the mysterious father he never knew, or possibly a malignant doppelgänger, are pulling the strings. . . . [Straub's] evocative prose, a seamless splice of clipped hard-boiled banter and poetic reflection, contributes to the thick atmosphere of apprehension that makes this one of the most invigorating horror reads of the year." Publ Wkly

Mystery. Dutton 1990 548p il o.p.

* LC 89-7734

Second title in the author's Blue rose trilogy. "When a traffic accident nearly ends his young life, Tom Pasmore experiences all the usual near-death sensations: warm lights at the end of tunnels and friendly faces beckoning him onward. But by cheating death, his life is forever changed. Tom becomes obsessed with murder, with detection, and especially with a recent killing on

Mill Walk, the fictional Caribbean island where his family lives. Tom's sleuthing mania is fed by an eccentric neighbor, Lamont von Heilitz, a famous retired detective. . . . The remarkable depth of characterization make apparent the fact that *Mystery* is meant to be much more than a conventional shocker. For the most part, Straub delivers the goods." Booklist

(ed) Poe's children. See Poe's children

(jt. auth) King, S. Black house

Strauss, Darin

More than it hurts you; a novel. Dutton 2008 401p $24.95

ISBN 978-0-525-95070-7; 0-525-95070-2

LC 2007-43742

This is "the story of Josh Goldin, a handsome young husband, father and successful advertising man. Everyone likes Josh, and his life is close to perfect until the day his wife, Dori, calls him at work from the hospital. Their baby is in intensive care, having 'coded' shortly after having been brought in for what seemed like a fairly routine stomach upset. The baby recovers, but some wheels have been set in motion. The young black female doctor who's in charge of the pediatric ICU is suspicious of the baby's condition and the mother's behavior. Soon the family must endure home visits from representatives of Child Placement Services, and eventually the police arrive and take the baby into protective custody. Josh struggles with his anger and pain and his vacillation between supporting his wife and suspecting her. At the same time, the reader is brought into the turbulent life of the doctor, Darlene Stokes, a single mother whose long-missing, drug-dealing father has just been released from prison and wants contact with her." Rocky Mountain News

The "novel is most effective not in its sweeping, occasionally grandiloquent observations about society as a whole, but in its mastery of personal, domestic issues, the disturbing, soul-searching, what-if questions Strauss raises about marriage, parenthood, loyalty and responsibility." Chicago Tribune

The real McCoy; a novel. Dutton 2002 326p

ISBN 0-525-94651-9   LC 2002-23545

"It's the end of the nineteenth century, and Kid McCoy—a small-time boxer long past his prime—comes to young Virgil Selby's town. McCoy is beaten so badly that he dies. Virgil drags the dying man to the forest, learns the location of Kid McCoy's next fight, and then—poof—becomes Kid McCoy, Kid, née Virgil, ends up in a Chinese railroad worker community, where he meets Johnny Gold, a first-rate flimflam man with a habit of not finishing his . . . McCoy and Gold team up, and eventually McCoy cons his way to a world boxing title, becoming the toast of New York society." Booklist

The author has "taken the tale of an all-but-forgotten boxer and used it as his jumping-off point to worry questions of identity and the thin, often nonexistent lines between filmflamming and lying and storytelling itself." N Y Times Book Rev

Strayed, Cheryl

Torch. Houghton 2005 322p $24

ISBN 0-618-47217-7   LC 2005-10333

Strayed, Cheryl—*Continued*

"Teresa Rae Wood is famous in her small town of Midden, Minnesota, for hosting Modern Pioneers, a local radio program that gives tips on living off the land. At the age of 38, she is diagnosed with a virulent form of cancer and dies within months. Her common-law husband, Bruce, and her children, 20-year-old Claire and 18-year-old Josh, are left reeling. Bruce abruptly marries his next-door neighbor, Josh becomes heavily involved in dealing methamphetamine, and Claire single-mindedly devotes herself to keeping her mother's memory alive." Booklist

"A beautiful book, expansive in its treatment of tragedy and grief, but equally attentive to all of the most telling details. The language is lovely, offering delicious, compelling imagery without being heavy-handed." Providence Journal

Strieber, Whitley

2012: the war for souls. Tor 2007 319p $24.95
ISBN 978-0-7653-1896-1; 0-7653-1896-2
LC 2007-17374

"A Tom Doherty Associates book"

This sequel to The Grays "blends equal parts science fiction thriller, supernatural horror and provocative spiritual speculation. As struggling author Wylie Dale works on his latest novel, which revolves around an upcoming date when the earth crosses both the galactic equator and the solar ecliptic—a time that the Maya predicted would mark the cataclysmic end of this age—he begins to uncover evidence that what he's writing about is actually happening on a parallel earth. If nothing is done, on December 21, 2012, gateways will open into this world and reptilian invaders will not only enslave humanity but feast on their succulent souls as well. While Strieber's exploration into the existence and import of the soul isn't exactly profound, it is wildly entertaining." Publ Wkly

The forbidden zone. Dutton 1993 309p
ISBN 0-525-93683-1
LC 93-6726

"Not long after physicist Brian Kelly and his pregnant wife hear human screams coming from within a dirt mound, inhabitants of their upstate New York town are attacked by wasp-like fireflies, women transformed into grub-like creatures are dug from the earth and an otherworldly being terrorizes motorists from its Dodge Viper. Brian theorizes that somehow the space-time fabric has been breached, and before long he and a few companions are engaged in a classic battle with an army of ancient demons." Publ Wkly

"The action and danger in this novel are exciting, and while the physics and the explanation for the horrific events are rather muddy, the story works well as a Lovecraft-style tale brought into modern times." Libr J

The Grays. Tor 2006 335p $24.95
ISBN 0-765-31389-8
LC 2005-34494

"A Tom Doherty Associates book"

"Danny and Katelyn Callaghan are a happily married couple oblivious that both took a saucer ride as kids—until a UFO sighting in their Indiana town awakens subliminal memories and excites their genius teenage son, Conner. Meanwhile, in a secret facility in Colorado, Air Force Lt. Lauren Glass learns that the Roswell incident really happened, and that for decades the surviving ETs have been sharing their advanced science with us. In ex-

change, these 'Grays' have sought to rejuvenate their dying species by genetically manipulating human receptacles for their DNA. But some military hard-liners see this as a betrayal of humanity, and they launch a manhunt that brings them to Indiana and the Callaghans' doorstep. . . . [The author's] depiction of black ops intrigue and military espionage is a first-rate exercise in literary paranoia." Publ Wkly

The hunger. Pocket Books 1981 357p pa $24.95
ISBN 978-1-416-58374-5

First published 1981 by Morrow

Miriam Blaylock, an ancient vampire, sets out to find a new human companion when her current one begins to age rapidly.

Followed by The last vampire

The last vampire. Pocket Bks. 2001 303p $24.95
ISBN 0-7434-1720-8
LC 2001-21013

Sequel to The hunger (1981)

Miriam Blaylock "plans to attend various conclaves of the Keepers, as vampires refer to themselves. What none of them anticipates, however, is that their human prey has discovered their existence and, what is worse, has the means to eradicate them. First in Thailand, then in France, whole lairs are destroyed by a group of vampire slayers led by CIA agent Paul Ward. Only Miriam manages to escape the slaughter. She flees back to her nest in New York City. Paul wants to follow only to be told by his superiors that the President has decided that vampires have human rights, which means that Paul may be guilty of murder." Libr J

"There's much here to admire, not least Strieber's expert modulation of tone and dialogue as POV shifts from Miriam (fluid, refined) to Paul (muscular, slangy)." Publ Wkly

Majestic. Putnam 1989 317p o.p.
LC 89-8495

The author "combines fictitious confessions and military documents with genuine newspaper reports to depict a reputed encounter with alien beings near New Mexico's Roswell Army Air Field in 1947. What appears to be a disabled U.F.O. is discovered, and a paranoid military appoints a man named Will Stone to direct the investigation—and to conceal the incident in an operation code named Majestic. Forty years later, Stone reveals the cover-up to a shocked reporter, Nicholas Duke, who narrates the tale." N Y Times Book Rev

"Strieber has managed to weave two major themes in ufology (crashes and abductions) into an intriguing and unconventional tale that has both the dialogue and flavor of postwar America as well as the surrealistic aura of contemporary fiction." Booklist

Warday; and the journey onward; [by] Whitley Strieber and James W. Kunetka. Holt, Rinehart & Winston 1984 374p o.p.
LC 83-18678

"On Oct. 28, 1988, the Soviet Union launches a surprise attack on the United States. Ten-megaton atomic bombs detonate over Washington, San Antonio and the eastern edge of Queens. Smaller bombs strike the Minuteman and MX missile fields spread out across the northern plains. Washington and San Antonio are 'instantly vaporized.' Manhattan escapes destruction but is abandoned. Five years later, two writers brave the hazards of post-Warday travel to report back to us on how surviving America 'feels and tastes and smells.'" NY Times Book Rev

Strieber, Whitley—*Continued*

The Wolfen. Morrow 1978 252p o.p.

* LC 78-7482

"Two cops are brutally killed and their guts are devoured by what appears to be a pack of wild animals. The police in charge, a middle-aged slob and a newly fledged woman detective, bicker endlessly through the killings of a blind man, a couple of junkies, and more, while the pack, mutant wolves, kill for food and to keep their secret from being discovered. This is a very specialized form of animal disaster novel, but much more suspenseful and imaginative than most. The windup is total thrill." Libr J

Stroby, Wallace

The barbed-wire kiss. St. Martin's Minotaur 2003 340p $24.95

ISBN 0-312-30034-4   LC 2002-35879

"Ex-cop Harry Rane, recovering from the death of his wife and forced into semi-retirement by a bullet wound, comes to the rescue of his longtime friend Bobby. Bobby has made a big mistake: he has invested money with a partner for a 'one-time' drug buy. The partner has disappeared with the cash, but the supplier, a suspicious character under scrutiny by New Jersey cops, still wants his money." Libr J

"Although the story advances predictably. . . . Stroby does wonders with his blue-collar characters, the hardworking fishermen and mechanics and bar waitresses who put their hand to petty crime the way they play the lottery—to try their luck and get a thrill, the way they did when the seashore was a kinder place to live." N Y Times Book Rev

Stross, Charles

Accelerando. Ace Books; distributed by us 2005 390p

ISBN 0-441-01284-1   LC 2005-42815

"Expanded from several stories originally published in *Asimov's Science Fiction*, . . . [this] novel follows several generations of the Macx family through the rapidly transforming, Internet-enabled global economy of the early twenty-first century to the human and transhuman populated worlds of the outer solar system a half century later. . . . Stross has his thumb squarely on the pulse of technology's leading edge and exults in extrapolating mere glimmers of ideas out to their mind-bending limits." Booklist

Glasshouse. Ace Books 2006 335p $24.95

ISBN 0-44101-403-8   LC 2006-4358

This novel offers a "glimpse at life in the twenty-seventh century. In an era of virtual immortality, where computer backups of human consciousness have become as routine as unlimited body modification, Robin is a patient in a rehab clinic for convalescents of voluntary memory erasure. With only scant clues, contained in a letter from his former self, to his previous and possibly espionage-related career, Robin quickly discovers his new identity offers little protection from several would-be assassins. Seizing the chance to evade his pursuers for good, he volunteers for a three-year experiment, devised by history professors, to simulate the 'dark ages' of early-twenty-first-century society." Publ Wkly

The novel "gives in a little to convention near the end, as the story inevitably progresses toward a rebellion plot, but even here, Stross keeps the sweet little surprises coming. . . . Mostly, Glasshouse is an incisive look into societies that allow themselves, for whatever reason, to be guided not by cooperation and the greater good but by fear and mistrust." SF Reviews.net

Halting state. Ace Books 2007 351p $24.95

ISBN 978-0-441-01498-9; 0-441-01498-4

LC 2007-15872

"The setting is a virtual world called Avalon Four; the year, 2018. Sgt. Sue Smith, an Edinburgh constable, takes on a special case: a bank robbery committed by a team of Orcs with a dragon for backup. As Smith delves further into the case, both in the real and in the virtual worlds, she uncovers evidence that the crime is more than simply a robbery." Libr J

"Brimming with suspense and awash in contemporary references — evidently, iPods and Starbucks will still be popular in 2018 — Stross' storytelling is not only edgy and smart but grounded in human concerns, making State perfect fodder for n00bs and old-timers alike." Wired

Iron sunrise. Ace Bks. 2004 355p $23.95

ISBN 0-441-01159-4

"When the explosion of a G2 star destroys the planet Moscow, the survivors send a counterattack against the suspected attackers, the New Dresden system. When New Dresden denies responsibility, Old Earth agent Rachel Mansour investigates to stave off outright war. Only a teenager named Wednesday knows what's been going on, but she is unaware of her knowledge." Libr J

"Stross skillfully balances suspense and humor throughout, offering readers—especially fans of Iain M. Banks and Ken MacLeod—a fascinating future that seems more than possible." Publ Wkly

The Jennifer morgue; plus bonus story "Pimpf" and afterword: The golden age of spying. Golden Gryphon Press 2006 313p $25.95

ISBN 1-930846-45-2   LC 2006-11154

"Bob Howard is a computer übergeek employed by the Laundry, a secret British agency assigned to clean up incursions from other realities caused by the inadvertent manipulation of complex mathematical equations: in other words, magic. In 1975, the CIA used Howard Hughes's Glomar Explorer in a bungled attempt to raise a sunken Soviet submarine in order to access the Jennifer Morgue, an occult device that allows communication with the dead. Now a ruthless billionaire intends to try again, even if by doing so he awakens the Great Old Ones, who thwarted the earlier expedition. It's up to Bob and a collection of British eccentrics even Monty Python would consider odd to stop the bad guy and save the world, while getting receipts for all expenditures or else face the most dreaded menace of all: the Laundry's own auditors. Stross has a marvelous time making eldritch horror appear commonplace in the face of bureaucracy." Publ Wkly

Saturn's children; a space opera. Ace Books 2008 323p $24.95

ISBN 978-0-441-01594-8   LC 2008-8228

"After the extinction of the human race in the 23rd century, robots and androids continue to function, forming their own stratified society to carry out their creators'

Stross, Charles—*Continued*

dreams of space colonization. Freya Nakamichi 47a femmebot designed as a concubine for a race that no longer exists-occupies a place in society midway between the elite Aristos and the slave-chipped worker robots. Having to make her own way, she accepts a commission to deliver a small package from Mercury to Mars, unaware of the trouble that awaits her as humanoid factions vie for the contents of the package." Libr J

"Stross tosses out ideas aplenty. Since his robots know they were created by humans, for example, they consider evolution heretical. It isn't a relaxing bedtime read, but it is the sort of mind-expanding adventure that made 'hard' science fiction famous." New Scientist

Strout, Elizabeth

Abide with me; a novel. Random 2006 294p $24.95

ISBN 1-4000-6207-1   LC 2005-50380

"The handsome minister Tyler Caskey, of West Annett, Maine, is beloved by his parishioners because he really does think they're all God's children. But in the bleak autumn of 1959, more than a year after the death of his wife, Tyler is still awash in grief. The man who once held them rapt from the pulpit now appears ridiculous up there—'like a big tractor being driven by a teenage kid, slipping in and out of gear'—and his daughter has started screaming and spitting in kindergarten. How can he lead them if he himself is lost? Just as she did in her first novel, 'Amy and Isabelle,' Strout has created an absorbing world peopled by characters who argue the merits of canned cranberry sauce and using one's turn signal; meanwhile, dark fears about Freud and Khrushchev run beneath the surface of their lives like water under ice. With superlative skill, Strout challenges us to examine what makes a good story—and what makes a good life." New Yorker

Amy and Isabelle. Random House 1999 303p $22.95

ISBN 0-375-50134-7   LC 98-19995

"Amy Goodrow, 16, is the shy only child of Isabelle, single mother. Isabelle's shame over the secret of her daughter's illegitimacy and her hunger for respectability keep her painfully isolated from the community of the New England mill town where she has made her home. Even before Amy's relations with her teacher become known, her beauty and her burgeoning sexuality arouse uncomfortable feelings of competitiveness in Isabelle, as well as dread at the prospect of her daughter's flight from Isabelle's carefully constructed nest." Publ Wkly

"As the cacophony of disaster grows ever louder in contemporary culture, Strout has written an excellent novel about enduring the banalities of ordinary life." New Yorker

Olive Kitteridge. Random House 2008 270p $25

ISBN 978-1-4000-6208-9; 1-4000-6208-X

       LC 2007-16999

Contents: Pharmacy; Incoming tide; The piano player; A little burst; Starving; A different road; Winter concert; Tulips; Basket of trips; Ship in a bottle; Security; Criminal; River

"These linked stories introduce the inhabitants of Crosby, Maine, where the pull of domestic tragedy is stronger for rarely being spoken of. Angela doesn't mention the bruises she's noticed on her mother's arm at the nursing home; Marlene learns of her husband's infidelity only after her funeral; Kevin plans to shoot himself, like his mother before him. And there in every story, like a tree that's been blackened by lightning but still leafs in the spring, stands Olive Kitteridge, a retired math teacher who loves her tulips, bullies her husband, and barks at anyone foolish enough to irritate her. You loathe this woman at the book's beginning; you long for her at its finish. Strout makes us experience not only the terrors of change but also the terrifying hope that change can bring: she plunges us into these churning waters and we come up gasping for air." New Yorker

Stuart, Ian, 1922-1987 *See* MacLean, Alistair, 1922-1987

Stubbs, Harry Clement *See* Clement, Hal, 1922-2003

Stubbs, Jean, 1926-

Family games. St. Martin's Press 1994 294p o.p.   LC 93-44054

The Malpas family assembles for Christmas at their Cornwall farmhouse: "headstrong daughter Blanche, an unwed mother, brings her infant son and temporarily abandons her feud with her father, the brilliant and irascible Anthony; recently separated son Edward, still reeling from his wife's departure, arrives with his two children; and beautiful, dependent daughter Lydia surprises the others by bringing a likable woman friend instead of another one of a parade of 'moneyed and moronic' male beaux. At the close of the Malpases' impromptu Christmas Eve open house, three unexpected visitors appear, Magi-like, at the door. One is Natalie, Anthony's imperious twin sister; another is Katrina, Edward's estranged wife; the third is Daniel Kidd, the father of Blanche's child." Publ Wkly

"The writer appears fully in control of this entertaining romp concerning one very dysfunctional, if provocative, family." Booklist

Like we used to be. St. Martin's Press 1990 c1989 387p o.p.   LC 89-27133

First published 1989 in the United Kingdom

"This is the story of Leila and Zoe Gideon, sisters who are in every way different, yet who love each other and their marvelous British family unreservedly. The story begins with Zoe's wedding and Leila's first love affair in the summer of 1953, and spans the next 15 years. Zoe struggles to create a loving home with her difficult husband, Matthew. Leila, the rebellious sister, makes an independent life for herself as an artist in London. Told alternately by Leila and Zoe, the book has leisurely pace filled with emotional detail. This will appeal to lovers of old-fashioned family novels." Libr J

"Social ferment and family history are vigorously blended in a dramatic style characteristic of a master storyteller." Publ Wkly

Stumpf, Douglas

Confessions of a Wall Street shoeshine boy; [by] Doug Stumpf. HarperCollins Publishers 2007 290p $24.95

ISBN 978-0-06-088953-1; 0-06-088953-5

LC 2006-53546

This satirical "novel views corruption at Wall Street's highest levels through the eyes of two outsiders. Gil, who immigrated to New York from São Paulo as a child and retains a Portuguese-flavored grammar, overhears tales of life on the trading floor while shining some of the nicest shoes in business. He absorbs the particulars of a world where jockeying banter about sex, drugs, and pushup contests is interspersed with long hours of watching numbers on a screen, and where the appeal of insider trading as a way to break the tedium becomes unignorable. Stumpf switches between Gil's voice and that of a magazine writer in need of a big story who fastens onto him as a source. As they become entangled in mounting financial and sexual scandals, Stumpf exposes the sordidness in both the financial and the journalistic worlds." New Yorker

Styron, Alexandra

All the finest girls; a novel. Little, Brown 2001 259p $23.95

ISBN 0-316-89080-4

LC 00-50051

"Addy Abraham is 32, single, childless and dissatisfied with her work restoring paintings for a Manhattan museum. Addy is somewhat estranged from her father (a well-known philosophy professor) and from her mother, who relegated a good deal of Addy's upbringing to a Caribbean nanny named Louise; much of the novel takes place on the island of St. Clair, where Addy has traveled for Louise's funeral." N Y Times Book Rev

Styron "beautifully juxtaposes Addy's past and the present on St. Claire, dealing deftly with a series of ironies. Although some readers may find Addy slow to catch on, Styron's gift is to make the reader feel real grief for her characters and real relief for Addy when she begins to make a peace with herself and her parents." Publ Wkly

Styron, William, 1925-2006

The confessions of Nat Turner. Modern Lib. 1994 xliv, 428p hardcover o.p. pa $14

ISBN 0-679-60101-5; 0-679-73663-8 (pa)

* LC 94-9393

A reissue of the title first published 1967 by Random House

This "account of an actual person and event is based on the brief contemporary pamphlet of the same title presented to a trial court as evidence and published in Virginia a year after the revolt of fellow slaves led by Turner in 1831. Imagining much of Turner's youth and early manhood before the rebellion that he headed at the age of 31, Styron in frequently rhetorical and pseudo-Biblical style has Turner recall his religious faith and his power of preaching to other slaves." Oxford Companion to Am Lit. 5th edition

Lie down in darkness. Bobbs-Merrill 1951 400p o.p.

"Mr. Styron takes a marriage for the framework of his story, the journey of a hearse to the cemetery for his action, and the suicide of a young woman for his impetus, his mood, and his climax. The marriage is that of Milton and Helen Loftis, a Virginia couple, and the hearse, which they follow in separate limousines, carries the remains of their daughter Peyton, who is in death, as she was in life, only a symbol of her parents' mutual hatred, their despair, and their overpowering self-pity." New Yorker

"The book is not bleakly written. On the contrary, it is richly and even (in the best sense) poetically written. . . . If the parts seem to succeed each other with no apparent logic or dialectic, each part is brilliantly made and lovingly accomplished." Atlantic

Set this house on fire. Random House 1960 507p o.p.

"The narrator, Peter Leverett, a government employee returning to the U.S., stops in the little Italian village of Sambuco to see his old schoolmate Mason Flagg. The next morning the satyrical Flagg is found dead at the base of a cliff, a peasant girl has been raped and beaten until she dies, and Cass Kinsolving, a drunken, psychoneurotic American painter and the butt of Flagg's devilish humor, has temporarily disappeared. Though the case is written off as one of murder and suicide, the remainder of the novel probes minutely the past lives of the main characters, focusing through Peter's concern and his desire to know the whole truth. A large part of the action takes place in the Mediterranean village, but the novel is also one of contemporary America and Americans; of a world of conflict, too much wealth, too much sex and commercialism, too prevalent shallowness and lack of values." Libr J

Sophie's choice. Modern Lib. 1998 599p $22; pa $14

ISBN 0-679-60289-5; 0-679-73637-9 (pa)

* LC 97-36895

A reissue of the title first published 1979

"Sophie Zawistowska is a Polish Catholic who has somehow survived Auschwitz and resettled in America after the war. Here, in a Jewish boarding house in Flatbush, she meets two men—Nathan Landau, a brilliant but dangerously unstable Jew who becomes her lover; and Stingo, a young Southern writer (and autobiographical simulacrum of Styron himself). The novel traces Stingo's intense involvement with the lovers—their euphoric highs as well as their cataclysmic descents into psychopathy—and his growing fascination with the horror of Sophie's past." Libr J

"It was a daring act for Styron, whose sensibilities are wholly Southern, to venture into the territory of the American Jew, to say nothing of his plunge into European history. The book is powerfully moving." Burgess. 99 Novels

Sullivan, Eleanor

(ed) Fifty years of the best from Ellery Queen's Mystery Magazine. See Fifty years of the best from Ellery Queen's Mystery Magazine

Sundaresan, Indu

In the Convent of Little Flowers; stories. Atria Books 2008 216p $22

ISBN 978-1-4165-8609-8; 1-4165-8609-1

LC 2008-34437

Contents: Shelter of rain; Three and a half seconds; The faithful wife; Fire; The most unwanted; The key club; Bedside dreams; The chosen one; Hunger

Sundaresan "bluntly questions how evolved the globalized world truly is in these stories of individuals trapped between India's archaic traditions and blitz into modernity. . . . Sundaresan (The Twentieth Wife) bluntly questions how evolved the globalized world truly is in these stories of individuals trapped between India's archaic traditions and blitz into modernity." Publ Wkly

The splendor of silence; a novel. Atria Books 2006 403p $25

ISBN 978-0-7432-8367-0; 0-7432-8367-8

LC 2006-48364

"Flashbacks to 1940s India occur when Olivia receives a mysterious trunk that promises to explain who she is. The trunk arrives on the same day that her father, Sam, dies and contains information about her biological mother, Mila. Through a letter hidden among the keepsakes in the box, Olivia learns that her father spent time in India searching for his missing brother. While there, he fell in love with Mila, the daughter of the local political agent and fiancée of a prince. It was also there that he got to know Mila's brothers, who knew the whereabouts of his own brother. A series of events leads to the arrival of the trunk for Olivia years later. Sundaresan's descriptive writing style makes for a colorful, engrossing read, and while the story does hop between time periods and locations, the reader is never lost along the way." Libr J

Suri, Manil

The age of Shiva; a novel. W. W. Norton 2008 455p $24.95

ISBN 978-0-393-06569-5; 0-393-06569-3

LC 2007-37322

"Coming of age in Delhi in the fifties, Meera takes her father's atheism and progressive attitudes for granted, but she keenly resents the tyrannies of her favored older sister, who forces Meera to play the go-between in her romance with the handsome Dev. When Dev is dumped for a more suitable fiancé, Meera rashly attempts to console him; soon she is stuck with yet another of her sister's hand-me-downs—this time, forever. Dev drinks too much, and his family lives in a one-bedroom flat by the railroad tracks. Only when Meera conceives a child will she truly have something to call her own. Suri's . . . novel is a sensuous, nuanced portrait of motherhood, but it also sparks with the frictions of being female in an India where television soaps and political slogans compete noisily with Hindu myth." New Yorker

The death of Vishnu. Norton 2001 295p $24.95

ISBN 0-393-05042-4　　　　LC 00-58414

"The lives and loves of residents of an apartment house in Bombay unfold as Vishnu, a drunk, lies dying on the steps that serve as his home. As his neighbors argue over the cost of an ambulance, the sick man drifts in and out of consciousness, reflecting on the meaning of his life." Libr J

"Its clever structure allows [this book] to display a manageable cross-section of contemporary Indian life, including class and religious frictions. But Suri . . . has more to offer here than gentle social comedy. During the course of the novel, Vishnu's soul disentangles itself from his earthly remains and begins ascending the apartment house stairs. As this spirit looks back on the life just ending, Suri's novel achieves an eerie and memorable transcendence." Time

Süskind, Patrick

Perfume: the story of a murderer; translated from the German by John E. Woods. Knopf 1986 255p o.p.

* LC 86-45419

Original German edition, 1985

Set in eighteenth-century France, Perfume relates the "tale of Jean-Baptiste Grenouille, a person as gifted as he was abominable. Born without a smell of his own but endowed with an extraordinary sense of smell, Grenouille becomes obsessed with procuring the perfect scent that will make him fully human." Libr J

"Those readers who feel they are wasting their time with novels unless they are picking up facts will welcome Süskind's encyclopedic overview of the methods of making perfume. Like the best scents, there is something fundamentally formulaic about this novel, but its effects will linger long after it has been stoppered." Time

Sutcliff, Rosemary, 1920-1992

Sword at sunset. Coward-McCann 1963 495p o.p.

A novel based on historical facts about the legendary Arthur. "The time is the century after the last Roman legions leave Britain, and Arthur is desperately striving to hold Britain against the Saxons, Picts, and other invading savage tribes. [This is] the story of his tragic fate, his good times and bad." Publ Wkly

Sutherland, J. A. See Sutherland, John, 1938-

Sutherland, John, 1938-

(ed) The Oxford book of English love stories. See The Oxford book of English love stories

Svevo, Italo, 1861-1928

Zeno's conscience; translated from the Italian by William Weaver with an introduction by Elizabeth Hardwick. Knopf 2001 xlix, 437p $20 o.p.

ISBN 0-375-41330-8

* LC 2001-40821

"Everyman's library"

Original Italian edition, 1923; previous English translations had title: The confessions of Zeno

"Confessions of Zeno is disguised as the story of [the author's] life as prepared by a psychoanalyst's patient for his doctor, and it is a masterpiece of sleepy wit and biting irony. Zeno is a foolish fellow. He is lazy, inquisitive, a master of indecision, always planning to give up his pet vices, always trying new careers, always expecting to do great things at something else, salving his con-

Svevo, Italo, 1861-1928—*Continued*

science after each relapse and failure in the most mischievous, comic and natural ways. There is no describable plot to Zeno's confessions." Outlook

This is "a highly human story and its material is fundamentally as sound as its method. . . . The work of a man who wrote to please himself, it has an individuality and originality you cannot escape noticing, and it has, too, a fine and comprehensive knowledge of its character." N Y Times Book Rev

Swain, James

Midnight rambler; a novel of suspense. Ballantine Books 2007 350p $24.95

ISBN 978-0-345-47546-6; 0-345-47546-1

LC 2007-28324

"As a specialist in finding missing children, Jack [Carpenter] occasionally picks up jobs from South Florida police departments and distraught parents, but that barely pays the bills. He trades his services as a security guard for part of the rent on a studio apartment above a bar in Dania Beach where he lives with a terrific dog. Once one of Broward's finest who hunted down the area's most notorious criminals, Jack was fired for assaulting a prisoner. A civil lawsuit left him nearly broke and he's separated from his wife. But his greatest fear is not his living situation — it's that Simon Skell, a killer known as the Midnight Rambler whom Jack helped to convict, will be released on a technicality. When evidence starts to indicate that Simon may be innocent, Jack goes into hyper mode. The police won't help him, but Jack finds an unusual ally in a FBI agent whose own daughter vanished." South Florida Sun-Sentinel

"No one would accuse James Swain of writing mandarin prose; in fact, he uses language with such blunt force he could be hammering in nails." N Y Times Book Rev

Swann, Maxine

Flower children. Riverhead Books 2007 211p $21.95

ISBN 978-1-594-48945-7; 1-594-48945-9

LC 2006-39269

This novel is "made up of vignettes about four sibling 'flower children' whose parents are Pennsylvania farm country back-to-the-land hippies. Swann portrays the free-floating '70s coming-of-age of these four siblings— Lu, Maeve (who narrates much of the novel), Tuck and Clyde—who delight in running freely in the countryside, but grow embarrassed by the unconventional practices of their politically active, casual-dressing parents. Their parents, Sam, a Harvard graduate, and Dee, a gardener and artist, built their own house, and though they aim to raise their children in an ideal world 'in which nothing is lied about, whispered about, and nothing is ever concealed,' the parents separate, and subsequent storylike chapters delineate their children's sometimes rocky confrontation with the world of TVs, junk food and schoolyard cliques." Publ Wkly

"Swann evokes the wonder of childhood with an almost hallucinatory precision." Vogue

Swanwick, Michael

The best of Michael Swanwick. Subterranean Press 2008 469p $38

ISBN 978-1-59606-178-1; 1-59606-178-2

Contents: The feast of Saint Janis Ginungagap; Trojan horse; A midwinter's tale; The edge of the world; Griffin's egg; The changeling's tale; North of Diddy-Wah-Diddy; Radio waves; The dead; Mother Grasshopper; Radiant doors; The very pulse of the machine; Wild minds; Scherzo with tyannosaur; The raggle taggle gypsy-o; The dog said bowwow; Slow life; Legions in time; Triceratops summer; From Babel's fall'n glory we fled

"More than a quarter century's worth of short fiction is gathered in this comprehensive collection of stories. . . . The tales run the gamut from strict space adventures like 'The Very Pulse of the Machine' to deceptively complex ghost stories like 'Radio Waves.' . . . Swanwick's blend of savvy science fiction, Freudian fantasy and topnotch storytelling both chills and charms." Publ Wkly

Bones of the earth. HarperCollins Pubs. 2002 335p

ISBN 0-380-97836-9

LC 2001-40196

"Swanwick writes about paleontologists who travel back to the Mesozoic to study dinosaurs firsthand, with a technology supplied by enigmatic aliens. . . . His focus never strays far from the two reluctant collaborators, Griffin and the Old Man, who have transformed paleontology into an experimental science. The air of competence they adopt in their day-to-day operations cannot mask their anxiety over who ultimately are the experimenters and who are the subjects." N Y Times Book Rev

The dog said bow-wow. Tachyon Publications 2007 296p pa $14.95

ISBN 978-1-892391-52-0; 1-892391-52-X

Contents: "Hello," said the stick; The dog said bow-wow; Slow life; Triceratops summer; Tin marsh; An episode of stardust; The skysailor's tale; Legions in time; The little cat laughed to see such sport; The bordello in Faerie; The last geek; Gils and boys, come out to play; A great day for brontosaurs; Dirty little war; A small room in Koboldtown; Urdumheim

"There is a camaraderie about the stories Michael Swanwick has assembled in The Dog Said Bow-Wow, a willingness to share their deepest ingenuities with the reader, that makes the book almost tingle in the mind: wagging its tale to tell more. What the stories in this collection are so good at doing, to put it another way, is being stories. They wear their hearts on their sleeves. This is not exactly to say that Michael Swanwick does the same. The other side of the exuberance of The Dog Said Bow-Wow is a severe chastity of reticence. Michael Swanwick is a teller, but he does not tell himself. But we cannot fault a writer for selecting his remit. And the polished variousness of Swanwick's gift is in itself gift enough." Sci Fi Wkly

Swarthout, Glendon Fred

Bless the beasts and children; [by] Glendon Swarthout. Doubleday 1970 205p o.p.

*

"Six rich teenagers, rejected by their parents and avoided by their peers, group together at Box Canyon Summer Boys' Camp. Fragile egos and self-destructive personalities begin to heal under the leadership of Cotton, who gently pokes fun at their soft spots while building up their self-esteem. An effort on the part of the

Swarthout, Glendon Fred—*Continued*

group to stop the wanton slaughter of buffalo provides a high point of suspense." Shapiro. Fic for Youth. 3d edition

The shootist; [by] Glendon Swarthout. Doubleday 1975 186p o.p.

"J. B. Books, last of the West's big-time gunfighters and stoic sufferer of terminal cancer, plays out his death rites. Ensconced in a boarding house in El Paso, Books is approached by a host of exploiters who desire to use his impending death to enhance their own reputations and monetary status; the shootist, however, plans otherwise. He maneuvers his adversaries' self-aggrandizing behavior to his advantage, engineering them to carry out his desire; a quick and respectable death by bullet." Booklist

"This is definitely more than a Western; the characterization is flawless, the plot absorbing and convincing." Libr J

Swerling, Beverly

Shadowbrook; a novel of love and war; Beverly Swerling. Simon & Schuster 2004 490p il $24.95
  ISBN 0-7432-2812-X   LC 2003-64127

"Covering the years 1754-1760, with the British, French and Indians slaughtering each other for king and empire, Swerling tells of two men who straddle the white and red man's worlds, desperate to preserve the best of each culture, but fearful they will lose everything they love. Quentin Hale is a gentleman turned scout whose family owns a prosperous New York plantation called Shadowbrook. He is white, but also follows the Indian ways of his adopted tribe, the Potawatomi. Cormac Shea is part-Irish and part-Indian, nearly a brother to Hale, but he wants all whites driven from Canada. Together these men find themselves caught up in a bloody war neither wants, but they must fight to save the plantation and create a homeland for the Indians. . . . Surrounding them are colorful historical figures like the young George Washington, the hapless General Braddock and the powerful Ottawa chief, Pontiac." Publ Wkly

Swift, Graham, 1949-

Last orders. Knopf 1996 294p o.p.
                                      * LC 96-13726

"On a bleak spring day, four men meet in their favorite pub in a working-class London neighborhood. They are about to begin a pilgrimage to scatter the ashes of a fifth man, Jack Dodds, friend since WWII of three of them, adoptive father to the fourth. By the time they reach the seaside town where Jack's 'last orders' have sent them, the tangled relationship among the men, their wives and their children has obliquely been revealed." Publ Wkly

"The narrative is parceled out among . . . four men, as well as Amy, the widow, Vince's wife, Mandy, and Jack, the dead man. The accent is flat London vernacular, and the tone varies between mordant humor, gentle regret, and deep sorrow. Swift carries off this feat of ventriloquism with admirable skill." N Y Rev Books

Tomorrow. Alfred A. Knopf 2007 255p $23.95
  ISBN 978-0-307-26690-3   LC 2007-18684

This novel "has its roots in the 1960s sexual awakening and takes place over the course of a sleepless night in June 1995. Paula Campbell Hook lies awake beside her sleeping husband, Mike, and worries about the shocking revelation that she and Mike will make to their 16-year-old twins tomorrow." Publ Wkly

"The need to hold our interest is more than adequately covered by Paula's poignant account of what was required of her and Mike when she resolved to become pregnant, and the psychological adjustments subsequently required of both of them; this is Graham Swift at his impressive best in entering the minds of people with whom he can have little genuine connection or affinity." Times Lit Suppl

Waterland. Poseidon Press 1984 309p il
  ISBN 0-671-49863-0
                                      * LC 83-21248

This novel "concerns Tom Crick, an English history teacher in his mid-50s who, as the novel opens, has just been forced to accept early retirement. In response to his students' belief that history is a 'fairy-tale' and only the 'here and now' matters, Crick has abandoned the formal curriculum to tell stories about his childhood in East England's Fens. The headmaster, a physicist, shares the students' opinion of the past, and Crick's 'trying to put himself into history' is the last straw. But Crick won't go–his students are for once interested in his 'crazy yarns' until one day his wife goes mad and steals a baby from a supermarket shopping cart. The prospect of retirement gives Crick the freedom to tell his pupils the lurid story that lies behind his wife's theft." Nation

"The novel exceeds credibility and attenuates our tolerance in exactly the same degree as it creates, through [Swift's] own words, the portrait of a man who is deeply disturbed, and who is vainly attempting to build a structure from these words which will protect him from his childlessness, from his failure to create the future." Times Lit Suppl

Swift, Jonathan, 1667-1745

Gulliver's travels; with an introduction by Pat Rogers. Knopf 1991 xlv, 318p map $20
  ISBN 0-679-40545-3
                                      * LC 91-53011

"Everyman's library"
First published 1726

"In the account of his four wonder-countries Swift satirizes contemporary manners and morals, art and politics—in fact the whole social scheme—from four different points of view. The huge Brobdingnagians reduce man to his natural insignificance, the little people of Lilliput parody Europe and its petty broils, in Laputa philosophers are ridiculed, and finally all Swift's hatred and contempt find their satisfaction in degrading humanity to a bestial condition." Baker. Guide to the Best Fic

Swift, Margaret *See* Drabble, Margaret, 1939-

Symons, Julian, 1912-1994

The Kentish manor murders. Viking 1988 191p
o.p.   LC 87-40460
"A Viking novel of mystery and suspense"

"The detective in this book is an actor famous for his Sherlock Holmes readings. A reclusive billionaire en-

Symons, Julian, 1912-1994—*Continued*
gages him for a private reading. It seems that the man is a Conan Doyle enthusiast and a collector of Holmesiana. It seems also that an unknown Sherlock Holmes story has just turned up and the actor is asked to be a go-between in a sale to the billionaire. But is he really the billionaire? Or is he an impersonator? Fun and games, in Mr. Symons' best style." N Y Times Book Rev

Something like a love affair. Mysterious Press 1992 199p o.p.   LC 92-5980
"Judith is in bad shape long before she finds out the sordid truth about her husband, a successful architect of perfectionist temperament. Bored to distraction by her doll-like existence in a Sussex suburb . . . she has been writing herself passionate love letters cribbed from historical romances. When that mute cry for attention goes unnoticed, Judith throws herself into an obsessive affair with the loutish youth who has been giving her driving lessons. The next step is murder." N Y Times Book Rev
"Symons' tale is chillingly and compellingly told. Exploring the dark underside of the human spirit, it's story of a desperate woman who can no longer cope." Booklist

Szirtes, George, 1948-

(tr) Karinthy, F. Metropole

T

Tabucchi, Antonio, 1943-

It's getting later all the time; a novel in the form of letters; translated from the Italian by Alastair McEwen. New Directions 2006 232p pa $15.95
ISBN 978-0-8112-1546-6; 0-8112-1546-6
LC 2006-7369
Original Italian edition, 2001
"This epistolary novel is composed of 18 love letters; the fictional authors are 17 men and one woman, whose sweeping, summative voice closes the collection abruptly. . . . Written from places all over Europe, the letters are intimate and often exquisite, lingering over transcendent details of landscape, or ruefully soliloquizing on memory. One rancorous letter, 'A Good Man Like You,' recalls a betrayal seven years in the past, while another contemplates a journey never taken: 'Do you remember when we didn't go to Samarkand?' The whole makes for delicious voyeurism, leavened with pointed bafflement at these partially rendered relationships: just as the reader wishes for all the gaps to be filled in, the letter writers wish to recompose fractured relationships." Publ Wkly

Tademy, Lalita

Cane River. Warner Bks. 2001 418p il
ISBN 0-446-53052-2   LC 00-43682
"Five generations and a hundred years in the life of a matriarchal black Louisiana family are encapsulated in this . . . novel that is based in part upon the lives, as preserved in both historical record and oral tradition, of the author's ancestors. . . . Her frank observations about

black racism add depth to the tale, and she demonstrates that although the practice of slavery fell most harshly upon blacks, and especially women, it also constricted the lives and choices of white men. Photos of and documents relating to Tademy's ancestors add authenticity to a fascinating story." Publ Wkly

Talarigo, Jeff, 1961-

The ginseng hunter. Nan A. Talese 2007 177p $21.95
ISBN 978-0-385-51739-3; 0-385-51739-4
LC 2007-11395
"A nameless middle-aged Chinese man-whose mother was Chinese and father was Korean-maintains a quiet, relatively stable life gathering the valuable ginseng root. In strict adherence to family traditions, he takes only a single root a day when he can find them; once a month he stays overnight in the city of Yanji, at Miss Wong's bordello. On one such trip, he spends the night with a young North Korean refugee who tells a harrowing story of oppression. Alternating with her story is the tale of a North Korean mother and young daughter who are forcibly separated during famine." Publ Wkly
"From the smallest flowers to the majestic mountain landscape, Talarigo unobtrusively pays homage to the expansive beauty that still exists all around, as if gently buffering the pain of the landscape's inhabitants. . . . While Talarigo is an expert at luring us out of our comfort zones to bear witness with him, he also gives us quiet heroes who do not give in, who do not give up." Christ Sci Monit

Tallis, Frank

A death in Vienna. Grove Press 2006 c2005 458p $22
ISBN 0-8021-1815-1   LC 2005-50318
First published 2005 in the United Kingdom with title: Mortal mischief
A "whodunit set in turn-of-the-century Vienna. The circumstances of medium Charlotte Lowenstein's murder befuddle Detective Oskar Rheinhardt from the start: her body is found in a room locked from the inside. She has been shot, but there's evidence of neither a bullet nor a gun. Rheinhardt decides to consult his longtime friend, psychoanalyst Max Liebermann. Although all signs point to a supernatural killer, Liebermann, who puts a premium on hypnosis, dreams, and accidental utterances (Freudian slips), isn't so sure." Booklist
"Tallis deftly brings to life a city of contrasts, caught between polite manners and virulent antiSemitism. This first volume in a new historical series should appeal to Sherlock Holmes fans as well as those of John Dixon Carr's locked-room puzzlers." Libr J

Tan, Amy

The bonesetter's daughter. Putnam 2001 353p
ISBN 0-399-14643-1   LC 00-62673
The novel "is divided into three sections. The first, set in present-day California, introduces us to Ruth Young, a Chinese-American woman whose 10-year relationship with the man she loves is deteriorating for reasons she doesn't understand. . . .The middle section of the novel is the memoir written a few years earlier by Ruth's

Tan, Amy—*Continued*

mother, LuLing, so that her daughter will know the truth about LuLing's life in China. The third section focuses once more on Ruth, and what she will do with the knowledge she has gained." N Y Times Book Rev

"A fine and highly readable novel, The Bonesetter's Daughter is essentially about writing and the act of writing, what fuels it and how it is created. More specifically still, it is about how we, as women creatively express ourselves via language." Women's Rev Books

The hundred secret senses. Putnam 1995 358p o.p.   LC 95-31791

"Nearing divorce from her husband, Simon, Olivia Yee is guided by her elder half-sister, the irrepressible Kwan, into the heart of China. Olivia was five when 18-year-old Kwan first joined her family in the United States, and though always irritated by Kwan's oddities, Olivia was entranced by her eerie dreams of the ghost World of Yin. Only when visiting Kwan's home in Changmian does Olivia realize the dreams are, in Kwan's mind, memories from past lives. . . . Tan tells a mysterious, believable story and delivers Kwan's clipped, immigrant voice and engaging personality with charming clarity." Libr J

The Joy Luck Club. Putnam 1989 288p $24.95 ISBN 0-399-13420-4

*   * LC 88-26492

"Four aging Chinese women who knew life in China before 1949 and now live in San Francisco meet regularly to play mah-jongg and share thoughts about their American-born children. In alternating sections we learn about the cultural differences between the elderly 'aunties' and the younger generation. When one of the older women dies, her daughter is pressed to take her place in the Joy Luck Club. Her feeling of being out of place gradually gives way to an understanding of the need to retain cultural continuity and an appreciation for the strength and endurance of the older women." Shapiro. Fic for Youth. 3d edition

The kitchen god's wife. Putnam 1991 415p o.p.
*   * LC 91-7828

"Pressed to tell her American-born daughter the truth about her life in China, Winnie unburdens herself of old angers and fears, recounting her violent, war-wrenched youth and the barbaric tyranny of her arranged marriage." Am Libr

"Within the peculiar construction of Amy Tan's second novel is a harrowing, compelling and at times bitterly humorous tale in which an entire world unfolds in a Tolstoyan tide of event and detail." N Y Times Book Rev

Saving fish from drowning. Putnam 2005 474p $26.95

ISBN 0-399-15301-2   LC 2005-48724

"On an ill-fated art expedition into the southern Shan state of Burma, eleven Americans leave their Floating Island Resort for a Christmas-morning tour-and disappear. . . . They find themselves deep in the jungle, where they encounter a tribe awaiting the return of the leader and the mythical book of wisdom that will protect them from the ravages and destruction of the Myanmar military regime." Publisher's note

"Amy Tan has created a meta-fable of Orwellian stature, where Americans abroad think they know best, yet follow others blindly; where illusions and assumptions meet self-righteousness and arrogance." Ms.

Tanenbaum, Robert

Act of revenge; a novel; [by] Robert K. Tannenbaum. HarperCollins Pubs. 1999 402p $25

ISBN 0-06-019218-6   LC 98-54268

"Butch Karp, chief assistant New York DA, and his cohorts are trying to figure out the who and why of an important mafioso's murder. Karp's wife, security consultant Marlene Ciampi, is puzzling over a case of her own involving a Mafia wife and is almost killed in the process. Karp's 12-year-old genius daughter, Lucy, a language whiz and as inscrutable as her Chinese friends, turns out to be important to both cases and at serious risk." Booklist

"Tanenbaum has crafted a believably twisted gem of a gangster tale with visceral action and smooth comic relief in a technicolor, Big Apple setting that waxes nostalgic for the 'gentleman' killers of yesteryear." Publ Wkly

Corruption of blood; [by] Robert K. Tanenbaum. Dutton 1995 347p

ISBN 0-525-93870-2

*   * LC 95-12803

When Butch Karp "is lured from his unhappy berth in the Manhattan District Attorney's office to assist in the recently reopened Kennedy investigation, he must wade through conspiracy theories, stale evidence and the perennial Washington quagmire. . . . Karp's wife, the formidable Marlene Ciampi . . . joins her husband in the capital. Marlene, reluctant to join the 'wife-of' set, soon takes up an avenue of inquiry seemingly unrelated to the Kennedy conundrum when she sets out to clear the besmirched name of Richard Dobbs, the father of Karp's Congressional sponsor, who died in 1963. As in all good thrillers, everything that rises must converge, and so it is with Marlene's sleuthing and her husband's." N Y Times Book Rev

Falsely accused; [by] Robert K. Tanenbaum. Dutton 1996 304p

ISBN 0-525-94168-1   LC 96-17305

A legal thriller featuring married lawyers Butch Karp and Marlene Ciampi. In this episode "Bruce has spent over a year as the well-compensated pit bull litigator for a downtown law firm, and Marlene is getting antsy after a year-plus as a full-time mom. Soon Marlene partners with cop Harry Bello in a PI firm, and Karp sues New York City for former Chief Medical Examiner Murray Selig, fired at the urging of Manhattan DA (and Karp/Ciampi nemesis) Sanford Bloom. Tanenbaum draws together subplots involving political and police corruption, domestic violence, and illegal immigration in an involving tale that also illuminates Karp's and Ciampi's romantic and parental challenges." Booklist

Hoax; a novel; [by] Robert K. Tanenbaum. 1st Atria Books hardcover ed. Atria Books 2004 490p $25.95

ISBN 0-7434-5288-7   LC 2004-47941

A suspense novel featuring New York District Attorney Butch Karp. "The vicious murder of a West Coast rapper sets things in motion, unleashing a white-hot cascade of events that expose violence, greed, and corruption not only at the NYPD and the DA's office but also at the city's Catholic archdiocese. Tanenbaum . . . rentlessly builds suspense and gets ever closer to the hearts and minds of his singular characters." Booklist

Tanenbaum, Robert—*Continued*

Immoral certainty; [by] Robert K. Tanenbaum. Dutton 1991 282p

ISBN 0-525-24941-9 LC 90-13841

"The action is set mainly in the wilds of New York City's East Village, where a serial killer who brutalizes children is on the rampage. There's also a messy Mob hit in Little Italy to complicate the lives of no-nonsense D.A. Butch Karp and his colleague and 'occasional main squeeze,' Marlene. Are the cases related? And just how involved is one Felix Tighe, an ambitious yet minor-league criminal with a major-league mother fixation. The novel boasts a wealth of well-developed characters (the principals as well as the minor players); a slew of gallows humor; and a visceral prose style ideally suited to dealing with the sickening brutality of child abuse." Booklist

Irresistible impulse; [by] Robert K. Tanenbaum. Dutton 1997 346p

ISBN 0-525-94310-2 LC 97-16331

A legal thriller featuring NYDA Butch Karp and his wife Marlene Ciampi, the head of her own PI firm. "Against the advice of everyone from his boss to his secretary, Karp takes on the prosecution of a high-visibility defendant: a young white man charged with the brutal murders of elderly black women. Meanwhile, Marlene's cases win more publicity than she needs, as well as threats to her safety and that of her family." Booklist

Tanenbaum's "authentic background detail and his likable characters provide irresistible entertainment." Publ Wkly

Reckless endangerment; [by] Robert K. Tanenbaum. Dutton 1998 324p $23.95

ISBN 0-525-94347-1 LC 98-4902

This thriller "pits Deputy DA Karp, his detective cronies Raney and Fulton and his security-expert wife, Marlene, against an amorphous army of Palestinians terrorizing New York." Publ Wkly

"Tanenbaum controls the strands of his complex plot and maintains readers' interest in the growing Karp-Ciampi clan." Booklist

Reversible error; [by] Robert K. Tanenbaum. Dutton 1992 294p

ISBN 0-525-93423-5 LC 91-34464

New York "assistant D.A. Butch Karp faces a dilemma. A rogue cop is on the streets, taking out drug dealers, but Karp's investigation is brought to a halt when he is asked to suppress evidence. Sharing center stage with Karp's case is that of the D.A.'s colleague and lover, Marlene, who is on the trail of a rapist who wraps a pair of panty hose around each victim. With some unexpected help, Marlene spots a similarity in the victims. . . . With twin plots sizzling and exploding, the novel takes us inside the psyches of its characters, revealing the crime fighters' dark humor, rigid notions of right and wrong, and righteous anger." Booklist

True justice; [by] Robert K. Tanenbaum. Pocket Bks. 2000 374p il

ISBN 0-7434-0589-7 LC 00-708721

"Butch Karp, New York's assistant district attorney, and wife Marlene Ciampi, who heads an agency concerned with protecting battered women, find themselves in the middle of a crisis-and at each other's throats-when a newborn is murdered and the public demands that the teenaged mother be held accountable. Then their precocious daughter, Lucy gets involved." Libr J

"Each of the deftly drawn characters wrestles with the moral dilemmas raised by the intertwined plots in a believable way, and readers will close *True Justice's* final page satisfied they've wrestled with those dilemmas a bit themselves." Booklist

Tanizaki, Jun'ichirō, 1886-1965

The Makioka sisters; translated and introduced by Edward G. Seidensticker. Knopf 1993 xxxv,498p $20

ISBN 0-679-943452-0

* LC 92-55051

"Everyman's library"

Original Japanese edition, 1949; this translation first published 1957

"The four Makioka sisters represent the upper middle-class Japanese tradition and customs, though their circumstances leave them little substance to support this way of life. Two of the four sisters are unmarried. The elder, Yukiko, is retiring and highly conscious of her place in society. The younger, Taeko, is more susceptible to pernicious influences of a changing society. The conflict of personalities and environmental adjustments provide the motivating center for this novel." Libr J

"The narrative is very quiet, very leisurely. At times it seems interminable, but it is like the pigment used by a Renaissance painter to build up his picture. It is done with utmost skill and results in a dignified masterpiece of great beauty and quality." Chicago Sunday Trib

Tanner, Edward Everett *See* Dennis, Patrick, 1921-1976

Tapply, William G.

Bitch Creek; a novel. Lyon's Press 2004 292p $22.95

ISBN 1-592-28435-3 LC 2004-48954

"Stoney Calhoun works in Kate Balaban's bait/tackle shop in small-town Maine but has gaps in his memory after five years in an institution. When mutual friend and fishing guide Lyle goes missing, Stoney searches, finding the man's 'secret' trout stream and the man himself suspiciously drowned. Lyle's client, meanwhile, has disappeared. Aided by determination, logic, a psychic vision or two, and Kate's love, Stoney discovers that he was the intended target and that he's really an experienced investigator." Libr J

The author "mixes crisp plotting and character development with a subtle sense of time and place." Booklist

Client privilege. Delacorte Press 1990 260p o.p.

LC 89-23729

"Acting on behalf of his client and best friend, Judge Popowski (Pops) [Boston attorney] Coyne meets a TV reporter, Wayne Churchill, who threatens the judge's virtually certain appointment to the federal courts. Implicitly trusting the judge's statement that the newsman has no real grounds for blackmail, Coyne refuses Churchill's demand of $10,000 for his silence. The reporter's murder that same night brings the police to question the attorney, who, standing on client privilege, withholds Pops's name

Tapply, William G.—*Continued*

and therefore risks his own arrest as the killer. The circumstances force Coyne to search for the guilty party in order to clear himself." Publ Wkly

Close to the bone. St. Martin's Press 1996 208p o.p.   LC 96-18990

"A Thomas Dunne book"

Boston lawyer Brady Coyne "recommends Paul Cizek, a fishing buddy and a defense attorney with a reputation as a miracle worker, to defend a client's son involved in a fatal DUI rap. Cizek takes and wins the case, but privately explains to Coyne how his victories are eating at him. He detests the people he is defending—the child molester, the Mafia hit man and now an unremorseful alcoholic. When Cizek, depressed and separated from his wife, disappears and his empty boat is found drifting in a storm, the police assume accident or suicide. But Coyne's investigation, undertaken at the behest of Cizek's wife, and accruing dead bodies suggest more sinister possibilities. . . . Tapply treats his characters and his readers with respect." Publ Wkly

Cutter's run; a Brady Coyne novel. St. Martin's Press 1998 274p $23.95

ISBN 0-312-18561-8   LC 98-5331

"Boston lawyer Brady Coyne, in rural Maine for the weekend to visit his 'virtual spouse' Alex, stops and offers Charlotte Gillespie, a middle-aged black woman, a ride. In short order, someone poisons her dog and paints swastikas on her cabin door. Then Charlotte disappears. Brady explores the obvious: wanna-be klansmen and skinheads. Brady eventually realizes it may have been Carlotte's past and not her present—as an unwelcome resident in an unfriendly town—that resulted in her disappearance. Brady also realizes his relationship with Alex may not be as rock solid as he thought. . . . [This] mystery reaffirms Tapply's reputation for sound plotting, sterling dialogue, and poignant glimpses into the heart of a lonely man." Booklist

Dead meat; a Brady Coyne mystery. Scribner 1987 213p o.p.   LC 86-26143

"Heeding the call of one of his eccentric, well-to-do clients, Brady packs rod and reel and journeys to Raven Lake Lodge in the wilds of Maine, where his friend Tiny Wheeler, the lodge's owner, is trying to cope with the disappearance of a guest and a takeover bid by a group of Indian activists, who contend that the lodge is situated on sacred tribal ground. It doesn't take Brady long to realize that the situations are inextricably linked in a web of intrigue that points toward organized crime." Booklist

Dead winter; a Brady Coyne novel. Delacorte Press 1989 230p o.p.   LC 88-13867

"A friend's daughter-in-law has been murdered on board the family yacht and Brady Coyne, the attorney-turned-sleuth, is called in when all fingers point to the victim's husband. This is the first in a trio of murders in which Brady becomes involved. A mysterious bald man is murdered in a nearby town and a young waitress with a brutal husband is slain locally. Yet only Brady sees the connections and starts a search to find out not only who-dun-it, but how these three unrelated murders are connected." West Coast Rev Books

"The plot takes some gothic turns—bastardy, incest, and earlier violent death—but Tapply never neglects his nicely defined characterizations or loses his cool control over narrative tension in this very satisfying caper." Publ Wkly

First light; the first ever Brady Coyne/J.W. Jackson novel; [by] William G. Tapply and Philip R. Craig. Scribner 2002 351p $24

ISBN 0-7432-2208-3   LC 2001-49053

This mystery, set on Martha's Vineyard, features "Boston lawyer Brady Coyne and former cop J.W. Jackson. . . . When tough businessman Jack Bannerman's wife goes missing, he hires private detective Jackson to find her. A parallel missing person's case develops when Coyne, Jackson's buddy, arrives for a fishing derby, only to see his elderly client Sarah Fairchild's private nurse vanish mysteriously in the midst of a nasty dispute over the future of ailing Mrs. Fairchild's sizable beachfront property." Publ Wkly

Muscle memory; a Brady Coyne novel. St. Martin's Press 1999 257p $23.95

ISBN 0-312-20563-5   LC 99-22042

When Boston "lawyer Brady Coyne agrees to handle a divorce case, he opens the door to trouble. His client, in hock to the mob, disappears, and his client's wife is found murdered." Libr J

Tapply "integrates Coyne's personal travails and his professional obligations, marking this novel as a model addition in a mature series: smoothly written, accessible to new readers and solidly plotted." Publ Wkly

Past tense; a Brady Coyne novel. St. Martin's Minotaur 2001 292p

ISBN 0-312-28442-X   LC 2001-41943

"Brady Coyne and girlfriend Evie . . . become prime suspects when a stalker from Evie's past winds up dead outside the couple's rented Cape Cod cottage. Evie's subsequent disappearance sends the Boston attorney into investigative mode." Libr J

Scar tissue. St. Martin's Minotaur 2000 276p $24.95

ISBN 0-312-26679-0

* LC 00-40229

Once Boston attorney Brady Coyne's "suspicions are aroused about a tragic road accident that swept two teenagers to their deaths in an icy river, he handles the sleazy business of small-town rot with the commitment and discretion that distinguish him as a sleuth. Tapply's understated style may forever condemn Coyne to a dull love life; but it serves the sordid nature of the story and well suits the hero." N Y Times Book Rev

Tight lines; a Brady Coyne novel. Delacorte Press 1992 277p o.p.   LC 91-31880

Brady Coyne, "a Boston lawyer whose client base is profoundly rich if not famous, is called to the side of Susan Ames, a wealthy widow dying of cancer. Using the pretense of establishing ground rules for the disposition of the historically significant family estate, she asks Brady to find the daughter she hasn't seen in 11 years." Booklist

A void in hearts; a Brady Coyne mystery. Scribner 1988 198p o.p.   LC 88-12203

"A marginally unscrupulous private eye, Les Katz, gets himself killed after blackmailing a client. Brady is called to the sleuth's deathbed but arrives too late, leaving him no choice but to figure out what happened." Booklist

Tapply, William G.—*Continued*
(jt. auth) Craig, P. R. Third strike

Tarkington, Booth, 1869-1946

Alice Adams; illustrated by Arthur William Brown. Doubleday, Page 1921 434p il o.p.

*

"A social climber, the title character is ashamed of her unsuccessful family. Hoping to attract a wealthy husband, she lies about her background, but she is found out and is shunned by those whom she sought to attract. At the novel's end, she knows her chances for happiness and a successful marriage are bleak, but she remains unbowed." Merriam-Webster's Ency of Lit

The magnificent Ambersons. Modern Library 1998 268p pa $12.95
ISBN 0-375-75250-1

* LC 98-19552

First published 1918 by Doubleday, Page
"The novel traces the growth of the United States through the decline of the once-powerful, socially prominent Amberson family. Their fall is contrasted with the rise of new industrial tycoons and land developers, whose power comes not through family connections but through financial dealings and modern manufacturing." Merriam-Webster's Ency of Lit

Tarr, Judith, 1955-

Lady of horses. Forge 2000 415p $25.95
ISBN 0-312-86114-1   LC 00-27653
"A Tom Doherty Associates book"
This prehistoric epic's "heroine, Sparrow, possesses the gift of divination, but as a girl in a culture that only values males, she is compelled to conceal it. She must also hide her forbidden passion for horses. When she and her sister-in-law, Keen, are discovered with the horse herd, they flee taking the king stallion with them. They end up in a land where females are not stigmatized, and where they are free to worship the Horse Goddess. . . . Tarr blends mythology and fantasy to make an unrecorded era of time vibrant and alive while brilliantly depicting nomadic cultures." Booklist

Pillar of fire. Forge 1995 448p o.p.
                                      LC 95-6315
"A Tom Doherty Associates book"
"This narrative is based on an intriguing premise: What if Moses, patriarch of monotheism, and the Pharaoh Akhenaten, who forbade the Egyptians from worshiping any god save the sun god Aten, were one and the same? After all, Akhenaten's body disappeared after his death, and Moses rose to prominence shortly thereafter. The third-person narration sticks close to the point of view of Nofret, a young Hittite slave girl who serves the Pharaoh's third daughter." Publ Wkly
"Tarr makes of this intriguing speculation an exhilarating ride, powerfully written, through a lost world of chariot races, royalty, revolt, and enduring loyalty that is sure to please many readers." Booklist

Queen of swords. Forge 1997 464p o.p.
                                      LC 96-33220
"A Tom Doherty Associates book"
This historical novel "focuses on the reign of Melisende, the oldest daughter of Baldwin II, King of Je-

rusalem. She ruled from 1129 to 1153, first as queen to Fulk of Anjou, who succeeded her father, then as regent to her son. When he reached his majority, she refused to relinquish her power until he forced her from the throne. The story is told from the viewpoints of her son and a lady-in-waiting, Richildis, and her family. Richildis came to the Holy Land on the ship with Fulk searching for her brother. She stayed on to serve the queen." Libr J
"A richly textured tapestry steeped in history and fraught with romance, adventure, and intrigue." Booklist

Queen of the Amazons. Tor Bks. 2004 320p $23.95
ISBN 0-7653-0395-7   LC 2003-61396
"After refusing to kill her newborn daughter, proclaimed 'soulless' by the Seer, Amazon Queen Hyppolyta vows that only her child will succeed her as ruler of her people. With her customary storytelling skill, the author of Lord of the Two Lands portrays the life and times of one of ancient history's most enigmatic and compelling women, reputedly the lover of Alexander the Great and the leader of a fierce army of female warriors. Tarr's elegant style and historical accuracy, along with her ability to construct believable characters, make this tale a strong addition to most libraries and essential for fans of historical fantasy." Libr J

Tarr, Rodger L.

(ed) Rawlings, M. K. Short stories

Tartt, Donna

The little friend. Knopf 2002 555p $26
ISBN 0-679-43938-2   LC 2002-66878
"The death of nine-year-old Robin Cleve Dufresnes, found hanging from a tree in his own backyard in Alexandria, Miss., has never been solved. The crime destroyed his family: it turned his mother into a lethargic recluse; his father left town; and the surviving siblings, Allison and Harriet, are now, 12 years later—it is the early '70s—largely being raised by their black maid and a matriarchy of female relatives. . . . [Harriet] vows to solve the mystery of her brother's death and unmask the killer, whom she decides, without a shred of evidence, is Danny Ratliff, a member of a degenerate, redneck family of hardened criminals." Publ Wkly
Tartt's "book is a ruthlessly precise reckoning of the world as it is—drab, ugly, scary, inconclusive—filtered through the bright colors and impossible demands of childhood perception. It grips you like a fairy tale, but denies you the consoling assurance that it's all just make-believe." N Y Times Book Rev

The secret history. Knopf 1992 523p
ISBN 0-679-41032-5

* LC 92-53053

This novel "is set on a small college campus in Vermont. Dissatisfied with the crass values of their fellow students, a small corps of undergraduates groups itself around a favored professor of classics, who nurtures both their sense of moral elevation and an insularity from conventional college life that ultimately proves fatal. Among Prof. Julian Morrow's followers are Henry Winter, a tall scion of a wealthy St. Louis family, . . . the twins Charles and Camilla Macaulay, both intellectually gifted and eccentric only in their excessive mutual devotion;

Tartt, Donna—*Continued*

Francis Abernathy, a dandyish homosexual slowly awakening to his sexuality; and Edmund (Bunny) Corcoran, . . . [who] becomes the group's victim." N Y Times Book Rev

"Tartt records the aftereffects of unpunished crime with great skill." New Repub

Tate, Ellalice, 1906-1993

For works written by this author under other names see Holt, Victoria, 1906-1993; Plaidy, Jean, 1906-1993

Tax, Meredith

Rivington Street. Morrow 1982 431p o.p.
LC 81-22587

"This is the story of Russian immigrant men and women caught up in the social upheavals at the beginning of this century. Set on the Lower East Side of New York, the book concerns strong-willed Hannah Levy, her daughters, Sarah, a social activist, and Ruby, a creative designer of clothes, and their beautiful and romantic friend, Rachel Cohen. It is the women who dominate this book. Their struggle to survive the terrible working conditions and low pay of jobs in the garment industry and the violence that comes when they demand a better life make an absorbing story. Tax has used real incidents— the fire at the Triangle Waist factory, a strike of garment workers, and the jailing of suffragists—to add color and authenticity to the story." Libr J

Followed by Union Square

Taylor, Benjamin, 1952-

The book of getting even; a novel. Steerforth Press 2008 166p $23.95
ISBN 978-1-58642-143-4   LC 2008-5834

Gabriel Geismar "is the son of a domineering rabbi growing up in nineteen-fifties New Orleans. Homosexual, suffering from a physical deformity (he has a supernumerary thumb), and enthralled by mathematics—'calculability, sweet detachment from the corporeal universe'— Gabriel has 'a furious craving for other, nobler origins.' In college, he meets Marghie and Danny Hundert, whose famous physicist father is one of his heroes, and adopts the family as his own. The book explores the tortured and often misguided process by which children attempt to define themselves in relation to their parents (one iteration of the 'getting even' of the title), a process from which Danny and Marghie, as Gabriel slowly discovers, are not exempt. Taylor captures their quests for identity in pitch-perfect dialogue and lengthy meditative passages; his elegant plotting feels at once deliberate and improvised." New Yorker

Taylor, Elizabeth, 1912-1975

Mrs. Palfrey at the Claremont. Viking 1971 178p o.p.
                                                                 *

"A tale about an elderly British widow who takes up residence in one of those shabby, genteel hotels along London's Cromwell Road. She is at a desperate loss for what to do with herself to fill in the time and try to make her fellow lodgers believe she still has some semblance of a personal life. The portraits of the elderly and crotchety residents are drawn with a pen only lightly tipped in acid, and Mrs. Palfrey herself is very human and endearing. She finds her real hope for the future in pretending that a rather callow but not unkind casual acquaintance is really her grandson." Publ Wkly

Taylor, Kamala Purnaiya *See* Markandaya, Kamala, 1924-2004

Taylor, M. Glenn

The ballad of Trenchmouth Taggart. Vandalia Press 2008 276p pa $16.50
ISBN 978-1-933202-31-0; 1-933202-31-9
                                                  LC 2008-927388

"Meet Trenchmouth Taggart, a man born and orphaned in 1903, a man nicknamed for his lifelong oral affliction. In the West Virginia coal mine wars, a boy hardens quick when he picks up a gun. Exile is his trophy, and he spends his adult years on the run. He changes his name and plays a mean mouth harp, and he keeps on running from his past, all the way to Chicago." Publisher's note

"Taylor's prose is so fluid and seemingly effortless that The Ballad of Trenchmouth Taggart bridges the usually irreconcilable gap between popular fiction and literary fiction. It's that rare creature — a literary page-turner — and it will please both the casual reader and the college professor . . . . [This] is a stunning, fully realized, unique and ambitious book that proves there's still passion, fire and brilliance in the American novel." Houston Chron

Taylor, Peter Hillsman, 1917-1994

A summons to Memphis; [by] Peter Taylor. Knopf 1986 209p o.p.
                                          * LC 86-45417

"A son, now a grown man, recounts the family's subservience to a strong-willed father. Against a background of Southern manners in Memphis and Nashville, the Carver daughters and sons experience frustration of their hopes to marry and enjoy family lives of their own. The mother, soon after her marriage to George Carver, withdraws from resisting his authority. The daughters never find suitors who suit their father. One brother, escaping to war, is killed and the narrator, Philip, a bachelor still at 49, is summoned home by his sisters to prevent their father, at 81, from remarrying. The seemingly selfless care given by the daughters might stem from self-interest rather than filial devotion." Shapiro. Fic for Youth. 3d edition

Taylor, Robert Lewis

The travels of Jaimie McPheeters. Doubleday 1958 544p o.p.

"Fourteen-year old Jaimie McPheeters, the son of Sardius McPheeters, an unsuccessful, windy-minded doctor who is given to gambling and drink, sets out with his father from their Louisville home in the spring of 1849 for the California gold fields, and in the course of the next three years or so is kidnapped by outlaws; is captured by Indians; witnesses a lot of brutality, including a duel,

Taylor, Robert Lewis—*Continued*

fires, killings, and some startling Indian cruelty; suffers semi-starvation and degradation; and in the end, after his father's death, becomes part owner of a handsome California ranch, where he settles with his mother, his sisters, and his Indian sweetheart." New Yorker

"The piquant combination of solid historical content, satisfying adventure, good literary style, sophisticated wit and humor will give this book wide appeal." Libr J

Tea, Michelle

Rose of no man's land; a novel. MacAdam/Cage Pub. 2006 306p $22

ISBN 1-59692-160-9   LC 2005-224876

"There's nothing that Trisha, a 14-year-old loner in the beaten-down town of Mogsfield, Massachusetts, likes better than to listen to music and drink beer in bed. With a couch potato for a mother, a white-trash live-in boyfriend who doesn't exactly uplift the household, and a carbophobic sister obsessed with being on MTV's Real World, Trisha expects nothing from the summer ahead. Then, at a mall job gone bad, she meets the rebellious mall rat Rose, and her 24-hour adventure begins—from friendship to crystal meth to tattoos to wild sexual adventures on a golf course to, finally, finding herself." Bookmarks Magazine

This novel is "both a riotously funny coming-of-age story and a poignant cautionary tale that smacks of 'there but for the grace of God' heartbreak. . . . But Trisha's cynical, wisecracking descriptions are almost too brilliantly evocative, too clever as she illuminates the story's small cast of characters with vivid, telling details." Boston Globe

Tearne, Roma

Mosquito. Europa Editions 2008 c2007 299p pa $16.95

ISBN 978-1-933372-57-0; 1-933372-57-5

First published 2007 in the United Kingdom

"Set adrift by the recent death of his wife, Theo Samarajeeva abandons his comfortable writer's life in London and returns to Sri Lanka, his war torn homeland. There he meets Nulani, a talented and enigmatic young artist. An unorthodox and tenuous love blossoms between this unlikely pair. Nulani finally feels love, and Theo sees hope in his future. But when the insurgency explodes, their precarious world is torn apart. Theo is held captive and stripped of everything he once held dear. Nulani is forced into exile." Publisher's note

"Flashes of true beauty, along with an impressively sustained forward drive, are enough to make Mosquito an engaging and thought-provoking novel." Times Lit Suppl

Temple, Peter, 1946-

The broken shore. Farrar, Straus and Giroux 2007 357p $25

ISBN 978-0-374-11693-4; 0-374-11693-8

LC 2006-32983

First published 2005 in Australia

"Melbourne homicide detective Joe Cashin has been temporarily assigned to his hometown, dinky Port Monro. Rehabilitating (with aspirin and whiskey, mostly)

from injuries only slowly explained, he broods over family history and mistakes made. But when a local eminence is assaulted—and an attempt to detain the suspect goes fatally wrong—Cashin finds that small-town crimes offer complications worthy of the big city." Booklist

"Flinty, funny, subtle, and smart, The Broken Shore sags under the burden of a few too many narrative complications and, like many a top-drawer mystery, collapses toward the end, as the haunting questions, so elegantly posed, are suddenly and a little awkwardly answered. But this is a hazard of the genre, and Temple ranks among its very best practitioners." Entertainment Wkly

Templeton, Edith, 1916-

Gordon. Pantheon Bks. 2001 226p $22

ISBN 0-375-42194-7   LC 2002-70427

First published 1966 in the United Kingdom under the pseudonym Louise Walbrook

"This eerie tale of sexual obsession is narrated by a young woman adrift in London just after the Second World War. She meets a 'frightening, sinister, implacable' psychiatrist who, over all protest, invades her, body and mind, arousing previously unsuspected tastes for submission and humiliation. One part 'Story of O' to two parts Muriel Spark, the book beautifully evokes the tightened belts and loose morals of postwar London." New Yorker

Tennant, Emma, 1937-

Pemberley; or Pride and prejudice continued. St. Martin's Press 1993 184p $18.95

ISBN 0-312-10793-5

* LC 94-171082

"It is the Christmas season, and Elizabeth Darcy (Elizabeth Bennet of *Pride and Prejudice*) now the uneasy mistress of the great estate of Pemberley, anticipates the holidays with growing trepidation. Her foolish widowed mother and two of her sisters, flighty Kitty and pedantic Mary, are soon to descend upon the household. Adding to the guest list, as well as the complications, are her husband's formidable aunt, Lady Catherine de Bourgh, and the Wickhams (the cad who eloped with Elizabeth's sister after his unsuccessful attempt to run off with her sister-in-law). Sweet-tempered Jane will also be present, but her imminent confinement is a constant reminder to Elizabeth of her own barrenness." Libr J

The author's "narrative is made uncomfortably compelling by her utter mastery of Austen's style. In its pace and sensibility, the text virtually breathes Jane Austen; the malaise that Ms. Tennant so powerfully exploits is solidly rooted in her model." N Y Times Book Rev

Followed by An unequal marriage

An unequal marriage; or, Pride and prejudice twenty years later. St. Martin's Press 1994 186p

ISBN 0-312-11533-4   LC 94-26108

"In this sequel-to-the-sequel, {Elizabeth and Darcy} experience the mixed blessings children can bring. At 17, Miranda is lovely, competent, and her father's pride and joy, but heir-apparent Edward, a student at Eton, has long been a problem. As guests gather for the wedding of close friend Colonel Fitzwilliam, reports come that Edward has fallen under bad influences in London and gambled away part of the family estate. Cold disciplinar-

Tennant, Emma, 1937-—_Continued_

ian Darcy acts, while compassionate chatelaine Elizabeth is distraught and susceptible to the admiring glances of handsome Mr. Gresham." Libr J

Tepper, Sheri S.

The gate to Women's Country. Doubleday 1988 278p o.p.

* LC 88-387

"A Foundation book"

"A feminist fable set somewhere in the Pacific Northwest 300 years after a nuclear holocaust. Men and women now live in separate but adjacent communities. Although the men are organized into military garrisons, the women appear to have the upper hand in government, deciding matters of trade and law and, most important, reproduction. . . . The elaborate society that the author takes such pains to describe is based on a big lie; the story she tells is part of the deception. Some will find this narrative strategy as distasteful as the secret it conceals. But Ms. Tepper is not afraid to ask hard questions, beginning with this: If biology is destiny, how can society hope to control its self-destructive tendencies without controlling biology as well?" N Y Times Book Rev

Grass. Doubleday 1989 426p o.p.

* LC 89-30105

"A Foundation book"

In this first volume of a trilogy "diplomats are dispatched to the planet Grass in search of the cure for a deadly disease that is spreading throughout inhabited space. The human settlers, xenophobic and conservative landed gentry, lead an existence tightly structured around the Hunt, a complex and violent ritual involving the use of alien mounts that seem nearly demonic in their malevolence. The presence of a number of not particularly sympathetic religious groups adds complexity to the situation. This is a beautifully written novel with well-developed characters and a number of very interesting aliens." Anatomy of Wonder 4

Followed by Raising the stones

The Margarets. Eos 2007 508p il $26.95

ISBN 978-0-06-117065-2; 0-06-117065-8

LC 2006-47079

"Margaret is the only kid on a research colony orbiting Mars. Smart, bored and profoundly lonely, she begins to create alter egos for fun. . . . As Margaret grows into a smart and lonely teenager her family must return to the grim, environmentally ravished Earth, where the only economically viable product for interplanetary export is human slaves. Facing a series of blind choices that pull her in two directions, she begins to shed the imaginary Margarets. The Margarets scatter off to other settled worlds, unaware of their other selves. Each Margaret struggles to survive by her (or his) wits, and to understand the growing threats to Earth and humanity. . . . [This novel] incorporates a grab bag of creatures, cultures, psychological metaphors, characters, commentaries and predicaments. The result is a delightful variation on the kind of novel with disparate characters and plot threads that somehow come together at the end. In this tale, they are together in the mind of a child at the beginning." Salon.com

Raising the stones. Doubleday 1990 453p o.p.

LC 90-30191

"A Foundation book"

In this second volume of the trilogy set in a far away galaxy "a community of good people (who live in peace and harmony under the subtle mind control of an alien intelligence they refer to as 'the God') are threatened by a sect of religious fanatics (whose megalomaniacal creed not only permits the enslavement of unbelievers but 'insists' on it)." N Y Times Book Rev

This is a "complicated, exciting narrative that explores central questions of religion and faith, and of the dangers and usefulness of technology." Women's Rev Books

Followed by Sideshow

Sideshow. Bantam Bks. 1992 467p o.p.

LC 91-40420

In this concluding volume of the trilogy begun with Grass, "a sentient fungus has infested most of the galaxy, reworking the life forms it inhabits to enhance their physical and spiritual comfort. The people of the planet Elsewhere, however, see the fungus's contented hosts as slaves; to preserve free will on Elsewhere, the rulers have imposed absolute cultural relativity within which pleasant and unsavory societies coexist, their integrity rigidly maintained by Enforcers. But powers have arisen to challenge the status quo." Publ Wkly

"Tepper's imaginative vision holds forth and delivers one of her most challenging works." Libr J

Singer from the sea. Avon Eos 1999 426p $24

ISBN 0-380-97480-0

LC 99-10231

"Despite her status as a young noblewoman of the planet Haven, Genevieve rebels against the strict regulations concerning highborn women. Defying her father's wishes, she seeks her own forbidden destiny and discovers the dark secrets that lie at the heart of her world and its forgotten history. Tepper . . . continues to explore the intricacies of human societal structures and the complex connections between humans and their environment, combining stylistic grace with imaginative insight." Libr J

The visitor; a novel. Eos 2002 407p

ISBN 0-380-97905-5

LC 2001-40197

"Dismé Latimer is an orphan, tyrannized by an evil stepmother and stepsister who deprive her of her heritage. Her rigid, corrupt society is ruled by a bureaucracy that keeps its people in line through a systematic and legally sanctioned use of torture, as its leaders pursue the black arts in their quest for power. Dismé secretly possesses a forbidden book, the memoir of her ancestor, Nell Latimer, who was a scientist at the time of The Happening. A thousand years earlier, an asteroid (the 'Visitor') hit Earth, nearly wiping out the human race and causing huge changes in geography and climate." SLJ

"Tepper has created a mesmerizing story full of intriguing characters, resonant images and powerful themes." Publ Wkly

Terrell, Whitney

The huntsman. Viking 2001 358p il

ISBN 0-670-89465-6

Terrell, Whitney—*Continued*

"Stan Granger, loner and fisherman, pulls the body of a young white woman from the Missouri River. It's not his first encounter with a waterlogged corpse, but this time it's someone he knows. She was Clarissa Sayers, the strange and wild daughter of a federal judge, and her death was caused not by drowning but by a blow to the head. Suspicion centers on Booker Short, a young black parole violator from Oklahoma with whom she'd been having an affair." Libr J

Terrell provides a "Dreiseresque study of Kansas City in the nineties, in all its complicated manners and minutiae. An unsung corner of the American landscape, the city is the real hero here, as white and black, rich and poor, old and young collide." New Yorker

Tevis, Walter S., 1928-1984

The queen's gambit; [by] Walter Tevis. Random House 1983 243p o.p.

                    * LC 82-15058

This "is the story of an orphan girl who is taught to play chess by the janitor of her orphanage. Beth Harmon has genius; she wins her first tournament when she is 14, becomes American champion at 18 and starts the international circuit. She may well be the second best player in the world. Only the world champion, a Russian . . . is stronger than she, and she is scared to death of him. The climax of the book comes when they meet over the board in a Moscow tournament." N Y Times Book Rev

"Familiarity with chess is not needed in order to enjoy this book though aficionados will delight in its evocation of their esoteric freemasonry." Times Lit Suppl

Texier, Catherine

Victorine. Pantheon Books 2004 324p $24

  ISBN 0-375-42124-6   LC 2003-54860

The author "imagines the life of her great-grandmother, who left her husband and two children in a French provincial town in the late 1890's and supposedly ran off to Indochina with a customs officer. The affair might have lasted a year and a half; in 1900, Victorine returned to her husband in France and gave birth to a third child." N Y Times Book Rev

"With lush, vivid description, Texier brings to life both the world around Victorine and the woman herself." Libr J

Tey, Josephine, 1896-1952

Brat Farrar. Macmillan 1950 c1949 219p o.p.

First published 1949 in the United Kingdom

"The scene is an English country home owned by the orphaned Ashby children and managed for them by their aunt, who has made a success of the horses she bred and exhibited. Simon, charming and spoiled, is about to take over as he comes of age, when a well-coached imposter arrives and claims to be the elder brother who had disappeared eight years before, leaving a suicide note." Booklist

  also in Tey, J. Three by Tey

The daughter of time. Macmillan 1952 c1951 204p o.p.

First published 1951 in England

"Alan Grant, injured policeman hospitalized and bored, is diverted by a photograph of Richard III, commonly conceded murderer of the princes in the Tower. With the invaluable assistance of a research student, Grant's convalescence becomes a lively pursuit of the truth as shown by records in Richard's time." Libr J

The author "not only reconstructs the probably historical truth, she re-creates the intense dramatic excitement of the scholarly research necessary to unveil it." N Y Times Book Rev

  also in Tey, J. Four, five and six by Tey

Four, five and six by Tey. Macmillan 1958 3v in 1 o.p.

"Murder revisited series"

An omnibus edition of three complete Scotland Yard mysteries in which Inspector Alan Grant solves the crimes. Includes The singing sands (1952) and The daughter of time (1951) and A shilling for candles (1936), about a film star whose death by strangulation is the focus of Grant's investigation

The Franchise affair. Macmillan 1948 238p o.p.

"A lawyer in an English country town answers an appeal for help from two women who, having only recently inherited a home, were still outsiders to the townspeople and, being independent, reserved, and unusual, were called witches. When a girl in another town accused them of imprisoning, starving, and beating her in their attic, they were helpless, for the circumstantial evidence seemed indisputable. Good characterization, good writing, and to the lawyer's surprise, an emotional involvement for him." Booklist

  also in Tey, J. Three by Tey

The man in the queue. Macmillan 1953 213p o.p.

First published 1929 by Dutton under the pseudonym Gordon Daviot

A man is stabbed to death waiting in the ticket line of a popular London musical, and Inspector Grant of the C.I.D. is assigned to the case

"Every detail of the discovery of first the identity and then the murderer of the knifed man is admirably invented, and the story, at first sight a simple build-up . . . turns out to be a serious inductive exercise." Springfield Repub

Miss Pym disposes. Macmillan 1948 213p o.p.

First published 1946 in the United Kingdom

An English woman psychologist delivers a lecture at a physical training college and decides to stay a little longer. She becomes very friendly with some of the seniors, and eventually finds herself involved in an "accident" which turns out to be a murder

  also in Tey, J. Three by Tey

A shilling for candles

  In Tey, J. Four, five and six by Tey

The singing sands. Macmillan 1953 c1952 221p o.p.

First published 1952 in the United Kindgom. Variant title: Grant's last case

A cryptic fragment of verse, found near a dead man on a train en route to Scotland is Inspector Grant's only clue to the identity of the man's murderer

  also in Tey, J. Four, five and six by Tey

Tey, Josephine, 1896-1952—*Continued*

Three by Tey; Miss Pym disposes; The Franchise affair [and] Brat Farrar; with an introduction by James Sandoe. Macmillan 1954 3v in 1 o.p.

"Murder revisited series. A Cock Robin mystery"

An omnibus edition of three titles entered separately

Thackeray, William Makepeace, 1811-1863

Vanity fair; [by] W.M. Thackeray; edited with an introduction by John Sutherland; with 193 illustrations by the author. Oxford University Press 2008 c2003 lviii, 949p il (Oxford world's classics) pa $8.95

ISBN 978-0-19-953762-4; 0-19-953762-3

First published 1848

"The book is a densely populated, multi-layered panorama of manners and human frailties. . . . The novel deals mainly with the interwoven fortunes of two women, the wellborn, passive Amelia Sedley and the ambitious, essentially amoral Becky Sharp, the latter perhaps the most memorable character Thackeray created. The adventuress Becky is the character around whom all the men play their parts." Merriam-Webster's Ency of Lit

The Virginians; introduction by M. R. Ridley. Dutton 1965 2v o.p.

First published 1857; first United States edition published 1869 by Fields, Osgood & Co.

"A sequel to 'Henry Esmond', it relates the story of George and Harry Warrington, the twin grandsons of Colonel Henry Esmond. The novel follows the brothers from boyhood in America, through various experiences in England, and finally through the American Revolution, in which George fights on the British side and Harry on the side of his friend George Washington." Reader's Ency. 4th edition

Thayer, Nancy, 1943-

An act of love. St. Martin's Press 1997 245p $22.95

ISBN 0-312-15471-2   LC 97-14404

"Owen and Linda McFarland, both novelists, have been married for seven years and reside on a Massachusetts farm with Bruce and Emily, the children from each of their respective first marriages. Their uneventful existence is disrupted, however, when Emily, now a teenager attending the same boarding school as Bruce, attempts suicide. After voluntarily staying on at the psychiatric hospital, Emily whose recent behavioral changes include sudden weight gain and newfound religious devotion, reveals in therapy that the reason behind her despair is that her stepbrother raped her, a charge that Bruce vehemently denies." Publ Wkly

"Thayer's prose is fluid and concise, her characters rich and human, her dialogue easy and believable." Booklist

Belonging. St. Martin's Press 1995 341p o.p.
LC 95-15457

"Joanna Jones is the single and successful star of a television show, *Joanna Jones' Fabulous Homes*. Her romantic involvement with the show's married coproducer, Carter Amberson, suits her just fine until, nearly 40, she discovers that she is pregnant with Carter's twins. Understanding that Carter refuses to divorce his wife and fearing that he might convince her to have an abortion, she takes a leave of absence from her work and escapes to a creaking old house she discovered and bought in Nantucket." Libr J

"The story surely captivates at moments and mostly satisfies. Except for the overattention to material and social superficiality, Thayer's story of a woman's quest for self-identity and self-affirmation does inspire." Booklist

Between husbands and friends; a novel. St. Martin's Press 1999 241p $22.95

ISBN 0-312-20613-5   LC 99-27233

"Narrator Lucy West, 37, is a self-employed mother of two; her husband, Max, edits the local newspaper in Sussex, a Boston suburb. Suave, irreverent Kate Cunningham and her husband, Chip, an attorney, move to Sussex in 1987; Kate and Lucy meet at their children's preschool and become fast friends. Soon the couples summer together on Nantucket, and their lives grow ever more entwined. Thayer's narrative jumps back and forth between the couples' present and their shared past. . . . Readers prepared for the slow pace of Thayer's plot will appreciate her detailed, realistic records of motherhood, child-rearing and domestic routine in Sussex and Nantucket." Publ Wkly

Everlasting. Viking 1991 322p o.p.
LC 90-50462

"Catherine Eliot, at 18, is aimless until she falls into a job in a flower shop and realizes that this is the business she was born for. Though her social register family has cut her off, she uses her own social connections to build her business into a giant. This rejected daughter does all she can to rescue her family from financial and emotional distress. Though her help is neither understood nor appreciated, Catherine eventually finds contentment in herself, her marriage, and her business. An absorbing story and heroine." Libr J

Family secrets. Viking 1993 338p o.p.
LC 92-50746

At the center of this novel is "Diane, driven, successful, and suffering the disillusionment of mid-life crisis. The FBI contacts her in an attempt to locate her recently widowed mother, who they believe possesses top-secret information. At the same time, Julia, her unhappily college-bound daughter who's desperately in love with the boy next door and more desperately in need of breaking away from her mother's expectations, runs off to be married. Meanwhile, Diane's mother, Jean, captures the foregone dream of her youth: traveling through Europe with no itinerary, enjoying only quiet, anonymous days of her very own. Gradually, gently, the lives of these women unfold before us and Jean's mysterious secret is revealed." Booklist

My dearest friend. Scribner 1989 342p o.p.
LC 89-6276

"Divorcée Daphne Miller is the mother of a 16-year-old daughter who takes off abruptly for California to live with a father she has not heard from for 14 years. Deprived of child support payments, Daphne moves into a country shack. Once a college professor like her ex-husband and two married swains, she is now a lowly but plucky department secretary. Flashbacks reveal her best friend's betrayal and its impact on Daphne's marriage,

Thayer, Nancy, 1943—*Continued*

and counterpoint her slow recovery during which Daphne again allows friends to play key roles in her life." Publ Wkly

Thayer, Steve

The leper. North Star 2008 389p map $24.95
ISBN 978-0-87839-266-7

This is the story of "the life of soldier turned schoolteacher John Eric Severson, from World War I to the mid-1970s. . . . Severson, soon after his return to the U.S. from the war, is diagnosed with leprosy and sent to a Louisiana leper colony. He never sees his home, his family, or the woman he loves again. . . . The book is filled with engaging, memorable supporting players, and Severson himself is such a vividly drawn character that readers may have to remind themselves that he is a fictional character." Booklist

The weatherman; a novel. Viking 1995 452p $21.95
ISBN 0-670-84958-8　　　　　　　LC 94-20142

"Dixon Bell is a television meteorologist with an eerie gift for reading the weather. Rick Beanblossom is a news producer who hides his disfigured face behind a mask. Andrea Labore is the beautiful cop turned reporter whom they both love. Meanwhile, the Calendar Killer is strangling a woman each season during a significant weather event. When Bell is arrested and accused of the murders, Beanblossom and Labore join forces to prove his innocence. The novel's characters are deeply developed, and the riveting plot is cloaked in descriptive episodes of weather. Additionally, readers will receive a fascinating view of the intense machinations of television news productions." Libr J

Theorin, Johan, 1963-

Echoes from the dead. Delacorte Press 2008 388p pa $12
ISBN 978-0-385-34221-6; 0-385-34221-7
　　　　　　　　　　　　　　　　LC 2008-6631

Original Swedish edition, 2007

This novel "set on the desolate Baltic island of Öland, a 'summer place' which is almost uninhabited for the rest of the year. Julia Davidsson has never come to terms with the disappearance of her five-year-old son 20 years previously. No trace of the child has ever been found; until Julia's father, a retired sea captain who lives on the island, receives one of the boy's shoes in the post. Together, father and daughter begin to piece together fragments of the past. Yes, there's plenty of etiolated Nordic gloom, but Theorin's prose is wonderfully descriptive and he writes so well about the natural world that the island is as much a character as the people who live there. The exposition of history and the nature of memory is haunting and lyrical, but never impedes a cracking good plot." Guardian

Theroux, Alexander, 1939-

Darconville's cat. Doubleday 1981 704p
ISBN 0-385-15951-X　　　　　　　LC 80-00629

"The hero works as English lecturer in an American Southern women's college and falls in love with a student. Marriage is proposed and arranged, but the false hilding falls for another man. Revenge is planned and curses are articulated, but Darconville meets natural death in Venice. This simple tale easily fills 704 pages, for, in the Rabelaisian manner, it is decorated with monstrous catalogues, liturgies, baroque pastiches, diaries—anything, in fact, to prevent the story from moving fast" Burgess. 99 Novels

Laura Warholic; or, The sexual intellectual. Fantagraphics 2007 878p $29.95
ISBN 978-1-56097-798-8; 1-56097-798-1

"Eugene Eyestones is an erudite man of taste and refinement earning his keep by writing an intellectual yet nonetheless scandalous sex column for a Boston magazine published by the grotesquely fat and foul Minot Warholic. Laura, Warholic's homely, straw-thin, slutty, rock-and-roll-fanatic ex-wife, serves as gentlemanly Eugene's unlikely muse, while he dreams of Rapunzel, a fair lady working in a bakery. Weary of the anti-Semitic, racist, misogynist, and homophobic tirades and insults habitually spewed by his cartoonishly vituperative colleagues, Eugene goes on the road with obtuse Laura, touring America's grand spectrum of tackiness." Booklist

"A remarkable achievement, a bombastic, squirm-inducing, and belief-rattling satire on political correctness shown through the lens of a sexless love story between two of the most unlovable (if not repulsive) characters in recent American letters. It takes an author like Theroux, who is as established as he is antiestablishment, to pull off a novel that for many other authors would be career suicide." Believer

Theroux, Paul

The collected stories. Viking 1997 660p o.p.
　　　　　　　　　　　　　　* LC 96-52417

Contents: World's end; Zombies; The imperial icehouse; Yard sale; Algebra; The English adventure; After the war; Words are deeds; White lies; Clapham Junction; The odd-job man; Portrait of a lady; The prison diary of Jack Faust; A real Russian ikon; A political romance; Sinning with Annie; A love knot; What have you done to our Leo?; Memories of a curfew; Biographical notes for four American poets; Hayseed; A deed without a name; You make me mad; Dog days; A burial at Surabaya; Polvo; Low tide; Jungle bells; Warm dogs; The consul's file; Dependent wife; White Christmas; Pretend I'm not here; Loser wins; The flower of Malaya; The Autumn dog; Dengué fever; The South Malaysia Pineapple Growers' Association; The butterfly of the laruts; The tennis court; Reggie Woo; Conspirators; The Johore murders; The tiger's suit; Coconut gatherer; The last colonial; Triad; Diplomatic relations; Dear William; Volunteer speaker; Reception; Namesake; An English unofficial rose; Children; Charlie Hogle's earring; The exile; Tomb with a view; The man on the Clapham omnibus; Sex and its substitutes; The honorary Siberian; Gone West; A little flame; Fury; Neighbors; Fighting talk; The Winfield wallpaper; Dancing on the radio; Memo

Doctor DeMarr
In Theroux, P. Half Moon Street

Doctor Slaughter
In Theroux, P. Half Moon Street

Theroux, Paul—*Continued*

The elephant god
In Theroux, P. The Elephanta suite

The Elephanta suite. Houghton Mifflin 2007 274p $25

ISBN 978-0-618-94332-6; 0-618-94332-3
LC 2007-13978

"The dismayed, disoriented American travelers in this trio of stereotype-shattering novellas . . . lament the missing 'solemn pieties' and 'virtuous peasants' of the India they read about in novels. In 'Monkey Hill,' a wealthy ugly American-type husband and wife take pampered health spa treatment at the foot of the Himalayas to be their due. But when the couple presume that the sybaritic care they're paying for includes invitations for sex with masseurs and waiters, their idyllic holiday takes a tragic turn. In 'The Gateway of India,' a fast-track Boston capitalist finds his loathing for the squalor of Mumbai's slums tempered by how easy it is to buy the affections of young women; meanwhile, his once obsequious Indian assistant is usurping his power. In 'The Elephant God,' a college graduate on her own encounters a young man whose call-center mastery of American dialect somehow rewires him from overly friendly striver to malevolent stalker." Publ Wkly

"Together, the three novellas of 'The Elephanta Suite' render India as a mass of contradictions: both a testing ground for patience and a training ground for serenity, if you're an American. The stories also recall the best of the author's earlier psychosexual parables ('Doctor Slaughter,' 'Chicago Loop'), blending Theroux the traveler and Theroux the connoisseur of our most wanton instincts into one." Seattle Times

The gateway of India
In Theroux, P. The Elephanta suite

Half Moon Street; two short novels. Houghton Mifflin 1984 219p o.p. LC 84-10495

This work "contains two novellas on a single theme: the terrors of leading a double life. In 'Doctor DeMarr,' the shorter work, a man who believes his twin brother to be dead steps into his brother's life. . . . [In 'Doctor Slaughter,' an] American woman on a study grant in London finds nothing working well for her until she sells her talents to an 'escort service.'" Newsweek

"Theroux endows these two cautionary tales with a palpable sense of danger and a trenchant wit that are both disturbing and enticing." Booklist

Hotel Honolulu. Houghton Mifflin 2001 424p $26

ISBN 0-618-09501-2 LC 00-54125

"The episodic narrative is presided over by two protagonists: the unnamed narrator, a has-been writer who leaves the mainland to manage the seedy Hotel Honolulu, and raucous millionaire Buddy Hamstra, the hotel's owner and former manager, who fired himself to give the narrator his job." Publ Wkly

"The book brims with eccentric characters and their wild, usually morbid tales." Atl Mon

Kowloon Tong. Houghton Mifflin 1997 243p o.p. LC 96-29717

"Neville 'Bunt' Mullard is a quintessential Englishman: he likes eating at Fatty's Chophouse, going to the races, and having tea and oaties with Mum. Only Bunt was born and bred in Hong Kong, where he now runs a factory that his father established with Mr. Chuck, who has just died and left his shares to the Mullard family. Bunt is trying to ignore the imminent Chinese takeover of Hong Kong, but then Mr. Hung arrives from the mainland, demanding to buy the well-situated factory—and backing up his demands with some ugly tactics." Libr J

Monkey Hill
In Theroux, P. The Elephanta suite

The Mosquito Coast; a novel; with woodcuts by David Frampton. Houghton Mifflin 1982 374p o.p.
* LC 81-6787

"Allie Fox, a cantankerous Yankee inventor fed up with an America gone soft, pursues his obsession with total self-sufficiency to the wild coast of Honduras, dragging his devoted but uneasy family behind. His aim is to make a 'slightly better job than God' of this poisoned world, as far from cheeseburgers and drive-in churches as possible. And his ingenious pioneer Eden actually works, until his swelling egomania finally topples it." Libr J

"The physical impact of the style, the exact observation, the occasional intrusion of the hallucinatory make this a remarkable work of art; its philosophical content is profound." Burgess. 99 Novels

My secret history. Putnam 1989 511p o.p.
* LC 88-32182

"From an early adolescence torn between a call to the priesthood and the call of the flesh, through late-adolescent sexual initiation and a young adult's escapades as a teacher in Africa, to a grown man's crisis in marriage, Theroux recounts the 'secret history' of Andy Parent, a writer suspiciously resembling Theroux himself." Libr J

"'My secret history' is about the permanence of marriage in the face of mistrust and infidelity; it's about the wisdom of women and the foolishness of men; and it's about mature love as the necessary and sometimes successful antidote to youthful selfishness." N Y Times Book Rev

Picture palace; a novel. Houghton Mifflin 1978 359p

ISBN 0-395-26475-8
* LC 77-18725

"At seventy, Maude Pratt is a world famous photographer. . . . As the book opens, a young man is sifting through her photographs to prepare a retrospective of her work. The images bring up buried memories of her photographic adventures, her incestuous longings for her brother, and the many self-deceptions that marked her life." Saturday Rev

Picture palace "is an elaborate visual conceit, a sublime meditation on seeing and knowing. Confident and commanding, the author displays his narrative gifts which range from the laconic to the lyrical, the telescopic to the microscopic. This is a novel which, like a photograph, one will return to again and again." Christ Sci Monit

Thin, D.

(tr) Simenon, G. The man who watched trains go by

Thin, Douglas *See* Thin, D.

Thom, James Alexander

Panther in the sky. Ballantine Bks. 1989 655p il
o.p.   LC 88-48012
The "portrait of Tecumseh, the renowned Shawnee
chief and warrior who established a confederacy of tribes
in order to resist U.S. encroachment into the Ohio valley,
is suitably suffused with fascinating elements of native
American lore, legend, and culture. . . . Action and reflection are juxtaposed in a riveting narrative that animates a remarkable cast of celebrated characters and vivifies recorded events. This respectful version of the life
of a heroic and courageous native American represents
historical fiction at its finest." Booklist

The red heart. Ballantine Bks. 1997 454p map
$25
   ISBN 0-345-41719-4   LC 97-18577
A "novel based on the well-known true life story of
Frances Slocum. The five-year-old daughter of a Pennsylvania Quaker family, Slocum was kidnapped by Delaware Indians in 1778 and adopted by an Indian woman
who raised the child as her own. In Thom's telling of her
story, we see Slocum grow into a respected figure among
the Miamis, becoming Maconakwa—Little Bear Woman—and raising a family on her own. The events of her
life are set against the gradual destruction of Indian life
on the early U.S. frontier. . . . Thom's research is exhaustive, his eye for detail impressive." Publ Wkly

Thomas, Craig, 1942-

Firefox. Holt, Rinehart & Winston 1977 288p
   ISBN 0-03-020791-6   LC 77-71356
"When intelligence leaks out that the Soviets have de-
veloped an incredibly sophisticated warplane code-named
Firefox, with a speed of Mach 5, the Western allies, who
couldn't match it in years, decide to 'steal' the plane
during its first test flight. The CIA and Britain's SIS join
forces, and they pick Vietnam vet Mitchell Gant—emo-
tionally unstable, but a superb pilot—to nab Firefox."
Publ Wkly
"Suspenseful to the end, the psychological ups and
downs are well handled, as are the flight sequences."
Booklist
Followed by Firefox down (1983)

Thomas, D. M.

The white hotel. Viking 1981 274p o.p.
                                        * LC 80-52004
This novel "tells the story of 'Anna G.,' a fictitious patient of Freud's. Anna, an intelligent and sensitive musician, suffers from recurring pains in her left breast and
ovary, with no organic cause. The 'white hotel' is the
setting of Anna's vivid sexual fantasies and visions of
death. Anna's poetry and journal, as well as Freud's covering letters and his case history of her analysis, are followed by a narrative history of Elisabeth Erdman ('Anna
G.')." Libr J
"Repetition, stunningly enacted in imagery that continually circles in on itself, is the method by which Thomas
binds us to his prose. The white hotel is the leitmotif.
. . . The richness of this book is reminiscent of a painstakingly woven tapestry; one can focus on the details but
must be absorbed by the whole." New Repub

Thomas, Dylan, 1914-1953

The collected stories. New Directions 1984 362p
o.p.
                                        * LC 84-6822
Contents: After the fair; The tree; The true story; The
enemies; The dress; The visitor; The vest; The burning
baby; The orchards; The end of the river; The lemon;
The horse's ha; The school for witches; The mouse and
the woman; A prospect of the sea; The holy six; Pro-
logue to an adventure; The map of love; In the direction
of the beginning; An adventure from a work in progress
Portrait of the artist as a young dog: The peaches; A
visit to grandpa's; Patricia, Edith, and Arnold; The fight;
Extraordinary little cough; Just like little dogs; Where
Tawe flows; Who do you wish was with us; Old Garbo;
One warm Saturday
A fine beginning; Plenty of furniture; Four lost souls;
Quite early one morning; A child's Christmas in Wales;
Holiday memory; The crumbs of one man's year; Return
journey; The followers; A story; Brember; Jarley's; In
the garden; Gasper, Melchior, Balthasar

Portrait of the artist as a young dog
   In Thomas, D. The collected stories p122-238

Thomas, Elizabeth Marshall, 1931-

Reindeer Moon. Houghton Mifflin 1987 338p
o.p.   LC 86-18530
"A Peter Davison book"
"We meet the protagonist, Yanan, as a young girl, living with her family in what is now Siberia. Just a few
chapters into the narrative, she dies and becomes a spirit
who must serve the members of her lodge by finding
food for them, often by taking on the form and behavioral characteristics of animals or birds. The story proceeds
in flashback as Yanan relates the memories of her
youth." Publ Wkly
"What makes the reader care for this young girl so far
removed from us by time and distance is that in telling
her story the author conveys sentiments and feelings not
remote from our own today." N Y Times Book Rev

Thomas, Michael M.

Black money. Crown 1994 309p o.p.
                                        LC 93-33813
This novel "tracks a criminal scam from its detection
in a small California mall through its connections to
South American drug cartels, the Mafia, and the highest
reaches of the U.S. government. A middle-level federal
bureaucrat and the socially well-connected editor of a
muckraking magazine join forces to expose an enormously complicated scheme for laundering drug money."
Booklist
Thomas "writes a very exciting and almost-too-
believable tale of power politics and international crime."
Libr J

Hanover Place. Warner Bks. 1990 479p $19.45
   ISBN 0-446-51330-X   LC 89-40038
"Hanover Place, in 1924, is the site of a moderately
successful brokerage house owned by the Warringtons.
Thomas' novel charts the triumphs, losses, and peccadil-
loes of the Warringtons and their kind, also serving up
a portrait of the world of high finance, from the rudi-

Thomas, Michael M.—*Continued*

mentary days of stocks (and the Depression) to the modern age of junk bonds, forced mergers, unfriendly takeovers, and so on. One prominent theme here is anti-Semitism, symbolized by a bright young Jewish clerk who is upgraded into the partners' circle, yet must endure the bigotry of the WASPish men and women who dominate high-level New York society. Later, financial revenge is wrought. A big tale of Americans and their money certain to entertain." Booklist

Thomas, Rosie

All my sins remembered. Bantam Bks. 1992 c1991 548p o.p.   LC 92-8547

First published 1991 in the United Kingdom

This "tale revolves around interviews biographer Elizabeth Ainger records with her grandmother's elderly cousin, Clio, an accomplished novelist. Once three generations of family history are reconstructed, Elizabeth's project has revealed much more than girlish crushes and failed love affairs. This rousing, thoroughly engaging read moves from Victorian drawing rooms to bohemian Bloomsbury and Nazi Germany, with painful secrets and bittersweet betrayals revealed at every turn." Booklist

Other people's marriages. Morrow 1994 c1993 425p o.p.   LC 93-8885

First published 1993 in the United Kingdom

"Within a few weeks of her arrival in the London suburb of Grafton, a young widow begins an affair with a married man. The affair is soon discovered, however, and it sets off a chain reaction of infidelities through five married couples." N Y Times Book Rev

"Effective, precise details vivify physical settings (various homes are as acutely rendered as the cathedral, the novel's central symbol), and the characters, some unappealing but all understandable, are well drawn." Libr J

Thomas, Ross, 1926-1995

Ah, treachery!. Mysterious Press 1994 274p o.p.   LC 94-15118

"In 1989, army major Edd 'Twodees' Partain took part in an illegal operation in El Salvador that his former comrades now want expunged from the record. Meanwhile, top political fund-raiser Millicent Altford needs to recover $1.2 million in stolen under-the-table contributions. These two scenarios dovetail as Altford engineers to have Partain, who was drummed out of the service for assaulting a superior officer, fired from his job in a Wyoming gun store in order to hire him to 'ride shotgun' as she goes after the loot. . . . Thomas's yarn reaffirms his expertise at the black-humored political thriller." Publ Wkly

The fourth Durango. Mysterious Press 1989 312p o.p.   LC 89-3091

Durango, California is "the ideal hideout for a man with a price on his life. For a fee, the shrewd mayor and her loyal chief of police offer sanctuary to a judge who has just done time on a cooked-up bribery charge. The judge and his son-in-law, a disbarred lawyer, move into 'the only money-losing Holiday Inn west of Beirut' and devise a plan for smoking out the person with the vendetta against the judge. For an even bigger fee, the may-

or and her top cop are game to conspire in the scheme—until an extremely ugly man comes to town and starts shooting up the citizenry." N Y Times Book Rev

Voodoo, Ltd. Mysterious Press 1992 282p $19.95

ISBN 0-89296-451-0   LC 91-51185

"Ione Gamble, an actress 'with a face known throughout the world,' is in a real jam. The police think she murdered her former lover, Billy Rice, a dissolute publishing heir and independent movie producer, at his Malibu beach house. Gamble isn't so sure about that, since she was blind drunk at the time. Desperate, she hires Enno Glimm, who will spare no expense in recruiting a discreet hypnotist to probe her alcoholic blackout for the truth without concurrently selling her story to the tabloids. Glimm's company, based in Germany, is a sort of global office-temp agency that fills unusual short-term employment requirements." N Y Times Book Rev

Thomas, Sherree

(ed) Dark matter. See Dark matter

Thomas, Sherry

Private arrangements. Bantam Books 2008 351p pa $6.99

ISBN 978-0-440-24431-8; 0-440-24431-5
                                            LC 2008-577025

"Camden Saybrook, Lord Tremaine, returns to late 19th-century England to confront his wife, Gigi, about her petition for divorce. Still bitter from Gigi's machinations to snare him as her husband, Camden will grant the divorce under one condition—Gigi must give him an heir within a year. Sparks fly as the two embark on heated attempts to put the bun in the oven, despite Gigi's fear that her next conquest, the insipid Lord Frederick, will discover her duplicitously lusty reunion. A captivating subplot emerges when Gigi's mother, Mrs. Rowland, sets her own plan in motion for Gigi's next nuptials. Thomas propels the plot forward with revealing repartee and gives the leads real nuance." Publ Wkly

Thomas, Thomas T.

(jt. auth) Pohl, F. Mars Plus

Thomason, Dustin

(jt. auth) Caldwell, I. The rule of four

Thompson, Jean, 1950-

Wide blue yonder; a novel. Simon & Schuster 2002 367p $24

ISBN 0-7432-0512-X   LC 2001-34157

"It's summer 1999 in Springfield, IL, and Harvey Sloan's sole interest in life continues to be the Weather Channel. His great-niece, Josie, possessed by a hopeless teenage love, confides in Abe Lincoln. Her divorced mother, Elaine, starts to believe that a good or bad day is indicated by her car's service engine light. Meanwhile, Rolando Gottschalk, armed with a gun and an unknown agenda, seems to be headed to Springfield from Los Angeles, leaving a wake of random destruction. Add Mitch, a gorgeous cop, and Rosa, a Mexican cleaning woman, to the mix and you have a novel with characters both memorable and believable." Libr J

Thompson, Jim

The killer inside me
In Crime novels: American noir of the 1950s

Thornton, Tim, 1973-

The alternative hero. Alfred A. Knopf 2009
403p $24.95
ISBN 978-0-307-27109-9   LC 2009-14054

"As a schoolboy in the late '80s, Clive Beresford is a
devoted fan of indie band the Thieving Magpies. Lance
Webster, the band's frontman, becomes Clive's hero, a
pop culture god Clive follows from gig to gig. After
Lance publicly self-destructs and disappears from the
public eye, Clive stumbles into an adulthood of failed romance and dismal job prospects and wonders if he'll
ever get out of his rut. But after he discovers his former
idol living a few doors down the street, Clive makes
painfully awkward contact, and the two begin an unlikely
friendship with Clive pretending to be clueless about
who his neighbor is while secretly intent on writing a
tell-all book." Publ Wkly

"Clive's first-person melodramatics strike a deep and
resonant chord, not because they revolve around any particular band, but because they're about those of us who
live and die for music. . . . Those particular teenage
heart-scars still pain us decades later, seething to a beat
that goes on and on and on, even when our own lives
seem to have come to a full stop. Thornton's peculiar genius is in marking those teenage tablatures and playing
them all the way through, a music fan's grace note, a
love song to what was and may yet still be." Austin
Chron

Tillman, Lynne

American genius; a comedy. Soft Skull Press
2006 292p pa $15
ISBN 1-933368-44-6   LC 2006-04047

This novel "presents an unnamed woman of a certain
age, who lingers in a spa (or is it a madhouse?), digressing with authority on loneliness, denim, Eames chairs,
the history of silk, the vicissitudes of friendship, Puritanism, the blissfulness of sleep and the pleasures of 100%
cotton socks. Dialogue is virtually absent, as is plot;
most everything—a painful childhood, beloved pets, a
dead father and brother and a troubled mother—is revealed through the woman's first-person recollections and
observations. Eventually, it appears the narrator is resident in a New Age, claustrophobia-inducing colony,
where she sharply observes her strange fellows and attends absurd guest lectures." Publ Wkly

"Every book is an experiment. What emerges here is
a bold showcase of a novel, a cabinet of curiosity, a proposal for what fiction could be—a statement of intent,
perhaps, rather than a fully formed artifact." N Y Times
Book Rev

Timm, Uwe, 1940-

Morenga; translated from the German by Breon
Mitchell. New Directions 2003 340p $25.95
ISBN 0-8112-1514-8
                                        * LC 2002-15248

Original German edition, 1978
This novel is "an oddly fragmented montage that offers
a . . . view of the title figure, a charismatic black South-
West African who led the Hottentot and Herero uprising
against the Germans after the Boer War. The initial protagonist is a fictional German military veterinarian . . . .
The early chapters concern the mysterious fate of a colleague who disappears from [the veterinarian's] unit.
From there, Timm turns to the uprising itself, his depiction of Morenga's role broken up by snapshots of secondary characters." Publ Wkly

The "fragmentary approach has great cumulative moral
power, making us consider all sides of the story without
forgetting that there were victims who deserve some remembrance." N Y Times Book Rev

Tinti, Hannah

Animal crackers. Dial Press 2004 197p $22.95
ISBN 0-385-33743-4   LC 2003-70125

Contents: Animal crackers; Home sweet home; Reasonable terms; Preservation; Slim's last ride; Hit man of
the year; Talk turkey; How to revitalize the snake in
your life; Gallus, gallus; Bloodworks; Miss Waldron's
red colobus

"Tinti boldly parses primal emotions in her stealthy
short stories, which, like cats' paws, conceal weapons of
great precision. Each tale posits interaction between animals and humans, which, rather than offering cuddly moments, lead to vicious or spooky confrontations. Zoos
make perfect theaters for Tinti's creepy and caustic satires. . . . Tinti's fables are dark and wily, grim yet morbidly fascinating exposures of both our animal selves and
our uniquely human psychoses." Booklist

The good thief. Dial Press 2008 327p $25
ISBN 978-0-385-33745-8   LC 2008-13507

This "novel is an homage to old-fashioned boy's-own
adventure stories, and unfolds like a Robert Louis Stevenson tale retold amid the hardscrabble squalor of Colonial New England. The sheer strangeness of the story is
beguiling: a one-handed boy, tainted by his upbringing in
a Catholic orphanage and with little to offer but a head
full of lice, is adopted by a con artist, and enters an underworld of ruthless mousetrap-manufacturing barons,
feisty chimney-dwelling dwarves, and, perhaps most terrifying of all, black-market dentists. In keeping with the
gothic tradition, Tinti writes with an arch, almost camp
sensibility. While on a nocturnal grave-digging excursion
to procure bodies for a crazy scientist, for instance, the
pair encounter an assassin, who tells the twelve-year-old
hero that he's 'made for killing.' Will the boy ever
discover the truth of his past? It's good fun watching
him find out." New Yorker

Tiptree, James, 1916-1987

The girl who was plugged in
In The Hugo winners p397-434

Houston, Houston, do you read?
In The Hugo winners p200-56

Tirone Smith, Mary-Ann, 1944-

Love her madly; a novel. Holt & Co. 2002 307p
$25
ISBN 0-8050-6648-9   LC 2001-39306

Tirone Smith, Mary-Ann, 1944-—*Continued*

This thriller "introduces Poppy Rice, FBI agent and brassy gal all around, who blusters her way into a capital punishment case obviously inspired by that of real-life convicted killer Karla Faye Tucker, executed a few years ago. Rona Leigh Glueck awaits the execution chamber, 'about to be the first woman put to death by the people of Texas since the Civil War,' but Poppy deduces that Ms. Glueck's wrists were too dainty to have wielded a heavy ax in a double homicide." Publ Wkly

"Smith delivers a smart, irreverent heroine; pitch-perfect Texan dialogue; gasp-worthy plot twists; and quite a bit of substance along with the action. Poppy has some serious and scathing things to say about the death penalty, religion, and Texas politics." Booklist

She smiled sweetly; a Poppy Rice mystery; Mary-Ann Tirone Smith. 1st ed. Holt & Co. 2004 275p $25

ISBN 0-8050-7224-1   LC 2003-55757

FBI agent Poppy Rice "agrees to help a friend's mom find closure in the case of the death of a pregnant woman in her native Ireland during the 1970s, but before you can say 'Erin go bragh,' the body of another pregnant young woman with an Irish link washes up on a beach in Boston Harbor. Police detective and Hindu/Catholic Rocky Patel heads the Beantown investigation of the American victim, and his coolness and wisdom complement Poppy's no-nonsense professionalism." Publ Wkly

She's not there; a Poppy Rice novel. Holt & Co. 2003 317p map $25

ISBN 0-8050-7223-3   LC 2002-68592

"FBI agent Poppy Rice is taking some time off with boyfriend Joe at his vacation home on Block Island. . . . Her enforced relaxation falls by the wayside after only a few days when she stumbles across the body of a teenage girl from the island's summer weight-loss camp." Booklist

"The ease with which Poppy gets technical support from Washington and manpower from the Rhode Island mainland is some stretch, but that doesn't take away from her shrewd analysis of the isolationist island mentality or her understanding of teenage behavior." N Y Times Book Rev

Titmarsh, Michael Angelo *See* Thackeray, William Makepeace, 1811-1863

Toer, Pramoedya Ananta, 1925-2006

All that is gone; translated from the Indonesian by Willem Samuels. Hyperion East 2004 255p $23.95

ISBN 1-401-36663-5   LC 2003-56675

Contents: All that is gone; Inem; In twilight born; Circumcision; Revenge; Independence Day; Acceptance; The rewards of marriage

"A sense of duty is perhaps natural for a writer who spent nearly two decades as a political prisoner under three different regimes. But the striking achievement of these stories is an unshakable innocence of voice and a willingness to leave judgment to the reader. Pramoedya's art is made more of sadness than of anger, and he is particularly adept at narrating from a child's perspective—as when a six-year-old boy sees his best friend, a girl of eight, married off, beaten by her husband, and, after she flees, made a social outcast." New Yorker

The girl from the coast; translated by Willem Samuels. Hyperion 2002 280p $22.95

ISBN 0-7868-6820-1   LC 2002-69063

Original Indonesian edition, 1987

In this "tale of feudal Java, a beautiful young woman from a poor fishing village has the misfortune of catching the eye of a Muslim aristocrat who asks to marry her, but who, after a brief ceremony in which a dagger takes the place of the groom, merely installs her in his bleak residence as a lowly concubine. . . . As Toer unfurls this entrancing, indelible tale based on his grandmother's hard life, he deftly dissects the conventions that enable a brutal few to oppress the suffering many." Booklist

Toews, Miriam, 1964-

A complicated kindness; a novel; Miriam Toews. Counterpoint 2004 246p $23

ISBN 1-582-43321-6   LC 2004-7960

"Sixteen-year-old Nomi Nichol is a Mennonite, which, she wryly observes, 'is the most embarrassing subsect of people to belong to if you're a teenager.' Because Mennonites shun modern ways, Nomi's repressively fundamentalist community on the plains of Manitoba is a tourist attraction for Americans searching 'for a glimpse backwards in time.' Half of Nomi's family, 'the better-looking half' as she puts it, is missing. Her older sister has fled the stifling strictures of their hometown, while her mother has also vanished after having been excommunicated by her own brother, the local minister, whom Nomi dubs 'The Mouth of Darkness.' That leaves the 16-year-old to look after her gentle, bewildered father and to deal with her own loneliness and persistent memories of how her family came undone." Booklist

"Nomi's hunger for life prevents the novel from being as bleak as her situation might suggest; her account of her trials is veined with a dark humor that glints with the glee of payback." N Y Times Book Rev

Tóibín, Colm, 1955-

The blackwater lightship; a novel. Scribner 2000 273p

ISBN 0-684-87389-3   LC 00-21036

First published 1999 in the United Kingdom

Helen O'Doherty is a school principal living in Dublin, Ireland, whose brother Declan is "dying of AIDS. Declan's wish is to be moved to the home of their acerbic grandmother, Dora, who lives on a cliff overlooking the sea. Guiltstricken to discover that her brother has been ill for years and never confided in her, Helen moves in as well, . . . along with her mother, Lily, and Declan's friends, Larry and Paul." N Y Times Book Rev

"The novel shows us discreetly what a practical, complicated matter dying is, how much logistics and paraphernalia it requires, and its unflinchingly exact style is a kind of respect paid to this. The commonplce and the catastropic lie cheek-by-jowl." London Rev Books

Brooklyn; a novel. Scribner 2009 262p $25

ISBN 978-1-4391-3831-1   LC 2009-10753

"A diligent young woman with few opportunities in nineteen-fifties Ireland is packed off by her family to Brooklyn, where she works in a department store, goes to church and night school, and acquires a boyfriend, be-

Tóibín, Colm, 1955-—_Continued_
fore a family crisis presents her with a stark choice between her new life and her old one. Within these confines, Tóibín creates a narrative of remarkable power, writing with a spareness and intensity that give the minutest shades of feeling immense emotional impact. Seen through his protagonist's cautious eyes, even hackneyed tropes of Brooklyn life, such as trips to Ebbets Field and Coney Island, take on a subtle strangeness. Purging the immigrant novel of all swagger and sentimentality, Tóibín leaves us with a renewed understanding that to emigrate is to become a foreigner in two places at once." New Yorker

The heather blazing. Viking 1993 245p
ISBN 0-670-84789-5

* LC 92-50350
First published 1992 in the United Kingdom
The novel "explores the rigidly controlled mind and soul of a high court Dublin judge, Eamon Redmond. Toibin . . . [presents the] particulars of Redmond's life: his devotion to the law, his daughter's out-of-wedlock pregnancy, his controversial decision in a case concerning the expulsion of a pregnant high school student, and his wrenching memories of his motherless childhood and his father's debilitation after a stroke." Booklist
"Toibin weaves past and present together in a way designed to extract the maximum resonance from the juxtaposition. One of the book's surprises is its subtle humor, its awareness of small ironies." Voice Lit Suppl

The master. Scribner 2004 338p $25
ISBN 0-7432-5040-0

* LC 2003-67376
This novel depicts the writer Henry James during his middle years. "What Toibin has so boldly done—and so brilliantly and successfully—is forge a sympathetic imagining of James' interior life. . . . Even the reader who knows little about Henry James or his work can enjoy this marvelously intelligent and engaging novel, which presents not on a silver platter but in tender, opened hands a beautifully nuanced psychological portrait." Booklist

Mothers and sons; stories. Scribner 2007 271p $24
ISBN 978-1-4165-3465-5; 1-4165-3465-2

LC 2006-47181
First published 2006 in the United Kingdom
Contents: The use of reason; A song; The name of the game; Famous blue raincoat; A priest in the family; A journey; Three friends; A summer job; A long winter
"So flawless and unshowy is the language in Mothers and Sons that only on reflection does it sink in how varied the tone is among these stories. Yes, they're nearly all melancholic, but every shade in the rainbow of melancholy is represented, and the perspective shifts from mother to son to omniscient with no discernible change in authority." Montreal Gazette

Tolkien, J. R. R. (John Ronald Reuel), 1892-1973

The book of lost tales; part I-II; edited by Christopher Tolkien. Houghton Mifflin 1984 2v (History of Middle Earth) o.p.   LC 83-12782
Part one first published 1983 in the United Kingdom
Contents: pt. 1 The cottage of lost play; The music of the Ainur; The coming of the Valar and the building of Valinor; The chaining of Melko; The coming of the Elves and the making of Kôr; The theft of Melko and the darkening of Valinor; The flight of the Noldoli; The tale of the Sun and Moon; The hiding of Valinor; Gilfanon's tale: the travail of the Noldoli and the coming of Mankind
pt. II: The tale of Tinúviel; Turambar and the Foalókë; The fall of Gondolin; The Nauglafring; The tale of Eärendel; The history of Eriol; AElfwine of England
"These fascinating stories of fairies and elves battling evil creatures shed considerable light on the evolution of Tolkien's elaborate fictional world." Booklist

The fellowship of the ring; being the first part of The lord of the rings. 2nd ed. Houghton Mifflin 1986 c1965 423p il $21.95
ISBN 0-395-48931-8

* LC 88-120282
First published 1954
"Frodo, a home-loving young hobbit, inherits the magic ring which his uncle Bilbo brought back from the adventures described in the juvenile fantasy 'The hobbit'. This sequel, expressly addressed to adults, is the first of a three-part saga that tells of Frodo's valiant journey undertaken to prevent the ring from falling into the hands of the powers of darkness. Elves, dwarfs, hobbits, men, and sundry evil beings, each as real as the other, populate an allegorical tale that shows how power corrupts." Booklist
Followed by The two towers

also in Tolkien, J. R. R. The lord of the rings

The hobbit; or, There and back again; illustrated by Michael Hague. Houghton Mifflin 1984 290p il $29.95
ISBN 0-395-36290-3

* LC 84-9023
First published 1937 in the United Kingdom; first United States edition 1938
"This fantasy features the adventures of hobbit Bilbo Baggins, who joins a band of dwarves led by Gandalf the Wizard. Together they seek to recover the stolen treasure that is hidden in Lonely Mountain and guarded by Smaug the Dragon. This book precedes the _Lord of the Rings_ trilogy." Shapiro. Fic for Youth. 3d edition
"It must be understood that this is a children's book only in the sense that the first of many readings can be undertaken in the nursery. . . . [The hobbit] will be funniest to its youngest readers, and only years later, at a tenth or twentieth reading, will they begin to realize what deft scholarship and profound reflection have gone to make everything in it so ripe, so friendly, and in its own way so true." Times Lit Suppl

Tolkien, J. R. R. (John Ronald Reuel), 1892-1973—*Continued*

The lord of the rings. 2nd ed. Houghton Mifflin 1986 c1966 3v

The trilogy was first published 1954-55 in the United Kingdom. This revised edition first published 1966 in the United Kingdom

Contents: v1 The fellowship of the ring; v2 The two towers; v3 The return of the king

"This is a tale of imaginary gnomelike creatures who battle against evil. Led by Frodo, the hobbits embark on a journey to prevent a magic ring from falling into the grasp of the powers of darkness. The forces of good succeed in their fight against the Dark Lord of evil, and Frodo and Sam bring the Ring to Mount Doom, where it is destroyed." Shapiro. Fic for Youth. 3d edition

Narn i chîn Húrin; the tale of the children of Húrin; edited by Christopher Tolkien ; illustrated by Alan Lee. Houghton Mifflin 2007 313p il map $26

ISBN 978-0-618-89464-2; 0-618-89464-0

LC 2007-1420

A "tale of Middle-earth's First Age, which appeared in incomplete forms in the posthumously published The Silmarillion and Unfinished Tales. . . . [This is] the tragic story of Túrin and Niënor, the children of Húrin, the lord of Dor-lómin, who achieved renown for having confronted Morgoth, who was the master of Sauron, the manifestation of evil in the Lord of the Rings. The lengthy and fatiguing battle against Morgoth forms the backdrop for the moving account of the life of Húrin's eldest son, Túrin, a valiant but proud warrior whose all too human frailties augur an unhappy end." Publ Wkly

"If anyone still labors under the delusion that J. R. R. Tolkien was a writer of twee fantasies for children, this novel should set them straight. A bleak, darkly beautiful tale played out against the background of the First Age of Tolkien's Middle Earth, The Children of Hurin possesses the mythic resonance and grim sense of inexorable fate found in Greek tragedy." Washington Post Book World

The return of the king; being the third part of The lord of the rings. 2nd ed. Houghton Mifflin 1986 c1965 440p $21.95

ISBN 0-395-48930-X

* LC 88-195987

First published 1955 in the United Kingdom

In the concluding volume of the trilogy "The dark lord of evil is overthrown, the rightful king comes into his own, and the Age of Men begins." Booklist

also in Tolkien, J. R. R. The lord of the rings

The Silmarillion; edited by Christopher Tolkien. Houghton Mifflin 1977 365p o.p.   LC 77-8025

Contents: Ainulindale; Valaquenta; Quenta Silmarillion: Of the beginning of days; Quenta Silmarillion: Of Autë and Yavanna; Quenta Silmarillion: Of the coming of the elves and the captivity of Melkor; Quenta Silmarillion: Of Thingol and Melian; Quenta Silmarillion: Of Eldamar and the princes of the Eldalië; Quenta Silmarillion: Of Fëanor and the unchaining of Melkor; Quenta Silmarillion: Of the Silmarils and the unrest of the Noldor; Quenta Silmarillion: Of the darkening of Valinor; Quenta Silmarillion: Of the flight of the Noldor; Quenta Silmarillion: Of the Sindar; Quenta Silmarillion: Of the sun and moon and the hiding of Valinor; Quenta Silmarillion: Of men; Quenta Silmarillion: Of the return of the Noldor; Quenta Silmarillion: Of Beleriand and its realms; Quenta Silmarillion: Of the Noldor in Beleriand; Quenta Silmarillion: Of Maeglin; Quenta Silmarillion: Of the coming of men into the West; Quenta Silmarillion: Of the ruin of Beleriand and the fall of Fingollin; Quenta Silmarillion: Of Beren and Lúthien; Quenta Silmarillion: Of the fifth battle: Niraeth Arnoediad; Quenta Silmarillion: Of Turin Turambar; Quenta Silmarillion: Of the ruin of Doriath; Quenta Silmarillion: Of Tuor and the fall of Gondolin; Quenta Silmarillion: Of the voyage of Eärendil and the war of wrath; Akallabeth; Of the Rings of Power and the Third Age

"Tolkien began writing these introductory legends in 1917 and, sporadically throughout his life, continued adding to them; his son Christopher has edited and compiled the various versions into a single cohesive work. Two brief tales, which outline the origin of the world and describe the gods who create and rule, precede the title story about the Silmarils—three brilliant, jewel-like creatures who are desired and fought over, setting up a clash between good and evil." Booklist

The two towers; being the second part of The lord of the rings. 2nd ed. Houghton Mifflin 1986 c1965 352p $21.95

ISBN 0-395-48933-4

* LC 88-195969

First published 1954

"Here the Companions of the Ring, separated, meet Saruman the wizard, cross the Dead Marshes, and prepare for the Great War in which the power of the Ring will be undone." Libr J

Followed by The return of the king

also in Tolkien, J. R. R. The lord of the rings

Tolkien, John Ronald Reuel *See* Tolkien, J. R. R. (John Ronald Reuel), 1892-1973

Tolstaia, Tat´iana, 1951-

The slynx; [by] Tatyana Tolstaya; translated by Jamey Gambrell. Houghton Mifflin 2003 278p $24

ISBN 0-618-12497-7   LC 2002-27627

Original Russian edition, 2000

In a postapocalyptic Russia, "in a society turned primitive by nuclear holocaust, people hunt mice and tremble at the mention of a mysterious forest creature called the slynx; of course, they are utterly ignorant, as books are banned. . . . Benedikt, scribe to the tyrant who rules this sorry land . . . has yet to read a book, but in the course of the novel he discovers the libraries owned by the Olders, those who recall the world before the fateful blast. Not surprisingly, he finds that literature is both liberating and dangerous." Libr J

"It takes some time for a plot to develop, but Tolstaya sketches a vivid picture of life in this permanent winter. . . . In this extended fable, she captures the Russian yearning for culture, even in desperate circumstances. Gambrell ably translates the mix of neologisms and plain speech with which Tolstaya describes this devastated world." Publ Wkly

Tolstaia, Tat´iana, 1951——*Continued*
White walls; collected stories; [by] Tatyana
Tolstaya; translated by Antonina W. Bouis [and]
Jamey Gambrell. New York Review Books 2007
404p (New York Review Books classics) pa
$16.95
ISBN 978-1-59017-197-4; 1-59017-197-7

LC 2007-5450
Contents: Loves me, loves me not; Okkervil River;
Sweet Shura; On the golden porch; Hunting the wooly
mammoth; The circle; A clean sheet; Fire and dust; Date
with a bird; Sweet dreams, son; Sonya; The fakir; Peters;
Sleepwalker in a fog; Serafim; The moon came out;
Night; Heavenly flame; Most beloved; The poet and the
muse; Limpopo; Yorick; White walls; See the other side
"Angels, imaginary friends, near-saints, shades and
über-ogres fall to Earth among ordinary Russians and
routinely succeed in whetting the imagination in this
sparkling collection from Tolstoy's great-grandniece. . . .
It includes her two previous story collections, On the
Golden Porch and Sleepwalker in a Fog, along with
more recent work. . . . Beautiful, imaginative and disconcerting, Tolstaya's Russia is a labyrinth of treasures
and horrors." Publ Wkly

Tolstoy, Leo, graf, 1828-1910

Anna Karenina; edited and introduced by Leonard J. Kent and Nina Berberova. Modern Lib.
1993 xxvii, 927p $22.95
ISBN 0-679-60079-5

* LC 93-43634
Written in 1873-1876
This novel "is the story of a tragic, adulterous love.
Anna meets and falls in love with Aleksei Vronski, a
handsome young officer. She abandons her child and
husband in order to be with Vronski. When she thinks
Vronski has tired of her, she kills herself by leaping under a train. The idea for the story reputedly came to Tolstoy after he had viewed the body of a young woman
who committed a similar suicide. A subplot concerns the
contrasting happy marriage of Konstantin Levin and his
young wife Kitty. Levin's search for meaning in his life
and his love for a natural, simple existence on his estate
are reflections of Tolstoy's own moods and thoughts of
the time." Reader's Ency. 4th edition

Childhood, Boyhood and Youth; translated from
the Russian by C. J. Hogarth. Knopf 1991 314p
$17
ISBN 0-679-40578-X

LC 91-52984
"Everyman's library"
Originally published separately, 1852, 1854 and 1857
respectively; this edition first published 1912
"An autobiographical trilogy. . . . 'Childhood' was the
first of Tolstoy's works to receive wide attention. The
descriptions of life on a provincial estate are among the
best depictions of nature in Russian literature." Reader's
Ency. 4th edition

The Cossacks
In Tolstoy, L., graf. The short novels of
Tolstoy

The death of Iván Ilyitch
In Tolstoy, L., graf. The short novels of
Tolstoy

The death of Ivan Ilyitch, and other stories; a
new translation from the Russian by Constance
Garnett. Dodd, Mead 1927 362p o.p.
Contents: The death of Ivan Ilyitch; Family happiness;
Polikushka; Two hussars; The snowstorm; Three deaths

The Devil
In Tolstoy, L., graf. The Kreutzer sonata, The
Devil, and other tales
In Tolstoy, L., graf. The short novels of
Tolstoy

Divine and human and other stories; new translations by Peter Sekirin. Zondervan 2000 211p
$19.99
ISBN 0-310-22367-9

LC 00-20791
Contents: The son of a thief; The repentant sinner; The
archangel Gabriel; The prayer; The poor people; A cof-
feehouse in the city of Surat; Kornei Vasiliev; A grain
of rye the size of a chicken egg; The berries; Stones;
The big dipper; The power of childhood; Why did it
happen?; Divine and human; The requirements of love;
Sisters
"These 16 selections from Tolstoy's final eclectic collection of tales titled *The Sunday Reading Stories* represent the Russian novelist's turn away from the troubling
human condition in *Anna Karenina* toward a growing
preoccupation with moral issues." Publ Wkly

Family happiness
In Tolstoy, L., graf. The Kreutzer sonata, The
Devil, and other tales
In Tolstoy, L., graf. The short novels of
Tolstoy

Father Sergius
In Tolstoy, L., graf. The Kreutzer sonata, The
Devil, and other tales

Hadji Murád
In Tolstoy, L., graf. The short novels of
Tolstoy

The Kreutzer sonata, The Devil, and other tales;
translation of Family happiness, by J. D. Duff, and
of other stories by Aylmer Maude; with an introduction by Aylmer Maude. Oxford Univ. Press
1957 xxi, 375p o.p.
Contents: Family happiness; The Kreutzer sonata; The
Devil; Father Sergius; François; The porcelain doll

Master and man
In Tolstoy, L., graf. The short novels of
Tolstoy

Polikúshka
In Tolstoy, L., graf. The short novels of
Tolstoy

Resurrection; a new translation, with an introduction, by Anthony Briggs. Penguin Books 2009
xxxiv, 520p (Penguin classics) pa $16
ISBN 978-0-14-042463-8; 0-14-042463-6
Original Russian edition, 1899
"The story deals with the spiritual regeneration of a
young nobleman, Prince Nekhlyudov. In his earlier years,

Tolstoy, Leo, graf, 1828-1910—*Continued*

he seduced a young girl, Katyusha Maslova. She became a prostitute and later became involved with a man she is accused of poisoning. Nekhlyudov, serving on the jury, recognizes her and decides that he is morally guilty for her predicament. He decides to marry her, and when she is convicted he follows her to Siberia to accomplish his aim. Maslova is repelled by his reforming zeal. She marries another prisoner, but is finally convinced of Nekhlyudov's sincerity and accepts his friendship." Reader's Ency. 4th edition

The short novels of Tolstoy; selected with an introduction by Philip Rahv; translated by Aylmer Maude. Dial Press 1946 xx, 716p o.p.

Contents: Two hussars; Family happiness; The Cossacks; Polikúshka; The death of Iván Ilyitch; The Devil; Master and man; Hadji Murád

Short stories; selected and introduced by Ernest J. Simmons. Modern Lib. 1964-1965 2v o.p.

Contents: v 1: A history of yesterday; The raid; A billiard-markers' notes; The wood-felling; Sevastopol in December 1854; Sevastopol in May 1855; Sevastopol in August 1855; Meeting a Moscow acquaintance in the detachment; The snow storm; Lucerne; Albert; Three deaths; Strider; The porcelain doll

v2: God sees the truth, but waits; A prisoner in the Caucasus; The bearhunt; What men live by; A spark neglected burns the house; Two old men; Where love is, God is; Evil allures, but good endures; Little girls wiser than men; Elias; The story of Iván, the Fool; The repentant sinner; The three hermits; The imp and the crust; How much land does a man need; A grain as big as a hen's egg; The godson; The empty drum; Esarhaddon, King of Assyria; Work, death and sickness; Three questions; The memoirs of a madman; After the ball; Fëdor Kuzmich; Alyósha

Two hussars

In Tolstoy, L., graf. The short novels of Tolstoy

War and peace; translated by Richard Pevear and Larissa Volokhonsky. Knopf 2007 1273p $37

ISBN 978-0-307-26693-4; 0-307-26693-1

LC 2007-15989

Original Russian edition, 1864-1869

"Stressing that their War and Peace sticks more closely to the Russian text than any other, including Louise and Aylmer Maude's semi-canonical 1923 version, Pevear and Volokhonsky retain the considerable amount of French used by Tolstoy's counts and princesses, preserve the author's penchant for word repetition and aim to match his tidy syntactic conciseness. The result certainly reads smoothly, its English being neither egregiously contemporary nor inappropriately old-fashioned." Washington Post Book World Modern Lib. 1994 1386p $25.95

ISBN 0-679-60084-1

* LC 93-38836

Original Russian edition, 1864-1869

"The story covers roughly the years between 1805 and 1820, centering on the invasion of Russia by Napoleon's army in 1812 and the Russian resistance to the invader. Over five hundred characters, all carefully rendered, populate the pages of the novel. Every social level, from Na-

poleon himself to the peasant Platon Karatayev, is represented. Interwoven with the story of the war are narrations of the lives of several main characters, especially those of Natasha Rostova, Prince Andrey Bolkonsky, and Pierre Bezukhov. These people are shown as they progress from youthful uncertainties and searchings toward a more mature understanding of life." Reader's Ency. 4th edition

Toole, F. X., 1930-2002

Pound for pound; a novel. Ecco 2006 366p $25.95

ISBN 978-0-06-088133-7   LC 2005-49508

This is the "story of Eduardo 'Chicky' Garza, a young San Antonio fighter and grandson of onetime contender Eloy 'Texas Wolf' Garza. When Chicky is cheated out of a shot at the Olympic team, his grandfather encourages him to move to Los Angeles and find trainer Dan Cooley, a former boxer who lost to the grandfather 40 years earlier in a fixed fight. Though struggling with a deep depression brought on by the accidental death of his young grandson, Cooley decides to take Chicky on, paving the way for him to face the fighter who cheated him. The result is powerful and very readable, if somewhat sentimental, and Toole's deep love of boxing's rituals, traditions, and code of honor shines through." Libr J

Toole, John Kennedy, 1937-1969

A confederacy of dunces; foreword by Walker Percy. Louisiana State Univ. Press 1980 338p $24.95

ISBN 0-8071-0657-7

* LC 79-20190

The protagonist of this novel set in New Orleans is Ignatius J. Reilly, "a medievalist whose fortunes take a downward turn when he is nearly arrested for being a 'suspicious character.' Things only get worse when he and his mother (leaving the Night of Joy bar, where they've gone to soothe their nerves after the near-arrest) run their car into a building, and Ignatius is forced to find a job to pay for the damages." Christ Sci Monit

"At the heart of this splendid mock-heroic with its blundering and canniness, its falstaffian excesses and 'Alice in Wonderland' wit, lies a profound sense of solitude. Like everything else in Ignatuis J. Reilly's world, the absence of love is larger than life." Newsweek

Torday, Paul, 1946-

Salmon fishing in the Yemen. Harcourt 2007 333p $24

ISBN 978-0-15-101276-3   LC 2006-33713

"Dr. Alfred Jones is a henpecked, slightly pompous middle-aged scientist at the National Centre for Fisheries Excellence in London when he is approached by a mysterious sheikh about an outlandish plan to introduce the sport of salmon fishing into the Yemen. Dr. Jones refuses, but the project, however scientifically absurd, catches the eye of British politicians, who pressure him to work on it. His diaries of the Yemen Salmon Project, from beginning to . . . end, form the narrative backbone of this novel." Publisher's note

This is an "oddball piece of fiction that—despite being told through dry diary extracts, e-mails and reports—is

Torday, Paul, 1946——*Continued*

an amusing satire on the tensions between the West and the Middle East, and a commentary on the value of belief to mankind. . . . The success of the book lies in the charm of Mr. Torday's storyline—his love of salmon fishing shines through his text—and his skill at portraying the petty officialdom and manipulativeness of modern government." Economist

Torsvan, Berick Traven *See* Traven, B.

Torsvan, Traven *See* Traven, B.

Tournier, Michel

Friday; translated from the French by Norman Denny. Johns Hopkins University Press 1997 c1969 235p pa $25
ISBN 0-8018-5592-6
* LC 96-45295
Original French edition, 1967; this translation first published 1969 by Doubleday
A retelling of the legend of Robinson Crusoe. "Cast away on a tropical island . . . Crusoe sets out to tame it, to remake it in the image of the civilization he has left behind. Alone and against incredible odds, he almost succeeds. Then a mulatto named Friday appears and teaches Robinson that there are, aftere all, better things in life than civilization." Publisher's note

"M. Tournier is a cultivated and disciplined writer, and his Robinson, the son of a Yorkshire draper, is most likable. . . . The castaway has that quaint and peculiarly English stolidity that seems to exist only in the imagination of the French." New Yorker

The ogre; translated from the French by Barbara Bray. Johns Hopkins University Press 1997 c1972 373p pa $19.95
ISBN 0-8018-5590-x
* LC 96-46778
Original French edition, 1970; this translation first published 1972 by Doubleday and in the United Kingdom by Collins with title: The Erl-king
This novel "traces the life of Abel Tiffauges, a huge French garage mechanic, from his childhood memories . . . to his 1940-4 experience as a prisoner of war, ending up working at a training camp for young boys at Kaltenborn." Good Fiction Guide
A work that "bears patently the marks of greatness. It relentlessly pushes individual idiosyncrasy to–and even beyond–the point of universality. It covers simultaneously the events inside one head and one continent. It uses documentary knowledge–minute and encyclopedic knowledge of photography, history, zoology, anthropometry, weaponry– to illustrate the otherwise undocumentable progress of a human obsession." New Yorker

Tower, Wells, 1973-

Everything ravaged, everything burned. Farrar, Straus and Giroux 2009 238p $24
ISBN 978-0-374-29219-5; 0-374-29219-1
LC 2008-42757

Contents: The brown coast; Retreat; Executors of important energies; Down through the valley; Leopard; Door in your eye; Wild America; On the show; Everything ravaged, everything burned

"Holy hell! After enduring years of literary atrophy, mostly reading stories by authors so alienated from what the majority of actual human beings suffer, they compensate for a lack of authentic visceral insight with decorative, purple prose and quirky coincidences, now an author emerges who again dares to pierce the heart of modern realism, revealing the conflicted spirit of middle-America, a troubling yet real place populated by lonely divorcees, hormonal teens, Alzheimer-afflicted fathers and the sons who can't care for them, each person searching for the treasure chest of meaning in a landscape that's already been pillaged, the earth salted." PopMatters

Townsend, Sue

Adrian Mole; the Cappucino years. Soho Press 2000 c1999 390p
ISBN 1-56947-204-1
LC 99-87241
First published 1999 in the United Kingdom
"Now in his 'cappucino years,' Adrian is a single father and chef who struggles financially. His personal life continues to be complicated by his dysfunctional family, his still unrequited love for Pandora Braithwaite, and the revelation that he is father to not one but two sons." Libr J

"Adrian is a comic Job in a world gone mad with irony and greed. But his confused heart brims with love and good intentions, and Townsend skewers end-of-the millennium Britain with acumen and glee." Booklist

The Adrian Mole diaries. Grove Press 1986 c1985 342p
ISBN 0-394-55298-9
* LC 86-226
First published 1985 in the United Kingdom; A combined edition of two titles: The secret diary of Adrian Mole, age 13 ¾ (1982); and Growing pains (1984)
"The messy, inconsistent world of adulthood is seen through the eyes of a 14-year-old aspiring intellectual and poet. Adrian Mole begins his diary when spots appear on his face and his parents' marriage dissolves. By the diary's end he has been in love, become helpmate to a feisty 89-year-old, and held his mother's hand during the birth of his sister. Adrian's pithy commentary records the ludicrousness of school and state bureaucracy and the aberrations of the nuclear age." Booklist
Followed by Adrian Mole: the lost years

Adrian Mole: the lost years. Soho Press 1994 309p $22
ISBN 1-56947-014-6
LC 94-11276
"Portions of this text appeared in *The True Confessions of Adrian Albert Mole,* while @Adrian Mole and the Small Amphibians' appeared in *Adrian Mole, From Minor to Major. Adrian Mole, The Wilderness Years* appears in its entirety. All were first published in Great Britain." Verso of title page
"Adrian's latest diaries chronicle his mighty struggle to survive the adolescent and postpubescent years. His outrageous clothes and strong views about everything from the government to unwed mothers can't disguise the angst he suffers: he's still trying to find a niche for his

Townsend, Sue—*Continued*

unrecognized genius. . . . Townsend is a satirist of the first order, offering brilliantly witty humor peppered with sobering insights into the troubles and traumas of working-class Brits." Booklist

Growing pains
In Townsend, S. The Adrian Mole diaries

Number 10; Sue Townsend. Soho 2003 277p $24

ISBN 1-569-47349-8   LC 2003-50562

This novel combines "social satire with an odd-couple road trip. The buddy team includes Jack, a policeman who grew up on the edge of squalor but manages to emerge a decent and levelheaded man. The other half is Edward, reared in privilege to take his all-but-predestined place as prime minister. Struck with the realization that he has no idea what life is like for ordinary citizens, Edward sets off, incognito, for a week-long safari into the land of the common folk, with Jack as his escort. Because it's hard for the prime minister to travel unnoticed, he does what any sensible man would do—slips into a wig and high heels and becomes 'Edwina.' The book doesn't lack for skewering observations of the upper and lower classes, but Edward and Jack are both such well-meaning characters, the book comes off ultimately as more affirming than biting." Booklist

The secret diary of Adrian Mole, age 13¾
In Townsend, S. The Adrian Mole diaries

Tracy, P. J.

Monkeewrench. Putnam 2003 373p $23.95
ISBN 0-399-14978-3   LC 2002-68139
"When people start dying in strange ways in Minneapolis, everyone wonders what the murderer will do next—everyone except the employees of Monkeewrench Software, who are all too aware that their new serial-killer computer game is the model for the crimes. They go to the police with the what, where, and when of the next murders and quickly become suspects themselves." Booklist

"Unlike the conventionally dimwitted cops and hick sheriff's deputies, Grace and her four geek partners in the software company . . . add real flavor to the proceedings with their colorful jargon and quirky personas. These techno-nerds may be freaks—and one of them may even be a killer—but they have style." N Y Times Book Rev

Traven, B.

The treasure of the Sierra Madre. Knopf 1935 366p o.p.
*

Original German edition, 1927
This novel analyzes the "psychology of greed in telling of three Americans searching for a lost gold mine in Mexican mountains." Oxford Companion to Am Lit. 6th edition

Traver, Robert, 1903-1991

Anatomy of a murder. St. Martin's Press 1958 437p o.p.
*

"Not the usual murder mystery but a review by the lawyer for the defense from the time he takes the case of an army lieutenant who admits to having killed the man who raped his wife, until the end of the trial. Much attention is given to establishing the fact of rape. Although the recital is wordy it maintains suspense in showing the legal and personal resources the lawyer calls on to build his defense and the way that rivalry between prosecution and defense shapes the trial." Booklist

Tremain, Rose

The color. Farrar, Straus & Giroux 2003 382p $25
ISBN 0-374-12605-4   LC 2002-192528
This novel, set in the mid-19th century, centers on Joseph and Harriet Blackstone, who have married and emigrated to New Zealand in search of a better life. "Together with Joseph's mother, they attempt to build a farm on the flats outside of Christchurch, but when Joseph finds gold in the creek, he becomes obsessed by 'the color', as the fabulous metal is known. Abandoning both women, he travels by ship to the west coast, where he encounters hundreds of other desperate men and the clamorous, filthy, dehumanizing conditions in which they live. . . . By the time [Harriet] does join him, each of them despises the other, yet the discovery of gold binds them in a new way." Publ Wkly

"As the story gathers momentum, it widens . . . . Tremain's excursions into the minds of her Maori and Chinese characters are written with a blend of sympathy and irony that sabotages our expectations of things exotic and inscrutable." N Y Times Book Rev

Music & silence. Farrar, Straus & Giroux 2000 485p
ISBN 0-374-19989-2   LC 99-42880
First published 1999 in the United Kingdom
"British lutenist Peter Claire arrives in Copenhagen in 1629 to join the orchestra of King Christian IV. Depressed after a doomed love affair with a soulful Irish countess, Peter finds his melancholy mood mirrored by that of the king, who is beset by both financial and marital crises. That fruitless wars and profligate spending by the Danish nobility have depleted the country's coffers is the king's public woe; privately, his heart is anguished by the behavior of his consort, Kristen Munk, who despises her own children, keeps her spouse from her bed and is carrying on with a German mercenary." Publ Wkly

"So hypnotic are Rose Tremain's seductive paragraphs that we are borne along without effort in a world which is neither fact nor fiction but has the strengths of both, with a uniquely sensitive imagination at work." N Y Rev Books

The road home. Little, Brown 2008 432p $24.99
ISBN 978-0-316-00261-5; 0-316-00261-5
     LC 2008-921700
First published 2007 in the United Kingdom
"Lev has left his mother and child in his village in Eastern Europe to seek work in London, bringing with

Tremain, Rose—*Continued*
him an E.U. passport, a handful of English phrases, and a small stash of cash and vodka. At first, he is repelled by what he finds: the shaved heads, the greasy food in disposable packaging, the women thrusting their breasts at him from the pages of the daily paper. But opportunities also push themselves forward in this cold new world; soon he is scheming for a way to unite his future and his past. At once timeless and bitingly contemporary, this novel explores the life now lived by millions—when one's hope lies in one country and one's heart in another." New Yorker

Sacred country. Atheneum Pubs. 1993 c1992 323p $21
ISBN 0-689-12170-9   LC 92-21457
First published 1992 in the United Kingdom
"At the age of six, Mary Ward, standing with her family in a wintry Suffolk field to observe a two-minute silence in honor of the death of King George VI, comes to the realization that she was meant to be a boy. From this beginning in 1952 until 1980, Tremain tells the evocative tale of Mary's lonely quest to transform herself into Martin. Emotionally abandoned by her parents, Mary finds refuge first with her grandfather, Cord, and later with her schoolteacher, Miss McRae." Libr J
The author "gives us a precisely imagined landscape and a complicated group of characters that we come to care deeply about." N Y Times Book Rev

The way I found her. Farrar, Straus & Giroux 1998 358p $25
ISBN 0-374-28666-3
                                      * LC 97-32676
First published 1997 in the United Kingdom
"Thirteen-year-old Lewis Little—dog-lover, chess player, amateur detective—joins his mother on a summer translating job in Paris to see the city and improve his French. But when he meets their glamorous hostess, Valentina Gavrilovich, with her infectious laugh, her cerise lipstick, and her large white breasts, his life is changed forever. And when Valentina vanishes he dedicates himself, like a knight from one of the medieval romances he writes, to rescuing her. Lewis's own narrative of innocence and experience is curiously reminiscent of the nineteen-fifties, and the effect is one of pleasurable nostalgia." New Yorker

Trenhaile, John

The gates of exquisite view. Dutton 1988 374p o.p.   LC 87-13630
"Saga of English capitalist Simon Young, his Hong Kong enterprise, and the secrets in his supercomputer." Smith. Cloak and Dagger Fic
"Trenhaile craftily weaves a portentous web of political intrigue, masking until the final pages the exact nature of his characters' intentions and loyalties. . . . Neatly paced suspense from a master of the genre." Booklist

Treuer, David

The translation of Dr Apelles; a love story. Graywolf 2006 344p $23
ISBN 978-1-55597-451-0; 1-55597-451-1
                            LC 2006-924339

This "novel is a metaphysical blending of two love stories, one mythological, the other very much in the urban present. Dr Apelles is a Native American translator of ancient Native American texts—every other Friday. The rest of his time is spent in a vast library, sorting an endless succession of obscure books. He feels that no one would notice if he disappeared, and knows that he takes too much comfort in 'the bouquet of languages he holds so dear.' Then a new translation he is working on sends him into a tailspin. It's a mythological tale of two orphaned Native Americans from different tribes who fall in love, suffer hardships, and eventually marry. Dr Apelles becomes immersed in his translation, seeing his own life as pale and loveless in comparison. As he becomes romantically involved with a coworker, the translation becomes the story he tells her of his own life. Treuer's novel comprises an intricate and provocative labyrinth that challenges the reader at every turn." Booklist

Trevanian

The Eiger sanction. Crown 1972 316p o.p.
                                      *
"American art professor-mountain climber Dr. Jonathan Hemlock moonlights as an assassin in the employ of the Search and Sanction Division of the mythical counter-assassination bureau known as C-11. In his last mission before retirement, he is sent along on a top-flight mountain climbing expedition in Switzerland with orders to liquidate one of three companions known to have killed an unlucky C-11 agent in Montreal. Not knowing the identity of the assassin Hemlock ruthlessly plans to bump off all three." Smith. Cloak and Dagger Fic

Incident at Twenty Mile. St. Martin's Press 1998 308p $24.95
ISBN 0-312-19233-9   LC 98-19401
"Matthew Dubcheck wanders into the dying silver-mining town of Twenty-Mile, Wyoming, and declares himself the Ringo Kid, after the hero of his favorite dime novels. The romanticized West clashes with the real West when an escaped con comes to town, befriends Matthew, and the wheels begin to turn toward an inevitably tragic conclusion. The anti-western is also a staple of the genre, and this tragicomic tale takes its place alongside such similar efforts as *True Git* and poet David Waggoner's delightful *Where Is My Wandering Boy Tonight?*" Booklist

The Loo sanction; a novel. Three Rivers Press 2005 294p pa $13.95
ISBN 1-4000-9828-9; 978-1-4000-9828-6
                            LC 2004-29743
First published 1973
"Jonathan Hemlock, American art expert whose past has included espionage work, is dragooned and blackmailed by British intelligence into trying to infiltrate a vicious gang that specializes in kinky sex, drugs and incriminating photos of British VIP's." Publ Wkly
"The plot, though fast-moving, is not the most sophisticated, yet there is a certain excitement in this descendant of James Bond, and it works despite one's better judgment." Libr J

Trevanian—_Continued_

Shibumi. Crown 1979 374p o.p.

LC 78-20950

This novel relates the "feats of Hel, the world's highest-paid assassin. Hel guns down political terrorists of the CIA, PLO, and various other organizations, then takes on the superpower of espionage agencies, the Mother Company." Publ Wkly

The summer of Katya. Crown 1983 242p o.p.

* LC 83-1790

"The time is 1914 and the story takes place in a small French Basque village. Dr. Jean-Marc Montjean, young and newly graduated from medical school, meets and falls in love with Katya, a beautiful young girl. Their encounter comes by way of an accident that befalls Katya's brother Paul, to whom she is very attached. Jean-Marc becomes involved with their family and begins to pay court to Katya. He is warned that any romantic attachment is out of the question because of her delicate health. A mystery in the background of the family hangs over all their relationships, and in a final meeting there is a shocking climax that leaves the reader stunned." Shapiro. Fic for Youth. 3d edition

Trevor, Elleston, 1920-1995

For works written by this author under other names see Hall, Adam, 1920-1995

Trevor, William, 1928-

A bit on the side. Viking 2004 244p $24.95

ISBN 0-670-91507-6   LC 2004-42035

Contents: Sitting with the dead; Traditions; Justina's priest; An evening out; Graillis's legacy; Solitude; Sacred statues; Rose wept; Big bucks; On the streets; The dancing-master's music; A bit on the side

The author "reveals his native Ireland as a world sandwiched between modernity and its accompanying wealth, secularism and vulgarity, and a past that was more soulful and pious but also more restrictive. . . . Trevor . . . explores the many sources and shadings of regret with his usual delicate but brilliant psychological nuance, brightened occasionally by nostalgia for the lost love that once impelled his characters forward." Publ Wkly

Cheating at canasta. Viking 2007 231p $24.95

ISBN 978-0-670-01837-6   LC 2007-13499

Contents: The dressmaker's child; The room; Men of Ireland; Cheating at canasta; Bravado; An afternoon; At Olivehill; A perfect relationship; The children; Old flame; Faith; Folie à deux

"While many story collections suffer from repetitiveness when read in rapid succession, Trevor's scope is sufficiently broad to avoid this pitfall. . . . His characters are filled with yearning but, stymied by forces beyond their control, must resign themselves to stasis. If this sounds less than chipper, it is offset by the beauty and solace to be found in the deep level of understanding Trevor brings to his characters." Christ Sci Monit

The collected stories. Viking 1992 1261p o.p.

* LC 92-54071

Contents: A meeting in middle age; Access to the children; The general's day; Memories of Youghal; The table; A school story; The penthouse apartment; In at the birth; The introspections of J. P. Powers; The day we got drunk on cake; Miss Smith; The Hotel of the Idle Moon; Nice day at school; The original sins of Edward Tripp; The forty-seventh Saturday; The ballroom of romance; A happy family; The grass widows; The Mark-2 wife; An evening with John Joe Dempsey; Kinkies; Going home; A choice of butchers; O fat white woman; Raymond Bamber and Mrs. Fitch; The distant past; In Isfahan; Angels at the Ritz; The death of Peggy Meehan; Mrs. Silly; A complicated nature; Teresa's wedding; Office romances; Mr. McNamara; Afternoon dancing; Last wishes; Mrs. Acland's ghosts; Another Christmas; Broken homes; Matilda's England; Torridge; Death in Jerusalem; Lovers of their time; The raising of Elvira Tremlett; Flights of fancy; Attracta; A dream of butterflies; The bedroom eyes of Mrs. Vansittart; Downstairs at Fitzgerald's; Mulvihill's memorial; Beyond the pale; The blue dress; The teddy-bears' picnic; The time of year; Being stolen from; Mr. Tennyson; Autumn sunshine; Sunday drinks; The Paradise Lounge; Mags; The news from Ireland; On the Zattere; The wedding in the garden; Lunch in winter; The property of Colette Nervi; Running away; Cocktails at Doney's; Her mother's daughter; Bodily secrets; Two more gallants; The smoke trees of San Pietro; Virgins; Music; Events at Drimaghleen; Family sins; A trinity; The third party; Honeymoon in Tramore; The printmaker; In love with Ariadne; A husband's return; Coffee with Oliver; August Saturday; Children of the headmaster; Kathleen's field

Death in summer. Viking 1998 214p $23.95

ISBN 0-670-88202-X

* LC 98-21569

"A sudden death brings together a rootless, shifty young woman named Pettie and the recently widowed Thaddeus Davenant, who is trying to find a nanny for his baby daughter. With a badly typed letter of reference and threadbare clothing, Pettie is quickly turned away, but not before she has formed an irresistible (if deceived) impression of the life she could share with Thaddeus. Trevor inhabits his characters so fully that they seem present before us, and his exploration of their accidental connections demonstrates, yet again, his ability to imbue the most casual actions with unsettling significance." New Yorker

Felicia's journey. Viking 1995 c1994 212p

ISBN 0-670-85745-9

* LC 94-32413

First published 1994 in the United Kingdom

"When handsome Johnny Lysaght, home from England to visit his mother, first catches sight of Felicia, she is standing outside Hickey's Hotel in a bridesmaid's dress. When the famously fat and affable Mr. Hilditch first catches sight of her, a few months later, she is pregnant and desperate, asking for directions outside a Midlands factory, with her grandmother's stolen pension money stuffed in her plastic carrier bag. Hilditch can tell at a glance that the Irish girl needs a special friend. . . . The insignificance of Felicia's ever-narrowing life is challenged by our terror that she will lose it." New Yorker

"Trevor is chilling and precise in his evocation of the loss of innocence, loss of heart, while he highlights the dismal features of contemporary society. Felicia's journey proceeds in an inimical atmosphere in which disquiet and corruption are the order of the day." New Statesman Soc

Fools of fortune. Viking 1983 238p

ISBN 0-670-32355-1   LC 83-47867

Trevor, William, 1928-——_Continued_

"Willie Quinton tells of an idyllic childhood on his family's small estate, an ordered life shattered by the uprising, by the division of Irish society and, finally, by murder and destruction of their home. Uprooted to Cork, Willie lives with his widowed, alcoholic mother; goes to school; and eventually meets Marianne, a distant cousin from England. Their brief love is eclipsed by Willie's vengeance on his family's destroyer, shattering all their lives until his gentle daughter, Imelda, resumes the thread." Libr J

The hill bachelors. Viking 2000 244p

ISBN 0-670-89373-0   LC 00-32485

Contents: Three people; Of the cloth; Good news; The mourning; A friend in the trade; Low Sunday, 1950; Le visiteur; The Virgin's gift; Death of a professor; Against the odds; The telephone game; The hill bachelors

"All the stories deal with the major disappointments and small rewards that life brings, particularly within the arena of love. No story here is less that a bravura performance." Booklist

Love and summer. Viking 2009 211p $25.95

ISBN 978-0-670-02123-9; 0-670-02123-7

     LC 2009-18184

A novel about the "summer love that blooms between Ellie Dillahan, an orphan who has become a farmer's wife, and Florian Kilderry, a bachelor haunted by his muse yet lacking any means of expressing his art. Ellie and Florian meet in Rathmoye, a small Irish town where the influential and tragic Connulty family owns several concerns, including a burned-out cinema and a boarding house. Only Miss Connulty and her brother, Joseph Paul, remain to enact the final scene of their family's drama, into which the young lovers have unwittingly stumbled." Libr J

"The speech in this novel, bare and unvarnished, is a constant joy, partly because [Trevor's] characters tend to reticence, to a reluctance to reveal themselves in what they say, and yet do so time and again, even in conversations in which nothing is said openly, but only obliquely, indeed especially in such conversations. His sympathy extends, with rare art, to them all." Scotsman

(ed) The Oxford book of Irish short stories. See The Oxford book of Irish short stories

The silence in the garden. Viking 1988 204p o.p.

     * LC 87-40662

"Told in an elliptical, slow-moving narrative is this tale of the Rolleston family, a once vital aristocratic Irish family who peters away into seemingly inexplicable hopelessness. The elder sons remain bachelors. . . . The beautiful daughter withers, as she tosses away one fiancé and, in her mid-30s, chooses a man too old for her and incapable of siring children. As poor relation Sarah discovers at last, this is voluntary self-punishment for a shared act of cruelty that had violent repercussions." Libr J

"While the subject might seem common, Trevor's treatment is a dazzling tour de force of epigrammatic detail and psychological insinuation as the writer reconstructs whole lives through the telling deployment of a single episode. Moreover, there is a tissue of lies, secrets, and deceptions that is gradually revealed in the progress of these people's stories. Trevor captures the contradictions and subtle ironies brilliantly." Booklist

Trial and error; an Oxford anthology of legal stories; edited by Fred R. Shapiro and Jane Garry. Oxford Univ. Press 1997 479p $35

ISBN 0-19-509547-2   LC 97-19789

Contents: The two drovers, by W. Scott; Bleak house, by C. Dickens; Adam Bede, by G. Eliot; Roughing it, by M. Twain; Lady Anna, by A. Trollope; Billy Budd, by H. Melville; Weir of Hermiston, by R. L. Stevenson; The cop and the anthem, by O. Henry; The Forsyte saga, by J. Galsworthy; A Jury of her peers, by S. Glaspell; The witness for the prosecution, by A. Christie; The letter, by W. S. Maugham; The majesty of the law, by F. O'Connor; Shooting an elephant, by G. Orwell; Tomorrow, by W. Faulkner; And/or, by S. A. Brown; Happy event, by N. Gordimer; Greenhouse with cyclamens I, by R. West; The floating opera, by J. Barth; Eli, the fanatic, by P. Roth; To kill a mockingbird, by H. Lee; Mr. Portway's practice, by M. Gilbert; The senior partner's ghosts, by L. Auchincloss; The naked civil servant, by Q. Crisp; The French lieutenant's woman, by J. Fowles; An act of prostitution, by J. A. McPherson; A gentleman's agreement, by E. Jolley; The sorcerer of Bolinas Reef, by C. A. Reich; The good mother, by S. Miller; The bonfire of the vanities, by T. Wolfe; American appetites, by J. C. Oates; A lesson before dying, by E. J. Gaines

"The stories treat the human dimension of the law, focusing on the institutions, legal rules, and legal actors. . . . The wide range of situations, predicaments, and interpretation make this a fascinating compilation." Libr J

Trigiani, Adriana

Big Cherry Holler; a Big Stone Gap novel. Random House 2001 272p

ISBN 0-375-50617-9   LC 2001-18599

It is "now the late 1980s, and Ave Maria and Jack MacChesney have been married 11 years. They have a ten-year-old daughter, Etta, but lost their younger child, Joe, a few years earlier. This loss and other marital stresses have tested their relationship, but the summer brings on the biggest trial yet. As Jack tries to launch a new construction business in Big Stone Gap, VA, Ave Maria and Etta take off for Italy." Libr J

"Although readers of _Big Stone Gap_ are going to find this novel more serious, they should rest assured that most of the old favorite small town characters are still there. Catching an earful, usually unsolicited, of their views and advice on life, marriage, and love is a part of the charm of both the predecessor and this follow-up." Booklist

Big Stone Gap; a novel. Random House 2000 272p

ISBN 0-375-50403-6   LC 99-43306

This novel is about Ave Maria Mulligan, a "35-year-old pharmacist and self-proclaimed town spinster, who is hankering for a bigger, better world than her own in the Blue Ridge Mountains of Virginia in the late 1970s." N Y Times Book Rev

"One chapter, which is based on a real-life campaign visit from John Warner and his then-wife Elizabeth Taylor is a hoot. And you don't want to miss Ave Maria's friend, the sexy Iva Lou Wade, one of the best fictional librarians to come along in years." Libr J

Trigiani, Adriana—*Continued*

Milk glass moon; a Big Stone Gap novel. Random House 2002 256p

  ISBN 0-375-50618-7   LC 2002-17945

Final volume in the Big Stone Gap trilogy featuring former spinster and town pharmacist Ave Maria MacChesney. "Learning to reconcile her own personal desires with those of her beloved husband and daughter, a middle-aged Ave Maria 'redreams' her future and explores another life path." Booklist

"The folksy dialogue and unabashed sentimentalism can be cloying, but Ave's astringent insights and critical self-appraisal sharpen the tale." Publ Wkly

Very Valentine. HarperCollins Publishers 2009 371p $25.95

  ISBN 978-0-06-125705-6; 0-06-125705-2

                           LC 2008-34314

In this first book in a projected trilogy, Valentine Roncalli struggles to save her decades-old family business, finding love and the life she wants along the way.

"Food, shoes and romance feature prominently in this zesty novel of an Italian-American family. . . . Rich descriptions of beautiful things—a Greenwich Village rooftop garden, the Blue Grotto of Capri, a bounty of well-made meals, sexy men in sweaters—create a (not quite) fairy tale of guilty pleasures." Kirkus

Trocheck, Kathy Hogan

  See also Andrews, Mary Kay, 1954-

Trollip, Stanley *See* Stanley, Michael

Trollope, Anthony, 1815-1882

Barchester Towers. Knopf 1992 xxxiii, 277p (Chronicles of Barsetshire) $20

  ISBN 0-679-40587-9

                           * LC 91-53197

First published 1857. Second of the Chronicles of Barsetshire

"Continues the picture of clerical society with its peculiar humors and foibles. The chief incidents are connected with the appointment of a new bishop, the troubles and disappointments this involves, and the intrigues and jealousies of the clergy: the henpecked bishop, the ambitious archdeacon, and the dean, canons, and others, with their wives. The picture of the eccentric Stanhope family is particularly delicious." Lenrow. Reader's Guide to Prose Fic

Followed by Doctor Thorne

Can you forgive her?; with an introduction by A.O.J. Cockshut. Knopf 1994 xxxiii, 447p $23

  ISBN 0-679-43595-6   LC 94-6553

"Everyman's library"

First published 1864-65

This first of the Palliser novels "tells the interwoven stories of two women, Alice Vavasor and Lady Glencora M'Cluskie, who struggle to come to terms with the choices available to them concerning marriage." Merriam-Webster's Ency of Lit

Can you forgive her? [abridged]

  In Trollope, A. The Pallisers p11-115

The complete shorter fiction; edited by Julian Thompson. Carroll & Graf Pubs. 1992 959p o.p.

Includes the following stories: Relics of General Chassé, a tale of Antwerp; The courtship of Susan Bell; The O'Conors of Castle Conor, County Mayo; La Mère Bauche; An unprotected female at the pyramids; The chateau of Prince Polignac; Miss Sarah Jack of Spanish Town, Jamaica; John Bull on the Guadalquivir; A ride across Palestine; Mrs. General Talboys; The parson's daughter of Oxney Colne; Returning home; The man who kept his money in a box; Aaron Trow; The House of Heine Brothers in Munich; George Walker at Suez; The mistletoe bough; The journey to Panama; The widow's mite; The two generals; Miss Ophelia Gledd; Malachi's Cove; Father Giles of Ballymoy; The geltle Euphemia; Lotta Schmidt; The adventures of Fred Pickering; The last Austrian who left Venice; The Turkish bath; Mary Gresley; Josephine de Montmorenci; The Panjandrum; The spotted dog; Mrs. Brumby; Christmas day at Kirkby Cottage; Christmas at Thompson Hall; Why Frau Frohmann raised her prices; The telegraph girl; The lady of Launay; Alice Dugdale; Catherine Carmichael; or, Three years running; The two heroines of Plumplington; Not if I know it

Doctor Thorne; with an introduction by N. John Hall. Knopf 1993 xxxi, 319p (Chronicles of Barsetshire) $20

  ISBN 0-679-42304-4   LC 93-1853

"Everyman's library"

First published 1858. Third of the Chronicles of Barsetshire

"A story of quiet country life; and the interest of the book lies in the character studies rather than in the plot. The scene is laid in the west of England about 1854. The heroine, Mary Thorne, is a sweet, modest girl, living with her kind uncle Doctor Thorne, in the village of Greshambury, where Frank Gresham, the young heir of Greshambury Park, falls in love with her." Keller. Reader's Dig of Books

Followed by Framley parsonage

The Duke's children [abridged]

  In Trollope, A. The Pallisers p387-437

The Eustace diamonds. Knopf 1992 xxxi, 249p $20

  ISBN 0-679-41745-1

                           * LC 92-52910

"Everyman's library"

First published 1872

The third Palliser novel. "The story follows two contrasting women and their courtships. Lizzie Eustace and Lucy Morris are both hampered in their love affairs by their lack of money. Lizzie's trickery and deceit, however, contrast with Lucy's constancy. Trollope was understood to be commenting on the malaise in Victorian England that allowed a character like Lizzie, who marries for money, steals the family diamonds, and behaves despicably throughout, to rise unscathed in society." Merriam-Webster's Ency of Lit

The Eustace diamonds [abridged]

  In Trollope, A. The Pallisers p189-264

Trollope, Anthony, 1815-1882—*Continued*

Framley parsonage; with an introduction by Graham Handley. Knopf 1994 xxxi, 587p (Chronicles of Barsetshire) $20

ISBN 0-679-43133-0

"Everyman's library"

First published 1861. Fourth of the Chronicles of Barsetshire

"The vicar of Framley, a weak but honest young man, is led astray and into debt by a spendthrift M. P., and finds himself in a false position. The other branch of the story deals with his sister's chequered love affair and marriage to young Lord Lufton. A great crowd of characters are engaged in the social functions, the intrigues and the match making, the general effect of which is comic, though graver interest is never far off, and there are situations of deepest pathos." Baker. Guide to the Best Fic

Followed by The small house at Allington

The last chronicle of Barset; with an introduction by Graham Handley. Knopf 1995 xxix, 983p (Chronicles of Barsetshire) $24

ISBN 0-679-44366-5   LC 95-75205

"Everyman's library"

First published 1867. Sixth in the Chronicles of Barsetshire

"The ecclesiastical society of 'The Warden,' Mr. Harding, Mrs. Proudie, and the rest make their last appearance. The dominant situation is one of intense anguish. A poor country clergyman, proud, learned, sternly conscientious is accused of a felony, and the pressure of family want makes his guilt seem only too probable." Baker. Guide to the Best Fic

The Pallisers; abridged and introduced by Michael Hardwick. Coward, McCann & Geoghegan 1975 c1974 436p o.p.

One volume abridgment of six "parliamentary novels"

Contents: Can you forgive her; Phineas Finn; The Eustace diamonds; Phineas Redux; The prime minister; The Duke's children

Phineas Finn [abridged]

In Trollope, A. The Pallisers p117-88

Phineas Redux [abridged]

In Trollope, A. The Pallisers p265-323

The prime minister. Oxford University Press 2009 xxiv, 438p il (Oxford world's classics) pa $14.95

ISBN 978-0-19-953775-4; 0-19-953775-5

First published 1876

"Considered by modern critics to represent the apex of the 'Palliser novels', it is the fifth in the series and sustains two plot lines. One records the clash between the Duke of Omnium, now prime minister of a coalition government, and his high-spirited wife, Lady Glencora, whose drive to become the most brilliant hostess in society causes embarrassment for her husband and eventually contributes to his downfall. The second plot reveals the machinations of Ferdinand Lopez, an ambitious social climber who wins the support of Lady Glencora—but not her husband—for an election campaign. The novel brilliantly dissects the politics of both marriage and government." Merriam-Webster's Ency of Lit

The prime minister [abridged]

In Trollope, A. The Pallisers p325-85

The small house at Allington; with an introduction by A.O.J. Cockshut. Knopf 1997 xxix, 740p (Chronicles of Barsetshire) $23

ISBN 0-375-40067-2

"Everyman's library"

"Country life, its quiet, its pleasures and troubles, monotony and dullness, and with digressions into boarding-house life in London and into high society. Many old friends appear in the usual concourse of characters, among whom stand out Mr. Crosbie, a snobbish and cowardly trifler. . . . Lily Dale, the jilted maiden, amiable and weak Johnny Eames, and the aristocratic doll, Lady Dumbello; all closely copied from life." Baker. Guide to the Best Fic

Followed by The last chronicle of Barset

The warden; introduction by Louis Auchincloss; notes by Andrew Maunder. Modern Library 2003 230p (Chronicles of Barsetshire) pa $11

ISBN 0-8129-6704-6   LC 2002-24533

"Modern Library classics"

First published 1855. First of the Chronicles of Barsetshire

"The Reverend Septimus Harding, the conscientious warden of a charitable retirement home for men, resigns after being accused of making too much profit from the sinecure." Merriam-Webster's Ency of Lit

Followed by Barchester Towers

Trollope, Joanna

The best of friends. Viking 1998 293p $23.95

ISBN 0-670-87973-8   LC 97-49162

First published 1995 in the United Kingdom

"Whittingbourne is one of those charming English towns where families live happily ever after. Gina and Fergus, Hillary and Laurance have grown up, married, and raised their children in the warmth of amiable friendship. But one day it all unravels as Fergus calmly leaves Gina to share his life with a young man in London, and Laurance nearly chucks it all to move to France with Gina in the heat of passion. Their children are devastated and beset with emerging passions of their own." Libr J

"Trollope's facility at spinning an intricate story is enhanced by light-fingered dialogue, and the lesson she spins in this tale of easy pleasure and its complicated aftermath is both sobering and hopeful." Publ Wkly

Brother and sister. Bloomsbury 2004 311p $23.95

ISBN 1-582-34400-0   LC 2003-62649

"Born to two different mothers but adopted together and raised as brother and sister, David and Nathalie are fiercely close. Even their spouses acknowledge their unique bond, forged by the belief that they are special— 'chosen' by each other, though born to different parents. They aren't much concerned about the circumstances of their births until the girlfriend of David's colleague asks them to contact their birth mothers as part of her thesis research. Their decision to do so profoundly affects their lives and the lives of those close to them. When their mothers, who have gone on to have families, finally acknowledge their youthful indiscretions and meet David and Nathalie as adults, it sets off a ripple effect that

Trollope, Joanna—*Continued*

nearly destroys all the families involved." Libr J

"Trollope is a pointillist of domestic relationships, and she has built an impressive body of work addressing powerful tensions like those that animate Brother and Sister. With well-placed strokes, she brings to life all of her characters, including the complex lives of the birth mothers. She's especially accomplished in her portrayals of children by turns humorous, frustrating or heartbreaking, but never precious." Washington Post Book World

The choir. Random House 1995 261p o.p.

* LC 95-11612

First published 1993 in the United Kingdom

"The all-boy choir at Aldminster Cathedral is blessed with a cheerfully ferocious choirmaster, a magnificent seventeenth-century organ, and a celestial new treble in the earthly guise of eleven-year-old Henry Ashworth. But the choir also costs the diocese more than fifty thousand pounds a year, which the dean thinks might be better spent elsewhere—on new lighting, perhaps—and a delicious cathedral-town battle about tradition and privilege ensues. Almost all the characters in this companionable novel are on speaking terms with God, but His will, while frequently consulted, is variously interpreted." New Yorker

Friday nights; a novel. Bloomsbury 2008 330p $24.99

ISBN 978-1-59691-407-0; 1-59691-407-6

LC 2007-37579

"Retiree Eleanor often sees Paula and Lindsay, two harried young mothers, passing on the street and decides they should have time to relax. Paula and Lindsay, who have never met each other before, turn down Eleanor's offer of babysitting but are flustered enough to accept her invitation to visit her one Friday evening. The group soon expands to include Blaise, Eleanor's neighbor; Karen, Blaise's coworker; and Jules, Lindsay's younger sister. Trollope outlines each woman's history, deftly interweaving their individual stories with those of the new connections growing among them. When Paula begins dating Jackson Miller, the equilibrium of the group is altered, and as Jackson becomes a part of all of their lives, events occur that will change the group forever. Trollope's novel rings true, portraying the complexities of contemporary women's lives without sentimentality or melodrama." Libr J

Legacy of love; {by} Joanna Trollope writing as Caroline Harvey. Viking 2000 385p

ISBN 0-670-89181-9   LC 00-36791

"A novel in three parts featuring three generations of daring Englishwomen from the same family who challenge societal mores to pursue love and passion. Although unexceptional in its writing and plot, the book reveals Harvey's vast knowledge of travel and history, from Victorian England and British-ruled Afghanistan to World War II." Libr J

Marrying the mistress. Viking 2000 293p

ISBN 0-670-89150-9   LC 99-462175

"When a respectable judge named Guy Stockdale decides to leave his 40-year marriage to take up with his longtime mistress, his grown sons warily prepare to weather the consequences. Simon, his mother's favorite, takes her side, and Alan, Simon's gay brother, assumes

his usual posture of good-natured temperance. But neither Guy's mistress, Merrion, nor Laura, his left-behind wife, are conventional types, and neither plays her expected role." N Y Times Book Rev

"None of the themes here . . . are terribly unusual, but Trollope's proven ability to present them intelligently, as moral and emotional tangles faced by thinking, interesting people, satisfyingly combines the universally recognizable and the intellectually engaging." Publ Wkly

The men and the girls. Random House 1993 c1992 248p o.p.   LC 93-18421

First published 1992 in the United Kingdom

Oxford is the setting for a "story of the intimate and suddenly volatile relationships of two former school friends, now past 60 years of age. James lives with Kate (who is thirtysomething), her teenage daughter (nose earring, shorn head, black boots, etc.), and crochety Uncle Leonard. Hugh's wife, Julia, also thirtyish, is the mother of young twins. Into the very settled lives of these two households comes Beatrice, an elderly spinster, knocked off her bicycle by James' car." Booklist

"One of the pleasures in good contemporary British fiction like 'The Men and the Girls' is the writing itself—deft, fluid, perceptive and concise. Another is the wonderfully wry humor, particularly when its objects are sacred cows. Like Muriel Spark, Joanna Trollope is hilarious about old people, for instance." N Y Times Book Rev

Next of kin. Viking 2001 289p $23.95

ISBN 0-670-89999-2   LC 2001-17743

This novel begins "with the funeral of Caro Meredith, wife of a dairy farmer in the English Midlands. Caro's death is merely the prelude, however, to a series of shattering events for those she left behind—from husband Robin and daughter Judy, a magazine 'subeditor,' to brother-in-law Joe and his wife, Lyndsay, to Robin's parents, Dilys and Harry. The arrival of Judy's unconventional roommate, Zoe, brings a measure of openness to this emotionally closed family and gives Robin some small amount of the love that he lacked throughout his marriage." Libr J

"In addition to crafting an absorbing narrative, Trollope charms with her depiction of several young children, whose speech and behavior are captured with clarity and endearing fidelity." Publ Wkly

Other people's children. Viking 1999 294p $23.95

ISBN 0-670-88513-4

* LC 98-40004

"Falling in love with a man does not mean falling in love with his children: that is the premise of this story of linked and sundered families. Josie's second marriage includes three stepchildren, whose loyalty to their inadequate mother makes them hate Josie for her very competence; Elizabeth's beloved fiancé comes with a son she adores and a grown daughter determined to oust her. Trollope may not aim high, but she aims for the heart, and she hits it." New Yorker

The rector's wife. Random House 1994 287p o.p.

* LC 94-20625

First published 1991 in the United Kingdom

The provincial English "rector in The Rector's Wife, Peter Bouverie, has spent his life and defined his minis-

Trollope, Joanna—*Continued*

try according to what other people think, and he expects his family to do the same. . . . The turning point comes early in the story, when Peter is passed over for a much hoped-for appointment to the position of archdeacon. When his career hits dead end, it becomes bitterly clear that he has no inner resources or satisfying relationships to fall back on. In his marriage and ministry, Peter has dried up. Anna, too, is on the verge of either drying up or going mad. As her frustration deepens over Peter's disappointment and the estrangement between them, she decides to change her life. She begins to carve out small spaces of independence from the parish by transferring their daughter to a Catholic school, taking a job at a local supermarket and, finally, seeking the love absent in her marriage with the brother of the new archdeacon." Christ Century

Second honeymoon; a novel. Bloomsbury 2006 323p $23.95

ISBN 978-1-59691-038-6; 1-59691-038-0

LC 2005-57011

"Ben Boyd is leaving home. At twenty-two, he's the youngest of the family and the last to leave. His mother Edie, an actress, is distraught. His father Russell, a theatrical agent, is hoping to get his wife back after decades of family life. Ben's brother, Matthew, is wrestling with a relationship in which he earns less than his successful girlfriend. Their sister Rosa is wrestling with debt, and the end of a turbulent love affair. . . . Rosa is the first of the Boyd children to think she may have to move back in with her parents-just until she can make ends meet again." Publisher's note

The author "excels at middle-class family dramas, and [this] is a welcome entry in her canon. Like an overzealous housewife who just can't step away from the vacuum, she succumbs to the impulse to tidy up all the subplots. But Edie, Russell, and their brood are winning enough that fans will want to move in right along with the kids." Christ Sci Monit

A Spanish lover. Random House 1996 c1993 334p o.p.

LC 96-24846

First published 1993 in the United Kingdom

"Lizzie has been rather smug about her thriving marriage, her four children, her successful shop, and her big house, but she becomes unconscionably jealous when Frances, her quiet, devoted twin, finds love with the sexy, supportive, but married—and foreign—Luis. This British author excels at setting up the stuff of female fantasy and, from those worn materials, making something that draws you in and slams you with a thud of emotion so authentic it becomes your own." New Yorker

Tropper, Jonathan

How to talk to a widower. Delacorte Press 2007 341p $20

ISBN 978-0-385-33890-5; 0-385-33890-2

LC 2006-28678

"Since magazine columnist Doug Parker's wife died in a plane crash one year ago, he's been caught in the whirlpool of his grief. The bigger world, though, is trying to pull him back out. Doug's teen stepson is getting into trouble at school, and his little sister is getting married soon. Meanwhile, his other sister is trying to set him up with every woman in town. What ensues is equal parts hilarity and despair—often, both at once. As always, Jonathan Tropper cares deeply for his characters, warts and all, and writes very sweetly about the fragile yet resilient world they inhabit." PopMatters

Trotter, William R.

The sands of pride; a novel of the Civil War. Carroll & Graf Pubs. 2002 754p $28

ISBN 0-7867-1013-6

LC 2002-22697

"Opening on New Year's Eve 1860, almost six months before North Carolina's grudging decision to secede from the Union of May 20, 1861, this sprawling account revolves around the bustling seaport of Wilmington, which serves as the lifeline of the Confederacy, Jefferson Davis; the architect of Fort Fisher, Col. William Lamb; Lafayette Baker, deputy director of the fledgling Secret Service; Gen. Robert E. Lee; Gen. Ambrose Burnside; and the naval commander William Barker Cushing are some of the real-life historic figures that are artfully integrated with an extensive dramatis personae of flamboyant and idiosyncratic fictional character." Publ Wkly

Trueblood, Valerie

Seven loves; a novel. Little, Brown and Co. 2006 232p $23.95

ISBN 978-0-316-05893-3

LC 2005-26604

This "novel follows the story of 74-year-old May Nilsson, a retired English teacher and widow, who finds herself belonging to the country of old women and reminiscing on a past defined by love. May remembers the difficult and pleasurable years of her marriage to a doctor as well as the excitement and pain of an extramarital affair. She reflects on a young coworker's elementary nature, her son's capriciousness, and her mother's political convictions. Each chapter presents an impressionistic view of May's family, friends, and lovers and their varying degrees of longing and happiness. Gently told, Trueblood's first work is poetic, contemplative, and tender." Booklist

Truman, Margaret, 1924-2008

Murder at Ford's Theatre. Ballantine Bks. 2002 326p $24.95

ISBN 0-345-44489-2

LC 2002-74748

"When the body of congressional intern Nadia Zarinski turns up outside the stage door of Ford's Theatre, D.C. police detectives Mo Johnson and Rick Klayman, who happens to be a Lincoln buff, are assigned the case. Nadia worked in the office of Senator Bruce Lerner, ex-husband of Clarise Emerson, head of Ford's Theatre and nominee for chair of the National Endowment for the Arts. Once Clarise determines with Klayman's help that her son, Jeremiah, was the last to see Nadia alive, she appeals to former attorney Mackensie 'Mac' Smith to represent him." Publ Wkly

Murder at the Library of Congress. Random House 1999 322p $25

ISBN 0-375-50068-5

LC 99-14953

"Pre-Columbian art expert Annabel Smith has been asked to write an article on a second diary of Columbus' voyage—if such an artifact really exists. Her research takes her into the inner workings of LC and leads to the discovery of illicit payoffs and the solutions to a pair of murders, one old, one new." Booklist

Truman, Margaret, 1924-2008—*Continued*

Murder in the White House; a novel. Arbor House 1980 235p o.p.   LC 79-54004

"When Secretary of State Blaine is murdered in the Lincoln Sitting Room of the White House, President Webster orders Special Counsel Fairchild to coordinate efforts to solve the case with the authorities. The lawyer turned detective begins investigating everyone with access to the White House, including Webster, the First Lady and her daughter Lynne." Publ Wkly

Murder on Capitol Hill; a novel. Arbor House 1981 255p o.p.   LC 80-70223

"Lawyer Lydia James agrees to the request of Veronica Caldwell to act as counsel for the senatorial committee investigating the killing of her husband, Senate Majority leader Cale Caldwell. He has been stabbed at a reception honoring him, where his black-sheep son Mark, member of a fanatical cult, is among the 200 or more guests. Mark is arrested for the murder, and also on suspicion of having killed Jimmye, Veronica's niece, years earlier, an unsolved crime. His mother and brother, Cale Jr., sorrowfully agree that Mark is guilty, but Lydia believes the charges are trumped up. She gets herself into dicey situations, chasing clues." Publ Wkly

Trumbo, Dalton, 1905-1976

Johnny got his gun. Lippincott 1939 309p o.p.
                                                    *

"Far more than an antiwar polemic, this compassionate description of the effects of war on one soldier is a poignant tribute to the human instinct to survive. Badly mutilated, blind, and deaf, Johnny fights to communicate with an uncomprehending medical world debating his fate." Shapiro. Fic for Youth. 3d edition

Truong, Monique T. D.

The book of salt; [by] Monique Truong. Houghton Mifflin 2003 261p $24
    ISBN 0-618-30400-2   LC 2002-192152
"From a few lines in The Alice B. Toklas Cook Book, Truong reimagines the Vietnamese cook who was hired by the famous residents at 27 Rue de Fleurus. Binh, as he calls himself, is an exile from his homeland, where he was denounced because of a homosexual relationship and banished by his brutal father. After three years at sea, Binh ends up in Paris, where he answers Toklas's ad. . . and enters the household of Gertrude Stein." Publ Wkly

"Truong is tapping some trendy territory here: the postcolonial perspective; the book derived from a minor character in another well-known book. . .; the gay novel; the novel of exile. And Truong's central character, the gay Asian houseboy, is something of a stereotype in itself. But nothing in this distinctive novel feels secondhand." N Y Times Book Rev

Truscott, Lucian K., 1947-

Heart of war. Dutton 1997 370p o.p.
                                                    LC 96-29876
The protagonist of this thriller is "Maj. Kara Guldry, a lawyer and West Point graduate who is assigned to investigate the murder of a Lt. Sheila Worthy. Kara soon discovers that the young woman's lover was none other

than General Beckwith, the base commander. After her friend, Lannie Love, another Beckwith mistress, is stabbed in a similar manner, Kara is convinced that Beckwith is the key to the murders." Libr J

"Despite some occasionally breathy prose, Truscott's novel provides a fascinating peek behind the olive drab curtain, blending a solid plot with a piercing critique of hypocrisy, power politics and sexual misconduct in today's armed forces." N Y Times Book Rev

Tryon, Thomas

In the fire of spring. Knopf 1991 609p o.p.
                                                    LC 91-414
In this sequel to The wings of the morning "a runaway slave, Rose Mills, is helped to safety by the abolitionist Appleton Talcott and two of his daughters as they return home to Pequot Landing. . . . The Talcotts and the slave-owning Grimes family are still feuding, but it's now 1841, and fuel has been added to the fire. First of all, the Talcotts open a school for young black women, which gives the Grimeses something new to holler about. Second, Appleton's wife, Mabel Talcott, is secretly dying. As she ponders her mortality and worries about her children, her dying wish is granted: daughter Aurora, abroad for years with husband and child, returns home. Mab's heart breaks as she learns of her daughter's travails and of her undying love for the true father of her child—none other than the swashbuckling, lady-killing Sinjin Grimes." Booklist

The other. Knopf 1971 280p o.p.
                                                    *

"Bizarre events occur in and around the once-prosperous Perry family in Connecticut during the 1930s. The men have all died mysteriously and brutally. Niles and Holland, 12-year-old twins, seem to be linked to the ghastly deaths and disasters. A compassionate Russian grandmother plays along with Niles's deception and tries to protect him." Shapiro. Fic for Youth. 3d edition

The wings of the morning. Knopf 1990 567p o.p.   LC 89-39513
"Set in the 1820s and 1830s in the small Connecticut town of Pequot Landing, the novel tells of the feud between the town's two first families—the Talcotts and the Grimeses. The link between the two families is the miller's daughter, Georgie Ross—childhood friend to the rakish Sinjin Grimes and former servant and close friend to the Talcotts. Georgie is a levelheaded, independent heroine and her experiences highlight the conditions of women in that time." Libr J

"Unalloyed pleasure for fans of this genre, Tryon's literate 19th-century soap opera is steeped in the rhythms of Trollope and Scott." Publ Wkly

Followed by In the fire of spring

Ts'an-hsüeh, 1953-

Blue light in the sky & other stories; [by] Can Xue; translated by Karen Gernant and Chen Zeping. New Directions 2006 212p pa $14.95
    ISBN 978-0-8112-1648-7; 0-8112-1648-9
                                                    LC 2006-9091
    Contents: Blue light in the sky; The bizarre wooden building; A negligible game on the journey; Helin; The lure of the sea; Snake Island; Night in the mountain vil-

Ts'an-hsüeh, 1953—_Continued_

lage; Scenes inside the dilapidated walls; Burial; The
spring; The little monster; My brother; Top floor; Mosquitoes and mountain ballads

Can Xue "writes in the artless prose of fairy tales and
employs a curious dreamlike logic in her narratives.
Characters witness grotesque illnesses, dodge natural catastrophes and endlessly wander through dark labyrinths
of misunderstanding. . . . [One of her narrator's] says of
fishing nets, 'Only a random string is needed-the less related, the better,' and it's a deft description of Can Xue's
eccentric storytelling." Publ Wkly

Tsukiyama, Gail

Dreaming water. St. Martin's Press 2002 288p
$23.95

ISBN 0-312-20607-0   LC 2001-58896

"At 38, Hana Murayama is dying of Werner's syndrome, a genetic defect that causes premature aging.
Hana is almost totally dependent on her mother, Cata,
who at 62 is still recovering from the sudden death of
her husband, Max. . . . Over the course of two days,
Hana and Cate retrace in memory their lives and Max's.
Their scattered and sometimes conflicting expectations
are brought into sharp focus when Hana's best friend,
Laura, now a successful East Coast lawyer, arrives with
her two daughters, Hana's godchildren, allowing Hana
and Cate to find a measure of the reconciliation that has
eluded them." Publ Wkly

The street of a thousand blossoms. St. Martin's
Press 2007 422p $24.95

ISBN 978-0-312-27482-5; 0-312-27482-3

LC 2007-21012

"Set in Japan and spanning over 25 years (1939-66),
the novel unravels the hardships and triumphs of two
brothers raised by their loving maternal grandparents following the loss of their parents in a tragic accident. The
dreams of older brother Hiroshi of becoming a sumotori
(a sumo wrestler) and younger brother Kenji of becoming a Noh theater mask artisan are quelled by the onset
of World War II. Passages describing the devastation
wrought by the atomic bombings upon their lives and of
those close to them, particularly the family of sisters
Haru and Aki, who later becomes Hiroshi's wife, are
well written and emotionally gripping." Libr J

T͡Sypkin, Leonid, 1926-1982

Summer in Baden-Baden; a novel; translated
from the Russian by Roger and Angela Keys; introduction by Susan Sontag. New Directions 2001
xxi, 146p $23.95

ISBN 0-8112-1484-2

* LC 2001-32658

Originally serialized 1982 in Russian emigré weekly;
this translation first published 1987 in the United Kingdom

This novel "opens with the unnamed narrator
(Tsypkin) bound once more for Leningrad. . . . A century earlier, in the hot summer of 1867, the Dostoyevskys
headed for the writers much coveted roulette tables at a
German spa in the same carriage that is now taking the
narrator across frosty Russia. Tsypkin's story shifts back
and forth in time and crosses the borders of several

genres." New Leader

"Tsypkin's stream-of-consciousness prose style is associative, inclusive, allusive, detached and yet humane." N
Y Times Book Rev

Tucker, Todd, 1968-

Over and under. Thomas Dunne Books/St.
Martin's Press 2008 275p $23.95

ISBN 978-0-312-37990-2; 0-312-37990-0

LC 2008-12472

"A bitter 1979 labor strike at southern Indiana's Borden Casket Company serves as the volatile backdrop for
this haunting coming-of-age novel. . . . With their fathers on opposite sides of the dispute, Andrew Jackson
Gray and Thomas Jefferson Kruer, both 14, learn there
is more to life than exploring caves, shooting targets
with their prized M-6 Scout rifles and sneaking out on
starry nights to run through the woods. . . . Tucker convincingly makes Andy's voice at once eloquent and gritty, and makes the rural Indiana landscape palpable." Publ
Wkly

Turgenev, Ivan Sergeevich, 1818-1883

Fathers and sons; a new translation by Michael
R. Katz. Norton 1994 157p $25

ISBN 0-393-03559-X

* LC 92-40010

Original Russian edition, 1862. Variant title: Fathers
and children

This novel "concerns the inevitable conflict between
generations and between the values of traditionalists and
intellectuals. The physician Bazarov, the novel's protagonist, is the most powerful of Turgenev's creations. He is
a nihilist, denying the validity of all laws save those of
the natural sciences. Uncouth and forthright in his opinions, he is nonetheless susceptible to love and by that
fact doomed to unhappiness. In sociopolitical terms he
represents the victory of the revolutionary nongentry intelligentsia over the gentry intelligentsia to which Turgenev belonged." Merriam-Webster's Ency of Lit

First love and other stories; [by] Ivan Turgenev;
translated by Isaiah Berlin and Leonard Schapiro;
introduced by V.S. Pritcett. Knopf 1994 xxxvii,
253p $17

ISBN 0-679-43594-8   LC 94-6233

"Everyman's library"

Contents: First love; Spring torrents; A fire at sea

Spring torrents [variant title: The torrents of
spring]

_In_ Turgenev, I. S. First love and other stories

The torrents of spring; [by] Ivan Turgenev; illustrated by Valentin Popov; translated by Ivy and
Tatiana Litvonov. Grove Press 1996 174p il $25

ISBN 0-8021-1594-2

* LC 96-14697

Original Russian edition, 1872. Variant title: Spring
torrents

This classic Russian novel "is a love story beautifully
and simply told: a young Russian nobleman, Dimitry
Sanin, falls in love with a pure and sweet girl, Gemma,
but through unforeseen circumstances and his own weak-

Turgenev, Ivan Sergeevich, 1818-1883—Continued

ness he forsakes her for a sensual woman of the world, Maria Nikolayevna, for whom men are mere playthings of the moment. He does so in spite of being fully aware that this liaison will bring him nothing but ruin and humiliation. . . . This short novel has no political overtones and deals only with the emotional experiences of the characters." Libr J

Turner, Frederick W., 1937-

1929; [by] Frederick Turner. Counterpoint Bks. 2003 390p $25

ISBN 1-58243-265-1

                  * LC 2002-154007

"A brilliant cornet player with an amazing ear, [Bix Beiderbecke] drank himself to death at the age of 28 with illegal Prohibition liquor. . . . Turner offers a fictional take on Beiderbecke's life, giving readers a . . . picture of what life was like for jazz musicians in the years leading up to the Great Depression." Publ Wkly

"Written in a period-appropriate overheated, romantic prose, and incorporating memorable appearances by Capone, Bing Crosby, Maurice Ravel, Paul Whiteman, and Clara Bow, the book is by turns corny, intoxicating, and ineffably sad, like the 'hot' music it is designed to evoke." New Yorker

Redemption. Harcourt 2006 348p $24

ISBN 978-0-15-101470-5; 0-15-101470-1

                  LC 2006-9241

"Turner's slow, humid tale, punctuated by indescribable violence, sexual and otherwise, unrolls in 1913, along the streets of Storyville, New Orleans. Every night, Francis Muldoon, a.k.a Fast-Mail, a former cop whose gunshot injury has put him out of commission, keeps an eye on business for Tom Anderson, whose fiefdom extends from swank saloons to two-bit whorehouses. Turner's subject is the way a district's history of poverty, defilement, and petty retribution can coexist with, and be elevated by, its trade in beauty and every kind of physical and spiritual release." New Yorker

Turner, Nancy E., 1953-

These is my words; the diary of Sarah Agnes Prine, 1881-1901. ReganBooks 1998 384p $23

ISBN 0-06-039225-8   LC 97-37622

"Based on the real-life exploits of the author's great-grandmother, this fictionalized diary . . . details one woman's struggles with life and love in frontier Arizona at the end of the last century. When she begins recording her life, Sarah Prine is an intelligent, headstrong 18-year-old capable of holding her own on her family's settlement near Tucson. Her skill with a rifle fends off a constant barrage of Indian attacks and outlaw assaults. it also attracts a handsome Army captain named Jack Elliot. By the time she's 21, Sarah has recorded her loveless marriage to a family friend, the establishment of a profitable ranch, the birth of her first child—and the death of her husband. The love between Jack and Sarah, which dominates the rest of the tale, has begun to blossom." Publ Wkly

"The language is rich and fine, sounding true to its time without being precious." Booklist

Turow, Scott

The burden of proof. Farrar, Straus & Giroux 1990 515p $22.95

ISBN 0-374-11734-9   LC 90-33593

Lawyer Sandy Stern featured in Presumed innocent "returns home to find his wife has committed suicide. Stern is currently involved in the defense of his brother-in-law, Dixon, who is accused of shady doings on the commodities market; also involved are Stern's daughter and her husband." Libr J

"The plotting is clear and clean, spun out with Greek inevitability and the niceties of law and finance are lucidly, smoothly, explained. Stern's complex character is well-drawn . . . and the members of his family are individualized and believable. The Federal judges and prosecutors have unique backgrounds and prejudices. Even the minor characters are given faces and personalities." America

The laws of our fathers. Farrar, Straus & Giroux 1996 533p $26.95

ISBN 0-374-18423-2   LC 96-16104

In this legal thriller, "the wife of a state senator has been killed in a drive-by shooting, and Judge Sonia Klonsky is presiding over the trial of the victim's son, who has been accused of masterminding the murder. Most of the protagonists have crossed paths decades before, when they were campus radicals, and there are some distinctly unconvincing flashbacks to the apocalyptic days of '69. Still, as the novel gathers momentum it reveals a complex portrait, in which children are forced to live in the shadow of their parents, and chastened middle-aged idealists must reckon with the enthusiasms and sins of their youth." New Yorker

Limitations. Picador 2006 197p pa $13

ISBN 978-0-312-42645-3; 0-312-42645-3

                  LC 2006-50345

First published in serial form in the New York Times Magazine

"The action centers on the fictional Kindle County in Illinois, and [Turow] revives some familiar characters, including George Mason from Personal Injuries and Rusty Sabich, the hero of . . . Presumed Innocent. Mason is now an appellate judge, faced with the challenge of crafting the decision in a high-profile case involving a sexual assault that reawakens his long-suppressed guilt over his role in a similar incident decades before. To compound his inner turmoil, Mason finds himself the object of threatening e-mails from an unknown source. . . . Turow's writing is assured as ever." Publ Wkly

Ordinary heroes. Farrar, Straus & Giroux 2005 384p $25

ISBN 0-374-18421-6   LC 2005-11824

"Stewart Dubinsky is not especially close to his father, David Dubin. Even their names are different, yet David's death prompts Stewart to try and find out more about this enigmatic man. He uncovers some startling information: that his father was engaged to another woman before his mother, and that he was court-martialed during the Battle of the Bulge. Dubinsky decides to write a family history, starts digging, and uncovers a manuscript his father wrote about his war experiences that is alternately moving and horrifying, vindicating, and vilifying and shines light on a side of his parents that he never knew.

Turow, Scott—*Continued*

While some of the historical facts presented are not 100 percent accurate, the book's emotional wallop more than justifies the literary license and should secure its place in the canon of World War II literature." Libr J

Personal injuries. Farrar, Straus & Giroux 1999 403p $27

ISBN 0-374-28194-7   LC 99-30829

"U.S. Attorney Stan Sennett has set his sights on a powerful group of corrupt judges, vowing to prosecute them at any cost. With the help of the FBI, he devises a set of legal traps designed to produce the evidence he needs to convict. The centerpiece of this subversion is Robbie Feaver, a Kindle County personal injury lawyer nabbed for tax evasion by Sennett. . . . Densely packed and tightly constructed, this tangle of human relationships and legal machinations will have Turow fans burning the midnight oil." SLJ

Presumed innocent. Farrar, Straus & Giroux 1987 431p $30

ISBN 0-374-23713-1

    * LC 87-368

"Rusty Sabich, the chief deputy prosecuting attorney assigned to investigate the murder of his co-worker and former lover, Carolyn Polhemus, is the narrator who draws us into the world of big-city crime and law enforcement as seen through a lawyer's eyes. Because his boss, Raymond Horgan, the Prosecuting Attorney in this unnamed Midwestern city, is up for re-election, Carolyn's murder has become a political issue, and the heat is on Rusty to bring in the killer as soon as he can." N Y Times Book Rev

This novel contains "high drama and suspense, as scenes in and out of the courtroom crackle with the amazing interactions of complex, fascinating characters. This is a great book." Libr J

Reversible errors. Farrar, Straus & Giroux 2002 433p il $28

ISBN 0-374-28160-2

    * LC 2002-70891

"In 1991, three people were brutally murdered in a Kindle County diner. Prosecutor Muriel Wynn and detective Larry Starczek ferreted out Rommy Gandolf, who soon confessed to the crime. Ten years later, Rommy is on death row, just weeks away from his execution. Arthur Raven has been appointed as his lawyer, but he can't imagine that anything new will turn up despite Rommy's claims of innocence. Then Erno Erdai steps forward." Booklist

"What Turow has done, in book after book, is to give us page turners that are also pleasing literary artifacts, mysteries that are also investigations into coomplex human emotions." N Y Times Book Rev

Turtledove, Harry

Into the darkness. Doherty Assocs. 1999 540p

ISBN 0-312-86895-2   LC 98-43610

"A Tom Doherty Associates book"

First title in the author's Alternate world fantasy series. "In the beginning, militarily efficient Algarve occupies the Duchy of Bari . . . and is quickly followed by one of Algarve's traditional foes, Unkerlant. . . . Throughout, World War II buffs will search for further reflections in

Turtledove's fantastic mirror, but they will also, like other readers, be quickly caught up in the sheer ingenuity of the tale, in which dragons provide airpower, behemoths (think rhinoceroses the size of elephants) are tanks, magic wands take the place of rifles, and submarine warfare is in the hands of leviathan-riders." Booklist

Rulers of the darkness. TOR Bks. 2002 576p il $27.95

ISBN 0-7653-0036-2   LC 2001-58465

"A Tom Doherty Associates book"

Sequel to : Through the darkness

"The fourth volume of the alternate-history saga Darkness deals with the fourth year of a World War II. . . . Kuusamo's sorcerous Manhattan Project has the potential to generate destructive energy by drawing on the past and the future, which is the same way the Algarvians use the life energy of murdered Kaunians. Meanwhile, more conventional counteroffensives against Algarve are in progress, with Unkerlant and Algarve reaching a gigantic confrontation in a battle recognizable as a re-imagining of the Battle of Kursk. One need not, however, be able to run down all of Turtledove's real-world parallels to appreciate how well he presents the human dilemmas of global warfare." Booklist

Tussing, Justin

The best people in the world. HarperCollins 2006 336p $24.95

ISBN 0-06-081533-7   LC 2005-46064

"It's the early 1970s, a time when lofty ideals such as peace, love, and understanding are awakening passions in the young and impressionable. When 17-year-old Thomas falls in love with Alice, his 25-year-old teacher, they escape the suffocating confines of Paducah, Kentucky, in the company of Shiloh, an eccentric drifter who serves as a guide as they set up a squatter's camp in the isolated Vermont mountains." Booklist

"The scenes between Alice and Thomas are almost absurdly lyrical and chaste. . . . But Tussing's indexes and inventories of Actual Things, circa 1972, are mercifully never more than a page or two away. At his best, Tussing is a kind of Wacko-Thoreau, and 'The Best People in the World' is one bright book of exuberant American life." N Y Times Book Rev

Twain, Mark, 1835-1910

The adventures of Huckleberry Finn. Modern Library 1993 xx, 433p $16.95

ISBN 0-679-42470-9

    * LC 92-51065

First published 1885. This is a companion volume to: The adventures of Tom Sawyer

This novel "begins with Huck's escape from his drunken, brutal father to the river, where he meets up with Jim, a runaway slave. The story of their journey downstream, with occasional forays into the society along the banks, is an American classic that captures the smells, rhythms, and sounds, the variety of dialects and the human activity of life on the great river. It is also a penetrating social commentary that reveals corruption, moral decay, and intellectual impoverishment through Huck and Jim's encounters with traveling actors and con men, lynch mobs, thieves, and Southern gentility." Reader's Ency. 4th edition

Twain, Mark, 1835-1910—*Continued*

also in Twain, M. Mississippi writings

The adventures of Tom Sawyer; [illustrated by True W. Williams]; foreword and notes by John C. Gerber; text established by Paul Baender. University of California Press 2002 c1982 274p il pa $14.95

ISBN 0-520-23575-4

*

First published 1876. This is a companion volume to: The adventures of Huckleberry Finn

"Tom, a shrewd and adventurous boy, is at home in the respectable world of his Aunt Polly, as well as in the self-reliant, parentless world of Huck Finn. The two friends, out in the cemetery under a full moon, attempt to cure warts with a dead cat. They accidentally witness a murder, of which Muff Potter is later wrongly accused. Knowing that the true murderer is Injun Joe, the boys are helpless with fear; they decide to run away to Jackson's Island. After a few pleasant days of smoking and swearing, they realize that the townspeople believe them dead. Returning in time to hear their funeral eulogies, they become town heroes. At the trial of Muff Potter, Tom, unable to let an innocent person be condemned, reveals his knowledge. Injun Joe flees. Later Tom and his sweetheart, Becky Thatcher, get lost in the cave in which the murderer is hiding. They escape, and Tom and Huck return to find the treasure Joe has buried." Reader's Ency. 4th edition

also in Twain, M. The adventures of Tom Sawyer, Tom Sawyer abroad, Tom Sawyer, detective p31-236
also in Twain, M. Mississippi writings

The adventures of Tom Sawyer, Tom Sawyer abroad, Tom Sawyer, detective; edited by John C. Gerber, Paul Baender, and Terry Firkins. University of Calif. Press 1980 717p il o.p.

LC 76-47974

A combined edition of three Tom Sawyer titles first published 1876, 1894 and 1896, respectively

The American claimant

In Twain, M. The gilded age and later novels

The complete novels of Mark Twain; edited with an introduction by Charles Neider. Doubleday 1964 2v o.p.

Contents: v1: The gilded age (1873); The adventures of Tom Sawyer (1876); The prince and the pauper (1881); Adventures of Huckleberry Finn (1881)

v2: A Connecticut Yankee in King Arthur's court (1889); The American claimant (1892); Tom Sawyer abroad (1894); Pudd'nhead Wilson (1894); Those extraordinary twins (1894); Personal recollections of Joan of Arc (1896); Tom Sawyer, detective (1896)

The complete short stories of Mark Twain; now collected for the first time; edited with an introduction by Charles Neider. Doubleday 1957 xxiv, 676p pa $15.95 hardcover o.p.

ISBN 0-06-058697-4 (pa)

Contents: The notorious jumping frog of Calaveras County; The story of the bad little boy; Cannibalism in the cars; A day at Niagara; Legend of the Capitoline Ve-

nus; Journalism in Tennessee; A curious dream; The facts in the great beef contract; How I edited an agricultural paper; A medieval romance; My watch; Political economy; Science vs. Luck; The story of the good little boy; Buck Fanshaw's funeral; The story of the Old Ram; Tom Quartz; A trial; The trials of Simon Erickson; A true story; Experience of the McWilliamses with membranous croup; Some learned fables for good old boys and girls; The canvasser's tale; The loves of Alonzo Fitz Clarence and Rosannah Ethelton; Edward Mills and George Benton: a tale; The man who put up at Gadsby's; Mrs. McWilliams and the lightning; What stumped the blue jays; A curious experience; The invalid's story; The McWilliamses and the burglar alarm; The stolen White Elephant; A burning brand; A dying man's confession; The professor's yarn; A ghost story; Luck; Playing courier; The Californian's tale; The diary of Adam and Eve; The Esquimau maiden's romance; Is he living or is he dead?; The £1,000,000 bank-note; Cecil Rhodes and the shark; The joke that made Ed's fortune; A story without an end; The man that corrupted Hadleyburg; The death disk; Two little tales; The belated Russian passport; A double-barreled detective story; The five boons of life; Was it Heaven? or Hell?; A dog's tale; The $30,000 bequest; A horse's tale; Hunting the deceitful turkey; Extract from Captain Stormfield's visit to heaven; A fable; The mysterious stranger

"The sixty pieces which are here hospitably called short stories illustrate both the weaknesses and the strengths of Mark Twain as a writer of fiction." N Y Times Book Rev

A Connecticut Yankee in King Arthur's court; edited by Bernard L. Stein; with an introd. by Henry Nash Smith. Published for the Iowa Center for Textual Studies by the University of California Press 1979 827p il $75

ISBN 0-520-03621-2

* LC 77-91761

First published 1889; published in the United Kingdom with title: Yankee at the court of King Arthur

This satiric novel is a "tale of a commonsensical Yankee who is carried back in time to Britain in the Dark Ages, and it celebrates homespun ingenuity and democratic values in contrast to the superstitious ineptitude of a feudal monarchy." Merriam-Webster's Ency of Lit

also in Twain, M. Historical romances

The gilded age

also in Twain, M. The gilded age and later novels

The gilded age and later novels. Library of America 2002 1053p $40

ISBN 1-931082-10-3   LC 2001-38053

Contents: The gilded age; The American claimant; Tom Sawyer abroad; Tom Sawyer, detective; No. 44, the mysterious stranger

The gilded age (1873), written with Charles Dudley Warner, is a panorama of an age in which the nation's capital teemed with would-be power brokers and vast fortunes piled up amid thriving corruption. In The American claimant (1892), an English viscount travels to America in search of an heir to his father's earldom. There he meets the primary claimant to the title, an eccentric yet good natured inventor, Colonel Mulberry

Twain, Mark, 1835-1910—*Continued*

Sanders. In Tom Sawyer abroad (1994), Tom, Huck Finn, and Jim take a trip via balloon across the Atlantic to the Sahara desert. In Tom Sawyer, detective (1896), Tom and Huck solve a complex murder mystery involving a diamond theft and Tom's Uncle Silas. No. 44, the mysterious stranger (1969) is a different version of the posthumously published The mysterious stranger, based on Twain's final manuscript. This version, set in Eseldorf, Austria in 1490, features "a likable young printer's devil, called only No. 44, who is possessed of satanic powers that allow him to master the craft of printing in a few hours. Singlehandedly he speedily produces a Bible and magically summons up phantasmagoric people to print innumerable copies." Oxford Companion to Am Lit. 6th edition

Historical romances; The prince and the pauper, A Connecticut Yankee in King Arthur's court, Personal recollections of Joan of Arc; [notes by Susan K. Harris] Library of Am. 1994 1029p maps (Library of America, 71) $35

ISBN 0-940450-82-8   LC 93-40246

Contents: The prince and the pauper; A Connecticut Yankee in King Arthur's court; Personal recollections of Joan of Arc

In The prince and the pauper (1882), a prince, Edward VI, switches clothes with Tom Canty, a poor boy who looks exactly like him. When the two are discovered, Edward is mistakenly driven from the castle and forced to endure Tom's harsh, impoverished life while Tom experiences Edward's life as royalty. A Connecticut Yankee in King Arthur's court and Personal recollections of Joan of Arc are entered separately.

The man that corrupted Hadleyburg, and other stories and essays. Harper 1900 364p o.p.

Contents: The man that corrupted Hadleyburg; My début as a literary person; £1,000,000 bank-note; Esquimau maiden's romance; My first lie, and how I got out of it; Belated Russian passport; Two little tales; About playacting; Diplomatic pay and clothes; Is he living or is he dead?; My boyhood dreams; Austrian Edison keeping school again; Death disk; Double-barreled detective story; Petition to the Queen of England

Mississippi writings. Literary Classics of the United States 1982 1084p $30

ISBN 0-940450-07-0   LC 82-9917

Contents: The adventures of Tom Sawyer; Life on the Mississippi; Adventures of Huckleberry Finn; Pudd'nhead Wilson

The adventures of Tom Sawyer, The adventures of Huckleberry Finn, and Pudd'nhead Wilson are entered separately. Life on the Mississippi (1883) is an autobiographical narrative that focuses on the author's childhood near the river.

Mysterious stranger, and other stories. Harper 1922 324p il o.p.

Contents: Mysterious stranger; Horse's tale; Extract from Captain Stormfield's visit to Heaven; Fable; My platonic sweetheart; Hunting the deceitful turkey; McWilliamses and the burglar alarm

No. 44, The mysterious stranger

In Twain, M. The gilded age and later novels

Personal recollections of Joan of Arc; by the Sieur Louis de Conte (her page and secretary); illustrated by G. B. Cutts. Harper 1926 596p il o.p.

First published 1896

"De Conte, who tells the story in the first person, has been reared in the same village with its subject, has been her daily playmate there, and has followed her fortunes in later life, serving her to the end, his being the friendly hand that she touches last. After her death, he comes to understand her greatness; he calls hers 'the most noble life that was ever born into this world save only One.' Beginning with a scene in her childhood that shows her innate sense of justice, goodness of heart, and unselfishness, the story follows her throughout her stormy career. We have her audiences with the king; her marches with her army; her entry into Orleans; her fighting; her trial; her execution; all simply and naturally and yet vividly told. The historical facts are closely followed." Keller. Reader's Dig of Books

also in Twain, M. Historical romances

The prince and the pauper

In Twain, M. Historical romances

Pudd'nhead Wilson;; and, Those extraordinary twins; introduction by Ron Powers; illustrations by F.M. Senior and C.H. Warren. Modern Library 2002 xvi, 263p il (Modern Library classics)

ISBN 0-81296-622-8   LC 2002-66002

Pudd'nhead Wilson was first published 1894 with title: The tragedy of Pudd'nhead Wilson. The short story Those extraordinary twins is about conjoined twins of completely opposite philosophy and temperament

"David Wilson is called 'Pudd'nhead' by the townspeople, who fail to understand his combination of wisdom and eccentricity. He redeems himself by simultaneously solving a murder mystery and a case of transposed identities. The mystery revolves around two children, a white boy and a mulatto, who are born on the same day. . . . The book is an implicit condemnation of a society that allows slavery. It also includes a series of brilliant epigrams which are distillations of Twain's wit and wisdom." Reader's Ency. 4th edition

also in Twain, M. Mississippi writings

Tom Sawyer abroad

In Twain, M. The adventures of Tom Sawyer, Tom Sawyer abroad, Tom Sawyer, detective p251-341

In Twain, M. The gilded age and later novels

Tom Sawyer, detective

In Twain, M. The adventures of Tom Sawyer, Tom Sawyer abroad, Tom Sawyer, detective p357-415

In Twain, M. The gilded age and later novels

Tweedsmuir, John Buchan, Baron *See* Buchan, John, 1875-1940

Two hundred years of great American short stories. See 200 years of great American short stories

Tyler, Anne, 1941-

The accidental tourist. Knopf 1985 355p o.p.

* LC 85-40161

"After 20 years of marriage, Macon and Sarah separate. Thus, a man used to intense order in his life finds his existence thrown into disorder; forced to create a new life for himself, Macon must overcome numerous obstacles—particularly his inability to communicate, to relate to other people's needs and problems." Booklist

"Thanks to her inimitable mix of an extraordinary inventiveness with characters and a profound humanity, Tyler makes this book a joy to read." Wilson Libr Bull

The amateur marriage; a novel. Knopf 2004 306p $24.95

ISBN 1-400-04207-0

* LC 2003-59536

This novel presents a portrait of the six-decade marriage of a Baltimore couple, Michael and Pauline Anton. "Although acquaintances like to think of them as a perfect couple, Pauline and Michael are constantly bickering, sulking and fighting at home. . . . [Yet] Pauline and Michael are also tied to each other by their children, by shared adventures and, as the years pass, by bonds of memory and inertia. Caring for aging parents, witnessing the illnesses and travails of friends, adapting to a move to the suburbs—these are all experiences that bind Pauline and Michael to each other, even as their very different temperaments and interests increasingly pull them apart." N Y Times (N Y Late Ed)

"In order to illuminate every facet of the couple's interactions and personalities, the story is told from several points of view: those of Michael and Pauline and two of their three children. Although Tyler's prose occasionally slips into banality, she never falters in creating vivid characters whose weaknesses are both credible and compelling." New Yorker

Back when we were grownups; a novel. Knopf 2001 273p $25

ISBN 0-375-41253-0   LC 2001-88107

"After recovering from the shock of becoming a widow in her mid-twenties, Rebecca 'Beck' Davitch has spent several busy decades occupied with managing both her quirky clan of in-laws and their party-hosting business. . . . At 53, Beck is feeling a little rundown herself. She wonders what became of the serious college student she once was and whether she took the right path when she followed her heart to the altar at 19. Beck thus embarks on a quixotic interior journey." Libr J

This "is as perceptive, as full of gentle comedy and human warmth as any of Ms Tyler's previous novels. She manages her quirky, engagingly named characters (Patch, Biddy, NoNo, Jeep, Zeb) beautifully, spinning a web of family tensions with a wonderful lightness of touch—in this, Ms Tyler is matchless." Economist

Breathing lessons. Knopf 1988 327p o.p.

* LC 88-45260

"Maggie and Ira Moran, late middle-aged, travel from their home in Baltimore to a friend's funeral in Pennsylvania. The expedition precipitates an introspective journey into their individual and collective pasts and presents and futures." Booklist

This novel has "irresistibly funny passages you want to read out loud and poignant insights that illuminate the serious business of sharing lives in an unsettling world." Publ Wkly

Celestial navigation. Knopf 1974 273p o.p.

Set in Baltimore, this novel tells of artist Jeremy Pauling's attempts to overcome his comfortable isolation and make contact with others

The author "is especially gifted in the art of freeing her characters and then keeping track of them as they move in their unique and often solitary orbits. . . . She has a way of transcribing their peculiarities with such loving wholeness that when we examine them we keep finding more and more pieces of ourselves." N Y Times Book Rev

The clock winder. Knopf 1972 312p o.p.

"It all starts when Elizabeth Abbott agrees to become Mrs. Emerson's handyman for the summer. Before it's over, one of the Emersons (Timothy) kills himself, another (Andrew) shoots Elizabeth, and Mrs. Emerson has a stroke. The 'handyman' finds herself holding the family together and ultimately stays on to become an Emerson herself by marrying Matthew." Libr J

The author has a "remarkable understanding of the intricacies of family life, a sympathy for odd-ball characters who never become merely southern grotesques . . . but are observed so gently that the term 'neurotic' seems equally inappropriate for them." New Repub

Digging to America; a novel. Knopf 2006 277p $24.95

ISBN 0-307-26394-0   LC 2005-52963

This "novel tells the story of two Baltimore families—the all-American Donaldsons and the Iranian-born Yazdans—who become the closest of friends after they both adopt baby girls from Korea." N Y Times (Late N Y Ed)

With this novel, "Tyler has delivered something startlingly fresh while retaining everything we love about her work . . . . Her success at portraying culture clash and the complex longings and resentments of those new to America confirms what we knew, or should have known, all along: There's nothing small about Tyler's world, nothing precious about her attention to the hopes and fears of ordinary people." Washington Post Book World

Dinner at the Homesick Restaurant. Knopf 1982 303p hardcover o.p. pa $14.95

ISBN 0-394-52381-4; 0-449-91159-4 (pa)

* LC 81-13694

"Pearl Tull, an angry woman who vacillates between excesses of maternal energy and spurts of terrifying rage, has been deserted by her husband and has brought up her three children alone. Cody, the eldest, is handsome, wild, and in a lifelong battle of jealousy with his young brother, the sweet-tempered and patient Ezra. Their sister Jenny tries, through three marriages, to find a stability which was never present in Pearl's home. Ezra also tries to achieve a permanence through his homey Homesick Restaurant in Baltimore, but he is cruelly tricked by his brother and is unable to establish any unity in the family." Shapiro. Fic for Youth. 3d edition

Earthly possessions. Knopf 1977 197p

ISBN 0-394-4114-7   LC 76-41222

This "novel concerns Charlotte Emory, a 35-year-old woman who goes to her bank in Clarion, Md., one morning to withdraw enough cash to leave her husband. Instead, she is hustled off as hostage to a bank robber and peripatetic demolition-derby rider named Jake Simms.

Tyler, Anne, 1941——*Continued*

Simms needs funds to get to Florida and take his girlfriend out of a home for unwed mothers. All that he and Charlotte share, apart from the stolen car they are riding in, is a distrust of 'closed-in spaces'—for him, the prison he has just escaped; for her, a household that includes a gaunt preacher husband, two children, three brothers-in-law and a procession of itinerant sinners, soldiers and salesmen." Newsweek

"The book is contrapuntal, alternating chapters of the present action with chapters of first-person flashback. . . . The dialogue has perfect pitch, the visual detail seems astonishing yet apt." New Repub

Ladder of years. Knopf 1995 325p $24

ISBN 0-679-43941-2   LC 94-38909

This novel's protagonist is forty-year-old Delia Grinstead. "Feeling unappreciated and unnoticed by her husband, a family doctor who took over Delia's father's practice, and increasingly unnecessary in the lives of her nearly grown children, Delia wanders off during a family beach vacation and starts a new life in a small town. She's sad and uncertain about her break with her previous life but oddly determined." Libr J

"'Ladder of Years' feels, indeed, like the story of a woman who thought she could prune her life down to a short story, only to find it blooming, unexpectedly, into an Anne Tyler novel. There can be few more delightful revelations." New Yorker

Morgan's passing. Knopf 1980 311p o.p.

LC 79-20272

"A young girl-wife goes into labor while she and her boy-husband are putting on a puppet-show of Cinderella at a church fair in Baltimore in 1967. Her baby is delivered en route to the hospital by a member of the audience who claims to be a doctor. . . . The fake doctor—who lives in a tumultuous . . . cluttered house with an imperturbable wife, seven daughters, his half-senile mother, and crackpot sister—attaches himself to the young couple and their child, following them, popping up at odd moments. Later, after they have all become friends, this attachment narrows, focusing upon the young wife, with unsettling consequences for everyone." New Repub

A patchwork planet. Knopf 1998 287p $24

ISBN 0-375-40256-X   LC 98-84431

This novel, set in Baltimore, "tells the story of a year in the life of 30-year-old Barnaby Gaitlin who, despite coming from a wealthy family, works as an odd-job man. Barnaby is an ordinary and somewhat bewildered man whose life turns on a chance encounter with a woman who may represent the angel that brings change and gives direction to his life." Libr J

"For some readers, the story may indeed be too quiltlike—cozy and cute. But unlike the patchwork it depicts, it is a wonder of construction: everything fits; it's seamless." New Yorker

Saint maybe. Knopf 1991 337p $22

ISBN 0-679-40361-2

* LC 91-52704

This novel tells the story of "Ian Bedloe, who believes himself responsible for the death of his older brother, Danny, killed in a late-night car crash after an angry confrontation with Ian. Danny's wife, grief-stricken and unstable, soon commits suicide, leaving behind three children (two from her previous marriage, to a man who has vanished). Overwhelmed by guilt, Ian takes . . . measures to redeem himself." N Y Times Book Rev

"Tyler's remarkable novel pulls at the heart strings and jogs the memories of forgotten youth. . . . While the majority of YA readers lack enough life experiences to appreciate the pure joy of Tyler's descriptions and thoughts, not to steer them in her direction would be a shame." SLJ

Searching for Caleb. Knopf 1976 c1975 309p

ISBN 0-394-49848-8

"The Pecks of Baltimore are wealthy, stand-offish, stolidly self-satisfied. In their suburban enclave . . . four generations have lived quietly together . . . [presided over by the] grandfather, Daniel. Only two have rebelled: Caleb, Daniel's dreamy, cello-playing brother who disappeared without a trace 60 years ago, and Duncan, Daniel's grandson. . . . When Duncan marries his cousin Justine, hitherto an ardent Peck, she begins to discover her own thirst for adventure. . . . And so, when Daniel decides to find his lost brother, Justine is the one who joins him." N Y Times Book Rev

"Anne Tyler's tone is understated, ironic, and elliptical, which suits her characters well. Searching for Caleb rarely gives us heights and depths of emotion or the excitement of discovery, but it does offer the very welcome old-fashioned virtues of a patient, thoughtful chronicle." Saturday Rev

A slipping-down life. Knopf 1970 214p o.p.

"Evie Decker, unattractive and unpopular, and Drumsticks Casey, an unknown rock musician, are misfits living in a small Southern town. They are drawn together in a union which is more bizarre than romantic. It is a union, however, that seems to fulfill the needs of each and makes for a marriage that is marked by quiet desperation." Shapiro. Fic for Youth. 3d edition

The tin can tree. Knopf 1965 273p o.p.

"Six-year-old Janie Rose Pike was killed in a fall from a tractor, an accident which shook but does not really change the little world in which she lived. Mrs. Pike, left stunned and silent by her daughter's death, is too apathetic to pay attention to her 10-year-old son, Simon. Her grown-up niece, who lives with the family, tries to take care of Simon and at the same time to cope with her own problems. It is Simon himself . . . who finally awakens his mother to the need for life to continue." Libr J

U

Uhnak, Dorothy

Codes of betrayal. St. Martin's Press 1997 293p $23.95

ISBN 0-312-15582-4   LC 97-23598

"Nick O'Hara was raised by his uncle Frank, an Irish cop, but his mother was a Ventura, daughter of an underworld crime boss. Nick follows his uncle into the NYPD, juggling professional life and family ties, until his son is killed in a sour drug deal while hanging out with a Ventura cousin. Then he learns his own father was a victim of the Ventura crime family. Marriage on the skids, Nick

Uhnak, Dorothy—*Continued*

turns to gambling, loses big, rips off a drug dealer to pay his debts, and winds up snared by the Feds, who offer a deal: exploit his family connection and help bring down the Venturas." Booklist

"This work effectively portrays one man's agony with life gone wrong and the decline of mobster power as the century ends." Libr J

The investigation; a novel. Simon & Schuster 1977 344p o.p.

* LC 77-7981

Sgt. Joe Peters is "a detective on the Queens County district attorney's squad. He accompanies his partner one morning on a house call involving two missing children. The distraught parents are George and Kitty Keeler. George is 'an obese, balding, sloppy middle-aged man' who owns a bar. Kitty, more than twenty years his junior, is a 'very beautiful kid' who manages a health spa owned by a small-time gangster. The Keeler marriage is shaky, and Kitty accuses George of having taken the boys. But when their bodies are found in a nearby park and Kitty's account of her actions begins to sound suspicious, she is indicted for murder. . . . Out of curiosity and an attraction to Kitty, [Peters] sets out to investigate on his own." Newsweek

Victims; a novel. Simon & Schuster 1986 c1985 316p o.p.   LC 85-26246

"Young nurse Anna Grace is stabbed to death on a street in Queens in full view of scores of apartment dwellers who decide not to get involved. Tough, good-looking NYPD detective Miranda Torres investigates the crime in association with bigshot newspaper columnist Mike Stein, whose only goal is to show the insensitivities of modern society without caring who the criminal is or why poor Anna was his victim. Miranda stays honest in trying to do her job, but finds that the well-spring of corruption in law enforcement is so powerful that it even touches her friends in the highest levels of government." Booklist

Ulinich, Anya, 1973-

Petropolis. Viking 2007 324p $24.95
ISBN 978-0-670-03819-0; 0-670-03819-9
LC 2006-41356

"Sasha Goldberg is the ultimate outsider: she's a chubby, biracial Jewish girl from the Siberian town of Asbestos 2. . . . Following her heart gets her into trouble at home, so she flees Russia as a mail-order bride and lands in suburban Arizona. Sasha manages to escape her Red Lobster-loving fiance and embarks on a misadventure-filled journey across America in search of her father." Publisher's note

"In the end, [the author] ties a neat bow around Sasha's serious coming-of-age problems, but bittersweetness lingers. Petropolis bursts with artful details of an immigrant's peripatetic youth and quest for home-the grappling for the strong woman inside of the lost girl." Ms.

Umrigar, Thrity N.

The space between us; a novel; [by] Thrity Umrigar. William Morrow 2005 321p
ISBN 0-06-07915-5-1   LC 2005-50510

"Sera Dubash is an upper-middle-class Parsi housewife in modern-day Bombay. Bhima is her domestic servant. Though they inhabit dramatically different worlds, the two women have much in common. Both married men they alternately love and loathe: Sera's moody husband frequently beats her, and Bhima's betrothed falls into an alcohol-drenched depression after losing his job. Sera's civil treatment of her servant—she overlooks Bhima's frequent tardiness and treats her like an equal—dismays her neighbors and friends. She also offers to fund the college education of Bhima's granddaughter, Maya, whom Bhima adopted when the girl's mother died of AIDS. The bond between the two women deepens when Sera (whose own daughter is happily wed and expecting her first child) arranges an abortion for unmarried Maya." Booklist

"The life of the privileged is harshly measured against the life of the powerless, but empathy and compassion are evoked by both strong women, each of whom is forced to make a separate choice. Umrigar is a skilled storyteller, and her memorable characters will live on for a long time." Washington Post Book World

The weight of heaven; a novel; [by] Thrity Umrigar. Harper 2009 365p $25.99
ISBN 978-0-06-147254-1

* LC 2008-32950

"Frank and Ellie Benton, grappling with the death of their seven-year-old son, move from Ann Arbor, Mich., to Girbaug, India, where Frank takes a job running a factory. While he tackles the barriers faced by an educated, wealthy American in charge of a Third World work force, Ellie, a psychologist, makes inroads with the impoverished locals at a health clinic. Frank has a difficult time adjusting at work, and at home he takes an interest in their housekeepers' son, Ramesh, and begins tutoring him. While Frank buries his grief by helping Ramesh, he ends up in competition with the boy's bitter father, Prakash, and further damaging his already troubled marriage." Publ Wkly

This is "is a bold, beautifully rendered tale of cultures that clash and coalesce." Booklist

Under African skies; modern African stories; edited and with an introduction by Charles R. Larson. Farrar, Straus & Giroux 1997 315p $25
ISBN 0-374-21178-7   LC 96-48601

Contents: The complete gentleman, by A. Tutuola; The eyes of the statue, by C. Laye; Sarzan, by B. Diop; Black girl, by S. Ousmane; Papa, snake & I, by L. B. Honwana; A meeting in the dark, by Ngugi wa Thiong'o; A handful of dates, by T. Salih; Mrs. Plum, by E. Mphahlele; Tekayo, by G. Ogot; Two sisters, by A. A. Aidoo; Girls at war, by C. Achebe; The prisoner who wore glasses, by B. Head; In the hospital, by S. M. Cordor; The true martyr is me, by R. Philombe; Innocent terror, by T. M. Sallah; Africa kills her sun, by K. Saro-Wiwa; Afrika road, by D. Mattera; Why don't you carve other animals, by Y. Vera; The magician and the girl, by V. Tadjo; A prayer from the living, by B. Okri; Effortless tears, by A. Kanengoni; Give me a chance, by M. Nhlapo; Taken, by S. Chimombo; I'm not talking about that, now, by S. Magona; My father, the Englishman, and I, by N. Farah; A gathering of bald men, by M. Langa

Under African skies—*Continued*

An "impressive collection of short stories from sub-Saharan Africa. Published between 1952 and 1996, some translated from French, Portuguese, and Arabic, these stories share a common outrage against Africa's decay, whether from oppressive colonialism and corruption or the repression of tradition and ignorance. These are not folk tales about great chiefs but heart-rending stories about ordinary people . . . trying to make a life for their families, caught up in the political and spiritual struggle for Africa." Libr J

Undset, Sigrid, 1882-1949

The bridal wreath
In Undset, S. Kristin Lavransdatter

The cross
In Undset, S. Kristin Lavransdatter

Kristin Lavransdatter; translated from the Norwegian. Knopf 1935 3v in 1 $50
ISBN 0-394-43262-2
*

Contains three novels originally published separately in Norway in 1920, 1921, and 1922 respectively; first United States publication with titles: The bridal wreath (1923); The mistress of Husaby (1925); The cross (1927)

Although the "action takes place in the fourteenth century, the lives of the characters are marked by almost the same problems depicted in modern novels: passion, adultery, premarital pregnancy, ambition, conflict. Kristin, daughter of Lavrans and Ragnfrid, is betrothed to Simon Andressön but falls in love with Erlend Nikulassön and finally wins her father's approval to marry him. Her father realizes on their wedding night that they are already lovers. The book follows Kristin's life as she tries to manage her estate and as her husband loses his lands and leaves her after a bitter quarrel. After several attempts at reconciliation, Erlend returns, only to be killed in a fight. The six sons of Kristin follow different paths. Two die during the Black Plague, which was so dreadful a scourge in that era. The portrayal of this Norwegian woman is vivid and human." Shapiro. Fic for Youth. 3d edition

The mistress of Husaby
In Undset, S. Kristin Lavransdatter

Unferth, Deb Olin

Vacation. McSweeney's 2008 215p $22
ISBN 978-1-93478-109-8; 1-93478-109-6
"The novel follows a woman who finds out her husband's deepest secret: he once jumped out of a window in pursuit of a bird who flew into the room. The deadpan humor continues as the woman decides to harbor her own secret: she has an affair, which consists entirely of trailing of a random man whom she never seeks to meet. The prose is highly stylized and full of devastating wit. Each sentence springs from an almost visual idiom. . . . Funny, bleak, often brilliant, Vacation once again proves that Unferth can preform a linguistic high-wire act all her own." Esquire

The **Unforgetting** heart: an anthology of short stories by African American women (1859-1993); edited by Asha Kanwar. Aunt Lute Bks. 1993 xxi, 292p
ISBN 1-879960-31-1   LC 93-3240

Contents: The two offers, by F. E. W. Harper; Aunt Lindy: a story founded on real life, by V. E. Matthews; Tony's wife, by A. Dunbar; A dash for liberty, by P. E. Hopkins; The octoroon's revenge, by R. D. Todd; After many days: a Christmas story, by F. B. Williams; The preacher at Hill Station, by K. D. C. Tillman; Guests unexpected: a Thanksgiving story, by M. K. Griffin; The judgment of Roxenie, by E. W. Smith; Breaking the color-line, by A. McCary; Mammy: a story, by A. F. Ries; Mary Elizabeth: a story, by J. Fauset; Goldie, by A. W. Grimké; Isis, by Z. N. Hurston; Sanctuary, by N. Larsen; Doby's gone, by A. Petry; In the laundry room, by A. Childress; Brooklyn, by P. Marshall; The funeral, by A. A. Shockley; A happening in Barbados, by L. M. Meriwether; Mom Luby and the social worker, by K. Hunter; The library, by N. Giovanni; After Saturday night comes Sunday, by S. Sanchez; Nineteen fifty-five, by A. Walker; The lesson, by T. C. Bambara; Kiswana Browne, by G. Naylor; Johnnieruth, by B. Birtha; Fifth Sunday, by R. Dove; The life you live (may not be your own), by J. C. Cooper; Ma'Dear, by T. McMillan; Emerald City: Third & Pike, by C. W. Sherman; Croon, by W. Coleman

Unsworth, Barry, 1930-

After Hannibal. Talese 1997 250p il
ISBN 0-385-48651-0
* LC 96-20856
First published 1996 in the United Kingdom
In this novel "five sets of outsiders invade Umbria by renovating houses along a country track. Trouble is made for them by local peasants and by an exploitative speculating Brit, but the real story is the way their various hopes and intrigues retrace ingrained historical patterns. Recognizing these patterns and, in a sense, presiding over them is an Italian lawyer so shrewd and wizardly that he seems supernatural." New Yorker

Land of marvels; a novel. Nan A. Talese 2009 287p $26
ISBN 978-0-385-52007-2   LC 2008-09201
"It is 1914, and, after three years in the deserts of Mesopotamia, the British archeologist John Somerville believes he is on the brink of a great discovery. Before he can uncover what he thinks was the residence of the last Assyrian king, Somerville must fight off plans for a railway that will encroach on his dig site, and thwart the efforts of Elliot, a charismatic, straight-talking American (in British historical novels there is rarely any other kind) who is bent on finding oil and on destroying what remains of Somerville's marriage. There is something of E. M. Forster in Unsworth's knowing depiction of a decaying empire run by upper-class incompetents, and in his generous and sympathetic portrayal of women caught between cultures." New Yorker

Losing Nelson; a novel. Talese 1999 338p $23.95
ISBN 0-385-48652-9   LC 99-28757

Unsworth, Barry, 1930-—*Continued*

"Charles Cleasby, a reclusive amateur historian, is obsessed with Lord Admiral Horatio Nelson, hero of the Battle of Trafalgar. Cleasby is fascinated with every detail of his hero's life: myriad historical anniversaries, details of his personal life, and accounts of famous battles that Cleasby reenacts with ship models in his basement. In short, Cleasby is living vicariously through Nelson's life, his hero's exploits compensating for his mundane existence. To assert his divine image of Nelson, Cleasby is determined to disprove Nelson's involvement in a brutal massacre." Booklist

"Unsworth is in complete control of his material, effortlessly sustaining an almost unbearable level of tension that is suddenly resolved in an unusually effective surprise ending." Libr J

Morality play. Talese 1995 192p o.p.

LC 95-4106

This novel, set in 14th century England, is narrated by "Nicholas Barber, a young monk who has forsaken his calling and joined an itinerant troupe of players that gets caught up in the real-life drama of a small-town murder. The crime presents Barber and his fellows with an opportunity to attract a larger-than-usual audience, and they turn sleuths, weaving the bits of information yielded by their investigation into an improvised play that eventually reveals the surprising, sordid truth. Rich in historical detail, Unsworth's well-told tale explores some timeless moral dilemmas and reads like a modern page-turner." Libr J

The ruby in her navel; a novel of love and intrigue in the twelfth century. Nan A. Talese 2006 399p $26

ISBN 0-385-50963-4   LC 2006-40370

"Set in the Kingdom of Sicily in the mid-12th century, this tale of romance, intrigue, and betrayal focuses on Thurstan Beauchamp, the landless son of a Norman knight. Thurstan serves Roger II, the illustrious but warlike Norman King of Sicily, as the Purveyor of Pleasures and Shows in a secretive royal chancery whose functions range from espionage to royal entertainments. Yusuf, a Muslim Arab who runs this operation from the glittering royal palace in Palermo, sends Thurstan on a mysterious mission to Bari to meet a Serbian insurgent fighting against Sicily's rival, the Byzantine Empire. Thurstan then becomes unwittingly entangled with the religious, political, and ethnic tensions festering in a polyglot culture caught between a brash Christian Europe and an entrenched Muslim civilization." Libr J

"Like the best historical fiction writers, Unsworth tells his story while also fleshing out the backdrop with details that ground us in the moment and make it tangibly real. He makes his characters' individual experiences representative of larger concerns." Washington Post Book World

Sacred hunger. Doubleday 1992 629p o.p.

LC 91-33237

A novel about the 18th century slave trade. "William Kemp hopes to recoup his losses in cotton speculation by entering the Triangular Trade. As ship's doctor, his nephew Matthew experiences firsthand the horrors of shipboard life, ultimately leading a revolt that lands the crew and remaining slaves on the southeastern coast of Florida. Here they try to establish 'a paradise place'." Libr J

"Deftly utilizing a flood of period detail, Unsworth has written a book whose stately pace, like the scope of its meditations, seems accurately to evoke the age. Tackling here a central perversity of our history—the keeping of slaves in a land where 'all men are created equal'—Unsworth illuminates the barbaric cruelty of slavery, as well as the subtler habits of politics and character that it creates." Publ Wkly

The songs of the kings; a novel. Doubleday 2003 338p $26

ISBN 0-385-50114-5

* LC 2002-66845

"A stubborn wind from the northeast ushers in rough times for the House of Atreus, and the Greek ships, en route to Troy, remain trapped in the straits at Aulis. Unsworths' retelling of the story, familiar from Euripides, of the sacrifice of Iphigeneia to appease the gods so that the boats can sail is a bold, modern tale with cynical riffs on the themes of duty and power, truth and fiction. His Greek warriors are schemers and media-savvy self-promoters who are desperate to look good in the sung reports that are their equivalent of the news media—songs that are, we realize, the seeds of the Homeric tradition." New Yorker

Stone virgin. Houghton Mifflin 1986 309p

ISBN 0-395-35412-9

* LC 85-24897

"Simon Raikes is given the task of restoring a 15th-century sculpture of the Madonna on a church in Venice. A frustrated artist himself, Simon is compelled to solve certain mysteries: Who was the sculptor? Why was the work suppressed for two centuries? How did it earn consecration? As he begins to painstakingly shear away corrosion, the statue apparently confronts him with visions and stirs his passions. His search for answers leads to a local sculptor's wife, with whom Simon falls in love, and eventually to a new mystery." Libr J

"The strength of Unsworth's novel doesn't lie simply in its critique of masculine love, courtly and carnal, sacred and profane. For Stone Virgin is also a murder mystery, a reflection on mediaevalism versus Renaissance humanism, creator versus critic and—last but not least–an elegy to Venice, its water and stone." New Statesman

Upadhyay, Samrat

The guru of love. Houghton Mifflin 2003 290p $23

ISBN 0-618-24727-0   LC 2002-32234

Ramchandra, a math teacher in 1990s Kathmandu, Nepal, has "become infatuated with one of his tutees, 15-year-old single mother Malati. Unable to endure his obsession, his wife, Goma, has fled to her parents' home with pubescent Sanu and her younger brother, Rakesh. But nothing—neither infidelity nor her rich parents' scorn for a son-in-law who can barely afford a dilapidated apartment with outdoor plumbing—diminishes Goma's love for Ramchandra." Publ Wkly

The author "excels at depicting the thousand small cuts that afflict a middle-class married man having an affair. . . . The writing is emotionally restrained and doesn't call attention to itself. There are no lyrical bursts of exuberance over the country's beauty or the torments of love. At points the novel is excessively terse; when three

Upadhyay, Samrat—_Continued_
words would have sufficed, Upadhyay uses two. In spite
of that it is gripping, because you like the characters so
much, and wish them well." N Y Times Book Rev

Updike, John, 1932-2009

The afterlife and other stories. Knopf 1994 316p
$24

ISBN 0-679-43583-2   LC 94-9818
Contents: The afterlife; Wildlife; Brother grasshopper;
Conjunction; The journey to the dead; The man who became a soprano; Short Easter; A sandstone farmhouse;
The other side of the street; Tristan and Iseult; George
and Vivian: Aperto, Chiuso, Bluebeard in Ireland; Farrell's caddie; The rumor; Falling asleep up North; The
brown chest; His mother inside him; Baby's first step;
Playing with dynamite; The black room; Cruise; Grand-
parenting
"In these mellow, reflective stories, where parents die
and grandchildren are born, Updike's heroes are acutely
aware of lost glory yet discover the strength to persevere." Libr J

Bech: a book. Knopf 1970 206p o.p.

Contents: Bech in Russia; Bech in Rumania; The Bulgarian poetess; Bech takes pot luck; Bech panics; Bech
swings; Bech enters Heaven
"In seven episodes presented in the guise of lectures
with a spurious bibliography, the work reveals the literary and personal life of Henry Bech, a distinguished
Jewish author of New York. Revelatory incidents include
Bech's travels in the 1960s as a kind of cultural ambassador in Russia and Eastern Europe, his visit as a lecturer to adulatory pupils at a girls' school, his diverse romantic affairs, his difficulties in writing as he ages, and
his ultimate enshrinement as a major American author."
Oxford Companion to Am Lit. 6th edition

Bech at bay; a quasi-novel. Knopf 1998 240p
$23

ISBN 0-375-40368-X   LC 98-27868
Contents: Bech in Czech; Bech presides; Bech pleads
guilty; Bech noir; Bech and the bounty of Sweden
This book "brings readers amusingly up to date on the
life and times of Bech, a neurotic Jewish novelist. Skipping merrily along, the real author describes the imaginary author's trip to Czechoslovakia, his stint as head of
a pretentious and marginal writers' group, a period of
true weirdness in which he literally murders his critics,
his late arrival at fatherhood and his receipt of a Nobel
prize." Economist

Bech is back. Knopf 1982 195p o.p.

LC 82-161
Contents: Three illuminations in the life of an Ameri-
can author; Bech third-worlds it; Australia and Canada;
The Holy Land; Macbech; Bech wed; White on white
Further episodes in the life of Henry Bech. "The no-
vella-length 'Bech Wed' finds him married to suburban
Bea who provides three teenagers, a dog, and a house in
Ossining where Bech finally finishes his fourth novel,
'Think Big,' which is hyped and heralded after his 15-
year silence: 'The squalid book we all deserve,' said Al-
fred Kazin in the 'New York Times Book Review.' In
the other stories . . . Bech tours Third-World countries;

writes his name 28,500 times for a new signed edition of
an old novel; is interviewed in Canada and Australia; and
visits Israel with his Episcopalian bride. An atmospheric
travelogue and funny satire of the literary scene." Libr J

Brazil. Knopf 1994 260p $23
ISBN 0-679-43071-7   LC 93-28632
"Tristão Raposo, a nineteen-year-old black child of the
Rio slums, and Isabel Leme, an eighteen-year-old upper-
class white girl, meet on Copacabana Beach; their flight
into marriage takes them to the farthest reaches of Brazil's wild west. Privation, violence, captivity, and reversals of fortune afflict them; his mother curses them, her
father harries them with hirelings, and neither lover is
absolutely faithful. Yet Tristão and Isabel hold to the
faith that each is the other's fate for life." Publisher's
note
This novel, "for all its political incorrectness, seems
good-natured and bent on self-parody. . . . If the book's
surface is sometimes a little sticky, its allegorical underpinnings are graceful and firm." N Y Times Book Rev

The centaur. Knopf 1963 302p $24.95
ISBN 0-394-41881-6

"Utilizing a contemporay setting in Olinger, Pennsylvania, Updike attempts to retell the myth of Chiron, wisest
of the centaurs, a creature who gave up his immortality
on behalf of Prometheus. In this modern version, Chiron
is a high-school science teacher, George Caldwell, and
Prometheus is his 15-year-old son, Peter. The story revolves around three critical days in their lives." Shapiro.
Fic for Youth. 3d edition

Gertrude and Claudius. Knopf 2000 212p $23
ISBN 0-375-40908-4   LC 99-57601
"Updike turns to Shakespeare's 'Hamlet,' exploring the
origin of Gertrude and Claudius' 'reechy kisses.' When
the sixteen-year-old Gertrude is unwillingly betrothed to
the elder Hamlet, Horwendil, by her father . . . she
quickly falls for his brother, Claudius. The two honorably resist their feelings until they are beset by the anxieties of aging; as it turns out, the murder of Horwendil
is an act of emotional (and political) desperation rather
than cold calculation. Likewise, Updike's portrayal of
Gertrude and Claudius' thwarted affections is not just a
deft literary exercise but an affecting—and funny—invo-
cation of the abundant desires of what Hamlet called
'this too too solid flesh." New Yorker

In the beauty of the lilies. Knopf 1996 491p
$25.95
ISBN 0-679-44640-0   LC 95-23467
The novel "opens in Paterson, New Jersey, in 1910.
'At the moment Mary Pickford fainted' while making a
movie close by, Presbyterian minister Clarence Wilmot
loses his faith. That loss precipitates another loss: his
job. Since 'now he was free—free to sink,' he turns to
selling encyclopedias door to door and to an addictive
habit of watching the fabulous new medium, moving pictures. Updike then tells of the following three generations of Clarence's family. . . . Updike's soaring novel
becomes an extended yet taut metaphor for the secular-
ization of religion and the concomitant infatuation with
movies as a substitute for religion." Booklist

Licks of love; short stories and a sequel. Knopf
2000 359p $25
ISBN 0-375-41113-5   LC 00-34906

Updike, John, 1932-2009—*Continued*

Contents: The women who got away; Lunch hour; New York girl; My father on the verge of disgrace; The cats; Oliver's evolution; Natural color; Licks of love in the heart of the cold war; His oeuvre; How was it, really?; Scenes from the fifties; Metamorphosis; Rabbit remembered

"This book of stories, mostly about old wives and girlfriends recollected in middle-aged tranquillity, also includes a novella—a return to the world of Harry Angstrom, Updike's unlikely alter ego. In 'Rabbit Remembered,' it turns out that Rabbit's untimely demise has not diminished his ability to shake up the lives of those around him. His family may not miss him, exactly, but, like the rest of us, they still can't get over him." New Yorker

Memories of the Ford Administration; a novel. Knopf 1992 371p

ISBN 0-679-41681-1   LC 92-52955

Professor Alfred Clayton "has received a request from the Northern New England Association of American Historians for his memories and impressions of the Gerald Ford Administration (1974-77). 'Alf' obliges with his memories of a turbulent period in his personal history, as well as pages of an unpublished book he was writing at the time, on the life of James Buchanan, the fifteenth President of the United States (1857-61)." Publisher's note

"Updike's elegant, yet slangy portrait of the Ford era demonstrates considerable finesse. Even more impressive is his authentic, yet unstilted, evocation of Buchanan's era." Christ Sci Monit

My father's tears and other stories. Alfred A. Knopf 2009 292p $25.95

ISBN 978-0-307-27156-3; 0-307-27156-0
                                  LC 2008-54376

Contents: Morocco; Personal archaeology; Free; The walk with Elizanne; The guardians; The laughter of the gods; Varieties of religious experience; Spanish prelude to a second marriage; Delicate wives; The accelerating expansion of the universe; German lessons; The road home; My father's tears; Kinderszenen; The apparition; Blue light; Outage; The full glass

"A perfect bookend to Pigeon Feathers, the precocious collection of stories that nearly five decades ago announced their 30-year-old writer's discovery of his own inimitable voice. . . . Mr. Updike writes in these stories . . . with the quiet assurance of someone in complete control of his craft." N Y Times (Late N Y Ed)

Pigeon feathers, and other stories. Knopf 1962 278p $29.95; pa $14

ISBN 0-394-44056-0; 0-449-91225-6 (pa)

Contents: Walter Briggs; The persistence of desire; Still life; Flight; Should wizard hit mommy?; A sense of shelter; Dear Alexandros; Wife-wooing; Pigeon feathers; Home; Archangel; You'll never know, dear, how much I love you; The astronomer; A & P; The doctor's wife; Lifeguard; The crow in the woods; The blessed man of Boston, my grandmother's thimble, and Fanning Island; Packed dirt, churchgoing, a dying cat, a traded car

These stories "are filled with gentle humor and irony. Youth, marriage, and family life provide most of the themes." Cincinnati Public Libr

The poorhouse fair. Knopf 1959 c1958 185p o.p.

A reissue with a new introduction of the title first published 1959

This novel concerns the lives of a handful of marvelously eccentric and understandable people in a poorhouse on the undulating plains of central New Jersey. It begins on the morning of the annual Fair, an innovation of Conner, the new and very ambitious prefect. Conner's struggle to institutionalize old age inevitably meets the stiff opposition of those who want to individualize it

"This is a wise book with much to say on individualism and conformity, mechanization and craftsmanship, the 'welfare state' and the 'old days'—and, foremost, on 'death' as it is looked upon by the aged and the young. Updike's old people are memorable." Libr J

Rabbit Angstrom; a tetralogy; with an introduction by author. Knopf 1995 xxxi, 1519p $30

ISBN 0-679-44459-9

Contents: Rabbit, run (1960); Rabbit redux (1971); Rabbit is rich (1981); Rabbit at rest (1990)

Rabbit at rest. Knopf 1990 512p

ISBN 0-394-58815-0   LC 90-52953

Sequel to Rabbit is rich

"In John Updike's fourth and final novel about ex-basketball player Harry 'Rabbit' Angstrom, the hero has acquired heart trouble, a Florida condo, and a second grandchild. His son, Nelson, is behaving erratically; his daughter-in-law, Pru, is sending out mixed signals; and his wife, Janice, decides in midlife to become a working girl." Publisher's note

"The being that most illuminates the Rabbit quartet is not finally Harry Angstrom himself but the world through which he moves in his slow downward slide, meticulously recorded by one of our most gifted American realists." N Y Times Book Rev

also in Updike, J. Rabbit Angstrom

Rabbit is rich. Knopf 1981 467p $30

ISBN 0-394-52087-4   LC 81-1287

Sequel to Rabbit redux

"Rabbit and Janice have now inherited a half interest in his late father-in-law's business and, having found a kind of place in society, he is a member of the local country club. He is resigned to good relations with Stavros, and he sees Ruth to determine if a chance acquaintance is their daughter. Rabbit finds that the girl is not his daughter, but he does become involved in paternal problems with his son Nelson, now in college, who has gotten his girl friend pregnant." Oxford Companion to Am Lit. 5th edition

"A superlative comic novel that is also an American romance." Time

Followed by Rabbit at rest

also in Updike, J. Rabbit Angstrom

Rabbit redux. Knopf 1971 406p

ISBN 0-394-47273-X

Sequel to Rabbit, run

"Updike profiles Harry (Rabbit) Angstrom, 10 years after his first appearance, as a conservative suburbanite no longer running away from responsibilities but unable to resolve the anxieties that are brought to him from outside. His wife takes a lover and, after decrying Rabbit's lack of will to keep her, leaves their home. Rabbit and

Updike, John, 1932-2009—*Continued*

his thirteen-year-old son Nelson become involved with Jill Pendleton, a young hippie girl whom Rabbit takes into his house; to him she is a sometimes baffling sexual partner, to Nelson an older sister. Jill's friend Skeeter then arrives, a black man of devastating wit and antic humor who initiates Rabbit to marijuana and encourages him to read black history." Booklist

"There are some structural faults, and moments when characters don't ring true. But I can think of no stronger vindication of the claims of essentially realistic fiction than this extraordinary synthesis of the disparate elements of contemporary experience." N Y Times Book Rev

Followed by Rabbit is rich

also in Updike, J. Rabbit Angstrom

Rabbit remembered
In Updike, J. Licks of love p177-359

Rabbit, run. Knopf 1960 307p o.p.
$\qquad$ *

"Contemporary in setting and tone, and brilliant in its evocation of everyday life in America, the novel is about Harry Angstrom ('Rabbit'), a salesman who, on an impulse, leaves home, his alcoholic wife, Janice, and his child, Nelson, to find freedom. After several escapades and a liaison with an ex-prostitute, he returns to his wife and child and attempts to settle down again. In this novel, Updike conveys the longings and frustrations of family life. Rabbit's malaise is not so much a yearning for freedom as, perhaps, a yearning for guiding spiritual values and meaning. At the end, still dissatisfied and guilt-ridden because of the responsibility he feels for the death of his second child, he begins running again." Reader's Ency. 3d edition

Followed by Rabbit redux

also in Updike, J. Rabbit Angstrom

Roger's version. Knopf 1986 328p
ISBN 0-394-55435-3
$\qquad$ * LC 86-45298

"Divinity professor Roger Lambert is visited by Dale Kohler, an earnest young student who wants a grant to prove the existence of God by computer. The visit disrupts Roger's ordinary existence, bringing him into contact with . . . Verna (his half-sister's daughter), and leading to his wife's affair with Dale." Libr J

This novel "succeeds in spite of its symbolic structure. Its power and charm lie in the terrific appeal it makes to our capacity for intellectual wonderment. It's rather thrilling to watch Updike assimilate the new vocabularies of particle physics and computer technology—and then fuse them with the ancient vocabulary of religious belief." Newsweek

S. Knopf 1988 279p o.p.   LC 87-40496

This novel "concerns Sarah Worth, a latter-day Hester Prynne who has become enamored of a Hindu religious leader called the Arhat. A New Englander, she goes west to join his commune in Arizona, and there mingles with the other sannyasins (pilgrims) in the . . . attempt to subdue ego and achieve moksha (salvation, release from illusion)." Publisher's note

This "is an acid comedy of illusions and delusions told entirely in the words of a woman who is both deceived and deceiver." Atlantic

Seek my face. Knopf 2002 276p $23
ISBN 0-375-41490-8   LC 2002-18442

"The action of the novel, such as it is, takes place over a single early-April day at the house in the Vermont countryside of the septuagenarian Hope Chafetz, an artist in her own right and, more famously, widow of the action painter Zack McCoy and ex-wife of the Pop artist Guy Holloway. Kathryn, an ambitious young journalist, has come up from New York to interview this living repository of the history of postwar American art. Through the course of the long day the two women talk, attended by a tape recorder, that ubiquitous tool of contemporary journalism." N Y Times Book Rev

"Despite its uncomplicated premise, the novel achieves a remarkable depth of characterization and a glowing beauty in its articulation of the artistic sensibility." Booklist

Terrorist. Alfred A. Knopf 2006 320p $24.95
ISBN 0-307-26465-3   LC 2005-57985

This novel tells the story "of eighteen-year-old Ahmad Ashmawy Mulloy and his devotion to Allah and the words of the Holy Qur'an, as expounded to him by a local mosque's imam. The son of an Irish-American mother and an Egyptian father who disappeared when he was three, Ahmad turned to Islam at the age of eleven. He feels his faith threatened by the materialistic, hedonistic society he sees around him in the slumping factory town of New Prospect, in northern New Jersey. . . . When he finds employment in a furniture store owned by a family of recently immigrated Lebanese, the threads of a plot gather around him, with reverberations that rouse the Department of Homeland Security." Publisher's note

"The last part of the novel is suspenseful. It brings together a serviceable plot, which leans a little heavily on coincidental connections, a questionable provocation and some broadly motivated acts of heroism. It seems meant as a fable, and any good fable requires some derring-do. The most satisfactory elements in 'Terrorist' are those that remind us that no amount of special pleading can set us free of history, no matter how oblivious and unresponsive to it we may be." N Y Times Book Rev

Toward the end of time. Knopf 1997 334p $25
ISBN 0-375-40006-0   LC 97-5167

The protagonist, Ben Turnbull, "is a sixty-six-year-old retired investment counselor living north of Boston in the year 2020. A recent war between the United States and China has thinned the population and brought social chaos. . . . Nevertheless, Ben's life, traced by his journal entries over the course of a year, retains many of its accustomed comforts. . . . Something of a science buff, he finds his personal history caught up in the disjunctions and vagaries of the 'many-worlds' hypothesis derived from the indeterminacy of quantum theory." Publisher's note

"Like Updike, Ben can write elegant sentences. Although his temporal excursions (and Updike's researched inventions) at first seem random, they fit together into a paranoid structure by novel's end. Ben's report from the body front and reflections on his failures . . . are simultaneously sad and comic, often worthy of that old endgamer Beckett." Nation

Updike, John, 1932-2009—*Continued*

Trust me; short stories. Knopf 1987 302p o.p.
LC 86-46018

Contents: Trust me; Killing; Still of some use; The city; The lovely troubled daughters of our old crowd; Unstuck; A constellation of events; Deaths of distant friends; Pygmalion; More stately mansions; Learn a trade; The ideal village; One more interview; The other; Slippage; Poker night; Made in heaven; Getting into the set; The wallet; Leaf season; Beautiful husbands; The other woman

Villages. Knopf 2004 321p $25
ISBN 1-400-04290-9   LC 2004-43845

This novel "follows its hero, Owen Mackenzie, from his birth in the semirural Pennsylvania town of Willow to his retirement in the rather geriatric community of Haskells Crossing, Massachusetts. In between these two settlements comes Middle Falls, Connecticut, where Owen, an early computer programmer, founds with a partner, Ed Mervine, the successful firm of E-O Data, which is housed in an old gun factory on the Chunkaunkabaug River. Owen's education is not merely technical but liberal, as the humanity of his three villages, especially that of their female citizens, works to disengage him from his youthful innocence." Publisher's note

"Owen's obsession with women's bodies and blithe ignorance of their inner lives can sometimes read like a tedious parody of Updike's earlier work, without a sense of humor to imply the author is in on the joke. Yet Updike still writes lovely sentences and creates a believable portrait of the American village, concealing dark secrets but providing a limited stability." Publ Wkly

The widows of Eastwick. Knopf 2008 308p $24.95
ISBN 978-0-307-26960-7; 0-307-26960-4
LC 2008-18513

In the early chapters of this sequel Updike's "three coven members from 'The Witches of Eastwick' (1984), try to cope with the recent deaths of their husbands by visiting exotic and distant lands. . . . Soon the novel settles in one locale as the three witches, no longer the supple, self-confident, gorgeous young women of the earlier novel, return to Eastwick ostensibly to rediscover their powers so that they can 'give something back' to this city where they once so memorably applied their witchery to ignoble ends." San Antonio Express-News

"One wonders whether anybody has ever described the small physical indignities of the aging process with as much tenderness and good humor as Updike. . . . Now the witches' sex lives are over, but their lives aren't, and you sense Updike's twinkly eyes peering cautiously into the darkness, beyond the glow of the merely fleshly, trying to make out what the world beyond might look like." Time

The witches of Eastwick. Knopf 1984 307p o.p.
* LC 83-49048

"A novel about three Rhode Island women whose marriages have collapsed and who turn to devil worship and witchcraft." Reader's Ency. 4th edition

"While not a typical Updike narrative, the author's glittering wit, pungent observations, and fabled legerdemain at tabulating mundane particulars reach their peaks in the first half of the novel. Only in the last sections does the reader's attention flag." Booklist

Ure, Louise

The fault tree. St. Martin's Minotaur 2008 336p $24.95
ISBN 978-0-312-37585-0; 0-312-37585-9
LC 2007-38730

"Cadence Moran, a blind auto mechanic in Tucson, Ariz., has an uncanny ability to pinpoint engine problems by sound. Her skill soon becomes a key element in solving a series of gruesome murders." Publ Wkly

Ure "makes a convincing case for a woman who overcomes her overwhelming sense of inadequacy to become a heroine. Heart-stopping suspense that builds to a crescendo and well-defined characters make this a topnotch mystery." Libr J

Uris, Leon, 1924-2003

Armageddon; a novel of Berlin. Doubleday 1964 632p o.p.

Berlin from the close of World War II to the end of the airlift is the setting of this novel. Sean O'Sullivan, an American captain responsible for the military government of the city of Rombaden, nurses a fierce hatred of the Germans, and is faced with a dilemma when he falls in love with a German girl

The author "provides a broad and moving panorama of the rebuilding of postwar Germany at the time when the Allies and the Russians first came to clash over Berlin and its routes of access." Atlantic

Battle cry. Putnam 1953 505p o.p.

"Taking an average group of American boys from their home environment through the ordeal of boot camp, to the battlefields of Guadalcanal, Tarawa, and Saipan, the author fills in a detailed picture of Marine training and traditions." Booklist

Exodus. Doubleday 1958 626p il hardcover o.p. pa $7.99
ISBN 0-385-05082-8; 0-553-25847-8 (pa)
*

"Following World War II the British forbade immigration of the Jews to Israel. European Jewish underground groups, aided by Palestinian agent Ari Ben Canaan, made every effort to aid these unfortunate victims of Nazi persecution. The novel provides insight into the heritage of the Jews and understanding of the danger involved in helping them reach a safe haven. It also includes the warm love story of Ari and a gentile nurse, Kitty Fremont, who cared very much for the welfare of the Jewish children caught in this nightmare." Shapiro. Fic for Youth. 3d edition

Mila 18. Doubleday 1961 539p $19.95
ISBN 0-385-02076-7

"Mila 18 was the actual command post of the resistance movement organized by the Warsaw Jews. . . . [This is the story] of the handful of men and women who, knowing they had to die, defied the whole German Army with their homemade weapons, and won the respect of the world." N Y Times Book Rev

"Uris' major talent is that he is a master storyteller. And in 'Mila 18' he uses this talent fully and unhampered, in a straight narrative that generates an almost unbelievable dramatic intensity." San Francisco Chron

Uris, Leon, 1924-2003—*Continued*

QB VII. Doubleday 1970 504p o.p.
This novel is "about the trial of an American novelist in Queen's Bench 7 for libeling a Polish surgeon by contending he performed experimental sterilizations of Jews in a concentration camp." Oxford Companion to Am Lit. 5th edition
"Two thirds of this jumbo novel are concerned with the trial, Kelna versus Cady. The judge allows this and overrules that. Dramatic, impassioned confrontations before the Queen's Bench alternate with contributory scenes: the two principals surrounded by worried families, mistresses and friends, the police pressing their search for missing witnesses, the speculation about who's guilty and who's innocent." N Y Times Book Rev

Redemption; a novel. HarperCollins Pubs. 1995 827p
ISBN 0-06-018333-0   LC 95-10834
The focus of this sequel is "the conflict between two of the three dominant families of *Trinity*, the tempestuous Larkins and their staid British counterparts, the Hubbles. . . . Uris begins by tracing the Larkin legacy from patriarch Liam's exile to New Zealand, where he becomes squire of a sheep farm; his brother, Conor, becomes a legendary Irish revolutionary. Another Larkin progeny, Liam's son Rory, is acclaimed as a war hero after fighting with the British at Gallipoli, while Rory's brother Dary takes Catholic clerical vows, only to have a powerful love drive him to question both celibacy and his calling. Uris balances the struggles of the Larkins with the more repressed travails of Caroline Hubble, who battles the efforts of her husband to oppress the Irish after losing a pair of sons in the disastrous British battle against the Turks." Publ Wkly

Trinity. Doubleday 1976 751p il $21.95
ISBN 0-385-03458-X
                                                              *
This novel is set in Ireland between the 1840's and 1916. "The trinity includes the Larkin clan of Ballyutogue, Catholic hill-farmers who have eked out a bare subsistence in County Donegal for generations; the powerful Hubble dynasty, British aristocracy which has dominated the area for three centuries; and the McLeods of Belfast, shipyard workers whose Scottish Presbyterian forebears were planted there by the British to solidify the power of the Crown." Christ Sci Monit
"The story has a kind of relentless power, based on the real tragedy of Ireland, and Uris's achievement is that he has neither cheapened nor trivialized that tragedy." N Y Times Book Rev

Urquhart, Jane, 1949-

Away; a novel. Viking 1994 c1993 356p o.p.
                                      LC 94-178660
The "saga of a family who must leave Ireland for Canada during the potato famine of the 1840's. As a young girl in Ireland, Mary is taken 'away' to the faeries after a young sailor (a faerie-daemon) whom she rescued dies in her arms. Although she does eventually marry, have a family, and start a new life in the Canadian wilderness, Mary still hears the call of her sailor and finally leaves her family to live the rest of her life alone by a lake. Her daughter Eileen, in turn, falls in love with an Irish na-

tionalist whose passion is only for his cause; she spends the rest of her life 'away' in thoughts of him." Libr J
"Urquhart's blending of the spiritual and political sides of the Irish makes an amazing story told in a language that is melodious and laden with complex imagery." Booklist

A map of glass. MacAdam/Cage Pub. 2006 371p $25
ISBN 1-596921-70-6   LC 2006-360
First published 2005 in Canada
"Set in present-day Toronto and in the 19th-century world of rural Ontario timber barons, [this novel] opens with the wintry death of Alzheimer's sufferer Andrew, whose body, borne by an ice floe, runs aground on the small Lake Ontario island where artist Jerome McNaughton is seeking inspiration. The story steps back a century, to when Andrew's ancestors, owners of the same island, razed forests to build ships, then it jumps forward a year from the opening scene of Andrew's death, to when Sylvia, Andrew's married lover of 20 years, sets out to meet with Jerome, who discovered Andrew's body, and, through Jerome, to reconnect one last time with Andrew. Meanwhile, Jerome, the relationship-shy adult child of an abusive, alcoholic father, is slowly coming to trust that girlfriend Mira's love for him is real. Urquhart reveals all of their haunted personal histories in the lyrical first and third parts of the novel. But it's in the compact family-saga middle, where a slew of Andrew's memorable forebears take the stage, that this novel's luminous heart truly lies." Publ Wkly

The underpainter. Viking 1997 340p o.p.
                                      * LC 97-225317
This is a "symbolic tale about the life of a famous American artist. Austin spends his summers painting in a small Canadian town, and his winters showing off in New York City, a split-down-the-middle life indicative of his disconnectedness. Turned off to emotion at an early age, Austin is unable to return the love of his muse and model, a graceful and mystically self-sufficient woman, or the generosity of his only true friend, a sensitive man who suffers a broken heart and the horrors of war with valor and compassion." Booklist
"Urquhart writes forcefully; her imagery is vivid, and her evocation of time and place is accomplished and assured. There is an impressive density of character and narrative, and her use of illustrative detail is, at times, striking." Times Lit Suppl

Urrea, Luis Alberto

Into the beautiful North; a novel. Little, Brown and Company 2009 342p $24.99
ISBN 978-0-316-02527-0; 0-316-02527-5
                                      LC 2008-39962
This novel is "about Nayeli, who is 19 years old and working in a taco shop in what would conventionally be referred to as a 'sleepy Mexican village.' The town is not as sleepy as the residents would like. Bandidos — drug dealers — have appeared and are threatening their way of life. There aren't enough men left in town to defend the women, children and old people from their incursions. Nayeli comes up with a solution after seeing 'The Magnificent Seven' at the local cinema. . . . She decides to go to the United States and find seven men to bring back home. They will marry, start families and

Urrea, Luis Alberto—*Continued*

be the salvation of the village. Their mere presence will deter bandidos. Her Tia Irma won't let her go alone, so she takes Irma's American Express card; Tacho, the gay owner of the taco shop; and her two best friends, Yolo, the reader, and Veronica, the goth girl. So begins their picaresque adventure. The escapades of these four and the people they meet, who help or hinder them, are alternately hilarious, poignant, scary and sad." Seattle Times

V

Vachss, Andrew H.

Another life; a Burke novel. Pantheon Books 2008 271p $24.95

ISBN 978-0-307-37741-8; 0-307-37741-5

LC 2008-00213

"When a sniper shoots Burke's father, the Prof, the Prof's uneasy relationship with the law means that his life-threatening wounds can't be treated at a hospital. While his father's fate remains uncertain, a shadowy figure connected with U.S. intelligence draws Burke, an ex-con turned avenging angel for hire, into a kidnapping case. Early one morning, somebody removed the infant son of a Saudi prince from his father's custom Rolls, parked near an abandoned pier near the Hudson River, after the prince was serviced by a prostitute, who didn't realize the child was in the back seat. Burke visits his usual seamy corners of New York City in the ensuing investigation." Publ Wkly

Choice of evil; [by] Andrew Vachss. Knopf 1999 305p $23

ISBN 0-375-40647-6

LC 99-61596

"At a gay rally in New York City, Burke's friend Crystal Beth is killed in a drive-by shooting. Burke and his tribe of shadowy, semicriminal associates set out to track down the killer, but their investigation is soon impeded by a retaliatory series of murders perpetrated against known gay bashers. . . . Vachss creates a gun-metal gray, paranoid milieu where few can be trusted, where to be mainstream is to be compromised, and where children and women are always—yes, always—at risk." Booklist

Dead and gone; [by] Andrew Vachss. Knopf 2000 333p

ISBN 0-375-41121-6

LC 00-40565

"Professional killers ambush Burke late one night, putting a bullet in his head and killing his beloved dog, Pansy. Physically, Vachss's self-professed 'outlaw' is a changed man when he finally sneaks out of the hospital. But he's still the same old Burke on the inside. He wants revenge—but he has no idea who masterminded the attack. Thus begins a months-long odyssey that takes him all over the country." Publ Wkly

"The left-for-dead-but-back-for-revenge plot is an old one, but Vachss manages to give it new life. Burke isn't quite as dark as he's been in the past, finding time to wax poetic on Chicago bluesman Son Seals and to discuss hot cars with other gear heads. But the message is the same: no mercy for the exploiters of children." Booklist

Down here; [by] Andrew Vachss. Knopf 2004 289p $19.95

ISBN 1-400-04173-2

LC 2003-58860

Burke "returns from the 'dead' to help a former colleague arrested for attempting to kill a suspected serial rapist. As Burke begins to pull in old favors and reveal his still-living status to select individuals, he discovers obvious holes in the prosecution's theory. The recent overturning of the alleged rapist's conviction makes all of his victims potential murder suspects." Libr J

"This is yet another carefully crafted descent into a hellish environment in which sexual predators roam virtually unchecked, at least until targeted by Burke. One would think the same revenge plot would get old when recast again and again, but, amazingly, Vachss adds enough subtle differences to keep each novel unique and engaging." Booklist

Down in the zero; a novel; by Andrew Vachss. Knopf 1994 259p o.p.

LC 94-12312

In this mystery Burke is "confronted with young adult suicides and sexual blackmail in an affluent Connecticut suburb. Hired to watch the young son of a former lover, Burke is drawn into a bizarre situation populated by characters almost as strange as his friends. The suicides and the sadomasochistic sex, which are weirdly connected, force Burke to enlist his usual cohorts. Fans will want this crisply written work." Libr J

Footsteps of the hawk; [by] Andrew Vachss. Knopf 1995 237p o.p.

LC 95-17596

"The action begins when Burke is approached by a female police officer, Belinda, who wants him to exonerate her lover, now serving time as a serial killer. Belinda contends that the real killer is still on the loose; her lover is a connected guy who probably deserves to be in prison, but he's no killer. So she says. She also pins the cover-up on Morales, a psycho cop with a desire to send Burke to prison for his role in the violent breakup of a child pornography ring. Burke employs his familiar Fagin's army of street types to discover the real killer and the real motives behind the crime. As always in Vachss' work, New York's underbelly is vividly evoked." Booklist

Hard candy; a novel; by Andrew Vachss. Knopf 1989 241p o.p.

LC 89-45272

In this "novel featuring unlicensed New York private eye Burke, word is out that the ex-con PI has become a gun-for-hire. Besides coping with this crazy rumor, Burke contends with two figures from his youth who suddenly turn up. One of them, Candy, now a mini-skirted call girl fond of whips and leashes, wants Burke to rescue her teenaged daughter from a cult in Brooklyn; the other, Wesley, an Uzi-toting hit man, already has the cult's leader, Train, in his sights. When Burke learns that the cult safehouse is a baby-breeding operation, vigilante-style justice ensues." Publ Wkly

Pain management; [by] Andrew Vachss. Knopf 2001 307p

ISBN 0-375-41322-7

LC 2001-29868

Burke "resurfaces in Portland, Oregon, after an assassin left him for dead in New York. He's living from hand to mouth when he stumbles into a missing-child case. Burke suspects parental involvement in the disappearance of young teen Rosa, but nothing supports the

Vachss, Andrew H.—*Continued*

theory. The trail leads first to Portland's red light district, where he hears about a serial killer whom the cops seem unwilling or unable to catch." Booklist

"Vachss finally lets his secondary characters speak for themselves, as opposed to being wholly defined by Burke's inner growl." Publ Wkly

Sacrifice; a novel; by Andrew Vachss. Knopf 1991 271p o.p.

* LC 90-53582

"Super-tough Manhattan maverick PI Burke works both sides of the law to save Luke, an eight-year-old suspect in a series of baby murders." Publ Wkly

"Vachss' clipped, blunt, ocassionally overly melodramatic sentences may, in some way, be ripe for parody (à la Mickey Spillane), but they also convey the frightening impact of the somber, shocking, emotionally deadening hellholes that Burke, breaking every civilized rule, battles gamely through." Booklist

Safe house; [by] Andrew Vachss. Knopf 1998 291p o.p.

LC 97-50557

"At the request of Crystal Beth, operator of a Manhattan safe house, Burke agrees to take the case of a mother being stalked by her estranged husband, the leader of a neo-Nazi cell. As Burke untangles the web that connects the white supremacists to protectors in the federal government, he helps foil a terrorist plot that echoes the real Oklahoma City bombing. As always, Burke's exploits are an occasion to provide updates on Max the Silent, Michelle the transsexual and other veterans of his guerrilla underground—and to offer a quick study of the ways in which the justice system fails victims of crime." Publ Wkly

Two trains running; [by] Andrew Vachss. Pantheon Books 2005 447p $25

ISBN 0-4000-4381-6

* LC 2004-60127

"Locke City, a Southern mill town turned tourist mecca, is controlled by the firm but benevolent hand of local crime tsar Royal Beaumont. When the New York mafia arrives, he hires former undercover FBI agent Walker Dett to protect his interests. In short snippets of action and dialog, Vachss . . . creates a broad picture of crime in Locke City, from teenage street gangs to crooked national politicians, with the Ku Klux Klan, militant African Americans, and other factions woven into a shocking climax. A riveting page-turner that marks a definite change of direction from the author's dark Burke thrillers." Libr J

Valdes-Rodriguez, Alisa

Dirty girls on top. St. Martin's Press 2008 324p $24.95

ISBN 978-0-312-34967-7; 0-312-34967-X

LC 2008-12930

Sequel to: The Dirty Girls Social Club (2003)

"The six sucias (dirty girls) return with hilarious and raunchy tales of Latina-tinged love, marriage, and sex told from each character's point of view. Pop star Cuicatl likens the touch of one of her groupie lovers to 'uncooked tofu from the refrigerator,' while man-izer Usnavys describes her husband's wardrobe style as 'like a college student on welfare cheese.' Despite a plot full of guilty-pleasure material, Dirty Girls admirably dives into darker areas like infidelity, mortality, addiction, and abuse. Hey, life can't be a fiesta 24/7." Entertainment Wkly

Vallgren, Carl-Johan

The horrific sufferings of the mind-reading monster Hercules Barefoot; his wonderful love and his terrible hatred. HarperCollins 2006 288p $23.95

ISBN 0-06-084199-0   LC 2005-52695

Original Swedish edition, 2002

"Set in the early 1800s, the story follows Hercule Barfuss, who is born deaf, dumb and grotesquely misshapen, with a 'dark red cavity' for a face, in a German whorehouse. But he has a gentle, intelligent nature and a budding gift of telepathy, which reveals people's innermost, unacknowledged desires. Reared in the brothel, Hercule forms a deep bond with a beautiful girl, Henriette Vogel, who was born there the same night he was. After the loving pair is tragically separated at age 10, Hercule traverses Europe–living in a Jesuit monastery, an asylum and with a traveling freak show–persecuted everywhere as he seeks out Henriette. Along with Hercule's relentless search for Henriette, it is a sadistic cardinal's pursuit of Hercule ('a demon') that propels the novel." Publ Wkly

"Overflowing with engrossing drama and superlative characterizations, Vallgren's novel is a masterful meditation on the triumph of love over human degradation." Booklist

Van de Wetering, Janwillem, 1931-2008

The Amsterdam cops; collected stories. Soho Crime 1999 254p $22

ISBN 1-56947-171-1   LC 99-23243

Contents: The deadly egg; Six this, six that; The sergeant's cat; There goes ravelaar; The letter in the peppermint jar; Heron Island; Letter present; Houseful of mussels; Holiday patrol; Sure, blue, and dead, too; Hup three; The machine gun and the mannequin; The bongo bungler

"Written during the past 16 years, the stories feature the Amsterdam Murder Brigade's cynical, jowly Detective-Adjutant Henk Grijpstra and his handsome assistant Detective-Sergeant Rinus de Gier." Publ Wkly

The blond baboon; a novel. Houghton Mifflin 1978 194p o.p.   LC 77-17338

"Elaine Carnet, one-time chanteuse, is found by her daughter at the bottom of the stairs leading to the garden. Elaine, retired from the cabaret world, has run a profitable furniture business for some years now. It is not clear who might wish her dead, if anyone did. But . . . [detectives Grijpstra and de Gier] feel Carnet's daughter and her explanation of the events don't ring true." Publ Wkly

The hollow-eyed angel. Soho Press 1996 282p $22

ISBN 1-56947-056-1

* LC 95-26296

"A young gay reserve policeman asks the commissaris, who happens to be going to a conference in New York, to investigate the mysterious death of his uncle in Central Park. Rinus de Gier follows the commissaris, who is

Van de Wetering, Janwillem, 1931-2008—*Continued*

now very old and nods off during lectures. Meanwhile, Henk Grijpstra investigates the death of a baron on a golf course as a possible homicide." Murphy. Ency of Murder and Mystery

Just a corpse at twilight. Soho Press 1994 265p $20

ISBN 1-56947-016-2   LC 94-9499

"Responding to de Gier's trans-Atlantic call for help, Grijpstra leaves the cozy embrace of his mistress, Nellie, for a daunting journey to a small coastal island in Maine where his former partner has gone to seek solitude and wisdom . . . and is being blackmailed for having pushed a local woman, his sometime lover, over a cliff to her death. . . . More than one drug-running operation, a money-making scam of lesser proportion, gratuitous cruelty, venality, a Papuan rite of revenge and intelligent, unpredictable humor wrap up this narrative delight." Publ Wkly

The perfidious parrot. Soho Press 1997 280p $22

ISBN 1-56947-102-9

* LC 97-2548

In this novel "Grijpstra and de Gier have retired and started a private detective agency. A sleazy character named Carl Ambagt twists their arms into investigating piracy on the high seas—the theft of a chartered oil tanker in the Caribbean. The case takes them to Key West and The Perfidious Parrot, a lap dancing bar, then on to St. Eustatius. Van de Wetering's ribald streak is getting stronger and stronger, his writing looser and looser; in *The Perfidious Parrot*, he writes like a Dutch Carl Hiaasen." Murphy. Ency of Murder and Mystery

Van Gelder, Gordon

(ed) The Best from fantasy & science fiction: the fiftieth anniversary anthology. See The Best from fantasy & science fiction: the fiftieth anniversary anthology

Van Gulik, Robert *See* Gulik, Robert Hans van, 1910-1967

Van Slyke, Helen, 1919-1979

Public smiles, private tears; [by] Helen Van Slyke with James Elward. Harper & Row 1982 250p

ISBN 0-06-014961-2   LC 81-47794

"Beverly Thyson Richmond is an ambitious career woman in the 1940s and 1950s, a time when most women were homemakers and those with careers were viewed skeptically. Beverly chooses to work in a large department store rather than attend college. With the assistance of her mentor, Beverly develops a retailing career that eventually dominates her life." Libr J

"On her death in 1979 Van Slyke . . . left the uncompleted first half of a novel that has now been completed by Elward, a playwright and author of three pseudonymous novels. The result is an expert combination; one cannot tell where the splice occurs, and the spirit and tone are consistent." Publ Wkly

Van Vogt, A. E. (Alfred Elton), 1912-2000

Slan. An Orb ed. Orb 1998 255p pa $13.95

ISBN 0-312-85236-3

* LC 97-38438

"A Tom Doherty Associates book"
First published 1940

"One of the landmark novels of the genre, Van Vogt's 1940 tale follows the 'Slan,' a new breed of telepathic humans and their search for a society free from persecution. Essential for all libraries." Libr J

Followed by Slan hunter

Slan hunter; [by] A.E. van Vogt and Kevin J. Anderson. TOR 2007 270p $24.95

ISBN 978-0-7653-1675-2; 0-7653-1675-7

LC 2007-8357

"A Tom Doherty Associates book"
This sequel finds "true mutant (or slan) Jommy Cross trying to head off the impending invasion of Earth by the Mars-based group of slan without tendrils. Opposing him again are John Petty, head of the secret police and chief slan hunter, and Jem Lorry, traitorous presidential adviser and leader of the invasion. Seeking his dead father's hidden retreat, Jommy hopes to uncover the origins of both the true and the tendrilless slan, to stop their internecine war and to relieve human fears of being replaced by artificially created supermen." Publ Wkly

"This sequel to the late Van Vogt's cult sf classic Slan [1940] combines notes from the author and his son Greg with the storytelling skill of sf veteran Anderson, working with the Van Vogt family's permission. [The result is] a blend of astute social commentary and pulp sf action/adventure." Libr J

Van Vogt, Alfred Elton *See* Van Vogt, A. E. (Alfred Elton), 1912-2000

Vance, Jack, 1916-

The last castle
In The Hugo winners p245-305

Vanderbes, Jennifer

Easter Island; a novel. Dial Press (NY) 2003 304p $24.95

ISBN 0-385-33673-X   LC 2002-31588

This novel "parallels two stories: that of Elsa Pendleton, who travels to Easter Island in 1913 with her much older husband and her mentally impaired sister to study the toppled moai statues, and of Dr. Greer Farraday, who in the 1970s escapes grief after the death of her famed scientist husband, accused of fraud, by studying ancient pollen on the island. Both women have been suppressed by circumstance—Elsa, always her sister's caretaker, has made a bid for security by marrying a colleague of her father after his death, and Greer battles prejudice against women scientists." Libr J

"Vanderbes knows how to craft suspense, and the narratives—while packed with vivid historical and scientific detail—move forward on the strength of her fully realized characters." Publ Wkly

Vanderhaeghe, Guy, 1951-

The last crossing. Alantic Monthly Press 2004 393p $24

    ISBN 0-87113-912-X   LC 2003-60152

"Centered on three English brothers who venture to the American West—one as a missionary, the two others in pursuit when he disappears—this saga encompasses a wide range of characters through alternating narrative voices. In a panorama of late-nineteenth-century Montana and western Canada, Vanderhaeghe details the lawlessness of the early frontier towns and the desperate ferocity of the dying indigenous tribes. He dwells with particular pathos on the children of white traders and Native American women, who are caught between two cultures. The prose can be overripe, particularly in the opening chapters, and moments of historical exposition are clumsily inserted. However, the sweep of the narrative gradually overcomes these missteps, and as the various searches for revenge or redemption get under way the writing achieves unforced grace and power." New Yorker

Vann, David

Legend of a suicide. University of Massachusetts Press 2008 172p $24.95

    ISBN 978-1-55849-672-9; 1-55849-672-6

                    LC 2008-35381

Contents: Ichthyology; Rhoda; A legend of good men; Sukkwan Island; Ketchikan; The higher blue

This "collection, five stories and a novella, . . . revolves obsessively around the suicide of an Alaskan father. Hopscotching through time, each tale examines the father's death from the perspective of his young son, Roy. . . . Vann uses startling powers of observation to create strong characters, tense scenes and genuine surprises, leading to a ghastly conclusion that's sure to linger." Publ Wkly

Vapnyar, Lara, 1971-

Broccoli and other tales of food and love. Pantheon Books 2008 148p $20

    ISBN 978-0-375-42487-8; 0-375-42487-3

                    LC 2007-41537

Contents: A bunch of broccoli on the third shelf; Borscht; Puffed rice and meatballs; Salad Olivier; Luda and Milena; Slicing sautéed spinach

"This slim collection of six short stories (plus recipes) focuses on Russian and Eastern European immigrants to the US. They are lonely, they are disoriented, and they hope dinner will assuage their longings. Food is the slender thread that connects their pasts to their presents. Vapnyar's characters are funny, vulnerable, somewhat deluded, but also courageous. . . . [They] drift wistfully through landscapes they have not yet learned how to embrace. Yet Vapnyar's sly humor keeps her narratives light along with their poignance." Christ Sci Monit

Vargas Llosa, Mario, 1936-

Aunt Julia and the scriptwriter; translated by Helen R. Lane. Farrar, Straus & Giroux 1982 374p o.p.

                        * LC 82-5159

Original Spanish edition, 1977

In this novel Vargas Llosa "draws on memories of his youth during the mid-1950s, namely his marriage to an aunt despite strong family opposition, and the action-packed soap operas penned by a mad colleague at a Lima radio station where Vargas Llosa was employed. The work's overriding irony stems from the juxtaposition of the two plot lines, the first based on fact and the second on imaginary events. The end result is a kind of metanovel in which the author sees the objective account of his courtship and marriage gradually assume the characteristics of melodrama." Ency of World Lit in the 20th Century

The bad girl; translated from the Spanish by Edith Grossman. Farrar, Straus & Giroux 2007 276p $25

    ISBN 978-0-374-18243-4   LC 2007-04941

Original Spanish edition, 2006

This novel "spans 1950s Lima, 1960s revolutionary Paris, 1970s hippie London, 1980s swinging Tokyo and 1990s theatrical Spain. . . . Each of its seven long chapters, separated by years, relates a new episode in the lurching, on-again-off-again saga of Ricardo Somocurcio and the bad girl, who sports a new identity each time he encounters her." San Francisco Chron

"Each chapter in Ricardo's life, in Edith Grossman's tart, fluent translation, is a small novel unto itself with its own amiable or striking protagonists, offering a whole fabric of reality waiting to be shredded to pieces by the reappearance of the bad girl. In this way, Vargas Llosa lures us into the world of Latin American revolutionaries; the tony equestrian crowd of Norfolk, England; the denizens of sex clubs in Tokyo; and much more. . . . Vargas Llosa, pulling back one illusory screen after another, eventually reveals the bad girl's true story in a manner that couldn't be more satisfying." Seattle Times

Captain Pantoja and the Special Service; translated from the Spanish by Gregory Kolovakos and Ronald Christ. Harper & Row 1978 244p

    ISBN 0-06-014494-7   LC 76-26280

Original Spanish edition, 1973

"Pantoja is a diligent young army officer who is sent to the Peruvian tropics to organize a squadron of prostitutes and thus make life more bearable for lonely soldiers stationed in remote out-posts. Because of his puritanical nature and zealously analytical approach to his assignment, Pantoja elicits the reader's guffaws from the beginning, but ultimately he comes to typify the absurd hero who continues to struggle against overwhelming odds. The theme of absurdity is underscored, moreover, by the hilarious parodies of military procedures, the clashing montage of incompatible episodes, and generous doses of irony and the grotesque." Ency of World Lit in the 20th Century

Death in the Andes; translated by Edith Grossman. Farrar, Straus & Giroux 1996 275p o.p.

                      LC 95-40883

Original Spanish edition, 1993

"Guerrillas, army officers, environmentalists, a bizarre witch and her equally strange husband, and even a couple of French tourists all have their roles to play as the author fashions a plot centering on the mysterious killing of three men in a remote village. Finding the killer is the framework upon which the author develops a pageant of contemporary Peruvian society." Booklist

This novel "begins with a mystery. . . . It concludes with an enigma: How slender is the boundary between

Vargas Llosa, Mario, 1936----*Continued*

civilization and tenebrous horror? The novel's indecipherable mystery is exquisitely attractive to the clear, transparent country that is a genial reader's mind." Atl Mon

The Feast of the Goat; translated from the Spanish by Edith Grossman. Farrar, Straus & Giroux 2001 404p $25; pa $14

ISBN 0-374-15476-7; 0-312-42027-7 (pa)

LC 2001-33480

Original Spanish edition, 2000

"This fictional portrait of ruthless Dominican Republic dictator Rafael Trujillo focuses on the end of the old 'goat's' life. . . . Vargas Llosa relates Trujillo's story from the perspective of Urania Cabral, a successful New York lawyer who has spent a lifetime in exile but returns to her homeland when the tyrant is finally murdered. Urania hopes to rid herself of the demons that have possessed her since 1961, when as a teenager she was battered and humiliated by the impotent and vindictive old dictator." Libr J

The notebooks of Don Rigoberto; translated by Edith Grossman. Farrar, Straus & Giroux 1998 259p il $23

ISBN 0-374-22327-0

* LC 98-70961

Original Spanish edition, 1997

This novel is set in Lima, Peru. "Don Rigoberto and his beautiful wife, Lucrecia, are separated, driven apart by an obscure sexual encounter between Lucrecia and her stepson, the prepubescent Fonchito, who may or may not be a little devil in disguise. Because he misses her so, Don Rigoberto fills notebooks with his graphic longings, while Fonchito visits Lucrecia in the hope of effecting a reconciliation—and in the meantime discusses frankly his identification with the artist Egon Schiele, whose sexual excesses he details with wide-eyed wonder." Libr J

"Vargas Llosa's complex, gorgeous prose, heroically translated by Edith Grossman, sweeps the reader into a rich confusion of art and fact, fiction and reality, fantasy and deed, where there are no vices and the only virtue is imagination." N Y Times Book Rev

The way to paradise; translated by Natasha Wimmer. Farrar, Straus & Giroux 2003 373p $25

ISBN 0-374-22803-5

* LC 2003-56379

This is a dual fictional biography of "early-nineteenth-century French-Peruvian workers' rights activist Flora Tristan and her grandson, famous painter Paul Gauguin. In alternating chapters, the author. . . fashions portraits of these two vibrant individuals as he follows Flora in touring France to carry out her campaign to promote labor organization and equality in marriage, and Paul in awakening to his innate sexuality, to say nothing of tapping into his formidable artistic talent, by abandoning France for the South Pacific." Booklist

"A whiff of the lecture hall is detectable all through this book. (Some passages have more dates than an almanac.) But the juxtaposition of Tristan's and Gauguin's stories is fascinating all the same. In their different ways, both were moralists and proselytizers." N Y Time Book Rev

Varley, John, 1947-

Demon. Putnam 1984 464p o.p.

LC 84-4814

The author "concludes his trilogy about Gaea, the sentient asteroid circling Titan. Cirocco Jones and her allies, including various Titanides and a Terran bodybuilder, struggle to provide the last refuge for fugitives from an Earth devastated by nuclear war." Booklist

The golden globe. Ace Bks. 1998 425p $22.95

ISBN 0-441-00558-6

LC 98-14612

"Galactic actor and con man Sparky Valentine runs afoul of the Charonese Mafia on Pluto and takes on the most important role of his long and illustrious career—that of a desperate survivor. Varley . . . artfully combines a rousing sf adventure with generous doses of Shakespearean lore and theater history, all of which serve as an elaborate backdrop for a moving portrait of a child actor who never quite grew up." Libr J

The persistence of vision

In The Hugo winners p459-507

Red lightning. Ace Books 2006 330p $24.95

ISBN 0-441-01364-3

LC 2005-34226

The protagonist of this sequel to Red thunder is "Ray Garcia-Strickland, son of Martian explorer and hotel owner Manny Garcia. The family still has connections to Earth, though, and when an unidentified object strikes the Atlantic, destroying a huge percentage of the U.S. East Coast and several Caribbean islands, they head for Florida to get Grandmother, who owns a hotel on the coast, out of the disaster zone. Then there's mad genius Uncle Jubal, singlehandedly responsible for the incomprehensible Squeezers technology that creates incredibly cheap energy and makes space travel possible, who lives surrounded by a web of 'security' in the Falklands. Just as the family thinks the worst is over, Jubal vanishes, and there are earthly powers that will stop at nothing to find him." Booklist

"Drawing unabashedly on current events from 9/11 to Hurricane Katrina, the author mixes space opera-esque adventure and merriment with uncensored images of disaster areas and teenage sex. At his Heinlein-channeling best, Varley preaches the gospel of individual responsibility with all the fervor of a space-age libertarian revival preacher." Publ Wkly

Red thunder. Ace Bks. 2003 411p $23.95

ISBN 0-441-01015-4

LC 2002-38231

"When a Chinese spacecraft, Heavenly Harmony, threatens to land on Mars a few days before the U.S. shuttle vehicle Ares Seven, washed-up ex-astronaut Travis Broussard, his brilliant but uncoventional cousin, Jubal, and four kids from Florida decide to build their own private spaceship, Red Thunder, and get there first in this riveting SF thriller. . . . With hilarious, well-drawn characters, extraordinary situations presented plausibly, plus exciting action and adventure, this book should do thunderously well." Publ Wkly

Rolling thunder. Ace Books 2008 344p $24.95

ISBN 978-0-441-01563-4; 0-441-01563-8

LC 2007-46581

"In the distant future, Mars is a colony of Earth, and Lt. Patricia Podkayne is a third-generation Martian with something to prove. As a member of the Music, Arts,

Varley, John, 1947-—*Continued*

and Drama Division of the Martian Navy, she accepts an assignment as an entertainer on the planet Europa, not realizing that trouble is brewing on that world. . . . Varley's style of future sf is immediate and gritty, filled with realistic details and believable characters. His conclusion to a trilogy begun with Red Lightning and Red Thunder demonstrates his skill as both raconteur and master of science-based fiction." Libr J

Titan; illustrated by Freff. Berkley Pub. Corp. 1979 302p il o.p.

* LC 78-23865

The first volume of a trilogy that includes Wizard and Demon

"The heroine finds an artificial world among the satellites of Saturn and becomes an agent of its resident intelligence, the godlike Gaea, before being forced to turn against 'her.' Conscientiously nonsexist action-adventure SF." Anatomy of Wonder. 3d edition

Followed by Wizard

Wizard; illustrated by Freff. Berkley Pub. Corp. 1980 354p il o.p.   LC 79-24871

"In this sequel to . . . 'Titan,' Varley continues his exploration of the sentient, wheel-shaped world called Gaea. Twenty years have passed, and now that Earth is aware of her, Gaea has tried to protect herself by becoming valuable to humanity—offering us 'miracles' based on her immense scientific knowledge. Two supplicants for such boons are the central characters: Chris, a man from Earth, and Robin, a woman from the Coven, an all-female orbital colony. To earn their miracles, Gaea requires them to become heroes. To achieve this, they accompany Rocky and Gaby (heroines of the first book, back in supporting roles) on a dangerous odyssey through Gaea's rebellious regions and learn that Gaea herself is the real enemy." Publ Wkly

Followed by Demon

Vassanji, M. G. (Moyez G.), 1950-

The assassin's song. Alfred A. Knopf 2007 313p $25

ISBN 978-1-4000-4217-3; 1-400-04217-8

LC 2007-8562

"Karsan Dargawalla is destined from boyhood to succeed his father and his father's father as avatar of Pirbaag, a 13th-century Sufi shrine. As the novel unfolds in fits and starts, Karsan rejects his spiritual inheritance and decamps for Harvard in 1970, against his chagrined father's wishes. The three decades of stubborn self-exile that follow represent a sorrowful generational rift between father and son that ends when Karsan returns home after his ascetic father's death." Publ Wkly

"Vassanji eloquently details the sufferings of Karsan's family as the price of his individual freedom, but suggests that this abandonment was necessary, and that tradition, in the face of India's 'ancient animosities,' must be engaged with critically and in the context of the wider world." New Yorker

The in-between world of Vikram Lall. Knopf 2004 369p $25

ISBN 1-400-04216-X   LC 2004-48967

"In this novel set among Kenya's Indian diaspora, two ill-fated loves—Vikram Lall's for a young English girl, his sister's for a young African man—symbolize their family's tenuous social position as neither privileged oppressor nor righteous oppressed. Vikram, now in exile in Canada, recounts Kenya's painful process of decolonization and his own role laundering money for government officials, an activity that he justifies as the survival tactic of one considered 'inherently disloyal' because of his race. . . . The book admirably captures the tenor of the postcolonial period: the predicament of the Asian minority, the corruption that marred Kenya's fledgling independence, and the individual tragedies that were the cost of revolution." New Yorker

Vassanji, Moyez G. *See* Vassanji, M. G. (Moyez G.), 1950-

Vennewitz, Leila

(tr) Böll, H. The clown

Verghese, Abraham, 1955-

Cutting for stone; a novel. Alfred A. Knopf 2009 541p $26.95

ISBN 978-0-375-41449-7; 0-375-41449-5

LC 2008-28252

A "novel about identical twin boys born in Addis Ababa in 1954 and instantly orphaned—their mother dies, their father flees. Raised by doctors at the hospital, Shiva and Marion soon begin practicing medicine themselves, but their lives unhappily diverge. . . . Verghese, a doctor, has an affinity for unstinting detail and unscientific intuition. The exhaustive gore of the medical procedures is matched by a poetic perception of the outside world—arriving in New York, Marion misses the cacophony of Addis Ababa's roads, observing that in America 'the cars were near silent, like a school of fish.' Verghese bends history and coincidence to his narrative needs—characters cross paths when they should and find the information they seek—creating a story much like the human bodies Marion painstakingly describes: beautiful, amazing, and a bit of a mess." New Yorker

Verissimo, Luis Fernando, 1936-

Borges and the eternal orangutans; translated from the Portuguese by Margaret Jull Costa. New Directions 2005 c2004 135p pa $13.95

ISBN 0-8112-1592-x   LC 2004-28203

Original Portuguese edition, 2000

"Vogelstein is a loner who has always lived among books. Suddenly, fate grabs hold if his insignificant life and carries him off to Buenos Aires, to a conference on Edgar Allan Poe, the inventor of the modern detective story. There Vogelstein meets his idol, Jorge Luis Borges, and for reasons that a mere passion for literature cannot explain, he finds himself at the center of a murder investigation that involves arcane demons, the mysteries of the Kabbala, the possible destruction of the world, and the Elizabethan magus John Dee's 'Eternal Orangutan,' which, given all the time in the world, would end up writing all the known books in the cosmos." Publisher's note

Verissimo, Luis Fernando, 1936——Continued

"Most writers feel passionate about Borges, but few would have the temerity to put the enigmatic sage into their fiction. That's because evoking Borges's presence would likely overwhelm any meager thoughts of their own. Yet Brazilian novelist Luis Fernando Verissimo has such temerity, as well as the talent to pull it off." Washington Post Book World

Verne, Jules, 1828-1905

Around the world in eighty days; translated with an introduction and notes by William Butcher. Oxford University Press 1999 xlv, 247p pa $9.95

ISBN 0-19-283778-8

Original French edition, 1873

"The hero, Phileas Fogg, undertakes his hasty world tour as the result of a bet made at his London club. He and his French valet Passepartout, meet with some fantastic adventures, but these are overcome by the loyal servant and the endlessy inventive Fogg. The feat they perform is incredible for its day; Fogg wins his bet, having circled the world in only eighty days." Reader's Ency. 4th edition

From the earth to the moon, and Round the moon; With pictures of the author and his environment and illus. of the setting of the book, together with an introd. by Arthur C. Clarke. Dodd, Mead 1962 308p il (Great illustrated classics) o.p.

LC 63-07412

The two books comprising this volume were first published 1865 and 1872 respectively

These titles provide a "striking example of early hard SF, detailing with great precision the preparations and scientific premises (still mostly correct, apart from the deadly effect of acceleration on the passengers) for a voyage to the moon." New Ency of Sci Fic

A journey to the centre of the earth; introduction by David Brin. Modern Library 2003 195p pa $8.95

ISBN 0-8129-7009-8

* LC 2003-59947

Original French edition, 1864. Variant title: A trip to the center of the earth

"More than half the book is given to the preliminaries before the actual descent begins, the first two chapters relying on a standard point of departure, the discovery of a manuscript giving the location of the caverns in Iceland. The narrative shows Verne's intense care in presenting the latest scientific thought of his age, while the sighting of the plesiosaurus and the giant humanoid shepherding mammoths indicates how well he incorporated lengthy imaginary episodes to flesh out the factual report." Anatomy of Wonder 4

The mysterious island; pictures by N. C. Wyeth. Scribner 1988 c1918 493p il $25.95

ISBN 0-684-18957-7

LC 88-3167

Sequel to Twenty thousand leagues under the sea

Original French edition, 1874; first United States edition published 1883 by J. W. Lovell; this is a reissue of the 1918 edition

A story of adventure in three parts: Dropped from the clouds; Abandoned; and The secret of the island

"Five men and a dog are carried out to sea in a balloon and drop from the clouds on the mysterious island. Their Crusoe-like resourcefulness and adventures are the theme of the book." Toronto Public Libr

Paris in the twentieth century; translated by Richard Howard; introduction by Eugen Weber. Random House 1996 222p il $21

ISBN 0-679-44434-3

LC 95-31750

Written in 1863; original French edition published 1994

Set in the 1960s, "the novel depicts Michel Dufrenoy as a poet and humanities scholar at sea in a crass commercial world that has strong overtones of Soviet realism. He befriends a young musician with whom he works; reconnects with his long-lost uncle, a literature professor; and even falls in love with the professor's granddaughter. But despite the kindnesses of his friends, Michel fails to succeed with the technological culture around him. Notable are the predictions about the subway, electric lights, and electronic music." Libr J

Round the moon

In Verne, J. From the earth to the moon, and Round the moon

Twenty thousand leagues under the sea; translated with an introduction and notes by William Butcher. Oxford University Press 1998 xlviii, 445p pa $10.95

ISBN 0-19-282839-8

* LC 97-29726

Original French edition, 1870

"The voyage of the Nautilus permitted Verne to describe the wonders of an undersea world almost totally unknown to the general public of the period. Indebted to literary tradition for his Atlantis, he made his major innovation in having the submarine completely powered by electricity, although the interest in electrical forces goes back to Poe and Shelley. So far as the enigmatic ending is concerned, his readers had to wait for the three-part The Mysterious Island (1874-1875) to learn that Nemo had been the Indian warrior-prince Dakkar, who had been involved in the Sepoy Mutiny of 1857." Anatomy of Wonder 4

Vernon, Olympia

Eden. Grove Press 2003 272p $23

ISBN 0-8021-1728-7

LC 2002-33863

"Fourteen-year-old Maddy Dangerfield is called upon to help her cancer-afflicted aunt Pip live out her last days. Maddy's mother, Faye, can't forgive her sister's betrayal of her with her own husband. Maddy is caught in the vortex of unresolved conflicts among the adults: a stoic, overworked mother who can't make peace with a dying sister; an alcoholic husband addicted to gambling; and a fiery aunt who has lived her life on her own terms. The small black community of Pyke County, Mississippi, is also saturated with unresolved conflicts, seething resentments, and violence. . . .Vernon's writing is lyrical and emotionally powerful." Booklist

A killing in this town. Grove Press 2006 246p $22

ISBN 0-8021-1813-5

LC 2005-52547

Vernon, Olympia—_Continued_

"Told as an allegory, this novel . . . presents a story of racism and hatred in a Mississippi town controlled by the Ku Klux Klan. In this town, a rite of passage for a 13-year-old boy involves summoning a black man from his house, tying him to a pulley, and dragging him behind a horse until dead." Libr J

"The novel shows the debilitating cancer of hatred and prejudice and the beauty of the effort to stop the violence. In language reminiscent of Toni Morrison and William Faulkner, Vernon weaves a powerful yet dreamlike story of our not-too-distant past." Booklist

The **vicious** circle; mystery and crime stories by members of the Algonquin Round Table; edited by Otto Penzler. Pegasus Books 2007 205p $25; pa $13.95

ISBN   978-1-933648-67-5;   1-933648-67-8; 978-1-605980-24-9 (pa); 1-605980-24-2 (pa)

Contents: Coroner's inquest, by M. Connelly; The mystery of the poisoned kipper, by R. Benchley; Farewell, my lovely appetizer, by S. J. Perelman; Haircut, by R. Lardner; Moonlight sonata, by A. Woollcott; The great Warburton mystery, by G. S. Kaufman and H. Dietz; Big blonde, by D. Parker; Up the close and down the stair, by S. J. Perelman; The man who came back, by E. Ferber; Rien ne va plus, by A. Woollcott; Four-and-twenty blackjacks, by S. J. Perelman; Stop me-if you've heard this one, by R. Lardner

"As mystery expert Penzler admits in his introduction, this volume contains 'little classic detection . . . and less nail-biting suspense' than the usual crime fiction anthology, but those curious about the legendary figures of the Algonquin Round Table—a group of New York City writers and critics from the 1920s, many affiliated with the New Yorker—will get at least a taste of the wit and sophistication for which they were known." Publ Wkly

Vida, Vendela

And now you can go; a novel. Knopf 2003 189p $19.95

ISBN 1-400-04027-2   LC 2002-35688

"An armed man waylays a twenty-one-year-old woman, Ellis, in Riverside Park, seeking a partner in suicide, but she survives. . . . Ellis alternately fends off and submits to the consolations of various men; thinks about the child an infertile couple conceived with her eggs; broods over her father's four-year disapearance and unexplained return; jets off to the Philippines on a volunteer mission; then, back in Manhattan, cuts her hair into a mullet. There's plenty of mordant humor along the way." New Yorker

Let the Northern Lights erase your name; a novel. Ecco 2007 226p $23.95

ISBN 978-0-06-082837-0; 0-06-082837-4
                                LC 2006-45030

In this novel, "a twenty-eight-year-old editor of film subtitles discovers on her father's death that he is not her biological parent: her mother, who abandoned her as a teenager, had been married to another man. Feeling betrayed by her fiancé, who has known about the deception for years, she abruptly leaves him to search for her real father in the northern reaches of Finland. Vida gives the icy landscape an eerie, forbidding beauty, and her writing

has moments of great emotional acuity. Her heroine is inexplicable and often unlikable, but Vida skillfully draws a parallel between her harsh and thoughtless behavior and that of her mother." New Yorker

Vidal, Gore, 1925-

1876; a novel. Modern Lib. 1998 524p $22.95

ISBN 0-679-60294-1   LC 98-21216

A volume in the author's American chronicle series

A reissue of the title first published 1976 by Random House

"As in 'Burr,' Charles Schuyler, hinted-at as the illegitimate son of Aaron Burr, again narrates. Now a respected and popular journalist-historian, Schuyler at 63 has returned, after years abroad, to the U.S. in the company of his widowed daughter, the Princess d'Agrigente, who is in need of a well-connected husband—thereby giving Vidal another occasion to crash society's party as he follows Schuyler on his journalistic assignments through New York, the city of Washington, later to Philadelphia for the Centennial, then Cincinnati for the Republican Convention." Publ Wkly

Burr. Modern Lib. 1998 697p $20

ISBN 0-679-60285-2   LC 97-39825

A volume in the author's American chronicle series

"_Burr_ is a novel in the form of a memoir told in part by Burr and in part by the young journalist Charles Schuyler, a fictional creation and Vidal's strongest character." Choice

The city and the pillar. Vintage 2003 207p pa $15

ISBN 1-4000-3037-4; 978-1-4000-3037-8

First published 1948 by Dutton

"Jim, a handsome, all-American athlete, has always been shy around girls. But when he and his best friend, Bob, partake in 'awful kid stuff,' the experience forms Jim's ideal of spiritual completion. Defying his parents' expectations, Jim strikes out on his own, hoping to find Bob and rekindle their amorous friendship. Along the way he struggles with what he feels is his unique bond with Bob and with his persistent attraction to other men." Publisher's note

Clouds and eclipses; the collected short stories. Carroll & Graf 2006 166p pa $13.95

ISBN 0-78671-810-2

Contents: Three stratagems; The robin; A moment of green laural; The Zenner Trophy; Erlinda and Mr. Coffin; Pages from an abandoned journal; The ladies in the library; Clouds and eclipses

"This volume collects the short fiction of Vidal . . ., including the recently rediscovered story from which the book takes its title. All eight pieces date to the author's early career and, with the exception of the title story, were previously published in 1956. Diverse, engaging, and full of surprising twists and turns, the stories take the general theme of homosexual encounter from various points of view. The writing is crisp; the images, crystal clear and often breathtaking." Libr J

Creation; a novel. Random House 1981 510p il o.p.   LC 79-5528

"The narrator, old and blind and finishing out his days as Persian ambassador to Pericles' Athens, is recounting his life's experiences, mostly as acquired in the service

Vidal, Gore, 1925-—*Continued*

of Darius the Great and his son Xerxes. . . . In particular, he describes his special missions to India, where, as well as meeting a variety of world princes, he converses with the Buddha, and to what is now China, where he becomes a friend and admirer of Confucius." Publ Wkly

Empire; a novel. Modern Lib. 1998 651p $23.95
ISBN 0-679-60293-3

* LC 98-21224

A volume in the author's American chronicle series

A reissue of the title first published 1987 by Random House

"The core of Vidal's story is the inexorable march of one Caroline Sanford, newspaper owner, into the inner circle of the Washington, D.C., power elite." Booklist

"Interesting and well-developed real-life characters abound, including, most memorably, Secretary of State and Lincoln's old friend John Hay. Intermixed with the well-researched backdrop of historical characters and events is Caroline's personal story." Libr J

The golden age; a novel. Doubleday 2000 467p $27.50
ISBN 0-385-50075-0   LC 00-43071

Seventh and final volume in the author's American chronicle series. Set chronologically after Washington, D.C.

"The primary figure around which Vidal spins his . . . story is Caroline Sanford, an actress turned Washington newspaper publisher who is also a friend of Franklin Delano Roosevelt. As Vidal's tale opens, we see political Washington divided over the issue of whether to aid the Allies in their fight against German aggression. His large cast of characters includes both real and fictional politicians, moviemakers, and writers." Booklist

"Vidal is best on the surface. His account of the 1940 conventions is a real romp. He depicts F.D.R. with irreverent skill. . . . It's good to know how badly Wendell Willkie could give a public speech; and there are some wonderful scenes in which Eleanor Roosevelt skillfully manipulates her husband and the bosses of the old Democratic Party." N Y Times Book Rev

Hollywood; a novel of America in the 1920s. Modern Lib. 1999 558p $24.95
ISBN 0-679-60292-5   LC 98-46174

A volume in the author's American chronicle series

A reissue of the title first published 1990 by Random House

The main characters, newspaper publishers Blaise and Caroline Stanford, first appeared in Washington, D.C. "Assigned to travel to Hollywood [in 1917] to help pull the infant 'photo play' industry behind the war effort, Caroline discovers that, at the age of 40, she has the looks and potential to become a film star. Sold to a world-wide audience as 'Emma Traxler', she begins to understand that cinema has the power to re-shape the world. . . . [Meanwhile], President Wilson is struggling to win support for his vision of a League of Nations. When he fails, the way is open for the Republican Warren Harding to assume power. The ensuing corruption scandals culminate in the Tea Pot Dome affair." New Statesman Soc

Vidal's "highly polished prose style, in part the fruit of his classical training, is a constant delight." N Y Times Book Rev

Lincoln. Modern Lib. 1993 712p o.p.
* LC 92-27273

A reissue of the title first published 1984 by Random House

"In the atmosphere of intrigue that permanently settled over Washington City during the Civil War, the initially unpromising Lincoln, an unlikely hero, rises to greatness; despite almost insurmountable troubles that deteriorate his physical and mental well-being, Lincoln shows his true mastery of crisis leadership, necessary not only to save the Union but to refashion it." Booklist

This novel "is not so much an imaginative reconstruction of an era as an intelligent, lucid and highly informative transcript of it, never less than workmanlike in its blocking out of scenes and often extremely compelling." N Y Times Book Rev

Myra Breckinridge

In Vidal, G. Myra Breckinridge [and] Myron p1-213

Myra Breckinridge [and] Myron. Random House 1986 417p $19.95
ISBN 0-394-55376-4

* LC 86-11423

Combined edition of two titles first published 1968 and 1974 respectively

In the first novel, Myra who was once Myron seduces both Rusty Godowsky and his girlfriend Mary-Ann Pringle. The sequel is set in 1973. Myron Breckinridge, the alter ego of the transsexual heroine, is pushed through his television screen and onto the set of a 1948 film "Siren of Babylon" starring Maria Montez. He has difficulty in getting out. Myra periodically takes command of Myron's body. She attempts to save the world from overpopulation by altering the male sex

Myron

In Vidal, G. Myra Breckinridge [and] Myron p217-417

The Smithsonian Institution; a novel. Random House 1998 260p $23
ISBN 0-375-50121-5   LC 97-38615

"On Good Friday, 1939, 13-year-old T. is summoned from his D.C. boarding school to the Mall for a mysterious meeting. It seems the outwardly average (if unusually attractive) young man has scribbled, in the margins of a math test, an equation that may be essential to the upcoming war effort. Cloistered with Oppenheimer, Einstein, Charles Lindbergh, the Founding Fathers and other historical personages who have been kept alive in the Smithsonian's magical exhibits, T. struggles to solve the mysteries of space-time, prevent the coming war (in which he is doomed to die) and hold on to cradle-robbing Frankie Cleveland, the immortal 22-year-old version of Grover's First Lady." Publ Wkly

"Fans of Vidal's comic novels can expect the usual mixture of earthiness and erudition, though on a more restrained level; the novel provides the author with the chance to put words in the mouths of a dozen presidents, noted scientists, and pop culture heroes." Libr J

Washington, D.C.; a novel. Modern Lib. 1999 422p $24.95
ISBN 0-679-60291-7   LC 98-46173

Vidal, Gore, 1925-—*Continued*

A volume in the author's American chronicle series

Set from the New Deal to the McCarthy years this "political novel features the ambitions of both a senator and his young secretary for the Presidency. The senator loses his chance for the Democratic nomination when Roosevelt decides to run for a third term. The secretary, mapping his course to the top, with the help of a journalist invents a non-happening which makes him a national hero. He then blackmails the senator into withdrawing from the race and wins the senatorial seat for himself." Booklist

Vila-Matas, Enrique, 1948-

Montano's malady; translated from the Spanish by Jonathan Dunne. New Directions 2007 $14.95p pa $14.95

ISBN 978-0-8112-1628-9; 0-8112-1628-4
                          * LC 2006-102330

Original Spanish edition, 2002

"Written in the form of a journal, which becomes a novel, then a dictionary of writers' journals, then a lecture on the writing of such journals, Montano tells of its narrator's obsession with literature. Middle-aged and married to Rosa, he has become 'a walking dictionary of quotations', unable to do anything without it triggering a memory of something he's read or, worse, something remembered by a writer that he's read, which in turn recalls a thought from the head of yet another writer. Following him and his overactive brain from his native Barcelona to Nantes, Chile, the Azores, Lisbon and Budapest — via Walter Benjamin, Kafka, W. G. Sebald, Pessoa and Robert Walser among others — is like playing a mental version of Twister. . . . Shunning narrative, the book continues to seduce with writerly observations — both the narrator's, and quotations from other writers." Telegraph (London)

Villars, Elizabeth, 1941-

The Normandie affair. Doubleday 1982 319p o.p.
                          LC 81-43727

This novel is "set aboard an opulent cruise liner, the 'Normandie,' in the days when luxury and sumptuousness were taken for granted. Villars' story covers six days of irrevocable change in the lives of several passengers crossing from New York to France in 1936. At the center of this drama is mysterious Anson Sherwood, a wealthy Bostonian with a passion for and inordinate knowledge of the 'Normandie.' Sherwood turns out to be a dedicated meddler who interferes in the lives of his fellow passengers, involving himself in both romantic entanglements and political intrigues, usually with fortuitous results. Neatly bundling drama and romance, Villars has captured the dichotomous nature of shipboard life." Booklist

Vine, Barbara, 1930-

See also Rendell, Ruth, 1930-

Anna's book; [by] Ruth Rendell writing as Barbara Vine. Harmony Bks. 1993 394p o.p.
                          LC 92-34309

This "tale of psychological suspense revolves around a woman's discovery that the published memoirs of her deceased grandmother hid evidence of an elderly woman's murder and the disappearance of a little girl." Libr J

"Vine's story is utterly riveting, rich and multifaceted in its complexity. Her characters are wonderfully real and fascinatingly unconventional." Booklist

The blood doctor; a novel. Crown 2002 369p il $25

ISBN 1-400-04504-5   LC 2002-18491

"Martin Nanther—biographer and member of the House of Lords—discovers some blighted roots on his family tree while researching the life of his great-great-grandfather, Henry, an expert on hemophilia and physician to Queen Victoria. Martin contacts long-lost relatives who help him uncover some puzzling events in Henry's life." Publ Wkly

"The story lacks the usual page-turner suspense of the Rendell/Vine novels but makes up for that with unusually detailed glimpses into Victorian life and the inner workings of the House of Parliament, which American readers will find particularly intriguing." Libr J

The brimstone wedding. Harmony Bks. 1996 330p $24

ISBN 0-517-70339-4   LC 95-30280

In this novel, "two women, divided by age and class, share their deepest secrets in an English nursing home in which one cares for the other. There is a sense of secrecy from the start, as Jenny Warner tells dying Stella Newland about her love affair and Stella shares with Jenny the location of her secret house." Libr J

"Both Jenny and Stella embrace their pain with the sense of fatalism that has always been Ms. Vine's literary hallmark. The wonder is that they can speak their hearts in such clear and distinctive voices and yet retain their interior mystery." N Y Times Book Rev

The chimney sweeper's boy; a novel. Harmony Bks. 1998 344p $24

ISBN 0-609-60287-X
                          * LC 98-10567

This novel revolves around the "sudden death of Gerald Candless, a celebrated English novelist who lived on the Devon coast with his wife, Ursula, and two daughters to whom he was conspicuously devoted. When one daughter, Sarah, starts researching her father's early history for the biography she has been asked to write, she discovers that he was living under a false identity for most of his life. As more facts emerge from Sarah's research, they both illuminate and contradict the dark views of Gerald's personality supplied by his bitter wife and the deep, if ambiguous, insights contained in his own novels." N Y Times Book Rev

Gallowglass. Harmony Bks. 1990 272p $19.95

ISBN 0-517-57744-5
                          * LC 89-29026

In this novel the "reader comes to know the perversities of lamebrain Joe and his malicious friend, Sandor, who concoct—Sandor actually drawing up the plans, Joe just following along out of dumb adoration—a scheme to kidnap a wealthy woman. Events transpiring in the woman's household—particularly, her relations with and the backgrounds of the people in her domestic employ—add double and triple layers to the conflict." Booklist

"Miss Vine's most penetrating foray yet into the dark mysteries of the heart's obsessions, this haunting novel examines love in many guises—romantic, parental, idola-

Vine, Barbara, 1930-—*Continued*

trous, possessive, selfless, erotic, platonic and sick. The scope of observation is dazzling; the tone, remarkably nonjudgmental." N Y Times Book Rev

Grasshopper; a novel. Harmony Bks. 2000 392p $25

ISBN 0-609-60789-8   LC 00-38281

This novel focuses on "the lonely life of 19-year-old Clodagh Brown in Maida Vale, a fictional north London suburb. Haunted by tragedy in her young life, she befriends a group of equally damaged and alienated youths. Their nocturnal habit is to climb onto the roof and roam on the tops of buildings, from one to another. It is all a daring adventure, until the motives of the various characters collide." Libr J

"Only a handful of writers, in any genre, can match Barbara Vine for imaginative originality and ingenuity. . . . Grasshopper is about good intentions gone wrong, violence, innocence and an encounter with true evil. . . . To say that a book can open your eyes to a different world is a cliché, but rarely has it been more apt than in describing this novel." New Statesman (Engl)

The house of stairs; [by] Ruth Rendell writing as Barbara Vine. Harmony Bks. 1989 c1988 277p o.p.   LC 88-38303

First published 1988 in the United Kingdom

"Elizabeth Vetch, a writer, recalls her adolescence and young womanhood living with her cousin Cosette in a big, eccentric house in the Notting Hill section of London. Lots of people besides Elizabeth and Cosette lived in the House of Stairs, though; it was nest to many of their friends as well. Cosette is intent on recovering her lost youth, and because of her vulnerability in that direction, two residents conspire against her to gain her money. The consequence is violent death, with Elizabeth losing the one person she truly loved. A complex, eloquent novel—sure to retain Vine's large readership and undoubtedly gain her even more followers." Booklist

King Solomon's carpet. Harmony Bks. 1992 c1991 355p o.p.   LC 91-43668

First published 1991 in the United Kingdom

"Tom, a brain-damaged flutist who plays aviary music in the London Underground, is obsessed with Alice, a violinist obsessed with Axel, whose own obsession is with bombs and death. Along with Jed, who loves no one but his pet hawk, and Jasper, a 9-year-old boy who rides the tops of subway cars and loves the danger, they all live in a rotting old Victorian mansion owned by Jarvis Stringer, who has the most interesting obsession of all: the master study he is compiling on the world's subway systems." N Y Times Book Rev

The author "displays her remarkable ability to spot and dissect the terrifying beneath the ordinary, to imbue a setting with its own, almost palpable terror, and to construct in the process a narrative maze filled with constant, fearful surprise." Booklist

The minotaur; a novel. Shaye Areheart Books 2005 341p $25

ISBN 0-307-23760-5   LC 2005-10837

"In this novel, set in the late 1960s, an autistic man, a dysfunctional family, and an innocent young woman become entangled in a web of deceit. Swedish nursing student Kerstin Kvist comes to Essex, England, to care

for 39-year-old John Cosway, who is being heavily sedated for a mental illness he doesn't actually have. John's mother and sisters live with him on a drafty estate at the mercy of a trust. Naturally inquisitive, Kerstin wants to explore the bizarre, labyrinthine library built on the estate but ends up coming across secrets best left hidden." Libr J

"This is very satisfying reading, a sort of blend of Edgar Allan Poe and Anthony Trollope." Booklist

No night is too long. Harmony Bks. 1995 c1994 315p $23

ISBN 0-517-79964-2

                                        * LC 94-13064

First published 1994 in the United Kingdom

The narrator of this novel, Tim Cornish, a student of creative writing at an English university, is "filled with remorse. . . . Friendless, indifferent to his future, he lives alone in the rotting old house where he grew up, conjuring up the ghost of [Dr Ivo Steadman], the lover he knocked unconscious and left for dead on a desert island. His only correspondent is a mysterious letter writer who taunts him with true stories of castaways who survived." New Statesman Soc

"This is a novel about the effects of passion in which the mood is as bleak as the cold North Sea; a murder mystery in which the crucial killing is imaginary, and the actual killing arbitrary. . . . Nevertheless—the novel does grip and its scheme is impressive; it is hard to withhold applause from an author so lavishly endowed with the capacity to invent interlocking segments of plot." Times Lit Suppl

Vinge, Joan D., 1948-

The Snow Queen. Dial Press (NY) 1980 536p o.p.

                                        * LC 79-20555

"A Quantum novel"

"An amalgam of SF and heroic fantasy borrowing the structure of Hans Christian Andersen's famous story, set on a barbarian world exploited by technologically superior outworlders, against the background of a fallen galactic empire." Anatomy of Wonder 4

Followed by World's end

The Summer Queen. Warner Bks. 1991 670p o.p.   LC 90-50521

Sequel to World's end

"As the Summer Star ascends in the skies above the planet Tiamat, marking the end of more than a century of exploitation by the technologically advanced Hegemony, Moon Dawntreader—the Summer Queen appointed to lead her people back to their traditional ways—breaks with ancient custom, choosing instead to prepare to meet the Hegemony's inevitable return on equal terms." Libr J

"Plots and subplots proliferate, and although the prose is sometimes florid and the romance and sex scenes overly sentimental, the book is so full of drama, conflict and tragedy that it justifies its length." Publ Wkly

World's end. Bluejay Bks. 1984 230p o.p.   LC 83-21374

In this novel "BZ Gundhalinu, a police inspector who played a minor role in . . . [The Snow Queen] is the central character. Having left Carbuncle at the time of

Vinge, Joan D., 1948-—_Continued_

the Change he has traveled to World's End in search of his two irresponsible older brothers. World's End, a barely habitable frontier planet, is center of a 'Company' mining operation but also contains Fire Lake, an unexplained anomaly that appears to drive those who approach it insane." Voice Youth Advocates

Followed by: The Summer Queen

Vinge, Vernor

A deepness in the sky. TOR Bks. 1999 606p

ISBN 0-312-85683-0   LC 98-43457

"A Tom Doherty Associates book"

Prequel to A fire upon the deep

"Representatives of the Qeng Ho, a galactic trading consortium, and the Emergents, a group of long-isolated humans with strange powers, vie for control of one another and for the opportunity to exploit a planet of intelligent nonhumans, called Spiders, who are just reaching their technological maturity." N Y Times Book Rev

Vinge "is among the very best of the current crop of hard SF writers, producing work that is not only fast-paced and intellectually challenging, but also stylishly written and centered on carefully drawn characters." Publ Wkly

A fire upon the deep. TOR Bks. 1992 391p o.p.

* LC 91-39020

"A Tom Doherty Associates book"

"Fleeing a menace of galactic proportions, a spaceship crashes on an unfamiliar world, leaving the survivors—a pair of children—to the not-so-tender mercies of a medieval, lupine race. Responding to the crippled ship's distress signal, a rescue mission races against time to retrieve the children and recover the weapon they need to prevent the universe from being forever changed." Libr J

"Thoughtful space opera at its best, this book delivers everything it promises in terms of galactic scope, audacious concepts and believable characters both human and nonhuman." N Y Times Book Rev

Rainbows end. Tor 2006 364p $25.95

ISBN 0-312-85684-9   LC 2006-278136

"A Tom Doherty Associates book"

This hard SF novel is set in San Diego, California. "Circa 2025, people use high-tech contact lenses to interface with computers in their clothes. 'Silent messaging' is so automatic that it feels like telepathy. Robert Gu, a talented Chinese-American poet, has missed much of this revolution due to Alzheimer's, but now the wonders of modern medicine have rehabilitated his mind. Installed in remedial classes at the local high school, he tries to adjust to this brave new world, but soon finds himself enmeshed in a somewhat quixotic plot by elderly former University of California-San Diego faculty members to protest the destruction of the university library, now rendered superfluous by the ubiquitous online databanks. Unbeknownst to Robert, he's also a pawn in a dark international conspiracy to perfect a deadly biological weapon." Publ Wkly

"Vinge's world is saturated with the logical extensions of current R&D. He has thought long and hard about how pervasive and ubiquitous information technology will transform our lives." Sci Fic Wkly

Viswanathan, Padma, 1968-

The toss of a lemon. Harcourt 2008 619p il $26

ISBN 978-0-15-101533-7; 0-15-101533-3

LC 2008-13369

This "novel spans 66 years-from 1896 to 1962—in the life of one Tamil family. The matriarch of the clan, Sivakami, a Brahmin, was married at ten and widowed at 18. Already a mother of two, Sivakami was determined to set a pious example. This meant that she shaved her head, wore only white, and touched no one, not even her children or grandchildren, between dusk and dawn. What's more, she obeyed the custom of staying inside her home, venturing outdoors only three times in the many decades before her death. Sivakami's proscribed world is portrayed in amazing detail, and the life of the Brahmin elite is vividly captured. . . . Gender rules, class relations, and the political castes of late 19th- and early to mid-20th-century India are well presented, making this an important work of historical fiction." Libr J

Vlautin, Willy

Northline; a novel. Harper Perennial 2008 192, 18p pa $14.95

ISBN 978-0-06-145652-7; 0-06-145652-7

LC 2008-297989

Allison Johnson, the protagonist of this novel, is a "hard luck gal who leaves Las Vegas and runs north to Reno to break free of her abusive skinhead boyfriend. Allison hates herself. She drinks until she passes out and suffers from panic attacks so severe that the only way to calm her nerves is by slicing her body, biting her cheek, or putting cigarettes out on her arm. It would have been easier to give up, but she doesn't and that's what this book is really about. Instead of letting the darkness swallow her whole, Allison gets out of bed every day and throws herself into the world, and eventually she meets another crippled soul named Dan Mahony. Together they pull each other up. They learn to trust and eventually allow a sliver of hope to release them of their pasts." Blurt

"Vlautin's writing style is perfectly suited to his material: Things happen the way they happen, slowly but inexorably, with the significance of any moment rarely evident until after the fact, or maybe never evident at all. There are no epiphanies here; new lives are built one unassuming sentence at a time." Portland Mercury

Voelker, John Donaldson _See_ Traver, Robert, 1903-1991

Voïnovich, Vladimir, 1932-

Monumental propaganda; translated by Andrew Bromfield. Knopf 2004 365p $25

ISBN 0-375-41235-2   LC 2003-60476

Original Russian edition, 2000

This novel "centers on Aglaya Stepanovna Revkina, a true believer in Stalin, who finds herself bewildered and beleaguered in the relative openness of the Khrushchev era. She believes her greatest achievement was to have browbeaten her community into building an iron statue of the supreme leader, which she moves into her apartment after his death. And despite the ebb and flow of political ideology in her provincial town, she stubbornly,

Voĭnovich, Vladimir, 1932-—*Continued*
and at all costs, centers her life on her private icon."
Publisher's note

"If Frank Capra had been an acerbic Russian novelist
and not a sunny American filmmaker, he might have
written novels like Vladimir Voinovich's: funny, antic
works that pit the little man against the system, ordinary
folks against bureaucratic institutions and corrupt authorities." N Y Times (Late N Y Ed)

Vollmann, William T.

Argall. Viking 2001 746p il $40
ISBN 0-670-91030-9   LC 2001-17744
"A novel about the founding of the Virginia colony,
this is the third volume in Vollmann's . . . historical
'Seven Dreams' series. . . . The book is divided into
two sections, the first focusing mainly on John Smith,
the second on Pocahontas. Both parts are told in the
voice of the dreamer William the Blind, who for this occasion adopts his own weird version of Elizabethan English." Libr J

"The eponymous Captain Argall edges into the foreground in the second part, succeeding Smith as James-
town's leading spirit; he has the sinister bearing of some
Jacobean theater devil—like Iago, there's menace in his
meanings. He kidnaps Pokahuntas and manipulates her
assimilation into settler culture. Vollman's ability to
write in Smith's English and endow it with a contemporary snap is an extraordinary feat." Publ Wkly

Butterfly stories; a novel. Grove Press 1993
279p il
ISBN 0-8021-1502-0
                                           * LC 93-2489
The protagonist of this novel, "known as 'the butterfly
boy' in grade school but now simply called 'the journalist,' travels to Southeast Asia to investigate the prostitution problem, accompanied by a photographer. The latter
proves to be an impeccable sex tourist, but the journalist
is inept. He forgets to use a condom the very first night
and suffers from an ever-worsening barrage of fevers and
infections thereafter. Then he falls in love with one of
the prostitutes and decides to marry." Libr J

There is "great tenderness in Vollman, and wit, and he
seems to know his settings intimately; in Butterfly Stories, one enters a vast, introverted, nearly psychotic
mind, and the effect is hypnotic." Booklist

Europe central. Viking 2005 832p il $39.95
ISBN 0-670-03392-8
                                           * LC 2004-61170
A novel about the "warring authoritarian cultures of
Germany and the USSR in the twentieth century. . . .
Vollmann compares and contrasts the moral decisions
made by various figures from this period some famous,
some infamous, some unknown. Also explored in this
book are the fates of artists and poets ranging from
Kathe Kollwitz and Anna Akhmatova to Marina
Tsvetaeva and Van Cliburn. A series of stories examine
the complex and elusive Soviet composer Dmitri Shosta-
kovich and the constant Stalinist assaults upon his work
and life." Publisher's note

"What sets 'Europe Central' apart from Vollmann's
other large-scale historical productions is its strong narrative lines. The pieces are dated and arranged
chronologically to give the book a plot that arcs from

prewar political machinations to Germany's surge east to
Russia's counteroffensive, and that ends with cold war
politics in divided Berlin." N Y Times Book Rev

Fathers and crows. Viking 1992 990p
ISBN 0-670-84333-4
                                           * LC 92-18315
This second title in the author's Seven dreams series
"is set in the 17th century as Jesuit priests begin their
work of converting the Indians to Christianity. . . . The
narrator, William the Blind, urges us to approach his narrative by immersing ourselves in the Stream of Time,
which will carry us back to the moment when the French
first landed on Canadian soil." N Y Times Book Rev

The language "moves interestingly between contemporary colloquial, Hollywood historical, Middle High
Tolkientalk, and a quirky and enjoyable poetry: never
less than vigorous and inventive. . . . Despite nudges,
the narrative grips." Times Lit Suppl

The ice-shirt. Viking 1990 415p il maps
ISBN 0-670-83239-1   LC 90-50051
This is "the first of seven planned novels in William
T. Vollmann's 'symbolic history' of North America, a
. . . fusion of Norse myth and legend dealing with the
arrival of the first colonists and their encounters with the
native Indian and Inuit peoples. Occasionally interrupted
by his own travel observations of Greenland, Iceland and
the Canadian subarctic—the book is illustrated by sketches and maps the author made during his researches
there–his sources are the Greenlandic and Icelandic sagas, the chronicles of travellers, but also Butler's
Erewhon, tourism brochures and conversations." New
Statesman Soc

"Without apparent strain, the story interweaves numerous characters, sea voyages, murders and supernatural
horrors, digressing with relish. . . . 'The Ice-Shirt' impresses mightily in its scope, its scene-painting and its
enciphered social messages." N Y Times Book Rev

The rifles. Viking 1994 411p il maps
ISBN 0-670-84856-5   LC 93-31577
This is the third installment in the author's Seven
Dreams series of novels, a symbolic history of North
America. This novel, to be volume six in the completed
series, "revolves around the fourth Arctic expedition of
British explorer Sir John Franklin. This doomed voyage
to find the Northwest Passage took place between 1845
and 1848 and resulted in death from starvation or exposure for each of the more than a hundred men involved.
Equally important . . . are the adventures of one Captain
Subzero, . . . who in the late 1980s travels to the Canadian Arctic towns of Resolute Bay and Pond Inlet, where
he falls in love with an Inuit woman named Reepah and
discovers that, although more than 140 years separate
them, he and John Franklin are one and the same." Nation

"What The Rifles demonstrates, and what magnetizes
the narrative's scattered contexts is the real and binding
continuity between nineteenth and twentieth-century patterns of mind-above all, this terrible insistence on our
will to power over the world." Yale Rev

The royal family. Viking 2000 780p $40
ISBN 0-670-89167-3   LC 99-56587
This novel is "the story of Henry Tyler, a private detective nursing a penchant for the seedy side of life and
an unrequited infatuation with the wife of his brother,

Vollmann, William T.—_Continued_

John, a . . . contract attorney. Henry is hired by a crude tycoon named Brady to search the Tenderloin, San Francisco's skid row, for an underworld character called the Queen of the Whores." N Y Times Book Rev

"Vollmann is after large-scale social chronicle; he includes characters from nearly every walk of life, and trains his attentions on processes not often seen by the faint of heart. . . . But this hypperrealistic novelist also aims to present a metaphysics: the two brothers stand for two kinds of human being, the chosen and the outcast. As in all Vollmann's novels, the author's encyclopedic ambition sometimes overwhelms the human scale; some supporting characters, though, do stay vivid. Vollmann avoids simply glamorizing the outcasts but remains, deep down, a Blakean romantic: prostitution is for him not only the universal indictment of the human race but also, paradoxically, the only paradise we can actually visit." Publ Wkly

Volokhonsky, Larissa

(tr) Chekhov, A. P. Complete short novels

(tr) Tolstoy, L., graf. War and peace

Volpi, Jorge

In search of Klingsor; translated by Kristina Cordero. Scribner 2002 414p $26

ISBN 0-7432-0118-3   LC 2002-17582

Original Spanish edition published 1999 in Mexico

This novel operates "at several levels—as a thriller about a U.S. military officer seeking to ferret out the identity of the scientist who directed Nazi research during WWII, as a scientific search for truth by a physicist who encounters Einstein, Von Neumann, Schrödinger, Neils Bohr and other great minds of the 20th century and as a literary novel about a moral quest to destroy an evil that dates back to ancient German folklore." Publ Wkly

The author "delivers a novel that manages to function as a crackling spy thriller while delivering a thoughtful treatist on the nature of love and deception." Booklist

Voltaire, 1694-1778

Candide; translated by Peter Constantine. Modern Library 2005 119p hardcover o.p. pa $8.95

ISBN 0-679-64313-3; 0-812-97201-5 (pa)
                                   * LC 2004-55244

Original French edition, 1759

"In this philosophical fantasy, naive Candide sees and suffers such misfortune that he ultimately rejects the philosophy of his tutor Doctor Pangloss, who claims that 'all is for the best in this best of all possible worlds.' Candide and his companions—Pangloss, his beloved Cunegonde, and his servant Cacambo—display an instinct for survival that provides them hope in an otherwise somber setting. When they all retire together to a simple life on a small farm, they discover that the secret of happiness is 'to cultivate one's garden,' a practical philosophy that excludes excessive idealism and nebulous metaphysics." Merriam-Webster's Ency of Lit

also in Voltaire. Candide and other stories
also in Voltaire. Voltaire's Candide, Zadig, and selected stories p3-101

Candide and other stories; translated from the French, with an introduction and notes, by Roger Pearson. Knopf 1992 307p $17

ISBN 0-679-41746-X
"Everyman's library"
Contents: Candide; Micromegas; Zadig; The ingenu; The white bull

Voltaire's Candide, Zadig, and selected stories; translated with an introduction by Donald M. Frame. Candide illustrations by Paul Klee. Indiana Univ. Press 1961 351p il o.p.

Contains 14 satiric tales in addition to Candide (1759) and Zadig (1748)

Contents: Candide; Zadig; Micromegas; The world as it is; Memnon; Bababec and the fakirs; History of Scarmentado's travels; Plato's dream; Account of the sickness, confession, death, and apparition of the Jesuit Berthier; Story of a good Brahman; Jeannot and Colin; An Indian adventure; Ingenuous; The one-eyed porter; Memory's adventure; Court Chesterfield's ears and Chaplain Goudman

Zadig
_In_ Voltaire. Candide and other stories
_In_ Voltaire. Voltaire's Candide, Zadig, and selected stories p102-72

Von Goethe, Johann Wolfgang _See_ Goethe, Johann Wolfgang von, 1749-1832

Vonnegut, Kurt, 1922-2007

Armageddon in retrospect; and other new and unpublished writings on war and peace; [illustrations by the author; introduction by Mark Vonnegut] G. P. Putnam's Sons 2008 232p il $24.95

ISBN 978-0-399-15508-6; 0-399-15508-2

Of the 13 pieces included in this volume, 10 are short stories: Great day; Guns before butter; Happy birthday, 1951; Brighten up; The unicorn trap; Unknown soldier; Spoils; Just you and me, Sammy; Commandant's desk; Armageddon in retrospect

"Only a few of the . . . stories rely on the twists of reality and narrative present in Vonnegut's novels; the majority are carried by the characters' struggle with the absurdities of war and peace. Vonnegut's World War II experience as a prisoner of war in Dresden haunts the work, with multiple stories featuring American POWs in Germany. . . . Readers of Vonnegut's books won't find any surprises here, but because he is at his sardonic best when working in short form, they won't be let down by his humor and poignancy, either." Libr J

Bagombo snuff box: uncollected short fiction. Putnam 1999 295p hardcover o.p. pa $13.95

ISBN 0-399-14505-2; 0-425-17446-8 (pa)
                                   LC 99-13665

Contents: Thanasphere; Mnemonics; Any reasonable offer; The package; The no-talent kid; Poor little rich town; Souvenir; The cruise of The Jolly Roger; Custom-made bride; Ambitious sophomore; Bagombo snuff box; The powder-blue dragon; A present for Big Saint Nick; Unpaid consultant; Der Arme Dolmetscher; The boy who hated girls; This son of mine; A night for love; Find me

Vonnegut, Kurt, 1922-2007—*Continued*
a dream; Runaways; 2BRO2B; Lovers Anonymous; Hal Irwin's magic lamp

"The 23 stories in this collection were published in magazines . . . during the Fifties and are collected here for the first time. The topics covered include space travel ('Thanasphere'), which describes the first manned orbit of Earth; finding the American dream ('The package'), about a new home full of the latest accessories; and an attempt to impress an old girlfriend (the title story). . . . Although many of the stories are topically dated, the ironic insights and illumination of character are timeless, and no one does it better than Vonnegut." Libr J

Breakfast of champions; or, Goodbye blue Monday!; by Kurt Vonnegut, Jr; with drawings by the author. Delacorte Press 1973 295p il o.p.
*

"In this novel Pontiac dealer Dwayne Hoover, science fiction writer Kilgore Trout, artist Rabo Karabekian and others play out a drama that runs the gamut from race tensions and sexual fantasies to pollution, the power 'bad chemicals' can exert over a human being, the sheer insanity of trying to prove you are a human being when you suspect you are just another machine in a machine-mad world." Publ Wkly

"In this novel Vonnegut is . . . clearing his head by throwing out acquired ideas, and also liberating some of the characters from his previous books. . . . This explosive meditation ranks with Vonnegut's best." N Y Times Book Rev

Cat's cradle; by Kurt Vonnegut, Jr. Holt, Rinehart & Winston 1963 233p o.p.
*

"In this mordant satire on religion, research, government, and human nature, a free-lance writer becomes the catalyst in a chain of events that unearths the secret of ice-nine. This is an element potentially more lethal than that produced by nuclear fission. The search leads to a mythical island, San Lorenzo, where the writer also discovers the leader of a new religion, Bokonon." Shapiro. Fic for Youth. 3d edition

Deadeye Dick. Delacorte Press/Seymour Lawrence 1982 240p
ISBN 0-440-01780-7   LC 82-13024
"In Midland City, Ohio, the [Waltz] family is isolated and scorned by the community for patriarch Otto's ersatz career as an artist and his strident support for Nazi policies. Their wealth and what's left of their social position is decimated when younger son Rudy (Deadeye Dick) accidently shoots a pregnant woman. Father pleads guilty to the crime, Rudy becomes a night-shift pharmacist, author of the prize-winning but unsuccessful play 'Katmandu' and cook and maid for his useless mother. Brother Felix becomes the president of NBC, and mother dies of radiation emitted from the fireplace of their 'shitbox' home. The entire populace is eventually exterminated . . . by the inadvertent dropping of a neutron bomb." SLJ

Galápagos; a novel. Delacorte Press/Seymour Lawrence 1985 295p o.p.
* LC 85-4581
"A group of tourists on a cruise survive the end of the world, settling on a small Galapagos Island and beginning a new evolutionary sequence. The ghostly narrator looks back on things from a perspective one million years later." Anatomy of Wonder 4

God bless you, Mr. Rosewater; or, Pearls before swine; by Kurt Vonnegut, Jr. Holt, Rinehart & Winston 1965 217p o.p.
"With a satirist's eye for the meanness of man, especially his greed, Vonnegut tells the story of Eliot Rosewater, president of the Rosewater Foundation, who uses his position to help all petitioners. Discovering a plot to remove him from authority Rosewater gives all his money to over 50 children he is falsely accused of fathering." Booklist

Hocus pocus. Putnam 1990 302p o.p.
LC 90-34535
This novel is set in an America of the future. The story is told by Eugene Debs Hartke, a West Point graduate and Vietnam veteran, as he awaits trial for complicity in a mass escape from a black prison where he has been teaching inmates to read. It is 2001: "most of the United States has been sold to foreigners, and what is left is broken down and depleted. Black markets, race war, martial law, tuberculosis and AIDS are all somewhere between endemic and epidemic." N Y Times Book Rev

"Vonnegut remains an effectual stylist, combining deadpan irony and *faux naiveté*. As usual, his central narrative winds through a mosaic of aphorisms, verbal tics, digressions, homilies, obscure facts. . . . This compendium of devices and concerns may have hardened into a formula, but it has not yet ceased to be a diverting one." Times Lit Suppl

Jailbird; a novel; by Kurt Vonnegut, Jr. Delacorte Press/Seymour Lawrence 1979 246p
ISBN 0-440-05449-4   LC 79-12881
This novel "opens with Walter F. Starbuck, a 64-year-old victim of Watergate, about to be released from a Georgia prison for white-collar workers. Bereft of fortune and family (his wife is dead, his son is ungrateful) Starbuck retreats to the past via flashbacks of World War II, old love affairs, and past occupations. Eventually he regains respectability in the ubiquitous RAMJAC Corporation . . . which owns 19% of America and continues to swallow every major enterprise in its path." Libr J

Player piano; by Kurt Vonnegut, Jr. Scribner 1952 295p o.p.
*

"Paul Proteus, engineer, leads revolt against machine-computer conformist civilization, only to find that when it succeeds, people wish for the machines again. In order or in chaos, mob psychology is stupid. Modern civilization has hate-love affinity for machines. Incisive satire; a classic modern dystopia." Anatomy of Wonder. 3d edition

The sirens of Titan; by Kurt Vonnegut, Jr. Houghton Mifflin 1961 c1959 319p o.p.
*

First published 1959 in paperback by Dell
This novel "attacks the concept of causality and the confusion of luck with God's will [and] reveals human

Vonnegut, Kurt, 1922-2007—*Continued*
history as a trivial incident manipulated by the alien
Tralfamadorians to further an equally trivial scheme."
New Ency of Sci Fic

Slapstick; or, Lonesome no more! a novel.
Delacorte Press/Seymour Lawrence 1976 243p o.p.

In this satirical fantasy, President of the United States
Dr. Wilbur Daffodil-11 Swain sits in the ruins of Manhattan's Skycraper National Park writing his memoirs. As
deformed children, he and his twin sister were separately
regarded as idiots but discovered that together they were
super-intelligent and went on to write a best-selling
child-rearing manual. As president, Wilbur instituted a
program to combat loneliness by forming artificial extended families

"Slapstick is a deceptively short and simple book. Its
readability should not distract one from the fact that
Vonnegut has found a fictional situation which considers
serious human problems." New Repub

Slaughterhouse-five; or, The children's crusade:
a duty-dance with death. 25th anniversary ed.
Delacorte Press 1994 205p il $22.50; pa $6.99
ISBN 0-385-31208-3; 0-440-18029-5 (pa)
* LC 94-171120
A reissue of the title first published 1969

This novel "mixes a fictionalized account of the author's experience of the fire bombing of Dresden with a
compensatory fantasy of the planet Tralfamadore, the science-fiction element is progressively dominated by the
overall concerns of satire, black humor, and absurdism."
Reader's Ency. 3d edition

"A masterpiece, in which Vonnegut penetrated to the
heart of the issues developed in his earlier absurdist
fabulations. A key work of modern SF." Anatomy of
Wonder 4

Timequake. Putnam 1997 219p il $23.95
ISBN 0-399-13737-8   LC 97-14508
"The cataclysm of the title—in 2001, time undergoes a
tremor, and everyone must relive the nineties—provides
an excuse for Vonnegut and his longtime alter ego, Kilgore Trout, to trade rants: on desert camouflage, thirties
socialism, the joys of waiting in line at the post office,
the traitorousness of Dillinger's Hungarian girlfriend,
semicolons. The resulting quilt of snippets is equal parts
memoir, literary charm, self-congratulation, humanist sermon, randy geriatric fantasy, and toastmasterly jokefest."
New Yorker

Welcome to the monkey house; a collection of
short works; by Kurt Vonnegut, Jr. Delacorte Press
1968 298p o.p.
"A Seymour Lawrence book"

Contents: Where I live; Harrison Bergeron; Who am I
this time?; Welcome to the monkey house; Long walk to
forever; The Foster portfolio; Miss Temptation; All the
king's horses; Tom Edison's shaggy dog; New dictionary; Next door; More stately mansions; The Hyannis
Port story; D.P.; Report on the Barnhouse Effect; The
euphio question; Go back to your precious wife and son;
Deer in the works; The lie; Unready to wear; The kid
nobody could handle; The manned missiles; EPICAC;
Adam; Tomorrow and tomorrow and tomorrow

Vreeland, Susan

Girl in hyacinth blue. MacMurray & Beck 1999
242p $17.50
ISBN 1-87844-890-0   LC 99-27405
This novel "follows the trail of an 'unknown' painting
by the Dutch master Vermeer—*The Girl in Hyacinth
Blue*—from the time of its creation in seventeenth-
century Holland to the present day. In each of the eight
independent but chronologically linked chapters, the
painting shows up as a prop in the lives of different
owners, and in telling the circumstances under which
these people acquire or lose the painting, Vreeland gives
the readers a sense of the evolution of Dutch social history." Booklist

"Vreeland strikes a pleasing balance between the timeless world of the painting as a work of art and the finite
worlds of its possessors and admirers—not to mention
the world of its subject and its creator. Intelligent,
searching and unusual, the novel is filled with luminous
moments; like the painting it describes so well, it has a
way of lingering in the reader's mind." N Y Times Book
Rev

Luncheon of The Boating Party. Viking 2007
434p il map
ISBN 978-0-670-03854-1; 0-670-03854-7
LC 2006-35324
In this novel Vreeland turns "to French impressionist
master Auguste Renoir's famous painting Luncheon of
the Boating Party, which depicts a group of people (in
1880) enjoying leisure time on the terrace of a riverside
restaurant. The current conditions in the life of the painter himself launch the author on an amazingly engrossing
reinvigoration of the lives of the individuals who modeled for Renoir for that work, all of whom were actual
people, and all are given a third dimension in Vreeland's
lovely prose." Booklist

The passion of Artemesia. Viking 2002 288p
ISBN 0-670-89449-4   LC 2001-26119
Narrated in the "first-person voice of Italian painter
Artemisia Gentileschi (1593-1653), the novel tells the
story of Gentileschi's life and career in Renaissance Italy. Publicly humiliated and scorned in Rome after her
participation as defendant in a rape trial in which the accused is her painting teacher (and father's friend)
Agostino Tassi, Artemisia accepts a hastily arranged marriage at the age of 18 to Pietro Stiatessi, an artist in Florence." Publ Wkly

"Vreeland palpably captures Artemisia's joy as she
blends colors and watches her artistic imaginings take
shape. . . . Although her final confrontation with her father, artist Orazio Gentileschi, feels forced, the novel
brilliantly captures the life of an extraordinary artist."
Libr J

W

Wagner, Bruce

The chrysanthemum palace. Simon & Schuster
2005 210p $23
ISBN 0-7432-4339-0   LC 2004-43059

Wagner, Bruce—*Continued*

"On the set of a schlocky TV space opera called 'Starwatch,' three children of wealthy and talented parents struggle to attain success of their own. The narrator, Bertie, is the son of the show's creator, and his current acting job is the nadir in a career of ever-shrinking ambition. His companions are Clea, the pill-popping daughter of a sexy actress who died young, and Thad, who is plagued by a personality disorder and the outsized legend of his father, an award-winning author. Suffering in the shadow of parental fame is a familiar trope of tabloid pathos, and the parents here are predictably malevolent. . . . [Wagner's] ability to eviscerate the absurdities of Hollywood, while occasionally hinting at its basic humanity, remains undiminished." New Yorker

Wahlöö, Maj Sjöwall *See* Sjöwall, Maj, 1935-

Wahlöö, Per, 1926-1975

(jt. auth) Sjöwall, M. Cop killer

(jt. auth) Sjöwall, M. The laughing policeman

(jt. auth) Sjöwall, M. The locked room

(jt. auth) Sjöwall, M. Murder at the Savoy

Wakefield, Dan

Starting over. Delacorte Press/Seymour Lawrence 1973 290p o.p.

      *

"Phil Potter, this book's hero, is 34, a failed actor who has become a successful New York public-relations executive. His four-year marriage to Jessica, a lovely model and closet alcoholic, has ended in divorce, and everyone tells him how lucky he is. Lucky? Being alone, he discovers, can be as bad as a homicidal marriage. So Potter decides to fashion a new life. He moves to Boston, takes a job teaching 'Communications' at Gilpen Junior College and prescribes sexual encounters with every available New England divorcee and matron as the perfect anodyne to his painful isolation." Newsweek

"A powerful, naturalistic depiction of the agony suffered by a man whose affluence merely conceals an utter absence of value and direction." Libr J

Walbert, Kate

The gardens of Kyoto; a novel. Scribner 2001 288p

  ISBN 0-684-86948-9   LC 2001-18876

"Ellen, the self-effacing narrator, mourns the disappearance of her cousin on Iwo Jima during the Second World War, and tries to decipher a book he has left her about the Kyoto gardens. The beauty of these landscapes lies in their impenetrability: one, made up entirely of shadows, must be viewed at night; another may be seen only through a window whose blind is forever drawn. Similarly, Ellen stands on the fringes of other, more dramatic lives, first befriending a fellow-coed whose affair with a married professor ends in an illegal abortion, then falling in love with a traumatized veteran of the Korean War. In precise, delicate prose, the author renders with equal power the quiet desperation of a girl growing up in nineteen-fifies America . . . and the ethereal." New Yorker

Our kind. Scribner 2004 195p $23

  ISBN 0-7432-4559-8   LC 2003-66294

"This novel is narrated collectively by a group of older women who have been friends since they were young. . . . The affluent East Coast suburban protagonists of 'Our Kind' came of age in the late 40's and early 50's." N Y Times Book Rev

"Walbert's characters are caught like insects in amber as they make late-in-life discoveries no school could ever teach. Brittle, funny and poignant, this is a prickly treat." Publ Wkly

A short history of women; a novel. Scribner 2009 239p $24

  ISBN 978-1-4165-9498-7; 1-4165-9498-1

                    LC 2008-38312

This novel follows five generations of women as each "tries (or declines) to find balance between career, marriage and motherhood. Dorothy Trevor is a suffragette in early World War I England who starves herself to death for her cause, leaving her young children behind. Her daughter, Evelyn Townsend, makes her way to America and academia, focusing her life on her work. Evelyn's niece Dorothy Townsend endures 1970s consciousness-raising, a lost child and a marriage that grows stale. Dorothy's daughter Liz, a privileged Manhattan mom, seeks reassurance from her 6-year-old. And Liz's niece Dora, set to graduate as part of Yale's class of 2011, is introduced to us via her Facebook profile and a few impatient words on the phone." Seattle Times

"Characters are recognizable but not clichéd and will stay with readers as wise, if also flawed and struggling, exemplars of political and intellectual engagement." Libr J

Walbrook, Louise *See* Templeton, Edith, 1916-

Walker, Alice, 1944-

By the light of my father's smile; a novel. Random House 1998 222p $22.95

  ISBN 0-375-50152-5   LC 98-5464

"Susannah and Magdalena are sisters estranged from each other and their parents since adolescence, after Magdalena is beaten by their father for having sex. As each woman expresses her loneliness and anger—Susannah through sexual exploration, Magdalena through food—they are observed by their father's ghost, who seeks a reconciliation with them that comes only after their deaths." Libr J

"Walker has created a romantic but propagandistic fairy tale that veers disconcertingly from the facile to the heartfelt." Booklist

The color purple. 10th anniversary ed. Harcourt Brace Jovanovich 1992 290p il $24; pa $14

  ISBN 0-15-119154-9; 0-15-602835-2 (pa)

                    * LC 91-47202

A reissue of the title first published 1982

"A feminist novel about an abused and uneducated black woman's struggle for empowerment, the novel was praised for the depth of its female characters and for its eloquent use of black English vernacular." Merriam-Webster's Ency of Lit

Now is the time to open your heart; a novel. Random House 2004 240p $24.95

  ISBN 1-400-06173-3   LC 2003-54766

Walker, Alice, 1944——*Continued*

"A well-published author, married many times, [Kate] has lived a life rich with explorations of the natural world and the human soul. Now, at fifty-seven, she leaves her lover, Yolo, to embark on a new excursion, one that begins on the Colorado River, proceeds through the past, and flows, inexorably, into the future. As Yolo begins his own parallel voyage, Kate encounters celibates and lovers, shamans and snakes, memories of family disaster and marital discord, and emerges at a place where nothing remains but love." Publisher's note

"Walker's dreamlike novel incorporates the political and spiritual consciousness and emotional style for which she is known and appreciated." Booklist

Possessing the secret of joy. Harcourt Brace Jovanovich 1992 286p $25

ISBN 0-15-173152-7   LC 92-6883

"Walker details the life of Tashi, a woman who grew up in the Olinka tribe in Africa but spent most of her adult life in the U.S. As a child, when the custom of circumcision is ordinarily carried out among Olinka females, Tashi was spared; later, though, her muddled need to reidentify with her origins causes her to submit to the tribal circumciser's blade. Rather than reknitting her soul to that of her people, the episode and its disastrous consequences alienate her body from sexuality and her mind from reality." Booklist

"The people in Ms. Walker's book are archetypes rather than characters as we have come to expect them in the 20th-century novel, and this is by defiant intention. . . . When the novel is operating genuinely on this archetypal level, it has a mythic strength. Its many voices are not rendered as stream-of-consciousness monologues, nor are they made to belong to distinct individuals. Instead, they are highly stylized, operatic, prophetic—and powerfully poetic." N Y Times Book Rev

The temple of my familiar. Harcourt Brace Jovanovich 1989 416p $19.95

ISBN 0-15-188533-8   LC 88-7995

"Time and place range from precolonial Africa to post-slavery North Carolina to modern-day San Francisco; and the characters themselves change and evolve as their stories are told, their myriad histories revealed. Most often present are Miss Lissie, an old woman with a fascinating host of former lives; her companion, the gentle Mr. Hal; Arveyda, a soul-searching musician; his wife Carlotta, who was born in the South American jungle; Fanny, a young woman who has a tendency to fall in love with spirits; and her husband Suwelo, who tries hard but simply does not understand her." Libr J

This is a "novel only in a loose sense. Rather, it is a mixture of mythic fantasy, revisionary history, exemplary biography and sermon. It is short on narrative tension, long on inspirational message." N Y Times Book Rev

The way forward is with a broken heart. Random House 2000 200p $23.95

ISBN 0-679-45587-6   LC 00-27172

Includes the following stories: To my young husband; Kindred spirits; Olive oil; Cuddling; Charms; There was a river; Uncle Loaf and Auntie Putt-Putt; Blaze; Growing out; Conscious birth; This is how it happened; The brotherhood of the saved

"In seven beautifully written and astoundingly perceptive short stories—admittedly based in fact, then fictionalized—[Walker] homes in on the problems endemic to interracial romance and offers a near stream-of-consciousness reflection on her own ten-year marriage to a white civil rights attorney." Libr J

You can't keep a good woman down; stories. Harcourt Brace Jovanovich 1981 167p o.p.

LC 80-8761

Contents: Nineteen fifty-five; How did I get away with killing one of the biggest lawyers in the States? It was easy; Elethia; The lover; Petunias; Coming apart Fame; The abortion; Porn; Advancing Luna—and Ida B. Wells; Laurel; A letter of the times; or, Should this sado-masochism be saved; A sudden trip home in the spring; Source

Walker, Dale L.

(ed) Westward. See Westward

Walker, Margaret, 1915-1998

Jubilee. Houghton Mifflin 1966 497p o.p.
*

"Vyry was a slave and the daughter of a slave. She suffered slavery's tribulations and looked forward to the time of freedom to bring her a home of her own and provide an education for her children. The Civil War and the Reconstruction period brought the possibility of that day of jubilation, but the attainment of her two desires still seemed remote. The author gives a clear picture of the everyday life of slaves, their modes of behavior, and the patterns and rhythms of their speech." Shapiro. Fic for Youth. 3d edition

Walker, Mary Willis

All the dead lie down. Doubleday 1998 308p $22.95

ISBN 0-385-47858-5   LC 97-24131

"Several topics concern magazine writer Molly Cates: the upcoming concealed handgun bill in the Texas legislature, the plight of homeless women in Austin, and her refusal to believe her father's suicide some 28 years earlier. So Molly learns how to shoot, interviews bag ladies, and pursues a new source of material about her father. Literate prose, in-depth characterization, and a cleverly manipulated plot." Libr J

Under the beetle's cellar. Doubleday 1995 311p

ISBN 0-385-46859-8   LC 95-10708

Crime reporter Molly Cates confronts "cult leader Samuel Mordecai, whose Austin, Texas, compound is just as bound-for-tragedy as David Koresh's. Mordecai believes the end of the world is imminent, and according to a divine vision he's received, he must sacrifice a group of purified 'lambs of God' who'll serve as his ticket into Heaven. To that end, he's kidnapped a school bus driver and 11 children and kept them hostage in a buried bus for 46 days." Booklist

"If there can be such a thing as a heartwarming suspense thriller, then Mary Willis Walker has written a nifty one. . . . The real drama is played underground, where the heroic bus driver draws on his war experiences in Vietnam and every bit of his strength to comfort the children and prepare them for what may well be the end of their world." N Y Times Book Rev

Wall, Kathryn R.

The Mercy Oak. St. Martin's Minotaur 2008
310p $24.95

ISBN 978-0-312-37534-8; 0-312-37534-4

LC 2008-3304

In this episode, South Carolina Lowcountry PI Bay
Tanner "must tackle two cases that hit close to home.
Her housekeeper's son disappears after the suspicious
hit-and-run death of a young Hispanic woman who had
been advocating for the rights of illegal immigrants.
Then, during a bank robbery, Lavinia, the woman who
raised Bay and still lives with her father, tries to help an
old man who has recognized one of the robbers. At the
risk of her own life, Bay is desperate to keep those she
cares about safe. Sue Grafton, Sara Paretsky, and Marcia
Muller come to mind as the quintessential writers of the
modern female private eye novel. Wall, in a quiet and
unassuming way, has produced a body of work of equal
quality as she tackles complex modern issues that trouble
her very human characters." Libr J

Wall, P. S. (Paula S.), 1954-

The Wilde women; a novel; [by] Paula Wall.
Atria Books 2007 310p

ISBN 978-0-7434-9621-6; 0-7434-9621-3

LC 2006-48023

Having left her southern hometown of Five Points five
years earlier after discovering that her sister and fiancé
had been having an affair, unpredictable Pearl Wilde returns home to exact revenge.

"Each and every character in Wall's tall tale has a
uniquely flawed personality, and Wall has a wonderful
sense of place and an adept way with words, adding up
to an enthralling novel." Booklist

Wall, Paula S. *See* Wall, P. S. (Paula S.), 1954-

Wallace, Daniel, 1959-

Big fish; a novel of mythic proportions.
Algonquin Bks. 1998 180p

ISBN 1-56512-217-8

* LC 98-26216

"William Bloom's father, Edward, is dying. He dies in
fact in four different takes, all of which have William
and his mother waiting outside a bedroom door as the
family doctor tells them it's time to say their goodbyes.
He intersperses the four takes with stories (all filtered
through William's mind and voice) about the elusive Edward. . . . In a plainspoken style dotted with transcendent passages, Wallace mixes the mundane and the
mythical. His chapters have the transformative quality of
fable and fairy tale, and the novel's roomy structure allows the mystery and lyricism of the story to coalesce."
Publ Wkly

Mr. Sebastian and the Negro magician; a novel.
Doubleday 2007 257p

ISBN 978-0-385-52109-3; 0-385-52109-X

LC 2006-28103

"An inept African-American illusionist is dogged by
the deal he struck with the devil in Wallace's . . . novel,
a circus picaresque that barnstorms its way through the
1950s American South. Henry Walker, once the 'greatest

magician in the world,' has been reduced to a minstrel
show-like novelty act in a traveling circus. Henry's story, told by a succession of narrators—including members
of the circus and a private detective—begins during the
Depression, when Henry's family fell on hard times.
While down and out, Henry meets and apprentices with
the devilish magician Mr. Sebastian. Henry learns the secrets of magic, but his ambition and ability are crimped
when his beloved sister, Hannah, disappears." Publ Wkly

"The unraveling of a man's myth to illuminate the essence of his life is the charm of this accomplished and
inventive novel." Paste

The Watermelon King. Houghton Mifflin 2003
226p $23

ISBN 0-618-22138-7

LC 2002-75941

"Lucy Rider drives into Ashland, AL, on a hot day in
1982 and unintentionally changes the nature of the quiet
little town forever . . . . Known as the Watermelon Capital of the World, Ashland celebrates each watermelon
crop with a festival, crowning a watermelon king and or-
chestrating his performance in a fertility rite for the following year's crop. The fertility ritual leads to Lucy's
death and to the gradual decline of the town. Eighteen
years later, Thomas Rider drives into Ashland, seeking
information about his mother and his own roots, and
Ashland again takes a Rider to its collective hearts, again
leading to tragedy and loss." Libr J

"This is a unique and spellbinding novel, an unforgettable southern tall tale with extraordinary characters."
Booklist

Wallace, David Foster

Infinite jest; a novel. Little, Brown 1996 1079p
$29.95

ISBN 0-316-92004-5

* LC 95-30619

This novel is "set sometime in the next century, on the
grounds of a New England tennis academy and in a
rehab clinic. Among other things, the book contains perhaps the most moving and hypnotic writing on the psychology of addiction and recovery to be found in modern
fiction. There are obsessive riffs on sports, on drugs, and
on the hidden horrors of entertainment: the title of the
novel refers to the title of a movie that is said to be so
'terminally compelling' that viewers will watch it passively and repeatedly to the point of death. Comparisons
with Pynchon are inevitable, and in this case they are
fully justified." New Yorker

Oblivion; stories. Little, Brown 2004 329p
$25.95

ISBN 0-316-91981-0

Contents: Mister Squishy; The soul is not a smithy; Incarnations of burned children; Another pioneer; Good old
neon; Philosophy and the mirror of nature; Oblivion; The
Suffering Channel

"Unpacking our inner lives with empathy and care,
Oblivion showcases the incredibly rich textures and crystalline clarity of Wallace's prose, confirming the singular
genius of his expansive imagination and resonating with
the complexities of minds in motion." American Book
Review

Wallace, Irving, 1916-1990

The man; a novel. Simon & Schuster 1964 766p o.p.

This is the story of a black Senator who becomes the first black President of the United States after the deaths, in rapid succession, of first the Vice President and then both the President and the Speaker of the House

The portrayal of the "President as a man, an able, intelligent, politically moderate man who has never been to the fore but must take responsibility overnight, is excellent. With a huge cast of characters and one crisis after another in the plot, this makes an absorbing story." Publ Wkly

The prize. Simon & Schuster 1962 768p o.p.

This novel is an "inquiry into the private lives of a batch of Nobel Prize winners. . . . The prize winners are . . . a French husband-and-wife team of chemists whose marriage is collapsing, a neurotic American heart surgeon broodingly resentful that he must share the award in medicine with an Italian doctor, a gentle German-born physicist from Atlanta who is being wooed by the Communists of East Germany, and an American novelist who is just coming out of a long alcoholic trance. Wallace . . . assembles them all in Stockholm and embarks them on the frenzied series of public and private events that surround Nobel award weeks in the Swedish capital." NY Her Trib Books

Wallace, Lew, 1827-1905

Ben-Hur; a tale of the Christ. Harper 1880 552p o.p.

This novel "depicts the oppressive Roman occupation of ancient Palestine and the origins of Christianity. The Jew Judah Ben-Hur is wrongly accused by his former friend, the Roman Messala, of attempting to kill a Roman official. He is sent to be a slave and his mother and sister are imprisoned. Years later he returns, wins a chariot race against Messala, and is reunited with his now leprous mother and sister. Mother and daughter are cured on the day of the Crucifixion, and the family is converted to Christianity." Merriam-Webster's Ency of Lit

Wallach, Janet, 1942-

Seraglio. Talese 2003 316p $24.95

ISBN 0-385-49046-1   LC 2002-28698

Based on fact, "this book traces the life of Aimée du Buc de Rivery . . . who was kidnapped at age 13 en route to her home in Martinique. Her pirate captors take her to the Turkish sultan, who enslaves her in the seraglio . . . . There, Aimée befriends Tulip, the black eunuch responsible for her welfare. Tulip recounts Aimée's reluctant initiation into the harem as Nakshidil, her dramatic development from slave girl to woman of pleasure, and her incredible transformation into the valide sultan (mother of the sultan) . . . assisting him in his controversial attempt to westernize 19th-century Turkey." Libr J

"It is to Wallach's credit that at no point does her story seem preposterous. The intrigue and drama of the palace are balanced by capable, authoritative prose and admirable restraint, resulting in a novel at once serious and enchanting." Publ Wkly

Wallant, Edward Lewis, 1926-1962

The pawnbroker; [by] Edward L. Wallant. Harcourt, Brace & World 1961 279p o.p.

"Sol Nazerman is a survivor of the Holocaust. In the past he had been a university teacher in Poland; now he runs a pawnshop in Harlem in which Murillio, a ruthless racketeer, has a financial interest. Into Nazerman's shop come people who are sad, sick, or criminal. He also meets Marilyn Birchfield, a friendly social worker who tries to get past the frozen outward indifference of the pawnbroker. In flashbacks that describe the horror and torture suffered by Nazerman and his family, the reader begins to understand his withdrawal from humanity. The relationship between him and his young, ambitious, and confused assistant, Jesus Ortiz, provides the novel's shattering climax." Shapiro. Fic for Youth. 3d edition

Waller, Robert James, 1939-

The bridges of Madison County. Warner Bks. 1992 171p il o.p.

* LC 91-50416

"This is the story of four days that change forever the lives of two lonely people. Robert Kincaid is a roving photographer for *National Geographic* and Francesca Johnson is a housewife whose marriage suffers from a lack of romance. Francesca's family is out of town when Kincaid arrives on the scene, and the pair are instantly attracted. They soon become lovers, and Kincaid asks Francesca to run away with him, but she refuses. Francesca stays loyal to her family, and memories of Kincaid are all that remain." Libr J

"An erotic, bittersweet tale of lingering memories and forsaken possibilities." Publ Wkly

Walser, Robert, 1878-1956

The assistant; translated from the German by Susan Bernofsky. New Directions 2007 302p pa $16.95

ISBN 978-0-8112-1590-9; 0-8112-1590-3

LC 2007-6865

Original German edition, 1908

The "novel tells the story of Joseph Marti, a plain and impressionable young man who comes to work for the Tobler family in their large villa near the German town of Barenswil. Marti's floundering attempts to ingratiate himself with this peculiar clan, and the response his efforts elicit from the hapless patriarch, Karl Tobler, lay at the heart of this baggy, rambling, digressive beast of a novel." Village Voice

"Walser's clerks and layabouts are perhaps the nicest, most considerate people you can meet in modernist fiction, but they can also be cuttingly ironic in the way of only the very polite. . . . Susan Bernofsky reproduces this effect and others with impressive fluency and naturalness." New Yorker

Walsh, Helen, 1977-

Brass. Canongate 2004 296p pa $14

ISBN 1-8419-5484-5 (pa)   LC 2005-415744

In this novel set in Liverpool, "nineteen-year-old university student Millie O'Reilley has not taken the news of the impending nuptials of her best mate, 28-year-old

Walsh, Helen, 1977——*Continued*

Jamie Keeley, very well. Drinking and drugging her way through the evenings, she usually ends up trolling the seedy section of town in search of female prostitutes (the 'brass' of the title). Jamie is growing increasingly impatient with and worried by Millie's behavior and is at a loss to explain their relationship to his dim-witted, social-climbing fiancee. What sets this first novel apart within a burgeoning subgenre is Walsh's lyrical prose. Her evocative phrasing both contains and stands in direct contrast to incredibly graphic scenes of depravity, and the result is both disturbing and compelling." Booklist

Walsh, Jill Paton See Paton Walsh, Jill, 1937-

Walsh, Pearl S. *See* Buck, Pearl S. (Pearl Sydenstricker), 1892-1973

Waltari, Mika, 1908-1979

The Roman; The memoirs of Minutus Launsus Manilianus, who has won the Insignia of a Triumph, who has the rank of consul, who is chairman of the Priests' Collegium of the god Vespasian and a member of the Roman Senate; English version by Joan Tate. Putnam 1966 637p o.p.

This is the final volume of the trilogy, the first being The Egyptian, and the second, The Etruscan

Original Finnish edition, 1964

The story is set in the first century A.D. during the reigns of Claudius and Nero. Minutus is born in Antioch, comes to Rome at the age of fifteen, visits Jerusalem and Britain with the army, and wins honors and power and has several love affairs. He becomes intimate with Nero and helps him persecute the Christians

"Though Minutus is somewhat wooden, his adventures are astonishing. Waltari shuttles his hero around the empire, from Britain to Ephesus, in order to describe the growing decadence of Rome, the rise of Christianity, and the existence of other religions. Waltari's sense of humor and irony points up his pageant of Roman life." Publ Wkly

Walters, Minette

The breaker. Putnam 1999 351p $23.95

ISBN 0-399-14492-7　　　　　　LC 98-51836

As this psychological thriller opens "the corpse of an attractive and pregnant woman is discovered washed ashore on the rocky Dorset coast in England. She has been drugged and sexually assaulted, her fingers deliberately broken, her body lashed to a dinghy to ensure her slow and painful death. What resident of the seaside village could be capable of such an atrocious crime?" Libr J

"Walters limits the suspects to two men with sufficient reason (and appropriate perversions) to have wanted the victim dead—the husband she betrayed and the lover she betrayed him with. Instead of making it easier to identify the killer, the narrow field only intensifies the challenge by demanding closer analysis." N Y Times Book Rev

The dark room. Putnam 1995 381p o.p.

　　　　　　　　　　　　* LC 95-10616

In this novel, "Jinx Kingsley, daughter of millionaire Adam Kingsley, wakes up in a hospital. Not only is she suffering from amnesia, but she is swathed in bandages

after an unsuccesful suicide attempt—her second in as many weeks—in apparent reaction to the news that her fiancé Leo has jilted her and disappeared with Jinx's best friend, Meg. Then Meg's and Leo's . . . bodies are discovered, and Jinx becomes the number-one murder suspect." Booklist

"Motivation is at the heart of The Dark Room. Like all the best detective fiction it challenges readers to work out how a particular character would act faced with specific circumstances. . . . The quest for truth is punctuated by touches of humanity that lift this novel way above others of its genre." New Statesman Soc

The devil's feather. Alfred A. Knopf 2006 349p $24

ISBN 0-307-26462-9　　　　　　LC 2006-41033

First published 2005 in the United Kingdom

In this "thriller, Connie Burns, a white Zimbabwean war correspondent for Reuters, investigates five gruesome murders in Sierra Leone and follows a hunch, convinced that a British mercenary is using the mayhem of war zones to disguise his taste for raping and killing women. After a mysterious assailant kidnaps her and holds her prisoner for three days in Iraq, she becomes convinced that her quarry is now hunting her. She flees to Dorset, rents an isolated house that turns out to have a troubled history, and is befriended by a reclusive neighbor who, some years before, lost her entire family in a car crash. Given the ultra-contemporary world of the early part of the novel, the scenes in Dorset . . . seem parochial, but this does not lessen Walters's ability to use horror-movie logic to terrifying effect." New Yorker

The echo. Putnam 1997 338p o.p.

　　　　　　　　　　　　　LC 96-37485

"The discovery of a homeless man's body in the garage of a banker's wife leads her—and a journalist interested in the homeless—to find out more about the man. They also reinvestigate the disappearance, years ago, of the banker and a sizable sum of cash. . . . Well-crafted psychological suspense from a master." Libr J

The sculptress. St. Martin's Press 1993 308p o.p.　　　　　　　　　　　　LC 93-21527

"Roz Leigh, an author embittered by the tragic death of a child and a split from her husband, agrees to write the story of Olive Martin, a grossly fat, untidy woman serving a long prison sentence for the particularly grisly murder of her mother and sister. Visiting Olive in jail, Roz finds herself drawn to the woman, and despite the fact that 'the sculptress' readily confessed to the crime, she begins to find odd discrepancies in the evidence against her." Publ Wkly

"Walters mesmerizes her readers with a sleek, exciting tale whose slick veneer disguises a sinister, menacing evil." Booklist

The shape of snakes. Putnam 2001 384p $24.95

ISBN 0-399-14733-0　　　　　　LC 00-65319

The novel's protagonist "was traumatized in 1978 by the violent death of a London neighbor who suffered from Tourette's syndrome. 'I could never decide whether 'Mad Annie' was murdered because she was mad or because she was black,' she says. But the cruel nature of the woman's death and the torments she endured from prejudiced neighbors have haunted Mrs. Ranelagh for 20 years. And now it is time for the reckoning. Although the narrator obviously has a hidden agenda, the master

Walters, Minette—*Continued*

manipulator here is Walters, whose commanding control over her inflammatory material—and her readers—distracts the eye from potential murder suspects and directs the mind to the everyday acts of casual inhumanity that are the real issue." N Y Times Book Rev

Walton, Jo

Farthing. Tor 2006 319p $25.95

ISBN 0-765-31421-5   LC 2005-34487

"A Tom Doherty Associates book"

"In an alternate reality in which a group of English nobles overthrew Winston Churchill and made peace with Adolf Hitler in 1941, a murder is committed at the home of Lord and Lady Eversley, and suspicion falls on David Kahn, the Jewish husband of Lucy Eversley. Only Inspector Carmichael of Scotland Yard believes that something else might be at work and that the Kahns could, in fact, be victims themselves. . . . An excellent example of alternate history." Libr J

Half a crown. Tor 2008 316p $25.95

ISBN 978-0-7653-1621-9; 0-7653-1621-8

LC 2008-31019

"A Tom Doherty Associates book"

Conclusion of the author's Small Change alternative-history trilogy; earlier titiles: Farthing and Ha'penny

"Former Scotland Yarder Peter Carmichael, now head of the secret police organization known as the Watch, must prepare for a peace conference to be held in London two decades after Britain reached an accommodation with Hitler's Germany in the early 1940s. Carmichael also has to worry about his sexual relationship with his valet, Jack, and the covert unit within the Watch he's created to smuggle British Jews out of the country. Then his naïve 18-year-old ward, Elvira Royston, who's about to be presented to the queen, overhears a conversation that could compromise her protector. Elvira, who winds up in police custody after attending a political rally that turns violent, accepts her authoritarian society with a casualness that's truly chilling." Publ Wkly

"A difficult — and important — book to read about a world gone mad. The characterization is first-rate, the plot is compelling and most important of all, even in this world, there is hope." Romantic Times

Ha'penny. Tor 2007 319p $25.95

ISBN 978-0-7653-1853-4; 0-7653-1853-9

LC 2007-21113

"A Tom Doherty Associates Book"

Sequel to: Farthing

This second volume of the author's Small Change trilogy "delves deeper into the intrigue and paranoia of 1940s fascist Great Britain. Denied help from the United States, England negotiated the Farthing Peace with the Nazis to end WWII, surrendering freedom for a narrow kind of safety. Eight years later, Scotland Yard investigators like Inspector Carmichael spend as much time monitoring the activities of gays, Jews and foreigners as they do hunting criminals. Carmichael, outed to his superiors as a homosexual and blackmailed into keeping deadly political secrets, plans to retire after his current case, a bombing at the country house of respected actress Lauria Gilmore. Meanwhile, Viola Lark is preparing for the role of her life as a female Hamlet when she's coerced into a plot to kill the prime minister and Hitler on opening

night. World Fantasy Award-winner Walton masterfully illustrates how fear can overwhelm common sense." Publ Wkly

Wambaugh, Joseph

The blue knight. Little, Brown 1972 338p o.p.

*

"An Atlantic Monthly Press book"

A novel about "Bumper Morgan, a fat Irish cop at 50, dyspeptic, lusty, tough, egotistic, with only two days to go before his planned retirement from the Los Angeles police department." Libr J

"The caricature is deliberate; the author means to endow a stereotype with complexity and sentiment. Bumper has his own street ethics. . . . The book tends to be a bit ostentatious in such honesties, as if they established Bumper's credibility. In the end, Wambaugh sentimentalizes Bumper as a sort of repellently lovable super-cop who, whenever he is not strongarming 'pukepots,' is bantering in Yiddish, Spanish or Arabic with the ethnics on the beat." Time

Finnegan's week. Morrow 1993 348p o.p.

LC 93-24890

"The owner of a waste-hauling firm shaves costs by mislabeling drums of highly toxic pesticide and dumping them illegally. When two deaths result, Fin Finnegan teams up with civilian and Navy investigators to solve the series of related crimes." SLJ

"There is a boyish excessiveness to Mr. Wambaugh's writing that produces an odd synergy with his carefully constructed plots and his colorful characters." N Y Times Book Rev

Floaters. Bantam Bks. 1996 293p o.p.

LC 95-26625

In this novel, "two clumsy conspirators try to fix the America's Cup race. A hot number named Blaze Duvall does the grunt work of seducing a dumb sailor into sabotaging the Black Magic, the formidable New Zealand contender. Blaze stands to make a buck from this scheme, but it is really a crime of passion devised by Ambrose Lutterworth, the keeper of the cup, who can't bear to give up his beloved charge. As a spy, the flame-haired Blaze is a bit conspicuous, catching the eye of Fortney and Leeds, a couple of calloused veterans with the harbor police unit that cruises Mission Bay in San Diego." N Y Times Book Rev

Hollywood crows; a novel. Little, Brown 2008 343p $26.99

ISBN 978-0-316-02528-7; 0-316-02528-3

LC 2007-33059

"Nathan Weiss, known as Hollywood Nate for his acting ambitions, and his friend Bix Ramstead are now assigned to the LAPD's Community Relations Office, which handles quality-of-life issues and whose members are referred to as Crows. Weiss and Ramstead both become ensnared by a stunning femme fatale, Margot Aziz, who's in the middle of a contentious divorce. Aziz is trying to gain the upper hand over her husband, who operates a seedy nightclub but stays on the good side of law enforcement with well-timed donations to police charities." Publ Wkly

"Wambaugh is an important writer not simply because he's ambitious and technically accomplished, but also be-

Wambaugh, Joseph—*Continued*

cause he 'owns' a critical slice of L.A.'s literary real estate: the Los Angeles Police Department not just its inner workings, but also its relationship to the city's political establishment and to its intricately enmeshed social classes." Los Angeles Times Book Rev

Hollywood Station; a novel. Little, Brown and Co. 2006 340p $24.99

ISBN 9780316066143; 0-316-06614-1

* LC 2006-15759

This novel about the LAPD focuses on "an understaffed office at Hollywood Station, where cops mix with drugged-out lowlifes, prostitutes, and gullible tourists along the Hollywood Walk of Fame. The 68-year-old sergeant, nicknamed 'the Oracle,' keeps an eye on his own strange squad—a new, lactating mother; a college dropout; and two 30-something surfer dudes, among others—as they get caught up in the Hollywood underworld of Russian mobsters, druggies, and murderers." Bookmarks Magazine

"Wambaugh has his finger on the pulse of today's police force in a way that most other authors simply can't match, and that makes his work a delight to read." Chicago Sun-Times

The new centurions. Little, Brown 1971 c1970 376p o.p.

"An Atlantic Monthly Press book"

The author "shows us the excitement, danger and sordidness found in the daily work of three young Los Angeles policemen. From the police academy to the first foot patrol, from the first patrol-car duty to the first promotion, Wambaugh follows his three main characters in their professional and personal lives, and shows us that police work, like the ministry, medicine or the military, is a profession demanding 24-hour dedication, determination, discipline and often a frustrating acceptance of defeat." Natl Rev

"As a novel the book has lapses, it wears its exposition on its sleeve—necessarily, perhaps, in view of what it's trying to do—and the three protagonists, though very different in type, are perhaps not sufficiently different in sensibility. . . . But never mind that. What he knows Wambaugh tells truly, perceptively, and well." Book World

Wander, Fred, 1917-2006

The seventh well; translated by Michael Hofmann. W.W. Norton & Co. 2008 160p $23.95; pa $13.95

ISBN 978-0-393-06538-1; 0-393-06538-3; 978-0-393-33362-6 (pa); 0-393-33362-0 (pa)

LC 2007-28897

Original German edition, 1971

This is a "novel narrated by a young man who attempts to maintain his own sanity in the death camps by immersing himself in the lives of his fellow prisoners. Originally published in 1971, it is now available in a superb new translation by Michael Hofmann. Wander does not guide the reader on his own journey from boxcar to barbed wire, as Elie Wiesel and Primo Levi have done. Rather, his anonymous narrator undergoes a sort of spiritual education as he studies the doomed men and boys

around him. The result is an indirect portrait of a man trying to grasp an unthinkable trauma." N Y Times Book Rev

Wang, An-i *See* Wang Anyi, 1954-

Wang Anyi, 1954-

The song of everlasting sorrow; a novel of Shanghai; translated by Michael Berry and Susan Chan Egan. Columbia University Press 2008 440p (Weatherhead books on Asia) $29.95

ISBN 978-0-231-14342-4; 0-231-14342-7

LC 2007-10812

Original Chinese edition, 1996

"Enamored by Hollywood in prerevolutionary China, Wang Qiyao serendipitously poses for a photograph that is chosen for the cover of Shanghai Life magazine. Dubbed A Proper Young Lady of Shanghai, she wins second runner-up in a 1946 beauty pageant and is soon mistress to a wealthy benefactor. After his death, marriage in her fallen state is out of the question, and Wang Qiyao embarks on a lonely, decades-long journey through Shanghai's myriad longtang, or vast neighborhoods inside enclosed alleys." Publ Wkly

"Michael Berry and Susan Chang Egan's graceful translation, only rarely marred by jarring Americanisms ('grunt work,' 'deal breaker'), helps us understand why Wang Anyi is one of the most critically acclaimed writers in the Chinese-speaking world. . . . [As the novel] moves toward its violent, melodramatic and distressingly appropriate ending, readers may feel a Proustian nostalgia for the novel's lost time, a sadness that mirrors the melancholy that haunts Wang Qiyao and pervades the fascinating, mostly vanished longtang of Shanghai." N Y Times Book Rev

Ward, Amanda Eyre, 1972-

Forgive me; a novel. Random House 236p $23.95

ISBN 978-0-345-49446-7; 0-345-49446-6

LC 2006-50436

The protagonist of this novel is "Nadine, a fly-by-night journalist in her mid-30s who can't quite focus on anything beyond the next hot story. Continually jetting off for international trouble spots, Nadine is thoroughly unwilling to recognize just how utterly, and ultimately rather despicably, addicted she is to other peoples' misery. It doesn't help that she's also the kind of person who will harp on about troubles in faraway lands while remaining utterly blind to those existing right before her nose. After a troubled recovery in her home town of Nantucket (she got in over her head in Mexico, not surprisingly), Nadine heads off to South Africa, where she had once spent some time, to cover the Truth and Reconciliation Commission hearings on apartheid atrocities, and confronts some ugly truths about herself. Ward's plotting may not always be the best, this is a start-and-stop kind of book, but her sharp evocation of Nadine—newsgatherer as self-absorbed vampire—is one that's hard to forget." PopMatters

Ward, Liza

Outside valentine. Holt & Co. 2004 301p $23

ISBN 0-8050-7598-4

Ward, Liza—*Continued*

"Crosscutting between the late 1950s and the year 1991, and told in a trio of voices, the novel tracks the murderous acts of Charles Starkweather and his 14-year-old girlfriend, Caril Ann Fugate, and their impact on Lowell Bowman, who was orphaned by their rampage." Booklist

"A gifted writer, Ward uses simple imagery to chilling effect. A dog with a broken neck hiding under the bed after its owner has been murdered and a dead schoolgirl with her skirt pulled up—Starkweather says he just wanted to look—are as vivid as anything filmmakers have fashioned from the same raw material." Washington Post Book World

Ward, Mary Jane, 1905-

The snake pit. Random House 1946 278p o.p.
Related in the first person, this tells of the experiences undergone by the patient, Virginia Cunningham, in a state mental hospital. It follows the course of her insanity from her commitment to her final release. It also takes the reader through mental hospital routine in all its reality

"Chronicled so quietly and unemphatically, the horrors of asylum life become infinitely more poignant than they appear in the hands of grimmer writers who are out to shock. Obviously an incomplete picture, but an extraordinarily moving one." New Yorker

Warren, Robert Penn, 1905-1989

All the king's men. Harcourt Brace Jovanovich 1990 c1946 531p $19
ISBN 0-15-104772-3
* LC 90-36181

"An HBJ modern classic"
First published 1946
"In the South during the 1920s a young journalist, Jack Burden, becomes involved in the drive for political power by soon-to-be governor Willie Stark. The journey is a rocky, disillusioning one, and involves exploitation, deceit, and violence. When asked by Stark to uncover a scandal in the past of Judge Irwin, Jack must weigh the many consequences of such action." Shapiro. Fic for Youth. 3d edition

Band of angels. Random House 1955 375p o.p.
*

"A lush, full-bodied Civil War story about a Kentucky plantation owner's daughter sold into slavery whose fight becomes an inquiry into the nature of freedom and the quest for individual identity." Oxford Companion to Am Lit. 6th edition

World enough and time; a romantic novel. Random House 1950 512p o.p.
*

"The murder in Kentucky of Col. Solomon P. Sharp by Jeroboam O. Beauchamp, whose trial was the sensation of 1826, has been a popular theme for novelists ever since. Warren's version in this novel is based on *The Confession*, which Beauchamp published in 1826. Warren introduced many variations, however, and his quotations from documents are his own inventions." Benet's Reader's Ency of Am Lit

Waters, Sarah

Fingersmith. Riverhead Bks. 2002 511p
ISBN 1-573-22203-8
LC 2001-51053
"Sue Trinder, who also goes by a number of other names, appears to be a foundling, left for safekeeping at Mrs. Sucksby's baby farm by her thieving mother. . . . Raised by Mrs. Sucksby as her own, Sue picks up a few tricks from a crooked locksmith. . . . One day a young man, Richard Rivers, known as Gentleman, comes knocking at the door with a scheme to marry himself off to a lonely heiress, Maud Lilly, then have her shut up in a madhouse once her money is his. He enlists Sue to be the young woman's maid, promising her a cut of the proceeds. But having attached herself to Maud for the sake of the money, Sue finds herself drawn into an unexpected and fearful intimacy." N Y Times Book Rev

The little stranger. Riverhead Books 2009 466p $26.95
ISBN 978-1-59448-880-1; 1-59448-880-0
LC 2009-09338
"In post-World War II Britain, the financially struggling Dr. Faraday is called to Hundreds Hall, home of the upper-class Ayreses, now fallen on hard times. Ostensibly there to treat Roderick Ayres for a war injury, Faraday soon sees signs of mental decline—first in Roderick and later in his mother, Mrs. Ayres. Waters builds the suspense slowly, with the skeptical Faraday refusing to accept the explanations of Roderick or of the maid Betty, who believe that there is a supernatural presence in the house. Meanwhile, Faraday becomes enamored of Roderick's sister Caroline and begins to dream of building a family within the confines of the ruined Hundreds Hall. This spooky, satisfying read has the added pleasure of effectively detailing postwar village life, with its rationing, social strictures, and gossip." Libr J

The night watch. Riverhead Books 2006 450p $25.95
ISBN 1-59448-905-X
LC 2005-44927
"In the fall of 1947, an androgynous woman walks aimlessly through the scarred streets of London, adjusting her cufflinks. An ambulance driver during the Blitz, she now does nothing more dramatic than go to the cinema, arriving midway through a film and watching the second half first—'People's pasts, you know, being so much more interesting than their futures.' Likewise, this historical novel begins at the end and moves backward, tracing the lives of its characters from peacetime Britain to the early years of the war. The centerpiece of the book is set in 1944, when the characters come fully alive, creeping through blackout London—an apocalyptic landscape of rubble and ash, searchlights and fires. Waters, acclaimed for her Victorian-era romps, has done meticulous research, and renders wartime scenes with unnerving authenticity." New Yorker

Watkins, Paul, 1964-

The forger. Picador 2000 322p $25
ISBN 0-312-26593-X
* LC 00-33631
"Shortly before WWII, David Halifax, a young American painter, receives a mysterious scholarship to study in Paris with the eccentric genius Alexander Pankratov. Halifax supplements his scholarship income by selling

Watkins, Paul, 1964-—*Continued*

his sketches through a charming and unscrupulous art dealer, Guillaume Fleury. When war is declared, the three are enlisted by the French government in an elaborate scheme to prevent classic works of art from falling into German hands." Publ Wkly

"Watkins is an extremely facile writer. His novels are thrilling, fast-paced, intricately plotted and extraordinarily atmospheric. Cerebral in the manner of Graham Greene, . . . Watkins, like Greene, can create a wartime sensibility in which every footfall on the stairs has you holding your breath in anticipation. In 'The Forger', he has created a shifting—and shifty—cast of characters whose loyalties and alliances keep changing as the events of the war advance." N Y Times Book Rev

The ice soldier. H. Holt 2006 341p $25

ISBN 0-8050-7867-3   LC 2005-46237

"Narrator William Bromley leads a quiet, isolated life in England circa 1950, socializing only with his similarly inclined friend and mountaineering partner Stanley Carton. Much to the dismay of Stanley's uncle Henry (who not only inspired them to become climbers but was also the first to climb a peak in the Italian Alps, which was named Carton Peak after him), both have given up mountaineering. When a former friend and mountaineer, Sturges, shows up, William begins having flashbacks to his mission as an ice soldier during World War II. The death of Uncle Henry forces both William and Stanley to confront their pasts in a dramatic fashion. With a narrative so strong in imagery and detail that the reader can almost feel the gusts of an Alpine blizzard, this adventurous tale builds to a final climax on Carton Peak, where William's horrific wartime experience occurred." Libr J

Watson, Brad

The heaven of Mercury. Norton 2002 333p $23.95

ISBN 0-393-04757-1

In this "southern gothic tale, Finus Bates, an 89-year-old radio announcer, reflects on his thwarted love affair with Birdie Wells. As a child, Finus falls in love with the winsome Birdie when he spies her executing a naked cartwheel. Despite their mutual attraction, Birdie and Finus end up betrothed to others: Birdie to the lecherous son of one of the town's wealthiest families, and Finus to Birdie's best friend, a severe woman with unexpected reservoirs of strength. As Watson traces the lovers' sad histories, he flips to the present day, when Finus investigates the decades-old poisoning of Birdie's husband." Booklist

"Watson lays bare the lives and most intimate secrets of the richest and poorest families in Mercury, MS. The characters' racism may offend some readers, but it is an essential element of that particular time and place." Libr J

Watson, Jan Elizabeth, 1972-

Asta in the wings. Tin House Books 2009 314p (Tin House new voice) pa $14

ISBN 978-0-9802436-1-1; 0-9802436-1-0

LC 2008-40525

This is the "story of what happens when the outside world discovers that a widowed mother in Maine has removed her two children, seven-year-old Asta and her nine-year-old brother, Orion, from any contact with the outside world. Unaware that their mother is delusional, the two children do not feel deprived under her care, appreciating her for what she is able to provide. When their isolated living situation is discovered, the children find themselves at the mercy of kind yet sometimes misguided adults. Asta emerges as the stronger, more communicative child. Bright and sometimes wily, she remains steadfastly devoted to her gifted yet now mute brother." Libr J

"Watson hasn't set herself an easy task for her debut. The success of the novel rests entirely on her main character's sparrow-sized shoulders. Fortunately, Asta has reserves of intelligence and resourcefulness to spare and her voice is unforgettable." Christ Sci Monit

Watts, Peter 1958-

Starfish. Tor 1999 317p hardcover o.p. pa $14.95

ISBN 978-0-7653-1596-0; 0-7653-1596-3

LC 99-22967

"A Tom Doherty Associates book"

First title in the author's Rifter's trilogy

"In the near future, energy comes from the geothermal waters of the deep ocean, but the cost of providing power for the surface has a price-the sanity of the physically modified humans ('rifters') who live in an alien and dangerous environment. Watts's first novel elegantly captures the isolation and claustrophobia of the lightless ocean depths, smoothly blending psychological suspense with high-tech sf adventure." Libr J

Followed by: Maelstrom (2001) and Behemoth (2004)

Blindsight. Tor 2006 384p $25.95

ISBN 978-0-7653-1218-1; 0-7653-1218-2

LC 2006-5917

"A Tom Doherty Associates book"

"A swarm of Fireflies—lighted alien objects in the sky—now orbits Earth, speaking among themselves and ignoring human attempts at communication. In desperation, a group consisting of a linguist with multiple personality disorder, a biologist more machine than man, a paleogenetic vampire, and a pacifist is sent to confront this unfathomable alien presence." Libr J

Watts "remains one of the most exacting hard SF writers in the field, with a meticulous approach to the science in his works." Sci Fi Wkly

Waugh, Evelyn, 1903-1966

Brideshead revisited; with an introduction by Frank Kermode. Knopf 1993 xxxvii, 315p $17

ISBN 0-679-42300-1

* LC 93-1854

"Everyman's library"

A reissue of the title first published 1945 by Little, Brown

"The novel, which takes the form of an extended flashback, is narrated by Charles Ryder, an army officer billeted at the eponymous country house, owned by an aris-

Waugh, Evelyn, 1903-1966—*Continued*

tocratic Roman Catholic family headed by Lord and Lady Marchmain. Charles had visited Brideshead with Sebastian Flyte, the Marchmains' younger son, when both were Oxford undergraduates. In the course of the narrative Ryder conveys his fascination with the family, all of whom are eccentric or unhappy in some way." Oxford Companion to 20th Cent Lit in Engl

The complete stories of Evelyn Waugh. Little, Brown 1999 535p $29.95

ISBN 0-316-92546-2

* LC 99-20837

Contents: The balance; A house of gentlefolks; The manager of "The Kremlin"; Love in the slump; Too much tolerance; Excursion in reality; Incident in Azania; Bella Fleace gave a party; Cruise; The man who liked Dickens; Out of depth; By special request; Period piece; On guard; Mr. Loveday's little outing; Winner takes all; An Englishman's home; The sympathetic passenger; My father's house; Lucy Simmonds; Charles Ryder's schooldays; Scott-King's modern Europe; Tactical exercise; Compassion; Love among the ruins; Basil Seal rides again; The curse of the horse race; Fidon's confetion; Multa Pecunia; Fragment of a novel; Essay; The house: an anti-climax; Portrait of young man with career; Antony, who sought things that were lost; Edward of unique achievement; Fragments: they dine with the past; Conspiracy to murder; Unacademic exercise: a nature story; The national game

"These 39 stories span Waugh's writing career, and to a one they demonstrate his trademark wit and sophistication." Booklist

Decline and fall. Doubleday, Doran 1929 c1928 293p o.p.

First published 1928 in the United Kingdom

This novel "recounts the chequered career of Paul Pennyfeather, sent down from Scone College, Oxford, for 'indecent behaviour', as the innocent victim of a drunken orgy. Thus forced to abandon a career in the church, he becomes a schoolmaster at Llanabba Castle, where he encounters headmaster Fagan and his daughters, the dubious, bigamous, and reappearing Captain Grimes, and young Beste-Chetwynde, whose glamorous mother Margot carries him off to the dangerous delight of high society. They are about to be married when Paul is arrested at the Ritz and subsequently imprisoned for Margot's activities in the white slave trade." Oxford Companion to Engl Lit. 6th edition

The end of the battle. Little, Brown 1962 c1961 319p o.p.

Sequel to Officers and gentlemen

First published 1961 in the United Kingdom with title: Unconditional surrender

In this final volume of the trilogy "Guy volunteers for service in Italy with the military government, and he eventually goes to Yugoslavia as a liaison officer with the Partisans. Virginia gives birth to a son (not Guy's) and is killed in an air raid. At the end of the book Guy has again asserted himself, in the rescue of a group of Jewish refugees, and realizes what kind of man he used to be: one who believed that his private honour would be satisfied by war. In an Epilogue we learn that he has remarried and surrounded himself with a family." Camb Guide to Lit in Engl

The loved one; an Anglo-American tragedy. Little, Brown 1948 164p pa $13.95 hardcover o.p.

ISBN 0-316-92608-6

"Depicting romance in a mortuary could be gruesome but the author succeeds both in poking satirical fun at the maudlin pretentiousness of the funeral industry and in delighting the reader with a hilarious love story." Shapiro. Fic for Youth. 3d edition

Men at arms. Little, Brown 1952 o.p.

This is the first volume of the trilogy that includes Officers and gentlemen and The end of the battle

This novel "introduces 35-year-old divorced Catholic Guy Crouchback, who after much effort succeeds in enlisting in the Royal Corps of Halberdiers just after the outbreak of the Second World War. Much of the plot revolves around his eccentric fellow officer Apthorpe, an old Africa hand who suffers repeatedly from 'Bechuana tummy', is deeply devoted to his 'thunder box' (or chemical closet), and dies in West Africa at the end of the novel of some unspecified tropical disease, aggravated by Guy's thoughtful gift of a bottle of whisky. Other characters include Guy's ex-wife, the beautiful socialite Virginia Troy, her second (but not her final) husband, Tommy Blackhouse, and the ferocious one-eyed Brigadier Ritchie-Hook, who involves Guy in a near-disastrous escapade." Oxford Companion to Engl Lit. 6th edition

Followed by Officers and gentlemen

Officers and gentlemen. Little, Brown 1955 339p o.p.

Sequel to Men at arms

This novel "continues Waugh's semi-satiric, semiemotional portrayal of civilian and military life with an account of Guy's training on the Hebridean island of Mugg with a commando unit, and of the exploits of exhairdresser Trimmer, now Captain McTavish, which include an affair with Virginia and the blowing up of a French railway; the action moves to Alexandria, then to the withdrawal from Crete, with all but four of 'Hookforce' taken prisoner." Oxford Companion to Engl Lit. 6th edition

Followed by The end of the battle

Vile bodies. Little, Brown 1930 321p o.p.

*

"Set in England between the wars, the novel examines the frenetic but empty lives of the Bright Young Things, young people who indulge in constant party-going, heavy drinking, and promiscuous sex. At the novel's end, the realities of the world intrude, with Adam Fenwick-Symes, the protagonist, serving on a battlefield at the onset of another world war." Merriam-Webster's Ency of Lit

Weaver, Michael, 1929-

Deceptions. Warner Bks. 1995 454p o.p.

LC 94-17382

"The story concerns two boys who grew up in the Mob's shadow. One is now an artist, the other a hit man. When the hit man fails to kill one victim (because of true love, we learn), powerful forces of vengeance are unleashed. The artist, challenged to rat on his childhood buddy, draws upon murderous resources." Libr J

"Enhanced by strong, sinewy writing, numerous plot twists and a potent melding of sex and violence, this ex-

Weaver, Michael, 1929- —*Continued*
pertly wrought novel proves that Weaver knows what
most thriller fans want—and can deliver it in spades."
Publ Wkly

Weaver, William, 1923-

(tr) Bassani, G. The garden of the Finzi-Continis

Webb, James H. *See* Webb, Jim

Webb, Jim

A sense of honor. Prentice-Hall 1981 308p o.p.
LC 80-25852
"Plebe life at Annapolis in 1968 proceeds as normal
while the specter of Vietnam haunts the routine of mid-
shipmen and the careers of recent graduates. Traditional
military ways begin to yield to changing times and altered perceptions; on a personal level this conflict is captured in the relationship between a fourth-year student
and a plebe who questions the rigid code of honor and
unblinking acceptance of the hazing ritual." Booklist
"In this powerful novel, Webb . . . a graduate of the
Academy, pulls the reader right into the caldron of Annapolis for a vivid picture of heroes and martinets living
according to their various interpretations of 'honor'; and
he illuminates the mystique that makes men voluntarily
stay in such a meat grinder." Publ Wkly

Weber, David, 1952-

Off Armageddon Reef. Tor 2007 605p $25.95
ISBN 978-0-7653-1500-7; 0-7653-1500-9
LC 2006-25838
"A Tom Doherty Associates book"
The author launches an epic series with this far-future
saga, "which springboards off the near-destruction of humanity in a massive war with the alien Gbaba. The survivors of the human race retreat to the planet Safehold,
where they sacrifice basic human rights—and an accurate
memory of the Gbaba—for the preservation of the species. The colony's founders psychologically program the
colonists to prevent the re-emergence of scientific inquiry, higher mathematics or advanced technology, which
the Gbaba would detect and destroy. Centuries later, cultural stagnation on this feudal but thriving planet is enforced by the all-powerful Church of God Awaiting. But
one kingdom—with the aid of the war's last survivor, a
cybernetic avatar that awakens to reinvent itself as a man
named Merlin Athrawes—risks committing the ultimate
heresy. Shifting effortlessly between battles among warp-
speed starships and among oar-powered galleys, Weber
brings the political maneuvering, past and future technologies, and vigorous protagonists together for a cohesive,
engrossing whole." Publ Wkly

Weber, Katharine

The little women. Farrar, Straus & Giroux 2003
240p $22
ISBN 0-374-18959-5
LC 2003-44062
In a story narrated by 16-year-old Joanna, the modern-
day Little Women of the title "grow up in New York
City in cozy upper-middle-class bliss, their perfect family

the envy of all. But their smug contentment is shattered
when they discover their mother's affair; their father's
blasé reaction is almost worse. In protest, Joanna and
Amy move in with Meg and her roommate, Teddy Bell,
at their off-campus apartment near Yale University. . . .
Comments from Meg and Amy pepper the text, contest-
ing the structure of Joanna's story and arguing with her
about her perspective and her version of reality." Publ
Wkly
"In places, the readers' and author's notes do cause the
pace to drag. But fortunately, the story of three teenage
girls making a go of living in a New Haven apartment
with a cute male roommate is lively, interesting and funny enough to carry one over the sluggish bits. . . . Novels with spurious critical apparatus don't often wear it
lightly, but Weber's use of the form is both easy and
playful." N Y Times Book Rev

The Music Lesson. Crown 1999 178p
ISBN 0-609-60317-5
LC 98-9346
"Patricia Dolan is a fortysomething art history librarian
at the Frick Museum in New York when she's accosted
by a dangerously charming young Irish cousin. Swept up
in a gust of passion, she moves with him to a remote
Irish village. Exploiting her knowledge, cousin Michael
and his IRA splinter group steal a priceless Vermeer, *The
Music Lesson*, for which they hope to extract a ransom
from the British monarchy." Libr J
This "mystery is as intricate as an acrostic. A trio of
clues—the motives of the narrator, who is a woman recovering from the accidental death of her child; the
paintings of Vermeer, and the ideals of Irish nationalism—yield, by the book's close, an almost perfect, if
chilling, answer." New Yorker

Weiner, Jennifer, 1970-

Certain girls; a novel. Atria Books 2008 386p
$26.95
ISBN 978-0-7432-9425-6; 0-7432-9425-4
LC 2007-38373
In this sequel to Good in bed (2001), Weiner revisits
"the memorable and feisty Candace 'Cannie' Shapiro.
Flashing forward 13 years, the novel follows Cannie as
she navigates the adolescent rebellion of her about-tobe
bat mitzvahed daughter, Joy, and juggles her writing career; her relationship with her physician husband, Peter
Krushelevansky; her ongoing weight struggles; and the
occasional impasse with Joy's biological father, Bruce
Guberman." Publ Wkly
This is the "kind of book that gets under your skin, reminding you what it felt like to listen to your friend snap
her retainer in the dark during a sleepover when you
were 13 and capturing exactly what it feels like now,
watching your child grow away from you and praying
that someday she comes back." Washington Post Book
World

Good in bed; a novel. Pocket Books 2001 376p
ISBN 0-7434-1816-6
LC 00-68212
"Cannie Shapiro is in her late twenties, funny, independent, and a talented reporter for the Philadelphia Inquirer. After a 'temporary' breakup with her boyfriend of
three years, she reads his debut column, 'Good in Bed,'
in the women's magazine *Moxie*. Titled 'Loving a Larger
Woman,' this very personal piece triggers events that
completely transform her and those around her. Cannie's

Weiner, Jennifer, 1970-—*Continued*

adventures will strike a chord with all young women struggling to find their place in the world, especially those larger than a size eight." Libr J

In her shoes; a novel. Atria Books 2002 424p $25

ISBN 0-7434-1819-0   LC 2003-537614

"Meet plump, dependable Rose Feller and her gorgeous, out-of-control sister, Maggie. As children, they lost their mother and contact with grandmother Ella. Now, 20 years later, we follow their struggles to forgive the past, reclaim each other's love, and become their best selves. . . . Reworking the age-old theme that self-knowledge and acceptance are needed before love and happiness can be achieved, Weiner embroiders serious matters with threads of humor to produce a novel full of memorable characters and situations." Libr J

Little earthquakes. Atria Bks. 2004 417p $26

ISBN 0-7434-7009-5

This is the "story of four women in Philadelphia who bond over pregnancy and motherhood. Becky, Kelly, and Ayinde meet in yoga class, and the three become friends when Ayinde's water breaks one day after class and they take her to the hospital. Becky is a chef with an adoring husband and an annoying mother-in-law; Kelly is frustrated when her husband loses his job and drags his feet looking for another; Ayinde's husband is a famous basketball player whom she suspects of infidelity. What brings the women together is their love for their newborns. The fourth woman, Lia, watches the group from afar; she's an actress who walked out on her husband after a devastating tragedy. Weiner seamlessly and gracefully weaves the four women's stories together." Booklist

Weinstein, Debra, 1961-

Apprentice to the flower poet Z. Random House 2004 242p $23.95

ISBN 1-400-06155-5

A novel about New York's academic poetry scene. "Z. writes sexy if vapid poems about flowers and love and is hell bent on protecting her turf, pleasing her politically well placed lover, avoiding her actor-writer husband, showcasing her Harvard-bound daughter, and taking full advantage of Annabelle, her initially enthralled, soon disillusioned assistant. An undergraduate steeped in Emily Dickinson, entangled in a weird affair, in debt to her therapist, and eager to learn from the master, Annabelle finds herself doing Z.'s housework, running dubious errands, and, in effect, writing Z.'s poems." Booklist

"What's sharpest about Weinstein's well-metered wit is the way she sinks down into this elite subculture. The whole shameful business has been presatirzed for decades, but Weinstein, a published poet herself, knows where all the bodies are buried." Christ Sci Monit

Weir, Alison

Innocent traitor; a novel of Lady Jane Grey. Ballantine Books 2007 c2006 402p $24.95

ISBN 0-345-49485-7   LC 2006-49860

"Lady Jane, known to history as the Nine Days Queen, is a tragic and appealing figure. Abused by her parents, this talented and intelligent girl was bullied into a hateful marriage and pushed into accepting the Crown after the death of King Edward VI. Edward's older sister, Princess Mary (later known as Bloody Mary, and for good reason), rightfully claimed the Crown as her own, and Jane was sent to the Tower of London and eventually executed. Weir tells the story of Jane's short life from multiple viewpoints, which might initially confuse readers unfamiliar with the history, but this is a small fault in an otherwise entertaining and moving novel." Libr J

The Lady Elizabeth; a novel. Ballantine Books 2008 480p $25

ISBN 978-0-345-49535-8; 0-345-49535-7

     LC 2008-284

A novel about the life of the young Elizabeth Tudor before she ascended to the throne. "From the time of her mother's death when she was three to her inheritance of the throne in her twenties, danger always came at Elizabeth from some corner. Early in her life, she was stripped of her title of princess; later, she had to defend her virtue from the roving eyes and hands of her stepfather; and, finally, she had to navigate the deadly waters between her Protestant faith and her sister's fanatical Catholicism. Several times Elizabeth barely escaped alive; hers was not a life that could be borne by the average person. Weir successfully depicts this extraordinary young woman who beat the odds to become one of the world's greatest rulers." Libr J

Weisgall, Deborah

The world before her. Houghton Mifflin 2008 278p $25

ISBN 978-0-618-74657-6; 0-618-74657-9

     LC 2008-4734

"Mary Ann Evans, known to the world as George Eliot, the author of such great works as Middlemarch, is in Venice in 1880, to spend her honeymoon with Johnnie Cross, an uxorious American banker. Mary Ann had a long, passionate affair with philosopher and critic George Lewes, who was married to another woman. The two lived together until Lewes' death in 1878. . . . The other story is of Caroline Edgar Spingold, who arrives in Venice exactly a century after Evans, in 1980, on a business trip with her husband, Malcolm. He is 'commerce,' taking care of the finances, while she is 'art,' capricious and impulsive. Her views on marriage are tainted by her father's long-ago desertion of her mother. Describing the stories of Mary Ann and Caroline in alternate chapters, Weisgall draws parallel portraits of marital dissatisfaction and the attraction of the fleeting past to nullify the dreariness of the present. Her writing is tender, drowning you in its drunken energy, with the city of Venice providing a tasteful backdrop." St. Petersburg Times

Welch, James, 1940-2003

The heartsong of Charging Elk; a novel. Doubleday 2000 440p $24.95

ISBN 0-385-49674-5

     * LC 99-58875

"As a young Oglala Sioux, Charging Elk saw the massacre of General Custer's forces at Little Big Horn. . . . Now in his early 20s and on a tour of Europe as part of Buffalo Bill Cody's 'Wild West show' in the 1890s, Charging Elk has become stranded in Marseille, France." Christ Sci Monit

Welch, James, 1940-2003—*Continued*

The author "estranges our vision. We have no choice but to feel, as we look through Charging Elk's eyes, what it is like to live in a no man's land forever." N Y Times Book Rev

The Indian lawyer. Norton 1990 349p
ISBN 0-393-02896-8

* LC 90-6894

"Sylvester Yellow Calf, the hero of this novel, has fought his way, despite the odds, to a top post in a prestigious Montana law firm and now is being wooed as a candidate for Congress by political power brokers. Sylvester, ex-basketball star and Stanford Law School graduate, recognizes that such a move could put him in a position to help his fellow Native Americans and at the same time to work for the preservation of the environment. While his responsibilities are all too clear to him, Yellow Calf hesitates, and, as he ponders his decision, he is drawn by a convict into a web that nearly strangles him." Choice

"The novel contains good, fast-paced action with succinct insight into our ordinary dilemmas." Nation

Welcome, John, 1914-

(ed) The Dick Francis treasury of great racing stories. See The Dick Francis treasury of great racing stories

(ed) The New treasury of great racing stories. See The New treasury of great racing stories

Weldon, Fay

Big girls don't cry. Atlantic Monthly Press 1998 345p $24
ISBN 0-87113-720-8   LC 98-35702
First published 1997 in the United Kingdom with title: Big women

This novel looks back "at the early days of feminism as experienced by four Londoners. In 1971 Layla, Zoe and Alice gather in Stephie's living room to engage in consciousness-raising while, in an upstairs bedroom, Stephie's husband, Hamish, deprograms a convert. The women, discover this sexual betrayal just as Zoe's abusive husband, Bull, arrives to save her soul from women's lib. Provoked by these outrages, the remaining three decide to establish Medusa, a publishing house devoted to women's works." Publ Wkly

"Just when Weldon's wit starts to sound like fingernails on a blackboard, she relents and reminds us that even in comedy, she's dead serious. . . . It's tempting to find the zany conclusion unsatisfying because it leaves no answers, but that's the privilege of smart satire." Christ Sci Monit

A hard time to be a father. St. Martin's Press 1999 242p $23.95
ISBN 1-58234-011-0

Contents: What the papers say; The ghost of potlatch past; Once in love in Oslo; GUP—or falling in love in Helsinki; Come on, everyone!; Percentage trust; Inside the whale—or, I don't know but I've been told; Move out: move on; New Year's Day; Inspector remorse; My mother said; A libation of blood; Pyroclastic flow; Spirits fly south; Stasi; A great antipodean scandal; New advances; Noisy into the night; A hard time to be a father

Weldon "is at her wry, risk-taking best in this broad collection of 19 stories. . . . In her signature style, Weldon peoples many of these pieces with women who wreak catastrophe in ways that thrill the misanthropic reader." Publ Wkly

The life and loves of a she-devil. Pantheon Bks. 1984 c1983 241p o.p.

* LC 84-7070

First published 1983 in the United Kingdom

"A fable about female power and powerlessness, telling the story of Ruth, an ugly woman married to a philandering man, who transforms herself by sheer strength of will into the image of her hated rival." Oxford Companion to 20th-Century Lit in Engl

Rhode Island blues. Atlantic Monthly Press 2000 325p $24
ISBN 0-87113-775-5   LC 00-38576

"Felicity Moore is an attractive, sexually active octogenarian grandmother who has decided to move into the Golden Bowl Complex for Creative Retirement. . . . Felicity's granddaughter, Sophia King, is a 34-year-old British film editor. . . . When Sophia comes to New England to help Felicity settle into the Golden Bowl, she learns that her grandmother had another daughter whom she gave up for adoption more than a half century earlier. While Sophia returns to London in search of her long-lost aunt, Felicity falls in love with a compulsive gambler and together they outsmart the evil and sadistic Nurse Dawn." Publ Wkly

"Weldon employs a merciless form of satire here; she also takes on favorite themes: love and the war between the sexes. But 'Rhode Island Blues'—is about more than that. Just how much more, in fact, is staggering. Here's a short list of topics covered: rape, adoption, prostitution, murder, romance between the elderly, compulsive gambling, family bonds, madness Hollywood, immigration and sadomasochism." N Y Time Book Rev

She may not leave. Atlantic Monthly Press 2006 c2005 284p $24
ISBN 0-8711-3942-1   LC 2005-7227

"In their mid-thirties—handsome, healthy, and well educated—literary agent Hattie and crusading journalist Martyn have been thrown off their game by the arrival of their infant daughter. While on maternity leave, Hattie feels particularly oppressed by the domestic routine. . . . She suggests they hire an au pair, but Martyn has serious qualms about the ethics of having a servant. However, once Martyn experiences the calming effect the Polish nanny has on his household—which allows him to sleep late and eat gourmet meals, not to mention witness demonstrations of her belly-dancing lessons—his political principles crumble, but so does his relationship with Hattie. Narrating the whole turn of events is Hattie's 72-year-old grandmother, Frances, a character who allows Weldon to describe the changing attitudes toward children and marriage over four generations. . . . Throwing in one final unexpected but delicious twist at the end, Weldon delivers another of her trademark takes on the domestic wars." Booklist

Worst fears; a novel. Atlantic Monthly Press 1996 200p o.p.   LC 95-52367

The protagonist of this novel is "Alexandra Ludd, a successful stage actress who is performing in Ibsen's *A Doll's House* when her husband, Ned, a theater critic,

Weldon, Fay—*Continued*

dies in their country house. Alexandra takes a leave of absence from the London production, only to find that her friends in the country all seem to be engaged in some kind of cover-up regarding the circumstances of Ned's death. It gradually becomes clear to Alexandra that her husband lived a very different and more promiscuous life than she'd ever suspected." Publ Wkly

Fay Weldon is the "quintessential anti-romance novelist and always will be. But she's filed down a few sharp edges in 'Worst Fears,' and that makes it one of her best novels yet." N Y Times Book Rev

Wellesley, Charles *See* Brontë, Charlotte, 1816-1855

Wellington, David

Monster Island; a zombie novel. Thunder's Mouth 2006 282p pa $13.95

ISBN 1-56025-850-0

In this first volume of a projected horror trilogy, "most of the world has fallen to the undead, with pockets of survivors clinging to a precarious existence. At the behest of the leader of the Free Women's Republic of Somaliland, a shipload of those makes the ludicrous trip from Africa to New York in a desperate quest for medicine. New York is a wasteland, and everything depends on a small, incredibly dedicated band of teenage girls, armed to the teeth, and native guide Dekalb, formerly a UN arms inspector. Also, in NYC there is Gary, a zombie who, completely unexpectedly, retains live human mental faculties. . . . There are many layers to this zombie apocalypse, and this book just gets things rolling." Booklist

Wells, H. G. (Herbert George), 1866-1946

The complete short stories of H. G. Wells. St. Martin's Press 1987 c1927 1038p $19.95

ISBN 0-312-15855-6   LC 87-27478

First published 1927 in the United Kingdom with title: The short stories of H. G. Wells

Short stories included are: The empire of the ants; A vision of judgment; The land ironclads; The beautiful suit; The door in the wall; The pearl of love; The country of the blind; The stolen bacillus; The flowering of the strange orchid; In the Avu observatory; The triumphs of a taxidermist; A deal in ostriches; Through a window; The temptation of Harringay; The flying man; The diamond maker; Æpyornis Island; The remarkable case of Davidson's eyes; The Lord of the Dynamos; The Hammerpond Park burglary; The moth; The treasure in the forest; The Plattner story; The Argonauts of the air; The story of the late Mr. Elvesham; In the abyss; The apple; Under the knife; The sea raiders; Pollock and the Porroh man; The red room; The cone; The purple pileus; The jilting of Jane; In the modern vein; A catastrophe; A slip under the microscope; The reconciliation; My first aeroplane; Little mother up the Morderberg; The story of the last trump; The grisly folk; The crystal egg; The star; A story of the stone age; A story of the days to come; The man who could work miracles; Filmer; The magic shop; The valley of spiders; The truth about Pyecraft; Mr. Skelmersdale in Fairyland; The inexperienced ghost;

Jimmy Goggles the god; The new accelerator; Mr. Ledbetter's vacation; The stolen body; Mr. Brisher's treasure; Miss Winchelsea's heart; A dream of Armageddon

A collection of 62 short stories and the complete work: The time machine, first published 1895

"A fat, heavy volume packed with humour, strangeness, horror and imaginative stimulus." Daily Telegraph

The first men in the moon
   In Wells, H. G. Seven famous novels

The food of the gods
   In Wells, H. G. Seven famous novels

In the days of the comet
   In Wells, H. G. Seven famous novels

The invisible man. Penguin 2005 xxiv, 161p pa $6

ISBN 0-14-143998-X
             *

First published 1897

"The story concerns the life and death of a scientist named Griffin who has gone mad. Having learned how to make himself invisible, Griffin begins to use his invisibility for nefarious purposes, including murder. When he is finally killed, his body becomes visible again." Merriam-Webster's Ency of Lit

   also in Wells, H. G. Seven famous novels

The island of Doctor Moreau; edited by Patrick Parrinder; with an introduction by Margaret Atwood and notes by Steven McLean. Penguin Books 2005 xxxiv, 139p (Penguin classics)

ISBN 0-14-144102-X
             *

First published 1896

This is "an evolutionary fantasy about a shipwrecked naturalist who becomes involved in an experiment to 'humanize' animals by surgery." Oxford Companion to Engl Lit. 6th edition

   also in Wells, H. G. Seven famous novels

The island of Dr. Moreau
   In Wells, H. G. Seven famous novels

Seven famous novels; with a preface by the author. Knopf 1934 860p o.p.

Contents: The time machine (1895); The island of Dr. Moreau (1896); The invisible man (1897); The war of the worlds (1898); The first men in the moon (1901); The food of the gods (1904); In the days of the comet (1906)

The time machine. Penguin 2005 xxviii, 104p pa $9

ISBN 0-14-143997-1
             *

First published 1895

"Wells advanced his social and political ideas in this narrative of a nameless Time Traveller who is hurtled into the year 802,701 by his elaborate ivory, crystal, and brass contraption. The world he finds is peopled by two races: the decadent Eloi, fluttery and useless, are dependent for food, clothing, and shelter on the simian subterranean Morlocks, who prey on them. The two races—whose names are borrowed from the Biblical Eli and Moloch—symbolize Wells's vision of the eventual result

Wells, H. G. (Herbert George), 1866-1946—
Continued
of unchecked capitalism: a neurasthenic upper class that
would eventually be devoured by a proletariat driven to
the depths." Merriam-Webster's Ency of Lit

> *also in* Wells, H. G. The complete short
> stories of H. G. Wells
>
> *also in* Wells, H. G. Seven famous novels

Tono-Bungay; edited by Patrick Parrinder; with
an introduction and notes by Edward Mendelson.
Penguin 2005 xxxiii, 414p pa $14
  ISBN 0-14-144111-9
  First published 1908
"The narrator is George Ponderevo, son of the housekeeper on a large estate, who is apprenticed to his uncle,
Edward Ponderevo, a small-town druggist. His fantastic
uncle soon moves to London and makes a fortune from
his quack medicine Tono-Bungay. George helps his uncle, ironically observes his rise in the world, and uses
some of his money to set himself up as an airplane designer. George resembles H. G. Wells himself—the son
of a housekeeper, apprenticed to a druggist, a socialist,
and a man with a vision of progress through properly
used science." Reader's Ency. 4th edition

The war of the worlds; illustrated by Edward
Gorey. New York Review Books [2005] c1960
251p il $16.95
  ISBN 1-59017-158-6
                                    * LC 2005-3693
  First published 1898
"The inhabitants of Mars, a loathsome though highly
organized race, invade England, and by their command
of superior weapons subdue and prey on the people." Baker. Guide to the Best Fic

In this novel the author "introduced the 'Alien' being
into the role which became a cliché—a monstrous invader of Earth, a competitor in a cosmic struggle for existence. Though the Martians were a ruthless and terrible
enemy, HGW was careful to point out that Man had
driven many animal species to extinction, and that human invaders of Tasmania had behaved no less callously
in exterminating their cousins." Sci Fic Ency

> *also in* Wells, H. G. Seven famous novels

Wells, Herbert George *See* Wells, H. G. (Herbert
George), 1866-1946

Wells, Ken

Crawfish mountain; a novel. Random House
2007 364p $25.95
  ISBN 978-0-375-50876-9; 0-375-50876-7
                                    LC 2007-5612
"When Justin Pitre inherited Crawfish Mountain, a
500-acre tract of beautiful bayou wetland, he vowed to
maintain it in its pristine condition. However, Tom Huff,
regional vice president of Standard of Texas Company, is determined to run a pipeline through the land, and
uses threats, intimidation, and political clout to get his
way. As Justin and his wife, Grace, plot a strategy to
save their land, which takes an unplanned turn toward revenge, some of Huff's activities-illegal dumping of toxic
waste, bribery of state officials, and plans for cutting a

shipping channel through the bayous-come to light." Libr
J

A "cautionary tale about the environment, set five
years before Hurricane Katrina. It's both a political satire
and a page-turning mystery. Like the best jambalaya, it's
liberally spiced. Readers can almost taste the boiled
crawfish and oyster po' boys with extra pickles and may-
onnaise (pronounced MY-Nez, by one character). Wells
. . . makes the most of Louisiana's legendary political
corruption and its roguish politicians." USA Today

Welsh, Irvine

Porno. Norton 2002 483p $24.95
  ISBN 0-393-05723-2   LC 2002-26362
  Sequel to: Trainspotting (1994)
"Things are looking up for Simon David Williamson
('Sick Boy'), who has inherited a pub in his native Edinburgh. He's also ready to break into the movies, specifically that branch identified as the 'adult entertainment industry'. . . . The big issue is whether Simon will meet
the psychotic Begbie, to whom he mails unsolicited gay
porn in jail." Libr J

This novel "signals, if not a return to form, then at
least a return to enthusiastic formlessness—to something
like the raw, jagged energy of old." N Y Times Book
Rev

Trainspotting. W.W. Norton 2002 343p $23.95
  ISBN 0-393-05724-0
  First published 1993 in the United Kingdom
This novel is set in a working class neighborhood in
Edinburgh. Narrator Mark Renton tells the story "of
young junkies in their 20s living on the dole, fending off
adulthood and trying to escape from a world of AIDS,
death and national despair." New Repub

Welsh, Louise

The cutting room. Canongate 2002 294p $24
  ISBN 1-8419-5280-X   LC 2002-437974
"Gay auctioneer Rilke agrees to pack up and sell off
an enormous quantity of high-quality goods in an inordi-
nately short amount of time, no questions asked. . . .
While clearing out the attic, he discovers a horrfying
packet of snuff pornography. Depite his own proclivities
for promiscuous, anonymous sex, he is haunted by the
woman portrayed in the photographs and determined to
discover whether the events depicted actually happened."
Booklist

"A remarkable first novel. Like all the best exponents
of the genre, Louise Welsh sets up her template and then
manipulates it, using the glamour of crime to examine
more humdrum kinds of suffering and loss. She piles on
atmosphere to produce a Glasgow that is predictably dark
and yet still plausible." N Y Times Book Rev

Welty, Eudora, 1909-2001

The collected stories of Eudora Welty. Harcourt
Brace Jovanovich 1980 622p hardcover o.p. pa
$16
  ISBN 0-15-118994-3; 0-15-618921-6 (pa)
                                    * LC 80-7947
Contents: Lily Daw and the three ladies; A piece of
news; Petrified man; The key; Keela, the outcast Indian
maiden; Why I live at the P.O.; The whistle; The hitch-

Welty, Eudora, 1909-2001—*Continued*

hikers; A memory; Clytie; Old Mr. Marblehall; Flowers for Marjorie; A curtain of green; A visit of charity; Death of a traveling salesman; Powerhouse; A worn path; First love; The wide net; A still moment; Asphodel; The winds; The purple hat; Livvie; At the landing; Shower of gold; June recital; Sir Rabbit; Moon Lake; The whole world knows; Music from Spain; The wanderers; No place for you, my love; The burning; The bride of the Innisfallen; Ladies in spring; Circe; Kin; Going to Naples; Where is the voice coming from?; The demonstrators

This volume contains four previously published collections: A curtain of green, and other stories; The wide net, and other stories; The golden apples and The bride of the Innisfallen, and other stories. Also included in this volume are two uncollected pieces: Where is the voice coming from? and The demonstrators.

Complete novels. Library of Am. 1998 1009p $35
ISBN 1-883011-54-X

* LC 97-46702
Contents: The robber bridegroom; Delta wedding; The Ponder heart; Losing battles; The optimist's daughter

Delta wedding; a novel. Harcourt Brace & Co. 1946 247p o.p.

*

A "portrait of a Southern plantation family in 1923. Set in the context of the wedding of one of the daughters, the novel explores the relationships among members of the Fairchild family, most of whom have been sheltered from any contact with the world outside the Mississippi Delta. Although they quarrel among themselves, they also unite against any threats to the family's status, honoring the belief in the family as a sacred and unchanging entity." Merriam-Webster's Ency of Lit

also in Welty, E. Complete novels

The golden apples
In Welty, E. The collected stories of Eudora Welty

Losing battles. Random House 1970 436p il o.p.
"At a large family gathering in Banner, Mississippi, the Renfro and Beecham families have assembled to celebrate Granny's ninetieth birthday. They are also celebrating Jack Renfro's return from the prison farm. As one might expect, the day is made up of reminiscences and recountings of earlier events, so that the novel actually spans many years. One of the key figures is Gloria, an orphan. She is frequently teased about being the daughter of another orphan, Rachel Sojourner, and of one of the Beecham boys who died in World War I. Gloria, who had married Jack just prior to his imprisonment, feels that they must get away from the clan, all of whom seem proud of their ignorance in spite of Miss Julia Mortimer's lifelong struggle to teach them something. It was a losing battle, probably even for Gloria." Shapiro. Fic for Youth. 3d edition

also in Welty, E. Complete novels

The optimist's daughter. Random House 1972 180p o.p.
"This novel is considered the high point of Welty's lengthy career. The strong character study examines 45-year-old Laurel McKelva Hand, who returns from Chica-

go to Mississippi, where her father is dying. She is forced to consider her complex and ambiguous emotions about her powerful and dynamic father, the impact of this relationship on her life, and her puzzlement at his late marriage to a coarse and shallow woman who is Laurel's own age." Shapiro. Fic for Youth. 3d edition

also in Welty, E. Complete novels

The Ponder heart; drawings by Joe Krush. Harcourt Brace & Co. 1954 156p il o.p.

*

"Cast as a monologue, [this comic novella] is rich with colloquial speech and descriptive imagery. The narrator of the story is Miss Edna Earle Ponder, one of the last living members of a once-prominent family, who manages the Beulah Hotel in Clay, Miss. She tells a traveling salesman the history of her family and fellow townsfolk." Merriam-Webster's Ency of Lit

also in Welty, E. Complete novels

The robber bridegroom; designed and illustrated by Barry Moser. Harcourt Brace Jovanovich 1987 c1942 134p il $19.95
ISBN 0-15-178318-7

* LC 87-21195
A reissue of the title first published 1942 by Doubleday
"A novelette combining fairy tale and ballad form, telling of the wooing of Rosamond, the daughter of a Mississippi planter, by a bandit chief." Oxford Companion to Am Lit. 6th edition
"Miss Welty uses the magic of metaphor and simile like a lyric poet, and writes with a limpid purity, and exquisite sense of descriptive coloring that gives a warm glow of beauty to a fantastic, and unfortunately sometimes tiresome story." Springfield Repub

also in Welty, E. Complete novels

Stories, essays & memoir; [selected and annotated by Richard Ford and Michael Kreyling] Library of Am. 1998 976p il $35
ISBN 1-88301-155-8   LC 97-46691

The wide net and other stories
In Welty, E. The collected stories of Eudora Welty

Wenner, Kate, 1947-

Dancing with Einstein; a novel; Kate Wenner. Scribner 2004 223p $24
ISBN 0-7432-5164-4   LC 2003-65681
"Marea Hoffman, now approaching 30, arrives in New York after years of backpacking around the world. She quickly locates an apartment in Greenwich Village, gets a night job in an organic bakery, and sets to work on unpacking the emotional baggage of her childhood. The daughter of a Princeton physicist, Marea harbors affectionate memories of her surrogate 'grandpa,' Albert Einstein. But her father's work on the hydrogen bomb alienated him from both the pacifist Einstein and Marea's mother, who was raised Quaker. Marea's parents were on the verge of divorce when her father died in a car accident. Determined to deal with her father's death, Marea signs on with four therapists: a Freudian analyst, a New Age Jungian, a feminist, and one, found by chance, with-

Wenner, Kate, 1947-—*Continued*
out any evident personal agenda." Libr J
"Despite the occasional awkward piece of dialogue,
Marea's tortured path to peace, stillness and purpose
rings true." Publ Wkly

Werfel, Franz

The forty days of Musa Dagh. Viking 1934
824p o.p.

          *

Original German edition, 1933; published in the United
Kingdom with title: The forty days
"Gabriel Bagradian returns to his ancestral village in
Syria, where he learns that the Turks are disarming the
Armenians and sending them into exile. Gabriel plans the
resistance to the Turks and directs the fortification of the
mountain Musa Dagh. The Turks are successfully re-
pulsed a number of times but at great cost in lives to the
Armenians on the mountain. On the fortieth day the rem-
nant of the Armenian force is rescued by the French."
Shapiro. Fic for Youth. 3d edition

The song of Bernadette; translated by Ludwig
Lewisohn. Viking 1942 575p o.p.

Original German edition, 1941
A slightly fictionalized version of "the life of Saint
Bernadette of Lourdes. While it is not exactly a religious
work, it is truly reverent in its approach to the inscrutable, the unfathomable, the divine. There is an engrossing
picture of emperor, bishops, priests, nuns, merchants and
artisans. A living pageant of the second Empire in
France." Ont Libr Rev

Wesley, Mary

Part of the furniture. Viking 1997 c1996 256p
o.p.   LC 96-46226
This novel is set in World War II England. "Seventeen-year-old Juno Marlowe has always worshiped the
rich young cousins who live next door, but they treat her
as though she were 'part of the furniture.' After losing
her virginity to them during a rough, crude night of sex,
she sees them off at the train station and is caught in an
air raid. Taking refuge with an astute stranger, she promises to deliver a letter to his family. And so she ends up
living on the estate of widower Robert Copplestone,
where she is treated with care and kindness. Forty years
Juno's senior, Robert is mortified when he realizes that
he is in love with her, but Juno soon forgets her childish
fixation on the cousins and talks Robert into marrying
her." Booklist
"Wesley's skill with character development and her
subtle, amusing dissection of that paramount British preoccupation, family background and breeding, endow this
novel with the charm of a comedy of manners and the
enduring appeal of a satisfying love story." Publ Wkly

Wesselmann, Debbie Lee, 1959-

Captivity. John F. Blair, Publisher 2008 295p
$22.95
   ISBN 978-089587-353-8; 0-89587-353-2
                      LC 2007-37816

"Primatologist Dana Armstrong is passionate about
making a difference in the lives of the animals living at
a South Carolina chimpanzee sanctuary. But a break-in
resulting in the escape of numerous chimpanzees forces
Dana to not only determine who was responsible for the
vandalism but also deal with her traumatic memories of
the past—for Dana is a survivor of a psychological experiment, raised as a child with a chimp named Annie.
She now faces opposition from the local community, political pressure from her university, and a ghost from her
past who is bent upon her destruction. . . . [The author
combines] a riveting plot with exciting characters to hold
you spellbound until the last page." Libr J

West, Dorothy, 1907-1998

The wedding. Doubleday 1995 240p hardcover
o.p. pa $12.95
   ISBN 0-385-47143-2; 0-385-47144-0 (pa)
                    * LC 94-27285
This novel is "set on Martha's Vineyard during the
1950s and focuses on the black bourgeois community
known as the Oval. Dr. Clark Coles and his wife, Cor-
rine, highly respected Ovalites, are preparing for the
wedding of their youngest daughter, Shelby, who, much
to their consternation, is marrying a white jazz musician.
Lute McNeil, a compulsive womanizer who has recently
made a fortune in the furniture business, is determined to
stop Shelby's wedding; he is confident that he can convince Shelby to marry him, which would bring him the
social acceptance he has always craved." Booklist
"Through the ancestral histories of the Coles family,
West . . . subtly reveals the ways in which color can
burden and codify behavior. The author makes her points
with a delicate hand, maneuvering with confidence and
ease through a sometimes incendiary subject." Publ Wkly

West, Jessamyn, 1902-1984

Collected stories of Jessamyn West. Harcourt
Brace Jovanovich 1986 480p o.p.
                      LC 86-12031
Contents: Probably Shakespeare; A time of learning;
The mysteries of life in an orderly manner; Love, death,
and the ladies' drill team; Homecoming; The battle of
the suits; Tom Wolfe's my name; Learn to say good-bye;
A little collar for the monkey; Public-address system;
Foot-shaped shoes; Horace Chooney, M.D.; The linden
trees; Breach of promise; The singing lesson; The Calla
Lilly Cleaners & Dyers; The wake; Grand opening; Alo-
ha, farewell to thee; Reverdy; Up a tree; There ought to
be a judge; Gallup Poll; Alive and real; I'll ask him to
come sooner; Hunting for hoot owls; Crimson Ramblers
of the world, farewell; Night piece for Julia; Live life
deeply; Mother's Day; The heavy stone; 99.6; The day
of the hawk; Like visitant of air; The condemned librarian; Child of the century; Flow gently, sweet aspirin; The
second (or perhaps third) time round

The friendly persuasion. Harcourt 1945 214p
hardcover o.p. pa $13
   ISBN 0-15-133605-9; 0-15-602909-X (pa)
                             *
"The Birdwell family of Indiana led a quiet life until
the Civil War came into their lives. They were Quakers
and tried to live according to the teachings of William

West, Jessamyn, 1902-1984—*Continued*

Penn. Jess Birdwell, a nurseryman, loved a fast horse as well as his trees and the people he knew. Eliza, his wife, was a Quaker minister and a gentle, albeit strict, soul. When the war reached Indiana, Josh, the oldest son, was torn between his Quaker upbringing and his belief in the rightness of the Union cause; Mattie was at that difficult age between childhood and womanhood; and Little Jess, the youngest, ran into trouble with Eliza's geese. This is a wonderful family chronicle, with the laughter, tears, and tenderness that can be found in many families." Shapiro. Fic for Youth. 3d edition

West, Mary Jessamyn *See* West, Jessamyn, 1902-1984

West, Morris L., 1916-1999

The clowns of God; [by] Morris West. St. Martin's Press 1990 c1981 370p $19.95

ISBN 0-312-04459-3

* LC 89-70344

A reissue of the title first published 1981 by Morrow

This novel takes place in the last decade of the 20th century. As the story opens, "Jean Marie Barette, lately Pope, has been forced into abdication because the cardinals don't know how else to cope with his apocalyptic vision of the approaching end of the world and the second coming of Jesus Christ. What follows [concerns his efforts] . . . to find a way to proclaim his vision without sending his cherished world into a tailspin of chaos and hysteria." Christ Sci Monit

"The fugitive ex-pope posits all the fearful questions about life that have perplexed us since Hiroshima. West's ultimate answers will disturb some and be dismissed by others, but no one will be left unmoved. The sheer power of his prose and his keen understanding of human nature make this novel a stunning accomplishment." Libr J

Followed by Lazarus

The devil's advocate. Morrow 1959 319p o.p.

In this novel "the plot concerns a British Monsignor who investigates the petition for canonization of a man who died before a partisan firing squad in Calabria during World War II. As the investigation progresses, he learns a great deal about the man, his family, the village in which he lived and, especially, about himself." Publ Wkly

"The characters all are firmly, brightly established. The writing, without fanciness or flourish, goes along with a fine, steady drive. There are no profound insights, no remarkable illuminations. But there is an engrossing story, expertly told, about a set of fascinating people whose lives are viewed as meaningful." Chicago Sunday Trib

Lazarus; [by] Morris West. St. Martin's Press 1990 293p o.p.   LC 89-77919

Concluding volume of the author's Vatican trilogy. "Pope Leo XIV faces death from heart disease as the novel opens and is targeted for assassination by a fundamentalist group, but he realizes a need for tolerance and begins to undo the very policies that have made him a reactionary." Smith. Cloak and Dagger Fic

"A tense and exciting thriller, Lazarus also explores world crises and theological politics quite as fascinating to non-Catholics as to Catholics. . . . While the book can be read as a complement to the other two novels, it stands alone as a superb, absorbing novel." Libr J

Masterclass; [by] Morris West. St. Martin's Press 1991 330p o.p.   LC 90-28090

Max Mather "served as the paleographer (manuscript archivist) for a well-known Italian family. But when he comes into possession of two Raphael originals, Max becomes incredibly wily, both about the effect his discovery will have on the international art world and about his prospects for cashing in. Big-time collectors, dealers, and auctioneers are drawn into Mather's game, with the players flitting easily from New York to Zurich to Florence to Amsterdam and back again. Amid all the artsy oneupmanship, West gives us a subplot involving the murder of a Manhattan painter whose brilliance extended from her way with palette and brush to kinky, omnivorous sex. Solid plotting and interesting characters make this flashy novel of intrigue fully enjoyable." Booklist

The shoes of the fisherman; a novel. Morrow 1963 374p o.p.

In this first title in the author's Vatican trilogy, "a humble Ukrainian pope finds himself the central negotiator in an attempt to prevent the United States and the Soviet Union from starting World War III. During the negotiations, the pope must confront the Russian who once tortured him. The work, a popular and critical success, demonstrates West's concern with modern man's inability to communicate with his brother." McCormick and Fletcher. Spy Fic

Followed by The clowns of God

West, Nathanael, 1903-1940

A cool million
In West, N. Novels and other writings

The day of the locust
In West, N. Miss Lonelyhearts & The day of the locust
In West, N. Novels and other writings

The dream life of Balso Snell
In West, N. Novels and other writings

Miss Lonelyhearts. Liveright 1933 213p o.p.
                                                                      *

"The story of a man who writes an 'advice to the lovelorn' column, the theme of the book is the loneliness of the individual in modern society. The hero tries to live the role of omniscient counselor he has assumed for the paper, but his attempts to reach out to suffering humanity are twisted by circumstances, and he is finally murdered by a man he has tried to help." Reader's Ency. 4th edition

also in West, N. Miss Lonelyhearts & The day of the locust
also in West, N. Novels and other writings

Miss Lonelyhearts & The day of the locust. Modern Lib. 1998 289p $15.50

ISBN 0-679-60278-X   LC 97-39828

Combined edition of two titles first published 1933 and 1939 respectively. The day of the locust is about Hollywood and the misfits who flock to it in search of the American dream

West, Nathanael, 1903-1940—*Continued*

Novels and other writings. Library of Am. 1997 829p $35

ISBN 1-88301-128-0   LC 96-49007

"Each of West's novels is distinct in style and theme. In the Dada-inspired The Dream Life of Balso Snell (1931), he freely mixes high-flown literary and religious allusions with erotic and scatological humor. Miss Lonelyhearts (1933) presents, in a series of grotesque, starkly etched episodes, the spiritual breakdown of a newspaper columnist overwhelmed by his readers' suffering. By contrast, A Cool Million (1934) reduces the eternal optimism of Horatio Alger's novels to a brutal, cartoonish farce. In his last work, The Day of the Locust (1939), West renders with hallucinatory precision the reverse side of the Hollywood dream, as he choreographs a cast of failures, has-beens, and deluded glamourseekers in what becomes an apocalyptic dance of death. Also included is a generous sampling of West's other surviving work, ranging from freewheeling improvisations and grotesque comic tales to more mainstream work written with Hollywood or Broadway in mind." Publisher's note

West, Paul, 1930-

Lord Byron's doctor; a novel. Doubleday 1989 277p

ISBN 0-385-26129-2

        * LC 89-7735

"Lord Byron's doctor was John Polidori, whom he hired as a traveling companion on his trip to the Continent in 1816. West's novel recreates the diary that Polidori had been commissioned to keep but that never saw print." Libr J

"Through Polidori, West compiles a lurid case history on the cruelty of genius. Shelley may have been 'polite to God and pious towards women,' but Byron was arrogant about both. His disdain toward lesser literary figures was godlike, and his venery demonic. . . . Romanticism and egoism normally go hand in hand. Here they are passionately entwined. Rocking and rolling in Byron's carriage, sailing through storms, discussing the uses of opium or exchanging ghost stories at the Villa Diodati, the group is principally concerned with who will be favored by the muse." Time

Love's mansion. Random House 1992 339p

ISBN 0-394-58734-0

        * LC 92-6804

"Set in England, the story moves from the late Victorian era to mid-century, telling the story of two lovers, Harry and Hilly, whose lives are irrevocably changed by World War I. Tantalizingly, the novel's point of view is that of the couple's son, who must look back in time, guessing at motives, imagining dialog, intuiting emotions." Libr J

"As Mr. West has made vividly clear, we have much to learn from the Moxons and their changing world. It is perhaps unfashionable to write about the pain and transformations that characterize the love of a long-married couple, but Mr. West is concerned with something much more personal than literary fashion. At times the astounding 'diligence of human memory' takes off in his book and produces passages that are close to poetry, almost always when his style is at its least extended and inclusive." N Y Times Book Rev

O.K.; the corral, the Earps, and Doc Holliday: a novel. Scribner 2000 302p $24

ISBN 0-684-84865-1   LC 99-89924

"On his way from Georgia to the healthier climate of Colorado, consumptive dentist Dr. John Henry Holliday visits Dallas, East Las Vegas and Dodge, gradually abandoning dentistry as he discovers his prowess as a gunfighter and his Keatsian obsession with death. Along the way, he saves the life of Wyatt Earp, marshal and gunman. The two become fast friends and eventually land in Tombstone, Ariz., where they take part in the almost mythical 1881 gunfight between the Clanton Gang and the Earp family at the O.K. Corral." Publ Wkly

West "cares more about character and color than action, and his prose can at times be ponderous. But although some details, like those of Doc's ravaging consumption, require a strong stomach, they serve to depict Holliday as a moving and complex character." N Y Times Book Rev

Sporting with Amaryllis. Overlook Press 1996 158p $19.95

ISBN 0-87951-666-6   LC 96-22766

"In this novel, West presents a fictive portrait of the poet John Milton as a brilliant, virginal, and very curious 17-year-old. On holiday from Cambridge, Milton is picked up on a bustling London street by a dark-skinned [woman] . . . who turns out to be his muse. Obsessed with Virgil, he calls her Amaryllis . . . and embarks on a magical journey that lasts a day but shapes a lifetime." Booklist

"Readers who accept unreservedly Milton's solemn, extravagant sense of his destiny are not likely to be amused by West's conception of how muse Amaryllis worked over youth Milton. West makes the muse anything but 'thankless.' But one doesn't have to swallow a word of West's flamboyant writing to find it piquant. It's pleasanter and more comfortable, certainly, to imagine Milton exuberantly enjoying, and benefiting from, fleshly indulgence than to endure seeing him cruelly cartooned as a bigoted thug and assassin." American Scholar

West, Dame Rebecca, 1892-1983

The birds fall down. Viking 1966 435p o.p.

        LC 67-10214

In this novel "Count Diakonov, an exiled aristocrat, and Chubinov, an informant and revolutionary, are the central characters. Their long dialogue explores the mystique of pre-Revolutionary Russia and provides a philosophical basis for a complex story of intrigue and treason." Cincinnati Public Libr

"This is a great work of literature. . . . Rebecca West was fascinated by espionage and from her knowledge of Russian emigres she created a comprehensive picture of their preoccupations and torments at the turn of the century." McCormick and Fletcher. Spy Fic

West, V. Sackville- *See* Sackville-West, V. (Victoria), 1892-1962

Westerfeld, Scott

The killing of worlds. TOR Bks. 2003 336p

ISBN 0-7653-0850-9   LC 2003-56304

Westerfeld, Scott—*Continued*
"A Tom Doherty Associates book"
Sequel to The risen empire
"Captain Laurent Zai demonstrates his strategic cleverness as well as an unusual amount of luck, when he unexpectedly defeats the Rix ship he was sent to destroy—
an assignment intended to be a suicide mission. Meanwhile, in the imperial senate, Nara Oxham walks a fine
line between treason and her party's agenda as she fights
the emperor himself. . . . [This is] a rip-roaring space
opera, with its strength residing in the characters, all of
them involved in believable dilemmas." Booklist

The risen empire. TOR Bks. 2003 304p $24.95
ISBN 0-7653-0555-0   LC 2002-42952
"A Tom Doherty Associates book"
"In an interstellar empire of 80 human worlds, ruled
by an emperor who lets selected humans cheat death,
tensions between most humans and the resurrected elite,
aka the Risen, are increasing. The Rix, a cult of cyborgs
who worship compound AI minds, hunger to liberate the
empire's worlds from mere human control. When a Rix
raiding party captures the emperor's sister, Capt. Laurent
Zai of the Imperial Navy must save her." Publ Wkly
"Westerfeld's speculations about the rise and fall of
civilizations are appealingly quirky . . . and his action
scenes have a breathless realism that does not gloss over
the bloody nature of combat. Perhaps most important, his
moral calculus never lapses into Q.E.D. As the narrative
jumps from intimate glimpses of the Empire to the Rix
Cult and back again, we grow less and less clear about
whom we are rooting for." N Y Times Book Rev

Westheimer, David, 1917-2005

Von Ryan's Express. Doubleday 1964 327p o.p.
                                                    *
"Colonel Joseph Ryan is shot down over Italy and is
sent to a prisoner-of-war camp, where he imposes military discipline upon the other prisoners. After Italy's surrender, when the prisoners are put on a train for Germany, Ryan plans a daring takeover of the train and gets
the men to Switzerland." Shapiro. Fic for Youth. 2d edition
Followed by Von Ryan's return (1980)

Westlake, Donald E.
*For works written by this author under other
names see* Stark, Richard

The ax. Mysterious Press 1997 273p o.p.
                                       * LC 96-52068
This novel "takes a familiar plight—Burke Devore, a
middle-level executive at a paper company, has been
downsized out of what he had imagined was a secure
lifetime job—and gives it a terrifying twist. Not content
quietly to abandon his decently prosperous existence,
Devore searches out the ideal job at the ideal company
and then identifies a half-dozen unemployed potential rivals for the spot and sets out to murder them one by
one." Publ Wkly
"As novels go, 'The Ax' is pretty much flawless, with
a surprise ending that will unplug your expectations.
Burke Devore is American Man at the millennium—as
emblematic of his time as George F. Babbitt and Holden
Caulfield and Capt. John Yossarian were of theirs. Westlake has written a remarkable book. If you can't relate
to it, be thankful." N Y Times Book Rev

Baby, would I lie?; a romance of the Ozarks.
Mysterious Press 1994 291p o.p.
                                             LC 93-40485
This comic mystery, featuring characters from the author's Trust me on this, "is set in 'the new Nashville':
Branson, Missouri. Singer Ray Jones is accused of one
murder and then of a second. Out on bail, he continues
to entertain in this theater. Meanwhile, an army of troops
from the sleazy tabloid *Weekly Galaxy* descends to bug
offices, lie, infiltrate, and do anything else necessary to
get some sort of story on the upcoming trial. Also arriving are reporters Sara and Jack, lovers and representatives of a trendy New York magazine called *Trend: The
Magazine for the Way We Live This Instant.* The action
is jet-fast, and the satiric commentary on country western
stars and fans is wonderfully wicked." Libr J

Bad news; by Donald Westlake. Mysterious
Press 2001 342p $30
ISBN 0-89296-717-X   LC 00-45592
In this comic caper "Andy Kelp, Tiny Bulcher and the
Murches (Stan and Mom) join Dortmunder in horning in
on another crew's scam—cheating two Native American
tribes out of one-third of the take from a lucrative Indian
casino in upstate New York. Fitzroy Guilderpost, mastermind of the con . . . has enlisted Little Feather Redcorn,
a Las Vegas card dealer and showgirl, to pose as the last
living member of an extinct tribe with a claim to the casino." Publ Wkly
"Westlake has a genius for comic strategy, and the
complications he devises when the casino operators initiate a counterplot to discredit Little Feather have a lunatic
brilliance worthy of Abbott and Costello. But Westlake
is also a card with characters, and he flashes that talent
to terrific effect here." N Y Times Book Rev

Bank shot. Simon & Schuster 1972 224p o.p.
                                                    *
In this novel "criminal mastermind Dortmunder . . .
plans to rob a Long Island suburban bank by stealing the
whole bank—a mobile trailer home being used temporarily while the new bank building is under construction.
Dortmunder's cohorts include Victor, a former FBI agent
ousted because he thought the FBI ought to have a secret
hand-shake; Herman X, a black militant lock expert; and
a female cab driver who wears a neck brace while trying
to collect a phoney insurance claim." Booklist
It is Westlake's "triumph that whereas on one hand the
reader knows he simply can't take the characters and situations seriously, those characters are so deftly drawn
that they are eminently believable." N Y Times Book
Rev

Don't ask. Mysterious Press 1993 327p $18.95
ISBN 0-89296-469-3   LC 92-53721
In this novel John Dormunder "and his cohorts agree
to steal a religious relic, the femur of a thirteenth-century
saint, that is a bone of contention between two fledgling
Eastern European countries. Possession of the bone will
lead to a seat in the United Nations." Booklist
"If the plot is of no great concern, it is the effortlessness, wit, and sheer good-heartedness of the telling that
make 'Don't Ask' such a consistent delight." N Y Times
Book Rev

Drowned hopes. Mysterious Press 1990 422p
ISBN 0-89296-178-3   LC 89-35859

Westlake, Donald E.—*Continued*

In this "comedy-mystery, ex-con John Dortmunder and his benevolent criminal cohorts are continuously frustrated in their attempts to recover $700,000 in stolen money from a 50-foot-deep reservoir in upper New York State." Booklist

Get real. Grand Central Publishing 2009 278p $23.99

ISBN 978-0-446-17860-0; 0-446-17860-8

LC 2008-933234

"When Dortmunder and his associates—okay, his criminal gang—are offered a role on a reality show dramatizing their exploits, they initially think it's a terrible idea. However, they soon see it as an opportunity to aid in their usual criminal pursuits. While the producers of their show believe that the group is staging a smalltime robbery, they're actually working on a way to find what they believe is a large amount of money being housed by the production company." Libr J

"A rollicking crime caper that pulls the pants right off the reality TV industry." N Y Times Book Rev

Good behavior. Mysterious Press 1985 244p

ISBN 0-89296-240-2

LC 85-43178

"John Archibald Dortmunder runs across several Manhattan rooftops after trying to pull a break-in. He ends up on the roof of a building in a newly trendy but unsettled neighborhood, then falls through a skylight into a covey of cloistered nuns, who see the thief as an answer to their prayers." Booklist

The author "manages to create characters who are a curious mixture of stereotypes and archetypes. If he is a master of the comic crime caper, and he is, he also does what the best comic writers throughout history have done—make a comment on society." N Y Times Book Rev

The hook. Mysterious Press 2000 280p $30

ISBN 0-89296-588-6

LC 99-36273

"Frustrated by what he sees as outrageous monetary demands from his ex-wife, successful author Bryce Proctorr hires an old acquaintance, Wayne Prentice, to kill her. In a variation on the murder-for-hire theme, Proctorr offers Prentice, also a struggling author, both money and the opportunity to publish under his name. While the arrangement seems ideal for both parties, it soon becomes evident that such is not the case." Libr J

"Westlake salts the stew with lots of fascinating publishing shoptalk, and his portrayal of the psychological unraveling of a writer is made all the more chilling by the quiet realism of its presentation. A fine thriller." Booklist

The hot rock. Simon & Schuster 1970 249p o.p.

*

"The hot rock is the Balambo Emerald, part of an African exhibit at the New York Coliseum, owned by Akinzi, and coveted by the breakaway state of Talabwo. Major Iko of Talabwo selects John Dortmunder as the mastermind for the heist. But lifting the stone from the Coliseum is only the first caper for Dortmunder's carefully chosen crew." Libr J

This novel "comes awesomely close to the ultimate in comic, big-caper novels; it's . . . filled with mocking style and action and imagination." N Y Times Book Rev

Money for nothing. Mysterious Press 2003 294p $24.95

ISBN 0-89296-787-0

LC 2002-35888

"New York advertising executive Josh Redmont finds himself in the middle of an espionage drama, cast as the hero but utterly unprepared for the role. Seven years earlier, Redmont began receiving $1,000 checks, issued by 'United States Agent'; after trying unsuccessfully to track down the source of the checks, Redmont began depositing them and has been doing so ever since. His 'found money,' however, comes with very big strings, as Josh learns when he is approached by an unassuming-looking man who announces, 'I am from United States Agent. You are now active.'" Booklist

"Although Westlake has written funnier books and his characters could use more dimension, 'Money for Nothing' has all of his trademarks: an ample supply of silliness and suspense wrapped up in a wacky plot." N Y Times Book Rev

Put a lid on it. Mysterious Press 2002 247p $23.95

ISBN 0-89296-718-8

LC 2001-51435

Francis Meehan "is in federal prison for hijacking a mail truck he thought contained computer chips. A presidential reelection official offers him a pardon with a Watergate-type scheme: Meehan must steal a video that, if made public, may prevent the president's reelection." Publ Wkly

This is a "crime caper that also gets some nice digs in as political satire. . . . Although Meehan isn't quite as ingenious a thief as some of Westlake's other criminal protagonists, he's a born philosopher." N Y Times Book Rev

The road to ruin. Mysterious Press 2004 342p $25

ISBN 0-89296-801-X

LC 2003-65007

In this Dortmunder caper the "conspicuous target of larcenous intent is one Monroe Hall, the broadly drawn, babyish CEO and chief perpetrator of an Enron-like financial debacle, which has made him a pariah to friends and potential employees but still rich in funds and enemies. When a disgruntled former chauffeur hires Dortmunder and his crew to steal Hall's classic-car collection for the insurance, together with all the swag they can haul, our clumsy confederation of bandits decides to sidestep the estate's elaborate security system by hiring themselves on as staff, with rumpled second-story man Dortmunder in the unlikely role of butler." Booklist

"Ingenuity fuels the plot, but what puts the match to the comedy is the moral outrage of the furiously funny characters." N Y Times Book Rev

Smoke. Mysterious Press 1995 454p

ISBN 0-89296-534-7

LC 94-48254

"Freddie Noon is a sharp, likable burglar whose mistake is to break into the offices of two doctors doing socalled research for the Tobacco Institute. Catching him, they make him a human guinea pig for one of their formulas, and—meet disappearing Freddie. Naturally, his life as a burglar gets much easier, but his girlfriend, Peg, isn't too comfortable with an invisible lover." Publ Wkly

"Though Mr. Westlake is a virtuoso plotter, the point of his books, here as ever, is to be found in the interstices. Wicked one-liners and testy miniature monologues about whatever happens to be on the author's mind are

Westlake, Donald E.—*Continued*

scattered generously throughout. The implications of invisibility are played for laughs with near-arrogant skill." N Y Times Book Rev

Thieves' dozen. Mysterious Press 2004 183p pa $12.95

ISBN 0-446-69302-2 (pa)   LC 2003-70612

Contents: Ask a silly question; Horse laugh; Too many crooks; A midsummer's daydream; The Dortmunder workout; Party animal; Give till it hurts; Jumble sale; Now what; Art and craft; Fugue for felons

A collection of Dortmunder stories. "The swift succession of heists, getaways, scrapes, and screwups gathered in Thieves' Dozen epitomizes the venal joys of the comic caper. . . . The short-story form is well suited to Westlake's sly shenanigans, and he even finds room for snippets of the Runyonesque repartee that gives this inspired nonsense just the right touch of absurd panache." Booklist

Trust me on this. Mysterious Press 1988 293p o.p.   LC 87-22098

"As a young and comely reporter is driving down that highway on route to reporting for her new job at the 'Weekly [Galaxy]' she finds a bloody corpse hanging half-out of a Buick Riviera. When she is assigned to her new editor, a driven personality, as are all who are employed at this paper, she tells him about the corpse on the road thinking he will assign her to the story. But this kind of story is not what interests that kind of paper—the corpse is probably a nobody, the car he was in was surely a nothing. But Sara Joslyn is haunted by what she saw even though she hasn't the time or freedom to look into the matter further." West Coast Rev Books

"In between stories about space battles, 100-year-old twins, dead country music stars and bizarre medical happenings, Mr. Westlake has sandwiched a nice romance and a fairish murder mystery." N Y Times Book Rev

Watch your back. Mysterious Press 2005 310p $24.95

ISBN 0-89296-802-8   LC 2004-61064

"Arnie Albright, a fence so obnoxious his family intervened and sent him to Club Med in hopes he'd become more likable, has returned from the resort minimally improved, but having met the man of his dreams Preston Fareweather, a millionaire who's as comically distasteful as Arnie and who, more importantly, plans to be away from his art-filled New York penthouse indefinitely, on the run from hordes of furious ex-wives. Albright calls in Dortmunder and his pals to take advantage of Fareweather's absence. . . . Events unfold in a delicious sequence, and every step is complemented by great writing." Publ Wkly

What's so funny? Warner 2007 359p $24.99

ISBN 9780446582407; 0-446-58240-9

"Perennially star-crossed thief John Dortmunder is blackmailed by Johnny Eppick, a retired New York City cop. After careful study, Eppick has concluded that Dortmunder is the finest thief not already in jail. So, unless Dortmunder steals an 800-pound gold-and-jewel-encrusted chess set intended for Russia's last czar, he's off to prison again. But the job, in Dortmunder's very professional opinion, is impossible. The chess set is in the basement vault of a Manhattan bank building, and

it's been there—safe—for 60 years." Booklist

This caper has "an ending so laden with irony it almost has you thinking that crime doesn't pay. But of course it does pay, in those laughs that land on every page." N Y Times Book Rev

What's the worst that could happen? Mysterious Press 1996 373p o.p.   LC 96-12770

"In the midst of burglarizing a Long Island mansion, Dortmunder is caught by billionaire Fairbanks, who claims to the police that Dortmunder's lucky ring (given to Dortmunder by his girlfriend, May) actually belongs to him. Unluckily for Fairbanks, he has robbed the wrong man. Determined to get the ring back, Dortmunder enlists his old cronies in pursuing Fairbanks from Washington's notorious Watergate . . . to a glitzy Las Vegas casino where Dortmunder exacts a satisfying vengeance." Libr J

"Although the gang's dirty tricks are wonderfully ingenious, the characters deliver the real razzle-dazzle. A grandiose guy like Max is cut to order for Mr. Westlake's droll comic style, which reflects a kind of gleeful horror at the schlocky esthetics of the rich and the morally damned." N Y Times Book Rev

Westmacott, Mary, 1890-1976

See also Christie, Agatha, 1890-1976

Westward; a fictional history of the American West: 28 original stories celebrating the 50th anniversary of the Western Writers of America; edited by Dale L. Walker. Forge 2003 432p $25.95

ISBN 0-7653-0451-1   LC 2002-45481

"A Tom Doherty Assiates book"

Contents: First horse, by Coldsmith, D.; Encounter on Horse-Killed Creek, by Gulick, B.; York's story, by Walker, D. L.; Melodies the song dogs sing, by Blevins, W.; Gabe and the doctor, by House, R. C.; A man alone, by Breen, J. V.; Jonas Crag, by Jakes, J.; Inquest in Zion, by Blum, I. B.; Dead Man's Hollow, by Reasoner, J.; The hundred day men, by Black M.;Leaving Paradise, by Carroll, L.; Miss Libbie tells all, by Salzer, S. K.; How I happened to put on the blue, by Carney, O.; The stand, by Braun, M.; The square reporter, by Wheeler, R. S.; Betrayal, by Sandifer, L.; Thirty rangers, by Smith, C.; The whispering, by Graebner, J. E.; The fevers, by Eckhardt, C. F.; I killed King Fisher, by Froh, R.; Noah, by Mehok, E. L.; The big die-up, by Smith, T. D.; Do the dark dance, by Knight, A. W.; Letters to the stove, by Long, E.; East breeze, by Aadland, D.; Big Tim Magoon and the wild west, by Estleman, L. D.; The true facts about the death of Wes Hardin, by Crider, B.

"The collection reveals both the vitality and the diversity of the western genre as well as the enduring appeal of the short story." Booklist

Wharton, Edith, 1862-1937

The age of innocence. D. Appleton & Co. 1920 364p o.p.

New York City in the 1870s "was a place of tight social stratification with rituals for everything from romance to etiquette at the opera. The young attorney

Wharton, Edith, 1862-1937—*Continued*
Newland Archer was engaged to lovely, socially acceptable May Welland. He faced the power of family and social mores when he became attracted to May's bohemian
cousin, Ellen." Shapiro. Fic for Youth. 3d edition

   also in Wharton, E. New York novels
     p689-958
   also in Wharton, E. Novels

A backward glance
In Wharton, E. Novellas and other writings

The children. Scribner 282p $25
   ISBN 0-684-18453-2
First published 1928 by D. Appleton & Co.
   Standing at the rail of the liner, Martin Boyne sur-
veyed his fellow-passengers in the act of coming aboard.
'Not a soul I shall want to speak to—as usual!' was his
comment. Then he saw Judy Wheater carrying a fat, rosy
baby up the gang plank and he changed his mind. Judy
was only sixteen, but there was nothing inexperienced in
the way she herded her troupe of brothers and sisters and
'steps' over to Europe while her father and mother
played at divorce and remarriage. For a whole summer,
Martin, old bachelor that he was, joined forces with Judy
in her gallant attempt to keep her flock together

Collected stories, 1891-1910; [Maureen Howard
selected the contents and wrote the notes for this
volume] Library of Am. 2001 928p $35
   ISBN 1-88301-193-0   LC 00-57596
   Contents: Mrs. Manstey's view; The fulness of life;
The lamp of psyche; The valley of childish things, and
other emblems; The muse's tragedy; A journey; The pelican; Souls belated; The twilight of the God; A cup of
cold water; The touchstone; The Duchess at prayer; The
angel at the grave; The recovery; The Rembrandt; The
moving finger; Sanctuary; The descent of man; The mission of Jane; The other two; The reckoning; Expiation;
The lady's maid's bell; The house of the dead hand; The
introducers; The hermit and the wild woman; The last asset; The pretext; The pot-boiler; The best man; His father's son; The daunt Diana; The debt; Full circle; The
legend; The eyes

Collected stories, 1911-1937; edited by Maureen
Howard. Library of Am. 2001 848p $35
   ISBN 1-88301-194-9   LC 00-57595
   Contents: Xingu; Coming home; Autres temps . . .;
Kerfol; The long run; The triumph of night; Bunner sis-
ters; Writing a war story; The Marne [novelette]; Miss
Mary Pask; The young gentlemen; Bewitched; The seed
of the faith; Velvet ear-pads; Atrophy; A bottle of
Perrier; After Holbein; Mr. Jones; Her son; The day of
the funeral; A glimpse; Joy in the house; Charm incorpo-
rated; Pomegranate seed; Confession; Roman fever; The
looking-glass; Duration; All souls'

The custom of the country. Scribner 594p $55
   ISBN 0-684-14655-X
   "Hudson River editions"
First published 1913
   "The story of Undine Spragg, a young woman with social aspirations who convinces her nouveau riche parents
to leave the Midwest and settle in New York. There she
captures and marries a young man from New York's
high society. This and each subsequent relationship she

engineers prove unsatisfactory, chiefly because of her
greed and great ambition." Merriam-Webster's Ency of
Lit

   also in Wharton, E. New York novels
     p325-688
   also in Wharton, E. Novels

Ethan Frome. Scribner 1911 195p pa $13
hardcover o.p.
   ISBN 0-684-82591-0
                                            *
   This is "an ironic tragedy of love, frustration, jealousy,
and sacrifice. The scene is a New England village, where
Ethan barely makes a living out of a stony farm and is
at odds with his wife Zeena (short for Zenobia), a whin-
ing hypochondriac. Mattie, a cousin of Zeena's comes to
live with them, and love develops between her and
Ethan. They try to end their impossible lives by steering
a bobsled into a tree; instead ending up crippled and tied
for the rest of their unhappy time on earth to Zeena and
the barren farm. Zeena, however, is transformed into a
devoted nurse and Mattie becomes the nagging invalid."
Benet's Reader's Ency of Am Lit

   also in Wharton, E. Novellas and other
     writings

False dawn
In Wharton, E. Novellas and other writings

The house of mirth. Scribner 329p $50
   ISBN 0-684-14658-4
                                            *
   "Hudson River editions"
First published 1905
   "The story concerns the tragic fate of the beautiful and
well-connected but penniless Lily Bart, who at age 29
lacks a husband to secure her position in society. Maneuvering to correct this situation, she encounters both Simon Rosedale, a rich man outside her class, and Lawrence Selden, who is personally appealing and socially
acceptable but not wealthy. She becomes indebted to an
unscrupulous man, has her reputation sullied by a promiscuous acquaintance, and slides into genteel poverty.
Unable or unwilling to ally herself with either Rosedale
or Selden, she finally despairs and takes an overdose of
pills." Merriam-Webster's Ency of Lit

   also in Wharton, E. New York novels p1-324
   also in Wharton, E. Novels

Madame de Treymes
In Wharton, E. Novellas and other writings

Madame de Troyes
In Wharton, E. Novellas and other writings

The Marne
In Wharton, E. Collected stories, 1911-1937

The mother's recompense
In Wharton, E. Novellas and other writings

New Year's Day
In Wharton, E. Novellas and other writings

New York novels; foreword by Louis Auchincloss. Modern Lib. 1998 xxi, 958p $27.95
   ISBN 0-679-60302-6   LC 98-5465
   Contents: The house of mirth (1905); The custom of
the country (1913); The age of innocence (1920)

Wharton, Edith, 1862-1937—*Continued*

Novellas and other writings. Library of Am. 1990 1137p il $45

ISBN 0-940450-53-4   LC 89-62930

Contents: Madame de Treymes; Ethan Frome; Summer; Old New York; The mother's recompense; A backward glance

In Madame de Treymes (1907), an American woman living in Paris tries to break her engagement with a local aristocrat. Ethan Frome is entered separately. Summer (1917) tells the story of Charity Royall, an adopted New England girl in a poor village who falls in love with a young architect from the city. Old New York (1924) is a collection of four novellas, each set in four different decades: False dawn, The old maid, The spark, and New Year's Day. In The mother's recompense (1925), a promiscuous mother moves in with her daughter only to discover her daughter's fiancee was once one of her own lovers. A backward glance (1934) is the author's autobiography.

Novels. Library of America 1985 1328p $40

ISBN 0-940450-31-3   LC 85-191816

Contents: The house of mirth; The reef; The custom of the country; The age of innocence

The house of mirth, The custom of the country, and the age of innocence are entered separately. In the reef (1912), the "action is confined almost exclusively to a chateau in France and the issue narrowed to a psychological struggle in the mind of the heroine, Anna Leath, who discovers that the man she has agreed to marry has had an affair with the young woman who is about to marry her stepson." Ref Guide to Am Lit. 2d edition

The old maid

In Wharton, E. Novellas and other writings

Old New York

In Wharton, E. Novellas and other writings

The reef

In Wharton, E. Novels

Sanctuary

In Wharton, E. Collected stories, 1891-1910

The selected short stories of Edith Wharton; introduced and edited by R.W.B. Lewis. Scribner 1991 xxi, 390p $24.95

ISBN 0-684-19304-3   LC 91-11433

Contents: A journey; The pelican; Souls belated; The descent of man; The mission of Jane; The other two; The dilettante; The lady's maid's bell; The legend; The eyes; Xingu; Autres temps . . .; Kerfol; The long run; A bottle of Perrier; After Holbein; Mr. Jones; Pomegranate seed; Roman fever; Duration; All Souls'

A "collection of 21 of the author's best stories. Lewis' excellent introduction explains Wharton's appeal and provides a brief overview of her life and prolific literary output." Booklist

The spark

In Wharton, E. Novellas and other writings

Summer

In Wharton, E. Novellas and other writings

The touchstone

In Wharton, E. Collected stories, 1891-1910

Wharton, William

Birdy. Knopf 1979 c1978 309p

ISBN 0-394-42569-3

* LC 77-28023

"At the close of World War II, in the mental ward of a veteran's hospital, there is a patient whose behavior quite baffles the psychiatrists. The patient's only childhood friend, another soldier who has a severe facial wound, is transferred to the hospital in the hope he may be of help. The friend instantly recognizes that the patient is behaving exactly like a bird. (The keeping of birds had always been an obsession of the patient throughout his adolescence.)" Choice

"Only the most rigorous imagination can make a story of this sort work for a reader who is generally indifferent to birds. Wharton has just such an imagination." Newsweek

Dad; a novel. Knopf 1981 449p o.p.

LC 80-2725

"Jack Tremont is a fifty-two year old American artist who lives in Paris. He is called home to care for his parents, both of whom have recently become ill. His nineteen year old son shows up also, since his grandparent's home is so convenient to the California State University that he has just left. We meet father and son after they leave California and begin a cross country drive. We move back and forth from past to present, comparing and contrasting the perceptions, concerns, and needs of three generations in one family. Each chapter presents a different character's point of view." Best Sellers

"It's an old story, this man-in-the-middle business, but fresh in Wharton's telling because he lets experience—lunch, a crisis, baseball on TV—accumulate as naturally and surely as aging itself." Saturday Rev

Wheeler, Harvey, 1918-2004

(jt. auth) Burdick, E. Fail-safe

Wheeler, Richard S.

The canyon of bones. Forge 2007 330p $24.95

ISBN 978-0-7653-1324-9; 0-7653-1324-3

LC 2006-102846

"A Tom Doherty Associates book"

Another of the author's westerns featuring "redoubtable mountain man Barnaby Skye. It is the late 1850s and Skye, a deserter from the Royal Navy, and his Crow Indian wife, Victoria, agree that Skye should take a second Indian wife to produce a son. Skye marries Blue Dawn, a beautiful, young Shoshone woman, and the trio is hired to guide brash English explorer and journalist Graves Duplessis Mercer to see a mysterious canyon full of dinosaur bones." Publ Wkly

"Overall, this is genial, character-driven western writing with plenty of action and appreciation for Native American customs. Skye's foulmouthed Crow wife, Victoria, is absolutely delightful, and even his cantankerous horse, Jawbone, has more personality than most western leads. Not just for fans of the series, this will appeal to anyone in search of solidly adventuresome tales." Booklist

Eclipse. Forge 2002 380p $27.95

ISBN 0-312-87846-X   LC 2001-58978

Wheeler, Richard S.—*Continued*

"A Tom Doherty Associates book"

After returning home to a hero's welcome in 1806 "Meriwether Lewis floundered as the governor of the Louisiana Territory, Beset by financial and political difficulties, a depressed and despondent Lewis apparently either committed suicide or was murdered in the Tennessee backwoods in 1809. Wheeler ponders that puzzle, constructing a chilling scenario in which a delusional, syphilis-wracked Lewis feels duty bound to end his fife rather than bring shame upon his name, his family, and his beloved Corps of Discovery. A riveting re-creation of the tragic final years of an American legend." Booklist

North Star; a Barnaby Skye novel. Forge 2009 320p $25.95

ISBN 978-0-7653-1663-9; 0-7653-1663-3

LC 2009-278179

"A Tom Doherty Associates Book"

This novel in the author's series "featuring venerable mountain man Barnaby Skye, finds Skye—after more than 50 years of trapping beaver, hunting bear, fighting Indians and living outdoors—in constant rheumatic pain, losing his eyesight and wishing to live out his days in a house with a roof, a floor and a real bed. It is 1870, the fur business is dead and white men are taking all the Indian lands. His two Indian wives, Victoria and Mary, have different feelings about these changes. Victoria dreads leaving her Indian family for a white man's life, and Mary longs to see her son, Dirk, whom Skye had sent away to school several years earlier. There is little gun smoke, but plenty of suspense as Skye and Victoria confront brutal Texas cattlemen and cheating Indian agents, and Mary travels to St. Louis to find her son." Publ Wkly

Whetstone, Diane McKinney- *See* McKinney-Whetstone, Diane

Whitaker, Rodney *See* Trevanian

White, Bailey

Quite a year for plums; a novel. Knopf 1998 220p $22

ISBN 0-679-44531-5   LC 97-41124

"The women in town are worried about Roger, the peanut virologist. Hilma and Meade discuss him at their weekly readings. Eula frets over his welfare—not to mention his appetite. And everyone else just seems to be content with giving opinions on his budding romance with the strange bird artist, Della. . . . [The author] will make the reader care about this nurturing gaggle of women and other community members in a small, sleepy town in southern Georgia." Libr J

White, Edmund, 1940-

The beautiful room is empty. Knopf 1988 227p o.p.   LC 87-40495

In this sequel to A boy's own story, the author "follows our nameless hero from his final year at prep school in the mid-1950s through his cruisy but self-deprecating college years to the 'turning point' in his life—the famous Stonewall uprising of 1969 in which the clients of a New York gay bar stood up to the policemen

trying to close it down. What emerges is the picture of a young man desperately struggling to come to terms with himself, a struggle that is a universal even if the context for every individual is different. Artfully constructed, this work clearly transcends its 'gay' theme." Libr J

Followed by The farewell symphony

A boy's own story. Dutton 1982 217p o.p.
                              * LC 82-9536

In this first volume of an autobiographical trilogy, a nameless narrator reminisces about his homosexual childhood and his conflicting emotions in coming of age during the 1950s. At fifteen years of age, the boy hopes that "he is just passing through a homosexual 'stage.' At prep school he goes to a . . . psychiatrist who pops pills and talks of his own problems—and with no help from this man he begins slowly to see the real dimensions of his own life." Newsweek

This first-person novel is "written with the flourish of a master stylist. . . . It is an endearing portrait of a child's longing to be charming, popular, powerful, and loved, and of his struggles with adults . . . {told with} sensitivity and elegance." Harpers

Followed by The beautiful room is empty (1988) and The farewell symphony (1997)

Hotel de Dream; a New York novel. Ecco 2007 225p $23.95

ISBN 978-0-06-085225-2; 0-06-085225-9

LC 2007-29872

"The American novelist Stephen Crane, according to an unreliable contemporary, began a book about a male prostitute. As no such manuscript survives, White steps in with an artfully pulpy tale about Elliott, a teenage newsboy in New York, who is kept by a married banker. As frame and counterpoint, he shows us Crane, terminally tubercular, summoning his remaining strength to dictate "The Painted Boy" to his common-law wife, who transports him from England to the Black Forest in a vain search for a cure. White illuminates Crane's literary milieu, the urban gay subculture of his time, and the relationship of a writer's experience to his fiction." New Yorker

The married man; a love story. Knopf 2000 321p $25

ISBN 0-375-40005-2   LC 99-53980

This is the "tale of Austin Smith, an expatriated scion of decayed Southern gentry, who lives on Ile Saint Louis, in Paris. Austin, an expert on 18th-century French furniture, is HIV positive but healthy when he becomes the lover of Julien, a married architect more than 20 years Austin's junior who is in the process of divorcing his wife." Publ Wkly

"A shrewd social observer with a great gift for dialogue, White composes quicksilver scenes bright with wit, then sets aside comedy-of-manners for the luster of tragedy." Booklist

White, Kate

A body to die for. Warner Bks. 2003 294p $23.95

ISBN 0-446-53148-0   LC 2003-41081

White, Kate—*Continued*

"Depressed by her nonexistent love life, Bailey, a free-lance true-crime writer for 'Gloss' magazine, leaves Manhattan for some R&R at the Cedar Inn and Spa in Warren, Mass., owned and run by an old friend of her mother's. Her first night there, however, she stumbles on the corpse of one of the inn's female therapists—wrapped in silver Mylar paper. [The therapist's] murder, on top of the accidental death of a male client some months earlier, could spell doom for the inn, unless Bailey can get to the bottom of things." Publ Wkly

"Once again, White's background as editor-in-chief of 'Cosmopolitan' shines through in her snappy dialog, tight plotting, and insider humor. . . . A breezy beach read for mystery fans." Libr J

Lethally blond. Warner Books 2007 323p $24.99

ISBN 978-0-446-57795-3; 0-446-57795-2

LC 2007-447

"When former fling and sweet stud Chris Wickersham asks Bailey [Weggins] to look into the disappearance of a fellow actor on his TV show, Morgue, she agrees. Someone else might make a couple of phone calls, but rather inexplicably Bailey drives upstate to the missing man's country home. He's there, dead in the bathtub, where he's been for a couple of weeks. Not pretty. That puts Bailey right in the middle of a mystery teeming with TV types, actors, producers, and PR people, one of whom seriously wants Bailey dead." Booklist

"White's flair for pop culture and affection for single career women make this trendy romantic suspense cocktail an addictive read." Publ Wkly

White, Patrick, 1912-1990

The eye of the storm. Viking 1974 c1973 608p o.p.

First published 1973 in the United Kingdom

"Elizabeth Hunter, once a brilliant socialite and a rich, sensual, materialistic woman, now into her eighties, is dying in her Sydney mansion, perceived as a house-shrine by the nurses and servants who devotedly revolve around her. Mrs. Hunter's crucial experience, during the eye of a cyclone, of harmony between her inner, essential self and the outer void has determined the rest of her life, especially the act of dying. Flawed as she is, her strength and intense authenticity of being is communicated in varying degrees to her servants, her lawyer and to her two inauthentic children, the Princess de Lascabanes and Sir Basil Hunter. The comic brilliance of White's conception of Sir Basil, the weary actor for whom life and acting are perpetually fused, is one of the novel's highlights." Oxford Companion to Australian Lit

White, Phyllis Dorothy James *See* James, P. D.

White, Randy Wayne

Black widow. G.P. Putnam's Sons 2008 337p $24.95

ISBN 978-0-399-15456-0; 0-399-15456-6

LC 2008-859

Doc Ford, "a marine biologist and covert operative who lives on Florida's Sanibel Island, is busy serving his shadowy U.S. government masters by researching the potential use by terrorists of jellyfish and other venomous sea creatures when he receives a desperate appeal for help from an old friend. Shay Money, a successful 26-year-old businesswoman who's about to be married, fears her future happiness is in jeopardy because an extortionist has videotaped her and three female friends in sexually compromising situations. While Ford manages to get the tape in exchange for a sizable payment, his suspicions that the criminal isn't done with Money are soon confirmed." Publ Wkly

"Like Robert B. Parker and John D. MacDonald at their best, White draws readers into his world with characters you'd pay just to hang out with and then hooks us with straight-ahead action. It's an old-school combination, but it still works just fine." Booklist

White, Stephen Walsh

Dry ice; a novel. Dutton 2007 401p $25.95

ISBN 978-0-525-94997-8

LC 2006-26771

Sequel to Kill me

"Psychologist Alan Gregory has a secret, and one of his former patients, a deranged killer, is taunting him with it. Michael McClelland . . . has escaped a mental institution and is coming after Gregory's friends and family, including his wife, a deputy district attorney suffering from multiple sclerosis. Gregory becomes a suspect in a series of crimes ranging from the murder of a new patient on a neighbor's property to the disappearance of a star witness in his wife's current grand jury case." Libr J

"Contemporary cerebral thrillers don't get much better than . . . [this novel], which deftly combines complex characterization and intricate plotting." Publ Wkly

Kill me; a novel; [by] Stephen White. Dutton 2006 402p $25.95

ISBN 0-525-94930-5

LC 2005-24296

"In this installment of the . . . series starring clinical psychologist Dr. Alan Gregory, the setting remains the picturesque Colorado countryside, but White sends Dr. Gregory to the background and instead features one of his patients, an unnamed, happily married businessman with an adventurous streak. After a near-fatal crash during a Canadian skiing expedition, coupled with a friend's accident, our hero begins to question his own mortality and vows never to be a burden to his family. When he gets word of an organization that, for a hefty fee, will end your life should you become 'a burden,' he rather hastily signs up.But what if you discover you have a slowly ticking time bomb in your head, and while death could come at any moment, it might not be right away? How do you say not quite yet to your personal hit men?. . . . Bizarre, thrilling, and oh so much fun." Booklist

Missing persons; [by] Stephen White. Dutton 2005 391p $25.95

ISBN 0-525-94859-7

LC 2004-27172

"Eight years to the day after JonBenet Ramsey was murdered, her childhood friend and neighbor, Mallory, winds up missing. At first, her disappearance seems unconnected to the disappearance of Diane, one of Boulder (Colorado) psychologist Alan Gregory's colleagues, or the apparent murder of Diane's friend Hannah. But noth-

White, Stephen Walsh—*Continued*

ing is coincidental in a White murder mystery, and once again, he expertly places the good doctor in the middle of one doozy of a whodunit." Booklist

White, T. H. (Terence Hanbury), 1906-1964

The book of Merlyn; the unpublished conclusion to The once and future king; prologue by Sylvia Townsend Warner; illustrated by Trevor Stubley. University of Tex. Press 1977 xx, 137p il o.p.

LC 77-3454

Sequel to The once and future king
"White, who believed that the central theme of Malory's 'Morte d'Arthur' was to find an antidote to war, pursues that theme here, going to the animals for his answer. Old and defeated King Arthur is led by magician Merlyn into a badger's sett where a group of animals are discussing people. It's Merlyn, however, who becomes chief orator. Publ Wkly
"Writing during World War II, White vented his feelings about the futility of war with a fierceness that sometimes overwhelms the intriguing mixture of fantasy, humor, and rationality which pervaded the tetralogy." Booklist

The candle in the wind
    In White, T. H. The once and future king

The ill-made knight
    In White, T. H. The once and future king

The once and future king. Putnam 1958 677p $25.95

ISBN 0-399-10597-2

* LC 58-10760

An omnibus edition of four novels; The sword in the stone (1939), The witch in the wood (1939, now called The Queen of Air and Darkness) and The ill-made knight (1940). A number of alterations have been made in the earlier books. Previously unpublished, The candle in the wind "deals with the plotting of Mordred and his kinsmen of the house of Orkney, and their undying enmity to King Arthur." Times Lit Suppl
"White's contemporary retelling of Malory's Le Morte d'Arthur is both romantic and exciting." Shapiro. Fic for Youth. 3d edition

The Queen of Air and Darkness
    In White, T. H. The once and future king

The sword in the stone; with decorations by the author and end papers by Robert Lawson. Putnam 1939

First published 1938 in the United Kingdom
An "account of everyday life in a great medieval manor, with two boys, Kay and Wart (who turns out to be King Arthur) learning the code of being a gentleman, busy with hawking, jousting, sword play, and hunting. The whole trend of the story is how the boy Wart was made worthy to become a king." Ont Libr Rev
"Delightful, fantastic, satirical nonsense, for the reader with a background of Arthurian legend." Wis Libr Bull
Followed by The witch in the wood
    In White, T. H. The once and future king

The witch in the wood
    In White, T. H. The once and future king

White, Terence Hanbury *See* White, T. H. (Terence Hanbury), 1906-1964

Whitehead, Colson, 1969-

Apex hides the hurt. Doubleday 2006 212p $22.95

ISBN 0-385-50795-X   LC 2005-49391

A "tale about a man who comes up with catchy product names. A consultant who names things yet who remains nameless, his claim to fame is the brand name Apex for multiculturally hued Band-Aids. Curiously, he has lost a toe under peculiar circumstances that jibe with the cost of hiding the hurt, per the Apex tagline, and now, limping and moody, he arrives in Winthrop, a small town determined to rename itself. He visits with the last Winthrop, the eccentric descendant of the family that once bankrolled the town with its barbed-wire factory, and is schmoozed by Lucky, CEO of the town's current money magnet, a software company, and Regina, the town's mayor, who traces her roots to the freed slaves who founded the town and called it Freedom." Booklist
"A secretive narrator often means the story is weak and has to be puffed up with mystery, but Whitehead's gorgeous, expertly crafted sentences help the reader past the novel's slow start. . . . We are slowly filled in on the limp, the misfortune, the meaning of the title–and we're treated to an eloquent novel about racial identity in America. . . . What could have been an academic exercise becomes a smart tale about who we are under our labels." Newsweek

The intuitionist; a novel. Anchor Bks. (NY) 1999 255p $19.95

ISBN 0-385-49299-5   LC 98-6756

This "novel follows the travails of the redoubtable Lila Mae Watson, the first black woman Elevator Inspector in a nameless city very much like New York. Caught between the political machinations of the two factions of the Elevator Guild (the Intuitionists, like Lila, inspect the elevators by a sort of sympathetic insight, whereas the Empiricists actually examine the cables and helical springs), Lila Mae finds herself in the midst of a murky underground war for control over the kingdom of Vertical Transport. Whitehead's prose is graceful and often lyrical and his elevator underworld is a complex, lovingly realized creation." New Yorker

John Henry Days; a novel. Doubleday 2001 389p $24.95

ISBN 0-385-49819-5   LC 00-43143

This is a "character study surrounding the legend of folk hero John Henry. A John Henry festival in a small West Virginia town draws a diverse crowd, including J. Sutter, a freelance writer going from one event to another in search of free food and paid expenses; and Pamela Street, a restless woman grieving for her father. Both are forced to reevaluate their lives, brought together by bonds of race and history." Libr J
"Whitehead relishes slashing through the mindlessness of the age in a voice so intelligent and an idiom so imaginative that it can lift a reader right out of his chair. But he is not remorseless. He likes these people and respects their longings. They have no moral compass, but he has, so we can laugh at them but still grieve for the loss of so much possibility." N Y Times Book Rev

Whitehead, Colson, 1969—*Continued*

Sag Harbor; a novel. Doubleday 2009 288p $24.95

ISBN 978-0-385-52765-1; 0-385-52765-9

LC 2008-13510

"Here we find Benji, a black kid from New York City, who attends a fancy private high school, 15 years old in the summer of 1985. His family owns a beach house in Sag Harbor, N.Y., where the book is set. . . . The summer over which the novel takes place, Benji and his brother Reggie are at that crucial stage of transition, where the 'who' you are begins flirting with the more permanent 'who' you will become. Benji has tried to step up a rung on the high school ladder-of-cool, but failed when he let slip a couple of contaminating remnants of his upbringing in Nerdville. . . . Benji spends much of his summer working at a local ice cream shop, going to the beach, talking about girls, staging BB-gun fights (with disastrous results) with his friends, and hanging out in his house, which is left without parents during the week." San Francisco Chron

The author "serves up whole sundaes worth of riffs on the quotidian, all hung on the skinny frame of a 15-year-old everyman virgin and his marginally less distinct friends, give or take a repressive father and a particularly evocative shoreline landscape." Village Voice

Whitney, Phyllis A., 1903-2008

Amethyst dreams. Crown 1997 276p $25

ISBN 0-517-70759-4

LC 97-5000

"When Hallie Knight receives a summons to Topsail Island by the grandfather of her college roommate, she immediately responds. Knowing that Susan has disappeared without a trace piques her curiosity, but she's also glad of the opportunity to escape the pain caused by her husband's infidelity. She never expects to become the catalyst for unraveling the strange fate of her friend or find the courage to reexamine her own life." Booklist

"What matters here are the characters' wonderfully wrought temperaments—no sinners, no saints, but ultimately lots of forgiveness—and the subtle, little glimpses of fear that keep readers looking for answers right up to the satisfying conclusion." Libr J

Domino. Doubleday 1979 351p o.p.

LC 79-7331

"Domino is a ghost town, an abandoned silver mine camp in the Colorado Rockies that holds the secret to young Laurie Morgan's psychic wound. During the 20 years since she left her grandmother's mansion, she has endured nightmarish recollections of a peripheral role in her father's shooting. Now Laurie is summoned to the bedside of that imperious old woman, who needs the assistance of a blood relative if the Morgan territory is to resist the overtures of opportunist land developers." Publ Wkly

Poinciana. Doubleday 1980 345p o.p.

LC 80-949

"Poinciana is the exquisite Palm Beach estate to which young and naive Sharon comes as chatelaine. Married at a vulnerable period in her life to Ross Logan, 60-year-old robber baron, she becomes another of his possessions, a beautiful object like the netsuke collection in his museum-home. There are counterforces in ex-wives, a senile mother, a scheming daughter and Logan's death before Sharon develops her own resources." Publ Wkly

The singing stones. Doubleday 1990 507p o.p.

LC 89-37137

Lynn McLeod "is an ombudsman for terminally ill children who is suddenly summoned to assist the daughter of her first husband. But the child is not physically ill. She is haunted by the near-fatal accident that crippled her father and the threatening presence of her wicked stepmother (whom everyone believes to be the epitome of quiet kindness). Lynn enters the complicated family situation with great reluctance, bewitched by the spiritualist philosophies of one character yet driven by her own sympathy for a child in distress. A terrific work of romantic suspense in a contemporary setting." Booklist

Spindrift. Doubleday 1975 301p o.p.

This novel is set in Newport, Rhode Island. "Christy Moreland, having recovered from a breakdown after the apparent suicide of her father, newspaperman Adam Keene, arrives at 'Spindrift,' her domineering mother-in-law's estate. Theo [her mother-in-law] is set on keeping young Peter, son of Christy and her passive husband, Joel. Christy is equally determined to get the boy back and to prove her father was murdered. She suspects Theo and others in the lush company, except strong, personable Bruce Perry. With her marriage failing, Christy turns to Bruce who she hopes will help her and with whom she feels she's falling in love." Publ Wkly

Whyte, Jack

The singing sword. Forge 1996 383p o.p.

LC 96-19966

"A Tom Doherty Associates book"

"As the novel progresses, and the Roman Empire continues to decay, the colony of Camulod flourishes. But the lives of the colony's main characters, Gaius Publius Varrus—ironsmith, innovator and soldier—and his brother-in-law, former Roman Senator Caius Britannicus, are not trouble-free, especially when their most bitter enemy, Claudius Seneca, reappears. . . . Whyte provides rich detail about the forging of superior weaponry, the breeding of horses, the training of cavalrymen, the growth of a lawmaking body within the community and the origins of the Round Table." Publ Wkly

Followed by The eagles' brood

Wibberley, Leonard, 1915-1983

The mouse that roared. Little, Brown 1955 279p o.p.

* LC 54-8294

"The 'Tiny Twenty' overtake the major powers of the world after plotting a bold maneuver to steal the atomic secrets of the United States. Centuries of industrialization and sophistication separate the tiny European nation from the enraged larger countries, who must acquiesce to the will of the former. Underneath this lighthearted tale is a serious warning about the dangers of nuclear power." (Shapiro. Fic for Youth. 3d edition)

Wideman, John Edgar

The cattle killing. Houghton Mifflin 1996 212p o.p.

* LC 96-19305

Set in Philadelphia, this novel "begins inside the head of a black novelist who processes images of the city as it is now and as it was when he was growing up. . . .

Wideman, John Edgar—*Continued*

[He] dreams his way back to 1793. A plague is sweeping through the City of Brotherly Love, giving its white citizens feverish delusions that the pestilence is the sinister work of the blacks in their midst, who are themselves immune. Bearing witness to this madness is a young itinerant minister of mixed racial origins who . . . freed his mother from slavery. He wanders about, working at odd jobs, preaching the Gospel. His faith, however sturdy, cannot protect him from the perils of a landscape agitated by disease and race hate." Nation

"Wideman hauntingly evokes the tragic consequences of racial prejudice. Brimming with mysteries and shadowy secrets, the narrative winds elliptically among the stories of blacks whose attempts to rise above bigotry and lead free lives come to heartbreaking conclusions." Publ Wkly

Fanon. Houghton Mifflin 2008 240p $24
ISBN 978-0-618-94263-3; 0-61894-263-7
LC 2007-9420

This novel is "narrated by Thomas, who's trying to write a book about political activist Frantz Fanon (1925-61), author of The Wretched of the Earth. The story also revolves around Thomas's aging mother and his brother, who's serving time in Pennsylvania." Libr J

"This is Wideman's mulligan stew—on the one hand, the Homewood boy who went on scholarship to Penn, and from Penn to Oxford, and from Oxford to the Iowa Writers' Workshop, nods his head to Marx, Freud, Yeats, Sartre, Joyce, Nabokov, and Baudelaire; on the other, the novelist and college professor who still feels guilty about going to Europe instead of jail signifies his solidarity with W.E.B. DuBois, James Baldwin, and Frantz Fanon by riff, scat, and Igbo. How this mixture works is mysterious, but it always has." Harper's

God's gym; John Edgar Wideman. Houghton Mifflin 2005 175p $23
ISBN 0-618-51525-9
LC 2004-54071
Contents: Weight; Hunters; Sharing; The silence of Thelonious Monk; Are dreams faster than the speed of light; Who invented the jump shot; What we cannot speak about we must pass over in silence; Fanon; Who weeps when one of us goes down blues; Sightings

The author "offers ten stories that range widely from family and basketball to illness and death. In addition, race is an important element. . . . Wideman's stories are feasts of language offering up new metaphors and original imagery. He often uses a dreamlike, stream-of-consciousness style, wandering seemingly far from the original story but eventually resolving back to the starting elements. Each story is a gem that grows more brilliant with rereading." Libr J

Philadelphia fire; a novel. Holt & Co. 1990 199p o.p.
* LC 90-30590
This novel "is, as the title reflects, centered on the 1985 destruction of the Philadelphia headquarters of an organization called MOVE. The narrator is a black American who has removed himself from his homeland and taken refuge from the cares of life on an easygoing island in the Aegean. Nevertheless, when news of the MOVE incident reaches him, he becomes obsessed with its meaning—to him personally, to black Americans in general." Booklist

"Wideman is best when he is most personal. . . . By turns brilliant and murky, seamless and ragged, Philadelphia Fire is on to something big. Wideman's vision of racism in the U.S. suggests nothing less than a genetic disorder present at the birth of the nation." Time

The stories of John Edgar Wideman. Pantheon Bks. 1992 432p o.p.
LC 91-50839
Contents: All stories are true; Casa Grande; Backseat; Loon man; Everybody knew Bubba Riff; Signs; What he saw; A voice foretold; Newborn thrown in trash and dies; Welcome; Doc's story; The Statue of Liberty; Valaida; Hostages; Surfiction; Rock River; When it's time to go; Concert; Presents; The tambourine lady; Little Brother; Fever; Damballah; Daddy Garbage; Lizabeth: the caterpillar story; Hazel; The Chinaman; The watermelon story; The songs of Reba Love Jackson; Across the wide Missouri; Rashad; Tommy; Solitary; The beginning of Homewood

"The 25 stories pulled together here demonstrate [the author's] eloquence in picturing various elements in the constant friction between black and white societies in the U.S. Family and place are, thus, two prominent themes. He writes lushly, beautifully, yet loudly as well; his voice is deep, rich, booming." Booklist

Two cities. Houghton Mifflin 1998 242p $24
ISBN 0-395-85730-9
LC 98-22915
"Kassima, her husband and sons dead, meets Robert Jones in her native Pittsburgh, sleeps with him, and spends much of the rest of the book doing her best to avoid him: this is a cautious love story. The narrative's anchor is Kassima's elderly tenant, who wanders about Pittsburgh and Philadelphia with a camera, making the invisible visible. Wideman, similarly, is a writer who shows you things you would never have seen without him; his prose at once bears the weight of a brutal, complex legacy and exults in a sort of weightlessness." New Yorker

Wiesel, Elie, 1928-

The accident
In Wiesel, E. Night, Dawn, The accident: three tales p205-318

A beggar in Jerusalem; a novel; translated from the French by Lily Edelman and the author. Random House 1970 211p o.p.
Original French edition, 1969
"This novel consists of the stories of the characters who have gathered at the Wailing Wall in Jerusalem. A 'beggar' named David loiters and waits, in the aftermath of the Six-Day War, in the company of . . . [a] crew of 'beggars.' . . . He is waiting—or passively searching—for his friend Katriel, who has died in the fighting, and for Katriel's widow, Malka. At the same time the 'beggar' is certainly no beggar; his name may not be David. . . . The war is not only the Six-Day War—it is every action in which the Jews have been threatened with destruction. And Katriel may not be dead at all." Book World

"Reading Elie Wiesel is not an easy experience. It is certainly by no means an act of escape, the traditional function of literary entertainment. His works touch all of one's fibers. . . . After we have listened to what Wiesel has to say, other literature seems meaningless." Saturday Rev

Wiesel, Elie, 1928——*Continued*

Dawn; translated from the French by Frances Frenaye. Hill & Wang 1961 89p o.p.

*

Original French edition, 1960

"Elisha, a young Jewish terrorist fighting for the creation of Israel in the 1940s, is faced with an agonizing moral dilemma. He is to be the executioner of a British officer in reprisal for the hanging of a captured terrorist. A survivor of the concentration camps and a victim all of his life, Elisha considers whether he is any different from his oppressors if he can execute a helpless prisoner in cold blood." Shapiro. Fic for Youth. 3d edition

also in Wiesel, E. Night, Dawn, The accident: three tales

The forgotten; translated by Stephen Becker. Summit Bks. 1992 237p o.p.   LC 91-46826

Original French edition, 1989

Holocaust "survivor Elhanan Rosenbaum, now living in New York and a distinguished professor with a psychiatric practice, is tragically losing his prodigious memory. While he can still remember, he creates a 'backup' by bequeathing to his son, Malkiel, his stories of the martyred death of his father in his Carpathian village (for whom his son is named); his teenage stint in the army and his return to a ghetto empty of Jews; his adventures in the underground partisan movement; and his love of Talia, the extraordinary woman who rescued him and who died giving birth to his only son." Libr J

"Mr. Wiesel is a writer of contention and his characters, even when affectionate, speak with a bitter music. The most loving—and the saddest—of these sounds occur in the dark duets between father and son, especially as Elhanan admits to Malkiel that he 'cannot recall the essential thing that I want so much to pass on to you.' Elhanan's faith, his temptation to faith . . . is as stunning as the loss he confronts." N Y Times Book Rev

The Golem; the story of a legend; as told by Elie Wiesel and illustrated by Mark Podwal; translated by Anne Borchardt. Summit Bks. 1983 105p il o.p.   LC 83-9304

"The Golem exists only to save his people, the Jews of sixteenth century Prague in this case, from the heinous, antisemitic acts of the gentile population. Mute, made of clay, and given life through the faith of Rabbi Yehuda Loew, the Golem goes about Prague in secret, uncovering the trumped up charges of the gentiles against individual members of the local community. Eventually, at the behest of the Rabbi, the Golem leaves. The narrator asks for his return, knowing the Golem's work is not done." Best Sellers

"This fable is eloquently presented through the combination of Wiesel's facile storytelling skills and Mark Podwal's evocative line drawings." Booklist

The judges; a novel; translated from the French by Geoffrey Strachan. Knopf 2002 209p $24

ISBN 0-375-40909-2   LC 2002-25462

Original French edition, 1999

"A plane bound from New York to Israel is forced to land in a snowstorm in Connecticut, and five passengers are taken to the house of a local man who has the delusion that he is a judge in a capital case. As the guests respond to the judge's more and more personal and insinuating questions, their characters are revealed." Publ Wkly

As the characters "talk about themselves and remember crucial turning points in their lives. Wiesel weaves in Jewish history and mysticism with the characters' personal memories, and he raises the big existential questions about life and death and memory and guilt and forgiveness, with lots of metaphors about scapegoat, fellow traveler, messenger, etc." Booklist

Night

In Wiesel, E. Night, Dawn, The accident: three tales

Night, Dawn, The accident: three tales. Hill & Wang 1972 318p pa $14 hardcover o.p.

ISBN 0-374-52140-9

In Dawn, Elisha, a young Jewish terrorist fighting for the creation of Israel in the 1940s is faced with an agonizing moral dilemma. He is to be the executioner of a British officer in reprisal for the hanging of a captured terrorist. A survivor of the concentration camps and a victim all of his life, Elisha considers whether he is any different from his oppressors if he can execute a helpless prisoner in cold blood. Night is a memoir. The accident concerns a survivor of Auschwitz who, recovering from a near-fatal accident, questions the meaning of man's existence and purpose, and death

The oath; translated from the French by Marion Wiesel. Random House 1973 283p

ISBN 0-394-48779-6

*

"Azriel meets a young man attempting to commit suicide. Azriel tries to take the man's mind off his plight by interesting him in a story. It is the story of Kolvillag, where all Jews (but one) were killed on the merest pretext by those whose excuse was the charge of Christ-killers. All of the Jews, however, had taken an oath (of the title) never to tell how they suffered—a kind of weapon of silence against their persecutors. Azriel is now faced with breaking that vow to help save the would-be suicide's life. He tells the tale." America

A "powerful novel, interwoven with threads of Hasidic tales, cabalistic mysticism, Talmudic sayings, and pietistic folklore." Libr J

The testament; a novel; translated from the French by Marion Wiesel. Summit Bks. 1981 346p

ISBN 0-671-44833-1   LC 80-27251

Original French edition, 1980

"In modern-day Israel, awaiting his mother's arrival on a plane filled with Russian immigrants, [Grisha] reflects on his childhood and youth and rereads the 'testament of Paltiel Kossover,' a confession/autobiography written by his father in prison shortly before his execution in 1947. The manuscript (which was smuggled out by a stenographer) reveals an idealist dedicated to perfecting humanity, an innocent victim of the machinations of the Soviet regime." Libr J

"In none of Wiesel's earlier novels are the characters so earthy, so real, so finely chiseled, as in this one. Women advance more fully to center stage and play more dominant roles. . . . The almost photographic realism of the narrative gives it a cumulative power that is overwhelming." Christ Century

Wiesel, Elie, 1928- —*Continued*

Twilight; translated from the French by Marion Wiesel. Summit Bks. 1988 217p o.p.

LC 88-2634

Original French edition, 1987

"Raphael is a professor on sabbatical studying at an exclusive upstate New York asylum (the Mountain Clinic, which caters to patients whose 'schizophrenia is linked to Ancient History, to Biblical times'). Wiesel's portraits of these descendants of Adam (one actually believes himself to be Adam) bring a dark humor to this otherwise somber story. Raphael studies not only the patients and staff, but also his own past, reliving the effect of the Holocaust on his family, his own escape, and the loss of his savior, Pedro. . . . Raphael's guilt at having survived has begun to smother him, yet it is his struggle that prompts him to ask such probing questions about God, life, and death." Booklist

"Despite the Holocaust and its atrocities, so specially devised to destroy human life and dignity, we experience in Mr. Wiesel's novel how good the family is, how good people are. Utterly without sentimentality, he gives us a small but real measure of what the world's loss has been." N Y Times Book Rev

Wiesel, Eliezer *See* Wiesel, Elie, 1928-

Wiggen, Henry W. *See* Harris, Mark, 1922-2007

Wiggins, Marianne

Evidence of things unseen; a novel. Simon & Schuster 2003 383p $25

ISBN 0-684-86969-1   LC 2003-45611

"Born in Kitty Hawk, where the Wright brothers first rose towards the sun, Ray Foster, or 'Fos', . . . is fascinated by radiance. A portrait photographer who deals with the dynamics of light, Fos . . . keeps a lump of phosphorous glowing in a fish tank by his bedside. . . . After signing on as an official photographer for the Tennessee Valley Authority–hence becoming complicit in kicking countless farmers off their ancestral lands to make way for hydroelectric dams–Fos assumes a similar recordkeeping role at the Oak Ridge Laboratory in Tennessee, one of three research sites for the Manhattan project." Economist

"Wiggins fits her lyrical prose to a distinctly rural, Southern cadence, easily blending the vernacular with luminous imagery, adding bits of poetry, passages explaining scientific phenomena, interpolations about the Scopes trial and even references to Moby-Dick, which serves as a leitmotif." Publ Wkly

John Dollar. Harper & Row 1989 214p o.p.

* LC 88-45538

"Just after World War I, Charlotte Lewes, a 25-year-old schoolteacher raised on Kipling, is sent to Rangoon to instill British values in the children of English colonists. During a festive sailing expedition, a tidal wave strands her and seaman John Dollar on an island with eight schoolgirls." Libr J

"Writing with an impressive degree of control and sophistication, Marianne Wiggins investigates the ghastly processes which crush the marooned children. . . . The phenomenon that particularly fascinates Wiggins in the spiritual disintegration she depicts as the consequence of this spectacle is the growth of a parodic religion." London Rev Books

The shadow catcher. Simon & Schuster 2007 323p il $25

ISBN 978-0-7432-6520--1; 0-7432-6520-3

LC 2007-11842

A fictionalization of the life of photographer Edward Sheriff Curtis. "Digging into the photographer's past in a parallel story line is the modern-day, fictional Marianne Wiggins, an Angeleno who has written a novel about Curtis and is resisting Hollywood's attempts to glamorize him. . . . This faux Wiggins—the real one thanks her sister in the acknowledgments for 'license to decorate our shared history'—stumbles into a mystery involving her family, but the personal developments are considerably less interesting than the detailed reconstruction of Curtis' wife Clara. . . . The beautifully rendered Clara gives resonant shape to Wiggins' musings on the enigmatic Curtis—wayward husband, absent father, acquaintance of Teddy Roosevelt, emblem of a great national restlessness—and leads the author to intriguing insights into sexual politics, the mythology of the West and the relationship between physical and emotional distance." PopMatters

Wiggs, Susan

The ocean between us. Mira 2004 382p $19.95

ISBN 0-7783-2035-9   LC 2004-557716

"Steve Bennett is a perfect navy officer with a perfect navy family, and he's confident that his world is just the way it should be. But his son wants to be an artist instead of attending the U.S. Naval Academy, and his stalwart and capable wife of 20 years, Grace, is tired of being the perfect navy wife. She wants her own home, and she wants her own career. She's feeling altogether unsettled, but nothing is more unsettling than the secret her husband has hidden from her their entire marriage. Nothing, that is, until the accident on the carrier. Wiggs has done an excellent job of depicting what lies beneath the surfaces of relationships—assumptions, misunderstandings, and expectations." Booklist

Wignall, Kevin

For the dogs. Simon & Schuster 2004 209p $22

ISBN 0-7432-4756-6   LC 2004-45386

"Stephen Lucas, a recently retired, emotionally stunted hit man, emerges from his Swiss hideaway as a favor to old friend Londoner Mark Hatto, who hires Lucas to surreptitiously guard his daughter, bright, extroverted Ella, while she's vacationing in Italy with her boyfriend. After Ella's entire family is murdered, Lucas foils several serious attempts on Ella's life, and the two of them form an odd, almost familial relationship. The boyfriend soon drops out of the picture as the hit man reluctantly helps Ella exact revenge on those who killed her family. There's plenty of action, but it's the twisting, turning, complicated relationship between Ella and Lucas that forms the core of this compelling novel." Publ Wkly

Wilcken, Hugo, 1964-

The execution; a novel. HarperCollins Pubs. 2002 213p $23.95

ISBN 0-06-018823-5   LC 2001-42410

Wilcken, Hugo, 1964--—*Continued*

"Matthew Bourne's life is changed the day he is asked to identify the body of a dead colleague's wife. That cataclysmic event transforms him from a good-looking man with a loving partner, a sweet daughter, plenty of friends, and a good job that supports a cause he believes in to a haggard, hopeless shadow who loses his grip on life." Booklist

"Wilcken can be forgiven for resolving knotty plot problems with a well-timed coincidence here and there; his book is an exciting, nervy thriller that fulfills the demands of the genre while resonating on deeper frequencies." N Y Times Book Rev

Wilcox, Collin

Dead center. Holt & Co. 1992 262p o.p.

LC 91-31076

In this Frank Hastings mystery "a series of powerful and wealthy men are shot to death on the street, the weapon the .22 favored by professional hitmen. The cops finally connect the victims as rather nasty members of the ultra-exclusive Rabelais Club. . . . Old scandals (a hooker's death covered up, a notorious high-stakes poker circle), heavy political and media pressure and glimpses (for us) of the killer's mind-set lead up to Hastings's harrowing, climactic confrontation with the murderer." Publ Wkly

Except for the bones. Doherty Assocs. 1991 282p o.p.

LC 91-21579

"A TOR book"

"Detective Alan Bernhardt looks into the suspicious death of a New York real estate tycoon's latest girlfriend—a death secretly witnessed by the man's estranged stepdaughter in Cape Cod." Libr J

"Wilcox delivers a taut, suspenseful mystery with credible dialogue and good local color." Publ Wkly

Find her a grave. Forge 1993 288p o.p.

LC 93-26557

"A Tom Doherty Associates book"

"Alan Bernhardt is a San Francisco stage director who moonlights as a private eye. He's hired to help the illegitimate daughter of a late Mafia chieftain collect her inheritance, which is buried by the headstone of her mother's grave." Booklist

The author "gradually establishes an authentic mobster milieu, offering the required mix of brutality and honor." Publ Wkly

Full circle. Forge 1994 352p o.p.

LC 94-32703

"A Tom Doherty Associates book"

In Bernhardt's Edge (1988) San Francisco sleuth Alan Bernhardt "saved the life of art expert Betty Giles who, along with her boyfriend, was blackmailing aged millionaire Raymond DuBois, owner of several pieces of stolen art. Now the FBI is putting heat on Bernhardt to reveal Betty's whereabouts, while DuBois, who would like to preserve his reputation by returning the purloined pieces to their rightful owners, hires Bernhardt to do so." Publ Wkly

"This is cleverly plotted and populated with a half-dozen self-serving, potentially lethal characters. A truly engrossing read." Booklist

Switchback. Holt & Co. 1993 256p o.p.

LC 93-18197

San Francisco's Lt. Frank Hastings "pursues the murderer of a beautiful but selfish young woman who revelled in controlling others. Hastings questions both Haight-Ashbury acquaintances and Nob Hill lovers; meanwhile, constant erotic tension flows from the mutual attraction between Hastings (who lives with divorcée Ann) and bunco squad cop Janet. Wilcox's practiced hand lends a deft descriptive touch, whether to setting, plot or character: add this to the better police procedurals list." Libr J

Wilcox, James, 1949-

Heavenly days; a novel. Viking 2003 199p $23.95

ISBN 0-670-03247-6   LC 2003-50164

A novel set in the small Louisiana town of Tula Springs. "Lou Jones, moving through her fifties at too rapid a pace, is unhappy: her husband lost his job and moved out of their $300,000 'Cajun cabin' and is now living in his parents' house. Plus, Lou, who minds everyone's business except her own, has a doctorate in music but makes more money working as the receptionist for a fundamentalist health club than she could ever earn at the state college. Wilcox adds in some dizzying subplots involving Lou's oldest friend, a scandal at the college, a group of militant lesbians, and marital infidelity." Booklist

Hunk City; a novel. Viking 2007 199p $25.95

ISBN 978-0-670-03152-8; 0-670-03152-6

LC 2006-48687

This novel is set "in the small fictional town of Tula Springs, Louisiana. . . . Burma Van Buren, assistant manager of Redds Dollar Store and heir to her late husband's $35 million fortune, is having a terrible time figuring out which organizations most deserve her contribution. She's a diehard liberal, much to the consternation of her corrupt Republican accountant and her feisty gun-toting mother. Meanwhile, her love life is nonexistent: her handsome landscaper is gay, and her lifelong love, Mr. Pickens, is still married to a scheming Evangelical." Booklist

"Wilcox has always been about more than broad comedy. His men and women, though often clownish, are rarely cartoonish. He has a Dickensian knack for animating minor characters and an eye for the telling detail." N Y Times Book Rev

Wilde, Oscar, 1854-1900

The picture of Dorian Gray. Modern Library 1992 254p $16.95

ISBN 0-679-60001-9

* LC 92-11593

First published 1891 in the United Kingdom; first United States edition published 1895 by G. Munro's Sons

"An archetypal tale of a young man who purchases eternal youth at the expense of his soul, the novel was a romantic exposition of Wilde's Aestheticism. Dorian Gray is a wealthy Englishman who gradually sinks into a life of dissipation and crime. Despite his unhealthy behavior, his physical appearance remains youthful and un-

Wilde, Oscar, 1854-1900—*Continued*
marked by dissolution. Instead, a portrait of himself
catalogues every evil deed by turning his once handsome
features into a hideous mask." Merriam-Webster's Ency
of Lit

Wilder, Elly *See* Robb, J. D., 1950-

Wilder, Thornton, 1897-1975

The bridge of San Luis Rey; illustrated by Amy
Drevenstedt. Boni, A. C. 1967 c1927 235p il o.p.

First published 1927
"On Friday, July 20, 1714, high in the Andes of Peru,
the famous bridge of San Luis Rey collapsed, killing the
five people who were crossing it. A priest who was witness to the event decided that the tragedy provided the
chance to prove the wisdom of God in that instance, and
thereafter spent years investigating the lives of the people
who had been killed." Shapiro. Fic for Youth. 3d edition

> *also in* Wilder, T. The bridge of San Luis
> Rey and other novels 1926-1948

The bridge of San Luis Rey and other novels
1926-1948; [edited by J. D. McClatchy] Library of
America 2009 731p $35
ISBN 978-1-59853-045-2
In addition to the novels: The cabala;The bridge at San
Luis Rey; The woman of Andros; Heaven's my destina-
tion; The ides of March; this collection contains several
essays on fiction and the following early short stories:
The marriage of Zabett; "Spiritus valet"; Eddy Greater;
Précautions inutiles; A diary: first and last entry; The
warship
The cabala (1926) is a tale of youthful enchantment
with Rome in the form of a fictitious memoir of an
American student. Set in 18th-century Peru, The bridge
of San Luis Rey (1927), "is a kind of theological detective story concerning a friar's investigations into the lives
of five individuals before they were killed in a bridge
collapse. . . . The Woman of Andros [1930], based on
the Andria of Roman writer Terence, is a consideration
of the ancient world filtered through the sensibility of a
meditative courtesan; Heaven's My Destination [1935], a
departure from Wilder's historical themes, is a picaresque
romp through Depression-era America; and The Ides of
March [1948] takes up the story of Julius Caesar's assassination by imagining the exchange of letters among such
prominent ancient figures as Catullus, Cleopatra, Cicero,
and Caesar himself." Publisher's note

The cabala
> *In* Wilder, T. The bridge of San Luis Rey and
> other novels 1926-1948

The eighth day. Harper & Row 1967 435p o.p.
"A chronicle of two early 20th-century Midwestern
families and their involvement in a murder case raising
serious questions about human nature." Oxford Companion to Am Lit. 6th edition

Heaven's my destination
> *In* Wilder, T. The bridge of San Luis Rey and
> other novels 1926-1948

The ides of March. Harper 1948 246p o.p.
This novel offers "divergent views of Caesar's last
months seen through letters and documents." Oxford
Companion to Am Lit. 6th edition

> *also in* Wilder, T. The bridge of San Luis
> Rey and other novels 1926-1948

Theophilus North. Harper & Row 1973 374p
o.p.

"A Cass Canfield book"
"In the summer of 1926, a 30-year-old teacher named
Theophilus North comes to Newport, R.I., to tutor the
children of the fashionably rich and to read out loud.
. . . In Newport he discovers nine separate cities differing in age and social class. In these stories of which this
novel is composed, North marches through them all—careers and cities—healing the sick, repairing marriages,
rescuing a damsel from injustice, restoring life and health
to the old and frail, and freedom to the confined."
Newsweek

The woman of Andros
> *In* Wilder, T. The bridge of San Luis Rey and
> other novels 1926-1948

Wilhelm, Kate

The best defense. St. Martin's Press 1994 342p
o.p.   LC 94-2039
In this legal thriller Barbara Holloway "defends Paula
Kennerman, a battered wife accused of killing her daughter and burning down the safe house in which they had
been sheltered. . . . The Holloways' crack team of private investigators assures that important clues are developed in time to use as evidence as Barbara skillfully
conducts the defense in a suspenseful trial. The ambitious plot-subplot net threads together abortion rights,
antifeminist backlash, and the inequities of legal aid for
rich and poor." Libr J

Death qualified; a mystery of chaos. St.
Martin's Press 1991 438p o.p.   LC 90-27504
"Nell Kendricks is charged with murdering her estranged husband, Lucas, who disappeared years ago
while working on a top-secret experiment attempting to
use chaos theory to change the observer's perception of
the universe. Now it appears that Lucas had spent the intervening years drugged and amnesiac, a handyman at
the university where the studies had taken place. Attorney Barbara Holloway, who is 'death qualified' (i.e., legally permitted to act in capital cases), agrees to defend
Nell, despite having left the profession, disillusioned by
its practices." Publ Wkly
"It is difficult to describe the novel's many dimensions, ranging from tense courtroom scenes to the almost
fantastic descriptions of the scientific study. Most astonishing is the author's ability to peel off one layer after
another, revealing new ways of looking at the same
facts." Libr J

The deepest water. St. Martin's Minotaur 2000
279p $23.95
ISBN 0-312-26143-8
*LC 00-31724

Wilhelm, Kate—*Continued*

"Abby Connors is mourning the death of her father, bestselling novelist Jud Vickers, at the age of 48. Jud was a womanizing former ne'er-do-well who had recently found success, only to be murdered at his remote lakefront cabin. The local police baffled, Abby soon finds herself doing her own sleuthing, much to the dismay of her husband, Brice, a financial planner who was always jealous of Jud's primary place in Abby's heart. As Abby investigates further, she discovers secrets in Jud's past as well as an unfinished novel." Publ Wkly

Wilhelm's "characters are well drawn, the setting is real, and the pace keeps the reader raptly involved to the last page." Libr J

Defense for the devil. St. Martin's Press 1999 389p $24.95

ISBN 0-312-19854-X LC 98-44576

"Mitch Arno is a spouse abuser, small-time thug, and general ne'er-do-well. When he trashes wife Maggie's cozy Oregon B&B after his latest 'job,' she kicks him out, and he heads for his brother's house. Meanwhile, Maggie turns to attorneys Barbara Holloway and her father, Frank, to get a restraining order against Mitch and file for damages. Then Mitch turns up dead, and brother Ray is arrested for murder. Maggie persuades Barbara to defend Ray, placing her and her father in the middle of a deadly web of deception and greed." Libr J

"The nuances of courtroom procedure are compellingly presented, . . . including a sophisticated look at the complex psychology of a jury." Publ Wkly

Desperate measures. St. Martin's Minotaur 2001 387p

ISBN 0-312-27663-X

Barbara Holloway's "latest client is a brilliant young man named Alex Feldman, who has been left hideously deformed by a birth defect. He is accused of killing his next-door neighbor, Gus Marchand, a tyrannical religious Zealot who saw Alex's deformity as the mark of the devil. There is little evidence against him, but Marchand has created such hostility and fear toward Alex in their small, rural community that it seems likely he will be convicted on the basis of his appearance alone. . . . Readers are given all the necessary facts and Alex is an excellent character. Wilhelm does a good job of conveying his anguish and isolation." Publ Wkly

The good children. St. Martin's Press 1998 246p $22.95

ISBN 0-312-17914-6 LC 97-37101

"The McNairs' move into a home of their own near Portland, Oregon, seems too good to be true. All the kids have rooms of their own and the promise from their father of no more transfers. But their idyll is soon shattered; father Will is killed in an industrial accident. Though left relatively financially secure, the family is not the same. Mother Lee can't cope and becomes increasingly reclusive. The four kids must manage the house, their mother, and themselves. Then, one day, they come home to find her dead on the patio. Fearful of being separated, the kids construct a complex scheme to keep their home intact." Libr J

"Brilliantly plotted, lyrically written, alluring and magical, mesmerizing, terrifying, and heartbreakingly funny, Wilhelm's story is a wrenching masterpiece about love,

loyalty, and lies that will lodge itself in readers' psyches long after they've finished the last, stunning chapter." Booklist

The Hamlet trap. St. Martin's Press 1987 234p o.p. LC 87-16368

"Ashland, Oregon, home of the Oregon Shakespearean Festival, provides the setting for this [mystery]. . . . The action centers on the fictional Harley Theatre, a repertory group coexisting in Ashland with the more famous Shakespeare company. When a new director arrives on the scene and selects a controversial winner in a new-playwright's contest, trouble brews. Soon corpses dot the tranquil southern Oregon community, and the niece of the theater's owner is about to be indicted for murder. To the rescue comes an engaging pair of sleuths—ex-cop Charlie Meiklejohn and his psychologist wife Constance Leidl." Booklist

This "is a psychological mystery, and a classic murder puzzle as well. Constance and Charlie are a loving couple and skillful detectives; good company for one another and for the reader." Wilson Libr Bull

Justice for some. St. Martin's Press 1993 260p o.p. LC 93-15046

"Heading for a family gathering at her father's home/water garden business in rural California, widowed Sarah Drexler anticipates a respite from her work as an Oregon state judge. Instead she finds her deductive skills challenged and the lives of those dearest to her threatened. Joining the tense family dinner is Fran Donatio, a woman whose presence Sarah's father Ralph does not explain. The next morning, after Ralph's body is pulled from a lily pond, police Lt. Arthur Fernandez arrives with questions on another matter. . . . This tale . . . offers a bonus in Fernandez who, running his own, equally intelligent investigation in the background, provides a welcome change from the expected solitary-sleuth plot structure." Publ Wkly

Malice prepense. St. Martin's Press 1996 412p o.p. LC 96-1190

"Attorney Barbara Holloway is hired to defend a 28-year-old brain-injured man who is accused of murdering an Oregon Congressman. With only a pile of rocks found at the murder scene tying the young man to the crime, Holloway skillfully clears him, but her client's father then becomes the prime suspect. Her defense of the now-accused father is much more complex." Libr J

"As Wilhelm spins her riveting tale, she not only makes the legal system comprehensible and compelling but also makes her readers care about her characters, particularly the efficient yet vulnerable Barbara." Publ Wkly

No defense. St. Martin's Press 2000 376p $24.95

ISBN 0-312-20953-3 LC 99-56355

In this legal thriller Oregon attorney Barbara Holloway defends "Lara Jessup, a young widow accused of murdering her much older husband, Vinny, a man with a large insurance policy, a terminal case of cancer, and some very powerful enemies. Jessup's alibi begins to evaporate when her adolescent son contradicts her story, and Holloway is left with no way to defend her except to expose those powerful enemies. . . . Although there is nothing particularly original or surprising here, this well-written novel skillfully captures small-town life in a rural western community with all its benefits and drawbacks." Booklist

Wilhelm, Kate—*Continued*

Sweet, sweet poison. St. Martin's Press 1990 262p o.p.   LC 89-77847

The first victim in this "mystery is a watchdog named Sadie, owned by Al and Sylvie Zukal, two likable, spectacularly vulgar *kvetches* from the Bronx who invested some recent lottery winnings in a rural estate in Spender's Ferry, N.Y. After the Zukals' young friend David dies, the well-oiled, older detective team of Charlie Meiklejohn and Constance Leidl . . . begins to question the conclusions of the local sheriff, who labels these and additional inventive killings—by poison, drugs, bees and gas—accident or suicide." Publ Wkly

Wilhelm "offers studied prose, an almost too heavy dose of local color, and tightly knit plotting in a novel that isn't like most mysteries. Here, hidden fantasies emerge from the subtext, and narrative detours that would lose most crime writers are handled adroitly." Booklist

Where late the sweet birds sang. Harper & Row 1976 251p o.p.

*

"Pollution and pestilence are the consequences of a war that destroys most of the earth and its inhabitants. The elder Sumners have created a scientific research center whose goal is to perfect a technique for cloning since, among the other results of the world disaster, men and women have become sterile. The younger Sumners are victimized by these clones, who perpetuate the form of humans but have no humaneness or humanity." Shapiro. Fic for Youth. 3d edition

Wilkins, Kim

Veil of gold. Tor 2008 c2005 495p $25.95
ISBN 978-0-7653-2006-3; 0-7653-2006-1

First published 2005 in Australia with title: Rosa and the veil of gold

"The discovery of an ancient gold bear hidden in the walls of a St. Petersburg bathhouse brings researchers Daniel St. Clair and Em Hayward to verify its age. On their way to the university in Arkhangelsk, however, they lose their way; maps become useless, and they have no choice but to venture on—and into an unfamiliar, strange Russia. Seeking Daniel, his lost love Rosa ventures forth into her own mystical journey, confronting her past in an attempt to save Daniel's—and possibly the world's—future." Libr J

"Wilkins's human characters are endearing and her mythic monsters spring into vibrant life. Adult fairy tales don't come any better than this." Publ Wkly

Wilkinson, Tim

(tr) Kertész, I. Detective story

Willard, Tom

Buffalo soldiers. Forge 1996 331p $22.95
ISBN 0-312-86041-2

* LC 95-53295

"A Tom Doherty Associates book"

"Held captive by the Kiowa and then bartered to a white buffalo hunter, Augustus Sharps is freed in 1869 by troopers of the all-black Tenth U.S. Cavalry, in which he enlists. First in a series chronicling African American contributions to U.S. military history, Willard's . . . well-researched novel traces Augustus's soldiering from Fort Wallace, Kansas, until his retirement to an Arizona ranch." Libr J

Willeford, Charles Ray, 1919-1988

Pick-up
In Crime novels: American noir of the 1950s

Willetts, H. T.

(tr) Solzhenitsyn, A. In the first circle

Williams, Joy, 1944-

Honored guest; stories. Knopf 2004 213p
ISBN 0-679-44647-8   LC 2004-44199

Contents: Honored guest; Congress; Marabou; The visiting privilege; Substance; Anodyne; The other week; Claro; Charity; ACK; Hammer; Fortune

"The troubled characters in Williams' latest short stories, set in locales as diverse as Maine and Mexico, don't have the wherewithal to do anything but brood, with the exception of a forensic anthropologist who solves the mysteries of scattered bones, hair, and teeth, a feat not unlike the one Williams pulls off in these canny and dissecting tales of fractured lives." Booklist

Williams, Niall, 1958-

John; a novel. Bloomsbury 2008 276p $24.95
ISBN 978-1-59691-467-4; 1-59691-467-X
LC 2007-25810

"A fictional portrayal of the last years of John, Williams' story explores the exiled Christian community on the island of Patmos. In his hope to preserve the message of love before his own death and the extermination of Christianity, the aging apostle records his encounters with Jesus amid the turmoil of the Roman Empire in the first century." BookPage

"This novel will appeal to readers who like imaginative and gritty sagas of the lives of key Christians in the early church as well as those who value lyricism." Publ Wkly

Williams, Tennessee, 1911-1983

Collected stories; with an introduction by Gore Vidal. New Directions 1985 xxv, 574p o.p.
* LC 85-10642

Contents: The angel in the alcove; Chronicle of a demise; Completed; Desire and the black masseur; Field of blue children; "Grand"; Happy August the Tenth; The important thing; The inventory at Fontana Bella; The killer chicken and the closet queen; The kingdom of earth; The knightly quest; The malediction; Mama's old stucco house; Man bring this up road; The mattress by the tomato patch; Miss Coynte of Greene; The mysteries of the Joy Rio; The night of the Iguana; One arm; Oriflamme; The poet; Portrait of a girl in glass; Resemblance between a violin case and a coffin; Sabbatha and solitude; Three players of a summer game; Two on a party; The vengence of Nitocris; The vine; The yellow

Williams, Tennessee, 1911-1983—*Continued*

bird; A lady's beaded bag; Something by Tolstoi; Big Black; A Mississippi idyll; The accent of a coming foot; Twenty-seven wagons full of cotton; Sand; Ten minute stop; Gift of an apple; In memory of an aristocrat; The dark room; The interval; Tent worms; Something about him; Rubio y Morena; The coming of something to Widow Holly; Hard candy; A recluse and his guest; Das Wasser ist Kalt; Mother Yaws

The Roman spring of Mrs. Stone. New Directions 1950 148p o.p.

                                             *

A wealthy widowed American ex-actress is the heroine of this short novel. At fifty Mrs. Stone is losing her beauty, her stage career is ended, and she finds herself just 'drifting' through an aimless existence in Rome. When an unscrupulous countess introduces a handsome young gigolo to Mrs. Stone it is the beginning of the end

"There are many superb moments, scenes which move with a dramatist's ease. There is a hard candor about Mrs. Stone, about all people who fail at real living and attempt a life of fantasy and fail at that, leaving them vulnerable to annihilation. . . . This different version of Mr. Williams' repeated theme has resulted in a sharp, witty and moving novel." Chicago Sunday Trib

Williams, Thomas Lanier *See* Williams, Tennessee, 1911-1983

Williamson, Penelope

Heart of the west; a novel. Simon & Schuster 1995 591p o.p.
                           LC 94-33487

"A tale of the settling of the West told from a woman's perspective—three women actually. Clementine Kennicutt is a proper Bostonian lady until she literally bumps into Gus McQueen and elopes with him to Montana. Hannah Yorke is the town prostitute who becomes a prosperous landowner, though she is forever marked by her past. And Erlan Woo is a young Chinese picture bride whose heart remains in China. These three seemingly mismatched characters become fast friends." SLJ

"Williamson gives these characters convincing voices . . . and demonstrates how women could bond and find new identities on the frontier. Williamson tells her story with brio, if a little too much florid prose." Publ Wkly

The outsider. Simon & Schuster 1996 464p o.p.
                           LC 96-7291

"Rachel Yoder is a young widow with a son trying to survive on a Montana sheep farm in the 1880s. She still grieves for her husband, murdered by the local cattleman's association, but her faith carries her through. As a member of a religious community called the Plain people, she believes that one must not question God's workings. Her beliefs are about to be challenged when a wounded gunfighter named Johnny Cain stumbles onto the Yoder cabin in the midst of a severe snowstorm." Booklist

"This is rich, wonderful reading sure to please any fan of good old-fashioned storytelling." Libr J

Willig, Lauren

The seduction of the crimson rose. Dutton 2008 385p $24.95; pa $15
   ISBN   978-0-525-95033-2;   0-525-95033-8; 978-0-451-22441-5 (pa); 0-451-22441-8 (pa)
                          LC 2007-43044

"Determined to secure another London season without assistance from her new brother-in-law, Mary Alsworthy accepts a secret assignment from Lord Vaughn on behalf of the Pink Carnation. She must infiltrate the ranks of the dreaded French spy, the Black Tulip, before he and his master can stage their planned invasion of England. . . . And as our modern-day heroine, Eloise Kelly, digs deeper into England's Napoleonic-era espionage, she becomes even more entwined with Colin Selwick, the descendant of her spy subjects." Publisher's note

"The flower-named spies of Regency England return as Willig's smart, sassy style cleverly incorporates a modern-day historian's hunt for information with Regency characters and events. Willig switches from a historical voice to a modern tone with ease, drawing readers back and forth in time as they hold their breath to see what happens next." Romantic Times

Willis, Connie

Doomsday book. Bantam Bks. 1992 445p
   ISBN 0-553-08131-4
                             * LC 91-42819

"Kivrin, a student of medieval history, is sent back in time to 14th-century Oxfordshire to do some hands-on study. Meanwhile, in the near-future present day of the book, an old disease comes back to smite Oxford. In the resultant chaos, no one realises that because of a slip-up, Kivrin has arrived bang in the middle of the Black Death." New Statesman Soc

"As much as I enjoyed [Willis's] story, . . . the time travel device is given no justification, and none of the paradoxical implications of time travel are explored. Doomsday Book is a historical novel with tenuous SF connections. . . . Warts and all, though, this is a cracking good story, and that is the bottom line criterion for any novel, SF or other." New Scientist

Passage. Bantam Bks. 2001 594p
   ISBN 0-553-11124-8   LC 00-68052

This novel "concerns the scientific study of near death experiences (NDEs). . . . Psychologist Joanna Lander, an NDE specialist, joins neurologist Richard Wright in a research project employing a psychoactive drug to simulate NDEs. When most of the volunteer subjects drop out, Joanna agrees to go under and finds herself aboard the *Titanic*. She returns time after time to the ill-fated ship and becomes increasingly obsessed with the experience and why it seems so real and familiar. . . . With memorable characters, believable science, and convincing hospital ambiance, an initially slow-moving yarn turns into a page-turner whose explosive climax will rock readers back on their heels." Booklist

To say nothing of the dog; or, How we found the bishop's bird stump at last. Bantam Bks. 1998 434p hardcover o.p. pa $7.99
   ISBN 0-553-09995-7; 0-553-57538-4 (pa)
                             LC 97-16002

Willis, Connie—*Continued*

"Rich dowager Lady Schrapnell has invaded Oxford University's time travel research project in 2057, promising to endow it if they help her rebuild Coventry Cathedral, destroyed by a Nazi air raid in 1940. . . . Time traveler Ned Henry is suffering from advanced time lag and has been sent, he thinks, for rest and relaxation to 1888, where he connects with time traveler Verity Kindle and discovers that he is actually there to correct an incongruity created when Verity inadvertently brought something forward from the past." Booklist

"No one mixes scientific mumbo jumbo and comedy of manners with more panache than Willis." N Y Times Book Rev

Willis, Mary

See also Walker, Mary Willis

Willocks, Tim

The religion. Sarah Crichton Books 2007 618p $26

ISBN 978-0-374-24865-9; 0-374-24865-6

LC 2006-30419

First published 2006 in the United Kingdom

This novel is "set against the backdrop of the 1565 Turkish invasion of Malta. . . . Adventurer Mattias Tannhauser unwittingly agrees to accompany beautiful noblewoman Carla La Penautier from Sicily to Malta. Their mission is to find the illegitimate son whom Carla was forced to abandon at birth and to save the boy from a horrible fate that will inevitably befall the Christian survivors after the anticipated Turkish victory. Upon their arrival on Malta and despite his aversion to religious fanatics and his cynical view of political causes, Mattias serves as military advisor to the besieged Knights of Saint John the Baptist, a.k.a. 'The Religion.' However, a mysterious inquisitor and devout monk named Ludovico seeks to sabotage Mattias and Carla—as well as the Christian forces on Malta." Libr J

The author is "especially convincing on the battle lust which overtakes both sides, and vividly places us among the besieged. If you don't mind a bit of romance tacked around the fighting, it is a gripping story with reliable factual underpinnings: history as heroics." Times Lit Suppl

Wilson, A. N. (Andrew Norman), 1950-

Winnie and Wolf. Farrar, Straus & Giroux 2008 c2007 363p $25

ISBN 978-0-374-29096-2

LC 2008-932297

First published 2007 in the United Kingdom

"The book chronicles the putative love affair between the grotesquely cuddly Adolf 'Wolf' Hitler and Winnie Wagner, the opera-managing daughter-in-law of the infamous composer. . . . The story is told in retrospect, in the 1980s, by Herr N——, a onetime Wagner family assistant, true believer in the Master (the composer, not the genocidal mastermind) and classically unreliable narrator. Now marooned in East Germany, N—— revisits the pre-war glory days in Bayreuth, his hometown and the site of Wagner's self-built concert hall. N—— is writing an extended letter to his adopted daughter, Senta, in an attempt to explain the truth about her birth and parentage (look to the title for clues). Wrestling with Winnie's role

in Wolf's rise—'love and death, inextricably mixed'—the narrator skirts around his own culpability in the destruction of his family and country, and of the Jews and 'pansies' who once peopled Bayreuth's musical sphere." Time Out N Y

This is a "remarkable effort, simultaneously dazzling and sluggish. Wilson pulls off a daring risk in seeking to humanize an unspeakable monster by giving him a domestic life and a mundane past, because he realizes that to explain is not to exonerate." Denver Post

Wilson, Andrew Norman *See* Wilson, A. N. (Andrew Norman), 1950-

Wilson, F. Paul (Francis Paul)

Conspiracies; a Repairman Jack novel. Forge 2000 317p

ISBN 0-312-86797-2

LC 99-52372

"A Tom Doherty Associates book"

"Jack, a fix-it man who specializes in problems that frequently require him to face powerful foes and slip into the world of the supernatural, is hired to locate the missing wife of a businessman. This time he must find a missing woman who happens to be one of the world's leading conspiracy theorists (she was preparing to reveal her Grand Unification Theory, which would explain the truth behind all manner of strange goings-on). To find her, Jack must attend a convention of conspiracy buffs, most of whom seem more than a little strange. . . . Those who look at conspiracy theories with a skeptical eye will have a great time, as will anyone who likes a well-plotted, spooky thriller. Wilson tells a great story." Booklist

Deep as the marrow. Forge 1997 352p $24.95

ISBN 0-312-86264-4

LC 96-30502

"A Tom Doherty Associates book"

"When President Thomas Winston announces a plan to attack the drug problem by making drugs legal, he's met first with public outrage, then with an assassination plot involving his boyhood friend and personal physician, Dr. John VanDuyne. In a plan masterminded by a Colombian drug lord, six-year-old Katie VanDuyne is kidnapped to persuade her father to give the president an antibiotic that will destroy his bone marrow. The kidnapping goes awry early on, because of the doctor's ethics and a kidnapper's attachment to Katie, but Wilson spins out the action to the last pages, making some persuasive arguments for drug legalization along the way." Libr J

The haunted air; a Repairman Jack novel. Forge 2002 415p $24.95

ISBN 0-312-87868-0

LC 2002-72059

"A Tom Doherty Associates book"

This Repairman Jack novel "teams the righteous urban mercenary with his strangest bedfellows yet: a pair of sham spirit mediums who openly operate their occult con game out of a brownstone in Queens. . . . Jack takes the case of brothers Lyle and Charlie Kenton, who've been threatened by other Big Apple pseudo-psychics for horning in on the lucrative seance scene. No sooner has Jack begun . . . than real ghosts begin popping up along with a secret cult of ritual child murderers. . . . Above all, the novel enhances the enigma of Jack, a hero who commands respect despite his curmudgeonly disdain for

Wilson, F. Paul (Francis Paul)—*Continued*
contemporary culture, his morally ambiguous work-for-hire ethic and his unsettling appeal to the vigilante in every reader." Publ Wkly

Legacies. Forge 1998 381p $24.95
ISBN 0-312-86414-0   LC 98-14322
"A Tom Doherty Associates book"
"Jack, a fix-it man who specializes in solving people's problems (and who, as far as the authorities are concerned, doesn't even exist), does a favor for a friend—he recovers some toys stolen from a hospital—and winds up helping a woman solve a deadly mystery from her past. Repairman Jack is a strong man whose moments of compassion don't seem forced, an enigma without being annoyingly mysterious." Booklist

Wilson, Francis Paul *See* Wilson, F. Paul (Francis Paul)

Wilson, John Anthony Burgess *See* Burgess, Anthony, 1917-1993

Wilson, Robert, 1957-

The blind man of Seville. Harcourt 2003 434p $26
ISBN 0-15-100835-3   LC 2002-68495
"Javier Falcón, chief homicide detective in Seville, has a ghastly murder to solve, one that inexplicably strikes into the depths of his being. When two similar murders follow, Falcón finds himself facing a midlife crisis as he penetrates his own past to find connections between the victims and his recently deceased father, a famous painter who lived a life of hidden depravity." Libr J
"Wilson . . . is able to hold reader interest at an almost unbearable pitch of excitement throughout this shocker with exquisite plot pacing and intriguing character revelations." Booklist

The hidden assassins. Harcourt 2006 453p $25
ISBN 978-0-15-101239-8; 0-15-101239-3
                              LC 2006-17507
"A mutilated, faceless, scalped, and headless body of a male appears in the city dump. The violence escalates when a bomb destroys a mosque, an apartment building, and a preschool. Fueled by public pressure, Seville homicide detective Jefe Javier Falcón . . . starts to investigate the complex motives behind these acts of terror." Bookmarks Magazine
"Falcón is smart and relentless and thoroughly decent, which makes him a capable, if less than captivating, guide through the complicated tangle of motives and suspects. . . . [The novel] is smart and challenging, a mystery that demonstrates the flexibility of a genre that is too often constrained by convention and stereotypes." Cleveland Plain Dealer

Wilson, Robert Charles, 1953-

Blind Lake. TOR Bks. 2003 399p $24.95
ISBN 0-7653-0262-4   LC 2003-47345
"A Tom Doherty Associates book"
"When the research facility at Blind Lake, MN, is placed under military blockade and quarantine, the scientists and workers . . . can only connect their enforced isolation with their research on a newly discovered form of alien life on a distant planet. Journalist Chris Carmody, trapped in Blind Lake, finds his life transformed by his chance encounter with researcher Marguerite Hauser and her troubled daughter, Tessa, a young girl whose unusual mind may hold the key to unraveling the alien mystery." Libr J
"No one knows better than Wilson how to manipulate the language of science to suggest the essential unknowability of the universe. . . . The drama at Blind Like gradually expands to encompass humans and aliens in entirely unforeseen ways." N Y Times Book Rev

Julian Comstock; a story of 22nd-century America. Tor Bks. 2009 413p $25.95
ISBN 978-0-7653-1971-5; 0-7653-1971-3
                              LC 2008-53400
"A Tom Doherty Associates book"
This novel is "set in a postcollapse, imperial United States returned to 19th-century technology and mores. Julian Comstock, the disgraced nephew of the tyrannical American president, grows up in a small town in what was formerly northern Canada. Adam Hazzard, Julian's working-class friend, and Sam Godwin, a bluff old retainer and secret Jew, struggle to keep Julian alive despite his uncle's hatred and Julian's proclivity for annoying the repressive Dominion Church. When Julian is drafted to fight the invading Dutch in Labrador, exaggerated tales of his heroism, written by would-be novelist Adam, catapult the young aristocrat to unwanted fame." Publ Wkly
The narrative is "beautifully written, populated with engaging and sympathetic, if conflicted, characters, and unlike anything else [Wilson's] done to date . . . . It's also a fascinating example of SF's ongoing negotiations with ideas of history and identity, and a good deal more complex than its faux-naif narrative voice and boys'-book adventure plotting would seem to suggest." Locus

Spin. Tor 2005 364p
ISBN 0-7653-0938-6   LC 2004-58862
"The narrative time oscillates effortlessly between Tyler Dupree's early adolescence and his near-future young manhood haunted by the impending death of the sun and the earth. Tyler's best friends, twins Diane and Jason Lawton, take two divergent paths: Diane into a troubling religious cult of the end, Jason into impassioned scientific research to discover the nature of the galactic Hypotheticals whose 'Spin' suddenly sealed Earth in a 'cosmic baggie,' making one of its days equal to a hundred million years in the universe beyond. As convincing as Wilson's scientific hypothesizing is—biological, astrophysical, medical—he excels even more dramatically with the infinitely intricate, minutely nuanced relationships among Jason, Diane and Tyler, whose older self tries to save them both with medicines from Mars, terraformed through Jason's genius into an incubator for new humanity." Publ Wkly

Wilson, Sloan, 1920-2003

The man in the gray flannel suit. Simon & Schuster 1955 304p o.p.
                                              *
The man of the title is the ordinary, upper middle class New York business employee, who at five o'clock heads for his home, wife, and children in Connecticut. Thomas

Wilson, Sloan, 1920-2003—*Continued*

Rath is his name in this book. Tom joins a large corporation, does an honest job, and is evidently headed for bigger money. As an undercurrent to his daily life Tom remembers his war service, the girl he met in Rome, and his illegitimate son

"Thoughtful, searching novel. . . . Sloan Wilson manages to hold the reader's interest and at the same time to solve Rath's problems without distorting his character." N Y Her Trib Books

Wiltse, David

Blown away. Putnam 1996 343p o.p.

LC 96-2387

In this novel, "Karl Atlee, alias Jason Cole, unleashes a series of bombings. . . . After blowing up Cornell University's suicide bridge and killing a student, the madman with a mission bombs the Roosevelt Island tram, the Triborough Bridge, and the Holland Tunnel, taking many more innocent lives. Special Agents John Becker and Pegeen Haddad have been assigned to stop Atlee." Libr J

"Wiltse illuminates a broad spectrum of heroism and villainy with a colorful, often humorous cast of characters that makes agent Becker seem drab by comparison. These engaging folk will hold readers in thrall through a fastpaced, cleverly plotted tale that features plenty of action, on the street and off, and that will leave readers just as the title says." Publ Wkly

Bone deep. Putnam 1995 340p o.p.

LC 95-11089

This suspense novel features FBI agent John Becker. Connecticut's "rain-swollen Saugatuck River floats a bone into a local backyard, prompting the attention of the vacationing Becker and his old friend 'Tee' Terhune, the town's police chief. . . . After marks on the bone reveal that the body it belongs to was cut in pieces before burial, an upriver search turns up a charnel house of companion bones in the loose soil of a Christmas tree farm. A prime suspect arises when Tee gets anonymous tips that one of his officers, the loathsome McNeil, who likes to sleep with high-school girls, is involved in the killings." Publ Wkly

Wimberley, Darryl

The king of Colored Town. Toby 2007 353p $24.95

ISBN 978-1-59264-181-9; 1-59264-181-4

This "novel explores school integration in Florida in the 1960s through the eyes of tall, musically gifted Cilla Handsom, the black teenage daughter of an autistic mother who requires a lot of care. The section of Laureate, where she lives, is dubbed 'Colored Town' and lacks running water and music, but for one well and radio. Cilla's old life of toting water and helping her mother perform at church is interrupted by the arrival of charismatic Joe Billy King by train one day and by her teacher's request that she join the marching band at the county's formerly all-white school in exchange for music lessons." Libr J

"An impassioned and eloquent piece of storytelling set in the last days of the Jim Crow South." Texas Monthly

Wimmer, Natasha

(tr) Bolaño, R. 2666

Windling, Terri, 1958-

(ed) Snow white, blood red. See Snow white, blood red

Winegardner, Mark, 1961-

The Godfather returns. Random House 2004 430p $26.95

ISBN 1-400-06101-6   LC 2004-51380

This is a sequel to Mario Puzo's 1969 novel. "It is 1955. Michael Corleone has won a bloody victory in the war among New York's crime families. Now he wants to consolidate his power, save his marriage, and take his family into legitimate businesses. To do so, he must confront his most dangerous adversary yet, Nick Geraci, a former boxer who worked his way through law school as a Corleone street enforcer, and who is every bit as deadly and cunning as Michael. Their personal cold war will run from 1955 to 1962, exerting immense influence on the lives of America's most powerful criminals and their loved ones." Publisher's note

"This is a phenomenally entertaining, psychologically rich saga that spans the entire Godfather years imagined in novel and film by Mario Puzo (the latter via his screenplays), filling in the blanks, fleshing out the characters, focusing primarily on the time (mid 1950s-early '60s) between when Puzo's landmark novel ended and the film Godfather II begins." Publ Wkly

Wingate, Steven

Wifeshopping; stories. Houghton Mifflin 2008 190p pa $13.95

ISBN 978-0-547-05365-3   LC 2008-4733

"A Mariner original"

Contents: Beaching it ;Me and Paul; The Balkan house; Inside the hole; A story about two prisoners; Meeting Grace; Faster; Dig for dollars; Bill; Three a.m. ambulance driver; Knuckles; Our last garage sale; In Flagstaff

"One of the cruelest ironies of modern letters is that so many books are written about male insecurity — consider the oeuvres of Bellow and Updike, and work down from there — and yet so few readers of serious fiction seem to be men. This irony is especially piquant in the case of Steven Wingate's new story collection, 'Wifeshopping.' Trust me, fellas, even if you think you'e been a bad boyfriend, the protagonists assembled here could teach you a thing or two about despicable conduct. Nearly all are in the thrall of misguided wooing. They want sex (naturally) and companionship (to some vague extent), but mostly they want to bask in the glamorous notion that they are the marrying kind. It's almost sweet, really — until it turns toxic." Los Angeles Times Book Rev

Winkler, Anthony C.

Dog war. Akashic Books 2007 195p pa $14.95

ISBN 978-1-93335-428-6; 1-93335-428-3

LC 2006-936538

Winkler, Anthony C.—*Continued*

"Newly widowed, Precious, an upstanding Jamaican with practical ideas and a conversational relationship with Jesus, becomes a maid in a Miami mansion for a pampered dog, who soon develops overfond feelings for her person. The dog belongs to the spiritually questing Mistress Lucy, a multimillionaire among whose most pressing concerns is whether to have her Rolls 'decowed'—the leather removed on moral grounds. Winkler has a fine ear for patois and dialogue, and a love of language that makes bawdy jokes crackle." New Yorker

Winslow, Don, 1953-

The Dawn Patrol. Alfred A. Knopf 2008 303p $23.95

ISBN 978-0-307-26620-0; 0-307-26620-6

LC 2008-6531

"Winslow horses around early with a lightweight plot about San Diego cop turned PI Boone Daniels searching for an AWOL stripper scheduled to testify against a nightclub owner running an insurance scam. Riotous beach-rat banter abounds, and the 'endless summer' vibe is blissful. But a dreadful undercurrent emerges in which Winslow's amiable 'Dawn Patrol' (the day's earliest surfers) see their carefree lifestyle threatened by the modern virus of gangs, drugs and violence. Winslow transforms his blithe trifle into an elegiac riff on the Pacific Coast's paradise lost, and produces a classic. If you haven't read Winslow yet, get to it." San Francisco Chron

The winter of Frankie Machine. Alfred A. Knopf 2006 299p $23.95

ISBN 1-4000-4498-7

LC 2006-45263

"Frank Machianno, a retired mob hit man known as Frankie Machine as a tribute to his efficiency, has put his past behind him and is living a tranquil life in San Diego running a bait shop and supplying restaurants with linens and seafood. When the son of a local mob boss asks for his backup in resolving a dispute with the Detroit mob, Frank agrees, only to find that he's been set up as the intended victim of a hit. Using his survival skills and street smarts, the executioner follows a trail of bodies to identify which of his past crimes has caught up with him. While the plot is familiar, Winslow has created plausible characters and taut scenes of suspense that will keep readers turning pages." Publ Wkly

Winspear, Jacqueline, 1955-

Among the mad; a Maisie Dobbs novel. Henry Holt and Company 2009 303p $25

ISBN 978-0-8050-8216-6; 0-8050-8216-6

LC 2008-32576

Sequel to: An incomplete revenge (2008)

This "novel opens on Christmas Eve 1931, as Maisie witnesses an injured war veteran-turned-beggar blow himself up on a crowded London street. This tragic event turns sinister the next day when the prime minister receives a menacing letter that demands the government immediately render aid to alleviate the suffering of the unemployed, particularly war veterans who served their country dutifully. If no action is taken within 48 hours, there will be consequences." Libr J

"The lamentation over economic crisis, terrorism and traumatized veterans feels both true to its setting and disquietingly contemporary. Well-crafted and well worth reading." Kirkus

Birds of a feather; a novel. Soho Press 2004 311p $25

ISBN 1-569-47368-4

LC 2003-25732

"A Maisie Dobbs novel"

Sequel to Maisie Dobbs (2003)

P.I. Maisie Dobbs "has been hired to find the missing daughter of a wealthy London magnate. As Maisie and her Cockney assistant, Billy Beale, try to track Charlotte Waite down, they discover that three of her old friends have been murdered-poisoned and then bayoneted." Libr J

"The period touches, from clothing to manners, are not only elegantly presented but unostentatious." Booklist

Followed by Pardonable lies (2005)

An incomplete revenge; a Maisie Dobbs novel. H. Holt 2008 306p $24; pa $14

ISBN 978-0-8050-8215-9; 0-8050-8215-8; 978-0-312-42818-1 (pa); 0-312-42818-9 (pa)

LC 2007-40639

Sequel to Messenger of truth (2006)

In this episode "Maisie is employed by James Compton to investigate a number of strange fires that break out in a Kent village around harvest time each year when the community is bustling with locals, Londoners, and Gypsies. Compton's company is interested in buying the local brickwork manufacturer, but he wants to make certain the purchase won't cause any ill effects to his company. Maisie soon senses that the villagers know more than they will say about the mysterious fires. . . . Maisie is absolutely compelling not only as an investigator but also as a psychologist while she probes the hearts and minds of those she meets." Libr J

Followed by Among the mad (2009)

Maisie Dobbs; a novel. Soho Press 2003 294p $24

ISBN 1-56947-330-7

* LC 2002-44656

In this novel "set in WWI-era England, humble housemaid Maisie Dobbs climbs . . . up Britain's social ladder, becoming in turn a university student, a wartime nurse and ultimately a private investigator. . . . Her first sleuthing case, which begins as a simple marital infidelity investigation, leads to a trail of war-wounded soldiers lured to a remote convalescent home in Kent from which no one seems to emerge alive." Publ Wkly

"For a clever and resourceful young woman who has just set herself up in business as a private investigator, Maisie seems a bit too sober and much too sad. Romantic readers sensing a story-within-a-story won't be disappointed. But first, they must prepare to be astonished at the sensitivity and wisdom with which Maisie resolves her first professional assignment." N Y Times Book Rev

Messenger of truth; a Maisie Dobbs novel. H. Holt 2006 322p $24; pa $14

ISBN 978-0-8050-7898-5; 0-8050-7898-3; 978-0-312-42685-9 (pa); 0-312-42685-2 (pa)

LC 2006-43626

Winspear, Jacqueline, 1955-—*Continued*

Sequel to Pardonable lies (2005)

This installment in the historical mystery series "finds our fearless psychologist/inquiry agent investigating the death of artist Nick Bassington-Hope. According to Detective Inspector Stratton, Nick's fall from a set of scaffolding was merely a tragic accident. Nick's twin sister, Georgina, however, insists he was murdered and hires Maisie to discover the truth. . . . The mystery itself is rather transparent, but what makes this book delightful is how Winspear shows Maisie's emotional development amid the bitter legacy of the Great War." Libr J

Followed by An incomplete revenge (2008)

Pardonable lies; a Maisie Dobbs novel. Henry Holt 2005 342p $23

ISBN 0-8050-7897-5   LC 2005-46388

Sequel to Birds of a feather (2004)

In this installment, "British psychologist and investigator Maisie Dobbs, who attended university after serving as a nurse in France during World War I, tackles a trio of cases that ranges from the unsettling to the surreal. There's 13-year-old Avril Jarvis, accused of first-degree murder. And Sir Cecil Lawton, QC, who is attempting to honor his late wife's request to determine if their fighter-pilot son is living or dead. And Maisie's rich, trendy friend, Priscilla, desperate for details about her brother, who was killed in the Great War. Maisie pursues clues with the help of her Cockney assistant, Billy, and wisdom imparted by her elegant, if enigmatic, mentor, Maurice. . . . A trip to France reveals a startling connection between the cases but proves traumatic for the former nurse still haunted by her experiences tending to wounded soldiers during the war." Booklist

Followed by Messenger of truth (2006)

Winston, Lolly

Good grief. Warner Books 2004 344p $18

ISBN 0-446-53304-1   LC 2003-15207

After thirty-six-year-old Sophie Stanton's husband Ethan dies of cancer, she leaves her job with a technology company in Silicon Valley and winds up in Oregon where she reinvents herself as a baker and finds a new love interest

"Throughout this heartbreaking, gorgeous look at loss, Winston imbues her heroine and her narrative with the kind of grace, bitter humor and rapier-sharp realness that will dig deep into a reader's heart and refuse to let go. Sophie is wounded terribly, but she's also funny, fresh and utterly believable." Publ Wkly

Winterson, Jeanette, 1959-

Oranges are not the only fruit. Grove Press 1997 176p pa $14

ISBN 0-8021-3516-1

First published 1985 in the United Kingdom

"Raised by an oppressively evangelical mother, Jeanette grows up a good little Christian soldier, even going so far as to stitch samplers whose apocalyptic themes terrify her classmates. . . . Jeanette would have remained in the fold but for her unconventional desires; though she can reconcile her love of women with her love of God, the church cannot. It could have been a grim tale, but this [novel] . . . is in fact a wry and tender telling of a young girl's triumphantly coming into her own." Libr J

Sexing the cherry. Atlantic Monthly Press 1990 167p

ISBN 0-87113-350-4

* LC 90-30682

This is a novel "about a prodigious giantess and her explorer son in 17th-century London. Jordan fetches the first pineapple to the court of Charles II, while his mother, The Dog Woman, wreaks vengeance upon Puritans in a brothel. The plague; the flying princesses who defy laws of the courts and gravity; Jordan's travels to the floating city and the botanical wonders of the New World–the tale . . . [involves both] history and fantasy. The two characters eventually merge into the grievously polluted life of modern London." Libr J

"Winterson, whose work is full of profound truths disguised as simple statements, is at her epigrammatic best on the subject of romantic love." Quill Quire

The stone gods. Harcourt 2008 c2007 206p $24

ISBN 978-0-15-101491-0; 0-15-101491-4

LC 2007-47079

First published 2007 in the United Kingdom

"Heroine Billie Crusoe appears in three different end-of-the-world scenarios, allowing Winterson to explore the repetitive and destructive nature of human history and an inability (or unwillingness) of people to learn from previous mistakes. In the first section, inhabitants of the pollution-choked planet Orbus have discovered Planet Blue (Earth), and soon set about launching an asteroid at it to kill the dinosaurs that would prevent them from colonizing the planet. The second and third sections are set on Earth in 1774 and then in the Post-3 War era." Publ Wkly

"A playful but impassioned novel. Winterson cloaks her disillusionment without political excesses in a sustained imaginative jeu d'esprit. Her writing is funny and beautiful." London Times

Winthrop, Elizabeth

Island justice. Morrow 1998 356p $25

ISBN 0-688-15920-6   LC 97-36566

A novel about "secret and not-so-secret lives on a small New England island. There's Maggie Hammond, thirtysomething international furniture surveyor, drawn back to the island to sell the house she's inherited from her godmother; Anna Craven, a woman stifled by her overbearing, emotionally abusive husband; Erin Craven, grappling with adolescence; and Sam Matera, local naturalist and science teacher whose love complicates Maggie's decision." Libr J

"Along with the satisfying plot . . . readers are also provided with a good deal of information about the flora and fauna of coastal New England and the delicate balance of its human society. 'Island Justice' is the kind of book that used to be called a 'good read'—and sometimes there's nothing better." N Y Times Book Rev

Winthrop, Elizabeth Hartley, 1979-

December. Alfred A. Knopf 2008 239p $23.95

ISBN 978-0-307-26830-3; 0-307-26830-6

LC 2007-37095

"It's December, and 11-year-old Isabelle hasn't spoken in eight months. Her puzzled parents have been in turn patient, forceful, despairing, and supportive, trying every method they can think of to get Isabelle to talk. She has

Winthrop, Elizabeth Hartley, 1979——*Continued*
seen four psychologists without improvement, and now
her private school has issued an ultimatum: Isabelle will
be expelled if she doesn't start speaking when school resumes in January." Libr J

"To appreciate December, which offers the pleasures
of beautifully composed scenes and, when it shifts to Isabelle's point of view, an exact rendering of a child's
acute perceptions, the reader must accept that Isabelle
has fallen under a sort of existential spell. The fact that
her father, Wilson, calls her Belle bolsters the impression
that this is a modern fairy tale, and so does the novel's
deadline-driven structure. . . . December posits the old-
fashioned thesis that family love can conquer many ills.
Some may discount this notion as too hopeful, but others
will find, in Winthrop's exact but tender portraits of domestic rituals, enough evidence to support it." N Y
Times Book Rev

Winton, Tim

Breath; a novel. Farrar, Straus and Giroux 2008
320p $23
ISBN 978-0-374-11634-7; 0-374-11634-2
　　　　　　　　　　　　　　　LC 2007-47879
"Narrated retrospectively by its protagonist, Bruce
Pike, when he is in his fifties, [this novel] is set in the
tiny sawmilling town of Sawyer, and tells the story of
the friendship between 11-year-old Bruce (aka Pikelet)
and the slightly older Loonie, a wildly reckless and daring boy. They are both bound together by their obsession
with surfing, and when Sando, an older pro with an aura
of mystique, takes them under his wing, the obsession
comes closer to something more elemental, more dangerous. Under Sando's tutelage, Pikelet surfs the dangerous
bombora, Old Smoky, but it is left to Loonie and Sando
to do the lethal Nautilus as Pikelet chickens out. The
skittering dynamic within the trio, already unstable,
changes irrevocably after this, and especially when the
fourth character, Sando's unhappy wife Eva, enters the
picture." Scotland on Sunday

"The novel's complexity is poetic, psychological and
ethical. Winton's descriptions of changing seas and
changing seasons are outstanding. His insights into what
motivates people like the bitter Eva or the profoundly irresponsible Sando disclose unsettling ethical implications
with a sure hand." Sydney Morning Herald

Dirt music; a novel. Scribner 2002 411p $26
ISBN 0-7432-2802-2　　　　　LC 2002-17583
First published 2001 in Australia
"At 40, Georgie Jutland, former nurse, inveterate risk-
taker, incipient alcoholic and lifelong rebel against her
prominent family, has moved in with widowed lobster
fisherman Jim Buckridge, "the uncrowned prince" of the
western seaside community of White Point. Although
Georgie devotes herself to Jim's two young sons, their
relationship is uneasy and somehow empty. When she's
drawn to shamateur (fish poacher) Luther Fox, who
breaks the law to keep his mind from tragic memories,
the lives of all three begin to unravel." Publ Wkly

"As well as offering nuanced portraits of three very
different characters, [this] is a cracking page-turner
which deftly splices together separate narrative threads
without ever losing its headlong momentum. . . . Mr
Winton comes from Western Australia, a vast state of
exceptional natural beauty. . . . He brilliantly conjures

its hostile desert spaces and its magnificent coastline. His
characters, like the landscape they inhabit, are by turns
callous and poetic, vulgar and seductive." Economist

Wishingrad, Jay

(ed) Legal fictions. See Legal fictions

Witchel, Alex

The spare wife. Alfred A. Knopf 2008 286p
$23.95
ISBN 978-1-4000-4149-7; 1-4000-4149-X
　　　　　　　　　　　　　　　LC 2007-40320
"Former model, widow, and sometime lawyer Ponce
Morris (named for Ponce de León and his fountain of
youth) has made it perfectly clear that she isn't interested
in sex and romance anymore. So her girlfriends don't
mind when she acts as a 'spare wife' and attends events
and such with their husbands. The wives benefit from
Ponce's friendship, too, in the form of girl talk and shopping expositions. But when Babette, a young aspiring
writer and editorial assistant, discovers that Ponce is having an affair with one of the husbands, she finds herself
with a scoop that could kick her writing career into high
gear." Libr J

"Witchel's drama-filled portrait of 40-something socialites in the Paris Hilton era has scandalous affairs and social to-dos to spare. It's extravagant and shallow, closely
observed and entertaining." Publ Wkly

Witt, Martha

Broken as things are; a novel. Henry Holt 2004
293p $23
ISBN 0-8050-7595-X　　　　　LC 2003-57003
Fourteen-year-old "Morgan-Lee and her handsome,
'unwell' 15-year-old brother, Ginx, are as emotionally
close as twins. They have a secret language—a nonsensi-
cal patois that Ginx created—and share a running story
about a brother and sister who are given permission to
love each other forever and ever. Their mother is an
overdelicate flower who's taken to her bed rather than
face her son's problems; their father is kind but incapable of taking control; and their younger sister, Dana, has
all but abandoned the family, moving into her aunt and
uncle's house next door. Everything is proceeding as
well as can be expected . . . until Morgan-Lee falls in
love with her childhood friend, Billy. Neither sibling is
prepared for the inevitable as Morgan-Lee's adolescence
strains the family bonds and pitches the household into
full-blown crisis." Publ Wkly

"Witt's image-laden prose navigates the obvious territory between sanity and craziness but also beautifully
evokes that time in childhood when boundaries between
fantasy and reality are not yet clear." Libr J

Wittenborn, Dirk

Pharmakon. Viking 2008 406p $25.95
ISBN 978-0-670-01942-7; 0-670-01942-9
　　　　　　　　　　　　　　　LC 2007-40456
"William Friedrich, an ambitious professor of psychology at Yale in 1952, has stumbled upon a drug that
promises happiness—and that can make him a famous
man. When his experiment goes awry, and a research
subject commits murder, the consequences will haunt

Wittenborn, Dirk—*Continued*

him and his family forever. . . . [The book] follows the Friedrichs from the well-ordered suburban life of postwar America through the chaos and freedom of the counterculture, into the drug-fueled, media-crazed eighties and beyond." Publisher's note

This is a "smart, eccentric coming-of-age story about an entire culture's maturation process, not just one about the workings of a single family. And Mr. Wittenborn is able to channel a lifetime's worth of psychiatric symptoms into one improbably universal story." N Y Times (Late N Y Ed)

Wodehouse, P. G. (Pelham Grenville), 1881-1975

The code of the Woosters. Doubleday, Doran 1938 298p o.p.

"It was only the fact that Jeeves belonged to an exclusive club of gentlemen's personal gentlemen, where all the secrets in the lives of employers were filed for reference, that saved Bertie Wooster when the disappearance of an eighteenth-century silver cows-creamer threatened to land him in jail. Two rival collectors who coveted the piece of silver, and two pairs of bickering lovers, made Bertie's life a burden until Jeeves unearthed evidence that was a weapon." Booklist

The inimitable Jeeves. Autograph ed. British Bk. Centre 1956 192p o.p.

First published 1923 in the United Kingdom

The resourceful valet again takes command of a typical Wodehouse situation

Tales from the Drones Club. International Polygonics 1991 352p o.p.   LC 91-8386

First published 1982 in the United Kingdom

Contents: Fate; Tried in the furnace; Trouble down at Tudsleigh; The amazing hat mystery; Goodbye to all cats; The luck of the Stiffhams; Noblesse oblige; Uncle Fred flits by; The masked troubadour; All's well with Bingo; Bingo and the Peke crisis; The editor regrets; Sonny boy; The shadow passes; Bramley is so bracing; The fat of the land; The word in season; Leave it to Algy; Oofy, Freddie and the beef trust; Bingo bans the bomb; Stylish stouts

A Wodehouse bestiary; edited and with a preface by D.R. Bensen; foreword by Howard Phipps, Jr. Ticknor & Fields 1985 329p o.p.

LC 85-7999

Contents: Unpleasantness at Bludleigh Court; Sir Roderick comes to lunch; Something squishy; Pig-Hoo-o-o-o-ey; Comrade Bingo; Monkey business; Jeeves and the impending doom; Open house; Ukridge's dog college; The story of Webster; The go-getter; Jeeves and the old school chum; Uncle Fred flits by; The mixer

"An anthology of tales featuring animals of all sorts wreaking havoc in the lives of Bertie Wooster, the indomitable Jeeves, Mr. Muliner's various relations, and other familiar characters from the madcap Wodehousian world. The numerous mishaps, involving snakes, pigs, gorillas, swans, dogs, and cats, prove as amusing as ever." Booklist

The world of Jeeves. Harper & Row 1988 c1967 654p o.p.

* LC 88-45072

First published 1967 in the United Kingdom

Contents: Jeeves takes charge; Jeeves in the springtime; Scoring off Jeeves; Sir Roderick comes to lunch; Aunt Agatha takes the count; The artistic career of Corky; Jeeves and Chump Cyril; Jeeves and the unbidden guest; Jeeves and the hard-boiled egg; The aunt and the sluggard; Comrade Bingo; The great sermon handicap; The purity of the turf; The metropolitan touch; The delayed exit of Claude and Eustace; Bingo and the little woman; The rummy affair of Old Biffy; Without the option; Fixing it for Freddie; Clustering round young Bingo; Jeeves and the impending doom; The inferiority complex of Old Sippy; Jeeves and the Yule-tide spirit; Jeeves and the song of songs; Episode of the dog Mcintosh; The spot of art; Jeeves and the kid Clementina; The love that purifies; Jeeves and the old school chum; Indian summer of an uncle; The ordeal of young Tuppy; Bertie changes his mind; Jeeves makes an omelette; Jeeves and the greasy bird

Wodehouse, Pelham Grenville *See* Wodehouse, P. G. (Pelham Grenville), 1881-1975

Wolcott, James

The catsitters; a novel. HarperCollins Pubs. 2001 314p $25

ISBN 0-06-019414-6   LC 00-50635

"Johnny Downs is a New York bartender who longs to be a successful actor. Dumped by his girlfriend for reasons that he can't quite grasp, Johnny licks his wounds and takes solace from Darlene Ryder, a straight-talking graduate student whose interest in Johnny is romantic without being sexual: Darlene becomes a kind of relationship coach, offering him counsel in matters of the heart." New Yorker

"This novel has so many hilarious twists and turns that it keeps even the most jaded romance reader turning the pages. Wolcott expertly blends his careening plot with wit, sarcasm, and insight." Libr J

Wolfe, Gene, 1931-

The best of Gene Wolfe; a definitive retrospective of his finest short fiction. Tor 2009 478p $27.95

ISBN 978-0-7653-2135-0; 0-7653-2135-1

* LC 2009-12889

"A Tom Doherty Associates book"

Contents: The island of Doctor Death and other stories; The toy theater; The fifth head of Cerberus; Beech Hill; The recording; Hour of trust; The death of Dr. Island; La Befana; Forlesen; Westwind; The hero as werewolf; The marvelous chessplaying automaton; Straw; The eyeflash miracles; Seven American nights; The detective of dreams; Kevin Malone; The god and his man; On the train; From the desk of Gilmer C. Merton; Death of the island doctor; Redbeard; The boy who hooked the sun; Parkroads: a review; Game in the pope's head; And when they appear; Bed and breakfast; Petting zoo; The tree is my hat; Has anybody seen Junie Moon?; A cabin on the coast

Wolfe, Gene, 1931——*Continued*

A "retrospective from this writer's writer, comprising 31 tales, 1970-1999, ranging from a few pages to novella length, selected by the author (with one exception, included at his agents' behest) and arranged chronologically." Kirkus

This "is a highly flattering career retrospective of a postmodern fabulist disguised as a mild-mannered SF writer." Publ Wkly

Castleview. Doherty Assocs. 1990 278p o.p.
* LC 89-25712

"A TOR book"

"The inhabitants of the small town of Castleview, in a 'forgotten and countrified corner of upstate Illinois,' have grown accustomed to glimpsing a 'mirage' that resembles a medieval castle suspended in air. With the arrival in town of Will E. Shields, who has just bought a local automobile dealership, mysteries multiply like goose bumps. The town's hospital and funeral home fill with the victims of peculiar accidents, unsavory strangers knock on doors or peer through windows or suddenly appear on rainy highways riding horses with too many legs—and you just know Castleview is in for a major crisis." N Y Times Book Rev

Wolfe's "deceptively simple prose masks a wealth of complexity." Libr J

The Citadel of the Autarch. Timescape Bks. 1983 317p (Book of the new Sun, v4) o.p.
LC 82-5964

In this concluding volume of the tetralogy "Severian, the exiled torturer . . . attains the destiny hinted at since the first book and becomes the Autarch, 'who in one body is a thousand,' ruler of the Commonwealth and potential saviour of a dying Earth waiting for its reddened sun to go out." Publ Wkly

"Wolfe plays with the language like a master wordsmith, yet never loses control of the multi-layered story he's weaving. His style is paradoxically both baroque and simple—the lush beauty of the words never renders the tale impenetrable." Best Sellers

The claw of the conciliator. Timescape Bks. 1981 303p (Book of the new Sun, v2) o.p.
LC 80-20569

In this second volume of the series "Severian, a journeyman torturer, struggles to return the magical Claw of the Conciliator to its guardians. His quest is delayed when men under the leadership of the bandit Vodalus capture him to prevent the execution of a comrade. Severian and his companion Jonas win their freedom by agreeing to carry a message to an agent of Vodalus' at the Castle Absolute, seat of power for the ruling Autarch. Severian has no intention of carrying the promise through, in spite of his admiration for Vodalus. His intention to find his lover and continue his personal quest suffers a temporary setback at the hands of Castle guards." West Coast Rev Books

Followed by The sword of the Lictor

An evil guest. Tor 2008 304p $25.95
ISBN 978-0-7653-2133-6; 0-7653-2133-5
LC 2008-28716

"A Tom Doherty Associates book"

"A century from now, in a world not so different from our own, Cassie, an actress, falls in love with two men,

a private detective with mysterious powers and a powerful and wealthy man who has visited the human colonies in space. One transforms her into her true self, while the other becomes her stage angel and backs her career. Yet both men know that all is not as it seems and beneath the facade of everyday life there lurk strange, elder beings whose horrors only wait to be unleashed." Libr J

The novel is set in the "future, but despite the holographic video broadcasts and intergalactic space transports, the world feels like that of the 1930s, complete with tough-talking cops, wily dames and shady operatives; it's more pulp thriller than Space Age adventure. Though this results in a future with some oddly old-fashioned gender roles, it allows Wolfe to mine his many sources and inspirations—from the detective novels of Raymond Chandler to the fantastic tales of H.P. Lovecraft—to dazzling effect." BookPage

Pirate freedom. Tor 2007 320p il $24.95
ISBN 978-0-7653-1878-7; 0-7653-1878-4
LC 2007-14348

This is the "story of the two lives of Father Christopher, a Catholic priest in the contemporary world and a successful pirate on the Spanish Main three centuries earlier. . . . Piratical Christopher certainly takes advantage of his chosen career to free himself of many of the restrictions of his era, though he did also take a wife and father a child, both of whom he lost in his passage to the future." Booklist

"The one issue Wolfe tap-dances around is slavery. Chris treats slaves as fellow men and frees them whenever possible without anything more than the occasional light question from others. Wolfe's writing is reminiscent of Carol Emshwiller. . . . There's the same concrete level of detail mixed with an occasionally hazy sense of time and events. The novel is as simple as Wolfe's straightforward, lean prose and easily pulls the reader through to an enjoyable circular ending." BookPage

The shadow of the torturer. Simon & Schuster 1980 303p (Book of the new Sun, v1) o.p.
LC 79-22371

"A TOR book"

A novel about "the experiences of Severian, a young man apprenticed to a legally sanctioned guild of torturers. . . . When Severian breaks the rules of the guild by allowing a 'client' to commit suicide, he is sent from his strange home, the only place he has known, on a journey through an inhospitable and dangerous world." Libr J

"The book combines elements of fantasy and sf, and the slow pacing is balanced by the excellent characterization and the richly detailed, thoroughly compelling future world." Booklist

Followed by The claw of the conciliator

The sword of the Lictor. Timescape Bks. 1981 302p (Book of the new Sun, v3) o.p.
LC 81-9427

In this third volume of the series "Severian, the torturer demoted to executioner, has reached Thrax, city of his exile, only to find that he can no longer do his work. He lets a prisoner escape rather than kill her (his original crime was to offer a prisoner the escape of death) and flees to the mountains. He meets the Alzabo, a terrifying creature in whom those eaten seem to live on, adopts a son and loses him, fights a revivified tyrant of the past and wins, helps the people of the floating islands, meets

Wolfe, Gene, 1931-—*Continued*
aliens and learns something of their true nature. The magical jewel called the Claw of the Conciliator is smashed, but Severian finds its essential heart, which is indeed a claw." Publ Wkly

Followed by The Citadel of the Autarch

The Urth of the new sun. Doherty Assocs. 1987 372p (Book of the new Sun) o.p.

LC 87-50478

"A TOR book"

This sequel to the four-volume Book of the new Sun continues "the story of Severian, a one-time torturers' apprentice who becomes Autarch and then leaves Urth to find the 'new sun' that alone can rejuvenate an exhausted humanity." N Y Times Book Rev

For all its obvious unity, the book also has a strongly picaresque quality, with many episodes and characters developed as lovingly and skillfully as Wolfe can manage—which is very well indeed." Booklist

Wolfe, Inger Ash

The calling. Harcourt 2008 371p $24

ISBN 978-0-15-101347-0   LC 2007-29290

This mystery "opens with the grisly slaying of an elderly cancer sufferer in Port Dundas, a remote Ontario town that has gone years without a homicide. The murder hits at a particularly tough time for 61-year-old Det. Insp. Hazel Micallef, who's struggling to come to terms with a surprise divorce and battles daily with her acerbic 87-year-old mother. A serious staff shortage and an injured back add to the department commander's woes. A second, even more disturbing killing raises the ante for Micallef, who's already doubtful she can solve the first case. As Micallef marshals her forces, Wolfe fans the already high suspense by cutting between them and their elusive quarry. With the body count climbing, the detective puts herself increasingly at risk in a desperate attempt to foil the grand, demented plan that the killer regards as a mission." Publ Wkly

"An excellent literary thriller, both riveting and precise. The ending is a shocker." Libr J

Wolfe, Thomas, 1900-1938

The complete short stories of Thomas Wolfe; edited by Francis E. Skipp; foreword by James Dickey. Scribner 1987 xxix, 621p pa $27.50 hardcover o.p.

ISBN 0-02-040891-9 (pa)   LC 86-13782

Contents: An angel on the porch; The train and the city; Death the proud brother; No door; The four lost men; Boom town; The sun and the rain; The house of the far and lost; Dark in the forest, strange as time; For professional appearance; The names of the nation; One of the girls in our party; Circus at dawn; His father's earth; Old Catawba; Arnold Pentland; The face of the war; Gulliver, the story of a tall man; In the park; Only the dead know Brooklyn; Polyphemus; The far and the near; The bums at sunset; The bell remembered; Fame and the poet; Return; Mr. Malone; Oktoberfest; 'E: a recollection; April, late April; The child by tiger; Katamoto; The lost boy; Chickamauga; The company; A prologue to America; Portrait of a literary critic; The birthday; A note on experts: Dexter Vespasian Joyner; Three o'clock;

The winter of our discontent; The dark Messiah; The hollyhock sowers; Nebraska Crane; So this is man; The promise of America; The hollow men; The anatomy of loneliness; The lion at morning; The plumed knight; The newspaper; No cure for it; On leprechauns; The return of the prodigal; Old Man Rivers; Justice is blind; No more rivers; The Spanish letter

"All 58 of Wolfe's short stories . . . have been edited by Skipp in a way that represents what Wolfe himself may have wanted his audience to read." Booklist

Look homeward, angel; a story of the buried life; with an introduction by Maxwell E. Perkins. Scribner 563p $45; pa $14

ISBN 0-684-15158-8; 0-684-80443-3 (pa)

First published 1929

This novel, autobiographical in character, "describes the childhood and youth of Eugene Gant in the town of Altamont, state of Catawba (said to be Asheville, North Carolina). As Gant grows up, he becomes aware of the relations among his family, meets the eccentric people of the town, goes to college, discovers literature and ideas, has his first love affairs, and at last sets out alone on a mystic and romantic 'pilgrimage.'" Reader's Ency. 4th edition

Followed by Of time and the river (1935)

O lost; a story of the buried life; text established by Arlyn and Matthew J. Bruccoli. Centenary ed. University of S.C. Press 2000 xli, 694p il $34.95

ISBN 1-57003-369-2   LC 00-9503

"The reinsertion of expurgated material puts the marrow back in the novel's bones, making for a richer reading experience." Libr J

Of time and the river; a legend of man's hunger in his youth. Scribner 912p $35

ISBN 0-684-14739-4

First published 1935

In this sequel to Look homeward, angel, "Eugene Gant, the hero, spends two years as a graduate student at Harvard, returns home for the dramatic death of his father, and teaches literature in New York City at the 'School for Utility Culture' (New York University). Eventually he tours France, returning home financially and emotionally exhausted." Reader's Ency. 4th edition

The web and the rock. Harper 1939 695p o.p.

This "is an autobiographical account of a successful young writer from North Carolina living in New York City in the early 20th century. The main character, George Webber, bears many similarities to Eugene Gant, the soul-searching protagonist of Wolfe's earlier novels." Merriam-Webster's Ency of Lit

"Wolfe's large scheme has the scope, massive detail and sense of space and time of an epic structure, but also the redundancy of its cyclic conception. The interest lies with the accurate dialogues, realistic descriptions and passages of poetic rhetoric sometimes of considerable power." Penguin Companion to Am Lit

Followed by You can't go home again

Wolfe, Thomas, 1900-1938—*Continued*

You can't go home again. Harper 1940 743p o.p.

                                                  *

"This sequel to The web and the rock "deals with George's life after his return to the U.S.: his continued unsatisfactory romance; his success in writing novels reminiscent of Wolfe's own; his kindly relation and later dissatisfaction with an internationally famous but disillusioned novelist and with his editor, who fatalistically accepts the sickness of civilization; his unsuccessful attempt to return to the roots of his hometown, whose morality has become shoddy during the prosperous decade of the '20s; and his horrid discovery of the destruction of the Germany he had once loved." Oxford Companion to Am Lit. 6th edition

Wolfe, Tom

The bonfire of the vanities. Farrar, Straus & Giroux 1987 659p $25
  ISBN 0-374-11534-6
                                  * LC 87-17691

"The novel relates the fall of Sherman McCoy, an investment banker making a million a year who seems blind to everything except appearances, sex and money. He lives in the middle of New York City without knowing New York City. He seems barely to know his decorative wife, his decorative daughter or his libidinous mistress, to say nothing of himself. He's all surface is Sherman, and when he blunders off the expressway into the welfare jungle of the South Bronx in his $48,000 Mercedes, into the biggest trouble of his heretofore charmed life, he is without reserves of experience, imagination or moral awareness with which to guide himself." N Y Times Book Rev

"Erupting from the first line with noise, color, tension and immediacy, this immensely entertaining novel accurately mirrors a system that has broken down: from the social code of basic good manners to the fair practices of the law." Publ Wkly

I am Charlotte Simmons. Farrar, Straus and Giroux 2004 676p $28.95
  ISBN 0-374-28158-0   LC 2004-47131

"Dupont University–the Olympian halls of learning housing the cream of America's youth, the roseate Gothic spires and manicured lawns suffused with tradition . . . Or so it appears to beautiful, brilliant Charlotte Simmons, a sheltered freshman from North Carolina. But Charlotte soon learns, to her mounting dismay, that for the uppercrust coeds of Dupont, sex, Cool, and kegs trump academic achievement every time. As Charlotte encounters Dupont's privileged elite . . . she gains a new, revelatory sense of her own power, that of her difference and of her very innocence, but little does she realize that she will act as a catalyst in all of their lives." Publisher's note

"Tom Wolfe can make words dance and sing and perform circus tricks, he can make the reader sigh with pleasure before his arias of coloratura description, he can do just about anything in these pages with words, including exaggerate, distort and rant." Washington Post Book World

A man in full; a novel. Farrar, Straus & Giroux 1998 742p $28.95
  ISBN 0-374-27032-5
                                * LC 98-29842

"Set in Atlanta, the plot primarily follows 'Cap'm' Charlie Croaker, an aging ol' boy alpha male real estate tycoon who's a Georgia cracker through and through and a bull in the China closet of life. Croaker's empire begins crumbling when he defaults on a $500-million loan and is besieged by the bank's pit bull repo squad. Add in an OJ-esque college football star accused of raping a white debutante, the mayor and a preacher who try to defend him, and a philosophical convict, all of whom are on a crash course with each other." Libr J

"Among all the animal appetites that are slaked or comically thwarted during the novel there appears one new to Wolfe's fiction. For all their affluence, or their pained lack of same, his chief characters hunger for a code of conduct or a framework of beliefs that will make sense of their lives right now, a blink before the millennium. At its heart, A Man in Full is a cliff-hanging morality tale." Time

Wolff, Maritta M., 1918-2002

Sudden rain; [by] Maritta Wolff. Scribner 2005 434p $26
  ISBN 0-7432-5482-1   LC 2004-52149

"Written in the prefeminist early 1970s, this novel features an Alice Adams like cast of well-heeled West Coast characters. The men go off to work, have casual affairs, and come home for cocktail hour expecting their pampered wives to tolerate their indiscretions and look after their homes and children without complaint. The leisurely plot deals with four interconnected couples whose relationships undergo dramatic changes as a Santa Ana wind blows through town. During a four-day weekend of drinking, smoking, and conversation, a long-estranged father and daughter come together, an aerospace engineer resolves to end his fractious marriage and marry his longtime mistress, and a newly divorced young couple attempt a reconciliation. When Wolff . . . died in 2002, her husband found this manuscript in their refrigerator, and it thaws out like a well-preserved artifact." Libr J

Wolff, Tobias, 1945-

Old school; a novel. Knopf 2003 195p $22
  ISBN 0-375-40146-6
                                * LC 2003-52930

"It is 1960, and the narrator is beginning his final year at a private school of strong literary traditions. Aspiring writers edit the literary journal and compete to win private audiences with visiting luminaries of letters. This year, the guests are to be Robert Frost, Ayn Rand, and Ernest Hemingway. The narrator is a scholarship student, and though his school prides itself on class blindness, his classmates are well versed in spotting the subtle indicators of economic background. Longing to fit in, he dissembles, cultivating an 'easy disregard' by which he hopes to imply his own privilege. But this doubleness leads him toward an unexpected decision with far-reaching consequences for his future." Booklist

"A fine offering, manly in spirit and style . . . Wolff

Wolff, Tobias, 1945-—*Continued*

displays exceptional skill in capturing the small sights and sensations that evoke the whole rarefied world he's taking us back to." Atl Mon (1993)

Our story begins; new and selected stories. Alfred A. Knopf 2008 379p $26.95

ISBN 978-1-4000-4459-7   LC 2007-44262

Contents: In the garden of the North American martyrs; Next door; Hunters in the snow; The liar; Soldier's joy; The rich brother; Leviathan; Desert breakdown, 1968; Say yes; Mortals; Flyboys; Sanity; The other Miller; Two boys and a girl; The chain; Smorgasbord; Lady's dream; powder;The night in question; Firelight; Bullet in the brain; That room; Awaiting orders; A white Bible; Her dog; A mature student; The deposition; Down to bone; Nightingale; The benefit of doubt; Deep kiss

"It does not seem coincidental that Wolff's most protean narratives draw heavily upon his autobiographical experiences. Wolff, at his best, is truly a novelist of himself. His feats of self-invention offer a compelling rebuttal both to the fabulists whose stories fall so short of reality that they have to borrow the truth guarantee of memoir—if the lies rang truer, they could be published as fiction—and to those who denounce the faking of memoir as some sort of heinous crime, rather than the failed act of literature it is." Slate

Wolitzer, Hilma

Hearts. Farrar, Straus & Giroux 1980 342p o.p.
     * LC 80-18556

"Widowed at 26 after six weeks of marriage, Linda Reismann finds herself pregnant and saddled with her husband's 13-year-old daughter, whom she hardly knows. Robin, a perpetually sullen and hostile child who already looks like a woman, is her stepmother's natural antagonist. . . . Taking only what she can stow in the trunk of her car, Linda drives Robin west from New Jersey. She has three items on her agenda: an abortion, the surrender of Robin to her grandfather in Iowa, and her own new life in California. . . . Robin has her own agenda: to find and take revenge on her mother, who ran out on her when she was 5." Newsweek

"This is a comedy about the heart-wrenching process of growth; it is written with great skill and no condescension. Few readers will fail to be moved." New Repub

Summer reading; a novel. Ballantine Books 2007 251p $24.95

ISBN 978-0-345-48586-1; 0-345-48586-6
     LC 2006-35771

This novel "opens as Alyssa (Lissy) Snyder—trophy second wife, reluctant stepmom, and major dyslexic—hosts a summer book discussion group. She's hoping to catch the attention of Ardith Templeton, who initiated the group and who, with her husband Larry, commands center stage in the tony Hamptons social scene. Retired English professor Angela Graves conducts the group, assigns the readings and tries to inspire her charges to take life lessons from the likes of Jane Eyre and Madame Bovary. . . . First-person chapters alternate among Lissy, Angela (who picks over old regrets), and Michelle Cutty, a young local who works as Lissy's summer maid." Publ Wkly

"Maintaining three perspectives throughout a compara-tively short book without labored or slick effect is no mean feat. But once she gets things up and running, Wolitzer accomplishes it with unforced smoothness." N Y Times Book Rev

Tunnel of love. HarperCollins Pubs. 1994 376p o.p.
     LC 93-51064

"Michael di Capua books"

"Linda Reismann is a 24-year-old widow, saddled with an unborn child and teenage Robin, the daughter of her former husband. She travels from Newark to Los Angeles looking for a new start. An aging liquor-store owner hires her, proposes marriage, then is shot by a robber. A Latino dance instructor helps her get work at an upscale aerobic salon, but he turns out to be married. Cynthia Sterling, a wealthy soap-opera producer, hires her as a personal trainer; she supplies incredible medical care and moral support in the aftermath of a terrible car accident (caused by Robin), then files suit for custody of Linda's baby, calling her an unfit mother." Booklist

"The reader is shocked at first by the similarities between this novel and an earlier one, 'Hearts.' . . . In fiction, however, as in nature, God resides in the details. Besides which, while Robin is almost a butterfly in parts of 'Hearts,' here she has advanced backward to become a great fat caterpillar, a gorgeous carbuncle on a solid and good-hearted novel." N Y Times Book Rev

Wolitzer, Meg, 1959-

Surrender, Dorothy; a novel. Scribner 1999 224p $22

ISBN 0-684-84844-9   LC 98-47007

In this novel "three Wesleyan alums—Peter, Maddy, and Adam—react to the sudden death of a beautiful and beloved fourth, Sara. The four had planned to share an August beach house rental. Now, Adam's lover, Shawn, takes her place, the only one not part of the decade-long hermetically sealed group until Sara's death brings them her distraught mother Natalie." Libr J

"Buried within this affecting novel is the troubling question of whether close friendships and close family ties can keep a person from finding romantic intimacy. Wolitzer's Sara didn't live long enough to explore that possibility; perhaps her survivors will be luckier." N Y Times Book Rev

The ten-year nap. Riverhead Books 2008 351p $24.95

ISBN 978-1-59448-978-5; 1-59448-978-5
     LC 2007-38759

This novel "tells the story of a group of formerly high-achieving women who forsook their careers when they had children. Ten years later, as the book's title implies, these mothers are waking up, and realizing that they are bored, directionless, worried about money, and perhaps overinvested in the lives of their husbands, their children and their friends. At their center is Amy Lamb, a former lawyer whose mother, a successful, and very happy, novelist, incessantly nudges her daughter about getting back to work. Amy considers returning to the law, but is crippled by the insecurity born of being out of the workforce, away from the technological innovations that have transformed her profession. Listless, with a 10-year-old who is no longer dependent on her, Amy becomes embroiled in the entanglements of another mother — a working mother — whom she meets at her son's prep

Wolitzer, Meg, 1959-—*Continued*

school. 'The Ten-Year Nap' is an engrossing, juicy read about girlfriends, marriages, jealousies and money. But it's also an occasionally brutal dissection of the habits and hang-ups of a rarefied group of mega-mamas." Salon.com

The wife; a novel. Scribner 2003 219p $23
ISBN 0-684-86940-3   LC 2002-36660

"Joan Castleman is en route to Finland to watch her husband, the renowned author Joe Castleman, win the Helsinki Prize when she decides to leave him. What follows is Joan's fascinating recollection of their marriage, his career, and her fading dreams. Telling her story in alternating segments, she starts in the 1950s with the beginning of the couple's professor-student relationship and continues through to the present, their 40 years of marriage stacking up unspoken regrets." Libr J

"Wolitzer's crisp pacing and dry wit carry us headlong into a devastating message about the price of love and fame." Publ Wkly

A **Woman's** eye; edited by Sara Paretsky. Delacorte Press 1991 448p o.p.
        LC 90-28102

Stories included are: Lucky dip, by L. Cody; Murder without a text, by A. Cross; The puppet, by D. S. Davis; Death and diamonds, by S. Dunlap; Getting to know you, by A. Fraser; Full circle, by S. Grafton; Her good name, by C. G. Hart; That summer at Quichiquois, by D. B. Hughes; Discards, by F. Kellerman; Deborah's judgement, by M. Maron; Benny's space, by M. Muller; Where are you, Monica?, by M. A. Oliver; Settled score, by S. Paretsky; The scar, by N. Pickard; A man's home, by S. Singer; Looking for Thelma, by G. Slovo; A match made in hell, by J. Smith; The cutting edge, by M. Wallace; Ghost station, by C. Wheat; Theft of the poet, by B. Wilson; Kill the man for me, by M. Wings

Woo, Sung J.

Everything Asian. Thomas Dunne Books 2009 328p $23.95
ISBN 978-0-312-53885-9; 0-312-53885-5
        LC 2008-37673

"David Kim, formerly known as Dae Joon, has just turned 12 years old and moved to New Jersey from Korea. After five years of living with his mother and his older, moody sister, he must reconnect with a father he does not remember and get used to his American life, which consists of going to school and working at his parents' shop, East Meets West. In a series of interwoven short stories, Woo captures both the difficulty of transitioning from adolescence into adulthood and the additional challenges of making that transition in a new country." Libr J

"A charming tale of family, community and the struggle for understanding. . . . Woo eschews immigrant clichés to focus on complicated familial relationships and surprising, sympathetic characters. Alternating between humor and melancholy, Woo's text strikes a true chord." Publ Wkly

Wood, Barbara, 1947-

The dreaming; a novel of Australia. Random House 1991 453p o.p.   LC 90-52883

"After her parents tragic deaths in 1871, Joanna Drury leaves her native India for Australia, to unlock the secret past that haunted her mother, Lady Emily, and led to her mysterious, sudden death at age 40. In Melbourne, Joanna meets dashing and sensitive frontiersman Hugh Westbrook, and together they build Hugh's sheep station into a thriving enterprise, all the while looking for the source of the 'curse' on Joanna's family that took hold in an ancient time the aborigines call 'the dreaming.' . . . Wood's soft-edged prose, likable characters, and period details are always a big hit with her many fans." Booklist

Perfect Harmony; a novel. Little, Brown 1998 429p $23.95
ISBN 0-316-81653-1   LC 97-37623

"Charlotte Lee is the head of Harmony, a major player in the international herbal-medicine industry. Charlotte has taken the ancient Chinese remedies once concocted in her grandmother's kitchen and turned them into a multimillion-dollar business. But now three people have died after taking Harmony products, and when Charlotte receives a series of threatening e-mail messages, it's clear someone is out to ruin the company. Enter Jonathan Sutherland former FBI agent, computer whiz, and—coincidentally—the man Charlotte has loved since she was a teenager." Booklist

Vital signs. Doubleday 1985 326p o.p.
        * LC 84-13639

"Three women share an apartment and their dreams in medical school in the late 1960s, each of them driven: Sondra by her suspected black ancestry, Ruth by the father she could never please, Mickey by the birthmark that scarred her psyche more than her face. Each has professional success and personal heartache in the 18-year span of the novel, Sondra working at a medical mission in Kenya, Ruth with a fertility clinic and a large family to juggle, and Mickey, her own scar eradicated, as a plastic surgeon to the rich and famous." Libr J

"Wood's expert knowledge of medicine and her deft interplay of plot and character make this a richly textured and quite credible story that is delightfully unpredictable from the first page through the last." Booklist

Woodrell, Daniel

The death of sweet mister; a novel. Putnam 2001 196p $23.95
ISBN 0-399-14751-9
        * LC 00-45972

"A Marian Wood book"

Set in the Missouri hill country, this novel "presents one eventful summer in the life of Shug, a friendless, overweight 13-year-old living with his mother in the caretaker's cottage at the local cemetery. Glenda flirts incessantly, even with her son, who is becoming increasingly aware of her charms. Glenda's husband, Red (who may or may not be Shug's father), comes and goes, bringing money occasionally and strife a lot more often. . . . Shug's efforts to protect his mother from Red, from other admirers, and from her own rash decisions come to a head one hot summer night." Libr J

Woodrell, Daniel—*Continued*

"Woodrell's merciless realism is shot through with humor and rural wisdom; his work may not be to everyone's taste, but his bleak world is rendered with consummate artistry." Publ Wkly

Give us a kiss; a country noir. Holt & Co. 1996 237p

ISBN 0-8050-2298-8

* LC 95-23458

A "novel set in the Missouri Ozarks, this is the . . . tale of tough-guy midlist novelist Doyle Redmond's transformation into the writer he only dreamed of being. Escaping from trendy California in his estranged wife's Volvo, Doyle reconnects with his roughneck heritage: gun-crazy grandpa and older brother, . . . marijuana farms, and a 50-year-old blood feud with the infamous Dolly clan." Libr J

The author creates a "vanishing South with an accuracy and understanding beyond any genre writer's capability. . . . If one is tempted to hear echoes of William Faulkner, Erskine Caldwell or Andrew Lytle in such themes, no matter. Mr. Woodrell isn't imitating any of them. He's only drawing from the same well they did, but with a different take, a different voice, a sharper sense of irony and satire." N Y Times Book Rev

Winter's bone; a novel. Little, Brown and Co. 2006 193p $22.95

ISBN 0-316-05755-X

LC 2005-17349

"Sixteen-year-old Ree Dolly has a plan. She's going to join the army as soon as she can free herself from her complicated family obligations. Unfortunately, her father, part of a large extended Dolly family crystal meth enterprise, is missing. Her mother's mind is gone, and two little brothers worship at Ree's feet. Ree gets word that her father has skipped bail; if he doesn't meet his court date, the family loses its home, and there's nowhere to go. Ree begins a journey through the savage poverty of a brutally cold Ozarks winter to deliver her father before his court date." Libr J

"Like his characters, and especially his teen characters, Woodrell's prose mixes tough and tender so thoroughly yet so delicately that we never taste even a hint of false bravado, on the one hand, or sentimentality, on the other. And Ree is one of those heroines whose courage and vulnerability are both irresistible and completely believable—think of not just Mattie Ross in True Grit but also Scout in To Kill a Mockingbird or even Eliza Naumann in Bee Season. One runs out of superlatives to describe Woodrell's fiction." Booklist

Woods, John E. (John Edwin)

(tr) Mann, T. Doctor Faustus

(tr) Schulze, I. New lives

Woods, Sara

The lie direct. St. Martin's Press 1983 191p o.p.

LC 83-2982

London barrister/detective "Maitland agrees to defend John Ryder, on trial for treason, in spite of the overwhelming evidence against him. Dr. Boris Gollnow defects from Russia and identifies Ryder as the man who has been selling secrets to the Soviets. Winifred Paull, who claims Ryder has married her in a bigamous ceremony, confirms the identification and so do others. Only the accused's legal wife, Carol, and Antony believe in him. Maitland . . . turns detective and searches for proof of perjury by the witnesses for the prosecution. When Winifred is murdered and Carol is charged with that crime, the lawyer's problems magnify." Publ Wkly

Naked villainy. St. Martin's Press 1987 269p o.p.

LC 86-27925

This case featuring barrister-sleuth Antony Maitland, "begins with one of Maitland's friends telling him about cosmetics king Georges Letendre, who, while visiting his sister in London, found a photograph of her naked on an altar at the climactic moment of a Black Mass. Letendre is subsequently murdered, and Maitland is asked to defend the chief suspect, the dead man's son. Maitland delves deeply into the occult and financial chicanery before putting together a brilliant Old Bailey performance." Booklist

Woods, Stuart

Chiefs. Norton 1981 427p

ISBN 0-03-901461-4

* LC 80-27350

"Set in the small town of Delano, Ga., the novel tells of three Delano police chiefs—a farmer, a sadistic racist and a black—who must deal with the same case: the disappearances and murders of a number of white, teenaged boys over the course of 40 years. The mystery—readers will discern the killer's identity quite early—is played against the South in transition as local politics acquire national prominence when the son of the first chief becomes a candidate for governor and is eyed by the JFK White House as a potential running mate in the reelection campaign." Publ Wkly

Choke; a novel. HarperCollins Pubs. 1995 280p o.p.

LC 95-37300

Chuck Chandler "teaches tennis at an exclusive club in Key West and meets his 'match' in gorgeous Claire Carras and her much older, wealthy husband, Harry. Chuck boats, wines, and dines with the Carrases, beds Claire, then finds himself accused of Harry's apparent murder. . . . Enter Tommy Sculley, formerly with the New York Police Department, now augmenting his pension working for the Key West police. Tommy is streetwise and intelligent, and he won't quit until he finds the truth." Libr J

"Mr. Woods knows how to keep the narrative pace in overdrive, and the twists of the plot, if not always surprising, are satisfactorily developed." N Y Times Book Rev

Cold paradise. Putnam 2001 326p

ISBN 0-399-14736-5

LC 00-45974

When millionaire Thad Shames asks Stone Barrington "to go to Palm Beach to track down a mysterious woman he met at a party, Barrington sees the mission as little more than a wild goose chase. . . . To his surprise, it doesn't take long to find the woman, but it's an even bigger shock to him to discover that she is Allison Manning, now calling herself Liz, whom he helped when she was accused of killing her husband. . . . That husband is still very much alive, and Liz wants to pay him to leave her alone with some of the money from the insurance scam they pulled off together." Booklist

Woods, Stuart—*Continued*

Dead eyes. HarperCollins Pubs. 1994 303p o.p.
LC 93-14221

"Young Hollywood actress Chris Callaway is poised at the brink of stardom when her world collapses. Shortly after she begins receiving disquieting letters signed 'Admirer,' she is nearly blinded in a fall at the construction site of her new Malibu home. As Admirer becomes a menacing stalker, sending gifts and a gruesome photo and calling on the phone, Chris is stoutly guarded by her best friend and confidant, hairdresser Danny Devere. Also on duty is Beverly Hills police detective and stalker expert Jon Larsen. . . . Woods's style is lean and staccato, if unsubtle, and he's a pro at turning up the suspense." Publ Wkly

Dead in the water; a novel. HarperCollins Pubs. 1997 325p o.p.
LC 97-14255

"City Attorney Stone Barrington is on the small island of St. Marks off the coast of Antigua for vacation. His live-in girlfriend is unable to join him. Since he is at loose ends, he attends the coroner's inquest into the death of Paul Manning, a famous mystery writer who was sailing across the Atlantic when, according to his wife, he died. She is arrested for murder because the island prosecutor has political ambitions of being the next prime minister, and a good murder case is just what he needs. Manning was heavily insured, and within a day or so, $15 million is paid to his estate and then transferred to a Cayman Island account. Barrington takes on Allison Manning's defense with the help of a local barrister." Libr J

"This is a cleverly plotted, witty crime caper with a dash of sex, a likably roughish hero, and a surprising twist at the finish." Booklist

Dirt; a novel. HarperCollins Pubs. 1996 272p o.p.
LC 96-199910

In this novel, "Stone Barrington, a retired police detective turned lawyer/investigator, aids Amanda Dart, a famous gossip columnist, who receives a FAX that threatens to expose her. The FAX, entitled 'Dirt,' is sent not only to Amanda but to much of New York society. Although Amanda makes a living destroying other people's lives, she carefully guards her own reputation. Barrington is brought in to discover the author of 'Dirt,' which exposes the lives of other unscrupulous characters as well." Libr J

"Dripping with name-dropping, haute couture and pricey playthings, and spiced with hormonal aerobics as Stone trolls the siren-infested waters of upscale Manhattan, the narrative rockets toward an abrupt but absolutely stunning denouement." Publ Wkly

Dirty work. Putnam 2003 322p $25.95
ISBN 0-399-14982-1   LC 2002-32975

"Suave cop-turned-lawyer Stone Barrington is asked to hire someone to take photos of Lawrence Fortescue, the husband of a wealthy socialite, with a woman who is presumably his mistress. Stone hires the nephew of an old friend, who proves to be grossly incompetent when he falls through the skylight onto the man he's supposed to be photographing. Fortescu ends up dead, the supposed mistress disappears, and the photographer is charged with manslaughter. As Stone digs deeper, he discovers that Fortescue wasn't killed by the photographer's

fall, but by an injection of poison. Enter Carpenter, aka Felicity Devonshire, Stone's contact in British intelligence. Carpenter suspects the woman involved with Fortescue is actually . . . a trained assassin with a grudge." Booklist

Grass roots; a novel. Simon & Schuster 1989 459p
ISBN 0-671-66739-4   LC 89-32198

"After years as chief of staff for a venerable Georgia senator, Will Lee decides to run for the seat himself when a stroke cripples his mentor. Standing in his way are an ambitious governor in the Democratic primary and, possibly, a far-right fundamentalist in the general election. In addition, Will must interrupt his campaign to serve as the defense lawyer in a controversial race-murder trial, while elsewhere, a dedicated ex-cop pursues the head of a Klan-like vigilante group that's been carrying out gangland-style killings." Publ Wkly

"A consummate storyteller, Woods . . . demonstrates his narrative ability by intertwining contemporary southern politics and the murder trial into a most satisfying tale." Libr J

Heat. HarperCollins Pubs. 1994 346p
ISBN 0-06-017776-4   LC 94-4175

"Unjustly imprisoned, bereft of wife and daughter, ex-DEA agent Jesse Warden is offered a daring gamble: if he can infiltrate and destroy a heavily armed religious cult, he can win his freedom." Libr J

"Despite a few momentary lapses into banal predictability, Woods has concocted a high-octane story filled with nail-biting suspense and enough unusual twists to keep even experienced puzzle-solvers guessing." Booklist

Imperfect strangers. HarperCollins Pubs. 1995 269p o.p.
LC 94-34506

"Woods' 'imperfect' strangers meet on an airplane. Sandy Kinsolving is an attractive, well-dressed man of means. He's flying from London to New York because his father-in-law, who's bankrolled his lucrative wine-selling business, has just had a stroke. Sandy and his wife are far from close, and he's concerned that his father-in-law's death will have unpleasant financial consequences. His seatmate, Peter Martindale, also a well-dressed man of means, is a gallery owner based in San Francisco. It seems that he and his wife are also on the outs, and he, too, stands to lose his livelihood. . . . Peter proposes that they murder each other's wives. The trick here is to complicate matters, and Woods succeeds admirably." Booklist

L.A. dead. Putnam 2000 338p
ISBN 0-399-14664-4   LC 00-28059

This Stone Barrington thriller "finds the lawyer/sleuth from New York back in Los Angeles on a murder case. . . . His ex-lover, Arrington Calder, stands accused of murdering her husband, movie star and renowned man-about-town Vance Calder, found dead of a gunshot wound in the couple's Bel Air mansion. Upon hearing the news, Barrington, in Italy for his imminent wedding to the lovely but unpredictable Dolce Bianchi, rushes to L.A. to take over Arrington's defense." Publ Wkly

L.A. Times; a novel. HarperCollins Pubs. 1993 329p o.p.
LC 92-54724

"Vincente Michaele Callabrese works as a shakedown artist for the mob in New York City's Little Italy, but moviegoing is his passion. Early in the story, he changes

Woods, Stuart—*Continued*

his name to Michael Vincent and makes a break for L.A., where with the help of powerful studio head Leo Goldman he fulfills his dream of becoming a big-time producer. Vincent's *cosa nostra* connections keep in touch, particularly old pal Tommy Provenzano whose rise to power in New York parallels Vincent's in Hollywood. Eventually, Vincent's desire to bring a gentle turn-of-the-century novel to the screen leads him to employ the sorts of techniques and friends that served him in his mafia days." Publ Wkly

New York dead. HarperCollins Pubs. 1991 303p o.p.   LC 90-56374

A mystery "set in Manhattan's Upper East Side, the stomping ground of Stone Barrington, a well-bred but unpretentious detective. . . . Late one evening, as Stone trudges home from Elaine's Restaurant, popular TV newscaster Sasha Nijinsky plummets 12 stories from her terrace and lands on a heap of dirt 20 yards away from him—remarkably, still alive. Stone fails to apprehend the person who flees Sasha's penthouse and, after the ambulance carrying her collides with a fire truck, Sasha herself disappears. Despite the fact that no corpse is in evidence, the baffled NYPD eagerly pins a murder rap on Sasha's distraught lesbian lover. Stone refuses to accept his colleagues' pat solution." Publ Wkly

Orchid Beach. HarperCollins Pubs. 1998 325p $25
ISBN 0-06-019181-3   LC 98-23628
"Army Sergeant Holly Barker has just lost a sexual-harassment case against Colonel Bruno, her former boss. . . . Fortunately, her father, a soon-to-retire master sergeant, knows Chet Marley, the chief of police in Orchid Beach, Florida. Chet is looking for a new deputy chief. It sounds good to Holly, so she packs her gear and sets off for Florida. But when she arrives, she steps into big trouble. The night before, Chet Marley and his best friend were murdered. Shocked at such brutality in peaceful-looking Orchid Beach, Holly sets out to find the killer, only to run into an elaborate conspiracy plot." Booklist
"The story gets extra bite from Holly's intriguing relationship with an inherited canine named Daisy, the clairvoyant Doberman that belonged to her mentor." Publ Wkly

Palindrome. Harper & Row 1991 344p
ISBN 0-06-017911-2   LC 90-55587
"When Liz Barwick is beaten nearly to death by her steroid-crazed husband, Baker Ramsey, a star NFL running back, she quickly divorces him, takes a large cash settlement and disappears from public view. Liz, whose book of sports photographs has just been released, takes advantage of her publisher's offer to live in his cottage on an isolated private island off the Georgia coast. But when Ramsey goes on a murderous rampage, Liz's lawyer and publisher and his wife are among his victims. Meanwhile other events are unfolding on Cumberland Island, where Liz becomes involved with the Drummond family." Publ Wkly

Reckless abandon. G.P. Putnam's Sons 2004 289p $25.95
ISBN 0-399-15151-6   LC 2003-64799

This thriller features cop-turned-lawyer Stone Barrington and Holly Barker, chief of the Orchid Beach, Florida, police department. "Holly's come to New York hot on the trail of Trini Rodriguez, a bad guy she thought she'd stabbed to death in an earlier adventure. He's currently wanted for (among other things) blowing up a dozen people by hiding bombs in the caskets of two of his earlier victims and detonating them at the funeral. But finding him won't be so simple: he's been placed in the FBI Witness Protection Program and is working with the Feds and the CIA to catch an Arab terrorist group trying to employ the Mafia in a money-laundering scheme. Shortly after Holly takes up residence in Stone's guest room, the two of them are hip deep in the dangerous case and likewise each other. . . . Cross-pollinating all these characters from various books makes for some heavyhanded background exposition at times, but readers with no previous experience will still enjoy this amusing, full-throttle sex and crime romp." Publ Wkly

The run. HarperCollins Pubs. 2000 356p
ISBN 0-06-019187-2
Sequel to Grass roots (1989)
"Will and Kate Lee, now a Washington power couple, decide to go for broke in their service to the country. Will, a popular senator from Georgia, jumps into the race for the presidency, while Kate, a deputy director at the CIA, cheers him on. . . . The candidate's liberal leanings are anathema to a right-wing militia group from Idaho, whose leader, Zeke Tennant, tracks Will from one campaign stop to another with a duffel bag full of weapons. In a final showdown, Tennant makes one last assassination attempt." Publ Wkly
"A clever, well-constructed story of political ambition and behind-the-scenes skulduggery." Booklist

Santa Fe rules. HarperCollins Pubs. 1992 303p o.p.   LC 91-58476
"You're a rich, successful Hollywood producer who awakens the morning before Thanksgiving in your Santa Fe home with no memory of the previous night. Ignoring your dog's attempts to get you to visit the guest wing of the house, you leave and fly your private plane to Los Angeles. But you never get there: a breakdown forces you to spend the holiday isolated in a small airport town. When you finally see the newspaper the next day, you read that the bodies of your wife, your business partner and a third man—assumed to be you—have been found in the guest room of the Santa Fe residence. . . . Wolf Willett decides to stay 'dead' for a while and finish work on his new film, then hires a top defense attorney and turns himself in." Publ Wkly

The short forever. Putnam 2002 321p $24.95
ISBN 0-399-14868-X   LC 2001-48725
Mogul John Bartholomew hires Stone Barrington "to fly to London and persuade his niece, Erica, to leave her cocaine-smuggling boyfriend, Lance Cabot, and to make sure Lance winds up in jail. Dapper Stone charms Erica, who offers to set him up with her sister, Monica, and then introduces him to Lance. With help from two British investigators, Stone learns John Bartholomew is not who he seems." Publ Wkly
"Filling his story with enough twists and turns to dizzy even the most seasoned reader, Woods keeps the tension high until the last page." Booklist

Woods, Stuart—*Continued*

Short straw. G. P. Putnam's Sons 2006 289p $25.95

ISBN 0-399-15368-3　　　　　　LC 2006-41643

When Santa Fe defense lawyer Ed Eagle "wakes up on the morning of his fiftieth birthday, he discovers his wife has left him and taken him for a cool million. The second shock Eagle receives is news that a local lawyer has blown his brains out in the courthouse, after murdering his wife and children. The plot races off in two directions: with two edgy characters, an ex-LAPD detective and an Apache Indian tracker, whom Eagle hires to find his wife in Mexico; and with Eagle's efforts to clear a man wrongly charged, he believes, with a triple homicide. Woods keeps the wattage high as the two plots intersect, and Eagle finds himself more and more entangled in a deadly criminal scheme. The homicidal desperation of Eagle's wife and the dodginess of the men he sends after her keep the surprises coming." Booklist

Swimming to Catalina; a novel. HarperCollins Pubs. 1998 311p o.p.　　　　LC 97-51173

Former NYPD cop turned lawyer Stone "Barrington's former girlfriend Arrington has married Barrington's friend Vance Calder, Hollywood's hottest actor. Three months into the marriage, Arrington's been kidnapped, and Vance calls Barrington to beg for his help. Barrington comes to L.A. only to find a hornet's nest. . . . Despite the fact that this book is definitely politically incorrect and Barrington has apparently never heard of safe sex, it's a highly entertaining read that's chock-full of slam-bang action, fast cars, beautiful women, fine wine, and tart, tongue-in-cheek humor." Booklist

Two-dollar bill. G.P. Putnam's Sons 2005 298p $25.95

ISBN 0-399-15251-2　　　　　　LC 2004-60068

Stone Barrington "becomes involved with a loud-talking Texan improbably named Billy Bob Barnstormer. It isn't long before Stone regrets ever being introduced to Billy Bob, especially when he leaves a dead body in Stone's guest room. But that is only the beginning of a tale that finds Stone, along with his best friend, Dino Bacchetti, following a twisted trail as they attempt to capture Billy Bob, who, it turns out, is much more dangerous than Stone could ever have imagined. Narrator Roberts slips comfortably into his performance, bringing a nice, down-to-earth quality to his portrayal of Stone." Publ Wkly

Worst fears realized. HarperCollins Pubs. 1999 332p $25

ISBN 0-06-019182-1　　　　　　LC 98-52924

In this Stone Barrington adventure, "the Manhattan lawyer turned investigator faces an indictment for the murder of a woman he's just met. When other brutal murders quickly pile up—all women connected to him or his best friend, Dino Bacchetti of the 19th Precinct—Stone knows that one of a cop's worst fears has been realized: a con with a grudge is bent on vengeance. While trying to save the lives of the women he cares about, Stone struggles to track down the killer and head off a DA who's out to get him for murder." Libr J

Woolf, Virginia, 1882-1941

Between the acts. Harcourt Brace & Co. 1941 219p o.p.

This novel "describes a pageant on English history, written and directed by Miss La Trobe, and its effects on the people who watch it. Most of the audience misunderstand it in various ways; a clergyman reduces its vision to a sermon. But, for a moment, Woolf implies art, has imposed order on the chaos of human life" Reader's Ency. 4th edition

The complete shorter fiction of Virginia Woolf; edited by Susan Dick. Harcourt Brace Jovanovich 1985 313p o.p.

Contents: Phyllis and Rosamond; The mysterious case of Miss V.; The journal of Mistress Joan Martyn; Memoirs of a novelist; The mark on the wall; Kew Gardens; The evening party; Solid objects; Sympathy; An unwritten novel; A haunted house; A society; Monday or Tuesday; The string quartet; Blue & green; A woman's college from outside; In the orchard; Mrs. Dalloway in Bond Street; Nurse Lugton's curtain; The widow and the parrot: a true story; The new dress; Happiness; Ancestors; The introduction; Together and apart; The man who loved his kind; A simple melody; A summing up; Moments of being: 'Slater's pins have no points'; The lady in the looking-glass: a reflection; The fascination of the pool; Three pictures; Scenes from the life of a British naval officer; Miss Pryme; Ode written partly in prose on seeing the name of Cutbush above a butcher's shop in Pentonville; Portraits; Uncle Vanya; The Duchess and the jeweller; The shooting party; Lappin and Lapinova; The searchlight; Gipsy, the mongrel; The legacy; The symbol; The watering place

"Woolf's 46 short stories demonstrate her fondness for experimenting with narrative forms and voices. Arranged chronologically, the pieces range from tales with traditional plot lines to denser interior monologues, and enable the reader to appreciate Woolf's development as a writer of fiction." Publ Wkly

Jacob's room. Harcourt Brace & Co. 1923 303p o.p.

First published 1922 in the United Kingdom

"The life story, character, and friends of Jacob Flanders are presented in a series of separate scenes and moments. The story of this sensitive, promising young man carries him from his childhood, through college at Cambridge, love affairs in London, and travels in Greece, to his death in the war. At the end, instead of describing his death, Virginia Woolf describes his empty room." Reader's Ency. 4th edition

Mrs. Dalloway. Knopf 1993 xxviii, 219p $16
ISBN 0-679-42042-8

　　　　　　　　　　　　　* LC 92-54300

"Everyman's library"

A reissue of the title first published 1925 by Harcourt Brace & Co.

"In this stream-of-consciousness novel all action takes place on a single day. By probing the thoughts and memories of various characters, the author has encompassed several people's lives. Clarissa has a party planned for the evening and is thinking of her daughter's involvement with a religious fanatic. Also in her thoughts are old friends like Sally Seton, who drops by at the party,

Woolf, Virginia, 1882-1941—*Continued*

and Clarissa's former lover, Peter Walsh, who is drawn to Sally, much to Clarissa's chagrin. When a noted psychiatrist arrives late at the party because one of his patients, Septimus Smith, has committed suicide, Clarissa is affected, not because she knew the victim, but because suicide is tantamount to wastefulness." Shapiro. Fic for Youth. 3d edition

Orlando; a biography. Harcourt Brace & Co. 1928 333p il o.p.

"Orlando begins as a young Elizabethan nobleman and ends, three hundred years later, as a contemporary young woman, based on the author's friend Victoria Sackville-West. The novel contains a great deal of literary history and brilliant, ironic insights into the social history of the ages through which Orlando lives. Orlando starts life as a male poet and ends as an equally intense and able woman poet, in order to emphasize the author's belief that women are intellectually men's equals." Reader's Ency. 4th edition

To the lighthouse. Harcourt Brace & Co. 1927 310p $17; pa $9

ISBN 0-15-190737-4; 0-15-690739-9 (pa)

*

Arranged in three sections, the first "called 'The window,' describes a day during Mr. and Mrs. Ramsay's house party at their country home by the sea. Mr. Ramsay is a distinguished scholar . . . whose mind works rationally, heroically and rather icily. . . . The Ramsays have arranged to take a boat out to the lighthouse, the next morning, and their little son James is bitterly disappointed when a change in weather makes it impossible. The second section, called 'Time passes' describes the seasons and the house, unused and decaying, in the years after Mrs. Ramsay's death. In the third section, the 'Lighthouse,' Mr. Ramsay and his friends are back at the house. He takes the postponed trip to the lighthouse with his now 16-year-old son, who is at last able to communicate silently with him and forgive him for being different from his mother." Reader's Ency. 4th edition

The voyage out. Modern Lib. 2000 xliv, 473p $17.95

ISBN 0-679-64028-2   LC 99-54259

First published 1915 in the United Kingdom; first United States edition 1920 by Harcourt Brace & Co.

"The story concerns a young woman of 24, Rachel Vinrace, an innocent, 'unlicked' girl who voyages to South America on board her father's ship, the *Euphrosyne*. Accompanying her are her aunt, Helen Ambrose, and uncle Ridley, together with an assortment of English characters whose social interaction is delicately observed. In South America Rachel meets a young Englishman, Terence Hewet, an aspiring writer working on his first novel. . . . He and Rachel fall in love and become engaged, determined to establish their future marriage on a new basis of equality. However, during an expedition Rachel contracts an unspecified disease and is confined to her bed with a fever. After a fortnight's illness she dies." Camb Guide to Lit in Engl

The waves. Harcourt Brace & Co. 1931 297p o.p.

*

"Highly original, unconventional, and poetic, it describes the characters, lives, and relationships of six persons living in England. The book is composed of interior monologues, spoken by the six characters in rotation, and of interludes describing the ascent and descent of the sun, the rise and fall of the waves, and the passing of the seasons. These natural cycles symbolize the progress of time, which carries the individual from birth to death." Reader's Ency. 4th edition

The years. Harcourt Brace & Co. 1937 435p o.p.

*

This novel "traces the history of a family, opening in 1880 as the children of Colonel and Mrs. Pargiter, living together in a large Victorian London house (later described by one of them as 'Hell') wait for their mother's death and the freedom it will bring; it takes them through several carefully dated and documented sections to the 'Present Day' of 1936, and a large family reunion, where two generations gather." Oxford Companion to Engl Lit. 6th edition

Woolrich, Cornell, 1903-1968

I married a dead man

In Crime novels: American noir of the 1930s and 40s

Wouk, Herman, 1915-

The Caine mutiny; a novel of World War II. Doubleday 1951 494p o.p.

*

"The old American mine sweeper 'Caine' patrols the Pacific during World War II. The action shifts from the bridge of the ship to the wardroom and from scenes of petty tyranny on the part of the skipper to incidents of fierce action and heroism on the part of the men. Ensign Willie Keith is assigned to the ship and leads a mutiny against paranoid Captain Queeg, who is eventually brought to trial in a scene that poses the difficulty of weighing evidence to prove that the takeover by the men was justifiable." Shapiro. Fic for Youth. 3d edition

A hole in Texas. Little, Brown 2004 278p $25

ISBN 0-316-52590-1

"Unassuming NASA physicist Guy Carpenter, who abandoned his hunt for a particle called the Higgs Boson, is suddenly in the limelight when the Chinese claim they've made the discovery." Libr J

"The plot is busy but secondary to Carpenter's banter and romantic escapades. Occasionally corny but also playful, thoughtful and passionate." Publ Wkly

Marjorie Morningstar. Doubleday 1955 565p o.p.

*

"The story of a middle-class Jewish girl who temporarily rejects her upbringing in her infatuation with the world of show business." Reader's Ency. 4th edition

War and remembrance; a novel. Little, Brown 1978 1042p

ISBN 0-316-95501-9

* LC 78-17746

Wouk, Herman, 1915-—*Continued*

Sequel to The winds of war

This book "covers the events of 1941-1945. particularly as experienced by the fictional Henry family, Captain Victor ('Pug') Henry, continuing his remarkable naval career which brings him into contact with President Roosevelt and other historical luminaries, ends up an admiral. His marriage to Rhoda, however, finally comes undone for good and their oldest son, Warren, is killed at Midway. Byron, the Henrys' other son, eventually commands a submarine in the Pacific, but his Jewish wife, Natalie, their infant son, and her famous uncle, Aaron Jastow, are irresistibly sucked into the clutches of the Nazis." Libr J

Wouk's "work is a journey of extraordinary emotional riches. Quantity in time becomes quality, movement becomes scope, and history becomes human yearning." NY Times Book Rev

The winds of war; a novel. Little, Brown 1971 885p pa $16.99 hardcover o.p.

ISBN 0-316-95266-8

"On the broadest of tapestries, Wouk weaves the effect of the preparation and the actual outbreak of World War II upon the family of Commander 'Pug' Henry. The affairs of the Henry family became intertwined with those of others, in such varying scenes as Washington, Berlin, Rome, London, and Moscow. . . . Despite the novel's breadth, the development of Henry's character as the middle-class military leader America needed in the 1940's is surprisingly credible." Choice

Wray, John, 1971-

Canaan's tongue. Alfred A. Knopf 2005 341p $25

ISBN 1-400-04086-8   LC 2004-64902

"Loosely based on the story of pre-Civil War slave stealer John Murrell, a.k.a. 'The Redeemer,' and his 'Mystic Clan' gang, this novel centers on the relationship between gang member Virgil Ball and charismatic leader Thaddeus Morelle. Ball, the son of a Kansas preacher, is simultaneously captivated and repelled by the criminal Morelle. Though he quickly becomes part of the gang's inner circle, he finds himself deeply conflicted about his involvement, a tension that will eventually lead to a violent act of expiation. Yet, in the end, even murder will not free him from the sway of a power older and deeper than Morelle. Wray has crafted an ambitious and strongly allegorical tale about the ability of belief to structure reality." Libr J

Lowboy. Farrar, Straus and Giroux 2009 258p $25

ISBN 978-0-374-19416-1; 0-374-19416-5
                           LC 2008-17921

"Will Heller, aka Lowboy, is a brilliant but troubled 16-year-old paranoid schizophrenic in New York City. Recently escaped from a mental hospital and obsessed with the notion that the world is about to be destroyed by global warming, he boards the subway one morning seeking to save the world in the only way he believes it can be-by having sex with a woman. He attempts to locate former girlfriend Emily Wallace, whom he has not seen since he pushed her onto the subway tracks a year earlier, the act that led to his stay in a mental hospital.

Throughout his daylong adventures in the tunnels and streets, he is pursued by police detective Ali Lateef and his mother, Violet, a woman with her own secrets, who seek to bring him home before he harms himself or others." Libr J

This is a "brilliant and gutsy performance but a cryptic one. It expresses its meanings in hallucinated events that seem to vibrate on the page. At certain moments the book feels like a runaway subway car; you want it to slow down for you." Buffalo News

Wright, Alexis, 1950-

Carpentaria; a novel. Atria Books 2009 c2006 517p $26

ISBN 978-1-4165-9310-2; 1-4165-9310-1

First published 2006 in Australia

"In the sparsely populated northern Queensland town of Desperance, loyalties run deep and battle lines have been drawn between the powerful Phantom family, leaders of the Westend Pricklebush people, and Joseph Midnight's renegade Eastend mob, and their disputes with the white officials of neighboring towns." Publisher's note

"This book is a sprawling, surreal anti-*Odyssey* in which time and space contract and expand and experience takes place in the Dreamtime, on the sea, and on and under the continent of Australia. . . . [This novel] will surely stand as a masterpiece of modern English-language literature." Libr J

Wright, Eric, 1929-

The last hand. Thomas Dunne Bks. 2002 231p

ISBN 0-312-28330-X   LC 2001-51295

Toronto's Charlie Salter "has reached 60, the limit for Canadian police to retire from active service, but he's lost none of his smarts as he looks into the murder of a prominent lawyer found stabbed to death in his apartment, which a woman, who neighbors say dressed like a prostitute, was seen to leave." Publ Wkly

"As usual, Salter has an insight that proves the unraveling of the unconventional case. The real action, however, is internal, as Salter faces down his own fears. A sensitive end to a marvelous series." Booklist

Wright, John C.

The golden age; a romance of the far future. TOR Bks. 2002 336p

ISBN 0-312-84870-6   LC 2001-58468

"A Tom Doherty Associates book"

In this future novel, the first of a projected two-volume saga, Phaethon Radamanthus, the 3,000 year-old scion of one of Earth's most powerful families begins a search for his lost memories

The author "chooses simple pulp-fiction plots to drive us through the technological complexities of Phaethon's world. The hero's quest to regain his lost memories, learn his true identity and reach the stars is undeniably compelling. As a result, having to wait for the next volume is frustrating. Wright's ornate and conceptually dense prose will not be to everyone's taste but, for those willing to be challenged, this is a rare and mind-blowing treat." Publ Wkly

Wright, Richard, 1908-1960

Black boy
also in Wright, R. Works

Eight men. World Pub. 1961 250p o.p.
Contents: The man who was almost a man; The man who lived underground; Big black good man; The man who saw the flood; Man, God ain't like that . . .; The man who killed a shadow; The man who went to Chicago

Lawd today!
In Wright, R. Works

Native son. Harper & Brothers 1940 359p o.p.
*
"Bigger Thomas is black. He is driven by anger, hate, and frustration, which are born out of the poverty that has dominated his life. When he gets a job with the Daltons, a white family, he is confused by their behavior and misinterprets their patronizing friendship. Tragedy follows when he accidentally kills Mary Dalton and escalates when Bigger murders his black girlfriend, Bessie." Shapiro. Fic for Youth. 3d edition
also in Wright, R. Works

The outsider. Harper & Row 1953 440p o.p.
"Cross Damon, a black man who works in the Chicago post office, is caught in a subway accident but escapes without serious injury, though because of a mistaken identity his death is announced. He decides to take advantage of this error to start life anew and thus free himself of his entanglements with women and debts. He goes to New York to live under an assumed name and before long becomes enmeshed in the Communist party. By it he is used as a murderer, until he is himself killed by a Party member." Oxford Companion to Am Lit. 6th edition
In Wright, R. Works

Uncle Tom's children; five long stories. Harper & Row 1938 xxx, 384p pa $13.95 hardcover o.p.
ISBN 0-06-058714-8 (pa)
Contents: Big boy leaves home; Down by the riverside; Long black song; Fire and cloud; Bright and morning star
The stories in this collection deal with conflicts between whites and blacks in the South.
also in Wright, R. Works

Works. Library of Am. 1991 2v ea $35
ISBN 0-940450-66-6 (v1); 0-940450-67-4 (v2)
LC 91-60540
Contents: v1 Early works; v2 Later works
This set contains the complete novels Native son; The outsider (1953); and Lawd today! (1963); the story collection Uncle Tom's children; and the memoir Black boy

Wright, Stephen, 1946-

The Amalgamation Polka. Knopf 2006 323p $24.95
ISBN 0-679-45117-X   LC 2005-938382
This novel tells the "story of a man caught between the fierce abolitionist sentiments of his parents and his maternal grandparents' equally ferocious allegiance to the Confederacy." N Y Times (Late N Y Ed)

"Wright is nothing if not ambitious, and the energy with which he throws himself into this world which bears only a passing resemblance to 19th-century America is a wonder to behold. The novel overflows with charlatans, whores, preachers, soldiers-of-fortune, madmen and even a handful of pirates, all of them declaiming, at the tops of their lungs, in language that often borders on free verse. The prose is unapologetically purple." Washington Post Book World

Going native; a novel. Farrar, Straus & Giroux 1994 305p
ISBN 0-374-16490-8
* LC 93-10944
This novel explores the "psyches of various distressed characters. The first belongs to an unhappy Chicago-area suburbanite whose husband, Wylie, an average-looking guy with an enigmatic and elusive temperament, disappears one evening while they're entertaining their friends Gerri and Tom H'anna. End of first chapter. Next, Wright thrusts us into the manic realm of Wylie's slovenly crack-head neighbors, who alternate bouts of rough sex with chaotic outings in a beat-up Ford Galaxy. This car reappears in the following chapter when its driver picks up a hitchhiker, who, incidentally, has just stabbed a trucker to death. When the driver introduces himself as Tom Hanna, we realize we've picked up Wylie's trail. He's heading West, and his trip is a grim one." Booklist
"'Going Native' is less a portrait of a potential psychopath than a panoramic dive into a world in which the protagonist blurs to become just one more figure in the landscape. Stephen Wright's America is a paranoiac's, and a satirist's, dream come true." N Y Times Book Rev

Meditations in green. Scribner 1983 342p
ISBN 0-684-18010-3
* LC 83-11666
This is a novel about the Vietnam War. "Stationed with the 1069th Intelligence Unit, James Griffin believed he could keep himself detached from the war, viewing it almost as a movie, but instead the war became more real and he became less so until his former life and persona seemed only a fantasy. Back home, he attempts to find some sense of himself again-as he learns how to meditate like a plant, is befriended by a part-time social worker, and tries to deal with a psychotic friend who is seeking revenge on his sergeant." Libr J
"The narrative works several time frames and points of view into a mesmerizing mosaic of men in combat. . . . The absence of feasible political and military goals turns these soldiers in on themselves, and they take out their frustrations on each other rather than an intangible enemy. Exactly how and why this happens is made graphically clear in this superb [novel]." Quill Quire

Wroblewski, David

The story of Edgar Sawtelle; a novel. Ecco 2008 566p $25.95; pa $16.99
ISBN 978-0-06-137422-7;   0-06-137422-9; 978-0-06-137423-4 (pa); 0-06-137423-7 (pa)
"Set in rural nineteen-seventies Wisconsin, this loose retelling of Hamlet focusses on Edgar, a boy born mute and with a preternatural ability to commune with the dogs whose breeding and training is his family's business. Idyllic routine is threatened when Edgar's ne'er-do-well uncle comes to live with the family, and the menace

Wroblewski, David—*Continued*

persists even after his sudden departure. Soon afterward, Edgar's father dies of an apparent aneurysm; Edgar becomes convinced, but can't prove, that his uncle—who soon inserts himself back into the family—is to blame. In this début novel, Wroblewski illustrates the relationship between man and canine (at times, from the dog's point of view) in a way that is both lyrical and unsentimental, and demonstrates an ability to create a coherent, captivating fictional world in which even supernatural elements feel entirely persuasive." New Yorker

Wurlitzer, Rudolph

Drop edge of yonder; a novel. Two Dollar Radio 2008 304p pa $15

ISBN 978-0-9763895-5-2; 0-9763895-5-X
* LC 2007-924062

"The novel tracks the wayward drift of a mountain man named Zebulon Shook, who is cursed by his dying Shoshone lover—named Not Here Not There—to 'drift like a blind man between the worlds, not knowing if you're dead or alive, or if the unseen world exists, or if you're dreaming.' With the collapse of the fur trade, Zebulon quits the mountains, crawls out of an arroyo after being shot in the heart and left for dead, and becomes an outlaw. In seedy Vera Cruz, he runs into a Russian count and his mysterious half-Abyssinian consort, Delilah, who pay him to sail with them to the gold fields of northern California. The story ends in the Pacific Northwest, at the Trail's End Saloon, but before we get there, we are treated to a Wunderkammer of western tropes and historical residues: wardens and wanted posters, rancheros and opium dens, freedom and fate, the Great Spirit and the Colt .45. Wurlitzer trots through this magic theater like a restless auteur. Chapters are short, the dialogue tangy and declarative, and scenes established and characters described with the visual fetishism of a Leone film." Bookforum

Y

Yan Ni *See* Shan Sa, 1972-

Yancey, Richard

The highly effective detective; a Teddy Ruzak novel. Thomas Dunne Books/St Martin's Minotaur 2006 294p $23.95

ISBN 0-312-34752-9
LC 2006-42512

"When his mother dies and leaves him quite a bit of money, night security officer Theodore Ruzak opens a detective agency with no license and no clients. Teddy may be overweight and uneducated, but he has heart and good moral character. He also has flashes of insight and keen powers of observation, making him just the person to consult when you witness the SUV hit-and-run slaughter of a family of geese or your stepmom goes missing the same day as the avian murders. The city of Knoxville will never be the same. Yancey . . . introduces a colorful, memorable detective and tells a suspenseful story full of great humor and careful plotting." Libr J

Yarbro, Chelsea Quinn, 1942-

Blood roses; a novel of Saint-Germain. TOR Bks. 1998 382p $24.95

ISBN 0-312-86529-5
LC 98-23671

"A Tom Doherty Associates book"

"As an exiled foreigner living in the village of Orgon in the midst of 14th-century France, the 3000-year-old vampire Saint-Germain . . . has enough trouble at the best of times convincing the locals that his unusual habits and interests are no threat. . . . Yet even the purest motives aren't enough to withstand the suspicion of the church when Saint-Germain uses his medical skills to heal the Vidame Saint Joachim of a wound no other healer has been able to diagnose. When the church accuses Saint-Germain of helping to spread the plague, the vampire is forced to flee as his lands and goods are seized." Publ Wkly

Yarbro "balances description, action, and romance excellently, producing a briskly paced, highly readable historical fantasy and the only recent series installment that is a good starting point for entering the St. Germain saga." Booklist

Come twilight; a novel of Saint-Germain. TOR Bks. 2000 479p il

ISBN 0-312-87330-1
LC 00-31710

"A Tom Doherty Associates book"

"While traveling through Spain in the seventh century, Saint-Germain, against his better judgment, saves the life of the mortally wounded Csimenae through a mingling of their blood. Despite his efforts to instruct her in the necessity of unobtrusive coexistence with humans, the haughty, impetuous Csimenae intimidates her countrymen into worshiping her and her son, Aulutis, eventually driving her vampire mentor away. Over the next 500 years, Saint-Germain's travels bring him into contact several times with Csimenae, who engenders a personal vampire army that preys on both unwary pilgrims and invading Moors. . . . Though the incessant details of daily life in the Dark Ages can grow wearisome, they are offset by Saint-Germain's poignant moments of soul-searching over his rare, regrettable moment of fallibility." Publ Wkly

Communion blood; a novel of Saint-Germain. TOR Bks. 1999 477p $26.95

ISBN 0-312-86793-X
LC 99-38760

"A Tom Doherty Associates book"

The vampire Count "Saint-Germain is in late-seventeenth-century Italy after the true death of his beloved Olivia Clemens. Trying to settle her affairs as she would have wished, he has to fight fraudulent efforts to settle her estate on an imposter instead of on her faithful servant. Meanwhile, he inevitably runs afoul of the church, this time in the person of a cardinal who is scheming to increase the power of the Papal States and, on the side, abusing his sister. All this makes for quite lively reading in its own right, but the romance's real strength . . . lies in the meticulously researched and vividly written depiction of a long-ago and largely long-forgotten time and place." Booklist

Night blooming. Aspect 2002 429p map $24.95

ISBN 0-446-52981-8
LC 2002-16876

Yarbro, Chelsea Quinn, 1942-—*Continued*

"Yarbro's vampire hero Saint-Germain continues his wanderings through history, this time in the late eighth century. The great French king Karl-lo-Magne summons Saint-Germain, here known as Hiernom Rakoczy, to his court. On the way, Rakoczy and his entourage meet Gynethe Mehaut, a young albino afflicted with a stigmata and awaiting news of her fate at a convent. . . . Volunteering to accompany [Gynethe] to the papal court in Rome, Rakoczy soon finds himself haunting his old haunts and falling in love with his charge. But Gynethe . . . is in great danger from those who feel threatened by her, and all Rakoczy's efforts may not be enough to save her." Booklist

"Richly rewarding for longtime readers, the novel also provides a good entry point for new recruits with its subtly supplied back story." Publ Wkly

Yarbrough, Steve, 1956-

The end of California. Knopf 2006 303p $23.95
ISBN 1-4000-4438-3   LC 2005-57750

In this "novel, a 42-year-old doctor named Pete Barrington returns from California to his little home town in Mississippi. He started there as a poor farm boy, but brains, looks and football talent helped him advance to college, medical school and a good life out West. An adulterous affair with a patient ended that, and now he, his wife and their 15-year-old daughter are starting over back home. Yarbrough's story blends elements we have seen in other novels—the small-town South, the football hero grown up, passions that reach back to high school, a little incest and a lot of extramarital sex, racial tensions, hypocrisy among the pious—but it all works because Yarbrough knows his characters so well, cares for them so deeply and writes of them in prose that is graceful, precise and packed with surprises." Washington Post Book World

Prisoners of war; a novel. Knopf 2004 287p $23
ISBN 0-375-41478-9
                         * LC 2003-40071

"In 1943, Dan Timms awaits being drafted away from the memory of his father's recent suicide, the guilt and sorrow of his mother, and the protection of his enterprising uncle, for whom he and a young black man called L.C. drive a 'rolling store' through the Delta, its plantations now worked by German soldiers whose fighting days are over. As they would seem to be for Dan's friend Marty Stark, returned mysteriously from the front and reassigned to guard men he had been trained to kill. But for L.C., a danger more immediate than the one looming overseas is the society into which he was born." Publisher's note

"Yarbrough writes with quiet compassion about Loring's black population, its reluctance to fight for a country that has so consistently betrayed its democratic promise. To this combustible setting will come a peculiar prisoner, one with an 'angry purple stain, either a birthmark or a rash,' who speaks broken English and haunts one of the Loring natives assigned to guard him. It is the fate of this mysterious captive that once again forces the people of Loring to confront what it means to be American, and all the unexpected and often unwarranted sacrifices that identity might comprise." N Y Times Book Rev

Yates, Richard, 1926-1992

The collected stories of Richard Yates; introduction by Richard Russo. Holt & Co. 2001 xx, 472p
ISBN 0-8050-6693-4
                         * LC 00-61400

Contents: Doctor Jack-o'-lantern; The best of everything; Jody rolled the bones; No pain whatsoever; A glutton for punishment; A wrestler with sharks; Fun with a stranger; The B.A.R. Man; A really good jazz piano; Out with the old; Builders; Oh, Joseph, I'm so tired; A natural girl; Trying out for the race; Liars in love; A compassionate leave; Regards at home; Saying goodbye to Sally; The canal; A clinical romance; Bells in the morning; Evening on the Cote d'Azur; Thieves; A private possession; The comptroller and the wild wind; A last fling, like; A convalescent ego

"Bitterness, loneliness and lack of fulfillment are the central themes of this grim posthumous collection." Publ Wkly

The **Year's** best fantasy. See The Year's best fantasy and horror

The **Year's** best fantasy and horror; 1st-21st annual collections; edited by Ellen Datlow and Kelly Link & Gavin J. Grant. St. Martin's Press 1988-2008 21v

First two annual compilations published with title: The Year's best fantasy

Each annual collection includes short stories, poems, and essays. The nonfiction sections cover such topics as trends in fantasy and horror publishing; fantasy and horror films, television and comics; nonprint media; and obituaries. Over the years contributors of stories have included Charles De Lint, Steve Rasnic Tem, Garry Kilworth, Angela Carter, Karel Capek, Isabel Allende, Stephen King, Jane Yolen, Thomas Ligotti, Clive Barker, Glen Hirshberg, Ted Chiang, and Elizabeth Hand

Year's best science fiction; 1st-26th annual collections; edited by Gardner Dozois. St. Martin's Press 1984-2009

First three annual collections published by Bluejay Books

Each annual collection contains stories, a summation of developments in the field, and a list of honorable mentions. Over the years contributors have included Michael Swanwick, Maureen F. McHugh, Charles Sheffield, Cory Doctorow, Kage Baker, Brian Stableford, Gene Wolfe, Nancy Kress, Gregory Benford, Stephen Baxter, Elizabeth Bear, Paolo Bacigalupi, Jay Lake, and Mary Rosenblum

Yehoshua, Abraham B.

A woman in Jerusalem; [by] A.B. Yehoshua; translated from the Hebrew by Hillel Halkin. Harcourt, Inc. 2006 237p $25
ISBN 1-870015-98-3   LC 2005-33435
Original Hebrew edition, 2004

"He doesn't know it, but the manager of the human resources division of a bakery in Jerusalem is about to launch on a journey. A woman killed in a terrorist bombing has been traced to the bakery by a pay stub, and a

Yehoshua, Abraham B.—*Continued*

nasty newspaper story condemns the owner's insensitivity in letting her languish nameless in the morgue. In fact, she's not currently an employee, but it's up to the manager to fix this public relations disaster, an assignment that leads him from the victim's shabby home all the way to Russia to deliver her body to her mother and son. While surmounting bureaucratic hurdles, the manager wrestles with issues of doing good. He's also painfully reminded of his strained relationships with his daughter and ex-wife." Libr J

The author "has long been described as the Hebrew Faulkner. Indeed, the plot of his eighth novel uses a bold and often funny improvisation on William Faulkner's 1930 classic, 'As I Lay Dying', to explore guilt, penance and public relations in Israel's underbelly. . . . His evocation of what it means to be human is drawn in the subtlest strokes." Economist

Yoder, Lauren

(tr) Halter, M. Messiah

Yolen, Jane

Briar Rose. Doherty Assocs. 1992 190p (Fairy tale series) hardcover o.p. pa $6.99

ISBN 0-312-85135-9; 0-7653-4230-8 (pa)

LC 92-25456

"A TOR book"

"Yolen takes the story of Briar Rose (commonly known as Sleeping Beauty) and links it to the Holocaust. . . . Rebecca Berlin, a young woman who has grown up hearing her grandmother Gemma tell an unusual and frightening version of the Sleeping Beauty legend, realizes when Gemma dies that the fairy tale offers one of the very few clues she has to her grandmother's past. . . . By interpolating Gemma's vivid and imaginative story into the larger narrative, Yolen has created an engrossing novel." Publ Wkly

Yoon, Paul

Once the shore; stories. Sarabande Books 2009 270p pa $15.95

ISBN 978-1-932511-70-3; 1-932511-70-9

LC 2008-19331

Contents: Once the shore; Among the wreckage; Faces to the fire; So that they do not hear us; The woodcarver's daughter; Look for me in the camphor tree; And we will be here; The hanging lanterns of Ido

"Yoon's collection of eight richly textured stories explore the themes of family, lost love, silence, alienation and the effects of the Japanese occupation and the Korean War on the poor communities of a small South Korean island." Publ Wkly

Yorke, Margaret

Act of violence. St. Martin's Press 1998 282p $22.95

ISBN 0-312-18522-7　　　　LC 98-16546

First published 1997 in the United Kingdom

In this mystery, "a small English village shudders after a murderous rampage by two school-boys, but a manipulative local therapist seems unperturbed." Libr J

"The tension leading to the young toughs' arrest is taut, and the identity of the murderess-turned-counselor kept cleverly obscured until the very end." Publ Wkly

Almost the truth. Mysterious Press 1995 c1994 278p o.p.　　　　LC 94-36601

First published 1994 in the United Kingdom

"Hannah's rape during the course of a burglary shatters her family's happiness, but she makes matters worse by blaming her father. Her father, in turn, seeks a singular and surprising revenge on the rapist, released after a very short prison term." Libr J

"Without sacrificing entertainment to message, this absorbing, utterly unsentimental narrative reminds us that behind crime-related headlines live real people whose futures are marked by the crimes' effects." Publ Wkly

Criminal damage. Mysterious Press 1992 248p o.p.　　　　LC 91-51182

"Mrs. Newton, a widow, enjoys a quiet and determinedly tidy life in the picturesque English village of Middle Bardolph, but storms are brewing that seem likely to unsettle it. Geoffrey, her boring and not very pleasant son, thinks his mother should underwrite the larger home his ambitious wife demands. Temperamental daughter Jennifer is increasingly obsessed with her former lover and his new fiancée and seems bent on disrupting their lives. . . . Yorke . . . mixes this deftly drawn, untrustworthy cast with robbery, violence and a hidden past, keeping readers guessing about what will be done and who will do it." Publ Wkly

False pretences. St. Martin's Press 1999 310p $23.95

ISBN 0-312-19975-9　　　　LC 98-51198

First published 1998 in the United Kingdom

This psychological thriller, set in a small English village, traces "the local secrets exposed by a stranger and the aftermath when her true identity is discovered. Captivating and full-bodied." Libr J

The price of guilt. St. Martin's Press 2000 297p $24.95

ISBN 0-312-25332-X　　　　LC 99-88102

First published 1999 in the United Kingdom

"Louise Widdows's mentally abusive husband disappears the same night she suffers injuries in a hit-and-run accident. About the same time, Louise learns she has inherited a cottage, so she moves, hoping to start anew and perhaps locate the son she gave up for adoption 30-odd years earlier." Libr J

"Yorke is a master at making the reader care about meek and lonely middle-aged women. While the latter part of the novel largely fills in the motivations of minor characters in flashback, Colin's fate remains up in the air until the very end—and is as ironic as Louise's, if more just." Publ Wkly

A question of belief. Mysterious Press 1997 282p o.p.

* LC 97-20833

First published 1996 in the United Kingdom

In this novel of psychological suspense, an English "department store executive is falsely accused of sexual harassment by a vindictive customer. After losing both his job and the trust of his family, the poor chump fakes his suicide and tramps off to a little village where nobody knows of his shame. Here his fate intersects with

Yorke, Margaret—*Continued*

that of another outcast, an illiterate teenager who has been shabbily manipulated by a militant animal rights activist with a hidden agenda. Several other folks come out of the woods to play, and although their convergences are strictly contrived, their characters are sharply defined in this fatalistic tale of modern morality in tatters." N Y Times Book Rev

Yoshimoto, Banana, 1964-

Asleep; translated from the Japanese by Michael Emmerich. Grove Press 2000 177p

ISBN 0-8021-1669-8   LC 99-88699

Contents: Night and night's travelers; Love songs; Asleep

This volume consists "of three novellas, each telling a somewhat mystical tale of haunted slumber. In the first story, a woman mourning a dead lover finds herself sleepwalking; in the next, a woman involved in a relationship with a man, whose wife is in a coma, realizes that she is unable to remain awake; and in the third, a woman finds her dreams inhabited by a dead woman, her former rival in a love triangle. The stories flow easily and quietly from one to the next, and while they have a lyrical, almost poetic, quality, they remain gripping, dramatic, intense, and real." Booklist

Asleep [a novella]
In Yoshimoto, B. Asleep p105-77

Goodbye Tsugumi; a novel; translated from the Japanese by Michael Emmerich. Grove Press 2002 186p $23

ISBN 0-8021-1638-8   LC 2001-58460

Original Japanese edition, 1999

"Maria Shirakawa is a thoughtful young woman thrown by family circumstance (her parents never married; with her mother, she is waiting for her father's divorce from his current wife) into growing up with her cousin, Tsugumi Yamamoto, in her aunt and uncle's small inn. Tsugumi, who is chronically ill, possesses a mischievous charm that both maddens and amuses her family. . . . Tsugumi's tenuous health seems to free her from the behavioral norms that govern Maria and Tsugumi's long-suffering older sister, Yoko, allowing her to curse, flirt with boys, concoct elaborate pranks and shock adults in a way Maria resents, envies and admires." Publ Wkly

Kitchen; translated from the Japanese by Megan Backus. Grove Press 1993 152p o.p.

* LC 92-12871

Original Japanese edition, 1987

The volume comprises two works of fiction, the title novella and a short story. "Both 'Kitchen' and 'Moonlight Shadow,' each narrated by young women, are about loss. In the longer story, Mikage, the female narrator, moves into the house of Yuichi and his mother/father [a transexual] after the death of her grandmother; in the second, the girl has lost a boyfriend in a car crash, and is granted a vision of her beloved by a mysterious lady on a bridge." Times Lit Suppl

"In supple, precise prose Yoshimoto conveys her protagonists' emotional states by according them unusual sensitivity to the natural world; they share an enhanced vision that makes things shine with luminous clarity or emanate the gloom of mortality." Publ Wkly

Kitchen [novella]
In Yoshimoto, B. Kitchen

Love songs
In Yoshimoto, B. Asleep p67-103

Night and night's travelers
In Yoshimoto, B. Asleep p1-65

Youmans, Marly

The wolf pit. Farrar, Straus & Giroux 2001 342p $24

ISBN 0-374-29195-0

* LC 2001-42278

This Civil War novel focuses on "Robin, a young Confederate soldier, and Agate, a mulatto slave girl. In his . . . double tale, each of the characters suffers untold miseries. Robin's are endured in the heat of battle and the horrors of prison camp. while Agate must bear the indignities of slavery. . . . The novel's many dramatic and traumatic events will keep the reader breathless, while the haunting, lyrical language and the fierce intelligence behind it reminds us we are reading a writer and storyteller of the first order." Publ Wkly

Yourcenar, Marguerite

Memoirs of Hadrian; translated from the French by Grace Frick in collaboration with the author. Farrar, Straus and Young 1954 313p o.p.

*

Original French edition, 1951

"The memoirs portray the emperor on the eve of his death and describe his reflections as he gazes out upon the city that seemed to him indestructible and that he now fears will fall. As with most of her work, the book is a minutely researched reconstruction of actual events in the distant past through which she develops penetrating and fully credible portraits of the people she describes." Reader's Ency. 4th edition

Yrsa Sigurðardóttir

Last rituals; an Icelandic novel of secret symbols, medieval witchcraft, and modern murder; translated from the Icelandic by Bernard Scudder. HarperCollins Publishers 2007 314p $23.95

ISBN 978-0-06-114336-6; 0-06-114336-7

Original Icelandic edition, 2005

"Thóra is a thirtysomething divorcée, mother of two, and a partner in a small law firm. She is reluctantly drawn into a murder investigation when approached by the Guntlieb family, whose son, Harald, was killed at the university. With the pay at twice her usual rate and the assistance of Matthew Reich, the Guntlieb family representative, Thóra can't refuse, even though the gruesome murder appalls her. To find the murderer, Thóra and Matthew must delve into Harald's interests in witchcraft and witch burnings and investigate his university friends. Scudder provides such a smooth translation, right down to the slang used by Harald's college friends, that an engaged reader can easily forget this was originally written in Icelandic." Libr J

Yu Hua

Brothers; translated from the Chinese by Eileen Chow and Carlos Rojas. Pantheon Books 2009 641p $29.95

ISBN 978-0-375-42499-1; 0-375-42499-7

LC 2008-21617

Original Chinese edition, 2005

This novel, "a family history documenting four decades of profound social and cultural transformation in China, begins on a toilet. In a sleepy rural outpost known as Liu Town, fourteen-year-old Baldy Li is caught peeping at women's bottoms in a latrine. He becomes known as a compulsive public masturbator, and his obsession continues into adulthood: he ends up hosting a beauty pageant for virgins (all of whom rely on doctored hymens to gain entrance). The book has sold more than a million copies in China, despite its irreverent take on everything from the Cultural Revolution to the capitalist boom." New Yorker

Yunis, Alia

The night counter; a novel. Shaye Areheart Books 2009 365p $24

ISBN 978-0-307-45362-4; 0-307-45362-6

LC 2009-281269

"Fatima is an elderly Lebanese woman living in Los Angeles with her favorite grandson, Amir. She moved to Detroit from Lebanon seven decades ago and has since had two husbands, 10 children, and 14 grandchildren. At this point, she's ready to say goodbye to all of it. Or almost ready, that is. First, she must find a wife for wannabe actor Amir (blithely overlooking his constant insistence that he's gay) and then arrange for him to inherit her beloved mother's house in Lebanon. In the meantime, as the successful conclusion of that task drags on, Fatima is content to stay alive for another 1,001 days, spending each night telling her stories to Scheherazade." Christ Sci Monit

This "novel, mixes equal parts of magical realism, social commentary, family drama and light-hearted humor to create a delicious and intriguing indulgence worth savoring." Minneapolis Star Trib

Z

Zabytko, Irene

When Luba leaves home; a profile in stories. Algonquin Bks. 2003 230p $22.95

ISBN 1-56512-332-8

LC 2002-38525

"A Shannon Ravenel book"

Contents: Steve's bar; My black valiant; The celebirty; Saint Sonya; The last boat; Obligation; Pani Ryhotska in love; Lavender soap; The prodigal son enters heaven; John Mars, All-American

"Occasionally awkward, but often shining with quiet grace, these 10 interconnected stories by Zabytko. . . follow the childhood-to-young-adulthood trajectory of Luba Vovkovych, who lives with her Ukrainian immigrant parents in Chicago in the 1900s." Publ Wkly

Zafón, Carlos Ruiz *See* Ruiz Zafón, Carlos, 1964-

Zahn, Timothy

The last command. Bantam Bks. 1993 407p (Star wars, v3) o.p.

LC 92-43876

Earlier titles in the author's Thrawn trilogy: Heir to empire (1991); Dark force rising (1992)

In this concluding volume of the Star wars trilogy "Thrawn mounts a final siege against the Republic. While Han and Chewbacca struggle to form a wary alliance of smugglers in a last-ditch attack against the Empire, Leia keeps the Alliance together and prepares for the birth of her Jedi twins. But the Empire has too many ships and too many clones to combat. The Republic's only hope lies in sending a small force, led by Luke, into the very stronghold that houses Thrawn's terrible cloning machines." Publisher's note

Zamíàtin, Evgeniĭ Ivanovich, 1884-1937

We; [by] Yevgeny Zamyatin; translated by Mirra Ginsburg. Viking 1972 204p o.p.

First translation published 1924

"The ultimate dystopian novel, presenting a vision of the United States: a society whose suppression of individuality in the cause of order proceeds to the logical limit of eliminating the imagination. Its origin, and the fact that it circulated surreptitiously in Russia as a samizdat publication, encourages a reading that construes it as an attack on Soviet communism, but it actually refers to a much more fundamental tendency in human nature towards conformity and autmatism. Not published in Russia until 1988." Anatomy of Wonder. 5th edition

Zamyatin, Yevgeny Ivanovich *See* Zamíàtin, Evgeniĭ Ivanovich, 1884-1937

Zelazny, Roger

Blood of Amber. Arbor House 1986 215p

ISBN 0-87795-829-7

LC 86-3530

"A Del Rey book"

Sequel to Trumps of doom

In this seventh installment in the author's Amber fantasy series "the sorcerer Merlin of Amber—aka Merle Corey of San Francisco—learns the identities of two would-be assassins but makes a truce with one to pursue the greater, more dangerous power beyond them. Once again, the limited plot is enlivened by Zelazny's irony, his bravura sequences . . . and his laconic sense of the incongruous." Publ Wkly

Followed by Sign of chaos

The courts of chaos. Doubleday 1978 183p

ISBN 0-385-13685-4

LC 78-3263

Sequel to The hand of Oberon

This fifth title in the author's "Amber fantasy series answers many of the questions central to previous installments; the nature of the magical kingdom of Amber and the tangents it sometimes forms with the real world; the mystery behind the disappearance of Oberon the King—which forms the plot of the stories—and the machinations of Corwin, Prince of Amber, and his siblings, who thrive on intrigue." Booklist

Followed by Trumps of doom

The dead man's brother. Hard Case Crime 2009 256p pa $6.99

ISBN 978-0-8439-6115-7; 0-8439-6115-5

Zelazny, Roger—*Continued*

"The story follows Ovid Wiley, a former art smuggler turned respectable gallery owner who finds his former smuggling partner dead in his place of work. He is quickly picked up by the police, and then the CIA, which offers to make his trouble go away for a price. Wiley must track down a priest who has absconded with $3 million of the Vatican's dollars. This unwelcome assignment takes Wiley to Rome, where he meets up with his smuggling partner's ex-girlfriend, and then to Brazil, where he and Maria end up involved in local politics. The story is solid, but not spectacular. Zelazny keeps everything moving along nicely, but it's all territory that's been trod before. It's entertaining, and it shows Zelazny could have easily branched out into other genres, but The Dead Man's Brother is remarkable mainly for it's status as a forgotten novel." Independent Crime

Donnerjack; [by] Roger Zelazny, Jane Lindskold. Avon Bks. 1997 503p $24

ISBN 0-380-97326-X   LC 96-48705

"One hundred years ago, the World Net crashed, creating a separate virtual-reality universe complete with its own gods, its own civilizations, its own magic. Virtù can be accessed for recreation or business from our own world, Verité, through virtual bodies. Non of the self-aware programs of Virtù can visit Verité, however, and the more powerful of them deeply resent it. John D'Arcy Donnerjack, instrumental in creating Virtù and among the foremost explorers of its wonders, has fallen in love with an artificial intelligence named Ayradyss. When she dies, Donnerjack follows her to Death's realm and demands her back." Publ Wkly

"The late Zelazny's last novel, completed by Lindskold, is one of his largest and most ambitious. . . . All the mythic resonances we have come to expect from Zelazny are here in abundance." Booklist

The guns of Avalon. Doubleday 1972 180p (Amber) o.p.

Sequel to Nine princes in Amber

In this second volume of the author's Amber series Corwin "again walks the shadow worlds in search of his stolen birthright and encounters dreaded forces of evil conjured up by his own terrible curse." Booklist

Followed by Sign of the unicorn

The hand of Oberon. Doubleday 1976 181p

ISBN 0-385-08541-9

"The fourth title in Zelazny's epic fantasy of the world called Amber picks up in mid-dialogue form the conclusion of the previous novel 'Sign of the Unicorn.'" Booklist

"Oberon, the royal leader of the land of Amber, is unexpectedly missing, and his large family of sons and daughters is engaged in searching for him, or else trying to keep him missing." Publ Wkly

Followed by The courts of chaos

Home is the hangman

In The Hugo winners p5-67

Knight of shadows. Morrow 1989 251p (Amber) o.p.   LC 89-34658

Sequel to Sign of chaos

"The ninth book in Zelazny's Amber sagas. . . . Merlin, son of Corwin, escapes at the last minute from the Citadel of the FourWorlds. He is immediately plunged

into intrigue and adventure. By book's end, it is apparent that his travels are not yet complete. Zelazny's pacing and the ingenious games he plays with magic continue to be rewarding." Booklist

Followed by Prince of chaos

Lord of light. Doubleday 1967 257p o.p.   *

This novel "describes a planet colonized by refugees from India who are tyrannized by a few of their fellow citizens who have assumed the guise and powers of the Hindu gods. Instead of easing his readers into the strange setting and unfamiliar mythology, Zelazny began the story in the middle, centuries after the initial landing; that the reader can absorb—and care to absorb—the complexities of the plot and setting is a tribute to the author's storytelling ability." New Ency of Sci Fic

Nine princes in Amber. Doubleday 1970 188p (Amber) o.p.   *

This tale, the first in the author's Amber series, is a fantasy and adventure story about Corwin, who, following an attack of amnesia, realizes that he is one of nine princes in the kingdom of Amber. Each one of the nine princes and four princesses wants the throne, and war breaks out between the brothers

Followed by The guns of Avalon

Prince of chaos. Morrow 1991 225p (Amber) o.p.   LC 91-17296

Sequel to Knight of shadows

The tenth book in the Amber sagas "takes Merlin Corey to the actual Courts of Chaos, which have figured as offstage presences in the series beginning with *Trumps of Doom*. We now see the Courts from the inside, and a certain amount of the mystery about Corey's world and future is dispelled, although not without the usual quota of intrigues and dangers. The finer nuances of the series are becoming a little hard to appreciate without having followed it from the beginning. The vivid imagination and high command of language, however, can still be enjoyed on a volume-by-volume basis." Booklist

Sign of chaos. Arbor House 1987 214p (Amber) o.p.   LC 87-14509

Sequel to Blood of Amber

In the eighth volume of the author's Amber fantasy series "Merlin Corey follows a confused trail to the Keep of Four Worlds, where he learns the secret of the involvement of the Courts of Chaos in all the intrigues and wars to which he is heir." Booklist

Followed by Knight of shadows

Sign of the unicorn. Doubleday 1975 186p (Amber) o.p.

Sequel to The guns of Avalon

"Third in a series of science fiction-fantasy adventures featuring Corwin, Prince of Amber. . . . Court intrigue is rampant among the surviving princes and princesses of Amber, all of whom weave in and out of Shadow, a multi-dimensional world they can manipulate, and unite to rescue a brother imprisoned by evil beings threatening the kingdom. This, though action packed, does not advance the fortunes of Corwin to any extent but does fill in background." Booklist

Followed by The hand of Oberon

Zelazny, Roger—*Continued*

Trumps of doom. Arbor House 1985 183p

ISBN 0-87795-718-5   LC 84-299

Sequel to The courts of chaos

"A new sequence [in the Amber fantasy series] begins in this sixth volume centering on Corwin's son Merlin, a sorcerer who has followed the father he barely knew from their powerful realm of Amber to an Earth that is one of Amber's many shadowy alternate worlds. Attempts on Merlin's life force him to return to Amber, where he becomes embroiled once more in family quarrels and finally confronts the man who has been stalking him. This fast-paced, colorful tale is enriched by Zelazny's literary analogs of his alternate worlds as he flips from one frame of reference to another (tarot, computers, lawyerly logic) and from one voice to another (hard-boiled detective, classical allusions, high fantasy)." Publ Wkly

Followed by Blood of Amber

Zeltserman, Dave

Small crimes. Serpent's Tail 2008 263p pa $14.95

ISBN 978-1-85242-971-3; 1-85242-971-2

"This tale is told by one of fortune's fools: Joe Denton is a crooked ex-cop in Vermont who's just been released from jail after serving seven years for stabbing the local district attorney in the face. Since what's past is never truly past in crime noir, no sooner does Joe step out of the slammer than cosmic IOU's begin to rain down on his head. First, the disfigured DA cheerfully greets Joe outside the prison and announces that a local crime kingpin (and Joe's secret boss) is dying of cancer and has found religion. The kingpin's expected confession should send Joe straight back behind bars. Then, the local sheriff (also crooked) orders Joe to murder the DA before the crime kingpin can confess. The plot of Small Crimes ricochets out from this claustrophobic opening, and it's a thing of sordid beauty." NPR

Zimler, Richard

The last kabbalist of Lisbon. Overlook Press 1998 318p $24.95

ISBN 0-87951-834-0

      * LC 97-46184

"A young manuscript illuminator, fruitseller and secretly practicing Jew and kabbalist searches for the murderer of his uncle in this . . . [novel] set during the horrific 1506 Lisbon Inquisition. Outwardly Christian converts, Berekiah Zarco and his family practice Judaism clandestinely and study the Kabbalah, the mystical Jewish philosophy that sees God's presence in all things. Tragedy strikes when Berekiah discovers the naked, bloody bodies of his Kabbalist Uncle Abraham and a young girl, their throats slit, in a secret prayer cellar." Publ Wkly

This novel "first published in Portuguese, vividly recreates the world of ancient Lisbon, presenting Berekiah's mysticism in graceful, albeit occasionally florid, prose. Zimler's portrait of the city (and the New Christians' uneasy place within it) enriches his many-layered narrative, in which a suitably complex cast of characters plays a dangerous game with fate." N Y Times Book Rev

Zipes, Jack David

(tr & ed) Hesse, H. The fairy tales of Hermann Hesse

Zola, Émile, 1840-1902

Germinal; translated with an introduction and notes by Roger Pearson. Penguin Books 2004 xlv, 546p (Penguin classics) pa $10

ISBN 978-0-14-044742-2; 0-14-044742-3

      *

Original French edition, 1885, one of the Rougon-Macquart series

"A study of life in the mines. . . . Étienne Lanier, a socialist, is forced to work in the mines. Low wages and fines cause a strike, of which Lanier is one of the leaders. He counsels moderation; but hunger drives the miners to desperation, and force is met by force. Several are killed, Lanier is deported, and the miners fall back into their old slavery." Keller. Reader's Dig of Books

Nana; translated with an introduction by Douglas Parmée. Oxford University Press 1998 c1992 xxix, 430p (Oxford world's classics)

ISBN 0-19-283670-6

      *

Original French edition, 1880, one of the Rougon-Macquart series

"The title character grows up in the slums of Paris. She has a brief career as an untalented actress before finding success as a courtesan. Although vulgar and ignorant, she has a destructive sexuality that attracts many rich and powerful men. Cruelly contemptuous of her lovers' emotions, Nana wastes their fortunes, driving many of them to ruin and even suicide." Merriam-Webster's Ency of Lit

Three faces of love; especially translated for this volume by Roland Gant. Vanguard Press 1969 c1968 151p o.p.

These three early Zola stories explore different kinds of love. In For One Night of Love "Zola tells of a dullard whose passion leads to suicide through his having been accessory in the murder of his rival, killed by the girl, a marquise. 'Round Trip' is a lyric of youthful sensuality triumphing over middle-aged insensitivity. In 'Winkles for M. Chabre' Zola deals with a triangle (aging husband, young wife, young man); the husband has been told to expect a child if he follows a diet of shellfish; he gets the child, unaware that it is not because of winkles. Slight things, these stories, but welcome additions to the austere works usually associated with Zola." Libr J

Zuber, Isabel

Salt. Picador 2002 352p

ISBN 0-312-28133-1   LC 2001-54892

The author depicts "one woman's life in the American South at the turn of the 20th century. . . . Central to her portrait are the relationships between Anna Maud Stockton Bayley, her adulterous, twice-married husband, John, and their offspring. Forced into marriage after John seduces her, Anna makes the best of it, sewing, gardening and keeping house in the small town of Faith, N.C. Still,

Zuber, Isabel—*Continued*

she dreams of music, singing, travel and love. But single-minded John, who is avid to increase his land, children and stock, is less interested in his young wife's desires than his own personal gain." Publ Wkly

"Zuber gets the historical details right, and her characters' emotions (especially Anna's—romantic, tender and full of quiet desperation) are handled just as deftly." N Y Times Book Rev

Zumas, Leni, 1972-

Farewell navigator; stories. Open City Books 2008 168p pa $14

ISBN 978-1-890447-49-6; 1-890447-49-8

LC 2008-5955

Contents: Farewell navigator; Dragons may be the way forward; The everything hater; Heart sockets; How he was a wicked son; Thieves and mapmakers; Waste no time if this method faiels; Handfasting; Blotilla takes the cake; Leopard arms

"Zumas's penchant for rhythmic language and experimentation is paralleled (and possibly influenced) by her work as a drummer. . . . [She focuses] on the culture of rebellious musicians, rock clubs and 'trapped people.' Zumas's stories deal with suicide and bleeding rectums, and take place in rehab centers and towns that don't exist on maps—microcosms of the great community of solitude. Like powerful music, the phenomenon of Zumas's fiction happens when the rhythms are perfectly in time with the pitch of loneliness. She pounds away at her words until they make a melancholy sound." Paste

TITLE AND SUBJECT INDEX

This index to the books listed in part 1 includes title and subject entries, arranged in one alphabet. Full information for each book is given in part 1 under the main entry, which is usually the author.

Title entries. Novels are listed under title. Analytical entries are made for novels published in omnibus editions and for novelettes. Such entries carry *In* or *also in* designations and usually include the page numbers in the book where the item is to be found.

Subject entries. Subject headings are printed in capital letters. The listing of a work under a subject indicates that a major portion of the work is about that subject. Under genre headings, such as SCIENCE FICTION or PHILOSOPHICAL NOVELS, works of that genre are listed. Under the heading DETECTIVES a list of individual fictional detectives makes reference to the authors of the detective novels in which they appear. Subdivisions under headings are given first by chronological period, then by topic, and then by place name.

1st to die. Patterson, J.
3 by Irving. Irving, J.
3: This gun for hire, The confidential agent, The ministry of fear. Greene, G.
10 lb. penalty. Francis, D.
The 14 sisters of Emilio Montez O'Brien. See Hijuelos, O. The fourteen sisters of Emilio Montez O'Brien
Twenty fragments of a ravenous youth. Guo Xiaolu
20th century ghosts. Hill, J.
The 27 ingredient chili con carne murders. Pickard, N.
The 42nd parallel. Dos Passos, J.
    also in Dos Passos, J. U.S.A.
The 47th samurai. Hunter, S.
82 Desire. Smith, J.
101 Reykjavik. Hallgrímur Helgason
The 158-pound marriage. Irving, J.
    In Irving, J. 3 by Irving p561-718
200 years of great American short stories. Entered in Part I under title
1876. Vidal, G.
1916. Llywelyn, M.
1919. Dos Passos, J.
    also in Dos Passos, J. U.S.A.
1921. Llywelyn, M.
1929. Turner, F. W.
1940. Neugeboren, J.
1949. Llywelyn, M.
1972. Llywelyn, M.
2001: a space odyssey. Clarke, A. C.
2010: odyssey two. Clarke, A. C.
2012: the war for souls. Strieber, W.
2061: odyssey three. Clarke, A. C.
2666. Bolaño, R.
3001: the final odyssey. Clarke, A. C.
30,000 on the hoof. See Grey, Z. Woman of the frontier

A

"A" is for alibi. Grafton, S.
The A.B.C. murders. Christie, A.
Abandon. Iyer, P.
ABANDONED CHILDREN
    See also Orphans
    Quindlen, A. Blessings
    Shreve, A. Light on snow
ABANDONED TOWNS See Extinct cities
The Abbess of Crewe. Spark, M.
ABBESSES See Nuns
ABBEYS
    See also Cathedrals; Churches; Convent life; Monasticism and religious orders
    Austen, J. Northanger Abbey
ABDUCTION See Kidnapping
The abduction. Grippando, J.

ABEL (BIBLICAL FIGURE)
                    About
    Maine, D. Fallen
Abide with me. Strout, E.
Ablutions. DeWitt, P.
ABNORMALITIES AND DEFORMITIES See Deformities; Dwarfs; Face—Abnormalities and deformities; Monsters
ABOLITIONISTS
    See also Slavery; Underground railroad
    Banks, R. Cloudsplitter
    Stowe, H. B. Uncle Tom's cabin
    Tryon, T. In the fire of spring
    Wright, S. The Amalgamation Polka
ABORIGINES, AUSTRALIAN See Australian aborigines
ABORTION
    Irving, J. The cider house rules
    McKinney-Whetstone, D. Leaving Cecil Street
    Patterson, R. N. No safe place
    Patterson, R. N. Protect and defend
    Piercy, M. Braided lives
    Pottinger, S. The fourth procedure
    Searles, J. Boy still missing
About a boy. Hornby, N.
About face. Leon, D.
Above suspicion. MacInnes, H.
Absalom, Absalom! Faulkner, W.
    also in Faulkner, W. Novels, 1936-1940 p1-315
Absolute friends. Le Carré, J.
An absolute gentleman. Kinder, R. M.
Absolute power. Baldacci, D.
Absolute truths. Howatch, S.
The abstinence teacher. Perrotta, T.
Absurdistan. Shteyngart, G.
Abundance. Naslund, S. J.
ABUSE OF CHILDREN See Child abuse
Abuse of power. Rosenberg, N. T.
ABUSED WIVES See Wife abuse
ABYSSINIA See Ethiopia
Acacia. Durham, D. A.
ACADIANS
                    Louisiana
    See Cajuns
Accelerando. Stross, C.
Acceptance. Coll, S.
The acceptance world. Powell, A.
    In Powell, A. A dance to the music of time
The accident. Wiesel, E.
    In Wiesel, E. Night, Dawn, The accident: three tales p205-318
The accidental. Smith, A.
ACCIDENTAL DEATH See Accidents
An accidental man. Murdoch, I.
The accidental time machine. Haldeman, J. W.
The accidental tourist. Tyler, A.

ACCIDENTS

See also Drowning; Fires; Industrial accidents; Shipwrecks and castaways; Traffic accidents

Aira, C. An afternoon in the life of a landscape painter
Brown, R. Tender mercies
Carroll, J. The ghost in love
De los Santos, M. Belong to me
Delinsky, B. The summer I dared
Evans, N. The horse whisperer
Hamilton, J. When Madeline was young
Hériz, E. d. Lies
King, S. Duma Key
Lawrence, S. The lightning keeper
Mawer, S. The fall
Oates, J. C. American appetites
Packer, A. The dive from Clausen's pier
Proulx, A. Postcards
Roy, A. The god of small things
Spark, M. Reality and dreams
Steel, D. The house on Hope Street
Trollope, J. The men and the girls
Vonnegut, K. Deadeye Dick

ACCIDENTS, INDUSTRIAL *See* Industrial accidents

Accordion crimes. Proulx, A.

ACCORDIONISTS

Proulx, A. Accordion crimes

ACCOUNTANTS

Pronzini, B. The crimes of Jordan Wise

ACCULTURATION

See also Americanization; Race relations
Momaday, N. S. House made of dawn

The **accusers**. Davis, L.

ACHILLES (LEGENDARY CHARACTER)

Cook, E. Achilles

Achilles. Cook, E.
Acorna. McCaffrey, A.
Acorna's people. McCaffrey, A.
Acorna's quest. McCaffrey, A.
Acorna's rebels. McCaffrey, A.
Acorna's search. McCaffrey, A.
Acorna's triumph. McCaffrey, A.
Acorna's world. McCaffrey, A.
Across open ground. Parkinson, H.
Across the river and into the trees. Hemingway, E.
An **act** of love. Thayer, N.
Act of revenge. Tanenbaum, R.
Act of violence. Yorke, M.
Active service. Crane, S.
In Crane, S. The complete novels of Stephen Crane p429-592

ACTORS

See also Motion picture actors and actresses; Strolling players; Theater life

Baldwin, J. Tell me how long the train's been gone
Bernhard, T. Woodcutters
Carroll, J. Fault lines
Davies, R. World of wonders
Estleman, L. D. The adventures of Johnny Vermillion
Frey, J. Bright shiny morning
Irving, J. A son of the circus
Irving, J. Until I find you
Isaacs, S. Almost paradise
Kaplow, R. Me and Orson Welles
Korda, M. Curtain
L'Engle, M. Certain women
L'Engle, M. A live coal in the sea
Leonard, E. Get Shorty
Lessing, D. M. Love, again
Lott, B. Ancient highway
Martin, V. The confessions of Edward Day
Matheson, R. Hunted past reason
McCoy, H. They shoot horses, don't they?
McLarty, R. Traveler
Miller, W. M. The darfsteller
Nye, R. The late Mr. Shakespeare
Roth, P. The humbling
Simmons, D. Muse of fire
Varley, J. The golden globe
Wagner, B. The chrysanthemum palace
West, N. The day of the locust
Westlake, D. E. Money for nothing

Wolcott, J. The catsitters

Actress in the house. McElroy, J.

ACTRESSES

See also Motion picture actors and actresses; Strolling players; Theater life

Baldwin, J. Tell me how long the train's been gone
Blatty, W. P. The exorcist
Buruma, I. The China lover
Clark, M. H. Weep no more, my lady
Cohen, L. H. House lights
Didion, J. Play it as it lays
Goudge, E. Such devoted sisters
Grøndahl, J. C. Lucca
Harris, E. L. Not a day goes by
Iyer, P. Abandon
Korda, M. Curtain
Leonard, E. LaBrava
Lipman, E. The family man
Lord, B. B. The middle heart
McElroy, J. Actress in the house
McPhee, J. A man of no moon
Michael, J. Acts of love
Oates, J. C. Blonde
Pilcher, R. Winter solstice
Sontag, S. In America
Steel, D. Sunset in St. Tropez
Tey, J. A shilling for candles
Thomas, R. Voodoo, Ltd
Trollope, J. Second honeymoon
Walton, J. Ha'penny
Weldon, F. Worst fears
West, N. The day of the locust
Williams, T. The Roman spring of Mrs. Stone
Wolfe, G. An evil guest

Acts of faith. Caputo, P.
Acts of love. Michael, J.
Ada. Nabokov, V. V.
also in Nabokov, V. V. Novels, 1969-1974

ADAM (BIBLICAL FIGURE)
About

Maine, D. Fallen

Adam and Eve and Pinch me. Rendell, R.
Adam Bede. Eliot, G.

ADAMS, ABIGAIL, 1744-1818
About

Hambly, B. Patriot hearts

ADAMS, JOHN QUINCY, 1767-1848
About

Pesci, D. Amistad

Addie Pray. Brown, J. D.

ADELAIDE (AUSTRALIA) *See* Australia—Adelaide

ADIRONDACK MOUNTAINS (N.Y.)

Doctorow, E. L. Loon Lake
Robinson, R. Sweetwater

Admiral Hornblower in the West Indies. Forester, C. S.

ADOLESCENCE

See also Boys; Girls; Youth
Abraham, P. The romance reader
Aciman, A. A. Call me by your name
Alexie, S. Flight
Barbery, M. The elegance of the hedgehog
Bassani, G. The garden of the Finzi-Continis
Berg, E. We are all welcome here
Betts, D. Souls raised from the dead
Bock, C. Beautiful children
Brown, L. Joe
Burns, O. A. Cold Sassy tree
Chevalier, T. Burning bright
Coe, J. The Rotters' Club
Cohen, L. H. Heart, you bully, you punk
Colette. Claudine at school
Colette. Gigi
Colette. The tender shoot
Dallas, S. Tallgrass
De Gramont, N. Gossip of the starlings
Dean, M. L. The time it takes to fall
DeLillo, D. Ratner's star
Desai, K. The inheritance of loss
Díaz, J. The brief wondrous life of Oscar Wao
Doctorow, E. L. Billy Bathgate
Doig, I. English Creek
Dragomán, G. The white king

ADOPTION—Continued

D'Amato, B. White male infant
Goudge, E. Trail of secrets
Hagen, G. The Laments
Hallinan, T. A nail through the heart
James, P. D. Innocent blood
Kingsolver, B. Pigs in heaven
Lee, C.-R. A gesture life
Mishima, Y. The decay of the angel
Moore, L. A gate at the stairs
Morrison, T. A mercy
Mortman, D. True colors
Parker, T. J. Silent Joe
Patchett, A. Run
Reed, K. The baby merchant
Tevis, W. S. The queen's gambit
Trollope, J. Brother and sister
Tyler, A. Digging to America
Umrigar, T. N. The weight of heaven
Wharton, E. Summer

Adrian Mole. Townsend, S.
The **Adrian** Mole diaries. Townsend, S.
Adrian Mole: the lost years. Townsend, S.
Adrift just off the Islets of Langerhans: latitude 38° 54′ N, longitude 77° 00′ 13″ W. Ellison, H.
In The Hugo winners p547-81

ADULTERY *See* Marriage problems
Adulthood rites. Butler, O. E.

ADVENTURE

See also Buried treasure; Escapes; International intrigue; Manhunts; Picaresque novels; Pirates; Science fiction; Sea stories; Soldiers of fortune; Spies; Voyages and travels; Western stories

Allende, I. Daughter of fortune
Bainbridge, B. The birthday boys
Barone, S. Dawn of empire
Barone, S. Empire rising
Bates, H. E. Fair stood the wind for France
Benchley, P. Jaws
Berger, T. Little Big Man
Buchan, J. The thirty-nine steps
Caldwell, I. The rule of four
Caputo, P. Horn of Africa
Carlson, R. The signal
Cervantes Saavedra, M. d. Don Quixote de la Mancha
Clavell, J. Gai-Jin
Clavell, J. Shogun
Clavell, J. Tai-Pan
Clavell, J. Whirlwind
Conrad, J. The Nigger of the Narcissus
Conrad, J. Nostromo
Cooper, J. F. The last of the Mohicans
Cooper, J. F. The Leatherstocking tales
Cooper, J. F. The Pathfinder
Cooper, J. F. The prairie
Cornwell, B. The archer's tale
Cornwell, B. Sharpe's battle
Cornwell, B. Sharpe's devil
Cornwell, B. Sharpe's fortress
Cornwell, B. Sharpe's fury
Cornwell, B. Sharpe's havoc
Cornwell, B. Sharpe's prey: Richard Sharpe and the Expedition to Copenhagen, 1807
Cornwell, B. Sharpe's Trafalgar
Cornwell, B. Sharpe's Waterloo
Crichton, M. Sphere
Cussler, C. Atlantis found
Cussler, C. Black wind
Cussler, C. The chase
Cussler, C. Fire ice
Cussler, C. Inca gold
Cussler, C. Lost city
Cussler, C. Plague ship
Cussler, C. Sahara
Cussler, C. Valhalla rising
Cussler, C. White death
Darnton, J. Neanderthal
Dickey, J. Deliverance
Doyle, Sir A. C. The lost world
Du Maurier, Dame D. Jamaica Inn
Dumas, A. The Count of Monte Cristo
Dumas, A. The last cavalier
Dumas, A. The three musketeers
Dunnett, D. Checkmate

Dunnett, D. Pawn in frankincense
Eco, U. Baudolino
Finney, P. Gloriana's torch
Forester, C. S. Admiral Hornblower in the West Indies
Forester, C. S. The African Queen
Forester, C. S. Beat to quarters
Forester, C. S. Commodore Hornblower
Forester, C. S. Flying colours
Forester, C. S. Hornblower and the Atropos
Forester, C. S. Hornblower and the Hotspur
Forester, C. S. Hornblower during the crisis, and two stories: Hornblower's temptation and The last encounter
Forester, C. S. The last nine days of the Bismarck
Forester, C. S. Lieutenant Hornblower
Forester, C. S. Lord Hornblower
Forester, C. S. Ship of the line
Forester, C. S. To the Indies
Forsyth, F. The day of the jackal
Forsyth, F. The whispering wind
Fraser, G. M. The reavers
Gear, K. O. People of the masks
Gear, K. O. People of the mist
Gear, W. M. People of the thunder
Ghosh, A. Sea of poppies
Gilman, D. The amazing Mrs. Pollifax
Gilman, D. The elusive Mrs. Pollifax
Gilman, D. A palm for Mrs. Pollifax
Gilman, D. The unexpected Mrs. Pollifax
Greene, G. Our man in Havana
Greene, G. Travels with my aunt
Grimes, M. Biting the moon
Grisham, J. The testament
Haggard, H. R. King Solomon's mines
Haggard, H. R. She
Harrison, H. The Stainless Steel Rat joins the circus
Harrison, H. The Stainless Steel Rat sings the blues
Hesse, H. Narcissus and Goldmund
Higgins, J. Flight of eagles
Higgins, J. Storm warning
Hilton, J. Lost horizon
Hoffman, A. The probable future
Holland, C. The angel and the sword
Holland, C. The firedrake
Holland, C. Jerusalem
Hope, A. The prisoner of Zenda
Hughes, R. A. W. A high wind in Jamaica
Iagnemma, K. The expeditions
Innes, H. The wreck of the Mary Deare
Jakes, J. American dreams
Jakes, J. California gold
Jennings, G. Raptor
Johnston, T. C. Dance on the wind
Johnston, T. C. Wind walker
Keneally, T. To Asmara
Lackey, M. Firebird
Lambdin, D. King's captain
L'Amour, L. Last of the breed
L'Amour, L. May there be a road
L'Amour, L. The walking drum
Lebbon, T. Fallen
Llywelyn, M. Druids
Llywelyn, M. The last prince of Ireland
Llywelyn, M. Pride of lions
Llywelyn, M. Red Branch
London, J. The Sea-Wolf
Lowell, E. Pearl Cove
Lustbader, E. V. Floating city
Lustbader, E. V. Second skin
MacInnes, H. Above suspicion
MacInnes, H. The Venetian affair
MacLean, A. Force 10 from Navarone
MacLean, A. The guns of Navarone
MacLean, A. Ice Station Zebra
MacLean, A. Night without end
MacLean, A. When eight bells toll
Marías, J. Voyage along the horizon
Martel, Y. Life of Pi
Martin, G. R. R. Hunter's run
McCammon, R. R. Gone south
McCutchan, P. Apprentice to the sea
McCutchan, P. Cameron's crossing
McCutchan, P. The last farewell
McCutchan, P. The new lieutenant
McCutchan, P. The second mate

AFRICA—Native peoples—*Continued*

Hulme, K. The nun's story

Ruark, R. Uhuru

Timm, U. Morenga

Politics

See Politics—Africa

Race relations

Gordimer, N. A guest of honor

AFRICA, CENTRAL *See* Central Africa

AFRICA, EAST *See* East Africa

AFRICA, GERMAN EAST *See* East Africa

AFRICA, SOUTH *See* South Africa

AFRICA, WEST *See* West Africa

AFRICAN AMERICAN CHILDREN

Morrison, T. A mercy

AFRICAN AMERICAN SERVANTS

Epstein, L. San Remo Drive

Watson, B. The heaven of Mercury

AFRICAN AMERICAN SOLDIERS

Katzenbach, J. Hart's war

McBride, J. Miracle at St. Anna

AFRICAN AMERICAN WOMEN

Cooper, J. C. The future has a past

Hurston, Z. N. Their eyes were watching God

Larsen, N. Passing

Marshall, P. Brown girl, brownstones

McMillan, T. The interruption of everything

AFRICAN AMERICANS

See also African American children; African American servants; African American soldiers; African American women; Blacks; Mulattoes; Slavery

Baldwin, J. Early novels and stories

Baldwin, J. Going to meet the man

Bambara, T. C. Gorilla, my love

Barrett, W. E. The lilies of the field

Busch, F. The night inspector

Calling the wind

Campbell, B. M. Brothers and sisters

Campbell, B. M. Your blues ain't like mine

Carter, S. L. The emperor of Ocean Park

Carter, S. L. New England white

Carter, S. L. Palace council

Cleage, P. Babylon sisters

Cooper, J. C. The wake of the wind

Cooper, J. C. Wild stars seeking midnight suns

Crafts, H. The bondswomans narrative

Dexter, P. Train

Doctorow, E. L. Ragtime

Doig, I. Prairie nocturne

Due, T. My soul to keep

Durham, D. A. Gabriel's story

Durham, D. A. A walk through darkness

Estleman, L. D. Black powder, white smoke

Everett, P. L. I am Not Sidney Poitier

Faulkner, W. The reivers

Gaines, E. J. The autobiography of Miss Jane Pittman

Gibbons, K. On the occasion of my last afternoon

Gurganus, A. Saint monster

Haley, A. Mama Flora's family

Hamilton, J. When Madeline was young

Harris, E. L. And this too shall pass

Harris, E. L. If this world were mine

Harris, E. L. Not a day goes by

Harris, M. Bang the drum slowly

Himes, C. The collected stories of Chester Himes

Hughes, L. Laughing to keep from crying

Hughes, L. Not without laughter

Hughes, L. Short stories of Langston Hughes

Hughes, L. Simple speaks his mind

Hughes, L. Simple stakes a claim

Hughes, L. Simple takes a wife

Hughes, L. Simple's Uncle Sam

Hurston, Z. N. The complete stories

Hurston, Z. N. Jonah's gourd vine

Hurston, Z. N. Moses, man of the mountain

Hurston, Z. N. Novels and stories

Jiles, P. The color of lightning

Joe, Y. My fine lady

Jones, E. P. All Aunt Hagar's children

Jones, E. P. The known world

Kidd, S. M. The secret life of bees

Laken, V. Dream house

Lee, H. To kill a mockingbird

Mansbach, A. The end of the Jews

Mansbach, A. Shackling water

Marshall, P. Praisesong for the widow

Martin, V. Property

McCullers, C. Clock without hands

McCullers, C. The member of the wedding

McMillan, T. A day late and a dollar short

McMillan, T. How Stella got her groove back

McMillan, T. Waiting to exhale

Mitcham, J. Sabbath Creek

Morrison, T. Jazz

Morrison, T. Love

Morrison, T. Song of Solomon

Morrison, T. Tar baby

Mosley, W. The man in my basement

Mosley, W. RL's dream

Naylor, G. Bailey's Café

Naylor, G. Linden Hills

Naylor, G. Mama Day

Naylor, G. The men of Brewster Place

Naylor, G. The women of Brewster Place

Oates, J. C. Black girl/White girl

Parks, G. The learning tree

Parks, S.-L. Getting mother's body

Patchett, A. Run

Petry, A. L. The street

Phillips, C. Crossing the river

Phillips, C. Dancing in the dark

Powers, R. The time of our singing

Price, R. The good priest's son

Price, R. Clockers

Reed, I. Japanese by spring

Roth, P. The human stain

Rush, N. Mortals

Sanders, D. Clover

Shange, N. Sassafrass, Cypress & Indigo

The Sleeper wakes

Smith, L. E. Strange fruit

Southgate, M. The fall of Rome

Stowe, H. B. Uncle Tom's cabin

Strauss, D. More than it hurts you

Styron, W. The confessions of Nat Turner

The Unforgetting heart: an anthology of short stories by African American women (1859-1993)

Unsworth, B. Sacred hunger

Vernon, O. Eden

Walker, A. By the light of my father's smile

Walker, A. Possessing the secret of joy

Walker, A. The temple of my familiar

Walker, A. The way forward is with a broken heart

Walker, A. You can't keep a good woman down

Walker, M. Jubilee

Wallace, D. Mr. Sebastian and the Negro magician

Wallace, I. The man

Whitehead, C. The intuitionist

Whitehead, C. John Henry Days

Whitehead, C. Sag Harbor

Wideman, J. E. God's gym

Wideman, J. E. Philadelphia fire

Wideman, J. E. The stories of John Edgar Wideman

Willard, T. Buffalo soldiers

Wolfe, T. A man in full

Wright, R. Eight men

Wright, R. Native son

Wright, R. The outsider

Wright, R. Uncle Tom's children

Wright, R. Works

Youmans, M. The wolf pit

Civil rights

Berg, E. We are all welcome here

Johnson, C. R. Dreamer

Naslund, S. J. Four spirits

Ridley, J. A conversation with the Mann

Straight, S. I been in sorrow's kitchen and licked out all the pots

Relations with Jews

Malamud, B. The tenants

AGING

Lodge, D. Deaf sentence
Maupin, A. Michael Tolliver lives
Roth, P. Everyman
Roth, P. The humbling

AGNOSTICISM

Joyce, J. A portrait of the artist as a young man
The **agony** and the ecstasy. Stone, I.

AGORAPHOBIA

Reynolds, M. The Starlite Drive-in
The **Aguero** sisters. García, C.
Ah, but your land is beautiful. Paton, A.
Ah, treachery! Thomas, R.
Ahab's wife; or, The star-gazer. Naslund, S. J.
Aiding and abetting. Spark, M.

AIDS (DISEASE)

Cleage, P. What looks like crazy on an ordinary day—
Cunningham, M. The hours
Due, T. Blood colony
Gaitskill, M. Veronica
Hoffman, A. At risk
Monette, P. Afterlife
Peterson, P. W. Women in the grove
Price, R. The promise of rest
Self, W. Dorian
Tóibín, C. The blackwater lightship
Vollmann, W. T. Butterfly stories
White, E. The married man
Ain't she sweet. Phillips, S. E.

AIR MAIL SERVICE

Saint-Exupéry, A. d. Night flight

AIR PILOTS

Bates, H. E. Fair stood the wind for France
Bohjalian, C. A. Skeletons at the feast
Coonts, S. Final flight
Coonts, S. Flight of the Intruder
Griffin, W. E. B. The aviators
Griffin, W. E. B. By order of the President
Heller, J. Catch-22
Higgins, J. Flight of eagles
Jakes, J. American dreams
L'Amour, L. Last of the breed
Michener, J. A. The bridges at Toko-ri
Michener, J. A. Sayonara
Mosher, H. F. On Kingdom Mountain
Nance, J. J. Fire flight
Nance, J. J. The last hostage
Nance, J. J. Medusa's child
Saint-Exupéry, A. d. Night flight
Shreve, A. The pilot's wife
Shreve, A. Resistance
Thomas, C. Firefox

AIR TRAVEL

Miles, J. Dear American Airlines
AIR WARFARE See Military aeronautics; World War, 1939-
1945—Aerial operations

AIRCRAFT CARRIERS

Michener, J. A. The bridges at Toko-ri

AIRLINES

See also Airports

Flight attendants

See Flight attendants
AIRMEN See Air pilots

AIRPLANE CARRIERS See Aircraft carriers

AIRPLANES

Nance, J. J. Pandora's clock
Thomas, C. Firefox

Pilots

See Air pilots
Airport. Hailey, A.

AIRPORTS

Hailey, A. Airport
Airs above the ground. Stewart, M.

AIX-EN-PROVENCE (FRANCE) See France—Aix-en-
Provence

AIYANGAR, SRINIVASA RAMANUJAN See Ramanujan
Aiyangar, Srinivasa, 1887-1920
AKHENATON, KING OF EGYPT, FL. CA. 1388-1358 B.C.
About
Tarr, J. Pillar of fire
**AL-WAZZAN, AL-HASSAN IBN MUHAMMAD IBN
AHMAD** See Leo Africanus, ca. 1492-ca. 1550

ALABAMA

Atkins, A. Wicked city
Childress, M. Crazy in Alabama
Cook, T. H. Breakheart Hill
Flagg, F. Fried green tomatoes at the Whistle-Stop Cafe
Franklin, T. Hell at the breech
Franklin, T. Smonk; or, Widow town
Kincaid, N. Verbena
Lee, H. To kill a mockingbird
McCammon, R. R. Boy's life
McFarland, D. Letter from Point Clear
Wallace, D. The Watermelon King

Birmingham

Naslund, S. J. Four spirits

Mobile

Howard, R. Like trees, walking
Kerley, J. The hundredth man

Montgomery

Brown, R. M. Southern discomfort

ALAMO (SAN ANTONIO, TEX.)

Siege, 1836

Harrigan, S. The gates of the Alamo
Alas, Babylon. Frank, P.

ALASKA

Brand, M. Chinook
Kantner, S. Ordinary wolves
Kesey, K. Sailor song
Michener, J. A. Alaska
Rice, L. The letters
Vann, D. Legend of a suicide

Frontier and pioneer life

See Frontier and pioneer life—Alaska

Anchorage

Harrison, K. The seal wife
Alaska. Michener, J. A.

ALBANIA

Gilman, D. The unexpected Mrs. Pollifax
Kadare, I. Agamemnon's daughter [novella]
Kadare, I. The general of the dead army
Kadare, I. Spring flowers, spring frost
Kadare, I. The Successor
Kadare, I. The three-arched bridge
ALBANY (N.Y.) See New York (State)—Albany
The **Albertine** notes. Moody, R.
In Moody, R. Right livelihoods

ALBINOS

Yarbro, C. Q. Night blooming

ALCHEMY

Redfern, E. Auriel rising
Stott, R. Ghostwalk
Alchemy of stone. Sedia, E.

ALCOHOLICS See Alcoholism

ALCOHOLISM

Allison, D. Bastard out of Carolina
Banks, R. Affliction
Breslin, J. Table money
Brontë, A. The tenant of Wildfell Hall
Brown, L. Joe
Coetzee, J. M. Age of iron
Conroy, P. Beach music
Dee, E. The con man's daughter
DeWitt, P. Ablutions
Doyle, R. Paula Spencer
Doyle, R. The woman who walked into doors
Erdrich, L. Four souls
Faulks, S. On Green Dolphin Street

ALCOHOLISM—*Continued*
Frey, J. Bright shiny morning
Goudge, E. Thorns of truth
Hannah, K. On Mystic lake
Hatoum, M. The brothers
Hemingway, E. Islands in the stream
Hemingway, E. The torrents of spring
Høeg, P. The woman and the ape
Huneven, M. Blame
Jackson, C. The lost weekend
Johnston, W. The colony of unrequited dreams
Kinder, C. Honeymooners
Korda, M. Curtain
Lowry, M. Under the volcano
McDermott, A. Charming Billy
McFarland, D. The music room
McMillan, T. Disappearing acts
McMurtry, L. Buffalo girls
Miles, J. Dear American Airlines
Minot, S. Monkeys
Moody, R. The Omega Force
O'Hara, J. Appointment in Samarra
Paretsky, S. Ghost country
Richler, M. Solomon Gursky was here
Rinehart, S. Built in a day
Rossner, J. Perfidia
Saul, J. The right hand of evil
Spanidou, I. Before
Stirling, J. The island wife
Styron, W. Set this house on fire
Suri, M. The death of Vishnu
Turner, F. W. 1929
Willeford, C. R. Pick-up
Woodrell, D. The death of sweet mister
Yoshimoto, B. Love songs

ALEUTS
Harrison, S. Call down the stars
Harrison, S. Cry of the wind
Harrison, S. Song of the river

ALEXANDER, THE GREAT, 356-323 B.C.
About
Doherty, P. C. The gates of hell
Doherty, P. C. The godless man
Doherty, P. C. The house of death
Renault, M. Funeral games
Renault, M. The Persian boy
Tarr, J. Queen of the Amazons
Alexander Pushkin: complete prose fiction. Pushkin, A. S.
ALEXANDRIA (EGYPT) *See* Egypt—Alexandria
The **Alexandria** quartet: Justine; Balthazar; Mountolive [and] Clea. Durrell, L.

ALGERIA

Oran
Camus, A. The plague
ALGONQUIAN INDIANS
See also Shawnee Indians
Gear, K. O. People of the mist
Alias Grace. Atwood, M.
The **alibi**. Brown, S.
Alice Adams. Tarkington, B.
Alice in exile. Read, P. P.
Alice in jeopardy. McBain, E.
An **alien** heat. Moorcock, M.
ALIENATION (SOCIAL PSYCHOLOGY)
See also Social isolation
Adams, P. The sister
Burroughs, W. S. Naked lunch
Ford, R. Independence Day
Ford, R. The lay of the land
Heinemann, L. Paco's story
Høeg, P. Borderliners
Hoffman, A. Skylight confessions
Kantner, S. Ordinary wolves
Klíma, I. No saints or angels
Lessing, D. M. Ben, in the world
Lessing, D. M. The fifth child
McGinniss, J. The delivery man
Picoult, J. Nineteen minutes
Qashu, S. Dancing Arabs
Spiegelman, I. Everyone's burning
Trevor, W. Felicia's journey

Vine, B. Grasshopper
Wideman, J. E. Philadelphia fire
Winton, T. Dirt music
The **alienist**. Carr, C.
ALIENS, ILLEGAL *See* Undocumented aliens
ALIENS, UNDOCUMENTED *See* Undocumented aliens
Alive in Necropolis. Dorst, D.
All aboard. Porter, J. A.
All about Lulu. Evison, J.
All Aunt Hagar's children. Jones, E. P.
All for love. Jacobson, D.
All hat. Smith, B.
All he ever wanted. Shreve, A.
All in the family. O'Connor, E.
All is vanity. Schwarz, C.
All mortal flesh. Spencer-Fleming, J.
All my sins remembered. Thomas, R.
All or nothing. Adler, E.
All other nights. Horn, D.
All passion spent. Sackville-West, V.
All quiet on the western front. Remarque, E. M.
All souls. Marías, J.
All souls' day. Nooteboom, C.
All souls' rising. Bell, M. S.
All that I have. Freeman, C.
All that is gone. Toer, P. A.
All the days and nights. Maxwell, W.
All the dead lie down. Walker, M. W.
All the finest girls. Styron, A.
All the flowers are dying. Block, L.
All the king's men. Warren, R. P.
All the little live things. Stegner, W. E.
All the names. Saramago, J.
All the pretty horses. McCarthy, C.
All the sad young literary men. Gessen, K.
All the Weyrs of Pern. McCaffrey, A.
All the windwracked stars. Bear, E.
All things, all at once. Abbott, L. K.

ALLEGORIES
See also Fables; Fantasies; Good and evil; Parables; Symbolism
Abe, K. The woman in the dunes
Adams, R. Watership Down
Aira, C. Ghosts
Anderson, P. Goat song
Atwood, M. The Handmaid's tale
Auster, P. In the country of last things
Barth, J. Giles goat-boy
Beagle, P. S. The last unicorn
Berry, J. The manual of detection
Brooks, T. The sword of Shannara
Bunyan, J. The pilgrim's progress
Calvino, I. Mr. Palomar
Camus, A. The fall
Cheever, J. Oh, what a paradise it seems
Coetzee, J. M. Life & times of Michael K.
De Lint, C. Trader
Drabble, M. The witch of Exmoor
Elkin, S. Stanley Elkin's The magic kingdom
Ellison, H. The deathbird
Faulkner, W. A fable
Flanagan, R. Gould's book of fish
García Márquez, G. The autumn of the patriarch
García Márquez, G. One hundred years of solitude
Golding, W. Darkness visible
Golding, W. The inheritors
Golding, W. Lord of the flies
Grass, G. Cat and mouse
Grass, G. The flounder
Hansen, E. F. Tales of protection
Hesse, H. Narcissus and Goldmund
Hesse, H. Siddhartha
Hoban, R. Riddley Walker
Hrabal, B. Too loud a solitude
Irving, J. A prayer for Owen Meany
Kadare, I. Spring flowers, spring frost
Kafka, F. The castle
Kafka, F. The trial
King, S. The stand
Krüger, M. The cello player
Le Guin, U. K. The beginning place
Lessing, D. M. Shikasta
Lewis, C. S. Out of the silent planet

ALLEGORIES—*Continued*

Lewis, C. S. Perelandra
Lewis, C. S. That hideous strength
Lewis, C. S. Till we have faces
Maḥfūẓ, N. Children of the alley
Malamud, B. The natural
Martin, V. Mary Reilly
Melville, H. Mardi: and a voyager thither
Murdoch, I. The green knight
Oates, J. C. Black water
O'Connor, F. The violent bear it away
Ōe, K. Nip the buds, shoot the kids
Orwell, G. Animal farm
Ozick, C. The Messiah of Stockholm
Percy, W. Lancelot
Porter, K. A. Ship of fools
Powers, R. Operation wandering soul
Robbins, T. Jitterbug perfume
Robbins, T. Still life with Woodpecker
Rushdie, S. Haroun and the sea of stories
Rushdie, S. Midnight's children
Saramago, J. All the names
Saramago, J. Blindness
Saramago, J. The cave
Saramago, J. Seeing
Silko, L. Gardens in the dunes
Steinbeck, J. Burning bright
Stevenson, R. L. The strange case of Dr. Jekyll and Mr. Hyde
Tepper, S. S. The visitor
Theroux, P. The Mosquito Coast
Tolkien, J. R. R. The fellowship of the ring
Tolkien, J. R. R. The hobbit
Tolkien, J. R. R. The lord of the rings
Tolkien, J. R. R. The return of the king
Tolkien, J. R. R. The Silmarillion
Tolkien, J. R. R. The two towers
Updike, J. Brazil
Updike, J. The witches of Eastwick
Vernon, O. A killing in this town
Whitehead, C. The intuitionist
Wiggins, M. John Dollar
Wilde, O. The picture of Dorian Gray
Alley Kat blues. Kijewski, K.
The **almost** moon. Sebold, A.
Almost paradise. Isaacs, S.
An **almost** perfect moment. Kirshenbaum, B.
Almost the truth. Yorke, M.

ALMSHOUSES

Trollope, A. The warden
Aloft. Lee, C.-R.
Alone. Gardner, L.
Alone in the crowd. García-Roza, L. A.
Along came a spider. Patterson, J.
Alphabet of thorn. McKillip, P. A.

ALPS

Johnson, D. L'affaire
Mann, T. The magic mountain
Mawer, S. The fall
Parks, T. Cleaver
Parks, T. Rapids
Watkins, P. The ice soldier
Already dead. Huston, C.
Altered carbon. Morgan, R. K.
Altered states. Chayefsky, P.
The **alternative** hero. Thornton, T.
Alternatives to sex. McCauley, S.
ALUMNI, COLLEGE *See* College alumni
Alva & Irva. Carey, E.
Alvin Journeyman. Card, O. S.
Always outnumbered, always outgunned. Mosley, W.

ALZHEIMER'S DISEASE

Cumyn, A. Losing it
Dean, L. Becoming strangers
Gutcheon, B. R. Five fortunes
Hays, T. The pleasure was mine
O'Farrell, M. The vanishing act of Esme Lennox
Robinson, R. Cost
Sparks, N. The notebook
Amagansett. Mills, M.
The **Amalgamation** Polka. Wright, S.
The **amateur** marriage. Tyler, A.

The **amateur** spy. Fesperman, D.

AMATEUR THEATRICALS

House, T. The beginning of calamities
The **amazing** adventures of Kavalier and Clay. Chabon, M.
Amazing grace. Steel, D.
The **amazing** Mrs. Pollifax. Gilman, D.

AMAZON RIVER VALLEY

Cussler, C. Inca gold
Hamilton-Paterson, J. Gerontius
King, R. The sound of butterflies
Walker, A. Now is the time to open your heart
AMBASSADORS *See* Diplomatic life
The **ambassadors.** James, H.

AMBITION

See also Self-made men
Adiga, A. The white tiger
Archer, J. As the crow flies
Auchincloss, L. Her infinite variety
Blackwell, E. Grub
Bradford, B. T. The Ravenscar dynasty
Bradford, B. T. A woman of substance
Caldwell, T. Captains and kings
Carter, S. L. The emperor of Ocean Park
Daley, R. Wall of brass
Dexter, P. The paperboy
Dunne, D. The two Mrs. Grenvilles
Estleman, L. D. Gas City
Finder, J. Killer instinct
Fuentes, C. The death of Artemio Cruz
Jakes, J. California gold
Laker, R. Banners of silk
Millhauser, S. Martin Dressler
Narayan, R. K. The financial expert
Narayan, R. K. Mr. Sampath—the printer of Malgudi
Rand, A. The fountainhead
Ridley, J. A conversation with the Mann
Ross-Macdonald, M. The rich are with you always
Ross-Macdonald, M. Tamsin Harte
Ross-Macdonald, M. The world from rough stones
Schulberg, B. What makes Sammy run?
Stendhal. The red and the black
Trollope, A. The Eustace diamonds
Vidal, G. Washington, D.C.
Warren, R. P. All the king's men
West, N. A cool million
Woods, S. L.A. Times

AMERICA

See also Central America; South America

Discovery and exploration

Forester, C. S. To the Indies
America. Coonts, S.
America America. Canin, E.
The **American.** James, H.
American appetites. Oates, J. C.
AMERICAN CIVIL WAR, 1861-1865 *See* United States—Civil War, 1861-1865
The **American** claimant. Twain, M.
In Twain, M. The gilded age and later novels
American desert. Everett, P. L.
American detective. Estleman, L. D.
American dreams. Jakes, J.
American fantastic tales: terror and the uncanny from Poe to the pulps. Entered in Part I under title
American fantastic tales: terror and the uncanny from the 1940s to now. Entered in Part I under title
American genius. Tillman, L.
American gods. Gaiman, N.

AMERICAN LOYALISTS

Cooper, J. F. The spy
Hill, L. Someone knows my name
Roberts, K. L. Oliver Wiswell

AMERICAN MUSEUM OF NATURAL HISTORY

Preston, D. The cabinet of curiosities
American pastoral. Roth, P.
American purgatorio. Haskell, J.
AMERICAN REVOLUTION, 1775-1783 *See* United States—Revolution, 1775-1783
American rust. Meyer, P.
AMERICAN SOLDIERS *See* Soldiers—United States

American tabloid. Ellroy, J.

An **American** tragedy. Dreiser, T.

American West: twenty new stories from the Western Writers of America. Entered in Part I under title

AMERICANIZATION

Alvarez, J. How the García girls lost their accents

Cather, W. My Ántonia

Cather, W. O pioneers!

Jen, G. Mona in the promised land

Jen, G. Typical American

Rølvaag, O. E. Peder Victorious

AMERICANS

Ivory Coast

D'Souza, T. Whiteman

Afghanistan

Fesperman, D. The warlord's son

Michener, J. A. Caravans

Africa

Bellow, S. Henderson the rain king

Hamilton, M. The camel bookmobile

Rush, N. Mating

Australia

Nordhoff, C. Botany Bay

Belgium

Shreve, A. Resistance

Botswana

Rush, N. Mortals

Burma

Tan, A. Saving fish from drowning

Cambodia

Long, J. The reckoning

Canada

Freedman, B. Mrs. Mike

Urquhart, J. The underpainter

Caribbean region

Marshall, P. Praisesong for the widow

Styron, A. All the finest girls

Central America

Bowles, P. Up above the world

Didion, J. A book of common prayer

Stone, R. A flag for sunrise

Central Europe

Egan, J. The keep

China

Hersey, J. A single pebble

Michael, J. A certain smile

Colombia

Grippando, J. A king's ransom

Cuba

Kushner, R. Telex from Cuba

Czech Republic

Roth, P. The Prague orgy

Eastern Europe

Mewshaw, M. Shelter from the storm

Ecuador

Kunkel, B. Indecision

Egypt

Ducornet, R. Gazelle

England

Fyfield, F. Undercurrents

Galsworthy, J. Maid in waiting

Griesemer, J. Signal & noise

Hale, S. Austenland

Higgins, J. The eagle has landed

Hornby, N. Juliet, naked

James, H. The author of "Beltraffio"

James, H. The golden bowl

James, H. An international episode

James, H. Lady Barberina

Leimbach, M. Daniel isn't talking

Lurie, A. Foreign affairs

McFarland, D. A face at the window

McGowan, H. Schooling

McMurtry, L. Buffalo girls

Melville, H. Israel Potter

Messud, C. The hunters [novelette]

Michaels, B. The dancing floor

Murdoch, I. An accidental man

Roth, P. Deception

Theroux, P. Doctor Slaughter

Woods, S. The short forever

Europe

Cather, W. One of ours

Folsom, A. R. The day after tomorrow

Hemingway, E. The sun also rises

Highsmith, P. The boy who followed Ripley

Hunter, E. Lizzie

James, H. The portrait of a lady

James, H. The pupil

James, H. The siege of London

James, H. The wings of the dove

Lewis, S. Dodsworth

Maugham, W. S. The razor's edge

McCarthy, M. Birds of America

McPhee, M. L'America

Pynchon, T. Gravity's rainbow

Wharton, E. The children

Wolfe, T. Of time and the river

Wolfe, T. The web and the rock

Wolfe, T. You can't go home again

France

Baldwin, J. Giovanni's room

Barnes, D. Nightwood

Daley, R. Nowhere to run

Highsmith, P. The talented Mr. Ripley

James, H. The ambassadors

James, H. The American

James, H. Madame de Mauves

Johnson, D. Le divorce

Johnson, D. L'affaire

Johnson, D. Le mariage

Just, W. S. Forgetfulness

Kay, G. G. Ysabel

Krantz, J. Mistral's daughter

Marshall, P. The fisher king

Mathews, H. My life in CIA

Maxwell, W. The chateau

McGowan, K. The expected one

Miller, H. Tropic of Cancer

Nin, A. Children of the albatross

Nin, A. The four-chambered heart

Nin, A. Ladders to fire

Shaw, I. Evening in Byzantium

Steel, D. Sunset in St. Tropez

Truong, M. T. D. The book of salt

Watkins, P. The forger

Welch, J. The heartsong of Charging Elk

Wharton, E. Madame de Treymes

White, E. The married man

Germany

Barnes, D. Nightwood

Deaver, J. Garden of beasts

Ford, R. The student conductor

Isaacs, S. Shining through

Just, W. S. The weather in Berlin

Kanon, J. The good German

O'Connor, R. Buffalo soldiers

Uris, L. Armageddon

Vonnegut, K. Slaughterhouse-five

Greece

Murray, S. Forgery

Guatemala

Henley, P. Hummingbird house

Honduras

Theroux, P. The Mosquito Coast

AMERICANS—*Continued*

Hungary

Phillips, A. Prague

India

Sinha, I. Animal's people
Sundaresan, I. The splendor of silence
Theroux, P. The elephant god
Theroux, P. The Elephanta suite
Theroux, P. The gateway of India
Theroux, P. Monkey Hill
Umrigar, T. N. The weight of heaven

Iraq

Unsworth, B. Land of marvels

Ireland

Labiner, N. Miniatures
Lordan, B. But come ye back
Weber, K. The Music Lesson

Islands of the Pacific

Melville, H. Omoo: a narrative of adventures in the South
Seas

Israel

Miller, R. Welcome to Heavenly Heights
Stone, R. Damascus Gate
Uris, L. Exodus

Italy

Aciman, A. A. Call me by your name
Bausch, R. Peace
Epstein, L. The eighth wonder of the world
Goodman, C. The night villa
Greeley, A. M. Irish stew!
Grisham, J. The broker
Grisham, J. Playing for pizza
Gruber, M. The forgery of Venus
Hawthorne, N. The marble faun
Hayter, S. Bandit queen boogie
Hellenga, R. The Italian lover
Hemingway, E. Across the river and into the trees
Hemingway, E. A farewell to arms
Howells, W. D. A foregone conclusion
Howells, W. D. Indian summer
James, H. The Aspern papers
James, H. Daisy Miller
James, H. Roderick Hudson
Leonard, E. Pronto
Martin, M. Vatican
Martin, V. Italian fever
McBride, J. Miracle at St. Anna
McPhee, J. A man of no moon
Rabb, J. The book of Q
Rice, L. The deep blue sea for beginners
Russo, R. Bridge of sighs
Scott, J. Tourmaline
Spencer, E. Knights and dragons
Spencer, E. The light in the piazza
Styron, W. Set this house on fire
Wilder, T. The cabala
Williams, T. The Roman spring of Mrs. Stone

Japan

Bird, S. The Yokota Officers Club
Dickey, J. To the white sea
Lee, D. Country of origin
Murakami, R. In the miso soup
Smith, M. C. December 6

Marquesas Islands

Melville, H. Typee: a peep at Polynesian life

Mexico

Christensen, K. Trouble
D'Erasmo, S. The sky below
Doerr, H. Consider this, señora
Doerr, H. Stones for Ibarra
Fuentes, C. The old gringo
Hambly, B. Days of the dead
Hansen, R. Atticus
Johansen, I. And then you die—
Kellerman, J. Sunstroke
Kerouac, J. Tristessa
Michener, J. A. Mexico

Nin, A. Seduction of the Minotaur
Portis, C. Gringos
Smith, S. The ruins
Traven, B. The treasure of the Sierra Madre

Middle East

Menendez, A. The last war

Morocco

Johnson, D. Lulu in Marrakech

North Africa

Bowles, P. Let it come down
Bowles, P. The sheltering sky

Peru

Lynn, A. Now you see it

Portugal

L'Engle, M. The love letters

Romania

Marks, J. Fangland
Wiesel, E. The forgotten

Russia

D'Amato, B. White male infant
DeMille, N. The charm school
Harris, R. Archangel
L'Amour, L. Last of the breed
Shonk, K. The red passport

Rwanda

Leonard, E. Pagan babies

Sicily

Hersey, J. A bell for Adano

Singapore

Clavell, J. King Rat

South Africa

Ward, A. E. Forgive me

Southeast Asia

Vollmann, W. T. Butterfly stories

Switzerland

Ludlum, R. The Sigma protocol

Thailand

Berlinski, M. Fieldwork
Hallinan, T. A nail through the heart

Ukraine

Foer, J. S. Everything is illuminated

Uruguay

Cameron, P. The city of your final destination

Vietnam

Greene, G. The quiet American
Henley, P. In the river sweet

West Africa

Patterson, R. N. Eclipse

Zaire

Kingsolver, B. The poisonwood Bible
Stevens, M. The curve of the world
Amerika. Kafka, F.
Amethyst dreams. Whitney, P. A.

AMISH

Williamson, P. The outsider

AMISTAD (SCHOONER)

Pesci, D. Amistad
Amistad. Pesci, D.

AMNESIA

Barnard, R. Out of the blackout
Brown, S. The witness
Eco, U. The mysterious flame of Queen Loana
Fielding, J. See Jane run
Greene, G. The ministry of fear
Grimes, M. Biting the moon
Grimes, M. Dakota
Hall, S. The raw shark texts

ANNE BOLEYN, QUEEN, CONSORT OF HENRY VIII, KING OF ENGLAND, 1507-1536
About
Gregory, P. The other Boleyn girl
Maxwell, R. The secret diary of Anne Boleyn
Plaidy, J. Murder most royal

ANNE OF CLEVES, QUEEN, CONSORT OF HENRY VIII, KING OF ENGLAND, 1515-1557
About
Gregory, P. The Boleyn Inheritance
Annie John. Kincaid, J.
Annie Kilburn. Howells, W. D.
In Howells, W. D. Novels, 1886-1888
The **Anodyne** Necklace. Grimes, M.

ANOREXIA NERVOSA
Levenkron, S. The best little girl in the world
Another country. Baldwin, J.
also in Baldwin, J. Early novels and stories
Another life. Vachss, A. H.

ANSON, GEORGE ANSON, BARON, 1697-1762
About
O'Brian, P. The golden ocean
The **answer** is always yes. Ferrell, M.

ANTARCTIC REGIONS
See also Arctic regions
Bainbridge, B. The birthday boys
Cussler, C. Shock wave
Robinson, K. S. Antarctica
Antarctica. Robinson, K. S.
Anthem. Rand, A.
The **anthologist**. Baker, N.

ANTHROPOLOGISTS
Berlinski, M. Fieldwork
Jackson, S. The haunting of Hill House
Johnson, A. Parasites like us
Lively, P. Spiderweb
Oliver, C. From other shores
Oliver, C. Shadows in the sun
Oliver, C. The shores of another sea
Oliver, C. Unearthly neighbors
Ondaatje, M. Anil's ghost
Pym, B. An unsuitable attachment
Vanderbes, J. Easter Island

ANTIETAM, BATTLE OF, 1862
Reasoner, J. Antietam
Antietam. Reasoner, J.

ANTIGUA AND BARBUDA
Kincaid, J. Annie John
Kincaid, J. Mr. Potter

ANTIQUE DEALERS
See also Art dealers
McMurtry, L. Cadillac Jack
Pym, B. The sweet dove died
Welsh, L. The cutting room

ANTIQUES
See also Antiquities
Neville, K. The eight
Neville, K. The fire
Pye, M. The pieces from Berlin

ANTIQUITIES
See also Archeology
Khemir, S. The blue manuscript
Mosse, K. Labyrinth

ANTISEMITISM
See also Holocaust, Jewish (1933-1945); Jews—Persecutions
Bassani, G. The garden of the Finzi-Continis
Baxter, C. Saul and Patsy
Bellow, S. The victim
Epstein, L. The eighth wonder of the world
Franklin, A. Mistress of the art of death
Greenberg, J. I never promised you a rose garden
Hamill, P. Snow in August
Hill, R. When all is said and done
Hobson, L. K. Z. Gentleman's agreement
Isaacs, S. Red, white and blue
Lipman, E. The Inn at Lake Devine
Malamud, B. The fixer
Oates, J. C. The gravedigger's daughter

Pears, I. The dream of Scipio
Richler, M. Solomon Gursky was here
Roth, P. The plot against America
Schwarz-Bart, A. The last of the just
Thomas, M. M. Hanover Place
Walton, J. Farthing
The **antisocial** behaviour of Horace Rumpole. See Mortimer, J. Rumpole misbehaves

ANTONIUS, MARCUS, CA. 83-30 B.C.
About
George, M. The memoirs of Cleopatra

ANTS
Byatt, A. S. Morpho Eugenia
The **Anubis** slayings. Doherty, P. C.
Anvil of stars. Bear, G.

ANXIETY *See* Fear
The **anxiety** of everyday objects. Sheehan, A.
Anything considered. Mayle, P.
Anything for Billy. McMurtry, L.
Anything you say can and will be used against you. Drummond, L. L.
Anywhere but here. Simpson, M.

APACHE INDIANS
Fergus, J. The wild girl: the notebooks of Ned Giles, 1932 [y]
Littell, R. Walking back the cat
Rosenberg, R. This is not civilization
Apaches. Carcaterra, L.

APARTHEID *See* South Africa—Race relations

APARTMENT HOUSES
Aira, C. Ghosts
Barbery, M. The elegance of the hedgehog
Gilb, D. The flowers
Hegi, U. The vision of Emma Blau
Malamud, B. The tenants
McCall Smith, A. Love over Scotland
McCall Smith, A. The world according to Bertie
Mistry, R. Family matters
Perec, G. Life
Rinaldi, N. Between two rivers
Saul, J. Midnight voices
Schwartz, L. S. In the family way
Suri, M. The death of Vishnu

APARTMENTS *See* Apartment houses

APES
Boulle, P. Planet of the apes
Høeg, P. The woman and the ape
Apex hides the hurt. Whitehead, C.
The **apocalypse** watch. Ludlum, R.
The **Apostle**. Asch, S.

APOTHECARIES *See* Pharmacists

APPALACHIAN MOUNTAINS
See also Blue Ridge Mountains
McCrumb, S. The ballad of Frankie Silver
McCrumb, S. The hangman's beautiful daughter
McCrumb, S. The rosewood casket
McCrumb, S. She walks these hills

APPALACHIAN REGION
Adams, S. K. My old true love
Kingsolver, B. Prodigal summer
Laskas, G. M. The midwife's tale
Marshall, C. Christy
McCrumb, S. Foggy Mountain breakdown and other stories
Smith, L. Fair and tender ladies
Smith, L. Oral history
Appaloosa. Parker, R. B.
Apparition alley. Forrest, K. V.
Appassionata. Hoffman, E.
The **appeal**. Grisham, J.
Apple tree lean down. [omnibus volume] Pearce, M. E.
Apple tree lean down [novel] Pearce, M. E.
In Pearce, M. E. Apple tree lean down
Appleseed. Clute, J.
Appointment in Samarra. O'Hara, J.
The **apprentice**. Gerritsen, T.
The **apprentice** lover. Parini, J.
Apprentice to the flower poet Z. Weinstein, D.
Apprentice to the sea. McCutchan, P.

APPRENTICES
Andersen Nexø, M. Pelle the conqueror: v2 Apprenticeship
April Fool's Day. Novakovich, J.
April hopes. Howells, W. D.
  In Howells, W. D. Novels, 1886-1888
Apt pupil. King, S.
  In King, S. Different seasons p103-296
The **Aquitaine** progression. Ludlum, R.

ARAB AMERICANS
Abu-Jaber, D. Crescent
Fesperman, D. The amateur spy
Yunis, A. The night counter
ARAB-ISRAELI CONFLICT, 1948-1949 *See* Israel-Arab War, 1948-1949
ARAB-JEWISH RELATIONS *See* Jewish-Arab relations
ARABS
  See also Jewish-Arab relations; Palestinian Arabs
Higgins, J. Edge of danger
Spark, M. The Mandelbaum Gate
United States
Adams, L. Harbor
ARBUCKLE, FATTY, 1887-1933
About
Atkins, A. Devil's garden
ARBUCKLE, ROSCOE *See* Arbuckle, Fatty, 1887-1933
Arch of triumph. Remarque, E. M.
Archangel. Harris, R.
ARCHEOLOGICAL SPECIMENS *See* Antiquities
ARCHEOLOGISTS
  See also Women archeologists
Ackroyd, P. The fall of Troy
Darnton, J. Neanderthal
Faber, M. The hundred and ninety-nine steps
Galsworthy, J. Maid in waiting
Goodman, C. The night villa
Khemir, S. The blue manuscript
Long, J. The reckoning
Michael, J. Sleeping beauty
Ondaatje, M. Anil's ghost
Unsworth, B. Land of marvels
ARCHEOLOGY
  See also Antiquities; Prehistoric man; Stone Age
Crichton, M. Timeline
Cussler, C. Inca gold
Archer in Hollywood. Macdonald, R.
Archer in jeopardy. Macdonald, R.
The **archer's** tale. Cornwell, B.
ARCHERY
Cornwell, B. The archer's tale
Cornwell, B. Vagabond
Archform. Modesitt, L. E., Jr.
ARCHITECTS
  See also Building
Barbash, T. The last good chance
Berne, S. A perfect arrangement
Boyle, T. C. The women
Dickens, C. Martin Chuzzlewit
Epstein, L. The eighth wonder of the world
Ferber, E. So Big
Greene, G. A burnt-out case
Hoffman, A. Skylight confessions
Horan, N. Loving Frank
Hunter, E. Candyland
Miller, S. The distinguished guest
Rand, A. The fountainhead
Rayner, R. The cloud sketcher
Wharton, E. Sanctuary
White, E. The married man
The **archivist**. Cooley, M.
ARCHIVISTS
Holland, T. The archivist's story
The **archivist's** story. Holland, T.
ARCTIC REGIONS
  See also Alaska; Antarctic regions; Greenland
Faber, M. The Fahrenheit twins
Johnston, W. The navigator of New York
MacLean, A. Ice Station Zebra
McGregor, E. The ice child

Mowat, F. The Snow Walker
Nichols, P. Voyage to the North Star
Simmons, D. The terror
Vollmann, W. T. The rifles
ARGALL, SIR SAMUEL, CA. 1572-CA. 1626
About
Vollmann, W. T. Argall
Argall. Vollmann, W. T.
ARGENTINA
  See also Patagonia (Argentina and Chile)
Griffin, W. E. B. Blood and honor
Griffin, W. E. B. Honor bound
19th century
Fuentes, C. The campaign
Prisoners and prisons
  See Prisoners and prisons—Argentina
Rural life
Greene, G. The honorary consul
Buenos Aires
Aira, C. Ghosts
Cortázar, J. Hopscotch
Englander, N. The Ministry of Special Cases
Puig, M. Kiss of the spider woman
Saint-Exupéry, A. d. Night flight
ARGENTINE REPUBLIC *See* Argentina
ARGENTINES
France
Cortázar, J. Hopscotch
ARGENTINIANS *See* Argentines
ARISTOCRACY
  See also Courts and courtiers; Society novels
England
Balogh, M. Simply perfect
Colegate, I. The shooting party
Gee, S. The scandal of the season
Hardwick, M. The Duchess of Duke Street
James, H. An international episode
James, H. Lady Barberina
Riley, J. M. The serpent garden
Sackville-West, V. The Edwardians
Wodehouse, P. G. The code of the Woosters
Wodehouse, P. G. Tales from the Drones Club
France
Dickens, C. A tale of two cities
Haasse, H. S. In a dark wood wandering
James, H. The American
Laker, R. To dance with kings
Orczy, E., Baroness. Adventures of the Scarlet Pimpernel
Orczy, E., Baroness. The elusive Pimpernel
Orczy, E., Baroness. The Scarlet Pimpernel
Proust, M. The Guermantes way
Proust, M. Sodom and Gomorrah
Riley, J. M. The serpent garden
Stendhal. The red and the black
Italy
Bassani, G. The garden of the Finzi-Continis
Stendhal. The charterhouse of Parma
Japan
Mishima, Y. Spring snow
Schwartz, J. B. The commoner
Russia
West, Dame R. The birds fall down
Scotland
Coleridge, N. Godchildren
Sicily
Unsworth, B. The ruby in her navel
ARIZONA
Bull, E. Territory
Jance, J. A. Kiss of the bees
Kingsolver, B. Animal dreams
Kingsolver, B. The bean trees
Kingsolver, B. Pigs in heaven

ARIZONA—Continued
  Mapson, J.-A. Loving Chloe
  Preston, D. Blasphemy
  Rosenberg, R. This is not civilization

19th century
  Silko, L. Gardens in the dunes
  Turner, N. E. These is my words

Frontier and pioneer life
  See Frontier and pioneer life—Arizona

Phoenix
  McMillan, T. Waiting to exhale

Tucson
  Cullin, M. Undersurface
  Kingsolver, B. Pigs in heaven
  Ure, L. The fault tree
The **ark** builder. Potok, C.
  In Potok, C. Old men at midnight

ARKANSAS
  Brandon, J. Arkansas
  Grisham, J. A painted house
  Harington, D. With
  Hunter, S. Black light
  McFadden, B. L. Sugar
  Paddock, J. A secret word

Farm life
  See Farm life—Arkansas

Hot Springs
  Hunter, S. Hot Springs
Arkansas. Brandon, J.
Arlington Park. Cusk, R.

ARMADA, 1588
  Finney, P. Gloriana's torch
Armageddon. Uris, L.
Armageddon in retrospect. Vonnegut, K.

ARMAMENTS
  Pears, I. Stone's fall
  Silva, D. Moscow rules

ARMED FORCES

United States
  See United States—Armed forces
ARMENIAN GENOCIDE, 1915-1923 See Armenian massacres, 1915-1923

ARMENIAN MASSACRES, 1915-1923
  Shafak, E. The bastard of Istanbul
  Werfel, F. The forty days of Musa Dagh

ARMENIANS

Syria
  Werfel, F. The forty days of Musa Dagh

Turkey
  Shafak, E. The bastard of Istanbul

United States
  Shafak, E. The bastard of Istanbul
ARMIES
  See also Great Britain. Army
The **armies** of memory. Barnes, J.
ARMS AND ARMOR
  See also Swords
Arms and the women. Hill, R.
ARMY HOSPITALS See Hospitals and sanatoriums
An **army** of angels. Marcantel, P.
ARMY OFFICERS See Germany—Army—Officers; Peru—Army—Officers; Russia—Army—Officers
ARNOLD, BENEDICT, 1741-1801
About
  Roberts, K. L. Arundel
  Roberts, K. L. Rabble in arms
Around the time of Clemente Colling. Hernández, F.
  In Hernández, F. and Allen, E. Lands of memory
Around the world in eighty days. Verne, J.
Arrest Sitting Bull. Jones, D. C.
Arrowsmith. Lewis, S.
  also in Lewis, S. Arrowsmith; Elmer Gantry; Dodsworth

Arrowsmith; Elmer Gantry; Dodsworth. Lewis, S.
ARSON
  Chazin, S. Flashover
  Clarke, B. An arsonist's guide to writers' homes in New England
  Emerson, E. W. Pyro
  Emerson, E. W. Vertical burn
  Grant, S. Map of Ireland
  Jones, S. Outcast
  Mishima, Y. The temple of the golden pavilion
  Spencer, S. Endless love
An **arsonist's** guide to writers' homes in New England. Clarke, B.
ART
  Dean, D. The madonnas of Leningrad
  Huddle, D. La Tour dreams of the wolf girl
  Hustvedt, S. What I loved
  Stone, I. The agony and the ecstasy
ART COLLECTORS
  Davies, R. What's bred in the bone
  Kurzweil, A. The grand complication
  Murray, S. Forgery
ART CRITICS
  Farmer, P. J. Riders of the purple wage
  Hoban, R. Angelica's Grotto
ART DEALERS
  See also Antique dealers
  Krentz, J. A. Lost and found
  Lindsey, D. L. The color of night
  Lowell, E. Die in plain sight
  MacInnes, H. Prelude to terror
  Mayle, P. Chasing Cézanne
  West, M. L. Masterclass
  Woods, S. Imperfect strangers
ART FORGERIES See Forgery of works of art
ART GALLERIES AND MUSEUMS
  Kellerman, J. The genius
Art in America. McLarty, R.
ART OBJECTS
  See also Antiques
  Archer, J. A matter of honor
  James, H. The spoils of Poynton
The **art** of deception. Pearson, R.
The **art** of losing. Dixon, K.
The **art** of racing in the rain. Stein, G.
The **Art** of the story. Entered in Part I under title
ARTAGNAN, CHARLES DE BATZ-CASTELMORE, COMTE D', 1613?-1673
About
  Dumas, A. The man in the iron mask [variant title: The iron mask]
  Dumas, A. Twenty years after
ARTHUR, KING
About
  Berger, T. Arthur Rex
  Bradley, M. Z. The mists of Avalon
  Cornwell, B. Enemy of God
  Cornwell, B. Excalibur
  Cornwell, B. The winter king
  Lawhead, S. Avalon
  Stewart, M. Mary Stewart's Merlin trilogy
  Stewart, M. The wicked day
  Sutcliff, R. Sword at sunset
  Twain, M. A Connecticut Yankee in King Arthur's court
  White, T. H. The book of Merlyn
  White, T. H. The once and future king
  White, T. H. The sword in the stone
Arthur Mervyn. Brown, C. B.
  In Brown, C. B. Three Gothic novels
Arthur Rex. Berger, T.

ARTIFICIAL INTELLIGENCE
  Anderson, P. Genesis
  Darnton, J. Mind catcher
  Iles, G. The footprints of God
  Palwick, S. Shelter
  Powers, R. Galatea 2.2
  Rucker, R. v. B. Postsingular
  Stross, C. Accelerando

ASTRONOMERS

Greer, A. S. The path of minor planets
Grenville, K. The lieutenant
Hazzard, S. The transit of Venus
Mallon, T. Two moons

ASTROPHYSICISTS

Bova, B. Jupiter
Asylum. McGrath, P.
At end of day. Higgins, G. V.
At fault. Chopin, K.
In Chopin, K. Complete novels and stories
At home in Thrush Green. Read, Miss
At Lady Molly's. Powell, A.
In Powell, A. A dance to the music of time
At risk. Hoffman, A.
At swim-two-birds. O'Brien, F.
In O'Brien, F. The complete novels
At swim, two boys. O'Neill, J.
At the mountains of madness, and other novels. Lovecraft, H. P.
At weddings and wakes. McDermott, A.

ATATÜRK, KEMAL, 1881-1938
About

De Bernières, L. Birds without wings

ATHENS (GREECE) *See* Greece—Athens

ATHLETES

See also Olympic Games
Coldsmith, D. The long journey home
Deford, F. The entitled
Grisham, J. Playing for pizza
Lupica, M. Wild pitch
Patterson, J. Hide & seek
Phillips, S. E. Natural born charmer
Starr, J. Lights out

ATLANTA (GA.) *See* Georgia—Atlanta

ATLANTIC CITY (N.J.) *See* New Jersey—Atlantic City

ATLANTIC OCEAN

World War, 1939-1945

See World War, 1939-1945—Atlantic Ocean

ATLANTIS

Cussler, C. Atlantis found
Milligan, J. Jack Fish
Atlantis found. Cussler, C.
Atlas shrugged. Rand, A.
Atmospheric disturbances. Galchen, R.

ATOMIC BOMB

Bock, D. The ash garden
Burdick, E. Fail-safe
Dick, P. K. Dr. Bloodmoney
Follett, K. Triple
Golding, W. Lord of the flies
Griffin, W. E. B. The last heroes
Griffin, W. E. B. The secret warriors
Griffin, W. E. B. The soldier spies
Kanon, J. Los Alamos
Krauss, N. Man walks into a room
McMahon, T. A. Principles of American nuclear chemistry
Smith, M. C. Stallion Gate
Snow, C. P. The new men
Strieber, W. Warday
Vonnegut, K. Cat's cradle
Wenner, K. Dancing with Einstein
Wibberley, L. The mouse that roared
Wiggins, M. Evidence of things unseen

ATOMIC SUBMARINES *See* Nuclear submarines

ATOMIC WARFARE *See* Nuclear warfare

ATONEMENT

Greene, G. Brighton rock
Howatch, S. The heartbreaker
Nooteboom, C. Lost paradise
Pelecanos, G. P. The way home
Picoult, J. Change of heart
Seymour, G. Rat run
Atonement. McEwan, I.

ATROCITIES

See also Holocaust, Jewish (1933-1945); Jews—Persecutions; Massacres; Torture; World War, 1939-1945—Atrocities
Alarcón, D. Lost City Radio

Castellanos Moya, H. Senselessness
Attachment. Fonseca, I.

ATTEMPTED MURDER *See* Murder stories

ATTEMPTED SUICIDE *See* Suicide

Atticus. Hansen, R.

ATTITUDE (PSYCHOLOGY)

See also Prejudices
The **attorney.** Martini, S. P.

ATTORNEYS *See* Law and lawyers

AU PAIRS

Berne, S. A perfect arrangement
Kincaid, J. Lucy
Moore, L. A gate at the stairs
Prose, F. Primitive people
Weldon, F. She may not leave

AUCTIONS

Welsh, L. The cutting room
August. Rossner, J.
Augusta Locke. Henderson, W. H.

AUGUSTUS, EMPEROR OF ROME, 63 B.C.-14 A.D.
About

Graves, R. I, Claudius
Aunt Dimity digs in. Atherton, N.
Aunt Julia and the scriptwriter. Vargas Llosa, M.
Auntie Mame. Dennis, P.

AUNTS

See also Nieces
Braybrooke, J. Every eye
Childress, M. Crazy in Alabama
Dennis, P. Auntie Mame
Dickens, C. David Copperfield
Gaffney, P. Flight lessons
Gibbons, K. Divining women
Goudge, E. Such devoted sisters
Greene, G. Travels with my aunt
Gurganus, A. The practical heart [novelette]
Heyer, G. Black sheep
Lodge, D. Paradise news
McDermott, A. At weddings and wakes
O'Farrell, M. The vanishing act of Esme Lennox
Pérez Galdós, B. Doña Perfecta
Proulx, A. The shipping news
Purdy, J. The nephew
Smith, S. Novel on yellow paper
Vargas Llosa, M. Aunt Julia and the scriptwriter
Vernon, O. Eden
Auriel rising. Redfern, E.

AUSCHWITZ (POLAND: CONCENTRATION CAMP)

Wander, F. The seventh well

AUSTEN, JANE, 1775-1817
About

Fowler, K. J. The Jane Austen book club
Parodies, imitations, etc.

Hale, S. Austenland
Tennant, E. Pemberley
Tennant, E. An unequal marriage
Austenland. Hale, S.
Austerlitz. Sebald, W. G.

AUSTRALIA

See also Tasmania (Australia)
Coetzee, J. M. Elizabeth Costello
De Kretser, M. The lost dog
Flanagan, R. The unknown terrorist
Hospital, J. T. Oyster
Keneally, T. A family madness
Keneally, T. Office of innocence
Keneally, T. River town
Keneally, T. Woman of the inner sea
London, J. The good parents
Malouf, D. The complete stories
McCullough, C. The thorn birds
McGahan, A. The white earth
McInerney, M. Upside down, inside out
Nooteboom, C. Lost paradise
Perlman, E. Seven types of ambiguity
White, P. The eye of the storm
Winton, T. Breath
Winton, T. Dirt music

TITLE AND SUBJECT INDEX

AUTHORS—*Continued*

King, S. Salem's Lot
Koontz, D. R. Relentless
Kotzwinkle, W. The bear went over the mountain
Krauss, N. The history of love
Kundera, M. Slowness
Labiner, N. Miniatures
Leavitt, D. Martin Bauman
Leavitt, D. While England sleeps
Lelchuk, A. Ziff
Lodge, D. Therapy
Lodge, D. Thinks—
London, J. Martin Eden
Lopez, B. H. Resistance
Mailer, N. Tough guys don't dance
Malamud, B. The tenants
Mann, T. Death in Venice
Mansbach, A. The end of the Jews
Marías, J. Voyage along the horizon
Markson, D. The last novel
Markson, D. Vanishing point
Matheson, R. Hunted past reason
Mathews, H. My life in CIA
Maugham, W. S. Cakes and ale
Maxwell, W. Bright center of heaven
McCauley, S. True enough
McEwan, I. The child in time
McLarty, R. Art in America
Michener, J. A. The novel
Miller, A. Oxygen
Mortimer, J. Felix in the underworld
Muñoz Molina, A. A manuscript of ashes
Murdoch, I. The book and the brotherhood
Nabokov, V. V. Look at the harlequins!
Nabokov, V. V. The real life of Sebastian Knight
Naipaul, V. S. Half a life
Naipaul, V. S. Magic seeds
Naipaul, V. S. A way in the world
O'Brien, F. At swim-two-birds
Õe, K. A quiet life
O'Neill, J. Kilbrack; or, Who is Nancy Valentine?
Parini, J. The apprentice lover
Pearl, M. The Dante Club
Pouncey, P. R. Rules for old men waiting
Powell, A. Books do furnish a room
Powers, K. Capote in Kansas
Powers, R. Galatea 2.2
Price, N. Night woman
Price, R. Samaritan
Prose, F. Blue angel
Pyper, A. The killing circle
Read, P. P. A season in the West
Reuss, F. Mohr
Rich, N. The mayor's tongue
Richler, M. Barney's version
Roberts, N. Angel's fall
Roberts, N. River's end
Rosales, G. The halfway house
Rosenblatt, R. Lapham rising
Roth, H. From bondage
Roth, H. Requiem for Harlem
Roth, P. The anatomy lesson
Roth, P. Deception
Roth, P. Exit ghost
Roth, P. The ghost writer
Roth, P. My life as a man
Roth, P. The Prague orgy
Roth, P. Zuckerman bound
Roth, P. Zuckerman unbound
Ruiz Zafón, C. The angel's game
Schwarz, C. All is vanity
Smith, A. The accidental
Spark, M. Loitering with intent
Spencer, S. Willing
Stone, K. Happy endings
Straub, P. The Hellfire Club
Straub, P. In the night room
Straub, P. Lost boy lost girl
Strieber, W. 2012: the war for souls
Strieber, W. Warday
Styron, W. Sophie's choice
Tearne, R. Mosquito
Theroux, P. Hotel Honolulu
Theroux, P. My secret history

Tyler, A. The accidental tourist
Updike, J. Bech: a book
Updike, J. Bech at bay
Updike, J. Bech is back
Uris, L. QB VII
Vargas Llosa, M. Aunt Julia and the scriptwriter
Vidal, G. Burr
Vine, B. The blood doctor
Vine, B. The chimney sweeper's boy
Vonnegut, K. Breakfast of champions
Vonnegut, K. Timequake
Wallace, I. The prize
West, P. Lord Byron's doctor
Westlake, D. E. The hook
Wideman, J. E. The cattle killing
Wideman, J. E. Fanon
Wilhelm, K. The deepest water
Wolfe, T. Of time and the river
Wolfe, T. The web and the rock
Wolfe, T. You can't go home again
Wolff, T. Old school
Wolitzer, M. The wife
Woodrell, D. Give us a kiss

AUTHORSHIP

See also Authors

Auster, P. Oracle night
Carey, P. My life as a fake
Christensen, I. Azorno
Clarke, B. An arsonist's guide to writers' homes in New England
Coetzee, J. M. Diary of a bad year
Coetzee, J. M. Elizabeth Costello
DeWitt, P. Ablutions
Hellenga, R. The Italian lover
Marías, J. Dark back of time
Martini, S. P. The list
Saramago, J. The history of the siege of Lisbon
Savage, S. The cry of the sloth
Spark, M. The finishing school
Vila-Matas, E. Montano's malady
Weber, K. The little women
White, E. Hotel de Dream

AUTISM

Koontz, D. R. By the light of the moon
Moon, E. The speed of dark

AUTISTIC CHILDREN

Haddon, M. The curious incident of the dog in the night-time
Leimbach, M. Daniel isn't talking
Miller, S. Family pictures
Rucker, R. v. B. Postsingular
Silver, M. The god of war

AUTOBIOGRAPHICAL STORIES

Agee, J. The morning watch
Baldwin, J. Go tell it on the mountain
Ballard, J. G. Empire of the Sun
Bao Ninh. The sorrow of war
Butler, S. The way of all flesh
Colette. The complete Claudine
Colette. Music-hall sidelights
Crafts, H. The bondswomans narrative
Dennis, P. Auntie Mame
Dexter, P. Spooner
Dickens, C. David Copperfield
Disch, T. M. Word of God: or, Holy writ rewritten
Dische, I. The Empress of Weehawken
Dostoyevsky, F. The gambler
Dufresne, J. Requiem, Mass.
Eliot, G. Middlemarch
Ellis, B. E. Lunar Park
Eve, N. The family orchard
Gao Xingjian. Soul mountain
Godwin, G. Queen of the underworld
Goethe, J. W. v. The sorrows of young Werther
Guo Xiaolu. Twenty fragments of a ravenous youth
Halter, M. The book of Abraham
Hawthorne, N. The Blithedale romance
Hemingway, E. The garden of Eden
Hemingway, E. True at first light
Hernández, F. Lands of memory [novelette]
Himes, C. Yesterday will make you cry
Jhabvala, R. P. My nine lives
Johnson, B. S. The unfortunates

AVIATORS *See* Air pilots
The **aviators**. Griffin, W. E. B.
Avon historical romance [series]
    Lindsey, J. Gentle rogue
Await your reply. Chaon, D.
Awake. Graver, E.
The **awakening**. Chopin, K.
    In Chopin, K. Complete novels and stories
The **awakening** land. Richter, C.
Away. Urquhart, J.
The **ax**. Westlake, D. E.
Azorno. Christensen, I.
Aztec. Jennings, G.
Aztec blood. Jennings, G.

AZTECS

    Falconer, C. Feathered serpent
    Jennings, G. Aztec
    Jennings, G. Aztec blood
    Sherwood, F. Night of sorrows

B

"**B**" is for burglar. Grafton, S.
Babbitt. Lewis, S.
    also in Lewis, S. Main Street & Babbitt
BABEL´, I. (ISAAC), 1894-1940
          About
    Holland, T. The archivist's story
BABEL´, ISAAC *See* Babel´, I. (Isaac), 1894-1940
Babi Yar. Anatoli, A.

BABI YAR MASSACRE, 1941

    Anatoli, A. Babi Yar

BABOONS

    Oliver, C. The shores of another sea
The **baby** merchant. Reed, K.

BABY SITTERS

    Iles, G. Turning angel
Baby, would I lie? Westlake, D. E.
Babylon sisters. Cleage, P.
The **bachelor** of arts. Narayan, R. K.
    In Narayan, R. K. Swami and friends, The bachelor of arts,
    The dark room, The English teacher
BACHELORS *See* Single men
The **bachelors**. Spark, M.
The **Bachman** books: four early novels by Stephen King. King, S.
Back roads. O'Dell, T.
Back story. Parker, R. B.
Back when we were grownups. Tyler, A.
A **backward** glance. Wharton, E.
    In Wharton, E. Novellas and other writings
Bad blood. Fairstein, L.
Bad Boy Brawly Brown. Mosley, W.
Bad company. Higgins, J.
The **bad** detective. Keating, H. R. F.
Bad dirt. Proulx, A.
The **bad** girl. Vargas Llosa, M.
Bad Girl Creek. Mapson, J.-A.
Bad love. Kellerman, J.
Bad luck and trouble. Child, L.
Bad men. Connolly, J.
Bad monkeys. Ruff, M.
Bad news. Westlake, D. E.
The **bad** place. Koontz, D. R.
The **bad** seed. March, W.
Bad things happen. Dolan, H.
Badenheim 1939. Appelfeld, A.
Badger boy. Kelton, E.
Badlands. Bowen, P.
BAG LADIES *See* Homeless persons
Bag of bones. King, S.
Bagombo snuff box: uncollected short fiction. Vonnegut, K.
BAHIA (BRAZIL) *See* Brazil—Bahia

BAIL

    Leonard, E. Rum punch
Bailey's Café. Naylor, G.

BAJA CALIFORNIA (MEXICO: PENINSULA) *See* Mexico—Baja California
The **baked** bean supper murders. Rich, V.

BAKER, CHET

          About
    Moody, B. Looking for Chet Baker
Baker towers. Haigh, J.
Balance of power. Patterson, R. N.

BALL GAMES

         See also Baseball; Football; Tennis
The **ballad** of Frankie Silver. McCrumb, S.
The **ballad** of Peckham Rye. Spark, M.
    also in Spark, M. A Muriel Spark trio p233-386
The **ballad** of the sad café [novelette] McCullers, C.
    In McCullers, C. Collected stories p195-253
    In McCullers, C. Complete novels
The **ballad** of Trenchmouth Taggart. Taylor, M. G.

BALLET

         See also Dancers
    Godden, R. Pippa passes
    McCann, C. Dancer

BALLOONS

    Twain, M. Tom Sawyer abroad
BALLS (PARTIES) *See* Parties
Balthasar's odyssey. Maalouf, A.
Balthazar. Durrell, L.
    also in Durrell, L. The Alexandria quartet: Justine;
    Balthazar; Mountolive [and] Clea p205-390
BALTIMORE (MD.) *See* Maryland—Baltimore
Band of angels. Warren, R. P.
Bandbox. Mallon, T.
Bandit queen boogie. Hayter, S.
BANDITS *See* Brigands and robbers
Bandits. Leonard, E.

BANDS (MUSIC)

    Wimberley, D. The king of Colored Town
Bang the drum slowly. Harris, M.
BANGKOK (THAILAND) *See* Thailand—Bangkok
Bangkok 8. Burdett, J.
Bangkok haunts. Burdett, J.
Bangkok Tattoo. Burdett, J.

BANGLADESHIS

          England
    Ali, M. Brick lane
Banishing Verona. Livesey, M.
BANK CLERKS *See* Clerks

BANK ROBBERS

    Anderson, E. Thieves like us
    Black, L. Takeover
    Connelly, J. Crumbtown
    Cussler, C. The chase
    Estleman, L. D. The adventures of Johnny Vermillion
    Higgins, G. V. The friends of Eddie Coyle
    Stross, C. Halting state
    Tyler, A. Earthly possessions
    Westlake, D. E. Bank shot
Bank shot. Westlake, D. E.

BANKERS

    Dickens, C. Hard times
    Higgins, G. V. The Mandeville talent
    Le Carré, J. Single & Single
    Plain, B. Tapestry
    Sarton, M. Anger
    Wolfe, T. The bonfire of the vanities

BANKS

         See also Bankers
    Browne, M. Eye of the abyss
    Campbell, B. M. Brothers and sisters
    Dickens, C. Hard times
    Le Carré, J. A most wanted man
Banners of silk. Laker, R.

BARABBAS (BIBLICAL FIGURE)

          About
    Lagerkvist, P. Barabbas
Barabbas. Lagerkvist, P.
The **barbarous** coast. Macdonald, R.
    In Macdonald, R. Archer in Hollywood p171-346

The **beginning** place. Le Guin, U. K.
BEHAVIOR MODIFICATION
    See also Brainwashing
The **behaviour** of moths. See Adams, P. The sister
BEHN, APHRA, 1640-1689
        About
    Stevenson, J. The shadow king
BEIDERBECKE, BIX, 1903-1931
        About
    Turner, F. W. 1929
BEIJING (CHINA) *See* China—Beijing
Beijing coma. Ma Jian
Being dead. Crace, J.
Being invisible. Berger, T.
Being there. Kosinski, J. N.
BEIRUT (LEBANON) *See* Lebanon—Beirut
Bel canto. Patchett, A.
Bel Ria. Burnford, S.
BELFAST (NORTHERN IRELAND) *See* Northern Ireland—Belfast
BELGIAN CONGO *See* Zaire
BELGIANS

                Japan
    Nothomb, A. Tokyo fiancee
BELGIUM
    Shreve, A. Resistance

            19th century
    Stone, I. Lust for life

            Flanders
    Dunnett, D. Niccolò rising
Belgrave Square. Perry, A.
The **believers**. Heller, Z.
BELL, GERTRUDE MARGARET LOWTHIAN, 1868-1926
        About
    Russell, M. D. Dreamers of the day
The **bell**. Murdoch, I.
A **bell** for Adano. Hersey, J.
The **bell** jar. Plath, S.
BELL-RINGERS *See* Bells and bell ringers
Bella Poldark. Graham, W.
The **Bellarosa** connection. Bellow, S.
Belle ruin. Grimes, M.
Bellefleur. Oates, J. C.

BELLS AND BELL RINGERS
    Hersey, J. A bell for Adano
    Hugo, V. The hunchback of Notre Dame
Belong to me. De los Santos, M.
Belonging. Thayer, N.
Ben-Hur. Wallace, L.
Ben, in the world. Lessing, D. M.
BENARES (INDIA) *See* India—Benares
A **bend** in the river. Naipaul, V. S.
A **bend** in the road. Sparks, N.
Bend sinister. Nabokov, V. V.
    In Nabokov, V. V. Novels and memoirs, 1941-1951
Bendigo Shafter. L'Amour, L.
Beneath the skin. French, N.
The **benediction** of Brother Cadfael. Peters, E.
BENTEEN, FREDERICK WILLIAM, 1834-1898
        About
    Falconer, D. The lost thoughts of soldiers
BEREAVEMENT
    Banks, R. The sweet hereafter
    Boswell, R. Century's son
    Fitch, J. Paint it black
    Gottlieb, E. Now you see him
    Haig, M. The possession of Mr Cave
    Hall, S. The raw shark texts
    Hart, J. The truth about love
    Hawkes, J. Second skin
    Hearon, S. Footprints
    Hegi, U. The worst thing I've done
    Hood, A. The knitting circle
    Joss, M. The night following
    Kallos, S. Sing them home
    Keegan, N. Swimming

    King, S. Lisey's story
    Land, B. Pilgrims upon the earth
    McCann, C. Let the great world spin
    McFarland, D. Singing boy
    Miller, S. Lost in the forest
    Moloney, S. The dwelling
    Monette, P. Afterlife
    Morley, I. Come Sunday
    Naylor, P. R. After
    Ōe, K. An echo of heaven
    Ozick, C. Rosa
    Petterson, P. In the wake
    Prose, F. Goldengrove
    Rice, L. Last kiss
    Rice, L. The letters
    Romano, T. When the world was young
    Schwartz, J. B. Reservation Road
    Sebold, A. The lovely bones
    Shreve, A. Light on snow
    Shreve, S. R. A student of living things
    Steel, D. The house on Hope Street
    Strayed, C. Torch
    Strout, E. Abide with me
    Tropper, J. How to talk to a widower
    Umrigar, T. N. The weight of heaven
    Walbert, K. The gardens of Kyoto
    Winston, L. Good grief
    Wolitzer, M. Surrender, Dorothy
    Yoshimoto, B. Kitchen
    Yoshimoto, B. Night and night's travelers
BERLIN (GERMANY) *See* Germany—Berlin
Berlin game. Deighton, L.
The **Berlin** memorandum. See Hall, A. The Quiller memorandum
The **Berlin** stories. Isherwood, C.
BERNADETTE, SAINT, 1844-1879
        About
    Werfel, F. The song of Bernadette
Berserker fury. Saberhagen, F.
Berserker's star. Saberhagen, F.
Bertie and the seven bodies. Lovesey, P.
Best American mystery stories [date] Entered in Part I under title
The **Best** American mystery stories of the century. Entered in Part I under title
The **Best** American short stories. Entered in Part I under title
The **best** defense. Wilhelm, K.
Best enemies. Heller, J.
The **Best** from Fantasy & Science Fiction. Entered in Part I under title
The **Best** from fantasy & science fiction: the fiftieth anniversary anthology. Entered in Part I under title
The **best** is yet to come. Gould, J.
The **best** little girl in the world. Levenkron, S.
The **best** of Damon Knight. Knight, D. F.
The **best** of Ellery Queen. Queen, E.
The **best** of friends. Trollope, J.
The **best** of Gene Wolfe. Wolfe, G.
The **best** of Lucius Shepard. Shepard, L.
The **best** of Michael Moorcock. Moorcock, M.
The **best** of Michael Swanwick. Swanwick, M.
The **best** of Sholom Aleichem. Sholem Aleichem
Best of the Best American short stories, 1915-1950. Entered in Part I under title
The **best** people in the world. Tussing, J.
The **best** science fiction of Arthur Conan Doyle. Doyle, Sir A. C.
The **best** short stories of Bret Harte. Harte, B.
The **best** short stories of Dostoevsky. Dostoyevsky, F.
The **best** short stories of O. Henry. Henry, O.
The **best** short stories of Ring Lardner. Lardner, R.
The **best** short stories of W. Somerset Maugham. Maugham, W. S.
The **best** stories of Sarah Orne Jewett. Jewett, S. O.
The **best** western stories of John Jakes. Jakes, J.
Bet me. Crusie, J.
BETHLEM ROYAL HOSPITAL (LONDON, ENGLAND)
    Hollingshead, G. Bedlam
Betrayals. Le Guin, U. K.
    In Le Guin, U. K. Four ways to forgiveness p1-34
BETROTHALS
    Hardy, T. Under the greenwood tree
    Wharton, E. The mother's recompense

Bitch Creek. Tapply, W. G.
Biting the moon. Grimes, M.
Bitten. Armstrong, K.
Bitter medicine. Paretsky, S.
Bitter sweet. Spencer, L.
Black & white. Shapiro, D.
Black and blue. Quindlen, A.
Black and blue. Rankin, I.
Black and white and dead all over. Darnton, J.
Black Betty. Mosley, W.
Black Blade. Lustbader, E. V.
The **black** book. Rankin, I.
Black boy. Wright, R.
   also in Wright, R. Works
Black cherry blues. Burke, J. L.
BLACK CHILDREN *See* African American children
Black cross. Iles, G.
The **black** dahlia. Ellroy, J.
Black dogs. McEwan, I.
Black flies. Burke, S.
Black girl/White girl. Oates, J. C.
Black hats. Collins, M. A.

BLACK HOLES (ASTRONOMY)
   Egan, G. Incandescence
Black house. King, S.

BLACK HUMOR *See* Humor; Satire
The **black** ice. Connelly, M.

BLACK-JEWISH RELATIONS *See* African Americans—Relations with Jews
Black light. Hunter, S.

BLACK MAGIC *See* Witchcraft
Black man. See Morgan, R. K. Thirteen
Black maps. Spiegelman, P.

BLACK MARKETS
   Clavell, J. King Rat
Black money. Thomas, M. M.
Black Mountain. Standiford, L.
Black Narcissus. Godden, R.
The **black** opal. Holt, V.
Black orchids; &, the silent speaker. Stout, R.
Black powder, white smoke. Estleman, L. D.
Black robe. Moore, B.

BLACK SERVANTS *See* African American servants
Black sheep. Heyer, G.
Black ships. Graham, J.

BLACK SOLDIERS *See* African American soldiers
Black storm. Poyer, D.
Black Sunday. Harris, T.
The **black** swan. Mann, T.
Black swan green. Mitchell, D.
The **black** tower. Bayard, L.
The **black** tower. James, P. D.
Black water. Oates, J. C.
Black water. Parker, T. J.
Black widow. White, R. W.
Black wind. Cussler, C.

BLACK WOMEN *See* African American women
Blackbird house. Hoffman, A.
The **blackboard** jungle. Hunter, E.
Blackest bird. Rose, J.
Blacklist. Paretsky, S.

BLACKMAIL
   See also Extortion
   Abbott, M. E. The song is you
   Baldacci, D. Absolute power
   Clark, M. The legal limit
   Cornwell, B. Sharpe's fury
   Ellis, D. Life sentence
   Fesperman, D. The amateur spy
   Goddard, R. Into the blue
   Greene, G. The heart of the matter
   Grippando, J. Found money
   Grisham, J. The brethren
   Higgins, J. The president's daughter
   Hill, S. Mrs. de Winter
   Meltzer, B. The first counsel
   Meltzer, B. The tenth justice
   Richards, D. A. The bay of love and sorrows
   Riordan, R. Cold Springs
   Roberts, N. Honest illusions
   Shelby, P. Days of drums

   Spark, M. The bachelors
   Woods, S. Dirt

BLACKS
   See also African Americans
   Bell, M. S. All souls' rising
   Condé, M. I, Tituba, black witch of Salem
   Conrad, J. The Nigger of the Narcissus
   Hill, L. Someone knows my name
   Kincaid, J. Autobiography of my mother
   Nunez, E. Grace
   Phillips, C. A distant shore

England
   Phillips, C. Foreigners

BLACKSMITHS
   Pearce, M. E. Cast a long shadow
The **blackwater** lightship. Tóibín, C.
Blackwater sound. Hall, J. W.
Blackwater spirits. Monfredo, M. G.
Blackwood Farm. Rice, A.
The **blade** itself. Abercrombie, J.
The **blade** itself. Sakey, M.

BLAKE, WILLIAM, 1757-1827
About
   Chevalier, T. Burning bright
Blame. Huneven, M.
Blanche cleans up. Neely, B.
Blasphemy. Preston, D.
Blaze. King, S.
Bleak House. Dickens, C.
Bleeding hearts. Haddam, J.
Bleeding Kansas. Paretsky, S.
Bless the beasts and children. Swarthout, G. F.
Blessed assurance: a moral tale. Gurganus, A.
   In Gurganus, A. White people p192-252

BLESSED VIRGIN MARY, SAINT *See* Mary, Blessed Virgin, Saint
The **blessing** way. Hillerman, T.
   also in Hillerman, T. The Joe Leaphorn mysteries
Blessings. Plain, B.
Blessings. Quindlen, A.

BLIND
   Brontë, C. Jane Eyre
   Flagg, F. Standing in the rainbow
   Grøndahl, J. C. Lucca
   Hernández, F. Around the time of Clemente Colling
   Kelman, J. How late it was, how late
   London, J. The Sea-Wolf
   Sheehan, A. The anxiety of everyday objects
   Shreve, A. Eden Close
   Ure, L. The fault tree
   Varley, J. The persistence of vision
   West, P. Love's mansion
   Woods, S. Dead eyes
Blind alley. Johansen, I.
The **blind** assassin. Atwood, M.
Blind date. Fyfield, F.
Blind Lake. Wilson, R. C.
The **blind** man of Seville. Wilson, R.
Blind willow, sleeping woman. Murakami, H.
Blindness. Saramago, J.
Blindsight. Watts, P.
Blindspot. Kamensky, J.
The **Blithedale** romance. Hawthorne, N.
   also in Hawthorne, N. Collected novels

BLIZZARDS *See* Storms

BLOCH, EDUARD
About
   Neugeboren, J. 1940

BLOCK ISLAND (R.I.)
   Tirone Smith, M.-A. She's not there
The **blond** baboon. Van de Wetering, J.
Blonde. Oates, J. C.
Blonde roots. Evaristo, B.
Blood & orchids. Katkov, N.
Blood and gold. Rice, A.
Blood and honor. Griffin, W. E. B.
Blood and iron. Bear, E.
Blood and rubles. Kaminsky, S. M.
Blood canticle. Rice, A.
Blood colony. Due, T.

The **blood** doctor. Vine, B.
Blood kin. Dovey, C.
Blood lines. Harrod-Eagles, C.
Blood lines. Rendell, R.
Blood memory. Coel, M.
Blood meridian. McCarthy, C.
Blood money. Perry, T.
Blood mud. Constantine, K. C.
Blood music. Bear, G.
    In Bear, G. The collected stories of Greg Bear
Blood of Amber. Zelazny, R.
The **blood** of Caesar. Bell, A. A.
The **blood** of flowers. Amirrezvani, A.
Blood of victory. Furst, A.
Blood on the moon. Ellroy, J.
    In Ellroy, J. L.A. noir p1-206
Blood on the wood. Linscott, G.
The **blood** oranges. Hawkes, J.
Blood rain. Dibdin, M.
Blood relations. Parker, B.
Blood roses. Yarbro, C. Q.
Blood shot. Paretsky, S.
Blood sins. Hooper, K.
Blood trail. Box, C. J.
Blood Trillium. May, J.
Blood type. Greenleaf, S.
Blood will tell. See Christie, A. Mrs. McGinty's dead
Blood work. Connelly, M.
Bloodhounds. Lovesey, P.
Blood's a rover. Ellroy, J.
A **Bloodsmoor** romance. Oates, J. C.
Blown away. Wiltse, D.
Blue angel. Prose, F.
Blue at the mizzen. O'Brian, P.
Blue Calhoun. Price, R.
Blue collar blues. McMillan, R.
Blue corn murders. Pickard, N.
Blue death. O'Donnell, L.
Blue Deer thaw. Harrison, J.
Blue diary. Hoffman, A.
Blue dog, green river. Brower, B.
The **blue** door. Fulmer, D.
The **blue** flower. Fitzgerald, P.
The **blue** hour. Parker, T. J.
The **blue** knight. Wambaugh, J.
Blue light in the sky & other stories. Ts'an-hsüeh
Blue lonesome. Pronzini, B.
The **blue** manuscript. Khemir, S.
Blue Mars. Robinson, K. S.
Blue moon. Rice, L.
Blue plate special. Runyon, D.
    In Runyon, D. Guys and dolls p345-505
Blue Ridge. Pearson, T. R.

BLUE RIDGE MOUNTAINS

    Hamner, E. The homecoming
    Hamner, E. Spencer's Mountain
Blue shoe. Lamott, A.
Blue shoes and happiness. McCall Smith, A.
The **blue** star. Earley, T.
Bluebirds used to croon in the choir. Meno, J.
Bluegate Fields. Perry, A.
Blues dancing. McKinney-Whetstone, D.
The **bluest** blood. Roberts, G.
The **bluest** eye. Morrison, T.

BOARDERS *See* Boarding houses

BOARDING HOUSES

    Balzac, H. d. Père Goriot (Old Goriot)
    Egolf, T. Skirt and the fiddle
    Levy, A. Small island
    Naylor, G. Bailey's Café
    Ross-Macdonald, M. Tamsin Harte
    Spark, M. A far cry from Kensington
    Tyler, A. Celestial navigation

BOARDING SCHOOLS *See* School life

BOATS AND BOATING

    See also Rafting (Sports); Sailing vessels
The **bodies** left behind. Deaver, J.
The **body.** King, S.
    In King, S. Different seasons p299-451
Body and soil. McInerny, R. M.
The **body** artist. DeLillo, D.
Body count. Kienzle, W. X.

Body double. Gerritsen, T.
The **body** in the Big Apple. Page, K. H.
The **body** in the bog. Page, K. H.
The **body** in the bookcase. Page, K. H.
The **body** in the library. Christie, A.
The **body** in the vestibule. Page, K. H.
The **body** of David Hayes. Pearson, R.
Body of lies. Ignatius, D.
Body surfing. Shreve, A.
A **body** to die for. White, K.

BODYGUARDS

    Parker, R. B. Double play
    Parker, T. J. Storm runners

BOERS *See* Afrikaners

BOHEMIANISM

    Kerouac, J. And the hippos were boiled in their tanks
    Kerouac, J. The Dharma bums
    Kerouac, J. On the road
    Kerouac, J. On the road: the original scroll
    Kerouac, J. Road novels 1957-1960
    Kerouac, J. The subterraneans
    Kerouac, J. Tristessa
    Maugham, W. S. Of human bondage
    McCarthy, M. A charmed life
    Powell, A. Casanova's Chinese restaurant
    Powell, A. Hearing secret harmonies

BOHEMIANS

United States

    See Czechs—United States

BOLEYN, ANNE *See* Anne Boleyn, Queen, consort of Henry VIII, King of England, 1507-1536

BOLEYN, JANE, VISCOUNTESS ROCHFORD, D. 1542
About
    Gregory, P. The Boleyn Inheritance

BOLEYN, MARY, CA. 1500-1543
About
    Gregory, P. The other Boleyn girl
The **Boleyn** Inheritance. Gregory, P.

BOLÍVAR, SIMÓN, 1783-1830
About
    García Márquez, G. The general and his labyrinth

BOLSHEVISM *See* Communism
Bolt. Francis, D.
Bomb grade. Freemantle, B.

BOMBAY (INDIA) *See* India—Bombay
Bomber's law. Higgins, G. V.

BOMBING MISSIONS *See* World War, 1939-1945—Aerial operations

BOMBS

    See also Atomic bomb
    Choi, S. A person of interest
    Crais, R. Demolition angel
    Grisham, J. The chamber
    Knox, E. Billie's kiss
    Lutz, J. Final seconds
    Nance, J. J. Medusa's child
    Snyder, D. J. Night crossing
    Wiltse, D. Blown away
Bon voyage. Coward, N.
    In Coward, N. The collected stories of Noël Coward p562-630

BONANNO, JOSEPH, 1905-2002
About
    Latour, J. The Havana World Series

BONAPARTE, NAPOLEON *See* Napoleon I, Emperor of the French, 1769-1821
The **bondswomans** narrative. Crafts, H.
Bone. Ng, F. M.
Bone by bone. Matthiessen, P.
Bone deep. Wiltse, D.
Bone Key. Standiford, L.
The **bone** people. Hulme, K.
The **bone** vault. Fairstein, L.
Bones. Kellerman, J.
Bones. Pronzini, B.
Bones and silence. Hill, R.
Bones of the earth. Swanwick, M.
The **bonesetter's** daughter. Tan, A.
Boneshaker. Priest, C.

The **bonfire** of the vanities. Wolfe, T.
Bonjour tristesse. Sagan, F.
BONN (GERMANY) *See* Germany—Bonn
The **book** about Blanche and Marie. Enquist, P. O.
The **book** and the brotherhood. Murdoch, I.
The **book** class. Auchincloss, L.
The **book** of Abraham. Halter, M.
The **book** of air and shadows. Gruber, M.
A **book** of common prayer. Didion, J.
The **book** of Dahlia. Albert, E.
The **book** of Daniel. Doctorow, E. L.
The **Book** of Dave. Self, W.
The **book** of evidence. Banville, J.
The **book** of getting even. Taylor, B.
BOOK OF KELLS
    Gill, B. Death in Dublin
The **book** of kills. McInerny, R. M.
The **book** of knowledge. Grumbach, D.
The **book** of laughter and forgetting. Kundera, M.
The **book** of lies. Meltzer, B.
The **book** of lost tales. Tolkien, J. R. R.
The **book** of lost things. Connolly, J.
The **book** of Merlyn. White, T. H.
The **book** of night women. James, M.
The **book** of Q. Rabb, J.
The **book** of salt. Truong, M. T. D.
The **book** of Samson. Maine, D.
The **book** of splendor. Sherwood, F.
The **book** of words. Erpenbeck, J.
BOOK RARITIES *See* Rare books
BOOK SHOPS *See* Booksellers and bookselling
Booked to die. Dunning, J.
The **bookman's** wake. Dunning, J.
BOOKS
    See also Books and reading; Manuscripts; Rare books
BOOKS, RARE *See* Rare books
BOOKS AND READING
    Brooks, G. People of the book
    Connolly, J. The book of lost things
    Domínguez, C. M. The house of paper
    Fforde, J. The Eyre affair
    Fforde, J. Thursday Next in Lost in a good book
    Fforde, J. Thursday Next in Something rotten
    Fforde, J. Thursday Next in The well of lost plots
    Fowler, K. J. The Jane Austen book club
    Hamilton, M. The camel bookmobile
    Hrabal, B. Too loud a solitude
    Jones, L. Mister Pip
    Maalouf, A. Balthasar's odyssey
    Ruiz Zafón, C. The angel's game
    Ruiz Zafón, C. The shadow of the wind
    Savage, S. Firmin
    Schlink, B. The reader
    Shaffer, M. A. The Guernsey Literary and Potato Peel Pie Society
    Tolstaia, T. The slynx
    Vila-Matas, E. Montano's malady
    Wolitzer, H. Summer reading
Books do furnish a room. Powell, A.
    In Powell, A. A dance to the music of time
The **books** of blood. Barker, C.

BOOKSELLERS AND BOOKSELLING
    Berry, S. The Charlemagne pursuit
    Brookner, A. Undue influence
    Eco, U. The mysterious flame of Queen Loana
    Glass, J. Three Junes
    Grossman, D. Be my knife
    Gruber, M. The book of air and shadows
    Martin, W. Harvard Yard
    Pipkin, J. Woodsburner
    Schine, C. The love letter
Boone's Lick. McMurtry, L.
Bootlegger's daughter. Maron, M.
BOOTLEGGING *See* Liquor traffic
BORDEN, LIZZIE, 1860-1927
About
    Hunter, E. Lizzie
BORDER PATROL AGENTS
    Lynch, J. Border songs
Border songs. Lynch, J.

Borderliners. Høeg, P.
Bordersnakes. Crumley, J.
BORGES, JORGE LUIS, 1899-1986
About
    Verissimo, L. F. Borges and the eternal orangutans
Borges and the eternal orangutans. Verissimo, L. F.
BORGIA FAMILY
About
    Puzo, M. The family
BORMANN, MARTIN, 1900-1945
About
    Lindgren, T. Hash
Born to run. Grippando, J.
Borrowed hearts. DeMarinis, R.

BOSNIA AND HERCEGOVINA
    Stanišic, S. How the soldier repairs the gramophone
Sarajevo
    Hemon, A. Nowhere man
BOSNIANS

United States
    Hemon, A. Nowhere man
BOSTON (MASS.) *See* Massachusetts—Boston
The **Bostonians**. James, H.
BOTANISTS
    Hay, E. A student of weather
    Humphreys, H. The lost garden
    Vanderbes, J. Easter Island
Botany Bay. Nordhoff, C.
Both ends of the night. Muller, M.

BOTSWANA
    Rush, N. Mating
    Rush, N. Mortals
The **bottoms**. Lansdale, J. R.
BOUNTY (SHIP)
    Nordhoff, C. The Bounty trilogy

    Nordhoff, C. Men against the sea
    Nordhoff, C. Mutiny on the Bounty
The **Bounty** trilogy. Nordhoff, C.
BOURGEOISIE *See* Middle classes
The **Bourne** identity. Ludlum, R.
The **Bourne** supremacy. Ludlum, R.
The **Bourne** ultimatum. Ludlum, R.
BOW AND ARROW *See* Archery
Bowl of cherries. Kaufman, M.

BOXING
    DeVido, B. Every time I talk to Liston
    Lee, G. China boy
    Lovesey, P. The detective wore silk drawers
    Toole, F. X. Pound for pound
The **boy** detective fails. Meno, J.
The **boy** on the bus. Schupack, D.
Boy still missing. Searles, J.
The **boy** who followed Ripley. Highsmith, P.
The **boy** who would live forever. Pohl, F.
Boyos. Marinick, R.
BOYS
    See also Adolescence; Children; Youth
    Abani, C. GraceLand
    Ansay, A. M. River angel
    Ballard, J. G. Empire of the Sun
    Bradbury, R. Dandelion wine
    Bradbury, R. Something wicked this way comes
    Carey, P. His illegal self
    Chekhov, A. P. The steppe
    Childress, M. Crazy in Alabama
    Clinch, J. Finn
    Coe, J. The Rotters' Club
    Connelly, K. The lizard cage
    Connolly, J. The book of lost things
    Conroy, P. The lords of discipline
    Couto, M. Sleepwalking land
    Deane, S. Reading in the dark
    Dickens, C. David Copperfield
    Dickens, C. Dombey and Son
    Dickens, C. Oliver Twist

Breakfast at Tiffany's: a short novel and three stories. Capote, T.
Breakfast of champions. Vonnegut, K.
Breakfast with Buddha. Merullo, R.
Breakheart Hill. Cook, T. H.
Breaking news. MacNeil, R.
Breaking the tongue. Loh, V.
Breaking up is hard to do. Gorman, E.
Breakout. Stark, R.
The **breast.** Roth, P.
   In Roth, P. Novels, 1967-1972
Breath. Winton, T.
A **breath** of snow and ashes. Gabaldon, D.
Breathing lessons. Tyler, A.
The **breathing** method. King, S.
   In King, S. Different seasons p453-518
BRÉBEUF, JEAN DE, SAINT, 1593-1649
      About
   Vollmann, W. T. Fathers and crows
The **brethren.** Grisham, J.
Brewing up a storm. Lathen, E.
Briar Rose. Coover, R.
Briar Rose. Yolen, J.

BRIBERY
   Keating, H. R. F. The bad detective
Bribery, corruption also. Keating, H. R. F.
Brick lane. Ali, M.
The **bridal** wreath. Undset, S.
   In Undset, S. Kristin Lavransdatter
The **bride.** Garwood, J.
The **bride** from Odessa. Cozarinsky, E.
The **bride** of Lammermoor. Scott, Sir W.
Bride of Pendorric. Holt, V.
The **bridegroom.** Ha Jin
Brideshead revisited. Waugh, E.
The **bridesmaid.** Rendell, R.
The **bridge** of San Luis Rey. Wilder, T.
   also in Wilder, T. The bridge of San Luis Rey and other novels 1926-1948
The **bridge** of San Luis Rey and other novels 1926-1948. Wilder, T.
Bridge of sand. Burroway, J.
Bridge of sighs. Russo, R.
The **Bridge** of Sighs. Steinhauer, O.
The **bridge** over the River Kwai. Boulle, P.
BRIDGEPORT (CONN.) *See* Connecticut—Bridgeport

BRIDGES
   Barton, E. Brookland
   Boulle, P. The bridge over the River Kwai
   Kadare, I. The three-arched bridge
The **bridges** at Toko-ri. Michener, J. A.
The **bridges** of Madison County. Waller, R. J.
Bridget Jones: the edge of reason. Fielding, H.
Bridget Jones's diary. Fielding, H.
The **brief** history of the dead. Brockmeier, K.
Brief lives. Brookner, A.
The **brief** wondrous life of Oscar Wao. Díaz, J.

BRIGANDS AND ROBBERS
   See also Outlaws; Robbery
   Blackmore, R. D. Lorna Doone
   Puzo, M. The Sicilian
   Urrea, L. A. Into the beautiful North
Bright center of heaven. Maxwell, W.
   In Maxwell, W. Early novels and stories
Bright lights, big city. McInerney, J.
Bright shiny morning. Frey, J.
Brightness reef. Brin, D.
BRIGHTON (ENGLAND) *See* England—Brighton
Brighton rock. Greene, G.
Brimstone. Parker, R. B.
Brimstone. Preston, D.
The **brimstone** wedding. Vine, B.

BRITISH

      Afghanistan
   Hensher, P. The Mulberry empire
   Trollope, J. Legacy of love

      Africa
   Conrad, J. Heart of darkness
   Gordimer, N. A guest of honor

   Lessing, D. M. The sweetest dream
   Ruark, R. Uhuru

      Argentina
   Greene, G. The honorary consul

      Asia
   Gardam, J. Old Filth

      Austria
   Stewart, M. Airs above the ground

      Belgium
   Faber, M. The courage consort [novelette]

      Brazil
   Hamilton-Paterson, J. Gerontius
   King, R. The sound of butterflies
   Lessing, D. M. Ben, in the world

      Burma
   Ghosh, A. The glass palace
   Mason, D. The piano tuner

      Caribbean region
   Dean, L. Becoming strangers

      China
   Ballard, J. G. Empire of the Sun
   Ishiguro, K. When we were orphans

      Crete
   Stewart, M. The moon-spinners

      Croatia
   Seymour, G. The heart of danger

      Denmark
   Tremain, R. Music & silence

      Egypt
   Deighton, L. City of gold
   Durrell, L. Mountolive

      Ethiopia
   Gibb, C. Sweetness in the belly

      France
   Bates, H. E. Fair stood the wind for France
   Cornwell, B. Vagabond
   Faulks, S. Birdsong
   Freeling, N. One more river
   Godden, R. The greengage summer
   Graham, W. Bella Poldark
   Hemingway, E. The sun also rises
   Laker, R. Banners of silk
   Lessing, D. M. Ben, in the world
   Mayle, P. Anything considered
   Mayle, P. A good year
   Mayle, P. Hotel Pastis
   Orczy, E., Baroness. Adventures of the Scarlet Pimpernel
   Orczy, E., Baroness. The elusive Pimpernel
   Orczy, E., Baroness. The Scarlet Pimpernel
   Rhys, J. Quartet
   Stewart, M. Nine coaches waiting
   Stewart, M. Thunder on the right
   Tremain, R. The way I found her

      Germany
   Hall, A. The Quiller memorandum
   Isherwood, C. The last of Mr. Norris
   Le Carré, J. The spy who came in from the cold
   MacLean, A. Where eagles dare
   Shakespeare, N. Snowleg

      Greece
   Fowles, J. The magus
   Goddard, R. Into the blue
   Stewart, M. My brother Michael

      Hong Kong
   Clavell, J. Tai-Pan
   Lanchester, J. Fragrant Harbor
   Lee, J. Y. K. The piano teacher
   Theroux, P. Kowloon Tong

      India
   Dyer, G. Jeff in Venice, death in Varanasi

BRUTUS, LUCIUS JUNIUS
About
Massie, A. Caesar
BUBONIC PLAGUE *See* Plague
BUCHANAN, JAMES, 1791-1868
About
Updike, J. Memories of the Ford Administration
Bucking the sun. Doig, I.
Buckingham Palace gardens. Perry, A.
BUDAPEST (HUNGARY) *See* Hungary—Budapest
Buddenbrooks. Mann, T.
Buddha Da. Donovan, A.
The **Buddha** of suburbia. Kureishi, H.
BUDDHISM
See also Zen Buddhism
Burdett, J. Bangkok 8
Burdett, J. Bangkok haunts
Burdett, J. Bangkok Tattoo
Donovan, A. Buddha Da
Endō, S. Deep river
Hesse, H. Siddhartha
Merullo, R. Breakfast with Buddha
Mishima, Y. The Temple of Dawn
Mishima, Y. The temple of the golden pavilion
Pattison, E. The skull mantra
Zelazny, R. Lord of light
BUENOS AIRES (ARGENTINA) *See* Argentina—Buenos Aires
BUFFALO, AMERICAN *See* Bison
BUFFALO (N.Y.) *See* New York (State)—Buffalo
BUFFALO BILL, 1846-1917
About
McMurtry, L. Buffalo girls
McMurtry, L. Telegraph days
BUFFALO BILL'S WILD WEST COMPANY
Welch, J. The heartsong of Charging Elk
Buffalo girls. McMurtry, L.
Buffalo soldiers. O'Connor, R.
Buffalo soldiers. Willard, T.
BUILDING
Follett, K. Pillars of the earth
Hodgins, E. Mr. Blandings builds his dream house
Built in a day. Rinehart, S.
BULGARIA
Sofia
Gilman, D. The elusive Mrs. Pollifax
BULIMIA
Minot, E. The Brambles
The **bull** from the sea. Renault, M.
BULL RUN, 1ST BATTLE, 1861
Cornwell, B. Rebel
Bullet Park. Cheever, J.
also in Cheever, J. Complete novels
BULLFIGHTERS AND BULLFIGHTING
Hemingway, E. The sun also rises
Michener, J. A. Mexico
BULLFIGHTING *See* Bullfighters and bullfighting
BULLYING
Picoult, J. Nineteen minutes
Bum steer. Pickard, N.
BUNKER, CHANG, 1811-1874
About
Slouka, M. God's fool
BUNKER, ENG, 1811-1874
About
Slouka, M. God's fool
Burden of desire. MacNeil, R.
The **burden** of proof. Turow, S.
BUREAUCRACY
See also Civil service
Bulgakov, M. A. The master and Margarita
Grushin, O. The dream life of Sukhanov
Torday, P. Salmon fishing in the Yemen
Whitehead, C. The intuitionist
The **burglar** in the library. Block, L.
BURGLARS *See* Thieves

BURIAL *See* Funeral rites and ceremonies
Buried evidence. Rosenberg, N. T.
BURIED TREASURE
Conrad, J. Nostromo
Cussler, C. Inca gold
DeMille, N. Plum Island
Forester, C. S. Hornblower and the Atropos
Mosher, H. F. On Kingdom Mountain
Preston, D. Riptide
BURMA
Connelly, K. The lizard cage
Ghosh, A. The glass palace
Mason, D. The piano tuner
Tan, A. Saving fish from drowning
Burn. Lutz, J.
BURN CARE UNITS
Davidson, A. The gargoyle
Burn marks. Paretsky, S.
Burn out. Muller, M.
BURNES, SIR ALEXANDER, 1805-1841
About
Hensher, P. The Mulberry empire
The **burning** bride. Lawrence, M. K.
Burning bright. Chevalier, T.
Burning bright. Steinbeck, J.
In Steinbeck, J. Travels with Charley and later novels, 1947-1962
The **burning** city. Niven, L.
The **burning** man. Margolin, P.
Burning Marguerite. Inness-Brown, E.
Burning your boats. Carter, A.
A **burnt-out** case. Greene, G.
BURR, AARON, 1756-1836
About
Vidal, G. Burr
Burr. Vidal, G.
BURYING GROUNDS *See* Cemeteries
BUSES
Steinbeck, J. The wayward bus
Accidents
See Traffic accidents
BUSINESS
See also Advertising; Department stores; Merchants
Barry, M. Company
Bradford, B. T. The Ravenscar dynasty
Finder, J. Vanished
Heffernan, W. The Dinosaur Club
Howells, W. D. The rise of Silas Lapham
Norris, F. The pit
O'Hara, J. From the terrace
Park, E. Personal days
Tarkington, B. The magnificent Ambersons
Theroux, P. Kowloon Tong
Vonnegut, K. Jailbird
Wilson, S. The man in the gray flannel suit
Unscrupulous methods
Baldacci, D. Total control
Clavell, J. Noble house
Dunne, D. An inconvenient woman
Finder, J. Killer instinct
Galgut, D. The impostor
Goddard, R. Into the blue
Grisham, J. The appeal
Ignatius, D. A firing offense
Larsson, S. The girl with the dragon tattoo
Le Carré, J. The constant gardener
Martin, C. W. How to sell
Norris, F. The octopus
Wells, H. G. Tono-Bungay
BUSINESS DEPRESSION, 1929
Adams, A. A southern exposure
Algren, N. A walk on the wild side
Brown, J. D. Addie Pray
Doctorow, E. L. Loon Lake
Doig, I. Bucking the sun
Hamner, E. The homecoming
Kennedy, W. Ironweed

BUSINESSMEN

Adiga, A. The white tiger
Atwood, M. The blind assassin
Collins, J. Beginner's Greek
DeLillo, D. Cosmopolis
Finder, J. Company man
Finder, J. Power play
Gurganus, A. He's one, too
Harrison, C. Afterburn
Ignatius, D. The Sun King
Korda, M. Worldly goods
Lanchester, J. Fragrant Harbor
Leithauser, B. A few corrections
Lewis, S. Babbitt
Lightman, A. P. The diagnosis
McGuane, T. Nothing but blue skies
Millhauser, S. Martin Dressler
Percy, W. The moviegoer
Powell, D. Angels on toast
Roth, P. American pastoral
Theroux, P. The gateway of India
Updike, J. Villages
Westlake, D. E. The ax

BUSINESSWOMEN

Auchincloss, L. Her infinite variety
Bradford, B. T. A woman of substance
Bushnell, C. Lipstick jungle
Campbell, B. M. Brothers and sisters
Cleage, P. Babylon sisters
Hill, R. When all is said and done
McMillan, T. How Stella got her groove back
McNaught, J. Paradise
Michael, J. A certain smile
Michaels, F. Celebration
Sheldon, S. Master of the game
Thayer, N. Everlasting
Van Slyke, H. Public smiles, private tears
Vidal, G. Empire
Wood, B. Perfect Harmony
Busman's honeymoon. Sayers, D. L.
The **bust** of the emperor. Roth, J.
  In Roth, J. The collected stories of Joseph Roth
Busy bodies. Hess, J.
But come ye back. Lordan, B.
But I wouldn't want to die there. Pickard, N.
The **butcher** boy. McCabe, P.

BUTCHERS

Doenges, J. God of gods

BUTLERS

Ishiguro, K. The remains of the day
McGrath, P. The grotesque
Wodehouse, P. G. The world of Jeeves
Butterfield 8. O'Hara, J.

BUTTERFLIES

King, R. The sound of butterflies
Butterfly stories. Vollmann, W. T.
A **buyer's** market. Powell, A.
  In Powell, A. A dance to the music of time
Buying a fishing rod for my grandfather. Gao Xingjian
Buzz cut. Hall, J. W.
By any other name. Robinson, S.
  In The Hugo winners p141-97
By George. Harding, J. W.
By love possessed. Cozzens, J. G.
By night in Chile. Bolaño, R.
By order of the President. Griffin, W. E. B.
By sorrow's river. McMurtry, L.
By the lake. McGahern, J.
By the light of my father's smile. Walker, A.
By the light of the moon. Koontz, D. R.

BYRON, GEORGE GORDON BYRON, 6TH BARON, 1788-1824

About

Crowley, J. Lord Byron's novel
West, P. Lord Byron's doctor

C

"C" is for corpse. Grafton, S.

CAB DRIVERS

O'Dell, T. Sister mine
Self, W. The Book of Dave
The **cabal** and other stories. Gilchrist, E.
The **cabala**. Wilder, T.
  In Wilder, T. The bridge of San Luis Rey and other novels 1926-1948
Cabbages and kings. Henry, O.
  In Henry, O. The complete works of O. Henry p551-679
The **cabinet** of curiosities. Preston, D.

CABLES, SUBMARINE

Griesemer, J. Signal & noise
The **cadence** of grass. McGuane, T.
Cadillac Jack. McMurtry, L.
Caedmon's song. See Robinson, P. The first cut

CAESAR, JULIUS, 100-44 B.C.

About

George, M. The memoirs of Cleopatra
Massie, A. Caesar
McCullough, C. Caesar
McCullough, C. Caesar's women
McCullough, C. Fortune's favorites
Saylor, S. The triumph of Caesar
Wilder, T. The ides of March
Caesar. Massie, A.
Caesar. McCullough, C.
Caesar's women. McCullough, C.
CAFÉS See Restaurants, lunchrooms, etc.

CAIN (BIBLICAL FIGURE)

About

Maine, D. Fallen
Cain his brother. Perry, A.
The **Caine** mutiny. Wouk, H.
CAIRO (EGYPT) See Egypt—Cairo

CAJUNS

Gaines, E. J. A gathering of old men
Wells, K. Crawfish mountain
Cakes and ale. Maugham, W. S.
CALABRIA (ITALY) See Italy—Calabria

CALAMITY JANE, 1852-1903

About

McMurtry, L. Buffalo girls
CALCUTTA (INDIA) See India—Calcutta

CALIFORNIA

See also Death Valley (Calif. and Nev.)
Brownrigg, S. Morality tale
Cunningham, M. The hours
Deaver, J. Roadside crosses
Dick, P. K. The transmigration of Timothy Archer
Ginsberg, D. The grift
Goudge, E. One last dance
Goudge, E. Stranger in paradise
Gutcheon, B. R. Saying grace
Hall, A. L. The rhythm of the road
Huneven, M. Blame
Huston, C. The shotgun rule
Jakes, J. California gold
Kinder, C. Honeymooners
Klein, M. Con ed
Koontz, D. R. Brother Odd
Koontz, D. R. The darkest evening of the year
Koontz, D. R. False memory
Koontz, D. R. Fear nothing
Koontz, D. R. The husband
Koontz, D. R. Intensity
Koontz, D. R. Seize the night
Koontz, D. R. The taking
Koontz, D. R. Velocity
Lazar, Z. Sway
Lee, C. Y. The flower drum song
Lemann, N. Malaise
Leonard, E. Mr. Majestyk
Leonard, E. Road dogs
Mapson, J.-A. Bad Girl Creek
Martini, S. P. The judge
McMillan, T. The interruption of everything
Miller, S. Lost in the forest
Muller, M. Cyanide Wells
Otsuka, J. When the emperor was divine
Otto, W. How to make an American quilt

CALIFORNIA—San Francisco—*Continued*
Lee, C. Y. The flower drum song
Lee, G. China boy
Lescroart, J. T. The first law
Lescroart, J. T. Guilt
Lescroart, J. T. The hearing
Lescroart, J. T. The mercy rule
Lescroart, J. T. Nothing but the truth
Lescroart, J. T. The oath
Lescroart, J. T. The second chair
Maupin, A. Michael Tolliver lives
Moore, C. A dirty job
Ng, F. M. Bone
Norris, F. McTeague
Palwick, S. Shelter
Patterson, J. 1st to die
Patterson, R. N. Degree of guilt
Patterson, R. N. Eyes of a child
Paul, J. Elsewhere in the land of parrots
Richmond, M. No one you know
Shafak, E. The bastard of Istanbul
Siegel, S. Final verdict
Steel, D. Amazing grace
Tan, A. The bonesetter's daughter
Tan, A. The Joy Luck Club
Vollmann, W. T. The royal family

Santa Barbara
Iyer, P. Abandon
Rosenberg, N. T. Buried evidence

Santa Monica
Smith, A. Good morning, killer
California girl. Parker, T. J.
California gold. Jakes, J.
The **Californios**. L'Amour, L.
Call down the stars. Harrison, S.
Call it sleep. Roth, H.
Call me by your name. Aciman, A. A.
The **call** of the toad. Grass, G.
The **call** of the wild. London, J.
    also in London, J. Novels & stories
Callahan's con. Robinson, S.
CALLENDER, JAMES THOMSON, 1758-1803
    About
Safire, W. Scandalmonger
The **calligrapher**. Docx, E.

CALLIGRAPHERS
Docx, E. The calligrapher
The **calling**. Wolfe, I. A.
Calling the wind. Entered in Part I under title
Calpurnia. Scott, A.
Calumet City. Newton, C.

CAMBODIA
Hall, A. Quiller Salamander
CAMBRIDGE (ENGLAND) *See* England—Cambridge
CAMBRIDGE (MASS.) *See* Massachusetts—Cambridge
CAMBRIDGE UNIVERSITY *See* University of Cambridge
The **camel** bookmobile. Hamilton, M.
The **camelia-lady**. See Dumas, A. Camille
Cameron's crossing. McCutchan, P.
Camille. Dumas, A.
The **campaign**. Fuentes, C.

CAMPAIGNS, PRESIDENTIAL

United States
See Presidents—United States—Election

CAMPING
    See also Wilderness survival

CAMPS, SUMMER *See* Summer camps

CAMPUS LIFE *See* College life
Can you forgive her? Trollope, A.
Can you forgive her? [abridged] Trollope, A.
    In Trollope, A. The Pallisers p11-115
Canaan's tongue. Wray, J.

CANADA
Adamson, G. The outlander
Atwood, M. The blind assassin
Cather, W. Shadows on the rock
Cumyn, A. Losing it

Davies, R. The cunning man
Davies, R. Fifth business
Davies, R. The manticore
Davies, R. Murther & walking spirits
Davies, R. What's bred in the bone
Findley, T. The piano man's daughter
Hay, E. Garbo laughs
Itani, F. Remembering the bones
L'Amour, L. The haunted mesa
Munro, A. Friend of my youth
Munro, A. The moons of Jupiter
Munro, A. Open secrets
Ondaatje, M. In the skin of a lion
Pohl, F. Chernobyl
Shields, C. The stone diaries
Urquhart, J. Away

To 1763 (New France)
Cather, W. Shadows on the rock
Moore, B. Black robe

19th century
Atwood, M. Alias Grace
Brand, M. The Stingaree
Penney, S. The tenderness of wolves

College life
See College life—Canada

Farm life
See Farm life—Canada

Frontier and pioneer life
See Frontier and pioneer life—Canada

Politics
See Politics—Canada

Rural life
Davies, R. World of wonders
Munro, A. Lives of girls & women

British Columbia
Anderson-Dargatz, G. A recipe for bees

Halifax
Norman, H. The museum guard

Manitoba
Norman, H. The haunting of L
Toews, M. A complicated kindness

Montreal
Reichs, K. J. Déjà dead
Richler, M. Barney's version
Richler, M. Solomon Gursky was here

New Brunswick
Richards, D. A. The bay of love and sorrows

Newfoundland
Johnston, W. The colony of unrequited dreams
Johnston, W. The custodian of paradise
Norman, H. The bird artist
Proulx, A. The shipping news

Northwest Territories
Freedman, B. Mrs. Mike
Hay, E. Late nights on air
Patterson, K. Consumption
Vollmann, W. T. The rifles

Nova Scotia
MacDonald, A.-M. Fall on your knees
MacLeod, A. Island
MacNeil, R. Burden of desire

Ontario
Burnford, S. The incredible journey
Davies, R. Fifth business
De la Roche, M. Jalna
De Lint, C. Memory and dream
Itani, F. Deafening
Lawson, M. Crow Lake
MacDonald, A.-M. The way the crow flies
Penney, S. The tenderness of wolves
Shields, C. Unless

CAPOTE, TRUMAN, 1924-1984
About
Powers, K. Capote in Kansas
Capote in Kansas. Powers, K.

CAPRI
Goodman, C. The night villa
Parini, J. The apprentice lover
Rice, L. The deep blue sea for beginners
Caprice and Rondo. Dunnett, D.
Captain Alatriste. Pérez-Reverte, A.
The **captain** and the enemy. Greene, G.
Captain Blood. Sabatini, R.
Captain Newman, M.D. Rosten, L.
Captain Pantoja and the Special Service. Vargas Llosa, M.
Captain Saturday. Inman, R.
Captains and kings. Caldwell, T.
The **captain's** daughter. Pushkin, A. S.
   In Pushkin, A. S. Alexander Pushkin: complete prose fiction p266-357

CAPTAINS OF SHIPS *See* Shipmasters
The **captive**. Proust, M.
   In Proust, M. The captive [and] The fugitive
   In Proust, M. Remembrance of things past p1-422
The **captive** [and] The fugitive. Proust, M.
The **captive** Queen of Scots. Plaidy, J.
Captivity. Wesselmann, D. L.
¡**Caramba**!. Martínez, N. M.
The **Caravaggio** obsession. Banks, O. T.
Caravans. Michener, J. A.
A **cardinal** offense. McInerny, R. M.
The **cardinal** virtues. Greeley, A. M.

CARDINALS
Vallgren, C.-J. The horrific sufferings of the mind-reading monster Hercules Barefoot
Cardington Crescent. Perry, A.

CAREGIVERS
Berg, E. We are all welcome here
Careless in red. George, E.
Caribbean. Michener, J. A.

CARIBBEAN ISLANDS *See* West Indies

CARIBBEAN REGION
   See also Spanish Main
Buffett, J. A salty piece of land
Dean, L. Becoming strangers
Green cane and juicy flotsam
Hemingway, E. Islands in the stream
Kincaid, J. Autobiography of my mother
Matthiessen, P. Far Tortuga
Michener, J. A. Caribbean
Mitchard, J. Still summer
Nunez, E. Anna in-between
Stone, R. Bay of souls
Styron, A. All the finest girls
Vonnegut, K. Cat's cradle
Wolfe, G. Pirate freedom
Woods, S. Dead in the water
Carioca Fletch. Mcdonald, G.
   In Mcdonald, G. The Fletch chronicles
Carmen. Mérimée, P.

CARNARVON, HENRY HOWARD MOLYNEUX HERBERT, 4TH EARL OF, 1831-1890
About
Holland, C. Valley of the Kings

CARNIVALS (CIRCUS) *See* Amusement parks
Carolina moon. McCorkle, J.

CARPATHIAN MOUNTAINS
Wiesel, E. The oath
Carpentaria. Wright, A.

CARPENTERS
Eliot, G. Adam Bede
Carrie. King, S.
Carried away. Munro, A.

CARRIERS, AIRCRAFT *See* Aircraft carriers
A **carrion** death. Stanley, M.
Carry me down. Hyland, M. J.

CARS (AUTOMOBILES) *See* Automobiles

CARTER, HOWARD
About
Holland, C. Valley of the Kings

CARTOGRAPHERS
Humphreys, H. Afterimage

CARTOONISTS
Ha Jin. In the pond
Jacobson, H. Kalooki nights
The **caryatids**. Sterling, B.
Casanova's Chinese restaurant. Powell, A.
   In Powell, A. A dance to the music of time
The **case** has altered. Grimes, M.
Case histories. Atkinson, K.
A **case** of exploding mangoes. Hanif, M.
The **case** of the missing books. Sansom, I.
Cashelmara. Howatch, S.
Casino Royale. Fleming, I.
Cast a long shadow. Pearce, M. E.
Cast the first stone. See Himes, C. Yesterday will make you cry

CASTE
India
Mistry, R. A fine balance
Roy, A. The god of small things
Viswanathan, P. The toss of a lemon
The **castle**. Kafka, F.
Castle. Lennon, J. R.
The **castle** in the forest. Mailer, N.
Castle Rackrent. Edgeworth, M.

CASTLES
Egan, J. The keep
Holt, V. Bride of Pendorric
Stewart, M. Nine coaches waiting
Castleview. Wolfe, G.

CASTRATI *See* Eunuchs

CASTRO, FIDEL, 1926-
About
Block, L. Killing Castro
Hunter, S. Havana
Cat & mouse. Patterson, J.
Cat and mouse. Grass, G.
   also in Grass, G. The Danzig trilogy
Cat chaser. Leonard, E.
Cat in a midnight choir. Douglas, C. N.
Cat in a neon nightmare. Douglas, C. N.
The **cat** who ate Danish modern. Braun, L. J.
The **cat** who brought down the house. Braun, L. J.
The **cat** who sang for the birds. Braun, L. J.
The **cat** who smelled a rat. Braun, L. J.
The **cat** who went underground. Braun, L. J.
Catalyst. Hoffman, N. K.

CATASTROPHES *See* Disasters
The **catch**. Mayor, A.
Catch-22. Heller, J.
The **catcher** in the rye. Salinger, J. D.

CATHARINE HOWARD, QUEEN, CONSORT OF HENRY VIII, KING OF ENGLAND, D. 1542
About
Gregory, P. The Boleyn Inheritance
Plaidy, J. Murder most royal

CATHEDRAL LIFE
Dickens, C. The mystery of Edwin Drood
Hugo, V. The hunchback of Notre Dame
L'Engle, M. A severed wasp
Palliser, C. The unburied
Trollope, A. Barchester Towers
Trollope, J. The choir

CATHEDRAL TOWNS
   See also Cathedral life

CATHEDRALS
Dickens, C. The mystery of Edwin Drood
Follett, K. Pillars of the earth
Follett, K. World without end
L'Engle, M. A severed wasp

CATHERINE, OF ARAGON, QUEEN, CONSORT OF HENRY VIII, KING OF ENGLAND, 1485-1536
About
Gregory, P. The other Boleyn girl

CATHERINE, OF BRAGANZA, QUEEN, CONSORT OF CHARLES II, KING OF GREAT BRITAIN, 1638-1705
About
Koen, K. Dark angels

CELTS

Kay, G. G. Ysabel
Llywelyn, M. Druids
Llywelyn, M. The horse goddess

CEMETERIES

Dorst, D. Alive in Necropolis
King, S. Pet sematary
Reynolds, S. A gracious plenty
The **centaur**. Updike, J.
Centennial. Michener, J. A.
The **center** of everything. Moriarty, L.

CENTRAL AFRICA

Ballard, J. G. The day of creation

CENTRAL AMERICA

Forester, C. S. Beat to quarters
Stone, R. A flag for sunrise

Politics

See Politics—Central America

CENTRAL EUROPE

Egan, J. The keep
Korda, M. Worldly goods

CENTRAL INTELLIGENCE AGENCY (U.S.) *See* United
States. Central Intelligence Agency
A **Century** of great Western stories. Entered in Part I under title

**CENTURY OF PROGRESS INTERNATIONAL EXPOSI-
TION (1933-1934: CHICAGO, ILL.)**

Brown, C. The hatbox baby
Century's son. Boswell, R.

CEPHALONIA ISLAND (GREECE)

De Bernières, L. Corelli's mandolin

CEREBROVASCULAR DISEASE

Albert, E. The book of Dahlia
Ha Jin. The crazed
Heller, Z. The believers
Piercy, M. Three women

CEREMONIES *See* Rites and ceremonies
Certain girls. Weiner, J.
A **certain** justice. James, P. D.
Certain prey. Sandford, J.
A **certain** smile. Michael, J.
Certain women. L'Engle, M.

CERVANTES SAAVEDRA, MIGUEL DE, 1547-1616
Parodies, imitations, etc.

Greene, G. Monsignor Quixote

CEYLON *See* Sri Lanka

CHAGALL, MARC, 1887-1985
About

Horn, D. The world to come
Chain of evidence. Pearson, R.
Chains of command. Caunitz, W. J.

CHALLENGER (SPACE SHUTTLE)

Dean, M. L. The time it takes to fall
Challenger Park. Harrigan, S.
The **chamber**. Grisham, J.
Chance. Parker, R. B.

CHANCELLORSVILLE, BATTLE OF, 1863

Crane, S. The red badge of courage

CHANDLER, RAYMOND, 1888-1959
Parodies, imitations, etc.

Parker, R. B. Perchance to dream
A **change** of gravity. Higgins, G. V.
Change of heart. Picoult, J.
A **changed** man. Prose, F.

CHANNEL ISLANDS
See also Guernsey (Channel Islands)
Goudge, E. Green Dolphin Street
Chaos of crime. Shannon, D.
Chaos theory. Krist, G.

CHAPLIN, CHARLIE, 1889-1977
About

Gold, G. D. Sunnyside
Chapterhouse: Dune. Herbert, F.

CHARBONNEAU, JEAN-BAPTISTE, 1805-1866
About

Sargent, C. Museum of human beings

CHARITIES *See* Endowments
Charity girl. Lowenthal, M.
The **Charlemagne** pursuit. Berry, S.

CHARLES II, KING OF GREAT BRITAIN, 1630-1685
About

Koen, K. Dark angels

CHARLES, D'ORLÉANS, 1394-1465
About

Haasse, H. S. In a dark wood wandering
A **Charles** Dickens Christmas. Dickens, C.

CHARLESTON (S.C.) *See* South Carolina—Charleston
Charleston. Jakes, J.
Charley Bland. Settle, M. L.
Charley's web. Fielding, J.
Charlie's chance. See Freemantle, B. Bomb grade
Charlotte Gray. Faulks, S.
The **Charlotte** Perkins Gilman reader. Gilman, C. P.
Charlotte Perkins Gilman's Utopian novels. Gilman, C. P.
The **charm** school. DeMille, N.
A **charmed** life. McCarthy, M.
Charming Billy. McDermott, A.
Charms for the easy life. Gibbons, K.
The **charterhouse** of Parma. Stendhal

CHARWOMEN
See also Cleaning women
The **chase**. Cussler, C.

CHASIDISM *See* Hasidism
Chasing Cézanne. Mayle, P.
Chasing darkness. Crais, R.
Chat. Mayor, A.
The **chateau**. Maxwell, W.
In Maxwell, W. Later novels and stories

CHATEAUX *See* Castles
The **Chatham** School affair. Cook, T. H.

CHAUFFEURS

Adiga, A. The white tiger
Cheating at canasta. Trevor, W.
Cheating at solitaire. Haddam, J.
Cheating death. Keating, H. R. F.
Checkmate. Dunnett, D.

CHEERFUL STORIES

Austen, J. Emma
Benson, E. F. Make way for Lucia
Colwin, L. Happy all the time
Davies, V. Miracle on 34th Street
Heyer, G. The grand Sophy
Karon, J. A common life
Karon, J. In this mountain
Karon, J. A new song
Karon, J. Out to Canaan
Keillor, G. Lake Wobegon days
Keillor, G. Lake Wobegon summer 1956
Powers, J. R. Do black patent-leather shoes really reflect up?
Powers, J. R. The last Catholic in America
Read, Miss. Affairs at Thrush Green
Read, Miss. At home in Thrush Green
Read, Miss. Chronicles of Fairacre
Read, Miss. Farewell to Fairacre
Read, Miss. Friends at Thrush Green
Read, Miss. Mrs. Pringle
Read, Miss. Return to Thrush Green
Read, Miss. Thrush Green
West, J. The friendly persuasion
White, B. Quite a year for plums
Wodehouse, P. G. The code of the Woosters
Wodehouse, P. G. The inimitable Jeeves
Wodehouse, P. G. Tales from the Drones Club
Wodehouse, P. G. A Wodehouse bestiary
Wodehouse, P. G. The world of Jeeves

CHEESEMAKERS

Milton, G. Edward Trencom's nose

CHEMICALS

Grisham, J. The appeal

CHEMISTS
See also Medicines, Patent, proprietary, etc.
Deighton, L. Funeral in Berlin
Levi, P. The monkey's wrench
O'Connell, J. The resurrectionist
Wallace, I. The prize

CLARK, WILLIAM, 1770-1838
About
Hall, B. I should be extremely happy in your company
Sargent, C. Museum of human beings
A **clash** of kings. Martin, G. R. R.
CLASS DISTINCTION
See also Middle classes; Social classes
Bainbridge, B. Every man for himself
Brown, R. M. Southern discomfort
Chevalier, T. Girl with a pearl earring
Crane, S. Active service
Crane, S. The third violet
Cusk, R. Arlington Park
Dreiser, T. An American tragedy
Dunne, D. People like us
Forster, E. M. A room with a view
Greene, G. The tenth man
Grisham, J. A painted house
Harris, J. Gentlemen and players
Hijuelos, O. Empress of the splendid season
Ishiguro, K. The remains of the day
James, H. The American
Leavitt, D. While England sleeps
McNaught, J. Paradise
Paddock, J. A secret word
Quindlen, A. Blessings
Restrepo, L. Delirium
Rice, A. The Feast of All Saints
Richler, M. Solomon Gursky was here
Stirling, J. The marrying kind
Tarkington, B. Alice Adams
Umrigar, T. N. The space between us
Wolff, T. Old school
Class reunion. Jaffe, R.
Classic lines: more great racing stories. See The New treasury of
great racing stories
The **classic** Philip José Farmer, 1952-1964—1964-1973. Farmer,
P. J.
Claudine and Annie. Colette
In Colette. The complete Claudine p516-632
Claudine at school. Colette
In Colette. The complete Claudine p1-206
In Colette. Six novels p1-234
Claudine in Paris. Colette
In Colette. The complete Claudine p209-364
Claudine married. Colette
In Colette. The complete Claudine p367-510
CLAUDIUS, EMPEROR OF ROME, 10 B.C.-54
About
Graves, R. Claudius, the god and his wife Messalina
Graves, R. I, Claudius
Claudius, the god and his wife Messalina. Graves, R.
The **claw** of the conciliator. Wolfe, G.
Clea. Durrell, L.
also in Durrell, L. The Alexandria quartet: Justine;
Balthazar; Mountolive [and] Clea p653-884
CLEANING WOMEN
See also Maids (Servants)
Doyle, R. Paula Spencer
Hijuelos, O. Empress of the splendid season
Hunt, S. The invention of everything else
Messud, C. A simple tale
Clear and present danger. Clancy, T.
Clear light of day. Desai, A.
Cleaver. Parks, T.
CLEMENS, SAMUEL LANGHORNE *See* Twain, Mark, 1835-
1910
CLEOPATRA, QUEEN OF EGYPT, D. 30 B.C.
About
Essex, K. Kleopatra
Essex, K. Pharaoh
George, M. The memoirs of Cleopatra
Cleopatra's sister. Lively, P.
CLERGY
See also Evangelists; Rabbis
Baker, K. Strivers Row
Baldwin, J. Go tell it on the mountain
Doctorow, E. L. City of God
Guterson, D. Our Lady of the Forest
Harington, D. The pitcher shower
Hawthorne, N. The scarlet letter
Heinlein, R. A. Job: a comedy of justice
Howells, W. D. Annie Kilburn

Howells, W. D. The minister's charge
Hurston, Z. N. Jonah's gourd vine
Iagnemma, K. The expeditions
Lehrer, J. The special prisoner
Lewis, S. Elmer Gantry
MacDonald, J. D. One more Sunday
McFarland, D. Letter from Point Clear
Miller, S. While I was gone
Morley, I. Come Sunday
Pipkin, J. Woodsburner
Price, R. The good priest's son
Robinson, M. Gilead
Robinson, M. Home
Smith, M. C. Rose
Stirling, J. The workhouse girl
Strout, E. Abide with me
Trollope, A. The warden
Wideman, J. E. The cattle killing
CLERGY, ANGLICAN AND EPISCOPAL *See* Anglican and
Episcopal clergy
CLERGY, CATHOLIC *See* Catholic priests
CLERGY, ITINERANT *See* Itinerant clergy
CLERKS
See also Civil service
Camus, A. The stranger
Kafka, F. The trial
Pym, B. Quartet in autumn
The **client.** Grisham, J.
Client privilege. Tapply, W. G.
The **clinic.** Kellerman, J.
CLIPPER SHIPS *See* Sailing vessels
The **cloak** and the staff. Dickson, G. R.
In The Hugo winners p209-43
The **clock** winder. Tyler, A.
Clock without hands. McCullers, C.
In McCullers, C. Complete novels
Clockers. Price, R.
CLOCKS AND WATCHES
Kurzweil, A. The grand complication
A **clockwork** orange. Burgess, A.
CLONES *See* Asexual reproduction
CLONING
Sterling, B. The caryatids
Close combat. Griffin, W. E. B.
Close quarters. Golding, W.
Close range. Proulx, A.
Close relations. Isaacs, S.
A **close** run thing. Mallinson, A.
Close to the bone. Tapply, W. G.
The **closed** circle. Coe, J.
The **closers.** Connelly, M.
Closing time. Heller, J.
CLOTHING INDUSTRY
Laker, R. Banners of silk
Tax, M. Rivington Street
CLOTHING WORKERS *See* Clothing industry
Cloud atlas. Mitchell, D.
Cloud chamber. Dorris, M.
The **cloud** of unknowing. Cook, T. H.
The **cloud** sketcher. Rayner, R.
Clouds and eclipses. Vidal, G.
Clouds of witness. See Sayers, D. L. Clouds of witnesses
Clouds of witnesses. Sayers, D. L.
Cloudsplitter. Banks, R.
Clover. Sanders, D.
The **clown.** Böll, H.
CLOWNS
Böll, H. The clown
Høeg, P. The quiet girl
The **clowns** of God. West, M. L.
The **Club** Dumas. Pérez-Reverte, A.
CLUBS
Auchincloss, L. The book class
Dickens, C. The posthumous papers of the Pickwick Club
King, S. The breathing method
Santmyer, H. H. "—and ladies of the club"
Spark, M. The girls of slender means
Tan, A. The Joy Luck Club

CLUBS—*Continued*
  Wodehouse, P. G. Tales from the Drones Club
COACHING (ATHLETICS)
  Perrotta, T. The abstinence teacher
Coal black horse. Olmstead, R.
COAL MINERS *See* Coal mines and mining
COAL MINES AND MINING
  O'Dell, T. Coal Run
  O'Dell, T. Sister mine
  Pancake, A. Strange as this weather has been
England
  Smith, M. C. Rose
France
  Zola, É. Germinal
Wales
  Llewellyn, R. How green was my valley
Coal Run. O'Dell, T.
COAL TOWNS *See* Coal mines and mining
COAST GUARD (U.S.) *See* United States. Coast Guard
Coastliners. Harris, J.
COBBETT, WILLIAM, 1763-1835
About
  Safire, W. Scandalmonger
The **Cobra** event. Preston, R.
COCAINE
  See also Crack (Drug)
  McCann, C. Let the great world spin
  Pelecanos, G. P. The sweet forever
  Price, R. Clockers
COCKROACHES
  Lashner, W. Kockroach
COCKTAIL PARTIES *See* Parties
CODE DECIPHERING *See* Cryptography
Code of the West. Latham, A.
The **code** of the Woosters. Wodehouse, P. G.
Code sixty-one. Harstad, D.
Codes of betrayal. Uhnak, D.
The **codex.** Preston, D.
CODRINGTON, SIR HENRY JOHN, 1808-1877
About
  Donoghue, E. The sealed letter
CODY, WILLIAM FREDERICK *See* Buffalo Bill, 1846-1917
Coffee will make you black. Sinclair, A.
The **Coffin** Dancer. Deaver, J.
Coinspinner's story. See Saberhagen, F. The fifth book of lost
  swords: Coinspinner's story
Cold blood. La Plante, L.
Cold case. Barnes, L.
Cold company. Henry, S.
Cold Flat Junction. Grimes, M.
Cold Harbour. Higgins, J.
Cold heaven. Moore, B.
Cold in hand. Harvey, J.
Cold is the grave. Robinson, P.
Cold light. Harvey, J.
Cold Mountain. Frazier, C.
Cold paradise. Woods, S.
Cold pursuit. Parker, T. J.
A **cold** red sunrise. Kaminsky, S. M.
Cold Sassy tree. Burns, O. A.
Cold service. Parker, R. B.
The **cold** six thousand. Ellroy, J.
Cold Springs. Riordan, R.
The **coldest** blood. Kelly, J.
Coldheart Canyon. Barker, C.
COLLABORATIONISTS *See* World War, 1939-1945—Collab-
  orationists
Collected fictions. Borges, J. L.
Collected novellas. García Márquez, G.
Collected novels. Hawthorne, N.
The **collected** short fiction of C.J. Cherryh. Cherryh, C. J.
Collected short stories. Huxley, A.
The **collected** short stories. Rhys, J.
Collected stories. Carver, R.
Collected stories. Dahl, R.
Collected stories. García Márquez, G.
Collected stories. Greene, G.

Collected stories. Kafka, F.
Collected stories. Kipling, R.
Collected stories. Lawrence, D. H.
Collected stories. McCullers, C.
The **collected** stories. Michaels, L.
Collected stories. O'Connor, F.
The **collected** stories. Paley, G.
The **collected** stories. Price, R.
Collected stories. Rendell, R.
The **collected** stories. Theroux, P.
The **collected** stories. Thomas, D.
The **collected** stories. Trevor, W.
Collected stories. Williams, T.
Collected stories & later writings. Bowles, P.
Collected stories, 1891-1910. Wharton, E.
Collected stories, 1911-1937. Wharton, E.
Collected stories, 1948-1986. Morris, W.
Collected stories: A friend of Kafka to Passions. Singer, I. B.
Collected stories and other writings. Cheever, J.
Collected stories and other writings. Porter, K. A.
Collected stories: Gimpel the fool to The letter writer. Singer, I.
  B.
The **collected** stories of Amanda Cross. Cross, A.
The **collected** stories of Amy Hempel. Hempel, A.
The **collected** stories of André Maurois. Maurois, A.
The **collected** stories of Arthur C. Clarke. Clarke, A. C.
The **collected** stories of Chester Himes. Himes, C.
The **collected** stories of Colette. Colette
The **collected** stories of Eudora Welty. Welty, E.
The **collected** stories of Greg Bear. Bear, G.
The **collected** stories of Hortense Calisher. Calisher, H.
The **collected** stories of Jack Schaefer. Schaefer, J. W.
The **collected** stories of Jean Stafford. Stafford, J.
Collected stories of Jessamyn West. West, J.
Collected stories of John O'Hara. O'Hara, J.
The **collected** stories of Joseph Roth. Roth, J.
The **collected** stories of Katherine Anne Porter. Porter, K. A.
The **collected** stories of Lydia Davis. Davis, L.
The **collected** stories of Max Brand. Brand, M.
The **collected** stories of Noël Coward. Coward, N.
The **collected** stories of Philip K. Dick. Dick, P. K.
The **collected** stories of Richard Yates. Yates, R.
The **collected** stories of Robert Silverberg. Silverberg, R.
The **collected** stories of Seán O'Faoláin. O'Faoláin, S.
Collected stories of Wallace Stegner. Stegner, W. E.
Collected stories of William Faulkner. Faulkner, W.
Collected stories: One night in Brazil to The death of Methuse-
  lah. Singer, I. B.
Collected tales. De la Mare, W.
The **collected** tales and poems of Edgar Allan Poe. Poe, E. A.
The **collected** tales of E. M. Forster. Forster, E. M.
The **collected** tales of Nikolai Gogol. Gogol´, N. V.
Collected works. O'Connor, F.
COLLECTIVE SETTLEMENTS
  Carey, P. His illegal self
  Gardam, J. Faith Fox
  McPhee, M. Gorgeous lies
  Raymond, J. The half-life
  Sontag, S. In America
  Updike, J. S
  Varley, J. The persistence of vision
The **collector** of hearts. Oates, J. C.
COLLECTORS AND COLLECTING
  Chatwin, B. Utz
  Doctorow, E. L. Homer & Langley
  Domínguez, C. M. The house of paper
  Hornby, N. High fidelity
  Smith, Z. The autograph man
COLLEGE ALUMNI
  Jaffe, R. Class reunion
COLLEGE LIFE
  See also College students; School life; Students; Teachers
  Barth, J. Giles goat-boy
Canada
  Davies, R. The lyre of Orpheus
  Davies, R. The rebel angels
England
  Amis, K. Lucky Jim
  Lewis, C. S. That hideous strength
  Lodge, D. Nice work

COLLEGE LIFE—England—*Continued*
Lodge, D. Thinks—
Marías, J. All souls
Snow, C. P. The masters

France
McCarthy, M. Birds of America

Ireland
Binchy, M. Circle of friends

United States
Carter, S. L. New England white
Collins, M. Death of a writer
Fitzgerald, F. S. This side of paradise
Godwin, G. The good husband
Hassler, J. The dean's list
Hassler, J. Rookery blues
Hynes, J. The lecturer's tale
Jaffe, R. Class reunion
Lasdun, J. The horned man
Leebron, F. G. In the middle of all this
Lipman, E. My latest grievance
Maxwell, W. The folded leaf
McCarthy, M. The groves of Academe
Nabokov, V. V. Pnin
Nichols, J. T. The sterile cuckoo
Oates, J. C. Black girl/White girl
Perrotta, T. Joe College
Powers, R. Galatea 2.2
Prose, F. Blue angel
Reed, I. Japanese by spring
Roth, P. Indignation
Roth, P. Letting go
Russo, R. The straight man
Salinger, J. D. Franny & Zooey
Sarton, M. A small room
Shulman, M. The many loves of Dobie Gillis
Smiley, J. Moo
Smith, B. Joy in the morning
Tartt, D. The secret history
Theroux, A. Darconville's cat
Updike, J. Memories of the Ford Administration
Wolfe, T. Of time and the river

COLLEGE STUDENTS
See also College life
Auster, P. Invisible
Caldwell, I. The rule of four
Coll, S. Acceptance
Cooley, M. The archivist
Ferrell, M. The answer is always yes
Grossman, L. The magicians
Kay, G. G. The summer tree
Moore, L. A gate at the stairs
Nicholls, D. A question of attraction
Noel, K. Halfway house
Nunez, S. The last of her kind
Oates, J. C. Black girl/White girl
Roth, H. Requiem for Harlem
Sittenfeld, C. The man of my dreams
Stade, G. Love is war
Vida, V. And now you can go
Weber, K. The little women
Weinstein, D. Apprentice to the flower poet Z
Wolfe, T. I am Charlotte Simmons

COLLEGE TEACHERS *See* Teachers

COLLINS, WILKIE, 1824-1889
About
Simmons, D. Drood
The **colloquy** of the dogs. Cervantes Saavedra, M. d.
In Cervantes Saavedra, M. d. Three exemplary novels p125-217

COLLYER, HOMER, 1881-1947
About
Doctorow, E. L. Homer & Langley

COLLYER, LANGLEY, 1885-1947
About
Doctorow, E. L. Homer & Langley

COLOMBIA
García Márquez, G. The general and his labyrinth
Grippando, J. A king's ransom
Restrepo, L. Delirium

Rural life
García Márquez, G. Chronicle of a death foretold
García Márquez, G. Collected novellas
García Márquez, G. In evil hour
García Márquez, G. Leaf storm, and other stories
García Márquez, G. One hundred years of solitude

COLONIAL UNITED STATES *See* United States—To 1776
COLONIALISM *See* Imperialism
COLONIES

Great Britain
See Great Britain—Colonies

COLONIES, ARTIST *See* Artist colonies
The **colony** of unrequited dreams. Johnston, W.
The **color**. Tremain, R.
The **color** of a dog running away. Gwyn, R.
The **color** of lightning. Jiles, P.
The **color** of magic. Pratchett, T.
The **color** of night. Lindsey, D. L.
The **color** purple. Walker, A.

COLORADO
Borland, H. When the legends die
Carter, S. L. Jericho's fall
Cather, W. The song of the lark
Dallas, S. Tallgrass
Haruf, K. Eventide
Haruf, K. Plainsong
King, S. The shining
Kyle, A. The god of animals
McLarty, R. Art in America
Michener, J. A. Centennial
White, S. W. Dry ice
White, S. W. Missing persons
Whitney, P. A. Domino

19th century
Dallas, S. The diary of Mattie Spenser

Frontier and pioneer life
See Frontier and pioneer life—Colorado

Aspen
Ducker, B. Dizzying heights

Denver
Coel, M. Blood memory

COLUMBUS, CHRISTOPHER
About
Dorris, M. The crown of Columbus
Forester, C. S. To the Indies

COLUMBUS (OHIO) *See* Ohio—Columbus
COLUMNISTS *See* Journalists

COMA
Ma Jian. Beijing coma
Coma. Cook, R.

COMANCHE INDIANS
Kelton, E. Badger boy
Kelton, E. Slaughter
Kelton, E. The way of the coyote
McMurtry, L. Comanche moon
Comanche moon. McMurtry, L.
Come along with me. Jackson, S.
Come back to Sorrento. Powell, D.
In Powell, D. Novels, 1930-1942
Come Sunday. Morley, I.
Come twilight. Yarbro, C. Q.
Come with me to Babylon. Levitt, P. M.
Comeback. Stark, R.

COMEDIANS
Houellebecq, M. The possibility of an island
McCracken, E. Niagara Falls all over again
Ridley, J. A conversation with the Mann
Shreve, S. R. Plum & Jaggers
The **comedians**. Greene, G.

COMETS
Greer, A. S. The path of minor planets
Niven, L. Lucifer's hammer

COMFORT WOMEN
Lee, C.-R. A gesture life

The **comforters**. Spark, M.
  In Spark, M. A Muriel Spark trio p13-228
The **comforts** of a muddy Saturday. McCall Smith, A.

COMIC BOOKS, STRIPS, ETC.
  Chabon, M. The amazing adventures of Kavalier and Clay
  O'Connell, J. The resurrectionist
The **coming**. Haldeman, J. W.
Coming home. Pilcher, R.

COMING OF AGE STORIES *See* Adolescence; Youth

COMMANCHE INDIANS *See* Comanche Indians
The **command**. Poyer, D.

COMMERCIAL AERONAUTICS
  See also Air mail service
  Saint-Exupéry, A. d. Night flight

COMMERCIAL AVIATION *See* Commercial aeronautics
The **commissariat** of enlightenment. Kalfus, K.

COMMISSION FOR TRUTH AND RECONCILIATION
(SOUTH AFRICA) *See* South Africa. Commission for Truth
  and Reconciliation
The **commodore**. O'Brian, P.
Commodore Hornblower. Forester, C. S.
A **common** life. Karon, J.
The **commoner**. Schwartz, J. B.

COMMUNES *See* Collective settlements

COMMUNICATION
  Lem, S. Fiasco
  Pynchon, T. The crying of lot 49
Communion blood. Yarbro, C. Q.

COMMUNISM
  See also Totalitarianism
  Esterházy, P. Celestial harmonies
  Greene, G. Monsignor Quixote
  McEwan, I. Black dogs
  Shakespeare, N. Snowleg
  Vollmann, W. T. Europe central
  Wright, R. The outsider

China
  Ha Jin. The crazed
  Ha Jin. In the pond
  Ha Jin. Waiting
  Han, S. Till morning comes
  Lord, B. B. The middle heart
  Min, A. Becoming Madame Mao

Czechoslovakia
  Kundera, M. The joke

England
  Lessing, D. M. The golden notebook
  Snow, C. P. The conscience of the rich

Germany
  Higgins, J. Day of judgment

Russia
  Furnivall, K. The red scarf
  Koestler, A. Darkness at noon
  Littell, R. The Stalin epigram
  Makine, A. Music of a life
  Pasternak, B. L. Doctor Zhivago
  Rand, A. We the living
  Sholokhov, M. A. And quiet flows the Don
  Sholokhov, M. A. The Don flows home to the sea
  Solzhenitsyn, A. Cancer ward
  Wiesel, E. The testament

South Africa
  Lessing, D. M. Landlocked
  Lessing, D. M. A ripple from the storm

United States
  Doctorow, E. L. The book of Daniel
  Roth, P. I married a communist

Vietnam
  Greene, G. The quiet American

COMMUNISTS *See* Communism

COMPANIONS
  Marías, J. The man of feeling
  Quick, A. I thee wed

  Quick, A. The paid companion
Company. Barry, M.
The **company**. Littell, R.
The **company**. Parker, K. J.
Company man. Finder, J.
The **company** of women. Gordon, M.
The **company** you keep. Gordon, N.
Compelling evidence. Martini, S. P.

COMPETITION
  Coll, S. Acceptance
The **complete** Claudine. Colette
Complete collected stories. Pritchett, V. S.
The **complete** ghost stories of Charles Dickens. Dickens, C.
Complete novels. Hammett, D.
Complete novels. McCullers, C.
The **complete** novels. O'Brien, F.
Complete novels. Welty, E.
Complete novels and stories. Chopin, K.
The **complete** novels of Mark Twain. Twain, M.
The **complete** novels of Stephen Crane. Crane, S.
The **complete** Sherlock Holmes. Doyle, Sir A. C.
The **complete** short fiction of Joseph Conrad. Conrad, J.
Complete short novels. Chekhov, A. P.
Complete short stories. Graves, R.
Complete short stories. Maugham, W. S.
The **complete** short stories. Stevenson, R. L.
The **complete** short stories & sketches of Stephen Crane. Crane,
  S.
The **complete** short stories of Ambrose Bierce. Bierce, A.
The **complete** short stories of H. G. Wells. Wells, H. G.
The **complete** short stories of Jack London. London, J.
The **complete** short stories of Marcel Proust. Proust, M.
The **complete** short stories of Mark Twain. Twain, M.
Complete short stories of Nathaniel Hawthorne. Hawthorne, N.
The **complete** short stories of Robert Louis Stevenson. Steven-
  son, R. L.
The **complete** short stories of Thomas Wolfe. Wolfe, T.
The **complete** shorter fiction. Melville, H.
The **complete** shorter fiction. Trollope, A.
The **complete** shorter fiction of Virginia Woolf. Woolf, V.
The **complete** stories. Asimov, I.
The **complete** stories. Hurston, Z. N.
The **complete** stories. Kafka, F.
The **complete** stories. Malamud, B.
The **complete** stories. Malouf, D.
The **complete** stories. O'Connor, F.
Complete stories, 1864-1874. James, H.
Complete stories, 1874-1884. James, H.
Complete stories, 1884-1891. James, H.
Complete stories, 1892-1898. James, H.
Complete stories, 1898-1910. James, H.
Complete stories and poems of Edgar Allan Poe. Poe, E. A.
The **complete** stories of Evelyn Waugh. Waugh, E.
The **complete** stories of Truman Capote. Capote, T.
The **complete** tales and poems of Edgar Allan Poe. See Poe, E.
  A. The collected tales and poems of Edgar Allan Poe
The **complete** tales of Henry James. James, H.
The **complete** tales of Washington Irving. Irving, W.
The **complete** twenty thousand leagues under the sea. See Verne,
  J. Twenty thousand leagues under the sea
The **complete** Western stories of Elmore Leonard. Leonard, E.
The **complete** works of Isaac Babel. Babel´, I.
The **complete** works of O. Henry. Henry, O.
A **complicated** kindness. Toews, M.

COMPOSERS
  Frame, R. The lantern bearers
  Galloway, J. Clara
  Hesse, H. Gertrude
  Hijuelos, O. A simple Habana melody: from when the world
    was good
  Krüger, M. The cello player
  Mann, T. Doctor Faustus
  McEwan, I. Amsterdam
  Öe, K. A quiet life
  Piercy, M. Summer people
Compromising positions. Isaacs, S.
Compulsion. Ablow, K. R.
Compulsion. Levin, M.

COMPULSORY MILITARY SERVICE *See* Draft

COMPUTER GAMES
  Stross, C. Halting state

COMPUTER HACKERS

Gibson, W. Neuromancer
Larsson, S. The girl who played with fire
Larsson, S. The girl with the dragon tattoo
Stross, C. The Jennifer morgue

COMPUTER PROGRAMMING *See* Programming (Computers)

COMPUTER SIMULATION *See* Virtual reality

COMPUTERS

See also Programming (Computers)
Anderson, P. Goat song
Brunner, J. Stand on Zanzibar
Card, O. S. Earthfall
Costello, M. Big if
Crumey, A. Mr. Mee
Danvers, D. The fourth world
Darnton, J. Mind catcher
Heinlein, R. A. The moon is a harsh mistress
Iles, G. The footprints of God
Iles, G. Mortal fear
Kunzru, H. Transmission
Lustbader, E. V. Second skin
Nance, J. J. Medusa's child
Powers, R. The gold bug variations
Saul, J. Shadows
Stephenson, N. Cryptonomicon
Thomas, M. M. Black money
Trenhaile, J. The gates of exquisite view
Updike, J. Roger's version
Updike, J. Villages
Wilhelm, K. Death qualified
Wood, B. Perfect Harmony

COMSTOCK, ANTHONY, 1844-1915
About
Piercy, M. Sex wars

Con ed. Klein, M.

The **con** man's daughter. Dee, E.

CON MEN *See* Swindlers and swindling

CONCENTRATION CAMPS

See also Auschwitz (Poland: Concentration camp); Political prisoners; World War, 1939-1945—Prisoners and prisons
Iles, G. Black cross
Otsuka, J. When the emperor was divine
Styron, W. Sophie's choice

A **concise** Chinese-English dictionary for lovers. Guo Xiaolu

The **condition**. Haigh, J.

CONDUCT OF LIFE *See* Ethics

CONDUCTORS (MUSIC)

Ford, R. The student conductor

CONFEDERACY *See* Confederate States of America

A **confederacy** of dunces. Toole, J. K.

CONFEDERATE AGENTS *See* Spies

CONFEDERATE STATES OF AMERICA

Kantor, M. Andersonville
Wright, S. The Amalgamation Polka

CONFEDERATE STATES OF AMERICA. ARMY

Bahr, H. The Judas Field
Cornwell, B. Rebel
Shaara, J. Gods and generals
Shaara, J. The last full measure
Youmans, M. The wolf pit

Confess, Fletch. Mcdonald, G.

In Mcdonald, G. The Fletch chronicles

CONFESSION

Banville, J. The book of evidence

Confession. Pickard, N.

Confessional. Higgins, J.

Confessions of a Wall Street shoeshine boy. Stumpf, D.

Confessions of an ugly stepsister. Maguire, G.

The **confessions** of Edward Day. Martin, V.

Confessions of Felix Krull, confidence man. Mann, T.

The **confessions** of Nat Turner. Styron, W.

The **confessions** of Zeno. See Svevo, I. Zeno's conscience

The **confidence-man**: his masquerade. Melville, H.

also in Melville, H. Pierre; or, The ambiquities, Israel Potter: his fifty years of exile, The piazza tales, The confidence-man: his masquerade, Uncollected prose, Billy Budd, Sailor: (an inside narrative)

The **confidential** agent. Greene, G.

In Greene, G. 3: This gun for hire, The confidential agent, The ministry of fear

CONFLICT OF GENERATIONS

Cummins, A. Yellowcake
Cunningham, M. Flesh and blood
Jen, G. Mona in the promised land
Lee, C. Y. The flower drum song
Lurie, A. The war between the Tates
Meloy, M. Liars and saints
Read, P. P. The professor's daughter
Stegner, W. E. All the little live things
Thayer, N. Family secrets
Trollope, J. The men and the girls
Turgenev, I. S. Fathers and sons
Tyler, A. A slipping-down life
Vassanji, M. G. The assassin's song
West, D. The wedding
Wharton, W. Dad

CONFORMITY

See also Individualism
Berger, T. Neighbors
Høeg, P. Borderliners
Lewis, S. Babbitt
McCann, C. Zoli
McNicholl, D. A son called Gabriel
Trollope, J. The rector's wife
Wilson, S. The man in the gray flannel suit

CONGO (DEMOCRATIC REPUBLIC) *See* Zaire

The **conjugial** angel. Byatt, A. S.

In Byatt, A. S. Angels and insects

CONNECTICUT

Clark, M. H. Two little girls in blue
Hobson, L. K. Z. Gentleman's agreement
Hodgins, E. Mr. Blandings builds his dream house
Hoffman, A. Skylight confessions
Lawrence, S. The lightning keeper
O'Nan, S. Last night at the Lobster
O'Nan, S. The night country
Rice, L. Last kiss
Rice, L. Safe harbor
Schine, C. The love letter
Schwartz, J. B. Reservation Road
Shulman, M. Rally round the flag, boys!
Straub, P. The Hellfire Club
Tryon, T. The other
Updike, J. Villages
Westlake, D. E. The ax
Wittenborn, D. Pharmakon

19th century
Tryon, T. In the fire of spring
Tryon, T. The wings of the morning

Bridgeport
Howard, M. Natural history

Hartford
Pearson, R. Chain of evidence

New Haven
Mattison, A. The wedding of the two-headed woman
Perrotta, T. Joe College
Weber, K. The little women

A **Connecticut** Yankee in King Arthur's court. Twain, M.

also in Twain, M. Historical romances

CONRAD, JOSEPH, 1857-1924
About
Ozick, C. Dictation [novelette]

Cons, scams & grifts. Gores, J.

CONSCIENCE

See also Ethics; Guilt
Conrad, J. Lord Jim
Dostoyevsky, F. Crime and punishment
Hawthorne, N. The marble faun
Hawthorne, N. The scarlet letter
Wharton, E. The touchstone

The **conscience** of the rich. Snow, C. P.

CONSCIENTIOUS OBJECTORS

Barker, P. The eye in the door

Consequences. Lively, P.

CONSERVATION OF NATURE *See* Nature conservation

TITLE AND SUBJECT INDEX

The **conservationist**. Gordimer, N.

CONSERVATIONISTS

Cheever, J. Oh, what a paradise it seems
Consider this, señora. Doerr, H.
Consolation. Redhill, M.

CONSPIRACIES

Abrahams, P. Hard rain
Baldacci, D. The simple truth
Baldacci, D. Total control
Barbash, T. The last good chance
Carter, S. L. Palace council
Cook, R. Marker
Cook, R. Seizure
Cook, R. Vector
Costello, M. Big if
Crichton, M. Prey
Cussler, C. Fire ice
Cussler, C. Flood tide
Cussler, C. Plague ship
Cussler, C. Sahara
Cussler, C. White death
Danvers, D. The fourth world
Darnton, J. The experiment
DeLillo, D. Libra
DeMille, N. Wild fire
Due, T. Blood colony
Eco, U. Foucault's pendulum
Ellroy, J. The cold six thousand
Emerson, E. W. Vertical burn
Ferrigno, R. Prayers for the assassin
Fleming, T. J. When this cruel war is over
Folsom, A. R. The day after tomorrow
Folsom, A. R. Day of confession
Fraser, G. M. The reavers
Freely, M. Enlightenment
Freemantle, B. Dead men living
Greeley, A. M. Irish lace
Grippando, J. Found money
Hanif, M. A case of exploding mangoes
Harris, R. Fatherland
Harrison, C. The finder
Higgins, J. The eagle has flown
Higgins, J. The White House connection
Høeg, P. Smilla's sense of snow
Hospital, J. T. Due preparations for the plague
Hospital, J. T. Oyster
Hunter, S. Pale horse coming
Ignatius, D. A firing offense
Johansen, I. And then you die—
Johansen, I. The face of deception
Johnson, C. R. Dreamer
Koontz, D. R. Dark rivers of the heart
Koontz, D. R. Fear nothing
Kress, N. Dogs
Krist, G. Chaos theory
Le Carré, J. Absolute friends
Le Carré, J. The mission song
Le Carré, J. The tailor of Panama
Littell, R. The company
Ludlum, R. The apocalypse watch
Ludlum, R. The Aquitaine progression
Ludlum, R. The Holcroft covenant
Ludlum, R. The Prometheus deception
Ludlum, R. The Sigma protocol
Lustbader, E. V. Black Blade
Lynch, S. The lies of Locke Lamora
Martin, M. Windswept House
Marusek, D. Counting heads
Massie, A. Caesar
McAuley, P. J. White devils
McDonell, N. An expensive education
McGowan, N. The expected one
McNamer, D. Red rover
Meltzer, B. The book of lies
Meltzer, B. The first counsel
Moody, R. The Omega Force
Moore, B. The statement
Morgan, R. K. Broken angels
Niven, L. Saturn's race
Palmer, M. The fifth vial
Patterson, J. Four blind mice
Patterson, R. N. Eclipse
Pottinger, S. The fourth procedure

Poyer, D. Down to a sunless sea
Rabb, J. The book of Q
Redfern, E. Auriel rising
Reed, B. The indictment
Reich, C. Rules of deception
Ricks, T. E. A soldier's duty
Ruiz, L. M. Only one thing missing
Shelby, P. Days of drums
Sheldon, S. The doomsday conspiracy
Sheldon, S. Windmills of the gods
Siegel, J. Deceit
Silva, D. The mark of the assassin
Snyder, D. J. Night crossing
Stephenson, N. Cryptonomicon
Strieber, W. The Grays
Tanenbaum, R. Corruption of blood
Thomas, M. M. Black money
Vinge, V. Rainbows end
Walton, J. Farthing
Walton, J. Ha'penny
West, M. L. Masterclass
Wood, B. Perfect Harmony
Woods, S. Orchid Beach
Conspiracies. Wilson, F. P.
The **constant** gardener. Le Carré, J.
CONSTANTINOPLE See Turkey—Istanbul

CONSTRUCTION INDUSTRY

Clark, M. H. Before I say goodbye
Kelly, T. Empire rising
Ondaatje, M. In the skin of a lion
Trigiani, A. Big Cherry Holler
CONSULS See Diplomatic life
Consumption. Patterson, K.
Contact. Sagan, C.
Contagious. Sigler, S.

CONTENTMENT

See also Happiness

CONTESTS

Drayson, N. Guide to the birds of East Africa
Parkhurst, C. Lost and found
Contract null & void. Gores, J.
The **contract** surgeon. O'Brien, D.

CONVENT LIFE

See also Abbeys; Nuns
Godden, R. Black Narcissus
Gregory, P. The wise woman
Hansen, R. Mariette in ecstasy
Hulme, K. The nun's story
L'Engle, M. The love letters
Roberts, M. Reader, I married him
Spark, M. The Abbess of Crewe
Stewart, M. Thunder on the right
Westlake, D. E. Good behavior
A **conventional** corpse. Hess, J.
CONVENTS See Convent life
CONVENTS AND NUNNERIES See Convent life

CONVERSATION

Murdoch, I. A fairly honourable defeat
Segal, E. Love story
A **conversation** with the Mann. Ridley, J.

CONVERSION

Baldwin, J. Go tell it on the mountain
Cooley, M. The archivist
Galsworthy, J. Flowering wilderness
Conviction. Patterson, R. N.
CONVICTS See Crime and criminals; Ex-convicts; Prisoners and prisons
CONVICTS, ESCAPED See Escaped convicts

COOK, FREDERICK ALBERT, 1865-1940
About
Johnston, W. The navigator of New York

COOKERY

Esquivel, L. Like water for chocolate
Harris, J. Five quarters of the orange
Lanchester, J. The debt to pleasure
The **cooking** school murders. Rich, V.

COOKS

Ali, M. In the kitchen

COOKS—*Continued*

Desai, K. The inheritance of loss
Dovey, C. Blood kin
Faulkner, W. The sound and the fury
Glass, J. The whole world over
Hardwick, M. The Duchess of Duke Street
Howatch, S. The wonder-worker
Lipman, E. The Inn at Lake Devine
McCullers, C. The member of the wedding
Ólafur Jóhann Ólafsson. The journey home
Raymond, J. The half-life
Roberts, N. Angel's fall
Townsend, S. Adrian Mole
Truong, M. T. D. The book of salt
A **cool** million. West, N.
In West, N. Novels and other writings

COOPERATIVE SOCIETIES

Chute, C. The school on Heart's Content Road
Hawthorne, N. The Blithedale romance
The **Cooperman** variations. Engel, H.
COOPERSTOWN (N.Y.) *See* New York (State)—Cooperstown
Cop killer. Sjöwall, M.
Copy Kat. Kijewski, K.
Corelli's mandolin. De Bernières, L.
CORINTH (N.Y.) *See* New York (State)—Corinth
CORK (IRELAND: COUNTY) *See* Ireland—Cork (County)
CORNWALL (ENGLAND) *See* England—Cornwall
CORONERS

See also Medical examiners
Franklin, A. Mistress of the art of death
Franklin, A. The serpent's tale
CORPORATIONS *See* Business
CORPULENCE *See* Obesity
The **corrections**. Franzen, J.
Corridors of power. Snow, C. P.
CORRUPTION (IN POLITICS)

See also Bribery; Political ethics
Adams, H. Democracy
Atkins, A. Wicked city
Bolaño, R. The skating rink
Diehl, W. Reign in hell
Dovey, C. Blood kin
Ellis, D. Life sentence
Ellroy, J. American tabloid
Ellroy, J. The cold six thousand
Estleman, L. D. Gas City
Estleman, L. D. Port hazard
Goddard, R. Into the blue
Greeley, A. M. Irish lace
Grisham, J. The brethren
Grisham, J. The pelican brief
Hiaasen, C. Sick puppy
Hiaasen, C. Strip tease
Higgins, G. V. A change of gravity
Isegawa, M. Snakepit
Kadare, I. Spring flowers, spring frost
Kelly, T. Empire rising
Kennedy, W. Roscoe
Koontz, D. R. Dark rivers of the heart
Meltzer, B. The zero game
Moore, B. The statement
Oates, J. C. The falls
Parker, B. Blood relations
Parker, T. J. The fallen
Patterson, R. N. Dark lady
Patterson, R. N. Eyes of a child
Puzo, M. The godfather
Reed, B. The indictment
Rogers, R. Devil's Cape
Rosenberg, N. T. Abuse of power
Silva, D. The mark of the assassin
Tanenbaum, R. Corruption of blood
Tanenbaum, R. Falsely accused
Tanenbaum, R. Reversible error
Thomas, R. Ah, treachery!
Thomas, R. The fourth Durango
Turow, S. Presumed innocent
Twain, M. The gilded age
Vachss, A. H. Two trains running
Vassanji, M. G. The in-between world of Vikram Lall
Vidal, G. Hollywood

Vonnegut, K. Jailbird
Warren, R. P. All the king's men
Wells, K. Crawfish mountain
Wolfe, T. A man in full
Corruption of blood. Tanenbaum, R.
CORSAIRS *See* Pirates
CORTÉS, HERNÁN, 1485-1547
About
Falconer, C. Feathered serpent
Sherwood, F. Night of sorrows
COSA NOSTRA *See* Mafia
Cosmopolis. DeLillo, D.
COSSACKS

Pushkin, A. S. The captain's daughter
Sholokhov, M. A. And quiet flows the Don
Sholokhov, M. A. The Don flows home to the sea
Sienkiewicz, H. With fire and sword
Tolstoy, L., graf. The Cossacks
The **Cossacks**. Tolstoy, L., graf
In Tolstoy, L., graf. The short novels of Tolstoy
Cost. Robinson, R.
COSTUME PARTIES *See* Parties
Coswell's guide to Tambralinga. Landers, S.
COTSWOLDS (ENGLAND)

Lively, P. Passing on
Pilcher, R. The shell seekers
Cotton comes to Harlem. Himes, C.
The **Count** of Monte Cristo. Dumas, A.
COUNTER CULTURE

Abrahams, P. Hard rain
Gordon, N. The company you keep
Lazar, Z. Sway
Lessing, D. M. The good terrorist
Nunez, S. The last of her kind
Pynchon, T. Vineland
Robbins, T. Still life with Woodpecker
Swann, M. Flower children
COUNTER-REFORMATION *See* Reformation
COUNTERESPIONAGE *See* International intrigue; Spies
COUNTERFEITERS

Kerr, P. Dark matter
The **counterfeiters** (Les faux-monnayeurs). Gide, A.
The **counterlife**. Roth, P.
also in Roth, P. Novels and other narratives 1986-1991
Counting heads. Marusek, D.
The **country** doctor. Balzac, H. d.
The **country** girls. O'Brien, E.
In O'Brien, E. The country girls trilogy and epilogue p3-175
The **country** girls trilogy and epilogue. O'Brien, E.
COUNTRY LIFE

See also Farm life; Mountain life; Plantation life; Ranch life; Small town life
Allison, D. Bastard out of Carolina
Chute, C. The school on Heart's Content Road
Gloss, M. The hearts of horses
Pilcher, R. Winter solstice
Rhodes, D. Driftless
Taylor, M. G. The ballad of Trenchmouth Taggart
Wiggins, M. Evidence of things unseen
COUNTRY MUSIC

Hall, A. L. The rhythm of the road
Portis, C. Norwood
Smith, L. The devil's dream
Spencer, L. Small town girl
Westlake, D. E. Baby, would I lie?
A **country** of old men. Hansen, J.
Country of origin. Lee, D.
A **country** of our own. Poyer, D.
A **country** of strangers. Shreve, S. R.
The **country** of the pointed firs. Jewett, S. O.
also in Jewett, S. O. The best stories of Sarah Orne Jewett
also in Jewett, S. O. The country of the pointed firs and other stories p1-139
The **country** of the pointed firs and other stories. Jewett, S. O.
COUPS D'ÉTAT

Dovey, C. Blood kin
Forsyth, F. The dogs of war
Knebel, F. Seven days in May

COURAGE

See also Heroism

Forester, C. S. The last nine days of the Bismarck
Hemingway, E. The old man and the sea
Hersey, J. The wall
Nordhoff, C. Men against the sea
Saint-Exupéry, A. d. Night flight
Uris, L. Mila 18
The **courage** consort. Faber, M.
The **courage** consort [novelette] Faber, M.
  In Faber, M. The courage consort
COURT LIFE *See* Courts and courtiers
The **court-martial** of George Armstrong Custer. Jones, D. C.

COURTESANS

See also Prostitutes

Dumas, A. Camille
Dunant, S. In the company of the courtesan
Wilder, T. The woman of Andros
COURTROOM SCENES *See* Trials

COURTS AND COURTIERS

See also names of individual kings, queens, and rulers;
  also subdivision Kings and rulers under names of countries
Hope, A. The prisoner of Zenda
Tarr, J. Queen of swords

Denmark

Tremain, R. Music & silence
Updike, J. Gertrude and Claudius

Egypt

Smith, W. A. River god

England

Gregory, P. Earthly joys
Holt, V. My enemy the Queen
Koen, K. Dark angels
Mantel, H. Wolf Hall
Maxwell, R. The Queen's bastard
Maxwell, R. The secret diary of Anne Boleyn
Penman, S. K. Devil's brood
Penman, S. K. Falls the shadow
Penman, S. K. Here be dragons
Penman, S. K. The reckoning
Penman, S. K. The sunne in splendour
Penman, S. K. Time and chance
Penman, S. K. When Christ and his saints slept
Plaidy, J. The captive Queen of Scots
Plaidy, J. Murder most royal
Plaidy, J. The pleasures of love
Plaidy, J. William's wife
Riley, J. M. The serpent garden
Seton, A. Katherine
Weir, A. Innocent traitor
Weir, A. The Lady Elizabeth

France

Davis, K. Versailles
Dumas, A. The man in the iron mask [variant title: The iron mask]
Dumas, A. The three musketeers
Haasse, H. S. In a dark wood wandering
Laker, R. To dance with kings
Naslund, S. J. Abundance
Riley, J. M. The serpent garden

Italy

Sontag, S. The volcano lover
Stendhal. The charterhouse of Parma

Japan

Mishima, Y. Spring snow
Murasaki Shikibu. The tale of Genji

Scotland

Dunnett, D. Gemini

Turkey

Wallach, J. Seraglio

COURTS-MARTIAL

DeMille, N. Word of honor
Jones, D. C. The court-martial of George Armstrong Custer
Nordhoff, C. Mutiny on the Bounty
Poyer, D. The circle
The **courts** of chaos. Zelazny, R.

COURTSHIP

Colette. Claudine in Paris
Colette. Gigi
Colwin, L. Happy all the time
Gee, S. The scandal of the season
James, H. Daisy Miller
James, H. Washington Square
Purdy, J. In a shallow grave
Stowe, H. B. The minister's wooing
Cousin Bette. Balzac, H. d.

COUSINS

Balzac, H. d. Cousin Bette
Bradford, B. T. The Ravenscar dynasty
Chabon, M. The amazing adventures of Kavalier and Clay
Coe, J. The rain before it falls
Colwin, L. Happy all the time
Dew, R. F. The evidence against her
Egan, J. The keep
Faulkner, W. The mansion
Hamilton, J. When Madeline was young
Jakes, J. American dreams
James, H. The Europeans
McCorkle, J. Ferris Beach
McDermott, A. Child of my heart
Mitford, N. Love in a cold climate
Mitford, N. The pursuit of love
Morris, M. M. Fiona Range
Pearson, T. R. Blue Ridge
Robards, K. Ghost moon
Seton, A. Dragonwyck
Siddons, A. R. Nora, Nora
Stewart, M. The Gabriel hounds
Thomas, R. All my sins remembered
Walbert, K. The gardens of Kyoto
Weber, K. The Music Lesson
Yoshimoto, B. Goodbye Tsugumi
Yoshimoto, B. Night and night's travelers
The **covenant**. Michener, J. A.
Coventry. Humphreys, H.

COVINGTON, SYMS, 1813-1861
About
McDonald, R. Mr. Darwin's shooter

COWARDICE

Conrad, J. Lord Jim
Crane, S. The red badge of courage

COWBOYS

Clark, W. V. T. The Ox-bow incident
Durham, D. A. Gabriel's story
Evans, N. The horse whisperer
Houston, P. Cowboys are my weakness
Kittredge, W. The Willow Field
McCarthy, C. All the pretty horses
Schaefer, J. W. Monte Walsh
Cowboys are my weakness. Houston, P.
COWHANDS *See* Cowboys
COWS *See* Cattle
Coyote. Steele, A. M.
Coyote summer. Gear, W. M.
Coyote waits. Hillerman, T.

COYOTES

Kingsolver, B. Prodigal summer
Crabwalk. Grass, G.

CRACK (DRUG)

Burke, S. Black flies
Carcaterra, L. Apaches
The **cradle**. Somerville, P.
The **cradle** will fall. Clark, M. H.

CRANE, CORA HOWARTH STEWART TAYLOR, 1868-1910
About
White, E. Hotel de Dream

CRANE, STEPHEN, 1871-1900
About
White, E. Hotel de Dream
Cranford. Gaskell, E. C.
Crawfish mountain. Wells, K.
The **crazed**. Ha Jin

CRAZY HORSE, SIOUX CHIEF, CA. 1842-1877
About
    O'Brien, D. The contract surgeon
Crazy in Alabama. Childress, M.
Crazybone. Pronzini, B.

CREATION (LITERARY, ARTISTIC, ETC.)
    See also Authorship
    Ishiguro, K. The unconsoled
Creation. Vidal, G.
Creatures of the kingdom. Michener, J. A.
CREDIBILITY *See* Truthfulness and falsehood
A **creek** called Wounded Knee. Jones, D. C.
Creek Mary's blood. Brown, D. A.

CREOLES
    Hambly, B. Days of the dead
    Hambly, B. Dead water
    Hambly, B. A free man of color
    Hambly, B. Graveyard dust
    Hambly, B. Sold down the river
    Hambly, B. Die upon a kiss
    Hambly, B. Wet grave
    Tademy, L. Cane River
Crescent. Abu-Jaber, D.
Crescent City. Plain, B.
Crescent city kill. Smith, J.

CRETE
    Kazantzakis, N. Zorba the Greek
    Renault, M. The king must die
    Stewart, M. The moon-spinners

CRICKET
    Gunesekera, R. The match
    O'Neill, J. Netherland
The **cricket** on the hearth. Dickens, C.
    also in Dickens, C. A Charles Dickens Christmas p205-308

CRICKETS
    Dickens, C. The cricket on the hearth

CRIME AND CRIMINALS
    See also Arson; Atrocities; Bank robbers; Brigands and robbers; Child abuse; Counterfeiters; Escaped convicts; Extortion; Gangs; Gangsters; Hostages; Juvenile delinquency; Kidnapping; Mafia; Murder stories; Rape; Smuggling; Swindlers and swindling; Thieves; Underworld; War criminals; Wife abuse
Abani, C. GraceLand
Adams, L. Harbor
Atkins, A. White shadow
Atkins, A. Wicked city
Baldacci, D. Absolute power
Brandon, J. Arkansas
Breslin, J. The gang that couldn't shoot straight
Camus, A. The plague
Carcaterra, L. Apaches
Cheever, J. Falconer
Clark, M. H. The cradle will fall
Connelly, M. The brass verdict
Connelly, M. The Lincoln lawyer
Daley, R. Nowhere to run
Dee, E. The con man's daughter
Defoe, D. Moll Flanders
Dickens, C. Great expectations
Dickens, C. Oliver Twist
Dixon, K. The art of losing
Dostoyevsky, F. Crime and punishment
Dreiser, T. An American tragedy
Drury, T. The driftless area
Durham, M. The man who loved Cat Dancing
Ellroy, J. Because the night
Ellroy, J. Blood on the moon
Ellroy, J. L.A. confidential
Ellroy, J. L.A. noir
Ellroy, J. Suicide hill
Ellroy, J. White jazz
Estleman, L. D. Jitterbug
Faulkner, W. Intruder in the dust
Forsyth, F. The day of the jackal
Freeman, C. All that I have
George, E. What came before he shot her
Godey, J. The taking of Pelham one two three
Goodis, D. Down there
Goodis, D. Nightfall

Gores, J. Cons, scams & grifts
Gores, J. Contract null & void
Green, N. Shooting Dr. Jack
Greene, G. Brighton rock
Grisham, J. The brethren
Hage, R. De Niro's game
Hallinan, T. A nail through the heart
Hamill, P. Snow in August
Harrison, C. Afterburn
Harrison, C. The finder
Hayter, S. Bandit queen boogie
Hemingway, E. To have and have not
Hiaasen, C. Lucky you
Hiaasen, C. Native tongue
Hiaasen, C. Skin tight
Hiaasen, C. Skinny dip
Hiaasen, C. Stormy weather
Hiaasen, C. Strip tease
Higgins, G. V. At end of day
Higgins, G. V. Bomber's law
Higgins, G. V. The friends of Eddie Coyle
Highsmith, P. The boy who followed Ripley
Highsmith, P. Ripley under ground
Highsmith, P. Ripley's game
Highsmith, P. The talented Mr. Ripley
Highsmith, P. The talented Mr. Ripley; Ripley under ground; Ripley's game
Holden, C. The jazz bird
Hugo, V. Les misérables
Hunter, S. Black light
Hunter, S. Dirty white boys
Huston, C. Caught stealing
Huston, C. The mystic arts of erasing all signs of death
Isaacs, S. Lily White
James, P. D. Innocent blood
Johnson, D. Nobody move
Katkov, N. Blood & orchids
Katzenbach, J. Just cause
Keating, H. R. F. The bad detective
King, S. Blaze
Klein, M. Con ed
Krist, G. Chaos theory
Latour, J. The Havana World Series
Leiber, F. Ill met in Lankhmar
Leonard, E. Be cool
Leonard, E. Freaky Deaky
Leonard, E. Get Shorty
Leonard, E. The hot kid
Leonard, E. Killshot
Leonard, E. Maximum Bob
Leonard, E. Mr. Majestyk
Leonard, E. Mr. Paradise
Leonard, E. Out of sight
Leonard, E. Pagan babies
Leonard, E. Pronto
Leonard, E. Riding the rap
Leonard, E. Road dogs
Leonard, E. Rum punch
Leonard, E. Split images
Leonard, E. Stick
Leonard, E. Tishomingo blues
Levin, M. Compulsion
Lindsey, D. L. The rules of silence
Livesey, M. Criminals
Ludlum, R. The Matlock paper
Lustbader, E. V. Dark homecoming
Mailer, N. The executioner's song
Marinick, R. Boyos
Marks, J. Fangland
Mason, D. A far country
Mayle, P. Anything considered
Mayle, P. Hotel Pastis
McEwan, I. Saturday
Monaghan, N. The killing jar
Oates, J. C. Rape
Parker, B. Criminal justice
Parker, T. J. L.A. outlaws
Patterson, J. Along came a spider
Pelecanos, G. P. The big blowdown
Pelecanos, G. P. Drama city
Pelecanos, G. P. Shame the devil
Pelecanos, G. P. The sweet forever
Pelecanos, G. P. The turnaround
Perry, T. Blood money

Cry of the wind. Harrison, S.
Cry, the beloved country. Paton, A.
The **crying** of lot 49. Pynchon, T.

CRYPTOGRAPHY

Brown, D. The Da Vinci code
Harris, R. Enigma
Stephenson, N. Cryptonomicon
Cryptonomicon. Stephenson, N.
The **crystal** cave. Stewart, M.
    In Stewart, M. Mary Stewart's Merlin trilogy
The **crystal** frontier. Fuentes, C.
Crystal line. McCaffrey, A.
Crystal singer. McCaffrey, A.

CUBA

Block, L. Killing Castro
García, C. The Aguero sisters
García, C. Monkey hunting
Hemingway, E. Islands in the stream
Hemingway, E. To have and have not
Hijuelos, O. A simple Habana melody: from when the world
    was good
Kushner, R. Telex from Cuba

Havana

García, C. Dreaming in Cuba
Greene, G. Our man in Havana
Hemingway, E. The old man and the sea
Hunter, S. Havana
Latour, J. The Havana World Series
Montero, M. Dancing to "Almendra"
Sanchez, T. King Bongo

CUBAN AMERICANS

Deford, F. The entitled
García, C. A handbook to luck
García, C. Monkey hunting
Hijuelos, O. Empress of the splendid season
Hijuelos, O. The fourteen sisters of Emilio Montez O'Brien
Mestre-Reed, E. The second death of Única Aveyano
Parker, B. Suspicion of deceit

CUBAN MISSILE CRISIS, OCT. 1962

Crowley, J. The translator

CUBAN REFUGEES

Bell, C. The Perez family

CUBANS

Africa

Smith, W. A. Golden fox

England

Oyeyemi, H. The opposite house

France

Hijuelos, O. A simple Habana melody: from when the world
    was good

United States

Atkins, A. White shadow
Bell, C. The Perez family
García, C. The Aguero sisters
García, C. Dreaming in Cuba
Hijuelos, O. The Mambo Kings play songs of love
Rosales, G. The halfway house

CUCHULAIN (LEGENDARY CHARACTER)

Llywelyn, M. Red Branch
Cujo. King, S.

CULTS

Atwood, M. The year of the flood
Cussler, C. Plague ship
DeLillo, D. The names
Goodman, C. The night villa
Hooper, K. Blood sins
Hospital, J. T. Oyster
Houellebecq, M. The possibility of an island
Jhabvala, R. P. Shards of memory
King, L. R. A darker place
Koontz, D. R. One door away from heaven
LaValle, V. D. Big machine
McGowan, K. The expected one
Õe, K. An echo of heaven

Õe, K. Somersault
Prose, F. Hunters and gatherers
Rabb, J. The book of Q
Sidor, S. The mirror's edge
Tirone Smith, M.-A. Love her madly
Walker, M. W. Under the beetle's cellar
Wilson, R. C. Spin
Woods, S. Heat

CULTURE CONFLICT

    See also East and West

Achebe, C. Things fall apart
Alvarez, J. How the García girls lost their accents
Condé, M. I, Tituba, black witch of Salem
De Bernières, L. Birds without wings
Doerr, H. Consider this, señora
Doerr, H. Stones for Ibarra
D'Souza, T. The Konkans
Erdrich, L. Love medicine
Erdrich, L. Tracks
García, C. Dreaming in Cuban
Gordimer, N. The pickup
Grenville, K. The secret river
Guo Xiaolu. A concise Chinese-English dictionary for lovers
Han, S. Till morning comes
Ishiguro, K. An artist of the floating world
Jen, G. Mona in the promised land
Jennings, G. Aztec
Johnson, D. Le divorce
Kingsolver, B. Pigs in heaven
Lahiri, J. The namesake
Lee, C. Y. The flower drum song
Lee, D. Country of origin
Lee, G. China boy
Malouf, D. Remembering Babylon
Michael, J. A certain smile
Michener, J. A. Caribbean
Momaday, N. S. House made of dawn
Moore, B. Black robe
Naipaul, V. S. A way in the world
Ng, F. M. Bone
Nunez, E. Anna in-between
Patterson, K. Consumption
Phillips, A. Prague
Power, S. The grass dancer
Richter, C. The light in the forest
Rosenberg, R. This is not civilization
Shafak, E. The bastard of Istanbul
Silko, L. Gardens in the dunes
Sundaresan, I. The splendor of silence
Tan, A. The Joy Luck Club
Theroux, P. Monkey Hill
Thom, J. A. The red heart
Tyler, A. Digging to America
Updike, J. Terrorist
Wharton, E. Madame de Treymes

CULTURE CONTACT *See* Acculturation
The **cunning** man. Davies, R.

CURIE, MARIA SKLODOWSKA *See* Curie, Marie, 1867-1934

CURIE, MARIE, 1867-1934
About

Enquist, P. O. The book about Blanche and Marie
The **curious** incident of the dog in the night-time. Haddon, M.
The **curse** of the appropriate man. Freed, L.
Curse of the Spellmans. Lutz, L.

CURSES

Díaz, J. The brief wondrous life of Oscar Wao
King, S. Thinner
Robbins, T. Fierce invalids home from hot climates

CURSES, FAMILY *See* Family curses
Curtain. Christie, A.
Curtain. Korda, M.

CURTIS, EDWARD S., 1868-1952
About

Wiggins, M. The shadow catcher
The **curve** of the world. Stevens, M.

CUSTER, GEORGE ARMSTRONG, 1839-1876
About

Jones, D. C. The court-martial of George Armstrong Custer
The **custodian** of paradise. Johnston, W.

CUSTODY OF CHILDREN

Martini, S. P. The attorney

Dark matter. Kerr, P.
Dark places. Flynn, G.
Dark rivers of the heart. Koontz, D. R.
The **dark** room. Narayan, R. K.
In Narayan, R. K. Swami and friends, The bachelor of arts, The dark room, The English teacher
The **dark** room. Walters, M.
Dark Rosaleen. Brand, M.
In Brand, M. Max Brand's best western stories
The **dark** tower and other stories. Lewis, C. S.
Dark voyage. Furst, A.
The **dark** wind. Hillerman, T.
also in Hillerman, T. The Jim Chee mysteries
A **darker** place. King, L. R.
The **darkest** evening of the year. Koontz, D. R.
Darkest fear. Coben, H.
Darkly dreaming Dexter. Lindsay, J. P.
Darkmans. Barker, N.
Darkness. Saul, J.
Darkness and light. Harvey, J.
Darkness at noon. Koestler, A.
Darkness falls. Murphy, M.
A **darkness** more than night. Connelly, M.
Darkness visible. Golding, W.
Darkside. Deutermann, P. T.
The **dart** league king. Morris, K. L.

DARTS PLAYERS
Morris, K. L. The dart league king

DARWIN, CHARLES, 1809-1882
About
McDonald, R. Mr. Darwin's shooter
Darwin's wink. Anderson, A.

DATING (SOCIAL CUSTOMS)
Clark, M. H. Loves music, loves to dance
Crusie, J. Bet me
Tropper, J. How to talk to a widower
Daughter of fortune. Allende, I.
Daughter of the forest. Marillier, J.
The **daughter** of time. Tey, J.
also in Tey, J. Four, five and six by Tey

DAUGHTERS See Fathers and daughters; Mothers and daughters; Stepdaughters
The **daughters** of Cain. Dexter, C.
Daughters of the new world. Shreve, S. R.

DAVID, KING OF ISRAEL
About
Edghill, I. Queenmaker
L'Engle, M. Certain women
David Copperfield. Dickens, C.

DAVID KALAKAUA, KING OF HAWAII See Kalakaua, David, King of Hawaii, 1836-1891
Dawn. Butler, O. E.
Dawn. Wiesel, E.
also in Wiesel, E. Night, Dawn, The accident: three tales
Dawn of empire. Barone, S.
The **Dawn** Patrol. Winslow, D.
The **Dawson** pedigree. Sayers, D. L.
The **day** after tomorrow. Folsom, A. R.
A **day** late and a dollar short. McMillan, T.
A **day** no pigs would die. Peck, R. N.
Day of atonement. Kellerman, F.
Day of confession. Folsom, A. R.
The **day** of creation. Ballard, J. G.
Day of judgment. Higgins, J.
Day of reckoning. Higgins, J.
The **day** of the jackal. Forsyth, F.
The **day** of the locust. West, N.
In West, N. Miss Lonelyhearts & The day of the locust
In West, N. Novels and other writings
The **day** of the scorpion. Scott, P.
also in Scott, P. The Raj quartet
The **day** the rabbi resigned. Kemelman, H.
The **daybreakers.** L'Amour, L.
In L'Amour, L. The Sacketts: beginnings of a dynasty
Daylight. Knox, E.
Days of drums. Shelby, P.
Days of hope. See Malraux, A. Man's hope
Days of the dead. Hambly, B.

DE BRÉBEUF, JEAN See Brébeuf, Jean de, Saint, 1593-1649

DEACONS
Chekhov, A. P. The duel

DEAD
See also Funeral rites and ceremonies
Dorst, D. Alive in Necropolis
James, H. The beast in the jungle
King, S. The dark half
King, S. Pet sematary
Moloney, S. The dwelling
Reynolds, S. A gracious plenty
Stross, C. The Jennifer morgue
Dead and gone. Simpson, D.
Dead and gone. Vachss, A. H.
Dead as a dodo. Langton, J.
Dead by morning. Simpson, D.
Dead center. Wilcox, C.
Dead crazy. Pickard, N.
Dead end. See Harrod-Eagles, C. Grave music
Dead even. Meltzer, B.
Dead eyes. Woods, S.
The **dead** fathers club. Haig, M.
The **dead** fish museum. D'Ambrosio, C., Jr.
The **dead** hour. Mina, D.
Dead in the water. Woods, S.
Dead languages. Shields, D.
The **dead** man's brother. Zelazny, R.
Dead man's ransom. Peters, E.
Dead man's walk. McMurtry, L.
Dead meat. Tapply, W. G.
Dead men living. Freemantle, B.
Dead midnight. Muller, M.
Dead north. Henry, S.
The **dead** of winter. Gosling, P.
Dead ringer. Scottoline, L.
The **dead** sit round in a ring. Lawrence, D.
Dead souls. Gogol', N. V.
Dead souls. Rankin, I.
Dead to rights. Jance, J. A.
Dead water. Hambly, B.
Dead water. Marsh, Dame N.
Dead winter. Tapply, W. G.
The **dead** zone. King, S.
Deadeye Dick. Vonnegut, K.
Deadly décisions. Reichs, K. J.
Deadly rich. Stewart, E.
A **deadly** shade of gold. MacDonald, J. D.
Deadwood. Dexter, P.

DEAF
Greenberg, J. In this sign
Itani, F. Deafening
Lodge, D. Deaf sentence
McCullers, C. The heart is a lonely hunter
Seth, V. An equal music
Deaf sentence. Lodge, D.
Deafening. Itani, F.

DEAFNESS See Deaf
Deal on ice. Standiford, L.
Deal with the dead. Standiford, L.
Dealings with the firm of Dombey and Son. See Dickens, C. Dombey and Son

DEANS (CATHEDRAL AND COLLEGIATE) See Anglican and Episcopal clergy
The **dean's** list. Hassler, J.
Dear American Airlines. Miles, J.
Dear and glorious physician. Caldwell, T.
Dear husband. Oates, J. C.
Dear John. Sparks, N.
The **dearly** departed. Lipman, E.
Dearly devoted Dexter. Lindsay, J. P.

DEATH
See also Bereavement; Dead; Deathbed scenes
Agee, J. A death in the family
Banks, R. The sweet hereafter
Bausch, R. Peace
Betts, D. Souls raised from the dead
Brockmeier, K. The brief history of the dead
Cather, W. Lucy Gayheart
Coetzee, J. M. Age of iron
Crace, J. Being dead
Davies, R. The cunning man
DeLillo, D. White noise
Duncan, G. Death of an ordinary man
Garner, H. The spare room
Gatewood, R. The sound of the trees
Glass, J. Three Junes

TITLE AND SUBJECT INDEX

DETECTIVES—*Continued*

Leaphorn, Lieutenant Joe. See stories by Hillerman, T.
Lennox, Charles. See stories by Finch, C.
Lieberman, Abe. See stories by Kaminsky, S. M.
Lieberman, Max. See stories by Tallis, F.
Lightfoot, Marie. See stories by Pickard, N.
Linton, Sara. See stories by Slaughter, K.
Little, Bernie. See stories by Abrahams, P.
Liu Hulan. See stories by See, L.
Lloyd, Chief Inspector. See stories by McGown, J.
Longmire, Walt. See stories by Johnson, C.
Lovejoy. See stories by Gash, J.
Loy, Ed. See stories by Hughes, D.
Lynley, Thomas. See stories by George, E.
MacAlister, Marti. See stories by Bland, E. T.
Macbeth, Hamish. See stories by Beaton, M. C.
MacPherson, Elizabeth. See stories by McCrumb, S.
Maigret, Chief Inspector. See stories by Simenon, G.
Maitland, Antony. See stories by Woods, S.
Mallory, Kathleen. See stories by O'Connell, C.
Malloy, Claire. See stories by Hess, J.
Mancuso, Dante. See stories by Stansberry, D.
Manfredi, Egidio. See stories by McInerny, R. M.
March, John. See stories by Spiegelman, P.
Marlowe, Philip. See stories by Chandler, R.
Marlowe, Philip. See stories by Parker, R. B.
Marple, Miss Jane. See stories by Christie, A.
Marsala, Cat. See stories by D'Amato, B.
McCain, Sam. See stories by Gorman, E.
McCone, Sharon. See stories by Muller, M.
McGarr, Chief Inspector Peter. See stories by Gill, B.
McGee, Travis. See stories by MacDonald, J. D.
McGill, Leonid. See stories by Mosley, W.
McKee, Bergen. See stories by Hillerman, T.
McLeish, Chief Inspector John. See stories by Neel, J.
McNally, Archy. See stories by Sanders, L.
McRae, Detective Sergeant Logan. See stories by MacBride, S.
Meehan, Paddy. See stories by Mina, D.
Meiklejohn, Charlie. See stories by Wilhelm, K.
Mendoza, Lieutenant Luis. See stories by Shannon, D.
Meren, Lord. See stories by Robinson, L. S.
Millhone, Kinsey. See stories by Grafton, S.
Milodragovitch, Milo. See stories by Crumley, J.
Mingus, Max. See stories by Stone, N.
Minton, Paris. See stories by Mosley, W.
Molloy, Claire. See stories by Hess, J.
Monaghan, Tess. See stories by Lippman, L.
Monk, Inspector William. See stories by Perry, A.
Montero, Britt. See stories by Buchanan, E.
Moodrow, Stanley. See stories by Solomita, S.
Moon, Charlie. See stories by Doss, J. D.
Morse, Inspector. See stories by Dexter, C.
Mulcahaney, Lieutenant Norah. See stories by O'Donnell, L.
Mulheisen, Fang. See stories by Jackson, J. A.
Nudger, Alo. See stories by Lutz, J.
Oliver, Gideon. See stories by Elkins, A. J.
O'Malley, Father John. See stories by Coel, M.
Otani, Superintendent Tetsuo. See stories by Melville, J.
Page, Lorraine. See stories by La Plante, L.
Pamplemousse, Monsieur. See stories by Bond, M.
Pargeter, Mrs. Melita. See stories by Brett, S.
Paris, Charles. See stories by Brett, S.
Parker, Charlie. See stories by Connolly, J.
Pascoe, Inspector. See stories by Hill, R.
Peabody, Amelia. See stories by Peters, E.
Peace, Charlie. See stories by Barnard, R.
Pepper, Amanda. See stories by Roberts, G.
Perry, Lincoln. See stories by Koryta, M.
Peters, Sergeant Joe. See stories by Uhnak, D.
Peters, Toby. See stories by Kaminsky, S. M.
Petrovich, Porfiry. See stories by Morris, R. N.
Pickett, Joe. See stories by Box, C. J.
Pigeon, Anna. See stories by Barr, N.
Pike, Joe. See stories by Crais, R.
Pine, Leonard. See stories by Lansdale, J. R.
Pitt, Inspector. See stories by Perry, A.
Pitt, Joe. See stories by Huston, C.
Pliny, the Younger. See stories by Bell, A. A.
Plum, Stephanie. See stories by Evanovich, J.
Poirot, Hercule. See stories by Christie, A.
Pollifax, Mrs. Emily. See stories by Gilman, D.
Portal, Ellis. See stories by Aubert, R.
Potter, Eugenia. See stories by Pickard, N.

Potter, Eugenia. See stories by Rich, V.
Queen, Ellery. See stories by Queen, E.
Queen, Inspector Richard. See stories by Queen, E.
Quinn, Terry. See stories by Pelecanos, G. P.
Quirke, Garret. See stories by Banville, J.
Qwilleran, Jim. See stories by Braun, L. J.
Raisin, Agatha. See stories by Beaton, M. C.
Ramadge, Gwenn. See stories by O'Donnell, L.
Ramotswe, Precious. See stories by McCall Smith, A.
Randall, Sunny. See stories by Parker, R. B.
Rane, Harry. See stories by Stroby, W.
Rawlins, Easy. See stories by Mosley, W.
Reacher, Jack. See stories by Child, L.
Rebus, Inspector. See stories by Rankin, I.
Reilly, Regan. See stories by Clark, C. H.
Renko, Arkady. See stories by Smith, M. C.
Repairman Jack. See stories by Wilson, F. P.
Resnick, Inspector Charlie. See stories by Harvey, J.
Reynolds, Ali. See stories by Jance, J. A.
Rheinhardt, Oskar. See stories by Tallis, F.
Rhodenbarr, Bernie. See stories by Block, L.
Rhyme, Lincoln. See stories by Deaver, J.
Robicheaux, Dave. See stories by Burke, J. L.
Roosevelt, Eleanor. See stories by Roosevelt, E.
Rostnikov, Inspector Porfiry. See stories by Kaminsky, S. M.
Ruso, Gaius Petreius. See stories by Downie, R.
Russell, Mary. See stories by King, L. R.
Ruzak, Teddy. See stories by Yancey, R.
Ryan, Blackie. See stories by Greeley, A. M.
Salter, Inspector Charlie. See stories by Wright, E.
Schulz, Goldy. See stories by Davidson, D. M.
Scudder, Matthew. See stories by Block, L.
Seddon, Carole. See stories by Brett, S.
Self, Gerhard. See stories by Schlink, B.
Serrailler, Detective Chief Inspector Simon. See stories by Hill, S.
Sewell, Hitchcock. See stories by Cockey, T.
Shandy, Peter. See stories by MacLeod, C.
Shimura, Rei. See stories by Massey, S.
Shugak, Kate. See stories by Stabenow, D.
Sixsmith, Joe. See stories by Hill, R.
Slider, Inspector Bill. See stories by Harrod-Eagles, C.
Small, Rabbi David. See stories by Kemelman, H.
Smith, Bill. See stories by Rozan, S. J.
Smith, Mac. See stories by Truman, M.
Spade, Sam. See stories by Hammett, D.
Spenser. See stories by Parker, R. B.
Stone, Jesse. See stories by Parker, R. B.
Strange, Derek. See stories by Pelecanos, G. P.
Stride, Jonathan. See stories by Freeman, B.
Sughrue, C. W. See stories by Crumley, J.
Tacitus, Cornelius. See stories by Bell, A. A.
Tanner, Bay. See stories by Wall, K. R.
Tanner, John Marshall. See stories by Greenleaf, S.
Taylor, Jack. See stories by Bruen, K.
Thanet, Detective Inspector Luke. See stories by Simpson, D.
Thatcher, John Putnam. See stories by Lathen, E.
Thorn. See stories by Hall, J. W.
Tibbs, Virgil. See stories by Ball, J. D.
Tolliver, Jeffrey. See stories by Slaughter, K.
Tryon, Glynis. See stories by Monfredo, M. G.
Turner, John. See stories by Sallis, J.
Valentino. See stories by Estleman, L. D.
Van Alstyne, Russ. See stories by Spencer-Fleming, J.
Van der Valk, Inspector. See stories by Freeling, N.
Walker, Amos. See stories by Estleman, L. D.
Wallander, Kurt. See stories by Mankell, H.
Warshawski, V. I. See stories by Paretsky, S.
Weaver, Benjamin. See stories by Liss, D.
Weggins, Bailey. See stories by White, K.
Wexford, Chief Inspector. See stories by Rendell, R.
White, Blanche. See stories by Neely, B.
Wimsey, Lord Peter. See stories by Sayers, D. L.
Wolfe, Nero. See stories by Goldsborough, R.
Wolfe, Nero. See stories by Stout, R.
Zen, Aurelio. See stories by Dibdin, M.
Zondi, Detective Sergeant Mickey. See stories by McClure, J.

DETECTIVES, PRIVATE

Adler, E. All or nothing
Barnes, J. The somnambulist
Berry, J. The manual of detection
Collins, M. A. Black hats
Cunningham, E. Shadows in the starlight

DICTATORS

See also Fascism; Totalitarianism

García Márquez, G. The autumn of the patriarch
Greene, G. The comedians
Kadare, I. Agamemnon's daughter [novella]
Keneally, T. The tyrant's novel
Lewis, S. It can't happen here
Orwell, G. Animal farm
Steinbeck, J. The moon is down
Vargas Llosa, M. The Feast of the Goat

DICTATORSHIP *See* Dictators

DIDEROT, DENIS, 1713-1784
About
Bradbury, M. To the Hermitage

DIETING *See* Reducing

Different seasons. King, S.

Digging to America. Tyler, A.

DINAH (BIBLICAL FIGURE)
Fiction
Diamant, A. The red tent

Dinner at the Homesick Restaurant. Tyler, A.

DINNER PARTIES *See* Dinners

DINNERS

Bernhard, T. Woodcutters
The **Dinosaur** Club. Heffernan, W.

DINOSAURS

Crichton, M. Jurassic Park
Doyle, Sir A. C. The lost world
Foster, A. D. Dinotopia lost
Preston, D. Tyrannosaur Canyon
Swanwick, M. Bones of the earth
Dinotopia lost. Foster, A. D.

DIPLOMATIC LIFE

Durrell, L. Mountolive
Faulks, S. On Green Dolphin Street
Greene, G. The honorary consul
Le Carré, J. The constant gardener
Michener, J. A. Caravans
Rushdie, S. Shalimar the clown
Sheldon, S. Windmills of the gods
Sontag, S. The volcano lover
Wouk, H. The winds of war

DIPLOMATS *See* Diplomatic life

DIRECTORS, MOTION PICTURE *See* Motion picture producers and directors

Dirt. Woods, S.

Dirt music. Winton, T.

The **dirty** dozen. Nathanson, E. M.

The **Dirty** Duck. Grimes, M.

Dirty girls on top. Valdes-Rodriguez, A.

A **dirty** job. Moore, C.

Dirty money. Stark, R.

The **Dirty** Secrets Club. Gardiner, M.

Dirty white boys. Hunter, S.

Dirty work. Woods, S.

DISAPPEARANCES *See* Missing persons

Disappearing acts. McMillan, T.

DISASTERS

See also Earthquakes; Epidemics; Famines; Floods; Industrial accidents; Shipwrecks and castaways
Leiber, F. The Wanderer
Lessing, D. M. The memoirs of a survivor
MacNeil, R. Burden of desire

DISC JOCKEYS

Beatty, P. Slumberland

DISEASES

See also AIDS (Disease); Alzheimer's disease; Sexually transmitted diseases; Tuberculosis
Brown, C. B. Arthur Mervyn
Cussler, C. Sahara
Huyler, F. The laws of invisible things
Koontz, D. R. Fear nothing
Marks, J. Fangland
Palahniuk, C. Rant
Shreve, S. R. The visiting physician
Disgrace. Coetzee, J. M.

DISGUISES *See* Impersonations

DISNEY WORLD (FLA.) *See* Walt Disney World (Fla.)

DISNEYWORLD (FLA.) *See* Walt Disney World (Fla.)

Disobedience. Hamilton, J.

A **disorder** peculiar to the country. Kalfus, K.

DISORDERS OF PERSONALITY *See* Personality disorders

The **dispossessed**. Le Guin, U. K.

DISSENTERS

Holland, T. The archivist's story
The **dissident**. Freudenberger, N.

DISSIDENTS *See* Dissenters

The **distant** echo. McDermid, V.

A **distant** shore. Phillips, C.

Distant star. Bolaño, R.

DISTILLERIES

Barton, E. Brookland

DISTILLING, ILLICIT *See* Moonshiners

The **distinguished** guest. Miller, S.

DISTRICT OF COLUMBIA *See* Washington (D.C.)

Disturbances in the field. Schwartz, L. S.

The **dive** from Clausen's pier. Packer, A.

Divine and human and other stories. Tolstoy, L., graf

The **divine** invasion. Dick, P. K.

In Dick, P. K. VALIS and later novels

Divine justice. Baldacci, D.

A **diving** rock on the Hudson. Roth, H.

Divining women. Gibbons, K.

A **division** of the spoils. Scott, P.

also in Scott, P. The Raj quartet

DIVORCE

See also Divorced persons; Marriage problems
Banks, R. Affliction
Donoghue, E. The sealed letter
Galsworthy, J. In chancery
Galsworthy, J. Over the river
Godden, R. The battle of the Villa Fiorita
Haigh, J. The condition
Howells, W. D. A modern instance
Isaacs, S. Close relations
Johnson, D. Le divorce
Kalfus, K. A disorder peculiar to the country
King, T. Survivor
Meloy, M. A family daughter
Michaels, B. Shattered silk
Miller, S. The distinguished guest
Miller, S. The good mother
O'Nan, S. Snow angels
Robinson, R. Cost
Trollope, J. Other people's children
Tyler, A. The amateur marriage
Wakefield, D. Starting over
Wharton, E. The custom of the country
Le **divorce**. Johnson, D.

DIVORCED PERSONS

Barthelme, F. Waveland
Beattie, A. Picturing Will
Betts, D. Souls raised from the dead
Carlson, R. The signal
DeLillo, D. Falling man
DeMille, N. The gate house
Ferrante, E. The lost daughter
Ford, R. Independence Day
Ford, R. The lay of the land
Goldsmith, O. The First Wives Club
Grenville, K. The idea of perfection
Grøndahl, J. C. Lucca
Harrison, J. The English major
Hart, J. The reconstructionist
Hearon, S. Year of the dog
Hiaasen, C. Strip tease
Hoffman, A. Second nature
Hoffman, A. Seventh heaven
Hoffman, A. Turtle Moon
Lamb, W. I know this much is true
Lamott, A. Blue shoe
Leithauser, B. A few corrections
Lipman, E. The family man
Mantel, H. Beyond black
McCabe, P. Winterwood
McGrath, P. Trauma
McMillan, T. How Stella got her groove back
Miller, S. Lost in the forest
Miller, S. The world below

Down there. Goodis, D.
   In Crime novels: American noir of the 1950s
Down to a soundless sea. Steinbeck, T.
Down to a sunless sea. Poyer, D.
Down town. Sams, F.
Downtown owl. Klosterman, C.
Downward to the Earth. Silverberg, R.
   In Silverberg, R. A Robert Silverberg omnibus
DOYLE, SIR ARTHUR CONAN, 1859-1930
      Parodies, imitations, etc.
   Cullin, M. A slight trick of the mind
   Hockensmith, S. Holmes on the range
   Hockensmith, S. On the wrong track
   King, L. R. The beekeeper's apprentice, or, On the segregation of the queen
   King, L. R. The game
   King, L. R. Justice Hall
   King, L. R. A letter of Mary
   King, L. R. Locked rooms
   King, L. R. The moor
   King, L. R. O Jerusalem
   Meyer, N. The seven-per-cent solution
   Meyer, N. The West End horror
   Pirie, D. The patient's eyes
DOYLE, CONAN *See* Doyle, Sir Arthur Conan, 1859-1930
Dr. Bloodmoney. Dick, P. K.
   In Dick, P. K. Five novels of the 1960s & 70s
Dr. Death. Kellerman, J.
Dr. Jekyll and Mr. Hyde [variant title: The strange case of Dr. Jekyll and Mr. Hyde] Stevenson, R. L.
   In Stevenson, R. L. The complete short stories p102-64
Dr. Jekyll and Mr. Hyde. See Stevenson, R. L. The strange case of Dr. Jekyll and Mr. Hyde
Dr. King's refrigerator and other bedtime stories. Johnson, C. R.
Dracula. Stoker, B.

DRAFT
   Bellow, S. Dangling man
   Carroll, J. Fault lines
DRAFT, MILITARY *See* Draft
DRAFT RESISTERS *See* Draft
Dragon bones. See, L.
Dragonflight. McCaffrey, A.
Dragonquest. McCaffrey, A.
Dragonriders of Pern [series]
   McCaffrey, A. Dragonquest
   McCaffrey, A. The white dragon
DRAGONS
   Lackey, M. Joust
   McCaffrey, A. All the Weyrs of Pern
   McCaffrey, A. Dragonflight
   McCaffrey, A. Dragonquest
   McCaffrey, A. Dragon's Kin
   McCaffrey, A. Dragonsdawn
   McCaffrey, A. Dragonseye
   McCaffrey, A. The girl who heard dragons [novelette]
   McCaffrey, A. The Masterharper of Pern
   McCaffrey, A. The renegades of Pern
   McCaffrey, A. The skies of Pern
   McCaffrey, A. Wehr search
   McCaffrey, A. The white dragon
   Norton, A. The elvenbane
   Norton, A. Elvenblood
   Novik, N. His majesty's dragon
Dragon's Kin. McCaffrey, A.
Dragon's lair. Penman, S. K.
Dragonsdawn. McCaffrey, A.
Dragonseye. McCaffrey, A.
Dragonwyck. Seton, A.
The **draining** lake. Arnaldur Indriðason
Drama city. Pelecanos, G. P.
DRAMATISTS
   Hazzard, S. The transit of Venus
   Lessing, D. M. Love, again
   Murdoch, I. The sea, the sea
The **dreadful** lemon sky. MacDonald, J. D.
Dream house. Laken, V.
The **dream** life of Balso Snell. West, N.
   In West, N. Novels and other writings
The **dream** life of Sukhanov. Grushin, O.
Dream of darkness. Hill, R.
The **dream** of Scipio. Pears, I.

The **dream** stalker. Coel, M.
Dreamcatcher. King, S.
Dreamer. Johnson, C. R.
Dreamers of the day. Russell, M. D.
The **dreaming.** Wood, B.
Dreaming in Cuban. García, C.
The **dreaming** void. Hamilton, P. F.
Dreaming water. Tsukiyama, G.

DREAMS
   Hill, R. Dream of darkness
   Le Guin, U. K. The lathe of heaven
   O'Brien, T. Going after Cacciato
   Ruiz, L. M. Only one thing missing
   West, N. The dream life of Balso Snell
Dreams of glory. Fleming, T. J.
Dreams of my Russian summers. Makine, A.
Dreamsnake. McIntyre, V. N.
The **dreamthief's** daughter. Moorcock, M.
DRESDEN (GERMANY) *See* Germany—Dresden
Dress her in indigo. MacDonald, J. D.

DRESSMAKERS
   Peebles, F. d. P. The seamstress
The **drifters.** Michener, J. A.
The **drifter's** wheel. DePoy, P.
Driftless. Rhodes, D.
The **driftless** area. Drury, T.
Drink with the Devil. Higgins, J.
Drinking coffee elsewhere. Packer, Z.

DRIVE-IN THEATERS
   Lansdale, J. R. A fine dark line
The **driver's** seat. Spark, M.
Drood. Simmons, D.
Drop edge of yonder. Wurlitzer, R.
Drown. Díaz, J.
Drowned hopes. Westlake, D. E.
The **drowned** life. Ford, J.

DROWNING
   Ferrante, E. Troubling love
   Grimes, M. Hotel Paradise
   Hamilton, J. A map of the world
   Hough, R. The stowaway
   Oates, J. C. Black water
   O'Nan, S. Snow angels
   Rash, R. Saints at the river
   Rice, L. Safe harbor
   Schwarz, C. Drowning Ruth
Drowning lessons. Selgin, P.
The **drowning** pool. Macdonald, R.
Drowning Ruth. Schwarz, C.
The **drowning** tree. Goodman, C.
DRUG ABUSE
   See also Drugs
   Welsh, I. Porno

DRUG ADDICTION
   Cheever, J. Falconer
   Docx, E. Pravda
   Grossman, D. Someone to run with
   Hoffman, A. Skylight confessions
   Kerouac, J. And the hippos were boiled in their tanks
   Maḥfūẓ, N. Midaq Alley
   McKinney-Whetstone, D. Blues dancing
   Meyer, N. The seven-per-cent solution
   Miller, R. The private lives of Pippa Lee
   Monaghan, N. The killing jar
   Mrazek, R. J. Unholy fire
   O'Connor, R. Buffalo soldiers
   Robinson, R. Cost
   Simmons, D. Drood
   Wallace, D. F. Infinite jest

DRUG ADDICTS
   Burroughs, W. S. Naked lunch
   Frey, J. Bright shiny morning
   LaValle, V. D. Big machine
   Maazel, F. Last last chance
   Welsh, I. Trainspotting

DRUG INDUSTRY *See* Pharmaceutical industry

DRUG TRAFFIC
   Baldacci, D. Divine justice

EARTH, DESTRUCTION OF—*Continued*
Bear, G. The forge of God
Hoban, R. Riddley Walker
Niven, L. Lucifer's hammer
Earth. Brin, D.
Earth abides. Stewart, G. R.
Earthfall. Card, O. S.
Earthly joys. Gregory, P.
Earthly possessions. Tyler, A.
Earthquake weather. Lankford, T.

EARTHQUAKES
See also Disasters
Gardiner, M. The Dirty Secrets Club
Rosenberg, R. This is not civilization
Steel, D. Amazing grace

EAST AFRICA
Hemingway, E. True at first light

EAST AND WEST
See also Acculturation
Clavell, J. Gai-Jin
Clavell, J. Noble house
Clavell, J. Shogun
Endō, S. Silence
Forster, E. M. A passage to India
Han, S. Till morning comes
Hersey, J. A single pebble
Rushdie, S. The ground beneath her feet
Scott, P. The day of the scorpion
Scott, P. The jewel in the crown
Tan, A. The Joy Luck Club
East and West. Maugham, W. S.
In Maugham, W. S. Complete short stories

EAST EUROPEANS

England
Tremain, R. The road home

EAST INDIANS

Africa
Naipaul, V. S. A bend in the river
Naipaul, V. S. Half a life

Canada
Alam, S. The groom to have been
Vassanji, M. G. The assassin's song

England
Kunzru, H. The impressionist
Kureishi, H. The Buddha of suburbia
Leavitt, D. The Indian clerk
Naipaul, V. S. Half a life
Naipaul, V. S. Magic seeds
Seton, A. Green darkness

Italy
Ondaatje, M. The English patient

Malaysia
Samarasan, P. Evening is the whole day

Trinidad and Tobago
Naipaul, V. S. A house for Mr. Biswas

United States
D'Souza, T. The Konkans
Lahiri, J. Interpreter of maladies
Lahiri, J. The namesake
Lahiri, J. Unaccustomed earth
East into Upper East. Jhabvala, R. P.
East is east. Lathen, E.
East of Eden. Steinbeck, J.
also in Steinbeck, J. Novels, 1942-1952
East of the mountains. Guterson, D.

EAST SIDE, LOWER (NEW YORK, N.Y.) *See* New York
(N.Y.)—Lower East Side

EAST TIMOR (INDONESIA)
Lee, M. The canal house
East, west. Rushdie, S.

EASTER ISLAND
Vanderbes, J. Easter Island
Easter Island. Vanderbes, J.

EASTER REBELLION, 1916 *See* Ireland—Sinn Fein Rebellion,
1916

EASTERN EUROPE
Kostova, E. The historian
Mewshaw, M. Shelter from the storm
Easy meat. Harvey, J.
Easy prey. Sandford, J.
Eat the document. Spiotta, D.

ECCENTRICS AND ECCENTRICITIES
See also Recluses
Barker, N. Darkmans
Binchy, M. Whitethorn Woods
Boyle, T. C. Road to Wellville
Cadwalladr, C. The family tree
Carey, E. Alva & Irva
Childress, M. Crazy in Alabama
Clark, N. The Hills at home
Crews, H. A feast of snakes
Cusk, R. In the fold
Dallas, S. The Persian Pickle Club
Davis-Goff, A. This cold country
Dennis, P. Auntie Mame
Diamant, A. Last days of Dogtown
Doctorow, E. L. Homer & Langley
Drabble, M. The witch of Exmoor
D'Souza, T. The Konkans
Dufresne, J. Deep in the shade of paradise
Dufresne, J. Requiem, Mass.
Erdrich, L. The Beet Queen
Gardam, J. Faith Fox
Gay, W. Twilight
Goldberg, M. Bee season
Hansen, E. F. Tales of protection
Hansen, R. Isn't it romantic?
Hiaasen, C. Nature girl
Hiaasen, C. Stormy weather
Howatch, S. The wonder-worker
Irving, J. A son of the circus
Irving, J. A widow for one year
Jackson, J. Between, Georgia
Kallos, S. Broken for you
Kay, T. Shadow song
Kurzweil, A. The grand complication
Labiner, N. Miniatures
Lansdale, J. R. Sunset and sawdust
Larsen, R. The selected works of T. S. Spivet
Leonard, E. Maximum Bob
Lindgren, T. Hash
Liss, D. The ethical assassin
Marías, J. All souls
Martin, S. The pleasure of my company
Martínez, N. M. ¡Caramba!
McCorkle, J. Carolina moon
McCrumb, S. St. Dale
McGahern, J. By the lake
McMahon, T. A. Ira Foxglove
McMurtry, L. By sorrow's river
McMurtry, L. Folly and glory
McMurtry, L. Loop group
McMurtry, L. Sin killer
McMurtry, L. The wandering hill
Milton, G. Edward Trencom's nose
Mitford, N. Love in a cold climate
Mitford, N. The pursuit of love
Mosher, H. F. On Kingdom Mountain
Murakami, H. The wind-up bird chronicle
Novakovich, J. April Fool's Day
O'Neill, J. Kilbrack; or, Who is Nancy Valentine?
Ozick, C. Heir to the glimmering world
Paasilinna, A. The howling miller
Pearson, T. R. A short history of a small place
Pessl, M. Special topics in calamity physics
Portes, A. Hick
Portis, C. The dog of the South
Portis, C. Gringos
Portis, C. Masters of Atlantis
Portis, C. Norwood
Ramsland, M. Doghead
Reuss, F. Horace afoot
Robbins, T. Villa incognito
Rosenblatt, R. Lapham rising
Smith, D. Pictures from an expedition
Smith, D. I capture the castle

ELECTRICITY

Lawrence, S. The lightning keeper

ELECTRONIC COMPUTERS *See* Computers

ELECTRONIC MAIL MESSAGES

Hamilton, J. Disobedience

ELECTRONIC SURVEILLANCE

Raban, J. Surveillance

The **elegance** of the hedgehog. Barbery, M.

The **elementals**. Llywelyn, M.

The **elephant** god. Theroux, P.

   In Theroux, P. The Elephanta suite

The **elephant** keeper. Nicholson, C.

The **Elephanta** suite. Theroux, P.

ELEPHANTS

Gruen, S. Water for elephants

Nicholson, C. The elephant keeper

Theroux, P. The elephant god

ELEVATORS

Whitehead, C. The intuitionist

Eleven on top. Evanovich, J.

The **eleventh** man. Doig, I.

ELGAR, EDWARD, 1857-1934
About

Hamilton-Paterson, J. Gerontius

ELIOT, GEORGE, 1819-1880
About

Weisgall, D. The world before her

ELIOT, T. S. (THOMAS STEARNS), 1888-1965
About

Cooley, M. The archivist

ELIZABETH I, QUEEN OF ENGLAND, 1533-1603
About

Gregory, P. The queen's fool

Harper, K. The Poyson garden

Harper, K. The queene's Christmas

Harper, K. The tidal poole

Holt, V. My enemy the Queen

Maxwell, R. The Queen's bastard

Maxwell, R. The secret diary of Anne Boleyn

Maxwell, R. The wild Irish

Plaidy, J. The captive Queen of Scots

Weir, A. The Lady Elizabeth

ELIZABETH, QUEEN, CONSORT OF FREDERICK V, KING OF BOHEMIA, 1596-1662
About

Stevenson, J. The winter queen

Elizabeth Costello. Coetzee, J. M.

Ellen Foster. Gibbons, K.

Ellen Gilchrist: collected stories. Gilchrist, E.

Ellis Island. Helprin, M.

   In Helprin, M. Ellis Island & other stories p128-96

Ellis Island. Stewart, F. M.

Ellis Island & other stories. Helprin, M.

Elmer Gantry. Lewis, S.

   also in Lewis, S. Arrowsmith; Elmer Gantry; Dodsworth

Elmore Leonard's Dutch treat: 3 novels. Leonard, E.

Elsewhere in the land of parrots. Paul, J.

The **elusive** Mrs. Pollifax. Gilman, D.

The **elusive** Pimpernel. Orczy, E., Baroness

The **elvenbane**. Norton, A.

Elvenblood. Norton, A.

Elvis in the morning. Buckley, W. F.

EMBEZZLEMENT

Clark, M. H. The second time around

Johnson, D. Nobody move

Ludlum, R. The Scarlatti inheritance

Perry, T. Dance for the dead

Pronzini, B. The crimes of Jordan Wise

EMERALDS

Westlake, D. E. The hot rock

EMERGENCY MEDICAL TECHNICIANS

Burke, S. Black flies

EMERSON, RALPH WALDO, 1803-1882
About

Pearl, M. The Dante Club

The **emigrants**. Moberg, V.

The **emigrants**. Sebald, W. G.

EMIGRÉS *See* Refugees

Emily Dickinson is dead. Langton, J.

Emma. Austen, J.

Emma. Brontë, C.

Emmeline. Rossner, J.

EMOTIONALLY DISTURBED CHILDREN

Clark, M. H. No place like home

Levenkron, S. The best little girl in the world

Potok, C. The promise

EMPATHY

Katzenbach, J. The madman's tale

The **emperor** of Ocean Park. Carter, S. L.

The **emperor's** children. Messud, C.

Empire. Vidal, G.

Empire Falls. Russo, R.

The **empire** of ice cream. Ford, J.

Empire of lies. Klavan, A.

Empire of the Sun. Ballard, J. G.

Empire rising. Kelly, T.

EMPIRE STATE BUILDING (NEW YORK, N.Y.)

Kelly, T. Empire rising

Empress of the splendid season. Hijuelos, O.

The **Empress** of Weehawken. Dische, I.

Empress Orchid. Min, A.

The **enchantress**. Han, S.

The **enchantress** of Florence. Rushdie, S.

Enclave. Reed, K.

The **end** of all songs. Moorcock, M.

The **end** of California. Yarbrough, S.

The **end** of my career. Franklin, M.

The **end** of sleep. Somerville, R.

The **end** of the affair. Greene, G.

The **end** of the alphabet. Richardson, C. S.

The **end** of the battle. Waugh, E.

End of the chapter. Galsworthy, J.

End of the drive. L'Amour, L.

The **end** of the Jews. Mansbach, A.

END OF THE WORLD

   See also Earth, Destruction of

Adrian, C. The children's hospital

Butler, O. E. Adulthood rites

Butler, O. E. Dawn

Butler, O. E. Imago

Ellison, H. The deathbird

Gaiman, N. Good omens

Glavinic, T. Night work

Percy, W. Love in the ruins

Shute, N. On the beach

Updike, J. Toward the end of time

West, M. L. The clowns of God

Wilson, R. C. Spin

ENDANGERED SPECIES

Anderson, A. Darwin's wink

Millet, L. How the dead dream

Ender's game. Card, O. S.

Ender's shadow. Card, O. S.

Endless love. Spencer, S.

Endless night. Christie, A.

ENDOWMENTS

Vonnegut, K. God bless you, Mr. Rosewater

Enduring love. McEwan, I.

Endymion. Simmons, D.

Enemies, a love story. Singer, I. B.

The **enemy**. Child, L.

Enemy mine. Longyear, B. B.

   In The Hugo winners p5-67

Enemy of God. Cornwell, B.

Enemy women. Jiles, P.

ENGAGEMENTS *See* Betrothals

ENGINEERS

Griesemer, J. Signal & noise

Harris, R. Pompeii

Hersey, J. A single pebble

Levi, P. The monkey's wrench

Vonnegut, K. Player piano

ENGLAND

   See also Cotswolds (England); Lake District (England); Stonehenge (England)

Archer, J. As the crow flies

ENGLAND—16th century—*Continued*
Gregory, P. The other Boleyn girl
Gregory, P. The queen's fool
Gregory, P. The wise woman
Holt, V. My enemy the Queen
L'Amour, L. To the far blue mountains
Mantel, H. Wolf Hall
Maxwell, R. The Queen's bastard
Maxwell, R. The secret diary of Anne Boleyn
Maxwell, R. The wild Irish
Nye, R. The late Mr. Shakespeare
Plaidy, J. The captive Queen of Scots
Plaidy, J. Murder most royal
Riley, J. M. The serpent garden
Seton, A. Green darkness
Twain, M. The prince and the pauper
Weir, A. Innocent traitor
Weir, A. The Lady Elizabeth

17th century
Barth, J. The sot-weed factor
Blackmore, R. D. Lorna Doone
Brooks, G. Year of wonders
Chevalier, T. Burning bright
Defoe, D. Moll Flanders
Du Maurier, Dame D. Frenchman's Creek
Dumas, A. Twenty years after
Gregory, P. Earthly joys
Gregory, P. Virgin earth
Koen, K. Dark angels
Morrow, J. The last witchfinder
Nye, R. The late Mr. Shakespeare
Pears, I. An instance of the fingerpost
Plaidy, J. The pleasures of love
Plaidy, J. William's wife

18th century
Brontë, C. Emma
Chase, L. L. Lord of scoundrels
Fielding, H. The history of the adventures of Joseph Andrews
    and of his friend Mr. Abraham Adams and, An apology for
    the life of Mrs. Shamela Andrews
Fielding, H. The history of Tom Jones, a foundling
Koen, K. Through a glass darkly
Nicholson, C. The elephant keeper
Richardson, S. Pamela
Smollett, T. G. The expedition of Humphry Clinker
Thackeray, W. M. The Virginians

19th century
Austen, J. Emma
Austen, J. Mansfield Park
Austen, J. Northanger Abbey
Austen, J. Persuasion
Austen, J. Pride and prejudice
Balogh, M. More than a mistress
Balogh, M. Seducing an angel
Balogh, M. Simply love
Balogh, M. Simply magic
Balogh, M. Simply perfect
Balogh, M. Slightly dangerous
Byatt, A. S. Angels and insects
Chase, L. L. The last hellion
Cornwell, B. The archer's tale
Cox, M. The glass of time
Cox, M. The meaning of night
Dickens, C. Barnaby Rudge
Dickens, C. Bleak House
Dickens, C. A Charles Dickens Christmas
Dickens, C. A Christmas carol
Dickens, C. The cricket on the hearth
Dickens, C. David Copperfield
Dickens, C. Dombey and Son
Dickens, C. Great expectations
Dickens, C. Hard times
Dickens, C. Little Dorrit
Dickens, C. Nicholas Nickleby
Dickens, C. The old curiosity shop
Dickens, C. The posthumous papers of the Pickwick Club
Donoghue, E. The sealed letter
Eliot, G. Adam Bede
Eliot, G. Middlemarch
Eliot, G. The mill on the Floss
Forester, C. S. Commodore Hornblower
Forester, C. S. Lord Hornblower

Fowles, J. The French lieutenant's woman
Gaskell, E. C. Cranford
Graham, W. Bella Poldark
Hardy, T. Under the greenwood tree
Hawthorne, N. Doctor Grimshawe's secret
Hensher, P. The Mulberry empire
Heyer, G. Black sheep
Heyer, G. Frederica
Heyer, G. The grand Sophy
Holt, V. The black opal
Holt, V. Mistress of Mellyn
Holt, V. Secret for a nightingale
Humphreys, H. Afterimage
James, H. The spoils of Poynton
James, H. The turn of the screw
Lofts, N. Gad's Hall
Mallinson, A. A close run thing
Palliser, C. The unburied
Pearce, M. E. Cast a long shadow
Quick, A. I thee wed
Quick, A. Late for the wedding
Quick, A. The paid companion
Richler, M. Solomon Gursky was here
Rogers, J. Mr. Wroe's virgins
Ross-Macdonald, M. For they shall inherit
Ross-Macdonald, M. The rich are with you always
Ross-Macdonald, M. The Trevarton inheritance
Ross-Macdonald, M. The world from rough stones
Smith, M. C. Rose
Tennant, E. Pemberley
Tennant, E. An unequal marriage
Thackeray, W. M. Vanity fair
Thomas, S. Private arrangements
Trollope, A. Barchester Towers
Trollope, A. Doctor Thorne
Trollope, A. The Eustace diamonds
Trollope, A. Framley parsonage
Trollope, A. The last chronicle of Barset
Trollope, A. The Pallisers
Trollope, A. The prime minister
Trollope, A. The small house at Allington
Trollope, A. The warden
Vine, B. The blood doctor
Willig, L. The seduction of the crimson rose
Willis, C. To say nothing of the dog; or, How we found the
    bishop's bird stump at last

Aristocracy
See Aristocracy—England

Civil War
See England—17th century

Coal mines and mining
See Coal mines and mining—England

College life
See College life—England

Communism
See Communism—England

Courts and courtiers
See Courts and courtiers—England

Farm life
See Farm life—England

Kings and rulers
Gregory, P. The Boleyn Inheritance
Gregory, P. The other Boleyn girl
Gregory, P. The queen's fool

Politics
See Politics—England

Prisoners and prisons
See Prisoners and prisons—England

Race relations
Levy, A. Fruit of the lemon
Levy, A. Small island
Phillips, C. Foreigners

ENGLAND—London—*Continued*

Beckett, S. Murphy
Bowen, E. The heat of the day
Bradford, B. T. The Ravenscar dynasty
Brookner, A. Family and friends
Brookner, A. Undue influence
Byatt, A. S. Possession
Cary, J. The horse's mouth
Chevalier, T. Burning bright
Clark, M. H. The Anastasia syndrome
Coe, J. The closed circle
Coe, J. The rain before it falls
Cox, M. The meaning of night
Cronin, A. J. The citadel
Dark, A. E. Think of England
De Bernières, L. A partisan's daughter
Docx, E. The calligrapher
Donoghue, E. The sealed letter
Faulks, S. Engleby
Fielding, H. Bridget Jones: the edge of reason
Fielding, H. Bridget Jones's diary
Fonseca, I. Attachment
Ford, F. M. A man could stand up
Frayn, M. Spies
French, N. Beneath the skin
French, N. Land of the living
Fresán, R. Kensington Gardens
Fyfield, F. Blind date
Galsworthy, J. End of the chapter
Galsworthy, J. A modern comedy
Galsworthy, J. To let
Gardam, J. The queen of the tambourine
George, E. What came before he shot her
Gibb, C. Sweetness in the belly
Gibson, W. Pattern recognition
Greene, G. The end of the affair
Greene, G. The human factor
Greene, G. The ministry of fear
Guo Xiaolu. A concise Chinese-English dictionary for lovers
Hambly, B. Those who hunt the night
Hand, E. Mortal love
Hardwick, M. The Duchess of Duke Street
Hart, J. The reconstructionist
Hilton, J. Random harvest
Hoban, R. Her name was Lola
Høeg, P. The woman and the ape
Hoffman, A. The third angel
Hornby, N. About a boy
Hornby, N. High fidelity
Hornby, N. How to be good
Hornby, N. A long way down
Howatch, S. The heartbreaker
Howatch, S. The high flyer
Huxley, A. Point counter point
Kavenna, J. Inglorious
Keyes, M. Last Chance Saloon
Korda, M. Curtain
Kureishi, H. The Buddha of suburbia
Kureishi, H. Something to tell you
Laird, N. Utterly monkey
Le Carré, J. The looking glass war
Leavitt, D. While England sleeps
Lebrecht, N. The song of names
Leebron, F. G. In the middle of all this
Lessing, D. M. Ben, in the world
Lessing, D. M. The four-gated city
Lessing, D. M. The good terrorist
Lessing, D. M. Love, again
Lessing, D. M. The sweetest dream
Levy, A. Fruit of the lemon
Levy, A. Small island
Lively, P. Consequences
Livesey, M. Banishing Verona
Livesey, M. The house on Fortune Street
Livesey, M. The missing world
Lovesey, P. On the edge
Lurie, A. Foreign affairs
Marías, J. Your face tomorrow: volume one: Fever and spear
Marías, J. Your face tomorrow: volume two: Dance and dream
Maugham, W. S. Of human bondage
Mawer, S. The fall
McCarthy, T. Remainder
McEwan, I. Amsterdam

McEwan, I. Saturday
McGrath, P. Spider
Milton, G. Edward Trencom's nose
Moorcock, M. The end of all songs
Mortimer, J. Felix in the underworld
Mortimer, J. Rumpole misbehaves
Murdoch, I. An accidental man
Murdoch, I. A fairly honourable defeat
Murdoch, I. The green knight
Murdoch, I. The nice and the good
Murdoch, I. Nuns and soldiers
Naipaul, V. S. Half a life
Niffenegger, A. Her fearful symmetry
O'Brien, E. Girls in their married bliss
O'Brien, E. Time and tide
Pearl, M. The last Dickens
Phillips, M. Gods behaving badly
Powell, A. At Lady Molly's
Powell, A. The military philosophers
Pym, B. Excellent women
Pym, B. The sweet dove died
Pym, B. An unsuitable attachment
Pynchon, T. Gravity's rainbow
Read, P. P. A season in the West
Rendell, R. Adam and Eve and Pinch me
Rendell, R. The bridesmaid
Rendell, R. Going wrong
Rendell, R. The keys to the street
Rendell, R. Thirteen steps down
Rendell, R. The tree of hands
Roth, P. Deception
Rutherfurd, E. London
Sackville-West, V. All passion spent
Self, W. The Book of Dave
Seymour, G. Rat run
Shaffer, M. A. The Guernsey Literary and Potato Peel Pie Society
Shriver, L. The post-birthday world
Snow, C. P. The conscience of the rich
Snow, C. P. Homecoming
Spark, M. Aiding and abetting
Spark, M. The bachelors
Spark, M. The ballad of Peckham Rye
Spark, M. A far cry from Kensington
Spark, M. The girls of slender means
Spark, M. Loitering with intent
Steel, D. The kiss
Taylor, E. Mrs. Palfrey at the Claremont
Templeton, E. Gordon
Theroux, P. Doctor Slaughter
Thomas, R. All my sins remembered
Torday, P. Salmon fishing in the Yemen
Tremain, R. The road home
Trevanian. The Loo sanction
Trollope, J. Second honeymoon
Unsworth, B. Losing Nelson
Vargas Llosa, M. The bad girl
Vine, B. Anna's book
Vine, B. Grasshopper
Vine, B. The house of stairs
Vine, B. King Solomon's carpet
Walters, M. The shape of snakes
Waters, S. Fingersmith
Waters, S. The night watch
Waugh, E. Vile bodies
Weldon, F. Big girls don't cry
Weldon, F. Rhode Island blues
Weldon, F. She may not leave
Willig, L. The seduction of the crimson rose
Winterson, J. Sexing the cherry
Woolf, V. Mrs. Dalloway

London—16th century

Kellerman, F. The quality of mercy

London—17th century

Kerr, P. Dark matter
Redfern, E. Auriel rising
Stevenson, J. The shadow king

London—Plague, 1665

Defoe, D. A journal of the plague year

London—18th century

Dickens, C. A tale of two cities

TITLE AND SUBJECT INDEX

ESCAPED CONVICTS
Baldacci, D. The simple truth
Hunter, S. Dirty white boys
Leonard, E. Up in Honey's room
Maynard, J. Labor Day
McCrumb, S. She walks these hills
Escapement. Lake, J.

ESCAPES
Bates, H. E. Fair stood the wind for France
Dumas, A. The Count of Monte Cristo
Forester, C. S. Flying colours
Forester, C. S. Hornblower and the Atropos
Hersey, J. The wall
King, S. Rita Hayworth and Shawshank redemption
Stark, R. Breakout
Westheimer, D. Von Ryan's Express
The **Escher** twist. Langton, J.

ESKIMOS *See* Aleuts; Inuit

ESP *See* Extrasensory perception

ESPIONAGE *See* International intrigue; Spies

ESSEX, THOMAS CROMWELL, EARL OF *See* Cromwell, Thomas, Earl of Essex, 1485?-1540

ESSEX (ENGLAND) *See* England—Essex

The **estate**. Singer, I. B.

ESTATES *See* Houses

The **eternal** moment. See Forster, E. M. The collected tales of E. M. Forster

Ethan Frome. Wharton, E.
also in Wharton, E. Novellas and other writings

The **ethical** assassin. Liss, D.

ETHICS
See also Conscience; Medical ethics; Political ethics; Sin; Truthfulness and falsehood; Utilitarianism
Barbash, T. The last good chance
Canin, E. America America
Caputo, P. Horn of Africa
Clark, M. The legal limit
Dexter, P. The paperboy
Ducker, B. Dizzying heights
Haig, M. The Labrador Pact
Horn, D. All other nights
Reed, B. The choice
Reuland, R. Semiautomatic
Shreve, A. Strange fits of passion
Snow, C. P. The new men
Steinbeck, J. The winter of our discontent
Wharton, E. Sanctuary

ETHIOPIA
Gibb, C. Sweetness in the belly
Keneally, T. To Asmara
Verghese, A. Cutting for stone

Politics
See Politics—Ethiopia

ETHIOPIANS

United States
Mengestu, D. The beautiful things that heaven bears
Eucalyptus. Bail, M.

EUNUCHS
King, R. Domino
Smith, W. A. River god

EUROPE
See also Central Europe; Eastern Europe
Archer, J. A matter of honor
Greene, G. Orient Express
Ishiguro, K. The unconsoled
Pynchon, T. Gravity's rainbow
Sartre, J. P. The reprieve
Tournier, M. The ogre
West, Dame R. The birds fall down

To 476
Llywelyn, M. The horse goddess

392-814
Jennings, G. Raptor
Yarbro, C. Q. Night blooming

11th century
Holland, C. The firedrake

12th century
Eco, U. Baudolino
L'Amour, L. The walking drum

15th century
Dunnett, D. Caprice and Rondo
Dunnett, D. Niccolò rising
Dunnett, D. Race of scorpions
Dunnett, D. Scales of gold
Dunnett, D. The spring of the ram
Dunnett, D. To lie with lions
Dunnett, D. The unicorn hunt

16th century
Dunnett, D. Checkmate
Halter, M. Messiah

17th century
Maalouf, A. Balthasar's odyssey

19th century
Cornwell, B. Sharpe's battle
James, H. The portrait of a lady
Vallgren, C.-J. The horrific sufferings of the mind-reading monster Hercules Barefoot

Politics
See Politics—Europe

EUROPE, CENTRAL *See* Central Europe

EUROPE, EASTERN *See* Eastern Europe

Europe central. Vollmann, W. T.

EUROPEANS

Africa
Forsyth, F. The dogs of war

The **Europeans**. James, H.

The **Eustace** diamonds. Trollope, A.

The **Eustace** diamonds [abridged] Trollope, A.
In Trollope, A. The Pallisers p189-264

EUTHANASIA
Lescroart, J. T. The mercy rule
Quindlen, A. One true thing
White, S. W. Kill me

Eva Luna. Allende, I.

Eva moves the furniture. Livesey, M.

EVANGELISTS
Leonard, E. Touch
Lester, J. Do Lord remember me
Lewis, S. Elmer Gantry
MacDonald, J. D. One more Sunday
Perrotta, T. The abstinence teacher
Smith, L. Saving Grace

EVE (BIBLICAL FIGURE)
About
Maine, D. Fallen

Even money. Francis, D.

Evening. Minot, S.

Evening in Byzantium. Shaw, I.

Evening is the whole day. Samarasan, P.

The **evening** star. McMurtry, L.

Evensong. Godwin, G.

Eventide. Haruf, K.

EVERGLADES (FLA.)
Matthiessen, P. Bone by bone
Matthiessen, P. Lost Man's River
Matthiessen, P. Shadow country

Evergreen. Plain, B.

Everlasting. Thayer, N.

Every crooked nanny. Andrews, M. K.

Every eye. Braybrooke, J.

Every fear. Mofina, R.

Every good boy does fine. Laskowski, T.

Every last cuckoo. Maloy, K.

Every last drop. Huston, C.

Every man dies alone. Fallada, H.

Every man for himself. Bainbridge, B.

Every time I talk to Liston. DeVido, B.

Everybody loves somebody. Scott, J.

Everyman. Roth, P.

Everyone dies. McGarrity, M.

Everyone's burning. Spiegelman, I.

EXPERIMENTAL STORIES—*Continued*

Sinisalo, J. Troll
Sorrentino, G. A strange commonplace
Steinbeck, J. Burning bright
Tillman, L. American genius
TSypkin, L. Summer in Baden-Baden
Unferth, D. O. Vacation
Vila-Matas, E. Montano's malady
Vollmann, W. T. The ice-shirt
Walker, A. The temple of my familiar
Wallace, D. F. Infinite jest
Wideman, J. E. The cattle killing
Wideman, J. E. Philadelphia fire

EXPERIMENTS, SCIENTIFIC See Scientific experiments
Exploration team. Jenkins, W. F.
In The Hugo winners p95-142

EXPLORERS

Bainbridge, B. The birthday boys
Forester, C. S. To the Indies
Gilman, C. P. Herland
Gilman, C. P. Moving the mountain
Gilman, C. P. With her in Ourland
Hall, B. I should be extremely happy in your company
Johnston, W. The navigator of New York
Maalouf, A. Leo Africanus
McDonald, R. Mr. Darwin's shooter
Poe, E. A. The journal of Julius Rodman
Vollmann, W. T. Argall
Vollmann, W. T. The rifles
Wheeler, R. S. Eclipse
The **exquisite**. Hunt, L.

EXTERMINATION, JEWISH See Holocaust, Jewish (1933-1945)

EXTINCT CITIES

See also Pompeii (Ancient city); Troy (Ancient city)
Whitney, P. A. Domino

EXTORTION

Dickens, C. Our mutual friend
Godey, J. The taking of Pelham one two three
Gruber, M. The forgery of Venus
Leonard, E. Freaky Deaky
Leonard, E. LaBrava
Lindsey, D. L. The rules of silence
Siegel, J. Derailed
Trevanian. The Loo sanction
Weber, K. The Music Lesson

EXTRASENSORY PERCEPTION

See also Clairvoyance; Telepathy
Anderson, P. The Saturn game
Greeley, A. M. Irish cream
Greeley, A. M. Irish stew!
Høeg, P. The quiet girl
Hooper, K. Stealing shadows
King, S. The dead zone
King, S. The shining
Koontz, D. R. The bad place
Krentz, J. A. Running hot
Le Guin, U. K. The left hand of darkness
Lessing, D. M. The four-gated city
Lustbader, E. V. Black Blade
Stewart, M. Touch not the cat
Wilson, R. C. Blind Lake
Extremely loud & incredibly close. Foer, J. S.
The **eye** in the door. Barker, P.
Eye of the abyss. Browne, M.
The **eye** of the leopard. Mankell, H.
Eye of the needle. Follett, K.
Eye of the storm. Higgins, J.
The **eye** of the storm. White, P.
Eyes of a child. Patterson, R. N.
Eyesores. Shade, E.

EYEWITNESSES See Witnesses
The **Eyre** affair. Fforde, J.

F

"**F**" is for fugitive. Grafton, S.
A **fable**. Faulkner, W.
also in Faulkner, W. Novels, 1942-1954 p665-1072

FABLES

See also Allegories
Haig, M. The Labrador Pact
Ozick, C. The Puttermesser papers
Paasilinna, A. The howling miller
Rushdie, S. Haroun and the sea of stories
Sinisalo, J. Troll
Tan, A. Saving fish from drowning
The **fabulous** riverboat. Farmer, P. J.
Fabulous small Jews. Epstein, J.

FACE

Abnormalities and deformities

Busch, F. The night inspector
Kellogg, M. Tell me that you love me, Junie Moon
The **face**. Koontz, D. R.
A **face** at the window. McFarland, D.
The **face-changers**. Perry, T.
The **face** of a stranger. Perry, A.
The **face** of deception. Johansen, I.
The **face** of trespass. Rendell, R.
The **face** on the wall. Langton, J.

FACTORIES

See also Clothing industry; Labor and laboring classes
Crowley, J. Four freedoms
Lodge, D. Nice work
Theroux, P. Kowloon Tong

FACULTY (EDUCATION) See Teachers
Fahrenheit 451. Bradbury, R.
The **Fahrenheit** twins. Faber, M.
In Faber, M. The courage consort
The **Fahrenheit** twins. See Faber, M. Vanilla bright like Eminem
Fail-safe. Burdick, E.

FAILURE

DeMarinis, R. Sky full of sand
Lipsyte, S. Home land
Miles, J. Dear American Airlines
Scott, J. Tourmaline
Wheeler, R. S. Eclipse
Fair and tender ladies. Smith, L.
Fair stood the wind for France. Bates, H. E.

FAIRIES

Bull, E. War for the Oaks
Crowley, J. Little, big
A **fairly** honourable defeat. Murdoch, I.

FAIRS

Read, Miss. Thrush Green
Updike, J. The poorhouse fair
The **fairy** godmother. Lackey, M.

FAIRY TALES See Fantasies
Allen, S. A. The sugar queen
Maguire, G. Confessions of an ugly stepsister
Maguire, G. Mirror mirror
The **fairy** tales of Hermann Hesse. Hesse, H.

FAITH

Ansay, A. M. River angel
Cooley, M. The archivist
Davies, R. The cunning man
Endō, S. Deep river
Godwin, G. Evensong
Grisham, J. The testament
Guterson, D. Our Lady of the Forest
Hansen, R. Mariette in ecstasy
Hoffman, A. The third angel
Howatch, S. Absolute truths
Howatch, S. Glamorous powers
Howatch, S. Mystical paths
Howatch, S. Scandalous risks
Howatch, S. Ultimate prizes
Howatch, S. The wonder-worker
L'Engle, M. Certain women
Maine, D. The preservationist
Marcantel, P. An army of angels
McDonald, R. Mr. Darwin's shooter
McEwan, I. Enduring love
Picoult, J. Keeping Faith
Robinson, M. Home
Rogers, J. Mr. Wroe's virgins
Russell, M. D. Children of God
Russell, M. D. The sparrow

TITLE AND SUBJECT INDEX

FAITH CURE
Bambara, T. C. The salt eaters
Leonard, E. Touch
Faith Fox. Gardam, J.
FAITH HEALERS *See* Faith cure
FAITHFULL, EMILY, 1835-1895
                About
Donoghue, E. The sealed letter
Faithless. Oates, J. C.
Faking it. Crusie, J.
Falconer. Cheever, J.
   also in Cheever, J. Complete novels
The **fall**. Camus, A.
The **fall**. Mawer, S.
A **fall** from grace. Barnard, R.
The **fall** of Hyperion. Simmons, D.
The **fall** of Rome. Southgate, M.
The **fall** of Troy. Ackroyd, P.
Fall on your knees. MacDonald, A.-M.
Fallen. Lebbon, T.
Fallen. Maine, D.
The **fallen**. Parker, T. J.
The **fallen** curtain and other stories. Rendell, R.
   In Rendell, R. Collected stories p1-135
Fallen into the pit. Peters, E.
The **fallen** man. Hillerman, T.
Falling man. DeLillo, D.
The **falls**. Oates, J. C.
The **falls**. Rankin, I.
Falls the shadow. Penman, S. K.

FALSE ACCUSATION
Baldwin, J. If Beale Street could talk
Eliot, G. Silas Marner
Gaines, E. J. A lesson before dying
Hamilton, J. A map of the world
Holt, V. The black opal
Katkov, N. Blood & orchids
Katzenbach, J. Hart's war
Lee, H. To kill a mockingbird
Lewin, M. Z. Oh Joe
Malamud, B. The fixer
McEwan, I. Atonement
Mina, D. Deception
Parker, B. Suspicion of vengeance
Patterson, R. N. Eclipse
Richmond, M. No one you know
Rosenfelt, D. Don't tell a soul
Tey, J. The Franchise affair
Wilder, T. The eighth day
Yorke, M. A question of belief
False conception. Greenleaf, S.
False dawn. Wharton, E.
   In Wharton, E. Novellas and other writings
False memory. Koontz, D. R.
False pretences. Yorke, M.
False scent. Marsh, Dame N.
Falsely accused. Tanenbaum, R.

FAME
Blackwell, E. Grub
Dunne, J. G. Nothing lost
Gold, G. D. Sunnyside
Leonard, E. The hot kid
McCrumb, S. St. Dale
Oates, J. C. Blonde
Powell, D. The locusts have no king
Rebeck, T. Three girls and their brother
The **family**. Puzo, M.
Family and friends. Brookner, A.

FAMILY CHRONICLES
   See also Family life
Allende, I. The house of the spirits
Archer, J. As the crow flies
Baldwin, J. Go tell it on the mountain
Battle, L. Southern women
Boyle, T. C. World's end
Bradford, B. T. The Ravenscar dynasty
Breslin, J. Table money
Brown, D. A. Creek Mary's blood
Butler, S. The way of all flesh
Carter, S. L. The emperor of Ocean Park
Cheever, J. The Wapshot chronicle
Cheever, J. The Wapshot scandal

Cooper, J. C. The wake of the wind
Cunningham, M. Flesh and blood
Davidar, D. The house of blue mangoes
Davies, R. The manticore
Davies, R. Murther & walking spirits
De la Roche, M. Jalna
Delbanco, N. What remains
Doig, I. Bucking the sun
Dorris, M. Cloud chamber
Dorris, M. A yellow raft in blue water
Dunne, D. A season in purgatory
Dunnett, D. Niccolò rising
Dunnett, D. Race of scorpions
Dunnett, D. The spring of the ram
Edgeworth, M. Castle Rackrent
Esterházy, P. Celestial harmonies
Eve, N. The family orchard
Faulkner, W. Flags in the dust
Faulkner, W. Sartoris
Galsworthy, J. End of the chapter
Galsworthy, J. The Forsyte saga
Galsworthy, J. A modern comedy
García, C. The Aguero sisters
García, C. Dreaming in Cuban
García, C. Monkey hunting
García Márquez, G. One hundred years of solitude
Gibbons, K. Charms for the easy life
Gilmore, J. Golden country
Graham, W. Bella Poldark
Grau, S. A. The keepers of the house
Haley, A. Mama Flora's family
Halter, M. The book of Abraham
Harrison, J. The road home
Hawthorne, N. The House of the Seven Gables
Hegi, U. The vision of Emma Blau
Hijuelos, O. The fourteen sisters of Emilio Montez O'Brien
Hill, R. B. Hanta yo
Høeg, P. The history of Danish dreams
Houston, J. D. Bird of another heaven
Howard, M. Natural history
Howatch, S. Cashelmara
Howatch, S. Penmarric
Howatch, S. The wheel of fortune
Hunter, E. The Chisholms
Isaacs, S. Almost paradise
Isaacs, S. Red, white and blue
Jakes, J. American dreams
Jakes, J. Charleston
Jakes, J. Heaven and hell
Jakes, J. Love and war
Jakes, J. North and South
Jennings, G. Aztec
Jhabvala, R. P. Shards of memory
Kennedy, W. Very old bones
Kesey, K. Sometimes a great notion
Kittredge, W. The Willow Field
Krantz, J. Mistral's daughter
Laker, R. To dance with kings
L'Amour, L. The Sacketts: beginnings of a dynasty
Laskas, G. M. The midwife's tale
Lawrence, D. H. The rainbow
L'Engle, M. Certain women
Lessing, D. M. The sweetest dream
Lott, B. Ancient highway
Maḥfūz, N. Palace of desire
Maḥfūz, N. Palace walk
Maḥfūz, N. Sugar Street
Manicka, R. The rice mother
Mann, T. Buddenbrooks
Mansbach, A. The end of the Jews
Martin, W. Annapolis
Martin, W. Cape Cod
McCrumb, S. The songcatcher
McCullough, C. The thorn birds
Michener, J. A. Chesapeake
Michener, J. A. Mexico
Michener, J. A. Poland
Miller, S. Family pictures
Morrison, T. Song of Solomon
Nabokov, V. V. Ada
Naylor, G. Linden Hills
Ng, F. M. Bone
Oates, J. C. Bellefleur
Pearce, M. E. Apple tree lean down [omnibus volume]

FAMILY CHRONICLES—*Continued*

Piercy, M. Three women
Pilcher, R. September
Pilcher, R. The shell seekers
Plain, B. Evergreen
Plain, B. The golden cup
Plain, B. Harvest
Plain, B. Random winds
Plain, B. Tapestry
Powers, R. The time of our singing
Price, E. Savannah
Puzo, M. The family
Richler, M. Solomon Gursky was here
Ross-Macdonald, M. For they shall inherit
Ross-Macdonald, M. The rich are with you always
Ross-Macdonald, M. The world from rough stones
Rushdie, S. The Moor's last sigh
Rutherfurd, E. Russka
Rutherfurd, E. Sarum
Scott, Sir W. The bride of Lammermoor
Seth, V. A suitable boy
Shange, N. Betsey Brown
Shaw, I. Beggarman, thief
Shaw, I. Rich man, poor man
Sheldon, S. Master of the game
Shreve, S. R. Daughters of the new world
Simpson, M. Anywhere but here
Singer, I. B. The family Moskat
Smith, L. The devil's dream
Smith, L. Family linen
Smith, L. Oral history
Smith, Z. White teeth
Stegner, W. E. Angle of repose
Steinbeck, J. East of Eden
Tademy, L. Cane River
Tarkington, B. The magnificent Ambersons
Thackeray, W. M. The Virginians
Thomas, M. M. Hanover Place
Trevor, W. Fools of fortune
Trollope, J. Legacy of love
Tryon, T. In the fire of spring
Tryon, T. The wings of the morning
Tyler, A. Dinner at the Homesick Restaurant
Tyler, A. Searching for Caleb
Undset, S. Kristin Lavransdatter
Updike, J. In the beauty of the lilies
Uris, L. Trinity
Urquhart, J. Away
Welty, E. Losing battles
West, D. The wedding
Woolf, V. The years
Yunis, A. The night counter

FAMILY CURSES

Caldwell, T. Captains and kings
Hawthorne, N. The House of the Seven Gables
Holt, V. Bride of Pendorric
Smith, L. Oral history
Wood, B. The dreaming
A **family** daughter. Meloy, M.
Family games. Stubbs, J.
Family happiness. Colwin, L.
Family happiness. Tolstoy, L., graf
    In Tolstoy, L., graf. The Kreutzer sonata, The Devil, and
        other tales
    In Tolstoy, L., graf. The short novels of Tolstoy
Family honor. Parker, R. B.

FAMILY LIFE

    See also Aunts; Brothers; Brothers and sisters; Family
    chronicles; Fathers; Fathers and sons; Fathers-in-law;
    Grandchildren; Granddaughters; Grandfathers; Grandmoth-
    ers; Grandparents; Grandsons; Half-brothers; Half-sisters;
    Marriage; Marriage problems; Mothers and daughters;
    Mothers and sons; Mothers-in-law; Nephews; Nieces; Par-
    ent and child; Sisters; Stepbrothers; Stepchildren; Step-
    daughters; Stepfathers; Stepmothers; Stepsisters; Stepsons;
    Twins; Uncles
Abraham, P. The romance reader
Adams, A. After the war
Adams, A. A southern exposure
Adams, S. K. My old true love
Agee, J. A death in the family
Aira, C. Ghosts
Alcott, L. M. Jo's boys

Alcott, L. M. Little women
Allende, I. The house of the spirits
Allende, I. Portrait in sepia
Allison, D. Bastard out of Carolina
Alvarez, J. How the García girls lost their accents
Austen, J. Emma
Austen, J. Mansfield Park
Austen, J. Northanger Abbey
Austen, J. Sense and sensibility
Auster, P. The Brooklyn follies
Balzac, H. d. Cousin Bette
Bassani, G. The garden of the Finzi-Continis
Bausch, R. Thanksgiving night
Bellow, S. Henderson the rain king
Bellow, S. Mr. Sammler's planet
Berne, S. A perfect arrangement
Betts, D. Souls raised from the dead
Binchy, M. Silver wedding
Bird, S. The Yokota Officers Club
Bradbury, R. Dandelion wine
Brookner, A. Family and friends
Brown, R. Before and after
Buck, P. S. The good earth
Byatt, A. S. The children's book
Cadwalladr, C. The family tree
Caldwell, T. Captains and kings
Cartwright, J. The promise of happiness
Casey, J. Spartina
Chaudhuri, A. The immortals
Cheever, J. Bullet Park
Chekhov, A. P. Three years
Christensen, L. S. The half brother
Chute, C. The Beans of Egypt, Maine
Clark, N. The Hills at home
Cohen, L. H. House lights
Colwin, L. A big storm knocked it over
Colwin, L. Family happiness
Connell, E. S. Mr. Bridge
Connell, E. S. Mrs. Bridge
Conroy, P. Beach music
Conroy, P. The prince of tides
Cook, T. H. The cloud of unknowing
Cummins, A. Yellowcake
Cunningham, M. Flesh and blood
Cusk, R. In the fold
Dark, A. E. Think of England
De la Roche, M. Jalna
Dean, M. L. The time it takes to fall
Deane, S. Reading in the dark
Delbanco, N. What remains
DeLillo, D. White noise
Demetz, H. The house on Prague Street
Desai, A. Clear light of day
Dew, R. F. The truth of the matter
Díaz, J. The brief wondrous life of Oscar Wao
Doig, I. Dancing at the Rascal Fair
Doig, I. English Creek
Donovan, A. Buddha Da
Doyle, R. Paddy Clarke, ha ha ha
Doyle, R. The woman who walked into doors
Drabble, M. The witch of Exmoor
D'Souza, T. The Konkans
Dufresne, J. Deep in the shade of paradise
Dufresne, J. Requiem, Mass.
Dunn, K. Geek love
Eliot, G. The mill on the Floss
Ellis, B. E. Lunar Park
Enright, A. The gathering
Epstein, L. San Remo Drive
Faulkner, W. As I lay dying
Faulkner, W. Flags in the dust
Faulkner, W. The mansion
Faulkner, W. Sartoris
Faulkner, W. The sound and the fury
Faulkner, W. The town
Ferber, E. So Big
Flynn, G. Sharp objects
Forster, E. M. Howards End
Franzen, J. The corrections
Freda, J. The patience of rivers
Freudenberger, N. The dissident
Fuentes, C. Happy families
Galsworthy, J. The Forsyte saga
Gibbons, K. Sights unseen

FAMILY LIFE—*Continued*

Roy, A. The god of small things
Runcie, J. Canvey Island
Russo, R. Nobody's fool
Salinger, J. D. Franny & Zooey
Salinger, J. D. Raise high the roof beam, carpenters, and Seymour: an introduction
Samarasan, P. Evening is the whole day
Sanders, L. Guilty pleasures
Saroyan, W. The human comedy
Schwartz, J. B. Reservation Road
Schwartz, L. S. Disturbances in the field
Schwartz, L. S. In the family way
Scott, J. Tourmaline
Searles, J. Boy still missing
Sebold, A. The lovely bones
Settle, M. L. Charley Bland
Shafak, E. The bastard of Istanbul
Sharpe, M. The sleeping father
Shaw, I. Bread upon the waters
Shepard, L. Softspoken
Shields, D. Dead languages
Shreve, A. Body surfing
Shreve, A. The weight of water
Shreve, S. R. A student of living things
Siddons, A. R. Sweetwater Creek
Sinclair, A. Coffee will make you black
Singer, I. B. The estate
Singer, I. B. The family Moskat
Smiley, J. A thousand acres
Smith, A. The accidental
Smith, B. A tree grows in Brooklyn
Smith, D. I capture the castle
Smith, R. K. Jane's house
Smith, Z. On beauty
Snow, C. P. The conscience of the rich
Snow, C. P. Last things
Snow, C. P. Time of hope
Sofer, D. The Septembers of Shiraz
Spencer, S. Endless love
Starr, J. Panic attack
Stead, C. The man who loved children
Stefaniak, M. H. The Turk and my mother
Stegner, W. E. The Big Rock Candy Mountain
Stein, G. The art of racing in the rain
Steinbeck, J. The grapes of wrath
Stirling, J. The penny wedding
Straight, S. The gettin place
Strayed, C. Torch
Stubbs, J. Family games
Stubbs, J. Like we used to be
Styron, A. All the finest girls
Styron, W. Lie down in darkness
Tanizaki, J. The Makioka sisters
Tarkington, B. Alice Adams
Tartt, D. The little friend
Taylor, B. The book of getting even
Taylor, P. H. A summons to Memphis
Tennant, E. An unequal marriage
Thayer, N. An act of love
Thompson, J. Wide blue yonder
Tóibín, C. The blackwater lightship
Tóibín, C. The heather blazing
Townsend, S. The Adrian Mole diaries
Trevor, W. The silence in the garden
Trollope, A. The Duke's children [abridged]
Trollope, A. Phineas Redux [abridged]
Trollope, J. Brother and sister
Trollope, J. Marrying the mistress
Trollope, J. The men and the girls
Trollope, J. Next of kin
Trollope, J. Other people's children
Trollope, J. The rector's wife
Trollope, J. Second honeymoon
Tryon, T. The other
Turow, S. The burden of proof
Twain, M. The adventures of Tom Sawyer
Tyler, A. The amateur marriage
Tyler, A. Back when we were grownups
Tyler, A. Breathing lessons
Tyler, A. The clock winder
Tyler, A. Digging to America
Tyler, A. Dinner at the Homesick Restaurant
Tyler, A. Earthly possessions

Tyler, A. Ladder of years
Tyler, A. Morgan's passing
Tyler, A. Saint maybe
Tyler, A. The tin can tree
Updike, J. Rabbit at rest
Updike, J. Rabbit is rich
Updike, J. Rabbit remembered
Vernon, O. Eden
Viswanathan, P. The toss of a lemon
Weiner, J. In her shoes
Welty, E. Delta wedding
Welty, E. Losing battles
Welty, E. The optimist's daughter
West, J. The friendly persuasion
Wharton, E. The children
Wiggs, S. The ocean between us
Wilder, T. The eighth day
Wilhelm, K. The good children
Winterson, J. Oranges are not the only fruit
Witt, M. Broken as things are
Wittenborn, D. Pharmakon
Wolfe, T. Look homeward, angel
Wolfe, T. O lost
Woo, S. J. Everything Asian
Woodrell, D. The death of sweet mister
Woolf, V. To the lighthouse
Wouk, H. Marjorie Morningstar
Family linen. Smith, L.
A **family** madness. Keneally, T.
The **family** man. Lipman, E.
Family matters. Mistry, R.
The **family** Moskat. Singer, I. B.
The **family** orchard. Eve, N.
Family pictures. Miller, S.
FAMILY SAGAS *See* Family chronicles
Family secrets. Thayer, N.
The **family** tree. Cadwalladr, C.
Family values. Constantine, K. C.

FAMINES

Buck, P. S. The good earth
A **fanatic** heart. O'Brien, E.

FANATICISM

Banks, R. Cloudsplitter
Boyle, T. C. Road to Wellville
Brown, C. B. Wieland
DeLillo, D. Libra
Evenson, B. The open curtain
Everett, P. L. American desert
Heinlein, R. A. Job: a comedy of justice
Hospital, J. T. Oyster
King, S. Insomnia
Meek, J. The people's act of love
Moulessehoul, M. The swallows of Kabul
Yorke, M. A question of belief

FANATICS *See* Fanaticism
Fangland. Marks, J.
FANON, FRANTZ, 1925-1961
                                    About
Wideman, J. E. Fanon
Fanon. Wideman, J. E.
Fanshawe. Hawthorne, N.
    In Hawthorne, N. Collected novels

FANTASIES

    See also Allegories; End of the world; Experimental stories; Future; Science fiction; Utopias
Abercrombie, J. Before they are hanged
Abercrombie, J. Last argument of kings
Abercrombie, J. The blade itself
Abraham, D. An autumn war
Abraham, D. A shadow in summer
Adams, R. Watership Down
Adrian, C. The children's hospital
Aira, C. Ghosts
American fantastic tales: terror and the uncanny from Poe to the pulps
American fantastic tales: terror and the uncanny from the 1940s to now
Anderson, P. War of the Gods
Anthony, P. Split infinity
Anthony, P. Virtual mode
Baker, K. The house of the stag
Baker, K. Mother Aegypt and other stories

FANTASIES—*Continued*

McCaffrey, A. The Masterharper of Pern
McCaffrey, A. Pegasus in space
McCaffrey, A. The renegades of Pern
McCaffrey, A. The skies of Pern
McCaffrey, A. The white dragon
McDermott, J. M. Last dragon
McKillip, P. A. Alphabet of thorn
McKillip, P. A. The sorceress and the Cygnet
McMullen, S. Glass dragons
Miéville, C. The city & the city
Miéville, C. Perdido Street Station
Miéville, C. The scar
Miller, W. M. A canticle for Leibowitz
Millhauser, S. Martin Dressler
Milligan, J. Jack Fish
Modesitt, L. E., Jr. Viewpoints critical
Moning, K. M. The immortal highlander
Moon, E. Moon flights
Moorcock, M. An alien heat
Moorcock, M. The best of Michael Moorcock
Moorcock, M. The dreamthief's daughter
Moorcock, M. The end of all songs
Moorcock, M. The hollow lands
Moorcock, M. The skrayling tree
Mosse, K. Labyrinth
Nabokov, V. V. Pale fire
Nathan, R. Portrait of Jennie
Nebula Awards showcase [date]
Niven, L. The burning city
Norton, A. The elvenbane
Norton, A. Elvenblood
Norton, A. Golden Trillium
Novik, N. His majesty's dragon
O'Brien, F. The Dalkey archive
O'Connell, J. The resurrectionist
Odom, M. The destruction of the books
Orwell, G. Animal farm
The Oxford book of modern fairy tales
Parker, K. J. The company
Parker, K. J. Devices and desires
Pelevin, V. The sacred book of the werewolf
Phillips, M. Gods behaving badly
Piercy, M. Woman on the edge of time
Powers, T. Three days to never
Pratchett, T. The color of magic
Pratchett, T. The fifth elephant
Pratchett, T. Going postal
Pratchett, T. Monstrous regiment
Pratchett, T. Thief of time
Pratchett, T. Thud!
Pratchett, T. The truth
Putney, M. J. A kiss of fate
Rand, A. Atlas shrugged
Riley, J. M. The serpent garden
Robbins, T. Jitterbug perfume
Robbins, T. Villa incognito
Robson, J. Keeping it real
Roth, J. The leviathan
Ruiz Zafón, C. The angel's game
Ruiz Zafón, C. The shadow of the wind
Rushdie, S. The Moor's last sigh
Rushdie, S. The satanic verses
Saberhagen, F. The fifth book of lost swords: Coinspinner's story
Saberhagen, F. The first book of lost swords: Woundhealer's story
Saberhagen, F. The fourth book of lost swords: Farslayer's story
Saberhagen, F. The last book of swords: Shieldbreaker's story
Saberhagen, F. The second book of lost swords: Sightblinder's story
Saberhagen, F. The seventh book of lost swords: Wayfinder's story
Saberhagen, F. The sixth book of lost swords: Mindsword's story
Saberhagen, F. The third book of lost swords: Stonecutter's story
Saint, H. F. Memoirs of an invisible man
Salvatore, R. A. Immortalis
Sanderson, B. Elantris
Sanderson, B. Mistborn: the final empire
Savage, S. Firmin
Sedia, E. Alchemy of stone

Silverberg, R. Lord Valentine's castle
Sinisalo, J. Troll
Snow white, blood red
Spark, M. The ballad of Peckham Rye
Steinbeck, J. The short reign of Pippin IV
Swanwick, M. The best of Michael Swanwick
Swift, J. Gulliver's travels
Tarr, J. Lady of horses
Tarr, J. Queen of the Amazons
Tolkien, J. R. R. The book of lost tales
Tolkien, J. R. R. The fellowship of the ring
Tolkien, J. R. R. The hobbit
Tolkien, J. R. R. The lord of the rings
Tolkien, J. R. R. Narn i chîn Húrin
Tolkien, J. R. R. The return of the king
Tolkien, J. R. R. The Silmarillion
Tolkien, J. R. R. The two towers
Turtledove, H. Into the darkness
Turtledove, H. Rulers of the darkness
Twain, M. A Connecticut Yankee in King Arthur's court
Vinge, J. D. The Snow Queen
Vinge, J. D. The Summer Queen
Vonnegut, K. Cat's cradle
Vonnegut, K. Slapstick
Wallace, D. The Watermelon King
Welty, E. The robber bridegroom
White, T. H. The book of Merlyn
White, T. H. The once and future king
White, T. H. The sword in the stone
Wibberley, L. The mouse that roared
Wilkins, K. Veil of gold
Winterson, J. Sexing the cherry
Wolfe, G. The best of Gene Wolfe
Wolfe, G. Castleview
Wolfe, G. The Citadel of the Autarch
Wolfe, G. The claw of the conciliator
Wolfe, G. An evil guest
Wolfe, G. Pirate freedom
Wolfe, G. The shadow of the torturer
Wolfe, G. The sword of the Lictor
Wolfe, G. The Urth of the new sun
Woolf, V. Orlando
The Year's best fantasy and horror
Yolen, J. Briar Rose
Zelazny, R. Blood of Amber
Zelazny, R. The courts of chaos
Zelazny, R. The guns of Avalon
Zelazny, R. The hand of Oberon
Zelazny, R. Knight of shadows
Zelazny, R. Nine princes in Amber
Zelazny, R. Prince of chaos
Zelazny, R. Sign of chaos
Zelazny, R. Sign of the unicorn
Zelazny, R. Trumps of doom

FANTASTIC FICTION *See* Fantasies; Science fiction
A **far** country. Mason, D.
A **far** cry from Kensington. Spark, M.
Far from the madding crowd. Hardy, T.
The **far** pavilions. Kaye, M. M.
The **far** side of the dollar. Macdonald, R.
Far Tortuga. Matthiessen, P.
Farewell, my lovely. Chandler, R.
  In Chandler, R. Stories and early novels p765-984
Farewell navigator. Zumas, L.
A **farewell** to arms. Hemingway, E.
Farewell to Fairacre. Read, Miss

FARM LIFE
  See also Peasant life
Dallas, S. Tallgrass
Markandaya, K. Nectar in a sieve

Arkansas
Grisham, J. A painted house

California
Mapson, J.-A. Bad Girl Creek
Norris, F. The octopus
Steinbeck, J. To a god unknown

Canada
Anderson-Dargatz, G. A recipe for bees
Lawson, M. Crow Lake

China
Buck, P. S. The good earth

FATHERS AND DAUGHTERS—*Continued*

Hall, A. L. The rhythm of the road
Hannah, K. On Mystic lake
Harris, J. Coastliners
Hellenga, R. Philosophy made simple
Hunter, S. Night of thunder
Ishiguro, K. An artist of the floating world
James, H. The golden bowl
James, H. Washington Square
Kafka, K. Miranda's vines
Kimmel, H. Something rising (light and swift)
Kincaid, J. Mr. Potter
Kingsolver, B. Animal dreams
Le, T. D. T. The gangster we are all looking for
Lee, H. To kill a mockingbird
L'Engle, M. Certain women
Lipman, E. The family man
Lively, P. The road to Lichfield
Livesey, M. The house on Fortune Street
McGrath, P. Martha Peake
McNaught, J. Paradise
McPhee, M. Gorgeous lies
Miles, J. Dear American Airlines
Moore, C. A dirty job
Oates, J. C. Black girl/White girl
Oates, J. C. The model
Pears, I. Stone's fall
Pessl, M. Special topics in calamity physics
Picoult, J. Vanishing acts
Pronzini, B. In an evil time
Proulx, A. The shipping news
Read, P. P. The professor's daughter
Rendell, R. Heartstones
Reuss, F. Mohr
Robinson, M. Home
Rock, P. My abandonment
Roth, P. American pastoral
Russo, R. Empire Falls
Sagan, F. Bonjour tristesse
Sakamoto, K. One hundred million hearts
Saramago, J. The cave
Scottoline, L. Moment of truth
Segal, E. Love story
Shreve, A. Light on snow
Sittenfeld, C. The man of my dreams
Smiley, J. A thousand acres
Smith, L. Saving Grace
Spark, M. Reality and dreams
Stevens, M. Useful girl
Strout, E. Abide with me
Toews, M. A complicated kindness
Trevor, W. Death in summer
Trollope, J. Next of kin
Ulinich, A. Petropolis
Undset, S. The bridal wreath
Undset, S. The mistress of Husaby
Vidal, G. 1876
Vine, B. The chimney sweeper's boy
Walker, A. By the light of my father's smile
Wenner, K. Dancing with Einstein
Wiggins, M. The shadow catcher
Wilhelm, K. The deepest water
Woodrell, D. Winter's bone
Yehoshua, A. B. A woman in Jerusalem
Yorke, M. Almost the truth

FATHERS AND SONS

See also Fathers and daughters; Parent and child

Abani, C. GraceLand
Akst, D. The Webster chronicle
Andersen Nexø, M. Pelle the conqueror: v1 Childhood
Banks, R. Cloudsplitter
Barker, N. Darkmans
Barthelme, F. Waveland
Berry, S. The Charlemagne pursuit
Bragg, M. The soldier's return
Bragg, M. A son of war
Chaon, D. Await your reply
Chekhov, A. P. My life
Cook, T. H. Master of the delta
Cusk, R. In the fold
Darnton, J. Mind catcher
De los Santos, M. Belong to me
Deb, S. The point of return
Dexter, P. The paperboy

Dexter, P. Spooner
Dickens, C. Dombey and Son
Doig, I. Mountain time
Dostoyevsky, F. The brothers Karamazov
Dragomán, G. The white king
Elkin, S. The MacGuffin
Ellis, B. E. Lunar Park
Enger, L. Undiscovered country
Epstein, L. San Remo Drive
Foer, J. S. Extremely loud & incredibly close
Ford, R. Independence Day
Forsyth, F. Avenger
García, C. A handbook to luck
Glass, J. Three Junes
Gordimer, N. The conservationist
Gordimer, N. My son's story
Griffin, W. E. B. Blood and honor
Griffin, W. E. B. Honor bound
Griffin, W. E. B. Secret honor
Grippando, J. Born to run
Grippando, J. A king's ransom
Grisham, J. The summons
Gunesekera, R. The match
Gurganus, A. Saint monster
Habila, H. Measuring time
Hadley, T. The master bedroom
Haig, M. The dead fathers club
Hansen, R. Atticus
Harding, P. Tinkers
Hart, J. Down river
Hart, J. The king of lies
Hart, J. Damage
Havazelet, E. Bearing the body
Hemingway, E. Islands in the stream
Hofmann, G. Luck
Homes, A. M. This book will save your life
Hunter, S. Black light
Iagnemma, K. The expeditions
Irving, J. Last night in Twisted River
Irving, J. Until I find you
Johnson, W. The devil you know
Johnston, W. The navigator of New York
Judd, A. Legacy
Just, W. S. Exiles in the garden
Just, W. S. An unfinished season
Kennedy, W. Very old bones
Kertész, I. Detective story
Klein, M. Con ed
Kureishi, H. The Buddha of suburbia
Land, B. Pilgrims upon the earth
Lansdale, J. R. The bottoms
Le Carré, J. Single & Single
Lee, C. Y. The flower drum song
Leithauser, B. A few corrections
Lewis, J. The king is dead
Lodge, D. Deaf sentence
Lodge, D. Paradise news
Lupica, M. Wild pitch
Lychack, W. The wasp eater
Marías, J. A heart so white
Marlette, D. Magic time
McCarthy, C. The road
McCrumb, S. The rosewood casket
McMahon, T. A. Principles of American nuclear chemistry
Melnyczuk, A. The house of widows
Meredith, G. The ordeal of Richard Feverel
Mitchell, D. Number9dream
Murdoch, I. The good apprentice
Naipaul, V. S. Half a life
Narayan, R. K. The financial expert
O'Connell, J. The resurrectionist
Ōe, K. The pinch runner memorandum
Okuizumi, H. The stones cry out
O'Nan, S. The names of the dead
Parker, T. J. Silent Joe
Parks, T. Cleaver
Parry, R. The winter wolf
Pearson, T. R. Blue Ridge
Peck, R. N. A day no pigs would die
Pelecanos, G. P. The way home
Potok, C. The chosen
Potok, C. My name is Asher Lev
Potok, C. The promise
Pouncey, P. R. Rules for old men waiting

FIFTH CENTURY, B.C.

Vidal, G. Creation
The **fifth** child. Lessing, D. M.

FIFTH COLUMN *See* World War, 1939-1945—Collaborationists

The **fifth** elephant. Pratchett, T.
The **Fifth** Floor. Harvey, M. T.
The **fifth** vial. Palmer, M.
Fifty years of the best from Ellery Queen's Mystery Magazine. Entered in Part I under title

FIGURINES *See* Art objects

FIJI

Johnson, S. The sailmaker's daughter

FIJI ISLANDS *See* Fiji

FILICIDE

McCabe, P. Winterwood
Moore, S. The big girls
Fima. Oz, A.
The **final** country. Crumley, J.
Final flight. Coonts, S.
The **final** judgment. Patterson, R. N.
The **final** martyrs. Endō, S.
Final payments. Gordon, M.
Final seconds. Lutz, J.
Final target. Johansen, I.
Final verdict. Siegel, S.

FINANCE

See also Banks
Thomas, M. M. Hanover Place
The **financial** expert. Narayan, R. K.
In Narayan, R. K. Mr. Sampath—the printer of Malgudi, The financial expert, Waiting for the Mahatma

FINANCIERS *See* Capitalists and financiers

Find her a grave. Wilcox, C.
The **finder**. Harrison, C.
Finders keepers. Michaels, F.
Finding Laura. Hooper, K.
Finding Nouf. Ferraris, Z.
A **fine** and bitter snow. Stabenow, D.
A **fine** and private place. Queen, E.
A **fine** balance. Mistry, R.
A **fine** dark line. Lansdale, J. R.
Fine just the way it is. Proulx, A.
Fingersmith. Waters, S.
The **finishing** school. Godwin, G.
The **finishing** school. Spark, M.
Finity's End. Cherryh, C. J.

FINLAND

Rayner, R. The cloud sketcher
Finn. Clinch, J.
Finnegans wake. Joyce, J.
Finnegan's week. Wambaugh, J.

FINNS

United States

Rayner, R. The cloud sketcher
Fiona Range. Morris, M. M.
The **fire**. Neville, K.
Fire down below. Golding, W.
Fire flight. Nance, J. J.
Fire ice. Cussler, C.
Fire in the blood. Némirovsky, I.
Fire in the steppe. Sienkiewicz, H.
Fire logic. Marks, L. J.
Fire on the mountain. Desai, A.
Fire on the waters. Poyer, D.
Fire sale. Paretsky, S.
A **fire** upon the deep. Vinge, V.

FIREARMS

Dickinson, P. Some deaths before dying
Patterson, R. N. Balance of power
Firebird. Garcia y Robertson, R.
Firebird. Lackey, M.
The **firedrake**. Holland, C.

FIREFIGHTERS

Chazin, S. Flashover
Emerson, E. W. Pyro
Emerson, E. W. Vertical burn

Harrison, C. The finder
Nance, J. J. Fire flight
Firefox. Thomas, C.
The **fireman's** fair. Humphreys, J.

FIRES

See also Arson; Disasters
Crane, S. The monster
Hospital, J. T. Oyster
Pipkin, J. Woodsburner
Wideman, J. E. Philadelphia fire
Firestarter. King, S.
Firewall. Mankell, H.
A **firing** offense. Ignatius, D.
The **firm**. Grisham, J.
Firmin. Savage, S.
The **first** book of lost swords: Woundhealer's story. Saberhagen, F.
The **first** counsel. Meltzer, B.
The **first** cut. Robinson, P.
The **first** deadly sin. Sanders, L.
The **first** desire. Reisman, N.
The **first** eagle. Hillerman, T.
First king of Shannara. Brooks, T.
The **first** law. Lescroart, J. T.
First light. Tapply, W. G.
First love and other stories. Turgenev, I. S.
The **first** man in Rome. McCullough, C.
The **first** men in the moon. Wells, H. G.
In Wells, H. G. Seven famous novels
First offense. Rosenberg, N. T.
The **first** victim. Pearson, R.
The **first** wave. Benn, J. R.
The **First** Wives Club. Goldsmith, O.
The **fisher** king. Marshall, P.

FISHERIES

Torday, P. Salmon fishing in the Yemen

FISHERMEN

See also Fishing
Casey, J. Spartina
Grass, G. The flounder
Guterson, D. Snow falling on cedars
Mills, M. Amagansett
Mishima, Y. The sound of waves
Rice, L. Blue moon
Winton, T. Dirt music

FISHES

Grass, G. The flounder

FISHING

See also Fishermen; Pearl fishing; Salmon fishing
Hemingway, E. Islands in the stream
McGuane, T. Ninety-two in the shade
The **Fitzgerald** reader. Fitzgerald, F. S.
The **five** bells and bladebone. Grimes, M.
Five fortunes. Gutcheon, B. R.
Five novels of the 1960s & 70s. Dick, P. K.
Five quarters of the orange. Harris, J.
The **five** red herrings. Sayers, D. L.
Five skies. Carlson, R.
The **fixer**. Malamud, B.
A **flag** for sunrise. Stone, R.
Flags in the dust. Faulkner, W.
also in Faulkner, W. Novels, 1926-1929

FLAMENCO DANCERS *See* Dancers

FLANDERS (BELGIUM) *See* Belgium—Flanders

FLANNIGAN, KATHERINE MARY O'FALLON
About

Freedman, B. Mrs. Mike
Flappers and philosophers. Fitzgerald, F. S.
In Fitzgerald, F. S. Novels and stories, 1920-1922 p249-433
Flashover. Chazin, S.

FLEMING, IAN, 1908-1964
Parodies, imitations, etc.

Faulks, S. Devil may care
Flesh and blood. Cunningham, M.
Flesh and blood. Harvey, J.
Flesh house. MacBride, S.
Flesh wounds. Greenleaf, S.
Fletch. Mcdonald, G.
also in Mcdonald, G. The Fletch chronicles
Fletch and the man who. Mcdonald, G.
In Mcdonald, G. The Fletch chronicles

The **food** of the gods. Wells, H. G.
  In Wells, H. G. Seven famous novels
Fools of fortune. Trevor, W.
Fools rush in. Gorman, E.
FOOTBALL
  See also Super Bowl Game (Football)
  Grisham, J. Playing for pizza
  Harris, E. L. And this too shall pass
  Phillips, S. E. It had to be you
Footprints. Hearon, S.
The **footprints** of God. Iles, G.
Footsteps of the hawk. Vachss, A. H.
For love. Miller, S.
For the dogs. Wignall, K.
For they shall inherit. Ross-Macdonald, M.
The **forbidden** zone. Strieber, W.
Force 10 from Navarone. MacLean, A.

FORCED LABOR
  Solzhenitsyn, A. One day in the life of Ivan Denisovich
FORD, GERALD R., 1913-2006
            About
  Updike, J. Memories of the Ford Administration
FORD, ROBERT, 1862-1892
            About
  Hansen, R. The assassination of Jesse James by the coward
    Robert Ford

FORECASTING
  Othmer, J. P. The futurist
A **foregone** conclusion. Howells, W. D.
  In Howells, W. D. Novels, 1875-1886
Foreign affairs. Lurie, A.
Foreign affairs and other stories. O'Faoláin, S.
  In O'Faoláin, S. The collected stories of Seán O'Faoláin
    p1061-1226
The **foreign** correspondent. Furst, A.
FOREIGN SERVICE *See* Diplomatic life

FOREIGN VISITORS
  Silber, J. The size of the world
Foreigner. Cherryh, C. J.
Foreigners. Phillips, C.

FORENSIC SCIENTISTS
  Abu-Jaber, D. Origin
  Black, L. Takeover
  Gardiner, M. The Dirty Secrets Club
  Lindsay, J. P. Dearly devoted Dexter
  Lindsay, J. P. Dexter in the dark
The **foreseeable** future. Price, R.
The **forest**. Rutherfurd, E.
FORESTS AND FORESTRY
  See also Wilderness areas
  Le Guin, U. K. The word for world is forest
Forever. Hamill, P.
Forever free. Haldeman, J. W.
Forever peace. Haldeman, J. W.
The **forever** war. Haldeman, J. W.
The **forge** of God. Bear, G.
The **forger**. Watkins, P.
Forgery. Murray, S.
The **forgery** of Venus. Gruber, M.

FORGERY OF WORKS OF ART
  Crusie, J. Faking it
  Davies, R. The lyre of Orpheus
  Davies, R. What's bred in the bone
  Gaddis, W. The recognitions
  Gruber, M. The forgery of Venus
  Krentz, J. A. Lost and found
  Mayle, P. Chasing Cézanne
  Watkins, P. The forger
Forgetfulness. Just, W. S.
Forgive me. Ward, A. E.
Forgiveness day. Le Guin, U. K.
  In Le Guin, U. K. Four ways to forgiveness p35-92
Forgiving. Spencer, L.
The **forgotten**. Kellerman, F.
The **forgotten**. Wiesel, E.
The **forgotten** man. Crais, R.
The **Forsyte** saga. Galsworthy, J.
The **fortress** of solitude. Lethem, J.
Fortunate son. Mosley, W.

The **fortune**. Korda, M.
Fortune is a woman. Adler, E.
FORTUNES *See* Wealth
The **fortunes** and misfortunes of the famous Moll Flanders. See
    Defoe, D. Moll Flanders
Fortune's favorites. McCullough, C.
Fortune's Rocks. Shreve, A.
The **forty** days of Musa Dagh. Werfel, F.
Forward, Gunner Asch! Kirst, H. H.
Forward the Foundation. Asimov, I.

FOSSILS
  Doyle, Sir A. C. The lost world
  Smith, D. Pictures from an expedition
FOSTER CHILDREN
  See also Adoption
  Alexie, S. Flight
  Austen, J. Mansfield Park
  Eliot, G. Silas Marner
  Fitch, J. White oleander
  Gibbons, K. Ellen Foster
  March, W. The bad seed
  McKinney-Whetstone, D. Tempest rising
  Rinehart, S. Built in a day
Foucault's pendulum. Eco, U.
Foul matter. Grimes, M.
Found money. Grippando, J.
Foundation. Asimov, I.
Foundation and earth. Asimov, I.
Foundation and empire. Asimov, I.
FOUNDATIONS (ENDOWMENTS) *See* Endowments
Foundation's edge. Asimov, I.
Foundation's fear. Benford, G.
FOUNDLINGS *See* Abandoned children
The **fountainhead**. Rand, A.
Four blind mice. Patterson, J.
The **four-chambered** heart. Nin, A.
  In Nin, A. Cities of the interior p239-358
Four, five and six by Tey. Tey, J.
Four freedoms. Crowley, J.
The **four-gated** city. Lessing, D. M.
  In Lessing, D. M. Children of violence
The **four** million. Henry, O.
  In Henry, O. The complete works of O. Henry p1-108
Four novels of the 1960s. Dick, P. K.
Four past midnight. King, S.
Four souls. Erdrich, L.
Four spirits. Naslund, S. J.
Four ways to forgiveness. Le Guin, U. K.
The **fourteen** sisters of Emilio Montez O'Brien. Hijuelos, O.
The **fourth** book of lost swords: Farslayer's story. Saberhagen,
    F.
The **fourth** deadly sin. Sanders, L.
The **fourth** Durango. Thomas, R.
The **fourth** hand. Irving, J.

FOURTH OF JULY
  Lockridge, R. Raintree County
  Lurie, A. Only children
The **fourth** procedure. Pottinger, S.
The **fourth** protocol. Forsyth, F.
The **fourth** world. Danvers, D.

FOX, GEORGE, 1624-1691
            About
  De Hartog, J. The peaceable kingdom
FOX, MARGARET ASKEW FELL, 1614-1702
            About
  De Hartog, J. The peaceable kingdom
Foxfire. Oates, J. C.
Foxmask. Marillier, J.
Fragile things. Gaiman, N.
Fragrant Harbor. Lanchester, J.
Frames. Estleman, L. D.
Framley parsonage. Trollope, A.

FRANCE
  Cocteau, J. The impostor
  Colette. The complete Claudine
  Colette. Music-hall sidelights
  Dufossé, C. School's out
  Furst, A. Kingdom of shadows
  Guène, F. Kiffe kiffe tomorrow
  Harris, J. Chocolat

FRANCE—Paris—*Continued*

Marshall, P. The fisher king
McCarthy, M. Birds of America
Miller, A. Oxygen
Miller, H. Tropic of Cancer
Nin, A. Children of the albatross
Nin, A. The four-chambered heart
Nin, A. Ladders to fire
Remarque, E. M. Arch of triumph
Rhys, J. Quartet
Richler, M. Barney's version
Sartre, J. P. The age of reason
Stamm, P. On a day like this
Steinbeck, J. The short reign of Pippin IV
Tremain, R. The way I found her
Truong, M. T. D. The book of salt
Vargas Llosa, M. The bad girl
Verne, J. Paris in the twentieth century
Watkins, P. The forger
White, E. The married man

Paris—9th century

Holland, C. The angel and the sword

Paris—15th century

Hugo, V. The hunchback of Notre Dame

Paris—18th century

Dickens, C. A tale of two cities
Sabatini, R. Scaramouche

Paris—19th century

Balzac, H. d. Cousin Bette
Balzac, H. d. Père Goriot (Old Goriot)
Dumas, A. The Count of Monte Cristo
James, H. The ambassadors
James, H. The American
Laker, R. Banners of silk
Zola, É. Nana

Provence

Mayle, P. Anything considered
Mayle, P. A good year
Mayle, P. Hotel Pastis
Pears, I. The dream of Scipio

Saint-Tropez

Steel, D. Sunset in St. Tropez

Versailles

Davis, K. Versailles
Laker, R. To dance with kings
Naslund, S. J. Abundance
The **Franchise** affair. Tey, J.
    also in Tey, J. Three by Tey
FRANK, ANNE, 1929-1945
About
Lourie, R. A hatred for tulips

FRANKENSTEIN (FICTITIOUS CHARACTER)

Sheck, L. A monster's notes
Frankenstein; or, The modern Prometheus. Shelley, M. W.
FRANKLIN, BENJAMIN, 1706-1790
About
Morrow, J. The last witchfinder
Shaara, J. The glorious cause
Shaara, J. Rise to rebellion
FRANKLIN, JANE GRIFFIN, LADY, 1792-1875
About
Flanagan, R. Wanting
FRANKLIN, SIR JOHN, 1786-1847
About
Flanagan, R. Wanting
Simmons, D. The terror
Vollmann, W. T. The rifles
Franny & Zooey. Salinger, J. D.

FRATRICIDE

Cheever, J. Falconer
Wroblewski, D. The story of Edgar Sawtelle

FRAUD

Iles, G. Third degree
Freaky Deaky. Leonard, E.
Frederica. Heyer, G.

FREDERICK I, HOLY ROMAN EMPEROR, CA. 1123-1190
About
Eco, U. Baudolino
Free fall in crimson. MacDonald, J. D.
A **free** life. Ha Jin
A **free** man of color. Hambly, B.
FREEDOM *See* Liberty
Freedom. Safire, W.
Freedomland. Price, R.
Freedom's landing. McCaffrey, A.
Freedom's ransom. McCaffrey, A.

FREEMASONS

Brown, D. The lost symbol
Kurtz, K. Two crowns for America
FREIGHTERS *See* Ships
FRENCH, PAUL *See* Asimov, Isaac, 1920-1992

FRENCH

Algeria

Camus, A. The stranger

Canada

Cather, W. Shadows on the rock

Egypt

Roiphe, A. R. An imperfect lens

England

Du Maurier, Dame D. Frenchman's Creek

Indochina

Texier, C. Victorine

Ireland

Flanagan, T. The year of the French

Poland

Furst, A. The spies of Warsaw

Russia

Bradbury, M. To the Hermitage
Makine, A. Dreams of my Russian summers

United States

Cather, W. Death comes for the archbishop
Hansen, R. Isn't it romantic?
FRENCH AND INDIAN WAR, 1755-1763 *See* United States—
    French and Indian War, 1755-1763
The **French** lieutenant's woman. Fowles, J.
FRENCH REVOLUTION *See* France—1789-1799
FRENCH RIVIERA *See* Riviera (France and Italy)
FRENCH SOLDIERS *See* Soldiers—France
Frenchman's Creek. Du Maurier, Dame D.
FREUD, SIGMUND, 1856-1939
About
Meyer, N. The seven-per-cent solution
Thomas, D. M. The white hotel
FREYTAG-LORINGHOVEN, ELSA VON, BARONESS, 1874-1927
About
Steinke, R. Holy skirts
Friday. Heinlein, R. A.
Friday. Tournier, M.
Friday nights. Trollope, J.
Friday the rabbi slept late. Kemelman, H.
Fried green tomatoes at the Whistle-Stop Cafe. Flagg, F.
A **friend** of Kafka and other stories. Singer, I. B.
    In Singer, I. B. Collected stories: A friend of Kafka to Passions
Friend of mankind and other stories. Mazor, J.
Friend of my youth. Munro, A.
The **friendly** persuasion. West, J.
FRIENDS *See* Friendship
FRIENDS, SOCIETY OF *See* Society of Friends
Friends at Thrush Green. Read, Miss
The **friends** of Eddie Coyle. Higgins, G. V.

FRIENDSHIP

See also Love
Adler, E. Fortune is a woman

TITLE AND SUBJECT INDEX

FRONTIER AND PIONEER LIFE—*Continued*

Middle Western States

Cooper, J. F. The prairie

Minnesota

Moberg, V. The last letter home
Moberg, V. Unto a good land

Montana

Williamson, P. Heart of the west
Williamson, P. The outsider

Nebraska

Cather, W. My Ántonia
Cather, W. O pioneers!

New York (State)

Cooper, J. F. The Deerslayer
Cooper, J. F. The last of the Mohicans
Cooper, J. F. The Leatherstocking tales
Cooper, J. F. The Pathfinder
Cooper, J. F. The pioneers
Edmonds, W. D. Drums along the Mohawk

New Zealand

Goudge, E. Green Dolphin Street

Ohio

Richter, C. The awakening land
Swerling, B. Shadowbrook

Ohio River Valley

Settle, M. L. O Beulah Land

Oklahoma

Ferber, E. Cimarron

Pennsylvania

Larsen, D. The white
Liss, D. The whiskey rebels

South Dakota

Dexter, P. Deadwood
Rølvaag, O. E. Giants in the earth
Rølvaag, O. E. Peder Victorious

Southwestern States

Brand, M. In the hills of Monterey

Texas

Michener, J. A. Texas
Sherman, J. The Baron war

Virginia

L'Amour, L. To the far blue mountains

Western States

Berger, T. Little Big Man
Coldsmith, D. Tallgrass
Guthrie, A. B. The big sky
Guthrie, A. B. The way West
Henderson, W. H. Augusta Locke
Holland, C. An ordinary woman
Hunter, E. The Chisholms
Johnston, T. C. Dance on the wind
Johnston, T. C. Wind walker
L'Amour, L. The Cherokee Trail
L'Amour, L. End of the drive
L'Amour, L. Jubal Sackett
L'Amour, L. The Sacketts: beginnings of a dynasty
McMurtry, L. Boone's Lick
McMurtry, L. Buffalo girls
McMurtry, L. Comanche moon
McMurtry, L. Dead man's walk
McMurtry, L. Lonesome dove
McMurtry, L. Zeke and Ned
Portis, C. True grit
Schaefer, J. W. The collected stories of Jack Schaefer
Taylor, R. L. The travels of Jaimie McPheeters
Vanderhaeghe, G. The last crossing
Willard, T. Buffalo soldiers

Wyoming

L'Amour, L. Bendigo Shafter
Frost. Bernhard, T.
Fruit of the lemon. Levy, A.

FRUIT PICKERS *See* Migrant labor
The **frumious** Bandersnatch. McBain, E.

FUGATE, CARIL ANN
About
Ward, L. Outside valentine
Fugitive. Margolin, P.
The **fugitive** [variant title: The sweet cheat gone] Proust, M.
  In Proust, M. The captive [and] The fugitive
  In Proust, M. Remembrance of things past p425-706
Fugitive colors. Maron, M.
Fugitive pieces. Michaels, A.

FUGITIVE SLAVES
Crafts, H. The bondswomans narrative
Durham, D. A. A walk through darkness
McBride, J. Song yet sung
Tryon, T. In the fire of spring
Twain, M. The adventures of Huckleberry Finn

FUGITIVES
  See also Escaped convicts; Fugitive slaves; Manhunts;
  Outlaws
Ablow, K. R. Compulsion
Anderson, E. Thieves like us
Coben, H. Gone for good
Furnivall, K. The red scarf
Irving, J. Last night in Twisted River
Meek, J. The people's act of love
Moore, B. The statement
Piercy, M. Vida
Riordan, R. Cold Springs
Saint, H. F. Memoirs of an invisible man
Smith, A. Good morning, killer
Spark, M. Aiding and abetting
Spiotta, D. Eat the document
Woodrell, D. Winter's bone
Wray, J. Canaan's tongue
Fugitives' fire. Brand, M.
Full circle. Wilcox, C.

FUNDAMENTALISM *See* Fundamentalists

FUNDAMENTALISTS
Paretsky, S. Bleeding Kansas
Wilcox, J. Hunk City
Winterson, J. Oranges are not the only fruit

FUNERAL DIRECTORS *See* Undertakers and undertaking
Funeral games. Renault, M.
Funeral in Berlin. Deighton, L.
Funeral in blue. Perry, A.

FUNERAL RITES AND CEREMONIES
Agee, J. A death in the family
Duncan, G. Death of an ordinary man
Faulkner, W. As I lay dying
Lipman, E. The dearly departed
Styron, A. All the finest girls
Styron, W. Lie down in darkness
Tyler, A. Breathing lessons
Waugh, E. The loved one
Welty, E. Losing battles
Welty, E. The optimist's daughter

FUR TRADE
Guthrie, A. B. The big sky
The **further** adventures of Menachem-Mendl. Sholem Aleichem

FUTURE
  See also Science fiction
Amis, M. London fields
Anderson, P. Genesis
Anderson, P. Goat song
Asaro, C. Primary inversion
Asimov, I. Forward the Foundation
Asimov, I. Foundation
Asimov, I. Foundation and earth
Asimov, I. Foundation and empire
Asimov, I. Foundation's edge
Asimov, I. Prelude to Foundation
Asimov, I. Second Foundation
Atwood, M. The Handmaid's tale
Atwood, M. The year of the flood
Auster, P. In the country of last things
Banks, I. Matter
Barnes, J. The armies of memory
Bear, G. Anvil of stars
Bear, G. The forge of God

GAMBLING

See also Lotteries

Amado, J. Dona Flor and her two husbands
Atkins, A. White shadow
Dickens, C. The old curiosity shop
Dixon, K. The art of losing
Dostoyevsky, F. The gambler
Fleming, I. Casino Royale
Francis, D. Even money
Iles, G. The devil's punchbowl
Johnson, D. Nobody move
Latour, J. The Havana World Series
Leiber, F. Gonna roll the bones
Rigosi, G. Night bus
Robbins, H. Sin city
Schwegel, T. Person of interest
Westlake, D. E. Bad news
The **game**. King, L. R.
A **game** of thrones. Martin, G. R. R.
Game over. Harrod-Eagles, C.

GAMES

See also Video games

Shan Sa. The girl who played go

GANDHI, MAHATMA, 1869-1948
About
Narayan, R. K. Waiting for the Mahatma

GANDHI, MOHANDAS KARAMCHAND *See* Gandhi, Mahatma, 1869-1948

The **gang** that couldn't shoot straight. Breslin, J.

GANGS

See also Juvenile delinquency

Bell, M. S. Ten Indians
Fairstein, L. Killer heat
Grossman, D. Someone to run with
Oates, J. C. Foxfire
Wray, J. Canaan's tongue
The **gangster** we are all looking for. Le, T. D. T.

GANGSTERS

See also Mafia

Atkins, A. White shadow
Collins, M. A. Black hats
Dezenhall, E. Money wanders
Doctorow, E. L. Billy Bathgate
Dunne, D. An inconvenient woman
Gilmore, J. Golden country
Gruber, M. The book of air and shadows
Hunter, S. Hot Springs
Lashner, W. Kockroach
Leonard, E. Get Shorty
Lustbader, E. V. Second skin
Parker, R. B. Double play
Rayner, R. The cloud sketcher
Shteyngart, G. The Russian debutante's handbook
Tanenbaum, R. Act of revenge
Turner, F. W. 1929
Garbo laughs. Hay, E.
Garden of beasts. Deaver, J.
A **garden** of earthly delights. Oates, J. C.
The **garden** of Eden. Hemingway, E.
The **garden** of evil. Hewson, D.
The **garden** of last days. Dubus, A.
Garden of lies. Goudge, E.
The **Garden** of Rama. Clarke, A. C.
The **garden** of the Finzi-Continis. Bassani, G.

GARDEN PARTIES *See* Parties

The **garden** party and other stories. Mansfield, K.

GARDENERS

Coetzee, J. M. Life & times of Michael K.
Gregory, P. Earthly joys
Gregory, P. Virgin earth
Kosinski, J. N. Being there
Laker, R. The golden tulip

GARDENING *See* Gardens

GARDENS

Humphreys, H. The lost garden
Gardens in the dunes. Silko, L.
Gardens of Covington. Medlicott, J. A.
The **gardens** of Kyoto. Walbert, K.
The **gargoyle**. Davidson, A.

GARMENT WORKERS *See* Clothing industry
Gas City. Estleman, L. D.

GASCONY (FRANCE) *See* France—Gascony
A **gate** at the stairs. Moore, L.
The **gate** house. DeMille, N.
Gate of the sun. Khoury, E.
The **gate** to Women's Country. Tepper, S. S.
Gatekeeper. Shelby, P.
The **gates** of exquisite view. Trenhaile, J.
The **gates** of hell. Doherty, P. C.
The **gates** of the Alamo. Harrigan, S.
Gateway. Pohl, F.
The **gateway** of India. Theroux, P.
In Theroux, P. The Elephanta suite
The **gathering**. Enright, A.
The **gathering**. Kienzle, W. X.
A **gathering** of old men. Gaines, E. J.
Gaudy Night. Sayers, D. L.

GAUGUIN, PAUL, 1848-1903
About
Maugham, W. S. The moon and sixpence
Vargas Llosa, M. The way to paradise

GAUL

Llywelyn, M. Druids

GAULLE, CHARLES DE, 1890-1970
About
Forsyth, F. The day of the jackal

GAULS *See* Celts

GAUSS, CARL FRIEDRICH, 1777-1855
About
Kehlmann, D. Measuring the world

GAUTAMA BUDDHA
About
Mishima, Y. The Temple of Dawn
Mishima, Y. The temple of the golden pavilion

GAY MEN *See* Homosexuality

GAY WOMEN *See* Lesbianism

Gazelle. Ducornet, R.

GDANSK (POLAND) *See* Poland—Gdansk

Geek love. Dunn, K.

GEISHAS

Golden, A. Memoirs of a geisha
Kawabata, Y. Snow country
Gemini. Dunnett, D.
The **Gemini** contenders. Ludlum, R.

GEMS *See* Diamonds; Emeralds

GENEALOGY

Groff, L. The monsters of Templeton
Halter, M. The book of Abraham
The **general** and his labyrinth. García Márquez, G.
The **general** of the dead army. Kadare, I.

GENERALS

Griffin, W. E. B. Secret honor
Massie, A. Caesar
Ricks, T. E. A soldier's duty
The **general's** daughter. DeMille, N.

GENERATION GAP *See* Conflict of generations
Generation loss. Hand, E.
Generosity. Powers, R.
Generous death. Pickard, N.
Genesis. Anderson, P.

GENETIC ENGINEERING

Morgan, R. K. Thirteen
Scalzi, J. The ghost brigades

GENETIC EXPERIMENTATION *See* Genetics
GENETIC RESEARCH *See* Genetics

GENETICS

Crichton, M. Jurassic Park
Cussler, C. Atlantis found
Darnton, J. The experiment
DeMille, N. Plum Island
Dick, P. K. Flow my tears, the policeman said
Herbert, F. Dune
Herbert, F. Dune messiah
Herbert, F. Heretics of Dune
Hoffman, E. The secret
Johansen, I. Long after midnight
Koontz, D. R. Watchers

GERMANY—14th century—*Continued*
Flynn, M. Eifelheim

15th century

Gross, C. Scholarium

18th century

Fitzgerald, P. The blue flower
Hofmann, G. Lichtenberg and the little flower girl

19th century

Galloway, J. Clara
Mann, T. Buddenbrooks

1918-1945

Bohjalian, C. A. Skeletons at the feast
Browne, M. Eye of the abyss
Deaver, J. Garden of beasts
Fallada, H. Every man dies alone
Grass, G. Crabwalk
Grass, G. Dog years
Grass, G. The tin drum
Hansen, R. Hitler's niece
Isherwood, C. The Berlin stories
Remarque, E. M. The road back
Remarque, E. M. A time to love and a time to die
Reuss, F. Mohr

1945-

Anthony, E. The Janus imperative
Ford, R. The student conductor
Forsyth, F. The Odessa file
Grass, G. The call of the toad
Grass, G. Dog years
Grass, G. Too far afield
Handke, P. The left-handed woman
Harris, R. Fatherland
Higgins, J. Day of judgment
Kanon, J. The good German
Krüger, M. The cello player
Schlink, B. The reader
Shakespeare, N. Snowleg
Uris, L. Armageddon

American occupation, 1945-1955

See Germany—1945-

Army

Anatoli, A. Babi Yar
Kirst, H. H. Forward, Gunner Asch!
Remarque, E. M. All quiet on the western front

Army—Officers

Kirst, H. H. The return of Gunner Asch

Communism

See Communism—Germany

World War, 1939-1945

See World War, 1939-1945—Germany

Bavaria

MacLean, A. Where eagles dare

Berlin

Barnes, D. Nightwood
Beatty, P. Slumberland
Deaver, J. Garden of beasts
Deighton, L. Berlin game
Deighton, L. Funeral in Berlin
Deighton, L. London match
Fallada, H. Every man dies alone
Grass, G. Too far afield
Isherwood, C. The Berlin stories
Just, W. S. The weather in Berlin
Kanon, J. The good German
McEwan, I. The innocent
Nabokov, V. V. King, queen, knave
Nooteboom, C. All souls' day
Pye, M. The pieces from Berlin
Uris, L. Armageddon

Bonn

Böll, H. The clown

Cologne

Böll, H. The silent angel

Gross, C. Scholarium

Dresden

Vonnegut, K. Slaughterhouse-five

Düsseldorf

Mann, T. The black swan

Hamburg

Le Carré, J. A most wanted man
Germinal. Zola, É.
GERMS *See* Microorganisms
Gerontius. Hamilton-Paterson, J.
GERONTOLOGISTS *See* Physicians
Gertrude. Hesse, H.
Gertrude and Claudius. Updike, J.
GESTAPO *See* National socialism
A **gesture** life. Lee, C.-R.
Get a life. Gordimer, N.
Get real. Westlake, D. E.
Get Shorty. Leonard, E.
The **gettin** place. Straight, S.
Getting mother's body. Parks, S.-L.

GETTYSBURG, BATTLE OF, 1863

Gingrich, N. Gettysburg
Olmstead, R. Coal black horse
Shaara, M. The killer angels
Gettysburg. Gingrich, N.
GHETTOS *See* Jews—Segregation
The **ghost**. Harris, R.
Ghost. Lightman, A. P.
The **ghost** brigades. Scalzi, J.
Ghost country. Paretsky, S.
The **ghost** in love. Carroll, J.
Ghost moon. Robards, K.
The **ghost** road. Barker, P.

GHOST STORIES

See also Gothic romances; Horror stories; Supernatural
    phenomena
Aira, C. Ghosts
Byatt, A. S. The conjugial angel
Carroll, J. The ghost in love
The dark
Davies, R. Murther & walking spirits
DeLillo, D. The body artist
Dickens, C. A Christmas carol
Dickens, C. The complete ghost stories of Charles Dickens
Ellis, B. E. Lunar Park
Gutcheon, B. R. More than you know
Haig, M. The dead fathers club
Hansen, E. F. Tales of protection
Harwood, J. The ghost writer
Hill, J. 20th century ghosts
Hill, J. Heart-shaped box
Hoffman, A. The third angel
Hooper, K. Haunting Rachel
Jackson, S. The haunting of Hill House
James, H. The turn of the screw
Kallos, S. Broken for you
King, S. Bag of bones
Lightman, A. P. Ghost
Livesey, M. Eva moves the furniture
Lofts, N. Gad's Hall
Long, D. The inhabited world
Lovecraft, H. P. The mound
Lurie, A. Women and ghosts
McFarland, D. A face at the window
Moloney, S. The dwelling
Niffenegger, A. Her fearful symmetry
O'Nan, S. The night country
The Oxford book of English ghost stories
The Oxford book of twentieth-century ghost stories
Saul, J. Second child
See, L. Peony in love
Shepard, L. Softspoken
Steel, D. Johnny Angel
Straub, P. Ghost story
Tan, A. The hundred secret senses
Ghost story. Straub, P.
Ghost town. Coover, R.

GHOST TOWNS *See* Extinct cities
The **ghost** walker. Coel, M.
The **ghost** writer. Harwood, J.

GRANDFATHERS—*Continued*

Foer, J. S. Extremely loud & incredibly close
Grisham, J. The chamber
Gurganus, A. A hog loves its life: something about my grand-
    father
Kring, S. Thank you for all things
Lowell, E. Die in plain sight
McGuane, T. Nobody's angel
Paretsky, S. Ghost country
Stanišic, S. How the soldier repairs the gramophone
Toole, F. X. Pound for pound

GRANDMOTHERS

Allende, I. Portrait in sepia
Cohen, L. H. House lights
Colette. Gigi
De la Roche, M. Jalna
Desai, A. Fire on the mountain
Dische, I. The Empress of Weehawken
Jhabvala, R. P. Heat and dust
L'Engle, M. A live coal in the sea
Makine, A. Dreams of my Russian summers
Miller, S. The world below
Narayan, R. K. Waiting for the Mahatma
Read, Miss. Thrush Green
Ross-Macdonald, M. The Trevarton inheritance
Scott, J. Follow me
Tóibín, C. The blackwater lightship
Tryon, T. The other
Weiner, J. In her shoes
Weldon, F. Rhode Island blues
Weldon, F. She may not leave
Whitney, P. A. Domino
Yolen, J. Briar Rose
The **grandmother's** tale and selected stories. Narayan, R. K.

GRANDPARENTS

Benioff, D. City of thieves
Gardam, J. Faith Fox
Kelman, J. Kieron Smith, boy
Mitchard, J. A theory of relativity
Wright, S. The Amalgamation Polka

GRANDSONS

Hays, T. The pleasure was mine

GRANT, ULYSSES S. (ULYSSES SIMPSON), 1822-1885
About

Byrd, M. Grant
Gingrich, N. Grant comes east
Shaara, J. The last full measure
Grant. Byrd, M.
Grant comes east. Gingrich, N.
Grant's last case. See Tey, J. The singing sands
The **grapes** of wrath. Steinbeck, J.
Grass. Tepper, S. S.
The **grass** crown. McCullough, C.
The **grass** dancer. Power, S.
The **grass** harp. Capote, T.
The **grass** is singing. Lessing, D. M.
Grass roots. Woods, S.
Grasshopper. Vine, B.
Grave mistake. Marsh, Dame N.
Grave music. Harrod-Eagles, C.
Grave secrets. Reichs, K. J.
Grave tattoo. McDermid, V.
Grave undertakings. McInerny, R. M.
Gravedigger. Hansen, J.
The **gravedigger's** daughter. Oates, J. C.
Graveyard dust. Hambly, B.
The **graveyard** game. Baker, K.
GRAVEYARDS *See* Cemeteries
Gravity's rainbow. Pynchon, T.
The **Grays.** Strieber, W.
The **great** American novel. Roth, P.
    also in Roth, P. Novels, 1973-1977
GREAT AUNTS *See* Aunts

GREAT BRITAIN

    See also England; Northern Ireland; Scotland; Wales
McCullough, C. The song of Troy

Armed forces

    See also Great Britain. Army

Colonies

Clavell, J. Tai-Pan

GREAT BRITAIN. AIR FORCE *See* Great Britain. Royal Air
    Force

GREAT BRITAIN. ARMY

Cornwell, B. Sharpe's battle
Cornwell, B. Sharpe's fortress
Cornwell, B. Sharpe's fury
Cornwell, B. Sharpe's prey: Richard Sharpe and the Expedi-
    tion to Copenhagen, 1807
Cornwell, B. Sharpe's Trafalgar
Kaye, M. M. The far pavilions
Kaye, M. M. Shadow of the moon
Waugh, E. Men at arms
Waugh, E. Officers and gentlemen

Officers

Forester, C. S. Hornblower and the Atropos
Forester, C. S. Ship of the line
Mallinson, A. A close run thing
Waugh, E. The end of the battle
Boulle, P. The bridge over the River Kwai

GREAT BRITAIN. NAVY *See* Great Britain. Royal Navy

GREAT BRITAIN. ROYAL AIR FORCE

Goddard, R. Never go back

GREAT BRITAIN. ROYAL FLYING CORPS

    See also Great Britain. Royal Air Force

GREAT BRITAIN. ROYAL NAVAL AIR SERVICE

    See also Great Britain. Royal Air Force

GREAT BRITAIN. ROYAL NAVY

Forester, C. S. Admiral Hornblower in the West Indies
Forester, C. S. Beat to quarters
Forester, C. S. Flying colours
Forester, C. S. Mr. Midshipman Hornblower
Lambdin, D. King's captain
McCutchan, P. The new lieutenant
Monsarrat, N. The cruel sea
O'Brian, P. The hundred days
O'Brian, P. The unknown shore
O'Brian, P. The yellow admiral
Unsworth, B. Losing Nelson

Officers

Forester, C. S. Hornblower and the Hotspur
Forester, C. S. Hornblower during the crisis, and two stories:
    Hornblower's temptation and The last encounter
Forester, C. S. Lieutenant Hornblower
McCutchan, P. Cameron's crossing
Novik, N. His majesty's dragon
O'Brian, P. Blue at the mizzen
O'Brian, P. The commodore
O'Brian, P. The wine-dark sea
Reeman, D. A ship must die
Great dream of heaven. Shepard, S.
Great expectations. Dickens, C.
The **great** fire. Hazzard, S.
The **great** Gatsby. Fitzgerald, F. S.
    also in Fitzgerald, F. S. The Fitzgerald reader p105-238
The **great** man. Christensen, K.
The **great** perhaps. Meno, J.
Great racing stories. See The Dick Francis treasury of great rac-
    ing stories
Great short works of Joseph Conrad. Conrad, J.
Great stories of the American West. Entered in Part I under title
The **greatest** evil. Kienzle, W. X.
Greatest hits. Entered in Part I under title
The **greatest** love [novelette] McCaffrey, A.
    In McCaffrey, A. The girl who heard dragons p169-225

GRECO-TURKISH WAR, 1921-1922

Karnezis, P. The maze

GREECE

    See also Cephalonia Island (Greece); Lesbos Island
    (Greece)
Cook, E. Achilles
Crane, S. Active service
Doherty, P. C. The godless man
Doherty, P. C. The house of death
Fowles, J. The magus
Glass, J. Three Junes
Goddard, R. Into the blue
Jong, E. Sappho's leap
Michaels, A. Fugitive pieces
Murray, S. Forgery
Renault, M. The bull from the sea
Renault, M. Funeral games

GUILT—*Continued*

Schwartz, J. B. Reservation Road
Schwarz, C. Drowning Ruth
Shakespeare, N. Snowleg
Shreve, A. The weight of water
Smith, S. A simple plan
Styron, W. Sophie's choice
Trevor, W. The silence in the garden
Tyler, A. Saint maybe
Ward, A. E. Forgive me
Wiesel, E. Twilight
Guilt. Lescroart, J. T.
Guilty as sin. Hoag, T.
Guilty pleasures. Sanders, L.
The **gulf.** Poyer, D.

GULF STREAM

Hemingway, E. The old man and the sea
Gulliver's travels. Swift, J.
GUNBOATS *See* Warships
Gunman's rhapsody. Parker, R. B.
Gunner Asch goes to war. *See* Kirst, H. H. Forward, Gunner Asch!
GUNS *See* Firearms
The **guns** of Avalon. Zelazny, R.
The **guns** of Navarone. MacLean, A.
The **guru** of love. Upadhyay, S.
Guys and dolls. Runyon, D.

GYPSIES

Gores, J. Cons, scams & grifts
Hugo, V. The hunchback of Notre Dame
King, S. Thinner
McCann, C. Zoli
Mérimée, P. Carmen
The **Gyrth** chalice mystery. Allingham, M.
In Allingham, M. Three cases for Mr. Campion p421-604

H

"**H**" is for homicide. Grafton, S.
H. P. Lovecraft. Lovecraft, H. P.
The **ha-ha.** King, D.
Hadji Murád. Tolstoy, L., graf
In Tolstoy, L., graf. The short novels of Tolstoy
HADRIAN, EMPEROR OF ROME, 76-138
About
Yourcenar, M. Memoirs of Hadrian
HAITI

Danticat, E. The dew breaker
Danticat, E. Krik? Krak!
Greene, G. The comedians

Revolution, 1791-1804

Bell, M. S. All souls' rising
Roberts, K. L. Lydia Bailey

Port-au-Prince

Greene, G. The comedians

HAITIANS

Dominican Republic

Danticat, E. The farming of bones

United States

Danticat, E. The dew breaker
Prose, F. Primitive people
Half a crown. Walton, J.
Half a heart. Brown, R.
Half a life. Naipaul, V. S.
Half asleep in frog pajamas. Robbins, T.
The **half** brother. Christensen, L. S.

HALF-BROTHERS

Christensen, L. S. The half brother
Evenson, B. The open curtain
Kesey, K. Sometimes a great notion
Murdoch, I. The good apprentice
Smith, W. A. Power of the sword
Smith, W. A. Rage

HALF-CASTES *See* Mixed bloods

The **half-life.** Raymond, J.
Half Moon Street. Perry, A.
Half Moon Street. Theroux, P.
Half of a yellow sun. Adichie, C. N.

HALF-SISTERS

Fielding, J. Missing pieces
García, C. The Aguero sisters
Half the blood of Brooklyn. Huston, C.
Halfway house. Noel, K.
The **halfway** house. Rosales, G.

HALIFAX (N.S.) *See* Canada—Halifax
HALLET, ELIZABETH FONES WINTHROP FEAKE, B. 1610
About
Seton, A. The Winthrop woman
HALLUCINATIONS AND ILLUSIONS
See also Personality disorders
Dick, P. K. Now wait for last year
Halting state. Stross, C.
HAMILTON, ALEXANDER, 1757-1804
About
Liss, D. The whiskey rebels
HAMILTON, LADY EMMA, 1761?-1815
About
Sontag, S. The volcano lover
HAMILTON, SIR WILLIAM, 1730-1803
About
Sontag, S. The volcano lover
The **Hamilton** case. De Kretser, M.
The **hamlet.** Faulkner, W.
also in Faulkner, W. Novels, 1936-1940 p727-1075
also in Faulkner, W. Snopes p1-349
The **Hamlet** trap. Wilhelm, K.
The **hammer** of God. Clarke, A. C.
Hammerheads. Brown, D.
HAMMETT, DASHIELL, 1894-1961
About
Atkins, A. Devil's garden
HAMMETT, SAMUEL DASHIELL *See* Hammett, Dashiell, 1894-1961
HAMPSHIRE (ENGLAND) *See* England—Hampshire
HAND

Irving, J. The fourth hand
The **hand** I fan with. Ansa, T. M.
Hand of evil. Jance, J. A.
The **hand** of Oberon. Zelazny, R.
A **handbook** to luck. García, C.
The **Handmaid's** tale. Atwood, M.
The **handyman.** See, C.
HANDYMEN *See* Hired men
HANDYWOMEN *See* Hired women
The **hangman's** beautiful daughter. McCrumb, S.
Hangman's holiday. Sayers, D. L.
Hannibal. Harris, T.
Hannibal rising. Harris, T.
Hanover Place. Thomas, M. M.
Hanta yo. Hill, R. B.
Ha'penny. Walton, J.

HAPPINESS

Powers, R. Generosity
Happy all the time. Colwin, L.
Happy endings. Stone, K.
Happy families. Fuentes, C.
Happy to be here. Keillor, G.
HARASSMENT, SEXUAL *See* Sexual harassment
Harbor. Adams, L.
Hard candy. Vachss, A. H.
Hard currency. Kaminsky, S. M.
Hard eight. Evanovich, J.
Hard evidence. D'Amato, B.
The **hard** life. O'Brien, F.
In O'Brien, F. The complete novels
Hard rain. Abrahams, P.
Hard revolution. Pelecanos, G. P.
Hard road. D'Amato, B.
Hard stop. Knopf, C.
Hard time. Paretsky, S.
A **hard** time to be a father. Weldon, F.

HEBRIDES (SCOTLAND)
> *See also* Skye (Scotland)
> Stewart, M. The stormy petrel
> Woolf, V. To the lighthouse

HEDONISM
> Colette. Claudine married
> Kazantzakis, N. Zorba the Greek
> Kundera, M. Slowness
> See, C. The handyman

Heechee rendezvous. Pohl, F.

Heir to the glimmering world. Ozick, C.

HEIRESSES *See* Inheritance and succession; Wealth

HEIRS *See* Inheritance and succession; Wealth

Helen hath no fury. Roberts, G.

HELEN OF TROY (LEGENDARY CHARACTER)
> George, M. Helen of Troy

Helen of Troy. George, M.

HELL
> Butler, R. O. Hell

Hell. Butler, R. O.

Hell at the breech. Franklin, T.

Hell to pay. Pelecanos, G. P.

The **Hellfire** Club. Straub, P.

Helliconia spring. Aldiss, B. W.

Helliconia summer. Aldiss, B. W.

Helliconia winter. Aldiss, B. W.

Hello goodbye. Chenoweth, E.

Help the poor struggler. Grimes, M.

Helpless. Gowdy, B.

HEMINGS, SALLY, 1773-1835
> **About**
> Chase-Riboud, B. Sally Hemings
> Hambly, B. Patriot hearts

The **Hemingway** reader. Hemingway, E.

Henderson the rain king. Bellow, S.
> *also in* Bellow, S. Novels, 1956-1964

HENRY II, KING OF ENGLAND, 1133-1189
> **About**
> Franklin, A. Mistress of the art of death
> Franklin, A. The serpent's tale
> Penman, S. K. Devil's brood
> Penman, S. K. Time and chance
> Penman, S. K. When Christ and his saints slept

HENRY III, KING OF ENGLAND, 1207-1272
> **About**
> Penman, S. K. Falls the shadow

HENRY VIII, KING OF ENGLAND, 1491-1547
> **About**
> Gregory, P. The Boleyn Inheritance
> Gregory, P. The other Boleyn girl
> Mantel, H. Wolf Hall
> Maxwell, R. The secret diary of Anne Boleyn
> Plaidy, J. Murder most royal

The **Henry** James reader. James, H.

Henry of Atlantic City. Reuss, F.

Her fearful symmetry. Niffenegger, A.

Her infinite variety. Auchincloss, L.

Her mother's daughter. French, M.

Her name was Lola. Hoban, R.

HERCEGOVINA *See* Bosnia and Hercegovina

HERCULANEUM (ANCIENT CITY)
> Goodman, C. The night villa

Here be dragons. Penman, S. K.

Here lies. Parker, D.

Here on Earth. Hoffman, A.

The **heretic's** daughter. Kent, K.

Heretics of Dune. Herbert, F.

Herland. Gilman, C. P.
> *also in* Gilman, C. P. The Charlotte Perkins Gilman reader
> *also in* Gilman, C. P. Charlotte Perkins Gilman's Utopian novels p150-269

HERMAPHRODITISM
> Eugenides, J. Middlesex
> Jennings, G. Raptor

The **hermit** of Eyton Forest. Peters, E.

HERMITAGE (SAINT PETERSBURG, RUSSIA)
> Dean, D. The madonnas of Leningrad

HERMITS
> *See also* Recluses
> Guterson, D. The other

HEROES
> *See also* Heroism
> Grossman, A. Soon I will be invincible
> Rogers, R. Devil's Cape

HEROIN
> Robbins, T. Villa incognito
> Robinson, R. Cost

HEROISM
> *See also* Courage; Heroes
> Keneally, T. Flying hero class

Herzog. Bellow, S.
> *also in* Bellow, S. Novels, 1956-1964

He's one, too. Gurganus, A.
> *In* Gurganus, A. The practical heart

The **heyday** of the insensitive bastards. Boswell, R.

Hick. Portes, A.

HICKOK, WILD BILL, 1837-1876
> **About**
> Dexter, P. Deadwood

The **hidden** assassins. Wilson, R.

Hidden prey. Sandford, J.

Hide & seek. Patterson, J.

High country. Barr, N.

High country fall. Maron, M.

High fidelity. Hornby, N.

The **high** flyer. Howatch, S.

High lonesome. Oates, J. C.

HIGH SCHOOLS *See* School life

A **high** wind in Jamaica. Hughes, R. A. W.

The **high** window. Chandler, R.
> *also in* Chandler, R. Stories and early novels p985-1177

Highgate rise. Perry, A.

The **highly** effective detective. Yancey, R.

Highwire moon. Straight, S.

HIJACKING OF AIRPLANES
> Griffin, W. E. B. By order of the President
> Hospital, J. T. Due preparations for the plague
> Keneally, T. Flying hero class
> Nance, J. J. The last hostage

HIJACKING OF SHIPS
> Coonts, S. America
> Follett, K. Triple
> MacLean, A. When eight bells toll

HIJACKING OF SUBWAYS
> Godey, J. The taking of Pelham one two three

The **hill** bachelors. Trevor, W.

The **Hills** at home. Clark, N.

HIMALAYA MOUNTAINS
> Godden, R. Black Narcissus

HINDUISM
> Narayan, R. K. The bachelor of arts

HINDUS
> Kaye, M. M. The far pavilions
> Seth, V. A suitable boy

> **England**
> *See also* East Indians—England

HIPPIES
> *See also* Bohemianism
> Carey, P. His illegal self
> Dierbeck, L. One pill makes you smaller
> McPhee, M. L'America
> Powell, A. Hearing secret harmonies
> Swann, M. Flower children

HIPPOLYTA (LEGENDARY CHARACTER)
> Tarr, J. Queen of the Amazons

The **hippopotamus** pool. Peters, E.

HIRED KILLERS
> Brown, S. The crush
> Estleman, L. D. Something borrowed, something black
> Gay, W. Twilight
> Greatest hits
> Hunter, S. Havana

HOLOCAUST SURVIVORS—*Continued*
Wiesel, E. Twilight
Holy fire. Sterling, B.
HOLY GRAIL *See* Grail
Holy skirts. Steinke, R.
The **holy** thief. Peters, E.

HOLY WEEK
Faulkner, W. A fable
Home. Robinson, M.
Home fires. Rice, L.
Home fires burning. Maron, M.
Home is the hangman. Zelazny, R.
  In The Hugo winners p5-67
Home land. Lipsyte, S.
Home safe. Berg, E.
The **homecoming**. Hamner, E.
Homecoming. Schlink, B.
Homecoming. Snow, C. P.

HOMECOMINGS
Faulkner, W. Soldiers' pay
Settle, M. L. The killing ground
Homegoing. Pohl, F.

HOMELESS PERSONS
Auster, P. In the country of last things
Bock, C. Beautiful children
Coetzee, J. M. Age of iron
Frey, J. Bright shiny morning
Grisham, J. The street lawyer
Hendrie, L. Remember me
Howells, W. D. The minister's charge
Kennedy, W. Ironweed
Lessing, D. M. Ben, in the world
Piercy, M. The longings of women
Rendell, R. The keys to the street
Rock, P. My abandonment
Walters, M. The echo
Homely girl, a life, and other stories. Miller, A.

HOMER
Parodies, imitations, etc.
Ehrenreich, B. The suitors
Simmons, D. Ilium
Simmons, D. Olympos
Homer & Langley. Doctorow, E. L.

HOMES *See* Houses

HOMES FOR THE ELDERLY *See* Old age homes

HOMESTEADING
  See also Frontier and pioneer life
Doig, I. Dancing at the Rascal Fair
Stegner, W. E. The Big Rock Candy Mountain
The **homing**. Saul, J.

HOMING PIGEONS
Shalev, M. A pigeon and a boy

HOMOSEXUALITY
  See also Bisexuality; Lesbianism
Aciman, A. A. Call me by your name
Baldwin, J. Tell me how long the train's been gone
Barker, P. The eye in the door
Buruma, I. The China lover
Cullin, M. Undersurface
Cunningham, M. Flesh and blood
D'Erasmo, S. The sky below
Dickinson, P. Some deaths before dying
Doenges, J. God of gods
Durrell, L. Clea
Forster, E. M. Maurice
Frame, R. The lantern bearers
Frey, J. Bright shiny morning
Gide, A. The counterfeiters (Les faux-monnayeurs)
Gide, A. The immoralist
Glass, J. Three Junes
Glass, J. The whole world over
Grant, S. Map of Ireland
Greer, A. S. The story of a marriage
Gregory, P. Earthly joys
Grumbach, D. The book of knowledge
Gurganus, A. He's one, too
Gurganus, A. Preservation news
Haddon, M. A spot of bother
Hamilton, J. The short history of a prince

Harris, E. L. And this too shall pass
Himes, C. Yesterday will make you cry
House, T. The beginning of calamities
James, H. The pupil
Kerouac, J. And the hippos were boiled in their tanks
Keyes, M. Last Chance Saloon
Leavitt, D. The lost language of cranes
Leavitt, D. Martin Bauman
Leavitt, D. While England sleeps
Lessing, D. M. The good terrorist
Lipman, E. The family man
Mallon, T. Fellow travelers
Mann, T. Death in Venice
Maupin, A. Michael Tolliver lives
McCauley, S. Alternatives to sex
McCauley, S. True enough
McEwan, I. Enduring love
McFarland, D. Letter from Point Clear
McNicholl, D. A son called Gabriel
Monette, P. Afterlife
Murdoch, I. The bell
Murdoch, I. A fairly honourable defeat
O'Neill, J. At swim, two boys
Penguin book of gay short fiction
Price, R. Kate Vaiden
Price, R. The promise of rest
Puig, M. Kiss of the spider woman
Purdy, J. The nephew
Pym, B. The sweet dove died
Renault, M. The Persian boy
Rush, N. Mortals
Self, W. Dorian
Spark, M. The finishing school
Taylor, B. The book of getting even
Tóibín, C. The blackwater lightship
Trollope, J. The best of friends
Truong, M. T. D. The book of salt
Truscott, L. K. Heart of war
Vidal, G. The city and the pillar
Vine, B. No night is too long
Welsh, L. The cutting room
White, E. The beautiful room is empty
White, E. A boy's own story
White, E. Hotel de Dream
White, E. The married man

HOMOSEXUALS *See* Homosexuality; Lesbianism

HONDURAS
Theroux, P. The Mosquito Coast
Honest doubt. Cross, A.
Honest illusions. Roberts, N.

HONESTY
  See also Truthfulness and falsehood
Honeymooners. Kinder, C.

HONEYMOONS
McEwan, I. On Chesil Beach

HONG KONG
Adler, E. Fortune is a woman
Clavell, J. Noble house
Clavell, J. Tai-Pan
Harrison, C. Afterburn
Lanchester, J. Fragrant Harbor
Lee, J. Y. K. The piano teacher
Theroux, P. Kowloon Tong
Trenhaile, J. The gates of exquisite view

HONGKONG *See* Hong Kong
Honky tonk Kat. Kijewski, K.

HONOLULU (HAWAII) *See* Hawaii—Honolulu

HONOR
Eng, T. T. The gift of rain
Honor bound. Griffin, W. E. B.
The **honorary** consul. Greene, G.
Honored guest. Williams, J.
The **honourable** schoolboy. Le Carré, J.
The **hook**. Westlake, D. E.
Hopalong Cassidy and the trail to Seven Pines. See L'Amour, L.
  The trail to Seven Pines

HOPKINS, GERARD MANLEY, 1844-1889
About
Hansen, R. Exiles
Hopscotch. Cortázar, J.

Horace afoot. Reuss, F.
Horn of Africa. Caputo, P.
Hornblower and the Atropos. Forester, C. S.
Hornblower and the Hotspur. Forester, C. S.
Hornblower during the crisis, and two stories: Hornblower's temptation and The last encounter. Forester, C. S.
The **horned** man. Lasdun, J.
Hornet flight. Follett, K.
The **horrific** sufferings of the mind-reading monster Hercules Barefoot. Vallgren, C.-J.
The **horror** in the museum, and other revisions. Lovecraft, H. P.

HORROR STORIES
    See also Ghost stories; Gothic romances; Murder stories; Supernatural phenomena; Vampires; Werewolves
    American fantastic tales: terror and the uncanny from Poe to the pulps
    American fantastic tales: terror and the uncanny from the 1940s to now
    Barker, C. The books of blood
    Barker, C. Coldheart Canyon
    Bradbury, R. Something wicked this way comes
    Clark, M. H. A cry in the night
    Du Maurier, Dame D. Daphne du Maurier's classics of the macabre
    Due, T. Blood colony
    Due, T. The good house
    Due, T. My soul to keep
    Gallagher, S. The kingdom of bones
    Gregory, D. Pandemonium
    Hambly, B. Those who hunt the night
    Hambly, B. Traveling with the dead
    Hill, J. Heart-shaped box
    Jackson, S. The haunting of Hill House
    Jackson, S. We have always lived in a castle
    James, H. The turn of the screw
    King, S. Black house
    King, S. The breathing method
    King, S. Carrie
    King, S. Cell
    King, S. Christine
    King, S. Cujo
    King, S. The dark half
    King, S. Desperation
    King, S. Everything's eventual: 14 dark tales
    King, S. Firestarter
    King, S. Four past midnight
    King, S. From a Buick 8
    King, S. Gerald's game
    King, S. Insomnia
    King, S. It
    King, S. Just after sunset
    King, S. Needful things
    King, S. Night shift
    King, S. Pet sematary
    King, S. The regulators
    King, S. Salem's Lot
    King, S. The shining
    King, S. Skeleton crew
    King, S. The stand
    King, S. Thinner
    Koontz, D. R. The bad place
    Koontz, D. R. Strangers
    Koontz, D. R. Watchers
    Lebbon, T. Fallen
    Levin, I. Rosemary's baby
    Levin, I. The Stepford wives
    The living dead
    Lovecraft, H. P. H. P. Lovecraft
    Lovecraft, H. P. The horror in the museum, and other revisions
    Lovecraft, H. P. Tales of H.P. Lovecraft
    MacAlister, K. A girl's guide to vampires
    March, W. The bad seed
    Marks, J. Fangland
    Martin, V. Mary Reilly
    Matheson, R. I am legend
    McCammon, R. R. Boy's life
    Moloney, S. The dwelling
    Moody, D. Hater
    O'Connor, F. The violent bear it away
    The Oxford book of gothic tales
    Pekearo, N. T. The wolfman
    Poe's children
    Preston, D. Reliquary

    Pyper, A. The killing circle
    Rice, A. Blackwood Farm
    Rice, A. Blood and gold
    Rice, A. Blood canticle
    Rice, A. Interview with the vampire
    Rice, A. Lasher
    Rice, A. Memnoch the Devil
    Rice, A. The queen of the damned
    Rice, A. The tale of the body thief
    Rice, A. Taltos
    Rice, A. The vampire Armand
    Rice, A. The vampire Lestat
    Rice, A. Vittorio the vampire
    Rice, A. The witching hour
    Saul, J. Darkness
    Saul, J. The homing
    Saul, J. Midnight voices
    Saul, J. The presence
    Saul, J. Second child
    Saul, J. Shadows
    Shelley, M. W. Frankenstein; or, The modern Prometheus
    Shepard, L. Softspoken
    Sigler, S. Contagious
    Sigler, S. Infected
    Simmons, D. The terror
    Smith, M. M. The intruders
    Smith, S. The ruins
    Stevenson, R. L. The strange case of Dr. Jekyll and Mr. Hyde
    Stoker, B. The Bram Stoker bedside companion
    Stoker, B. Dracula
    Stoker, B. Midnight tales
    Straub, P. Ghost story
    Straub, P. The Hellfire Club
    Straub, P. In the night room
    Straub, P. Lost boy lost girl
    Straub, P. Magic terror
    Straub, P. Mr. X
    Strieber, W. The forbidden zone
    Strieber, W. The hunger
    Strieber, W. The last vampire
    Strieber, W. The Wolfen
    Stross, C. The Jennifer morgue
    Tryon, T. The other
    Wellington, D. Monster Island
    The Year's best fantasy and horror

HORSE FARMS
    Hoag, T. Dark horse
The **horse** goddess. Llywelyn, M.
Horse heaven. Smiley, J.

HORSE RACING
    See also Jockeys
    The Dick Francis treasury of great racing stories
    Dixon, K. The art of losing
    Francis, D. 10 lb. penalty
    Francis, D. Bolt
    Francis, D. Even money
    Francis, D. Field of thirteen
    Francis, D. Longshot
    Francis, D. Nerve
    Francis, D. Smokescreen
    Francis, D. Whip hand
    The New treasury of great racing stories
    Shoemaker, B. Stalking horse
    Smiley, J. Horse heaven
    Smith, B. All hat
The **horse** whisperer. Evans, N.
The **Horse** You Came In On. Grimes, M.

HORSES
    See also Lippizaner horses
    Brand, M. Dark Rosaleen
    Evans, N. The horse whisperer
    Gloss, M. The hearts of horses
    McCarthy, C. All the pretty horses
    Meyers, K. The work of wolves
    Olmstead, R. Coal black horse
    Steinbeck, J. The red pony
    Tarr, J. Lady of horses
The **horse's** mouth. Cary, J.

HOSPITALERS OF ST. JOHN IN JERUSALEM *See* Knights of Malta

HOSPITALS AND SANATORIUMS
    See also Burn care units
    Adrian, C. The children's hospital

HOSPITALS AND SANATORIUMS—*Continued*

Barker, P. The eye in the door
Barker, P. The ghost road
Barker, P. Regeneration
Clark, M. H. The cradle will fall
Cook, R. Coma
Cook, R. Godplayer
Greene, G. A burnt-out case
Hemingway, E. A farewell to arms
Hooker, R. MASH
Hulme, K. The nun's story
Jackson, C. The lost weekend
Jones, J. Whistle
Kesey, K. One flew over the cuckoo's nest
Mann, T. The magic mountain
Mason, B. A. Spence + Lila
McCullough, C. An indecent obsession
O'Connell, J. The resurrectionist
Powers, R. Operation wandering soul
Rosten, L. Captain Newman, M.D.
Sanders, L. The sixth commandment
See, C. There will never be another you
Simon, C. The trolley
Solzhenitsyn, A. Cancer ward
Wharton, W. Birdy
Willis, C. Passage
The **host**. Meyer, S.

HOSTAGES

Black, L. Takeover
Dovey, C. Blood kin
Finder, J. Power play
Green, G. D. Ravens
Greene, G. The tenth man
Grisham, J. The street lawyer
Herron, M. Reconstruction
Iles, G. Third degree
King, S. Misery
Lively, P. Cleopatra's sister
O'Brien, E. House of splendid isolation
Palmer, M. The patient
Patchett, A. Bel canto
Patterson, J. Roses are red
Powers, R. Plowing the dark
Tyler, A. Earthly possessions
Wiesel, E. Dawn
Wiesel, E. The judges
The **hot** kid. Leonard, E.
The **hot** rock. Westlake, D. E.
Hot six. Evanovich, J.
Hot Springs. Hunter, S.
Hotel. Hailey, A.
Hotel de Dream. White, E.
Hotel du Lac. Brookner, A.
Hotel Honolulu. Theroux, P.
The **Hotel** New Hampshire. Irving, J.
Hotel Paradise. Grimes, M.
Hotel Pastis. Mayle, P.

HOTELS, TAVERNS, ETC.

Ali, M. In the kitchen
Amado, J. Gabriela, clove and cinnamon
Brookner, A. Hotel du Lac
Conrad, J. Victory
DeWitt, P. Ablutions
Du Maurier, Dame D. Jamaica Inn
Egan, J. The keep
Gilman, D. A palm for Mrs. Pollifax
Godden, R. The greengage summer
Goodman, C. The seduction of water
Grimes, M. Belle ruin
Grimes, M. Hotel Paradise
Haig, M. The dead fathers club
Hailey, A. Hotel
Hardwick, M. The Duchess of Duke Street
Hoffman, A. The third angel
Holland, C. Pacific Street
Hunt, S. The invention of everything else
Irving, J. The Hotel New Hampshire
King, S. The shining
Lent, J. Lost nation
Mayle, P. Hotel Pastis
Mehta, G. A river Sutra
Meyer, C. Brown eyes blue
Ólafur Jóhann Ólafsson. The journey home

Robinson, S. Callahan's con
Sparks, N. Nights in Rodanthe
Taylor, E. Mrs. Palfrey at the Claremont
Theroux, P. Hotel Honolulu
The **hound** of the Baskervilles. Doyle, Sir A. C.
The **hours**. Cunningham, M.
The **hours** of the virgin. Estleman, L. D.
The **house** at Riverton. Morton, K.
A **house** for Mr. Biswas. Naipaul, V. S.
House lights. Cohen, L. H.
House made of dawn. Momaday, N. S.
The **house** of blue mangoes. Davidar, D.
House of blues. Smith, J.
The **house** of death. Doherty, P. C.
House of many gods. Davenport, K.
House of meetings. Amis, M.
The **house** of mirth. Wharton, E.
   also in Wharton, E. New York novels p1-324
   also in Wharton, E. Novels
The **house** of paper. Domínguez, C. M.
House of reeds. Harlan, T.
House of splendid isolation. O'Brien, E.
The **house** of stairs. Vine, B.
The **House** of the Seven Gables. Hawthorne, N.
   also in Hawthorne, N. Collected novels
The **house** of the spirits. Allende, I.
The **house** of the stag. Baker, K.
The **house** of the Vestals. Saylor, S.
The **house** of widows. Melnyczuk, A.
The **house** on Fortune Street. Livesey, M.
The **house** on Hope Street. Steel, D.
The **house** on Mango Street. Cisneros, S.
The **house** on Prague Street. Demetz, H.
The **house** sitter. Lovesey, P.

HOUSEHOLD EMPLOYEES

   See also Au pairs; Butlers; Cooks; Hired men; Hired women; Housekeepers; Maids (Servants); Nursemaids; Valets

Ozick, C. Heir to the glimmering world
Umrigar, T. N. The space between us
Household saints. Prose, F.
The **housekeeper** and the professor. Ogawa, Y.

HOUSEKEEPERS

Adams, A. After the war
Doig, I. The whistling season
Labiner, N. Miniatures
McBain, E. Alice in jeopardy
McFarland, D. School for the blind
Ogawa, Y. The housekeeper and the professor
Piercy, M. The longings of women
Stein, G. Three lives
Winkler, A. C. Dog war

HOUSEMAIDS *See* Maids (Servants)

HOUSES

   See also Apartment houses

Clark, M. H. No place like home
De la Roche, M. Jalna
Delinsky, B. Flirting with Pete
Forster, E. M. Howards End
Gurganus, A. Preservation news
Hawthorne, N. The House of the Seven Gables
Hodgins, E. Mr. Blandings builds his dream house
Howatch, S. Cashelmara
Howatch, S. Penmarric
Howatch, S. The wheel of fortune
James, H. The spoils of Poynton
Laken, V. Dream house
Lofts, N. Gad's Hall
Moloney, S. The dwelling
Naipaul, V. S. A house for Mr. Biswas
Rendell, R. Thirteen steps down
Rosenblatt, R. Lapham rising
Scott, A. Calpurnia
Stewart, M. Touch not the cat
Swerling, B. Shadowbrook
Unsworth, B. After Hannibal
Houses of stone. Michaels, B.

HOUSTON (TEX.) *See* Texas—Houston
Houston, Houston, do you read? Tiptree, J.
   In The Hugo winners p200-56
How far is the ocean from here. Shearn, A.
How green was my valley. Llewellyn, R.

HUMOR—*Continued*

Spark, M. The prime of Miss Jean Brodie
Steinbeck, J. Cannery Row
Steinbeck, J. Sweet Thursday
Stevenson, R. L. The misadventures of John Nicholson
Svevo, I. Zeno's conscience
Swarthout, G. F. Bless the beasts and children
Taylor, R. L. The travels of Jaimie McPheeters
Thornton, T. The alternative hero
Toole, J. K. A confederacy of dunces
Townsend, S. Adrian Mole
Townsend, S. The Adrian Mole diaries
Townsend, S. Adrian Mole: the lost years
Trollope, A. The Duke's children [abridged]
Tropper, J. How to talk to a widower
Twain, M. The adventures of Huckleberry Finn
Twain, M. The adventures of Tom Sawyer
Wallace, D. Big fish
Waugh, E. Decline and fall
Waugh, E. The loved one
Waugh, E. Men at arms
Waugh, E. Officers and gentlemen
Weiner, J. Good in bed
Weiner, J. In her shoes
Welsh, I. Trainspotting
Welty, E. The Ponder heart
West, J. The friendly persuasion
Westlake, D. E. Bad news
Westlake, D. E. Bank shot
Westlake, D. E. Don't ask
Westlake, D. E. Drowned hopes
Westlake, D. E. Get real
Westlake, D. E. Good behavior
Westlake, D. E. The hot rock
Westlake, D. E. Money for nothing
Westlake, D. E. Put a lid on it
Westlake, D. E. The road to ruin
Westlake, D. E. Smoke
Westlake, D. E. Thieves' dozen
Westlake, D. E. Watch your back
Westlake, D. E. What's so funny?
Westlake, D. E. What's the worst that could happen?
White, B. Quite a year for plums
Wibberley, L. The mouse that roared
Wilcox, J. Heavenly days
Wilcox, J. Hunk City
Winkler, A. C. Dog war
Wodehouse, P. G. The code of the Woosters
Wodehouse, P. G. The inimitable Jeeves
Wodehouse, P. G. Tales from the Drones Club
Wodehouse, P. G. A Wodehouse bestiary
Yunis, A. The night counter

HUMOROUS STORIES *See* Humor
The **hunchback** of Notre Dame. Hugo, V.

HUNCHBACKS

Hugo, V. The hunchback of Notre Dame
McCullers, C. The ballad of the sad café [novelette]
The **hundred** and ninety-nine steps. Faber, M.
  In Faber, M. The courage consort
A **hundred** camels in the courtyard. Bowles, P.
  In Bowles, P. Collected stories & later writings
The **hundred** days. O'Brian, P.
The **hundred** secret senses. Tan, A.

HUNDRED YEARS' WAR, 1339-1453

Cornwell, B. The archer's tale
Cornwell, B. Vagabond
Doyle, Sir A. C. The White Company
Haasse, H. S. In a dark wood wandering
The **hundredth** man. Kerley, J.

HUNGARIANS

France

Furst, A. Kingdom of shadows
Miller, A. Oxygen

HUNGARY

Esterházy, P. Celestial harmonies
Furst, A. Kingdom of shadows

World War, 1939-1945

See World War, 1939-1945—Hungary

Budapest

Phillips, A. Prague
The **hunger**. Strieber, W.
Hunk City. Wilcox, J.
The **hunt** for Red October. Clancy, T.
The **hunted**. Leonard, E.
  In Leonard, E. Elmore Leonard's Dutch treat: 3 novels
Hunted past reason. Matheson, R.
The **hunter**. Stark, R.
HUNTERS *See* Hunting
The **hunters**. Messud, C.
The **hunters** [novelette] Messud, C.
  In Messud, C. The hunters
Hunters and gatherers. Prose, F.
Hunter's moon. Anderson, P.
  In The Hugo winners p510-50
Hunter's moon. Stabenow, D.
Hunter's run. Martin, G. R. R.

HUNTING

  See also Trappers and trapping; Whaling
Colegate, I. The shooting party
Cooper, J. F. The pioneers
Guterson, D. East of the mountains
Guthrie, A. B. The big sky
King, S. Dreamcatcher
Nichols, P. Voyage to the North Star
Thomas, E. M. Reindeer Moon

Africa

Hemingway, E. True at first light
Smith, W. A. A time to die
Hunting badger. Hillerman, T.
The **huntsman**. Terrell, W.

HURRICANE KATRINA, 2005

Burke, J. L. The tin roof blowdown
Piazza, T. City of refuge

HURRICANES

Hiaasen, C. Stormy weather
The **husband**. Koontz, D. R.

HUSBAND AND WIFE

  See also Marriage
Abrahams, P. Nerve damage
Ackroyd, P. The fall of Troy
Chenoweth, E. Hello goodbye
Crace, J. Being dead
Hays, T. The pleasure was mine
Hollingshead, G. Bedlam
James, H. The author of "Beltraffio"
King, R. The sound of butterflies
Lewis, S. Dodsworth
Martin, C. Where the river ends
Mason, B. A. Spence + Lila
Maxwell, W. The chateau
McEwan, I. On Chesil Beach
McFarland, D. A face at the window
Oates, J. C. American appetites
Rash, R. Serena
Reuss, F. Mohr
Richardson, C. S. The end of the alphabet
Roth, J. The triumph of beauty
Shaley, T. Husband and wife
Sparks, N. The notebook
Strauss, D. More than it hurts you
Theroux, P. Monkey Hill
Tremain, R. The color
Unferth, D. O. Vacation
Wiggins, M. Evidence of things unseen
Wiggins, M. The shadow catcher
Wolitzer, M. The wife
Husband and wife. Shaley, T.
Hush money. Parker, R. B.
The **Hyde** Park headsman. Perry, A.
The **Hyde** Park murder. Roosevelt, E.

HYDROGEN BOMB *See* Atomic bomb

HYDROPHOBIA *See* Rabies
Hyperion. Simmons, D.

HYPNOSIS *See* Hypnotism

HYPNOTISM

Koontz, D. R. False memory
Stoker, B. Dracula

HYPNOTISM—*Continued*
Thomas, R. Voodoo, Ltd

HYPOCHONDRIA
Roth, J. The triumph of beauty

HYPOCRISY
Collins, M. Lost souls
Dickens, C. Martin Chuzzlewit
Ellis, W. Crooked little vein

I

I. Dixon, S.
I am Charlotte Simmons. Wolfe, T.
I am legend. Matheson, R.
I am no one you know. Oates, J. C.
I am not a cop! Belzer, R.
I am Not Sidney Poitier. Everett, P. L.
I am the only running footman. Grimes, M.
I been in sorrow's kitchen and licked out all the pots. Straight, S.
I capture the castle. Smith, D.
I, Claudius. Graves, R.
I hate to see that evening sun go down. Gay, W.
"I" is for innocent. Grafton, S.
I know this much is true. Lamb, W.
I lock my door upon myself. Oates, J. C.
I married a communist. Roth, P.
I married a dead man. Woolrich, C.
In Crime novels: American noir of the 1930s and 40s
I never promised you a rose garden. Greenberg, J.
I remember! I remember! O'Faoláin, S.
In O'Faoláin, S. The collected stories of Seán O'Faoláin p544-699
I, robot. Asimov, I.
I sailed with Magellan. Dybek, S.
I see you everywhere. Glass, J.
I served the King of England. Hrabal, B.
I should be extremely happy in your company. Hall, B.
I, the jury. Spillane, M.
In Spillane, M. The Mike Hammer collection [v1]
I thee wed. Quick, A.
I, Tituba, black witch of Salem. Condé, M.
I wish I had a red dress. Cleage, P.

IBIZA (SPAIN)
Braybrooke, J. Every eye

IBO (AFRICAN PEOPLE)
Achebe, C. Things fall apart
Ice. McBain, E.
Ice. Sorokin, V.

ICE AGE *See* Prehistoric times
The ice child. McGregor, E.

ICE HOCKEY *See* Hockey
The ice queen. Hoffman, A.
The ice-shirt. Vollmann, W. T.

ICE SKATING
Bolaño, R. The skating rink
The ice soldier. Watkins, P.
Ice Station Zebra. MacLean, A.

ICELAND
Ólafur Jóhann Ólafsson. The journey home

10th century
Seton, A. Avalon

Reykjavik
Bragi Ólafsson. The pets
Hallgrímur Helgason. 101 Reykjavik
Yrsa Sigurðardóttir. Last rituals

ICELANDERS

England
Ólafur Jóhann Ólafsson. The journey home

IDAHO
Carlson, R. Five skies
Parkinson, H. Across open ground

Woods, S. Heat
The idea of perfection. Grenville, K.
Ideas of heaven. Silber, J.

IDENTITY *See* Personality

IDENTITY (PSYCHOLOGY)
Harding, P. Tinkers
Larsen, N. Passing
Vida, V. Let the Northern Lights erase your name
Identity. Kundera, M.

IDENTITY THEFT
Chaon, D. Await your reply
The ides of March. Wilder, T.
also in Wilder, T. The bridge of San Luis Rey and other novels 1926-1948
The idiot. Dostoyevsky, F.
If Beale Street could talk. Baldwin, J.
If ever I return, pretty Peggy-O. McCrumb, S.
If I forget thee, Jerusalem. Faulkner, W.
In Faulkner, W. Novels, 1936-1940 p493-726
If I'd killed him when I met him. McCrumb, S.
If not now, when? Levi, P.
If on a winter's night a traveler. Calvino, I.
If this world were mine. Harris, E. L.

IGBO (AFRICAN PEOPLE) *See* Ibo (African people)
Ignorance. Kundera, M.
Ilium. Simmons, D.
The **ill-made** knight. White, T. H.
In White, T. H. The once and future king
Ill met in Lankhmar. Leiber, F.
In The Hugo winners p55-115
The **Illearth** war. Donaldson, S. R.

ILLEGAL ALIENS *See* Undocumented aliens

ILLEGITIMACY
See also Unmarried mothers
Allison, D. Bastard out of Carolina
Brown, R. Half a heart
Cheever, J. Bullet Park
Chen, D. Brothers
Dickens, C. Bleak House
Dreiser, T. Jennie Gerhardt
Dunnett, D. Pawn in frankincense
Faulkner, W. The sound and the fury
Fielding, H. The history of Tom Jones, a foundling
Findley, T. The piano man's daughter
Hawthorne, N. The scarlet letter
Henley, P. In the river sweet
Higgins, J. The president's daughter
Howatch, S. Penmarric
Jennings, G. Aztec blood
Kennedy, W. Very old bones
Krantz, J. Mistral's daughter
Kunzru, H. The impressionist
L'Engle, M. A live coal in the sea
Lofts, N. Gad's Hall
Maxwell, R. The Queen's bastard
Oates, J. C. A garden of earthly delights
Plain, B. Blessings
Rash, R. Serena
Rossner, J. Emmeline
Stirling, J. The workhouse girl
Strout, E. Amy and Isabelle
Stubbs, J. Family games
Tryon, T. In the fire of spring
Updike, J. Rabbit remembered
Vida, V. Let the Northern Lights erase your name
Vine, B. Anna's book

ILLINOIS
Bradbury, R. Dandelion wine
Dickinson, C. A shortcut in time
Hamilton, J. When Madeline was young
Hoffman, E. The secret
Maxwell, W. So long, see you tomorrow
Maxwell, W. Time will darken it
Powers, R. Prisoner's dilemma
Straub, P. Mr. X
Thompson, J. Wide blue yonder
Turow, S. Limitations
Wilder, T. The eighth day

19th century
Dickens, C. Martin Chuzzlewit

ILLINOIS—19th century—*Continued*
Diehl, W. Reign in hell

Farm life

See Farm life—Illinois

Chicago

Algren, N. The man with the golden arm
Bellow, S. The adventures of Augie March
Bellow, S. Dangling man
Bellow, S. Humboldt's gift
Brown, C. The hatbox baby
Butcher, J. Small favor
Campbell, B. M. Your blues ain't like mine
Cisneros, S. The house on Mango Street
Diehl, W. Primal fear
Diehl, W. Show of evil
Doenges, J. God of gods
Dreiser, T. Jennie Gerhardt
Dreiser, T. Sister Carrie
D'Souza, T. The Konkans
Dybek, S. I sailed with Magellan
Ellis, D. Life sentence
Farrell, J. T. Studs Lonigan
Fielding, J. Tell me no secrets
Greeley, A. M. Irish cream
Greeley, A. M. Irish lace
Greeley, A. M. Irish stew!
Greeley, A. M. Second spring
Greeley, A. M. September song
Greeley, A. M. Younger than springtime
Hailey, A. Airport
Hamilton, J. Disobedience
Harris, E. L. And this too shall pass
Hemon, A. The Lazarus project
Hemon, A. Nowhere man
Just, W. S. An unfinished season
Maxwell, W. The folded leaf
Meno, J. The great perhaps
Miller, S. The distinguished guest
Miller, S. Family pictures
Mitchard, J. The deep end of the ocean
Newton, C. Calumet City
Norris, F. The pit
Paretsky, S. Ghost country
Phillips, S. E. It had to be you
Powers, R. Generosity
Romano, T. When the world was young
Sakey, M. The blade itself
Schwegel, T. Person of interest
Sidor, S. The mirror's edge
Sinclair, A. Coffee will make you black
Sinclair, U. The jungle
Spencer, S. Endless love
Turner, F. W. 1929
Wright, R. Native son
Wright, R. The outsider

ILLNESS

See also Invalids; Mental illness; Terminal illness
Betts, D. Souls raised from the dead
Elkin, S. Stanley Elkin's The magic kingdom
James, H. The pupil
James, H. The wings of the dove
Klein, R. The moth diaries
Lightman, A. P. The diagnosis
Martin, V. Italian fever
Powers, R. Operation wandering soul
Powers, R. Prisoner's dilemma
Sarton, M. A reckoning
Shaley, T. Husband and wife
Illumination night. Hoffman, A.
Illuminations. See Hoffman, E. Appassionata
Illusions. Pronzini, B.
The **illustrated** man. Bradbury, R.

ILLUSTRATORS

Bock, C. Beautiful children
Neugeboren, J. 1940
Norman, H. The bird artist
Shriver, L. The post-birthday world
Smith, D. Pictures from an expedition
I'm so happy for you. Rosenfeld, L.
The **image** and other stories. Singer, I. B.
   In Singer, I. B. Collected stories: One night in Brazil to The death of Methuselah

IMAGINARY CITIES

Calvino, I. Invisible cities
Carey, E. Alva & Irva

IMAGINARY KINGDOMS

Anthony, P. Split infinity
Barker, C. Weaveworld
Brooks, T. The druid of Shannara
Brooks, T. First king of Shannara
Brooks, T. The sword of Shannara
Hope, A. The prisoner of Zenda
Pohl, F. Beyond the blue event horizon
Silverberg, R. Lord Valentine's castle
Swift, J. Gulliver's travels
Tolkien, J. R. R. The hobbit
Tolkien, J. R. R. The lord of the rings
Tolkien, J. R. R. The return of the king
Tolkien, J. R. R. The Silmarillion
Tolkien, J. R. R. The two towers
Vinge, J. D. The Snow Queen
Vinge, J. D. The Summer Queen
Vinge, J. D. World's end
The **imaginary** voyages: The narrative of Arthur Gordon Pym; The unparalleled adventure of one Hans Pfaall; The journal of Julius Rodman. Poe, E. A.
Imago. Butler, O. E.
Imajica. Barker, C.
The **immaculate** deception. Pears, I.

IMMIGRANTS

Adams, L. Harbor
Ali, M. Brick lane
Boyle, T. C. The tortilla curtain
Cather, W. My Ántonia
Cleage, P. Babylon sisters
Cleave, C. Little Bee
Cunningham, M. Flesh and blood
Delbanco, N. What remains
Doctorow, E. L. Ragtime
D'Souza, T. The Konkans
Gilmore, J. Golden country
Hegi, U. The vision of Emma Blau
Helprin, M. Ellis Island
Hemon, A. The Lazarus project
Hemon, A. Love and obstacles
Hemon, A. Nowhere man
Hershon, J. The German bride
Jen, G. Typical American
Keneally, T. River town
King, R. A girl from Zanzibar
Levitt, P. M. Come with me to Babylon
Levy, A. Fruit of the lemon
Levy, A. Small island
Manseau, P. Songs for the butcher's daughter
McCann, C. Let the great world spin
Mengestu, D. The beautiful things that heaven bears
O'Neill, J. Netherland
Oyeyemi, H. The opposite house
Piercy, M. Sex wars
Pipkin, J. Woodsburner
Powers, R. Generosity
Powers, R. The time of our singing
Proulx, A. Accordion crimes
Raban, J. Waxwings
Reyn, I. What happened to Anna K.
Roth, H. A star shines over Mt. Morris Park
Samarasan, P. Evening is the whole day
See, L. Shanghai girls
Sinclair, U. The jungle
Slouka, M. The visible world
Smith, Z. White teeth
Stewart, F. M. Ellis Island
Tan, A. The bonesetter's daughter
Tóibín, C. Brooklyn
Tremain, R. The road home
Ulinich, A. Petropolis
Vapnyar, L. Broccoli and other tales of food and love
Yehoshua, A. B. A woman in Jerusalem
Immoral certainty. Tanenbaum, R.
The **immoralist**. Gide, A.
The **immortal** highlander. Moning, K. M.
Immortalis. Salvatore, R. A.

IMMORTALITY

Doctorow, C. Down and out in the Magic Kindgom

Indemnity only. Paretsky, S.

INDEPENDENCE DAY (UNITED STATES) *See* Fourth of July

Independence Day. Ford, R.

INDIA

Davidar, D. The house of blue mangoes
Hesse, H. Siddhartha
Markandaya, K. Nectar in a sieve
McDonald, I. River of gods
Mehta, G. A river Sutra
Narayan, R. K. Mr. Sampath—the printer of Malgudi, The financial expert, Waiting for the Mahatma
Sinha, I. Animal's people
Viswanathan, P. The toss of a lemon
Zelazny, R. Lord of light

British occupation, 1765-1947

Cornwell, B. Sharpe's fortress
Forster, E. M. A passage to India
Ghosh, A. The glass palace
Godden, R. Black Narcissus
Jhabvala, R. P. Heat and dust
Kaye, M. M. The far pavilions
Kaye, M. M. Shadow of the moon
Kunzru, H. The impressionist
Mehta, G. Raj
Narayan, R. K. The bachelor of arts
Narayan, R. K. The dark room
Narayan, R. K. The English teacher
Narayan, R. K. Swami and friends
Narayan, R. K. Swami and friends, The bachelor of arts, The dark room, The English teacher
Narayan, R. K. Waiting for the Mahatma
Scott, P. The day of the scorpion
Scott, P. A division of the spoils
Scott, P. The jewel in the crown
Scott, P. The Raj quartet
Scott, P. The towers of silence
Sundaresan, I. The splendor of silence

1947-

Adiga, A. The white tiger
Chatterjee, U. English, August
Deb, S. The point of return
Desai, A. Clear light of day
Desai, A. Fire on the mountain
Dyer, G. Jeff in Venice, death in Varanasi
Endō, S. Deep river
Jhabvala, R. P. Out of India
Naipaul, V. S. Magic seeds
Narayan, R. K. The financial expert
Narayan, R. K. Mr. Sampath—the printer of Malgudi
Narayan, R. K. Under the banyan tree and other stories
Roy, A. The god of small things
Rushdie, S. Midnight's children
Rushdie, S. Shalimar the clown
Scott, P. Staying on
Seth, V. A suitable boy
Sundaresan, I. In the Convent of Little Flowers
Suri, M. The age of Shiva
Theroux, P. The elephant god
Theroux, P. The Elephanta suite
Theroux, P. The gateway of India
Theroux, P. Monkey Hill
Vassanji, M. G. The assassin's song

Politics

See Politics—India

Race relations

Forster, E. M. A passage to India

Rural life

Jhabvala, R. P. Heat and dust
Narayan, R. K. The grandmother's tale and selected stories
Narayan, R. K. Malgudi days

Benares

Mishima, Y. The Temple of Dawn

Bombay

Chaudhuri, A. The immortals
Irving, J. A son of the circus
Mistry, R. Family matters
Mistry, R. A fine balance

Rushdie, S. The ground beneath her feet
Rushdie, S. Midnight's children
Rushdie, S. The Moor's last sigh
Suri, M. The death of Vishnu
Umrigar, T. N. The space between us

Calcutta

Ghosh, A. Sea of poppies

Delhi

Desai, A. Clear light of day
The **Indian** clerk. Leavitt, D.
Indian killer. Alexie, S.
The **Indian** lawyer. Welch, J.
INDIAN OCEAN *See* World War, 1939-1945—Indian Ocean
Indian summer. Howells, W. D.
    In Howells, W. D. Novels, 1875-1886
The **Indian** summer of a Forsyte. Galsworthy, J.
    In Galsworthy, J. The Forsyte saga p313-59

INDIANA

Collins, M. Lost souls
Henley, P. In the river sweet
Kimmel, H. Something rising (light and swift)
Kimmel, H. The used world
Reynolds, M. The Starlite Drive-in
Tarkington, B. Alice Adams
Tucker, T. Over and under
Vonnegut, K. God bless you, Mr. Rosewater

19th century

Fleming, T. J. When this cruel war is over
Lockridge, R. Raintree County
Tarkington, B. The magnificent Ambersons
West, J. The friendly persuasion

Indianapolis

Lewin, M. Z. Oh Joe

INDIANAPOLIS (IND.) *See* Indiana—Indianapolis

INDIANS OF CENTRAL AMERICA

    See also Mayas

INDIANS OF MEXICO

    See also Aztecs; Incas
Danvers, D. The fourth world

INDIANS OF NORTH AMERICA

    See also names of specific tribes or nations
Alexie, S. Flight
Baker, K. Sky coyote
Brand, M. Beyond the outposts
Brown, C. B. Edgar Huntly
Brown, D. A. Creek Mary's blood
Coel, M. Blood memory
Coldsmith, D. The long journey home
Coldsmith, D. Tallgrass
Cooper, J. F. The last of the Mohicans
Cooper, J. F. The Leatherstocking tales
Cooper, J. F. The pioneers
Dorris, M. The crown of Columbus
Erdrich, L. The red convertible
Gear, K. O. People of the masks
Gear, K. O. People of the owl
Gear, W. M. Coyote summer
Gear, W. M. People of the thunder
Gregory, P. Virgin earth
Guthrie, A. B. The big sky
Guthrie, A. B. The way West
Harrison, S. Brother Wind
Harrison, S. Call down the stars
Harrison, S. Cry of the wind
Harrison, S. Mother earth, father sky
Harrison, S. My sister the moon
Harrison, S. Song of the river
Hill, R. B. Hanta yo
Humphreys, J. Nowhere else on earth
Johnston, T. C. Lay the mountains low
Kingsolver, B. Animal dreams
L'Amour, L. The haunted mesa
L'Amour, L. Jubal Sackett
L'Amour, L. Last of the breed
McCarthy, C. Blood meridian
McMurtry, L. Buffalo girls
Meyers, K. The work of wolves
Michener, J. A. Centennial
Momaday, N. S. House made of dawn

Innocent blood. James, P. D.
Innocent grave. Robinson, P.
Innocent traitor. Weir, A.
The **innocent** voyage. See Hughes, R. A. W. A high wind in Jamaica
The **innocent** wife. See Colette. Claudine and Annie
INNS See Hotels, taverns, etc.

INQUISITION

Lewis, M. G. The monk
The **inquisitors'** manual. Antunes, A. L.

INSANE, CRIMINAL AND DANGEROUS

See also Insanity; Mentally ill
Clark, M. H. A cry in the night
Clark, M. H. A stranger is watching
Connelly, M. Void moon
Crais, R. Demolition angel
Diehl, W. Show of evil
Hall, J. W. Rough draft
Harris, T. Hannibal
Harris, T. Hannibal rising
Harris, T. Red Dragon
Harris, T. The silence of the lambs
Johansen, I. The killing game
Katzenbach, J. The analyst
Katzenbach, J. Just cause
Katzenbach, J. The madman's tale
Katzenbach, J. The wrong man
King, S. Misery
King, S. Rage
Koontz, D. R. False memory
Koontz, D. R. Intensity
Koontz, D. R. Velocity
Lehane, D. Shutter Island
Leonard, E. Glitz
Lutz, J. Dancing with the dead
Meltzer, B. Dead even
O'Brien, E. In the forest
Patterson, J. Along came a spider
Patterson, J. Cat & mouse
Patterson, J. Cross
Patterson, J. Jack and Jill
Patterson, J. Kiss the girls
Patterson, J. Pop! goes the weasel
Patterson, J. Roses are red
Perry, T. Fidelity
Rendell, R. Live flesh
Straub, P. The Hellfire Club
Thompson, J. The killer inside me

INSANE ASYLUMS See Mentally ill—Care and treatment

INSANITY

See also Insane, Criminal and dangerous; Mental illness; Personality disorders
Brontë, C. Jane Eyre
Cheever, J. Bullet Park
Evenson, B. The open curtain
Faulkner, W. The sound and the fury
Galsworthy, J. Maid in waiting
Jackson, S. We have always lived in a castle
Keneally, T. A family madness
King, S. Roadwork
McCabe, P. Winterwood
McGrath, P. Asylum
Melville, H. Pierre
Nin, A. The four-chambered heart
Rendell, R. Adam and Eve and Pinch me
Stevenson, R. L. The merry men
Ward, M. J. The snake pit
West, M. L. The clowns of God
Wiesel, E. Twilight
Insect dreams. Estrin, M.

INSECTS

Estrin, M. Insect dreams
Kafka, F. Metamorphosis
Saul, J. The homing

INSOMNIA

Cohen, R. Inspired sleep
Insomnia. King, S.
Inspector Ghote trusts the heart. Keating, H. R. F.
Inspector Maigret and the killers. Simenon, G.
INSPIRATION See Creation (Literary, artistic, etc.)
Inspired sleep. Cohen, R.

An **instance** of the fingerpost. Pears, I.
The **instant** enemy. Macdonald, R.
In Macdonald, R. Archer in jeopardy
INSTRUCTORS See Teachers
Instruments of night. Cook, T. H.

INSURANCE AGENTS

Moody, R. K&K

INSURANCE BROKERS

Cain, J. M. Double indemnity
Gurganus, A. Blessed assurance: a moral tale
Shreve, A. Where or when

INTELLECTUALS

See also Scholars
Davies, R. The cunning man
Kundera, M. Slowness
Mendelson, C. Morningside Heights
Oz, A. Fima

INTELLIGENCE AGENTS See Secret service
Intensity. Koontz, D. R.
INTER-RACIAL MARRIAGE See Interracial marriage
Interest of justice. Rosenberg, N. T.

INTERFAITH MARRIAGE

Powers, R. The time of our singing
Roth, P. Letting go
An **international** episode. James, H.
In James, H. Complete stories, 1874-1884
In James, H. The complete tales of Henry James

INTERNATIONAL INTRIGUE

See also Adventure; Secret service; Spies
Anthony, E. The Janus imperative
Archer, J. A matter of honor
Buchan, J. The thirty-nine steps
Buckley, W. F. Mongoose, R.I.P
Clancy, T. Clear and present danger
Clancy, T. The hunt for Red October
Clancy, T. Patriot games
Clavell, J. Noble house
Cussler, C. Fire ice
Cussler, C. Sahara
Deighton, L. Berlin game
Deighton, L. Funeral in Berlin
Deighton, L. The Ipcress file
Deighton, L. London match
Deighton, L. Mexico set
Didion, J. The last thing he wanted
Durrell, L. Mountolive
Fleming, I. Casino Royale
Fleming, I. Doctor No
Fleming, I. From Russia, with love
Fleming, I. Goldfinger
Fleming, I. The man with the golden gun
Fleming, I. On Her Majesty's Secret Service
Fleming, I. You only live twice
Follett, K. Lie down with lions
Follett, K. Triple
Folsom, A. R. The day after tomorrow
Forsyth, F. The day of the jackal
Forsyth, F. The dogs of war
Forsyth, F. The fourth protocol
Francis, C. Wolf winter
Freemantle, B. Bomb grade
Furst, A. The spies of Warsaw
Gilman, D. The amazing Mrs. Pollifax
Gilman, D. The elusive Mrs. Pollifax
Gilman, D. A palm for Mrs. Pollifax
Gilman, D. The unexpected Mrs. Pollifax
Goldman, W. Marathon man
Grady, J. Six days of the condor
Greene, G. 3: This gun for hire, The confidential agent, The ministry of fear
Greene, G. The captain and the enemy
Greene, G. The ministry of fear
Greene, G. Our man in Havana
Greene, G. The quiet American
Greene, G. Travels with my aunt
Grisham, J. The broker
Hall, A. The Quiller memorandum
Hall, A. Quiller Salamander
Hall, A. Quiller solitaire
Harris, R. Fatherland
Harris, T. Black Sunday

Intruder in the dust. Faulkner, W.
  also in Faulkner, W. Novels, 1942-1954 p283-470
The **intruders**. Smith, M. M.
Intuition. Goodman, A.
The **intuitionist**. Whitehead, C.

INUIT

Mowat, F. The Snow Walker
Patterson, K. Consumption
Simmons, D. The terror
Vollmann, W. T. The rifles

INVALIDS

See also Paraplegics
Cather, W. Sapphira and the slave girl
Dickens, C. Dombey and Son
Elkin, S. Stanley Elkin's The magic kingdom
Nin, A. The four-chambered heart
Wharton, E. Ethan Frome
Invasion of privacy. Healy, J. F.
Invasion of privacy. O'Shaughnessy, P.
Inventing the Abbotts and other stories. Miller, S.
The **invention** of everything else. Hunt, S.

INVENTORS

Fishburne, R. Going to see the elephant
Hunt, S. The invention of everything else
Theroux, P. The Mosquito Coast
The **investigation**. Uhnak, D.

INVESTMENTS

Ducker, B. Dizzying heights

INVISIBILITY

Berger, T. Being invisible
Saint, H. F. Memoirs of an invisible man
Westlake, D. E. Smoke
Invisible. Auster, P.
Invisible cities. Calvino, I.
Invisible man. Ellison, R.
The **invisible** man. Wells, H. G.
  also in Wells, H. G. Seven famous novels
Iodine. Kimmel, H.

IONIAN ISLANDS (GREECE)

See also Cephalonia Island (Greece)

IOWA

Drury, T. The driftless area
Harstad, D. Code sixty-one
Robinson, M. Gilead
Smiley, J. A thousand acres
Waller, R. J. The bridges of Madison County

Farm life

See Farm life—Iowa
The **Ipcress** file. Deighton, L.

IPHIGENIA (LEGENDARY CHARACTER)

Unsworth, B. The songs of the kings
IRA *See* Irish Republican Army
Ira Foxglove. McMahon, T. A.

IRAN

17th century

Amirrezvani, A. The blood of flowers

IRAN

Clavell, J. Whirlwind

To 640 A.D.

Vidal, G. Creation

Prisoners and prisons

See Prisoners and prisons—Iran

Tehran

García, C. A handbook to luck
Ignatius, D. The increment
Sofer, D. The Septembers of Shiraz

IRANIAN AMERICANS

Tyler, A. Digging to America

IRAQ

Unsworth, B. Land of marvels

Baghdad

Menendez, A. The last war

IRAQ WAR, 2003-

Paretsky, S. Bleeding Kansas

IRELAND

See also Northern Ireland
Banville, J. The book of evidence
Banville, J. The sea
Binchy, M. Circle of friends
Binchy, M. The glass lake
Crane, S. The O'Ruddy
Donovan, G. Young Irelanders
Doyle, R. The deportees and other stories
Doyle, R. A star called Henry
French, T. In the woods
French, T. The likeness
Hart, J. The truth about love
Higgins, J. Confessional
Higgins, J. Drink with the Devil
Hyland, M. J. Carry me down
Joyce, J. Dubliners
Llywelyn, M. 1921
Llywelyn, M. 1949
O'Brien, E. House of splendid isolation
O'Brien, E. Lantern slides
O'Brien, F. The complete novels
O'Brien, F. The Dalkey archive
O'Brien, F. The hard life
O'Connor, F. Collected stories
O'Faoláin, S. The collected stories of Seán O'Faoláin
The Oxford book of Irish short stories
Parsons, J. Mary, Mary
Powell, A. The valley of bones
Rutherfurd, E. The princes of Ireland
Rutherfurd, E. The rebels of Ireland
Tóibín, C. The blackwater lightship
Trevor, W. Fools of fortune
Uris, L. Redemption
Uris, L. Trinity
Weber, K. The Music Lesson

To 1172

Llywelyn, M. Pride of lions
Llywelyn, M. Red Branch

17th century

Llywelyn, M. The last prince of Ireland

18th century

Edgeworth, M. Castle Rackrent

French invasion, 1798

Flanagan, T. The year of the French

19th century

Flanagan, T. The tenants of time
Howatch, S. Cashelmara
Mallinson, A. A close run thing

Sinn Fein Rebellion, 1916

Llywelyn, M. 1916
O'Neill, J. At swim, two boys

College life

See College life—Ireland

Farm life

See Farm life—Ireland

Peasant life

See Peasant life—Ireland

Politics

See Politics—Ireland

Rural life

Binchy, M. Whitethorn Woods
Davis-Goff, A. This cold country
McCabe, E. Heaven lies about us
McCabe, P. The butcher boy
McCabe, P. Winterwood
McGahern, J. By the lake
O'Brien, E. The country girls
O'Brien, E. In the forest
O'Brien, E. Wild Decembers
O'Brien, F. The poor mouth
O'Neill, J. Kilbrack; or, Who is Nancy Valentine?
Trevor, W. Love and summer

JAPAN—1945—*Continued*

Ōe, K. Somersault
Okuizumi, H. The stones cry out
Schwartz, J. B. The commoner
Yoshimoto, B. Asleep [a novella]
Yoshimoto, B. Goodbye Tsugumi
Yoshimoto, B. Kitchen
Yoshimoto, B. Love songs
Yoshimoto, B. Night and night's travelers

Aristocracy

See Aristocracy—Japan

Courts and courtiers

See Courts and courtiers—Japan

Rites and ceremonies

See Rites and ceremonies—Japan

Rural life

Abe, K. The woman in the dunes

Hiroshima

Bock, D. The ash garden
Pywell, S. L. What happened to Henry

Kamakura

Kawabata, Y. The sound of the mountain

Kyoto

Walbert, K. The gardens of Kyoto

Okinawa

Bird, S. The Yokota Officers Club

Tokyo

Hill, T. The love of stones
Hunter, S. The 47th samurai
Kawabata, Y. The sound of the mountain
Lee, D. Country of origin
Mishima, Y. Spring snow
Mitchell, D. Number9dream
Murakami, H. After dark
Murakami, R. In the miso soup
Nothomb, A. Tokyo fiancee
Peace, D. Tokyo year zero
Perdue, L. Slatewiper
Smith, M. C. December 6
Tsukiyama, G. The street of a thousand blossoms
Vargas Llosa, M. The bad girl

JAPANESE

Canada

Sakamoto, K. One hundred million hearts

China

Ballard, J. G. Empire of the Sun
Shan Sa. The girl who played go

Hawaii

Michener, J. A. Hawaii

India

Endō, S. Deep river

Mexico

Ōe, K. An echo of heaven

United States

Ōe, K. An echo of heaven
Reed, I. Japanese by spring

JAPANESE AMERICANS

Guterson, D. Snow falling on cedars
Lee, C.-R. A gesture life

Evacuation and relocation, 1942-1945

Dallas, S. Tallgrass
Otsuka, J. When the emperor was divine
Japanese by spring. Reed, I.
JAPANESE SOLDIERS *See* Soldiers—Japan
Jaws. Benchley, P.
Jayber Crow. Berry, W.
Jazz. Morrison, T.
The **jazz** bird. Holden, C.
Jazz funeral. Smith, J.

JAZZ MUSIC

Baker, D. Young man with a horn
Faulks, S. On Green Dolphin Street
Goonan, K. A. In war times
Hassler, J. Rookery blues
Joe, Y. My fine lady
Mackey, N. Bass cathedral
Mansbach, A. The end of the Jews
Marshall, P. The fisher king
Turner, F. W. 1929

JEALOUSY

Balzac, H. d. Cousin Bette
Barker, N. Darkmans
Cather, W. Sapphira and the slave girl
Chevalier, T. Girl with a pearl earring
Eliot, G. Middlemarch
Essex, K. Leonardo's swans
Goudge, E. Such devoted sisters
Hart, J. Sin
Hatoum, M. The brothers
Hawkes, J. The blood oranges
Hegi, U. The worst thing I've done
Iles, G. Third degree
Klein, R. The moth diaries
Lebrecht, N. The song of names
Mann, T. Young Joseph
Muñoz Molina, A. In her absence
Norman, H. The haunting of L
Oates, J. C. The falls
Pirandello, L. The outcast
Proust, M. The captive
Proust, M. The fugitive [variant title: The sweet cheat gone]
Rendell, R. Going wrong
Rosenfeld, L. I'm so happy for you
Shreve, A. Body surfing
Shreve, A. The weight of water
Spark, M. The finishing school
Starr, J. Lights out

JEANNE D'ARC, SAINT *See* Joan, of Arc, Saint, 1412-1431
Jeff in Venice, death in Varanasi. Dyer, G.
JEFFERSON, THOMAS, 1743-1826
About
Chase-Riboud, B. Sally Hemings
JEMISON, MARY, 1743-1833
About
Larsen, D. The white
Jennie Gerhardt. Dreiser, T.
    also in Dreiser, T. Sister Carrie; Jennie Gerhardt; Twelve men
The **Jennifer** morgue. Stross, C.
Jericho's fall. Carter, S. L.

JERUSALEM

Bulgakov, M. A. The master and Margarita
Eve, N. The family orchard
Grossman, D. Be my knife
Grossman, D. Someone to run with
Holland, C. Jerusalem
Oz, A. Fima
Oz, A. Panther in the basement
Qashu, S. Dancing Arabs
Spark, M. The Mandelbaum Gate
Stone, R. Damascus Gate
Tarr, J. Queen of swords
Wiesel, E. A beggar in Jerusalem
Yehoshua, A. B. A woman in Jerusalem
Jerusalem. Holland, C.
Jerusalem Inn. Grimes, M.

JESUITS

Blatty, W. P. The exorcist
Eco, U. The island of the day before
Hansen, R. Exiles
Higgins, J. Day of judgment
McDonald, I. Brasyl
Russell, M. D. Children of God
Russell, M. D. The sparrow
Vollmann, W. T. Fathers and crows

JESUS CHRIST

About

Asch, S. The Nazarene
Bulgakov, M. A. The master and Margarita
Crace, J. Quarantine

JEWS—*Continued*

New Jersey

Dezenhall, E. Money wanders
Roth, P. American pastoral

New York (N.Y.)

Bellow, S. Mr. Sammler's planet
Bellow, S. The victim
Chabon, M. The amazing adventures of Kavalier and Clay
Colwin, L. Family happiness
Hamill, P. Snow in August
Helprin, M. Ellis Island
Kirshenbaum, B. An almost perfect moment
Malamud, B. The assistant
Mirvis, T. The outside world
Ozick, C. Heir to the glimmering world
Ozick, C. The Puttermesser papers
Plain, B. The golden cup
Potok, C. The chosen
Potok, C. The gift of Asher Lev
Potok, C. My name is Asher Lev
Potok, C. The promise
Reyn, I. What happened to Anna K.
Rosen, J. Joy comes in the morning
Roth, H. Call it sleep
Roth, H. A diving rock on the Hudson
Roth, H. From bondage
Roth, H. Requiem for Harlem
Roth, H. A star shines over Mt. Morris Park
Sholem Aleichem. The adventures of Mottel, the cantor's son
Singer, I. B. Shadows on the Hudson
Stern, S. The angel of forgetfulness
Styron, W. Sophie's choice
Tax, M. Rivington Street
Wallant, E. L. The pawnbroker
Wiesel, E. The accident
Wouk, H. Marjorie Morningstar

New York (State)

Abraham, P. The romance reader
Kay, T. Shadow song
Reisman, N. The first desire
Wiesel, E. Twilight

Palestine

Asch, S. The Apostle
Mann, T. The tales of Jacob
Mann, T. Young Joseph
Wallace, L. Ben-Hur
Wiesel, E. Dawn

Poland

Hersey, J. The wall
Ozick, C. The Messiah of Stockholm
Singer, I. B. The estate
Singer, I. B. The family Moskat
Singer, I. B. The magician of Lublin
Singer, I. J. The brothers Ashkenazi
Uris, L. Mila 18
Yolen, J. Briar Rose

Portugal

Zimler, R. The last kabbalist of Lisbon

Rome

Asch, S. The Apostle

Russia

Amis, M. House of meetings
Anatoli, A. Babi Yar
Malamud, B. The fixer
Potok, C. The war doctor
Richler, N. Your mouth is lovely
Sholem Aleichem. The adventures of Menahem-Mendl
Sholem Aleichem. The further adventures of Menachem-Mendl
Sholem Aleichem. The nightingale
Sholem Aleichem. Tevye's daughters
Wiesel, E. The testament

United States

Bellow, S. The adventures of Augie March
Bellow, S. Herzog
Bellow, S. Mr. Sammler's planet
Chabon, M. The Yiddish policemen's union

Delbanco, N. What remains
Doctorow, E. L. The book of Daniel
Doctorow, E. L. Ragtime
Epstein, J. Fabulous small Jews
Gilmore, J. Golden country
Goldberg, M. Bee season
Havazelet, E. Bearing the body
Heller, J. Good as Gold
Hobson, L. K. Z. Gentleman's agreement
Horn, D. All other nights
Levitt, P. M. Come with me to Babylon
Lipman, E. The Inn at Lake Devine
Mansbach, A. The end of the Jews
Manseau, P. Songs for the butcher's daughter
Melman, P. C. Landsman
Plain, B. Crescent City
Plain, B. Evergreen
Plain, B. Harvest
Plain, B. Tapestry
Powers, R. The time of our singing
Reich, T. My Holocaust
Roth, P. The anatomy lesson
Roth, P. The ghost writer
Roth, P. Goodbye, Columbus
Roth, P. Goodbye, Columbus, and five short stories
Roth, P. I married a communist
Roth, P. Indignation
Roth, P. Letting go
Roth, P. My life as a man
Roth, P. Novels & stories, 1959-1962
Roth, P. The plot against America
Roth, P. Portnoy's complaint
Roth, P. The professor of desire
Roth, P. Zuckerman bound
Roth, P. Zuckerman unbound
Shaw, I. The young lions
Styron, W. Sophie's choice

JIANG QING, 1914-1991
About
Min, A. Becoming Madame Mao
The **Jim** Chee mysteries. Hillerman, T.
Jim the boy. Earley, T.
Jitterbug. Estleman, L. D.
Jitterbug perfume. Robbins, T.

JOAN, OF ARC, SAINT, 1412-1431
About
Marcantel, P. An army of angels
Twain, M. Personal recollections of Joan of Arc
Job: a comedy of justice. Heinlein, R. A.

JOCKEYS
Francis, D. Bolt
Francis, D. Nerve
Francis, D. Whip hand
Smith, B. All hat
Joe. Brown, L.
Joe College. Perrotta, T.
The **Joe** Leaphorn mysteries. Hillerman, T.

JOHANNESBURG (SOUTH AFRICA) *See* South Africa—Johannesburg

JOHN, KING OF ENGLAND, 1167-1216
About
Penman, S. K. Here be dragons

JOHN, OF GAUNT, DUKE OF LANCASTER, 1340-1399
About
Seton, A. Katherine

JOHN, THE APOSTLE, SAINT
About
Williams, N. John

JOHN, THE EVANGELIST, SAINT *See* John, the Apostle, Saint
John. Williams, N.

JOHN BROWN'S RAID, HARPERS FERRY, W.VA., 1859
See Harpers Ferry (W.Va.)—John Brown's raid, 1859
John Dollar. Wiggins, M.
John Henry Days. Whitehead, C.
Johnny Angel. Steel, D.
Johnny got his gun. Trumbo, D.
Johnny One-Eye. Charyn, J.
The **joke.** Kundera, M.
Jonah's gourd vine. Hurston, Z. N.
In Hurston, Z. N. Novels and stories p1-171

Jubal Sackett. L'Amour, L.
Jubilee. Dann, J.
Jubilee. Walker, M.
Jubilee Trail. Bristow, G.

JUDAH LOEW BEN BEZALEL, CA. 1525-1609
About
Sherwood, F. The book of splendor
Wiesel, E. The Golem

JUDAISM
See also Hasidism; Jews; Zionism
Agnon, S. Y. Only yesterday
Brooks, G. People of the book
Jen, G. Mona in the promised land
Mirvis, T. The outside world
Potok, C. The chosen
Potok, C. The gift of Asher Lev
Potok, C. My name is Asher Lev
Potok, C. The promise
Roiphe, A. R. Lovingkindness
Singer, I. B. The estate
Singer, I. B. The magician of Lublin
Wiesel, E. The Golem
Zimler, R. The last kabbalist of Lisbon
Judas child. O'Connell, C.
The **Judas** Field. Bahr, H.
Judas horse. Smith, A.

JUDAS ISCARIOT
About
Asch, S. The Nazarene
Kazantzakis, N. The last temptation of Christ
The **Judas** judge. McGarrity, M.
The **Judas** kiss. Holt, V.
Judas Priest. McInerny, R. M.
Jude the obscure. Hardy, T.
JUDEA *See* Palestine—To 70 A.D.
The **judge.** Martini, S. P.

JUDGES
Carter, S. L. The emperor of Ocean Park
Coulter, C. The target
Desai, K. The inheritance of loss
Grisham, J. The appeal
Grisham, J. The brethren
Leonard, E. Maximum Bob
Margolin, P. After dark
Marlette, D. Magic time
Martini, S. P. The judge
Patterson, R. N. Protect and defend
Picoult, J. Nineteen minutes
Pottinger, S. The fourth procedure
Rosenberg, N. T. Interest of justice
Schwartz, L. Angels Crest
Tóibín, C. The heather blazing
Trollope, J. Marrying the mistress
Turow, S. Limitations
The **judges.** Wiesel, E.
Judgment day. Farrell, J. T.
In Farrell, J. T. Studs Lonigan
A **judgment** in stone. Rendell, R.
The **judgment** of Caesar. Saylor, S.
Judith Hearne. See Moore, B. The lonely passion of Judith Hearne
The **jugger.** Stark, R.
Julian Comstock. Wilson, R. C.
Juliet, naked. Hornby, N.
JULY FOURTH *See* Fourth of July
July's people. Gordimer, N.
Jump and other stories. Gordimer, N.
The **jungle.** Sinclair, U.

JUNGLES
Conrad, J. Heart of darkness
Forester, C. S. The African Queen
Hamilton-Paterson, J. Gerontius
King, R. The sound of butterflies
Salak, K. The white Mary

JUPITER (PLANET)
Bova, B. Jupiter
Jupiter. Bova, B.
Jupiter's bones. Kellerman, F.
Jurassic Park. Crichton, M.
The **juror.** Green, G. D.
The **jury.** Martini, S. P.

JURY DUTY *See* Trials
Just a corpse at twilight. Van de Wetering, J.
Just after sunset. King, S.
Just an ordinary day. Jackson, S.
Just cause. Katzenbach, J.
Just one look. Coben, H.

JUSTICE
Spark, M. Aiding and abetting
Justice. Kellerman, F.
Justice for some. Wilhelm, K.
Justice Hall. King, L. R.
Justine. Durrell, L.
also in Durrell, L. The Alexandria quartet: Justine; Balthazar; Mountolive [and] Clea p11-203

JUVENILE DELINQUENCY
Burgess, A. A clockwork orange
Edgerton, C. Walking across Egypt
Garigliano, J. Dogface
Hunter, E. The blackboard jungle
Levin, M. Compulsion
Ōe, K. Nip the buds, shoot the kids

K

"K" is for killer. Grafton, S.
K&K. Moody, R.
In Moody, R. Right livelihoods
KAFIRS (AFRICAN PEOPLE) *See* Zulus (African people)
KAFKA, FRANZ, 1883-1924
Parodies, imitations, etc.
Estrin, M. Insect dreams
Lashner, W. Kockroach
Kafka on the shore. Murakami, H.
KALAKAUA, DAVID, KING OF HAWAII, 1836-1891
About
Houston, J. D. Bird of another heaven
Kaleidoscope. Gilman, D.
Kalooki nights. Jacobson, H.
KAMAKURA (JAPAN) *See* Japan—Kamakura
KAMPUCHEA *See* Cambodia

KĀNCHENJUNGA (NEPAL AND INDIA)
Desai, K. The inheritance of loss

KANSAS
Dallas, S. The Persian Pickle Club
Flynn, G. Dark places
Hughes, L. Not without laughter
Moriarty, L. The center of everything
Paretsky, S. Bleeding Kansas
Parks, G. The learning tree
Preston, D. Still life with crows

19th century
Durham, D. A. Gabriel's story
Parker, R. B. Gunman's rhapsody

Frontier and pioneer life
See Frontier and pioneer life—Kansas
KANSAS CITY (MO.) *See* Missouri—Kansas City
KARATE
See also Tae kwon do
Kartography. Shamsie, K.
Kat scratch fever. Kijewski, K.
Kate Vaiden. Price, R.
KATHERINE, DUCHESS OF LANCASTER, 1350-1403
About
Seton, A. Katherine
Katherine. Seton, A.
Kat's cradle. Kijewski, K.

KAYAKING
Parks, T. Rapids
The **keep.** Egan, J.
Keep the change. McGuane, T.
Keeper of dreams. Card, O. S.
The **keepers** of the house. Grau, S. A.
The **keeper's** son. Hickam, H. H.
Keeping Faith. Picoult, J.

Killing grounds. Stabenow, D.
A killing in this town. Vernon, O.
The killing jar. Monaghan, N.
Killing Mister Watson. Matthiessen, P.
The killing of worlds. Westerfeld, S.
Killing the lawyers. Hill, R.
Killing time. Harrod-Eagles, C.
Killshot. Leonard, E.
Kilo class. Robinson, P.
The kindly ones. Littell, J.
The kindly ones. Powell, A.
    In Powell, A. A dance to the music of time
The kindness of strangers. Smith, J.
Kindred. Butler, O. E.
Kinds of love. Sarton, M.
KING, ADA See Lovelace, Ada King, Countess of, 1815-1852
KING, AUGUSTA ADA See Lovelace, Ada King, Countess of, 1815-1852
KING, MARTIN LUTHER, JR., 1929-1968
                About
    Johnson, C. R. Dreamer
King Bongo. Sanchez, T.
The king in the tree. Millhauser, S.
    In Millhauser, S. The king in the tree: three novellas
The king in the tree: three novellas. Millhauser, S.
The king is dead. Lewis, J.
King Kelson's bride. Kurtz, K.
The king must die. Renault, M.
The king of Colored Town. Wimberley, D.
The king of lies. Hart, J.
The king of swords. Stone, N.
King, queen, knave. Nabokov, V. V.
King Rat. Clavell, J.
King Solomon's carpet. Vine, B.
King Solomon's mines. Haggard, H. R.
The kingdom of bones. Gallagher, S.
Kingdom of shadows. Furst, A.
Kingdoms of light. Foster, A. D.
KINGS AND RULERS
    See also Courts and courtiers; names of kings and rulers
    Anderson, P. War of the Gods
    Tremain, R. Music & silence
    Wallach, J. Seraglio
King's captain. Lambdin, D.
Kings of infinite space. Hynes, J.
A king's ransom. Grippando, J.
Kinshu: Autumn brocade. Miyamoto, T.

KIOWA INDIANS
    Momaday, N. S. The ancient child
Kiss. McBain, E.
The kiss. Steel, D.
A kiss before dying. Levin, I.
Kiss me, deadly. Spillane, M.
    In Spillane, M. The Mike Hammer collection [v2]
A kiss of fate. Putney, M. J.
Kiss of the bees. Jance, J. A.
Kiss of the spider woman. Puig, M.
Kiss the girls. Patterson, J.
Kissed a sad goodbye. Crombie, D.
Kissing the gunner's daughter. Rendell, R.
Kitchen. Yoshimoto, B.
Kitchen [novella] Yoshimoto, B.
    In Yoshimoto, B. Kitchen
The kitchen god's wife. Tan, A.
The kite runner. Hosseini, K.
KKK See Ku Klux Klan
Kleopatra. Essex, K.
The knife thrower and other stories. Millhauser, S.
Knight of shadows. Zelazny, R.
KNIGHTHOOD See Knights and knighthood
Knights and dragons. Spencer, E.
    In Spencer, E. The stories of Elizabeth Spencer p127-218
KNIGHTS AND KNIGHTHOOD
    See also Chivalry; Middle Ages
    Berger, T. Arthur Rex
    Cervantes Saavedra, M. d. Don Quixote de la Mancha
    Connell, E. S. Deus lo volt!
    Cornwell, B. Enemy of God
    Cornwell, B. Excalibur
    Cornwell, B. The winter king
    Doyle, Sir A. C. The White Company
    Follett, K. World without end

Holland, C. The angel and the sword
Holland, C. The firedrake
Holland, C. Jerusalem
Kurtz, K. The temple and the stone
Scott, Sir W. Ivanhoe
White, T. H. The once and future king
KNIGHTS OF MALTA
    Willocks, T. The religion
KNIGHTS OF RHODES See Knights of Malta
KNIGHTS OF ST. JOHN See Knights of Malta
KNITTING
    Hood, A. The knitting circle
The knitting circle. Hood, A.
Knockemstiff. Pollock, D. R.
KNOLLYS, LETTICE
                About
    Holt, V. My enemy the Queen
Knots. Farah, N.
The known world. Jones, E. P.
KNOXVILLE (TENN.) See Tennessee—Knoxville
Kockroach. Lashner, W.

KOKNAS (INDIC PEOPLE)
    D'Souza, T. The Konkans
The Konkans. D'Souza, T.

KOREA
    Yoon, P. Once the shore
KOREA (NORTH)
    Talarigo, J. The ginseng hunter
KOREAN AMERICANS
    Choi, S. A person of interest
    Kim, S. The interpreter
KOREAN WAR, 1950-1953
    Griffin, W. E. B. Under fire
    Ha Jin. War trash
    Hooker, R. MASH
    Michener, J. A. The bridges at Toko-ri
    Morris, W. Taps

                Casualties
    Phillips, J. A. Lark and Termite
KOREANS

                United States
    Woo, S. J. Everything Asian
KOSOVO (SERBIA)
    Fleishman, J. Promised virgins
Kowloon Tong. Theroux, P.
The Kreutzer sonata, The Devil, and other tales. Tolstoy, L., graf
Krik? Krak! Danticat, E.
KRIS KRINGLE See Santa Claus
Kristin Lavransdatter. Undset, S.
KU KLUX KLAN
    Doig, I. Prairie nocturne
    Ellroy, J. The cold six thousand
    Grisham, J. The chamber
    Howard, R. Like trees, walking
    Marlette, D. Magic time
    Vernon, O. A killing in this town
KUBLAI KHAN, 1216-1294
                About
    Calvino, I. Invisible cities
KURSK, BATTLE OF, RUSSIA, 1943
    Robbins, D. L. The last citadel
Kushiel's dart. Carey, J.
KYOTO (JAPAN) See Japan—Kyoto
KYRGYZSTAN
    Rosenberg, R. This is not civilization

L

L.A. confidential. Ellroy, J.

L.A. dead. Woods, S.
L.A. noir. Ellroy, J.
L.A. outlaws. Parker, T. J.
L.A. requiem. Crais, R.
L.A. Times. Woods, S.
"L" is for lawless. Grafton, S.
LA TOUR, GEORGES DE, 1593-1652
    About
  Huddle, D. La Tour dreams of the wolf girl
LABOR AND LABORING CLASSES
  See also Apprentices; Labor unions; Migrant labor; Prole-
tarian novels; Strikes and lockouts

    Denmark
  Andersen Nexø, M. Pelle the conqueror: v2 Apprenticeship

    England
  Pearce, M. E. Apple tree lean down [omnibus volume]
  Sillitoe, A. Saturday night and Sunday morning
  Swift, G. Last orders

    France
  Zola, É. Germinal

    Pennsylvania
  Poyer, D. Thunder on the mountain

    Poland
  Singer, I. J. The brothers Ashkenazi

    United States
  Doig, I. Bucking the sun
  Hemingway, E. The torrents of spring
  Lehane, D. The given day
  Steinbeck, J. In dubious battle
  Tax, M. Rivington Street

    Wales
  Llewellyn, R. How green was my valley
Labor Day. Maynard, J.

LABOR DISPUTES
  Tucker, T. Over and under
LABOR UNIONS
  See also Labor and laboring classes; Strikes and lockouts
  Lehane, D. The given day
  Poyer, D. Thunder on the mountain
  Schulberg, B. Waterfront
The **Labrador** Pact. Haig, M.
LaBrava. Leonard, E.
Labyrinth. Mosse, K.
The **labyrinthine** ways. See Greene, G. The power and the glory
The **lace** reader. Barry, B.
The **lacquer** screen. Gulik, R. H. v.
Ladder of years. Tyler, A.
Ladders to fire. Nin, A.
  In Nin, A. Cities of the interior p1-127
The **ladies'** man. Lipman, E.
The **ladies** of Covington send their love. Medlicott, J. A.
Lady Barberina. James, H.
  In James, H. Complete stories, 1874-1884
  In James, H. The complete tales of Henry James
Lady Chatterley's lover. Lawrence, D. H.
The **Lady** Elizabeth. Weir, A.
The **lady** in the lake. Chandler, R.
  In Chandler, R. Later novels and other writings
Lady Lazarus. Altschul, A. F.
Lady of horses. Tarr, J.
Lady with the camellias. See Dumas, A. Camille
L'affaire. Johnson, D.
LAGOS (NIGERIA) *See* Nigeria—Lagos
Laguna heat. Parker, T. J.
LAHORE (PAKISTAN) *See* Pakistan—Lahore
LAKE DISTRICT (ENGLAND)
  McDermid, V. Grave tattoo
Lake news. Delinsky, B.
LAKE ONTARIO (N.Y. AND ONT.)
  Cooper, J. F. The Pathfinder
LAKE TAHOE (CALIF. AND NEV.)
  O'Shaughnessy, P. Breach of promise
  O'Shaughnessy, P. Invasion of privacy
  O'Shaughnessy, P. Motion to suppress

  O'Shaughnessy, P. Obstruction of justice
  O'Shaughnessy, P. Writ of execution
  Pronzini, B. Step to the graveyard easy
Lake Wobegon days. Keillor, G.
Lake Wobegon summer 1956. Keillor, G.
LAMAS
  Hilton, J. Lost horizon
Lamb in love. Brown, C.
The **Laments**. Hagen, G.
L'America. McPhee, M.
The **Lamorna** wink. Grimes, M.
The **lamplighter**. O'Neill, A.
LANCASHIRE (ENGLAND) *See* England—Lancashire
LANCELOT (LEGENDARY CHARACTER)
  White, T. H. The candle in the wind
Lancelot. Percy, W.
Land of marvels. Unsworth, B.
Land of the living. French, N.
LAND REFORM *See* Land tenure
LAND SPECULATION *See* Speculation
LAND TENURE
  McGahan, A. The white earth
  McLarty, R. Art in America
  O'Brien, E. Wild Decembers
LANDLADIES *See* Landlord and tenant
Landlocked. Lessing, D. M.
  In Lessing, D. M. Children of violence
LANDLORD AND TENANT
  See also Tenant farming
  Rendell, R. Thirteen steps down
  Wideman, J. E. Two cities
LANDLORDS *See* Landlord and tenant
Lando. L'Amour, L.
  In L'Amour, L. The Sacketts: beginnings of a dynasty
Lands of memory. Hernández, F.
Lands of memory [novelette] Hernández, F.
  In Hernández, F. and Allen, E. Lands of memory
LANDSCAPE GARDENING
  See also Trees
Landsman. Melman, P. C.
LANGUAGE AND LANGUAGES
  Barbery, M. The elegance of the hedgehog
  Barker, N. Darkmans
  Castellanos Moya, H. Senselessness
  Clement, H. Noise
  Finch, S. The guild of xenolinguists
  Hoban, R. Riddley Walker
LANSKY, MEYER, 1902-1983
    About
  Latour, J. The Havana World Series
The **lantern** bearers. Frame, R.
Lantern slides. O'Brien, E.
Lapham rising. Rosenblatt, R.
LAPLAND
  Paasilinna, A. The howling miller
  Vida, V. Let the Northern Lights erase your name
LARCENY *See* Theft
Lark and Termite. Phillips, J. A.
LAS VEGAS (NEV.) *See* Nevada—Las Vegas
Lasher. Rice, A.
Last act in Palmyra. Davis, L.
Last argument of kings. Abercrombie, J.
The **last** book of swords: Shieldbreaker's story. Saberhagen, F.
The **last** camel died at noon. Peters, E.
Last car to Elysian Fields. Burke, J. L.
The **last** castle. Vance, J.
  In The Hugo winners p245-305
The **last** Catholic in America. Powers, J. R.
The **last** cavalier. Dumas, A.
Last chance for glory. Solomita, S.
Last Chance Saloon. Keyes, M.
The **last** child. Hart, J.
The **last** chronicle of Barset. Trollope, A.
The **last** citadel. Robbins, D. L.
The **last** command. Zahn, T.
The **last** crossing. Vanderhaeghe, G.
The **last** dance. McBain, E.
Last days of Dogtown. Diamant, A.

The **last** days of Pompeii. Lytton, E. B. L., Baron
The **last** detective. Crais, R.
The **last** detective. Lovesey, P.
The **last** Dickens. Pearl, M.
Last ditch. Marsh, Dame N.
The **last** Don. Puzo, M.
Last dragon. McDermott, J. M.
The **last** empress. Min, A.
The **last** enchantment. Stewart, M.
In Stewart, M. Mary Stewart's Merlin trilogy
The **last** English king. Rathbone, J.
Last evenings on Earth. Bolaño, R.
Last family in England. See Haig, M. The Labrador Pact
The **last** farewell. McCutchan, P.
The **last** full measure. Shaara, J.
The **last** gentleman. Percy, W.
The **last** girls. Smith, L.
The **last** good chance. Barbash, T.
The **last** good kiss. Crumley, J.
The **last** hand. Wright, E.
The **last** hellion. Chase, L. L.
The **last** heroes. Griffin, W. E. B.
The **last** hostage. Nance, J. J.
The **last** hurrah. O'Connor, E.
The **last** judgment. Pears, I.
The **last** juror. Grisham, J.
The **last** kabbalist of Lisbon. Zimler, R.
Last kiss. Rice, L.
Last last chance. Maazel, F.
The **last** letter home. Moberg, V.
The **last** light of the sun. Kay, G. G.
The **last** Nazi. Pottinger, S.
Last night. Salter, J.
Last night at the Lobster. O'Nan, S.
Last night in Twisted River. Irving, J.
The **last** nine days of the Bismarck. Forester, C. S.
The **last** novel. Markson, D.
The **last** of Chéri. Colette
In Colette. Six novels p535-648
The **last** of her kind. Nunez, S.
The **last** of Mr. Norris. Isherwood, C.
In Isherwood, C. The Berlin stories
Last of the breed. L'Amour, L.
The **last** of the just. Schwarz-Bart, A.
The **last** of the Mohicans. Cooper, J. F.
also in Cooper, J. F. The Leatherstocking tales
The **last** of the wine. Renault, M.
Last orders. Swift, G.
The **last** post. Ford, F. M.
In Ford, F. M. Parade's end
The **last** prince of Ireland. Llywelyn, M.
The **last** refuge. Knopf, C.
The **last** report on the miracles at Little No Horse. Erdrich, L.
The **last** resort. Lurie, A.
Last rites. Harvey, J.
Last rituals. Yrsa Sigurðardóttir
Last seen alive. Simpson, D.
The **last** suppers. Davidson, D. M.
The **last** temptation of Christ. Kazantzakis, N.
The **last** thing he wanted. Didion, J.
Last things. McInerny, R. M.
Last things. Snow, C. P.
The **last** time they met. Shreve, A.
The **last** town on earth. Mullen, T.
The **last** tycoon. Fitzgerald, F. S.
The **last** unicorn. Beagle, P. S.
The **last** vampire. Strieber, W.
The **last** war. Menendez, A.
The **last** witchfinder. Morrow, J.
The **last** word and other stories. Greene, G.
Late for the wedding. Quick, A.
The **late** Mr. Shakespeare. Nye, R.
Late nights on air. Hay, E.
Later novels. Cather, W.
Later novels and other writings. Chandler, R.
Later novels and stories. Maxwell, W.
Later short stories, 1888-1903. Chekhov, A. P.
The **lathe** of heaven. Le Guin, U. K.

LATIN AMERICA

Allende, I. Eva Luna
García Márquez, G. Love in the time of cholera
Kertész, I. Detective story
Naipaul, V. S. A way in the world

The Oxford book of Latin American short stories

Politics

See Politics—Latin America

LATIN AMERICANS

Europe

García Márquez, G. Strange pilgrims
LATINOS (U.S.) *See* Hispanic Americans
Laughable loves. Kundera, M.
Laughing Boy. La Farge, O.
The **laughing** policeman. Sjöwall, M.
Laughing to keep from crying. Hughes, L.
Laura Warholic; or, The sexual intellectual. Theroux, A.

LAVEAU, MARIE, 1794-1881

About

Rhodes, J. P. Voodoo dreams

LAW AND LAWYERS

See also Judges; Trials; Women lawyers

Baldacci, D. Absolute power
Baldacci, D. The simple truth
Banks, R. The sweet hereafter
Bernhardt, W. Dark justice
Brown, S. The alibi
Camus, A. The fall
Carter, S. L. The emperor of Ocean Park
Clark, M. The legal limit
Clark, M. H. Remember me
Connell, E. S. Mr. Bridge
Connell, E. S. Mrs. Bridge
Connelly, M. The brass verdict
Connelly, M. The Lincoln lawyer
Cook, R. Crisis
Cozzens, J. G. By love possessed
Davies, R. The manticore
De Kretser, M. The Hamilton case
DeLillo, D. Falling man
DeMille, N. The gate house
DeMille, N. The Gold Coast
Dickens, C. Bleak House
Dickens, C. The posthumous papers of the Pickwick Club
Diehl, W. Primal fear
Diehl, W. Reign in hell
Diehl, W. Show of evil
Ducker, B. Dizzying heights
Dunne, J. G. Nothing lost
Ellis, D. Life sentence
Fairstein, L. Bad blood
Fairstein, L. Killer heat
Folsom, A. R. Day of confession
Forsyth, F. Avenger
Gaddis, W. A frolic of his own
Gardam, J. Old Filth
Gordon, N. The company you keep
Greene, G. The tenth man
Grippando, J. Born to run
Grippando, J. Hear no evil
Grippando, J. A king's ransom
Grippando, J. Lying with strangers
Grisham, J. The appeal
Grisham, J. The chamber
Grisham, J. The client
Grisham, J. The firm
Grisham, J. The last juror
Grisham, J. The partner
Grisham, J. The pelican brief
Grisham, J. The rainmaker
Grisham, J. The runaway jury
Grisham, J. The street lawyer
Grisham, J. The summons
Grisham, J. The testament
Grisham, J. A time to kill
Gruber, M. The book of air and shadows
Hart, J. The king of lies
Higgins, G. V. The Mandeville talent
Hoag, T. Guilty as sin
Hoffman, J. Retribution
Humphreys, J. The fireman's fair
Iles, G. Turning angel
Isaacs, S. Shining through
Katzenbach, J. Hart's war
Kaufman, S. Diary of a mad housewife
Kennedy, D. The big picture

Legacies. Wilson, F. P.
Legacy. Judd, A.
Legacy of love. Trollope, J.
Legal fictions. Entered in Part I under title
The **legal** limit. Clark, M.
LEGAL PROFESSION *See* Law and lawyers
LEGAL STORIES *See* Law and lawyers
Legal tender. Scottoline, L.
Legend of a suicide. Vann, D.
LEGENDS AND FOLK TALES
    See also Grail
  Benét, S. V. The Devil and Daniel Webster
  Berger, T. Arthur Rex
  Bradley, M. Z. The mists of Avalon
  Lewis, C. S. Till we have faces
  Llywelyn, M. The horse goddess
  Mailer, N. Ancient evenings
  Mehta, G. A river Sutra
  Renault, M. The bull from the sea
  Renault, M. The king must die
  Schwarz-Bart, A. The last of the just
  Steinbeck, J. The pearl
  Stewart, M. The hollow hills
  Stewart, M. The last enchantment
  Stewart, M. The wicked day
  Sutcliff, R. Sword at sunset
  Updike, J. The centaur
  Welty, E. The robber bridegroom
  White, T. H. The once and future king
  White, T. H. The sword in the stone
  Wiesel, E. The Golem
LEICESTER, ROBERT DUDLEY, EARL OF, 1532?-1588
    About
  Gregory, P. The queen's fool
  Maxwell, R. The Queen's bastard
Lélia. Sand, G.
LENIN, VLADIMIR IL'ICH, 1870-1924
    About
  Kalfus, K. The commissariat of enlightenment
LENINGRAD (SOVIET UNION) *See* Russia—St. Petersburg
LENO, DAN, 1860-1904
    About
  Ackroyd, P. The trial of Elizabeth Cree
LEO AFRICANUS, CA. 1492-CA. 1550
    About
  Maalouf, A. Leo Africanus
Leo Africanus. Maalouf, A.
Leo the African. See Maalouf, A. Leo Africanus
LEONARDO, DA VINCI, 1452-1519
    About
  Brown, D. The Da Vinci code
  Essex, K. Leonardo's swans
Leonardo's swans. Essex, K.
LEOPOLD, NATHAN FREUNDENTHAL, 1904 OR 5-1971
    About
  Levin, M. Compulsion
The **leper**. Thayer, S.
LEPROSY
  Greene, G. A burnt-out case
  Thayer, S. The leper
LESBIANISM
    See also Homosexuality
  Barnes, D. Nightwood
  Colette. Claudine married
  Grant, S. Map of Ireland
  Grumbach, D. The book of knowledge
  Hall, R. The well of loneliness
  Hallgrímur Helgason. 101 Reykjavik
  Henley, P. In the river sweet
  Humphreys, H. Afterimage
  Hunter, E. Lizzie
  Lurie, A. The last resort
  Meyer, C. Brown eyes blue
  Muller, M. Cyanide Wells
  Naylor, G. The women of Brewster Place
  Nin, A. Ladders to fire
  Parks, S.-L. Getting mother's body
  The Penguin book of lesbian short stories
  Schwartz, L. Angels Crest
  Schwartz, L. S. In the family way

Shreve, A. Body surfing
Tea, M. Rose of no man's land
Truong, M. T. D. The book of salt
Vine, B. The house of stairs
Walsh, H. Brass
Waters, S. Fingersmith
Winterson, J. Oranges are not the only fruit
LESBOS ISLAND (GREECE)
  Jong, E. Sappho's leap
A **lesson** before dying. Gaines, E. J.
Let it come down. Bowles, P.
  In Bowles, P. The sheltering sky; Let it come down; The spider's house
Let me sing you gentle songs. See Olsson, L. Astrid & Veronika
Let the great world spin. McCann, C.
Let the Northern Lights erase your name. Vida, V.
Let us now praise famous men; A death in the family, and shorter fiction. Agee, J.
Lethally blond. White, K.
Letter from home. Hart, C. G.
Letter from Point Clear. McFarland, D.
A **letter** of Mary. King, L. R.
The **letter** of the law. Green, T.
LETTERS (STORIES ABOUT)
  Bellow, S. Herzog
  Coetzee, J. M. Age of iron
  French, N. Beneath the skin
  Kundera, M. Identity
  Labiner, N. Miniatures
  L'Engle, M. The love letters
  Michael, J. Acts of love
  Purdy, J. In a shallow grave
  Schine, C. The love letter
  Sparks, N. Message in a bottle
  Wharton, E. The touchstone
LETTERS (STORIES IN LETTER FORM)
  Adiga, A. The white tiger
  Davies, R. Fifth business
  Fuentes, C. The eagle's throne
  Gardam, J. The queen of the tambourine
  Goethe, J. W. v. The sorrows of young Werther
  Grass, G. Dog years
  Grossman, D. Be my knife
  Hailey, E. F. A woman of independent means
  Kingsolver, B. The poisonwood Bible
  Lardner, R. You know me, Al
  Mackey, N. Bass cathedral
  Miles, J. Dear American Airlines
  Miyamoto, T. Kinshu: Autumn brocade
  Murdoch, I. An accidental man
  Poe, E. A. The unparalleled adventure of one Hans Pfaall
  Price, R. Blue Calhoun
  Rice, L. The letters
  Richardson, S. Clarissa
  Richardson, S. Pamela
  Richler, N. Your mouth is lovely
  Robinson, E. The true and outstanding adventures of the Hunt sisters
  Robinson, M. Gilead
  Savage, S. The cry of the sloth
  Schulze, I. New lives
  Shaffer, M. A. The Guernsey Literary and Potato Peel Pie Society
  Sholem Aleichem. The adventures of Menahem-Mendl
  Sholem Aleichem. The further adventures of Menachem-Mendl
  Shriver, L. We need to talk about Kevin
  Smith, L. Fair and tender ladies
  Smollett, T. G. The expedition of Humphry Clinker
  Tabucchi, A. It's getting later all the time
  Updike, J. S
  Walker, A. The color purple
The **letters**. Rice, L.
Letters from the underworld. See Dostoyevsky, F. Notes from underground
Letting go. Roth, P.
  also in Roth, P. Novels & stories, 1959-1962
LEUKEMIA
  Doerr, H. Stones for Ibarra
  Picoult, J. My sister's keeper

LIFE ON OTHER PLANETS—*Continued*
Westerfeld, S. The risen empire
Wilson, R. C. Blind Lake
Life sentence. Ellis, D.
Life, the universe, and everything. Adams, D.
The **light** and the dark. Snow, C. P.
LIGHT HOUSES *See* Lighthouses
Light in August. Faulkner, W.
also in Faulkner, W. Novels, 1930-1935
The **light** in the forest. Richter, C.
The **light** in the piazza. Spencer, E.
In Spencer, E. The southern woman p258-311
Light music. Goonan, K. A.
Light on snow. Shreve, A.
Light thickens. Marsh, Dame N.
The **lighthouse**. James, P. D.

LIGHTHOUSES
Hansen, E. F. Tales of protection

LIGHTNING
Hoffman, A. The ice queen
Lightning. Koontz, D. R.
Lightning. Lutz, J.
Lightning. McBain, E.
The **lightning** keeper. Lawrence, S.
Lights out. Starr, J.
Like trees, walking. Howard, R.
Like water for chocolate. Esquivel, L.
Like we used to be. Stubbs, J.
Like you'd understand, anyway. Shepard, J.
The **likeness**. French, T.
The **lilies** of the field. Barrett, W. E.
Lily White. Isaacs, S.
LIMA (PERU) *See* Peru—Lima
Limitations. Turow, S.
The **limits** of enchantment. Joyce, G.

LINCOLN, ABRAHAM, 1809-1865
About
Safire, W. Freedom
Stone, I. Love is eternal
Vidal, G. Lincoln

LINCOLN, MARY TODD, 1818-1882
About
Newman, J. C. Mary
Stone, I. Love is eternal
The **Lincoln** lawyer. Connelly, M.

LINDBERGH, CHARLES, 1902-1974
About
Roth, P. The plot against America
Linden Hills. Naylor, G.
Line of fire. Griffin, W. E. B.
Linger awhile. Hoban, R.

LINGUISTS
Karinthy, F. Metropole
Links. Farah, N.
A **lion** among men. Maguire, G.
Lion in the valley. Peters, E.

LIONS
Maguire, G. A lion among men
The **lion's** game. DeMille, N.

LIPPIZANER HORSES
Stewart, M. Airs above the ground
Lipstick jungle. Bushnell, C.
LIQUOR INDUSTRY *See* Liquor traffic

LIQUOR TRAFFIC
See also Moonshiners
Francis, D. Proof
LISBON (PORTUGAL) *See* Portugal—Lisbon
Lisey's story. King, S.
The **list**. Martini, S. P.
The **list** of Adrian Messenger. MacDonald, P.
Listen to the silence. Muller, M.
Listening woman. Hillerman, T.
also in Hillerman, T. The Joe Leaphorn mysteries

LITERARY CRITICS
Koontz, D. R. Relentless
Nooteboom, C. Lost paradise

LITERARY LIFE
See also Authors
Barnes, D. Nightwood
Blackwell, E. Grub
Bolaño, R. By night in Chile
Byatt, A. S. Possession
Gessen, K. All the sad young literary men
Keillor, G. Love me
Lelchuk, A. Ziff
Martin, V. Italian fever
McInerney, J. Bright lights, big city
Michener, J. A. The novel
Parini, J. The apprentice lover
Powell, D. Turn, magic wheel
Roth, P. The counterlife
Savage, S. The cry of the sloth
Wolitzer, M. The wife

LITHUANIANS
United States
Sinclair, U. The jungle
LITTLE, MALCOLM *See* Malcolm X, 1925-1965
Little Bee. Cleave, C.
Little, big. Crowley, J.

LITTLE BIG HORN, BATTLE OF THE, 1876
Falconer, D. The lost thoughts of soldiers
Little Big Man. Berger, T.
Little bird of heaven. Oates, J. C.
Little children. Perrotta, T.
The **little** dog laughed. Hansen, J.
Little Dorrit. Dickens, C.
The **little** drummer girl. Le Carré, J.
Little earthquakes. Weiner, J.
Little face. Hannah, S.
The **little** friend. Tartt, D.
The **little** giant of Aberdeen County. Baker, T.
Little men. Alcott, L. M.
In Alcott, L. M. Little women; Little men; Jo's boys
The **little** prince. Saint-Exupéry, A. d.
Little Saigon. Parker, T. J.
The **little** sister. Chandler, R.
In Chandler, R. Later novels and other writings
The **little** stranger. Waters, S.
Little tiny teeth. Elkins, A. J.
Little women. Alcott, L. M.
In Alcott, L. M. Little women; Little men; Jo's boys
The **little** women. Weber, K.
Little women; Little men; Jo's boys. Alcott, L. M.
A **little** yellow dog. Mosley, W.
A **live** coal in the sea. L'Engle, M.
Live flesh. Rendell, R.
LIVERPOOL (ENGLAND) *See* England—Liverpool
Lives of girls & women. Munro, A.

LIVIA, EMPRESS, CONSORT OF AUGUSTUS, EMPEROR OF ROME, 58? B.C.-29
About
Graves, R. I, Claudius
The **living** dead. Entered in Part I under title
Living next door to the god of love. Robson, J.
The **lizard** cage. Connelly, K.
Lizzie. Hunter, E.

LLEWELYN AP IORWERTH, D. 1240
About
Penman, S. K. Here be dragons

LLYWELYN AP GRUFFYDD, D. 1282
About
Penman, S. K. The reckoning

LOANS
See also Moneylenders
Local girls. Hoffman, A.
The **locked** room. Sjöwall, M.
Locked rooms. King, L. R.
The **locusts** have no king. Powell, D.
In Powell, D. Novels, 1944-1962
LODZ (POLAND) *See* Poland—Lodz

LOEB, RICHARD A., 1905-1936
About
Levin, M. Compulsion

LOGGERS
Guterson, D. Our Lady of the Forest

LOUIS XIV, KING OF FRANCE, 1638-1715
About
Dumas, A. The man in the iron mask [variant title: The iron mask]
Laker, R. To dance with kings

LOUIS XV, KING OF FRANCE, 1710-1774
About
Laker, R. To dance with kings

LOUIS XVI, KING OF FRANCE, 1754-1793
About
Laker, R. To dance with kings

LOUISE
About
Jacobson, D. All for love

LOUISIANA

Chopin, K. At fault
Dufresne, J. Deep in the shade of paradise
Gaines, E. J. A gathering of old men
Gautreaux, T. The missing
Gear, K. O. People of the owl
Martin, V. Property
McCammon, R. R. Gone south
Robards, K. Ghost moon
Rogers, R. Devil's Cape
Tademy, L. Cane River
Wells, K. Crawfish mountain
Wilcox, J. Heavenly days
Wilcox, J. Hunk City

19th century

Chopin, K. Complete novels and stories
Gaines, E. J. The autobiography of Miss Jane Pittman
Straight, S. A million nightingales

New Orleans

Algren, N. A walk on the wild side
Chopin, K. The awakening
Faulkner, W. If I forget thee, Jerusalem
Faulkner, W. Mosquitoes
Hailey, A. Hotel
Hambly, B. Dead water
Hambly, B. A free man of color
Hambly, B. Graveyard dust
Hambly, B. Sold down the river
Hambly, B. Die upon a kiss
Hambly, B. Wet grave
Harris, T. Black Sunday
Inness-Brown, E. Burning Marguerite
Melman, P. C. Landsman
Percy, W. Lancelot
Percy, W. The moviegoer
Piazza, T. City of refuge
Plain, B. Crescent City
Rhodes, J. P. Voodoo dreams
Rhodes, J. P. Yellow moon
Rice, A. The Feast of All Saints
Roberts, N. Honest illusions
Roberts, N. Midnight Bayou
Robison, M. One D.O.A., one on the way
Taylor, B. The book of getting even
Toole, J. K. A confederacy of dunces
Turner, F. W. Redemption
Warren, R. P. Band of angels
Louisiana hotshot. Smith, J.

LOVE

Helprin, M. A soldier of the great war
Sarton, M. Kinds of love
Love. Morrison, T.

LOVE AFFAIRS
See also Courtship; Love stories; Lovers; Marriage problems
Adams, A. After the war
Adler, E. Now or never
Alvarez, J. How the García girls lost their accents
Amis, K. The Russian girl
Atwood, M. The blind assassin
Atwood, M. Life before man
Baker, N. The anthologist
Baldwin, J. Another country
Bank, M. The girls' guide to hunting and fishing
Beattie, A. My life, starring Dara Falcon
Betts, D. Souls raised from the dead

Bowen, E. The heat of the day
Boyle, T. C. The women
Braybrooke, J. Every eye
Brown, R. M. Southern discomfort
Bushnell, C. Lipstick jungle
Casey, J. Spartina
Cather, W. Lucy Gayheart
Chase-Riboud, B. Sally Hemings
Cheever, J. Oh, what a paradise it seems
Chekhov, A. P. The duel
Chopin, K. At fault
Coe, J. The closed circle
Cohen, L. H. House lights
Colette. Chéri
Colette. The last of Chéri
Colwin, L. Family happiness
Cook, T. H. The Chatham School affair
Doig, I. Prairie nocturne
Dostoyevsky, F. The gambler
Dunne, D. An inconvenient woman
Eco, U. The mysterious flame of Queen Loana
Enquist, P. O. The book about Blanche and Marie
Faulkner, W. If I forget thee, Jerusalem
Faulks, S. Birdsong
Faulks, S. On Green Dolphin Street
Fielding, H. The history of Tom Jones, a foundling
Fielding, J. Missing pieces
Findley, T. The piano man's daughter
Fonseca, I. Attachment
French, M. The women's room
Gander, F. As a friend
Gordimer, N. The conservationist
Gordimer, N. A guest of honor
Gordimer, N. My son's story
Gordon, M. The company of women
Gordon, M. Final payments
Gottlieb, E. Now you see him
Graver, E. Awake
Greene, G. The end of the affair
Greer, A. S. The path of minor planets
Griesemer, J. Signal & noise
Grossman, D. Be my knife
Ha Jin. Waiting
Hadley, T. The master bedroom
Hamilton, J. Disobedience
Hannah, S. The wrong mother
Harrigan, S. Challenger Park
Hart, J. Sin
Hazzard, S. The transit of Venus
Hellenga, R. The Italian lover
Heller, Z. What was she thinking?
Hemingway, E. The garden of Eden
Henley, P. In the river sweet
Hooper, C. A child's book of true crime
Horan, N. Loving Frank
Hornby, N. Juliet, naked
Howatch, S. Mystical paths
Howatch, S. Penmarric
Howatch, S. Scandalous risks
Howatch, S. Ultimate prizes
Huddle, D. La Tour dreams of the wolf girl
Hunter, E. Privileged conversation
Irving, J. A widow for one year
Isaacs, S. Close relations
Jacobson, D. All for love
James, H. The ambassadors
James, H. In the cage
James, H. What Maisie knew
Jen, G. Typical American
Jhabvala, R. P. Heat and dust
Johnson, D. L'affaire
Johnson, D. Lulu in Marrakech
Jones, J. From here to eternity
Kadare, I. Agamemnon's daughter [novella]
Kawabata, Y. Snow country
Kawabata, Y. Thousand cranes
Keneally, T. A family madness
Kerouac, J. The subterraneans
Kerouac, J. Tristessa
Keyes, M. Last Chance Saloon
Keyes, M. The other side of the story
Kim, S. The interpreter
King, T. Survivor
Korda, M. Curtain

Love songs. Yoshimoto, B.
In Yoshimoto, B. Asleep p67-103
LOVE STORIES
    See also Courtship; Gothic romances; Love affairs; Lovers. Your scandalous ways
Abu-Jaber, D. Crescent
Adams, S. K. My old true love
Adler, E. Fortune is a woman
Agnon, S. Y. Only yesterday
Alam, S. The groom to have been
Allen, S. A. The sugar queen
Allende, I. Daughter of fortune
Allende, I. Eva Luna
Amis, M. House of meetings
Anderson, A. Darwin's wink
Anderson, P. The Saturn game
Austen, J. Emma
Austen, J. Mansfield Park
Austen, J. Persuasion
Austen, J. Sense and sensibility
Bail, M. Eucalyptus
Baker, K. In the garden of Iden
Baldwin, J. If Beale Street could talk
Balogh, M. More than a mistress
Balogh, M. Seducing an angel
Balogh, M. Simply love
Balogh, M. Simply magic
Balogh, M. Simply perfect
Balogh, M. Slightly dangerous
Battle, L. Bed & breakfast
Baxter, C. The feast of love
Berry, W. Jayber Crow
Binchy, M. The glass lake
Binchy, M. Whitethorn Woods
Bolaño, R. The skating rink
Böll, H. The silent angel
Bourne, J. My lord and spymaster
Bourne, J. The spymaster's lady
Brand, M. Dust across the range
Brontë, A. The tenant of Wildfell Hall
Brontë, C. Jane Eyre
Brontë, E. Wuthering Heights
Brookner, A. Brief lives
Brown, C. The hatbox baby
Brown, C. Lamb in love
Burroway, J. Bridge of sand
Byatt, A. S. Possession
Cameron, P. The city of your final destination
Carroll, J. The ghost in love
Chase, L. L. The last hellion
Chase, L. L. Lord of scoundrels
Chen, D. Brothers
Cleage, P. I wish I had a red dress
Coetzee, J. M. Diary of a bad year
Cohen, L. H. Heart, you bully, you punk
Colette. The kepi
Collins, J. Beginner's Greek
Colwin, L. Happy all the time
Conley, R. J. Mountain windsong
Cook, T. H. Breakheart Hill
Coward, N. Bon voyage
Crace, J. The pesthouse
Crane, S. Active service
Crane, S. The third violet
Crowley, J. Little, big
Crowley, J. The translator
Crusie, J. Bet me
Crusie, J. Faking it
Dai Sijie. Once on a moonless night
Danielewski, M. Z. Only revolutions
Davies, P. H. The Welsh girl
De Bernières, L. Corelli's mandolin
De los Santos, M. Belong to me
De los Santos, M. Love walked in
Delinsky, B. Lake news
Delinsky, B. The summer I dared
Delson, R. Maynard and Jennica
Dew, R. F. The evidence against her
Dickens, C. Barnaby Rudge
Dickens, C. Great expectations
Docx, E. The calligrapher
Doig, I. Dancing at the Rascal Fair
Dorris, M. The crown of Columbus
Drabble, M. The sea lady

Drayson, N. Guide to the birds of East Africa
Du Maurier, Dame D. Frenchman's Creek
Dunn, S. The big love
Durham, M. The man who loved Cat Dancing
Earley, T. The blue star
Esquivel, L. Like water for chocolate
Evans, N. The horse whisperer
Faulks, S. Charlotte Gray
Finney, J. Time and again
Fishburne, R. Going to see the elephant
Fitch, J. Paint it black
Fitzgerald, P. The blue flower
Fleming, T. J. When this cruel war is over
Follett, K. Lie down with lions
Ford, R. The student conductor
Fowles, J. The French lieutenant's woman
Frazier, C. Cold Mountain
Frazier, C. Thirteen moons
Freda, J. The patience of rivers
Freud, E. Love falls
Furnivall, K. The red scarf
Gaffney, P. Circle of three
Gaffney, P. Flight lessons
García Márquez, G. Love in the time of cholera
Garwood, J. The bride
George, M. Helen of Troy
Gibb, C. Sweetness in the belly
Godden, R. Pippa passes
Goethe, J. W. v. The sorrows of young Werther
Golden, A. Memoirs of a geisha
Goudge, E. Garden of lies
Goudge, E. Stranger in paradise
Goudge, E. Such devoted sisters
Goudge, E. Trail of secrets
Goudge, E. Green Dolphin Street
Gould, J. The best is yet to come
Gould, J. A moment in time
Gowdy, B. The romantic
Grass, G. The call of the toad
Greeley, A. M. Irish lace
Greeley, A. M. Younger than springtime
Grenville, K. The idea of perfection
Grøndahl, J. C. Lucca
Gruen, S. Water for elephants
Guo Xiaolu. A concise Chinese-English dictionary for lovers
Gutcheon, B. R. More than you know
Gwyn, R. The color of a dog running away
Hallinan, T. A nail through the heart
Handler, D. Adverbs
Hannah, K. On Mystic lake
Hansen, R. Isn't it romantic?
Harington, D. The pitcher shower
Harris, E. L. And this too shall pass
Harrison, J. The English major
Harrison, K. The seal wife
Hassler, J. The dean's list
Hassler, J. Rookery blues
Hawke, E. Ash Wednesday
Hawthorne, N. Fanshawe
Hay, E. A student of weather
Hazzard, S. The great fire
Hearon, S. Year of the dog
Helprin, M. Ellis Island
Hemingway, E. A farewell to arms
Henley, P. Hummingbird house
Hewson, D. Lucifer's shadow
Heyer, G. Black sheep
Heyer, G. The grand Sophy
Hilton, J. Random harvest
Hoban, R. Her name was Lola
Hoban, R. Linger awhile
Høeg, P. The woman and the ape
Hoffman, A. Here on Earth
Hoffman, A. The ice queen
Hoffman, A. The third angel
Hoffman, A. Turtle Moon
Hofmann, G. Lichtenberg and the little flower girl
Holt, V. The black opal
Holt, V. Secret for a nightingale
Hornby, N. High fidelity
Hospital, J. T. Orpheus lost
House, S. A parchment of leaves
Howatch, S. Glittering images
Howatch, S. Penmarric

LOVE STORIES—*Continued*

Roiphe, A. R. An imperfect lens
Ross-Macdonald, M. Tamsin Harte
Ross-Macdonald, M. The Trevarton inheritance
Rush, N. Mating
Rushdie, S. The ground beneath her feet
Russell, M. D. Dreamers of the day
Saint, H. F. Memoirs of an invisible man
Sand, G. Marianne
Saramago, J. The history of the siege of Lisbon
Sayers, D. L. Busman's honeymoon
Schickler, D. Sweet and vicious
Schine, C. The love letter
Schine, C. The New Yorkers
Scott, Sir W. Rob Roy
See, L. Peony in love
Segal, E. Love story
Seth, V. An equal music
Shakespeare, N. Secrets of the sea
Shakespeare, N. Snowleg
Shalev, M. A pigeon and a boy
Shan Sa. The girl who played go
Sherwood, F. The book of splendor
Shields, C. The republic of love
Sholem Aleichem. The nightingale
Shreve, A. Eden Close
Shreve, A. Resistance
Sienkiewicz, H. The deluge
Sittenfeld, C. The man of my dreams
Skármeta, A. The dancer and the thief
Slouka, M. The visible world
Smith, M. C. Rose
Smith, W. A. Golden fox
Sparks, N. A bend in the road
Sparks, N. Dear John
Sparks, N. The guardian
Sparks, N. Message in a bottle
Sparks, N. Nights in Rodanthe
Sparks, N. The notebook
Sparks, N. A walk to remember
Spencer, E. The light in the piazza
Spencer, L. Bitter sweet
Spencer, L. Forgiving
Spencer, L. Morning glory
Spencer, L. Small town girl
Spencer, L. That Camden summer
Spencer, S. Endless love
Stamm, P. On a day like this
Starr, J. Lights out
Steel, D. Amazing grace
Steel, D. The house on Hope Street
Steel, D. Journey
Steel, D. The kiss
Steel, D. No greater love
Stevens, M. Useful girl
Stevenson, J. The winter queen
Stevenson, R. L. The story of a lie
Stewart, M. The stormy petrel
Stirling, J. The marrying kind
Stirling, J. The penny wedding
Stone, K. Happy endings
Styron, W. Sophie's choice
Sundaresan, I. The splendor of silence
Tabucchi, A. It's getting later all the time
Tearne, R. Mosquito
Tennant, E. An unequal marriage
Thayer, N. Family secrets
Theroux, A. Darconville's cat
Thomas, R. All my sins remembered
Tremain, R. Music & silence
Treuer, D. The translation of Dr Apelles
Trevanian. The summer of Katya
Trevor, W. Love and summer
Trigiani, A. Very Valentine
Trollope, J. Friday nights
Trueblood, V. Seven loves
Tryon, T. The wings of the morning
Turgenev, I. S. First love and other stories
Turgenev, I. S. Spring torrents [variant title: The torrents of spring]
Turgenev, I. S. The torrents of spring
Turner, N. E. These is my words
Tussing, J. The best people in the world
Unsworth, B. Stone virgin

Updike, J. Brazil
Uris, L. Redemption
Urquhart, J. Away
Urquhart, J. A map of glass
Vallgren, C.-J. The horrific sufferings of the mind-reading monster Hercules Barefoot
Vargas Llosa, M. Aunt Julia and the scriptwriter
Vargas Llosa, M. The bad girl
Villars, E. The Normandie affair
Vine, B. The brimstone wedding
Wall, P. S. The Wilde women
Waller, R. J. The bridges of Madison County
Watson, B. The heaven of Mercury
Weiner, J. Good in bed
Wesley, M. Part of the furniture
Wharton, E. Summer
Wharton, E. The touchstone
Wideman, J. E. Two cities
Williamson, P. Heart of the west
Williamson, P. The outsider
Willig, L. The seduction of the crimson rose
Winthrop, E. Island justice
Wood, B. Perfect Harmony
Wood, B. Vital signs
Love story. Segal, E.
Love walked in. De los Santos, M.
The **love** wife. Jen, G.
The **loved** one. Waugh, E.

LOVELACE, ADA KING, COUNTESS OF, 1815-1852
About
Crowley, J. Lord Byron's novel
The **lovely** bones. Sebold, A.

LOVERS
Ehrenreich, B. The suitors
Kundera, M. Identity
McGowan, H. Duchess of nothing
Piercy, M. Summer people
Trueblood, V. Seven loves
Lovers crossing. Mitchell, J. C.
Love's mansion. West, P.
Loves music, loves to dance. Clark, M. H.
Loving Chloe. Mapson, J.-A.
Loving Frank. Horan, N.
Lovingkindness. Roiphe, A. R.
Lowboy. Wray, J.

LOWELL (MASS.) *See* Massachusetts—Lowell

LOWER EAST SIDE (NEW YORK, N.Y.) *See* New York (N.Y.)—Lower East Side

LOYALISTS, AMERICAN *See* American loyalists

LUCAN, RICHARD JOHN BINGHAM, EARL OF, 1934-
About
Spark, M. Aiding and abetting
Lucca. Grøndahl, J. C.
Lucia in London. Benson, E. F.
In Benson, E. F. Make way for Lucia p179-358

LUCIANO, LUCKY, 1897-1962
About
Higgins, J. Luciano's luck
Luciano's luck. Higgins, J.
Lucia's progress. See Benson, E. F. The worshipful Lucia
Lucifer's hammer. Niven, L.
Lucifer's shadow. Hewson, D.
Luck. Hofmann, G.
The **Luck** of Roaring Camp, and other tales. Harte, B.
Lucky girls. Freudenberger, N.
Lucky Jim. Amis, K.
The **lucky** ones. Mortman, D.
Lucky you. Hiaasen, C.
Lucy. Kincaid, J.
Lucy Gayheart. Cather, W.
In Cather, W. Later novels

LUKE, SAINT
About
Caldwell, T. Dear and glorious physician
Lullaby. McBain, E.
Lullaby. Palahniuk, C.
Lulu in Marrakech. Johnson, D.

LUMBER INDUSTRY
See also Loggers
Bernhardt, W. Dark justice
Kesey, K. Sometimes a great notion

M

MAIDS (SERVANTS)
See also Cleaning women
Bird, S. The Yokota Officers Club
Chevalier, T. Girl with a pearl earring
Cox, M. The glass of time
Danticat, E. The farming of bones
Frey, J. Bright shiny morning
Humphreys, H. Afterimage
Richardson, S. Pamela
Stirling, J. The workhouse girl
Wolitzer, H. Summer reading
Maigret and the black sheep. Simenon, G.
Maigret and the fortune-teller. Simenon, G.
Maigret and the gangsters. See Simenon, G. Inspector Maigret and the killers
Maigret and the madwoman. Simenon, G.
Maigret and the Saturday caller. Simenon, G.
Maigret and the toy village. Simenon, G.
Maigret and the wine merchants. Simenon, G.
Maigret bides his time. Simenon, G.
Maigret goes home. Simenon, G.
Maigret in Holland. Simenon, G.
Maigret's memoirs. Simenon, G.
Maigret's war of nerves. See Simenon, G. A man's head
Main Street. Lewis, S.
also in Lewis, S. Main Street & Babbitt
Main Street & Babbitt. Lewis, S.

MAINE
Carroll, J. Fault lines
Chute, C. The Beans of Egypt, Maine
Chute, C. The school on Heart's Content Road
Connolly, J. Bad men
Cook, T. H. Places in the dark
Delinsky, B. The summer I dared
Gutcheon, B. R. More than you know
Hand, E. Generation loss
Harding, P. Tinkers
Irving, J. The cider house rules
Jewett, S. O. The country of the pointed firs
Jewett, S. O. The country of the pointed firs and other stories
King, S. Bag of bones
King, S. The body
King, S. Carrie
King, S. Cujo
King, S. Dolores Claiborne
King, S. Dreamcatcher
King, S. Insomnia
King, S. It
King, S. Lisey's story
King, S. Needful things
King, S. Pet sematary
King, S. Rita Hayworth and Shawshank redemption
King, S. Salem's Lot
King, T. Survivor
Ogilvie, E. When the music stopped
Rickards, J. Winter's end
Robinson, L. Water dogs
Robinson, R. Cost
Russo, R. Empire Falls
Shreve, A. Strange fits of passion
Spencer, L. That Camden summer
Strout, E. Abide with me
Strout, E. Olive Kitteridge
Watson, J. E. Asta in the wings
Winthrop, E. Island justice

18th century
Lawrence, M. K. The burning bride
Lawrence, M. K. Hearts and bones

19th century
Rossner, J. Emmeline
Mainspring. Lake, J.
Maisie Dobbs. Winspear, J.
Majestic. Strieber, W.
Make way for Lucia. Benson, E. F.
The **Makioka** sisters. Tanizaki, J.

MALADJUSTED CHILDREN *See* Emotionally disturbed children
Malaise. Lemann, N.
A **Malamud** reader. Malamud, B.

MALARIA
Mallon, T. Two moons

MALAYA
See also Malaysia
Eng, T. T. The gift of rain

MALAYSIA
Conrad, J. Lord Jim
Manicka, R. The rice mother
Samarasan, P. Evening is the whole day

MALCOLM X, 1925-1965
About
Baker, K. Strivers Row
The **male** impersonator. Benson, E. F.
In Benson, E. F. Make way for Lucia p535-48
Malgudi days. Narayan, R. K.
Malice domestic. Hardwick, M.
Malice prepense. Wilhelm, K.
MALINCHE *See* Marina, ca. 1505-ca. 1530
MALINTZIN *See* Marina, ca. 1505-ca. 1530
Mallory's oracle. O'Connell, C.
Malone dies. Beckett, S.
In Beckett, S. Molloy, Malone dies, The unnamable

MALPRACTICE
Cook, R. Crisis

MALTA
Willocks, T. The religion
MALTA, KNIGHTS OF *See* Knights of Malta
The **Maltese** falcon. Hammett, D.
also in Hammett, D. Complete novels
Mama Day. Naylor, G.
Mama Flora's family. Haley, A.
The **Mambo** Kings play songs of love. Hijuelos, O.
MAMMALS, FOSSIL *See* Fossils
MAN, PREHISTORIC *See* Prehistoric man; Prehistoric times
The **man**. Wallace, I.
A **man** could stand up. Ford, F. M.
In Ford, F. M. Parade's end
A **man** in full. Wolfe, T.
The **man** in my basement. Mosley, W.
The **man** in the gray flannel suit. Wilson, S.
The **man** in the high castle. Dick, P. K.
also in Dick, P. K. Four novels of the 1960s

MAN IN THE IRON MASK
About
Dumas, A. The man in the iron mask [variant title: The iron mask]
The **man** in the iron mask. [variant title: The iron mask] Dumas, A.
The **man** in the maze. Silverberg, R.
In Silverberg, R. A Robert Silverberg omnibus
The **man** in the queue. Tey, J.
The **man** of feeling. Marías, J.
Man of glass. Cervantes Saavedra, M. d.
In Cervantes Saavedra, M. d. Three exemplary novels p75-121
The **man** of my dreams. Sittenfeld, C.
A **man** of no moon. McPhee, J.
The **man** of property. Galsworthy, J.
also in Galsworthy, J. The Forsyte saga p3-309
A **man** of the people. Le Guin, U. K.
In Le Guin, U. K. Four ways to forgiveness p93-144
The **man** on the balcony. Sjöwall, M.
Man Plus. Pohl, F.
The **man** that corrupted Hadleyburg, and other stories and essays. Twain, M.
Man walks into a room. Krauss, N.
The **man** who cast two shadows. O'Connell, C.
The **man** who could fly and other stories. Anaya, R. A.
The **man** who loved Cat Dancing. Durham, M.
The **man** who loved children. Stead, C.
The **man** who loved God. Kienzle, W. X.
The **man** who smiled. Mankell, H.
The **man** who walked like a bear. Kaminsky, S. M.
The **man** who watched trains go by. Simenon, G.
The **man** with a load of mischief. Grimes, M.
The **man** with the golden arm. Algren, N.
The **man** with the golden gun. Fleming, I.
The **man** without a country. Hale, E. E.
The **man** without qualities. Musil, R.

MANASSAS, BATTLES OF *See* Bull Run, 1st Battle, 1861
MANCHESTER (ENGLAND) *See* England—Manchester
The **mandarins**. Beauvoir, S. d.

MARRIAGE—*Continued*

James, H. The spoils of Poynton
James, H. The wings of the dove
Joss, M. The night following
Karon, J. Out to Canaan
Kinder, C. Honeymooners
King, S. Lisey's story
Kittredge, W. The Willow Field
Koen, K. Through a glass darkly
Leebron, F. G. In the middle of all this
Lodge, D. Deaf sentence
Lordan, B. But come ye back
Marías, J. A heart so white
Mason, B. A. Spence + Lila
McEwan, I. Black dogs
McEwan, I. On Chesil Beach
McFarland, D. Letter from Point Clear
Meloy, M. Liars and saints
Meltzer, B. Dead even
Miller, S. The senator's wife
Minot, E. The Brambles
Minot, S. Folly
Morley, I. Come Sunday
Narayan, R. K. The dark room
Nunez, E. Anna in-between
Oates, J. C. The falls
O'Nan, S. The good wife
Pouncey, P. R. Rules for old men waiting
Price, R. Roxanna Slade
Pym, B. Civil to strangers
Rice, L. Blue moon
Russo, R. Bridge of sighs
Russo, R. That old Cape magic
Sarton, M. Anger
Seth, V. A suitable boy
Shakespeare, N. Secrets of the sea
Shreve, A. All he ever wanted
Shreve, A. Sea glass
Stegner, W. E. Crossing to safety
Stirling, J. The piper's tune
Stone, R. Outerbridge Reach
Suri, M. The age of Shiva
Swift, G. Tomorrow
Tennant, E. An unequal marriage
Thayer, N. Between husbands and friends
Thayer, N. Family secrets
Theroux, P. My secret history
Toer, P. A. The girl from the coast
Trollope, J. The men and the girls
Trollope, J. Next of kin
Tyler, A. The amateur marriage
Tyler, A. Breathing lessons
Vidal, G. 1876
Weiner, J. Little earthquakes
West, P. Love's mansion
Wolff, M. M. Sudden rain
Wolitzer, M. The ten-year nap
Wood, B. The dreaming

MARRIAGE, CHILDLESS *See* Childless marriage

MARRIAGE, INTERFAITH *See* Interfaith marriage

MARRIAGE, INTERRACIAL *See* Interracial marriage

MARRIAGE BROKERS

Pym, B. Jane and Prudence

MARRIAGE COUNSELING *See* Marriage problems

Marriage is murder. Pickard, N.

MARRIAGE PROBLEMS

See also Divorce; Family life; Interfaith marriage; Love
affairs

Adams, A. After the war
Akst, D. The Webster chronicle
Allison, D. Bastard out of Carolina
Amado, J. Dona Flor and her two husbands
Amis, K. The Russian girl
Anderson-Dargatz, G. A recipe for bees
Atwood, M. Life before man
Bausch, R. Thanksgiving night
Beattie, A. Chilly scenes of winter
Beattie, A. My life, starring Dara Falcon
Beauvoir, S. d. The mandarins
Bellow, S. Herzog
Berne, S. A perfect arrangement
Boswell, R. Century's son

Bowles, P. The sheltering sky
Breslin, J. Table money
Brontë, A. The tenant of Wildfell Hall
Brown, R. Tender mercies
Brownrigg, S. Morality tale
Bushnell, C. Lipstick jungle
Cain, J. M. Mildred Pierce
Cain, J. M. The postman always rings twice
Casey, J. Spartina
Cather, W. A lost lady
Choi, S. A person of interest
Chopin, K. The awakening
Cleave, C. Little Bee
Coe, J. The closed circle
Colette. Claudine and Annie
Colette. The last of Chéri
Colwin, L. Family happiness
Cronin, A. J. The citadel
Cumyn, A. Losing it
Cunningham, M. The hours
Cusk, R. In the fold
Dallas, S. The diary of Mattie Spenser
Dark, A. E. Think of England
De la Roche, M. Jalna
Dean, M. L. The time it takes to fall
DeMille, N. The Gold Coast
Dickens, C. Hard times
Dillard, A. The Maytrees
Donovan, A. Buddha Da
Dreiser, T. Sister Carrie
Durrell, L. Justine
Durrell, L. Mountolive
Eliot, G. Middlemarch
Elkin, S. The MacGuffin
Emmons, C. His mother's son
Erdrich, L. Four souls
Fielding, J. See Jane run
Fitzgerald, F. S. The beautiful and damned
Fitzgerald, F. S. The Great Gatsby
Flaubert, G. Madame Bovary
Fonseca, I. Attachment
Ford, F. M. No more parades
French, M. The women's room
Freudenberger, N. The dissident
Fromm, P. As cool as I am
Galsworthy, J. The Forsyte saga
Galsworthy, J. Swan song
Galsworthy, J. The white monkey
García Márquez, G. Chronicle of a death foretold
Gibbons, K. Divining women
Glass, J. The whole world over
Godden, R. The battle of the Villa Fiorita
Godwin, G. Evensong
Godwin, G. The good husband
Goldsmith, O. Young wives
Gordon, M. Final payments
Gottlieb, E. Now you see him
Goudge, E. One last dance
Goudge, E. Trail of secrets
Grau, S. A. The keepers of the house
Graver, E. Awake
Greene, G. The end of the affair
Greene, G. The heart of the matter
Greer, A. S. The story of a marriage
Gregory, P. Virgin earth
Griesemer, J. Signal & noise
Grippando, J. Lying with strangers
Grossman, D. Be my knife
Grushin, O. The dream life of Sukhanov
Ha Jin. Waiting
Haddon, M. A spot of bother
Haigh, J. Mrs. Kimble
Hamilton, J. Disobedience
Handke, P. The left-handed woman
Hannah, S. Little face
Hardy, T. The return of the native
Harrigan, S. Challenger Park
Hart, J. The king of lies
Hart, J. Damage
Haruf, K. Plainsong
Hawkes, J. The blood oranges
Hawthorne, N. The scarlet letter
Hazzard, S. The transit of Venus
Hearon, S. Footprints

MARRIAGE PROBLEMS—*Continued*

Stegner, W. E. Angle of repose
Stirling, J. The workhouse girl
Stone, R. Bay of souls
Stubbs, J. Family games
Stubbs, J. Like we used to be
Styron, W. Lie down in darkness
Swann, M. Flower children
Symons, J. Something like a love affair
Tanizaki, J. The Makioka sisters
Thayer, N. My dearest friend
Thomas, R. Other people's marriages
Thomas, S. Private arrangements
Tolstoy, L., graf. Anna Karenina
Tremain, R. The color
Trigiani, A. Big Cherry Holler
Trollope, A. The prime minister
Trollope, J. The best of friends
Trollope, J. Marrying the mistress
Trollope, J. The rector's wife
Trollope, J. A Spanish lover
Tyler, A. The accidental tourist
Tyler, A. The amateur marriage
Tyler, A. Earthly possessions
Tyler, A. Ladder of years
Tyler, A. Morgan's passing
Umrigar, T. N. The weight of heaven
Upadhyay, S. The guru of love
Updike, J. Rabbit redux
Updike, J. Rabbit, run
Vargas Llosa, M. The notebooks of Don Rigoberto
Vine, B. The chimney sweeper's boy
Waller, R. J. The bridges of Madison County
Watson, B. The heaven of Mercury
Weber, K. The little women
Weisgall, D. The world before her
Weldon, F. The life and loves of a she-devil
Wharton, E. The custom of the country
Wharton, E. Ethan Frome
Wharton, E. Madame de Treymes
Whitney, P. A. Amethyst dreams
Whitney, P. A. Poinciana
Whitney, P. A. Spindrift
Wiggs, S. The ocean between us
Wilhelm, K. The deepest water
Wolitzer, M. The wife
Wood, B. Vital signs
Woods, S. Imperfect strangers
Woods, S. Short straw
Yarbrough, S. The end of California
Zuber, I. Salt
Marriages and infidelities. Oates, J. C.
The **married** man. White, E.
The **marrying** kind. Stirling, J.
Marrying the mistress. Trollope, J.

MARS (PLANET)

Barnes, J. The sky so big and black
Bova, B. Mars
Bova, B. Mars life
Bova, B. Return to Mars
Bradbury, R. The Martian chronicles
Dick, P. K. Martian time-slip
Friedman, M. Martian Dawn
Haldeman, J. W. Marsbound
Lewis, C. S. Out of the silent planet
Pohl, F. Man Plus
Pohl, F. Mars Plus
Robinson, K. S. Blue Mars
Robinson, K. S. Green Mars [novelette]
Robinson, K. S. The Martians
Robinson, K. S. Red Mars
Simmons, D. Ilium
Simmons, D. Olympos
Tepper, S. S. The Margarets
Varley, J. Red lightning
Varley, J. Rolling thunder
Mars. Bova, B.
Mars life. Bova, B.
Mars Plus. Pohl, F.
Marsbound. Haldeman, J. W.
Martha Peake. McGrath, P.
Martha Quest. Lessing, D. M.
In Lessing, D. M. Children of violence

MARTHA'S VINEYARD (MASS.)

Carter, S. L. The emperor of Ocean Park
Harris, R. The ghost
Hoffman, A. Illumination night
West, D. The wedding

MARTIAL ARTS

Donohue, J. J. Sensei
The **Martian** chronicles. Bradbury, R.
Martian Dawn. Friedman, M.
Martian time-slip. Dick, P. K.
In Dick, P. K. Five novels of the 1960s & 70s

MARTIANS

See also Interplanetary visitors; Mars (Planet)
Heinlein, R. A. Stranger in a strange land
The **Martians**. Robinson, K. S.

MARTIN, VICTORIA C. WOODHULL *See* Woodhull, Victoria C., 1838-1927
Martin Bauman. Leavitt, D.
Martin Chuzzlewit. Dickens, C.
Martin Dressler. Millhauser, S.
Martin Eden. London, J.

MARY I, QUEEN OF ENGLAND, 1516-1558
About
Gregory, P. The queen's fool
Harper, K. The Poyson garden

MARY II, QUEEN OF GREAT BRITAIN, 1662-1694
About
Plaidy, J. William's wife

MARY, BLESSED VIRGIN, SAINT
About
Guterson, D. Our Lady of the Forest
Kirshenbaum, B. An almost perfect moment

MARY, QUEEN OF SCOTS, 1542-1587
About
Plaidy, J. The captive Queen of Scots
Mary. Newman, J. C.

MARY MAGDALENE, SAINT
About
McGowan, K. The expected one
Mary, Mary. Parsons, J.
Mary Reilly. Martin, V.
Mary Stewart's Merlin trilogy. Stewart, M.

MARY TUDOR *See* Mary I, Queen of England, 1516-1558
Marya. Oates, J. C.

MARYLAND

See also Chesapeake Bay (Md. and Va.)
Gaffney, P. Flight lessons
McBride, J. Song yet sung
Michener, J. A. Chesapeake
Tyler, A. Searching for Caleb

17th century
Barth, J. The sot-weed factor

Annapolis
Deutermann, P. T. Darkside
Martin, W. Annapolis

Baltimore
Bell, M. S. Ten Indians
Lippman, L. Scratch a woman
Lippman, L. What the dead know
Tyler, A. The amateur marriage
Tyler, A. Back when we were grownups
Tyler, A. Celestial navigation
Tyler, A. The clock winder
Tyler, A. Digging to America
Tyler, A. Dinner at the Homesick Restaurant
Tyler, A. Ladder of years
Tyler, A. Morgan's passing
Tyler, A. A patchwork planet
Tyler, A. Saint maybe
MASH. Hooker, R.

MASOCHISM

Templeton, E. Gordon

MASON, CHARLES, 1730-1787
About
Pynchon, T. Mason & Dixon
Mason & Dixon. Pynchon, T.

MATTACHICH, GEZA VON
About
Jacobson, D. All for love
Matter. Banks, I.
A **matter** of honor. Archer, J.
MAU MAU
Ruark, R. Uhuru
Maurice. Forster, E. M.
Maurice. Shelley, M. W.
Max Brand's best western stories. Brand, M.
Maximum Bob. Leonard, E.

MAY DAY
Kadare, I. Agamemnon's daughter [novella]
Read, Miss. Thrush Green
May Day. Fitzgerald, F. S.
In Fitzgerald, F. S. The Fitzgerald reader p3-53
May there be a road. L'Amour, L.
May we borrow your husband? Greene, G.
In Greene, G. Collected stories p1-161

MAYAS
Smith, S. The ruins
Maynard and Jennica. Delson, R.
MAYO (IRELAND) *See* Ireland—Mayo
The **Mayor** of Casterbridge. Hardy, T.

MAYORS
Barbash, T. The last good chance
Hardy, T. The Mayor of Casterbridge
Iles, G. The devil's punchbowl
Nersesian, A. The swing voter of Staten Island
The **mayor's** tongue. Rich, N.
The **Maytrees**. Dillard, A.
The **maze**. Coulter, C.
The **maze**. Karnezis, P.
A **maze** of death. Dick, P. K.
In Dick, P. K. VALIS and later novels

MCCOY, KID, 1872-1940
About
Strauss, D. The real McCoy
McNally's dilemma. Sanders, L.
McNally's gamble. Sanders, L.
McNally's luck. Sanders, L.
McNally's puzzle. Sanders, L.
McNally's secret. Sanders, L.
McNally's trial. Sanders, L.
McTeague. Norris, F.
also in Norris, F. Novels and essays
Me and Orson Welles. Kaplow, R.
Mean woman blues. Smith, J.
The **meaning** of night. Cox, M.
The **means** of escape. Fitzgerald, P.
Means of evil, five mystery stories. Rendell, R.
In Rendell, R. Collected stories p137-262
Measuring the world. Kehlmann, D.
Measuring time. Habila, H.

MEAT INDUSTRY
Sinclair, U. The jungle

MEDICAL ETHICS
Iles, G. The footprints of God
Lescroart, J. T. The oath
Michener, J. A. Recessional
Moon, E. The speed of dark
Picoult, J. My sister's keeper

MEDICAL EXAMINERS
Cook, R. Crisis
Cook, R. Marker
Patterson, J. 1st to die
MEDICAL LIFE *See* Physicians
MEDICAL RESEARCH *See* Medicine—Research
MEDICAL STUDENTS *See* Students
MEDICINE
See also Surgery
Caldwell, T. Testimony of two men

Research
Martini, S. P. The jury
Palmer, M. The fifth vial
Sanders, L. The sixth commandment
Saul, J. Shadows

Uris, L. QB VII
MEDICINE, EXPERIMENTAL *See* Medicine—Research
MEDICINE, PRACTICE OF *See* Physicians
MEDICINES, PATENT, PROPRIETARY, ETC.
Capote, T. The grass harp
Wells, H. G. Tono-Bungay
Medicus. Downie, R.
MEDIEVAL LIFE *See* Middle Ages
Meditations in green. Wright, S.

MEDITERRANEAN REGION
Dunnett, D. Pawn in frankincense
MEDIUMS *See* Spiritualism
MEDUSA (FRIGATE)
Edge, A. The god of spring
Medusa. Dibdin, M.
Medusa's child. Nance, J. J.

MEGALITHIC MONUMENTS
Cornwell, B. Stonehenge, 2000 B.C.

MELANCHOLY
Snow, C. P. The light and the dark
Melancholy baby. Parker, R. B.
MELBOURNE (AUSTRALIA) *See* Australia—Melbourne
MELISINDA, QUEEN, CONSORT OF FULK V, KING OF JERUSALEM, D. 1160
About
Tarr, J. Queen of swords
The **Mellstock** quire. See Hardy, T. Under the greenwood tree
Melmoth the wanderer. Maturin, C. R.
MELVILLE, HERMAN, 1819-1891
About
Busch, F. The night inspector
Parodies, imitations, etc.
Naslund, S. J. Ahab's wife; or, The star-gazer
The **member** of the wedding. McCullers, C.
also in McCullers, C. Collected stories p255-392
also in McCullers, C. Complete novels
Memento mori. Spark, M.
also in Spark, M. A Muriel Spark trio p393-608
Memnoch the Devil. Rice, A.
Memoirs from underground. See Dostoyevsky, F. Notes from underground
Memoirs of a geisha. Golden, A.
Memoirs of a space traveler. Lem, S.
The **memoirs** of a survivor. Lessing, D. M.
Memoirs of an ex-prom queen. Shulman, A. K.
Memoirs of an invisible man. Saint, H. F.
The **memoirs** of Cleopatra. George, M.
Memoirs of Hadrian. Yourcenar, M.
Memories of my melancholy whores. García Márquez, G.
Memories of the Ford Administration. Updike, J.
MEMORY
See also Amnesia
Amis, M. House of meetings
Banville, J. The sea
Carroll, J. The ghost in love
Coe, J. The rain before it falls
Dean, D. The madonnas of Leningrad
Delbanco, N. What remains
Drabble, M. The sea lady
Flynn, G. Dark places
Hamilton-Paterson, J. Gerontius
Harding, P. Tinkers
Harrison, J. Returning to earth
Itani, F. Remembering the bones
Johnston, W. The custodian of paradise
Kay, T. Shadow song
Krauss, N. Man walks into a room
Lightman, A. P. Reunion
Lourie, R. A hatred for tulips
Makine, A. Dreams of my Russian summers
Maxwell, W. So long, see you tomorrow
McCarthy, T. Remainder
McFarland, D. School for the blind
McNamer, D. Red rover
Mestre-Reed, E. The second death of Única Aveyano
Michaels, A. Fugitive pieces
Minot, S. Evening
Morton, K. The house at Riverton
Murakami, H. South of the border, west of the sun

METAMORPHOSIS

Chayefsky, P. Altered states
Metamorphosis. Kafka, F.
  also in Kafka, F. Collected stories p73-128
  also in Kafka, F. The complete stories
  also in Kafka, F. The metamorphosis and other stories p117-92
  also in Kafka, F. The penal colony: stories and short pieces
  also in Kafka, F. Selected short stories of Franz Kafka
The **metamorphosis** and other stories. Kafka, F.

METEOROLOGISTS

Galchen, R. Atmospheric disturbances
Harrison, K. The seal wife
Metropole. Karinthy, F.

MEXICAN AMERICANS
See also Mexicans—United States
Anaya, R. A. The man who could fly and other stories
Boyle, T. C. The tortilla curtain
Cisneros, S. The house on Mango Street
Forbes, C. The good works of Ayela Linde
Frey, J. Bright shiny morning
Gilb, D. The flowers
Martínez, N. M. ¡Caramba!
Nichols, J. T. The Milagro beanfield war
Piercy, M. Woman on the edge of time
Toole, F. X. Pound for pound

MEXICAN WAR, 1845-1848 *See* United States—War with Mexico, 1845-1848

MEXICANS

United States
Urrea, L. A. Into the beautiful North

MEXICO
See also Sierra Madre Mountains (Mexico)
Bolaño, R. 2666
Cussler, C. Inca gold
Danvers, D. The fourth world
Doerr, H. Consider this, señora
Doerr, H. Stones for Ibarra
Esquivel, L. Like water for chocolate
Fuentes, C. The eagle's throne
Fuentes, C. The old gringo
Fuentes, C. The years with Laura Diaz
Greene, G. The power and the glory
Hansen, R. Atticus
Howard, L. Cry no more
Johansen, I. And then you die—
Lowry, M. Under the volcano
McCarthy, C. All the pretty horses
Michener, J. A. Mexico
Nin, A. Seduction of the Minotaur
Portis, C. Gringos
Smith, S. The ruins
Urrea, L. A. Into the beautiful North

16th century
Falconer, C. Feathered serpent
Jennings, G. Aztec
Jennings, G. Aztec blood
Sherwood, F. Night of sorrows

19th century
Fuentes, C. The death of Artemio Cruz
Hambly, B. Days of the dead

Politics
See Politics—Mexico

Baja California
Steinbeck, J. The pearl

Juarez
McCarthy, C. Cities of the plain

Mexico City
Bolaño, R. Amulet
Christensen, K. Trouble
Gilman, D. The unexpected Mrs. Pollifax
Kerouac, J. Tristessa
Mexico. Michener, J. A.

MEXICO CITY (MEXICO) *See* Mexico—Mexico City
Mexico set. Deighton, L.

MIAMI (FLA.) *See* Florida—Miami

MIAMI INDIANS
Thom, J. A. The red heart
Michael Tolliver lives. Maupin, A.

MICHAL
About
Edghill, I. Queenmaker

MICHELANGELO BUONARROTI, 1475-1564
Fiction
Stone, I. The agony and the ecstasy

MICHIGAN
Baxter, C. Saul and Patsy
Cleage, P. I wish I had a red dress
Cleage, P. What looks like crazy on an ordinary day—
Eugenides, J. The virgin suicides
Finder, J. Company man
Harrison, J. Returning to earth
Iagnemma, K. The expeditions
Mallon, T. Dewey defeats Truman
Traver, R. Anatomy of a murder

Ann Arbor
Baxter, C. The feast of love
Dolan, H. Bad things happen
Laken, V. Dream house

Battle Creek
Boyle, T. C. Road to Wellville

Detroit
Arnow, H. L. S. The dollmaker
Bolaño, R. 2666
Estleman, L. D. Jitterbug
Eugenides, J. Middlesex
Hirshberg, G. The Snowman's children
Leonard, E. Freaky Deaky
Leonard, E. Mr. Paradise
Leonard, E. Pagan babies
Leonard, E. Up in Honey's room
McMillan, R. Blue collar blues
Oates, J. C. Them
Piercy, M. Braided lives
Yunis, A. The night counter

MICROORGANISMS
Crichton, M. The Andromeda strain
Midaq Alley. Maḥfūẓ, N.

MIDDLE AGE
See also Aging
Brown, C. Lamb in love
Cather, W. The professor's house
Christensen, K. Trouble
Colette. Chéri
Connell, E. S. Mr. Bridge
Connell, E. S. Mrs. Bridge
Elkin, S. The MacGuffin
Ford, R. The lay of the land
Harrison, J. The English major
Heller, J. Something happened
Lessing, D. M. The memoirs of a survivor
Lewis, S. Dodsworth
Lodge, D. Therapy
Mann, T. The black swan
McMurtry, L. The desert rose
McMurtry, L. Texasville
Oates, J. C. Middle age
Phillips, A. The song is you
Price, R. The good priest's son
Savage, S. The cry of the sloth
Spark, M. The prime of Miss Jean Brodie
Tyler, A. The accidental tourist
Tyler, A. Breathing lessons
Tyler, A. Ladder of years
Updike, J. Rabbit at rest
Updike, J. Rabbit is rich
Updike, J. Rabbit redux
Williams, T. The Roman spring of Mrs. Stone
Middle age. Oates, J. C.

MIDDLE AGES
See also Europe—392-814; Chivalry; Feudalism; Knights and knighthood
Anderson, P. War of the Gods
Connell, E. S. Deus lo volt!
Cornwell, B. Enemy of God

MISTRESSES—*Continued*
Gould, J. The best is yet to come
Gregory, P. The other Boleyn girl
King, R. Domino
Martin, V. Property
Trollope, J. Marrying the mistress
The **mists** of Avalon. Bradley, M. Z.
MITCHELL, MARGARET, 1900-1949
Parodies, imitations, etc.
Randall, A. The wind done gone
Mitigating circumstances. Rosenberg, N. T.
Mitsou. Colette
In Colette. Six novels p339-410
MIXED BLOODS
See also Mulattoes
Alexie, S. Flight
Eng, T. T. The gift of rain
Erdrich, L. The Beet Queen
Houston, J. D. Bird of another heaven
Humphreys, J. Nowhere else on earth
Jennings, G. Aztec blood
Murr, N. The perfect man
Powers, R. The time of our singing
MOBILE (ALA.) *See* Alabama—Mobile
Moby-Dick; or, The whale. Melville, H.
also in Melville, H. Redburn, his first voyage; White-jacket, or, The world in a man-of-war; Moby-Dick, or, The whale
The **mocking** program. Foster, A. D.
The **model.** Oates, J. C.
In Oates, J. C. Haunted p99-144
MODELS, ARTISTS' *See* Artists' models
MODELS, FASHION *See* Fashion models
A **modern** comedy. Galsworthy, J.
A **modern** instance. Howells, W. D.
In Howells, W. D. Novels, 1875-1886
MOGUL EMPIRE
Rushdie, S. The enchantress of Florence
MOHAMMEDANISM *See* Islam
MOHAMMEDANS *See* Muslims
MOHAWK VALLEY (N.Y.)
Edmonds, W. D. Drums along the Mohawk
MOHEGAN INDIANS
Cooper, J. F. The last of the Mohicans
MOHICAN INDIANS *See* Mohegan Indians
MOHR, MAX, 1891-1937
About
Reuss, F. Mohr
Mohr. Reuss, F.
MOLINA, RAFAEL LEÓNIDAS TRUJILLO *See* Trujillo Molina, Rafael Leónidas, 1891-1961
Moll Flanders. Defoe, D.
Molloy. Beckett, S.
In Beckett, S. Molloy, Malone dies, The unnamable
Molloy, Malone dies, The unnamable. Beckett, S.
Moment in Peking. Lin Yutang
A **moment** in time. Gould, J.
Moment of truth. Scottoline, L.
A **moment** on the edge. Entered in Part I under title
The **moment** she was gone. Hunter, E.
Mona in the promised land. Jen, G.
MONACO
Mayle, P. Anything considered
The **monarch** of the glen. Gaiman, N.
In Gaiman, N. Fragile things
MONASTERIES *See* Monasticism and religious orders
MONASTICISM AND RELIGIOUS ORDERS
See also Abbeys; Convent life; Jesuits; Monks
Gulik, R. H. v. The haunted monastery
Miller, W. M. A canticle for Leibowitz
Monday mourning. Reichs, K. J.
Monday the rabbi took off. Kemelman, H.
MONET, CLAUDE, 1840-1926
About
Jakeman, J. In the Kingdom of mists
MONEY
See also Finance
Grippando, J. Found money

Grisham, J. The summons
Thomas, M. M. Black money
Money for nothing. Westlake, D. E.
Money from home. Runyon, D.
In Runyon, D. Guys and dolls p167-337
Money shot. Faust, C.
Money wanders. Dezenhall, E.
MONEYLENDERS
See also Pawnbrokers
Dickens, C. Nicholas Nickleby
Pérez Galdós, B. Torquemada
MONGOLIA
Jiang Rong. Wolf totem
Mongoose, R.I.P. Buckley, W. F.
The **monk.** Lewis, M. G.
Monkeewrench. Tracy, P. J.
Monkey Hill. Theroux, P.
In Theroux, P. The Elephanta suite
Monkey hunting. García, C.
Monkey planet. See Boulle, P. Planet of the apes
Monkeys. Minot, S.
The **monkey's** wrench. Levi, P.
MONKS
See also Monasticism and religious orders
Eco, U. The name of the rose
Hesse, H. Narcissus and Goldmund
Kadare, I. The three-arched bridge
Kidd, S. M. The mermaid chair
Lewis, M. G. The monk
McCann, C. Let the great world spin
Pattison, E. The skull mantra
Preston, D. The wheel of darkness
Rathbone, J. The last English king
Unsworth, B. Morality play
Monk's-hood. Peters, E.
MONMOUTH'S REBELLION, 1685
Blackmore, R. D. Lorna Doone
MONOLOGUES
Bernhard, T. Frost
Hamid, M. The reluctant fundamentalist
MONROE, MARILYN, 1926-1962
About
Korda, M. The immortals
Oates, J. C. Blonde
Monsieur Pamplemousse. Bond, M.
Monsignor Quixote. Greene, G.
Monsoon. Smith, W. A.
The **monster.** Crane, S.
In Crane, S. Prose and poetry
Monster. Kellerman, J.
Monster Island. Wellington, D.
MONSTERS
Gaiman, N. The monarch of the glen
Groff, L. The monsters of Templeton
A **monster's** notes. Sheck, L.
The **monsters** of St. Helena. Hansen, B.
The **monsters** of Templeton. Groff, L.
Monstrous regiment. Pratchett, T.
MONTANA
Blew, M. C. Jackalope dreams
Davis, C. Winter range
Doig, I. Bucking the sun
Doig, I. Dancing at the Rascal Fair
Doig, I. The eleventh man
Doig, I. English Creek
Doig, I. Mountain time
Doig, I. Prairie nocturne
Doig, I. Ride with me, Mariah Montana
Doig, I. The whistling season
Evans, N. The horse whisperer
Fromm, P. As cool as I am
Kennedy, D. The big picture
Kittredge, W. The Willow Field
Laskowski, T. Every good boy does fine
McGuane, T. The cadence of grass
McGuane, T. Keep the change
McGuane, T. Nobody's angel
McGuane, T. Nothing but blue skies
McNamer, D. Red rover

MOTHERS AND DAUGHTERS—*Continued*

Davenport, K. House of many gods
Didion, J. A book of common prayer
Dische, I. The Empress of Weehawken
Doerr, H. Consider this, señora
Dorris, M. A yellow raft in blue water
Dubus, A. The garden of last days
Erdrich, L. The painted drum
Evans, N. The horse whisperer
Ferrante, E. The lost daughter
Ferrante, E. Troubling love
Fitch, J. White oleander
French, M. Her mother's daughter
Gaffney, P. Circle of three
García, C. Dreaming in Cuban
Gibbons, K. Charms for the easy life
Gibbons, K. Sights unseen
Godwin, G. A mother and two daughters
Goodman, C. The seduction of water
Goudge, E. Garden of lies
Goudge, E. Stranger in paradise
Goudge, E. Such devoted sisters
Goudge, E. Trail of secrets
Gowdy, B. Helpless
Griesemer, J. Signal & noise
Gutcheon, B. R. Five fortunes
Gutcheon, B. R. Saying grace
Hadley, T. The master bedroom
Hannah, S. Little face
Harris, J. Chocolat
Harris, J. Five quarters of the orange
Harris, J. The girl with no shadow
Henderson, W. H. Augusta Locke
Henley, P. In the river sweet
Hoffman, A. Here on Earth
Hoffman, A. The probable future
Hoffman, A. The story sisters
Hoffman, E. The secret
Hood, A. The knitting circle
Jackson, J. Between, Georgia
Jakes, J. Savannah; or, A gift for Mr. Lincoln
James, P. D. Innocent blood
Johnson, S. The sailmaker's daughter
Jones, L. Mister Pip
Joyce, G. The limits of enchantment
Karbo, K. Motherhood made a man out of me
Kent, K. The heretic's daughter
Keyes, M. The other side of the story
Kidd, S. M. The mermaid chair
Kincaid, J. Annie John
Kincaid, J. Autobiography of my mother
Kingsolver, B. Pigs in heaven
Kirshenbaum, B. An almost perfect moment
Krantz, J. Mistral's daughter
Lamott, A. Blue shoe
Laskas, G. M. The midwife's tale
Leroy, M. Postcards from Berlin
Lively, P. Consequences
Lively, P. Heat wave
Lively, P. Passing on
Manicka, R. The rice mother
Maxwell, R. The secret diary of Anne Boleyn
McCann, C. Let the great world spin
McMurtry, L. Buffalo girls
McMurtry, L. The desert rose
McMurtry, L. Terms of endearment
Meyer, C. Brown eyes blue
Miller, S. The good mother
Mitchard, J. Still summer
Moravia, A. Two women
Moriarty, L. The center of everything
Morley, I. Come Sunday
Morrison, T. A mercy
Nunez, E. Anna in-between
Oates, J. C. Marya
Oates, J. C. Missing mom
Oates, J. C. Rape
Ozick, C. Rosa
Packer, A. Songs without words
Parkhurst, C. Lost and found
Parsons, J. Mary, Mary
Phillips, J. A. MotherKind
Picoult, J. Keeping Faith
Piercy, M. Three women

Plain, B. Blessings
Powell, S. The Mushroom Man
Quindlen, A. Object lessons
Quindlen, A. One true thing
Rendell, R. The crocodile bird
Rendell, R. The water's lovely
Rice, L. The deep blue sea for beginners
Rice, L. The geometry of sisters
Rice, L. Home fires
Rice, L. Summer light
Richler, N. Your mouth is lovely
Robards, K. Ghost moon
Roiphe, A. R. Lovingkindness
Rosenberg, N. T. Buried evidence
Rosenberg, N. T. Mitigating circumstances
Ross-Macdonald, M. Tamsin Harte
Rossner, J. Perfidia
Schwarz, C. Drowning Ruth
Sebold, A. The almost moon
Shapiro, D. Black & white
Shields, C. Unless
Shreve, A. Eden Close
Shreve, A. The pilot's wife
Shreve, A. Strange fits of passion
Shreve, S. R. Daughters of the new world
Simpson, M. Anywhere but here
Somerville, P. The cradle
Sparks, N. Nights in Rodanthe
Spencer, E. The light in the piazza
Spencer, L. Bitter sweet
Spencer, L. That Camden summer
Straight, S. Highwire moon
Straight, S. A million nightingales
Strout, E. Amy and Isabelle
Talarigo, J. The ginseng hunter
Tan, A. The bonesetter's daughter
Tan, A. The Joy Luck Club
Tan, A. The kitchen god's wife
Thayer, N. Family secrets
Thayer, N. My dearest friend
Tóibín, C. The blackwater lightship
Trigiani, A. Milk glass moon
Tsukiyama, G. Dreaming water
Urquhart, J. Away
Vine, B. Anna's book
Walbert, K. The gardens of Kyoto
Watson, J. E. Asta in the wings
Weiner, J. Certain girls
Wharton, E. The mother's recompense
Wolitzer, H. Tunnel of love
Wolitzer, M. Surrender, Dorothy

MOTHERS AND SONS
    See also Parent and child
Beattie, A. Chilly scenes of winter
Carey, P. His illegal self
Coetzee, J. M. Life & times of Michael K.
Coupland, D. Eleanor Rigby
Crane, S. George's mother
De Kretser, M. The lost dog
Emmons, C. His mother's son
Erdrich, L. Four souls
Ferber, E. So Big
Fielding, J. Charley's web
Findley, T. The piano man's daughter
Fitch, J. Paint it black
Flagg, F. Standing in the rainbow
Gatewood, R. The sound of the trees
Glass, J. The whole world over
Graver, E. Awake
Green, G. D. The juror
Greer, A. S. The story of a marriage
Hallgrímur Helgason. 101 Reykjavik
Hamilton, J. Disobedience
Harrison, J. The road home
Harwood, J. The ghost writer
Hassler, J. The dean's list
Hoffman, A. Seventh heaven
Hoffman, A. Turtle Moon
Humphreys, H. Coventry
Irving, J. The world according to Garp
James, H. The siege of London
James, H. The spoils of Poynton
Jönsson, R. My life as a dog
Kafka, K. Miranda's vines

MOUNTAINS

See also Adirondack Mountains (N.Y.); Andes; Appalachian Mountains; Catskill Mountains (N.Y.); Himalaya Mountains; Sierra Madre Mountains (Mexico); Volcanoes

Mountolive. Durrell, L.

also in Durrell, L. The Alexandria quartet: Justine; Balthazar; Mountolive [and] Clea p391-652

Mourners. Pronzini, B.

MOURNING See Bereavement

MOURNING CUSTOMS See Funeral rites and ceremonies

The **mouse** that roared. Wibberley, L.

The **mousetrap**. See Christie, A. Three blind mice

The **moviegoer**. Percy, W.

MOVING PICTURE INDUSTRY See Motion pictures

MOVING PICTURES See Motion pictures

The **moving** target. Macdonald, R.

In Macdonald, R. Archer in Hollywood p3-169

Moving the mountain. Gilman, C. P.

In Gilman, C. P. The Charlotte Perkins Gilman reader

In Gilman, C. P. Charlotte Perkins Gilman's Utopian novels p37-149

MOZAMBIQUE

Couto, M. Sleepwalking land

Mr. Blandings builds his dream house. Hodgins, E.

Mr. Bridge. Connell, E. S.

Mr. Darwin's shooter. McDonald, R.

Mr. Majestyk. Leonard, E.

In Leonard, E. Elmore Leonard's Dutch treat: 3 novels

Mr. Mee. Crumey, A.

Mr. Midshipman Hornblower. Forester, C. S.

Mr. Norris changes trains. See Isherwood, C. The last of Mr. Norris

Mr. Palomar. Calvino, I.

Mr. Paradise. Leonard, E.

Mr. Potter. Kincaid, J.

Mr. Sammler's planet. Bellow, S.

Mr. Sampath—the printer of Malgudi. Narayan, R. K.

In Narayan, R. K. Mr. Sampath—the printer of Malgudi, The financial expert, Waiting for the Mahatma

Mr. Sampath—the printer of Malgudi, The financial expert, Waiting for the Mahatma. Narayan, R. K.

Mr. Sebastian and the Negro magician. Wallace, D.

Mr. Wroe's virgins. Rogers, J.

Mr. X. Straub, P.

Mrs. Bridge. Connell, E. S.

Mrs. Dalloway. Woolf, V.

Mrs. de Winter. Hill, S.

Mrs. Kimble. Haigh, J.

Mrs. McGinty's dead. Christie, A.

Mrs. Mike. Freedman, B.

Mrs. Palfrey at the Claremont. Taylor, E.

Mrs. Pargeter's package. Brett, S.

Mrs. Pollifax and the whirling dervish. Gilman, D.

Mrs. Pollifax, innocent tourist. Gilman, D.

Mrs. Pollifax pursued. Gilman, D.

Mrs. Pringle. Read, Miss

Ms. Hempel chronicles. Bynum, S. S.-L.

Mudbound. Jordan, H.

The **mugger**. McBain, E.

MULATTOES

Brown, R. Half a heart

Cather, W. Sapphira and the slave girl

Larsen, N. Passing

McCaig, D. Jacob's ladder

Mda, Z. The Madonna of Excelsior

Rice, A. The Feast of All Saints

Straight, S. A million nightingales

Walker, M. Jubilee

Warren, R. P. Band of angels

Youmans, M. The wolf pit

The **Mulberry** empire. Hensher, P.

MULTIPLE PERSONALITY

See also Dual personality; Personality disorders

MULTIPLE SCLEROSIS

Coupland, D. Eleanor Rigby

Price, R. The good priest's son

A **multitude** of sins. Ford, R.

The **mummers'** curse. Roberts, G.

The **mummy** case. Peters, E.

Mummy dearest. Hess, J.

MUNCHAUSEN SYNDROME BY PROXY

Strauss, D. More than it hurts you

Murder and the First Lady. Roosevelt, E.

Murder at Ford's Theatre. Truman, M.

Murder at midnight. Roosevelt, E.

Murder at Monticello. Langton, J.

Murder at Monticello; or, Old sins. Brown, R. M.

Murder at the feast of rejoicing. Robinson, L. S.

Murder at the God's gate. Robinson, L. S.

Murder at the Library of Congress. Truman, M.

Murder at the old vicarage. McGown, J.

Murder at the palace. Roosevelt, E.

Murder at the Savoy. Sjöwall, M.

The **murder** at the vicarage. Christie, A.

The **murder** book. Kellerman, J.

A **murder** in Mayfair. Barnard, R.

Murder in the Blue Room. Roosevelt, E.

Murder in the Calais coach. [variant title: Murder on the Orient Express] Christie, A.

Murder in the hearse degree. Cockey, T.

Murder in the map room. Roosevelt, E.

Murder in the Oval Office. Roosevelt, E.

Murder in the Rose Garden. Roosevelt, E.

Murder in the White House. Truman, M.

A **murder** is announced. Christie, A.

Murder most royal. Plaidy, J.

Murder must advertise. Sayers, D. L.

The **murder** of Roger Ackroyd. Christie, A.

Murder on Capitol Hill. Truman, M.

Murder on the Iditarod Trail. Henry, S.

Murder on the Leviathan. Akunin, B.

Murder on the Orient Express. See Christie, A. Murder in the Calais coach [variant title: Murder on the Orient Express]

Murder on the Trans-Siberian Express. Kaminsky, S. M.

Murder on the Yukon Quest. Henry, S.

MURDER STORIES

See also Assassination; Crime and criminals; Filicide; Fratricide; Infanticide; International intrigue; Murderers; Mystery and detective stories; Parricide; Poisons; Violence

Ablow, K. R. Compulsion

Ackroyd, P. The trial of Elizabeth Cree

Adiga, A. The white tiger

Adler, E. Now or never

Alexie, S. Indian killer

Amis, M. London fields

Atkins, A. White shadow

Atkins, A. Wicked city

Atwood, M. Alias Grace

Baldacci, D. Absolute power

Baldacci, D. The simple truth

Banville, J. The book of evidence

Barnard, R. A murder in Mayfair

Barry, B. The lace reader

Berlinski, M. Fieldwork

Bernhardt, W. Dark justice

Bolaño, R. 2666

Bolaño, R. The skating rink

Brown, C. B. Edgar Huntly

Brown, D. The Da Vinci code

Brown, R. Before and after

Brown, S. The alibi

Brown, S. The witness

Burdett, J. Bangkok 8

Burdett, J. Bangkok haunts

Burdett, J. Bangkok Tattoo

Burke, J. L. Rain gods

Cain, C. Heartsick

Cain, J. M. Double indemnity

Cain, J. M. The postman always rings twice

Campbell, B. M. Your blues ain't like mine

Camus, A. The stranger

Carr, C. The alienist

Carter, S. L. New England white

Childress, M. Crazy in Alabama

Clark, M. The legal limit

Clark, M. H. The cradle will fall

Clark, M. H. Daddy's little girl

Clark, M. H. Loves music, loves to dance

Clark, M. H. Nighttime is my time

Clark, M. H. On the street where you live

Coben, H. Gone for good

Coben, H. Hold tight

Coben, H. The innocent

Collins, M. Death of a writer

MURDER STORIES—*Continued*

King, S. Rage
Knode, H. The ticket out
Koontz, D. R. From the corner of his eye
Koontz, D. R. Intensity
Koontz, D. R. Velocity
Lankford, T. Earthquake weather
Lansdale, J. R. The bottoms
Lansdale, J. R. A fine dark line
Lansdale, J. R. Leather maiden
Lansdale, J. R. Sunset and sawdust
Larsson, S. The girl who played with fire
Lashner, W. A killer's kiss
Lawrence, M. K. The burning bride
Lawrence, M. K. Hearts and bones
Le Carré, J. The constant gardener
Lehane, D. Mystic river
Leonard, E. Split images
Lescroart, J. T. The first law
Lescroart, J. T. Guilt
Lescroart, J. T. The hearing
Lescroart, J. T. The mercy rule
Lescroart, J. T. Nothing but the truth
Lescroart, J. T. The oath
Lescroart, J. T. The second chair
Letts, B. Shoot the moon
Levin, I. A kiss before dying
Lewin, M. Z. Oh Joe
Lewis, J. The king is dead
Lewis, M. G. The monk
Lindsey, D. L. The color of night
Lippman, L. Scratch a woman
Logan, C. South of Shiloh
Lovesey, P. On the edge
Lowell, E. Die in plain sight
Ludlum, R. The Sigma protocol
Lustbader, E. V. Black Blade
Lustbader, E. V. Floating city
Lutz, J. Dancing with the dead
Lutz, J. Final seconds
MacLean, A. Night without end
Mailer, N. The executioner's song
Mailer, N. Tough guys don't dance
March, W. The bad seed
Margolin, P. After dark
Margolin, P. The burning man
Margolin, P. Fugitive
Margolin, P. Wild justice
Martini, S. P. The attorney
Martini, S. P. The judge
Martini, S. P. Prime witness
Martini, S. P. Undue influence
Matthiessen, P. Bone by bone
Matthiessen, P. Killing Mister Watson
Matthiessen, P. Lost Man's River
Matthiessen, P. Shadow country
Maxwell, W. So long, see you tomorrow
McCabe, P. The butcher boy
McCammon, R. R. Boy's life
McCorkle, J. Carolina moon
McCoy, H. They shoot horses, don't they?
McCrumb, S. The hangman's beautiful daughter
McCrumb, S. If ever I return, pretty Peggy-O
McDermid, V. The distant echo
McEwan, I. The innocent
McFarland, D. School for the blind
McFarland, D. Singing boy
McGrath, P. The grotesque
Meltzer, B. The book of lies
Meltzer, B. The first counsel
Melville, H. Pierre
Meyer, P. American rust
Michener, J. A. The novel
Miéville, C. The city & the city
Miller, S. While I was gone
Mills, M. Amagansett
Mina, D. Deception
Morrison, T. Jazz
Mortimer, J. Felix in the underworld
Mortman, D. True colors
Muller, M. Cyanide Wells
Muñoz Molina, A. A manuscript of ashes
Murdoch, I. The green knight
Murray, S. Forgery

Nabokov, V. V. King, queen, knave
Nabokov, V. V. Transparent things
Nasaw, J. L. Twenty-seven bones
Norman, H. The bird artist
Norris, F. McTeague
Oates, J. C. Because it is bitter, and because it is my heart
Oates, J. C. Broke heart blues
Oates, J. C. Little bird of heaven
Oates, J. C. Missing mom
Oates, J. C. The model
Ogilvie, E. When the music stopped
O'Hara, J. Butterfield 8
O'Nan, S. Snow angels
O'Neill, A. The lamplighter
O'Shaughnessy, P. Invasion of privacy
O'Shaughnessy, P. Motion to suppress
O'Shaughnessy, P. Unlucky in law
Palliser, C. The unburied
Palmer, M. The society
Pamuk, O. My name is Red
Parker, B. Blood relations
Parker, B. Suspicion of vengeance
Parker, T. J. Black water
Parker, T. J. California girl
Parker, T. J. Cold pursuit
Parker, T. J. The fallen
Parker, T. J. Silent Joe
Parsons, J. Mary, Mary
Patterson, J. 1st to die
Patterson, J. Cat & mouse
Patterson, J. Cross
Patterson, J. Four blind mice
Patterson, J. Hide & seek
Patterson, J. Jack and Jill
Patterson, J. Kiss the girls
Patterson, J. Pop! goes the weasel
Patterson, R. N. Dark lady
Patterson, R. N. Degree of guilt
Patterson, R. N. Eyes of a child
Patterson, R. N. The final judgment
Patterson, R. N. Silent witness
Pattison, E. The skull mantra
Pawel, R. Death of a nationalist
Peace, D. Tokyo year zero
Pearl, M. The Dante Club
Pearl, M. The last Dickens
Pears, I. An instance of the fingerpost
Pearson, R. The angel maker
Pearson, R. Beyond recognition
Pearson, R. Chain of evidence
Pearson, R. The first victim
Pearson, R. No witnesses
Pearson, R. Undercurrents
Pearson, T. R. Blue Ridge
Pearson, T. R. Cry me a river
Pelecanos, G. P. The night gardener
Pelecanos, G. P. Shame the devil
Penney, S. The tenderness of wolves
Pérez-Reverte, A. The fencing master
Pessl, M. Special topics in calamity physics
Porter, K. A. Noon wine
Pottinger, S. The fourth procedure
Poyer, D. Down to a sunless sea
Poyer, D. Thunder on the mountain
Preston, D. Brimstone
Preston, D. The cabinet of curiosities
Preston, D. Reliquary
Preston, D. The wheel of darkness
Price, R. Clockers
Pronzini, B. In an evil time
Pronzini, B. Step to the graveyard easy
Pronzini, B. A wasteland of strangers
Quick, A. Late for the wedding
Reed, B. The indictment
Reichs, K. J. Déjà dead
Rendell, R. Adam and Eve and Pinch me
Rendell, R. The crocodile bird
Rendell, R. The face of trespass
Rendell, R. A judgment in stone
Rendell, R. The keys to the street
Rendell, R. A sight for sore eyes
Rendell, R. Thirteen steps down
Rendell, R. The water's lovely
Reuland, R. Semiautomatic

MURDERERS—*Continued*

Walters, M. The devil's feather
Westlake, D. E. The ax
Murder@maggody.com. Hess, J.
A **Muriel** Spark trio. Spark, M.
Murphy. Beckett, S.
Murther & walking spirits. Davies, R.
Muscle memory. Tapply, W. G.
Muse of fire. Simmons, D.
The **museum** guard. Norman, H.
Museum of human beings. Sargent, C.
The **museum** of innocence. Pamuk, O.
The **Mushroom** Man. Powell, S.

MUSIC

Mann, T. Tristan
Powers, R. The time of our singing
Music & silence. Tremain, R.

MUSIC HALL ENTERTAINERS *See* Entertainers

Music-hall sidelights. Colette
In Colette. Six novels p237-337

MUSIC HALLS (VARIETY THEATERS, CABARETS, ETC.)

See also Vaudeville
The **Music** Lesson. Weber, K.
Music of a life. Makine, A.
The **music** room. McFarland, D.

MUSIC TEACHERS

Chaudhuri, A. The immortals
Doig, I. Prairie nocturne
Hernández, F. Around the time of Clemente Colling
Lee, J. Y. K. The piano teacher
Powell, D. Come back to Sorrento

MUSICIANS

See also Accordionists; Cellists; Conductors (Music); Drummers; Flutists; Pianists; Saxophonists; Trumpet players; Violinists
Baldwin, J. Another country
Beatty, P. Slumberland
Cather, W. Lucy Gayheart
Davies, R. The lyre of Orpheus
Flagg, F. Standing in the rainbow
Hassler, J. Rookery blues
Hesse, H. Gertrude
Hewson, D. Lucifer's shadow
Hijuelos, O. The Mambo Kings play songs of love
Hornby, N. High fidelity
Hospital, J. T. Orpheus lost
L'Engle, M. A severed wasp
Lethem, J. You don't love me yet
MacDonald, A.-M. Fall on your knees
Mackey, N. Bass cathedral
Maxwell, W. Bright center of heaven
McEwan, I. On Chesil Beach
McGuane, T. Panama
Mendelson, C. Morningside Heights
Mosley, W. RL's dream
Murakami, H. After dark
Romano-Lax, A. The Spanish bow
Sarton, M. Anger
Seth, V. An equal music
Smith, L. The devil's dream
Taylor, M. G. The ballad of Trenchmouth Taggart
Tremain, R. Music & silence
Turner, F. W. 1929
Tyler, A. Searching for Caleb
Tyler, A. A slipping-down life
Wimberley, D. The king of Colored Town

MUSLIMS

See also Islam
Caputo, P. Acts of faith
De Bernières, L. Birds without wings
D'Souza, T. Whiteman
Gibb, C. Sweetness in the belly
Guène, F. Kiffe kiffe tomorrow
Kureishi, H. Something to tell you
Pamuk, O. My name is Red
Seth, V. A suitable boy
Unsworth, B. The ruby in her navel
Updike, J. Terrorist

MUSSOLINI, BENITO, 1883-1945
About

Epstein, L. The eighth wonder of the world

MUSTAFA KEMAL *See* Atatürk, Kemal, 1881-1938

MUTATION (BIOLOGY)

See also Albinos
Anderson, P. The sharing of flesh
Bear, G. Blood music

MUTE PERSONS

Barnes, J. The somnambulist
Coulter, C. The target
Harrison, K. The seal wife
King, D. The ha-ha
Reuss, F. The wasties
Winthrop, E. H. December
Wroblewski, D. The story of Edgar Sawtelle

MUTINY

Faulkner, W. A fable
Nordhoff, C. Mutiny on the Bounty
Pesci, D. Amistad
Unsworth, B. Sacred hunger
Wouk, H. The Caine mutiny
Mutiny on the Bounty. Nordhoff, C.
also in Nordhoff, C. and Hall, J. N. The Bounty trilogy
My abandonment. Rock, P.
My Antonia. Cather, W.
also in Cather, W. Early novels and stories p707-938
My big apartment. Oster, C.
My brilliant career. Franklin, M.
My brother Michael. Stewart, M.
My career goes bung. Franklin, M.
My century. Grass, G.
My dearest friend. Thayer, N.
My enemy the Queen. Holt, V.
My father's tears and other stories. Updike, J.
My fine lady. Joe, Y.
My friend Maigret. Simenon, G.
My gun is quick. Spillane, M.
In Spillane, M. The Mike Hammer collection [v1]
My Holocaust. Reich, T.
My home is far away. Powell, D.
In Powell, D. Novels, 1944-1962
My last movie star. Sherrill, M.
My latest grievance. Lipman, E.
My life. Chekhov, A. P.
In Chekhov, A. P. Complete short novels
My life as a dog. Jönsson, R.
My life as a fake. Carey, P.
My life as a man. Roth, P.
also in Roth, P. Novels, 1973-1977
My life in CIA. Mathews, H.
My life, starring Dara Falcon. Beattie, A.
My lord and spymaster. Bourne, J.
My mistress's sparrow is dead. Entered in Part I under title
My name is Asher Lev. Potok, C.
My name is Red. Pamuk, O.
My nine lives. Jhabvala, R. P.
My old true love. Adams, S. K.
My revolutions. Kunzru, H.
My secret history. Theroux, P.
My sister the moon. Harrison, S.
My sister's keeper. Picoult, J.
My son's story. Gordimer, N.
My soul to keep. Due, T.
My sweet untraceable you. Scoppettone, S.
Myra Breckinridge. Vidal, G.
In Vidal, G. Myra Breckinridge [and] Myron p1-213
Myra Breckinridge [and] Myron. Vidal, G.
Myron. Vidal, G.
In Vidal, G. Myra Breckinridge [and] Myron p217-417
The **mysteries** of Udolpho. Radcliffe, A. W.
The **mysterious** flame of Queen Loana. Eco, U.
The **mysterious** island. Verne, J.
Mysterious stranger, and other stories. Twain, M.
The **Mysterious** West. Entered in Part I under title
Mystery. Straub, P.

MYSTERY AND DETECTIVE STORIES

See also Crime and criminals; Gothic romances; International intrigue; Murder stories
Akunin, B. Murder on the Leviathan
Berry, J. The manual of detection
Best American mystery stories [date]
Christie, A. Murder in the Calais coach [variant title: Murder on the Orient Express]
Clark, C. H. Decked

MYSTERY AND DETECTIVE STORIES—England—Continued

Gash, J. A rag, a bone, and a hank of hair
George, E. Careless in red
George, E. A traitor to memory
Giroux, E. X. A death for a dancer
Grimes, M. The Anodyne Necklace
Grimes, M. The case has altered
Grimes, M. The Deer Leap
Grimes, M. The Dirty Duck
Grimes, M. The five bells and bladebone
Grimes, M. Help the poor struggler
Grimes, M. I am the only running footman
Grimes, M. Jerusalem Inn
Grimes, M. The Lamorna wink
Grimes, M. The man with a load of mischief
Grimes, M. The Old Contemptibles
Grimes, M. The old fox deceiv'd
Grimes, M. The Old Silent
Grimes, M. The Old Wine Shades
Grimes, M. The Stargazey
Grimes, M. The winds of change
Hardwick, M. Malice domestic
Hardwick, M. Parson's pleasure
Harper, K. The Poyson garden
Harper, K. The queene's Christmas
Harper, K. The tidal poole
Harrod-Eagles, C. Blood lines
Harrod-Eagles, C. Death to go
Harrod-Eagles, C. Death watch
Harrod-Eagles, C. Game over
Harrod-Eagles, C. Grave music
Harrod-Eagles, C. Killing time
Harrod-Eagles, C. Orchestrated death
Harrod-Eagles, C. Shallow grave
Harvey, J. Cold in hand
Harvey, J. Cold light
Harvey, J. Darkness and light
Harvey, J. Easy meat
Harvey, J. Flesh and blood
Harvey, J. Last rites
Harvey, J. Still waters
Harvey, J. Wasted years
Haymon, S. T. Death of a hero
Hill, R. Arms and the women
Hill, R. Bones and silence
Hill, R. Child's play
Hill, R. Death comes for the Fat Man
Hill, R. Good morning, midnight
Hill, R. Killing the lawyers
Hill, R. Pictures of perfection
Hill, R. Singing the sadness
Hill, R. The wood beyond
Hill, S. The pure in heart
Hill, S. The various haunts of men
James, P. D. The black tower
James, P. D. A certain justice
James, P. D. Devices and desires
James, P. D. The lighthouse
James, P. D. Original sin
James, P. D. The private patient
James, P. D. The skull beneath the skin
James, P. D. A taste for death
James, P. D. An unsuitable job for a woman
Keating, H. R. F. The good detective
Keating, H. R. F. The soft detective
Kelly, J. The coldest blood
King, L. R. The beekeeper's apprentice, or, On the segregation of the queen
King, L. R. Justice Hall
King, L. R. A letter of Mary
King, L. R. The moor
Langton, J. Dead as a dodo
Lawrence, D. The dead sit round in a ring
Linscott, G. Blood on the wood
Liss, D. A spectacle of corruption
Lovesey, P. Bertie and the seven bodies
Lovesey, P. Bloodhounds
Lovesey, P. The detective wore silk drawers
Lovesey, P. Diamond dust
Lovesey, P. The house sitter
Lovesey, P. The last detective
Lovesey, P. Rough cider
Lovesey, P. Upon a dark night

Lovesey, P. The vault
Lovesey, P. Waxwork
MacDonald, P. The list of Adrian Messenger
Macdonald, R. The drowning pool
Marsh, Dame N. Dead water
Marsh, Dame N. False scent
Marsh, Dame N. Grave mistake
Marsh, Dame N. Last ditch
Marsh, Dame N. Light thickens
Marston, E. The Bawdy basket
Marston, E. The Devil's apprentice
Marston, E. The roaring boy
Marston, E. The stallions of Woodstock
Marston, E. The vagabond clown
Marston, E. The wanton angel
Marston, E. The wildcats of Exeter
McCrumb, S. Missing Susan
McGown, J. Murder at the old vicarage
McGown, J. Picture of innocence
McGown, J. Plots and errors
McGown, J. The stalking horse
McGown, J. Verdict unsafe
Meyer, N. The West End horror
Neel, J. To die for
Penman, S. K. Cruel as the grave
Penman, S. K. The queen's man
Perry, A. Bedford Square
Perry, A. Belgrave Square
Perry, A. Bluegate Fields
Perry, A. A breach of promise
Perry, A. Buckingham Palace gardens
Perry, A. Cain his brother
Perry, A. Cardington Crescent
Perry, A. A dangerous mourning
Perry, A. Death of a stranger
Perry, A. Defend and betray
Perry, A. The face of a stranger
Perry, A. Farriers' Lane
Perry, A. Funeral in blue
Perry, A. Half Moon Street
Perry, A. Highgate rise
Perry, A. The Hyde Park headsman
Perry, A. Paragon Walk
Perry, A. Pentecost Alley
Perry, A. Resurrection row
Perry, A. Seven dials
Perry, A. The silent cry
Perry, A. The sins of the wolf
Perry, A. Slaves of obsession
Perry, A. Southampton Row
Perry, A. Traitor's gate
Perry, A. The twisted root
Perry, A. Weighed in the balance
Perry, A. The Whitechapel conspiracy
Peters, E. The deeds of the disturber
Peters, E. The last camel died at noon
Peters, E. The benediction of Brother Cadfael
Peters, E. Brother Cadfael's penance
Peters, E. Dead man's ransom
Peters, E. Fallen into the pit
Peters, E. The hermit of Eyton Forest
Peters, E. The holy thief
Peters, E. Monk's-hood
Peters, E. The pilgrim of hate
Peters, E. The potter's field
Peters, E. A rare Benedictine
Peters, E. The rose rent
Peters, E. Saint Peter's Fair
Peters, E. The sanctuary sparrow
Peters, E. The summer of the Danes
Peters, E. The virgin in the ice
Pickard, N. Bum steer
Pirie, D. The patient's eyes
Rendell, R. Collected stories
Rendell, R. Harm done
Rendell, R. Kissing the gunner's daughter
Rendell, R. Not in the flesh
Rendell, R. Road rage
Rendell, R. Simisola
Rendell, R. A sleeping life
Robb, C. M. The riddle of St. Leonard's
Robinson, P. Cold is the grave
Robinson, P. Innocent grave
Robinson, P. Piece of my heart

MYSTERY AND DETECTIVE STORIES—Russia—*Continued*

Kaminsky, S. M. Death of a Russian priest
Kaminsky, S. M. The dog who bit a policeman
Kaminsky, S. M. The man who walked like a bear
Kaminsky, S. M. Murder on the Trans-Siberian Express
Kaminsky, S. M. Rostnikov's vacation
Morris, R. N. The gentle axe
Smith, M. C. Gorky Park
Smith, M. C. Polar Star
Smith, M. C. Red Square
Smith, M. C. Stalin's ghost
Smith, M. C. Wolves eat dogs

Saudi Arabia

Ferraris, Z. Finding Nouf

Scotland

Atkinson, K. When will there be good news?
Beaton, M. C. Death of a hussy
Beaton, M. C. Death of a macho man
MacBride, S. Flesh house
McCall Smith, A. The comforts of a muddy Saturday
McCall Smith, A. The lost art of gratitude
Mina, D. The dead hour
Mina, D. Slip of the knife
Rankin, I. Black and blue
Rankin, I. The black book
Rankin, I. Dead souls
Rankin, I. Exit music
Rankin, I. The falls
Rankin, I. The naming of the dead
Rankin, I. A question of blood
Rankin, I. Resurrection men
Rankin, I. Set in darkness
Sayers, D. L. The five red herrings

South Africa

Francis, D. Smokescreen
McClure, J. The steam pig
Meyer, D. Devil's peak

Sweden

Eriksson, K. The princess of Burundi
Jungstedt, M. The inner circle
Mankell, H. Before the frost
Mankell, H. Dogs of Riga
Mankell, H. Firewall
Mankell, H. The man who smiled
Mankell, H. One step behind
Mankell, H. The return of the dancing master
Sjöwall, M. Cop killer
Sjöwall, M. The laughing policeman
Sjöwall, M. The locked room
Sjöwall, M. The man on the balcony
Sjöwall, M. Murder at the Savoy

United States

Abrahams, P. Dog on it
Albert, S. W. Rosemary remembered
Andrews, M. K. Every crooked nanny
Andrews, M. K. Irish eyes
Ball, J. D. In the heat of the night
Banks, O. T. The Caravaggio obsession
Barnes, L. Cold case
Barnes, L. The snake tattoo
Barr, N. High country
Barr, N. Winter study
Belzer, R. I am not a cop!
The Best American mystery stories of the century
Bland, E. T. See no evil
Block, L. All the flowers are dying
Block, L. The burglar in the library
Block, L. Eight million ways to die
Block, L. The sins of the fathers
Block, L. A ticket to the boneyard
Block, L. When the sacred ginmill closes
Bowen, P. Badlands
Box, C. J. Blood trail
Box, C. J. Savage run
Boyer, R. The Daisy Ducks
Braun, L. J. The cat who ate Danish modern
Braun, L. J. The cat who brought down the house
Braun, L. J. The cat who sang for the birds
Braun, L. J. The cat who smelled a rat
Braun, L. J. The cat who went underground

Brown, R. M. Murder at Monticello; or, Old sins
Brown, R. M. Wish you were here
Buchanan, E. Love kills
Buchanan, E. Suitable for framing
Buchanan, E. You only die twice
Burke, A. Angel's tip
Burke, J. L. Black cherry blues
Burke, J. L. Heaven's prisoners
Burke, J. L. Last car to Elysian Fields
Burke, J. L. A stained white radiance
Burke, J. L. The tin roof blowdown
Burke, J. Remember me, Irene
Carr, C. The alienist
Caunitz, W. J. Chains of command
Caunitz, W. J. One Police Plaza
Chabon, M. The Yiddish policemen's union
Chandler, R. The big sleep
Chandler, R. The high window
Chandler, R. The lady in the lake
Chandler, R. Later novels and other writings
Chandler, R. The little sister
Chandler, R. The long goodbye
Chandler, R. Playback
Chandler, R. Raymond Chandler
Chandler, R. Stories and early novels
Child, L. Bad luck and trouble
Child, L. Echo burning
Child, L. The enemy
Child, L. The hard way
Child, L. Nothing to lose
Child, L. One shot
Child, L. Persuader
Child, L. Without fail
Clark, M. H. Weep no more, my lady
Coben, H. Darkest fear
Coben, H. One false move
Cockey, T. Hearse case scenario
Cockey, T. Murder in the hearse degree
Coel, M. The dream stalker
Coel, M. The ghost walker
Connelly, M. The black ice
Connelly, M. Blood work
Connelly, M. City of bones
Connelly, M. The closers
Connelly, M. A darkness more than night
Connelly, M. Echo Park
Connelly, M. Lost light
Connelly, M. The narrows
Connelly, M. The overlook
Connolly, J. The unquiet
Constantine, K. C. Blood mud
Constantine, K. C. Brushback
Constantine, K. C. Family values
Constantine, K. C. Grievance
Constantine, K. C. Saving room for dessert
Craig, P. R. A shoot on Martha's Vineyard
Craig, P. R. Third strike
Craig, P. R. Vineyard enigma
Craig, P. R. A vineyard killing
Crais, R. Chasing darkness
Crais, R. The forgotten man
Crais, R. Indigo slam
Crais, R. L.A. requiem
Crais, R. The last detective
Crais, R. The watchman
Cross, A. The collected stories of Amanda Cross
Cross, A. Honest doubt
Cross, A. An imperfect spy
Cross, A. The puzzled heart
Crumley, J. Bordersnakes
Crumley, J. The final country
Crumley, J. The last good kiss
Crumley, J. The wrong case
D'Amato, B. Hard evidence
D'Amato, B. Hard road
Dams, J. M. Death in lacquer red
Davidson, D. M. Killer pancake
Davidson, D. M. The last suppers
Davidson, D. M. Prime cut
Deaver, J. The broken window
Deaver, J. The Coffin Dancer
Deaver, J. The vanished man
DePoy, P. The drifter's wheel
Dobyns, S. Saratoga strongbox

MYSTERY AND DETECTIVE STORIES—United States—
Continued

Kaminsky, S. M. Dancing in the dark
Kaminsky, S. M. A fatal glass of beer
Kaminsky, S. M. Lieberman's choice
Kaminsky, S. M. Lieberman's day
Kaminsky, S. M. Lieberman's folly
Kaminsky, S. M. Lieberman's thief
Kaminsky, S. M. Not quite kosher
Kaminsky, S. M. Retribution
Kaminsky, S. M. Terror town
Kaminsky, S. M. To catch a spy
Kaminsky, S. M. Tomorrow is another day
Kaminsky, S. M. Vengeance
Kellerman, F. Day of atonement
Kellerman, F. The forgotten
Kellerman, F. Grievous sin
Kellerman, F. Jupiter's bones
Kellerman, F. Justice
Kellerman, F. Milk and honey
Kellerman, F. Moon music
Kellerman, F. Prayers for the dead
Kellerman, F. Sanctuary
Kellerman, F. Serpent's tooth
Kellerman, F. Stone kiss
Kellerman, F. Street dreams
Kellerman, J. Bad love
Kellerman, J. Billy Straight
Kellerman, J. Bones
Kellerman, J. The clinic
Kellerman, J. Devil's waltz
Kellerman, J. Dr. Death
Kellerman, J. Gone
Kellerman, J. Monster
Kellerman, J. The murder book
Kellerman, J. Private eyes
Kellerman, J. Self-defense
Kellerman, J. Survival of the fittest
Kellerman, J. Therapy
Kellerman, J. Time bomb
Kellerman, J. The web
Kellerman, J. When the bough breaks
Kemelman, H. The day the rabbi resigned
Kemelman, H. Friday the rabbi slept late
Kemelman, H. Saturday the rabbi went hungry
Kemelman, H. Sunday the rabbi stayed home
Kemelman, H. Thursday the rabbi walked out
Kemelman, H. Wednesday the rabbi got wet
Kienzle, W. X. Assault with intent
Kienzle, W. X. Body count
Kienzle, W. X. The gathering
Kienzle, W. X. The greatest evil
Kienzle, W. X. The man who loved God
Kienzle, W. X. The rosary murders
Kijewski, K. Alley Kat blues
Kijewski, K. Copy Kat
Kijewski, K. Honky tonk Kat
Kijewski, K. Kat scratch fever
Kijewski, K. Kat's cradle
Kijewski, K. Stray Kat waltz
King, L. R. Locked rooms
Knopf, C. Hard stop
Knopf, C. Head wounds
Knopf, C. The last refuge
Knopf, C. Two time
Koryta, M. The silent hour
Koryta, M. Tonight I said goodbye
La Plante, L. Cold blood
Langton, J. The deserter
Langton, J. Emily Dickinson is dead
Langton, J. The Escher twist
Langton, J. The face on the wall
Langton, J. Murder at Monticello
Lansdale, J. R. Vanilla Ride
Lathen, E. Brewing up a storm
Lathen, E. Going for the gold
Lathen, E. Right on the money
Lathen, E. Something in the air
Lehane, D. Prayers for rain
Lehane, D. Sacred
Leonard, E. When the women come out to dance, and other stories
Lethem, J. Motherless Brooklyn
Lippman, L. Hardly knew her

Lippman, L. No good deeds
Lovesey, P. Skeleton Hill
Lutz, J. Burn
Lutz, J. Death by jury
Lutz, J. Lightning
Lutz, J. Oops!
Lutz, L. Curse of the Spellmans
Lutz, L. Revenge of the Spellmans
Lutz, L. The Spellman files
MacDonald, J. D. Cinnamon skin
MacDonald, J. D. A deadly shade of gold
MacDonald, J. D. The deep blue good-by
MacDonald, J. D. The dreadful lemon sky
MacDonald, J. D. Free fall in crimson
MacDonald, J. D. The green ripper
MacDonald, J. D. The lonely silver rain
MacDonald, J. D. The long lavender look
MacDonald, J. D. One fearful yellow eye
MacDonald, J. D. A purple place for dying
MacDonald, J. D. The scarlet ruse
MacDonald, J. D. The turquoise lament
Macdonald, R. Archer in Hollywood
Macdonald, R. Archer in jeopardy
Macdonald, R. The far side of the dollar
Macdonald, R. The Galton case
Macdonald, R. The goodbye look
Macdonald, R. Sleeping beauty
Macdonald, R. The underground man
MacLeod, C. Exit the milkman
MacLeod, C. The Gladstone bag
MacLeod, C. Rest you merry
MacLeod, C. Vane pursuit
MacLeod, C. The withdrawing room
Maron, M. Bootlegger's daughter
Maron, M. Fugitive colors
Maron, M. High country fall
Maron, M. Home fires burning
Maron, M. Killer market
Maron, M. Shooting at loons
Maron, M. Slow dollar
Maron, M. Southern discomfort
Maron, M. Storm track
Maron, M. Uncommon clay
Maron, M. Up jumps the Devil
Massey, S. The pearl diver
Mathews, F. Death in a cold hard light
Mathews, F. Death in a mood indigo
Mayor, A. The catch
Mayor, A. Chat
Mayor, A. Occam's razor
Mayor, A. The sniper's wife
McBain, E. The big bad city
McBain, E. Eight black horses
McBain, E. Fat Ollie's book
McBain, E. Fiddlers
McBain, E. The frumious Bandersnatch
McBain, E. Hark!
McBain, E. Heat
McBain, E. Ice
McBain, E. Kiss
McBain, E. The last dance
McBain, E. Learning to kill
McBain, E. Lightning
McBain, E. Lullaby
McBain, E. Mischief
McBain, E. The mugger
McBain, E. Nocturne
McBain, E. Poison
McBain, E. There was a little girl
McBain, E. Three blind mice
McBain, E. Tricks
McBain, E. Vespers
McBain, E. Widows
McCammon, R. R. The Queen of Bedlam
McCrumb, S. If I'd killed him when I met him
McCrumb, S. MacPherson's lament
McCrumb, S. The Windsor knot
Mcdonald, G. Fletch
Mcdonald, G. The Fletch chronicles
Mcdonald, G. Son of Fletch
McGarrity, M. The big gamble
McGarrity, M. Death song
McGarrity, M. Everyone dies
McGarrity, M. The Judas judge

MYSTERY AND DETECTIVE STORIES—United States—
Continued

Sandford, J. Chosen prey
Sandford, J. Easy prey
Sandford, J. Hidden prey
Sandford, J. Mind prey
Sandford, J. Mortal prey
Sandford, J. Naked prey
Sandford, J. Night prey
Sandford, J. Rules of prey
Sandford, J. Silent prey
Sandford, J. Sudden prey
Sandford, J. Winter prey
Scoppettone, S. Everything you have is mine
Scoppettone, S. Gonna take a homicidal journey
Scoppettone, S. My sweet untraceable you
Shannon, D. Chaos of crime
Shoemaker, B. Stalking horse
Slaughter, K. Beyond reach
Smith, A. North of Montana
Smith, J. 82 Desire
Smith, J. Crescent city kill
Smith, J. House of blues
Smith, J. Jazz funeral
Smith, J. The kindness of strangers
Smith, J. Louisiana hotshot
Smith, J. Mean woman blues
Smith, J. New Orleans beat
Solomita, S. Damaged goods
Solomita, S. A good day to die
Solomita, S. Last chance for glory
Spencer-Fleming, J. All mortal flesh
Spencer-Fleming, J. In the bleak midwinter
Spiegelman, P. Black maps
Spiegelman, P. Red cat
Spillane, M. The Goliath bone
Spillane, M. The Mike Hammer collection [v1]
Spillane, M. The Mike Hammer collection [v2]
Stabenow, D. A deeper sleep
Stabenow, D. A fine and bitter snow
Stabenow, D. Hunter's moon
Stabenow, D. Killing grounds
Stabenow, D. The singing of the dead
Stabenow, D. So sure of death
Stabenow, D. Whisper to the blood
Standiford, L. Bone Key
Standiford, L. Deal on ice
Standiford, L. Deal with the dead
Stansberry, D. The ancient rain
Stewart, E. Deadly rich
Stone, N. The king of swords
Stout, R. Black orchids; &, the silent speaker
Stout, R. The doorbell rang
Stout, R. Fer-de-lance; &, The league of frightened men
Stout, R. Gambit
Stout, R. The rubber band & The red box
Stout, R. Some buried Caesar & The golden spiders
Stout, R. Too many cooks; & champagne for one
Stroby, W. The barbed-wire kiss
Tapply, W. G. Bitch Creek
Tapply, W. G. Client privilege
Tapply, W. G. Close to the bone
Tapply, W. G. Cutter's run
Tapply, W. G. Dead meat
Tapply, W. G. Dead winter
Tapply, W. G. First light
Tapply, W. G. Muscle memory
Tapply, W. G. Past tense
Tapply, W. G. Scar tissue
Tapply, W. G. Tight lines
Tapply, W. G. A void in hearts
Truman, M. Murder at Ford's Theatre
Truman, M. Murder at the Library of Congress
Truman, M. Murder in the White House
Truman, M. Murder on Capitol Hill
Twain, M. Tom Sawyer, detective
Uhnak, D. The investigation
Vachss, A. H. Another life
Vachss, A. H. Choice of evil
Vachss, A. H. Dead and gone
Vachss, A. H. Down here
Vachss, A. H. Down in the zero
Vachss, A. H. Footsteps of the hawk
Vachss, A. H. Hard candy

Vachss, A. H. Pain management
Vachss, A. H. Sacrifice
Vachss, A. H. Safe house
Van de Wetering, J. Just a corpse at twilight
Walker, M. W. All the dead lie down
Wall, K. R. The Mercy Oak
Westlake, D. E. Baby, would I lie?
Westlake, D. E. Trust me on this
White, K. A body to die for
White, K. Lethally blond
Wilcox, C. Dead center
Wilcox, C. Except for the bones
Wilcox, C. Find her a grave
Wilcox, C. Full circle
Wilcox, C. Switchback
Wilhelm, K. The Hamlet trap
Wilhelm, K. Justice for some
Wilhelm, K. Sweet, sweet poison
Wilson, F. P. Conspiracies
Wilson, F. P. The haunted air
Wilson, F. P. Legacies
Winslow, D. The Dawn Patrol
Woods, S. Chiefs
Woods, S. New York dead
Yancey, R. The highly effective detective

Wales

Penman, S. K. Dragon's lair
Robb, C. M. A gift of sanctuary
The **mystery** of Edwin Drood. Dickens, C.
The **mystic** arts of erasing all signs of death. Huston, C.
Mystic river. Lehane, D.
Mystical paths. Howatch, S.

MYSTICISM

Erdrich, L. Four souls
Hesse, H. Siddhartha
Llywelyn, M. Druids
Martin, G. R. R. A song for Lya
McEwan, I. Black dogs
Wiesel, E. Twilight
Zimler, R. The last kabbalist of Lisbon

MYTHICAL ANIMALS

See also Dragons; Unicorns; Vampires; Werewolves

MYTHOLOGY

See also Helen of Troy (Legendary character); Theseus (Greek mythology)

Gaiman, N. American gods
Lewis, C. S. Till we have faces
Momaday, N. S. The ancient child
Murdoch, I. The green knight
Simmons, D. Ilium
Simmons, D. Olympos

N

"N" is for noose. Grafton, S.
A **nail** through the heart. Hallinan, T.
The **naked** and the dead. Mailer, N.
Naked in death. Robb, J. D.
Naked lunch. Burroughs, W. S.
Naked prey. Sandford, J.
The **naked** sun. Asimov, I.
In Asimov, I. The rest of the robots
Naked villainy. Woods, S.
The **name** of the rose. Eco, U.
The **name** of the wind. Rothfuss, P.
The **names**. DeLillo, D.
The **names** of the dead. O'Nan, S.
The **namesake**. Lahiri, J.

NAMIBIA

Brink, A. P. The other side of silence
Timm, U. Morenga
The **naming** of the dead. Rankin, I.
Nana. Zola, É.
Nancy Culpepper. Mason, B. A.

NANNIES *See* Governesses; Nursemaids
The **nanny** diaries. McLaughlin, E.

NANOTECHNOLOGY

Stross, C. Accelerando

NAVAL BATTLES—*Continued*

Forester, C. S. The last nine days of the Bismarck
Forester, C. S. Ship of the line
Martin, W. Annapolis
McCutchan, P. Cameron's crossing
The **navigator** of New York. Johnston, W.
The **Nazarene**. Asch, S.
Nazi literature in the Americas. Bolaño, R.

NAZIS *See* National socialism

NAZISM *See* National socialism
Neanderthal. Darnton, J.

NEANDERTHAL RACE

See also Prehistoric man
Golding, W. The inheritors

NEAR-DEATH EXPERIENCES

Davis, K. The thin place
Willis, C. Passage

NEAR EAST *See* Middle East
The **near** future. Porter, J. A.

NEBRASKA

Cather, W. A lost lady
Cather, W. One of ours
Hansen, R. Isn't it romantic?
Harrison, J. The road home
Kallos, S. Sing them home
Powers, R. The echo maker
Ward, L. Outside valentine

19th century

Cather, W. My Ántonia
Cather, W. O pioneers!

Farm life

See Farm life—Nebraska

Frontier and pioneer life

See Frontier and pioneer life—Nebraska

Nebula Awards showcase [date] Entered in Part I under title
Necrochip. See Harrod-Eagles, C. Death to go
Nectar in a sieve. Markandaya, K.
Needful things. King, S.

NEEDLEWORK

Hendrie, L. Remember me

NEGROES *See* African Americans

NEIGHBORS

Baxter, C. The feast of love
Berger, T. Neighbors
Cheever, J. Bullet Park
Gowdy, B. The romantic
Hamilton, J. A map of the world
Hoffman, A. Illumination night
Lively, P. Spiderweb
McFadden, B. L. Sugar
McKinney-Whetstone, D. Leaving Cecil Street
Mendelson, C. Morningside Heights
Mengestu, D. The beautiful things that heaven bears
Messud, C. The hunters [novelette]
Miller, S. For love
Parker, T. J. California girl
Schine, C. The New Yorkers
Shreve, A. Eden Close
Thornton, T. The alternative hero
Unsworth, B. After Hannibal
Neighbors. Berger, T.
Nekropolis. McHugh, M. F.

NELSON, HORATIO NELSON, VISCOUNT, 1758-1805

About

Sontag, S. The volcano lover
Unsworth, B. Losing Nelson

NEO-NAZIS *See* Skinheads

NEPAL

Kathmandu

Upadhyay, S. The guru of love
The **nephew**. Purdy, J.

NEPHEWS

Dennis, P. Auntie Mame
Nabokov, V. V. King, queen, knave

Rosenberg, N. T. Interest of justice

NERO, EMPEROR OF ROME, 37-68

About

Sienkiewicz, H. Quo Vadis
Nerve. Francis, D.
Nerve damage. Abrahams, P.

NERVOUS BREAKDOWN

Kavenna, J. Inglorious
Marlette, D. Magic time
Wilson, R. The blind man of Seville

NERVOUS SYSTEM

Diseases

Kellogg, M. Tell me that you love me, Junie Moon
Netherland. O'Neill, J.

NETHERLANDS

MacLean, A. Floodgate
Maguire, G. Confessions of an ugly stepsister
Simenon, G. The man who watched trains go by
Vreeland, S. Girl in hyacinth blue

17th century

Chevalier, T. Girl with a pearl earring
Laker, R. The golden tulip
Moggach, D. Tulip fever
Stevenson, J. The winter queen

Amsterdam

Camus, A. The fall
Lourie, R. A hatred for tulips
Moggach, D. Tulip fever

NETHERLANDS EAST INDIES *See* Indonesia

NEURASTHENIA *See* Nervous breakdown

NEUROLOGISTS

Powers, R. The echo maker
Willis, C. Passage
Neuromancer. Gibson, W.

NEUROSES

Rossner, J. August

NEUROTICS *See* Neuroses

NEVADA

See also Death Valley (Calif. and Nev.)
Crichton, M. Prey
King, S. Desperation
Kittredge, W. The Willow Field
Krauss, N. Man walks into a room

19th century

Clark, W. V. T. The Ox-bow incident

Las Vegas

Bock, C. Beautiful children
Connelly, M. Void moon
Ellroy, J. Blood's a rover
García, C. A handbook to luck
McGinniss, J. The delivery man
McMurtry, L. The desert rose
Pronzini, B. The other side of silence
Puzo, M. The last Don
Robbins, H. Sin city

Reno

Vlautin, W. Northline
Never go back. Goddard, R.
Never let me go. Ishiguro, K.

NEW BRUNSWICK *See* Canada—New Brunswick
The **new** centurions. Wambaugh, J.

NEW ENGLAND

Amidon, S. Security
Berne, S. A perfect arrangement
Brown, R. Tender mercies
Carter, S. L. New England white
Cheever, J. The Wapshot chronicle
Cheever, J. The Wapshot scandal
Clarke, B. An arsonist's guide to writers' homes in New England
Cozzens, J. G. By love possessed
Erdrich, L. The painted drum
Hawthorne, N. Twice-told tales

NEW YORK (N.Y.)—*Continued*

Godey, J. The taking of Pelham one two three
Goudge, E. Garden of lies
Goudge, E. Trail of secrets
Grant, M. Officer down
Hamill, P. Forever
Heller, J. Closing time
Helprin, M. Winter's tale
Hijuelos, O. Empress of the splendid season
Hobson, L. K. Z. Gentleman's agreement
Hunter, E. The blackboard jungle
Hunter, E. Candyland
Hustvedt, S. What I loved
Isaacs, S. Shining through
Jackson, C. The lost weekend
Jen, G. Typical American
Kaplow, R. Me and Orson Welles
Kelly, T. Empire rising
Kelman, J. Summer of storms
Kerouac, J. And the hippos were boiled in their tanks
Klavan, A. Empire of lies
Larsen, N. Passing
Leavitt, D. The lost language of cranes
Marshall, P. Brown girl, brownstones
McInerney, J. Bright lights, big city
Moody, R. The Albertine notes
Nathan, R. Portrait of Jennie
Nersesian, A. The swing voter of Staten Island
Nin, A. A spy in the house of love
Ozick, C. The Puttermesser papers
Piercy, M. Braided lives
Plath, S. The bell jar
Preston, D. Reliquary
Preston, R. The Cobra event
Rand, A. The fountainhead
Rayner, R. The cloud sketcher
Rebeck, T. Three girls and their brother
Robb, J. D. Naked in death
Rossner, J. August
Roth, H. A diving rock on the Hudson
Roth, H. From bondage
Roth, H. Requiem for Harlem
Roth, P. The dying animal
Runyon, D. Guys and dolls
Saint, H. F. Memoirs of an invisible man
Salinger, J. D. The catcher in the rye
Salinger, J. D. Franny & Zooey
Salinger, J. D. Raise high the roof beam, carpenters, and Seymour: an introduction
Sanders, L. The sixth commandment
Schwartz, L. S. The fatigue artist
Shaw, I. Bread upon the waters
Shelby, P. Gatekeeper
Sheldon, S. Rage of angels
Singer, I. B. Shadows on the Hudson
Slattery, B. F. Spaceman blues
Tanenbaum, R. Act of revenge
Tanenbaum, R. Hoax
Trigiani, A. Very Valentine
Uhnak, D. Codes of betrayal
Van Slyke, H. Public smiles, private tears
Wellington, D. Monster Island
Westlake, D. E. Don't ask
Westlake, D. E. The hook
Westlake, D. E. Money for nothing
Westlake, D. E. Smoke
Wharton, E. The house of mirth
Wolcott, J. The catsitters
Wolfe, T. The web and the rock
Wolfe, T. You can't go home again
Wolfe, T. The bonfire of the vanities
Wray, J. Lowboy
Wright, R. The outsider

18th century

Charyn, J. Johnny One-Eye
Liss, D. The whiskey rebels

19th century

Busch, F. The night inspector
Carr, C. The alienist
Crane, S. Maggie: a girl of the streets (a story of New York)
Doctorow, E. L. The waterworks
Finney, J. Time and again
Melville, H. Pierre

Millhauser, S. Martin Dressler
Piercy, M. Sex wars
Rose, J. Blackest bird
Vidal, G. 1876
Wharton, E. The age of innocence
Wharton, E. Old New York

Bronx

Doctorow, E. L. Billy Bathgate
McCann, C. Let the great world spin
Neugeboren, J. 1940
Verghese, A. Cutting for stone

Brooklyn

Auster, P. The Brooklyn follies
Barton, E. Brookland
Breslin, J. The gang that couldn't shoot straight
Christensen, K. The great man
Cohen, L. H. Heart, you bully, you punk
Danticat, E. The dew breaker
García, C. Dreaming in Cuban
Gilmore, J. Golden country
Green, N. The angel of Montague Street
Green, N. Shooting Dr. Jack
Hamill, P. Snow in August
Kirshenbaum, B. An almost perfect moment
Lethem, J. The fortress of solitude
Malamud, B. The assistant
Marshall, P. The fisher king
Maynard, J. The usual rules
McDermott, A. At weddings and wakes
Miller, H. Tropic of Capricorn
Milligan, J. Jack Fish
Mirvis, T. The outside world
Nunez, E. Grace
Potok, C. The chosen
Potok, C. The gift of Asher Lev
Potok, C. My name is Asher Lev
Reuland, R. Semiautomatic
Rosenfeld, L. I'm so happy for you
Schwartz, L. S. The writing on the wall
Singer, I. B. Enemies, a love story
Smith, B. A tree grows in Brooklyn
Starr, J. Lights out
Styron, W. Sophie's choice
Tóibín, C. Brooklyn

Greenwich Village

Cunningham, M. The hours
Glass, J. The whole world over
Hunt, L. The exquisite
Powell, D. The golden spur
Powell, D. The wicked pavilion
Spanidou, I. Before
Steinke, R. Holy skirts
Weinstein, D. Apprentice to the flower poet Z
Wenner, K. Dancing with Einstein
White, E. The beautiful room is empty
Wolitzer, M. The wife

Harlem

Baker, K. Strivers Row
Baldwin, J. Go tell it on the mountain
Baldwin, J. If Beale Street could talk
Baldwin, J. Tell me how long the train's been gone
Burke, S. Black flies
Hughes, L. Simple speaks his mind
Hughes, L. Simple stakes a claim
Hughes, L. Simple takes a wife
Hughes, L. Simple's Uncle Sam
Mansbach, A. Shackling water
Morrison, T. Jazz
Petry, A. L. The street
Ridley, J. A conversation with the Mann
Roth, H. A star shines over Mt. Morris Park
Wallant, E. L. The pawnbroker

Lower East Side

Crane, S. Maggie: a girl of the streets (a story of New York)
Huston, C. Caught stealing
Mosley, W. RL's dream
Price, R. Lush life
Roth, H. Call it sleep
Stern, S. The angel of forgetfulness
Tax, M. Rivington Street

NEW YORK (STATE)—*Continued*
Perry, T. Shadow woman
Perry, T. Vanishing act
Prose, F. Goldengrove
Prose, F. Primitive people
Puzo, M. The godfather
Quindlen, A. Object lessons
Russo, R. Bridge of sighs
Russo, R. Nobody's fool
Russo, R. The risk pool
Shreve, A. Eden Close
Shriver, L. We need to talk about Kevin
Straub, P. Ghost story
Strieber, W. The forbidden zone
Westlake, D. E. Drowned hopes
Winegardner, M. The Godfather returns

18th century
Cooper, J. F. The Deerslayer
Cooper, J. F. The last of the Mohicans
Cooper, J. F. The Pathfinder
Cooper, J. F. The spy

19th century
Crane, S. The monster
Seton, A. Dragonwyck

Frontier and pioneer life
See Frontier and pioneer life—New York (State)

Politics
See Politics—New York (State)

Albany
Kennedy, W. Ironweed
Kennedy, W. Roscoe
Kennedy, W. Very old bones

Buffalo
Baxter, C. The soul thief
Reisman, N. The first desire

Cooperstown
Cooper, J. F. The pioneers

Corinth
Lurie, A. The war between the Tates

Ithaca
O'Nan, S. The names of the dead

New York City
See New York (N.Y.)

Niagara Falls
Oates, J. C. The falls
Oates, J. C. Rape

Syracuse
Abu-Jaber, D. Origin

Westchester County
Boyle, T. C. World's end
Green, G. D. The juror
Jen, G. Mona in the promised land
New York dead. Woods, S.
New York novels. Wharton, E.
New York Review Books classics [series]
Simenon, G. The man who watched trains go by
Simenon, G. Strangers in the house

NEW YORKER (PERIODICAL)
Keillor, G. Love me
The **New** Yorkers. Schine, C.

NEW ZEALAND
Hulme, K. The bone people
Tremain, R. The color
Uris, L. Redemption

19th century
Goudge, E. Green Dolphin Street

Frontier and pioneer life
See Frontier and pioneer life—New Zealand

NEW ZEALANDERS

England
Frame, J. Towards another summer

France
Knox, E. Daylight

NEWARK (N.J.) *See* New Jersey—Newark
NEWFOUNDLAND *See* Canada—Newfoundland
NEWPORT (R.I.) *See* Rhode Island—Newport
NEWSPAPER PUBLISHERS *See* Publishers and publishing
NEWSPAPERMEN *See* Journalists

NEWSPAPERS
Akst, D. The Webster chronicle
Darnton, J. Black and white and dead all over
Rand, A. The fountainhead
Schulberg, B. What makes Sammy run?
Spencer, L. Forgiving
Vidal, G. Empire

NEWTON, SIR ISAAC, 1642-1727
About
Kerr, P. Dark matter
Morrow, J. The last witchfinder
Stott, R. Ghostwalk
Next of kin. Trollope, J.

NEZ PERCE INDIANS
Johnston, T. C. Lay the mountains low

NIAGARA FALLS (N.Y.) *See* New York (State)—Niagara Falls
Niagara Falls all over again. McCracken, E.

NICARAGUA
Didion, J. The last thing he wanted

NICARAGUANS
United States
Leonard, E. Bandits
Niccolò rising. Dunnett, D.
The **nice** and the good. Murdoch, I.
Nice work. Lodge, D.
Nicholas Nickleby. Dickens, C.
The **Nick** Adams stories. Hemingway, E.

NIECES
Hansen, E. F. Tales of protection
Hansen, R. Hitler's niece
Rice, L. Safe harbor

NIGERIA
Habila, H. Measuring time

19th century
Achebe, C. Things fall apart

Civil War, 1967-1970
Adichie, C. N. Half of a yellow sun

Politics
See Politics—Nigeria

Lagos
Abani, C. GraceLand

NIGERIANS
England
Cleave, C. Little Bee
The **Nigger** of the Narcissus. Conrad, J.
also in Conrad, J. Great short works of Joseph Conrad p21-140
also in Conrad, J. The portable Conrad p292-453

NIGHT
Murakami, H. After dark
Night. Wiesel, E.
In Wiesel, E. Night, Dawn, The accident: three tales
Night and night's travelers. Yoshimoto, B.
In Yoshimoto, B. Asleep p1-65
Night blooming. Yarbro, C. Q.
Night bus. Rigosi, G.

NIGHT CLUBS
Ferrell, M. The answer is always yes
Hiaasen, C. Strip tease
Smith, M. C. December 6
The **night** counter. Yunis, A.
The **night** country. O'Nan, S.
Night crossing. Snyder, D. J.
Night, Dawn, The accident: three tales. Wiesel, E.

Night flight. Saint-Exupéry, A. d.
The **night** following. Joss, M.
The **night** gardener. Pelecanos, G. P.
The **night** in Lisbon. Remarque, E. M.
The **night** inspector. Busch, F.
The **night** manager. Le Carré, J.
Night of sorrows. Sherwood, F.
Night of the fox. Higgins, J.
Night of the jaguar. Gruber, M.
Night of thunder. Hunter, S.
Night passage. Parker, R. B.
Night prey. Sandford, J.
Night shift. King, S.
Night sins. Hoag, T.
Night train to Memphis. Peters, E.
The **night** villa. Goodman, C.
The **night** visitor. Doss, J. D.
The **night** watch. Waters, S.
Night without end. MacLean, A.
Night woman. Price, N.
Night work. Glavinic, T.
Nightcrawlers. Pronzini, B.
Nightfall. Goodis, D.
The **nightingale**. Sholem Aleichem
The **nightingales** of Troy. Fulton, A.
Nightlife. Perry, T.
Nightmare alley. Gresham, W. L.
    In Crime novels: American noir of the 1930s and 40s
Nightmare town. Hammett, D.
Nightmares & dreamscapes. King, S.
Nights at the circus. Carter, A.
Nights in Rodanthe. Sparks, N.
Nighttime is my time. Clark, M. H.
Nightwings [novelette] Silverberg, R.
    In The Hugo winners p503-57
    In Silverberg, R. A Robert Silverberg omnibus
Nightwood. Barnes, D.
NIHILISM
    See also Anarchism and anarchists
    Pynchon, T. V.
    Styron, W. Set this house on fire
    Tolstoy, L., graf. War and peace
    Turgenev, I. S. Fathers and sons
Nimitz class. Robinson, C.
Nine coaches waiting. Stewart, M.
Nine princes in Amber. Zelazny, R.
Nine stories. Salinger, J. D.
The **nine** tailors. Sayers, D. L.
Nineteen eighty-four. Orwell, G.
Nineteen minutes. Picoult, J.
Ninety-two in the shade. McGuane, T.
Nip the buds, shoot the kids. Ōe, K.
De **Niro's** game. Hage, R.
NIXON, RICHARD M. (RICHARD MILHOUS), 1913-1994
                About
    Roth, P. Our gang
No. 44, The mysterious stranger. Twain, M.
    In Twain, M. The gilded age and later novels
No birds sing. Bannister, J.
No body. Pickard, N.
No country for old men. McCarthy, C.
No defense. Wilhelm, K.
No good deeds. Lippman, L.
No graves as yet. Perry, A.
No greater love. Steel, D.
No laughing matter. Simpson, D.
No man's dog. Jackson, J. A.
No more parades. Ford, F. M.
    In Ford, F. M. Parade's end
No night is too long. Vine, B.
No one belongs here more than you. July, M.
No one writes to the colonel. García Márquez, G.
    In García Márquez, G. Collected novellas p107-66
No one you know. Richmond, M.
No ordinary matter. McPhee, J.
No place like home. Clark, M. H.
No safe place. Patterson, R. N.
No saints or angels. Klíma, I.
No second chance. Coben, H.
No time to wave goodbye. Mitchard, J.
No witnesses. Pearson, R.
NOAH (BIBLICAL FIGURE)
                About
    Maine, D. The preservationist

NOBEL PRIZES
    Wallace, I. The prize
NOBILITY *See* Aristocracy
Noble house. Clavell, J.
Nobody move. Johnson, D.
Nobody's angel. McGuane, T.
Nobody's fool. Russo, R.
Nocturne. McBain, E.
Noise. Clement, H.
The **nonborn** king. May, J.
None to accompany me. Gordimer, N.
Noon wine. Porter, K. A.
    In Porter, K. A. Collected stories and other writings
    In Porter, K. A. Pale horse, pale rider: three short novels
Nora, Nora. Siddons, A. R.
NORFOLK (ENGLAND) *See* England—Norfolk
NORMANDIE (STEAMSHIP)
    Villars, E. The Normandie affair
The **Normandie** affair. Villars, E.
NORMANDY (FRANCE) *See* France—Normandy
NORTH AFRICA
    See also Sahara
North and South. Jakes, J.

NORTH CAROLINA
    Adams, A. After the war
    Adams, A. A southern exposure
    Adams, S. K. My old true love
    Allen, S. A. The sugar queen
    Betts, D. Souls raised from the dead
    Dierbeck, L. One pill makes you smaller
    Earley, T. The blue star
    Earley, T. Jim the boy
    Edgerton, C. The Bible salesman
    Edgerton, C. Walking across Egypt
    Gibbons, K. Charms for the easy life
    Gibbons, K. Divining women
    Gibbons, K. Sights unseen
    Godwin, G. Evensong
    Godwin, G. A mother and two daughters
    Gurganus, A. Blessed assurance: a moral tale
    Gurganus, A. He's one, too
    Gurganus, A. A hog loves its life: something about my grand-
        father
    Gurganus, A. The oldest living Confederate widow tells all
    Gurganus, A. The practical heart [novelette]
    Gurganus, A. Preservation news
    Gurganus, A. Saint monster
    Hart, J. Down river
    Hart, J. The king of lies
    Hart, J. The last child
    Hickam, H. H. The keeper's son
    Hooper, K. Blood sins
    Hooper, K. Stealing shadows
    Huyler, F. The laws of invisible things
    Inman, R. Captain Saturday
    McCorkle, J. Carolina moon
    McCrumb, S. The songcatcher
    Medlicott, J. A. Gardens of Covington
    Medlicott, J. A. The ladies of Covington send their love
    Patterson, J. Four blind mice
    Pearson, T. R. A short history of a small place
    Percy, W. The second coming
    Pessl, M. Special topics in calamity physics
    Price, R. Blue Calhoun
    Price, R. The good priest's son
    Price, R. Kate Vaiden
    Price, R. The promise of rest
    Price, R. Roxanna Slade
    Price, R. The tongues of angels
    Rash, R. Serena
    Ross, A. B. Miss Julia throws a wedding
    Smith, L. On Agate Hill
    Sparks, N. A bend in the road
    Sparks, N. The guardian
    Sparks, N. Nights in Rodanthe
    Sparks, N. The notebook
    Sparks, N. A walk to remember
    Tyler, A. A slipping-down life
    Tyler, A. The tin can tree
    Wolfe, T. The web and the rock
    Zuber, I. Salt

NORTH CAROLINA—*Continued*
18th century
Gabaldon, D. A breath of snow and ashes
Gabaldon, D. An echo in the bone

19th century
Crafts, H. The bondswomans narrative
Humphreys, J. Nowhere else on earth
Slouka, M. God's fool
Trotter, W. R. The sands of pride

Farm life
See Farm life—North Carolina

NORTH DAKOTA
Erdrich, L. The Beet Queen
Erdrich, L. The last report on the miracles at Little No Horse
Erdrich, L. The Master Butchers Singing Club
Erdrich, L. The plague of doves
Erdrich, L. Tracks
Grimes, M. Dakota
Klosterman, C. Downtown owl
Power, S. The grass dancer

19th century
Jones, D. C. Arrest Sitting Bull
North of Montana. Smith, A.
North of nowhere, south of loss. Hospital, J. T.
North Star. Wheeler, R. S.
Northanger Abbey. Austen, J.

NORTHERN IRELAND
Deane, S. Reading in the dark
Llywelyn, M. 1972
McNicholl, D. A son called Gabriel
Snyder, D. J. Night crossing

Belfast
Dean, L. This human season
Moore, B. The lonely passion of Judith Hearne
Rankin, I. Watchman

NORTHERN RHODESIA *See* Zambia
Northline. Vlautin, W.
NORTHMEN *See* Vikings
NORTHUMBERLAND (ENGLAND) *See* England—Northumberland
NORTHWEST, OLD *See* Old Northwest
NORTHWEST, PACIFIC *See* Pacific Northwest
Northwest Passage. Roberts, K. L.
NORTHWEST TERRITORIES *See* Canada—Northwest Territories
The **Norton** book of science fiction. Entered in Part I under title

NORWAY
Francis, C. Wolf winter
Hansen, E. F. Tales of protection
Hermans, W. F. Beyond sleep
Petterson, P. In the wake

To 1397
Undset, S. Kristin Lavransdatter

Farm life
See Farm life—Norway

Rural life
Undset, S. Kristin Lavransdatter

NORWEGIANS
See also Vikings

United States
Rølvaag, O. E. Giants in the earth
Rølvaag, O. E. Peder Victorious
Norwood. Portis, C.

NOSTALGIA
Kundera, M. Ignorance
Nostromo. Conrad, J.
Not a day goes by. Harris, E. L.
Not before sundown. See Sinisalo, J. Troll
Not in the flesh. Rendell, R.
Not quite kosher. Kaminsky, S. M.
Not the end of the world. Atkinson, K.
Not without laughter. Hughes, L.

The **notebook.** Sparks, N.
The **notebooks** of Don Rigoberto. Vargas Llosa, M.
Notes from underground. Dostoyevsky, F.
    also in Dostoyevsky, F. The best short stories of Dostoevsky p115-260
Nothing but blue skies. McGuane, T.
Nothing but the truth. Lescroart, J. T.
Nothing but trouble. McGarrity, M.
Nothing but you. Entered in Part I under title
Nothing lost. Dunne, J. G.
Nothing to lose. Child, L.
NOTRE DAME UNIVERSITY *See* University of Notre Dame
NOTTINGHAM (ENGLAND) *See* England—Nottingham
NOTTINGHAMSHIRE (ENGLAND) *See* England—Nottinghamshire
NOVA SCOTIA *See* Canada—Nova Scotia
Nova swing. Harrison, M. J.

NOVALIS, 1772-1801
About
Fitzgerald, P. The blue flower
The **novel.** Michener, J. A.
Novel on yellow paper. Smith, S.

NOVELETTES
    See also Short stories
Aira, C. An afternoon in the life of a landscape painter
Aira, C. Ghosts
Appelfeld, A. Badenheim 1939
Barrett, W. E. The lilies of the field
Bellow, S. The Bellarosa connection
Bellow, S. Seize the day [novelette]
Benét, S. V. The Devil and Daniel Webster
Bolaño, R. By night in Chile
Bolaño, R. Distant star
Brand, M. Dark Rosaleen
Brand, M. Dust across the range
Brand, M. Outcasts
Byatt, A. S. Angels and insects
Calvino, I. Mr. Palomar
Capote, T. Breakfast at Tiffany's: a short novel and three stories
Castellanos Moya, H. Senselessness
Cervantes Saavedra, M. d. Three exemplary novels
Cheever, J. Oh, what a paradise it seems
Chekhov, A. P. Complete short novels
Chekhov, A. P. The duel
Chekhov, A. P. My life
Chekhov, A. P. The steppe
Chekhov, A. P. The story of an unknown man
Chekhov, A. P. Three years
Christensen, I. Azorno
Christie, A. Three blind mice
Cisneros, S. The house on Mango Street
Clark, M. H. The Anastasia syndrome
Cocteau, J. The impostor
Colette. The kepi
Colette. Six novels
Colette. The tender shoot
Conrad, J. Heart of darkness
Conrad, J. Youth
Cook, E. Achilles
Coover, R. Briar Rose
Coover, R. Ghost town
Coward, N. Bon voyage
Crane, S. The complete novels of Stephen Crane
Davies, V. Miracle on 34th Street
DeLillo, D. The body artist
Desai, A. Fire on the mountain
Dickens, C. A Charles Dickens Christmas
Dickens, C. A Christmas carol
Dickens, C. The cricket on the hearth
Doenges, J. God of gods
Domínguez, C. M. The house of paper
Dostoyevsky, F. The gambler
Dostoyevsky, F. Notes from underground
Erpenbeck, J. The book of words
Faber, M. The courage consort
Faber, M. The courage consort [novelette]
Faber, M. The Fahrenheit twins
Faber, M. The hundred and ninety-nine steps
Ferrante, E. The lost daughter
Ferrante, E. Troubling love
Fitzgerald, F. S. May Day

TITLE AND SUBJECT INDEX

NOVELETTES—*Continued*

Williams, T. The Roman spring of Mrs. Stone
Yoshimoto, B. Asleep
Yoshimoto, B. Kitchen [novella]
Yoshimoto, B. Love songs
Yoshimoto, B. Night and night's travelers

NOVELISTS *See* Authors

Novella. Goethe, J. W. v.
In Goethe, J. W. v. The sorrows of young Werther, and Novella p169-201

NOVELLAS *See* Novelettes

Novellas and other writings. Wharton, E.

NOVELS, UNFINISHED *See* Unfinished novels

Novels. Wharton, E.

Novels & stories. London, J.

Novels & stories, 1959-1962. Roth, P.

Novels, 1955-1962. Nabokov, V. V.

Novels, 1969-1974. Nabokov, V. V.

Novels, 1875-1886. Howells, W. D.

Novels, 1886-1888. Howells, W. D.

Novels, 1920-1925. Dos Passos, J.

Novels, 1926-1929. Faulkner, W.

Novels, 1930-1935. Faulkner, W.

Novels, 1930-1942. Powell, D.

Novels, 1936-1940. Faulkner, W.

Novels, 1942-1952. Steinbeck, J.

Novels, 1942-1954. Faulkner, W.

Novels, 1944-1953. Bellow, S.

Novels, 1944-1962. Powell, D.

Novels, 1956-1964. Bellow, S.

Novels, 1957-1962. Faulkner, W.

Novels, 1967-1972. Roth, P.

Novels, 1973-1977. Roth, P.

Novels and essays. Norris, F.

Novels and other narratives 1986-1991. Roth, P.

Novels and other writings. West, N.

Novels and stories. Hurston, Z. N.

Novels and stories, 1920-1922. Fitzgerald, F. S.

Novels and stories, 1932-1937. Steinbeck, J.

Now and then. Parker, R. B.

Now is the time to open your heart. Walker, A.

Now or never. Adler, E.

Now wait for last year. Dick, P. K.
In Dick, P. K. Five novels of the 1960s & 70s

Now you see him. Gottlieb, E.

Now you see it. Lynn, A.

The **nowhere** city. Lurie, A.

Nowhere else on earth. Humphreys, J.

Nowhere man. Hemon, A.

Nowhere to run. Daley, R.

NUCLEAR BOMB *See* Atomic bomb

NUCLEAR POWER PLANTS

Pohl, F. Chernobyl

NUCLEAR SUBMARINES

Clancy, T. The hunt for Red October
Coonts, S. America
MacLean, A. Ice Station Zebra

NUCLEAR WARFARE

See also Atomic bomb

Burdick, E. Fail-safe
Frank, P. Alas, Babylon
Shute, N. On the beach
West, M. L. The clowns of God

NUCLEAR WEAPONS

DeMille, N. Wild fire
Forsyth, F. The fourth protocol
Ignatius, D. The increment
Martini, S. P. Critical mass
Robinson, P. Nimitz class
Scholz, C. Radiance

Number 10. Townsend, S.

Number9dream. Mitchell, D.

NUNS

See also Ex-nuns

Barrett, W. E. The lilies of the field
Coben, H. The innocent
Godden, R. Black Narcissus
Hulme, K. The nun's story
Lanchester, J. Fragrant Harbor
L'Engle, M. The love letters

Robbins, T. Fierce invalids home from hot climates
Roberts, M. Reader, I married him
Salzman, M. Lying awake
Spark, M. The Abbess of Crewe
Steel, D. Amazing grace

Nuns and soldiers. Murdoch, I.

The **nun's** story. Hulme, K.

NUREYEV, RUDOLF, 1938-1993
About

McCann, C. Dancer

NURSEMAIDS

Styron, A. All the finest girls

NURSES AND NURSING

Coetzee, J. M. Slow man
Faulkner, W. Soldiers' pay
Hamilton, J. A map of the world
Hemingway, E. A farewell to arms
Holt, V. Secret for a nightingale
Hulme, K. The nun's story
Kesey, K. One flew over the cuckoo's nest
McCullough, C. An indecent obsession
McEwan, I. Atonement
Ondaatje, M. The English patient
Rinehart, M. R. Miss Pinkerton: adventures of a nurse detective
Straub, P. The Hellfire Club
Vine, B. The minotaur

NURSING HOMES

Lindgren, T. Hash
Mestre-Reed, E. The second death of Única Aveyano
Weldon, F. Rhode Island blues

O

"**O**" is for outlaw. Grafton, S.

O.K.. West, P.

O Beulah Land. Settle, M. L.

O Jerusalem. King, L. R.

O pioneers! Cather, W.
also in Cather, W. Early novels and stories

The **oath**. Lescroart, J. T.

The **oath**. Wiesel, E.

OBESITY

LaValle, V. D. The ecstatic
Walters, M. The sculptress
Weiner, J. Good in bed

Psychological aspects

See also Anorexia nervosa

Object lessons. Quindlen, A.

Oblivion. Wallace, D. F.

OBSESSIONS

Ackroyd, P. The fall of Troy
Bolaño, R. The skating rink
Erickson, S. Zeroville
King, R. The sound of butterflies
McCauley, S. Alternatives to sex
Moody, R. K&K
Pamuk, O. The museum of innocence
Phillips, A. The song is you
Vargas Llosa, M. The bad girl

OBSESSIVE-COMPULSIVE DISORDER

Martin, S. The pleasure of my company

OBSTETRICIANS *See* Physicians

Obstruction of justice. O'Shaughnessy, P.

Occam's razor. Mayor, A.

OCCULTISM

See also Alchemy; Supernatural phenomena; Superstition; Witchcraft

Eco, U. Foucault's pendulum
Gallagher, S. The kingdom of bones
Howe, K. The physick book of Deliverance Dane
King, S. Firestarter
Kurtz, K. Two crowns for America
LaValle, V. D. Big machine
Shannon, D. The Manson curse

TITLE AND SUBJECT INDEX

OCEAN

Verne, J. Twenty thousand leagues under the sea
The **ocean** between us. Wiggs, S.

OCEAN TRAVEL

See also Whaling; Yachts and yachting
Bainbridge, B. Every man for himself
Coward, N. Bon voyage
Galbraith, D. The rising sun
Golding, W. Close quarters
Golding, W. Fire down below
Golding, W. Rites of passage
McCutchan, P. The last farewell
Moberg, V. The emigrants
Porter, K. A. Ship of fools
Preston, D. The wheel of darkness
Villars, E. The Normandie affair
Woolf, V. The voyage out

OCEANIA *See* Islands of the Pacific
The **October** horse. McCullough, C.
The **octopus**. Norris, F.
   also in Norris, F. Novels and essays
The **Odessa** file. Forsyth, F.
Of human bondage. Maugham, W. S.
Of mice and men. Steinbeck, J.
   also in Steinbeck, J. Novels and stories, 1932-1937
Of time and the river. Wolfe, T.
Off Armageddon Reef. Weber, D.
Off Keck Road. Simpson, M.
Off the chart. Hall, J. W.
Office of innocence. Keneally, T.

OFFICE WORKERS

Hynes, J. Kings of infinite space
Moon, E. The speed of dark
Park, E. Personal days
Officer down. Grant, M.
Officers and gentlemen. Waugh, E.

OGLALA INDIANS

O'Brien, D. The contract surgeon
Welch, J. The heartsong of Charging Elk
The **ogre**. Tournier, M.
Oh Joe. Lewin, M. Z.
Oh, what a paradise it seems. Cheever, J.
   also in Cheever, J. Complete novels

OHIO

Dew, R. F. The evidence against her
Dew, R. F. The truth of the matter
King, S. The regulators
Morrison, T. The bluest eye
Morrison, T. Sula
O'Nan, S. Songs for the missing
Patterson, R. N. Silent witness
Pollock, D. R. Knockemstiff
Powell, D. Come back to Sorrento
Powell, D. Dance night
Powell, D. My home is far away
Roth, P. Indignation
Santmyer, H. H. "—and ladies of the club"
Shreve, S. R. The visiting physician
Smith, S. A simple plan
Vonnegut, K. Deadeye Dick

18th century
Richter, C. The awakening land

19th century
Anderson, S. Winesburg, Ohio
Richter, C. The awakening land

Frontier and pioneer life
See Frontier and pioneer life—Ohio

Cincinnati
Holden, C. The jazz bird

Columbus
Crusie, J. Faking it

OHIO RIVER VALLEY

Settle, M. L. O Beulah Land

Frontier and pioneer life
See Frontier and pioneer life—Ohio River Valley

OIL INDUSTRY *See* Petroleum industry
OIL WELLS *See* Petroleum industry
OJIBWA INDIANS *See* Chippewa Indians
OKINAWA (JAPAN) *See* Japan—Okinawa

OKLAHOMA

Anderson, E. Thieves like us
Crowley, J. Four freedoms
Hart, C. G. Letter from home
Hunter, S. Dirty white boys
Letts, B. Shoot the moon
Morrison, T. Paradise

19th century
Ferber, E. Cimarron

Frontier and pioneer life
See Frontier and pioneer life—Oklahoma

Politics
See Politics—Oklahoma

Tulsa
Straight, S. The gettin place

OLD AGE

See also Aging
Cary, J. The horse's mouth
Cheever, J. Oh, what a paradise it seems
Christensen, K. The great man
Coe, J. The rain before it falls
Coetzee, J. M. Age of iron
Coetzee, J. M. Diary of a bad year
Cooper, J. F. The prairie
Dean, D. The madonnas of Leningrad
Dickinson, P. Some deaths before dying
Dixon, S. Old friends
Edgerton, C. Walking across Egypt
Galsworthy, J. The Indian summer of a Forsyte
Galsworthy, J. Swan song
García Márquez, G. Memories of my melancholy whores
García Márquez, G. No one writes to the colonel
Gordon, M. Final payments
Gurganus, A. The oldest living Confederate widow tells all
Harding, P. Tinkers
Hassler, J. The Staggerford flood
Hemingway, E. The old man and the sea
Hilton, J. Good-bye Mr. Chips
Itani, F. Remembering the bones
Kawabata, Y. The sound of the mountain
King, S. Insomnia
Krauss, N. The history of love
Lindgren, T. Hash
Maloy, K. Every last cuckoo
McFarland, D. School for the blind
McMurtry, L. The evening star
McNamer, D. Red rover
Medlicott, J. A. Gardens of Covington
Medlicott, J. A. The ladies of Covington send their love
Messud, C. A simple tale
Mestre-Reed, E. The second death of Única Aveyano
Michener, J. A. Recessional
Miller, S. The distinguished guest
Mistry, R. Family matters
Mosley, W. RL's dream
Olsson, L. Astrid & Veronika
Porter, J. A. The near future
Pouncey, P. R. Rules for old men waiting
Price, R. The good priest's son
Purdy, J. The nephew
Quindlen, A. Blessings
Roth, P. Exit ghost
Roth, P. Sabbath's theater
Sackville-West, V. All passion spent
Sarton, M. As we are now
Sarton, M. Kinds of love
Scott, A. Calpurnia
Scott, P. Staying on
Simon, C. The trolley
Spark, M. Memento mori
Sparks, N. The notebook
Taylor, E. Mrs. Palfrey at the Claremont
Taylor, M. G. The ballad of Trenchmouth Taggart
Trollope, J. The men and the girls
Trueblood, V. Seven loves

OLD AGE—*Continued*
Tyler, A. A patchwork planet
Updike, J. The poorhouse fair
Updike, J. Seek my face
Updike, J. The widows of Eastwick
Weldon, F. Rhode Island blues
Wharton, W. Dad
White, P. The eye of the storm
Wiesel, E. The forgotten

OLD AGE HOMES
See also Nursing homes; Retirement communities
Sarton, M. As we are now
Updike, J. The poorhouse fair
Old boys. McCarry, C.
The **Old** Contemptibles. Grimes, M.
The **old** curiosity shop. Dickens, C.
Old Filth. Gardam, J.
Old flames. Lawton, J.
The **old** fox deceiv'd. Grimes, M.
Old friends. Dixon, S.
Old Goriot. See Balzac, H. d. Père Goriot (Old Goriot)
The **old** gringo. Fuentes, C.

OLD LADIES *See* Old age
Old Love. Singer, I. B.
In Singer, I. B. Collected stories: One night in Brazil to The death of Methuselah
The **old** maid. Wharton, E.
In Wharton, E. Novellas and other writings

OLD MAIDS *See* Single women
The **old** man and the sea. Hemingway, E.
Old man's war. Scalzi, J.

OLD MEN *See* Old age
Old men at midnight. Potok, C.
Old morality. Porter, K. A.
In Porter, K. A. Collected stories and other writings
Old mortality. Porter, K. A.
In Porter, K. A. Pale horse, pale rider: three short novels
Old New York. Wharton, E.
In Wharton, E. Novellas and other writings

OLD NORTHWEST
Roberts, K. L. Northwest Passage
Old school. Wolff, T.
The **Old** Silent. Grimes, M.

OLD SOUTHWEST
Richter, C. The sea of grass

OLD WOMEN *See* Old age
The **oldest** living Confederate widow tells all. Gurganus, A.
Oldtown folks. Stowe, H. B.
In Stowe, H. B. Uncle Tom's cabin: or, Life among the lowly; The minister's wooing; Oldtown folks p877-1468
Olive Kitteridge. Strout, E.
Oliver Twist. Dickens, C.
Oliver Wiswell. Roberts, K. L.

OLUWALE, DAVID, 1930 OR 1-1969
About
Phillips, C. Foreigners

OLYMPIC GAMES
Keegan, N. Swimming
Olympos. Simmons, D.

O'MALLEY, GRACE, 1530?-1603?
About
Maxwell, R. The wild Irish
The **Omega** Force. Moody, R.
In Moody, R. Right livelihoods
Omoo: a narrative of adventures in the South Seas. Melville, H.
also in Melville, H. Typee: a peep at Polynesian life; Omoo: a narrative of adventures in the South Seas; Mardi: and a voyager thither
On a day like this. Stamm, P.
On Agate Hill. Smith, L.
On beauty. Smith, Z.
On Chesil Beach. McEwan, I.
On Green Dolphin Street. Faulks, S.
On Her Majesty's Secret Service. Fleming, I.
On Kingdom Mountain. Mosher, H. F.
On Mystic lake. Hannah, K.
On secret service. Jakes, J.
On the beach. Shute, N.
On the edge. Lovesey, P.

On the nature of human romantic interaction. Iagnemma, K.
On the occasion of my last afternoon. Gibbons, K.
On the river Styx and other stories. Matthiessen, P.
On the road. Kerouac, J.
also in Kerouac, J. Road novels 1957-1960
On the road: the original scroll. Kerouac, J.
On the street where you live. Clark, M. H.
On the wrong track. Hockensmith, S.
Once a hero. Moon, E.
The **once** and future king. White, T. H.
Once on a moonless night. Dai Sijie
Once the shore. Yoon, P.
Once too often. Simpson, D.
One corpse too many. Peters, E.
also in Peters, E. The benediction of Brother Cadfael p211-348
One D.O.A., one on the way. Robison, M.
One day in the life of Ivan Denisovich. Solzhenitsyn, A.
One door away from heaven. Koontz, D. R.
One false move. Coben, H.
One fearful yellow eye. MacDonald, J. D.
One fine day the rabbi bought a cross. Kemelman, H.
One flew over the cuckoo's nest. Kesey, K.
One for the money. Evanovich, J.
One hundred million hearts. Sakamoto, K.
One hundred years of solitude. García Márquez, G.
One last dance. Goudge, E.
One lonely night. Spillane, M.
In Spillane, M. The Mike Hammer collection [v2]
One man's initiation: 1917. Dos Passos, J.
In Dos Passos, J. Novels, 1920-1925
One more river. Freeling, N.
One more river. See Galsworthy, J. Over the river
One more Sunday. MacDonald, J. D.
One of ours. Cather, W.
In Cather, W. Early novels and stories
One pill makes you smaller. Dierbeck, L.
One Police Plaza. Caunitz, W. J.
One shot. Child, L.
One step behind. Mankell, H.
The **One** Tree. Donaldson, S. R.
One true thing. Quindlen, A.
Only children. Lurie, A.
Only one thing missing. Ruiz, L. M.
Only revolutions. Danielewski, M. Z.
Only yesterday. Agnon, S. Y.

ONTARIO *See* Canada—Ontario
Oops!. Lutz, J.
The **open** curtain. Evenson, B.
Open secrets. Munro, A.
Open to the public. Spark, M.

OPERA
Davies, R. The lyre of Orpheus
Hambly, B. Die upon a kiss
Marías, J. The man of feeling
Parker, B. Suspicion of deceit
See, L. Peony in love
Operation wandering soul. Powers, R.

OPERATIONS, SURGICAL *See* Surgery

OPIUM
Hannan, C. Missy

OPIUM TRADE
Ghosh, A. Sea of poppies

OPIUM WAR, 1840-1842 *See* China—War of 1840-1842

OPPENHEIMER, J. ROBERT, 1904-1967
About
Smith, M. C. Stallion Gate
The **opposite** house. Oyeyemi, H.
The **optimist's** daughter. Welty, E.
also in Welty, E. Complete novels
Options. Henry, O.
In Henry, O. The complete works of O. Henry p680-810
Oracle night. Auster, P.

ORACLES
Graham, J. Black ships
Oral history. Smith, L.

ORAN (ALGERIA) *See* Algeria—Oran
Oranges are not the only fruit. Winterson, J.
Orchestrated death. Harrod-Eagles, C.
Orchid Beach. Woods, S.

The **overlook**. Connelly, M.
The **Ox-bow** incident. Clark, W. V. T.
OXFORD (ENGLAND) *See* England—Oxford
The **Oxford** book of American detective stories. Entered in Part I under title
The **Oxford** book of American short stories. Entered in Part I under title
The **Oxford** book of English ghost stories. Entered in Part I under title
The **Oxford** book of English love stories. Entered in Part I under title
The **Oxford** book of English short stories. Entered in Part I under title
The **Oxford** book of gothic tales. Entered in Part I under title
The **Oxford** book of Irish short stories. Entered in Part I under title
The **Oxford** book of Jewish stories. Entered in Part I under title
The **Oxford** book of Latin American short stories. Entered in Part I under title
The **Oxford** book of modern fairy tales. Entered in Part I under title
The **Oxford** book of science fiction stories. Entered in Part I under title
The **Oxford** book of short stories. Entered in Part I under title
The **Oxford** book of spy stories. Entered in Part I under title
The **Oxford** book of travel stories. Entered in Part I under title
The **Oxford** book of twentieth-century ghost stories. Entered in Part I under title
OXFORD UNIVERSITY *See* University of Oxford
OXFORDSHIRE (ENGLAND) *See* England—Oxfordshire
Oxygen. Miller, A.
Oyster. Hospital, J. T.

OZ (IMAGINARY PLACE)

Maguire, G. A lion among men
Maguire, G. Wicked

OZARK MOUNTAINS REGION

Harington, D. The pitcher shower
Woodrell, D. Winter's bone

P

"**P**" is for peril. Grafton, S.
The **Pacific** and other stories. Helprin, M.
Pacific beat. Parker, T. J.

PACIFIC NORTHWEST

Fowler, K. J. Sarah Canary
Priest, C. Boneshaker
Raymond, J. The half-life

PACIFIC OCEAN

Watts, P. Starfish

World War, 1939-1945

See World War, 1939-1945—Pacific Ocean
Pacific Street. Holland, C.
PACIFISM *See* Conscientious objectors
Pack of cards and other stories. Lively, P.
Paco's story. Heinemann, L.
Paddy Clarke, ha ha ha. Doyle, R.
Pagan babies. Leonard, E.

PAGANISM

Renault, M. The king must die
Sienkiewicz, H. Quo Vadis
Steinbeck, J. To a god unknown

PAGEANTS

Woolf, V. Between the acts
The **paid** companion. Quick, A.
Pain management. Vachss, A. H.
Paint it black. Fitch, J.
The **painted** bird. Kosinski, J. N.
The **painted** drum. Erdrich, L.
A **painted** house. Grisham, J.
The **painter** of battles. Pérez-Reverte, A.

PAINTERS

Cary, J. The horse's mouth
Clark, M. H. A cry in the night
Colwin, L. Family happiness
Crane, S. The third violet
Dovey, C. Blood kin
Durrell, L. Clea
Farmer, P. J. Riders of the purple wage
Gruber, M. The forgery of Venus
Hawthorne, N. The marble faun
Hemingway, E. Islands in the stream
Ishiguro, K. An artist of the floating world
James, H. The Europeans
Just, W. S. Forgetfulness
Kamensky, J. Blindspot
Krantz, J. Mistral's daughter
Maugham, W. S. The moon and sixpence
Momaday, N. S. The ancient child
Murdoch, I. Nuns and soldiers
Nathan, R. Portrait of Jennie
Perec, G. Life
Potok, C. The gift of Asher Lev
Potok, C. My name is Asher Lev
Roberts, K. L. Northwest Passage
Stone, I. Lust for life
Styron, W. Set this house on fire
Urquhart, J. The underpainter
Wharton, W. Dad

PAINTINGS

Banks, O. T. The Caravaggio obsession
Edge, A. The god of spring
Frayn, M. Headlong
Horn, D. The world to come
Johnson, D. Le divorce
King, S. Duma Key
Lowell, E. Die in plain sight
Mayle, P. Chasing Cézanne
Norman, H. The museum guard
Price, R. The good priest's son
Vreeland, S. Girl in hyacinth blue
Watkins, P. The forger
Weber, K. The Music Lesson

PAKISTAN

Hanif, M. A case of exploding mangoes
Mueenuddin, D. In other rooms, other wonders

Karachi

Shamsie, K. Kartography

Lahore

Hamid, M. The reluctant fundamentalist

PAKISTANIS

United States

Hamid, M. The reluctant fundamentalist
Palace council. Carter, S. L.
Palace of desire. Maḥfūẓ, N.
The **palace** thief. Canin, E.
Palace walk. Maḥfūẓ, N.
The **paladin** of souls. Bujold, L. M.
Pale fire. Nabokov, V. V.
    also in Nabokov, V. V. Novels, 1955-1962
The **pale** horse. Christie, A.
Pale horse coming. Hunter, S.
Pale horse, pale rider [novelette] Porter, K. A.
    In Porter, K. A. Collected stories and other writings
    In Porter, K. A. Pale horse, pale rider: three short novels
Pale horse, pale rider: three short novels. Porter, K. A.
    In Porter, K. A. Collected stories and other writings
    also in Porter, K. A. The collected stories of Katherine Anne Porter p173-317

PALEONTOLOGISTS

Lively, P. Cleopatra's sister
Preston, D. Tyrannosaur Canyon
Smith, D. Pictures from an expedition
Swanwick, M. Bones of the earth
Vine, B. No night is too long

PALESTINE

See also Israel; Jerusalem
Agnon, S. Y. Only yesterday
Eve, N. The family orchard

PARENT AND CHILD—*Continued*
Lipman, E. My latest grievance
London, J. The good parents
Lott, B. Ancient highway
Lurie, A. Only children
Lurie, A. The war between the Tates
Matar, H. In the country of men
Maynard, J. The usual rules
McDermott, A. Child of my heart
McEwan, I. The child in time
Meloy, M. Liars and saints
Michaels, F. Finders keepers
Miller, S. Family pictures
Miller, S. Lost in the forest
Minot, E. The Brambles
Mirvis, T. The outside world
Mistry, R. Family matters
Oates, J. C. Middle age
O'Nan, S. Songs for the missing
Palwick, S. Shelter
Parks, T. Destiny
Parks, T. Rapids
Patchett, A. Run
Perrotta, T. Little children
Picoult, J. Nineteen minutes
Powell, P. Edisto
Price, R. Blue Calhoun
Price, R. Roxanna Slade
Pronzini, B. The other side of silence
Rash, R. Saints at the river
Rice, L. The letters
Robinson, R. Cost
Romano, T. When the world was young
Roth, P. Everyman
Schwartz, L. Angels Crest
Schwegel, T. Person of interest
See, C. There will never be another you
Sharpe, M. The sleeping father
Shattuck, J. Perfect life
Slouka, M. The visible world
Straight, S. I been in sorrow's kitchen and licked out all the
  pots
Strauss, D. More than it hurts you
Sundaresan, I. The splendor of silence
Swann, M. Flower children
Swift, G. Tomorrow
Tarkington, B. Alice Adams
Taylor, B. The book of getting even
Thayer, N. Between husbands and friends
Trollope, J. The best of friends
Trollope, J. Other people's children
Trollope, J. Second honeymoon
Trueblood, V. Seven loves
Turow, S. The laws of our fathers
Tyler, A. The clock winder
Tyler, A. Dinner at the Homesick Restaurant
Vida, V. Let the Northern Lights erase your name
Wagner, B. The chrysanthemum palace
Weber, K. The little women
Weiner, J. Little earthquakes
Weldon, F. She may not leave
West, P. Love's mansion
Winthrop, E. H. December
Wolitzer, H. Hearts

PARIS (FRANCE) *See* France—Paris
Paris in the twentieth century. Verne, J.
Paris Trout. Dexter, P.
PARKER, JANE *See* Boleyn, Jane, Viscountess Rochford, d.
  1542

PARKINSONISM
Esquivel, L. Swift as desire
Franzen, J. The corrections
Miller, S. The distinguished guest
Mistry, R. Family matters

PARKS
  See also Amusement parks; Wilderness areas; Zoos
PARMA (ITALY) *See* Italy—Parma
PAROCHIAL SCHOOLS *See* Church schools
PARODIES
  See also names of prominent authors with the subdivision
  Parodies, imitations, etc.
  Berger, T. Arthur Rex

Coover, R. Ghost town
Fielding, H. The history of the adventures of Joseph Andrews
  and of his friend Mr. Abraham Adams and, An apology for
  the life of Mrs. Shamela Andrews
Hemingway, E. The torrents of spring
Nabokov, V. V. Lolita
O'Brien, F. The hard life

PARRICIDE
Rossner, J. Perfidia
Sebold, A. The almost moon

PARROTS
Paul, J. Elsewhere in the land of parrots
The **Parsifal** mosaic. Ludlum, R.
Parson's pleasure. Hardwick, M.
Part of the furniture. Wesley, M.

PARTIES
  See also Dinners
  Pilcher, R. September

PARTISANS *See* Guerrillas
A **partisan's** daughter. De Bernières, L.
The **partner**. Grisham, J.
Passage. Willis, C.
A **passage** to India. Forster, E. M.
Passing. Larsen, N.
Passing on. Lively, P.
The **passion** of Artemesia. Vreeland, S.
PASSION WEEK *See* Holy Week
Passions and other stories. Singer, I. B.
  In Singer, I. B. Collected stories: A friend of Kafka to Pas-
  sions
Past tense. Greenleaf, S.
Past tense. Tapply, W. G.
PASTORS *See* Clergy
The **pastures** of heaven. Steinbeck, J.
  In Steinbeck, J. Novels and stories, 1932-1937

PATAGONIA (ARGENTINA AND CHILE)
O'Brian, P. The unknown shore
A **patchwork** planet. Tyler, A.
PATENT MEDICINES *See* Medicines, Patent, proprietary, etc.
The **path** of minor planets. Greer, A. S.
The **Pathfinder**. Cooper, J. F.
  also in Cooper, J. F. The Leatherstocking tales
PATHOLOGISTS *See* Physicians
The **patience** of Maigret. See Simenon, G. A man's head
The **patience** of rivers. Freda, J.
The **patient**. Palmer, M.
The **patient's** eyes. Pirie, D.
Patriot games. Clancy, T.
Patriot hearts. Hambly, B.

PATRIOTISM
Doyle, R. A star called Henry
Forester, C. S. The last nine days of the Bismarck
Hale, E. E. The man without a country
Mishima, Y. Runaway horses
Pattern recognition. Gibson, W.
PAUL, THE APOSTLE, SAINT
  About
  Asch, S. The Apostle
Paul of Dune. Herbert, B.
Paula Spencer. Doyle, R.
Pawn in frankincense. Dunnett, D.
The **pawnbroker**. Wallant, E. L.

PAWNBROKERS
Wallant, E. L. The pawnbroker

PAWNEE INDIANS
Coldsmith, D. Tallgrass
Payback. See Stark, R. The hunter
Peace. Bausch, R.
Peace breaks out. Knowles, J.

PEACE CORPS (U.S.)
Rosenberg, R. This is not civilization
The **peaceable** kingdom. De Hartog, J.
The **pearl**. Steinbeck, J.
  also in Steinbeck, J. Novels, 1942-1952
Pearl Cove. Lowell, E.
The **pearl** diver. Massey, S.

PEARL FISHING

Steinbeck, J. The pearl

PEARLS

Lowell, E. Pearl Cove
Steinbeck, J. The pearl

PEASANT LIFE

China

Buck, P. S. The good earth

Ireland

Uris, L. Trinity

Italy

Silone, I. Bread and wine

Russia

Sholokhov, M. A. The Don flows home to the sea

Sicily

Puzo, M. The Sicilian

Peder Victorious. Rølvaag, O. E.

PEDIATRICIANS See Physicians

Pegasus in space. McCaffrey, A.

PEKING (CHINA) See China—Beijing

The **pelican** brief. Grisham, J.

Pelle the conqueror: v1 Childhood. Andersen Nexø, M.

Pelle the conqueror: v2 Apprenticeship. Andersen Nexø, M.

Pemberley. Tennant, E.

Pen pals. Goldsmith, O.

The **penal** colony: stories and short pieces. Kafka, F.

Penguin book of gay short fiction. Entered in Part I under title

The **Penguin** book of lesbian short stories. Entered in Part I under title

Penguin classics [series]
Cooper, J. F. The Deerslayer

Penhallow. Heyer, G.

PENINSULAR WAR, 1807-1814

Cornwell, B. Sharpe's battle
Cornwell, B. Sharpe's Waterloo
Forester, C. S. Commodore Hornblower
Forester, C. S. Hornblower and the Hotspur
Forester, C. S. Lieutenant Hornblower
Forester, C. S. Ship of the line

Penmarric. Howatch, S.

Pennies on a dead woman's eyes. Muller, M.

PENNSYLVANIA

Brown, C. B. Edgar Huntly
Brown, C. B. Wieland
Caldwell, T. Testimony of two men
Dark, A. E. Think of England
Donohue, K. Angels of destruction
Haigh, J. Baker towers
Hijuelos, O. The fourteen sisters of Emilio Montez O'Brien
Hornby, N. Juliet, naked
King, S. Christine
King, S. From a Buick 8
Leebron, F. G. In the middle of all this
Meyer, C. Brown eyes blue
Meyer, P. American rust
Michener, J. A. The novel
O'Dell, T. Back roads
O'Dell, T. Coal Run
O'Dell, T. Sister mine
O'Hara, J. From the terrace
O'Hara, J. Ten North Frederick
O'Nan, S. Snow angels
Poyer, D. Thunder on the mountain
Russo, R. The straight man
Scott, R. Follow me
Smiley, J. Good faith
Swann, M. Flower children
Updike, J. The centaur
Updike, J. Rabbit Angstrom
Updike, J. Rabbit at rest
Updike, J. Rabbit is rich
Updike, J. Rabbit redux
Updike, J. Rabbit, run
Wharton, W. Birdy

18th century

De Hartog, J. The peaceable kingdom

Larsen, D. The white
Liss, D. The whiskey rebels

19th century

Jakes, J. Heaven and hell
Jakes, J. Love and war
Jakes, J. North and South

Frontier and pioneer life

See Frontier and pioneer life—Pennsylvania

Philadelphia

Brown, C. B. Arthur Mervyn
De los Santos, M. Belong to me
De los Santos, M. Love walked in
Dunn, S. The big love
Durham, D. A. A walk through darkness
Fulmer, D. The blue door
Gallagher, S. The kingdom of bones
Goodis, D. Down there
Lashner, W. A killer's kiss
Liss, D. The whiskey rebels
McKinney-Whetstone, D. Leaving Cecil Street
McKinney-Whetstone, D. Tempest rising
Morrow, J. The last witchfinder
Scott, A. Calpurnia
Scottoline, L. Dead ringer
Scottoline, L. Legal tender
Scottoline, L. Mistaken identity
Scottoline, L. Rough justice
Scottoline, L. The vendetta defense
Weiner, J. Certain girls
Weiner, J. Good in bed
Weiner, J. Little earthquakes
Wideman, J. E. The cattle killing
Wideman, J. E. Philadelphia fire
Wideman, J. E. Two cities

Pittsburgh

Wideman, J. E. Two cities

The **penny** wedding. Stirling, J.

Pentecost Alley. Perry, A.

Peony in love. See, L.

People like us. Dunne, D.

People of Darkness. Hillerman, T.
also in Hillerman, T. The Jim Chee mysteries

People of the book. Brooks, G.

People of the masks. Gear, K. O.

People of the mist. Gear, K. O.

People of the owl. Gear, K. O.

People of the thunder. Gear, W. M.

The **people** on Privilege Hill and other stories. Gardam, J.

The **people's** act of love. Meek, J.

Perchance to dream. Parker, R. B.

Perdido Street Station. Miéville, C.

Père Goriot (Old Goriot). Balzac, H. d.

Perelandra. Lewis, C. S.

The **Perez** family. Bell, C.

A **perfect** arrangement. Berne, S.

Perfect Harmony. Wood, B.

Perfect life. Shattuck, J.

The **perfect** man. Murr, N.

A **perfect** spy. Le Carré, J.

A **perfect** stranger. Robinson, R.

Perfidia. Rossner, J.

The **perfidious** parrot. Van de Wetering, J.

PERFORMANCE ART

DeLillo, D. Falling man
Nooteboom, C. Lost paradise

PERFORMERS See Entertainers

Perfume: the story of a murderer. Süskind, P.

PERFUMES

Faber, M. The crimson petal and the white

PERIODICALS

Bushnell, C. Lipstick jungle
Dolan, H. Bad things happen
Mallon, T. Bandbox

PERSECUTION

See also Atrocities; Jews—Persecutions
Vallgren, C.-J. The horrific sufferings of the mind-reading monster Hercules Barefoot

PERSIA See Iran

The **Persian** boy. Renault, M.
The **Persian** Pickle Club. Dallas, S.
The **persistence** of vision. Varley, J.
   In The Hugo winners p459-507
A **person** of interest. Choi, S.
Person of interest. Schwegel, T.

PERSONAL BEAUTY
Maguire, G. Confessions of an ugly stepsister
Personal days. Park, E.
Personal injuries. Turow, S.
Personal recollections of Joan of Arc. Twain, M.
   also in Twain, M. Historical romances

PERSONALITY
Baxter, C. The soul thief
Dick, P. K. Flow my tears, the policeman said
Ludlum, R. The Bourne identity
Ludlum, R. The Bourne supremacy
McCarthy, T. Remainder
Moon, E. The speed of dark
Theroux, P. Doctor DeMarr
Theroux, P. Doctor Slaughter
Tyler, A. Morgan's passing

PERSONALITY DISORDERS
   See also Dual personality; Insane, Criminal and dangerous
Conroy, P. The prince of tides
Faulks, S. Engleby
Levenkron, S. The best little girl in the world
Percy, W. Lancelot
Rendell, R. A sight for sore eyes
Thomas, D. M. The white hotel
Unsworth, B. Losing Nelson
Persuader. Child, L.
Persuasion. Austen, J.

PERU
Redfield, J. The celestine prophecy
Vargas Llosa, M. Captain Pantoja and the Special Service
Vargas Llosa, M. Death in the Andes

18th century
Wilder, T. The bridge of San Luis Rey

Army—Officers
Vargas Llosa, M. Captain Pantoja and the Special Service

Lima
Vargas Llosa, M. Aunt Julia and the scriptwriter
Vargas Llosa, M. The notebooks of Don Rigoberto
Wilder, T. The bridge of San Luis Rey
The **pesthouse**. Crace, J.
Pet sematary. King, S.

PETIT, PHILIPPE, 1949-
About
McCann, C. Let the great world spin

PETRE, ROBERT PETRE, BARON, 1689-1713
About
Gee, S. The scandal of the season

PETROLEUM INDUSTRY
Cussler, C. Valhalla rising
Estleman, L. D. Gas City
Ferber, E. Cimarron
Furst, A. Blood of victory
McMurtry, L. Texasville
Patterson, R. N. Eclipse
Poyer, D. Thunder on the mountain
Unsworth, B. Land of marvels
Wells, K. Crawfish mountain
Petropolis. Ulinich, A.
The **pets**. Bragi Ólafsson
Pharaoh. Essex, K.

PHARISEES
Asch, S. The Nazarene

PHARMACEUTICAL INDUSTRY
Le Carré, J. The constant gardener
Palmer, M. Miracle cure
Preston, D. The codex
Reed, B. The choice
Wood, B. Perfect Harmony

PHARMACISTS
   See also Medicines, Patent, proprietary, etc.
Amado, J. Dona Flor and her two husbands

Cather, W. Shadows on the rock
Hearon, S. Year of the dog
McCullers, C. Clock without hands
Redhill, M. Consolation
Pharmakon. Wittenborn, D.
PHILADELPHIA (PA.) *See* Pennsylvania—Philadelphia
Philadelphia fire. Wideman, J. E.
PHILANTHROPY *See* Endowments

PHILIPPINES
Manila
Holthe, T. U. When the elephants dance

PHILOSOPHERS
Hellenga, R. Philosophy made simple
Morrow, J. The philosopher's apprentice
Murdoch, I. The philosopher's pupil
The **philosopher's** apprentice. Morrow, J.
The **philosopher's** pupil. Murdoch, I.

PHILOSOPHICAL NOVELS
Aira, C. An afternoon in the life of a landscape painter
Amis, M. House of meetings
Amis, M. Time's arrow
Barker, P. The eye in the door
Barker, P. The ghost road
Barker, P. Regeneration
Barnes, J. A history of the world in 10½ chapters
Beauvoir, S. d. The mandarins
Bellow, S. Henderson the rain king
Bellow, S. Herzog
Bellow, S. Mr. Sammler's planet
Bernhard, T. Frost
Brooks, G. Year of wonders
Bulgakov, M. A. The master and Margarita
Busch, F. The night inspector
Byatt, A. S. Morpho Eugenia
Calvino, I. If on a winter's night a traveler
Calvino, I. Mr. Palomar
Camus, A. The fall
Cervantes Saavedra, M. d. The colloquy of the dogs
Cervantes Saavedra, M. d. Man of glass
Coetzee, J. M. Age of iron
Coetzee, J. M. Elizabeth Costello
Coetzee, J. M. Foe
Cooley, M. The archivist
Crace, J. Being dead
Crumey, A. Mr. Mee
Cunningham, M. Specimen days
Darnton, J. Mind catcher
Davies, R. The cunning man
Davies, R. The rebel angels
DeLillo, D. The body artist
DeLillo, D. The names
Doctorow, E. L. City of God
Doctorow, E. L. The waterworks
Dostoyevsky, F. Notes from underground
Drabble, M. The witch of Exmoor
Eco, U. Baudolino
Eco, U. The island of the day before
Endō, S. Deep river
Esterházy, P. Celestial harmonies
Fuentes, C. The campaign
Gaddis, W. Agapé agape
Gaddis, W. The recognitions
Gao Xingjian. Soul mountain
García Márquez, G. The general and his labyrinth
Glavinic, T. Night work
Golding, W. Close quarters
Golding, W. Fire down below
Golding, W. The inheritors
Golding, W. Rites of passage
Grass, G. Crabwalk
Greene, G. Monsignor Quixote
Guterson, D. East of the mountains
Guterson, D. The other
Handke, P. Crossing the Sierra de Gredos
Hansen, E. F. Tales of protection
Hansen, R. Atticus
Hansen, R. Mariette in ecstasy
Harrar, G. The spinning man
Harrison, J. The English major
Hazzard, S. The great fire
Helprin, M. A soldier of the great war

PHYSICALLY HANDICAPPED—*Continued*
Rendell, R. Live flesh
Reynolds, S. A gracious plenty
Stewart, M. Nine coaches waiting
Trumbo, D. Johnny got his gun

PHYSICALLY HANDICAPPED CHILDREN
Graver, E. Awake
Koontz, D. R. One door away from heaven
Phillips, J. A. Lark and Termite

PHYSICIANS
See also Psychiatrists; Surgeons; Veterinarians; Women physicians
Amis, M. Time's arrow
Aslam, N. The wasted vigil
Balzac, H. d. The country doctor
Brown, C. The hatbox baby
Caldwell, T. Dear and glorious physician
Caldwell, T. Testimony of two men
Camus, A. The plague
Céline, L.-F. Journey to the end of the night
Chekhov, A. P. The duel
Clark, M. H. The cradle will fall
Cook, R. Coma
Cook, R. Crisis
Cook, R. Godplayer
Cook, R. Marker
Cook, R. Seizure
Cook, T. H. Breakheart Hill
Cronin, A. J. The citadel
Darnton, J. Mind catcher
Davies, R. The cunning man
De Bernières, L. Corelli's mandolin
De los Santos, M. Belong to me
Doctorow, E. L. The waterworks
Eliot, G. Middlemarch
Faulkner, W. If I forget thee, Jerusalem
Flaubert, G. Madame Bovary
Fleming, I. Doctor No
García Márquez, G. Leaf storm
Gibbons, K. On the occasion of my last afternoon
Gray, A. Poor things
Greene, G. The honorary consul
Grøndahl, J. C. Lucca
Ha Jin. Waiting
Hambly, B. Days of the dead
Hambly, B. Dead water
Hambly, B. Graveyard dust
Hambly, B. Sold down the river
Hambly, B. Die upon a kiss
Hambly, B. Wet grave
Hamilton, J. When Madeline was young
Holt, V. Secret for a nightingale
Hooker, R. MASH
Huyler, F. The laws of invisible things
Iles, G. Black cross
Iles, G. Third degree
Iles, G. Turning angel
Irving, J. The cider house rules
Irving, J. A son of the circus
James, H. Lady Barberina
Khoury, E. Gate of the sun
Lewis, S. Arrowsmith
MacLean, A. Ice Station Zebra
Margolin, P. Wild justice
Martin, V. Mary Reilly
Martini, S. P. The jury
Maugham, W. S. Of human bondage
McEwan, I. Saturday
McPhee, J. No ordinary matter
Michener, J. A. Recessional
Neugeboren, J. 1940
O'Brien, D. The contract surgeon
Ondaatje, M. Anil's ghost
Palmer, M. Miracle cure
Palmer, M. The society
Pasternak, B. L. Doctor Zhivago
Patterson, K. Consumption
Plain, B. Random winds
Potok, C. The war doctor
Powers, R. Operation wandering soul
Read, Miss. Thrush Green
Reed, B. The indictment
Reich, C. Rules of deception

Remarque, E. M. Arch of triumph
Reuss, F. Mohr
Rosten, L. Captain Newman, M.D.
Rush, N. Mortals
Sabatini, R. Captain Blood
Sanders, L. The sixth commandment
Shreve, A. Fortune's Rocks
Sparks, N. Nights in Rodanthe
Steel, D. The house on Hope Street
Stevenson, R. L. The strange case of Dr. Jekyll and Mr. Hyde
Taylor, R. L. The travels of Jaimie McPheeters
Theroux, P. Doctor DeMarr
Trevanian. The summer of Katya
Trollope, A. Doctor Thorne
Unsworth, B. Sacred hunger
Verghese, A. Cutting for stone
Vine, B. The blood doctor
Wallace, I. The prize
Waters, S. The little stranger
Wilson, F. P. Deep as the marrow
Yarbrough, S. The end of California

PHYSICISTS
Benford, G. Timescape
Bock, D. The ash garden
Flynn, M. Eifelheim
Hofmann, G. Lichtenberg and the little flower girl
Le Guin, U. K. The dispossessed
McMahon, T. A. Principles of American nuclear chemistry
Preston, D. Blasphemy
Scholz, C. Radiance
Snow, C. P. The new men
Somoza, J. C. Zig Zag
Strieber, W. The forbidden zone
Wallace, I. The prize
Wouk, H. A hole in Texas
The **physick** book of Deliverance Dane. Howe, K.

PHYSICS
Kehlmann, D. Measuring the world

PHYSIOLOGICAL PSYCHOLOGY
Keyes, D. Flowers for Algernon

PIANISTS
Bernhard, T. The loser
Docx, E. Pravda
Galloway, J. Clara
Goodis, D. Down there
Hambly, B. A free man of color
Hambly, B. Die upon a kiss
Hamilton, J. Disobedience
Hernández, F. Around the time of Clemente Colling
Hoffman, E. Appassionata
Ishiguro, K. The unconsoled
L'Engle, M. A severed wasp
Makine, A. Music of a life
Romano-Lax, A. The Spanish bow
The **piano** man's daughter. Findley, T.
The **piano** teacher. Lee, J. Y. K.
The **piano** tuner. Mason, D.

PIANO TUNERS
Mason, D. The piano tuner
The **piazza** tales. Melville, H.
    In Melville, H. Pierre; or, The ambiguities, Israel Potter: his fifty years of exile, The piazza tales, The confidence-man: his masquerade, Uncollected prose, Billy Budd, Sailor: (an inside narrative)

PICARESQUE NOVELS
See also Adventure
Adamson, G. The outlander
Barth, J. The sot-weed factor
Bellow, S. The adventures of Augie March
Berger, T. Little Big Man
Bolaño, R. The savage detectives
Brown, J. D. Addie Pray
Cervantes Saavedra, M. d. Don Quixote de la Mancha
Cervantes Saavedra, M. d. Rinconete and Cortadillo
Charyn, J. Johnny One-Eye
Crace, J. The pesthouse
Defoe, D. Moll Flanders
Dexter, P. Spooner
Dickens, C. The posthumous papers of the Pickwick Club
Doctorow, E. L. Billy Bathgate

POLICE—Miami (Fla.)—*Continued*
Hoffman, J. Retribution
Leonard, E. Glitz

Michigan

Finder, J. Company man

Minnesota

Hoag, T. Dust to dust
Hoag, T. Night sins
Tracy, P. J. Monkeewrench

Mississippi

Logan, C. South of Shiloh

Nevada

King, S. Desperation

New Jersey

Price, R. Clockers
Price, R. Freedomland
Price, R. Samaritan
Rosenfelt, D. Don't tell a soul

New Orleans (La.)

Turner, F. W. Redemption

New York (N.Y.)

Carcaterra, L. Apaches
Carr, C. The alienist
Caunitz, W. J. Chains of command
Caunitz, W. J. One Police Plaza
Chazin, S. Flashover
Daley, R. Wall of brass
Dee, E. The con man's daughter
DeMille, N. The lion's game
DeMille, N. Plum Island
DeMille, N. Wild fire
Doctorow, E. L. The waterworks
Fairstein, L. The bone vault
Fairstein, L. Entombed
Goodis, D. Nightfall
Grant, M. Officer down
Hunter, E. Candyland
Lustbader, E. V. Black Blade
Preston, D. Reliquary
Price, R. Lush life
Quindlen, A. Black and blue
Sanders, L. The first deadly sin
Sanders, L. The second deadly sin
Sanders, L. The third deadly sin
Standiford, L. Black Mountain
Strieber, W. The Wolfen
Tanenbaum, R. Falsely accused
Tanenbaum, R. Reversible error
Uhnak, D. Codes of betrayal
Uhnak, D. The investigation
Uhnak, D. Victims

New York (State)

Mills, M. Amagansett
O'Connell, C. Judas child

North Carolina

Betts, D. Souls raised from the dead

Oklahoma

Hunter, S. Dirty white boys

Paris (France)

Forsyth, F. The day of the jackal

Pennsylvania

Constantine, K. C. Saving room for dessert
King, S. From a Buick 8

Philadelphia (Pa.)

Scottoline, L. Legal tender
Scottoline, L. Mistaken identity

Portland (Ore.)

Cain, C. Heartsick
Perry, T. Nightlife

San Diego (Calif.)

Parker, T. J. Cold pursuit
Parker, T. J. The fallen

Wambaugh, J. Floaters

San Francisco (Calif.)

Dorst, D. Alive in Necropolis
Gardiner, M. The Dirty Secrets Club
Lescroart, J. T. The first law
Lescroart, J. T. Guilt
Lescroart, J. T. The hearing
Lescroart, J. T. The second chair
Patterson, J. 1st to die

Seville (Spain)

Wilson, R. The blind man of Seville
Wilson, R. The hidden assassins

South Africa

Paton, A. Too late the phalarope

Texas

Lansdale, J. R. The bottoms
Lansdale, J. R. Sunset and sawdust

Tokyo (Japan)

Lee, D. Country of origin
Peace, D. Tokyo year zero

Virginia

Pearson, T. R. Cry me a river

Washington (D.C.)

Patterson, J. Four blind mice
Patterson, J. London bridges
Patterson, J. Roses are red
Pelecanos, G. P. The night gardener
Pelecanos, G. P. Right as rain

Washington (State)

Pearson, R. The angel maker
Pearson, R. The art of deception
Pearson, R. Beyond recognition
Pearson, R. The body of David Hayes
Pearson, R. The first victim
Pearson, R. Middle of nowhere
Pearson, R. No witnesses
Pearson, R. Undercurrents

Wisconsin

Tracy, P. J. Monkeewrench

POLICEWOMEN

Deaver, J. The bodies left behind
Deaver, J. Roadside crosses
Dolan, H. Bad things happen
Hayder, M. Ritual
Newton, C. Calumet City
Robb, J. D. Naked in death
Wolfe, I. A. The calling

POLIDORI, JOHN WILLIAM, 1795-1821
About
West, P. Lord Byron's doctor
Polikúshka. Tolstoy, L., graf
In Tolstoy, L., graf. The short novels of Tolstoy

POLIOMYELITIS
Berg, E. We are all welcome here

POLISH AMERICANS
Maillard, K. The clarinet polka
Political animal. Mizner, D.

POLITICAL CAMPAIGNS *See* Politics

POLITICAL CORRUPTION *See* Corruption (in politics)

POLITICAL CRIMES AND OFFENSES
See also Assassination; Political prisoners; Terrorism

POLITICAL DEFECTORS *See* Defectors

POLITICAL ETHICS
See also Power (Social sciences)
O'Connor, E. All in the family

POLITICAL INTRIGUE *See* International intrigue; Politics

POLITICAL PRISONERS
Connelly, K. The lizard cage
Haasse, H. S. In a dark wood wandering
Higgins, J. Day of judgment
Holland, T. The archivist's story
Kertész, I. Detective story

POLITICS—United States—1900—_Continued_
Higgins, G. V. A change of gravity
Klein, J. Primary colors
Knebel, F. Seven days in May
Lehrer, J. Purple dots
Lewis, S. It can't happen here
Mallon, T. Dewey defeats Truman
Mallon, T. Fellow travelers
Mizner, D. Political animal
Mortman, D. The lucky ones
Nersesian, A. The swing voter of Staten Island
O'Brien, T. In the Lake of the Woods
O'Connor, E. All in the family
O'Connor, E. The last hurrah
Patterson, R. N. No safe place
Patterson, R. N. Protect and defend
Roth, P. I married a communist
Roth, P. Our gang
Thomas, R. Ah, treachery!
Vidal, G. The golden age
Vidal, G. Hollywood
Vidal, G. Washington, D.C.
Vonnegut, K. Jailbird
Wallace, I. The man
West, N. A cool million
Woods, S. The run

West Indies

Naipaul, V. S. Guerrillas

POLLUTION

Benford, G. Timescape
Burnside, J. Glister
Cussler, C. Sahara
Oates, J. C. The falls

POLO, MARCO, 1254-1323?
About
Calvino, I. Invisible cities

POLYGAMY
See also Mormons and Mormonism
Ebershoff, D. The 19th wife

POLYNESIA
See also Pitcairn Island

POLYNESIANS
See also Maoris
Michener, J. A. Hawaii
Nordhoff, C. Pitcairn's Island

POMPEII (ANCIENT CITY)

Harris, R. Pompeii
Lytton, E. B. L., Baron. The last days of Pompeii
Pompeii. Harris, R.
The **Ponder** heart. Welty, E.
also in Welty, E. Complete novels
POOR _See_ Poverty
The **poor** mouth. O'Brien, F.
_In_ O'Brien, F. The complete novels
Poor things. Gray, A.
The **poorhouse** fair. Updike, J.
Pop! goes the weasel. Patterson, J.
POPE, ALEXANDER, 1688-1744
About
Gee, S. The scandal of the season

POPES

Greeley, A. M. White smoke
Martin, M. Vatican
Martin, M. Windswept House
West, M. L. The clowns of God
West, M. L. Lazarus
West, M. L. The shoes of the fisherman
Porno. Welsh, I.

PORNOGRAPHY

Faust, C. Money shot
Hoban, R. Angelica's Grotto
Rosenberg, N. T. Interest of justice
Welsh, I. Porno
Welsh, L. The cutting room
PORT-AU-PRINCE (HAITI) _See_ Haiti—Port-au-Prince
Port hazard. Estleman, L. D.
The **portable** Conrad. Conrad, J.
The **portable** Stephen Crane. Crane, S.

PORTLAND (OR.) _See_ Oregon—Portland
Portnoy's complaint. Roth, P.
also in Roth, P. Novels, 1967-1972
Portrait in sepia. Allende, I.
The **portrait** of a lady. James, H.
Portrait of an artist, as an old man. Heller, J.
Portrait of Jennie. Nathan, R.
Portrait of the artist as a young dog. Thomas, D.
_In_ Thomas, D. The collected stories p122-238
A **portrait** of the artist as a young man. Joyce, J.

PORTUGAL

Antunes, A. L. The inquisitors' manual
Cornwell, B. Sharpe's havoc

Rural life
L'Engle, M. The love letters

Lisbon
Saramago, J. The history of the siege of Lisbon
Zimler, R. The last kabbalist of Lisbon

PORTUGUESE

Japan
Endō, S. Silence
Poseidon's gold. Davis, L.
The **possessed.** Dostoyevsky, F.
Possessing the secret of joy. Walker, A.
POSSESSION, DEMONIAC _See_ Demoniac possession
Possession. Byatt, A. S.
The **possession** of Mr Cave. Haig, M.
The **possibility** of an island. Houellebecq, M.
The **post-birthday** world. Shriver, L.

POSTAL SERVICE
See also Air mail service
Brown, C. Lamb in love
Wright, R. Lawd today!
Postcards. Proulx, A.
Postcards from Berlin. Leroy, M.
Posthumous papers. See Barnard, R. Death of a literary widow
The **posthumous** papers of the Pickwick Club. Dickens, C.
The **postman** always rings twice. Cain, J. M.
_In_ Crime novels: American noir of the 1930s and 40s
_In_ Cain, J. M. The postman always rings twice, double indemnity, Mildred Pierce and selected stories
The **postman** always rings twice, double indemnity, Mildred Pierce and selected stories. Cain, J. M.
Postsingular. Rucker, R. v. B.
Postures. See Rhys, J. Quartet
POTATO FAMINE _See_ Famines
Potshot. Parker, R. B.
The **potter's** field. Peters, E.
Pound for pound. Toole, F. X.

POVERTY

Adiga, A. The white tiger
Allison, D. Bastard out of Carolina
Amirrezvani, A. The blood of flowers
Boyle, T. C. The tortilla curtain
Bragg, M. A son of war
Brown, L. Joe
Caldwell, E. Tobacco road
Chute, C. The Beans of Egypt, Maine
Cisneros, S. The house on Mango Street
Davenport, K. House of many gods
Dickens, C. Little Dorrit
Donoghue, E. Slammerkin
García, C. A handbook to luck
García Márquez, G. No one writes to the colonel
George, E. What came before he shot her
Hardy, T. Jude the obscure
Hijuelos, O. Empress of the splendid season
Hugo, V. Les misérables
Hurston, Z. N. Seraph on the Suwanee
Laskas, G. M. The midwife's tale
Lawson, M. Crow Lake
Maḥfūẓ, N. Children of the alley
Maḥfūẓ, N. Midaq Alley
Mason, D. A far country
Melville, H. Israel Potter
Morris, M. M. The lost mother
Morris, M. M. Songs in ordinary time
Morrison, T. The bluest eye
Morrison, T. Sula

PRESIDENTS—United States—Election—*Continued*
Patterson, R. N. No safe place
Westlake, D. E. Put a lid on it
The **president's** daughter. Higgins, J.
PRESLEY, ELVIS, 1935-1977
About
Abani, C. GraceLand
Buckley, W. F. Elvis in the morning
PRESLEY, PRISCILLA BEAULIEU
About
Buckley, W. F. Elvis in the morning
PRESTER JOHN
About
Eco, U. Baudolino
Presumed innocent. Turow, S.
The **pretender**. See Stevenson, J. The shadow king
Prey. Crichton, M.
Prey dancing. Gash, J.
The **price** of blood. Hughes, D.
The **price** of guilt. Yorke, M.
Pride and prejudice. Austen, J.
Pride of lions. Llywelyn, M.
PRIESTS *See* Anglican and Episcopal clergy; Catholic priests;
Clergy
PRIESTS, CATHOLIC *See* Catholic priests
Primal fear. Diehl, W.
Primary colors. Klein, J.
Primary inversion. Asaro, C.

PRIMATOLOGISTS
Wesselmann, D. L. Captivity
Prime cut. Davidson, D. M.
The **prime** minister. Trollope, A.
The **prime** minister [abridged] Trollope, A.
In Trollope, A. The Pallisers p325-85

PRIME MINISTERS
Harris, R. The ghost
Townsend, S. Number 10
The **prime** of Miss Jean Brodie. Spark, M.
Prime witness. Martini, S. P.
PRIMITIVE CHRISTIANITY *See* Church history—Primitive
and early church
Primitive people. Prose, F.
PRIMITIVE RELIGION *See* Religion
The **prince** and the pauper. Twain, M.
In Twain, M. Historical romances
Prince of chaos. Zelazny, R.
Prince of Fire. Silva, D.
The **prince** of tides. Conroy, P.

PRINCES
See also Princesses
The **princes** of Ireland. Rutherfurd, E.
The **princess** of Burundi. Eriksson, K.

PRINCESSES
Holland, C. The angel and the sword
Lee, T. White as snow
Mehta, G. Raj
Mishima, Y. The Temple of Dawn
Sherwood, F. Night of sorrows
PRINCETON UNIVERSITY
Caldwell, I. The rule of four
Principles of American nuclear chemistry. McMahon, T. A.
PRINE, SARAH AGNES
About
Turner, N. E. These is my words

PRINTERS AND PRINTING
Lovric, M. The floating book
Twain, M. No. 44, The mysterious stranger
PRINTING *See* Printers and printing
PRISON CAMPS *See* World War, 1939-1945—Prisoners and
prisons
PRISON ESCAPES *See* Escapes
The **prisoner** of Zenda. Hope, A.
PRISONERS, POLITICAL *See* Political prisoners
PRISONERS AND PRISONS
See also Ex-convicts; Political prisoners; Prisoners of war
Egan, J. The keep
Eskridge, K. Solitaire

Hale, E. E. The man without a country
Hope, A. The prisoner of Zenda
Koestler, A. Darkness at noon
London, J. The star rover
Miéville, C. The scar
Argentina
Puig, M. Kiss of the spider woman
Australia
Flanagan, R. Gould's book of fish
Grenville, K. The lieutenant
McCullough, C. Morgan's run
China
Pattison, E. The skull mantra
England
Defoe, D. Moll Flanders
Dickens, C. Little Dorrit
Dickens, C. The posthumous papers of the Pickwick Club
Fyfield, F. Undercurrents
Walters, M. The sculptress
France
Dumas, A. The Count of Monte Cristo
Iran
Sofer, D. The Septembers of Shiraz
Northern Ireland
Dean, L. This human season
Russia
See also Prisoners and prisons—Siberia (Russia)
Furnivall, K. The red scarf
Solzhenitsyn, A. In the first circle
Siberia (Russia)
Amis, M. House of meetings
Solzhenitsyn, A. One day in the life of Ivan Denisovich
United States
Baldwin, J. If Beale Street could talk
Cain, C. Heartsick
Cheever, J. Falconer
Clark, M. The legal limit
Faulkner, W. If I forget thee, Jerusalem
Fitch, J. White oleander
Gaines, E. J. A lesson before dying
Goldsmith, O. Pen pals
Grisham, J. The brethren
Grisham, J. The chamber
Himes, C. Yesterday will make you cry
Huneven, M. Blame
Hunter, S. Pale horse coming
Kantor, M. Andersonville
Katzenbach, J. Just cause
King, S. Rita Hayworth and Shawshank redemption
Lowenthal, M. Charity girl
Mailer, N. The executioner's song
Moore, S. The big girls
O'Nan, S. The good wife
Picoult, J. Change of heart
Quindlen, A. One true thing
Siegel, J. Derailed
Turow, S. Reversible errors
Vonnegut, K. Jailbird
Woods, S. Heat
Prisoner's dilemma. Powers, R.
PRISONERS OF WAR
See also Concentration camps; World War, 1939-1945—
Prisoners and prisons
Ha Jin. War trash
Kantor, M. Andersonville
Novakovich, J. April Fool's Day
Vonnegut, K. Slaughterhouse-five
Prisoners of war. Yarbrough, S.
PRISONS *See* Prisoners and prisons
Private arrangements. Thomas, S.
PRIVATE DETECTIVES *See* Detectives, Private
PRIVATE EYE STORIES *See* Detectives, Private; Mystery and
detective stories
Private eyes. Kellerman, J.
The **private** lives of Pippa Lee. Miller, R.

PSYCHOLOGICAL NOVELS

Ablow, K. R. Compulsion
Abu-Jaber, D. Origin
Adams, P. The sister
Aira, C. An afternoon in the life of a landscape painter
Amis, M. House of meetings
Amis, M. Time's arrow
Antunes, A. L. The inquisitors' manual
Atwood, M. Alias Grace
Atwood, M. Cat's eye
Atwood, M. Life before man
Auster, P. Invisible
Auster, P. Oracle night
Bacon, C. Split estate
Bahr, H. The Judas Field
Bainbridge, B. The birthday boys
Bambara, T. C. The salt eaters
Banks, R. Affliction
Banks, R. Cloudsplitter
Barker, P. Double vision
Barker, P. The eye in the door
Barker, P. The ghost road
Barker, P. Regeneration
Barnard, R. Out of the blackout
Barnes, D. Nightwood
Barry, B. The lace reader
Baxter, C. The soul thief
Beattie, A. My life, starring Dara Falcon
Beattie, A. Picturing Will
Bellow, S. Dangling man
Bellow, S. The victim
Berlinski, M. Fieldwork
Bernhard, T. Frost
Bock, C. Beautiful children
Bock, D. The ash garden
Bolaño, R. The skating rink
Brookner, A. Brief lives
Brown, R. Before and after
Brown, R. Tender mercies
Brownrigg, S. The delivery room
Caputo, P. Acts of faith
Carroll, J. Fault lines
Cartwright, J. The promise of happiness
Cheever, J. Falconer
Chenoweth, E. Hello goodbye
Clark, M. H. No place like home
Clark, M. H. Remember me
Clark, W. V. T. The Ox-bow incident
Cleave, C. Little Bee
Coben, H. Gone for good
Coetzee, J. M. Diary of a bad year
Coetzee, J. M. Disgrace
Coetzee, J. M. Slow man
Collins, M. Lost souls
Conrad, J. Lord Jim
Conroy, P. Beach music
Cook, T. H. The cloud of unknowing
Cook, T. H. The fate of Katherine Carr
Cook, T. H. Instruments of night
Cooley, M. The archivist
Cox, M. The glass of time
Crane, S. The red badge of courage
Cullin, M. Undersurface
Dark, A. E. Think of England
Darnton, J. Mind catcher
Davenport, K. House of many gods
Davidson, A. The gargoyle
Davies, P. H. The Welsh girl
Davis, K. The thin place
Dean, D. The madonnas of Leningrad
DeLillo, D. Falling man
Delinsky, B. The summer I dared
D'Erasmo, S. The sky below
Desai, K. The inheritance of loss
Dew, R. F. The evidence against her
Dew, R. F. The truth of the matter
Dick, P. K. The transmigration of Timothy Archer
Dick, P. K. Valis
Diehl, W. Primal fear
Diehl, W. Show of evil
Dixon, S. Interstate
Dostoyevsky, F. The brothers Karamazov
Dostoyevsky, F. Crime and punishment
Dostoyevsky, F. The idiot

Doyle, R. Paula Spencer
Doyle, R. The woman who walked into doors
Dreiser, T. An American tragedy
Dubus, A. The garden of last days
Dufossé, C. School's out
Duisberg, K. W. The good patient
Duncan, G. Death of an ordinary man
Egan, J. The keep
Ellis, B. E. Lunar Park
Eskridge, K. Solitaire
Eugenides, J. The virgin suicides
Evans, N. The horse whisperer
Everett, P. L. The water cure
Faulkner, W. The mansion
Faulks, S. Engleby
Ferrante, E. The lost daughter
Ferrante, E. Troubling love
Fielding, J. See Jane run
Findley, T. The piano man's daughter
Fitch, J. Paint it black
Flaubert, G. Madame Bovary
Flynn, G. Dark places
Flynn, G. Sharp objects
Foer, J. S. Extremely loud & incredibly close
Ford, F. M. The good soldier
Forster, E. M. A passage to India
Frame, J. Towards another summer
Freeling, N. One more river
Freemantle, B. Mind/reader
French, N. Beneath the skin
French, N. Land of the living
French, T. In the woods
French, T. The likeness
Freudenberger, N. The dissident
Fugard, L. Skinner's drift
Fyfield, F. Blind date
Fyfield, F. Undercurrents
Gaddis, W. Agapé agape
Gaitskill, M. Veronica
Galchen, R. Atmospheric disturbances
García Márquez, G. Chronicle of a death foretold
García Márquez, G. The general and his labyrinth
Gardam, J. Old Filth
Gardam, J. The queen of the tambourine
Gibbons, K. Sights unseen
Gide, A. The counterfeiters (Les faux-monnayeurs)
Gide, A. The immoralist
Godden, R. Black Narcissus
Godwin, G. The finishing school
Golding, W. Darkness visible
Goodman, C. The drowning tree
Goodman, C. The seduction of water
Gordimer, N. None to accompany me
Gordimer, N. The pickup
Gottlieb, E. Now you see him
Gowdy, B. Helpless
Grass, G. The tin drum
Green, G. D. The juror
Green, G. D. Ravens
Greene, G. Brighton rock
Greene, G. The end of the affair
Greer, A. S. The path of minor planets
Greer, A. S. The story of a marriage
Grenville, K. The secret river
Gresham, W. L. Nightmare alley
Grippando, J. The informant
Grossman, L. The magicians
Guterson, D. The other
Guterson, D. Our Lady of the Forest
Haig, M. The possession of Mr Cave
Haigh, J. The condition
Hamilton, J. Disobedience
Hamilton, J. A map of the world
Hamilton, J. When Madeline was young
Hamilton-Paterson, J. Gerontius
Handke, P. The left-handed woman
Handke, P. Repetition
Hannah, S. Little face
Hannah, S. The wrong mother
Hansen, R. Mariette in ecstasy
Harding, P. Tinkers
Hardy, T. Jude the obscure
Hardy, T. The return of the native
Harrar, G. The spinning man

PSYCHOLOGICAL NOVELS—*Continued*

McPhee, M. L'America
Melnyczuk, A. The house of widows
Meloy, M. Liars and saints
Mendelson, C. Morningside Heights
Meno, J. The boy detective fails
Meredith, G. The ordeal of Richard Feverel
Miller, R. The private lives of Pippa Lee
Miller, S. The distinguished guest
Miller, S. Family pictures
Miller, S. For love
Miller, S. Lost in the forest
Millet, L. How the dead dream
Millhauser, S. Martin Dressler
Minot, E. The Brambles
Minot, S. Folly
Mishima, Y. Spring snow
Mishima, Y. The temple of the golden pavilion
Mitchard, J. The deep end of the ocean
Mitchard, J. No time to wave goodbye
Miyamoto, T. Kinshu: Autumn brocade
Moore, B. The statement
Morley, I. Come Sunday
Morris, K. L. The dart league king
Morris, M. M. The lost mother
Morrison, T. Jazz
Morrison, T. Love
Moses, K. Wintering
Mosley, W. Fortunate son
Muñoz Molina, A. In her absence
Murdoch, I. The bell
Murdoch, I. The philosopher's pupil
Murdoch, I. The sea, the sea
Murphy, M. Darkness falls
Murray, S. Forgery
Naipaul, V. S. Guerrillas
Naipaul, V. S. Half a life
Naipaul, V. S. Magic seeds
Naylor, P. R. After
Neugeboren, J. 1940
Nin, A. Cities of the interior
Norman, H. The museum guard
Nunez, E. Anna in-between
Nunez, S. The last of her kind
Oates, J. C. Black girl/White girl
Oates, J. C. Black water
Oates, J. C. Broke heart blues
Oates, J. C. The gravedigger's daughter
Oates, J. C. Missing mom
Oates, J. C. Rape
Oates, J. C. Them
Oates, J. C. We were the Mulvaneys
O'Brien, E. In the forest
O'Brien, T. In the Lake of the Woods
O'Connell, C. Judas child
O'Connell, J. The resurrectionist
O'Dell, T. Back roads
Ōe, K. The pinch runner memorandum
Ōe, K. A quiet life
O'Farrell, M. The vanishing act of Esme Lennox
O'Hara, J. Appointment in Samarra
O'Hara, J. From the terrace
Okuizumi, H. The stones cry out
Ólafur Jóhann Ólafsson. The journey home
O'Nan, S. The names of the dead
O'Nan, S. Songs for the missing
Ondaatje, M. Anil's ghost
Ondaatje, M. The English patient
Oster, C. My big apartment
Oyeyemi, H. The opposite house
Oz, A. Fima
Palahniuk, C. Diary
Pamuk, O. The museum of innocence
Parker, T. J. California girl
Parkhurst, C. The dogs of Babel
Parks, T. Cleaver
Parks, T. Destiny
Parks, T. Rapids
Parsons, J. Mary, Mary
Patterson, J. Hide & seek
Pérez Galdós, B. Torquemada
Pérez-Reverte, A. The painter of battles
Perlman, E. Seven types of ambiguity
Petterson, P. In the wake

Phillips, A. The song is you
Plain, B. Looking back
Pohl, F. Gateway
Powell, P. Edisto revisited
Price, R. The good priest's son
Pronzini, B. The crimes of Jordan Wise
Pronzini, B. In an evil time
Proust, M. The captive
Proust, M. The captive [and] The fugitive
Proust, M. The fugitive [variant title: The sweet cheat gone]
Proust, M. The Guermantes way
Proust, M. Remembrance of things past
Proust, M. Sodom and Gomorrah
Proust, M. Swann's way
Proust, M. Time regained [variant title: The past recaptured]
Proust, M. Within a budding grove
Purdy, J. In a shallow grave
Pywell, S. L. What happened to Henry
Qashu, S. Dancing Arabs
Raban, J. Surveillance
Remarque, E. M. The road back
Rendell, R. Adam and Eve and Pinch me
Rendell, R. The bridesmaid
Rendell, R. The crocodile bird
Rendell, R. The face of trespass
Rendell, R. Going wrong
Rendell, R. Heartstones
Rendell, R. A judgment in stone
Rendell, R. The keys to the street
Rendell, R. Live flesh
Rendell, R. A sight for sore eyes
Rendell, R. Thirteen steps down
Rendell, R. The tree of hands
Rendell, R. The water's lovely
Restrepo, L. Delirium
Reuss, F. Henry of Atlantic City
Reuss, F. The wasties
Reynolds, M. The Starlite Drive-in
Reynolds, S. A gracious plenty
Rice, L. The geometry of sisters
Rinehart, S. Built in a day
Robards, K. Ghost moon
Robinson, L. Water dogs
Robinson, P. The first cut
Robinson, R. Sweetwater
Rølvaag, O. E. Giants in the earth
Rosales, G. The halfway house
Rossner, J. August
Rossner, J. Perfidia
Roth, P. The humbling
Roth, P. When she was good
Runcie, J. Canvey Island
Saint-Exupéry, A. d. Night flight
Sakamoto, K. One hundred million hearts
Salinger, J. D. The catcher in the rye
Sanders, L. The first deadly sin
Sanders, L. The third deadly sin
Sarton, M. A reckoning
Saul, J. The right hand of evil
Schupack, D. The boy on the bus
Schwartz, J. B. Reservation Road
Schwartz, L. S. The writing on the wall
Sebold, A. The almost moon
Sebold, A. The lovely bones
Self, W. Dorian
Shakespeare, N. Snowleg
Shaley, T. Husband and wife
Shapiro, D. Black & white
Shaw, I. Evening in Byzantium
Shepard, L. Softspoken
Shields, C. Unless
Shreve, A. Body surfing
Shreve, A. Eden Close
Shreve, A. Light on snow
Shreve, A. The pilot's wife
Shreve, A. The weight of water
Shreve, S. R. A student of living things
Shriver, L. We need to talk about Kevin
Siegel, J. Derailed
Singer, I. B. Shadows on the Hudson
Smith, A. The accidental
Smith, L. The last girls
Snow, C. P. Homecoming
Stamm, P. On a day like this

PUBS *See* Hotels, taverns, etc.
Pudd'nhead Wilson; Twain, M.
 also in Twain, M. Mississippi writings
PUGILISM *See* Boxing

PUNS
 Farmer, P. J. Riders of the purple wage
The **pupil**. James, H.
 In James, H. Complete stories, 1884-1891
 In James, H. The complete tales of Henry James
 In James, H. Short novels of Henry James p355-405
 In James, H. What Maisie knew, In the cage, The pupil
The **puppet** masters. Heinlein, R. A.

PUPPETS AND PUPPET PLAYS
 Tyler, A. Morgan's passing
The **pure** in heart. Hill, S.

PURITANISM
 Seton, A. The Winthrop woman

PURITANS
 Condé, M. I, Tituba, black witch of Salem
 Hawthorne, N. The House of the Seven Gables
 Hawthorne, N. The scarlet letter
Purity of blood. Pérez-Reverte, A.
Purple dots. Lehrer, J.
A **purple** place for dying. MacDonald, J. D.
A **purse** of coppers. O'Faoláin, S.
 In O'Faoláin, S. The collected stories of Seán O'Faoláin
 p163-319
Pursuit. Perry, T.
The **pursuit** of Alice Thrift. Lipman, E.
The **pursuit** of love. Mitford, N.
 In Mitford, N. The pursuit of love & Love in a cold climate
 p{1}-283
The **pursuit** of love & Love in a cold climate. Mitford, N.
Pushover. O'Donnell, L.
Put a lid on it. Westlake, D. E.
The **Puttermesser** papers. Ozick, C.

PUZO, MARIO, 1920-1999
Parodies, imitations, etc.
 Winegardner, M. The Godfather returns
The **puzzled** heart. Cross, A.
Pylon. Faulkner, W.
 also in Faulkner, W. Novels, 1930-1935
Pyro. Emerson, E. W.

PYTHAGORAS
About
 Goodman, C. The night villa

Q

"**Q**" is for quarry. Grafton, S.
QB VII. Uris, L.

QUADRIPLEGICS
 Brown, R. Tender mercies

QUADROONS *See* Mulattoes
The **quality** of mercy. Kellerman, F.
Quarantine. Crace, J.
Quarry. Pronzini, B.
Quartet. Rhys, J.
Quartet in autumn. Pym, B.
QUÉBEC (PROVINCE) *See* Canada—Québec (Province)
QUÉBEC (QUÉBEC) *See* Canada—Québec (Québec)
Queen Lucia. Benson, E. F.
 In Benson, E. F. Make way for Lucia p1-178
The **Queen** of Air and Darkness. Anderson, P.
 In The Hugo winners p143-90
The **Queen** of Air and Darkness. White, T. H.
 In White, T. H. The once and future king
The **Queen** of Bedlam. McCammon, R. R.
Queen of swords. Tarr, J.
Queen of the Amazons. Tarr, J.
The **queen** of the damned. Rice, A.
The **queen** of the tambourine. Gardam, J.
Queen of the underworld. Godwin, G.
The **queene's** Christmas. Harper, K.
Queenmaker. Edghill, I.

QUEENS
 See also Courts and courtiers

QUEENS (NEW YORK, N.Y.) *See* New York (N.Y.)—Queens
The **Queen's** bastard. Maxwell, R.
The **queen's** fool. Gregory, P.
The **queen's** gambit. Tevis, W. S.
The **queen's** man. Penman, S. K.

QUEENSLAND (AUSTRALIA) *See* Australia—Queensland
The **quest** for Saint Camber. Kurtz, K.
A **question** of attraction. Nicholls, D.
A **question** of belief. Yorke, M.
A **question** of blood. Rankin, I.
A **question** of upbringing. Powell, A.
 In Powell, A. A dance to the music of time
The **quiet** American. Greene, G.
A **quiet** flame. Kerr, P.
The **quiet** girl. Høeg, P.
A **quiet** life. Ōe, K.
Quiller Balalaika. Hall, A.
The **Quiller** memorandum. Hall, A.
Quiller Salamander. Hall, A.
Quiller solitaire. Hall, A.

QUILTS
 Dallas, S. The Persian Pickle Club
 Michaels, B. Stitches in time
 Otto, W. How to make an American quilt
The **quincunx**. Palliser, C.

QUINTUPLETS
 Mason, B. A. Feather crowns
QUISLINGS *See* World War, 1939-1945—Collaborationists
Quite a year for plums. White, B.
Quite honestly. Mortimer, J.
Quo Vadis. Sienkiewicz, H.

R

"**R**" is for ricochet. Grafton, S.

RABBIS
 Abraham, P. The romance reader
 Doctorow, E. L. City of God
 Hamill, P. Snow in August
 Kemelman, H. The day the rabbi resigned
 Kemelman, H. Friday the rabbi slept late
 Kemelman, H. Monday the rabbi took off
 Kemelman, H. One fine day the rabbi bought a cross
 Kemelman, H. Saturday the rabbi went hungry
 Kemelman, H. Sunday the rabbi stayed home
 Kemelman, H. Thursday the rabbi walked out
 Kemelman, H. Wednesday the rabbi got wet
 Littell, R. Vicious circle
 Potok, C. The promise
 Rosen, J. Joy comes in the morning
Rabbit Angstrom. Updike, J.
Rabbit at rest. Updike, J.
 also in Updike, J. Rabbit Angstrom
Rabbit is rich. Updike, J.
 also in Updike, J. Rabbit Angstrom
Rabbit redux. Updike, J.
 also in Updike, J. Rabbit Angstrom
Rabbit remembered. Updike, J.
 In Updike, J. Licks of love p177-359
Rabbit, run. Updike, J.
 also in Updike, J. Rabbit Angstrom

RABBITS
 Adams, R. Watership Down
Rabble in arms. Roberts, K. L.

RABIES
 King, S. Cujo
Race of scorpions. Dunnett, D.
RACE PROBLEMS *See* Race relations
RACE RELATIONS
 See also African Americans; African Americans—Relations with Jews; Antisemitism; Culture conflict; Interracial marriage; Miscegenation; Prejudices
 Beatty, P. Slumberland
 D'Souza, T. Whiteman
 Evaristo, B. Blonde roots
 Vassanji, M. G. The in-between world of Vikram Lall

RAPE—*Continued*
Rosenberg, N. T. Buried evidence
Rosenberg, N. T. Mitigating circumstances
Scott, P. The day of the scorpion
Scott, P. The jewel in the crown
Thayer, N. An act of love
Theroux, P. The elephant god
Traver, R. Anatomy of a murder
Turow, S. Limitations
Wolfe, T. A man in full
Yorke, M. Almost the truth
Rape. Oates, J. C.
Rapids. Parks, T.

RAPPE, VIRGINIA, 1895-1921
About
Atkins, A. Devil's garden
Raptor. Jennings, G.
Rapture. Minot, S.
A **rare** Benedictine. Peters, E.

RARE BOOKS
Pérez-Reverte, A. The Club Dumas
Rat run. Seymour, G.
Ratner's star. DeLillo, D.

RATS
Savage, S. Firmin

RAUBAL, GELI, 1908-1931
About
Hansen, R. Hitler's niece
Ravens. Green, G. D.
The **Ravenscar** dynasty. Bradford, B. T.
The **raw** shark texts. Hall, S.
Raymond Chandler. Chandler, R.
The **razor's** edge. Maugham, W. S.
RCAF *See* Canada. Royal Canadian Air Force
The **reader**. Schlink, B.
Reader, I married him. Roberts, M.
Reading in the dark. Deane, S.
The **real** cool killers. Himes, C.
In Crime novels: American noir of the 1950s

REAL ESTATE
See also Speculation
Ducker, B. Dizzying heights
Ford, R. Independence Day
Ford, R. The lay of the land
Hiaasen, C. Native tongue
Hiaasen, C. Sick puppy
Lennon, J. R. Castle
Medlicott, J. A. Gardens of Covington
Smiley, J. Good faith

REAL ESTATE BUSINESS
McCauley, S. Alternatives to sex
Millet, L. How the dead dream
The **real** life of Sebastian Knight. Nabokov, V. V.
In Nabokov, V. V. Novels and memoirs, 1941-1951
The **real** McCoy. Strauss, D.
REAL PROPERTY *See* Real estate
Reality and dreams. Spark, M.
The **reavers**. Fraser, G. M.
Rebecca. Du Maurier, Dame D.
Rebel. Cornwell, B.
The **rebel** angels. Davies, R.
REBELLIONS *See* Revolutions
The **rebels**. Kelton, E.
The **rebels** of Ireland. Rutherfurd, E.
Recalled to life. Hill, R.
Recessional. Michener, J. A.
A **recipe** for bees. Anderson-Dargatz, G.
Reckless abandon. Woods, S.
Reckless endangerment. Tanenbaum, R.
The **reckoning**. Long, J.
The **reckoning**. Penman, S. K.
A **reckoning**. Sarton, M.

RECLUSES
See also Hermits
Doctorow, E. L. Homer & Langley
The **recognitions**. Gaddis, W.

RECONSTRUCTION
See also United States—1865-1898
Mitchell, M. Gone with the wind
Smith, L. On Agate Hill

Twain, M. The gilded age
RECONSTRUCTION (1865-1876)
See also Ku Klux Klan

RECONSTRUCTION (1939-1951)
Sicily
Hersey, J. A bell for Adano
Reconstruction. Herron, M.
The **reconstructionist**. Hart, J.
RECTORS *See* Anglican and Episcopal clergy; Catholic priests
The **rector's** wife. Trollope, J.
The **red** and the black. Stendhal
Red angel. Heffernan, W.
RED ARMY (SOVIET UNION) *See* Russia—Army
The **red** badge of courage. Crane, S.
also in Crane, S. The complete novels of Stephen Crane p197-299
also in Crane, S. The portable Stephen Crane p189-318
also in Crane, S. Prose and poetry
also in Crane, S. The red badge of courage and other stories
The **red** badge of courage and other stories. Crane, S.
Red Branch. Llywelyn, M.
Red cat. Spiegelman, P.
The **red** convertible. Erdrich, L.
A **red** death. Mosley, W.
Red Dragon. Harris, T.
Red gold. Furst, A.
Red harvest. Hammett, D.
In Hammett, D. Complete novels
The **red** heart. Thom, J. A.
Red lightning. Varley, J.
Red mandarin dress. Qiu Xiaolong
Red Mars. Robinson, K. S.
The **red** passport. Shonk, K.
The **Red** Pavilion. Gulik, R. H. v.
The **red** pony. Steinbeck, J.
In Steinbeck, J. The long valley
The **red** rover. Cooper, J. F.
In Cooper, J. F. Sea tales: The pilot, The red rover
Red rover. McNamer, D.
The **red** scarf. Furnivall, K.
Red sky at night. Hall, J. W.
Red Square. Smith, M. C.
The **red** tent. Diamant, A.
Red thunder. Varley, J.
The **red** tree. Kiernan, C. R.
Red, white and blue. Isaacs, S.
The **redbreast**. Nesbø, J.
Redburn, his first voyage. Melville, H.
In Melville, H. Redburn, his first voyage; White-jacket; or, The world in a man-of-war; Moby-Dick; or, The whale
Redburn, his first voyage; White-jacket; or, The world in a man-of-war; Moby-Dick; or, The whale. Melville, H.
REDEMPTION *See* Atonement
Redemption. Turner, F. W.
Redemption. Uris, L.
Redemption. *See* McGown, J. Murder at the old vicarage
Redline the stars. Norton, A.

REDUCING
Levenkron, S. The best little girl in the world
The **reef**. Wharton, E.
In Wharton, E. Novels
Reflections in a golden eye. McCullers, C.
also in McCullers, C. Complete novels

REFORMATION
See also Europe—16th century
Maxwell, R. The secret diary of Anne Boleyn

REFORMERS
See also Abolitionists

REFUGEES
See also Exiles
Bellow, S. The Bellarosa connection
Brookner, A. Family and friends
Couto, M. Sleepwalking land
Eggers, D. What is the what
Hein, C. Settlement
Hoffman, E. Appassionata
Kosinski, J. N. The painted bird
Le, T. D. T. The gangster we are all looking for
Ozick, C. Heir to the glimmering world

REFUGEES, CUBAN *See* Cuban refugees

RESTAURANTS, LUNCHROOMS, ETC.—*Continued*

O'Nan, S. Last night at the Lobster
Powell, A. Casanova's Chinese restaurant
Rice, L. Blue moon
Russo, R. Empire Falls
Steinbeck, J. Sweet Thursday
Steinbeck, J. The wayward bus

RESTORATION ENGLAND *See* England—17th century

RESURRECTION

Amado, J. Dona Flor and her two husbands
Farmer, P. J. The dark design
Farmer, P. J. The fabulous riverboat
Farmer, P. J. Gods of Riverworld
Farmer, P. J. The magic labyrinth
Farmer, P. J. To your scattered bodies go
Resurrection. Tolstoy, L., graf
Resurrection men. Rankin, I.
Resurrection row. Perry, A.
The **resurrectionist**. O'Connell, J.

RETIREMENT

See also Old age

Lee, C.-R. A gesture life
Pym, B. Quartet in autumn
Stegner, W. E. All the little live things

RETIREMENT COMMUNITIES

Michener, J. A. Recessional
Retribution. Hoffman, J.
Retribution. Kaminsky, S. M.
Retro. Estleman, L. D.

RETROSPECTIVE STORIES

Gardam, J. Old Filth
The **return** of Gunner Asch. Kirst, H. H.
The **return** of Santiago. Resnick, M.
The **return** of the dancing master. Mankell, H.
The **return** of the king. Tolkien, J. R. R.
    also in Tolkien, J. R. R. The lord of the rings
The **return** of the native. Hardy, T.
Return to Mars. Bova, B.
Return to Thrush Green. Read, Miss
Returning to earth. Harrison, J.
Reunion. Lightman, A. P.

REUNIONS

Clark, M. H. Nighttime is my time
Drabble, M. The sea lady
Goddard, R. Never go back
Goodman, C. The drowning tree
Jaffe, R. Class reunion
McCrumb, S. If ever I return, pretty Peggy-O
Siddons, A. R. Outer banks
Smith, L. The last girls

REUVENI, DAVID, 1490-CA. 1535
About
Halter, M. Messiah

REVENGE

Alexie, S. Flight
Amis, K. The Russian girl
Anderson, P. The sharing of flesh
Archer, J. As the crow flies
Baker, K. The house of the stag
Balzac, H. d. Cousin Bette
Bear, G. Anvil of stars
Bradford, B. T. The Ravenscar dynasty
Brand, M. Outcasts
Brink, A. P. The other side of silence
Brontë, E. Wuthering Heights
Carter, S. L. The emperor of Ocean Park
Chen, D. Brothers
Conrad, J. Victory
Cornwell, B. Vagabond
Cox, M. The meaning of night
Davis, C. Winter range
DeMille, N. The lion's game
Dickens, C. Great expectations
Dickens, C. A tale of two cities
Dumas, A. The Count of Monte Cristo
Enger, L. Undiscovered country
Estleman, L. D. Gas City
Everett, P. L. The water cure
Fairstein, L. Killer heat

Faust, C. Money shot
Franklin, T. Hell at the breech
French, A. Billy
Galgut, D. The impostor
García Márquez, G. Chronicle of a death foretold
George, E. What came before he shot her
Goddard, R. Beyond recall
Goldsmith, O. The First Wives Club
Goldsmith, O. Young wives
Gould, J. The best is yet to come
Grisham, J. The last juror
Grisham, J. A time to kill
Haig, M. The dead fathers club
Harris, J. Gentlemen and players
Harris, T. Hannibal rising
Harrison, S. Cry of the wind
Harrison, S. Song of the river
Heffernan, W. The Dinosaur Club
Hiaasen, C. Skinny dip
Higgins, J. Bad company
Higgins, J. Day of reckoning
Higgins, J. Edge of danger
Higgins, J. Midnight runner
Hill, J. Heart-shaped box
Hill, S. Mrs. de Winter
Hunter, S. The 47th samurai
Hunter, S. Black light
Hunter, S. Time to hunt
Huston, C. The shotgun rule
Isegawa, M. Snakepit
James, P. D. Innocent blood
Jance, J. A. Kiss of the bees
Jiles, P. The color of lightning
Johansen, I. The ugly duckling
Just, W. S. Forgetfulness
Katzenbach, J. The analyst
Kellerman, J. Sunstroke
King, S. Bag of bones
King, S. Rose Madder
Korda, M. Worldly goods
Le Carré, J. The night manager
Lebrecht, N. The song of names
Lehane, D. Mystic river
Lehrer, J. The special prisoner
Leonard, E. Glitz
Lindsey, D. L. The color of night
Margolin, P. Fugitive
McDermid, V. The distant echo
McEwan, I. Amsterdam
Melville, H. Moby-Dick; or, The whale
Michael, J. Sleeping beauty
Murdoch, I. The green knight
Nance, J. J. The last hostage
Norman, H. The haunting of L
Parker, T. J. Silent Joe
Parsons, J. Mary, Mary
Pearce, M. E. Cast a long shadow
Pelecanos, G. P. Drama city
Pelecanos, G. P. Shame the devil
Percy, W. Lancelot
Pérez Galdós, B. Doña Perfecta
Perry, T. Pursuit
Roberts, N. Honest illusions
Robinson, P. The first cut
Rosenberg, N. T. Mitigating circumstances
Savage, S. The cry of the sloth
Schwartz, J. B. Reservation Road
Scottoline, L. The vendetta defense
Shaw, I. Beggarman, thief
Siegel, J. Derailed
Skármeta, A. The dancer and the thief
Smith, W. A. Birds of prey
Starr, J. Lights out
Starr, J. Panic attack
Tartt, D. The little friend
Theroux, A. Darconville's cat
Wall, P. S. The Wilde women
Warren, R. P. World enough and time
Weaver, M. Deceptions
Weldon, F. The life and loves of a she-devil
Westlake, D. E. What's the worst that could happen?
Wignall, K. For the dogs
Woods, S. Dirty work
Woods, S. Palindrome

RIVERS

See also Mississippi River; Missouri River; Yangtze River (China)

Ballard, J. G. The day of creation
Brower, B. Blue dog, green river
Scott, J. Follow me
River's end. Roberts, N.

RIVIERA (FRANCE AND ITALY)

Sagan, F. Bonjour tristesse
Rivington Street. Tax, M.
RL's dream. Mosley, W.
The **road**. McCarthy, C.
The **road** back. Remarque, E. M.
Road dogs. Leonard, E.
The **road** home. Harrison, J.
The **road** home. Tremain, R.
Road rage. Rendell, R.
The **road** to Lichfield. Lively, P.
The **road** to ruin. Westlake, D. E.
Road to Wellville. Boyle, T. C.
Roads of destiny. Henry, O.
In Henry, O. The complete works of O. Henry p355-550
Roadside crosses. Deaver, J.
Roadwork. King, S.
In King, S. The Bachman books: four early novels by Stephen King
The **roaring** boy. Marston, E.

ROB ROY, 1671-1734
About
Scott, Sir W. Rob Roy
Rob Roy. Scott, Sir W.

ROBBER BARONS *See* Capitalists and financiers
The **robber** bridegroom. Welty, E.
also in Welty, E. Complete novels

ROBBERS *See* Brigands and robbers; Robbery

ROBBERY

See also Bank robbers; Theft

Barfoot, J. Critical injuries
Durham, M. The man who loved Cat Dancing
Latour, J. The Havana World Series
Malamud, B. The assistant
Pelecanos, G. P. Shame the devil
Roberts, N. Honest illusions
Stark, R. Comeback
Westlake, D. E. The hot rock
Westlake, D. E. Put a lid on it
Westlake, D. E. What's the worst that could happen?
A **Robert** Silverberg omnibus. Silverberg, R.

ROBINSON, JACKIE, 1919-1972
About
Parker, R. B. Double play
Robinson Crusoe. Defoe, D.

ROBOTS

Asimov, I. The Bicentennial Man
Asimov, I. The caves of steel
Asimov, I. I, robot
Asimov, I. The naked sun
Asimov, I. The rest of the robots
Martinez, A. L. The automatic detective
Miller, W. M. The darfsteller
Sedia, E. Alchemy of stone
Stross, C. Saturn's children
Tiptree, J. The girl who was plugged in
Winterson, J. The stone gods
Zelazny, R. Home is the hangman

ROCHFORD, JANE BOLEYN *See* Boleyn, Jane, Viscountess Rochford, d. 1542

ROCK MUSIC

Alexie, S. Reservation blues
Bull, E. War for the Oaks
Hiaasen, C. Basket case
Hill, J. Heart-shaped box
Hornby, N. High fidelity
Hornby, N. Juliet, naked
Lazar, Z. Sway
Lethem, J. You don't love me yet
McGuane, T. Panama
Parker, B. Criminal justice
Rushdie, S. The ground beneath her feet
Thornton, T. The alternative hero

ROCK MUSICIANS *See* Rock music

ROCKY MOUNTAINS

Poe, E. A. The journal of Julius Rodman

RODEOS

Borland, H. When the legends die
Roderick Hudson. James, H.
Roger Caras' Treasury of great cat stories. Entered in Part I under title
Roger Caras' Treasury of great dog stories. Entered in Part I under title

ROGERS, MARY, 1820-1841
About
Rose, J. Blackest bird

ROGERS, ROBERT, 1731-1795
About
Roberts, K. L. Northwest Passage
Roger's version. Updike, J.

ROGUES AND VAGABONDS

Brown, J. D. Addie Pray
Colette. The tender shoot
Doctorow, E. L. Loon Lake
Fraser, G. M. The reavers
Kerouac, J. The Dharma bums
Kerouac, J. On the road
Kerouac, J. On the road: the original scroll
Mann, T. Confessions of Felix Krull, confidence man
Steinbeck, J. Cannery Row
Steinbeck, J. Sweet Thursday
Steinbeck, J. Tortilla Flat
Tinti, H. The good thief

ROLLING STONES

Lazar, Z. Sway
Rolling stones. Henry, O.
In Henry, O. The complete works of O. Henry p941-1060
Rolling thunder. Varley, J.
Roma. Saylor, S.
Roma eterna. Silverberg, R.
The **Roman**. Waltari, M.

ROMAN CATHOLIC CHURCH *See* Catholic faith
ROMAN CATHOLIC RELIGION *See* Catholic faith
ROMAN EMPIRE *See* Rome
The **Roman** hat mystery. Queen, E.
ROMAN SOLDIERS *See* Soldiers—Rome
The **Roman** spring of Mrs. Stone. Williams, T.
The **romance** of Monte Beni. See Hawthorne, N. The marble faun
The **romance** reader. Abraham, P.

ROMANCES (GOTHIC) *See* Gothic romances
ROMANCES (LOVE STORIES) *See* Love affairs; Love stories

ROMANIA

Furst, A. Blood of victory
Marks, J. Fangland
Wiesel, E. The forgotten
The **romantic**. Gowdy, B.

ROME

Saylor, S. Roma
Silverberg, R. Roma eterna

510-30 B.C.

Davis, L. The accusers
Davis, L. Three hands in the fountain
Harris, R. Imperium
Massie, A. Caesar
McCullough, C. Caesar
McCullough, C. Caesar's women
McCullough, C. The first man in Rome
McCullough, C. Fortune's favorites
McCullough, C. The grass crown
McCullough, C. The October horse
Saylor, S. The house of the Vestals
Saylor, S. The judgment of Caesar
Saylor, S. A mist of prophecies
Saylor, S. Rubicon
Saylor, S. The triumph of Caesar
Wilder, T. The ides of March

30 B.C.-476 A.D.

Asch, S. The Nazarene

RUSSIA—*Continued*

Tolstaia, T. The slynx
Voĭnovich, V. Monumental propaganda
Vollmann, W. T. Europe central
Wiesel, E. The testament
Wilkins, K. Veil of gold

18th century

Pushkin, A. S. The captain's daughter

19th century

Chekhov, A. P. Complete short novels
Chekhov, A. P. The duel
Chekhov, A. P. Early short stories, 1883-1888
Chekhov, A. P. Later short stories, 1888-1903
Chekhov, A. P. Longer stories from the last decade
Chekhov, A. P. My life
Chekhov, A. P. The steppe
Chekhov, A. P. The story of an unknown man
Chekhov, A. P. Three years
Dostoyevsky, F. The best short stories of Dostoevsky
Dostoyevsky, F. The brothers Karamazov
Dostoyevsky, F. Crime and punishment
Dostoyevsky, F. The gambler
Dostoyevsky, F. The idiot
Dostoyevsky, F. Notes from underground
Dostoyevsky, F. The possessed
Gogol´, N. V. The collected tales of Nikolai Gogol
Gogol´, N. V. Dead souls
Gogol´, N. V. The overcoat, and other tales of good and evil
Gorky, M. Selected short stories
Pushkin, A. S. Alexander Pushkin: complete prose fiction
Sholem Aleichem. The nightingale
Tolstoy, L., graf. Anna Karenina
Tolstoy, L., graf. Childhood, Boyhood and Youth
Tolstoy, L., graf. The death of Ivan Ilyitch, and other stories
Tolstoy, L., graf. The Kreutzer sonata, The Devil, and other tales
Tolstoy, L., graf. Resurrection
Tolstoy, L., graf. The short novels of Tolstoy
Tolstoy, L., graf. Short stories
Tolstoy, L., graf. War and peace
Turgenev, I. S. Fathers and sons
Turgenev, I. S. First love and other stories

Aristocracy

See Aristocracy—Russia

Army—Officers

Uris, L. Armageddon

Communism

See Communism—Russia

Navy

Clancy, T. The hunt for Red October

Peasant life

See Peasant life—Russia

Politics

See Politics—Russia

Prisoners and prisons

See Prisoners and prisons—Russia

Rural life

Chekhov, A. P. Three years
Makine, A. The woman who waited
Rutherfurd, E. Russka
Sholokhov, M. A. And quiet flows the Don
Sholokhov, M. A. The Don flows home to the sea
Solzhenitsyn, A. Cancer ward

Leningrad

See Russia—St. Petersburg

Moscow

Bulgakov, M. A. The master and Margarita
Freemantle, B. Dead men living
Silva, D. Moscow rules
Tolstoy, L., graf. Childhood, Boyhood and Youth

St. Petersburg

Benioff, D. City of thieves
Dean, D. The madonnas of Leningrad
Docx, E. Pravda

Dostoyevsky, F. Crime and punishment
Dostoyevsky, F. The idiot
The **Russia** house. Le Carré, J.

RUSSIAN AMERICANS

Boswell, R. Century's son
Dean, D. The madonnas of Leningrad
Shteyngart, G. The Russian debutante's handbook
The **Russian** debutante's handbook. Shteyngart, G.
The **Russian** girl. Amis, K.

RUSSIAN REFUGEES

Bosse, M. J. The warlord
Nabokov, V. V. Look at the harlequins!
Nabokov, V. V. Pnin

RUSSIAN SOLDIERS *See* Soldiers—Russia

RUSSIANS

Australia

Keneally, T. A family madness

Canada

Messud, C. A simple tale

England

Amis, K. The Russian girl
Judd, A. Legacy
Lawton, J. Old flames

Germany

Turgenev, I. S. Spring torrents [variant title: The torrents of spring]
Turgenev, I. S. The torrents of spring
Uris, L. Armageddon

United States

Benioff, D. City of thieves
Crowley, J. The translator
Nabokov, V. V. Pnin
Piercy, M. Sex wars
Reyn, I. What happened to Anna K.
Shames, L. Mangrove squeeze
Ulinich, A. Petropolis
Russka. Rutherfurd, E.
Rustler roundup. L'Amour, L.
   In L'Amour, L. End of the drive p93-239
Ryan's rules. See Leonard, E. Swag

S

S. Updike, J.
S is for Silence. Grafton, S.
SAAVEDRA, MIGUEL DE CERVANTES *See* Cervantes Saavedra, Miguel de, 1547-1616
Sabbath Creek. Mitcham, J.
Sabbath's theater. Roth, P.

SABOTAGE

MacLean, A. Force 10 from Navarone
MacLean, A. The guns of Navarone
Vonnegut, K. Player piano

SABOTEURS *See* Sabotage

SACAGAWEA, B. 1786

About

Hall, B. I should be extremely happy in your company
Sargent, C. Museum of human beings

SACAJAWEA *See* Sacagawea, b. 1786
Sackett. L'Amour, L.
   In L'Amour, L. The Sacketts: beginnings of a dynasty
The **Sacketts:** beginnings of a dynasty. L'Amour, L.
Sacred. Lehane, D.
The **sacred** book of the werewolf. Pelevin, V.
Sacred clowns. Hillerman, T.
Sacred country. Tremain, R.
Sacred hunger. Unsworth, B.
SACRIFICE, HUMAN *See* Human sacrifice
Sacrifice. Vachss, A. H.

SADISM

See also Cruelty
Templeton, E. Gordon

SAFARIS *See* Hunting—Africa

Safe harbor. Rice, L.
Safe house. Vachss, A. H.
Sag Harbor. Whitehead, C.

SAHARA

Bowles, P. The sheltering sky
Cussler, C. Sahara
Sahara. Cussler, C.

SAIGON (VIETNAM) *See* Vietnam—Ho Chi Minh City

SAILING VESSELS

Higgins, J. Storm warning
Stone, R. Outerbridge Reach
The **sailmaker's** daughter. Johnson, S.
Sailor song. Kesey, K.

SAILORS *See* Seamen

SAINT HELENA

Hansen, B. The monsters of St. Helena
SAINT LOUIS (MO.) *See* Missouri—Saint Louis
Saint maybe. Tyler, A.
Saint monster. Gurganus, A.
In Gurganus, A. The practical heart
Saint Peter's Fair. Peters, E.

SAINT PETERSBURG (RUSSIA) *See* Russia—St. Petersburg

SAINTS

West, M. L. The devil's advocate
Saints at the river. Rash, R.
SALAZAR, ANTONIO DE OLIVEIRA, 1889-1970
About
Antunes, A. L. The inquisitors' manual
SALEM (MASS.) *See* Massachusetts—Salem
Salem's Lot. King, S.

SALES PERSONNEL AND SELLING

Edgerton, C. The Bible salesman
Flagg, F. Standing in the rainbow
Gurganus, A. Blessed assurance: a moral tale
Gurganus, A. Saint monster
Kafka, F. Metamorphosis
Liss, D. The ethical assassin
Updike, J. Rabbit is rich
Vonnegut, K. Breakfast of champions
SALESMEN AND SALESMANSHIP *See* Sales personnel and selling
Sally Hemings. Chase-Riboud, B.

SALMON FISHING

Torday, P. Salmon fishing in the Yemen
Salmon fishing in the Yemen. Torday, P.
Salt. Zuber, I.
The **salt** eaters. Bambara, T. C.
Salt River. Sallis, J.
A **salty** piece of land. Buffett, J.

SALVAGE

Cussler, C. Inca gold
Innes, H. The wreck of the Mary Deare

SALVATION

See also Atonement
Samaritan. Price, R.
The **same** sea. Oz, A.

SAMSON (BIBLICAL FIGURE)
About
Maine, D. The book of Samson

SAMURAI

Clavell, J. Gai-Jin
Clavell, J. Shogun
Mishima, Y. Runaway horses
SAN FRANCISCO (CALIF.) *See* California—San Francisco

SAN JACINTO, BATTLE OF, TEX., 1836

Kelton, E. Massacre at Goliad
San Remo Drive. Epstein, L.
SANATORIUMS *See* Hospitals and sanatoriums
Sanctuary. Faulkner, W.
also in Faulkner, W. Novels, 1930-1935
Sanctuary. Kellerman, F.
Sanctuary. Wharton, E.
In Wharton, E. Collected stories, 1891-1910
The **sanctuary** sparrow. Peters, E.

Sand castles. Freeling, N.
Sandkings. Martin, G. R. R.
In The Hugo winners p70-132
The **sands** of pride. Trotter, W. R.
SANDSTORMS *See* Storms
SANTA BARBARA (CALIF.) *See* California—Santa Barbara

SANTA CLAUS

Davies, V. Miracle on 34th Street
SANTA FE (N.M.) *See* New Mexico—Santa Fe
Santa Fe rules. Woods, S.

SANTA FE TRAIL

Bristow, G. Jubilee Trail
SANTA MONICA (CALIF.) *See* California—Santa Monica

SANTERIA

Oyeyemi, H. The opposite house
Sapphira and the slave girl. Cather, W.
also in Cather, W. Later novels

SAPPHO
About
Jong, E. Sappho's leap
Sappho's leap. Jong, E.

SARAH (BIBLICAL FIGURE)
About
Halter, M. Sarah
Sarah. Halter, M.
Sarah Canary. Fowler, K. J.
SARAJEVO (BOSNIA AND HERCEGOVINA) *See* Bosnia and Hercegovina—Sarajevo
Saratoga strongbox. Dobyns, S.

SARGENT, JOHN SINGER, 1856-1925
About
Gurganus, A. The practical heart [novelette]
Sartoris. Faulkner, W.
Sartoris {uncut version}. See Faulkner, W. Flags in the dust
Sarum. Rutherfurd, E.
SASKATCHEWAN *See* Canada—Saskatchewan
Sassafrass, Cypress & Indigo. Shange, N.

SASSOON, SIEGFRIED, 1886-1967
About
Barker, P. The eye in the door
Barker, P. Regeneration
The **satanic** verses. Rushdie, S.

SATANISM

See also Demoniac possession
Ruiz, L. M. Only one thing missing

SATIRE

See also Humor; Irony; Parodies
Adams, D. The hitchhiker's guide to the galaxy
Adams, D. Life, the universe, and everything
Adams, D. The restaurant at the end of the universe
Adams, D. So long, and thanks for all the fish
Adiga, A. The white tiger
Amis, K. The Russian girl
Austen, J. Northanger Abbey
Austen, J. Sense and sensibility
Barry, M. Company
Barth, J. Giles goat-boy
Barth, J. The sot-weed factor
Bellow, S. Humboldt's gift
Berger, T. Arthur Rex
Berger, T. Neighbors
Bernhard, T. Woodcutters
Blackwell, E. Grub
Bolaño, R. Nazi literature in the Americas
Boulle, P. The bridge over the River Kwai
Boulle, P. Planet of the apes
Boyle, T. C. Road to Wellville
Brooks, M. World War Z
Burgess, A. A clockwork orange
Butler, S. The way of all flesh
Castellanos Moya, H. Senselessness
Cervantes Saavedra, M. d. Don Quixote de la Mancha
Chabon, M. The Yiddish policemen's union
Chatterjee, U. English, August
Cheever, J. The Wapshot chronicle
Cheever, J. The Wapshot scandal
Clarke, B. An arsonist's guide to writers' homes in New England
Coe, J. The closed circle

SATIRE—*Continued*

Coe, J. The Rotters' Club
Cohen, R. Inspired sleep
Coleridge, N. Godchildren
Coll, S. Acceptance
Collins, J. Beginner's Greek
Collins, M. Death of a writer
Connell, E. S. Mr. Bridge
Connelly, J. Crumbtown
Coover, R. Pinocchio in Venice
Coupland, D. Eleanor Rigby
Cusk, R. In the fold
Davies, R. The lyre of Orpheus
Davies, R. Murther & walking spirits
De Bernières, L. Corelli's mandolin
DeLillo, D. Ratner's star
DeLillo, D. White noise
DeMille, N. The gate house
DeMille, N. The Gold Coast
Díaz, J. The brief wondrous life of Oscar Wao
Dickens, C. Bleak House
Dickens, C. Hard times
Dickens, C. Little Dorrit
Disch, T. M. Word of God: or, Holy writ rewritten
Dos Passos, J. The 42nd parallel
Dos Passos, J. 1919
Dos Passos, J. U.S.A.
Drabble, M. The sea lady
Drabble, M. The witch of Exmoor
Ducker, B. Dizzying heights
Dunn, K. Geek love
Dunne, D. People like us
Dunne, J. G. Nothing lost
Eco, U. Foucault's pendulum
Egolf, T. Skirt and the fiddle
Ehrenreich, B. The suitors
Elkin, S. The MacGuffin
Ellis, W. Crooked little vein
Epstein, L. The eighth wonder of the world
Everett, P. L. American desert
Everett, P. L. I am Not Sidney Poitier
Farmer, P. J. Riders of the purple wage
Faulkner, W. Mosquitoes
Fielding, H. The history of the adventures of Joseph Andrews
    and of his friend Mr. Abraham Adams and, An apology for
    the life of Mrs. Shamela Andrews
Fielding, H. The history of Tom Jones, a foundling
Fowler, K. J. Sarah Canary
Fowler, K. J. Sister Noon
Franzen, J. The corrections
Friedman, M. Martian Dawn
Fuentes, C. The eagle's throne
Gaddis, W. A frolic of his own
Gaddis, W. The recognitions
García Márquez, G. In evil hour
García Márquez, G. One hundred years of solitude
Gardam, J. Faith Fox
Gessen, K. All the sad young literary men
Gilman, C. P. Herland
Gilman, C. P. Moving the mountain
Gilman, C. P. With her in Ourland
Gogol', N. V. Dead souls
Golding, W. The inheritors
Gordon, E. F. It will come to me
Grass, G. The call of the toad
Grass, G. Dog years
Grass, G. The tin drum
Gray, A. Poor things
Greene, G. Our man in Havana
Grimes, M. Foul matter
Ha Jin. In the pond
Haig, M. The Labrador Pact
Haldeman, J. W. The coming
Hanif, M. A case of exploding mangoes
Harris, R. The ghost
Hašek, J. The good soldier Svejk
Heinlein, R. A. Job: a comedy of justice
Heinlein, R. A. The moon is a harsh mistress
Heinlein, R. A. Stranger in a strange land
Heller, J. Closing time
Heller, J. Good as Gold
Heller, Z. The believers
Hemingway, E. The torrents of spring
Hesse, H. The glass bead game (Magister Ludi)

Hiaasen, C. Native tongue
Hiaasen, C. Nature girl
Hiaasen, C. Sick puppy
Hiaasen, C. Stormy weather
Hiaasen, C. Strip tease
Hodgins, E. Mr. Blandings builds his dream house
Høeg, P. The history of Danish dreams
Høeg, P. The woman and the ape
Homes, A. M. This book will save your life
Hornby, N. About a boy
Houellebecq, M. The possibility of an island
Hrabal, B. I served the King of England
Hughes, R. A. W. A high wind in Jamaica
Huxley, A. Brave new world
Huxley, A. Point counter point
Hynes, J. Kings of infinite space
Hynes, J. The lecturer's tale
Inman, R. Captain Saturday
Irving, J. A prayer for Owen Meany
Irving, J. The world according to Garp
Isaacs, S. After all these years
Isaacs, S. Close relations
Ishiguro, K. The remains of the day
Jacobson, H. Kalooki nights
James, H. The Bostonians
Jen, G. Mona in the promised land
Johnson, A. Parasites like us
Johnson, D. L'affaire
Kadare, I. Spring flowers, spring frost
Kafka, F. Amerika
Kalfus, K. The commissariat of enlightenment
Kalfus, K. A disorder peculiar to the country
Kaufman, B. Up the down staircase
Kaufman, M. Bowl of cherries
Keillor, G. Love me
King, S. The running man
Kirst, H. H. Forward, Gunner Asch!
Kirst, H. H. The return of Gunner Asch
Kirst, H. H. The revolt of Gunner Asch
Klein, J. Primary colors
Kosinski, J. N. Being there
Kotzwinkle, W. The bear went over the mountain
Krauss, N. The history of love
Kunkel, B. Indecision
Laird, N. Utterly monkey
Lasdun, J. The horned man
Le Carré, J. The tailor of Panama
Leavitt, D. Martin Bauman
Lehrer, J. Purple dots
Lelchuk, A. Ziff
Lem, S. Memoirs of a space traveler
Lethem, J. Chronic city
Lewis, C. S. That hideous strength
Lewis, S. Babbitt
Lewis, S. Dodsworth
Lewis, S. Elmer Gantry
Lewis, S. It can't happen here
Lewis, S. Main Street
Lipman, E. My latest grievance
Lodge, D. Nice work
Lodge, D. Paradise news
Lodge, D. Therapy
Lurie, A. The war between the Tates
Maguire, G. Son of a witch
Mantel, H. Beyond black
Marías, J. All souls
Martin, C. W. How to sell
Martin, V. Italian fever
Martini, S. P. The list
Maugham, W. S. Cakes and ale
Mayle, P. Hotel Pastis
McCarthy, M. Birds of America
McCarthy, M. A charmed life
McCarthy, M. The group
McCarthy, M. The groves of Academe
McEwan, I. Amsterdam
McGrath, P. The grotesque
McLaughlin, E. The nanny diaries
Melville, H. The confidence-man: his masquerade
Messud, C. The emperor's children
Mitford, N. Love in a cold climate
Mitford, N. The pursuit of love
Mo Yan. Life and death are wearing me out
Moody, R. The Omega Force

SATIRE—*Continued*

Wibberley, L. The mouse that roared
Wolcott, J. The catsitters
Wolfe, T. The bonfire of the vanities
Wolfe, T. I am Charlotte Simmons
Wolfe, T. A man in full
Wolitzer, M. The wife
Woodrell, D. Give us a kiss
Wright, S. Going native
Yu Hua. Brothers

Saturday. McEwan, I.
Saturday night and Sunday morning. Sillitoe, A.
Saturday the rabbi went hungry. Kemelman, H.

SATURN (PLANET)

Bova, B. Saturn
Saturn. Bova, B.
The **Saturn** game. Anderson, P.
In The Hugo winners p269-325
Saturn's children. Stross, C.
Saturn's race. Niven, L.

SAUDI ARABIANS

United States

Dubus, A. The garden of last days
Saul and Patsy. Baxter, C.

SAUNDERS, MARY

About

Donoghue, E. Slammerkin
The **savage** detectives. Bolaño, R.
Savage run. Box, C. J.
Savages. Pronzini, B.
SAVANNAH (GA.) *See* Georgia—Savannah
Savannah. Price, E.
Savannah; or, A gift for Mr. Lincoln. Jakes, J.
Save the last dance for me. Gorman, E.
Saving fish from drowning. Tan, A.
Saving Grace. Smith, L.
Saving room for dessert. Constantine, K. C.

SAVONAROLA, GIROLAMO, 1452-1498

About

Eliot, G. Romola

SAXONS *See* Anglo-Saxons

SAXOPHONISTS

Mansbach, A. Shackling water
Saying grace. Gutcheon, B. R.
Sayonara. Michener, J. A.
Scales of gold. Dunnett, D.

SCANDAL

O'Hagan, A. Be near me
Shreve, A. Testimony
Scandal in Fair Haven. Hart, C. G.
The **scandal** of Father Brown. Chesterton, G. K.
In Chesterton, G. K. The Father Brown omnibus p815-974
The **scandal** of the season. Gee, S.
Scandalmonger. Safire, W.
Scandalous risks. Howatch, S.
A **scanner** darkly. Dick, P. K.
In Dick, P. K. Five novels of the 1960s & 70s
The **scar**. Miéville, C.
Scar tissue. Tapply, W. G.
Scaramouche. Sabatini, R.
The **scarecrow**. Connelly, M.
The **Scarlatti** inheritance. Ludlum, R.
The **scarlet** letter. Hawthorne, N.
also in Hawthorne, N. Collected novels
The **Scarlet** Pimpernel. Orczy, E., Baroness
The **scarlet** ruse. MacDonald, J. D.
Scavenger. Morrell, D.

SCHEHERAZADE (LEGENDARY CHARACTER)

Yunis, A. The night counter
Schild's ladder. Egan, G.

SCHINDLER, OSKAR, 1908-1974

About

Keneally, T. Schindler's list
Schindler's list. Keneally, T.
Schismatrix plus. Sterling, B.

SCHIZOPHRENIA

See also Dual personality; Personality disorders
Chaon, D. Await your reply

Cook, T. H. The cloud of unknowing
Greenberg, J. I never promised you a rose garden
Hunter, E. The moment she was gone
Lamb, W. I know this much is true
LaValle, V. D. The ecstatic
Moore, S. The big girls
Rosales, G. The halfway house
Vine, B. The minotaur
Wray, J. Lowboy
Scholarium. Gross, C.

SCHOLARS

See also Intellectuals
Aciman, A. A. Call me by your name
Amis, K. The Russian girl
Bellow, S. Herzog
Bulgakov, M. A. The master and Margarita
Cather, W. The professor's house
Crumey, A. Mr. Mee
Davies, R. The rebel angels
Dorris, M. The crown of Columbus
Drabble, M. The sea lady
Eco, U. Foucault's pendulum
Frayn, M. Headlong
Gross, C. Scholarium
Gruber, M. The book of air and shadows
Hawthorne, N. Fanshawe
Hesse, H. The glass bead game (Magister Ludi)
Hill, R. The Stranger House
Hofmann, G. Lichtenberg and the little flower girl
Langton, J. Emily Dickinson is dead
Marías, J. All souls
McDermid, V. Grave tattoo
Messud, C. The hunters [novelette]
Michaels, B. Houses of stone
Powell, D. The locusts have no king
Powers, R. Galatea 2.2
Redhill, M. Consolation
Snow, C. P. The light and the dark
Stott, R. Ghostwalk
Updike, J. Roger's version
Verissimo, L. F. Borges and the eternal orangutans
White, E. The married man
School days. Parker, R. B.
School for the blind. McFarland, D.

SCHOOL LIFE

Agee, J. The morning watch
Reed, K. Enclave
Spark, M. The finishing school

Denmark

Høeg, P. Borderliners

England

Brontë, C. Emma
Delderfield, R. F. To serve them all my days
Dickens, C. David Copperfield
Dickens, C. Nicholas Nickleby
Faulks, S. Engleby
Harding, J. W. By George
Harris, J. Gentlemen and players
Hilton, J. Good-bye Mr. Chips
Ishiguro, K. Never let me go
McGowan, H. Schooling
Read, Miss. Chronicles of Fairacre
Swift, G. Waterland

France

Colette. Claudine at school
Dufossé, C. School's out
Flaubert, G. Sentimental education

India

Narayan, R. K. Swami and friends

Ireland

O'Brien, E. The country girls

Scotland

Spark, M. The prime of Miss Jean Brodie

United States

Alcott, L. M. Jo's boys
Alcott, L. M. Little men
Bynum, S. S.-L. Ms. Hempel chronicles
Coll, S. Acceptance

SCIENCE FICTION—*Continued*

Egan, G. Incandescence
Egan, G. Schild's ladder
Emshwiller, C. The secret city
Farmer, P. J. The classic Philip José Farmer, 1952-1964—
   1964-1973
Farmer, P. J. The dark design
Farmer, P. J. The fabulous riverboat
Farmer, P. J. Gods of Riverworld
Farmer, P. J. The magic labyrinth
Farmer, P. J. To your scattered bodies go
Feeling very strange
Finch, S. The guild of xenolinguists
Flynn, M. Eifelheim
Flynn, M. The January dancer
Foster, A. D. Dinotopia lost
Gaiman, N. American gods
Gibson, W. Neuromancer
Goonan, K. A. In war times
Goonan, K. A. Light music
Grimsley, J. The ordinary
Haldeman, J. W. The accidental time machine
Haldeman, J. W. The coming
Haldeman, J. W. Forever free
Haldeman, J. W. Forever peace
Haldeman, J. W. The forever war
Haldeman, J. W. Marsbound
Hamilton, P. F. The dreaming void
Hamilton, P. F. Pandora's star
Harkaway, N. The gone-away world
Harlan, T. House of reeds
Harrison, H. The Stainless Steel Rat joins the circus
Harrison, H. The Stainless Steel Rat sings the blues
Harrison, H. Stainless steel visions
Harrison, M. J. Nova swing
Heinlein, R. A. Citizen of the galaxy
Heinlein, R. A. Friday
Heinlein, R. A. The moon is a harsh mistress
Heinlein, R. A. The puppet masters
Heinlein, R. A. Starship troopers
Heinlein, R. A. Stranger in a strange land
Herbert, B. Dune: House Atreides
Herbert, B. Dune: House Corrino
Herbert, B. Dune: House Harkonnen
Herbert, B. Dune: The Butlerian jihad
Herbert, B. Paul of Dune
Herbert, F. Chapterhouse: Dune
Herbert, F. Children of Dune
Herbert, F. Dune
Herbert, F. Dune messiah
Herbert, F. God Emperor of Dune
Herbert, F. Heretics of Dune
Høeg, P. The woman and the ape
Hoffman, N. K. Catalyst
Houellebecq, M. The possibility of an island
The Hugo winners
Ishiguro, K. Never let me go
Jenkins, W. F. Exploration team
Kelly, J. P. The wreck of the Godspeed
Kerr, K. Snare
Kessel, J. The Baum plan for financial independence and oth-
   er stories
Keyes, D. Flowers for Algernon
Knight, D. F. The best of Damon Knight
Koontz, D. R. Strangers
Kotzwinkle, W. E.T.
Kress, N. Beggars & choosers
Kress, N. Beggars in Spain
Kress, N. Beggars ride
Kress, N. Probability moon
Kress, N. Probability sun
Kress, N. Steal across the sky
Lake, J. Escapement
Lake, J. Mainspring
Le Guin, U. K. Betrayals
Le Guin, U. K. The birthday of the world and other stories
Le Guin, U. K. The dispossessed
Le Guin, U. K. Forgiveness day
Le Guin, U. K. Four ways to forgiveness
Le Guin, U. K. The lathe of heaven
Le Guin, U. K. The left hand of darkness
Le Guin, U. K. A man of the people
Le Guin, U. K. The telling
Le Guin, U. K. A woman's liberation

Leiber, F. The Wanderer
Lem, S. Eden
Lem, S. Fiasco
Lem, S. His Master's Voice
Lem, S. Memoirs of a space traveler
Lem, S. Solaris
Lessing, D. M. Mara and Dann
Lessing, D. M. Shikasta
Levi, P. The sixth day, and other tales
Lewis, C. S. Out of the silent planet
Lewis, C. S. Perelandra
London, J. The star rover
Martin, G. R. R. Hunter's run
Martinez, A. L. The automatic detective
Marusek, D. Counting heads
Matheson, R. I am legend
May, J. The adversary
May, J. Diamond mask
May, J. The golden torc
May, J. Jack the bodiless
May, J. Magnificat
May, J. The many-colored land
May, J. The nonborn king
McAllister, B. The girl who loved animals and other stories
McAuley, P. J. White devils
McCaffrey, A. Acorna
McCaffrey, A. Acorna's people
McCaffrey, A. Acorna's quest
McCaffrey, A. Acorna's rebels
McCaffrey, A. Acorna's search
McCaffrey, A. Acorna's triumph
McCaffrey, A. Acorna's world
McCaffrey, A. All the Weyrs of Pern
McCaffrey, A. The city who fought
McCaffrey, A. Dragonflight
McCaffrey, A. Dragonquest
McCaffrey, A. Dragon's Kin
McCaffrey, A. Dragonsdawn
McCaffrey, A. Dragonseye
McCaffrey, A. Freedom's landing
McCaffrey, A. Freedom's ransom
McCaffrey, A. The greatest love [novelette]
McCaffrey, A. The Masterharper of Pern
McCaffrey, A. The renegades of Pern
McCaffrey, A. The skies of Pern
McCaffrey, A. The white dragon
McDonald, I. River of gods
McDonald, I. Brasyl
McHugh, M. F. Nekropolis
McIntyre, V. N. Dreamsnake
McMullen, S. Souls in the great machine
Meyer, S. The host
Miéville, C. The city & the city
Miéville, C. Iron council
Miller, W. M. A canticle for Leibowitz
Modesitt, L. E., Jr. Archform
Modesitt, L. E., Jr. Viewpoints critical
Moon, E. Moon flights
Moon, E. Once a hero
Moorcock, M. An alien heat
Moorcock, M. The best of Michael Moorcock
Moorcock, M. The end of all songs
Moorcock, M. The hollow lands
Morgan, R. K. Altered carbon
Morgan, R. K. Broken angels
Morgan, R. K. Thirteen
Nebula Awards showcase [date]
The new space opera
Niven, L. Lucifer's hammer
Niven, L. The Mote in God's Eye
Niven, L. Ringworld
Niven, L. The Ringworld engineers
Niven, L. The Ringworld throne
Niven, L. Ringworld's children
Niven, L. Saturn's race
Norton, A. Beast Master's ark
Norton, A. Redline the stars
The Norton book of science fiction
Oliver, C. From other shores
The Oxford book of science fiction stories
Palwick, S. Shelter
Pohl, F. The annals of the Heechee
Pohl, F. Beyond the blue event horizon
Pohl, F. The boy who would live forever

The **scorpio** illusion. Ludlum, R.

SCOTLAND

    See also Hebrides (Scotland); Skye (Scotland)

Cronin, A. J. The keys of the kingdom
Gaiman, N. The monarch of the glen
Garwood, J. The bride
Glass, J. Three Junes
Knox, E. Billie's kiss
Livesey, M. Criminals
McDermid, V. The distant echo
O'Farrell, M. The vanishing act of Esme Lennox
O'Hagan, A. Be near me
Pilcher, R. A risk worth taking
Pilcher, R. September
Yorke, M. Almost the truth

To 1603

Dunnett, D. Gemini
Kurtz, K. The temple and the stone

16th century

Plaidy, J. The captive Queen of Scots

17th century

Galbraith, D. The rising sun

18th century

Scott, Sir W. The bride of Lammermoor
Scott, Sir W. Rob Roy
Smollett, T. G. The expedition of Humphry Clinker

19th century

Stevenson, R. L. The merry men
Stirling, J. The workhouse girl

Aristocracy

    See Aristocracy—Scotland

Courts and courtiers

    See Courts and courtiers—Scotland

Rural life

Buchan, J. The thirty-nine steps
Livesey, M. Eva moves the furniture
MacLean, A. When eight bells toll
Pilcher, R. Winter solstice
Stirling, J. The island wife
Stirling, J. The wind from the hills

Edinburgh

McCall Smith, A. Love over Scotland
McCall Smith, A. The world according to Bertie
O'Neill, A. The lamplighter
Spark, M. The prime of Miss Jean Brodie
Stross, C. Halting state
Welsh, I. Porno
Welsh, I. Trainspotting

Glasgow

Donovan, A. Buddha Da
Gray, A. Poor things
Kelman, J. How late it was, how late
Kelman, J. Kieron Smith, boy
Mina, D. Deception
Stirling, J. The marrying kind
Stirling, J. The penny wedding
Stirling, J. The piper's tune
Welsh, L. The cutting room

SCOTS

England

Spark, M. The ballad of Peckham Rye

France

Faulks, S. Charlotte Gray

Panama

Galbraith, D. The rising sun

United States

Doig, I. Dancing at the Rascal Fair
Glass, J. Three Junes
Kamensky, J. Blindspot
Pouncey, P. R. Rules for old men waiting

SCOTT, ROBERT FALCON, 1868-1912
About
Bainbridge, B. The birthday boys

SCOTT, WINFIELD, 1786-1866
About
Shaara, J. Gone for soldiers

SCOUTS AND SCOUTING

Berger, T. Little Big Man
Cooper, J. F. The Deerslayer
Cooper, J. F. The last of the Mohicans
Cooper, J. F. The Leatherstocking tales
Forsyth, F. The whispering wind

Scratch a woman. Lippman, L.
    In Lippman, L. Hardly knew her

SCRIPTWRITERS *See* Authors

SCULPTORS

Abrahams, P. Nerve damage
Barker, P. Double vision
Davidson, A. The gargoyle
Hawthorne, N. The marble faun
Hesse, H. Narcissus and Goldmund
James, H. Roderick Hudson
Murray, S. Forgery
Piercy, M. Summer people
Stone, I. The agony and the ecstasy
Unsworth, B. Stone virgin
Weisgall, D. The world before her

The **sculptress**. Walters, M.

SCULPTURE

    See also Statues; Wood carving

SCYTHIANS

Llywelyn, M. The horse goddess

SEA *See* Ocean

The **sea**. Banville, J.

SEA CAPTAINS *See* Seamen; Shipmasters

Sea change. Parker, R. B.

Sea glass. Shreve, A.

The **sea** lady. Drabble, M.

The **sea** of grass. Richter, C.

Sea of poppies. Ghosh, A.

SEA STORIES

    See also Seamen; Whaling; names of wars with the subdivision Naval operations

Beach, E. L. Run silent, run deep
Conrad, J. Lord Jim
Conrad, J. The Nigger of the Narcissus
Conrad, J. Typhoon
Conrad, J. Youth
Cooper, J. F. The pilot
Cooper, J. F. The red rover
Cooper, J. F. Sea tales: The pilot, The red rover
Cussler, C. Plague ship
Forester, C. S. Admiral Hornblower in the West Indies
Forester, C. S. Beat to quarters
Forester, C. S. Commodore Hornblower
Forester, C. S. Flying colours
Forester, C. S. Hornblower and the Atropos
Forester, C. S. Hornblower and the Hotspur
Forester, C. S. Hornblower during the crisis, and two stories: Hornblower's temptation and The last encounter
Forester, C. S. The last nine days of the Bismarck
Forester, C. S. Lieutenant Hornblower
Forester, C. S. Lord Hornblower
Forester, C. S. Mr. Midshipman Hornblower
Forester, C. S. Ship of the line
Heggen, T. Mister Roberts
Higgins, J. Storm warning
Hough, R. The stowaway
Innes, H. The wreck of the Mary Deare
Lambdin, D. King's captain
Lindsey, J. Gentle rogue
London, J. The Sea-Wolf
MacLean, A. When eight bells toll
Marías, J. Voyage along the horizon
Martel, Y. Life of Pi
Martin, W. Annapolis
Matthiessen, P. Far Tortuga
McCutchan, P. Apprentice to the sea
McCutchan, P. Cameron's crossing
McCutchan, P. The last farewell
McCutchan, P. The new lieutenant
McCutchan, P. The second mate
Melville, H. Billy Budd, sailor
Melville, H. Moby-Dick; or, The whale

SECRET SERVICE—*Continued*

Higgins, J. Confessional
Higgins, J. Day of judgment
Higgins, J. Drink with the Devil
Higgins, J. The eagle has landed
Higgins, J. Eye of the storm
Higgins, J. Night of the fox
Higgins, J. The president's daughter
Higgins, J. Rough justice
Higgins, J. Touch the devil
Ignatius, D. The increment
Lawton, J. Old flames
Le Carré, J. The honourable schoolboy
Le Carré, J. The little drummer girl
Le Carré, J. The mission song
Le Carré, J. A most wanted man
Le Carré, J. Our game
Le Carré, J. Smiley's people
Le Carré, J. The spy who came in from the cold
Le Carré, J. The tailor of Panama
Le Carré, J. Tinker, tailor, soldier, spy
Ludlum, R. The apocalypse watch
Ludlum, R. The Janson directive
Ludlum, R. The Matarese Circle
Ludlum, R. The Parsifal mosaic
Ludlum, R. The Prometheus deception
Ludlum, R. The Scarlatti inheritance
MacInnes, H. Above suspicion
MacInnes, H. Ride a pale horse
MacLean, A. When eight bells toll
McDonell, N. An expensive education
Morrell, D. The brotherhood of the rose
Sansom, C. J. Winter in Madrid
Shelby, P. Days of drums
Shelby, P. Gatekeeper
Smith, T. R. Child 44
Smith, T. R. The secret speech
Smith, W. A. Golden fox
Snyder, D. J. Night crossing
Stewart, M. Airs above the ground
Stross, C. The Jennifer morgue

SECRET SOCIETIES
    See also Freemasons
Baldacci, D. Divine justice
Bear, E. Ink and steel
Ludlum, R. The Matarese Circle
Neville, K. The eight
Neville, K. The fire
Portis, C. Masters of Atlantis
The **secret** speech. Smith, T. R.
The **secret** warriors. Griffin, W. E. B.
A **secret** word. Paddock, J.

SECRETARIES

Ozick, C. Dictation [novelette]
Sheehan, A. The anxiety of everyday objects
Secrets of the sea. Shakespeare, N.

SECTS

Rogers, J. Mr. Wroe's virgins
Security. Amidon, S.
Seducing an angel. Balogh, M.

SEDUCTION

Colette. Mitsou
Dierbeck, L. One pill makes you smaller
Kundera, M. Slowness
Mawer, S. The fall
Nabokov, V. V. Lolita
Tolstoy, L., graf. Resurrection
The **seduction** of the crimson rose. Willig, L.
Seduction of the Minotaur. Nin, A.
    In Nin, A. Cities of the interior p463-589
The **seduction** of water. Goodman, C.
See Jane run. Fielding, J.
See no evil. Bland, E. T.
Seeing. Saramago, J.
Seeing a large cat. Peters, E.
Seek my face. Updike, J.
SEGREGATION *See* Race relations
Seize the day. Bellow, S.
    also in Bellow, S. Novels, 1956-1964
Seize the day [novelette] Bellow, S.
    In Bellow, S. Seize the day

Seize the night. Koontz, D. R.
Seizure. Cook, R.
Selected short stories. Gorky, M.
The **selected** short stories of Edith Wharton. Wharton, E.
Selected short stories of Franz Kafka. Kafka, F.
Selected stories. Munro, A.
The **selected** stories of Patricia Highsmith. Highsmith, P.
The **selected** works of T. S. Spivet. Larsen, R.

SELF-DEFENSE *See* Martial arts
Self-defense. Kellerman, J.
Self help. See Docx, E. Pravda

SELF-MADE MEN
    See also Success
Caldwell, T. Captains and kings
James, H. The American
West, N. A cool million

SELF-SACRIFICE

Dickens, C. A tale of two cities
French, M. Her mother's daughter
Tolstoy, L., graf. Resurrection
Wolitzer, M. The wife

SELFISHNESS

Balzac, H. d. Père Goriot (Old Goriot)
Self's punishment. Schlink, B.

SELIM III, SULTAN OF TURKEY, 1761-1808
About
Wallach, J. Seraglio
Semiautomatic. Reuland, R.
The **senator's** wife. Miller, S.

SENECA INDIANS

Larsen, D. The white
Sense and sensibility. Austen, J.
A **sense** of honor. Webb, J.
A **sense** of reality. Greene, G.
    In Greene, G. Collected stories p164-323
Sensei. Donohue, J. J.
Senselessness. Castellanos Moya, H.

SENSES

Smith, D. The beautiful miscellaneous
Sentimental education. Flaubert, G.
A **sentimental** journey through France and Italy. Sterne, L.
    In Sterne, L. The life and opinions of Tristram Shandy, gentleman and A sentimental journey through France and Italy p691-832
A **separate** peace. Knowles, J.
SEPOY REBELLION *See* India—British occupation, 1765-1947
September. Pilcher, R.

SEPTEMBER 11 TERRORIST ATTACKS, 2001

DeLillo, D. Falling man
Foer, J. S. Extremely loud & incredibly close
Kalfus, K. A disorder peculiar to the country
Maynard, J. The usual rules
McCauley, S. Alternatives to sex
McInerney, J. The good life
McPhee, M. L'America
Messud, C. The emperor's children
Price, R. The good priest's son
Schwartz, L. S. The writing on the wall
The **September** Society. Finch, C.
September song. Greeley, A. M.
The **Septembers** of Shiraz. Sofer, D.
Seraglio. Wallach, J.
Seraph on the Suwanee. Hurston, Z. N.
    In Hurston, Z. N. Novels and stories p597-920

SERBIA
    See also Kosovo (Serbia)
Novakovich, J. April Fool's Day

SERBIANS

England
Brownrigg, S. The delivery room
De Bernières, L. A partisan's daughter

United States
Lawrence, S. The lightning keeper
Serena. Rash, R.
SERGEANTS *See* Soldiers

SEX—*Continued*

Vidal, G. Myra Breckinridge [and] Myron
Vollmann, W. T. Butterfly stories
Vollmann, W. T. The royal family
Wallace, D. The Watermelon King
Walsh, H. Brass
Weaver, M. Deceptions
West, P. Sporting with Amaryllis
Winton, T. Breath
Wolfe, T. I am Charlotte Simmons
Woods, S. Dirt
Woods, S. Reckless abandon
Wright, S. Going native
Yarbrough, S. The end of California
Yu Hua. Brothers

SEX PROBLEMS

See also Hermaphroditism; Incest; Marriage problems;
Sexual perversion; Transsexuals

Hawkes, J. The blood oranges
Huxley, A. Point counter point
Irving, J. The water-method man
Nabokov, V. V. Lolita
Rossner, J. Looking for Mr. Goodbar
Roth, P. My life as a man
Roth, P. Portnoy's complaint
Thomas, D. M. The white hotel
Tolstoy, L., graf. The Kreutzer sonata, The Devil, and other
tales
Tremain, R. Sacred country
Woolf, V. The voyage out
Sex wars. Piercy, M.
Sexing the cherry. Winterson, J.

SEXUAL HARASSMENT

Prose, F. Blue angel

SEXUAL INSTINCT

Ducornet, R. Gazelle
Fromm, P. As cool as I am
Mitchell, D. Black swan green

SEXUAL PERVERSION

Gay, W. Twilight

SEXUALLY TRANSMITTED DISEASES

Lowenthal, M. Charity girl
Seymour: an introduction. Salinger, J. D.
In Salinger, J. D. Raise high the roof beam, carpenters, and
Seymour: an introduction p1
Shackling water. Mansbach, A.
The **shadow** catcher. Wiggins, M.
Shadow country. Matthiessen, P.
A **shadow** in summer. Abraham, D.
The **shadow** king. Stevenson, J.
Shadow of the moon. Kaye, M. M.
The **shadow** of the torturer. Wolfe, G.
The **shadow** of the wind. Ruiz Zafón, C.
Shadow song. Kay, T.
Shadow woman. Perry, T.
The **shadow** year. Ford, J.
Shadowbrook. Swerling, B.
Shadows. Saul, J.
Shadows in the starlight. Cunningham, E.
Shadows in the sun. Oliver, C.
In Oliver, C. From other shores
Shadows on the Hudson. Singer, I. B.
Shadows on the rock. Cather, W.
also in Cather, W. Later novels

SHAKERS

Peck, R. N. A day no pigs would die

SHAKESPEARE, WILLIAM, 1564-1616
About

Bear, E. Ink and steel
Gruber, M. The book of air and shadows
Kellerman, F. The quality of mercy
Martin, W. Harvard Yard
Nye, R. The late Mr. Shakespeare
Simmons, D. Muse of fire

Macbeth

Marsh, Dame N. Light thickens

Parodies, imitations, etc.

Craig, A. Love in idleness
Haig, M. The dead fathers club
Updike, J. Gertrude and Claudius

Shakespeare's kitchen. Segal, L. G.
Shalimar the clown. Rushdie, S.
Shallow grave. Harrod-Eagles, C.
Shallow graves. Healy, J. F.
The **shaman's** bones. Doss, J. D.
Shame the devil. Pelecanos, G. P.
Shane. Schaefer, J. W.

SHANGHAI (CHINA) See China—Shanghai

Shanghai girls. See, L.
The **shape** of dread. Muller, M.
The **shape** of snakes. Walters, M.
The **shape** shifter. Hillerman, T.
Shards of memory. Jhabvala, R. P.

SHARECROPPERS See Tenant farming

The **sharing** of flesh. Anderson, P.
In The Hugo winners p558-94
A **shark** out of water. Lathen, E.

SHARKS

Benchley, P. Jaws
Sharp objects. Flynn, G.
Sharpe's battle. Cornwell, B.
Sharpe's devil. Cornwell, B.
Sharpe's fortress. Cornwell, B.
Sharpe's fury. Cornwell, B.
Sharpe's havoc. Cornwell, B.
Sharpe's prey: Richard Sharpe and the Expedition to Copenha-
gen, 1807. Cornwell, B.
Sharpe's Trafalgar. Cornwell, B.
Sharpe's Waterloo. Cornwell, B.
Shattered. Francis, D.
Shattered silk. Michaels, B.

SHAW, THOMAS EDWARD See Lawrence, T. E. (Thomas
Edward), 1888-1935

The **shawl**. Ozick, C.

SHAWNEE INDIANS

Thom, J. A. Panther in the sky
She. Haggard, H. R.
She may not leave. Weldon, F.
She smiled sweetly. Tirone Smith, M.-A.
She walks these hills. McCrumb, S.

SHEEP

Hardy, T. Far from the madding crowd
Parkinson, H. Across open ground

SHEEP FARMING See Sheep

SHEHU, MEHMET, 1913-1981
About

Kadare, I. The Successor
The **shell** seekers. Pilcher, R.
Shelter. Palwick, S.
Shelter from the storm. Mewshaw, M.
The **sheltering** sky. Bowles, P.
also in Bowles, P. The sheltering sky; Let it come down;
The spider's house
The **sheltering** sky; Let it come down; The spider's house.
Bowles, P.
The **shepherd**. Girzone, J. F.

SHEPHERDS

Stirling, J. The island wife
Sheriff Larrabee's prisoner. Brand, M.
In Brand, M. Stolen gold: a western trio

SHERIFFS

Burke, J. L. Rain gods
Davis, C. Winter range
Estleman, L. D. Port hazard
Freeman, C. All that I have
Grimes, M. Belle ruin
Grimes, M. Cold Flat Junction
Grimes, M. Hotel Paradise
Letts, B. Shoot the moon
McCarthy, C. No country for old men
McCrumb, S. The ballad of Frankie Silver
McCrumb, S. The hangman's beautiful daughter
McCrumb, S. If ever I return, pretty Peggy-O
McCrumb, S. She walks these hills
McLarty, R. Art in America
McMurtry, L. Telegraph days
Meyer, P. American rust
Parker, R. B. Appaloosa
Parker, R. B. Brimstone

SHORT STORIES—_Continued_

Capote, T. Breakfast at Tiffany's: a short novel and three stories

Capote, T. The complete stories of Truman Capote

Card, O. S. Keeper of dreams

Card, O. S. Maps in a mirror

Carter, A. Burning your boats

Carver, R. Collected stories

Cather, W. The troll garden

Cather, W. Willa Cather's collected short fiction, 1892-1912

A Century of great Western stories

Chandler, R. Raymond Chandler

Chandler, R. Stories and early novels

Cheever, J. Collected stories and other writings

Chekhov, A. P. Early short stories, 1883-1888

Chekhov, A. P. Later short stories, 1888-1903

Chekhov, A. P. Longer stories from the last decade

Cherryh, C. J. The collected short fiction of C.J. Cherryh

Chesterton, G. K. Father Brown mystery stories

Chesterton, G. K. The Father Brown omnibus

Chesterton, G. K. The innocence of Father Brown

Chopin, K. Complete novels and stories

Christie, A. Three blind mice and other stories

Clark, M. H. The Anastasia syndrome and other stories

Clarke, A. C. The collected stories of Arthur C. Clarke

Colette. The collected stories of Colette

Connell, E. S. Lost in Uttar Pradesh

Conrad, J. Great short works of Joseph Conrad

Conrad, J. The portable Conrad

Cooper, J. C. The future has a past

Cooper, J. C. Wild stars seeking midnight suns

Coward, N. The collected stories of Noël Coward

Cozarinsky, E. The bride from Odessa

Crane, E. You must be this happy to enter

Crane, S. The complete short stories & sketches of Stephen Crane

Crane, S. The portable Stephen Crane

Crane, S. Prose and poetry

Crane, S. The red badge of courage and other stories

Cross, A. The collected stories of Amanda Cross

Dahl, R. Collected stories

D'Ambrosio, C., Jr. The dead fish museum

Dann, J. Jubilee

Danticat, E. Krik? Krak!

The dark

Dark matter

Davis, L. The collected stories of Lydia Davis

Day, C. The circus in winter

De la Mare, W. Collected tales

DeMarinis, R. Borrowed hearts

Dexter, C. Morse's greatest mystery and other stories

Díaz, J. Drown

The Dick Francis treasury of great racing stories

Dickens, C. The complete ghost stories of Charles Dickens

Dinesen, I. Seven Gothic tales

Dinesen, I. Winter's tales

Disch, T. M. The wall of America

Doctorow, C. Overclocked

Doctorow, E. L. Sweet land stories

Doenges, J. What she left me: stories and a novella

Doerr, H. The tiger in the grass

Donoghue, E. Touchy subjects

Donovan, G. Young Irelanders

Dostoyevsky, F. The best short stories of Dostoevsky

Doyle, Sir A. C. The best science fiction of Arthur Conan Doyle

Doyle, Sir A. C. The complete Sherlock Holmes

Doyle, R. The deportees and other stories

Drake, D. Grimmer than hell

Drummond, L. L. Anything you say can and will be used against you

Du Maurier, Dame D. Daphne du Maurier's classics of the macabre

Dumas, A. Short stories

Dybek, S. I sailed with Magellan

Effinger, G. A. George Alec Effinger live! from planet Earth

Eisenberg, D. Twilight of the superheroes

Endō, S. The final martyrs

Engel, M. P. Strangers and sojourners

Enright, A. Yesterday's weather

Epstein, J. Fabulous small Jews

Erdrich, L. The red convertible

Faber, M. Vanilla bright like Eminem

Farmer, P. J. The classic Philip José Farmer, 1952-1964— 1964-1973

Faulkner, W. Collected stories of William Faulkner

Faulkner, W. The Faulkner reader

Faulkner, W. Go down, Moses

Faulkner, W. Uncollected stories of William Faulkner

Faulkner, W. The unvanquished

Feeling very strange

Fifty years of the best from Ellery Queen's Mystery Magazine

Finch, S. The guild of xenolinguists

Fitzgerald, F. S. The Fitzgerald reader

Fitzgerald, F. S. Flappers and philosophers

Fitzgerald, F. S. The short stories of F. Scott Fitzgerald

Fitzgerald, F. S. Six tales of the jazz age, and other stories

Fitzgerald, F. S. The stories of F. Scott Fitzgerald

Fitzgerald, F. S. Tales of the jazz age

Fitzgerald, P. The means of escape

Ford, J. The drowned life

Ford, J. The empire of ice cream

Ford, R. A multitude of sins

Ford, R. Women with men

Forester, C. S. Mr. Midshipman Hornblower

Forster, E. M. The collected tales of E. M. Forster

Forsyth, F. The veteran

Francis, D. Field of thirteen

Freed, L. The curse of the appropriate man

Freudenberger, N. Lucky girls

Fuentes, C. The crystal frontier

Fuentes, C. Happy families

Fulton, A. The nightingales of Troy

Gaiman, N. Fragile things

Gaitskill, M. Don't cry

Gao Xingjian. Buying a fishing rod for my grandfather

García Márquez, G. Collected stories

García Márquez, G. Leaf storm, and other stories

García Márquez, G. Strange pilgrims

Gardam, J. The people on Privilege Hill and other stories

Gardiner, J. R. The Magellan House

Gay, W. I hate to see that evening sun go down

Gifford, B. The stars above Veracruz

Gilchrist, E. The age of miracles

Gilchrist, E. The cabal and other stories

Gilchrist, E. Ellen Gilchrist: collected stories

Gilchrist, E. Flights of angels

Gilman, C. P. The Charlotte Perkins Gilman reader

Gogol', N. V. The collected tales of Nikolai Gogol

Gogol', N. V. The overcoat, and other tales of good and evil

Gordimer, N. Beethoven was one-sixteenth black

Gordimer, N. Jump and other stories

Gordimer, N. Loot, and other stories

Gorky, M. Selected short stories

Great stories of the American West

Greatest hits

Green cane and juicy flotsam

Greene, G. Collected stories

Greene, G. The last word and other stories

Groff, L. Delicate edible birds and other stories

Gurganus, A. White people

Ha Jin. The bridegroom

Hadley, T. Sunstroke and other stories

Hammett, D. Crime stories and other writings

Hammett, D. Nightmare town

Hardy, T. Wessex tales

Harrison, H. Stainless steel visions

Harte, B. The best short stories of Bret Harte

Harte, B. The Luck of Roaring Camp, and other tales

Hawthorne, N. Complete short stories of Nathaniel Hawthorne

Hawthorne, N. Mosses from an old manse

Hawthorne, N. The snow-image

Hawthorne, N. Tales and sketches, including Twice-told tales, Mosses from an old manse, and The snow-image; A wonder book for girls and boys; Tanglewood tales for girls and boys, being a second Wonder book

Hawthorne, N. Twice-told tales

Helprin, M. Ellis Island & other stories

Helprin, M. The Pacific and other stories

Hemingway, E. The Hemingway reader

Hemingway, E. In our time

Hemingway, E. Men without women

Hemingway, E. The Nick Adams stories

Hemingway, E. The short stories

Hemingway, E. The snows of Kilimanjaro and other stories

Hemon, A. Love and obstacles

Hempel, A. The collected stories of Amy Hempel

SHORT STORIES—*Continued*

Mortimer, J. The second Rumpole omnibus
Mosley, W. Always outnumbered, always outgunned
Mosley, W. Six easy pieces
Mosley, W. Walkin' the dog
Mowat, F. The Snow Walker
Mueenuddin, D. In other rooms, other wonders
Munro, A. Carried away
Munro, A. Friend of my youth
Munro, A. Hateship, friendship, courtship, loveship, marriage
Munro, A. The love of a good woman
Munro, A. The moons of Jupiter
Munro, A. Open secrets
Munro, A. Runaway
Munro, A. Selected stories
Munro, A. The view from Castle Rock
Murakami, H. Blind willow, sleeping woman
My mistress's sparrow is dead
The Mysterious West
Nabokov, V. V. The stories of Vladimir Nabokov
Narayan, R. K. The grandmother's tale and selected stories
Narayan, R. K. Malgudi days
Narayan, R. K. Under the banyan tree and other stories
Nebula Awards showcase [date]
The new space opera
New stories from the South: the year's best [date]
The New treasury of great racing stories
The Norton book of science fiction
Nothing but you
Oates, J. C. The collector of hearts
Oates, J. C. Dear husband,
Oates, J. C. Faithless
Oates, J. C. Haunted
Oates, J. C. Heat, and other stories
Oates, J. C. High lonesome
Oates, J. C. I am no one you know
Oates, J. C. Marriages and infidelities
Oates, J. C. Where are you going, where have you been?
Oates, J. C. Where is here?
Oates, J. C. Wild nights!
Oates, J. C. Will you always love me? and other stories
O'Brien, E. A fanatic heart
O'Brien, E. Lantern slides
O'Brien, T. The things they carried
O'Connor, F. The complete stories
O'Connor, F. Everything that rises must converge
O'Connor, F. A good man is hard to find and other stories
O'Connor, F. Collected stories
O'Faoláin, S. The collected stories of Seán O'Faoláin
O'Hara, J. Collected stories of John O'Hara
Olsen, T. Tell me a riddle
The Oxford book of American detective stories
The Oxford book of American short stories
The Oxford book of English ghost stories
The Oxford book of English love stories
The Oxford book of English short stories
The Oxford book of gothic tales
The Oxford book of Irish short stories
The Oxford book of Jewish short stories
The Oxford book of Latin American short stories
The Oxford book of modern fairy tales
The Oxford book of science fiction stories
The Oxford book of short stories
The Oxford book of spy stories
The Oxford book of travel stories
The Oxford book of twentieth-century ghost stories
Ozick, C. Dictation
Packer, Z. Drinking coffee elsewhere
Paley, G. The collected stories
Paretsky, S. Windy City blues
Parker, D. Here lies
Paton, A. Tales from a troubled land
Penguin book of gay short fiction
The Penguin book of lesbian short stories
Peters, E. A rare Benedictine
Peterson, P. W. Women in the grove
Pilcher, R. Flowers in the rain & other stories
Pirandello, L. Short stories
Poe, E. A. Complete stories and poems of Edgar Allan Poe
Poe's children
Pollock, D. R. Knockemstiff
Porter, J. A. All aboard
Porter, K. A. Collected stories and other writings
Porter, K. A. The collected stories of Katherine Anne Porter

Porter, K. A. Flowering Judas and other stories
Porter, K. A. The leaning tower, and other stories
Price, R. The collected stories
Price, R. The foreseeable future
Pritchett, V. S. Complete collected stories
Proulx, A. Bad dirt
Proulx, A. Close range
Proulx, A. Fine just the way it is
Proust, M. The complete short stories of Marcel Proust
Pushkin, A. S. Alexander Pushkin: complete prose fiction
Pym, B. Civil to strangers and other writings
Queen, E. The best of Ellery Queen
Rawlings, M. K. Short stories
Rendell, R. Blood lines
Rendell, R. Collected stories
Rhys, J. The collected short stories
Robinson, K. S. The Martians
Robinson, R. A perfect stranger
Roger Caras' Treasury of great cat stories
Roger Caras' Treasury of great dog stories
Roth, J. The collected stories of Joseph Roth
Roth, P. Goodbye, Columbus
Roth, P. Goodbye, Columbus, and five short stories
Roth, P. Novels & stories, 1959-1962
Runyon, D. Guys and dolls
Rushdie, S. East, west
Russell, K. St. Lucy's home for girls raised by wolves
Russo, R. The whore's child
Saki. The short stories of Saki
Salinger, J. D. Nine stories
Salter, J. Last night
Sartre, J. P. Intimacy, and other stories
Saunders, G. In persuasion nation
Sayers, D. L. Hangman's holiday
Sayers, D. L. In the teeth of the evidence and other stories
Sayers, D. L. Lord Peter
Saylor, S. The house of the Vestals
Schaefer, J. W. The collected stories of Jack Schaefer
Scholz, C. The amount to carry
Scott, J. Everybody loves somebody
Segal, L. G. Shakespeare's kitchen
Seiffert, R. Field study
Selgin, P. Drowning lessons
Shabtai, Y. Uncle Peretz takes off
Shade, E. Eyesores
Shaw, I. Short stories: five decades
Shepard, J. Like you'd understand, anyway
Shepard, L. The best of Lucius Shepard
Shepard, S. Great dream of heaven
Sholem Aleichem. The best of Sholom Aleichem
Sholem Aleichem. Tevye the dairyman and The railroad stories
Sholem Aleichem. Tevye's daughters
Shonk, K. The red passport
Shulman, M. The many loves of Dobie Gillis
Silber, J. Ideas of heaven
Sillitoe, A. The loneliness of the long-distance runner
Silverberg, R. The collected stories of Robert Silverberg
Simpson, H. In the driver's seat
Singer, I. B. Collected stories: A friend of Kafka to Passions
Singer, I. B. Collected stories: Gimpel the fool to The letter writer
Singer, I. B. Collected stories: One night in Brazil to The death of Methuselah
Singer, I. B. A crown of feathers and other stories
Singer, I. B. A friend of Kafka and other stories
Singer, I. B. Gimpel the fool and other stories
Singer, I. B. The image and other stories
Singer, I. B. An Isaac Bashevis Singer reader
Singer, I. B. Old Love
Singer, I. B. Passions and other stories
Singer, I. B. The séance & other stories
Singer, I. B. Short Friday & other stories
Singer, I. B. The Spinoza of Market Street
Škvorecký, J. When Eve was naked
The Sleeper wakes
Smiley, J. The age of grief
Snow white, blood red
Sorrentino, G. The moon in its flight
Spark, M. Open to the public
Spencer, E. The southern woman
Spencer, E. The stories of Elizabeth Spencer
Stafford, J. The collected stories of Jean Stafford
Stegner, W. E. Collected stories of Wallace Stegner

TITLE AND SUBJECT INDEX

SIERRA MADRE MOUNTAINS (MEXICO)

Traven, B. The treasure of the Sierra Madre
A **sight** for sore eyes. Rendell, R.
Sightblinder's story. See Saberhagen, F. The second book of lost swords: Sightblinder's story
Sights unseen. Gibbons, K.
The **Sigma** protocol. Ludlum, R.
Sign of chaos. Zelazny, R.
The **sign** of four. Doyle, Sir A. C.
The **sign** of the book. Dunning, J.
Sign of the unicorn. Zelazny, R.
The **signal**. Carlson, R.
Signal & noise. Griesemer, J.
Signed, Mata Hari. Murphy, Y.
Silas Marner. Eliot, G.
Silence. Endō, S.
The **silence** in the garden. Trevor, W.
The **silence** of the lambs. Harris, T.
The **silence** of the rain. García-Roza, L. A.
The **silent** angel. Böll, H.
The **silent** cry. Perry, A.
The **silent** hour. Koryta, M.
Silent Joe. Parker, T. J.
Silent prey. Sandford, J.
Silent witness. Patterson, R. N.
Silk road. Larsen, J.
The **Silmarillion**. Tolkien, J. R. R.

SILVER MINES AND MINING

Conrad, J. Nostromo
Trevanian. Incident at Twenty Mile
The **silver** spoon. Galsworthy, J.
In Galsworthy, J. A modern comedy
The **silver** swan. Banville, J.
Silver wedding. Binchy, M.
The **silver** wolf. Borchardt, A.
Silverlight. Llywelyn, M.
Simisola. Rendell, R.
A **simple** Habana melody: from when the world was good. Hijuelos, O.
A **simple** plan. Smith, S.
Simple speaks his mind. Hughes, L.
Simple stakes a claim. Hughes, L.
Simple takes a wife. Hughes, L.
A **simple** tale. Messud, C.
In Messud, C. The hunters
The **simple** truth. Baldacci, D.
Simple's Uncle Sam. Hughes, L.
Simply love. Balogh, M.
Simply magic. Balogh, M.
Simply perfect. Balogh, M.

SIN

Greene, G. Brighton rock
Sin. Hart, J.
Sin city. Robbins, H.
Sin killer. McMurtry, L.
Sing them home. Kallos, S.

SINGAPORE

Boulle, P. The bridge over the River Kwai
Clavell, J. King Rat
Loh, V. Breaking the tongue
Singer from the sea. Tepper, S. S.

SINGERS

Cather, W. The song of the lark
Doig, I. Prairie nocturne
Erdrich, L. The Master Butchers Singing Club
Faber, M. The courage consort [novelette]
Grossman, D. Someone to run with
Hall, A. L. The rhythm of the road
Hesse, H. Gertrude
Hijuelos, O. A simple Habana melody: from when the world was good
Jackson, S. Caught up in the rapture
Joe, Y. My fine lady
King, R. Domino
Marías, J. The man of feeling
McCrumb, S. If ever I return, pretty Peggy-O
McCrumb, S. The songcatcher
Patchett, A. Bel canto
Patterson, J. Hide & seek
Phillips, A. The song is you
Powers, R. The time of our singing

Pynchon, T. The crying of lot 49
Rushdie, S. The ground beneath her feet
Sarton, M. Anger
Smith, L. The devil's dream
Spencer, L. Small town girl
Steel, D. Amazing grace
Thomas, D. M. The white hotel
Tyler, A. A slipping-down life
Weiner, J. In her shoes
Singing boy. McFarland, D.
The **singing** of the dead. Stabenow, D.
The **singing** sands. Tey, J.
also in Tey, J. Four, five and six by Tey
The **singing** stones. Whitney, P. A.
The **singing** sword. Whyte, J.
Singing the sadness. Hill, R.
Single & Single. Le Carré, J.

SINGLE MEN

See also Widowers
Alam, S. The groom to have been
Hornby, N. About a boy
Lee, C.-R. A gesture life
Lipman, E. The ladies' man
Narayan, R. K. The bachelor of arts
Pym, B. Quartet in autumn
Sams, F. Down town
Spark, M. The bachelors
Stamm, P. On a day like this
Talarigo, J. The ginseng hunter
Wolcott, J. The catsitters

SINGLE-PARENT FAMILY

Dorris, M. The crown of Columbus
Morris, M. M. The lost mother
Petry, A. L. The street
Smith, R. K. Jane's house
A **single** pebble. Hersey, J.
Single wife. Solomon, N.

SINGLE WOMEN

See also Unmarried mothers; Widows
Abu-Jaber, D. Crescent
Albert, E. The book of Dahlia
Allen, S. A. The sugar queen
Ansa, T. M. The hand I fan with
Balzac, H. d. Cousin Bette
Bank, M. The girls' guide to hunting and fishing
Barbery, M. The elegance of the hedgehog
Blew, M. C. Jackalope dreams
Brookner, A. Hotel du Lac
Brookner, A. Undue influence
Bynum, S. S.-L. Ms. Hempel chronicles
Capote, T. The grass harp
Clark, M. H. The Anastasia syndrome
Cox, M. The glass of time
Crouch, K. Girls in trucks
Davenport, K. House of many gods
Davies, P. H. The Welsh girl
Dunn, S. The big love
Faber, M. The hundred and ninety-nine steps
Faulkner, W. Intruder in the dust
Fielding, H. Bridget Jones: the edge of reason
Fielding, H. Bridget Jones's diary
Fielding, J. Charley's web
Fitch, J. Paint it black
Forester, C. S. The African Queen
Fowler, K. J. Sister Noon
Freeman, C. Go with me
Gaffney, P. Flight lessons
Gaskell, E. C. Cranford
Gloss, M. The hearts of horses
Goodman, A. Paradise park
Gordon, M. Final payments
Gould, J. A moment in time
Graham, W. Bella Poldark
Grimes, M. The train now departing: two novellas
Grimes, M. When the mousetrap closes
Groff, L. The monsters of Templeton
Guo Xiaolu. Twenty fragments of a ravenous youth
Guo Xiaolu. A concise Chinese-English dictionary for lovers
Gurganus, A. The practical heart [novelette]
Guterson, M. Gone to the dogs
Hale, S. Austenland
Hannan, C. Missy
Hayter, S. Bandit queen boogie

SISTERS—*Continued*

Tan, A. The hundred secret senses
Tanizaki, J. The Makioka sisters
Tea, M. Rose of no man's land
Trollope, J. A Spanish lover
Vanderbes, J. Easter Island
Walker, A. By the light of my father's smile
Walker, A. The color purple
Wall, P. S. The Wilde women
Weber, K. The little women
Weiner, J. In her shoes

SISTERS AND BROTHERS *See* Brothers and sisters

SISTERS-IN-LAW

Colette. Claudine and Annie
Kingsolver, B. Prodigal summer

SITTING BULL, DAKOTA CHIEF, 1831-1890
About

Jones, D. C. Arrest Sitting Bull

SIX-DAY WAR *See* Israel-Arab War, 1967

Six days of the condor. Grady, J.
Six early stories. Mann, T.
Six easy pieces. Mosley, W.
Six novels. Colette
Six tales of the jazz age, and other stories. Fitzgerald, F. S.
Sixes and sevens. Henry, O.
In Henry, O. The complete works of O. Henry p811-940
The **sixth** book of lost swords: Mindsword's story. Saberhagen, F.
The **sixth** commandment. Sanders, L.
The **sixth** day, and other tales. Levi, P.
Sixty stories. Barthelme, D.
The **size** of the world. Silber, J.
The **skating** rink. Bolaño, R.
Skeleton canyon. Jance, J. A.
Skeleton crew. King, S.
Skeleton dance. Elkins, A. J.
Skeleton Hill. Lovesey, P.
Skeletons at the feast. Bohjalian, C. A.
The **skies** of Pern. McCaffrey, A.
Skin River. Sidor, S.
Skin tight. Hiaasen, C.

SKINHEADS

Prose, F. A changed man
Skinner's drift. Fugard, L.
Skinny dip. Hiaasen, C.
Skinny legs and all. Robbins, T.
Skinwalkers. Hillerman, T.
Skirt and the fiddle. Egolf, T.
The **skrayling** tree. Moorcock, M.
Skulduggery. Hart, C. G.
The **skull** beneath the skin. James, P. D.
The **skull** mantra. Pattison, E.
The **sky** below. D'Erasmo, S.
Sky coyote. Baker, K.
Sky full of sand. DeMarinis, R.
The **sky** so big and black. Barnes, J.

SKYE (SCOTLAND)

Stewart, M. Wildfire at midnight
Skylight confessions. Hoffman, A.
Slammerkin. Donoghue, E.
Slan. Van Vogt, A. E.
Slan hunter. Van Vogt, A. E.
Slapstick. Vonnegut, K.
Slatewiper. Perdue, L.
Slaughter. Kelton, E.
Slaughterhouse-five. Vonnegut, K.

SLAVE TRADE

Evaristo, B. Blonde roots
Johnson, C. R. Middle passage
Phillips, C. Crossing the river
Unsworth, B. Sacred hunger
Wray, J. Canaan's tongue

SLAVERY

See also Abolitionists; African Americans; Fugitive slaves; Slave trade; Underground railroad
Bell, M. S. All souls' rising
Butler, O. E. Kindred
Caputo, P. Acts of faith
Cather, W. Sapphira and the slave girl
Chase-Riboud, B. Sally Hemings

Condé, M. I, Tituba, black witch of Salem
Crafts, H. The bondswomans narrative
Durham, D. A. A walk through darkness
Fuller, D. Sweetsmoke
Gaines, E. J. The autobiography of Miss Jane Pittman
García, C. Monkey hunting
Gibbons, K. On the occasion of my last afternoon
Hambly, B. Sold down the river
Hansen, B. The monsters of St. Helena
Heidish, M. A woman called Moses
Heinlein, R. A. Citizen of the galaxy
Hill, L. Someone knows my name
Jakes, J. Charleston
James, M. The book of night women
Jones, E. P. The known world
L'Engle, M. The other side of the sun
Martin, V. Property
McCaig, D. Jacob's ladder
Morrison, T. A mercy
Pesci, D. Amistad
Phillips, C. Crossing the river
Plain, B. Crescent City
Rhodes, J. P. Voodoo dreams
Smith, W. A. River god
Stowe, H. B. Uncle Tom's cabin
Straight, S. A million nightingales
Stross, C. Saturn's children
Styron, W. The confessions of Nat Turner
Tademy, L. Cane River
Twain, M. Pudd'nhead Wilson
Vance, J. The last castle
Walker, M. Jubilee
Wallach, J. Seraglio
Warren, R. P. Band of angels
Wright, S. The Amalgamation Polka
Youmans, M. The wolf pit

SLAVES *See* Slavery
Slaves of obsession. Perry, A.

SLED DOG RACING

Henry, S. Murder on the Iditarod Trail

SLEEP

Kress, N. Beggars & choosers
Kress, N. Beggars in Spain
Yoshimoto, B. Asleep [a novella]
The **Sleeper** wakes. Entered in Part I under title
Sleeping beauty. Macdonald, R.
Sleeping beauty. Michael, J.
Sleeping bones. Forrest, K. V.
Sleeping dogs. Gorman, E.
The **sleeping** father. Sharpe, M.
A **sleeping** life. Rendell, R.
Sleeping with the enemy. Price, N.
Sleepwalking land. Couto, M.
A **slight** trick of the mind. Cullin, M.
Slightly dangerous. Balogh, M.
Slightly shady. Quick, A.
Slip of the knife. Mina, D.
A **slipping-down** life. Tyler, A.

SLOVAKIA

McCann, C. Zoli
Slow dollar. Maron, M.
Slow man. Coetzee, J. M.
Slowness. Kundera, M.

SLUM LIFE

Abani, C. GraceLand
Algren, N. A walk on the wild side
Bellow, S. The adventures of Augie March
Crane, S. George's mother
Crane, S. Maggie: a girl of the streets (a story of New York)
Dickens, C. Oliver Twist
Farrell, J. T. Studs Lonigan
Naylor, G. The men of Brewster Place
Naylor, G. The women of Brewster Place
Oates, J. C. Them
Petry, A. L. The street
Sinha, I. Animal's people
Smith, B. A tree grows in Brooklyn
Theroux, P. The gateway of India
Wright, R. Native son
Slumberland. Beatty, P.

SLUMS *See* Slum life

SMALL TOWN LIFE—*Continued*

Rash, R. Saints at the river
Reuss, F. Horace afoot
Reynolds, S. A gracious plenty
Richards, D. A. The bay of love and sorrows
Rinehart, S. Built in a day
Roth, P. When she was good
Russo, R. Bridge of sighs
Russo, R. Empire Falls
Russo, R. Nobody's fool
Russo, R. The risk pool
Sams, F. Down town
Santmyer, H. H. "—and ladies of the club"
Saroyan, W. The human comedy
Sarton, M. Kinds of love
Schupack, D. The boy on the bus
Schwartz, J. B. Reservation Road
Settle, M. L. Charley Bland
Sholem Aleichem. The nightingale
Shreve, A. Strange fits of passion
Shreve, S. R. The visiting physician
Siddons, A. R. Nora, Nora
Simpson, M. Off Keck Road
Smith, L. Family linen
Sparks, N. A bend in the road
Spencer, L. Bitter sweet
Spencer, L. Morning glory
Spencer, L. That Camden summer
Steinbeck, J. East of Eden
Stowe, H. B. Oldtown folks
Strout, E. Amy and Isabelle
Strout, E. Olive Kitteridge
Tarkington, B. Alice Adams
Thomas, R. The fourth Durango
Trigiani, A. Big Cherry Holler
Trigiani, A. Big Stone Gap
Trigiani, A. Milk glass moon
Tryon, T. In the fire of spring
Tryon, T. The wings of the morning
Twain, M. Pudd'nhead Wilson
Updike, J. Villages
Vernon, O. A killing in this town
Wallace, D. The Watermelon King
Watson, B. The heaven of Mercury
Welty, E. Losing battles
Welty, E. The optimist's daughter
White, B. Quite a year for plums
Whitehead, C. Apex hides the hurt
Wilcox, J. Heavenly days
Wilcox, J. Hunk City
Winthrop, E. Island justice
Wolfe, T. Look homeward, angel
Wolfe, T. O lost
Woods, S. Chiefs
Yarbrough, S. The end of California
Yarbrough, S. Prisoners of war
Zuber, I. Salt
Small vices. Parker, R. B.

SMALLWOOD, JOSEPH R., 1900-1991
About
Johnston, W. The colony of unrequited dreams

SMELL

Milton, G. Edward Trencom's nose
A **smile** on the face of the tiger. Estleman, L. D.
Smiley's people. Le Carré, J.
Smilla's sense of snow. Høeg, P.

SMITH, JOHN, 1580-1631
About
Vollmann, W. T. Argall

SMITHSONIAN INSTITUTION
Vidal, G. The Smithsonian Institution
The **Smithsonian** Institution. Vidal, G.
Smoke. Westlake, D. E.
Smoke in mirrors. Krentz, J. A.
Smokescreen. Francis, D.

SMOKING

Gutcheon, B. R. Five fortunes

SMUGGLERS *See* Smuggling

SMUGGLING

Cussler, C. Flood tide
Cussler, C. Inca gold

Du Maurier, Dame D. Jamaica Inn
Hemingway, E. To have and have not
Howard, L. Cry no more
Spark, M. The comforters
Stone, R. Dog soldiers
The **snake** pit. Ward, M. J.
The **snake** tattoo. Barnes, L.
The **snake**, the crocodile, and the dog. Peters, E.
Snakepit. Isegawa, M.

SNAKES

Parker, T. J. Where serpents lie
Snare. Kerr, K.
The **sniper's** wife. Mayor, A.
Snopes. Faulkner, W.
Snow. Pamuk, O.
Snow angels. O'Nan, S.
Snow country. Kawabata, Y.
In Kawabata, Y. Snow country, and Thousand cranes p1-175
Snow country, and Thousand cranes. Kawabata, Y.
Snow falling on cedars. Guterson, D.
The **snow-image**. Hawthorne, N.
In Hawthorne, N. Tales and sketches, including Twice-told tales, Mosses from an old manse, and The snow-image; A wonder book for girls and boys; Tanglewood tales for girls and boys, being a second Wonder book
Snow in August. Hamill, P.
The **Snow** Queen. Vinge, J. D.

SNOW STORMS *See* Storms
The **Snow** Walker. Mowat, F.

Snow white, blood red. Entered in Part I under title
Snowleg. Shakespeare, N.
The **Snowman's** children. Hirshberg, G.
The **snows** of Kilimanjaro and other stories. Hemingway, E.

SNOWSTORMS *See* Storms
So Big. Ferber, E.
So long, and thanks for all the fish. Adams, D.
So long, see you tomorrow. Maxwell, W.
In Maxwell, W. Later novels and stories
So sure of death. Stabenow, D.

SOCIAL CLASSES
See also Class distinction; Society novels
Auchincloss, L. Her infinite variety
Bellow, S. The adventures of Augie March
Boyle, T. C. The tortilla curtain
Canin, E. America America
Colegate, I. The shooting party
Coleridge, N. Godchildren
Doctorow, E. L. Ragtime
Ghosh, A. Sea of poppies
Hosseini, K. The kite runner
James, H. In the cage
James, H. The portrait of a lady
Keneally, T. River town
Lodge, D. Nice work
Oates, J. C. Because it is bitter, and because it is my heart
O'Hara, J. Ten North Frederick
Taylor, P. H. A summons to Memphis
Waugh, E. Decline and fall
Wilder, T. Theophilus North
Wolfe, T. I am Charlotte Simmons

SOCIAL CONDITIONS *See* Social problems

SOCIAL ISOLATION

Desai, A. Fire on the mountain
Handke, P. The left-handed woman
Silverberg, R. The man in the maze
Watson, J. E. Asta in the wings

SOCIAL PROBLEMS
See also Child labor; Crime and criminals; Divorce; Drug abuse; Drug addiction; Homeless persons; Juvenile delinquency; Poverty; Prejudices; Prostitution; Race relations; Slum life; Suicide; Technology and civilization; Unemployed; Violence
Calvino, I. Invisible cities
Cronin, A. J. The citadel
De Hartog, J. The peaceable kingdom
Doctorow, E. L. Ragtime
Dos Passos, J. The 42nd parallel
Dos Passos, J. 1919
Dos Passos, J. Manhattan transfer
Dos Passos, J. U.S.A.
Dreiser, T. An American tragedy

TITLE AND SUBJECT INDEX

SOCIAL PROBLEMS—*Continued*

Dreiser, T. Jennie Gerhardt
Forster, E. M. A passage to India
Girzone, J. F. Joshua and the city
Hugo, V. Les misérables
Kingsolver, B. Animal dreams
Maḥfūẓ, N. Midaq Alley
Momaday, N. S. House made of dawn
Morrison, T. Sula
Musil, R. The man without qualities
Rossner, J. Looking for Mr. Goodbar
Sinclair, U. The jungle
Smith, B. A tree grows in Brooklyn
Smith, L. E. Strange fruit
Smith, M. C. Rose
Steinbeck, J. The grapes of wrath
Styron, W. Set this house on fire
Tolstoy, L., graf. Childhood, Boyhood and Youth
Turgenev, I. S. Fathers and sons
Wells, H. G. Tono-Bungay
Wouk, H. Marjorie Morningstar
Wright, R. Native son
Wright, R. The outsider

SOCIAL SATIRE *See* Satire

SOCIAL WORKERS

Cleage, P. I wish I had a red dress
Martin, S. The pleasure of my company
Shaley, T. Husband and wife

SOCIALISM

Hawthorne, N. The Blithedale romance
Zola, É. Germinal
The **society**. Palmer, M.

SOCIETY NOVELS

See also Aristocracy
Auchincloss, L. The book class
Auchincloss, L. Her infinite variety
Benson, E. F. Make way for Lucia
Dunne, D. An inconvenient woman
Dunne, D. People like us
Dunne, D. The two Mrs. Grenvilles
Galsworthy, J. The silver spoon
Howells, W. D. The rise of Silas Lapham
Huxley, A. Point counter point
Jacobson, D. All for love
James, H. The Europeans
James, H. The spoils of Poynton
Minot, S. Folly
Mitford, N. Love in a cold climate
Mitford, N. The pursuit of love
Musil, R. The man without qualities
Powell, A. A dance to the music of time
Proust, M. The Guermantes way
Sackville-West, V. The Edwardians
Thackeray, W. M. Vanity fair
Tolstoy, L., graf. Anna Karenina
Trollope, A. Framley parsonage
Trollope, A. The prime minister
Vidal, G. 1876
Waugh, E. Brideshead revisited
Waugh, E. Vile bodies
Wharton, E. The age of innocence
Wharton, E. The children
Wharton, E. The house of mirth

SOCIETY OF FRIENDS

De Hartog, J. The peaceable kingdom
Jiles, P. The color of lightning
The **Society** of S. Hubbard, S.

SOCRATES

About

Renault, M. The last of the wine
Sodom and Gomorrah. Proust, M.
SOFIA (BULGARIA) *See* Bulgaria—Sofia
The **soft** detective. Keating, H. R. F.
Softspoken. Shepard, L.
Solar barque. See Nin, A. Seduction of the Minotaur
Solaris. Lem, S.
Sold down the river. Hambly, B.
A **soldier** of the great war. Helprin, M.
The **soldier** spies. Griffin, W. E. B.

SOLDIERS

See also Women soldiers
De Bernières, L. Corelli's mandolin
Dickson, G. R. Lost Dorsai
Habila, H. Measuring time
Jennings, G. Raptor
Kadare, I. The general of the dead army
Karnezis, P. The maze
Meek, J. The people's act of love
Scalzi, J. Old man's war

Australia
McCullough, C. An indecent obsession

Austria
Hašek, J. The good soldier Svejk

Canada
MacNeil, R. Burden of desire

France
Balzac, H. d. The country doctor
Colette. The kepi
Faulkner, W. A fable
Flanagan, T. The year of the French

Germany
Böll, H. The silent angel
Higgins, J. The eagle has landed
Kirst, H. H. Forward, Gunner Asch!
Kirst, H. H. The return of Gunner Asch
Kirst, H. H. The revolt of Gunner Asch
Remarque, E. M. All quiet on the western front
Remarque, E. M. A time to love and a time to die
Robbins, D. L. War of the rats
Shaw, I. The young lions

Great Britain
Barker, P. The eye in the door
Barker, P. The ghost road
Barker, P. Regeneration
Boulle, P. The bridge over the River Kwai
Cornwell, B. Sharpe's battle
Cornwell, B. Sharpe's fortress
Cornwell, B. Sharpe's fury
Cornwell, B. Sharpe's havoc
Cornwell, B. Sharpe's prey: Richard Sharpe and the Expedition to Copenhagen, 1807
Cornwell, B. Sharpe's Trafalgar
Cornwell, B. Sharpe's Waterloo
Ford, F. M. A man could stand up
Ford, F. M. No more parades
MacLean, A. Force 10 from Navarone
MacLean, A. The guns of Navarone
Mallinson, A. A close run thing
Ondaatje, M. The English patient
Scott, P. A division of the spoils
Waugh, E. Men at arms
Waugh, E. Officers and gentlemen

Israel
Leshem, R. Beaufort

Japan
Shan Sa. The girl who played go

Rome
Llywelyn, M. Druids

Russia
See also Cossacks
Robbins, D. L. War of the rats
Tolstoy, L., graf. War and peace

United States
See also African American soldiers
Bausch, R. Peace
Clavell, J. King Rat
Crane, S. The red badge of courage
Dos Passos, J. Three soldiers
Fleming, T. J. Dreams of glory
Gold, G. D. Sunnyside
Goonan, K. A. In war times
Griffin, W. E. B. The aviators
Griffin, W. E. B. Special ops
Hawke, E. Ash Wednesday

SOLDIERS—United States—*Continued*
Hersey, J. A bell for Adano
Higgins, J. Night of the fox
Hooker, R. MASH
Johnson, D. Tree of smoke
Jones, J. From here to eternity
Jones, J. The thin red line
Jones, J. Whistle
Mailer, N. The naked and the dead
Melman, P. C. Landsman
Melville, H. Israel Potter
Nathanson, E. M. The dirty dozen
O'Brien, T. Going after Cacciato
Purdy, J. The nephew
Ricks, T. E. A soldier's duty
Shaara, J. Gone for soldiers
Shaw, I. The young lions
Shulman, M. Rally round the flag, boys!
Sparks, N. Dear John
Sundaresan, I. The splendor of silence
Willard, T. Buffalo soldiers
Wright, S. Meditations in green

Vietnam

Bao Ninh. The sorrow of war
SOLDIERS, BLACK *See* African American soldiers
The **soldier's** art. Powell, A.
In Powell, A. A dance to the music of time
A **soldier's** duty. Ricks, T. E.

SOLDIERS OF FORTUNE

Caputo, P. Horn of Africa
Cussler, C. Plague ship
Forsyth, F. The dogs of war
Walters, M. The devil's feather
Soldiers' pay. Faulkner, W.
also in Faulkner, W. Novels, 1926-1929
The **soldier's** return. Bragg, M.
SOLICITORS *See* Law and lawyers
Solitaire. Eskridge, K.

SOLITUDE

Parks, T. Cleaver
Solomon Gursky was here. Richler, M.

SOLOMON ISLANDS

See also World War, 1939-1945—Solomon Islands
London, J. South Sea tales

SOMALIA

Farah, N. Knots
Farah, N. Links
McDonell, N. An expensive education
Some bitter taste. Nabb, M.
Some buried Caesar & The golden spiders. Stout, R.
Some deaths before dying. Dickinson, P.
Some do not. Ford, F. M.
In Ford, F. M. Parade's end
Somebody else's music. Haddam, J.
Someone knows my name. Hill, L.
Someone to run with. Grossman, D.
Someplace to be flying. De Lint, C.
Somersault. Ōe, K.
SOMERSET (ENGLAND) *See* England—Somerset
Something borrowed, something black. Estleman, L. D.
Something happened. Heller, J.
Something in the air. Lathen, E.
Something like a love affair. Symons, J.
Something rising (light and swift). Kimmel, H.
Something special. Murdoch, I.
Something to tell you. Kureishi, H.
Something wicked this way comes. Bradbury, R.
Sometimes a great notion. Kesey, K.

SOMNAMBULISM

Brown, C. B. Edgar Huntly
The **somnambulist.** Barnes, J.
A **son** called Gabriel. McNicholl, D.
Son of a witch. Maguire, G.
Son of Fletch. Mcdonald, G.
A **son** of the circus. Irving, J.
A **son** of war. Bragg, M.
A **song** for Lya. Martin, G. R. R.
In The Hugo winners p483-544
The **song** is you. Abbott, M. E.

The **song** is you. Phillips, A.
The **song** of Bernadette. Werfel, F.
The **song** of everlasting sorrow. Wang Anyi
Song of ice and fire [series]
Martin, G. R. R. A feast for crows
The **song** of names. Lebrecht, N.
Song of Solomon. Morrison, T.
The **song** of the lark. Cather, W.
In Cather, W. Early novels and stories
Song of the river. Harrison, S.
The **song** of Troy. McCullough, C.
Song yet sung. McBride, J.
The **songcatcher.** McCrumb, S.

SONGS

McCrumb, S. The songcatcher
Songs for the butcher's daughter. Manseau, P.
Songs for the missing. O'Nan, S.
Songs in ordinary time. Morris, M. M.
The **songs** of the kings. Unsworth, B.
Songs without words. Packer, A.
SONGWRITERS *See* Composers
SONS *See* Fathers and sons; Mothers and sons; Stepsons
Sons and lovers. Lawrence, D. H.

SONS-IN-LAW

Saramago, J. The cave
The **sons** of heaven. Baker, K.
Sons of Texas: the rebels. See Kelton, E. The rebels
Soon I will be invincible. Grossman, A.
Sophie's choice. Styron, W.
The **sorceress** and the Cygnet. McKillip, P. A.
SORCERY *See* Witchcraft
The **sorrow** of war. Bao Ninh
The **sorrowing** wind. Pearce, M. E.
In Pearce, M. E. Apple tree lean down p333-494
The **sorrows** of an American. Hustvedt, S.
The **sorrows** of young Werther. Goethe, J. W. v.
In Goethe, J. W. v. The sorrows of young Werther, and Novella p1-167
The **sorrows** of young Werther, and Novella. Goethe, J. W. v.
The **sot-weed** factor. Barth, J.

SOUL

See also Transmigration
Soul circus. Pelecanos, G. P.
Soul mountain. Gao Xingjian
The **soul** thief. Baxter, C.
Souls in the great machine. McMullen, S.
Souls raised from the dead. Betts, D.
The **sound** and the fury. Faulkner, W.
also in Faulkner, W. The Faulkner reader p5-251
also in Faulkner, W. Novels, 1926-1929
The **sound** of butterflies. King, R.
The **sound** of the mountain. Kawabata, Y.
The **sound** of the trees. Gatewood, R.
The **sound** of trumpets. Mortimer, J.
The **sound** of waves. Mishima, Y.
SOUTH (U.S.) *See* Southern States

SOUTH AFRICA

See also Africa
Galgut, D. The impostor
Gordimer, N. The conservationist
Gordimer, N. Get a life
Gordimer, N. July's people
Gordimer, N. Jump and other stories
Gordimer, N. None to accompany me
Gordimer, N. The pickup
Lessing, D. M. Children of violence
Lessing, D. M. The grass is singing
Mda, Z. The whale caller
Michener, J. A. The covenant
Morley, I. Come Sunday
Paton, A. Ah, but your land is beautiful
Paton, A. Cry, the beloved country
Paton, A. Tales from a troubled land
Sheldon, S. Master of the game
Smith, W. A. Golden fox
Smith, W. A. Power of the sword
Smith, W. A. A time to die
Ward, A. E. Forgive me

19th century

Harries, A. Manly pursuits

SOUTHERN STATES—*Continued*

Reynolds, S. A gracious plenty
Siddons, A. R. Heartbreak Hotel
Siddons, A. R. Outer banks
Smith, L. The devil's dream
Smith, L. Oral history
Smith, L. Saving Grace
Spencer, E. The southern woman
Tyler, A. Earthly possessions
Walker, A. The color purple
Wallace, D. Mr. Sebastian and the Negro magician
White, B. Quite a year for plums
Woods, S. Chiefs

19th century

Gibbons, K. On the occasion of my last afternoon
Mitchell, M. Gone with the wind
Price, E. Savannah
Walker, M. Jubilee

Farm life

See Farm life—Southern States

Mountain life

See Mountain life—Southern States

Politics

See Politics—Southern States
The **southern** woman. Spencer, E.
Southern women. Battle, L.

SOUTHWEST, NEW *See* Southwestern States

SOUTHWEST, OLD *See* Old Southwest

SOUTHWESTERN STATES

See also Santa Fe Trail
Anaya, R. A. The man who could fly and other stories
Barrett, W. E. The lilies of the field

Frontier and pioneer life

See Frontier and pioneer life—Southwestern States

SOVIET UNION *See* Russia

Space. Michener, J. A.

SPACE AND TIME

See also Time travel
Benford, G. Timescape
Heinlein, R. A. Job: a comedy of justice
The **space** between us. Umrigar, T. N.

SPACE COLONIES

Anderson, P. The sharing of flesh
Clement, H. Noise
Dick, P. K. Martian time-slip
Dick, P. K. A maze of death
Haldeman, J. W. Marsbound
Hamilton, P. F. The dreaming void
Heinlein, R. A. The moon is a harsh mistress
Jenkins, W. F. Exploration team
Le Guin, U. K. The word for world is forest
Martin, G. R. R. Hunter's run
McCaffrey, A. Freedom's landing
McCaffrey, A. Freedom's ransom
McDevitt, J. Infinity beach
Niven, L. Ringworld
Niven, L. The Ringworld engineers
Niven, L. The Ringworld throne
Niven, L. Ringworld's children
Pohl, F. Man Plus
Pohl, F. Mars Plus
Robinson, K. S. Blue Mars
Robinson, K. S. The Martians
Robinson, K. S. Red Mars
Scalzi, J. Old man's war
Steele, A. M. Coyote
Varley, J. Rolling thunder

SPACE FLIGHT

See also Astronauts; Interplanetary voyages; Science fiction
Pohl, F. Beyond the blue event horizon
Pohl, F. Gateway
Pohl, F. Heechee rendezvous
Sher, I. Gentlemen of space

SPACE FLIGHT TO MARS

Varley, J. Red thunder

SPACE FLIGHT TO THE MOON

Michener, J. A. Space
The **space** merchants. Pohl, F.

SPACE PROBES

Crichton, M. The Andromeda strain

SPACE SHIPS

Anderson, P. The longest voyage
Clarke, A. C. The Garden of Rama
Clarke, A. C. Rama II
Clarke, A. C. Rama revealed
Clarke, A. C. Rendezvous with Rama
Crichton, M. Sphere
Leiber, F. Ship of shadows
Lem, S. Fiasco
McCaffrey, A. The city who fought
Pohl, F. Homegoing
Varley, J. Red thunder
Westerfeld, S. The killing of worlds

SPACE STATIONS

Bova, B. Jupiter
Harrigan, S. Challenger Park

SPACE TRAVEL *See* Space flight

Spaceman blues. Slattery, B. F.

SPAIN

Bolaño, R. The skating rink
Greene, G. Monsignor Quixote
Handke, P. Crossing the Sierra de Gredos
Hemingway, E. The sun also rises
Malraux, A. Man's hope
Mérimée, P. Carmen
Muñoz Molina, A. In her absence
Muñoz Molina, A. A manuscript of ashes

To 711

Yarbro, C. Q. Come twilight

16th century

Cervantes Saavedra, M. d. Don Quixote de la Mancha

17th century

Cervantes Saavedra, M. d. Three exemplary novels
Pérez-Reverte, A. Captain Alatriste
Pérez-Reverte, A. Purity of blood

19th century

Cornwell, B. Sharpe's fury
Pérez Galdós, B. Doña Perfecta
Pérez Galdós, B. Torquemada
Pérez-Reverte, A. The fencing master

Civil War, 1936-1939

Leavitt, D. While England sleeps
Pawel, R. Death of a nationalist
Sansom, C. J. Winter in Madrid

Politics

See Politics—Spain

Rural life

Pérez Galdós, B. Doña Perfecta

Barcelona

Gwyn, R. The color of a dog running away
Hériz, E. d. Lies
Mortman, D. True colors
Pérez-Reverte, A. The nautical chart
Ruiz Zafón, C. The angel's game
Ruiz Zafón, C. The shadow of the wind

Madrid

Lewis, M. G. The monk
Pérez Galdós, B. Torquemada
Pérez-Reverte, A. The Club Dumas
Romano-Lax, A. The Spanish bow
Ruiz, L. M. Only one thing missing
Vargas Llosa, M. The bad girl

Seville

Cervantes Saavedra, M. d. Man of glass
Cervantes Saavedra, M. d. Rinconete and Cortadillo
Wilson, R. The blind man of Seville
Wilson, R. The hidden assassins

SPANIARDS

England

Hill, R. The Stranger House
Marías, J. All souls
Marías, J. Dark back of time
Marías, J. Your face tomorrow: volume one: Fever and spear
Marías, J. Your face tomorrow: volume two: Dance and dream

Mexico

Falconer, C. Feathered serpent
Sherwood, F. Night of sorrows

SPANISH ARMADA, 1588 *See* Armada, 1588
The **Spanish** bow. Romano-Lax, A.
SPANISH CIVIL WAR, 1936-1939 *See* Spain—Civil War, 1936-1939
SPANISH INQUISITION *See* Inquisition
A **Spanish** lover. Trollope, J.

SPANISH MAIN

Sabatini, R. Captain Blood
The **spare** room. Garner, H.
The **spare** wife. Witchel, A.
The **spark**. Wharton, E.
   In Wharton, E. Novellas and other writings
SPARKS, TIMOTHY *See* Dickens, Charles, 1812-1870
The **sparrow**. Russell, M. D.
Spartina. Casey, J.
SPAS *See* Health resorts
Special ops. Griffin, W. E. B.
The **special** prisoner. Lehrer, J.
Special topics in calamity physics. Pessl, M.
Specimen days. Cunningham, M.
A **spectacle** of corruption. Liss, D.

SPECULATION

Moggach, D. Tulip fever
Norris, F. The pit

SPEECH DISORDERS

   See also Stuttering
The **speed** of dark. Moon, E.
The **Spellman** files. Lutz, L.
Spence + Lila. Mason, B. A.
   In Mason, B. A. Nancy Culpepper
Spencer's Mountain. Hamner, E.
Sphere. Crichton, M.
Spider. McGrath, P.
The **spider's** house. Bowles, P.
   In Bowles, P. The sheltering sky; Let it come down; The spider's house
Spiderweb. Lively, P.

SPIES

   See also International intrigue; Secret service. Your scandalous ways
Abrahams, P. Hard rain
Bourne, J. My lord and spymaster
Bourne, J. The spymaster's lady
Bowen, E. The heat of the day
Buchan, J. The thirty-nine steps
Buckley, W. F. Mongoose, R.I.P
Charyn, J. Johnny One-Eye
Clancy, T. The hunt for Red October
Clavell, J. Noble house
Cooper, J. F. The spy
Cornwell, B. Sharpe's havoc
Davies, R. What's bred in the bone
Deaver, J. Garden of beasts
Deighton, L. Berlin game
Deighton, L. City of gold
Deighton, L. Funeral in Berlin
Deighton, L. The Ipcress file
Deighton, L. London match
Deighton, L. Mexico set
DeMille, N. The charm school
Doctorow, E. L. The book of Daniel
Dunning, J. Two o'clock, eastern wartime
Faulks, S. Devil may care
Fesperman, D. The amateur spy
Finney, P. Gloriana's torch
Fleming, I. Casino Royale
Fleming, I. Doctor No
Fleming, I. From Russia, with love

Fleming, I. Goldfinger
Fleming, I. The man with the golden gun
Fleming, I. On Her Majesty's Secret Service
Fleming, I. You only live twice
Fleming, T. J. Dreams of glory
Follett, K. Eye of the needle
Follett, K. Hornet flight
Follett, K. Lie down with lions
Francis, C. Wolf winter
Freemantle, B. Bomb grade
Freemantle, B. Dead men living
Furst, A. Dark voyage
Furst, A. The spies of Warsaw
Gilman, D. The amazing Mrs. Pollifax
Gilman, D. The elusive Mrs. Pollifax
Gilman, D. A palm for Mrs. Pollifax
Gilman, D. The unexpected Mrs. Pollifax
Goldman, W. Marathon man
Grady, J. Six days of the condor
Greene, G. 3: This gun for hire, The confidential agent, The ministry of fear
Greene, G. The human factor
Greene, G. The ministry of fear
Greene, G. Our man in Havana
Hall, A. Quiller Balalaika
Hall, A. The Quiller memorandum
Hall, A. Quiller Salamander
Hall, A. Quiller solitaire
Higgins, J. The eagle has flown
Higgins, J. The eagle has landed
Horn, D. All other nights
Ignatius, D. Body of lies
Ignatius, D. The increment
Isaacs, S. Shining through
Jakes, J. On secret service
Johnson, D. Tree of smoke
Johnson, D. Lulu in Marrakech
Judd, A. Legacy
Koontz, D. R. Watchers
Le Carré, J. Absolute friends
Le Carré, J. The honourable schoolboy
Le Carré, J. The little drummer girl
Le Carré, J. The looking glass war
Le Carré, J. The night manager
Le Carré, J. Our game
Le Carré, J. A perfect spy
Le Carré, J. The Russia house
Le Carré, J. The secret pilgrim
Le Carré, J. Smiley's people
Le Carré, J. The spy who came in from the cold
Le Carré, J. The tailor of Panama
Le Carré, J. Tinker, tailor, soldier, spy
Leonard, E. Up in Honey's room
Lindsey, D. L. The color of night
Littell, R. The company
Littell, R. Walking back the cat
Ludlum, R. The Bourne identity
Ludlum, R. The Bourne supremacy
Ludlum, R. The Bourne ultimatum
Ludlum, R. The Parsifal mosaic
MacInnes, H. Prelude to terror
MacInnes, H. Ride a pale horse
MacLean, A. Ice Station Zebra
MacLean, A. Where eagles dare
Mailer, N. Harlot's ghost
Marías, J. Your face tomorrow: volume one: Fever and spear
Marías, J. Your face tomorrow: volume two: Dance and dream
Mathews, H. My life in CIA
McCarry, C. Old boys
McEwan, I. The innocent
Morrell, D. The brotherhood of the rose
Murphy, Y. Signed, Mata Hari
Ondaatje, M. The English patient
The Oxford book of spy stories
Rankin, I. Watchman
Sansom, C. J. Winter in Madrid
Smith, M. C. Stallion Gate
Steinhauer, O. The tourist
Sundaresan, I. The splendor of silence
Trenhaile, J. The gates of exquisite view
Trevanian. The Eiger sanction
Trevanian. The Loo sanction
West, Dame R. The birds fall down

STOUT, REX, 1886-1975
Parodies, imitations, etc.
Goldsborough, R. The missing chapter
The **stowaway**. Hough, R.

STOWAWAYS
Hough, R. The stowaway
The **straight** man. Russo, R.
Strange as this weather has been. Pancake, A.
The **strange** case of Dr. Jekyll and Mr. Hyde. Stevenson, R. L.
   also in Stevenson, R. L. The complete short stories of Robert Louis Stevenson
   also in Stevenson, R. L. The strange case of Dr. Jekyll and Mr. Hyde, and other famous tales p1-69
The **strange** case of Dr. Jekyll and Mr. Hyde, and other famous tales. Stevenson, R. L.
A **strange** commonplace. Sorrentino, G.
Strange fits of passion. Shreve, A.
Strange fruit. Smith, L. E.
The **strange** mutiny of Gunner Asch. See Kirst, H. H. The revolt of Gunner Asch
Strange pilgrims. García Márquez, G.
The **stranger**. Camus, A.
The **Stranger** House. Hill, R.
Stranger in a strange land. Heinlein, R. A.
Stranger in paradise. Goudge, E.
A **stranger** is watching. Clark, M. H.
Strangers. Koontz, D. R.
Strangers and brothers. Snow, C. P.
Strangers and sojourners. Engel, M. P.
Strangers in the house. Simenon, G.
Strawberry Sunday. Greenleaf, S.
Stray Kat waltz. Kijewski, K.

STREAM OF CONSCIOUSNESS
Antunes, A. L. The inquisitors' manual
Barnes, D. Nightwood
Bolaño, R. By night in Chile
Böll, H. The clown
Faulkner, W. As I lay dying
Ford, F. M. The last post
Gaddis, W. Agapé agape
García Márquez, G. The autumn of the patriarch
Joyce, J. Finnegans wake
Joyce, J. Ulysses
Lessing, D. M. The golden notebook
Lowry, M. Under the volcano
McGowan, H. Schooling
Parks, T. Destiny
Percy, W. Lancelot
Porter, K. A. Pale horse, pale rider [novelette]
Proust, M. The captive
Proust, M. The captive [and] The fugitive
Proust, M. The fugitive [variant title: The sweet cheat gone]
Proust, M. The Guermantes way
Proust, M. Remembrance of things past
Proust, M. Sodom and Gomorrah
Proust, M. Swann's way
Proust, M. Time regained [variant title: The past recaptured]
Proust, M. Within a budding grove
Pynchon, T. Gravity's rainbow
Styron, W. Lie down in darkness
TSypkin, L. Summer in Baden-Baden
Woolf, V. Jacob's room
Woolf, V. Mrs. Dalloway
Woolf, V. To the lighthouse
Woolf, V. The waves
Woolf, V. The years
The **street**. Petry, A. L.
Street dreams. Kellerman, F.
The **street** lawyer. Grisham, J.
The **street** of a thousand blossoms. Tsukiyama, G.
Streets of Laredo. McMurtry, L.
Strictly business. Henry, O.
   In Henry, O. The complete works of O. Henry p1484-1631

STRIKES AND LOCKOUTS
Galsworthy, J. Swan song
Poyer, D. Thunder on the mountain
Shreve, A. Sea glass
Steinbeck, J. In dubious battle
Strip tease. Hiaasen, C.
Stripped. Freeman, B.

STRIPTEASERS
Bock, C. Beautiful children
Dubus, A. The garden of last days
Flanagan, R. The unknown terrorist
Strivers Row. Baker, K.
STROKE *See* Cerebrovascular disease

STROLLING PLAYERS
Sabatini, R. Scaramouche
Strong as death. Newman, S.
Strong poison. Sayers, D. L.
The **student** conductor. Ford, R.
A **student** of living things. Shreve, S. R.
A **student** of weather. Hay, E.
STUDENTS
   See also College life; College students; School life; Youth
Baxter, C. The soul thief
Cather, W. The professor's house
Cook, R. Coma
Dufossé, C. School's out
Goldman, W. Marathon man
James, H. The pupil
King, S. Rage
Knowles, J. Peace breaks out
Stirling, J. The marrying kind
Studs Lonigan. Farrell, J. T.
A **study** in scarlet. Doyle, Sir A. C.

STUTTERING
Shields, D. Dead languages
SUBMARINE WARFARE *See* World War, 1939-1945—Naval operations—Submarine

SUBMARINES
   See also Nuclear submarines
Beach, E. L. Run silent, run deep
Hemingway, E. Islands in the stream
McCutchan, P. The last farewell
Robinson, P. Kilo class
Robinson, P. Nimitz class
Verne, J. Twenty thousand leagues under the sea
The **subterraneans**. Kerouac, J.
   In Kerouac, J. Road novels 1957-1960

SUBURBAN LIFE
Berger, T. Neighbors
Berne, S. A perfect arrangement
Cheever, J. Bullet Park
Coben, H. Hold tight
Connell, E. S. Mr. Bridge
Connell, E. S. Mrs. Bridge
Cusk, R. Arlington Park
Ford, R. Independence Day
Gardam, J. The queen of the tambourine
Hamilton, J. When Madeline was young
Hill, R. When all is said and done
Hoffman, A. Seventh heaven
Just, W. S. An unfinished season
Levin, I. The Stepford wives
Lippman, L. Scratch a woman
McDermott, A. That night
McMillan, T. The interruption of everything
Oates, J. C. American appetites
Oates, J. C. Middle age
Oates, J. C. Missing mom
Perrotta, T. The abstinence teacher
Perrotta, T. Little children
Powers, J. F. Wheat that springeth green
Roth, P. American pastoral
Shulman, M. Rally round the flag, boys!
Stead, C. The man who loved children
Tropper, J. How to talk to a widower
Tyler, A. The amateur marriage
Updike, J. Rabbit is rich
Updike, J. Rabbit redux
Wilson, S. The man in the gray flannel suit
SUBURBS *See* Suburban life
SUBVERSIVE ACTIVITIES
   See also Terrorism

SUBWAYS
Godey, J. The taking of Pelham one two three
Preston, D. Reliquary
Vine, B. King Solomon's carpet

SUPERNATURAL PHENOMENA—*Continued*

Bradbury, R. Something wicked this way comes
Brower, B. Blue dog, green river
Bull, E. Territory
Clark, M. H. Before I say goodbye
Clark, M. H. Remember me
Connolly, J. Bad men
Davies, R. What's bred in the bone
Donohue, K. Angels of destruction
Drury, T. The driftless area
Due, T. The good house
Due, T. My soul to keep
Fishburne, R. Going to see the elephant
Ford, J. The drowned life
Ginsberg, D. The grift
Gregory, D. Pandemonium
Gruber, M. Night of the jaguar
Hawthorne, N. Twice-told tales
Hill, R. The Stranger House
Hooper, K. Blood sins
James, H. The turn of the screw
Johansen, I. Final target
King, S. Carrie
King, S. Christine
King, S. The dark half
King, S. Desperation
King, S. Duma Key
King, S. Firestarter
King, S. From a Buick 8
King, S. Insomnia
King, S. Lisey's story
King, S. Needful things
King, S. The regulators
King, S. Rose Madder
King, S. Salem's Lot
Koontz, D. R. Brother Odd
Koontz, D. R. By the light of the moon
Koontz, D. R. The darkest evening of the year
Koontz, D. R. From the corner of his eye
L'Amour, L. The haunted mesa
LaValle, V. D. Big machine
Leiber, F. Gonna roll the bones
Levin, I. Rosemary's baby
Lewis, M. G. The monk
Lofts, N. Gad's Hall
Lovecraft, H. P. At the mountains of madness, and other novels
Lovecraft, H. P. The Dunwich horror, and others
Michaels, B. The dancing floor
Michaels, B. Stitches in time
Moloney, S. The dwelling
Naylor, G. Mama Day
Picoult, J. Change of heart
Poe, E. A. The narrative of Arthur Gordon Pym of Nantucket
Power, S. The grass dancer
Powers, T. Three days to never
Preston, D. The wheel of darkness
Reynolds, S. A gracious plenty
Rice, A. Lasher
Rice, A. Taltos
Rice, A. The witching hour
Richardson, K. Greywalker
Riley, J. M. In pursuit of the green lion
Roberts, N. Midnight Bayou
Rogers, R. Devil's Cape
Shepard, L. Softspoken
Simmons, D. Drood
Stoker, B. Dracula
Stott, R. Ghostwalk
Straub, P. Ghost story
Straub, P. Mr. X
Strieber, W. The forbidden zone
Thomas, E. M. Reindeer Moon
Wallace, D. The Watermelon King
Waters, S. The little stranger
Whitney, P. A. The singing stones
Wilde, O. The picture of Dorian Gray
Wolfe, G. Castleview

SUPERSTITION

See also Occultism; Vampires; Voodooism; Werewolves
Naylor, G. Mama Day
Stevenson, R. L. The beach of Falesá

SUPREME COURT (U.S.) *See* United States. Supreme Court

SÛRETÉ, FRENCH *See* Police—Paris (France)

SURFERS

Winslow, D. The Dawn Patrol
Winton, T. Breath
The **surgeon**. Gerritsen, T.

SURGEONS

See also Physicians; Women physicians
Fielding, J. See Jane run
Hiaasen, C. Skin tight
Irving, J. The fourth hand
Kundera, M. The unbearable lightness of being
Uris, L. QB VII

SURGERY

See also Transplantation of organs, tissues, etc.
Cook, R. Coma
Cook, R. Godplayer
Cook, R. Marker
Palmer, M. The patient

SURREALISM

Berry, J. The manual of detection
Bolaño, R. By night in Chile
Burroughs, W. S. Naked lunch
Childress, M. Crazy in Alabama
DeLillo, D. Ratner's star
Ellis, B. E. Lunar Park
Erickson, S. Zeroville
Foer, J. S. Everything is illuminated
García Márquez, G. The autumn of the patriarch
Grushin, O. The dream life of Sukhanov
Harkaway, N. The gone-away world
Høeg, P. The quiet girl
Hoffman, A. Seventh heaven
Ishiguro, K. The unconsoled
Ishiguro, K. When we were orphans
Lethem, J. Chronic city
Lethem, J. The fortress of solitude
Muñoz Molina, A. In her absence
Murakami, H. Kafka on the shore
Murakami, H. South of the border, west of the sun
Murakami, H. The wind-up bird chronicle
O'Brien, F. The third policeman
Pelevin, V. The sacred book of the werewolf
Saramago, J. Blindness
Shteyngart, G. The Russian debutante's handbook
Wright, S. Going native
Surrender, Dorothy. Wolitzer, M.

SURREY (ENGLAND) *See* England—Surrey

SURROGATE MOTHERS

McCaffrey, A. The greatest love [novelette]
Shearn, A. How far is the ocean from here
Surveillance. Raban, J.

SURVEYORS

Pynchon, T. Mason & Dixon

SURVIVAL (AFTER AIRPLANE ACCIDENTS, SHIP-WRECKS, ETC.)

See also Shipwrecks and castaways; Wilderness survival
Defoe, D. Robinson Crusoe
Dick, P. K. Dr. Bloodmoney
Dickey, J. To the white sea
Frank, P. Alas, Babylon
Golding, W. Lord of the flies
MacLean, A. Night without end
Martel, Y. Life of Pi
McCarthy, C. The road
O'Brian, P. The unknown shore
Simmons, D. The terror
Strieber, W. Warday
Tournier, M. Friday
Vonnegut, K. Galápagos
Wiggins, M. John Dollar
The **survival** of Juan Oro. Brand, M.
Survival of the fittest. Kellerman, J.
Survivor. King, T.

SURVIVORS, HOLOCAUST *See* Holocaust survivors

SUSPENSE NOVELS

See also Adventure; Conspiracies; Gothic romances; Horror stories; Kidnapping; Murder stories; Mystery and detective stories; Psychological novels; Secret service; Spies; Terrorism
Abrahams, P. Hard rain
Abrahams, P. Nerve damage

SUSPENSE NOVELS—*Continued*

Gardner, L. Alone
Gerritsen, T. The apprentice
Gerritsen, T. Body double
Gerritsen, T. The sinner
Gerritsen, T. The surgeon
Gibson, W. Spook country
Gilman, D. The amazing Mrs. Pollifax
Gilman, D. The elusive Mrs. Pollifax
Goddard, R. Into the blue
Goddard, R. Never go back
Godey, J. The taking of Pelham one two three
Goldman, W. Marathon man
Gowdy, B. Helpless
Grady, J. Six days of the condor
Grant, M. Officer down
Green, G. D. The juror
Green, G. D. Ravens
Gregory, P. The wise woman
Griffin, W. E. B. By order of the President
Griffin, W. E. B. The last heroes
Griffin, W. E. B. The secret warriors
Griffin, W. E. B. The soldier spies
Grippando, J. The abduction
Grippando, J. Born to run
Grippando, J. Found money
Grippando, J. Hear no evil
Grippando, J. The informant
Grippando, J. A king's ransom
Grippando, J. Lying with strangers
Grisham, J. The brethren
Grisham, J. The broker
Grisham, J. The client
Grisham, J. The firm
Grisham, J. The last juror
Grisham, J. The partner
Grisham, J. The pelican brief
Grisham, J. The rainmaker
Grisham, J. The runaway jury
Grisham, J. The street lawyer
Gruber, M. The book of air and shadows
Gruber, M. The forgery of Venus
Gruber, M. Night of the jaguar
Gruber, M. Valley of bones
Gutcheon, B. R. More than you know
Hailey, A. Detective
Hall, A. Quiller Balalaika
Hall, A. The Quiller memorandum
Hall, A. Quiller Salamander
Hall, A. Quiller solitaire
Hall, J. W. Rough draft
Hall, S. The raw shark texts
Hallinan, T. A nail through the heart
Hambly, B. Days of the dead
Hambly, B. Dead water
Hambly, B. A free man of color
Hambly, B. Graveyard dust
Hambly, B. Sold down the river
Hambly, B. Die upon a kiss
Hambly, B. Wet grave
Hand, E. Generation loss
Hannah, S. Little face
Hannah, S. The wrong mother
Harrar, G. The spinning man
Harris, R. Archangel
Harris, R. Enigma
Harris, R. Fatherland
Harris, R. The ghost
Harris, R. Pompeii
Harris, T. Black Sunday
Harris, T. Hannibal
Harris, T. Hannibal rising
Harris, T. Red Dragon
Harris, T. The silence of the lambs
Harrison, C. Afterburn
Harrison, C. The finder
Harrison, C. The Havana room
Hart, J. The king of lies
Hart, J. The last child
Hayder, M. Ritual
Henry, A. Learning to fly
Herron, M. Reconstruction
Hewson, D. Lucifer's shadow
Hiaasen, C. Lucky you

Higgins, J. Bad company
Higgins, J. Cold Harbour
Higgins, J. Confessional
Higgins, J. Day of judgment
Higgins, J. Day of reckoning
Higgins, J. Drink with the Devil
Higgins, J. Edge of danger
Higgins, J. Eye of the storm
Higgins, J. Luciano's luck
Higgins, J. Midnight runner
Higgins, J. Night of the fox
Higgins, J. The president's daughter
Higgins, J. Rough justice
Higgins, J. Touch the devil
Higgins, J. The White House connection
Highsmith, P. The boy who followed Ripley
Highsmith, P. Ripley under ground
Highsmith, P. Ripley's game
Highsmith, P. The talented Mr. Ripley
Highsmith, P. The talented Mr. Ripley; Ripley under ground;
    Ripley's game
Hill, R. Dream of darkness
Hill, R. The Stranger House
Hill, S. Mrs. de Winter
Hirshberg, G. The Snowman's children
Hoag, T. Dark horse
Hoag, T. Dust to dust
Hoag, T. Guilty as sin
Hoag, T. Kill the messenger
Hoag, T. Night sins
Høeg, P. The quiet girl
Høeg, P. Smilla's sense of snow
Hoffman, J. Retribution
Hooper, K. Blood sins
Hooper, K. Finding Laura
Hooper, K. Haunting Rachel
Hooper, K. Stealing shadows
Hospital, J. T. Due preparations for the plague
Hospital, J. T. Orpheus lost
Howatch, S. The high flyer
Hunter, E. Privileged conversation
Hunter, S. The 47th samurai
Hunter, S. Black light
Hunter, S. Dirty white boys
Hunter, S. Havana
Hunter, S. Night of thunder
Hunter, S. Time to hunt
Huston, C. Caught stealing
Huston, C. The shotgun rule
Huyler, F. The laws of invisible things
Ignatius, D. A firing offense
Iles, G. Black cross
Iles, G. The devil's punchbowl
Iles, G. The footprints of God
Iles, G. Mortal fear
Iles, G. Third degree
Iles, G. Turning angel
Jance, J. A. Kiss of the bees
Johansen, I. And then you die—
Johansen, I. Blind alley
Johansen, I. The face of deception
Johansen, I. Final target
Johansen, I. The killing game
Johansen, I. Long after midnight
Johansen, I. The ugly duckling
Johnson, W. The devil you know
Judd, A. Legacy
Kanon, J. The good German
Kanon, J. Los Alamos
Katzenbach, J. The analyst
Katzenbach, J. Just cause
Katzenbach, J. The madman's tale
Katzenbach, J. State of mind
Katzenbach, J. The wrong man
Kellerman, F. The quality of mercy
Kellerman, J. The genius
Kellerman, J. Sunstroke
Kelman, J. Summer of storms
Kerley, J. The hundredth man
Khemir, S. The blue manuscript
Kinder, R. M. An absolute gentleman
King, L. R. A darker place
King, L. R. Keeping watch
King, S. The dead zone

TITLE AND SUBJECT INDEX

SUSPENSE NOVELS—*Continued*

Palmer, M. The society
Parker, B. Blood relations
Parker, B. Criminal justice
Parker, B. Suspicion of betrayal
Parker, B. Suspicion of deceit
Parker, B. Suspicion of vengeance
Parker, T. J. Black water
Parker, T. J. The blue hour
Parker, T. J. California girl
Parker, T. J. Cold pursuit
Parker, T. J. The fallen
Parker, T. J. L.A. outlaws
Parker, T. J. Little Saigon
Parker, T. J. Silent Joe
Parker, T. J. Storm runners
Parker, T. J. Where serpents lie
Parsons, J. Mary, Mary
Patterson, J. 1st to die
Patterson, J. Along came a spider
Patterson, J. Cat & mouse
Patterson, J. Cross
Patterson, J. Four blind mice
Patterson, J. Hide & seek
Patterson, J. Jack and Jill
Patterson, J. Kiss the girls
Patterson, J. London bridges
Patterson, J. Pop! goes the weasel
Patterson, J. Roses are red
Patterson, R. N. Balance of power
Patterson, R. N. Conviction
Patterson, R. N. Dark lady
Patterson, R. N. Eclipse
Patterson, R. N. The final judgment
Patterson, R. N. No safe place
Patterson, R. N. Silent witness
Pattison, E. The skull mantra
Pearl, M. The Dante Club
Pearson, R. The angel maker
Pearson, R. The art of deception
Pearson, R. Beyond recognition
Pearson, R. The body of David Hayes
Pearson, R. Chain of evidence
Pearson, R. The first victim
Pearson, R. Middle of nowhere
Pearson, R. No witnesses
Pelecanos, G. P. Shame the devil
Pelecanos, G. P. The sweet forever
Perdue, L. Slatewiper
Pérez-Reverte, A. The nautical chart
Perry, T. Blood money
Perry, T. Dance for the dead
Perry, T. The face-changers
Perry, T. Fidelity
Perry, T. Nightlife
Perry, T. Pursuit
Perry, T. Runner
Perry, T. Shadow woman
Perry, T. Vanishing act
Picoult, J. Vanishing acts
Pottinger, S. The fourth procedure
Pottinger, S. The last Nazi
Poyer, D. Down to a sunless sea
Preston, D. Blasphemy
Preston, D. Brimstone
Preston, D. The cabinet of curiosities
Preston, D. The codex
Preston, D. Reliquary
Preston, D. Still life with crows
Preston, D. Tyrannosaur Canyon
Preston, D. The wheel of darkness
Preston, R. The Cobra event
Price, N. Night woman
Pronzini, B. The crimes of Jordan Wise
Pronzini, B. In an evil time
Pronzini, B. The other side of silence
Pronzini, B. Step to the graveyard easy
Pronzini, B. A wasteland of strangers
Pyper, A. The killing circle
Quick, A. I thee wed
Quick, A. Late for the wedding
Quick, A. Slightly shady
Quick, A. Wicked widow
Rabb, J. The book of Q

Rankin, I. Watchman
Redfern, E. Auriel rising
Reich, C. Rules of deception
Reichs, K. J. Déjà dead
Rendell, R. The bridesmaid
Rendell, R. Heartstones
Rendell, R. A judgment in stone
Rendell, R. The keys to the street
Rendell, R. Live flesh
Rendell, R. A sight for sore eyes
Rendell, R. Thirteen steps down
Rendell, R. The water's lovely
Reuland, R. Semiautomatic
Rigosi, G. Night bus
Riordan, R. Cold Springs
Robards, K. Ghost moon
Robards, K. To trust a stranger
Robbins, D. L. War of the rats
Robbins, H. Sin city
Roberts, N. Angel's fall
Roberts, N. Honest illusions
Roberts, N. Midnight Bayou
Roberts, N. River's end
Robinson, P. Kilo class
Robinson, P. Nimitz class
Robinson, P. The first cut
Rosenberg, N. T. Buried evidence
Rosenberg, N. T. First offense
Rosenberg, N. T. Interest of justice
Rosenberg, N. T. Sullivan's law
Rosenfelt, D. Don't tell a soul
Ruiz, L. M. Only one thing missing
Ruiz Zafón, C. The shadow of the wind
Sanchez, T. King Bongo
Sanders, L. The first deadly sin
Sanders, L. Guilty pleasures
Sanders, L. The second deadly sin
Sanders, L. The sixth commandment
Sanders, L. Sullivan's sting
Sanders, L. The tenth commandment
Sanders, L. The third deadly sin
Sansom, C. J. Winter in Madrid
Saul, J. The presence
Saul, J. Shadows
Schickler, D. Sweet and vicious
Schwegel, T. Person of interest
Scottoline, L. Legal tender
Scottoline, L. Mistaken identity
Scottoline, L. Moment of truth
Scottoline, L. Rough justice
Seymour, G. Killing ground
Seymour, G. Rat run
Shannon, D. The Manson curse
Shelby, P. Days of drums
Shelby, P. Gatekeeper
Sheldon, S. The doomsday conspiracy
Shreve, A. Resistance
Shreve, A. Testimony
Shreve, A. The weight of water
Shreve, S. R. A student of living things
Sidor, S. Skin River
Siegel, J. Deceit
Siegel, J. Derailed
Siegel, S. Final verdict
Sigler, S. Contagious
Sigler, S. Infected
Silva, D. The mark of the assassin
Silva, D. The messenger
Silva, D. Moscow rules
Silva, D. Prince of Fire
Silva, D. The secret servant
Simmons, D. Drood
Smith, A. Good morning, killer
Smith, A. Judas horse
Smith, M. C. December 6
Smith, M. M. The intruders
Smith, S. The ruins
Smith, S. A simple plan
Smith, T. R. Child 44
Smith, T. R. The secret speech
Smith, W. A. Golden fox
Smith, W. A. The seventh scroll
Snyder, D. J. Night crossing
Sparks, N. A bend in the road

TITLE AND SUBJECT INDEX

SUSPENSE NOVELS—*Continued*
Sparks, N. The guardian
Standiford, L. Black Mountain
Stark, R. Ask the parrot
Stark, R. Breakout
Stark, R. Dirty money
Stark, R. The hunter
Stark, R. The jugger
Starr, J. Panic attack
Steinhauer, O. The Bridge of Sighs
Steinhauer, O. The tourist
Stephenson, N. Cryptonomicon
Stevens, M. The curve of the world
Stewart, M. Airs above the ground
Stewart, M. The moon-spinners
Stewart, M. My brother Michael
Stewart, M. The stormy petrel
Stone, R. Damascus Gate
Strieber, W. Majestic
Swain, J. Midnight rambler
Tanenbaum, R. Act of revenge
Tanenbaum, R. Corruption of blood
Tanenbaum, R. Falsely accused
Tanenbaum, R. Hoax
Tanenbaum, R. Irresistible impulse
Tanenbaum, R. Reckless endangerment
Tanenbaum, R. True justice
Tartt, D. The secret history
Theorin, J. Echoes from the dead
Thomas, C. Firefox
Thomas, M. M. Black money
Thomas, R. Ah, treachery!
Thomas, R. The fourth Durango
Tirone Smith, M.-A. Love her madly
Tirone Smith, M.-A. She smiled sweetly
Tirone Smith, M.-A. She's not there
Tracy, P. J. Monkeewrench
Trenhaile, J. The gates of exquisite view
Trevanian. The Eiger sanction
Trevanian. The Loo sanction
Trevor, W. Felicia's journey
Truscott, L. K. Heart of war
Turow, S. The laws of our fathers
Turow, S. Personal injuries
Turow, S. Reversible errors
Uhnak, D. Codes of betrayal
Ure, L. The fault tree
Vargas Llosa, M. Death in the Andes
Vine, B. Gallowglass
Vine, B. Grasshopper
Vine, B. King Solomon's carpet
Vine, B. The minotaur
Vine, B. No night is too long
Volpi, J. In search of Klingsor
Walker, M. W. Under the beetle's cellar
Wallace, I. The man
Walters, M. The breaker
Walters, M. The dark room
Walters, M. The devil's feather
Walters, M. The echo
Walters, M. The sculptress
Walters, M. The shape of snakes
Watkins, P. The forger
Weaver, M. Deceptions
West, M. L. The clowns of God
West, M. L. Masterclass
Westlake, D. E. Money for nothing
White, S. W. Dry ice
White, S. W. Kill me
White, S. W. Missing persons
Whitney, P. A. Amethyst dreams
Whitney, P. A. Domino
Whitney, P. A. The singing stones
Whitney, P. A. Spindrift
Wilcken, H. The execution
Wilhelm, K. The best defense
Wilhelm, K. The deepest water
Wilhelm, K. Defense for the devil
Wilhelm, K. Desperate measures
Wilhelm, K. Malice prepense
Wilhelm, K. No defense
Wilson, F. P. Deep as the marrow
Wilson, R. The blind man of Seville
Wilson, R. The hidden assassins

Wiltse, D. Blown away
Wiltse, D. Bone deep
Winslow, D. The winter of Frankie Machine
Wolfe, I. A. The calling
Wood, B. Perfect Harmony
Woods, S. Choke
Woods, S. Cold paradise
Woods, S. Dead eyes
Woods, S. Dead in the water
Woods, S. Dirt
Woods, S. Dirty work
Woods, S. Grass roots
Woods, S. Heat
Woods, S. Imperfect strangers
Woods, S. L.A. dead
Woods, S. L.A. Times
Woods, S. Orchid Beach
Woods, S. Reckless abandon
Woods, S. The run
Woods, S. Santa Fe rules
Woods, S. The short forever
Woods, S. Short straw
Woods, S. Swimming to Catalina
Woods, S. Two-dollar bill
Woods, S. Worst fears realized
Wouk, H. A hole in Texas
Yorke, M. Almost the truth
Yorke, M. The price of guilt
Yorke, M. A question of belief
Suspicion of betrayal. Parker, B.
Suspicion of deceit. Parker, B.
Suspicion of vengeance. Parker, B.
Suspicious characters. See Sayers, D. L. The five red herrings
SUSSEX (ENGLAND) See England—Sussex
Suzanne's diary for Nicholas. Patterson, J.
Swag. Leonard, E.
  In Leonard, E. Elmore Leonard's Dutch treat: 3 novels
The **swallows** of Kabul. Moulessehoul, M.
Swami and friends. Narayan, R. K.
  In Narayan, R. K. Swami and friends, The bachelor of arts,
    The dark room, The English teacher
Swami and friends, The bachelor of arts, The dark room, The
  English teacher. Narayan, R. K.
Swan song. Galsworthy, J.
  In Galsworthy, J. A modern comedy
Swann's way. Proust, M.
  also in Proust, M. Remembrance of things past p3-462
Sway. Lazar, Z.
SWEDEN
  See also Lapland
  Christensen, L. S. The half brother
  Larsson, S. The girl who played with fire
  Larsson, S. The girl with the dragon tattoo
  Lindgren, T. Hash
  Olsson, L. Astrid & Veronika
  Theorin, J. Echoes from the dead

19th century
  Moberg, V. The emigrants

Farm life
  See Farm life—Sweden

Rural life
  Jönsson, R. My life as a dog

Stockholm
  Ozick, C. The Messiah of Stockholm
SWEDES
  See also Vikings

Denmark
  Andersen Nexø, M. Pelle the conqueror: v1 Childhood
  Andersen Nexø, M. Pelle the conqueror: v2 Apprenticeship

England
  Vine, B. The minotaur

Islands of the Pacific
  Conrad, J. Victory

United States
  Cather, W. O pioneers!
  Cather, W. The song of the lark
  Moberg, V. The emigrants

SWEDES—United States—*Continued*
Moberg, V. The last letter home
Moberg, V. Unto a good land

Zambia

Mankell, H. The eye of the leopard
Sweet and vicious. Schickler, D.
The **sweet** dove died. Pym, B.
The **sweet** forever. Pelecanos, G. P.
The **sweet** hereafter. Banks, R.
Sweet land stories. Doctorow, E. L.
Sweet, sweet poison. Wilhelm, K.
Sweet Thursday. Steinbeck, J.
   also in Steinbeck, J. Travels with Charley and later novels,
    1947-1962
The **sweetest** dream. Lessing, D. M.
Sweetness in the belly. Gibb, C.
Sweetsmoke. Fuller, D.
Sweetwater. Robinson, R.
Sweetwater Creek. Siddons, A. R.
Swift as desire. Esquivel, L.

SWIMMING

Keegan, N. Swimming
Swimming. Keegan, N.
Swimming to Catalina. Woods, S.

SWINDLERS AND SWINDLING

   See also Business—Unscrupulous methods
Brown, C. B. Arthur Mervyn
Brown, J. D. Addie Pray
Dickens, C. Martin Chuzzlewit
Ginsberg, D. The grift
Green, G. D. Ravens
Haigh, J. Mrs. Kimble
Hiaasen, C. Stormy weather
Leonard, E. Road dogs
Lynch, S. The lies of Locke Lamora
Melville, H. The confidence-man: his masquerade
Porter, J. A. The near future
Portes, A. Hick
Smiley, J. Good faith
Smith, B. All hat
Strauss, D. The real McCoy
Tinti, H. The good thief
The **swing** voter of Staten Island. Nersesian, A.

SWISS

France

Stamm, P. On a day like this
SWISS ALPS *See* Alps
Switchback. Wilcox, C.

SWITZERLAND

Brookner, A. Hotel du Lac
Gilman, D. A palm for Mrs. Pollifax
Reich, C. Rules of deception
Spark, M. The finishing school
Wharton, E. The children

Geneva

Ludlum, R. The Sigma protocol

Zurich

Davies, R. The manticore
Pye, M. The pieces from Berlin
Sword at sunset. Sutcliff, R.
The **sword** in the stone. White, T. H.
   In White, T. H. The once and future king
Sword of honour. See Waugh, E. Men at arms
The **sword** of Shannara. Brooks, T.
The **sword** of the Lictor. Wolfe, G.

SWORDS

Hunter, S. The 47th samurai

SYMBOLISM

   See also Allegories; Parables
Ballard, J. G. The day of creation
Barth, J. Giles goat-boy
Bellow, S. Henderson the rain king
Coetzee, J. M. Foe
Conrad, J. The Nigger of the Narcissus
Doctorow, E. L. Loon Lake
Faulkner, W. A fable
Fowles, J. The magus

Fuentes, C. The campaign
García, C. The Aguero sisters
Gordimer, N. The conservationist
Grass, G. Cat and mouse
Grass, G. The Danzig trilogy
Grass, G. Dog years
Grass, G. The tin drum
Handke, P. The left-handed woman
Hawthorne, N. The scarlet letter
Helprin, M. A soldier of the great war
Hesse, H. Demian
Hesse, H. The glass bead game (Magister Ludi)
Hesse, H. Narcissus and Goldmund
Hesse, H. Steppenwolf
Høeg, P. The history of Danish dreams
Hulme, K. The bone people
Irving, J. A prayer for Owen Meany
Joyce, J. Ulysses
Kafka, F. Metamorphosis
Kafka, F. The trial
Kawabata, Y. Thousand cranes
Kingsolver, B. Animal dreams
Mann, T. The black swan
Mann, T. Death in Venice
Mann, T. The magic mountain
Melville, H. Billy Budd, sailor
Melville, H. Mardi: and a voyager thither
Melville, H. Moby-Dick; or, The whale
Momaday, N. S. The ancient child
Murakami, H. The wind-up bird chronicle
Murdoch, I. Nuns and soldiers
Nabokov, V. V. Ada
Nabokov, V. V. Pale fire
O'Brien, T. In the Lake of the Woods
Õe, K. An echo of heaven
Õe, K. The pinch runner memorandum
Okuizumi, H. The stones cry out
Percy, W. Lancelot
Poe, E. A. The narrative of Arthur Gordon Pym of Nantucket
Porter, K. A. Ship of fools
Powers, R. Operation wandering soul
Pynchon, T. V.
Roth, P. The breast
Roy, A. The god of small things
Rushdie, S. The ground beneath her feet
Rushdie, S. The satanic verses
Silverberg, R. Downward to the Earth
Tan, A. The bonesetter's daughter
Theroux, P. The Mosquito Coast
Thomas, D. M. The white hotel
Updike, J. Roger's version
Urquhart, J. The underpainter
Walbert, K. The gardens of Kyoto
Wiesel, E. A beggar in Jerusalem
Woolf, V. Between the acts
Woolf, V. The waves

SYMPATHY

   See also Empathy

SYRIA

Caldwell, T. Dear and glorious physician
Werfel, F. The forty days of Musa Dagh

SYRIANS

Brazil

Amado, J. Gabriela, clove and cinnamon
The **syringa** tree. Gien, P.

T

T is for trespass. Grafton, S.
Table money. Breslin, J.
TABOO *See* Superstition
TACITUS, CORNELIUS
About
Bell, A. A. The blood of Caesar
TADZHIKISTAN *See* Tajikistan
TAE KWON DO
Bell, M. S. Ten Indians

TAHITI

Maugham, W. S. The moon and sixpence
Melville, H. Omoo: a narrative of adventures in the South Seas

TAHOE, LAKE (CALIF. AND NEV.) *See* Lake Tahoe (Calif. and Nev.)

Tai-Pan. Clavell, J.

The **tailor** of Panama. Le Carré, J.

TAJIKISTAN

Darnton, J. Neanderthal

Takeover. Black, L.

The **taking**. Koontz, D. R.

The **taking** of Pelham one two three. Godey, J.

TALAVERA CAMPAIGN, 1809 *See* Peninsular War, 1807-1814

The **tale** of Genji. Murasaki Shikibu

The **tale** of the body thief. Rice, A.

A **tale** of two cities. Dickens, C.

The **talented** Mr. Ripley. Highsmith, P.
In Crime novels: American noir of the 1950s
In Highsmith, P. The talented Mr. Ripley; Ripley under ground; Ripley's game

The **talented** Mr. Ripley; Ripley under ground; Ripley's game. Highsmith, P.

Tales and sketches, including Twice-told tales, Mosses from an old manse, and The snow-image; A wonder book for girls and boys; Tanglewood tales for girls and boys, being a second Wonder book. Hawthorne, N.

Tales from a troubled land. Paton, A.

Tales from the Drones Club. Wodehouse, P. G.

Tales of good and evil. See Gogol', N. V. The overcoat, and other tales of good and evil

Tales of H.P. Lovecraft. Lovecraft, H. P.

The **tales** of Jacob. Mann, T.
In Mann, T. Joseph and his brothers p3-258

Tales of protection. Hansen, E. F.

Tales of the jazz age. Fitzgerald, F. S.
In Fitzgerald, F. S. Novels and stories, 1920-1922 p797-1054

Tales of the night. Høeg, P.

TALIBAN (AFGHANISTAN)

Hosseini, K. The kite runner

Talking God. Hillerman, T.

The **talking** trees and other stories. O'Faoláin, S.
In O'Faoláin, S. The collected stories of Seán O'Faoláin p889-1060

Tallgrass. Coldsmith, D.

Tallgrass. Dallas, S.

Taltos. Rice, A.

Taming a sea-horse. Parker, R. B.

TAMPA (FLA.) *See* Florida—Tampa

Tamsin Harte. Ross-Macdonald, M.

Tapestry. Plain, B.

Taps. Morris, W.

Tar baby. Morrison, T.

The **target**. Coulter, C.

TASMANIA (AUSTRALIA)

Flanagan, R. Wanting
Hooper, C. A child's book of true crime
Shakespeare, N. Secrets of the sea

A **taste** for death. James, P. D.

TAVERNS *See* Hotels, taverns, etc.

TAYLOR, CORA HOWARTH STEWART *See* Crane, Cora Howarth Stewart Taylor, 1868-1910

TEACHERS

See also Students; Tutors

Abe, K. The woman in the dunes
Amis, K. Lucky Jim
Balogh, M. Simply love
Balogh, M. Simply magic
Baxter, C. Saul and Patsy
Blew, M. C. Jackalope dreams
Boswell, R. Century's son
Bynum, S. S.-L. Ms. Hempel chronicles
Carter, S. L. The emperor of Ocean Park
Chaon, D. Await your reply
Cheever, J. Falconer
Choi, S. A person of interest
Coetzee, J. M. Disgrace
Cohen, L. H. Heart, you bully, you punk

Cohen, R. Inspired sleep
Colette. Claudine at school
Collins, M. Death of a writer
Cook, T. H. The Chatham School affair
Cook, T. H. Master of the delta
Cumyn, A. Losing it
Davies, R. Fifth business
Delderfield, R. F. To serve them all my days
DeLillo, D. White noise
Dickens, C. Nicholas Nickleby
Doig, I. The whistling season
Dufossé, C. School's out
Durrell, L. Balthazar
Durrell, L. Clea
Durrell, L. Justine
Fielding, J. Heartstopper
Fowles, J. The magus
Gaines, E. J. A lesson before dying
Godwin, G. The good husband
Goodman, C. The night villa
Goodman, C. The seduction of water
Gordimer, N. My son's story
Gordon, E. F. It will come to me
Gordon, M. The company of women
Grant, S. Map of Ireland
Greene, G. The confidential agent
Guterson, D. The other
Ha Jin. The crazed
Haldeman, J. W. The coming
Hamilton, J. The short history of a prince
Hardy, T. Under the greenwood tree
Harrar, G. The spinning man
Harris, J. Gentlemen and players
Harrison, J. The English major
Haruf, K. Plainsong
Hassler, J. The dean's list
Hassler, J. Rookery blues
Heller, J. Good as Gold
Heller, Z. What was she thinking?
Herron, M. Reconstruction
Hilton, J. Good-bye Mr. Chips
Hooper, C. A child's book of true crime
Huddle, D. La Tour dreams of the wolf girl
Huneven, M. Blame
Hunter, E. The blackboard jungle
Hynes, J. The lecturer's tale
Kaufman, B. Up the down staircase
Kincaid, N. Verbena
Kinder, R. M. An absolute gentleman
Kingsolver, B. Animal dreams
Kirshenbaum, B. An almost perfect moment
Knowles, J. Peace breaks out
Knowles, J. A separate peace
Krauss, N. Man walks into a room
Lasdun, J. The horned man
Leavitt, D. Martin Bauman
Leebron, F. G. In the middle of all this
Lightman, A. P. Reunion
Lipman, E. My latest grievance
Lockridge, R. Raintree County
Lodge, D. Deaf sentence
Lodge, D. Nice work
Lodge, D. Thinks—
Ludlum, R. The Matlock paper
Lurie, A. Foreign affairs
Lurie, A. The war between the Tates
MacDonald, A.-M. The way the crow flies
MacInnes, H. Above suspicion
Marshall, C. Christy
McCarthy, M. The groves of Academe
McGowan, H. Schooling
McKinney-Whetstone, D. Blues dancing
Meno, J. The great perhaps
Nabokov, V. V. Ada
Nabokov, V. V. Bend sinister
Nabokov, V. V. Pale fire
Nabokov, V. V. Pnin
Narayan, R. K. The English teacher
Nunez, E. Grace
Parker, T. J. L.A. outlaws
Patton, F. G. Good morning, Miss Dove
Pearce, M. E. Apple tree lean down [omnibus volume]
Piercy, M. The longings of women
Potok, C. The troupe teacher

TEXAS—*Continued*

Walker, M. W. Under the beetle's cellar

19th century

Harrigan, S. The gates of the Alamo

Jiles, P. The color of lightning

Kelton, E. Badger boy

Kelton, E. The rebels

Kelton, E. Slaughter

Kelton, E. The way of the coyote

Latham, A. Code of the West

Sherman, J. The Baron war

Farm life

See Farm life—Texas

Frontier and pioneer life

See Frontier and pioneer life—Texas

Politics

See Politics—Texas

Alamo

See Alamo (San Antonio, Tex.)

El Paso

DeMarinis, R. Sky full of sand

Houston

Brown, R. Half a heart

McMurtry, L. The evening star

McMurtry, L. Terms of endearment

Texas. Michener, J. A.

TEXAS RANGERS

Kelton, E. Texas vendetta

Kelton, E. The way of the coyote

McMurtry, L. Comanche moon

Texas sunrise. Kelton, E.

Texas vendetta. Kelton, E.

Texasville. McMurtry, L.

TEXTILE INDUSTRY

See also Weavers

Singer, I. J. The brothers Ashkenazi

THAILAND

Berlinski, M. Fieldwork

18th century

Han, S. The enchantress

Bangkok

Burdett, J. Bangkok 8

Burdett, J. Bangkok haunts

Burdett, J. Bangkok Tattoo

Hallinan, T. A nail through the heart

Mishima, Y. The Temple of Dawn

Thale's Folly. Gilman, D.

Thank you for all things. Kring, S.

THANKSGIVING DAY

Bausch, R. Thanksgiving night

Ford, R. The lay of the land

Thanksgiving night. Bausch, R.

That Camden summer. Spencer, L.

That distant land. Berry, W.

That hideous strength. Lewis, C. S.

That night. McDermott, A.

That old ace in the hole. Proulx, A.

That old Cape magic. Russo, R.

The 19th wife. Ebershoff, D.

THEATER LIFE

See also Actors; Actresses; Strolling players; Vaudeville; names of actors and actresses

Colette. Music-hall sidelights

Davies, R. World of wonders

Dickens, C. Nicholas Nickleby

Dreiser, T. Sister Carrie

Gallagher, S. The kingdom of bones

L'Engle, M. Certain women

Lessing, D. M. Love, again

Michael, J. Acts of love

Miller, W. M. The darfsteller

Nye, R. The late Mr. Shakespeare

Singer, I. B. The magician of Lublin

Unsworth, B. Morality play

Zola, É. Nana

THEATRICAL TROUPES *See* Strolling players; Theater life

THEFT

See also Embezzlement; Robbery; Thieves

Eliot, G. Silas Marner

Leonard, E. Bandits

Pérez-Reverte, A. The fencing master

Westlake, D. E. Don't ask

Their eyes were watching God. Hurston, Z. N.

also in Hurston, Z. N. Novels and stories p173-333

Them. Oates, J. C.

THEODORIC, KING OF THE OSTROGOTHS, 454?-526
About

Jennings, G. Raptor

Theophilus North. Wilder, T.

A **theory** of relativity. Mitchard, J.

Therapy. Kellerman, J.

Therapy. Lodge, D.

There was a little girl. McBain, E.

There will never be another you. See, C.

There's something in a Sunday. Muller, M.

These is my words. Turner, N. E.

THESEUS (LEGENDARY CHARACTER)

Renault, M. The bull from the sea

Renault, M. The king must die

They came like swallows. Maxwell, W.

In Maxwell, W. Early novels and stories

They shoot horses, don't they? McCoy, H.

In Crime novels: American noir of the 1930s and 40s

Thicker than water. McInerny, R. M.

A **thief** of time. Hillerman, T.

Thief of time. Pratchett, T.

The **thief** of Venice. Langton, J.

THIEVES

See also Theft

Cervantes Saavedra, M. d. Rinconete and Cortadillo

Connelly, M. Void moon

Crusie, J. Faking it

Cussler, C. Inca gold

Defoe, D. Moll Flanders

Dickens, C. Oliver Twist

Gilman, D. A palm for Mrs. Pollifax

Herlihy, J. L. Midnight cowboy

Horn, D. The world to come

Keating, H. R. F. The bad detective

Leiber, F. Ill met in Lankhmar

Leonard, E. Swag

Parker, T. J. L.A. outlaws

Roberts, N. Honest illusions

Schickler, D. Sweet and vicious

Skármeta, A. The dancer and the thief

Smith, S. A simple plan

Thomas, C. Firefox

Waters, S. Fingersmith

Westlake, D. E. Smoke

Woodrell, D. The death of sweet mister

Thieves' dozen. Westlake, D. E.

Thieves like us. Anderson, E.

In Crime novels: American noir of the 1930s and 40s

Thin air. Parker, R. B.

The **thin** man. Hammett, D.

also in Hammett, D. Complete novels

The **thin** place. Davis, K.

The **thin** red line. Jones, J.

The **thing** around your neck. Adichie, C. N.

Things fall apart. Achebe, C.

Things gone and things still here. Bowles, P.

In Bowles, P. Collected stories & later writings

The **things** they carried. O'Brien, T.

Think of England. Dark, A. E.

Thinks—. Lodge, D.

Thinner. King, S.

The **third** angel. Hoffman, A.

The **third** book of lost swords: Stonecutter's story. Saberhagen, F.

The **third** deadly sin. Sanders, L.

Third degree. Iles, G.

The **third** policeman. O'Brien, F.

In O'Brien, F. The complete novels

Third strike. Craig, P. R.

The **third** violet. Crane, S.

In Crane, S. The complete novels of Stephen Crane p349-428

In Crane, S. Prose and poetry

Tinker, tailor, soldier, spy. Le Carré, J.
Tinkers. Harding, P.
TIRO, M. TULLIUS
About
Harris, R. Imperium
Tishomingo blues. Leonard, E.
Titan. Varley, J.
TITANIC (STEAMSHIP)
Bainbridge, B. Every man for himself
Finney, J. From time to time
Willis, C. Passage
Titmuss regained. Mortimer, J.
TITUBA
About
Condé, M. I, Tituba, black witch of Salem
To a god unknown. Steinbeck, J.
In Steinbeck, J. Novels and stories, 1932-1937
To Asmara. Keneally, T.
To catch a spy. Kaminsky, S. M.
To dance with kings. Laker, R.
To die for. Neel, J.
To have and have not. Hemingway, E.
To kill a mockingbird. Lee, H.
To let. Galsworthy, J.
In Galsworthy, J. The Forsyte saga p665-921
To lie with lions. Dunnett, D.
To say nothing of the dog; or, How we found the bishop's bird stump at last. Willis, C.
To serve them all my days. Delderfield, R. F.
To the far blue mountains. L'Amour, L.
To the Hermitage. Bradbury, M.
To the Indies. Forester, C. S.
To the lighthouse. Woolf, V.
To the nines. Evanovich, J.
To the white sea. Dickey, J.
To trust a stranger. Robards, K.
To your scattered bodies go. Farmer, P. J.
TOBACCO HABIT *See* Smoking

TOBACCO INDUSTRY
Grisham, J. The runaway jury
Tobacco road. Caldwell, E.
TOKLAS, ALICE B.
About
Truong, M. T. D. The book of salt
TOKYO (JAPAN) *See* Japan—Tokyo
Tokyo fiancee. Nothomb, A.
Tokyo year zero. Peace, D.
TOLSTOY, LEO, GRAF, 1828-1910
About
Kalfus, K. The commissariat of enlightenment
Parodies, imitations, etc.
Reyn, I. What happened to Anna K.
Tom Chatto. See McCutchan, P. Apprentice to the sea
Tom Chatto, RNR. See McCutchan, P. The new lieutenant
Tom Chatto, second mate. See McCutchan, P. The second mate
Tom Jones. See Fielding, H. The history of Tom Jones, a foundling
Tom Sawyer abroad. Twain, M.
In Twain, M. The adventures of Tom Sawyer, Tom Sawyer abroad, Tom Sawyer, detective p251-341
In Twain, M. The gilded age and later novels
Tom Sawyer, detective. Twain, M.
In Twain, M. The adventures of Tom Sawyer, Tom Sawyer abroad, Tom Sawyer, detective p357-415
In Twain, M. The gilded age and later novels
Tomorrow. Swift, G.
Tomorrow is another day. Kaminsky, S. M.
The tongues of angels. Price, R.
Tonight I said goodbye. Koryta, M.
Tonio Kröger. Mann, T.
In Mann, T. Stories of three decades
Tono-Bungay. Wells, H. G.
Too far afield. Grass, G.
Too late the phalarope. Paton, A.
Too loud a solitude. Hrabal, B.
Too many cooks; & champagne for one. Stout, R.
Torch. Strayed, C.
TORIES, AMERICAN *See* American loyalists
TORONTO (ONT.) *See* Canada—Toronto
Torquemada. Pérez Galdós, B.

Torquemada and Saint Peter. Pérez Galdós, B.
In Pérez Galdós, B. Torquemada p405-569
Torquemada at the stake. Pérez Galdós, B.
In Pérez Galdós, B. Torquemada p1-60
Torquemada in Purgatory. Pérez Galdós, B.
In Pérez Galdós, B. Torquemada p221-404
Torquemada on the cross. Pérez Galdós, B.
In Pérez Galdós, B. Torquemada p61-220
The torrents of spring. Hemingway, E.
also in Hemingway, E. The Hemingway reader p25-86
The torrents of spring. Turgenev, I. S.
The torso in the town. Brett, S.
The tortilla curtain. Boyle, T. C.
Tortilla Flat. Steinbeck, J.
also in Steinbeck, J. Novels and stories, 1932-1937
TORTURE
Danticat, E. The dew breaker
Everett, P. L. The water cure
Kertész, I. Detective story
Lehrer, J. The special prisoner
The toss of a lemon. Viswanathan, P.
Total control. Baldacci, D.
Total recall. Paretsky, S.
TOTALITARIANISM
See also Communism; Dictators; Fascism; National socialism
Antunes, A. L. The inquisitors' manual
Bolaño, R. By night in Chile
Chatwin, B. Utz
Connelly, K. The lizard cage
Danticat, E. The dew breaker
Dragomán, G. The white king
Englander, N. The Ministry of Special Cases
Erpenbeck, J. The book of words
Farah, N. Links
Hall, S. Daughters of the north
Hrabal, B. I served the King of England
Isegawa, M. Snakepit
Kadare, I. Agamemnon's daughter
Kadare, I. The Successor
Keneally, T. The tyrant's novel
Koestler, A. Darkness at noon
Kundera, M. The joke
Matar, H. In the country of men
McCann, C. Zoli
Moulessehoul, M. The swallows of Kabul
Nabokov, V. V. Bend sinister
Orwell, G. Animal farm
Orwell, G. Nineteen eighty-four
Saramago, J. The cave
Smith, T. R. Child 44
Sorokin, V. Ice
Steele, A. M. Coyote
Vollmann, W. T. Europe central
Zamîatin, E. I. We
Touch. Leonard, E.
Touch not the cat. Stewart, M.
Touch the devil. Higgins, J.
Touched by the dead. See Barnard, R. A murder in Mayfair
The touchstone. Wharton, E.
In Wharton, E. Collected stories, 1891-1910
Touchy subjects. Donoghue, E.
Tough guys don't dance. Mailer, N.
La Tour dreams of the wolf girl. Huddle, D.
The tourist. Steinhauer, O.
TOURIST TRADE
Bowles, P. Up above the world
Harris, J. Coastliners
Lodge, D. Paradise news
Tan, A. Saving fish from drowning
TOURISTS *See* Tourist trade
Tourmaline. Scott, J.
TOUSSAINT LOUVERTURE, 1743?-1803
About
Bell, M. S. All souls' rising
Toward the end of time. Updike, J.
Towards another summer. Frame, J.
Towards zero. Christie, A.
TOWER OF LONDON (ENGLAND)
Kerr, P. Dark matter
The towers of silence. Scott, P.
also in Scott, P. The Raj quartet

TRIALS—*Continued*

Connelly, M. The Lincoln lawyer
Cook, R. Crisis
Cozzens, J. G. By love possessed
De Kretser, M. The Hamilton case
Dexter, P. Paris Trout
Dickens, C. Bleak House
Dickens, C. The posthumous papers of the Pickwick Club
Dickens, C. A tale of two cities
Diehl, W. Primal fear
Donoghue, E. The sealed letter
Dostoyevsky, F. The brothers Karamazov
Dreiser, T. An American tragedy
Dunne, J. G. Nothing lost
Faulkner, W. The mansion
Faulkner, W. Requiem for a nun
Fielding, J. Tell me no secrets
French, A. Billy
Galsworthy, J. Maid in waiting
Galsworthy, J. Over the river
Galsworthy, J. The silver spoon
Green, G. D. The juror
Green, T. The letter of the law
Grippando, J. Hear no evil
Grisham, J. The appeal
Grisham, J. The partner
Grisham, J. The rainmaker
Grisham, J. The runaway jury
Grisham, J. A time to kill
Guterson, D. Snow falling on cedars
Hamilton, J. A map of the world
Hoag, T. Guilty as sin
Holden, C. The jazz bird
Howe, K. The physick book of Deliverance Dane
Hunter, E. Lizzie
Iles, G. Turning angel
Jones, D. C. The court-martial of George Armstrong Custer
Katkov, N. Blood & orchids
Katzenbach, J. Hart's war
Kent, K. The heretic's daughter
Koestler, A. Darkness at noon
Lawrence, M. K. Hearts and bones
Lehrer, J. The special prisoner
Lescroart, J. T. The hearing
Lescroart, J. T. The mercy rule
Levin, M. Compulsion
Margolin, P. After dark
Margolin, P. The burning man
Margolin, P. Fugitive
Marlette, D. Magic time
Martini, S. P. Compelling evidence
Martini, S. P. The judge
Martini, S. P. The jury
Martini, S. P. Prime witness
Martini, S. P. Undue influence
Meltzer, B. Dead even
Miller, S. The good mother
Morrow, J. The last witchfinder
Oates, J. C. American appetites
O'Shaughnessy, P. Breach of promise
O'Shaughnessy, P. Invasion of privacy
O'Shaughnessy, P. Motion to suppress
O'Shaughnessy, P. Obstruction of justice
O'Shaughnessy, P. Writ of execution
Parker, B. Blood relations
Patterson, J. Hide & seek
Patterson, R. N. Degree of guilt
Patterson, R. N. Eyes of a child
Patterson, R. N. The final judgment
Patterson, R. N. Silent witness
Pesci, D. Amistad
Picoult, J. My sister's keeper
Reed, B. The choice
Reuland, R. Semiautomatic
Scottoline, L. Mistaken identity
Scottoline, L. Rough justice
Scottoline, L. The vendetta defense
Siegel, S. Final verdict
Traver, R. Anatomy of a murder
Turow, S. The laws of our fathers
Turow, S. Limitations
Turow, S. Presumed innocent
Uris, L. QB VII
Warren, R. P. World enough and time

Welty, E. The Ponder heart
Wilhelm, K. The best defense
Wilhelm, K. Death qualified
Wilhelm, K. Defense for the devil
Wilhelm, K. Desperate measures
Wilhelm, K. Malice prepense
Wilhelm, K. No defense
Woods, S. Dead in the water
Woods, S. Grass roots

TRIBES

Berlinski, M. Fieldwork
Darnton, J. Neanderthal
Tricks. McBain, E.
The **trimmed** lamp. Henry, O.
   In Henry, O. The complete works of O. Henry p1365-1483

TRINIDAD AND TOBAGO

Naipaul, V. S. A house for Mr. Biswas
Naipaul, V. S. A way in the world
Trinity. Uris, L.
A **trip** to the center of the earth. *See* Verne, J. A journey to the centre of the earth
Triple. Follett, K.

TRIPLETS

Powell, S. The Mushroom Man

TRIPOLITAN WAR, 1801-1805 *See* United States—Tripolitan War, 1801-1805

TRISTAN, FLORA, 1803-1844
About
Vargas Llosa, M. The way to paradise

TRISTAN (LEGENDARY CHARACTER)

Millhauser, S. The king in the tree
Tristan. Mann, T.
   In Mann, T. Stories of three decades
Tristessa. Kerouac, J.
   In Kerouac, J. Road novels 1957-1960
Tristram Shandy. *See* Sterne, L. The life and opinions of Tristram Shandy, gentleman
The **triumph** of beauty. Roth, J.
   In Roth, J. The collected stories of Joseph Roth
The **triumph** of Caesar. Saylor, S.
A **triumph** of souls. Foster, A. D.
Trojan gold. Peters, E.

TROJAN WAR

George, M. Helen of Troy
McCullough, C. The song of Troy
Simmons, D. Ilium
Simmons, D. Olympos
Unsworth, B. The songs of the kings
Troll. Sinisalo, J.
The **troll** garden. Cather, W.
   In Cather, W. Early novels and stories
   In Cather, W. Willa Cather's collected short fiction, 1892-1912
The **trolley**. Simon, C.

TROLLS *See* Fairies
Trophies and dead things. Muller, M.
Tropic of Cancer. Miller, H.
Tropic of Capricorn. Miller, H.
Trouble. Christensen, K.
Trouble for Lucia. Benson, E. F.
   In Benson, E. F. Make way for Lucia p941-1119
Trouble in Paradise. Parker, R. B.
Troubled sleep. Sartre, J. P.
Troubling love. Ferrante, E.
The **troupe** teacher. Potok, C.
   In Potok, C. Old men at midnight

TROY (ANCIENT CITY)
   See also Trojan War
Ackroyd, P. The fall of Troy
George, M. Helen of Troy

TRUCK DRIVERS

Hall, A. L. The rhythm of the road
TRUCKS
Accidents
   See Traffic accidents
The **true** and outstanding adventures of the Hunt sisters. Robinson, E.

True at first light. Hemingway, E.
True believers. Haddam, J.
True colors. Mortman, D.
True confessions. Dunne, J. G.
True enough. McCauley, S.
True grit. Portis, C.
True justice. Tanenbaum, R.

TRUJILLO MOLINA, RAFAEL LEÓNIDAS, 1891-1961
About
Vargas Llosa, M. The Feast of the Goat

TRUMPET PLAYERS
Baker, D. Young man with a horn
Trumps of doom. Zelazny, R.
Trust me. Updike, J.
Trust me on this. Westlake, D. E.
The **truth**. Pratchett, T.
The **truth** about love. Hart, J.

TRUTH AND RECONCILIATION COMMISSION (SOUTH AFRICA) *See* South Africa. Commission for Truth and Reconciliation
The **truth** hurts. Pickard, N.
The **truth** of the matter. Dew, R. F.

TRUTHFULNESS AND FALSEHOOD
Eco, U. Baudolino
Hyland, M. J. Carry me down
Smith, A. The accidental

TUAMOTU ISLANDS *See* Islands of the Pacific

TUBERCULOSIS
Conrad, J. The Nigger of the Narcissus
Gide, A. The immoralist
Mann, T. The magic mountain
Patterson, K. Consumption

TUBMAN, HARRIET, 1820?-1913
About
Heidish, M. A woman called Moses

TUDOR ENGLAND *See* England—16th century
Tulip fever. Moggach, D.

TULIP MANIA, 17TH CENTURY
Moggach, D. Tulip fever

TULSA (OKLA.) *See* Oklahoma—Tulsa
Tunnel of love. Wolitzer, H.
Tunnel vision. Paretsky, S.
The **Turk** and my mother. Stefaniak, M. H.

TURKEY
De Bernières, L. Birds without wings
Freely, M. Enlightenment
Karnezis, P. The maze
Pamuk, O. Snow

19th century
Wallach, J. Seraglio

Istanbul
Gilman, D. The amazing Mrs. Pollifax
Hill, T. The love of stones
L'Amour, L. The walking drum
Menendez, A. The last war
Pamuk, O. The museum of innocence
Pamuk, O. My name is Red
Rosenberg, R. This is not civilization
Shafak, E. The bastard of Istanbul

TURKO-GREEK WAR, 1921-1922 *See* Greco-Turkish War, 1921-1922
Turn, magic wheel. Powell, D.
In Powell, D. Novels, 1930-1942
The **turn** of the screw. James, H.
also in James, H. Complete stories, 1892-1898
also in James, H. The complete tales of Henry James
also in James, H. The Henry James reader p255-356
also in James, H. Short novels of Henry James p407-530
The **turnaround**. Pelecanos, G. P.

TURNCOATS *See* Defectors

TURNER, NAT, 1800?-1831
About
Styron, W. The confessions of Nat Turner

TURNER, TED, 1938-
About
Everett, P. L. I am Not Sidney Poitier

TURNER'S SYNDROME
Haigh, J. The condition
Turning angel. Iles, G.

TURPIN, RANDY, 1928-1966
About
Phillips, C. Foreigners
The **turquoise** lament. MacDonald, J. D.
Turtle Moon. Hoffman, A.

TUSCANY (ITALY) *See* Italy—Tuscany

TUTANKHAMEN, KING OF EGYPT
About
Holland, C. Valley of the Kings

TUTORS
Barth, J. The sot-weed factor
Desai, K. The inheritance of loss
James, H. The pupil
Mann, T. The black swan
Shreve, A. Body surfing
Upadhyay, S. The guru of love
Voltaire. Candide
Wilder, T. Theophilus North

TWAIN, MARK, 1835-1910
Parodies, imitations, etc.
Clinch, J. Finn
Twelve times blessed. Mitchard, J.
Twentieth century ghosts. See Hill, J. 20th century ghosts
Twenty-one stories. Greene, G.
In Greene, G. Collected stories p325-562
Twenty-seven bones. Nasaw, J. L.
The **twenty-seven** ingredient chili con carne murders. See Pickard, N. The 27 ingredient chili con carne murders
Twenty thousand leagues under the sea. Verne, J.
Twenty years after. Dumas, A.
Twice-told tales. Hawthorne, N.
also in Hawthorne, N. Tales and sketches, including Twice-told tales, Mosses from an old manse, and The snow-image; A wonder book for girls and boys; Tanglewood tales for girls and boys, being a second Wonder book
Twilight. Gay, W.
Twilight. Wiesel, E.
Twilight of the superheroes. Eisenberg, D.

TWINS
See also Siamese twins
Ablow, K. R. Compulsion
Adichie, C. N. Half of a yellow sun
Barth, J. The sot-weed factor
Carey, E. Alva & Irva
Chaon, D. Await your reply
Clark, M. H. Two little girls in blue
Docx, E. Pravda
Faber, M. The Fahrenheit twins
Golding, W. Darkness visible
Habila, H. Measuring time
Hart, J. The last child
Hatoum, M. The brothers
Higgins, J. Flight of eagles
Hunter, E. The moment she was gone
Irving, J. A son of the circus
Lamb, W. I know this much is true
Michael, J. Deceptions
Niffenegger, A. Her fearful symmetry
Robison, M. One D.O.A., one on the way
Roy, A. The god of small things
Singer, I. J. The brothers Ashkenazi
Thackeray, W. M. The Virginians
Theroux, P. Doctor DeMarr
Trevanian. The summer of Katya
Trollope, J. A Spanish lover
Tryon, T. The other
Verghese, A. Cutting for stone
Woods, S. Palindrome
The **twisted** root. Perry, A.
Two cities. Wideman, J. E.
Two crowns for America. Kurtz, K.
Two-dollar bill. Woods, S.
Two for the dough. Evanovich, J.
Two hundred years of great American short stories. See 200 years of great American short stories
Two hussars. Tolstoy, L., graf
In Tolstoy, L., graf. The short novels of Tolstoy
Two little girls in blue. Clark, M. H.
The **two** minute rule. Crais, R.

Two moons. Mallon, T.
The **two** Mrs. Grenvilles. Dunne, D.
Two o'clock, eastern wartime. Dunning, J.
Two thousand and one: a space odyssey. See Clarke, A. C. 2001: a space odyssey
Two thousand sixty-one: odyssey three. See Clarke, A. C. 2061: odyssey three
Two thousand ten: odyssey two. See Clarke, A. C. 2010: odyssey two
Two time. Knopf, C.
The **two** towers. Tolkien, J. R. R.
    also in Tolkien, J. R. R. The lord of the rings
Two trains running. Vachss, A. H.
Two women. Moravia, A.
TYCOONS *See* Millionaires
Typee: a peep at Polynesian life. Melville, H.
    also in Melville, H. Typee: a peep at Polynesian life; Omoo: a narrative of adventures in the South Seas; Mardi: and a voyager thither
Typee: a peep at Polynesian life; Omoo: a narrative of adventures in the South Seas; Mardi: and a voyager thither. Melville, H.
Typhoon. Conrad, J.
    In Conrad, J. Great short works of Joseph Conrad p259-328
    In Conrad, J. The portable Conrad p192-287

TYPHOONS

    Conrad, J. Typhoon
Typical American. Jen, G.
Tyrannosaur Canyon. Preston, D.
The **tyrant's** novel. Keneally, T.
TZ'U-HSI, EMPRESS DOWAGER OF CHINA, 1835-1908
About
    Min, A. Empress Orchid
    Min, A. The last empress

U

U-BOATS *See* Submarines
U.F.O.'S *See* Flying saucers
U.S.A.. Dos Passos, J.
Ubik. Dick, P. K.
    In Dick, P. K. Four novels of the 1960s

UGANDA

    Isegawa, M. Snakepit
The **ugly** duckling. Johansen, I.
Uhuru. Ruark, R.

UKRAINE

    Foer, J. S. Everything is illuminated
Kiev
    Anatoli, A. Babi Yar
    Malamud, B. The fixer

UKRAINIANS

England
    Lewycka, M. A short history of tractors in Ukrainian
Ultimate prizes. Howatch, S.
Ulysses. Joyce, J.
Unaccustomed earth. Lahiri, J.
The **unbearable** lightness of being. Kundera, M.
The **unburied.** Palliser, C.
Uncle Peretz takes off. Shabtai, Y.
Uncle Tom's cabin. Stowe, H. B.
    also in Stowe, H. B. Uncle Tom's cabin: or, Life among the lowly; The minister's wooing; Oldtown folks p1-519
Uncle Tom's cabin: or, Life among the lowly; The minister's wooing; Oldtown folks. Stowe, H. B.
Uncle Tom's children. Wright, R.
    also in Wright, R. Works

UNCLES

    See also Nephews
    Abu-Jaber, D. Crescent
    Dickens, C. Nicholas Nickleby
    Enger, L. Undiscovered country
    Haig, M. The dead fathers club
    Jackson, S. We have always lived in a castle
    McGahan, A. The white earth
    McGuane, T. Keep the change

    Meloy, M. A family daughter
    Mitchard, J. A theory of relativity
    Norman, H. The bird artist
    Norman, H. The museum guard
    Trollope, J. The men and the girls
    Welty, E. The Ponder heart
    Wroblewski, D. The story of Edgar Sawtelle
Uncollected stories of William Faulkner. Faulkner, W.
Uncommon clay. Maron, M.
Unconditional surrender. See Waugh, E. The end of the battle
The **unconsoled.** Ishiguro, K.
Under African skies. Entered in Part I under title
Under fire. Griffin, W. E. B.
Under the banyan tree and other stories. Narayan, R. K.
Under the beetle's cellar. Walker, M. W.
Under the color of law. McGarrity, M.
Under the greenwood tree. Hardy, T.
Under the volcano. Lowry, M.
Undercurrents. Fyfield, F.
Undercurrents. Pearson, R.
The **underground** man. Macdonald, R.
UNDERGROUND MOVEMENTS (WORLD WAR, 1939-1945) *See* World War, 1939-1945—Underground movements

UNDERGROUND RAILROAD

    Heidish, M. A woman called Moses
    Stowe, H. B. Uncle Tom's cabin
The **underpainter.** Urquhart, J.
Undersurface. Cullin, M.

UNDERTAKERS AND UNDERTAKING

    Gay, W. Twilight

UNDERWORLD

    See also Crime and criminals; Gangsters; Mafia
    Algren, N. The man with the golden arm
    Busch, F. The night inspector
    DeMarinis, R. Sky full of sand
    Dickens, C. Oliver Twist
    Dos Passos, J. U.S.A.
    Ellroy, J. American tabloid
    Ellroy, J. Blood's a rover
    Ellroy, J. The cold six thousand
    Ellroy, J. L.A. confidential
    Ellroy, J. White jazz
    Faust, C. Money shot
    Hiaasen, C. Stormy weather
    Higgins, G. V. At end of day
    Johansen, I. Final target
    Mortimer, J. Felix in the underworld
    Pelecanos, G. P. The big blowdown
    Puzo, M. The godfather
    Puzo, M. The last Don
    Sanchez, T. King Bongo
    Steinbeck, J. Cannery Row
    Turner, F. W. Redemption
    Wambaugh, J. Hollywood crows
    Wambaugh, J. Hollywood Station
    Weaver, M. Deceptions
    Winegardner, M. The Godfather returns
Underworld. DeLillo, D.
Undiscovered country. Enger, L.

UNDOCUMENTED ALIENS

    Adams, L. Harbor
    Boyle, T. C. The tortilla curtain
    Cleave, C. Little Bee
    Cussler, C. Flood tide
    Prose, F. Primitive people
    Straight, S. Highwire moon
Undue influence. Brookner, A.
Undue influence. Martini, S. P.
Unearthly neighbors. Oliver, C.
    In Oliver, C. From other shores

UNEMPLOYED

    Minot, E. The Brambles
    Pilcher, R. A risk worth taking
    Steinbeck, J. Cannery Row
    Steinbeck, J. The grapes of wrath
    Steinbeck, J. Sweet Thursday
    Westlake, D. E. The ax
    Wolitzer, M. The ten-year nap
An **unequal** marriage. Tennant, E.
The **unexpected** Mrs. Pollifax. Gilman, D.

UNFINISHED NOVELS

Crane, S. The O'Ruddy
Dickens, C. The mystery of Edwin Drood
Dumas, A. The last cavalier
Fitzgerald, F. S. The last tycoon
Forester, C. S. Hornblower during the crisis, and two stories: Hornblower's temptation and The last encounter
Hawthorne, N. Doctor Grimshawe's secret
Hemingway, E. The garden of Eden
Hemingway, E. True at first light
Jones, J. Whistle
Kafka, F. Amerika
Kafka, F. The castle
Kafka, F. The trial
Mann, T. Confessions of Felix Krull, confidence man
Musil, R. The man without qualities
Sterne, L. A sentimental journey through France and Italy
An **unfinished** season. Just, W. S.
The **Unforgetting** heart: an anthology of short stories by African American women (1859-1993). Entered in Part I under title
An **unfortunate** prairie occurrence. Harrison, J.
The **unfortunates**. Johnson, B. S.
Unholy fire. Mrazek, R. J.
The **unicorn** hunt. Dunnett, D.

UNICORNS

Beagle, P. S. The last unicorn

UNIDENTIFIED FLYING OBJECTS

Strieber, W. Majestic

UNIDENTIFIED FLYING SAUCERS See Flying saucers
Uniform justice. Leon, D.

UNITED STATES

See also Middle Western States; Southern States; Southwestern States; Western States; names of individual states
Céline, L.-F. Journey to the end of the night
Crane, S. The red badge of courage
DeLillo, D. Libra
DeLillo, D. Underworld
Doctorow, E. L. Ragtime
Dos Passos, J. The 42nd parallel
Dos Passos, J. 1919
Dos Passos, J. U.S.A.
Ellroy, J. American tabloid
Ellroy, J. The cold six thousand
James, H. What Maisie knew, In the cage, The pupil
Kerouac, J. On the road
Kerouac, J. On the road: the original scroll
Kosinski, J. N. Being there
Nabokov, V. V. Lolita
Sandburg, C. Remembrance Rock
Sayers, D. L. Busman's honeymoon
Sayers, D. L. The unpleasantness at the Bellona Club
Stewart, F. M. Ellis Island
Vidal, G. The Smithsonian Institution
Vonnegut, K. Hocus pocus
Vonnegut, K. Jailbird
Wilson, R. C. Julian Comstock
Wright, S. Going native

To 1776

Defoe, D. Moll Flanders
Gabaldon, D. A breath of snow and ashes
L'Amour, L. To the far blue mountains
Morrison, T. A mercy
Pynchon, T. Mason & Dixon
Richter, C. The light in the forest

18th century

Thackeray, W. M. The Virginians
Thom, J. A. The red heart
Vidal, G. Burr

French and Indian War, 1755-1763

Cooper, J. F. The last of the Mohicans
Cooper, J. F. The Leatherstocking tales
Cooper, J. F. The Pathfinder
Roberts, K. L. Northwest Passage
Swerling, B. Shadowbrook

Revolution, 1775-1783

See also American loyalists
Charyn, J. Johnny One-Eye
Cooper, J. F. The spy

Edmonds, W. D. Drums along the Mohawk
Fleming, T. J. Dreams of glory
Gabaldon, D. An echo in the bone
Hambly, B. Patriot hearts
Hill, L. Someone knows my name
Jakes, J. Charleston
Kurtz, K. Two crowns for America
McGrath, P. Martha Peake
Roberts, K. L. Arundel
Shaara, J. The glorious cause
Shaara, J. Rise to rebellion

Revolution, 1775-1783—Campaigns

Roberts, K. L. Oliver Wiswell
Roberts, K. L. Rabble in arms

Revolution, 1775-1783—Naval operations

Cooper, J. F. The pilot

1783-1809

Roberts, K. L. Lydia Bailey

1783-1815

Hambly, B. Patriot hearts
Safire, W. Scandalmonger

19th century

Hill, R. B. Hanta yo
Kantor, M. Andersonville
Lockridge, R. Raintree County
Mitchell, M. Gone with the wind
Oates, J. C. A Bloodsmoor romance
Plain, B. Crescent City
Sontag, S. In America
Stone, I. Love is eternal
Thom, J. A. The red heart
Twain, M. The gilded age
Vidal, G. 1876
Vidal, G. Burr
Vidal, G. Empire
Vidal, G. Lincoln

Tripolitan War, 1801-1805

Roberts, K. L. Lydia Bailey

War of 1812

Brown, R. M. Dolley

1815-1861

Stowe, H. B. Uncle Tom's cabin
Updike, J. Memories of the Ford Administration

War with Mexico, 1845-1848

Kelton, E. The rebels
Shaara, J. Gone for soldiers

Civil War, 1861-1865

Adams, S. K. My old true love
Bahr, H. The Judas Field
Byrd, M. Grant
Cornwell, B. Rebel
Doctorow, E. L. The march
Faulkner, W. The unvanquished
Fleming, T. J. When this cruel war is over
Frazier, C. Cold Mountain
Gibbons, K. On the occasion of my last afternoon
Gingrich, N. Gettysburg
Gingrich, N. Grant comes east
Greeley, A. M. Irish lace
Griesemer, J. Signal & noise
Gurganus, A. The oldest living Confederate widow tells all
Horn, D. All other nights
Humphreys, J. Nowhere else on earth
Jakes, J. Charleston
Jakes, J. Love and war
Jakes, J. North and South
Jakes, J. On secret service
Jakes, J. Savannah; or, A gift for Mr. Lincoln
Jiles, P. Enemy women
Kantor, M. Andersonville
Logan, C. South of Shiloh
McCaig, D. Jacob's ladder
Melman, P. C. Landsman
Mitchell, M. Gone with the wind
Mrazek, R. J. Unholy fire
Olmstead, R. Coal black horse

UNITED STATES—Civil War, 1861-1865—*Continued*
Plain, B. Crescent City
Poyer, D. Fire on the waters
Reasoner, J. Antietam
Safire, W. Freedom
Shaara, J. Gods and generals
Shaara, J. The last full measure
Shaara, M. The killer angels
Trotter, W. R. The sands of pride
Vidal, G. Lincoln
Warren, R. P. Band of angels
Wray, J. Canaan's tongue
Wright, S. The Amalgamation Polka
Youmans, M. The wolf pit

Civil War, 1861-1865—Naval operations
Poyer, D. A country of our own

1865-1898
Jakes, J. Heaven and hell
Twain, M. The gilded age
Wharton, E. The age of innocence

Civil War, 1861-1865
Crane, S. The red badge of courage

Armed forces
Knebel, F. Seven days in May

College life
See College life—United States

Communism
See Communism—United States

Fascism
See Fascism—United States

Politics
See Politics—United States

Presidents
See Presidents—United States

Prisoners and prisons
See Prisoners and prisons—United States

Race relations
Alexie, S. Indian killer
Baker, K. Strivers Row
Baldwin, J. Another country
Baldwin, J. If Beale Street could talk
Bambara, T. C. The salt eaters
Bell, M. S. Ten Indians
Berg, E. We are all welcome here
Brown, R. M. Southern discomfort
Brown, R. Half a heart
Brown, S. The witness
Burroway, J. Bridge of sand
Campbell, B. M. Brothers and sisters
Campbell, B. M. Your blues ain't like mine
Childress, M. Crazy in Alabama
Clinch, J. Finn
Cooper, J. C. The wake of the wind
Dexter, P. Paris Trout
Doctorow, E. L. Ragtime
Doig, I. Prairie nocturne
Dunne, J. G. Nothing lost
Ellison, R. Invisible man
Epstein, L. San Remo Drive
Everett, P. L. I am Not Sidney Poitier
Faulkner, W. Intruder in the dust
Faulkner, W. Light in August
Fowler, K. J. Sarah Canary
French, A. Billy
Gaines, E. J. A gathering of old men
Gaines, E. J. A lesson before dying
Gibbons, K. Divining women
Gilb, D. The flowers
Grant, S. Map of Ireland
Grau, S. A. The keepers of the house
Greer, A. S. The story of a marriage
Grisham, J. The chamber
Grisham, J. A painted house
Grisham, J. A time to kill
Gurganus, A. Blessed assurance: a moral tale

Haley, A. Mama Flora's family
Hambly, B. A free man of color
Howard, R. Like trees, walking
Hughes, L. Not without laughter
Hughes, L. Simple speaks his mind
Hughes, L. Simple stakes a claim
Hughes, L. Simple takes a wife
Hughes, L. Simple's Uncle Sam
Jordan, H. Mudbound
Kay, T. The runaway
Kidd, S. M. The secret life of bees
Laken, V. Dream house
Lansdale, J. R. The bottoms
Lansdale, J. R. A fine dark line
Lansdale, J. R. Sunset and sawdust
Lee, H. To kill a mockingbird
Lehane, D. The given day
L'Engle, M. The other side of the sun
Lethem, J. The fortress of solitude
Marlette, D. Magic time
Matthiessen, P. Bone by bone
Matthiessen, P. Shadow country
McCullers, C. Clock without hands
Mengestu, D. The beautiful things that heaven bears
Michener, J. A. Chesapeake
Miller, S. The distinguished guest
Morrison, T. A mercy
Morrison, T. Tar baby
Mosley, W. Fortunate son
Naslund, S. J. Four spirits
Nordan, L. Wolf whistle
Oates, J. C. Because it is bitter, and because it is my heart
Oates, J. C. Black girl/White girl
Parker, R. B. Double play
Parks, G. The learning tree
Parks, S.-L. Getting mother's body
Pelecanos, G. P. The night gardener
Pelecanos, G. P. Right as rain
Pelecanos, G. P. The turnaround
Phillips, C. Crossing the river
Phillips, C. Dancing in the dark
Powell, P. Edisto
Powers, R. The time of our singing
Price, R. The promise of rest
Price, R. Freedomland
Randall, A. The wind done gone
Rhodes, J. P. Voodoo dreams
Rice, A. The Feast of All Saints
Ridley, J. A conversation with the Mann
Robinson, M. Gilead
Roth, P. The human stain
Shreve, S. R. A country of strangers
Siddons, A. R. Nora, Nora
Smith, L. E. Strange fruit
Southgate, M. The fall of Rome
Straight, S. The gettin place
Straight, S. A million nightingales
Styron, W. The confessions of Nat Turner
Tademy, L. Cane River
Terrell, W. The huntsman
Vachss, A. H. Two trains running
Vernon, O. Eden
Vernon, O. A killing in this town
Wallace, I. The man
Warren, R. P. Band of angels
West, D. The wedding
Whitehead, C. Apex hides the hurt
Whitehead, C. The intuitionist
Wideman, J. E. The cattle killing
Wideman, J. E. Philadelphia fire
Wimberley, D. The king of Colored Town
Wolfe, T. A man in full
Woods, S. Chiefs
Wright, R. Native son
Yarbrough, S. Prisoners of war

UNITED STATES. AIR FORCE
Dickey, J. To the white sea
Heller, J. Catch-22
Rosten, L. Captain Newman, M.D.
Officers
L'Amour, L. Last of the breed
Westheimer, D. Von Ryan's Express

UNITED STATES. ARMY
DeMille, N. The general's daughter

UNITED STATES NAVAL ACADEMY—*Continued*
Webb, J. A sense of honor

UNITED STATES NAVAL OBSERVATORY
Mallon, T. Two moons

UNIVERSE
Lake, J. Mainspring

UNIVERSITY LIFE *See* College life

UNIVERSITY OF CAMBRIDGE
Leavitt, D. The Indian clerk
Snow, C. P. The light and the dark
Snow, C. P. The masters

UNIVERSITY OF NOTRE DAME
McInerny, R. M. The book of kills
McInerny, R. M. Celt and pepper
McInerny, R. M. Irish coffee
McInerny, R. M. Irish tenure

UNIVERSITY OF OXFORD
Marías, J. All souls
Marías, J. Dark back of time
Sayers, D. L. Gaudy Night

UNIVERSITY STUDENTS *See* College life
The **unknown** shore. O'Brian, P.
The **unknown** terrorist. Flanagan, R.
Unless. Shields, C.
Unlucky in law. O'Shaughnessy, P.

UNMARRIED COUPLES
Hawke, E. Ash Wednesday
Mapson, J.-A. Loving Chloe
McMillan, T. Disappearing acts
Shriver, L. The post-birthday world
Walker, A. Now is the time to open your heart
Weldon, F. She may not leave

UNMARRIED MOTHERS
Gordon, M. The company of women
Llywelyn, M. 1949
Reed, K. The baby merchant
Richler, N. Your mouth is lovely
Sheldon, S. Rage of angels
Shreve, A. Fortune's Rocks
Straight, S. I been in sorrow's kitchen and licked out all the pots
Thayer, N. Belonging
Upadhyay, S. The guru of love
The **unnamable**. Beckett, S.
In Beckett, S. Molloy, Malone dies, The unnamable
Unnatural death. See Sayers, D. L. The Dawson pedigree
Unnatural selection. Elkins, A. J.
The **unparalleled** adventure of one Hans Pfaall. Poe, E. A.
In Poe, E. A. The collected tales and poems of Edgar Allan Poe p3-41
In Poe, E. A. The imaginary voyages: The narrative of Arthur Gordon Pym; The unparalleled adventure of one Hans Pfaall; The journal of Julius Rodman p366-506
The **unpleasantness** at the Bellona Club. Sayers, D. L.
The **unquiet**. Connolly, J.
An **unsuitable** attachment. Pym, B.
An **unsuitable** job for a woman. James, P. D.
Until I find you. Irving, J.
Unto a good land. Moberg, V.
The **unvanquished**. Faulkner, W.
also in Faulkner, W. Novels, 1936-1940 p317-492
UNWED MOTHERS *See* Unmarried mothers
Up above the world. Bowles, P.
In Bowles, P. Collected stories & later writings
Up in Honey's room. Leonard, E.
Up jumps the Devil. Maron, M.
Up the down staircase. Kaufman, B.
Upon a dark night. Lovesey, P.
Die **upon** a kiss. Hambly, B.
Upside down, inside out. McInerney, M.

URANIUM
Cummins, A. Yellowcake
The **Urth** of the new sun. Wolfe, G.

URUGUAY
Cameron, P. The city of your final destination
The **used** world. Kimmel, H.
Useful girl. Stevens, M.
The **uses** of enchantment. Julavits, H.

The **usual** rules. Maynard, J.

UTAH
Ebershoff, D. The 19th wife
Evenson, B. The open curtain
Mailer, N. The executioner's song

19th century
Grey, Z. Riders of the purple sage

UTE INDIANS
Borland, H. When the legends die
Doss, J. D. The night visitor
Doss, J. D. The shaman's bones

UTILITARIANISM
Dickens, C. Hard times

UTOPIAS
Gilman, C. P. Herland
Gilman, C. P. Moving the mountain
Gilman, C. P. With her in Ourland
Hawthorne, N. The Blithedale romance
Hesse, H. The glass bead game (Magister Ludi)
Huxley, A. Brave new world
Le Guin, U. K. The dispossessed
Murdoch, I. The bell
Piercy, M. Woman on the edge of time
Rush, N. Mating
Skinner, B. F. Walden two
Unsworth, B. Sacred hunger
Wells, H. G. In the days of the comet
Utterly monkey. Laird, N.
Utz. Chatwin, B.

V

V.. Pynchon, T.
Vacation. Unferth, D. O.

VACATIONS
Brookner, A. Hotel du Lac
Chenoweth, E. Hello goodbye
Dean, L. Becoming strangers
Mortimer, J. Summer's lease
Raucher, H. Summer of '42
Spark, M. The driver's seat
Steel, D. Sunset in St. Tropez
Vagabond. Cornwell, B.
The **vagabond** clown. Marston, E.

VAGABONDS *See* Rogues and vagabonds
VAGRANTS *See* Homeless persons
The **vagrants**. Li Yiyun

VALETS
Chekhov, A. P. The story of an unknown man
Verne, J. Around the world in eighty days
Wodehouse, P. G. The code of the Woosters
Wodehouse, P. G. The inimitable Jeeves
Valhalla rising. Cussler, C.
Valis. Dick, P. K.
In Dick, P. K. VALIS and later novels
VALIS and later novels. Dick, P. K.
Valley of bones. Gruber, M.
The **valley** of bones. Powell, A.
In Powell, A. A dance to the music of time
The **valley** of fear. Doyle, Sir A. C.
Valley of the Kings. Holland, C.

VALPARAISO (CHILE)

Valparaiso (Chile)
See Chile—Valparaiso
The **vampire** Armand. Rice, A.
The **vampire** Lestat. Rice, A.

VAMPIRES
Hambly, B. Those who hunt the night
Hambly, B. Traveling with the dead
Hubbard, S. The Society of S
Huston, C. Already dead
Huston, C. Every last drop
Huston, C. Half the blood of Brooklyn

VETERANS (VIETNAMESE WAR, 1961-1975)—*Continued*
McFarland, D. Singing boy
Morris, M. M. Fiona Range
O'Brien, T. In the Lake of the Woods
O'Nan, S. The names of the dead
Pekearo, N. T. The wolfman
Stone, R. Dog soldiers
Thayer, S. The weatherman
Thomas, R. Ah, treachery!
Vonnegut, K. Hocus pocus
Walker, M. W. Under the beetle's cellar
Webb, J. A sense of honor

VETERANS (WORLD WAR, 1914-1918)
Erdrich, L. The Master Butchers Singing Club
Faulkner, W. Soldiers' pay
Ford, F. M. The last post
Gautreaux, T. The missing
Parkinson, H. Across open ground
Remarque, E. M. The road back
Thayer, S. The leper
Wiggins, M. Evidence of things unseen

VETERANS (WORLD WAR, 1939-1945)
Algren, N. The man with the golden arm
Böll, H. The silent angel
Bragg, M. The soldier's return
Bragg, M. A son of war
Dickinson, P. Some deaths before dying
Greeley, A. M. Younger than springtime
Greer, A. S. The story of a marriage
Guterson, D. Snow falling on cedars
Hawkes, J. Second skin
Hazzard, S. The great fire
Heller, J. Closing time
Hunter, S. Hot Springs
Jones, J. Whistle
Jordan, H. Mudbound
Knowles, J. Peace breaks out
Lee, C.-R. A gesture life
Lehrer, J. The special prisoner
Levy, A. Small island
McEwan, I. Atonement
McNamer, D. Red rover
Okuizumi, H. The stones cry out
Pouncey, P. R. Rules for old men waiting
Turow, S. Ordinary heroes
Watkins, P. The ice soldier
Wharton, W. Birdy
Wilson, S. The man in the gray flannel suit

VETERANS DAY
Ford, F. M. A man could stand up

VETERINARIANS
Deb, S. The point of return
Gould, J. A moment in time
Gruen, S. Water for elephants
Miller, S. While I was gone
Stewart, M. Airs above the ground
The **vicious** circle. Entered in Part I under title
Vicious circle. Littell, R.
The **victim**. Bellow, S.
In Bellow, S. Novels, 1944-1953
Victims. Uhnak, D.
VICTORIAN ENGLAND *See* England—19th century
Victorine. Texier, C.
Victory. Conrad, J.
Vida. Piercy, M.

VIDEO GAMES
Tracy, P. J. Monkeewrench
VIDOCQ, EUGÈNE FRANÇOIS, 1775-1857
About
Bayard, L. The black tower
VIDOCQ, FRANÇOIS *See* Vidocq, Eugène François, 1775-1857

VIENNA (AUSTRIA) *See* Austria—Vienna

VIETNAM
Bao Ninh. The sorrow of war
Communism
See Communism—Vietnam

Ho Chi Minh City
Greene, G. The quiet American
Saigon
See Vietnam—Ho Chi Minh City

VIETNAMESE
France
Truong, M. T. D. The book of salt
United States
Parker, T. J. Little Saigon

VIETNAMESE AMERICANS
Vietnamese Americans
Le, T. D. T. The gangster we are all looking for
VIETNAMESE SOLDIERS *See* Soldiers—Vietnam

VIETNAMESE WAR, 1961-1975
Bao Ninh. The sorrow of war
Coonts, S. Flight of the Intruder
DeMille, N. Word of honor
Griffin, W. E. B. The aviators
Heinemann, L. Paco's story
Henley, P. In the river sweet
Johnson, D. Tree of smoke
King, S. Hearts in Atlantis
Long, J. The reckoning
Mason, B. A. In country
McCann, C. Let the great world spin
McDermott, A. After this
O'Brien, T. Going after Cacciato
O'Brien, T. The things they carried
O'Nan, S. The names of the dead
Parini, J. The apprentice lover
Pouncey, P. R. Rules for old men waiting
Robbins, T. Villa incognito
Wright, S. Meditations in green
The **view** from Castle Rock. Munro, A.
The **view** from the seventh layer. Brockmeier, K.
Viewpoints critical. Modesitt, L. E., Jr.

VIGILANTES
Franklin, T. Hell at the breech
Peebles, F. d. P. The seamstress
Slattery, B. F. Liberation

VIKINGS
Anderson, P. War of the Gods
Kay, G. G. The last light of the sun
Marillier, J. Foxmask
Seton, A. Avalon
Smiley, J. The Greenlanders
Vollmann, W. T. The ice-shirt
Vile bodies. Waugh, E.
Villa incognito. Robbins, T.
Village diary. Read, Miss
In Read, Miss. Chronicles of Fairacre p177-360
The **village** school. Read, Miss
In Read, Miss. Chronicles of Fairacre p9-176
Villages. Updike, J.
VINCI, LEONARDO DA *See* Leonardo, da Vinci, 1452-1519
Vineland. Pynchon, T.
Vineyard enigma. Craig, P. R.
A **vineyard** killing. Craig, P. R.
VINEYARDS *See* Wine and wine making
VIOLENCE
See also Child abuse; Terrorism; Wife abuse
Alexie, S. Flight
Banks, R. Affliction
Barfoot, J. Critical injuries
Barker, C. Imajica
Bell, M. S. All souls' rising
Bell, M. S. Ten Indians
Brandon, J. Arkansas
Brink, A. P. The other side of silence
Brown, L. Joe
Caputo, P. Horn of Africa
Carcaterra, L. Apaches
Coetzee, J. M. Disgrace
Coetzee, J. M. Life & times of Michael K.
Crews, H. A feast of snakes
Dean, L. This human season

VIRUSES—*Continued*
DeMille, N. Plum Island
Koontz, D. R. Seize the night
Kress, N. Dogs
Maazel, F. Last last chance
Nance, J. J. Pandora's clock
Pottinger, S. The last Nazi
Preston, R. The Cobra event
The **visible** world. Slouka, M.
The **vision** of Emma Blau. Hegi, U.
A **vision** of light. Riley, J. M.

VISIONS
See also Dreams
Dick, P. K. Martian time-slip
McBride, J. Song yet sung
The **visiting** physician. Shreve, S. R.
The **visitor**. Tepper, S. S.
VISITORS, FOREIGN *See* Foreign visitors
VISITORS FROM OUTER SPACE *See* Interplanetary visitors
Vital signs. Wood, B.
VITICULTURE *See* Wine and wine making
VITORIA CAMPAIGN, 1813 *See* Peninsular War, 1807-1814
Vittorio the vampire. Rice, A.
VIVISECTION *See* Medicine—Research
The **voice** of the city. Henry, O.
In Henry, O. The complete works of O. Henry p1253-1364
Voices in summer. Pilcher, R.
A **void**. Perec, G.
A **void** in hearts. Tapply, W. G.
Void moon. Connelly, M.
The **volcano** lover. Sontag, S.

VOLCANOES
Harris, R. Pompeii
Lytton, E. B. L., Baron. The last days of Pompeii
Verne, J. A journey to the centre of the earth
Voltaire's Candide, Zadig, and selected stories. Voltaire

VOLUNTEER WORKERS
See, C. There will never be another you
VON FREYTAG-LORINGHOVEN, ELSA *See* Freytag-Loringhoven, Elsa von, Baroness, 1874-1927
Von Ryan's Express. Westheimer, D.
Voodoo dreams. Rhodes, J. P.
Voodoo, Ltd. Thomas, R.

VOODOOISM
See also Zombies
Due, T. The good house
Rhodes, J. P. Voodoo dreams
Rhodes, J. P. Yellow moon
Stone, R. Bay of souls
Voyage along the horizon. Marías, J.
The **voyage** out. Woolf, V.
Voyage to the North Star. Nichols, P.

VOYAGES AND TRAVELS
See also Adventure; Air travel; Railroads—Travel; Sea stories; Tourist trade; Travelers
Conrad, J. Youth
Dunnett, D. Caprice and Rondo
Dunnett, D. Scales of gold
Dunnett, D. To lie with lions
Dunnett, D. The unicorn hunt
Ghosh, A. Sea of poppies
Golding, W. Close quarters
Golding, W. Fire down below
Golding, W. Rites of passage
Halter, M. Messiah
Higgins, J. Storm warning
Johnson, C. R. Middle passage
Larsen, R. The selected works of T. S. Spivet
Lodge, D. Paradise news
Marías, J. Voyage along the horizon
McCarthy, C. The road
McCutchan, P. Apprentice to the sea
McCutchan, P. The second mate
Melnyczuk, A. The house of widows
Moberg, V. The emigrants
Nichols, P. Voyage to the North Star
O'Brian, P. The golden ocean
The Oxford book of travel stories
Poe, E. A. The imaginary voyages: The narrative of Arthur Gordon Pym; The unparalleled adventure of one Hans Pfaall; The journal of Julius Rodman

Seton, A. Avalon
Stone, R. Outerbridge Reach
Verne, J. Around the world in eighty days
Villars, E. The Normandie affair
Vollmann, W. T. The ice-shirt
Wright, S. Going native
Vurt. Noon, J.

W

WAGNER, WINIFRED, 1897-1980
About
Wilson, A. N. Winnie and Wolf

WAGON TRAINS
Guthrie, A. B. The way West
Waifs and strays. Henry, O.
In Henry, O. The complete works of O. Henry p1632-92
The **wailing** wind. Hillerman, T.
Waiting. Ha Jin
Waiting for the Mahatma. Narayan, R. K.
In Narayan, R. K. Mr. Sampath—the printer of Malgudi, The financial expert, Waiting for the Mahatma
Waiting to exhale. McMillan, T.

WAITRESSES
De los Santos, M. Belong to me
Hemingway, E. The torrents of spring
O'Nan, S. Last night at the Lobster
Robbins, T. Skinny legs and all
Schwartz, L. Angels Crest
Vlautin, W. Northline
The **wake** of the wind. Cooper, J. C.
Walden two. Skinner, B. F.

WALES
Cronin, A. J. The citadel
Hadley, T. The master bedroom
Kay, G. G. The last light of the sun
Mawer, S. The fall
Powell, A. The valley of bones
Smollett, T. G. The expedition of Humphry Clinker

5th century
Stewart, M. The crystal cave
Stewart, M. Mary Stewart's Merlin trilogy

13th century
Penman, S. K. Here be dragons
Penman, S. K. The reckoning

19th century
Llewellyn, R. How green was my valley

Coal mines and mining
See Coal mines and mining—Wales

Rural life
Davies, P. H. The Welsh girl
Howatch, S. The wheel of fortune
Powell, S. The Mushroom Man
Sheers, O. Resistance
A **walk** on the wild side. Algren, N.
A **walk** through darkness. Durham, D. A.
A **walk** through the fire. Muller, M.
A **walk** to remember. Sparks, N.
Walkin' the dog. Mosley, W.
Walking across Egypt. Edgerton, C.
Walking back the cat. Littell, R.
The **walking** drum. L'Amour, L.
Walking shadow. Parker, R. B.
The **wall**. Hersey, J.
The **wall**, and other stories. See Sartre, J. P. Intimacy, and other stories
The **wall** of America. Disch, T. M.
Wall of brass. Daley, R.

WALL STREET (NEW YORK, N.Y.)
See also Stock exchange
Goldsmith, O. Pen pals
Stumpf, D. Confessions of a Wall Street shoeshine boy
Thomas, M. M. Hanover Place

WALT DISNEY WORLD (FLA.)
Doctorow, C. Down and out in the Magic Kingdom

WASHINGTON (STATE)

Alexie, S. Reservation blues
Bernhardt, W. Dark justice
Guterson, D. East of the mountains
Guterson, D. The other
Guterson, D. Our Lady of the Forest
Guterson, D. Snow falling on cedars
Hannah, K. On Mystic lake
Long, D. The inhabited world
Lynch, J. Border songs
Mullen, T. The last town on earth
Roberts, N. River's end
Smith, M. M. The intruders

Seattle

Alexie, S. Indian killer
Doig, I. Mountain time
Emerson, E. W. Pyro
Emerson, E. W. Vertical burn
Kallos, S. Broken for you
Martini, S. P. The list
Pearson, R. The angel maker
Pearson, R. The art of deception
Pearson, R. Beyond recognition
Pearson, R. The body of David Hayes
Pearson, R. The first victim
Pearson, R. Middle of nowhere
Pearson, R. No witnesses
Pearson, R. Undercurrents
Powers, R. Plowing the dark
Raban, J. Surveillance
Raban, J. Waxwings
Robbins, T. Half asleep in frog pajamas
Washington, D.C. Vidal, G.
Washington Square. James, H.
  also in James, H. The Henry James reader p1-163
  also in James, H. Short novels of Henry James p59-256
The **wasp** eater. Lychack, W.
The **wasted** vigil. Aslam, N.
Wasted years. Harvey, J.
A **wasteland** of strangers. Pronzini, B.
The **wasties**. Reuss, F.
Watch your back. Westlake, D. E.
Watchers. Koontz, D. R.
The **watchman**. Crais, R.
Watchman. Rankin, I.
Water. Miller, A. L.
The **water** cure. Everett, P. L.
Water dogs. Robinson, L.
Water for elephants. Gruen, S.
Water like a stone. Crombie, D.
The **water-method** man. Irving, J.
  In Irving, J. 3 by Irving p285-560
Waterfront. Schulberg, B.
Waterland. Swift, G.

WATERLOO, BATTLE OF, 1815

Cornwell, B. Sharpe's Waterloo
The **Watermelon** King. Wallace, D.

WATERMELONS

Wallace, D. The Watermelon King
The **water's** lovely. Rendell, R.
Watership Down. Adams, R.
The **waterworks**. Doctorow, E. L.

WATSON, EDGAR J., 1855-1910
About

Matthiessen, P. Bone by bone
Matthiessen, P. Killing Mister Watson
Matthiessen, P. Shadow country
Waveland. Barthelme, F.
The **waves**. Woolf, V.
Waxwings. Raban, J.
Waxwork. Lovesey, P.
The **way** forward is with a broken heart. Walker, A.
The **way** home. Pelecanos, G. P.
The **way** I found her. Tremain, R.
A **way** in the world. Naipaul, V. S.
The **way** of all flesh. Butler, S.
The **way** of the coyote. Kelton, E.
The **way** some people die. Macdonald, R.
  In Macdonald, R. Archer in Hollywood p347-528
The **way** the crow flies. MacDonald, A.-M.
The **way** through the woods. Dexter, C.

The **way** to paradise. Vargas Llosa, M.
The **way** up. See Hardwick, M. The Duchess of Duke Street
The **way** West. Guthrie, A. B.
Wayfinder's story. See Saberhagen, F. The seventh book of lost
  swords: Wayfinder's story
The **wayward** bus. Steinbeck, J.
  also in Steinbeck, J. Travels with Charley and later novels,
    1947-1962
We. Zamíàtin, E. I.
We are all welcome here. Berg, E.
We are now beginning our descent. Meek, J.
We have always lived in a castle. Jackson, S.
We need to talk about Kevin. Shriver, L.
We the living. Rand, A.
We were the Mulvaneys. Oates, J. C.

WEALTH

  See also Capitalists and financiers; Millionaires
Adichie, C. N. Half of a yellow sun
Atwood, M. The blind assassin
Boyle, T. C. The tortilla curtain
Canin, E. America America
Coleridge, N. Godchildren
Cusk, R. In the fold
De Gramont, N. Gossip of the starlings
DeLillo, D. Cosmopolis
DeMille, N. The gate house
DeMille, N. The Gold Coast
Dickens, C. Great expectations
Doctorow, E. L. The waterworks
Dunne, D. An inconvenient woman
Dunne, D. A season in purgatory
Dunne, D. The two Mrs. Grenvilles
Everett, P. L. I am Not Sidney Poitier
Fitzgerald, F. S. The beautiful and damned
Fitzgerald, F. S. The Great Gatsby
Fitzgerald, F. S. The rich boy
Galgut, D. The impostor
Gould, J. The best is yet to come
Gould, J. A moment in time
Hemmings, K. H. The descendants
Hijuelos, O. Empress of the splendid season
Ignatius, D. The Sun King
Isaacs, S. After all these years
Jakes, J. California gold
Johnson, D. L'affaire
Klein, M. Con ed
Korda, M. The fortune
Korda, M. Worldly goods
Kosinski, J. N. The devil tree
Lemann, N. Malaise
Lindsey, D. L. The rules of silence
Ludlum, R. The Scarlatti inheritance
McCarthy, T. Remainder
McLaughlin, E. The nanny diaries
McNaught, J. Paradise
McPhee, M. L'America
Michael, J. Sleeping beauty
Michaels, F. Finders keepers
Mitford, N. Love in a cold climate
Mitford, N. The pursuit of love
Morrison, T. Love
O'Hara, J. From the terrace
Pears, I. Stone's fall
Pilcher, R. September
Prose, F. Primitive people
Quindlen, A. Blessings
Rosenblatt, R. Lapham rising
Sanders, L. Guilty pleasures
Shaw, I. Bread upon the waters
Spencer, S. Willing
Steel, D. Amazing grace
Steel, D. Sunset in St. Tropez
Stone, K. Happy endings
Thayer, N. Everlasting
Thomas, M. M. Hanover Place
Tyler, A. A patchwork planet
Vonnegut, K. God bless you, Mr. Rosewater
West, M. L. Masterclass
Whitney, P. A. Amethyst dreams
Whitney, P. A. Poinciana
Wilder, T. Theophilus North
Winkler, A. C. Dog war
Witchel, A. The spare wife
Wolfe, T. A man in full

White butterfly. Mosley, W.
The White Company. Doyle, Sir A. C.
White death. Cussler, C.
White devils. McAuley, P. J.
The white dragon. McCaffrey, A.
The white earth. McGahan, A.
White elephant dead. Hart, C. G.
White Fang. London, J.
   also in London, J. Novels & stories
   also in London, J. White Fang, and other stories p1-230
White Fang, and other stories. London, J.
White gold wielder. Donaldson, S. R.
The white hotel. Thomas, D. M.
The White House connection. Higgins, J.
The White House pantry murder. Roosevelt, E.
White-jacket: or, The world in a man-of-war. Melville, H.
   In Melville, H. Redburn, his first voyage; White-jacket; or,
     The world in a man-of-war; Moby-Dick; or, The whale
White jazz. Ellroy, J.
The white king. Dragomán, G.
White male infant. D'Amato, B.
The white Mary. Salak, K.
The white monkey. Galsworthy, J.
   In Galsworthy, J. A modern comedy
White noise. DeLillo, D.
White oleander. Fitch, J.
White people. Gurganus, A.
White shadow. Atkins, A.
White smoke. Greeley, A. M.
WHITE SUPREMACY MOVEMENTS *See* Skinheads
White teeth. Smith, Z.
The white tiger. Adiga, A.
White walls. Tolstaia, T.
The Whitechapel conspiracy. Perry, A.
Whiteman. D'Souza, T.
Whitethorn Woods. Binchy, M.
WHITMAN, WALT, 1819-1892
        About
Cunningham, M. Specimen days
WHITTLING *See* Wood carving
WHODUNITS *See* Mystery and detective stories
The whole truth. Pickard, N.
The whore's child. Russo, R.
Who's Irish? Jen, G.
Whose body? Sayers, D. L.
Wicked. Maguire, G.
Wicked city. Atkins, A.
The wicked day. Stewart, M.
The wicked pavilion. Powell, D.
   In Powell, D. Novels, 1944-1962
Wicked widow. Quick, A.
Wickett's remedy. Goldberg, M.
Widdershins. De Lint, C.
Wide blue yonder. Thompson, J.
The wide net and other stories. Welty, E.
   In Welty, E. The collected stories of Eudora Welty
Wide Sargasso Sea. Rhys, J.
A widow for one year. Irving, J.

WIDOWERS

Bacon, C. Split estate
Banville, J. The sea
Coben, H. No second chance
Cooley, M. The archivist
De Bernières, L. A partisan's daughter
Doig, I. The whistling season
Drayson, N. Guide to the birds of East Africa
Finder, J. Company man
Gardam, J. Old Filth
Glass, J. Three Junes
Guterson, D. East of the mountains
Haig, M. The possession of Mr Cave
Harrigan, S. Challenger Park
Hellenga, R. Philosophy made simple
Hoban, R. Linger awhile
Hoffman, A. Skylight confessions
Joss, M. The night following
Kawabata, Y. The sound of the mountain
Keneally, T. The tyrant's novel
King, S. Bag of bones
Lemann, N. Malaise
Lively, P. The photograph
McElroy, J. Actress in the house

Moore, C. A dirty job
Narayan, R. K. The English teacher
Naylor, P. R. After
Nooteboom, C. All souls' day
Parkhurst, C. The dogs of Babel
Parks, T. Rapids
Pilcher, R. Winter solstice
Proulx, A. The shipping news
Rinehart, S. Built in a day
Sagan, F. Bonjour tristesse
Saramago, J. The cave
Shreve, A. Light on snow
Smith, R. K. Jane's house
Sparks, N. Message in a bottle
Strout, E. Abide with me
Tremain, R. The road home
Trevor, W. Death in summer
Trollope, J. Next of kin
Tropper, J. How to talk to a widower
Wesley, M. Part of the furniture

WIDOWS

Abe, K. The woman in the dunes
Adamson, G. The outlander
Atwood, M. The blind assassin
Baldacci, D. Total control
Barker, P. Double vision
Battle, L. Bed & breakfast
Berg, E. Home safe
Böll, H. The silent angel
Bowen, E. The heat of the day
Brooks, G. Year of wonders
Burroway, J. Bridge of sand
Chopin, K. At fault
Christensen, K. The great man
Cleage, P. I wish I had a red dress
Cleage, P. What looks like crazy on an ordinary day—
Cleave, C. Little Bee
DeLillo, D. The body artist
Dew, R. F. The truth of the matter
Dickinson, P. Some deaths before dying
Donohue, K. Angels of destruction
Doyle, R. Paula Spencer
Edgerton, C. Walking across Egypt
Faulkner, W. Soldiers' pay
Gaffney, P. Circle of three
Goldberg, M. Wickett's remedy
Goudge, E. Stranger in paradise
Goudge, E. Thorns of truth
Gould, J. The best is yet to come
Green, J. The beach house
Gurganus, A. The oldest living Confederate widow tells all
Gutcheon, B. R. Five fortunes
Harris, J. Chocolat
Harris, J. Five quarters of the orange
Howatch, S. The heartbreaker
Humphreys, H. Coventry
Hustvedt, S. The sorrows of an American
Irving, J. The fourth hand
Kincaid, N. Verbena
King, S. Lisey's story
Kingsolver, B. Prodigal summer
Korda, M. The fortune
L'Amour, L. The Cherokee Trail
L'Engle, M. A severed wasp
Lessing, D. M. Love, again
Lodge, D. Thinks—
Mallon, T. Two moons
Maloy, K. Every last cuckoo
Mann, T. The black swan
Marshall, P. Praisesong for the widow
Mawer, S. The fall
McBain, E. Alice in jeopardy
McFarland, D. Singing boy
McMurtry, L. The evening star
McMurtry, L. Loop group
McMurtry, L. Terms of endearment
Medlicott, J. A. Gardens of Covington
Medlicott, J. A. The ladies of Covington send their love
Michael, J. A certain smile
Millhauser, S. Revenge
Mitchard, J. Twelve times blessed
Murdoch, I. Nuns and soldiers
Oates, J. C. The falls

WIDOWS—*Continued*

O'Brien, E. House of splendid isolation
Perry, T. Fidelity
Powell, S. The Mushroom Man
Purdy, J. In a shallow grave
Quick, A. Wicked widow
Quindlen, A. Blessings
Raucher, H. Summer of '42
Redhill, M. Consolation
Riley, J. M. The serpent garden
Roberts, M. Reader, I married him
Robinson, R. Sweetwater
Ruiz, L. M. Only one thing missing
Russo, R. Empire Falls
Sackville-West, V. All passion spent
Sarton, M. A reckoning
See, C. There will never be another you
Shreve, A. Body surfing
Shreve, A. The pilot's wife
Spark, M. A far cry from Kensington
Sparks, N. The guardian
Spencer, L. Bitter sweet
Spencer, L. Morning glory
Steel, D. The house on Hope Street
Trueblood, V. Seven loves
Tyler, A. Back when we were grownups
Tyler, A. The clock winder
Updike, J. Seek my face
Updike, J. The widows of Eastwick
Viswanathan, P. The toss of a lemon
Weldon, F. Worst fears
Welty, E. The optimist's daughter
Wideman, J. E. Two cities
Williams, T. The Roman spring of Mrs. Stone
Williamson, P. The outsider
Winkler, A. C. Dog war
Winston, L. Good grief
Wolitzer, H. Hearts
Wolitzer, H. Tunnel of love
Widows. McBain, E.
The **widows** of Eastwick. Updike, J.
Widow's walk. Parker, R. B.
Wieland. Brown, C. B.
   In Brown, C. B. Three Gothic novels
The **wife**. Wolitzer, M.

WIFE ABUSE

Clark, M. H. No place like home
Doyle, R. The woman who walked into doors
Ferrante, E. Troubling love
King, S. Dolores Claiborne
King, S. Insomnia
King, S. Rose Madder
Oates, J. C. The gravedigger's daughter
Price, N. Sleeping with the enemy
Quindlen, A. Black and blue
Shreve, A. Strange fits of passion
Steel, D. Journey
Wilhelm, K. The best defense

WIFE AND HUSBAND *See* Husband and wife

WIFE BEATING *See* Wife abuse

WIFE SWAPPING *See* Marriage problems

Wifeshopping. Wingate, S.
A **wild** and lonely place. Muller, M.
Wild Decembers. O'Brien, E.
Wild fire. DeMille, N.
The **wild** girl: the notebooks of Ned Giles, 1932. [y] Fergus, J.
The **wild** Irish. Maxwell, R.
Wild justice. Margolin, P.

WILD MEN

Hoffman, A. Second nature
Wild nights! Oates, J. C.
The **wild** palms. See Faulkner, W. If I forget thee, Jerusalem
Wild pitch. Lupica, M.
Wild stars seeking midnight suns. Cooper, J. C.
The **wildcats** of Exeter. Marston, E.

WILDE, OSCAR, 1854-1900
Parodies, imitations, etc.

Self, W. Dorian
The **Wilde** women. Wall, P. S.

WILDERNESS AREAS

Henderson, W. H. Augusta Locke

Lent, J. Lost nation
McCarthy, C. The crossing
Standiford, L. Black Mountain

WILDERNESS SURVIVAL

Barnes, J. The sky so big and black
Brockmeier, K. The brief history of the dead
Brower, B. Blue dog, green river
Johnson, W. The devil you know
King, S. The girl who loved Tom Gordon
Long, J. The reckoning
Matheson, R. Hunted past reason
Perry, T. Vanishing act
Riordan, R. Cold Springs
Schwartz, L. Angels Crest
Stevens, M. The curve of the world
Wildfire at midnight. Stewart, M.
Will you always love me? and other stories. Oates, J. C.
Willa Cather's collected short fiction, 1892-1912. Cather, W.

WILLIAM III, KING OF GREAT BRITAIN, 1650-1702
About

Plaidy, J. William's wife

WILLIAM, OF WYKEHAM, BISHOP OF WINCHESTER, 1324-1404
About

Robb, C. M. The cross-legged knight

WILLIAMS, BERT, 1874-1922
About

Phillips, C. Dancing in the dark

WILLIAMS, WINIFRED *See* Wagner, Winifred, 1897-1980

William's wife. Plaidy, J.
Willing. Spencer, S.
The **Willow** Field. Kittredge, W.
The **willow** pattern. Gulik, R. H. v.

WILLS

Mortimer, J. Paradise postponed
WILTSHIRE (ENGLAND) *See* England—Wiltshire
The **wind** done gone. Randall, A.
The **wind** from the hills. Stirling, J.
The **wind-up** bird chronicle. Murakami, H.
Wind walker. Johnston, T. C.
Windmills of the gods. Sheldon, S.
The **winds** of change. Grimes, M.
Winds of fate. Lackey, M.
Winds of fury. Lackey, M.
The **winds** of war. Wouk, H.
The **Windsor** knot. McCrumb, S.
Windswept House. Martin, M.
Windy City blues. Paretsky, S.

WINE AND WINE MAKING

Francis, D. Proof
Kafka, K. Miranda's vines
Mayle, P. A good year
Woods, S. Imperfect strangers
The **wine-dark** sea. O'Brian, P.
Winesburg, Ohio. Anderson, S.
The **wings** of the dove. James, H.
The **wings** of the morning. Tryon, T.
Winnie and Wolf. Wilson, A. N.
WINNIPEG (MAN.) *See* Canada—Winnipeg
Winter and night. Rozan, S. J.
Winter in Madrid. Sansom, C. J.
Winter journey. Colegate, I.
The **winter** king. Cornwell, B.
The **winter** of Frankie Machine. Winslow, D.
The **winter** of our discontent. Steinbeck, J.
   also in Steinbeck, J. Travels with Charley and later novels, 1947-1962
Winter prey. Sandford, J.
The **winter** queen. Stevenson, J.
Winter range. Davis, C.
Winter solstice. Pilcher, R.
Winter study. Barr, N.
The **winter** wolf. Parry, R.
Wintering. Moses, K.
Winter's bone. Woodrell, D.
Winter's end. Rickards, J.
Winter's tale. Helprin, M.
Winter's tales. Dinesen, I.
Winterwood. McCabe, P.
The **Winthrop** woman. Seton, A.

WOMEN—*Continued*

L'Engle, M. Certain women
Lively, P. Consequences
Lively, P. Moon tiger
Manicka, R. The rice mother
Markson, D. Wittgenstein's mistress
McCauley, S. True enough
McDermott, A. At weddings and wakes
McMillan, T. How Stella got her groove back
Mehta, G. Raj
Momaday, N. S. The ancient child
Morrison, T. Paradise
Munro, A. Open secrets
Naylor, G. The women of Brewster Place
Nin, A. Cities of the interior
Otto, W. How to make an American quilt
Oyeyemi, H. The opposite house
Paddock, J. A secret word
Paretsky, S. Ghost country
Pilcher, R. September
Pilcher, R. The shell seekers
Powell, D. Come back to Sorrento
Powell, D. A time to be born
Pym, B. Excellent women
Read, P. P. Alice in exile
Ross, A. B. Miss Julia throws a wedding
Rushdie, S. The enchantress of Florence
Scott, J. Follow me
See, L. Peony in love
Sheldon, S. Windmills of the gods
Shields, C. The stone diaries
Shreve, S. R. Daughters of the new world
Siddons, A. R. Islands
Sienkiewicz, H. Fire in the steppe
Steel, D. Amazing grace
Strout, E. Olive Kitteridge
Thayer, N. My dearest friend
Theroux, P. Doctor Slaughter
Thomas, E. M. Reindeer Moon
Trollope, J. Legacy of love
Trueblood, V. Seven loves
Turner, N. E. These is my words
Updike, J. S
Vine, B. The brimstone wedding
Walbert, K. The gardens of Kyoto
Walbert, K. Our kind
Walbert, K. A short history of women
Walker, A. Possessing the secret of joy
Wallach, J. Seraglio
Williamson, P. Heart of the west
Winthrop, E. Island justice

Employment

Crowley, J. Four freedoms
Wilcox, J. Heavenly days

Psychology

Alarcón, D. Lost City Radio
Anderson-Dargatz, G. A recipe for bees
Barfoot, J. Critical injuries
Berg, E. What we keep
Braybrooke, J. Every eye
Brownrigg, S. Morality tale
Byatt, A. S. The conjugial angel
Chopin, K. The awakening
Clark, M. H. Remember me
Cleage, P. What looks like crazy on an ordinary day—
Cline, R. What to keep
Coetzee, J. M. Age of iron
Cohen, R. Inspired sleep
Colwin, L. Goodbye without leaving
Coupland, D. Eleanor Rigby
Cristofano, D. The girl she used to be
Cunningham, M. The hours
Cusk, R. Arlington Park
Dallas, S. The diary of Mattie Spenser
De Bernières, L. A partisan's daughter
Delinsky, B. Flirting with Pete
Delinsky, B. The summer I dared
Doyle, R. Paula Spencer
Doyle, R. The woman who walked into doors
Duisberg, K. W. The good patient
Emmons, C. His mother's son
Enright, A. The gathering
Erdrich, L. Four souls

Faber, M. The courage consort [novelette]
Ferrante, E. The lost daughter
Ferrante, E. Troubling love
Fielding, J. Missing pieces
Findley, T. The piano man's daughter
Fonseca, I. Attachment
French, N. Land of the living
Fyfield, F. Blind date
Gardam, J. The queen of the tambourine
Gibbons, K. On the occasion of my last afternoon
Godwin, G. Evensong
Gowdy, B. The romantic
Graver, E. Awake
Greer, A. S. The story of a marriage
Hadley, T. The master bedroom
Hamilton, J. A map of the world
Hannah, K. On Mystic lake
Hannah, S. The wrong mother
Hansen, R. Mariette in ecstasy
Harrigan, S. Challenger Park
Hart, J. Sin
Hearon, S. Footprints
Hearon, S. Year of the dog
Hegi, U. Stones from the river
Hill, R. When all is said and done
Høeg, P. Smilla's sense of snow
Hoffman, A. Skylight confessions
Hoffman, E. The secret
Hood, A. Places to stay the night
Howatch, S. The high flyer
Huneven, M. Blame
Inness-Brown, E. Burning Marguerite
Isaacs, S. Lily White
Johnston, W. The custodian of paradise
Joss, M. The night following
Kallos, S. Broken for you
Kasischke, L. The life before her eyes
Kavenna, J. Inglorious
Kelman, J. Summer of storms
Kidd, S. M. The mermaid chair
Kimmel, H. Iodine
Kincaid, J. Autobiography of my mother
Kincaid, J. Lucy
King, S. Dolores Claiborne
King, S. Gerald's game
King, S. Rose Madder
King, T. Survivor
Kingsolver, B. Animal dreams
Klíma, I. No saints or angels
Kundera, M. Identity
Lamott, A. Blue shoe
Lemann, N. Malaise
Lessing, D. M. The good terrorist
Lessing, D. M. Love, again
Lipman, E. The pursuit of Alice Thrift
Lively, P. The road to Lichfield
Lively, P. Spiderweb
Livesey, M. Criminals
Livesey, M. Eva moves the furniture
MacDonald, A.-M. Fall on your knees
Mapson, J.-A. Loving Chloe
Martin, V. Italian fever
Martin, V. Trespass
Mason, B. A. Feather crowns
Mattison, A. The wedding of the two-headed woman
McGowan, H. Duchess of nothing
Menendez, A. The last war
Michael, J. Sleeping beauty
Michaels, F. Celebration
Miller, R. The private lives of Pippa Lee
Miller, S. For love
Miller, S. While I was gone
Miller, S. The world below
Minot, S. Evening
Morley, I. Come Sunday
Morris, M. M. A dangerous woman
Nooteboom, C. Lost paradise
Oates, J. C. Blonde
Oates, J. C. The falls
Oates, J. C. The gravedigger's daughter
Oates, J. C. I lock my door upon myself
O'Brien, E. House of splendid isolation
O'Brien, E. Time and tide
Ōe, K. An echo of heaven

WOMEN—Social conditions—*Continued*

Oates, J. C. A Bloodsmoor romance
Oates, J. C. Marya
O'Farrell, M. The vanishing act of Esme Lennox
Piercy, M. Braided lives
Piercy, M. Gone to soldiers
Piercy, M. The longings of women
Piercy, M. Sex wars
Price, N. Sleeping with the enemy
Price, R. Kate Vaiden
Prose, F. Household saints
Richardson, S. Clarissa
Richardson, S. Pamela
Riley, J. M. In pursuit of the green lion
Riley, J. M. A vision of light
Ross-Macdonald, M. The Trevarton inheritance
Sand, G. Lélia
Santmyer, H. H. "—and ladies of the club"
Schwartz, J. B. The commoner
See, L. Shanghai girls
Shange, N. Sassafrass, Cypress & Indigo
Shulman, A. K. Memoirs of an ex-prom queen
Silko, L. Gardens in the dunes
Spencer, L. That Camden summer
Stein, G. Three lives
Stirling, J. The marrying kind
Stirling, J. The workhouse girl
Straight, S. I been in sorrow's kitchen and licked out all the
  pots
Straight, S. A million nightingales
Sundaresan, I. In the Convent of Little Flowers
Suri, M. The age of Shiva
Tademy, L. Cane River
Tax, M. Rivington Street
Toer, P. A. The girl from the coast
Trollope, A. Can you forgive her? [abridged]
Trollope, J. The rector's wife
Tryon, T. The wings of the morning
Umrigar, T. N. The space between us
Undset, S. Kristin Lavransdatter
Van Slyke, H. Public smiles, private tears
Viswanathan, P. The toss of a lemon
Vreeland, S. The passion of Artemesia
Walker, A. The color purple
Walker, A. The temple of my familiar
Wang Anyi. The song of everlasting sorrow
Wharton, E. The custom of the country
Wharton, E. The house of mirth
Zola, É. Nana
Zuber, I. Salt

WOMEN, BLACK *See* African American women

WOMEN, JEWISH *See* Jewish women

The **women**. Boyle, T. C.

Women and ghosts. Lurie, A.

WOMEN ARCHEOLOGISTS

Preston, D. The cabinet of curiosities
Smith, W. A. The seventh scroll

WOMEN ARTISTS

Atwood, M. Cat's eye
Barker, P. Double vision
De Lint, C. Memory and dream
Dunant, S. The birth of Venus
Green, G. D. The juror
Hegi, U. The worst thing I've done
Hooper, K. Finding Laura
Kelly, T. Empire rising
Meyer, C. Brown eyes blue
Mortman, D. True colors
Palahniuk, C. Diary
Riley, J. M. The serpent garden
Tearne, R. Mosquito
Updike, J. Seek my face
Weisgall, D. The world before her

WOMEN ASTRONAUTS

Harrigan, S. Challenger Park

WOMEN AUTHORS

Alvarez, J. Yo!
Atwood, M. The blind assassin
Battle, L. Southern women
Berg, E. Home safe

Brookner, A. Hotel du Lac
Byatt, A. S. The children's book
Carroll, J. Fault lines
Cline, R. What to keep
Coetzee, J. M. Elizabeth Costello
Coetzee, J. M. Slow man
Coward, N. Bon voyage
Doig, I. Bucking the sun
Drabble, M. The witch of Exmoor
Frame, J. Towards another summer
Gordon, E. F. It will come to me
Hall, J. W. Rough draft
Hay, E. Garbo laughs
Irving, J. A widow for one year
Keyes, M. The other side of the story
Lessing, D. M. The golden notebook
Lively, P. Heat wave
McEwan, I. Atonement
McGowan, K. The expected one
Meloy, M. A family daughter
Miller, S. The distinguished guest
Oates, J. C. Marya
Ogilvie, E. When the music stopped
Olsson, L. Astrid & Veronika
Piercy, M. The longings of women
Potok, C. The troupe teacher
Robinson, P. The first cut
Schwartz, L. S. The fatigue artist
Settle, M. L. Charley Bland
Settle, M. L. The killing ground
Shaffer, M. A. The Guernsey Literary and Potato Peel Pie Society
Shields, C. Unless
Shreve, A. Strange fits of passion
Stegner, W. E. Angle of repose
Thomas, R. All my sins remembered
Tremain, R. The way I found her
Weiner, J. Certain girls
Wiggins, M. The shadow catcher

WOMEN EDITORS

Carey, P. My life as a fake
Evans, N. The horse whisperer
Spark, M. A far cry from Kensington

WOMEN IN BUSINESS *See* Businesswomen

Women in love. Lawrence, D. H.

WOMEN IN POLITICS

Clark, M. H. Before I say goodbye
Didion, J. A book of common prayer
Ferber, E. Cimarron
Grippando, J. The abduction
Gutcheon, B. R. Five fortunes
Mortman, D. The lucky ones

Women in the grove. Peterson, P. W.

WOMEN JOURNALISTS

Adler, E. Now or never
Buruma, I. The China lover
Cain, C. Heartsick
Clark, M. H. Daddy's little girl
Clark, M. H. The second time around
Coel, M. Blood memory
D'Amato, B. White male infant
Didion, J. The last thing he wanted
Flynn, G. Sharp objects
Godwin, G. Queen of the underworld
Hart, C. G. Letter from home
Isaacs, S. Red, white and blue
Johnston, W. The colony of unrequited dreams
Kavenna, J. Inglorious
Lively, P. Cleopatra's sister
MacInnes, H. Ride a pale horse
Mortman, D. The lucky ones
Patterson, J. 1st to die
Patterson, R. N. Degree of guilt
Porter, K. A. Pale horse, pale rider [novelette]
Pottinger, S. The fourth procedure
Price, R. Freedomland
Raban, J. Surveillance
Salak, K. The white Mary
Sparks, N. Message in a bottle
Steel, D. Journey
Thomas, M. M. Black money
Updike, J. Seek my face

WORLD WAR, 1914-1918—*Continued*

Porter, K. A. Pale horse, pale rider [novelette]
Pouncey, P. R. Rules for old men waiting
Sholokhov, M. A. And quiet flows the Don
Trumbo, D. Johnny got his gun
Urquhart, J. The underpainter
West, P. Love's mansion

Naval operations

Forester, C. S. The last nine days of the Bismarck
McCutchan, P. The last farewell
McCutchan, P. The new lieutenant

Secret service

Murphy, Y. Signed, Mata Hari

Africa

Forester, C. S. The African Queen

Canada

MacNeil, R. Burden of desire

England

Barker, P. The eye in the door
Barker, P. The ghost road
Barker, P. Regeneration
Byatt, A. S. The children's book
Hilton, J. Random harvest
Morton, K. The house at Riverton
Perry, A. No graves as yet

France

Céline, L.-F. Journey to the end of the night
Cocteau, J. The impostor
Colette. Mitsou
Dos Passos, J. One man's initiation: 1917
Faulkner, W. A fable
Faulks, S. Birdsong
Ford, F. M. No more parades
Proust, M. Time regained [variant title: The past recaptured]
Remarque, E. M. All quiet on the western front
Wharton, E. The Marne

Germany

Remarque, E. M. The road back

Italy

Helprin, M. A soldier of the great war
Hemingway, E. A farewell to arms

Middle East

Werfel, F. The forty days of Musa Dagh

Turkey

De Bernières, L. Birds without wings

United States

Dos Passos, J. 1919
Dos Passos, J. Manhattan transfer
Gold, G. D. Sunnyside
Mullen, T. The last town on earth
Parkinson, H. Across open ground

WORLD WAR, 1939-1945

Bock, D. The ash garden
Burnford, S. Bel Ria
Delderfield, R. F. To serve them all my days
Doig, I. The eleventh man
Griffin, W. E. B. The last heroes
Griffin, W. E. B. The secret warriors
Griffin, W. E. B. The soldier spies
Higgins, J. The eagle has flown
Jones, J. The thin red line
Lee, C.-R. A gesture life
Ólafur Jóhann Ólafsson. The journey home
Piercy, M. Gone to soldiers
Slouka, M. The visible world
Steinbeck, J. The moon is down
Turow, S. Ordinary heroes
Volpi, J. In search of Klingsor
Walbert, K. The gardens of Kyoto
Waugh, E. The end of the battle
Waugh, E. Men at arms
Waugh, E. Officers and gentlemen
Wouk, H. War and remembrance
Wouk, H. The winds of war

Aerial operations

Heller, J. Catch-22
Higgins, J. Flight of eagles
Vonnegut, K. Slaughterhouse-five

Atrocities

See also Holocaust, Jewish (1933-1945)
Anatoli, A. Babi Yar
Hersey, J. The wall
Littell, J. The kindly ones
Uris, L. QB VII

Collaborationists

Eng, T. T. The gift of rain
Shreve, A. Resistance

Jews

See also Holocaust, Jewish (1933-1945)
Keneally, T. Schindler's list
Levi, P. If not now, when?
Remarque, E. M. The night in Lisbon
Wander, F. The seventh well

Naval operations

Furst, A. Dark voyage
Heggen, T. Mister Roberts
Hickam, H. H. The keeper's son
McCutchan, P. Cameron's crossing
Reeman, D. A ship must die

Naval operations—Submarine

Beach, E. L. Run silent, run deep

Prisoners and prisons

See also Concentration camps
Ballard, J. G. Empire of the Sun
Boulle, P. The bridge over the River Kwai
Clavell, J. King Rat
Davies, P. H. The Welsh girl
Katzenbach, J. Hart's war
Keneally, T. Schindler's list
Lehrer, J. The special prisoner
Nathanson, E. M. The dirty dozen
Vonnegut, K. Slaughterhouse-five
Westheimer, D. Von Ryan's Express
Yarbrough, S. Prisoners of war

Secret service

Follett, K. Eye of the needle
Follett, K. Jackdaws
Griffin, W. E. B. Secret honor
Higgins, J. Cold Harbour
Iles, G. Black cross
Ludlum, R. The Rhinemann exchange

Underground movements

Fallada, H. Every man dies alone
Faulks, S. Charlotte Gray
Follett, K. Hornet flight
Follett, K. Jackdaws
Furst, A. Blood of victory
Furst, A. The foreign correspondent
Furst, A. Red gold
Shreve, A. Resistance
Uris, L. Mila 18

Algeria

Benn, J. R. The first wave

Argentina

Griffin, W. E. B. Blood and honor
Griffin, W. E. B. Honor bound
Griffin, W. E. B. Secret honor

Atlantic Ocean

Monsarrat, N. The cruel sea

Australia

Keneally, T. Office of innocence
McCullough, C. An indecent obsession

Belgium

Hulme, K. The nun's story
Shreve, A. Resistance

Canada

Norman, H. The museum guard

World War Z. Brooks, M.
World without end. Follett, K.
Worldly goods. Korda, M.
World's end. Boyle, T. C.
World's end. Vinge, J. D.
The **worshipful** Lucia. Benson, E. F.
    In Benson, E. F. Make way for Lucia p763-940
Worst fears. Weldon, F.
Worst fears realized. Woods, S.
The **worst** thing I've done. Hegi, U.

WOUNDED KNEE CREEK, BATTLE OF, 1890
    Jones, D. C. A creek called Wounded Knee
The **wounded** Land. Donaldson, S. R.
Woundhealer's story. See Saberhagen, F. The first book of lost
    swords: Woundhealer's story

WOUNDS AND INJURIES
    Crane, S. The monster
    Laskowski, T. Every good boy does fine
The **wreck** of the Godspeed. Kelly, J. P.
The **wreck** of the Mary Deare. Innes, H.

WRIGHT, FRANK LLOYD, 1867-1959
        About
    Boyle, T. C. The women
    Horan, N. Loving Frank
Writ of execution. O'Shaughnessy, P.
WRITERS *See* Authors
The **writing** on the wall. Schwartz, L. S.

WROE, JOHN, 1782-1863
        About
    Rogers, J. Mr. Wroe's virgins
The **wrong** case. Crumley, J.
The **wrong** man. Katzenbach, J.
The **wrong** mother. Hannah, S.
Wuthering Heights. Brontë, E.

WYOMING
    Bacon, C. Split estate
    Carlson, R. The signal
    Isaacs, S. Red, white and blue
    Roberts, N. Angel's fall
    Standiford, L. Black Mountain

        19th century
    Durham, M. The man who loved Cat Dancing
    L'Amour, L. Bendigo Shafter
    Schaefer, J. W. Shane
    Trevanian. Incident at Twenty Mile

        Frontier and pioneer life
    See Frontier and pioneer life—Wyoming

X

The **XYZ** murders. Queen, E.

Y

YACHTS AND YACHTING
    Wambaugh, J. Floaters
YAMAGUCHI, SHIRLEY *See* Yamaguchi, Yoshiko, 1920-
YAMAGUCHI, YOSHIKO, 1920-
        About
    Buruma, I. The China lover

YANGTZE RIVER (CHINA)
    Hersey, J. A single pebble
Yankee at the court of King Arthur. See Twain, M. A Connecti-
    cut Yankee in King Arthur's court
Yankee Doodle dead. Hart, C. G.
Year of the dog. Hearon, S.
The **year** of the flood. Atwood, M.
The **year** of the French. Flanagan, T.
Year of wonders. Brooks, G.
The **years**. Woolf, V.
The **Year's** best fantasy. See The Year's best fantasy and horror
The **Year's** best fantasy and horror. Entered in Part I under title

Year's best science fiction. Entered in Part I under title
The **years** of rice and salt. Robinson, K. S.
The **years** with Laura Diaz. Fuentes, C.
The **yellow** admiral. O'Brian, P.
Yellow moon. Rhodes, J. P.
A **yellow** raft in blue water. Dorris, M.
The **yellow** room conspiracy. Dickinson, P.
Yellowcake. Cummins, A.

YELLOWSTONE NATIONAL PARK
    Nance, J. J. Fire flight

YEMEN
    Torday, P. Salmon fishing in the Yemen
Yesterday will make you cry. Himes, C.
Yesterday's weather. Enright, A.
The **Yiddish** policemen's union. Chabon, M.
Yo!. Alvarez, J.
The **Yokota** Officers Club. Bird, S.

YORKSHIRE (ENGLAND) *See* England—Yorkshire
You can't go home again. Wolfe, T.
You can't keep a good woman down. Walker, A.
You don't love me yet. Lethem, J.
You know me, Al. Lardner, R.
    In Lardner, R. Ring around the bases
You must be this happy to enter. Crane, E.
You only die twice. Buchanan, E.
You only live twice. Fleming, I.
You suck. Moore, C.

YOUNG, ANN ELIZA, B. 1844
        About
    Ebershoff, D. The 19th wife
The **young** Apollo and other stories. Auchincloss, L.
Young Irelanders. Donovan, G.
Young Joseph. Mann, T.
    In Mann, T. Joseph and his brothers p261-444
The **young** lions. Shaw, I.
Young Lonigan. Farrell, J. T.
    In Farrell, J. T. Studs Lonigan
Young man with a horn. Baker, D.
The **young** manhood of Studs Lonigan. Farrell, J. T.
    In Farrell, J. T. Studs Lonigan
Young wives. Goldsmith, O.
Younger than springtime. Greeley, A. M.
Your blues ain't like mine. Campbell, B. M.
Your face tomorrow: volume one: Fever and spear. Marías, J.
Your face tomorrow: volume two: Dance and dream. Marías, J.
Your mouth is lovely. Richler, N.
Your scandalous ways.

YOUTH
        See also Adolescence; Boys; Girls; Students
    Barfoot, J. Critical injuries
    Colette. Chéri
    Conrad, J. Youth
    Cook, T. H. Breakheart Hill
    Ferrell, M. The answer is always yes
    Fitzgerald, F. S. The beautiful and damned
    Fitzgerald, F. S. This side of paradise
    Freda, J. The patience of rivers
    Galsworthy, J. The white monkey
    Gardam, J. The flight of the maidens
    Gessen, K. All the sad young literary men
    Godden, R. Pippa passes
    Guest, J. Ordinary people
    Guo Xiaolu. Twenty fragments of a ravenous youth
    Hesse, H. Demian
    Huston, C. The shotgun rule
    Jones, S. Outcast
    Kay, G. G. Ysabel
    Krist, G. Chaos theory
    McCarthy, M. Birds of America
    Michener, J. A. The drifters
    Mishima, Y. The sound of waves
    Nichols, J. T. The sterile cuckoo
    O'Hagan, A. Be near me
    Salinger, J. D. The catcher in the rye
    Siddons, A. R. Heartbreak Hotel
    Sillitoe, A. Saturday night and Sunday morning
    Smith, B. Joy in the morning
    Sparks, N. A walk to remember
    Spencer, S. Endless love
    Stirling, J. The marrying kind
    Stirling, J. The penny wedding
    Tarkington, B. Alice Adams